BUSINESS STATISTICS

OF THE UNITED STATES

PATTERNS OF ECONOMIC CHANGE

12th EDITION
2007

Edited by Cornelia J. Strawser

Associate Editors
Mary Meghan Ryan
Daniel Coleman
Katherine A. DeBrandt
Mark Siegal

BERNAN PRESS
Lanham, MD

ISBN: 978-1-59888-078-6

ISSN: 1086-8488

Printed by Automated Graphic Systems, Inc., White Plains, MD, on acid-free paper that meets the American National Standards Institute Z39-48 standard.

2008 2007   4 3 2 1

BERNAN PRESS
4611-F Assembly Drive
Lanham, MD 20706
800-274-4447
email: info@bernan.com
www.bernan.com

BUSINESS STATISTICS
OF THE
UNITED STATES

PATTERNS OF ECONOMIC CHANGE

12th Edition
2007

CONTENTS

ACKNOWLEDGMENTS

The data tables and figures in this book were compiled by associate editors Mary Meghan Ryan, Daniel Coleman, and Mark Siegal, under the supervision of Bernan Press managing editor Katherine DeBrandt. The editor is indebted to them for the knowledge, experience, judgment, and technical and organizational skills that they brought to bear on this massive and complex task.

Bernan's editorial and production departments, under the overall direction of Kenneth Lawrence, did the copyediting, layout, and graphics preparation. Lateef Padgett prepared the layout and graphics, under the supervision of Bernan Press production team leader Jo A. Wilson. Shana Hertz served as the lead copyeditor. Shana, Jo, and Lateef capably handled all editorial and production aspects of this edition.

Finally, special thanks are due to the many federal agency personnel who, as always, responded generously to our frequent need for assistance in obtaining data and background information.

ACKNOWLEDGMENTS

PREFACE

Business Statistics of the United States: Patterns of Economic Change, 12th Edition, 2007 is a basic desk reference for anyone requiring statistics on the U.S. economy. It contains about 3,500 economic time series in all, which portray the period since World War II in comprehensive detail, and, in the case of 144 key series, the period from 1929 through 1948. The data are predominantly from federal government sources. Of equal importance to the data are the extensive background notes for each chapter, which help users understand the data, use them appropriately, and, if desired, seek additional information from the source agencies.

THE 2007 EDITION

The 2007 edition of *Business Statistics*, like the 2006, 2005, and 2004 editions, is intended to provide a rich, deep, and comprehensive picture of the American economy. The subtitle introduced with the 2004 edition—*Patterns of Economic Change*—acknowledges the increased resources made available for analyzing the economic history of the past half-century and more, observing past trends, and providing the basis for projecting such trends into the future.

- Whereas editions prior to 2004 typically presented data for only the latest 30 years, *Business Statistics* now presents annual data for an entire half-century, with summary data going back to 1929 where available. This allows users to refer to earlier periods of depression, war, recession, expansion, and cycles of inflation and disinflation.
- New data using the new North American Industry Classification System (NAICS) give a much clearer picture of the most dynamic sectors of the "new economy."

As always, each table in the 2007 edition has been updated through the latest full year for which data were available (usually 2005) and all historical revisions to the data available as of November 2006 have been incorporated.

THE PLAN OF THE BOOK

The history of the U.S. economy in the period since World War II is told in the major U.S. government sets of statistical data: the national income and product accounts compiled by the Bureau of Economic Analysis (BEA); the data on labor force, employment, hours, earnings, and productivity compiled by the Bureau of Labor Statistics (BLS); the price indexes collected by BLS; and the financial market data compiled primarily by the Board of Governors of the Federal Reserve System (FRB). All of these sets exist in annual and either monthly or quarterly form beginning in 1946, 1947, or 1948.

In Part A, *Business Statistics* presents all annual values for major indicators and their significant components back to 1950, where possible, along with recent quarterly or monthly data. This enables easy calculation of growth rates for periods or subperiods and more flexible comparisons of recent values with historical data.

However, historical data with a higher frequency than annual are required for many purposes, including comparison of activity before and after business cycle turning points and observation of the effects of the outbreak or the end of war. For the main series presented in Part A, historical quarterly or monthly data are presented in Part C that go all the way back to the beginning of the postwar period, where available. Part C also includes, for some important series, annual values for the years between the end of World War II and 1949 (which had to be dropped from the tables in Part A).

In both Part A and Part C, the presentations begin with the national income and product accounts, or NIPAs. The NIPAs comprise a comprehensive, thorough, and internally consistent data set. They measure the value of the total output of the U.S. economy (the gross domestic product, or GDP) and they allocate that value between its quantity, or "real," and price components. They show how the value of output is distributed among consumers, business investors, government, and foreign customers, and how the income generated in producing that output is distributed between labor and capital.

Production estimates for the "industrial" sectors of the economy—manufacturing, mining, and utilities—follow the presentation of the overall accounts.

Then, more detail is presented for the final demand components of production. GDP by definition consists of the sum of consumption expenditures, business investment, government purchases of goods and services, and exports minus imports—the elementary economics blackboard equation "GDP = C + I + G + X - M." Chapters on each of these demand components are presented in Part A.

Following these chapters, there is a chapter on prices, two chapters on the compensation of labor and capital inputs and the amount and productivity of labor input, one chapter on energy inputs into production and consumption, and one chapter on money and financial markets.

While GDP is initially defined and measured by adding up its final demand categories, this output is produced in industries—some in the old-line heavy industries such as manufacturing, mining, and utilities, but an increasing share in the huge and heterogeneous group known as "service-providing" industries. Part A gives a number of summary measures of activity classified by industry or industrial sector: industrial production, profits, and employment-related data.

Industry data are presented in more detail in Part B. However, users will not find the same degree of historical continuity as in Part A. The pace of technological and organizational change that the American economy has experienced over the past half-century has been so rapid that the statistical industry definitions have had difficulty keeping up. It has proved impossible in many cases to produce historical data series that cover the entire postwar period and also meaningfully reflect the detailed industrial structure of the economy as it exists today.

The industries that have been used to categorize data during most of the postwar period were originally defined in the 1930s and have been modified only modestly since then. They do not provide an adequate framework for analyzing economic activity in the twenty-first century. An up-to-date system, called the North American Industry Classification System (NAICS), was put into effect beginning in 1997 and was slightly modified in 2002. It has now been incorporated into nearly all of the government's statistical series. However, this system required breaks with the past at many disaggregated reporting levels, and data collected under the earlier Standard Industrial Classification (SIC) system are, in many areas, not easily convertible to the new system.

Different statistical agencies have dealt with this problem in different ways, and *Business Statistics* provides both detailed information for recent data and as much historical comparability as possible. For industrial production, the Federal Reserve Board has been able to carry estimates on the NAICS basis back to at least 1972 (estimates go back to 1967 for some higher-level aggregates); these are shown in Chapters 2 and 20. BLS has calculated employment and related data back to 1939 for NAICS "supersectors," and these are shown in Chapters 10 and 18. On the other hand, the Census Bureau's Capital Expenditures Survey gives data by NAICS industries beginning only in 1998 (Chapter 5.)

In Part B, *Business Statistics* first presents a general description of NAICS and its differences from SIC, followed by a table summarizing the structure of the U.S. economy as specified in NAICS. This table indicates how the NAICS statistical system is organized and shows—very roughly, in some cases—how each NAICS industry relates to the earlier SIC industries. In this part's chapters, *Business Statistics* presents detailed industry data on a NAICS basis as far back as it is available. BLS employment and related data are available back to 1990. Census Bureau data on manufacturers' shipments, orders, and inventories, and wholesale and retail sales and stocks, begin in 1992. For these data, *Business Statistics* shows roughly comparable data for earlier years, with an overlap shown in the year 1992, making comparisons at a broad level observable. For selected service industries, NAICS data are available only from 1998 forward. NIPA data by industry are presented on a NAICS basis as far back as available and on a SIC basis for earlier years.

Part C, Historical Data, begins with a table summarizing annual values for important economic aggregates for the years 1929 through 1948, giving some information about the enormous changes the economy went through as it experienced the Great Depression and the New Deal,

mobilized for World War II, and subsequently demobilized. In the subsequent two chapters, postwar annual and quarterly or monthly values for the most important NIPA series and other major indicators provide opportunities to observe changes associated with all of the 10 complete (peak-to-peak) business cycles that have been identified for this period.

Part D, State and Regional Data, now includes both data by state and region on personal income and employment back to 1958, and values and quantity indexes for GDP by state and region back to 1977.

Notes and definitions. Productive use of economic data requires accurate knowledge of the sources and meaning of the data. The notes and definitions for each chapter, shown immediately after that chapter's tables, contain definitions, descriptions of recent data revisions, and references to sources of additional technical information. They also include information about data availability and revision and release schedules, which allows users to readily access the latest current values if they need to keep up with the data month by month or quarter by quarter.

THE HISTORY OF BUSINESS STATISTICS

The history of *Business Statistics* began with the publication, many years ago, of the first edition of a volume with the same name and general purpose by the U.S. Department of Commerce's Bureau of Economic Analysis (BEA). After 27 periodic editions, the last of which appeared in 1992, BEA found it necessary (for budgetary and other reasons) to discontinue both the publication and the maintenance of the database from which the publication was derived.

The individual statistical series gathered together here are publicly available. However, the task of gathering them from the numerous sources within the government and assembling them into one coherent database is impractical for most data users. Even when current data are readily available, obtaining the full historical time series is often time-consuming and difficult. Definitions and other documentation can also be inconvenient to find. Believing that a *Business Statistics* compilation was too valuable to be lost to the public, Bernan Press published the first edition of the present publication, edited by Dr. Courtenay M. Slater, in 1995. The first edition received a warm welcome from users of economic data. Dr. Slater, formerly chief economist of the Department of Commerce, continued to edit and improve *Business Statistics* through four subsequent annual editions. The current editor worked with Dr. Slater on the fourth and fifth editions. In subsequent editions, she has continued in the tradition established by Dr. Slater of ensuring high-quality data while revising and expanding the book's scope to include significant new aspects of the U.S. economy and longer historical background.

Nearly all of the statistical data in this book are from federal government sources and are available in the public domain. Sources and restrictions, if any, are given in the applicable notes and definitions.

The data in this volume meet the publication standards of the federal statistical agencies from which they were obtained. Every effort has been made to select data that are accurate, meaningful, and useful. All statistical data are subject to error arising from sampling variability, reporting errors, incomplete coverage, imputation, and other causes. The responsibility of the editor and publisher of this volume is limited to reasonable care in the reproduction and presentation of data obtained from established sources.

The 2007 edition has been edited by Cornelia J. Strawser, in association with Mary Meghan Ryan, Daniel Coleman, and Katherine A. DeBrandt. Mark Siegal, the associate editor of the 2006 edition, contributed at early stages of preparation.

Dr. Strawser is the senior economic consultant to Bernan Press. She edited the seventh, eighth, ninth, tenth, and eleventh editions and was the co-editor of two previous editions of *Business Statistics*. She was co-editor of *Foreign Trade of the United States, 2001*, and also worked on the *Handbook of U.S. Labor Statistics*. She was formerly a senior economist for the U.S. House of Representatives Budget Committee and has also served at the Senate Budget Committee, the Congressional Budget Office, and the Federal Reserve Board staff. Her fields of special concentration were analysis of current business conditions, including issues of economic measurement; monetary and fiscal policy; and income distribution and poverty.

Mary Meghan Ryan is a research editor with Bernan Press. She received her bachelor's degree in economics from the University of Maryland and is a former economist with the American Economics Group. Ms. Ryan has also worked as a research assistant for FRANDATA. She is the associate editor of the *Handbook of U.S. Labor Statistics* and of *Vital Statistics of the United States*, both published by Bernan Press.

Daniel Coleman, a research editor with Bernan Press, also served as an associate editor on this edition of *Business Statistics*. He received his B.A. in Philosophy and English from Calvin College in Grand Rapids, MI and has worked as an editor for several years in the Washington, D.C. area.

The editor assumes full responsibility for the interpretations presented in this volume.

New and updated information that may be helpful to users of *Business Statistics* is discussed in this article in five categories: (I) new data included in this edition; (II) effects of hurricanes and other disasters as reflected in the national income and product accounts (NIPAs); (III) early warnings of impending upward revisions in payroll employment and reporting changes in worker hours and earnings; (IV) some common issues and pitfalls encountered in day-to-day use of current economic data; and (V) updated information about saving by nonprofit institutions as it affects the frequently cited "personal" saving statistics.

I. NEW DATA INCLUDED IN THIS EDITION

As the economy changes and the statistical system strives to keep abreast, new statistical series become available and new interest may be directed at particular existing series. The following series—some new, some not—are introduced in this edition of *Business Statistics*.

Median usual weekly earnings of full-time wage and salary workers

Data on the "median usual weekly earnings" of workers have been collected and published as a part of the CPS (the Current Population Survey, which is the monthly "household" survey) since 1979. Earnings from this report covering full-time wage and salary workers have been added to *Business Statistics* in this edition because they may complement an imminent change in reporting of hourly and weekly earnings in the CES (the Current Employment Survey, which is the monthly "payroll" survey of employers).

The change in the CES is described below in section III, "Early Warnings." The data on the number, hours, and earnings of "production or nonsupervisory workers" will be replaced by data on the hours and "regular" earnings of all employees, supplemented by data on gross monthly earnings including "irregular payments." ("Production or nonsupervisory workers" is a term that needs elaboration. A precise explanation can be found in the notes and definitions for Tables 10-7 through 10-12. Briefly, this reporting category comprises production workers in manufacturing and mining, construction workers in construction, and nonsupervisory workers in all other industries.)

This change will certainly increase the timeliness and accuracy of U.S. aggregate income estimates, but it may also lose some useful information.

Some users value the production/nonsupervisory worker data precisely because the higher echelons of supervision are not included. Such users may take a particular interest in the welfare of typical working people.[1] They may hold that cost pressures arising from management salaries are less important in the inflationary process than cost pressures arising from worker wages. Or they may fear that inclusion of very high salaries for a few managers will bias upward the measures of earnings per employee, making them less useful as gauges of living standards for typical workers. (See "Whose Standard of Living?" in the following article, "Using the Data.")

Median usual weekly earnings from the CPS, presented in Table 10-13, provide an alternative source of data on the earnings of typical workers. Median weekly earnings are not an exact substitute for the to-be-discontinued earnings data. They are published quarterly rather than monthly and only provide data on weekly earnings, whereas the CES provides both hourly and weekly earnings. *Business Statistics* publishes the median earnings data for full-time workers only, which makes it more likely that the trends of hourly and weekly earnings will be similar. CPS earnings are collected by interviews with household members rather than from employer payroll records. They are tabulated by age group, allowing a focus on adult workers who are more likely to be breadwinners; they can also be examined by sex, race, and Hispanic origin. And, of course, they represent medians—not an average (see "Whose Standard of Living?"). For illustration and further discussion of the median weekly earnings data, see Figure 10-5 and the notes and definitions for Chapter 10.

For users concerned with labor cost pressures, the editor would not recommend the use of either of the earnings series just discussed, but would suggest focusing on appropriate components of the Employment Cost Index (ECI), which is presented in Chapter 9 and also discussed below in the "Issues and Pitfalls" section under the "Measures of Employee Compensation" heading.

Smoothed estimates of labor force and employment

The official estimates of total civilian labor force and total civilian employment that are collected in the CPS and shown in Tables 10-1 and 10-2 of *Business Statistics* are characterized by the discontinuities that occur when new population controls are introduced, which takes place in January of most years. Population controls are the estimates of the population universe that the CPS sample is designed to represent. These controls change not only with the introduction of new decennial census data, but also with new intercensal estimates of births, deaths, and migration. They are enumerated and further discussed in the notes and definitions for Tables 10-1 through 10-5 and below in the "Issues and Pitfalls" section of this article, under the "Measures of Employment" heading.

For users who would like to have historical monthly series for total civilian labor force and total civilian employment that represent the best estimates of changes over time without these discontinuities, the Bureau of Labor Statistics (BLS) has estimated a smoothed time series for the years 1990 through 2005, which is presented in Table 20-3A and described in the notes and definitions for Chapter 20.

Quarterly data for services and e-commerce

The Census Bureau has instituted a quarterly survey of selected service industries, previously covered only in annual surveys, to improve the quality of quarterly estimates of gross domestic product (GDP). Beginning with the fourth quarter of 2003, revenues for firms with employees are collected for about two dozen service industries. This provides published data for individual industries and for three important industry groups: Information; Professional, scientific, and technical services; and Administrative and support and waste management and remediation. Hospitals and nursing and residential care facilities are also covered. These data were presented in an article in the 2006 edition of *Business Statistics* and are now incorporated into Chapter 17 as Table 17-17.

The Census Bureau also collects quarterly data on e-commerce in retail sales, beginning with the fourth quarter of 1999. These are now incorporated into Chapter 17 as Table 17-10. They were also presented in an article in the 2006 edition of *Business Statistics*.

Software in capital expenditures

In its comprehensive revision of the NIPAs in 2003, BEA added computer software to its estimates of business and government investment in producers' durable equipment, and this change has been reflected in the NIPA tables contained in *Business Statistics* since that time. This year, for the first time, the Census Survey of Capital Spending published separate values of capitalized computer software included in their reported values of investment in equipment. These data are now shown in Table 5-10.

II. EFFECTS OF HURRICANES AND OTHER DISASTERS

With the publication of the NIPA data for 2005 in this edition of *Business Statistics*, it is important to explain how the accounts reflect the effects of Hurricane Katrina in the third quarter of that year. The same principles of measurement apply to the NIPA treatment of other hurricanes, earthquakes, and the terror attacks of September 11, 2001.

As the Bureau of Economic Analysis (BEA), the government agency that compiles the NIPAs, explains, "Gross domestic product (GDP) is not directly affected by the destruction of previously produced property." ("The Impact of the Third-Quarter Hurricanes on the NIPAs," *Survey of Current Business*, December 2005, p. 4). Some commentators like to point out that GDP can even be, perversely, increased by an episode of destruction, once people start buying and producing to replace the lost assets.

What these observers may not realize is that the NIPAs also include series that do recognize destruction of capital, namely several income measures and the net national product (NNP). BEA statisticians estimate the amount of loss in such disasters that is over and above normal depreciation and include it in "consumption of fixed capital" (CFC), which is deducted from GDP to yield NNP. See

Table 1-9 in Chapter 1 and the associated notes and definitions for the relationship of gross and net product and income. Since personal income and net factor incomes are also measured net of CFC, the dip in NNP caused by the destruction of assets also causes a dip in income.

In Table 1-9, users of this volume will be able to spot the Katrina-caused upward bump in CFC and the resulting decline in NNP in the third quarter of 2005. In Tables 1-10, 1-11, and 4-1, it will be seen that total national net "rental income of persons," which includes the imputed rent on owner-occupied homes, was actually negative in the third quarter of 2005, as the value of hurricane destruction of property exceeded the entire national value of rentals paid or imputed on the equity value of the remaining owner-occupied residential stock. Smaller declines in that quarter can also be seen in corporate profits and proprietors' income.

Insurance payments ameliorate some of the economic losses to individuals. The insurance payments do not of themselves restore the assets; that happens only when new construction and other investment start to take place. The insurance payments appear in non-production income components of the NIPAs as transfer payments of various kinds, and they appear when the insured losses occur, not when the actual monetary payments are made. For example, in Table 4-1, the user will note a sharp upward bump in "personal current transfer receipts from business" in the third quarter of 2005. Thus, personal income in total declined not by the amount of the total property loss as recorded in the rental payment component but by the value of the uninsured loss—the property loss minus the insurance receipts.

For the impact on business transfer payments, in Table 1-11, the user can see the spike in the third quarter of 2005 in business insurance transfers to persons and a minus entry in business transfer payments to government, which indicates net receipts of insurance payments by business from government. Not shown separately in Table 1-11 but included in total business current transfer payments is a minus entry in payments to the rest of the world, indicating net receipts from overseas reinsurance companies. (See the notes and definitions for Tables 7-9 through 7-16 for a discussion of the treatment of international insurance service flows.)

BEA has made disaster adjustments of this nature for Hurricanes Andrew and Iniki in 1992; the Midwest floods and the East Coast storms in 1993; the California Northridge earthquake in 1994; Hurricane Opal in 1995; Hurricane Floyd in 1999; Tropical Storm Allison in 2001; the terrorist attacks of September 11, 2001; Hurricanes Charley, Frances, Ivan, and Jeanne in 2004; and Hurricanes Katrina, Rita, and Wilma in 2005. These adjustments apply to the national figures and to state and local estimates (such as those shown in Chapter 21 of this book).

References (all available on the BEA Web site)

Further information can be found in the following resources: "The Impact of the Third-Quarter Hurricanes on the NIPAs," *Survey of Current Business*, December 2005, p. 4; "Final Estimates for the Third Quarter of 2005," *Survey of Current Business*, January 2006, p. 1–3; "Disaster Adjustments," in "XI. Technical Notes," April 2006, <http://www.bea.gov/bea/regional/articles/lapi2004/technote.pdf> (Accessed Jan. 4, 2007); and "Frequently Asked Questions," *How Are Disasters (Such as Hurricanes and Earthquakes) Treated in the National Accounts?*, <http://www.bea.gov/bea/faq/national/0805PIKtnaffects.htm> (Accessed Jan. 4, 2007).

III. EARLY WARNINGS

Substantial benchmark revision to payroll employment

Each year, the Current Employment Statistics (CES) monthly survey data on nonfarm payroll employment are benchmarked to comprehensive counts of employment for the month of March. These comprehensive counts are derived from state unemployment insurance tax records that nearly all employers are required to file.

BLS announced, on October 6, 2006, a preliminary estimate of the annual benchmark revision to establishment survey employment. This revision is scheduled for February 2, 2007, and is not embodied in the data published in this edition of *Business Statistics*. For March 2006, there is estimated to be an unusually large upward revision of 810,000 workers, or 0.6 percent—exceeding in absolute and percentage terms any benchmark revision in the preceding 10 years.

The monthly CES survey is collected from employers. This collection method has a known downward bias because business "deaths" drop out of the sample immediately, while business "births" are not immediately incorporated. To correct for this, the CES has long used a model-based procedure each month to estimate the employment resulting from the births of new firms.

In most recent years, the benchmark data have indicated that the bias correction procedure has been working reasonably well. In the 10 years through March 2005, the largest upward revisions were 0.4 percent in 1997 and 2000. There were small downward revisions in 2001 through 2003 and in 2005. For total national employment, the revisions averaged plus or minus 0.2 percent.

Any model-based procedure is based on average performance and is not likely to catch sizeable cyclical shifts. For that reason, even with the correction procedure, an unusually large upward benchmark adjustment would be expected at some point in a cyclical recovery—indeed, part of the surprise is that this one took so long to arrive, in a cyclical recovery that according to the National Bureau of Economic Research began in November 2001.

BLS is studying the 2006 benchmark revision and can be expected to do its best to put any lessons learned to work in future CES estimation procedures.

In the following article "Using the Data: The U.S. Economy in the New Century," the discussions of recent cyclical behavior of employment and productivity include consideration of the effects of the expected benchmark revisions.

Change in reporting of hours and earnings

According to BLS, CES data on hours and earnings of production or nonsupervisory workers "have become increasingly difficult to collect, because these categorizations are not meaningful to survey respondents. Many survey respondents report that it is not possible to tabulate their payroll records based on the production/nonsupervisory definitions." Consequently, BLS has begun to collect data on the hours and regular earnings of *all* employees and, in addition but separately, data on gross monthly earnings including "irregular payments." Publication of these new series on an experimental basis is scheduled for early 2007, while publication of official series on the new basis is scheduled for mid-2007. Publication of the series on hours and earnings of production or nonsupervisory workers is to be discontinued in early 2010. ("Changes to the Current Employment Statistics Survey." [January 18, 2006. <http://www.bls.gov/CES>. Accessed June 8, 2006.])

Possible consequences of this change and alternatives for users of the current production/nonsupervisory worker hours and earnings series are discussed previously in this article under the "New Data: Median Usual Weekly Earnings of Full-time Wage and Salary Workers" heading.

IV. ISSUES AND PITFALLS

Almost every day, some new reading on the state of the economy is released—a new estimate of the latest quarter's GDP, new figures on employment and unemployment, or a new month's inflation rate. Politicians, pundits, and stock market gurus give instant opinions on the significance of the new numbers. One of the purposes of *Business Statistics* is to provide background information and perspective on this daily stream of new and updated economic data, and thus to help users of this book make their own informed judgments.

Sometimes the very richness of U.S. economic data makes comparison and analysis difficult for people who are not already familiar with the intricacies of the system. For example, one government agency issues two different estimates each month of what at first glance would seem to be the same thing, "employment." More generally, the constant labors of statistical agencies to incorporate new information and new understanding of the economy lead to frequent revisions of data.

To help users with these difficulties, the notes and definitions at the end of each chapter in *Business Statistics* explain concepts, definitions, measurement methods, and revision procedures. Here, the editor will further expand the discussion of two important issues: the measurement of employment and the measurement of employee compensation per hour.

Measures of employment

Each month, BLS updates two distinct measures of aggregate employment in the U.S. economy.

One measure, total civilian employment, is a count of the number of civilians holding jobs. It is derived from a large sample survey of households (the Current Population Survey, or CPS) and periodically benchmarked to population levels or "controls" established by the decennial census and other, more comprehensive data.

The other measure is nonfarm payroll employment. It is derived from a very large sample of employers (Current Employment Statistics, or CES) and is benchmarked each year to a comprehensive, near-complete count of employment from the records of the unemployment insurance system. It is a count of jobs rather than of persons employed, so that multiple jobholders ("moonlighters") are counted at each job rather than as one person employed.

Financial market participants and other instant analysts typically read the CES numbers—specifically, the change in total payroll employment and/or the change in private payroll employment—as key indicators of the current course of the economy. This survey's large sample size and consequent relative stability make it relatively easy to distinguish the "signal" from the "noise." According to BLS calculations, the size of the over-the-month change in employment required to be statistically significant is plus or minus 436,000 in the CPS series, but only plus or minus 99,000 in the CES series.

In recent years, some analysts have noticed that the CPS has shown a stronger employment trend and have suggested that it is a better measure of employment. They hold that because the CPS is a survey of households, it is not subject to the potential failure of the employer survey to pick up an adequate estimate of new business formation. The upcoming benchmark revision in payroll employment discussed above seems to supply some reinforcement for this view. In addition, analysts who give preference to CPS employment point out that it includes self-employment, which is omitted by definition from the CES. (Self-employment is shown in Table 10-2 in this volume.)

However, there is also an important point to be made about potential bias and distortion in the CPS, which arises from the fact that it is anchored in projections of the total population. If these projections are in error—and they have been in the past, due to misestimates of international migration—then the errors will carry through to the estimates of the number employed. (On the subject of population projections and revisions, see the box entitled "A Note of Caution About Data Revisions" in the following article, "Using the Data: The U.S. Economy in the New Century.")

Another problem with the use of CPS employment is that when the population controls are revised to reflect new information from the decennial census or new migration estimates, the adjustments are introduced in a lump sum in a single month (usually January). This makes for a discontinuity between the two adjoining months, instead of spreading the correction over the months or years during which the misstatement emerged. The notes and definitions for Tables 10-1 through 10-5 explain the adjustments that have been made from 1953 through 2005, including

the size and direction of each adjustment. As detailed previously in the "New Data" section, this edition of *Business Statistics* includes smoothed monthly estimates for the years 1990 through 2005 in Table 20-3A.

CES benchmark adjustments, on the other hand, are immediately "wedged" back to the previous benchmark month as part of the benchmarking process, resulting in a smoother and more realistic pattern of revision. In addition, because the CES is a survey of employers, it will not be biased by errors in population estimates due to faulty estimates of migration. In the late 1990s, unlike in the more recent period, the CES showed greater employment growth than the CPS—a difference that was narrowed when new population numbers caused upward adjustment of CPS employment and supported the accuracy of the CES estimates.

Each month, BLS publishes—along with the release of the latest monthly employment and labor force data—an extensive article on its Web site that details the characteristics of both employment series and calculates, for comparison with the CES payroll employment series, an "adjusted household survey"; this survey makes all feasible adjustments for definitional differences and smooths the population control revisions. As *Business Statistics* went to press, the most current article available was "Employment from the BLS Household and Payroll Surveys: Summary of Recent Trends," December 8, 2006. This version is the source for the estimates of statistical significance cited previously and for the BLS judgments quoted in the following paragraphs.

According to BLS, the adjustments for definitional differences and population control smoothing "provide a partial explanation for the employment trend differences." Other differences remain, some of which are not readily measured or quantified; these differences continue to be explored. BLS concludes that "both the payroll and household surveys are needed for a complete picture of the labor market. The payroll survey provides a highly reliable gauge of monthly change…[and] offers industry and geographic information at very detailed levels. The household survey provides a broader picture of employment including agriculture and the self employed, as well as detailed information on the demographic composition of the employed and the unemployed."

The editor of *Business Statistics* agrees with these judgments, and also agrees with the large number of practiced analysts who treat the change in payroll employment as an essential barometer of the health of the U.S. economy.

Measures of employee compensation

Hourly earnings, wages, salaries, and compensation—each of these terms is used to describe at least one data series in the U.S. statistical system, and each appears in at least one of three different data sets presented in *Business Statistics*. Additional, more detailed data on labor compensation are presented in the *Handbook of U.S. Labor Statistics*, also published by Bernan Press. It is important for the user to understand the characteristics of each of these series in order to select the one most suited for his or her purpose.

Wages typically means "gross" amounts per hour paid to hourly workers. "Gross" in this context indicates non-exclusion of the values of withheld income and payroll taxes, dues, and any other withheld amounts. Gross wages do not include the employer share of payroll taxes for social insurance or the cost of employer-provided benefits, such as pensions and health insurance. Indexes for hourly wages and salaries are presented in Table 9-2, and measures of hourly and weekly earnings are presented in Tables 10-11 and 10-12, with precise definitions of each in the notes and definitions for those chapters.

Salaries represent "gross" amounts paid to those who are paid by the week, month, or year, rather than by the hour. Indexes for hourly wages and salaries are presented in Table 9-2, and salaried production or nonsupervisory workers are included in the hourly and weekly earnings measures in Tables 10-11 and 10-12. As with wages, salaries do not exclude personal and payroll taxes on the individual or other amounts withheld, but do exclude the cost of employer-paid benefits and payroll taxes.

Compensation includes wages and salaries as defined previously, plus the employer-paid payroll taxes and benefit costs. This term appears in two different data sets in this volume, both of which are presented in Chapter 9. Table 9-1 presented weighted indexes of compensation per hour in the Employment Cost Index (ECI), and Table 9-3 shows indexes for the benefits. Table 9-4 presents aggregate average measures of compensation per hour as part of the set of data known as productivity and costs.

Compensation thus represents the total cost of labor to the employer. Wages and salaries represent the gross taxable income to the employees. Note that neither concept represents worker take-home pay.

Only one measure in this book represents net spendable income after all income and payroll taxes—disposable personal income, which can be found in Table 4-1. Disposable personal income includes not only labor income but also all forms of capital income. It is not available by industry or by income level. It is shown on a per capita basis, with the denominator being the total U.S. population. Like all other income averages, per capita disposable income is a mean, and because of the skewed distribution of income, is biased upward as a measure of the income of a typical or median individual. (See "Whose Standard of Living?" in the following article, "Using the Data.") There are no currently reported measures of the narrower concept of "worker take-home pay."

The probable principal use for *compensation* series—the use emphasized by Federal Reserve economists—is as an indicator of inflationary cost pressure. Labor costs represent about two-thirds of the cost of production. If labor costs rise faster than productivity, either from the effects of a tight labor market or from some external cause, such as a rise in payroll taxes or health benefit costs, the result can be a rise in unit labor costs and upward pressure on prices. For this reason, unit labor costs is a widely-watched indicator.

In evaluating trends in compensation for this purpose, the differences between the two series presented in Chapter 9 are important. The notes and definitions for that chapter explain each one in a general chapter note and in the specific notes for each table.

The compensation per hour component of the productivity and costs measures (Table 9-4) is simply an average of all compensation divided by all labor input, and will increase if there is a shift in the composition of output toward industries that pay their employees more, even if no individual worker experiences any increase in his or her hourly compensation. However, high-pay industries are typically high-productivity industries, and a shift toward those industries will also register as an increase in productivity even if productivity is unchanged in each individual industry. Thus, such a shift in the composition of *output* will not increase *labor cost per unit of output* or the inflationary pressure that unit labor cost is assumed to measure.

In contrast, the Employment Cost Index (ECI) (Tables 9-1 through 9-3) holds constant the composition of employment in order to isolate trends in hourly wages, salary rates, and compensation rates for individual occupations. One appropriate use of ECI measures would be to test the relationship of the unemployment rate or other measures of labor market tightness to the rate of change in the cost of a unit of labor. Compensation per hour from the productivity and cost data set would not be appropriate for such uses because of its susceptibility to distortion from changes in the industry mix.

The ECI includes sales commissions in its measures of wages and salaries. Since these are subject to temporary fluctuations that may not reflect underlying cost trends, ECIs excluding the sales occupations are also calculated and published.

Currently, the cost of stock options issued to employees is not included in the ECI, and is included in the compensation component of the productivity measures only with a lag. As illustrated in the notes and definitions, this has led to large revisions in compensation per hour in some recent periods. Whether this is a significant failing in the ECI depends on the extent to which employees accept stock options as a substitute for demanding higher salaries and/or benefits. Obviously, stock options can be a significant addition to employee income and wealth, and their addition to employee purchasing power should be recognized (subject to the definition of income in the national income and product accounts [NIPAs], which excludes the capital gains component of any stock-market-related transaction). However, for many businesses and economists, the whole point of using stock options or stock for compensation is that they do not become part of the permanent labor cost structure in the way that an increase in wage rates does. If this is the motivation or result of using stock options, such increases in compensation should not be considered to be a rise in inflationary cost pressures.

Hourly earnings, as presented in Chapter 10, are a major source for the aggregate compensation measures in productivity and costs. They are reported monthly at the beginning of the following month—far more promptly than the quarterly measures—and they currently represent the production or nonsupervisory workers that make up about four-fifths of the labor force. They are based on the very large sample survey of employers (the CES survey, which is described in the preceding section). Hourly earnings are described in the notes and definitions for Chapter 10; they exclude stock options and fluctuate as the composition of output and employment fluctuates between high- and low-pay industries. Weekly earnings, based on these hourly earnings data, are an important component of personal income and thus a major determinant of consumer income and purchasing power.

With the change from production/nonsupervisory workers to all employees in the CES monthly hourly and weekly earnings series (described previously in the "Early Warnings" section), the weekly earnings series will provide a more reliable indicator of total income, but hourly earnings could become less useful as a measure of inflationary pressure because they will reflect a more heterogeneous employee mix.

V. NONPROFIT INSTITUTIONS

In the NIPAs, the personal sector includes not only households, but also "nonprofit institutions serving households" (NPISHs). This comprises all nonprofit institutions except those that are considered to be serving government and business, such as chambers of commerce and trade associations. Those institutions are included in the business sector instead.

For annual (not quarterly) data for years 1992 through 2005, BEA now compiles and makes available tables showing personal income and its disposition for households and

NPISHs separately. Each major type of income and expenditure is estimated separately for the two groups. Household receipts from NPISHs, purchases from NPISHs, and contributions to NPISHs are identified separately instead of being netted out as they are in the current quarterly accounts. These data provide answers to questions about how much of "personal" saving is in fact accounted for by NPISHs, and whether these institutions are a factor in the observed changes in personal saving behavior. Saving estimates from these tables are shown in Table A-1.

These results indicate that NPISHs accounted for a surprisingly large proportion of "personal" saving in the stock-market boom years of 1999 and 2000. More recently, the amount and share of NPISH saving has subsided but remains positive. As a result, when the NPISH saving is removed from the household accounts, it can be seen that dis-saving—that is, net borrowing and spending down of assets to finance current consumption—by the household sector in 2005 was even greater than the published quarterly data suggested.

These data and the data on income and outlays for the household and nonprofit sectors on which they are based are available in Table 2.9 in the NIPA tables, which can be found on the BEA Web site at <http://www.bea.gov>. An article by Marshall B. Reinsdorf, entitled "Alternative Measures of Personal Saving," *Survey of Current Business*, September 2004; and an article from the April 2003 *Survey*, "Income and Outlays of Households and of Nonprofit Institutions Serving Households," can also be found on the BEA Web site.

ENDNOTES

[1]Federal Reserve Chairman Alan Greenspan cited the contrast between the growth in the earnings of production/nonsupervisory workers and those of supervisory and professional workers in a discussion of the "bivariate income distribution," a phenomenon that he regards as "not healthful." (Answers to the questions of members of Congress in "Monetary Policy and the State of the Economy: Hearing Before the Committee on Financial Services, U.S. House of Representatives, July 20, 2005," Serial No.109-47, U.S. Government Printing Office. <http://www.access.gpo.gov/congress/house/house03ch109.html>. [p. 37])

Table A-1. Personal Saving: Households and Nonprofit Institutions Serving Households (NPISHs)

Year	Personal saving (billions of dollars)			NPISH saving as a percent of total personal saving	Saving as a percent of disposable income	
	Total personal	Household	NPISH		Total personal	Household
1992	366.0	352.6	13.5	3.7	7.7	7.5
1993	284.0	271.4	12.6	4.4	5.8	5.6
1994	249.5	238.8	10.6	4.2	4.8	4.7
1995	250.9	235.7	15.2	6.1	4.6	4.4
1996	228.4	206.9	21.6	9.5	4.0	3.7
1997	218.3	176.5	41.8	19.1	3.6	3.0
1998	276.8	240.3	36.5	13.2	4.3	3.8
1999	158.6	114.0	44.6	28.1	2.4	1.7
2000	168.5	116.6	51.9	30.8	2.3	1.6
2001	132.3	107.8	24.5	18.5	1.8	1.4
2002	184.7	168.6	16.2	8.8	2.4	2.2
2003	174.9	166.4	8.5	4.9	2.1	2.0
2004	174.3	162.6	11.8	6.8	2.0	1.9
2005	-34.8	-49.6	14.8	. . .	-0.4	-0.5

. . . = Not available.

This edition of *Business Statistics of the United States* provides a summary economic record of the years from 1929 through the end of World War II and extensive detail about the entire, remarkable period from the end of that war through the first five years of the 21st century.

Business Statistics enables its users to undertake many different types of analysis. They can look at the postwar period as a whole, perhaps comparing it with the years 1929 through 1948. They can examine the performance of the U.S. economy in different wars, both large and small. They can compare economic performance in each of 13 business cycles, including or excluding the "Great Depression" of the 1930s. They can compare the beginnings of previous expansions with the period of growth, still under way at the time of this writing, that began the expansion phase of the 11th postwar cycle. They can examine the entire history of the cycle of inflation and disinflation that occurred from the 1960s through the 1990s, and contrast it with the deflation of the early 1930s and wartime inflations.

To assist the users of these statistics, the editor begins this article by providing some examples of important analytical techniques for extracting a message from a column of figures. Following that section, and illustrating the use of the techniques described, is a comparison of some important indicators for the most recent period of recession, recovery, and expansion (from 2000 through 2005) with long-term averages and with the five years beginning with the 1990–1991 recession. Subsequent sections deal with standard-of-living issues and with the relation between inflation and unemployment. Following these sections are brief mentions of wartime comparisons, business cycle comparisons, and other possible uses.

Analytical techniques

In assessing the performance of an economy over longer periods of time, it is important to use analytical techniques that highlight the most important attributes of the series. In this article and in the graphs and text that accompany nearly every *Business Statistics* data chapter, the editor will frequently make use of three useful tools: the ratio-scale graph, the calculation of compound annual growth rates, and the use of cyclically comparable years to estimate trends and to separate trend from cyclical behavior. Econometricians use more elaborate methods of statistical analysis to estimate relationships and construct models, but much can be discerned by using these relatively simple techniques.

Ratio-scale graphs. The beginning of Chapter 1 (Figure 1-1) is a time series graph of output per capita from 1946 through 2005, drawn on a ratio scale. Output per capita is the constant-dollar value of each year's U.S. gross domestic product (GDP), divided by the size of that year's U.S. population.

The reader will quickly see that equal distances on the vertical scale of this graph do not represent equal 2000-dollar differences in values. However, equal vertical distances do represent equal percent changes. Any upward-sloping straight line plotted on this scale represents a constant percentage rate of growth over the period, and any downward-sloping straight line represents a constant percentage rate of decline.

This ratio-scale graph was produced by the following three steps: (1) The values to be graphed were converted into natural (base e) logarithms. (2) The natural logarithms were graphed. (3) For ease in interpretation, the vertical scale on this graph of the logarithms was relabeled, replacing the actual numerical value of the logarithm that was plotted with the numerical value of its antilog—that is, the original value.

This technique is only valid for data series that do not include zeroes or negative numbers, for which logarithms do not exist. Because percentage values, such as the unemployment rate, and percent changes, such as the inflation rate, are already in percentage terms, and because percent changes may include zero and/or negative values, they are not graphed in this fashion.

Compound annual growth rates. In the text of this article and in the highlights pages that precede and accompany most of the chapters, the editor often uses compound annual growth rates to summarize the history of important economic processes, such as economic and demographic growth and inflation.

The compound annual growth rate is the percentage rate which, when compounded annually, would cause a quantity "X(t)" observed in a period "t" to grow (or decline) to a quantity "X(t+i)" over a period of "i" years. Using this procedure, growth percentages for different periods spanning different numbers of years can be reduced to a common scale—the annual rate—for comparison. The formula for calculating such a growth rate, "r," is as follows:

$$r = \left(\sqrt[i]{X(t+i) \Big/ X(t)} - 1 \right) \times 100 \, .$$

When growth rates are functionally related to each other, such as the growth rates for output, hours worked, and output per hour worked (productivity), those rates will be arithmetically consistent as in the following formula, where "o" is the percentage growth rate for output, "h" the rate for hours worked, and "p" the growth rate for output per hour worked:

$$p = [[(100 + o) / (100 + h)] - 1] \times 100$$

When the percentage growth rates are not very far from zero, relationships of this kind can be approximated or verified by simple addition or subtraction of the relevant percentage rates. For example, the productivity growth rate of 2.2 percent shown in Table B-1 (output per hour, nonfarm business, 1948–2000) is (approximately) the difference between the output growth rate of 3.7 percent and the hours growth rate of 1.5 percent.

Using cyclically comparable end points. For economic processes that have significant business-cycle components, such as output and employment, it is important to use comparable points in the business cycle for estimating underlying growth rates. (For an explanation and enumeration of business cycles, see the notes and definitions for Table 1-8.) One commonly used method is simply to calculate growth rates between years with similar, high rates of resource utilization. The broadest readily available measure of resource utilization is the unemployment rate, which was 3.8 percent in 1948 and 4.0 percent in 2000.[1] Hence, in the analysis that follows, postwar long-term growth rates are, where possible, calculated as the rates for the 52-year period from 1948 to 2000.

For comparisons using monthly or quarterly data, calculations can be somewhat more precisely made by using the dates of business cycle peaks, which are shown in the notes and definitions for Table 1-8, as beginning and end points.

The year 2005, the last shown in this book, cannot be treated as if it were a business cycle peak. The expansion is continuing at this writing (late in 2006) and shows no signs of an imminent downturn. Hence, it does not tell the whole story to compare the most recent five years with a long-term, peak-to-peak performance such as that seen from 1948 to 2000. Instead, for cyclically sensitive indicators such as GDP and employment, the editor will compare the 2000–2005 period with a cyclically similar period, the years 1990–1995.

The year 1990 represented a high point in the annual average for real GDP, which declined in 1991 because of a recession that ran from July 1990 to March 1991. Similarly, the year 2000 was a year of high growth, followed by very slow growth in 2001 associated with the recession that ran from March to November of 2001. This suggests that it is appropriate to compare the 2000–2005 period with 1990–1995, bearing in mind that each includes a recession period but not a full period of expansion. Hence, both periods can be expected to show slower growth than any period that runs all the way from one cycle peak to the next.[2]

Assessing growth and labor compensation, long-term and early expansion

Table B-1 displays growth rates and related variables for some major economic indicators over the entire 1948–2000 period and for two periods of recession and partial recovery (1990–1995 and 2000–2005). Also included is a shorter "long-term" period, 1979–2000, which is the longest peak-to-peak span that can also yield comparisons using the Employment Cost Index (ECI). For each indicator, a reference is given to the source tables in *Business Statistics*.

A NOTE OF CAUTION ABOUT DATA REVISIONS

Although these data, like all of the data in *Business Statistics*, come from the world's best national statistical operations, they also pertain to the world's largest and most complex economy. The data are approximations, and the more recent data are preliminary approximations. Many important series have already been revised several times and will be revised again. Here are some examples of recent data revisions:

- *Population growth.* Before the results of Census 2000 became available, population growth was estimated at 0.97 percent per year from 1990 to 2000. The actual results of Census 2000 came in higher, and the year 2000 and the intervening years were revised accordingly. Population growth from 1990 to 2000 is now measured at 1.22 percent.
- *GDP* is revised every year for at least three preceding years. Before the July 2005 revision, growth in real GDP from 2000 to 2004 was estimated at 2.51 percent per year. With the July 2005 and 2006 revisions, incorporated in this volume of *Business Statistics*, growth over those same 4 years is estimated at an annual rate of 2.18 percent. Downward revisions in GDP growth were reflected in similar downward revisions in productivity growth and upward revisions in unit labor costs.
- *Payroll employment* is subject to benchmark revision each year. The March 2005 benchmark, the latest included in this volume, was a downward revision of 0.1 percent, and the average revision for the 10 years ending in 2005 was plus or minus 0.2 percent. However, the Bureau of Labor Statistics announced in October 2006 a preliminary estimate that total employment reported for March 2006 will be revised upward by an unusually large 0.6 percent when the final benchmark revisions are published on February 2, 2007. (See the "Early Warnings" section in the preceding article, "Topics of Current Interest.") Since benchmark adjustments are "wedged" back to the previous benchmark, this means that 2005 employment data for the months of April through December, and therefore the 2005 annual average, will also be revised upward. This suggests a more optimistic recent employment picture than portrayed by the data in this volume. On the other hand, it could lead to downward revisions in productivity growth, since payroll employment is multiplied by hours per employee to yield total hours worked, the denominator of output per hour.
- *Labor compensation* as measured in the productivity and costs reporting system has been subject to significant revisions lately, apparently reflecting new information about bonuses, stock options, and other one-time payments. See the general note at the beginning of the notes and definitions for Chapter 9 and the "Issues and Pitfalls" section in the preceding article, "Topics of Current Interest."

Table B-1. Rates of Growth and Compensation: Long-Term and Early Expansion

(Percent change, annual rate, except as noted.)

Classification	Long-term		Recession and early expansion	
	1948–2000	1979–2000	1990–1995	2000–2005
OUTPUT, POPULATION, AND EMPLOYMENT				
Real GDP (Tables 1-2 and 19-2)	3.5	3.1	2.5	2.4
Population (Tables 1-7 and 19-7)	1.3	1.1	1.3	1.0
GDP per capita (Tables 1-7 and 19-7)	2.2	2.0	1.2	1.4
Civilian labor force (Tables 10-1 and 20-3)	1.7	1.5	1.0	0.9
Labor force participation rate (Table 10-1)	[1]8.3	[1]3.4	[1]0.1	[1]-1.1
Civilian employment (Table 10-2)	1.7	1.6	1.0	0.7
Unemployment rate (Table 10-4)	[1]0.2	[1]-1.8	[1]0.0	[1]1.1
Nonfarm payroll employment (Table 10-7)	2.1	1.8	1.4	0.3
NONFARM BUSINESS PRODUCTIVITY AND UNIT LABOR COSTS (TABLES 9-4 AND 9-13)				
Output	3.7	3.4	2.9	2.6
Hours of all persons	1.5	1.6	1.3	-0.5
Output per hour	2.2	1.7	1.5	3.1
Labor costs per unit of output	3.3	3.1	1.6	0.8
EMPLOYMENT COST INDEX (ECI) AND PRICES				
Compensation per hour	. . .	4.6	3.2	3.6
Wages and salaries (Table 9-2)	. . .	4.3	3.0	2.9
Benefits (Table 9-3)	. . .	5.3	4.4	5.4
CPI-U-RS (Table 8-2)	. . .	3.8	2.6	2.5
Real compensation per hour, based on ECI and CPI-U-RS ...	. . .	0.8	0.6	1.1
Wages and salaries	. . .	0.5	0.4	0.4
Benefits	. . .	1.5	1.8	2.9

[1]Percentage point difference over total period, not at an annual rate.

. . . = Not available.

Real GDP grew at a 3.5 percent annual rate from 1948 to 2000. As would be expected, growth from 2000 to 2005 was slower, at an annual rate of 2.4 percent. This was almost the same as the 1990–1995 period of recession and early recovery, when growth averaged 2.5 percent.

Population growth is estimated to have slowed in the 21st century (although this judgment might be viewed with some skepticism, in the light of the scale of revision noted in the preceding box). Accepting the current estimate of population growth, however, it appears that real GDP per capita rose a little faster in the recent period than in the early 1990s, although it increased more slowly than the long-term average of 2.2 percent per year.

Increases in real GDP per capita can happen if work input increases more than population, if more output can be produced by each unit of work input (that is, if productivity rises), or a combination of both. Taking the half-century ending in 2000 as a whole, both factors were at work. Some interesting differences can be seen in the first five years of this century, compared with the preceding half-century and with the previous cyclically comparable five-year period.

Labor force, employment, and unemployment. From 1948 to 2000, the labor force and total employment grew at a 1.7 percent rate—much faster than the population growth rate of 1.3 percent—because of a large increase in the labor force participation rate. Women of working age increasingly entered the work force, and their numbers far exceeded the numbers of men who left it. (For detailed

statistics on labor force participation rates by sex, age, race, and Hispanic origin, see Bernan Press's *Handbook of U.S. Labor Statistics.*)

Labor force growth was slower in 1990–1995 than its long-term average, and slowed slightly further in the most recent five years. Adult women's participation in the labor force grew more slowly in the last decade of the century and actually declined between 1999 and 2004. However, this group's participation recovered in 2005, and by 2006 (according to the latest data available at this writing) had reached its 1999 high. The labor force participation rates of both adult men and teenagers in 2005 and 2006 were not as high as their rates in 1990. (Table 10-1)

In the 1990–1995 period, growth of total civilian employment kept pace with labor force growth and the unemployment rate was the same at the end of the five-year span as it was at the beginning. Over the more recent period, employment growth did not keep up with labor force growth and the unemployment rate increased.

Growth in nonfarm payroll employment in the first five years of this century slowed much more sharply than total civilian employment. This would still be true even allowing for the expected upward revision of the payroll employment series (see the "Early Warnings" section in the preceding article, "Topics of Current Interest.")

Productivity. Growth in GDP that exceeds employment growth mainly implies growth in output per hour worked, known as productivity. (The other link in the chain, hours worked per employee, can also change but has been a relatively minor factor.) The 1948–2000 average rate of growth for output per hour in U.S. nonfarm business was 2.2 percent. Productivity grew more slowly from 1990 to 1995, which was expected, based on previous experience, in a period that included a recession but not a full recovery.

Confounding expectations, productivity growth from 2000 to 2005 was 3.1 percent per year, significantly *higher* than the long-term average. This made it possible to increase GDP and GDP per capita with an actual decrease in labor input (hours worked). Allowing for the impact on 2005 data of the expected upward revision in 2006 payroll employment would indicate a slightly smaller decline in hours and increase in productivity over the five-year period, but the difference from the 1990–1995 period would still be striking.

Productivity growth is also considered to be a major determinant of the real wage, since it allows increases in compensation without increases in labor cost. The preferred measures of nominal labor compensation—the Employment Cost Index (ECI) measures—are shown in Table B-1. (See the preceding article, "Topics of Current Interest" and its "Issues and Pitfalls" section for explanation of why the ECI is preferred to other compensation measures.) ECI measures are only available beginning in 1979, which is why a column showing growth from 1979 to 2000 appears in this table. (The years 1979 and 2000 are roughly comparable in cyclical terms, so that they can be used to suggest a trend. The 1979 unemployment rate of 5.8 percent was substantially higher than in 2000, but it nevertheless represented a cyclical low, a point that would be not be reached again until 1988.)

The first thing to notice is the increased disparity between the growth rate of wages and salaries—the pre-tax compensation that workers see on their pay stubs—and the growth rate of total compensation, which also takes account of all "fringe benefits" including the employer Social Security tax and the cost of employer-paid medical benefits. (Table 9-3) Health care costs are driving this increasing gap between what the employer pays in total for his or her workers and what workers see as their wages or salaries. This gap is also part of the reason that average hourly earnings for production or nonsupervis-

ory workers (Table 10-11), which also exclude the cost of fringe benefits, have fallen so far behind the growth rate of productivity.

But even taking benefit costs into account by using the ECI index for total compensation, it appears that real compensation is falling behind productivity at a greater rate than it did during the early 1990s. In the last portion of Table B-1, the rate of increase in the CPI-U-RS is subtracted from the nominal ECI rates of increase to show the rate of change in real ECI measures. (The CPI-U-RS is a version of the Consumer Price Index that is also used to deflate other compensation and income measures used in this article. See the notes and definitions for Chapter 8.) From 1990 to 1995, real compensation grew 0.6 percent per year, compared with a productivity increase of 1.5 percent. From 2000 to 2005, real compensation grew 1.1 percent per year, compared with a productivity increase of 3.1 percent. As will be shown below, only part of these recent gaps between productivity and real compensation can be explained "technically" by the difference between the price index used for productivity and that used for compensation.

A more complete accounting of the costs of production, taking capital as well as labor costs into account, can be observed in the productivity and cost data for nonfinancial corporations. These are only available back to 1958. The earliest year in that span with an unemployment rate comparable to 2000 is 1967 (3.8 percent, the same as 1948 and only slightly different from 2000's 4.0 percent). Table B-2 compares nonfinancial corporation indicators for 1967–2000 and the two five-year recession-recovery periods. (Table 9-4)

The 33-year span from 1967 to 2000 excludes many years of high productivity growth, and the productivity growth rate of 1.8 percent shown in the first column of this table is accordingly lower than the longer-term rate of 2.2 percent shown in the first column of Table B-1, but similar to the 1979–2000 rate in the second column of that table. From 1990 to 1995, productivity growth in this sector was about the same as for all nonfarm business; from 2000 to 2005, it was even higher.

From 1967 to 2000, nominal compensation per hour at nonfinancial corporations rose at a 5.8 percent average

Table B-2. Productivity and Related Data, Nonfinancial Corporations

(Percent change, annual rate.)

Classification	1967–2000	1990–1994	2000–2004
Output per hour worked	1.8	1.6	3.4
Compensation per hour	5.8	2.9	3.9
Real compensation per hour	0.9	0.3	1.3
Unit labor costs	3.9	1.3	0.5
Unit non-labor costs	4.5	0.8	1.3
Unit profits	1.8	7.2	7.3
Implicit price deflator	3.7	1.8	1.3
Consumer price deflator for real compensation	4.9	2.6	2.5
Real compensation-productivity gap	0.9	1.3	2.1
Portion of gap explained by deflator difference	1.2	0.8	1.2

annual rate. With productivity growing at a 1.8 percent rate, unit labor cost increased at a 3.9 percent rate. Unit non-labor costs (capital consumption, interest, and indirect taxes) rose at a 4.5 percent rate and unit profits at a 1.8 percent rate. Over this longer term, the relative decline in profits and rise in unit non-labor costs echoes the rise in interest and fall in profits indicated in the national income and product accounts (NIPAs), which in turn reflects the rise in corporate indebtedness. (Tables 1-13 and 12-5). The implicit price deflator for the sector, or the total price of a unit of output—which is the sum of the unit labor and nonlabor costs and unit profits growth rates, weighted by their shares—rose at a 3.7 percent rate, about the same as the rise in unit labor cost.

Yet despite the fact that unit labor costs rose at about the same rate as prices, "real" compensation per hour, as calculated and published by the Bureau of Labor Statistics and shown here, fell short of productivity growth in the 1967–2000 period. This is because of a substantial difference in price trends between the "market basket" that workers consume and the "market basket" that U.S. corporations produce. Business sector output includes a substantial proportion of high-tech products, which have had dramatic price declines. Workers, on the other hand, *buy* proportionately fewer computers and other high-tech products and more commodity-based products, including imports. They did not get less than their proportionate share of the current-dollar value of the sector's output, but what they earned lost ground in *relative* purchasing power. As the table demonstrates, the difference between the output price deflator for the sector and the consumer price deflator used for real compensation more than explains the gap between productivity and real compensation for the 1967–2000 period as a whole.

However, the deflator difference falls short of explaining the gap in the 1990–1995 period and even more so in the 2000–2005 period.

Whose standard of living?

So far, this article has been concerned with averages—average GDP per capita, average output and real compensation per hour worked, and the like. It is important to note that the average, known technically to statisticians as a "mean," is only one way of describing the central tendency of any set of statistical data, and is not necessarily the method that produces the most representative number.

A researcher interested in the economic well-being of a typical American family (or household) would probably judge that the best single number to characterize that well-being would be the standard of living of a family (or household) situated at the middle of the income distribution. Half of all families would have higher incomes and half would have lower incomes. This is the measure known as the "median." Medians are not the same as averages or means, and in the case of income distributions, they are invariably lower.

This difference is sometimes illustrated by the image of a billionaire walking into a working-class bar. The "average income" (mean income) of each person in the bar would jump, as a billion dollars was added to the numerator of the average and just one unit was added to the denominator. However, the median would be little if at all changed—at most, the addition of one person to the group might mean that the median income moved up from one worker to the next best-paid worker—and this would accord with an accurate perception that the *typical* person in that bar had not experienced any significant increase in his income.

Furthermore, if the incomes of people at the upper end of the distribution increase faster than the incomes of those at the middle and bottom of the distribution (which is what happens when the income distribution becomes more unequal), then the means will also *increase* more than the medians.

Once a year, as a supplement to the Current Population Survey, the Census Bureau collects income data from its large sample of households that are used to produce a report on median incomes, the distribution of income, and the poverty rate, providing a rich picture of the well-being of households and individuals throughout the income distribution. Data for families has been available since 1947, though it is currently less emphasized than the data on households, which is available from 1967 through 2005. Tables based on these data are presented in Chapter 3.

Looking at the half-century trend, Chapter 3 shows that real median family cash income increased 1.9 percent from 1948 to 2000. This is less than the increases in mean per capita incomes that can be derived from the NIPAs— 2.2 percent in real per capita GDP and 2.3 percent in real per capita disposable personal income during that period. It is also less than the 2.1 percent increase in real mean family income that can be derived from the Census Bureau income data itself. Had the median income increased as fast as the Census mean—implying no change in the income distribution, which would result if incomes for all income levels rose at the same rate—the median family would have had over $6,000 more income in 2000, in that year's dollars.

Increasing inequality in income distribution can also be seen by comparing the 1948 and 2000 income shares shown in Chapter 3. The top 20 percent of families received 47.7 percent of all income in 2000, compared with 42.4 percent in 1948. The shares of each of the lower four quintiles declined. There is also a more comprehensive measure of income inequality known as the "Gini coefficient," which is discussed and shown in Chapter 3 and its notes and definitions; it ranges from 0 to 1.000 and rises when inequality increases. For families, the Gini coefficient rose from 0.371 in 1948 to 0.433 in 2000.

It can be argued that the postwar growth in real income and productivity required increasing rewards for the successful—increasing absolutely, and also increasing relative to other workers—so that the hypothetical potential increase calculated for the median family could never actually occur. This is not a question that can be definitively answered—certainly not based on the kind of data available here—but it might be noted that productivity increases were quite rapid during the earlier postwar years, *before* the trend toward a more unequal income distribution began. (Chapters 3 and 9)

"Households" is a broader and more comprehensive category than families, comprising family households, nonfamily households, and unrelated individuals. The Census Bureau has collected income data for households since 1967. These data are the basis for the reports on median income and poverty that are released and widely discussed in the late summer each year. These are also presented and described in Chapter 3 and its notes and definitions.

Data on households and on year-round, full-time workers from the Census Bureau's income and poverty reports are shown in Table B-3, which again uses 1967–2000 for the longer-run trend and compares the two most recent five-year recession-recovery periods.

The use of household and family data from the Census Bureau for longer-term comparisons has been criticized on the grounds that household and family size have been declining over time; because of this, the median household or family may have fewer earners and may support fewer people than in earlier years. To the extent that this is true, conclusions about changes in well being based on median income may be unwarranted. However, this is insignificant in the case of the five-year growth calculations shown here. From 1990 to 1995, according to data available on the Census Bureau Web site, average household size actually increased—from 2.63 to 2.65 persons. From 2000 to 2005, average size declined slightly, from 2.58 to 2.57 persons. Family size also would not be a factor in the comparison above between mean and median family incomes for the 1948–2000 period, since the increase in the mean is for the exact same families as the increase in the median.

From 1967 to 2000, real median household income grew at a 0.9 percent annual rate. This was actually the same rate as real (mean) compensation at nonfinancial corporations, as shown in Table B-2. This similarity of growth rates is far from a foregone conclusion, since the two series share only one component, though a major one—wages and salaries. Both measures are before taxes on wages and other income. Compensation includes fringe benefits, as men-

tioned above, but household income does not. Household income includes Social Security payments and other non-wage sources of income, such as welfare payments, interest, and dividends. See the notes and definitions for Chapter 3 for more information.

For the two recession-recovery periods, household income changes and median earnings changes for full-time workers can be compared with the real (mean) wages and salaries changes shown in Table B-1.

From 1990 to 1995, real wages and salaries as measured by the ECI deflated by PCE rose at a 0.4 percent rate. The ECI is a weighted average, which is a type of mean. It holds the occupational composition of employment constant, while the Census median measures reflect the actual changing composition of employment. In that period, median earnings and household income were stagnant and the poverty rate rose slightly.

From 2000 to 2005, the real ECI for wages and salaries was again up at an 0.4 percent annual rate, falling far short of productivity growth by more than can be accounted for by deflator differences and fringe benefits. Real median household income and real earnings for full-time male workers did even worse, declining at a rate of about half a percent. Only full-time female workers saw increases in real earnings. The poverty rate rose 1.3 percentage points.

It has been recently argued that median income and poverty lag behind the business cycle. Examination of Figures 3-1 and 3-2 will show that while this is indeed the case, the lags have been getting longer in recent years. Real household income finally rose in 2005, but the years 2000–2004 comprised the first span in which median income declined four years in a row.

Inflation and unemployment

A number of important price indicators are presented in *Business Statistics*, both in Chapter 8: Prices and Table 1-5, which shows chain-type price indexes for GDP and various subsectors. Users should note that price <u>indexes</u> measure the average <u>level</u> of prices, relative to some base year that is set to equal 100, while "inflation" is the annual percent <u>rate of change</u> in a price index.

Accurate measurement of prices is challenging in a dynamic economy. Frequently, biases have been identified in the most widely used price indicators, the official

Table B-3. Trend and Cycle in Household Income and Poverty

(Percent change, annual rate, except as noted.)

Classification	1967–2000	1990–1995	2000–2005
Real median household income	0.9	0.0	-0.5
Real median earnings of full-time, year-round workers			
Male	0.5	0.0	-0.4
Female	1.3	-0.1	0.5
Percent of population in poverty	[1]-2.9	[1]0.3	[1]1.3

[1]Percentage point difference over total period, not at an annual rate.

Consumer Price Index for All Urban Consumers (CPI-U) and its close relative, the Consumer Price Index for Urban Wage Earners and Clerical Workers (CPI-W). Improved methods to remove these biases are frequently introduced into the calculation of the indexes going forward, but the official indexes are not retroactively corrected. However, there are some alternative versions of the CPI that carry the current improved methodologies back for some historical period. These are presented in *Business Statistics*; see Tables 8-2 and 8-3 and their associated notes and definitions. One of these alternatives, the CPI-U-RS, is used by the Bureau of Labor Statistics to calculate historical values of real compensation (Chapter 9), and by the Census Bureau to calculate historical values of real median income (Chapter 3).

Because of this and other perceived shortcomings of the official CPIs, economists at the Federal Reserve, among others, pay particular attention to the chain-type price indexes for personal consumption expenditures in the NIPAs. The NIPA indexes use many of the same basic price observations that are collected for the CPIs. However, the NIPA indexes are defined to cover a somewhat broader universe of prices. In compiling the NIPA indexes, the Bureau of Economic Analysis processes the data in a more consistent fashion and regularly revises past data to correct biases. (See Table 1-5 and the notes and definitions to Chapter 1.)

Still, all of these indexes tell a similar story about the behavior of inflation over the postwar period. As Figure 8-1 in Chapter 8 shows, inflation was high in 1946 and 1947 as World War II price controls were dismantled and pent-up purchasing power from the war period was released. Prices declined in the 1949 recession but rose sharply in 1950 and 1951 with recovery and the outbreak of the Korean War. Inflation was negative again in 1955 in the aftermath of that war's end and the 1954 recession. Inflation rose during two recoveries in 1956–1957 and 1960, but fell back to about 1 percent—generally judged to represent price stability because of remaining and irremediable biases in the price indexes—in the slack years of 1961 and 1962.

However, as the 1960s progressed, the federal government embarked on a stimulative fiscal policy with the intent of attaining an unemployment rate lower than those observed in the 1950s and early 1960s. (Tables 10-3 and 10-4) As the buildup in military spending for the Vietnam War progressed, fiscal policy became even more stimulative, without any attempt to raise taxes or cut back on other spending until late in the decade. (Chapter 6) Monetary policy tended to support the fiscal policy. An attempt was made to hold wages and prices down using voluntary "guidelines" in the early 1960s, but the guidelines collapsed in 1966, and inflation continued to accelerate during the sustained period of high employment through 1969.

The 1970 recession failed to bring inflation down, and the 1971 recovery was weak. New moves to accelerate the recovery, including monetary stimulus and depreciation of the dollar, were undertaken. New price controls and guidelines were introduced, with some initial effect on inflation. But the 1972 decline in inflation was short-lived, followed by new highs as the price controls collapsed and commodity prices soared. The severe 1975–1976 recession provided only a temporary and incomplete respite from inflation, which soared to double digits in 1979 through 1981 with recovery and new commodity price shocks.

Finally, under the impact of a tough monetary policy that led to the 1981–1982 recession—the most severe of the postwar period—inflation ratcheted down to a core rate of about 4 percent during the 1982–1990 expansion. A recession in 1990 ushered in even lower inflation rates throughout the rest of the 1990s, despite the achievement in the late 1990s of the lowest unemployment rates since 1969.

As the above narrative indicates, the 1950s and 1960s were characterized by an apparent inverse relationship, often interpreted as a "trade-off," between inflation and high employment, with inflation falling as an apparent consequence of unemployment rising. By the 1970s, inflation became more stubborn and failed to respond proportionately and negatively to increases in unemployment. Indeed, at times inflation and unemployment rose together, a phenomenon known as "stagflation." This has often been ascribed to "supply shocks"—for example, bad harvests, oil embargoes, and OPEC price increases—which, unlike decreases in aggregate demand, tend to increase inflation even while depressing output. In retrospect, some supply shocks should perhaps be considered as delayed reactions to demand shocks. To give an important example, oil prices tend to increase when the dollar has declined, and they tend to fall during worldwide recessions—as they did in 1986. (See the general price data in Chapter 8, the oil price data in Chapter 11, and the data on the international value of the dollar in Table 13-6.) Since a decline in the dollar is an expected consequence of expansionary monetary policy, the resulting increase in the price of oil could be considered part of the inflationary effect of such a policy.

In attempting to explain stagflation, economists now take account of the role of expectations—especially worker expectations about future inflation—in maintaining the momentum of a given inflation rate even in the presence of unemployment. This mechanism is believed by many to explain the worsening of the tradeoff in the 1970s.

Many economists were again surprised by the combination of low unemployment and low inflation in the late 1990s. The surprise was greater among those economists who looked to the unemployment rate as the sole measure of resource utilization. In fact, the level of capacity utilization also plays a role in determining to what extent changes in aggregate demand affect prices and to what extent they lead to expanded volume of production instead. Capacity utilization measures are not available for all sectors of the economy, but the Federal Reserve Board does maintain utilization series for the industrial sector, as seen in Table 2-3. Average utilization of manufacturing capacity declined between the last three major business cycle peaks—from 1979 to 1989 and again from 1989 to

2000. This indicated less pressure on prices from one cycle to the next, helping to offset the effect of lower unemployment rates over the same intervals.

The issues involved in the relationships between inflation, economic growth, and unemployment are far from settled. Debate continues about the relative roles of monetary policy, tax rates and other aspects of fiscal policy, global competition, other supply considerations, labor market institutions, and expectations.

With respect to monetary policy, *Business Statistics* provides data on the monetary and reserve aggregates in Tables 12-1 through 12-3. Rates of change in money and reserves have provided increasingly inaccurate forecasts of inflation and are not widely considered to be valid indicators of the state of monetary policy any more. In fact, the Federal Reserve has discontinued publication of M3, the broadest monetary aggregate. The data on interest rates provided in Table 12-9—especially the federal funds rate, which is directly controlled by the Federal Reserve—are currently the subject of more attention in assessing the monetary policy stance. Table 12-9 now includes an estimate of the "real" (inflation-adjusted) federal funds rate. A real rate near or below zero suggests that Federal Reserve policy is stimulative and potentially inflationary, while high positive rates such as those observed in the early 1980s suggest contraction and disinflation. A market-based, longer-term real rate is included as well.

War and the economy

Figure 6-3 suggests the rather modest impact that federal spending on the wars in Afghanistan and Iraq is likely to have had on the U.S. economy as of fiscal year 2005. Relative to the value of GDP, defense spending increased from 3.0 percent during the period 1999–2001 to 4.0 percent in 2005, but was not much higher than at the low point of the post-World-War-II demobilization (3.5 percent). It was lower than Korean War (1950–1953) levels, Vietnam War (1964–1975) levels, and 1980s defense buildup levels. Its increase was not as rapid as the 1980s buildup, which went from 4.6 percent of GDP in 1980 to 6.1 percent in 1983.

(The 1990–1991 Gulf War was largely financed by U.S. allies, leading to a slight *decline* in the defense/GDP ratio.)

Business cycle comparisons

Business Statistics now also provides expanded data on earlier cyclical recoveries that users may compare with current data. The reference dates for business cycles from 1927 to date are shown in the notes and definitions for Table 1-8. Monthly and quarterly data for major indicators such as output, employment, and unemployment for the entire postwar period are shown in Chapters 19 and 20. In Chapters 18, 19, and 20, annual data are provided from 1929 through 1949, and annual data for 1950 through 2005 are shown throughout the earlier chapters.

...and more

This article has provided examples of the kinds of data analysis newly possible with this expanded version of *Business Statistics*. Many other possibilities are available. Detail by industry is shown in Chapters 2, 9, 10, and 15 through 17. State and regional detail is shown in Chapter 21. Information about business and consumer balance sheets can be found in Chapter 12.

The editor anticipates that users will find this volume even more useful than previous editions, and welcomes input on ways to make it even more helpful. The editor can be contacted via e-mail at <cstrawser@bernan.com>.

ENDNOTES

[1]Some economists assert that 2000 does not represent a sustainable level of economic activity. One definition of sustainability is a level of activity that does not cause inflation to accelerate. There was some rise in inflation in 2000, but it was modest compared with the acceleration in 1948. (See Table 8-3.) If both peaks were somewhat above sustainability, it would not necessarily invalidate the calculation of growth rates between them.

[2]In earlier years, it would not have been surprising to have a full peak-to-peak cycle included within a 5-year span. Of the 8 complete cycles between 1945 and 1981, 6 were less than 60 months from peak to peak. However, the 2 complete cycles since that time lasted 108 months (July 1981 to July 1990) and 128 months (July 1990 to March 2001). After the severe 1981–1982 recession, which wrung out the inflation of the 1970s, recessions have become less frequent and changes in both directions have become less volatile. See the business cycle chronology in the notes and definitions for Chapter 1 and Figures 1-1, 1-3, 2-1, and 8-1.

These notes provide general information about the data in Tables 1-1 through 21-2. Specific notes with information about data sources, definitions, methodology, revisions, and sources of additional information follow the tables in each chapter.

Main divisions of the book

The tables are divided into four main parts:

Part A (Tables 1-1 through 13-6) pertains to the U.S. economy as a whole. Generally, each table presents annual averages back to 1950, or as far back as available, and quarterly or monthly values for the most recent year or years. (Full quarterly and monthly histories and annual averages before 1950 for major series are shown in Part C.) Some chapters present data for the United States only in aggregate, while others—such as the chapters concerning industrial production and capacity utilization (Chapter 2), capital expenditures (Chapter 5), profits (Chapter 9), and employment, hours, and earnings (Chapter 10)—also have detail for major industry groups.

Data by industry on industrial production and capacity utilization (Tables 2-2 and 2-3), capital expenditures (Table 5-11), profits (Table 9-6), and payroll employment, hours, and earnings (Tables 10-7 through 10-12) are classified using the new North American Industry Classification System (NAICS), as far back as such data are made available by the source agencies. In the case of corporate profits, for which the NAICS data do not go back far, data for preceding years using the older classification system (Standard Industrial Classification, or SIC) are shown with an overlap.

Part B focuses on the individual industries that together produce the gross domestic product (GDP).

- Chapter 14 provides an overview of NAICS, presenting the overall structure of the classification system, the definition of each major industry group, and the approximate relationships of each group to the industries in SIC.
- Chapter 15 contains data on value added (GDP) by industry, using NAICS for the years 1998 through 2005 and SIC for the years 1987 through 2000.
- Chapter 16 provides further detail on payroll employment, hours, and earnings classified according to NAICS.
- Chapter 17 presents various data sets for key economic sectors. Some of the tables are based on definitions of products, rather than of producing establishments, and are valid for either classification system. This is the case for Tables 17-1, Petroleum and Petroleum Products; 17-2, New Construction; 17-3, Housing Starts and Building Permits, New House Sales, and Prices; and 17-8, Motor Vehicle Sales and Inventories. Tables 17-4 through 17-7 and 17-9, 17-11,

and 17-12, which cover manufacturing and retail and wholesale trade, show overlapping data for the year 1992 using the old and new classification systems. This preserves the old-basis historical record for the years prior to 1992. Tables 17-15 through 17-17 for services industries also present data on the NAICS basis, while Tables 17-13 and 17-14 show overlapping data for earlier years using SIC.

The 1987 SIC is published in the *Standard Industrial Classification Manual, 1987*, by the Executive Office of the President, Office of Management and Budget (Washington, DC: U.S. Government Printing Office, 1988). NAICS is fully described in U.S. Office of Management and Budget's *North American Industry Classification System: United States, 2002*, which was published by Bernan Press in 2003. Additional information is available on the Census Bureau Web site <http://www.census.gov>.

Part C presents further historical detail. Chapter 18 shows selected data for the years 1929 through 1948. These are shown on an annual basis only, as many of the series are not available in quarterly or monthly detail. Chapters 19 and 20 present quarterly or monthly data back to the earliest postwar year available for major series, along with available annual data for 1946 through 1949; the remaining annual values are shown in Part A.

Part D presents data by state and region, calculated by the Bureau of Economic Analysis; data are available on an annual basis only. Table 21-1 contains data on GDP and Table 21-2 shows data on personal income, population, and employment.

Characteristics of the tables and the data

The subtitles or column headings for the data tables normally indicate that the data are *seasonally adjusted* or *not seasonally adjusted* or *at a seasonally adjusted annual rate*. These headings refer to the monthly or quarterly data, rather than the annual data. Annual data by definition require no seasonal adjustment. Annual values are normally calculated as totals or averages (as appropriate) of unadjusted data. Such annual values are shown in either or both adjusted or unadjusted data columns.

Seasonal adjustment removes from the time series the average impact of variations that normally occur at about the same time each year, due to occurrences such as weather, holidays, and tax payment dates.

A simplified example of the process of seasonal adjustment, or deseasonalizing, can indicate its importance in the interpretation of economic time series. Statisticians compare actual monthly data for a number of years with "moving average" trends of the monthly data for the 12 months centered on each month's data. For example, they may find that in November, sales values are usually about 95 percent of the moving average, while in December, usual sales values are 110 percent of the average. Suppose that actual November sales in the current year are $100 and December sales are $105. The seasonally adjusted value for November will be $105 ($100/0.95) while the value for December will be $95 ($105/1.10). Thus, an apparent increase in the unadjusted data turns out to be a decrease when adjusted for the usual seasonal pattern.

The statistical method used to achieve the seasonal adjustment may vary from one data set to another. Many of the data are adjusted by a computer method known as X-12-ARIMA, developed by the Census Bureau. A description of the method is found in "New Capabilities and Methods of the X-12-ARIMA Seasonal Adjustment Program," by David F. Findley, Brian C. Monsell, William R. Bell, Mark C. Otto and Bor-Chung Chen (*Journal of Business and Economic Statistics*, April 1998). This article can be downloaded from the Census Bureau Web site at <http://www.census.gov>.

Data presented at *annual rates* show values at their annual equivalents—the values that would be registered if the rate of activity measured during a particular month or quarter were maintained for a full year. Specifically, seasonally adjusted monthly values are multiplied by 12 and quarterly values by 4 to yield seasonally adjusted annual rates. See the preceding article, "Using the Data," for an explanation of annual *growth* rates.

Indexes. Aggregate measures of prices and quantities are expressed in the form of indexes in many of the data sets presented in this volume. The most basic and familiar form of index, the original Consumer Price Index, begins with a "market basket" of goods and services purchased in a base period. Each component of the market basket is moved forward by the observed change in the price of the item selected to represent that component. These weighted component prices—the quantities in the base period repriced in the prices of subsequent periods—are aggregated, divided by the base period aggregate, and multiplied by 100 to provide an index number. An index calculated in this way is known as a Laspeyres index. In general, economists believe that Laspeyres price indexes tend to have an upward bias, showing more price increase than if account were taken of consumers' ability to change spending patterns and maintain the same level of satisfaction in response to changing relative prices.

A *Paasche index* is one that uses the weights of the current period. Since the weights in the Paasche index change in each period, Paasche indexes only provide acceptable indications of change relative to the base period. Paasche indexes for two periods neither of which is the base period cannot be correctly compared: for example, a Paasche price index might change even if no prices changed because of a change in the composition of output toward prices that had previously increased more from the base period. When the national income and product account (NIPA) measures of real output were Laspeyres measures, using the weights of a single base year, the implicit deflators (current-dollar values divided by constant-dollar values) were Paasche indexes. Just as Laspeyres price indexes are upward-biased, Paasche price indexes are downward-biased because they overestimate consumers' ability to maintain the same level of satisfaction by changing spending patterns.

In recent years, government statisticians (with the aid of elaborate computer programs) have developed measures of real output and prices that minimize bias by using the weights of both periods and updating the weights for each period-to-period comparison. Such measures are described as chained indexes and are used in the NIPAs, the index of industrial production, and an experimental consumer price index. Chained measures are discussed more fully in the notes and definitions for Chapter 1, Chapter 2, and Chapter 8. The "Fisher Ideal" index, the "superlative" index, and the "Tornqvist formula" are all types of chained indexes that use weights for both periods under comparison.

Detail may not sum to totals due to rounding. Since annual data are typically calculated by source agencies as the annual totals or averages of not-seasonally-adjusted data, they therefore will not be precisely equal to the annual totals or averages of monthly seasonally-adjusted data. Seasonal adjustment procedures are typically multiplicative rather than additive, and as a result, seasonally-adjusted data may not add or average to the annual figure.

Most of the data in this volume are from federal government sources and may be reproduced freely. A few series are from private sources and are used with permission; further use may be subject to copyright restrictions. A list of data sources is shown below.

The tables in this volume incorporate data revisions and corrections released by the source agencies through November 2006.

Data sources

Most of the data in this volume are from the government agencies and private sources listed below. The specific source(s) for each individual data set is identified at the beginning of the notes and definitions for the relevant data pages.

Board of Governors of the Federal Reserve System
20th Street & Constitution Avenue NW
Washington, DC 20551

Data Inquiries and Publication Sales:
    Publications Services
    Mail Stop 127
    Board of Governors of the Federal Reserve System
    Washington, DC 20551
    Phone: (202) 452-3245

Quarterly Publication:
    As of 2006, the *Federal Reserve Bulletin* is available free of charge and only on the Federal Reserve Web site.

URL:
    http://www.federalreserve.gov

Bureau of Economic Analysis (BEA)
U.S. Department of Commerce
1441 L Street, NW
Washington, DC 20230

Data Inquiries:
Public Information Office
Phone: (202) 606-9900

Monthly Publication:
Survey of Current Business
Available by subscription; call (202) 512-1800 or visit
http://bookstore.gpo.gov

URL:
http://www.bea.gov

Bureau of Labor Statistics (BLS)
U.S. Department of Labor
2 Massachusetts Avenue NE
Washington, DC 20212-0001
(202) 691-5200

URL:
http://www.bls.gov

Data Inquiries:
Blsdata_staff@bls.gov

Monthly Publications:
Monthly Labor Review
Employment and Earnings
Compensation and Working Conditions
Producer Price Indexes
CPI Detailed Report
Available by subscription from the Superintendent
of Documents, Government Printing Office
(see address for the Superintendent of Documents).

Census Bureau
U.S. Department of Commerce
4700 Silver Hill Road
Washington, DC 20233

URL:
http://www.census.gov

Ordering Data Products:
Call Center: (301) 763-INFO (4636)

E-mail Questions:
webmaster@census.gov

E-sales:
http://www.census.gov/mp/www/censtore.html

Conference Board, The
845 Third Avenue
New York, NY 10022

URL:
http://www.tcb-indicators.org

Monthly Publication:
Business Cycle Indicators Report, available by
subscription from the address listed above.

Employment and Training Administration
U.S. Department of Labor
200 Constitution Avenue NW
Washington, DC 20210
(877) US2-JOBS

URLs:
http://www.doleta.gov
http://www.itsc.state.md.us

Energy Information Administration (EIA)
U.S. Department of Energy
1000 Independence Avenue SW
Washington, DC 20585

Data Inquiries and Publications:
National Energy Information Center
Phone: (202) 586-8800
E-mail: infoctr@eia.doe.gov

Monthly Publication:
Monthly Energy Review, as of 2007 available only on
the EIA Web site, free of charge.

URL:
http://www.eia.doe.gov

National Agricultural Statistics Service (NASS)
U.S. Department of Agriculture
14th Street & Independence Avenue SW
Washington, DC 20250

Data Inquiries:
Information Hotline: (800) 727-9540 or (202) 720-3878

Publication Sales:
Phone: (800) 999-6779
Fax: (703) 834-0110

URL:
http://www.usda.gov/nass/

To order government publications
Superintendent of Documents
Government Printing Office
Washington, DC 20402
(202) 512-1800

URL:
http://bookstore.gpo.gov

Office of Federal Housing Enterprise Oversight
(OFHEO)
1700 G Street NW
4th Floor
Washington, DC 20552
(202) 414-3800

URL:
http://www.ofheo.gov

U.S. Department of the Treasury
Office of International Affairs
Treasury International Capital System

URL:
http://www.treas.gov/tic

PART A

THE U.S. ECONOMY

CHAPTER 1: NATIONAL INCOME AND PRODUCT AND CYCLICAL INDICATORS

Section 1a: Gross Domestic Product: Values, Quantities, and Prices

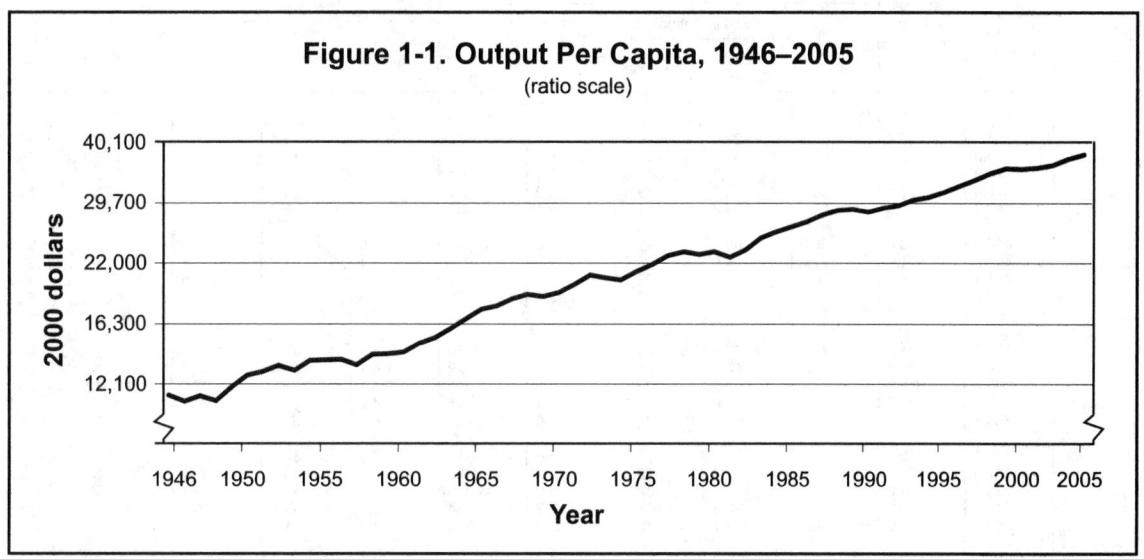

Figure 1-1. Output Per Capita, 1946–2005
(ratio scale)

- Output of goods and services in the United States, expressed in constant 2000-value dollars to remove the effect of inflation (real gross domestic product, or GDP), rose from $1.64 trillion in 1948 to $9.82 trillion in 2000—comparable high points in the business cycle. (Tables 1-2 and 19-2) This was a nearly sixfold increase in real value over the 52-year period, with an average growth rate of 3.5 percent per year. From 2000 to 2005, the rate of annual growth was 2.4 percent.

- Real GDP per capita—the constant-dollar average value of production for each man, woman, and child in the population—rose from $11,206 (2000 dollars) in 1948 to $34,759 in 2000, a rate of 2.2 percent per year. From 2000 to 2005, the annual growth rate was 1.4 percent. (Tables 1-7 and 19-7) This value is charted in the figure above. It is graphed on a "ratio scale," with equal vertical distances signifying equal percent changes.

- The figure above indicates that growth is not always smooth or uninterrupted. There are times when output levels off or declines, marking the periods identified as recessions in economic activity. (Table 1-8 and the associated notes and definitions)

- Measured in current dollars, the value of GDP rose even faster, reflecting increases in the average price level. Current-dollar GDP rose from $269 billion in 1948 to over $12 trillion in 2005. (Tables 1-1 and 19-1) The price level in 2005 was nearly 7 times that in 1948, reflecting an average inflation rate of 3.4 percent per year. (Tables 1-5 and 19-5) Annual rates of increase in the chain-type price index for GDP ranged from 9 percent or more in 1947, 1974–1975, and 1980–1981 to changes of no more than 1.2 percent in 1949–1950, 1954, 1959, 1961, 1963, and 1998. Over the last 10 years, inflation averaged 2.0 percent per year.

Table 1-1. Gross Domestic Product

(Billions of dollars, quarterly data are at seasonally adjusted annual rates.)   NIPA Tables 1.1.5, 5.6.5A, 5.6.5B

Year and quarter	Gross domestic product	Personal consump-tion expen-ditures	Gross private domestic investment						Exports and imports of goods and services			Government consumption expenditures and gross investment		
			Total	Fixed investment		Change in private inventories			Net exports	Exports	Imports	Total	Federal	State and local
				Nonresi-dential	Residential	Nonfarm	Farm							
1950	293.8	192.2	54.1	27.8	20.5	5.9	-0.1		0.7	12.4	11.6	46.8	26.0	20.7
1951	339.3	208.5	60.2	31.8	18.4	8.9	1.0		2.5	17.1	14.6	68.1	45.1	23.0
1952	358.3	219.5	54.0	31.9	18.6	2.1	1.4		1.2	16.5	15.3	83.6	59.2	24.4
1953	379.4	233.1	56.4	35.1	19.4	1.2	0.7		-0.7	15.3	16.0	90.6	64.4	26.1
1954	380.4	240.0	53.8	34.7	21.1	-2.1	0.2		0.4	15.8	15.4	86.2	57.3	28.9
1955	414.8	258.8	69.0	39.0	25.0	5.6	-0.6		0.5	17.7	17.2	86.5	54.9	31.6
1956	437.5	271.7	72.0	44.5	23.6	4.9	-1.0		2.4	21.3	18.9	91.4	56.7	34.7
1957	461.1	286.9	70.5	47.5	22.2	0.7	0.1		4.1	24.0	19.9	99.7	61.3	38.3
1958	467.2	296.2	64.5	42.5	22.3	-2.3	2.0		0.5	20.6	20.0	106.0	63.8	42.2
1959	506.6	317.6	78.5	46.5	28.1	5.5	-1.6		0.4	22.7	22.3	110.0	65.4	44.7
1960	526.4	331.7	78.9	49.4	26.3	2.7	0.6		4.2	27.0	22.8	111.6	64.1	47.5
1961	544.7	342.1	78.2	48.8	26.4	2.1	0.9		4.9	27.6	22.7	119.5	67.9	51.6
1962	585.6	363.3	88.1	53.1	29.0	5.5	0.6		4.1	29.1	25.0	130.1	75.3	54.9
1963	617.7	382.7	93.8	56.0	32.1	5.1	0.5		4.9	31.1	26.1	136.4	76.9	59.5
1964	663.6	411.4	102.1	63.0	34.3	6.0	-1.2		6.9	35.0	28.1	143.2	78.5	64.8
1965	719.1	443.8	118.2	74.8	34.2	8.4	0.8		5.6	37.1	31.5	151.5	80.4	71.0
1966	787.8	480.9	131.3	85.4	32.3	14.1	-0.5		3.9	40.9	37.1	171.8	92.5	79.2
1967	832.6	507.8	128.6	86.4	32.4	9.0	0.9		3.6	43.5	39.9	192.7	104.8	87.9
1968	910.0	558.0	141.2	93.4	38.7	7.7	1.4		1.4	47.9	46.6	209.4	111.4	98.0
1969	984.6	605.2	156.4	104.7	42.6	9.2	0.0		1.4	51.9	50.5	221.5	113.4	108.2
1970	1 038.5	648.5	152.4	109.0	41.4	2.8	-0.8		4.0	59.7	55.8	233.8	113.5	120.3
1971	1 127.1	701.9	178.2	114.1	55.8	6.6	1.7		0.6	63.0	62.3	246.5	113.7	132.8
1972	1 238.3	770.6	207.6	128.8	69.7	8.8	0.3		-3.4	70.8	74.2	263.5	119.7	143.8
1973	1 382.7	852.4	244.5	153.3	75.3	14.4	1.5		4.1	95.3	91.2	281.7	122.5	159.2
1974	1 500.0	933.4	249.4	169.5	66.0	16.8	-2.8		-0.8	126.7	127.5	317.9	134.6	183.4
1975	1 638.3	1 034.4	230.2	173.7	62.7	-9.6	3.4		16.0	138.7	122.7	357.7	149.1	208.7
1976	1 825.3	1 151.9	292.0	192.4	82.5	18.0	-0.8		-1.6	149.5	151.1	383.0	159.7	223.3
1977	2 030.9	1 278.6	361.3	228.7	110.3	17.8	4.5		-23.1	159.4	182.4	414.1	175.4	238.7
1978	2 294.7	1 428.5	438.0	280.6	131.6	24.4	1.4		-25.4	186.9	212.3	453.6	190.9	262.6
1979	2 563.3	1 592.2	492.9	333.9	141.0	14.4	3.6		-22.5	230.1	252.7	500.8	210.6	290.2
1980	2 789.5	1 757.1	479.3	362.4	123.2	-0.2	-6.1		-13.1	280.8	293.8	566.2	243.8	322.4
1981	3 128.4	1 941.1	572.4	420.0	122.6	21.0	8.8		-12.5	305.2	317.8	627.5	280.2	347.3
1982	3 255.0	2 077.3	517.2	426.5	105.7	-20.7	5.8		-20.0	283.2	303.2	680.5	310.8	369.7
1983	3 536.7	2 290.6	564.3	417.2	152.9	9.6	-15.4		-51.7	277.0	328.6	733.5	342.9	390.5
1984	3 933.2	2 503.3	735.6	489.6	180.6	59.7	5.7		-102.7	302.4	405.1	797.0	374.4	422.6
1985	4 220.3	2 720.3	736.2	526.2	188.2	16.1	5.8		-115.2	302.0	417.2	879.0	412.8	466.2
1986	4 462.8	2 899.7	746.5	519.8	220.1	8.0	-1.5		-132.7	320.5	453.3	949.3	438.6	510.7
1987	4 739.5	3 100.2	785.0	524.1	233.7	33.6	-6.4		-145.2	363.9	509.1	999.5	460.1	539.4
1988	5 103.8	3 353.6	821.6	563.8	239.3	30.4	-11.9		-110.4	444.1	554.5	1 039.0	462.3	576.7
1989	5 484.4	3 598.5	874.9	607.7	239.5	27.7	0.0		-88.2	503.3	591.5	1 099.1	482.2	616.9
1990	5 803.1	3 839.9	861.0	622.4	224.0	12.2	2.4		-78.0	552.4	630.3	1 180.2	508.3	671.9
1991	5 995.9	3 986.1	802.9	598.2	205.1	0.9	-1.3		-27.5	596.8	624.3	1 234.4	527.7	706.7
1992	6 337.7	4 235.3	864.8	612.1	236.3	10.1	6.2		-33.2	635.3	668.6	1 271.0	533.9	737.0
1993	6 657.4	4 477.9	953.4	666.6	266.0	27.0	-6.2		-65.0	655.8	720.9	1 291.2	525.2	766.0
1994	7 072.2	4 743.3	1 097.1	731.4	301.9	51.8	12.1		-93.6	720.9	814.5	1 325.5	519.1	806.3
1995	7 397.7	4 975.8	1 144.0	810.0	302.8	42.2	-11.1		-91.4	812.2	903.6	1 369.2	519.2	850.0
1996	7 816.9	5 256.8	1 240.3	875.4	334.1	22.1	8.6		-96.2	868.6	964.8	1 416.0	527.4	888.6
1997	8 304.3	5 547.4	1 389.8	968.7	349.1	68.8	3.2		-101.6	955.3	1 056.9	1 468.7	530.9	937.8
1998	8 747.0	5 879.5	1 509.1	1 052.6	385.8	69.4	1.4		-159.9	955.9	1 115.9	1 518.3	530.4	987.9
1999	9 268.4	6 282.5	1 625.7	1 133.9	424.9	69.6	-2.7		-260.5	991.2	1 251.7	1 620.8	555.8	1 065.0
2000	9 817.0	6 739.4	1 735.5	1 232.1	446.9	57.8	-1.3		-379.5	1 096.3	1 475.8	1 721.6	578.8	1 142.8
2001	10 128.0	7 055.0	1 614.3	1 176.8	469.3	-31.7	0.0		-367.0	1 032.8	1 399.8	1 825.6	612.9	1 212.8
2002	10 469.6	7 350.7	1 582.1	1 066.3	503.9	14.4	-2.5		-424.4	1 005.9	1 430.3	1 961.1	679.7	1 281.5
2003	10 960.8	7 703.6	1 664.1	1 077.4	572.4	13.9	0.4		-499.4	1 040.8	1 540.2	2 092.5	756.4	1 336.0
2004	11 712.5	8 211.5	1 888.0	1 155.3	675.3	49.0	8.4		-613.2	1 178.1	1 791.4	2 226.2	825.9	1 400.3
2005	12 455.8	8 742.4	2 057.4	1 265.7	770.4	21.0	0.3		-716.7	1 303.1	2 019.9	2 372.8	878.3	1 494.4
2003														
1st quarter	10 705.6	7 548.1	1 606.4	1 044.0	539.3	19.1	3.9		-499.3	1 012.4	1 511.7	2 050.3	725.9	1 324.4
2nd quarter	10 831.8	7 628.4	1 617.1	1 067.4	553.2	-3.8	0.3		-501.3	1 010.8	1 512.1	2 087.7	762.2	1 325.5
3rd quarter	11 086.1	7 782.6	1 690.5	1 093.3	585.4	12.2	-0.4		-495.2	1 040.7	1 535.9	2 108.2	764.8	1 343.3
4th quarter	11 219.5	7 855.3	1 742.3	1 104.8	611.6	28.1	-2.2		-501.8	1 099.1	1 600.9	2 123.7	772.8	1 350.9
2004														
1st quarter	11 430.9	8 018.0	1 781.9	1 112.1	631.8	32.2	5.8		-543.4	1 135.1	1 678.5	2 174.4	808.2	1 366.3
2nd quarter	11 649.3	8 148.1	1 892.2	1 137.6	675.2	56.4	22.9		-606.2	1 166.3	1 772.5	2 215.1	823.8	1 391.4
3rd quarter	11 799.4	8 265.0	1 917.7	1 170.0	692.9	46.6	8.2		-630.7	1 185.3	1 815.9	2 247.3	838.4	1 409.0
4th quarter	11 970.3	8 414.8	1 960.2	1 201.5	701.4	60.7	-3.4		-672.7	1 225.8	1 898.5	2 268.0	833.2	1 434.8
2005														
1st quarter	12 173.2	8 519.7	2 013.5	1 230.0	724.1	58.5	0.8		-676.2	1 254.0	1 930.2	2 316.2	862.9	1 453.3
2nd quarter	12 346.1	8 674.6	2 009.1	1 251.8	764.9	-0.9	-6.7		-686.4	1 293.8	1 980.2	2 348.9	868.4	1 480.5
3rd quarter	12 573.5	8 847.3	2 052.6	1 276.7	791.2	-16.6	1.3		-728.8	1 312.4	2 041.2	2 402.4	895.8	1 506.6
4th quarter	12 730.5	8 927.8	2 154.5	1 304.3	801.5	42.8	5.8		-775.4	1 352.4	2 127.8	2 423.6	886.2	1 537.4

Table 1-2. Real Gross Domestic Product

(Billions of chained [2000] dollars, quarterly data are at seasonally adjusted annual rates.) **NIPA Tables 1.1.6, 5.6.6A, 5.6.6B**

Year and quarter	Gross domestic product	Personal consumption expenditures	Gross private domestic investment						Exports and imports of goods and services			Government consumption expenditures and gross investment			Residual
			Total	Fixed investment		Change in private inventories		Net exports	Exports	Imports	Total	Federal	State and local	
				Nonresidential	Residential	Nonfarm	Farm								
1950	1 777.3	1 152.8	227.7	...	...	20.8	-0.3	...	50.3	59.3	405.3	...	...	0.5
1951	1 915.0	1 171.2	228.3	...	...	25.8	1.7	...	61.7	61.7	553.5	...	...	-38.0
1952	1 988.3	1 208.2	206.5	...	...	6.7	2.5	...	59.0	67.1	666.3	...	...	-84.6
1953	2 079.5	1 265.7	216.2	...	...	4.1	1.6	...	55.1	73.4	713.9	...	...	-98.0
1954	2 065.4	1 291.4	206.1	...	...	-6.8	0.4	...	57.7	69.8	665.1	...	...	-85.1
1955	2 212.8	1 385.5	256.2	...	...	17.0	-1.5	...	63.9	78.2	640.7	...	...	-55.3
1956	2 255.8	1 425.4	252.7	...	...	14.2	-2.6	...	74.4	84.5	641.0	...	...	-53.2
1957	2 301.1	1 460.7	241.7	...	...	2.2	0.4	...	80.9	88.1	669.5	...	...	-63.6
1958	2 279.2	1 472.3	221.7	...	...	-7.0	4.7	...	70.0	92.3	690.9	...	...	-83.4
1959	2 441.3	1 554.6	266.7	...	...	17.9	-3.8	...	77.2	101.9	714.3	...	...	-69.6
1960	2 501.8	1 597.4	266.6	...	...	8.8	1.4	...	90.6	103.3	715.4	...	...	-64.9
1961	2 560.0	1 630.3	264.9	...	...	7.0	2.1	...	91.1	102.6	751.3	...	...	-75.0
1962	2 715.2	1 711.1	298.4	...	...	18.3	1.4	...	95.7	114.3	797.6	...	...	-73.3
1963	2 834.0	1 781.6	318.5	...	...	17.0	1.2	...	102.5	117.3	818.1	...	...	-69.4
1964	2 998.6	1 888.4	344.7	...	...	19.7	-3.1	...	114.6	123.6	836.1	...	...	-61.6
1965	3 191.1	2 007.7	393.1	...	...	27.4	2.0	...	117.8	136.7	861.3	...	...	-52.1
1966	3 399.1	2 121.8	427.7	...	...	45.2	-1.1	...	126.0	157.1	937.1	...	...	-56.4
1967	3 484.6	2 185.0	408.1	...	...	28.4	2.1	...	128.9	168.5	1 008.9	...	...	-77.8
1968	3 652.7	2 310.5	431.9	...	...	23.7	3.3	...	139.0	193.6	1 040.5	...	...	-75.6
1969	3 765.4	2 396.4	457.1	...	...	27.8	0.0	...	145.7	204.6	1 038.0	...	...	-67.2
1970	3 771.9	2 451.9	427.1	...	...	7.8	-1.9	...	161.4	213.4	1 012.9	...	...	-68.0
1971	3 898.6	2 545.5	475.7	...	...	18.5	3.3	...	164.1	224.7	990.8	...	...	-52.8
1972	4 105.0	2 701.3	532.1	...	...	24.2	0.3	...	176.5	250.0	983.5	...	...	-38.4
1973	4 341.5	2 833.8	594.4	...	...	36.6	1.5	...	209.7	261.6	980.0	...	...	-14.8
1974	4 319.6	2 812.3	550.6	...	...	35.1	-3.6	...	226.3	255.7	1 004.7	...	...	-18.6
1975	4 311.2	2 876.9	453.1	...	...	-19.2	4.7	...	224.9	227.3	1 027.4	...	...	-43.8
1976	4 540.9	3 035.5	544.7	...	...	34.0	-1.3	...	234.7	271.7	1 031.9	...	...	-34.2
1977	4 750.5	3 164.1	627.0	...	...	32.1	5.9	...	240.3	301.4	1 043.3	...	...	-22.8
1978	5 015.0	3 303.1	702.6	...	...	40.9	1.7	...	265.7	327.6	1 074.0	...	...	-2.8
1979	5 173.4	3 383.4	725.0	...	...	21.5	3.5	...	292.0	333.0	1 094.1	...	...	11.9
1980	5 161.7	3 374.1	645.3	...	...	0.0	-5.8	...	323.5	310.9	1 115.4	...	...	14.3
1981	5 291.7	3 422.2	704.9	...	...	25.5	8.2	...	327.4	319.1	1 125.6	...	...	30.7
1982	5 189.3	3 470.3	606.0	...	...	-24.6	6.1	...	302.4	315.0	1 145.4	...	...	-19.8
1983	5 423.8	3 668.6	662.5	...	...	10.2	-14.2	...	294.6	354.8	1 187.3	...	...	-34.4
1984	5 813.6	3 863.3	857.7	...	...	66.5	5.1	...	318.7	441.1	1 227.0	...	...	-12.0
1985	6 053.7	4 064.0	849.7	...	...	17.5	5.7	...	328.3	469.8	1 312.5	...	...	-31.0
1986	6 263.6	4 228.9	843.9	...	...	10.1	-1.8	...	353.7	510.0	1 392.5	...	...	-45.4
1987	6 475.1	4 369.8	870.0	...	...	37.7	-7.4	...	391.8	540.2	1 426.7	...	...	-43.0
1988	6 742.7	4 546.9	890.5	...	...	32.7	-10.7	...	454.6	561.4	1 445.1	...	...	-33.0
1989	6 981.4	4 675.0	926.2	...	...	28.8	0.0	...	506.8	586.0	1 482.5	...	...	-23.1
1990	7 112.5	4 770.3	895.1	595.1	298.9	13.2	2.1	-54.7	552.5	607.1	1 530.0	659.1	868.4	-91.1
1991	7 100.5	4 778.4	822.2	563.2	270.2	1.0	-1.5	-14.6	589.1	603.7	1 547.2	658.0	886.8	-96.0
1992	7 336.6	4 934.8	889.0	581.3	307.6	10.3	5.8	-15.9	629.7	645.6	1 555.3	646.6	906.5	-89.1
1993	7 532.7	5 099.8	968.3	631.9	332.7	27.7	-6.1	-52.1	650.0	702.1	1 541.1	619.6	919.5	-78.6
1994	7 835.5	5 290.7	1 099.6	689.9	364.8	52.0	11.2	-79.4	706.5	785.9	1 541.3	596.4	943.3	-63.7
1995	8 031.7	5 433.5	1 134.0	762.5	353.1	41.3	-10.6	-71.0	778.2	849.1	1 549.7	580.3	968.3	-51.1
1996	8 328.9	5 619.4	1 234.3	833.6	381.3	21.7	6.8	-79.6	843.4	923.0	1 564.9	573.5	990.5	-38.5
1997	8 703.5	5 831.8	1 387.7	934.2	388.6	68.5	2.9	-104.6	943.7	1 048.3	1 594.0	567.6	1 025.9	-23.8
1998	9 066.9	6 125.8	1 524.1	1 037.8	418.3	71.2	1.4	-203.7	966.5	1 170.3	1 624.4	561.2	1 063.0	-14.6
1999	9 470.3	6 438.6	1 642.6	1 133.3	443.6	71.5	-3.0	-296.2	1 008.2	1 304.4	1 686.9	573.7	1 113.2	-5.8
2000	9 817.0	6 739.4	1 735.5	1 232.1	446.9	57.8	-1.3	-379.5	1 096.3	1 475.8	1 721.6	578.8	1 142.8	0.2
2001	9 890.7	6 910.4	1 598.4	1 180.5	448.5	-31.8	0.0	-399.1	1 036.7	1 435.8	1 780.3	601.4	1 179.0	1.6
2002	10 048.8	7 099.3	1 557.1	1 071.5	469.9	15.2	-2.5	-471.3	1 013.3	1 484.6	1 858.8	643.4	1 215.4	3.0
2003	10 301.0	7 295.3	1 613.1	1 081.8	509.4	14.0	0.4	-518.9	1 026.1	1 545.0	1 904.8	687.1	1 217.8	3.4
2004	10 703.5	7 577.1	1 770.6	1 145.8	559.9	47.0	6.1	-590.9	1 120.4	1 711.3	1 940.6	716.6	1 223.9	0.4
2005	11 048.6	7 841.2	1 866.3	1 223.8	608.0	19.6	0.2	-619.2	1 196.1	1 815.3	1 958.0	727.5	1 230.4	-10.5
2003														
1st quarter	10 126.0	7 184.9	1 561.8	1 047.5	484.1	19.2	4.8	-507.2	1 003.3	1 510.5	1 879.3	662.5	1 216.9	7.2
2nd quarter	10 212.7	7 249.3	1 574.4	1 074.5	496.3	-3.2	0.4	-526.9	999.0	1 525.9	1 907.5	693.0	1 214.4	6.9
3rd quarter	10 398.7	7 352.9	1 639.7	1 098.8	521.8	12.0	-1.2	-513.8	1 026.3	1 540.0	1 914.5	693.7	1 220.8	-0.5
4th quarter	10 467.0	7 394.3	1 676.5	1 106.5	535.2	28.1	-2.4	-527.8	1 075.8	1 603.6	1 918.0	699.0	1 219.0	0.9
2004														
1st quarter	10 566.3	7 479.8	1 696.4	1 111.2	539.2	32.1	3.9	-548.5	1 094.8	1 643.2	1 931.8	711.3	1 220.4	1.4
2nd quarter	10 671.6	7 534.4	1 781.9	1 130.7	564.1	54.5	17.9	-593.9	1 111.3	1 705.2	1 942.6	715.7	1 226.8	4.9
3rd quarter	10 753.3	7 607.1	1 790.8	1 158.8	568.6	44.8	5.9	-599.4	1 124.3	1 723.7	1 948.7	724.5	1 224.1	0.9
4th quarter	10 822.9	7 687.1	1 813.4	1 182.3	567.7	56.5	-3.3	-621.9	1 151.3	1 773.1	1 939.3	714.9	1 224.3	-4.7
2005														
1st quarter	10 913.8	7 739.4	1 849.6	1 199.7	582.8	54.9	0.7	-626.4	1 164.5	1 790.9	1 947.2	720.8	1 226.3	-5.7
2nd quarter	11 001.8	7 819.8	1 832.6	1 214.8	609.9	-1.0	-5.8	-606.1	1 191.0	1 797.1	1 952.6	721.6	1 230.9	-10.3
3rd quarter	11 115.1	7 895.3	1 855.9	1 232.4	620.4	-14.0	1.1	-607.6	1 200.5	1 808.1	1 968.8	738.2	1 230.5	-17.0
4th quarter	11 163.8	7 910.2	1 927.0	1 248.2	618.9	38.6	4.8	-636.6	1 228.4	1 865.0	1 963.5	729.6	1 233.7	-8.8

Note: Chained (2000) dollar series are calculated as the product of the chain-type quantity index and the 2000 current-dollar value of the corresponding series, divided by 100. Because the formula for the chain-type quantity indexes uses weights from more than one period, the corresponding chained-dollar estimates are usually not additive. The residual line is the difference between the first line and the sum of the most detailed lines shown in the Bureau of Economic Analysis (BEA) published data.

. . . = Not available.

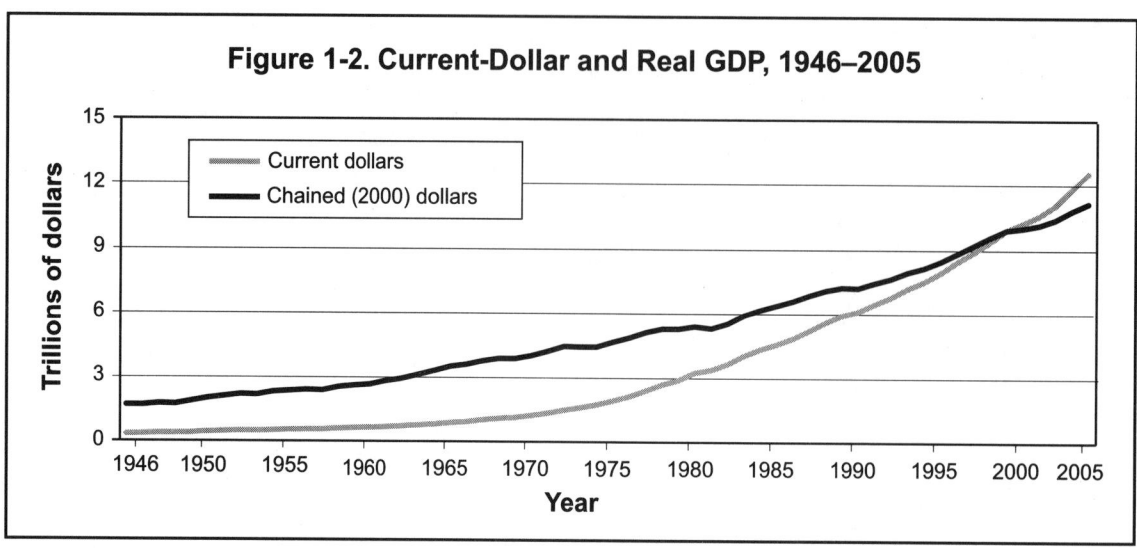

Figure 1-2. Current-Dollar and Real GDP, 1946–2005

•Figure 1-2 graphs the value of gross domestic product (GDP) in both current dollars and real terms (chained 2000 dollars). Since real GDP is expressed in dollar values from the year 2000, the two are the same in that year. As prices increase in nearly every year, the current-dollar measure grows faster than the measure of real, or constant-dollar, GDP. (Tables 1-1, 19-1, 1-2, and 19-2)

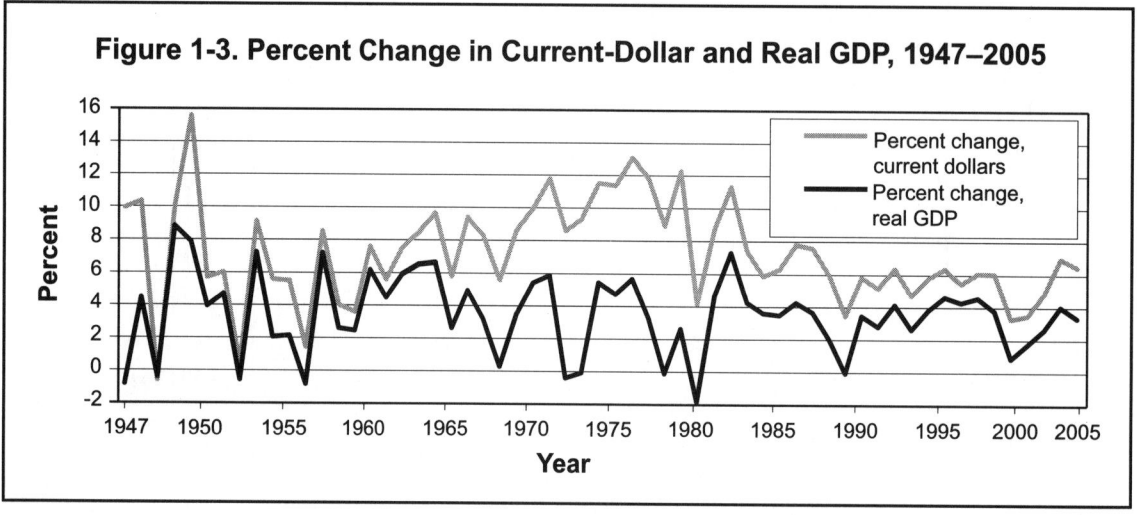

Figure 1-3. Percent Change in Current-Dollar and Real GDP, 1947–2005

•The arithmetic scale used in Figure 1-2 seems to suggest ever-accelerating growth in GDP, but it should not be interpreted in this way. (See "Using the Data: The U.S. Economy in the New Century" in the introductory material to this book.) Figure 1-3 depicts the same data in the form of year-to-year percent changes. The annual changes in real GDP, though quite variable, fluctuate around a value of 3.5 percent, the average rate between the business cycle peak years of 1948 and 2000. The changes in nominal GDP, which are roughly the sum of the real change and the inflation rate, are more volatile. During years of low inflation, they are quite similar to (though somewhat higher than) the changes in real GDP. In years of high inflation, they are far above the changes in real GDP. Some years of high nominal change, notably 1974 and 1975, have seen the real GDP actually decline. (Tables 1-1, 19-1, 1-3, and 19-3)

Table 1-3. Contributions to Percent Change in Real Gross Domestic Product

(Percent, percentage points.)

NIPA Table 1.1.2

Year and quarter	Percent change at seasonally adjusted annual rate, GDP	Personal consumption expenditures	Gross private domestic investment				Exports and imports of goods and services			Government consumption expenditures and gross investment		
			Total	Fixed investment		Change in private inventories	Net exports	Exports	Imports	Total	Federal	State and local
				Nonresidential	Residential							
1950	8.7	4.28	5.74	0.86	2.03	2.84	-1.31	-0.66	-0.65	0.02	-0.56	0.58
1951	7.7	1.05	0.05	0.44	-1.14	0.75	0.81	0.98	-0.17	5.84	5.78	0.06
1952	3.8	1.95	-1.65	-0.18	-0.10	-1.37	-0.59	-0.22	-0.37	4.11	4.00	0.11
1953	4.6	2.91	0.70	0.80	0.18	-0.28	-0.70	-0.31	-0.39	1.67	1.33	0.34
1954	-0.7	1.25	-0.69	-0.20	0.42	-0.91	0.40	0.19	0.21	-1.64	-2.25	0.60
1955	7.1	4.57	3.45	1.01	0.90	1.54	-0.04	0.44	-0.48	-0.84	-1.39	0.55
1956	1.9	1.79	-0.23	0.55	-0.49	-0.29	0.37	0.70	-0.33	0.01	-0.24	0.25
1957	2.0	1.53	-0.71	0.16	-0.32	-0.54	0.25	0.43	-0.18	0.93	0.46	0.47
1958	-1.0	0.50	-1.25	-1.12	0.05	-0.18	-0.89	-0.69	-0.20	0.69	-0.01	0.70
1959	7.1	3.55	2.80	0.73	1.21	0.86	0.00	0.45	-0.45	0.76	0.42	0.34
1960	2.5	1.73	0.00	0.52	-0.39	-0.13	0.72	0.78	-0.06	0.03	-0.35	0.39
1961	2.3	1.30	-0.10	-0.06	0.01	-0.05	0.06	0.03	0.03	1.07	0.51	0.56
1962	6.1	3.11	1.81	0.78	0.46	0.57	-0.21	0.25	-0.47	1.36	1.07	0.29
1963	4.4	2.56	1.00	0.50	0.58	-0.08	0.24	0.35	-0.12	0.58	0.01	0.57
1964	5.8	3.71	1.25	1.07	0.30	-0.13	0.36	0.59	-0.23	0.49	-0.17	0.65
1965	6.4	3.91	2.16	1.65	-0.15	0.66	-0.30	0.15	-0.45	0.65	0.00	0.66
1966	6.5	3.50	1.44	1.29	-0.43	0.58	-0.29	0.36	-0.65	1.87	1.24	0.63
1967	2.5	1.81	-0.76	-0.15	-0.13	-0.49	-0.22	0.12	-0.34	1.68	1.17	0.51
1968	4.8	3.50	0.90	0.46	0.53	-0.10	-0.30	0.41	-0.70	0.73	0.10	0.63
1969	3.1	2.27	0.90	0.78	0.13	0.00	-0.04	0.25	-0.29	-0.06	-0.42	0.37
1970	0.2	1.42	-1.04	-0.06	-0.26	-0.73	0.34	0.56	-0.22	-0.55	-0.86	0.31
1971	3.4	2.38	1.67	0.00	1.10	0.58	-0.19	0.10	-0.29	-0.50	-0.85	0.36
1972	5.3	3.80	1.87	0.92	0.89	0.06	-0.21	0.42	-0.63	-0.16	-0.42	0.26
1973	5.8	3.05	1.96	1.50	-0.04	0.50	0.82	1.12	-0.29	-0.08	-0.41	0.33
1974	-0.5	-0.47	-1.30	0.09	-1.13	-0.27	0.75	0.58	0.18	0.52	0.08	0.44
1975	-0.2	1.42	-2.98	-1.14	-0.57	-1.27	0.89	-0.05	0.94	0.48	0.03	0.45
1976	5.3	3.48	2.84	0.52	0.90	1.41	-1.08	0.37	-1.45	0.10	0.00	0.09
1977	4.6	2.68	2.43	1.19	0.99	0.25	-0.72	0.20	-0.92	0.23	0.19	0.04
1978	5.6	2.76	2.16	1.69	0.35	0.12	0.05	0.82	-0.78	0.60	0.22	0.38
1979	3.2	1.52	0.61	1.23	-0.21	-0.41	0.66	0.82	-0.16	0.37	0.20	0.17
1980	-0.2	-0.17	-2.12	-0.04	-1.17	-0.91	1.68	0.97	0.71	0.38	0.39	-0.01
1981	2.5	0.90	1.59	0.74	-0.35	1.20	-0.15	0.12	-0.27	0.19	0.42	-0.23
1982	-1.9	0.87	-2.55	-0.51	-0.71	-1.34	-0.60	-0.73	0.12	0.35	0.35	0.01
1983	4.5	3.65	1.45	-0.16	1.33	0.29	-1.35	-0.22	-1.13	0.77	0.63	0.13
1984	7.2	3.44	4.63	2.05	0.64	1.95	-1.58	0.63	-2.21	0.70	0.30	0.40
1985	4.1	3.31	-0.17	0.82	0.07	-1.06	-0.42	0.23	-0.65	1.41	0.74	0.67
1986	3.5	2.62	-0.12	-0.36	0.55	-0.32	-0.30	0.54	-0.84	1.27	0.55	0.71
1987	3.4	2.17	0.51	-0.01	0.10	0.42	0.17	0.78	-0.61	0.52	0.36	0.17
1988	4.1	2.66	0.39	0.57	-0.05	-0.14	0.82	1.24	-0.42	0.27	-0.15	0.42
1989	3.5	1.86	0.64	0.61	-0.14	0.17	0.52	0.99	-0.47	0.52	0.14	0.39
1990	1.9	1.34	-0.53	0.05	-0.37	-0.21	0.43	0.81	-0.39	0.64	0.18	0.46
1991	-0.2	0.11	-1.20	-0.57	-0.37	-0.26	0.69	0.63	0.06	0.23	-0.02	0.24
1992	3.3	2.18	1.07	0.32	0.47	0.29	-0.04	0.68	-0.72	0.11	-0.15	0.26
1993	2.7	2.23	1.21	0.83	0.31	0.07	-0.59	0.32	-0.91	-0.18	-0.35	0.17
1994	4.0	2.52	1.93	0.91	0.39	0.63	-0.43	0.85	-1.29	0.00	-0.30	0.30
1995	2.5	1.81	0.48	1.08	-0.14	-0.46	0.11	1.04	-0.93	0.10	-0.20	0.30
1996	3.7	2.31	1.35	1.01	0.33	0.02	-0.14	0.91	-1.05	0.18	-0.08	0.26
1997	4.5	2.54	1.95	1.33	0.08	0.54	-0.34	1.30	-1.64	0.34	-0.07	0.41
1998	4.2	3.36	1.63	1.28	0.32	0.03	-1.16	0.27	-1.43	0.34	-0.07	0.41
1999	4.5	3.44	1.33	1.09	0.27	-0.03	-0.99	0.47	-1.46	0.67	0.14	0.54
2000	3.7	3.17	0.99	1.06	0.03	-0.10	-0.86	0.93	-1.79	0.36	0.05	0.31
2001	0.8	1.74	-1.39	-0.52	0.02	-0.88	-0.20	-0.60	0.40	0.60	0.23	0.37
2002	1.6	1.90	-0.41	-1.06	0.22	0.43	-0.69	-0.23	-0.46	0.80	0.43	0.37
2003	2.5	1.94	0.54	0.10	0.41	0.04	-0.44	0.12	-0.56	0.47	0.44	0.02
2004	3.9	2.71	1.49	0.58	0.53	0.38	-0.65	0.88	-1.53	0.36	0.30	0.06
2005	3.2	2.44	0.87	0.67	0.50	-0.30	-0.26	0.68	-0.94	0.17	0.11	0.06
2003												
1st quarter	1.2	1.41	-0.16	-0.24	0.20	-0.12	0.21	-0.53	0.74	-0.26	0.01	-0.27
2nd quarter	3.5	2.53	0.51	1.01	0.51	-1.01	-0.73	-0.16	-0.57	1.16	1.26	-0.10
3rd quarter	7.5	4.13	2.56	0.92	1.08	0.56	0.51	1.02	-0.51	0.29	0.03	0.26
4th quarter	2.7	1.59	1.39	0.29	0.55	0.56	-0.47	1.81	-2.29	0.14	0.21	-0.07
2004												
1st quarter	3.9	3.30	0.74	0.18	0.16	0.40	-0.73	0.69	-1.42	0.55	0.49	0.06
2nd quarter	4.0	2.07	3.17	0.69	1.03	1.44	-1.62	0.60	-2.22	0.43	0.18	0.25
3rd quarter	3.1	2.74	0.32	0.97	0.18	-0.84	-0.20	0.46	-0.66	0.24	0.34	-0.10
4th quarter	2.6	2.97	0.82	0.81	-0.04	0.05	-0.81	0.96	-1.77	-0.37	-0.38	0.01
2005												
1st quarter	3.4	1.94	1.32	0.59	0.63	0.09	-0.16	0.47	-0.63	0.31	0.23	0.08
2nd quarter	3.3	2.94	-0.61	0.51	1.11	-2.23	0.72	0.94	-0.22	0.21	0.03	0.18
3rd quarter	4.2	2.76	0.84	0.59	0.43	-0.18	-0.06	0.33	-0.39	0.64	0.66	-0.01
4th quarter	1.8	0.53	2.51	0.52	-0.06	2.05	-1.07	0.97	-2.04	-0.21	-0.33	0.13

Table 1-4. Chain-Type Quantity Indexes for Gross Domestic Product and Domestic Purchases

(Index numbers, 2000 = 100.)

NIPA Tables 1.1.3, 1.4.3, 2.3.3

Year and quarter	Gross domestic product, total	Personal consumption expenditures		Private fixed investment			Exports and imports of goods and services		Government consumption expenditures and gross investment			Gross domestic purchases
		Total	Excluding food and energy	Total	Nonresidential	Residential	Exports	Imports	Total	Federal	State and local	
1950	18.1	17.1	13.7	13.0	8.6	32.3	4.6	4.0	23.5	35.6	17.5	17.7
1951	19.5	17.4	13.8	12.4	9.0	27.0	5.6	4.2	32.2	59.0	17.6	18.9
1952	20.3	17.9	14.2	12.2	8.8	26.6	5.4	4.5	38.7	76.8	17.9	19.7
1953	21.2	18.8	14.9	13.0	9.6	27.5	5.0	5.0	41.5	82.9	18.8	20.8
1954	21.0	19.2	15.2	13.3	9.4	29.8	5.3	4.7	38.6	72.0	20.5	20.6
1955	22.5	20.6	16.5	15.0	10.4	34.6	5.8	5.3	37.2	65.5	21.9	22.0
1956	23.0	21.2	16.9	15.0	11.0	31.8	6.8	5.7	37.2	64.3	22.6	22.4
1957	23.4	21.7	17.3	14.9	11.2	29.8	7.4	6.0	38.9	66.6	24.0	22.8
1958	23.2	21.8	17.4	13.8	10.0	30.2	6.4	6.3	40.1	66.6	26.0	22.8
1959	24.9	23.1	18.6	15.7	10.8	37.8	7.0	6.9	41.5	68.7	27.0	24.4
1960	25.5	23.7	19.2	15.9	11.4	35.1	8.3	7.0	41.6	66.8	28.2	24.8
1961	26.1	24.2	19.7	15.8	11.3	35.2	8.3	7.0	43.6	69.6	29.9	25.4
1962	27.7	25.4	20.9	17.2	12.3	38.6	8.7	7.7	46.3	75.5	30.8	27.0
1963	28.9	26.4	22.0	18.6	13.0	43.2	9.4	8.0	47.5	75.5	32.7	28.1
1964	30.5	28.0	23.5	20.4	14.5	45.7	10.5	8.4	48.6	74.5	34.9	29.7
1965	32.5	29.8	25.1	22.5	17.0	44.3	10.7	9.3	50.0	74.5	37.3	31.7
1966	34.6	31.5	26.6	23.7	19.2	40.4	11.5	10.6	54.4	82.7	39.6	33.8
1967	35.5	32.4	27.6	23.3	18.9	39.1	11.8	11.4	58.6	91.0	41.6	34.8
1968	37.2	34.3	29.2	24.9	19.7	44.4	12.7	13.1	60.4	91.7	44.0	36.6
1969	38.4	35.6	30.4	26.5	21.2	45.7	13.3	13.9	60.3	88.5	45.5	37.7
1970	38.4	36.4	31.0	25.9	21.1	43.0	14.7	14.5	58.8	82.0	46.8	37.6
1971	39.7	37.8	32.5	27.9	21.1	54.8	15.0	15.2	57.6	75.7	48.2	39.0
1972	41.8	40.1	34.7	31.2	23.1	64.5	16.1	16.9	57.1	72.6	49.3	41.1
1973	44.2	42.0	36.9	34.1	26.4	64.1	19.1	17.7	56.9	69.5	50.7	43.1
1974	44.0	41.7	36.9	32.0	26.7	50.9	20.6	17.3	58.4	70.1	52.6	42.6
1975	43.9	42.7	37.7	28.5	24.0	44.3	20.5	15.4	59.7	70.4	54.5	42.1
1976	46.3	45.0	39.8	31.4	25.2	54.7	21.4	18.4	59.9	70.4	54.9	44.9
1977	48.4	47.0	41.8	35.9	28.0	66.4	21.9	20.4	60.6	71.9	55.1	47.3
1978	51.1	49.0	44.1	40.2	32.2	70.6	24.2	22.2	62.4	73.7	56.9	49.8
1979	52.7	50.2	45.5	42.5	35.5	68.0	26.6	22.6	63.5	75.5	57.8	51.1
1980	52.6	50.1	45.4	39.7	35.4	53.6	29.5	21.1	64.8	79.0	57.7	50.1
1981	53.9	50.8	46.4	40.6	37.4	49.3	29.9	21.6	65.4	82.8	56.6	51.4
1982	52.9	51.5	47.1	37.7	36.0	40.4	27.6	21.3	66.5	86.0	56.6	50.8
1983	55.2	54.4	50.3	40.5	35.5	57.1	26.9	24.0	69.0	91.7	57.3	53.7
1984	59.2	57.3	53.6	47.3	41.8	65.6	29.1	29.9	71.3	94.6	59.3	58.4
1985	61.7	60.3	56.9	49.8	44.6	66.6	30.0	31.8	76.2	102.0	63.0	61.0
1986	63.8	62.7	59.6	50.4	43.3	74.8	32.3	34.6	80.9	107.8	67.1	63.2
1987	66.0	64.8	61.8	50.7	43.3	76.3	35.7	36.6	82.9	111.7	68.0	65.2
1988	68.7	67.5	64.4	52.4	45.5	75.5	41.5	38.0	83.9	109.9	70.6	67.3
1989	71.1	69.4	66.4	53.9	48.1	73.2	46.2	39.7	86.1	111.6	73.0	69.2
1990	72.5	70.8	67.8	52.8	48.3	66.9	50.4	41.1	88.9	113.9	76.0	70.2
1991	72.3	70.9	67.9	49.4	45.7	60.5	53.7	40.9	89.9	113.7	77.6	69.6
1992	74.7	73.2	70.6	52.3	47.2	68.8	57.4	43.7	90.3	111.7	79.3	72.0
1993	76.7	75.7	73.2	56.8	51.3	74.4	59.3	47.6	89.5	107.1	80.5	74.3
1994	79.8	78.5	76.2	62.1	56.0	81.6	64.4	53.3	89.5	103.1	82.5	77.6
1995	81.8	80.6	78.6	66.1	61.9	79.0	71.0	57.5	90.0	100.3	84.7	79.4
1996	84.8	83.4	81.7	72.0	67.7	85.3	76.9	62.5	90.9	99.1	86.7	82.4
1997	88.7	86.5	85.3	78.7	75.8	86.9	86.1	71.0	92.6	98.1	89.8	86.4
1998	92.4	90.9	90.1	86.7	84.2	93.6	88.2	79.3	94.4	97.0	93.0	90.9
1999	96.5	95.5	95.2	93.9	92.0	99.3	92.0	88.4	98.0	99.1	97.4	95.8
2000	100.0	100.0	100.0	100.0	100.0	100.0	100.0	100.0	100.0	100.0	100.0	100.0
2001	100.8	102.5	102.9	97.0	95.8	100.4	94.6	97.3	103.4	103.9	103.2	100.9
2002	102.4	105.3	105.9	92.0	87.0	105.1	92.4	100.6	108.0	111.2	106.4	103.2
2003	104.9	108.2	109.0	95.1	87.8	114.0	93.6	104.7	110.6	118.7	106.6	106.1
2004	109.0	112.4	113.5	102.1	93.0	125.3	102.2	116.0	112.7	123.8	107.1	110.7
2005	112.5	116.3	117.3	109.7	99.3	136.1	109.1	123.0	113.7	125.7	107.7	114.4
2003												
1st quarter	103.1	106.6	107.1	91.5	85.0	108.3	91.5	102.4	109.2	114.5	106.5	104.2
2nd quarter	104.0	107.6	108.3	93.8	87.2	111.1	91.1	103.4	110.8	119.7	106.3	105.3
3rd quarter	105.9	109.1	109.9	96.9	89.2	116.8	93.6	104.4	111.2	119.9	106.8	107.0
4th quarter	106.6	109.7	110.6	98.2	89.8	119.8	98.1	108.7	111.4	120.8	106.7	107.8
2004												
1st quarter	107.6	111.0	111.9	98.8	90.2	120.7	99.9	111.3	112.2	122.9	106.8	108.9
2nd quarter	108.7	111.8	112.8	101.5	91.8	126.2	101.4	115.5	112.8	123.7	107.3	110.4
3rd quarter	109.5	112.9	114.1	103.4	94.1	127.2	102.6	116.8	113.2	125.2	107.1	111.3
4th quarter	110.2	114.1	115.1	104.7	96.0	127.0	105.0	120.2	112.6	123.5	107.1	112.2
2005												
1st quarter	111.2	114.8	115.7	106.7	97.4	130.4	106.2	121.4	113.1	124.5	107.3	113.1
2nd quarter	112.1	116.0	117.0	109.3	98.6	136.5	108.6	121.8	113.4	124.7	107.7	113.8
3rd quarter	113.2	117.2	118.1	111.0	100.0	138.8	109.5	122.5	114.4	127.5	107.7	114.9
4th quarter	113.7	117.4	118.2	111.8	101.3	138.5	112.1	126.4	114.0	126.1	108.0	115.7

Table 1-5. Chain-Type Price Indexes for Gross Domestic Product and Domestic Purchases

(Index numbers, 2000 = 100.)   NIPA Tables 1.1.4, 1.6.4, 2.3.4

Year and quarter	Gross domestic product, total	Personal consumption expenditures		Private fixed investment			Exports and imports of goods and services		Government consumption expenditures and gross investment			Gross domestic purchases
		Total	Excluding food and energy	Total	Nonresidential	Residential	Exports	Imports	Total	Federal	State and local	
1950	16.5	16.7	16.8	22.2	26.3	14.2	24.5	19.6	11.5	12.6	10.4	16.2
1951	17.6	17.8	17.8	24.1	28.8	15.2	27.7	23.7	12.3	13.2	11.4	17.4
1952	18.0	18.2	18.2	24.7	29.5	15.7	27.9	22.8	12.6	13.3	11.9	17.7
1953	18.2	18.4	18.6	24.9	29.7	15.8	27.8	21.8	12.7	13.4	12.2	17.9
1954	18.4	18.6	18.9	25.1	30.0	15.8	27.4	22.1	13.0	13.7	12.4	18.1
1955	18.7	18.7	19.1	25.5	30.4	16.2	27.7	22.0	13.5	14.5	12.6	18.4
1956	19.4	19.1	19.6	27.0	32.8	16.6	28.6	22.4	14.3	15.2	13.4	19.0
1957	20.0	19.6	20.2	27.9	34.5	16.6	29.7	22.6	14.9	15.9	14.0	19.7
1958	20.5	20.1	20.6	28.0	34.7	16.6	29.4	21.7	15.3	16.6	14.2	20.1
1959	20.8	20.4	21.0	28.3	35.1	16.6	29.4	21.9	15.4	16.5	14.5	20.4
1960	21.0	20.8	21.4	28.4	35.3	16.7	29.8	22.1	15.6	16.6	14.7	20.6
1961	21.3	21.0	21.6	28.3	35.1	16.8	30.3	22.1	15.9	16.9	15.1	20.9
1962	21.6	21.2	21.9	28.3	35.1	16.8	30.4	21.8	16.3	17.2	15.6	21.1
1963	21.8	21.5	22.2	28.3	35.1	16.7	30.3	22.3	16.7	17.6	15.9	21.4
1964	22.1	21.8	22.5	28.4	35.3	16.8	30.6	22.7	17.1	18.2	16.2	21.7
1965	22.5	22.1	22.8	28.9	35.7	17.3	31.5	23.1	17.6	18.7	16.7	22.1
1966	23.2	22.7	23.2	29.5	36.2	17.9	32.5	23.6	18.3	19.3	17.5	22.7
1967	23.9	23.2	23.9	30.4	37.1	18.5	33.7	23.7	19.1	19.9	18.5	23.4
1968	24.9	24.2	24.9	31.6	38.4	19.5	34.5	24.0	20.1	21.0	19.5	24.4
1969	26.2	25.3	26.1	33.1	40.0	20.9	35.6	24.7	21.3	22.1	20.8	25.6
1970	27.5	26.4	27.3	34.6	41.9	21.5	37.0	26.1	23.1	23.9	22.5	27.0
1971	28.9	27.6	28.5	36.3	43.9	22.8	38.4	27.7	24.9	26.0	24.1	28.4
1972	30.2	28.5	29.5	37.9	45.4	24.2	40.1	29.7	26.8	28.5	25.5	29.6
1973	31.9	30.1	30.5	40.0	47.1	26.3	45.4	34.8	28.7	30.4	27.5	31.3
1974	34.7	33.2	32.8	43.9	51.7	29.0	56.0	49.8	31.6	33.2	30.5	34.5
1975	38.0	36.0	35.5	49.4	58.8	31.7	61.7	54.0	34.8	36.6	33.5	37.8
1976	40.2	37.9	37.7	52.2	62.0	33.7	63.7	55.6	37.1	39.2	35.6	39.9
1977	42.8	40.4	40.1	56.3	66.3	37.1	66.3	60.5	39.7	42.2	37.9	42.6
1978	45.8	43.2	42.8	61.1	70.7	41.7	70.3	64.8	42.2	44.8	40.4	45.7
1979	49.6	47.1	45.7	66.6	76.4	46.4	78.8	75.9	45.8	48.2	43.9	49.7
1980	54.1	52.1	49.9	72.9	83.2	51.4	86.8	94.5	50.8	53.3	48.9	54.9
1981	59.1	56.7	54.2	79.7	91.2	55.6	93.2	99.6	55.8	58.5	53.7	59.9
1982	62.7	59.9	57.8	84.0	96.3	58.6	93.6	96.2	59.4	62.4	57.1	63.3
1983	65.2	62.4	60.8	83.9	95.4	59.9	94.0	92.6	61.8	64.6	59.7	65.5
1984	67.7	64.8	63.4	84.4	95.2	61.6	94.9	91.8	65.0	68.4	62.3	67.8
1985	69.7	66.9	65.8	85.5	95.9	63.2	92.0	88.8	67.0	70.0	64.7	69.8
1986	71.3	68.6	68.2	87.5	97.6	65.9	90.6	88.9	68.2	70.4	66.6	71.3
1987	73.2	70.9	70.8	89.1	98.4	68.6	92.9	94.3	70.1	71.2	69.4	73.5
1988	75.7	73.8	73.8	91.4	100.6	70.9	97.7	98.8	71.9	72.7	71.5	76.0
1989	78.6	77.0	76.9	93.6	102.7	73.2	99.3	100.9	74.1	74.7	73.9	78.9
1990	81.6	80.5	80.2	95.5	104.7	74.9	100.0	103.8	77.1	77.1	77.4	82.1
1991	84.5	83.4	83.3	97.0	106.3	75.9	101.3	103.4	79.8	80.2	79.7	84.8
1992	86.4	85.8	86.1	96.7	105.4	76.8	100.9	103.6	81.7	82.6	81.3	86.8
1993	88.4	87.8	88.3	97.8	105.5	79.9	100.9	102.7	83.8	84.8	83.3	88.7
1994	90.3	89.7	90.4	99.1	106.0	82.8	102.0	103.6	86.0	87.1	85.5	90.6
1995	92.1	91.6	92.4	100.3	106.2	85.8	104.4	106.4	88.4	89.5	87.8	92.5
1996	93.9	93.5	94.1	100.0	105.0	87.6	103.0	104.5	90.5	92.0	89.7	94.1
1997	95.4	95.1	95.6	99.8	103.7	89.8	101.2	100.8	92.1	93.5	91.4	95.4
1998	96.5	96.0	96.9	98.9	101.4	92.2	98.9	95.4	93.5	94.5	92.9	96.1
1999	97.9	97.6	98.3	98.9	100.1	95.8	98.3	96.0	96.1	96.9	95.7	97.6
2000	100.0	100.0	100.0	100.0	100.0	100.0	100.0	100.0	100.0	100.0	100.0	100.0
2001	102.4	102.1	101.9	101.0	99.7	104.6	99.6	97.5	102.5	101.9	102.9	102.0
2002	104.2	103.5	103.7	101.7	99.5	107.2	99.3	96.3	105.5	105.6	105.4	103.6
2003	106.4	105.6	105.2	103.3	99.6	112.4	101.4	99.7	109.8	110.1	109.7	106.0
2004	109.4	108.4	107.3	106.8	100.8	120.6	105.2	104.7	114.7	115.2	114.4	109.2
2005	112.7	111.5	109.6	110.5	103.4	126.7	108.9	111.3	121.2	120.7	121.5	113.0
2003												
1st quarter	105.7	105.1	104.6	103.1	99.7	111.4	100.9	100.1	109.1	109.6	108.8	105.4
2nd quarter	106.1	105.2	104.9	102.9	99.3	111.5	101.2	99.1	109.4	110.0	109.1	105.6
3rd quarter	106.6	105.9	105.4	103.2	99.5	112.2	101.4	99.7	110.1	110.3	110.0	106.2
4th quarter	107.2	106.2	105.8	104.1	99.8	114.3	102.2	99.8	110.7	110.6	110.8	106.7
2004												
1st quarter	108.2	107.2	106.5	105.2	100.1	117.2	103.7	102.2	112.6	113.6	112.0	107.8
2nd quarter	109.2	108.2	107.1	106.4	100.6	119.8	105.0	104.0	114.0	115.1	113.4	108.9
3rd quarter	109.7	108.7	107.5	107.3	101.0	121.9	105.4	105.4	115.3	115.7	115.1	109.6
4th quarter	110.6	109.5	108.2	108.3	101.6	123.6	106.5	107.1	117.0	116.6	117.2	110.6
2005												
1st quarter	111.6	110.1	108.8	109.2	102.5	124.3	107.7	107.8	119.0	119.7	118.5	111.4
2nd quarter	112.2	110.9	109.3	109.9	103.1	125.5	108.6	110.2	120.3	120.4	120.3	112.4
3rd quarter	113.1	112.1	109.7	110.9	103.6	127.6	109.3	112.9	122.0	121.4	122.4	113.6
4th quarter	114.0	112.9	110.4	112.2	104.5	129.5	110.1	114.1	123.4	121.5	124.6	114.5

Table 1-6. Final Sales

(Quarterly dollar data are at seasonally adjusted annual rates.)   **NIPA Tables 1.4.4, 1.4.5, 1.4.6**

Year and quarter	Final sales of domestic product			Final sales to domestic purchasers		
	Billions of dollars	Billions of chained (2000) dollars	Chain-type price index, 2000 = 100	Billions of dollars	Billions of chained (2000) dollars	Chain-type price index, 2000 = 100
1950	288.0	1 763.8	16.3	287.3	1 787.4	16.1
1951	329.4	1 889.4	17.4	326.9	1 900.0	17.2
1952	354.8	1 990.0	17.8	353.7	2 013.6	17.6
1953	377.4	2 087.7	18.1	378.1	2 127.1	17.8
1954	382.3	2 092.5	18.3	381.9	2 123.4	18.0
1955	409.8	2 209.2	18.6	409.3	2 242.8	18.3
1956	433.5	2 259.0	19.2	431.2	2 285.0	18.9
1957	460.3	2 316.9	19.9	456.2	2 338.3	19.5
1958	467.6	2 299.0	20.3	467.0	2 341.1	20.0
1959	502.7	2 442.7	20.6	502.3	2 487.4	20.2
1960	523.2	2 506.8	20.9	519.0	2 534.8	20.5
1961	541.7	2 566.8	21.1	536.8	2 594.6	20.7
1962	579.5	2 708.6	21.4	575.4	2 744.8	21.0
1963	612.1	2 830.3	21.6	607.2	2 862.4	21.2
1964	658.8	2 999.9	22.0	651.9	3 024.5	21.6
1965	709.9	3 173.8	22.4	704.3	3 211.2	21.9
1966	774.2	3 364.8	23.0	770.3	3 415.5	22.6
1967	822.7	3 467.6	23.7	819.2	3 528.1	23.2
1968	900.9	3 640.3	24.8	899.6	3 715.3	24.2
1969	975.4	3 753.7	26.0	974.0	3 832.6	25.4
1970	1 036.5	3 787.7	27.4	1 032.6	3 854.0	26.8
1971	1 118.9	3 893.4	28.7	1 118.2	3 969.3	28.2
1972	1 229.2	4 098.6	30.0	1 232.6	4 186.9	29.4
1973	1 366.8	4 315.9	31.7	1 362.7	4 373.4	31.2
1974	1 486.0	4 305.5	34.5	1 486.8	4 329.7	34.3
1975	1 644.6	4 352.5	37.8	1 628.6	4 338.2	37.5
1976	1 808.2	4 522.3	40.0	1 809.8	4 556.2	39.7
1977	2 008.6	4 721.6	42.5	2 031.7	4 789.5	42.4
1978	2 268.9	4 981.6	45.6	2 294.3	5 047.9	45.5
1979	2 545.3	5 161.2	49.3	2 567.9	5 194.2	49.4
1980	2 795.8	5 196.7	53.8	2 808.9	5 142.8	54.6
1981	3 098.6	5 265.1	58.9	3 111.2	5 217.9	59.6
1982	3 269.9	5 233.4	62.5	3 289.9	5 218.2	63.1
1983	3 542.4	5 454.0	65.0	3 594.1	5 507.3	65.3
1984	3 867.8	5 739.2	67.4	3 970.5	5 877.3	67.6
1985	4 198.4	6 042.1	69.5	4 313.6	6 204.2	69.5
1986	4 456.3	6 271.8	71.1	4 589.0	6 452.0	71.1
1987	4 712.3	6 457.2	73.0	4 857.5	6 626.5	73.3
1988	5 085.3	6 734.5	75.5	5 195.7	6 849.7	75.9
1989	5 456.7	6 962.2	78.4	5 544.8	7 041.6	78.8
1990	5 788.5	7 108.5	81.4	5 866.5	7 157.4	82.0
1991	5 996.3	7 115.0	84.3	6 023.8	7 115.2	84.7
1992	6 321.4	7 331.1	86.2	6 354.7	7 333.0	86.7
1993	6 636.6	7 522.3	88.2	6 701.6	7 566.4	88.6
1994	7 008.4	7 777.8	90.1	7 102.0	7 853.6	90.4
1995	7 366.5	8 010.2	92.0	7 457.9	8 076.8	92.3
1996	7 786.1	8 306.5	93.7	7 882.3	8 383.1	94.0
1997	8 232.3	8 636.6	95.3	8 333.9	8 740.4	95.3
1998	8 676.2	8 997.6	96.4	8 836.2	9 203.2	96.0
1999	9 201.5	9 404.0	97.8	9 462.0	9 701.3	97.5
2000	9 760.5	9 760.5	100.0	10 140.0	10 140.0	100.0
2001	10 159.7	9 920.9	102.4	10 526.7	10 320.5	102.0
2002	10 457.7	10 036.5	104.2	10 882.1	10 505.3	103.6
2003	10 946.5	10 285.1	106.4	11 445.9	10 799.5	106.0
2004	11 655.1	10 648.3	109.5	12 268.4	11 231.1	109.2
2005	12 434.6	11 025.2	112.8	13 151.3	11 636.1	113.0
2003						
1st quarter	10 682.6	10 100.9	105.8	11 181.8	10 603.9	105.5
2nd quarter	10 835.4	10 213.7	106.1	11 336.7	10 735.6	105.6
3rd quarter	11 074.3	10 385.9	106.6	11 569.5	10 895.9	106.2
4th quarter	11 193.6	10 440.0	107.2	11 695.4	10 962.4	106.7
2004						
1st quarter	11 392.9	10 528.7	108.2	11 936.4	11 070.8	107.8
2nd quarter	11 569.9	10 596.1	109.2	12 176.1	11 181.5	108.9
3rd quarter	11 744.6	10 700.1	109.8	12 375.3	11 291.0	109.6
4th quarter	11 913.0	10 768.2	110.6	12 585.7	11 381.1	110.6
2005						
1st quarter	12 113.8	10 856.5	111.6	12 790.0	11 473.9	111.5
2nd quarter	12 353.7	11 005.3	112.3	13 040.2	11 603.2	112.4
3rd quarter	12 588.8	11 123.5	113.2	13 317.6	11 722.8	113.6
4th quarter	12 681.9	11 115.5	114.1	13 457.3	11 744.6	114.6

Table 1-7. Per Capita Product and Income and U.S. Population

(Dollars, except as noted; quarterly data are at seasonally adjusted annual rates.)

NIPA Table 7.1

Year and quarter	Current dollars							Chained (2000) dollars						Population (mid-period, thousands)
	Gross domestic product	Personal income	Dispos-able personal income	Personal consumption expenditures				Gross domestic product	Dispos-able personal income	Personal consumption expenditures				
				Total	Durable goods	Nondur-able goods	Services			Total	Durable goods	Nondur-able goods	Services	
1950	1 937	1 510	1 385	1 267	203	648	417	11 717	8 306	7 600	509	3 324	3 607	151 684
1951	2 199	1 672	1 497	1 352	194	708	450	12 412	8 408	7 591	456	3 354	3 728	154 287
1952	2 283	1 754	1 550	1 399	187	731	481	12 668	8 534	7 698	436	3 427	3 826	156 954
1953	2 378	1 829	1 621	1 461	205	738	517	13 032	8 802	7 932	482	3 477	3 923	159 565
1954	2 342	1 813	1 627	1 478	196	737	545	12 719	8 757	7 952	472	3 460	4 011	162 391
1955	2 509	1 913	1 714	1 566	235	755	576	13 389	9 177	8 383	566	3 564	4 148	165 275
1956	2 601	2 019	1 801	1 615	227	777	611	13 410	9 450	8 474	534	3 621	4 279	168 221
1957	2 692	2 094	1 867	1 675	233	800	641	13 435	9 508	8 528	529	3 622	4 365	171 274
1958	2 683	2 119	1 898	1 701	215	814	672	13 088	9 433	8 455	479	3 597	4 456	174 141
1959	2 860	2 218	1 979	1 793	241	838	714	13 782	9 685	8 776	527	3 682	4 612	177 130
1960	2 912	2 277	2 022	1 835	240	846	750	13 840	9 735	8 837	527	3 662	4 721	180 760
1961	2 965	2 335	2 078	1 862	227	852	782	13 932	9 901	8 873	499	3 669	4 838	183 742
1962	3 139	2 448	2 171	1 947	251	872	823	14 552	10 227	9 170	549	3 727	5 000	186 590
1963	3 263	2 534	2 246	2 022	273	888	861	14 971	10 455	9 412	594	3 751	5 153	189 300
1964	3 458	2 681	2 410	2 144	295	931	918	15 624	11 061	9 839	640	3 880	5 393	191 927
1965	3 700	2 860	2 563	2 283	325	986	972	16 420	11 594	10 331	712	4 035	5 610	194 347
1966	4 007	3 072	2 734	2 446	347	1 062	1 037	17 290	12 065	10 793	763	4 208	5 821	196 599
1967	4 189	3 262	2 895	2 555	354	1 092	1 108	17 533	12 457	10 994	767	4 228	6 039	198 752
1968	4 533	3 547	3 114	2 780	402	1 174	1 203	18 196	12 892	11 510	843	4 377	6 292	200 745
1969	4 857	3 840	3 324	2 985	424	1 249	1 313	18 573	13 163	11 820	864	4 449	6 529	202 736
1970	5 064	4 090	3 587	3 162	414	1 326	1 421	18 391	13 563	11 955	826	4 504	6 712	205 089
1971	5 427	4 350	3 860	3 379	467	1 375	1 538	18 771	14 001	12 256	928	4 528	6 886	207 692
1972	5 899	4 729	4 140	3 671	526	1 467	1 678	19 555	14 512	12 868	1 001	4 677	7 200	209 924
1973	6 524	5 241	4 616	4 022	583	1 619	1 820	20 484	15 345	13 371	1 094	4 784	7 466	211 939
1974	7 013	5 716	5 010	4 364	572	1 798	1 994	20 195	15 094	13 148	1 009	4 645	7 570	213 898
1975	7 586	6 181	5 498	4 789	618	1 948	2 223	19 961	15 291	13 320	999	4 668	7 775	215 981
1976	8 369	6 762	5 972	5 282	728	2 102	2 452	20 822	15 738	13 919	1 116	4 848	8 012	218 086
1977	9 219	7 414	6 517	5 804	823	2 257	2 725	21 565	16 128	14 364	1 207	4 915	8 274	220 289
1978	10 307	8 255	7 224	6 417	906	2 472	3 039	22 526	16 704	14 837	1 258	5 046	8 569	222 629
1979	11 387	9 161	7 967	7 073	952	2 774	3 347	22 982	16 931	15 030	1 240	5 123	8 734	225 106
1980	12 249	10 134	8 822	7 716	940	3 057	3 719	22 666	16 940	14 816	1 129	5 057	8 785	227 726
1981	13 601	11 266	9 765	8 439	1 006	3 299	4 134	23 007	17 217	14 879	1 132	5 066	8 844	230 008
1982	14 017	11 951	10 426	8 945	1 034	3 392	4 519	22 346	17 418	14 944	1 120	5 065	8 944	232 218
1983	15 092	12 635	11 131	9 775	1 198	3 547	5 030	23 146	17 828	15 656	1 272	5 187	9 349	234 333
1984	16 638	13 915	12 319	10 589	1 381	3 742	5 466	24 593	19 011	16 343	1 445	5 346	9 644	236 394
1985	17 695	14 787	13 037	11 406	1 524	3 894	5 988	25 382	19 476	17 040	1 577	5 443	10 098	238 506
1986	18 542	15 466	13 649	12 048	1 674	3 982	6 391	26 024	19 906	17 570	1 714	5 587	10 302	240 683
1987	19 517	16 255	14 241	12 766	1 736	4 181	6 849	26 664	20 072	17 994	1 728	5 670	10 652	242 843
1988	20 827	17 358	15 297	13 685	1 851	4 421	7 413	27 514	20 740	18 554	1 816	5 802	10 983	245 061
1989	22 169	18 545	16 257	14 546	1 907	4 716	7 923	28 221	21 120	18 898	1 839	5 907	11 205	247 387
1990	23 195	19 500	17 131	15 349	1 895	4 996	8 457	28 429	21 281	19 067	1 813	5 932	11 398	250 181
1991	23 650	19 923	17 609	15 722	1 790	5 068	8 864	28 007	21 109	18 848	1 688	5 840	11 438	253 530
1992	24 668	20 870	18 494	16 485	1 882	5 179	9 424	28 556	21 548	19 208	1 763	5 878	11 680	256 922
1993	25 578	21 356	18 872	17 204	2 024	5 300	9 881	28 940	21 493	19 593	1 877	5 956	11 855	260 282
1994	26 844	22 176	19 555	18 004	2 210	5 455	10 339	29 741	21 812	20 082	2 009	6 088	12 058	263 455
1995	27 749	23 078	20 287	18 665	2 294	5 571	10 800	30 128	22 153	20 382	2 073	6 147	12 228	266 588
1996	28 982	24 176	21 091	19 490	2 419	5 767	11 304	30 881	22 546	20 835	2 209	6 230	12 443	269 714
1997	30 424	25 334	21 940	20 323	2 538	5 931	11 854	31 886	23 065	21 365	2 370	6 321	12 705	272 958
1998	31 674	26 880	23 161	21 291	2 717	6 096	12 478	32 833	24 131	22 183	2 608	6 498	13 090	276 154
1999	33 181	27 933	23 968	22 491	2 927	6 461	13 103	33 904	24 564	23 050	2 880	6 718	13 454	279 328
2000	34 759	29 847	25 472	23 862	3 057	6 895	13 911	34 759	25 472	23 862	3 057	6 895	13 911	282 429
2001	35 491	30 571	26 235	24 722	3 097	7 068	14 557	34 659	25 697	24 215	3 156	6 962	14 098	285 371
2002	36 321	30 813	27 164	25 501	3 205	7 215	15 081	34 861	26 235	24 629	3 347	7 067	14 225	288 253
2003	37 651	31 478	28 039	26 463	3 238	7 524	15 701	35 385	26 553	25 060	3 506	7 224	14 355	291 114
2004	39 847	33 108	29 536	27 937	3 355	7 979	16 603	36 415	27 254	25 778	3 694	7 414	14 710	293 933
2005	41 984	34 513	30 458	29 468	3 482	8 559	17 426	37 241	27 318	26 430	3 861	7 674	14 954	296 677
2003														
1st quarter	36 913	31 026	27 499	26 026	3 143	7 444	15 439	34 914	26 176	24 773	3 349	7 146	14 286	290 025
2nd quarter	37 259	31 341	27 820	26 240	3 224	7 414	15 602	35 129	26 437	24 936	3 474	7 169	14 314	290 717
3rd quarter	38 033	31 575	28 341	26 700	3 309	7 605	15 786	35 675	26 776	25 226	3 601	7 283	14 377	291 485
4th quarter	38 393	31 966	28 492	26 881	3 276	7 630	15 975	35 818	26 819	25 303	3 598	7 297	14 441	292 226
2004														
1st quarter	39 033	32 432	28 962	27 379	3 317	7 802	16 260	36 081	27 018	25 541	3 643	7 360	14 574	292 853
2nd quarter	39 686	32 842	29 322	27 758	3 326	7 930	16 503	36 355	27 113	25 667	3 650	7 373	14 678	293 539
3rd quarter	40 093	33 190	29 583	28 084	3 367	8 004	16 713	36 538	27 228	25 848	3 717	7 421	14 752	294 301
4th quarter	40 572	33 960	30 271	28 521	3 411	8 178	16 932	36 683	27 654	26 055	3 763	7 501	14 837	295 037
2005														
1st quarter	41 175	33 990	30 073	28 818	3 427	8 288	17 103	36 916	27 319	26 178	3 777	7 582	14 867	295 643
2nd quarter	41 669	34 296	30 273	29 277	3 518	8 467	17 293	37 132	27 290	26 392	3 884	7 656	14 918	296 289
3rd quarter	42 331	34 551	30 461	29 786	3 560	8 703	17 524	37 421	27 183	26 581	3 959	7 702	14 997	297 027
4th quarter	42 756	35 210	31 020	29 985	3 424	8 777	17 783	37 494	27 484	26 567	3 822	7 757	15 035	297 748

Table 1-8. Composite Indexes of Economic Activity and Selected Index Components

Year and month	Cyclical composite indexes, 1996 = 100				Selected components of leading index		Selected component of coincident index	Selected component of lagging index
	Leading	Coincident	Lagging	Ratio, coincident to lagging	Vendor performance (slower deliveries, diffusion index, percent)	Interest rate spread, 10-year Treasury bond less federal funds [1]	Personal income less transfer payments (billions of 2000 dollars)	Consumer installment credit outstanding (percent of personal income)
1959	42.0	37.0	36.5	101.5	60.6	1.03	1 803.8	13.3
1960	41.6	37.8	38.4	98.4	35.7	0.90	1 857.5	14.2
1961	43.9	38.0	38.7	98.2	48.1	1.93	1 904.0	14.2
1962	46.4	39.8	39.8	99.9	48.8	1.24	2 007.7	14.3
1963	49.0	41.1	41.4	99.3	51.1	0.82	2 083.0	15.1
1964	51.8	42.9	43.1	99.6	62.8	0.69	2 208.0	15.9
1965	54.5	45.5	45.3	100.3	66.6	0.21	2 350.4	16.5
1966	55.3	48.2	48.1	100.3	73.0	-0.19	2 489.7	16.5
1967	55.4	49.6	49.9	99.4	44.0	0.85	2 583.1	16.1
1968	58.0	51.7	51.4	100.5	52.6	-0.01	2 715.4	15.7
1969	58.1	53.7	54.0	99.5	65.2	-1.53	2 835.3	15.8
1970	54.5	53.8	55.4	97.0	50.3	0.17	2 889.1	15.4
1971	58.1	54.6	54.8	99.5	48.0	1.50	2 956.8	15.5
1972	63.4	57.6	55.1	104.5	62.7	1.78	3 135.9	15.8
1973	64.8	60.8	58.4	104.1	88.0	-1.89	3 317.4	16.3
1974	58.2	61.2	62.2	98.5	65.8	-2.95	3 282.7	16.1
1975	56.0	59.1	61.1	96.7	30.2	2.16	3 239.7	14.9
1976	62.4	61.9	60.1	103.0	54.4	2.57	3 400.7	14.6
1977	66.4	65.0	61.7	105.3	55.7	1.88	3 559.8	14.9
1978	67.7	68.5	64.9	105.6	60.5	0.48	3 763.4	15.5
1979	65.9	70.7	69.0	102.5	57.9	-1.75	3 881.8	16.0
1980	62.2	70.5	71.3	98.8	40.6	-1.90	3 894.8	15.2
1981	60.8	71.4	72.2	99.0	46.3	-2.47	4 006.5	14.0
1982	59.6	70.0	72.3	96.8	43.5	0.74	4 043.8	13.8
1983	66.5	71.2	70.6	100.9	56.8	2.02	4 126.6	13.8
1984	70.5	75.8	74.8	101.3	57.3	2.21	4 458.4	14.6
1985	73.6	78.1	78.4	99.6	48.0	2.52	4 633.7	16.0
1986	77.3	79.8	80.5	99.2	50.6	0.88	4 770.8	17.0
1987	80.7	82.4	81.9	100.6	57.4	1.73	4 904.1	16.9
1988	83.0	85.5	84.5	101.2	57.7	1.28	5 093.4	16.8
1989	82.5	87.5	87.9	99.5	47.6	-0.72	5 254.2	16.8
1990	81.1	88.5	89.5	98.8	47.9	0.45	5 321.1	16.5
1991	81.5	87.5	89.1	98.1	47.3	2.17	5 256.0	15.9
1992	85.9	88.8	86.9	102.2	50.2	3.49	5 374.1	14.9
1993	90.5	90.7	88.3	102.7	51.5	2.85	5 430.4	15.0
1994	95.4	94.1	91.1	103.2	60.1	2.88	5 593.4	15.9
1995	97.2	97.2	97.0	100.2	52.8	0.74	5 759.9	17.5
1996	100.0	100.0	100.0	100.0	50.5	1.14	5 981.1	18.5
1997	105.3	103.6	102.9	100.7	53.9	0.89	6 269.4	18.6
1998	109.0	108.0	107.1	100.9	51.1	-0.09	6 714.1	18.5
1999	112.9	111.6	111.2	100.4	53.3	0.67	6 948.4	19.0
2000	115.0	115.4	116.7	98.8	53.3	-0.21	7 345.3	19.2
2001	112.9	114.7	117.2	97.9	48.0	1.13	7 376.4	20.4
2002	118.4	114.1	116.4	98.0	53.3	2.94	7 336.0	21.3
2003	124.3	114.5	116.4	98.4	53.0	2.89	7 412.5	21.5
2004	133.5	117.5	116.4	100.9	62.6	2.93	7 648.7	21.1
2005	136.6	120.1	120.5	99.7	54.1	1.08	7 814.1	20.8
2004								
January	130.3	115.8	115.6	100.2	61.6	3.15	7 540.0	21.3
February	130.6	116.1	115.4	100.6	62.9	3.07	7 551.4	21.2
March	132.4	116.6	115.0	101.4	66.6	2.83	7 561.5	21.2
April	132.5	116.8	115.1	101.5	67.1	3.35	7 570.0	21.1
May	133.3	117.2	115.4	101.6	68.5	3.72	7 592.6	21.1
June	133.7	117.1	115.9	101.0	66.9	3.70	7 589.2	21.1
July	134.2	117.5	116.9	100.5	64.5	3.24	7 634.0	21.1
August	134.4	117.8	117.1	100.6	62.9	2.85	7 650.1	21.1
September	134.4	117.8	117.6	100.2	59.7	2.52	7 635.3	21.2
October	134.4	118.3	118.1	100.2	58.8	2.34	7 714.1	21.1
November	135.2	118.5	118.0	100.4	56.6	2.26	7 717.5	21.1
December	136.1	119.9	117.1	102.4	55.5	2.07	8 028.2	20.4
2005								
January	135.8	119.2	118.5	100.6	54.1	1.94	7 784.0	20.9
February	136.3	119.3	119.2	100.1	54.1	1.67	7 780.5	20.9
March	135.4	119.4	119.3	100.1	52.7	1.87	7 766.1	20.9
April	135.5	119.5	119.8	99.7	52.1	1.55	7 770.4	20.9
May	135.6	119.8	120.2	99.7	51.2	1.14	7 788.4	20.8
June	137.1	120.2	120.3	99.9	53.1	0.96	7 835.8	20.8
July	136.9	120.5	120.6	99.9	52.3	0.92	7 881.4	20.8
August	137.0	119.5	121.1	98.7	50.6	0.76	7 548.6	21.3
September	135.8	120.1	120.9	99.3	58.6	0.58	7 842.4	20.7
October	136.9	120.5	121.8	98.9	60.8	0.68	7 870.2	20.5
November	138.2	121.2	122.0	99.3	56.9	0.54	7 925.6	20.5
December	138.5	121.6	121.8	99.8	52.9	0.31	7 976.0	20.4

[1]Not seasonally adjusted.

Section 1b: Income and Value Added

Figure 1-4. Factor Income by Type, 1948 and 2005

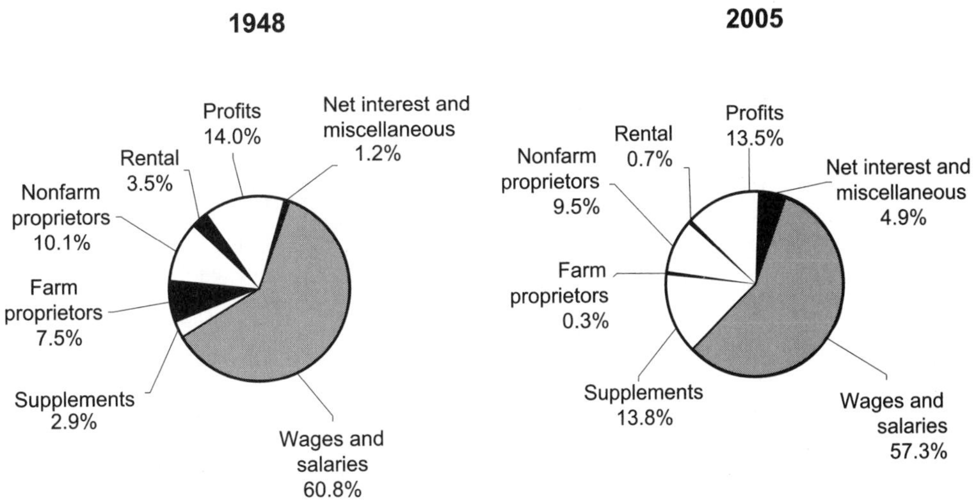

1948

- Profits 14.0%
- Net interest and miscellaneous 1.2%
- Rental 3.5%
- Nonfarm proprietors 10.1%
- Farm proprietors 7.5%
- Supplements 2.9%
- Wages and salaries 60.8%

2005

- Rental 0.7%
- Nonfarm proprietors 9.5%
- Profits 13.5%
- Net interest and miscellaneous 4.9%
- Farm proprietors 0.3%
- Supplements 13.8%
- Wages and salaries 57.3%

- The changing distribution of the national income over the postwar period is shown in the figure above, based on data in Tables 1-11 and 19-8.

- The total income concept is called "net national factor income," formerly known as simply "national income," and is the sum of the income components illustrated in the graph. The cost of all forms of labor compensation rose from 63.7 percent of the total in 1948 to 71.1 percent of the total in 2004. However, the wage and salary share declined from 60.8 percent to 57.3 percent. The increase in the total labor share is entirely accounted for by supplements to wages and salaries, which are the costs of fringe benefits, including health insurance, and taxes ("employer contributions") to pay for Social Security and Medicare.

- The farm proprietors' share dropped from 7.5 percent in 1948 to less than 1 percent in 2005. Shares going to nonfarm proprietors also declined slightly. Proprietors' income includes the return to their labor input as well as to their land and other capital, so it cannot be unequivocally attributed to either capital or labor.

- The share of rental income of persons declined from 3.5 percent in 1948 to less than 1 percent in 2005. This seems surprising, as the share includes the imputed rental income of homeowners, and homeownership has been increasing. However, the rental income imputed to homeowners is net of all the costs of owning a home, including interest, depreciation, taxes, and purchased inputs. Table 12-7 shows that home mortgage debt has been increasing relative to real estate value. Accordingly, interest costs in recent years have absorbed a much greater share of the gross rental value of homeownership than in 1948, leaving a smaller return to the homeowner's equity.

- The share of capital incomes other than rental income rose from 15.2 percent to 18.4 percent, with the interest portion rising as the corporate profits portion declined. Corporations, like homeowners, have increased their debt relative to their equity.

Table 1-9. Relation of Gross Domestic Product, Gross and Net National Product, National Income, and Personal Income

(Billions of dollars, quarterly data are at seasonally adjusted annual rates.)

NIPA Table 1.7.5

Year and quarter	Gross domestic product	Plus: Income receipts from the rest of the world	Less: Income payments to the rest of the world	Equals: Gross national product	Less: Consumption of fixed capital									Equals: Net national product
					Total	Private					Government			
						Total	Domestic business			House-holds and institutions	Total	General govern-ment	Govern-ment enter-prises	
							Total	Capital consump-tion allow-ances	Less: Capital consump-tion ad-justment					
1950	293.8	2.2	0.7	295.2	29.4	21.5	18.1	14.9	-3.2	3.3	8.0	7.5	0.5	265.8
1951	339.3	2.8	0.9	341.2	33.2	24.6	20.7	17.1	-3.6	3.8	8.7	8.1	0.6	308.0
1952	358.3	2.9	0.9	360.3	35.7	26.1	21.9	18.8	-3.1	4.2	9.6	8.9	0.6	324.6
1953	379.4	2.8	0.9	381.3	37.8	27.3	22.9	21.0	-1.9	4.4	10.5	9.8	0.7	343.5
1954	380.4	3.0	0.9	382.5	39.9	28.7	24.1	23.0	-1.1	4.7	11.2	10.4	0.7	342.6
1955	414.8	3.5	1.1	417.2	42.1	30.3	25.3	25.7	0.4	5.0	11.8	11.0	0.8	375.1
1956	437.5	3.9	1.1	440.3	46.4	33.6	28.1	27.9	-0.2	5.5	12.8	11.9	0.9	393.9
1957	461.1	4.3	1.2	464.1	49.9	36.3	30.4	30.3	-0.1	5.8	13.6	12.7	0.9	414.3
1958	467.2	3.9	1.2	469.8	52.0	38.1	32.1	31.6	-0.4	6.1	13.9	12.9	1.0	417.8
1959	506.6	4.3	1.5	509.3	53.0	38.6	32.2	33.5	1.4	6.4	14.5	13.5	1.0	456.3
1960	526.4	4.9	1.8	529.5	55.6	40.5	33.9	35.3	1.4	6.7	15.0	13.9	1.1	473.9
1961	544.7	5.3	1.8	548.2	57.2	41.6	34.7	36.7	2.0	6.9	15.6	14.4	1.2	491.0
1962	585.6	5.9	1.8	589.7	59.3	42.8	35.6	41.0	5.4	7.2	16.5	15.3	1.2	530.5
1963	617.7	6.5	2.1	622.2	62.4	44.9	37.5	43.5	6.0	7.5	17.5	16.2	1.3	559.8
1964	663.6	7.2	2.3	668.5	65.0	46.9	39.0	46.2	7.2	7.9	18.1	16.7	1.4	603.5
1965	719.1	7.9	2.6	724.4	69.4	50.5	41.9	49.5	7.6	8.5	18.9	17.4	1.5	655.0
1966	787.8	8.1	3.0	792.9	75.6	55.5	46.3	53.5	7.2	9.2	20.1	18.5	1.6	717.3
1967	832.6	8.7	3.3	838.0	81.5	59.9	50.0	57.9	7.8	9.9	21.6	19.8	1.8	756.5
1968	910.0	10.1	4.0	916.1	88.4	65.2	54.4	62.6	8.2	10.8	23.1	21.1	2.0	827.7
1969	984.6	11.8	5.7	990.7	97.9	73.1	61.2	68.9	7.7	12.0	24.8	22.6	2.2	892.8
1970	1 038.5	12.8	6.4	1 044.9	106.7	80.0	67.2	73.9	6.7	12.9	26.7	24.2	2.5	938.2
1971	1 127.1	14.0	6.4	1 134.7	115.0	86.7	72.5	79.5	6.9	14.2	28.3	25.5	2.8	1 019.7
1972	1 238.3	16.3	7.7	1 246.8	126.5	97.1	80.9	88.9	8.1	16.2	29.5	26.4	3.1	1 120.3
1973	1 382.7	23.5	10.9	1 395.3	139.3	107.9	89.9	97.0	7.1	18.0	31.4	27.8	3.5	1 256.0
1974	1 500.0	29.8	14.3	1 515.5	162.5	126.6	105.9	107.6	1.7	20.7	35.9	31.6	4.3	1 353.0
1975	1 638.3	28.0	15.0	1 651.3	187.7	147.8	124.4	118.5	-5.9	23.4	40.0	34.9	5.1	1 463.6
1976	1 825.3	32.4	15.5	1 842.1	205.2	162.5	136.9	128.6	-8.3	25.6	42.6	37.1	5.5	1 637.0
1977	2 030.9	37.2	16.9	2 051.2	230.0	184.3	155.3	146.2	-9.1	29.0	45.7	39.7	6.0	1 821.2
1978	2 294.7	46.3	24.7	2 316.3	262.3	212.8	179.3	165.5	-13.7	33.6	49.5	42.8	6.7	2 054.0
1979	2 563.3	68.3	36.4	2 595.3	300.1	245.7	206.9	190.0	-16.9	38.8	54.5	46.9	7.6	2 295.1
1980	2 789.5	79.1	44.9	2 823.7	343.0	281.1	236.8	217.1	-19.8	44.3	61.8	53.1	8.8	2 480.7
1981	3 128.4	92.0	59.1	3 161.4	388.1	317.9	268.9	269.3	0.4	49.0	70.1	60.2	10.0	2 773.3
1982	3 255.0	101.0	64.5	3 291.5	426.9	349.8	297.3	309.4	12.1	52.5	77.1	66.3	10.9	2 864.6
1983	3 536.7	101.9	64.8	3 573.8	443.8	362.1	307.4	347.8	40.4	54.7	81.7	70.2	11.5	3 130.0
1984	3 933.2	121.9	85.6	3 969.5	472.6	385.6	328.0	393.4	65.4	57.6	87.0	74.8	12.2	3 496.9
1985	4 220.3	112.4	85.9	4 246.8	506.7	414.0	353.0	445.4	92.4	61.0	92.7	79.8	12.9	3 740.1
1986	4 462.8	111.4	93.6	4 480.6	531.3	431.8	366.9	458.4	91.5	64.9	99.5	85.7	13.8	3 949.3
1987	4 739.5	123.2	105.3	4 757.4	561.9	455.3	385.7	475.1	89.4	69.5	106.7	92.1	14.6	4 195.4
1988	5 103.8	152.1	128.5	5 127.4	597.6	483.5	408.9	501.0	92.1	74.6	114.1	98.4	15.6	4 529.8
1989	5 484.4	177.7	151.5	5 510.6	644.3	522.1	440.6	523.1	82.5	81.5	122.2	105.3	16.9	4 866.3
1990	5 803.1	189.1	154.3	5 837.9	682.5	551.6	466.4	521.1	54.7	85.1	130.9	113.1	17.9	5 155.4
1991	5 995.9	168.9	138.5	6 026.3	725.9	586.9	497.4	530.1	32.7	89.5	139.1	120.2	18.8	5 300.4
1992	6 337.7	152.7	123.0	6 367.4	751.9	607.3	510.5	544.9	34.4	96.8	144.6	124.8	19.8	5 615.5
1993	6 657.4	156.2	124.3	6 689.3	776.4	624.7	524.6	569.3	44.7	100.1	151.8	130.6	21.1	5 912.9
1994	7 072.2	186.4	160.2	7 098.4	833.7	675.1	568.0	615.1	47.1	107.1	158.6	135.9	22.7	6 264.7
1995	7 397.7	233.9	198.1	7 433.4	878.4	713.4	600.2	651.8	51.6	113.2	165.0	141.4	23.6	6 555.1
1996	7 816.9	248.7	213.7	7 851.9	918.1	748.8	630.7	696.7	66.1	118.2	169.3	144.6	24.6	6 933.8
1997	8 304.3	286.7	253.7	8 337.3	974.4	800.3	675.2	756.5	81.3	125.1	174.1	148.2	25.9	7 362.8
1998	8 747.0	287.1	265.8	8 768.3	1 030.2	851.2	718.3	809.6	91.4	132.9	179.0	151.9	27.1	7 738.2
1999	9 268.4	320.8	287.0	9 302.2	1 101.3	914.3	769.8	883.6	113.7	144.5	187.0	158.4	28.6	8 200.9
2000	9 817.0	382.7	343.7	9 855.9	1 187.8	990.8	836.1	943.9	107.8	154.8	197.0	166.4	30.6	8 668.1
2001	10 128.0	322.4	278.8	10 171.6	1 281.5	1 075.5	903.7	1 028.7	124.9	171.7	206.0	172.7	33.3	8 890.2
2002	10 469.6	305.7	275.0	10 500.2	1 292.0	1 080.3	893.6	1 109.3	215.7	186.8	211.6	178.3	33.4	9 208.3
2003	10 960.8	336.8	280.0	11 017.6	1 336.5	1 118.3	916.6	1 123.6	207.0	201.7	218.2	183.2	35.0	9 681.1
2004	11 712.5	410.2	363.9	11 758.7	1 436.2	1 205.4	969.5	1 155.9	186.4	235.9	230.8	192.7	38.0	10 322.6
2005	12 455.8	513.3	481.5	12 487.7	1 604.8	1 352.6	1 059.1	953.1	-106.1	293.5	252.2	207.2	45.1	10 882.9
2003														
1st quarter	10 705.6	315.6	276.2	10 744.9	1 317.0	1 101.1	906.1	1 093.5	187.4	195.0	215.9	181.6	34.2	9 427.9
2nd quarter	10 831.8	323.6	267.0	10 888.4	1 329.5	1 111.7	912.7	1 129.5	216.9	199.1	217.7	183.0	34.7	9 558.9
3rd quarter	11 086.1	337.2	283.6	11 139.8	1 342.6	1 123.6	919.9	1 137.0	217.2	203.7	219.0	183.8	35.2	9 797.2
4th quarter	11 219.5	370.8	293.1	11 297.3	1 357.0	1 136.7	927.7	1 134.5	206.8	209.0	220.2	184.5	35.8	9 940.3
2004														
1st quarter	11 430.9	376.1	305.6	11 501.5	1 373.2	1 150.3	934.5	1 143.2	208.8	215.8	223.0	186.5	36.4	10 128.3
2nd quarter	11 649.3	398.3	357.8	11 689.7	1 394.5	1 166.4	945.0	1 143.7	198.7	221.3	228.1	190.7	37.5	10 295.2
3rd quarter	11 799.4	415.1	369.2	11 845.3	1 534.9	1 301.9	1 027.1	1 189.7	162.6	274.8	233.0	194.5	38.6	10 310.3
4th quarter	11 970.3	451.2	423.1	11 998.5	1 442.0	1 203.1	971.5	1 147.0	175.4	231.6	238.9	199.2	39.7	10 556.4
2005														
1st quarter	12 173.2	472.2	437.9	12 207.5	1 467.8	1 225.7	990.1	924.1	-66.0	235.6	242.1	202.0	40.2	10 739.7
2nd quarter	12 346.1	489.0	460.6	12 374.6	1 491.1	1 244.9	1 004.5	926.9	-77.5	240.4	246.2	205.1	41.0	10 883.5
3rd quarter	12 573.5	527.2	475.0	12 625.7	1 898.0	1 632.3	1 197.6	1 019.7	-177.9	434.7	265.7	209.1	56.6	10 727.7
4th quarter	12 730.5	564.9	552.4	12 743.0	1 562.5	1 307.5	1 044.4	941.5	-102.9	263.1	255.0	212.4	42.6	11 180.5

Table 1-9. Relation of Gross Domestic Product, Gross and Net National Product, National Income, and Personal Income—Continued

(Billions of dollars, quarterly data are at seasonally adjusted annual rates.)

NIPA Table 1.7.5

Year and quarter	Net national product	Less: Statistical discrepancy	Equals: National income	Corporate profits with IVA and CCAdj	Taxes on production and imports less subsidies	Contributions for government social insurance	Net interest and miscellaneous payments on assets	Business current transfer payments, net	Current surplus of government enterprises	Wage accruals less disbursements	Personal income receipts on assets	Personal current transfer receipts	Equals: Personal income	Addendum: Gross national income
							Less:				Plus:			
1950	265.8	1.4	264.4	36.0	22.4	5.5	3.2	0.9	. . .	0.0	18.6	14.0	229.0	293.8
1951	308.0	3.6	304.3	41.2	24.0	6.6	3.7	1.2	. . .	0.1	19.1	11.4	258.0	337.6
1952	324.6	2.8	321.8	39.3	26.7	6.9	4.1	1.3	. . .	0.0	19.9	11.9	275.4	357.5
1953	343.5	4.0	339.5	39.7	29.0	7.1	4.7	1.2	. . .	-0.1	21.6	12.5	291.9	377.2
1954	342.6	3.2	339.4	38.8	29.0	8.1	5.6	1.0	. . .	0.0	23.2	14.3	294.5	379.3
1955	375.1	2.5	372.7	49.5	31.7	9.1	6.2	1.4	. . .	0.0	25.7	15.7	316.1	414.8
1956	393.9	-1.7	395.6	48.5	33.9	10.0	6.9	1.7	. . .	0.0	28.2	16.8	339.6	441.9
1957	414.3	0.0	414.3	48.4	36.0	11.4	8.0	1.9	. . .	0.0	30.6	19.5	358.7	464.1
1958	417.8	1.0	416.8	43.5	36.8	11.4	9.5	1.8	. . .	0.0	31.9	23.5	369.0	468.8
1959	456.3	0.5	455.8	55.7	40.0	13.8	9.6	1.8	1.0	0.0	34.6	24.2	392.8	508.9
1960	473.9	-0.9	474.9	53.8	43.4	16.4	10.6	1.9	0.9	0.0	37.9	25.7	411.5	530.4
1961	491.0	-0.6	491.6	54.9	45.0	17.0	12.5	2.0	0.8	0.0	40.1	29.5	429.0	548.8
1962	530.5	0.4	530.1	63.3	48.2	19.1	14.2	2.2	0.9	0.0	44.1	30.4	456.7	589.4
1963	559.8	-0.8	560.6	69.0	51.2	21.7	15.2	2.7	1.4	0.0	47.9	32.2	479.6	623.0
1964	603.5	0.8	602.7	76.5	54.6	22.4	17.4	3.1	1.3	0.0	53.8	33.5	514.6	667.7
1965	655.0	1.6	653.4	87.5	57.8	23.4	19.6	3.6	1.3	0.0	59.4	36.2	555.7	722.8
1966	717.3	6.3	711.0	93.2	59.3	31.3	22.4	3.5	1.0	0.0	64.1	39.6	603.9	786.6
1967	756.5	4.6	751.9	91.3	64.2	34.9	25.5	3.8	0.9	0.0	69.0	48.0	648.3	833.4
1968	827.7	4.6	823.2	98.8	72.3	38.7	27.1	4.3	1.2	0.0	75.2	56.1	712.0	911.5
1969	892.8	3.2	889.7	95.4	79.4	44.1	32.7	4.9	1.0	0.0	84.1	62.3	778.5	987.6
1970	938.2	7.3	930.9	83.6	86.7	46.4	39.1	4.5	0.0	0.0	93.5	74.7	838.8	1 037.6
1971	1 019.7	11.6	1 008.1	98.0	95.9	51.2	43.9	4.3	-0.2	0.6	101.0	88.1	903.5	1 123.1
1972	1 120.3	9.1	1 111.2	112.1	101.4	59.2	47.9	4.9	0.5	0.0	109.6	97.9	992.7	1 237.7
1973	1 256.0	8.6	1 247.4	125.5	112.1	75.5	55.2	6.0	-0.4	-0.1	124.7	112.6	1 110.7	1 386.7
1974	1 353.0	10.9	1 342.1	115.8	121.7	85.2	70.8	7.1	-0.9	-0.5	146.4	133.3	1 222.6	1 504.6
1975	1 463.6	17.7	1 445.9	134.8	131.0	89.3	81.6	9.4	-3.2	0.1	162.2	170.0	1 335.0	1 633.6
1976	1 637.0	25.1	1 611.8	163.3	141.5	101.3	85.5	9.5	-1.8	0.1	178.4	184.0	1 474.8	1 817.0
1977	1 821.2	22.3	1 798.9	192.4	152.8	113.1	101.1	8.4	-2.6	0.1	205.3	194.2	1 633.2	2 028.9
1978	2 054.0	26.6	2 027.4	216.6	162.2	131.3	115.0	10.6	-1.9	0.3	234.8	209.6	1 837.7	2 289.7
1979	2 295.1	46.0	2 249.1	223.2	171.9	152.7	138.9	13.0	-2.6	-0.2	274.7	235.3	2 062.2	2 549.2
1980	2 480.7	41.4	2 439.3	201.1	190.9	166.2	181.8	14.4	-4.8	0.0	338.7	279.5	2 307.9	2 782.3
1981	2 773.3	30.9	2 742.4	226.1	224.5	195.7	232.3	17.6	-4.9	0.1	421.9	318.4	2 591.3	3 130.4
1982	2 864.6	0.3	2 864.3	209.7	226.4	208.9	271.1	20.1	-4.0	0.0	488.4	354.8	2 775.3	3 291.2
1983	3 130.0	45.7	3 084.2	264.2	242.5	226.0	285.3	22.5	-3.1	-0.4	529.6	383.7	2 960.7	3 528.0
1984	3 496.9	14.6	3 482.3	318.6	269.3	257.5	327.1	30.1	-1.9	0.2	607.9	400.1	3 289.5	3 954.9
1985	3 740.1	16.7	3 723.4	330.3	287.3	281.4	341.3	34.8	0.8	-0.2	654.0	424.9	3 526.7	4 230.1
1986	3 949.3	47.0	3 902.3	319.5	298.9	303.4	366.8	36.6	1.3	0.0	695.5	451.0	3 722.4	4 433.6
1987	4 195.4	21.7	4 173.7	368.8	317.7	323.1	366.4	33.8	1.2	0.0	717.0	467.6	3 947.4	4 735.7
1988	4 529.8	-19.5	4 549.4	432.6	345.5	361.5	385.3	34.0	2.5	0.0	769.3	496.6	4 253.7	5 147.0
1989	4 866.3	39.7	4 826.6	426.6	372.1	385.2	432.1	39.2	4.9	0.0	878.0	543.4	4 587.8	5 470.9
1990	5 155.4	66.2	5 089.1	437.8	398.7	410.1	442.2	39.4	1.6	0.1	924.0	595.2	4 878.6	5 771.6
1991	5 300.4	72.5	5 227.9	451.2	430.2	430.2	418.2	39.9	5.7	-0.1	932.0	666.4	5 051.0	5 953.8
1992	5 615.5	102.7	5 512.8	479.3	453.9	455.0	388.5	42.4	7.6	-15.8	910.9	749.4	5 362.0	6 264.7
1993	5 912.9	139.5	5 773.4	541.9	467.0	477.7	365.7	40.7	7.2	6.4	901.8	790.1	5 558.5	6 549.8
1994	6 264.7	142.5	6 122.3	600.3	513.5	508.2	366.4	43.3	8.6	17.6	950.8	827.3	5 842.5	6 955.9
1995	6 555.1	101.2	6 453.9	696.7	524.2	532.8	367.1	46.9	11.4	16.4	1 016.4	877.4	6 152.3	7 332.3
1996	6 933.8	93.7	6 840.1	786.2	546.8	555.2	376.2	53.1	12.7	3.6	1 089.2	925.0	6 520.6	7 758.2
1997	7 362.8	70.7	7 292.2	868.5	579.1	587.2	415.6	49.9	12.6	-2.9	1 181.7	951.2	6 915.1	8 266.6
1998	7 738.2	-14.6	7 752.8	801.6	604.4	624.2	487.1	64.7	10.3	-0.7	1 283.2	978.6	7 423.0	8 783.0
1999	8 200.9	-35.7	8 236.7	851.3	629.8	661.4	495.4	67.4	10.1	5.2	1 264.2	1 022.1	7 802.4	9 337.9
2000	8 668.1	-127.2	8 795.2	817.9	664.6	702.7	559.0	87.1	5.3	0.0	1 387.0	1 084.0	8 429.7	9 983.1
2001	8 890.2	-89.6	8 979.8	767.3	673.3	731.1	566.3	92.8	-1.4	0.0	1 380.0	1 193.9	8 724.1	10 261.3
2002	9 208.3	-21.0	9 229.3	886.3	724.4	750.0	520.9	84.3	0.9	0.0	1 333.2	1 286.2	8 881.9	10 521.2
2003	9 681.1	48.8	9 632.3	993.1	759.3	778.6	524.7	83.8	1.7	15.0	1 336.6	1 351.0	9 163.6	10 968.8
2004	10 322.6	66.7	10 255.9	1 182.6	819.4	826.4	485.1	85.5	-5.0	-15.0	1 427.9	1 426.5	9 731.4	11 692.0
2005	10 882.9	71.0	10 811.8	1 330.7	865.1	880.6	483.4	74.2	-15.4	0.0	1 519.4	1 526.6	10 239.2	12 416.6
2003														
1st quarter	9 427.9	21.3	9 406.7	923.6	745.5	765.4	529.1	84.1	5.4	11.4	1 329.1	1 327.0	8 998.2	10 723.7
2nd quarter	9 558.9	21.1	9 537.9	956.2	744.6	775.0	529.6	83.8	2.5	13.6	1 334.9	1 344.0	9 111.3	10 867.3
3rd quarter	9 797.2	97.9	9 699.3	1 016.2	766.4	782.1	526.4	84.1	0.5	25.0	1 339.5	1 365.5	9 203.6	11 041.9
4th quarter	9 940.3	54.9	9 885.4	1 076.5	780.7	791.9	513.7	83.3	-1.5	10.0	1 343.1	1 367.6	9 341.3	11 242.4
2004														
1st quarter	10 128.3	43.9	10 084.3	1 158.1	801.7	810.8	501.8	85.4	-2.3	-3.5	1 366.1	1 399.3	9 497.7	11 457.6
2nd quarter	10 295.2	88.2	10 207.0	1 183.3	815.4	819.8	493.4	86.1	-3.6	-21.5	1 389.8	1 416.7	9 640.5	11 601.5
3rd quarter	10 310.3	66.8	10 243.5	1 154.0	822.9	831.8	475.7	79.1	-5.6	-25.0	1 415.7	1 441.7	9 767.9	11 778.4
4th quarter	10 556.4	67.8	10 488.6	1 234.9	837.4	843.1	469.4	91.2	-8.6	-10.0	1 539.8	1 448.4	10 019.4	11 930.6
2005														
1st quarter	10 739.7	37.4	10 702.3	1 320.0	849.4	863.6	483.7	97.6	-9.1	0.0	1 464.3	1 487.3	10 048.8	12 170.1
2nd quarter	10 883.5	88.1	10 795.4	1 342.9	864.7	871.5	477.1	99.9	-11.3	0.0	1 500.5	1 510.1	10 161.5	12 286.5
3rd quarter	10 727.7	84.5	10 643.2	1 266.3	872.1	888.5	482.9	0.2	-27.7	0.0	1 532.7	1 569.0	10 262.7	12 541.2
4th quarter	11 180.5	74.3	11 106.2	1 393.5	874.2	898.9	490.0	99.1	-13.3	0.0	1 580.2	1 539.8	10 483.7	12 668.7

. . . = Not available.

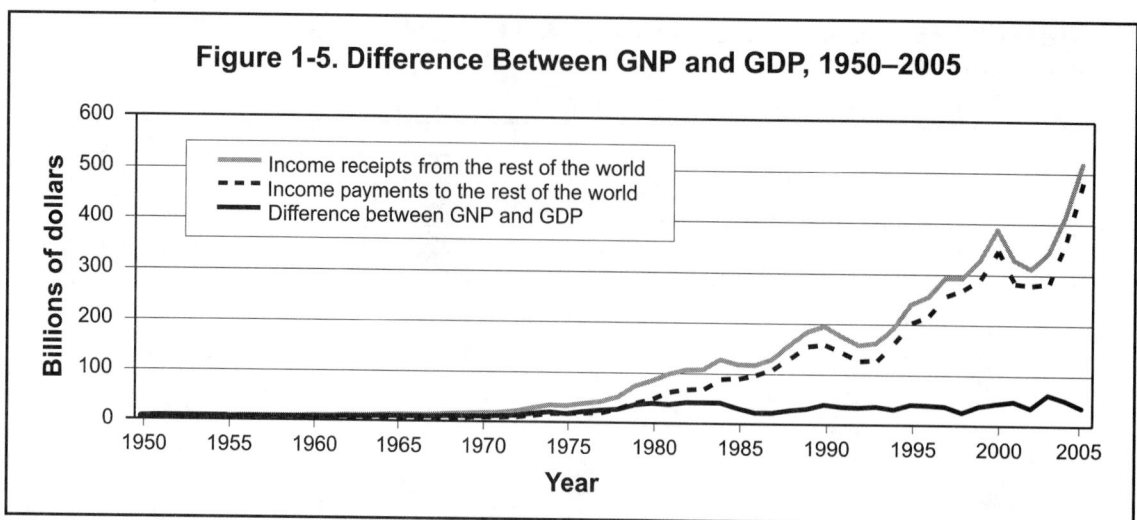

Figure 1-5. Difference Between GNP and GDP, 1950–2005

•Over the postwar period, income receipts by U.S. residents from the rest of the world have consistently exceeded income payments from U.S. industries to the rest of the world. In other words, U.S. residents have had more income to spend than was generated by production within the country's boundaries. This was indicated by an excess of gross national product (GNP) over gross domestic product (GDP). (Table 1-9)

•Through the early 1980s, the excess of receipts over payments was growing relative to GDP, rising from 0.5 percent in 1950 to 1.2 percent in 1979 and 1980. However, it shrank rapidly to 0.4 percent in 1986 and has fluctuated around that level ever since. (Table 1-9)

•This relative decline in the gap reflects the deteriorating international investment position of the United States. The excess of U.S. assets abroad over foreign-owned assets in the United States peaked in 1980. The investment position then declined rapidly and became negative in 1986. At the end of 2005, the value of foreign-owned assets in the United States exceeded the value of U.S.-owned assets abroad by $2.7 trillion, as a result of balance of payments deficits and the associated inflows of foreign capital. (Table 7-8) This net indebtedness amounted to 21.6 percent of GDP.

•The gap between GNP and GDP reflects differences in three income components: compensation, net interest and miscellaneous payments, and corporate profits. Comparison between those elements, as shown in Table 1-10 (domestic income) and Table 1-11 (national income), illustrates that profits earned by U.S. corporations still exceed those generated in the domestic economy, but net payments of interest by domestic industry are increasingly going to overseas lenders.

Table 1-10. Gross Domestic Income by Type of Income

(Billions of dollars, quarterly data are at seasonally adjusted annual rates.)

NIPA Tables 1.1.5, 1.10

Year and quarter	Gross domestic income	Compensation of employees			Taxes on production and imports	Less: Subsidies	Net operating surplus					
								Private enterprises				
		Total	Wage and salary accruals	Supplements to wages and salaries			Total	Total	Net interest and miscellaneous payments, domestic industries	Business current transfer payments, net	Proprietors' income with IVA and CCAdj	Rental income of persons with CCAdj
1950	292.4	155.2	147.2	8.0	23.0	0.6	. . .	85.4	3.1	0.9	37.6	9.2
1951	335.7	181.4	171.6	9.8	24.8	0.7	. . .	97.0	3.5	1.2	42.7	10.1
1952	355.6	196.2	185.6	10.5	27.1	0.4	. . .	97.0	4.0	1.3	43.1	11.2
1953	375.3	210.2	199.0	11.2	29.1	0.1	. . .	98.4	4.6	1.2	42.1	12.5
1954	377.2	209.2	197.3	11.9	28.9	-0.1	. . .	99.1	5.4	1.0	42.3	13.5
1955	412.3	225.8	212.2	13.5	31.5	-0.2	. . .	112.8	6.1	1.4	44.3	13.9
1956	439.2	244.6	229.1	15.5	34.3	0.4	. . .	114.3	6.8	1.7	45.8	14.2
1957	461.1	257.6	240.0	17.6	36.6	0.7	. . .	117.6	8.0	1.9	47.9	14.6
1958	466.2	259.6	241.4	18.2	37.7	0.9	. . .	117.7	9.4	1.8	50.1	15.4
1959	506.1	281.1	259.9	21.1	41.1	1.1	132.0	131.0	9.5	1.8	50.7	16.2
1960	527.3	296.6	273.0	23.6	44.6	1.1	131.8	130.8	10.4	1.9	50.8	17.1
1961	545.3	305.4	280.7	24.8	47.0	2.0	137.6	136.8	12.1	2.0	53.2	17.9
1962	585.3	327.2	299.5	27.8	50.4	2.3	150.6	149.7	13.8	2.2	55.4	18.8
1963	618.5	345.3	314.9	30.4	53.4	2.2	159.6	158.3	14.7	2.7	56.5	19.5
1964	662.8	370.7	337.8	32.9	57.3	2.7	172.4	171.1	16.9	3.1	59.4	19.6
1965	717.5	399.5	363.8	35.7	60.8	3.0	190.9	189.6	19.1	3.6	63.9	20.2
1966	781.5	442.6	400.3	42.3	63.3	3.9	204.0	203.0	21.9	3.5	68.2	20.8
1967	828.0	475.1	429.0	46.1	68.0	3.8	207.2	206.2	24.9	3.8	69.8	21.2
1968	905.4	524.3	472.0	52.3	76.5	4.2	220.5	219.3	26.7	4.3	74.3	20.9
1969	981.4	577.6	518.3	59.3	84.0	4.5	226.5	225.5	33.2	4.9	77.4	21.2
1970	1 031.2	617.2	551.5	65.7	91.5	4.8	220.6	220.6	39.9	4.5	78.4	21.4
1971	1 115.5	658.9	584.5	74.4	100.6	4.7	245.7	245.9	44.2	4.3	84.8	22.4
1972	1 229.2	725.1	638.8	86.4	108.1	6.6	276.1	275.6	48.9	4.9	95.9	23.4
1973	1 374.1	811.2	708.8	102.5	117.3	5.2	311.4	311.8	57.5	6.0	113.5	24.3
1974	1 489.1	890.3	772.3	118.0	125.0	3.3	314.6	315.6	72.7	7.1	113.1	24.3
1975	1 620.6	949.2	814.9	134.3	135.5	4.5	352.7	356.0	83.2	9.4	119.5	23.7
1976	1 800.1	1 059.4	899.8	159.6	146.6	5.1	394.1	396.0	85.2	9.5	132.2	22.3
1977	2 008.7	1 180.6	994.2	186.4	159.9	7.1	445.3	447.9	99.8	8.4	145.7	20.7
1978	2 268.1	1 336.2	1 121.3	214.9	171.2	8.9	507.4	509.3	116.2	10.6	166.6	22.1
1979	2 517.3	1 500.8	1 255.9	245.0	180.4	8.5	544.4	547.0	141.5	13.0	180.1	23.8
1980	2 748.1	1 651.9	1 377.7	274.2	200.7	9.8	562.3	567.2	183.0	14.4	174.1	30.0
1981	3 097.5	1 826.0	1 517.7	308.3	236.0	11.5	658.9	663.9	228.9	17.6	183.0	38.0
1982	3 254.7	1 926.0	1 593.9	332.1	241.3	15.0	675.4	679.4	267.0	20.1	176.3	38.8
1983	3 490.9	2 042.8	1 684.8	358.0	263.7	21.2	761.9	765.0	283.1	22.5	192.5	37.8
1984	3 918.6	2 255.8	1 855.3	400.5	290.2	21.0	920.9	922.8	327.1	30.1	243.3	40.2
1985	4 203.6	2 424.9	1 995.7	429.2	308.5	21.3	984.7	983.9	352.6	34.8	262.3	41.9
1986	4 415.8	2 571.9	2 116.6	455.3	323.7	24.8	1 013.7	1 012.4	386.6	36.6	275.7	33.5
1987	4 717.8	2 751.6	2 272.1	479.5	347.9	30.2	1 086.6	1 085.4	395.1	33.8	302.2	33.5
1988	5 123.3	2 968.1	2 453.8	514.2	374.9	29.4	1 212.1	1 209.6	417.8	34.0	341.6	40.6
1989	5 444.7	3 146.5	2 597.6	548.9	399.3	27.2	1 281.8	1 276.9	471.7	39.2	363.3	43.1
1990	5 736.8	3 340.5	2 756.3	584.2	425.5	26.8	1 315.1	1 313.5	481.1	39.4	380.6	50.7
1991	5 923.4	3 448.0	2 825.7	622.3	457.5	27.3	1 319.3	1 313.6	461.6	39.9	377.1	60.3
1992	6 235.0	3 638.4	2 967.5	670.9	483.8	29.9	1 390.8	1 383.2	428.9	42.4	427.6	78.0
1993	6 517.9	3 804.7	3 092.5	712.2	503.4	36.4	1 469.7	1 462.4	407.4	40.7	453.8	95.6
1994	6 929.7	4 001.2	3 253.8	747.5	545.6	32.2	1 581.3	1 572.8	413.3	43.3	473.3	119.7
1995	7 296.5	4 197.4	3 439.8	757.7	558.2	34.0	1 696.4	1 685.0	420.0	46.9	492.1	122.1
1996	7 723.2	4 394.7	3 627.3	767.3	581.1	34.3	1 863.6	1 850.9	438.9	53.1	543.2	131.5
1997	8 233.7	4 666.1	3 879.1	787.0	612.0	32.9	2 014.1	2 001.5	489.2	49.9	576.0	128.8
1998	8 761.6	5 023.9	4 187.3	836.7	639.8	35.4	2 103.1	2 092.8	564.1	64.7	627.8	137.5
1999	9 304.1	5 362.3	4 476.6	885.7	674.0	44.2	2 210.7	2 200.6	577.9	67.4	678.3	147.3
2000	9 944.1	5 787.3	4 833.8	953.4	708.9	44.3	2 304.5	2 299.1	661.2	87.1	728.4	150.3
2001	10 217.6	5 947.2	4 947.9	999.3	728.6	55.3	2 315.6	2 317.0	687.2	92.8	771.9	167.4
2002	10 490.6	6 096.6	4 986.3	1 110.3	762.8	38.4	2 377.6	2 376.8	640.7	84.3	768.4	152.9
2003	10 912.0	6 331.1	5 133.4	1 197.7	807.2	47.9	2 485.1	2 483.4	627.6	83.8	811.3	133.0
2004	11 645.8	6 656.3	5 383.2	1 273.2	864.0	44.7	2 733.9	2 738.9	609.0	85.5	911.1	127.0
2005	12 384.8	7 036.6	5 671.1	1 365.5	922.4	57.3	2 878.2	2 893.6	642.3	74.2	970.7	72.8
2003												
1st quarter	10 684.3	6 208.3	5 038.2	1 170.0	787.5	42.0	2 413.5	2 408.2	633.1	84.1	779.1	137.4
2nd quarter	10 810.8	6 294.6	5 104.3	1 190.3	800.2	55.6	2 442.1	2 439.6	626.3	83.8	801.6	130.5
3rd quarter	10 988.2	6 371.5	5 164.9	1 206.6	812.9	46.5	2 507.7	2 507.3	630.2	84.1	823.5	116.3
4th quarter	11 164.7	6 450.0	5 226.1	1 223.9	828.0	47.3	2 577.0	2 578.5	620.9	83.3	840.8	147.6
2004												
1st quarter	11 387.0	6 527.8	5 282.3	1 245.5	845.4	43.7	2 684.2	2 686.5	610.1	85.4	877.5	140.1
2nd quarter	11 561.0	6 596.3	5 334.3	1 262.1	858.2	42.8	2 754.8	2 758.4	616.6	86.1	910.2	132.0
3rd quarter	11 732.6	6 695.5	5 414.0	1 281.5	867.2	44.3	2 679.2	2 684.8	606.5	79.1	915.1	112.7
4th quarter	11 902.5	6 805.7	5 502.1	1 303.5	885.2	47.8	2 817.4	2 825.9	602.7	91.2	941.5	123.4
2005												
1st quarter	12 135.8	6 895.8	5 561.9	1 333.9	901.6	52.3	2 922.9	2 932.0	626.2	97.6	952.8	118.5
2nd quarter	12 258.1	6 959.9	5 607.5	1 352.4	920.2	55.6	2 942.4	2 953.8	627.6	99.9	965.8	102.8
3rd quarter	12 489.0	7 100.1	5 721.7	1 378.4	930.2	58.1	2 618.9	2 646.6	647.7	0.2	967.3	-11.5
4th quarter	12 656.2	7 190.7	5 793.3	1 397.4	937.3	63.1	3 028.8	3 042.1	667.5	99.1	996.8	81.5

. . . = Not available.

Table 1-10. Gross Domestic Income by Type of Income—Continued

(Billions of dollars, quarterly data are at seasonally adjusted annual rates.)

NIPA Tables 1.1.5, 1.10

Year and quarter	Net operating surplus—Continued					Current surplus of government enterprises	Consumption of fixed capital			Statistical discrepancy	Gross domestic product
	Private enterprises—Continued										
	Corporate profits with IVA and CCAdj, domestic industries										
			Profits after tax								
	Total	Taxes on corporate income	Total	Net dividends	Undistributed corporate profits		Total	Private	Government		
1950	34.7	17.9	16.8	7.9	9.0	...	29.4	21.5	8.0	1.4	293.8
1951	39.5	22.6	16.9	7.4	9.5	...	33.2	24.6	8.7	3.6	339.3
1952	37.4	19.4	18.0	7.5	10.5	...	35.7	26.1	9.6	2.8	358.3
1953	37.9	20.3	17.6	7.8	9.9	...	37.8	27.3	10.5	4.0	379.4
1954	36.9	17.6	19.3	7.9	11.4	...	39.9	28.7	11.2	3.2	380.4
1955	47.2	22.0	25.1	8.9	16.2	...	42.1	30.3	11.8	2.5	414.8
1956	45.7	22.0	23.7	9.5	14.2	...	46.4	33.6	12.8	-1.7	437.5
1957	45.3	21.4	23.8	9.9	14.0	...	49.9	36.3	13.6	0.0	461.1
1958	41.0	19.0	22.0	9.8	12.2	...	52.0	38.1	13.9	1.0	467.2
1959	53.0	23.7	29.2	10.7	18.5	1.0	53.0	38.6	14.5	0.5	506.6
1960	50.6	22.8	27.9	11.4	16.4	0.9	55.6	40.5	15.0	-0.9	526.4
1961	51.5	22.9	28.6	11.5	17.1	0.8	57.2	41.6	15.6	-0.6	544.7
1962	59.5	24.1	35.4	12.4	23.0	0.9	59.3	42.8	16.5	0.4	585.6
1963	64.9	26.4	38.5	13.6	25.0	1.4	62.4	44.9	17.5	-0.8	617.7
1964	72.0	28.2	43.8	15.0	28.9	1.3	65.0	46.9	18.1	0.8	663.6
1965	82.8	31.1	51.7	16.9	34.8	1.3	69.4	50.5	18.9	1.6	719.1
1966	88.7	33.9	54.8	17.8	37.0	1.0	75.6	55.5	20.1	6.3	787.8
1967	86.6	32.9	53.7	18.3	35.3	0.9	81.5	59.9	21.6	4.6	832.6
1968	93.2	39.6	53.5	20.2	33.4	1.2	88.4	65.2	23.1	4.6	910.0
1969	88.8	40.0	48.8	20.4	28.4	1.0	97.9	73.1	24.8	3.2	984.6
1970	76.5	34.8	41.8	20.4	21.4	0.0	106.7	80.0	26.7	7.3	1 038.5
1971	90.2	38.2	52.0	20.3	31.7	-0.2	115.0	86.7	28.3	11.6	1 127.1
1972	102.6	42.3	60.2	21.9	38.3	0.5	126.5	97.1	29.5	9.1	1 238.3
1973	110.6	50.0	60.6	23.1	37.5	-0.4	139.3	107.9	31.4	8.6	1 382.7
1974	98.3	52.8	45.5	23.5	22.1	-0.9	162.5	126.6	35.9	10.9	1 500.0
1975	120.2	51.6	68.6	26.4	42.2	-3.2	187.7	147.8	40.0	17.7	1 638.3
1976	146.8	65.3	81.5	30.1	51.4	-1.8	205.2	162.5	42.6	25.1	1 825.3
1977	173.3	74.4	98.9	33.7	65.2	-2.6	230.0	184.3	45.7	22.3	2 030.9
1978	193.8	84.9	108.9	39.6	69.3	-1.9	262.3	212.8	49.5	26.6	2 294.7
1979	188.6	90.0	98.6	41.5	57.1	-2.6	300.1	245.7	54.5	46.0	2 563.3
1980	165.7	87.2	78.5	47.3	31.1	-4.8	343.0	281.1	61.8	41.4	2 789.5
1981	196.4	84.3	112.1	58.3	53.8	-4.9	388.1	317.9	70.1	30.9	3 128.4
1982	177.1	66.5	110.6	61.3	49.2	-4.0	426.9	349.8	77.1	0.3	3 255.0
1983	229.2	80.6	148.5	71.3	77.2	-3.1	443.8	362.1	81.7	45.7	3 536.7
1984	282.0	97.5	184.5	78.5	106.0	-1.9	472.6	385.6	87.0	14.6	3 933.2
1985	292.2	99.4	192.8	85.7	107.1	0.8	506.7	414.0	92.7	16.7	4 220.3
1986	280.0	109.7	170.4	88.3	82.1	1.3	531.3	431.8	99.5	47.0	4 462.8
1987	320.8	130.4	190.4	95.6	94.8	1.2	561.9	455.3	106.7	21.7	4 739.5
1988	375.7	141.6	234.0	98.0	136.0	2.5	597.6	483.5	114.1	-19.5	5 103.8
1989	359.5	146.1	213.4	126.4	87.0	4.9	644.3	522.1	122.2	39.7	5 484.4
1990	361.7	145.4	216.3	144.1	72.2	1.6	682.5	551.6	130.9	66.2	5 803.1
1991	374.7	138.6	236.1	156.4	79.8	5.7	725.9	586.9	139.1	72.5	5 995.9
1992	406.2	148.7	257.5	159.9	97.7	7.6	751.9	607.3	144.6	102.7	6 337.7
1993	465.0	171.0	294.0	182.2	111.7	7.2	776.4	624.7	151.8	139.5	6 657.4
1994	523.2	193.7	329.5	197.4	132.0	8.6	833.7	675.1	158.6	142.5	7 072.2
1995	603.9	218.7	385.2	221.6	163.7	11.4	878.4	713.4	165.0	101.2	7 397.7
1996	684.3	231.7	452.6	257.3	195.3	12.7	918.1	748.8	169.3	93.7	7 816.9
1997	757.5	246.1	511.5	283.9	227.6	12.6	974.4	800.3	174.1	70.7	8 304.3
1998	698.7	248.3	450.4	309.2	141.2	10.3	1 030.2	851.2	179.0	-14.6	8 747.0
1999	729.8	258.6	471.1	295.7	175.5	10.1	1 101.3	914.3	187.0	-35.7	9 268.4
2000	672.2	265.2	407.0	348.4	58.6	5.3	1 187.8	990.8	197.0	-127.2	9 817.0
2001	597.6	204.1	393.5	330.1	63.4	-1.4	1 281.5	1 075.5	206.0	-89.6	10 128.0
2002	730.5	192.6	537.9	351.3	186.5	0.9	1 292.0	1 080.3	211.6	-21.0	10 469.6
2003	827.7	243.3	584.4	392.8	191.6	1.7	1 336.5	1 118.3	218.2	48.8	10 960.8
2004	1 006.3	300.1	706.2	492.7	213.6	-5.0	1 436.2	1 205.4	230.8	66.7	11 712.5
2005	1 133.7	399.3	734.4	338.7	395.7	-15.4	1 604.8	1 352.6	252.2	71.0	12 455.8
2003											
1st quarter	774.4	234.1	540.3	342.5	197.8	5.4	1 317.0	1 101.1	215.9	21.3	10 705.6
2nd quarter	797.3	228.9	568.5	431.4	137.1	2.5	1 329.5	1 111.7	217.7	21.1	10 831.8
3rd quarter	853.1	245.5	607.6	393.3	214.3	0.5	1 342.6	1 123.6	219.0	97.9	11 086.1
4th quarter	885.9	264.7	621.2	403.9	217.3	-1.5	1 357.0	1 136.7	220.2	54.9	11 219.5
2004											
1st quarter	973.3	281.3	692.0	457.0	235.0	-2.3	1 373.2	1 150.3	223.0	43.9	11 430.9
2nd quarter	1 013.4	303.0	710.4	421.2	289.2	-3.6	1 394.5	1 166.4	228.1	88.2	11 649.3
3rd quarter	971.4	297.8	673.6	468.4	205.1	-5.6	1 534.9	1 301.9	233.0	66.8	11 799.4
4th quarter	1 067.0	318.1	748.9	624.0	125.0	-8.6	1 442.0	1 203.1	238.9	67.8	11 970.3
2005											
1st quarter	1 136.9	400.9	736.0	470.5	265.5	-9.1	1 467.8	1 225.7	242.1	37.4	12 173.2
2nd quarter	1 157.7	392.8	764.9	411.5	353.4	-11.3	1 491.1	1 244.9	246.2	88.1	12 346.1
3rd quarter	1 042.9	378.9	664.0	237.9	426.1	-27.7	1 898.0	1 632.3	265.7	84.5	12 573.5
4th quarter	1 197.2	424.6	772.6	234.9	537.7	-13.3	1 562.5	1 307.5	255.0	74.3	12 730.5

. . . = Not available.

Table 1-11. National Income by Type of Income

(Billions of dollars, quarterly data are at seasonally adjusted annual rates.)

NIPA Tables 1.7.5, 1.12

Year and quarter	National income, total	Compensation of employees Total	Wage and salary accruals Total	Government	Other	Supplements to wages and salaries Total	Employer contributions for: Employee pension and insurance funds	Government social insurance	Proprietors' income with IVA and CCAdj Total	Farm	Nonfarm	Rental income of persons with CCAdj
1950	264.4	155.3	147.3	22.6	124.6	8.0	4.7	3.4	37.6	12.9	24.7	9.2
1951	304.3	181.4	171.6	29.2	142.4	9.8	5.7	4.1	42.7	15.3	27.4	10.1
1952	321.8	196.2	185.6	33.4	152.3	10.5	6.4	4.1	43.1	14.3	28.8	11.2
1953	339.5	210.2	199.0	34.3	164.7	11.2	7.0	4.2	42.1	12.1	30.0	12.5
1954	339.4	209.2	197.3	34.9	162.4	11.9	7.3	4.6	42.3	11.7	30.6	13.5
1955	372.7	225.7	212.2	36.6	175.6	13.5	8.4	5.2	44.3	10.6	33.7	13.9
1956	395.6	244.5	229.0	38.8	190.2	15.5	9.8	5.7	45.8	10.5	35.4	14.2
1957	414.3	257.5	240.0	41.0	198.9	17.6	11.2	6.4	47.9	10.4	37.4	14.6
1958	416.8	259.5	241.3	44.1	197.2	18.2	11.9	6.3	50.1	12.3	37.8	15.4
1959	455.8	281.0	259.8	46.1	213.8	21.1	13.3	7.9	50.7	10.0	40.6	16.2
1960	474.9	296.4	272.9	49.2	223.7	23.6	14.3	9.3	50.8	10.5	40.3	17.1
1961	491.6	305.3	280.5	52.5	228.0	24.8	15.2	9.6	53.2	11.0	42.2	17.9
1962	530.1	327.1	299.4	56.3	243.0	27.8	16.6	11.2	55.4	11.0	44.4	18.8
1963	560.6	345.2	314.9	60.0	254.8	30.4	18.0	12.4	56.5	10.8	45.7	19.5
1964	602.7	370.7	337.8	64.9	272.9	32.9	20.3	12.6	59.4	9.6	49.8	19.6
1965	653.4	399.5	363.8	69.9	293.8	35.7	22.7	13.1	63.9	11.8	52.1	20.2
1966	711.0	442.7	400.3	78.4	321.9	42.3	25.5	16.8	68.2	12.8	55.4	20.8
1967	751.9	475.1	429.0	86.5	342.5	46.1	28.1	18.0	69.8	11.5	58.4	21.2
1968	823.2	524.3	472.0	96.7	375.3	52.3	32.4	20.0	74.3	11.5	62.8	20.9
1969	889.7	577.6	518.3	105.6	412.7	59.3	36.5	22.8	77.4	12.6	64.7	21.2
1970	930.9	617.2	551.6	117.2	434.3	65.7	41.8	23.8	78.4	12.7	65.7	21.4
1971	1 008.1	658.9	584.5	126.8	457.8	74.4	47.9	26.4	84.8	13.2	71.6	22.4
1972	1 111.2	725.1	638.8	137.9	500.9	86.4	55.2	31.2	95.9	16.8	79.1	23.4
1973	1 247.4	811.2	708.8	148.8	560.0	102.5	62.7	39.8	113.5	28.9	84.6	24.3
1974	1 342.1	890.2	772.3	160.5	611.8	118.0	73.3	44.7	113.1	23.2	89.9	24.3
1975	1 445.9	949.1	814.8	176.2	638.6	134.3	87.6	46.7	119.5	21.7	97.8	23.7
1976	1 611.8	1 059.3	899.7	188.9	710.8	159.6	105.2	54.4	132.2	17.0	115.2	22.3
1977	1 798.9	1 180.5	994.2	202.6	791.6	186.4	125.3	61.1	145.7	15.7	130.0	20.7
1978	2 027.4	1 336.1	1 121.2	220.0	901.2	214.9	143.4	71.5	166.6	19.6	147.1	22.1
1979	2 249.1	1 500.8	1 255.8	237.1	1 018.7	245.0	162.4	82.6	180.1	21.8	158.3	23.8
1980	2 439.3	1 651.8	1 377.6	261.5	1 116.2	274.2	185.2	88.9	174.1	11.3	162.8	30.0
1981	2 742.4	1 825.8	1 517.5	285.8	1 231.7	308.3	204.7	103.6	183.0	18.7	164.3	38.0
1982	2 864.3	1 925.8	1 593.7	307.5	1 286.2	332.1	222.4	109.8	176.3	13.1	163.3	38.8
1983	3 084.2	2 042.6	1 684.6	324.8	1 359.8	358.0	238.1	119.9	192.5	6.0	186.5	37.8
1984	3 482.3	2 255.6	1 855.1	348.1	1 507.0	400.5	261.5	139.0	243.3	20.6	222.7	40.2
1985	3 723.4	2 424.7	1 995.5	373.9	1 621.6	429.2	281.5	147.7	262.3	20.8	241.5	41.9
1986	3 902.3	2 570.1	2 114.8	397.0	1 717.9	455.3	297.5	157.9	275.7	22.6	253.1	33.5
1987	4 173.7	2 750.2	2 270.7	422.6	1 848.1	479.5	313.2	166.3	302.2	28.7	273.5	33.5
1988	4 549.4	2 967.2	2 452.9	451.3	2 001.6	514.2	329.6	184.6	341.6	26.8	314.7	40.6
1989	4 826.6	3 145.2	2 596.3	480.2	2 116.2	548.9	355.2	193.7	363.3	33.0	330.3	43.1
1990	5 089.1	3 338.2	2 754.0	517.7	2 236.3	584.2	377.8	206.5	380.6	31.9	348.7	50.7
1991	5 227.9	3 445.2	2 823.0	546.8	2 276.2	622.3	407.1	215.1	377.1	26.7	350.4	60.3
1992	5 512.8	3 635.4	2 964.5	569.2	2 395.3	670.9	442.5	228.4	427.6	34.5	393.0	78.0
1993	5 773.4	3 801.4	3 089.2	586.8	2 502.4	712.2	472.4	239.8	453.8	31.2	422.6	95.6
1994	6 122.3	3 997.2	3 249.8	606.2	2 643.5	747.5	493.3	254.1	473.3	33.9	439.4	119.7
1995	6 453.9	4 193.3	3 435.7	625.5	2 810.2	757.7	493.6	264.0	492.1	22.7	469.5	122.1
1996	6 840.1	4 390.5	3 623.2	644.4	2 978.8	767.3	492.5	274.9	543.2	37.3	505.9	131.5
1997	7 292.2	4 661.7	3 874.7	668.1	3 206.6	787.0	497.5	289.5	576.0	34.2	541.8	128.8
1998	7 752.8	5 019.4	4 182.7	697.3	3 485.5	836.7	529.7	307.0	627.8	29.4	598.4	137.5
1999	8 236.7	5 357.1	4 471.4	729.3	3 742.1	885.7	562.4	323.3	678.3	28.6	649.7	147.3
2000	8 795.2	5 782.7	4 829.2	774.7	4 054.5	953.4	609.9	343.5	728.4	22.7	705.7	150.3
2001	8 979.8	5 942.1	4 942.8	815.9	4 126.9	999.3	642.7	356.6	771.9	19.7	752.2	167.4
2002	9 229.3	6 091.2	4 980.9	865.9	4 115.0	1 110.3	745.1	365.2	768.4	10.6	757.8	152.9
2003	9 632.3	6 325.4	5 127.7	904.4	4 223.3	1 197.7	815.6	382.1	811.3	29.2	782.1	133.0
2004	10 255.9	6 650.3	5 377.1	941.8	4 435.3	1 273.2	866.1	407.1	911.1	36.2	874.9	127.0
2005	10 811.8	7 030.3	5 664.8	977.7	4 687.1	1 365.5	933.2	432.3	970.7	30.2	940.4	72.8
2003												
1st quarter	9 406.7	6 202.4	5 032.4	895.2	4 137.2	1 170.0	795.1	374.9	779.1	21.8	757.4	137.4
2nd quarter	9 537.9	6 289.0	5 098.7	903.1	4 195.6	1 190.3	810.1	380.3	801.6	30.5	771.2	130.5
3rd quarter	9 699.3	6 365.8	5 159.3	907.1	4 252.2	1 206.6	822.5	384.1	823.5	32.1	791.5	116.3
4th quarter	9 885.4	6 444.3	5 220.4	912.2	4 308.2	1 223.9	834.7	389.2	840.8	32.5	808.3	147.6
2004												
1st quarter	10 084.3	6 521.9	5 276.4	931.3	4 345.1	1 245.5	846.1	399.4	877.5	38.1	839.4	140.1
2nd quarter	10 207.0	6 590.2	5 328.1	939.1	4 389.1	1 262.1	858.2	403.8	910.2	39.5	870.6	132.0
3rd quarter	10 243.5	6 689.6	5 408.1	944.8	4 463.3	1 281.5	871.7	409.8	915.1	32.9	882.2	112.7
4th quarter	10 488.6	6 799.4	5 495.8	952.1	4 543.8	1 303.5	888.3	415.3	941.5	34.3	907.3	123.4
2005												
1st quarter	10 702.3	6 889.6	5 555.7	968.4	4 587.3	1 333.9	909.8	424.1	952.8	33.9	918.9	118.5
2nd quarter	10 795.4	6 953.7	5 601.3	973.7	4 627.6	1 352.4	924.7	427.7	965.8	28.7	937.1	102.8
3rd quarter	10 643.2	7 093.6	5 715.2	980.6	4 734.6	1 378.4	942.1	436.3	967.3	29.7	937.7	-11.5
4th quarter	11 106.2	7 184.4	5 787.0	988.1	4 798.9	1 397.4	956.1	441.3	996.8	28.7	968.1	81.5

Table 1-11. National Income by Type of Income—Continued

(Billions of dollars, quarterly data are at seasonally adjusted annual rates.)

NIPA Tables 1.7.5, 1.12

| Year and quarter | Corporate profits with IVA and CCAdj | | | | | Net interest and miscellaneous payments | Taxes on production and imports | Less: Subsidies | Business current transfer payments, net | | | Current surplus of government enterprises | Addendum: Net national factor income |
| | Total | Taxes on corporate income | Profits after tax | | | | | | | | | | |
			Total	Net dividends	Undistributed corporate profits				Total [1]	To persons	To government		
1950	36.0	17.9	18.1	8.8	9.3	3.2	23.0	0.6	0.9	0.6	0.3	. . .	241.2
1951	41.2	22.6	18.6	8.6	10.1	3.7	24.8	0.7	1.2	0.9	0.3	. . .	279.1
1952	39.3	19.4	19.9	8.6	11.3	4.1	27.1	0.4	1.3	0.9	0.4	. . .	293.9
1953	39.7	20.3	19.4	8.9	10.6	4.7	29.1	0.1	1.2	0.8	0.4	. . .	309.3
1954	38.8	17.6	21.2	9.3	11.9	5.6	28.9	-0.1	1.0	0.6	0.4	. . .	309.4
1955	49.5	22.0	27.5	10.5	17.0	6.2	31.5	-0.2	1.4	0.9	0.4	. . .	339.6
1956	48.5	22.0	26.5	11.3	15.3	6.9	34.3	0.4	1.7	1.2	0.5	. . .	359.9
1957	48.4	21.4	26.9	11.7	15.2	8.0	36.6	0.7	1.9	1.4	0.5	. . .	376.4
1958	43.5	19.0	24.5	11.6	13.0	9.5	37.7	0.9	1.8	1.2	0.6	. . .	378.1
1959	55.7	23.7	32.0	12.6	19.4	9.6	41.1	1.1	1.8	1.3	0.4	1.0	413.1
1960	53.8	22.8	31.0	13.4	17.6	10.6	44.6	1.1	1.9	1.3	0.5	0.9	428.7
1961	54.9	22.9	32.0	13.9	18.1	12.5	47.0	2.0	2.0	1.4	0.7	0.8	443.7
1962	63.3	24.1	39.2	15.0	24.1	14.2	50.4	2.3	2.2	1.5	0.7	0.9	478.8
1963	69.0	26.4	42.6	16.2	26.4	15.2	53.4	2.2	2.7	1.9	0.8	1.4	505.3
1964	76.5	28.2	48.3	18.2	30.1	17.4	57.3	2.7	3.1	2.2	0.9	1.3	543.6
1965	87.5	31.1	56.4	20.2	36.2	19.6	60.8	3.0	3.6	2.3	1.4	1.3	590.7
1966	93.2	33.9	59.3	20.7	38.7	22.4	63.3	3.9	3.5	2.1	1.4	1.0	647.2
1967	91.3	32.9	58.4	21.5	36.9	25.5	68.0	3.8	3.8	2.3	1.5	0.9	683.0
1968	98.8	39.6	59.2	23.5	35.6	27.1	76.5	4.2	4.3	2.8	1.5	1.2	745.4
1969	95.4	40.0	55.4	24.2	31.2	32.7	84.0	4.5	4.9	3.3	1.6	1.0	804.3
1970	83.6	34.8	48.9	24.3	24.6	39.1	91.5	4.8	4.5	2.9	1.6	0.0	839.7
1971	98.0	38.2	59.9	25.0	34.8	43.9	100.6	4.7	4.3	2.7	1.6	-0.2	908.1
1972	112.1	42.3	69.7	26.8	42.9	47.9	108.1	6.6	4.9	3.1	1.8	0.5	1 004.4
1973	125.5	50.0	75.5	29.9	45.6	55.2	117.3	5.2	6.0	3.9	2.0	-0.4	1 129.7
1974	115.8	52.8	63.0	33.2	29.8	70.8	125.0	3.3	7.1	4.7	2.4	-0.9	1 214.2
1975	134.8	51.6	83.2	33.0	50.2	81.6	135.5	4.5	9.4	6.8	2.6	-3.2	1 308.8
1976	163.3	65.3	98.1	39.0	59.0	85.5	146.6	5.1	9.5	6.7	2.8	-1.8	1 462.7
1977	192.4	74.4	118.0	44.8	73.2	101.1	159.9	7.1	8.4	5.1	3.3	-2.6	1 640.4
1978	216.6	84.9	131.8	50.8	81.0	115.0	171.2	8.9	10.6	6.5	4.1	-1.9	1 856.5
1979	223.2	90.0	133.2	57.5	75.7	138.9	180.4	8.5	13.0	8.2	4.8	-2.6	2 066.8
1980	201.1	87.2	113.9	64.1	49.9	181.8	200.7	9.8	14.4	8.6	5.7	-4.8	2 238.9
1981	226.1	84.3	141.8	73.8	68.0	232.3	236.0	11.5	17.6	11.2	6.4	-4.9	2 505.2
1982	209.7	66.5	143.2	77.7	65.4	271.1	241.3	15.0	20.1	12.4	7.8	-4.0	2 621.8
1983	264.2	80.6	183.6	83.5	100.1	285.3	263.7	21.2	22.5	13.8	8.7	-3.1	2 822.4
1984	318.6	97.5	221.1	90.8	130.3	327.1	290.2	21.0	30.1	19.7	10.4	-1.9	3 184.8
1985	330.3	99.4	230.9	97.6	133.4	341.3	308.5	21.3	34.8	22.3	12.6	0.8	3 400.5
1986	319.5	109.7	209.8	106.2	103.7	366.8	323.7	24.8	36.6	22.9	13.6	1.3	3 565.6
1987	368.8	130.4	238.4	112.3	126.1	366.4	347.9	30.2	33.8	20.2	13.6	1.2	3 821.1
1988	432.6	141.6	291.0	129.9	161.1	385.3	374.9	29.4	34.0	20.6	13.4	2.5	4 167.3
1989	426.6	146.1	280.5	158.0	122.6	432.1	399.3	27.2	39.2	23.5	15.7	4.9	4 410.3
1990	437.8	145.4	292.4	169.1	123.3	442.2	425.5	26.8	39.4	22.2	17.2	1.6	4 649.4
1991	451.2	138.6	312.6	180.7	131.9	418.2	457.5	27.3	39.9	17.9	22.0	5.7	4 752.1
1992	479.3	148.7	330.6	187.9	142.7	388.5	483.8	29.9	42.4	19.6	24.5	7.6	5 008.8
1993	541.9	171.0	370.9	202.8	168.1	365.7	503.4	36.4	40.7	14.4	26.6	7.2	5 258.4
1994	600.3	193.7	406.5	234.7	171.8	366.4	545.6	32.2	43.3	15.1	28.6	8.6	5 556.9
1995	696.7	218.7	478.0	254.2	223.8	367.1	558.2	34.0	46.9	19.0	26.5	11.4	5 871.4
1996	786.2	231.7	554.5	297.6	256.9	376.2	581.1	34.3	53.1	22.9	31.1	12.7	6 227.6
1997	868.5	246.1	622.4	334.5	287.9	415.6	612.0	32.9	49.9	19.4	29.7	12.6	6 650.6
1998	801.6	248.3	553.3	351.6	201.7	487.1	639.8	35.4	64.7	26.0	35.0	10.3	7 073.3
1999	851.3	258.6	592.6	337.4	255.3	495.4	674.0	44.2	67.4	34.1	35.9	10.1	7 529.4
2000	817.9	265.2	552.7	377.9	174.8	559.0	708.9	44.3	87.1	42.4	43.7	5.3	8 038.3
2001	767.3	204.1	563.2	370.9	192.3	566.3	728.6	55.3	92.8	50.0	47.5	-1.4	8 215.0
2002	886.3	192.6	693.7	399.2	294.5	520.9	762.8	38.4	84.3	37.3	46.6	0.9	8 419.8
2003	993.1	243.3	749.9	424.7	325.1	524.7	807.2	47.9	83.8	34.3	47.9	1.7	8 787.4
2004	1 182.6	300.1	882.5	539.5	343.0	485.1	864.0	44.7	85.5	28.1	49.8	-5.0	9 356.1
2005	1 330.7	399.3	931.4	576.9	354.5	483.4	922.4	57.3	74.2	45.7	30.1	-15.4	9 887.9
2003													
1st quarter	923.6	234.1	689.5	411.7	277.8	529.1	787.5	42.0	84.1	36.4	46.8	5.4	8 571.7
2nd quarter	956.2	228.9	727.4	417.4	310.0	529.6	800.2	55.6	83.8	35.6	47.5	2.5	8 706.9
3rd quarter	1 016.2	245.5	770.7	427.1	343.6	526.4	812.9	46.5	84.1	33.9	48.3	0.5	8 848.4
4th quarter	1 076.5	264.7	811.8	442.8	369.0	513.7	828.0	47.3	83.3	31.2	48.9	-1.5	9 022.8
2004													
1st quarter	1 158.1	281.3	876.8	475.5	401.3	501.8	845.4	43.7	85.4	25.6	50.1	-2.3	9 199.5
2nd quarter	1 183.3	303.0	880.2	503.0	377.2	493.4	858.2	42.8	86.1	23.7	50.9	-3.6	9 309.0
3rd quarter	1 154.0	297.8	856.2	529.0	327.2	475.7	867.2	44.3	79.1	38.4	46.4	-5.6	9 347.1
4th quarter	1 234.9	318.1	916.8	650.5	266.2	469.4	885.2	47.8	91.2	24.8	51.8	-8.6	9 568.6
2005													
1st quarter	1 320.0	400.9	919.0	554.3	364.7	483.7	901.6	52.3	97.6	31.0	51.9	-9.1	9 764.5
2nd quarter	1 342.9	392.8	950.1	568.2	381.9	477.1	920.2	55.6	99.9	33.0	53.2	-11.3	9 842.2
3rd quarter	1 266.3	378.9	887.5	584.0	303.5	482.9	930.2	58.1	0.2	79.8	-34.3	-27.7	9 798.7
4th quarter	1 393.5	424.6	968.9	601.0	367.9	490.0	937.3	63.1	99.1	39.0	49.4	-13.3	10 146.2

[1]Includes net transfer payments to the rest of the world, not shown separately.
. . . = Not available.

Table 1-12. Gross and Net Value Added of Domestic Corporate Business

(Billions of dollars, quarterly data are at seasonally adjusted annual rates.)   **NIPA Table 1.14**

Year and quarter	Gross value added of corporate business, total	Consumption of fixed capital	Net value added											Gross value added of financial corporate business
			Total	Compensation of employees	Taxes on production and imports less subsidies	Net operating surplus								
						Total	Net interest and miscellaneous payments	Business current transfer payments	Corporate profits with IVA and CCAdj					
									Total	Taxes on corporate income	Profits after tax			
											Total	Net dividends	Undistributed	
1950	160.4	11.6	148.8	98.7	14.8	35.3	-0.1	0.7	34.7	17.9	16.8	7.9	9.0	7.3
1951	183.9	13.2	170.7	114.6	15.9	40.3	-0.2	1.1	39.5	22.6	16.9	7.4	9.5	8.2
1952	192.6	14.0	178.6	123.0	17.3	38.2	-0.2	1.1	37.4	19.4	18.0	7.5	10.5	9.2
1953	206.2	14.8	191.4	134.0	18.5	38.9	0.0	1.0	37.9	20.3	17.6	7.8	9.9	10.2
1954	203.6	15.7	188.0	132.2	17.9	37.8	0.2	0.8	36.9	17.6	19.3	7.9	11.4	10.8
1955	229.5	16.6	212.9	144.6	19.8	48.5	0.2	1.2	47.2	22.0	25.1	8.9	16.2	11.8
1956	245.6	18.7	226.9	158.2	21.5	47.2	0.0	1.5	45.7	22.0	23.7	9.5	14.2	12.9
1957	256.9	20.5	236.4	166.5	22.8	47.1	0.2	1.7	45.3	21.4	23.8	9.9	14.0	13.8
1958	251.8	21.6	230.2	164.0	23.1	43.0	0.6	1.5	41.0	19.0	22.0	9.8	12.2	14.7
1959	281.9	21.8	260.1	180.3	25.6	54.2	-0.2	1.5	53.0	23.7	29.2	10.7	18.5	15.9
1960	293.9	23.3	270.6	190.7	27.8	52.0	-0.2	1.6	50.6	22.8	27.9	11.4	16.4	17.5
1961	302.1	23.9	278.2	195.6	28.9	53.7	0.4	1.8	51.5	22.9	28.6	11.5	17.1	18.4
1962	329.0	24.6	304.4	211.0	31.2	62.2	0.7	2.0	59.5	24.1	35.4	12.4	23.0	19.3
1963	349.5	26.0	323.5	222.7	33.2	67.7	0.4	2.4	64.9	26.4	38.5	13.6	25.0	19.7
1964	377.7	27.2	350.4	239.2	35.6	75.7	0.8	2.9	72.0	28.2	43.8	15.0	28.9	21.6
1965	414.4	29.4	385.0	259.9	37.8	87.3	1.2	3.3	82.8	31.1	51.7	16.9	34.8	23.2
1966	454.1	32.7	421.4	288.5	38.9	94.0	2.3	3.0	88.7	33.9	54.8	17.8	37.0	25.1
1967	479.3	35.6	443.6	308.4	41.4	93.8	4.0	3.3	86.6	32.9	53.7	18.3	35.3	28.1
1968	529.1	39.1	490.1	341.3	47.8	100.9	3.9	3.8	93.2	39.6	53.5	20.2	33.4	31.3
1969	576.7	44.2	532.5	378.6	52.9	101.0	7.8	4.4	88.8	40.0	48.8	20.4	28.4	36.2
1970	597.8	48.9	548.9	400.2	57.0	91.7	11.3	3.9	76.5	34.8	41.8	20.4	21.4	39.4
1971	646.1	52.9	593.2	425.3	62.8	105.2	11.5	3.5	90.2	38.2	52.0	20.3	31.7	43.1
1972	716.8	59.1	657.7	472.5	67.3	117.9	11.3	4.0	102.6	42.3	60.2	21.9	38.3	47.3
1973	802.6	65.9	736.6	533.9	74.1	128.6	13.0	5.0	110.6	50.0	60.6	23.1	37.5	51.8
1974	869.9	78.2	791.7	587.4	78.6	125.6	20.7	6.6	98.3	52.8	45.5	23.5	22.1	60.0
1975	944.4	92.9	851.6	614.9	84.5	152.2	23.4	8.6	120.2	51.6	68.6	26.4	42.2	67.8
1976	1 062.9	102.8	960.1	695.2	91.4	173.5	18.8	7.9	146.8	65.3	81.5	30.1	51.4	73.2
1977	1 205.2	117.4	1 087.8	784.8	100.0	203.0	23.3	6.4	173.3	74.4	98.9	33.7	65.2	85.8
1978	1 376.4	136.0	1 240.4	901.9	108.7	229.8	27.5	8.5	193.8	84.9	108.9	39.6	69.3	103.6
1979	1 530.7	157.2	1 373.4	1 023.4	115.0	235.0	34.9	11.5	188.6	90.0	98.6	41.5	57.1	114.7
1980	1 666.0	180.1	1 485.8	1 122.6	128.6	234.6	55.9	13.0	165.7	87.2	78.5	47.3	31.1	128.8
1981	1 893.3	205.3	1 688.0	1 243.9	154.4	289.7	77.7	15.6	196.4	84.3	112.1	58.3	53.8	147.3
1982	1 971.4	227.5	1 743.9	1 297.5	161.3	285.2	90.0	18.1	177.1	66.5	110.6	61.3	49.2	165.2
1983	2 121.0	236.0	1 885.0	1 371.2	177.4	336.3	86.6	20.6	229.2	80.6	148.5	71.3	77.2	188.0
1984	2 378.0	252.9	2 125.1	1 520.3	195.6	409.2	98.8	28.3	282.0	97.5	184.5	78.5	106.0	210.5
1985	2 535.3	274.0	2 261.3	1 630.9	209.0	421.4	96.9	32.3	292.2	99.4	192.8	85.7	107.1	233.3
1986	2 649.8	284.4	2 365.4	1 728.6	219.6	417.2	107.0	30.1	280.0	109.7	170.4	88.3	82.1	262.3
1987	2 837.9	300.0	2 537.9	1 849.8	233.4	454.8	108.3	25.6	320.8	130.4	190.4	95.6	94.8	280.8
1988	3 071.3	318.9	2 752.3	1 988.9	252.0	511.4	108.7	27.1	375.7	141.6	234.0	98.0	136.0	299.7
1989	3 235.0	344.6	2 890.4	2 097.6	267.5	525.3	129.4	36.5	359.5	146.1	213.4	126.4	87.0	322.7
1990	3 382.0	367.5	3 014.5	2 208.1	284.5	521.9	125.3	34.9	361.7	145.4	216.3	144.1	72.2	340.5
1991	3 468.9	395.7	3 073.2	2 253.0	307.9	512.3	101.7	35.8	374.7	138.6	236.1	156.4	79.8	369.2
1992	3 643.1	408.7	3 234.4	2 377.0	325.9	531.5	79.3	46.0	406.2	148.7	257.5	159.9	97.7	407.1
1993	3 824.8	421.3	3 403.5	2 489.2	343.5	570.8	72.1	33.7	465.0	171.0	294.0	182.2	111.7	427.0
1994	4 103.4	456.6	3 646.9	2 633.0	375.6	638.3	74.9	40.2	523.2	193.7	329.5	197.4	132.0	433.9
1995	4 354.5	486.9	3 867.6	2 774.1	384.1	709.3	66.4	39.1	603.9	218.7	385.2	221.6	163.7	475.0
1996	4 626.5	513.6	4 112.9	2 916.1	397.4	799.4	70.0	45.1	684.3	231.7	452.6	257.3	195.3	517.0
1997	4 983.6	553.6	4 430.0	3 125.0	415.7	889.3	95.4	36.3	757.5	246.1	511.5	283.9	227.6	581.8
1998	5 313.6	589.0	4 724.6	3 397.6	429.8	897.2	143.3	55.2	698.7	248.3	450.4	309.2	141.2	658.6
1999	5 655.0	632.0	5 023.0	3 645.2	449.4	928.4	142.3	56.3	729.8	258.6	471.1	295.7	175.5	704.1
2000	6 051.8	690.0	5 361.8	3 957.7	477.1	926.9	178.1	76.6	672.2	265.2	407.0	348.4	58.6	779.6
2001	6 099.4	752.5	5 346.9	4 016.7	473.6	856.6	171.3	87.7	597.6	204.1	393.5	330.1	63.4	805.9
2002	6 225.8	742.1	5 483.7	4 044.5	502.7	936.5	135.9	70.1	730.5	192.6	537.9	351.3	186.5	854.1
2003	6 456.9	759.8	5 697.1	4 156.9	528.8	1 011.4	120.8	63.0	827.7	243.3	584.4	392.8	191.6	898.5
2004	6 873.2	796.2	6 077.1	4 354.6	567.0	1 155.4	78.3	70.8	1 006.3	300.1	706.2	492.7	213.6	940.3
2005	7 357.0	856.8	6 500.2	4 612.5	604.9	1 282.7	56.3	92.7	1 133.7	399.3	734.4	338.7	395.7	987.3
2003														
1st quarter	6 358.0	752.1	5 605.8	4 076.1	518.6	1 011.2	170.4	66.5	774.4	234.1	540.3	342.5	197.8	914.0
2nd quarter	6 403.5	757.0	5 646.5	4 131.0	516.8	998.7	137.2	64.1	797.3	228.9	568.5	431.4	137.1	901.9
3rd quarter	6 492.7	762.3	5 730.5	4 183.6	535.9	1 011.0	95.7	62.1	853.1	245.5	607.6	393.3	214.3	889.4
4th quarter	6 573.3	767.9	5 805.4	4 237.0	543.8	1 024.6	79.7	59.1	885.9	264.7	621.2	403.9	217.3	888.7
2004														
1st quarter	6 698.2	771.9	5 926.3	4 266.3	555.0	1 105.1	73.7	58.0	973.3	281.3	692.0	457.0	235.0	918.0
2nd quarter	6 805.6	779.8	6 025.9	4 310.8	563.3	1 151.8	81.0	57.3	1 013.4	303.0	710.4	421.2	289.2	926.7
3rd quarter	6 939.9	832.3	6 107.5	4 382.0	569.1	1 156.5	79.6	105.5	971.4	297.8	673.6	468.4	205.1	946.9
4th quarter	7 049.2	800.7	6 248.5	4 459.3	580.8	1 208.4	78.8	62.5	1 067.0	318.1	748.9	624.0	125.0	969.6
2005														
1st quarter	7 192.6	816.3	6 376.3	4 511.9	591.4	1 273.0	63.4	72.7	1 136.9	400.9	736.0	470.5	265.5	998.7
2nd quarter	7 271.6	827.9	6 443.7	4 556.4	603.5	1 283.8	50.6	75.5	1 157.7	392.8	764.9	411.5	353.4	947.2
3rd quarter	7 424.5	927.2	6 497.3	4 658.7	610.1	1 228.6	54.3	131.4	1 042.9	378.9	664.0	237.9	426.1	998.8
4th quarter	7 539.4	856.0	6 683.4	4 723.2	614.8	1 345.4	57.1	91.2	1 197.2	424.6	772.6	234.9	537.7	1 004.5

Table 1-13. Gross Value Added of Nonfinancial Domestic Corporate Business in Current and Chained Dollars

(Billions of dollars, quarterly data are at seasonally adjusted annual rates.)   NIPA Table 1.14

Year and quarter	Current-dollar gross value added													Gross value added in billions of chained (2000) dollars
	Total	Consumption of fixed capital	Net value added											
			Total	Compensation of employees	Taxes on production and imports less subsidies	Net operating surplus								
						Total	Net interest and miscellaneous payments	Business current transfer payments	Corporate profits with IVA and CCAdj					
									Total	Taxes on corporate income	Profits after tax			
											Total	Net dividends	Undistributed	
1950	153.1	11.3	141.8	94.4	14.4	33.1	0.9	0.6	31.6	16.8	14.8	7.4	7.4	675.3
1951	175.7	12.9	162.9	109.8	15.4	37.7	1.0	0.8	35.9	21.1	14.8	7.0	7.7	714.0
1952	183.4	13.6	169.7	117.8	16.8	35.2	1.2	0.9	33.1	17.7	15.5	7.1	8.4	738.8
1953	195.9	14.4	181.6	128.2	17.9	35.5	1.3	1.0	33.2	18.4	14.9	7.2	7.6	792.6
1954	192.9	15.2	177.7	125.9	17.3	34.4	1.6	0.9	31.9	15.5	16.4	7.4	9.0	783.0
1955	217.7	16.1	201.7	137.9	19.2	44.6	1.6	1.0	41.9	20.1	21.8	8.4	13.4	878.0
1956	232.7	18.1	214.6	150.8	20.8	43.0	1.8	1.1	40.2	19.9	20.2	9.0	11.2	907.2
1957	243.1	19.9	223.2	158.4	22.0	42.7	2.2	1.2	39.4	19.0	20.4	9.2	11.2	919.1
1958	237.1	21.0	216.2	155.2	22.3	38.6	2.8	1.2	34.6	16.1	18.6	9.1	9.5	882.5
1959	266.0	21.1	244.9	170.8	24.4	49.7	2.9	1.3	45.5	20.7	24.8	9.8	15.0	980.4
1960	276.4	22.6	253.8	180.4	26.6	46.8	3.2	1.4	42.2	19.1	23.1	10.5	12.6	1 012.0
1961	283.7	23.2	260.5	184.5	27.6	48.4	3.7	1.5	43.2	19.4	23.8	10.6	13.2	1 033.6
1962	309.8	23.9	285.9	199.3	29.9	56.8	4.3	1.7	50.8	20.6	30.2	11.6	18.6	1 120.7
1963	329.9	25.2	304.7	210.1	31.7	62.9	4.7	1.7	56.5	22.8	33.8	12.4	21.3	1 186.7
1964	356.1	26.4	329.7	225.7	33.9	70.2	5.2	2.0	63.0	23.9	39.2	14.0	25.2	1 270.3
1965	391.2	28.4	362.8	245.4	36.0	81.4	5.8	2.2	73.3	27.1	46.2	16.2	30.0	1 375.1
1966	429.0	31.5	397.4	272.9	37.0	87.6	7.0	2.7	77.9	29.5	48.4	16.8	31.6	1 472.6
1967	451.2	34.3	416.8	291.1	39.3	86.4	8.4	2.8	75.2	27.8	47.3	17.3	30.1	1 508.9
1968	497.8	37.6	460.2	321.9	45.5	92.8	9.7	3.1	80.0	33.5	46.5	19.0	27.5	1 604.8
1969	540.5	42.4	498.1	357.1	50.2	90.8	12.7	3.2	74.9	33.3	41.6	19.0	22.5	1 667.6
1970	558.3	46.8	511.5	376.5	54.2	80.7	16.6	3.3	60.9	27.3	33.6	18.3	15.3	1 649.9
1971	603.0	50.7	552.4	399.4	59.5	93.4	17.6	3.7	72.1	30.0	42.1	18.1	24.0	1 716.6
1972	669.5	56.4	613.2	443.9	63.7	105.6	18.6	4.0	83.0	33.8	49.2	19.7	29.5	1 846.4
1973	750.8	62.7	688.1	502.2	70.1	115.8	21.8	4.7	89.4	40.4	49.0	20.8	28.2	1 957.7
1974	809.8	74.1	735.7	552.2	74.4	109.1	27.5	4.1	77.5	42.8	34.7	21.5	13.1	1 925.4
1975	876.7	87.9	788.7	575.5	80.2	133.1	28.4	5.0	99.6	41.9	57.7	24.6	33.2	1 898.8
1976	989.7	97.0	892.7	651.4	86.7	154.7	26.0	7.0	121.7	53.5	68.2	27.8	40.5	2 050.0
1977	1 119.4	110.5	1 008.8	735.3	94.6	178.9	28.5	9.0	141.4	60.6	80.9	30.9	50.0	2 200.0
1978	1 272.9	127.8	1 145.1	845.3	102.7	197.0	33.4	9.5	154.1	67.6	86.6	35.9	50.6	2 344.1
1979	1 415.9	147.3	1 268.6	959.9	108.8	200.0	41.8	9.5	148.8	70.6	78.1	37.6	40.5	2 418.7
1980	1 537.1	168.2	1 368.9	1 049.8	121.5	197.6	54.2	10.2	133.2	68.2	65.0	44.7	20.4	2 394.6
1981	1 746.0	191.5	1 554.5	1 161.5	146.7	246.4	67.2	11.4	167.7	66.0	101.7	52.5	49.2	2 491.5
1982	1 806.2	211.2	1 594.9	1 203.9	152.9	238.1	77.4	8.8	151.9	48.8	103.1	54.1	49.0	2 430.6
1983	1 933.0	217.6	1 715.4	1 266.9	168.0	280.5	77.0	10.5	192.9	61.7	131.2	63.2	68.0	2 545.1
1984	2 167.5	230.7	1 936.8	1 406.1	185.0	345.7	86.0	11.7	248.0	75.9	172.0	67.2	104.8	2 772.8
1985	2 302.0	247.4	2 054.6	1 504.2	196.6	353.8	91.5	16.1	246.3	71.1	175.2	72.0	103.2	2 896.3
1986	2 387.5	255.3	2 132.2	1 583.1	204.6	344.5	95.1	27.3	222.1	76.2	145.9	72.9	73.0	2 963.3
1987	2 557.1	266.5	2 290.6	1 687.8	216.8	386.0	96.4	29.9	259.7	94.2	165.5	76.3	89.2	3 119.6
1988	2 771.6	281.6	2 490.0	1 812.8	233.8	443.4	109.8	27.4	306.2	104.0	202.3	82.2	120.1	3 300.7
1989	2 912.3	301.6	2 610.7	1 914.7	248.2	447.9	142.0	23.0	282.9	101.2	181.7	105.4	76.4	3 361.8
1990	3 041.5	319.2	2 722.3	2 012.9	263.5	445.8	146.2	25.4	274.3	98.5	175.8	118.3	57.5	3 404.0
1991	3 099.7	341.4	2 758.3	2 048.4	285.7	424.2	135.9	26.7	261.5	88.6	172.9	125.5	47.4	3 376.2
1992	3 236.0	353.6	2 882.3	2 154.1	302.5	425.7	111.3	25.2	289.2	94.4	194.8	134.1	60.7	3 479.5
1993	3 397.8	363.4	3 034.4	2 244.8	318.8	470.8	102.0	29.6	339.2	108.0	231.2	149.1	82.1	3 575.5
1994	3 669.5	391.5	3 278.0	2 381.5	349.6	546.9	101.0	30.0	415.9	132.9	283.1	157.9	125.2	3 797.9
1995	3 879.5	415.0	3 464.5	2 509.8	356.9	597.8	115.2	30.2	452.5	141.0	311.4	178.0	133.5	3 977.4
1996	4 109.5	436.5	3 673.0	2 630.8	369.1	673.1	111.9	38.0	523.2	153.1	370.1	197.5	172.6	4 196.4
1997	4 401.8	467.1	3 934.7	2 812.9	385.5	736.3	124.0	39.0	573.4	161.9	411.5	215.9	195.6	4 469.3
1998	4 655.0	493.3	4 161.7	3 045.6	398.7	717.4	143.8	35.2	538.3	158.6	379.7	241.0	138.7	4 725.4
1999	4 950.8	523.8	4 427.0	3 267.7	416.6	742.7	160.2	45.0	537.6	171.2	366.3	224.6	141.7	5 011.0
2000	5 272.2	567.8	4 704.3	3 544.4	443.4	716.5	191.7	48.4	476.4	170.2	306.2	251.3	54.8	5 272.2
2001	5 293.5	646.8	4 646.7	3 595.9	439.1	611.6	204.0	50.6	357.2	111.7	245.5	245.4	0.1	5 224.5
2002	5 371.7	643.6	4 728.2	3 611.9	465.5	650.8	167.4	54.0	429.4	97.0	332.3	254.8	77.5	5 269.7
2003	5 558.4	657.5	4 900.9	3 703.2	488.5	709.2	152.6	64.4	492.1	135.7	356.4	292.7	63.8	5 382.1
2004	5 932.9	686.2	5 246.7	3 873.4	522.9	850.4	137.8	60.0	652.6	185.3	467.4	366.9	100.5	5 654.5
2005	6 369.7	739.7	5 630.1	4 099.7	558.1	972.2	156.6	51.4	764.2	251.4	512.9	228.5	284.4	5 959.9
2003														
1st quarter	5 443.9	651.8	4 792.1	3 631.3	479.2	681.6	167.2	61.0	453.4	129.4	324.0	245.5	78.5	5 293.8
2nd quarter	5 501.6	655.5	4 846.1	3 680.1	476.9	689.1	155.5	63.8	469.8	123.5	346.4	333.1	13.3	5 337.8
3rd quarter	5 603.3	659.3	4 944.0	3 727.0	495.3	721.8	147.2	66.0	508.6	135.8	372.7	292.7	80.0	5 417.8
4th quarter	5 684.6	663.4	5 021.2	3 774.5	502.4	744.2	140.6	66.9	536.6	154.0	382.7	299.6	83.1	5 479.0
2004														
1st quarter	5 780.2	666.0	5 114.1	3 794.8	511.8	807.5	135.4	66.5	605.6	164.3	441.3	340.8	100.4	5 554.5
2nd quarter	5 878.9	672.3	5 206.6	3 834.5	519.5	852.7	137.5	66.6	648.7	186.0	462.7	298.3	164.4	5 603.9
3rd quarter	5 992.9	716.8	5 276.1	3 897.7	524.8	853.6	137.8	40.4	675.4	199.2	476.2	339.2	137.0	5 707.4
4th quarter	6 079.6	689.7	5 389.9	3 966.5	535.6	887.7	140.3	66.5	681.0	191.6	489.4	489.3	0.1	5 752.0
2005														
1st quarter	6 193.9	703.3	5 490.6	4 010.2	545.6	934.7	148.8	66.4	719.4	238.4	481.0	364.6	116.5	5 829.7
2nd quarter	6 324.4	713.2	5 611.3	4 049.9	556.8	1 004.6	152.9	67.3	784.3	244.9	539.4	303.0	236.5	5 935.2
3rd quarter	6 425.7	804.9	5 620.8	4 140.7	562.9	917.3	159.3	11.1	746.8	255.8	491.0	126.3	364.7	5 994.5
4th quarter	6 534.8	737.2	5 797.6	4 198.0	567.2	1 032.4	165.1	60.9	806.4	266.4	540.0	120.1	419.9	6 079.8

NOTES AND DEFINITIONS

TABLES 1-1 THROUGH 1-7, 1-9 THROUGH 1-13, AND 19-1 THROUGH 19-5
NATIONAL INCOME AND PRODUCT

SOURCE: U.S. DEPARTMENT OF COMMERCE, BUREAU OF ECONOMIC ANALYSIS (BEA)

All data on these pages are from the national income and product accounts (NIPAs). The data are as published in the 2003 comprehensive NIPA revisions and have been subsequently updated and revised in each annual revision through August 2006.

See the article entitled "Topics of Current Interest" at the beginning of this book for an explanation of how Hurricane Katrina and other disasters are reflected in the NIPAs.

Definitions and notes on the data:
Basic concepts of total output and income

The NIPAs depict the U.S. economy in several different dimensions. The basic concept is gross domestic product (GDP), which is the market value of all goods and services produced by labor and property located in the United States.

In principle, GDP can be measured by summing the values created by each industry in the economy. However, it can more readily be measured by summing up all the final demands for the economy's output. This final demand approach also has the advantage of depicting the origins of demand for economic production, whether from consumers, businesses, or government.

Since production for the market necessarily generates incomes equal to its value, there is also an income total that corresponds to the production value total. This income can be measured so as to depict the distribution of value among labor, capital, and other income recipients.

The structure and relationships of several of these major concepts are illustrated in Tables 1-9 and 1-10. The definitions of these concepts are as follows:

Gross domestic product (GDP), the featured measure of the value of U.S. output, is the market value of the goods and services produced by labor and property located in the United States. Market values represent output valued at the prices paid by the final customer, and therefore include taxes on production and imports, such as customs duties and taxes on sales and property.

GDP is "gross" product in the sense that capital consumption allowances (economic depreciation) have not been deducted.

GDP is primarily measured by summing the values of personal consumption expenditures (PCE), gross private domestic investment (including change in private inventories and before deduction of charges for consumption of fixed capital), net exports of goods and services, and government consumption expenditures and gross investment. GDP measured in this way excludes duplication involving "intermediate" purchases of goods and services (which are goods and services purchased by industries and used in production), the value of which is already included in the value of the final products. Production of any intermediate goods unused in production in the current period is captured in the measurement of inventory change.

In concept, GDP is equal to the sum of the economic value added by (formerly referred to as "gross product originating in") all industries in the United States. This, in turn, also makes it the conceptual equivalent of *gross domestic income (GDI)*, a new concept introduced in the 2003 revision. GDI is the sum of the incomes earned in each domestic industry, plus the taxes on production and imports and less the subsidies that account for the difference between output value and factor input value. This derivation is shown in Table 1-10. Since the incomes and taxes can be measured directly, they can be summed to a total that is equivalent to GDP in concept, but differs due to imperfections in measurement. The difference between the two is known as the *statistical discrepancy*. It is expressed as GDP minus GDI.

Gross national product (GNP) refers to all goods and services produced by labor and property supplied by U.S. residents, whether located in the United States or abroad, expressed at market prices. It is equal to GDP, plus income receipts from the rest of the world, less income payments to the rest of the world. *Domestic* production and income refer to the location of the factors of production, with only factors located in the United States included; *national* production and income refer to the ownership of the factors of production, with only factors owned by United States residents included.

Before the comprehensive NIPA revisions made in 1991, GNP was the commonly used measure of U.S. production. (The terminology survives in popular cultural references such as the name of a musical group and the "Gross National Parade.") However, GDP is clearly preferable when it is compared with indicators such as employment, hours worked, and capital utilized—for example, in the calculation of labor and capital productivity—because it is confined to production taking place within the borders of the United States. It is also the measure used by almost all other countries, thus facilitating international comparisons.

The income-side aggregate corresponding to GNP is *gross national income*, shown as an addendum to Table 1-9. It consists of gross domestic income plus income receipts from the rest of the world, less income payments to the rest of the world. It is used as the denominator for a national saving/income ratio, presented in Chapter 5.

National income is the preferred measure for calculating and comparing saving, since it is the income aggregate from which that saving arises. As with GDP and gross domestic income, the statistical discrepancy indicates the difference between the product-side and income-side measurement of the same concept.

Net national product is the market value, net of depreciation, of goods and services attributable to the labor and property supplied by U.S. residents. It is equal to GNP minus the *consumption of fixed capital (CFC)*. CFC relates only to fixed capital located in the United States. (Investment in that capital is measured by private fixed investment and government gross investment.) In periods in which extraordinary property destruction occurs, such as a severe hurricane or a terror attack, normal capital consumption is augmented by the estimated value of the lost assets.

National income has been redefined and now includes all net incomes (net of the consumption of fixed capital) earned in production. It now includes not only "factor incomes"—net incomes received by labor and capital as a result of their participation in the production process, but also "nonfactor charges"—taxes on production and imports, business transfer payments, and the current surplus of government enterprises, less subsidies. This change has been made to conform with the international guidelines for national accounts, *System of National Accounts (SNA) 1993*. According to SNA 1993, these charges cannot be eliminated from the input and output prices.

Since national income now includes the nonfactor charges, it is conceptually equivalent to net national product and differs only by the amount of the statistical discrepancy.

The concept formerly known as "national income" is still included in the accounts as an addendum item called "net national factor income." It is shown in Table 1-11 and used as the denominator in Figure 1-4. *Net national factor income* consists of compensation of employees, proprietors' income with inventory valuation and capital consumption adjustments, rental income of persons with capital consumption adjustment, corporate profits with inventory valuation and capital consumption adjustments, and net interest.

By definition, national income and its components exclude all income from capital gains—that is, increases in the value of owned assets. Such increases have no counterpart on the production side of the accounts. This exclusion is partly accomplished by means of the inventory valuation and capital consumption adjustments, which will be described below in the definitions of the components of product and income.

Definitions and notes on the data:
Imputation

The term *imputation* will appear from time to time in the following definitions of product and income components.

Imputed values are values estimated by BEA statisticians for certain important product and income components that are not explicitly valued in the source data, usually because a market transaction in money terms is not involved. Imputed values appear on both the product and income side of the accounts; they add equal amounts to income and spending, so that no imputed saving is created.

One important example is the imputed rent on owner-occupied housing. The building of such housing is counted as investment, yet in the monetary accounts of the household sector, there is no income from that investment nor rental paid for it. In the NIPAs, the rent that each such dwelling would earn if rented is estimated and added to both national and personal income, as part of rental income receipts, and to personal consumption expenditures as part of expenditures on housing services.

Another important example is imputed interest. For example, an individual keeps a monetary balance in a bank or other financial institution. He or she receives either no interest or below-market interest, but receives the institution's services, such as clearing checks and otherwise facilitating payments, with little or no charge. Where is the product generated by the institution's workers and capital? In the NIPAs, the depositor is imputed a market-rate-based interest return on his or her balance, which is then imputed as a service charge paid to the institution, and therefore included in the value of the institution's output.

Definitions and notes on the data:
Components of product

Personal consumption expenditures (PCE) is goods and services purchased by persons residing in the United States. PCE consists mainly of purchases of new goods and services by individuals from businesses. It includes purchases that are financed by insurance—for example, by government-provided and private medical insurance. In addition, PCE includes purchases of new goods and services by nonprofit institutions, net purchases of used goods ("net" here indicates purchases of used goods from business less sales of used goods to business) by individuals and nonprofit institutions, and purchases abroad of goods and services by U.S. residents traveling or working in foreign countries. PCE also includes purchases for certain goods and services provided by government agencies. (See notes and definitions for Tables 4-1 through 4-5 for additional information.) New annual accounts separate household and nonprofit institution expenditures and incomes; these are presented in the article at the beginning of this volume.

Gross private domestic investment consists of private fixed investment and change in private inventories.

Private fixed investment consists of both nonresidential and residential fixed investment. The term "residential" refers to the construction and equipping of living quarters for permanent occupancy. Hotels and motels are included in *nonresidential fixed investment*, as described below.

Private fixed investment consists of purchases of fixed assets, which are commodities that will be used in a production process for more than one year, including replacements and additions to the capital stock. It is measured "gross," before a deduction for consumption of existing fixed capital. It covers all investment by private businesses and nonprofit institutions in the United States, regardless of whether the investment is owned by U.S. residents. The residential component includes investment in owner-occupied housing; the homeowner is treated equivalently to a business in these investment accounts. (However, when GDP by sector is calculated, owner-occupied housing is no longer included in the business sector. It is allocated to the households and institutions sector.) Private fixed investment does not include purchases of the same types of equipment and structures by government agencies, which are included in government gross investment, nor does it include investment by U.S. residents in other countries.

Nonresidential fixed investment is the total of nonresidential structures and nonresidential equipment and software.

Nonresidential structures consists of new construction, brokers' commissions on sales of structures, and net purchases of used structures by private business and by nonprofit institutions from government agencies (that is, purchases of used structures from government minus sales of used structures to government). New construction also includes hotels and motels, as well as mining exploration, shafts, and wells.

Nonresidential equipment and software consists of private business purchases on capital account of new machinery, equipment, and vehicles; purchases and in-house production of software; dealers' margins on sales of used equipment; and net purchases of used equipment from government agencies, persons, and the rest of the world (that is, purchases of such equipment minus sales of such equipment). It does not include the estimated personal-use portion of equipment purchased for both business and personal use, which is allocated to PCE.

Residential private fixed investment consists of both residential structures and residential producers' durable equipment (equipment such as appliances owned by landlords and rented to tenants). Investment in structures consists of new units, improvements to existing units, purchases of manufactured homes, brokers' commissions on the sale of residential property, and net purchases of used residential structures from government agencies (that is, purchases of such structures from government minus sales of such structures to government). As noted above, it includes investment in owner-occupied housing.

Change in private inventories is the change in the physical volume of inventories held by businesses, with that change being valued at the average price of the period. It differs from the change in the book value of inventories reported by most businesses; an *inventory valuation adjustment (IVA)* converts book value change using historical cost valuations to the change in physical volume, valued at average replacement cost.

Net exports of goods and services is *exports of goods and services* less *imports of goods and services*. It does not include income payments or receipts or transfer payments to and from the rest of the world.

Government consumption expenditures is the estimated value of the services produced by governments (federal, state, and local) for current consumption. Since these are generally not sold, there is no market valuation, and they are priced at the cost of inputs. The input costs consist of the compensation of general government employees; the estimated consumption of general government fixed capital, including software (CFC, or economic depreciation); and the cost of goods and services purchased by government less the value of sales to other sectors. The value of investment in equipment and structures produced by government workers and capital is also subtracted, and is instead included in government investment. Government sales to other sectors consist primarily of receipts of tuition payments for higher education and receipts of charges for medical care.

This definition of government consumption expenditures differs in concept, but not in the amount contributed to GDP, from the treatment in existence before the 2003 revision. In the new definition, goods and services purchased by government are considered to be intermediate output. In the previous definition, they were considered as final sales. Since their value is added to the other components to yield total government consumption expenditures, the dollar total contributed to GDP is the same. The only practical difference is that the goods purchased disappear from the goods account, appearing in the services account instead. In the industry sector accounts, the value added by government is also unchanged. It continues to be measured as the sum of compensation and CFC, or equivalently as gross government output less the value of goods and services purchased. The new definition increases conformity with SNA 1993.

Gross government investment consists of general government and government enterprise expenditures for fixed assets (structures and equipment and software). Government inventory investment is included in government consumption expenditures.

Definitions and notes on the data:
Real values, quantity and price indexes

Real, or chained (2000) dollar, estimates are estimates from which the effect of price change has been removed. Prior to the 1996 comprehensive revision, constant-dollar measures were obtained by combining real output measures for different goods and services using the relative prices of a single year as weights for the entire time span of the series. In the recent environment of rapid technological change, which has caused the prices of computers and electronic components to decline dramatically relative to other prices, this method distorts the measurement of economic growth and causes excessive revisions of growth rates at each benchmark revision. The current, chained-dollar measure changes the relative price weights each year, as relative prices shift over time. As a result, historical growth rates have not been revised as a result of recent changes in relative prices.

Chained-dollar estimates, although expressed as if they had occurred according to the prices of a single year (currently 2000) for continuity's sake, are usually not additive. This means that because of the changes in price weights each year, the chained (2000) dollar components in any given table for any year other than 2000 usually do not add to the chained (2000) dollar total. The amount of the difference for the major components of GDP is called the residual and is shown in Table 1-2. In time periods close to the base year, the residual is usually quite small; over longer periods, the differences become much larger. For this reason, BEA no longer publishes chained-dollar estimates prior to 1990, except for selected aggregate series. For the more detailed components, historical trends and fluctuations in real volumes are represented by *chain-type quantity indexes*, which are presented in Tables 1-4, 4-4, 5-4, 5-6, and 19-2.

Chain-weighting leads to complexity in estimating the contribution of economic sectors to an overall change in output; it becomes difficult for someone without access to the complicated statistical methods used to find the correct answers to questions such as "How much is the rise in defense spending contributing to GDP growth?" Because of this, BEA is now calculating and publishing such estimates; *Business Statistics* reproduces these calculations in Tables 1-3 and 19-3. To calculate contributions to growth for longer periods than those published by BEA, see J. Steven Landefeld and Robert P. Parker, "BEA's Chain Indexes, Time Series, and Measures of Long-Term Economic Growth," *Survey of Current Business*, May 1997; and "Preview of the Comprehensive Revision of the National Income and Product Accounts: BEA's New Featured Measures of Output and Prices," *Survey of Current Business*, July 1995.

GDP price indexes measure price changes between any two adjacent years (or quarters) for a fixed "market basket" of goods and services consisting of the average quantities purchased in those two years (or quarters). The annual measures are chained together to form an index with prices in 2000 set to equal 100. Using average quantities as weights and changing weights each year eliminates the substitution bias that arises in more conventional indexes, in which weights are taken from a single base period that is usually early in the period under measurement. Generally, this bias leads to an overstatement of price increase. (The CPI-U and the CPI-W are examples

of such conventional indexes, technically known as "Laspeyres" indexes. See "General Notes" at the beginning of this volume and the notes and definitions for Chapter 8 for further explanation.)

The chain-type formula guarantees that a GDP price index change will differ only trivially from the change in the implicit deflator (ratio of current-dollar to real value). Therefore, *Business Statistics* is no longer publishing a separate table of implicit deflators.

Definitions and notes on the data:
Aggregates of sales and purchases

Final sales of domestic product is GDP minus change in private inventories. It is the sum of personal consumption expenditures, gross private domestic fixed investment, government consumption expenditures and gross investment, and net exports of goods and services.

Gross domestic purchases is the market value of goods and services purchased by U.S. residents, regardless of where those goods and services were produced. It is GDP minus net exports (that is, minus exports plus imports) of goods and services; equivalently, it is the sum of personal consumption expenditures, gross private domestic investment, and government consumption expenditures and gross investment. The price index for gross domestic purchases is therefore a measure of price change for goods and services purchased by (rather than produced by) U.S. residents.

Final sales to domestic purchasers is gross domestic purchases minus change in private inventories.

Definitions and notes on the data:
Per capita product and income estimates

In Table 1-7, annual and quarterly measures of product, income, and consumption spending are expressed in per capita terms—the aggregate dollar amount divided by the U.S. population. Population data from 1991 forward reflect the results of Census 2000.

National per capita totals, as shown in Table 1-7, are based on definitions of income and population that differ slightly from the sum of the states shown in Table 21-2. See the notes and definitions for Chapter 21 for further explanation.

Definitions and notes on the data:
Components of income

There are now two different presentations of aggregate income for the United States: *gross domestic income* (Table 1-10) and *national income* (Table 1-11). As noted above, domestic income refers to income generated from production within the United States, while national income refers to income received by residents of the United States. This means that some of the income components differ between the two tables. Domestic income payments include payments to the rest of the world from domestic industries. National income payments exclude payments to the rest of the world but include payments received by U.S. residents from the rest of the world. These differences are seen in employee compensation, interest, and corporate profits. Taxes on production, imports, and corporate profits, business transfer payments, subsidies, proprietors' income, rental income, and the current surplus of government enterprises are the same in both accounts.

A third income aggregate is *personal income*. The derivation of this well-known statistic from national income is shown in Table 1-9. Personal income will be discussed and defined in more detail in Chapter 4.

Compensation of employees is the income accruing to employees as remuneration for their work. It is the sum of wage and salary accruals and supplements to wages and salaries. In the domestic income account, it is called "compensation of employees, paid." It refers to all payments generated by domestic production, including those to workers residing in the "rest of the world." In the national and personal income accounts, it is a different amount labeled "compensation of employees, received"—that is, received by U.S. residents—including from the rest of the world.

Wage and salary accruals consists of the monetary remuneration of employees, including the compensation of corporate officers; corporate directors' fees paid to directors who are also employees of the corporation; commissions, tips, and bonuses; voluntary employee contributions to certain deferred compensation plans, such as 401(k) plans; and receipts in kind that represent income. As of the 2003 revision, it also includes judicial fees to jurors and witnesses, compensation of prison inmates, and marriage fees to justices of the peace, all of which were formerly included in "other labor income."

In concept, wage and salary accruals include the value of the exercise by employees of "nonqualified stock options," in which an employee is allowed to buy stock for less than its current market price. (Actual measurement of these values involves a number of problems, particularly in the short run. Such stock options are not included in the monthly wage data from the Bureau of Labor Statistics, which are the main source for current extrapolations of wages and salaries, and are not consistently reported in corporate financial statements. They are, however, generally included in the unemployment insurance wage data that are used to correct the preliminary wage and salary estimates.) Another form of stock option, the "incentive stock option," leads to a capital gain only and is thus not included in the definition of wages and salaries.

Wage and salary accruals include retroactive wage payments for the period in which they were earned, not for the period in which they were paid. In the NIPAs, wages accrued is the appropriate measure for both domestic and national income. Wages disbursed is the appropriate measure for personal income, since the latter concept focuses on what individuals receive. The difference, *wage accruals less disbursements*, is shown in Table 1-7. Substantial entries appear for this item in 2003 and 2004 because there were 53 Fridays instead of 52 Fridays in the latter year. As a result, some of the wages disbursed in 2004 were actually accrued in 2003.

Supplements to wages and salaries consists of *employer contributions for employee pension and insurance funds* and *employer contributions for government social insurance.*

Employer contributions for employee pension and insurance funds consists of employer payments (including payments-in-kind) to private pension and profit-sharing plans, private group health and life insurance plans, privately administered workers' compensation plans, government employee retirement plans, and supplemental unemployment benefit plans. This includes the major part of the former category "other labor income." The remainder of "other labor income" has been reclassified as wages and salaries (as noted above).

Employer contributions for government social insurance consists of employer payments under the following federal, state, and local government programs: old-age, survivors, and disability insurance (Social Security); hospital insurance (Medicare); unemployment insurance; railroad retirement; pension benefit guaranty; veterans' life insurance; publicly administered workers' compensation; military medical insurance; and temporary disability insurance.

Taxes on production and imports is included in the gross domestic income account to make it comparable in concept to gross domestic product. It consists of federal excise taxes and customs duties and of state and local sales taxes, property taxes (including residential real estate taxes), motor vehicle license taxes, severance taxes, special assessments, and other taxes. It is equal to the former "indirect business taxes and nontax liabilities" less most of the nontax liabilities, which have now been reclassified as "business transfer payments."

Subsidies (payments by government to business other than purchases of goods and services) are now presented separately from the current surplus of government enterprises, which is presented as a component of net operating surplus. However, for the years prior to 1959, subsidies continue to be presented as net of the current surplus of government enterprises, since detailed data to separate the series for this period are not available.

Net operating surplus is a new aggregate introduced in the 2003 revision—a grouping of the business income components of the gross domestic income account. It reflects the net income accruing to business capital, showing business income after subtracting the costs of compensation of employees, taxes on production and imports (less subsidies), and consumption of fixed capital (CFC) from gross domestic product, before subtracting financing costs (such as net interest) and business transfer payments. Net operating surplus consists of the net operating surplus of private enterprises and the current surplus of government enterprises.

Net interest and miscellaneous payments, domestic industries consists of interest paid by domestic private enterprises and of rents and royalties paid by private enterprises to government, less interest received by domestic private enterprises. Interest received does not include interest received by noninsured pension plans, which are recorded as being directly received by persons in personal income. Both interest categories include monetary and imputed interest. In the *national* account, interest paid to the rest of the world is subtracted, and interest received from the rest of the world is added. Interest payments on mortgage and home improvement loans and on home equity loans are included as net interest in the private enterprises account.

It should be noted that net interest does not include interest paid by federal, state, or local governments. In fact, government interest does not enter into the national and domestic income accounts, though it does appear as a component of personal income. The NIPAs draw a distinction between interest paid by government and that paid by business.

The reasoning behind this distinction is that interest paid by business is one of the income counterparts of the production side of the account. The value of business production (as measured by its output of goods and services) includes the value added by business capital, and interest paid by business to its lenders is part of the total return to business capital.

However, there is no product flow in the accounts that is a counterpart to the payment of interest by government. The output of government does not have a market value. For purposes of GDP measurement, BEA estimates its contribution to GDP as the sum of compensation of employees, purchases of goods and services, and consumption of government fixed capital. (See above, and also the notes and definitions to Chapter 6.) This implies an estimate (described as "conservative" by BEA) that the net return to government capital is zero. Consequently, this assumption generates no income corresponding to the interest payment.

Supporting the distinction between business and government interest payments, it may be pointed out that most federal government debt was not incurred to finance investment, but rather to finance wars, to avoid tax increases and spending cuts during recessions, or to stimulate the economy. Some of the largest and most productive government investments—investments for highways—are typically financed by taxes on a pay-as-you-go basis, and not by borrowing.

Business current transfer payments, *net* consists of payments to persons, to government, and to the rest of the world by private business for which no current services are performed. Net insurance settlements—actual insured losses (or claims payable) less a normal level of losses—are treated as transfer payments. Payments to government consist of federal deposit insurance premiums, fines, regulatory and inspection fees, tobacco settlements, and other miscellaneous payments previously classified as "nontaxes." Taxes paid by domestic corporations to foreign governments, formerly classified as transfer payments, are now counted as taxes on corporate income.

In the NIPAs, capital income other than interest—corporate profits, proprietors' income, and rental income—is converted from the basis usually shown in the books of business and reported to the Internal Revenue Service to a basis that more closely represents income from current production. In the business accounts that provide the source data, depreciation of structures and equipment typically reflects a historical cost basis and a possibly arbitrary service life allowed by law to be used for tax purposes. BEA adjusts these values to reflect the average actual life of the capital goods and the cost of replacing them in the current period's prices. This conversion is done for all three forms of capital income. In addition, corporate and proprietors' incomes also require an adjustment for inventory valuation to exclude any profits or losses that might appear in the books, should the cost of inventory acquisition not be valued in the current period's prices. These two adjustments are called the *capital consumption adjustment (CCAdj)* and the *inventory valuation adjustment (IVA)*. They will be described in more detail below.

Proprietors' income with inventory valuation and capital consumption adjustments is the current-production income (including income-in-kind) of sole proprietorships and partnerships and of tax-exempt cooperatives. The imputed net rental income of owner-occupants of farm dwellings is included, but the imputed net rental income of owner-occupants of nonfarm dwellings is included in rental income of persons. Fees paid to outside directors of corporations are included. Proprietors' income excludes dividends and monetary interest received by nonfinancial business and rental incomes received by persons not primarily engaged in the real estate business; these incomes are included in dividends, net interest, and rental income of persons.

Rental income of persons with capital consumption adjustment is the net current-production income of persons from the rental of real property (except for the income of persons primarily engaged in the real estate business), the imputed net rental income of owner-occupants of nonfarm dwellings, and the royalties received by persons from patents, copyrights, and rights to natural resources. Consistent with the classification of investment in owner-occupied housing as business investment, the homeowner is considered to be paying himself or herself the rental value of the house (classified as PCE for services) and retaining as net income the amount of that rental remaining after paying interest and other costs.

Corporate profits with inventory valuation and capital consumption adjustments (often referred to as "economic profits") is the current-production income, net of economic depreciation, of organizations treated as corporations in the NIPAs. These organizations consist of all entities required to file federal corporate tax returns, including mutual financial institutions and cooperatives subject to federal income tax; private noninsured pension funds; nonprofit institutions that primarily serve business; Federal Reserve Banks, which accrue income stemming from the conduct of monetary policy; and federally-sponsored credit agencies. With several differences, this income is measured as receipts less expenses as defined in federal tax law. Among these differences: receipts exclude capital gains and dividends received, expenses exclude depletion and capital losses and losses resulting from bad debts, inventory withdrawals are valued at replacement cost, and depreciation is on a consistent accounting basis and is valued at replacement cost. Since *national* income is defined as the income of U.S. residents, its profits component includes income earned abroad by U.S. corporations and excludes income earned by the rest of the world within the United States.

Taxes on corporate income consists of taxes on corporate income paid to government and to the rest of the world.

Taxes on corporate income paid to government (formerly "profits tax liability") is the sum of federal, state, and local income taxes on all income subject to taxes. This income includes capital gains and other income excluded from profits before tax. These taxes are measured on an accrual basis, net of applicable tax credits.

Taxes on corporate income paid to the rest of the world consists of nonresident taxes, which are those paid by domestic corporations to foreign governments. These taxes were formerly classified as business transfer payments to the rest of the world.

Profits after tax is total corporate profits with IVA and CCAdj less taxes on corporate income. It consists of dividends and undistributed corporate profits.

Dividends is payments in cash or other assets, excluding the corporations' own stock, that are made by corporations to stockholders. In the domestic account, these are payments by domestic industries to stockholders in the United States and abroad; in the national account, these are all dividends received by U.S. residents. The payments are measured net of dividends received by U.S. corporations. Dividends paid to state and local government social insurance funds and general government are included.

Undistributed profits is corporate profits after tax with IVA and CCAdj less dividends.

The *inventory valuation adjustment (IVA)* for corporations is the difference between the cost of inventory withdrawals as valued in the source data used to determine profits before tax and the cost of withdrawals valued at replacement cost. In the NIPAs, inventory profits or losses are shown as adjustments to business income (corporate profits and nonfarm proprietors' income). These are shown as the IVA with the sign reversed. No adjustment is needed for farm proprietors' income, as farm inventories are measured on a current-market-cost basis.

Consumption of fixed capital (CFC) is a charge for the using-up of private and government fixed capital located in the United States. It is not based on the depreciation schedules allowed in tax law, but instead on studies of prices of used equipment and structures in resale markets. In periods in which extraordinary property destruction occurs, such as the damage caused by a severe hurricane or a terror attack, normal capital consumption is augmented by the estimated value of the lost assets.

For general government and for nonprofit institutions that primarily serve individuals, CFC on their capital assets is recorded in government consumption expenditures and in personal consumption expenditures, respectively. It is considered to be the value of the current services of the fixed capital assets owned and used by these entities.

Private capital consumption allowances consists of tax-return-based depreciation charges for corporations and nonfarm proprietorships and of historical-cost depreciation (calculated by BEA using a geometric pattern of price declines) for farm proprietorships, rental income of persons, and nonprofit institutions.

The private capital consumption adjustment (CCAdj) is the difference between private capital consumption allowances and private consumption of fixed capital. It therefore reflects the net effect of the two adjustments made to reported nonfarm business profits that convert historical to replacement costs and incorporate actual (rather than tax-based) service lives.

Definitions and notes on the data:
Gross value added of domestic corporate business

Gross value added is the term now used for what was formerly called "gross domestic product originating." It represents that share of the GDP produced in the specified sector or industry. Tables 1-12 and 1-13 show the current-dollar value of gross value added for all domestic corporate business and its financial and nonfinancial components. For the total and for nonfinancial corporations, consumption of fixed capital and net value added are shown, as is the allocation of net value added among employee compensation, taxes and transfer payments, and capital income. Constant-dollar values are also shown for nonfinancial corporations.

The data for nonfinancial corporations are often considered to be somewhat sturdier than data for the other sectors of the economy, since they exclude sectors whose outputs are difficult to evaluate—households, institutions, general government, and financial business—as well as excluding all noncorporate business.

Revisions

NIPA data normally undergo revision at the end of every July. These annual revisions typically cover annual and quarterly data for the previous three years. They may also include more limited revisions to data for earlier years. The NIPA data undergo "benchmark" revision approximately once every five years. At these times, definitional or other comprehensive changes may affect data back to 1929—the earliest year for which official national accounts data are available. The latest comprehensive revision of the NIPAs was released in 2003.

In mid-2002, BEA inaugurated a new revision schedule for wages and salaries and related income-side components of the NIPAs. When "final" estimates of GDP are released each quarter, wages and salaries and related data will be revised for both the "GDP" quarter and the previous quarter. Since these revisions only affect income-side components, GDP itself will not be revised for that previous quarter (and the statistical discrepancy will therefore change). The purpose of this schedule change is to achieve a more timely incorporation of the Bureau of Labor Statistics's quarterly tabulations of employees covered by state unemployment insurance. Previously, revisions based on these data were not incorporated until July of the following year. The same revision schedule will also be used in the monthly estimates of personal income.

Data availability

Annual data are available beginning with 1929. Quarterly data begin with 1946 for current-dollar values and 1947 for quantity and price measures, such as real GDP and the GDP price index. Not all data are available for all time periods.

New data are normally released toward the end of each month. The first estimates for each calendar quarter are released in the month after the quarter's end. Revisions for the most recent quarter are released in the second and third months after the quarter's end. As described above, wage and salary and related income-side components may be revised for previous quarters as well.

The most recent data are published each month in the *Survey of Current Business*. Current and historical data may be obtained from the BEA Web site at <http://www.bea.gov> and the STAT-USA subscription Web site at <http://www.stat-usa.gov>.

References

Articles describing and presenting the NIPAs are found in the *Survey of Current Business*, available by mail subscription and on the BEA Web site. The latest revision is described in Eugene P. Seskin and Shelly Smith's article, "Annual Revision of the National Income and Product Accounts: Annual Estimates for 2003–2005, Quarterly Estimates for 2003:I–2006:I," August 2006, Vol. 86 Number 8. Previous annual revisions are described in articles in earlier August issues.

The comprehensive 2003 revision is presented and described in several articles in the *Survey of Current Business*: "Improved Estimates of the National Income and Product Accounts for 1929–2002: Results of the Comprehensive Revision," February 2004; "Preview of the 2003 Comprehensive Revision of the National Income and Product Accounts: Statistical Changes," September 2003; "Preview of the 2003 Comprehensive Revision of the National Income and Product Accounts: New and Redesigned Tables," August 2003; "Preview of the 2003 Comprehensive Revision of the National Income and Product Accounts: Changes in Definitions and Classifications," June 2003; "Income and Outlays of Households and of Nonprofit Institutions Serving Households," April 2003; "Preview of Revised NIPA Estimates for 1997: Effects of Incorporating the 1997 Benchmark I-O Accounts and Proposed Definitional and Statistical Changes," January 2003; "Note on the Upcoming Comprehensive Revision of the National Income and Product Accounts," November 2002; and "Selected Issues in the Measurement of U.S. International Services," June 2002.

The previous comprehensive revision was presented in "Improved Estimates of the National Income and Product Accounts for 1929–99: Results of the Comprehensive Revision," April 2000.

The most recent description of NIPA methods and sources is found in the *Survey of Current Business*, "Updated Summary NIPA Methodologies," November 2005. Other papers on methodology can be found on the BEA Web site under "National Economic Accounts/Methodologies."

The treatment of employee stock options is discussed in Carol Moylan, "Treatment of Employee Stock Options in the U.S. National Economic Accounts," available on the BEA Web site at <http://www.bea.gov>.

TABLES 1-8 AND 20-7
COMPOSITE INDEXES OF ECONOMIC ACTIVITY

Source: The Conference Board

The composite indexes of leading, coincident, and lagging indicators are intended to help predict and identify peaks and troughs in the business cycle. They are calculated from sets of component series selected for their utility as indicators of stages of the business cycle. The component series originate from a variety of sources, as indicated below. A few component series that are not published elsewhere in this volume appear on the page with the composites. For other components, references to related tables in *Business Statistics* are given below.

The classification of indicators into leading, coincident, and lagging series grew out of an approach to the study of economic fluctuations that was pioneered by Wesley C. Mitchell and Arthur F. Burns early in the twentieth century and carried on by other researchers affiliated with the National Bureau of Economic Research (NBER). It was observed that indicators of business activity tended to move up and down over periods that were longer than a year and were therefore not accounted for by seasonal variation. Although these periods of expansion and contraction were not uniform in length, their recurrent nature caused them to be called "business cycles."

Furthermore, researchers have discovered that some indicators of the general state of business activity, such as different measures of production and income, tend to move together. Their peaks occur within a few months of each other and their low points, or troughs, also tend to occur close together. These are the *coincident indicators*. Other indicators move cyclically, but their peaks and troughs come noticeably before the peaks and troughs in the coincident indicators. These are the *leading indicators*, which are of great interest to anyone with a stake in the future performance of the economy. Finally, still other indicators have peaks and troughs that occur noticeably later than those in the coincident indicators; these are the *lagging indicators*. Lagging indicators can be valuable in observing whether cyclical imbalances have increased or are being corrected, suggesting that preconditions may exist for a new cycle phase. The *ratio of coincident to lagging indicators* is therefore of some interest as a leading indicator in its own right, although one that is even less regular than the leading index itself.

The first NBER-established business cycle dates were published in 1929. Currently, the dates are established by the NBER Business Cycle Dating Committee, first formed in 1978. Business cycle dates are based on monthly data, and the identification of a recession does not always follow the common definition of recession as two consecutive quarters of decline in real GDP. In all, the NBER has identified 31 cycles since December 1854.

The monthly and quarterly dates of the cycles from before the Great Depression to the latest announced turning point—the trough, or end of the recession, in November 2001—are shown in the table below. Quarterly turning points are identified by Roman numerals. NBER considers the trough month to be both the end of the decline and the beginning of the recovery, based on the concept that the actual turning point was some particular day within that month. Thus, the latest recession ended in November 2001, and the recovery also began in November 2001.

Similarly, the peak month of March 2001 was both the last month of expansion and the first month of recession.

BUSINESS CYCLE REFERENCE DATES
1927–2001

TROUGH	PEAK
November 1927 (IV)	August 1929 (III)
March 1933 (I)	May 1937 (II)
June 1938 (II)	February 1945 (I)
October 1945 (IV)	November 1948 (IV)
October 1949 (IV)	July 1953 (II)
May 1954 (II)	August 1957 (III)
April 1958 (II)	April 1960 (II)
February 1961 (I)	December 1969 (IV)
November 1970 (IV)	November 1973 (IV)
March 1975 (I)	January 1980 (I)
July 1980 (III)	July 1981 (III)
November 1982 (IV)	July 1990 (III)
March 1991 (I)	March 2001 (I)
November 2001 (IV)	

For additional information on NBER and its business cycle studies, see the NBER Web site at <http://www.nber.org/cycles>.

The composite indexes were originally compiled and published by BEA. In 1995, responsibility for compilation and publication was transferred to The Conference Board, a not-for-profit business research organization.

It is often said that the leading indicator index is designed to predict turning points in business activity 6 months in advance. This needs to be taken with a grain of salt. The current version of the leading index leads the 7 business cycle peaks that have occurred since the first month of the index by an average of 11 months; the shortest lead was 8 months and the longest was 18 months. It also predicted one recession that did not occur, in 1966–1967. The current leading index leads the 7 business cycle troughs by an average of 6 months, with a range from 2 to 11 months. This experience suggests that users need to be careful about relying on any mechanical interpretation of the leading index.

Index components

The *index of leading economic indicators* consists of the following 10 components; monthly data are seasonally adjusted, except as noted.

- *Average weekly hours* is average hours worked per week by production workers in manufacturing. Source: Bureau of Labor Statistics. (Table 10-9)

- *Initial claims, unemployment insurance* is average weekly claims for unemployment insurance under state programs. For inclusion in the leading index, the signs of the month-to-month changes are reversed, as claims increase when employment conditions worsen. Source: U.S. Department of Labor, Employment and Training Administration. (Table 10-6)

• *Manufacturers' new orders, consumer goods and materials* is new orders (net of order cancellations), expressed in constant dollars. Source: Census Bureau, with inflation adjustment by The Conference Board. (See Table 17-6 for current-dollar data.)

• *Vendor performance, slower deliveries diffusion index* tracks the relative speed with which goods-producing companies receive deliveries from their suppliers. An increase in this series indicates a slowdown in deliveries and is generally caused by increased demand for manufacturing materials. The survey asks purchasing managers if their suppliers' deliveries were obtained faster, slower, or at the same rate as the previous month's deliveries. The index records the percentage reporting slower deliveries plus half of the percentage reporting no change in delivery speed. Source: National Association of Purchasing Management. (Table 1-8)

• *Manufacturers' new orders, nondefense capital goods* is new orders (net of order cancellations), in constant dollars. Source: Census Bureau, with inflation adjustment by The Conference Board. (See Table 17-6 for new orders for nondefense capital goods in current dollars.)

• *Building permits, new private housing units* is the number of new private housing units authorized by local building permits. Source: Census Bureau. (Table 17-3)

• *Stock prices: 500 common stocks* is an index based on 1941–1943 = 10, not seasonally adjusted. Source: Standard and Poor's Corporation. (Table 12-10)

• *Money supply (M2)* is in billions of chained 2000 dollars. Source: Federal Reserve Board of Governors, with inflation adjustment by The Conference Board. (See Table 12-1 for the M2 money supply in current dollars.)

• *Interest rate spread* is equal to the rate on 10-year U.S. Treasury bonds less the rate on federal funds. The interest rate series are not seasonally adjusted. Source: Federal Reserve Board of Governors. (Table 12-9)

• *Index of consumer expectations* is based on the first quarter of 1966 = 100. The monthly data are not seasonally adjusted. Source: University of Michigan, Survey Research Center. This is a copyrighted series; it may not be reproduced without written permission from the source.

The *index of coincident economic indicators* consists of the following four components, with monthly data seasonally adjusted:

• *Employees on nonagricultural payrolls* is total wage and salary employees, in thousands. Source: Bureau of Labor Statistics. (Table 10-7)

• *Personal income less transfer payments* is in billions of chained 2000 dollars (seasonally adjusted annual rate). Source: Bureau of Economic Analysis, with inflation adjustment by The Conference Board, using the implicit deflator for personal consumption expenditures (PCE). (See Table 4-1 for total personal income and transfer payments in current dollars, and Table 1-5 for the price index for PCE, which is usually the same as the implicit deflator.)

• *Index of industrial production* is an index of the output of the mining, manufacturing, and utility sectors of the U.S. economy. The index is based on 1997 = 100. Source: Federal Reserve Board of Governors. (Table 2-1)

• *Manufacturing and trade sales* is in millions of chained 2000 dollars. Source: Bureau of Economic Analysis. (Table 5-9)

The *index of lagging economic indicators* consists of the following seven components, with monthly data seasonally adjusted, except as noted.

• *Average duration of unemployment* is in weeks. As with initial claims, the signs of the month-to-month changes are reversed. Source: Bureau of Labor Statistics. (Table 10-5)

• *Ratio: manufacturing and trade inventories to sales* is calculated from sales and inventories in chained 2000 dollars. Source: Bureau of Economic Analysis. (Table 5-9)

• *Manufacturing labor cost per unit of output* is the percent change over a six-month span in a monthly index constructed by The Conference Board. (See Table 9-4 for the Bureau of Labor Statistics's quarterly index of manufacturing unit labor cost.)

• *Average prime interest rate* is an average percentage rate per annum used by banks to price short-term business loans; not seasonally adjusted. Source: Federal Reserve Board of Governors. (Table 12-9)

• *Commercial and industrial loans outstanding* is in billions of chained 2000 dollars. Sources: Federal Reserve Board of Governors, with inflation adjustment by The Conference Board. (See Table 12-4 for current-dollar data.)

• *Consumer credit outstanding* is expressed as a percent of personal income. Sources: Bureau of Economic Analysis (Table 4-1) and Federal Reserve Board of Governors. (Table 12-8)

• *Consumer price index for services* is the percent change over the last six months, expressed at an annual rate, of the services component of the Consumer Price Index. Source: Bureau of Labor Statistics. (Table 8-1)

Notes on the data

Each composite index is scaled so that its average monthly value equals 100 in the base year, which is currently 1996. Changes in the components are calculated and standardized, using the standard deviation of each component, to equalize the volatility of each component in an index. Indicators that are not available at publication time are estimated using statistical imputation (an autoregressive model). In subsequent months, the imputations are replaced by the actual reported data. This imputation procedure allows an earlier release each month of preliminary values for the composite indexes.

Two major revisions in the calculation of the composite indexes were introduced with the preliminary index for June 2005 (along with some minor technical modifications).

• Trend adjustments were introduced—or re-introduced, since they had been a feature of some earlier versions of the composites. The entire history of the leading and lagging indexes was revised to give each the same time trend as the coincident composite. The trend adjustment is accomplished by adding an adjustment factor to the monthly growth rate of the index, and the same adjustment factor is used in each month's estimation of the current index. The adjustment factors are updated once a year during the regular annual benchmark revisions, which are usually made in January.

• The way that the yield spread is incorporated in the index was also changed. The contribution of the yield spread to the change in the leading index is now calculated from the value of the spread itself in the given month rather than as the change in the spread from the previous month. The new measure will contribute negatively only when the yield spread inverts (the long rate is less than the short rate).

The latest annual revision was made in January 2006, when the standardization factors were revised, resulting in the revision of historical values for all three composites. The most recent comprehensive revisions, which included the addition and deletion of components, were introduced in 1996.

Data availability

Data are published each month by The Conference Board. Its monthly report, *Business Cycle Indicators*, is available by subscription from The Conference Board, 845 Third Avenue, New York, NY 10022. A monthly press release from The Conference Board, with information about the indexes and their components, is available at <http://www.tcb-indicators.org>. The full historical database (with monthly data back to 1959) is available by subscription from the same Web site.

References

In addition to The Conference Board's *Business Cycle Indicators* (referenced above), see the *Survey of Current Business* article entitled "Business Cycle Indicators: Upcoming Revision of the Composite Indexes" (October 1993).

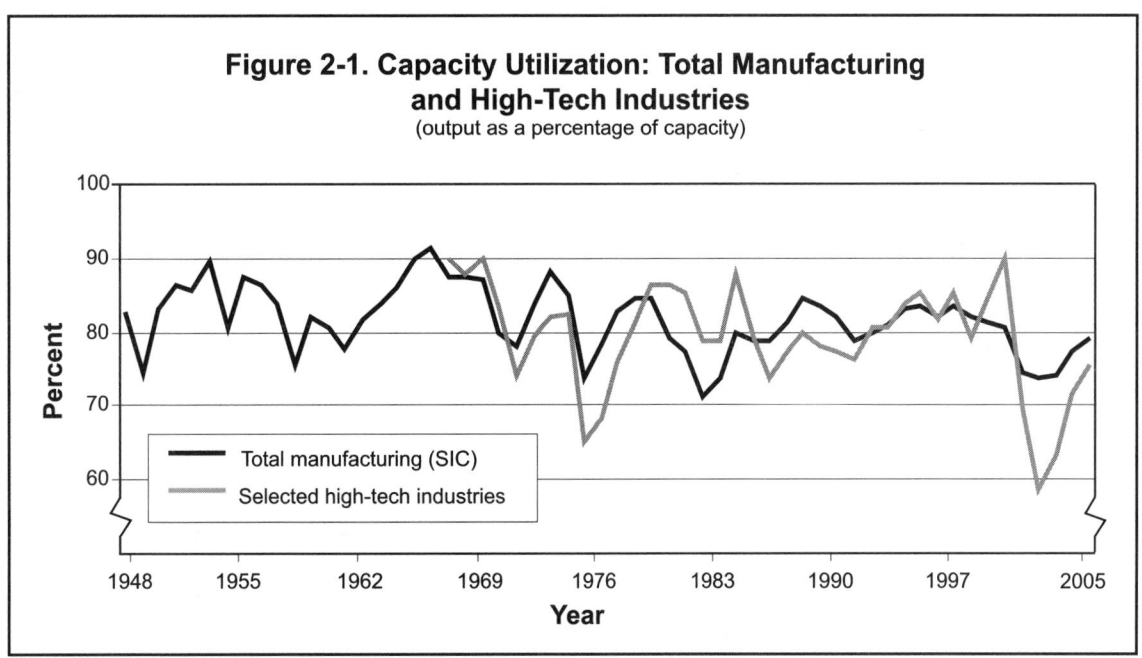

Figure 2-1. Capacity Utilization: Total Manufacturing and High-Tech Industries
(output as a percentage of capacity)

- Manufacturing capacity utilization is a key statistic for the U.S. economy, despite being limited to a sector that by some measures is diminishing in importance. (The Federal Reserve also provides measures of capacity utilization for "total industry"—manufacturing, mining, and utilities. However, mining and utilities are less significant in the context of business cycle analysis, and much of the variation in capacity use by utilities is a result of transitory weather variations, not economic factors.) Manufacturing utilization is an important indicator of inflationary pressure and measures an element in the demand for new capital goods. (Table 2-3)

- Capacity utilization in the high-tech industries (computers and office equipment, communications equipment, and semiconductors and related electronic components) has been more volatile than in the rest of industry, as seen in Figure 2-1. High-tech cycles were also not precisely synchronized with the overall cycle. At the height of the dot-com boom in 2000, high-tech utilization soared to 89.5 percent, while capacity use declined elsewhere. In 2002, high-tech industries used only 58.2 percent of capacity; however, their recovery started in 2003, ahead of the rest of manufacturing. (Table 2-3)

- Industrial production increased 176 percent from 1967 to 2005, which translates into an annual average growth rate of 2.7 percent. High-tech industries grew at an annual rate of 18.2 percent, while the rest of the manufacturing, mining, and utilities industries grew at a rate of 1.8 percent. (Tables 2-1 and 2-2)

Table 2-1. Industrial Production Indexes by Market Groups

(Seasonally adjusted, 2002 = 100.)

Year and month	Total industrial production	Final products and nonindustrial supplies Total	Consumer goods Total	Durable consumer goods Total	Automotive products	Home electronics	Appliances, furniture, and carpeting	Miscellaneous durable goods	Nondurable consumer goods Total
1967	39.2	39.2	44.9	30.7	29.7	1.1	43.2	47.4	52.0
1968	41.4	41.1	47.6	34.2	35.4	1.2	46.3	50.5	54.1
1969	43.3	42.6	49.4	35.6	35.6	1.3	48.9	54.6	55.9
1970	41.9	41.3	48.8	32.9	29.9	1.1	48.4	52.7	56.9
1971	42.5	41.9	51.6	37.2	38.1	1.3	51.1	55.6	58.5
1972	46.6	45.8	55.8	41.7	41.1	1.4	60.0	62.4	62.2
1973	50.4	49.2	58.3	44.8	44.7	1.7	64.8	65.2	64.2
1974	50.2	49.0	56.6	40.8	38.6	1.5	58.9	62.9	64.2
1975	45.7	45.5	54.4	37.0	37.1	1.3	50.4	55.9	63.1
1976	49.3	48.7	58.8	41.8	42.3	1.6	57.0	62.2	67.0
1977	53.1	52.7	62.5	47.0	47.9	1.9	64.0	68.9	69.5
1978	56.0	55.8	64.5	48.1	47.6	2.1	67.4	71.2	71.9
1979	57.7	57.7	63.5	46.4	42.9	2.1	67.6	71.7	71.5
1980	56.2	56.8	61.1	40.3	33.0	2.1	62.9	65.7	71.6
1981	56.9	58.0	61.5	40.9	34.1	2.2	62.1	66.6	71.9
1982	54.0	56.5	61.3	38.5	33.1	2.0	56.1	63.0	73.1
1983	55.4	57.9	63.6	42.8	38.4	2.8	62.0	64.8	74.0
1984	60.4	62.9	66.5	47.9	43.0	3.4	69.0	71.6	75.5
1985	61.2	64.5	67.1	47.9	43.0	3.6	68.5	71.7	76.4
1986	61.8	65.8	69.5	51.0	46.2	4.7	71.9	74.0	78.2
1987	64.9	68.9	72.3	53.9	49.2	4.6	75.8	78.6	81.0
1988	68.2	72.1	75.1	56.8	51.9	6.0	76.9	82.1	83.7
1989	68.8	72.8	75.4	58.1	53.9	6.3	77.7	82.6	83.4
1990	69.4	73.6	75.8	56.4	50.5	7.2	75.8	81.8	84.8
1991	68.3	72.4	75.7	53.9	47.2	8.6	70.5	79.0	86.0
1992	70.3	74.2	77.9	59.2	55.2	9.4	74.6	81.5	86.7
1993	72.6	76.7	80.6	64.8	61.0	14.7	78.8	85.0	87.9
1994	76.5	80.1	84.4	71.7	68.3	21.9	84.5	89.8	90.1
1995	80.2	83.2	86.9	75.0	70.4	32.5	84.0	92.4	92.2
1996	83.6	86.4	88.7	78.0	72.6	40.5	85.0	95.5	93.4
1997	89.7	91.9	91.9	83.3	78.0	55.0	88.7	97.8	95.6
1998	94.9	97.2	95.1	88.9	83.2	69.3	94.6	101.0	97.7
1999	99.3	100.1	97.1	95.5	91.2	90.3	97.8	103.4	97.7
2000	103.5	103.4	99.0	98.3	93.4	98.7	100.5	106.3	99.2
2001	99.9	100.5	97.8	94.1	90.5	98.8	96.2	98.8	99.3
2002	100.0	100.0	100.0	100.0	100.0	100.0	100.0	100.0	100.0
2003	100.6	100.8	101.0	104.0	107.1	112.1	99.6	99.4	99.8
2004	104.7	104.8	103.1	106.9	109.3	113.6	103.9	103.2	101.6
2005	108.1	109.1	105.3	109.0	111.8	119.2	105.5	104.0	103.9
2003									
January	100.5	100.4	100.5	103.8	106.5	113.2	98.1	100.5	99.2
February	100.6	100.6	100.9	101.8	104.0	103.5	97.8	99.5	100.6
March	100.4	100.7	101.0	101.9	104.5	103.5	97.3	99.5	100.7
April	99.6	99.7	100.3	101.6	104.1	107.4	97.4	98.3	99.8
May	99.5	99.7	100.0	101.5	103.3	105.0	99.0	98.9	99.4
June	99.8	100.1	100.5	103.2	105.5	115.2	99.8	99.1	99.4
July	100.3	100.6	101.3	105.1	109.2	113.3	100.4	98.6	99.7
August	100.4	100.7	100.9	103.7	106.2	117.7	100.1	99.1	99.8
September	101.0	101.3	101.8	107.3	112.8	119.9	100.6	98.8	99.6
October	101.1	101.1	101.1	105.3	109.0	113.7	101.1	99.4	99.4
November	102.0	102.3	102.0	106.5	110.0	116.1	102.2	100.8	100.2
December	102.3	102.4	102.2	106.5	110.3	116.4	101.8	100.7	100.4
2004									
January	102.7	102.8	102.7	108.2	111.6	119.5	104.4	102.2	100.5
February	103.5	103.7	103.4	107.9	111.2	123.3	103.9	101.9	101.5
March	103.2	103.3	102.5	107.2	110.4	125.3	102.1	101.7	100.6
April	104.0	104.2	103.2	107.9	110.7	116.7	104.6	103.0	101.3
May	105.0	105.0	103.8	107.1	108.8	115.4	104.8	103.8	102.5
June	104.4	104.3	102.4	105.1	105.8	109.7	103.6	104.0	101.3
July	105.0	104.9	102.3	105.0	105.7	102.3	103.8	104.7	101.2
August	105.3	105.4	103.2	107.2	109.5	109.9	104.0	104.0	101.7
September	105.1	105.0	102.6	105.4	107.0	108.2	103.2	103.2	101.4
October	105.8	106.0	103.6	107.7	110.7	114.3	104.0	103.3	101.9
November	106.0	106.2	103.7	107.3	109.9	112.6	104.4	103.2	102.2
December	106.7	106.9	104.1	107.3	110.1	106.6	104.1	103.4	102.9
2005									
January	106.9	107.1	103.9	106.3	108.2	108.2	104.2	103.6	102.9
February	107.4	107.6	104.7	109.7	113.9	115.0	104.5	103.8	102.8
March	107.3	107.7	104.6	107.7	110.3	113.1	105.5	102.9	103.4
April	107.2	107.7	104.1	106.0	107.8	115.2	102.9	103.0	103.3
May	107.4	108.1	104.6	107.1	109.3	124.7	104.0	102.5	103.5
June	108.3	109.0	105.8	108.5	111.7	120.4	105.6	102.5	104.7
July	108.3	109.1	105.2	107.1	109.5	116.1	105.2	102.3	104.4
August	108.6	109.5	105.6	110.1	114.4	113.6	106.5	103.1	103.9
September	107.2	109.1	106.4	112.7	117.8	113.5	108.5	104.9	103.9
October	108.4	111.0	106.5	113.1	117.3	125.3	108.4	106.3	103.9
November	109.4	111.3	105.7	110.1	111.7	132.1	106.2	106.6	103.9
December	110.4	112.0	106.6	109.0	110.1	133.4	104.7	106.7	105.5

Table 2-1. Industrial Production Indexes by Market Groups—Continued

(Seasonally adjusted, 2002 = 100.)

Year and month	Final products and nonindustrial supplies—Continued												
	Consumer goods—Continued						Business equipment				Defense and space equipment	Construction supplies	Business supplies
	Nondurable consumer goods—Continued												
	Nondurable non-energy consumer goods					Consumer energy products	Total	Transit	Information processing	Industrial and other			
	Total	Foods and tobacco	Clothing	Chemical products	Paper products								
1967	53.8	57.5	159.0	24.6	52.0	43.1	22.4	77.3	2.0	53.5	92.0	50.2	33.1
1968	55.6	59.0	164.7	26.8	51.5	46.1	23.4	86.2	2.3	53.4	92.2	52.8	35.2
1969	57.2	60.6	167.2	28.2	53.3	49.4	24.9	85.0	2.6	56.9	87.8	55.1	37.4
1970	57.8	61.4	162.3	30.6	51.4	52.2	24.0	74.5	2.7	54.9	74.3	53.1	37.5
1971	59.3	63.3	161.4	32.3	52.5	54.7	22.9	72.1	2.5	52.5	66.8	54.8	38.7
1972	63.2	66.9	175.6	35.3	52.9	57.7	26.0	78.7	2.9	59.7	65.0	62.2	42.6
1973	65.2	68.7	179.1	38.0	54.7	58.8	30.0	93.5	3.4	68.0	71.5	67.5	45.2
1974	64.9	69.0	167.9	40.1	53.8	60.3	31.7	91.2	4.0	70.9	73.9	65.9	45.1
1975	63.2	67.9	163.1	38.6	50.8	61.6	28.0	79.8	3.6	62.2	74.9	55.8	41.6
1976	67.3	72.3	171.8	42.0	52.8	64.8	29.7	82.3	4.2	64.7	72.8	60.2	44.2
1977	69.8	73.7	180.2	43.7	57.7	67.4	34.3	98.1	5.6	70.5	65.1	65.6	47.9
1978	72.5	76.5	184.5	46.4	60.6	68.6	38.8	114.7	7.0	75.5	65.6	69.3	50.5
1979	71.5	76.0	174.3	46.5	61.2	70.4	43.8	134.5	8.8	80.2	70.3	71.0	52.3
1980	72.3	77.1	177.4	46.3	62.0	67.8	44.5	126.6	10.8	77.7	83.9	65.7	51.0
1981	72.9	77.5	177.3	47.0	63.6	67.4	45.8	118.6	12.7	77.5	91.2	64.5	52.3
1982	74.3	80.0	176.8	47.1	65.2	67.8	41.9	90.3	14.4	67.1	109.1	58.6	51.7
1983	75.2	80.1	181.7	47.6	68.0	68.4	41.8	88.3	16.2	62.1	109.7	62.6	54.1
1984	76.6	81.1	182.3	48.7	71.4	70.5	48.2	91.4	20.3	70.9	124.6	68.2	58.8
1985	77.7	83.5	174.4	49.2	75.1	70.4	50.2	94.5	22.0	71.8	139.6	69.9	60.4
1986	79.7	84.9	174.2	53.0	76.1	71.8	49.3	86.4	22.1	71.4	148.2	72.3	62.4
1987	82.5	86.9	175.5	57.1	80.5	74.5	52.4	88.0	24.8	73.9	151.1	76.7	66.1
1988	84.8	89.4	172.7	60.5	82.7	78.4	57.2	97.3	27.1	80.3	152.0	78.4	68.6
1989	84.3	88.7	164.7	61.7	83.0	78.8	59.0	101.6	27.7	83.0	152.0	78.0	69.6
1990	86.3	91.2	161.3	64.0	84.6	78.3	61.0	110.3	29.5	82.4	145.8	77.3	71.3
1991	87.2	91.6	160.7	66.2	85.0	80.7	59.8	115.1	29.4	78.0	135.2	73.0	70.4
1992	88.3	92.9	164.2	66.0	86.1	79.6	62.1	110.6	33.2	79.4	125.5	76.0	72.1
1993	88.9	92.1	167.3	67.8	88.1	83.1	64.5	102.1	35.5	84.7	118.6	79.4	74.4
1994	91.4	95.9	170.2	69.2	87.2	84.2	68.2	94.7	39.7	90.4	111.5	85.2	77.3
1995	93.5	98.3	169.5	72.2	87.7	86.4	73.8	90.8	47.0	96.1	108.2	87.0	80.7
1996	94.1	98.0	164.9	75.6	87.4	90.2	80.5	94.7	56.6	99.5	104.5	90.9	83.6
1997	96.9	99.5	164.0	79.9	95.1	89.6	92.3	113.7	70.7	105.6	102.2	95.3	89.7
1998	99.5	102.0	154.2	83.9	100.4	89.6	102.8	136.4	83.8	109.0	105.9	100.2	95.0
1999	98.8	100.1	148.2	85.1	102.7	92.7	108.6	135.1	101.4	106.5	103.1	102.7	99.3
2000	100.2	101.6	141.2	88.2	103.7	94.9	116.6	117.5	123.2	112.6	92.2	105.0	104.0
2001	100.0	101.5	120.5	92.9	100.9	96.0	108.4	111.9	117.7	101.7	100.1	100.2	99.8
2002	100.0	100.0	100.0	100.0	100.0	100.0	100.0	100.0	100.0	100.0	100.0	100.0	100.0
2003	99.7	100.6	92.2	100.3	96.7	100.6	100.0	96.6	103.4	99.3	105.0	99.1	100.7
2004	101.5	102.7	88.2	102.2	99.6	101.9	109.4	105.6	113.8	108.2	113.1	104.6	103.9
2005	103.8	104.4	85.2	104.5	105.2	104.2	119.2	116.7	133.6	112.8	125.2	108.7	107.6
2003													
January	99.0	98.3	97.2	100.7	98.5	100.1	99.0	95.7	100.7	99.2	103.7	99.1	101.4
February	99.8	100.0	95.4	100.7	98.0	104.4	99.4	94.4	102.7	99.3	104.1	98.1	101.0
March	100.5	101.3	95.2	100.3	99.0	101.4	99.7	95.2	103.2	99.2	103.4	97.8	101.2
April	100.0	101.3	94.3	100.2	95.9	98.7	98.3	94.1	101.7	97.8	103.1	96.9	99.8
May	99.1	100.4	94.1	98.6	95.9	100.6	98.2	93.6	102.2	97.5	103.5	98.1	100.1
June	99.8	100.4	92.6	100.6	97.9	97.2	98.8	94.2	102.7	98.2	103.9	98.8	99.8
July	99.7	100.8	91.7	100.1	96.7	99.9	99.1	95.7	103.0	98.0	104.5	98.4	100.3
August	99.3	100.5	88.4	100.4	95.8	101.7	100.3	96.0	104.8	99.1	105.4	99.3	100.3
September	99.4	100.9	88.7	100.1	94.6	100.6	100.9	99.6	104.6	99.2	106.2	99.2	100.3
October	99.3	100.6	89.6	99.7	95.5	99.8	100.9	98.5	105.4	99.1	107.1	100.2	100.7
November	100.3	101.4	90.1	101.2	96.4	99.9	102.8	100.7	104.8	102.4	107.8	101.6	101.7
December	100.0	101.2	89.2	101.1	96.2	102.2	102.9	101.1	105.0	102.3	107.2	102.0	101.7
2004													
January	99.7	100.8	89.3	100.7	95.6	104.1	103.7	101.8	106.5	102.6	106.4	102.4	101.7
February	100.8	102.3	89.8	100.6	98.0	104.9	105.3	102.9	108.3	104.4	108.6	102.3	102.8
March	100.8	102.0	90.2	101.3	97.8	99.8	105.7	102.4	108.7	105.0	109.5	102.7	102.2
April	101.7	103.0	90.7	102.2	98.8	99.7	107.2	104.5	109.1	106.9	110.9	103.5	103.2
May	102.8	104.8	89.9	102.2	99.8	101.5	108.3	103.9	111.1	108.2	112.1	104.9	104.1
June	100.8	102.2	88.8	100.8	98.7	103.3	108.8	103.7	112.5	108.5	112.0	104.6	103.8
July	101.1	102.2	86.4	102.0	99.6	101.5	111.3	105.4	114.9	111.3	114.2	105.7	104.3
August	102.1	103.2	85.2	102.8	101.9	100.0	110.9	106.4	115.9	109.7	114.6	105.7	104.5
September	101.7	102.6	86.7	102.9	100.2	100.4	111.3	106.1	117.3	109.7	116.1	104.9	104.2
October	102.2	102.7	86.7	104.0	100.7	101.0	112.6	108.7	118.6	110.7	116.7	106.1	104.7
November	102.3	103.0	87.7	103.3	101.1	102.1	112.9	110.2	119.9	110.0	117.6	105.7	105.0
December	102.6	103.0	87.0	103.7	103.4	104.1	114.1	110.6	122.6	110.8	119.0	106.1	106.2
2005													
January	103.1	103.5	86.0	103.8	105.6	102.0	115.2	111.8	124.4	111.5	119.4	106.0	106.7
February	103.2	103.0	85.8	105.5	104.5	101.1	115.9	114.8	125.5	111.2	121.6	106.4	106.1
March	103.1	103.2	85.1	104.7	105.2	104.6	116.3	115.1	126.3	111.4	122.5	106.2	106.5
April	103.3	103.2	85.4	105.2	105.6	103.1	116.8	116.4	127.4	111.3	124.5	107.3	106.7
May	103.9	104.2	83.3	105.4	106.2	102.0	117.9	118.7	129.2	111.7	124.1	107.5	106.7
June	104.0	104.7	82.9	105.2	105.6	107.2	118.4	119.3	131.0	111.6	124.9	106.9	107.6
July	103.8	104.7	84.7	104.2	104.7	107.1	120.0	118.5	133.9	113.4	126.8	107.5	107.4
August	103.2	103.8	85.0	103.8	104.4	106.5	120.1	118.7	136.1	112.5	127.4	108.2	107.9
September	103.7	104.5	85.7	104.2	103.9	105.0	115.1	88.9	138.1	113.1	124.6	109.8	107.8
October	104.2	105.3	85.4	104.1	105.3	102.7	123.1	121.5	141.3	114.5	127.8	112.4	108.4
November	104.4	105.7	86.2	103.8	104.9	102.3	125.8	127.9	144.9	115.5	128.6	113.4	109.1
December	105.1	106.7	86.5	104.1	106.4	107.2	126.4	129.4	144.8	116.0	129.9	113.1	110.3

Table 2-1. Industrial Production Indexes by Market Groups—Continued

(Seasonally adjusted, 2002 = 100.)

Year and month	Total	Non-energy materials Total	Durable Total	Durable Consumer parts	Durable Equipment parts	Durable Other	Nondurable Total	Nondurable Textile	Nondurable Paper	Nondurable Chemical	Energy materials
1967	38.3	31.5	25.0	48.2	7.1	58.1	47.7	80.1	49.9	33.3	68.4
1968	40.8	33.8	26.4	54.3	7.3	61.1	52.4	88.4	52.2	38.7	71.6
1969	43.2	35.9	27.8	54.7	7.8	65.1	56.7	90.8	56.7	43.0	75.2
1970	41.7	33.8	25.3	45.9	7.1	60.8	57.0	87.5	56.2	44.0	78.9
1971	42.4	34.4	25.4	50.8	7.1	58.5	59.4	91.6	58.7	46.6	79.6
1972	46.6	38.5	28.7	56.5	8.2	66.2	65.5	96.5	62.6	54.2	82.6
1973	50.8	42.7	32.7	65.7	9.7	73.3	68.8	93.8	67.5	59.8	84.7
1974	50.7	42.6	32.4	58.1	10.2	73.3	69.7	87.7	70.9	61.5	84.3
1975	45.2	36.6	27.1	46.8	8.8	61.3	62.5	85.9	61.7	51.5	83.5
1976	49.2	40.8	30.3	59.8	9.5	65.8	69.2	95.7	67.8	59.0	85.4
1977	52.6	44.2	33.1	65.5	10.8	69.7	74.2	102.0	70.9	65.6	88.1
1978	55.2	47.1	35.7	69.3	12.1	74.3	77.0	100.9	74.3	69.5	89.1
1979	56.8	48.4	36.9	65.5	13.4	76.1	78.4	100.1	77.3	72.3	91.6
1980	54.6	45.5	34.2	50.5	13.7	70.4	75.9	97.7	77.9	66.9	92.3
1981	54.9	45.7	34.3	48.0	14.1	70.5	76.4	95.5	79.4	67.4	93.2
1982	50.7	41.2	29.9	40.8	12.9	59.5	72.4	87.2	80.1	60.4	89.2
1983	52.1	44.0	31.9	49.6	13.2	62.3	77.6	97.8	85.2	66.8	86.4
1984	57.0	49.1	37.1	58.9	15.9	68.9	81.0	97.6	90.4	71.0	91.8
1985	57.0	49.1	37.3	61.3	16.0	68.5	80.3	92.3	89.9	69.7	91.3
1986	57.0	50.1	37.8	60.8	16.3	69.8	82.8	96.2	93.8	73.1	87.7
1987	60.0	53.4	40.5	62.4	17.8	74.6	87.8	108.0	98.4	79.5	89.8
1988	63.3	56.8	43.7	67.5	19.4	80.0	91.1	107.0	101.7	84.3	92.9
1989	63.8	57.2	43.9	64.0	20.1	80.3	91.9	109.3	101.6	85.4	93.8
1990	64.2	57.3	44.0	59.7	20.8	80.8	92.1	103.9	102.0	86.3	95.7
1991	63.3	56.1	42.8	56.4	20.8	77.3	91.1	103.8	99.8	85.0	95.8
1992	65.4	58.9	45.7	63.3	22.1	81.3	93.4	109.8	102.2	87.2	94.9
1993	67.6	61.6	48.8	71.9	23.5	84.5	94.5	114.3	102.2	87.7	95.1
1994	72.1	66.7	54.4	83.3	26.8	90.8	97.2	121.3	106.1	90.4	96.7
1995	76.3	71.4	60.3	86.6	33.1	94.2	98.2	119.3	108.8	91.1	98.1
1996	80.0	75.6	66.3	89.0	40.0	97.0	97.3	116.0	105.3	91.5	99.6
1997	86.7	83.9	75.8	95.8	51.3	101.9	101.9	121.4	106.5	98.1	99.5
1998	92.0	90.3	84.3	98.8	63.6	104.7	103.3	120.4	107.4	98.5	99.9
1999	98.0	97.8	94.4	108.8	78.9	106.3	104.8	117.4	109.5	101.6	99.7
2000	103.7	104.5	104.5	108.8	100.1	107.4	104.7	112.6	108.3	102.4	101.1
2001	99.0	98.6	99.0	95.9	99.6	99.9	98.1	99.6	101.8	95.4	100.0
2002	100.0	100.0	100.0	100.0	100.0	100.0	100.0	100.0	100.0	100.0	100.0
2003	100.4	100.6	102.3	97.7	109.6	98.7	97.8	94.4	95.0	99.4	99.6
2004	104.6	106.5	110.4	99.9	125.8	103.7	100.1	89.2	96.7	104.2	99.6
2005	106.6	110.2	117.1	101.6	144.0	105.1	99.2	84.5	97.2	100.8	97.8
2003											
January	100.8	100.9	101.9	101.3	104.9	99.7	99.2	97.1	98.6	100.1	100.2
February	100.5	100.4	101.3	98.4	105.7	99.0	98.9	98.3	96.2	100.3	100.9
March	100.0	100.2	100.8	96.8	106.5	98.2	99.0	97.4	97.6	99.8	99.3
April	99.5	99.4	100.1	95.4	106.4	97.2	98.2	96.8	95.1	99.7	99.6
May	99.3	99.4	100.8	95.7	107.3	98.0	97.1	95.0	95.2	97.5	98.9
June	99.4	99.7	101.3	97.1	107.8	98.2	97.0	93.7	94.6	97.1	98.7
July	99.8	99.9	101.7	97.3	109.3	97.7	96.9	90.8	94.3	98.2	99.3
August	99.8	99.7	101.6	95.4	110.3	97.7	96.5	90.9	93.3	98.1	100.0
September	100.6	100.8	102.8	99.0	111.8	97.7	97.4	92.1	93.6	99.6	99.8
October	101.1	101.5	103.9	97.7	113.5	99.2	97.5	92.7	93.0	100.1	100.0
November	101.7	102.6	105.3	98.9	115.3	100.6	98.1	93.8	93.7	100.6	99.3
December	102.1	103.1	106.0	99.7	116.3	100.9	98.3	93.7	94.2	101.1	99.3
2004											
January	102.5	103.2	106.3	100.4	117.2	100.6	98.2	93.0	94.4	100.8	100.6
February	103.2	104.3	107.7	101.6	119.6	101.5	98.7	90.5	94.6	101.3	100.2
March	103.1	104.6	108.1	100.4	120.7	102.1	98.8	90.0	94.6	102.3	99.3
April	103.8	105.2	108.6	99.8	121.5	102.9	99.7	88.9	95.9	103.4	99.8
May	104.9	106.3	109.9	99.6	124.0	104.1	100.3	88.3	96.8	104.3	101.0
June	104.5	106.3	110.1	98.4	125.5	104.0	100.1	88.7	97.2	104.6	99.8
July	105.1	107.2	111.1	97.7	127.5	105.1	100.8	89.4	98.1	105.0	99.7
August	105.2	107.8	112.0	99.9	129.0	104.9	101.0	89.8	97.6	105.8	98.4
September	105.1	107.7	112.1	99.3	130.6	104.3	100.7	89.0	97.6	105.4	98.2
October	105.6	108.3	112.8	100.9	130.3	105.2	101.0	88.0	97.4	105.6	98.5
November	105.9	108.3	112.8	100.4	130.8	105.2	101.0	87.1	98.0	105.9	99.3
December	106.5	108.8	113.4	100.8	132.5	105.1	101.3	87.4	98.4	106.3	100.4
2005											
January	106.8	109.6	114.7	100.8	136.4	105.3	101.3	87.6	98.4	104.6	99.4
February	107.0	109.7	115.2	102.4	138.0	104.6	101.0	85.4	98.6	104.9	99.7
March	106.8	109.4	114.8	100.4	137.8	104.8	100.7	85.1	98.6	103.9	99.8
April	106.5	109.2	114.9	99.1	139.7	104.5	100.1	83.5	97.5	103.7	99.2
May	106.5	109.3	115.2	99.5	141.0	104.1	99.8	83.6	96.4	102.6	99.2
June	107.3	109.5	115.5	102.4	141.7	103.0	99.7	84.4	97.2	102.9	101.3
July	107.2	109.8	115.9	101.1	143.4	103.2	100.0	85.3	96.1	103.3	100.3
August	107.4	110.2	117.0	101.6	145.7	104.0	99.3	84.5	96.0	102.1	100.0
September	104.5	109.4	118.8	103.3	147.2	105.8	94.8	84.3	95.7	90.8	92.8
October	104.9	110.9	120.1	104.4	149.1	107.0	96.4	84.4	97.1	92.9	90.9
November	106.9	112.1	120.9	102.1	153.1	107.2	98.3	83.7	96.4	98.4	94.3
December	108.3	113.0	121.8	102.0	155.3	107.7	99.2	82.6	98.0	99.2	96.8

Table 2-1. Industrial Production Indexes by Market Groups—Continued

(Seasonally adjusted, 2002 = 100.)

Year and month	Special aggregates											
	Energy						Non-energy					Total non-energy, excluding high-tech
									Selected high-tech			
	Total	Consumer energy products	Commercial energy products	Oil and gas well drilling	Converted fuels	Primary energy	Total	Total	Computers and office equipment	Communications equipment	Semiconductors and related components	
1967	57.5	43.1	30.7	. . .	57.1	79.0	35.9	0.3	. . .	. . .	. . .	52.7
1968	60.6	46.1	33.3	. . .	61.2	81.2	37.9	0.3	. . .	. . .	. . .	55.6
1969	63.9	49.4	35.1	. . .	65.4	84.0	39.6	0.3	. . .	. . .	. . .	57.9
1970	66.9	52.2	37.7	. . .	68.8	88.1	37.8	0.3	. . .	. . .	. . .	55.1
1971	68.2	54.7	39.7	. . .	70.7	87.4	38.4	0.3	. . .	. . .	. . .	56.2
1972	71.3	57.7	41.8	97.2	75.1	88.8	42.4	0.4	0.1	11.1	0.1	61.8
1973	73.1	58.8	44.1	91.5	78.0	89.9	46.3	0.4	0.1	12.1	0.2	67.1
1974	73.5	60.3	44.2	106.3	76.9	90.2	46.0	0.5	0.2	12.3	0.2	66.3
1975	73.7	61.6	45.8	119.9	74.2	91.0	41.1	0.5	0.2	10.7	0.2	59.2
1976	76.1	64.8	48.1	135.0	78.3	91.1	44.7	0.6	0.3	10.9	0.2	64.1
1977	79.1	67.4	49.8	171.5	81.1	93.7	48.5	0.8	0.4	13.4	0.3	69.0
1978	80.4	68.6	51.3	191.0	80.5	96.0	51.6	1.0	0.6	14.7	0.4	72.8
1979	82.8	70.4	53.7	203.7	83.5	98.1	53.2	1.3	0.8	17.6	0.5	74.1
1980	83.1	67.8	52.8	240.9	81.8	100.1	51.4	1.5	1.2	19.3	0.5	70.6
1981	84.4	67.4	54.2	289.4	80.7	102.1	52.0	1.8	1.6	20.1	0.6	70.8
1982	81.3	67.8	54.9	254.7	74.2	99.2	49.1	2.1	1.9	21.3	0.7	66.0
1983	78.9	68.4	56.0	197.3	74.1	94.9	51.3	2.5	2.7	20.7	0.8	68.4
1984	83.6	70.5	59.0	214.9	78.8	100.9	56.5	3.3	3.9	23.4	1.1	74.3
1985	83.3	70.4	61.2	196.8	78.5	100.3	57.5	3.5	4.5	23.6	1.2	75.3
1986	80.5	71.8	62.9	95.4	75.7	96.1	58.8	3.6	4.9	22.2	1.3	77.0
1987	82.8	74.5	66.2	91.8	79.6	96.8	62.1	4.3	6.3	22.7	1.6	80.6
1988	86.0	78.4	68.5	111.1	83.2	99.4	65.4	5.0	7.7	24.1	1.8	84.2
1989	86.9	78.8	71.0	96.4	86.3	98.8	66.0	5.3	8.1	24.2	2.0	84.6
1990	88.3	78.3	73.0	102.5	87.1	101.5	66.4	6.0	8.7	26.9	2.3	84.7
1991	88.8	80.7	74.1	80.1	87.1	101.6	65.1	6.4	9.0	26.8	2.7	82.5
1992	87.6	79.6	73.6	55.6	88.7	99.0	67.6	7.7	11.3	30.8	3.3	84.7
1993	89.2	83.1	75.8	77.3	90.4	98.2	70.0	9.1	14.0	35.2	3.8	86.9
1994	91.0	84.2	78.8	92.0	91.8	99.9	74.3	11.8	17.4	43.6	5.1	90.7
1995	92.9	86.4	81.6	89.6	93.2	101.4	78.2	16.6	24.3	51.5	7.9	93.0
1996	95.2	90.2	84.2	96.1	94.8	102.8	81.8	23.3	34.4	62.5	11.8	94.5
1997	95.6	89.6	87.6	110.1	96.3	101.6	88.9	34.6	48.7	82.1	18.9	99.2
1998	96.0	89.6	89.1	103.2	97.5	101.7	94.9	48.4	67.1	94.4	29.1	102.8
1999	96.8	92.7	92.6	80.7	99.1	100.1	99.8	70.5	88.1	118.3	48.2	104.1
2000	99.2	94.9	96.4	114.3	101.5	101.0	104.4	100.7	102.8	158.9	77.4	105.0
2001	99.3	96.0	98.1	138.7	97.7	101.2	100.0	102.6	103.7	142.8	85.2	99.8
2002	100.0	100.0	100.0	100.0	100.0	100.0	100.0	100.0	100.0	100.0	100.0	100.0
2003	100.8	100.6	105.1	116.2	99.9	99.5	100.6	117.6	108.9	100.1	130.7	99.4
2004	101.5	101.9	107.4	126.9	101.6	98.6	105.4	141.2	110.7	116.7	168.8	103.2
2005	101.5	104.2	110.8	142.5	102.5	95.7	109.6	172.0	119.9	144.5	211.4	106.1
2003												
January	101.3	100.1	107.8	103.0	102.5	99.0	100.4	107.4	107.2	92.3	114.7	99.9
February	102.5	104.4	105.7	107.7	103.0	99.7	100.2	110.9	109.1	97.8	117.9	99.4
March	100.7	101.4	104.7	110.5	98.5	99.7	100.3	112.6	109.1	99.9	120.2	99.5
April	100.2	98.7	103.5	113.4	98.4	100.3	99.5	112.9	108.2	99.0	121.9	98.6
May	100.3	100.6	104.2	117.2	96.7	100.0	99.4	114.1	108.1	98.9	124.5	98.4
June	99.0	97.2	101.3	118.9	97.1	99.5	100.0	115.7	109.7	100.5	126.1	98.9
July	100.4	99.9	105.0	117.9	99.8	99.0	100.2	118.3	111.9	99.1	131.3	99.0
August	101.4	101.7	105.3	119.0	101.3	99.4	100.1	120.7	112.6	101.7	134.5	98.8
September	101.0	100.6	105.0	119.8	99.5	100.0	101.0	122.1	110.7	101.5	138.5	99.6
October	101.0	99.8	105.2	121.5	100.6	99.7	101.1	124.3	107.7	103.5	143.4	99.6
November	100.7	99.9	106.3	122.0	100.5	98.7	102.3	125.3	105.9	102.9	146.8	100.8
December	101.5	102.2	107.9	123.0	100.7	98.6	102.4	127.0	107.0	104.3	148.8	100.8
2004												
January	102.5	104.1	106.5	122.8	101.9	99.9	102.7	130.5	109.7	108.1	152.4	101.0
February	102.7	104.9	108.4	123.1	102.5	99.1	103.7	133.5	111.9	109.9	156.6	101.8
March	100.7	99.8	105.8	124.4	99.1	99.3	103.8	135.0	112.2	109.6	159.6	101.8
April	101.1	99.7	106.7	124.3	101.4	99.1	104.7	135.5	111.1	109.7	161.0	102.7
May	102.4	101.5	107.6	123.6	105.1	99.0	105.5	138.3	109.8	111.8	166.1	103.5
June	101.9	103.3	106.9	125.0	102.0	98.7	104.9	140.4	109.2	114.4	169.1	102.8
July	101.4	101.5	106.3	126.6	100.9	99.1	105.8	142.4	109.2	117.1	171.7	103.6
August	100.1	100.0	105.5	127.6	98.9	98.1	106.5	145.7	109.7	119.3	177.0	104.1
September	100.4	100.4	107.2	128.2	100.5	97.1	106.1	147.6	110.3	120.9	179.6	103.6
October	100.6	101.0	107.1	128.9	100.8	97.3	107.0	147.0	110.9	123.7	176.4	104.6
November	101.7	102.1	109.0	133.2	102.2	97.8	107.0	147.8	111.7	126.9	175.9	104.5
December	103.1	104.1	111.2	134.7	103.6	98.8	107.5	151.0	112.6	129.3	180.5	104.9
2005												
January	101.7	102.0	108.6	136.3	101.9	98.1	108.1	157.8	113.6	133.3	191.8	105.2
February	101.6	101.1	107.7	138.2	101.2	98.9	108.7	160.4	114.7	134.3	196.0	105.7
March	102.8	104.6	109.5	140.0	103.5	98.1	108.3	160.4	115.8	133.6	195.8	105.3
April	102.0	103.1	109.1	140.1	101.9	97.9	108.4	163.1	117.0	134.9	200.0	105.2
May	101.5	102.0	108.4	135.7	102.1	97.8	108.8	166.2	118.5	138.3	203.8	105.5
June	104.8	107.2	113.7	140.6	107.2	98.7	109.0	167.9	120.1	139.7	205.7	105.7
July	103.9	107.1	111.5	143.6	105.9	97.8	109.2	171.6	120.0	145.3	209.9	105.7
August	103.7	106.5	112.4	146.2	105.3	97.5	109.7	176.7	121.0	147.2	218.9	106.0
September	98.6	105.0	111.6	146.0	101.1	89.2	109.2	179.6	122.1	151.2	221.9	105.4
October	96.8	102.7	111.0	149.3	98.4	87.6	111.3	181.3	123.0	156.3	221.9	107.4
November	99.0	102.3	111.5	147.9	99.8	91.9	111.9	188.0	125.4	160.6	232.2	107.9
December	101.9	107.2	114.2	146.4	101.8	94.5	112.5	191.1	127.2	159.8	238.3	108.3

. . . = Not available.

Table 2-2. Industrial Production Indexes by NAICS Industry Groups

(Seasonally adjusted, 2002 = 100.)

Year and month	Total industrial production	Manu-facturing (SIC)	Manufacturing (NAICS)										
			Total	Durable goods manufacturing									
				Total	Wood products	Nonmetallic mineral products	Primary metals	Fabricated metal products	Machinery	Computer and electronic products	Electrical equipment, appliances, and components	Motor vehicles and parts	Aerospace and miscella-neous transport equipment
1967	39.2	36.1	...	...	...	...	...	...	...	...	...	...	...
1968	41.4	38.1	...	...	...	...	...	...	...	...	...	...	...
1969	43.3	39.8	...	...	...	...	...	...	...	...	...	...	...
1970	41.9	38.0	...	...	...	...	...	...	...	...	...	...	...
1971	42.5	38.6	...	...	...	...	...	...	...	...	...	...	...
1972	46.6	42.7	41.7	31.6	73.5	74.1	120.9	69.3	68.4	1.5	71.9	44.2	72.7
1973	50.4	46.5	45.5	35.5	71.1	79.6	140.6	76.6	79.0	1.7	80.9	50.6	82.9
1974	50.2	46.4	45.4	35.3	64.6	78.7	144.2	75.4	82.9	1.9	78.9	43.4	84.2
1975	45.7	41.5	40.5	30.6	59.9	70.5	111.8	65.1	72.3	1.7	63.3	37.8	80.0
1976	49.3	45.2	44.2	33.4	67.5	74.5	118.7	69.8	75.5	2.0	71.5	48.3	74.9
1977	53.1	49.1	48.0	36.7	72.8	79.3	119.8	75.7	82.4	2.5	78.8	55.0	75.5
1978	56.0	52.1	51.0	39.6	73.7	84.6	127.4	79.4	88.8	3.1	83.6	57.3	83.2
1979	57.7	53.7	52.6	41.6	71.3	84.4	130.4	82.9	93.8	3.8	87.1	52.5	97.2
1980	56.2	51.7	50.5	39.7	66.0	76.0	114.4	78.2	89.3	4.6	81.9	38.6	104.8
1981	56.9	52.3	51.1	40.2	64.6	72.8	114.6	77.7	88.4	5.3	80.9	37.6	100.3
1982	54.0	49.5	48.2	36.7	57.9	64.5	80.9	69.6	74.0	6.0	72.9	33.9	93.5
1983	55.4	51.7	50.4	38.5	67.2	69.4	82.8	70.2	66.9	6.9	75.4	43.3	89.1
1984	60.4	56.9	55.5	44.0	71.9	74.8	90.8	76.4	77.9	8.6	84.9	52.0	94.4
1985	61.2	57.9	56.5	45.0	72.7	76.2	83.9	77.5	78.1	9.2	83.6	54.0	101.0
1986	61.8	59.1	57.7	45.8	79.1	79.4	81.9	77.0	76.9	9.6	85.1	53.9	106.2
1987	64.9	62.4	60.9	48.4	86.2	83.7	88.2	78.4	78.3	10.8	86.3	55.9	110.0
1988	68.2	65.6	64.2	51.8	86.1	85.4	98.8	82.4	86.2	11.9	90.4	59.7	115.7
1989	68.8	66.1	64.8	52.4	84.8	84.6	96.6	81.7	89.3	12.2	89.0	59.1	122.7
1990	69.4	66.6	65.3	52.5	83.9	83.4	95.4	80.7	87.1	13.2	86.7	55.5	123.2
1991	68.3	65.3	64.1	50.9	78.5	76.8	89.5	77.0	81.8	13.7	82.2	53.1	118.9
1992	70.3	67.7	66.7	53.5	82.8	80.2	91.7	79.4	81.6	15.5	87.2	60.4	110.0
1993	72.6	70.1	69.1	56.5	83.7	82.0	96.1	82.4	87.6	17.1	92.7	66.8	102.6
1994	76.5	74.3	73.5	61.5	88.7	86.5	103.5	89.6	96.0	20.3	99.5	76.7	92.1
1995	80.2	78.3	77.6	66.8	90.8	89.1	104.5	95.1	102.7	26.4	101.7	79.0	87.5
1996	83.6	81.8	81.4	72.4	93.8	94.8	107.0	98.6	106.2	33.6	104.9	79.6	90.9
1997	89.7	88.8	88.3	81.2	96.6	98.0	111.6	103.0	112.2	45.2	108.8	85.8	101.5
1998	94.9	94.7	94.2	89.8	100.9	102.9	113.5	106.3	115.0	58.3	112.8	90.2	117.6
1999	99.3	99.7	99.3	97.6	105.1	103.8	113.2	107.1	112.7	77.2	114.8	100.1	113.4
2000	103.5	104.3	104.0	105.3	103.6	103.8	109.5	111.3	118.4	102.5	120.6	99.5	99.7
2001	99.9	99.9	99.7	100.2	97.0	99.9	99.1	103.2	104.8	103.6	108.3	90.6	105.9
2002	100.0	100.0	100.0	100.0	100.0	100.0	100.0	100.0	100.0	100.0	100.0	100.0	100.0
2003	100.6	100.5	100.7	102.3	98.8	100.1	97.6	98.6	99.0	112.6	97.8	104.0	97.3
2004	104.7	105.4	105.8	109.8	104.9	105.4	103.4	103.2	110.7	130.7	101.5	108.0	100.7
2005	108.1	109.4	109.9	116.8	107.6	107.1	100.6	106.5	116.1	156.7	106.6	111.3	109.3
2003													
January	100.5	100.3	100.4	101.5	97.9	99.2	100.8	99.8	98.3	106.2	97.7	105.2	97.5
February	100.6	100.1	100.2	100.9	97.6	98.0	98.7	98.8	98.7	107.8	98.4	101.8	97.0
March	100.4	100.3	100.4	100.7	96.2	99.3	94.0	98.6	99.0	108.8	97.7	101.4	97.1
April	99.6	99.5	99.6	100.0	96.4	97.9	95.2	97.6	97.5	108.5	96.8	100.5	96.9
May	99.5	99.4	99.5	100.4	96.6	100.4	94.7	98.2	97.6	109.7	97.8	99.9	96.5
June	99.8	99.9	100.0	101.4	97.3	100.3	98.5	98.1	97.5	110.9	98.5	101.8	96.5
July	100.3	100.2	100.4	102.0	98.9	100.1	95.4	98.2	97.1	112.6	96.2	104.9	96.9
August	100.4	100.1	100.3	102.1	98.3	100.8	95.6	97.7	98.5	114.8	98.1	102.3	97.2
September	101.0	101.0	101.3	103.6	99.1	100.0	94.2	98.4	99.4	116.0	97.0	109.2	97.0
October	101.1	101.1	101.4	103.7	100.6	101.3	98.5	99.0	98.5	117.7	98.2	105.9	97.4
November	102.0	102.3	102.6	105.3	103.9	102.2	101.0	99.7	102.6	118.7	98.7	107.0	98.6
December	102.3	102.3	102.7	105.6	102.9	101.7	104.2	99.8	103.4	119.4	98.2	107.6	98.4
2004													
January	102.7	102.6	103.1	106.2	103.2	102.7	98.5	100.7	104.1	121.3	99.0	109.0	98.0
February	103.5	103.6	104.0	107.4	103.9	102.2	101.2	101.2	107.4	123.6	99.1	109.3	99.3
March	103.2	103.7	104.1	107.6	103.4	104.7	101.6	100.9	108.0	125.0	98.6	108.6	98.9
April	104.0	104.6	105.0	108.4	105.2	104.9	101.6	102.3	109.3	125.3	100.4	108.9	99.6
May	105.0	105.5	105.9	109.2	106.3	105.1	103.2	103.4	110.6	128.2	101.0	107.2	99.6
June	104.4	104.9	105.3	109.0	104.3	104.5	103.4	103.5	111.0	129.8	101.6	104.9	99.6
July	105.0	105.7	106.2	110.2	106.1	106.0	106.4	104.0	113.5	131.9	102.1	104.5	101.4
August	105.3	106.4	106.8	111.0	105.6	106.6	104.7	104.3	111.8	134.4	102.7	108.4	101.3
September	105.1	106.0	106.4	110.9	103.7	107.1	105.2	103.8	112.8	136.1	102.8	106.5	100.9
October	105.8	106.9	107.4	112.1	105.9	107.0	105.3	104.8	113.3	136.4	103.2	109.8	102.2
November	106.0	106.9	107.4	112.1	105.3	106.0	105.8	104.6	113.1	136.9	103.6	109.2	103.6
December	106.7	107.5	107.9	112.9	105.4	107.7	104.4	104.6	113.1	139.7	103.6	110.0	104.2
2005													
January	106.9	108.1	108.4	113.7	108.7	106.3	103.8	105.4	114.1	144.3	104.3	108.6	104.2
February	107.4	108.6	109.0	114.8	105.7	106.4	101.9	105.3	114.0	146.8	103.7	113.4	106.3
March	107.3	108.2	108.6	114.2	104.9	105.1	102.3	105.0	114.3	147.4	103.6	109.8	107.5
April	107.2	108.3	108.6	114.3	104.8	105.7	99.5	105.5	114.3	149.5	103.5	107.9	109.5
May	107.4	108.7	109.0	115.0	105.9	105.9	98.9	105.7	114.5	152.2	104.4	108.8	110.4
June	108.3	109.0	109.4	115.5	104.4	106.4	95.5	105.6	115.0	153.6	105.1	111.4	110.2
July	108.3	109.1	109.6	115.9	104.9	105.9	95.3	106.1	116.3	156.5	106.3	109.2	110.9
August	108.6	109.5	110.1	117.3	104.0	105.9	98.2	106.6	114.1	160.1	107.2	113.1	111.7
September	107.2	108.9	109.5	117.5	107.2	107.2	101.8	106.8	116.1	162.1	108.8	116.3	94.2
October	108.4	110.9	111.5	120.7	112.7	108.8	102.7	109.0	119.0	165.0	110.9	116.3	112.2
November	109.4	111.7	112.4	121.2	114.0	111.6	103.5	109.1	120.2	170.7	110.5	110.9	116.4
December	110.4	112.2	112.8	121.4	113.4	109.6	104.0	108.5	121.8	172.5	110.6	109.5	118.4

... = Not available.

Table 2-2. Industrial Production Indexes by NAICS Industry Groups—Continued

(Seasonally adjusted, 2002 = 100.)

| Year and month | Durable goods manufacturing—Continued | | Manufacturing (NAICS)—Continued | | | | | | | | | Other manufacturing (non-NAICS) |
| | | | Nondurable goods manufacturing | | | | | | | | | |
	Furniture and related products	Miscellaneous manufacturing	Total	Food, beverage, and tobacco products	Textile and product mills	Apparel and leather	Paper	Printing and support	Petroleum and coal products	Chemical	Plastics and rubber products	
1967	. . .	. . .	. . .	. . .	. . .	. . .	. . .	. . .	. . .	. . .	. . .	. . .
1968	. . .	. . .	. . .	. . .	. . .	. . .	. . .	. . .	. . .	. . .	. . .	. . .
1969	. . .	. . .	. . .	. . .	. . .	. . .	. . .	. . .	. . .	. . .	. . .	. . .
1970	. . .	. . .	. . .	. . .	. . .	. . .	. . .	. . .	. . .	. . .	. . .	. . .
1971	. . .	. . .	. . .	. . .	. . .	. . .	. . .	. . .	. . .	. . .	. . .	. . .
1972	54.2	41.2	61.0	65.8	86.8	179.5	66.1	51.5	73.6	48.3	35.2	65.6
1973	56.7	42.4	63.8	66.5	85.9	182.6	71.4	54.1	72.3	52.9	39.6	67.6
1974	52.2	41.5	64.1	67.5	79.0	171.7	74.5	52.5	78.0	55.0	38.6	68.0
1975	44.5	38.8	59.5	66.3	76.4	167.2	64.6	49.0	76.9	48.3	33.0	64.8
1976	49.6	42.2	64.9	70.8	85.1	176.0	71.1	52.6	85.2	54.1	36.5	66.8
1977	56.9	45.8	69.4	72.4	93.0	184.5	74.2	57.0	91.2	58.8	42.9	73.2
1978	61.4	46.8	71.8	75.0	92.7	188.6	77.6	60.3	92.1	61.7	44.4	75.7
1979	60.9	46.9	72.2	74.6	92.6	177.1	78.7	62.1	98.4	63.1	43.8	77.3
1980	58.8	44.4	70.0	75.8	88.8	180.5	78.6	62.6	87.2	59.6	39.0	79.9
1981	58.3	46.1	70.6	76.6	86.9	180.4	79.6	64.2	83.2	60.5	41.3	81.8
1982	54.9	46.6	69.6	78.8	80.6	179.3	78.4	69.0	79.5	56.7	40.5	82.8
1983	60.2	46.5	72.8	79.0	90.9	184.2	83.4	74.2	80.8	60.6	44.1	85.0
1984	67.6	50.4	76.2	80.1	93.2	184.0	87.6	80.8	82.6	64.1	50.9	88.9
1985	68.0	51.1	76.6	82.7	90.0	175.9	85.9	84.0	81.3	63.6	52.9	92.4
1986	71.1	52.3	78.9	83.7	93.8	175.1	89.4	88.2	80.9	66.5	55.1	94.2
1987	76.1	56.4	83.1	85.4	103.4	176.8	92.4	94.8	84.8	71.8	61.0	99.7
1988	75.2	61.8	85.9	87.8	102.6	173.5	96.1	97.8	87.4	75.8	63.7	99.3
1989	74.8	62.6	86.4	87.3	104.4	165.9	97.1	98.2	86.5	77.3	65.9	97.8
1990	73.2	65.7	87.8	89.7	100.2	162.0	97.0	101.9	86.6	79.1	67.7	96.7
1991	67.6	67.0	87.4	90.4	98.8	160.9	97.3	98.7	85.3	78.8	67.0	92.8
1992	73.0	69.9	89.7	91.6	104.2	165.2	99.6	104.1	84.9	80.0	72.1	91.0
1993	76.1	73.9	91.0	91.3	108.2	168.6	100.8	104.4	85.5	81.0	77.2	91.8
1994	78.7	74.4	94.1	94.4	114.2	170.5	105.1	105.5	87.9	83.0	83.6	90.9
1995	80.0	77.2	95.8	97.1	113.1	169.3	106.7	107.1	89.5	84.4	85.7	90.9
1996	80.6	81.0	96.1	96.3	110.5	165.3	103.3	107.9	91.6	86.1	88.6	90.2
1997	89.3	83.2	99.6	98.4	116.6	164.6	105.5	110.0	94.6	91.2	94.0	97.7
1998	95.7	88.1	101.1	101.3	115.7	155.2	106.4	111.2	92.8	92.7	97.4	104.1
1999	98.9	89.9	101.8	99.5	115.5	148.6	107.2	112.3	96.7	94.6	102.5	107.4
2000	100.4	94.9	102.4	100.9	113.3	141.7	105.0	113.0	96.6	96.0	103.6	109.5
2001	94.0	93.7	99.0	100.7	101.6	120.4	99.0	106.0	96.0	94.3	97.6	103.1
2002	100.0	100.0	100.0	100.0	100.0	100.0	100.0	100.0	100.0	100.0	100.0	100.0
2003	98.3	102.0	98.9	100.5	95.9	92.1	95.9	95.8	98.3	99.7	99.4	97.0
2004	101.4	105.5	101.0	102.3	93.1	88.4	98.0	96.0	103.7	102.8	102.5	98.8
2005	100.7	110.3	101.8	104.4	91.4	85.9	98.1	97.4	103.8	102.5	104.7	101.8
2003												
January	98.4	102.0	99.1	98.5	97.1	97.1	99.4	97.0	99.2	100.3	99.7	98.6
February	98.0	101.4	99.4	100.0	98.1	95.3	96.9	96.9	98.3	100.6	99.8	98.7
March	97.3	101.6	99.8	101.2	98.3	95.2	98.3	97.4	99.6	100.0	99.9	99.5
April	95.3	100.7	99.1	101.2	97.9	94.2	96.0	95.6	96.6	100.0	98.4	96.7
May	97.1	100.9	98.4	100.3	95.7	93.8	95.9	95.8	98.5	98.2	99.2	96.6
June	98.1	102.5	98.3	100.4	95.2	92.2	95.6	95.6	95.6	98.9	98.5	98.4
July	99.1	102.3	98.4	100.6	93.9	91.5	95.1	95.4	96.1	99.2	98.5	96.8
August	98.4	101.4	98.2	100.3	93.9	88.3	94.5	94.8	97.6	99.2	98.9	95.8
September	98.8	101.8	98.6	100.8	93.6	88.6	94.7	95.1	98.9	99.6	99.3	94.9
October	99.4	102.1	98.6	100.5	94.8	89.5	93.9	95.6	99.4	99.4	99.7	95.7
November	100.4	104.0	99.3	101.1	96.4	89.9	94.8	95.4	99.6	100.3	100.8	96.6
December	99.7	103.0	99.2	100.9	95.3	89.2	95.7	94.8	100.6	100.6	99.7	96.1
2004												
January	100.1	103.9	99.3	100.8	97.4	89.4	95.5	95.2	100.3	100.5	100.1	95.5
February	99.5	104.0	99.8	102.2	94.1	89.8	95.9	95.4	100.3	100.8	100.9	97.6
March	100.2	103.7	99.9	101.7	91.6	90.4	95.7	94.9	102.5	101.5	101.0	97.5
April	101.7	104.9	100.8	102.6	92.5	90.9	97.5	95.3	101.7	102.5	102.3	98.6
May	103.0	105.9	101.8	104.2	93.2	90.0	98.4	95.9	102.8	102.9	102.5	99.2
June	101.9	105.1	100.8	101.8	92.3	89.0	98.5	96.2	103.8	102.3	103.5	98.2
July	101.6	105.9	101.3	101.8	94.5	86.7	99.5	96.7	105.4	103.1	103.5	99.0
August	102.0	106.0	101.6	102.6	93.3	85.4	98.6	96.6	105.8	103.8	103.0	101.1
September	101.1	105.2	101.1	102.2	92.4	86.9	98.7	95.6	103.1	103.4	102.3	99.3
October	101.5	106.6	101.8	102.4	93.5	87.2	99.2	96.2	104.7	104.4	103.6	99.0
November	102.0	107.0	101.8	102.6	91.4	88.2	99.1	96.8	106.4	104.1	102.8	99.1
December	102.7	107.5	101.9	102.6	90.5	87.4	99.0	97.2	107.2	104.5	103.3	101.1
2005												
January	102.5	108.5	102.1	103.4	92.6	86.4	99.9	97.9	105.3	103.8	104.0	102.5
February	102.2	108.9	102.2	103.0	91.6	86.1	99.6	97.0	107.6	104.6	103.7	101.5
March	101.6	108.8	101.9	103.3	91.5	85.5	99.8	96.4	105.7	103.8	103.5	102.4
April	100.0	108.9	101.9	103.2	89.6	85.8	98.2	96.5	106.9	104.1	103.8	102.5
May	100.3	109.0	101.9	104.3	89.8	83.9	96.8	97.0	105.5	103.9	103.1	103.2
June	99.9	109.7	102.1	104.5	90.8	83.6	97.8	96.5	107.9	103.9	102.9	102.0
July	99.8	109.7	102.1	104.8	91.9	85.5	96.6	97.9	105.6	103.7	103.2	101.0
August	100.2	111.6	101.5	103.9	91.9	85.9	96.2	97.2	104.2	102.7	104.1	100.9
September	101.7	111.9	100.1	104.6	92.6	86.7	96.5	97.9	98.5	97.5	106.5	100.4
October	100.5	112.6	100.7	105.5	93.2	86.5	98.8	98.2	95.4	98.8	106.2	101.4
November	100.2	112.2	102.0	105.8	91.6	87.5	97.2	98.3	101.9	101.3	107.4	101.1
December	99.4	111.7	102.7	106.9	89.7	87.7	99.3	98.4	101.7	101.9	108.4	102.3

. . . = Not available.

Table 2-2. Industrial Production Indexes by NAICS Industry Groups—Continued

(Seasonally adjusted, 2002 = 100.)

Year and month	Mining	Utilities			Selected high-tech industries	Excluding selected high-tech industries	Stage-of-process groups		
		Total	Electric	Natural gas			Crude	Primary and semi-finished	Finished
1967	. . .	. . .	. . .	. . .	0.3	53.9	71.8	. . .	. . .
1968	. . .	. . .	. . .	. . .	0.3	56.8	77.6	. . .	. . .
1969	. . .	. . .	. . .	. . .	0.3	59.3	83.0	. . .	. . .
1970	. . .	. . .	. . .	. . .	0.3	57.2	85.0	. . .	. . .
1971	. . .	. . .	. . .	. . .	0.3	58.3	86.2	. . .	. . .
1972	106.8	50.3	40.9	110.3	0.4	63.6	93.4	44.8	39.1
1973	107.4	53.2	44.6	105.8	0.4	68.6	97.2	48.9	42.2
1974	105.8	53.0	44.8	102.3	0.5	67.9	98.7	48.3	42.4
1975	103.3	54.0	46.8	95.6	0.5	61.9	91.4	42.8	39.9
1976	104.0	56.4	49.7	94.6	0.6	66.5	95.5	46.7	42.7
1977	106.4	58.7	52.9	91.4	0.8	71.0	100.2	50.4	46.4
1978	109.8	60.2	54.6	92.2	1.0	74.4	102.8	52.8	49.9
1979	113.1	61.6	55.8	94.6	1.3	76.0	105.5	54.0	52.1
1980	115.1	62.0	56.7	92.6	1.5	73.3	106.3	50.5	52.7
1981	118.1	62.9	58.2	90.5	1.8	73.7	108.9	50.5	54.0
1982	112.3	60.9	56.8	85.0	2.1	69.3	102.8	46.4	53.5
1983	106.4	61.4	58.5	79.6	2.5	70.6	99.8	48.7	55.0
1984	113.3	65.0	61.8	84.5	3.3	76.1	106.7	53.5	60.0
1985	111.1	66.4	64.1	81.0	3.5	76.9	104.5	54.0	61.9
1986	103.0	67.0	65.4	77.0	3.6	77.6	99.2	55.0	63.5
1987	103.9	70.1	68.5	80.6	4.3	80.9	102.3	58.2	66.4
1988	106.5	74.1	72.4	85.5	5.0	84.4	105.8	61.3	69.9
1989	105.3	76.4	74.6	88.6	5.3	84.9	105.9	61.7	70.8
1990	106.9	77.9	76.7	85.6	6.0	85.2	107.5	61.8	72.0
1991	104.5	79.8	78.5	87.9	6.4	83.5	104.7	60.9	71.1
1992	102.2	79.7	78.1	90.4	7.7	85.1	103.8	63.4	72.8
1993	102.2	82.6	80.9	93.8	9.1	87.2	102.5	66.4	74.9
1994	104.6	84.2	82.7	94.4	11.8	90.7	104.7	71.0	78.1
1995	104.4	87.2	85.7	96.9	16.6	92.9	105.2	75.2	81.7
1996	106.2	89.7	87.9	101.5	23.3	94.5	104.9	79.2	84.9
1997	108.0	89.7	88.2	99.5	34.6	98.5	107.7	85.6	91.4
1998	106.4	92.0	91.8	93.1	48.4	101.5	105.8	91.3	97.5
1999	101.2	94.7	94.5	95.7	70.5	102.8	104.2	97.7	100.2
2000	103.5	97.4	97.2	98.6	100.7	103.9	104.2	103.2	103.8
2001	104.5	97.0	96.9	97.2	102.6	99.7	101.4	98.6	101.1
2002	100.0	100.0	100.0	100.0	100.0	100.0	100.0	100.0	100.0
2003	99.8	102.0	102.1	101.2	117.6	99.7	98.7	100.5	101.2
2004	99.5	103.1	104.1	98.2	141.2	102.9	99.7	105.1	105.6
2005	97.4	105.7	107.2	98.3	172.0	105.2	97.1	108.8	110.5
2003									
January	99.7	102.8	102.8	102.7	107.4	100.1	99.3	100.9	100.4
February	100.1	104.5	103.5	109.7	110.9	99.9	99.6	100.8	100.4
March	100.0	101.2	101.1	101.8	112.6	99.7	99.7	100.2	100.8
April	99.8	100.7	100.8	100.1	112.9	98.8	99.0	99.1	100.3
May	99.2	101.2	101.2	101.4	114.1	98.7	98.1	99.6	99.8
June	99.6	99.1	98.9	99.8	115.7	98.9	98.4	99.3	100.7
July	99.1	102.0	102.3	100.1	118.3	99.3	97.9	99.9	101.3
August	99.6	103.2	103.9	99.4	120.7	99.2	98.1	100.2	101.1
September	100.7	101.6	101.9	99.7	122.1	99.9	98.9	100.5	102.2
October	100.4	101.7	102.1	100.1	124.3	99.9	98.7	101.2	101.7
November	99.6	101.9	102.5	98.8	125.3	100.8	98.2	102.1	102.9
December	99.4	103.5	103.9	101.4	127.0	100.9	98.0	102.7	102.8
2004									
January	101.0	104.2	104.4	103.4	130.5	101.2	99.2	102.9	103.3
February	99.8	105.4	105.0	107.7	133.5	101.9	98.7	104.0	104.2
March	100.0	101.0	102.5	93.3	135.0	101.9	99.3	103.3	104.2
April	99.7	102.0	103.1	96.2	135.5	102.4	99.6	104.0	105.1
May	99.8	104.4	105.9	96.3	138.3	103.3	100.0	105.4	105.8
June	99.4	103.9	105.4	96.0	140.4	102.6	99.9	105.2	104.5
July	100.3	102.2	103.0	97.8	142.4	103.1	100.7	105.5	105.5
August	99.3	100.5	100.8	98.5	145.7	103.3	100.0	105.7	106.2
September	97.2	103.1	104.1	97.9	147.6	103.0	98.6	105.8	105.9
October	97.9	102.8	104.4	94.6	147.0	103.8	99.2	106.2	107.2
November	99.9	103.0	104.1	97.1	147.8	104.0	100.8	106.2	107.3
December	100.4	105.2	106.2	99.8	151.0	104.6	101.1	107.2	107.7
2005									
January	99.9	102.9	104.0	97.3	157.8	104.5	100.6	107.4	108.1
February	100.9	101.7	102.9	95.6	160.4	104.9	101.2	107.1	109.3
March	100.4	104.8	105.5	101.1	160.4	104.8	100.8	107.4	109.0
April	100.5	103.1	104.1	98.3	163.1	104.6	100.3	107.3	108.9
May	99.8	102.9	103.2	101.1	166.2	104.7	99.6	107.3	109.8
June	100.8	108.3	109.7	101.2	167.9	105.5	100.4	108.5	110.3
July	99.8	108.1	109.6	100.9	171.6	105.4	99.4	108.6	110.5
August	99.2	108.4	110.1	100.4	176.7	105.5	98.5	109.1	111.0
September	90.3	108.1	110.5	96.5	179.6	104.0	88.7	109.4	110.4
October	89.1	105.9	109.5	89.6	181.3	105.2	88.6	110.1	112.8
November	93.1	104.8	107.3	93.0	188.0	106.0	92.7	110.8	113.0
December	95.5	109.2	110.0	104.3	191.1	107.0	95.1	112.0	113.4

. . . = Not available.

Table 2-3. Capacity Utilization by NAICS Industry Groups

(Output as a percentage of capacity, seasonally adjusted.)

Year and month	Total industry	Total manufacturing (SIC)	Manufacturing (NAICS)											
			Total	Durable goods manufacturing									
				Total	Wood products	Nonmetallic mineral products	Primary metals	Fabricated metal products	Machinery	Computer and electronic products	Electrical equipment, appliances, and components	Motor vehicles and parts	Aircraft and miscellaneous transportation equipment
1967	87.0	87.2	. . .	87.5	. . .	75.7	85.0	86.4	90.4	. . .	. . .	78.9	94.1
1968	87.3	87.1	. . .	87.3	. . .	78.4	84.8	87.3	85.1	. . .	. . .	90.0	89.2
1969	87.4	86.6	. . .	86.9	. . .	79.7	88.2	86.2	86.8	. . .	. . .	86.5	83.6
1970	81.2	79.4	. . .	77.5	. . .	73.9	79.3	78.5	79.9	. . .	. . .	66.1	71.4
1971	79.6	77.9	. . .	75.1	. . .	75.6	72.8	78.5	74.0	. . .	. . .	78.6	62.2
1972	84.6	83.3	83.2	81.8	92.2	79.7	82.7	85.1	83.1	81.0	89.8	84.1	64.0
1973	88.4	87.6	87.7	88.5	87.7	84.4	94.6	91.0	92.3	85.1	97.7	91.7	72.9
1974	85.2	84.4	84.5	84.7	77.9	82.3	96.5	85.9	91.9	83.1	91.5	76.6	74.2
1975	75.6	73.5	73.4	71.6	71.1	73.3	75.0	71.9	77.7	68.4	70.6	65.6	70.4
1976	79.6	78.1	78.1	76.2	80.4	77.8	78.5	75.4	79.7	71.2	78.9	81.9	65.5
1977	83.1	82.2	82.2	80.9	86.4	82.4	79.1	79.6	84.9	77.4	85.6	90.0	65.5
1978	84.8	84.3	84.3	83.9	85.3	85.9	84.2	80.6	88.7	81.6	87.9	90.7	71.5
1979	85.0	84.2	84.1	84.5	80.6	83.9	86.0	81.6	90.9	86.0	89.3	81.1	81.3
1980	80.7	78.7	78.4	77.6	73.1	74.5	76.1	75.5	84.4	86.0	82.3	59.1	84.6
1981	79.7	77.1	76.7	75.3	70.9	71.1	77.2	73.5	81.4	83.9	79.3	57.3	77.6
1982	73.7	71.0	70.5	66.6	63.3	63.4	55.3	65.4	67.2	80.7	69.8	51.4	70.0
1983	74.7	73.4	72.9	68.4	74.0	69.3	59.0	66.4	61.1	80.1	72.7	67.4	66.4
1984	80.4	79.4	79.0	76.7	78.9	75.3	69.2	73.3	71.8	87.1	82.1	81.3	69.2
1985	79.4	78.3	77.8	75.8	78.2	75.6	67.1	74.0	71.5	81.0	78.8	83.1	71.8
1986	78.6	78.3	77.9	75.3	83.1	78.2	69.5	73.7	70.8	77.5	79.9	78.2	73.4
1987	81.2	81.0	80.5	77.6	87.8	81.5	79.5	75.3	72.3	79.5	82.0	77.2	74.9
1988	84.2	84.0	83.8	82.0	86.4	83.3	90.2	79.9	80.4	80.8	86.8	82.3	79.4
1989	83.6	83.1	83.0	81.4	84.1	82.2	86.5	79.7	83.6	78.3	85.9	79.2	84.9
1990	82.4	81.6	81.4	79.1	82.1	80.0	84.2	77.6	80.9	78.4	83.6	70.6	85.7
1991	79.6	78.3	78.2	75.0	76.8	73.6	78.9	74.0	76.0	76.8	78.9	63.6	83.5
1992	80.4	79.6	79.5	77.1	81.1	77.2	81.6	76.3	75.4	78.7	82.1	72.4	77.4
1993	81.4	80.4	80.3	78.8	81.5	78.7	86.2	77.2	79.2	78.0	86.6	78.6	73.0
1994	83.6	82.8	82.8	82.1	84.2	82.3	91.7	81.6	84.3	80.3	91.9	87.2	66.7
1995	83.9	83.0	83.0	82.4	83.1	83.3	89.4	83.7	85.8	82.9	91.5	83.4	64.3
1996	83.0	81.8	81.8	81.4	82.8	86.9	88.0	83.3	83.7	80.2	90.4	80.8	67.1
1997	83.9	83.0	82.8	82.5	82.3	86.5	87.6	82.2	82.7	82.8	88.7	82.5	74.1
1998	82.7	81.7	81.4	80.9	83.5	86.6	85.5	80.2	80.3	77.8	86.5	79.5	83.6
1999	81.9	80.8	80.5	80.5	83.3	83.6	83.4	77.9	76.8	80.3	84.5	85.5	77.9
2000	81.8	80.3	79.9	80.3	79.2	81.3	80.2	78.8	78.9	84.7	86.9	83.4	66.5
2001	76.3	74.1	73.6	71.7	72.6	77.2	73.9	72.4	69.3	69.2	77.1	74.0	69.2
2002	75.1	73.3	72.9	70.0	75.0	77.7	77.3	70.3	66.8	60.5	73.4	79.6	64.4
2003	75.7	73.7	73.3	70.7	75.3	78.2	77.0	69.4	67.2	64.7	74.6	79.5	61.8
2004	78.6	77.1	76.8	75.0	80.5	81.7	83.4	72.8	76.3	71.2	79.1	79.8	63.8
2005	80.0	78.9	78.5	77.4	82.6	81.6	81.3	74.8	80.5	76.3	84.1	80.1	68.2
2003													
January	75.5	73.5	73.1	70.6	74.2	77.5	78.8	70.2	66.2	62.5	73.4	82.3	62.2
February	75.6	73.4	72.9	70.1	74.0	76.6	77.3	69.5	66.5	63.2	74.2	79.4	61.8
March	75.4	73.5	73.0	69.9	73.1	77.7	73.7	69.3	66.8	63.5	73.9	78.7	61.8
April	74.9	72.9	72.4	69.3	73.3	76.6	74.8	68.6	65.9	63.0	73.4	77.7	61.6
May	74.9	72.8	72.4	69.5	73.6	78.5	74.5	69.0	66.1	63.4	74.4	76.9	61.4
June	75.1	73.2	72.7	70.1	74.1	78.5	77.6	69.0	66.1	63.8	75.1	78.0	61.3
July	75.4	73.4	73.0	70.4	75.5	78.3	75.3	69.0	66.0	64.5	73.5	80.1	61.6
August	75.5	73.4	72.9	70.4	75.1	78.9	75.6	68.7	67.0	65.5	75.1	77.7	61.7
September	76.0	74.0	73.7	71.4	75.7	78.2	74.7	69.2	67.7	66.0	74.4	82.7	61.6
October	76.1	74.1	73.7	71.5	77.0	79.2	78.2	69.6	67.2	66.7	75.5	79.9	61.8
November	76.8	75.0	74.6	72.5	79.6	79.8	80.5	70.1	70.1	67.0	76.0	80.4	62.6
December	76.9	75.1	74.7	72.7	78.8	79.3	83.2	70.3	70.8	67.2	75.8	80.5	62.5
2004													
January	77.2	75.3	74.9	73.0	79.1	80.1	78.8	70.9	71.4	68.0	76.6	81.3	62.2
February	77.8	76.0	75.6	73.8	79.6	79.6	81.1	71.3	73.7	69.1	76.7	81.3	63.1
March	77.6	76.1	75.7	73.9	79.3	81.5	81.6	71.1	74.3	69.6	76.5	80.6	62.8
April	78.1	76.7	76.3	74.4	80.7	81.6	81.8	72.1	75.2	69.5	78.0	80.7	63.2
May	78.8	77.3	76.9	74.9	81.6	81.7	83.2	72.9	76.3	70.7	78.6	79.4	63.2
June	78.4	76.9	76.5	74.7	80.1	81.1	83.4	73.0	76.6	71.3	79.1	77.5	63.1
July	78.8	77.4	77.1	75.4	81.5	82.2	85.9	73.4	78.4	72.0	79.7	77.1	64.2
August	79.0	77.9	77.5	75.9	81.0	82.6	84.6	73.6	77.3	72.9	80.2	79.9	64.1
September	78.7	77.5	77.2	75.6	79.6	82.8	85.1	73.3	78.0	73.3	80.4	78.4	63.8
October	79.2	78.1	77.8	76.3	81.3	82.6	85.1	74.0	78.4	72.8	80.8	80.7	64.5
November	79.3	78.0	77.7	76.1	80.8	81.7	85.6	73.8	78.3	72.5	81.2	80.2	65.3
December	79.7	78.3	77.9	76.4	80.9	82.9	84.4	73.9	78.3	73.3	81.3	80.6	65.7
2005													
January	79.8	78.6	78.2	76.8	83.5	81.7	83.9	74.4	79.0	75.0	81.9	79.4	65.6
February	80.0	78.9	78.5	77.3	81.1	81.7	82.4	74.2	79.0	75.5	81.6	82.8	66.8
March	79.9	78.5	78.1	76.7	80.5	80.5	82.7	73.9	79.2	75.0	81.5	79.9	67.5
April	79.7	78.4	78.0	76.5	80.5	80.9	80.4	74.3	79.2	75.2	81.6	78.4	68.6
May	79.8	78.6	78.1	76.7	81.3	80.9	79.9	74.4	79.4	75.7	82.3	78.7	69.1
June	80.3	78.7	78.2	76.8	80.2	81.2	77.1	74.2	79.7	75.5	82.9	80.4	68.8
July	80.2	78.6	78.2	76.8	80.6	80.6	76.9	74.5	80.6	76.0	83.9	78.5	69.2
August	80.3	78.8	78.4	77.4	79.9	80.5	79.2	74.7	79.1	76.7	84.8	81.1	69.5
September	79.1	78.2	77.8	77.2	82.3	81.4	82.1	74.8	80.5	76.8	86.1	83.1	58.5
October	79.9	79.4	79.1	79.1	86.6	82.5	82.9	76.3	82.5	77.1	87.8	82.8	69.7
November	80.5	79.9	79.6	79.2	87.6	84.5	83.6	76.2	83.3	78.8	87.6	78.7	72.1
December	81.1	80.1	79.7	79.0	87.1	82.8	84.0	75.8	84.5	78.6	87.7	77.4	73.3

. . . = Not available.

Table 2-3. Capacity Utilization by NAICS Industry Groups—Continued

(Output as a percentage of capacity, seasonally adjusted.)

| Year and month | Durable goods manufacturing—Continued | | Manufacturing (NAICS)—Continued | | | | | | | | | Other manufacturing (non-NAICS) |
| | | | Nondurable goods manufacturing | | | | | | | | | |
	Furniture and related products	Miscellaneous manufacturing	Total	Food, beverage, and tobacco products	Textile and product mills	Apparel and leather	Paper	Printing and support	Petroleum and coal products	Chemical	Plastics and rubber products	
1967	91.9	. . .	86.3	85.0	. . .	. . .	89.7	. . .	94.9	78.9	88.3	. . .
1968	91.5	. . .	86.5	84.8	. . .	. . .	89.3	. . .	95.8	80.1	91.2	. . .
1969	93.0	. . .	86.2	85.1	. . .	. . .	91.0	. . .	96.4	79.1	90.4	. . .
1970	84.5	. . .	82.2	84.1	. . .	. . .	86.1	. . .	96.8	76.1	79.5	. . .
1971	85.5	. . .	81.9	84.0	. . .	. . .	86.8	. . .	95.7	75.4	80.1	. . .
1972	94.2	80.4	85.3	85.1	89.3	81.8	91.4	92.4	93.6	80.2	88.8	85.7
1973	95.4	79.3	86.6	84.8	86.2	82.0	94.9	94.0	90.4	83.9	92.5	84.7
1974	82.3	74.4	84.2	83.8	76.0	76.2	95.1	88.1	92.8	84.3	84.2	82.7
1975	68.0	67.9	76.0	80.1	72.1	74.5	80.8	79.6	83.6	71.7	70.0	77.2
1976	75.6	72.4	80.9	83.3	80.6	77.7	87.6	82.2	86.0	77.5	77.2	77.4
1977	83.9	77.5	84.1	82.8	88.1	81.8	90.1	86.0	87.7	80.8	88.5	83.4
1978	85.1	79.1	84.9	83.5	87.8	84.1	92.2	87.4	86.4	81.7	88.4	85.1
1979	79.5	78.9	83.6	81.3	87.5	79.0	91.0	86.0	89.8	81.6	83.4	85.3
1980	74.0	74.4	79.4	81.2	83.4	80.5	88.2	83.8	76.7	75.6	73.1	87.3
1981	71.7	75.9	78.8	80.9	80.7	79.9	86.8	81.2	73.5	75.4	76.3	87.7
1982	66.9	73.6	76.7	81.9	74.6	79.7	84.0	82.3	73.6	69.0	72.9	86.8
1983	73.1	70.5	79.8	81.3	83.9	83.6	88.2	84.7	77.8	73.0	79.9	87.4
1984	80.1	75.6	82.4	81.6	85.5	83.8	90.7	87.7	81.6	76.1	90.0	89.6
1985	77.9	74.1	80.8	82.9	81.4	80.0	87.2	86.1	81.9	73.6	86.1	90.5
1986	79.8	73.5	81.8	82.8	83.6	81.2	89.2	86.4	81.6	75.9	84.6	88.8
1987	83.3	76.9	84.8	83.6	91.1	82.8	90.4	89.6	84.4	81.1	89.1	90.7
1988	80.4	81.6	86.3	85.0	88.7	82.8	92.1	90.2	87.1	84.3	88.8	88.5
1989	78.5	79.6	85.2	83.5	88.3	80.9	91.2	88.4	86.8	83.8	86.4	85.4
1990	75.5	79.9	84.4	84.3	83.3	79.5	89.2	89.1	86.7	83.3	82.9	83.9
1991	70.5	78.3	82.3	83.2	81.5	81.2	87.2	84.2	84.4	81.0	77.9	81.6
1992	77.3	77.2	82.5	82.2	85.5	83.6	87.5	86.0	85.0	79.8	81.2	80.8
1993	80.2	78.3	82.2	80.4	87.7	84.9	87.0	85.0	86.8	78.9	85.6	82.5
1994	81.8	78.6	83.8	82.2	89.7	86.1	88.8	85.3	88.7	79.5	90.4	82.2
1995	81.5	80.4	83.9	83.1	86.4	85.6	88.8	84.9	89.3	79.7	88.8	82.1
1996	79.9	81.4	82.4	81.3	83.4	83.4	84.3	84.0	90.6	79.2	87.6	80.9
1997	83.6	79.4	83.3	81.8	85.7	82.2	85.1	82.8	92.2	81.2	88.2	85.1
1998	83.7	79.8	82.1	82.7	83.0	77.8	85.8	80.7	86.9	79.1	86.7	86.8
1999	81.4	76.4	80.5	79.2	81.7	76.7	86.5	79.4	88.2	77.5	86.2	86.9
2000	78.8	76.4	79.4	78.8	79.8	75.9	84.8	79.6	87.5	76.3	82.5	87.5
2001	71.5	72.3	76.2	77.9	72.8	68.4	80.9	75.9	86.4	72.6	76.5	82.7
2002	73.9	73.9	76.9	77.5	74.0	63.5	83.5	73.2	87.0	75.3	78.6	81.9
2003	72.4	74.2	76.7	78.0	73.6	65.7	81.8	71.4	86.6	74.3	79.7	82.1
2004	74.9	76.0	79.1	79.2	74.8	70.6	84.4	73.5	91.5	76.4	84.1	84.4
2005	73.9	77.9	80.0	80.7	76.3	76.3	84.6	76.2	91.1	75.7	86.6	86.4
2003												
January	72.2	74.5	76.4	76.5	73.2	65.9	83.9	71.7	86.6	75.0	78.9	82.2
February	71.9	73.9	76.7	77.7	74.2	65.3	82.0	71.7	86.0	75.1	79.1	82.5
March	71.5	74.0	77.2	78.6	74.5	65.8	83.3	72.2	87.3	74.7	79.4	83.5
April	70.0	73.3	76.7	78.6	74.5	65.7	81.5	71.0	84.9	74.6	78.4	81.4
May	71.4	73.5	76.2	77.9	73.1	66.1	81.6	71.2	86.7	73.2	79.3	81.6
June	72.2	74.5	76.2	78.0	73.0	65.6	81.5	71.2	84.3	73.7	78.9	83.3
July	73.0	74.4	76.4	78.1	72.2	65.7	81.2	71.2	84.9	73.9	79.2	82.1
August	72.5	73.7	76.3	77.9	72.4	63.9	80.8	70.8	86.3	73.8	79.7	81.5
September	72.9	73.9	76.7	78.2	72.5	64.8	81.1	71.2	87.5	74.1	80.2	80.8
October	73.4	74.1	76.7	78.0	73.7	66.0	80.5	71.7	88.0	73.9	80.8	81.7
November	74.2	75.5	77.4	78.5	75.3	67.0	81.4	71.7	88.2	74.6	81.8	82.5
December	73.7	74.7	77.4	78.2	74.7	67.1	82.2	71.4	89.1	74.8	81.1	82.2
2004												
January	74.0	75.3	77.5	78.1	76.6	67.8	82.2	71.9	88.8	74.7	81.7	81.7
February	73.6	75.3	78.0	79.2	74.4	68.8	82.5	72.2	88.8	74.9	82.4	83.6
March	74.1	75.1	78.1	78.8	72.7	69.9	82.4	72.1	90.6	75.5	82.6	83.5
April	75.2	75.9	78.8	79.5	73.7	70.9	84.0	72.5	89.8	76.2	83.8	84.4
May	76.1	76.5	79.7	80.8	74.6	70.9	84.8	73.2	90.8	76.5	85.0	84.9
June	75.3	75.9	78.9	78.8	74.1	70.7	84.9	73.6	91.6	76.0	84.9	84.0
July	75.0	76.3	79.4	78.9	76.2	69.6	85.8	74.2	93.0	76.5	85.0	84.6
August	75.2	76.3	79.6	79.5	75.5	69.2	85.0	74.3	93.3	77.1	84.6	86.3
September	74.5	75.6	79.2	79.2	75.0	71.0	85.1	73.7	90.9	76.7	84.1	84.7
October	74.8	76.5	79.8	79.3	76.2	72.0	85.6	74.3	92.2	77.5	85.2	84.3
November	75.1	76.7	79.8	79.4	74.7	73.4	85.5	75.0	93.6	77.2	84.6	84.4
December	75.5	76.9	80.0	79.4	74.2	73.5	85.3	75.4	94.3	77.4	85.1	86.0
2005												
January	75.4	77.5	80.2	80.0	76.2	73.2	86.1	76.1	92.6	76.9	85.7	87.2
February	75.1	77.6	80.2	79.7	75.5	73.6	85.9	75.5	94.6	77.4	85.4	86.2
March	74.7	77.4	80.0	79.9	75.7	73.7	86.1	75.2	92.9	76.8	85.4	87.0
April	73.5	77.3	80.0	79.8	74.3	74.6	84.7	75.3	93.9	77.0	85.7	87.0
May	73.6	77.2	80.0	80.7	74.7	73.5	83.5	75.8	92.7	76.8	85.1	87.6
June	73.4	77.5	80.2	80.8	75.7	73.9	84.4	75.5	94.7	76.7	85.0	86.6
July	73.3	77.4	80.2	81.0	76.8	76.2	83.3	76.6	92.6	76.5	85.4	85.7
August	73.5	78.5	79.7	80.3	76.9	77.2	83.1	76.1	91.4	75.7	86.2	85.6
September	74.6	78.5	78.7	80.8	77.7	78.5	83.3	76.8	86.3	71.9	88.2	85.1
October	73.7	78.9	79.2	81.5	78.4	78.9	85.3	77.1	83.6	72.7	88.0	85.9
November	73.5	78.4	80.2	81.7	77.3	80.5	84.0	77.3	89.3	74.6	89.1	85.7
December	72.9	77.9	80.8	82.5	75.9	81.4	85.8	77.4	89.1	74.9	90.0	86.7

. . . = Not available.

Table 2-3. Capacity Utilization by NAICS Industry Groups—Continued

(Output as a percentage of capacity, seasonally adjusted.)

Year and month	Mining	Utilities	Selected high-technology industries				Measures excluding selected high-technology industries		Stage-of-process groups		
			Total	Computers and office equipment	Communications equipment	Semiconductors and related electronic components	Total industry	Manufacturing	Crude	Primary and semi-finished	Finished
1967	81.2	94.5	89.4	. . .	. . .	. . .	86.9	86.8	81.1	85.0	88.2
1968	83.6	95.1	87.6	. . .	. . .	. . .	87.2	87.0	83.4	86.8	87.0
1969	86.8	96.8	89.5	. . .	. . .	. . .	87.1	86.4	85.7	88.1	85.4
1970	89.3	96.3	83.1	. . .	. . .	. . .	80.9	79.2	85.2	81.5	77.9
1971	88.0	94.7	73.9	. . .	. . .	. . .	79.9	78.2	84.4	81.6	75.3
1972	90.9	95.2	79.0	84.5	72.5	85.1	84.8	83.5	88.6	88.1	79.4
1973	92.0	94.3	81.7	81.9	75.3	91.6	88.6	87.9	90.6	92.2	83.0
1974	91.1	87.4	82.0	88.3	73.5	87.7	85.3	84.5	91.3	87.4	80.2
1975	89.2	84.5	64.7	69.1	62.0	63.7	76.0	73.9	83.9	75.1	73.5
1976	89.7	85.2	67.8	73.6	61.8	70.0	80.0	78.6	87.1	80.0	76.4
1977	89.7	85.3	75.4	74.3	72.9	79.8	83.4	82.6	89.0	84.3	79.5
1978	89.8	84.2	80.9	82.3	77.0	83.6	85.0	84.5	88.3	85.9	82.1
1979	91.1	85.5	86.0	81.5	87.7	90.3	84.9	84.1	89.3	85.8	82.0
1980	91.5	85.1	86.0	84.4	89.9	84.2	80.5	78.3	89.1	78.6	79.6
1981	91.4	84.3	85.1	86.3	87.3	81.7	79.5	76.6	89.5	77.1	78.0
1982	83.7	80.4	78.3	70.5	87.2	81.3	73.5	70.6	82.0	70.4	73.6
1983	78.5	79.7	78.4	74.7	80.4	80.9	74.5	73.0	78.7	74.2	73.4
1984	84.7	82.9	87.6	86.0	86.0	90.4	80.0	78.8	84.9	81.1	77.6
1985	83.3	83.1	78.8	78.2	82.7	76.3	79.4	78.3	83.1	79.9	77.1
1986	76.5	82.3	73.4	73.9	76.8	70.5	78.9	78.7	78.4	79.9	77.1
1987	79.6	83.9	77.1	74.8	77.5	79.3	81.4	81.3	82.7	83.0	78.5
1988	83.6	86.1	79.3	77.2	79.7	81.1	84.5	84.4	86.5	86.0	81.3
1989	84.9	86.6	77.6	74.7	78.1	79.7	84.0	83.6	87.2	84.9	81.0
1990	86.9	86.0	77.1	70.9	80.6	80.8	82.7	81.9	88.2	82.6	80.3
1991	84.9	86.8	75.9	71.9	74.4	79.8	79.8	78.5	85.3	79.7	77.9
1992	84.4	85.2	80.1	80.4	79.3	79.9	80.4	79.5	85.2	81.3	78.1
1993	85.8	87.7	80.3	80.1	78.5	81.2	81.5	80.4	85.3	83.6	78.0
1994	87.6	88.8	83.4	81.4	82.8	84.7	83.6	82.8	87.4	86.7	79.1
1995	87.9	89.9	85.0	81.3	79.7	89.2	83.8	82.8	88.5	86.7	79.4
1996	90.3	90.4	81.3	80.6	76.7	84.1	83.2	81.8	88.2	85.6	78.7
1997	91.3	89.1	85.0	86.0	79.5	87.9	83.8	82.7	89.7	85.8	80.2
1998	89.1	91.1	78.9	81.6	79.9	76.9	83.1	81.9	87.0	83.9	80.4
1999	86.3	92.4	83.7	84.2	84.5	83.0	81.8	80.5	86.6	84.1	78.5
2000	90.9	92.2	89.5	77.7	91.3	94.5	81.2	79.4	88.4	84.4	77.3
2001	90.9	88.7	68.9	68.1	69.9	69.0	76.9	74.6	85.6	77.5	72.8
2002	86.7	87.5	58.2	68.7	44.9	62.1	76.5	74.7	84.0	77.1	71.2
2003	88.0	86.2	63.0	76.4	45.2	69.7	76.5	74.6	84.9	77.4	71.7
2004	88.1	84.7	71.3	76.5	53.7	79.8	79.0	77.6	86.8	80.6	74.3
2005	87.0	86.0	75.3	78.8	67.3	78.3	80.4	79.3	85.5	81.8	76.9
2003											
January	87.6	88.1	59.8	74.9	41.4	65.8	76.7	74.7	84.6	77.7	71.3
February	88.0	89.3	61.3	76.4	43.9	66.7	76.6	74.4	85.0	77.6	71.3
March	88.0	86.3	61.7	76.4	44.9	67.1	76.4	74.5	85.3	77.1	71.5
April	88.0	85.6	61.4	75.9	44.5	67.1	75.8	73.9	84.9	76.4	71.1
May	87.6	85.9	61.6	75.8	44.6	67.6	75.8	73.8	84.3	76.7	70.8
June	88.0	83.8	62.1	77.0	45.3	67.6	76.0	74.2	84.7	76.5	71.4
July	87.6	86.1	63.1	78.6	44.8	69.4	76.3	74.3	84.4	77.0	71.7
August	88.0	86.9	64.0	79.0	46.0	70.3	76.3	74.1	84.6	77.2	71.6
September	89.0	85.3	64.4	77.7	46.0	71.6	76.8	74.8	85.4	77.4	72.3
October	88.7	85.3	65.3	75.5	47.0	73.4	76.8	74.8	85.3	78.0	71.9
November	88.0	85.2	65.6	74.3	46.8	74.5	77.5	75.7	84.9	78.7	72.8
December	87.8	86.3	66.2	74.9	47.5	74.9	77.6	75.8	84.9	79.1	72.6
2004											
January	89.2	86.7	67.7	76.8	49.3	76.1	77.8	75.9	85.9	79.3	72.9
February	88.2	87.4	69.1	78.2	50.2	77.6	78.4	76.5	85.6	80.0	73.5
March	88.3	83.6	69.6	78.3	50.2	78.5	78.1	76.6	86.1	79.5	73.4
April	88.1	84.1	69.6	77.4	50.3	78.6	78.7	77.2	86.5	80.0	74.1
May	88.2	85.9	70.8	76.3	51.3	80.4	79.3	77.8	87.0	81.0	74.5
June	87.9	85.3	71.5	75.7	52.6	81.1	78.8	77.2	86.9	80.8	73.6
July	88.8	83.7	72.2	75.6	54.0	81.5	79.2	77.8	87.6	80.9	74.2
August	88.0	82.1	73.4	75.6	55.0	83.0	79.3	78.2	87.2	81.0	74.7
September	86.2	84.2	73.7	75.8	55.8	83.1	79.0	77.8	86.0	81.0	74.4
October	86.9	83.8	72.8	76.0	57.2	80.4	79.6	78.5	86.6	81.2	75.2
November	88.7	83.9	72.4	76.3	58.8	78.7	79.7	78.5	88.2	81.0	75.2
December	89.3	85.6	73.2	76.6	59.9	79.2	80.2	78.8	88.5	81.7	75.5
2005											
January	88.9	83.7	75.5	76.9	61.8	82.4	80.1	78.9	88.2	81.8	75.6
February	89.9	82.7	75.7	77.2	62.4	82.3	80.3	79.2	88.8	81.4	76.4
March	89.5	85.2	74.6	77.6	62.1	80.3	80.3	78.9	88.5	81.4	76.1
April	89.7	83.8	74.7	78.1	62.7	79.9	80.1	78.8	88.2	81.2	76.0
May	89.1	83.7	74.9	78.6	64.3	79.2	80.1	79.0	87.6	81.0	76.5
June	90.0	88.0	74.4	79.2	65.0	77.7	80.7	79.1	88.4	81.7	76.8
July	89.1	88.0	74.8	78.8	67.7	77.1	80.6	79.0	87.6	81.6	76.8
August	88.6	88.2	75.6	79.0	68.6	78.1	80.7	79.2	86.8	81.8	77.1
September	80.7	88.0	75.5	79.3	70.5	76.8	79.5	78.6	78.2	81.9	76.6
October	79.6	86.2	74.9	79.4	72.9	74.6	80.3	80.0	78.2	82.2	78.2
November	83.2	85.4	76.2	80.6	75.0	75.7	80.9	80.4	81.8	82.5	78.3
December	85.4	89.0	76.1	81.3	74.6	75.4	81.6	80.6	84.0	83.2	78.4

. . . = Not available.

NOTES AND DEFINITIONS

TABLES 2-1 THROUGH 2-3 AND 20-1
INDUSTRIAL PRODUCTION AND CAPACITY UTILIZATION

SOURCE: BOARD OF GOVERNORS OF THE FEDERAL RESERVE SYSTEM

The *industrial production index* measures changes in the physical volume or quantity of output of manufacturing, mining, and electric and gas utilities. *Capacity utilization* is calculated by dividing a seasonally adjusted industrial production index for an industry or group of industries by a related index of productive capacity.

Around the 15th day of each month, the Federal Reserve issues estimates of industrial production and capacity utilization for the previous month. The production estimates are in the form of index numbers (currently 2002 = 100) that reflect the monthly levels of total output of the nation's factories, mines, and gas and electric utilities expressed as a percent of the monthly average in the 2002 base year. Capacity estimates are expressed as index numbers, 2002 output = 100 (not 2002 capacity), and capacity utilization is measured by the production index as a percent of the capacity index. Since the bases of those two indexes are the same for each industry, this procedure yields production as a percent of capacity. Monthly estimates are subject to revision in each of the three subsequent months, as well as to annual and comprehensive revisions in subsequent years. Monthly series are seasonally adjusted using the Census X-12-ARIMA program.

In 2006, the annual revision of the industrial production and capacity utilization figures was released on December 11, too late to be tabulated for this edition of *Business Statistics*. Mainly the revisions affect data from 2003 forward, but smaller revisions are made all the way back to 1972. The revised data are not continuous with the data shown in this volume, though the picture of the economy that they show is essentially the same in its cyclical and trend behavior. Among major groups, the only striking difference is a downward revision in output of defense and space equipment beginning in mid-2003. For revised data, users should refer to the Federal Reserve Web site at <http://www.federalreserve. gov> and look under the "Economic Research and Data" heading.

Definitions and notes on the data

The index of industrial production measures a large portion of the goods output of the national economy on a monthly basis. That portion, together with construction, has also accounted for the bulk of the variation in output over the course of many historical business cycles. The substantial industrial detail included in the index illuminates structural developments in the economy.

The total industrial production index and the indexes for its major components are constructed from individual industry series (300 series for data from 1997 forward) based on the 2002 North American Industry Classification System (NAICS). See Chapter 14 of this publication for a description of NAICS and a table that outlines its structure.

The Federal Reserve has been able to provide a much longer continuous historical series on the NAICS basis than other government agencies. In a major research effort, the Fed and the Census Bureau's Center for Economic Studies re-coded data from seven Censuses of Manufactures, beginning in 1963, to establish benchmark NAICS data for output, value added, and capacity utilization. The resulting indexes are shown annually for the last 34 years (39 years for aggregate levels) in Tables 2-1 through 2-3.

The Fed's featured indexes for total industry and total manufacturing on the Standard Industrial Classification (SIC) basis do not observe the reclassifications under NAICS of the logging industry to the Agriculture sector and the publishing industry to the Information sector. (The reason cited by the Fed was to avoid "changing the scope or historical continuity of these statistics.") One advantage of the SIC index for capacity utilization is that it is a continuous series back to 1947 (shown in Table 20-1). On the new NAICS basis, production and capacity utilization are shown back to 1972 in Tables 2-2 and 2-3.

The individual series components of the indexes are grouped in two ways: market groups and industry groups.

Market groups. For analyzing market trends and product flows, the individual series are grouped into two major divisions: *final products and nonindustrial supplies* and *materials. Final products* consists of products purchased by consumers, businesses, or government for final use. *Nonindustrial supplies* are expected to become inputs in nonindustrial sectors: the two major subgroups are *construction supplies* and *business supplies. Materials* comprises industrial output that requires further processing within the industrial sector. This twofold division distinguishes between products that are ready to ship outside the industrial sector and those that will stay within the sector for further processing.

Final products are divided into *consumer goods* and *equipment*, and equipment is divided into *business equipment* and *defense and space equipment*. Further subdivisions of each market group are based on type of product and the market destination for the product.

Industry groups are typically groupings by 3-digit NAICS industries and major aggregates of these industries—for example, *durable goods* and *nondurable goods manufacturing, mining*, and *utilities*. Indexes are also calculated for *stage-of-process* industry groups—*crude, primary and semi-finished*, and *finished* processing. The stage-of-process grouping was a new feature in the 2002 revision, replacing the two narrower and less refined "primary processing manufacturing" and "advanced processing manufacturing" groups that were previously published. *Crude processing* consists of logging, much of mining, and certain basic manufacturing activities in the chemical, paper, and metals industries. *Primary and semifinished processing* represents industries that produce materials and parts used as inputs by other industries. *Finished processing* includes industries that produce goods in their finished form for use by consumers, business investments, or government.

The indexes of industrial production are constructed with data from a variety of sources. Current monthly estimates of production are based on measures of physical output where possible and appropriate. For a few high-tech industries, the estimated value of nominal output is deflated by a corresponding price index. For industries in which such direct measurement is not possible on a monthly basis, output is inferred from production-worker hours, adjusted for trends in worker productivity derived from annual and benchmark revisions. (Between the 1960s and 1997, electric power consumption was used as a monthly output indicator for some industries instead of hours. However, the coverage of the survey deteriorated, and in the 2005 revision, the decision was made to resume the use of hours in those industries, beginning with the data for 1997.)

In annual and benchmark revisions, the individual indexes are revised using data from the quinquennial Censuses of Manufactures and Mineral Industries and the Annual Survey of Manufactures and Survey of Plant Capacity, prepared by the Census Bureau; deflators from the Producer Price Indexes and other sources; the *Minerals Yearbook*, prepared by the Department of the Interior; publications from the Department of Energy; and other sources.

The weights used in computing the indexes are based on Census value added—the difference between the value of production and the cost of materials and supplies consumed. (Census value added differs in some respects from the economic concept of industry value added used in the national income and product accounts [NIPAs]. Industry value added as defined in the NIPAs is not available in sufficient detail for the industrial production indexes. See Chapter 15 for data and a description of NIPA value added by major industry group.) Before 1972, a linked-Laspeyres formula is used. Beginning with 1972, the index uses a version of the Fisher-ideal index formula—a chain-weighting system similar to that in the NIPAs. See the "General Notes" article at the front of this book and the notes and definitions for Chapter 1 for more information. Chain-weighting keeps the index from being distorted by the use of obsolete relative prices.

For the purpose of these value-added weights, value added per unit of output is based on data from the Censuses of Manufacturing and Mineral Industries, the Census Bureau's

Annual Survey of Manufactures, and revenue and expense data reported by the Department of Energy and the American Gas Association, which are projected into recent years by using changes in relevant Producer Price Indexes.

To separate seasonal movements from cyclical patterns and underlying trends, each component of the index is seasonally adjusted by the Census X-12-ARIMA method.

The index does not cover production on farms, in the construction industry, in transportation, or in various trade and service industries. A number of groups and subgroups include data for individual series not published separately.

Capacity utilization is calculated for the manufacturing, mining, and electric and gas utilities industries. Output is measured by seasonally adjusted indexes of industrial production. The capacity indexes attempt to capture the concept of sustainable maximum output, which is defined as the greatest level of output that a plant can maintain within the framework of a realistic work schedule, taking account of normal downtime and assuming sufficient availability of inputs to operate the machinery and equipment in place. The 85 individual industry capacity indexes are based on a variety of data, including capacity data measured in physical units compiled by government agencies and trade associations, Census Bureau surveys of utilization rates and investment, and estimates of growth of the capital stock.

Revisions

Revisions normally occur annually, late in the year, and incorporate the additional source data that have become available. In November 2005, the latest annual revision was released, and its results are presented in this volume. In addition to the usual revisions of recent years, the indexes were all rebased from 1997 = 100 to 2002 = 100.

A previous comprehensive revision in 1997 moved the reference year from 1987 to 1992 = 100 and introduced annual (instead of quinquennial) updating of the value-added weights for each industry. In the January 2001 revision, recalculation of the value-added weights each month was introduced.

Data availability

Data are available monthly in Federal Reserve release G.17. Selected data are subsequently published monthly in the *Statistical Supplement to the Federal Reserve Bulletin*. Historical data may be purchased on diskette from Publications Services, Board of Governors of the Federal Reserve System (the full address is shown below). Current and historical data and background information are available on the Federal Reserve Web site at <http://www.federalreserve.gov>. The total Industrial Production Index extends back to 1919.

Chain-weighting makes it difficult for the user to analyze in detail the sources of aggregate output change. An

"Explanatory Note," included in each month's index release, provides some assistance for the user, including a reference to an Internet location with the exact contribution of a monthly change in a component index to the monthly change in the total index.

References

The G.17 release each month contains extensive explanatory material, as well as references for further detail. The 2005 revision is described in "Industrial Production and Capacity Utilization: The 2005 Annual Revision," issued on November 7, 2005.

An earlier detailed description of the industrial production index, together with a history of the index, a glossary of terms, and a bibliography is presented in *Industrial Production—1986 Edition*, available from Publication Services, Mail Stop 127, Board of Governors of the Federal Reserve System, Washington, DC 20551.

CHAPTER 3: INCOME DISTRIBUTION AND POVERTY

Section 3a: Household and Family Income

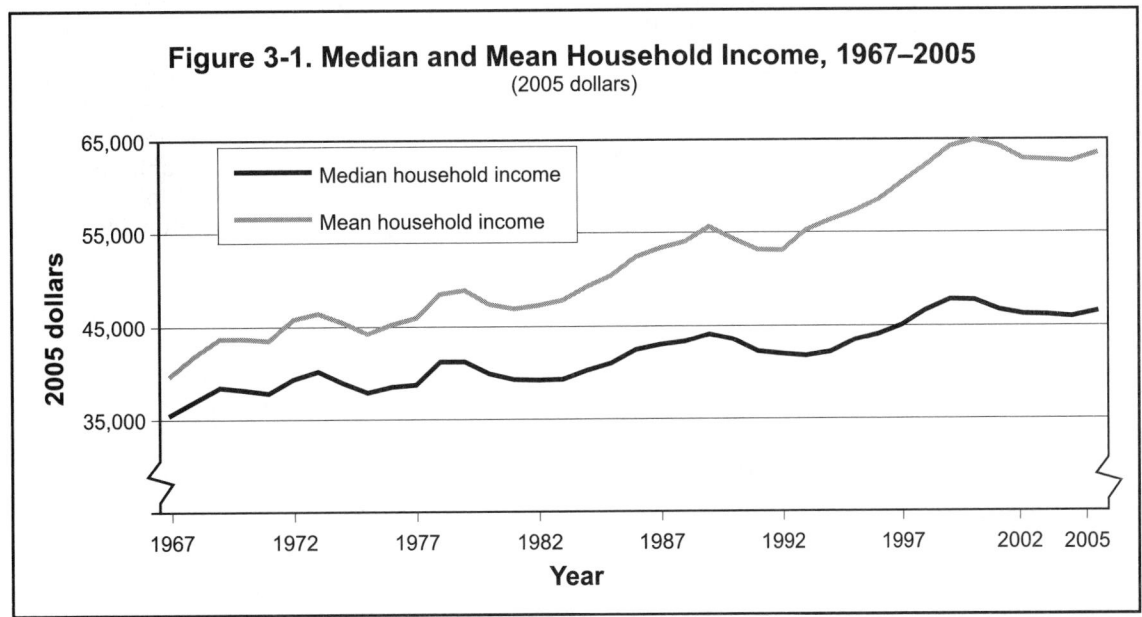

Figure 3-1. Median and Mean Household Income, 1967–2005
(2005 dollars)

- Measured as cash income before taxes, median household income in 2005 was $46,326, up from its level in 2004 but down 2.8 percent in constant (2005) dollars from the 1999 all-time high of $47,671. Between the 1969 business cycle peak and 1999, real median household income rose an average 0.7 percent per year. (Table 3-1)

- The Census Bureau also tabulates "mean income," which is the sum of all the reported household incomes divided by the number of households. Mean income is higher than median income when the distribution of income is skewed upward, with very large incomes at the top of the distribution. It rises faster than median income when the income distribution becomes more unequal. (See "Whose Standard of Living?" in the article "Using the Data: The U.S. Economy in the New Century" at the beginning of this book.) Mean household income peaked one year later in 2000, rose at a 1.3 percent annual rate from 1969 to 2000, and declined 2.2 percent from 2000 to 2005. (Table 3-1)

- Measures of household income distribution confirm an increase in income inequality. The "Gini coefficient" has risen from 0.386 in 1968 to a new high of 0.469 in 2005. (Table 3-4)

- The ratio of women's to men's earnings for year-round, full-time workers increased from 0.607 in 1960 to 0.770 in 2005. Men's earnings in 2005 were at the same level as in 1972, in real terms, while women's real earnings increased 33 percent over the same period. (Table 3-1)

Table 3-1. Median and Mean Household Income and Median Earnings

(2005 dollars, ratio.)

Year	Median household income						Mean household income, all races	Median earnings of year-round, full-time workers		
	All races	White		Black	Asian [1]	Hispanic (any race)		Male workers	Female workers	Ratio, female to male
		Total	Not Hispanic							
1960	. . .	. . .	. . .	. . .	. . .	. . .	. . .	29 983	18 192	0.607
1961	. . .	. . .	. . .	. . .	. . .	. . .	. . .	30 947	18 336	0.592
1962	. . .	. . .	. . .	. . .	. . .	. . .	. . .	31 520	18 690	0.593
1963	. . .	. . .	. . .	. . .	. . .	. . .	. . .	32 322	19 052	0.589
1964	. . .	. . .	. . .	. . .	. . .	. . .	. . .	33 087	19 570	0.591
1965	. . .	. . .	. . .	. . .	. . .	. . .	. . .	33 508	20 079	0.599
1966	. . .	. . .	. . .	. . .	. . .	. . .	. . .	34 994	20 141	0.576
1967	35 379	36 895	. . .	21 422	. . .	. . .	39 569	35 572	20 555	0.578
1968	36 873	38 392	. . .	22 639	. . .	. . .	41 716	36 497	21 225	0.582
1969	38 282	39 953	. . .	24 150	. . .	. . .	43 553	38 584	22 712	0.589
1970	38 026	39 606	. . .	24 107	. . .	. . .	43 542	39 036	23 175	0.594
1971	37 634	39 364	. . .	23 253	. . .	. . .	43 283	39 181	23 315	0.595
1972	39 216	41 141	41 727	24 014	. . .	31 047	45 642	41 258	23 872	0.579
1973	40 008	41 929	42 299	24 681	. . .	30 995	46 268	42 573	24 110	0.566
1974	38 774	40 550	40 896	24 115	. . .	30 840	45 343	41 080	24 136	0.588
1975	37 736	39 463	39 760	23 691	. . .	28 350	44 065	40 800	23 998	0.588
1976	38 368	40 192	41 012	23 899	. . .	28 941	45 131	40 694	24 495	0.602
1977	38 585	40 575	41 380	23 944	. . .	30 269	45 772	41 582	24 501	0.589
1978	41 061	42 686	43 490	25 652	. . .	32 173	48 328	42 877	25 486	0.594
1979	41 015	43 004	43 609	25 248	. . .	32 496	48 722	42 393	25 293	0.597
1980	39 739	41 925	42 667	24 153	. . .	30 631	47 263	41 763	25 125	0.602
1981	39 125	41 338	41 935	23 197	. . .	31 384	46 741	41 558	24 617	0.592
1982	39 064	40 896	41 582	23 178	. . .	29 394	47 078	40 819	25 204	0.617
1983	39 081	40 972	. . .	23 192	. . .	29 367	47 617	40 685	25 873	0.636
1984	40 079	42 282	43 160	24 087	. . .	30 383	49 107	41 515	26 427	0.637
1985	40 868	43 100	44 069	25 642	. . .	30 221	50 295	41 866	27 035	0.646
1986	42 309	44 480	45 491	25 626	. . .	31 186	52 270	42 919	27 584	0.643
1987	42 827	45 123	46 364	25 755	52 959	31 776	53 261	42 638	27 791	0.652
1988	43 168	45 635	46 893	26 015	51 163	32 281	53 938	42 266	27 916	0.660
1989	43 946	46 227	47 221	27 492	54 887	33 327	55 522	41 552	28 535	0.687
1990	43 366	45 232	46 266	27 048	55 687	32 340	54 171	40 086	28 708	0.716
1991	42 108	44 125	45 179	26 287	50 946	31 716	53 005	41 123	28 728	0.699
1992	41 774	43 919	45 393	25 573	51 544	30 812	52 960	41 175	29 146	0.708
1993	41 562	43 849	45 463	25 986	51 016	30 447	55 115	40 453	28 932	0.715
1994	42 038	44 336	45 767	27 397	52 745	30 516	56 199	40 201	28 932	0.720
1995	43 346	45 496	47 292	28 485	51 662	29 079	57 163	40 064	28 617	0.714
1996	43 967	46 034	48 049	29 089	53 609	30 853	58 375	39 819	29 371	0.738
1997	44 883	47 269	49 215	30 383	54 882	32 297	60 271	40 843	30 289	0.742
1998	46 508	48 933	50 759	30 321	55 780	33 884	62 021	42 274	30 932	0.732
1999	47 671	49 580	51 726	32 694	59 695	36 016	64 119	42 629	30 827	0.723
2000	47 599	49 782	51 717	33 630	63 205	37 598	64 767	42 228	31 130	0.737
2001	46 569	49 093	51 065	32 499	59 148	37 015	64 191	42 209	32 218	0.763
2002	46 036	. . .	. . .	. . .	. . .	35 934	62 800	42 801	32 786	0.766
2003	45 970	. . .	. . .	. . .	. . .	35 017	62 683	43 158	32 605	0.755
2004	45 817	. . .	. . .	. . .	. . .	35 417	62 488	42 160	32 285	0.766
2005	46 326	. . .	. . .	. . .	. . .	35 967	63 344	41 386	31 858	0.770
By race										
Race alone										
2002	. . .	48 942	50 911	31 509	57 127	. . .	. . .	. . .	. . .	. . .
2003	. . .	48 424	50 702	31 460	59 109	. . .	. . .	. . .	. . .	. . .
2004	. . .	48 218	50 546	31 101	59 427	. . .	. . .	. . .	. . .	. . .
2005	. . .	48 554	50 784	30 858	61 094	. . .	. . .	. . .	. . .	. . .
Race alone or in combination										
2002	. . .	. . .	. . .	31 672	56 757	. . .	. . .	. . .	. . .	. . .
2003	. . .	. . .	. . .	31 506	58 645	. . .	. . .	. . .	. . .	. . .
2004	. . .	. . .	. . .	31 246	59 370	. . .	. . .	. . .	. . .	. . .
2005	. . .	. . .	. . .	30 954	61 048	. . .	. . .	. . .	. . .	. . .

[1] For 1987 through 2001, Asian and Pacific Islander.
. . . = Not available.

Table 3-2. Median Income and Poverty Rates by Race and Hispanic Origin Using 3-Year Moving Averages

(Income in 2005 dollars, percent of population.)

Race and Hispanic origin	Median household income				Poverty rate			
	2000–2002	2001–2003	2002–2004	2003–2005	2000–2002	2001–2003	2002–2004	2003–2005
All Races	46 735	46 192	45 941	46 038	11.7	12.1	12.4	12.6
White alone or in combination	49 228	48 755	48 438	48 316	9.9	10.3	10.6	10.7
White alone	49 272	48 828	48 528	48 399	9.9	10.2	10.5	10.6
Not Hispanic	51 231	50 893	50 720	50 677	7.7	8.0	8.3	8.4
Black alone or in combination	32 600	31 892	31 475	31 235	23.0	23.6	24.3	24.6
Black alone	32 546	31 823	31 357	31 140	23.1	23.7	24.4	24.7
American Indian and Alaskan Native alone or in combination	35 943	36 867	37 458	37 217	21.6	20.0	19.2	19.7
American Indian and Alaskan Native alone	35 474	35 045	34 165	33 627	23.1	23.3	24.3	25.3
Asian alone or in combination	59 703	58 183	58 257	59 688	10.0	10.7	10.5	10.8
Asian alone	59 827	58 461	58 554	59 877	10.1	10.7	10.6	10.9
Native Hawaiian and Other Pacific Islander alone or in combination	. . .	. . .	53 889	53 606	. . .	. . .	. . .	. . .
Native Hawaiian and Other Pacific Islander alone	. . .	. . .	53 374	54 318	. . .	. . .	. . .	. . .
Hispanic (any race)	36 849	35 989	35 456	35 467	21.6	21.9	22.1	22.0

. . . = Not available.

Table 3-3. Median Family Income by Type of Family

(2004 dollars.)

Year	All families	Married couple			Male householder [1]	Female householder [1]	4-person family
		Total	Wife in paid labor force	Wife not in paid labor force			
1947	21 771	. . .	. . .	. . .	. . .	. . .	23 646
1948	21 177	. . .	. . .	. . .	. . .	. . .	23 045
1949	20 898	. . .	. . .	. . .	. . .	. . .	22 721
1950	22 055	22 898	26 600	22 028	20 699	12 772	24 420
1951	22 827	23 614	28 501	22 365	21 245	13 663	25 368
1952	23 468	24 500	29 561	22 997	21 809	13 484	26 382
1953	25 424	26 197	32 395	24 675	24 651	14 714	. . .
1954	24 759	25 745	31 705	24 070	23 850	13 630	. . .
1955	26 364	27 444	33 549	25 815	25 004	14 746	29 354
1956	28 098	29 232	35 016	27 304	24 494	16 189	31 266
1957	28 285	29 372	34 977	27 527	26 092	15 737	31 258
1958	28 158	29 420	34 396	27 582	23 580	15 172	31 468
1959	29 804	31 152	36 891	29 254	25 381	15 208	33 397
1960	30 374	31 742	37 293	29 834	26 267	16 041	34 023
1961	30 695	32 311	38 471	29 929	27 130	16 019	34 452
1962	31 570	33 198	39 548	30 553	30 272	16 596	35 811
1963	32 683	34 482	40 737	31 584	29 864	16 794	37 332
1964	33 905	35 778	42 168	32 713	29 895	17 848	38 648
1965	35 311	36 875	43 635	33 459	31 205	17 927	39 590
1966	37 200	38 712	45 666	35 205	31 767	19 805	41 196
1967	38 020	40 455	47 716	36 477	32 657	20 580	43 105
1968	39 777	42 136	49 242	37 855	33 735	20 630	45 315
1969	41 654	44 162	51 351	39 207	36 827	21 293	46 908
1970	41 568	44 302	51 717	39 196	37 966	21 456	47 045
1971	41 487	44 331	51 845	39 305	35 182	20 628	46 896
1972	43 499	46 579	54 382	41 308	40 326	20 904	50 121
1973	44 381	47 979	56 114	42 049	39 560	21 349	50 490
1974	43 232	46 653	54 353	40 984	39 064	21 740	50 158
1975	42 453	46 006	53 340	39 461	40 213	21 179	49 041
1976	43 776	47 420	54 818	40 770	37 636	21 104	50 674
1977	44 041	48 462	55 757	41 438	39 939	21 362	51 507
1978	46 527	51 011	58 314	42 613	42 112	22 517	53 881
1979	47 225	51 666	59 941	42 690	40 525	23 821	54 277
1980	45 647	50 245	58 362	41 193	38 038	22 599	52 831
1981	44 437	49 750	58 051	40 342	39 477	21 754	52 150
1982	43 913	48 759	56 860	39 914	37 742	21 521	51 757
1983	44 225	49 093	57 767	39 385	39 304	21 211	52 508
1984	45 734	51 234	59 982	40 801	40 357	22 152	53 804
1985	46 439	52 073	60 999	41 116	37 878	22 872	54 881
1986	48 439	53 943	63 054	42 429	41 046	22 440	57 085
1987	49 248	55 464	64 801	42 362	40 085	23 349	58 973
1988	49 391	55 832	65 528	41 764	41 161	23 545	59 916
1989	50 332	56 707	66 592	42 290	40 966	24 188	59 967
1990	49 545	55 910	65 555	42 414	40 706	23 729	58 091
1991	48 608	55 446	65 149	40 677	38 345	22 576	58 234
1992	48 255	55 271	65 674	39 812	36 384	22 463	58 386
1993	47 578	55 361	65 916	38 900	34 071	22 455	58 137
1994	48 895	56 683	67 210	39 306	34 988	22 991	59 271
1995	49 987	57 927	68 711	39 849	37 367	24 237	61 158
1996	50 705	59 583	69 981	40 453	37 879	23 867	61 754
1997	52 307	60 549	71 203	42 283	38 683	24 673	62 613
1998	54 091	62 705	73 782	43 008	41 295	25 650	64 882
1999	55 350	64 044	75 353	43 617	42 324	26 934	67 732
2000	55 647	64 825	75 943	43 856	41 382	28 208	68 742
2001	54 857	64 384	75 587	43 519	39 045	27 473	67 524
2002	54 285	64 211	76 475	42 123	39 641	27 755	65 894
2003	54 096	63 955	77 190	42 227	39 054	27 264	66 842
2004	54 061	63 630	76 814	42 221	40 293	26 964	66 111

[1]No spouse present.
. . . = Not available.

Table 3-4. Shares of Aggregate Income Received by Each Fifth and Top 5 Percent of Households

Year	Number (thousands)	Share of aggregate income (percent)						Mean household income (2005 dollars)						Gini coefficient
		Lowest fifth	Second fifth	Third fifth	Fourth fifth	Highest fifth	Top 5 percent	Lowest fifth	Second fifth	Third fifth	Fourth fifth	Highest fifth	Top 5 percent	
1967	60 813	4.0	10.8	17.3	24.2	43.6	17.2	7 925	21 956	35 052	49 044	88 262	139 228	0.397
1968	62 214	4.2	11.1	17.6	24.5	42.6	16.3	8 600	23 058	36 573	51 017	88 652	135 535	0.386
1969	63 401	4.1	10.9	17.5	24.5	43.0	16.6	8 816	23 803	38 036	53 278	93 641	144 135	0.391
1970	64 778	4.1	10.8	17.4	24.5	43.3	16.6	8 673	23 493	37 830	53 325	94 402	144 897	0.394
1971	66 676	4.1	10.6	17.3	24.5	43.5	16.7	8 721	23 048	37 372	53 129	94 140	144 393	0.396
1972	68 251	4.1	10.4	17.0	24.5	43.9	17.0	9 233	23 848	38 920	55 877	100 314	155 483	0.401
1973	69 859	4.2	10.4	17.0	24.5	43.9	16.9	9 663	24 297	39 851	57 332	102 580	158 005	0.400
1974	71 163	4.3	10.6	17.0	24.6	43.5	16.5	9 637	23 953	38 600	55 748	98 771	150 132	0.395
1975	72 867	4.3	10.4	17.0	24.7	43.6	16.5	9 303	22 853	37 493	54 481	96 189	145 968	0.397
1976	74 142	4.3	10.3	17.0	24.7	43.7	16.6	9 533	23 340	38 384	55 741	98 655	150 316	0.398
1977	76 030	4.2	10.2	16.9	24.7	44.0	16.8	9 481	23 338	38 605	56 564	100 870	154 310	0.402
1978	77 330	4.2	10.2	16.8	24.7	44.1	16.8	10 045	24 668	40 731	59 668	106 527	162 146	0.402
1979	80 776	4.1	10.2	16.8	24.6	44.2	16.9	9 982	24 827	40 933	60 069	107 802	164 411	0.404
1980	82 368	4.2	10.2	16.8	24.7	44.1	16.5	9 671	24 070	39 719	58 516	104 334	155 914	0.403
1981	83 527	4.1	10.1	16.7	24.8	44.3	16.5	9 440	23 515	38 955	58 068	103 726	154 137	0.406
1982	83 918	4.0	10.0	16.5	24.5	45.0	17.0	9 277	23 474	38 857	57 790	105 991	160 155	0.412
1983	85 407	4.0	9.9	16.4	24.6	45.1	17.0	9 395	23 601	39 021	58 556	107 508	162 434	0.414
1984	86 789	4.0	9.9	16.3	24.6	45.2	17.1	9 720	24 210	40 120	60 407	111 075	167 673	0.415
1985	88 458	3.9	9.8	16.2	24.4	45.6	17.6	9 714	24 618	40 863	61 466	114 815	177 110	0.419
1986	89 479	3.8	9.7	16.2	24.3	46.1	18.0	9 812	25 240	42 237	63 628	120 434	188 668	0.425
1987	91 124	3.8	9.6	16.1	24.3	46.2	18.2	10 077	25 610	42 818	64 720	123 082	193 916	0.426
1988	92 830	3.8	9.6	16.0	24.2	46.3	18.3	10 251	25 872	43 273	65 413	124 881	196 957	0.426
1989	93 347	3.8	9.5	15.8	24.0	46.8	18.9	10 633	26 455	43 975	66 519	130 032	210 086	0.431
1990	94 312	3.8	9.6	15.9	24.0	46.6	18.5	10 378	26 113	43 132	65 030	126 200	200 959	0.428
1991	95 669	3.8	9.6	15.9	24.2	46.5	18.1	10 100	25 369	42 139	64 236	123 178	192 231	0.428
1992	96 426	3.8	9.4	15.8	24.2	46.9	18.6	9 894	24 791	41 767	64 115	124 233	197 180	0.433
1993	97 107	3.6	9.0	15.1	23.5	48.9	21.0	9 790	24 819	41 603	64 655	134 704	231 197	0.454
1994	98 990	3.6	8.9	15.0	23.4	49.1	21.2	10 051	25 048	42 195	65 661	138 039	238 494	0.456
1995	99 627	3.7	9.1	15.2	23.3	48.7	21.0	10 615	25 946	43 384	66 692	139 175	240 196	0.450
1996	101 018	3.6	9.0	15.1	23.3	49.0	21.4	10 647	26 135	43 959	68 036	143 096	249 267	0.455
1997	102 528	3.6	8.9	15.0	23.2	49.4	21.7	10 721	26 802	45 091	69 840	148 898	261 299	0.459
1998	103 874	3.6	9.0	15.0	23.2	49.2	21.4	11 031	27 854	46 606	72 081	152 530	265 861	0.456
1999	106 434	3.6	8.9	14.9	23.2	49.4	21.5	11 614	28 518	47 735	74 294	158 433	275 370	0.458
2000	108 209	3.6	8.9	14.8	23.0	49.8	22.1	11 514	28 749	47 874	74 422	161 272	286 114	0.462
2001	109 297	3.5	8.7	14.6	23.0	50.1	22.4	11 178	28 086	47 011	73 710	160 975	287 238	0.466
2002	111 278	3.5	8.8	14.8	23.3	49.7	21.7	10 844	27 572	46 463	73 084	156 037	272 479	0.462
2003	112 000	3.4	8.7	14.8	23.4	49.8	21.4	10 608	27 250	46 256	73 218	156 082	268 741	0.464
2004	113 343	3.4	8.7	14.7	23.2	50.1	21.8	10 587	27 089	45 896	72 368	156 502	272 721	0.466
2005	114 384	3.4	8.6	14.6	23.0	50.4	22.2	10 655	27 357	46 301	72 825	159 583	281 155	0.469

Table 3-5. Shares of Aggregate Income Received by Each Fifth and Top 5 Percent of Families

Year	Number of families (thousands)	Share of aggregate income (percent)						Mean family income (2005 dollars)						Gini coefficient
		Lowest fifth	Second fifth	Third fifth	Fourth fifth	Highest fifth	Top 5 percent	Lowest fifth	Second fifth	Third fifth	Fourth fifth	Highest fifth	Top 5 percent	
1947	37 237	5.0	11.9	17.0	23.1	43.0	17.5	. . .	. . .	. . .	. . .	. . .	. . .	0.376
1948	38 624	4.9	12.1	17.3	23.2	42.4	17.1	. . .	. . .	. . .	. . .	. . .	. . .	0.371
1949	39 303	4.5	11.9	17.3	23.5	42.7	16.9	. . .	. . .	. . .	. . .	. . .	. . .	0.378
1950	39 929	4.5	12.0	17.4	23.4	42.7	17.3	. . .	. . .	. . .	. . .	. . .	. . .	0.379
1951	40 578	5.0	12.4	17.6	23.4	41.6	16.8	. . .	. . .	. . .	. . .	. . .	. . .	0.363
1952	40 832	4.9	12.3	17.4	23.4	41.9	17.4	. . .	. . .	. . .	. . .	. . .	. . .	0.368
1953	41 202	4.7	12.5	18.0	23.9	40.9	15.7	. . .	. . .	. . .	. . .	. . .	. . .	0.359
1954	41 951	4.5	12.1	17.7	23.9	41.8	16.3	. . .	. . .	. . .	. . .	. . .	. . .	0.371
1955	42 889	4.8	12.3	17.8	23.7	41.3	16.4	. . .	. . .	. . .	. . .	. . .	. . .	0.363
1956	43 497	5.0	12.5	17.9	23.7	41.0	16.1	. . .	. . .	. . .	. . .	. . .	. . .	0.358
1957	43 696	5.1	12.7	18.1	23.8	40.4	15.6	. . .	. . .	. . .	. . .	. . .	. . .	0.351
1958	44 232	5.0	12.5	18.0	23.9	40.6	15.4	. . .	. . .	. . .	. . .	. . .	. . .	0.354
1959	45 111	4.9	12.3	17.9	23.8	41.1	15.9	. . .	. . .	. . .	. . .	. . .	. . .	0.361
1960	45 539	4.8	12.2	17.8	24.0	41.3	15.9	. . .	. . .	. . .	. . .	. . .	. . .	0.364
1961	46 418	4.7	11.9	17.5	23.8	42.2	16.6	. . .	. . .	. . .	. . .	. . .	. . .	0.374
1962	47 059	5.0	12.1	17.6	24.0	41.3	15.7	. . .	. . .	. . .	. . .	. . .	. . .	0.362
1963	47 540	5.0	12.1	17.7	24.0	41.2	15.8	. . .	. . .	. . .	. . .	. . .	. . .	0.362
1964	47 956	5.1	12.0	17.7	24.0	41.2	15.9	. . .	. . .	. . .	. . .	. . .	. . .	0.361
1965	48 509	5.2	12.2	17.8	23.9	40.9	15.5	. . .	. . .	. . .	. . .	. . .	. . .	0.356
1966	49 214	5.6	12.4	17.8	23.8	40.5	15.6	11 969	26 572	38 021	50 898	86 867	133 386	0.349
1967	50 111	5.4	12.2	17.5	23.5	41.4	16.4	12 164	27 202	39 099	52 437	92 591	146 494	0.358
1968	50 823	5.6	12.4	17.7	23.7	40.5	15.6	13 101	28 573	40 821	54 593	93 286	143 802	0.348
1969	51 586	5.6	12.4	17.7	23.7	40.6	15.6	13 530	29 881	42 759	57 280	98 099	150 674	0.349
1970	52 227	5.4	12.2	17.6	23.8	40.9	15.6	13 340	29 497	42 649	57 530	98 930	150 644	0.353
1971	53 296	5.5	12.0	17.6	23.8	41.1	15.7	13 344	29 047	42 499	57 556	99 134	151 154	0.355
1972	54 373	5.5	11.9	17.5	23.9	41.4	15.9	13 916	30 363	44 598	60 904	105 628	161 934	0.359
1973	55 053	5.5	11.9	17.5	24.0	41.1	15.5	14 280	30 930	45 446	62 108	106 561	160 818	0.356
1974	55 698	5.7	12.0	17.6	24.1	40.6	14.8	14 544	30 702	44 823	61 410	103 477	150 932	0.355
1975	56 245	5.6	11.9	17.7	24.2	40.7	14.9	13 966	29 524	43 899	60 106	101 289	148 584	0.357
1976	56 710	5.6	11.9	17.7	24.2	40.7	14.9	14 306	30 275	45 161	61 705	103 854	152 001	0.358
1977	57 215	5.5	11.7	17.6	24.3	40.9	14.9	14 235	30 429	45 764	63 129	106 351	155 043	0.363
1978	57 804	5.4	11.7	17.6	24.2	41.1	15.1	14 790	32 074	48 162	66 357	112 600	165 003	0.363
1979	59 550	5.4	11.6	17.5	24.1	41.4	15.3	14 945	32 312	48 730	67 088	115 070	170 331	0.365
1980	60 309	5.3	11.6	17.6	24.4	41.1	14.6	14 386	31 316	47 308	65 634	110 507	157 094	0.365
1981	61 019	5.3	11.4	17.5	24.6	41.2	14.4	13 954	30 346	46 413	65 163	109 337	152 779	0.369
1982	61 393	5.0	11.3	17.2	24.4	42.2	15.3	13 179	29 902	45 658	64 771	116 130	160 130	0.380
1983	62 015	4.9	11.2	17.2	24.5	42.4	15.3	12 992	29 891	45 990	65 545	113 649	163 860	0.382
1984	62 706	4.8	11.1	17.1	24.5	42.5	15.4	13 448	30 790	47 505	67 932	118 063	170 698	0.383
1985	63 558	4.8	11.0	16.9	24.3	43.1	16.1	13 616	31 245	48 241	69 149	122 889	183 646	0.389
1986	64 491	4.7	10.9	16.9	24.1	43.4	16.5	13 999	32 323	50 076	71 551	128 875	195 705	0.392
1987	65 204	4.6	10.7	16.8	24.0	43.8	17.2	13 980	32 721	50 809	72 718	132 895	208 039	0.393
1988	65 837	4.6	10.7	16.7	24.0	44.0	17.2	14 104	32 844	51 111	73 403	134 682	210 436	0.395
1989	66 090	4.6	10.6	16.5	23.7	44.6	17.9	14 388	33 474	52 004	74 820	140 877	225 673	0.401
1990	66 322	4.6	10.8	16.6	23.8	44.3	17.4	14 241	33 217	51 157	73 569	136 725	214 527	0.396
1991	67 173	4.5	10.7	16.6	24.1	44.2	17.1	13 606	32 295	50 110	72 678	133 526	206 610	0.397
1992	68 216	4.3	10.5	16.5	24.0	44.7	17.6	13 071	31 527	49 806	72 396	134 721	212 110	0.404
1993	68 506	4.1	9.9	15.7	23.3	47.0	20.3	12 956	31 117	49 311	73 098	147 694	254 915	0.429
1994	69 313	4.2	10.0	15.7	23.3	46.9	20.1	13 534	32 020	50 564	74 744	150 629	258 419	0.426
1995	69 597	4.4	10.1	15.8	23.2	46.5	20.0	14 329	33 016	51 692	75 631	151 948	260 593	0.421
1996	70 241	4.2	10.0	15.8	23.1	46.8	20.3	14 107	33 258	52 607	76 869	155 624	269 255	0.425
1997	70 884	4.2	9.9	15.7	23.0	47.2	20.7	14 624	34 266	54 064	79 278	162 872	285 053	0.429
1998	71 551	4.2	9.9	15.7	23.0	47.3	20.7	14 982	35 262	55 810	81 845	168 458	294 849	0.430
1999	73 206	4.3	9.9	15.6	23.0	47.2	20.3	15 589	36 236	57 196	84 420	173 019	298 316	0.429
2000	73 778	4.3	9.8	15.4	22.7	47.7	21.1	16 008	36 602	57 525	84 781	177 879	315 205	0.433
2001	74 340	4.2	9.7	15.4	22.9	47.7	21.0	15 462	35 803	56 836	84 525	176 054	309 126	0.435
2002	75 616	4.2	9.7	15.5	23.0	47.6	20.8	15 216	35 302	56 305	83 743	172 923	302 635	0.434
2003	76 232	4.1	9.6	15.5	23.2	47.6	20.5	14 720	34 910	56 261	84 593	173 320	298 698	0.436
2004	76 866	4.0	9.6	15.4	23.0	47.9	20.9	14 674	34 927	56 057	83 751	174 303	303 664	0.438
2005	77 418	4.0	9.6	15.3	22.9	48.1	21.1	14 767	35 137	56 227	84 095	176 292	308 636	0.440

. . . = Not available.

Table 3-6. Median Household Income by State

(2005 dollars.)

State	1990	1991	1992	1993	1994	1995	1996	1997	1998	1999	2000	2001	2002	2003	2004	2005
United States	43 366	42 108	41 774	41 562	42 038	43 346	43 967	44 883	46 508	47 671	47 599	46 569	46 036	45 970	45 817	46 326
Alabama	33 828	34 029	35 190	33 368	35 435	33 061	37 538	38 738	43 376	42 465	40 156	38 774	40 819	39 536	37 854	37 150
Alaska	56 915	56 765	56 999	57 114	59 110	60 999	65 382	58 211	60 630	60 206	59 906	63 260	57 288	55 010	56 904	55 891
Arizona	42 325	42 962	40 031	40 590	40 773	39 259	39 191	39 710	44 361	43 336	45 097	47 094	43 132	43 686	45 312	45 245
Arkansas	33 001	32 756	32 564	30 650	33 309	32 836	33 599	31 731	33 089	34 770	33 664	36 766	35 157	33 961	36 154	36 658
California	48 214	47 053	47 592	45 330	46 034	47 077	48 080	48 144	48 959	51 107	53 069	52 120	51 494	52 318	50 868	51 755
Colorado	44 510	44 027	44 294	45 882	49 294	51 779	50 728	52 437	55 735	56 435	54 684	54 475	52 425	52 997	52 588	50 449
Connecticut	56 295	58 920	55 689	52 571	53 547	51 191	52 176	53 349	55 626	56 874	59 265	56 831	57 953	58 330	56 943	56 835
Delaware	44 613	45 545	48 649	47 978	46 740	44 430	48 695	52 194	49 586	54 620	57 092	54 701	53 897	52 020	49 656	51 235
District of Columbia	39 672	41 771	41 243	36 324	39 239	39 113	39 599	38 642	39 987	41 753	41 973	44 046	40 165	41 276	41 358	41 891	44 993
Florida	38 648	38 091	37 292	37 982	38 168	37 837	37 957	39 364	41 753	41 973	44 046	40 165	41 276	41 358	41 891	42 990
Georgia	39 916	38 035	39 266	42 123	40 999	43 375	40 255	44 468	46 245	46 183	47 498	46 953	46 612	45 036	42 355	45 926
Hawaii	56 369	52 060	57 423	56 756	55 055	54 508	51 746	49 648	48 831	52 132	58 431	52 315	51 349	55 007	58 123	59 586
Idaho	36 649	36 503	37 776	41 255	41 089	41 565	42 997	40 515	43 871	41 936	42 635	42 172	40 941	44 966	45 841	44 176
Illinois	47 130	44 565	43 021	43 712	45 708	48 428	48 999	50 071	51 643	54 271	52 217	50 917	46 363	47 917	47 618	48 398
Indiana	39 000	37 863	38 902	39 213	36 297	42 467	43 539	47 168	47 520	47 838	46 323	44 530	44 558	45 022	43 745	42 437
Iowa	39 521	39 910	39 192	38 132	43 100	45 181	41 139	40 975	44 276	48 142	46 466	45 188	44 560	43 917	44 842	46 500
Kansas	43 329	40 947	41 378	39 605	36 902	38 595	40 366	44 235	43 908	43 750	46 543	45 672	46 264	46 940	42 439	42 027
Kentucky	35 889	33 216	32 023	32 429	34 652	34 652	37 919	40 153	40 573	39 521	41 109	42 388	39 906	39 197	36 801	36 699
Louisiana	32 449	35 361	34 687	35 005	33 454	35 552	37 488	40 341	37 957	38 251	34 821	36 747	36 917	35 558	37 647	37 236
Maine	39 776	38 952	40 384	36 503	39 500	43 069	42 981	39 749	42 627	45 523	42 244	40 375	40 005	39 385	42 711	43 923
Maryland	56 276	51 649	50 728	53 134	51 072	52 206	54 498	56 623	59 821	61 153	61 819	59 033	61 231	55 516	59 013	60 512
Massachusetts	52 496	49 919	49 577	49 309	52 769	49 068	48 924	50 969	50 647	53 989	52 998	57 624	49 678	46 368	47 778	43 669	45 933
Michigan	43 358	44 891	43 998	43 453	45 973	46 335	48 591	46 990	50 020	53 989	51 591	49 678	46 368	47 778	43 669	45 933
Minnesota	45 571	41 204	42 244	44 810	43 836	48 252	50 779	51 625	57 322	55 101	61 497	58 096	59 294	56 057	57 980	54 215
Mississippi	29 224	27 221	28 048	29 522	33 095	33 757	33 047	34 566	34 829	38 045	38 880	33 261	33 523	34 732	35 917	32 875
Missouri	39 585	39 033	37 308	38 158	39 336	44 299	42 447	44 335	48 082	48 476	51 121	45 588	46 435	46 441	43 546	42 986
Montana	33 854	34 702	36 168	35 215	36 001	35 308	35 533	35 431	37 768	36 358	37 155	35 428	37 814	36 196	35 092	37 313
Nebraska	39 802	41 302	40 972	41 252	41 425	41 887	42 136	42 077	43 552	45 247	47 327	48 094	46 456	46 666	45 250	47 923
Nevada	46 379	46 037	43 508	47 646	46 738	45 900	47 743	47 125	47 550	48 568	51 870	50 070	48 803	47 950	48 783	48 209
New Hampshire	59 098	50 363	53 773	50 506	45 922	49 827	48 817	49 726	53 772	53 949	57 728	56 607	60 053	58 969	58 715	56 984
New Jersey	56 098	55 978	53 178	53 880	55 088	55 088	55 873	58 802	58 244	59 594	58 259	57 138	57 093	59 235	59 476	57 124	63 368
New Mexico	36 264	37 096	35 261	35 598	35 055	33 061	31 076	36 491	37 727	38 157	39 780	36 529	38 490	37 254	40 885	38 947
New York	45 753	44 440	42 340	42 169	41 562	42 013	43 865	43 419	44 725	46 843	46 186	46 443	45 555	45 407	46 142	47 176
North Carolina	38 132	37 533	37 867	38 341	39 237	40 678	44 102	43 470	42 864	43 640	43 435	42 085	39 638	39 561	41 584	42 056
North Dakota	36 590	36 190	36 760	37 407	36 844	37 002	38 984	38 401	36 245	38 262	40 804	39 472	39 296	42 884	40 532	42 192
Ohio	43 468	41 639	42 821	41 621	41 505	44 446	42 205	43 826	46 556	46 258	48 701	46 080	46 335	46 184	44 495	44 203
Oklahoma	35 315	35 589	34 476	34 936	35 167	33 469	33 988	38 025	40 339	38 285	36 764	39 269	39 576	38 100	40 939	37 645
Oregon	42 407	42 198	43 534	44 086	40 985	46 269	43 967	45 176	46 726	47 581	48 176	45 516	45 377	44 187	42 365	44 159
Pennsylvania	42 008	42 445	40 746	41 235	41 780	43 916	43 232	45 504	46 664	44 230	47 810	47 970	46 133	45 561	45 581	46 300
Rhode Island	46 299	43 101	41 496	44 579	41 600	44 978	45 818	42 205	48 662	50 041	47 833	50 423	46 045	47 448	49 538	49 484
South Carolina	41 617	38 386	37 604	34 660	38 887	36 979	42 942	41 556	39 789	42 712	42 588	41 615	41 046	40 835	39 985	40 230
South Dakota	35 586	34 439	35 805	36 900	38 740	37 624	36 576	36 015	39 214	41 969	41 347	41 112	41 941	42 482	43 151
Tennessee	32 720	34 179	33 159	33 395	37 315	36 908	38 142	37 158	40 774	42 782	38 650	39 461	40 197	39 820	39 345	39 406
Texas	40 882	38 763	38 115	38 218	40 072	40 755	40 969	42 542	42 798	45 319	43 766	45 060	43 583	41 675	42 781	41 422
Utah	43 654	39 159	46 703	47 609	46 536	46 404	45 882	51 881	52 984	53 943	53 901	52 208	51 954	52 291	52 572	54 813
Vermont	45 039	40 751	44 663	41 328	46 648	43 025	40 084	42 515	47 091	48 712	44 883	44 987	46 677	45 909	48 912	50 704
Virginia	50 796	50 510	52 085	48 469	49 052	46 076	48 574	52 102	51 853	53 525	53 463	55 405	53 876	58 137	52 851	51 914
Washington	46 508	47 481	46 224	47 434	43 691	45 244	45 433	54 049	56 718	53 267	48 205	46 858	49 047	50 416	51 592	50 646
West Virginia	32 061	32 353	27 641	29 828	30 702	31 648	31 275	33 340	31 939	34 319	33 340	32 723	31 870	34 769	34 489	36 445
Wisconsin	44 479	43 516	45 417	42 261	46 108	52 096	49 552	48 024	49 429	53 495	51 111	50 007	49 829	49 101	47 261	44 650
Wyoming	42 667	40 604	41 191	39 169	43 179	40 106	38 344	40 538	42 161	43 632	44 922	43 802	43 164	45 160	46 915	44 718

Section 3b: Poverty

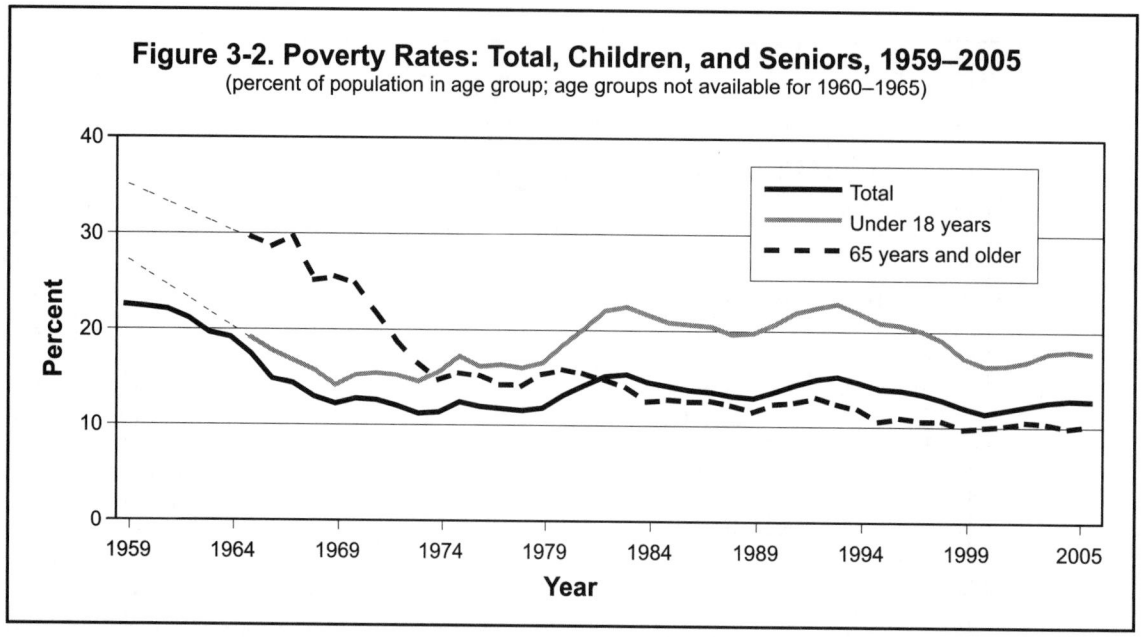

Figure 3-2. Poverty Rates: Total, Children, and Seniors, 1959–2005
(percent of population in age group; age groups not available for 1960–1965)

- The number of Americans with family incomes below the poverty line increased from 11.3 percent of the population in 2000 (which was near the all-time low reached in 1973) to 12.7 percent in 2004; the decline to 12.6 percent in 2005 was not statistically significant. (Table 3-8)

- The poverty rate for senior citizens (age 65 years and older) was 10.1 percent in 2005, lower than the rate for people age 18 to 64 years. This has not always been the case. In 1959, the first poverty rate calculations showed more than one-third of all seniors as living in poverty, compared with 17 percent of working-age adults. (Table 3-10) Between 1959 and 1974, ad hoc legislative changes raised Social Security benefits by a cumulative 104 percent—exceeding the 69 percent increase in consumer prices—and since then, each year's payments have been indexed to the rate of change in the Consumer Price Index, Urban Wage Earners and Clerical Workers (CPI-W). (See Chapter 8.) However, it should be noted that when medical expenses are taken into account, one set of recent Census Bureau estimates indicates that redefining both income and the poverty line would raise the poverty rate of the elderly above the poverty rate of working-age adults. (Table 3-17)

- The poverty rate for children, on the other hand, has always been higher than the average. The gap between the official poverty rates for children and for working-age adults has been as high as 10 percentage points (in 1959 and the early 1990s, for example) and as low as 5.3 percentage points (in 1969). (Table 3-10)

- Poverty among Hispanics (who may be of any race) was 21.8 percent in 2005, compared with 8.3 percent for non-Hispanic Whites. Poverty among Blacks was 24.9 percent and poverty among Asians was 11.1 percent. (Table 3-8)

Table 3-7. Weighted Average Poverty Thresholds by Family Size

(Dollars.)

Year	Unrelated individuals			Families of 2 people			Families, all ages								CPI-U, all items (1982–1984 = 100)
	All ages	Under 65 years	65 years and older	All ages	House-holder under 65 years	House-holder 65 years and older	3 people	4 people	5 people	6 people	7 people or more (before 1980)	7 people	8 people	9 people or more	
1959	1 467	1 503	1 397	1 894	1 952	1 761	2 324	2 973	3 506	3 944	4 849	. . .	. . .	. . .	29.2
1960	1 490	1 526	1 418	1 924	1 982	1 788	2 359	3 022	3 560	4 002	4 921	. . .	. . .	. . .	29.6
1961	1 506	1 545	1 433	1 942	2 005	1 808	2 383	3 054	3 597	4 041	4 967	. . .	. . .	. . .	29.9
1962	1 519	1 562	1 451	1 962	2 027	1 828	2 412	3 089	3 639	4 088	5 032	. . .	. . .	. . .	30.3
1963	1 539	1 581	1 470	1 988	2 052	1 850	2 442	3 128	3 685	4 135	5 092	. . .	. . .	. . .	30.6
1964	1 558	1 601	1 488	2 015	2 079	1 875	2 473	3 169	3 732	4 193	5 156	. . .	. . .	. . .	31.0
1965	1 582	1 626	1 512	2 048	2 114	1 906	2 514	3 223	3 797	4 264	5 248	. . .	. . .	. . .	31.5
1966	1 628	1 674	1 556	2 107	2 175	1 961	2 588	3 317	3 908	4 388	5 395	. . .	. . .	. . .	32.5
1967	1 675	1 722	1 600	2 168	2 238	2 017	2 661	3 410	4 516	5 550	. . .	. . .	. . .	33.4
1968	1 748	1 797	1 667	2 262	2 333	2 102	2 774	3 553	4 188	4 706	5 789	. . .	. . .	. . .	34.8
1969	1 840	1 893	1 757	2 383	2 458	2 215	2 924	3 743	4 415	4 958	6 101	. . .	. . .	. . .	36.7
1970	1 954	2 010	1 861	2 525	2 604	2 348	3 099	3 968	4 680	5 260	6 468	. . .	. . .	. . .	38.8
1971	2 040	2 098	1 940	2 633	2 716	2 448	3 229	4 137	4 880	5 489	6 751	. . .	. . .	. . .	40.5
1972	2 109	2 168	2 005	2 724	2 808	2 530	3 339	4 275	5 044	5 673	6 983	. . .	. . .	. . .	41.8
1973	2 247	2 307	2 130	2 895	2 984	2 688	3 548	4 540	5 358	6 028	7 435	. . .	. . .	. . .	44.4
1974	2 495	2 562	2 364	3 211	3 312	2 982	3 936	5 038	5 950	6 699	8 253	. . .	. . .	. . .	49.3
1975	2 724	2 797	2 581	3 506	3 617	3 257	4 293	5 500	6 499	7 316	9 022	. . .	. . .	. . .	53.8
1976	2 884	2 959	2 730	3 711	3 826	3 445	4 540	5 815	6 876	7 760	9 588	. . .	. . .	. . .	56.9
1977	3 075	3 152	2 906	3 951	4 072	3 666	4 833	6 191	7 320	8 261	10 216	. . .	. . .	. . .	60.6
1978	3 311	3 392	3 127	4 249	4 383	3 944	5 201	6 662	7 880	8 891	11 002	. . .	. . .	. . .	65.2
1979	3 689	3 778	3 479	4 725	4 878	4 390	5 784	7 412	8 775	9 914	12 280	. . .	. . .	. . .	72.6
1980	4 190	4 290	3 949	5 363	5 537	4 983	6 565	8 414	9 966	11 269	13 955	12 761	14 199	16 896	82.4
1981	4 620	4 729	4 359	5 917	6 111	5 498	7 250	9 287	11 007	12 449	. . .	14 110	15 655	18 572	90.9
1982	4 901	5 019	4 626	6 281	6 487	5 836	7 693	9 862	11 684	13 207	. . .	15 036	16 719	19 698	96.5
1983	5 061	5 180	4 775	6 483	6 697	6 023	7 938	10 178	12 049	13 630	. . .	15 500	17 170	20 310	99.6
1984	5 278	5 400	4 979	6 762	6 983	6 282	8 277	10 609	12 566	14 207	. . .	16 096	17 961	21 247	103.9
1985	5 469	5 593	5 156	6 998	7 231	6 503	8 573	10 989	13 007	14 696	. . .	16 656	18 512	22 083	107.6
1986	5 572	5 701	5 255	7 138	7 372	6 630	8 737	11 203	13 259	14 986	. . .	17 049	18 791	22 497	109.6
1987	5 778	5 909	5 447	7 397	7 641	6 872	9 056	11 611	13 737	15 509	. . .	17 649	19 515	23 105	113.6
1988	6 022	6 155	5 674	7 704	7 958	7 157	9 435	12 092	14 304	16 146	. . .	18 232	20 253	24 129	118.3
1989	6 310	6 451	5 947	8 076	8 343	7 501	9 885	12 674	14 990	16 921	. . .	19 162	21 328	25 480	124.0
1990	6 652	6 800	6 268	8 509	8 794	7 905	10 419	13 359	15 792	17 839	. . .	20 241	22 582	26 848	130.7
1991	6 932	7 086	6 532	8 865	9 165	8 241	10 860	13 924	16 456	18 587	. . .	21 058	23 582	27 942	136.2
1992	7 143	7 299	6 729	9 137	9 443	8 487	11 186	14 335	16 952	19 137	. . .	21 594	24 053	28 745	140.3
1993	7 363	7 518	6 930	9 414	9 728	8 740	11 522	14 763	17 449	19 718	. . .	22 383	24 838	29 529	144.5
1994	7 547	7 710	7 108	9 661	9 976	8 967	11 821	15 141	17 900	20 235	. . .	22 923	25 427	30 300	148.2
1995	7 763	7 929	7 309	9 933	10 259	9 219	12 158	15 569	18 408	20 804	. . .	23 552	26 237	31 280	152.4
1996	7 995	8 163	7 525	10 233	10 564	9 491	12 516	16 036	18 952	21 389	. . .	24 268	27 091	31 971	156.9
1997	8 183	8 350	7 698	10 473	10 805	9 712	12 802	16 400	19 380	21 886	. . .	24 802	27 593	32 566	160.5
1998	8 316	8 480	7 818	10 634	10 972	9 862	13 003	16 660	19 680	22 228	. . .	25 257	28 166	33 339	163.0
1999	8 499	8 667	7 990	10 864	11 213	10 075	13 289	17 030	20 128	22 730	. . .	25 918	28 970	34 436	166.6
2000	8 791	8 959	8 259	11 235	11 589	10 418	13 740	17 604	20 815	23 533	. . .	26 750	29 701	35 150	172.2
2001	9 039	9 214	8 494	11 569	11 920	10 715	14 128	18 104	21 405	24 195	. . .	27 517	30 627	36 286	177.1
2002	9 183	9 359	8 628	11 756	12 110	10 885	14 348	18 392	21 744	24 576	. . .	28 001	30 907	37 062	181.7
2003	9 393	9 573	8 825	12 015	12 384	11 133	14 680	18 810	22 245	25 122	. . .	28 544	31 589	37 656	184.0
2004	9 646	9 827	9 060	12 335	12 714	11 430	15 066	19 307	22 830	25 787	. . .	29 233	32 641	39 062	188.9
2005	9 973	10 160	9 367	12 755	13 145	11 815	15 577	19 971	23 613	26 683	. . .	30 249	33 610	40 288	195.3

. . . = Not available.

Table 3-8. Poverty Status of People by Race and Hispanic Origin

(Thousands of people, percent of population.)

Year	Number of people, all races	All races		White		White, not Hispanic		Black		Asian [1]		Hispanic (any race)	
		Number	Poverty rate (percent)	Number	Poverty rate (percent)	Number	Poverty rate (percent)	Number	Poverty rate (percent)	Number	Poverty rate (percent)	Number	Poverty rate (percent)
1959	176 557	39 490	22.4	28 484	18.1	. . .	. . .	9 927	55.1	. . .	. . .	. . .	. . .
1960	179 503	39 851	22.2	28 309	17.8	. . .	. . .	. . .	. . .	. . .	. . .	. . .	. . .
1961	181 277	39 628	21.9	27 890	17.4	. . .	. . .	. . .	. . .	. . .	. . .	. . .	. . .
1962	184 276	38 625	21.0	26 672	16.4	. . .	. . .	. . .	. . .	. . .	. . .	. . .	. . .
1963	187 258	36 436	19.5	25 238	15.3	. . .	. . .	. . .	. . .	. . .	. . .	. . .	. . .
1964	189 710	36 055	19.0	24 957	14.9	. . .	. . .	. . .	. . .	. . .	. . .	. . .	. . .
1965	191 413	33 185	17.3	22 496	13.3	. . .	. . .	. . .	. . .	. . .	. . .	. . .	. . .
1966	193 388	28 510	14.7	19 290	11.3	. . .	. . .	8 867	41.8	. . .	. . .	. . .	. . .
1967	195 672	27 769	14.2	18 983	11.0	. . .	. . .	8 486	39.3	. . .	. . .	. . .	. . .
1968	197 628	25 389	12.8	17 395	10.0	. . .	. . .	7 616	34.7	. . .	. . .	. . .	. . .
1969	199 517	24 147	12.1	16 659	9.5	. . .	. . .	7 095	32.2	. . .	. . .	. . .	. . .
1970	202 183	25 420	12.6	17 484	9.9	. . .	. . .	7 548	33.5	. . .	. . .	. . .	. . .
1971	204 554	25 559	12.5	17 780	9.9	. . .	. . .	7 396	32.5	. . .	. . .	. . .	. . .
1972	206 004	24 460	11.9	16 203	9.0	. . .	. . .	7 710	33.3	. . .	. . .	2 414	22.8
1973	207 621	22 973	11.1	15 142	8.4	12 864	7.5	7 388	31.4	. . .	. . .	2 366	21.9
1974	209 362	23 370	11.2	15 736	8.6	13 217	7.7	7 182	30.3	. . .	. . .	2 575	23.0
1975	210 864	25 877	12.3	17 770	9.7	14 883	8.6	7 545	31.3	. . .	. . .	2 991	26.9
1976	212 303	24 975	11.8	16 713	9.1	14 025	8.1	7 595	31.1	. . .	. . .	2 783	24.7
1977	213 867	24 720	11.6	16 416	8.9	13 802	8.0	7 726	31.3	. . .	. . .	2 700	22.4
1978	215 656	24 497	11.4	16 259	8.7	13 755	7.9	7 625	30.6	. . .	. . .	2 607	21.6
1979	222 903	26 072	11.7	17 214	9.0	14 419	8.1	8 050	31.0	. . .	. . .	2 921	21.8
1980	225 027	29 272	13.0	19 699	10.2	16 365	9.1	8 579	32.5	. . .	. . .	3 491	25.7
1981	227 157	31 822	14.0	21 553	11.1	17 987	9.9	9 173	34.2	. . .	. . .	3 713	26.5
1982	229 412	34 398	15.0	23 517	12.0	19 362	10.6	9 697	35.6	. . .	. . .	4 301	29.9
1983	231 700	35 303	15.2	23 984	12.1	19 538	10.8	9 882	35.7	. . .	. . .	4 633	28.0
1984	233 816	33 700	14.4	22 955	11.5	18 300	10.0	9 490	33.8	. . .	. . .	4 806	28.4
1985	236 594	33 064	14.0	22 860	11.4	17 839	9.7	8 926	31.3	. . .	. . .	5 236	29.0
1986	238 554	32 370	13.6	22 183	11.0	17 244	9.4	8 983	31.1	. . .	. . .	5 117	27.3
1987	240 982	32 221	13.4	21 195	10.4	16 029	8.7	9 520	32.4	1 021	16.1	5 422	28.0
1988	243 530	31 745	13.0	20 715	10.1	15 565	8.4	9 356	31.3	1 117	17.3	5 357	26.7
1989	245 992	31 528	12.8	20 785	10.0	15 599	8.3	9 302	30.7	939	14.1	5 430	26.2
1990	248 644	33 585	13.5	22 326	10.7	16 622	8.8	9 837	31.9	858	12.2	6 006	28.1
1991	251 192	35 708	14.2	23 747	11.3	17 741	9.4	10 242	32.7	996	13.8	6 339	28.7
1992	256 549	38 014	14.8	25 259	11.9	18 202	9.6	10 827	33.4	985	12.7	7 592	29.6
1993	259 278	39 265	15.1	26 226	12.2	18 882	9.9	10 877	33.1	1 134	15.3	8 126	30.6
1994	261 616	38 059	14.5	25 379	11.7	18 110	9.4	10 196	30.6	974	14.6	8 416	30.7
1995	263 733	36 425	13.8	24 423	11.2	16 267	8.5	9 872	29.3	1 411	14.6	8 574	30.3
1996	266 218	36 529	13.7	24 650	11.2	16 462	8.6	9 694	28.4	1 454	14.5	8 697	29.4
1997	268 480	35 574	13.3	24 396	11.0	16 491	8.6	9 116	26.5	1 468	14.0	8 308	27.1
1998	271 059	34 476	12.7	23 454	10.5	15 799	8.2	9 091	26.1	1 360	12.5	8 070	25.6
1999	276 208	32 791	11.9	22 169	9.8	14 735	7.7	8 441	23.6	1 285	10.7	7 876	22.7
2000	278 944	31 581	11.3	21 645	9.5	14 366	7.4	7 982	22.5	1 258	9.9	7 747	21.5
2001	281 475	32 907	11.7	22 739	9.9	15 271	7.8	8 136	22.7	1 275	10.2	7 997	21.4
2002	285 317	34 570	12.1	. . .	. . .	. . .	. . .	. . .	. . .	. . .	. . .	8 555	21.8
2003	287 699	35 861	12.5	. . .	. . .	. . .	. . .	. . .	. . .	. . .	. . .	9 051	22.5
2004	290 617	37 040	12.7	. . .	. . .	. . .	. . .	. . .	. . .	. . .	. . .	9 122	21.9
2005	293 135	36 950	12.6	. . .	. . .	. . .	. . .	. . .	. . .	. . .	. . .	9 368	21.8
By race													
Race alone													
2002	. . .	. . .	. . .	23 466	10.2	15 567	8.0	8 602	24.1	1 161	10.1	. . .	. . .
2003	. . .	. . .	. . .	24 272	10.5	15 902	8.2	8 781	24.4	1 401	11.8	. . .	. . .
2004	. . .	. . .	. . .	25 327	10.8	16 908	8.7	9 014	24.7	1 201	9.8	. . .	. . .
2005	. . .	. . .	. . .	24 872	10.6	16 227	8.3	9 168	24.9	1 402	11.1	. . .	. . .
Race alone or in combination													
2002	. . .	. . .	. . .	. . .	. . .	. . .	. . .	8 884	23.9	1 243	10.0	. . .	. . .
2003	. . .	. . .	. . .	. . .	. . .	. . .	. . .	9 108	24.3	1 527	11.8	. . .	. . .
2004	. . .	. . .	. . .	. . .	. . .	. . .	. . .	9 411	24.7	1 295	9.7	. . .	. . .
2005	. . .	. . .	. . .	. . .	. . .	. . .	. . .	9 517	24.7	1 501	10.9	. . .	. . .

[1] For 1987 through 2001, Asian and Pacific Islander.
. . . = Not available.

Table 3-9. Poverty Status of Families by Type of Family

(Thousands of families, percent)

Year	Married-couple families				Families with no spouse present						Unrelated individuals	
	Number of families		Poverty rate (percent)		Male householder			Female householder				
						Poverty rate (percent)			Poverty rate (percent)		Total below poverty level	Poverty rate
	Total	Total below poverty level	Total	With children under 18 years	Total below poverty level	Total	With children under 18 years	Total below poverty level	Total	With children under 18 years		
1959	39 335	. . .	. . .	. . .	. . .	. . .	. . .	1 916	42.6	59.9	4 928	46.1
1960	39 624	. . .	. . .	. . .	. . .	. . .	. . .	1 955	42.4	56.3	4 926	45.2
1961	40 405	. . .	. . .	. . .	. . .	. . .	. . .	1 954	42.1	56.0	5 119	45.9
1962	40 923	. . .	. . .	. . .	. . .	. . .	. . .	2 034	42.9	59.7	5 002	45.4
1963	41 311	. . .	. . .	. . .	. . .	. . .	. . .	1 972	40.4	55.7	4 938	44.2
1964	41 648	. . .	. . .	. . .	. . .	. . .	. . .	1 822	36.4	49.7	5 143	42.7
1965	42 107	. . .	. . .	. . .	. . .	. . .	. . .	1 916	38.4	52.2	4 827	39.8
1966	42 553	. . .	. . .	. . .	. . .	. . .	. . .	1 721	33.1	47.1	4 701	38.3
1967	43 292	. . .	. . .	. . .	. . .	. . .	. . .	1 774	33.3	44.5	4 998	38.1
1968	43 842	. . .	. . .	. . .	. . .	. . .	. . .	1 755	32.3	44.6	4 694	34.0
1969	44 436	. . .	. . .	. . .	. . .	. . .	. . .	1 827	32.7	44.9	4 972	34.0
1970	44 739	. . .	. . .	. . .	. . .	. . .	. . .	1 952	32.5	43.8	5 090	32.9
1971	45 752	. . .	. . .	. . .	. . .	. . .	. . .	2 100	33.9	44.9	5 154	31.6
1972	46 314	. . .	. . .	. . .	. . .	. . .	. . .	2 158	32.7	44.5	4 883	29.0
1973	46 812	2 482	5.3	. . .	154	10.7	. . .	2 193	32.2	43.2	4 674	25.6
1974	47 069	2 474	5.3	6.0	125	8.9	15.4	2 324	32.1	43.7	4 553	24.1
1975	47 318	2 904	6.1	7.2	116	8.0	11.7	2 430	32.5	44.0	5 088	25.1
1976	47 497	2 606	5.5	6.4	162	10.8	15.4	2 543	33.0	44.1	5 344	24.9
1977	47 385	2 524	5.3	6.3	177	11.1	14.8	2 610	31.7	41.8	5 216	22.6
1978	47 692	2 474	5.2	5.9	152	9.2	14.7	2 654	31.4	42.2	5 435	22.1
1979	49 112	2 640	5.4	6.1	176	10.2	15.5	2 645	30.4	39.6	5 743	21.9
1980	49 294	3 032	6.2	7.7	213	11.0	18.0	2 972	32.7	42.9	6 227	22.9
1981	49 630	3 394	6.8	8.7	205	10.3	14.0	3 252	34.6	44.3	6 490	23.4
1982	49 908	3 789	7.6	9.8	290	14.4	20.6	3 434	36.3	47.8	6 458	23.1
1983	50 350	3 488	6.9	9.4	292	13.1	18.1	3 498	34.5	45.7	6 740	23.1
1984	50 933	3 438	6.7	8.9	311	12.9	17.1	3 474	34.0	45.4	6 609	21.8
1985	50 081	3 815	7.6	10.1	268	13.2	20.2	3 564	36.0	47.1	6 725	21.5
1986	51 537	3 123	6.1	8.0	287	11.4	17.8	3 613	34.6	46.0	6 846	21.6
1987	51 675	3 011	5.8	7.7	340	12.0	16.8	3 654	34.2	45.5	6 857	20.8
1988	52 100	2 897	5.6	7.2	336	11.8	18.0	3 642	33.4	44.7	7 070	20.6
1989	52 317	2 931	5.6	7.3	348	12.1	18.1	3 504	32.2	42.8	6 760	19.2
1990	52 147	2 981	5.7	7.8	349	12.0	18.8	3 768	33.4	44.5	7 446	20.7
1991	52 457	3 158	6.0	8.3	392	13.0	19.6	4 161	35.6	47.1	7 773	21.1
1992	53 090	3 385	6.4	8.6	484	15.8	22.5	4 275	35.4	46.2	8 075	21.9
1993	53 181	3 481	6.5	9.0	488	16.8	22.5	4 424	35.6	46.1	8 388	22.1
1994	53 865	3 272	6.1	8.3	549	17.0	22.6	4 232	34.6	44.0	8 287	21.5
1995	53 570	2 982	5.6	7.5	493	14.0	19.7	4 057	32.4	41.5	8 247	20.9
1996	53 604	3 010	5.6	7.5	531	13.8	20.0	4 167	32.6	41.9	8 452	20.8
1997	54 321	2 821	5.2	7.1	507	13.0	18.7	3 995	31.6	41.0	8 687	20.8
1998	54 778	2 879	5.3	6.9	476	12.0	16.6	3 831	29.9	38.7	8 478	19.9
1999	56 290	2 748	4.9	6.4	485	11.8	16.3	3 559	27.8	35.7	8 400	19.1
2000	56 598	2 637	4.7	6.0	485	11.3	15.3	3 278	25.4	33.0	8 653	19.0
2001	56 755	2 760	4.9	6.1	583	13.1	17.7	3 470	26.4	33.6	9 226	19.9
2002	57 327	3 052	5.3	6.8	564	12.1	16.6	3 613	26.5	33.7	9 618	20.4
2003	57 725	3 115	5.4	7.0	636	13.5	19.1	3 856	28.0	35.5	9 713	20.4
2004	57 983	3 216	5.5	7.0	657	13.4	17.1	3 962	28.3	35.9	9 926	20.4
2005	58 189	2 944	5.1	6.5	669	13.0	17.6	4 044	28.7	36.2	10 425	21.1

. . . = Not available.

Table 3-10. Poverty Status of People by Sex and Age

(Thousands of people, percent of population.)

Year	Poverty status of people by sex				Poverty status of people by age					
	Males below poverty level		Females below poverty level		Children under 18 years below poverty level		People 18 to 64 years below poverty level		People 65 years and older below poverty level	
	Number (thousands)	Poverty rate (percent)	Number (thousands)	Poverty rate (percent)	Number (thousands)	Poverty rate (percent)	Number (thousands)	Poverty rate (percent)	Number (thousands)	Poverty rate (percent)
1959	. . .	. . .	. . .	. . .	17 552	27.3	16 457	17.0	5 481	35.2
1966	12 225	13.0	16 265	16.3	12 389	17.6	11 007	10.5	5 114	28.5
1967	11 813	12.5	15 951	15.8	11 656	16.6	10 725	10.0	5 388	29.5
1968	10 793	11.3	14 578	14.3	10 954	15.6	9 803	9.0	4 632	25.0
1969	10 292	10.6	13 978	13.6	9 691	14.0	9 669	8.7	4 787	25.3
1970	10 879	11.1	14 632	14.0	10 440	15.1	10 187	9.0	4 793	24.6
1971	10 708	10.8	14 841	14.1	10 551	15.3	10 735	9.3	4 273	21.6
1972	10 190	10.2	14 258	13.4	10 284	15.1	10 438	8.8	3 738	18.6
1973	9 642	9.6	13 316	12.5	9 642	14.4	9 977	8.3	3 354	16.3
1974	10 313	10.2	13 881	12.9	10 156	15.4	10 132	8.3	3 085	14.6
1975	10 908	10.7	14 970	13.8	11 104	17.1	11 456	9.2	3 317	15.3
1976	10 373	10.1	14 603	13.4	10 273	16.0	11 389	9.0	3 313	15.0
1977	10 340	10.0	14 381	13.0	10 288	16.2	11 316	8.8	3 177	14.1
1978	10 017	9.6	14 480	13.0	9 931	15.9	11 332	8.7	3 233	14.0
1979	10 535	10.0	14 810	13.2	10 377	16.4	12 014	8.9	3 682	15.2
1980	12 207	11.2	17 065	14.7	11 543	18.3	13 858	10.1	3 871	15.7
1981	13 360	12.1	18 462	15.8	12 505	20.0	15 464	11.1	3 853	15.3
1982	14 842	13.4	19 556	16.5	13 647	21.9	17 000	12.0	3 751	14.6
1983	15 182	13.5	20 084	16.8	13 911	22.3	17 767	12.4	3 625	13.8
1984	14 537	12.8	19 163	15.9	13 420	21.5	16 952	11.7	3 330	12.4
1985	14 140	12.3	18 923	15.6	13 010	20.7	16 598	11.3	3 456	12.6
1986	13 721	11.8	18 649	15.2	12 876	20.5	16 017	10.8	3 477	12.4
1987	14 029	12.0	18 518	15.0	12 843	20.3	15 815	10.6	3 563	12.5
1988	13 599	11.5	18 146	14.5	12 455	19.5	15 809	10.5	3 481	12.0
1989	13 366	11.2	18 162	14.4	12 590	19.6	15 575	10.2	3 363	11.4
1990	14 211	11.7	19 373	15.2	13 431	20.6	16 496	10.7	3 658	12.2
1991	15 082	12.3	20 626	16.0	14 341	21.8	17 586	11.4	3 781	12.4
1992	16 222	12.9	21 792	16.6	15 294	22.3	18 793	11.9	3 928	12.9
1993	16 900	13.3	22 365	16.9	15 727	22.7	19 781	12.4	3 755	12.2
1994	16 316	12.8	21 744	16.3	15 289	21.8	19 107	11.9	3 663	11.7
1995	15 683	12.2	20 742	15.4	14 665	20.8	18 442	11.4	3 318	10.5
1996	15 611	12.0	20 918	15.4	14 463	20.5	18 638	11.4	3 428	10.8
1997	15 187	11.6	20 387	14.9	14 113	19.9	18 085	10.9	3 376	10.5
1998	14 712	11.1	19 764	14.3	13 467	18.9	17 623	10.5	3 386	10.5
1999	14 079	10.4	18 712	13.2	12 280	17.1	17 289	10.1	3 222	9.7
2000	13 536	9.9	18 045	12.6	11 587	16.2	16 671	9.6	3 323	9.9
2001	14 327	10.4	18 580	12.9	11 733	16.3	17 760	10.1	3 414	10.1
2002	15 162	10.9	19 408	13.3	12 133	16.7	18 861	10.6	3 576	10.4
2003	15 783	11.2	20 078	13.7	12 866	17.6	19 443	10.8	3 552	10.2
2004	16 399	11.5	20 641	13.9	13 041	17.8	20 545	11.3	3 453	9.8
2005	15 950	11.1	21 000	14.1	12 896	17.6	20 450	11.1	3 603	10.1

. . . = Not available.

Table 3-11. Poverty Status of People Inside and Outside Metropolitan Areas, and People In and Near Poverty

(Thousands of people, percent of population.)

Year	Inside metropolitan areas		Central city		Outside central city		Outside metropolitan areas		Total in and near poverty (income below 1.25 times the poverty level)		Near poor (income between 1 and 1.25 times poverty level)	
	Number (thousands)	Poverty rate (percent)	Number (thousands)	Poverty rate (percent)	Number (thousands)	Poverty rate (percent)	Number (thousands)	Poverty rate (percent)	Number (thousands)	Percent	Number (thousands)	Percent
1959	17 019	15.3	10 437	18.3	6 582	12.2	21 747	33.2	54 942	31.1	15 452	8.7
1960	...	...	...	...	...	...	...	...	54 560	30.4	14 709	8.2
1961	...	...	...	...	...	...	...	...	54 280	30.0	14 652	8.1
1962	...	...	...	...	...	...	...	...	53 119	28.8	14 494	7.9
1963	...	...	...	...	...	...	...	...	50 778	27.1	14 342	7.7
1964	...	...	...	...	...	...	...	...	49 819	26.3	13 764	7.3
1965	...	...	...	...	...	...	...	...	46 163	24.1	12 978	6.8
1966	...	...	...	...	...	...	...	...	41 267	21.3	12 757	6.6
1967	13 832	10.9	8 649	15.0	5 183	7.5	13 936	20.2	39 206	20.0	11 437	5.8
1968	12 871	10.0	7 754	13.4	5 117	7.3	12 518	18.0	35 905	18.2	10 516	5.3
1969	13 084	9.5	7 993	12.7	5 091	6.8	11 063	17.9	34 665	17.4	10 518	5.3
1970	13 317	10.2	8 118	14.2	5 199	7.1	12 103	16.9	35 624	17.6	10 204	5.0
1971	14 561	10.4	8 912	14.2	5 649	7.2	10 999	17.2	36 501	17.8	10 942	5.3
1972	14 508	10.3	9 179	14.7	5 329	6.8	9 952	15.3	34 653	16.8	10 193	4.9
1973	13 759	9.7	8 594	14.0	5 165	6.4	9 214	14.0	32 828	15.8	9 855	4.7
1974	13 851	9.7	8 373	13.7	5 477	6.7	9 519	14.2	33 666	16.1	10 296	4.9
1975	15 348	10.8	9 090	15.0	6 259	7.6	10 529	15.4	37 182	17.6	11 305	5.4
1976	15 229	10.7	9 482	15.8	5 747	6.9	9 746	14.0	35 509	16.7	10 534	5.0
1977	14 859	10.4	9 203	15.4	5 657	6.8	9 861	13.9	35 659	16.7	10 939	5.1
1978	15 090	10.4	9 285	15.4	5 805	6.8	9 407	13.5	34 155	15.8	9 658	4.5
1979	16 135	10.7	9 720	15.7	6 415	7.2	9 937	13.8	36 616	16.4	10 544	4.7
1980	18 021	11.9	10 644	17.2	7 377	8.2	11 251	15.4	40 658	18.1	11 386	5.1
1981	19 347	12.6	11 231	18.0	8 116	8.9	12 475	17.0	43 748	19.3	11 926	5.3
1982	21 247	13.7	12 696	19.9	8 551	9.3	13 152	17.8	46 520	20.3	12 122	5.3
1983	21 750	13.8	12 872	19.8	8 878	9.6	13 516	18.3	47 150	20.3	11 847	5.1
1984	...	...	...	...	...	...	...	...	45 288	19.4	11 588	5.0
1985	23 275	12.7	14 177	19.0	9 097	8.4	9 789	18.3	44 166	18.7	11 102	4.7
1986	22 657	12.3	13 295	18.0	9 362	8.4	9 712	18.1	43 486	18.2	11 116	4.7
1987	23 054	12.3	13 697	18.3	9 357	8.3	9 167	17.0	43 032	17.9	10 811	4.5
1988	23 059	12.2	13 615	18.1	9 444	8.3	8 686	16.0	42 551	17.5	10 806	4.4
1989	22 917	12.0	13 592	18.1	9 326	8.0	8 611	15.7	42 653	17.3	11 125	4.5
1990	24 510	12.7	14 254	19.0	10 255	8.7	9 075	16.3	44 837	18.0	11 252	4.5
1991	26 827	13.7	15 314	20.2	11 513	9.6	8 881	16.1	47 527	18.9	11 819	4.7
1992	28 380	14.2	16 346	20.9	12 034	9.9	9 634	16.9	50 592	19.7	12 578	4.9
1993	29 615	14.6	16 805	21.5	12 810	10.3	9 650	17.2	51 801	20.0	12 536	4.8
1994	29 610	14.2	16 098	20.9	13 511	10.3	8 449	16.0	50 401	19.3	12 342	4.7
1995	28 342	13.4	16 269	20.6	12 072	9.1	8 083	15.6	48 761	18.5	12 336	4.7
1996	28 211	13.2	15 645	19.6	12 566	9.4	8 318	15.9	49 310	18.5	12 781	4.8
1997	27 273	12.6	15 018	18.8	12 255	9.0	8 301	15.9	47 853	17.8	12 280	4.6
1998	26 997	12.3	14 921	18.5	12 076	8.7	7 479	14.4	46 036	17.0	11 560	4.3
1999	25 278	11.3	13 404	16.5	11 874	8.3	7 513	14.3	45 030	16.3	12 239	4.4
2000	24 603	10.8	13 257	16.3	11 346	7.8	6 978	13.4	43 612	15.6	12 030	4.3
2001	25 446	11.1	13 394	16.5	12 052	8.2	7 460	14.2	45 320	16.1	12 413	4.4
2002	27 096	11.6	13 784	16.7	13 311	8.9	7 474	14.2	47 084	16.5	12 514	4.4
2003	28 367	12.1	14 551	17.5	13 816	9.1	7 495	14.2	48 687	16.9	12 826	4.5
2004	...	...	...	...	...	...	...	...	49 693	17.1	12 653	4.4
2005 [1]	30 098	12.2	15 966	17.0	14 132	9.3	6 852	14.5	49 327	16.8	12 377	4.2

[1]Data by residence for 2005 are based on new definitions of metropolitan and micropolitan statistical areas announced in 2003. The major categories are now entitled "inside metropolitan statistical areas" and "outside metropolitan statistical areas." The sub-categories within metropolitan statistical areas are now entitled "inside principal cities" and "outside principal cities." See "About Metropolitan and Micropolitan Statistical Areas" at <http://www.census.gov/population/www/estimates/aboutmetro.html>.
. . . = Not available.

Table 3-12. Poor People Age 16 Years and Older by Work Experience

(Thousands of people, percent of population [poverty rate], percent of total poor people.)

Year	Total number of poor people, 16 years and older	Worked		Worked year-round, full-time			Worked less than year-round or full-time			Did not work		
		Number	Percent of total poor	Number	Poverty rate (percent)	Percent of total poor	Number	Poverty rate (percent)	Percent of total poor	Number	Poverty rate (percent)	Percent of total poor
1978	16 914	6 599	39.0	1 309	. . .	7.7	5 290	. . .	31.3	10 315	. . .	61.0
1979	16 803	6 601	39.3	1 394	. . .	8.3	5 207	. . .	31.0	10 202	. . .	60.7
1980	18 892	7 674	40.6	1 644	. . .	8.7	6 030	. . .	31.9	11 218	. . .	59.4
1981	20 571	8 524	41.4	1 881	. . .	9.1	6 643	. . .	32.3	12 047	. . .	58.6
1982	22 100	9 013	40.8	1 999	. . .	9.0	7 014	. . .	31.7	13 087	. . .	59.2
1983	22 741	9 329	41.0	2 064	. . .	9.1	7 265	. . .	31.9	13 412	. . .	59.0
1984	21 541	8 999	41.8	2 076	. . .	9.6	6 923	. . .	32.1	12 542	. . .	58.2
1985	21 243	9 008	42.4	1 972	. . .	9.3	7 036	. . .	33.1	12 235	. . .	57.6
1986	20 688	8 743	42.3	2 007	. . .	9.7	6 736	. . .	32.6	11 945	. . .	57.7
1987	20 546	8 258	40.2	1 821	2.4	8.9	6 437	12.5	31.3	12 288	21.6	59.8
1988	20 323	8 363	41.2	1 929	2.4	9.5	6 434	12.7	31.7	11 960	21.2	58.8
1989	19 952	8 376	42.0	1 908	2.4	9.6	6 468	12.5	32.4	11 576	20.8	58.0
1990	21 242	8 716	41.0	2 076	2.6	9.8	6 640	12.6	31.3	12 526	22.1	59.0
1991	22 530	9 208	40.9	2 103	2.6	9.3	7 105	13.4	31.5	13 322	22.8	59.1
1992	23 951	9 739	40.6	2 211	2.7	9.2	7 528	14.1	31.4	14 212	23.7	59.3
1993	24 832	10 144	40.8	2 408	2.9	9.7	7 736	14.6	31.2	14 688	24.2	59.1
1994	24 108	9 829	40.8	2 520	2.9	10.5	7 309	13.9	30.3	14 279	23.6	59.2
1995	23 077	9 484	41.1	2 418	2.7	10.5	7 066	13.7	30.6	13 593	22.3	58.9
1996	23 472	9 586	40.8	2 263	2.5	9.6	7 323	14.1	31.2	13 886	22.7	59.2
1997	22 753	9 444	41.5	2 345	2.5	10.3	7 099	13.8	31.2	13 309	21.7	58.5
1998	22 256	9 133	41.0	2 804	2.9	12.6	6 329	12.7	28.4	13 123	21.1	59.0
1999	21 762	9 251	42.5	2 559	2.6	11.8	6 692	13.2	30.8	12 511	19.9	57.5
2000	21 080	8 511	40.4	2 439	2.4	11.6	6 072	12.1	28.8	12 569	19.8	59.6
2001	22 245	8 530	38.3	2 567	2.6	11.5	5 963	11.8	26.8	13 715	20.6	61.7
2002	23 601	8 954	37.9	2 635	2.6	11.2	6 318	12.4	26.8	14 647	21.0	62.1
2003	24 266	8 820	36.3	2 636	2.6	10.9	6 183	12.2	25.5	15 446	21.5	63.7
2004	25 256	9 384	37.2	2 891	2.8	11.4	6 493	12.8	25.7	15 871	21.7	62.8
2005	25 381	9 340	36.8	2 894	2.8	11.4	6 446	12.8	25.3	16 041	21.8	63.2

. . . = Not available.

Table 3-13. Poverty Rates by State

(Percent of population.)

State	1990	1991	1992	1993	1994	1995	1996	1997	1998	1999	2000	2001	2002	2003	2004	2005
United States	13.5	14.2	14.8	15.1	14.5	13.8	13.7	13.3	12.7	11.9	11.3	11.7	12.1	12.5	12.7	12.6
Alabama	19.2	18.8	17.3	17.4	16.4	20.1	14.0	15.7	14.5	15.2	13.3	15.9	14.5	15.0	16.9	16.7
Alaska	11.4	11.8	10.2	9.1	10.2	7.1	8.2	8.8	9.4	7.6	7.6	8.5	8.8	9.6	9.1	10.0
Arizona	13.7	14.8	15.8	15.4	15.9	16.1	20.5	17.2	16.6	12.2	11.7	14.6	13.5	13.5	14.4	15.2
Arkansas	19.6	17.3	17.5	20.0	15.3	14.9	17.2	19.7	14.7	14.7	16.5	17.8	19.8	17.8	15.1	13.8
California	13.9	15.7	16.4	18.2	17.9	16.7	16.9	16.6	15.4	14.0	12.7	12.6	13.1	13.1	13.2	13.2
Colorado	13.7	10.4	10.8	9.9	9.0	8.8	10.6	8.2	9.2	8.5	9.8	8.7	9.8	9.7	10.0	11.4
Connecticut	6.0	8.6	9.8	8.5	10.8	9.7	11.7	8.6	9.5	7.2	7.7	7.3	8.3	8.1	10.1	9.3
Delaware	6.9	7.5	7.8	10.2	8.3	10.3	8.6	9.6	10.3	10.4	8.4	6.7	9.1	7.3	9.0	9.2
District of Columbia	21.1	18.6	20.3	26.4	21.2	22.2	24.1	21.8	22.3	17.4	15.2	18.2	17.0	16.8	17.0	21.3
Florida	14.4	15.4	15.6	17.8	14.9	16.2	14.2	14.3	13.1	12.4	11.0	12.7	12.6	12.7	11.6	11.1
Georgia	15.8	17.2	17.7	13.5	14.0	12.1	14.8	14.5	13.5	12.8	12.1	12.9	11.2	11.9	13.0	14.4
Hawaii	11.0	7.7	11.2	8.0	8.7	10.3	12.1	13.9	10.9	10.8	8.9	11.4	11.3	9.3	8.6	8.6
Idaho	14.9	13.9	15.2	13.1	12.0	14.5	11.9	14.7	13.0	14.1	12.5	11.5	11.3	10.2	9.9	9.9
Illinois	13.7	13.5	15.6	13.6	12.4	12.4	12.1	11.2	10.1	9.9	10.7	10.1	12.8	12.6	12.3	11.5
Indiana	13.0	15.7	11.8	12.2	13.7	9.6	7.5	8.8	9.4	6.7	8.5	8.5	9.1	9.9	11.6	12.6
Iowa	10.4	9.6	11.5	10.3	10.7	12.2	9.6	9.6	9.1	7.4	8.3	7.4	9.2	8.9	10.9	11.3
Kansas	10.3	12.3	11.1	13.1	14.9	10.8	11.2	9.7	9.6	12.3	8.0	10.1	10.1	10.8	11.4	12.5
Kentucky	17.3	18.8	19.7	20.4	18.5	14.7	17.0	15.9	13.5	12.1	12.6	12.6	14.2	14.4	17.8	14.8
Louisiana	23.6	19.0	24.5	26.4	25.7	19.7	20.5	16.3	19.1	19.2	17.2	16.2	17.5	17.0	16.8	18.3
Maine	13.1	14.1	13.5	15.4	9.4	11.2	11.2	10.1	10.4	10.6	10.1	10.3	13.4	11.6	11.6	12.6
Maryland	9.9	9.1	11.8	9.7	10.7	10.1	10.3	8.4	7.2	7.3	7.4	7.2	7.4	8.6	9.9	9.7
Massachusetts	10.7	11.0	10.3	10.7	9.7	11.0	10.1	12.2	8.7	11.8	9.8	8.9	10.0	10.3	9.3	10.1
Michigan	14.3	14.1	13.6	15.4	14.1	12.2	11.2	10.3	11.0	9.7	9.9	9.4	11.6	11.4	13.3	12.0
Minnesota	12.0	12.9	13.0	11.6	11.7	9.2	9.8	9.6	10.3	7.3	5.7	7.4	6.5	7.4	7.0	8.1
Mississippi	25.7	23.7	24.6	24.7	19.9	23.5	20.6	16.7	17.6	16.2	14.9	19.3	18.4	16.0	18.7	20.1
Missouri	13.4	14.8	15.7	16.1	15.6	9.4	9.5	11.8	9.8	11.7	9.2	9.7	9.9	10.7	12.2	11.6
Montana	16.3	15.4	13.8	14.9	11.5	15.3	17.0	15.6	16.6	15.8	14.1	13.3	13.5	15.1	14.2	13.8
Nebraska	10.3	9.5	10.6	10.3	8.8	9.6	10.2	9.8	12.3	11.0	8.6	9.4	10.6	9.8	9.5	9.5
Nevada	9.8	11.4	14.7	9.8	11.1	11.1	8.1	11.0	10.6	11.3	8.8	7.1	8.9	10.9	10.9	10.6
New Hampshire	6.3	7.3	8.7	9.9	7.7	5.3	6.4	9.1	9.8	7.6	4.5	6.5	5.8	5.8	5.5	5.6
New Jersey	9.2	9.7	10.3	10.9	9.2	7.8	9.2	9.3	8.6	7.8	7.3	8.1	7.9	8.6	8.0	6.8
New Mexico	20.9	22.4	21.6	17.4	21.1	25.3	25.5	21.2	20.4	20.9	17.5	18.0	17.9	18.1	16.5	17.9
New York	14.3	15.3	15.7	16.4	17.0	16.5	16.7	16.5	16.7	14.2	13.9	14.2	14.0	14.3	15.0	14.5
North Carolina	13.0	14.5	15.8	14.4	14.2	12.6	12.2	11.4	14.0	13.8	12.5	12.5	14.3	15.7	14.6	13.1
North Dakota	13.7	14.5	12.1	11.2	10.4	12.0	11.0	13.6	15.1	13.1	10.4	13.8	11.6	9.7	9.7	11.2
Ohio	11.5	13.4	12.5	13.0	14.1	11.5	12.7	11.0	11.2	12.0	10.0	10.5	9.8	10.9	11.6	12.3
Oklahoma	15.6	17.0	18.6	19.9	16.7	17.1	16.6	13.7	14.1	12.8	14.9	15.1	14.1	12.8	10.8	15.6
Oregon	9.2	13.5	11.4	11.8	11.8	11.2	11.8	11.6	15.0	12.6	10.9	11.8	10.9	12.5	11.8	12.0
Pennsylvania	11.0	11.0	11.9	13.2	12.5	12.2	11.6	11.2	11.3	9.3	8.6	9.6	9.5	10.5	11.4	11.2
Rhode Island	7.5	10.4	12.4	11.2	10.3	10.6	11.0	12.7	11.6	10.0	10.2	9.6	11.0	11.5	11.5	12.1
South Carolina	16.2	16.4	19.0	18.7	13.8	19.9	13.0	13.1	13.7	11.7	11.1	15.1	14.3	12.7	14.9	15.0
South Dakota	13.3	14.0	15.1	14.2	14.5	14.5	11.8	16.5	10.8	7.7	10.7	8.4	11.5	12.7	13.5	11.8
Tennessee	16.9	15.5	17.0	19.6	14.6	15.5	15.9	14.3	13.4	11.9	13.5	14.1	14.8	14.0	15.9	14.9
Texas	15.9	17.5	18.3	17.4	19.1	17.4	16.6	16.7	15.1	15.2	15.5	14.9	15.6	17.0	16.5	16.2
Utah	8.2	12.9	9.4	10.7	8.0	8.4	7.7	8.9	9.0	5.7	7.6	10.5	9.9	9.1	10.1	9.2
Vermont	10.9	12.6	10.5	10.0	7.6	10.3	12.6	9.3	9.9	9.6	10.0	9.7	9.9	8.5	7.8	7.6
Virginia	11.1	9.9	9.5	9.7	10.7	10.2	12.3	12.7	8.8	7.9	8.3	8.0	9.9	10.0	9.4	9.2
Washington	8.9	9.5	11.2	12.1	11.7	12.5	11.9	9.2	8.9	9.6	10.8	10.7	11.0	12.6	11.4	10.2
West Virginia	18.1	17.9	22.3	22.2	18.6	16.7	18.5	16.4	17.8	15.7	14.7	16.4	16.8	17.4	14.2	15.4
Wisconsin	9.3	9.9	10.9	12.6	9.0	8.5	8.8	8.2	8.8	8.6	9.3	7.9	8.6	9.8	12.4	10.2
Wyoming	11.0	9.9	10.3	13.3	9.3	12.2	11.9	13.5	10.6	11.6	10.8	8.7	9.0	9.8	10.0	10.6

Section 3c: Alternative Measures of Income and Poverty

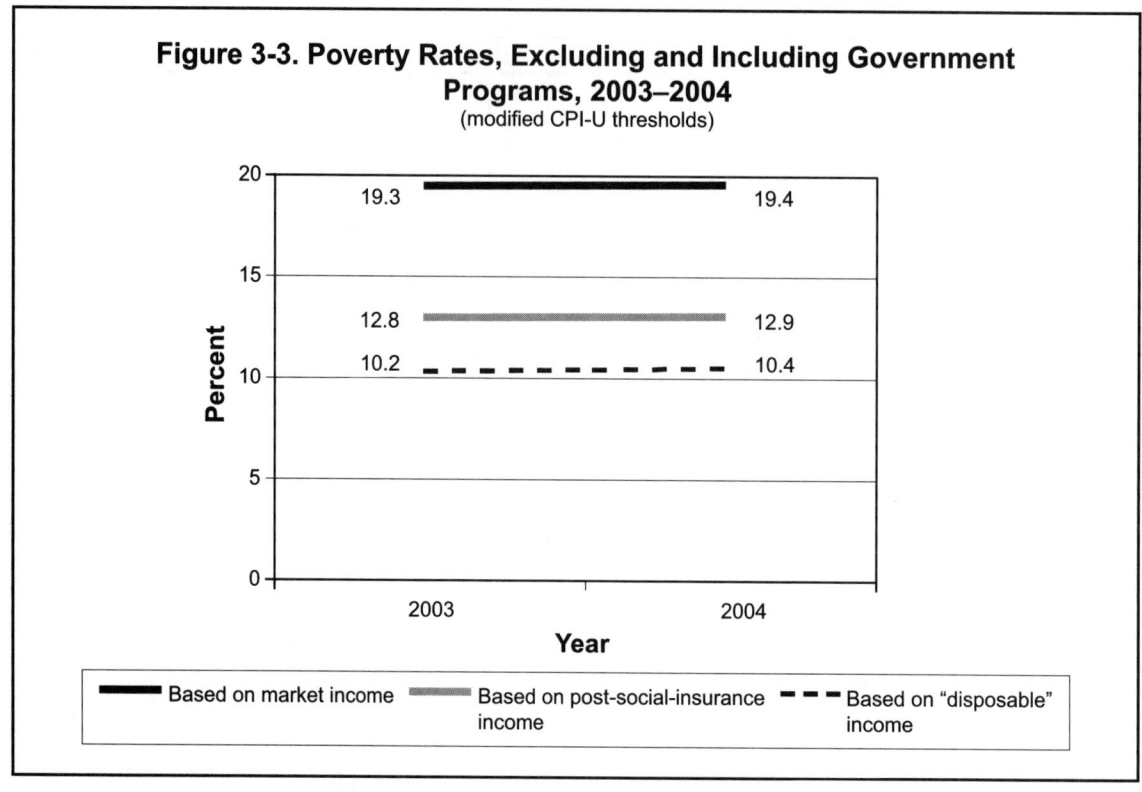

Figure 3-3. Poverty Rates, Excluding and Including Government Programs, 2003–2004
(modified CPI-U thresholds)

- The Census Bureau calculates "alternative" or "experimental" sets of income and poverty measures that change income and poverty definitions. Figure 3-3 above illustrates the differences in poverty estimates when the definition of income is varied. If family income is defined as "market income," including income generated by the economy but excluding government cash transfers such as Social Security and family assistance, much higher poverty rates are observed—19.3 percent in 2003 and 19.4 percent in 2004. (Table 3-15)

- Adding to market income the cash transfers from government social insurance programs such as Social Security, but not the "means-tested" programs such as family assistance for which only the poor are eligible, gives "post-social-insurance" poverty rates of 12.8 and 12.9 percent. (Table 3-15)

- Removing income, payroll, and property taxes; adding the Earned Income Tax Credit; and adding means-tested government transfers—family assistance, food stamps, housing, and nutrition aid—reduces measured poverty rates to 10.2 and 10.4 percent in 2003 and 2004. The percentage point reduction in poverty rates resulting from social insurance (from 19.4 percent to 12.9 percent in 2004) is more than twice the reduction resulting from the net effect of taxes and means-tested transfers (12.9 to 10.4 percent). (Table 3-15)

Table 3-14. Median Household Income and Poverty Rates for People, Based on Alternative Definitions of Income, 1979–2003

Year	Definition 1, MI: Money income excluding capital gains (current official measure)				Definition 4: Money income before taxes and cash transfers, plus realized capital gains (losses) and health insurance supplements			
	Median income (2003 dollars)	Poverty rate (percent)		Gini coefficient	Median income (2003 dollars) [2]	Poverty rate (percent)		Gini coefficient
		Official threshold	CPI-U-RS threshold [1]			Official threshold	CPI-U-RS threshold [1]	
1979	38 649	11.7	10.6	0.403	38 259	18.8	17.8	0.460
1980	37 447	13.0	11.5	0.401	36 346	20.1	19.0	0.462
1981	36 868	14.0	12.2	0.404	35 544	21.1	19.8	0.466
1982	36 811	15.0	13.2	0.409	35 118	22.0	20.6	0.475
1983	36 826	15.2	13.7	0.412	35 570	21.8	20.6	0.478
1984	37 767	14.4	12.8	0.413	36 739	20.8	19.5	0.477
1985	38 510	14.0	12.5	0.418	37 418	20.4	19.1	0.486
1986	39 868	13.6	12.2	0.423	38 937	19.9	18.7	0.505
1987	40 357	13.4	12.1	0.424	39 188	19.7	18.7	0.488
1988	40 678	13.0	11.7	0.425	39 727	19.7	18.5	0.489
1989	41 411	12.8	11.3	0.429	40 466	19.4	18.1	0.492
1990	40 865	13.5	11.9	0.426	39 348	19.9	18.7	0.487
1991	39 679	14.2	12.4	0.425	38 086	21.1	19.7	0.490
1992	39 364	14.8	13.1	0.430	37 679	22.1	20.6	0.497
1993	39 165	15.1	13.4	0.448	37 554	22.6	21.1	0.514
1994	39 613	14.5	12.6	0.450	38 438	22.0	20.3	0.515
1995	40 845	13.8	11.7	0.444	39 509	21.1	19.5	0.509
1996	41 431	13.7	11.6	0.447	40 300	20.8	19.1	0.511
1997	42 294	13.3	11.3	0.448	41 294	20.3	18.7	0.513
1998	43 825	12.7	10.6	0.446	42 643	19.3	17.4	0.509
1999	44 922	11.9	9.9	0.445	44 112	18.7	16.9	0.508
2000	44 853	11.3	9.7	0.447	44 197	18.0	16.5	0.506
2001	43 882	11.7	9.9	0.450	43 151	18.5	16.9	0.510
2002	43 381	12.1	10.1	0.448	42 422	19.0	17.4	...
2003	43 318	12.5	10.5	0.450	42 295	19.5	17.8	...

Year	Definition 14, MI - Tx + NC: Income after all taxes and transfers				Definition 15, MI - Tx + NC + HE: Income after all taxes and transfers, plus net imputed return on equity in own home			
	Median income (2003 dollars)	Poverty rate (percent)		Gini coefficient [3]	Median income (2003 dollars)	Poverty rate (percent)		Gini coefficient [3]
		Official threshold	CPI-U-RS threshold [1]			Official threshold	CPI-U-RS threshold [1]	
1979	35 435	8.9	7.9	0.359	37 776	7.5	6.7	0.352
1980	34 290	10.1	8.6	0.354	37 804	8.2	7.0	0.347
1981	33 505	11.5	9.8	0.358	39 199	8.7	7.3	0.350
1982	33 831	12.3	10.6	0.366	38 398	9.9	8.5	0.359
1983	34 359	12.7	11.0	0.374	38 203	10.4	9.0	0.368
1984	35 049	12.0	10.4	0.378	39 262	9.9	8.6	0.372
1985	35 709	11.7	10.1	0.385	39 410	9.9	8.6	0.381
1986	37 197	11.3	9.8	0.409	40 026	10.1	8.6	0.404
1987	37 696	11.0	9.5	0.382	41 065	9.7	8.2	0.380
1988	37 796	10.8	9.4	0.385	41 195	9.4	8.2	0.384
1989	38 556	10.4	8.8	0.389	41 662	9.1	7.6	0.387
1990	37 960	10.9	9.3	0.382	40 526	9.8	8.3	0.381
1991	37 443	11.4	9.7	0.380	40 127	10.3	8.6	0.379
1992	37 741	11.9	10.2	0.385	40 026	10.7	9.1	0.381
1993	38 104	12.1	10.3	0.398	40 230	11.2	9.4	0.395
1994	38 740	11.1	9.2	0.400	41 113	10.0	8.3	0.395
1995	39 922	10.3	8.5	0.394	42 263	9.4	7.6	0.388
1996	40 295	10.2	8.4	0.398	42 444	9.3	7.6	0.392
1997	40 985	10.0	8.2	0.403	43 000	9.2	7.5	0.397
1998	42 459	9.5	7.7	0.405	44 302	8.8	7.1	0.399
1999	43 328	8.9	7.2	0.408	45 354	8.2	6.5	0.402
2000	43 285	8.8	7.2	0.410	45 634	8.0	6.5	0.402
2001	43 369	9.0	7.3	0.412	45 126	8.3	6.7	0.407
2002	43 155	9.3	7.7	0.394	44 884	8.6	7.1	0.388
2003	43 629	9.7	7.9	0.394	45 154	9.0	7.4	0.390

Note: See notes and definitions for explanation of alternative definitions and thresholds and of the Gini coefficient.

[1] Before 1987, threshold based on CPI-U-X1.
[2] Years before 2002 linked by editor to Census 2002 figure based on changes in earlier Census Bureau estimates.
[3] Earlier years not comparable with 2002 and 2003 because of a change in tax estimating model.
. . . = Not available.

Table 3-15. Median Household Income and Poverty Rates with New Poverty Thresholds, Excluding and Including Effects of Government Programs, 2003–2004

Year	Based on money income				Based on market income			
	Median income (2004 dollars)	Poverty rate (percent)		Gini coefficient	Median income (2004 dollars)	Poverty rate (percent)		Gini coefficient
		CPI-U threshold	CPI-U-RS threshold			CPI-U threshold	CPI-U-RS threshold	
2003	44 483	12.5	10.4	0.450	41 983	19.3	17.3	0.492
2004	44 389	12.6	10.6	0.450	41 648	19.4	17.6	0.496

Year	Based on post-social-insurance income				Based on disposable income			
	Median income (2004 dollars)	Poverty rate (percent)		Gini coefficient	Median income (2004 dollars)	Poverty rate (percent)		Gini coefficient
		CPI-U threshold	CPI-U-RS threshold			CPI-U threshold	CPI-U-RS threshold	
2003	46 196	12.8	11.0	0.446	39 933	10.2	8.1	0.405
2004	45 968	12.9	11.2	0.449	39 754	10.4	8.3	0.400

Note: See notes and definitions for explanation of the income definitions and poverty thresholds.

Table 3-16. Official and National Academy of Sciences (NAS)–Based Poverty Rates, 1999–2004

(Percent of population.)

Measurement method	1999	2000	2001	2002 (new tax model)	2003 (revised)	2004
Official measure	11.9	11.3	11.7	12.1	12.5	12.7
MSI-GA-CPI	12.1	12.0	12.2	12.1	12.3	12.5
MIT-GA-CPI	12.7	12.5	12.5	12.6	12.7	13.0
CMB-GA-CPI	12.8	12.6	12.8	12.7	12.9	13.3
MSI-NGA-CPI	12.2	12.1	12.3	12.3	12.4	12.7
MIT-NGA-CPI	12.8	12.7	12.7	12.8	12.7	13.1
CMB-NGA-CPI	12.9	12.8	12.9	12.9	13.0	13.3
MSI-GA-CE	12.1	12.3	12.9	13.2	13.4	13.4
MIT-GA-CE	12.7	12.8	13.2	13.7	13.9	14.1
CMB-GA-CE	12.8	12.8	13.1	13.4	13.7	13.9
MSI-NGA-CE	12.2	12.5	13.0	13.4	13.5	13.4
MIT-NGA-CE	12.8	13.0	13.4	13.9	14.1	14.1
CMB-NGA-CE	12.9	13.0	13.2	13.7	13.9	13.9

Note: The Census Bureau changed the way it modeled taxes, effective with the revised 2002 estimates. Consequently, comparisons of 2002 and later data with earlier years may be affected.

MSI means "Medical out-of-pocket expenses subtracted from income."
MIT means "Medical out-of-pocket expenses in the thresholds."
CMB means "Combined methods."
GA means "Geographic adjustment (of poverty thresholds)."
NGA means "No geographic adjustment (of poverty thresholds)."
CPI means "Thresholds were adjusted since 1999 using the Consumer Price Index for All Urban Consumers."
CE means "Thresholds were recomputed since 1999 using data from the Consumer Expenditure Survey."

See notes and definitions for further explanation.

Table 3-17. Comparison of NAS-Based and Official Poverty Rates by Selected Characteristics, 2004

(Percent of population.)

Characteristic	Official poverty rate (no geographic adjustment)	NAS-based rate, MIT, CPI adjustment of 1999 thresholds	
		Without geographic adjustment	With geographic adjustment
All People	12.7	13.1	13.0
People in			
Married-couple families	6.4	6.9	7.0
Families with female householder, no husband present	30.5	28.1	27.3
By age			
Under 18 years	17.8	15.2	15.3
18 to 64 years	11.3	12.1	12.1
65 years and older	9.8	13.7	13.1
Race and Hispanic origin			
White alone	10.8	11.5	11.5
Non-Hispanic White alone	8.7	9.5	8.8
Black alone	24.7	22.9	22.0
Asian alone	9.8	11.1	13.4
Hispanic (any race)	21.9	21.7	25.3
Region			
Northeast	11.6	10.8	12.7
Midwest	11.6	12.0	10.2
South	14.1	15.1	12.8
West	12.6	12.9	16.5

Note: MIT means "Medical out-of-pocket expenses in the thresholds."

NOTES AND DEFINITIONS

TABLES 3-1 THROUGH 3-17
INCOME DISTRIBUTION AND POVERTY

SOURCE: U.S. DEPARTMENT OF COMMERCE, CENSUS BUREAU

All data in this chapter are derived from the Current Population Survey (CPS), which is also the source of the data on labor force, employment, and unemployment used in Chapter 10. (See the notes and definitions for Tables 10-1 through 10-5.) Early each year, the 60,000 households in this monthly survey are asked additional questions concerning earnings and other income in the previous year. This survey, informally known as the "March Supplement," is now formally known as the Current Population Survey Annual Social and Economic Supplement (CPS-ASEC). It was previously called the Annual Demographic Supplement.

The population represented by the survey is the civilian noninstitutional population of the United States and members of the armed forces in the United States living off post or with their families on post, but excluding all other members of the armed forces. As it is a survey of households, homeless persons are not included.

Racial classification and Hispanic origin

In 2002 and all earlier years, the CPS required respondents to report identification with only one race group. Since 2003, the CPS has allowed respondents to choose more than one race group. Income data for 2002 were collected in early 2003; thus, in the data for 2002 and all subsequent years, an individual could report identification with more than one race group. In the 2000 census, about 2.6 percent of people reported identification with more than one race.

Therefore, data from 2002 onward that are classified by race are not strictly comparable with race-classified data for 2001 and earlier years. As alternative approaches to dealing with this problem, the Census Bureau has tabulated two different race concepts for each racial category in a number of cases. In the case of Blacks, for example, this means there is one income measure for "Black alone," consisting of people who report Black and no other race, and one for "Black alone or in combination," which includes all the "Black alone" reporters plus those who report Black in combination with any other race. The tables in this volume show both the "alone" and the "alone or in combination" values where available.

The race classifications now used in the CPS are *White, Black, Asian, American Indian and Alaska Native,* and *Native Hawaiian and Other Pacific Islander.* The last two groups are too small to provide reliable data for a single year, but in a new Census Bureau table (reproduced here as Table 3-2), household income data for all five groups are presented in 2- and 3-year averages. Before 2002, the

---

The ACS: New Estimates of Income and Poverty for States and Smaller Areas

When the Census Bureau released the CPS data for 2005, it also released a report on income and poverty for states and smaller areas in 2005 based on a new, separate survey—the *American Community Survey* (ACS). According to the Census Bureau, "The ACS offers broad, comprehensive information on social, economic, and housing data and is designed to provide this information at many levels of geography, particularly for local communities." The ACS is designed to replace the decennial census "long form" questionnaire, which has been the source of decennial census data for small areas; the ACS will have the additional advantage of providing much more up-to-date information between censuses. The ACS is a much larger survey, reaching 250,000 addresses each month, but it is not designed to provide the same degree of continuity over time as the CPS. The release of the 2005 ACS data in August 2006 generated wide media interest. In many media outlets, ACS results were featured more prominently than the CPS findings, reflecting the ACS's abundance of local data.

ACS data are presented by Bernan Press in *County and City Extra.* These data, with their relatively short historical comparisons and their focus on small-area data, are outside the scope of *Business Statistics.* The Census Bureau recommends that the CPS data be used for national estimates, and *Business Statistics* will continue to present CPS data exclusively.

This volume also includes two tables of historical state data on household income and poverty based on CPS data. (Tables 3-6 and 3-13) While the CPS data are not as well designed for yielding accurate state-level estimates as the ACS data, they provide perspective on the behavior of these variables at the state level over longer periods of time. These tables should be used with caution. Typically, the Census Bureau presents CPS state data accompanied by estimates of their often-large standard errors and encourages users to reduce excessive random sampling variation by using two- or three-year moving averages.

An August 2006 press release entitled "Income Climbs, Poverty Stabilizes, Uninsured Rate Increases," available on the Census Bureau Web site, provides information about both surveys and additional references for users who require data from the ACS. It can be found at <http://www.census.gov/PressRelease/www/releases/archives/income_wealth/007419.html>. The ACS data are presented in report ACS-02 "Income, Earnings, and Poverty Data from the 2005 American Community Survey," issued August 2006, available on the Census Bureau Web site at <http://www.census.gov/prod/2006pubs/acs-02.pdf>.

category shown as "Asian" in Table 3-1 included the Native Hawaiian and Other Pacific Islander race group.

Hispanic origin is a separate question in the survey—not a racial classification—and Hispanics may be of any race. A subgroup of *White non-Hispanic* is shown in some tables. According to the Census Bureau, "Being Hispanic was reported by 12.1 percent of White householders who reported only one race, 2.9 percent of Black householders who reported only one race, 27.7 percent of American Indian and Alaska Native householders who reported only one race, and 9.5 percent of Native Hawaiian and Other Pacific Islander householders who reported only one race." ("Income, Poverty, and Health Insurance Coverage in the United States: 2005," p. 1) In an earlier report, the Census Bureau also said, "Data users should exercise caution when interpreting aggregate results for the Hispanic population or for race groups, because these populations consist of many distinct groups that differ in socioeconomic characteristics, culture, and recency of immigration." ("Income, Poverty, and Health Insurance Coverage in the United States: 2003," pp. 1-2)

Definitions

Households consists of all persons who occupy a housing unit. A household includes the related family members and all the unrelated persons, if any (such as lodgers, foster children, wards, or employees), who share the housing unit. A person living alone in a housing unit or a group of unrelated persons sharing a housing unit as partners is also counted as a household. The count of households excludes group quarters.

Earnings includes all income from work, including wages, salaries, armed forces pay, commissions, tips, piece-rate payments, and cash bonuses, before deductions such as taxes, bonds, pensions, and union dues. This category also includes net income from nonfarm self-employment and farm self-employment. Wage and salary supplements that are paid directly by the employer, such as the employer share of Social Security taxes and the cost of employer-provided health insurance, are not included.

Income, in the official definition used in the survey, is money income, including earnings from work as defined above; unemployment compensation; workers' compensation; Social Security; Supplemental Security Income; cash public assistance (welfare payments); veterans' payments; survivor benefits; disability benefits; pension or retirement income; interest income; dividends (but not capital gains); rents, royalties, and payments from estates or trusts; educational assistance, such as scholarships or grants; child support; alimony; financial assistance from outside of the household; and other cash income regularly received, such as foster child payments, military family allotments, and foreign government pensions. Receipts not counted as income include capital gains or losses, withdrawals of bank deposits, money borrowed, tax refunds, gifts, and lump-sum inheritances or insurance payments.

A *year-round, full-time worker* is a person who worked 35 or more hours per week and 50 or more weeks during the previous calendar year.

A *family* is a group of two or more persons related by birth, marriage, or adoption who reside together.

Unrelated individuals are persons 15 years old and older who are not living with any relatives. The poverty status of unrelated individuals is determined independently of and is not affected by the incomes of other persons with whom they may share a household.

Median income is the amount of income that divides the ranked income distribution into two equal groups, with half having incomes above the median and half having incomes below the median. The median income for persons is based on persons 15 years old and older with income.

Mean income is the amount obtained by dividing the total aggregate income of a group by the number of units in that group. Within the context of this survey, means are higher than medians because of the skewed nature of the income distribution; see the section "Whose Standard of Living?" in the article "Using the Data: The U.S. Economy in the New Century," which can be found at the beginning of this book.

Where available, historical income figures are shown in constant *2005 dollars*. Some data are shown in dollars for an earlier year if that year is the latest year for which the Census Bureau provided that particular data set. All constant-dollar figures are converted from current-dollar values using the *CPI-U-RS* (the Consumer Price Index, All Urban, Research Series), which measures changes in prices for past periods using the methodologies of the current CPI, and is similar in concept and behavior to the deflators used in the NIPAs for consumer income and spending. See Chapter 8 for CPI-U-RS data and the corresponding notes and definitions.

Income distribution

Income distribution is portrayed by dividing the total ranked distribution of families or households into *fifths* or *quintiles*, and also by separately tabulating the top 5 percent (which is included in the highest fifth). The households or families are arrayed from those with the lowest income to those with the highest income, then divided into five groups, with each group containing one-fifth of the total number of households. Within each quintile, incomes are summed and calculated as a share of total income for all quintiles, and are averaged to show the average or mean income within that quintile.

A statistical measure that summarizes the dispersion of income across the entire income distribution is the *Gini coefficient* (also known as Gini ratio, Gini index, or index of income concentration), which can take values ranging from 0 to 1. A Gini value of 1 indicates "perfect" inequality; that is, one household has all the income and the rest have none. A value of 0 indicates "perfect" equality, a situation in which all households have equal income.

There are small differences between the Gini coefficients presented in the report's main tables and those presented in the tables comparing alternative definitions of income. In the latter, the coefficients were recalculated, using a slightly different method for comparability with the other income definitions.

The *number of people below poverty level*, or the number of poor people, is the number of people with family or individual incomes below a specified level that is intended to measure the cost of a minimum standard of living. These minimum levels vary by size and composition of family and are known as *poverty thresholds.*

The official poverty thresholds are based on a definition developed in 1964 by Mollie Orshansky of the Social Security Administration. She calculated food budgets for families of various sizes and compositions, using an "economy food plan" developed by the U.S. Department of Agriculture (the cheapest of four plans developed). Reflecting a 1955 Department of Agriculture survey that found that families of three or more persons spent about one-third of their after-tax incomes on food, Orshansky multiplied the costs of the food plan by 3 to arrive at a set of thresholds for poverty income for families of three or larger. For 2-person families, the multiplier was 3.7; for 1-person families, the threshold was 80 percent of the 2-person threshold.

These poverty thresholds have been adjusted each year for price increases, using the percent change in the Consumer Price Index for All Urban Consumers (CPI-U).

For more information on the Orshansky thresholds (the description of which has been simplified here), see Gordon Fisher, "The Development of the Orshansky Thresholds and Their Subsequent History as the Official U.S. Poverty Measure" (May 1992), available on the Census Bureau Web site at <http://www.census.gov/hhes/poverty/povmeas/papers/orshansky.html>.

The *poverty rate* for a demographic group is the number of poor people or poor families in that group expressed as a percentage of the total number of people or families in the group.

Average poverty thresholds. The thresholds used to calculate poverty rates vary not only with the size of the family but with the number of children in the family. For example, the threshold for a 3-person family in 2005 was $15,277 if there were no children in the family but $15,735 if the family consisted of 1 adult and 2 children. For 2005, there are 48 different threshold values depending on size of household, number of children, and whether the householder is 65 years old or older (with lower thresholds for the older householders). The full matrix of thresholds is shown in the report referenced below. To give a general sense of the "poverty line," the Census Bureau also publishes the average threshold for each size family, based on the actual mix of family types in that year. These are the values shown in Table 3-7 to represent the history of poverty thresholds. The average value for 3-person families, as shown in Table 3-7, was $15,577, a weighted average of the values actually used for the 3 different possible family compositions.

Metropolitan area status. Poverty status by residence for people *inside metropolitan areas* and *outside metropolitan areas*, and with the metropolitan area group subdivided into *central city* and *outside central city*, is shown in Table 3-11 for the years 1959 and 1967–2003. Data for 2004 are not available because the sample for that year was a mixture of 1990 census–based sample design and 2000 census–based sample design, with different definitions for metropolitan areas. The data for 2005 shown in that table reflect new, somewhat different definitions, as explained in a corresponding footnote. The major categories are now entitled *inside metropolitan statistical areas* and *outside metropolitan statistical areas.* The sub-categories within the metropolitan statistical area group are now entitled *inside principal cities* and *outside principal cities.*

A person with *work experience* (Table 3-12) is one who, during the preceding calendar year and on a part-time or full-time basis, did any work for pay or profit or worked without pay on a family-operated farm or business at any time during the year. A *year-round* worker is one who worked for 50 weeks or more during the preceding calendar year. A person is classified as having worked *full time* if he or she worked 35 hours or more per week during a majority of the weeks worked. A *year-round, full-time worker* is a person who worked 35 or more hours per week and 50 or more weeks during the previous calendar year.

Toward better measures of income and poverty

The definition of the official poverty rate is established by the Office of Management of Budget in the Executive Office of the President and has not been substantially changed since 1969. Criticisms of the current definition are legion; in response to these criticisms, the Census Bureau has published extensive research work illustrating the effects of various ways of modifying income definitions and poverty thresholds. Some of the results of this work are published here in Tables 3-14 through 3-17 and explained in the notes and definitions below.

Major types of criticism

One type of criticism accepts the general concept of the Orshansky threshold but makes the income definition more realistic by including capital gains; taxes and tax credits; noncash food, housing, and health benefits provided by government and employers; and the value of home-ownership. There is debate about whether it is appropriate to use income data augmented in this way in conjunction with the official thresholds. The original 1964 thresholds made no allowance for health insurance or other health expenses—in effect, they assumed that the poor would get free medical care, or at least that the poverty calculation was not required to allow for medical needs—and it is not clear to what extent they include housing expenses in a way that is comparable with the inclusion of a homeownership component in income. Nevertheless, the Census Bureau has calculated and published income and poverty figures based on broadened income definitions and either the official thresholds or thresholds that are closely related to the official ones. Some of these calculations are presented in Tables 3-14 and 3-15 and described below.

Still accepting the validity of the basic Orshansky threshold concept, some critics have also argued that use of the CPI-U in the official measure to update the thresholds each year has overstated the price increase, and that an inflator such as the CPI-U-RS should be used instead. (See the notes and definitions for Chapter 8.) Use of the CPI-U-RS leads to lower poverty thresholds beginning in the late 1970s, when the CPI began to be distorted by housing and other biases subsequently corrected by new methods. Tables 3-14 and 3-15 also show poverty rates using the lower CPI-U-RS thresholds.

Another type of criticism argues that the official thresholds are no longer relevant to today's needs, and that the concepts of income (or "resources") and the threshold levels depicting adequate standards of living need to be rethought together. These critics cite the availability of more up-to-date information about consumer spending at various income levels. The Consumer Expenditure Survey (CEX), originally designed to provide the weights for the Consumer Price Index, is now conducted annually and provides extensive data on consumer spending patterns. To give just one example of the information available now that was not available to Orshansky, the CEX indicates that food now accounts for one-sixth, not one-third, of total family expenditures, even among low-income families. (For data and notes on the Consumer Expenditure Survey, see Bernan Press's *Handbook of U.S. Labor Statistics*.)

A special panel of the National Academy of Sciences (NAS) undertook a study that reconsidered both resources and thresholds. The Census Bureau now calculates and publishes poverty rates that have been developed following NAS recommendations, which are presented in Tables 3-16 and 3-17.

Alternative definitions of income with Orshansky-type poverty thresholds

The Census Bureau has calculated "alternative" income and poverty measures based on a number of different definitions of income. In many cases, these measures require simulation—use of data from sources other than the CPS to estimate elements of family and individual income as reported in the CPS. One system of alternatives was used for data through 2003, and another was introduced for 2004 data. Although these systems differed from each other in details, both provided poverty rates before and after the effects of various government programs, demonstrating the effects of these programs in alleviating poverty.

These alternative calculations also featured an alternative updating of poverty thresholds for price change, using the CPI-U-RS instead of the CPI-U. (See above and the notes and definitions for Chapter 8.) Use of the CPI-U-RS eliminates a presumed upward bias in the poverty rate relative to the poverty rates estimated before the bias emerged. This is a bias in the behavior of the time series given the concept of the Orshansky threshold, not necessarily a bias in the current level of poverty, since all the other criticisms of the Orshansky thresholds need to be considered when assessing the general adequacy of today's poverty measurements.

TABLE 3-14

Table 3-14 shows median household income and poverty rates according to a system of alternative income definitions that was last used in published reports for 2003 data, issued in June 2005. The income data are expressed in 2003 dollars. It is reprinted here from earlier editions of *Business Statistics* because it provides the longest time series for such comparisons.

Definition 1, also known as "MI," is the official Census Bureau definition of money income described above.

Definition 4 is Definition 1 income minus government cash transfers (Social Security, unemployment compensation, workers' compensation, veterans' payments, railroad retirement, Black Lung payments, government education assistance, Supplemental Security Income, and welfare payments), plus realized capital gains and employers' payments for health insurance coverage. Capital gains and health insurance are not collected in the CPS but are simulated using statistical data from the Internal Revenue Service and the National Medical Care Expenditure Survey. Definition 4 is the closest approach in this set of calculations to a measure of the income generated by the workings of the economy before government interventions in the form of taxes and transfer payments. Income according to this definition was only published by the Census Bureau for 2002 and 2003 in its last report using this framework. It has been extended back to 1979 on an estimated 2003-dollar basis by the editor, using estimates for the same concept of income published in earlier Census Bureau reports.

Definition 14, also known as "MI - Tx + NC," is income after all government income and earnings tax and transfer interventions. It consists of Definition 4 income minus payroll taxes and federal and state income taxes, plus the Earned Income Credit; plus all of the cash transfers listed above as being subtracted from money income to yield Definition 4; plus the "fungible" value of Medicare and

Medicaid (see below for definition); plus the value of regular-price school lunches provided by government; and plus the value of noncash transfers, including food stamps, rent subsidies, and free and reduced-price school lunches. The tax information is not collected in the CPS but is simulated using statistical data from the Internal Revenue Service, Social Security payroll tax formulas, and a model of each state's income tax regulations.

The "fungible" value approach to medical benefits counts such benefits as income only to the extent that they free up resources that would have been spent on medical care. Therefore, if family income is not sufficient to cover the family's basic food and housing requirements, Medicare and Medicaid are treated as having no income value. Data on average Medicare and Medicaid outlays per enrollee are used in the valuation process.

Food stamp values are reported in the March CPS. Estimates of other government subsidy payments use data from the Department of Agriculture (for school lunches) and the 1985 American Housing Survey.

Definition 15 ("MI - Tx + NC + HE") is Definition 14 income plus the net imputed return on equity in owner-occupied housing—the calculated annual benefit of converting one's home equity into an annuity, net of property taxes. This concept can be thought of as measuring the extent to which equity in the home relieves the owner of the need for rental or mortgage payments. Information from the 1987 American Housing Survey is used to assign values of home equity and amounts of property taxes. Since disposable personal income in the national income and product accounts (NIPAs) includes the imputed rent on owner-occupied housing plus most of the cash and in-kind transfers included in Definitions 14 and 15, Definition 15 is the Census Bureau income definition closest to the NIPA concept.

TABLE 3-15

For the years 2003 and 2004, the Census Bureau redefined alternative income measures—and modified the poverty thresholds as well—in a report issued in February 2006 entitled "The Effects of Government Taxes and Transfers on Income and Poverty: 2004," available on the Census Bureau Web site at <http://www.census.gov>. Selected statistics for 2003 and 2004 from this report are shown in Table 3-15.

In this report, the Orshansky poverty thresholds were modified using a more systematic formula to adjust the basic official 4-person, 2-child threshold for different family sizes and compositions. The distinction between families with householders over and under the age of 65 years was also dropped. Otherwise, these thresholds still conform to the basic Orshansky calculation of the costs of a food budget times multipliers derived from budgets observed in 1955. These modified thresholds were then inflated to 2003 and 2004 price levels on both a CPI-U and a CPI-U-RS basis.

Money income is the concept used in the official income and poverty measures, and consists of cash income before deductions for taxes and other expenses. It does not include lump-sum payments, capital gains, or noncash benefits such as food stamps.

Market income includes money income except government cash transfers; includes imputed realized capital gains and losses; includes the imputed rate of return on home equity; and subtracts imputed work expenses <u>other than child care</u>. As an approach to an estimate of income generated by the economy before any government interventions, it is somewhat similar to Definition 4 in the earlier measures, but differs in that it excludes health insurance, includes home equity return, and deducts certain work expenses.

Post-social-insurance income is market income plus government non-means-tested cash transfers, of which Social Security is the dominant example. It differs from the official money income measure in that it includes capital gains and losses and the return on home equity, is adjusted to exclude certain work expenses, and excludes means-tested cash transfers (family assistance, Supplemental Security Income, and means-tested veterans' payments).

Disposable income is post-social-insurance income plus means-tested cash transfers, plus the value of nonmedical means-tested noncash transfers (food stamps, public or subsidized housing, and free or reduced-price school lunches), minus federal payroll taxes, federal and state income taxes, and property taxes on owner-occupied homes. It also includes the Earned Income Tax Credit. Disposable income is roughly similar to Definition 15 in the earlier calculations defined above, except that neither health insurance nor government medical programs are included and work expenses are deducted.

Measures based on NAS recommendations—Tables 3-16 and 3-17

The alternative poverty rates shown in Tables 3-14 and 3-15, which use broader definitions of income and/or eliminate some price-index bias, seem to remedy some of the alleged shortcomings of the official definition. However, they do not reflect the now-available improved data that can be used to measure need in a much more precise way than Orshansky's method. The most recent calculations of experimental poverty measures that redefine both income and need are presented in "Alternative Poverty Estimates in the United States: 2003" (see below for complete reference) and updated through 2004 on the Census Bureau Web site at <http://www.census.gov>.

To derive these estimates, a baseline set of poverty thresholds for the year 1999, based on data from the CEX for the years 1997–1999, was developed as follows:

- A reference family type was selected: a 2-adult, 2-child family falling between the 30th and 35th percentile of the distribution of expenditures in the CEX. The value of expenditures on the total of food, clothing, shelter, and utilities by such families was multiplied by about 1.23 to account for other necessities, not including health care. For health care, three different treatments were developed; these treatments are described below.

- Equivalence scale adjustments were used to convert the threshold for the reference family to thresholds for other family sizes and compositions, accounting for the differing needs of adults and children and the economies of scale of living in larger families.

- For some of the experimental measures, thresholds were adjusted geographically to reflect differences in the cost of living (in practice, difference in housing costs) in different areas.

The family incomes to be compared with these poverty thresholds were defined and measured to include the effects of all taxes, tax credits, and in-kind benefits such as food stamps, but not the value of homeownership, and to allow for expenses such as child care that are necessary to hold a job.

The 12 measures shown in Table 3-16 are reprinted from Table B-3 in "Alternative Poverty Estimates in the United States: 2003," and updated from the table "Alternative Poverty Estimates Based on National Academy of Sciences Recommendations, by Geographic and Inflationary Adjustments: 2003 and 2004"; these sources are available on the Census Bureau Web site.

- *MSI* indicates that in calculating the poverty rate, medical out-of-pocket expenses are subtracted from family income before comparing that income to the family's threshold.

- *MIT* indicates that poverty thresholds were increased to take the family's potential medical out-of-pocket expenses into account, using the CEX and the 1996 Medical Expenditures Panel Survey, with the amounts depending on family size, age, and health insurance coverage.

- *CMB* indicates that expected medical out-of-pocket expenses were included in the thresholds, and the difference between each family's spending and the expected spending was subtracted from family income—and if the difference was negative, the amount was added to income. This way, families that were "unexpectedly healthy" were classified as better off.

- *GA* indicates that the thresholds were adjusted geographically. Measures labeled NGA were not.

- *CPI* indicates that the thresholds established for 1999 were updated to the four succeeding years using the percent change in the CPI-U. This means that the threshold

has been held constant in real (inflation-adjusted) terms since 1999, just as the official threshold was intended to be held constant in real terms since 1964.

- *CE* indicates that the thresholds were updated using median expenditures from the latest available 12 quarters of CEX data. This means that as the actual real living standards of the reference lower-middle-income family rises (or falls), the real standard of living represented by the poverty thresholds will rise (or fall) commensurately.

In Table 3-17, poverty rates for 2004 using one of the NAS-based concepts—adjustment with the CPI, with medical out-of-pocket expenses in the threshold—are shown with and without the geographic adjustment to demonstrate the impact of the new methods and the geographic adjustment.

Notes on the data

The following are the principal changes that may affect year-to-year comparability of all income and poverty data from the CPS.

- Beginning in 1952, the estimates are based on 1950 census population controls. Earlier figures were based on 1940 census population controls.

- Beginning in 1962, 1960 census–based sample design and population controls are fully implemented.

- With 1971 and 1972 data, 1970 census–based sample design and population controls were introduced.

- With 1983–1985 data, 1980 census–based sample design was introduced; 1980 population controls were introduced; and these were extended back to 1979 data.

- With 1993 data, there was a major redesign of the CPS, including the introduction of computer-assisted interviewing. The limits used to "code" reported income amounts were changed, resulting in reporting of higher income values for the highest-income families and, consequently, an exaggerated year-to-year increase in income inequality. (It is possible that this jump actually reflects in one year an increase that had emerged more gradually, so that the distribution measures for 1993 and later years may be properly comparable with data for decades earlier even if they should not be directly compared with 1992.) In addition, 1990 census–based population controls were introduced, and these were extended back to the 1992 data.

- With 1995 data, the 1990 census–based sample design was implemented and the sample was reduced by 7,000 households.

- Data for 2001 implemented population controls based on the 2000 census, which were carried back to 1999. Data from 2000 forward also incorporate results from a 28,000-household sample expansion.

For more information on these and other changes that could affect comparability, see "Current Population Survey Technical Paper 63RV: Design and Methodology" (March 2002), and footnotes to CPS historical income tables; both are available on the Census Bureau Web site at <http://www.census.gov/hhes/income>.

Data availability

Data embodying the official definitions of income and poverty are published annually in late summer or early fall by the Census Bureau, as part of a series with the general title *Current Population Reports: Consumer Income, P60*. Most of the data in this chapter were derived from report P60-231, "Income, Poverty, and Health Insurance Coverage in the United States: 2005" (August 2006).

All of the alternative income and poverty estimates through 2003 in this volume were published in two reports, both issued in June 2005: P60-228, "Alternative Income Estimates in the United States: 2003"; and P60-227, "Alternative Poverty Estimates in the United States: 2003." The NAS-based data for 2004 with revised estimates for 2003 are posted on the Census Bureau Web site under the title "Alternative Poverty Estimates Based on National Academy of Sciences Recommendations, by Geographic and Inflationary Adjustments: 2003 and 2004." The data in Table 3-15 are found in "The Effects of Government Taxes and Transfers on Income and Poverty: 2004" (February 2006). These reports and the related data, including historical tabulations, used in *Business Statistics* are available on the Census Bureau Web site at <http://www.census.gov>, under the general headings of "Income" and "Poverty."

References

Definitions and descriptions of the concepts and data of the official and alternative series are provided in the source documents listed above and in the references contained therein.

Additional descriptive material on the NAS-based experimental poverty measures is found in the Census report P60-216, "Experimental Poverty Measures: 1999" (October 2001), available at <http://www.census.gov/prod/2001pubs/p60-216.pdf>; and in Kathleen S. Short and Thesia I. Garner, "A Decade of Experimental Poverty Thresholds 1990 to 2000" (June 27, 2002), available at <http://www.census.gov/hhes/www/povmeas/papers/decade.pdf>.

CHAPTER 4: CONSUMER INCOME AND SPENDING

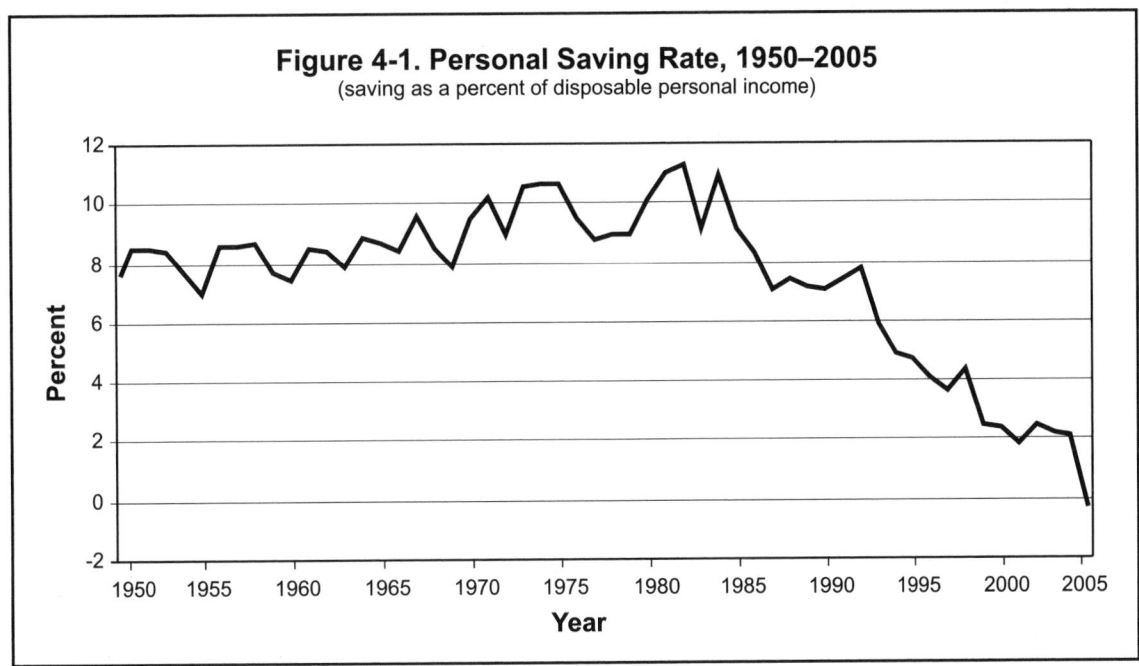

Figure 4-1. Personal Saving Rate, 1950–2005
(saving as a percent of disposable personal income)

- The personal saving rate—saving as a percent of disposable income—averaged 8 to 10 percent for much of the postwar period, but commenced a marked downtrend around 1987. From 1999 through 2004, the saving rate averaged only 2 percent. In 2005, for the first year since 1933 (the bottom of the Great Depression), personal saving was negative—consumers in the aggregate spent more than their income. (Tables 4-1, 18-1, and 19-6) Uninsured property losses caused by Hurricane Katrina provide only a partial explanation for the negative saving figure.

- It should be noted that personal income does not, by definition, include any capital gains. Despite that, the taxes on realized capital gains are deducted from personal income to get after-tax income (along with all other income taxes). Capital gains are a source of spending power in addition to current disposable income; they can be converted into cash by asset sales, refinancing, and home equity loans. Capital gains on common stock and housing have been particularly strong in recent years, but may not be a reliable source for continued gains in wealth and spending power in the future. (Table 12-10)

- Although low personal saving may not necessarily signal aggregate consumer impoverishment, due to the additional resources provided to consumers by capital gains, it still contributes to the need for foreign financing to fill the gap between investment and national saving. (Table 5-1)

- Labor compensation, excluding social insurance contributions, made up 60.1 percent of total personal income in 2005. This was about the same as in 2000, but was down from 65.4 percent in 1948. ("Contributions for social insurance," mainly Social Security taxes, are excluded from both the numerator and the denominator of this percentage.) Transfer payments accounted for a rising share of personal income over the period. It should be noted that, just as "consumption expenditures" in the national income and product accounts includes all spending financed by government health insurance programs such as Medicare and Medicaid, the transfer payment component of income (as defined here) includes the equivalent payments on behalf of persons by these same programs. Proprietors' and rental income made up a declining share of personal income, while the shares of dividends and interest (particularly the latter) rose. (Table 4-1)

Table 4-1. Personal Income and Its Disposition

(Billions of current dollars, except as noted; quarterly data are at seasonally adjusted annual rates.) **NIPA Table 2.1**

Year and quarter	Personal income													
	Total	Compensation of employees, received	Proprietors' income with IVA and CCAdj	Rental income of persons with CCAdj	Personal income receipts on assets			Personal current transfer receipts	Government social benefits to persons					
					Total	Personal interest income	Personal dividend income	Total	Total	Social Security and Medicare	Government unemployment insurance	Veterans	Family assistance	Other
1950	229.0	155.3	37.6	9.2	18.6	9.7	8.8	14.0	13.4	1.0	1.5	7.7	0.6	2.7
1951	258.0	181.4	42.7	10.1	19.1	10.5	8.6	11.4	10.5	1.9	0.9	4.6	0.6	2.6
1952	275.4	196.2	43.1	11.2	19.9	11.3	8.6	11.9	11.0	2.2	1.1	4.3	0.5	2.9
1953	291.9	210.3	42.1	12.5	21.6	12.7	8.9	12.5	11.7	3.0	1.0	4.1	0.5	3.0
1954	294.5	209.2	42.3	13.5	23.2	14.0	9.3	14.3	13.7	3.6	2.2	4.2	0.6	3.2
1955	316.1	225.7	44.3	13.9	25.7	15.2	10.5	15.7	14.8	4.9	1.5	4.4	0.6	3.3
1956	339.6	244.5	45.8	14.2	28.2	16.9	11.3	16.8	15.6	5.7	1.5	4.4	0.6	3.4
1957	358.7	257.5	47.9	14.6	30.6	18.9	11.7	19.5	18.1	7.3	1.9	4.5	0.7	3.7
1958	369.0	259.5	50.1	15.4	31.9	20.3	11.6	23.5	22.2	8.5	4.1	4.7	0.8	4.1
1959	392.8	281.0	50.7	16.2	34.6	22.0	12.6	24.2	22.9	10.2	2.8	4.6	0.9	4.5
1960	411.5	296.4	50.8	17.1	37.9	24.5	13.4	25.7	24.4	11.1	3.0	4.6	1.0	4.7
1961	429.0	305.3	53.2	17.9	40.1	26.2	13.9	29.5	28.1	12.6	4.3	5.0	1.1	5.1
1962	456.7	327.1	55.4	18.8	44.1	29.1	15.0	30.4	28.8	14.3	3.1	4.7	1.3	5.5
1963	479.6	345.2	56.5	19.5	47.9	31.7	16.2	32.2	30.3	15.2	3.0	4.8	1.4	5.9
1964	514.6	370.7	59.4	19.6	53.8	35.6	18.2	33.5	31.3	16.0	2.7	4.7	1.5	6.4
1965	555.7	399.5	63.9	20.2	59.4	39.2	20.2	36.2	33.9	18.1	2.3	4.9	1.7	7.0
1966	603.9	442.7	68.2	20.8	64.1	43.4	20.7	39.6	37.5	20.8	1.9	4.9	1.9	8.1
1967	648.3	475.1	69.8	21.2	69.0	47.5	21.5	48.0	45.8	25.8	2.2	5.6	2.3	9.9
1968	712.0	524.3	74.3	20.9	75.2	51.6	23.5	56.1	53.3	30.5	2.1	5.9	2.8	11.9
1969	778.5	577.6	77.4	21.2	84.1	59.9	24.2	62.3	59.0	33.1	2.2	6.7	3.5	13.4
1970	838.8	617.2	78.4	21.4	93.5	69.2	24.3	74.7	71.7	38.6	4.0	7.7	4.8	16.6
1971	903.5	658.3	84.8	22.4	101.0	75.9	25.0	88.1	85.4	44.7	5.8	8.8	6.2	20.0
1972	992.7	725.1	95.9	23.4	109.6	82.8	26.8	97.9	94.8	49.8	5.7	9.7	6.9	22.7
1973	1 110.7	811.3	113.5	24.3	124.7	94.8	29.9	112.6	108.6	60.9	4.4	10.4	7.2	25.7
1974	1 222.6	890.7	113.1	24.3	146.4	113.2	33.2	133.3	128.6	70.3	6.8	11.8	8.0	31.7
1975	1 335.0	949.0	119.5	23.7	162.2	129.3	32.9	170.0	163.1	81.5	17.6	14.5	9.3	40.2
1976	1 474.8	1 059.2	132.2	22.3	178.4	139.5	39.0	184.0	177.3	93.3	15.8	14.4	10.1	43.7
1977	1 633.2	1 180.4	145.7	20.7	205.3	160.6	44.7	194.2	189.1	105.3	12.7	13.8	10.6	46.7
1978	1 837.7	1 335.8	166.6	22.1	234.8	184.0	50.7	209.6	203.2	116.9	9.1	13.9	10.8	52.5
1979	2 062.1	1 501.0	180.1	23.8	274.7	217.3	57.4	235.3	227.1	132.5	9.4	14.4	11.1	59.6
1980	2 307.9	1 651.8	174.1	30.0	338.7	274.7	64.0	279.5	270.8	154.8	15.7	15.0	12.5	72.8
1981	2 591.3	1 825.7	183.0	38.0	421.9	348.3	73.6	318.4	307.2	182.1	15.6	16.1	13.1	80.2
1982	2 775.3	1 925.9	176.3	38.8	488.4	410.8	77.6	354.8	342.4	204.6	25.1	16.4	12.9	83.4
1983	2 960.7	2 043.0	192.5	37.8	529.6	446.3	83.3	383.7	369.9	222.2	26.2	16.6	13.8	91.0
1984	3 289.5	2 255.4	243.3	40.2	607.9	517.2	90.6	400.1	380.4	237.8	15.9	16.4	14.5	95.9
1985	3 526.7	2 424.9	262.3	41.9	654.0	556.6	97.4	424.9	402.6	253.0	15.7	16.7	15.2	102.0
1986	3 722.4	2 570.1	275.7	33.5	695.5	589.5	106.0	451.0	428.0	268.9	16.3	16.7	16.1	109.9
1987	3 947.4	2 750.2	302.2	33.5	717.0	604.9	112.2	467.6	447.4	282.6	14.5	16.6	16.4	117.3
1988	4 253.7	2 967.2	341.6	40.6	769.3	639.5	129.7	496.6	476.0	300.2	13.2	16.9	16.9	128.8
1989	4 587.8	3 145.2	363.3	43.1	878.0	720.2	157.8	543.4	519.9	325.6	14.3	17.3	17.5	145.3
1990	4 878.6	3 338.2	380.6	50.7	924.0	755.2	168.8	595.2	573.1	351.8	18.0	17.8	19.2	166.2
1991	5 051.0	3 445.3	377.1	60.3	932.0	751.7	180.3	666.4	648.5	381.7	26.6	18.3	21.1	200.8
1992	5 362.0	3 651.2	427.6	78.0	910.9	723.4	187.4	749.4	729.8	414.4	38.9	19.3	22.2	234.9
1993	5 558.5	3 794.9	453.8	95.6	901.8	699.6	202.2	790.1	775.7	443.4	34.1	20.1	22.8	255.3
1994	5 842.5	3 979.6	473.3	119.7	950.8	716.8	234.0	827.3	812.2	475.4	23.5	20.1	23.2	270.0
1995	6 152.3	4 177.0	492.1	122.1	1 016.4	763.2	253.2	877.4	858.4	506.8	21.4	20.9	22.6	286.7
1996	6 520.6	4 386.9	543.2	131.5	1 089.2	793.0	296.2	925.0	902.1	537.7	22.0	21.7	20.3	300.4
1997	6 915.1	4 664.6	576.0	128.8	1 181.7	848.7	333.0	951.2	931.8	563.2	19.9	22.5	17.9	308.3
1998	7 423.0	5 020.1	627.8	137.5	1 283.2	933.2	349.9	978.6	952.6	575.1	19.5	23.4	17.4	317.3
1999	7 802.4	5 352.0	678.3	147.3	1 264.2	928.6	335.6	1 022.1	988.0	588.9	20.3	24.3	17.9	336.7
2000	8 429.7	5 782.7	728.4	150.3	1 387.0	1 011.0	376.1	1 084.0	1 041.6	620.8	20.3	25.1	18.4	357.0
2001	8 724.1	5 942.1	771.9	167.4	1 380.0	1 011.0	369.0	1 193.9	1 143.9	668.5	31.7	26.7	18.1	398.9
2002	8 881.9	6 091.2	768.4	152.9	1 333.2	936.1	397.2	1 286.2	1 248.9	707.5	53.2	29.6	17.7	440.9
2003	9 163.6	6 310.4	811.3	133.0	1 336.6	914.1	422.6	1 351.0	1 316.7	741.3	52.8	32.0	18.4	472.2
2004	9 731.4	6 665.3	911.1	127.0	1 427.9	890.8	537.1	1 426.5	1 398.4	791.4	36.0	34.3	18.4	518.4
2005	10 239.2	7 030.3	970.7	72.8	1 519.4	945.0	574.4	1 526.6	1 480.9	844.9	31.3	36.8	18.3	549.4
2003														
1st quarter	8 998.2	6 191.0	779.1	137.4	1 329.1	919.7	409.4	1 327.0	1 290.5	728.7	50.9	31.5	18.1	461.3
2nd quarter	9 111.3	6 275.4	801.6	130.5	1 334.9	919.6	415.3	1 344.0	1 308.3	738.0	54.6	31.9	18.3	465.5
3rd quarter	9 203.6	6 340.8	823.5	116.3	1 339.5	914.6	424.9	1 365.5	1 331.6	744.7	54.3	32.3	18.5	481.8
4th quarter	9 341.3	6 434.3	840.8	147.6	1 343.1	902.4	440.7	1 367.6	1 336.4	753.9	51.4	32.3	18.5	480.3
2004														
1st quarter	9 497.7	6 525.4	877.5	140.1	1 366.1	892.8	473.4	1 399.3	1 373.7	774.2	43.0	33.7	18.4	504.4
2nd quarter	9 640.5	6 611.7	910.2	132.0	1 389.8	889.0	500.8	1 416.7	1 393.0	786.4	35.5	34.0	18.4	518.8
3rd quarter	9 767.9	6 714.6	915.1	112.7	1 415.7	889.1	526.6	1 441.7	1 403.2	796.5	33.3	34.5	18.4	520.6
4th quarter	10 019.4	6 809.4	941.5	123.4	1 539.8	892.3	647.5	1 448.4	1 423.5	808.4	32.3	34.9	18.3	529.7
2005														
1st quarter	10 048.8	6 889.6	952.8	118.5	1 464.3	912.3	552.0	1 487.3	1 456.3	832.2	32.8	36.4	18.3	536.6
2nd quarter	10 161.5	6 953.7	965.8	102.8	1 500.5	934.8	565.7	1 510.1	1 477.2	844.4	30.7	36.7	18.3	547.1
3rd quarter	10 262.7	7 093.6	967.3	-11.5	1 532.7	951.2	581.5	1 569.0	1 489.2	848.5	30.2	37.0	18.4	555.1
4th quarter	10 483.7	7 184.4	996.8	81.5	1 580.2	981.7	598.5	1 539.8	1 500.8	854.6	31.6	37.2	18.5	558.8

Table 4-1. Personal Income and Its Disposition—Continued

(Billions of current dollars, except as noted; quarterly data are at seasonally adjusted annual rates.) **NIPA Table 2.1**

Year and quarter	Personal current transfer receipts—Cont. From business, net	Less: Contributions for government social insurance	Less: Personal current taxes	Equals: Disposable personal income	Total	Personal consumption expenditures	Personal interest payments	Personal current transfer payments Total	To government	To the rest of the world, net	Saving Billions of dollars	Percent of disposable personal income	Disposable personal income, billions of chained (2000) dollars
1950	0.6	5.5	18.9	210.1	195.0	192.2	2.0	0.8	0.3	0.4	15.1	7.2	1 260.0
1951	0.9	6.6	27.1	231.0	211.5	208.5	2.2	0.7	0.3	0.4	19.5	8.4	1 297.3
1952	0.9	6.9	32.0	243.4	222.9	219.5	2.6	0.8	0.4	0.4	20.5	8.4	1 339.4
1953	0.8	7.1	33.2	258.6	237.1	233.1	3.2	0.9	0.4	0.5	21.5	8.3	1 404.5
1954	0.6	8.1	30.2	264.3	244.3	240.0	3.4	0.9	0.4	0.5	20.0	7.6	1 422.1
1955	0.9	9.1	32.9	283.3	263.6	258.8	4.0	0.8	0.4	0.4	19.7	6.9	1 516.7
1956	1.2	10.0	36.6	303.0	277.2	271.7	4.6	1.0	0.5	0.5	25.8	8.5	1 589.7
1957	1.4	11.4	38.9	319.8	292.8	286.9	4.9	1.1	0.6	0.5	27.0	8.5	1 628.5
1958	1.2	11.4	38.5	330.5	302.2	296.2	5.0	1.0	0.6	0.4	28.3	8.6	1 642.6
1959	1.3	13.8	42.3	350.5	323.9	317.6	5.5	0.8	0.3	0.5	26.7	7.6	1 715.5
1960	1.3	16.4	46.1	365.4	338.8	331.7	6.2	0.8	0.3	0.5	26.7	7.3	1 759.7
1961	1.4	17.0	47.3	381.8	349.6	342.1	6.5	1.0	0.5	0.5	32.2	8.4	1 819.2
1962	1.5	19.1	51.6	405.1	371.3	363.3	7.0	1.1	0.5	0.5	33.8	8.3	1 908.2
1963	1.9	21.7	54.6	425.1	391.8	382.7	7.9	1.2	0.5	0.7	33.3	7.8	1 979.1
1964	2.2	22.4	52.1	462.5	421.7	411.4	8.9	1.3	0.6	0.7	40.8	8.8	2 122.8
1965	2.3	23.4	57.7	498.1	455.1	443.8	9.9	1.4	0.6	0.8	43.0	8.6	2 253.3
1966	2.1	31.3	66.4	537.5	493.1	480.9	10.7	1.6	0.8	0.8	44.4	8.3	2 371.9
1967	2.3	34.9	73.0	575.3	520.9	507.8	11.1	2.0	1.0	1.0	54.4	9.5	2 475.9
1968	2.8	38.7	87.0	625.0	572.2	558.0	12.2	2.0	1.0	1.0	52.8	8.4	2 588.0
1969	3.3	44.1	104.5	674.0	621.4	605.2	14.0	2.2	1.1	1.1	52.5	7.8	2 668.7
1970	2.9	46.4	103.1	735.7	666.2	648.5	15.2	2.6	1.3	1.3	69.5	9.4	2 781.7
1971	2.7	51.2	101.7	801.8	721.2	701.9	16.6	2.8	1.5	1.3	80.6	10.1	2 907.9
1972	3.1	59.2	123.6	869.1	791.9	770.6	18.1	3.1	1.8	1.4	77.2	8.9	3 046.5
1973	3.9	75.5	132.4	978.3	875.6	852.4	19.8	3.4	1.8	1.5	102.7	10.5	3 252.3
1974	4.7	85.2	151.0	1 071.6	958.0	933.4	21.2	3.4	2.1	1.3	113.6	10.6	3 228.5
1975	6.8	89.3	147.6	1 187.4	1 061.9	1 034.4	23.7	3.8	2.5	1.3	125.6	10.6	3 302.6
1976	6.7	101.3	172.3	1 302.5	1 180.2	1 151.9	23.9	4.4	3.0	1.3	122.3	9.4	3 432.2
1977	5.1	113.1	197.5	1 435.7	1 310.4	1 278.6	27.0	4.8	3.5	1.3	125.3	8.7	3 552.9
1978	6.5	131.3	229.4	1 608.3	1 465.8	1 428.5	31.9	5.4	3.9	1.5	142.5	8.9	3 718.8
1979	8.2	152.7	268.7	1 793.5	1 634.4	1 592.2	36.2	5.9	4.3	1.6	159.1	8.9	3 811.2
1980	8.6	166.2	298.9	2 009.0	1 807.5	1 757.1	43.6	6.8	5.0	1.8	201.4	10.0	3 857.7
1981	11.2	195.7	345.2	2 246.1	2 001.8	1 941.1	49.3	11.4	6.0	5.5	244.3	10.9	3 960.0
1982	12.4	208.9	354.1	2 421.2	2 150.4	2 077.3	59.5	13.6	7.1	6.6	270.8	11.2	4 044.9
1983	13.8	226.0	352.3	2 608.4	2 374.8	2 290.6	69.2	15.0	8.1	6.9	233.6	9.0	4 177.7
1984	19.7	257.5	377.4	2 912.0	2 597.3	2 503.3	77.0	16.9	9.2	7.8	314.8	10.8	4 494.1
1985	22.3	281.4	417.4	3 109.3	2 829.3	2 720.3	90.4	18.6	10.4	8.2	280.0	9.0	4 645.2
1986	22.9	303.4	437.3	3 285.1	3 016.7	2 899.7	96.1	20.9	12.0	9.0	268.4	8.2	4 791.0
1987	20.2	323.1	489.1	3 458.3	3 216.9	3 100.2	93.6	23.1	13.2	9.9	241.4	7.0	4 874.5
1988	20.6	361.5	505.0	3 748.7	3 475.8	3 353.6	96.8	25.4	14.8	10.6	272.9	7.3	5 082.6
1989	23.5	385.2	566.1	4 021.7	3 734.5	3 598.5	108.2	27.8	16.5	11.4	287.1	7.1	5 224.8
1990	22.2	410.1	592.8	4 285.8	3 986.4	3 839.9	116.1	30.4	18.4	12.0	299.4	7.0	5 324.2
1991	17.9	430.2	586.7	4 464.3	4 140.1	3 986.1	118.5	35.6	22.6	13.0	324.2	7.3	5 351.7
1992	19.6	455.0	610.6	4 751.4	4 385.4	4 235.3	111.8	38.3	26.0	12.3	366.0	7.7	5 536.3
1993	14.4	477.7	646.6	4 911.9	4 627.9	4 477.9	107.3	42.7	28.5	14.2	284.0	5.8	5 594.2
1994	15.1	508.2	690.7	5 151.8	4 902.4	4 743.3	112.8	46.3	30.9	15.4	249.5	4.8	5 746.4
1995	19.0	532.8	744.1	5 408.2	5 157.3	4 975.8	132.7	48.9	32.6	16.2	250.9	4.6	5 905.7
1996	22.9	555.2	832.1	5 688.5	5 460.0	5 256.8	150.3	52.9	34.9	18.0	228.4	4.0	6 080.9
1997	19.4	587.2	926.3	5 988.8	5 770.5	5 547.4	163.9	59.2	38.2	21.0	218.3	3.6	6 295.8
1998	26.0	624.2	1 027.0	6 395.9	6 119.1	5 879.5	174.5	65.2	40.6	24.6	276.8	4.3	6 663.9
1999	34.1	661.4	1 107.5	6 695.0	6 536.4	6 282.5	181.0	73.0	44.7	28.3	158.6	2.4	6 861.3
2000	42.4	702.7	1 235.7	7 194.0	7 025.6	6 739.4	204.7	81.5	50.0	31.5	168.5	2.3	7 194.0
2001	50.0	731.1	1 237.3	7 486.8	7 354.5	7 055.0	212.2	87.2	54.2	33.0	132.3	1.8	7 333.3
2002	37.3	750.0	1 051.8	7 830.1	7 645.4	7 350.7	196.4	98.2	58.2	40.0	184.7	2.4	7 562.2
2003	34.3	778.6	1 001.1	8 162.5	7 987.7	7 703.6	182.5	101.5	61.3	40.2	174.9	2.1	7 729.9
2004	28.1	826.4	1 049.8	8 681.6	8 507.2	8 211.5	186.0	109.7	66.8	42.9	174.3	2.0	8 010.8
2005	45.7	880.6	1 203.1	9 036.1	9 070.9	8 742.4	209.4	119.2	72.0	47.1	-34.8	-0.4	8 104.6
2003													
1st quarter	36.4	765.4	1 022.7	7 975.5	7 826.4	7 548.1	179.1	99.1	59.5	39.6	149.1	1.9	7 591.7
2nd quarter	35.6	775.0	1 023.7	8 087.6	7 913.7	7 628.4	184.4	100.9	60.6	40.3	173.9	2.2	7 685.7
3rd quarter	33.9	782.1	942.6	8 261.0	8 067.0	7 782.6	184.6	99.8	61.8	38.0	194.0	2.3	7 804.8
4th quarter	31.2	791.9	1 015.4	8 326.0	8 143.5	7 855.3	181.9	106.3	63.2	43.1	182.5	2.2	7 837.3
2004													
1st quarter	25.6	810.8	1 016.0	8 481.6	8 302.7	8 018.0	177.3	107.4	64.7	42.7	178.9	2.1	7 912.4
2nd quarter	23.7	819.8	1 033.4	8 607.1	8 438.7	8 148.1	181.1	109.5	66.2	43.3	168.3	2.0	7 958.8
3rd quarter	38.4	831.8	1 061.6	8 706.3	8 565.1	8 265.0	189.3	110.7	67.6	43.2	141.2	1.6	8 013.3
4th quarter	24.8	843.1	1 088.2	8 931.2	8 722.3	8 414.8	196.2	111.2	68.9	42.4	208.9	2.3	8 158.8
2005													
1st quarter	31.0	863.6	1 157.9	8 890.9	8 838.5	8 519.7	199.8	119.0	69.9	49.0	52.5	0.6	8 076.6
2nd quarter	33.0	871.5	1 191.8	8 969.7	9 000.4	8 674.6	208.5	117.3	71.3	46.0	-30.8	-0.3	8 085.8
3rd quarter	79.8	888.5	1 215.0	9 047.7	9 180.3	8 847.3	214.6	118.5	72.7	45.8	-132.6	-1.5	8 074.1
4th quarter	39.0	898.9	1 247.6	9 236.1	9 264.5	8 927.8	214.9	121.8	74.2	47.6	-28.5	-0.3	8 183.3

Table 4-2. Personal Consumption Expenditures: Current Dollars, Constant Dollars, and Price Indexes

(Billions of dollars, except as noted; quarterly data are at seasonally adjusted annual rates.)   NIPA Tables 1.1.6, 2.3.4, 2.3.5, 2.3.6

Year and quarter	Personal consumption expenditures											
	Current dollars				Chained (2000) dollars				Chain-type price indexes (2000 = 100)			
	Total	Durable goods	Nondurable goods	Services	Total	Durable goods	Nondurable goods	Services	Total	Durable goods	Nondurable goods	Services
1950	192.2	30.7	98.2	63.3	1 152.8	...	...	...	16.7	39.8	19.5	11.6
1951	208.5	29.9	109.2	69.5	1 171.2	...	...	...	17.8	42.5	21.1	12.1
1952	219.5	29.3	114.7	75.4	1 208.2	...	...	...	18.2	42.9	21.3	12.6
1953	233.1	32.7	117.8	82.5	1 265.7	...	...	...	18.4	42.5	21.2	13.2
1954	240.0	31.9	119.7	88.4	1 291.4	...	...	...	18.6	41.6	21.3	13.6
1955	258.8	38.8	124.7	95.2	1 385.5	...	...	...	18.7	41.4	21.2	13.9
1956	271.7	38.1	130.8	102.8	1 425.4	...	...	...	19.1	42.5	21.5	14.3
1957	286.9	40.0	137.1	109.8	1 460.7	...	...	...	19.6	44.1	22.1	14.7
1958	296.2	37.4	141.7	117.0	1 472.3	...	...	...	20.1	44.9	22.6	15.1
1959	317.6	42.7	148.5	126.5	1 554.6	...	...	...	20.4	45.7	22.8	15.5
1960	331.7	43.3	152.8	135.6	1 597.4	...	...	...	20.8	45.4	23.1	15.9
1961	342.1	41.8	156.6	143.8	1 630.3	...	...	...	21.0	45.6	23.2	16.2
1962	363.3	46.9	162.8	153.6	1 711.1	...	...	...	21.2	45.8	23.4	16.5
1963	382.7	51.6	168.2	162.9	1 781.6	...	...	...	21.5	45.9	23.7	16.7
1964	411.4	56.7	178.6	176.1	1 888.4	...	...	...	21.8	46.1	24.0	17.0
1965	443.8	63.3	191.5	189.0	2 007.7	...	...	...	22.1	45.7	24.4	17.3
1966	480.9	68.3	208.7	203.8	2 121.8	...	...	...	22.7	45.5	25.2	17.8
1967	507.8	70.4	217.1	220.3	2 185.0	...	...	...	23.2	46.2	25.8	18.3
1968	558.0	80.8	235.7	241.6	2 310.5	...	...	...	24.2	47.7	26.8	19.1
1969	605.2	85.9	253.1	266.1	2 396.4	...	...	...	25.3	49.1	28.1	20.1
1970	648.5	85.0	272.0	291.5	2 451.9	...	...	...	26.4	50.1	29.4	21.2
1971	701.9	96.9	285.5	319.5	2 545.5	...	...	...	27.6	52.0	30.4	22.3
1972	770.6	110.4	308.0	352.2	2 701.3	...	...	...	28.5	52.5	31.4	23.3
1973	852.4	123.5	343.1	385.8	2 833.8	...	...	...	30.1	53.3	33.8	24.4
1974	933.4	122.3	384.5	426.6	2 812.3	...	...	...	33.2	56.7	38.7	26.3
1975	1 034.4	133.5	420.7	480.2	2 876.9	...	...	...	36.0	61.8	41.7	28.6
1976	1 151.9	158.9	458.3	534.7	3 035.5	...	...	...	37.9	65.3	43.3	30.6
1977	1 278.6	181.2	497.1	600.2	3 164.1	...	...	...	40.4	68.1	45.9	32.9
1978	1 428.5	201.7	550.2	676.6	3 303.1	...	...	...	43.2	72.0	49.0	35.5
1979	1 592.2	214.4	624.5	753.3	3 383.4	...	...	...	47.1	76.8	54.1	38.3
1980	1 757.1	214.2	696.1	846.9	3 374.1	...	...	...	52.1	83.3	60.4	42.3
1981	1 941.1	231.3	758.9	950.8	3 422.2	...	...	...	56.7	88.9	65.1	46.7
1982	2 077.3	240.2	787.6	1 049.4	3 470.3	...	...	...	59.9	92.4	67.0	50.5
1983	2 290.6	280.8	831.2	1 178.6	3 668.6	...	...	...	62.4	94.2	68.4	53.8
1984	2 503.3	326.5	884.6	1 292.2	3 863.3	...	...	...	64.8	95.6	70.0	56.7
1985	2 720.3	363.5	928.7	1 428.1	4 064.0	...	...	...	66.9	96.6	71.5	59.3
1986	2 899.7	403.0	958.4	1 538.3	4 228.9	...	...	...	68.6	97.7	71.3	62.0
1987	3 100.2	421.7	1 015.3	1 663.3	4 369.8	...	...	...	70.9	100.5	73.7	64.3
1988	3 353.6	453.6	1 083.5	1 816.5	4 546.9	...	...	...	73.8	101.9	76.2	67.5
1989	3 598.5	471.8	1 166.7	1 960.0	4 675.0	...	...	...	77.0	103.7	79.8	70.7
1990	3 839.9	474.2	1 249.9	2 115.9	4 770.3	453.5	1 484.0	2 851.7	80.5	104.6	84.2	74.2
1991	3 986.1	453.9	1 284.8	2 247.4	4 778.4	427.9	1 480.5	2 900.0	83.4	106.1	86.8	77.5
1992	4 235.3	483.6	1 330.5	2 421.2	4 934.8	453.0	1 510.1	3 000.8	85.8	106.8	88.1	80.7
1993	4 477.9	526.7	1 379.4	2 571.8	5 099.8	488.4	1 550.4	3 085.7	87.8	107.8	89.0	83.3
1994	4 743.3	582.2	1 437.2	2 723.9	5 290.7	529.4	1 603.9	3 176.6	89.7	110.0	89.6	85.7
1995	4 975.8	611.6	1 485.1	2 879.1	5 433.5	552.6	1 638.6	3 259.9	91.6	110.7	90.6	88.3
1996	5 256.8	652.6	1 555.5	3 048.7	5 619.4	595.9	1 680.4	3 356.0	93.5	109.5	92.6	90.8
1997	5 547.4	692.7	1 619.0	3 235.8	5 831.8	646.9	1 725.3	3 468.0	95.1	107.1	93.8	93.3
1998	5 879.5	750.2	1 683.6	3 445.7	6 125.8	720.3	1 794.4	3 615.0	96.0	104.2	93.8	95.3
1999	6 282.5	817.6	1 804.8	3 660.0	6 438.6	804.6	1 876.6	3 758.0	97.6	101.6	96.2	97.4
2000	6 739.4	863.3	1 947.2	3 928.8	6 739.4	863.3	1 947.2	3 928.8	100.0	100.0	100.0	100.0
2001	7 055.0	883.7	2 017.1	4 154.3	6 910.4	900.7	1 986.7	4 023.2	102.1	98.1	101.5	103.3
2002	7 350.7	923.9	2 079.6	4 347.2	7 099.3	964.8	2 037.1	4 100.4	103.5	95.8	102.1	106.0
2003	7 703.6	942.7	2 190.2	4 570.8	7 295.3	1 020.6	2 103.0	4 178.8	105.6	92.4	104.1	109.4
2004	8 211.5	986.3	2 345.2	4 880.1	7 577.1	1 085.7	2 179.2	4 323.9	108.4	90.8	107.6	112.9
2005	8 742.4	1 033.1	2 539.3	5 170.0	7 841.2	1 145.3	2 276.8	4 436.6	111.5	90.2	111.5	116.5
2003												
1st quarter	7 548.1	911.5	2 159.0	4 477.7	7 184.9	971.4	2 072.5	4 143.3	105.1	93.8	104.2	108.1
2nd quarter	7 628.4	937.3	2 155.4	4 535.6	7 249.3	1 009.8	2 084.2	4 161.3	105.2	92.8	103.4	109.0
3rd quarter	7 782.6	964.4	2 216.8	4 601.4	7 352.9	1 049.6	2 123.0	4 190.7	105.9	91.8	104.4	109.8
4th quarter	7 855.3	957.4	2 229.5	4 668.4	7 394.3	1 051.4	2 132.5	4 220.2	106.2	91.0	104.6	110.6
2004												
1st quarter	8 018.0	971.5	2 284.7	4 761.8	7 479.8	1 067.0	2 155.3	4 268.2	107.2	91.0	106.0	111.6
2nd quarter	8 148.1	976.2	2 327.8	4 844.2	7 534.4	1 071.4	2 164.3	4 308.4	108.2	91.1	107.6	112.4
3rd quarter	8 265.0	990.9	2 355.5	4 918.6	7 607.1	1 093.9	2 184.0	4 341.5	108.7	90.6	107.9	113.3
4th quarter	8 414.8	1 006.4	2 412.7	4 995.7	7 687.1	1 110.3	2 213.1	4 377.4	109.5	90.6	109.0	114.1
2005												
1st quarter	8 519.7	1 013.1	2 450.2	5 056.4	7 739.4	1 116.8	2 241.5	4 395.3	110.1	90.7	109.3	115.0
2nd quarter	8 674.6	1 042.3	2 508.6	5 123.7	7 819.8	1 150.8	2 268.4	4 420.0	110.9	90.6	110.6	115.9
3rd quarter	8 847.3	1 057.3	2 584.9	5 205.1	7 895.3	1 175.9	2 287.6	4 454.5	112.1	89.9	113.0	116.9
4th quarter	8 927.8	1 019.6	2 613.5	5 294.7	7 910.2	1 137.9	2 309.6	4 476.7	112.9	89.6	113.2	118.3

. . . = Not available.

Table 4-3. Personal Consumption Expenditures by Major Type of Product

(Billions of dollars, quarterly data are at seasonally adjusted annual rates.)

NIPA Table 2.3.5

Year and quarter	Personal consumption expenditures, total	Durable goods				Nondurable goods					
		Total	Motor vehicles and parts	Furniture and household equipment	Other durable goods	Total	Food	Clothing and shoes	Gasoline and oil	Fuel oil and coal	Other nondurable goods
1950	192.2	30.7	13.7	13.7	3.3	98.2	53.9	19.6	5.5	3.4	15.8
1951	208.5	29.9	12.2	14.1	3.6	109.2	60.7	21.3	6.1	3.5	17.6
1952	219.5	29.3	11.4	14.0	3.9	114.7	64.1	22.0	6.8	3.5	18.4
1953	233.1	32.7	13.9	14.7	4.1	117.8	65.4	22.2	7.4	3.4	19.4
1954	240.0	31.9	12.8	14.8	4.3	119.7	66.8	22.3	7.8	3.5	19.3
1955	258.8	38.8	17.7	16.4	4.6	124.7	68.6	23.3	8.6	3.8	20.4
1956	271.7	38.1	15.8	17.3	5.0	130.8	71.4	24.4	9.4	3.9	21.7
1957	286.9	40.0	17.6	17.2	5.2	137.1	75.1	24.5	10.2	4.1	23.2
1958	296.2	37.4	15.1	16.9	5.4	141.7	77.9	24.9	10.6	4.2	24.2
1959	317.6	42.7	18.9	18.1	5.7	148.5	80.6	26.4	11.3	4.0	26.1
1960	331.7	43.3	19.7	18.0	5.7	152.8	82.3	27.0	12.0	3.8	27.7
1961	342.1	41.8	17.8	18.3	5.7	156.6	84.0	27.6	12.0	3.8	29.2
1962	363.3	46.9	21.5	19.3	6.1	162.8	86.1	29.0	12.6	3.8	31.4
1963	382.7	51.6	24.4	20.7	6.6	168.2	88.2	29.8	13.0	4.0	33.1
1964	411.4	56.7	26.0	23.2	7.5	178.6	93.5	32.4	13.6	4.1	35.0
1965	443.8	63.3	29.9	25.1	8.2	191.5	100.7	34.1	14.8	4.4	37.6
1966	480.9	68.3	30.3	28.2	9.8	208.7	109.3	37.4	16.0	4.7	41.4
1967	507.8	70.4	30.0	30.0	10.4	217.1	112.4	39.2	17.1	4.8	43.5
1968	558.0	80.8	36.1	32.9	11.8	235.7	122.2	43.2	18.6	4.7	47.0
1969	605.2	85.9	38.4	34.7	12.9	253.1	131.5	46.5	20.5	4.6	50.2
1970	648.5	85.0	35.5	35.7	13.7	272.0	143.8	47.8	21.9	4.4	54.1
1971	701.9	96.9	44.5	37.8	14.6	285.5	149.7	51.7	23.2	4.6	56.4
1972	770.6	110.4	51.1	42.4	16.9	308.0	161.4	56.4	24.4	5.1	60.8
1973	852.4	123.5	56.1	47.9	19.5	343.1	179.6	62.5	28.1	6.3	66.6
1974	933.4	122.3	49.5	51.5	21.3	384.5	201.8	66.0	36.1	7.8	72.7
1975	1 034.4	133.5	54.8	54.5	24.2	420.7	223.2	70.8	39.7	8.4	78.5
1976	1 151.9	158.9	71.3	60.2	27.4	458.3	242.5	76.6	43.0	10.1	86.0
1977	1 278.6	181.2	83.5	67.2	30.5	497.1	262.6	84.1	46.9	11.1	92.4
1978	1 428.5	201.7	93.1	74.3	34.3	550.2	289.6	94.3	50.1	11.5	104.7
1979	1 592.2	214.4	93.5	82.7	38.2	624.5	324.7	101.2	66.2	14.4	118.0
1980	1 757.1	214.2	87.0	86.7	40.5	696.1	356.0	107.3	86.7	15.4	130.6
1981	1 941.1	231.3	95.8	92.1	43.4	758.9	383.5	117.2	97.9	15.8	144.5
1982	2 077.3	240.2	102.9	93.4	43.9	787.6	403.4	120.5	94.1	14.5	155.2
1983	2 290.6	280.8	126.5	106.6	47.7	831.2	423.8	130.9	93.1	13.6	169.8
1984	2 503.3	326.5	152.1	119.0	55.4	884.6	447.4	142.5	94.6	13.9	186.3
1985	2 720.3	363.5	175.9	128.5	59.0	928.7	467.6	152.1	97.2	13.6	198.2
1986	2 899.7	403.0	194.1	143.0	66.0	958.4	492.0	163.1	80.1	11.3	211.9
1987	3 100.2	421.7	195.0	153.4	73.2	1 015.3	515.2	174.4	85.4	11.2	229.1
1988	3 353.6	453.6	209.4	163.7	80.5	1 083.5	553.5	185.5	88.3	11.7	244.5
1989	3 598.5	471.8	215.3	171.6	84.9	1 166.7	591.6	198.9	98.6	11.9	265.7
1990	3 839.9	474.2	212.8	171.6	89.8	1 249.9	636.8	204.1	111.2	12.9	285.0
1991	3 986.1	453.9	193.5	171.7	88.7	1 284.8	657.5	208.7	108.5	12.4	297.8
1992	4 235.3	483.6	213.0	178.7	91.9	1 330.5	669.3	221.9	112.4	12.2	314.7
1993	4 477.9	526.7	234.0	193.4	99.3	1 379.4	691.9	229.9	114.1	12.4	331.1
1994	4 743.3	582.2	260.5	213.4	108.3	1 437.2	720.6	238.1	116.2	12.8	349.5
1995	4 975.8	611.6	266.7	228.6	116.3	1 485.1	740.9	241.7	120.2	13.1	369.2
1996	5 256.8	652.6	284.9	242.9	124.8	1 555.5	768.7	250.2	130.4	14.3	391.9
1997	5 547.4	692.7	305.1	256.2	131.4	1 619.0	796.2	258.1	134.4	13.3	416.9
1998	5 879.5	750.2	336.1	273.1	141.0	1 683.6	829.8	270.9	122.4	11.5	449.0
1999	6 282.5	817.6	370.8	293.9	153.0	1 804.6	873.1	286.3	137.9	11.9	495.6
2000	6 739.4	863.3	386.5	312.9	163.9	1 947.2	925.2	297.3	175.7	15.8	532.9
2001	7 055.0	883.7	407.9	312.1	163.7	2 017.1	967.9	297.7	171.6	15.4	564.4
2002	7 350.7	923.9	429.3	323.1	171.6	2 079.6	1 001.9	303.5	164.5	14.2	595.5
2003	7 703.6	942.7	431.7	331.5	179.4	2 190.2	1 046.0	310.9	192.7	16.9	623.7
2004	8 211.5	986.3	437.9	356.5	191.8	2 345.2	1 114.8	325.1	230.4	18.4	656.5
2005	8 742.4	1 033.1	448.2	377.2	207.7	2 539.3	1 201.4	341.8	280.2	21.9	694.0
2003											
1st quarter	7 548.1	911.5	419.3	320.2	172.0	2 159.0	1 026.8	303.0	200.1	18.1	611.0
2nd quarter	7 628.4	937.3	433.8	326.9	176.6	2 155.4	1 033.8	307.8	182.7	16.2	615.0
3rd quarter	7 782.6	964.4	443.3	337.2	183.8	2 216.8	1 056.6	316.8	195.8	16.5	631.2
4th quarter	7 855.3	957.4	430.4	341.7	185.4	2 229.5	1 066.7	316.1	192.2	16.9	637.7
2004											
1st quarter	8 018.0	971.5	433.8	348.8	188.9	2 284.7	1 089.4	323.8	213.0	17.6	641.0
2nd quarter	8 148.1	976.2	431.9	353.9	190.3	2 327.8	1 104.6	321.5	231.8	17.4	652.5
3rd quarter	8 265.0	990.9	438.6	359.7	192.6	2 355.5	1 119.3	325.1	230.4	18.6	662.0
4th quarter	8 414.8	1 006.4	447.4	363.6	195.4	2 412.7	1 145.9	330.1	246.5	19.9	670.4
2005											
1st quarter	8 519.7	1 013.1	443.6	368.4	201.2	2 450.2	1 165.3	335.5	249.3	20.5	679.6
2nd quarter	8 674.6	1 042.3	459.6	374.4	208.3	2 508.6	1 191.9	341.5	264.3	21.3	689.7
3rd quarter	8 847.3	1 057.3	468.1	380.0	209.2	2 584.9	1 214.7	341.3	308.2	22.8	698.0
4th quarter	8 927.8	1 019.6	421.6	386.0	212.0	2 613.5	1 233.7	349.1	299.1	23.0	708.6

Table 4-3. Personal Consumption Expenditures by Major Type of Product—Continued

(Billions of dollars, quarterly data are at seasonally adjusted annual rates.)

NIPA Table 2.3.5

Year and quarter	Services Total	Housing	Household operation Total	Electricity and gas	Other household operation	Transportation	Medical care	Recreation	Other services
1950	63.3	21.7	9.5	3.3	6.2	6.0	7.2	3.9	15.0
1951	69.5	24.3	10.4	3.7	6.7	7.0	7.7	4.0	16.0
1952	75.4	27.0	11.2	4.1	7.1	7.4	8.5	4.3	17.1
1953	82.5	29.9	12.1	4.5	7.6	8.0	9.5	4.5	18.5
1954	88.4	32.3	12.7	5.0	7.7	8.2	10.5	4.8	20.0
1955	95.2	34.4	14.2	5.5	8.7	8.6	11.2	5.2	21.7
1956	102.8	36.7	15.4	6.1	9.3	9.2	12.1	5.6	23.8
1957	109.8	39.3	16.4	6.5	9.9	9.7	13.4	5.6	25.4
1958	117.0	42.0	17.5	7.1	10.4	9.9	14.8	5.8	27.0
1959	126.5	45.0	18.7	7.6	11.1	10.6	16.4	6.4	29.4
1960	135.6	48.2	20.3	8.3	12.0	11.2	17.7	6.9	31.3
1961	143.8	51.2	21.2	8.8	12.4	11.6	19.0	7.4	33.3
1962	153.6	54.7	22.4	9.4	13.0	12.3	21.2	8.0	35.0
1963	162.9	58.0	23.6	9.9	13.8	12.9	23.0	8.5	36.9
1964	176.1	61.4	25.0	10.4	14.6	13.8	26.4	9.1	40.4
1965	189.0	65.4	26.5	10.9	15.6	14.7	28.6	9.6	44.2
1966	203.8	69.5	28.1	11.5	16.6	15.9	31.5	10.4	48.4
1967	220.3	74.1	30.0	12.2	17.8	17.4	34.7	11.1	53.0
1968	241.6	79.8	32.3	13.0	19.2	19.3	40.1	12.5	57.7
1969	266.1	86.9	35.0	14.1	21.0	21.6	45.8	13.8	62.9
1970	291.5	94.1	37.8	15.3	22.4	24.0	51.7	15.1	68.8
1971	319.5	102.8	41.1	16.9	24.2	26.8	58.4	16.3	74.0
1972	352.2	112.6	45.4	18.8	26.7	29.6	65.6	17.6	81.4
1973	385.8	123.3	49.9	20.4	29.5	31.6	73.3	19.7	88.0
1974	426.6	134.8	55.8	24.0	31.8	34.1	82.3	22.5	97.1
1975	480.2	147.7	64.0	29.2	34.8	37.9	95.6	25.4	109.7
1976	534.7	162.2	72.5	33.2	39.3	42.5	109.1	28.4	120.1
1977	600.2	180.2	81.8	38.5	43.3	48.7	125.3	31.4	132.8
1978	676.6	202.4	91.2	43.0	48.2	53.4	143.1	34.7	151.8
1979	753.3	227.3	100.3	47.8	52.5	59.9	161.0	38.8	166.2
1980	846.9	256.2	113.7	57.5	56.2	65.2	184.4	43.6	183.8
1981	950.8	289.7	126.8	64.8	62.0	70.3	216.7	50.6	196.7
1982	1 049.4	315.2	142.5	74.2	68.3	72.9	243.3	56.8	218.8
1983	1 178.6	341.0	157.0	82.4	74.6	81.1	274.3	63.6	261.6
1984	1 292.2	374.5	169.4	86.5	82.9	93.2	303.2	69.7	282.1
1985	1 428.1	412.7	181.8	90.8	91.1	104.5	331.5	77.7	319.8
1986	1 538.3	448.4	187.7	89.2	98.5	111.1	357.5	83.7	349.9
1987	1 663.5	483.7	195.4	90.9	104.5	120.9	392.2	90.0	381.2
1988	1 816.5	521.5	207.3	96.3	111.0	133.4	442.8	102.1	409.4
1989	1 960.0	557.4	221.1	101.0	120.0	142.0	492.5	114.3	432.8
1990	2 115.9	597.9	227.3	101.0	126.2	147.7	556.0	125.9	461.0
1991	2 247.4	631.1	238.6	107.4	131.2	145.3	608.9	132.9	490.6
1992	2 421.2	658.5	250.7	108.9	141.9	157.7	672.2	146.6	535.5
1993	2 571.8	683.9	269.9	118.2	151.7	172.7	715.1	160.4	569.8
1994	2 723.9	726.1	286.2	120.7	165.5	190.6	752.9	171.4	596.7
1995	2 879.1	764.4	298.7	122.2	176.5	207.7	797.9	187.9	622.5
1996	3 048.7	800.1	318.5	129.4	189.1	226.5	833.5	202.5	667.6
1997	3 235.8	842.6	337.0	131.3	205.6	245.7	873.0	215.1	722.4
1998	3 445.7	894.6	350.5	129.8	220.7	259.5	921.4	229.3	790.5
1999	3 660.0	948.4	364.8	130.6	234.1	276.4	961.1	248.6	860.7
2000	3 928.8	1 006.5	390.1	143.3	246.8	291.3	1 026.8	268.3	945.9
2001	4 154.3	1 073.7	409.0	156.7	252.3	292.8	1 113.8	284.1	980.7
2002	4 347.2	1 123.1	407.7	152.5	255.2	288.4	1 206.2	299.1	1 022.7
2003	4 570.8	1 161.8	429.4	167.3	262.1	297.3	1 300.5	317.7	1 064.0
2004	4 880.1	1 236.1	450.0	176.6	273.5	307.8	1 395.7	341.6	1 148.9
2005	5 170.0	1 304.1	483.0	199.8	283.2	320.4	1 493.4	360.6	1 208.4
2003									
1st quarter	4 477.7	1 142.3	424.4	164.4	260.0	293.0	1 267.5	309.6	1 040.8
2nd quarter	4 535.6	1 151.5	429.1	168.3	260.8	295.3	1 290.1	315.0	1 054.6
3rd quarter	4 601.4	1 167.2	429.9	167.2	262.7	299.2	1 311.5	320.3	1 073.2
4th quarter	4 668.4	1 186.2	434.1	169.2	264.8	301.6	1 333.0	325.9	1 087.6
2004									
1st quarter	4 761.8	1 206.0	441.2	173.9	267.2	303.7	1 357.6	333.6	1 119.7
2nd quarter	4 844.2	1 228.1	446.1	173.8	272.3	306.4	1 383.4	339.6	1 140.6
3rd quarter	4 918.6	1 247.0	451.7	174.6	277.1	308.7	1 409.5	344.5	1 157.3
4th quarter	4 995.7	1 263.2	461.1	183.9	277.2	312.3	1 432.5	348.6	1 178.0
2005									
1st quarter	5 056.4	1 280.8	467.2	187.6	279.6	314.7	1 456.3	354.3	1 183.1
2nd quarter	5 123.7	1 297.2	474.3	192.1	282.2	318.8	1 478.3	357.9	1 197.1
3rd quarter	5 205.1	1 311.7	484.3	199.4	285.0	322.3	1 505.0	362.6	1 219.1
4th quarter	5 294.7	1 326.6	506.1	219.9	286.2	325.9	1 534.0	367.7	1 234.4

Table 4-4. Chain-Type Quantity Indexes for Personal Consumption Expenditures by Major Type of Product

(Index numbers, 2000 = 100, seasonally adjusted.)

NIPA Table 2.3.3

Year and quarter	Personal consumption expenditures, total	Durable goods				Nondurable goods					
		Total	Motor vehicles and parts	Furniture and household equipment	Other durable goods	Total	Food	Clothing and shoes	Gasoline and oil	Fuel oil and coal	Other nondurable goods
1950	17.1	8.9	14.4	5.6	6.8	25.9	34.3	15.0	20.5	231.8	17.0
1951	17.4	8.1	12.2	5.3	6.9	26.6	35.2	14.9	22.3	231.2	17.7
1952	17.9	7.9	11.0	5.4	7.4	27.6	36.4	15.7	24.1	224.7	18.5
1953	18.8	8.9	13.6	5.6	7.7	28.5	37.7	15.9	25.4	217.2	19.2
1954	19.2	8.9	13.0	5.8	8.1	28.9	38.5	15.9	26.2	221.4	19.1
1955	20.6	10.8	17.8	6.5	8.9	30.3	40.1	16.7	28.5	235.3	20.1
1956	21.2	10.4	15.1	6.8	9.6	31.3	41.4	17.1	30.2	235.8	21.0
1957	21.7	10.5	15.8	6.6	9.7	31.9	42.2	17.0	31.4	233.8	21.7
1958	21.8	9.7	13.1	6.5	9.9	32.2	42.2	17.1	32.9	242.7	22.2
1959	23.1	10.8	15.6	7.0	10.5	33.5	43.7	18.0	34.6	231.8	23.5
1960	23.7	11.0	16.6	6.9	10.4	34.0	44.0	18.2	35.8	222.0	24.6
1961	24.2	10.6	14.9	7.0	10.3	34.6	44.5	18.5	36.1	211.4	25.9
1962	25.4	11.9	17.7	7.5	11.0	35.7	45.1	19.4	37.7	210.9	27.7
1963	26.4	13.0	20.0	8.0	11.7	36.5	45.6	19.7	38.8	221.3	29.0
1964	28.0	14.2	21.1	9.0	13.1	38.2	47.4	21.3	40.9	230.0	30.3
1965	29.8	16.0	24.5	9.9	14.5	40.3	50.0	22.1	42.9	240.8	32.1
1966	31.5	17.4	25.0	11.2	17.2	42.5	52.1	23.6	45.5	247.8	34.7
1967	32.4	17.6	24.4	11.7	18.0	43.2	52.8	23.8	47.0	247.9	35.6
1968	34.3	19.6	28.4	12.4	19.6	45.1	55.4	24.8	50.3	234.7	37.1
1969	35.6	20.3	29.6	12.8	20.5	46.3	56.8	25.2	53.7	222.4	38.2
1970	36.4	19.6	26.6	12.9	21.5	47.4	58.5	24.9	57.0	206.9	39.5
1971	37.8	21.6	31.7	13.4	21.8	48.3	59.1	26.1	59.8	199.9	39.7
1972	40.1	24.3	36.3	14.9	24.6	50.4	61.0	27.9	62.2	219.7	41.8
1973	42.0	26.8	39.6	16.5	27.7	52.1	61.2	29.8	65.4	238.6	44.6
1974	41.7	25.0	32.8	16.7	28.5	51.0	60.2	29.4	62.2	188.3	44.5
1975	42.7	25.0	33.0	16.3	29.6	51.8	61.7	30.4	64.1	184.8	43.0
1976	45.0	28.2	40.0	17.4	31.9	54.3	64.9	31.8	66.6	207.5	44.6
1977	47.0	30.8	44.2	18.9	34.2	55.6	66.1	33.6	68.7	200.9	45.3
1978	49.0	32.4	46.1	20.0	36.5	57.7	66.8	36.9	70.3	199.3	48.6
1979	50.2	32.3	43.1	21.1	37.9	59.2	68.1	38.8	69.3	185.2	51.4
1980	50.1	29.8	37.3	20.7	35.1	59.1	68.7	39.7	65.4	143.2	52.2
1981	50.8	30.1	38.1	20.7	35.6	59.8	68.8	42.2	66.3	120.1	53.3
1982	51.5	30.1	39.1	20.3	35.0	60.4	69.9	42.8	67.2	111.5	53.0
1983	54.4	34.5	46.7	23.1	37.0	62.4	71.9	46.0	68.7	111.6	54.3
1984	57.3	39.6	54.5	25.8	42.4	64.9	73.5	49.9	70.8	111.2	57.4
1985	60.3	43.6	61.6	28.1	44.4	66.7	75.2	52.2	72.2	112.5	58.8
1986	62.7	47.8	66.2	31.6	48.9	69.1	77.0	56.4	75.7	116.7	60.5
1987	64.8	48.6	63.8	33.9	52.0	70.7	78.0	58.4	77.8	115.1	62.9
1988	67.5	51.5	67.4	36.2	54.8	73.0	81.1	60.2	79.8	119.4	64.3
1989	69.4	52.7	67.3	38.1	56.0	75.0	82.5	63.6	81.5	116.5	66.4
1990	70.8	52.5	66.3	38.3	56.6	76.2	84.8	63.2	80.8	105.8	67.7
1991	70.9	49.6	58.6	38.7	54.1	76.0	84.7	63.4	79.9	104.8	67.4
1992	73.2	52.5	63.4	40.8	55.0	77.6	85.2	66.9	83.1	107.3	68.7
1993	75.7	56.6	67.1	45.1	59.2	79.6	86.7	69.7	85.2	109.6	71.1
1994	78.5	61.3	71.5	50.1	63.6	82.4	88.8	73.4	86.3	114.9	74.6
1995	80.6	64.0	70.4	55.4	67.8	84.2	89.4	76.4	87.9	118.2	77.7
1996	83.4	69.0	73.8	61.8	73.0	86.3	90.2	80.2	89.9	116.5	81.3
1997	86.5	74.9	78.8	69.1	77.7	88.6	91.4	82.6	92.7	107.0	85.7
1998	90.9	83.4	87.7	78.2	83.9	92.2	93.6	88.4	96.9	101.3	90.3
1999	95.5	93.2	96.4	89.7	92.6	96.4	96.6	95.0	100.4	103.7	95.4
2000	100.0	100.0	100.0	100.0	100.0	100.0	100.0	100.0	100.0	100.0	100.0
2001	102.5	104.3	105.0	106.0	99.6	102.0	101.6	102.0	101.5	95.8	103.1
2002	105.3	111.8	111.0	116.4	105.2	104.6	103.2	106.9	103.6	98.1	106.4
2003	108.2	118.2	114.4	127.1	111.8	108.0	105.7	112.3	104.3	97.4	111.3
2004	112.4	125.8	116.5	142.5	119.4	111.9	109.3	117.9	105.9	92.5	116.1
2005	116.3	132.7	117.2	156.8	129.7	116.9	115.2	125.2	105.8	86.8	120.8
2003											
1st quarter	106.6	112.5	109.9	119.3	106.7	106.4	104.8	108.8	103.4	98.5	109.2
2nd quarter	107.6	117.0	114.4	124.2	110.2	107.0	104.9	111.6	103.6	94.1	110.9
3rd quarter	109.1	121.6	117.7	131.0	114.4	109.0	106.5	114.5	104.7	97.5	112.3
4th quarter	109.7	121.8	115.5	133.9	115.9	109.5	106.6	114.2	105.5	99.5	113.8
2004											
1st quarter	111.0	123.6	116.2	137.5	117.5	110.7	108.0	117.5	105.9	94.8	113.8
2nd quarter	111.8	124.1	115.1	140.6	117.7	111.1	108.5	116.1	106.0	93.6	115.5
3rd quarter	112.9	126.7	116.8	144.8	120.0	112.2	109.3	117.9	105.5	93.3	117.1
4th quarter	114.1	128.6	118.1	147.3	122.2	113.7	111.3	120.0	106.1	88.3	117.9
2005											
1st quarter	114.8	129.4	115.8	150.6	126.1	115.1	112.8	121.9	107.4	90.9	119.0
2nd quarter	116.0	133.3	119.8	154.0	130.7	116.5	114.4	124.7	106.3	88.9	120.5
3rd quarter	117.2	136.2	122.8	159.1	130.0	117.5	116.2	125.6	104.9	86.1	121.4
4th quarter	117.4	131.8	110.3	163.5	132.0	118.6	117.3	128.7	104.7	81.2	122.4

Table 4-4. Chain-Type Quantity Indexes for Personal Consumption Expenditures by Major Type of Product
—Continued

(Index numbers, 2000 = 100, seasonally adjusted.)

NIPA Table 2.3.3

Year and quarter	Total	Housing	Services Household operation Total	Electricity and gas	Other household operation	Transportation	Medical care	Recreation	Other services
1950	13.9	15.0	14.2	14.1	13.6	18.7	10.0	10.0	15.4
1951	14.6	16.0	15.1	15.8	14.1	20.3	10.5	10.1	15.5
1952	15.3	17.1	15.6	17.2	14.0	20.6	11.0	10.3	16.1
1953	15.9	18.0	16.3	18.5	14.5	21.2	11.5	10.4	16.7
1954	16.6	18.9	17.0	20.3	14.5	20.9	12.3	10.6	17.4
1955	17.4	19.8	18.6	21.9	16.1	21.7	12.8	11.1	18.1
1956	18.3	20.8	19.9	23.8	17.1	22.6	13.6	11.7	18.8
1957	19.0	21.8	20.7	25.3	17.5	23.0	14.4	11.3	19.4
1958	19.8	22.9	21.4	26.7	17.9	22.6	15.3	11.3	20.2
1959	20.8	24.1	22.3	28.3	18.4	23.5	16.5	12.0	21.2
1960	21.7	25.4	23.4	29.9	19.2	24.3	17.1	12.7	21.9
1961	22.6	26.6	24.2	31.4	19.7	24.6	17.9	13.3	22.8
1962	23.7	28.1	25.4	33.6	20.4	25.5	19.4	14.0	23.3
1963	24.8	29.4	26.5	35.2	21.1	26.6	20.7	14.6	24.2
1964	26.3	30.8	27.8	37.1	22.1	28.0	23.0	15.2	25.8
1965	27.7	32.5	29.2	38.8	23.2	29.2	24.1	15.6	27.5
1966	29.1	34.0	30.6	41.0	24.3	30.8	25.4	16.3	28.9
1967	30.6	35.6	32.2	43.3	25.5	32.5	26.4	16.8	30.7
1968	32.1	37.4	33.6	45.8	26.3	34.5	28.4	17.8	31.8
1969	33.7	39.4	35.3	48.5	27.5	36.3	30.4	18.8	32.4
1970	35.0	40.8	36.6	50.8	28.3	37.3	32.1	19.6	33.7
1971	36.4	42.6	37.2	52.4	28.5	38.7	34.1	20.3	34.6
1972	38.5	45.1	39.2	55.5	29.9	41.1	36.5	21.3	36.2
1973	40.3	47.4	41.1	57.1	31.8	42.2	39.1	23.1	37.0
1974	41.2	49.8	41.6	57.8	32.1	42.5	40.5	24.7	36.1
1975	42.7	51.3	43.5	61.0	33.4	42.9	42.5	26.1	37.4
1976	44.5	52.8	45.3	63.2	34.9	44.2	44.5	27.9	39.1
1977	46.4	54.2	47.7	66.3	36.9	47.4	46.7	29.7	40.8
1978	48.6	56.8	50.2	69.2	39.1	49.0	48.9	31.1	42.6
1979	50.0	59.1	51.7	69.7	41.2	50.4	50.9	32.5	42.8
1980	50.9	60.9	53.1	71.6	42.2	47.9	52.7	34.1	42.5
1981	51.8	62.5	52.6	70.4	42.1	46.5	55.4	37.1	41.9
1982	52.9	62.8	53.0	71.3	42.3	45.9	56.2	39.7	44.5
1983	55.8	64.1	54.7	73.4	43.7	48.9	58.5	42.7	50.1
1984	58.0	66.8	56.1	73.9	45.8	53.6	60.2	44.8	52.0
1985	61.3	69.5	58.4	75.8	48.3	58.4	62.7	48.1	56.7
1986	63.1	71.3	59.4	75.0	50.5	60.7	65.2	49.9	58.1
1987	65.8	73.5	62.1	77.7	53.2	63.1	68.6	51.9	61.0
1988	68.5	75.8	65.0	81.6	55.4	66.3	72.0	56.7	62.5
1989	70.6	77.8	67.6	83.3	58.7	67.2	74.0	60.7	64.3
1990	72.6	79.7	68.3	81.9	60.5	67.2	77.7	63.6	65.7
1991	73.8	81.5	69.2	84.5	60.4	64.0	80.3	64.0	66.7
1992	76.4	82.7	71.1	84.0	63.8	66.7	84.1	68.6	69.1
1993	78.5	83.6	74.6	88.5	66.8	69.5	85.4	72.8	72.0
1994	80.9	86.4	77.8	89.9	70.9	75.0	86.4	76.3	73.6
1995	83.0	88.2	80.2	90.8	74.2	79.6	88.3	81.7	74.5
1996	85.4	89.5	83.9	94.0	78.2	85.0	89.8	85.2	77.2
1997	88.3	91.7	87.2	93.3	83.9	90.4	91.8	87.8	80.8
1998	92.0	94.3	91.5	95.4	89.4	93.4	94.5	91.3	86.9
1999	95.7	97.2	95.3	96.4	94.7	97.3	96.3	96.1	92.8
2000	100.0	100.0	100.0	100.0	100.0	100.0	100.0	100.0	100.0
2001	102.4	102.7	100.2	98.3	101.4	98.9	104.7	102.5	101.5
2002	104.4	103.5	100.8	101.1	100.6	96.2	110.7	104.8	102.2
2003	106.4	104.5	102.2	102.9	101.8	96.3	115.0	108.4	103.1
2004	110.1	108.5	104.9	104.6	105.1	97.5	118.6	113.6	107.4
2005	112.9	111.5	107.1	107.3	107.0	97.7	122.8	116.7	109.5
2003									
1st quarter	105.5	103.5	101.9	103.7	100.8	96.4	114.0	106.5	102.2
2nd quarter	105.9	104.0	101.9	102.4	101.6	96.1	114.7	107.8	102.6
3rd quarter	106.7	104.8	102.0	101.8	102.1	96.4	115.3	108.9	103.6
4th quarter	107.4	105.8	103.1	103.9	102.6	96.5	116.0	110.4	104.0
2004									
1st quarter	108.6	107.0	103.8	104.9	103.1	97.0	116.8	112.1	106.0
2nd quarter	109.7	108.0	104.5	103.8	104.9	97.6	117.9	113.4	107.2
3rd quarter	110.5	109.0	104.9	102.6	106.3	97.5	119.2	114.2	107.8
4th quarter	111.4	109.8	106.5	106.9	106.3	97.9	120.3	114.7	108.6
2005									
1st quarter	111.9	110.6	106.6	107.0	106.4	98.1	121.1	116.0	108.4
2nd quarter	112.5	111.3	106.9	106.9	106.8	97.8	122.1	116.5	109.0
3rd quarter	113.4	111.9	107.5	107.4	107.5	97.4	123.4	117.0	110.2
4th quarter	113.9	112.4	107.6	108.0	107.3	97.3	124.6	117.4	110.6

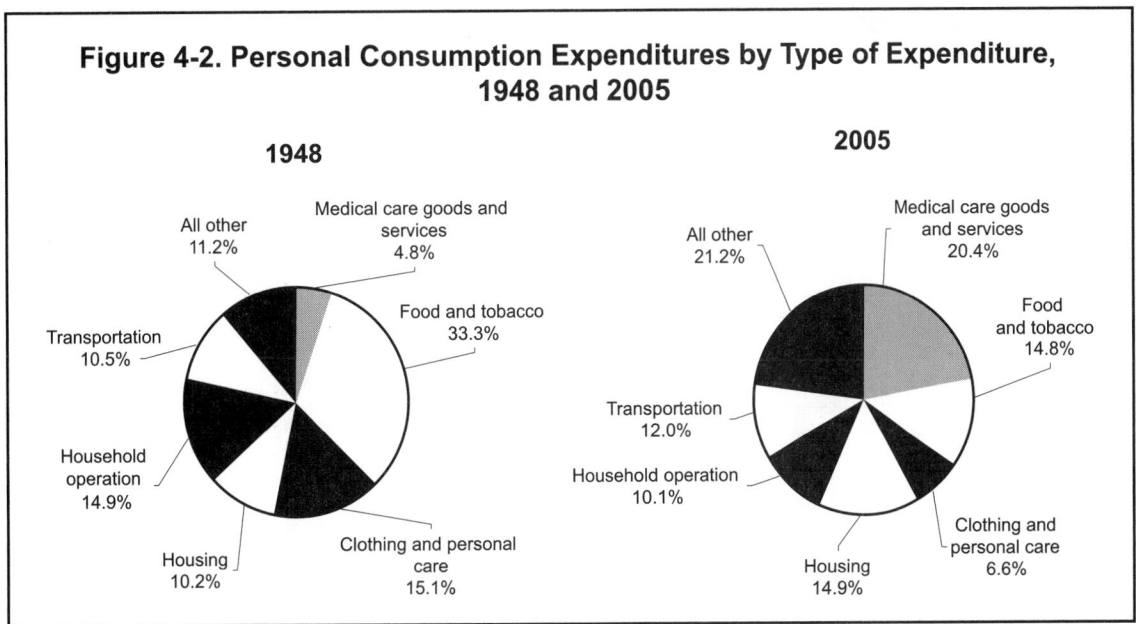

Figure 4-2. Personal Consumption Expenditures by Type of Expenditure, 1948 and 2005

- Spending for medical care goods and services in 2005 made up 20.4 percent of personal consumption spending—more than four times the percentage in 1948. This includes medical care payments made by government and private insurance on behalf of individuals, as well as out-of-pocket consumer payments. (Table 4-5)

- In 2005, much smaller shares were required for food and tobacco and for clothing and personal care than in 1948, as seen in the figure. Household operation claimed a smaller share of the total, but housing itself took a larger share. Transportation rose slightly, and the "all other" share nearly doubled. It should be noted that the nonprofit sector is included in this tabulation, and its spending on education, research, religious, and welfare activities is included in the "all other" category. (Table 4-5)

Table 4-5. Personal Consumption Expenditures by Type of Expenditure

(Billions of dollars.)

NIPA Table 2.5.5

Year	Personal consumption expenditures	Food and tobacco	Clothing, accessories, and jewelry	Personal care	Housing	Household operation	Medical care	Personal business	Transportation	Recreation	Education and research	Religious and welfare activities	Foreign travel and other, net
1939	67.2	20.9	8.4	1.0	9.4	9.6	3.1	3.0	6.5	3.5	0.7	1.0	0.2
1940	71.3	22.0	8.9	1.0	9.7	10.4	3.3	3.1	7.3	3.8	0.8	1.0	0.1
1941	81.1	25.4	10.5	1.2	10.4	11.8	3.6	3.2	8.6	4.3	0.8	1.1	0.1
1942	89.0	30.7	13.1	1.4	11.2	12.7	4.1	3.3	5.6	4.7	0.9	1.2	0.2
1943	99.9	35.8	16.0	1.6	11.8	13.1	4.5	3.7	5.6	5.0	1.1	1.5	0.3
1944	108.7	39.3	17.5	1.8	12.3	14.0	5.1	3.9	5.9	5.4	1.1	1.7	0.6
1945	120.0	43.5	19.6	2.0	12.8	15.5	5.4	4.1	6.8	6.2	1.1	1.8	1.2
1946	144.3	50.7	22.0	2.1	14.2	19.9	6.6	4.7	12.4	8.6	1.2	2.0	-0.1
1947	162.0	56.1	22.8	2.2	16.0	23.7	7.4	5.2	15.8	9.3	1.5	2.1	0.0
1948	175.0	58.2	24.2	2.3	17.9	26.1	8.4	5.6	18.4	9.7	1.7	2.3	0.3
1949	178.5	56.6	23.3	2.3	19.6	25.7	8.7	5.8	21.7	10.0	1.8	2.3	0.6
1950	192.2	58.1	23.7	2.4	21.7	29.1	9.4	6.4	25.2	11.2	1.9	2.4	0.7
1951	208.5	65.2	25.6	2.7	24.3	31.1	10.2	6.9	25.3	11.7	2.1	2.6	0.9
1952	219.5	69.0	26.6	2.9	27.0	31.5	11.2	7.2	25.6	12.3	2.2	3.0	1.1
1953	233.1	70.5	27.0	3.1	29.9	33.0	12.2	8.0	29.4	13.1	2.3	3.1	1.5
1954	240.0	71.7	27.2	3.4	32.3	33.7	13.3	8.8	28.8	13.6	2.5	3.3	1.5
1955	258.8	73.6	28.4	3.7	34.4	37.3	14.2	9.8	35.0	14.6	2.7	3.5	1.6
1956	271.7	76.7	29.7	4.1	36.7	39.8	15.5	10.7	34.4	15.5	3.0	3.9	1.7
1957	286.9	80.7	30.0	4.6	39.3	41.2	17.1	11.4	37.4	15.9	3.4	4.1	1.7
1958	296.2	83.9	30.3	4.9	42.0	42.4	18.7	12.2	35.5	16.3	3.7	4.4	1.9
1959	317.6	87.2	32.0	5.2	45.0	45.0	20.6	13.1	40.7	17.7	4.0	5.1	2.0
1960	331.7	89.2	32.7	5.6	48.2	46.7	22.2	14.1	42.8	18.5	4.4	5.2	2.1
1961	342.1	91.1	33.5	6.1	51.2	48.2	23.9	15.3	41.5	19.3	4.7	5.3	2.0
1962	363.3	93.3	35.0	6.7	54.7	51.0	26.5	15.9	46.4	20.8	5.1	5.5	2.3
1963	382.7	95.7	36.0	7.0	58.0	54.0	28.7	16.7	50.2	22.4	5.6	5.7	2.5
1964	411.4	101.1	39.1	7.5	61.4	58.4	32.3	18.4	53.3	24.6	6.2	6.6	2.6
1965	443.8	108.8	41.4	8.1	65.4	62.1	34.7	20.1	59.4	26.9	7.0	7.1	2.9
1966	480.9	117.8	45.5	9.0	69.5	67.2	38.0	22.0	62.2	30.9	8.0	7.7	3.1
1967	507.8	121.4	47.8	9.8	74.1	70.8	41.4	23.7	64.5	33.1	8.9	8.5	3.8
1968	558.0	131.6	52.5	10.5	79.8	76.3	47.7	26.0	73.9	36.7	10.1	9.3	3.7
1969	605.2	141.3	56.2	10.9	86.9	81.1	54.2	28.9	80.4	40.0	11.3	10.0	4.0
1970	648.5	154.6	57.6	11.5	94.1	84.8	61.3	31.8	81.5	43.1	12.7	11.0	4.5
1971	701.9	161.0	61.8	11.7	102.8	90.1	68.5	34.3	94.5	46.0	13.9	12.5	4.8
1972	770.6	173.6	67.1	12.3	112.6	99.5	76.7	37.7	105.1	51.5	15.3	14.0	5.2
1973	852.4	192.9	74.7	13.6	123.3	111.4	85.3	41.3	115.8	57.6	16.9	15.0	4.7
1974	933.4	215.9	79.3	14.8	134.8	123.6	95.5	46.6	119.7	63.4	18.5	16.7	4.7
1975	1 034.4	238.3	85.6	16.1	147.7	135.7	109.9	54.9	132.4	70.5	20.6	18.3	4.4
1976	1 151.9	259.3	93.7	17.5	162.2	152.0	124.7	60.5	156.8	78.2	22.5	20.8	3.8
1977	1 278.6	279.6	102.8	19.9	180.2	170.5	142.1	67.2	179.1	85.5	24.2	23.2	4.3
1978	1 428.5	307.8	115.1	21.9	202.4	189.6	162.3	78.9	196.7	96.1	26.8	26.6	4.3
1979	1 592.2	343.9	123.4	23.8	227.3	212.0	183.3	85.9	219.6	108.9	29.8	30.3	4.1
1980	1 757.1	376.8	132.3	25.5	256.2	233.3	209.6	95.2	238.9	117.5	33.5	34.8	3.5
1981	1 941.1	406.3	143.8	27.1	289.7	254.5	245.2	102.3	264.0	130.8	37.6	39.2	0.4
1982	2 077.3	427.7	147.0	28.0	315.2	271.9	274.8	115.1	270.0	140.9	41.3	43.0	2.5
1983	2 290.6	451.3	161.1	32.2	341.0	296.7	310.0	143.6	300.7	156.9	45.4	46.1	5.4
1984	2 503.3	476.6	175.8	35.5	374.5	322.8	343.7	151.8	339.9	174.8	49.4	51.8	6.6
1985	2 720.3	498.4	188.3	38.8	412.7	343.6	376.4	177.5	377.7	189.7	53.9	55.7	7.7
1986	2 899.7	524.2	204.1	42.3	448.4	359.6	407.4	198.3	385.2	206.9	58.1	61.9	3.3
1987	3 100.2	549.8	218.9	46.5	483.7	376.3	447.6	213.6	401.3	226.8	63.2	66.7	6.1
1988	3 353.6	588.2	235.7	50.1	521.5	398.6	505.0	224.2	431.1	251.7	70.2	74.4	2.8
1989	3 598.5	630.3	252.5	53.8	557.4	423.2	561.9	236.3	455.9	272.4	77.7	81.0	-3.7
1990	3 839.9	677.8	261.5	56.9	597.9	433.3	635.1	250.9	471.7	290.2	83.7	88.7	-7.7
1991	3 986.1	699.9	263.5	58.5	631.1	444.3	692.9	279.7	447.3	302.0	89.3	92.9	-15.2
1992	4 235.3	717.3	280.9	62.0	658.5	466.0	761.1	306.7	483.2	321.3	96.0	102.3	-20.0
1993	4 477.9	740.6	293.4	64.4	683.9	497.5	809.0	330.0	520.8	351.0	101.5	106.5	-20.6
1994	4 743.3	767.9	306.3	68.1	726.1	529.6	853.3	336.1	567.3	383.4	107.3	115.3	-17.4
1995	4 975.8	790.1	314.5	72.8	764.4	553.5	905.0	349.6	594.6	418.1	114.3	120.4	-21.4
1996	5 256.8	820.1	327.2	77.0	800.1	586.6	950.7	376.0	641.8	448.4	122.6	130.5	-24.2
1997	5 547.4	850.0	337.4	82.9	842.6	616.2	1 002.8	412.9	685.2	474.5	129.7	134.2	-21.1
1998	5 879.5	888.7	356.3	86.2	894.6	641.8	1 069.4	446.1	718.0	505.8	140.0	146.0	-13.3
1999	6 282.5	944.8	379.6	89.5	948.4	675.2	1 130.8	491.6	785.0	546.1	150.5	154.5	-13.5
2000	6 739.4	1 003.7	397.0	93.4	1 006.5	719.3	1 218.3	539.1	853.4	585.7	163.8	172.3	-13.0
2001	7 055.0	1 052.0	397.1	94.5	1 073.7	740.3	1 327.3	536.5	872.4	604.0	178.1	186.5	-7.4
2002	7 350.7	1 091.1	407.0	96.7	1 123.1	747.4	1 441.2	547.0	882.2	629.9	190.2	200.1	-5.1
2003	7 703.6	1 134.0	418.8	100.4	1 161.8	781.1	1 556.5	559.7	921.7	659.9	203.1	207.1	-0.5
2004	8 211.5	1 202.3	442.1	106.6	1 236.1	824.4	1 670.4	612.4	976.2	708.4	213.6	219.0	0.1
2005	8 742.4	1 291.4	464.8	112.2	1 304.1	881.7	1 784.1	647.9	1 048.9	756.3	226.5	224.5	0.0

NOTES AND DEFINITIONS

All personal income and personal consumption expenditure series are from the national income and product accounts (NIPAs). All quarterly series are shown at seasonally adjusted annual rates. Current and constant dollar values are in billions of dollars. Indexes of price and quantity are based on the average for the year 2000, which equals 100.

In all these tables, the personal sector includes nonprofit institutions serving households. Tables in which income, spending, and saving are estimated separately for households and for nonprofit institutions are also now available on an annual basis only, beginning with the year 1992. These data are presented and discussed in the article at the beginning of this book, "Topics of Current Interest." These tables are available on the BEA Web site at <http://www.bea.gov> as Table 2.9.

In several cases, the notes and definitions below will refer to *imputations* or *imputed values*. See the notes and definitions to Chapter 1 for an explanation of imputation and the role it plays in national and personal income measurement.

See "Topics of Current Interest" at the beginning of this book for an explanation of how Hurricane Katrina and other disasters are reflected in personal income.

TABLES 4-1 THROUGH 4-4 AND 19-6
SOURCES AND DISPOSITION OF PERSONAL INCOME; PERSONAL CONSUMPTION EXPENDITURES BY MAJOR TYPE OF PRODUCT

SOURCE: U.S. DEPARTMENT OF COMMERCE, BUREAU OF ECONOMIC ANALYSIS (BEA)

Definitions

Personal income is the income received by persons residing in the United States from participation in production, from government and business transfer payments, and from government interest, which is treated similarly to a transfer payment rather than as income from participation in production. *Persons* refers to individuals, nonprofit institutions that primarily serve individuals, private noninsured welfare funds, and private trust funds. All proprietors' income is treated as received by individuals. Life insurance carriers and private noninsured pension funds are not counted as persons, but their saving is credited to persons.

Personal income is the sum of compensation received by employees, proprietors' income with inventory valuation and capital consumption adjustments (IVA and CCAdj), rental income of persons with capital consumption adjustment, personal receipts on assets, and personal current transfer receipts, less contributions for social insurance.

Personal income differs from national income in that it includes current transfer payments and interest received by persons, regardless of source, while it excludes the following income components: employee and employer contributions for social insurance; business transfer payments, interest payments, and other payments on assets other than to persons; taxes on production and imports less subsidies; the current surplus of government enterprises; and undistributed corporate profits with IVA and CCAdj.

Compensation of employees, received is the sum of wage and salary accruals and supplements to wages and salaries, as defined in the *national* income account (see Table 1-7 and the notes and definitions to Chapter 1), minus an adjustment item *wage accruals less disbursements*. By subtracting this adjustment, BEA puts retroactive wage payments back into the quarter <u>in which</u> the wages were <u>received</u> by workers rather than the quarter <u>for which</u> they were <u>paid</u>. This adjustment item is zero in most quarters, but there are substantial entries in 2003 and 2004 because 53 Friday paydays fell in 2004 instead of the usual 52; see the notes and definitions for Chapter 1. *Wage accruals less disbursements* is shown in Table 1-7, but is not shown in Tables 4-1 or 19-6.

As in *national* income, *compensation of employees* refers to compensation received by residents of the United States, including compensation from the rest of the world, but excludes compensation from domestic industries to workers residing in the rest of the world.

Wage and salary disbursements consists of the monetary remuneration of employees, including the compensation of corporate officers; corporate directors' fees paid to directors who are also employees of the corporation; the value of employee exercise of "nonqualified stock options"; commissions, tips, and bonuses; voluntary employee contributions to certain deferred-compensation plans, such as 401(k) plans; receipts in kind that represent income; and judicial fees to jurors and witnesses, compensation of prison inmates, and marriage fees to justices of the peace, all of which were formerly included in "other labor income."

Supplements to wages and salaries consists of employer contributions to employee pension and insurance funds and to government social insurance funds.

The following two categories, *proprietors' income* and *rental income*, are both measured net of depreciation of the capital (structures and equipment) involved. BEA calculates normal depreciation, based on the estimated life of the capital, and subtracts it from the estimated value of receipts to yield net income. In the case of a major disaster, such as a severe hurricane or terrorist attack, the extraordinary loss of capital is also estimated and subtracted from receipts in the quarter in which it occurs.

Proprietors' income with inventory valuation and capital consumption adjustments is the current-production income (including income-in-kind) of sole proprietors and partnerships and of tax-exempt cooperatives. The imputed net rental income of owner-occupants of farm dwellings is included. Dividends and monetary interest received by proprietors of nonfinancial business and rental incomes received by persons not primarily engaged in the real estate business are excluded. These incomes are included in personal income receipts on assets and rental income of persons, respectively. Fees paid to outside directors of corporations are included. The two valuation adjustments are designed to obtain income measures that exclude any element of capital gains: inventory withdrawals are valued at replacement cost, rather than historical cost, and charges for depreciation are on an economically consistent accounting basis and are valued at replacement cost.

Rental income of persons with capital consumption adjustment consists of the net current-production income of persons from the rental of real property (other than the incomes of persons primarily engaged in the real estate business), the imputed net rental income of owner-occupants of nonfarm dwellings, and the royalties received by persons from patents, copyrights, and rights to natural resources. The capital consuption adjustment converts charges for depreciation to an economically consistent accounting basis valued at replacement cost.

Personal income receipts on assets consists of personal interest income and personal dividend income.

Personal interest income is the interest income (monetary and imputed) of persons from all sources, including interest paid by government to government employee retirement plans, as well as government interest paid directly to persons.

Personal dividend income is the dividend income of persons from all sources, excluding capital gains distributions. It equals net dividends paid by corporations (dividends paid by corporations minus dividends received by corporations) less a small amount of corporate dividends received by general government. Dividends received by government employee retirement systems are included in personal dividend income.

Personal current transfer receipts is income payments to persons for which no current services are performed. It consists of government social benefits to persons and net receipts from business.

Government social benefits to persons (formerly called "government transfer payments to persons") consists of benefits from the following categories of programs:

- *Social Security and Medicare*, consisting of federal old age, survivors, disability, and health insurance;

- *Unemployment insurance*;

- *Veterans' benefits*;

- *Family assistance*, which consists of Aid to Families with Dependent Children and (beginning in 1996) assistance programs operating under the Personal Responsibility and Work Opportunity Reconciliation Act of 1996;

- *Other*, which includes pension benefit guaranty, workers' compensation, military medical insurance, temporary disability insurance, food stamps, Black Lung benefits, supplemental security income, public assistance (including Medicaid), educational assistance, and the earned income credit. Government payments to nonprofit institutions, other than for work under research and development contracts, also are included. Payments from government employee retirement plans are not included.

Contributions for government social insurance, which is subtracted to arrive at personal income, includes payments by employers, employees, self-employed, and other individuals who participate in the following programs: old-age, survivors, and disability insurance (Social Security); hospital insurance and supplementary medical insurance (Medicare); unemployment insurance; railroad retirement; veterans' life insurance; and temporary disability insurance. Contributions to government employee retirement plans are not included in this item.

In the 2003 revision, there was a change in the tabular presentation of contributions for government social insurance, though not in the concept of personal income. Before the revision, the components of personal income included only wages and salaries and "other labor income." Personal contributions for social insurance were subtracted from that total. In the revision, the total compensation concept presented in the table contains wages and salaries and all supplements, including the employer social insurance payments. Both the employer and employee contributions are then subtracted to arrive at personal income. In either case, the effect is to end up with a personal income figure that is net of all social insurance taxes but not net of personal income taxes.

Personal current taxes is tax payments (net of refunds) by persons residing in the United States that are not chargeable to business expenses, including taxes on income, on realized net capital gains, and on personal property. As of the 1999 revisions, estate and gift taxes are classified as capital transfers and are not included in personal current taxes.

Disposable personal income is personal income minus personal current taxes. It is the income from current production that is available to persons for spending or saving. However, it is not the cash flow available, since it excludes capital gains. Disposable personal income in chained (2000) dollars represents the inflation-adjusted value of disposable personal income.

Personal outlays is the sum of *personal consumption expenditures* (defined below), *personal interest payments*, and *personal current transfer payments*.

Personal current transfer payments to government includes donations, fees, and fines paid to federal, state, and local governments. These were formerly classified as "personal nontax payments" and included in the old "personal tax and nontax payments" total.

Personal current transfer payments to the rest of the world (net) is personal remittances in cash and in kind to the rest of the world less such remittances from the rest of the world.

Personal saving is derived by subtracting personal outlays from disposable personal income. It is the current saving of individuals (including proprietors), nonprofit institutions that primarily serve individuals, life insurance carriers, retirement funds (including those of government employees), private noninsured welfare funds, and private trust funds. Conceptually, personal saving may also be viewed as the sum of the net acquisition of financial assets and the change in physical assets less the sum of net borrowing and consumption of fixed capital. In either case, it is defined to exclude both realized and unrealized capital gains.

Note that in the context of national income accounting, the term just defined is saving, not "savings." *Saving* refers to a <u>flow</u> of income during a particular time span (such as a year or a quarter) that is not consumed. It is therefore available to finance a commensurate <u>flow</u> of investment during that time span. Strictly defined, "savings" denotes an accumulated <u>stock</u> of monetary funds—possibly the cumulative effects of successive periods of *saving*—available to the owner in asset form, such as in a bank savings account.

Personal consumption expenditures (PCE) is goods and services purchased by persons residing in the United States. Persons are defined as individuals and nonprofit institutions that primarily serve individuals. PCE mostly consists of purchases of new goods and services by individuals from business, including purchases financed by insurance (such as medical insurance). In addition, PCE includes purchases of new goods and services by nonprofit institutions, net purchases of used goods by individuals and nonprofit institutions, and purchases abroad of goods and services by U.S. residents traveling or working in foreign countries. PCE also includes purchases for certain goods and services provided by the government, primarily tuition payments for higher education, charges for medical care, and charges for water and sanitary services. Finally, PCE includes imputed purchases that keep PCE invariant to changes in the way that certain activities are carried out. For example, to take account of the value of the services provided by owner-occupied housing, PCE includes an imputation equal to what (estimated) rent homeowners would pay if they rented their houses from themselves. (See the discussion of imputation in the notes and definitions for Chapter 1.) Actual purchases of residential structures by individuals are classified as gross private domestic investment.

Tables 4-3 and 4-4 present personal consumption expenditures classified by major type of product: *durable goods*, *nondurable goods*, and *services*. Each of these three major categories is then subdivided according to type of expenditure.

In general, *durable goods* are commodities that can be stored or inventoried and that have an average life of at least three years. *Nondurable goods* are all other commodities that can be stored or inventoried.

This classification system is not always helpful with respect to the objective of spending. For example, the *medical care* component of services does not include drugs and medicines, which are included in nondurable goods. For a more precise classification of consumption spending by objective, see Table 4-5 and its description below. This classification is only available on an annual basis.

Revisions

Data in this book reflect the 2003 comprehensive revisions to the NIPAs and all further revisions available through August 2006.

See the notes and definitions for Chapter 1 for an explanation of a new revision schedule for wages and salaries and related components of the income side of the NIPAs. This means quarterly revisions for as much as seven months of previous data, which affect income and saving while leaving PCE and other components of gross domestic product (GDP) untouched.

An important conceptual change was made in the 1999 comprehensive revision of the NIPAs, when it was decided to treat the retirement plans of federal, state, and local employees like private pensions. Previously, these employee retirement plans were treated as government social insurance programs. Both the employer contributions to and the dividends and interest received by these retirement funds are now treated as components of personal income, while benefits paid by the plans to retirees are treated as transactions within the personal sector rather than as transfer payments. This conceptual revision raised employer contributions for employee pension and insurance funds and dividends and interest, and reduced transfer payments received and personal contributions for social insurance. The effect was to move the accumulation of assets in these pension funds from the government surplus to personal saving.

Data availability

Monthly data are made available in a BEA press release, usually distributed the first business day following the monthly release of the latest NIPA estimates. Monthly and quarterly data are subsequently published each month in the BEA's *Survey of Current Business*. Current and historical data are available on the BEA Web site at <http://www.bea.gov>, and may also be obtained from the STAT-USA subscription Web site at <http://www.statusa. gov>.

References

The latest revision is presented and described in an article on the NIPAs in the August 2006 *Survey of Current Business*. Other references can be found in the notes and definitions for Chapter 1. A discussion of monthly estimates of personal income and its disposition appears in the November 1979 edition of the *Survey of Current Business*. A more detailed description of concepts, sources, and methods used in estimating personal consumption expenditures appears in *Personal Consumption Expenditures* (NIPA Methodology Paper No. 6, 1990), available on the BEA Web site from the National Technical Information Service (NTIS Accession No. PB 90-254244) available online at <http://www. bea.gov/bea/ARTICLES/NATION AL/NIPA/Methpap/methpap6.pdf>. Additional and more recent information can be found in the articles listed in the notes and definitions for Tables 1-1 through 1-7 and Tables 1-9 through 1-13.

TABLE 4-5
PERSONAL CONSUMPTION EXPENDITURES BY TYPE OF EXPENDITURE

SOURCE: BUREAU OF ECONOMIC ANALYSIS (BEA)

In this table, also derived from the NIPAs, annual estimates of the current-dollar value of PCE are presented by "type of expenditure" instead of by "type of product." The latter is the classification scheme used in Tables 4-3 and 4-4. The "type of expenditure" tabulations provide a more precise delineation of consumer spending by its ultimate objective. These tabulations cut across the categories of durable goods, nondurable goods, and services that are used in the quarterly estimates. The definitions of the expenditure types given below explain the relationship of each to the categories used in the "type of product" tables.

Definitions

Food and tobacco includes food, beverages (including alcoholic beverages), and tobacco products, whether purchased for home consumption or on the premises of eating and drinking places. All of these components are included in nondurable goods in the "major type of product" classification system.

Clothing, accessories, and jewelry includes clothing and shoes from the nondurable goods category, jewelry and watches from the durable goods category, and cleaning, storage, and repair of clothing and shoes from the services category.

Personal care includes toilet articles and preparations from nondurable goods and barbershops, beauty parlors, and health clubs from services.

Housing includes rents paid for rental housing, imputed rent of owner-occupied dwellings, and rent of hotels, motels, clubs, schools, and other group housing. All components are from the services group.

Household operation includes furniture, appliances, and other durable household goods from durable goods; "semidurable" furnishings (such as textile goods), household supplies, and stationery from nondurable goods; and utilities, communications, domestic service, maintenance, insurance, and miscellaneous services from services.

Medical care includes drug preparations and sundries from nondurable goods, ophthalmic and orthopedic products from durable goods, and the services of medical professionals, hospitals, nursing homes, and health insurance.

Personal business includes financial, legal, funeral, and miscellaneous services.

Transportation includes the purchase of motor vehicles and parts from the durable goods category, gasoline and oil from nondurable goods, and tolls, insurance, transit, taxi, rail, bus, airline, and other transportation services.

Recreation includes books, "wheel goods" (other than those classified in transportation), photo equipment, boats, pleasure aircraft, video, audio, musical instruments, computers, and software, all from durable goods; toys, sports supplies, flowers, seeds, and potted plants from nondurable goods; and a long list of recreational and cultural services, including legal gambling. (Goods and services that are illegal are outside the scope of the national income and product accounts.)

Education and research includes all education and research expenditures in the service category, including the research of nonprofit institutions.

Religious and welfare activities are all classified as services in the "major type of product" system. For nonprofits, this category equals current expenditures (including consumption of fixed capital) of religious, social welfare, foreign relief, and political organizations, and those of museums, libraries, and foundations. The expenditures are net of receipts—such as those from sales of meals, rooms, and entertainments—accounted for separately in consumer expenditures. They exclude relief payments within the United States and expenditures by foundations for education and research. For proprietary and government institutions, the value for this category equals receipts from users.

Foreign travel and other, net consists of foreign travel spending (services) and other expenditures abroad (nondurable goods) by U.S. residents minus expenditures in the United States by nonresidents (services) and personal remittances in kind to nonresidents (nondurable goods). Negative figures indicate that the sum of the first two terms is less than the sum of the second two terms.

Beginning with 1981, foreign travel spending by U.S. residents includes U.S. students' expenditures abroad, and expenditures in the United States by nonresidents includes nonresidents' student and medical care expenditures in the United States. Positive values for this category, indicating that U.S. residents spent more abroad than foreigners spent in the United States, appear in the 1980s when the dollar was strong against other major currencies. (The international value of the dollar is shown in Table 13-6.) Negative values in the 1990s are associated with a weaker dollar, which discourages U.S. residents' travel abroad and encourages tourism by foreigners in the United States. The negative sign does not indicate a drain on GDP, but rather indicates that the goods and services purchased by foreigners in the United States belong in the category of exports rather than in the consumption spending of U.S. residents.

Data availability and revisions

Data are published once a year in supplemental NIPA tables in the *Survey of Current Business* (most recently in August 2006), reflecting the most recent NIPA revisions. They are also available on the BEA Web site at <http://www.bea.gov>.

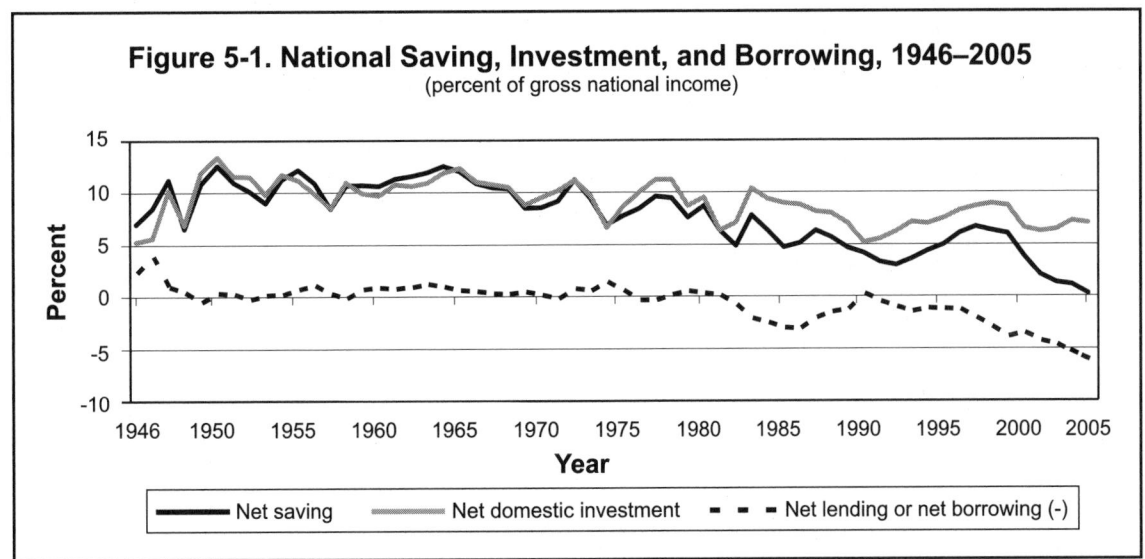

Figure 5-1. National Saving, Investment, and Borrowing, 1946–2005
(percent of gross national income)

- In 2005, there was no net saving (that is, no saving other than allowances for capital consumption) in the U.S. economy. The national saving rate had not been that low since the depression years of 1931–1934, when saving was negative. The federal government deficit on the NIPA basis was over $300 billion, even though the economy was in its fourth year of recovery. Individuals and state and local governments also spent more than their incomes. Only corporations were net savers in 2005. (Tables 5-1, 18-1, and 19-9)

- While net saving was falling toward zero, net domestic investment (gross investment minus depreciation) held at 6 to 7 percent of gross national income (GNI). This excess of investment over saving was financed by an increase in borrowing overseas (a larger negative entry on the figure above) from 4.0 percent in 2000 to 6.2 percent of GNI in 2005. (Table 5-1)

- In terms of physical quantities, total gross private fixed investment rose 9.7 percent between 2000 and 2005; this was entirely accounted for by a 36.1 percent rise in housing. Nonresidential investment fell 0.7 percent, with structures down 19.7 percent, while equipment and software rose 7.2 percent. (Tables 5-3 and 5-4)

Table 5-1. Saving and Investment

(Billions of dollars, except as noted; quarterly data are at seasonally adjusted annual rates.)   NIPA Tables 1.7.5, 5.1

Year and quarter	Gross saving												
		Net saving						Consumption of fixed capital					
			Private			Government			Private			Government	
	Total	Total	Total	Personal saving	Undistributed corporate profits with IVA and CCAdj	Federal	State and local	Total	Total	Domestic business	Households and institutions	Federal	State and local
1950	60.6	31.2	24.4	15.1	9.3	5.5	1.3	29.4	21.5	18.1	3.3	5.8	2.1
1951	75.0	41.8	29.6	19.5	10.1	9.6	2.6	33.2	24.6	20.7	3.8	6.1	2.6
1952	74.2	38.5	31.8	20.5	11.3	3.7	3.0	35.7	26.1	21.9	4.2	6.8	2.7
1953	75.1	37.4	32.1	21.5	10.6	1.8	3.5	37.8	27.3	22.9	4.4	7.6	2.8
1954	73.4	33.5	31.9	20.0	11.9	-1.6	3.2	39.9	28.7	24.1	4.7	8.3	2.9
1955	88.0	45.9	36.7	19.7	17.0	5.7	3.5	42.1	30.3	25.3	5.0	8.7	3.1
1956	99.4	53.0	41.0	25.8	15.3	7.6	4.4	46.4	33.6	28.1	5.5	9.3	3.5
1957	99.6	49.7	42.2	27.0	15.2	3.3	4.2	49.9	36.3	30.4	5.8	9.8	3.9
1958	90.8	38.8	41.3	28.3	13.0	-5.4	2.9	52.0	38.1	32.1	6.1	9.9	4.0
1959	106.2	53.2	46.0	26.7	19.4	3.3	3.8	53.0	38.6	32.2	6.4	10.2	4.2
1960	111.3	55.8	44.3	26.7	17.6	7.2	4.3	55.6	40.5	33.9	6.7	10.6	4.4
1961	114.3	57.1	50.2	32.2	18.1	2.6	4.3	57.2	41.6	34.7	6.9	10.9	4.7
1962	124.9	65.7	57.9	33.8	24.1	2.5	5.2	59.3	42.8	35.6	7.2	11.5	5.0
1963	133.2	70.8	59.7	33.3	26.4	5.4	5.7	62.4	44.9	37.5	7.5	12.1	5.4
1964	143.4	78.4	71.0	40.8	30.1	1.0	6.4	65.0	46.9	39.0	7.9	12.3	5.7
1965	158.5	89.1	79.2	43.0	36.2	3.3	6.5	69.4	50.5	41.9	8.5	12.7	6.2
1966	168.7	93.1	83.1	44.4	38.7	2.3	7.8	75.6	55.5	46.3	9.2	13.2	6.9
1967	170.5	89.0	91.4	54.4	36.9	-9.4	7.0	81.5	59.9	50.0	9.9	14.0	7.5
1968	182.0	93.6	88.4	52.8	35.6	-2.3	7.5	88.4	65.2	54.4	10.8	14.8	8.3
1969	198.3	100.4	83.7	52.5	31.2	8.7	8.0	97.9	73.1	61.2	12.0	15.5	9.3
1970	192.7	86.0	94.0	69.5	24.6	-15.2	7.1	106.7	80.0	67.2	12.9	16.1	10.6
1971	208.9	93.9	115.8	80.6	34.8	-28.4	6.5	115.0	86.7	72.5	14.2	16.5	11.8
1972	237.5	111.0	119.8	77.2	42.9	-24.4	15.6	126.5	97.1	80.9	16.2	16.6	12.8
1973	292.0	152.7	148.3	102.7	45.6	-11.3	15.7	139.3	107.9	89.9	18.0	17.1	14.3
1974	301.5	139.0	143.4	113.6	29.8	-13.8	9.3	162.5	126.6	105.9	20.7	18.2	17.7
1975	297.0	109.2	175.8	125.6	50.2	-69.0	2.5	187.7	147.8	124.4	23.4	19.7	20.2
1976	342.1	137.0	181.3	122.3	59.0	-51.7	7.4	205.2	162.5	136.9	25.6	21.4	21.3
1977	397.5	167.5	198.5	125.3	73.2	-44.1	13.1	230.0	184.3	155.3	29.0	23.1	22.6
1978	478.0	215.7	223.5	142.5	81.0	-26.5	18.7	262.3	212.8	179.3	33.6	25.0	24.5
1979	536.7	236.6	234.9	159.1	75.7	-11.3	13.0	300.1	245.7	206.9	38.8	27.0	27.5
1980	549.4	206.5	251.3	201.4	49.9	-53.6	8.8	343.0	281.1	236.8	44.3	30.1	31.8
1981	654.7	266.6	312.3	244.3	68.0	-53.3	7.6	388.1	317.9	268.9	49.0	33.8	36.3
1982	629.1	202.2	336.2	270.8	65.4	-131.9	-2.2	426.9	349.8	297.3	52.5	37.6	39.5
1983	609.4	165.6	333.7	233.6	100.1	-173.0	4.9	443.8	362.1	307.4	54.7	40.8	40.9
1984	773.4	300.9	445.0	314.8	130.3	-168.1	23.9	472.6	385.6	328.0	57.6	44.6	42.3
1985	767.5	260.7	413.4	280.0	133.4	-175.0	22.3	506.7	414.0	353.0	61.0	48.1	44.6
1986	733.5	202.2	372.0	268.4	103.7	-190.8	21.0	531.3	431.8	366.9	64.9	51.6	47.9
1987	796.8	234.9	367.4	241.4	126.1	-145.0	12.4	561.9	455.3	385.7	69.5	55.2	51.4
1988	915.0	317.4	434.0	272.9	161.1	-134.5	17.9	597.6	483.5	408.9	74.6	59.3	54.8
1989	944.7	300.4	409.7	287.1	122.6	-130.1	20.8	644.3	522.1	440.6	81.5	63.5	58.7
1990	940.4	258.0	422.7	299.4	123.3	-172.0	7.2	682.5	551.6	466.4	85.1	67.9	63.0
1991	964.1	238.2	456.1	324.2	131.9	-213.7	-4.2	725.9	586.9	497.4	89.5	72.2	66.9
1992	948.2	196.3	493.0	366.0	142.7	-297.4	0.7	751.9	607.3	510.5	96.8	74.7	69.9
1993	962.4	186.0	458.6	284.0	168.1	-273.5	0.9	776.4	624.7	524.6	100.1	77.9	73.8
1994	1 070.7	237.1	438.9	249.5	171.8	-212.3	10.5	833.7	675.1	568.0	107.1	80.2	78.5
1995	1 184.5	306.2	491.1	250.7	223.8	-197.0	12.0	878.4	713.4	600.2	113.2	81.9	83.1
1996	1 291.1	373.0	489.0	228.4	256.9	-141.8	25.8	918.1	748.8	630.7	118.2	82.0	87.2
1997	1 461.1	486.6	503.3	218.3	287.9	-55.8	39.1	974.4	800.3	675.2	125.1	82.5	91.6
1998	1 598.7	568.6	477.8	276.8	201.7	38.8	52.0	1 030.2	851.2	718.3	132.9	82.8	96.2
1999	1 674.3	573.0	419.0	158.6	255.3	103.6	50.4	1 101.3	914.3	769.8	144.5	84.8	102.1
2000	1 770.5	582.7	343.3	168.5	174.8	189.5	50.0	1 187.8	990.8	836.1	154.8	87.2	109.8
2001	1 657.6	376.1	324.6	132.3	192.3	46.7	4.8	1 281.5	1 075.5	903.7	171.7	88.2	117.8
2002	1 489.1	197.1	479.2	184.7	294.5	-247.9	-34.2	1 292.0	1 080.3	893.6	186.8	88.9	122.7
2003	1 459.0	122.5	515.0	174.9	325.1	-372.1	-20.4	1 336.5	1 118.3	916.6	201.7	90.4	127.8
2004	1 543.7	107.5	502.4	174.3	343.0	-382.0	-12.9	1 436.2	1 205.4	969.5	235.9	94.1	136.7
2005	1 612.0	7.2	319.7	-34.8	354.5	-309.2	-3.3	1 604.8	1 352.6	1 059.1	293.5	99.0	153.2
2003													
1st quarter	1 402.6	85.5	436.9	149.1	277.8	-290.2	-61.2	1 317.0	1 101.1	906.1	195.0	89.7	126.2
2nd quarter	1 435.6	106.2	498.9	173.9	310.0	-365.5	-27.2	1 329.5	1 111.7	912.7	199.1	90.6	127.2
3rd quarter	1 445.6	103.0	562.6	194.0	343.6	-451.4	-8.2	1 342.6	1 123.6	919.9	203.7	90.7	128.3
4th quarter	1 552.2	195.2	561.5	182.5	369.0	-381.5	15.2	1 357.0	1 136.7	927.7	209.0	90.7	129.5
2004													
1st quarter	1 532.7	159.5	575.2	178.9	401.3	-401.0	-14.7	1 373.2	1 150.3	934.5	215.8	91.8	131.2
2nd quarter	1 525.8	131.3	525.6	168.3	377.2	-380.6	-13.6	1 394.5	1 166.4	945.0	221.3	93.8	134.3
3rd quarter	1 575.4	40.5	443.4	141.2	327.2	-380.6	-22.3	1 534.9	1 301.9	1 027.1	274.8	94.5	138.6
4th quarter	1 540.6	98.6	465.2	208.9	266.2	-365.7	-0.9	1 442.0	1 203.1	971.5	231.6	96.2	142.7
2005													
1st quarter	1 608.4	140.5	417.2	52.5	364.7	-287.6	10.9	1 467.8	1 225.7	990.1	235.6	97.5	144.7
2nd quarter	1 565.0	74.0	351.1	-30.8	381.9	-289.6	12.4	1 491.1	1 244.9	1 004.5	240.4	98.2	147.9
3rd quarter	1 653.5	-244.5	170.9	-132.6	303.5	-396.0	-19.3	1 898.0	1 632.3	1 197.6	434.7	99.8	165.9
4th quarter	1 621.2	58.7	339.5	-28.5	367.9	-263.6	-17.2	1 562.5	1 307.5	1 044.4	263.1	100.7	154.3

Table 5-1. Saving and Investment—Continued

(Billions of dollars, except as noted; quarterly data are at seasonally adjusted annual rates.)　　　　NIPA Tables 1.7.5, 5.1

Year and quarter	Gross domestic investment, capital account transactions, and net lending, NIPAs						Statistical discrepancy	Net domestic investment	Gross national income	Gross saving as a percent of gross national income	Net saving as a percent of gross national income
	Total	Gross domestic investment			Capital account transactions, net	Net lending or net borrowing (-), NIPAs					
		Total	Private	Government							
1950	62.0	63.9	54.1	9.8	. . .	-1.8	1.4	34.4	293.8	20.6	10.6
1951	78.7	77.8	60.2	17.6	. . .	0.9	3.6	44.5	337.6	22.2	12.4
1952	77.0	76.3	54.0	22.3	. . .	0.6	2.8	40.6	357.5	20.7	10.8
1953	79.2	80.4	56.4	24.0	. . .	-1.3	4.0	42.7	377.2	19.9	9.9
1954	76.6	76.3	53.8	22.5	. . .	0.2	3.2	36.4	379.3	19.3	8.8
1955	90.5	90.0	69.0	21.0	. . .	0.4	2.5	47.9	414.8	21.2	11.1
1956	97.7	94.9	72.0	22.9	. . .	2.8	-1.7	48.5	441.9	22.5	12.0
1957	99.6	94.8	70.5	24.4	. . .	4.8	0.0	45.0	464.1	21.5	10.7
1958	91.9	91.0	64.5	26.5	. . .	0.9	1.0	38.9	468.8	19.4	8.3
1959	106.7	107.8	78.5	29.3	. . .	-1.2	0.5	54.8	508.9	20.9	10.4
1960	110.4	107.2	78.9	28.3	. . .	3.2	-0.9	51.6	530.4	21.0	10.5
1961	113.8	109.5	78.2	31.3	. . .	4.3	-0.6	52.3	548.8	20.8	10.4
1962	125.3	121.4	88.1	33.3	. . .	3.9	0.4	62.2	589.4	21.2	11.1
1963	132.4	127.4	93.8	33.6	. . .	5.0	-0.8	65.0	623.0	21.4	11.4
1964	144.2	136.7	102.1	34.6	. . .	7.5	0.8	71.7	667.7	21.5	11.7
1965	160.0	153.8	118.2	35.6	. . .	6.2	1.6	84.4	722.8	21.9	12.3
1966	175.0	171.1	131.3	39.8	. . .	3.9	6.3	95.5	786.6	21.4	11.8
1967	175.1	171.6	128.6	43.0	. . .	3.6	4.6	90.1	833.4	20.5	10.7
1968	186.6	184.8	141.2	43.6	. . .	1.7	4.6	96.5	911.5	20.0	10.3
1969	201.5	199.7	156.4	43.3	. . .	1.8	3.2	101.8	987.6	20.1	10.2
1970	200.0	196.0	152.4	43.6	. . .	4.0	7.3	89.3	1 037.6	18.6	8.3
1971	220.5	219.9	178.2	41.8	. . .	0.6	11.6	104.9	1 123.1	18.6	8.4
1972	246.6	250.2	207.6	42.6	. . .	-3.6	9.1	123.7	1 237.7	19.2	9.0
1973	300.7	291.3	244.5	46.8	. . .	9.3	8.6	152.1	1 386.7	21.1	11.0
1974	312.3	305.7	249.4	56.3	. . .	6.6	10.9	143.2	1 504.6	20.0	9.2
1975	314.7	293.3	230.2	63.1	. . .	21.4	17.7	105.6	1 633.6	18.2	6.7
1976	367.2	358.4	292.0	66.4	. . .	8.9	25.1	153.2	1 817.0	18.8	7.5
1977	419.8	428.8	361.3	67.5	. . .	-9.0	22.3	198.8	2 028.9	19.6	8.3
1978	504.6	515.0	438.0	77.1	. . .	-10.4	26.6	252.7	2 289.7	20.9	9.4
1979	582.8	581.4	492.9	88.5	. . .	1.4	46.0	281.2	2 549.2	21.1	9.3
1980	590.9	579.5	479.3	100.3	. . .	11.4	41.4	236.6	2 782.3	19.7	7.4
1981	685.6	679.3	572.4	106.9	. . .	6.3	30.9	291.2	3 130.4	20.9	8.5
1982	629.4	629.5	517.2	112.3	-0.2	0.0	0.3	202.6	3 291.2	19.1	6.1
1983	655.1	687.2	564.3	122.9	-0.2	-31.8	45.7	243.4	3 528.0	17.3	4.7
1984	788.0	875.0	735.6	139.4	-0.2	-86.7	14.6	402.4	3 954.9	19.6	7.6
1985	784.1	895.0	736.2	158.8	-0.3	-110.5	16.7	388.3	4 230.1	18.1	6.2
1986	780.5	919.7	746.5	173.2	-0.3	-138.9	47.0	388.4	4 433.6	16.5	4.6
1987	818.5	969.2	785.0	184.3	-0.4	-150.4	21.7	407.3	4 735.7	16.8	5.0
1988	895.5	1 007.7	821.6	186.1	-0.5	-111.7	-19.5	410.1	5 147.0	17.8	6.2
1989	984.3	1 072.6	874.9	197.7	-0.3	-88.0	39.7	428.4	5 470.9	17.3	5.5
1990	1 006.7	1 076.7	861.0	215.8	6.6	-76.6	66.2	394.2	5 771.6	16.3	4.5
1991	1 036.6	1 023.2	802.9	220.3	4.5	9.0	72.5	297.3	5 953.8	16.2	4.0
1992	1 051.0	1 087.9	864.8	223.1	0.6	-37.5	102.7	336.0	6 264.7	15.1	3.1
1993	1 102.0	1 172.4	953.4	219.0	1.3	-71.7	139.5	395.9	6 549.8	14.7	2.8
1994	1 213.2	1 318.4	1 097.1	221.4	1.7	-106.9	142.5	484.7	6 955.9	15.4	3.4
1995	1 285.7	1 376.7	1 144.0	232.7	0.9	-91.9	101.2	498.4	7 332.3	16.2	4.2
1996	1 384.8	1 485.2	1 240.3	244.9	0.7	-101.0	93.7	567.1	7 758.2	16.6	4.8
1997	1 531.7	1 641.9	1 389.8	252.2	1.0	-111.3	70.7	667.5	8 266.6	17.7	5.9
1998	1 584.1	1 771.5	1 509.1	262.4	0.7	-188.1	-14.6	741.3	8 783.0	18.2	6.5
1999	1 638.5	1 912.4	1 625.7	286.8	4.8	-278.7	-35.7	811.2	9 337.9	17.9	6.1
2000	1 643.3	2 040.0	1 735.5	304.5	0.8	-397.4	-127.2	852.1	9 983.1	17.7	5.8
2001	1 567.9	1 938.3	1 614.3	324.0	1.1	-371.5	-89.6	656.9	10 261.3	16.2	3.7
2002	1 468.1	1 926.4	1 582.1	344.3	1.4	-459.7	-21.0	634.4	10 521.2	14.2	1.9
2003	1 507.8	2 020.0	1 664.1	356.0	3.2	-515.5	48.8	683.5	10 968.8	13.3	1.1
2004	1 610.3	2 259.4	1 888.0	371.4	2.3	-651.3	66.7	823.2	11 692.0	13.2	0.9
2005	1 683.1	2 454.5	2 057.4	397.1	4.4	-775.8	71.0	849.7	12 416.6	13.0	0.1
2003											
1st quarter	1 423.8	1 954.6	1 606.4	348.2	1.7	-532.5	21.3	637.6	10 723.7	13.1	0.8
2nd quarter	1 456.7	1 969.6	1 617.1	352.5	6.4	-519.2	21.1	640.1	10 867.3	13.2	1.0
3rd quarter	1 543.5	2 053.4	1 690.5	362.8	3.3	-513.2	97.9	710.7	11 041.9	13.1	0.9
4th quarter	1 607.1	2 102.6	1 742.3	360.3	1.4	-496.9	54.9	745.6	11 242.4	13.8	1.7
2004											
1st quarter	1 576.7	2 140.2	1 781.9	358.3	1.8	-565.4	43.9	767.0	11 457.6	13.4	1.4
2nd quarter	1 614.0	2 263.8	1 892.2	371.7	1.6	-651.4	88.2	869.3	11 601.5	13.2	1.1
3rd quarter	1 642.2	2 293.6	1 917.7	375.9	3.7	-655.1	66.8	758.7	11 778.4	13.4	0.3
4th quarter	1 608.4	2 339.9	1 960.2	379.7	1.9	-733.4	67.8	897.9	11 930.6	12.9	0.8
2005											
1st quarter	1 645.7	2 397.1	2 013.5	383.6	10.8	-762.1	37.4	929.3	12 170.1	13.2	1.2
2nd quarter	1 653.1	2 404.4	2 009.1	395.3	2.4	-753.6	88.1	913.3	12 286.5	12.7	0.6
3rd quarter	1 737.9	2 452.9	2 052.6	400.3	2.2	-717.2	84.5	554.9	12 541.2	13.2	-1.9
4th quarter	1 695.4	2 563.6	2 154.5	409.1	2.1	-870.2	74.3	1 001.1	12 668.7	12.8	0.5

. . . = Not available.

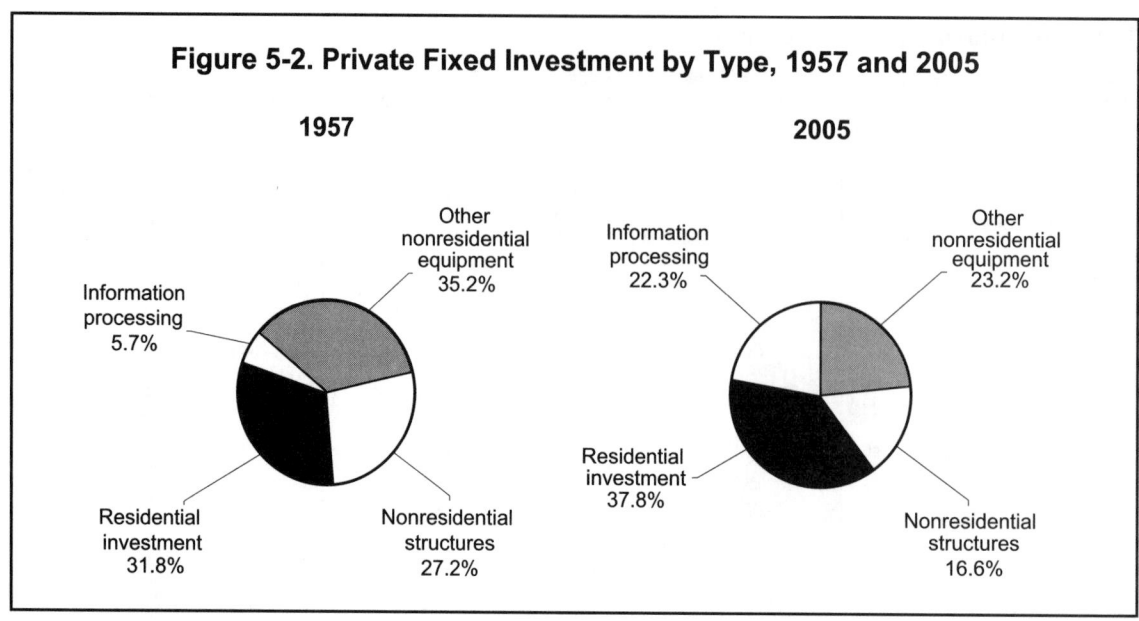

Figure 5-2. Private Fixed Investment by Type, 1957 and 2005

- Between 1957 (a high year in an early postwar business cycle) and 2005, the quantity of aggregate gross private fixed investment increased more than sevenfold, with an average annual growth rate of 4.2 percent. Every major type of investment, except for structures for manufacturing (i.e., building new factories), grew in real terms between those two years. (Table 5-4)

- However, the composition of this investment changed markedly. Information processing software and equipment rose from 5.7 percent to 22.3 percent of current-dollar value, while other equipment became relatively less important, decreasing from 35.2 percent to 23.2 percent of current-dollar value. Nonresidential structures also lost relative importance, falling from 27.3 percent to 16.6 percent of current-dollar value, while residential investment grew from 31.8 percent to 37.8 percent of current-dollar value. (Table 5-2)

Table 5-2. Gross Private Fixed Investment by Type

(Billions of dollars, quarterly data are at seasonally adjusted annual rates.) **NIPA Table 5.3.5**

Year and quarter	Total gross private fixed investment	Nonresidential									
		Total	Structures						Equipment and software		
			Total	Commercial and health care	Manufac-turing	Power and communi-cation	Mining exploration, shafts, and wells	Other non-residential structures	Total	Information processing equipment and software	
										Total	Computers and peripheral equipment
1950	48.3	27.8	10.0	1.8	1.1	2.8	1.4	2.9	17.8	1.8	. . .
1951	50.3	31.8	12.0	1.9	2.1	3.0	1.7	3.2	19.9	2.1	. . .
1952	50.5	31.9	12.2	1.6	2.3	3.1	2.0	3.3	19.7	2.4	. . .
1953	54.5	35.1	13.6	2.1	2.2	3.6	2.1	3.5	21.5	2.7	. . .
1954	55.8	34.7	13.9	2.6	2.0	3.3	2.3	3.6	20.8	2.4	. . .
1955	64.0	39.0	15.2	3.4	2.3	3.3	2.5	3.7	23.9	2.8	. . .
1956	68.1	44.5	18.2	4.2	3.2	4.1	2.7	4.0	26.3	3.4	. . .
1957	69.7	47.5	19.0	4.1	3.6	4.5	2.6	4.1	28.6	4.0	. . .
1958	64.9	42.5	17.6	4.2	2.4	4.4	2.4	4.2	24.9	3.6	. . .
1959	74.6	46.5	18.1	4.6	2.1	4.3	2.5	4.7	28.4	4.0	0.0
1960	75.7	49.4	19.6	4.8	2.9	4.4	2.3	5.2	29.8	4.9	0.2
1961	75.2	48.8	19.7	5.5	2.8	4.1	2.3	5.0	29.1	5.3	0.3
1962	82.0	53.1	20.8	6.2	2.8	4.1	2.5	5.2	32.3	5.7	0.3
1963	88.1	56.0	21.2	6.1	2.9	4.4	2.3	5.6	34.8	6.5	0.7
1964	97.2	63.0	23.7	6.8	3.6	4.8	2.4	6.2	39.2	7.4	0.9
1965	109.0	74.8	28.3	8.2	5.1	5.4	2.4	7.2	46.5	8.5	1.2
1966	117.7	85.4	31.3	8.3	6.6	6.3	2.5	7.8	54.0	10.7	1.7
1967	118.7	86.4	31.5	8.2	6.0	7.1	2.4	7.8	54.9	11.3	1.9
1968	132.1	93.4	33.6	9.4	6.0	8.3	2.6	7.3	59.9	11.9	1.9
1969	147.3	104.7	37.7	11.7	6.8	8.7	2.8	7.8	67.0	14.6	2.4
1970	150.4	109.0	40.3	12.5	7.0	10.2	2.8	7.8	68.7	16.6	2.7
1971	169.9	114.1	42.7	14.9	6.3	11.0	2.7	7.9	71.5	17.3	2.8
1972	198.5	128.8	47.2	17.6	5.9	12.1	3.1	8.6	81.7	19.5	3.5
1973	228.6	153.3	55.0	19.8	7.9	13.8	3.5	9.9	98.3	23.1	3.5
1974	235.4	169.5	61.2	20.6	10.0	15.1	5.2	10.3	108.2	27.0	3.9
1975	236.5	173.7	61.4	17.7	10.6	15.7	7.4	10.1	112.4	28.5	3.6
1976	274.8	192.4	65.9	18.1	10.1	18.2	8.6	11.0	126.4	32.7	4.4
1977	339.0	228.7	74.6	20.3	11.1	19.3	11.5	12.5	154.1	39.2	5.7
1978	412.2	280.6	93.6	25.3	16.2	21.4	15.4	15.2	187.0	48.7	7.6
1979	474.9	333.9	117.7	33.5	22.0	24.6	19.0	18.5	216.2	58.5	10.2
1980	485.6	362.4	136.2	41.0	20.5	27.3	27.4	20.0	226.2	68.8	12.5
1981	542.6	420.0	167.3	48.3	25.4	30.0	42.5	21.2	252.7	81.5	17.1
1982	532.1	426.5	177.6	55.8	26.1	29.6	44.8	21.3	248.9	88.3	18.9
1983	570.1	417.2	154.3	55.8	19.5	25.8	30.0	23.3	262.9	100.1	23.9
1984	670.2	489.6	177.4	70.6	20.9	26.5	31.3	28.1	312.2	121.5	31.6
1985	714.4	526.2	194.5	84.1	24.1	26.5	27.9	31.8	331.7	130.3	33.7
1986	739.9	519.8	176.5	80.9	21.0	28.3	15.7	30.7	343.3	136.8	33.4
1987	757.8	524.1	174.2	80.8	21.2	25.4	13.1	33.7	349.9	141.2	35.8
1988	803.1	563.8	182.8	86.3	23.2	25.0	15.7	32.5	381.0	154.9	38.0
1989	847.3	607.7	193.7	88.3	28.8	27.5	14.9	34.3	414.0	172.6	43.1
1990	846.4	622.4	202.9	87.5	33.6	26.3	17.9	37.6	419.5	177.2	38.6
1991	803.3	598.2	183.6	68.9	31.4	31.6	18.5	33.2	414.6	182.9	37.7
1992	848.5	612.1	172.6	64.5	29.0	33.9	14.2	31.0	439.6	199.9	44.0
1993	932.5	666.6	177.2	69.4	23.6	33.2	16.6	34.5	489.4	217.6	47.9
1994	1 033.3	731.4	186.8	75.4	28.9	31.2	16.4	34.9	544.6	235.2	52.4
1995	1 112.9	810.0	207.3	83.1	35.5	33.1	15.0	40.6	602.8	263.0	66.1
1996	1 209.5	875.4	224.6	91.5	38.2	29.2	16.8	49.0	650.8	290.1	72.8
1997	1 317.8	968.7	250.3	104.3	37.6	28.8	22.4	57.3	718.3	330.3	81.4
1998	1 438.4	1 052.6	275.2	115.4	40.5	33.6	23.4	62.3	777.3	363.4	87.2
1999	1 558.8	1 133.9	282.2	124.3	32.6	39.5	20.6	65.2	851.7	411.0	96.0
2000	1 679.0	1 232.1	313.2	137.6	31.8	46.8	27.2	69.9	918.9	467.6	101.4
2001	1 646.1	1 176.8	322.6	134.9	29.5	49.6	39.2	69.4	854.2	437.0	85.4
2002	1 570.2	1 066.3	279.2	116.8	17.8	49.5	35.6	59.5	787.1	399.4	77.2
2003	1 649.8	1 077.4	277.2	112.2	16.7	44.2	45.7	58.4	800.2	406.7	77.8
2004	1 830.6	1 155.3	300.8	122.3	18.5	41.7	54.9	63.5	854.5	431.6	82.3
2005	2 036.2	1 265.7	338.6	132.5	24.1	41.2	76.4	64.3	927.1	454.3	85.1
2003											
1st quarter	1 583.3	1 044.0	269.9	109.3	15.6	47.4	41.3	56.3	774.1	393.8	75.3
2nd quarter	1 620.6	1 067.4	279.2	110.4	17.0	45.4	46.7	59.7	788.2	394.9	73.5
3rd quarter	1 678.7	1 093.3	280.2	113.3	17.2	42.7	48.1	58.9	813.2	412.5	79.1
4th quarter	1 716.4	1 104.8	279.6	115.5	17.1	41.4	46.8	58.7	825.2	425.5	83.4
2004											
1st quarter	1 743.9	1 112.1	286.5	115.7	17.2	42.9	51.0	59.7	825.6	430.0	81.4
2nd quarter	1 812.8	1 137.6	296.8	123.3	17.0	38.7	53.9	63.9	840.8	428.1	79.0
3rd quarter	1 862.9	1 170.0	306.4	126.0	18.3	41.2	55.7	65.2	863.6	431.5	83.0
4th quarter	1 902.9	1 201.5	313.6	124.3	21.4	43.9	58.9	65.1	887.9	436.5	85.9
2005											
1st quarter	1 954.1	1 230.0	326.5	129.0	22.8	43.3	66.4	64.9	903.5	447.0	85.4
2nd quarter	2 016.7	1 251.8	332.0	131.2	22.8	41.8	73.1	63.1	919.8	452.3	85.3
3rd quarter	2 067.9	1 276.7	336.3	133.0	24.3	39.0	76.8	63.1	940.4	456.6	83.9
4th quarter	2 105.8	1 304.3	359.7	137.0	26.6	40.7	89.3	66.1	944.7	461.3	85.9

. . . = Not available.

Table 5-2. Gross Private Fixed Investment by Type—Continued

(Billions of dollars, quarterly data are at seasonally adjusted annual rates.)

NIPA Table 5.3.5

Year and quarter	Nonresidential—Continued: Equipment and software—Continued					Total	Residential						
	Information processing equipment and software—Continued		Industrial equipment	Transportation equipment	Other nonresidential equipment		Residential structures					Residential equipment
	Software [1]	Other information processing					Total	Permanent site: Total	Single family	Multifamily	Other residential structures	
1950	...	1.8	4.5	6.4	5.1	20.5	20.2	16.1	...	...	4.0	0.4
1951	...	2.1	5.7	6.6	5.5	18.4	18.1	13.8	...	...	4.3	0.4
1952	...	2.4	5.9	5.7	5.6	18.6	18.2	13.4	...	...	4.9	0.4
1953	...	2.7	6.7	6.6	5.6	19.4	19.0	13.9	...	...	5.1	0.4
1954	...	2.4	7.1	6.0	5.3	21.1	20.7	15.4	...	...	5.3	0.4
1955	...	2.8	7.3	7.5	6.3	25.0	24.6	18.6	...	...	6.0	0.4
1956	...	3.4	8.8	7.4	6.7	23.6	23.1	16.5	...	...	6.6	0.5
1957	...	4.0	9.6	8.3	6.7	22.2	21.7	15.1	...	...	6.6	0.5
1958	...	3.6	8.2	6.1	6.9	22.3	21.9	15.4	13.1	2.3	6.4	0.5
1959	0.0	4.0	8.5	8.3	7.6	28.1	27.5	19.7	16.7	3.0	7.9	0.6
1960	0.1	4.6	9.4	8.5	7.1	26.3	25.8	17.5	14.9	2.6	8.3	0.5
1961	0.2	4.8	8.8	8.0	7.0	26.4	25.9	17.4	14.1	3.3	8.5	0.5
1962	0.2	5.1	9.3	9.8	7.5	29.0	28.4	19.9	15.1	4.8	8.5	0.5
1963	0.4	5.4	10.0	9.4	8.8	32.1	31.5	22.4	16.0	6.4	9.1	0.6
1964	0.5	5.9	11.4	10.6	9.9	34.3	33.6	24.1	17.6	6.4	9.5	0.6
1965	0.7	6.7	13.7	13.2	11.0	34.2	33.5	23.8	17.8	6.0	9.7	0.7
1966	1.0	8.0	16.2	14.5	12.7	32.3	31.6	21.8	16.6	5.2	9.8	0.7
1967	1.2	8.2	16.9	14.3	12.4	32.4	31.6	21.5	16.8	4.7	10.1	0.7
1968	1.3	8.7	17.3	17.6	13.0	38.7	37.9	26.7	19.5	7.2	11.1	0.9
1969	1.8	10.4	19.1	18.9	14.4	42.6	41.6	29.2	19.7	9.5	12.4	1.0
1970	2.3	11.6	20.3	16.2	15.6	41.4	40.2	27.1	17.5	9.5	13.2	1.1
1971	2.4	12.2	19.5	18.4	16.3	55.8	54.5	38.7	25.8	12.9	15.8	1.3
1972	2.8	13.2	21.4	21.8	19.0	69.7	68.1	50.1	32.8	17.2	18.0	1.5
1973	3.2	16.3	26.0	26.6	22.6	75.3	73.6	54.6	35.2	19.4	19.0	1.7
1974	3.9	19.2	30.7	26.3	24.3	66.0	64.1	43.4	29.7	13.7	20.7	1.9
1975	4.8	20.2	31.3	25.2	27.4	62.7	60.8	36.3	29.6	6.7	24.5	1.9
1976	5.2	23.1	34.1	30.0	29.6	82.5	80.4	50.8	43.9	6.9	29.6	2.1
1977	5.5	28.0	39.4	39.3	36.3	110.3	107.9	72.2	62.2	10.0	35.7	2.4
1978	6.3	34.8	47.7	47.3	43.2	131.6	128.9	85.6	72.8	12.8	43.3	2.7
1979	8.1	40.2	56.2	53.6	47.9	141.0	137.8	89.3	72.3	17.0	48.6	3.2
1980	9.8	46.4	60.7	48.4	48.3	123.2	119.8	69.6	52.9	16.7	50.2	3.4
1981	11.8	52.5	65.5	50.6	55.2	122.6	118.9	69.4	52.0	17.5	49.5	3.6
1982	14.0	55.3	62.7	46.8	51.2	105.7	102.0	57.0	41.5	15.5	45.0	3.7
1983	16.4	59.8	58.9	53.5	50.4	152.9	148.6	95.0	72.5	22.4	53.7	4.2
1984	20.4	69.6	68.1	64.4	58.1	180.6	175.9	114.6	86.4	28.2	61.3	4.7
1985	23.8	72.9	72.5	69.0	59.9	188.2	183.1	115.9	87.4	28.5	67.2	5.1
1986	25.6	77.7	75.4	70.5	60.7	220.1	214.6	135.2	104.1	31.0	79.4	5.5
1987	29.0	76.4	76.7	68.1	63.9	233.7	227.9	142.7	117.2	25.5	85.2	5.8
1988	34.2	82.8	84.2	72.9	69.0	239.3	233.2	142.4	120.1	22.3	90.9	6.1
1989	41.9	87.6	93.3	67.9	80.2	239.5	233.4	143.2	120.9	22.3	90.1	6.1
1990	47.6	90.9	92.1	70.0	80.2	224.0	218.0	132.1	112.9	19.3	85.8	6.0
1991	53.7	91.5	89.3	71.5	70.8	205.1	199.4	114.6	99.4	15.1	84.8	5.7
1992	57.9	98.1	93.0	74.7	72.0	236.3	230.4	135.1	122.0	13.1	95.3	5.9
1993	64.3	105.4	102.2	89.4	80.2	266.0	259.9	150.9	140.1	10.8	109.0	6.1
1994	68.3	114.6	113.6	107.7	88.1	301.9	295.6	176.4	162.3	14.1	119.2	6.2
1995	74.6	122.3	129.0	116.1	94.7	302.8	296.5	171.4	153.5	17.9	125.1	6.3
1996	85.5	131.9	136.5	123.2	101.0	334.1	327.8	191.1	170.8	20.3	136.7	6.3
1997	107.5	141.4	140.4	135.5	112.1	349.1	342.8	198.1	175.2	22.9	144.8	6.3
1998	124.0	152.2	146.4	144.0	123.5	385.8	379.3	224.0	199.4	24.6	155.3	6.6
1999	152.6	162.4	147.0	167.6	126.0	424.9	417.8	251.3	223.8	27.4	166.6	7.0
2000	176.2	190.0	159.2	160.8	131.2	446.9	439.5	265.0	236.8	28.3	174.5	7.4
2001	174.7	177.0	146.7	141.7	128.8	469.3	461.9	279.4	249.1	30.3	182.5	7.4
2002	167.6	154.5	135.7	126.3	125.7	503.9	496.3	298.8	265.9	33.0	197.5	7.6
2003	171.4	157.5	140.7	118.3	134.5	572.4	564.5	345.7	310.6	35.1	218.8	7.9
2004	184.3	164.9	138.4	141.6	143.0	675.3	666.8	417.5	377.6	39.9	249.3	8.5
2005	194.0	175.2	155.1	158.3	159.4	770.4	761.3	481.7	433.5	48.2	279.6	9.1
2003												
1st quarter	166.1	152.4	141.1	110.4	128.8	539.3	531.8	326.0	291.0	35.0	205.8	7.5
2nd quarter	167.5	153.9	144.9	117.3	131.1	553.2	545.5	330.5	296.0	34.5	215.0	7.7
3rd quarter	174.6	158.8	141.3	121.3	138.1	585.4	577.4	349.8	314.2	35.5	227.6	8.0
4th quarter	177.4	164.7	135.4	124.3	139.9	611.6	603.5	376.5	341.0	35.5	227.0	8.1
2004												
1st quarter	181.6	167.0	134.5	122.9	138.2	631.8	623.5	390.5	353.5	37.0	233.0	8.3
2nd quarter	181.9	167.2	134.3	136.9	141.4	675.2	666.9	415.4	376.4	39.0	251.5	8.4
3rd quarter	185.4	163.1	140.9	146.6	144.6	692.9	684.4	430.5	388.9	41.6	253.9	8.5
4th quarter	188.3	162.3	143.7	159.8	147.9	701.4	692.7	433.6	391.5	42.1	259.0	8.7
2005												
1st quarter	189.7	171.8	150.1	155.5	150.9	724.1	715.3	452.4	407.4	45.0	262.8	8.9
2nd quarter	193.8	173.3	149.5	158.0	159.9	764.9	755.8	474.1	427.5	46.6	281.7	9.1
3rd quarter	195.6	177.2	157.0	165.0	161.8	791.2	782.0	493.1	443.6	49.5	288.9	9.2
4th quarter	196.9	178.4	163.9	154.6	164.9	801.5	792.1	507.3	455.5	51.8	284.8	9.4

[1] Excludes software "embedded," or bundled, in computers and other equipment.
... = Not available.

Table 5-3. Real Gross Private Fixed Investment by Type

(Billions of chained [2000] dollars, quarterly data are at seasonally adjusted annual rates.) NIPA Table 5.3.6

Year and quarter	Total gross private fixed investment	Nonresidential							Equipment and software		
		Total	Structures						Total	Information processing equipment and software	
			Total	Commercial and health care	Manufacturing	Power and communication	Mining exploration, shafts, and wells	Other nonresidential structures		Total	Computers and peripheral equipment [1]
1990	886.6	595.1	275.2	119.6	45.4	33.4	26.6	50.4	355.0	100.7	...
1991	829.1	563.2	244.6	92.9	41.8	39.6	26.0	43.8	345.9	105.9	...
1992	878.3	581.3	229.9	86.4	38.4	42.0	21.5	40.6	371.1	122.2	...
1993	953.5	631.9	228.3	89.9	30.2	39.3	24.8	43.8	417.4	138.2	...
1994	1 042.3	689.9	232.3	94.1	35.7	35.6	23.9	42.8	467.2	155.7	...
1995	1 109.6	762.5	247.1	99.7	42.1	36.3	20.3	47.9	523.1	182.7	...
1996	1 209.2	833.6	261.1	107.4	44.2	31.3	21.5	56.4	578.7	218.9	...
1997	1 320.6	934.2	280.1	118.6	42.3	30.1	25.3	63.9	658.3	269.9	...
1998	1 455.0	1 037.8	294.5	125.4	43.7	34.7	23.3	67.4	745.6	328.9	...
1999	1 576.3	1 133.3	293.2	129.4	33.9	40.8	21.3	67.9	840.2	398.5	...
2000	1 679.0	1 232.1	313.2	137.6	31.8	46.8	27.2	69.9	918.9	467.6	...
2001	1 629.4	1 180.5	306.1	130.3	28.5	48.2	32.0	66.6	874.2	459.0	...
2002	1 544.6	1 071.5	253.8	109.8	16.7	47.1	24.5	55.9	820.2	437.4	...
2003	1 596.9	1 081.8	243.5	102.6	15.4	41.0	29.0	53.4	843.1	462.7	...
2004	1 713.9	1 145.8	248.7	105.2	16.2	35.8	32.8	55.1	904.2	509.3	...
2005	1 842.0	1 223.8	251.5	104.4	19.6	33.5	36.4	52.2	984.9	552.6	...
1994											
1st quarter	1 011.6	665.9	222.4	87.7	31.4	36.2	23.7	43.1	452.1	149.0	...
2nd quarter	1 036.0	679.3	235.0	96.9	35.6	35.2	23.3	43.8	455.7	152.7	...
3rd quarter	1 046.4	692.0	234.7	96.0	36.6	35.4	23.8	42.7	467.4	157.1	...
4th quarter	1 075.1	722.6	237.1	95.8	39.1	35.6	25.0	41.7	493.7	164.0	...
1995											
1st quarter	1 099.6	752.1	243.1	99.0	40.0	37.2	22.0	44.4	516.5	171.6	...
2nd quarter	1 095.5	757.4	247.9	100.3	43.3	37.3	20.0	46.1	517.8	180.2	...
3rd quarter	1 110.1	762.5	249.8	100.1	43.0	36.4	19.6	49.7	521.2	184.1	...
4th quarter	1 133.3	777.9	247.7	99.3	42.0	34.4	19.6	51.5	537.0	194.8	...
1996											
1st quarter	1 161.8	797.1	252.1	99.6	44.3	32.8	20.4	54.4	551.6	205.1	...
2nd quarter	1 199.7	820.0	257.6	106.0	43.4	31.2	21.9	54.9	568.7	214.1	...
3rd quarter	1 227.4	847.3	260.7	109.4	42.5	30.1	21.9	56.8	591.8	224.3	...
4th quarter	1 247.8	870.1	273.8	114.5	46.8	30.9	22.1	59.3	602.9	232.0	...
1997											
1st quarter	1 272.0	892.2	276.2	119.4	42.4	29.1	24.8	60.7	621.8	246.6	...
2nd quarter	1 299.4	914.3	273.7	114.6	40.9	29.5	25.6	63.2	644.7	260.7	...
3rd quarter	1 349.6	961.1	284.2	120.9	43.6	30.6	25.1	64.1	680.5	280.6	...
4th quarter	1 361.4	969.0	286.3	119.4	42.2	31.3	25.7	67.8	686.3	291.5	...
1998											
1st quarter	1 402.4	1 001.6	286.7	120.8	44.8	34.0	23.6	63.5	717.2	309.9	...
2nd quarter	1 444.5	1 032.5	298.0	126.7	44.6	34.9	24.0	67.9	737.3	322.7	...
3rd quarter	1 465.1	1 042.4	295.5	124.7	43.2	35.1	23.9	68.6	749.1	332.2	...
4th quarter	1 507.7	1 074.7	297.6	129.5	42.1	35.0	21.8	69.5	778.6	350.7	...
1999											
1st quarter	1 531.0	1 094.0	292.0	128.4	38.1	36.7	20.0	68.9	802.7	369.5	...
2nd quarter	1 568.6	1 127.3	294.1	129.5	34.3	39.2	21.7	69.6	833.5	395.8	...
3rd quarter	1 598.6	1 154.4	291.8	129.9	32.6	42.6	20.5	66.2	862.4	412.8	...
4th quarter	1 606.9	1 157.3	294.8	129.9	30.5	44.8	22.8	66.9	862.3	415.8	...
2000											
1st quarter	1 651.1	1 196.7	299.9	130.8	31.0	44.7	24.2	69.2	896.7	442.9	...
2nd quarter	1 689.1	1 238.6	312.5	136.7	33.0	45.7	26.9	70.2	926.0	465.7	...
3rd quarter	1 686.4	1 245.2	319.7	140.8	31.6	47.8	28.2	71.3	925.5	473.8	...
4th quarter	1 689.4	1 247.9	320.6	141.9	31.6	49.0	29.4	68.8	927.3	488.1	...
2001											
1st quarter	1 678.2	1 234.4	313.8	140.8	32.4	44.1	31.7	64.6	920.8	485.7	...
2nd quarter	1 640.5	1 190.2	310.6	135.4	30.2	47.6	32.6	64.4	879.2	461.4	...
3rd quarter	1 621.9	1 169.3	315.1	126.1	28.9	49.1	34.1	76.1	852.9	447.3	...
4th quarter	1 577.0	1 128.2	284.9	118.9	22.6	52.2	29.7	61.1	843.8	441.7	...
2002											
1st quarter	1 551.5	1 090.3	270.3	116.5	19.3	53.5	24.0	57.9	820.9	435.0	...
2nd quarter	1 545.9	1 073.3	256.4	111.2	17.3	47.9	23.4	57.4	819.0	437.1	...
3rd quarter	1 543.2	1 068.0	245.8	107.3	15.2	43.2	25.4	54.5	825.7	444.2	...
4th quarter	1 537.8	1 054.5	242.5	104.2	14.9	43.8	25.4	53.8	815.4	433.3	...
2003											
1st quarter	1 536.3	1 047.5	238.2	100.2	14.4	44.4	26.5	51.7	813.3	442.1	...
2nd quarter	1 575.6	1 074.5	246.5	101.4	15.7	42.3	30.0	54.8	831.7	446.0	...
3rd quarter	1 626.7	1 098.8	246.0	103.9	15.9	39.5	30.3	53.9	857.8	470.4	...
4th quarter	1 648.9	1 106.5	243.1	104.7	15.7	37.9	29.2	53.2	869.5	492.4	...
2004											
1st quarter	1 658.0	1 111.2	245.0	103.0	15.5	38.7	31.5	53.2	872.0	501.8	...
2nd quarter	1 704.4	1 130.7	249.1	107.5	15.1	33.6	33.2	56.0	887.6	503.1	...
3rd quarter	1 736.1	1 158.8	251.0	107.2	15.9	34.8	33.3	56.1	915.1	510.3	...
4th quarter	1 757.1	1 182.3	249.7	103.2	18.3	36.3	33.3	55.0	942.0	521.8	...
2005											
1st quarter	1 790.6	1 199.7	253.0	105.0	19.1	35.6	34.9	54.1	956.5	537.4	...
2nd quarter	1 835.8	1 214.8	251.7	104.6	18.8	34.0	36.9	51.8	974.8	547.9	...
3rd quarter	1 864.2	1 232.4	247.1	103.6	19.6	31.6	36.0	50.9	1 000.6	557.7	...
4th quarter	1 877.3	1 248.2	254.2	104.4	21.0	32.6	37.9	52.2	1 007.6	567.3	...

[1]See notes and definitions.
. . . = Not available.

Table 5-3. Real Gross Private Fixed Investment by Type—Continued

(Billions of chained [2000] dollars, quarterly data are at seasonally adjusted annual rates.) **NIPA Table 5.3.6**

Year and quarter	Nonresidential—Continued — Equipment and software—Continued — Information processing equipment and software—Continued — Software[2]	Other information processing	Industrial equipment	Transportation equipment	Other nonresidential equipment	Residential — Total	Residential structures — Total	Permanent site — Total	Single family	Multifamily	Other residential structures	Residential equipment
1990	39.9	80.1	109.2	81.0	96.0	298.9	292.6	181.3	154.2	26.7	111.6	6.0
1991	45.1	79.6	102.2	78.8	82.0	270.2	264.0	156.1	135.1	20.6	107.8	5.8
1992	53.0	84.4	104.0	80.2	81.6	307.6	301.4	182.0	164.1	17.5	119.5	6.0
1993	59.3	90.9	112.9	95.1	89.3	332.7	326.4	194.3	179.7	14.1	132.1	6.1
1994	65.1	99.4	122.9	111.4	96.5	364.8	358.6	217.6	198.9	18.2	141.2	6.1
1995	71.6	107.0	134.9	120.6	101.7	353.1	346.8	203.2	180.6	22.6	143.4	6.2
1996	84.1	117.2	139.9	125.4	105.6	381.3	375.1	222.3	197.3	25.0	152.8	6.2
1997	108.8	127.3	143.0	135.9	115.8	388.6	382.4	223.5	196.6	26.9	158.8	6.1
1998	129.4	143.2	148.1	145.4	125.7	418.3	411.9	244.7	218.1	26.6	167.1	6.4
1999	157.2	158.0	147.9	167.7	126.7	443.6	436.6	262.9	234.2	28.7	173.6	7.0
2000	176.2	190.0	159.2	160.8	131.2	446.9	439.5	265.0	236.8	28.3	174.5	7.4
2001	173.8	181.7	145.7	142.8	126.9	448.5	441.1	266.6	237.1	29.5	174.5	7.4
2002	169.7	161.1	134.5	126.0	122.9	469.9	462.2	277.3	246.3	31.0	184.9	7.7
2003	177.3	167.1	138.4	113.8	130.4	509.4	501.2	304.5	272.6	31.9	196.7	8.1
2004	195.0	180.7	132.7	128.8	137.6	559.9	550.9	339.4	305.0	34.4	211.3	9.0
2005	206.2	193.6	143.5	145.4	147.3	608.0	598.5	375.5	336.3	39.2	222.5	9.4
1994												
1st quarter	63.0	96.5	119.7	109.3	94.1	358.8	352.8	213.3	197.5	15.2	139.6	6.0
2nd quarter	64.4	98.0	120.6	105.2	95.7	370.9	364.8	222.5	204.6	17.4	142.5	6.1
3rd quarter	66.0	100.1	123.9	108.0	97.0	367.0	360.9	219.7	199.7	19.6	141.4	6.1
4th quarter	67.1	102.9	127.6	123.2	99.3	362.3	355.9	214.8	193.8	20.7	141.3	6.3
1995												
1st quarter	68.1	106.6	133.2	130.5	102.3	354.2	347.9	208.2	186.2	21.8	139.8	6.2
2nd quarter	70.2	107.6	135.3	117.7	101.5	342.9	336.6	196.4	174.7	21.6	140.1	6.1
3rd quarter	72.7	105.8	136.2	115.4	101.1	353.6	347.2	200.5	177.2	23.2	146.6	6.2
4th quarter	75.6	108.0	135.0	118.6	102.1	361.6	355.3	207.9	184.1	23.8	147.3	6.2
1996												
1st quarter	78.6	113.0	138.2	117.1	103.0	371.1	364.9	215.2	190.4	24.8	149.7	6.1
2nd quarter	81.9	116.2	140.8	120.8	104.3	386.8	380.5	227.0	200.2	26.9	153.5	6.3
3rd quarter	85.4	119.6	139.5	132.0	107.1	385.7	379.6	225.1	201.1	23.8	154.5	6.1
4th quarter	90.3	120.1	141.2	131.8	108.0	381.8	375.5	221.9	197.4	24.5	153.6	6.2
1997												
1st quarter	99.8	120.9	140.5	132.2	110.6	383.1	377.0	221.4	195.1	26.3	155.5	6.1
2nd quarter	105.1	124.1	143.2	135.2	112.4	387.9	381.8	224.2	197.0	27.3	157.5	6.1
3rd quarter	111.8	131.1	143.9	142.3	119.4	389.7	383.5	222.2	196.0	26.2	161.1	6.1
4th quarter	118.7	133.1	144.2	133.8	120.8	393.6	387.5	226.2	198.4	27.9	161.1	6.2
1998												
1st quarter	122.1	139.5	151.1	134.7	125.0	401.8	395.5	232.9	205.0	27.9	162.6	6.3
2nd quarter	126.2	142.2	149.4	140.3	127.8	412.9	406.5	239.5	213.5	26.1	166.9	6.4
3rd quarter	131.5	143.1	145.9	146.8	126.5	424.1	417.7	249.3	223.3	26.0	168.4	6.5
4th quarter	137.8	148.1	146.2	159.8	123.8	434.3	427.7	257.2	230.6	26.6	170.6	6.6
1999												
1st quarter	144.9	149.8	145.6	161.4	127.5	438.1	431.3	261.1	232.5	28.6	170.3	6.7
2nd quarter	154.5	157.0	147.4	165.7	125.1	441.8	434.9	260.3	231.8	28.4	174.6	7.0
3rd quarter	162.2	162.8	149.2	174.6	126.1	444.5	437.3	262.0	232.8	29.2	175.3	7.2
4th quarter	167.2	162.4	149.3	169.1	128.2	449.9	442.7	268.4	239.6	28.8	174.4	7.2
2000												
1st quarter	171.4	179.9	156.3	166.1	131.3	454.5	447.1	272.6	243.5	29.0	174.6	7.3
2nd quarter	175.8	187.7	159.7	167.0	133.6	450.4	443.1	268.8	239.7	29.1	174.3	7.3
3rd quarter	176.2	192.3	161.9	159.5	130.4	441.2	433.8	259.3	232.4	26.8	174.5	7.4
4th quarter	181.2	200.2	159.0	150.7	129.6	441.6	434.2	259.5	231.5	28.0	174.6	7.4
2001												
1st quarter	181.4	193.7	159.3	145.3	130.9	444.0	436.6	263.7	234.6	29.1	172.8	7.4
2nd quarter	174.1	182.9	147.3	144.5	126.3	450.1	442.7	268.4	239.1	29.3	174.3	7.4
3rd quarter	172.3	177.8	140.6	137.6	127.6	452.1	444.8	269.7	240.3	29.4	175.1	7.3
4th quarter	167.4	172.2	135.4	144.0	122.8	447.8	440.4	264.6	234.5	30.1	175.8	7.5
2002												
1st quarter	166.3	162.9	135.8	130.4	120.3	459.0	451.4	268.7	238.0	30.8	182.7	7.6
2nd quarter	170.2	162.6	132.7	126.1	123.8	469.5	461.8	277.3	245.9	31.4	184.5	7.7
3rd quarter	173.4	161.7	134.7	124.1	123.6	471.8	464.2	280.1	248.9	31.2	184.1	7.6
4th quarter	168.7	157.1	134.9	123.5	124.1	479.3	471.6	283.3	252.4	30.8	188.3	7.7
2003												
1st quarter	170.4	160.2	139.1	108.3	125.1	484.1	476.4	289.0	257.4	31.6	187.4	7.7
2nd quarter	171.8	162.4	142.7	116.6	127.1	496.3	488.3	293.8	262.4	31.4	194.6	8.0
3rd quarter	180.6	168.7	138.9	116.8	133.8	521.8	513.5	309.4	276.9	32.5	204.1	8.3
4th quarter	186.3	177.0	132.8	113.5	135.5	535.2	526.7	325.8	293.6	32.0	200.7	8.5
2004												
1st quarter	191.3	181.5	130.6	111.7	134.4	539.2	530.5	327.5	294.8	32.6	202.8	8.7
2nd quarter	192.2	182.9	129.4	123.7	136.1	564.1	555.2	340.0	306.0	33.9	215.0	8.9
3rd quarter	195.8	179.1	134.7	134.3	139.0	568.6	559.4	345.8	310.2	35.5	213.4	9.1
4th quarter	200.7	179.2	136.1	145.3	141.1	567.7	558.4	344.2	308.7	35.4	214.0	9.3
2005												
1st quarter	201.7	189.3	140.4	141.4	141.3	582.8	573.5	358.7	321.1	37.5	214.4	9.3
2nd quarter	205.7	191.5	138.4	144.6	148.0	609.9	600.4	373.1	334.7	38.3	227.0	9.4
3rd quarter	208.0	196.0	144.9	152.3	148.8	620.4	610.8	382.6	342.6	39.9	227.8	9.4
4th quarter	209.5	197.5	150.4	143.2	151.2	618.9	609.2	387.8	346.6	41.1	220.9	9.7

[2]Excludes software "embedded," or bundled, in computers and other equipment.

Table 5-4. Chain-Type Quantity Indexes for Private Fixed Investment by Type

(Index numbers, 2000 = 100.)

NIPA Table 5.3.3

Year and quarter	Total gross private fixed investment	Nonresidential							Equipment and software		
		Total	Structures						Total	Information processing equipment and software	
			Total	Commercial and health care	Manufac-turing	Power and communi-cation	Mining exploration, shafts, and wells	Other non-residential structures		Total	Computers and peripheral equipment
1950	13.0	8.6	26.4	10.8	27.8	42.9	45.6	34.9	5.1	0.2	. . .
1951	12.4	9.0	28.4	10.4	48.8	43.1	47.9	34.1	5.3	0.2	. . .
1952	12.2	8.8	28.3	8.1	52.2	43.5	53.3	34.3	5.1	0.2	. . .
1953	13.0	9.6	30.8	11.1	49.9	47.8	58.2	35.6	5.6	0.3	. . .
1954	13.3	9.4	31.9	13.8	46.7	43.7	64.4	37.5	5.3	0.2	. . .
1955	15.0	10.4	34.2	17.9	51.1	41.6	69.3	37.6	6.0	0.3	. . .
1956	15.0	11.0	37.8	20.3	67.1	48.6	67.0	37.2	6.2	0.3	. . .
1957	14.9	11.2	37.7	19.3	71.2	50.5	63.3	37.2	6.3	0.3	. . .
1958	13.8	10.0	35.7	20.3	49.1	48.5	59.2	38.9	5.4	0.3	. . .
1959	15.7	10.8	36.5	22.0	43.8	46.5	60.7	42.9	6.1	0.3	0.0
1960	15.9	11.4	39.4	23.4	59.3	47.0	57.0	47.7	6.3	0.4	0.0
1961	15.8	11.3	40.0	26.7	58.0	44.0	58.1	46.6	6.2	0.4	0.0
1962	17.2	12.3	41.8	29.7	58.6	44.3	60.9	47.6	6.9	0.5	0.0
1963	18.6	13.0	42.2	28.7	58.8	47.2	57.2	50.3	7.5	0.6	0.0
1964	20.4	14.5	46.6	31.2	70.7	51.4	61.2	55.2	8.5	0.7	0.0
1965	22.5	17.0	54.1	36.6	97.8	56.9	60.5	62.0	10.0	0.8	0.0
1966	23.7	19.2	57.8	35.7	121.5	64.9	57.3	64.4	11.6	1.1	0.0
1967	23.3	18.9	56.3	34.3	106.9	71.0	54.8	63.0	11.5	1.1	0.0
1968	24.9	19.7	57.1	37.5	102.9	78.9	55.1	55.8	12.3	1.2	0.0
1969	26.5	21.2	60.2	43.3	108.2	78.9	57.5	55.4	13.3	1.5	0.0
1970	25.9	21.1	60.4	43.9	104.5	86.3	54.1	52.1	13.2	1.7	0.0
1971	27.9	21.1	59.4	47.9	86.3	87.0	50.0	48.8	13.3	1.8	0.0
1972	31.2	23.1	61.2	52.3	75.4	90.7	53.7	49.3	15.1	2.0	0.0
1973	34.1	26.4	66.2	54.7	93.4	96.5	57.3	53.1	17.8	2.4	0.0
1974	32.0	26.7	64.8	51.3	106.4	90.4	68.1	48.7	18.3	2.7	0.0
1975	28.5	24.0	58.0	39.9	102.0	83.1	79.5	43.0	16.5	2.7	0.0
1976	31.4	25.2	59.4	39.4	94.2	90.6	85.8	45.2	17.6	3.1	0.1
1977	35.9	28.0	61.8	41.5	96.8	89.2	96.9	47.7	20.2	3.8	0.1
1978	40.2	32.2	70.8	47.3	129.1	93.5	110.5	54.1	23.3	4.9	0.2
1979	42.5	35.5	79.7	56.4	158.6	97.0	117.7	59.5	25.3	5.9	0.3
1980	39.7	35.4	84.4	61.9	132.7	97.9	165.4	57.7	24.4	6.9	0.5
1981	40.6	37.4	91.1	66.9	150.6	100.4	192.3	55.8	25.4	8.0	0.7
1982	37.7	36.0	89.5	72.8	145.4	94.8	177.7	52.7	24.1	8.5	0.9
1983	40.5	35.5	79.9	70.7	105.2	81.6	147.2	55.6	25.4	10.0	1.3
1984	47.3	41.8	91.0	86.0	108.8	83.3	167.3	65.1	30.5	12.6	2.2
1985	49.8	44.6	97.5	99.3	121.7	82.4	149.1	71.7	32.4	14.1	2.7
1986	50.4	43.3	86.8	92.3	102.3	87.9	87.3	67.4	33.0	15.2	3.1
1987	50.7	43.3	84.3	89.0	99.7	78.2	85.4	71.4	33.5	16.1	3.9
1988	52.4	45.5	84.9	91.6	105.2	73.8	93.7	66.5	36.0	18.0	4.5
1989	53.9	48.1	86.6	90.5	126.0	76.6	84.7	67.9	38.6	20.5	5.5
1990	52.8	48.3	87.9	86.9	142.8	71.3	97.9	72.1	38.6	21.5	5.4
1991	49.4	45.7	78.1	67.5	131.5	84.7	95.7	62.6	37.6	22.6	5.9
1992	52.3	47.2	73.4	62.8	120.7	89.8	79.2	58.1	40.4	26.1	8.0
1993	56.8	51.3	72.9	65.3	94.8	83.9	91.3	62.7	45.4	29.6	10.3
1994	62.1	56.0	74.2	68.4	112.2	76.0	88.1	61.3	50.8	33.3	12.8
1995	66.1	61.9	78.9	72.5	132.3	77.6	74.7	68.6	56.9	39.1	19.3
1996	72.0	67.7	83.4	78.1	139.1	66.8	79.3	80.7	63.0	46.8	27.8
1997	78.7	75.8	89.4	86.2	132.9	64.4	93.0	91.5	71.6	57.7	40.3
1998	86.7	84.2	94.0	91.2	137.4	74.2	85.8	96.4	81.1	70.3	58.2
1999	93.9	92.0	93.6	94.1	106.5	87.2	78.3	97.2	91.4	85.2	82.5
2000	100.0	100.0	100.0	100.0	100.0	100.0	100.0	100.0	100.0	100.0	100.0
2001	97.0	95.8	97.7	94.7	89.7	103.0	117.8	95.3	95.1	98.2	102.4
2002	92.0	87.0	81.0	79.8	52.4	100.6	90.3	80.0	89.3	93.5	107.3
2003	95.1	87.8	77.7	74.6	48.5	87.7	106.7	76.5	91.7	99.0	121.3
2004	102.1	93.0	79.4	76.5	51.0	76.6	120.8	78.8	98.4	108.9	138.5
2005	109.7	99.3	80.3	75.9	61.8	71.5	134.1	74.8	107.2	118.2	163.3
2003											
1st quarter	91.5	85.0	76.1	72.8	45.2	94.8	97.5	74.0	88.5	94.5	113.6
2nd quarter	93.8	87.2	78.7	73.7	49.4	90.3	110.3	78.5	90.5	95.4	113.5
3rd quarter	96.9	89.2	78.6	75.5	50.1	84.4	111.4	77.2	93.3	100.6	124.4
4th quarter	98.2	89.8	77.6	76.1	49.5	81.1	107.6	76.2	94.6	105.3	133.7
2004											
1st quarter	98.8	90.2	78.2	74.9	48.8	82.6	115.9	76.2	94.9	107.3	132.4
2nd quarter	101.5	91.8	79.5	78.2	47.6	71.8	122.2	80.2	96.6	107.6	130.7
3rd quarter	103.4	94.1	80.1	78.0	50.1	74.3	122.6	80.3	99.6	109.1	141.1
4th quarter	104.7	96.0	79.7	75.0	57.5	77.6	122.5	78.7	102.5	111.6	149.8
2005											
1st quarter	106.7	97.4	80.8	76.3	60.1	76.0	128.5	77.4	104.1	114.9	154.9
2nd quarter	109.3	98.6	80.4	76.0	59.2	72.7	135.7	74.1	106.1	117.2	160.5
3rd quarter	111.0	100.0	78.9	75.3	61.6	67.6	132.6	72.8	108.9	119.3	163.8
4th quarter	111.8	101.3	81.2	75.9	66.1	69.6	139.5	74.8	109.7	121.3	173.9

. . . = Not available.

Table 5-4. Chain-Type Quantity Indexes for Private Fixed Investment by Type—Continued

(Index numbers, 2000 = 100.)

NIPA Table 5.3.3

Year and quarter	Nonresidential—Continued: Equipment and software—Continued: Information processing equipment and software—Continued: Software[1]	Other information processing	Industrial equipment	Transportation equipment	Other nonresidential equipment	Residential: Total	Residential structures: Total	Residential structures: Permanent site: Total	Single family	Multifamily	Other residential structures	Residential equipment
1950	...	2.3	22.1	18.5	24.6	32.3	33.3	45.3	...	...	15.9	9.0
1951	...	2.5	24.8	17.8	24.8	27.0	27.8	36.2	...	...	15.7	8.3
1952	...	2.9	25.7	14.7	25.0	26.6	27.3	34.1	...	...	17.4	8.3
1953	...	3.2	28.3	17.4	24.4	27.5	28.2	35.2	...	...	18.1	8.7
1954	...	2.9	29.2	15.3	23.0	29.8	30.6	38.7	...	...	18.9	8.9
1955	...	3.3	29.0	19.4	27.0	34.6	35.6	45.7	...	...	20.9	10.2
1956	...	3.8	32.0	17.5	27.9	31.8	32.6	39.6	...	...	22.3	11.3
1957	...	4.3	32.4	18.7	26.3	29.8	30.5	36.0	...	...	22.5	11.3
1958	...	3.9	27.0	13.6	26.7	30.2	30.8	36.9	34.6	51.8	21.9	12.0
1959	0.0	4.2	27.4	18.0	28.7	37.8	38.7	47.0	44.0	66.6	26.6	13.8
1960	0.1	4.9	29.6	18.6	26.3	35.1	36.0	41.5	38.9	58.6	27.7	13.0
1961	0.1	5.2	28.0	17.6	26.0	35.2	36.1	41.3	36.8	73.9	28.3	13.0
1962	0.1	5.5	29.4	21.7	27.8	38.6	39.5	47.1	39.3	107.4	28.5	13.8
1963	0.2	5.7	31.8	21.0	32.3	43.2	44.2	53.4	41.9	144.2	30.7	15.4
1964	0.2	6.2	35.9	23.7	35.8	45.7	46.8	57.0	46.0	143.2	31.8	16.5
1965	0.3	7.1	42.4	29.7	39.7	44.3	45.3	54.5	45.0	128.7	31.7	18.4
1966	0.5	8.3	48.7	32.7	44.7	40.4	41.1	47.8	40.0	107.9	31.3	18.8
1967	0.6	8.3	48.9	31.6	42.2	39.1	39.8	45.6	39.2	93.7	31.2	19.3
1968	0.6	8.6	47.9	38.0	42.7	44.4	45.2	53.6	43.1	135.4	32.8	23.0
1969	0.8	9.9	51.1	39.5	45.6	45.7	46.4	55.1	41.0	168.5	33.5	26.2
1970	1.1	10.7	51.9	32.4	47.6	43.0	43.4	49.9	35.6	164.9	33.9	28.6
1971	1.1	10.8	47.6	35.0	47.5	54.8	55.5	67.2	49.4	209.9	38.5	32.0
1972	1.3	11.5	51.3	40.7	53.8	64.5	65.4	81.3	58.7	262.8	42.2	38.4
1973	1.5	13.9	60.7	48.9	62.8	64.1	64.8	80.9	57.4	270.2	41.3	43.2
1974	1.8	15.4	65.4	44.3	62.0	50.9	51.1	58.6	44.1	174.0	40.2	44.0
1975	2.1	14.8	55.4	38.2	57.4	44.3	44.3	44.8	40.2	77.6	43.6	41.0
1976	2.3	16.2	55.7	42.4	57.9	54.7	55.0	58.9	56.0	75.2	49.3	43.1
1977	2.4	19.5	59.0	51.6	65.2	66.4	67.0	76.0	72.0	99.6	53.9	47.2
1978	2.8	23.2	65.7	57.0	71.8	70.6	71.2	79.5	74.4	112.2	59.1	51.3
1979	3.5	26.0	70.4	59.5	73.2	68.0	68.4	74.4	65.9	137.1	59.7	56.2
1980	4.1	28.0	67.4	48.6	65.8	53.6	53.6	52.3	43.3	122.7	55.7	56.3
1981	4.8	29.6	66.3	47.2	67.6	49.3	49.2	48.2	39.4	118.0	50.8	56.2
1982	5.5	29.8	60.5	41.8	58.5	40.4	40.0	37.6	30.2	96.2	43.8	54.0
1983	6.5	31.3	55.7	47.1	56.3	57.1	57.0	61.4	52.5	131.8	50.8	60.3
1984	8.3	35.7	63.8	56.1	63.8	65.6	65.6	72.1	60.9	161.0	56.1	66.8
1985	9.8	36.8	66.7	58.3	64.4	66.6	66.5	71.2	60.4	156.9	59.8	72.1
1986	11.0	38.3	66.4	56.1	63.2	74.8	74.7	79.5	69.1	161.5	67.9	78.0
1987	12.5	36.8	64.8	53.3	65.0	76.3	76.2	80.6	74.7	127.4	69.9	81.2
1988	14.9	39.3	68.0	56.2	68.1	75.5	75.3	77.7	73.8	108.7	72.0	83.9
1989	19.2	41.1	72.8	50.6	76.1	73.2	73.0	75.7	71.7	108.5	69.1	84.4
1990	22.6	42.1	68.6	50.4	73.2	66.9	66.6	68.4	65.1	94.6	64.0	81.9
1991	25.6	41.9	64.2	49.0	62.5	60.5	60.1	58.9	57.1	72.9	61.8	78.7
1992	30.1	44.4	65.3	49.9	62.2	68.8	68.6	68.7	69.3	62.0	68.5	81.1
1993	33.7	47.9	70.9	59.1	68.1	74.4	74.3	73.3	75.9	50.0	75.7	82.7
1994	37.0	52.3	77.2	69.3	73.6	81.6	81.6	82.1	84.0	64.5	80.9	83.2
1995	40.7	56.3	84.7	75.0	77.5	79.0	78.9	76.7	76.3	80.0	82.2	84.3
1996	47.7	61.7	87.9	78.0	80.5	85.3	85.3	83.9	83.3	88.5	87.6	83.9
1997	61.8	67.0	89.8	84.5	88.3	86.9	87.0	84.3	83.0	95.3	91.0	83.2
1998	73.5	75.4	93.0	90.4	95.8	93.6	93.7	92.3	92.1	94.2	95.8	87.6
1999	89.2	83.1	92.9	104.3	96.6	99.3	99.3	99.2	98.9	101.7	99.5	95.3
2000	100.0	100.0	100.0	100.0	100.0	100.0	100.0	100.0	100.0	100.0	100.0	100.0
2001	98.7	95.6	91.5	88.8	96.7	100.4	100.4	100.6	100.1	104.3	100.0	100.4
2002	96.3	84.8	84.5	78.3	93.7	105.1	105.2	104.6	104.0	109.8	106.0	104.1
2003	100.6	87.9	86.9	70.7	99.4	114.0	114.0	114.9	115.1	112.7	112.7	110.3
2004	110.7	95.1	83.4	80.1	104.9	125.3	125.3	128.1	128.8	121.6	121.1	122.1
2005	117.1	101.9	90.1	90.4	112.3	136.1	136.2	141.7	142.0	138.8	127.5	128.2
2003												
1st quarter	96.7	84.3	87.4	67.3	95.3	108.3	108.4	109.0	108.7	111.7	107.4	104.4
2nd quarter	97.5	85.5	89.6	72.5	96.9	111.1	111.1	110.8	110.8	111.1	111.5	108.3
3rd quarter	102.5	88.8	87.3	72.6	101.9	116.8	116.8	116.7	116.9	114.9	117.0	112.9
4th quarter	105.7	93.2	83.4	70.6	103.3	119.8	119.8	122.9	124.0	113.3	115.0	115.4
2004												
1st quarter	108.6	95.5	82.0	69.5	102.5	120.7	120.7	123.6	124.5	115.5	116.2	118.3
2nd quarter	109.1	96.3	81.3	76.9	103.7	126.2	126.3	128.3	129.3	119.8	123.2	120.4
3rd quarter	111.2	94.2	84.6	83.5	105.9	127.2	127.3	130.5	131.0	125.6	122.3	123.7
4th quarter	113.9	94.3	85.5	90.4	107.5	127.0	127.0	129.9	130.4	125.3	122.6	126.2
2005												
1st quarter	114.5	99.6	88.2	87.9	107.7	130.4	130.5	135.3	135.6	132.6	122.9	126.0
2nd quarter	116.8	100.8	86.9	89.9	112.8	136.5	136.6	140.8	141.3	135.6	130.1	127.5
3rd quarter	118.1	103.2	91.0	94.7	113.4	138.8	139.0	144.3	144.7	141.3	130.6	128.2
4th quarter	118.9	103.9	94.5	89.0	115.2	138.5	138.6	146.3	146.4	145.5	126.6	131.3

[1]Excludes software "embedded," or bundled, in computers and other equipment.
. . . = Not available.

Table 5-5. Current-Cost Net Stock of Fixed Assets

(Billions of dollars, year-end estimates.)

Year	Total	Private				Government				Private and government fixed assets				Government, by level	
		Total	Nonresidential		Residential	Total	Nonresidential		Residential	Total	Nonresidential		Residential	Federal	State and local
			Equipment and software	Structures			Equipment and software	Structures			Equipment and software	Structures			
1947	729.8	515.4	68.0	180.0	267.4	214.4	62.0	146.8	5.6	729.8	130.1	326.8	273.0	121.1	93.3
1948	774.6	560.0	82.2	189.8	288.0	214.6	52.2	157.4	5.0	774.6	134.4	347.3	293.0	113.0	101.6
1949	779.1	579.4	86.0	190.9	302.5	199.8	44.3	150.3	5.2	779.1	130.3	341.2	307.7	102.8	96.9
1950	864.7	653.2	99.4	214.1	339.6	211.5	40.5	164.6	6.4	864.7	140.0	378.8	346.0	102.3	109.3
1951	947.2	710.5	109.3	232.4	368.7	236.7	44.3	184.5	7.9	947.2	153.6	417.0	376.6	113.9	122.9
1952	1 001.7	747.6	114.8	245.3	387.4	254.1	50.7	195.9	7.4	1 001.7	165.6	441.3	394.8	123.9	130.2
1953	1 037.0	777.7	124.2	251.7	401.9	259.3	57.5	193.9	7.9	1 037.0	181.7	445.6	409.7	130.5	128.8
1954	1 084.4	809.2	127.7	258.0	423.4	275.2	64.1	200.6	10.6	1 084.4	191.8	458.6	434.0	140.7	134.5
1955	1 178.3	881.4	140.3	284.9	456.2	296.9	69.5	219.7	7.6	1 178.3	209.9	504.7	463.8	147.5	149.4
1956	1 277.6	948.4	157.3	312.9	478.2	329.1	74.1	246.1	8.9	1 277.6	231.4	559.0	487.2	159.8	169.3
1957	1 339.6	996.5	171.3	331.0	494.2	343.2	76.2	257.5	9.4	1 339.6	247.5	588.5	503.6	165.7	177.4
1958	1 381.9	1 020.6	176.7	334.8	509.2	361.3	77.9	273.2	10.2	1 381.9	254.6	607.9	519.4	171.7	189.5
1959	1 436.4	1 064.8	185.7	347.7	531.3	371.6	82.4	278.1	11.1	1 436.4	268.1	625.8	542.4	175.9	195.7
1960	1 481.9	1 096.8	191.6	353.0	552.2	385.1	85.2	288.1	11.8	1 481.9	276.9	641.1	564.0	180.0	205.1
1961	1 536.4	1 132.0	194.8	364.8	572.3	404.4	89.2	302.7	12.6	1 536.4	284.0	667.5	584.9	187.0	217.4
1962	1 604.0	1 173.3	202.2	377.7	593.4	430.7	96.5	320.8	13.5	1 604.0	298.7	698.4	606.9	197.9	232.8
1963	1 660.6	1 209.0	210.7	390.3	608.0	451.6	99.2	338.7	13.7	1 660.6	309.9	729.0	621.8	203.5	248.1
1964	1 767.2	1 293.6	223.4	413.3	657.0	473.7	102.0	357.1	14.6	1 767.2	325.4	770.3	671.6	209.0	264.7
1965	1 883.5	1 379.4	240.7	441.1	697.6	504.0	104.6	384.1	15.3	1 883.5	345.4	825.2	712.9	216.0	288.0
1966	2 041.8	1 496.9	268.2	474.4	754.4	544.9	109.8	418.7	16.4	2 041.8	378.0	893.0	770.8	226.7	318.2
1967	2 197.0	1 608.5	293.8	509.0	805.7	588.6	116.4	454.9	17.3	2 197.0	410.2	963.9	823.0	240.9	347.7
1968	2 411.6	1 772.7	323.9	558.7	890.2	638.9	120.9	498.6	19.4	2 411.6	444.8	1 057.3	909.6	253.0	385.9
1969	2 627.6	1 924.5	357.4	614.7	952.3	703.2	125.1	556.5	21.6	2 627.6	482.5	1 171.2	973.9	267.4	435.8
1970	2 860.8	2 078.4	392.2	678.0	1 008.2	782.4	131.1	628.2	23.1	2 860.8	523.4	1 306.3	1 031.2	285.3	497.1
1971	3 159.1	2 311.6	419.8	758.6	1 133.2	847.5	132.2	689.5	25.9	3 159.1	552.0	1 448.0	1 159.1	299.5	548.0
1972	3 474.0	2 550.6	452.8	830.4	1 267.4	923.4	134.0	760.4	29.0	3 474.0	586.8	1 590.8	1 296.4	322.5	600.9
1973	3 938.4	2 899.6	505.4	941.9	1 452.3	1 038.8	136.2	869.9	32.8	3 938.4	641.5	1 811.8	1 485.0	349.5	689.3
1974	4 692.4	3 415.8	623.4	1 139.6	1 652.7	1 276.6	149.7	1 090.3	36.6	4 692.4	773.1	2 229.9	1 689.4	403.3	873.3
1975	5 075.8	3 734.7	713.9	1 228.9	1 791.8	1 341.1	164.4	1 136.6	40.1	5 075.8	878.3	2 365.5	1 832.0	426.6	914.5
1976	5 533.8	4 115.7	790.4	1 336.5	1 988.9	1 418.1	178.7	1 194.6	44.8	5 533.8	969.1	2 531.1	2 033.6	462.8	955.3
1977	6 194.0	4 686.9	887.7	1 477.9	2 321.2	1 507.1	195.0	1 260.6	51.5	6 194.0	1 082.7	2 738.6	2 372.7	485.7	1 021.4
1978	7 012.2	5 364.2	1 014.2	1 673.0	2 677.0	1 648.0	207.8	1 380.7	59.6	7 012.2	1 222.0	3 053.6	2 736.5	524.0	1 124.0
1979	8 087.7	6 210.7	1 178.5	1 924.0	3 108.2	1 877.0	225.2	1 581.0	70.9	8 087.7	1 403.7	3 504.9	3 179.1	583.9	1 293.1
1980	9 216.7	7 067.8	1 367.4	2 195.8	3 504.6	2 148.9	251.5	1 819.7	77.8	9 216.7	1 618.9	4 015.5	3 582.3	648.0	1 501.0
1981	10 163.3	7 802.6	1 525.1	2 507.8	3 769.7	2 360.7	282.9	1 992.6	85.2	10 163.3	1 808.0	4 500.5	3 854.9	697.1	1 663.6
1982	10 720.3	8 229.0	1 615.8	2 672.6	3 940.6	2 491.3	307.5	2 093.4	90.3	10 720.3	1 923.4	4 766.0	4 030.9	735.5	1 755.8
1983	11 067.2	8 516.4	1 669.4	2 747.3	4 099.7	2 550.9	337.9	2 112.2	100.8	11 067.2	2 007.3	4 859.4	4 200.5	772.4	1 778.5
1984	11 661.4	9 011.2	1 760.7	2 919.4	4 331.1	2 650.3	360.9	2 184.7	104.6	11 661.4	2 121.6	5 104.2	4 435.7	810.6	1 839.7
1985	12 275.5	9 509.0	1 865.6	3 078.6	4 564.7	2 766.5	383.7	2 277.0	105.8	12 275.5	2 249.3	5 355.6	4 670.6	842.4	1 924.1
1986	13 046.3	10 110.1	1 970.1	3 210.1	4 929.9	2 936.2	411.5	2 414.9	109.7	13 046.3	2 381.6	5 625.0	5 039.6	885.2	2 051.0
1987	13 803.5	10 710.8	2 071.2	3 391.1	5 248.5	3 092.6	437.2	2 535.8	119.6	13 803.5	2 508.4	5 926.9	5 368.2	921.5	2 171.1
1988	14 642.9	11 391.6	2 198.7	3 618.5	5 574.3	3 251.3	471.1	2 645.0	135.2	14 642.9	2 669.9	6 263.5	5 709.5	977.3	2 274.0
1989	15 480.2	12 051.7	2 335.2	3 832.9	5 883.6	3 428.5	508.3	2 775.8	144.4	15 480.2	2 843.4	6 608.7	6 028.0	1 031.2	2 397.4
1990	16 211.5	12 610.9	2 469.1	4 030.8	6 111.0	3 600.7	551.1	2 900.4	149.2	16 211.5	3 020.2	6 931.1	6 260.2	1 078.9	2 521.8
1991	16 602.8	12 880.7	2 541.1	4 091.4	6 248.3	3 722.1	583.9	2 988.0	150.2	16 602.8	3 125.0	7 079.4	6 398.5	1 122.5	2 599.6
1992	17 323.9	13 438.8	2 613.9	4 224.9	6 599.9	3 885.1	613.3	3 112.8	159.0	17 323.9	3 227.2	7 337.8	6 758.9	1 169.4	2 715.7
1993	18 231.0	14 166.8	2 728.2	4 433.7	7 004.9	4 064.3	637.0	3 257.0	170.3	18 231.0	3 365.2	7 690.7	7 175.1	1 209.0	2 855.2
1994	19 352.0	15 056.7	2 880.6	4 670.7	7 505.4	4 295.2	665.8	3 447.7	181.7	19 352.0	3 546.4	8 118.4	7 687.1	1 260.7	3 034.5
1995	20 298.9	15 794.3	3 067.4	4 887.1	7 839.8	4 504.7	674.8	3 641.7	188.2	20 298.9	3 742.1	8 528.8	8 028.0	1 291.3	3 213.4
1996	21 299.9	16 618.1	3 233.1	5 114.3	8 270.6	4 681.8	674.8	3 810.5	196.5	21 299.9	3 907.9	8 924.9	8 467.1	1 315.5	3 366.3
1997	22 450.5	17 549.3	3 394.6	5 424.1	8 730.6	4 901.2	671.4	4 032.9	196.8	22 450.5	4 066.1	9 457.0	8 927.5	1 334.7	3 566.5
1998	23 721.6	18 620.5	3 583.8	5 736.6	9 300.1	5 101.1	677.1	4 217.1	206.9	23 721.6	4 260.9	9 953.7	9 507.0	1 355.8	3 745.3
1999	25 246.1	19 847.2	3 822.1	6 038.4	9 986.7	5 398.9	698.2	4 480.7	219.9	25 246.1	4 520.3	10 519.1	10 206.7	1 398.9	4 000.0
2000	26 902.2	21 189.5	4 077.3	6 436.5	10 675.7	5 712.7	703.0	4 778.0	231.7	26 902.2	4 780.3	11 214.5	10 907.4	1 424.6	4 288.1
2001	28 464.7	22 484.8	4 203.2	6 816.8	11 464.8	5 979.9	711.3	5 021.9	246.7	28 464.7	4 914.5	11 838.7	11 711.5	1 446.8	4 533.1
2002	29 788.3	23 522.7	4 270.8	7 058.8	12 193.1	6 265.6	723.2	5 278.8	263.6	29 788.3	4 994.0	12 337.6	12 456.7	1 469.9	4 795.7
2003	31 424.4	24 916.9	4 380.8	7 311.3	13 224.7	6 507.5	738.2	5 489.8	279.5	31 424.4	5 119.0	12 801.1	13 504.3	1 498.9	5 008.6
2004	34 421.1	27 192.8	4 553.6	7 979.4	14 659.8	7 228.3	786.5	6 138.0	303.7	34 421.1	5 340.2	14 117.4	14 963.6	1 593.2	5 635.1
2005	37 250.6	29 343.8	4 742.5	8 801.3	15 800.1	7 906.7	814.6	6 770.4	321.7	37 250.6	5 557.1	15 571.7	16 121.7	1 681.0	6 225.7

Table 5-6. Chain-Type Quantity Indexes for Net Stock of Fixed Assets

(Index numbers, 2000 = 100.)

Year	Total	Private				Government				Private and government fixed assets				Government, by level	
		Total	Nonresidential		Residential	Total	Nonresidential		Residential	Total	Nonresidential		Residential	Federal	State and local
			Equipment and software	Structures			Equipment and software	Structures			Equipment and software	Structures			
1947	20.83	18.35	9.13	24.33	19.73	30.29	50.32	26.13	16.37	20.83	14.98	25.14	19.67	67.93	17.25
1948	21.14	19.16	10.04	24.90	20.60	28.63	39.61	26.39	16.67	21.14	14.26	25.57	20.52	60.29	17.59
1949	21.55	19.81	10.56	25.42	21.36	28.08	34.03	26.91	17.68	21.55	13.94	26.09	21.29	56.40	18.16
1950	22.17	20.68	11.17	26.03	22.49	27.64	28.55	27.59	18.57	22.17	13.71	26.73	22.41	52.62	18.86
1951	23.01	21.45	11.79	26.72	23.37	28.73	30.50	28.44	19.96	23.01	14.52	27.49	23.31	54.76	19.57
1952	23.89	22.17	12.30	27.39	24.21	30.23	34.07	29.46	21.53	23.89	15.46	28.31	24.16	58.56	20.29
1953	24.84	22.95	12.90	28.15	25.07	31.83	37.84	30.55	22.94	24.84	16.51	29.21	25.04	62.46	21.10
1954	25.73	23.72	13.29	28.93	26.02	33.20	39.81	31.80	23.59	25.73	17.12	30.19	25.99	64.78	22.13
1955	26.70	24.65	13.86	29.79	27.17	34.34	40.62	33.05	24.09	26.70	17.73	31.21	27.11	65.96	23.26
1956	27.67	25.56	14.47	30.81	28.16	35.47	41.38	34.30	24.74	27.67	18.36	32.33	28.10	67.04	24.40
1957	28.58	26.41	15.07	31.79	29.06	36.61	41.87	35.59	25.92	28.58	18.95	33.44	29.00	67.90	25.63
1958	29.40	27.10	15.28	32.62	29.94	37.94	42.57	37.04	28.01	29.40	19.23	34.53	29.92	69.14	27.01
1959	30.44	28.00	15.66	33.48	31.15	39.50	44.37	38.49	30.35	30.44	19.81	35.63	31.15	71.20	28.40
1960	31.43	28.88	16.10	34.45	32.22	40.91	45.53	39.93	32.09	31.43	20.36	36.80	32.23	72.70	29.78
1961	32.44	29.72	16.44	35.42	33.27	42.57	47.40	41.50	34.20	32.44	20.91	38.02	33.30	74.84	31.28
1962	33.58	30.71	16.99	36.47	34.44	44.31	49.62	43.08	36.56	33.58	21.70	39.29	34.51	77.17	32.82
1963	34.79	31.81	17.66	37.49	35.80	45.96	50.99	44.82	37.78	34.79	22.47	40.62	35.86	78.72	34.52
1964	36.14	33.07	18.57	38.70	37.24	47.64	52.14	46.64	39.10	36.14	23.42	42.09	37.30	79.99	36.36
1965	37.63	34.50	19.90	40.23	38.60	49.30	52.66	48.58	40.50	37.63	24.64	43.79	38.66	80.79	38.33
1966	39.19	35.98	21.59	41.85	39.75	51.15	53.72	50.64	42.02	39.19	26.25	45.60	39.82	81.95	40.43
1967	40.64	37.31	23.00	43.37	40.84	53.08	55.12	52.71	43.73	40.64	27.67	47.35	40.92	83.06	42.67
1968	42.14	38.74	24.47	44.89	42.12	54.82	55.31	54.81	45.40	42.14	28.97	49.12	42.21	83.16	44.99
1969	43.66	40.27	26.10	46.52	43.44	56.30	54.96	56.68	47.52	43.66	30.32	50.85	43.54	82.79	47.12
1970	45.00	41.63	27.43	48.11	44.62	57.53	54.36	58.28	49.69	45.00	31.38	52.44	44.75	82.16	49.00
1971	46.37	43.13	28.57	49.61	46.28	58.43	52.17	59.81	51.79	46.37	32.03	53.95	46.41	80.59	50.74
1972	47.94	44.89	30.09	51.11	48.29	59.29	50.41	61.20	53.55	47.94	33.07	55.41	48.42	79.33	52.35
1973	49.68	46.87	32.30	52.80	50.26	60.22	49.08	62.55	55.21	49.68	34.74	56.95	50.38	78.41	53.92
1974	51.16	48.47	34.33	54.35	51.63	61.27	48.78	63.84	56.79	51.16	36.43	58.38	51.76	78.03	55.46
1975	52.28	49.62	35.47	55.57	52.70	62.33	48.77	65.07	58.68	52.28	37.41	59.59	52.85	77.87	56.92
1976	53.57	50.98	36.74	56.76	54.20	63.38	49.11	66.25	60.15	53.57	38.54	60.78	54.34	77.95	58.32
1977	55.15	52.74	38.58	58.03	56.17	64.30	49.38	67.27	61.55	55.15	40.16	61.94	56.31	78.06	59.53
1978	57.04	54.84	41.05	59.68	58.28	65.37	49.70	68.50	62.72	57.04	42.32	63.41	58.40	78.26	60.93
1979	59.02	57.01	43.75	61.67	60.26	66.59	50.72	69.76	63.84	59.02	44.78	65.10	60.36	78.70	62.43
1980	60.65	58.74	45.66	63.84	61.59	67.83	51.93	70.99	65.27	60.65	46.60	66.87	61.69	79.31	63.90
1981	62.22	60.44	47.52	66.30	62.70	68.93	53.33	72.01	66.96	62.22	48.39	68.72	62.82	80.21	65.06
1982	63.41	61.68	48.47	68.58	63.43	69.92	55.11	72.82	68.53	63.41	49.46	70.38	63.57	81.28	66.03
1983	64.78	63.11	49.52	70.29	64.86	71.05	57.86	73.59	70.41	64.78	50.76	71.69	65.01	82.89	66.99
1984	66.67	65.12	51.63	72.56	66.64	72.48	61.47	74.56	72.01	66.67	53.09	73.41	66.78	84.91	68.21
1985	68.71	67.24	53.69	75.18	68.43	74.24	66.21	75.73	73.97	68.71	55.54	75.42	68.58	87.54	69.67
1986	70.70	69.24	55.37	77.22	70.56	76.17	71.37	77.03	76.07	70.70	57.72	77.14	70.70	90.42	71.26
1987	72.64	71.18	56.77	79.20	72.72	78.13	76.59	78.40	78.25	72.64	59.64	78.85	72.87	93.45	72.87
1988	74.56	73.13	58.50	81.07	74.81	79.91	80.59	79.77	80.19	74.56	61.68	80.52	74.95	95.43	74.57
1989	76.44	75.04	60.40	82.87	76.75	81.70	84.95	81.12	81.89	76.44	63.92	82.12	76.89	97.24	76.36
1990	78.22	76.77	61.91	84.85	78.41	83.67	89.40	82.66	83.79	78.22	65.84	83.92	78.55	99.10	78.37
1991	79.61	78.03	62.87	86.21	79.76	85.52	92.68	84.27	85.42	79.61	67.11	85.38	79.91	100.45	80.38
1992	81.05	79.39	64.08	87.16	81.41	87.28	95.38	85.86	87.21	81.05	68.53	86.61	81.57	101.57	82.36
1993	82.72	81.12	66.23	88.23	83.32	88.74	96.57	87.36	88.73	82.72	70.55	87.86	83.46	101.92	84.21
1994	84.54	83.08	69.09	89.15	85.44	90.03	96.91	88.83	89.98	84.54	73.06	89.01	85.57	101.71	86.04
1995	86.57	85.27	72.66	90.48	87.47	91.45	97.11	90.46	91.49	86.57	76.16	90.47	87.59	101.56	88.01
1996	88.88	87.76	76.72	92.08	89.75	93.11	97.41	92.35	93.04	88.88	79.70	92.19	89.85	102.02	90.08
1997	91.35	90.47	81.60	93.89	92.04	94.63	97.23	94.17	95.82	91.35	83.86	94.01	92.12	101.35	92.36
1998	94.08	93.50	87.20	95.88	94.58	96.24	97.75	95.95	97.32	94.08	88.74	95.91	94.64	100.85	94.68
1999	96.99	96.69	93.47	97.80	97.29	98.09	98.94	97.92	98.81	96.99	94.27	97.85	97.32	100.54	97.26
2000	100.00	100.00	100.00	100.00	100.00	100.00	100.00	100.00	100.00	100.00	100.00	100.00	100.00	100.00	100.00
2001	102.54	102.67	103.88	101.91	102.68	102.03	101.17	102.18	101.43	102.54	103.48	102.03	102.66	99.46	102.88
2002	104.76	104.89	106.00	103.14	105.53	104.27	102.92	104.52	102.99	104.76	105.55	103.73	105.48	99.36	105.89
2003	107.06	107.20	107.92	104.23	108.71	106.52	104.71	106.88	104.45	107.06	107.45	105.35	108.62	99.45	108.85
2004	109.56	109.78	110.54	105.28	112.16	108.73	107.35	109.07	105.92	109.56	110.08	106.88	112.02	99.91	111.62
2005	112.10	112.47	114.00	106.22	115.62	110.71	110.52	110.93	107.22	112.10	113.50	108.22	115.44	100.48	114.04

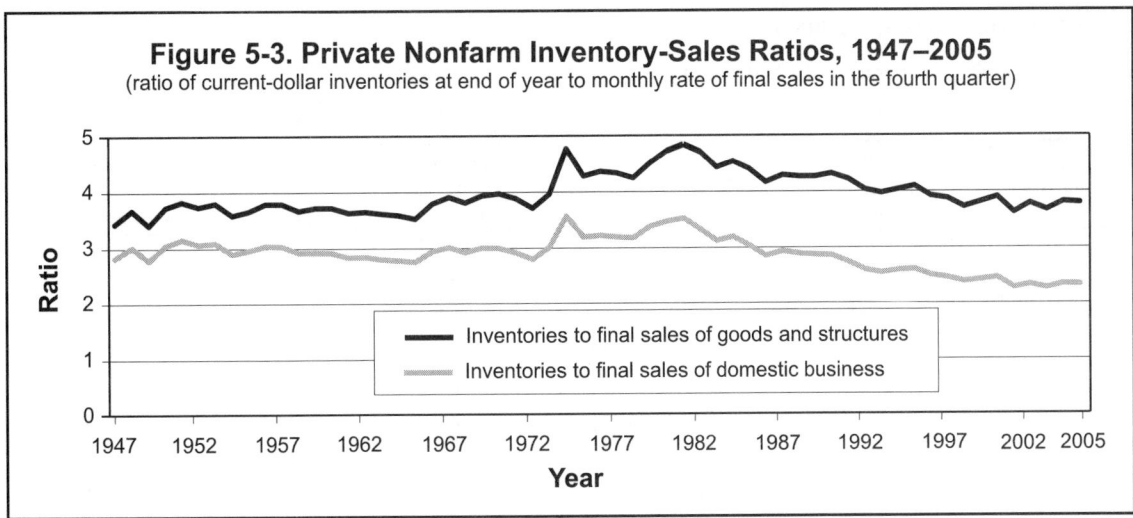

Figure 5-3. Private Nonfarm Inventory-Sales Ratios, 1947–2005
(ratio of current-dollar inventories at end of year to monthly rate of final sales in the fourth quarter)

- Inventories play a key role in the business cycle, and ratios of inventories to sales (I/S ratios) are important cyclical indicators. If production gets ahead of sales, or if sales take an unexpected dip, there can be "involuntary" inventory accumulation. In that case, I/S ratios rise and production has to be cut back. In the figure above, this can be seen most strikingly in the high ratios associated with the severe 1974–1975 and 1981–1982 recessions. By contrast, the 2001 recession was preceded by a very modest increase in I/S ratios. (Tables 5-7 and 19-7)

- In addition to these cyclical movements, the broadest ratios of inventories to monthly sales rates for total business show a downtrend over the postwar period. The lower line on the figure shows an example of such a broad ratio. The downtrend is summarized in the decline between the earliest and latest pre-recession ratios of nonfarm inventories to sales for domestic business; this ratio fell from 2.77 in 1947 to 2.37 in 1999. (Tables 5-7 and 19-7)

- However, this decline may simply reflect the shift in the composition of output toward services, which require relatively less inventory support. When nonfarm inventories are compared with final sales of goods and structures only, as in the higher line on the figure, the 1999 ratio is actually higher than in 1947. This suggests that although inventory efficiencies may well be achieved by individual firms or industries, they may not translate into inventory efficiency for the goods-and-structures economy as a whole. (Tables 5-7 and 19-7)

- Interrupting the trends in both ratios is a period of increase extending from about 1966 through the early 1980s. This coincides with a period of high and rising inflation, which may have given firms the incentive to hold inventory in excess of production needs as a hedge against—or a speculation on—price increases. (Table 5-7 and Chapter 8)

Table 5-7. Inventories to Sales Ratios

(Seasonally adjusted, ratio of inventories at end of quarter to monthly rate of sales during the quarter, annual data are for fourth quarter.)

NIPA Tables 5.7.5A, 5.7.5B, 5.7.6A, 5.7.6B

Year and quarter	Ratio, total private inventories to final sales of domestic business		Ratio, nonfarm inventories to final sales of domestic business		Ratio, nonfarm inventories to final sales of goods and structures	
	Current dollars	Chained (2000) dollars	Current dollars	Chained (2000) dollars	Current dollars	Chained (2000) dollars
1950	5.70	3.53	3.00	2.24	3.68	3.39
1951	5.76	3.62	3.11	2.40	3.78	3.61
1952	5.16	3.61	3.02	2.39	3.69	3.59
1953	4.96	3.61	3.04	2.39	3.75	3.59
1954	4.67	3.40	2.85	2.23	3.54	3.35
1955	4.36	3.33	2.91	2.24	3.61	3.36
1956	4.41	3.33	2.99	2.30	3.74	3.48
1957	4.39	3.36	2.98	2.32	3.74	3.52
1958	4.44	3.33	2.87	2.25	3.62	3.42
1959	4.20	3.26	2.87	2.27	3.67	3.48
1960	4.17	3.27	2.86	2.29	3.67	3.51
1961	4.07	3.20	2.78	2.24	3.58	3.45
1962	4.09	3.21	2.79	2.29	3.60	3.51
1963	3.91	3.15	2.75	2.27	3.56	3.49
1964	3.75	3.07	2.73	2.26	3.54	3.49
1965	3.73	2.99	2.70	2.24	3.47	3.42
1966	3.88	3.16	2.89	2.44	3.74	3.75
1967	3.87	3.25	2.96	2.54	3.86	3.92
1968	3.76	3.23	2.87	2.53	3.76	3.91
1969	3.85	3.30	2.95	2.62	3.89	4.08
1970	3.78	3.29	2.94	2.63	3.92	4.13
1971	3.73	3.24	2.86	2.59	3.83	4.07
1972	3.72	3.09	2.75	2.50	3.66	3.90
1973	4.18	3.13	2.96	2.57	3.91	4.01
1974	4.49	3.37	3.52	2.82	4.73	4.50
1975	4.02	3.17	3.14	2.62	4.24	4.17
1976	3.93	3.14	3.17	2.63	4.32	4.21
1977	3.86	3.13	3.14	2.62	4.29	4.18
1978	3.95	3.06	3.12	2.58	4.20	4.06
1979	4.17	3.08	3.33	2.60	4.47	4.08
1980	4.23	3.05	3.42	2.60	4.69	4.13
1981	4.15	3.20	3.47	2.71	4.80	4.31
1982	3.95	3.15	3.28	2.64	4.67	4.26
1983	3.68	2.91	3.07	2.49	4.39	3.98
1984	3.70	2.98	3.14	2.56	4.50	4.07
1985	3.49	2.92	2.99	2.50	4.36	4.03
1986	3.23	2.84	2.80	2.44	4.12	3.92
1987	3.31	2.84	2.88	2.47	4.25	3.99
1988	3.27	2.75	2.84	2.43	4.22	3.92
1989	3.22	2.75	2.82	2.44	4.22	3.94
1990	3.21	2.77	2.81	2.46	4.27	4.02
1991	3.04	2.77	2.69	2.46	4.17	4.07
1992	2.90	2.67	2.55	2.36	3.99	3.90
1993	2.83	2.63	2.50	2.35	3.92	3.86
1994	2.87	2.67	2.54	2.38	3.99	3.88
1995	2.86	2.63	2.56	2.38	4.05	3.88
1996	2.74	2.56	2.45	2.30	3.87	3.74
1997	2.68	2.60	2.41	2.34	3.82	3.78
1998	2.56	2.59	2.33	2.35	3.67	3.75
1999	2.59	2.60	2.37	2.37	3.76	3.79
2000	2.63	2.62	2.41	2.40	3.85	3.86
2001	2.44	2.55	2.23	2.33	3.57	3.74
2002	2.51	2.58	2.28	2.37	3.73	3.85
2003	2.45	2.49	2.22	2.28	3.62	3.67
2004	2.52	2.49	2.29	2.28	3.76	3.67
2005	2.51	2.42	2.28	2.22	3.74	3.55
2003						
1st quarter	2.53	2.57	2.30	2.36	3.78	3.83
2nd quarter	2.48	2.54	2.26	2.33	3.71	3.78
3rd quarter	2.44	2.49	2.21	2.28	3.59	3.66
4th quarter	2.45	2.49	2.22	2.28	3.62	3.67
2004						
1st quarter	2.47	2.48	2.23	2.28	3.66	3.67
2nd quarter	2.51	2.49	2.26	2.28	3.70	3.69
3rd quarter	2.51	2.49	2.28	2.28	3.73	3.66
4th quarter	2.52	2.49	2.29	2.28	3.76	3.67
2005						
1st quarter	2.53	2.48	2.30	2.28	3.77	3.66
2nd quarter	2.48	2.43	2.25	2.24	3.67	3.56
3rd quarter	2.47	2.40	2.25	2.20	3.66	3.51
4th quarter	2.51	2.42	2.28	2.22	3.74	3.55

Table 5-8. Manufacturing and Trade Sales and Inventories

Classification basis, year, and month	Sales, billions of dollars					Inventories, billions of dollars, end of period, seasonally adjusted				Ratios, inventories to sales, seasonally adjusted [1]			
	Not seasonally adjusted, total	Seasonally adjusted				Total	Manufacturing	Retail trade	Merchant wholesalers	Total	Manufacturing	Retail trade	Merchant wholesalers
		Total	Manufacturing	Retail trade	Merchant wholesalers								
SIC Basis													
1980	3 926.8	3 926.8	1 852.7	956.9	1 117.2	...	...	121.1	122.6	...	...	1.48	...
1981	4 269.9	4 269.9	2 017.5	1 038.2	1 214.2	...	...	132.7	129.7	...	...	1.49	1.25
1982	4 171.5	4 171.5	1 960.2	1 068.7	1 142.5	573.9	311.9	134.6	127.4	1.67	1.95	1.49	1.36
1983	4 431.4	4 431.4	2 070.6	1 170.2	1 190.7	590.3	312.4	147.8	130.1	1.56	1.78	1.44	1.28
1984	4 921.5	4 921.5	2 288.2	1 286.9	1 346.4	649.8	339.5	167.8	142.5	1.53	1.73	1.49	1.23
1985	5 071.0	5 071.0	2 334.5	1 375.0	1 361.5	664.0	334.7	181.9	147.4	1.55	1.73	1.52	1.28
1986	5 165.0	5 165.0	2 335.9	1 449.6	1 379.5	662.7	322.7	186.5	153.6	1.55	1.68	1.56	1.32
1987	5 492.8	5 492.8	2 475.9	1 541.3	1 475.6	709.8	338.1	207.8	163.9	1.50	1.59	1.55	1.29
1988	5 965.9	5 965.9	2 695.4	1 656.2	1 614.2	767.2	369.4	219.0	178.8	1.49	1.57	1.54	1.30
1989	6 324.5	6 324.5	2 840.4	1 759.0	1 725.1	815.5	391.2	237.2	187.0	1.52	1.63	1.58	1.28
1990	6 550.9	6 550.9	2 912.2	1 844.6	1 794.1	840.7	405.1	239.8	195.8	1.52	1.65	1.56	1.29
1991	6 513.8	6 513.8	2 878.2	1 855.9	1 779.7	834.7	391.0	243.4	200.4	1.53	1.65	1.54	1.33
1992	6 806.1	6 806.1	3 004.7	1 951.6	1 849.8	842.9	382.5	252.2	208.2	1.48	1.54	1.52	1.32
NAICS Basis													
1992	6 486.9	6 486.9	2 904.0	1 815.7	1 767.1	837.2	378.9	261.4	196.9	1.52	1.57	1.67	1.31
1993	6 811.0	6 811.0	3 020.5	1 942.2	1 848.2	864.2	379.8	279.5	204.8	1.50	1.51	1.69	1.31
1994	7 323.0	7 323.0	3 238.1	2 110.0	1 974.9	927.5	400.1	305.4	222.0	1.47	1.45	1.67	1.29
1995	7 861.2	7 861.2	3 479.7	2 222.5	2 159.0	986.3	425.0	322.9	238.4	1.48	1.44	1.73	1.30
1996	8 248.2	8 248.2	3 597.2	2 366.7	2 284.3	1 005.7	430.7	333.9	241.1	1.46	1.43	1.68	1.27
1997	8 686.5	8 686.5	3 834.7	2 474.0	2 377.8	1 046.9	443.8	344.6	258.5	1.42	1.37	1.65	1.26
1998	8 914.0	8 914.0	3 899.8	2 587.1	2 427.1	1 078.8	449.2	357.3	272.3	1.44	1.39	1.64	1.32
1999	9 439.6	9 439.6	4 031.9	2 808.6	2 599.2	1 139.2	463.7	385.1	290.4	1.41	1.35	1.60	1.30
2000	10 011.9	10 011.9	4 208.6	2 988.8	2 814.6	1 198.7	481.8	407.0	309.8	1.41	1.36	1.60	1.30
2001	9 875.8	9 875.8	4 022.9	3 067.7	2 785.2	1 141.2	447.9	395.0	298.4	1.44	1.40	1.59	1.33
2002	9 935.1	9 935.1	3 965.2	3 134.3	2 835.5	1 158.5	439.5	416.5	302.5	1.38	1.33	1.56	1.26
2003	10 199.9	10 199.9	3 972.1	3 265.5	2 962.3	1 147.1	406.8	432.3	308.0	1.36	1.28	1.57	1.23
2004	11 033.0	11 033.0	4 259.2	3 477.3	3 296.5	1 234.3	434.9	461.2	338.2	1.30	1.19	1.56	1.18
2005	11 814.1	11 814.1	4 544.8	3 719.2	3 550.1	1 288.0	452.0	473.9	362.1	1.29	1.18	1.51	1.19
2002													
January	750.2	812.9	327.3	256.8	228.8	1 139.1	444.4	397.2	297.5	1.40	1.36	1.55	1.30
February	751.4	813.7	325.2	258.4	230.1	1 132.7	438.9	398.9	294.9	1.39	1.35	1.54	1.28
March	835.7	816.6	328.3	258.0	230.3	1 128.3	435.9	397.4	295.1	1.38	1.33	1.54	1.28
April	825.8	826.5	331.0	261.8	233.8	1 126.5	435.3	397.2	293.9	1.36	1.32	1.52	1.26
May	859.8	828.2	335.3	257.8	235.2	1 130.4	433.8	402.2	294.4	1.36	1.29	1.56	1.25
June	844.1	828.7	331.5	260.2	237.0	1 132.5	434.2	402.8	295.5	1.37	1.31	1.55	1.25
July	813.9	832.0	331.2	263.2	237.7	1 138.6	434.0	406.8	297.9	1.37	1.31	1.55	1.25
August	865.6	840.5	334.2	265.6	240.7	1 141.3	435.1	407.2	299.0	1.36	1.30	1.53	1.24
September	834.6	834.8	333.6	261.3	239.9	1 148.6	436.6	411.6	300.4	1.38	1.31	1.58	1.25
October	862.2	835.2	333.7	262.3	239.2	1 150.6	437.1	413.8	299.7	1.38	1.31	1.58	1.25
November	825.3	837.1	331.0	263.7	242.4	1 151.7	436.2	415.3	300.2	1.38	1.32	1.58	1.24
December	866.4	832.0	326.0	266.0	240.1	1 158.5	439.5	416.5	302.5	1.39	1.35	1.57	1.26
2003													
January	781.2	840.0	329.0	267.5	243.5	1 156.0	435.6	418.3	302.1	1.38	1.32	1.56	1.24
February	772.8	837.4	330.0	263.9	243.5	1 162.8	437.6	422.0	303.2	1.39	1.33	1.60	1.25
March	865.3	845.9	331.1	268.7	246.1	1 161.5	433.5	423.9	304.1	1.37	1.31	1.58	1.24
April	832.0	832.8	323.9	267.6	241.2	1 159.9	431.1	424.1	304.7	1.39	1.33	1.58	1.26
May	855.6	833.5	325.2	267.6	240.7	1 153.8	427.7	423.1	303.0	1.38	1.32	1.58	1.26
June	865.2	841.4	327.6	269.9	243.9	1 149.0	423.2	423.5	302.3	1.37	1.29	1.57	1.24
July	838.2	855.4	334.5	274.2	246.7	1 146.0	418.6	425.0	302.3	1.34	1.25	1.55	1.23
August	862.5	853.2	328.3	278.3	246.6	1 139.0	415.8	421.4	301.8	1.33	1.27	1.51	1.22
September	872.1	859.7	335.5	276.3	247.9	1 141.4	412.1	426.0	303.3	1.33	1.23	1.54	1.22
October	894.8	862.8	336.9	274.6	251.3	1 145.8	411.0	429.2	305.6	1.33	1.22	1.56	1.22
November	836.8	866.7	334.5	278.5	253.7	1 146.4	408.4	431.5	306.6	1.32	1.22	1.55	1.21
December	923.4	870.9	337.6	277.2	256.0	1 147.1	406.8	432.3	308.0	1.32	1.20	1.56	1.20
2004													
January	802.8	871.8	336.6	278.9	256.2	1 147.1	406.5	432.6	307.9	1.32	1.21	1.55	1.20
February	825.3	878.6	335.4	281.7	261.5	1 156.0	408.5	435.3	312.2	1.32	1.22	1.54	1.19
March	956.1	907.5	350.4	286.8	270.4	1 164.1	410.2	440.2	313.8	1.28	1.17	1.53	1.16
April	908.1	904.4	349.8	283.5	271.1	1 171.3	412.0	445.2	314.0	1.30	1.18	1.57	1.16
May	917.3	912.6	350.5	289.2	272.8	1 179.9	415.3	446.8	317.8	1.29	1.18	1.54	1.16
June	951.5	910.2	353.8	282.9	273.5	1 192.1	419.2	452.2	320.7	1.31	1.18	1.60	1.17
July	894.5	917.9	355.1	288.7	274.1	1 204.7	422.6	456.3	325.8	1.31	1.19	1.58	1.19
August	944.9	926.9	361.2	288.4	277.4	1 216.0	425.8	461.1	329.2	1.31	1.18	1.60	1.19
September	942.5	928.7	357.6	293.9	277.2	1 214.9	426.2	458.5	330.1	1.31	1.19	1.56	1.19
October	942.9	937.9	363.0	295.5	279.4	1 221.2	430.1	456.8	334.2	1.30	1.19	1.55	1.20
November	937.8	945.0	365.3	296.2	283.5	1 233.2	434.4	460.6	338.2	1.30	1.19	1.56	1.19
December	1 009.4	952.4	367.0	299.9	285.4	1 234.3	434.9	461.2	338.2	1.30	1.18	1.54	1.18
2005													
January	863.5	955.6	370.9	298.7	286.0	1 244.5	440.5	461.8	342.2	1.30	1.19	1.55	1.20
February	877.8	954.5	367.0	301.6	285.9	1 250.3	443.0	463.3	344.1	1.31	1.21	1.54	1.20
March	1 011.6	962.5	373.7	302.3	286.6	1 254.7	445.2	464.6	344.9	1.30	1.19	1.54	1.20
April	965.1	970.2	372.6	307.0	290.6	1 259.1	445.7	465.3	348.1	1.30	1.20	1.52	1.20
May	987.5	972.1	376.0	305.7	290.4	1 260.2	444.9	466.7	348.6	1.30	1.18	1.53	1.20
June	1 023.8	977.9	374.9	311.3	291.6	1 259.4	444.9	463.9	350.7	1.29	1.19	1.49	1.20
July	946.9	988.6	375.8	318.1	294.7	1 255.7	447.6	456.5	351.6	1.27	1.19	1.43	1.19
August	1 034.4	994.9	384.2	312.0	298.7	1 260.6	446.4	460.9	353.2	1.27	1.16	1.48	1.18
September	1 018.2	1 001.1	383.1	313.1	304.9	1 266.8	446.2	464.7	355.9	1.27	1.16	1.48	1.17
October	1 012.7	1 007.7	386.0	313.7	308.0	1 272.3	449.3	465.9	357.1	1.26	1.16	1.49	1.16
November	1 001.7	1 009.3	387.4	315.6	306.4	1 278.9	450.0	470.2	358.7	1.27	1.16	1.49	1.17
December	1 071.0	1 021.3	394.5	316.8	310.0	1 288.0	452.0	473.9	362.1	1.26	1.15	1.50	1.17

[1] Annual data are averages of monthly ratios.
. . . = Not available.

Table 5-9. Real Manufacturing and Trade Sales and Inventories

(Billions of chained [1996 or 2000] dollars, ratios; seasonally adjusted; annual sales figures are averages of seasonally adjusted monthly data.)

Classification basis, year, and month	Sales, monthly average				Inventories, end of period				Ratios, end-of-period inventories to monthly average sales			
	Total	Manufac-turing	Retail trade	Merchant wholesalers	Total	Manufac-turing	Retail trade	Merchant wholesalers	Total	Manufac-turing	Retail trade	Merchant wholesalers
SIC Basis (1996 dollars)												
1975	376.2	179.0	110.1	87.5	546.6	295.2	135.3	107.1	1.45	1.65	1.23	1.22
1976	403.5	195.4	117.4	91.4	578.9	309.3	145.7	115.0	1.43	1.58	1.24	1.26
1977	431.8	211.2	123.2	98.0	607.3	317.9	153.9	127.2	1.41	1.51	1.25	1.30
1978	458.5	221.3	129.1	108.4	645.7	332.5	164.1	141.3	1.41	1.50	1.27	1.30
1979	469.5	224.2	131.3	114.0	666.7	345.3	164.1	148.9	1.42	1.54	1.25	1.31
1980	454.9	211.5	126.5	116.4	669.2	345.7	159.5	155.7	1.47	1.63	1.26	1.34
1981	457.7	213.1	127.0	117.1	685.7	350.3	168.4	159.5	1.50	1.64	1.33	1.36
1982	439.1	202.9	125.8	110.3	663.4	334.6	164.5	157.8	1.51	1.65	1.31	1.43
1983	460.7	212.4	135.1	113.5	675.3	334.2	177.9	157.9	1.47	1.57	1.32	1.39
1984	499.3	229.3	144.8	125.4	740.6	363.2	199.7	172.6	1.48	1.58	1.38	1.38
1985	513.8	233.5	151.2	129.4	755.3	356.9	215.1	180.6	1.47	1.53	1.42	1.40
1986	533.6	237.6	159.6	136.6	762.4	353.1	218.5	189.2	1.43	1.49	1.37	1.38
1987	553.2	248.0	164.2	141.3	799.5	361.6	239.7	197.6	1.45	1.46	1.46	1.40
1988	579.1	259.4	171.3	148.6	832.7	378.5	247.4	205.9	1.44	1.46	1.44	1.39
1989	590.5	261.9	175.6	153.1	864.6	392.7	261.9	209.2	1.46	1.50	1.49	1.37
1990	593.9	261.4	177.3	155.3	880.1	401.6	260.2	217.1	1.48	1.54	1.47	1.40
1991	586.4	257.1	174.0	155.3	878.2	394.9	260.8	221.9	1.50	1.54	1.50	1.43
1992	607.7	266.4	179.9	161.5	886.6	390.1	265.4	230.9	1.46	1.46	1.48	1.43
1993	632.7	274.5	188.7	169.4	912.0	393.7	280.8	237.3	1.44	1.43	1.49	1.40
1994	670.3	290.1	201.0	179.2	959.2	405.8	301.4	252.0	1.43	1.40	1.50	1.41
1995	699.5	301.1	208.2	190.2	996.4	419.9	313.6	263.0	1.42	1.39	1.51	1.38
1996	726.0	309.5	218.5	198.0	1 016.4	430.0	321.0	265.4	1.40	1.39	1.47	1.34
NAICS Basis (2000 dollars)												
1997	737.1	324.1	219.8	190.2	1 025.1	430.7	340.6	254.1	1.39	1.33	1.55	1.34
1998	774.7	335.6	234.2	203.2	1 081.4	449.3	357.9	274.4	1.40	1.34	1.53	1.35
1999	819.4	346.2	253.6	218.9	1 143.8	466.3	385.5	292.0	1.40	1.35	1.52	1.33
2000	844.8	350.2	265.9	228.7	1 188.3	474.2	407.1	307.0	1.41	1.35	1.53	1.34
2001	834.8	331.2	274.0	228.7	1 147.9	452.8	396.3	298.6	1.38	1.37	1.45	1.31
2002	845.0	327.7	284.5	232.9	1 168.4	447.0	420.6	300.5	1.38	1.36	1.48	1.29
2003	855.7	323.2	297.3	235.7	1 176.0	437.5	436.4	301.8	1.37	1.35	1.47	1.28
2004	889.0	329.8	313.0	248.1	1 214.6	437.1	458.4	319.4	1.37	1.33	1.46	1.29
2005	918.0	334.9	329.0	256.7	1 232.4	434.7	463.6	334.7	1.34	1.30	1.41	1.30
2002												
January	841.8	330.6	280.7	229.9	1 149.0	451.1	399.5	298.2	1.37	1.37	1.42	1.30
February	840.5	326.7	282.6	230.9	1 146.2	449.7	400.9	295.4	1.36	1.38	1.42	1.28
March	833.4	323.3	281.2	228.3	1 146.4	449.1	401.6	295.5	1.38	1.39	1.43	1.30
April	845.4	329.4	284.2	232.1	1 145.2	448.3	402.4	294.2	1.36	1.36	1.42	1.27
May	843.9	330.7	280.2	233.1	1 147.8	446.8	406.0	294.7	1.36	1.35	1.45	1.26
June	845.4	326.4	284.4	234.8	1 151.2	446.3	408.7	295.9	1.36	1.37	1.44	1.26
July	851.0	331.0	286.7	233.7	1 154.5	446.4	410.0	297.8	1.36	1.35	1.43	1.27
August	852.1	328.8	288.5	235.6	1 154.1	446.6	409.0	298.1	1.35	1.36	1.42	1.27
September	843.4	326.3	283.5	234.0	1 159.3	447.1	413.4	298.5	1.37	1.37	1.46	1.28
October	846.6	329.1	285.6	232.2	1 159.2	446.8	414.9	297.2	1.37	1.36	1.45	1.28
November	849.9	326.6	287.2	236.4	1 162.9	445.5	419.3	297.7	1.37	1.36	1.46	1.26
December	846.4	323.3	289.7	233.6	1 168.4	447.0	420.6	300.5	1.38	1.38	1.45	1.29
2003												
January	849.3	324.4	290.9	234.0	1 167.7	445.2	422.3	299.9	1.38	1.37	1.45	1.28
February	837.6	321.6	285.0	230.5	1 173.9	448.8	424.3	300.4	1.40	1.40	1.49	1.30
March	842.2	320.4	289.6	232.0	1 174.2	446.4	426.5	301.0	1.39	1.39	1.47	1.30
April	841.8	318.6	290.8	232.2	1 175.9	446.2	427.9	301.5	1.40	1.40	1.47	1.30
May	846.7	320.6	293.5	233.1	1 172.8	445.1	427.4	300.0	1.39	1.39	1.46	1.29
June	852.6	321.0	296.2	235.7	1 171.1	442.7	428.9	299.2	1.37	1.38	1.45	1.27
July	865.4	327.2	300.8	238.1	1 171.2	440.7	431.0	299.2	1.35	1.35	1.43	1.26
August	860.9	320.3	304.6	236.8	1 167.6	440.2	428.6	298.5	1.36	1.37	1.41	1.26
September	865.6	326.7	302.0	237.7	1 172.2	438.5	433.7	299.7	1.35	1.34	1.44	1.26
October	867.4	327.6	301.7	239.1	1 175.3	438.9	434.6	301.5	1.36	1.34	1.44	1.26
November	869.6	323.9	307.2	240.0	1 176.4	437.6	437.1	301.5	1.35	1.35	1.42	1.26
December	869.9	326.0	305.7	239.7	1 176.0	437.5	436.4	301.8	1.35	1.34	1.43	1.26
2004												
January	867.3	323.7	306.2	238.3	1 174.9	436.3	437.7	300.6	1.36	1.35	1.43	1.26
February	869.9	321.4	307.7	242.2	1 180.4	436.8	439.7	303.7	1.36	1.36	1.43	1.25
March	892.6	333.8	312.1	248.8	1 183.9	437.0	442.9	303.8	1.33	1.31	1.42	1.22
April	884.4	330.0	308.4	247.7	1 186.4	436.4	447.5	302.5	1.34	1.32	1.45	1.22
May	885.5	327.4	312.4	247.7	1 190.2	436.7	448.7	304.8	1.34	1.33	1.44	1.23
June	883.8	329.8	305.8	249.7	1 195.4	438.0	450.6	306.8	1.35	1.33	1.47	1.23
July	889.2	329.9	312.9	248.4	1 200.9	438.8	450.6	311.4	1.35	1.33	1.44	1.25
August	895.8	334.2	312.7	250.9	1 206.2	439.1	453.0	314.0	1.35	1.31	1.45	1.25
September	895.9	329.9	318.3	249.9	1 202.9	436.6	452.4	314.0	1.34	1.32	1.42	1.26
October	895.6	332.0	317.3	248.4	1 209.1	437.0	455.4	316.9	1.35	1.32	1.44	1.28
November	899.4	331.5	318.6	251.3	1 215.7	438.5	457.6	319.8	1.35	1.32	1.44	1.27
December	908.8	333.6	323.5	254.2	1 214.6	437.1	458.4	319.4	1.34	1.31	1.42	1.26
2005												
January	910.6	336.6	322.0	254.2	1 222.3	440.9	458.9	322.6	1.34	1.31	1.43	1.27
February	905.9	331.1	323.7	253.4	1 226.8	441.1	462.1	323.8	1.35	1.33	1.43	1.28
March	906.0	334.5	322.8	250.9	1 226.5	440.9	462.2	323.7	1.35	1.32	1.43	1.29
April	911.0	332.7	326.5	254.4	1 225.0	439.8	459.4	326.0	1.35	1.32	1.41	1.28
May	915.7	336.7	326.0	255.4	1 224.4	438.3	459.9	326.4	1.34	1.30	1.41	1.28
June	918.6	333.8	331.8	255.9	1 224.7	437.7	459.3	328.0	1.33	1.31	1.38	1.28
July	922.3	332.1	338.5	255.4	1 219.0	439.1	451.7	328.1	1.32	1.32	1.34	1.29
August	923.1	338.3	330.0	257.4	1 218.9	436.9	452.9	329.2	1.32	1.29	1.37	1.28
September	917.2	333.6	326.9	258.9	1 222.3	434.6	457.0	331.0	1.33	1.30	1.40	1.28
October	920.5	333.2	328.2	261.2	1 227.2	435.1	461.3	331.4	1.33	1.31	1.41	1.27
November	929.0	335.9	334.6	261.4	1 228.9	434.0	463.3	332.3	1.32	1.29	1.39	1.27
December	935.7	340.1	336.5	262.1	1 232.4	434.7	463.6	334.7	1.32	1.28	1.38	1.28

Table 5-10. Capital Expenditures

(Millions of dollars.)

Capital expenditures	All companies								
	1996	1997	1998	1999	2000	2001	2002	2003	2004
TOTAL	807 070	871 765	970 897	1 046 952	1 161 029	1 109 004	997 894	975 015	1 047 492
Structures	243 427	273 298	329 111	320 078	364 407	363 748	358 484	344 641	371 914
New	223 588	254 451	284 491	296 496	329 525	335 538	321 191	305 291	326 955
Used	19 839	18 849	44 620	23 583	34 882	28 210	37 293	39 350	44 959
Equipment	563 641	598 466	641 786	726 874	796 622	745 256	639 410	630 373	675 578
New	526 016	562 019	606 210	689 553	750 626	706 617	598 668	579 414	629 629
Used	37 625	36 447	35 577	37 321	45 996	38 639	40 741	50 960	45 949
Not distributed as structures or equipment	2	0	0	0	0	0	0	0	0
CAPITALIZED COMPUTER SOFTWARE [1]	...	...	...	...	...	...	...	...	...
Prepackaged	...	...	...	...	...	...	...	...	...
Vendor-customized	...	...	...	...	...	...	...	...	...
Internally-developed	...	...	...	...	...	...	...	...	...
CAPITAL LEASE AND CAPITALIZED INTEREST EXPENSES [1]									
Capital leases	15 675	16 066	16 533	17 140	19 545	15 529	15 334	15 641	17 996
Capitalized interest	...	...	...	...	...	...	...	...	...

Capital expenditures	Companies with employees								
	1996	1997	1998	1999	2000	2001	2002	2003	2004
TOTAL	707 110	772 343	896 452	974 631	1 089 862	1 052 344	917 490	886 846	958 603
Structures	204 345	236 166	300 283	293 787	338 120	346 221	325 168	314 021	338 612
New	191 867	225 107	260 008	276 094	309 541	323 871	299 941	281 892	302 646
Used	12 478	11 060	40 275	17 693	28 579	22 349	25 227	32 128	35 966
Equipment	502 762	536 177	596 169	680 843	751 742	706 123	592 321	572 825	619 991
New	481 785	515 965	570 397	656 344	718 227	679 090	564 218	540 611	589 148
Used	20 977	20 212	25 773	24 499	33 515	27 033	28 103	32 214	30 842
Not distributed as structures or equipment	2	0	0	0	0	0	0	0	0
CAPITALIZED COMPUTER SOFTWARE [1]	...	...	...	...	...	...	...	45 464	49 869
Prepackaged	...	...	...	...	...	...	...	15 900	17 307
Vendor-customized	...	...	...	...	...	...	...	14 603	15 554
Internally-developed	...	...	...	...	...	...	...	14 960	17 008
CAPITAL LEASE AND CAPITALIZED INTEREST EXPENSES [1]									
Capital leases	13 023	14 549	15 631	16 594	19 184	15 500	15 092	15 137	17 526
Capitalized interest	6 827	7 273	9 799	9 591	11 423	11 969	...	...	...

Capital expenditures	Companies without employees								
	1996	1997	1998	1999	2000	2001	2002	2003	2004
TOTAL	99 960	99 422	74 445	72 322	71 168	56 660	80 404	88 169	88 889
Structures	39 082	37 132	28 828	26 291	26 287	17 527	33 316	30 621	33 302
New	31 721	29 344	24 483	20 402	19 984	11 667	21 250	23 399	24 309
Used	7 361	7 789	4 345	5 889	6 303	5 860	12 066	7 222	8 993
Equipment	60 878	62 289	45 617	46 030	44 880	39 133	47 088	57 549	55 587
New	44 231	46 054	35 813	33 209	32 399	27 528	34 450	38 803	40 481
Used	16 648	16 235	9 804	12 821	12 481	11 605	12 638	18 746	15 106
Not distributed as structures or equipment	0	0	0	0	0	0	0	0	0
CAPITALIZED COMPUTER SOFTWARE [1]	...	...	...	...	...	...	...	...	...
Prepackaged	...	...	...	...	...	...	...	...	...
Vendor-customized	...	...	...	...	...	...	...	...	...
Internally-developed	...	...	...	...	...	...	...	...	...
CAPITAL LEASE AND CAPITALIZED INTEREST EXPENSES [1]									
Capital leases	2 652	1 517	902	546	361	29	242	504	469
Capitalized interest	...	...	...	...	...	...	...	...	...

[1]Included in structures and equipment data shown above.
. . . = Not available.

Table 5-11. Capital Expenditures for Structures and Equipment for Companies with Employees by Major NAICS Industry Sector

(Millions of dollars.)

Year and type of expenditure	Total	Forestry, fishing, and agricultural services (113–115)	Mining (21)	Utilities (22)	Construc- tion (23)	Manufacturing (31–33)			Wholesale trade (42)	Retail trade (44–45)	Transporta- tion and ware- housing (48–49)	Information (51)
						Total	Durable goods industries (321, 327, 33)	Nondurable goods industries (31, 322–326)				
1998												
Total expenditures	896 452	854	40 424	36 010	26 867	203 587	117 901	85 685	29 169	57 276	51 287	96 487
Structures, total	300 283	206	26 503	18 574	7 062	39 028	19 406	19 622	7 480	25 105	13 036	24 721
New	260 008	158	24 714	17 771	4 749	37 122	18 449	18 673	6 738	23 104	12 365	24 218
Used	40 275	49	1 789	804	2 313	1 906	957	949	742	2 001	671	503
Equipment, total	596 169	648	13 921	17 436	19 805	164 559	98 496	66 063	21 690	32 171	38 251	71 766
New	570 397	603	12 625	17 266	15 346	159 363	95 571	63 792	20 470	30 359	33 409	70 827
Used	25 773	46	1 296	170	4 458	5 196	2 925	2 271	1 220	1 812	4 842	939
1999												
Total expenditures	974 631	1 716	30 586	42 802	23 110	196 399	117 005	79 394	32 442	64 063	57 299	122 827
Structures, total	293 787	344	17 626	21 241	1 753	33 985	17 320	16 665	7 264	29 494	14 122	34 924
New	276 094	331	17 039	20 784	1 505	32 814	16 581	16 233	6 508	28 670	13 859	33 733
Used	17 693	13	587	457	248	1 171	739	432	756	824	263	1 191
Equipment, total	680 843	1 371	12 960	21 561	21 356	162 414	99 685	62 729	25 179	34 569	43 178	87 903
New	656 344	1 190	12 167	20 545	18 600	157 715	96 434	61 281	23 714	33 567	40 425	85 310
Used	24 499	182	793	1 016	2 756	4 699	3 251	1 448	1 465	1 002	2 752	2 593
2000												
Total expenditures	1 089 862	1 488	42 522	61 302	25 049	214 827	133 786	81 041	33 579	69 791	59 851	160 177
Structures, total	338 120	139	28 620	29 472	2 803	39 434	21 228	18 207	8 923	32 037	13 457	41 502
New	309 541	134	25 500	29 258	2 583	36 643	19 748	16 895	8 364	30 413	13 190	40 062
Used	28 579	5	3 120	214	220	2 791	1 480	1 312	559	1 624	267	1 440
Equipment, total	751 742	1 350	13 902	31 830	22 245	175 393	112 558	62 835	24 656	37 754	46 394	118 675
New	718 227	1 086	12 854	27 937	17 788	169 454	108 703	60 751	23 610	36 428	43 455	117 835
Used	33 515	264	1 048	3 893	4 458	5 939	3 856	2 083	1 046	1 326	2 938	841
2001												
Total expenditures	1 052 344	1 532	51 278	82 823	24 802	192 835	118 875	73 959	29 981	66 917	57 756	144 793
Structures, total	346 221	226	32 678	38 093	3 859	39 815	22 032	17 784	6 932	30 010	16 594	41 742
New	323 871	149	31 825	36 504	3 389	38 001	20 701	17 301	5 357	29 118	14 479	41 384
Used	22 349	77	853	1 588	470	1 814	1 331	483	1 575	892	2 116	358
Equipment, total	706 123	1 306	18 600	44 731	20 943	153 019	96 844	56 176	23 049	36 906	41 161	103 051
New	679 090	1 091	17 567	42 939	17 432	148 397	94 251	54 145	20 757	35 074	38 521	102 410
Used	27 033	215	1 033	1 792	3 511	4 623	2 592	2 030	2 292	1 833	2 640	641
2002												
Total expenditures	917 490	1 910	42 467	65 502	24 773	157 243	84 062	73 181	26 789	59 316	47 124	88 156
Structures, total	325 168	184	30 685	29 893	1 890	32 643	15 133	17 510	5 885	26 286	14 498	33 607
New	299 941	118	29 775	29 008	1 254	31 022	14 396	16 626	5 447	25 051	13 870	33 472
Used	25 227	66	910	886	456	1 622	737	885	438	1 234	628	135
Equipment, total	592 321	1 726	11 783	35 609	23 063	124 600	68 929	55 671	20 904	33 030	32 626	54 550
New	564 218	1 319	10 262	34 816	19 257	118 621	66 112	52 510	18 562	31 157	29 178	54 247
Used	28 103	407	1 520	793	3 806	5 978	2 817	3 161	2 342	1 873	3 447	303
2003												
Total expenditures	886 846	1 894	50 548	54 569	23 159	149 065	80 226	68 839	26 014	65 868	44 460	80 524
Structures, total	314 021	202	36 617	24 841	1 676	31 108	13 330	17 778	5 615	29 675	13 005	30 765
New	281 892	177	35 897	24 580	1 424	29 315	12 631	16 685	4 921	27 393	11 779	30 406
Used	32 128	25	720	261	251	1 793	700	1 093	694	2 282	1 226	358
Equipment, total	572 825	1 692	13 931	29 729	21 484	117 956	66 895	51 061	20 399	36 193	31 454	49 759
New	540 611	1 267	12 135	29 044	16 170	112 102	62 810	49 292	19 457	32 162	26 786	47 857
Used	32 214	425	1 796	685	5 313	5 855	4 086	1 769	942	4 031	4 668	1 902
2004												
Total expenditures	958 603	2 081	53 683	50 110	28 679	156 889	85 057	71 832	31 932	71 747	47 735	83 461
Structures, total	338 612	324	36 664	24 404	4 513	32 235	13 913	18 321	7 024	33 207	13 436	28 571
New	302 646	309	35 682	23 631	4 163	30 402	13 100	17 302	6 446	31 382	12 812	26 187
Used	35 966	15	982	772	351	1 833	813	1 019	578	1 824	624	2 384
Equipment, total	619 991	1 757	17 019	25 707	24 166	124 655	71 144	53 511	24 908	38 541	34 298	54 890
New	589 148	1 507	15 745	25 420	18 984	120 307	68 526	51 780	21 615	36 639	29 665	53 158
Used	30 842	250	1 274	286	5 182	4 348	2 617	1 731	3 293	1 902	4 633	1 732

Note: Detail may not sum to total because of rounding.

Table 5-11. Capital Expenditures for Structures and Equipment for Companies with Employees by Major NAICS Industry Sector—Continued

(Millions of dollars.)

Year and type of expenditure	Finance and insurance (52)	Real estate and rental and leasing (53)	Professional, scientific, and technical services (54)	Management of companies and enterprises (55)	Administrative and support and waste management (56)	Educational services (61)	Health care and social assistance (62)	Arts, entertainment, and recreation (71)	Accommodation and food services (72)	Other services, except public administration (81)	Structure and equipment expenditures serving multiple industries
1998											
Total expenditures	118 173	85 184	22 277	1 821	13 110	12 983	47 109	8 994	20 822	20 627	3 392
Structures, total	27 221	36 775	4 886	753	4 288	9 109	23 971	5 045	12 045	13 737	738
New	16 858	24 109	4 572	502	3 745	8 734	21 328	4 838	10 402	13 280	699
Used	10 362	12 666	314	251	543	374	2 643	206	1 643	457	39
Equipment, total	90 952	48 409	17 390	1 068	8 822	3 874	23 138	3 949	8 777	6 890	2 654
New	90 058	46 877	16 868	1 030	8 346	3 825	22 465	3 752	8 005	6 296	2 609
Used	894	1 532	522	38	476	49	672	197	772	594	46
1999											
Total expenditures	130 101	100 629	29 546	6 065	16 227	13 532	51 342	13 355	23 328	16 902	2 359
Structures, total	20 080	33 903	6 780	1 668	2 875	9 767	25 922	8 119	13 431	9 975	516
New	17 918	30 295	6 168	1 509	2 773	9 140	24 159	7 971	11 391	9 033	495
Used	2 162	3 608	613	159	102	627	1 763	148	2 040	941	21
Equipment, total	110 021	66 726	22 766	4 397	13 353	3 766	25 420	5 236	9 897	6 928	1 843
New	109 577	63 555	22 153	4 319	12 323	3 668	24 945	5 125	9 324	6 370	1 752
Used	444	3 171	613	78	1 029	97	475	111	573	558	91
2000											
Total expenditures	133 684	92 456	34 055	5 054	17 506	18 223	52 166	19 125	26 307	21 125	1 572
Structures, total	23 010	24 815	8 141	1 570	4 032	13 699	26 868	12 245	13 873	13 274	206
New	20 298	17 793	7 470	955	3 504	12 965	23 999	11 627	12 879	11 705	200
Used	2 712	7 022	671	615	528	735	2 869	618	993	1 569	6
Equipment, total	110 675	67 641	25 914	3 484	13 475	4 523	25 299	6 880	12 434	7 852	1 366
New	109 678	62 175	24 847	3 403	12 723	4 338	24 407	6 161	11 501	7 192	1 357
Used	997	5 466	1 067	81	752	186	892	719	933	659	10
2001											
Total expenditures	131 105	82 674	30 464	3 035	15 785	17 377	52 932	14 974	21 365	29 006	911
Structures, total	22 744	20 489	7 258	933	3 527	12 852	27 030	8 998	12 248	20 031	163
New	19 571	17 325	6 793	869	3 367	11 860	25 241	8 157	11 402	18 918	162
Used	3 173	3 164	465	64	160	991	1 789	841	846	1 112	0
Equipment, total	108 361	62 185	23 206	2 102	12 258	4 525	25 902	5 976	9 117	8 976	749
New	107 268	60 295	22 330	2 019	11 644	4 238	24 573	5 590	7 921	8 300	725
Used	1 093	1 891	876	83	613	287	1 329	386	1 196	676	24
2002											
Total expenditures	128 444	94 529	25 864	3 430	14 719	19 532	59 311	13 169	22 409	21 269	1 532
Structures, total	24 308	35 579	7 129	933	3 276	14 655	30 291	7 758	12 157	13 261	250
New	19 748	30 227	6 424	913	2 948	13 601	27 273	7 332	10 848	11 363	248
Used	4 739	5 352	706	21	328	1 055	3 018	425	1 309	1 899	2
Equipment, total	103 956	58 949	18 735	2 497	11 443	4 876	29 021	5 412	10 252	8 007	1 282
New	103 421	56 847	18 021	2 481	10 585	4 690	28 196	5 132	9 290	6 858	1 276
Used	535	2 102	714	16	857	186	825	280	962	1 149	6
2003											
Total expenditures	120 787	87 952	24 703	3 298	16 612	16 667	61 151	11 029	21 036	26 035	1 476
Structures, total	26 200	25 028	5 314	925	3 976	11 984	30 996	6 800	10 568	18 518	209
New	17 908	16 446	4 671	869	3 213	11 569	28 885	6 532	9 417	16 288	202
Used	8 292	8 583	643	56	763	415	2 111	268	1 151	2 230	7
Equipment, total	94 587	62 923	19 389	2 373	12 636	4 683	30 155	4 229	10 468	7 517	1 267
New	94 205	61 253	18 675	2 368	11 374	4 569	29 497	4 038	9 684	6 706	1 263
Used	383	1 671	714	5	1 262	114	658	192	783	811	4
2004											
Total expenditures	153 229	92 163	26 874	4 222	17 546	19 019	65 274	12 154	20 641	19 717	1 445
Structures, total	43 721	27 963	6 133	1 136	2 547	13 808	33 173	7 352	9 859	12 278	265
New	29 003	22 157	5 838	911	2 288	12 861	31 154	7 187	9 113	10 866	252
Used	14 718	5 806	295	225	259	947	2 019	165	746	1 412	13
Equipment, total	109 508	64 201	20 741	3 086	14 999	5 211	32 101	4 802	10 782	7 439	1 180
New	108 940	61 785	20 161	2 993	12 802	4 986	31 428	4 674	10 358	6 804	1 178
Used	567	2 416	580	93	2 197	225	673	128	424	635	2

Note: Detail may not sum to total because of rounding.

NOTES AND DEFINITIONS

TABLES 5-1 THROUGH 5-4 AND 5-7
GROSS SAVING AND INVESTMENT ACCOUNTS; INVENTORIES TO SALES RATIOS

Source: U.S. Department of Commerce, Bureau of Economic Analysis (BEA)

Revisions

Data in these tables reflect revisions to the national income and product accounts (NIPAs) available through August 2006.

Definitions: Table 5-1

Gross saving is saving before the deduction of allowances for the consumption of fixed capital. It represents the amount of saving available to finance gross investment. *Net saving* is gross saving less allowances for fixed capital consumption. It represents the amount of saving available for financing expansion of the capital stock.

Personal saving is derived by subtracting personal outlays from disposable personal income. (See Chapter 4 for more information.) It is the current net saving of individuals (including proprietors of unincorporated businesses), nonprofit institutions that primarily serve individuals, life insurance carriers, retirement funds, private noninsured welfare funds, and private trust funds. Conceptually, personal saving may also be viewed as the sum for all persons (including institutions as just defined) of the net acquisition of financial assets and the change in physical assets, less the sum of net borrowing and consumption of fixed capital. In either case, it is defined to exclude capital gains. That is, it excludes profits on the increase in the value of homes, securities, and other property—whether realized or unrealized—and includes the noncorporate inventory valuation and capital consumption adjustments (IVA and CCAdj). (See the notes and definitions for Tables 1-1 through 1-13.)

Undistributed profits are corporate profits after tax less dividends, with the corporate IVA and corporate CCAdj. (See the notes and definitions for Tables 1-1 through 1-13.)

Government net saving was formerly called "current surplus or deficit (-) of general government." (See Chapter 6 for further detail from the government accounts.) Where current receipts of government exceed current expenditures, government has a current surplus (indicated by a positive value) and saving is made available to finance investment by government or other sectors—for example, by the repayment of debt, which can free up funds for private investment. Where current expenditures exceed current receipts, there is a government deficit (indicated by a negative value) and government must borrow, drawing on funds that would otherwise be available for private investment.

Consumption of fixed capital is an accounting charge for the using-up of private and government fixed capital, including software, located in the United States. It is based on studies of prices of used equipment and structures in resale markets. For general government and nonprofit institutions primarily serving individuals, it is recorded in government consumption expenditures and in personal consumption expenditures (PCE), respectively, as the value of the current services of the fixed capital assets owned and used by these entities. *Private consumption of fixed capital* consists of tax-return-based depreciation charges for corporations and nonfarm proprietorships and of historical-cost depreciation (calculated by the Bureau of Economic Analysis [BEA] using a geometric pattern of price declines) for farm proprietorships, rental income of persons, and nonprofit institutions, minus the capital consumption adjustments. (In other words, in the NIPA treatment of saving, the amount of the CCAdj is taken out of book depreciation and added to income and profits—a reallocation from one form of gross saving to another.)

Gross private domestic investment consists of gross private fixed investment and change in private inventories. See the notes and definitions for Chapter 1.

Gross government investment consists of federal, state, and local general government and government enterprise expenditures for fixed assets (structures, equipment, and software). Government inventory investment is included in government consumption expenditures. For more detail, see Chapter 6.

Capital account transactions, net are the net cash or in-kind transfers between the United States and the rest of the world that are linked to the acquisition or disposition of an asset rather than the purchase or sale of currently-produced goods and services. When positive, it represents a net transfer from the United States to the rest of the world; when negative, it represents a net transfer to the United States from the rest of the world. This is a definitional category that was introduced in the 1999 revision. Estimates are available only from 1982 forward.

Net lending or net borrowing (-), NIPAs is equal to the international balance on current account as measured in the NIPAs (see Chapter 7) less capital account transactions, net. When positive, this represents net investment by the United States in the rest of the world; when negative, it represents net borrowing by the United States from the rest of the world. For data before 1982, net lending or net borrowing equals the NIPA balance on current account, as estimates of capital account transactions are not available.

By definition, gross national saving must equal the sum of gross domestic investment, capital account transactions, and net international lending or borrowing. In practice, due to differences in measurement, they differ by the same *statistical discrepancy* calculated in the product and income accounts. (See Chapter 1.) Where the statistical discrepancy is negative, it means that the sum of measured investment, capital transactions, and net international transactions has fallen short of measured saving.

Gross national income is national income plus the consumption of fixed capital. (See Chapter 1 for further information.) This is a new concept introduced in the 2003 revision. It is conceptually equal to gross national product, but differs by the statistical discrepancy. It is an appropriate denominator for the national saving ratios. Saving was previously shown as a percentage of gross national product; in the revision, it is instead shown as a percentage of the income-side equivalent of gross national product. Since saving is measured as a residual from income, it is appropriate to involve the same measurement imperfections in both the numerator and the denominator of the fraction.

Definitions: Tables 5-2 through 5-4

Gross private fixed investment comprises both nonresidential and residential fixed investment. It consists of purchases of fixed assets, which are commodities that will be used in a production process for more than one year, including replacements and additions to the capital stock. It is "gross" because it is measured before a deduction for consumption of fixed capital. It covers all investment by private businesses and nonprofit institutions in the United States, regardless of whether the investment is owned by U.S. residents. It does not include purchases of the same types of equipment and structures by government agencies, which are included in government gross investment, or investment by U.S. residents in other countries.

Gross nonresidential fixed investment consists of structures, equipment, and software not related to personal residences.

Nonresidential structures consists of new construction, brokers' commissions on sales of structures, and net purchases (purchases less sales) of used structures by private business and by nonprofit institutions from government agencies. New construction includes hotels, motels, and mining exploration, shafts, and wells.

Nonresidential equipment and software consists of private business purchases—on capital account—of new machinery, equipment, and vehicles; purchases and in-house production of software; dealers' margins on sales of used equipment; and net purchases (purchases less sales) of used equipment from government agencies, persons, and the rest of the world. (However, it does not include the personal-use portion of equipment purchased for both business and personal use. This is included in PCE.)

Residential private fixed investment consists of both *structures* and residential producers' durable *equipment*—that is, equipment owned by landlords and rented to tenants. Investment in structures consists of new units, improvements to existing units, manufactured homes, brokers' commissions on the sale of residential property, and net purchases (purchases less sales) of used structures from government agencies.

Real gross private investment (Table 5-3) and *chain-type quantity indexes for private fixed investment* (Table 5-4) are defined and explained in the notes and definitions to Chapter 1. The chained-dollar (2000) estimates in Table 5-3 are constructed by applying the changes in the chain-type quantity indexes as shown in Table 5-4 to the 2000 current-dollar values. Thus, they do not contain any information about time trends that is not already present in the quantity indexes.

As the quantity indexes are chain-weighted at the basic level of aggregation, chained constant-dollar components generally do not add to the chained constant-dollar totals. For this reason, BEA only makes available year-2000-dollar estimates back to 1990 (except for the very highest levels of aggregation of GDP), since the addition problem is less severe for years close to the base year. However, the addition problem is so severe for computers that BEA does not even publish recent year-2000-dollar values for this component. BEA notes that "The quantity index for computers can be used to accurately measure the real growth rate of this component. However, because computers exhibit rapid changes in prices relative to other prices in the economy, the chained-dollar estimates should not be used to measure the component's relative importance or its contribution to the growth rate of more aggregate series." (Footnote to BEA Table 5.3.6, *Survey of Current Business*, available on the BEA Web site at <http://www.bea.gov>.) Accurate estimates of these contributions are shown in BEA Table 5.3.2, which is published in the *Survey of Current Business* and can be found on the BEA Web site.

Definitions: Table 5-7

Inventories to sales ratios. The ratios shown in Table 5-7 are based on the inventory estimates underlying the measurement of inventory change in the NIPAs. They include data and estimates for not only the inventories held in manufacturing and trade (see the following Tables 5-8 and 5-9), but also stocks held by all other businesses in the U.S. economy.

For the current-dollar ratios, inventories at the end of each quarter are valued in the prices that prevailed at the end of that quarter. For the constant-dollar ratios, they are valued in chained (2000) dollars. In both cases, the inventory-sales ratio is the value of the inventories at the end of the quarter divided by quarterly total sales at *monthly* rates (quarterly totals divided by 3). In other words, they represent how many months' supply businesses had on hand at the end of the period. Annual data are for the fourth quarter.

Data availability

Current data for some of these series are included in the monthly release of the latest NIPA estimates. All of the series are subsequently published each month in BEA's *Survey of Current Business*. Current and historical data may be obtained from the BEA Web site at <http://www.bea.gov> or the STAT-USA subscription Web site at <http://www.stat-usa.gov>.

References

Sources of information about the NIPAs are listed in the notes and definitions for Tables 1-1 through 1-13.

TABLES 5-5 AND 5-6
CURRENT-COST NET STOCK OF FIXED ASSETS; CHAIN-TYPE QUANTITY INDEXES FOR NET STOCK OF FIXED ASSETS

SOURCE: U.S. DEPARTMENT OF COMMERCE, BUREAU OF ECONOMIC ANALYSIS *(BEA)*

The Bureau of Economic Analysis (BEA) calculates measurements, integrated with the NIPAs, of the level of the stock of fixed assets in the U.S. economy, or what is commonly called the "capital stock." (The fixed investment component of the GDP is a flow, or the increment of new capital goods into the capital stock.) Data on consumer stocks of durable goods are also included in the accounts, but not shown here. Historical data are available back to 1901, with detailed annual estimates of net stocks, depreciation, and investment by type and by NAICS industry; the conversion of the historical data to the NAICS basis was completed this year. This volume of *Business Statistics* presents time series data on the net stock of fixed assets valued in current dollars and constant-dollar quantity indexes. Data for 1947 through 2005 are presented in Tables 5-5 and 5-6, and data for 1929 through 1948 in Table 18-3.

Definitions and methods

The definitions of capital stock categories are the same as used in gross domestic product (GDP) investment categories. (See the notes and definitions to Tables 5-2 through 5-4.)

The values of fixed capital and depreciation typically reported by businesses are inadequate for economic analysis and are not typically used in these measures. In business reports, capital is generally valued at historical costs—each year's capital acquisition in the prices of the year acquired—and the totals thus represent a mixture of pricing bases. Reported depreciation is generally based on historical cost and on depreciation rates allowable by federal income tax law, rather than on a realistic rate of economic depreciation.

In these data, the *net stock of fixed assets* is measured by a perpetual inventory method. In other words, net stock at any given time is the cumulative value of past gross investment less the cumulative value of past depreciation, including damages from disasters and war losses that exceed normal depreciation (such as the terror attacks of September 11, 2001).

Gross investment is the gross fixed investment component of GDP. Depreciation for privately-owned assets is the value of "consumption of fixed capital" in the NIPAs, which is subtracted from GDP in order to yield net domestic product. For government assets, the published NIPA value of consumption of fixed capital does not include disaster and war loss damage. The value of these damages is calculated by BEA and subtracted from capital stock assets for the purpose of fixed asset measurement.

The initial calculations using this perpetual inventory method are performed in real terms for each type of asset. They are then aggregated to higher levels using an annual-weighted Fisher-type index. (See the definition of *real or chained-dollar estimates* in the notes and definitions for Chapter 1.) This provides the *chain-type quantity indexes* shown in Table 5-6. Growth rates in these indexes measure real growth in the capital stock.

The real values are then converted to a current-cost basis to yield the values shown in Table 5-5. They are converted by multiplying the real values by the appropriate price index for the period under consideration. A major use of the current-cost net stock figures is comparison with the value of output in that year; for example, the current-cost net stock of fixed assets for the total economy divided by the current-dollar value of GDP yields a capital-output ratio for the entire economy. Growth rates in current-cost values will reflect both the real growth measured by the quantity indexes and the increase in the value at current prices of the existing stock.

Data availability

Historical fixed asset values updated to the NAICS basis for 1901 through 1986 were published on the BEA Web site, <http://www.bea.gov>, in April 2006. Data for 1987 through 1993 were revised and published on the BEA Web site in March 2005, and values for 1994–2004 were published in the September 2005 issue of the *Survey of Current Business*. Values on the Web site were updated through 2005 and incorporate the results of the 2006 annual revision of the NIPAs, which was published in August 2006.

References

The latest comprehensive revision was presented and described in "Fixed Assets and Consumer Durable Goods for 1994–2004," *Survey of Current Business*, September 2005. Data for earlier years were presented and described in "Fixed Assets and Consumer Durable Goods: Preliminary Estimates for 2002 and Revised Estimates for 1925–2001," *Survey of Current Business*, May 2004. The fixed asset measures are described in *Fixed Assets and Consumer Durable Goods in the United States, 1925–97* (September 2003), available on the BEA Web site at <http://www.bea.gov>.

TABLES 5-8 AND 5-9
MANUFACTURING AND TRADE SALES AND INVENTORIES

SOURCES: U.S. DEPARTMENT OF COMMERCE, CENSUS BUREAU (CURRENT-DOLLAR SERIES) AND U.S. DEPARTMENT OF COMMERCE, BUREAU OF ECONOMIC ANALYSIS (BEA) (CONSTANT-DOLLAR SERIES)

The current-dollar data on these pages draw together summary data from the separate series on manufacturers' shipments, inventories, and orders; merchant wholesalers' sales and inventories; and retail sales and inventories, all of which are included in Part B of this book. Generally, current-dollar inventories are collected on a current cost (or pre-LIFO [last in, first out]) basis. See the notes and definitions for Tables 17-4, 17-5, and 17-9 through 17-12 for further information about these data.

Data for recent years are compiled using the new North American Industry Classification System (NAICS), replacing the old Standard Industrial Classification (SIC).

•The Census Bureau has restated the current-dollar historical data on the NAICS basis back to January 1992. To allow the user to observe the difference between the two systems, and to "link" the new data to older data if a longer time series is required, *Business Statistics* is republishing the previous SIC-based annual data up through 1992 to provide an overlap with the new data in that year.

•BEA has restated the constant-dollar data on the NAICS basis back to the beginning of 1997. *Business Statistics* is publishing the previous SIC-based annual data through 1996. BEA provides overlapping data on its Web site at <http://www.bea.gov>.

In the NAICS, a few major industries have been taken out of manufacturing and trade entirely. Publishing and aerospace research activities have been reclassified from manufacturing into the new information industry, and food services and drinking places have been reclassified from retail trade into a new services category—accommodation and food services—which also includes hotels and similar establishments. A number of other activities have been moved within the broad category of manufacturing and trade. Food items made in retail establishments have been reclassified into manufacturing. A significant number of businesses previously classified as wholesale have been shifted into retail. Finally, the retail trade data, and therefore the total manufacturing and trade data, are no longer subdivided into durable and nondurable goods.

Based on these current-dollar values and relevant price data, BEA makes estimates of real sales, inventories, and inventory-sales ratios. Note, however, that annual figures for sales are shown as annual <u>totals</u> in Table 5-8 but as <u>averages</u> of the monthly data in Table 5-9. Also note that constant-dollar detail may not add to constant-dollar totals because of the chain-weighting formula; see the discussion of chain-weighted measures in the notes and definitions for Chapter 1.

Inventory values are as of the end of the month or year. In Table 5-8, annual values for monthly current-dollar inventory-sales ratios are averages of seasonally adjusted monthly ratios. However, for the real ratios in Table 5-9, annual figures for inventory-sales ratios are calculated by BEA as year-end (December) inventories divided by the monthly average of sales for the entire year. In all cases, the ratios in these two tables (like those in Table 5-7) represent the number of months' sales on hand as inventory at the end of the reporting period.

Data availability

Sales, inventories, and inventory-sales ratios for manufacturers, merchant wholesalers, and retailers are published monthly by the Census Bureau in a press release entitled "Manufacturing and Trade Inventories and Sales." Recent data are available on the Census Bureau Web site at <http://www.census.gov/mtis/www/mtis.html>.

Sales and inventories in constant dollars are available on the BEA Web site at <http://www.bea.gov>. To locate these data on that site, click on "Gross Domestic Product." Then, under "Supplemental Estimates," click "Underlying Detail Tables," and then on "List of Underlying Detail Tables." For the most recent data, if there is more than one table with the same title, select the last table.

References

Further information comparing NAICS and SIC industries can be found on the Census Bureau Web site.

For information about the 1996 historical revisions to sales and inventories in constant dollars, see "Real Inventories, Sales, and Inventory-Sales Ratios for Manufacturing and Trade, 1977–95," *Survey of Current Business*, May 1996.

TABLES 5-10 AND 5-11
ANNUAL CAPITAL EXPENDITURES

SOURCE: U.S. DEPARTMENT OF COMMERCE, CENSUS BUREAU

These data are from the Census Bureau's Annual Capital Expenditures Survey (ACES). The survey provides detailed information on capital investment in new and used structures and equipment by nonfarm businesses for 1996 through 2004.

The survey is based on a sample of approximately 46,000 companies with employees and 15,000 non-employer businesses (businesses with an owner but no employees). For companies with employees, the Census Bureau reports data for the years 1998 through 2004 for 132 separate industry categories from the North American Industry Classification System (NAICS); Table 5-11 shows these data for the major NAICS sectors. Total capital expenditures, with no industry detail, are reported for the nonemployer businesses and are shown in Table 5-10, where they can be compared with the totals for companies with employees for the years 1996 through 2004.

Definitions

Capital expenditures includes all capitalized costs during the year for both new and used structures and equipment, including software, that were chargeable to fixed asset accounts for which depreciation or amortization accounts are ordinarily maintained. For projects lasting longer than one year, this definition includes gross additions to construction-in-progress accounts, even if the asset was not in use and not yet depreciated. For *capital leases*, the company using the asset (lessee) is asked to include the cost or present value of the leased assets in the year in which the lease was entered. Also included in capital expenditures are capitalized leasehold improvements and capitalized interest charges on loans used to finance capital projects.

Structures consists of the capitalized costs of buildings and other structures and all necessary expenditures to acquire, construct, and prepare the structure. The cost of any machinery and equipment that is an integral or built-in feature of the structure is classified as structures. Also included are major additions and alterations to existing structures and capitalized repairs and improvements to buildings.

New structures includes new buildings and other structures not previously owned, as well as buildings and other structures that have been previously owned but not used or occupied.

Used structures includes buildings and other structures that have been previously owned and occupied.

Equipment includes machinery, furniture and fixtures, computers, and vehicles used in the production and distribution of goods and services. Expenditures for machinery and equipment that is housed in structures and can be removed or replaced without significantly altering the structure are classified as equipment.

New equipment consists of machinery and equipment purchased new and equipment produced in the company for use by the company.

Used equipment is secondhand machinery and equipment.

Capital leases consists of new assets acquired under capital lease arrangements entered into during the year. Capital leases are defined by the criteria in the Financial Accounting Standards (FASB) Number 13.

Capitalized computer software consists of costs of materials and services directly related to the development or acquisition of software; payroll and payroll-related costs for employees directly associated with software development; and interest cost incurred while developing the software. Capitalized computer software is defined by the criteria in Statement of Position 98-1, Accounting for the Costs of Computer Software Developed or Obtained for Internal Use.

Prepackaged software is purchased off-the-shelf through retailers or other mass-market outlets for internal use by the company and includes the cost of licensing fees and service/maintenance agreements.

Vendor-customized software is externally developed by vendors and customized for the company's use.

Internally-developed software is developed by the company's employees for internal use and includes loaded payroll (salaries, wages, benefits, and bonuses related to all software development activities).

Data availability

The *Annual Capital Expenditure Survey: 2004* was published by the Census Bureau in March 2006 and, in addition to new data for 2004, contains revised data for 2003. Previous surveys using NAICS, each containing the latest year's data and revisions for the preceding year, were issued in February 2005, February 2004, January 2003, April 2002, and May 2001. The 1998 and 1997 surveys show data by industry using the 1987 Standard Industrial Classification (SIC) system. Current and past surveys are available on the Census Bureau Web site at <http://www.census.gov/csd/ace>.

CHAPTER 6: GOVERNMENT

Section 6a: Federal Government in the National Income and Product Accounts

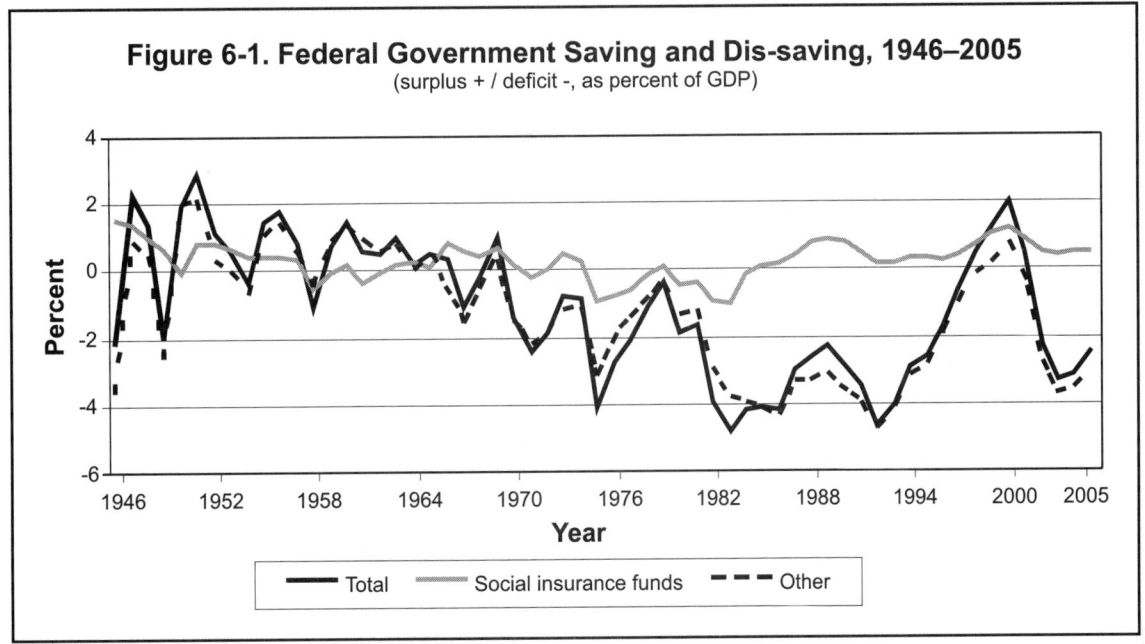

Figure 6-1. Federal Government Saving and Dis-saving, 1946–2005
(surplus + / deficit -, as percent of GDP)

- The non-social-insurance portion of the federal current budget has swung from large deficits to significant positive saving and back to deficit since the early 1980s. (Table 6-1)

- Total federal government current expenditures increased from 17.6 percent of gross domestic product (GDP) in 1953—the peak for Korean War spending— to 20.5 percent of GDP in 2005. The composition of expenditures changed significantly over that period. "Consumption" spending on defense and nondefense programs fell from 72 percent of total spending to 30 percent, while social benefits such as Social Security and Medicare rose from 13 percent to 42 percent. Grants to state and local governments increased from 3 percent to 14 percent, and interest outlays rose from 7 percent to 10 percent. (Tables 6-1 and 1-1)

- Federal government nondefense consumption spending, in real terms (as measured by the quantity index), increased at an annual rate of 2.5 percent from 1953 to 2005. Real federal nondefense gross investment spending rose 3.8 percent per year. (Table 6-6)

- Real defense consumption spending has jumped 29 percent in the five years since 2000, but in 2005 was still only 16 percent (an annual rate of 0.3 percent) above spending in 1953. Real defense investment spending was up 46 percent from 2000, but was only up 14 percent (an annual rate of 0.3 percent) from 1953. (Table 6-6)

Table 6-1. Federal Government Current Receipts and Expenditures

(National income and product accounts, calendar years, billions of dollars, quarterly data are at seasonally adjusted annual rates.)

NIPA Table 3.2

Year and quarter	Current receipts														
	Total	Tax receipts							Contributions for government social insurance	Income receipts on assets			Current transfer receipts	Current surplus of government enterprises
		Total 1	Personal current taxes	Taxes on production and imports		Taxes on corporate income				Total	Interest receipts	Rents and royalties		
				Total 1	Excise taxes	Total	Federal Reserve banks	Other						
1950	48.8	43.3	17.4	8.7	8.2	17.2	0.2	17.0	5.3	...	...	...	0.2	...
1951	62.9	56.3	25.4	9.2	8.6	21.7	0.3	21.4	6.4	...	...	...	0.3	...
1952	65.8	58.9	30.2	10.1	9.6	18.6	0.3	18.3	6.6	...	...	...	0.3	...
1953	68.6	61.5	31.3	10.7	10.2	19.5	0.3	19.1	6.8	...	...	...	0.3	...
1954	62.5	54.4	28.1	9.5	9.0	16.9	0.3	16.6	7.8	...	...	...	0.3	...
1955	71.1	62.0	30.5	10.4	9.8	21.1	0.3	20.8	8.8	...	...	...	0.3	...
1956	75.8	65.9	33.9	11.0	10.3	20.9	0.4	20.5	9.6	...	...	...	0.4	...
1957	79.3	67.9	36.0	11.5	10.8	20.4	0.5	19.9	11.0	...	...	...	0.4	...
1958	76.0	64.7	35.5	11.2	10.4	18.0	0.5	17.4	11.0	...	...	...	0.4	...
1959	87.0	73.3	38.5	12.2	11.2	22.5	0.9	21.6	13.4	0.0	...	0.0	0.4	-0.1
1960	93.9	76.5	41.8	13.1	12.0	21.4	0.9	20.6	16.0	1.4	1.3	0.0	0.4	-0.3
1961	95.5	77.5	42.7	13.2	12.2	21.5	0.7	20.8	16.5	1.5	1.4	0.1	0.5	-0.5
1962	103.6	83.3	46.5	14.2	13.0	22.5	0.8	21.7	18.6	1.7	1.6	0.1	0.5	-0.5
1963	111.8	88.6	49.1	14.7	13.5	24.6	0.9	23.7	21.0	1.8	1.7	0.1	0.6	-0.3
1964	111.8	87.8	46.0	15.5	14.2	26.1	1.6	24.6	21.7	1.8	1.7	0.1	0.7	-0.3
1965	120.9	95.7	51.1	15.5	13.9	28.9	1.3	27.6	22.7	1.9	1.8	0.1	1.1	-0.3
1966	137.9	104.8	58.6	14.5	12.6	31.4	1.6	29.8	30.5	2.1	2.0	0.1	1.2	-0.6
1967	146.9	109.9	64.4	15.2	13.3	30.0	1.9	28.1	34.0	2.5	2.3	0.2	1.1	-0.6
1968	171.2	129.8	76.4	17.0	14.7	36.1	2.5	33.6	37.8	2.9	2.7	0.2	1.1	-0.3
1969	192.5	146.1	91.7	17.9	15.5	36.1	3.0	33.0	43.1	2.7	2.5	0.2	1.1	-0.5
1970	186.0	138.0	88.9	18.2	15.7	30.6	3.5	27.1	45.3	3.1	2.8	0.2	1.1	-1.5
1971	191.7	138.7	85.8	19.1	16.0	33.5	3.4	30.1	50.0	3.5	3.1	0.3	1.1	-1.6
1972	220.1	158.4	102.8	18.6	15.6	36.6	3.2	33.4	57.9	3.6	3.3	0.4	1.3	-1.1
1973	250.4	173.1	109.6	19.9	16.7	43.3	4.3	38.9	74.0	3.8	3.4	0.4	1.3	-1.8
1974	279.5	192.2	126.5	20.2	16.5	45.1	5.6	39.6	83.5	4.2	3.6	0.5	1.4	-1.8
1975	277.2	187.0	120.7	22.2	16.4	43.6	5.4	38.2	87.5	4.9	4.3	0.6	1.5	-3.6
1976	322.5	218.1	141.2	21.6	17.0	54.6	5.9	48.7	99.1	5.9	5.2	0.7	1.6	-2.2
1977	363.4	247.4	162.2	22.9	17.5	61.6	5.9	55.7	110.3	6.7	5.8	0.9	1.9	-2.9
1978	423.5	286.9	188.9	25.6	18.5	71.4	7.0	64.4	127.9	8.5	7.4	1.1	2.4	-2.1
1979	486.2	326.2	224.6	26.0	18.5	74.4	9.3	65.1	148.9	10.7	9.2	1.5	2.8	-2.3
1980	532.1	355.9	250.0	34.0	26.9	70.3	11.7	58.6	162.6	13.7	11.3	2.3	3.5	-3.6
1981	619.4	408.1	290.6	50.3	41.7	65.7	14.0	51.7	191.8	18.3	14.8	3.5	3.8	-2.5
1982	616.6	386.8	295.0	41.4	32.8	49.0	15.2	33.8	204.9	22.2	18.3	3.8	5.2	-2.4
1983	642.3	393.6	286.2	44.8	35.7	61.3	14.2	47.1	221.8	23.8	20.4	3.5	6.0	-2.9
1984	709.0	425.7	301.4	47.8	35.9	75.2	16.1	59.2	252.8	26.6	22.8	3.9	7.3	-3.4
1985	773.3	460.6	336.0	46.4	34.3	76.3	17.8	58.5	276.5	29.1	25.7	3.5	9.4	-2.4
1986	815.2	479.6	350.1	44.0	30.3	83.8	17.8	66.0	297.5	31.4	29.0	2.4	8.2	-1.5
1987	896.6	544.0	392.5	46.3	30.7	103.2	17.7	85.4	315.9	27.9	25.6	2.3	10.7	-2.0
1988	958.2	566.7	402.9	50.3	33.9	111.1	17.4	93.8	353.1	30.0	28.0	2.0	10.8	-2.3
1989	1 037.4	621.7	451.5	50.2	32.7	117.2	21.6	95.6	376.3	28.6	26.5	2.1	12.4	-1.6
1990	1 081.5	642.8	470.2	51.4	33.9	118.1	23.6	94.5	400.1	30.2	27.6	2.6	13.5	-5.1
1991	1 101.3	636.1	461.3	62.2	45.3	109.9	20.8	89.2	418.6	30.1	27.4	2.8	17.9	-1.4
1992	1 147.2	660.4	475.3	63.7	45.4	118.8	16.8	102.0	441.8	25.7	23.1	2.6	19.4	-0.1
1993	1 222.5	713.4	505.5	66.7	46.9	138.5	16.0	122.5	463.6	26.2	23.5	2.7	21.1	-1.8
1994	1 320.8	781.9	542.7	79.4	57.9	156.7	20.5	136.3	493.7	23.4	20.6	2.7	22.3	-0.4
1995	1 406.5	845.1	586.0	75.9	56.1	179.3	23.4	155.9	519.2	23.7	21.2	2.5	19.1	-0.6
1996	1 524.0	932.4	663.4	73.2	54.0	190.6	20.1	170.5	542.8	26.9	23.0	4.0	23.1	-1.2
1997	1 653.1	1 030.6	744.3	78.2	58.6	203.0	20.7	182.3	576.4	25.9	21.4	4.5	19.9	0.3
1998	1 773.8	1 116.8	825.8	81.1	61.5	204.2	26.6	177.7	613.8	21.5	17.7	3.8	21.5	0.1
1999	1 891.2	1 195.7	893.0	83.9	64.7	213.0	25.4	187.6	651.6	21.5	18.0	3.5	22.7	-0.3
2000	2 053.8	1 313.6	999.1	87.8	66.7	219.4	25.3	194.1	691.7	25.2	20.1	5.1	25.7	-2.3
2001	2 016.2	1 252.2	994.5	85.8	65.2	164.7	27.1	137.6	717.5	24.9	18.4	6.5	27.1	-5.5
2002	1 853.2	1 075.5	830.5	87.3	67.4	150.5	24.5	126.0	734.3	20.2	15.4	4.9	24.8	-1.6
2003	1 879.9	1 070.8	774.5	89.7	68.2	197.8	22.0	175.8	758.9	22.9	16.4	6.5	25.0	2.3
2004	2 001.0	1 150.2	801.4	94.6	71.4	244.5	18.1	226.4	802.2	22.1	15.5	6.6	27.7	-1.2
2005	2 246.8	1 366.2	927.9	101.1	75.8	326.4	21.5	304.9	855.3	22.9	15.9	7.1	7.1	-4.9
2003														
1st quarter	1 888.9	1 092.7	804.4	90.0	68.5	190.8	23.9	166.9	747.6	19.8	15.0	4.7	24.2	4.6
2nd quarter	1 903.3	1 097.0	810.4	89.5	68.3	186.5	22.8	163.7	755.9	23.0	16.6	6.4	24.7	2.7
3rd quarter	1 817.3	1 004.5	708.2	88.8	67.3	199.6	21.4	178.2	761.7	24.2	16.9	7.3	25.4	1.5
4th quarter	1 910.2	1 089.1	774.7	90.3	68.8	214.3	20.0	194.3	770.3	24.8	17.2	7.6	25.7	0.4
2004														
1st quarter	1 945.4	1 108.6	776.0	93.6	71.4	229.4	17.2	212.2	787.8	22.2	15.3	7.0	26.7	0.1
2nd quarter	1 985.6	1 141.0	791.4	94.0	71.1	246.5	17.2	229.3	795.8	21.7	15.2	6.5	27.4	-0.3
3rd quarter	2 013.0	1 156.9	810.8	95.1	71.6	242.8	18.1	224.6	807.1	22.0	15.7	6.3	28.2	-1.3
4th quarter	2 059.9	1 194.3	827.5	95.8	71.4	259.3	19.8	239.5	817.9	22.5	15.9	6.5	28.6	-3.4
2005														
1st quarter	2 214.5	1 328.0	891.2	97.9	73.0	327.6	18.6	309.0	838.3	22.8	16.2	6.7	29.1	-3.7
2nd quarter	2 240.3	1 344.3	910.9	102.7	77.4	321.4	20.9	300.5	846.1	23.8	16.2	7.6	30.5	-4.5
3rd quarter	2 182.4	1 364.2	941.0	102.4	77.0	309.5	21.7	287.8	863.2	22.8	15.7	7.1	-61.7	-6.0
4th quarter	2 349.8	1 428.4	968.4	101.6	75.9	347.1	24.6	322.5	873.8	22.3	15.3	6.9	30.6	-5.4

1Includes components not shown separately.
. . . = Not available.

Table 6-1. Federal Government Current Receipts and Expenditures—Continued

(National income and product accounts, calendar years, billions of dollars, quarterly data are at seasonally adjusted annual rates.)

NIPA Table 3.2

Year and quarter	Current expenditures [1]		Government social benefits		Other current transfer payments		Interest payments			Subsidies	Net federal government saving, NIPA (surplus + / deficit -)		
	Total	Consumption expenditures	Total [1]	To persons	Total [1]	Grants-in-aid to state and local governments	Total	To persons and business	To the rest of the world		Total	Social insurance funds	Other
1950	43.3	22.1	10.2	10.2	5.5	1.9	4.5	...	0.0	1.0	5.5	-0.3	5.8
1951	53.3	34.4	7.9	7.9	5.2	2.0	4.6	...	0.0	1.2	9.6	2.6	7.0
1952	62.1	44.2	8.1	8.1	4.3	2.2	4.6	...	0.1	0.9	3.7	2.6	1.1
1953	66.8	48.3	8.7	8.7	4.3	2.3	4.7	...	0.1	0.7	1.8	2.1	-0.3
1954	64.2	43.9	10.7	10.7	4.1	2.3	4.8	...	0.1	0.6	-1.6	1.2	-2.8
1955	65.3	43.9	11.5	11.5	4.5	2.4	4.8	...	0.1	0.6	5.7	1.5	4.2
1956	68.3	45.1	12.3	12.3	4.4	2.5	5.2	...	0.2	1.2	7.6	1.7	5.9
1957	76.0	49.5	14.5	14.5	4.7	2.9	5.7	...	0.2	1.6	3.3	1.1	2.2
1958	81.4	50.9	18.2	18.2	5.2	3.3	5.4	...	0.1	1.8	-5.4	-2.7	-2.7
1959	83.6	50.0	18.6	18.6	7.6	3.8	6.3	...	0.3	1.1	3.3	-0.7	4.0
1960	86.7	49.8	20.1	19.9	7.4	4.0	8.4	8.0	0.3	1.1	7.2	0.4	6.8
1961	92.8	51.6	23.3	23.1	8.0	4.5	7.9	7.6	0.3	2.0	2.6	-2.3	5.0
1962	101.1	57.8	23.7	23.5	8.6	5.0	8.6	8.3	0.3	2.3	2.5	-0.6	3.1
1963	106.4	60.8	24.9	24.6	9.2	5.6	9.3	8.9	0.4	2.2	5.4	0.8	4.5
1964	110.8	62.8	25.4	25.2	9.8	6.5	10.0	9.6	0.5	2.7	1.0	1.3	-0.2
1965	117.6	65.7	27.6	27.3	10.7	7.2	10.6	10.1	0.5	3.0	3.3	0.5	2.9
1966	135.7	75.9	30.2	29.9	14.0	10.1	11.6	11.1	0.5	3.9	2.3	6.0	-3.7
1967	156.2	87.1	36.9	36.5	15.7	11.7	12.7	12.1	0.6	3.8	-9.4	4.1	-13.5
1968	173.5	95.4	42.2	41.9	17.1	12.7	14.6	13.9	0.7	4.1	-2.3	3.2	-5.5
1969	183.8	98.4	46.1	45.8	19.0	14.6	15.8	15.0	0.8	4.5	8.7	5.7	3.0
1970	201.1	98.6	56.1	55.6	23.9	19.3	17.7	16.7	1.0	4.8	-15.2	1.0	-16.2
1971	220.0	102.0	66.6	66.1	29.0	23.2	17.9	16.1	1.8	4.6	-28.4	-3.0	-25.3
1972	244.4	107.7	73.3	72.9	38.6	31.7	18.8	16.1	2.7	6.6	-24.4	-0.6	-23.8
1973	261.7	108.9	85.2	84.5	39.7	34.8	22.8	19.0	3.8	5.1	-11.3	5.8	-17.1
1974	293.3	118.0	103.9	103.3	41.8	36.3	26.0	21.7	4.3	3.2	-13.8	3.2	-17.0
1975	346.2	129.6	133.0	132.3	50.5	45.1	28.9	24.4	4.5	4.3	-69.0	-16.2	-52.9
1976	374.3	137.2	143.9	143.1	54.6	50.7	33.8	29.3	4.5	4.9	-51.7	-15.6	-36.1
1977	407.5	150.7	152.9	152.1	60.0	56.6	37.1	31.6	5.5	6.9	-44.1	-13.8	-30.2
1978	450.0	163.3	163.3	162.4	69.4	65.5	45.3	36.7	8.7	8.7	-26.5	-4.6	-21.9
1979	497.5	179.0	183.7	182.8	70.8	66.3	55.7	44.6	11.1	8.2	-11.3	0.2	-11.4
1980	585.7	207.5	220.7	219.6	78.4	72.3	69.7	57.0	12.7	9.4	-53.6	-15.5	-38.1
1981	672.7	238.3	251.4	250.1	78.2	72.5	93.9	76.6	17.3	11.1	-53.3	-13.8	-39.5
1982	748.5	263.3	282.4	281.2	76.4	69.5	111.8	92.5	19.3	14.5	-131.9	-33.8	-98.1
1983	815.4	286.5	304.3	303.0	78.7	71.6	124.6	105.6	19.0	20.8	-173.0	-37.3	-135.7
1984	877.1	310.0	310.5	309.2	86.0	76.7	150.3	129.1	21.2	20.6	-168.1	-8.7	-159.4
1985	948.2	338.4	326.6	325.4	92.7	80.9	169.4	146.3	23.1	20.9	-175.0	1.7	-176.7
1986	1 006.0	358.2	345.3	343.7	99.9	87.6	178.2	153.5	24.6	24.5	-190.8	6.4	-197.2
1987	1 041.6	374.3	358.2	356.7	94.7	83.9	184.6	158.4	26.2	29.9	-145.0	15.2	-160.2
1988	1 092.7	382.5	379.1	377.5	102.8	91.6	199.3	167.6	31.7	29.0	-134.5	39.7	-174.1
1989	1 167.5	399.2	412.2	410.6	109.8	98.3	219.3	181.0	38.4	26.8	-130.1	43.1	-173.2
1990	1 253.5	419.8	447.2	445.4	122.7	111.4	237.5	196.7	40.8	26.4	-172.0	43.0	-215.0
1991	1 315.0	439.5	494.2	492.0	103.5	131.6	250.9	210.1	40.9	26.9	-213.7	25.7	-239.4
1992	1 444.6	445.2	551.7	549.8	167.0	149.1	251.3	212.2	39.1	29.5	-297.4	6.5	-303.9
1993	1 496.0	441.9	582.4	580.5	182.3	163.7	253.4	214.0	39.4	36.0	-273.5	5.6	-279.1
1994	1 533.1	440.8	607.6	605.5	191.6	174.7	261.3	217.1	44.2	31.8	-212.3	17.9	-230.3
1995	1 603.5	440.5	642.7	640.8	196.3	184.1	290.4	236.6	53.8	33.7	-197.0	19.0	-216.0
1996	1 665.8	446.3	680.0	677.9	208.2	191.2	297.3	232.0	65.3	34.0	-141.8	13.9	-155.7
1997	1 708.9	457.7	706.3	704.2	212.5	198.6	300.0	221.3	78.6	32.4	-55.8	30.6	-86.4
1998	1 734.9	454.6	719.2	716.9	227.4	212.8	298.8	219.6	79.3	35.0	38.8	59.0	-20.2
1999	1 787.6	475.1	738.0	735.7	248.0	232.9	282.7	208.1	74.5	43.8	103.6	94.1	9.6
2000	1 864.4	499.3	772.5	770.0	265.6	247.3	283.3	200.3	83.0	43.8	189.5	112.3	77.1
2001	1 969.5	531.9	841.4	838.7	290.0	276.1	258.6	176.2	82.4	47.6	46.7	87.0	-40.3
2002	2 101.1	591.5	919.6	916.9	323.4	304.6	229.1	152.4	76.6	37.5	-247.9	48.9	-296.8
2003	2 252.1	662.7	966.5	963.7	362.2	338.5	212.9	139.0	73.9	47.8	-372.1	39.0	-411.1
2004	2 383.0	724.5	1 018.4	1 015.4	374.9	349.0	220.9	132.4	88.5	44.3	-382.0	50.3	-432.3
2005	2 555.9	768.6	1 081.7	1 078.6	395.0	361.1	253.8	140.3	113.6	56.9	-309.2	58.1	-367.3
2003													
1st quarter	2 179.0	636.9	948.0	945.3	337.0	311.9	216.6	144.1	72.5	41.9	-290.2	42.4	-332.6
2nd quarter	2 268.8	668.4	964.0	961.1	367.4	342.2	212.4	141.2	71.2	55.2	-365.5	37.4	-402.9
3rd quarter	2 268.8	669.1	972.7	969.8	369.4	345.9	210.0	135.3	74.7	47.5	-451.4	36.7	-488.1
4th quarter	2 291.7	676.5	981.5	978.6	374.8	354.2	212.5	135.4	77.1	46.4	-381.5	39.4	-420.8
2004													
1st quarter	2 346.4	712.2	1 003.7	1 000.8	373.0	339.5	215.6	136.4	79.2	43.4	-401.0	45.1	-446.1
2nd quarter	2 366.3	722.6	1 012.3	1 009.3	372.2	349.8	215.3	127.6	87.7	42.4	-380.6	49.2	-429.8
3rd quarter	2 393.6	734.8	1 022.2	1 019.2	367.8	345.7	224.8	133.1	91.7	43.9	-380.6	53.3	-433.9
4th quarter	2 425.6	728.3	1 035.6	1 032.4	386.6	361.2	227.7	132.5	95.2	47.4	-365.7	53.8	-419.5
2005													
1st quarter	2 502.0	758.0	1 065.9	1 062.9	395.2	355.9	230.9	128.8	102.2	51.9	-287.6	50.5	-338.1
2nd quarter	2 529.9	760.8	1 076.4	1 073.3	385.4	359.8	252.1	142.5	109.6	55.2	-289.6	49.4	-338.9
3rd quarter	2 578.5	784.3	1 087.8	1 084.7	393.5	361.9	255.2	137.9	117.2	57.7	-396.0	64.0	-460.0
4th quarter	2 613.3	771.1	1 096.7	1 093.5	405.7	366.8	277.1	151.8	125.3	62.7	-263.6	68.5	-332.0

[1]Includes components not shown separately.
. . . = Not available.

Table 6-2. Federal Government Consumption Expenditures and Gross Investment

(National income and product accounts, calendar years, billions of dollars, quarterly data are at seasonally adjusted annual rates.)

NIPA Tables 3.9.5, 3.10.5

Year and quarter	Total	Federal government consumption expenditures and gross investment											
		Consumption expenditures					Gross investment						
								National defense			Nondefense		
		Total	Compensation of general government employees	Consumption of general government fixed capital	Intermediate goods and services purchased [1]	Less: Own-account investment and sales to other sectors	Total	Total	Structures	Equipment and software	Total	Structures	Equipment and software
1950	26.0	22.1	11.1	5.8	5.7	0.4	3.9	2.4	0.5	1.9	1.6	1.2	0.4
1951	45.1	34.4	16.6	6.1	12.6	0.9	10.7	9.1	2.0	7.1	1.5	1.1	0.4
1952	59.2	44.2	19.3	6.8	18.7	0.6	15.0	13.4	3.3	10.1	1.6	1.1	0.5
1953	64.4	48.3	19.1	7.6	22.3	0.6	16.1	14.7	3.3	11.4	1.4	1.1	0.3
1954	57.3	43.9	18.3	8.2	18.1	0.7	13.3	12.1	2.7	9.4	1.2	0.9	0.3
1955	54.9	43.9	19.0	8.6	17.7	1.3	10.9	10.1	2.1	8.0	0.9	0.6	0.2
1956	56.7	45.1	19.6	9.2	17.1	0.8	11.6	10.5	2.1	8.4	1.2	0.9	0.3
1957	61.3	49.5	20.2	9.7	20.8	1.3	11.9	10.5	2.3	8.2	1.4	1.1	0.2
1958	63.8	50.9	21.3	9.8	21.1	1.3	12.9	11.3	2.6	8.7	1.6	1.4	0.2
1959	65.4	50.0	21.7	10.1	19.3	1.2	15.4	13.7	2.5	11.2	1.7	1.5	0.2
1960	64.1	49.8	22.6	10.5	17.8	1.1	14.3	12.3	2.2	10.1	2.0	1.7	0.3
1961	67.9	51.6	23.7	10.7	18.2	1.0	16.3	13.9	2.4	11.5	2.4	1.9	0.6
1962	75.3	57.8	25.2	11.3	22.4	1.1	17.4	14.5	2.0	12.5	2.9	2.1	0.8
1963	76.9	60.8	26.5	11.9	23.5	1.2	16.1	12.6	1.6	11.0	3.5	2.3	1.2
1964	78.5	62.8	28.5	12.2	23.3	1.2	15.6	11.5	1.3	10.2	4.2	2.5	1.6
1965	80.4	65.7	30.0	12.5	24.6	1.3	14.7	10.0	1.1	8.9	4.7	2.8	1.9
1966	92.5	75.9	34.3	13.0	30.3	1.7	16.7	11.8	1.3	10.5	4.9	2.8	2.1
1967	104.8	87.1	37.9	13.8	36.8	1.3	17.7	13.5	1.2	12.3	4.2	2.2	1.9
1968	111.4	95.4	41.9	14.5	40.3	1.3	16.0	12.2	1.2	10.9	3.8	2.1	1.7
1969	113.4	98.4	44.9	15.2	39.8	1.4	15.0	11.3	1.5	9.9	3.6	1.9	1.7
1970	113.5	98.6	48.3	15.8	35.9	1.4	14.8	11.1	1.3	9.8	3.8	2.1	1.7
1971	113.7	102.0	51.7	16.1	35.7	1.5	11.7	7.5	1.8	5.7	4.2	2.5	1.7
1972	119.7	107.7	55.4	16.2	38.4	2.3	12.0	7.5	1.8	5.7	4.5	2.7	1.8
1973	122.5	108.9	57.4	16.5	37.7	2.8	13.6	8.7	2.1	6.6	4.9	3.1	1.8
1974	134.6	118.0	62.0	17.6	41.7	3.4	16.6	11.1	2.2	8.9	5.6	3.4	2.2
1975	149.1	129.6	68.4	19.0	45.2	3.0	19.5	13.0	2.3	10.7	6.5	4.1	2.4
1976	159.7	137.2	73.3	20.5	46.2	2.8	22.6	15.3	2.1	13.2	7.3	4.6	2.7
1977	175.4	150.7	79.9	22.1	52.4	3.8	24.7	16.7	2.4	14.4	8.0	5.0	3.0
1978	190.9	163.3	85.8	24.0	58.2	4.5	27.6	17.8	2.5	15.3	9.8	6.1	3.7
1979	210.6	179.0	91.8	25.8	66.9	5.6	31.6	21.4	2.5	18.9	10.2	6.3	4.0
1980	243.8	207.5	102.5	28.7	82.3	6.2	36.3	24.3	3.2	21.1	12.0	7.1	4.9
1981	280.2	238.3	115.1	32.3	97.0	6.2	41.9	28.9	3.2	25.7	13.0	7.7	5.3
1982	310.8	263.3	125.3	36.0	108.2	6.1	47.5	34.7	4.0	30.8	12.7	6.8	6.0
1983	342.9	286.5	132.3	39.0	121.3	6.1	56.4	41.9	4.8	37.1	14.5	6.7	7.8
1984	374.4	310.0	149.4	42.8	124.5	6.7	64.4	48.7	4.9	43.8	15.7	7.0	8.7
1985	412.8	338.4	159.0	46.1	140.2	6.9	74.4	57.5	6.2	51.3	16.9	7.3	9.6
1986	438.6	358.2	163.1	49.6	152.4	6.9	80.4	62.9	6.8	56.1	17.5	8.0	9.5
1987	460.1	374.3	170.3	53.1	158.7	7.9	85.8	66.4	7.7	58.8	19.4	9.0	10.4
1988	462.3	382.5	178.0	56.9	156.4	8.7	79.8	61.3	7.4	53.9	18.6	6.8	11.7
1989	482.2	399.2	185.7	60.9	162.1	9.4	83.0	62.7	6.4	56.3	20.3	6.9	13.4
1990	508.3	419.8	193.9	65.1	171.2	10.3	88.5	65.9	6.1	59.8	22.6	8.0	14.6
1991	527.7	439.5	205.9	69.1	175.9	11.3	88.2	63.4	4.6	58.8	24.8	9.2	15.7
1992	533.9	445.2	210.7	71.4	174.3	11.3	88.8	61.6	5.2	56.3	27.2	10.3	16.9
1993	525.2	441.9	211.9	74.4	166.6	11.0	83.3	55.2	5.1	50.1	28.1	11.2	16.9
1994	519.1	440.8	209.8	76.4	167.6	13.0	78.3	52.9	5.7	47.2	25.4	10.5	14.9
1995	519.2	440.5	206.8	77.9	166.4	10.6	78.8	51.4	6.3	45.1	27.3	10.8	16.5
1996	527.4	446.3	210.7	78.0	168.8	11.1	81.1	52.1	6.7	45.4	29.1	11.2	17.9
1997	530.9	457.7	212.9	78.0	175.9	9.1	73.2	44.9	5.7	39.2	28.3	9.8	18.5
1998	530.4	454.6	215.1	78.0	171.5	9.9	75.8	45.0	5.1	39.9	30.8	10.6	20.2
1999	555.8	475.1	221.3	79.6	182.7	8.5	80.7	47.7	5.0	42.8	33.0	10.6	22.4
2000	578.8	499.3	233.8	81.6	193.8	9.8	79.5	48.8	5.0	43.8	30.7	8.3	22.3
2001	612.9	531.9	242.9	82.8	215.3	9.1	81.0	50.2	4.6	45.6	30.8	8.3	22.5
2002	679.7	591.5	269.4	83.5	248.0	9.4	88.1	55.4	4.4	51.0	32.7	9.9	22.8
2003	756.4	662.7	298.9	85.1	288.7	9.9	93.7	60.4	5.3	55.2	33.3	10.1	23.1
2004	825.9	724.5	323.0	88.6	323.4	10.5	101.4	67.5	5.1	62.4	33.9	9.6	24.3
2005	878.3	768.6	343.5	93.2	345.2	13.4	109.8	72.4	5.2	67.2	37.4	10.2	27.1
2003													
1st quarter	725.9	636.9	295.0	84.3	266.4	8.8	89.1	56.8	4.8	52.0	32.2	9.9	22.4
2nd quarter	762.2	668.4	299.6	85.2	294.6	10.9	93.8	60.0	5.0	55.0	33.8	10.4	23.4
3rd quarter	764.8	669.1	300.1	85.3	294.0	10.3	95.7	61.8	5.7	56.1	33.9	10.5	23.4
4th quarter	772.8	676.5	300.8	85.4	299.7	9.4	96.3	63.2	5.7	57.5	33.1	9.8	23.4
2004													
1st quarter	808.2	712.2	319.6	86.4	315.3	9.1	96.0	63.5	5.1	58.4	32.5	9.1	23.4
2nd quarter	823.8	722.6	322.6	88.4	321.4	9.7	101.2	67.0	4.7	62.3	34.2	9.9	24.3
3rd quarter	838.4	734.8	323.9	89.0	334.1	12.1	103.5	69.5	5.2	64.4	34.0	10.0	24.0
4th quarter	833.2	728.3	325.9	90.6	322.6	10.9	104.9	69.8	5.3	64.6	35.1	9.4	25.7
2005													
1st quarter	862.9	758.0	343.5	91.8	336.3	13.6	104.8	69.1	5.2	63.9	35.7	9.8	26.0
2nd quarter	868.4	760.8	342.6	92.5	337.4	11.7	107.6	72.2	5.0	67.2	35.4	9.2	26.2
3rd quarter	895.8	784.3	344.2	93.6	360.2	13.8	111.5	74.2	5.1	69.0	37.4	9.9	27.5
4th quarter	886.2	771.1	343.6	94.8	346.8	14.2	115.1	74.1	5.4	68.6	41.1	12.1	29.0

[1] Includes general government intermediate inputs for goods and services sold to other sectors and for own-account investment.

Table 6-3. Federal Government Defense and Nondefense Consumption Expenditures by Type

(National income and product accounts, calendar years, billions of dollars, quarterly data are at seasonally adjusted annual rates.)

NIPA Table 3.10.5

Year and quarter	Defense consumption expenditures [1]						Nondefense consumption expenditures [1]					
	Total	Compensation of general government employees	Consumption of general government fixed capital	Intermediate goods and services purchased [2]			Total	Compensation of general government employees	Consumption of general government fixed capital	Intermediate goods and services purchased [2]		
				Durable goods	Nondurable goods	Services				Durable goods	Nondurable goods	Services
1950	17.2	8.0	5.2	1.7	0.9	1.5	4.9	3.1	0.6	0.1	0.5	0.9
1951	30.1	13.5	5.4	4.4	2.3	5.0	4.3	3.1	0.6	0.1	0.1	0.7
1952	38.9	16.1	6.2	8.0	2.8	6.1	5.3	3.2	0.6	0.1	0.5	1.3
1953	41.2	16.0	6.9	9.1	4.2	5.1	7.1	3.1	0.6	0.1	2.4	1.3
1954	37.1	15.4	7.6	6.8	3.2	4.2	6.9	2.9	0.6	0.1	2.2	1.4
1955	36.9	15.8	8.0	6.0	1.7	5.9	7.1	3.2	0.6	0.1	2.5	1.6
1956	38.8	16.1	8.5	6.1	1.7	6.7	6.3	3.5	0.6	0.1	0.8	1.7
1957	43.2	16.5	9.0	6.7	2.2	9.3	6.3	3.7	0.6	0.1	0.8	1.8
1958	44.1	17.0	9.1	7.1	2.1	9.5	6.8	4.3	0.7	0.0	0.7	1.7
1959	40.1	17.3	9.5	5.1	1.8	6.9	9.8	4.4	0.7	0.0	3.3	2.1
1960	41.0	17.7	9.8	4.4	1.9	7.7	8.7	4.6	0.7	0.1	1.1	2.5
1961	42.7	18.3	10.0	3.6	2.3	8.8	9.0	5.4	0.7	0.1	0.4	3.0
1962	46.6	19.4	10.6	4.6	2.9	9.6	11.3	5.8	0.8	0.2	1.5	3.6
1963	48.3	20.1	11.1	4.7	2.7	10.2	12.4	6.4	0.9	0.3	1.2	4.5
1964	48.8	21.6	11.2	4.0	2.9	9.7	14.0	7.0	1.0	0.4	1.1	5.3
1965	50.6	22.6	11.3	4.2	3.2	9.9	15.1	7.4	1.2	0.5	1.1	5.7
1966	60.0	26.3	11.6	6.2	4.7	12.2	15.9	8.0	1.5	0.5	0.4	6.4
1967	70.0	29.3	12.1	6.2	7.3	15.5	17.1	8.6	1.7	0.4	1.2	6.2
1968	77.2	32.4	12.7	7.5	8.4	16.4	18.3	9.5	1.8	0.4	1.9	5.7
1969	78.2	34.7	13.2	6.5	7.6	16.5	20.2	10.1	2.0	0.3	3.0	5.9
1970	76.6	36.6	13.6	6.1	5.4	15.2	22.1	11.7	2.1	0.3	2.0	7.1
1971	77.1	38.2	13.8	4.6	4.4	16.3	24.9	13.4	2.3	0.3	2.1	8.1
1972	79.5	40.5	13.8	5.7	4.7	15.5	28.2	14.8	2.4	0.3	2.4	9.9
1973	79.4	41.4	14.0	5.5	4.3	15.3	29.4	16.0	2.5	0.2	1.9	10.4
1974	84.5	44.1	14.7	5.2	5.2	16.9	33.4	18.0	2.8	0.2	2.6	11.7
1975	90.9	47.9	15.7	6.0	5.1	17.4	38.7	20.5	3.2	0.2	2.8	13.7
1976	95.8	50.3	17.1	5.8	4.5	18.8	41.4	23.1	3.4	0.3	3.5	13.3
1977	104.2	53.6	18.4	8.0	4.5	20.4	46.5	26.3	3.7	0.3	4.4	14.7
1978	112.7	57.5	20.0	9.6	4.9	21.7	50.6	28.3	4.0	0.4	4.9	16.7
1979	123.8	61.7	21.3	11.3	6.2	24.2	55.1	30.1	4.5	0.5	5.2	19.4
1980	143.7	68.6	23.5	12.8	10.0	30.2	63.8	34.0	5.2	0.7	7.4	21.3
1981	167.3	78.8	26.3	16.2	11.8	35.8	71.0	36.3	6.0	0.6	11.2	21.4
1982	191.2	87.4	29.2	19.6	11.5	45.4	72.1	37.9	6.7	0.6	9.1	22.1
1983	208.8	92.4	31.7	25.1	11.3	49.5	77.7	39.9	7.3	0.9	10.6	23.9
1984	232.9	107.5	34.8	27.1	10.4	54.7	77.1	41.8	7.9	0.9	6.4	24.9
1985	253.7	115.3	37.5	29.3	10.0	63.4	84.7	43.6	8.7	1.0	9.5	27.1
1986	268.0	118.8	40.2	31.9	10.2	68.7	90.3	44.3	9.3	1.0	12.4	28.2
1987	283.6	123.5	43.0	33.8	10.3	75.1	90.6	46.8	10.1	1.1	6.9	31.6
1988	293.6	126.9	46.0	33.5	10.6	79.0	88.9	51.1	10.9	1.2	-0.1	32.2
1989	299.5	131.7	49.1	32.0	10.8	78.3	99.7	54.0	11.8	1.3	5.7	33.9
1990	308.1	134.5	52.4	31.6	11.0	81.8	111.7	59.3	12.7	1.5	5.7	39.6
1991	319.8	141.8	55.5	31.0	10.7	84.3	119.7	64.0	13.6	1.6	6.3	42.1
1992	315.3	143.0	57.3	28.4	9.4	81.3	129.8	67.7	14.2	1.7	6.9	46.7
1993	307.6	138.7	59.5	26.4	8.5	78.8	134.2	73.3	14.8	1.6	7.4	43.9
1994	300.7	134.7	61.0	22.9	7.6	80.5	140.1	75.1	15.3	1.6	7.0	48.1
1995	297.3	130.8	61.8	20.9	6.3	81.1	143.2	76.0	16.1	1.7	7.3	49.1
1996	302.5	133.3	61.2	20.8	7.6	83.6	143.8	77.3	16.7	1.8	7.2	47.8
1997	304.7	132.8	60.4	20.9	7.6	86.5	153.0	80.1	17.6	1.8	8.2	51.0
1998	300.7	131.6	59.6	21.0	7.0	84.7	153.9	83.5	18.4	1.7	8.2	49.0
1999	312.9	133.5	59.8	22.3	8.2	92.2	162.2	87.8	19.8	1.7	6.7	51.6
2000	321.5	138.9	60.2	22.3	10.4	92.7	177.8	94.8	21.4	1.8	8.5	58.1
2001	342.4	145.7	60.4	22.5	10.3	107.2	189.5	97.2	22.4	1.9	9.9	63.6
2002	381.7	163.1	60.5	23.4	11.5	127.4	209.9	106.3	22.9	2.2	11.3	72.2
2003	436.8	183.3	61.6	25.9	13.4	157.0	226.0	115.5	23.4	2.1	12.6	77.6
2004	483.7	200.2	64.5	28.8	16.9	177.9	240.7	122.8	24.1	2.4	13.9	83.5
2005	516.9	215.4	68.0	30.0	20.3	188.5	251.7	128.1	25.2	2.6	15.7	88.1
2003												
1st quarter	410.6	180.1	61.0	23.0	15.0	135.5	226.3	114.8	23.3	2.1	11.0	79.8
2nd quarter	446.9	183.6	61.8	26.7	14.1	165.7	221.6	116.1	23.4	2.1	12.6	73.3
3rd quarter	439.7	184.4	61.9	26.9	11.3	160.3	229.4	115.7	23.5	2.1	13.4	80.0
4th quarter	450.0	185.2	61.8	27.0	13.2	166.7	226.5	115.6	23.6	2.1	13.5	77.1
2004												
1st quarter	474.2	197.5	62.7	27.3	15.9	174.8	238.0	122.1	23.7	2.2	13.6	81.5
2nd quarter	481.0	199.2	64.4	29.2	16.7	176.1	241.5	123.4	24.0	2.4	14.0	83.0
3rd quarter	494.5	201.5	64.8	29.7	19.4	184.7	240.3	122.3	24.2	2.4	12.8	85.2
4th quarter	485.3	202.5	66.2	29.0	15.7	175.9	243.0	123.5	24.5	2.5	15.0	84.4
2005												
1st quarter	507.7	215.2	67.0	28.3	17.3	185.2	250.3	128.3	24.8	2.6	17.7	85.2
2nd quarter	512.1	214.9	67.5	29.5	20.2	185.3	248.7	127.7	25.1	2.6	13.7	86.1
3rd quarter	530.9	216.1	68.3	30.7	22.3	199.3	253.4	128.1	25.4	2.7	15.2	90.1
4th quarter	516.9	215.4	69.1	31.4	21.3	184.1	254.2	128.2	25.7	2.7	16.3	90.9

[1]Excludes government sales to other sectors and government own-account investment (construction and software).
[2]Includes general government intermediate inputs for goods and services sold to other sectors and for own-account investment.

Table 6-4. National Defense Consumption Expenditures and Gross Investment: Selected Detail

(National income and product accounts, calendar years, billions of dollars, quarterly data are at seasonally adjusted annual rates.)

NIPA Table 3.11.5

| Year and quarter | Compensation of general government employees | | Intermediate goods and services purchased [1] | | | | | | | Gross investment | | | |
| | | | Durable goods | Nondurable goods | | Services | | | | Equipment and software | | | |
	Military	Civilian	Aircraft	Petroleum products	Ammunition	Research and development	Installation support	Weapons support	Personnel support	Aircraft	Missiles	Ships	Electronics and software
1972	27.0	13.5	2.7	1.8	2.0	5.1	4.4	1.6	1.7	2.6	1.5	1.8	0.8
1973	27.6	13.8	2.4	1.7	1.7	5.3	4.3	1.6	1.5	2.3	1.5	1.6	0.9
1974	29.1	15.0	2.0	2.8	1.4	5.7	4.7	1.8	1.8	2.3	1.7	2.2	1.0
1975	31.1	16.8	2.1	2.9	1.1	5.9	4.9	1.7	2.1	3.6	1.3	2.2	1.2
1976	32.4	17.8	2.0	2.5	0.6	6.4	5.4	1.9	2.3	3.4	1.4	2.4	1.3
1977	34.0	19.7	3.3	2.4	0.8	6.8	6.2	2.1	2.2	3.7	1.2	3.1	1.5
1978	36.2	21.3	3.5	2.5	1.0	7.1	6.3	2.4	2.6	3.7	1.1	3.9	1.8
1979	38.7	22.9	4.8	3.6	1.2	7.7	7.3	2.9	2.7	4.8	1.8	4.3	2.1
1980	43.5	25.1	5.6	6.8	1.4	10.2	8.5	4.4	3.0	6.1	2.3	4.1	2.6
1981	50.5	28.3	7.8	7.7	1.6	12.4	9.3	5.2	4.0	7.5	2.8	5.1	3.2
1982	56.6	30.8	10.2	6.8	2.1	14.1	13.7	6.0	5.8	8.4	3.4	6.2	3.8
1983	59.8	32.7	13.6	6.4	2.5	14.5	15.5	7.3	6.4	10.1	4.6	7.1	4.6
1984	72.8	34.8	14.0	5.9	2.2	16.2	17.0	8.6	6.7	10.9	5.7	8.0	5.6
1985	78.2	37.2	15.4	5.8	1.3	21.7	17.2	9.8	8.4	13.4	6.6	9.0	7.0
1986	80.6	38.1	17.2	3.6	3.6	23.8	18.5	10.4	9.4	17.9	7.9	8.9	7.8
1987	83.7	39.8	18.2	3.9	2.8	27.0	19.1	11.0	10.9	17.6	8.7	8.8	8.7
1988	85.2	41.7	17.9	3.5	3.5	31.5	19.0	9.8	11.4	13.5	7.8	8.6	9.2
1989	87.4	44.3	16.4	4.2	3.1	28.6	19.0	10.3	12.4	12.2	8.8	10.0	9.6
1990	89.1	45.4	14.8	5.3	2.8	26.1	22.1	11.7	13.0	12.0	11.2	10.8	9.9
1991	93.8	48.0	13.6	4.7	2.7	21.9	23.8	10.2	12.7	9.2	10.8	10.2	9.7
1992	93.2	49.8	12.2	3.5	2.6	23.7	23.2	8.5	14.4	8.3	10.6	10.1	9.8
1993	88.0	50.7	10.7	3.2	2.5	22.9	25.4	7.5	13.7	9.3	7.9	8.7	9.9
1994	84.3	50.4	9.2	3.0	1.8	22.5	26.3	8.6	14.7	10.5	5.7	8.1	9.3
1995	81.3	49.5	8.9	2.8	1.2	21.7	25.8	9.1	16.1	9.0	4.7	8.0	8.8
1996	84.0	49.4	8.8	3.4	1.4	24.8	26.0	7.2	17.0	9.2	4.1	6.8	9.0
1997	83.8	49.0	9.4	2.9	1.7	26.3	25.3	8.4	18.5	5.8	2.9	6.1	9.0
1998	83.4	48.2	9.9	2.1	1.9	23.6	24.7	8.7	19.3	5.8	3.3	6.4	9.1
1999	85.2	48.3	10.5	2.6	1.9	26.6	25.0	9.3	22.4	7.0	2.8	6.8	9.8
2000	89.4	49.5	9.8	4.1	1.8	26.3	24.9	9.6	22.9	7.8	2.7	6.6	10.1
2001	95.4	50.3	9.8	4.2	2.1	30.6	27.3	12.0	27.5	8.5	3.3	7.2	9.8
2002	108.6	54.4	9.8	4.6	2.5	38.4	30.7	13.8	34.0	9.4	3.1	8.7	9.9
2003	125.7	57.7	11.2	5.3	2.6	47.1	35.9	16.6	41.2	9.2	3.3	9.5	10.6
2004	136.2	63.9	11.8	7.0	3.6	54.3	37.6	19.6	49.7	11.4	3.9	10.1	11.4
2005	146.9	68.4	10.7	10.2	4.0	56.3	38.9	20.2	55.2	13.5	4.2	9.8	12.8
1998													
1st quarter	83.9	49.0	9.1	2.3	1.6	20.1	24.4	7.5	17.0	4.2	2.9	6.3	9.0
2nd quarter	83.4	48.1	9.6	2.1	1.4	24.8	24.7	8.5	19.7	5.0	2.6	6.0	9.3
3rd quarter	83.5	48.3	10.0	2.0	2.5	22.6	25.4	8.6	20.2	6.7	4.6	6.5	9.2
4th quarter	82.9	47.4	10.8	1.8	2.0	26.8	24.3	10.0	20.1	7.2	2.9	6.9	9.0
1999													
1st quarter	85.0	48.2	9.5	1.7	1.7	27.4	24.4	8.2	20.9	5.9	2.8	6.8	8.6
2nd quarter	84.7	48.5	10.9	2.4	1.8	21.0	24.7	8.4	20.8	6.7	2.7	6.6	10.2
3rd quarter	85.1	48.7	11.5	3.5	2.3	25.6	25.0	9.0	22.4	8.7	2.8	6.5	10.4
4th quarter	85.9	48.0	10.0	2.6	1.8	32.1	26.0	11.4	25.5	6.6	3.1	7.1	9.9
2000													
1st quarter	88.6	49.4	10.5	4.1	1.6	23.7	23.9	6.8	20.5	9.3	2.3	6.1	9.9
2nd quarter	88.7	49.5	9.6	3.6	1.6	27.8	25.2	10.2	24.9	6.9	2.4	6.8	10.2
3rd quarter	90.5	49.7	10.2	4.1	2.1	24.1	25.5	10.3	23.8	8.1	2.2	6.7	9.9
4th quarter	90.0	49.5	9.1	4.4	1.9	29.4	25.1	11.0	22.6	6.8	3.9	6.8	10.3
2001													
1st quarter	94.2	49.3	8.8	4.4	1.9	30.2	27.3	12.3	27.2	6.8	3.6	7.2	9.8
2nd quarter	94.3	49.7	9.6	4.2	2.1	30.2	26.3	11.6	25.5	7.0	3.5	7.4	9.8
3rd quarter	95.3	50.9	11.2	4.2	2.2	28.9	26.8	10.9	26.8	10.7	3.0	6.9	9.7
4th quarter	97.9	51.2	9.4	4.0	2.1	33.2	28.6	13.3	30.6	9.5	3.1	7.3	9.8
2002													
1st quarter	106.0	54.2	9.2	3.6	2.4	33.8	29.4	12.5	31.0	7.3	3.4	8.1	9.9
2nd quarter	107.5	54.6	9.9	4.5	2.6	36.5	29.6	12.3	32.3	9.4	3.1	8.5	10.0
3rd quarter	108.0	54.5	10.2	4.3	2.7	35.7	31.2	14.1	35.2	10.2	2.9	8.9	10.2
4th quarter	113.0	54.4	9.9	5.9	2.4	47.5	32.6	16.1	37.7	10.5	3.1	9.0	9.6
2003													
1st quarter	122.6	57.5	9.7	8.0	2.1	37.3	32.9	13.5	36.1	9.4	2.7	8.5	10.4
2nd quarter	126.7	56.8	11.8	5.7	2.7	54.1	36.0	17.8	41.6	9.1	2.8	10.1	10.3
3rd quarter	126.7	57.7	11.4	3.0	2.8	45.1	37.1	17.7	42.9	8.5	3.3	10.1	11.1
4th quarter	126.6	58.5	11.8	4.5	2.9	52.0	37.5	17.5	44.2	9.9	4.3	9.4	10.6
2004													
1st quarter	135.2	62.3	11.2	6.5	3.4	53.4	38.9	19.1	47.5	9.0	3.7	10.0	10.7
2nd quarter	135.7	63.5	11.6	6.8	3.6	54.5	37.3	18.9	48.7	11.6	3.5	9.2	11.9
3rd quarter	136.5	65.1	12.5	9.2	3.8	55.2	38.2	21.6	52.5	11.1	4.2	11.5	11.4
4th quarter	137.5	64.9	12.0	5.7	3.8	53.9	36.2	18.6	50.1	13.8	4.1	9.6	11.7
2005													
1st quarter	147.7	67.5	10.7	6.9	3.7	55.9	38.0	20.0	53.0	12.7	3.4	9.9	11.6
2nd quarter	146.8	68.1	10.7	10.4	4.0	57.1	38.2	18.8	52.8	13.5	4.5	9.5	12.5
3rd quarter	146.7	69.4	10.6	12.2	4.2	59.4	40.5	22.6	59.2	14.0	3.7	10.6	13.3
4th quarter	146.6	68.8	11.0	11.2	4.2	52.7	38.9	19.2	55.6	13.9	5.2	9.2	13.5

[1] Includes general government intermediate inputs for goods and services sold to other sectors and for own-account investment.

Table 6-5. Federal Government Output, Lending and Borrowing, and Net Investment

(National income and product accounts, calendar years, billions of dollars, quarterly data are at seasonally adjusted annual rates.)

NIPA Tables 3.2, 3.10.5

Year and quarter	Output						Net lending (net borrowing -)							Net investment
	Gross		Value added		Intermediate goods and services purchased [1]		Net saving, current (surplus +, deficit -)	Plus: capital transfer receipts	Minus			Plus: Consumption of fixed capital	Equals: Net lending (borrowing -)	
	Defense	Non-defense	Defense	Non-defense	Defense	Non-defense			Gross investment	Capital transfer payments	Net purchases of non-produced assets			
1950	17.3	5.3	13.2	3.7	4.1	1.6	5.5	0.6	3.9	0.4	...	5.8	...	-1.9
1951	30.6	4.6	18.9	3.7	11.7	0.9	9.6	0.7	10.7	0.4	...	6.1	...	4.6
1952	39.1	5.7	22.3	3.8	16.9	1.9	3.7	0.8	15.0	0.5	...	6.8	...	8.2
1953	41.5	7.5	23.0	3.7	18.5	3.8	1.8	0.9	16.1	0.6	...	7.6	...	8.5
1954	37.3	7.3	23.0	3.5	14.3	3.8	-1.6	0.9	13.3	0.6	...	8.3	...	5.0
1955	37.3	7.9	23.7	3.8	13.6	4.1	5.7	1.0	10.9	0.7	...	8.7	...	2.2
1956	39.1	6.7	24.7	4.1	14.5	2.6	7.6	1.3	11.6	0.8	...	9.3	...	2.3
1957	43.7	7.1	25.5	4.4	18.1	2.7	3.3	1.4	11.9	1.3	...	9.8	...	2.1
1958	44.7	7.4	26.1	5.0	18.6	2.4	-5.4	1.3	12.9	2.3	...	9.9	...	3.0
1959	40.5	10.6	26.7	5.1	13.8	5.5	3.3	1.4	15.4	3.1	...	10.2	...	5.2
1960	41.5	9.4	27.4	5.6	14.0	3.7	7.2	1.8	14.3	2.6	0.5	10.6	2.1	3.7
1961	43.1	9.6	28.3	6.1	14.7	3.5	2.6	2.0	16.3	2.9	0.5	10.9	-4.2	5.4
1962	47.0	11.9	30.0	6.6	17.0	5.3	2.5	2.1	17.4	3.1	0.6	11.5	-5.0	5.9
1963	48.7	13.2	31.1	7.3	17.6	5.9	5.4	2.2	16.1	3.6	0.5	12.1	-0.5	4.0
1964	49.3	14.8	32.7	8.0	16.5	6.8	1.0	2.6	15.6	4.1	0.6	12.3	-4.4	3.3
1965	51.2	15.9	33.9	8.6	17.3	7.3	3.3	2.8	14.7	4.0	0.5	12.7	-0.4	2.0
1966	60.9	16.7	37.9	9.5	23.0	7.2	2.3	3.0	16.7	4.4	0.6	13.2	-3.2	3.5
1967	70.4	18.0	41.4	10.2	29.0	7.8	-9.4	3.1	17.7	4.3	-0.2	14.0	-14.0	3.7
1968	77.4	19.3	45.1	11.3	32.3	8.0	-2.3	3.1	16.0	6.0	-0.9	14.8	-5.4	1.2
1969	78.4	21.3	47.9	12.1	30.5	9.2	8.7	3.6	15.0	5.9	0.1	15.5	6.8	-0.5
1970	76.8	23.2	50.3	13.8	26.6	9.3	-15.2	3.7	14.8	5.3	-0.3	16.1	-15.2	-1.3
1971	77.3	26.1	52.0	15.7	25.3	10.4	-28.4	4.6	11.7	5.9	-0.4	16.5	-24.5	-4.8
1972	80.2	29.8	54.3	17.2	25.8	12.6	-24.4	5.4	12.0	6.0	-0.7	16.6	-19.7	-4.6
1973	80.5	31.2	55.4	18.6	25.1	12.6	-11.3	5.1	13.6	6.0	-3.2	17.1	-5.5	-3.5
1974	86.1	35.2	58.8	20.8	27.3	14.4	-13.8	4.8	16.6	7.9	-5.7	18.2	-9.6	-1.6
1975	92.1	40.4	63.7	23.7	28.5	16.8	-69.0	4.9	19.5	9.7	-0.4	19.7	-73.1	-0.2
1976	96.4	43.6	67.3	26.5	29.1	17.1	-51.7	5.6	22.6	10.6	-2.4	21.4	-55.5	1.2
1977	105.0	49.5	72.1	30.0	32.9	19.5	-44.1	7.2	24.7	11.1	-1.4	23.1	-48.3	1.6
1978	113.6	54.3	77.5	32.3	36.2	22.0	-26.5	5.2	27.6	11.9	-0.6	25.0	-35.1	2.6
1979	124.8	59.7	83.0	34.7	41.8	25.1	-11.3	5.5	31.6	14.4	-2.8	27.0	-22.0	4.6
1980	145.0	68.6	92.1	39.2	52.9	29.4	-53.6	6.5	36.3	16.6	-4.0	30.1	-65.9	6.2
1981	168.9	75.5	105.1	42.3	63.8	33.2	-53.3	6.9	41.9	15.6	-5.5	33.8	-64.6	8.1
1982	193.1	76.4	116.7	44.6	76.4	31.8	-131.9	7.5	47.5	14.6	-3.6	37.6	-145.1	9.9
1983	210.1	82.5	124.2	47.1	85.9	35.4	-173.0	5.8	56.4	15.5	-4.9	40.8	-193.5	15.6
1984	234.6	82.0	142.4	49.8	92.2	32.2	-168.1	6.0	64.4	17.7	-3.9	44.6	-195.6	19.8
1985	255.5	89.8	152.8	52.3	102.7	37.5	-175.0	6.4	74.4	19.4	-1.1	48.1	-213.2	26.3
1986	269.8	95.3	159.0	53.7	110.8	41.6	-190.8	7.0	80.4	20.0	-3.0	51.6	-229.6	28.8
1987	285.8	96.4	166.6	56.8	119.2	39.6	-145.0	7.2	85.8	19.0	-0.4	55.2	-186.9	30.6
1988	296.0	95.3	172.9	62.0	123.1	33.3	-134.5	7.6	79.8	19.6	-0.1	59.3	-166.9	20.5
1989	302.0	106.7	180.8	65.8	121.1	40.9	-130.1	8.9	83.0	20.1	-0.7	63.5	-160.1	19.5
1990	311.4	118.7	186.9	72.0	124.5	46.7	-172.0	11.6	88.5	28.1	-0.7	67.9	-208.3	20.6
1991	323.2	127.7	197.3	77.7	125.9	50.0	-213.7	11.0	88.2	26.3	0.2	72.2	-245.3	16.0
1992	319.4	137.1	200.3	81.8	119.1	55.3	-297.4	11.3	88.8	22.4	0.2	74.7	-322.9	14.1
1993	311.9	141.0	198.2	88.1	113.7	52.9	-273.5	12.9	83.3	24.5	0.2	77.9	-290.7	5.4
1994	306.7	147.1	195.7	90.5	111.0	56.7	-212.3	15.1	78.3	25.9	0.2	80.2	-221.4	-1.9
1995	301.0	150.2	192.6	92.1	108.3	58.1	-197.0	14.9	78.8	27.7	-7.4	81.9	-199.2	-3.1
1996	306.6	150.9	194.6	94.1	112.0	56.8	-141.8	17.5	81.1	28.2	-3.8	82.0	-147.8	-0.9
1997	308.1	158.6	193.2	97.7	115.0	60.9	-55.8	20.6	73.2	29.1	-7.6	82.5	-47.4	-9.3
1998	303.9	160.7	191.3	101.8	112.6	58.9	38.8	25.2	75.8	28.8	-5.6	82.8	47.8	-7.0
1999	315.9	167.6	193.3	107.6	122.7	60.0	103.6	28.8	80.7	36.1	-0.9	84.8	101.3	-4.1
2000	324.6	184.6	199.2	116.2	125.4	68.4	189.5	28.1	79.5	36.2	-0.3	87.2	189.4	-7.7
2001	345.9	195.1	206.0	119.6	139.9	75.4	46.7	28.0	81.0	40.8	-0.7	88.2	41.8	-7.2
2002	386.0	214.9	223.6	129.3	162.4	85.6	-247.9	25.3	88.1	48.4	0.3	88.9	-270.6	-0.8
2003	441.3	231.3	244.9	139.0	196.4	92.3	-372.1	22.0	93.7	62.4	-0.2	90.4	-415.6	3.3
2004	488.3	246.7	264.7	146.9	223.6	99.7	-382.0	24.6	101.4	63.1	0.0	94.1	-427.8	7.3
2005	522.1	259.8	283.4	153.3	238.7	106.5	-309.2	25.0	109.8	67.0	-0.6	99.0	-361.3	10.8
2003														
1st quarter	414.7	231.0	241.2	138.1	173.6	92.9	-290.2	22.5	89.1	54.0	-2.8	89.7	-318.3	-0.6
2nd quarter	451.8	227.6	245.3	139.5	206.5	88.1	-365.5	20.5	93.8	68.4	-0.7	90.6	-415.8	3.2
3rd quarter	444.7	234.7	246.2	139.2	198.5	95.5	-451.4	20.9	95.7	66.2	3.4	90.7	-505.2	5.0
4th quarter	453.9	232.0	247.0	139.2	206.9	92.8	-381.5	24.1	96.3	60.8	-0.7	90.7	-423.1	5.6
2004														
1st quarter	478.2	243.1	260.2	145.8	218.0	97.3	-401.0	23.2	96.0	60.8	0.0	91.8	-442.8	4.2
2nd quarter	485.5	246.8	263.5	147.4	222.0	99.4	-380.6	24.3	101.2	59.3	-0.7	93.8	-422.3	7.4
3rd quarter	500.1	246.8	266.3	146.5	233.8	100.3	-380.6	26.8	103.5	70.8	1.8	94.5	-435.5	9.0
4th quarter	489.3	249.9	268.6	147.9	220.7	101.9	-365.7	24.2	104.9	61.3	-1.0	96.2	-410.5	8.7
2005														
1st quarter	513.0	258.6	282.2	153.1	230.8	105.5	-287.6	23.9	104.8	71.6	0.3	97.5	-342.9	7.3
2nd quarter	517.4	255.2	282.4	152.8	235.0	102.4	-289.6	24.8	107.6	66.2	-0.6	98.2	-339.7	9.4
3rd quarter	536.6	261.5	284.4	153.5	252.2	108.0	-396.0	24.9	111.5	65.3	-2.3	99.8	-445.9	11.7
4th quarter	521.4	263.9	284.5	153.9	236.9	109.9	-263.6	26.3	115.1	64.8	0.0	100.7	-316.6	14.4

[1] Includes general government intermediate inputs for goods and services sold to other sectors and for own-account investment.
. . . = Not available.

Table 6-6. Chain-Type Quantity Indexes for Federal Government Defense and Nondefense Consumption Expenditures and Gross Investment

(Index numbers, 2000 = 100.)   NIPA Tables 3.9.3, 3.10.3

Year and quarter	Defense consumption expenditures [1] Total	Compensation of general government employees	Consumption of general government fixed capital	Intermediate goods and services purchased [2] Durable goods	Non-durable goods	Services	Defense gross investment	Nondefense consumption expenditures [1] Total	Compensation of general government employees	Consumption of general government fixed capital	Intermediate goods and services purchased [2] Durable goods	Non-durable goods excluding CCC inventory change	Services	Non-defense gross investment
1950	48.3	94.4	45.7	39.0	58.3	8.6	22.2	25.3	61.3	12.2	12.4	17.8	10.5	22.6
1951	82.1	163.5	44.7	93.4	153.0	24.7	78.8	21.1	56.3	12.4	12.3	31.3	7.7	20.3
1952	106.1	188.2	49.7	165.6	200.0	33.3	114.0	24.8	55.0	12.4	11.3	19.5	13.1	19.7
1953	110.8	184.3	55.5	185.4	321.2	26.8	127.7	32.3	50.4	12.4	10.4	19.5	13.1	17.3
1954	96.5	172.8	59.4	134.9	211.2	22.5	104.1	31.1	47.8	12.4	11.7	18.9	14.2	15.6
1955	90.2	164.0	60.6	114.4	97.0	29.4	84.1	30.5	48.4	12.3	9.7	21.8	14.7	11.1
1956	90.4	159.7	60.9	108.2	95.7	33.0	80.5	26.8	49.5	12.1	9.9	33.9	16.1	14.2
1957	96.5	157.5	61.2	113.3	115.7	44.3	76.3	25.9	50.9	12.0	9.1	46.9	15.8	15.9
1958	94.3	148.3	61.2	117.4	117.8	43.6	81.3	25.9	52.5	12.1	7.1	20.9	14.6	18.8
1959	87.2	144.3	62.5	83.9	98.5	39.2	97.0	37.5	52.6	12.0	5.4	57.5	19.1	18.9
1960	88.2	144.2	64.2	71.3	105.6	44.5	87.4	32.9	56.9	11.9	6.5	45.5	22.4	22.2
1961	90.4	147.1	65.4	58.5	130.3	48.7	96.9	32.5	58.3	12.1	11.7	53.1	26.5	26.9
1962	96.6	153.4	67.4	72.4	165.1	51.0	100.3	39.6	61.4	12.8	19.0	52.8	30.8	31.4
1963	97.6	150.7	69.1	73.0	153.6	54.8	86.6	43.2	65.0	14.1	26.4	58.8	38.7	36.9
1964	95.1	150.6	69.9	61.7	169.6	50.1	78.6	46.2	66.5	15.7	34.2	63.2	44.4	42.4
1965	95.4	150.8	69.8	63.9	183.2	49.7	68.6	48.3	67.7	18.0	43.7	63.5	45.8	48.4
1966	108.9	166.1	70.0	93.1	261.3	59.2	79.3	48.6	70.4	20.5	45.4	74.4	49.8	49.8
1967	123.1	180.7	71.3	91.9	401.9	70.4	89.5	50.8	73.9	22.5	39.8	80.4	45.9	40.4
1968	128.4	183.1	72.4	106.4	460.2	71.6	78.5	50.9	75.6	23.8	31.8	64.5	40.6	35.4
1969	123.3	183.3	72.1	88.8	408.4	67.7	69.5	53.5	76.3	24.7	27.7	81.1	39.6	32.1
1970	112.1	170.0	71.0	79.5	284.3	61.8	63.3	53.3	77.3	25.3	22.1	83.1	45.0	30.4
1971	103.4	157.1	68.0	57.2	232.4	61.8	40.3	55.8	79.9	25.5	21.2	79.1	49.1	31.9
1972	97.1	145.1	64.3	73.1	236.8	54.9	30.1	60.1	82.2	25.6	22.8	88.9	58.1	33.0
1973	90.0	137.6	61.3	67.6	176.0	51.4	33.9	59.4	82.4	25.9	18.0	76.8	58.3	34.0
1974	87.1	135.5	59.3	58.4	152.1	52.1	41.4	62.7	86.5	26.3	15.6	84.5	59.0	35.0
1975	85.0	133.6	58.5	60.7	126.0	48.9	46.0	64.8	88.0	26.8	16.7	63.9	62.1	36.3
1976	83.5	130.9	58.5	54.5	102.8	49.7	50.1	64.7	92.4	27.5	18.0	80.9	55.7	39.0
1977	84.4	129.8	58.8	69.0	96.0	50.4	51.2	67.4	94.5	28.3	20.7	92.5	59.0	41.0
1978	85.3	130.6	59.1	77.1	96.8	49.7	50.9	70.2	96.9	29.6	26.1	108.1	63.4	48.5
1979	86.4	129.5	59.7	83.3	99.7	51.5	58.1	71.4	96.8	31.2	31.5	108.2	67.9	47.3
1980	89.7	130.3	60.8	87.3	109.0	58.0	62.2	75.1	99.4	33.1	36.8	106.8	67.5	51.0
1981	94.8	134.3	62.3	101.8	115.3	63.8	68.6	76.3	96.5	35.2	32.7	177.1	61.4	50.8
1982	101.2	137.4	64.4	111.7	114.8	76.5	77.1	73.0	94.7	37.2	28.1	126.2	59.1	47.2
1983	106.6	139.5	67.5	132.0	120.2	81.0	90.5	75.7	96.0	39.8	42.8	132.1	62.0	53.6
1984	109.8	141.5	71.8	133.4	113.8	87.2	103.3	73.0	96.1	43.2	46.4	138.1	62.6	57.6
1985	116.4	144.1	77.5	143.2	111.8	99.1	124.4	77.1	96.3	46.6	47.4	121.1	65.5	61.5
1986	121.8	144.8	84.1	153.0	141.1	104.7	142.5	80.0	94.9	50.0	47.8	107.0	65.5	63.0
1987	126.3	146.1	90.6	162.5	138.2	111.1	155.6	78.8	96.6	53.2	53.5	121.9	72.2	69.1
1988	127.7	144.3	95.9	167.1	133.2	114.0	144.0	75.0	99.0	56.5	55.9	120.0	71.8	64.7
1989	126.8	144.3	100.1	160.4	129.0	110.3	144.9	81.4	99.6	59.8	61.5	106.5	72.8	69.0
1990	125.9	143.4	104.0	154.6	115.2	110.3	149.3	88.0	104.5	63.3	70.0	113.6	82.4	75.3
1991	125.8	142.9	107.0	147.6	117.3	110.0	140.7	89.1	104.2	66.9	72.1	96.8	84.8	81.5
1992	119.3	134.5	108.8	132.8	108.5	103.7	135.3	94.6	106.1	69.7	78.1	118.6	92.7	90.0
1993	114.2	128.7	109.2	120.8	99.5	98.4	118.3	93.4	106.0	72.2	76.0	118.5	85.6	92.1
1994	109.0	122.1	108.3	103.7	90.6	98.2	110.2	94.1	103.0	74.1	76.2	115.0	92.0	82.2
1995	105.2	115.4	106.7	94.2	74.3	96.6	104.3	92.6	98.9	76.3	78.4	112.7	92.0	87.1
1996	103.3	110.5	105.1	93.5	82.1	97.9	105.1	90.6	96.3	79.7	87.3	108.4	88.6	93.3
1997	102.1	106.5	103.5	93.9	82.7	99.2	92.4	93.7	95.7	83.6	92.4	116.8	92.3	92.0
1998	99.5	103.2	101.8	94.9	85.6	95.3	93.4	92.7	96.8	88.1	92.5	114.9	87.8	101.8
1999	101.0	100.7	100.8	100.8	95.3	102.2	97.6	94.5	97.0	94.3	92.3	91.8	91.0	108.9
2000	100.0	100.0	100.0	100.0	100.0	100.0	100.0	100.0	100.0	100.0	100.0	100.0	100.0	100.0
2001	103.9	100.7	99.8	100.9	104.7	112.2	104.1	104.5	99.9	103.9	112.5	118.6	107.3	100.3
2002	110.9	103.4	99.7	104.8	125.6	130.1	116.1	111.0	101.9	107.1	130.3	144.6	119.0	107.3
2003	120.5	107.1	100.5	115.3	129.1	154.9	126.3	115.0	104.4	109.2	129.6	158.6	125.3	109.4
2004	127.0	109.1	102.3	126.8	145.6	169.4	138.4	116.4	103.4	111.1	146.5	178.6	130.0	110.7
2005	128.6	109.4	104.9	129.8	141.1	173.2	145.9	116.6	103.2	114.1	163.8	182.5	131.0	119.7
2003														
1st quarter	113.9	105.9	100.0	102.5	136.8	135.4	118.8	115.8	104.4	108.5	129.6	140.1	129.7	105.9
2nd quarter	123.5	107.3	100.3	118.7	139.7	164.0	125.4	112.8	104.8	109.0	126.8	155.2	118.7	110.8
3rd quarter	121.1	107.6	100.6	119.7	111.2	157.5	129.1	116.5	104.3	109.5	131.3	168.8	129.0	111.6
4th quarter	123.5	107.5	101.0	120.2	128.9	162.8	131.9	114.8	104.0	109.9	130.7	170.3	123.7	109.2
2004														
1st quarter	126.6	108.8	101.4	121.0	154.9	168.6	132.0	116.4	103.4	110.3	135.6	183.0	128.9	106.6
2nd quarter	126.6	108.3	102.0	128.6	148.1	168.5	137.6	116.8	103.4	110.8	147.6	177.8	129.6	111.6
3rd quarter	129.1	109.3	102.5	130.6	159.6	175.1	142.3	115.9	102.9	111.4	148.2	174.7	131.8	110.8
4th quarter	125.7	109.8	103.1	126.9	119.6	165.5	141.6	116.6	103.8	112.1	154.7	178.7	129.6	113.7
2005														
1st quarter	127.6	109.9	103.8	123.1	133.3	171.9	139.3	116.4	103.7	112.9	157.4	188.6	128.1	115.0
2nd quarter	127.8	109.2	104.5	127.7	145.7	170.9	145.8	115.5	103.2	113.7	160.9	186.3	128.4	113.5
3rd quarter	131.2	109.2	105.2	132.6	147.4	182.3	149.9	116.7	102.5	114.5	167.7	175.3	133.7	119.4
4th quarter	127.5	109.3	105.8	135.8	138.2	167.6	148.7	117.4	103.2	115.3	169.0	179.9	133.8	130.8

[1] Excludes government sales to other sectors and government own-account investment (construction and software).
[2] Includes general government intermediate inputs for goods and services sold to other sectors and for own-account investment.

Table 6-7. Chain-Type Quantity Indexes for National Defense Consumption Expenditures and Gross Investment: Selected Detail

(Index numbers, 2000 = 100.)

NIPA Table 3.11.3

| Year and quarter | Compensation of general government employees | | Intermediate goods and services purchased [1] | | | | | | | Gross investment | | | |
| | | | Durable goods | Nondurable goods | | Services | | | | Equipment and software | | | |
	Military	Civilian	Aircraft	Petroleum products	Ammunition	Research and development	Installation support	Weapons support	Personnel support	Aircraft	Missiles	Ships	Electronics and software
1972	147.9	139.5	82.6	414.8	336.9	45.7	60.6	61.7	43.1	50.4	51.5	99.5	7.6
1973	139.5	133.7	69.0	262.5	262.8	45.7	55.2	58.0	34.8	44.3	53.8	84.0	8.3
1974	134.5	137.2	53.6	238.6	179.7	45.4	55.5	62.1	39.5	44.4	59.6	103.6	8.3
1975	131.6	137.2	49.4	200.8	125.1	43.5	52.9	54.1	39.4	67.2	43.5	92.7	9.6
1976	128.4	135.5	41.4	166.4	62.8	45.1	54.3	57.0	38.8	62.9	37.0	95.0	10.1
1977	127.3	134.2	63.2	141.5	85.8	46.6	57.1	56.7	34.2	65.7	29.0	110.9	11.2
1978	126.1	139.0	64.6	140.8	99.2	46.0	53.3	61.7	35.8	62.0	23.9	124.8	13.8
1979	124.1	139.6	80.4	143.2	110.2	47.6	56.9	67.8	34.2	77.7	48.1	128.4	15.1
1980	125.4	139.4	87.3	158.5	110.5	58.7	60.5	91.3	33.7	93.0	69.4	112.9	18.5
1981	129.4	143.4	112.5	155.7	124.8	68.0	62.1	97.6	41.3	107.6	80.5	128.7	22.0
1982	131.7	148.0	131.6	146.5	153.8	73.2	85.0	106.0	56.7	108.2	103.9	150.0	25.4
1983	134.0	149.8	160.2	156.9	180.4	72.3	93.1	123.2	60.6	122.9	131.5	166.7	31.0
1984	135.6	152.3	151.4	156.5	152.7	78.1	99.1	140.5	62.0	132.1	158.1	176.6	39.0
1985	137.6	156.4	162.7	159.2	91.1	103.1	97.3	155.5	75.7	180.4	180.3	194.1	49.9
1986	138.9	155.6	179.9	159.1	245.1	110.7	100.1	162.9	80.3	275.1	228.6	187.4	57.0
1987	140.6	156.0	192.7	163.4	186.0	124.6	99.9	168.4	87.5	315.6	260.0	182.3	65.2
1988	139.6	152.6	199.5	137.6	214.7	146.7	95.6	146.9	81.8	259.3	236.7	172.7	68.9
1989	138.9	154.1	188.1	151.1	179.6	130.9	94.8	148.4	83.6	237.2	271.1	191.7	72.1
1990	139.2	150.5	165.3	149.8	162.0	117.1	104.5	162.7	81.3	218.8	352.0	202.3	74.8
1991	140.7	145.8	147.9	148.0	152.8	96.6	110.6	135.6	74.6	157.4	354.0	181.5	73.6
1992	128.7	145.0	129.0	123.8	145.1	101.8	106.5	108.3	80.3	137.7	350.1	175.4	77.7
1993	122.1	141.0	111.8	119.0	144.0	96.8	114.9	91.4	74.4	148.8	254.0	147.9	78.3
1994	116.2	132.9	94.9	122.5	99.2	93.6	116.1	102.3	76.8	148.6	186.9	133.1	74.8
1995	110.2	125.0	90.4	111.2	63.5	90.0	109.8	106.1	81.0	120.1	158.1	125.3	71.6
1996	106.1	118.6	89.7	112.3	74.3	102.4	109.0	81.6	83.0	117.3	140.9	105.8	77.0
1997	103.3	112.4	95.8	100.9	91.3	105.9	105.2	92.9	88.5	81.6	104.2	93.8	80.9
1998	100.9	107.2	101.7	99.2	103.4	93.3	101.6	94.7	89.9	82.1	117.7	99.1	86.5
1999	99.1	103.4	107.4	108.5	105.2	103.4	101.9	99.3	101.5	85.4	105.7	105.0	95.7
2000	100.0	100.0	100.0	100.0	100.0	100.0	100.0	100.0	100.0	100.0	100.0	100.0	100.0
2001	102.0	98.3	98.6	122.0	114.3	114.5	106.4	122.2	115.3	116.8	126.9	109.6	99.0
2002	105.8	99.0	99.0	157.5	140.9	141.1	117.2	136.9	137.9	134.2	119.2	131.0	103.5
2003	111.5	98.8	111.2	135.2	143.7	168.1	131.9	160.9	161.8	133.0	122.8	142.0	113.2
2004	112.8	102.1	116.0	142.7	188.6	186.4	131.5	184.0	190.0	165.0	142.7	137.5	124.6
2005	112.2	104.4	104.2	135.9	199.2	184.7	130.5	183.7	205.9	200.8	151.8	125.8	141.4
1998													
1st quarter	101.9	108.8	93.8	102.7	86.1	80.1	101.7	82.5	80.6	61.9	106.4	96.9	83.9
2nd quarter	100.9	107.7	99.0	101.0	78.5	98.4	102.3	93.5	92.7	70.8	94.7	92.7	87.8
3rd quarter	101.0	107.2	102.7	99.9	137.4	89.4	103.8	94.0	93.9	97.1	163.2	100.3	87.4
4th quarter	100.0	105.1	111.5	93.1	111.6	105.5	98.8	108.6	92.5	98.4	106.6	106.6	87.0
1999													
1st quarter	99.1	104.3	97.7	99.2	92.8	107.8	99.8	88.8	95.8	72.3	101.6	106.4	83.9
2nd quarter	98.6	103.6	111.6	112.4	99.6	82.2	101.0	90.1	94.8	81.6	102.2	103.4	99.3
3rd quarter	99.6	102.9	118.2	136.6	127.8	99.6	101.4	96.9	101.5	106.7	104.3	100.8	102.1
4th quarter	99.3	102.9	102.2	85.7	100.6	124.0	105.2	121.5	113.8	81.1	114.5	109.5	97.6
2000													
1st quarter	99.2	100.5	106.9	110.5	90.1	91.2	96.9	72.3	90.4	116.6	83.4	92.6	98.5
2nd quarter	99.2	102.0	97.3	99.6	86.9	106.0	101.7	106.4	108.9	88.8	89.0	102.8	101.6
3rd quarter	100.6	99.6	103.4	97.6	116.1	91.6	101.6	107.1	103.4	105.8	80.6	101.0	97.7
4th quarter	101.1	98.0	92.4	92.3	107.0	111.2	99.8	114.1	97.2	88.8	147.0	103.6	102.3
2001													
1st quarter	101.8	98.0	89.0	111.3	103.5	113.6	107.4	125.5	115.4	91.4	136.6	109.0	98.4
2nd quarter	102.1	98.0	97.2	111.2	116.8	112.9	103.3	118.8	107.5	93.1	135.3	112.9	98.7
3rd quarter	101.7	99.3	113.5	116.0	119.4	107.9	104.0	110.4	111.9	144.7	115.4	104.4	99.0
4th quarter	102.5	98.0	94.9	149.3	117.4	123.5	111.0	134.2	126.3	137.9	120.2	112.0	100.1
2002													
1st quarter	105.3	97.6	93.0	148.9	133.8	125.2	114.3	125.5	126.9	105.8	129.1	124.2	102.0
2nd quarter	105.9	99.2	99.7	187.7	145.7	134.7	113.6	122.6	131.2	136.2	118.9	129.5	104.0
3rd quarter	106.2	100.0	103.0	127.1	148.9	131.0	118.0	140.4	142.2	145.5	110.8	134.5	107.2
4th quarter	105.8	99.4	100.3	166.4	135.1	173.4	122.8	159.3	151.4	149.5	117.8	135.9	100.8
2003													
1st quarter	109.6	99.1	97.0	184.8	116.4	134.7	122.4	132.0	143.1	135.7	103.8	127.3	110.2
2nd quarter	112.7	97.3	117.6	155.7	149.9	193.6	132.6	173.2	164.2	131.3	104.7	150.5	109.5
3rd quarter	112.3	98.8	112.9	81.6	153.5	160.2	136.4	171.2	167.8	122.2	122.4	150.5	118.8
4th quarter	111.6	100.0	117.2	118.7	155.1	184.0	136.4	167.3	172.1	143.0	160.4	139.7	114.5
2004													
1st quarter	113.4	100.1	110.8	172.2	180.1	186.4	138.3	182.1	183.1	131.2	137.4	143.3	115.9
2nd quarter	112.3	100.8	114.1	145.4	185.7	188.7	131.1	179.0	186.8	168.4	126.9	125.8	129.3
3rd quarter	112.2	103.9	122.0	166.2	194.6	188.5	132.7	201.9	200.2	162.3	155.5	154.8	125.0
4th quarter	113.3	103.5	117.2	87.0	193.9	182.1	124.1	173.0	190.1	198.2	150.8	125.8	128.2
2005													
1st quarter	113.3	103.5	103.6	113.3	185.6	185.8	127.7	184.5	199.0	183.3	124.1	127.2	128.1
2nd quarter	112.0	104.3	103.6	149.6	195.4	188.2	129.1	171.7	197.7	200.2	161.3	122.8	138.1
3rd quarter	111.5	105.1	102.9	148.6	208.7	194.2	135.8	205.6	220.5	211.1	132.7	137.6	148.4
4th quarter	111.8	104.7	106.5	132.3	207.1	170.6	129.5	173.3	206.5	208.4	189.3	115.7	151.2

Section 6b: State and Local Government in the National Income and Product Accounts

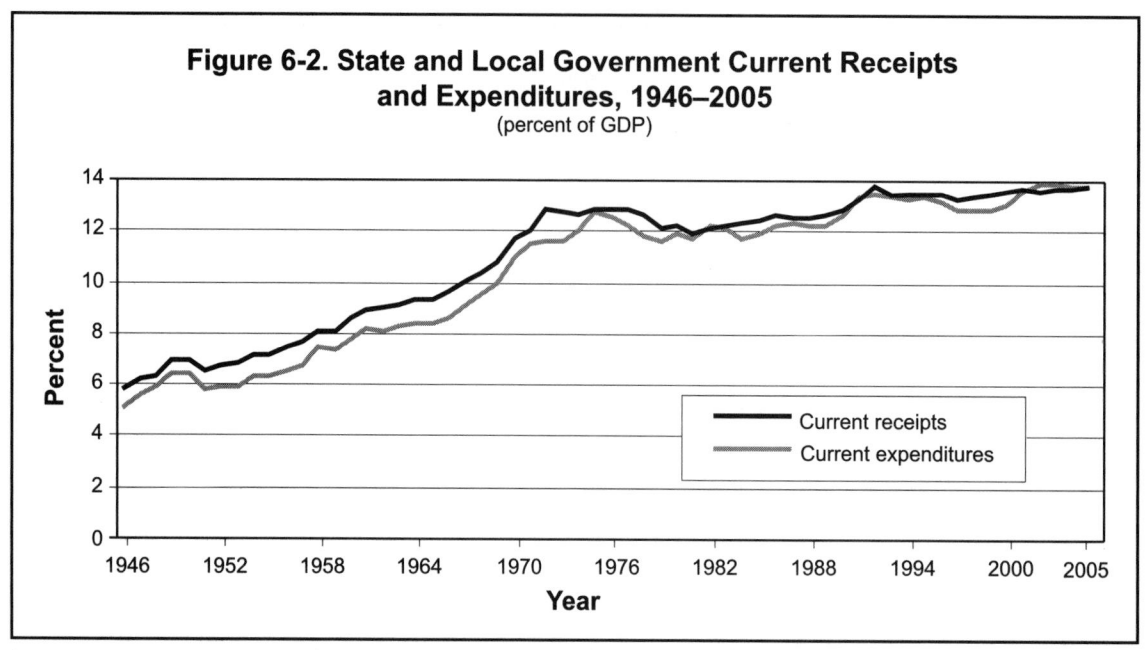

Figure 6-2. State and Local Government Current Receipts and Expenditures, 1946–2005
(percent of GDP)

- Both current receipts and current spending of state and local governments have increased as a share of gross domestic product (GDP) over the postwar period. State and local governments, unlike the federal government, are bound by constraints on deficit spending, and have generally run modest surpluses ("net saving") in their current accounts. In the early 2000s, however, state and local general fund ("other") deficits were larger and more persistent than in earlier periods of slack economic activity. (Tables 6-8 and 1-1)

- State and local gross investment rose at an annual rate of 3.3 percent in real terms from 1953 to 2005, compared with 3.8 percent for federal nondefense investment. (Tables 6-6 and 6-11)

- Though they are constrained against deficits in their annual budgets, state and local governments can and do borrow—for investment, or just to cover shortfalls in current accounts—by issuing bonds. (Usually, the permission of voters in the state or local jurisdiction is required.) Their net investment typically exceeds the sum of their current surpluses and their capital transfers (mainly federal highway money); consequently, they have usually been net borrowers from the rest of the economy, even before the deficits of the 2000s. (Table 6-10)

- For both state and local governments, transportation spending dominates the economic affairs function. For states, transportation and higher education together made up 43 percent of all spending in 2001. For local governments, transportation and elementary and secondary education accounted for 59 percent of their total spending in 2001. (Tables 6-14 and 6-15)

Table 6-8. State and Local Government Current Receipts and Expenditures

(National income and product accounts, calendar years, billions of dollars, quarterly data are at seasonally adjusted annual rates.)

NIPA Table 3.3

Year and quarter	Current receipts Total	Current tax receipts Total	Personal current taxes Total¹	Income taxes	Taxes on production and imports Total	Sales taxes	Property taxes	Other	Taxes on corporate income	Contributions for government social insurance	Income receipts on assets Total¹	Interest receipts	Rents and royalties
1950	20.0	16.5	1.5	0.8	14.2	4.8	7.1	2.3	0.8	0.2	0.5	0.3	0.2
1951	21.9	18.1	1.7	0.9	15.6	5.4	7.7	2.5	0.9	0.2	0.6	0.4	0.2
1952	23.7	19.7	1.8	1.0	17.0	5.8	8.4	2.8	0.8	0.3	0.7	0.4	0.2
1953	25.5	21.1	1.9	1.0	18.4	6.3	9.1	3.0	0.8	0.3	0.7	0.5	0.3
1954	26.9	22.2	2.1	1.1	19.4	6.5	9.7	3.2	0.8	0.3	0.8	0.5	0.3
1955	29.4	24.4	2.4	1.3	21.0	7.1	10.4	3.5	1.0	0.3	0.9	0.6	0.3
1956	32.4	27.0	2.7	1.6	23.3	8.0	11.5	3.8	1.0	0.4	1.0	0.7	0.3
1957	35.0	29.0	2.9	1.7	25.1	8.6	12.6	3.9	1.0	0.4	1.1	0.7	0.3
1958	37.1	30.6	3.1	1.8	26.5	10.0	13.8	2.8	1.0	0.4	1.1	0.8	0.4
1959	40.6	33.8	3.8	2.2	28.8	11.1	14.8	2.9	1.2	0.4	1.1	0.9	0.3
1960	44.5	37.0	4.2	2.5	31.5	12.2	16.2	3.1	1.2	0.5	1.3	1.0	0.3
1961	48.1	39.7	4.6	2.8	33.8	13.0	17.6	3.2	1.3	0.5	1.4	1.1	0.4
1962	52.0	42.8	5.0	3.2	36.3	14.0	19.0	3.3	1.5	0.5	1.5	1.1	0.4
1963	56.0	45.8	5.4	3.4	38.7	15.0	20.2	3.5	1.7	0.6	1.6	1.2	0.4
1964	61.3	49.8	6.1	4.0	41.8	16.5	21.7	3.7	1.8	0.7	1.9	1.5	0.4
1965	66.5	53.9	6.6	4.4	45.3	18.2	23.2	3.9	2.0	0.8	2.2	1.8	0.4
1966	74.9	58.8	7.8	5.4	48.8	20.0	24.5	4.3	2.2	0.9	2.6	2.1	0.5
1967	82.5	64.0	8.6	6.1	52.8	21.4	27.0	4.4	2.6	0.9	3.0	2.4	0.6
1968	93.5	73.4	10.6	7.8	59.5	25.1	29.9	4.6	3.3	0.9	3.5	2.8	0.7
1969	105.5	82.5	12.8	9.8	66.0	28.6	32.8	4.7	3.6	1.0	4.3	3.6	0.8
1970	120.1	91.3	14.2	10.9	73.3	31.6	36.7	5.0	3.7	1.1	5.2	4.3	0.8
1971	134.9	101.7	15.9	12.4	81.5	35.4	40.4	5.7	4.3	1.2	5.5	4.6	0.9
1972	158.4	115.6	20.9	17.2	89.4	39.8	43.2	6.4	5.3	1.3	5.9	4.9	1.0
1973	174.3	126.3	22.8	18.9	97.4	44.1	46.4	7.0	6.0	1.5	7.8	6.6	1.1
1974	188.1	136.0	24.5	20.4	104.8	48.2	49.0	7.7	6.7	1.7	10.2	8.9	1.3
1975	209.6	147.4	26.9	22.5	113.2	51.7	53.4	8.1	7.3	1.8	11.2	9.8	1.3
1976	233.7	165.7	31.1	26.3	125.0	57.8	58.2	9.0	9.6	2.2	10.4	9.0	1.3
1977	259.9	183.7	35.4	30.4	136.9	64.0	63.2	9.7	11.4	2.8	11.7	10.4	1.3
1978	287.6	198.2	40.5	35.0	145.6	71.0	63.7	10.9	12.1	3.4	14.7	13.3	1.3
1979	308.4	212.0	44.0	38.2	154.4	77.3	64.4	12.7	13.6	3.9	20.1	18.1	1.9
1980	338.2	230.0	48.9	42.6	166.7	82.9	68.8	15.0	14.5	3.6	26.3	23.1	3.1
1981	370.2	255.8	54.6	47.9	185.7	90.7	77.1	17.9	15.4	3.9	32.0	28.5	3.3
1982	391.4	273.2	59.1	51.9	200.0	96.2	85.3	18.5	14.0	4.0	36.7	33.1	3.5
1983	428.6	300.9	66.1	58.3	218.9	107.7	91.9	19.4	15.9	4.1	41.4	37.0	4.3
1984	480.2	337.3	76.0	67.5	242.5	121.0	99.7	21.8	18.8	4.7	47.7	42.6	4.9
1985	521.1	363.7	81.4	72.1	262.1	131.1	107.5	23.5	20.2	4.9	54.9	49.4	5.4
1986	561.6	389.5	87.2	77.4	279.7	139.9	116.2	23.7	22.7	6.0	58.4	52.0	6.2
1987	590.6	422.1	96.6	86.0	301.6	150.3	126.4	24.9	23.9	7.2	58.1	52.6	5.3
1988	635.5	452.8	102.1	90.6	324.6	162.4	136.5	25.7	26.0	8.4	60.5	55.9	4.4
1989	687.3	488.0	114.6	102.3	349.1	172.3	149.9	26.9	24.2	9.0	65.7	61.4	4.1
1990	737.8	519.1	122.6	109.6	374.1	184.3	161.5	28.3	22.5	10.0	68.4	64.1	4.2
1991	789.2	544.3	125.3	111.7	395.3	190.7	176.1	28.6	23.6	11.6	68.0	63.1	4.5
1992	845.7	579.8	135.3	120.4	420.1	204.3	184.7	31.1	24.4	13.1	64.8	59.6	4.8
1993	886.9	604.7	141.1	126.2	436.8	216.4	187.3	33.1	26.9	14.1	61.4	56.2	4.5
1994	942.9	644.2	148.0	132.2	466.3	231.4	199.4	35.5	30.0	14.5	63.2	57.9	4.5
1995	990.2	672.1	158.1	141.7	482.4	242.7	202.6	37.0	31.7	13.6	68.4	62.9	4.5
1996	1 043.3	709.6	168.7	152.3	507.9	256.2	212.4	39.4	33.0	12.5	73.3	67.3	4.6
1997	1 097.4	749.9	182.0	164.7	533.8	268.7	223.5	41.6	34.1	10.8	77.8	71.5	4.8
1998	1 163.2	794.9	201.2	183.0	558.8	283.9	231.0	43.9	34.9	10.4	80.9	74.6	4.6
1999	1 236.7	840.4	214.5	195.5	590.2	301.6	242.8	45.8	35.8	9.8	85.3	78.4	5.1
2000	1 319.5	893.2	236.6	217.3	621.1	316.6	254.6	49.9	35.5	11.0	92.2	84.0	6.3
2001	1 373.0	915.8	242.7	223.1	642.8	321.1	269.3	52.4	30.2	13.6	88.8	80.3	6.5
2002	1 410.1	929.0	221.3	200.8	675.5	330.2	290.1	55.2	32.2	15.8	78.2	69.6	6.6
2003	1 494.2	979.4	226.6	204.5	717.5	347.7	307.9	61.9	35.3	19.8	72.9	62.9	7.9
2004	1 592.6	1 060.9	248.4	225.1	769.4	370.3	329.8	69.3	43.1	24.2	73.3	62.1	8.7
2005	1 700.6	1 154.4	275.2	250.9	821.2	394.1	350.4	76.7	58.0	25.3	75.3	63.4	9.5
2003													
1st quarter	1 435.8	949.2	218.3	197.1	697.5	338.3	300.7	58.5	33.3	17.8	74.0	64.5	7.3
2nd quarter	1 474.2	956.8	213.2	191.4	710.7	344.7	305.2	60.7	32.9	19.1	73.0	63.1	7.7
3rd quarter	1 516.8	994.4	234.4	211.7	724.1	350.5	310.1	63.5	35.9	20.4	72.5	62.2	8.1
4th quarter	1 549.9	1 017.4	240.6	217.7	737.7	357.3	315.4	65.0	39.1	21.7	72.2	61.7	8.3
2004													
1st quarter	1 552.9	1 032.3	240.1	216.9	751.8	363.8	321.6	66.5	40.4	23.1	72.2	61.6	8.5
2nd quarter	1 582.9	1 049.8	242.0	219.0	764.1	368.5	327.1	68.5	43.7	24.0	72.9	62.1	8.6
3rd quarter	1 590.9	1 065.6	250.8	227.5	772.1	369.8	332.6	69.7	42.7	24.7	73.4	62.3	8.8
4th quarter	1 643.6	1 095.7	260.7	236.9	789.4	379.3	337.8	72.3	45.6	25.2	74.6	62.5	9.0
2005													
1st quarter	1 672.2	1 129.2	266.7	242.8	803.8	387.5	342.8	73.5	58.7	25.3	74.4	62.9	9.2
2nd quarter	1 702.9	1 155.6	280.9	256.9	817.5	393.7	347.9	76.0	57.1	25.3	75.0	63.2	9.4
3rd quarter	1 697.8	1 156.6	274.0	249.5	827.9	397.9	353.0	76.9	54.7	25.3	75.6	63.6	9.6
4th quarter	1 729.6	1 176.3	279.3	254.3	835.7	397.2	358.1	80.5	61.3	25.2	76.3	64.0	9.8

¹Includes components not shown separately.

Table 6-8. State and Local Government Current Receipts and Expenditures—Continued

(National income and product accounts, calendar years, billions of dollars, quarterly data are at seasonally adjusted annual rates.)

NIPA Table 3.3

Year and quarter	Current receipts—Continued					Current expenditures					Net state and local government saving, NIPA (surplus + / deficit -)		
	Current transfer receipts				Current surplus of government enterprises	Total [1]	Consumption expenditures	Government social benefits to persons	Interest payments	Subsidies	Total	Social insurance funds	Other
	Total	Federal grants-in-aid	From business, net	From persons									
1950	2.3	1.9	0.1	0.3	0.4	18.6	14.9	3.2	0.6	...	1.3	0.1	1.2
1951	2.5	2.0	0.1	0.3	0.5	19.4	16.1	2.6	0.6	...	2.6	0.1	2.5
1952	2.6	2.2	0.1	0.3	0.5	20.7	17.1	2.9	0.7	...	3.0	0.1	2.9
1953	2.8	2.3	0.1	0.3	0.6	22.0	18.2	3.0	0.8	...	3.5	0.1	3.4
1954	2.9	2.3	0.2	0.4	0.7	23.7	19.7	3.1	0.9	...	3.2	0.1	3.1
1955	3.0	2.4	0.2	0.4	0.8	25.9	21.6	3.3	1.1	...	3.5	0.1	3.4
1956	3.2	2.5	0.2	0.4	0.9	28.0	23.4	3.3	1.2	...	4.4	0.1	4.3
1957	3.6	2.9	0.2	0.5	0.9	30.8	25.8	3.6	1.4	...	4.2	0.1	4.1
1958	4.1	3.3	0.2	0.5	0.9	34.2	28.6	4.0	1.5	...	2.9	0.0	2.8
1959	4.2	3.8	0.1	0.3	1.1	36.9	30.7	4.3	1.8	0.0	3.8	0.0	3.8
1960	4.5	4.0	0.2	0.3	1.2	40.2	33.5	4.6	2.1	0.0	4.3	0.0	4.3
1961	5.2	4.5	0.2	0.4	1.3	43.8	36.6	5.0	2.2	0.0	4.3	0.0	4.3
1962	5.8	5.0	0.2	0.5	1.4	46.8	39.0	5.3	2.4	0.0	5.2	0.0	5.2
1963	6.4	5.6	0.3	0.5	1.6	50.3	41.9	5.7	2.7	0.0	5.7	0.0	5.7
1964	7.3	6.5	0.3	0.5	1.6	54.9	45.8	6.2	2.9	0.0	6.4	0.0	6.3
1965	8.0	7.2	0.3	0.5	1.7	60.0	50.2	6.7	3.1	0.0	6.5	0.1	6.4
1966	11.1	10.1	0.3	0.7	1.6	67.2	56.1	7.6	3.4	0.0	7.8	0.1	7.6
1967	13.1	11.7	0.5	0.9	1.5	75.5	62.6	9.2	3.7	0.0	7.0	0.1	6.9
1968	14.2	12.7	0.5	1.0	1.5	86.0	70.4	11.4	4.2	0.0	7.5	0.1	7.3
1969	16.2	14.6	0.5	1.1	1.5	97.5	79.9	13.2	4.4	0.0	8.0	0.2	7.8
1970	21.1	19.3	0.6	1.2	1.5	113.0	91.5	16.1	5.3	0.0	7.1	0.2	6.9
1971	25.2	23.2	0.6	1.4	1.4	128.5	102.7	19.3	6.5	0.0	6.5	0.2	6.2
1972	34.0	31.7	0.7	1.7	1.6	142.8	113.2	22.0	7.5	0.1	15.6	0.3	15.4
1973	37.3	34.8	0.9	1.7	1.5	158.6	126.0	24.1	8.5	0.1	15.7	0.3	15.4
1974	39.3	36.3	1.1	2.0	0.9	178.7	143.7	25.3	9.6	0.1	9.3	0.4	9.0
1975	48.7	45.1	1.2	2.4	0.4	207.1	165.1	30.8	11.1	0.2	2.5	0.5	2.0
1976	55.0	50.7	1.4	2.9	0.4	226.3	179.5	34.1	12.5	0.2	7.4	0.6	6.8
1977	61.4	56.6	1.6	3.3	0.3	246.8	195.9	37.0	13.7	0.2	13.1	1.0	12.2
1978	71.1	65.5	1.9	3.7	0.3	268.9	213.2	40.8	14.9	0.2	18.7	1.5	17.2
1979	72.7	66.3	2.2	4.1	-0.3	295.4	233.3	44.3	17.2	0.3	13.0	1.8	11.2
1980	79.5	72.3	2.5	4.7	-1.2	329.4	258.4	51.2	19.4	0.4	8.8	1.3	7.5
1981	81.0	72.5	2.9	5.7	-2.4	362.7	282.3	57.1	22.8	0.4	7.6	1.3	6.3
1982	79.1	69.5	3.2	6.4	-1.6	393.6	304.9	61.2	27.1	0.5	-2.2	1.2	-3.4
1983	82.4	71.6	3.6	7.2	-0.2	423.7	324.1	66.9	32.3	0.4	4.9	1.2	3.7
1984	89.0	76.7	4.2	8.1	1.5	456.2	347.7	71.2	37.0	0.4	23.9	1.4	22.5
1985	94.5	80.9	4.4	9.2	3.2	498.7	381.8	77.3	39.4	0.3	22.3	1.3	21.0
1986	105.0	87.6	6.7	10.6	2.8	540.7	417.9	84.3	38.2	0.3	21.0	1.9	19.1
1987	100.0	83.9	4.9	11.2	3.1	578.1	440.9	90.7	46.2	0.3	12.4	2.2	10.2
1988	109.0	91.6	5.4	12.0	4.8	617.6	470.4	98.5	48.4	0.4	17.9	2.5	15.4
1989	118.1	98.3	6.4	13.4	6.5	666.5	502.1	109.3	54.6	0.4	20.8	2.3	18.5
1990	133.5	111.4	7.1	14.9	6.7	730.5	544.6	127.7	57.9	0.4	7.2	2.0	5.3
1991	158.2	131.6	7.9	18.7	7.1	793.3	574.6	156.5	61.7	0.4	-4.2	2.4	-6.5
1992	180.3	149.1	9.2	21.9	7.7	845.0	602.7	180.0	61.9	0.4	0.7	3.1	-2.4
1993	197.7	163.7	10.5	23.5	9.0	886.0	630.3	195.2	60.2	0.4	0.9	4.2	-3.3
1994	211.9	174.7	12.0	25.2	9.0	932.4	663.3	206.7	62.0	0.3	10.5	4.6	5.8
1995	224.1	184.1	13.5	26.5	12.0	978.2	696.1	217.6	64.2	0.3	12.0	4.0	8.0
1996	234.1	191.2	15.2	27.8	13.9	1 017.5	724.8	224.3	68.1	0.3	25.8	2.8	23.0
1997	246.6	198.6	17.7	30.3	12.3	1 058.3	758.9	227.6	71.4	0.4	39.1	1.2	38.0
1998	266.8	212.8	22.1	31.9	10.2	1 111.2	801.4	235.8	73.6	0.4	52.0	1.7	50.3
1999	290.8	232.9	23.0	34.9	10.4	1 186.3	858.9	252.4	74.6	0.4	50.4	1.7	48.7
2000	315.4	247.3	28.8	39.2	7.7	1 269.5	917.8	271.7	79.5	0.5	50.0	2.0	47.9
2001	350.8	276.1	31.4	43.3	4.0	1 368.2	969.8	305.2	85.5	7.7	4.8	2.6	2.2
2002	384.7	304.6	32.6	47.5	2.5	1 444.3	1 025.3	332.0	86.0	0.9	-34.2	1.7	-35.9
2003	422.7	338.5	33.5	50.6	-0.6	1 514.5	1 073.8	353.0	87.7	0.1	-20.4	3.8	-24.1
2004	438.0	349.0	34.7	54.3	-3.8	1 605.5	1 130.3	382.9	91.8	0.4	-12.9	7.5	-20.4
2005	456.1	361.1	36.7	58.3	-10.5	1 703.9	1 207.2	402.3	94.2	0.4	-3.3	7.3	-10.6
2003													
1st quarter	394.0	311.9	32.6	49.5	0.7	1 497.0	1 065.2	345.3	86.4	0.1	-61.2	2.3	-63.5
2nd quarter	425.5	342.2	33.2	50.2	-0.2	1 501.4	1 066.7	347.2	87.1	0.3	-27.2	3.2	-30.4
3rd quarter	430.6	345.9	33.8	51.0	-1.1	1 525.0	1 076.2	361.8	88.1	-1.0	-8.2	4.3	-12.5
4th quarter	440.5	354.2	34.5	51.8	-1.8	1 534.8	1 086.9	357.8	89.2	0.9	15.2	5.3	9.9
2004													
1st quarter	427.6	339.5	35.3	52.8	-2.3	1 567.6	1 103.9	372.9	90.3	0.4	-14.7	6.6	-21.3
2nd quarter	439.8	349.8	35.9	53.8	-3.3	1 596.5	1 120.9	383.7	91.5	0.4	-13.6	7.4	-21.0
3rd quarter	431.4	345.7	31.0	54.8	-4.3	1 613.2	1 136.6	384.0	92.3	0.4	-22.3	7.9	-30.2
4th quarter	453.4	361.2	36.4	55.7	-5.2	1 644.5	1 160.0	391.2	93.0	0.4	-0.9	8.1	-9.0
2005													
1st quarter	448.7	355.9	36.1	56.7	-5.4	1 661.2	1 174.6	393.4	92.8	0.4	10.9	7.8	3.1
2nd quarter	453.8	359.8	36.3	57.7	-6.8	1 690.5	1 192.8	403.8	93.5	0.4	12.4	7.6	4.9
3rd quarter	462.0	361.9	41.4	58.8	-21.7	1 717.2	1 217.8	404.5	94.5	0.4	-19.3	7.2	-26.6
4th quarter	459.8	366.8	33.1	59.9	-7.9	1 746.8	1 243.4	407.3	95.8	0.4	-17.2	6.8	-24.0

[1] Includes components not shown separately.
. . . = Not available.

Table 6-9. State and Local Government Consumption Expenditures and Gross Investment

(National income and product accounts, calendar years, billions of dollars, quarterly data are at seasonally adjusted annual rates.)

NIPA Tables 3.9.5, 3.10.5

Year and quarter	Total	State and local government consumption expenditures and gross investment										
		Consumption expenditures [1]								Gross investment		
							Less					
		Total	Compensation of general government employees	Consumption of general government fixed capital	Intermediate goods and services purchased [2]	Own-account investment	Sales to other sectors			Total	Structures	Equipment and software
							Total [3]	Tuition and related educational charges	Health and hospital charges			
1950	20.7	14.9	10.1	1.7	4.9	0.3	1.6	0.1	0.3	5.9	5.4	0.5
1951	23.0	16.1	11.2	2.0	4.9	0.3	1.7	0.1	0.3	7.0	6.4	0.5
1952	24.4	17.1	12.3	2.2	4.9	0.4	1.8	0.2	0.3	7.3	6.7	0.6
1953	26.1	18.2	13.3	2.2	4.9	0.4	1.9	0.2	0.4	7.9	7.3	0.6
1954	28.9	19.7	14.7	2.2	5.2	0.4	2.0	0.2	0.4	9.2	8.5	0.7
1955	31.6	21.6	15.8	2.4	6.0	0.4	2.2	0.2	0.5	10.0	9.3	0.8
1956	34.7	23.4	17.6	2.8	5.9	0.5	2.4	0.2	0.6	11.3	10.4	0.9
1957	38.3	25.8	19.6	3.0	6.4	0.5	2.6	0.3	0.7	12.5	11.5	1.1
1958	42.2	28.6	21.6	3.1	7.5	0.6	3.0	0.3	0.9	13.5	12.5	1.1
1959	44.7	30.7	23.1	3.3	8.3	0.8	3.2	0.4	1.0	13.9	12.8	1.1
1960	47.5	33.5	25.5	3.5	8.9	0.8	3.5	0.4	1.0	13.9	12.7	1.2
1961	51.6	36.6	27.9	3.7	9.7	0.8	3.9	0.5	1.0	15.0	13.8	1.3
1962	54.9	39.0	30.2	3.9	10.1	0.9	4.4	0.6	1.3	15.9	14.5	1.3
1963	59.5	41.9	32.9	4.2	10.8	1.0	4.9	0.7	1.3	17.5	16.0	1.5
1964	64.8	45.8	35.9	4.5	11.9	1.0	5.5	0.8	1.5	19.0	17.2	1.8
1965	71.0	50.2	39.3	4.9	13.4	1.1	6.3	1.0	1.8	20.8	19.0	1.9
1966	79.2	56.1	44.1	5.5	14.9	1.2	7.2	1.2	2.1	23.1	21.0	2.1
1967	87.9	62.6	49.5	6.0	16.5	1.2	8.2	1.4	2.5	25.3	23.0	2.3
1968	98.0	70.4	55.9	6.6	18.7	1.3	9.5	1.6	3.2	27.7	25.2	2.4
1969	108.2	79.9	62.6	7.4	21.8	1.4	10.6	1.9	3.5	28.3	25.6	2.7
1970	120.3	91.5	71.1	8.4	25.4	1.5	11.8	2.4	3.8	28.7	25.8	3.0
1971	132.8	102.7	79.2	9.4	29.2	1.6	13.5	2.9	4.6	30.1	27.0	3.1
1972	143.8	113.2	87.7	10.2	32.2	1.7	15.2	3.2	5.6	30.6	27.1	3.5
1973	159.2	126.0	98.0	11.3	35.4	1.7	17.0	3.7	6.6	33.2	29.1	4.1
1974	183.4	143.7	107.7	14.1	42.7	2.1	18.7	4.0	7.4	39.6	34.7	4.9
1975	208.7	165.1	121.2	15.9	50.7	2.1	20.6	4.3	8.5	43.6	38.1	5.5
1976	223.3	179.5	133.0	16.6	55.2	2.0	23.3	4.7	9.9	43.8	38.1	5.7
1977	238.7	195.9	145.1	17.5	61.1	2.0	25.8	5.2	10.9	42.8	36.9	5.9
1978	262.6	213.2	158.9	18.9	66.9	2.3	29.2	5.8	12.7	49.5	42.8	6.6
1979	290.2	233.3	174.3	21.1	74.3	2.9	33.4	6.4	15.2	56.8	49.0	7.8
1980	322.4	258.4	193.0	24.3	82.0	3.3	37.6	7.2	17.3	64.0	55.1	8.9
1981	347.3	282.3	210.1	27.8	91.6	3.5	43.7	8.3	21.0	65.0	55.4	9.5
1982	369.7	304.9	227.4	30.3	100.6	3.7	49.7	9.4	24.5	64.8	54.2	10.6
1983	390.5	324.1	243.0	31.2	109.6	4.0	55.7	10.7	27.8	66.4	54.2	12.2
1984	422.6	347.7	261.1	32.0	119.0	4.6	59.8	11.7	29.4	75.0	60.5	14.4
1985	466.2	381.8	284.7	33.7	134.0	5.2	65.4	12.8	32.0	84.4	67.6	16.8
1986	510.7	417.9	307.3	36.2	151.6	5.7	71.5	13.9	34.8	92.8	74.2	18.6
1987	539.4	440.9	328.8	39.0	156.2	6.1	76.9	15.0	37.0	98.4	78.8	19.6
1988	576.7	470.4	353.7	41.5	166.0	6.7	84.1	16.6	40.3	106.3	84.8	21.5
1989	616.9	502.1	380.5	44.4	178.8	7.8	93.8	18.4	45.0	114.7	88.7	26.0
1990	671.9	544.6	414.6	48.0	194.0	8.6	103.5	20.3	50.0	127.2	98.5	28.7
1991	706.7	574.6	439.8	51.1	208.4	9.3	115.4	22.7	57.0	132.1	103.2	28.9
1992	737.0	602.7	463.9	53.4	224.0	9.5	129.1	25.5	65.3	134.3	104.2	30.1
1993	766.0	630.3	486.7	56.3	239.7	9.7	142.7	27.5	73.1	135.7	104.5	31.2
1994	806.3	663.3	511.2	59.5	256.0	10.1	153.3	29.4	78.8	143.0	108.7	34.3
1995	850.0	696.1	533.5	63.4	274.8	10.6	165.0	31.2	85.0	154.0	117.3	36.7
1996	888.6	724.8	552.7	66.7	289.6	11.0	173.2	33.0	86.6	163.8	126.8	36.9
1997	937.8	758.9	575.5	70.2	308.5	12.2	183.2	35.5	89.9	178.9	139.5	39.4
1998	987.9	801.4	603.3	73.9	331.4	12.6	194.6	38.1	95.9	186.5	143.6	43.0
1999	1 065.0	858.9	633.1	78.7	364.6	13.5	203.9	40.9	98.4	206.0	159.7	46.4
2000	1 142.8	917.8	669.4	84.8	399.0	14.9	220.6	44.3	105.5	225.0	176.0	49.0
2001	1 212.8	969.8	710.8	89.9	428.3	16.7	242.7	49.7	118.5	243.0	192.4	50.6
2002	1 281.5	1 025.3	754.2	94.8	452.9	17.0	259.5	53.6	128.4	256.1	205.9	50.2
2003	1 336.0	1 073.8	798.0	98.2	466.9	17.1	272.2	58.2	133.0	262.2	212.0	50.3
2004	1 400.3	1 130.3	832.7	104.1	500.3	17.7	289.0	62.3	139.9	270.0	218.4	51.6
2005	1 494.4	1 207.2	872.3	113.9	545.7	18.8	306.0	67.0	146.1	287.3	233.5	53.8
2003												
1st quarter	1 324.4	1 065.2	781.9	97.3	470.2	16.9	267.3	56.3	131.7	259.2	209.3	49.9
2nd quarter	1 325.1	1 066.7	793.8	97.8	462.1	16.8	270.1	57.5	132.2	258.7	209.1	49.7
3rd quarter	1 343.3	1 076.2	803.6	98.5	465.3	17.4	273.7	58.8	133.2	267.1	216.6	50.5
4th quarter	1 350.9	1 086.9	812.8	99.1	470.1	17.3	277.8	60.0	134.8	264.0	213.0	51.0
2004												
1st quarter	1 366.3	1 103.9	819.1	100.1	484.8	17.3	282.8	60.8	137.4	262.4	211.3	51.0
2nd quarter	1 391.4	1 120.9	828.1	102.3	495.6	17.8	287.3	61.9	139.3	270.5	219.3	51.1
3rd quarter	1 409.0	1 136.6	836.6	105.5	503.1	17.8	290.8	62.8	140.6	272.4	220.7	51.7
4th quarter	1 434.8	1 160.0	847.1	108.5	517.6	18.0	295.3	63.9	142.3	274.8	222.3	52.5
2005												
1st quarter	1 453.3	1 174.6	856.7	110.1	525.6	18.2	299.7	65.1	143.8	278.7	225.6	53.1
2nd quarter	1 480.5	1 192.8	866.5	112.6	536.0	18.8	303.5	66.2	145.1	287.7	234.0	53.7
3rd quarter	1 506.6	1 217.8	877.4	115.5	551.1	18.9	307.3	67.4	146.4	288.7	234.6	54.1
4th quarter	1 537.4	1 243.4	888.5	117.6	570.1	19.4	313.4	69.1	148.8	294.0	239.8	54.2

[1]Excludes government sales to other sectors and government own-account investment (construction and software).
[2]Includes general government intermediate inputs for goods and services sold to other sectors and for own-account investment.
[3]Includes components not shown seperately.

Table 6-10. State and Local Government Output, Lending and Borrowing, and Net Investment

(National income and product accounts, calendar years, billions of dollars, quarterly data are at seasonally adjusted annual rates.)

NIPA Tables 3.3, 3.10.5

Year and quarter	Output			Net lending (net borrowing -)							Net investment
	Gross	Value added	Intermediate goods and services purchased [1]	Net saving, current (surplus +, deficit -)	Plus: Capital transfer receipts	Minus			Plus: consumption of fixed capital	Equals: Net lending (borrowing -)	
						Gross investment	Capital transfer payments	Net purchases of nonproduced assets			
1950	16.7	11.8	4.9	1.3	0.6	5.9	. . .	0.3	2.1	-2.1	3.8
1951	18.1	13.2	4.9	2.6	0.7	7.0	. . .	0.3	2.6	-1.5	4.4
1952	19.3	14.4	4.9	3.0	0.7	7.3	. . .	0.3	2.7	-1.1	4.6
1953	20.5	15.5	4.9	3.5	0.8	7.9	. . .	0.3	2.8	-1.1	5.1
1954	22.1	16.9	5.2	3.2	0.8	9.2	. . .	0.4	2.9	-2.6	6.3
1955	24.2	18.2	6.0	3.5	1.0	10.0	. . .	0.6	3.1	-3.1	6.9
1956	26.3	20.4	5.9	4.4	1.1	11.3	. . .	0.7	3.5	-2.9	7.8
1957	29.0	22.6	6.4	4.2	1.6	12.5	. . .	0.7	3.9	-3.5	8.6
1958	32.2	24.7	7.5	2.9	2.7	13.5	. . .	0.8	4.0	-4.7	9.5
1959	34.8	26.5	8.3	3.8	3.5	13.9	. . .	0.8	4.2	-3.2	9.7
1960	37.9	28.9	8.9	4.3	3.0	13.9	. . .	0.9	4.4	-3.1	9.5
1961	41.3	31.6	9.7	4.3	3.3	15.0	. . .	1.0	4.7	-3.8	10.3
1962	44.3	34.2	10.1	5.2	3.5	15.9	. . .	1.1	5.0	-3.2	10.9
1963	47.9	37.1	10.8	5.7	4.1	17.5	. . .	1.2	5.4	-3.5	12.1
1964	52.3	40.4	11.9	6.4	4.7	19.0	. . .	1.3	5.7	-3.4	13.3
1965	57.6	44.2	13.4	6.5	4.7	20.8	. . .	1.3	6.2	-4.6	14.6
1966	64.5	49.6	14.9	7.8	5.1	23.1	. . .	1.4	6.9	-4.7	16.2
1967	72.0	55.5	16.5	7.0	5.1	25.3	. . .	1.4	7.5	-7.1	17.8
1968	81.2	62.5	18.7	7.5	6.8	27.7	. . .	1.4	8.3	-6.4	19.4
1969	91.9	70.0	21.8	8.0	6.8	28.3	. . .	1.0	9.3	-5.1	19.0
1970	104.9	79.5	25.4	7.1	6.2	28.7	. . .	1.1	10.6	-6.0	18.1
1971	117.9	88.6	29.2	6.5	7.0	30.1	. . .	1.6	11.8	-6.4	18.3
1972	130.0	97.9	32.2	15.6	7.3	30.6	. . .	1.7	12.8	3.4	17.8
1973	144.7	109.3	35.4	15.7	7.3	33.2	. . .	1.7	14.3	2.4	18.9
1974	164.5	121.8	42.7	9.3	9.2	39.6	. . .	1.9	17.7	-5.3	21.9
1975	187.9	137.1	50.7	2.5	11.0	43.6	. . .	1.9	20.2	-11.9	23.4
1976	204.8	149.7	55.2	7.4	12.0	43.8	. . .	1.7	21.3	-4.9	22.5
1977	223.7	162.6	61.1	13.1	13.1	42.8	. . .	1.6	22.6	4.5	20.2
1978	244.7	177.8	66.9	18.7	13.7	49.5	. . .	1.6	24.5	5.8	25.0
1979	269.6	195.4	74.3	13.0	16.2	56.8	. . .	1.7	27.5	-1.8	29.3
1980	299.3	217.3	82.0	8.8	18.6	64.0	. . .	1.8	31.8	-6.6	32.2
1981	329.5	237.9	91.6	7.6	17.8	65.0	. . .	2.0	36.3	-5.3	28.7
1982	358.3	257.7	100.6	-2.2	16.9	64.8	. . .	2.0	39.5	-12.6	25.3
1983	383.7	274.1	109.6	4.9	18.0	66.4	. . .	2.2	40.9	-4.9	25.5
1984	412.1	293.1	119.0	23.9	20.1	75.0	. . .	2.6	42.3	8.8	32.7
1985	452.4	318.4	134.0	22.3	22.0	84.4	. . .	3.1	44.6	1.5	39.8
1986	495.1	343.5	151.6	21.0	23.0	92.8	. . .	3.7	47.9	-4.6	44.9
1987	524.0	367.8	156.2	12.4	22.3	98.4	. . .	4.2	51.4	-16.4	47.0
1988	561.1	395.2	166.0	17.9	23.1	106.3	. . .	4.3	54.8	-14.8	51.5
1989	603.7	424.9	178.8	20.8	23.4	114.7	. . .	4.9	58.7	-16.6	56.0
1990	656.7	462.6	194.0	7.2	25.0	127.2	. . .	5.7	63.0	-37.7	64.2
1991	699.4	490.9	208.4	-4.2	25.8	132.1	. . .	5.8	66.9	-49.4	65.2
1992	741.3	517.3	224.0	0.7	26.9	134.3	. . .	5.9	69.9	-42.8	64.4
1993	782.7	543.0	239.7	0.9	28.6	135.7	. . .	5.8	73.8	-38.2	61.9
1994	826.7	570.7	256.0	10.5	29.9	143.0	. . .	6.2	78.5	-30.4	64.5
1995	871.7	596.9	274.8	12.0	32.4	154.0	. . .	6.6	83.1	-33.0	70.9
1996	908.9	619.3	289.6	25.8	33.9	163.8	. . .	6.1	87.2	-22.9	76.6
1997	954.3	645.8	308.5	39.1	35.3	178.9	. . .	5.8	91.6	-18.7	87.3
1998	1 008.6	677.2	331.4	52.0	36.0	186.5	. . .	7.5	96.2	-9.9	90.3
1999	1 076.4	711.8	364.6	50.4	39.9	206.0	. . .	8.6	102.1	-22.3	103.9
2000	1 153.2	754.2	399.0	50.0	43.7	225.0	. . .	8.8	109.8	-30.4	115.2
2001	1 229.1	800.8	428.3	4.8	48.6	243.0	. . .	9.2	117.8	-81.1	125.2
2002	1 301.8	848.9	452.9	-34.2	52.1	256.1	. . .	10.6	122.7	-126.1	133.4
2003	1 363.1	896.2	466.9	-20.4	51.6	262.2	. . .	10.9	127.8	-114.1	134.4
2004	1 437.1	936.8	500.3	-12.9	51.9	270.0	. . .	11.0	136.7	-105.3	133.3
2005	1 531.9	986.2	545.7	-3.3	53.9	287.3	. . .	11.6	153.2	-95.0	134.1
2003											
1st quarter	1 349.4	879.2	470.2	-61.2	45.7	259.2	. . .	10.9	126.2	-159.4	133.0
2nd quarter	1 353.7	891.6	462.1	-27.2	54.6	258.7	. . .	10.9	127.2	-115.1	131.5
3rd quarter	1 367.3	902.0	465.3	-8.2	55.2	267.1	. . .	10.8	128.3	-102.6	138.8
4th quarter	1 381.9	911.9	470.1	15.2	50.8	264.0	. . .	10.8	129.5	-79.3	134.5
2004											
1st quarter	1 404.0	919.2	484.8	-14.7	50.5	262.4	. . .	10.9	131.2	-106.3	131.2
2nd quarter	1 426.0	930.4	495.6	-13.6	48.9	270.5	. . .	11.0	134.3	-111.9	136.2
3rd quarter	1 445.1	942.1	503.1	-22.3	58.0	272.4	. . .	11.1	138.6	-109.2	133.8
4th quarter	1 473.2	955.6	517.6	-0.9	50.2	274.8	. . .	11.2	142.7	-94.0	132.1
2005											
1st quarter	1 492.5	966.9	525.6	10.9	52.3	278.7	. . .	11.3	144.7	-82.1	134.0
2nd quarter	1 515.1	979.1	536.0	12.4	55.2	287.7	. . .	11.5	147.9	-83.6	139.8
3rd quarter	1 544.0	992.9	551.1	-19.3	54.4	288.7	. . .	11.6	165.9	-99.4	122.8
4th quarter	1 576.2	1 006.0	570.1	-17.2	53.8	294.0	. . .	11.8	154.3	-114.9	139.7

[1]Includes general government intermediate inputs for goods and services sold to other sectors and for own-account investment.
. . . = Not available.

Table 6-11. Chain-Type Quantity Indexes for State and Local Government Consumption Expenditures and Gross Investment

(Index numbers, 2000 = 100.) NIPA Tables 3.9.3, 3.10.3

Year and quarter	Total	Consumption expenditures [1]								Gross investment		
		Total	Compensation of general government employees	Consumption of general government fixed capital	Intermediate goods and services purchased [2]	Less Own-account investment	Less Sales to other sectors Total	Tuition and related educational charges	Health and hospital charges	Total	Structures	Equipment and software
1950	17.5	17.7	22.5	11.9	8.7	18.1	9.6	5.6	5.8	17.3	24.2	2.7
1951	17.6	17.7	23.0	12.4	8.1	20.2	9.4	5.6	5.9	17.9	25.0	2.9
1952	17.9	17.9	23.8	12.9	7.9	23.8	9.6	5.9	6.0	18.3	25.5	3.1
1953	18.8	18.5	24.8	13.4	7.9	22.6	10.0	6.3	6.3	19.9	27.8	3.3
1954	20.5	19.3	25.9	14.1	8.2	23.6	10.6	6.9	6.9	23.8	33.4	3.6
1955	21.9	20.6	27.0	14.9	9.3	23.3	11.7	7.7	7.7	25.9	36.6	3.5
1956	22.6	21.3	28.8	15.7	9.0	26.1	12.2	8.8	8.8	26.5	37.2	4.0
1957	24.0	22.4	30.3	16.7	9.4	26.4	12.9	10.1	10.0	28.4	39.3	4.9
1958	26.0	24.2	32.2	17.7	10.8	28.3	14.4	11.5	12.6	31.2	43.6	4.9
1959	27.0	25.2	33.4	18.7	11.6	38.3	15.2	12.3	13.2	32.1	44.8	5.2
1960	28.2	26.6	35.2	19.8	12.2	35.9	15.7	13.6	12.2	32.5	44.9	5.9
1961	29.9	28.1	37.0	20.9	13.1	37.6	16.8	14.9	12.5	35.1	48.6	6.0
1962	30.8	28.9	38.2	22.0	13.6	40.0	18.7	16.9	14.6	36.4	50.2	6.5
1963	32.7	30.3	40.2	23.3	14.5	44.9	20.5	19.3	15.2	39.6	54.4	7.4
1964	34.9	32.3	42.6	24.7	15.8	44.4	22.5	22.6	16.4	42.4	58.0	8.4
1965	37.3	34.4	45.2	26.3	17.4	45.6	25.0	26.2	18.7	45.4	62.1	9.0
1966	39.6	36.5	47.9	28.0	18.8	48.1	27.3	29.7	21.3	48.4	66.0	9.9
1967	41.6	38.2	49.7	29.8	20.3	46.7	30.1	33.1	24.2	51.4	70.2	10.3
1968	44.0	40.7	52.7	31.6	22.3	49.2	33.0	37.2	28.3	53.7	73.4	10.8
1969	45.5	43.3	55.1	33.3	24.7	49.5	34.5	41.0	29.3	51.5	69.5	11.6
1970	46.8	45.9	57.5	34.9	27.2	50.1	36.2	47.7	29.8	48.3	64.4	12.1
1971	48.2	48.1	59.8	36.3	29.7	50.1	39.5	53.7	34.7	46.9	62.2	12.3
1972	49.3	49.9	61.9	37.6	31.5	48.8	42.3	57.0	39.8	45.4	59.2	13.7
1973	50.7	51.7	64.1	38.9	32.6	47.4	44.2	61.5	44.1	45.6	58.7	15.3
1974	52.6	54.0	66.4	40.3	34.4	50.5	44.2	61.3	45.5	46.0	58.5	16.7
1975	54.5	56.7	68.4	41.6	37.1	47.6	44.6	61.4	46.7	45.6	58.1	16.4
1976	54.9	57.5	69.2	42.8	38.2	42.0	47.1	63.4	49.7	44.8	57.0	16.1
1977	55.1	58.6	70.2	43.8	39.3	38.3	48.6	66.0	50.6	42.1	53.2	15.8
1978	56.9	59.7	71.8	44.7	40.3	41.3	50.9	69.6	54.1	45.9	58.3	16.7
1979	57.8	60.1	73.0	45.8	40.3	47.7	53.2	71.5	58.7	48.2	60.8	18.3
1980	57.7	60.0	73.9	47.0	39.0	49.7	54.1	73.9	59.2	48.4	60.5	19.5
1981	56.6	59.8	73.7	48.0	39.3	47.5	56.4	75.5	62.9	44.3	54.6	19.4
1982	56.6	60.7	74.0	48.9	41.0	47.9	58.1	75.4	64.8	41.6	50.1	20.6
1983	57.3	61.4	73.5	49.8	43.6	47.5	60.2	77.8	66.4	42.1	49.6	23.5
1984	59.3	62.5	73.8	51.1	45.4	52.8	60.0	77.7	64.9	47.3	55.0	27.5
1985	63.0	65.8	75.8	52.9	50.1	57.0	62.0	77.7	66.4	52.4	60.3	31.9
1986	67.1	69.9	77.9	55.0	56.7	61.0	64.1	78.3	68.1	56.0	64.1	34.9
1987	68.0	70.8	79.2	57.1	56.6	62.3	65.1	78.8	68.1	57.4	65.5	36.4
1988	70.6	73.2	81.9	59.5	58.1	65.2	66.4	81.3	68.2	60.4	68.4	39.4
1989	73.0	75.4	84.2	62.4	59.9	72.8	68.2	83.8	68.7	63.7	69.8	46.8
1990	76.0	77.8	86.5	65.7	61.8	76.3	69.5	85.6	69.4	68.7	75.0	51.1
1991	77.6	79.4	87.3	68.9	64.7	79.7	71.8	87.0	72.4	70.3	77.5	50.5
1992	79.3	81.3	88.5	71.9	68.1	78.9	75.0	88.7	76.6	71.2	77.8	52.9
1993	80.5	83.0	89.5	74.7	71.4	78.5	78.6	87.0	81.1	70.5	76.0	54.7
1994	82.5	85.1	90.8	77.4	74.9	79.3	81.4	87.7	84.3	72.5	76.6	60.2
1995	84.7	87.0	92.4	80.3	77.7	80.4	84.4	88.0	88.1	75.7	79.2	64.7
1996	86.7	88.6	93.6	83.3	79.5	81.4	86.0	88.2	87.7	79.1	83.1	66.7
1997	89.8	91.0	95.3	86.8	83.4	89.0	88.9	90.3	89.8	84.9	88.5	73.7
1998	93.0	94.4	96.9	90.9	90.0	90.7	92.9	92.9	94.9	87.4	88.4	84.1
1999	97.4	98.1	98.3	95.4	96.6	94.6	95.2	96.1	95.6	94.6	94.9	93.7
2000	100.0	100.0	100.0	100.0	100.0	100.0	100.0	100.0	100.0	100.0	100.0	100.0
2001	103.2	102.6	102.1	104.5	105.5	109.1	106.8	106.6	108.9	105.7	105.7	105.5
2002	106.4	105.6	103.8	109.0	110.8	108.8	110.3	107.7	114.2	109.4	109.9	107.1
2003	106.6	105.7	104.1	112.2	109.3	105.5	110.0	107.9	112.4	110.2	110.6	108.9
2004	107.1	106.7	104.3	115.3	111.5	105.5	111.0	105.6	113.1	108.5	107.7	112.2
2005	107.7	107.7	105.2	118.2	112.7	107.4	112.7	105.5	114.0	107.6	105.5	117.0
2003												
1st quarter	106.5	105.8	104.2	111.1	109.8	105.1	110.1	108.2	113.2	109.2	109.7	107.4
2nd quarter	106.3	105.6	104.1	111.9	109.2	104.3	110.0	108.6	112.2	108.9	109.3	107.5
3rd quarter	106.8	105.5	104.0	112.6	109.1	107.2	109.9	107.5	112.0	112.3	112.9	109.7
4th quarter	106.7	105.7	104.1	113.3	109.3	105.5	110.0	107.1	112.0	110.6	110.5	110.9
2004												
1st quarter	106.8	106.2	104.1	114.1	110.7	104.6	110.5	106.1	112.6	109.0	108.6	111.1
2nd quarter	107.3	106.6	104.2	114.9	111.5	106.5	110.9	106.0	113.0	110.3	110.1	111.2
3rd quarter	107.1	106.8	104.3	115.6	111.8	105.6	111.2	105.3	113.3	108.1	107.1	112.6
4th quarter	107.1	107.3	104.7	116.4	112.0	105.4	111.6	105.1	113.6	106.5	104.8	114.1
2005												
1st quarter	107.3	107.3	104.8	117.3	112.2	105.6	112.1	105.2	113.7	107.2	105.4	115.3
2nd quarter	107.7	107.4	105.0	117.9	112.4	108.0	112.5	105.0	114.0	108.7	107.0	116.6
3rd quarter	107.7	107.8	105.3	118.5	112.7	107.3	112.9	105.4	114.1	107.0	104.7	117.5
4th quarter	108.0	108.1	105.5	119.1	113.4	108.7	113.5	106.5	114.1	107.3	104.9	118.5

[1]Excludes government sales to other sectors and government own-account investment (construction and software).
[2]Includes general government intermediate inputs for goods and services sold to other sectors and for own-account investment.

Table 6-12. State Government Current Receipts and Expenditures

(National income and product accounts, calendar years, billions of dollars.) **NIPA Table 3.20**

Year	Current receipts												
		Current tax receipts								Contribu-tions for govern-ment social insurance	Income receipts on assets		
	Total ¹	Total	Personal current taxes		Taxes on production and imports				Taxes on corporate income		Total ¹	Interest receipts	Rents and royalties
			Total ¹	Income taxes	Total	Sales taxes	Property taxes	Other					
1959	21.8	16.7	3.1	2.0	12.5	10.0	0.5	2.0	1.1	0.4	0.5	0.3	0.2
1960	23.5	18.1	3.4	2.3	13.5	10.8	0.5	2.2	1.2	0.5	0.5	0.4	0.2
1961	25.2	19.3	3.7	2.5	14.4	11.6	0.5	2.3	1.3	0.5	0.6	0.4	0.2
1962	27.5	21.0	4.0	2.8	15.4	12.6	0.6	2.3	1.5	0.5	0.6	0.4	0.2
1963	29.6	22.4	4.3	3.1	16.4	13.4	0.6	2.4	1.6	0.6	0.6	0.4	0.2
1964	32.3	24.5	4.9	3.6	17.7	14.5	0.6	2.6	1.8	0.7	0.7	0.4	0.2
1965	35.8	26.9	5.4	3.9	19.6	16.1	0.7	2.8	1.9	0.8	0.8	0.5	0.3
1966	42.3	30.2	6.4	4.8	21.7	18.0	0.7	3.0	2.2	0.8	0.9	0.6	0.3
1967	46.5	32.7	7.0	5.3	23.3	19.4	0.7	3.1	2.5	0.9	1.1	0.8	0.3
1968	54.7	38.6	8.8	6.9	26.7	22.8	0.8	3.2	3.1	0.9	1.7	1.4	0.3
1969	62.6	44.0	10.8	8.6	29.9	25.7	0.9	3.3	3.4	1.0	2.1	1.8	0.3
1970	70.1	48.1	12.0	9.6	32.7	28.2	0.9	3.6	3.5	1.1	2.5	2.2	0.3
1971	79.4	53.8	13.4	11.0	36.3	31.4	1.0	3.9	4.0	1.2	2.7	2.3	0.4
1972	96.3	63.5	17.9	15.2	40.7	35.2	1.1	4.4	5.0	1.3	2.9	2.5	0.4
1973	104.5	70.2	19.8	16.8	44.7	38.8	1.2	4.7	5.7	1.5	3.9	3.3	0.5
1974	113.5	75.9	21.1	18.0	48.4	42.0	1.1	5.3	6.3	1.7	5.0	4.4	0.6
1975	127.4	81.9	23.2	19.9	51.8	44.7	1.4	5.6	6.9	1.8	5.6	5.0	0.6
1976	143.4	93.8	27.0	23.4	57.7	49.9	1.5	6.3	9.1	2.2	5.3	4.7	0.6
1977	160.0	105.1	30.9	27.2	63.4	55.0	1.5	6.9	10.8	2.8	6.1	5.4	0.6
1978	179.3	117.4	35.6	31.6	70.3	60.8	1.9	7.6	11.5	3.4	7.4	6.7	0.6
1979	197.3	128.9	38.9	34.6	77.1	65.7	2.3	9.0	12.9	3.9	10.3	9.2	1.1
1980	218.7	140.9	43.7	39.1	83.4	70.0	2.6	10.8	13.7	3.6	13.4	11.2	2.0
1981	239.5	155.6	48.5	43.6	92.7	76.5	2.7	13.6	14.5	3.9	15.6	13.2	2.2
1982	247.9	162.3	52.3	47.0	97.0	80.3	2.8	13.9	13.1	4.0	17.5	15.3	2.1
1983	272.9	180.5	58.9	53.2	106.8	90.0	3.0	13.8	14.9	4.1	19.5	17.2	2.2
1984	308.2	205.4	68.2	61.9	119.7	100.9	3.4	15.5	17.4	4.7	22.4	19.8	2.5
1985	333.1	220.9	73.2	66.1	129.0	109.0	3.5	16.5	18.7	4.9	25.9	23.1	2.6
1986	359.3	234.1	78.3	70.7	134.9	115.8	3.6	15.6	20.8	6.0	27.3	24.5	2.7
1987	380.4	253.6	87.5	79.1	144.3	124.6	3.7	16.0	21.8	7.2	28.2	25.5	2.6
1988	408.8	269.5	90.4	81.5	155.2	135.1	3.8	16.3	23.8	8.4	30.5	27.7	2.7
1989	441.4	288.1	102.4	92.9	163.5	142.3	4.3	17.0	22.2	9.0	32.4	29.8	2.4
1990	476.5	305.4	109.6	99.6	175.4	152.5	4.6	18.3	20.4	10.0	33.9	31.3	2.3
1991	512.3	314.1	111.8	101.4	180.8	157.5	4.9	18.3	21.5	11.6	34.4	31.4	2.6
1992	559.7	338.6	120.6	109.0	195.9	169.7	6.1	20.1	22.1	13.1	33.9	30.7	2.7
1993	593.9	356.9	126.3	114.9	206.3	179.4	5.9	21.0	24.3	14.1	32.6	29.5	2.5
1994	630.1	380.2	132.1	120.2	220.8	191.7	7.0	22.1	27.3	14.5	33.8	30.5	2.5
1995	662.8	401.4	140.9	128.4	231.3	200.5	7.2	23.6	29.1	13.6	36.6	33.1	2.6
1996	696.0	425.9	150.9	138.6	245.0	211.8	8.2	25.0	30.0	12.5	39.2	35.1	2.7
1997	731.1	449.0	162.7	149.7	255.4	221.3	8.1	26.0	30.8	10.8	41.6	37.4	2.7
1998	777.5	480.7	180.4	166.8	268.8	233.3	8.5	27.0	31.6	10.4	43.1	39.0	2.4
1999	826.2	508.0	192.5	178.4	283.0	245.9	9.1	27.9	32.5	9.8	46.7	42.4	2.6
2000	884.5	540.7	213.6	199.2	294.8	255.5	7.8	31.6	32.3	11.0	48.7	43.2	3.6
2001	922.0	547.2	219.9	205.5	300.1	259.6	7.9	32.6	27.2	13.6	46.6	41.0	3.7
2002	938.4	536.1	198.5	183.7	308.6	267.3	7.6	33.6	29.0	15.8	42.4	36.7	3.7
2003	990.2	562.6	202.2	186.2	328.6	281.8	9.3	37.5	31.8	19.8	41.6	34.9	4.5
2004	1 066.1	611.3	221.4	204.7	351.1	299.9	8.0	43.2	38.7	24.2	42.3	34.9	4.9
2005	1 144.3	675.3	246.1	228.6	377.1	319.1	8.5	49.5	52.1	25.3	43.6	35.7	5.5

¹ Includes components not shown separately.

Table 6-12. State Government Current Receipts and Expenditures—Continued

(National income and product accounts, calendar years, billions of dollars.)   **NIPA Table 3.20**

Year	Current receipts—Continued					Current expenditures					Net state government saving, NIPA (surplus + / deficit -)		
	Current transfer receipts												
	Total	Federal grants-in-aid	Local grants-in-aid	From business, net	From persons	Total ¹	Consumption expenditures	Government social benefits to persons	Grants-in-aid to local governments	Interest payments	Total	Social insurance funds	Other
1959	3.8	3.4	0.2	0.0	0.1	20.8	8.6	3.6	7.7	0.8	1.0	0.0	1.0
1960	3.9	3.5	0.2	0.0	0.1	22.6	9.3	3.8	8.6	0.9	0.9	0.0	0.9
1961	4.4	4.0	0.3	0.0	0.1	24.5	9.9	4.1	9.4	0.9	0.8	0.0	0.8
1962	4.9	4.4	0.3	0.1	0.2	26.6	10.7	4.4	10.3	1.0	0.9	0.0	0.9
1963	5.4	4.9	0.3	0.1	0.2	28.9	11.6	4.7	11.3	1.1	0.7	0.0	0.6
1964	5.9	5.4	0.3	0.1	0.2	31.4	12.5	5.1	12.4	1.2	0.9	0.0	0.9
1965	6.7	6.1	0.3	0.1	0.3	35.1	13.9	5.5	14.3	1.3	0.6	0.1	0.5
1966	9.6	8.9	0.4	0.1	0.3	40.2	15.6	6.4	16.7	1.4	2.1	0.1	2.0
1967	11.1	10.3	0.5	0.1	0.3	46.4	17.9	7.7	19.1	1.6	0.0	0.1	-0.1
1968	12.6	11.6	0.6	0.1	0.3	53.6	20.2	9.5	22.0	1.8	1.0	0.1	0.9
1969	14.6	13.3	0.8	0.1	0.4	61.4	23.2	10.8	25.4	1.8	1.1	0.2	1.0
1970	17.6	16.2	0.9	0.1	0.4	71.3	26.7	12.9	29.2	2.2	-1.2	0.2	-1.3
1971	21.0	19.4	1.0	0.1	0.4	81.1	29.8	15.3	33.0	2.8	-1.7	0.2	-2.0
1972	27.6	25.8	1.1	0.2	0.5	90.6	32.5	17.5	36.9	3.2	5.8	0.3	5.5
1973	27.9	25.8	1.2	0.2	0.7	101.2	36.5	19.4	41.1	3.6	3.3	0.3	3.0
1974	30.0	27.6	1.3	0.2	0.8	114.3	43.6	19.9	45.9	4.1	-0.8	0.4	-1.1
1975	36.9	33.9	1.7	0.2	1.0	132.3	51.0	24.2	51.4	4.7	-4.9	0.5	-5.4
1976	40.8	37.1	2.3	0.3	1.2	145.1	55.6	26.9	56.2	5.3	-1.8	0.6	-2.4
1977	44.6	40.6	2.4	0.3	1.4	157.4	60.6	29.1	60.7	5.8	2.5	1.0	1.6
1978	49.5	45.2	2.5	0.3	1.5	171.8	64.7	32.0	67.3	6.3	7.5	1.5	6.0
1979	52.4	48.3	2.2	0.4	1.6	191.9	72.0	35.4	75.4	7.3	5.3	1.8	3.6
1980	59.2	54.7	2.3	0.4	1.7	216.5	81.2	41.3	83.8	8.2	2.2	1.3	0.9
1981	62.8	57.7	2.7	0.5	2.0	238.7	89.8	46.7	90.4	9.4	0.8	1.3	-0.5
1982	61.9	56.0	3.1	0.6	2.3	255.9	96.6	51.0	94.5	11.3	-8.0	1.2	-9.2
1983	66.0	58.6	4.2	0.6	2.6	273.7	102.6	55.9	99.0	13.5	-0.8	1.2	-2.0
1984	72.1	63.3	5.0	0.8	3.0	297.3	110.2	59.8	108.7	15.5	10.9	1.4	9.5
1985	76.9	67.3	5.2	0.9	3.6	326.0	121.2	65.2	120.0	16.3	7.1	1.3	5.8
1986	86.7	74.5	5.3	2.8	4.1	350.2	131.3	71.4	128.9	15.0	9.0	1.9	7.2
1987	85.8	74.9	5.5	0.9	4.5	375.2	138.2	77.4	137.8	17.6	5.2	2.2	3.1
1988	93.9	82.1	5.6	1.1	5.2	404.6	148.8	84.4	148.1	18.4	4.3	2.5	1.7
1989	104.6	91.5	5.8	1.3	5.9	437.7	158.1	94.4	159.5	20.6	3.6	2.3	1.3
1990	119.5	104.7	6.2	1.6	6.9	479.6	171.4	111.0	169.4	22.3	-3.1	2.0	-5.1
1991	144.2	124.6	7.6	2.0	10.0	528.4	179.0	137.6	181.9	24.1	-16.1	2.4	-18.5
1992	165.4	141.8	9.0	2.6	12.1	570.4	186.1	159.5	194.8	24.0	-10.7	3.1	-13.8
1993	180.9	155.8	10.1	2.9	12.1	604.3	195.9	173.6	206.0	22.9	-10.4	4.2	-14.6
1994	191.7	164.9	11.0	3.4	12.4	639.5	206.5	184.4	218.9	23.5	-9.4	4.6	-14.0
1995	200.4	173.0	11.1	4.1	12.2	672.6	215.2	194.8	231.6	24.3	-9.8	4.0	-13.9
1996	206.8	177.7	12.0	5.0	12.0	699.4	221.2	202.5	242.4	25.6	-3.4	2.8	-6.2
1997	217.5	184.5	13.5	6.6	13.0	729.1	232.1	206.8	255.1	26.5	2.0	1.2	0.8
1998	231.3	194.9	13.3	9.8	13.2	773.5	249.0	214.6	273.9	27.1	4.0	1.7	2.3
1999	250.0	212.5	12.9	9.9	14.7	837.6	273.3	230.3	297.2	27.6	-11.4	1.7	-13.2
2000	273.4	227.4	14.0	14.7	17.3	898.7	291.5	248.7	319.4	29.3	-14.2	2.0	-16.2
2001	304.2	254.3	14.9	15.5	19.5	977.4	309.0	281.3	337.5	32.2	-55.4	2.6	-58.0
2002	334.3	280.6	15.5	16.3	21.9	1 029.3	326.2	306.6	352.6	32.2	-90.9	1.7	-92.6
2003	356.2	301.9	16.2	15.6	22.5	1 069.0	328.3	325.7	371.4	32.4	-78.8	3.8	-82.6
2004	377.7	321.7	16.6	15.6	23.7	1 130.2	339.1	354.3	390.8	33.9	-64.1	7.5	-71.6
2005	389.5	330.5	17.4	16.4	25.3	1 191.2	359.6	372.6	411.6	34.7	-47.0	7.3	-54.3

¹Includes components not shown separately.

Table 6-13. Local Government Current Receipts and Expenditures

(National income and product accounts, calendar years, billions of dollars.)   **NIPA Table 3.21**

Year	Current receipts Total [1]	Current tax receipts Total	Personal current taxes Total [1]	Personal current taxes Income taxes	Taxes on production and imports Total	Sales taxes	Property taxes	Other	Taxes on corporate income	Contributions for government social insurance	Income receipts on assets Total [1]	Interest receipts	Rents and royalties
1959	26.9	17.1	0.8	0.2	16.4	1.2	14.3	0.9	0.0	. . .	0.7	0.5	0.1
1960	29.9	18.8	0.8	0.3	18.0	1.3	15.7	0.9	0.0	. . .	0.8	0.7	0.1
1961	32.6	20.3	0.9	0.3	19.4	1.4	17.0	1.0	0.0	. . .	0.9	0.7	0.2
1962	35.2	21.8	1.0	0.3	20.8	1.5	18.4	1.0	0.0	. . .	1.0	0.8	0.2
1963	38.2	23.4	1.1	0.4	22.3	1.6	19.7	1.0	0.0	. . .	1.0	0.9	0.2
1964	41.8	25.3	1.2	0.5	24.1	1.9	21.1	1.1	0.0	. . .	1.3	1.1	0.2
1965	45.5	27.0	1.2	0.5	25.7	2.1	22.5	1.1	0.0	. . .	1.4	1.2	0.2
1966	49.9	28.5	1.4	0.6	27.1	2.0	23.8	1.3	0.0	. . .	1.7	1.4	0.3
1967	55.8	31.3	1.6	0.8	29.5	1.9	26.2	1.3	0.2	. . .	2.0	1.6	0.3
1968	61.7	34.8	1.7	0.9	32.8	2.3	29.1	1.4	0.3	. . .	1.7	1.4	0.4
1969	69.2	38.4	2.0	1.1	36.1	2.9	31.9	1.4	0.3	. . .	2.2	1.8	0.4
1970	80.3	43.2	2.3	1.3	40.6	3.5	35.7	1.5	0.2	. . .	2.6	2.2	0.5
1971	89.8	47.9	2.5	1.5	45.2	4.0	39.5	1.8	0.3	. . .	2.8	2.3	0.5
1972	100.5	52.0	3.0	2.0	48.8	4.6	42.2	2.0	0.3	. . .	3.0	2.4	0.6
1973	112.8	56.1	3.0	2.0	52.7	5.2	45.2	2.3	0.3	. . .	3.9	3.3	0.6
1974	122.6	60.2	3.4	2.3	56.4	6.1	47.9	2.4	0.3	. . .	5.2	4.5	0.7
1975	136.5	65.5	3.7	2.5	61.4	7.0	51.9	2.5	0.4	. . .	5.6	4.9	0.7
1976	150.1	71.9	4.1	2.8	67.3	7.9	56.7	2.7	0.5	. . .	5.1	4.4	0.7
1977	164.5	78.6	4.5	3.2	73.6	9.0	61.7	2.9	0.6	. . .	5.6	4.9	0.7
1978	179.6	80.8	4.9	3.4	75.3	10.2	61.8	3.3	0.6	. . .	7.2	6.5	0.7
1979	190.4	83.1	5.1	3.6	77.3	11.5	62.1	3.7	0.6	. . .	9.8	8.9	0.9
1980	207.6	89.1	5.1	3.5	83.3	12.8	66.2	4.2	0.7	. . .	12.9	11.8	1.1
1981	226.1	100.2	6.2	4.3	93.0	14.3	74.4	4.3	1.0	. . .	16.4	15.3	1.1
1982	243.7	110.8	6.9	4.9	103.0	15.9	82.5	4.6	1.0	. . .	19.2	17.8	1.4
1983	261.7	120.4	7.2	5.1	112.1	17.7	88.9	5.5	1.0	. . .	21.9	19.8	2.1
1984	288.9	131.9	7.8	5.6	122.7	20.1	96.3	6.3	1.4	. . .	25.2	22.8	2.4
1985	316.8	142.8	8.2	6.0	133.1	22.1	104.0	7.0	1.5	. . .	29.0	26.2	2.7
1986	340.9	155.4	8.9	6.8	144.7	24.1	112.6	8.1	1.8	. . .	31.1	27.5	3.5
1987	358.5	168.5	9.1	6.8	157.3	25.7	122.7	8.9	2.1	. . .	29.9	27.2	2.7
1988	386.1	183.3	11.7	9.1	169.4	27.2	132.7	9.4	2.2	. . .	30.0	28.3	1.7
1989	417.2	199.9	12.3	9.4	185.6	30.1	145.6	10.0	2.1	. . .	33.3	31.6	1.7
1990	443.3	213.7	12.9	10.0	198.7	31.8	157.0	9.9	2.1	. . .	34.5	32.7	1.8
1991	473.1	230.2	13.5	10.3	214.5	33.2	171.1	10.2	2.2	. . .	33.6	31.6	1.9
1992	496.7	241.2	14.7	11.4	224.2	34.6	178.6	11.0	2.3	. . .	30.9	28.8	2.0
1993	516.1	247.8	14.8	11.3	230.5	37.0	181.3	12.1	2.6	. . .	28.7	26.7	2.1
1994	550.0	264.0	15.9	12.0	245.4	39.7	192.4	13.3	2.7	. . .	29.4	27.4	2.0
1995	577.9	270.7	17.2	13.3	251.0	42.2	195.3	13.4	2.6	. . .	31.8	29.8	2.0
1996	610.4	283.7	17.8	13.7	262.9	44.4	204.2	14.4	3.0	. . .	34.1	32.2	2.0
1997	644.6	300.9	19.3	14.9	278.4	47.4	215.5	15.6	3.3	. . .	36.2	34.2	2.1
1998	682.9	314.2	20.9	16.2	290.0	50.6	222.5	16.9	3.3	. . .	37.8	35.6	2.2
1999	730.9	332.4	21.9	17.1	307.1	55.6	233.7	17.8	3.3	. . .	38.6	36.0	2.5
2000	779.2	352.6	23.1	18.0	326.2	61.1	246.8	18.3	3.3	. . .	43.5	40.8	2.7
2001	814.9	368.6	22.9	17.6	342.7	61.6	261.4	19.8	3.0	. . .	42.1	39.3	2.8
2002	851.9	392.9	22.8	17.1	366.9	62.8	282.6	21.5	3.2	. . .	35.8	32.9	2.9
2003	903.8	416.9	24.5	18.3	388.9	65.9	298.5	24.4	3.5	. . .	31.3	27.9	3.4
2004	946.8	449.5	27.0	20.4	418.2	70.4	321.7	26.1	4.3	. . .	31.0	27.2	3.8
2005	998.9	479.1	29.2	22.3	444.1	75.0	341.9	27.2	5.8	. . .	31.8	27.7	4.1

[1]Includes components not shown separately.
. . . = Not available.

Table 6-13. Local Government Current Receipts and Expenditures—Continued

(National income and product accounts, calendar years, billions of dollars.)

Year	Current receipts—Continued					Current expenditures					Net local government saving, NIPA (surplus + / deficit -)		
	Current transfer receipts												
	Total	Federal grants-in-aid	State grants-in-aid	From business, net	From persons	Total [1]	Consumption expenditures	Government social benefits to persons	Grants-in-aid to state governments	Interest payments	Total	Social insurance funds	Other
1959	8.3	0.4	7.7	0.1	0.1	24.1	22.1	0.7	0.2	1.0	2.8	...	2.8
1960	9.4	0.5	8.6	0.1	0.2	26.4	24.2	0.8	0.2	1.2	3.4	...	3.4
1961	10.4	0.6	9.4	0.2	0.3	29.1	26.6	0.9	0.3	1.3	3.5	...	3.5
1962	11.5	0.6	10.3	0.2	0.3	30.9	28.3	0.9	0.3	1.4	4.3	...	4.3
1963	12.6	0.8	11.3	0.2	0.3	33.2	30.4	1.0	0.3	1.5	5.0	...	5.0
1964	14.0	1.1	12.4	0.2	0.3	36.3	33.3	1.0	0.3	1.7	5.5	...	5.5
1965	15.9	1.1	14.3	0.3	0.3	39.6	36.3	1.1	0.3	1.8	5.9	...	5.9
1966	18.6	1.2	16.7	0.2	0.4	44.2	40.5	1.3	0.4	2.0	5.7	...	5.7
1967	21.6	1.5	19.1	0.4	0.6	48.9	44.7	1.6	0.5	2.1	7.0	...	7.0
1968	24.2	1.1	22.0	0.4	0.7	55.2	50.2	2.0	0.6	2.4	6.5	...	6.5
1969	27.7	1.3	25.4	0.4	0.7	62.4	56.6	2.4	0.8	2.5	6.8	...	6.8
1970	33.6	3.2	29.2	0.4	0.8	72.0	64.9	3.2	0.9	3.1	8.3	...	8.3
1971	38.2	3.8	33.0	0.5	0.9	81.6	72.9	4.0	1.0	3.8	8.2	...	8.2
1972	44.4	5.9	36.9	0.5	1.1	90.6	80.6	4.5	1.1	4.3	9.9	...	9.9
1973	51.8	9.0	41.1	0.7	1.0	100.4	89.5	4.7	1.2	4.9	12.4	...	12.4
1974	56.6	8.7	45.9	0.9	1.1	112.5	100.1	5.4	1.3	5.6	10.1	...	10.1
1975	65.0	11.2	51.4	1.0	1.4	129.1	114.1	6.6	1.7	6.4	7.4	...	7.4
1976	72.6	13.6	56.2	1.1	1.7	140.9	123.9	7.3	2.3	7.2	9.1	...	9.1
1977	79.9	16.0	60.7	1.3	1.9	153.9	135.3	8.0	2.4	7.9	10.6	...	10.6
1978	91.4	20.4	67.3	1.5	2.2	168.5	148.5	8.7	2.5	8.6	11.1	...	11.1
1979	97.8	18.1	75.4	1.8	2.6	182.8	161.3	8.9	2.2	9.9	7.7	...	7.7
1980	106.4	17.6	83.8	2.0	3.0	201.0	177.2	9.9	2.3	11.2	6.6	...	6.6
1981	111.3	14.8	90.4	2.4	3.7	219.4	192.6	10.4	2.7	13.4	6.8	...	6.8
1982	114.8	13.5	94.5	2.7	4.1	237.9	208.2	10.2	3.1	15.8	5.8	...	5.8
1983	119.5	13.0	99.0	3.0	4.5	256.0	221.5	11.0	4.2	18.8	5.7	...	5.7
1984	130.6	13.3	108.7	3.4	5.2	275.9	237.4	11.4	5.0	21.5	13.1	...	13.1
1985	142.7	13.6	120.0	3.5	5.7	301.6	260.6	12.1	5.2	23.0	15.2	...	15.2
1986	152.4	13.2	128.9	3.9	6.5	329.0	286.6	12.9	5.3	23.1	11.9	...	11.9
1987	157.4	9.0	137.8	4.0	6.7	351.3	302.7	13.4	5.5	28.6	7.2	...	7.2
1988	168.8	9.5	148.1	4.3	6.9	372.4	321.5	14.1	5.6	30.0	13.6	...	13.6
1989	178.8	6.8	159.5	5.1	7.5	400.0	344.1	15.0	5.8	34.0	17.2	...	17.2
1990	189.6	6.7	169.4	5.5	8.0	433.0	373.2	16.6	6.2	35.6	10.3	...	10.3
1991	203.5	7.0	181.9	5.9	8.7	461.2	395.6	18.9	7.6	37.7	11.9	...	11.9
1992	218.6	7.4	194.8	6.7	9.8	485.3	416.5	20.5	9.0	37.9	11.4	...	11.4
1993	232.9	7.9	206.0	7.7	11.4	504.7	434.4	21.6	10.1	37.2	11.4	...	11.4
1994	250.2	9.8	218.9	8.6	12.9	530.1	456.8	22.4	11.0	38.6	19.8	...	19.8
1995	266.4	11.1	231.6	9.4	14.3	556.0	480.8	22.9	11.1	39.9	21.9	...	21.9
1996	281.7	13.4	242.4	10.2	15.7	581.3	503.6	21.8	12.0	42.5	29.2	...	29.2
1997	297.7	14.1	255.1	11.1	17.3	607.5	526.8	20.8	13.5	44.9	37.1	...	37.1
1998	322.7	17.8	273.9	12.3	18.7	634.9	552.4	21.1	13.3	46.5	48.0	...	48.0
1999	350.9	20.3	297.2	13.1	20.2	669.1	585.6	22.1	12.9	47.0	61.8	...	61.8
2000	375.4	19.9	319.4	14.2	21.9	715.0	626.3	23.0	14.0	50.2	64.2	...	64.2
2001	399.0	21.7	337.5	15.8	23.9	754.7	660.7	24.0	14.9	53.4	60.2	...	60.2
2002	418.5	23.9	352.6	16.4	25.6	795.2	699.2	25.4	15.5	53.8	56.7	...	56.7
2003	454.0	36.6	371.4	17.9	28.1	845.4	745.5	27.3	16.2	55.3	58.5	...	58.5
2004	467.8	27.3	390.8	19.1	30.6	895.6	791.2	28.7	16.6	57.9	51.2	...	51.2
2005	495.5	30.6	411.6	20.3	33.0	955.2	847.5	29.7	17.4	59.5	43.7	...	43.7

[1]Includes components not shown separately.
... = Not available.

Table 6-14. State Government Consumption Expenditures and Gross Investment by Function

(National income and product accounts, calendar years, billions of dollars.)

Year	Consumption expenditures and gross investment												
	Total [1]	General public service	Public order and safety		Economic affairs		Housing and community services	Health	Education			Income security	
			Total [1]	Prisons	Total [1]	Transportation			Total [1]	Elementary and secondary	Higher	Total [1]	Welfare and social services
1959	15.4	1.2	0.8	0.5	8.7	7.2	0.0	1.8	2.6	0.2	2.1	0.4	0.3
1960	15.5	1.3	0.9	0.5	8.3	6.7	0.0	1.8	2.8	0.2	2.3	0.4	0.3
1961	17.0	1.4	0.9	0.5	9.2	7.4	0.0	2.0	3.2	0.2	2.6	0.3	0.3
1962	18.2	1.4	1.0	0.5	9.8	8.0	0.0	2.0	3.6	0.2	3.0	0.4	0.3
1963	20.1	1.5	1.1	0.6	10.7	8.9	0.0	2.2	4.2	0.2	3.6	0.4	0.3
1964	21.6	1.8	1.2	0.6	11.2	9.1	0.0	2.4	4.7	0.2	4.0	0.4	0.4
1965	23.6	2.0	1.3	0.7	11.9	9.7	0.0	2.5	5.3	0.2	4.4	0.5	0.4
1966	26.6	2.4	1.4	0.7	13.2	10.8	0.0	2.7	6.4	0.3	5.2	0.6	0.5
1967	29.7	2.6	1.6	0.8	14.1	11.3	0.0	3.0	7.6	0.4	6.2	0.7	0.6
1968	32.6	3.1	1.8	0.9	15.1	12.2	0.0	3.3	8.4	0.4	6.7	0.8	0.8
1969	36.2	3.9	2.1	1.0	16.0	12.8	0.0	3.8	9.4	0.4	7.5	1.0	0.9
1970	40.8	4.0	2.4	1.2	17.9	14.4	0.0	4.4	10.8	0.5	8.5	1.2	1.1
1971	44.9	4.4	2.7	1.3	19.3	15.4	0.0	5.0	11.9	0.5	9.3	1.5	1.4
1972	48.1	4.8	3.1	1.5	19.8	15.7	0.0	5.3	13.1	0.5	10.2	1.8	1.7
1973	52.8	5.8	3.5	1.7	20.7	16.3	0.0	5.5	14.7	0.5	11.7	2.4	2.2
1974	61.3	6.9	4.1	2.0	24.2	19.2	0.0	6.5	16.4	0.5	13.0	2.9	2.7
1975	68.9	7.9	4.7	2.3	26.4	20.8	0.3	7.4	18.2	0.7	14.1	3.5	3.3
1976	73.4	8.3	5.2	2.7	26.6	20.3	0.2	8.1	20.2	0.7	15.8	4.1	3.9
1977	77.8	9.0	5.8	3.1	27.1	20.5	0.2	9.0	21.3	0.7	16.7	4.7	4.4
1978	86.1	9.9	6.9	3.6	29.9	22.6	0.3	9.9	22.9	0.9	18.1	5.4	5.1
1979	97.6	11.6	8.2	4.2	34.4	26.3	0.3	11.0	25.3	1.0	20.1	6.0	5.7
1980	110.0	13.6	9.5	4.8	38.6	29.3	0.4	12.7	28.1	1.1	22.4	6.3	6.0
1981	119.1	14.4	10.6	5.5	41.3	31.1	0.3	13.6	31.0	1.2	25.1	7.0	6.6
1982	125.9	15.2	12.1	6.5	42.8	31.9	0.3	14.2	33.1	1.2	27.0	7.4	7.0
1983	133.1	16.9	13.5	7.4	44.7	33.6	0.2	13.9	34.5	1.1	28.4	8.5	8.1
1984	146.3	19.3	15.2	8.4	49.3	37.5	0.2	14.7	37.2	1.2	30.9	9.3	8.8
1985	161.5	21.4	17.5	10.0	53.8	41.2	0.2	16.0	41.2	1.3	34.3	10.1	9.6
1986	174.1	24.0	19.3	11.3	57.6	43.9	0.3	17.0	43.9	1.4	36.6	10.7	10.1
1987	185.4	25.8	21.5	12.7	60.7	46.2	0.5	18.3	45.7	1.5	37.7	11.4	10.7
1988	198.0	26.6	23.9	14.2	64.1	48.7	0.8	19.7	48.8	1.6	40.4	12.5	11.7
1989	210.8	28.6	26.6	16.1	65.4	48.9	1.1	20.7	52.7	1.8	43.4	13.7	12.8
1990	228.8	30.5	30.3	18.6	70.7	52.9	1.4	22.3	56.2	2.0	46.3	15.3	14.2
1991	238.4	31.8	32.5	20.1	72.9	54.4	1.7	22.4	57.9	2.2	47.9	16.9	15.6
1992	246.9	33.0	34.0	21.0	75.6	56.0	1.9	21.7	60.1	2.4	49.6	18.5	17.0
1993	258.9	34.2	36.2	22.6	78.9	58.4	2.0	21.8	63.5	2.4	52.6	20.2	18.5
1994	274.2	36.5	39.4	25.0	82.9	61.9	2.2	21.6	66.7	2.3	55.4	22.6	20.8
1995	287.1	37.4	42.8	27.2	85.9	64.1	2.5	22.0	69.6	2.7	57.3	24.4	22.2
1996	295.8	37.7	45.5	28.8	89.1	67.1	2.3	21.8	71.2	3.0	58.2	25.3	22.9
1997	310.3	40.9	48.5	30.4	93.6	71.1	2.2	20.5	74.5	3.2	61.1	27.1	24.4
1998	323.9	43.4	50.5	31.1	98.0	75.4	2.3	18.9	78.5	3.4	64.3	29.3	26.3
1999	351.4	47.4	55.1	33.7	106.6	82.3	2.6	21.2	83.6	3.6	68.5	31.7	28.8
2000	382.4	52.4	60.3	36.5	113.6	87.2	2.9	24.8	90.8	3.8	74.4	34.3	31.4
2001	410.4	57.0	64.5	38.8	121.5	94.5	2.8	27.0	97.5	4.0	80.1	36.3	33.3

Note: These data have not been updated consistent with recent revisions in the NIPAs and are reprinted as they appeared in the 9th, 10th, and 11th editions of *Business Statistics*.

[1]Includes components not shown separately.

Table 6-15. Local Government Consumption Expenditures and Gross Investment by Function

(National income and product accounts, calendar years, billions of dollars.)

Year	Consumption expenditures and gross investment												
	Total 1	General public service	Public order and safety		Economic affairs		Housing and community services	Health	Education			Income security	
			Total 1	Prisons	Total 1	Transpor-tation			Total 1	Elementary and secondary	Higher	Total	Welfare and social services
1959	29.7	2.3	3.3	0.2	4.6	3.9	2.7	1.3	14.5	14.0	0.3	0.3	0.3
1960	32.4	2.5	3.6	0.3	5.1	4.3	2.7	1.4	16.1	15.5	0.3	0.4	0.4
1961	35.0	2.8	3.8	0.3	5.2	4.4	2.9	1.5	17.6	17.0	0.3	0.4	0.4
1962	37.1	2.9	4.0	0.3	5.4	4.5	3.3	1.5	18.7	18.1	0.3	0.5	0.5
1963	39.8	3.1	4.2	0.3	6.0	4.9	3.0	1.6	20.5	19.7	0.4	0.5	0.5
1964	43.7	3.4	4.5	0.3	6.3	5.0	3.6	1.7	22.7	21.8	0.5	0.6	0.6
1965	48.1	3.8	4.8	0.4	7.1	5.4	3.8	1.8	25.1	24.0	0.6	0.7	0.7
1966	53.3	4.1	5.3	0.4	7.4	6.0	3.9	1.9	28.7	27.3	0.9	0.9	0.9
1967	58.8	4.6	5.8	0.4	8.2	6.5	4.1	2.1	31.7	30.1	1.1	1.0	1.0
1968	66.2	5.5	6.8	0.5	9.0	7.3	5.0	2.4	34.9	33.1	1.2	1.2	1.2
1969	72.2	6.0	7.5	0.5	9.4	7.6	4.9	2.7	38.6	36.5	1.4	1.5	1.5
1970	79.9	6.7	8.5	0.6	9.6	7.7	5.1	3.1	43.2	40.7	1.8	1.8	1.8
1971	88.6	7.6	9.7	0.8	10.0	8.0	5.5	3.7	47.9	45.0	2.1	2.1	2.1
1972	96.3	8.8	10.7	0.9	10.8	8.6	5.6	3.7	52.3	49.0	2.5	2.5	2.5
1973	107.3	10.3	11.9	1.0	11.9	9.5	6.3	4.2	57.6	53.9	2.8	2.7	2.7
1974	122.8	12.2	13.5	1.2	14.3	11.3	7.7	5.0	64.3	60.0	3.3	3.0	3.0
1975	140.1	14.7	15.5	1.4	15.8	12.7	8.6	5.3	73.6	68.6	3.8	3.3	3.3
1976	150.5	16.2	17.0	1.6	16.6	13.0	9.2	5.0	79.7	74.5	4.0	3.5	3.5
1977	161.5	18.1	18.5	1.8	17.7	13.7	9.0	5.5	85.4	79.7	4.4	3.9	3.9
1978	177.7	19.5	20.7	1.9	20.8	15.4	11.0	5.8	91.9	85.9	4.6	4.0	4.0
1979	194.3	20.5	22.6	2.1	23.4	17.3	12.3	5.7	101.1	94.7	4.9	4.4	4.4
1980	214.5	22.1	25.1	2.5	26.1	19.5	14.7	6.4	110.4	103.2	5.5	5.0	5.0
1981	230.5	23.9	28.3	2.8	28.8	21.1	14.5	6.5	117.9	110.1	6.0	5.5	5.5
1982	245.7	25.4	31.5	3.3	30.3	22.6	14.3	6.7	126.0	117.7	6.4	5.9	5.9
1983	258.4	26.9	33.9	3.8	31.3	23.6	13.8	6.4	133.5	125.2	6.1	6.7	6.7
1984	278.1	28.4	36.3	4.3	32.5	24.9	15.4	6.9	145.2	136.6	6.2	7.1	7.1
1985	303.3	31.0	40.1	4.9	35.5	26.4	16.7	7.4	157.7	148.4	6.6	7.8	7.8
1986	329.5	33.8	43.8	5.7	37.7	28.6	18.7	7.4	171.8	161.7	7.3	8.5	8.5
1987	352.1	35.3	47.4	6.6	38.1	30.1	20.7	8.4	184.8	173.9	7.8	9.0	9.0
1988	376.2	37.6	51.0	7.3	39.4	31.5	21.5	9.1	199.1	187.1	8.7	9.6	9.6
1989	406.9	41.0	56.3	8.5	41.6	33.7	22.2	9.9	215.6	202.4	9.5	10.7	10.7
1990	444.2	44.7	61.7	9.6	45.4	37.2	24.1	11.3	234.0	219.7	10.3	12.0	12.0
1991	469.8	47.7	66.3	10.4	47.1	38.8	24.9	11.6	247.8	232.7	10.8	12.9	12.9
1992	489.1	50.2	71.3	11.0	48.2	39.7	25.0	11.8	256.8	242.6	9.8	13.9	13.9
1993	506.8	52.8	74.6	11.4	50.8	42.3	23.6	10.8	267.5	252.4	10.5	14.7	14.7
1994	532.7	56.2	79.4	12.2	53.4	44.8	23.0	10.9	281.8	265.7	11.3	15.3	15.3
1995	563.4	59.3	84.2	12.9	54.8	45.7	24.0	9.7	302.2	285.5	11.6	15.6	15.6
1996	594.6	62.0	90.2	13.8	57.0	48.2	25.5	10.6	318.9	301.7	11.8	16.0	16.0
1997	639.4	70.6	95.7	14.3	63.6	52.5	27.0	10.1	340.5	321.8	12.6	16.5	16.5
1998	675.4	75.4	103.2	15.9	65.7	54.6	25.8	12.0	359.4	339.7	13.3	17.8	17.8
1999	724.6	82.3	109.5	17.0	70.8	58.4	25.4	14.4	385.6	364.8	14.0	19.1	19.1
2000	779.3	89.9	118.5	18.4	76.2	61.3	23.9	16.4	415.1	392.8	15.0	21.1	21.1
2001	819.5	90.5	127.9	19.6	77.4	64.9	25.4	16.9	439.8	416.5	15.6	22.5	22.5

Note: These data have not been updated consistent with recent revisions in the NIPAs and are reprinted as they appeared in the 9th, 10th, and 11th editions of *Business Statistics*.

1Includes components not shown separately.

Section 6c: Federal Government Budget Accounts

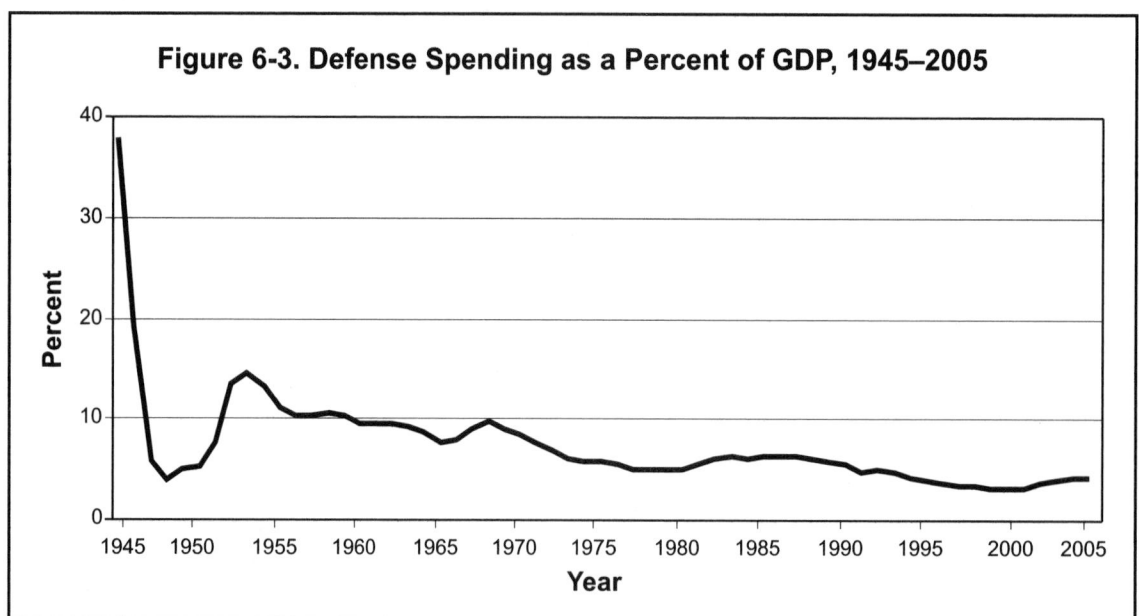

Figure 6-3. Defense Spending as a Percent of GDP, 1945–2005

- From fiscal year 2001 to fiscal year 2005, defense spending increased from 3.0 percent to 4.0 percent of gross domestic product (GDP). This was something like the increase at the beginning of the defense buildup of the 1980s, but less than the increases associated with the Korean and Vietnam Wars. The defense-to-GDP ratio remained low compared with the cold war decades from 1950 through 1990. Defense outlays as defined in the budget data used in this table include both consumption and investment spending and do not include an allowance for the consumption of fixed capital. (Table 6-16)

- After declining between 1993 and 2001, federal debt held by the public as a percent of GDP increased in the subsequent four fiscal years. While the level of this ratio appears low by average postwar standards, its direction of change may be more significant. Notably, although the ratio was over 100 percent in 1945 and 1946, its rapid decline in subsequent years left room for the rapid expansion of private debt that financed the postwar boom. A rising ratio, on the other hand, indicates an increasing federal presence as a credit market borrower, possibly crowding out domestic investment or absorbing increased capital inflows from abroad. (Table 6-17)

- Foreign and international investors bought all of the Treasury debt issued to finance the fiscal year 2004 deficit and four-fifths of the debt issued in fiscal year 2005. At the end of 2005, foreign and international investors held $2.1 trillion of Treasury debt, 45 percent of the $4.6 trillion total debt held by the public. (Table 6-17)

Table 6-16. Federal Government Receipts and Outlays by Fiscal Year [1]

(Budget accounts, millions of dollars.)

Year	Fiscal year GDP	Total receipts, net	Total outlays, net	Budget surplus or deficit (-) Total	On-budget	Off-budget	Borrowing from the public	Other financing	Individual income taxes	Corporate income taxes	Employment taxes and contributions	Unemployment insurance	Other retirement contributions
1939	89 100	6 295	9 141	-2 846	-3 362	516	...	...	1 029	1 127	1 593		
1940	96 800	6 548	9 468	-2 920	-3 484	564	...	...	892	1 197	725	1 015	45
1941	114 100	8 712	13 653	-4 941	-5 594	653	5 451	-510	1 314	2 124	827	1 056	57
1942	144 300	14 634	35 137	-20 503	-21 333	830	19 530	973	3 263	4 719	1 064	1 299	89
1943	180 300	24 001	78 555	-54 554	-55 595	1 041	60 013	-5 459	6 505	9 557	1 338	1 477	229
1944	209 200	43 747	91 304	-47 557	-48 735	1 178	57 030	-9 473	19 705	14 838	1 557	1 644	272
1945	221 400	45 159	92 712	-47 553	-48 720	1 167	50 386	-2 833	18 372	15 988	1 592	1 568	291
1946	222 700	39 296	55 232	-15 936	-16 964	1 028	6 679	9 257	16 098	11 883	1 517	1 316	282
1947	233 200	38 514	34 496	4 018	2 861	1 157	-17 522	13 504	17 935	8 615	1 835	1 329	259
1948	256 000	41 560	29 764	11 796	10 548	1 248	-8 069	-3 727	19 315	9 678	2 168	1 343	239
1949	271 100	39 415	38 835	580	-684	1 263	-1 948	1 368	15 552	11 192	2 246	1 205	330
1950	273 000	39 443	42 562	-3 119	-4 702	1 583	4 701	-1 582	15 755	10 449	2 648	1 332	358
1951	320 600	51 616	45 514	6 102	4 259	1 843	-4 697	-1 405	21 616	14 101	3 688	1 609	377
1952	348 600	66 167	67 686	-1 519	-3 383	1 864	432	1 087	27 934	21 226	4 315	1 712	418
1953	372 900	69 608	76 101	-6 493	-8 259	1 766	3 625	2 868	29 816	21 238	4 722	1 675	423
1954	377 300	69 701	70 855	-1 154	-2 831	1 677	6 116	-4 962	29 542	21 101	5 192	1 561	455
1955	394 600	65 451	68 444	-2 993	-4 091	1 098	2 117	876	28 747	17 861	5 981	1 449	431
1956	427 200	74 587	70 640	3 947	2 494	1 452	-4 460	513	32 188	20 880	7 059	1 690	571
1957	450 300	79 990	76 578	3 412	2 639	773	-2 836	-576	35 620	21 167	7 405	1 950	642
1958	460 500	79 636	82 405	-2 769	-3 315	546	7 016	-4 247	34 724	20 074	8 624	1 933	682
1959	491 500	79 249	92 098	-12 849	-12 149	-700	8 365	4 484	36 719	17 309	8 821	2 131	770
1960	517 900	92 492	92 191	301	510	-209	2 139	-2 440	40 715	21 494	11 248	2 667	768
1961	530 800	94 388	97 723	-3 335	-3 766	431	1 517	1 818	41 338	20 954	12 679	2 903	857
1962	567 600	99 676	106 821	-7 146	-5 881	-1 265	9 653	-2 507	45 571	20 523	12 835	3 337	875
1963	598 700	106 560	111 316	-4 756	-3 966	-789	5 968	-1 212	47 588	21 579	14 746	4 112	946
1964	640 400	112 613	118 528	-5 915	-6 546	632	2 871	3 044	48 697	23 493	16 959	3 997	1 007
1965	687 100	116 817	118 228	-1 411	-1 605	194	3 929	-2 518	48 792	25 461	17 358	3 803	1 081
1966	752 900	130 835	134 532	-3 698	-3 068	-630	2 936	762	55 446	30 073	20 662	3 755	1 129
1967	811 800	148 822	157 464	-8 643	-12 620	3 978	2 912	5 731	61 526	33 971	27 823	3 575	1 221
1968	866 600	152 973	178 134	-25 161	-27 742	2 581	22 919	2 242	68 726	28 665	29 224	3 346	1 354
1969	948 600	186 882	183 640	3 242	-507	3 749	-11 437	8 195	87 249	36 678	34 236	3 328	1 451
1970	1 012 200	192 807	195 649	-2 842	-8 694	5 852	5 090	-2 248	90 412	32 829	39 133	3 464	1 765
1971	1 079 900	187 139	210 172	-23 033	-26 052	3 019	19 839	3 194	86 230	26 785	41 699	3 674	1 952
1972	1 178 300	207 309	230 681	-23 373	-26 068	2 695	19 340	4 033	94 737	32 166	46 120	4 357	2 097
1973	1 307 600	230 799	245 707	-14 908	-15 246	338	18 553	-3 625	103 246	36 153	54 876	6 051	2 187
1974	1 439 300	263 224	269 359	-6 135	-7 198	1 063	2 789	3 346	118 952	38 620	65 888	6 837	2 347
1975	1 560 700	279 090	332 332	-53 242	-54 148	906	51 001	2 241	122 386	40 621	75 199	6 771	2 565
1976	1 736 500	298 060	371 792	-73 732	-69 427	-4 306	82 704	-8 972	131 603	41 409	79 901	8 054	2 814
TQ [1]	456 700	81 232	95 975	-14 744	-14 065	-679	18 105	-3 361	38 801	8 460	21 801	2 698	720
1977	1 974 300	355 559	409 218	-53 659	-49 933	-3 726	53 595	64	157 626	54 892	92 199	11 312	2 974
1978	2 217 000	399 561	458 746	-59 185	-55 416	-3 770	58 022	1 163	180 988	59 952	103 881	13 850	3 237
1979	2 500 700	463 302	504 028	-40 726	-39 633	-1 093	33 180	7 546	217 841	65 677	120 058	15 387	3 494
1980	2 726 700	517 112	590 941	-73 830	-73 141	-689	71 617	2 213	244 069	64 600	138 748	15 336	3 719
1981	3 054 700	599 272	678 241	-78 968	-73 859	-5 109	77 487	1 481	285 917	61 137	162 973	15 763	3 984
1982	3 227 600	617 766	745 743	-127 977	-120 593	-7 384	135 165	-7 188	297 744	49 207	180 686	16 600	4 212
1983	3 440 700	600 562	808 364	-207 802	-207 692	-110	212 693	-4 891	288 938	37 022	185 766	18 799	4 429
1984	3 840 200	666 486	851 853	-185 367	-185 269	-98	169 707	15 660	298 415	56 893	209 658	25 138	4 580
1985	4 141 500	734 088	946 396	-212 308	-221 529	9 222	200 285	12 023	334 531	61 331	234 646	25 758	4 759
1986	4 412 400	769 215	990 441	-221 227	-237 915	16 688	233 363	-12 136	348 959	63 143	255 062	24 098	4 742
1987	4 647 100	854 353	1 004 083	-149 730	-168 357	18 627	149 130	600	392 557	83 926	273 028	25 575	4 715
1988	5 008 600	909 303	1 064 481	-155 178	-192 265	37 087	161 863	-6 685	401 181	94 508	305 093	24 584	4 658
1989	5 400 500	991 190	1 143 829	-152 639	-205 393	52 754	139 100	13 539	445 690	103 291	332 859	22 011	4 546
1990	5 735 400	1 032 094	1 253 130	-221 036	-277 626	56 590	220 842	194	466 884	93 507	353 891	21 635	4 522
1991	5 935 100	1 055 093	1 324 331	-269 238	-321 435	52 198	277 441	-8 203	467 827	98 086	370 526	20 922	4 568
1992	6 239 900	1 091 328	1 381 649	-290 321	-340 408	50 087	310 738	-20 417	475 964	100 270	385 491	23 410	4 788
1993	6 575 500	1 154 471	1 409 522	-255 051	-300 398	45 347	248 659	6 392	509 680	117 520	396 939	26 556	4 805
1994	6 961 300	1 258 721	1 461 907	-203 186	-258 840	55 654	184 669	18 517	543 055	140 385	428 810	28 004	4 661
1995	7 325 800	1 351 932	1 515 884	-163 952	-226 367	62 415	171 313	-7 361	590 244	157 004	451 045	28 878	4 550
1996	7 694 100	1 453 177	1 560 608	-107 431	-174 019	66 588	129 695	-22 264	656 417	171 824	476 361	28 584	4 469
1997	8 182 400	1 579 423	1 601 307	-21 884	-103 248	81 364	38 271	-16 387	737 466	182 293	506 751	28 202	4 418
1998	8 627 900	1 721 955	1 652 685	69 270	-29 925	99 195	-51 245	-18 025	828 586	188 677	540 014	27 484	4 333
1999	9 125 300	1 827 645	1 702 035	125 610	1 920	123 690	-88 736	-36 874	879 480	184 680	580 880	26 480	4 473
2000	9 709 800	2 025 457	1 789 216	236 241	86 422	149 819	-222 559	-13 682	1 004 462	207 289	620 451	27 640	4 761
2001	10 057 900	1 991 426	1 863 190	128 236	-32 445	160 681	-90 189	-38 047	994 339	151 075	661 442	27 812	4 713
2002	10 377 400	1 853 395	2 011 153	-157 758	-317 417	159 659	220 812	-63 054	858 345	148 044	668 547	27 619	4 594
2003	10 805 500	1 782 532	2 160 117	-377 585	-538 418	160 833	373 016	4 569	793 699	131 778	674 981	33 366	4 631
2004	11 546 000	1 880 279	2 293 006	-412 727	-567 961	155 234	382 101	30 626	808 959	189 371	689 360	39 453	4 594
2005	12 290 400	2 153 859	2 472 205	-318 346	-493 611	175 265	296 685	21 661	927 222	278 282	747 664	42 002	4 459

[1] Fiscal years through 1976 are from July 1 through June 30. Beginning with October 1976 (fiscal year 1977), fiscal years are from October 1 through September 30. The period from July 1 through September 30, 1976, is a separate fiscal period known as the transition quarter (TQ) and is not included in any fiscal year.
. . . = Not available.

Table 6-16. Federal Government Receipts and Outlays by Fiscal Year [1]—Continued

(Budget accounts, millions of dollars.)

Year	Receipts by source—Continued				Outlays by function						
	Excise taxes	Estate and gift taxes	Customs deposits	Miscellaneous receipts	National defense	International affairs	General science, space, and technology	Energy	Natural resources and environment	Agriculture	Commerce and housing credit
1939	1 871		...		...	...	...	...	...	...	...
1940	1 977	353	331	14	1 660	51	...	88	997	369	550
1941	2 552	403	365	14	6 435	145	...	91	817	339	398
1942	3 399	420	369	11	25 658	968	4	156	819	344	1 521
1943	4 096	441	308	50	66 699	1 286	1	116	726	343	2 151
1944	4 759	507	417	48	79 143	1 449	48	65	642	1 275	624
1945	6 265	637	341	105	82 965	1 913	111	25	455	1 635	-2 630
1946	6 998	668	424	109	42 681	1 935	34	41	482	610	-1 857
1947	7 211	771	477	84	12 808	5 791	5	18	700	814	-923
1948	7 356	890	403	168	9 105	4 566	1	292	780	69	306
1949	7 502	780	367	241	13 150	6 052	48	341	1 080	1 924	800
1950	7 550	698	407	247	13 724	4 673	55	327	1 308	2 049	1 035
1951	8 648	708	609	261	23 566	3 647	51	383	1 310	-323	1 228
1952	8 852	818	533	359	46 089	2 691	49	474	1 233	176	1 278
1953	9 877	881	596	379	52 802	2 119	49	425	1 289	2 253	910
1954	9 945	934	542	429	49 266	1 596	46	432	1 007	1 817	-184
1955	9 131	924	585	341	42 729	2 223	74	325	940	3 514	92
1956	9 929	1 161	682	427	42 523	2 414	79	174	870	3 486	506
1957	10 534	1 365	735	573	45 430	3 147	122	240	1 098	2 288	1 424
1958	10 638	1 393	782	787	46 815	3 364	141	348	1 407	2 411	930
1959	10 578	1 333	925	662	49 015	3 144	294	382	1 632	4 509	1 933
1960	11 676	1 606	1 105	1 212	48 130	2 988	599	464	1 559	2 623	1 618
1961	11 860	1 896	982	918	49 601	3 184	1 042	510	1 779	2 641	1 203
1962	12 534	2 016	1 142	843	52 345	5 639	1 723	604	2 044	3 562	1 424
1963	13 194	2 167	1 205	1 022	53 400	5 308	3 051	530	2 251	4 384	62
1964	13 731	2 394	1 252	1 086	54 757	4 945	4 897	572	2 364	4 609	418
1965	14 570	2 716	1 442	1 594	50 620	5 273	5 823	699	2 531	3 954	1 157
1966	13 062	3 066	1 767	1 876	58 111	5 580	6 717	612	2 719	2 447	3 245
1967	13 719	2 978	1 901	2 107	71 417	5 566	6 233	782	2 869	2 990	3 979
1968	14 079	3 051	2 038	2 491	81 926	5 301	5 524	1 037	2 988	4 544	4 280
1969	15 222	3 491	2 319	2 909	82 497	4 600	5 020	1 010	2 900	5 826	-119
1970	15 705	3 644	2 430	3 424	81 692	4 330	4 511	997	3 065	5 166	2 112
1971	16 614	3 735	2 591	3 858	78 872	4 159	4 182	1 035	3 915	4 290	2 366
1972	15 477	5 436	3 287	3 632	79 174	4 781	4 175	1 296	4 241	5 227	2 222
1973	16 260	4 917	3 188	3 920	76 681	4 149	4 032	1 237	4 775	4 821	931
1974	16 844	5 035	3 334	5 368	79 347	5 710	3 980	1 303	5 697	2 194	4 705
1975	16 551	4 611	3 676	6 712	86 509	7 097	3 991	2 916	7 346	2 997	9 947
1976	16 963	5 216	4 074	8 027	89 619	6 433	4 373	4 204	8 184	3 109	7 619
TQ [1]	4 473	1 455	1 212	1 611	22 269	2 458	1 162	1 129	2 524	972	931
1977	17 548	7 327	5 150	6 531	97 241	6 353	4 736	5 770	10 032	6 734	3 093
1978	18 376	5 285	6 573	7 419	104 495	7 482	4 926	7 991	10 983	11 301	6 254
1979	18 745	5 411	7 439	9 252	116 342	7 459	5 234	9 179	12 135	11 176	4 686
1980	24 329	6 389	7 174	12 748	133 995	12 714	5 831	10 156	13 858	8 774	9 390
1981	40 839	6 787	8 083	13 790	157 513	13 104	6 468	15 166	13 568	11 241	8 206
1982	36 311	7 991	8 854	16 161	185 309	12 300	7 199	13 527	12 998	15 866	6 256
1983	35 300	6 053	8 655	15 600	209 903	11 848	7 934	9 353	12 672	22 814	6 681
1984	37 361	6 010	11 370	17 060	227 413	15 876	8 317	7 073	12 593	13 526	6 959
1985	35 992	6 422	12 079	18 571	252 748	16 176	8 626	5 608	13 357	25 477	4 337
1986	32 919	6 958	13 327	20 008	273 375	14 152	8 976	4 690	13 639	31 368	5 059
1987	32 457	7 493	15 085	19 518	281 999	11 649	9 215	4 072	13 363	26 513	6 435
1988	35 227	7 594	16 198	20 259	290 361	10 471	10 840	2 296	14 606	17 138	19 164
1989	34 386	8 745	16 334	23 328	303 559	9 585	12 837	2 705	16 182	16 861	29 710
1990	35 345	11 500	16 707	28 103	299 331	13 764	14 443	3 341	17 080	11 806	67 600
1991	42 402	11 138	15 949	23 675	273 292	15 851	16 110	2 436	18 559	15 056	76 271
1992	45 569	11 143	17 359	27 333	298 350	16 107	16 407	4 499	20 025	15 088	10 919
1993	48 057	12 577	18 802	19 535	291 086	17 248	17 029	4 319	20 239	20 246	-21 853
1994	55 225	15 225	20 099	23 258	281 642	17 083	16 226	5 218	21 026	14 915	-4 228
1995	57 484	14 763	19 301	28 663	272 066	16 434	16 723	4 936	21 915	9 672	-17 808
1996	54 014	17 189	18 670	25 649	265 753	13 496	16 708	2 839	21 524	9 036	-10 478
1997	56 924	19 845	17 928	25 596	270 505	15 228	17 173	1 475	21 227	8 890	-14 639
1998	57 673	24 076	18 297	32 815	268 456	13 109	18 217	1 270	22 300	12 078	1 010
1999	70 414	27 782	18 336	35 120	274 873	15 243	18 121	911	23 968	22 880	2 642
2000	68 865	29 010	19 914	43 065	294 495	17 216	18 633	-761	25 031	36 459	3 208
2001	66 232	28 400	19 369	38 044	304 880	16 493	19 784	9	25 623	26 253	5 739
2002	66 989	26 507	18 602	34 148	348 555	22 351	20 767	475	29 454	21 966	-399
2003	67 524	21 959	19 862	34 732	404 920	21 209	20 873	-735	29 703	22 497	735
2004	69 855	24 831	21 083	32 773	455 908	26 891	23 053	-166	30 725	15 440	5 273
2005	73 094	24 764	23 379	32 993	495 335	34 592	23 674	429	28 023	26 566	7 574

[1]Fiscal years through 1976 are from July 1 through June 30. Beginning with October 1976 (fiscal year 1977), fiscal years are from October 1 through September 30. The period from July 1 through September 30, 1976, is a separate fiscal period known as the transition quarter (TQ) and is not included in any fiscal year.
... = Not available.

Table 6-16. Federal Government Receipts and Outlays by Fiscal Year [1]—Continued

(Budget accounts, millions of dollars.)

Year	Outlays by function—Continued										
	Transportation	Community and regional development	Education, employment, and social services	Health	Medicare	Income security	Social Security	Veterans benefits and services	Administration of justice	General government	Net interest
1939	...	...	...	...	...	...	...	...	...	...	...
1940	392	285	1 972	55	...	1 514	28	570	81	274	899
1941	353	123	1 592	60	...	1 855	91	560	92	306	943
1942	1 283	113	1 062	71	...	1 828	137	501	117	397	1 052
1943	3 220	219	375	92	...	1 739	177	276	154	673	1 529
1944	3 901	238	160	174	...	1 503	217	-126	192	900	2 219
1945	3 654	243	134	211	...	1 137	267	110	178	581	3 112
1946	1 970	200	85	201	...	2 384	358	2 465	176	825	4 111
1947	1 130	302	102	177	...	2 820	466	6 344	176	1 114	4 204
1948	787	78	191	162	...	2 499	558	6 457	170	1 045	4 341
1949	916	-33	178	197	...	3 174	657	6 599	184	824	4 523
1950	967	30	241	268	...	4 097	781	8 834	193	986	4 812
1951	956	47	235	323	...	3 352	1 565	5 526	218	1 097	4 665
1952	1 124	73	339	347	...	3 655	2 063	5 341	267	1 163	4 701
1953	1 264	117	441	336	...	3 823	2 717	4 519	243	1 209	5 156
1954	1 229	100	370	307	...	4 434	3 352	4 613	257	799	4 811
1955	1 246	129	445	291	...	5 071	4 427	4 675	256	651	4 850
1956	1 450	92	591	359	...	4 734	5 478	4 891	302	1 201	5 079
1957	1 662	135	590	479	...	5 427	6 661	5 005	303	1 360	5 354
1958	2 334	169	643	541	...	7 535	8 219	5 350	325	655	5 604
1959	3 655	211	789	685	...	8 239	9 737	5 443	356	926	5 762
1960	4 126	224	968	795	...	7 378	11 602	5 441	366	1 184	6 947
1961	3 987	275	1 063	913	...	9 683	12 474	5 705	400	1 354	6 716
1962	4 290	469	1 241	1 198	...	9 207	14 365	5 619	429	1 049	6 889
1963	4 596	574	1 458	1 451	...	9 311	15 788	5 514	465	1 230	7 740
1964	5 242	933	1 555	1 788	...	9 657	16 620	5 675	489	1 518	8 199
1965	5 763	1 114	2 140	1 791	...	9 469	17 460	5 716	536	1 499	8 591
1966	5 730	1 105	4 363	2 543	64	9 678	20 694	5 916	564	1 603	9 386
1967	5 936	1 108	6 453	3 351	2 748	10 261	21 725	6 735	618	1 719	10 268
1968	6 316	1 382	7 634	4 390	4 649	11 816	23 854	7 032	659	1 757	11 090
1969	6 526	1 552	7 548	5 162	5 695	13 076	27 298	7 631	766	1 939	12 699
1970	7 008	2 392	8 634	5 907	6 213	15 655	30 270	8 669	959	2 320	14 380
1971	8 052	2 917	9 849	6 843	6 622	22 946	35 872	9 768	1 307	2 442	14 841
1972	8 392	3 423	12 529	8 674	7 479	27 650	40 157	10 720	1 684	2 960	15 478
1973	9 066	4 605	12 745	9 356	8 052	28 276	49 090	12 003	2 174	9 774	17 349
1974	9 172	4 229	12 457	10 733	9 639	33 713	55 867	13 374	2 505	10 032	21 449
1975	10 918	4 322	16 022	12 930	12 875	50 176	64 658	16 584	3 028	10 374	23 244
1976	13 739	5 442	18 910	15 734	15 834	60 799	73 899	18 419	3 430	9 706	26 727
TQ [1]	3 358	1 569	5 169	3 924	4 264	14 985	19 763	3 960	918	3 878	6 949
1977	14 829	7 021	21 104	17 302	19 345	61 060	85 061	18 022	3 701	12 791	29 901
1978	15 521	11 841	26 710	18 524	22 768	61 505	93 861	18 961	3 923	11 961	35 458
1979	18 079	10 480	30 223	20 494	26 495	66 376	104 073	19 914	4 286	12 241	42 633
1980	21 329	11 252	31 843	23 169	32 090	86 557	118 547	21 169	4 702	12 975	52 533
1981	23 379	10 568	33 151	26 866	39 149	100 299	139 584	22 973	4 908	11 374	68 766
1982	20 625	8 347	26 611	27 445	46 567	108 155	155 964	23 938	4 842	10 861	85 032
1983	21 334	7 564	26 196	28 641	52 588	123 031	170 724	24 824	5 246	11 182	89 808
1984	23 669	7 673	26 921	30 417	57 540	113 352	178 223	25 588	5 811	11 758	111 102
1985	25 838	7 680	28 593	33 542	65 822	128 979	188 623	26 262	6 426	11 521	129 478
1986	28 117	7 233	29 777	35 936	70 164	120 633	198 757	26 327	6 735	12 495	136 017
1987	26 222	5 051	28 922	39 967	75 120	124 088	207 353	26 750	7 715	7 494	138 611
1988	27 272	5 294	30 933	44 487	78 878	130 377	219 341	29 386	9 397	9 404	151 803
1989	27 608	5 362	35 330	48 390	84 964	137 426	232 542	30 031	9 644	9 323	168 981
1990	29 485	8 531	37 176	57 716	98 102	148 668	248 623	29 058	10 185	10 490	184 347
1991	31 099	6 810	41 234	71 183	104 489	172 462	269 015	31 305	12 487	11 582	194 448
1992	33 332	6 836	42 743	89 497	119 024	199 562	287 585	34 064	14 650	12 896	199 344
1993	35 004	9 146	47 376	99 415	130 552	209 969	304 585	35 671	15 193	12 968	198 713
1994	38 066	10 620	43 277	107 122	144 747	217 166	319 565	37 584	15 516	11 200	202 932
1995	39 350	10 746	51 020	115 418	159 855	223 799	335 846	37 890	16 509	13 834	232 134
1996	39 565	10 741	48 310	119 378	174 225	229 736	349 671	36 985	17 898	11 788	241 053
1997	40 767	11 049	48 961	123 843	190 016	235 032	365 251	39 313	20 618	12 587	243 984
1998	40 343	9 771	50 503	131 442	192 822	237 750	379 215	41 781	23 360	15 334	241 118
1999	42 532	11 865	50 591	141 074	190 447	242 478	390 037	43 212	26 536	15 315	229 755
2000	46 853	10 623	53 754	154 533	197 113	253 724	409 423	47 083	28 499	12 962	222 949
2001	54 447	11 773	57 143	172 270	217 384	269 774	432 958	45 039	30 202	14 263	206 167
2002	61 833	12 981	70 544	196 544	230 855	312 720	455 980	50 984	35 061	16 925	170 949
2003	67 069	18 850	82 568	219 576	249 433	334 632	474 680	57 022	35 340	23 054	153 073
2004	64 627	15 822	87 948	240 134	269 360	333 059	495 548	59 779	45 576	22 321	160 245
2005	67 894	26 264	97 526	250 612	298 638	345 847	523 305	70 151	40 019	16 994	183 986

[1]Fiscal years through 1976 are from July 1 through June 30. Beginning with October 1976 (fiscal year 1977), fiscal years are from October 1 through September 30. The period from July 1 through September 30, 1976, is a separate fiscal period known as the transition quarter (TQ) and is not included in any fiscal year.
. . . = Not available.

Table 6-17. Federal Government Debt by Fiscal Year [1]

(Billions of dollars, except as noted.)

Year	Federal government debt held by the public at end of fiscal year		Gross federal debt at end of fiscal year held by:						
	Debt held by the public	Debt/GDP ratio (percent)	Total	Social Security funds	Other U.S. government accounts	Federal Reserve System	Private investors		
							Total	Foreign and international investors	Domestic investors
1945	235	106.2	260	7	18	22	213	. . .	. . .
1946	242	108.6	271	8	21	24	218	. . .	. . .
1947	224	96.2	257	9	24	22	202	. . .	. . .
1948	216	84.5	252	10	26	21	195	. . .	. . .
1949	214	79.1	253	11	27	19	195	. . .	. . .
1950	219	80.2	257	13	25	18	201	. . .	. . .
1951	214	66.9	255	15	26	23	191	. . .	. . .
1952	215	61.6	259	17	28	23	192	. . .	. . .
1953	218	58.6	266	18	29	25	194	. . .	. . .
1954	224	59.5	271	20	26	25	199	. . .	. . .
1955	227	57.4	274	21	27	24	203	. . .	. . .
1956	222	52.0	273	23	28	24	198	. . .	. . .
1957	219	48.7	272	23	30	23	196	. . .	. . .
1958	226	49.2	280	24	29	25	201	. . .	. . .
1959	235	47.8	287	23	30	26	209	. . .	. . .
1960	237	45.7	291	23	31	27	210	. . .	. . .
1961	238	44.9	293	23	31	27	211	. . .	. . .
1962	248	43.7	303	22	33	30	218	. . .	. . .
1963	254	42.4	310	21	35	32	222	. . .	. . .
1964	257	40.1	316	22	37	35	222	. . .	. . .
1965	261	38.0	322	22	39	39	222	12	209
1966	264	35.0	328	22	43	42	222	12	210
1967	267	32.8	340	26	48	47	220	11	209
1968	290	33.4	369	28	51	52	237	11	227
1969	278	29.3	366	32	56	54	224	10	214
1970	283	28.0	381	38	60	58	225	14	211
1971	303	28.1	408	41	64	66	238	32	206
1972	322	27.4	436	44	70	71	251	49	202
1973	341	26.1	466	44	81	75	266	59	206
1974	344	23.9	484	46	94	81	263	57	206
1975	395	25.3	542	48	99	85	310	66	244
1976	477	27.5	629	45	107	95	383	70	313
TQ [1]	496	27.1	644	44	105	97	399	75	324
1977	549	27.8	706	40	118	105	444	96	349
1978	607	27.4	777	35	134	115	492	121	371
1979	640	25.6	829	33	156	116	525	120	404
1980	712	26.1	909	32	165	121	591	122	469
1981	789	25.8	995	27	178	124	665	131	534
1982	925	28.6	1 137	19	193	134	790	141	649
1983	1 137	33.1	1 372	32	202	156	982	160	822
1984	1 307	34.0	1 565	32	225	155	1 152	176	976
1985	1 507	36.4	1 817	40	270	170	1 337	223	1 115
1986	1 741	39.4	2 121	46	334	191	1 550	266	1 284
1987	1 890	40.7	2 346	65	391	212	1 678	280	1 398
1988	2 052	41.0	2 601	104	445	229	1 822	346	1 476
1989	2 191	40.6	2 868	157	520	220	1 971	395	1 576
1990	2 412	42.0	3 206	215	580	234	2 177	440	1 737
1991	2 689	45.3	3 598	268	641	259	2 430	477	1 953
1992	3 000	48.1	4 002	319	683	296	2 703	535	2 168
1993	3 248	49.4	4 351	366	737	326	2 923	591	2 331
1994	3 433	49.3	4 643	423	788	355	3 078	656	2 422
1995	3 604	49.2	4 921	483	833	374	3 230	800	2 430
1996	3 734	48.5	5 181	550	898	391	3 343	978	2 365
1997	3 772	46.1	5 369	631	966	425	3 348	1 218	2 130
1998	3 721	43.1	5 478	730	1 027	458	3 263	1 217	2 046
1999	3 632	39.8	5 606	855	1 118	497	3 136	1 281	1 854
2000	3 410	35.1	5 629	1 007	1 212	511	2 898	1 058	1 840
2001	3 320	33.0	5 770	1 170	1 280	534	2 785	1 006	1 780
2002	3 540	34.1	6 198	1 329	1 329	604	2 936	1 201	1 735
2003	3 913	36.2	6 760	1 485	1 362	656	3 257	1 454	1 803
2004	4 296	37.2	7 355	1 635	1 424	700	3 595	1 837	1 759
2005	4 592	37.4	7 905	1 809	1 504	736	3 856	2 070	1 786

[1]Fiscal years through 1976 are from July 1 through June 30. Beginning with October 1976 (fiscal year 1977), fiscal years are from October 1 through September 30. The period from July 1 through September 30, 1976, is a separate fiscal period known as the transition quarter (TQ) and is not included in any fiscal year.
. . . = Not available.

Section 6d: Government Output and Employment

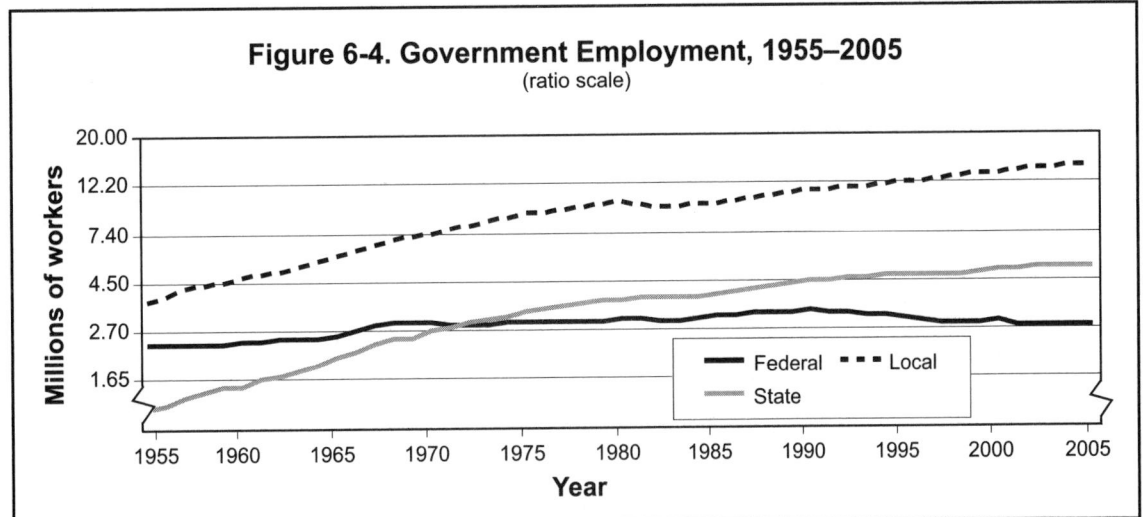

Figure 6-4. Government Employment, 1955–2005
(ratio scale)

- Since 1955, total reported employment of civilians by all levels of government has increased 211 percent—an annual rate of 2.3 percent per year—and its proportion of total payroll employment has risen from 13.8 percent to 16.3 percent. Federal employment rose 19 percent; state government employment rose 330 percent, with half of this increase due to education; and local government rose 319 percent, with 58 percent of this increase due to education. (Tables 6-19 and 10-7)

- Reported Department of Defense civilian employment has not increased in recent years, even as defense spending has been rising both absolutely and as a percentage of gross domestic product (GDP). It should be noted that the figures shown here are for civilian employees only, as compiled by the Bureau of Labor Statistics, and exclude the active-duty armed forces, defense contractors, and employees of the Central Intelligence Agency and the National Security Agency. (Table 6-19 and its notes and definitions)

- The real gross output of the federal government increased 123 percent from 1955 to 2004, with nondefense activity rising 253 percent and defense output rising 42 percent. The volume of intermediate goods and services purchased for nondefense purposes rose far faster than nondefense value added by government itself (where value added comprises the input of government employees and government-owned capital). For defense, government value added actually declined over that period, while purchases of intermediate goods and services rose 198 percent. (Table 6-18)

- Real gross output of state and local governments rose 463 percent over the same period, with value added rising 321 percent and goods and services purchased rising 1,112 percent. (Table 6-18)

Table 6-18. Chain-Type Quantity Indexes for Government Output

(Index numbers, 2000 = 100.)

NIPA Table 3.10.3

Year and quarter	Federal government									State and local government		
	Gross output of general government			Value added			Intermediate goods and services purchased [1]			Gross output of general government	Value added	Intermediate goods and services purchased [1]
	Total	Defense	Nondefense	Total	Defense	Nondefense	Total	Defense	Nondefense			
1950	39.7	48.1	26.2	66.6	78.6	47.2	15.7	19.4	10.2	16.5	21.0	8.7
1951	60.0	82.6	21.9	87.6	112.1	44.1	32.7	50.9	6.1	16.4	21.5	8.1
1952	75.7	105.4	25.6	97.6	127.8	43.3	50.2	76.6	11.7	16.7	22.2	7.9
1953	81.4	110.2	32.8	98.0	130.0	40.2	58.9	82.8	23.6	17.3	23.2	7.9
1954	72.1	96.0	31.8	95.5	127.1	38.5	46.0	61.4	23.1	18.0	24.2	8.2
1955	69.0	90.3	32.9	93.3	123.5	38.8	42.6	54.7	24.5	19.3	25.3	9.3
1956	67.0	90.3	27.5	92.3	121.6	39.5	40.2	56.2	16.1	20.0	26.9	9.0
1957	71.1	96.6	27.8	92.0	120.7	40.4	47.1	67.5	16.1	21.0	28.4	9.4
1958	69.7	94.8	27.3	89.4	116.1	41.5	46.8	68.1	14.4	22.7	30.1	10.8
1959	69.2	87.1	38.9	88.6	114.9	41.5	46.6	55.3	33.1	23.8	31.4	11.6
1960	68.1	88.2	33.9	90.3	115.9	44.4	43.1	56.4	22.6	25.1	33.0	12.2
1961	69.3	90.2	33.6	92.1	118.2	45.5	43.6	58.0	21.3	26.5	34.8	13.1
1962	75.8	96.5	40.5	95.9	122.8	47.9	52.0	65.5	31.2	27.5	36.0	13.6
1963	77.8	97.4	44.2	96.8	122.4	51.0	54.8	67.5	35.3	29.0	37.9	14.5
1964	77.3	95.0	46.9	97.7	122.9	52.7	53.0	62.4	38.5	31.0	40.2	15.8
1965	78.4	95.6	48.8	98.4	122.9	54.5	54.4	63.5	40.4	33.1	42.6	17.4
1966	87.2	109.5	49.1	104.9	131.4	57.5	65.1	82.5	38.4	35.3	45.2	18.8
1967	96.4	122.6	51.6	111.7	140.2	60.7	76.0	99.5	40.1	37.0	47.1	20.3
1968	99.5	127.6	51.9	113.5	142.1	62.5	80.2	107.3	39.0	39.6	49.9	22.3
1969	97.4	122.6	54.4	113.8	142.1	63.3	75.7	97.2	42.8	42.0	52.2	24.7
1970	90.4	111.5	54.2	109.0	133.9	64.2	66.8	83.1	41.6	44.4	54.5	27.2
1971	85.9	102.8	56.7	103.9	125.0	66.1	63.1	74.9	44.5	46.8	56.7	29.7
1972	84.2	97.1	61.5	98.9	116.1	67.8	65.4	73.3	52.3	48.7	58.6	31.5
1973	79.7	90.6	60.5	95.2	110.3	68.1	59.9	65.7	50.1	50.4	60.7	32.6
1974	79.2	88.0	63.6	94.9	108.1	71.2	59.2	62.6	53.2	52.4	62.9	34.4
1975	78.2	85.4	65.5	94.3	106.6	72.4	57.6	58.6	55.6	54.7	64.8	37.1
1976	77.0	83.3	65.8	94.5	105.0	75.8	54.9	56.0	52.7	55.6	65.7	38.2
1977	78.8	84.3	69.0	94.7	104.4	77.6	58.5	58.9	57.4	56.7	66.7	39.3
1978	80.5	85.2	72.2	95.9	105.1	79.8	60.9	60.1	61.5	58.0	68.2	40.3
1979	81.9	86.3	74.0	95.8	104.7	80.2	63.9	62.9	64.9	58.8	69.4	40.3
1980	85.2	89.8	77.0	97.4	105.7	82.7	69.1	69.3	68.2	58.8	70.4	39.0
1981	88.7	94.9	77.6	98.9	108.8	81.3	74.9	76.7	71.0	58.9	70.3	39.3
1982	91.6	101.3	74.1	100.5	111.6	80.6	79.2	87.2	64.4	59.9	70.8	41.0
1983	95.9	106.4	77.1	102.8	114.2	82.5	85.8	95.0	68.7	60.8	70.5	43.6
1984	97.2	109.7	74.6	105.1	117.2	83.6	85.9	98.8	62.2	61.8	70.9	45.4
1985	103.0	116.3	78.8	108.1	121.1	84.8	95.0	108.8	69.7	64.8	73.0	50.1
1986	107.4	121.6	81.8	110.0	124.0	84.7	102.8	117.2	76.0	68.7	75.1	56.7
1987	110.1	126.1	80.9	112.9	127.2	86.9	105.2	123.6	71.6	69.6	76.5	56.6
1988	110.0	127.7	77.6	114.3	128.0	89.7	102.9	126.1	60.9	71.8	79.1	58.1
1989	111.6	126.7	83.9	115.7	129.4	91.0	104.8	121.8	73.7	74.0	81.6	59.9
1990	113.3	126.2	90.1	117.8	130.2	95.7	106.1	119.4	81.8	76.2	84.0	61.8
1991	113.8	126.0	91.8	118.5	130.9	96.4	106.2	118.0	84.7	78.0	85.1	64.7
1992	111.3	119.7	96.4	116.0	126.0	98.5	103.8	109.8	92.7	80.1	86.5	68.1
1993	107.4	114.7	94.5	113.8	122.3	99.0	97.4	103.0	87.3	82.1	87.7	71.4
1994	104.8	110.2	95.2	110.1	117.5	97.1	96.4	98.8	92.0	84.3	89.2	74.9
1995	101.2	105.5	93.7	106.0	112.6	94.4	93.7	94.5	92.3	86.4	91.0	77.7
1996	99.4	103.8	91.6	103.0	108.8	93.0	93.5	95.9	89.2	88.0	92.4	79.5
1997	99.1	102.3	93.5	101.1	105.6	93.4	95.8	97.0	93.7	90.6	94.3	83.4
1998	97.3	99.6	93.2	100.0	102.7	95.1	92.9	94.6	90.0	94.1	96.2	90.0
1999	98.5	101.0	94.1	99.1	100.7	96.5	97.4	101.4	90.2	97.5	97.9	96.6
2000	100.0	100.0	100.0	100.0	100.0	100.0	100.0	100.0	100.0	100.0	100.0	100.0
2001	103.8	104.0	103.6	100.5	100.5	100.7	109.3	109.6	108.7	103.5	102.4	105.5
2002	110.5	111.1	109.5	102.5	102.3	102.8	123.8	125.3	121.0	106.6	104.4	110.8
2003	118.0	120.6	113.4	105.3	105.2	105.3	139.6	146.1	127.6	106.5	105.0	109.3
2004	122.7	127.0	115.0	106.3	107.1	104.7	150.7	160.2	133.1	107.5	105.5	111.5
2005	124.1	128.6	116.0	106.9	108.0	105.0	153.4	163.1	135.4	108.6	106.5	112.7
2003												
1st quarter	113.9	114.0	113.9	104.6	104.2	105.2	129.5	129.8	129.0	106.6	105.0	109.8
2nd quarter	119.4	123.7	111.6	105.4	105.4	105.6	143.0	154.3	122.1	106.4	105.0	109.2
3rd quarter	119.0	121.3	114.9	105.5	105.6	105.3	141.9	147.4	131.7	106.4	105.0	109.1
4th quarter	119.8	123.4	113.3	105.5	105.7	105.1	144.0	152.8	127.6	106.5	105.1	109.3
2004												
1st quarter	122.2	126.4	114.6	106.0	106.7	104.6	149.8	159.4	132.1	107.0	105.1	110.7
2nd quarter	122.4	126.5	115.0	105.8	106.5	104.7	150.6	160.1	133.2	107.4	105.3	111.5
3rd quarter	124.1	129.4	114.8	106.3	107.4	104.3	154.7	166.3	133.2	107.6	105.5	111.8
4th quarter	122.0	125.6	115.5	107.0	108.0	105.2	147.5	154.9	133.7	108.1	106.0	112.0
2005												
1st quarter	123.6	127.7	116.4	107.1	108.2	105.3	151.8	160.4	135.9	108.2	106.1	112.2
2nd quarter	123.0	127.9	114.3	106.8	107.9	105.0	150.6	161.5	130.6	108.4	106.4	112.4
3rd quarter	125.9	131.4	116.1	106.7	108.0	104.5	158.9	170.9	136.6	108.8	106.7	112.7
4th quarter	123.7	127.4	117.1	107.1	108.2	105.2	152.1	159.6	138.3	109.1	106.9	113.4

[1] Includes general government intermediate inputs for goods and services sold to other sectors and for own-account investment.

Table 6-19. Government Employment

(Calendar years; payroll employment, thousands, seasonally adjusted, except as noted.)

Year and month	Total government employment	Federal			State			Local		
		Total	Department of Defense (not seasonally adjusted)	Postal Service	Total	Education	State government hospitals (not seasonally adjusted)	Total	Education	Local government hospitals (not seasonally adjusted)
1950	6 120	2 023	533	516	. . .	. . .	. . .	. . .	. . .	. . .
1951	6 502	2 415	797	521	. . .	. . .	. . .	. . .	. . .	. . .
1952	6 727	2 539	868	542	. . .	. . .	. . .	. . .	. . .	. . .
1953	6 758	2 418	818	530	. . .	. . .	. . .	. . .	. . .	. . .
1954	6 858	2 295	744	533	. . .	. . .	. . .	. . .	. . .	. . .
1955	7 021	2 295	744	534	1 168	308	. . .	3 558	1 751	. . .
1956	7 386	2 318	749	539	1 249	334	. . .	3 819	1 884	. . .
1957	7 724	2 326	729	555	1 328	363	. . .	4 071	2 026	. . .
1958	7 946	2 298	695	567	1 415	389	. . .	4 232	2 115	. . .
1959	8 192	2 342	699	578	1 484	420	. . .	4 366	2 198	. . .
1960	8 464	2 381	681	591	1 536	448	. . .	4 547	2 314	. . .
1961	8 706	2 391	683	601	1 607	474	. . .	4 708	2 411	. . .
1962	9 004	2 455	697	601	1 669	511	. . .	4 881	2 522	. . .
1963	9 341	2 473	687	603	1 747	557	. . .	5 121	2 674	. . .
1964	9 711	2 463	676	604	1 856	609	. . .	5 392	2 839	. . .
1965	10 191	2 495	679	619	1 996	679	. . .	5 700	3 031	. . .
1966	10 910	2 690	741	686	2 141	775	. . .	6 080	3 297	. . .
1967	11 525	2 852	802	719	2 302	873	. . .	6 371	3 490	. . .
1968	11 972	2 871	801	729	2 442	958	. . .	6 660	3 649	. . .
1969	12 330	2 893	815	737	2 533	1 042	. . .	6 904	3 785	. . .
1970	12 687	2 865	756	741	2 664	1 104	. . .	7 158	3 912	. . .
1971	13 012	2 828	731	731	2 747	1 149	. . .	7 437	4 091	. . .
1972	13 465	2 815	720	703	2 859	1 188	459	7 790	4 262	467
1973	13 862	2 794	696	698	2 923	1 205	472	8 146	4 433	477
1974	14 303	2 858	698	710	3 039	1 267	483	8 407	4 584	483
1975	14 820	2 882	704	699	3 179	1 323	503	8 758	4 722	489
1976	15 001	2 863	693	676	3 273	1 371	518	8 865	4 786	492
1977	15 258	2 859	676	657	3 377	1 385	538	9 023	4 859	494
1978	15 812	2 893	661	660	3 474	1 367	541	9 446	4 958	535
1979	16 068	2 894	649	673	3 541	1 378	538	9 633	4 989	571
1980	16 375	3 000	645	673	3 610	1 398	530	9 765	5 090	604
1981	16 180	2 922	655	675	3 640	1 420	515	9 619	5 095	622
1982	15 982	2 884	690	684	3 640	1 433	494	9 458	5 049	635
1983	16 011	2 915	699	685	3 662	1 450	471	9 434	5 020	644
1984	16 159	2 943	716	706	3 734	1 488	459	9 482	5 076	623
1985	16 533	3 014	738	750	3 832	1 540	449	9 687	5 221	608
1986	16 838	3 044	736	792	3 893	1 561	438	9 901	5 358	601
1987	17 156	3 089	736	815	3 967	1 586	439	10 100	5 469	606
1988	17 540	3 124	719	835	4 076	1 621	446	10 339	5 590	619
1989	17 927	3 136	735	838	4 182	1 668	442	10 609	5 740	632
1990	18 415	3 196	722	825	4 305	1 730	426	10 914	5 902	646
1991	18 545	3 110	702	813	4 355	1 768	417	11 081	5 994	653
1992	18 787	3 111	702	800	4 408	1 799	419	11 267	6 076	665
1993	18 989	3 063	670	793	4 488	1 834	414	11 438	6 206	673
1994	19 275	3 018	657	821	4 576	1 882	407	11 682	6 329	673
1995	19 432	2 949	627	850	4 635	1 919	395	11 849	6 453	669
1996	19 539	2 877	597	867	4 606	1 911	376	12 056	6 592	648
1997	19 664	2 806	588	866	4 582	1 904	360	12 276	6 759	632
1998	19 909	2 772	550	881	4 612	1 922	346	12 525	6 921	630
1999	20 307	2 769	525	890	4 709	1 983	344	12 829	7 120	626
2000	20 790	2 865	510	880	4 786	2 031	343	13 139	7 294	622
2001	21 118	2 764	504	873	4 905	2 113	345	13 449	7 479	628
2002	21 513	2 766	499	842	5 029	2 243	349	13 718	7 654	642
2003	21 583	2 761	486	809	5 002	2 255	348	13 820	7 709	651
2004	21 621	2 730	473	782	4 982	2 238	348	13 909	7 765	656
2005	21 803	2 724	485	773	5 021	2 250	348	14 058	7 864	665
2005										
January	21 715	2 721	479	775	5 013	2 248	347	13 981	7 816	659
February	21 741	2 727	480	775	5 016	2 249	347	13 998	7 830	658
March	21 747	2 730	482	774	5 015	2 247	347	14 002	7 829	659
April	21 768	2 729	482	774	5 018	2 247	346	14 021	7 839	660
May	21 773	2 725	483	775	5 017	2 247	346	14 031	7 842	661
June	21 786	2 727	489	776	5 016	2 244	348	14 043	7 851	665
July	21 822	2 726	490	776	5 023	2 249	349	14 073	7 878	668
August	21 851	2 725	489	775	5 024	2 252	347	14 102	7 901	668
September	21 855	2 725	485	775	5 026	2 255	347	14 104	7 892	667
October	21 852	2 724	486	774	5 022	2 248	347	14 106	7 895	672
November	21 880	2 728	486	775	5 032	2 257	349	14 120	7 899	674
December	21 878	2 713	485	772	5 036	2 258	350	14 129	7 907	675

. . . = Not available.

NOTES AND DEFINITIONS

TABLES 6-1 THROUGH 6-11, 6-18, 19-10, AND 19-11 FEDERAL, STATE, AND LOCAL GOVERNMENT IN THE NATIONAL INCOME AND PRODUCT ACCOUNTS

SOURCE: U.S. DEPARTMENT OF COMMERCE, BUREAU OF ECONOMIC ANALYSIS (BEA)

These data are from the national income and product accounts (NIPAs), as published in the 2003 comprehensive NIPA revisions and as revised and updated through August 2006. For general information about the NIPAs and the 2003 revision, see the notes and definitions for Tables 1-1 through 1-7.

A new framework for the government accounts

In the 2003 revision, a new framework is used for government consumption expenditures—federal, state, and local—that explicitly recognizes the services produced by general government. Governments serve several functions in the economy. The functions recognized in the NIPAs are the production of nonmarket services; the consumption of these services, in that the value of the services provided to the general public is treated as government consumption expenditures; and the provision of transfer payments. These functions are financed through taxation, through contributions to social insurance funds, and in the world's capital markets.

In the new framework, the value of the government services produced and consumed (most of which are not sold in the market) is measured as the sum of the costs of the three major inputs: compensation of government employees, consumption of fixed capital (CFC), and intermediate goods and services purchased. The purchase from the private sector of goods and services by government, classified as final sales to government before the 2003 revision, is reclassified as intermediate purchases.

The value of government final purchases of consumption expenditures and gross investment, which constitutes the contribution of government demand to the gross domestic product (GDP), is not changed by this reclassification. It was previously defined as the sum of compensation, CFC, and goods and services purchased. However, the distribution of GDP by type of product is changed—final sales of goods are reduced by the amount of goods purchased by government, and services are increased by the same amount.

In addition to this change in the conceptual framework, a number of the categories of government receipts and expenditures have been redefined to make more precise distinctions. For example, items that used to be called "nontax payments" and included with taxes are now classified as transfer or fee payments and not included in taxes.

Finally, the concept previously known as "current surplus or deficit (-), national income and product accounts" has been renamed "net government saving." This recognizes, in part, the role of government in the capital markets. When government runs a current surplus, net government saving is positive and funds are made available (for example, by repayment of outstanding debt) to finance investment—both private-sector capital spending and government investment. When government runs a current deficit, or "dis-saves," it must borrow funds that would otherwise be available to finance investment.

However, net government saving does not give a complete picture of governments' role in capital markets, because it is based on current receipts and expenditures alone and does not include government investment activity.

The federal *budget* accounts (see Tables 6-16 and 6-17) do not draw a distinction between current and capital spending. The accounts of individual state and local governments typically separate capital from current spending and allow capital spending to be financed by borrowing—even when deficit financing of current spending is constitutionally forbidden. However, neither federal nor state and local government budget accounts typically show depreciation as a current expense in the way that is standard to private-sector accounting.

In the NIPAs, the capital spending of all levels of government is treated the same way as private investment spending. A depreciation entry for existing capital (CFC) is calculated, using estimated replacement costs and realistic depreciation rates, and entered as one element of government current expenditures and output. Capital spending is excluded from current expenditures but appears in the account for "net lending or borrowing (-)."

"Net lending or borrowing (-)" is shown along with its derivation in *Business Statistics* in Tables 6-5 (for the federal government) and 6-10 (for state and local governments). It consists of current net saving as defined above, plus the consumption of fixed capital (CFC, from the current expenditure account), minus gross investment, plus capital transfer receipts, and minus capital transfer payments and net purchases of non-produced assets. The logic is that when CFC exceeds actual investment expenditures, governments have positive saving and can lend (or repay debt); if gross investment exceeds CFC, government must borrow to finance the difference, indicating negative saving and requiring borrowing.

Notes on the data

Government receipts and expenditures data are derived from the U.S. government accounts and from Census Bureau censuses and surveys of government finances, which cover state and local governments. However, BEA makes a number of adjustments to the data to convert them from fiscal year to calendar year and quarter bases and to agree with the concepts of national income accounting. Data are converted from the cash basis usually found in financial statements to the timing bases required for the NIPAs. In the NIPAs, receipts from businesses are generally on an accrual basis, purchases of goods and services are recorded when delivered, and receipts from and transfer payments to persons are on a cash basis. The federal receipts and expenditure data from the NIPAs in Tables 6-1 through 6-7 therefore differ from the federal receipts and outlay data in Table 6-16. Among other differences, the latter are by fiscal year and are on a modified cash basis.

The NIPA data on government receipts and expenditures record transactions of governments (federal, state, and local) with other U.S. residents and foreigners. Each entry in the government receipts and expenditures account has a corresponding entry elsewhere in the NIPAs. Thus, for example, the sum of personal current taxes received by federal and state and local governments (Tables 6-1 and 6-8) is equal to personal current taxes paid, as shown in personal income (Table 4-1).

Definitions (general)

In the 2003 revision of the NIPAs, several items appear separately that were previously treated as "negative expenditures" and netted against other items on the expenditures side. This grossing-up of the accounts raises both receipts and outlays and has no effect on net saving. Grossing-up has been applied to taxes from the rest of the world, interest receipts (back to 1960 for the federal government and back to 1946 for state and local governments), dividends, and subsidies and the current surplus of government enterprises (back to 1959).

Definitions (current receipts)

Current tax receipts includes personal current taxes, taxes on production and imports, taxes on corporate income and (for the federal government only) taxes from the rest of the world. The taxes from the rest of the world are mostly income taxes and are not shown in the tables included in this chapter.

Personal current taxes is personal tax payments from residents of the United States that are not chargeable to business expense. Personal taxes consist of taxes on income, including on realized net capital gains, and on personal property. Personal contributions for social insurance are not included in this category. As of the 1999 revisions, estate and gift taxes are classified as capital transfers and are no longer included in personal current taxes. However, estate and gift taxes continue to be included in federal government receipts in Table 6-16.

Taxes on production and imports consists of federal excise taxes and customs duties and of state and local sales taxes, property taxes (including residential real estate taxes), motor vehicle licenses, severance taxes, other taxes, and special assessments. Before the 2003 revision, these taxes

were a component of "indirect business tax and nontax liabilities."

Taxes on corporate income covers federal, state, and local government income taxes on all corporate income subject to taxes. This income includes capital gains and other income excluded from the NIPA profits. The taxes are measured on an accrual basis, net of applicable tax credits.

Contributions for social insurance includes employer and personal contributions for Social Security, Medicare, unemployment insurance, and other government social insurance programs. As of the 1999 revisions, contributions to government employee retirement plans are no longer included in this category; these plans are now treated the same as private pension plans.

Income receipts on assets consists of *interest*, dividends (not shown separately here), and *rents and royalties*.

Interest receipts (1960 to the present for federal governments; 1946 to the present for state and local governments) consists of monetary and imputed interest received on loans and investments. In the NIPAs, this no longer includes interest received by government employee retirement plans, which is now credited to personal income. However, such interest received is still deducted from interest paid in the budget accounts that are shown in Table 6-16. Before the indicated years, receipts are deducted from aggregate interest payments in the NIPAs. Hence, they are not shown as receipts, and net interest is presented on the expenditure side. In the federal budget accounts in Table 6-16, net interest (total interest expenditures minus interest receipts) is the interest "expenditure" concept used throughout the period covered.

Current transfer receipts includes receipts in categories other than those specified above from persons and business. In the case of state and local government accounts (Table 6-8), it also includes *federal grants-in-aid*, a component of federal expenditures. Receipts from *business* and *persons* were previously included with income taxes in "tax and nontax payments." They consist of federal deposit insurance premiums and other nontaxes (largely fines and regulatory and inspection fees), state and local fines and other nontaxes (largely donations and tobacco settlements), and net insurance settlements paid to governments as policyholders.

The *current surplus of government enterprises* is the current operating revenue and subsidies received from other levels of government by such enterprises less their current expenses. No deduction is made for depreciation charges or net interest paid. Before 1959, this category of receipts is treated as a deduction from subsidies. In the <u>federal</u> NIPA accounts before 1959, there is no entry shown for the current surplus on the receipts side, and on the expenditure side, there is an entry for subsidies, which is net of the current surplus. (Subsidies are usually a larger amount than the enterprise surplus in the federal accounts.) In the state and local NIPA accounts before 1959, there is an entry for the surplus on the receipts side, which is net of subsidies. (Subsidies are typically smaller than the enterprise surplus in state and local finance.)

Definitions (consumption expenditures, saving, and gross investment)

Government consumption expenditures is expenditures by governments (federal or state and local) on services for current consumption. It includes *compensation of general government employees* (including employer contributions to government employee retirement plans, as of the 1999 revision); an allowance for *consumption of general government fixed capital (CFC)*, including software (depreciation); and *intermediate goods and services purchased*. (See the general discussion above for an explanation.) The estimated value of own-account investment—investment goods, including software, produced by government resources and purchased inputs—is subtracted here, and added to government gross investment. Sales to other sectors—primarily tuition payments received from individuals for higher education and charges for medical care to individuals—are also deducted.

Government social benefits consists of payments to individuals for which the individuals do not render current services. Examples are Social Security benefits, Medicare, Medicaid, unemployment benefits, and public assistance. Retirement payments to retired government employees from their pension plans are no longer included in this category.

Government social benefits to persons consists of payments to persons residing in the United States (with a corresponding entry of an equal amount in the personal income receipts accounts). Government social benefits to the rest of the world—not shown separately here—appear only in the federal government account, and are transfers, mainly retirement benefits, to former residents of the United States.

Other current transfer payments (federal account only) includes *grants-in-aid to state and local governments* and military and nonmilitary grants to foreign governments, not shown separately.

Federal grants-in-aid comprises net payments from federal to state and local governments that are made to help finance programs such as health (Medicaid), public assistance (the former Aid to Families with Dependent Children and the new Temporary Assistance for Needy Families), and education. Investment grants to state and local governments for highways, transit, air transportation, and water treatment plants are now classified as capital transfers and are no longer included in this category. However, such investment grants continue to be included as federal government outlays in Table 6-16.

Interest payments is monetary interest paid to U.S. and foreign persons and businesses and to foreign governments for public debt and other financial obligations. As noted above, from 1960 forward for the federal government and from 1946 forward for state and local governments, this represents gross total (not net) interest payments. Before those dates in the NIPAs, and throughout the federal budget accounts presented in Table 6-16, net instead of aggregate interest is shown; that is, gross total interest paid less interest received.

Subsidies are monetary grants paid by government to business, including to government enterprises at another level of government. Subsidies no longer include federal maritime construction subsidies, which are now classified as a capital transfer. For years prior to 1959, subsidies continue to be presented net of the *current surplus of government enterprises*, because detailed data to separate the series are not available for this period. See the above definition of current surplus of government enterprises for explanation of the pre-1959 treatment of this item in the federal accounts, which differs from the treatment in the state and local accounts.

Net saving, NIPA (surplus+/deficit-), is the sum of current receipts less the sum of current expenditures. This is shown separately for *social insurance funds* (which, in the case of the federal government, include Social Security and other trust funds) and *other* (all other government). As of the 1999 revisions, net government saving—particularly that of state and local governments—is measured as being significantly smaller than before the revision, as the net accumulations of government employee retirement plans (not Social Security) are now classified as personal saving rather than in the government sector.

Gross government investment consists of general government and government enterprise expenditures for fixed assets—structures, equipment, and software. The expenditures include the compensation of government employees and the purchase of goods and services as intermediate inputs associated with government production of fixed assets. Government inventory investment is included in government consumption expenditures.

Capital consumption. Consumption of fixed capital (CFC; economic depreciation) is included in government consumption expenditures as a partial measure of the value of the services of general government fixed assets, including structures, equipment, and software.

Definitions (output and net investment)

In Tables 6-5 and 6-10, current-dollar values of gross output and value added of government are presented, as described in the general discussion above. Gross output of government is the sum of the *intermediate goods and services purchased* by government and the value added by government as a producing industry. *Value added* consists of compensation of general government employees and consumption of general government fixed capital. Since this depreciation allowance is the only entry on the product side of the accounts measuring the output associated with such capital, a zero <u>net</u> return on these assets is implicitly assumed.

Gross output minus own-account investment and sales to other sectors (see the previous description) yields *government consumption expenditures*, which represents the contribution of government consumption spending to final demands in GDP.

The values of *net investment* shown in these tables are calculated by the editor, as gross investment minus the consumption of fixed capital.

Definitions (chain-type quantity indexes)

Chain-type quantity indexes represent changes over time in real values, removing the effects of inflation. Indexes for key categories in the government expenditure accounts, as well as for government gross output, value added, and intermediate goods and services purchased, use the chain formula described in the notes and definitions for Chapter 1 and are expressed as index numbers, with the average for the year 2000 = 100.

Data availability

The most recent data are published each month in the *Survey of Current Business*. Current and historical data may be obtained from the BEA Web site at <http://www.bea.gov> and the STAT-USA subscription Web site at <http://www.stat-usa.gov>.

References

See the references regarding the 2003 comprehensive revision of the NIPAs in the notes and definitions for Chapter 1.

For information about the classification of government expenditures into current consumption and gross investment, first undertaken in the 1996 comprehensive revisions, see the *Survey of Current Business* article, "Preview of the Comprehensive Revision of the National Income and Product Accounts: Recognition of Government Investment and Incorporation of a New Methodology for Calculating Depreciation," September 1995. Other sources of information about the NIPAs are listed in the notes and definitions for Tables 1-1 through 1-10.

TABLES 6-12 AND 6-13
STATE GOVERNMENT CURRENT RECEIPTS AND EXPENDITURES; LOCAL GOVERNMENT CURRENT RECEIPTS AND EXPENDITURES

SOURCE: BUREAU OF ECONOMIC ANALYSIS (BEA)

In the standard presentation of the national income and product accounts (NIPAs), such as in Tables 6-8 through 6-11 above, state and local governments are combined.

Annual measures for aggregate state governments and aggregate local governments are now available on the BEA Web site for the years 1959 through 2005. These measures are shown in Tables 6-12 and 6-13. The definitions are the same as in the other NIPA tables described above.

Two new categories appear in each table, detailing the inter-governmental flows that are consolidated in Table 6-8. State government receipts include not only *federal grants-in-aid* but also *local grants-in-aid*, and state government expenditures include *grants-in-aid to local governments*. Local government receipts include not only *federal grants-in-aid* but also *state grants-in-aid*, and local government expenditures include *grants-in-aid to state governments*. To make room for these columns, the components *current surplus of government enterprises* and *subsidies* are not shown, though they are included in total current receipts and total current expenditures respectively.

These measures are described in "Receipts and Expenditures of State Governments and of Local Governments," *Survey of Current Business*, October 2005. Data back to 1959 are available on the BEA Web site at <http://www.bea.gov>.

TABLES 6-14 AND 6-15
STATE GOVERNMENT CONSUMPTION EXPENDITURES AND GROSS INVESTMENT BY FUNCTION; LOCAL GOVERNMENT CONSUMPTION EXPENDITURES AND GROSS INVESTMENT BY FUNCTION

SOURCE: BUREAU OF ECONOMIC ANALYSIS (BEA)

As *Business Statistics* went to press, these data had not been revised to reflect the 2003 comprehensive revision of the NIPAs (as previously described in the notes and definitions for Chapter 1 and to Tables 6-1 through 6-11). They are reprinted as they appeared in the previous two editions of *Business Statistics*. They cover the years 1959 through 2001 and do not reflect new source data made available in the last three years. They follow the pre-2003 framework for government accounts. These two tables present only the total of consumption expenditures and gross investment, which is little affected by the 2003 conceptual revisions.

Definitions

The functions defined in Tables 6-14 and 6-15, which include consumption expenditures and gross investment combined, are roughly similar to the federal government spending concept and functions displayed in Table 6-16. Specifically:

- *General public service* includes executive and legislative functions, tax collection and financial management, and other services.

- *Public order and safety* includes police, fire, law courts, and *prisons*.

- *Economic affairs* includes general economic and labor affairs, agriculture, energy, natural resources, *transportation*, and other. *Transportation* includes highways, air transportation, water transportation, transit, and railroads.

- *Housing and community services* includes water, sewerage, sanitation, and other services.

- *Education* includes *elementary and secondary* and *higher* education, libraries, and other education services.

- *Income security* includes disability, *welfare and social services*, and other transfer payments to individuals.

- *Total consumption expenditures and gross investment* includes the groups listed above, *health*, and recreation and culture.

Data availability and references

These data were described and published in the *Survey of Current Business* article, "Receipts and Expenditures of State Government and of Local Governments, 1959–2001," June 2003.

TABLE 6-16
FEDERAL GOVERNMENT RECEIPTS AND OUTLAYS BY FISCAL YEAR

SOURCE: U.S. OFFICE OF MANAGEMENT AND BUDGET

These data on federal government receipts and outlays are on a modified cash basis and are from the *Budget of the United States Government: Historical Tables*. The data are by federal fiscal years: July 1 through June 30 through 1976 and October 1 through September 30 for 1977 and subsequent years. The period July 1 through September 30, 1976, is a separate fiscal period known as the transition quarter (TQ) and is not included in any fiscal year.

There are numerous differences in both timing and definition between these estimates and the NIPA estimates in Tables 6-1 through 6-7. See the notes and definitions for those tables for the definitional differences that were introduced with the 1999 comprehensive revision of the NIPAs.

Definitions

The definitions for this table are not affected by the 2003 or 1999 changes in the government sectors of the NIPAs.

Table references will be given indicating the source of each item in the *Historical Tables*; for example, "HT Table 1.1."

Receipts consist of gifts and other taxes or other compulsory payments to the government. Other types of payments to the government are netted against outlays. (HT Table 1.1)

Outlays occur when the federal government liquidates an obligation through a cash payment or when interest

accrues on public debt issues. Beginning with the data for 1992, outlays include the subsidy cost of direct and guaranteed loans made. Before 1992, the costs and repayments associated with such loans are recorded on a cash basis. As noted previously, various types of nontax receipts are netted against cash outlays. These accounts do not distinguish between investment outlays and current consumption and do not include allowances for depreciation. (HT Table 1.1)

The *total surplus (deficit-)* is receipts minus outlays. (HT Table 1.1)

On-budget and off-budget. By law, two government programs that are included in the federal receipts and outlays totals are "off-budget"—old-age, survivors, and disability insurance (Social Security) and the Postal Service. The former accounts for nearly all of the off-budget activity. The *surplus (deficit-)* not accounted for by these two programs is the on-budget surplus or deficit. (HT Table 1.1)

Sources of financing is the means by which the total deficit is financed or the surplus is distributed. By definition, sources of financing sum to the total deficit or surplus with the sign reversed. The principal source is *borrowing from the public*, shown as a positive number, that is, the increase in the debt held by the public. (Calculated as the change in the debt held by the public as shown in HT Table 7.1.) When there is a budget surplus, as in fiscal years 1998 to 2000, debt can be reduced, indicated by a minus sign in this column. *Other financing* includes drawdown (or buildup, shown here with a minus sign) in Treasury cash balances, seigniorage on coins, direct and guaranteed loan account cash transactions, and miscellaneous other transactions. (Calculated by subtracting borrowing from the public from the total deficit or surplus with the sign reversed.)

Some of the categories of *receipts by source* are self-explanatory. *Employment taxes and contributions* includes taxes for old-age, survivors, and disability insurance (Social Security), hospital insurance (Medicare), and railroad retirement funds. *Other retirement contributions* includes the employee share of payments for retirement pensions, mainly those for federal employees. *Excise taxes* includes federal taxes on alcohol, tobacco, telephone service, and transportation fuels, as well as taxes funding smaller programs such as black lung disability and vaccine injury compensation. *Miscellaneous receipts* includes deposits of earnings by the Federal Reserve system and all other receipts. (HT Tables 2.1, 2.4, and 2.5)

Outlays by function presents outlays according to the major purpose of the spending. Functional classifications cut across departmental and agency lines. Most categories of offsetting receipts are netted against cash outlays in the appropriate function, which explains how recorded outlays in *energy* and *commerce and housing credit* (which, as its name suggests, includes loan programs) can be negative. There is also a category of "undistributed offsetting receipts" (not shown), always with a negative sign, that includes proceeds from the sale or lease of assets and payments from federal agencies to federal retirement funds and the Social Security and Medicare trust funds. Note that *Social Security* is recorded separately from other *income security* outlays, and *Medicare* separately from other *health* outlays. (HT Table 3.1) For further explanation, consult the *Budget of the United States Government.*

In order to provide authoritative comparisons of these budget values with the overall size of the economy, a special calculation of gross domestic product by fiscal year (supplied to the Office of Management and Budget by BEA) is included in this table. (HT Table 1.2)

References

Definitions and budget concepts are discussed in *Budget of the United States: Historical Tables*, available from the Government Printing Office (GPO) and on the Web site listed in the next paragraph.

Data availability

The annual data are from the *Budget of the United States Government: Historical Tables* and are available on the GPO Web site at <http://www.gpo.gov/usbudget>.

Similarly defined data for the latest month, the year-ago month, and the current and year-ago fiscal year to date are published in the *Monthly Treasury Statement* prepared by the Financial Management Service, U.S. Department of the Treasury. For those who need up-to-date budget information, this publication is available on the Financial Management Service Web site at <http://www.fms.treas.gov>. As these monthly figures are never revised to agree with the final annual data, they are not published in this volume.

TABLE 6-17
FEDERAL GOVERNMENT DEBT BY FISCAL YEAR

Source: U.S. Office of Management and Budget

Debt outstanding at the end of each fiscal year is from the *Budget of the United States Government*. Most securities are recorded at sales price plus amortized discount or less amortized premium.

Definitions

Federal government debt held by the public consists of all federal debt held outside the federal government accounts—by individuals, financial institutions (including the Federal Reserve Banks), and foreign individuals, businesses, and central banks. It does not include federal debt held by federal government trust funds such as the Social Security trust fund. The level and change of the ratio of this debt to the value of gross domestic product (GDP) provide proportional measures of the impact of federal borrowing on credit markets. (HT Table 7.1) This measure of debt held by the public is very similar in concept and scope to the total federal government credit market debt

outstanding in the flow-of-funds accounts, shown in *Business Statistics* in Table 12-5; however, it is not identical, being priced somewhat differently, and is shown here in Chapter 6 on a fiscal year rather than calendar year basis.

Gross federal debt—total. This is the total debt owed by the U.S. Treasury. It includes a small amount of matured debt. (HT Table 7.1)

Debt held by Social Security funds is the sum of the end-year funds for old age and survivors insurance and disability insurance. (HT Table 13.1)

Debt held by other U.S. government accounts is calculated by subtracting the Social Security debt holdings from the total debt held by federal government accounts, which is shown in HT Table 7.1. It includes the balances in all the other trust funds, including the Medicare funds, federal employee retirement funds, and the highway trust fund.

Debt held by the Federal Reserve System is the total value of Treasury securities held by the 12 Federal Reserve Banks, which is acquired in open market operations that carry out monetary policy. (HT Table 7.1)

Debt held by private investors is calculated by subtracting the Federal Reserve debt from the total debt held by the public.

Debt held by foreign and international investors is based on surveys by the Treasury Department. Every few years there is a benchmark revision, which renders year-to-year changes invalid as measures of the borrowing during the year; such revisions occurred in 1979, 1985, 1990, 1995, 1999, 2000, and 2002. (Table 16-6, *Budget of the United States for Fiscal Year 2007: Analytical Perspectives*, pp. 233-234.)

Debt held by domestic investors is calculated by subtracting the foreign debt from the total debt held by private investors.

The "debt subject to statutory limitation," not shown here, is close to the gross federal debt in concept and size, but there are some relatively minor definitional differences specified by law. The debt limit can only be changed by an Act of Congress. For information about the debt subject to limit and other debt subjects, see the latest *Budget of the United States Government: Historical Statistics* and *Analytical Perspectives*.

Data availability

For the end-of-fiscal-year data, see *Historical Tables* and *Analytical Perspectives* in the *Budget of the United States Government*, which is available on the GPO Web site at <http://www.gpo.gov/usbudget>.

Recent quarterly data, but measured on a somewhat different basis, are found in the *Treasury Bulletin* in the chapter on "Ownership of Federal Securities (OFS)," in Tables

OFS-1 and OFS-2. The *Treasury Bulletin* can be accessed on the Internet at <http://www.fms.treas.gov/bulletin>. Holdings by Social Security funds are also available in the *Bulletin* in the chapter on "Federal Debt," Table FD-3. The disability fund is listed separately from the old-age and survivors fund.

TABLE 6-19
GOVERNMENT EMPLOYMENT

SOURCE: *U.S. DEPARTMENT OF LABOR, BUREAU OF LABOR STATISTICS*

See notes and definitions for Table 10-7.

Government payroll employment includes federal, state, and local activities such as legislative, executive, and judicial functions, as well as all government-owned and government-operated business enterprises, establishments, and institutions (arsenals, navy yards, hospitals, etc.), and government force account construction. The figures relate to civilian employment only. The Bureau of Labor Statistics (BLS) considers regular full-time teachers (private and government) to be employed during the summer vacation period, regardless of whether they are specifically paid in those months.

Employment in federal government establishments reflects employee counts as of the pay period containing the 12th of the month. Federal government employment excludes employees of the Central Intelligence Agency and the National Security Agency.

CHAPTER 7: U.S. FOREIGN TRADE AND FINANCE

Section 7a: Foreign Transactions in the National Income and Product Accounts

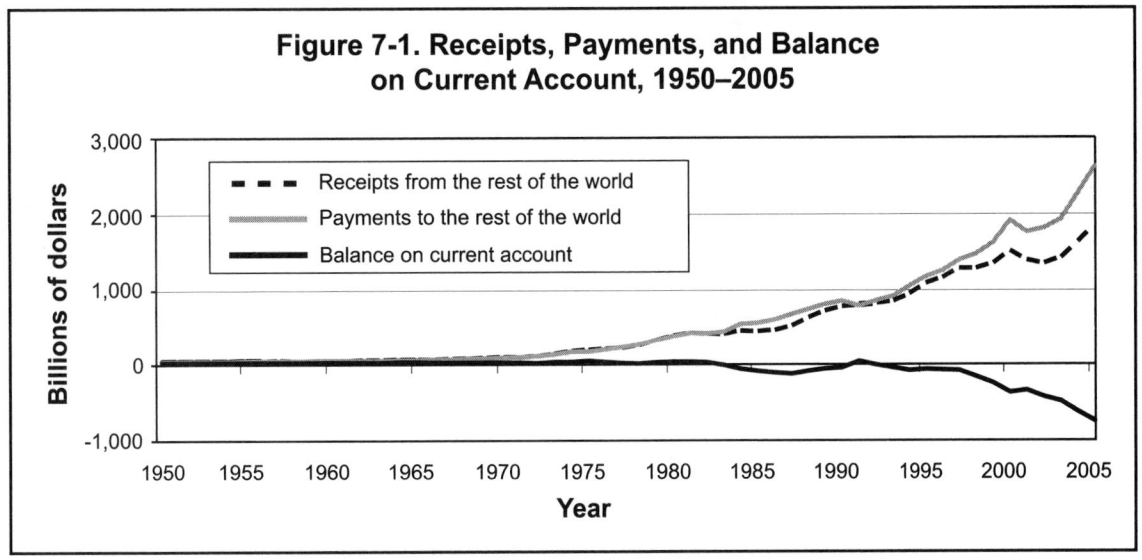

Figure 7-1. Receipts, Payments, and Balance on Current Account, 1950–2005

- For much of the early postwar period, U.S. current receipts from the rest of the world (exports and income receipts) and current payments to the rest of the world (imports, income payments, and net tax and transfer payments) were in rough balance. In most years through 1981, there was a surplus of receipts over payments—a positive balance on current account—that enabled the United States to invest in the economies of the rest of the world. (Table 7-1)

- However, beginning in 1983, large current-account deficits emerged, requiring capital inflows from abroad to finance them. The only current-account surplus since then occurred in 1991, when payments from other countries financed most of the cost of the first Gulf War. (Table 7-1)

- The NIPA current-account deficit of $771 billion in 2005 comprised a deficit of $792 billion on goods, a surplus of $75 billion on services, a surplus of $32 billion on income payments, and net payments of $87 billion in taxes and transfer payments. (Table 7-1)

- All the major categories of goods and services in Table 7-5 show long-term growth in quantity of both exports and imports. Between 1967 and 2005, the slowest-growing categories—exports and imports of foods and feeds—more than tripled, and the fastest-growing category—imports of capital goods, except automotive—was 157 times greater in real terms. The greatest growth in trade has been in capital goods and in "other private services" (financial, professional, and computer-related). In both of those categories, the quantity of imports has grown even faster than the quantity of exports. (Table 7-5)

Table 7-1. Foreign Transactions in the National Income and Product Accounts

(Billions of dollars, quarterly data are at seasonally adjusted annual rates.)

NIPA Table 4.1

Year and quarter	Current receipts from the rest of the world					Current payments to the rest of the world						Balance on current account, NIPAs	Net lending or net borrowing (-), NIPAs
	Exports of goods and services				Income receipts	Total	Imports of goods and services			Income payments	Current taxes and transfer payments, net		
	Total	Goods [1]		Services [1]			Goods [1]		Services [1]				
		Durable	Non-durable				Durable	Non-durable					
1950	14.5	5.1	5.1	2.1	2.2	16.4	3.0	6.1	2.5	0.7	4.0	-1.8	-1.8
1951	19.9	6.6	7.6	2.9	2.8	19.0	3.8	7.4	3.4	0.9	3.5	0.9	0.9
1952	19.3	6.9	6.5	3.0	2.9	18.7	4.1	6.7	4.5	0.9	2.5	0.6	0.6
1953	18.2	6.9	5.5	2.9	2.8	19.4	4.1	6.9	5.0	0.9	2.5	-1.3	-1.3
1954	18.9	7.1	5.8	2.9	3.0	18.6	3.6	6.7	5.1	0.9	2.3	0.2	0.2
1955	21.2	8.2	6.2	3.3	3.5	20.7	4.5	7.1	5.7	1.1	2.5	0.4	0.4
1956	25.2	9.8	7.8	3.7	3.9	22.5	5.2	7.6	6.1	1.1	2.4	2.8	2.8
1957	28.3	10.9	8.6	4.5	4.3	23.5	5.3	8.0	6.7	1.2	2.3	4.8	4.8
1958	24.4	9.0	7.4	4.1	3.9	23.5	5.0	8.0	7.1	1.2	2.3	0.9	0.9
1959	27.0	8.9	7.5	6.3	4.3	28.2	6.6	8.7	7.0	1.5	4.3	-1.2	-1.2
1960	31.9	11.3	9.2	6.6	4.9	28.7	6.4	8.9	7.6	1.8	4.1	3.2	3.2
1961	32.9	11.5	9.4	6.7	5.3	28.6	6.0	9.0	7.6	1.8	4.2	4.3	4.3
1962	35.0	12.0	9.7	7.4	5.9	31.1	6.9	9.9	8.1	1.8	4.3	3.9	3.9
1963	37.6	12.7	10.7	7.7	6.5	32.6	7.4	10.3	8.4	2.1	4.4	5.0	5.0
1964	42.3	14.7	12.0	8.3	7.2	34.7	8.4	11.0	8.7	2.3	4.3	7.5	7.5
1965	45.0	15.8	12.0	9.4	7.9	38.8	10.4	11.8	9.3	2.6	4.7	6.2	6.2
1966	49.0	17.5	13.2	10.2	8.1	45.1	13.3	13.1	10.7	3.0	5.0	3.9	3.9
1967	52.1	18.4	13.7	11.3	8.7	48.6	14.5	13.2	12.2	3.3	5.4	3.6	3.6
1968	58.0	21.0	14.3	12.6	10.1	56.3	18.8	15.1	12.6	4.0	5.7	1.7	1.7
1969	63.7	23.7	14.6	13.7	11.8	61.9	20.8	16.1	13.7	5.7	5.8	1.8	1.8
1970	72.5	27.1	17.4	15.2	12.8	68.5	22.8	18.1	14.9	6.4	6.3	4.0	4.0
1971	77.0	27.5	18.0	17.4	14.0	76.4	26.6	19.9	15.8	6.4	7.6	0.6	0.6
1972	87.1	31.0	20.8	19.0	16.3	90.7	33.3	23.6	17.3	7.7	8.8	-3.6	-3.6
1973	118.8	41.4	32.6	21.3	23.5	109.5	40.8	31.0	19.3	10.9	7.4	9.3	9.3
1974	156.5	56.5	44.5	25.7	29.8	149.8	50.3	54.2	22.9	14.3	8.1	6.6	6.6
1975	166.7	63.8	45.8	29.1	28.0	145.4	45.6	53.4	23.7	15.0	7.6	21.4	21.4
1976	181.9	69.0	48.7	31.7	32.4	173.0	56.8	67.8	26.5	15.5	6.3	8.9	8.9
1977	196.6	72.0	51.6	35.7	37.2	205.6	69.2	83.4	29.8	16.9	6.2	-9.0	-9.0
1978	233.1	85.3	60.1	41.5	46.3	243.6	89.0	88.4	34.8	24.7	6.7	-10.4	-10.4
1979	298.5	108.0	76.0	46.1	68.3	297.0	100.4	112.3	39.9	36.4	8.0	1.4	1.4
1980	359.9	133.3	92.5	55.0	79.1	348.5	111.9	136.6	45.3	44.9	9.8	11.4	11.4
1981	397.3	140.1	99.0	66.1	92.0	390.9	126.0	141.8	49.9	59.1	14.1	6.3	6.3
1982	384.2	124.7	90.3	68.2	101.0	384.4	125.1	125.4	52.6	64.5	16.7	-0.2	0.0
1983	378.9	120.4	86.9	69.7	101.9	410.9	147.3	125.4	56.0	64.8	17.5	-32.1	-31.8
1984	424.2	132.4	93.2	76.7	121.9	511.2	192.4	143.9	68.8	85.6	20.5	-86.9	-86.7
1985	414.5	137.2	85.0	79.8	112.4	525.3	204.2	139.1	73.9	85.9	22.2	-110.8	-110.5
1986	431.9	142.6	83.4	94.5	111.4	571.2	238.8	131.2	83.3	93.6	24.3	-139.2	-138.9
1987	487.1	162.9	94.6	106.4	123.2	637.9	264.2	150.6	94.3	105.3	23.5	-150.8	-150.4
1988	596.2	208.8	117.0	118.3	152.1	708.4	294.8	157.3	102.4	128.5	25.5	-112.2	-111.7
1989	681.0	239.8	129.5	134.0	177.7	769.3	310.4	174.4	106.7	151.5	26.4	-88.3	-88.0
1990	741.5	262.0	134.6	155.7	189.1	811.5	314.7	193.4	122.3	154.3	26.9	-70.1	-76.6
1991	765.7	282.3	141.3	173.3	168.9	752.3	315.7	185.0	123.6	138.5	-10.6	13.5	9.0
1992	788.0	300.6	147.4	187.4	152.7	824.9	346.9	198.1	123.6	123.0	33.4	-36.9	-37.5
1993	812.1	314.0	145.9	195.9	156.2	882.5	386.6	206.2	128.1	124.3	37.3	-70.4	-71.7
1994	907.3	349.7	160.4	210.8	186.4	1 012.5	454.2	222.6	137.7	160.2	37.8	-105.2	-106.9
1995	1 046.1	394.1	189.2	228.9	233.9	1 137.1	511.0	246.5	146.1	198.1	35.4	-91.0	-91.9
1996	1 117.3	421.8	196.6	250.2	248.7	1 217.6	533.6	273.8	157.4	213.7	39.1	-100.3	-101.0
1997	1 242.0	483.0	204.7	267.6	286.7	1 352.2	588.3	297.1	171.5	253.7	41.6	-110.2	-111.3
1998	1 243.1	487.1	193.8	275.1	287.1	1 430.5	636.5	292.5	186.9	265.8	48.8	-187.4	-188.1
1999	1 312.1	503.3	193.9	294.0	320.8	1 585.9	714.7	330.8	206.3	287.0	47.2	-273.9	-278.7
2000	1 478.9	569.2	215.1	311.9	382.7	1 875.6	820.7	422.8	232.3	343.7	56.1	-396.6	-397.4
2001	1 355.2	521.1	210.1	301.6	322.4	1 725.6	754.7	413.2	231.9	278.8	47.0	-370.4	-371.5
2002	1 311.6	487.2	210.4	308.4	305.7	1 769.9	770.0	419.4	241.0	275.0	64.5	-458.3	-459.7
2003	1 377.6	496.1	228.3	316.4	336.8	1 889.8	801.2	482.7	256.2	280.0	69.7	-512.3	-515.5
2004	1 588.3	561.8	257.1	359.3	410.2	2 237.4	929.9	565.3	296.2	363.9	82.1	-649.1	-651.3
2005	1 816.5	625.6	281.9	395.6	513.3	2 587.9	1 017.5	681.5	320.9	481.5	86.6	-771.4	-775.8
2003													
1st quarter	1 328.0	480.7	226.1	305.7	315.6	1 858.8	775.3	487.4	249.0	276.2	70.9	-530.8	-532.5
2nd quarter	1 334.4	485.1	222.3	303.3	323.6	1 847.2	790.8	476.0	245.3	267.0	68.1	-512.9	-519.2
3rd quarter	1 377.9	493.4	227.9	319.4	337.2	1 887.8	795.0	481.6	259.3	283.6	68.3	-509.9	-513.2
4th quarter	1 470.0	525.3	236.8	337.0	370.8	1 965.5	843.8	485.9	271.2	293.1	71.5	-495.5	-496.9
2004													
1st quarter	1 511.2	540.0	247.6	347.4	376.1	2 074.8	869.8	525.0	283.7	305.6	90.7	-563.6	-565.4
2nd quarter	1 564.6	555.8	254.5	356.1	398.3	2 214.4	926.1	554.3	292.1	357.8	84.1	-649.8	-651.4
3rd quarter	1 600.4	571.4	257.3	356.6	415.1	2 251.7	948.2	569.0	298.8	369.2	66.6	-651.4	-655.1
4th quarter	1 677.0	579.9	268.8	377.2	451.2	2 408.5	975.5	613.0	310.1	423.1	86.9	-731.5	-733.4
2005													
1st quarter	1 726.2	593.2	276.2	384.6	472.2	2 477.5	991.3	623.8	315.0	437.9	109.4	-751.3	-762.1
2nd quarter	1 782.8	615.8	286.8	391.2	489.0	2 534.1	1 007.7	654.7	317.8	460.6	93.3	-751.3	-753.6
3rd quarter	1 839.6	631.0	282.8	398.5	527.2	2 554.5	1 020.8	698.3	322.1	475.0	38.4	-714.9	-717.2
4th quarter	1 917.3	662.5	281.8	408.1	564.9	2 785.4	1 049.9	749.4	328.5	552.4	105.2	-868.2	-870.2

[1] Exports and imports of certain goods, primarily military equipment purchased and sold by the federal government, are included in services. Beginning with 1986, repairs and alterations of equipment are reclassified from goods to services.

Table 7-2. Chain-Type Quantity Indexes for Exports and Imports of Goods and Services

(Index numbers, 2000 = 100.)

Year and quarter	Exports of goods and services					Imports of goods and services				
	Total	Goods [1]			Services [1]	Total	Goods [1]			Services [1]
		Total	Durable	Nondurable			Total	Durable	Nondurable	
1967	11.76	10.64	7.47	20.84	14.91	11.42	9.40	5.12	20.74	22.89
1968	12.68	11.48	8.17	22.05	16.05	13.12	11.34	6.52	23.50	23.30
1969	13.29	12.08	8.83	22.26	16.65	13.87	11.96	6.97	24.37	24.77
1970	14.72	13.46	9.66	25.53	18.13	14.46	12.43	7.16	25.70	26.06
1971	14.97	13.41	9.59	25.56	19.53	15.23	13.47	7.89	27.29	25.32
1972	16.10	14.85	10.60	28.42	19.40	16.94	15.31	9.07	30.48	26.39
1973	19.13	18.26	13.20	34.31	20.78	17.73	16.39	9.66	32.87	25.50
1974	20.64	19.71	15.24	33.99	22.40	17.33	15.93	9.70	30.82	25.47
1975	20.51	19.25	14.92	33.09	23.77	15.40	13.92	7.92	28.60	24.37
1976	21.41	20.17	15.13	36.27	24.48	18.41	17.07	9.71	35.09	26.05
1977	21.92	20.43	15.10	37.54	26.06	20.43	19.15	10.98	39.08	27.35
1978	24.23	22.71	16.83	41.57	28.23	22.20	20.87	12.70	40.35	29.30
1979	26.64	25.40	19.16	45.32	29.10	22.57	21.23	12.99	40.82	29.70
1980	29.51	28.42	21.37	50.97	30.92	21.07	19.65	13.09	35.15	29.04
1981	29.87	28.11	20.60	52.30	34.21	21.62	20.06	14.18	34.09	30.71
1982	27.59	25.57	17.91	50.72	33.26	21.35	19.55	14.34	32.10	32.35
1983	26.88	24.84	17.54	48.69	32.71	24.04	22.21	17.28	34.19	34.96
1984	29.07	26.80	19.43	50.61	35.63	29.89	27.58	23.00	38.94	43.72
1985	29.95	27.79	21.00	49.29	36.05	31.83	29.31	25.30	39.41	47.05
1986	32.26	29.22	22.22	51.26	41.33	34.56	32.31	27.64	44.06	47.64
1987	35.74	32.46	25.37	54.32	45.50	36.60	33.81	28.87	46.28	53.21
1988	41.47	38.57	31.48	59.87	49.62	38.04	35.18	30.07	48.05	55.01
1989	46.23	43.17	35.91	64.72	54.72	39.71	36.69	31.42	49.93	57.68
1990	50.39	46.81	39.75	67.46	60.48	41.14	37.77	32.25	51.65	61.43
1991	53.74	50.04	42.70	71.44	64.08	40.91	37.74	32.43	51.07	59.85
1992	57.44	53.79	46.11	76.06	67.59	43.75	41.26	35.82	54.85	58.32
1993	59.29	55.53	48.51	75.51	69.73	47.58	45.42	40.07	58.66	60.03
1994	64.45	60.94	54.38	79.09	74.10	53.26	51.47	46.69	62.93	63.42
1995	70.98	68.07	62.13	84.20	78.79	57.54	56.10	52.04	65.52	65.49
1996	76.93	74.09	69.37	86.81	84.48	62.54	61.34	57.61	69.82	69.09
1997	86.08	84.72	81.90	92.35	89.51	71.04	70.17	67.05	77.20	75.60
1998	88.16	86.61	84.53	92.28	92.08	79.30	78.36	75.77	84.14	84.22
1999	91.97	89.91	88.48	93.77	97.21	88.39	88.08	86.73	90.90	90.04
2000	100.00	100.00	100.00	100.00	100.00	100.00	100.00	100.00	100.00	100.00
2001	94.57	93.87	91.73	99.59	96.30	97.29	96.83	93.76	102.90	99.71
2002	92.43	90.14	86.29	100.46	98.10	100.60	100.38	97.61	105.83	101.82
2003	93.60	91.77	87.81	102.39	98.15	104.69	105.29	101.79	112.16	101.86
2004	102.20	100.00	97.70	106.61	107.67	115.96	116.79	115.69	119.48	112.05
2005	109.11	107.51	107.10	109.80	113.12	123.01	124.64	125.52	124.27	115.17
2000										
1st quarter	96.77	95.86	95.51	96.81	99.06	95.64	95.47	95.68	94.97	96.60
2nd quarter	99.61	99.02	99.58	97.52	101.09	99.37	99.43	99.15	99.94	99.08
3rd quarter	102.16	103.27	103.06	103.81	99.38	102.70	102.76	102.60	103.08	102.40
4th quarter	101.46	101.85	101.85	101.86	100.47	102.29	102.35	102.57	102.01	101.92
2001										
1st quarter	100.08	100.44	100.03	101.52	99.19	101.33	101.46	99.05	106.14	100.62
2nd quarter	96.75	95.84	94.11	100.43	99.02	97.97	96.88	93.79	102.92	103.69
3rd quarter	92.01	90.64	87.91	97.90	95.44	95.35	94.73	91.67	100.77	98.59
4th quarter	89.42	88.57	84.87	98.49	91.56	94.52	94.26	90.51	101.78	95.92
2002										
1st quarter	90.56	88.21	84.00	99.53	96.39	97.17	96.36	93.72	101.55	101.36
2nd quarter	92.86	91.18	87.38	101.38	97.03	100.08	100.00	97.77	104.39	100.58
3rd quarter	93.52	91.67	88.22	100.92	98.12	101.47	101.58	99.23	106.24	101.00
4th quarter	92.78	89.52	85.59	100.01	100.87	103.69	103.57	99.72	111.12	104.37
2003										
1st quarter	91.52	89.97	85.09	102.88	95.39	102.36	102.56	98.70	110.07	101.49
2nd quarter	91.13	89.69	85.77	100.18	94.72	103.40	104.69	100.69	112.45	97.23
3rd quarter	93.61	91.60	87.41	102.78	98.62	104.35	104.85	100.90	112.51	102.02
4th quarter	98.14	95.83	92.96	103.74	103.87	108.67	109.09	106.85	113.63	106.69
2004										
1st quarter	99.86	97.48	94.79	105.03	105.77	111.35	111.75	109.10	117.09	109.49
2nd quarter	101.37	99.02	96.94	105.09	107.22	115.55	116.40	115.27	119.11	111.52
3rd quarter	102.56	101.00	99.08	106.71	106.45	116.80	117.73	117.59	118.80	112.37
4th quarter	105.02	102.51	100.00	109.63	111.23	120.15	121.27	120.79	122.92	114.83
2005										
1st quarter	106.23	103.89	101.68	110.25	112.03	121.36	122.74	121.98	124.86	114.76
2nd quarter	108.64	107.06	105.36	112.28	112.59	121.78	123.33	123.96	123.30	114.32
3rd quarter	109.50	108.05	108.10	109.29	113.16	122.52	124.16	126.30	121.91	114.65
4th quarter	112.05	111.03	113.26	107.39	114.69	126.38	128.33	129.83	127.00	116.95

[1]Exports and imports of certain goods, primarily military equipment purchased and sold by the federal government, are included in services. Beginning with 1986, repairs and alterations of equipment are reclassified from goods to services.

Table 7-3. Chain-Type Price Indexes for Exports and Imports of Goods and Services

(Index numbers, 2000 = 100.)

NIPA Table 4.2.4

Year and quarter	Exports of goods and services					Imports of goods and services				
	Total	Goods [1]			Services [1]	Total	Goods [1]			Services [1]
		Total	Durable	Nondurable			Total	Durable	Nondurable	
1967	33.73	38.56	43.39	30.65	24.29	23.69	23.75	34.60	15.07	22.86
1968	34.46	39.16	45.14	30.08	25.26	24.05	24.07	35.16	15.22	23.30
1969	35.63	40.37	47.11	30.44	26.31	24.68	24.75	36.28	15.58	23.78
1970	36.99	42.19	49.31	31.74	26.81	26.14	26.43	38.74	16.64	24.62
1971	38.36	43.32	50.45	32.76	28.58	27.74	27.78	41.10	17.29	26.85
1972	40.15	44.47	51.47	33.95	31.47	29.68	29.91	44.72	18.35	28.19
1973	45.43	51.62	55.04	44.13	32.94	34.84	35.26	51.48	22.33	32.61
1974	55.97	65.32	65.09	60.89	36.74	49.85	52.76	63.24	41.59	38.78
1975	61.68	72.60	75.12	64.38	39.21	54.00	57.18	70.19	44.14	41.92
1976	63.71	74.46	80.15	62.46	41.58	55.62	58.71	71.32	45.72	43.82
1977	66.30	77.17	83.82	63.92	43.92	60.52	64.08	76.76	50.50	46.93
1978	70.34	81.62	88.98	67.25	47.10	64.80	68.36	85.45	51.80	51.20
1979	78.81	92.40	99.03	77.99	50.77	75.88	80.61	94.25	65.09	57.82
1980	86.80	101.28	109.60	84.33	57.02	94.51	101.71	104.21	91.95	67.10
1981	93.22	108.43	119.47	87.98	61.97	99.59	107.38	108.33	98.36	70.01
1982	93.65	107.19	122.31	82.79	65.73	96.24	103.04	106.34	92.40	70.06
1983	94.02	106.41	120.58	82.98	68.31	92.63	98.73	103.87	86.72	68.91
1984	94.89	107.33	119.66	85.66	69.06	91.83	98.05	101.97	87.39	67.73
1985	91.98	101.96	114.83	80.17	70.94	88.81	94.19	98.34	83.51	67.65
1986	90.64	98.62	112.74	75.62	73.34	88.87	92.08	105.26	70.44	75.25
1987	92.87	101.17	112.81	80.98	74.94	94.25	98.65	111.52	76.97	76.32
1988	97.69	107.69	116.52	90.85	76.45	98.77	103.35	119.45	77.46	80.11
1989	99.31	109.08	117.32	93.04	78.50	100.94	106.27	120.39	82.61	79.66
1990	99.98	108.03	115.79	92.77	82.54	103.83	108.18	118.90	88.56	85.68
1991	101.31	107.91	116.12	91.94	86.69	103.42	106.70	118.63	85.70	88.88
1992	100.89	106.19	114.51	90.08	88.86	103.55	106.20	117.99	85.41	91.26
1993	100.90	105.59	113.73	89.83	90.07	102.67	104.95	117.56	83.14	91.87
1994	102.03	106.72	112.96	94.28	91.21	103.63	105.76	118.56	83.66	93.46
1995	104.38	109.25	111.44	104.46	93.14	106.41	108.57	119.65	88.98	96.06
1996	102.99	106.41	106.81	105.27	94.95	104.53	105.87	112.87	92.77	98.05
1997	101.23	103.50	103.60	103.05	95.86	100.82	101.47	106.90	91.01	97.69
1998	98.91	100.22	101.24	97.61	95.77	95.35	95.33	102.36	82.22	95.55
1999	98.31	98.87	99.94	96.11	96.97	95.96	95.46	100.41	86.07	98.63
2000	100.00	100.00	100.00	100.00	100.00	100.00	100.00	100.00	100.00	100.00
2001	99.62	99.32	99.80	98.08	100.39	97.50	97.00	98.09	94.98	100.13
2002	99.27	98.66	99.18	97.36	100.76	96.34	95.29	96.12	93.73	101.88
2003	101.43	100.64	99.26	103.64	103.33	99.69	98.06	95.92	101.80	108.29
2004	105.15	104.39	101.01	112.09	106.99	104.68	102.96	97.94	111.91	113.79
2005	108.95	107.63	102.62	119.36	112.12	111.27	109.62	98.77	129.72	119.93
2000										
1st quarter	99.46	99.64	99.85	99.10	99.01	99.32	99.18	100.30	97.05	100.05
2nd quarter	99.99	100.03	99.93	100.32	99.88	99.49	99.47	100.24	98.02	99.55
3rd quarter	100.22	100.12	100.17	99.98	100.49	100.51	100.57	100.03	101.62	100.16
4th quarter	100.33	100.21	100.06	100.59	100.63	100.69	100.77	99.43	103.31	100.23
2001										
1st quarter	100.35	100.17	100.17	100.15	100.78	99.93	99.80	99.30	100.68	100.61
2nd quarter	100.02	99.78	100.06	99.02	100.61	98.42	98.11	98.56	97.23	100.05
3rd quarter	99.51	99.13	99.66	97.76	100.45	97.09	96.47	97.70	94.16	100.34
4th quarter	98.62	98.17	99.31	95.39	99.74	94.56	93.61	96.79	87.86	99.51
2002										
1st quarter	98.36	97.83	99.26	94.43	99.65	94.15	93.14	96.22	87.53	99.43
2nd quarter	99.05	98.36	99.16	96.40	100.72	96.47	95.56	96.27	94.24	101.26
3rd quarter	99.77	99.16	99.21	98.95	101.25	97.30	96.18	96.20	96.07	103.24
4th quarter	99.91	99.29	99.08	99.66	101.42	97.44	96.27	95.79	97.08	103.59
2003										
1st quarter	100.92	100.17	99.24	102.15	102.74	100.08	99.01	95.71	104.75	105.64
2nd quarter	101.19	100.58	99.37	103.18	102.69	99.09	97.31	95.70	100.10	108.63
3rd quarter	101.42	100.41	99.16	103.10	103.86	99.73	97.91	96.01	101.21	109.45
4th quarter	102.18	101.41	99.28	106.15	104.04	99.84	98.03	96.24	101.12	109.45
2004										
1st quarter	103.70	103.03	100.10	109.65	105.33	102.19	100.42	97.18	106.10	111.59
2nd quarter	104.97	104.35	100.74	112.60	106.49	104.00	102.34	97.92	110.14	112.79
3rd quarter	105.44	104.63	101.32	112.13	107.40	105.41	103.69	98.27	113.36	114.50
4th quarter	106.49	105.56	101.88	113.97	108.72	107.13	105.40	98.41	118.04	116.27
2005										
1st quarter	107.70	106.71	102.49	116.46	110.07	107.82	105.88	99.02	118.21	118.20
2nd quarter	108.65	107.50	102.68	118.73	111.39	110.22	108.44	99.06	125.61	119.68
3rd quarter	109.34	107.85	102.55	120.28	112.92	112.92	111.38	98.47	135.49	120.95
4th quarter	110.11	108.45	102.75	121.96	114.08	114.12	112.79	98.53	139.57	120.91

[1]Exports and imports of certain goods, primarily military equipment purchased and sold by the federal government, are included in services. Beginning with 1986, repairs and alterations of equipment are reclassified from goods to services.

Table 7-4. Exports and Imports of Selected NIPA Types of Product

(Billions of dollars, quarterly data are at seasonally adjusted annual rates.) **NIPA Table 4.2.5**

Year and quarter	Exports Goods Foods, feeds, and beverages	Industrial supplies and materials	Capital goods, except auto-motive	Auto-motive vehicles, engines, and parts	Consumer goods, except auto-motive	Services Travel	Other private services (financial, profes-sional, etc.)	Imports Goods Foods, feeds, and beverages	Industrial supplies and materials, except petroleum and products	Petroleum and products	Capital goods, except auto-motive	Auto-motive vehicles, engines, and parts	Consumer goods, except auto-motive	Services Travel	Other private services (financial, profes-sional, etc.)
1967	5.0	10.0	9.9	2.8	2.1	1.6	0.7	4.6	9.9	2.1	2.5	2.4	4.2	3.2	0.4
1968	4.8	11.0	11.1	3.5	2.3	1.8	0.8	5.3	12.0	2.4	2.8	4.0	5.4	3.0	0.5
1969	4.7	11.7	12.4	3.9	2.6	2.0	0.9	5.2	11.7	2.6	3.4	5.1	6.5	3.4	0.6
1970	5.9	13.8	14.7	3.9	2.8	2.3	1.0	6.1	12.2	2.9	4.0	5.7	7.4	4.0	0.6
1971	6.1	12.6	15.4	4.7	2.9	2.5	1.3	6.4	13.6	3.7	4.3	7.6	8.4	4.4	0.7
1972	7.5	13.9	16.9	5.5	3.6	2.8	1.5	7.3	16.0	4.7	5.9	9.0	11.1	5.0	0.8
1973	15.2	19.7	22.0	7.0	4.8	3.4	1.7	9.1	19.2	8.4	8.3	10.7	12.9	5.5	0.9
1974	18.6	29.9	30.9	8.8	6.4	4.0	3.0	10.6	27.0	26.6	9.8	12.4	14.4	6.0	1.9
1975	19.2	29.3	36.6	10.8	6.6	4.7	3.7	9.6	23.6	27.0	10.2	12.1	13.2	6.4	2.3
1976	19.8	31.6	39.1	12.2	8.0	5.7	4.5	11.5	28.5	34.6	12.3	16.8	17.2	6.9	2.9
1977	19.7	33.2	39.8	13.5	8.9	6.2	4.9	14.0	33.4	45.0	14.0	19.4	21.8	7.5	3.2
1978	25.7	38.4	47.5	15.2	11.4	7.2	6.2	15.8	39.3	42.6	19.3	25.0	29.4	8.5	3.9
1979	30.5	53.3	60.2	17.9	14.0	8.4	7.3	18.0	45.0	60.4	24.6	26.6	31.3	9.4	4.6
1980	36.3	68.0	76.3	17.4	17.8	10.6	8.6	18.6	47.3	79.5	31.6	28.3	34.3	10.4	5.1
1981	38.8	65.7	84.2	19.7	17.7	12.9	13.2	18.6	52.0	78.4	37.1	31.0	38.4	11.5	6.3
1982	32.2	61.8	76.5	17.2	16.1	12.4	16.9	17.5	45.4	62.0	38.4	34.3	39.7	12.4	7.4
1983	32.1	57.1	71.7	18.5	14.9	10.9	17.6	18.8	51.1	55.1	43.7	43.0	47.3	13.2	7.3
1984	32.2	61.9	77.0	22.4	15.1	17.2	18.6	21.9	62.6	58.1	60.4	56.5	61.1	22.9	8.2
1985	24.6	59.4	79.3	24.9	14.6	17.8	19.4	21.8	59.2	51.4	61.3	64.9	66.3	24.6	9.4
1986	23.5	59.0	82.8	25.1	16.7	20.4	28.5	24.4	62.5	34.3	72.0	78.1	79.4	25.9	14.2
1987	25.2	67.4	92.7	27.6	20.3	23.6	29.8	24.8	66.1	42.9	85.1	85.2	88.8	29.3	17.7
1988	33.8	84.2	119.1	33.4	27.0	29.4	31.6	24.9	76.6	39.6	102.2	87.9	96.4	32.1	18.9
1989	36.3	95.3	136.9	35.0	36.0	36.2	37.2	24.9	78.8	50.9	112.4	87.2	103.6	33.4	20.4
1990	35.2	101.8	153.1	36.1	43.6	43.0	40.8	26.4	78.2	62.3	116.3	88.4	104.9	37.4	23.9
1991	35.8	106.1	166.6	39.7	46.7	48.4	48.3	26.2	75.6	51.7	121.0	85.7	107.6	35.3	27.6
1992	40.3	105.0	176.5	46.7	51.3	54.7	50.6	27.6	82.4	51.6	134.6	91.7	122.4	38.6	26.1
1993	40.6	102.8	182.9	51.3	54.6	57.9	53.8	27.9	88.7	51.5	152.9	102.4	133.7	40.7	28.7
1994	42.0	115.7	205.8	57.3	59.9	58.4	61.3	31.0	105.0	51.3	185.0	118.1	145.9	43.8	32.6
1995	50.5	141.3	234.5	61.3	64.3	63.4	65.5	33.2	119.9	56.0	222.2	123.6	159.4	44.9	36.2
1996	55.5	141.0	254.0	64.2	70.1	69.8	73.7	35.7	125.2	72.7	228.5	128.7	171.9	48.1	40.5
1997	51.5	152.6	295.9	73.3	78.0	73.4	84.5	39.7	135.3	71.7	253.4	139.5	194.1	52.1	44.6
1998	46.4	142.8	299.9	72.4	80.3	71.3	92.6	41.2	142.5	50.6	269.4	148.7	217.1	56.5	49.6
1999	46.0	142.4	311.2	75.3	80.9	74.8	105.2	43.6	147.9	67.8	295.7	179.0	242.0	59.0	58.1
2000	47.9	166.6	357.0	80.4	89.4	82.4	109.3	46.0	172.8	120.2	347.0	195.9	282.0	64.7	64.0
2001	49.4	155.3	321.7	75.4	88.3	71.9	116.3	46.6	164.8	103.6	298.0	189.8	284.5	60.2	70.9
2002	49.6	153.5	290.4	78.9	84.4	66.6	125.3	49.7	158.4	103.5	283.3	203.7	308.0	58.7	77.3
2003	55.0	168.3	293.7	80.6	89.9	64.3	130.7	55.8	174.4	133.1	295.9	210.1	334.0	57.4	80.2
2004	56.6	199.5	331.6	89.2	103.1	74.5	144.7	62.1	225.2	180.5	343.5	228.2	373.1	65.8	90.4
2005	59.0	227.5	362.7	98.6	115.7	81.7	158.2	68.1	264.9	251.9	379.2	239.5	407.3	69.2	98.7
2000 1st quarter	46.4	160.2	329.5	83.5	87.6	81.9	106.3	44.9	164.9	107.8	320.4	197.3	266.7	65.1	61.5
2nd quarter	47.9	163.3	356.4	80.2	88.8	84.1	108.0	45.9	169.9	117.9	346.2	195.4	280.0	64.6	62.6
3rd quarter	49.7	171.6	374.2	79.2	91.6	81.4	110.2	46.8	176.7	127.9	362.2	197.4	287.0	64.3	65.1
4th quarter	47.4	171.5	367.9	78.5	89.5	82.2	112.8	46.4	179.6	127.1	359.3	193.5	294.4	64.8	66.9
2001 1st quarter	49.7	165.2	364.2	73.5	92.7	82.9	114.1	45.7	186.2	125.3	339.4	189.1	291.7	63.5	68.2
2nd quarter	49.7	157.9	331.8	76.8	91.5	78.5	114.9	45.7	167.6	108.6	299.9	190.4	286.6	66.9	71.4
3rd quarter	49.3	151.5	302.1	76.5	85.1	69.5	116.4	48.0	157.0	97.1	280.0	191.6	282.4	58.4	72.0
4th quarter	49.0	146.6	288.8	74.9	84.0	56.7	119.8	47.1	148.4	83.4	272.8	188.0	277.3	51.9	72.0
2002 1st quarter	48.9	145.0	285.2	75.0	82.6	64.6	123.3	47.2	148.3	81.4	277.5	193.5	287.4	58.2	75.8
2nd quarter	49.2	154.7	293.5	81.0	84.3	64.6	124.8	49.0	156.9	104.0	285.5	203.5	305.9	58.0	75.1
3rd quarter	50.7	156.6	297.2	80.7	85.5	65.1	124.6	50.7	161.0	106.9	285.4	209.0	317.7	58.0	77.8
4th quarter	49.6	157.6	285.9	79.0	85.0	72.0	128.7	51.8	167.4	121.6	284.9	209.1	320.8	60.7	80.4
2003 1st quarter	52.6	167.0	282.8	79.7	86.8	63.2	126.6	53.9	170.6	142.1	285.7	205.4	326.3	58.0	78.6
2nd quarter	53.0	165.5	283.2	82.0	87.8	57.3	129.0	54.9	170.9	125.9	292.1	211.7	327.9	52.0	77.9
3rd quarter	55.5	166.8	293.1	78.4	91.1	64.7	131.2	56.4	177.1	131.2	294.1	205.0	333.9	58.6	79.6
4th quarter	59.0	173.8	315.5	82.5	93.9	72.1	136.2	58.1	178.9	133.1	311.5	218.4	348.0	61.3	84.6
2004 1st quarter	56.8	187.5	323.5	83.7	97.9	71.5	140.0	59.8	195.3	160.2	323.6	221.9	355.4	63.4	87.0
2nd quarter	56.2	196.3	328.7	87.5	101.9	74.7	143.0	62.4	221.8	167.8	340.8	230.4	375.9	65.8	88.8
3rd quarter	55.2	202.2	335.2	92.7	104.0	74.8	142.0	61.9	238.6	179.6	350.7	229.8	371.6	66.4	89.3
4th quarter	58.2	212.0	338.9	93.0	108.4	77.3	153.6	64.4	245.0	214.2	358.8	230.7	389.3	67.3	96.4
2005 1st quarter	56.8	219.9	343.6	94.2	112.6	79.9	153.3	65.6	250.1	212.6	362.8	231.8	403.1	69.1	94.8
2nd quarter	60.5	230.2	360.4	94.7	113.6	83.7	154.9	67.2	254.2	233.0	381.0	234.6	407.1	70.4	96.7
3rd quarter	58.7	230.0	362.4	100.9	116.6	81.6	158.1	69.0	261.6	269.1	383.2	241.2	403.8	68.7	100.0
4th quarter	59.8	230.0	384.3	104.5	120.0	81.5	166.6	70.6	293.6	292.6	389.9	250.4	415.3	68.5	103.4

Table 7-5. Chain-Type Quantity Indexes for Exports and Imports of Selected NIPA Types of Product

(Index numbers, 2000 = 100.)   NIPA Table 4.2.3

Year and quarter	Exports — Goods					Exports — Services		Imports — Goods						Imports — Services	
	Foods, feeds, and beverages	Industrial supplies and materials	Capital goods, except automotive	Automotive vehicles, engines, and parts	Consumer goods, except automotive	Travel	Other private services (financial, professional, etc.)	Foods, feeds, and beverages	Industrial supplies and materials, except petroleum and products	Petroleum and products	Capital goods, except automotive	Automotive vehicles, engines, and parts	Consumer goods, except automotive	Travel	Other private services (financial, professional, etc.)
1967	26.36	23.08	4.04	17.27	7.81	9.91	2.54	35.29	24.28	20.44	0.77	8.39	5.92	17.14	1.75
1968	25.94	26.26	4.16	21.28	8.49	10.24	2.63	40.04	28.90	23.54	0.88	13.06	7.48	15.53	1.98
1969	25.40	27.46	4.41	23.00	9.09	11.18	2.89	37.94	27.35	26.27	1.03	15.95	8.82	16.85	2.20
1970	30.65	30.75	4.93	22.47	9.64	12.06	3.09	40.53	27.64	28.37	1.07	16.31	9.49	19.44	2.30
1971	29.84	27.80	5.15	25.47	9.67	12.59	3.59	41.84	30.12	32.45	1.06	19.89	9.98	19.42	2.54
1972	35.22	29.61	5.64	28.59	11.30	13.52	4.00	44.54	33.05	39.63	1.36	21.55	12.17	21.01	2.62
1973	45.60	36.43	7.16	33.56	13.78	15.53	4.36	45.67	33.27	56.30	1.68	22.24	12.49	19.82	2.93
1974	40.86	37.49	8.94	37.44	17.14	16.90	7.12	42.25	32.41	54.20	1.79	23.62	11.24	17.79	5.90
1975	43.23	32.79	9.08	39.42	15.80	18.27	8.26	37.37	27.30	53.30	1.70	18.75	8.71	17.16	6.67
1976	49.05	35.42	8.96	41.21	17.82	20.82	9.56	42.54	33.25	64.27	2.06	24.84	11.24	18.25	8.01
1977	49.01	35.71	8.81	41.51	19.27	20.86	9.85	42.11	35.77	77.32	2.20	26.31	13.58	18.81	8.39
1978	60.55	39.47	10.06	42.62	22.25	22.41	11.67	47.28	39.17	73.10	2.84	28.47	16.68	19.43	9.80
1979	64.23	45.20	12.08	42.89	23.39	24.03	13.00	48.53	37.63	73.94	3.47	27.53	16.81	18.95	11.10
1980	72.41	51.30	14.10	36.12	28.35	26.84	13.89	42.24	32.84	59.72	4.09	27.28	16.93	18.93	11.33
1981	73.93	47.84	14.15	35.71	27.18	29.62	19.87	43.95	35.65	52.33	4.82	26.40	18.54	20.02	13.35
1982	69.46	46.40	12.51	29.26	24.46	26.41	23.96	44.80	32.32	45.00	5.24	28.25	19.38	23.74	15.14
1983	66.39	44.14	12.07	30.27	22.37	22.30	23.67	48.62	38.38	44.54	6.34	34.58	23.32	26.89	14.18
1984	64.60	46.40	13.37	35.72	22.26	33.26	24.00	55.08	47.60	47.05	9.48	44.44	29.44	49.15	15.89
1985	55.91	46.67	14.69	38.87	21.60	32.93	23.96	57.46	47.87	44.18	10.68	49.79	32.14	54.25	17.71
1986	57.68	48.75	16.03	38.23	23.89	36.74	34.02	58.82	50.41	54.62	12.12	53.90	35.61	50.43	25.44
1987	61.73	49.97	18.51	41.21	28.11	40.54	34.06	60.29	49.92	57.05	13.84	55.31	36.76	59.80	28.93
1988	67.84	56.33	23.53	48.91	35.91	48.91	35.63	57.90	50.46	63.10	15.96	53.92	37.30	61.45	30.85
1989	70.75	62.58	27.29	50.14	46.21	58.46	41.11	59.22	49.33	68.06	18.07	52.45	39.03	63.32	35.90
1990	73.20	66.23	31.59	50.17	54.13	65.94	43.21	61.49	50.07	68.97	19.48	52.72	38.34	67.65	38.87
1991	74.65	70.80	34.55	53.75	56.05	69.86	49.12	58.71	49.15	65.55	20.94	49.18	38.99	61.26	43.16
1992	84.50	72.10	37.86	62.03	60.35	77.51	50.06	61.98	54.04	67.94	24.26	51.72	43.05	63.07	40.76
1993	83.96	70.20	40.34	67.60	63.43	81.30	52.14	62.70	58.63	74.98	28.29	56.86	46.63	66.16	43.70
1994	83.99	74.12	46.54	74.75	69.35	81.70	58.50	64.13	67.37	79.61	34.76	63.56	50.52	68.51	49.82
1995	93.15	79.87	55.43	78.89	73.51	87.60	61.25	65.71	70.74	78.21	42.80	64.62	54.40	69.05	55.29
1996	91.66	83.60	64.24	81.83	79.08	94.21	67.64	72.26	74.90	84.38	50.29	66.84	58.49	71.76	61.10
1997	91.84	90.83	78.76	92.64	87.29	96.90	76.58	79.60	81.05	88.20	63.05	72.30	66.85	77.95	67.28
1998	90.93	89.84	82.12	91.39	89.90	93.09	83.98	85.42	89.81	93.94	72.46	76.96	75.79	88.11	76.53
1999	94.44	90.89	86.65	94.43	90.91	95.14	96.91	93.39	93.67	94.46	83.19	92.01	85.08	89.82	89.56
2000	100.00	100.00	100.00	100.00	100.00	100.00	100.00	100.00	100.00	100.00	100.00	100.00	100.00	100.00	100.00
2001	102.86	96.10	90.18	93.56	99.19	86.93	106.32	104.61	96.37	103.71	88.60	96.96	101.70	95.26	110.85
2002	100.78	96.40	82.36	97.41	95.21	81.20	114.72	110.13	99.12	101.08	87.16	103.78	111.25	90.22	118.35
2003	102.52	98.85	84.21	99.80	100.90	76.98	118.10	118.67	100.81	107.64	92.37	106.46	120.90	81.49	122.34
2004	96.07	105.12	95.13	108.46	114.59	86.25	126.92	125.49	116.57	114.69	108.41	113.68	134.13	86.96	135.97
2005	101.45	107.83	103.89	118.50	127.24	90.83	134.47	130.08	124.52	117.31	120.59	118.06	145.09	85.77	145.35
2000															
1st quarter	96.68	97.48	92.37	104.20	98.02	101.00	97.77	96.52	99.64	94.45	91.58	101.03	94.15	98.43	96.30
2nd quarter	98.49	97.94	100.02	99.87	99.26	102.02	99.11	99.21	99.73	102.82	99.39	99.74	99.26	99.42	98.20
3rd quarter	106.04	102.32	104.66	98.41	102.36	98.24	100.17	102.15	100.99	102.22	104.45	100.62	101.85	99.57	100.91
4th quarter	98.79	102.26	102.96	97.52	100.36	98.75	102.96	102.11	99.64	100.51	104.58	98.62	104.74	102.57	104.60
2001															
1st quarter	103.26	99.28	101.67	91.34	104.03	99.64	103.68	100.47	100.04	113.68	99.31	96.46	103.82	100.35	106.37
2nd quarter	104.26	96.18	92.69	95.16	103.01	94.06	105.18	102.51	95.12	102.52	88.75	97.36	102.36	106.38	111.91
3rd quarter	101.21	94.61	84.91	94.81	95.58	84.26	106.40	108.91	95.50	94.39	83.82	98.11	101.02	92.24	112.62
4th quarter	102.71	94.34	81.44	92.92	94.13	69.76	110.00	106.54	94.82	104.26	82.52	95.91	99.60	82.09	112.52
2002															
1st quarter	102.98	94.10	80.48	92.80	93.27	79.49	113.30	106.97	95.72	101.62	84.83	98.81	103.61	92.55	117.09
2nd quarter	102.67	97.66	83.12	100.17	95.37	78.75	113.93	109.51	97.96	98.90	87.50	103.80	110.60	89.94	114.22
3rd quarter	100.39	96.89	84.36	99.51	96.45	79.35	113.82	112.10	100.13	95.59	87.74	106.38	114.75	87.48	118.72
4th quarter	97.05	96.95	81.46	97.17	95.74	87.20	117.83	111.96	102.68	108.22	88.57	106.14	116.03	90.89	123.35
2003															
1st quarter	102.25	99.16	80.72	97.86	97.74	75.96	115.05	114.89	98.13	105.49	89.00	104.34	118.15	85.90	119.59
2nd quarter	100.55	97.44	80.90	100.55	98.69	69.24	116.81	117.11	99.47	108.61	91.07	107.39	118.68	72.15	118.56
3rd quarter	104.22	98.33	84.25	95.93	102.19	77.22	117.91	119.92	102.87	106.95	91.75	104.01	120.86	82.02	121.14
4th quarter	103.07	100.46	90.96	100.86	104.98	85.48	122.65	122.79	102.78	109.50	97.67	110.10	125.89	85.89	130.06
2004															
1st quarter	95.10	103.59	93.05	102.28	109.32	84.04	124.30	123.46	106.22	118.52	101.32	111.32	127.67	86.77	131.65
2nd quarter	89.07	105.39	94.35	106.45	113.64	86.46	125.73	126.37	115.67	111.06	107.49	115.11	135.23	87.79	133.63
3rd quarter	96.02	105.20	96.12	112.54	115.32	86.30	124.17	125.34	121.86	109.22	110.97	114.28	133.82	86.91	133.37
4th quarter	104.07	106.32	97.00	112.56	120.09	88.20	133.48	126.79	122.51	119.97	113.88	114.01	139.79	86.38	145.22
2005															
1st quarter	99.94	107.05	98.25	113.64	123.96	90.84	131.28	126.85	122.50	122.00	114.69	114.44	143.46	87.96	140.18
2nd quarter	103.38	110.03	103.04	114.03	124.97	93.87	131.94	128.00	122.70	114.96	120.44	115.73	144.89	86.01	142.22
3rd quarter	99.83	108.58	103.80	121.21	128.21	89.72	134.08	132.42	124.14	111.19	122.19	118.84	143.92	83.37	147.41
4th quarter	102.64	105.67	110.48	125.13	131.80	88.89	140.58	133.04	128.73	121.07	125.06	123.22	148.09	85.75	151.60

Section 7b: U.S. International Transactions Accounts

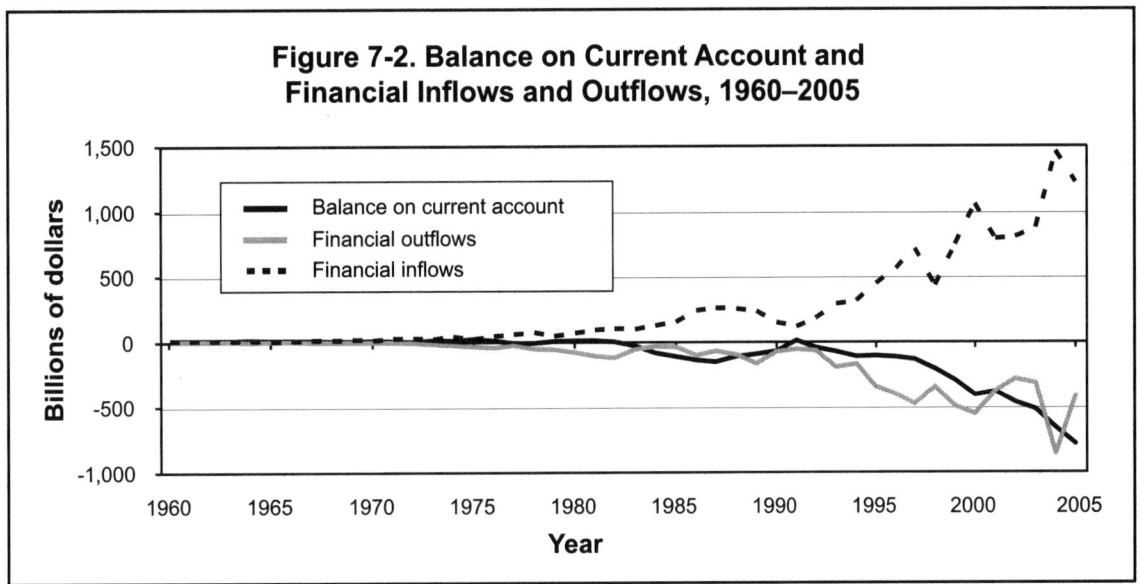

Figure 7-2. Balance on Current Account and Financial Inflows and Outflows, 1960–2005

- The U.S. current-account international balance is also recorded in the international transactions accounts (ITAs). The definitional differences between this balance and the balance in the national income and products accounts (NIPAs) are minor, and the trends in the two measures are similar. The ITAs measure the current account surplus or deficit (commonly known as the "balance of payments") and directly measure the financial flows required to finance it. (Table 7-6)

- Figure 7-2 above shows the current-account balance since 1960, culminating in a $792 billion deficit in 2005. U.S. investment in assets abroad contributed a further outflow, amounting to $427 billion in 2005. Financing the sum of these was a financial inflow, or an increase in foreign-owned assets in the United States, of $1.212 trillion. The financial outflows and inflows both fell back somewhat in 2005 after large increases in the previous year. The net of the financial flows does not exactly equal the current-account balance because of a capital transactions item and the ITA statistical discrepancy. (Table 7-6)

- The 2004 increase and subsequent fallback in U.S. investment abroad occurred mainly in direct investment and U.S. bank lending. The 2004 "bulge" in foreign investment in the United States was all in foreign official holdings. (Table 7-6)

- Before the 1980s, the United States was a net creditor with respect to the rest of the world. In other words, the value of the stock of U.S.-owned assets abroad exceeded the value of foreign-owned assets in the United States. Since then, the persistent net financial inflows associated with current-account deficits have cumulated, resulting in a growing net debtor status, with the value of foreign-owned assets in the United States exceeding the value of U.S.-owned assets abroad by $2.7 trillion as of the end of 2005. (Table 7-8)

Table 7-6. U.S. International Transactions

(Millions of dollars, seasonally adjusted.)

	Current account									
	Exports of goods and services and income receipts									
						Income receipts				
							Income receipts on U.S.-owned assets abroad			
Year and quarter	Total	Exports of goods and services	Exports of goods	Exports of services	Total	Total	Direct investment receipts	Other private receipts	U.S. government receipts	Compensation of employees
1960	30 556	25 940	19 650	6 290	4 616	4 616	3 621	646	349	. . .
1961	31 402	26 403	20 108	6 295	4 999	4 999	3 823	793	383	. . .
1962	33 340	27 722	20 781	6 941	5 618	5 618	4 241	904	473	. . .
1963	35 776	29 620	22 272	7 348	6 157	6 157	4 636	1 022	499	. . .
1964	40 165	33 341	25 501	7 840	6 824	6 824	5 106	1 256	462	. . .
1965	42 722	35 285	26 461	8 824	7 437	7 437	5 506	1 421	510	. . .
1966	46 454	38 926	29 310	9 616	7 528	7 528	5 260	1 669	599	. . .
1967	49 353	41 333	30 666	10 667	8 021	8 021	5 603	1 781	636	. . .
1968	54 911	45 543	33 626	11 917	9 367	9 367	6 591	2 021	756	. . .
1969	60 132	49 220	36 414	12 806	10 913	10 913	7 649	2 338	925	. . .
1970	68 387	56 640	42 469	14 171	11 748	11 748	8 169	2 671	907	. . .
1971	72 384	59 677	43 319	16 358	12 707	12 707	9 160	2 641	906	. . .
1972	81 986	67 222	49 381	17 841	14 765	14 765	10 949	2 949	866	. . .
1973	113 050	91 242	71 410	19 832	21 808	21 808	16 542	4 330	936	. . .
1974	148 484	120 897	98 306	22 591	27 587	27 587	19 157	7 356	1 074	. . .
1975	157 936	132 585	107 088	25 497	25 351	25 351	16 595	7 644	1 112	. . .
1976	172 090	142 716	114 745	27 971	29 375	29 375	18 999	9 043	1 332	. . .
1977	184 655	152 301	120 816	31 485	32 354	32 354	19 673	11 057	1 625	. . .
1978	220 516	178 428	142 075	36 353	42 088	42 088	25 458	14 788	1 843	. . .
1979	287 965	224 131	184 439	39 692	63 834	63 834	38 183	23 356	2 295	. . .
1980	344 440	271 834	224 250	47 584	72 606	72 606	37 146	32 898	2 562	. . .
1981	380 928	294 398	237 044	57 354	86 529	86 529	32 549	50 300	3 680	. . .
1982	366 983	275 236	211 157	64 079	91 747	91 747	29 469	58 160	4 118	. . .
1983	356 106	266 106	201 799	64 307	90 000	90 000	31 750	53 418	4 832	. . .
1984	399 913	291 094	219 926	71 168	108 819	108 819	35 325	68 267	5 227	. . .
1985	387 612	289 070	215 915	73 155	98 542	98 542	35 410	57 633	5 499	. . .
1986	407 098	310 033	223 344	86 689	97 064	96 156	36 938	52 806	6 413	908
1987	457 053	348 869	250 208	98 661	108 184	107 190	46 288	55 592	5 311	994
1988	567 862	431 149	320 230	110 919	136 713	135 718	58 445	70 571	6 703	995
1989	648 290	487 003	359 916	127 087	161 287	160 270	61 981	92 638	5 651	1 017
1990	706 975	535 233	387 401	147 832	171 742	170 570	65 973	94 072	10 525	1 172
1991	727 557	578 343	414 083	164 260	149 214	147 924	58 718	81 186	8 019	1 290
1992	750 648	616 882	439 631	177 251	133 767	131 971	57 539	67 316	7 115	1 796
1993	778 921	642 863	456 943	185 920	136 057	134 237	67 245	61 865	5 126	1 820
1994	869 775	703 254	502 859	200 395	166 521	164 578	77 344	83 106	4 128	1 943
1995	1 004 631	794 387	575 204	219 183	210 244	208 065	95 260	108 092	4 713	2 179
1996	1 077 731	851 602	612 113	239 489	226 129	223 948	102 505	116 852	4 591	2 181
1997	1 191 257	934 453	678 366	256 087	256 804	254 534	115 323	135 652	3 559	2 270
1998	1 194 993	933 174	670 416	262 758	261 819	259 382	103 963	151 818	3 601	2 437
1999	1 259 809	965 884	683 965	281 919	293 925	291 177	131 626	156 354	3 197	2 748
2000	1 421 515	1 070 597	771 994	298 603	350 918	348 083	151 839	192 398	3 846	2 835
2001	1 293 147	1 004 896	718 712	286 184	288 251	285 372	128 665	153 146	3 561	2 879
2002	1 245 373	974 721	682 422	292 299	270 652	267 841	145 590	118 948	3 303	2 811
2003	1 319 158	1 016 096	713 415	302 681	303 062	300 249	186 750	108 802	4 697	2 813
2004	1 526 855	1 151 942	807 516	344 426	374 913	372 035	226 224	142 813	2 998	2 878
2005	1 749 892	1 275 245	894 631	380 614	474 647	471 722	251 370	217 637	2 715	2 925
2001										
1st quarter	350 489	268 540	193 976	74 564	81 949	81 200	34 109	46 198	893	749
2nd quarter	334 968	259 140	185 030	74 110	75 828	75 123	33 106	41 240	777	705
3rd quarter	311 110	243 227	172 648	70 579	67 883	67 162	30 833	35 479	850	721
4th quarter	296 582	233 990	167 058	66 932	62 592	61 888	30 617	30 229	1 042	704
2002										
1st quarter	300 892	235 970	165 171	70 799	64 922	64 196	34 034	29 349	813	726
2nd quarter	312 379	244 423	172 131	72 292	67 956	67 265	35 931	30 628	706	691
3rd quarter	318 631	247 891	174 241	73 650	70 740	70 042	38 540	30 652	850	698
4th quarter	313 475	246 437	170 879	75 558	67 038	66 342	37 089	28 319	934	696
2003										
1st quarter	316 991	246 491	173 423	73 068	70 500	69 813	41 953	27 017	843	687
2nd quarter	319 380	246 866	174 438	72 428	72 514	71 839	44 351	26 247	1 241	675
3rd quarter	330 049	254 200	177 796	76 404	75 849	75 134	46 700	27 145	1 289	715
4th quarter	352 733	268 538	187 758	80 780	84 195	83 459	53 744	28 393	1 322	736
2004										
1st quarter	362 895	277 369	194 056	83 313	85 526	84 820	54 024	29 993	803	706
2nd quarter	375 770	284 893	199 617	85 276	90 877	90 191	55 831	33 647	713	686
3rd quarter	384 648	289 689	204 340	85 349	94 959	94 229	56 703	36 772	754	730
4th quarter	403 536	299 991	209 503	90 488	103 545	102 789	59 661	42 401	727	756
2005										
1st quarter	415 277	306 580	214 189	92 391	108 697	107 988	58 846	48 437	705	709
2nd quarter	429 326	316 645	222 591	94 054	112 681	111 952	60 572	50 674	706	729
3rd quarter	442 935	320 853	224 947	95 906	122 081	121 350	64 476	56 247	627	731
4th quarter	462 357	331 165	232 904	98 261	131 192	130 437	67 481	62 279	677	755

. . . = Not available.

Table 7-6. U.S. International Transactions—Continued

(Millions of dollars, seasonally adjusted.)

					Current account—Continued					
					Imports of goods and services and income payments [1]					
						Income payments				
							Income payments on foreign-owned assets in the U.S.			
Year and quarter	Total	Imports of goods and services	Imports of goods	Imports of services	Total	Total	Direct investment payments	Other private payments	U.S. government payments	Compensation of employees
1960	-23 670	-22 432	-14 758	-7 674	-1 238	-1 238	-394	-511	-332	...
1961	-23 453	-22 208	-14 537	-7 671	-1 245	-1 245	-432	-535	-278	...
1962	-25 676	-24 352	-16 260	-8 092	-1 324	-1 324	-399	-586	-339	...
1963	-26 970	-25 410	-17 048	-8 362	-1 560	-1 560	-459	-701	-401	...
1964	-29 102	-27 319	-18 700	-8 619	-1 783	-1 783	-529	-802	-453	...
1965	-32 708	-30 621	-21 510	-9 111	-2 088	-2 088	-657	-942	-489	...
1966	-38 468	-35 987	-25 493	-10 494	-2 481	-2 481	-711	-1 221	-549	...
1967	-41 476	-38 729	-26 866	-11 863	-2 747	-2 747	-821	-1 328	-598	...
1968	-48 671	-45 293	-32 991	-12 302	-3 378	-3 378	-876	-1 800	-702	...
1969	-53 998	-49 129	-35 807	-13 322	-4 869	-4 869	-848	-3 244	-777	...
1970	-59 901	-54 386	-39 866	-14 520	-5 515	-5 515	-875	-3 617	-1 024	...
1971	-66 414	-60 979	-45 579	-15 400	-5 435	-5 435	-1 164	-2 428	-1 844	...
1972	-79 237	-72 665	-55 797	-16 868	-6 572	-6 572	-1 284	-2 604	-2 684	...
1973	-98 997	-89 342	-70 499	-18 843	-9 655	-9 655	-1 610	-4 209	-3 836	...
1974	-137 274	-125 190	-103 811	-21 379	-12 084	-12 084	-1 331	-6 491	-4 262	...
1975	-132 745	-120 181	-98 185	-21 996	-12 564	-12 564	-2 234	-5 788	-4 542	...
1976	-162 109	-148 798	-124 228	-24 570	-13 311	-13 311	-3 110	-5 681	-4 520	...
1977	-193 764	-179 547	-151 907	-27 640	-14 217	-14 217	-2 834	-5 841	-5 542	...
1978	-229 870	-208 191	-176 002	-32 189	-21 680	-21 680	-4 211	-8 795	-8 674	...
1979	-281 657	-248 696	-212 007	-36 689	-32 961	-32 961	-6 357	-15 481	-11 122	...
1980	-333 774	-291 241	-249 750	-41 491	-42 532	-42 532	-8 635	-21 214	-12 684	...
1981	-364 196	-310 570	-265 067	-45 503	-53 626	-53 626	-6 898	-29 415	-17 313	...
1982	-355 975	-299 391	-247 642	-51 749	-56 583	-56 583	-2 114	-35 187	-19 282	...
1983	-377 488	-323 874	-268 901	-54 973	-53 614	-53 614	-4 120	-30 501	-18 993	...
1984	-473 923	-400 166	-332 418	-67 748	-73 756	-73 756	-8 443	-44 158	-21 155	...
1985	-483 769	-410 950	-338 088	-72 862	-72 819	-72 819	-6 945	-42 745	-23 129	...
1986	-530 142	-448 572	-368 425	-80 147	-81 571	-78 893	-6 856	-47 412	-24 625	-2 678
1987	-594 443	-500 552	-409 765	-90 787	-93 891	-91 553	-7 676	-57 659	-26 218	-2 338
1988	-663 741	-545 715	-447 189	-98 526	-118 026	-116 179	-12 150	-72 314	-31 715	-1 847
1989	-721 607	-580 144	-477 665	-102 479	-141 463	-139 177	-7 045	-93 768	-38 364	-2 286
1990	-759 290	-616 097	-498 438	-117 659	-143 192	-139 728	-3 450	-95 508	-40 770	-3 464
1991	-734 564	-609 479	-491 020	-118 459	-125 085	-121 059	2 265	-82 452	-40 872	-4 026
1992	-765 626	-656 094	-536 528	-119 566	-109 532	-104 780	-2 190	-63 509	-39 081	-4 752
1993	-823 914	-713 174	-589 394	-123 780	-110 741	-105 609	-7 943	-58 290	-39 376	-5 132
1994	-951 122	-801 747	-668 690	-133 057	-149 375	-143 423	-22 150	-77 081	-44 192	-5 952
1995	-1 080 124	-890 771	-749 374	-141 397	-189 353	-183 090	-30 318	-97 149	-55 623	-6 263
1996	-1 159 478	-955 667	-803 113	-152 554	-203 811	-197 511	-33 093	-97 800	-66 618	-6 300
1997	-1 286 597	-1 042 402	-876 470	-165 932	-244 195	-237 529	-42 950	-112 878	-81 701	-6 666
1998	-1 355 334	-1 097 780	-917 103	-180 677	-257 554	-250 560	-38 418	-127 988	-84 154	-6 994
1999	-1 509 207	-1 229 170	-1 029 980	-199 190	-280 037	-272 082	-53 437	-138 120	-80 525	-7 955
2000	-1 778 020	-1 448 156	-1 224 408	-223 748	-329 864	-322 345	-56 910	-180 918	-84 517	-7 519
2001	-1 630 811	-1 367 691	-1 145 900	-221 791	-263 120	-255 034	-12 783	-159 825	-82 426	-8 086
2002	-1 654 232	-1 395 789	-1 164 720	-231 069	-258 443	-250 063	-43 244	-130 177	-76 642	-8 380
2003	-1 777 462	-1 510 993	-1 260 717	-250 276	-266 469	-257 957	-73 961	-110 125	-73 871	-8 512
2004	-2 110 559	-1 763 238	-1 472 926	-290 312	-347 321	-338 400	-102 357	-147 569	-88 474	-8 921
2005	-2 455 328	-1 991 975	-1 677 371	-314 604	-463 353	-454 124	-116 953	-223 612	-113 559	-9 229
2001										
1st quarter	-442 851	-365 816	-309 396	-56 420	-77 035	-75 029	-7 556	-46 000	-21 473	-2 006
2nd quarter	-417 089	-347 792	-290 214	-57 578	-69 297	-67 291	-4 089	-41 944	-21 258	-2 006
3rd quarter	-401 111	-332 744	-277 881	-54 863	-68 367	-66 346	-7 084	-39 266	-19 996	-2 021
4th quarter	-369 764	-321 339	-268 409	-52 930	-48 425	-46 370	5 944	-32 615	-19 699	-2 055
2002										
1st quarter	-391 610	-329 136	-273 155	-55 981	-62 474	-60 380	-7 840	-32 770	-19 770	-2 094
2nd quarter	-416 841	-347 710	-291 124	-56 586	-69 131	-67 001	-13 212	-34 375	-19 414	-2 130
3rd quarter	-423 115	-355 148	-297 169	-57 979	-67 967	-65 923	-14 148	-32 785	-18 990	-2 044
4th quarter	-422 661	-363 794	-303 272	-60 522	-58 867	-56 757	-8 042	-30 247	-18 468	-2 110
2003										
1st quarter	-436 556	-370 708	-310 042	-60 666	-65 848	-63 701	-17 654	-27 934	-18 113	-2 147
2nd quarter	-433 578	-370 101	-310 279	-59 822	-63 477	-61 407	-17 263	-26 344	-17 800	-2 070
3rd quarter	-444 630	-377 175	-313 786	-63 389	-67 455	-65 330	-19 374	-27 285	-18 671	-2 125
4th quarter	-462 697	-393 008	-326 610	-66 398	-69 689	-67 520	-19 671	-28 562	-19 287	-2 169
2004										
1st quarter	-486 179	-413 517	-344 010	-69 507	-72 662	-70 490	-21 413	-29 279	-19 798	-2 172
2nd quarter	-521 646	-436 282	-364 709	-71 573	-85 364	-83 143	-27 479	-33 730	-21 934	-2 221
3rd quarter	-534 451	-446 361	-373 143	-73 218	-88 090	-85 888	-26 008	-36 945	-22 935	-2 202
4th quarter	-568 283	-467 077	-391 064	-76 013	-101 206	-98 879	-27 457	-47 615	-23 807	-2 327
2005										
1st quarter	-579 764	-474 688	-397 457	-77 231	-105 076	-102 817	-28 490	-48 786	-25 541	-2 259
2nd quarter	-599 390	-488 703	-410 811	-77 892	-110 687	-108 403	-29 520	-51 490	-27 393	-2 284
3rd quarter	-616 886	-502 645	-423 693	-78 952	-114 240	-111 887	-24 105	-58 479	-29 303	-2 353
4th quarter	-659 290	-525 939	-445 410	-80 529	-133 351	-131 018	-34 839	-64 857	-31 322	-2 333

[1]A minus sign indicates imports of goods and services or payments of incomes.
. . . = Not available.

Table 7-6. U.S. International Transactions—Continued

(Millions of dollars, seasonally adjusted.)

Year and quarter	Current account—Continued				Capital account transactions, net [2]	Financial account					
	Unilateral current transfers, net [2]					U.S.-owned assets abroad, net [2]					
		U.S. government					U.S. official reserve assets, net				
	Total	Grants	Pensions and other transfers	Private remittances and other transfers		Total	Total	Gold	Special drawing rights	Reserve position in the IMF	Foreign currencies
1960	-4 062	-3 367	-273	-423	. . .	-4 099	2 145	1 703	0	442	0
1961	-4 127	-3 320	-373	-434	. . .	-5 538	607	857	0	-135	-115
1962	-4 277	-3 453	-347	-477	. . .	-4 174	1 535	890	0	626	19
1963	-4 392	-3 479	-339	-575	. . .	-7 270	378	461	0	29	-112
1964	-4 240	-3 227	-399	-614	. . .	-9 560	171	125	0	266	-220
1965	-4 583	-3 444	-463	-677	. . .	-5 716	1 225	1 665	0	-94	-346
1966	-4 955	-3 802	-499	-655	. . .	-7 321	570	571	0	537	-538
1967	-5 294	-3 844	-571	-879	. . .	-9 757	53	1 170	0	-94	-1 023
1968	-5 629	-4 256	-537	-836	. . .	-10 977	-870	1 173	0	-870	-1 173
1969	-5 735	-4 259	-537	-939	. . .	-11 585	-1 179	-967	0	-1 034	822
1970	-6 156	-4 449	-611	-1 096	. . .	-8 470	3 348	787	16	389	2 156
1971	-7 402	-5 589	-696	-1 117	. . .	-11 758	3 066	866	486	1 350	382
1972	-8 544	-6 665	-770	-1 109	. . .	-13 787	706	547	7	153	-1
1973	-6 913	-4 748	-915	-1 250	. . .	-22 874	158	0	9	-33	182
1974	-9 249	-7 293	-939	-1 017	. . .	-34 745	-1 467	0	-172	-1 265	-30
1975	-7 075	-5 101	-1 068	-906	. . .	-39 703	-849	0	-66	-466	-317
1976	-5 686	-3 519	-1 250	-917	. . .	-51 269	-2 558	0	-78	-2 212	-268
1977	-5 226	-2 990	-1 378	-859	. . .	-34 785	-375	-118	-121	-294	158
1978	-5 788	-3 412	-1 532	-844	. . .	-61 130	732	-65	1 249	4 231	-4 683
1979	-6 593	-4 015	-1 658	-920	. . .	-64 915	6	-65	3	-189	257
1980	-8 349	-5 486	-1 818	-1 044	. . .	-85 815	-7 003	0	1 136	-1 667	-6 472
1981	-11 702	-5 145	-2 041	-4 516	. . .	-113 054	-4 082	*	-730	-2 491	-861
1982	-16 544	-6 087	-2 251	-8 207	199	-127 882	-4 965	0	-1 371	-2 552	-1 041
1983	-17 310	-6 469	-2 207	-8 635	209	-66 373	-1 196	0	-66	-4 434	3 304
1984	-20 335	-8 696	-2 159	-9 479	235	-40 376	-3 131	0	-979	-995	-1 156
1985	-21 998	-11 268	-2 138	-8 593	315	-44 752	-3 858	0	-897	908	-3 869
1986	-24 132	-11 883	-2 372	-9 877	301	-111 723	312	0	-246	1 501	-942
1987	-23 265	-10 309	-2 409	-10 548	365	-79 296	9 149	0	-509	2 070	7 588
1988	-25 274	-10 537	-2 709	-12 028	493	-106 573	-3 912	0	127	1 025	-5 064
1989	-26 169	-10 860	-2 775	-12 534	336	-175 383	-25 293	0	-535	471	-25 229
1990	-26 654	-10 359	-3 224	-13 070	-6 579	-81 234	-2 158	0	-192	731	-2 697
1991	9 904	29 193	-3 775	-15 514	-4 479	-64 389	5 763	0	-176	-366	6 307
1992	-35 100	-16 319	-4 043	-14 738	-557	-74 410	3 901	0	2 316	-2 691	4 276
1993	-39 811	-17 035	-4 104	-18 672	-1 299	-200 551	-1 379	0	-537	-43	-798
1994	-40 265	-14 978	-4 556	-20 731	-1 723	-178 937	5 346	0	-441	494	5 293
1995	-38 074	-11 190	-3 451	-23 433	-927	-352 264	-9 742	0	-808	-2 466	-6 468
1996	-43 017	-15 401	-4 466	-23 150	-735	-413 409	6 668	0	370	-1 280	7 578
1997	-45 062	-12 472	-4 191	-28 399	-1 027	-485 475	-1 010	0	-350	-3 575	2 915
1998	-53 187	-13 270	-4 305	-35 612	-766	-353 829	-6 783	0	-147	-5 119	-1 517
1999	-50 428	-13 774	-4 406	-32 248	-4 939	-504 062	8 747	0	10	5 484	3 253
2000	-58 645	-16 714	-4 705	-37 226	-1 010	-560 523	-290	0	-722	2 308	-1 876
2001	-51 295	-11 517	-5 798	-33 980	-1 270	-382 616	-4 911	0	-630	-3 600	-681
2002	-63 587	-17 097	-5 125	-41 365	-1 470	-294 646	-3 681	0	-475	-2 632	-574
2003	-69 210	-21 834	-5 341	-42 035	-3 321	-326 424	1 523	0	601	1 494	-572
2004	-81 582	-23 317	-6 264	-52 001	-2 261	-867 802	2 805	0	-398	3 826	-623
2005	-86 072	-31 362	-6 303	-48 407	-4 351	-426 801	14 096	0	4 511	10 200	-615
2001											
1st quarter	-15 171	-2 426	-1 316	-11 429	-301	-216 194	190	0	-189	574	-195
2nd quarter	-15 802	-2 479	-1 291	-12 032	-313	-86 702	-1 343	0	-156	-1 015	-172
3rd quarter	-2 941	-2 867	-1 305	1 231	-333	32 858	-3 559	0	-145	-3 242	-172
4th quarter	-17 374	-3 745	-1 886	-11 743	-323	-112 577	-199	0	-140	83	-142
2002											
1st quarter	-18 326	-6 397	-1 271	-10 658	-321	-84 841	390	0	-109	652	-153
2nd quarter	-14 764	-3 287	-1 279	-10 198	-333	-139 712	-1 843	0	-107	-1 607	-129
3rd quarter	-14 599	-3 075	-1 282	-10 242	-399	892	-1 416	0	-132	-1 136	-148
4th quarter	-15 897	-4 338	-1 292	-10 267	-417	-70 987	-812	0	-127	-541	-144
2003											
1st quarter	-17 598	-5 826	-1 320	-10 452	-450	-82 375	83	0	897	-644	-170
2nd quarter	-16 905	-5 855	-1 335	-9 715	-1 623	-158 245	-170	0	-102	86	-154
3rd quarter	-16 961	-5 435	-1 334	-10 192	-864	-847	-611	0	-97	-383	-131
4th quarter	-17 747	-4 718	-1 352	-11 677	-384	-84 954	2 221	0	-97	2 435	-117
2004											
1st quarter	-22 554	-7 744	-1 554	-13 256	-457	-309 212	557	0	-100	815	-158
2nd quarter	-20 895	-4 961	-1 556	-14 378	-399	-135 173	1 122	0	-90	1 345	-133
3rd quarter	-16 524	-4 911	-1 548	-10 065	-923	-144 528	429	0	-98	676	-149
4th quarter	-21 609	-5 701	-1 607	-14 301	-482	-278 884	697	0	-110	990	-183
2005											
1st quarter	-27 237	-9 221	-1 558	-16 458	-2 691	-87 391	5 331	0	1 713	3 763	-145
2nd quarter	-23 194	-5 780	-1 569	-15 845	-589	-196 376	-797	0	-97	-564	-136
3rd quarter	-9 464	-7 270	-1 584	-610	-557	-132 380	4 766	0	2 976	1 951	-161
4th quarter	-26 176	-9 091	-1 592	-15 493	-514	-10 656	4 796	0	-81	5 050	-173

[2]A minus sign indicates net unilateral transfers to foreigners, net capital or financial outflows, or increases in U.S. official assets.
. . . = Not available.
* = Less than $500,000 (+/-).

Table 7-6. U.S. International Transactions—Continued

(Millions of dollars, seasonally adjusted.)

Year and quarter	Financial account—Continued								
	U.S.-owned assets abroad, net [3]—Continued								
	U.S. government assets other than official reserve assets, net				U.S. private assets, net				
								U.S. claims	
	Total	U.S. credits and other long-term assets	Repayments on U.S. credits and other long-term assets	U.S. foreign currency holdings and short-term assets, net	Total	Direct investment	Foreign securities	On unaffiliated foreigners reported by U.S. nonbanking concerns	Reported by U.S. banks, not included elsewhere
1960	-1 100	-1 214	642	-528	-5 144	-2 940	-663	-394	-1 148
1961	-910	-1 928	1 279	-261	-5 235	-2 653	-762	-558	-1 261
1962	-1 085	-2 128	1 288	-245	-4 623	-2 851	-969	-354	-450
1963	-1 662	-2 204	988	-447	-5 986	-3 483	-1 105	157	-1 556
1964	-1 680	-2 382	720	-19	-8 050	-3 760	-677	-1 108	-2 505
1965	-1 605	-2 463	874	-16	-5 336	-5 011	-759	341	93
1966	-1 543	-2 513	1 235	-265	-6 347	-5 418	-720	-442	233
1967	-2 423	-3 638	1 005	209	-7 386	-4 805	-1 308	-779	-495
1968	-2 274	-3 722	1 386	62	-7 833	-5 295	-1 569	-1 203	233
1969	-2 200	-3 489	1 200	89	-8 206	-5 960	-1 549	-126	-570
1970	-1 589	-3 293	1 721	-16	-10 229	-7 590	-1 076	-596	-967
1971	-1 884	-4 181	2 115	182	-12 940	-7 618	-1 113	-1 229	-2 980
1972	-1 568	-3 819	2 086	165	-12 925	-7 747	-618	-1 054	-3 506
1973	-2 644	-4 638	2 596	-602	-20 388	-11 353	-671	-2 383	-5 980
1974	366	-5 001	4 826	541	-33 643	-9 052	-1 854	-3 221	-19 516
1975	-3 474	-5 941	2 475	-9	-35 380	-14 244	-6 247	-1 357	-13 532
1976	-4 214	-6 943	2 596	133	-44 498	-11 949	-8 885	-2 296	-21 368
1977	-3 693	-6 445	2 719	33	-30 717	-11 890	-5 460	-1 940	-11 427
1978	-4 660	-7 470	2 941	-131	-57 202	-16 056	-3 626	-3 853	-33 667
1979	-3 746	-7 697	3 926	25	-61 176	-25 222	-4 726	-5 014	-26 213
1980	-5 162	-9 860	4 456	242	-73 651	-19 222	-3 568	-4 023	-46 838
1981	-5 097	-9 674	4 413	164	-103 875	-9 624	-5 699	-4 377	-84 175
1982	-6 131	-10 063	4 292	-360	-116 786	-4 556	-7 983	6 823	-111 070
1983	-5 006	-9 967	5 012	-51	-60 172	-12 528	-6 762	-10 954	-29 928
1984	-5 489	-9 599	4 490	-379	-31 757	-16 407	-4 756	533	-11 127
1985	-2 821	-7 657	4 719	117	-38 074	-18 927	-7 481	-10 342	-1 323
1986	-2 022	-9 084	6 089	973	-110 014	-23 995	-4 271	-21 773	-59 975
1987	1 006	-6 506	7 625	-113	-89 450	-35 034	-5 251	-7 046	-42 119
1988	2 967	-7 680	10 370	277	-105 628	-22 528	-7 980	-21 193	-53 927
1989	1 233	-5 608	6 725	115	-151 323	-43 447	-22 070	-27 646	-58 160
1990	2 317	-8 410	10 856	-130	-81 393	-37 183	-28 765	-27 824	12 379
1991	2 923	-12 880	16 777	-974	-73 075	-37 889	-45 673	11 097	-610
1992	-1 667	-7 408	5 807	-67	-76 644	-48 266	-49 166	-387	21 175
1993	-351	-6 311	6 270	-310	-198 823	-83 951	-146 253	766	30 615
1994	-390	-5 383	5 088	-95	-183 893	-80 167	-63 190	-36 336	-4 200
1995	-984	-4 859	4 125	-250	-341 538	-98 750	-122 394	-45 286	-75 108
1996	-989	-5 025	3 930	106	-419 088	-91 885	-149 315	-86 333	-91 555
1997	68	-5 417	5 438	47	-484 533	-104 803	-116 852	-121 760	-141 118
1998	-422	-4 678	4 111	145	-346 624	-142 644	-130 204	-38 204	-35 572
1999	2 750	-6 175	9 559	-634	-515 559	-224 934	-122 236	-97 704	-70 685
2000	-941	-5 182	4 265	-24	-559 292	-159 212	-127 908	-138 790	-133 382
2001	-486	-4 431	3 873	72	-377 219	-142 349	-90 644	-8 520	-135 706
2002	345	-5 251	5 701	-105	-291 310	-154 460	-48 568	-50 022	-38 260
2003	537	-7 279	7 981	-165	-328 484	-149 897	-146 722	-18 851	-13 014
2004	1 710	-3 044	4 716	38	-872 317	-244 128	-146 549	-120 017	-361 623
2005	5 539	-2 255	5 603	2 191	-446 436	-9 072	-180 125	-44 221	-213 018
2001									
1st quarter	77	-1 094	1 071	100	-216 461	-35 381	-25 355	-46 769	-108 956
2nd quarter	-783	-1 330	573	-26	-84 576	-26 783	-50 200	-7 507	-86
3rd quarter	77	-1 011	1 118	-30	36 340	-44 327	11 639	1 824	67 204
4th quarter	143	-996	1 111	28	-112 521	-35 857	-26 728	43 932	-93 868
2002									
1st quarter	133	-853	994	-8	-85 364	-48 155	-9 012	-27 798	-399
2nd quarter	42	-565	566	41	-137 911	-36 163	-20 735	-13 680	-67 333
3rd quarter	-27	-1 375	1 452	-104	2 335	-33 165	4 884	-7 443	38 059
4th quarter	197	-2 458	2 689	-34	-70 372	-36 979	-23 705	-1 101	-8 587
2003									
1st quarter	53	-2 428	2 445	36	-82 511	-22 716	-31 947	1 757	-29 605
2nd quarter	310	-1 591	1 975	-74	-158 385	-46 590	-32 734	-15 829	-63 232
3rd quarter	483	-1 532	2 035	-20	-719	-40 689	-27 677	21 261	46 386
4th quarter	-309	-1 728	1 526	-107	-86 866	-39 899	-54 364	-26 040	33 437
2004									
1st quarter	727	-561	1 374	-86	-310 496	-56 127	-30 045	-55 101	-169 223
2nd quarter	-2	-668	544	122	-136 293	-53 196	-38 702	-4 969	-39 426
3rd quarter	484	-1 270	1 794	-40	-145 441	-38 774	-47 988	-3 501	-55 178
4th quarter	501	-545	1 004	42	-280 082	-96 026	-29 814	-56 446	-97 796
2005									
1st quarter	2 591	-519	1 083	2 027	-95 313	-31 259	-50 367	-67 170	53 483
2nd quarter	989	-708	1 586	111	-196 568	-33 957	-45 702	57 244	-174 153
3rd quarter	1 501	-518	1 957	62	-138 647	30 342	-36 790	-29 483	-102 716
4th quarter	459	-509	977	-9	-15 911	25 799	-47 266	-4 812	10 368

[3]A minus sign indicates financial outflows.

Table 7-6. U.S. International Transactions—Continued

(Millions of dollars, seasonally adjusted.)

Year and quarter	Total	Foreign official assets in the United States, net							Other foreign assets in the United States, net				
		Total	U.S. government securities			Other U.S. government liabilities	U.S. liabilities reported by U.S. banks, not included elsewhere	Other foreign official assets	Total	Direct investment	U.S. Treasury securities	U.S. securities other than Treasury securities	U.S. currency
			Total	U.S. Treasury securities	Other								
1960	2 294	1 473	655	655	. . .	215	603	. . .	821	315	-364	282	. . .
1961	2 705	765	233	233	. . .	25	508	. . .	1 939	311	151	324	. . .
1962	1 911	1 270	1 409	1 410	-1	152	-291	. . .	641	346	-66	134	. . .
1963	3 217	1 986	816	803	12	429	742	. . .	1 231	231	-149	287	. . .
1964	3 643	1 660	432	434	-2	298	930	. . .	1 983	322	-146	-85	. . .
1965	742	134	-141	-134	-7	65	210	. . .	607	415	-131	-358	. . .
1966	3 661	-672	-1 527	-1 548	21	113	742	. . .	4 333	425	-356	906	. . .
1967	7 379	3 451	2 261	2 222	39	83	1 106	. . .	3 928	698	-135	1 016	. . .
1968	9 928	-774	-769	-798	29	-15	10	. . .	10 703	807	136	4 414	. . .
1969	12 702	-1 301	-2 343	-2 269	-74	251	792	. . .	14 002	1 263	-68	3 130	. . .
1970	6 359	6 908	9 439	9 411	28	-456	-2 075	. . .	-550	1 464	81	2 189	. . .
1971	22 970	26 879	26 570	26 578	-8	-510	819	. . .	-3 909	367	-24	2 289	. . .
1972	21 461	10 475	8 470	8 213	257	182	1 638	185	10 986	949	-39	4 507	. . .
1973	18 388	6 026	641	59	582	936	4 126	323	12 362	2 800	-216	4 041	. . .
1974	35 341	10 546	4 172	3 270	902	301	5 818	254	24 796	4 760	697	378	1 100
1975	17 170	7 027	5 563	4 658	905	1 517	-2 158	2 104	10 143	2 603	2 590	2 503	1 500
1976	38 018	17 693	9 892	9 319	573	4 627	969	2 205	20 326	4 347	2 783	1 284	1 500
1977	53 219	36 816	32 538	30 230	2 308	1 400	773	2 105	16 403	3 728	534	2 437	1 900
1978	67 036	33 678	24 221	23 555	666	2 476	5 551	1 430	33 358	7 897	2 178	2 254	3 000
1979	40 852	-13 665	-21 972	-22 435	463	-40	7 213	1 135	54 516	11 877	4 060	1 351	3 000
1980	62 612	15 497	11 895	9 708	2 187	615	-159	3 145	47 115	16 918	2 645	5 457	4 500
1981	86 232	4 960	6 322	5 019	1 303	-338	-3 670	2 646	81 272	25 195	2 927	6 905	3 200
1982	96 589	3 593	5 085	5 779	-694	605	-1 747	-350	92 997	12 635	7 027	6 085	4 000
1983	88 694	5 845	6 496	6 972	-476	602	545	-1 798	82 849	10 372	8 689	8 164	5 400
1984	117 752	3 140	4 703	4 690	13	739	555	-2 857	114 612	24 468	23 001	12 568	4 100
1985	146 115	-1 119	-1 139	-838	-301	844	645	-1 469	147 233	19 742	20 433	50 962	5 200
1986	230 009	35 648	33 150	34 364	-1 214	2 195	1 187	-884	194 360	35 420	3 809	70 969	4 100
1987	248 634	45 387	44 802	43 238	1 564	-2 326	3 918	-1 007	203 247	58 470	-7 643	42 120	5 400
1988	246 522	39 758	43 050	41 741	1 309	-467	-319	-2 506	206 764	57 735	20 239	26 353	5 800
1989	224 928	8 503	1 532	149	1 383	160	4 976	1 835	216 425	68 274	29 618	38 767	5 900
1990	141 571	33 910	30 243	29 576	667	1 868	3 385	-1 586	107 661	48 494	-2 534	1 592	18 800
1991	110 809	17 388	16 147	14 846	1 301	1 367	-1 484	1 359	93 421	23 171	18 826	35 144	15 400
1992	170 663	40 476	22 403	18 454	3 949	2 190	16 571	-688	130 185	19 822	37 131	30 043	13 400
1993	282 041	71 753	53 014	48 952	4 062	1 313	14 841	2 585	210 288	51 363	24 381	80 092	18 900
1994	305 989	39 583	36 827	30 750	6 077	1 564	3 665	-2 473	266 406	46 121	34 274	56 971	23 400
1995	438 562	109 880	72 712	68 977	3 735	-105	34 008	3 265	328 682	57 776	91 544	77 249	12 300
1996	551 096	126 724	120 679	115 671	5 008	-982	5 704	1 323	424 372	86 502	147 022	103 272	17 362
1997	706 809	19 036	-2 161	-6 690	4 529	-881	22 286	-208	687 773	105 603	130 435	161 409	24 782
1998	423 569	-19 903	-3 589	-9 921	6 332	-3 326	-9 501	-3 487	443 472	179 045	28 581	156 315	16 622
1999	740 210	43 543	32 527	12 177	20 350	-2 863	12 964	915	696 667	289 444	-44 497	298 834	22 407
2000	1 046 896	42 758	35 710	-5 199	40 909	-1 825	5 746	3 127	1 004 138	321 274	-69 983	459 889	5 315
2001	782 859	28 059	54 620	33 700	20 920	-2 309	-29 978	5 726	754 800	167 021	-14 378	393 885	23 783
2002	797 813	115 945	90 971	60 466	30 505	137	21 221	3 616	681 868	84 372	100 403	283 299	21 513
2003	864 769	278 275	224 874	184 931	39 943	-517	48 643	5 275	586 494	63 961	91 455	220 705	16 640
2004	1 450 221	387 809	305 000	263 338	41 662	-139	69 245	13 703	1 062 412	133 162	102 940	381 493	14 827
2005	1 212 250	199 495	156 450	71 749	84 701	-488	24 275	19 258	1 012 755	109 754	199 491	474 140	19 416
2001													
1st quarter	332 155	21 333	19 590	16 016	3 574	-601	1 341	1 003	310 822	59 145	-17 659	129 474	2 311
2nd quarter	207 866	-19 965	-9 634	-19 566	9 932	-1 154	-10 205	1 028	227 831	59 338	-11 916	108 537	2 772
3rd quarter	22 936	15 653	14 545	14 761	-216	-205	-675	1 988	7 283	13 783	-7 998	60 748	8 203
4th quarter	219 902	11 038	30 119	22 489	7 630	-349	-20 439	1 707	208 864	34 755	23 195	95 126	10 497
2002													
1st quarter	174 113	12 801	10 337	4 420	5 917	-597	2 335	726	161 312	24 485	10 327	73 750	4 525
2nd quarter	231 296	53 312	25 942	19 374	6 568	365	26 099	906	177 984	7 194	18 830	99 689	7 183
3rd quarter	161 785	18 328	20 609	9 124	11 485	464	-3 590	845	143 457	13 929	54 060	43 282	2 556
4th quarter	230 618	31 504	34 083	27 548	6 535	-95	-3 623	1 139	199 114	38 763	17 186	66 578	7 249
2003													
1st quarter	242 159	50 622	41 461	30 277	11 184	-407	8 315	1 253	191 537	37 193	7 103	52 209	4 927
2nd quarter	220 780	66 889	47 550	42 668	4 882	-5	18 593	751	153 891	-5 420	49 717	81 187	1 458
3rd quarter	130 592	64 595	41 393	33 935	7 458	-118	21 981	1 339	65 997	-1 514	35 138	15 354	2 768
4th quarter	271 239	96 169	94 470	78 051	16 419	13	-246	1 932	175 070	33 703	-503	71 955	7 487
2004													
1st quarter	438 930	147 627	124 051	112 586	11 465	-225	22 058	1 743	291 303	23 627	31 976	47 862	-1 800
2nd quarter	314 152	79 944	66 043	62 841	3 202	-220	11 353	2 768	234 208	33 007	64 838	87 270	8 754
3rd quarter	260 132	71 285	63 125	51 193	11 932	476	4 317	3 367	188 847	36 844	-2 205	86 577	2 560
4th quarter	437 006	88 953	51 781	36 718	15 063	-170	31 517	5 825	348 053	39 683	8 331	159 784	5 313
2005													
1st quarter	224 128	18 965	33 007	9 226	23 781	-740	-15 814	2 512	205 163	30 539	86 108	77 412	1 072
2nd quarter	346 179	74 613	36 313	16 892	19 421	112	34 187	4 001	271 566	8 245	14 103	111 808	4 507
3rd quarter	388 592	33 983	25 926	8 213	17 713	395	824	6 838	354 609	44 459	37 239	153 049	4 679
4th quarter	253 350	71 934	61 204	37 418	23 786	-255	5 078	5 907	181 416	26 510	62 041	131 871	9 158

[4]A minus sign indicates financial outflows or a decrease in foreign official assets in the United States.
. . . = Not available.

Table 7-6. U.S. International Transactions—Continued

(Millions of dollars, seasonally adjusted.)

	Financial account—Continued										
Year and quarter	Foreign-owned assets in the United States, net 4—Cont.		Statistical discrepancy 5		Balance on goods	Balance on services	Balance on goods and services	Balance on income	Balance on goods, services, and income	Unilateral current transfers, net	Balance on current account
	Other foreign assets in the United States, net—Cont.		Total	Seasonal adjustment discrepancy							
	U.S. liabilities										
	To unaffiliated foreigners reported by U.S. nonbanking concerns	Reported by U.S. banks not included elsewhere									
1960	-90	678	-1 019	0	4 892	-1 385	3 508	3 379	6 887	-4 062	2 824
1961	226	928	-989	0	5 571	-1 376	4 195	3 755	7 950	-4 127	3 822
1962	-110	336	-1 124	0	4 521	-1 151	3 370	4 294	7 664	-4 277	3 387
1963	-37	898	-360	0	5 224	-1 014	4 210	4 596	8 806	-4 392	4 414
1964	75	1 818	-907	0	6 801	-779	6 022	5 041	11 063	-4 240	6 823
1965	178	503	-457	0	4 951	-287	4 664	5 350	10 014	-4 583	5 431
1966	476	2 882	629	0	3 817	-877	2 940	5 047	7 987	-4 955	3 031
1967	584	1 765	-205	0	3 800	-1 196	2 604	5 274	7 878	-5 294	2 583
1968	1 475	3 871	438	0	635	-385	250	5 990	6 240	-5 629	611
1969	792	8 886	-1 516	0	607	-516	91	6 044	6 135	-5 735	399
1970	2 014	-6 298	-219	0	2 603	-349	2 254	6 233	8 487	-6 156	2 331
1971	369	-6 911	-9 779	0	-2 260	957	-1 303	7 272	5 969	-7 402	-1 433
1972	815	4 754	-1 879	0	-6 416	973	-5 443	8 192	2 749	-8 544	-5 795
1973	1 035	4 702	-2 654	0	911	989	1 900	12 153	14 053	-6 913	7 140
1974	1 844	16 017	-2 558	0	-5 505	1 213	-4 292	15 503	11 211	-9 249	1 962
1975	319	628	4 417	0	8 903	3 501	12 404	12 787	25 191	-7 075	18 116
1976	-578	10 990	8 955	0	-9 483	3 401	-6 082	16 063	9 981	-5 686	4 295
1977	1 086	6 719	-4 099	0	-31 091	3 845	-27 246	18 137	-9 109	-5 226	-14 335
1978	1 889	16 141	9 236	0	-33 927	4 164	-29 763	20 408	-9 355	-5 788	-15 143
1979	1 621	32 607	24 349	0	-27 568	3 003	-24 565	30 873	6 308	-6 593	-285
1980	6 852	10 743	20 886	0	-25 500	6 093	-19 407	30 073	10 666	-8 349	2 317
1981	917	42 128	21 792	0	-28 023	11 852	-16 172	32 903	16 731	-11 702	5 030
1982	-2 383	65 633	36 630	0	-36 485	12 329	-24 156	35 164	11 008	-16 544	-5 536
1983	-118	50 342	16 162	0	-67 102	9 335	-57 767	36 386	-21 381	-17 310	-38 691
1984	16 626	33 849	16 733	0	-112 492	3 419	-109 073	35 063	-74 010	-20 335	-94 344
1985	9 851	41 045	16 478	0	-122 173	294	-121 880	25 723	-96 157	-21 998	-118 155
1986	3 325	76 737	28 590	0	-145 081	6 543	-138 538	15 494	-123 044	-24 142	-147 177
1987	18 363	86 537	-9 048	0	-159 557	7 874	-151 684	14 293	-137 391	-23 265	-160 655
1988	32 893	63 744	-19 289	0	-126 959	12 393	-114 566	18 687	-95 879	-25 274	-121 153
1989	22 086	51 780	49 605	0	-117 749	24 607	-93 142	19 824	-73 318	-26 169	-99 486
1990	45 133	-3 824	25 211	0	-111 037	30 173	-80 864	28 550	-52 314	-26 654	-78 968
1991	-3 115	3 994	-44 840	0	-76 937	45 802	-31 136	24 131	-7 005	9 904	2 897
1992	13 573	16 216	-45 617	0	-96 897	57 685	-39 212	24 235	-14 977	-35 100	-50 078
1993	10 489	25 063	4 617	0	-132 451	62 141	-70 311	25 316	-44 995	-39 811	-84 805
1994	1 302	104 338	-3 717	0	-165 831	67 338	-98 493	17 146	-81 347	-40 265	-121 612
1995	59 637	30 176	28 196	0	-174 170	77 786	-96 384	20 891	-75 493	-38 074	-113 567
1996	53 736	16 478	-12 188	0	-191 000	86 935	-104 065	22 318	-81 747	-43 017	-124 764
1997	116 518	149 026	-79 905	0	-198 104	90 155	-107 949	12 609	-95 340	-45 062	-140 402
1998	23 140	39 769	144 554	0	-246 687	82 081	-164 606	4 265	-160 341	-53 187	-213 528
1999	76 247	54 232	68 617	0	-346 015	82 729	-263 286	13 888	-249 398	-50 428	-299 826
2000	170 672	116 971	-70 213	0	-452 414	74 855	-377 559	21 054	-356 505	-58 645	-415 150
2001	66 110	118 379	-10 014	0	-427 188	64 393	-362 795	25 131	-337 664	-51 295	-388 959
2002	95 871	96 410	-29 251	0	-482 298	61 230	-421 068	12 209	-408 859	-63 587	-472 446
2003	96 526	97 207	-7 510	0	-547 302	52 405	-494 897	36 593	-458 304	-69 210	-527 514
2004	93 250	336 740	85 128	0	-665 410	54 114	-611 296	27 592	-583 704	-81 582	-665 286
2005	30 105	179 849	10 410	0	-782 740	66 011	-716 730	11 293	-705 437	-86 072	-791 508
2001											
1st quarter	112 097	25 454	-8 127	6 729	-115 420	18 144	-97 276	4 914	-92 362	-15 171	-107 533
2nd quarter	-173	69 273	-22 928	-2 608	-105 184	16 532	-88 652	6 531	-82 121	-15 802	-97 923
3rd quarter	-23 171	-44 282	37 481	-9 626	-105 233	15 716	-89 517	-484	-90 001	-2 941	-92 942
4th quarter	-22 643	67 934	-16 446	5 499	-101 351	14 002	-87 349	14 167	-73 182	-17 374	-90 556
2002											
1st quarter	57 788	-9 563	20 093	10 176	-107 984	14 818	-93 166	2 448	-90 718	-18 326	-109 044
2nd quarter	17 805	27 283	27 975	-2 208	-118 993	15 706	-103 287	-1 175	-104 462	-14 764	-119 226
3rd quarter	7 515	22 115	-43 195	-13 944	-122 928	15 671	-107 257	2 773	-104 484	-14 599	-119 083
4th quarter	12 763	56 575	-34 131	5 969	-132 393	15 036	-117 357	8 171	-109 186	-15 897	-125 083
2003											
1st quarter	68 460	21 645	-22 171	8 275	-136 619	12 402	-124 217	4 652	-119 565	-17 598	-137 163
2nd quarter	15 129	11 820	70 191	-1 477	-135 841	12 606	-123 235	9 037	-114 198	-16 905	-131 103
3rd quarter	9 137	5 114	2 661	-11 821	-135 990	13 015	-122 975	8 394	-114 581	-16 961	-131 542
4th quarter	3 800	58 628	-58 190	5 024	-138 852	14 382	-124 470	14 506	-109 964	-17 747	-127 711
2004											
1st quarter	42 419	147 219	16 577	10 471	-149 954	13 806	-136 148	12 864	-123 284	-22 554	-145 838
2nd quarter	2 840	37 499	-11 809	-2 405	-165 092	13 703	-151 389	5 513	-145 876	-20 895	-166 771
3rd quarter	13 353	51 718	51 646	-12 227	-168 803	12 131	-156 672	6 869	-149 803	-16 524	-166 327
4th quarter	34 638	100 304	28 716	4 163	-181 561	14 475	-167 086	2 339	-164 747	-21 609	-186 356
2005											
1st quarter	80 174	-70 142	57 678	13 192	-183 268	15 160	-168 108	3 621	-164 487	-27 237	-191 724
2nd quarter	-20 035	152 938	44 044	-4 862	-188 220	16 162	-172 058	1 994	-170 064	-23 194	-193 258
3rd quarter	20 271	94 912	-72 240	-17 549	-198 746	16 954	-181 792	7 841	-173 951	-9 464	-183 415
4th quarter	-50 305	2 141	-19 071	9 219	-212 506	17 733	-194 774	-2 159	-196 933	-26 176	-223 109

4A minus sign indicates financial outflows or a decrease in foreign official assets in the United States.
5Sum of credits and debits with the sign reversed.

Table 7-7. Foreigners' Transactions in Long-Term Securities with U.S. Residents

(Billions of dollars, not seasonally adjusted.)

Year and month	Gross purchases from U.S. residents	Gross sales to U.S. residents	Transactions in U.S. domestic securities between foreigners and U.S. residents						
				Net purchases					
			Total	Private					
				Total	Treasury bonds and notes	Government agency bonds	Corporate bonds	Equities	
1977	60.7	30.1	30.6	. . .	. . .	. . .	. . .	. . .	
1978	60.5	51.1	9.4	3.6	1.0	0.6	0.3	1.7	
1979	72.9	67.2	5.7	2.5	1.2	0.1	0.2	1.1	
1980	106.9	91.1	15.8	6.6	1.0	0.4	0.9	4.3	
1981	126.5	100.5	25.9	10.2	3.3	0.3	1.9	4.8	
1982	159.5	136.8	22.7	9.2	2.8	0.3	2.5	3.6	
1983	223.4	211.7	11.7	13.2	4.6	0.5	1.7	6.4	
1984	335.5	304.0	31.4	33.8	21.0	1.2	12.5	-0.9	
1985	667.2	588.9	78.3	71.9	21.1	4.6	41.4	4.8	
1986	1 355.4	1 266.9	88.6	76.4	5.2	8.2	45.1	18.0	
1987	1 692.1	1 623.0	69.1	37.5	-5.5	3.5	22.7	16.8	
1988	1 827.9	1 753.1	74.8	49.4	22.2	5.4	21.3	0.4	
1989	2 431.7	2 335.2	96.5	66.5	27.4	13.7	17.5	7.9	
1990	2 111.2	2 092.4	18.7	-3.6	-5.3	5.6	9.8	-13.7	
1991	2 382.1	2 324.0	58.1	54.3	18.7	8.9	16.5	10.1	
1992	2 677.8	2 604.6	73.2	63.1	32.4	14.3	20.0	-3.7	
1993	3 212.5	3 101.4	111.1	103.2	22.2	31.4	29.9	19.6	
1994	3 351.1	3 210.7	140.4	94.9	37.0	15.6	38.0	4.3	
1995	3 737.6	3 505.7	231.9	185.3	94.5	25.0	57.6	8.2	
1996	4 667.6	4 297.4	370.2	278.1	146.4	36.7	82.2	12.7	
1997	6 573.3	6 185.3	388.0	339.7	140.2	45.3	82.8	71.3	
1998	7 633.5	7 355.7	277.8	270.8	44.9	50.5	121.7	53.7	
1999	7 483.5	7 133.3	350.2	338.8	-0.1	71.9	158.8	108.2	
2000	8 684.1	8 226.3	457.8	420.1	-47.7	111.9	182.1	173.8	
2001	10 261.8	9 740.9	520.8	494.2	15.0	146.6	218.2	114.4	
2002	13 022.9	12 475.4	547.6	508.3	112.8	166.6	176.7	52.2	
2003	13 526.0	12 806.1	719.9	585.0	159.7	129.9	260.3	35.0	
2004	15 178.9	14 262.4	916.5	680.9	150.9	205.7	298.0	26.2	
2005	17 175.0	16 164.3	1 010.7	889.5	270.0	187.8	353.1	78.7	
2003									
January	949.9	903.8	46.1	38.7	-0.6	19.2	22.9	-2.9	
February	932.5	915.6	16.9	7.5	-7.5	4.5	12.6	-2.1	
March	1 196.3	1 125.0	71.3	70.0	27.0	13.8	26.4	2.8	
April	939.0	885.9	53.1	52.2	9.8	15.9	22.1	4.5	
May	1 252.3	1 150.8	101.5	87.3	28.4	25.0	27.2	6.7	
June	1 305.4	1 227.5	77.8	60.5	23.6	7.0	20.8	9.2	
July	1 287.9	1 208.4	79.5	67.4	39.1	12.2	25.6	-9.5	
August	1 266.8	1 213.1	53.7	56.8	21.2	7.9	16.1	11.6	
September	1 152.4	1 131.7	20.6	7.6	-3.9	-2.2	19.8	-6.1	
October	1 238.4	1 197.3	41.2	14.3	-13.1	8.5	20.0	-1.1	
November	986.3	904.2	82.1	60.5	16.6	7.4	27.6	8.9	
December	1 018.8	942.9	76.0	62.3	19.2	10.6	19.3	13.1	
2004									
January	1 137.8	1 043.6	94.2	64.1	19.2	22.4	10.7	11.8	
February	1 157.7	1 089.3	68.4	45.9	8.3	16.1	19.6	1.9	
March	1 393.5	1 326.1	67.3	29.4	17.6	-3.4	25.2	-10.1	
April	1 375.5	1 279.6	95.9	69.8	27.7	24.3	18.4	-0.6	
May	1 312.2	1 249.4	62.9	56.1	20.8	21.0	20.0	-5.7	
June	1 233.6	1 143.3	90.3	74.5	29.0	14.7	26.6	4.2	
July	1 202.9	1 135.0	67.8	58.5	6.7	16.8	27.7	7.3	
August	1 207.1	1 153.8	53.3	34.0	-2.1	14.9	23.7	-2.4	
September	1 250.7	1 183.5	67.2	52.6	6.2	6.0	43.8	-3.3	
October	1 193.8	1 130.0	63.8	48.9	3.6	22.9	18.9	3.6	
November	1 405.7	1 304.2	101.5	73.5	12.7	24.3	24.3	12.2	
December	1 308.5	1 224.6	83.8	73.6	1.4	25.6	39.3	7.3	
2005									
January	1 287.1	1 198.1	89.0	74.2	25.3	19.1	16.7	13.2	
February	1 364.7	1 273.4	91.4	73.1	32.3	10.6	28.9	1.2	
March	1 524.7	1 459.4	65.2	78.5	48.4	6.2	21.2	2.7	
April	1 407.3	1 348.6	58.6	47.7	16.5	8.5	17.8	4.9	
May	1 494.7	1 451.9	42.9	29.2	-6.3	17.5	17.6	0.4	
June	1 523.7	1 431.2	92.5	68.7	2.1	15.6	47.9	3.2	
July	1 287.0	1 192.5	94.5	83.9	23.6	30.5	22.0	7.8	
August	1 428.3	1 348.6	79.7	74.1	21.9	16.2	34.7	1.4	
September	1 668.0	1 559.5	108.5	104.7	23.3	17.5	41.8	22.1	
October	1 486.0	1 379.5	106.5	95.5	23.6	29.6	34.7	7.5	
November	1 465.5	1 358.3	107.2	97.4	48.0	8.1	36.5	4.8	
December	1 238.1	1 163.4	74.7	62.5	11.2	8.5	33.3	9.6	

. . . = Not available.

Table 7-7. Foreigners' Transactions in Long-Term Securities with U.S. Residents—Continued

(Billions of dollars, not seasonally adjusted.)

Year and month	Transactions in U.S. domestic securities between foreigners and U.S. residents—Continued					Transactions in foreign securities between foreigners and U.S. residents					Net long-term flows
	Net purchases—Continued					Gross purchases from U.S. residents	Gross sales to U.S. residents	Net purchases [1]			
	Official										
	Total	Treasury bonds and notes	Government agency bonds	Corporate bonds	Equities			Total	Bonds	Equities	
1977	. . .	. . .	. . .	. . .	. . .	10.3	15.8	-5.5	-5.1	-0.4	25.1
1978	5.8	3.7	0.7	0.7	0.7	14.8	18.5	-3.7	-4.2	0.5	5.7
1979	3.2	1.7	0.5	0.4	0.6	17.3	22.1	-4.8	-4.0	-0.8	0.9
1980	9.2	3.9	2.2	2.0	1.1	25.0	28.1	-3.1	-1.0	-2.1	12.6
1981	15.7	11.7	1.3	1.6	1.0	26.9	32.6	-5.7	-5.5	-0.2	20.2
1982	13.5	14.6	-0.7	-0.7	0.3	34.3	42.3	-8.0	-6.6	-1.3	14.7
1983	-1.5	0.8	-0.5	-0.8	-1.0	49.6	56.6	-7.0	-3.2	-3.8	4.7
1984	-2.3	0.5	0.0	-0.8	-2.1	70.8	75.9	-5.0	-3.9	-1.1	26.4
1985	6.4	8.1	-0.3	-1.6	0.1	102.1	110.0	-7.9	-4.0	-3.9	70.3
1986	12.1	14.2	-1.2	-1.6	0.7	216.1	221.7	-5.5	-3.7	-1.9	83.0
1987	31.6	31.1	1.6	-0.4	-0.6	294.5	301.4	-6.9	-8.0	1.1	62.3
1988	25.4	26.6	1.3	-0.1	-2.4	293.9	303.3	-9.4	-7.4	-2.0	65.4
1989	30.1	26.8	1.4	-0.2	2.0	344.6	363.2	-18.6	-5.5	-13.1	78.0
1990	22.3	23.3	0.7	-0.1	-1.4	437.7	468.9	-31.2	-21.9	-9.2	-12.4
1991	3.8	1.2	1.3	0.4	0.9	450.9	497.7	-46.8	-14.8	-32.0	11.3
1992	10.1	6.9	3.9	0.8	-1.5	663.6	711.5	-47.9	-15.6	-32.3	25.4
1993	7.9	1.3	4.0	0.6	2.0	991.4	1 134.5	-143.1	-80.4	-62.7	-31.9
1994	45.4	41.8	6.1	0.0	-2.5	1 234.5	1 291.8	-57.3	-9.2	-48.1	83.1
1995	46.6	39.6	3.7	0.2	3.0	1 235.1	1 333.8	-98.7	-48.4	-50.3	133.2
1996	92.1	85.8	5.0	1.5	-0.2	1 564.4	1 675.0	-110.6	-51.4	-59.3	259.6
1997	48.3	44.0	4.5	1.5	-1.7	2 207.7	2 296.8	-89.1	-48.1	-40.9	298.9
1998	7.0	4.1	6.3	0.2	-3.7	2 257.8	2 269.0	-11.1	-17.3	6.2	266.7
1999	11.4	-9.9	20.4	1.5	-0.6	1 975.6	1 965.6	10.0	-5.7	15.6	360.1
2000	37.7	-6.3	40.9	2.0	1.1	2 761.1	2 778.3	-17.1	-4.1	-13.1	440.7
2001	26.7	3.5	17.4	3.8	2.0	2 557.8	2 577.4	-19.6	30.5	-50.1	501.2
2002	39.3	7.1	28.6	5.6	-2.0	2 640.0	2 613.0	27.0	28.5	-1.5	574.6
2003	134.9	103.8	25.9	5.4	-0.3	2 761.8	2 818.4	-56.5	32.0	-88.6	663.3
2004	235.6	201.1	20.8	11.5	2.2	3 123.1	3 276.0	-152.8	-67.9	-85.0	763.6
2005	121.1	69.2	32.0	19.0	1.0	3 681.4	3 854.0	-172.6	-45.1	-127.5	838.1
2003											
January	7.4	2.4	4.5	0.5	0.0	213.2	214.7	-1.5	5.3	-6.8	44.6
February	9.4	4.3	4.8	0.2	0.0	187.4	179.6	7.8	11.9	-4.1	24.7
March	1.3	-0.1	0.9	0.5	0.0	231.6	236.7	-5.1	-0.2	-4.9	66.2
April	0.9	-1.1	2.1	0.0	0.0	201.3	195.6	5.7	3.4	2.3	58.9
May	14.2	13.4	0.7	0.2	-0.1	227.4	235.9	-8.5	3.3	-11.8	93.0
June	17.3	15.9	1.0	0.3	0.1	246.8	258.7	-11.9	-5.7	-6.2	65.9
July	12.1	11.6	0.0	0.5	0.0	259.2	256.3	2.9	11.5	-8.5	82.4
August	-3.0	-4.5	0.8	0.5	0.2	201.4	213.1	-11.6	2.8	-14.5	42.1
September	13.0	10.7	2.0	0.4	-0.1	260.7	261.6	-0.9	11.9	-12.8	19.7
October	26.9	23.6	2.8	0.7	-0.2	277.4	299.6	-22.2	-10.5	-11.6	19.0
November	21.7	19.0	1.9	1.0	-0.1	227.1	237.6	-10.5	-7.5	-2.9	71.7
December	13.7	8.7	4.4	0.7	-0.1	228.4	229.2	-0.8	5.9	-6.7	75.1
2004											
January	30.2	26.8	3.6	0.5	-0.7	271.9	285.7	-13.7	-3.5	-10.2	80.5
February	22.5	17.9	4.2	0.2	0.2	270.2	284.1	-13.9	-8.2	-5.7	54.4
March	38.0	33.6	2.8	1.3	0.3	329.5	326.7	2.8	0.8	1.9	70.1
April	26.2	22.7	1.8	0.6	1.1	260.7	264.5	-3.8	6.0	-9.9	92.1
May	6.8	7.9	-1.8	0.5	0.2	252.6	260.4	-7.8	-1.3	-6.5	55.1
June	15.8	16.3	-0.9	0.8	-0.5	250.1	259.4	-9.3	-1.1	-8.3	81.0
July	9.4	5.9	2.5	0.8	0.1	234.7	253.5	-18.9	-9.8	-9.1	49.0
August	19.3	15.5	2.6	1.1	0.1	233.7	242.1	-8.4	-7.6	-0.8	45.0
September	14.5	10.9	2.4	1.2	0.0	228.2	258.1	-29.9	-25.4	-4.5	37.3
October	14.9	15.6	-0.9	0.9	-0.7	254.9	270.7	-15.8	-5.6	-10.2	48.0
November	28.0	21.0	3.5	1.9	1.5	274.2	286.0	-11.8	-4.0	-7.8	89.7
December	10.3	7.0	1.0	1.6	0.6	262.5	284.9	-22.4	-8.3	-14.1	61.5
2005											
January	14.8	7.6	6.3	1.4	-0.5	243.2	250.4	-7.2	-1.7	-5.5	81.8
February	18.3	12.2	3.9	2.1	0.1	275.6	291.1	-15.5	-0.4	-15.1	75.9
March	-13.3	-14.2	1.3	-0.4	0.1	324.8	346.6	-21.8	-6.7	-15.1	43.5
April	11.0	13.2	-1.5	0.1	-0.7	284.9	293.6	-8.7	-6.2	-2.5	49.9
May	13.6	7.9	3.9	1.8	0.0	285.4	301.4	-16.0	-11.3	-4.7	26.9
June	23.8	17.6	3.1	2.6	0.5	305.9	323.4	-17.5	-5.0	-12.5	75.0
July	10.6	5.1	4.2	1.4	-0.1	271.6	289.3	-17.7	-8.9	-8.8	76.8
August	5.6	3.7	-0.4	2.0	0.3	308.5	308.9	-0.3	16.4	-16.7	79.4
September	3.8	-1.1	1.7	2.2	1.0	316.6	340.9	-24.3	-17.8	-6.5	84.2
October	11.0	6.0	3.2	1.6	0.2	379.2	383.1	-3.9	2.3	-6.2	102.6
November	9.9	4.8	3.2	1.8	0.1	342.0	359.4	-17.4	0.0	-17.3	89.8
December	12.2	6.5	3.2	2.5	0.0	343.6	365.9	-22.4	-5.7	-16.6	52.3

[1](-) indicates net U.S. acquisitions of foreign securities.
. . . = Not available.

Table 7-8. International Investment Position of the United States at Year-End

(Millions of dollars.)

Year	U.S. net international investment position — Direct investment at current cost	Direct investment at market value	U.S.-owned assets abroad — Total, direct investment at current cost	Total, direct investment at market value	Official reserve assets	Other U.S. government assets	Direct investment — Current cost	Market value	Foreign bonds	Foreign corporate stocks	U.S. nonbank claims	U.S. bank claims
1976	164 832	. . .	456 964	. . .	44 094	44 978	222 283	. . .	34 704	9 453	20 317	81 135
1977	171 440	. . .	512 278	. . .	53 376	48 567	246 078	. . .	39 329	10 110	22 256	92 562
1978	206 423	. . .	621 227	. . .	69 450	53 187	285 005	. . .	42 148	11 236	29 385	130 816
1979	316 926	. . .	786 701	. . .	143 260	58 851	336 301	. . .	41 966	14 803	34 491	157 029
1980	360 838	. . .	929 806	. . .	171 412	65 573	388 072	. . .	43 524	18 930	38 429	203 866
1981	339 767	. . .	1 001 667	. . .	124 568	70 893	407 804	. . .	45 675	16 467	42 752	293 508
1982	328 954	235 947	1 108 436	961 015	143 445	76 903	374 059	226 638	56 604	17 442	35 405	404 578
1983	298 304	257 393	1 210 974	1 129 673	123 110	81 664	355 643	274 342	58 569	26 154	131 329	434 505
1984	160 695	134 088	1 204 900	1 127 132	105 040	86 945	348 342	270 574	62 810	25 994	130 138	445 631
1985	54 343	96 886	1 287 396	1 302 712	117 930	89 792	371 036	386 352	75 020	44 383	141 872	447 363
1986	-36 209	100 782	1 469 396	1 594 652	139 875	91 850	404 818	530 074	85 724	72 399	167 392	507 338
1987	-80 007	50 529	1 646 527	1 758 711	162 370	90 681	478 062	590 246	93 889	94 700	177 368	549 457
1988	-178 470	10 466	1 829 665	2 008 365	144 179	87 892	513 761	692 461	104 187	128 662	197 757	653 227
1989	-259 506	-46 987	2 070 868	2 350 235	168 714	86 643	553 093	832 460	116 949	197 345	234 307	713 817
1990	-245 347	-164 495	2 178 978	2 294 085	174 664	84 344	616 655	731 762	144 717	197 596	265 315	695 687
1991	-309 259	-260 819	2 286 456	2 470 629	159 223	81 422	643 364	827 537	176 774	278 976	256 295	690 402
1992	-431 198	-452 305	2 331 696	2 656 496	147 435	83 022	663 830	798 630	200 817	314 266	254 303	668 023
1993	-306 956	-144 268	2 753 648	3 091 421	164 945	83 382	723 526	1 061 299	309 666	543 862	242 022	686 245
1994	-323 397	-135 251	2 987 118	3 315 135	163 394	83 908	786 565	1 114 582	310 391	626 762	322 980	693 118
1995	-458 462	-305 836	3 486 272	3 964 558	176 061	85 064	885 506	1 363 792	413 310	790 615	367 567	768 149
1996	-495 055	-360 024	4 032 307	4 650 837	160 739	86 123	989 810	1 608 340	481 411	1 006 135	450 578	857 511
1997	-820 682	-822 732	4 567 906	5 379 128	134 836	86 198	1 068 063	1 879 285	543 396	1 207 787	545 524	982 102
1998	-895 358	-1 070 769	5 095 546	6 179 126	146 006	86 768	1 196 021	2 279 601	594 400	1 474 983	588 322	1 009 046
1999	-766 237	-1 037 437	5 974 394	7 399 678	136 418	84 227	1 414 355	2 839 639	548 233	2 003 716	704 517	1 082 928
2000	-1 381 196	-1 581 007	6 238 785	7 401 192	128 400	85 168	1 531 607	2 694 014	572 692	1 852 842	836 559	1 231 517
2001	-1 919 430	-2 339 448	6 308 681	6 930 484	129 961	85 654	1 693 131	2 314 934	557 062	1 612 673	839 303	1 390 897
2002	-2 088 008	-2 454 328	6 652 248	6 807 793	158 602	85 309	1 867 043	2 022 588	705 226	1 374 665	901 946	1 559 457
2003	-2 131 170	-2 339 788	7 648 880	8 318 156	183 577	84 772	2 059 850	2 729 126	874 356	2 079 422	594 004	1 772 899
2004	-2 360 785	-2 448 744	9 186 661	10 075 337	189 591	83 062	2 399 224	3 287 900	992 969	2 560 418	733 538	2 227 859
2005	-2 693 799	-2 546 175	10 008 676	11 079 202	188 043	77 523	2 453 933	3 524 459	987 543	3 086 454	784 521	2 430 659

Year	Foreign-owned assets in the United States — Total, direct investment at current cost	Total, direct investment at market value	Foreign official assets	Direct investment in the United States — Current cost	Market value	U.S. Treasury securities	U.S. currency	Corporate and other bonds	Corporate stocks	U.S. nonbank liabilities	U.S. bank liabilities
1976	292 132	. . .	104 445	47 528	. . .	7 028	11 792	11 964	42 949	12 961	53 465
1977	340 838	. . .	140 867	55 413	. . .	7 562	13 656	11 456	39 779	11 921	60 184
1978	414 804	. . .	173 057	68 976	. . .	8 910	16 569	11 457	42 097	16 019	77 719
1979	469 775	. . .	159 852	88 579	. . .	14 210	19 552	10 269	48 318	18 669	110 326
1980	568 968	. . .	176 062	127 105	. . .	16 113	24 079	9 545	64 569	30 426	121 069
1981	661 900	. . .	180 425	164 623	. . .	18 505	27 295	10 694	64 391	30 606	165 361
1982	779 482	725 068	189 109	184 842	130 428	25 758	31 265	16 709	76 279	27 532	227 988
1983	912 670	872 280	194 468	193 708	153 318	33 846	36 776	17 454	96 357	61 731	278 330
1984	1 044 205	993 044	199 678	223 538	172 377	62 121	40 797	32 421	96 056	77 415	312 179
1985	1 233 053	1 205 826	202 482	247 223	219 996	87 954	46 036	82 290	125 578	86 993	354 497
1986	1 505 605	1 493 870	241 226	284 701	272 966	96 078	50 122	140 863	168 940	90 703	432 972
1987	1 726 534	1 708 182	283 058	334 552	316 200	82 588	55 584	166 089	175 643	110 187	518 833
1988	2 008 135	1 997 899	322 036	401 766	391 530	100 877	61 261	191 314	200 978	144 548	585 355
1989	2 330 374	2 397 222	341 746	467 886	534 734	166 541	67 118	231 673	251 191	167 093	637 126
1990	2 424 325	2 458 580	373 293	505 346	539 601	152 452	85 933	238 903	221 741	213 406	633 251
1991	2 595 715	2 731 448	398 538	533 404	669 137	170 295	101 317	274 136	271 872	208 908	637 245
1992	2 762 894	2 918 801	437 263	540 270	696 177	197 739	114 804	299 287	300 160	220 666	652 705
1993	3 060 604	3 235 689	509 422	593 313	768 398	221 501	133 734	355 822	340 627	229 038	677 147
1994	3 310 515	3 450 386	535 227	617 982	757 853	235 684	157 185	368 077	371 618	239 817	784 925
1995	3 944 734	4 270 394	682 873	680 066	1 005 726	326 995	169 484	459 080	510 769	300 424	815 043
1996	4 527 362	5 010 861	820 823	745 619	1 229 118	433 903	186 846	539 308	625 805	346 810	828 248
1997	5 388 588	6 201 860	873 716	824 136	1 637 408	538 137	211 628	618 837	893 888	459 407	968 839
1998	5 990 904	7 249 895	896 174	920 044	2 179 035	543 323	228 250	724 619	1 178 824	485 675	1 013 995
1999	6 740 631	8 437 115	951 088	1 101 709	2 798 193	440 685	250 657	825 175	1 526 116	578 046	1 067 155
2000	7 619 981	8 982 199	1 030 708	1 421 017	2 783 235	381 630	255 972	1 068 566	1 554 448	738 904	1 168 736
2001	8 228 111	9 269 932	1 109 072	1 518 473	2 560 294	375 059	279 755	1 343 071	1 478 301	798 314	1 326 066
2002	8 740 256	9 262 121	1 250 977	1 499 952	2 021 817	473 503	301 268	1 530 982	1 248 085	897 335	1 538 154
2003	9 780 050	10 657 944	1 562 770	1 576 983	2 454 877	527 223	317 908	1 710 787	1 712 069	450 884	1 921 426
2004	11 547 446	12 524 081	2 001 407	1 727 062	2 703 697	562 288	332 735	2 035 149	1 960 357	507 668	2 420 780
2005	12 702 475	13 625 377	2 216 123	1 874 263	2 797 165	704 875	352 151	2 275 197	2 115 485	563 749	2 600 632

. . . = Not available.

Section 7c: Exports and Imports

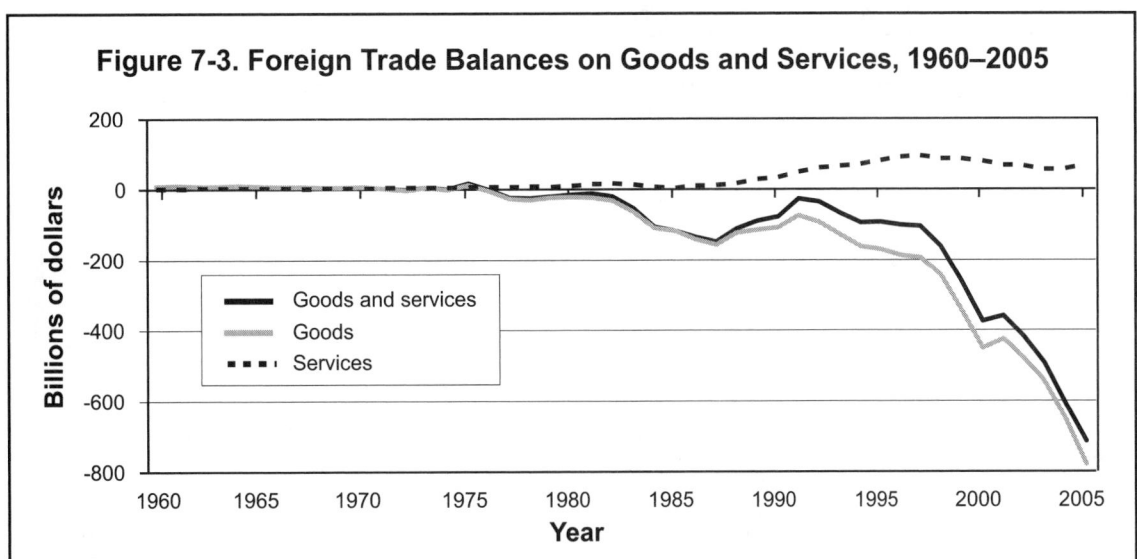

Figure 7-3. Foreign Trade Balances on Goods and Services, 1960–2005

- U.S. imports of goods and services exceeded exports by over $700 billion in 2005, setting yet another new record. Both exports and imports increased, but imports by more than exports—not only absolutely (in dollars) but also in terms of percentage rise. (Table 7-9)

- The trade deficit in goods also set a new record. Little of it was offset by the surplus in services trade, which rose somewhat in 2005 but remained below its 1997 peak of $90 billion. (Table 7-9)

- Canada and Mexico are the principal trading partners of the United States, with relations governed by the North American Free Trade Agreement (NAFTA). In 2005, U.S. exports to those two countries brought in $332 billion, compared with $186 billion in exports to the European Union and $184 billion in exports to China, Japan, and the newly industrialized countries of Asia (the NICS—Hong Kong, South Korea, Singapore, and Taiwan). (Table 7-13)

- U.S. imports from Canada and Mexico in 2005 amounted to $460 billion, compared with $309 billion from the European Union and $484 billion from China, Japan, and the Asian NICS. (Table 7-14)

- For U.S. services trade, "other private services" is the largest single category among both exports and imports. This includes such activities as education, financial services, and many other types of business and professional services. The United States had a surplus of $60 billion on "other private services" in 2005. The current-dollar value of this surplus has continued to increase and accounts for most of the total surplus on services. (Tables 7-15 and 7-16)

Table 7-9. U.S. Exports and Imports of Goods and Services

(Balance of payments basis; millions of dollars, seasonally adjusted.)

Year and month	Goods and services			Goods			Services		
	Exports	Imports	Balance	Exports	Imports	Balance	Exports	Imports	Balance
1960	25 940	22 432	3 508	19 650	14 758	4 892	6 290	7 674	-1 384
1961	26 403	22 208	4 195	20 108	14 537	5 571	6 295	7 671	-1 376
1962	27 722	24 352	3 370	20 781	16 260	4 521	6 941	8 092	-1 151
1963	29 620	25 410	4 210	22 272	17 048	5 224	7 348	8 362	-1 014
1964	33 341	27 319	6 022	25 501	18 700	6 801	7 840	8 619	-779
1965	35 285	30 621	4 664	26 461	21 510	4 951	8 824	9 111	-287
1966	38 926	35 987	2 939	29 310	25 493	3 817	9 616	10 494	-878
1967	41 333	38 729	2 604	30 666	26 866	3 800	10 667	11 863	-1 196
1968	45 543	45 293	250	33 626	32 991	635	11 917	12 302	-385
1969	49 220	49 129	91	36 414	35 807	607	12 806	13 322	-516
1970	56 640	54 386	2 254	42 469	39 866	2 603	14 171	14 520	-349
1971	59 677	60 979	-1 302	43 319	45 579	-2 260	16 358	15 400	958
1972	67 222	72 665	-5 443	49 381	55 797	-6 416	17 841	16 868	973
1973	91 242	89 342	1 900	71 410	70 499	911	19 832	18 843	989
1974	120 897	125 190	-4 293	98 306	103 811	-5 505	22 591	21 379	1 212
1975	132 585	120 181	12 404	107 088	98 185	8 903	25 497	21 996	3 501
1976	142 716	148 798	-6 082	114 745	124 228	-9 483	27 971	24 570	3 401
1977	152 301	179 547	-27 246	120 816	151 907	-31 091	31 485	27 640	3 845
1978	178 428	208 191	-29 763	142 075	176 002	-33 927	36 353	32 189	4 164
1979	224 131	248 696	-24 565	184 439	212 007	-27 568	39 692	36 689	3 003
1980	271 834	291 241	-19 407	224 250	249 750	-25 500	47 584	41 491	6 093
1981	294 398	310 570	-16 172	237 044	265 067	-28 023	57 354	45 503	11 851
1982	275 236	299 391	-24 156	211 157	247 642	-36 485	64 079	51 749	12 329
1983	266 106	323 874	-57 767	201 799	268 901	-67 102	64 307	54 973	9 335
1984	291 094	400 166	-109 072	219 926	332 418	-112 492	71 168	67 748	3 420
1985	289 070	410 950	-121 880	215 915	338 088	-122 173	73 155	72 862	294
1986	310 033	448 572	-138 538	223 344	368 425	-145 081	86 689	80 147	6 543
1987	348 869	500 552	-151 684	250 208	409 765	-159 557	98 661	90 787	7 874
1988	431 149	545 715	-114 566	320 230	447 189	-126 959	110 919	98 526	12 393
1989	487 003	580 144	-93 141	359 916	477 665	-117 749	127 087	102 479	24 607
1990	535 233	616 097	-80 864	387 401	498 438	-111 037	147 832	117 659	30 173
1991	578 344	609 479	-31 135	414 083	491 020	-76 937	164 261	118 459	45 802
1992	616 883	656 094	-39 212	439 631	536 528	-96 897	177 252	119 566	57 685
1993	642 863	713 173	-70 310	456 943	589 394	-132 451	185 920	123 779	62 141
1994	703 254	801 747	-98 493	502 859	668 690	-165 831	200 395	133 057	67 338
1995	794 387	890 771	-96 384	575 204	749 374	-174 170	219 183	141 397	77 786
1996	851 602	955 667	-104 065	612 113	803 113	-191 000	239 489	152 554	86 935
1997	934 453	1 042 402	-107 949	678 366	876 470	-198 104	256 087	165 932	90 155
1998	933 174	1 097 780	-164 606	670 416	917 103	-246 687	262 758	180 677	82 081
1999	965 884	1 229 170	-263 286	683 965	1 029 980	-346 015	281 919	199 190	82 729
2000	1 070 597	1 448 156	-377 559	771 994	1 224 408	-452 414	298 603	223 748	74 855
2001	1 004 896	1 367 691	-362 795	718 712	1 145 900	-427 188	286 184	221 791	64 393
2002	974 721	1 395 789	-421 067	682 422	1 164 720	-482 297	292 299	231 069	61 230
2003	1 016 096	1 510 993	-494 897	713 415	1 260 717	-547 302	302 681	250 276	52 405
2004	1 151 942	1 763 238	-611 296	807 516	1 472 926	-655 410	344 426	290 312	54 114
2005	1 275 245	1 991 975	-716 730	894 631	1 677 371	-782 740	380 614	314 604	66 011
2003									
January	81 821	122 857	-41 036	57 320	102 518	-45 198	24 501	20 339	4 162
February	82 448	122 014	-39 566	57 997	101 935	-43 938	24 451	20 079	4 372
March	82 222	125 837	-43 615	58 106	105 589	-47 483	24 116	20 248	3 868
April	80 884	123 145	-42 260	57 394	103 436	-46 041	23 490	19 709	3 781
May	81 802	122 795	-40 993	57 477	102 966	-45 489	24 325	19 829	4 496
June	84 180	124 162	-39 982	59 567	103 877	-44 310	24 613	20 285	4 328
July	84 795	126 315	-41 520	59 666	105 291	-45 625	25 129	21 024	4 105
August	83 666	123 568	-39 902	58 174	102 464	-44 290	25 492	21 104	4 388
September	85 738	127 293	-41 555	59 956	106 031	-46 075	25 782	21 262	4 520
October	88 119	129 146	-41 027	61 438	107 319	-45 881	26 681	21 827	4 854
November	90 328	129 974	-39 646	63 570	108 010	-44 440	26 758	21 964	4 794
December	90 090	133 888	-43 797	62 749	111 281	-48 531	27 341	22 607	4 734
2004									
January	89 357	134 313	-44 955	62 085	111 261	-49 175	27 272	23 052	4 220
February	92 643	137 080	-44 436	65 070	113 897	-48 826	27 573	23 183	4 390
March	95 368	142 125	-46 757	66 900	118 852	-51 952	28 468	23 273	5 195
April	94 487	142 343	-47 856	66 010	118 876	-52 866	28 477	23 467	5 010
May	96 255	144 818	-48 563	67 963	120 935	-52 972	28 292	23 883	4 409
June	94 152	149 121	-54 969	65 644	124 898	-59 254	28 508	24 223	4 285
July	95 639	147 121	-51 483	67 343	123 210	-55 868	28 296	23 911	4 385
August	96 146	150 041	-53 895	67 839	125 070	-57 231	28 307	24 971	3 336
September	97 905	149 198	-51 294	69 158	124 862	-55 705	28 747	24 336	4 411
October	99 445	153 744	-54 299	69 718	128 726	-59 008	29 727	25 018	4 709
November	99 022	157 429	-58 407	68 765	131 941	-63 176	30 257	25 488	4 769
December	101 524	155 903	-54 379	71 020	130 397	-59 377	30 504	25 506	4 998
2005									
January	101 900	158 537	-56 637	71 390	132 705	-61 315	30 510	25 832	4 678
February	101 760	159 283	-57 523	71 043	133 576	-62 533	30 717	25 707	5 010
March	102 919	156 868	-53 948	71 756	131 176	-59 419	31 163	25 692	5 471
April	105 333	162 342	-57 010	74 230	136 484	-62 255	31 103	25 858	5 245
May	105 363	161 992	-56 630	73 990	136 063	-62 074	31 373	25 929	5 444
June	105 950	164 369	-58 419	74 371	138 263	-63 892	31 579	26 106	5 473
July	106 536	164 616	-58 080	74 846	138 443	-63 597	31 690	26 173	5 517
August	107 992	166 734	-58 742	76 213	140 574	-64 361	31 779	26 160	5 619
September	106 327	171 295	-64 968	73 888	144 676	-70 788	32 439	26 619	5 820
October	108 593	175 191	-66 598	75 964	148 537	-72 573	32 629	26 654	5 975
November	110 006	174 008	-64 002	77 511	147 225	-69 714	32 495	26 783	5 712
December	112 567	176 741	-64 174	79 429	149 648	-70 219	33 138	27 093	6 045

Table 7-10. U.S. Exports of Goods by End-Use and Advanced Technology Categories

(Census basis, except as noted; billions of dollars; seasonally adjusted, except as noted.)

Year and month	Total exports of goods			Principal end-use category							Advanced technology products [1]
	Total, balance of payments basis	Net adjustments	Total, Census basis	Foods, feeds, and beverages	Industrial supplies and materials		Capital goods, except automotive	Automotive vehicles, engines, and parts	Consumer goods, except automotive	Other goods	
					Total	Petroleum and products					
1978	142.08	-1.59	143.66	25.68	39.59	1.95	47.50	15.16	11.38	...	...
1979	184.44	2.64	181.80	30.50	58.50	2.44	60.18	17.90	13.98	...	...
1980	224.25	3.55	220.70	36.28	72.09	3.57	76.28	17.44	17.75	...	...
1981	237.04	3.31	233.74	38.84	70.19	4.56	84.17	19.69	17.70	...	...
1982	211.16	-1.12	212.28	32.20	64.05	6.87	76.50	17.23	16.13	...	...
1983	201.80	0.09	201.71	32.09	58.94	5.59	71.66	18.46	14.93	...	...
1984	219.93	1.18	218.74	32.20	64.12	5.43	77.01	22.42	15.09	...	...
1985	215.92	3.29	212.62	24.57	61.16	5.71	79.32	24.95	14.59	...	...
1986	223.34	-3.13	226.47	23.52	64.72	4.43	82.82	25.10	16.73	...	...
1987	250.21	-3.70	253.90	25.23	70.05	4.63	92.71	27.58	20.31	...	...
1988	320.23	-3.11	323.34	33.77	90.02	4.48	119.10	33.40	26.98	...	...
1989	359.92	-3.08	363.00	36.34	98.36	6.46	136.94	35.05	36.01	...	...
1990	387.40	-5.57	392.97	35.18	105.55	8.36	153.07	36.07	43.60	20.73	...
1991	414.08	-7.77	421.85	35.79	109.69	8.40	166.72	39.72	46.65	23.66	...
1992	439.63	-8.54	448.17	40.34	109.59	7.62	176.50	46.71	51.31	24.39	...
1993	456.94	-7.92	464.86	40.59	111.89	7.49	182.85	51.35	54.56	23.89	...
1994	502.86	-9.77	512.63	41.96	121.55	6.97	205.82	57.31	59.86	26.50	...
1995	575.20	-9.54	584.74	50.47	146.37	8.10	234.46	61.26	64.31	28.72	...
1996	612.11	-12.96	625.08	55.53	147.98	9.63	253.99	64.24	70.11	33.85	...
1997	678.37	-10.82	689.18	51.51	158.32	10.42	295.87	73.30	77.96	33.51	...
1998	670.42	-11.72	682.14	46.40	148.31	8.08	299.87	72.39	80.29	35.44	...
1999	683.97	-11.83	695.80	45.98	147.52	8.62	310.79	75.26	80.92	35.32	...
2000	771.99	-9.92	781.92	47.87	172.62	12.01	356.93	80.36	89.38	34.77	227.39
2001	718.71	-10.39	729.10	49.41	160.10	10.64	321.71	75.44	88.33	34.11	199.63
2002	682.42	-10.68	693.10	49.62	156.81	10.34	290.44	78.94	84.36	32.94	178.57
2003	713.42	-11.36	724.77	55.03	173.04	12.69	293.67	80.63	89.91	32.49	180.21
2004	807.52	-11.26	818.78	56.57	203.96	17.08	331.56	89.21	103.08	34.40	201.42
2005	894.63	-11.35	905.98	58.96	233.08	22.66	362.69	98.58	115.72	36.96	216.06
2002											
January	55.21	-0.73	55.94	4.19	12.36	0.76	23.85	6.13	6.91	2.50	13.61
February	54.95	-0.77	55.72	4.16	12.25	0.78	23.46	6.28	6.98	2.58	12.96
March	55.02	-0.91	55.93	3.89	12.27	0.75	23.97	6.34	6.77	2.69	17.10
April	57.14	-0.82	57.96	3.97	12.98	0.80	24.48	6.71	7.07	2.77	14.40
May	57.02	-1.16	58.18	4.04	13.23	0.80	24.21	6.72	7.00	2.99	14.76
June	57.97	-0.80	58.77	4.30	13.34	0.81	24.69	6.83	7.01	2.60	16.41
July	58.21	-0.92	59.13	4.36	13.21	0.85	24.77	6.73	7.26	2.80	14.86
August	58.17	-1.00	59.17	4.23	13.45	0.93	24.74	6.79	7.10	2.87	15.13
September	57.86	-0.78	58.64	4.09	13.38	0.87	24.79	6.64	7.02	2.73	14.84
October	57.08	-0.99	58.07	3.84	13.15	0.91	24.37	6.65	7.18	2.87	15.73
November	57.92	-0.90	58.82	4.22	13.64	0.98	24.46	6.55	7.16	2.79	14.62
December	55.88	-0.91	56.79	4.35	13.56	1.10	22.65	6.56	6.91	2.77	14.15
2003											
January	57.32	-0.75	58.07	4.46	14.12	1.17	23.06	6.58	7.39	2.46	13.06
February	58.00	-0.85	58.85	4.37	14.02	1.20	24.19	6.63	7.05	2.60	13.53
March	58.11	-0.97	59.08	4.32	14.54	1.25	23.47	6.73	7.28	2.75	15.98
April	57.39	-1.18	58.57	4.37	14.13	1.06	23.27	6.74	7.14	2.93	13.95
May	57.48	-0.84	58.31	4.31	14.02	1.00	23.24	6.95	7.21	2.57	13.97
June	59.57	-1.02	60.58	4.58	14.60	1.07	24.29	6.80	7.60	2.72	15.42
July	59.67	-1.03	60.70	4.67	14.69	0.99	24.32	6.67	7.57	2.78	14.75
August	58.17	-1.00	59.17	4.56	14.07	0.91	24.06	6.20	7.52	2.77	14.47
September	59.96	-1.09	61.04	4.65	14.26	1.03	24.90	6.72	7.68	2.83	15.23
October	61.44	-0.77	62.20	4.82	14.66	0.97	25.64	6.92	7.66	2.51	16.29
November	63.57	-1.10	64.67	5.02	14.78	0.99	27.08	6.80	8.05	2.94	16.93
December	62.75	-0.79	63.54	4.91	15.16	1.06	26.16	6.90	7.77	2.63	16.63
2004											
January	62.09	-0.95	63.04	4.67	15.31	1.03	25.88	6.69	7.78	2.69	14.74
February	65.07	-0.94	66.01	4.73	15.91	1.18	27.38	7.01	8.13	2.85	15.96
March	66.90	-1.02	67.92	4.79	16.76	1.30	27.60	7.24	8.57	2.97	18.93
April	66.01	-0.94	66.95	4.75	16.43	1.27	27.04	7.26	8.52	2.96	16.34
May	67.96	-0.93	68.89	4.73	17.11	1.43	28.31	7.39	8.47	2.88	17.03
June	65.64	-1.05	66.69	4.57	16.42	1.37	26.82	7.21	8.49	3.18	17.47
July	67.34	-0.77	68.12	4.49	17.21	1.41	27.81	7.61	8.38	2.63	15.94
August	67.84	-0.84	68.68	4.45	17.00	1.55	27.93	7.76	8.78	2.75	16.00
September	69.16	-1.05	70.21	4.85	17.57	1.51	28.05	7.79	8.84	3.09	17.21
October	69.72	-0.96	70.67	4.82	18.06	1.68	28.28	7.74	8.97	2.81	17.67
November	68.77	-0.92	69.68	4.84	17.83	1.66	27.64	7.61	8.90	2.87	16.24
December	71.02	-0.89	71.91	4.88	18.35	1.70	28.82	7.90	9.23	2.73	17.90
2005											
January	71.39	-0.76	72.15	4.72	18.57	1.48	28.66	8.04	9.32	2.85	15.27
February	71.04	-0.78	71.82	4.69	18.85	1.85	28.30	7.78	9.44	2.77	14.79
March	71.76	-0.93	72.68	4.79	18.93	1.99	28.96	7.74	9.40	2.86	19.53
April	74.23	-0.94	75.17	4.88	19.60	2.12	30.27	7.95	9.32	3.14	18.66
May	73.99	-1.04	75.03	5.25	19.75	2.20	29.57	7.84	9.58	3.06	17.11
June	74.37	-1.04	75.41	5.01	19.57	2.05	30.25	7.89	9.52	3.17	19.30
July	74.85	-0.71	75.56	4.89	19.61	2.05	30.33	8.29	9.59	2.86	17.44
August	76.21	-1.08	77.30	4.92	20.03	1.98	31.08	8.43	9.64	3.20	18.58
September	73.89	-1.00	74.89	4.88	19.21	1.69	29.19	8.50	9.91	3.20	17.17
October	75.96	-0.92	76.89	5.04	19.30	1.62	31.22	8.53	9.54	3.25	18.93
November	77.51	-0.97	78.48	4.93	19.52	1.79	32.19	8.66	10.01	3.19	18.95
December	79.43	-1.16	80.59	4.98	20.15	1.84	32.66	8.94	10.46	3.41	20.33

[1]Not seasonally adjusted.
. . . = Not available.

Table 7-11. U.S. Imports of Goods by End-Use and Advanced Technology Categories

(Census basis, except as noted; billions of dollars; seasonally adjusted, except as noted.)

Year and month	Total imports of goods			Principal end-use category							Advanced technology products [1]
	Total, balance of payments basis	Net adjustments	Total, Census basis	Foods, feeds, and beverages	Industrial supplies and materials		Capital goods, except automotive	Automotive vehicles, engines, and parts	Consumer goods, except automotive	Other goods	
					Total	Petroleum and products					
1978	176.00	1.31	174.69	15.84	79.26	. . .	19.29	25.11	29.40	. . .	. . .
1979	212.01	2.60	209.41	18.01	102.67	. . .	24.49	26.51	31.22	. . .	. . .
1980	249.75	4.23	245.52	18.55	124.96	. . .	30.72	28.13	34.22	. . .	. . .
1981	265.07	3.76	261.31	18.53	131.10	. . .	36.86	30.80	38.30	. . .	. . .
1982	247.64	3.70	243.94	17.47	107.82	. . .	38.22	34.26	39.66	. . .	. . .
1983	268.90	7.18	261.72	18.56	105.63	. . .	42.61	42.04	46.59	. . .	. . .
1984	332.42	1.91	330.51	21.92	122.72	. . .	60.15	56.77	61.19	. . .	. . .
1985	338.09	1.71	336.38	21.89	112.48	. . .	60.81	65.21	66.43	. . .	. . .
1986	368.43	2.75	365.67	24.40	101.37	. . .	71.86	78.25	79.43	. . .	. . .
1987	409.77	3.48	406.28	24.81	110.67	. . .	84.77	85.17	88.82	. . .	. . .
1988	447.19	5.26	441.93	24.93	118.06	. . .	101.79	87.95	96.42	. . .	. . .
1989	477.37	3.72	473.65	25.08	132.40	. . .	112.45	87.38	102.26	. . .	. . .
1990	498.34	2.36	495.98	26.65	143.41	62.16	116.04	87.69	105.29	16.09	. . .
1991	490.98	2.53	488.45	26.21	131.38	51.78	120.80	84.94	107.78	15.94	. . .
1992	536.46	3.80	532.66	27.61	138.64	51.60	134.25	91.79	122.66	17.71	. . .
1993	589.44	8.78	580.66	27.87	145.61	51.50	152.37	102.42	134.02	18.39	. . .
1994	668.59	5.33	663.26	27.87	145.61	51.28	152.37	102.42	134.02	18.39	. . .
1995	749.57	6.03	743.54	33.18	181.85	56.16	221.43	123.80	159.91	23.39	. . .
1996	803.33	8.04	796.77	35.74	204.43	72.75	228.07	128.95	172.00	26.11	. . .
1997	876.37	6.66	869.70	39.69	213.77	71.77	253.28	139.81	193.81	29.34	. . .
1998	917.18	5.28	911.90	41.24	200.14	50.90	269.56	149.05	216.52	35.39	. . .
1999	1 029.99	5.37	1 024.62	43.60	221.39	67.81	295.72	178.96	241.91	43.04	. . .
2000	1 224.42	6.40	1 218.02	45.98	298.98	120.28	347.03	195.88	281.83	48.33	222.08
2001	1 145.90	4.90	1 141.00	46.64	273.87	103.59	297.99	189.78	284.29	48.42	195.18
2002	1 164.72	3.35	1 161.37	49.69	267.69	103.51	283.32	203.74	307.84	49.08	195.15
2003	1 260.72	3.60	1 257.12	55.83	313.82	133.10	295.87	210.14	333.88	47.59	207.03
2004	1 472.93	3.22	1 469.70	62.14	412.83	180.46	343.49	228.20	372.94	50.11	238.28
2005	1 677.37	3.92	1 673.46	68.09	523.88	251.86	379.23	239.51	407.17	55.57	259.74
2002											
January	89.68	0.23	89.44	3.88	19.55	6.92	22.84	15.72	23.45	4.01	14.78
February	91.76	0.22	91.54	3.97	19.47	6.39	23.13	16.44	24.54	3.99	14.50
March	91.72	0.27	91.45	3.95	19.72	7.04	23.41	16.22	23.85	4.30	16.20
April	96.29	0.31	95.97	4.02	22.52	8.98	23.73	16.94	24.75	4.01	15.53
May	96.69	0.30	96.40	4.10	22.37	8.77	23.68	16.79	25.36	4.09	15.63
June	98.14	0.30	97.85	4.14	21.91	8.26	23.96	17.13	26.35	4.36	16.37
July	97.48	0.28	97.20	4.23	22.17	8.60	23.85	16.87	26.03	4.05	16.96
August	100.02	0.29	99.72	4.26	23.10	9.11	23.73	17.71	26.90	4.03	16.55
September	99.67	0.31	99.36	4.20	23.15	9.02	23.76	17.65	26.47	4.13	16.83
October	97.18	0.32	96.86	4.10	24.10	10.09	22.39	17.09	25.17	4.02	17.39
November	102.40	0.29	102.12	4.38	24.42	10.07	24.37	17.56	27.42	3.98	17.60
December	103.69	0.23	103.46	4.47	25.22	10.26	24.47	17.62	27.57	4.11	16.80
2003											
January	102.52	0.23	102.28	4.48	25.69	11.20	24.32	17.09	26.75	3.96	15.41
February	101.94	0.22	101.72	4.39	26.08	11.87	23.46	16.90	26.98	3.91	14.32
March	105.59	0.25	105.34	4.61	27.91	12.46	23.65	17.36	27.82	4.00	16.82
April	103.44	0.26	103.18	4.64	25.79	11.02	24.27	17.20	27.36	3.92	16.35
May	102.97	0.35	102.61	4.63	24.71	9.89	24.33	17.60	27.51	3.85	15.85
June	103.88	0.48	103.40	4.47	25.27	10.58	24.42	18.13	27.07	4.04	17.28
July	105.29	0.21	105.08	4.64	26.56	11.23	24.40	17.80	27.65	4.04	17.49
August	102.46	0.47	101.99	4.62	25.87	10.79	24.01	15.93	27.77	3.79	16.24
September	106.03	0.31	105.72	4.84	26.29	10.79	25.12	17.53	28.02	3.92	18.80
October	107.32	0.28	107.04	4.80	25.95	10.40	25.49	17.96	28.83	4.01	19.96
November	108.01	0.27	107.74	4.88	25.81	10.78	25.73	18.21	29.05	4.06	18.63
December	111.28	0.26	111.02	4.85	27.90	12.10	26.67	18.43	29.08	4.10	19.87
2004											
January	111.26	0.25	111.02	4.81	28.73	12.76	26.79	17.81	28.86	4.01	16.75
February	113.90	0.23	113.66	5.02	30.60	13.46	26.53	18.61	28.78	4.13	16.66
March	118.85	0.30	118.56	5.12	31.43	13.83	27.56	19.06	31.18	4.20	20.40
April	118.88	0.26	118.62	5.09	30.86	12.98	27.90	19.19	31.40	4.18	19.57
May	120.94	0.26	120.67	5.27	32.72	13.66	28.11	19.29	31.12	4.17	18.63
June	124.90	0.27	124.63	5.25	35.41	15.32	29.21	19.12	31.42	4.22	21.10
July	123.21	0.31	122.90	5.24	34.30	14.21	29.04	19.17	31.00	4.15	19.55
August	125.07	0.27	124.80	5.20	36.66	15.77	29.01	18.73	30.94	4.28	20.14
September	124.86	0.25	124.61	5.05	35.33	14.92	29.63	19.54	30.93	4.12	20.40
October	128.73	0.28	128.45	5.28	38.01	17.14	29.99	19.36	31.64	4.18	22.05
November	131.94	0.30	131.64	5.41	40.35	19.35	29.74	19.13	32.87	4.14	21.97
December	130.40	0.26	130.14	5.41	38.42	17.06	29.98	19.18	32.80	4.34	21.05
2005											
January	132.70	0.29	132.41	5.47	38.42	16.93	30.86	19.65	33.50	4.51	18.95
February	133.58	0.29	133.29	5.42	39.36	17.87	29.94	19.47	34.72	4.38	18.10
March	131.18	0.28	130.90	5.51	39.64	18.35	29.91	18.82	32.50	4.52	21.09
April	136.48	0.41	136.07	5.55	41.44	19.46	31.72	19.10	33.60	4.66	20.89
May	136.06	0.31	135.75	5.62	40.42	18.62	31.28	19.80	34.00	4.63	21.01
June	138.26	0.27	137.99	5.63	41.59	20.19	32.25	19.76	34.15	4.61	22.87
July	138.44	0.38	138.06	5.64	42.80	20.86	31.73	19.83	33.44	4.63	21.45
August	140.57	0.31	140.26	5.74	44.51	22.64	31.82	20.31	33.36	4.54	21.73
September	144.68	0.35	144.33	5.88	47.08	23.78	32.24	20.17	34.13	4.83	22.68
October	148.54	0.34	148.20	5.79	50.22	25.03	32.16	20.72	34.53	4.78	23.67
November	147.22	0.32	146.90	5.90	49.08	24.41	32.34	20.75	34.01	4.83	23.84
December	149.65	0.36	149.29	5.96	49.32	23.72	32.98	21.14	35.23	4.66	23.46

[1] Not seasonally adjusted.
. . . = Not available.

Table 7-12. U.S. Exports and Imports of Goods by Principal End-Use Category in Constant Dollars

(Census basis; billions of 2000 chain-weighted dollars, except as noted; seasonally adjusted.)

Year and month	Exports							Imports						
	Total	Foods, feeds, and beverages	Industrial supplies and materials	Capital goods, except automotive	Automotive vehicles, engines, and parts	Consumer goods, except automotive	Other goods	Total	Foods, feeds, and beverages	Industrial supplies and materials	Capital goods, except automotive	Automotive vehicles, engines, and parts	Consumer goods, except automotive	Other goods
1986 [1]	227.20	22.30	57.30	75.80	21.70	...	...	365.40	24.40	101.30	71.80	78.20	79.40	...
1987 [1]	254.10	24.30	66.70	86.20	24.60	...	...	406.20	24.80	111.00	84.50	85.00	88.70	...
1988 [1]	322.40	32.30	85.10	109.20	29.30	...	...	441.00	24.80	118.30	101.40	87.70	95.90	...
1989 [1]	363.80	37.20	99.30	138.80	34.80	...	...	473.20	25.10	132.30	113.30	86.10	102.90	...
1990 [1]	393.60	35.10	104.40	152.70	37.40	39.22	18.70	495.30	26.60	146.20	116.40	87.30	105.70	14.46
1991 [1]	421.70	35.70	109.70	166.70	40.00	40.42	21.11	488.50	26.50	131.60	120.70	85.70	108.00	14.15
1992 [1]	448.20	40.30	109.10	175.90	47.00	43.60	21.71	532.70	27.60	138.60	134.30	91.80	122.70	15.46
1993 [1]	471.17	40.19	111.08	190.02	51.93	54.03	23.91	591.45	28.03	151.26	160.16	100.73	132.92	18.35
1994 [1]	522.29	40.43	114.17	225.76	56.54	58.97	26.41	675.05	29.52	168.80	199.56	112.13	144.22	20.82
1994	482.34	41.41	127.50	165.92	60.49	62.41	28.03	628.41	29.53	216.50	120.69	124.86	143.41	21.80
1995	531.74	45.70	136.13	192.70	64.02	66.02	28.79	682.73	30.28	222.84	145.53	126.99	154.37	23.01
1996	588.10	44.24	144.48	228.74	66.63	70.86	33.61	753.96	33.53	236.42	175.55	131.33	165.33	25.69
1997	666.61	44.12	156.35	280.22	75.18	77.82	33.38	858.67	36.75	252.73	219.82	141.98	188.23	29.06
1998	682.35	43.84	155.76	292.61	73.38	80.86	36.15	959.84	39.54	277.01	252.14	150.86	213.38	35.81
1999	704.29	45.35	156.88	308.44	75.99	81.42	36.12	1 075.39	43.18	281.43	289.21	180.17	239.60	43.70
2000	781.92	47.87	172.62	356.93	80.36	89.38	34.77	1 218.02	45.98	298.98	347.03	195.88	281.83	48.33
2001	733.58	49.14	164.85	321.92	75.13	88.38	34.15	1 177.64	47.76	297.51	306.31	189.86	286.48	48.79
2002	699.04	48.06	162.18	293.02	78.30	84.68	32.85	1 220.88	50.95	300.14	300.13	203.24	313.01	50.30
2003	716.76	48.90	169.20	298.57	79.57	89.30	31.49	1 284.63	55.65	312.13	317.04	208.48	339.95	47.88
2004	781.58	45.20	180.62	337.73	87.40	101.50	31.86	1 431.21	59.07	348.23	371.95	222.99	377.10	48.82
2005	837.34	47.47	185.69	368.49	95.58	112.43	32.78	1 529.88	61.17	363.84	413.31	231.69	408.07	52.30
2002														
January	56.93	4.14	13.24	24.01	6.09	6.93	2.52	96.53	3.96	25.00	24.02	15.73	23.73	4.12
February	56.85	4.24	13.14	23.60	6.24	7.02	2.61	99.06	4.19	24.90	24.38	16.41	24.91	4.12
March	56.86	3.92	13.08	24.04	6.30	6.80	2.71	97.70	4.10	23.68	24.73	16.22	24.26	4.44
April	58.73	3.98	13.57	24.63	6.67	7.11	2.78	100.79	4.13	25.18	25.04	16.92	25.18	4.11
May	58.92	4.05	13.76	24.40	6.67	7.05	3.00	100.89	4.18	24.59	25.03	16.80	25.82	4.20
June	59.40	4.25	13.76	24.96	6.78	7.05	2.59	102.57	4.30	24.25	25.31	17.09	26.82	4.47
July	59.42	4.18	13.46	25.01	6.69	7.29	2.78	101.67	4.36	24.32	25.26	16.83	26.46	4.15
August	59.38	4.01	13.72	24.97	6.74	7.11	2.84	103.96	4.40	25.01	25.11	17.66	27.32	4.12
September	58.67	3.75	13.58	25.05	6.59	7.03	2.69	103.15	4.27	24.60	25.19	17.60	26.93	4.22
October	58.09	3.61	13.27	24.64	6.58	7.19	2.84	100.20	4.14	25.17	23.92	16.97	25.60	4.10
November	58.83	3.89	13.83	24.74	6.48	7.17	2.75	106.54	4.44	26.31	26.02	17.48	27.94	4.06
December	56.95	4.04	13.77	22.98	6.49	6.92	2.74	107.82	4.49	27.16	26.12	17.53	28.06	4.19
2003														
January	58.03	4.13	14.24	23.33	6.50	7.39	2.42	104.64	4.46	25.71	25.96	17.02	27.21	4.01
February	58.42	4.07	13.81	24.45	6.54	7.02	2.54	102.53	4.37	24.56	25.08	16.81	27.52	3.94
March	58.48	4.02	14.12	23.76	6.65	7.25	2.67	105.32	4.56	25.54	25.32	17.26	28.36	3.99
April	58.08	4.05	13.84	23.55	6.66	7.12	2.85	105.91	4.60	26.12	25.97	17.09	27.88	3.95
May	57.75	3.87	13.80	23.52	6.87	7.18	2.51	106.43	4.63	25.99	26.07	17.49	28.05	3.89
June	59.94	4.12	14.30	24.62	6.72	7.54	2.64	106.26	4.50	25.75	26.10	18.00	27.52	4.07
July	60.08	4.21	14.47	24.60	6.58	7.51	2.70	107.64	4.64	26.72	26.10	17.68	28.11	4.07
August	58.78	4.17	13.78	24.56	6.11	7.47	2.69	104.36	4.64	25.81	25.71	15.82	28.28	3.82
September	60.40	4.05	13.90	25.51	6.63	7.62	2.73	108.32	4.84	26.36	26.93	17.42	28.54	3.94
October	61.31	4.11	14.21	26.25	6.82	7.58	2.41	109.94	4.79	26.24	27.46	17.75	29.39	4.04
November	63.35	4.11	14.22	27.66	6.70	7.95	2.81	110.23	4.84	25.87	27.64	17.99	29.54	4.08
December	62.15	4.00	14.49	26.77	6.80	7.68	2.51	113.05	4.77	27.47	28.72	18.17	29.56	4.10
2004														
January	61.24	3.78	14.28	26.47	6.59	7.70	2.55	111.57	4.72	27.17	28.78	17.53	29.16	3.97
February	63.81	3.75	14.70	27.92	6.90	8.05	2.68	113.60	4.85	28.43	28.51	18.30	29.08	4.07
March	65.23	3.67	15.26	28.14	7.13	8.48	2.77	117.73	4.94	28.55	29.62	18.73	31.49	4.13
April	64.00	3.52	14.88	27.54	7.13	8.42	2.75	117.19	4.86	27.42	30.16	18.83	31.73	4.10
May	65.67	3.48	15.36	28.84	7.25	8.37	2.66	117.97	5.07	27.87	30.39	18.91	31.51	4.08
June	63.83	3.51	14.80	27.34	7.06	8.40	2.95	121.66	5.04	29.93	31.71	18.72	31.83	4.12
July	64.92	3.51	15.23	28.33	7.46	8.24	2.43	120.07	5.02	29.13	31.53	18.73	31.40	4.04
August	65.63	3.75	14.94	28.45	7.59	8.62	2.55	120.43	4.99	29.85	31.48	18.27	31.34	4.15
September	66.88	4.02	15.32	28.58	7.62	8.68	2.85	119.78	4.76	28.45	32.21	19.03	31.33	4.00
October	66.88	4.05	15.35	28.76	7.56	8.81	2.57	121.89	4.88	29.35	32.69	18.80	32.01	4.05
November	65.76	4.04	15.05	28.10	7.43	8.73	2.62	124.88	5.00	31.28	32.36	18.55	33.20	3.97
December	67.76	4.12	15.45	29.25	7.70	9.02	2.48	124.46	4.95	30.82	32.51	18.58	33.03	4.15
2005														
January	67.58	3.97	15.37	29.05	7.82	9.06	2.58	126.81	5.06	31.09	33.39	19.05	33.59	4.30
February	67.21	3.97	15.52	28.68	7.57	9.19	2.50	126.80	4.97	31.22	32.42	18.87	34.73	4.17
March	67.47	3.90	15.30	29.36	7.52	9.15	2.56	122.34	4.87	29.77	32.44	18.24	32.50	4.29
April	69.47	3.97	15.61	30.68	7.73	9.05	2.79	125.37	4.93	29.71	34.35	18.49	33.63	4.40
May	69.53	4.18	15.96	29.98	7.60	9.31	2.72	126.00	4.99	29.68	33.88	19.17	34.04	4.38
June	69.89	3.93	15.84	30.70	7.66	9.27	2.83	127.75	5.08	30.18	34.96	19.12	34.20	4.37
July	69.83	3.83	15.71	30.80	8.05	9.34	2.54	126.41	5.12	29.74	34.64	19.18	33.53	4.39
August	71.39	3.87	16.01	31.54	8.17	9.38	2.84	126.74	5.19	29.65	34.76	19.63	33.50	4.30
September	68.73	3.90	14.94	29.68	8.23	9.61	2.81	127.35	5.32	29.15	35.32	19.49	34.20	4.52
October	70.22	4.02	14.75	31.78	8.24	9.24	2.84	129.76	5.19	30.41	35.31	20.01	34.62	4.42
November	72.08	3.94	15.16	32.85	8.36	9.69	2.80	130.76	5.25	31.17	35.56	20.03	34.16	4.47
December	73.94	4.00	15.52	33.40	8.64	10.13	2.98	133.82	5.20	32.07	36.29	20.41	35.36	4.30

[1]Data on the 2000 chain-weighted dollar basis are only available for 1994 to date. To provide more historical data, values in 1992 dollars are shown for the years 1986–1994.
. . . = Not available.

Table 7-13. U.S. Exports of Goods by Selected Regions and Countries

(Census f.a.s. basis; millions of dollars, not seasonally adjusted.)

Year and month	Total, all countries	Selected regions [1]					Selected countries					
		European Union, 15 countries	European Union, 25 countries	Euro area	Asian NICS	OPEC	Brazil	Canada	China	France	Germany, Federal Republic of	Hong Kong
1972	. . .	. . .	. . .	. . .	. . .	. . .	1 243	13 070	. . .	1 609	2 808	. . .
1973	. . .	. . .	. . .	. . .	. . .	. . .	1 916	16 146	. . .	2 263	3 756	. . .
1974	. . .	28 268	. . .	. . .	. . .	6 723	3 088	21 281	807	2 942	4 985	882
1975	. . .	22 862	. . .	. . .	. . .	10 767	3 056	22 948	304	3 031	5 194	808
1976	. . .	25 406	. . .	. . .	. . .	12 566	2 809	25 677	135	3 446	5 731	1 115
1977	. . .	26 476	. . .	. . .	. . .	14 019	2 490	27 738	171	3 503	5 989	1 292
1978	. . .	32 051	. . .	. . .	. . .	16 655	2 981	30 540	824	4 166	6 957	1 625
1979	. . .	42 582	. . .	. . .	. . .	15 051	3 442	37 599	1 724	5 587	8 478	2 083
1980	. . .	53 679	. . .	. . .	. . .	17 759	4 344	40 331	3 755	7 485	10 960	2 686
1981	. . .	52 363	. . .	. . .	. . .	21 533	3 798	44 602	3 603	7 341	10 277	2 635
1982	. . .	47 932	. . .	. . .	. . .	22 863	3 423	37 887	2 912	7 110	9 291	2 453
1983	201 708	44 311	. . .	. . .	. . .	16 905	2 557	43 345	2 173	5 961	8 737	2 564
1984	218 743	46 976	. . .	. . .	. . .	14 387	2 640	51 777	3 004	6 037	9 084	3 062
1985	212 621	48 994	. . .	. . .	16 918	12 480	3 140	53 287	3 856	6 096	9 050	2 786
1986	226 471	53 154	. . .	. . .	18 289	10 844	3 885	55 512	3 106	7 216	10 561	3 030
1987	253 904	60 575	. . .	. . .	23 548	11 058	4 040	59 814	3 497	7 943	11 748	3 983
1988	323 335	75 755	. . .	. . .	34 816	13 994	4 267	71 622	5 021	9 970	14 348	5 687
1989	363 836	86 331	. . .	. . .	38 404	13 196	4 804	78 809	5 755	11 579	16 862	6 246
1990	392 924	98 027	. . .	. . .	40 741	13 679	5 062	83 866	4 807	13 652	18 693	6 841
1991	421 764	103 123	. . .	. . .	45 628	19 054	6 148	85 150	6 278	15 346	21 302	8 137
1992	448 161	102 958	. . .	. . .	48 592	21 960	5 751	90 594	7 418	14 593	21 249	9 077
1993	465 090	96 973	. . .	. . .	52 502	19 500	6 058	100 444	8 763	13 267	18 932	9 874
1994	512 626	102 818	. . .	. . .	59 595	17 868	8 102	114 439	9 282	13 619	19 229	11 441
1995	584 742	123 671	. . .	. . .	74 234	19 533	11 439	127 226	11 754	14 245	22 394	14 232
1996	625 075	127 710	. . .	. . .	75 768	22 275	12 718	134 210	11 993	14 455	23 495	13 966
1997	689 182	140 773	. . .	. . .	78 225	25 526	15 915	151 767	12 862	15 965	24 458	15 117
1998	682 138	149 035	. . .	. . .	63 269	25 154	15 142	156 603	14 241	17 729	26 657	12 925
1999	695 797	151 814	. . .	. . .	70 989	20 166	13 203	166 600	13 111	18 877	26 800	12 652
2000	781 918	165 065	. . .	116 212	84 624	19 078	15 321	178 941	16 185	20 362	29 448	14 582
2001	729 100	158 768	. . .	112 903	71 982	20 053	15 880	163 424	19 182	19 865	29 995	14 028
2002	693 103	143 691	. . .	105 838	69 770	18 812	12 376	160 923	22 128	19 016	26 630	12 594
2003	724 771	151 731	. . .	113 132	71 601	17 279	11 211	169 924	28 368	17 053	28 832	13 521
2004	818 775	168 572	172 622	127 158	83 593	22 262	13 897	189 880	34 744	21 263	31 416	15 827
2005	905 978	181 718	186 437	137 497	86 828	32 074	15 372	211 899	41 925	22 410	34 184	16 351
2002												
January	52 667	11 408	. . .	8 249	5 216	1 238	1 016	12 062	1 569	1 543	2 022	900
February	53 061	12 153	. . .	8 983	4 619	1 348	1 004	12 368	1 530	1 872	2 183	911
March	60 728	13 298	. . .	9 842	6 289	1 431	1 076	13 954	1 621	1 801	2 530	1 134
April	58 146	12 079	. . .	8 758	5 819	1 591	1 059	14 114	1 545	1 578	2 133	1 043
May	59 884	11 948	. . .	8 829	5 817	2 043	969	14 586	1 774	1 570	2 084	1 054
June	59 920	11 908	. . .	8 578	6 408	1 431	1 017	14 214	2 206	1 532	2 197	1 135
July	55 032	10 537	. . .	7 722	6 313	1 569	970	11 607	1 848	1 249	1 990	1 035
August	59 491	11 752	. . .	8 460	6 246	1 492	1 134	13 913	1 840	1 287	2 147	1 113
September	57 277	11 571	. . .	8 521	5 813	1 924	1 053	13 334	2 024	1 503	2 328	1 117
October	61 975	13 015	. . .	9 748	6 078	1 646	1 159	14 702	1 963	1 993	2 402	1 009
November	59 671	12 470	. . .	9 470	5 614	1 641	1 037	13 908	2 161	1 704	2 419	1 089
December	55 249	11 553	. . .	8 679	5 539	1 459	882	12 161	2 049	1 384	2 194	1 055
2003												
January	54 854	11 823	. . .	8 809	5 064	1 126	809	12 890	2 070	1 369	2 160	947
February	55 917	12 091	. . .	8 936	5 704	1 358	812	13 293	2 049	1 314	2 426	954
March	63 524	13 884	. . .	10 084	6 265	1 562	937	15 360	2 423	1 717	2 803	1 183
April	59 162	12 929	. . .	9 823	5 366	1 279	847	14 646	2 122	1 568	2 477	1 061
May	59 984	12 709	. . .	9 377	5 399	1 242	882	15 208	1 984	1 458	2 490	1 063
June	61 570	12 678	. . .	9 359	6 092	1 624	942	15 003	2 120	1 521	2 262	1 078
July	57 010	11 553	. . .	8 564	6 226	1 387	951	12 030	2 067	1 193	2 210	1 075
August	58 611	11 962	. . .	8 757	6 391	1 449	1 031	12 990	2 034	1 265	2 315	1 147
September	60 239	12 159	. . .	9 190	5 753	1 640	924	14 518	2 091	1 331	2 191	1 218
October	66 389	13 575	. . .	10 329	6 481	1 514	1 034	15 555	2 778	1 439	2 659	1 288
November	64 492	13 627	. . .	10 379	6 155	1 514	1 001	14 598	3 320	1 418	2 470	1 189
December	62 959	12 742	. . .	9 525	6 705	1 584	1 040	13 834	3 310	1 460	2 370	1 318
2004												
January	59 083	12 480	12 772	9 288	5 655	1 423	1 043	13 316	2 629	1 484	2 310	1 072
February	63 418	13 612	14 065	10 251	6 572	1 401	1 317	14 399	2 979	1 581	2 503	1 259
March	74 195	15 773	16 165	11 763	7 722	1 815	1 281	17 227	3 375	2 112	2 838	1 385
April	67 770	14 439	14 829	10 801	6 595	1 559	1 104	16 027	2 735	1 741	2 558	1 267
May	69 615	14 498	14 870	10 857	7 532	1 797	1 153	16 311	2 874	1 827	2 724	1 263
June	68 747	13 636	13 912	10 392	7 098	2 013	1 072	16 433	2 791	1 856	2 493	1 331
July	64 240	12 750	13 046	9 526	6 988	1 825	1 160	13 864	2 668	1 407	2 421	1 338
August	67 571	13 258	13 545	9 884	7 370	1 810	1 231	16 070	2 675	1 471	2 618	1 339
September	69 561	13 940	14 219	10 606	7 230	1 960	1 131	16 633	2 862	1 817	2 780	1 431
October	73 490	15 016	15 341	11 499	6 965	2 280	1 181	16 969	2 947	2 085	2 862	1 403
November	69 613	14 196	14 544	10 777	6 271	2 030	1 110	16 676	2 965	1 964	2 573	1 300
December	71 473	14 974	15 315	11 514	7 596	2 350	1 115	15 956	3 246	1 918	2 738	1 440
2005												
January	66 328	13 793	14 111	10 525	6 697	1 992	1 051	15 568	2 609	1 764	2 507	1 125
February	68 441	14 680	15 005	11 079	6 538	2 008	1 109	16 092	3 108	1 925	2 702	1 221
March	79 954	16 551	16 985	12 518	8 044	2 902	1 222	18 920	3 336	2 026	3 127	1 523
April	76 424	15 993	16 473	12 005	7 197	2 716	1 218	18 105	3 372	2 047	2 790	1 439
May	76 073	15 650	16 061	11 554	7 243	2 567	1 300	18 327	3 237	1 848	2 951	1 281
June	78 052	15 265	15 659	11 507	7 325	2 536	1 331	18 685	3 431	1 998	2 705	1 378
July	70 609	13 935	14 297	10 491	7 148	2 499	1 365	14 720	3 632	1 601	2 654	1 332
August	77 373	14 051	14 460	10 519	7 776	2 893	1 373	18 250	3 889	1 522	2 888	1 429
September	74 381	14 341	14 718	10 876	7 046	2 578	1 286	18 368	3 209	1 726	2 890	1 586
October	79 552	15 531	15 939	11 671	7 591	3 060	1 308	18 747	3 948	1 858	2 859	1 313
November	78 879	15 900	16 298	12 362	6 562	3 035	1 282	18 417	3 890	2 119	3 093	1 299
December	79 910	16 027	16 432	12 391	7 661	3 288	1 528	17 700	4 265	1 977	3 017	1 425

[1] See notes and definitions for definitions of regions.
. . . = Not available.

Table 7-13. U.S. Exports of Goods by Selected Regions and Countries—Continued

(Census f.a.s. basis; millions of dollars, not seasonally adjusted.)

Year and month	Indonesia	Italy	Japan	Malaysia	Mexico	Netherlands	Singapore	South Korea	Taiwan	United Kingdom	Venezuela
1972	...	1 434	4 963	...	1 982	...	...	...	...	2 658	924
1973	...	2 119	8 313	...	2 937	...	...	...	...	3 564	1 033
1974	...	2 752	10 679	...	4 855	3 979	988	...	1 427	4 574	1 768
1975	...	2 867	9 563	...	5 141	4 183	994	...	1 660	4 527	2 243
1976	...	3 071	10 145	...	4 990	4 645	965	...	1 635	4 801	2 628
1977	...	2 790	10 529	...	4 806	4 796	1 172	...	1 798	5 951	3 171
1978	...	3 361	12 885	...	6 680	5 683	1 462	...	2 340	7 116	3 728
1979	...	4 362	17 581	...	9 847	6 907	2 331	...	3 271	10 635	3 934
1980	1 545	5 511	20 790	...	15 145	8 669	3 033	...	4 337	12 694	4 573
1981	1 302	5 360	21 823	...	17 789	8 595	3 003	...	4 305	12 439	5 445
1982	2 025	4 616	20 966	...	11 817	8 604	3 214	...	4 367	10 645	5 206
1983	1 466	3 908	21 894	...	9 082	7 767	3 759	...	4 667	10 621	2 811
1984	1 216	4 375	23 575	...	11 992	7 554	3 675	...	5 003	12 210	3 377
1985	795	4 625	22 631	...	13 635	7 269	3 476	5 956	4 700	11 273	3 399
1986	946	4 838	26 882	...	12 392	7 848	3 380	6 355	5 524	11 418	3 141
1987	767	5 530	28 249	...	14 582	8 217	4 053	8 099	7 413	14 114	3 586
1988	1 059	6 775	37 725	...	20 628	10 117	5 768	11 232	12 129	18 364	4 612
1989	1 247	7 215	44 494	...	24 982	11 364	7 345	13 478	11 335	20 837	3 025
1990	1 897	7 987	48 585	...	28 375	13 016	8 019	14 399	11 482	23 484	3 107
1991	1 891	8 570	48 125	3 900	33 277	13 511	8 804	15 505	13 182	22 046	4 656
1992	2 779	8 721	47 813	4 363	40 592	13 752	9 626	14 639	15 250	22 800	5 444
1993	2 770	6 464	47 892	6 064	41 581	12 839	11 678	14 782	16 168	26 438	4 590
1994	2 809	7 183	53 488	6 969	50 844	13 582	13 020	18 025	17 109	26 900	4 039
1995	3 360	8 862	64 343	8 816	46 292	16 558	15 333	25 380	19 290	28 857	4 640
1996	3 977	8 797	67 607	8 546	56 792	16 662	16 720	26 621	18 460	30 962	4 750
1997	4 522	8 995	65 549	10 780	71 388	19 827	17 696	25 046	20 366	36 425	6 602
1998	2 299	8 991	57 831	8 957	78 773	18 978	15 694	16 486	18 165	39 058	6 516
1999	2 038	10 091	57 466	9 060	86 909	19 437	16 247	22 958	19 131	38 407	5 354
2000	2 402	11 060	64 924	10 938	111 349	21 836	17 806	27 830	24 406	41 570	5 550
2001	2 521	9 916	57 452	9 358	101 297	19 485	17 652	22 181	18 122	40 714	5 642
2002	2 556	10 057	51 449	10 344	97 470	18 311	16 218	22 576	18 382	33 205	4 430
2003	2 516	10 561	52 004	10 914	97 412	20 695	16 560	24 073	17 448	33 828	2 831
2004	2 671	10 685	54 243	10 921	110 835	24 289	19 609	26 413	21 744	36 000	4 767
2005	3 054	11 524	55 485	10 461	120 365	26 485	20 642	27 765	22 069	38 588	6 421
2002											
January	136	714	3 945	726	7 734	1 460	1 386	1 706	1 224	2 764	374
February	198	797	3 862	688	7 250	1 480	1 069	1 487	1 152	2 771	379
March	201	885	4 744	1 253	7 624	1 710	1 705	1 877	1 573	2 985	365
April	195	824	3 901	960	8 258	1 714	1 329	1 931	1 516	2 957	320
May	222	933	4 262	856	8 530	1 593	1 235	1 991	1 538	2 702	677
June	195	775	4 670	1 003	8 088	1 531	1 538	1 975	1 760	2 966	272
July	198	836	4 493	828	7 963	1 353	1 323	1 890	2 066	2 456	304
August	282	823	4 791	907	8 559	1 514	1 600	1 919	1 614	2 914	329
September	187	679	4 138	798	8 283	1 505	1 133	1 974	1 588	2 643	400
October	212	977	4 151	874	9 221	1 476	1 583	1 982	1 504	2 904	374
November	268	914	4 412	723	8 606	1 490	1 302	1 800	1 423	2 619	470
December	262	901	4 082	728	7 354	1 484	1 015	2 044	1 425	2 524	165
2003											
January	238	956	3 919	719	7 780	1 529	1 069	1 726	1 322	2 670	121
February	207	752	4 136	689	7 093	1 550	1 425	2 162	1 163	2 781	188
March	233	849	4 470	848	7 805	1 861	1 566	2 182	1 335	3 300	183
April	194	787	4 475	917	7 816	1 816	1 146	1 919	1 240	2 729	179
May	192	1 071	4 562	983	8 082	1 590	1 312	1 825	1 199	2 939	182
June	200	866	4 403	896	8 012	1 667	1 341	2 115	1 559	2 949	218
July	184	746	4 238	976	7 904	1 524	1 599	1 949	1 604	2 655	279
August	195	736	4 298	913	7 941	1 610	1 847	1 860	1 538	2 818	288
September	173	748	4 163	970	8 534	1 586	1 258	1 885	1 391	2 577	241
October	193	1 110	4 384	998	9 520	2 031	1 450	2 111	1 633	2 821	308
November	248	961	4 481	946	8 621	2 081	1 262	2 199	1 504	2 806	348
December	260	979	4 475	1 058	8 304	1 850	1 286	2 139	1 962	2 782	296
2004											
January	192	761	3 975	929	8 097	1 635	1 231	1 831	1 520	2 814	281
February	215	773	4 117	908	8 073	2 073	1 389	2 273	1 651	2 895	291
March	261	954	5 121	1 020	9 712	2 088	1 964	2 350	2 023	3 400	398
April	191	1 007	4 772	918	9 342	2 155	1 670	1 971	1 686	3 078	389
May	223	1 037	4 353	920	9 216	2 017	1 857	2 503	1 909	3 143	377
June	218	870	4 792	811	9 172	1 928	1 742	2 133	1 892	2 887	393
July	245	782	4 567	855	8 781	1 768	1 781	2 171	1 699	2 856	404
August	188	734	4 291	846	9 512	2 028	2 023	2 374	1 635	2 926	414
September	208	869	4 453	872	9 635	2 079	1 687	2 254	1 859	2 904	409
October	254	963	5 102	898	10 076	2 244	1 541	2 091	1 931	3 051	486
November	223	962	4 254	915	9 996	1 925	1 309	2 025	1 636	3 017	461
December	253	973	4 448	1 030	9 224	2 351	1 415	2 438	2 304	3 030	464
2005											
January	249	896	3 984	685	9 217	2 098	1 559	2 215	1 799	2 807	513
February	311	951	4 133	773	9 010	2 109	1 564	2 243	1 511	3 100	473
March	324	1 091	4 967	837	9 914	2 384	2 105	2 372	2 044	3 490	481
April	292	1 042	4 569	800	9 840	2 314	1 610	2 126	2 022	3 493	495
May	226	972	4 151	832	9 929	2 240	1 766	2 169	2 026	3 623	530
June	263	935	5 034	898	10 114	2 226	1 696	2 482	1 768	3 287	500
July	218	877	4 783	888	9 220	2 105	1 588	2 431	1 798	3 057	522
August	193	804	4 939	962	10 665	1 955	1 744	2 379	2 224	3 119	571
September	243	907	4 440	947	10 285	2 086	1 715	2 137	1 607	3 029	592
October	239	957	4 871	1 013	10 961	2 385	1 977	2 569	1 733	3 333	567
November	244	994	4 632	894	10 979	2 155	1 605	2 016	1 642	3 102	563
December	253	1 098	4 981	933	10 231	2 428	1 713	2 628	1 895	3 149	613

... = Not available.

Table 7-14. U.S. Imports of Goods by Selected Regions and Countries

(Census Customs basis; millions of dollars, not seasonally adjusted.)

Year and month	Total, all countries	Selected regions [1]					Selected countries					
		European Union, 15 countries	European Union, 25 countries	Euro area	Asian NICS	OPEC	Brazil	Canada	China	France	Germany, Federal Republic of	Hong Kong
1972	...	...	...	...	...	...	942	14 927	...	1 369	4 250	...
1973	...	...	...	...	...	...	1 189	17 715	...	1 732	5 345	...
1974	...	19 035	...	...	...	...	1 700	21 924	...	2 257	6 324	...
1975	...	16 610	...	...	...	...	1 464	21 747	...	2 137	5 382	...
1976	...	17 848	...	...	...	...	1 737	26 237	...	2 509	5 592	...
1977	...	22 087	...	...	...	...	2 241	29 599	...	3 032	7 238	...
1978	...	29 009	...	...	...	...	2 826	33 525	...	4 051	9 962	...
1979	...	33 295	...	...	...	...	3 118	38 046	...	4 768	10 955	...
1980	...	35 958	...	...	...	...	3 715	41 455	...	5 247	11 681	...
1981	...	41 624	...	...	...	...	4 475	46 414	...	5 851	11 379	...
1982	...	42 509	...	...	...	...	4 285	46 477	...	5 545	11 975	...
1983	261 723	43 892	...	...	...	...	4 946	52 130	...	6 025	11 975	...
1984	330 510	57 360	...	...	...	...	7 621	66 478	...	8 113	16 996	...
1985	336 383	67 822		...	...	22 800	7 526	69 006	3 862	9 482	20 239	8 396
1986	365 672	75 736		...	...	19 750	6 813	68 253	4 771	10 129	25 124	8 891
1987	406 283	81 188		...	...	23 953	7 865	71 085	6 294	10 730	27 069	9 854
1988	441 926	84 939		...	...	22 962	9 294	81 398	8 511	12 509	26 362	10 238
1989	473 647	85 153		...	...	30 601	8 410	87 953	11 989	13 013	24 832	9 739
1990	495 980	91 868		...	...	38 017	7 976	91 372	15 224	13 124	28 109	9 488
1991	488 452	86 481		...	59 277	32 644	6 717	91 064	18 969	13 333	26 137	9 279
1992	532 663	93 993		...	62 384	33 200	7 609	98 630	25 728	14 797	26 137	9 793
1993	580 658	97 941		...	64 572	31 739	7 479	111 216	31 540	15 279	28 562	9 554
1994	663 256	110 875		...	71 388	31 685	8 683	128 406	38 787	16 699	31 744	9 696
1995	743 543	131 871		...	82 008	35 197	8 830	145 349	45 543	17 209	36 844	10 291
1996	795 289	142 947		...	82 770	44 285	8 773	155 893	51 513	18 646	38 945	9 865
1997	869 704	157 528		...	86 164	44 025	9 626	168 201	62 558	20 636	43 122	10 288
1998	911 896	176 380		...	85 961	33 925	10 102	173 256	71 169	24 016	49 842	10 538
1999	1 024 618	195 227		...	95 102	41 978	11 314	198 711	81 788	25 709	55 228	10 528
2000	1 218 022	220 019	...	163 520	111 438	67 090	13 853	230 838	100 018	29 800	58 513	11 449
2001	1 140 999	220 057	...	166 373	93 202	59 754	14 466	216 268	102 278	30 408	59 077	9 646
2002	1 161 366	225 771	...	172 573	91 850	53 245	15 781	209 088	125 193	28 240	62 506	9 328
2003	1 257 121	244 826	...	187 204	92 818	68 344	17 910	221 595	152 436	29 219	68 113	8 851
2004	1 469 704	272 439	281 959	209 606	105 476	94 105	21 160	256 360	196 682	31 606	77 266	9 314
2005	1 673 454	298 878	308 776	228 881	102 609	124 940	24 436	290 384	243 470	33 842	84 751	8 892
2003												
January	97 491	18 192	...	14 291	7 821	4 827	1 434	17 735	11 404	2 354	4 877	822
February	93 154	18 057	...	13 585	6 517	4 745	1 305	17 184	9 630	2 215	4 860	564
March	105 842	21 275	...	16 203	7 185	6 565	1 535	19 823	10 110	2 329	6 271	563
April	103 869	20 531	...	15 757	7 874	6 296	1 427	18 454	11 522	2 424	5 943	625
May	102 068	20 234	...	15 277	7 233	5 653	1 398	18 668	11 885	2 237	5 883	626
June	103 958	20 512	...	15 691	7 749	5 608	1 479	18 574	12 127	2 461	5 736	692
July	107 631	21 665	...	16 682	8 071	5 821	1 647	17 079	13 439	2 524	5 785	871
August	102 307	18 619	...	14 523	7 390	5 568	1 634	17 584	13 765	2 278	5 135	839
September	108 322	19 746	...	14 728	8 102	5 738	1 465	19 361	14 748	2 347	5 016	920
October	117 158	22 255	...	16 720	8 732	5 956	1 635	20 138	16 458	2 617	6 060	958
November	106 066	20 868	...	16 208	7 819	5 414	1 348	18 641	14 157	2 551	6 046	696
December	109 255	22 873	...	17 537	8 325	6 152	1 603	18 354	13 193	2 881	6 501	678
2004												
January	103 993	18 348	19 117	14 005	7 933	6 136	1 393	18 926	14 089	2 258	5 013	806
February	104 864	21 052	21 880	16 182	7 051	6 199	1 209	19 357	11 267	2 161	5 988	531
March	123 421	24 736	25 654	18 918	8 528	7 328	1 513	22 483	13 800	2 732	6 791	692
April	118 885	23 600	24 408	17 856	8 367	6 906	1 554	21 499	14 745	2 542	6 621	656
May	118 271	22 607	23 338	17 211	8 796	7 480	1 626	21 250	15 067	2 407	6 616	616
June	127 657	23 294	24 142	17 882	9 274	8 082	2 009	23 251	16 888	2 680	6 065	780
July	123 224	22 708	23 572	17 617	9 101	7 889	2 024	19 777	17 562	2 558	6 705	888
August	127 216	22 077	22 823	17 604	9 180	9 178	1 807	22 018	18 068	2 471	6 488	896
September	126 022	21 114	21 878	16 318	9 742	8 394	2 126	21 688	18 387	2 646	5 994	957
October	134 816	23 823	24 537	18 416	9 504	9 404	2 014	22 411	19 718	3 152	7 034	963
November	134 719	24 372	25 162	18 687	9 430	9 064	1 880	22 876	19 679	2 960	6 959	829
December	126 617	24 708	25 447	18 908	8 569	8 045	2 005	20 826	17 412	3 040	6 992	701
2005												
January	122 900	21 316	21 998	16 512	9 074	8 162	2 038	21 840	17 886	2 562	5 956	754
February	122 233	22 948	23 647	17 746	7 646	8 104	1 708	21 502	16 938	2 586	6 378	551
March	135 450	25 496	26 258	19 435	8 216	9 540	1 948	24 010	16 185	2 834	7 382	573
April	135 456	24 944	25 706	18 915	8 035	9 908	2 044	23 458	18 148	2 936	6 941	542
May	136 191	25 753	26 691	19 744	8 318	9 867	1 968	23 528	19 053	2 676	7 382	564
June	141 426	25 592	26 426	19 679	8 645	10 183	2 164	23 672	20 977	3 193	7 052	638
July	136 515	24 677	25 573	19 114	8 197	11 459	2 177	21 087	21 273	2 688	7 206	778
August	146 397	24 591	25 534	19 100	8 947	12 118	2 023	25 041	22 421	2 658	7 424	877
September	146 216	24 177	24 951	18 182	8 575	11 579	2 001	25 950	23 294	2 869	6 445	1 058
October	156 162	26 937	27 800	20 283	9 094	12 227	2 220	27 725	24 383	2 800	7 539	1 028
November	150 245	26 876	27 795	20 337	9 086	11 001	1 982	26 383	22 426	3 018	7 564	813
December	144 262	25 571	26 396	19 833	8 774	10 792	2 164	26 189	20 486	3 023	7 480	716

[1]See notes and definitions for definitions of regions.
. . . = Not available.

Table 7-14. U.S. Imports of Goods by Selected Regions and Countries—Continued

(Census Customs basis; millions of dollars, not seasonally adjusted.)

Year and month	Indonesia	Italy	Japan	Malaysia	Mexico	Netherlands	Singapore	South Korea	Taiwan	United Kingdom	Venezuela
						Selected countries—Continued					
1972	. . .	1 757	9 064	. . .	1 632	. . .	. . .	. . .	. . .	2 987	1 298
1973	. . .	2 002	9 676	. . .	2 306	. . .	. . .	. . .	. . .	3 657	1 787
1974	. . .	2 585	12 338	. . .	3 390	1 433	. . .	. . .	. . .	4 061	4 671
1975	. . .	2 397	11 268	. . .	3 059	1 083	. . .	. . .	. . .	3 784	3 624
1976	. . .	2 530	15 504	. . .	3 598	1 080	. . .	. . .	. . .	4 254	3 574
1977	. . .	3 037	18 550	. . .	4 694	1 477	. . .	. . .	. . .	5 141	4 084
1978	. . .	4 102	24 458	. . .	6 094	1 603	. . .	. . .	. . .	6 514	3 545
1979	. . .	4 918	26 248	. . .	8 800	1 852	. . .	. . .	. . .	8 028	5 166
1980	5 183	4 313	30 701	. . .	12 520	1 910	. . .	. . .	. . .	9 755	5 297
1981	6 022	5 189	37 612	. . .	13 765	2 366	. . .	. . .	. . .	12 835	5 566
1982	4 224	5 301	37 744	. . .	15 566	2 494	. . .	. . .	. . .	13 095	4 768
1983	5 285	5 455	41 183	. . .	16 776	2 970	. . .	. . .	. . .	12 470	4 938
1984	5 461	7 935	57 135	. . .	18 020	4 069	. . .	. . .	. . .	14 492	6 543
1985	4 569	9 674	68 783	. . .	19 132	4 081	4 260	10 031	16 396	14 937	6 537
1986	3 312	10 607	81 911	. . .	17 302	4 066	4 725	12 729	19 791	15 396	5 097
1987	3 394	11 040	84 575	. . .	20 271	3 964	6 201	16 987	24 622	17 341	5 579
1988	3 150	11 576	89 519	. . .	23 260	4 559	7 973	20 105	24 714	17 976	5 157
1989	3 529	11 933	93 586	. . .	27 162	4 810	8 950	19 742	24 326	18 319	6 771
1990	3 341	12 723	89 655		30 172	4 972	9 839	18 493	22 667	20 288	9 446
1991	3 241	11 764	91 511	6 102	31 130	4 811	9 957	17 019	23 023	18 413	8 179
1992	4 529	12 314	97 414	8 294	35 211	5 300	11 313	16 682	24 596	20 093	8 181
1993	5 435	13 216	107 246	10 563	39 917	5 443	12 798	17 118	25 102	21 730	8 140
1994	6 547	14 802	119 156	13 982	49 494	6 007	15 358	19 629	26 706	25 058	8 371
1995	7 435	16 348	123 479	17 455	61 684	6 405	18 560	24 184	28 972	26 930	9 721
1996	8 250	18 325	115 187	17 829	74 297	6 583	20 343	22 655	29 907	28 979	13 173
1997	9 188	19 408	121 663	18 027	85 938	7 293	20 075	23 173	32 629	32 659	13 477
1998	9 341	20 959	121 845	19 000	94 629	7 599	18 356	23 942	33 125	34 838	9 181
1999	9 525	22 357	130 864	21 424	109 721	8 475	18 191	31 179	35 204	39 237	11 335
2000	10 367	25 043	146 479	25 568	135 926	9 671	19 178	40 308	40 503	43 345	18 623
2001	10 104	23 790	126 473	22 340	131 338	9 515	15 000	35 181	33 375	41 369	15 251
2002	9 643	24 220	121 429	24 009	134 616	9 849	14 802	35 572	32 148	40 745	15 094
2003	9 515	25 414	118 037	25 440	138 060	10 953	15 138	37 229	31 599	42 795	17 136
2004	10 811	28 097	129 805	28 179	155 902	12 451	15 370	46 168	34 624	46 274	24 921
2005	12 014	31 009	138 004	33 685	170 109	14 862	15 110	43 781	34 826	51 033	33 978
2003											
January	728	2 003	9 110	1 891	10 831	883	1 421	2 861	2 717	3 003	400
February	715	1 808	9 441	1 651	10 958	849	1 106	2 643	2 204	3 493	690
March	810	2 291	10 435	1 936	11 783	959	1 231	2 897	2 494	3 729	1 458
April	855	2 118	10 333	2 041	11 155	951	1 333	3 342	2 574	3 515	1 648
May	793	2 054	9 106	1 990	11 495	825	1 285	2 751	2 571	3 559	1 581
June	761	2 109	9 739	2 169	11 420	935	1 365	3 070	2 622	3 525	1 533
July	868	2 487	10 129	2 331	11 125	955	1 239	3 241	2 720	3 711	1 539
August	797	2 169	9 089	2 223	11 403	878	1 065	2 776	2 709	3 171	1 706
September	799	1 779	9 442	2 297	11 817	917	1 346	3 023	2 815	3 647	1 620
October	949	2 105	10 787	2 435	12 966	1 011	1 342	3 674	2 758	4 136	1 648
November	767	2 157	10 187	2 228	11 693	941	1 124	3 397	2 602	3 430	1 539
December	673	2 334	10 241	2 249	11 417	849	1 281	3 555	2 812	3 876	1 773
2004											
January	774	2 003	9 172	2 112	11 201	853	1 148	3 365	2 615	3 203	1 765
February	763	2 092	10 238	1 894	11 709	929	1 140	3 086	2 294	3 495	1 706
March	932	2 484	11 792	2 224	13 594	1 035	1 274	3 742	2 820	4 234	2 058
April	869	2 295	11 230	2 277	12 576	976	1 249	3 652	2 810	4 168	1 956
May	853	2 181	9 841	2 133	13 050	959	1 289	4 040	2 851	3 891	2 117
June	992	2 559	11 038	2 387	13 850	1 034	1 329	4 090	3 075	3 960	2 187
July	1 075	2 547	11 045	2 393	12 213	1 020	1 410	3 829	2 975	3 760	2 022
August	949	2 442	10 651	2 586	13 279	1 110	1 373	3 803	3 109	3 456	2 323
September	1 009	2 167	10 510	2 612	13 521	1 030	1 378	4 393	3 014	3 496	1 929
October	950	2 292	11 440	2 685	14 475	1 256	1 405	4 096	3 040	4 062	2 519
November	892	2 380	11 636	2 391	13 909	1 156	1 219	4 317	3 066	4 196	2 275
December	753	2 656	11 212	2 485	12 526	1 092	1 158	3 757	2 953	4 355	2 065
2005											
January	896	2 353	10 154	2 328	12 074	1 036	1 237	4 124	2 959	3 545	2 518
February	913	2 262	10 993	2 101	12 607	962	1 136	3 411	2 548	3 705	2 154
March	1 050	2 659	12 779	2 454	14 114	1 162	1 164	3 696	2 784	4 333	2 852
April	957	2 515	11 793	2 715	14 282	1 193	1 269	3 465	2 760	4 323	2 655
May	908	2 673	10 756	2 712	14 414	1 286	1 231	3 627	2 896	4 326	2 841
June	984	2 696	12 004	2 951	14 849	1 146	1 254	3 806	2 946	4 138	2 964
July	1 014	2 865	11 394	3 094	12 710	1 218	1 189	3 324	2 907	4 035	3 218
August	1 098	2 872	11 457	3 102	14 896	1 236	1 338	3 661	3 071	4 139	3 056
September	1 109	2 166	10 838	3 000	14 518	1 412	1 259	3 343	2 915	4 352	3 317
October	1 135	2 754	12 173	3 246	15 720	1 518	1 313	3 727	3 027	4 914	2 798
November	1 020	2 688	11 946	2 880	15 499	1 489	1 322	3 901	3 050	4 969	2 625
December	930	2 506	11 715	3 102	14 427	1 204	1 399	3 697	2 963	4 255	2 980

. . . = Not available.

Table 7-15. U.S. Exports of Services

(Balance of payments basis, millions of dollars, seasonally adjusted.)

Year and month	Total	Travel	Passenger fares	Other transportation	Royalties and license fees	Other private services (financial, professional, etc.)	Transfers under U.S. military sales contracts [1]	U.S. government miscellaneous services
1960	6 290	919	175	1 607	837	570	2 030	153
1961	6 295	947	183	1 620	906	607	1 867	164
1962	6 941	957	191	1 764	1 056	585	2 193	195
1963	7 348	1 015	205	1 898	1 162	613	2 219	236
1964	7 840	1 207	241	2 076	1 314	651	2 086	265
1965	8 824	1 380	271	2 175	1 534	714	2 465	285
1966	9 616	1 590	317	2 333	1 516	814	2 721	326
1967	10 667	1 646	371	2 426	1 747	951	3 191	336
1968	11 917	1 775	411	2 548	1 867	1 024	3 939	353
1969	12 806	2 043	450	2 652	2 019	1 160	4 138	343
1970	14 171	2 331	544	3 125	2 331	1 294	4 214	332
1971	16 358	2 534	615	3 299	2 545	1 546	5 472	347
1972	17 841	2 817	699	3 579	2 770	1 764	5 856	357
1973	19 832	3 412	975	4 465	3 225	1 985	5 369	401
1974	22 591	4 032	1 104	5 697	3 821	2 321	5 197	419
1975	25 497	4 697	1 039	5 840	4 300	2 920	6 256	446
1976	27 971	5 742	1 229	6 747	4 353	3 584	5 826	489
1977	31 485	6 150	1 366	7 090	4 920	3 848	7 554	557
1978	36 353	7 183	1 603	8 136	5 885	4 717	8 209	620
1979	39 692	8 441	2 156	9 971	6 184	5 439	6 981	520
1980	47 584	10 588	2 591	11 618	7 085	6 276	9 029	398
1981	57 354	12 913	3 111	12 560	7 284	10 250	10 720	517
1982	64 079	12 393	3 174	12 317	5 603	17 444	12 572	576
1983	64 307	10 947	3 610	12 590	5 778	18 192	12 524	666
1984	71 168	17 177	4 067	13 809	6 177	19 255	9 969	714
1985	73 155	17 762	4 411	14 674	6 678	20 035	8 718	878
1986	86 689	20 385	5 582	15 438	8 113	28 027	8 549	595
1987	98 661	23 563	7 003	17 027	10 174	29 263	11 106	526
1988	110 919	29 434	8 976	19 311	12 139	31 111	9 284	664
1989	127 087	36 205	10 657	20 526	13 818	36 729	8 564	587
1990	147 832	43 007	15 298	22 042	16 634	40 251	9 932	668
1991	164 261	48 385	15 854	22 631	17 819	47 748	11 135	690
1992	177 252	54 742	16 618	21 531	20 841	50 292	12 387	841
1993	185 920	57 875	16 528	21 958	21 695	53 510	13 471	883
1994	200 395	58 417	16 997	23 754	26 712	60 841	12 787	887
1995	219 183	63 395	18 909	26 081	30 289	65 048	14 643	818
1996	239 489	69 809	20 422	26 074	32 470	73 340	16 446	928
1997	256 087	73 426	20 868	27 006	33 228	83 929	16 675	955
1998	262 758	71 325	20 098	25 604	35 626	91 774	17 405	926
1999	281 919	74 801	19 785	26 916	39 670	103 934	15 928	885
2000	298 603	82 400	20 687	29 803	43 233	107 904	13 790	786
2001	286 184	71 893	17 926	28 442	40 696	113 857	12 539	831
2002	292 299	66 605	17 046	29 195	44 508	122 207	11 943	795
2003	302 681	64 348	15 693	31 512	46 988	130 561	12 769	810
2004	344 426	74 547	18 851	37 436	52 512	144 654	15 467	959
2005	380 614	81 680	20 931	42 245	57 410	158 223	19 038	1 087
2003								
January	24 501	5 446	1 302	2 515	3 745	10 464	961	68
February	24 451	5 373	1 303	2 512	3 775	10 521	900	67
March	24 116	4 991	1 220	2 579	3 804	10 574	881	67
April	23 490	4 396	1 092	2 597	3 826	10 580	932	67
May	24 325	4 901	1 185	2 551	3 854	10 754	1 013	67
June	24 613	5 040	1 245	2 551	3 883	10 856	970	68
July	25 129	5 256	1 320	2 616	3 902	10 850	1 118	67
August	25 492	5 391	1 357	2 608	3 938	10 934	1 196	68
September	25 782	5 534	1 359	2 638	3 982	10 986	1 215	68
October	26 681	5 885	1 389	2 801	4 049	11 304	1 186	67
November	26 758	6 025	1 445	2 736	4 094	11 286	1 104	68
December	27 341	6 110	1 476	2 808	4 135	11 451	1 293	68
2004								
January	27 272	5 806	1 467	2 893	4 181	11 578	1 277	70
February	27 573	6 004	1 522	2 948	4 205	11 509	1 314	71
March	28 468	6 053	1 545	3 229	4 220	11 924	1 424	73
April	28 477	6 242	1 582	3 162	4 201	11 874	1 340	76
May	28 292	6 154	1 552	3 112	4 214	11 856	1 327	77
June	28 508	6 271	1 524	3 025	4 235	12 020	1 354	79
July	28 296	6 350	1 628	3 073	4 246	11 612	1 306	81
August	28 307	6 148	1 646	3 161	4 278	11 674	1 318	82
September	28 747	6 205	1 609	3 031	4 389	12 215	1 214	84
October	29 727	6 307	1 512	3 237	4 703	12 714	1 167	87
November	30 257	6 452	1 603	3 339	4 801	12 792	1 181	89
December	30 504	6 555	1 661	3 226	4 839	12 888	1 245	90
2005								
January	30 510	6 506	1 591	3 300	4 738	12 780	1 504	91
February	30 717	6 686	1 622	3 298	4 716	12 703	1 600	92
March	31 163	6 791	1 677	3 505	4 692	12 832	1 575	91
April	31 103	7 000	1 707	3 488	4 637	12 696	1 489	86
May	31 373	6 978	1 741	3 390	4 640	12 930	1 607	87
June	31 579	6 956	1 713	3 475	4 666	13 101	1 579	89
July	31 690	6 750	1 864	3 458	4 745	12 987	1 790	96
August	31 779	6 704	1 801	3 495	4 798	13 181	1 702	98
September	32 439	6 935	1 843	3 592	4 854	13 371	1 747	97
October	32 629	6 877	1 834	3 703	4 936	13 707	1 484	88
November	32 495	6 633	1 744	3 752	4 979	13 894	1 407	86
December	33 138	6 864	1 793	3 789	5 008	14 043	1 555	86

[1] Contains goods that cannot be separately identified.

Table 7-16. U.S. Imports of Services

(Balance of payments basis, millions of dollars, seasonally adjusted.)

Year and month	Total	Travel	Passenger fares	Other transportation	Royalties and license fees	Other private services (financial, professional, etc.)	Direct defense expenditures [1]	U.S. government miscellaneous services
1960	7 674	1 750	513	1 402	74	593	3 087	254
1961	7 671	1 785	506	1 437	89	588	2 998	268
1962	8 092	1 939	567	1 558	100	528	3 105	296
1963	8 362	2 114	612	1 701	112	493	2 961	370
1964	8 619	2 211	642	1 817	127	527	2 880	415
1965	9 111	2 438	717	1 951	135	461	2 952	457
1966	10 494	2 657	753	2 161	140	506	3 764	513
1967	11 863	3 207	829	2 157	166	565	4 378	561
1968	12 302	3 030	885	2 367	186	668	4 535	631
1969	13 322	3 373	1 080	2 455	221	751	4 856	586
1970	14 520	3 980	1 215	2 843	224	827	4 855	576
1971	15 400	4 373	1 290	3 130	241	956	4 819	592
1972	16 868	5 042	1 596	3 520	294	1 043	4 784	589
1973	18 843	5 526	1 790	4 694	385	1 180	4 629	640
1974	21 379	5 980	2 095	5 942	346	1 262	5 032	722
1975	21 996	6 417	2 263	5 708	472	1 551	4 795	789
1976	24 570	6 856	2 568	6 852	482	2 006	4 895	911
1977	27 640	7 451	2 748	7 972	504	2 190	5 823	951
1978	32 189	8 475	2 896	9 124	671	2 573	7 352	1 099
1979	36 689	9 413	3 184	10 906	831	2 822	8 294	1 239
1980	41 491	10 397	3 607	11 790	724	2 909	10 851	1 214
1981	45 503	11 479	4 487	12 474	650	3 562	11 564	1 287
1982	51 749	12 394	4 772	11 710	795	8 159	12 460	1 460
1983	54 973	13 149	6 003	12 222	943	8 001	13 087	1 568
1984	67 748	22 913	5 735	14 843	1 168	9 040	12 516	1 534
1985	72 862	24 558	6 444	15 643	1 170	10 203	13 108	1 735
1986	80 147	25 913	6 505	17 766	1 401	13 146	13 730	1 686
1987	90 787	29 310	7 283	19 010	1 857	16 485	14 950	1 893
1988	98 526	32 114	7 729	20 891	2 601	17 667	15 604	1 921
1989	102 479	33 416	8 249	22 172	2 528	18 930	15 313	1 871
1990	117 659	37 349	10 531	24 966	3 135	22 229	17 531	1 919
1991	118 459	35 322	10 012	24 975	4 035	25 590	16 409	2 116
1992	119 566	38 552	10 603	23 767	5 161	25 386	13 835	2 263
1993	123 779	40 713	11 410	24 524	5 032	27 760	12 086	2 255
1994	133 057	43 782	13 062	26 019	5 852	31 565	10 217	2 560
1995	141 397	44 916	14 663	27 034	6 919	35 199	10 043	2 623
1996	152 554	48 078	15 809	27 403	7 837	39 679	11 061	2 687
1997	165 932	52 051	18 138	28 959	9 161	43 154	11 707	2 762
1998	180 677	56 483	19 971	30 363	11 235	47 591	12 185	2 849
1999	199 190	58 963	21 315	34 139	13 107	55 510	13 335	2 821
2000	223 748	64 705	24 274	41 425	16 468	60 520	13 473	2 883
2001	221 791	60 200	22 633	38 682	16 538	66 021	14 835	2 882
2002	231 069	58 715	19 969	38 407	19 353	72 604	19 101	2 920
2003	250 276	57 444	20 957	44 705	19 033	79 710	25 296	3 131
2004	290 312	65 750	23 723	54 161	23 211	90 390	29 299	3 778
2005	314 604	69 175	26 066	62 107	24 501	98 714	30 062	3 979
2003								
January	20 339	5 007	1 715	3 556	1 508	6 452	1 850	251
February	20 079	4 825	1 672	3 459	1 496	6 467	1 907	253
March	20 248	4 661	1 620	3 776	1 495	6 480	1 961	255
April	19 709	4 146	1 583	3 788	1 516	6 405	2 015	256
May	19 829	4 331	1 603	3 603	1 537	6 440	2 057	258
June	20 285	4 512	1 689	3 698	1 564	6 472	2 090	260
July	21 024	4 810	1 846	3 872	1 617	6 533	2 084	262
August	21 104	4 979	1 875	3 630	1 642	6 590	2 125	263
September	21 262	4 849	1 791	3 792	1 663	6 722	2 180	265
October	21 827	5 003	1 853	3 800	1 655	6 952	2 300	264
November	21 964	5 036	1 894	3 699	1 662	7 055	2 349	269
December	22 607	5 285	1 816	4 032	1 678	7 143	2 378	275
2004								
January	23 052	5 347	1 899	4 240	1 718	7 210	2 347	291
February	23 183	5 346	1 914	4 266	1 747	7 246	2 364	300
March	23 273	5 167	1 927	4 406	1 778	7 301	2 388	306
April	23 467	5 309	1 883	4 341	1 824	7 354	2 446	310
May	23 883	5 558	1 950	4 339	1 846	7 405	2 470	315
June	24 223	5 588	2 049	4 476	1 860	7 448	2 483	319
July	23 911	5 531	1 984	4 422	1 833	7 339	2 479	323
August	24 971	5 550	1 997	4 558	2 650	7 412	2 479	325
September	24 336	5 520	1 921	4 632	1 894	7 569	2 475	325
October	25 018	5 548	2 031	4 735	2 000	7 937	2 448	319
November	25 488	5 585	2 066	4 957	2 028	8 079	2 452	321
December	25 506	5 701	2 102	4 789	2 032	8 090	2 468	324
2005								
January	25 832	5 713	2 060	5 356	1 965	7 896	2 506	336
February	25 707	5 729	2 064	5 211	1 956	7 892	2 517	338
March	25 692	5 828	2 089	5 050	1 959	7 911	2 519	336
April	25 858	5 884	2 177	5 027	1 978	7 977	2 494	321
May	25 929	5 868	2 177	5 019	1 998	8 057	2 491	319
June	26 106	5 837	2 201	5 089	2 028	8 136	2 493	322
July	26 173	5 732	2 220	5 025	2 102	8 247	2 511	336
August	26 160	5 677	2 164	5 017	2 124	8 324	2 514	340
September	26 619	5 772	2 270	5 163	2 130	8 430	2 514	340
October	26 654	5 739	2 204	5 348	2 052	8 477	2 503	331
November	26 783	5 620	2 229	5 422	2 076	8 605	2 501	330
December	27 093	5 776	2 211	5 380	2 133	8 764	2 499	330

[1]Contains goods that cannot be separately identified.

Table 7-17. U.S. Export and Import Price Indexes by End-Use Category

(2000 = 100, not seasonally adjusted.)

Year and month	Exports			Imports		
	All commodities	Agricultural	Nonagricultural	All commodities	Petroleum [1]	Nonpetroleum
1989	94.7	110.5	92.7	91.1	61.2	96.0
1990	95.5	105.1	94.4	94.0	75.5	97.1
1991	96.3	103.4	95.4	94.2	67.3	98.7
1992	96.3	102.5	95.7	94.9	62.9	100.0
1993	96.9	104.4	96.2	94.6	57.7	100.6
1994	98.9	109.4	98.0	96.2	54.3	103.2
1995	103.9	119.0	102.5	100.6	59.8	107.2
1996	104.5	132.6	101.6	101.6	71.1	106.4
1997	103.1	120.6	101.3	99.1	66.0	104.1
1998	99.7	108.8	98.8	93.1	44.8	100.4
1999	98.4	101.1	98.2	93.9	60.1	99.0
2000	100.0	100.0	100.0	100.0	100.0	100.0
2001	99.2	101.2	99.0	96.5	82.8	98.5
2002	98.2	103.2	97.8	94.1	85.3	96.2
2003	99.7	112.3	98.8	96.9	103.2	97.3
2004	103.6	123.4	102.1	102.3	134.6	99.8
2005	106.9	121.0	105.9	110.0	185.1	102.5
2001						
January	100.3	102.5	100.1	100.5	93.1	101.6
February	100.2	101.0	100.1	99.9	93.3	100.8
March	100.0	101.3	99.9	98.3	87.2	100.0
April	99.9	100.8	99.8	97.8	86.2	99.5
May	99.6	100.8	99.5	98.0	90.3	99.2
June	99.4	100.9	99.3	97.6	89.4	98.9
July	99.0	101.8	98.8	96.1	84.6	97.8
August	98.8	102.8	98.5	96.0	86.1	97.5
September	99.0	102.5	98.6	95.9	86.7	97.3
October	98.3	100.7	98.1	93.7	73.4	96.8
November	97.8	99.2	97.7	92.3	63.8	96.6
December	97.6	100.2	97.4	91.4	59.9	96.2
2002						
January	97.5	100.9	97.2	91.6	63.0	96.1
February	97.3	98.3	97.2	91.6	65.7	95.7
March	97.6	98.9	97.5	92.8	76.9	95.8
April	98.0	99.6	97.8	94.3	86.7	96.3
May	98.0	99.5	97.8	94.4	88.4	96.2
June	98.0	100.7	97.8	94.1	85.3	96.2
July	98.3	103.4	97.9	94.5	88.5	96.2
August	98.5	105.2	97.9	94.8	91.8	96.3
September	98.8	108.6	98.0	95.5	97.1	96.4
October	98.7	106.6	98.1	95.5	97.0	96.4
November	98.8	108.7	98.0	94.6	89.0	96.3
December	98.6	108.2	97.8	95.2	94.0	96.5
2003						
January	98.9	108.3	98.2	96.9	107.7	96.8
February	99.5	107.9	98.8	98.5	119.9	97.1
March	99.7	107.5	99.1	99.1	118.6	98.1
April	99.6	107.9	99.0	96.0	96.3	97.1
May	99.7	110.6	98.8	95.3	91.5	96.9
June	99.5	110.0	98.7	96.2	96.4	97.3
July	99.4	109.9	98.6	96.7	101.4	97.3
August	99.4	108.8	98.7	96.7	103.2	97.0
September	99.8	114.7	98.6	96.2	97.2	97.3
October	100.0	117.5	98.7	96.3	98.8	97.2
November	100.5	122.2	98.8	96.8	100.9	97.4
December	100.8	122.7	99.1	97.5	106.0	97.7
2004						
January	101.5	123.5	99.8	99.0	113.7	98.5
February	102.2	125.3	100.4	99.4	114.3	98.9
March	103.0	129.7	100.9	100.2	120.1	99.1
April	103.7	133.0	101.4	100.4	119.9	99.4
May	104.1	133.7	101.7	101.9	131.2	99.6
June	103.4	127.4	101.5	101.7	129.7	99.7
July	103.9	126.1	102.2	102.1	132.7	99.7
August	103.4	115.5	102.5	103.6	144.4	100.0
September	103.8	117.6	102.8	104.1	149.2	100.1
October	104.4	116.3	103.6	105.8	165.8	100.0
November	104.7	116.7	103.9	105.5	155.9	100.9
December	104.8	115.4	104.1	104.0	138.1	101.3
2005						
January	105.6	116.1	104.9	104.6	141.2	101.6
February	105.7	115.5	105.0	105.5	148.4	101.7
March	106.4	119.9	105.4	107.8	168.3	102.0
April	106.9	120.3	106.0	108.8	174.4	102.4
May	106.7	122.7	105.5	107.9	166.7	102.2
June	106.7	123.9	105.4	109.2	181.5	102.0
July	106.8	123.9	105.5	110.5	195.5	101.8
August	106.6	123.2	105.4	112.1	209.9	101.9
September	107.5	121.5	106.5	114.4	224.4	102.8
October	108.3	121.9	107.3	114.5	217.5	103.8
November	107.6	121.6	106.6	112.3	197.1	103.7
December	107.7	121.0	106.8	112.3	196.6	103.7

[1]Petroleum and petroleum products.

NOTES AND DEFINITIONS

This chapter presents data from two different data systems on international flows of goods, services, income payments, and financial transactions as they affect the U.S. economy. Tables 7-1 through 7-5 present data on the value, quantities, and prices of foreign transactions in the national income and product accounts (NIPAs). Tables 7-6 through 7-8 show foreign transactions and investment positions as depicted in the U.S. international transactions accounts (ITAs). Both sets of accounts are prepared by the Bureau of Economic Analysis (BEA) and draw on the same original source data. The source data for goods and services are presented in somewhat greater detail in Tables 7-9 through 7-16. Table 7-17 shows selected summary values for export and import price indexes compiled by the Bureau of Labor Statistics (BLS).

Further detail on U.S. foreign trade in goods and services by region, country, state, metropolitan area, product, and industry is published by Bernan online. For information, see: Diane Werneke. *United States Foreign Trade Highlights: Trends in the Global Market* (2nd edition). (Lanham, MD: Bernan Press, 2007. Bernan Press e-book.)

Due to a few differences in concept, scope, and definitions, the aggregate values of international transactions in the NIPAs (shown in Tables 7-1 and 7-4) are not exactly equal to the values for similar concepts in the ITAs or the Census values that serve as their sources, shown in Tables 7-6 through 7-16. The principal sources of differences are as follows:

- The NIPAs cover only the 50 states and the District of Columbia. The ITAs include the U.S. territories and Puerto Rico.

- Gold is treated differently.

- Services without payment by financial intermediaries except life insurance carriers (imputed interest) is treated differently.

A reconciliation of the two sets of international accounts is published regularly as part of the NIPAs. As of the time of writing, the most up-to-date reconciliation was Reconciliation Table 1, "Relation of Net Exports of Goods and Services and Net Receipts of Income in the NIPAs to Balance on Goods and Services and Income in the ITAs," which can be found in the *Survey of Current Business*, September 2006, page D-82.

In addition, certain conventions of presentation differ between the two sets of international accounts. In the NIPAs (Tables 7-1 through 7-5) and in Census tables of exports and imports of goods and services (Tables 7-9 through 7-16), values of imports are shown as positive values. In the ITA balance of payments (Table 7-6), however, values of imports of goods and services and of all other transactions that result in a payment to the rest of the world—income payments to foreigners, net transfers to foreigners, and net acquisition of assets from abroad—are presented with a minus sign.

TABLES 7-1 AND 7-4
FOREIGN TRANSACTIONS IN THE NATIONAL INCOME AND PRODUCT ACCOUNTS

SOURCE: U.S. DEPARTMENT OF COMMERCE, BUREAU OF ECONOMIC ANALYSIS

See the notes and definitions to Chapter 1 for an overview of the national income and product accounts (NIPAs).

In the 2003 comprehensive revision, the NIPA foreign transactions account was split into two accounts—the current account and the capital account. (This change had already been made in the ITAs.) Most international transactions fall into the current account, but occasionally there are substantial flows in the capital account when major already-existing assets are transferred. An example of this is the U.S. government's transfer of the Panama Canal to the Republic of Panama in 1999.

Definitions

In accordance with the split between current and capital account, there are now two NIPA measures of the balance of international transactions.

The *balance on current account, national income and product accounts* is *current receipts from the rest of the world* minus *current payments to the rest of the world*. A negative value indicates that current payments exceed current receipts.

Net lending or net borrowing (-), national income and product accounts is equal to the balance on current account less capital transfers to the rest of the world (net). Capital transfer payments to the rest of the world (net)—not shown separately in Table 7-1, although a similar measure is shown in the ITAs in Table 7-6—are cash or in-kind transfers linked to the acquisition or disposition of an existing asset. In contrast, the current account is limited to flows associated with current production of goods and services.

Net lending or net borrowing provides an indirect measure of the net acquisition of foreign assets by U.S. residents less the net acquisition of U.S. assets by foreign residents. These asset flows are measured directly in the ITAs. See Table 7-6 and its notes and definitions for a more extensive discussion of the relationship between the balances on current and capital account and international asset flows.

Current receipts from the rest of the world is *exports of goods and services* plus *income receipts*.

Current payments to the rest of the world is *imports of goods and services* plus *income payments* plus *current taxes and transfer payments (net)*.

Exports and imports of goods and services. Goods, in general, are products that can be stored or inventoried. Services, in general, are products that cannot be stored and are consumed at the place and time of their purchase. Goods include expenditures abroad by U.S. residents, except for travel. Services include foreign travel by U.S. residents, expenditures in the United States by foreign travelers, and exports and imports of certain goods—primarily military equipment purchased and sold by the federal government. See the following paragraph for the definition of travel.

Table 7-4 shows values for selected components of total goods and services; the components shown will not add to the total because of omitted items. In the case of goods, a miscellaneous "other" category is not shown. In the case of services, only two components are shown in this table. One is *travel*, which does not include passenger fares but includes as exports spending by foreign tourists in the United States, and includes as imports all other spending abroad by tourists from the United States. The other component shown here is a category called *other private services*, which includes the professional and financial services (for example, computer services) that have accounted for a large part of the long-term growth in the service category. The remaining components of total services are transfers under U.S. military agency sales contracts; passenger fares; other transportation; royalties and license fees; and a miscellaneous, smaller "other" category. They are shown separately in Tables 7-15 and 7-16.

Income receipts and payments. Income receipts—receipts from abroad of factor (labor or capital) income by U.S. residents—are analogous to exports and are combined with them to yield total *current receipts from the rest of the world. Income payments* by U.S. entities of factor income to entities abroad are analogous to imports.

Current taxes and transfer payments (net) consists of net payments between the United States and abroad that do not involve payment for the services of the labor or capital factors of production, purchase of currently-produced goods and services, or transfer of an existing asset. It includes net flows from persons, government, and business. The types of payments included are personal remittances from U.S. residents to the rest of the world, net of remittances from foreigners to U.S. residents; government grants; and transfer payments from businesses. Only the net payment to the rest of the world is shown. It is usually positive, with transfers from the United States to abroad exceeding the reverse flow. An exception came in 1991, when U.S. allies in the Gulf War reimbursed the United States for the cost of the war. This resulted in net payments to the United States from the rest of the world and appears as a negative entry in the net transfer payments column.

TABLES 7-2, 7-3 AND 7-5
CHAIN-TYPE QUANTITY AND PRICE INDEXES FOR NIPA FOREIGN TRANSACTIONS

These indexes represent the separation of the current-dollar values in Tables 7-1 and 7-4 into their real quantity and price trends components. See the notes and definitions to Chapter 1 for a general explanation of chained-dollar estimates of real output and prices. As those notes explain, quantity indexes are shown instead of constant-dollar estimates, because BEA no longer publishes its real output estimates before 1990 in any detail in the constant-dollar form. Therefore, quantity indexes are the only comprehensive source of information about longer-term trends in real volumes.

TABLES 7-6 AND 19-10
U.S. INTERNATIONAL TRANSACTIONS

Source: U.S. Department of Commerce, Bureau of Economic Analysis

The U.S. international transactions accounts, or "balance of payments," provide a comprehensive view of economic and financial transactions between the United States and foreign countries, measured in current dollars only (unlike the NIPAs, in which price and quantity trends are also estimated). Direct measurement of the values of financial asset flows further distinguishes this set of accounts from the NIPAs.

The international transactions accounts (ITAs) are subdivided into three sets of accounts, with each comprising credit and debit items. In concept, all of these items together provide a complete accounting for U.S. international transactions and should therefore sum to zero. In practice, there are substantial discrepancies due to measurement problems. See the definitions below for an explanation of the *statistical discrepancy* in these accounts, which is different from the measure of the same name in the NIPAs.

The *balance on current account* is the most frequently quoted statistic from these accounts, and is often, but imprecisely, called the "trade balance." (See the definitions below for the correct definitions of "trade balance" and "merchandise trade balance," both of which differ from the current account balance.) The current account includes exports and imports of goods and of travel, transportation, and other services; receipts and payments of income between U.S. and foreign residents; and foreign aid and other current transfers. The *financial account* covers most international flows of private and official capital, including direct investment. The *capital account*, which is small relative to the other two accounts, includes certain transactions in existing assets.

More detailed data on exports and imports of goods and services as measured in these accounts are shown in Tables 7-9 through 7-16.

Definitions

Unlike the practice in the NIPAs, each category of transaction in the ITAs is presented either as a *credit*, with an implicit plus sign, or as a *debit*, with a clearly marked minus sign. The signs indicate the direction of the ultimate impact on the overall balance.

Credits (+): The following items are treated as credits in the international transactions accounts: exports of goods and services and income receipts; unilateral current transfers to the United States; capital account transactions receipts; and financial inflows, which are increases in foreign-owned assets (U.S. liabilities) and decreases in U.S.-owned assets (U.S. claims). Credits represent payments of funds to U.S. entities.

Debits (-): The following items are treated as debits in the international transactions accounts, indicated by minus signs in the data cells: imports of goods and services and income payments; unilateral current transfers to foreigners; capital accounts transactions payments; financial outflows, which are decreases in foreign-owned assets (U.S. liabilities) and increases in U.S.-owned assets (U.S. claims). Debits represent requirements for U.S. entities to make payments to foreigners.

This convention of credits and debits is used only in the ITAs in Table 7-6 and the long-term flow data in Table 7-7 (see below). In Table 7-6, import values all have a negative sign. Import values are shown without negative signs both in the NIPA tables (Tables 7-1 and 7-4) and in the detailed tables from the Census Bureau on exports and imports of goods and services (Tables 7-9 through 7-16).

The *balance on goods* is the excess of exports of goods over imports of goods—the algebraic sum of the two, in ITA transactions accounting. A minus sign indicates an excess of imports over exports. A similar concept, which appears in monthly trade reports, is called the "merchandise trade balance."

The *balance on services* is the excess of service exports over service imports. A minus sign indicates an excess of imports over exports.

The *balance on goods and services* is the sum of the balance on goods and the balance on services. This concept is accurately described as the "balance of trade."

The *balance on income* is the excess of income receipts from abroad over income payments to foreigners. A minus sign indicates an excess of payments over receipts.

The *balance on goods, services, and income* is the excess of exports of goods, services, and income over imports of goods, services, and income. It is equal to the sum of the balance on goods and services and the balance on income. A minus sign indicates an excess of imports over exports.

The *balance on unilateral transfers* is equal to unilateral transfers, net, or transfers to the United States minus transfers from the United States. This category includes U.S. government grants, pensions, and other transfers, and private remittances and other transfers. It includes an adjustment for the difference between actual and normal insured losses. See the entry below, in the notes for Tables 7-9 through 7-16, concerning the measurement of insurance services.

The *balance on current account* is equal to the sum of the balance on goods, services, and income and the balance on unilateral transfers. It is the featured measure of the U.S. balance of payments.

The *capital account* covers net capital transfers and the acquisition and disposal of nonproduced nonfinancial assets. The major types of *capital transfers* are debt forgiveness and assets that accompany immigrants. *Nonproduced nonfinancial* assets include rights to natural resources, patents, copyrights, trademarks, franchises, and leases.

The *financial account* includes all other inflows and outflows of capital, or changes in U.S.-owned assets abroad and foreign-owned assets in the United States, including official reserve assets, direct investment, securities, currency, and bank deposits.

Direct investment financial flows are those associated with the acquisition of a significant interest (10 percent or more) in a business enterprise in one country by a resident of another country.

Foreign official assets in the United States. U.S. Treasury securities includes bills, certificates, marketable bonds and notes, and nonmarketable convertible and nonconvertible bonds and notes. Other U.S. *government securities* consists of U.S. Treasury and Export-Import Bank obligations, not included elsewhere, and of debt securities of U.S. government corporations and agencies. *Other U.S. government liabilities* primarily includes U.S. government liabilities to foreign official authorities associated with military agency sales contracts and other transactions arranged with or through foreign official agencies. *Other foreign official assets* consists of official investments in U.S. corporate stocks and in debt securities of private corporations and state and local governments.

In concept, the balance on current account is exactly offset by the net financial and capital inflow or outflow. For example, a U.S. current account deficit results in more dollars held by foreigners, which must be reflected in additional claims on the United States held by foreigners, whether in the form of U.S. currency, securities, loans, or other forms of ownership or obligation. However, because of different and incomplete data sources, the measured financial and capital accounts do not exactly offset the measured current account. The *statistical discrepancy* in the U.S. international accounts—the sum of all credits and debits, with the sign reversed—measures the amount by which the measured net financial and capital flow would have to be augmented (or diminished, in the case of a negative discrepancy) to exactly offset the current account balance. In the quarterly accounts, a part of this discrepancy, the *seasonal adjustment discrepancy*, results from separate seasonal adjustments of the components of the accounts. The statistical discrepancy in the international accounts is not the same as the statistical discrepancy in the national income and product accounts, which arises from measurement differences between domestic output and domestic income.

Notes on the data

Exports and imports of goods in the international transactions account excludes both exports of goods under U.S. military agency sales contracts identified in Census Bureau export documents and imports of goods under direct defense expenditures identified in import documents. They also reflect various other adjustments (for valuation, coverage, and timing) of Census Bureau statistics to a balance-of-payments basis. See Tables 7-10 and 7-11 and the associated notes and definitions for further information.

Services includes some goods, mainly military equipment (included in transfers under military agency sales contracts); major equipment, other materials, supplies, and petroleum products purchased abroad by U.S. military agencies (included in direct defense expenditures abroad); and fuels purchased by airline and steamship operators (included in other transportation).

U.S. government grants includes transfers of goods and services under U.S. military grant programs. The positive value in 1991 reflects net grants to the United States from other countries.

Beginning in 1982, *private remittances and other transfers* includes taxes paid by U.S. private residents to foreign governments and taxes paid by private nonresidents to the U.S. government.

At the present time, all U.S. Treasury-owned *gold* is held in the United States.

Repayments on U.S. credits and other long-term assets includes sales of foreign obligations to foreigners.

Beginning with the data for 1982, *direct investment income payments* and the reinvested earnings component of *direct investment* financial flows are measured on a current-cost (replacement-cost) basis after adjustment to reported depreciation, depletion, and expensed exploration and development costs. For prior years, depreciation is valued in terms of the historical cost of assets and reflects a mix of prices for the various years in which capital investments were made. See *Survey of Current Business*, July 1999, pages 65–67, and *Survey of Current Business*, June 1992, pages 72ff.

Estimates of *U.S. currency flows abroad* were introduced for the first time as part of the July 1997 revisions. Data for 1974 and subsequent years were affected (see *Survey of Current Business*, July 1997). Beginning with the 1998 revisions, currency flows are published separately from U.S. Treasury securities.

For 1978–1983, *U.S. Treasury securities* includes foreign-currency-denominated notes sold to private residents abroad.

Revisions

The international transactions accounts are revised annually each July. Changes in definitions and methodology and newly available source data may be introduced in these revisions.

Data availability

Quarterly and annual data are available from BEA. Data are first reported in a press release and subsequently published in the *Survey of Current Business*, which can be found on the BEA Web site at <http://www.bea.gov/bea/pubs.htm>. Revisions to historical data are published on an annual basis. The most recent historical revisions appear in the July 2006 issue of the *Survey of Current Business*. Complete historical data are available on the BEA Web site at <http://www.bea.gov/>.

References

Discussions of the impact of changes in methodology and incorporation of new data sources are found in the July issues (the June issues for 1995 and earlier years) of the *Survey of Current Business*, with the most recent article entitled "Annual Revision of the U.S. International Accounts, 1995–2005" (July 2006).

"The Balance of Payments of the United States: Concepts, Data Sources, and Estimating Procedures" (May 1990), available on the BEA Web site or from the National Technical Information Service (Accession No. PB 90-268715), describes the methodology in detail and provides a list of data sources.

TABLE 7-7
FOREIGNERS' TRANSACTIONS IN LONG-TERM SECURITIES WITH U.S. RESIDENTS

Source: U.S. Department of the Treasury

Some of the transactions that go into the ITA financial account are collected monthly. Since December 2003, these transactions have been reported by the Treasury Department in a monthly press release. They are presented in this edition of *Business Statistics* in Table 7-7.

These data cover transactions in long-term securities, measured at market value plus or minus commissions and fees, between foreigners and U.S. residents. They have more reporting gaps than the more comprehensive quarterly current account data in Table 7-6. These monthly data do not include direct investment, stock swaps, currency flows, changes in bank accounts, or transactions in short-term securities. They may be distorted by inappropriate reporting of repurchases and securities lending transactions. The data are more timely but less detailed than other information sources and are not reliable for country-by-country detail. They are based on a reporting panel of some 250 banks, securities dealers, and other enterprises with cross-border transactions of at least $50 million. This survey was designed to provide timely information for the balance of payments accounts, and its use for other applications—particularly those involving country detail—is less appropriate.

Definitions and notes on the data

U.S. residents includes any individual, corporation, or organization located in the United States (including branches, subsidiaries, and affiliates of foreign entities located in the United States) and any corporation incorporated in the United States, even if it has no physical presence in the country.

Gross purchases minus *gross sales* equals *net purchases*. As in the ITAs in Table 7-6, positive values for net purchases of U.S. securities by foreigners indicate capital inflows from foreigners to U.S. residents (and increased liabilities to foreigners on the part of the U.S. residents). Negative values for net purchases of foreign securities from U.S. residents indicate a capital outflow from U.S. residents to foreigners (and increased liabilities to U.S. residents on the part of foreigners). The algebraic sum of the two net purchases components gives *net long-term flows*. When positive, this indicates that the *net* capital inflows on U.S. securities exceed the net U.S. acquisitions of foreign securities.

Revisions

The monthly and annual data are revised frequently, when quarterly and annual benchmark data become available. The June release usually includes the final results from an annual survey of foreign holding of U.S. securities.

Data availability and references

Data for the latest month and recent historical data are published in a press release available around the middle of the second following month. The press release, supporting descriptions, references, and other relevant information concerning the Treasury International Capital System (TIC) can be found online at <http://www.treas. gov/tic>.

TABLE 7-8
INTERNATIONAL INVESTMENT POSITION OF THE UNITED STATES

Source: U.S. Department of Commerce, Bureau of Economic Analysis

The data presented in Tables 7-1 through 7-7 all represent <u>flows</u> of goods, services, and money over the designated time periods. Table 7-8, in contrast, is a measure of <u>stocks</u>, or total holdings of money and other claims. The data on the international investment position of the United States measure the extent to which the United States and its residents hold claims of ownership on foreigners or are creditors of foreigners; the extent to which foreigners, including foreign governments, hold claims of ownership on assets located in the United States or are creditors of U.S. residents and entities; and the net difference between the two amounts. This difference measures the amount by which the United States is a net creditor of the rest of the world or a net debtor to the rest of the world. A position of net U.S. indebtedness is represented by a minus sign in the net international investment position.

Changes in the net investment position can arise in two principal ways:

- The first way is through inflows or outflows of capital. A net inflow of capital increases U.S. indebtedness to foreigners, while a net outflow increases foreigners' indebtedness to the United States. A deficit in the U.S. international current account requires an equivalent inflow of foreign capital, while a surplus would require an equivalent outflow of U.S. capital; see notes for Table 7-6 for further explanation.

- The second way is through valuation adjustments, which are of several kinds: changes in market prices of assets; changes in exchange rates, which can cause revaluation of foreign-currency-denominated assets; and miscellaneous other adjustments due to changes in coverage, statistical discrepancies, and the like.

Definitions

Direct investment occurs when an individual or business in one country (the parent) obtains a lasting interest in, and a degree of influence over the management of, a business enterprise in another country (the affiliate). The U.S. data define this degree of interest to be ownership of at least 10 percent of the voting securities of an incorporated business enterprise or the equivalent interest in an unincorporated business enterprise.

When direct investment positions are valued at the historical costs carried on the books of the affiliated companies, much of the investment will reflect the price levels of earlier time periods. Therefore, before calculating the overall U.S. position, BEA re-estimates the <u>aggregate</u> direct investment totals using two alternative valuation bases. <u>Detailed</u> direct investment data by country and industry are available only on a historical cost basis.

At *current cost*, the portion of the direct investment position representing the parents' shares of their affiliates' tangible assets (property, plant, equipment, and inventories) is revalued to replacement cost in today's money, using a perpetual inventory model, appropriate price indexes, and appropriate depreciation allowances. (The same methodology is used for the U.S. stock of fixed assets; see the notes and definitions to Tables 5-5 and 5-6 for further information.) This is an adjustment made to the asset side of the balance sheet and reflects prices of tangible assets only.

The *market value* method revalues the owners' equity portion of the direct investment positions using general country indexes of stock market prices. This adjustment is made on the liability and owner's equity side of the balance sheet. Stock price changes reflect changes not only in the value of tangible assets, but also in the value of intangible assets and in the outlook for a country or industry.

Market values are more volatile than current cost, reflecting the nature of stock markets and the additional uncertainties concerning the intangibles included in the valuation. Typically, the total market value of direct investment is greater than the current replacement cost, though by varying proportions. However, in a few years (such as 1982 through 1984) aggregate market values fell below the estimated replacement cost.

U.S. official reserve assets includes gold, valued at the current market price; special drawing rights; the U.S. reserve position in the International Monetary Fund; and official holdings of foreign currencies.

Other U.S. government assets includes other U.S. government claims on foreigners and holdings of foreign currency and short-term assets.

U.S. nonbank claims includes U.S. claims on affiliated foreigners reported by U.S. nonbanking concerns.

U.S. bank claims consists of claims on foreigners, such as loans and commercial paper, held by U.S. banks and not reported elsewhere in the accounts.

Foreign official assets includes foreign government holdings of claims on the United States, including U.S. government securities and other liabilities and deposits held by such governments in U.S. banks.

Foreign-owned assets in the United States, other than official assets, also include *U.S. Treasury securities, U.S. currency, corporate and other bonds, corporate stocks, U.S. liabilities* (to foreigners) *reported by U.S. nonbanking concerns,* and *U.S. bank liabilities to foreigners* (such as deposits).

Data availability

The annual (year-end) data, along with revisions for earlier years and a descriptive article, are presented each year in the July issue of the *Survey of Current Business*. The articles and the data are available on the BEA Web site at <http://www.bea.gov>.

References

Relevant articles in the July 2006 Survey of Current Business include: "The International Investment Position of the United States at Yearend 2005" and "Direct Investment Positions for 2005: Country and Industry Detail." For background on the valuation of direct investment and other components, see "Valuation of the U.S. Net International Investment Position," *Survey of Current Business*, May 1991. Also see the references for Table 7-6.

TABLES 7-9 THROUGH 7-16
EXPORTS AND IMPORTS OF GOODS AND SERVICES

Sources: U.S. Department of Commerce, Census Bureau and Bureau of Economic Analysis

These tables present the source data used to build up the aggregate measures of goods and services flows shown in Tables 7-1 through 7-6. These data are compiled and published monthly, making trends evident before the publication of the quarterly aggregate estimates. They also provide more detail than the quarterly aggregates.

Monthly and annual data on exports and imports of *goods* are compiled by the Census Bureau from documents collected by the U.S. Customs Service. The Bureau of Economic Analysis (BEA) makes certain adjustments to these data (as described below) to place the estimates on a *balance of payments* basis for use in the national and international accounts.

Data on exports and imports of services are prepared by BEA from a variety of sources. Monthly data on services are available from January 1992. Annual and quarterly data for earlier years are available as part of the international transactions accounts. Current data on goods and services are available each month in a joint Census Bureau-BEA press release.

In the case of some of the detailed breakdowns of exports and imports, such as by end-use categories, monthly data may not sum exactly to annual totals. This is due to later revisions, which are made only to annual data and are not allocated to monthly data. Also, the constant-dollar figures expressed in 2000 dollars are calculated using chain weights. Therefore, the 2000-dollar detail will not add to the 2000-dollar totals.

In addition, monthly and annual data on exports and imports of goods for individual countries and various country groupings do not reflect subsequent revisions of annual total data. These country data are compiled by the Census Bureau for all countries, although this volume includes only a selection of the most significant ones. The full set of data can be accessed on the Census Bureau Web site at <http://www.census.gov>.

Definitions: Goods

Goods: Census basis. The Census basis goods data are compiled from documents collected by the U.S. Customs Service. They reflect the movement of goods between foreign countries and the 50 states, the District of Columbia,

Puerto Rico, the U.S. Virgin Islands, and U.S. Foreign Trade Zones. They include government and nongovernment shipments of goods, and exclude shipments between the United States and its territories and possessions; transactions with U.S. military, diplomatic, and consular installations abroad; U.S. goods returned to the United States by its armed forces; personal and household effects of travelers; and in-transit shipments. The general import values reflect the total arrival of merchandise from foreign countries that immediately enters consumption channels, warehouses, or Foreign Trade Zones.

For *imports*, the value reported is the U.S. Customs Service appraised value of merchandise (generally, the price paid for merchandise for export to the United States). Import duties, freight, insurance, and other charges incurred in bringing merchandise to the United States are excluded.

Exports are valued at the f.a.s. (free alongside ship) value of merchandise at the U.S. port of export, based on the transaction price including inland freight, insurance, and other charges incurred in placing the merchandise alongside the carrier at the U.S. port of exportation.

Goods: balance of payments (BOP) basis. Goods on a Census basis are adjusted by BEA to goods on a BOP basis to bring the data in line with the concepts and definitions used to prepare the international and national accounts. In general, the adjustments include changes in ownership that occur without goods passing into or out of the customs territory of the United States. These adjustments are necessary to supplement coverage of the Census basis data, to eliminate duplication of transactions recorded elsewhere in the international accounts, and to value transactions according to a standard definition.

The *export* adjustments include the following: (1) The deduction of *U.S. military sales contracts*. The Census Bureau has included these contracts in the goods data, but BEA includes them in the service category "Transfers Under U.S. Military Sales Contracts." BEA's source material for these contracts is more comprehensive but does not distinguish between goods and services. (2) The addition of *private gift* parcels mailed to foreigners by individuals through the U.S. Postal Service. Only commercial shipments are covered in Census goods exports. (3) The addition to *nonmonetary gold exports* of gold purchased by foreign official agencies from private dealers in the United States and held at the Federal Reserve Bank of New York. The Census data include only gold that leaves the customs territory. (4) *Smaller adjustments* includes deductions for repairs of goods, exposed motion picture film, and military grant aid, and additions for sales of fish in U.S. territorial waters, exports of electricity to Mexico, and vessels and oil rigs that change ownership without export documents being filed.

The *import* adjustments include the following: (1) On *inland freight in Canada*, the customs value for imports for certain Canadian goods is the point of origin in Canada.

BEA makes an addition for the inland freight charges of transporting these Canadian goods to the U.S. border. (2) An addition is made to *nonmonetary gold imports* for gold sold by foreign official agencies to private purchasers out of stock held at the Federal Reserve Bank of New York. The Census Bureau data include only gold that enters the customs territory. (3) A deduction is made for *imports* by U.S. *military agencies*. The Census Bureau has included these contracts in the goods data, but BEA includes them in the service category "Direct Defense Expenditures." BEA's source material is more comprehensive but does not distinguish between goods and services. (4) *Smaller adjustments* includes deductions for repairs of goods and for exposed motion picture film and additions for imported electricity from Mexico, conversion of vessels for commercial use, and repairs to U.S. vessels abroad.

Definitions: Services

The statistics are estimates of service transactions between foreign countries and the 50 states, the District of Columbia, Puerto Rico, the U.S. Virgin Islands, and other U.S. territories and possessions. Transactions with U.S. military, diplomatic, and consular installations abroad are excluded because they are considered to be part of the U.S. economy. Services are shown in the broad categories described below. For six of these categories, the definitions are the same for imports and exports. For the seventh, the export category is *transfers under U.S. military sales contracts*, while for imports, the category is *direct defense expenditures*.

Travel includes purchases of services and goods by U.S. travelers abroad and by foreign visitors to the United States. A traveler is defined as a person who stays for a period of less than one year in a country where the person is not a resident. Included are expenditures for food, lodging, recreation, gifts, and other items incidental to a foreign visit. Not included are the international costs of the travel itself, which are covered in *passenger fares* (see below).

Passenger fares consists of fares paid by residents of one country to residents in other countries. Receipts consist of fares received by U.S. carriers from foreign residents for travel between the United States and foreign countries and between two foreign points. Payments consist of fares paid by U.S. residents to foreign carriers for travel between the United States and foreign countries.

Break in series: travel and passenger fares. Beginning with data for 1984, these items incorporate results from a survey administered by the U.S. Travel and Tourism Administration. See *Survey of Current Business*, June 1989, pages 57ff.

Other transportation includes charges for the transportation of goods by ocean, air, waterway, pipeline, and rail carriers to and from the United States. Included are freight charges, operating expenses that transportation companies incur in foreign ports, and payments for vessel charter and aircraft and freight car rentals. (*Break in series*: Estimates of freight charges for the transportation of goods by truck between the United States and Canada are included in the data beginning with 1986. Reliable estimates for earlier years are not available. See *Survey of Current Business*, June 1994, pages 70ff.)

Royalties and license fees consists of transactions with foreign residents involving intangible assets and proprietary rights, such as the use of patents, techniques, processes, formulas, designs, know-how, trademarks, copyrights, franchises, and manufacturing rights. The term royalties generally refers to payments for the utilization of copyrights or trademarks, and the term license fees generally refers to payments for the use of patents or industrial processes.

Other private services includes transactions with "affiliated" foreigners for which no identification by type is available and transactions with unaffiliated foreigners.

The term "affiliated" refers to a direct investment relationship, which exists when a U.S. person has ownership or control (directly or indirectly) of 10 percent or more of a foreign business enterprise, or when a foreign person has a similar interest in a U.S. enterprise.

Transactions with "unaffiliated" foreigners in this "other private services" category consist of education services, financial services, insurance services, telecommunications services, and business, professional, and technical services. Included in the last group are advertising services; computer and data processing services; database and other information services; research, development, and testing services; management, consulting, and public relations services; legal services; construction, engineering, architectural, and mining services; industrial engineering services; installation, maintenance, and repair of equipment; and other services, including medical services and film and tape rental.

The insurance component of "other private services" was previously measured as premiums less actual losses paid or recovered. Furthermore, catastrophic losses were entered immediately when the loss occurred, rather than when the insurance claim was actually paid out. This led to sharp swings for any month in which catastrophic losses occurred, such as Hurricane Katrina in August 2005 or the September 11, 2001, terror attacks. In the accounts as revised in July 2003 and presented here, insurance services are now measured as premiums less "normal" losses. Normal losses consist of a measure of expected regularly occurring losses based on six years of past experience plus an additional allowance for catastrophic loss. Catastrophic losses, when they occur, are added in equal increments to the estimate of regularly occurring losses over the 20 years following the occurrence. As adoption of this methodology introduces a difference between actual and normal losses, an amount equal to the difference is entered in the international accounts as a current unilateral transfer.

BEA conducts surveys of international transactions in financial services and "selected services" (largely business, professional, and technical services). Beginning with data for 1986, *other private services* includes estimates of business, professional, and technical services from the BEA surveys of selected services. (See *Survey of Current Business*, June 1989, pages 57ff.)

Breaks in series: royalties and license fees and other private services. These items are presented on a gross basis beginning in 1982. The definition of exports is revised to exclude U.S. parents' payments to foreign affiliates and to include U.S. affiliates' receipts from foreign parents. The definition of imports is revised to include U.S. parents' payments to foreign affiliates and to exclude U.S. affiliates' receipts from foreign parents.

Transfers under U.S. military sales contracts (exports only) includes exports of goods and services in which U.S. government military agencies participate. This category includes both goods, such as equipment, and services, such as repair services and training, that cannot be separately identified. Transfers of goods and services under U.S. military grant programs are included.

Direct defense expenditures (imports only) consists of expenditures incurred by U.S. military agencies abroad, including expenditures by U.S. personnel, payments of wages to foreign residents, construction expenditures, payments for foreign contractual services, and procurement of foreign goods. Included are both goods and services that cannot be separately identified.

U.S. government miscellaneous services includes transactions of U.S. government nonmilitary agencies with foreign residents. Most of these transactions involve the provision of services to, or purchases of services from, foreigners. Transfers of some goods are also included.

Services estimates are based on quarterly, annual, and benchmark surveys and partial information generated from monthly reports. Service transactions are estimated at market prices. Estimates are seasonally adjusted when statistically significant seasonal patterns are present.

Definitions: Area groupings

The *European Union* originally included Austria, Belgium, Denmark, Finland, France, Germany, Greece, Ireland, Italy, Luxembourg, the Netherlands, Portugal, Spain, Sweden, and the United Kingdom. On May 1, 2004, the European Union expanded from 15 countries to 25 countries. The 10 countries added included Cyprus, the Czech Republic, Estonia, Hungary, Latvia, Lithuania, Malta, Poland, Slovakia, and Slovenia. Data are shown here for both the 15-country original group and the full 25-nation group.

The *Euro area* includes Austria, Belgium, Finland, France, Germany, Greece, Ireland, Italy, Luxembourg, the Netherlands, Portugal, and Spain. Greece entered the Euro area beginning in January 2001. Greece is included in the data for 2001 and later years but not in the data for 2000.

The *Asian Newly Industrialized Countries (NICS)* includes Hong Kong SAR, South Korea, Singapore, and Taiwan.

The *Organization of Petroleum Exporting Countries (OPEC)* consists of Algeria, Gabon, Indonesia, Iran, Iraq, Kuwait, Libya, Nigeria, Qatar, Saudi Arabia, the United Arab Emirates, and Venezuela.

Notes on the data

U.S./Canada data exchange and substitution. The data for U.S. exports to Canada are derived from import data compiled by Canada. The use of Canada's import data to produce U.S. export data requires several alignments in order to compare the two series.

• *Coverage*: Canadian imports are based on country of origin. U.S. goods shipped from a third country are included, but U.S. exports exclude these foreign shipments. U.S. export coverage also excludes certain Canadian postal shipments.

• *Valuation*: Canadian imports are valued at their point of origin in the United States. However, U.S. exports are valued at the port of exit in the United States and include inland freight charges, making the U.S. export value slightly larger. Canada requires inland freight to be reported.

• *Reexports*: U.S. exports include re-exports of foreign goods. Again, the aggregate U.S. export figure is slightly larger.

• *Exchange rate*: Average monthly exchange rates are applied to convert the published data to U.S. currency.

End-use categories and seasonal adjustment of trade in goods. Goods are initially classified under the Harmonized System, which describes and measures the characteristics of goods traded. Combining trade into approximately 140 export and 140 import end-use categories makes it possible to examine goods according to their principal uses. These categories are used as the basis for computing the seasonal and working-day adjusted data. Adjusted data are then summed to the six end-use aggregates for publication.

The seasonal adjustment procedure is based on a model that estimates the monthly movements as percentages above or below the general level of each end-use commodity series (unlike other methods that redistribute the actual series values over the calendar year). Imports of petroleum and petroleum products are adjusted for the length of the month.

Data availability

Data are released monthly in a joint Census Bureau-BEA press release (FT-900), which is published about six weeks after the end of the month to which the data pertain. The release and historical data are available on the Census Bureau Web site at <http://www.census.gov/foreigntrade/>.

Revisions

Data for recent years are normally revised annually. In some cases, revisions to annual totals are not distributed to monthly data; therefore, monthly data may not sum to the revised total shown. Data on trade in services may be subject to extensive revision as part of BEA's annual revision of the international transactions accounts (ITAs), usually released in July.

References

Discussion of the impact of changes in methodology and incorporation of new data sources are found in the discussions of annual revisions of the ITAs in the July issues of BEA's *Survey of Current Business.* The most recent pertinent article is "Annual Revision of the U.S. International Accounts, 1995–2005" (July 2006).

TABLE 7-17
EXPORT AND IMPORT PRICE INDEXES

SOURCE: U.S. DEPARTMENT OF LABOR, BUREAU OF LABOR STATISTICS

The International Price Program of the Bureau of Labor Statistics (BLS) collects price data for nonmilitary goods traded between the United States and the rest of the world and for selected transportation services in international markets. BLS aggregates the goods price data into export and import price indexes. Summary values of these price indexes for goods are presented in *Business Statistics.* For product and locality detail on international prices for both goods and services, see the *Handbook of U.S. Labor Statistics*, also published by Bernan Press.

Definitions

The *export* price index provides a measure of price change for all goods sold by U.S. residents (businesses and individuals located within the geographic boundaries of the United States, whether or not owned by U.S. citizens) to foreign buyers.

The *import* price index provides a measure of price change for goods purchased from other countries by U.S. residents.

Notes on the data

Published index series use a base year of 2000 = 100 whenever possible.

The product universe for both the import and export indexes includes raw materials, agricultural products, and manufactures. Price data are primarily collected by mail questionnaire, and directly from the exporter or importer in all but a few cases.

To the greatest extent possible, the data refer to prices at the U.S. border for exports and at either the foreign border or the U.S. border for imports. For nearly all products, the prices refer to transactions completed during the first week of the month and represent the actual price for which the product was bought or sold, including discounts, allowances, and rebates.

For the export price indexes, the preferred pricing basis is f.a.s. (free alongside ship) U.S. port of exportation. Where necessary, adjustments are made to reported prices to place them on this basis. An attempt is made to collect two prices for imports: f.o.b. (free on board) at the port of exportation and c.i.f. (cost, insurance, and freight) at the U.S. port of importation. Adjustments are made to account for changes in product characteristics in order to obtain a pure measure of price change.

The indexes are weighted indexes of the Laspeyres type. (See "General Notes" at the beginning of this volume for further explanation.) The values assigned to each weight category are based on trade value figures compiled by the Census Bureau. They are reweighted annually, with a two-year lag (as concurrent value data are not available) in revisions.

The merchandise price indexes are published using three different classification systems: the Harmonized System, the Bureau of Economic Analysis End-Use System, and the Standard International Trade Classification (SITC) system. The aggregate indexes shown here are from the End-Use System.

Data availability

Indexes are published monthly in a press release and a more detailed report. Selected data subsequently are published in BLS's *Monthly Labor Review*. Indexes are published for detailed product categories, as well as for all commodities. Aggregate import indexes by country or region of origin also are available, as are indexes for selected categories of internationally traded services. Additional information is available from the Division of International Prices in the Bureau of Labor Statistics. Complete historical data are available on the BLS Web site at <http://www.bls.gov>.

References

The indexes are described in "BLS to Produce Monthly Indexes of Export and Import Prices," *Monthly Labor Review* (December 1988), and Chapter 15, "International Price Indexes," *BLS Handbook of Methods*, Bulletin 2490 (April 1997).

CHAPTER 8: PRICES

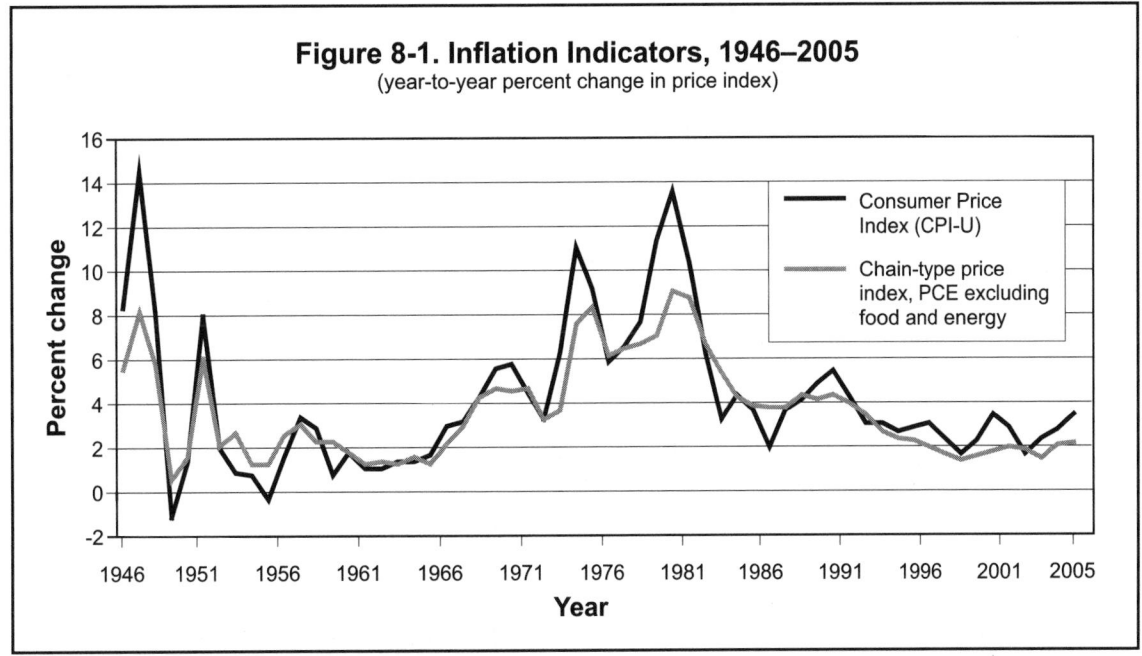

Figure 8-1. Inflation Indicators, 1946–2005
(year-to-year percent change in price index)

- Figure 8-1 shows annual rates of change in the Consumer Price Index for All Urban Consumers (CPI-U), the most widely used measure of the general price level, and in the chain-type price index for personal consumption expenditures (PCE) excluding food and energy, which provides one widely-used measure of the underlying rate of inflation. (Tables 8-1, 8-2, 8-3, 19-5, and 20-2)

- In the 1960s and 1970s, each recession left inflation significantly higher than before. Only after the inflation of the late 1970s and early 1980s, and the subsequent severe recession with its high rates of unemployment and low rates of capacity utilization (see Tables 10-3 and 2-3), has inflation subsided to levels comparable with the early postwar period. (Tables 8-1, 8-2, 8-3, 19-5, and 20-2)

- From 1960 to 2005, commodity prices in the CPI-U rose at an average rate of 3.5 percent per year, but service prices increased at an annual rate of 5.1 percent. (Table 8-1)

- The Producer Price Index (PPI) measures prices at the point of production, rather than at the consumer level. The most widely-used product of the PPI system—the PPI for finished goods—only covers commodities, whereas the CPI covers both commodities and services. For these reasons, the PPI for finished goods fluctuates more (both up and down) than the aggregate CPI-U, but has a less inflationary trend. (Table 8-4)

- The PPI data set also includes prices for intermediate materials, supplies, and components and crude materials for further processing. Intermediate materials prices fluctuate more than those of finished goods, and crude materials prices fluctuate most of all. (Table 8-4)

Table 8-1. Consumer Price Indexes, All Urban Consumers (CPI-U)

(1982–1984 = 100; seasonally adjusted, except as noted.)

Year and month	All items — Not seasonally adjusted	Seasonally adjusted — Index	Seasonally adjusted — Percent change	Food and beverages — Total	Food and beverages — Total food	Food at home — Total	Food at home — Cereals and bakery products	Food at home — Meats, poultry, fish, and eggs	Food at home — Dairy and related products	Food at home — Fruits and vegetables	Food at home — Non-alcoholic beverages	Food at home — Other food at home	Food away from home[1]	Alcoholic beverages[1]
1960	29.6	29.6	1.7	...	30.0	31.5	29.7	...	35.4	29.4	21.1	...	25.4	43.1
1961	29.9	29.9	1.0	...	30.4	31.8	30.3	...	35.9	29.5	21.1	...	26.0	43.3
1962	30.2	30.2	1.0	...	30.6	32.0	30.9	...	35.7	29.8	20.8	...	26.7	43.4
1963	30.6	30.6	1.3	...	31.1	32.4	31.4	...	35.6	31.5	21.1	...	27.3	43.8
1964	31.0	31.0	1.3	...	31.5	32.7	31.5	...	35.9	32.7	23.6	...	27.8	44.2
1965	31.5	31.5	1.6	...	32.2	33.5	31.9	...	36.0	32.6	23.4	...	28.4	44.6
1966	32.4	32.4	2.9	...	33.8	35.2	33.3	...	38.3	33.3	23.3	...	29.7	45.4
1967	33.4	33.4	3.1	35.0	34.1	35.1	34.0	38.0	40.0	33.3	23.1	29.3	31.3	46.4
1968	34.8	34.8	4.2	36.2	35.3	36.3	34.2	39.1	41.3	35.9	23.5	29.8	32.9	48.0
1969	36.7	36.7	5.5	38.1	37.1	38.0	35.2	42.6	42.7	36.4	24.2	30.7	34.9	49.7
1970	38.8	38.8	5.7	40.1	39.2	39.9	37.1	44.6	44.7	37.8	27.1	32.9	37.5	52.1
1971	40.5	40.5	4.4	41.4	40.4	40.9	38.8	44.1	46.1	39.7	28.1	34.3	39.4	54.2
1972	41.8	41.8	3.2	43.1	42.1	42.7	39.0	48.0	46.8	41.6	28.0	34.6	41.0	55.4
1973	44.4	44.4	6.2	48.8	48.2	49.7	43.5	60.9	51.2	47.4	30.1	36.7	44.2	56.8
1974	49.3	49.3	11.0	55.5	55.1	57.1	56.5	62.2	60.7	55.2	35.9	47.8	49.8	61.1
1975	53.8	53.8	9.1	60.2	59.8	61.8	62.9	67.0	62.6	56.9	41.3	55.4	54.5	65.9
1976	56.9	56.9	5.8	62.1	61.6	63.1	61.5	68.0	67.7	58.4	49.4	56.4	58.2	68.1
1977	60.6	60.6	6.5	65.8	65.5	66.8	62.5	67.4	69.5	63.8	74.4	68.4	62.6	70.0
1978	65.2	65.2	7.6	72.2	72.0	73.8	68.1	77.6	74.2	70.9	78.7	73.6	68.3	74.1
1979	72.6	72.6	11.3	79.9	79.9	81.8	74.9	89.0	82.8	76.6	82.6	79.0	75.9	79.9
1980	82.4	82.4	13.5	86.7	86.8	88.4	83.9	92.0	90.9	82.1	91.4	88.4	83.4	86.4
1981	90.9	90.9	10.3	93.5	93.6	94.8	92.3	96.0	97.4	92.0	95.3	94.9	90.9	92.5
1982	96.5	96.5	6.2	97.3	97.4	98.1	96.5	99.6	98.8	97.0	97.9	97.3	95.8	96.7
1983	99.6	99.6	3.2	99.5	99.4	99.1	99.6	99.2	100.0	97.3	99.8	99.5	100.0	100.4
1984	103.9	103.9	4.3	103.2	103.2	102.8	103.9	101.3	101.3	105.7	102.3	103.1	104.2	103.0
1985	107.6	107.6	3.6	105.6	105.6	104.3	107.9	100.1	103.2	108.4	104.3	105.7	108.3	106.4
1986	109.6	109.6	1.9	109.1	109.0	107.3	110.9	104.5	103.3	109.4	110.4	109.4	112.5	111.1
1987	113.6	113.6	3.6	113.5	113.5	111.9	114.8	110.5	105.9	119.1	107.5	110.5	117.0	114.1
1988	118.3	118.3	4.1	118.2	118.2	116.6	122.1	114.3	108.4	128.1	107.5	113.1	121.8	118.6
1989	124.0	124.0	4.8	124.9	125.1	124.2	132.4	121.3	115.6	138.0	111.3	119.1	127.4	123.5
1990	130.7	130.7	5.4	132.1	132.4	132.3	140.0	130.0	126.5	149.0	113.5	123.4	133.4	129.3
1991	136.2	136.2	4.2	136.8	136.3	135.8	145.8	132.6	125.1	155.8	114.1	127.3	137.9	142.8
1992	140.3	140.3	3.0	138.7	137.9	136.8	151.5	130.9	128.5	155.4	114.3	128.8	140.7	147.3
1993	144.5	144.5	3.0	141.6	140.9	140.1	156.6	135.5	129.4	159.0	114.6	130.5	143.2	149.6
1994	148.2	148.2	2.6	144.9	144.3	144.1	163.0	137.2	131.7	165.0	123.2	135.6	145.7	151.5
1995	152.4	152.4	2.8	148.9	148.4	148.8	167.5	138.8	132.8	177.7	131.7	140.8	149.0	153.9
1996	156.9	156.9	3.0	153.7	153.3	154.3	174.0	144.8	142.1	183.9	128.6	142.9	152.7	158.5
1997	160.5	160.5	2.3	157.7	157.3	158.1	177.6	148.5	145.5	187.5	133.4	147.3	157.0	162.8
1998	163.0	163.0	1.6	161.1	160.7	161.1	181.1	147.3	150.8	198.2	133.0	150.8	161.1	165.7
1999	166.6	166.6	2.2	164.6	164.1	164.2	185.0	147.9	159.6	203.1	134.3	153.5	165.1	169.7
2000	172.2	172.2	3.4	168.4	167.8	167.9	188.3	154.5	160.7	204.6	137.8	155.6	169.0	174.7
2001	177.1	177.1	2.8	173.6	173.1	173.4	193.8	161.3	167.1	212.2	139.2	159.6	173.9	179.3
2002	179.9	179.9	1.6	176.8	176.2	175.6	198.0	162.1	168.1	220.9	139.2	160.8	178.3	183.6
2003	184.0	184.0	2.3	180.5	180.0	179.4	202.8	169.3	167.9	225.9	139.8	162.6	182.1	187.2
2004	188.9	188.9	2.7	186.6	186.2	186.2	206.0	181.7	180.2	232.7	140.4	164.9	187.5	192.1
2005	195.3	195.3	3.4	191.2	190.7	189.8	209.0	184.7	182.4	241.4	144.4	167.0	193.4	195.9
2004														
January	185.2	185.9	0.4	183.8	183.4	183.2	204.4	179.8	172.0	226.1	140.1	162.7	184.9	189.4
February	186.2	186.5	0.3	184.4	183.9	183.7	204.3	179.6	171.7	229.5	140.4	163.5	185.5	189.9
March	187.4	187.3	0.4	184.8	184.3	184.2	204.9	179.4	172.1	230.2	140.1	164.9	185.8	190.8
April	188.0	187.5	0.1	185.2	184.7	184.5	205.1	179.8	174.8	230.0	139.4	165.0	186.2	191.8
May	189.1	188.6	0.6	186.5	186.0	186.5	205.4	181.7	186.1	230.1	140.2	165.4	186.7	191.7
June	189.7	189.2	0.3	187.0	186.5	187.1	206.0	182.3	190.5	227.9	140.2	165.9	187.0	192.4
July	189.4	189.2	0.0	187.3	186.8	187.2	206.3	183.6	188.2	226.6	140.4	166.0	187.8	192.2
August	189.5	189.4	0.1	187.5	187.0	187.0	206.4	183.4	184.8	228.1	140.8	166.1	188.4	192.5
September	189.9	189.7	0.2	187.4	186.9	186.4	206.7	183.0	181.5	228.7	140.6	165.0	188.9	193.4
October	190.9	190.8	0.6	188.3	187.9	187.8	207.3	182.8	181.2	240.2	140.5	165.3	189.4	193.6
November	191.0	191.2	0.2	188.8	188.3	188.3	207.9	182.3	180.4	247.8	140.3	164.8	189.6	194.0
December	190.3	191.2	0.0	188.8	188.3	188.2	207.9	183.1	179.3	246.0	141.3	164.1	189.9	193.9
2005														
January	190.7	191.4	0.1	189.1	188.6	188.0	208.1	183.4	182.9	236.5	141.5	165.6	190.8	194.3
February	191.8	192.1	0.4	189.2	188.6	187.7	208.3	183.9	181.4	234.7	141.4	165.0	191.4	195.2
March	193.3	193.2	0.6	189.6	189.0	188.1	208.6	184.3	181.6	233.9	142.9	165.5	191.7	195.7
April	194.6	194.1	0.5	190.9	190.4	190.2	208.7	185.3	182.9	242.2	144.5	167.5	192.1	195.9
May	194.4	194.0	-0.1	191.0	190.6	190.2	209.0	185.5	183.4	243.2	144.6	166.3	192.6	195.5
June	194.5	193.9	-0.1	191.0	190.6	189.7	208.6	185.2	182.7	239.8	144.4	166.9	193.2	195.9
July	195.4	195.1	0.6	191.4	190.9	190.0	208.5	184.5	182.2	242.7	144.8	167.5	193.6	195.8
August	196.4	196.2	0.6	191.5	191.1	189.9	209.3	184.1	182.7	241.2	144.8	167.7	194.2	195.9
September	198.8	198.6	1.2	192.0	191.5	190.3	208.7	184.8	181.6	243.9	145.6	167.6	194.6	196.6
October	199.2	199.1	0.3	192.4	192.0	190.7	209.7	184.5	181.7	245.6	145.6	168.2	195.2	196.8
November	197.6	197.8	-0.7	192.9	192.5	191.2	210.1	185.7	183.0	245.5	146.2	167.7	195.6	197.1
December	196.8	197.7	-0.1	193.1	192.7	191.4	209.9	185.7	182.5	247.2	146.1	168.1	196.0	196.4

[1]Not seasonally adjusted.
. . . = Not available.

Table 8-1. Consumer Price Indexes, All Urban Consumers (CPI-U)—Continued

(1982–1984 = 100, except as noted; seasonally adjusted, except as noted.)

Year and month	Total	Housing											
		Shelter						Fuels and utilities				Household furnishings and operations	
		Total	Rent of shelter [2]	Rent of primary residence	Lodging away from home [3]	Owners' equivalent rent of primary residence [2]	Tenants' and household insurance [1,3]	Total	Fuels		Water and sewer and trash collection services [3]	Total	Household operations [1,3]
									Fuel oils and other fuels	Gas (piped) and electricity			
1960	...	25.2	...	38.7	...	...	...	26.0	13.8	23.3	...	...	...
1961	...	25.4	...	39.2	...	...	...	26.3	14.1	23.5	...	...	...
1962	...	25.8	...	39.7	...	...	...	26.3	14.2	23.5	...	...	...
1963	...	26.1	...	40.1	...	...	...	26.6	14.4	23.5	...	...	...
1964	...	26.5	...	40.5	...	...	...	26.6	14.4	23.5	...	...	...
1965	...	27.0	...	40.9	...	...	...	26.6	14.6	23.5	...	...	...
1966	...	27.8	...	41.5	...	...	...	26.7	15.0	23.6	...	...	...
1967	30.8	28.8	...	42.2	...	...	...	27.1	15.5	23.7	...	42.0	...
1968	32.0	30.1	...	43.3	...	...	...	27.4	16.0	23.9	...	43.6	...
1969	34.0	32.6	...	44.7	...	...	...	28.0	16.3	24.3	...	45.2	...
1970	36.4	35.5	...	46.5	...	...	...	29.1	17.0	25.4	...	46.8	...
1971	38.0	37.0	...	48.7	...	...	...	31.1	18.2	27.1	...	48.6	...
1972	39.4	38.7	...	50.4	...	...	...	32.5	18.3	28.5	...	49.7	...
1973	41.2	40.5	...	52.5	...	...	...	34.3	21.1	29.9	...	51.1	...
1974	45.8	44.4	...	55.2	...	...	...	40.7	33.2	34.5	...	56.8	...
1975	50.7	48.8	...	58.0	...	...	...	45.4	36.4	40.1	...	63.4	...
1976	53.8	51.5	...	61.1	...	...	...	49.4	38.8	44.7	...	67.3	...
1977	57.4	54.9	...	64.8	...	...	...	54.7	43.9	50.5	...	70.4	...
1978	62.4	60.5	...	69.3	...	...	...	58.5	46.2	55.0	...	74.7	...
1979	70.1	68.9	...	74.3	...	...	...	64.8	62.4	61.0	...	79.9	...
1980	81.1	81.0	...	80.9	...	...	...	75.4	86.1	71.4	...	86.3	...
1981	90.4	90.5	...	87.9	...	...	...	86.4	104.6	81.9	...	93.0	...
1982	96.9	96.9	...	94.6	...	...	...	94.9	103.4	93.2	...	98.0	...
1983	99.5	99.1	102.7	100.1	...	102.5	...	100.2	97.2	101.5	...	100.2	...
1984	103.6	104.0	107.7	105.3	...	107.3	...	104.8	99.4	105.4	...	101.9	...
1985	107.7	109.8	113.9	111.8	...	113.2	...	106.5	95.9	107.1	...	103.8	...
1986	110.9	115.8	120.2	118.3	...	119.4	...	104.1	77.6	105.7	...	105.2	...
1987	114.2	121.3	125.9	123.1	...	124.8	...	103.0	77.9	103.8	...	107.1	...
1988	118.5	127.1	132.0	127.8	...	131.1	...	104.4	78.1	104.6	...	109.4	...
1989	123.0	132.8	138.0	132.8	...	137.4	...	107.8	81.7	107.5	...	111.2	...
1990	128.5	140.0	145.5	138.4	...	144.8	...	111.6	99.3	109.3	...	113.3	...
1991	133.6	146.3	152.1	143.3	...	150.4	...	115.3	94.6	112.6	...	116.0	...
1992	137.5	151.2	157.3	146.9	...	155.5	...	117.8	90.7	114.8	...	118.0	...
1993	141.2	155.7	162.0	150.3	...	160.5	...	121.3	90.3	118.5	...	119.3	...
1994	144.8	160.5	167.0	154.0	...	165.8	...	122.8	88.8	119.2	...	121.0	...
1995	148.5	165.7	172.4	157.8	...	171.3	...	123.7	88.1	119.2	...	123.0	...
1996	152.8	171.0	178.0	162.0	...	176.8	...	127.5	99.2	122.1	...	124.7	...
1997	156.8	176.3	183.4	166.7	...	181.9	...	130.8	99.8	125.1	...	125.4	...
1998	160.4	182.1	189.6	172.1	109.0	187.8	99.8	128.5	90.0	121.2	101.6	126.6	101.5
1999	163.9	187.3	195.0	177.5	112.3	192.9	101.3	128.8	91.4	120.9	104.0	126.7	104.5
2000	169.6	193.4	201.3	183.9	117.5	198.7	103.7	137.9	129.7	128.0	106.5	128.2	110.5
2001	176.4	200.6	208.9	192.1	118.6	206.3	106.2	150.2	129.3	142.4	109.6	129.1	115.6
2002	180.3	208.1	216.7	199.7	118.3	214.7	108.7	143.6	115.5	134.4	113.0	128.3	119.0
2003	184.8	213.1	221.9	205.5	119.3	219.9	114.8	154.5	139.5	145.0	117.2	126.1	121.8
2004	189.5	218.8	227.9	211.0	125.9	224.9	116.2	161.9	160.5	150.6	124.0	125.5	125.0
2005	195.7	224.4	233.7	217.3	130.3	230.2	117.6	179.0	208.6	166.5	130.3	126.1	130.3
2004													
January	186.9	216.0	224.8	208.2	122.5	222.4	114.8	157.4	148.3	147.0	120.6	125.2	122.7
February	187.2	215.9	224.8	208.6	120.6	222.7	115.0	159.4	148.8	149.0	121.8	125.4	123.4
March	187.7	216.9	226.0	209.1	123.7	223.2	115.1	158.2	146.7	147.6	121.9	125.5	123.6
April	188.3	217.7	226.7	209.7	124.7	224.0	115.7	158.4	146.0	147.9	122.2	125.2	123.8
May	188.9	218.4	227.5	210.3	126.0	224.4	116.1	159.7	149.1	148.9	123.3	125.3	124.0
June	189.5	218.8	228.0	210.9	125.9	224.9	116.2	161.7	152.3	151.0	123.8	125.5	124.7
July	189.9	219.3	228.5	211.3	126.6	225.3	116.1	162.6	155.9	151.6	124.5	125.2	125.5
August	190.2	219.6	228.7	212.0	125.8	225.8	116.3	163.6	162.8	152.2	125.0	125.0	126.1
September	190.8	220.4	229.5	212.4	129.0	226.1	116.6	163.3	164.9	151.5	125.6	125.3	126.1
October	191.1	220.7	229.9	212.9	128.8	226.4	116.3	163.4	178.7	150.7	126.0	126.3	126.2
November	191.7	220.9	230.0	213.1	128.4	226.7	117.7	167.1	188.0	154.5	126.4	125.9	127.0
December	192.1	221.4	230.4	213.8	128.6	227.1	118.7	167.6	185.5	155.2	126.5	125.9	127.0
2005													
January	192.4	221.8	230.8	214.4	128.2	227.6	118.5	168.0	180.0	155.8	127.6	126.0	127.9
February	193.0	222.5	231.7	214.8	129.7	228.2	118.7	169.0	181.3	156.6	128.5	125.8	128.6
March	193.9	223.5	232.9	215.4	133.4	228.6	119.0	169.9	188.6	157.2	128.6	125.9	128.3
April	194.3	223.6	233.0	216.0	131.4	229.1	118.2	172.5	195.1	159.9	129.0	125.9	129.1
May	194.5	223.7	233.0	216.5	129.4	229.5	118.0	173.4	192.6	160.9	129.5	126.6	129.7
June	194.7	224.1	233.4	217.0	129.7	229.9	118.0	173.2	197.0	160.2	130.1	125.9	130.1
July	195.5	224.7	234.2	217.6	130.6	230.4	118.1	175.7	208.8	162.3	130.9	126.0	130.3
August	195.8	224.9	234.3	218.1	129.6	230.8	117.8	177.5	216.5	163.9	131.0	126.1	130.7
September	196.8	224.7	234.1	218.6	126.5	231.2	116.6	185.3	239.7	171.9	131.4	126.0	131.0
October	198.6	225.8	235.2	219.4	130.4	231.6	115.8	193.7	242.1	181.8	131.9	126.1	131.6
November	199.4	226.5	235.9	219.9	131.8	232.1	115.9	196.0	233.0	185.1	132.6	126.2	132.5
December	199.7	227.2	236.6	220.4	132.8	232.7	116.1	193.5	230.7	182.1	133.1	126.8	133.3

[1] Not seasonally adjusted.
[2] December 1982 = 100.
[3] December 1997 = 100.
. . . = Not available.

Table 8-1. Consumer Price Indexes, All Urban Consumers (CPI-U)—Continued

(1982–1984 = 100, except as noted; seasonally adjusted, except as noted.)

Year and month	Apparel					Transportation								
							Private transportation						Motor vehicle parts and equipment [1]	Motor vehicle maintenance and repair
								New and used motor vehicles			Motor fuel			
	Total	Men's and boys' apparel	Women's and girls' apparel	Infants' and toddlers' apparel	Footwear	Total	Total	Total [3]	New vehicles	Used cars and trucks [1]	Total	Gasoline (all types)		
1960	45.7	47.2	56.7	36.8	41.1	29.8	30.6	. . .	51.6	25.0	24.4	24.4	. . .	26.5
1961	46.1	47.7	56.9	35.5	41.4	30.1	30.8	. . .	51.6	26.0	24.1	24.1	. . .	27.1
1962	46.3	48.0	56.8	34.8	42.0	30.8	31.4	. . .	51.4	28.4	24.3	24.3	. . .	27.5
1963	46.9	48.6	57.3	34.8	42.5	30.9	31.6	. . .	51.1	28.7	24.2	24.2	. . .	27.8
1964	47.3	49.3	57.6	34.9	42.6	31.4	32.0	. . .	50.9	30.0	24.1	24.1	. . .	28.2
1965	47.8	49.9	58.1	35.1	43.4	31.9	32.5	. . .	49.8	29.8	25.1	25.1	. . .	28.7
1966	49.0	51.2	59.2	35.4	46.0	32.3	32.9	. . .	48.9	29.0	25.6	25.6	. . .	29.2
1967	51.0	53.1	61.9	35.8	48.2	33.3	33.8	. . .	49.3	29.9	26.4	26.4	. . .	30.4
1968	53.7	56.1	65.6	37.3	50.8	34.3	34.8	. . .	50.7	. . .	26.8	26.8	. . .	32.1
1969	56.8	59.7	69.2	38.4	53.9	35.7	36.0	. . .	51.5	30.9	27.6	27.7	. . .	34.1
1970	59.2	62.2	71.8	39.2	56.8	37.5	37.5	. . .	53.1	31.2	27.9	27.9	. . .	36.6
1971	61.1	63.9	74.4	40.0	58.6	39.5	39.4	. . .	55.3	33.0	28.1	28.1	. . .	39.3
1972	62.3	64.7	76.2	41.1	60.3	39.9	39.7	. . .	54.8	33.1	28.4	28.4	. . .	41.1
1973	64.6	67.1	78.8	42.5	62.8	41.2	41.0	. . .	54.8	35.2	31.2	31.2	. . .	43.2
1974	69.4	72.4	83.5	54.2	66.6	45.8	46.2	. . .	58.0	36.7	42.2	42.2	. . .	47.6
1975	72.5	75.5	85.5	64.5	69.6	50.1	50.6	. . .	63.0	43.8	45.1	45.1	. . .	53.7
1976	75.2	78.1	87.9	68.0	72.3	55.1	55.6	. . .	67.0	50.3	47.0	47.0	. . .	57.6
1977	78.6	81.7	90.6	74.6	75.7	59.0	59.7	. . .	70.5	54.7	49.7	49.7	. . .	61.9
1978	81.4	83.5	92.4	77.4	79.0	61.7	62.5	. . .	75.9	55.8	51.8	51.8	77.6	67.0
1979	84.9	85.4	94.0	79.0	85.3	70.5	71.7	. . .	81.9	60.2	70.1	70.2	85.1	73.7
1980	90.9	89.4	96.0	85.5	91.8	83.1	84.2	. . .	88.5	62.3	97.4	97.5	95.3	81.5
1981	95.3	94.2	97.5	92.9	96.7	93.2	93.8	. . .	93.9	76.9	108.5	108.5	101.0	89.2
1982	97.8	97.6	98.5	96.3	99.1	97.0	97.1	. . .	97.5	88.8	102.8	102.8	103.6	96.0
1983	100.2	100.3	100.2	101.1	99.8	99.3	99.3	. . .	99.9	98.7	99.4	99.4	100.7	100.3
1984	102.1	102.1	101.3	102.6	101.1	103.7	103.6	. . .	102.6	112.5	97.9	97.8	95.6	103.8
1985	105.0	105.0	104.9	107.2	102.3	106.4	106.2	. . .	106.1	113.7	98.7	98.6	95.9	106.8
1986	105.9	106.2	104.0	111.8	101.9	102.3	101.2	. . .	110.6	108.8	77.1	77.0	95.4	110.3
1987	110.6	109.1	110.4	112.1	105.1	105.4	104.2	. . .	114.4	113.1	80.2	80.1	96.1	114.8
1988	115.4	113.4	114.9	116.4	109.9	108.7	107.6	. . .	116.5	118.0	80.9	80.8	97.9	119.7
1989	118.6	117.0	116.4	119.1	114.4	114.1	112.9	. . .	119.2	120.4	88.5	88.5	100.2	124.9
1990	124.1	120.4	122.6	125.8	117.4	120.5	118.8	. . .	121.4	117.6	101.2	101.0	100.9	130.1
1991	128.7	124.2	127.6	128.9	120.9	123.8	121.9	. . .	126.0	118.1	99.4	99.2	102.2	136.0
1992	131.9	126.5	130.4	129.3	125.0	126.5	124.6	. . .	129.2	123.2	99.0	99.0	103.1	141.3
1993	133.7	127.5	132.6	127.1	125.9	130.4	127.5	91.8	132.7	133.9	98.0	97.7	101.6	145.9
1994	133.4	126.4	130.9	128.1	126.0	134.3	131.4	95.5	137.6	141.7	98.5	98.2	101.4	150.2
1995	132.0	126.2	126.9	127.2	125.4	139.1	136.3	99.4	141.0	156.5	100.0	99.8	102.1	154.0
1996	131.7	127.7	124.7	129.7	126.6	143.0	140.0	101.0	143.7	157.0	106.3	105.9	102.2	158.4
1997	132.9	130.1	126.1	129.0	127.6	144.3	141.0	100.5	144.3	151.1	106.2	105.8	101.9	162.7
1998	133.0	131.8	126.0	126.1	128.0	141.6	137.9	100.1	143.4	150.6	92.2	91.6	101.1	167.1
1999	131.3	131.1	123.3	129.0	125.7	144.4	140.5	100.1	142.9	152.0	100.7	100.1	100.5	171.9
2000	129.6	129.7	121.5	130.6	123.8	153.3	149.1	100.8	142.8	155.8	129.3	128.6	101.5	177.3
2001	127.3	125.7	119.3	129.2	123.0	154.3	150.0	101.3	142.1	158.7	124.7	124.0	104.8	183.5
2002	124.0	121.7	115.8	126.4	121.4	152.9	148.8	99.2	140.0	152.0	116.6	116.0	106.9	190.2
2003	120.9	118.0	113.1	122.1	119.6	157.6	153.6	96.5	137.9	142.9	135.8	135.1	107.8	195.6
2004	120.4	117.5	113.0	118.5	119.3	163.1	159.4	94.2	137.1	133.3	160.4	159.7	108.7	200.2
2005	119.5	116.1	110.8	116.7	122.6	173.9	170.2	95.6	137.9	139.4	195.7	194.7	111.9	206.9
2004														
January	120.1	118.0	112.3	119.5	118.3	158.0	153.9	93.9	136.9	130.8	141.5	141.0	108.0	197.9
February	119.9	118.1	111.9	119.8	118.2	159.5	155.5	94.0	137.3	131.0	147.2	146.7	108.0	197.9
March	120.6	117.8	113.0	120.0	119.1	161.3	157.3	93.9	137.3	131.2	154.6	153.9	107.8	198.5
April	120.7	117.5	113.4	118.6	119.1	160.8	156.8	93.9	137.3	131.3	152.2	151.5	107.9	198.8
May	121.0	117.9	113.8	116.9	119.2	163.6	159.9	93.9	137.3	131.8	164.2	163.4	107.9	199.2
June	121.2	118.4	113.8	117.7	119.1	164.3	160.7	93.8	137.6	130.6	167.3	166.6	108.2	200.0
July	120.8	118.3	113.4	118.4	118.1	163.4	159.7	93.8	136.8	132.1	162.5	161.8	108.8	200.6
August	120.2	117.2	112.9	117.3	118.9	163.0	159.4	93.9	136.2	133.8	160.6	159.9	109.0	201.2
September	120.0	117.1	112.1	118.8	120.1	163.2	159.7	94.4	136.1	136.5	160.1	159.4	109.3	200.8
October	120.3	116.1	113.5	118.4	119.5	166.8	163.3	94.6	136.4	136.8	173.7	172.9	109.5	201.5
November	120.4	116.3	113.4	118.6	120.2	167.0	163.3	95.0	137.5	136.7	171.6	170.8	109.9	202.5
December	120.0	116.8	111.4	118.3	121.0	166.0	162.4	95.1	137.9	137.3	167.3	166.5	109.9	203.0
2005														
January	120.3	117.5	111.7	119.3	121.9	165.2	161.5	95.3	138.7	137.5	162.0	161.2	110.6	203.7
February	120.0	117.3	111.1	118.5	122.2	167.0	163.4	95.5	138.9	137.6	169.5	168.6	110.9	203.6
March	120.6	117.5	112.6	117.2	121.8	169.8	166.2	95.3	138.5	137.7	181.0	180.0	110.9	204.7
April	120.1	117.5	111.4	119.2	121.9	172.1	168.5	95.5	138.5	138.1	189.7	188.6	110.8	205.2
May	120.0	117.2	111.2	118.5	122.2	170.4	166.7	95.7	138.6	138.8	181.4	180.3	111.0	205.9
June	119.3	116.0	110.6	117.8	122.4	170.1	166.2	95.8	138.5	139.9	178.7	177.7	111.2	206.4
July	118.6	114.6	109.9	116.6	122.6	173.7	169.9	95.6	137.3	141.0	194.3	193.3	111.9	207.0
August	119.4	115.8	110.3	115.9	123.4	177.7	174.0	95.5	136.3	142.0	211.0	210.1	112.4	207.7
September	119.3	115.0	110.0	114.8	124.1	186.6	183.2	95.9	137.0	141.5	247.4	246.4	112.7	208.8
October	118.9	115.1	109.5	114.3	123.9	184.4	180.8	95.9	137.7	140.6	237.5	236.4	113.0	209.6
November	119.0	114.9	110.6	113.9	122.7	175.4	171.5	95.6	137.6	139.4	199.4	198.4	113.6	210.1
December	118.7	114.6	110.2	114.8	122.2	174.1	170.2	95.4	137.4	139.2	194.1	193.0	114.0	210.4

[1] Not seasonally adjusted.
[3] December 1997 = 100.
. . . = Not available.

Table 8-1. Consumer Price Indexes, All Urban Consumers (CPI-U)—Continued

(1982–1984 = 100, except as noted; seasonally adjusted.)

Year and month	Transportation—Continued		Medical care					Recreation		Education and communication			
					Medical care services						Education		
	Public transportation	Transportation services	Medical care, total	Medical care commodities	Total	Professional services	Hospital and related services	Total [3]	Video and audio [3]	Total [3]	Total [3]	Educational books and supplies	Tuition, other school fees, and childcare
1960	22.2	27.2	22.3	46.9	19.5	. . .	. . .	. . .	. . .	. . .	. . .	. . .	. . .
1961	23.2	27.8	22.9	46.3	20.2	. . .	. . .	. . .	. . .	. . .	. . .	. . .	. . .
1962	24.0	28.3	23.5	45.6	20.9	. . .	. . .	. . .	. . .	. . .	. . .	. . .	. . .
1963	24.3	28.6	24.1	45.2	21.5	. . .	. . .	. . .	. . .	. . .	. . .	. . .	. . .
1964	24.7	29.2	24.6	45.1	22.0	. . .	. . .	. . .	. . .	. . .	. . .	. . .	. . .
1965	25.2	30.3	25.2	45.0	22.7	. . .	. . .	. . .	. . .	. . .	. . .	. . .	. . .
1966	26.1	31.6	26.3	45.1	23.9	. . .	. . .	. . .	. . .	. . .	. . .	. . .	. . .
1967	27.4	32.6	28.2	44.9	26.0	30.9	. . .	. . .	. . .	. . .	. . .	33.7	. . .
1968	28.7	33.9	29.9	45.0	27.9	32.5	. . .	. . .	. . .	. . .	. . .	35.4	. . .
1969	30.9	36.3	31.9	45.4	30.2	34.7	. . .	. . .	. . .	. . .	. . .	37.4	. . .
1970	35.2	40.2	34.0	46.5	32.3	37.0	. . .	. . .	. . .	. . .	. . .	38.8	. . .
1971	37.8	43.4	36.1	47.3	34.7	39.4	. . .	. . .	. . .	. . .	. . .	41.4	. . .
1972	39.3	44.4	37.3	47.4	35.9	40.8	. . .	. . .	. . .	. . .	. . .	44.2	. . .
1973	39.7	44.7	38.8	47.5	37.5	42.2	. . .	. . .	. . .	. . .	. . .	45.6	. . .
1974	40.6	46.3	42.4	49.2	41.4	45.8	. . .	. . .	. . .	. . .	. . .	47.2	. . .
1975	43.5	49.8	47.5	53.3	46.6	50.8	. . .	. . .	. . .	. . .	. . .	50.3	. . .
1976	47.8	56.9	52.0	56.5	51.3	55.5	. . .	. . .	. . .	. . .	. . .	53.7	. . .
1977	50.0	61.5	57.0	60.2	56.4	60.0	. . .	. . .	. . .	. . .	. . .	56.9	. . .
1978	51.5	64.4	61.8	64.4	61.2	64.5	55.1	. . .	. . .	. . .	. . .	61.6	59.8
1979	54.9	69.5	67.5	69.0	67.2	70.1	61.0	. . .	. . .	. . .	. . .	65.7	64.7
1980	69.0	79.2	74.9	75.4	74.8	77.9	69.2	. . .	. . .	. . .	. . .	71.4	71.2
1981	85.6	88.6	82.9	83.7	82.8	85.9	79.1	. . .	. . .	. . .	. . .	80.3	79.9
1982	94.9	96.1	92.5	92.3	92.6	93.2	90.3	. . .	. . .	. . .	. . .	91.0	90.5
1983	99.5	99.1	100.6	100.2	100.7	99.8	100.5	. . .	. . .	. . .	. . .	100.3	99.7
1984	105.7	104.8	106.8	107.5	106.7	107.0	109.2	. . .	. . .	. . .	. . .	108.7	109.8
1985	110.5	110.0	113.5	115.2	113.2	113.5	116.1	. . .	. . .	. . .	. . .	118.2	119.7
1986	117.0	116.3	122.0	122.8	121.9	120.8	123.1	. . .	. . .	. . .	. . .	128.1	129.6
1987	121.1	121.9	130.1	131.0	130.0	128.8	131.6	. . .	. . .	. . .	. . .	138.1	140.0
1988	123.3	128.0	138.6	139.9	138.3	137.5	143.9	. . .	. . .	. . .	. . .	148.1	151.0
1989	129.5	135.6	149.3	150.8	148.9	146.4	160.5	. . .	. . .	. . .	. . .	158.0	162.7
1990	142.6	144.2	162.8	163.4	162.7	156.1	178.0	. . .	. . .	. . .	. . .	171.3	175.7
1991	148.9	151.2	177.0	176.8	177.1	165.7	196.1	. . .	. . .	. . .	. . .	180.3	191.4
1992	151.4	155.7	190.1	188.1	190.5	175.8	214.0	. . .	. . .	. . .	. . .	190.3	208.5
1993	167.0	162.9	201.4	195.0	202.9	184.7	231.9	90.7	96.5	85.5	78.4	197.6	225.3
1994	172.0	168.6	211.0	200.7	213.4	192.5	245.6	92.7	95.4	88.8	83.3	205.5	239.8
1995	175.9	175.9	220.5	204.5	224.2	201.0	257.8	94.5	95.1	92.2	88.0	214.4	253.8
1996	181.9	180.5	228.2	210.4	232.4	208.3	269.5	97.4	96.6	95.3	92.7	226.9	267.1
1997	186.7	185.0	234.6	215.3	239.1	215.4	278.4	99.6	99.4	98.4	97.3	238.4	280.4
1998	190.3	187.9	242.1	221.8	246.8	222.2	287.5	101.1	101.1	100.3	102.1	250.8	294.2
1999	197.7	190.7	250.6	230.7	255.1	229.2	299.5	102.0	100.7	101.2	107.0	261.7	308.4
2000	209.6	196.1	260.8	238.1	266.0	237.7	317.3	103.3	101.0	102.5	112.5	279.9	324.0
2001	210.6	201.9	272.8	247.6	278.8	246.5	338.3	104.9	101.5	105.2	118.5	295.9	341.1
2002	207.4	209.1	285.6	256.4	292.9	253.9	367.8	106.2	102.8	107.9	126.0	317.6	362.1
2003	209.3	216.3	297.1	262.8	306.0	261.2	394.8	107.5	103.6	109.8	134.4	335.4	386.7
2004	209.1	220.6	310.1	269.3	321.3	271.5	417.9	108.6	104.2	111.6	143.7	351.0	414.3
2005	217.3	225.7	323.2	276.0	336.7	281.7	439.9	109.4	104.2	113.7	152.7	365.6	440.9
2004													
January	210.8	219.3	303.8	265.8	314.0	266.0	408.7	108.0	103.7	110.9	139.6	345.1	402.2
February	210.8	219.4	305.2	266.6	315.6	267.5	410.3	108.3	103.8	111.2	140.3	346.2	404.2
March	211.2	219.6	306.6	267.3	317.3	269.0	411.8	108.6	104.0	111.3	141.1	347.2	406.6
April	210.9	219.7	307.7	268.5	318.3	269.7	413.2	108.7	104.3	111.3	141.8	349.0	408.6
May	208.5	219.6	308.6	269.0	319.4	270.2	415.5	108.7	104.3	111.2	142.5	350.1	410.6
June	208.0	219.9	309.8	269.3	320.9	271.1	417.9	108.9	104.4	111.5	143.3	351.0	412.9
July	208.4	220.7	310.8	269.5	322.1	271.9	419.5	108.7	104.4	111.6	143.9	351.1	414.9
August	206.8	220.8	311.8	269.9	323.4	273.3	420.1	108.5	104.2	111.6	144.9	354.6	417.6
September	205.1	220.8	312.9	270.8	324.5	273.8	422.1	108.7	104.3	112.0	145.6	351.3	420.2
October	207.0	221.6	314.0	271.7	325.7	274.3	423.9	108.8	104.4	111.8	146.2	352.4	422.1
November	211.3	222.7	314.6	271.4	326.7	275.2	424.3	108.9	104.2	112.2	147.1	355.8	424.4
December	209.8	222.3	315.8	271.1	328.4	275.9	428.0	108.8	104.4	112.3	147.8	358.5	426.5
2005													
January	209.3	222.5	317.0	272.0	329.7	276.8	430.0	109.0	104.3	112.5	148.4	357.2	428.3
February	209.0	222.5	318.4	272.7	331.4	278.0	432.3	108.9	104.0	112.8	149.2	357.6	430.7
March	211.4	223.2	319.8	273.2	333.0	278.9	434.8	108.9	104.3	113.0	149.9	358.9	433.0
April	214.2	224.1	320.7	273.5	334.2	280.0	436.6	109.0	104.4	113.4	150.8	360.7	435.4
May	215.7	224.7	321.9	274.5	335.4	280.8	438.1	109.3	104.3	113.4	151.6	362.7	437.9
June	217.8	225.4	322.6	275.3	336.1	281.3	438.9	109.0	103.1	113.5	152.4	363.9	440.1
July	219.5	226.1	323.8	276.0	337.5	282.1	441.0	109.1	103.2	113.6	153.2	365.7	442.4
August	220.2	227.1	324.2	276.7	337.7	282.4	441.4	109.4	104.4	113.6	153.7	365.9	444.1
September	220.8	227.8	325.2	277.6	338.8	283.5	442.0	109.8	104.7	114.3	154.6	370.8	446.4
October	223.1	227.7	327.0	278.9	340.7	284.6	445.4	110.0	104.6	114.3	155.3	372.4	448.3
November	223.4	228.3	328.7	280.5	342.5	285.6	448.7	109.9	104.4	114.8	156.1	374.9	450.5
December	222.3	228.3	329.4	281.1	343.2	286.3	449.7	110.0	104.4	115.0	156.8	376.9	452.7

[3]December 1997 = 100.
. . . = Not available.

Table 8-1. Consumer Price Indexes, All Urban Consumers (CPI-U)—Continued

(1982–1984 = 100, except as noted; seasonally adjusted, except as noted.)

Year and month	Education and communication—Continued					Other goods and services					Commodity and service groups of CPI-U	
	Communication					Total	Tobacco and smoking products [1]	Personal care			Commod-ities	Services
	Total [3]	Information and information processing						Total	Personal care products [1]	Personal care services [1]		
		Total [1,3]	Telephone services [1,3]	Information technology, hardware, and services								
				Total [1,4]	Personal computers and peripheral equipment [1,3]							
1960	. . .	. . .	. . .	. . .	. . .	. . .	29.1	34.6	38.2	31.0	33.6	24.1
1961	. . .	. . .	. . .	. . .	. . .	. . .	29.3	34.8	38.1	31.5	33.8	24.5
1962	. . .	. . .	. . .	. . .	. . .	. . .	29.5	35.4	38.5	32.2	34.1	25.0
1963	. . .	. . .	. . .	. . .	. . .	. . .	30.4	35.9	38.6	33.0	34.4	25.5
1964	. . .	. . .	. . .	. . .	. . .	. . .	31.2	36.3	38.6	33.9	34.8	26.0
1965	. . .	. . .	. . .	. . .	. . .	. . .	32.6	36.6	38.4	34.8	35.2	26.6
1966	. . .	. . .	. . .	. . .	. . .	. . .	34.2	37.3	38.0	36.4	36.1	27.6
1967	. . .	. . .	. . .	. . .	. . .	35.1	35.5	38.4	38.6	38.1	36.8	28.8
1968	. . .	. . .	. . .	. . .	. . .	36.9	37.8	40.0	39.8	40.1	38.1	30.3
1969	. . .	. . .	. . .	. . .	. . .	38.7	39.8	42.0	41.6	42.2	39.9	32.4
1970	. . .	. . .	. . .	. . .	. . .	40.9	43.1	43.5	42.7	44.2	41.7	35.0
1971	. . .	. . .	. . .	. . .	. . .	42.9	44.9	44.9	44.0	45.7	43.2	37.0
1972	. . .	. . .	. . .	. . .	. . .	44.7	47.4	46.0	45.2	46.8	44.5	38.4
1973	. . .	. . .	. . .	. . .	. . .	46.4	48.7	48.1	46.4	49.7	47.8	40.1
1974	. . .	. . .	. . .	. . .	. . .	49.8	51.1	52.8	51.5	53.9	53.5	43.8
1975	. . .	. . .	. . .	. . .	. . .	53.9	54.7	57.9	58.0	57.7	58.2	48.0
1976	. . .	. . .	. . .	. . .	. . .	57.0	57.0	61.7	61.3	61.9	60.7	52.0
1977	. . .	. . .	. . .	. . .	. . .	60.4	59.8	65.7	64.7	66.4	64.2	56.0
1978	. . .	. . .	. . .	. . .	. . .	64.3	63.0	69.9	68.2	71.3	68.8	60.8
1979	. . .	. . .	. . .	. . .	. . .	68.9	66.8	75.2	72.9	77.2	76.6	67.5
1980	. . .	. . .	. . .	. . .	. . .	75.2	72.0	81.9	79.6	83.7	86.0	77.9
1981	. . .	. . .	. . .	. . .	. . .	82.6	77.8	89.1	87.8	90.2	93.2	88.1
1982	. . .	. . .	. . .	. . .	. . .	91.1	86.5	95.4	95.1	95.7	97.0	96.0
1983	. . .	. . .	. . .	. . .	. . .	101.1	103.4	100.3	100.7	100.0	99.8	99.4
1984	. . .	. . .	. . .	. . .	. . .	107.9	110.1	104.3	104.2	104.4	103.2	104.6
1985	. . .	. . .	. . .	. . .	. . .	114.5	116.7	108.3	107.6	108.9	105.4	109.9
1986	. . .	. . .	. . .	. . .	. . .	121.4	124.7	111.9	111.3	112.5	104.4	115.4
1987	. . .	. . .	. . .	. . .	. . .	128.5	133.6	115.1	113.9	116.2	107.7	120.2
1988	. . .	. . .	. . .	. . .	. . .	137.0	145.8	119.4	118.1	120.7	111.5	125.7
1989	. . .	. . .	. . .	96.3	. . .	147.7	164.4	125.0	123.2	126.8	116.7	131.9
1990	. . .	. . .	. . .	93.5	. . .	159.0	181.5	130.4	128.2	132.8	122.8	139.2
1991	. . .	. . .	. . .	88.6	. . .	171.6	202.7	134.9	132.8	137.0	126.6	146.3
1992	. . .	. . .	. . .	83.7	. . .	183.3	219.8	138.3	135.5	140.0	129.1	152.0
1993	96.7	97.7	. . .	78.8	. . .	192.9	228.4	141.5	139.0	144.0	131.5	157.9
1994	97.6	98.6	. . .	72.0	. . .	198.5	220.0	144.6	141.5	147.9	133.8	163.1
1995	98.8	98.7	. . .	63.8	. . .	206.9	225.7	147.1	143.1	151.5	136.4	168.7
1996	99.6	99.5	. . .	57.2	. . .	215.4	232.8	150.1	144.3	156.6	139.9	174.1
1997	100.3	100.4	. . .	50.1	. . .	224.8	243.7	152.7	144.2	162.4	141.8	179.4
1998	98.7	98.5	100.7	39.9	78.2	237.7	274.8	156.7	148.3	166.0	141.9	184.2
1999	96.0	95.5	100.1	30.5	53.5	258.3	355.8	161.1	151.8	171.4	144.4	188.8
2000	93.6	92.8	98.5	25.9	41.1	271.1	394.9	165.6	153.7	178.1	149.2	195.3
2001	93.3	92.3	99.3	21.3	29.5	282.6	425.2	170.5	155.1	184.3	150.7	203.4
2002	92.3	90.8	99.7	18.3	22.2	293.2	461.5	174.7	154.7	188.4	149.7	209.8
2003	89.7	87.8	98.3	16.1	17.6	298.7	469.0	178.0	153.5	193.2	151.2	216.5
2004	86.7	84.6	95.8	14.8	15.3	304.7	478.0	181.7	153.9	197.6	154.7	222.8
2005	84.7	82.6	94.9	13.6	12.8	313.4	502.8	185.6	154.4	203.9	160.2	230.1
2004												
January	88.1	86.1	97.0	15.3	16.2	301.7	473.0	179.9	153.8	194.6	151.8	219.7
February	88.1	86.1	97.1	15.2	16.0	302.0	472.6	180.2	154.5	195.2	152.6	220.1
March	87.7	85.7	96.7	15.2	15.8	302.7	473.6	180.6	154.5	195.8	153.5	220.8
April	87.4	85.4	96.5	15.0	15.9	303.2	473.3	181.0	154.5	196.1	153.5	221.4
May	86.9	84.8	95.9	14.9	15.7	303.4	473.5	181.1	154.6	196.6	155.0	221.9
June	86.8	84.7	95.8	14.9	15.5	304.0	476.0	181.3	153.8	196.9	155.5	222.6
July	86.5	84.5	95.6	14.8	15.3	305.0	480.5	181.6	153.4	197.5	155.0	223.2
August	86.1	84.0	95.0	14.7	15.1	305.7	481.6	182.0	152.8	198.9	154.8	223.6
September	86.2	84.1	95.3	14.7	15.0	306.5	482.9	182.5	153.5	199.1	154.9	224.3
October	85.5	83.4	94.6	14.5	14.6	306.9	482.3	182.9	154.0	199.4	156.8	224.5
November	85.6	83.5	94.9	14.3	14.2	307.4	481.7	183.3	153.8	200.0	156.8	225.3
December	85.4	83.3	94.8	14.2	13.9	308.3	484.8	183.7	153.4	201.2	156.4	225.8
2005												
January	85.4	83.2	94.8	14.2	14.0	309.6	493.9	183.7	153.1	201.9	156.2	226.3
February	85.4	83.3	95.1	14.0	13.5	310.5	496.1	184.2	153.9	202.9	156.9	227.0
March	85.2	83.1	95.0	14.0	13.4	310.9	496.6	184.4	153.0	203.3	158.2	227.9
April	85.3	83.2	95.3	13.9	13.4	311.2	497.0	184.6	153.4	203.3	159.4	228.5
May	84.9	82.7	94.8	13.8	13.2	312.1	498.0	185.2	154.4	202.8	158.8	228.8
June	84.6	82.4	94.6	13.6	13.0	312.3	497.8	185.4	154.3	203.0	158.5	229.1
July	84.4	82.2	94.4	13.6	12.8	313.9	503.4	186.0	155.0	203.9	160.0	229.9
August	84.0	81.8	94.1	13.4	12.4	314.6	506.5	186.2	155.2	204.1	161.7	230.4
September	84.6	82.4	95.1	13.3	12.3	315.2	510.1	186.3	154.8	204.6	165.5	231.4
October	84.2	82.0	94.6	13.3	12.2	315.4	509.4	186.5	155.0	204.8	164.8	233.1
November	84.4	82.2	95.2	13.1	12.0	316.5	511.2	187.2	155.0	205.2	161.2	234.1
December	84.3	82.2	95.2	13.1	11.7	317.7	513.1	187.9	155.4	206.6	160.7	234.4

[1] Not seasonally adjusted.
[3] December 1997 = 100.
[4] December 1988 = 100.
. . . = Not available.

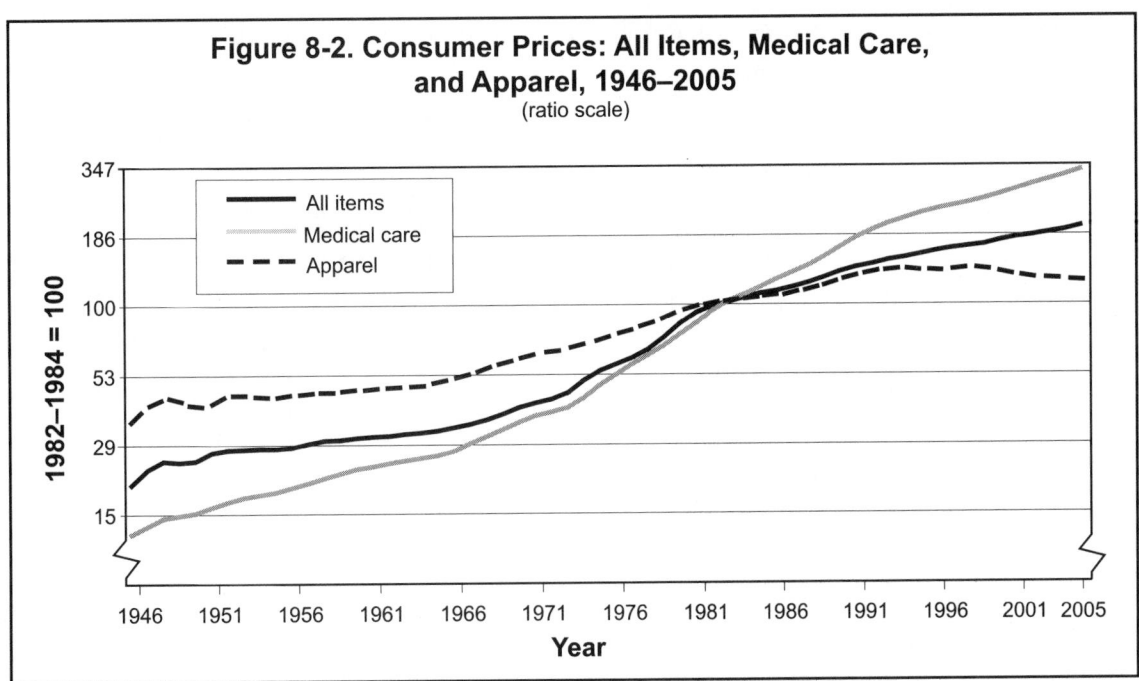

Figure 8-2. Consumer Prices: All Items, Medical Care, and Apparel, 1946–2005
(ratio scale)

- Figure 8-2 charts two components of the Consumer Price Index for All Urban Consumers (CPI-U), along with the all-items total. Since all three indexes have the base years 1982–1984, they converge in those years. However, over the postwar period, the trends of the two components are very different. (Tables 8-1 and 20-2)

- Apparel has been one of the areas most subject to international competition, and the apparel index shows far less growth than the overall average of prices. (Table 8-1)

- Medical care, on the other hand, has little price competition from producers in other countries. It is often paid for by third-party insurers, both government and private, rather than directly by consumers. Furthermore, it is characterized by trend growth in demand, due to rising income and expectations and to technological progress. All of these economic factors cause medical care prices to rise faster than the general price level. (Table 8-1)

- Medical care has arguably been overstated in the CPI due to the difficulties of making quality adjustments. Quality adjustments have been much improved in recent years, but such improvements are not retroactively introduced into the official CPIs.

Table 8-2. Alternative Measures of Total and Core Consumer Prices: Index Levels

(Various bases; monthly data seasonally adjusted, except as noted.)

Year and month	CPIs, all items					CPIs, all items less food and energy			Chain-type price indexes for personal consumption expenditures (PCE), 2000 = 100			
	CPI-U, 1982–1984 = 100	CPI-W, 1982–1984 = 100	CPI-U-X1, 1982–1984 = 100	CPI-U-RS, Dec. 1977 = 100, not seasonally adjusted	C-CPI-U, Dec. 1999 = 100, not seasonally adjusted	CPI-U, 1982–1984 = 100	CPI-U-RS, Dec. 1977 = 100, not seasonally adjusted	C-CPI-U, Dec. 1999 = 100, not seasonally adjusted	PCE, total	PCE, market-based	Excluding food and energy	
											PCE, total	PCE, market-based
1960	29.6	29.8	32.2	...	...	30.6	...	...	20.8	...	21.4	...
1961	29.9	30.1	32.5	...	...	31.0	...	...	21.0	...	21.6	...
1962	30.2	30.4	32.8	...	...	31.4	...	...	21.2	...	21.9	...
1963	30.6	30.8	33.3	...	...	31.8	...	...	21.5	...	22.2	...
1964	31.0	31.2	33.7	...	...	32.3	...	...	21.8	...	22.5	...
1965	31.5	31.7	34.2	...	...	32.7	...	...	22.1	...	22.8	...
1966	32.4	32.6	35.2	...	...	33.5	...	...	22.7	...	23.2	...
1967	33.4	33.6	36.3	...	...	34.7	...	...	23.2	...	23.9	...
1968	34.8	35.0	37.7	...	...	36.3	...	...	24.2	...	24.9	...
1969	36.7	36.9	39.4	...	...	38.4	...	...	25.3	...	26.1	...
1970	38.8	39.0	41.3	...	...	40.8	...	...	26.4	...	27.3	...
1971	40.5	40.7	43.1	...	...	42.7	...	...	27.6	...	28.5	...
1972	41.8	42.1	44.4	...	...	44.0	...	...	28.5	...	29.5	...
1973	44.4	44.7	47.2	...	...	45.6	...	...	30.1	...	30.5	...
1974	49.3	49.6	51.9	...	...	49.4	...	...	33.2	...	32.8	...
1975	53.8	54.1	56.2	...	...	53.9	...	...	36.0	...	35.5	...
1976	56.9	57.2	59.4	...	...	57.4	...	...	37.9	...	37.7	...
1977	60.6	60.9	63.2	...	...	61.0	...	...	40.4	...	40.1	...
1978	65.2	65.6	67.5	104.3	...	65.5	103.5	...	43.2	...	42.8	...
1979	72.6	73.1	74.0	114.1	...	71.9	110.7	...	47.1	...	45.7	...
1980	82.4	82.9	82.3	126.7	...	80.8	120.4	...	52.1	...	49.9	...
1981	90.9	91.4	90.1	138.6	...	89.2	131.4	...	56.7	...	54.2	...
1982	96.5	96.9	95.6	146.8	...	95.8	141.3	...	59.9	...	57.8	...
1983	99.6	99.8	99.6	152.9	...	99.6	149.0	...	62.4	...	60.8	...
1984	103.9	103.3	103.9	159.0	...	104.6	156.1	...	64.8	...	63.4	...
1985	107.6	106.9	107.6	164.3	...	109.1	162.8	...	66.9	...	65.8	...
1986	109.6	108.6	109.6	167.3	...	113.5	169.4	...	68.6	...	68.2	...
1987	113.6	112.5	113.6	173.0	...	118.2	176.0	...	70.9	...	70.8	...
1988	118.3	117.0	118.3	179.3	...	123.4	183.0	...	73.8	...	73.8	...
1989	124.0	122.6	124.0	187.0	...	129.0	190.3	...	77.0	...	76.9	...
1990	130.7	129.0	130.7	196.3	...	135.5	199.0	...	80.5	...	80.2	...
1991	136.2	134.3	136.2	203.4	...	142.1	207.4	...	83.4	...	83.3	...
1992	140.3	138.2	140.3	208.5	...	147.3	213.8	...	85.8	...	86.1	...
1993	144.5	142.1	144.5	213.7	...	152.2	219.8	...	87.8	...	88.3	...
1994	148.2	145.6	148.2	218.2	...	156.5	224.9	...	89.7	...	90.4	...
1995	152.4	149.8	152.4	223.5	...	161.2	230.6	...	91.6	...	92.4	...
1996	156.9	154.1	156.9	229.5	...	165.6	236.3	...	93.5	...	94.1	...
1997	160.5	157.6	160.5	234.4	...	169.5	241.5	...	95.1	95.8	95.6	96.6
1998	163.0	159.7	163.0	237.7	...	173.4	246.7	...	96.0	96.4	96.9	97.6
1999	166.6	163.2	166.6	242.7	...	177.0	251.7	...	97.6	97.7	98.3	98.6
2000	172.2	168.9	172.2	250.8	102.0	181.3	257.7	101.4	100.0	100.0	100.0	100.0
2001	177.1	173.5	177.1	257.8	104.3	186.1	264.5	103.5	102.1	101.9	101.9	101.7
2002	179.9	175.9	179.9	261.9	105.6	190.5	270.6	105.4	103.5	103.1	103.7	103.2
2003	184.0	179.8	184.0	267.9	107.8	193.2	274.6	106.6	105.6	105.0	105.2	104.3
2004	188.9	184.5	188.9	275.1	110.5	196.6	279.3	108.4	108.4	107.4	107.3	105.9
2005	195.3	191.0	195.3	284.3	[1]113.6	200.9	285.5	[1]110.4	111.5	110.3	109.6	107.7
2004												
January	185.9	181.4	185.9	269.7	108.5	194.6	275.7	107.0	106.8	106.0	106.2	105.0
February	186.5	182.1	186.5	271.2	109.1	194.8	277.0	107.5	107.2	106.3	106.4	105.2
March	187.3	182.9	187.3	272.9	109.7	195.4	277.0	108.1	107.6	106.7	106.7	105.4
April	187.5	183.1	187.5	273.8	110.0	195.9	279.3	108.3	107.8	106.8	106.9	105.6
May	188.6	184.2	188.6	275.3	110.6	196.2	279.3	108.3	108.2	107.3	107.1	105.7
June	189.2	184.8	189.2	276.2	110.8	196.6	279.3	108.2	108.5	107.6	107.3	105.9
July	189.2	184.8	189.2	275.9	110.7	196.8	279.4	108.3	108.6	107.6	107.4	106.0
August	189.4	184.9	189.4	275.9	110.7	197.0	279.7	108.4	108.6	107.6	107.5	106.0
September	189.7	185.3	189.7	276.5	111.0	197.6	280.6	108.8	108.8	107.7	107.7	106.1
October	190.8	186.4	190.8	278.0	111.6	197.9	281.6	109.2	109.3	108.3	108.0	106.4
November	191.2	186.8	191.2	278.2	111.6	198.3	281.6	109.2	109.6	108.5	108.2	106.6
December	191.2	186.8	191.2	277.1	111.2	198.5	281.1	109.0	109.6	108.4	108.3	106.6
2005												
January	191.4	186.9	191.4	277.6	[1]111.4	199.0	281.9	[1]109.3	109.7	108.6	108.6	106.9
February	192.1	187.7	192.1	279.3	[1]112.0	199.4	283.5	[1]109.8	110.0	108.9	108.8	107.1
March	193.2	188.7	193.2	281.4	[1]112.7	200.0	285.2	[1]110.3	110.5	109.4	109.0	107.3
April	194.1	189.7	194.1	283.3	[1]113.3	200.2	285.5	[1]110.5	110.9	109.8	109.1	107.4
May	194.0	189.5	194.0	283.1	[1]113.3	200.5	285.3	[1]110.5	110.9	109.8	109.3	107.6
June	193.9	189.5	193.9	283.2	[1]113.3	200.6	285.1	[1]110.3	111.0	109.8	109.4	107.6
July	195.1	190.8	195.1	284.5	[1]113.6	201.0	285.3	[1]110.2	111.4	110.3	109.5	107.7
August	196.2	192.1	196.2	285.9	[1]114.0	201.2	285.7	[1]110.3	111.9	110.7	109.7	107.8
September	198.6	194.8	198.6	289.4	[1]115.1	201.5	286.1	[1]110.6	112.9	111.8	110.0	108.0
October	199.1	195.1	199.1	290.1	[1]115.4	202.0	287.4	[1]111.1	113.2	112.0	110.2	108.2
November	197.8	193.5	197.8	287.8	[1]114.8	202.5	287.5	[1]111.1	112.7	111.5	110.4	108.4
December	197.7	193.3	197.7	286.5	[1]114.4	202.8	287.2	[1]111.0	112.7	111.4	110.6	108.5

[1]Interim values.
. . . = Not available.

Table 8-3. Alternative Measures of Total and Core Consumer Prices: Inflation Rates

(Percent changes from year earlier, except as noted; monthly data seasonally adjusted, except as noted.)

Year and month	CPIs, all items					CPIs, all items less food and energy			Chain-type price indexes for personal consumption expenditures (PCE), 2000 = 100			
	CPI-U, 1982–1984 = 100	CPI-W, 1982–1984 = 100	CPI-U-X1, 1982–1984 = 100	CPI-U-RS, Dec. 1977 = 100, not seasonally adjusted	C-CPI-U, Dec. 1999 = 100, not seasonally adjusted	CPI-U, 1982–1984 = 100	CPI-U-RS, Dec. 1977 = 100, not seasonally adjusted	C-CPI-U, Dec. 1999 = 100, not seasonally adjusted	PCE, total	PCE, market-based	Excluding food and energy	
											PCE, total	PCE, market-based
1960	1.7	1.7	1.9	...	...	1.3	...	...	1.6	...	1.7	...
1961	1.0	1.0	0.9	...	...	1.3	...	...	1.0	...	1.2	...
1962	1.0	1.0	0.9	...	...	1.3	...	...	1.2	...	1.3	...
1963	1.3	1.3	1.5	...	...	1.3	...	...	1.2	...	1.2	...
1964	1.3	1.3	1.2	...	...	1.6	...	...	1.4	...	1.5	...
1965	1.6	1.6	1.5	...	...	1.2	...	...	1.5	...	1.2	...
1966	2.9	2.8	2.9	...	...	2.4	...	...	2.5	...	2.1	...
1967	3.1	3.1	3.1	...	...	3.6	...	...	2.5	...	2.9	...
1968	4.2	4.2	3.9	...	...	4.6	...	...	3.9	...	4.2	...
1969	5.5	5.4	4.5	...	...	5.8	...	...	4.6	...	4.6	...
1970	5.7	5.7	4.8	...	...	6.3	...	...	4.7	...	4.5	...
1971	4.4	4.4	4.4	...	...	4.7	...	...	4.3	...	4.6	...
1972	3.2	3.4	3.0	...	...	3.0	...	...	3.5	...	3.2	...
1973	6.2	6.2	6.3	...	...	3.6	...	...	5.4	...	3.6	...
1974	11.0	11.0	10.0	...	...	8.3	...	...	10.3	...	7.5	...
1975	9.1	9.1	8.3	...	...	9.1	...	...	8.3	...	8.3	...
1976	5.8	5.7	5.7	...	...	6.5	...	...	5.5	...	6.1	...
1977	6.5	6.5	6.4	...	...	6.3	...	...	6.5	...	6.4	...
1978	7.6	7.7	6.8	...	...	7.4	...	...	7.0	...	6.6	...
1979	11.3	11.4	9.6	9.4	...	9.8	7.0	...	8.8	...	7.0	...
1980	13.5	13.4	11.2	11.0	...	12.4	8.8	...	10.7	...	9.0	...
1981	10.3	10.3	9.5	9.4	...	10.4	9.1	...	8.9	...	8.7	...
1982	6.2	6.0	6.1	5.9	...	7.4	7.5	...	5.5	...	6.6	...
1983	3.2	3.0	4.2	4.2	...	4.0	5.4	...	4.3	...	5.3	...
1984	4.3	3.5	4.3	4.0	...	5.0	4.8	...	3.8	...	4.2	...
1985	3.6	3.5	3.6	3.3	...	4.3	4.3	...	3.3	...	3.8	...
1986	1.9	1.6	1.9	1.8	...	4.0	4.1	...	2.4	...	3.7	...
1987	3.6	3.6	3.6	3.4	...	4.1	3.9	...	3.5	...	3.7	...
1988	4.1	4.0	4.1	3.6	...	4.4	4.0	...	4.0	...	4.3	...
1989	4.8	4.8	4.8	4.3	...	4.5	4.0	...	4.4	...	4.1	...
1990	5.4	5.2	5.4	5.0	...	5.0	4.6	...	4.6	...	4.3	...
1991	4.2	4.1	4.2	3.6	...	4.9	4.2	...	3.6	...	3.9	...
1992	3.0	2.9	3.0	2.5	...	3.7	3.1	...	2.9	...	3.4	...
1993	3.0	2.8	3.0	2.5	...	3.3	2.8	...	2.3	...	2.6	...
1994	2.6	2.5	2.6	2.1	...	2.8	2.3	...	2.1	...	2.3	...
1995	2.8	2.9	2.8	2.4	...	3.0	2.5	...	2.1	...	2.2	...
1996	3.0	2.9	3.0	2.7	...	2.7	2.5	...	2.2	...	1.9	...
1997	2.3	2.3	2.3	2.1	...	2.4	2.2	...	1.7	...	1.6	...
1998	1.6	1.3	1.6	1.4	...	2.3	2.2	...	0.9	0.6	1.3	1.0
1999	2.2	2.2	2.2	2.1	...	2.1	2.0	...	1.7	1.4	1.5	1.1
2000	3.4	3.5	3.4	3.3	...	2.4	2.4	...	2.5	2.4	1.7	1.4
2001	2.8	2.7	2.8	2.8	2.3	2.6	2.6	2.1	2.1	1.9	1.9	1.7
2002	1.6	1.4	1.6	1.6	1.2	2.4	2.3	1.8	1.4	1.1	1.8	1.5
2003	2.3	2.2	2.3	2.3	2.1	1.4	1.5	1.1	2.0	1.9	1.4	1.1
2004	2.7	2.6	2.7	2.7	2.5	1.8	1.7	1.7	2.6	2.3	2.0	1.5
2005	3.4	3.5	3.4	3.3	[1]2.8	2.2	2.2	[1]1.8	2.9	2.7	2.1	1.7
Percent change, annual rate												
1978–2005	4.1	4.0	4.0	3.8	...	4.2	3.8	...	3.6	...	3.5	...
2000–2005	2.5	2.5	2.5	2.5	2.2	2.1	2.1	1.7	2.2	2.0	1.9	1.5
2005												
January	3.0	3.0	3.0	2.9	[1]2.7	2.3	2.2	[1]2.1	2.7	2.4	2.2	1.8
February	3.0	3.1	3.0	3.0	[1]2.7	2.4	2.3	[1]2.1	2.6	2.4	2.2	1.8
March	3.2	3.2	3.2	3.1	[1]2.7	2.4	3.0	[1]2.0	2.7	2.5	2.2	1.8
April	3.5	3.6	3.5	3.5	[1]3.0	2.2	2.2	[1]2.0	2.9	2.8	2.1	1.7
May	2.9	2.9	2.9	2.8	[1]2.4	2.2	2.1	[1]2.0	2.5	2.3	2.1	1.8
June	2.5	2.5	2.5	2.5	[1]2.3	2.0	2.1	[1]1.9	2.3	2.1	2.0	1.7
July	3.1	3.2	3.1	3.1	[1]2.6	2.1	2.1	[1]1.8	2.6	2.5	2.0	1.7
August	3.6	3.9	3.6	3.6	[1]3.0	2.1	2.1	[1]1.8	3.0	2.9	2.0	1.8
September	4.7	5.1	4.7	4.7	[1]3.7	2.0	2.0	[1]1.7	3.8	3.9	2.1	1.8
October	4.4	4.7	4.4	4.4	[1]3.4	2.1	2.1	[1]1.7	3.5	3.5	2.1	1.7
November	3.5	3.6	3.5	3.5	[1]2.9	2.1	2.1	[1]1.7	2.9	2.8	2.1	1.7
December	3.4	3.5	3.4	3.4	[1]2.9	2.2	2.2	[1]1.8	2.9	2.8	2.1	1.8

[1] Interim values.
... = Not available.

Table 8-4. Producer Price Indexes and Purchasing Power of the Dollar

(1982 = 100, seasonally adjusted.)

Year and month	Finished goods		Finished consumer goods				Finished consumer goods, except foods			Capital equipment		
				Finished consumer foods								
	Total	Percent change from previous period	Total	Total	Crude	Processed	Total	Durable goods	Nondurable goods less foods	Total	Manu-facturing industries	Nonmanu-facturing industries
1960	33.4	0.9	33.6	35.5	39.8	35.2	33.5	43.8	28.4	32.8	30.2	34.8
1961	33.4	0.0	33.6	35.4	38.0	35.3	33.4	43.6	28.4	32.9	30.3	34.8
1962	33.5	0.3	33.7	35.7	38.4	35.6	33.4	43.4	28.4	33.0	30.5	34.9
1963	33.4	-0.3	33.5	35.3	37.8	35.2	33.4	43.1	28.5	33.1	30.6	34.8
1964	33.5	0.3	33.6	35.4	38.9	35.2	33.3	43.3	28.4	33.4	31.0	35.1
1965	34.1	1.8	34.2	36.8	39.0	36.8	33.6	43.2	28.8	33.8	31.5	35.4
1966	35.2	3.2	35.4	39.2	41.5	39.2	34.1	43.4	29.3	34.6	32.5	36.0
1967	35.6	1.1	35.6	38.5	39.6	38.8	34.7	44.1	30.0	35.8	33.8	37.0
1968	36.6	2.8	36.5	40.0	42.5	40.0	35.5	45.1	30.6	37.0	35.0	38.2
1969	38.0	3.8	37.9	42.4	45.9	42.3	36.3	45.9	31.5	38.3	36.2	39.5
1970	39.3	3.4	39.1	43.8	46.0	43.9	37.4	47.2	32.5	40.1	38.1	41.3
1971	40.5	3.1	40.2	44.5	45.8	44.7	38.7	48.9	33.5	41.7	39.6	43.0
1972	41.8	3.2	41.5	46.9	48.0	47.2	39.4	50.0	34.1	42.8	40.5	44.2
1973	45.6	9.1	46.0	56.5	63.6	55.8	41.2	50.9	36.1	44.2	42.2	45.3
1974	52.6	15.4	53.1	64.4	71.6	63.9	48.2	55.5	44.0	50.5	48.8	51.2
1975	58.2	10.6	58.2	69.8	71.7	70.3	53.2	61.0	48.9	58.2	56.5	58.9
1976	60.8	4.5	60.4	69.6	76.7	69.0	56.5	63.7	52.4	62.1	60.3	62.9
1977	64.7	6.4	64.3	73.3	79.5	72.7	60.6	67.4	56.8	66.1	64.5	66.8
1978	69.8	7.9	69.4	79.9	85.8	79.4	64.9	73.6	60.0	71.3	70.1	71.8
1979	77.6	11.2	77.5	87.3	92.3	86.8	73.5	80.8	69.3	77.5	77.1	77.7
1980	88.0	13.4	88.6	92.4	93.9	92.3	87.1	91.0	85.1	85.8	86.0	85.7
1981	96.1	9.2	96.6	97.8	104.4	97.2	96.1	96.4	95.8	94.6	94.9	94.4
1982	100.0	4.1	100.0	100.0	100.0	100.0	100.0	100.0	100.0	100.0	100.0	100.0
1983	101.6	1.6	101.3	101.0	102.4	100.9	101.2	102.8	100.5	102.8	102.3	103.0
1984	103.7	2.1	103.3	105.4	111.4	104.9	102.2	104.5	101.1	105.2	104.9	105.4
1985	104.7	1.0	103.8	104.6	102.9	104.8	103.3	106.5	101.7	107.5	107.4	107.6
1986	103.2	-1.4	101.4	107.3	105.6	107.4	98.5	108.9	93.3	109.7	109.7	109.7
1987	105.4	2.1	103.6	109.5	107.1	109.6	100.7	111.5	94.9	111.7	111.8	111.6
1988	108.0	2.5	106.2	112.6	109.8	112.7	103.1	113.8	97.3	114.3	115.5	113.9
1989	113.6	5.2	112.1	118.7	119.6	118.6	108.9	117.6	103.8	118.8	120.3	118.2
1990	119.2	4.9	118.2	124.4	123.0	124.4	115.3	120.4	111.5	122.9	124.5	122.2
1991	121.7	2.1	120.5	124.1	119.3	124.4	118.7	123.9	115.0	126.7	127.8	126.3
1992	123.2	1.2	121.7	123.3	107.6	124.4	120.8	125.7	117.3	129.1	129.3	129.0
1993	124.7	1.2	123.0	125.7	114.4	126.5	121.7	128.0	117.6	131.4	131.2	131.4
1994	125.5	0.6	123.3	126.8	111.3	127.9	121.6	130.9	116.2	134.1	133.2	134.3
1995	127.9	1.9	125.6	129.0	118.8	129.8	124.0	132.7	118.8	136.7	135.8	137.0
1996	131.3	2.7	129.5	133.6	129.2	133.8	127.6	134.2	123.3	138.3	137.2	138.6
1997	131.8	0.4	130.2	134.5	126.6	135.1	128.2	133.7	124.3	138.2	137.7	138.4
1998	130.7	-0.8	128.9	134.3	127.2	134.8	126.4	132.9	122.2	137.6	137.9	137.4
1999	133.0	1.8	132.0	135.1	125.5	135.9	130.5	133.0	127.9	137.6	138.5	137.3
2000	138.0	3.8	138.2	137.2	123.5	138.3	138.4	133.9	138.7	138.8	139.5	138.6
2001	140.7	2.0	141.5	141.3	127.7	142.4	141.4	134.0	142.8	139.7	140.4	139.4
2002	138.9	-1.3	139.4	140.1	128.5	141.0	138.8	133.0	139.8	139.1	140.0	138.7
2003	143.3	3.2	145.3	145.9	130.0	147.2	144.7	133.1	148.4	139.5	139.9	139.3
2004	148.5	3.6	151.7	152.7	138.2	153.9	150.9	135.0	156.6	141.4	142.4	141.0
2005	155.7	4.8	160.4	155.7	140.2	156.9	161.9	136.6	172.0	144.6	146.0	144.1
2004												
January	145.7	0.3	148.3	148.5	138.6	149.3	147.9	133.6	152.8	140.1	140.4	139.9
February	145.6	-0.1	148.3	148.6	134.8	149.7	147.8	133.7	152.6	139.9	140.7	139.6
March	146.3	0.5	149.1	150.9	146.4	151.2	148.0	134.4	152.6	140.4	141.3	140.0
April	147.4	0.8	150.4	152.9	133.8	154.5	149.1	134.3	154.3	140.6	141.9	140.0
May	148.6	0.8	152.0	155.0	132.6	156.9	150.5	134.9	156.0	140.9	142.2	140.3
June	148.5	-0.1	151.7	154.6	121.7	157.4	150.2	135.7	155.3	141.5	142.6	141.0
July	148.4	-0.1	151.5	151.9	121.3	154.5	151.1	134.8	156.9	141.3	142.7	140.7
August	148.5	0.1	151.5	151.8	128.4	153.7	151.1	134.9	156.9	141.8	142.8	141.3
September	148.6	0.1	151.6	152.4	138.8	153.5	150.9	135.3	156.4	142.1	143.1	141.6
October	150.8	1.5	154.5	154.7	159.3	154.2	154.0	135.9	160.7	142.5	143.5	142.1
November	152.2	0.9	156.2	155.1	156.7	154.9	156.3	136.3	163.8	142.9	143.6	142.5
December	151.5	-0.5	155.1	155.3	142.6	156.3	154.7	136.5	161.4	143.3	143.9	143.0
2005												
January	151.7	0.1	155.2	154.8	130.0	156.8	155.1	137.0	161.7	143.7	144.5	143.4
February	152.4	0.5	156.2	155.7	142.6	156.7	156.1	136.6	163.5	143.7	144.9	143.2
March	153.6	0.8	157.7	156.7	147.6	157.4	157.7	136.6	165.8	144.1	145.2	143.6
April	154.4	0.5	158.6	156.5	148.3	157.2	159.1	136.9	167.7	144.4	145.7	143.9
May	154.1	-0.2	158.1	156.2	139.8	157.5	158.5	136.9	166.8	144.8	146.0	144.3
June	154.2	0.1	158.4	155.1	138.2	156.5	159.3	136.4	168.2	144.6	146.0	144.0
July	155.4	0.8	159.8	154.0	131.5	155.9	161.7	137.0	171.5	145.0	146.2	144.5
August	156.2	0.5	161.0	153.7	127.7	155.9	163.5	136.8	174.2	145.0	146.3	144.4
September	158.4	1.4	164.0	155.6	141.2	156.7	166.8	137.3	178.9	145.3	146.6	144.7
October	159.6	0.8	165.6	155.7	135.7	157.3	169.1	136.2	182.7	145.0	146.9	144.3
November	158.8	-0.5	164.6	156.7	144.5	157.7	167.2	136.1	180.1	145.0	147.0	144.2
December	159.9	0.7	166.0	157.9	158.0	157.8	168.8	135.9	182.5	145.0	147.2	144.1

Table 8-4. Producer Price Indexes and Purchasing Power of the Dollar—Continued

(1982 = 100, seasonally adjusted.)

Year and month		Intermediate materials, supplies, and components											
	Total	Materials and components for manufacturing					Materials and components for construction	Processed fuels and lubricants			Containers, nonreturnable	Supplies	
		Total	Materials for food manufacturing	Materials for nondurable manufacturing	Materials for durable manufacturing	Components for manufacturing		Total	Manufacturing industries	Nonmanufacturing industries		Total	Manufacturing industries
1960	30.8	33.3	35.7	35.9	30.4	34.0	32.7	16.6	19.7	14.6	33.4	33.3	36.2
1961	30.6	32.9	36.9	35.1	30.0	33.7	32.2	16.8	19.9	14.8	33.2	33.7	35.8
1962	30.6	32.7	36.1	34.9	30.0	33.4	32.1	16.7	19.9	14.7	33.6	34.5	36.0
1963	30.7	32.7	37.9	34.6	30.0	33.4	32.2	16.6	19.8	14.5	33.2	35.0	35.8
1964	30.8	33.1	37.3	34.8	30.6	33.7	32.5	16.2	19.4	14.1	32.9	34.7	35.9
1965	31.2	33.6	38.3	35.2	31.2	34.2	32.8	16.5	19.6	14.4	33.5	35.0	36.1
1966	32.0	34.3	40.0	35.4	31.8	35.4	33.6	16.8	19.9	14.7	34.5	36.5	37.1
1967	32.2	34.5	39.2	35.2	32.3	36.5	34.0	16.9	20.1	14.8	35.0	36.8	37.6
1968	33.0	35.3	39.8	35.6	33.4	37.3	35.7	16.5	19.8	14.2	35.9	37.1	38.7
1969	34.1	36.5	42.0	36.0	35.2	38.5	37.7	16.6	20.0	14.4	37.2	37.8	39.8
1970	35.4	38.0	44.3	36.5	37.0	40.6	38.3	17.7	21.5	15.2	39.0	39.7	41.4
1971	36.8	38.9	45.7	37.0	38.1	41.9	40.8	19.5	23.6	16.6	40.8	40.8	42.5
1972	38.2	40.4	47.0	38.5	39.9	42.9	43.0	20.1	24.5	16.9	42.7	42.5	43.3
1973	42.4	44.1	57.2	42.6	43.1	44.3	46.5	22.2	26.4	19.4	45.2	51.7	45.6
1974	52.5	56.0	82.0	54.6	55.4	51.1	55.0	33.6	35.5	32.7	53.3	56.8	53.3
1975	58.0	61.7	82.1	61.4	60.8	57.8	60.1	39.4	41.9	38.0	60.0	61.8	59.4
1976	60.9	64.0	70.6	64.8	64.8	60.8	64.1	42.3	44.8	41.1	63.1	65.8	62.6
1977	64.9	67.4	71.9	66.8	70.2	64.5	69.3	47.7	51.0	46.2	65.9	69.3	66.6
1978	69.5	72.0	81.0	69.2	76.2	69.2	76.5	49.9	53.7	48.1	71.0	72.9	71.2
1979	78.4	80.9	89.9	78.3	87.3	75.8	84.2	61.6	64.3	60.4	79.4	80.2	78.1
1980	90.3	91.7	103.7	91.2	97.1	84.6	91.3	85.0	85.5	84.7	89.1	89.9	87.2
1981	98.6	98.7	102.1	100.5	100.7	94.7	97.9	100.6	100.2	101.0	96.7	96.9	95.2
1982	100.0	100.0	100.0	100.0	100.0	100.0	100.0	100.0	100.0	100.0	100.0	100.0	100.0
1983	100.6	101.2	101.3	98.5	103.0	102.4	102.8	95.4	96.2	94.9	100.4	101.8	101.5
1984	103.1	104.1	106.3	102.1	104.9	105.0	105.6	95.7	97.1	94.6	105.9	104.1	105.0
1985	102.7	103.3	101.5	100.5	103.3	106.4	107.3	92.8	93.8	92.0	109.0	104.4	107.3
1986	99.1	102.2	98.4	98.1	101.2	107.5	108.1	72.7	75.1	71.2	110.3	105.6	108.3
1987	101.5	105.3	100.8	102.2	106.2	108.8	109.8	73.3	75.9	71.7	114.5	107.7	110.0
1988	107.1	113.2	106.0	112.9	118.7	112.3	116.1	71.2	73.3	69.9	120.1	113.7	114.8
1989	112.0	118.1	112.7	118.5	123.6	116.4	121.3	76.4	78.3	75.3	125.4	118.1	119.8
1990	114.5	118.7	117.9	118.0	120.7	119.0	122.9	85.9	87.3	85.0	127.7	119.4	122.1
1991	114.4	118.1	115.3	116.7	117.2	121.0	124.5	85.3	88.4	83.4	128.1	121.4	124.4
1992	114.7	117.9	113.9	115.4	117.2	122.0	126.5	84.5	87.5	82.6	127.7	122.7	125.9
1993	116.2	118.9	115.6	115.5	119.1	123.0	132.0	84.7	88.1	82.6	126.4	125.0	128.5
1994	118.5	122.1	118.5	119.2	125.2	124.3	136.6	83.1	86.1	81.1	129.7	127.0	130.7
1995	124.9	130.4	119.5	135.1	135.6	126.5	142.1	84.2	87.1	82.3	148.8	132.1	137.0
1996	125.7	128.6	125.3	130.5	131.3	126.9	143.6	90.0	92.4	88.4	141.1	135.9	138.7
1997	125.6	128.3	123.2	129.6	132.8	126.4	146.5	89.3	92.0	87.6	136.0	135.9	139.4
1998	123.0	126.1	123.2	126.7	128.0	125.9	146.8	81.1	85.8	78.1	140.8	134.8	140.6
1999	123.2	124.6	120.8	124.9	125.1	125.7	148.9	84.6	87.9	82.5	142.5	134.2	140.7
2000	129.2	128.1	119.2	132.6	129.0	126.2	150.7	102.0	100.9	102.3	151.6	136.9	143.5
2001	129.7	127.4	124.3	131.8	125.1	126.4	150.6	104.5	105.7	103.5	153.1	138.7	145.4
2002	127.8	126.1	123.2	129.2	124.7	126.1	151.3	96.3	98.7	94.8	152.1	138.9	144.7
2003	133.7	129.7	134.4	137.2	127.9	125.9	153.6	112.6	116.0	110.5	153.7	141.5	146.5
2004	142.6	137.9	145.0	147.8	146.6	127.4	166.4	124.3	125.1	123.8	159.3	146.7	149.2
2005	154.0	146.0	146.0	163.2	158.3	129.9	176.6	150.0	148.6	150.9	167.1	151.9	155.7
2004													
January	136.4	131.9	139.2	140.2	133.1	125.9	156.3	117.6	119.6	116.3	153.8	143.1	146.8
February	137.5	133.2	139.9	140.9	137.3	126.2	159.1	117.8	120.2	116.3	153.6	143.8	147.1
March	138.4	134.2	142.1	141.3	140.6	126.5	161.9	117.4	119.8	115.9	154.1	144.8	147.5
April	140.2	136.1	146.7	143.4	144.1	127.0	164.5	118.9	120.4	118.0	154.9	146.3	147.9
May	142.0	137.3	151.6	144.5	146.6	127.2	166.7	122.6	123.5	122.0	156.7	147.2	148.2
June	142.5	137.6	151.3	145.9	145.7	127.5	166.8	123.6	126.6	121.8	158.9	147.3	148.8
July	143.2	138.0	146.4	147.3	147.2	127.5	167.4	125.3	126.2	124.7	159.7	148.0	149.4
August	144.6	139.4	144.2	149.9	150.3	127.7	169.8	127.7	128.5	127.3	162.0	147.6	149.6
September	144.8	140.7	144.0	152.7	152.1	128.0	170.9	124.5	124.8	124.4	163.6	148.0	150.3
October	146.3	141.5	143.9	154.5	153.0	128.2	170.9	129.6	127.2	131.2	164.7	148.0	151.2
November	147.6	142.1	144.6	155.6	153.7	128.4	170.8	134.5	132.3	136.0	164.9	148.2	151.6
December	147.5	142.9	146.1	156.8	155.4	128.6	171.6	131.2	131.1	131.3	165.3	148.5	152.3
2005													
January	148.3	144.0	146.6	157.9	157.5	129.2	173.3	130.5	130.2	130.8	165.4	149.6	153.3
February	149.2	144.5	146.2	158.1	159.2	129.4	174.8	132.4	131.0	133.4	166.1	150.0	153.7
March	150.6	145.1	146.9	160.3	159.0	129.5	175.0	137.1	134.6	138.7	166.9	150.7	154.3
April	151.6	144.8	146.2	159.5	158.3	129.6	175.2	142.1	139.4	143.8	167.5	151.0	154.6
May	151.1	144.5	146.7	159.7	156.7	129.6	174.8	140.1	139.5	140.5	167.3	151.3	154.9
June	151.4	144.2	145.0	159.4	156.1	129.6	175.4	142.0	139.3	143.8	167.4	151.7	155.2
July	152.9	144.6	144.2	160.8	155.4	129.9	175.7	148.2	145.4	149.9	166.8	152.0	155.3
August	153.7	144.4	143.8	161.2	153.9	130.0	175.4	152.5	150.5	153.7	166.8	152.2	155.6
September	157.3	146.7	145.1	166.7	156.8	130.1	176.9	163.6	162.5	164.4	166.1	152.5	156.1
October	162.0	149.3	146.4	173.0	159.9	130.2	179.3	177.9	176.3	179.0	166.9	153.6	157.8
November	159.9	149.5	147.3	170.9	162.4	130.8	181.0	166.2	168.1	165.0	168.4	153.8	158.8
December	160.3	150.0	147.2	170.8	164.6	130.9	182.0	165.5	165.2	165.8	170.0	154.2	159.9

Table 8-4. Producer Price Indexes and Purchasing Power of the Dollar—Continued

(1982 = 100, seasonally adjusted.)

Year and month	Intermediate materials, supplies, and components—Continued			Crude materials for further processing								
	Supplies—Continued					Nonfood materials						
	Nonmanufacturing industries			Total	Foodstuffs and feedstuffs	Total	Nonfood materials except fuel [1]			Crude fuel [2]		
	Total	Feeds	Other supplies				Total [1]	Manu-facturing [1]	Construc-tion	Total	Manu-facturing industries	Nonmanu-facturing industries
1960	32.1	37.2	33.2	30.4	38.4	...	26.9	26.3	35.9	10.5	9.0	11.8
1961	32.9	40.9	32.9	30.2	37.9	...	27.2	26.6	35.9	10.5	9.0	11.8
1962	33.8	43.6	33.2	30.5	38.6	...	27.1	26.5	36.1	10.4	8.9	11.8
1963	34.6	45.9	33.2	29.9	37.5	...	26.7	26.1	36.0	10.5	9.0	11.9
1964	34.1	45.0	32.9	29.6	36.6	...	27.2	26.6	35.9	10.5	9.0	11.9
1965	34.5	45.9	33.0	31.1	39.2	...	27.7	27.2	36.1	10.6	9.0	11.9
1966	36.2	50.0	33.8	33.1	42.7	...	28.3	27.8	36.3	10.9	9.3	12.3
1967	36.3	48.3	34.5	31.3	40.3	21.1	26.5	25.8	37.0	11.3	9.7	12.8
1968	36.4	46.5	35.4	31.8	40.9	21.6	27.1	26.3	38.4	11.5	9.9	13.1
1969	36.9	46.4	36.0	33.9	44.1	22.5	28.4	27.6	39.8	12.0	10.2	13.8
1970	38.9	49.9	37.6	35.2	45.2	23.8	29.1	28.3	42.1	13.8	11.3	16.6
1971	39.9	50.4	38.9	36.0	46.1	24.7	29.4	28.4	44.1	15.7	12.6	19.3
1972	42.0	56.1	39.8	39.9	51.5	27.0	32.3	31.5	45.0	16.8	13.5	20.6
1973	54.7	97.3	42.7	54.5	72.6	34.3	42.9	42.7	46.2	18.6	14.8	22.9
1974	58.4	90.2	50.5	61.4	76.4	44.1	54.5	55.0	50.0	24.8	19.1	31.8
1975	62.9	84.0	58.9	61.6	77.4	43.7	50.0	49.7	55.9	30.6	24.4	38.0
1976	67.3	95.1	62.0	63.4	76.8	48.2	54.9	54.7	59.6	34.5	29.0	40.5
1977	70.7	99.3	65.2	65.5	77.5	51.7	56.3	56.0	63.1	42.0	37.2	47.4
1978	73.8	95.5	69.7	73.4	87.3	57.5	61.9	61.5	68.7	48.2	43.1	53.8
1979	81.2	106.9	76.3	85.9	100.0	69.6	75.5	75.6	76.6	57.3	53.1	62.0
1980	91.1	110.6	87.5	95.3	104.6	84.6	91.8	92.3	87.9	69.4	66.7	72.5
1981	97.8	111.3	95.4	103.0	103.9	101.8	109.8	110.9	96.8	84.8	83.6	86.2
1982	100.0	100.0	100.0	100.0	100.0	100.0	100.0	100.0	100.0	100.0	100.0	100.0
1983	102.0	109.1	101.0	101.3	101.8	100.7	98.8	98.6	100.1	105.1	105.8	104.4
1984	103.7	104.2	103.7	103.5	104.7	102.2	101.0	100.8	103.1	105.1	105.6	104.6
1985	103.0	86.6	105.3	95.8	94.8	96.9	94.3	93.1	105.7	102.7	102.7	102.5
1986	104.2	90.5	106.2	87.7	93.2	81.6	76.0	72.6	106.5	92.2	91.1	93.6
1987	106.6	94.6	108.3	93.7	96.2	87.9	88.5	84.7	114.8	84.1	82.1	86.3
1988	113.2	115.0	112.7	96.0	106.1	85.5	85.9	81.5	126.5	82.1	80.1	84.5
1989	117.2	114.4	117.5	103.1	111.2	93.4	95.8	91.0	136.9	85.3	83.9	87.0
1990	118.0	102.8	120.2	108.9	113.1	101.5	107.3	102.5	145.2	84.8	82.9	87.0
1991	119.9	101.3	122.5	101.2	105.5	94.6	97.5	92.2	147.5	82.9	82.3	84.1
1992	121.1	103.0	123.7	100.4	105.1	93.5	94.2	87.9	162.1	84.0	83.1	85.2
1993	123.2	105.4	125.8	102.4	108.4	94.7	94.1	85.6	193.6	87.1	85.9	88.6
1994	125.1	105.8	127.9	101.8	106.5	94.8	97.0	88.3	199.1	82.4	81.7	83.6
1995	129.5	103.4	133.2	102.7	105.8	96.8	105.8	97.3	201.7	72.1	72.5	72.9
1996	134.4	133.1	134.6	113.8	121.5	104.5	105.7	97.6	195.7	92.6	90.7	94.3
1997	134.1	129.1	134.8	111.1	112.2	106.4	103.5	95.0	201.4	101.3	98.4	103.3
1998	132.2	100.2	136.2	96.8	103.9	88.4	84.5	76.7	196.0	86.7	84.8	88.5
1999	131.4	89.2	136.5	98.2	98.7	94.3	91.1	83.0	195.7	91.2	90.0	92.9
2000	134.1	94.6	138.8	120.6	100.2	130.4	118.0	108.7	193.4	136.9	136.9	139.3
2001	135.8	96.8	140.5	121.0	106.1	126.8	101.5	93.2	181.7	151.4	150.2	154.2
2002	136.3	98.1	140.9	108.1	99.5	111.4	101.0	92.5	181.4	117.3	113.4	119.8
2003	139.0	106.6	143.1	135.3	113.5	148.2	116.9	107.5	180.8	185.7	176.4	189.9
2004	144.9	119.1	148.4	159.0	127.0	179.2	149.2	137.7	191.8	211.4	200.5	216.2
2005	149.7	107.4	154.9	182.2	122.7	223.4	176.7	163.4	199.3	279.7	263.9	286.3
2004												
January	141.1	118.0	144.2	148.6	118.8	167.4	133.3	122.9	186.1	207.9	197.2	212.7
February	141.8	120.6	144.8	150.2	122.9	167.0	137.2	126.5	187.2	200.2	190.2	204.7
March	142.9	125.6	145.5	152.8	132.0	164.3	143.0	131.9	189.3	182.9	174.2	187.0
April	144.8	134.2	146.7	155.6	135.8	166.1	140.7	129.7	189.8	191.8	182.6	196.1
May	145.7	135.9	147.6	160.7	138.8	172.8	141.3	130.3	190.6	208.4	197.9	213.1
June	145.7	128.3	148.4	162.6	136.2	178.2	137.2	126.4	192.4	229.8	217.6	235.1
July	146.4	129.5	149.0	162.2	130.0	182.5	149.2	137.7	193.5	219.9	208.4	225.0
August	145.9	116.7	149.7	161.6	123.7	186.4	158.5	146.4	194.0	214.0	202.9	218.9
September	146.2	112.2	150.5	154.3	121.7	175.1	157.0	145.0	194.3	186.9	178.0	191.1
October	145.9	105.3	151.0	160.6	119.8	187.7	171.9	159.0	195.4	194.1	184.7	198.5
November	146.1	102.7	151.4	172.1	120.9	207.1	165.3	152.7	195.7	256.8	242.4	262.8
December	146.3	100.6	151.9	166.8	123.3	195.8	155.7	143.7	194.0	243.8	230.4	249.5
2005												
January	147.4	102.8	152.9	163.9	125.8	188.7	160.4	148.1	198.1	217.0	205.9	222.0
February	147.8	102.2	153.4	162.7	122.3	189.4	160.9	148.6	198.5	217.8	206.7	222.8
March	148.6	104.7	153.9	170.3	128.1	198.2	172.0	159.0	199.6	221.7	210.5	226.8
April	148.9	106.1	154.1	174.9	125.3	208.5	169.8	156.9	201.3	252.4	238.8	258.3
May	149.2	107.6	154.3	169.5	123.8	200.1	166.1	153.4	201.3	237.1	224.6	242.6
June	149.5	110.9	154.4	166.6	120.8	197.4	169.7	156.8	198.6	223.5	212.0	228.7
July	149.9	111.7	154.7	175.1	120.1	213.0	178.0	164.6	199.0	250.1	236.5	255.9
August	150.1	112.1	154.9	181.3	118.7	225.0	187.6	173.6	199.1	265.0	250.2	271.2
September	150.4	109.2	155.5	200.3	120.7	256.7	192.2	177.9	198.5	340.4	319.8	348.5
October	151.3	107.9	156.6	211.7	120.6	276.9	190.2	176.1	198.0	397.0	372.0	406.5
November	151.3	106.0	156.8	208.8	121.8	271.0	183.4	169.6	200.0	393.4	368.9	402.8
December	151.7	107.6	157.1	201.4	124.9	255.5	190.1	175.9	200.0	340.8	320.4	348.9

[1]Includes crude petroleum.
[2]Excludes crude petroleum.
. . . = Not available.

Table 8-4. Producer Price Indexes and Purchasing Power of the Dollar—Continued

(1982 = 100, seasonally adjusted.)

Year and month	Finished energy goods	Finished goods excluding:			Finished consumer goods excluding:		Intermediate materials		Intermediate materials less:			Crude materials		
		Foods	Energy	Foods and energy	Energy	Foods and energy	Foods and feeds	Energy goods	Foods and feeds	Energy	Foods and energy	Energy materials [1]	Less energy	Nonfood materials less energy [2]
1960	...	...	...	...	...	...	...	...	30.7	...	...	...	...	...
1961	...	...	...	...	...	...	...	...	30.3	...	...	...	...	...
1962	...	...	...	...	...	...	...	...	30.2	...	...	...	...	...
1963	...	...	...	...	...	...	...	...	30.1	...	...	...	...	...
1964	...	...	...	...	...	...	...	...	30.3	...	...	...	...	...
1965	...	...	...	...	...	...	...	...	30.7	...	...	...	...	...
1966	...	...	...	...	...	...	...	...	31.3	...	...	...	...	...
1967	...	35.0	...	...	...	...	41.8	...	31.7	...	...	...	...	...
1968	...	35.9	...	...	...	...	41.5	...	32.5	...	...	...	...	...
1969	...	36.9	...	...	...	...	42.9	...	33.6	...	...	...	...	...
1970	...	38.2	...	...	...	...	45.6	...	34.8	...	...	...	...	...
1971	...	39.6	...	...	...	...	46.7	...	36.2	...	...	...	...	...
1972	...	40.4	...	...	...	...	49.5	...	37.7	...	...	...	...	...
1973	...	42.0	...	48.1	...	50.4	70.3	...	40.6	...	44.3	...	...	70.8
1974	26.2	48.8	...	53.6	58.7	55.5	83.6	33.1	50.5	56.2	54.0	27.8	78.4	83.3
1975	30.7	54.7	62.4	59.7	63.9	60.6	81.6	38.7	56.6	61.7	60.2	33.3	75.9	69.3
1976	34.3	58.1	64.8	63.1	65.7	63.7	77.4	41.5	60.0	64.7	63.8	35.3	77.6	80.2
1977	39.7	62.2	68.6	66.9	69.4	67.3	79.6	46.8	64.1	68.5	67.6	40.4	78.1	79.8
1978	42.3	66.7	74.0	71.9	74.9	72.2	84.8	49.1	68.6	73.4	72.5	45.2	87.5	87.8
1979	57.1	74.6	80.7	78.3	81.7	78.8	94.5	61.1	77.4	81.7	80.7	54.9	101.5	106.2
1980	85.2	86.7	88.4	87.1	89.3	87.8	105.5	84.9	89.4	91.4	90.3	73.1	106.5	113.1
1981	101.5	95.6	95.4	94.6	95.7	94.6	104.6	100.5	98.2	98.2	97.7	97.7	105.7	111.7
1982	100.0	100.0	100.0	100.0	100.0	100.0	100.0	100.0	100.0	100.0	100.0	100.0	100.0	100.0
1983	95.2	101.8	102.5	103.0	102.4	103.1	103.6	95.3	100.5	101.7	101.6	98.7	102.6	105.3
1984	91.2	103.2	105.5	105.5	105.6	105.7	105.7	95.5	103.0	104.6	104.7	98.0	106.3	111.7
1985	87.6	104.6	107.2	108.1	107.0	108.4	97.3	92.6	103.0	104.7	105.2	93.3	97.0	104.9
1986	63.0	101.9	109.7	110.6	109.7	111.1	96.2	72.6	99.3	104.5	104.9	71.8	95.4	103.1
1987	61.8	104.0	112.3	113.3	112.5	114.2	99.2	73.0	101.7	107.3	107.8	75.0	100.9	115.7
1988	59.8	106.5	115.8	117.0	116.3	118.5	109.5	70.9	106.9	114.6	115.2	67.7	112.6	133.0
1989	65.7	111.8	121.2	122.1	122.1	124.0	113.8	76.1	111.9	119.5	120.2	75.9	117.7	137.9
1990	75.0	117.4	126.0	126.6	127.2	128.8	113.3	85.5	114.5	120.4	120.9	85.9	118.6	136.3
1991	78.1	120.9	129.1	131.1	130.0	133.7	111.1	85.1	114.6	120.8	121.4	80.4	110.9	128.2
1992	77.8	123.1	131.1	134.2	131.8	137.3	110.7	84.3	114.9	121.3	122.0	78.8	110.7	128.4
1993	78.0	124.4	132.9	135.8	133.5	138.5	112.7	84.6	116.4	123.2	123.8	76.7	116.3	140.2
1994	77.0	125.1	134.2	137.1	134.2	139.0	114.8	83.0	118.7	126.3	127.1	72.1	119.3	156.2
1995	78.1	127.5	136.9	140.0	136.9	141.9	114.8	84.1	125.5	134.0	135.2	69.4	123.5	173.6
1996	83.2	130.5	139.6	142.0	140.1	144.3	128.1	89.8	125.6	133.6	134.0	85.0	130.0	155.8
1997	83.4	130.9	140.2	142.4	141.0	145.1	125.4	89.0	125.7	133.7	134.2	87.3	123.5	156.5
1998	75.1	129.5	141.1	143.7	142.5	147.7	116.2	80.8	123.4	132.4	133.5	68.6	113.6	142.1
1999	78.8	132.3	143.0	146.1	145.2	151.7	111.1	84.3	123.9	131.7	133.1	78.5	107.9	135.2
2000	94.1	138.1	144.9	148.0	147.4	154.0	111.7	101.7	130.1	135.0	136.6	122.1	111.7	145.2
2001	96.7	140.4	147.6	150.0	150.8	156.9	115.9	104.1	130.5	135.1	136.4	122.3	112.2	130.7
2002	88.8	138.3	147.3	150.2	150.8	157.6	115.5	95.9	128.5	134.5	135.8	102.0	108.7	135.7
2003	102.0	142.4	149.0	150.5	153.1	157.9	125.9	111.9	134.2	137.7	138.5	147.2	123.4	152.5
2004	113.0	147.2	152.4	152.7	157.2	160.3	137.1	123.2	143.0	145.8	146.5	174.6	144.0	193.0
2005	132.6	155.5	155.9	156.4	160.8	164.3	133.8	149.2	155.1	153.3	154.6	234.0	143.5	202.4
2004														
January	107.8	144.7	150.4	151.4	154.8	159.0	132.9	116.5	136.7	139.8	140.4	163.5	134.4	179.3
February	107.4	144.6	150.4	151.4	154.9	159.1	134.1	116.8	137.8	141.1	141.7	158.9	140.0	188.9
March	107.3	144.9	151.3	151.8	156.0	159.5	137.3	116.4	138.6	142.4	142.8	153.0	147.8	193.5
April	109.5	145.7	152.0	152.0	157.0	159.8	143.2	117.8	140.2	144.3	144.5	158.8	148.5	186.0
May	112.5	146.7	152.7	152.3	157.9	160.0	147.2	121.4	141.9	145.6	145.6	172.1	148.4	177.5
June	111.3	146.7	152.9	152.8	158.0	160.4	144.4	122.4	142.5	145.9	146.1	180.0	146.4	177.2
July	113.7	147.2	152.0	152.5	156.7	160.0	141.5	124.0	143.4	146.4	146.8	177.9	147.0	196.2
August	113.4	147.4	152.3	152.9	156.9	160.3	135.8	126.4	145.1	147.5	148.3	181.9	143.5	200.0
September	112.3	147.3	152.7	153.2	157.4	160.7	134.1	123.5	145.4	148.6	149.5	166.6	141.5	197.8
October	118.8	149.6	153.7	153.7	158.6	161.2	131.8	128.8	147.1	149.0	150.1	181.8	142.0	204.7
November	123.3	151.2	154.1	154.1	159.0	161.7	131.3	133.3	148.5	149.5	150.7	208.3	143.7	208.0
December	119.1	150.3	154.4	154.5	159.3	162.1	131.6	130.6	148.4	150.0	151.2	192.7	145.0	206.4
2005														
January	118.1	150.7	154.9	155.4	159.9	163.3	132.8	130.0	149.1	151.1	152.3	183.9	146.0	203.3
February	120.4	151.3	155.2	155.5	160.3	163.4	132.3	131.5	150.0	151.9	153.1	186.6	142.3	199.1
March	124.0	152.5	155.7	155.7	160.7	163.5	133.6	136.0	151.5	152.5	153.7	199.7	146.2	198.2
April	126.6	153.5	155.9	156.1	160.9	164.0	133.5	140.4	152.5	152.5	153.8	212.6	145.4	202.5
May	124.6	153.3	156.1	156.4	161.0	164.3	134.4	139.1	151.9	152.2	153.4	203.1	142.7	196.7
June	126.5	153.7	155.7	156.3	160.6	164.3	134.3	141.4	152.3	152.1	153.3	202.1	138.7	189.7
July	131.4	155.5	155.8	156.8	160.5	164.8	134.0	147.6	153.9	152.3	153.5	224.0	138.5	190.9
August	135.4	156.6	155.7	156.8	160.4	164.9	133.9	152.1	154.8	152.2	153.4	237.5	139.8	199.6
September	142.7	158.9	156.4	157.1	161.3	165.2	133.8	163.4	158.5	153.7	154.9	278.2	144.4	210.8
October	148.8	160.3	156.1	156.6	160.9	164.5	134.3	177.7	163.3	155.8	157.1	308.6	143.4	207.6
November	144.2	159.1	156.4	156.8	161.5	164.7	134.3	165.5	161.2	156.4	157.8	298.0	145.6	212.6
December	147.7	160.1	156.8	156.8	161.9	164.8	134.7	164.9	161.5	157.0	158.4	274.0	148.9	216.6

[1] Includes crude petroleum.
[2] Excludes crude petroleum.
. . . = Not available.

Table 8-4. Producer Price Indexes and Purchasing Power of the Dollar—Continued

(1982 = 100, except as noted; not seasonally adjusted.)

Year and month	Total	Finished goods					Capital equipment	Intermediate materials, supplies, and components	Crude materials for further processing	Purchasing power of the dollar	
		Finished consumer goods								Producer prices for finished goods (1982–1984 = $1.00)	Consumer prices (CPI-U, 1982–1984 = $1.00)
		Total	Foods	Consumer goods except foods							
				Total	Durable goods	Nondurable goods less foods					
1960	33.4	33.6	35.5	33.5	43.8	28.4	32.8	30.8	30.4	3.047	3.378
1961	33.4	33.6	35.4	33.4	43.6	28.4	32.9	30.6	30.2	3.047	3.344
1962	33.5	33.7	35.7	33.4	43.4	28.4	33.0	30.6	30.5	3.038	3.311
1963	33.4	33.5	35.3	33.4	43.1	28.5	33.1	30.7	29.9	3.047	3.268
1964	33.5	33.6	35.4	33.3	43.3	28.4	33.4	30.8	29.6	3.038	3.226
1965	34.1	34.2	36.8	33.6	43.2	28.8	33.8	31.2	31.1	2.984	3.175
1966	35.2	35.4	39.2	34.1	43.4	29.3	34.6	32.0	33.1	2.891	3.086
1967	35.6	35.6	38.5	34.7	44.1	30.0	35.8	32.2	31.3	2.859	2.994
1968	36.6	36.5	40.0	35.5	45.1	30.6	37.0	33.0	31.8	2.781	2.874
1969	38.0	37.9	42.4	36.3	45.9	31.5	38.3	34.1	33.9	2.678	2.725
1970	39.3	39.1	43.8	37.4	47.2	32.5	40.1	35.4	35.2	2.589	2.577
1971	40.5	40.2	44.5	38.7	48.9	33.5	41.7	36.8	36.0	2.513	2.469
1972	41.8	41.5	46.9	39.4	50.0	34.1	42.8	38.2	39.9	2.435	2.392
1973	45.6	46.0	56.5	41.2	50.9	36.1	44.2	42.4	54.5	2.232	2.252
1974	52.6	53.1	64.4	48.2	55.5	44.0	50.5	52.5	61.4	1.935	2.028
1975	58.2	58.2	69.8	53.2	61.0	48.9	58.2	58.0	61.6	1.749	1.859
1976	60.8	60.4	69.6	56.5	63.7	52.4	62.1	60.9	63.4	1.674	1.757
1977	64.7	64.3	73.3	60.6	67.4	56.8	66.1	64.9	65.5	1.573	1.650
1978	69.8	69.4	79.9	64.9	73.6	60.0	71.3	69.5	73.4	1.458	1.534
1979	77.6	77.5	87.3	73.5	80.8	69.3	77.5	78.4	85.9	1.311	1.377
1980	88.0	88.6	92.4	87.1	91.0	85.1	85.8	90.3	95.3	1.156	1.214
1981	96.1	96.6	97.8	96.1	96.4	95.8	94.6	98.6	103.0	1.059	1.100
1982	100.0	100.0	100.0	100.0	100.0	100.0	100.0	100.0	100.0	1.018	1.036
1983	101.6	101.3	101.0	101.2	102.8	100.5	102.8	100.6	101.3	1.002	1.004
1984	103.7	103.3	105.4	102.2	104.5	101.1	105.2	103.1	103.5	0.981	0.962
1985	104.7	103.8	104.6	103.3	106.5	101.7	107.5	102.7	95.8	0.972	0.929
1986	103.2	101.4	107.3	98.5	108.9	93.3	109.7	99.1	87.7	0.986	0.912
1987	105.4	103.6	109.5	100.7	111.5	94.9	111.7	101.5	93.7	0.966	0.880
1988	108.0	106.2	112.6	103.1	113.8	97.3	114.3	107.1	96.0	0.942	0.845
1989	113.6	112.1	118.7	108.9	117.6	103.8	118.8	112.0	103.1	0.896	0.806
1990	119.2	118.2	124.4	115.3	120.4	111.5	122.9	114.5	108.9	0.854	0.765
1991	121.7	120.5	124.1	118.7	123.9	115.0	126.7	114.4	101.2	0.836	0.734
1992	123.2	121.7	123.3	120.8	125.7	117.3	129.1	114.7	100.4	0.826	0.713
1993	124.7	123.0	125.7	121.7	128.0	117.6	131.4	116.2	102.4	0.816	0.692
1994	125.5	123.3	126.8	121.6	130.9	116.2	134.1	118.5	101.8	0.811	0.675
1995	127.9	125.6	129.0	124.0	132.7	118.8	136.7	124.9	102.7	0.796	0.656
1996	131.3	129.5	133.6	127.6	134.2	123.3	138.3	125.7	113.8	0.775	0.637
1997	131.8	130.2	134.5	128.2	133.7	124.3	138.2	125.6	111.1	0.772	0.623
1998	130.7	128.9	134.3	126.4	132.9	122.2	137.6	123.0	96.8	0.779	0.613
1999	133.0	132.0	135.1	130.5	133.0	127.9	137.6	123.2	98.2	0.765	0.600
2000	138.0	138.2	137.2	138.4	133.9	138.7	138.8	129.2	120.6	0.737	0.581
2001	140.7	141.5	141.3	141.4	134.0	142.8	139.7	129.7	121.0	0.723	0.565
2002	138.9	139.4	140.1	138.8	133.0	139.8	139.1	127.8	108.1	0.733	0.556
2003	143.3	145.3	145.9	144.7	133.1	148.4	139.5	133.7	135.3	0.710	0.543
2004	148.5	151.7	152.7	150.9	135.0	156.6	141.4	142.6	159.0	0.685	0.529
2005	155.7	160.4	155.7	161.9	136.6	172.0	144.6	154.0	182.2	0.654	0.512
2004											
January	145.4	147.8	148.1	147.4	134.3	151.7	140.5	136.2	147.8	0.700	0.540
February	145.3	147.8	148.4	147.3	134.2	151.6	140.2	137.3	150.1	0.700	0.537
March	146.3	149.0	150.7	148.0	134.7	152.4	140.5	138.3	152.9	0.696	0.534
April	147.3	150.4	152.7	149.1	134.4	154.3	140.6	140.2	155.7	0.691	0.532
May	148.9	152.5	155.5	150.9	134.8	156.7	140.8	142.0	161.8	0.683	0.529
June	148.7	152.0	155.0	150.5	134.9	156.0	141.1	142.8	163.0	0.684	0.527
July	148.5	151.9	152.3	151.4	133.6	158.0	140.7	143.5	162.5	0.685	0.528
August	148.5	151.8	152.2	151.3	133.6	157.9	141.2	144.8	162.2	0.685	0.528
September	148.7	152.1	152.7	151.5	133.5	158.2	141.2	145.3	154.4	0.684	0.527
October	152.0	155.7	155.1	155.6	137.8	162.1	143.4	146.5	160.5	0.670	0.524
November	151.7	155.4	154.7	155.3	137.4	161.8	143.4	147.4	171.5	0.671	0.524
December	150.6	153.8	154.9	153.0	137.2	158.5	143.6	146.9	165.7	0.676	0.525
2005											
January	151.4	154.8	154.2	154.6	137.8	160.7	144.1	148.0	163.0	0.672	0.524
February	152.1	155.7	155.4	155.5	137.0	162.4	143.9	148.8	162.5	0.669	0.521
March	153.6	157.6	156.3	157.8	137.0	165.7	144.2	150.4	170.4	0.663	0.517
April	154.4	158.7	156.3	159.2	136.9	167.9	144.5	151.5	175.0	0.659	0.514
May	154.3	158.5	156.7	158.8	136.8	167.4	144.7	151.0	170.6	0.660	0.514
June	154.2	158.6	155.5	159.3	135.6	168.7	144.2	151.7	167.0	0.660	0.514
July	155.5	160.2	154.4	162.1	135.8	172.6	144.4	153.2	175.4	0.654	0.512
August	156.3	161.4	154.0	163.8	135.4	174.4	144.4	153.9	181.8	0.651	0.509
September	158.9	164.9	155.8	168.0	135.5	181.5	144.5	158.0	200.2	0.640	0.503
October	160.9	167.1	155.8	171.2	138.0	184.9	145.9	162.5	211.6	0.632	0.502
November	158.3	163.7	156.3	166.1	137.1	178.0	145.5	159.9	208.5	0.643	0.506
December	158.7	164.2	157.5	166.5	136.6	178.7	145.3	159.6	200.6	0.641	0.508

Table 8-5. Producer Price Indexes by Major Commodity Groups

(1982 = 100, not seasonally adjusted.)

Year and month	All commodities	Farm products	Processed foods and feeds	Industrial commodities													
				Total	Textile products and apparel	Hides, leather, and related products	Fuels and related products and power	Chemicals and related products	Rubber and plastics products	Lumber and wood products	Pulp, paper, and allied products	Metals and metal products	Machinery and metal equipment	Furniture and household durables	Nonmetallic mineral products	Transportation equipment	Miscellaneous products
1947	25.6	45.1	33.0	22.7	50.6	31.7	11.1	32.1	29.2	25.8	25.1	18.2	19.3	37.2	20.7	. . .	26.6
1948	27.7	48.5	35.3	24.6	52.8	32.1	13.1	32.8	30.2	29.5	26.2	20.7	20.9	39.4	22.4	. . .	27.7
1949	26.3	41.9	32.1	24.1	48.3	30.4	12.4	30.0	29.2	27.3	25.1	20.9	21.9	40.1	23.0	. . .	28.2
1950	27.3	44.0	33.2	25.0	50.2	32.9	12.6	30.4	35.6	31.4	25.7	22.0	22.6	40.9	23.5	. . .	28.6
1951	30.4	51.2	36.9	27.6	56.0	37.7	13.0	34.8	43.7	34.1	30.5	24.5	25.3	44.4	25.0	. . .	30.3
1952	29.6	48.4	36.4	26.9	50.5	30.5	13.0	33.0	39.6	33.2	29.7	24.5	25.3	43.5	25.0	. . .	30.2
1953	29.2	43.8	34.8	27.2	49.3	31.0	13.4	33.4	36.9	33.1	29.6	25.3	25.9	44.4	26.0	. . .	31.0
1954	29.3	43.2	35.4	27.2	48.2	29.5	13.2	33.8	37.5	32.5	29.6	25.5	26.3	44.9	26.6	. . .	31.3
1955	29.3	40.5	33.8	27.8	48.2	29.4	13.2	33.7	42.4	34.1	30.4	27.2	27.2	45.1	27.3	. . .	31.3
1956	30.3	40.0	33.8	29.1	48.2	31.2	13.6	33.9	43.0	34.6	32.4	29.6	29.3	46.3	28.5	. . .	31.7
1957	31.2	41.1	34.8	29.9	48.3	31.2	14.3	34.6	42.8	32.8	33.0	30.2	31.4	47.5	29.6	. . .	32.6
1958	31.6	42.9	36.5	30.0	47.4	31.6	13.7	34.9	42.8	32.5	33.4	30.0	32.1	47.9	29.9	. . .	33.3
1959	31.7	40.2	35.6	30.5	48.1	35.9	13.7	34.8	42.6	34.7	33.7	30.6	32.8	48.0	30.3	. . .	33.4
1960	31.7	40.1	35.6	30.5	48.6	34.6	13.9	34.8	42.7	33.5	34.0	30.6	33.0	47.8	30.4	. . .	33.6
1961	31.6	39.7	36.2	30.4	47.8	34.9	14.0	34.5	41.1	32.0	33.0	30.5	33.0	47.5	30.5	. . .	33.7
1962	31.7	40.4	36.5	30.4	48.2	35.3	14.0	33.9	39.9	32.2	33.4	30.2	33.0	47.2	30.5	. . .	33.9
1963	31.6	39.6	36.8	30.3	48.2	34.3	13.9	33.5	40.1	32.8	33.1	30.3	33.1	46.9	30.3	. . .	34.2
1964	31.6	39.0	36.7	30.5	48.5	34.4	13.5	33.6	39.6	33.5	33.0	31.1	33.3	47.1	30.4	. . .	34.4
1965	32.3	40.7	38.0	30.9	48.8	35.9	13.8	33.9	39.7	33.7	33.3	32.0	33.7	46.8	30.4	. . .	34.7
1966	33.3	43.7	40.2	31.5	48.9	39.4	14.1	34.0	40.5	35.2	34.2	32.8	34.7	47.4	30.7	. . .	35.3
1967	33.4	41.3	39.8	32.0	48.9	38.1	14.4	34.2	41.4	35.1	34.6	33.2	35.9	48.3	31.2	. . .	36.2
1968	34.2	42.3	40.6	32.8	50.7	39.3	14.3	34.1	42.8	39.8	35.0	34.0	37.0	49.7	32.4	. . .	37.0
1969	35.6	45.0	42.7	33.9	51.8	41.5	14.6	34.2	43.6	44.0	36.0	36.0	38.2	50.7	33.6	40.4	38.1
1970	36.9	45.8	44.6	35.2	52.4	42.0	15.3	35.0	44.9	39.9	37.5	38.7	40.0	51.9	35.3	41.9	39.8
1971	38.1	46.6	45.5	36.5	53.3	43.4	16.6	35.6	45.2	44.7	38.1	39.4	41.4	53.1	38.2	44.2	40.8
1972	39.8	51.6	48.0	37.8	55.5	50.0	17.1	35.6	45.3	50.7	39.3	40.9	42.3	53.8	39.4	45.5	41.5
1973	45.0	72.7	58.9	40.3	60.5	54.5	19.4	37.6	46.6	62.2	42.3	44.0	43.7	55.7	40.7	46.1	43.3
1974	53.5	77.4	68.0	49.2	68.0	55.2	30.1	50.2	56.4	64.5	52.5	57.0	50.0	61.8	47.8	50.3	48.1
1975	58.4	77.0	72.6	54.9	67.4	56.5	35.4	62.0	62.2	62.1	59.0	61.5	57.9	67.5	54.4	56.7	53.4
1976	61.1	78.8	70.8	58.4	72.4	63.9	38.3	64.0	66.0	72.2	62.1	65.0	61.3	70.3	58.2	60.5	55.6
1977	64.9	79.4	74.0	62.5	75.3	68.3	43.6	65.9	69.4	83.0	64.6	69.3	65.2	73.2	62.6	64.6	59.4
1978	69.9	87.7	80.6	67.0	78.1	76.1	46.5	68.0	72.4	96.9	67.7	75.3	70.3	77.5	69.6	69.5	66.7
1979	78.7	99.6	88.5	75.7	82.5	96.1	58.9	76.0	80.5	105.5	75.9	86.0	76.7	82.8	77.6	75.3	75.5
1980	89.8	102.9	95.9	88.0	89.7	94.7	82.8	89.0	90.1	101.5	86.3	95.0	86.0	90.7	88.4	82.9	93.6
1981	98.0	105.2	98.9	97.4	97.6	99.3	100.2	98.4	96.4	102.8	94.8	99.6	94.4	95.9	96.7	94.3	96.1
1982	100.0	100.0	100.0	100.0	100.0	100.0	100.0	100.0	100.0	100.0	100.0	100.0	100.0	100.0	100.0	100.0	100.0
1983	101.3	102.4	101.8	101.1	100.3	103.2	95.9	100.3	100.8	107.9	103.3	101.8	102.7	103.4	101.6	102.8	104.8
1984	103.7	105.5	105.4	103.3	102.7	109.0	94.8	102.9	102.3	108.0	110.3	104.8	105.1	105.7	105.4	105.2	107.0
1985	103.2	95.1	103.5	103.7	102.9	108.9	91.4	103.7	101.9	106.6	113.3	104.4	107.2	107.1	108.6	107.9	109.4
1986	100.2	92.9	105.4	100.0	103.2	113.0	69.8	102.6	101.9	107.2	116.1	103.2	108.8	108.2	110.0	110.5	111.6
1987	102.8	95.5	107.9	102.6	105.1	120.4	70.2	106.4	103.0	112.8	121.8	107.1	110.4	109.9	110.0	112.5	114.9
1988	106.9	104.9	112.7	106.3	109.2	131.4	66.7	116.3	109.3	118.9	130.4	118.7	113.2	113.1	111.2	114.3	120.2
1989	112.2	110.9	117.8	111.6	112.3	136.3	72.9	123.0	112.6	126.7	137.8	124.1	117.4	116.9	112.6	117.7	126.5
1990	116.3	112.2	121.9	115.8	115.0	141.7	82.3	123.6	113.6	129.7	141.2	122.9	120.7	119.2	114.7	121.5	134.2
1991	116.5	105.7	121.9	116.5	116.3	138.9	81.2	125.6	115.1	132.1	142.9	120.2	123.0	121.2	117.2	126.4	140.8
1992	117.2	103.6	122.1	117.4	117.8	140.4	80.4	125.9	115.1	146.6	145.2	119.2	123.4	122.2	117.3	130.4	145.3
1993	118.9	107.1	124.0	119.0	118.0	143.7	80.0	128.2	116.0	174.0	147.3	119.2	124.0	123.7	120.0	133.7	145.4
1994	120.4	106.3	125.5	120.7	118.3	148.5	77.8	132.1	117.6	180.0	152.5	124.8	125.1	126.1	124.2	137.2	141.9
1995	124.7	107.4	127.0	125.5	120.8	153.7	78.0	142.5	124.3	178.1	172.2	134.5	126.6	128.2	129.0	139.7	145.4
1996	127.7	122.4	133.3	127.3	122.4	150.5	85.8	142.1	123.8	176.1	168.7	131.0	126.5	130.4	131.0	141.7	147.7
1997	127.6	112.9	134.0	127.7	122.6	154.2	86.1	143.6	123.2	183.8	167.9	131.8	125.9	130.8	133.2	141.6	150.9
1998	124.4	104.6	131.6	124.8	122.9	148.0	75.3	143.9	122.6	179.1	171.7	127.8	124.9	131.3	135.4	141.2	156.0
1999	125.5	98.4	131.1	126.5	121.1	146.0	80.5	144.2	122.5	183.6	174.1	124.6	124.3	131.7	138.9	141.8	166.6
2000	132.7	99.5	133.1	134.8	121.4	151.5	103.5	151.0	125.5	178.2	183.7	128.1	124.0	132.6	142.5	143.8	170.8
2001	134.2	103.8	137.3	135.7	121.3	158.4	105.3	151.8	127.2	174.4	184.8	125.4	123.7	133.2	144.3	145.2	181.3
2002	131.1	99.0	136.2	132.4	119.9	157.6	93.2	151.9	126.8	173.3	185.9	125.9	122.9	133.5	146.2	144.6	182.4
2003	138.1	111.5	143.4	139.1	119.8	162.3	112.9	161.8	130.1	177.4	190.0	129.2	121.9	133.9	148.2	145.7	179.6
2004	146.7	123.3	151.2	147.6	121.0	164.5	126.9	174.4	133.8	195.6	195.7	149.6	122.1	135.1	153.2	148.6	183.2
2005	157.4	118.5	153.1	160.2	122.8	165.4	156.4	192.0	143.8	196.5	202.6	160.8	123.7	139.4	164.2	151.0	195.1
2005																	
January	150.9	118.8	151.8	152.7	122.1	165.3	132.3	185.5	139.7	194.6	200.8	160.1	123.1	137.5	159.2	151.9	189.5
February	151.6	117.6	152.3	153.6	122.1	165.5	134.2	186.4	140.6	198.2	201.5	160.5	123.3	138.2	160.3	151.0	191.5
March	153.7	123.0	153.4	155.6	122.3	165.6	140.9	188.9	141.2	198.6	202.1	160.4	123.5	138.6	160.8	151.0	192.2
April	155.0	120.7	153.3	157.2	122.5	164.8	146.5	189.0	141.7	198.3	202.1	161.1	123.7	138.7	162.1	151.0	192.8
May	154.3	121.5	154.3	156.3	122.6	164.8	143.7	188.4	141.9	195.2	202.2	159.4	123.7	139.2	162.7	151.0	193.4
June	154.3	118.3	153.2	156.6	122.8	165.7	146.0	187.2	142.4	197.6	202.6	157.6	123.7	139.3	163.1	149.7	194.4
July	156.3	116.3	153.0	159.1	122.7	165.8	154.8	189.3	142.4	196.0	202.6	157.4	123.8	139.8	164.8	150.1	195.3
August	157.6	114.5	152.7	160.8	122.8	165.6	160.7	189.9	142.4	194.1	202.3	158.4	123.9	139.6	165.4	150.0	196.1
September	162.2	116.8	153.1	166.0	123.3	165.3	177.6	194.9	143.7	197.4	202.9	161.1	123.8	139.6	166.5	150.2	196.8
October	166.2	115.7	153.9	170.6	123.3	165.3	190.7	202.3	146.8	198.0	203.5	161.9	123.9	140.0	167.4	152.9	198.0
November	163.7	117.5	153.2	167.6	123.4	165.4	177.4	201.4	151.0	194.1	203.8	165.0	123.8	140.8	169.1	151.8	200.3
December	163.0	121.1	153.5	166.5	123.4	165.0	172.1	201.3	151.9	195.2	204.3	166.7	123.7	141.1	169.5	151.2	200.9

. . . = Not available.

Table 8-6. Producer Price Indexes for the Net Output of Selected NAICS Industry Groups

(Various index bases, not seasonally adjusted.)

Year and month	Mining		Manufacturing (Dec. 1984 = 100)									
	Total (Dec. 1984 = 100)	Oil and gas extraction (Dec. 1985 = 100)	Total	Food manu-facturing	Leather and products	Petroleum and coal products	Chemicals	Plastics and rubber products	Nonmetallic mineral products	Primary metals	Fabricated metal products	Furniture and related products
1985	. . .	76.9	. . .	99.0	101.3	. . .	100.7	100.0	102.1	99.4	100.6	101.9
1986	77.0	76.9	98.4	100.3	103.0	66.6	100.5	100.3	103.8	97.0	101.0	103.9
1987	75.0	74.3	100.9	102.6	106.6	70.5	103.6	100.9	104.5	101.0	102.1	106.4
1988	70.6	68.5	104.4	107.1	113.4	67.7	113.0	106.7	105.8	113.0	107.4	111.4
1989	76.4	75.7	109.6	112.2	118.0	75.7	119.6	110.2	107.9	118.8	112.6	115.6
1990	81.8	82.7	114.5	116.2	122.6	91.4	121.0	111.3	110.0	116.5	115.1	119.1
1991	78.4	77.9	115.9	116.5	124.8	83.1	124.4	113.7	112.3	113.1	116.6	121.6
1992	76.9	76.5	117.4	116.9	127.0	80.3	125.8	114.2	112.8	111.7	117.2	122.9
1993	76.4	76.2	119.1	118.7	129.0	77.6	127.2	115.4	115.4	111.4	118.2	125.4
1994	73.3	71.1	120.7	120.1	130.6	74.8	130.0	117.1	119.6	117.0	120.3	129.7
1995	71.0	66.6	124.2	121.7	134.1	77.2	143.4	123.3	124.3	128.2	124.8	133.3
1996	84.4	84.8	127.1	127.1	134.7	87.4	145.8	123.1	125.8	123.7	126.2	136.2
1997	86.1	87.5	127.5	127.9	137.1	85.6	147.1	122.8	127.4	124.7	127.6	138.2
1998	70.8	68.3	126.2	126.3	137.1	66.3	148.7	122.1	129.3	120.9	128.7	139.7
1999	78.0	78.5	128.3	126.3	136.5	76.8	149.7	122.2	132.6	115.8	129.1	141.3
2000	113.5	126.8	133.5	128.5	137.9	112.8	156.7	124.6	134.7	119.8	130.3	143.3
2001	114.3	127.5	134.6	132.8	141.3	105.3	158.4	125.9	136.0	116.1	131.0	145.1
2002	96.6	107.0	133.7	132.0	141.1	98.8	157.3	125.5	137.1	116.2	131.7	146.3
2003	131.3	160.1	137.1	137.4	142.8	122.0	164.6	128.4	138.0	118.4	132.9	147.4
2004	153.4	192.7	142.9	144.3	143.6	149.9	172.8	131.7	142.7	142.8	141.3	151.5
2005	201.0	262.0	150.8	146.1	144.5	200.4	187.3	141.2	152.0	156.3	149.5	157.8
2005												
January	163.3	202.5	146.2	144.7	143.8	155.9	182.7	137.4	148.1	158.6	146.9	155.5
February	166.2	205.8	147.0	145.0	144.2	163.6	183.4	138.4	149.0	159.5	148.2	156.2
March	176.0	221.3	148.9	146.0	144.3	182.8	184.7	138.9	149.7	158.5	148.6	156.2
April	184.3	236.4	149.6	146.3	144.3	189.6	185.9	139.4	150.2	157.9	149.1	156.7
May	177.9	224.0	149.4	147.1	144.4	184.0	185.8	139.7	150.6	156.1	149.3	157.5
June	178.1	222.2	149.6	146.4	144.5	189.7	185.3	140.1	151.2	153.6	149.5	157.8
July	193.4	248.4	151.0	146.3	144.8	204.7	186.3	140.3	152.4	152.5	149.7	158.4
August	203.6	265.5	151.8	146.0	144.6	215.6	186.4	140.2	153.0	150.5	149.9	158.3
September	233.1	316.9	154.2	146.3	144.6	241.5	187.7	141.4	153.7	152.4	150.1	158.7
October	254.3	352.8	156.6	146.7	144.7	259.5	191.2	143.7	154.3	155.8	150.5	159.2
November	247.4	336.6	152.7	146.1	144.8	208.2	193.6	147.2	155.7	159.2	150.7	159.4
December	234.6	312.2	152.8	146.2	144.7	209.2	193.9	148.2	156.3	160.7	151.1	160.0

Year and month	Transportation and warehousing					Health care and social assistance			Other services industries (Dec. 1996 = 100)			
	Air transpor-tation (Dec. 1992 = 100)	Rail transpor-tation (Dec. 1996 = 100)	Pipeline transportation (June 1986 = 100)		Postal service (June 1989 = 100)	Offices of physicians (Dec. 1996 = 100)	Home health care (Dec. 1996 = 100)	Hospitals (Dec. 1992 = 100)	Legal services	Architec-tural, engineering, and related services	Employment services	Accom-modation
			Crude oil	Refined petroleum products								
1985	. . .	. . .	. . .	. . .	85.3	. . .	. . .	. . .	. . .	. . .	. . .	. . .
1986	. . .	. . .	. . .	. . .	86.5	. . .	. . .	. . .	. . .	. . .	. . .	. . .
1987	. . .	. . .	96.9	101.0	86.5	. . .	. . .	. . .	. . .	. . .	. . .	. . .
1988	. . .	. . .	92.7	100.9	96.6	. . .	. . .	. . .	. . .	. . .	. . .	. . .
1989	. . .	. . .	92.3	100.5	100.0	. . .	. . .	. . .	. . .	. . .	. . .	. . .
1990	. . .	. . .	94.2	100.8	100.0	. . .	. . .	. . .	. . .	. . .	. . .	. . .
1991	. . .	. . .	94.4	101.1	117.9	. . .	. . .	. . .	. . .	. . .	. . .	. . .
1992	. . .	. . .	94.8	101.2	119.8	. . .	. . .	. . .	. . .	. . .	. . .	. . .
1993	105.6	. . .	95.0	101.3	119.8	. . .	. . .	102.5	. . .	. . .	. . .	. . .
1994	108.5	. . .	102.5	103.4	119.8	. . .	. . .	106.2	. . .	. . .	. . .	. . .
1995	113.7	. . .	113.4	104.6	132.2	. . .	. . .	110.0	. . .	. . .	. . .	. . .
1996	121.1	. . .	104.7	104.3	132.3	. . .	. . .	112.6	. . .	. . .	. . .	. . .
1997	125.3	100.5	96.0	105.3	132.3	101.0	103.3	113.6	102.5	102.2	101.0	104.2
1998	124.5	101.7	96.8	104.8	132.3	103.2	106.2	114.4	106.1	105.1	103.2	108.1
1999	130.8	101.3	95.5	104.9	135.3	105.5	107.1	116.4	108.7	108.5	105.2	112.7
2000	147.7	102.6	101.0	105.3	135.2	107.3	111.1	119.4	112.5	111.8	107.3	116.2
2001	157.2	104.5	111.1	108.5	143.4	110.4	114.0	123.0	117.9	115.9	108.2	121.3
2002	157.8	106.6	112.3	111.0	150.2	110.3	116.6	127.5	121.7	121.1	108.9	121.3
2003	162.1	108.8	111.1	112.7	155.0	112.1	117.0	134.9	125.6	124.3	111.4	122.0
2004	162.3	113.4	115.2	116.0	155.0	114.3	119.8	141.5	131.8	126.8	113.9	125.2
2005	171.0	125.2	125.5	120.3	155.0	116.4	121.1	146.9	138.5	129.2	116.3	131.9
2005												
January	164.9	118.3	123.3	118.0	155.0	115.7	120.9	144.8	136.8	128.2	115.1	125.7
February	164.5	118.4	123.2	118.5	155.0	115.9	121.0	145.6	137.1	128.6	115.7	129.1
March	169.5	119.9	123.0	119.0	155.0	116.3	120.9	145.6	137.2	128.5	115.4	130.7
April	168.8	121.1	123.2	118.7	155.0	116.3	120.8	145.6	137.6	128.4	115.8	130.7
May	168.2	124.3	123.2	119.7	155.0	116.3	120.9	145.7	138.3	128.6	115.9	131.5
June	172.6	124.8	123.2	119.8	155.0	116.5	120.8	145.8	138.3	128.9	115.6	132.9
July	175.2	124.9	127.9	121.7	155.0	116.6	120.9	146.4	138.8	129.3	116.2	134.4
August	172.8	126.2	127.9	121.7	155.0	116.5	120.9	146.6	138.8	129.3	116.5	135.1
September	170.2	127.8	127.9	121.7	155.0	116.6	121.0	147.2	139.2	129.8	116.4	134.9
October	173.7	130.6	127.9	121.7	155.0	116.7	121.6	149.5	139.6	130.0	117.3	133.1
November	178.9	133.0	127.9	121.7	155.0	116.7	121.7	149.9	139.9	130.4	117.7	133.1
December	173.2	133.1	127.9	121.7	155.0	116.7	121.2	149.9	140.0	130.6	118.4	131.7

. . . = Not available.

Table 8-7. Prices Received and Paid by Farmers

(1990–1992 = 100, not seasonally adjusted.)

| Year and month | All farm products | Prices received by farmers — Crops | | | | | | | | | Livestock and products | | | | Food commodities | Prices paid by farmers [1] | | Ratio of prices received to prices paid |
		Total	Food grains	Feed grains and hay	Cotton	Tobacco	Oil-bearing crops	Fruit and nuts	Commercial vegetables	Potatoes and dry beans	Total	Meat animals	Dairy products	Poultry and eggs		All items	Production items	
1975	73	88	128	112	68	56	93	46	66	78	62	56	67	83	69	47	55	158
1976	75	87	105	105	99	63	97	45	67	75	64	57	74	83	71	50	59	150
1977	73	83	83	87	100	66	119	54	70	71	64	56	74	81	71	53	61	138
1978	83	89	102	88	91	72	110	72	74	73	78	75	81	87	83	58	67	144
1979	94	98	121	100	96	75	121	77	79	65	90	90	92	90	95	66	76	144
1980	98	107	136	115	114	80	118	73	80	93	89	84	100	91	96	75	85	131
1981	100	111	138	122	111	94	122	76	99	126	89	82	105	94	97	82	92	121
1982	94	98	119	103	92	99	103	78	92	88	90	86	104	89	93	86	94	109
1983	98	108	120	125	104	96	118	71	96	89	88	81	104	95	95	86	92	113
1984	101	111	117	127	108	98	125	85	97	111	91	83	103	109	98	89	94	114
1985	91	98	108	105	93	92	96	84	95	87	86	78	97	97	89	86	91	106
1986	87	87	89	84	91	82	89	83	92	81	88	80	96	105	87	85	86	103
1987	89	86	83	72	98	83	90	93	105	89	91	90	96	87	91	87	87	102
1988	99	104	113	102	95	86	126	96	104	88	93	91	93	98	99	91	90	108
1989	104	109	127	109	98	96	118	99	103	131	100	94	104	111	104	96	95	108
1990	104	103	100	105	107	97	105	97	102	133	105	105	105	105	104	99	99	105
1991	100	101	94	101	108	102	99	112	100	99	99	101	94	99	99	100	100	99
1992	98	101	113	98	88	101	100	99	111	88	97	96	100	97	99	101	101	97
1993	101	102	105	99	89	101	108	93	117	107	100	100	98	105	102	104	104	97
1994	100	105	119	106	109	102	110	90	109	110	95	90	99	106	98	106	106	94
1995	102	112	134	112	127	103	104	97	121	107	92	85	98	107	99	109	108	93
1996	112	127	157	146	122	105	128	118	111	114	99	87	114	120	108	115	115	98
1997	107	115	128	117	112	104	131	110	118	90	98	92	102	113	105	118	119	90
1998	102	107	103	100	107	104	107	112	123	99	97	79	119	117	101	115	113	89
1999	96	97	91	86	85	102	83	115	110	100	95	83	110	110	96	115	111	83
2000	96	96	85	86	82	107	85	98	121	93	97	94	94	106	97	120	116	80
2001	102	99	91	91	64	107	80	109	133	98	106	97	115	115	104	123	120	83
2002	98	105	104	100	56	108	88	105	137	129	90	87	93	94	97	124	119	79
2003	107	111	108	104	85	107	107	106	138	104	103	103	96	111	107	128	124	84
2004	119	117	120	109	91	94	134	120	137	102	122	116	123	132	122	134	131	89
2005	116	112	111	95	70	91	105	133	134	115	120	120	116	124	120	141	140	82
2003																		
January	99	103	117	105	75	120	99	79	112	105	96	93	90	108	97	126	122	79
February	99	103	106	106	77	119	100	79	113	110	95	95	87	104	96	127	123	78
March	99	106	102	106	80	104	101	87	123	112	93	93	84	104	96	128	124	77
April	100	109	99	107	75	70	104	95	129	117	93	96	84	99	98	128	124	78
May	105	115	102	109	76	. . .	109	107	138	117	96	100	84	103	104	127	123	83
June	107	117	102	110	75	. . .	109	116	152	110	99	101	84	109	106	127	123	84
July	105	109	98	102	76	103	104	121	119	113	101	101	93	109	104	127	123	83
August	109	113	110	102	76	104	101	125	138	96	105	104	102	112	110	127	123	86
September	111	111	111	101	92	108	97	126	144	90	110	108	111	115	112	128	125	87
October	113	111	113	96	112	109	111	127	143	87	116	115	115	118	116	129	126	88
November	116	116	119	99	104	114	121	121	156	95	117	116	110	124	120	129	126	90
December	115	117	124	103	104	115	127	100	175	97	112	110	106	121	117	129	126	89
2004																		
January	112	113	124	105	103	120	131	96	126	96	110	104	101	133	113	130	127	86
February	116	121	124	113	102	125	147	110	144	100	112	104	104	139	117	131	127	89
March	122	122	127	118	102	121	165	114	115	105	122	112	119	147	124	132	129	92
April	125	123	129	124	100	38	171	100	131	112	126	113	139	139	127	133	131	94
May	128	123	128	127	99	. . .	170	121	112	110	133	121	148	141	131	135	133	95
June	128	122	121	123	99	. . .	161	127	111	110	133	123	139	146	130	135	133	95
July	124	120	115	113	89	. . .	151	127	124	109	128	121	123	144	127	135	133	92
August	120	118	112	109	80	. . .	121	134	133	96	122	121	114	130	123	134	133	90
September	116	113	114	101	83	109	95	146	134	97	118	119	119	117	119	134	133	87
October	114	111	114	96	83	110	97	158	159	89	118	118	119	114	117	135	134	84
November	115	111	114	93	71	114	97	142	166	96	119	118	124	118	121	135	133	85
December	111	104	113	93	65	115	100	113	121	101	120	117	126	118	116	134	131	83
2005																		
January	111	102	114	95	64	123	100	114	95	105	121	121	123	122	116	137	134	81
February	114	107	109	91	63	127	99	126	121	106	119	119	118	120	118	137	134	83
March	119	116	111	95	67	84	107	119	164	114	121	122	119	122	123	139	136	86
April	121	120	109	96	68	84	108	105	183	112	122	125	116	121	125	140	138	86
May	119	116	109	99	65	. . .	111	119	134	122	121	125	113	122	122	140	138	85
June	119	120	108	103	69	. . .	119	143	140	133	117	119	110	123	121	141	140	84
July	117	116	107	105	68	. . .	119	142	114	147	117	115	113	126	119	141	140	83
August	116	115	108	100	69	. . .	109	146	119	117	117	116	113	125	120	141	141	82
September	116	111	111	94	73	. . .	93	153	132	104	122	119	117	134	121	143	142	81
October	111	103	112	85	80	. . .	97	152	114	96	122	121	119	125	116	145	145	77
November	113	105	115	83	80	. . .	98	152	118	106	121	120	116	127	120	143	143	79
December	115	110	117	90	79	. . .	102	121	169	115	120	121	113	123	122	144	143	80

[1] Includes commodities, services, interest, taxes, and wage rates.

. . . = Not available.

NOTES AND DEFINITIONS

TABLES 8-1 THROUGH 8-3 AND 20-2
CONSUMER PRICE INDEXES

SOURCES: U.S. DEPARTMENT OF LABOR, BUREAU OF LABOR STATISTICS (BLS) AND U.S. DEPARTMENT OF COMMERCE, BUREAU OF ECONOMIC ANALYSIS (BEA)

The Consumer Price Index (CPI), compiled by the Bureau of Labor Statistics (BLS), was originally conceived and compiled as a statistical measure of the average change in the cost to consumers of a market basket of goods and services purchased by urban wage earners and clerical workers. In 1978, its scope was broadened to also provide a measure of the change in cost of the average market basket for all urban consumers. There was still a demand for a wage-earner index, so both versions are calculated and published. The most commonly cited index is the Consumer Price Index for All Urban Consumers (CPI-U). The wage-earner alternative, used for calculating cost of living adjustments in many government programs (notably Social Security) and wage contracts, is called the Consumer Price Index for Urban Wage Earners and Clerical Workers (CPI-W). Both are presented by BLS back to 1919; however, the movements in the two indexes before 1978 are identical and are based on the wage-earner market basket.

These CPIs have typically been called "cost-of-living" indexes, even though the original fixed market basket concept does not correspond to economists' definition of a cost-of-living index. In recent years, the concept measured in practice in the CPI has developed into something a little closer to the theoretical definition of a cost-of-living index—that is, the cost of maintaining a constant standard of living or level of satisfaction rather than the cost of a fixed market basket. In addition, a new variation of the CPI—the Chained Consumer Price Index for All Urban Consumers (C-CPI-U)—provides a still closer approximation of a cost-of-living index.

The reference base for the total BLS index and most of its components is currently 1982–1984 = 100; however, new products that have been introduced into the index since January 1982 are shown on later reference bases, as is the entire C-CPI-U.

Price indexes for personal consumption expenditures (PCE) are calculated and published by the Bureau of Economic Analysis (BEA) as a part of the national income and product accounts (NIPAs). (See Chapters 1 and 4 and their notes and definitions.) The reference base for these indexes is the average in the NIPA base year, 2000. These indexes differ in a number of other respects from the CPIs, and are often emphasized by the Federal Reserve in its analyses of the nation's economy. They are also available monthly and are shown in Tables 8-2 and 8-3 for convenient comparison with the CPIs. See the definitions below for those tables below for further explanation.

The CPI-U and the CPI-W

All of the BLS consumer price indexes in Table 8-1 are components of the *CPI-U*. This index uses the consumption patterns for all urban consumers, who comprised about 87 percent of the noninstitutional population in the 1993–1995 period. Beginning with January 2006, the weights are based on consumer expenditures in the 2003–2004 period. From January 2004 to December 2005, the weights represented expenditures in the 2001–2002 period. From January 2002 to December 2003, the weights represented consumer expenditures in the 1999–2000 period. Between January 1998 and December 2001, weights from the 1993–1995 period were used. The weights will continue to be updated at two-year intervals. Previously, new weights were introduced only at the time of a major revision, which translated into a lag of a decade or more. See the notes on the CPI data, below, for further detail on the weights used in the periods before 1998.

A slightly different index that is widely used for adjusting wages and government benefits is the *CPI-W*, shown in Tables 8-2 and 8-3. It represents the buying habits of only urban wage earners and clerical workers—about 32 percent of the noninstitutional population in the 1993–1995 period. The weights are derived from the same Consumer Expenditure Surveys (CES) used for the CPI-U weights, and are changed on the same schedule, but include only consumers from the specified categories instead of all urban consumers.

The CPI was overhauled and updated in the latest major revision, which took effect in January 1998. In addition, new products and improved methods are regularly introduced into the index (usually in January).

The latest change in methods was the introduction of a geometric mean formula for calculating many of the basic components of the index. Beginning with the index for January 1999, this formula is used for categories comprising approximately 61 percent of total consumer spending. The new formula allows for the possibility that some consumers may react to changing relative prices within a category by substituting items whose relative prices have declined for products whose relative prices have risen, while maintaining their overall level of satisfaction. The geometric mean formula is not used for categories in which consumer substitution in the short term is not feasible.

The CPI-U was introduced in 1978. Before that time, only CPI-W data were available. The movements of the CPI-U before 1978 are therefore based on the changes in the CPI-W. The index levels are different, however, because the two indexes differed in the 1982–1984 base period.

Because the official CPI-U and CPI-W are so widely used in "escalation"—the calculation of cost-of-living adjustments for wages and for government payments and tax parameters—these price indexes are not retrospectively revised to incorporate new information and methods. (An exception is occasionally made for outright error, which happened in September 2000 and affected the data for January through August of that year.) Instead, the new information and methods of calculation are introduced in the current index and affect future index changes only. In Tables 8-2 and 8-3, special CPI and PCE indexes that are subject to retrospective revision are presented. These indexes can be used to provide more consistent historical information.

Notes on the CPI data

The CPI is based on prices of food, clothing, shelter, fuel, utilities, transportation, medical care, and other goods and services that people buy for day to day living. The quantity and quality of these items are kept essentially constant between revisions to ensure that only price changes will be measured. All taxes directly associated with the purchase and use of items, such as sales and property taxes, are included in the index; the effects of income and payroll tax changes are not included.

Data are collected from about 23,000 retail establishments and about 50,000 housing units in 87 urban areas across the country. These data are used to develop the U.S. city average.

Periodic major revisions of the indexes, in addition to revising the content and weights of the market basket of goods and services, update the statistical sample of urban areas, outlets, and unique items used in calculating the CPI and improve the statistical methods used. In addition, retail outlets and items are resampled on a rotating 5-year basis. Adjustments for changing quality are made at times of major product changes, such as the annual auto model changeover. Other methodological changes are introduced from time to time.

The CPI weights for 1964 through 1977 were derived from reported expenditures of a sample of wage earner and clerical worker families and individuals in 1960–1961 and adjusted for price changes between the survey dates and 1963. Weights for the 1978–1986 period were derived from a Consumer Expenditure Survey (CES) undertaken during the 1972–1974 period and adjusted for price change between the survey dates and December 1977. For 1987 through 1997, the spending patterns reflected in the CPI were derived from a CES undertaken during the 1982–1984 period. The reported expenditures were adjusted for price change between the survey dates and December 1986.

The CES is composed of two separate surveys: an interview survey and a diary survey, both of which are conducted by the Census Bureau for BLS. Each expenditure reported in the two surveys is coded to detailed categories, which are then combined into expenditure classes and ultimately into major expenditure groups. CPI data as of 1998 are grouped into eight such groups: (1) food and bever-

ages, (2) housing, (3) apparel, (4) transportation, (5) medical care, (6) recreation, (7) education and communication, and (8) other goods and services.

Seasonally adjusted national CPI indexes are published for selected series for which there is a significant seasonal pattern of price change. The factors currently in use were derived by the X-12-ARIMA seasonal adjustment method. Some series with extreme or sharp movements are seasonally adjusted using the X-12-ARIMA Intervention Analysis Seasonal Adjustment. Seasonally adjusted indexes and seasonal factors for the preceding five years are updated annually based on data through the previous December. Due to these revisions, BLS advises against the use of seasonally adjusted data for escalation. Detailed descriptions of seasonal adjustment procedures are available upon request from BLS.

CPI Definitions

Definitions of the major CPI groupings were modified beginning with the data for January 1998. These modifications were carried back to 1993. The definitions below are the current definitions currently used for the CPI components.

The *food and beverage index* includes both food at home and food away from home (restaurant meals and other food bought and eaten away from home).

The *housing index* measures changes in rental costs and expenses connected with the acquisition and operation of a home. The CPI-U, beginning with data for January 1983, and the CPI-W, beginning with data for January 1985, reflect a change in the methodology used to compute the homeownership component. A rental equivalence measure replaced an asset price approach. The central purpose of the change was to separate shelter costs from the investment component of homeownership, so that the index would only reflect the cost of shelter services provided by owner-occupied homes. In addition to these measures of the cost of shelter, the housing category includes insurance, fuel, utilities, and household furnishings and operations.

The *apparel index* includes the purchase of apparel and footwear.

The *private transportation index* includes prices paid by urban consumers for such items as new and used automobiles and other vehicles, gasoline, motor oil, tires, repairs and maintenance, insurance, registration fees, driver's licenses, parking fees, and the like. Auto finance charges, like mortgage interest payments, are considered to be a cost of asset acquisition, not of current consumption. Therefore, they are no longer included in the CPI. City bus, streetcar, subway, taxicab, intercity bus, airplane, and railroad coach fares are some of the components of the *public transportation index*.

The *medical care index* includes prices for professional medical services, hospital and related services, prescription and nonprescription drugs, and other medical care commodities. The portion of health insurance premiums used to cover the costs of these medical goods and services is distributed among the items; the portion of health insurance costs attributable to administrative expenses and profits of insurance providers constitutes a separate health insurance item. Effective with the January 1997 data, the method of calculating the hospital cost component was changed from the pricing of individual commodities and services to a more comprehensive cost-of-treatment approach.

Recreation includes components formerly listed in housing, apparel, entertainment, and "other goods and services."

Education and communication is a new group including components formerly categorized in housing and "other goods and services," such as telephone services and computers.

Other goods and services now includes tobacco, personal care, and miscellaneous.

Alternative price measures in Tables 8-2 and 8-3

Table 8-2 shows the all-items CPI-U and CPI-W, along with a number of other indexes that various analysts of price trends have preferred as measures of the price level. Table 8-3 shows the inflation rates (percent changes in price levels) implied by each of the indexes in Table 8-2.

As food and energy prices are volatile and frequently determined by forces separate from monetary aggregate demand pressures, many analysts prefer an index of prices excluding those components. Indexes *excluding food and energy* are known as *core* indexes, and inflation rates calculated from them are known as *core inflation rates*.

The *CPI-U-X1* is a special experimental version of the CPI that many researchers have used to provide a more historically consistent series. As explained above, the official CPI-U treated homeownership on an asset price basis until January 1983. It then changed to a rental equivalence method. The CPI-U-X1 also incorporates a rental equivalence approach to homeowners' costs for the years 1967–1982. It is rebased to the December 1982 value of the CPI-U (1982–1984 = 100); thus, it is identical to the CPI-U in December 1982 and all subsequent periods. For this reason, it is not updated or published in the CPI news release or on the BLS Web site.

The CPI-U-RS is a "research series" CPI that retroactively incorporates estimates of the effects of most of the methodological changes implemented since 1978, including the rental equivalence method, new or improved quality adjustments, and improvement of formulas to eliminate bias and allow for some consumer substitution within categories. This index is calculated from 1977 forward. Its reference base is December 1977 = 100. Thus, although it generally shows less *increase* than the official index, its current *levels* are considerably higher because the earlier reference base period had lower prices. Unlike the official CPIs and the CPI-U-X1, its historical values will be revised each time a significant change is made in the calculation of the current index. This index is not seasonally adjusted, and is not included in the CPI news release. It is available on the BLS Web site, along with an explanation and background material. The CPI-U-RS is used by BLS in the calculation of historical trends in real compensation per hour in its Productivity and Costs system; see Table 9-4 and its notes and definitions. It is also now used by the Census Bureau to convert household incomes into constant dollars, as seen in Chapter 3.

The C-CPI-U (Chained Consumer Price Index for All Urban Consumers) is a new, supplemental index that has been published in the monthly CPI news release since August 2002. It is available only from December 1999 to date and is calculated with the base December 1999 = 100; it is not seasonally adjusted. It is designed to be a still-closer approximation to a true cost-of-living index than the CPI-U and the CPI-W, assuming that consumers substitute between and within categories in response to changes in relative prices in order to maintain a fixed basket of "consumer satisfaction."

The C-CPI-U is a "superlative" index, using a method known as the "Tornqvist formula" to incorporate the composition of consumer spending in the current period as well as in the earlier base period. As it requires consumer expenditure data for the current as well as the earlier period, its final version can only be calculated after the expenditure data became available—about two years before the current period—and is approximated in more recent periods by making more extensive use of the geometric mean formula (see above). With the release of January 2006 data, the indexes for 2004 were revised to their final form, and the initial indexes for 2005 were revised. These 2005 indexes have the status of revised interim indexes.

Personal consumption expenditure (PCE) chain-type price indexes are calculated by the Bureau of Economic Analysis (BEA) in the framework of the national income and product accounts (NIPAs). (See the notes and definitions for Chapters 1 and 4.) The scope of NIPA PCE is broader than the scope of the CPI. PCE includes the rural as well as the urban population and the consumption spending of nonprofit entities. The CPI includes only consumer out-of-pocket cash spending, whereas PCE includes some imputed services and includes expenditures financed by government and private insurance, particularly in the medical care area. For this reason, there is a large difference between the relatively small weight of medical care spending in the CPI and the markedly greater percentage of PCE accounted for by total medical care spending. Housing, on the other hand, has a somewhat smaller weight in PCE and all non-housing components have a higher weight. It is believed that the CES tends to report housing expenditures accurately and somewhat underestimate other spending, which suggests that the weight of housing relative to all other products is overestimated in the CPI but measured more correctly in the PCE.

PCE chain-type indexes use the expenditure weights of both the earlier and the later period to determine the aggregate price change between the two periods. (See the notes and definitions for Chapter 1.) Thus, they are subject to revision as improved data on the composition of consumption spending become available, and in this respect resemble the C-CPI-U.

For a large share of PCE, the price movements for basic individual spending categories are determined by CPI components. The differences between the rates of change in the aggregate CPI and PCE indexes are in large part the result of the different weights, but also reflect the differences in scope discussed above and some alternative methodologies.

Market-based PCE indexes are based on household expenditures for which there are observable price measures. They exclude most implicit prices (for example, the services furnished without payment by financial intermediaries) and they exclude items not deflated by a detailed component of either the Consumer Price Index (CPI) or the Producer Price Index (PPI). This means that the price observations that make up these new aggregate measures are all based on observed market transactions. The new price measures are therefore known as "market-based price indexes." The imputed rent for owner-occupied housing is included in the market-based price index, since it is based on observed rentals of comparable homes. Household insurance premiums are also included in the market-based index, since they are deflated by the CPI for tenants' and household insurance. Excluded are services furnished without payment by financial intermediaries, most insurance purchases, expenses of NPISHs (nonprofit institutions serving households), gambling, margins on used light motor vehicles, and expenditures by U.S. residents working and traveling abroad. Also excluded are medical, hospitalization, and income loss insurance, expense of handling life insurance, motor vehicle insurance, and workers' compensation.

Inflation rates shown in Table 8-3 are percent changes in the price indexes shown in Table 8-2. For annual indexes, the rate is the percent change from the previous year. For monthly indexes, the rate is the percent change from the same month a year earlier. To give an indication of the longer-run implications of use of these different price indicators, compound annual inflation rates are also calculated by the editor for the 1978–2005 and 2000–2005 periods, using the growth rate formula presented in "Using the Data: The U.S. Economy in the New Century," which appears at the beginning of this volume.

Data availability and references

The CPI indexes are initially issued in a press release two to three weeks following the end of the month to which

the data pertain. This release and detailed and complete current and historical data on the CPI and its variants and components, along with extensive documentation, are available on the BLS Web site at <http://www.bls.gov/cpi>.

Information available at that site includes a fact sheet on seasonal adjustment; *BLS Handbook of Methods* Chapter 17, entitled "The Consumer Price Index"; a section entitled "Note on Chained Consumer Price Index for All Urban Consumers; a report entitled "CPI Research Series Using Current Methods"; and a number of explanatory CPI fact sheets on specific subjects.

The monthly PCE indexes are included in the monthly personal income report issued by BEA near the end of the following month. They are revised month-by-month, to reflect new information, and annually to reflect the annual and quinquennial benchmarking of the NIPAs. They can be found on the BEA Web site at <http://www.bea.gov>.

Two special issues of the *Monthly Labor Review* were devoted to CPI issues. The December 1996 issue describes the subsequently-implemented 1997 and 1998 revisions in a series of articles, and the December 1993 issue entitled *The Anatomy of Price Change* includes the following articles: "The Consumer Price Index: Underlying Concepts and Caveats"; "Basic Components of the CPI: Estimation of Price Changes"; "The Commodity Substitution Effect in CPI Data, 1982–1991"; and "Quality Adjustment of Price Indexes."

The new formula for calculating basic components is described in "Incorporating a Geometric Mean Formula into the CPI," *Monthly Labor Review*, October 1998. For a detailed discussion of the treatment of homeownership, see "Changing the Homeownership Component of the Consumer Price Index to Rental Equivalence," CPI Detailed Report, January 1983.

For a comprehensive, up-to-date professional review of CPI concepts and methodology, see Charles Schultze and Christopher Mackie, ed., *At What Price? Conceptualizing and Measuring Cost-of-Living and Price Indexes*, (Washington, DC: National Academy Press, 2001). Earlier discussions include: "Using Survey Data to Assess Bias in the Consumer Price Index," *Monthly Labor Review*, April 1998; Joel Popkin, "Improving the CPI: The Record and Suggested Next Steps," *Business Economics*, Vol. XXXII, No. 3 (July 1997), pages 42–47; *Measurement Issues in the Consumer Price Index* (Bureau of Labor Statistics, U.S. Department of Labor, June 1997); *Toward a More Accurate Measure of the Cost of Living, Final Report to the Senate Finance Committee from the Advisory Commission to Study the Consumer Price Index*, December 4, 1996 (the "Boskin Commission" report); and *Government Price Statistics*, U.S. Congress Joint Economic Committee, 87th Congress, 1st Session, January 24, 1961 (the "Stigler Committee" report).

TABLES 8-4 THROUGH 8-6 AND 20-2
PRODUCER PRICE INDEXES

Source: U.S. Department of Labor, Bureau of Labor Statistics

Producer Price Indexes (PPI) measure average changes in prices received by domestic producers. They are organized into three systems: by stage of processing, by commodity group, and by industry. Most of the indexes currently are published on a base of 1982 = 100. However, there are a number of exceptions for products and industries introduced into the index system since 1982. In this book, alternative base periods are identified in the column headings for the individual series.

Table 8-4 presents price indexes for commodities by stage of processing. Table 8-5 presents data by major commodity groups; this is the grouping that has the longest continuous history. In recent years, the major commodity groups—particularly the totals for all commodities and industrial commodities—have been de-emphasized, as they aggregate successive stages of processing and thus often exaggerate price trends. This effect was particularly acute in the energy price crisis of the early 1970s. To avoid this problem, the stage-of-processing groups were introduced in 1978. However, the individual commodity groups (for example, textile products and apparel) provide a much longer historical perspective on individual industrial sectors than is available in the current industry groupings. They are presented here for that reason.

Table 8-6 presents PPIs for the net output of selected industry groups. As the coverage of the PPI is expanded, indexes for additional industries are frequently introduced, and new industries may only go back to the most recent December. This volume includes only those industry groupings with at least nine years of historical data.

Definitions

The *stage-of-processing* PPI indexes organize commodities by class of buyer and degree of fabrication. These have been the featured measures since 1978. The three major indexes are: (1) *finished goods*, or commodities that will not undergo further processing and are ready for sale to the ultimate user (such as automobiles, meats, apparel, and machine tools); (2) *intermediate materials, supplies, and components*, or commodities that have been processed but require further processing before they become finished goods (such as steel mill products, cotton yarns, lumber, and flour), as well as physically complete goods that are purchased by business firms as inputs for their operations (such as diesel fuel and paper boxes); and (3) *crude materials* for further processing, or products entering the market for the first time that have not been manufactured or fabricated but will be processed before becoming finished goods (such as ores, scrap metals, crude petroleum, raw cotton, and livestock).

PPIs for the *net output* of industries and their products are grouped according to the North American Industry Classification System (NAICS). For each industry, they include both measures of price change for the products "primary" to that industry (products made primarily but not necessarily exclusively by that industry), and measures of changes in prices received by establishments classified in the industry for products or services chiefly made in some other industry. Thus, they are designed to be compatible with other economic time series organized by industry, such as data on shipments, employment, wages, and productivity.

Notes on the data

The probability sample used for calculating the PPI provides more than 100,000 price quotations per month, selected to represent the movement of prices of all commodities produced in the manufacturing; agriculture, forestry, and fishing; mining; and gas and electricity and public utility sectors. In addition, new PPIs are gradually being introduced for the products of industries in the transportation, trade, finance, and services sectors.

To the greatest extent possible, prices used in calculating the PPI represent prices received by domestic producers in the first important commercial transaction for each commodity. These indexes attempt to measure only price changes (changes in receipts per unit of measurement not influenced by changes in quality, quantity sold, terms of sale, or level of distribution). Most quotations are the selling prices of selected manufacturers or other producers, although a few prices are those quoted on organized exchanges or markets. Transaction prices are sought instead of list or book prices.

Price data are generally collected monthly, primarily by mail questionnaire. Most prices are obtained directly from producing companies on a voluntary and confidential basis. Prices are generally reported for the Tuesday of the week containing the 13th day of the month.

The name "Producer Price Index" became effective with the release of March 1978 data and replaced the term "Wholesale Price Index." The change was made to more accurately reflect the coverage of the data. At the same time, there was a shift in analytical emphasis from the All Commodities Index and other traditional commodity grouping indexes to the Finished Goods Index and other stage of processing indexes.

BLS revises the Producer Price Index weighting structure when data from economic censuses become available. Beginning with data for January 2002, the weights used to construct the PPI reflect 1997 shipments values as measured by the 1997 Economic Censuses and other sources. Data for 1996 through 2001 reflect 1992 shipments values; 1992 through 1995 reflect 1987 shipment values; 1987 through 1991 reflect 1982 values; 1976 through 1986 reflect 1972 values; and 1967 through 1975 reflect 1963 values.

BLS has been working for a number of years on a comprehensive overhaul of the theory, methodology, and procedures used to construct the PPI. One aspect of this overhaul was the previously mentioned shift in emphasis to the stage-of-processing measures, which began in 1978. Other changes phased in since 1978 include the replacement of judgment sampling with probability sampling techniques; expansion to systematic coverage of the net output of virtually all industries in the mining and manufacturing sectors; introduction of measures for selected services industries, including retail trade; a shift from a commodity to an industry orientation; and the exclusion of imports from, and the inclusion of exports in, the survey universe.

The commodity components of the stage-of-processing indexes, in addition to being available in unadjusted form, are also adjusted for seasonal variation using the X-12-ARIMA method. Since January 1988, BLS has also used Intervention Analysis Seasonal Adjustment for a small number of series to remove unusual values that might distort seasonal patterns before calculating the seasonal adjustment factors. Seasonal factors for the PPI are revised annually to take into account the most recent 12 months of data. Seasonally adjusted data for the previous 5 years are subject to these annual revisions. The industry net output indexes are not seasonally adjusted.

Data availability and references

The indexes are initially issued in a press release two to three weeks following the end of the month to which the data pertain. Data are subsequently published in greater detail in a monthly BLS publication, *PPI Detailed Report*. Each month, data for the fourth previous month (both unadjusted and seasonally adjusted) are revised to reflect late reports and corrections.

The press release, the *PPI Detailed Report*, detailed and complete current and historical data, and extensive documentation are available at <http://www.bls.gov/ppi>. The items available on this Web site include *BLS Handbook of Methods* Chapter 14, "Producer Price Indexes"; a selection of *Monthly Labor Review* articles on the PPI; and fact sheets on a number of issues and index components.

TABLE 8-4
PURCHASING POWER OF THE DOLLAR

Source: U.S. Department of Labor, Bureau of Labor Statistics; calculations by the editor

The purchasing power of the dollar measures changes in the quantity of goods and services a dollar will buy at a particular date compared with a selected base date. It must be defined in terms of the following: (1) the specific commodities and services that are to be purchased with the dollar; (2) the market level (producer, retail, etc.) at which they are purchased; and (3) the dates for which the comparison is to be made. Thus, the purchasing power of the dollar for a selected period, compared with another period, may be measured in terms of a single commodity or a large group of commodities, such as all goods and services purchased by consumers at retail or all finished commodities sold in primary markets.

Broad price indexes calculated by BLS that have been used to measure the purchasing power of the dollar in the United States include: (1) the Producer Price Index (PPI) for Finished Goods, which relates to prices received by the producers of finished commodities at the primary market level; and (2) two versions of the Consumer Price Index (the CPI-U and CPI-W), which measure average changes in retail prices of goods and services. These indexes are described above in the sections of the notes and definitions pertaining to the Producer Price Index and the Consumer Price Index, respectively.

The purchasing power of the dollar is computed by dividing the price index number for the base period by the price index number for the comparison date and expressing the result in dollars and cents. The base period is the period in which the price index equals 100; the purchasing power in that base period is therefore $1.00. In this book, 1982–1984 is used as the base period for the two indexes shown to enable ready comparisons.

Purchasing power estimates in terms of both the CPI-U and the CPI-W are calculated by BLS and published in the CPI press release. The CPI-U version is used here. The comparable purchasing power in terms of the finished goods PPI is calculated by the editor of *Business Statistics* after rebasing the index from its published 1982 base to 1982–1984 = 100. In all cases, the purchasing power measure is based on indexes not adjusted for seasonal variation.

TABLE 8-7
PRICES RECEIVED AND PAID BY FARMERS

Source: U.S. Department of Agriculture, National Agricultural Statistics Service (NASS)

The data on prices received and paid by farmers represent prices farmers received for commodities sold and prices paid for production input goods and services. Prices are weighted and aggregated into price indexes. These indexes provide measures of relative price changes for agricultural outputs and inputs. These price measures are based on voluntary reports from agribusiness firms, merchants, dealers, and farmers. Data are collected at regular intervals using mailed inquiries, telephone, and personal enumeration. In January 1995, these data were converted to a reference base of 1990–1992 = 100. Prices-paid indexes were only available quarterly for several years, but have been published monthly, beginning with January 1996, with monthly indexes for 1995 constructed for historical comparison.

Definitions

Prices received by farmers represents sales from producers to first buyers. They include all grades and qualities. The average commodity price from the survey multiplied by the total quantity marketed should theoretically give the total cash receipts for the commodity.

Prices paid by farmers represents the average costs of inputs purchased by farmers and ranchers to produce agricultural commodities. Conceptually, the average price when multiplied by quantity purchased should equal total producer expenditures for the item.

Ratio of prices received to prices paid is the ratio of the index of prices received for all farm products to the index of prices paid for all commodities and services. For some years, prices paid are available only for the first month of each quarter. Each month's ratio of prices received to prices paid is based on the latest data available.

Notes on the data

In 1995, the National Agricultural Statistics Service (NASS) reweighted and reconstructed the prices paid and received indexes. The indexes are now based on 5-year moving average weights compared with previous fixed weights. The changes in the construction of the indexes simplified updating component items and reference periods while maintaining appropriate weights. The overall changes to the weighting and construction of the indexes did not have a significant effect on the index levels. Therefore, they had little effect on the level of parity prices. Indexes are now published on a 1990–1992 = 100 base. As required by law, the parity ratio (ratio of prices received to prices paid) also continues to be published on a base of 1910–1914 = 100.

Prices paid. Since 1995, the Prices Paid Survey of items purchased by farm establishments has been conducted annually in April. Surveys are conducted for feed, seed, fertilizer, agricultural chemicals, fuel, and farm machinery. About 135 selected items are priced to represent groups of similar items purchased in order to make up the major production expenditure categories. The number of input items consumed on farms is so extensive that it is not feasible to collect price data for all of the inputs. Items on the questionnaire are described in the simplest way consistent with definite identification. Firms are requested to report prices for the most commonly sold item that meets the general specification on the questionnaire.

Reported data are summarized to regional estimates and then weighted to U.S. prices. Weights are based on available consumption or expenditure information. Average prices, including state and local taxes, are used in computing the indexes and are published in *Agricultural Prices* for the same month as the survey. Regional prices are published for feed, fuel, and fertilizer. U.S. prices are published for the remaining items surveyed.

BLS indexes are used to measure price change for the months when no survey data are collected. The BLS indexes measure price changes for farm supplies and repairs,

autos and trucks, building materials, and marketing containers. Before 1995, quarterly prices-paid surveys were conducted by NASS. Quarterly feeder livestock surveys are still conducted.

Revisions: prices paid. Any revisions are published in the monthly and annual issues of *Agricultural Prices*. The basis for revision must be supported by additional data that directly affect the level of the estimate. More revisions are likely to occur in April, when separate prices paid surveys are conducted.

Survey procedures: prices received. Primary sales data used to determine grain prices are obtained from probability samples of mills and elevators. These procedures ensure that virtually all grain moving into commercial channels has a chance of being included in the survey. Livestock prices are obtained from packers, stockyards, auctions, dealers, and market check data. Inter farm sales of grain and livestock are not included, as they represent very small percentages of total marketings. Grain marketed for seed is also excluded. Fruit and vegetable prices are obtained from sample surveys and market check data.

Summary and estimation procedures: prices received. Survey quantities sold are expanded by strata to state levels and used to weight average strata prices to a state average. State prices are then weighted to a U.S. price.

Revisions: prices received. For most items, the current month's price represents a three to five day period around the mid month. Previous month's prices represent actual dollars received for quantities sold during the entire month. Revisions are published in monthly issues of *Agricultural Prices* and in the annual summary published in July. A schedule of monthly revisions is published in the December issue of *Agricultural Prices* and in the July annual summary.

Reliability: prices received. U.S. price estimates generally have a sampling error of less than one-half percent for major commodities such as corn, wheat, soybeans, cotton, and rice.

Data availability

Prices paid and received by farmers are available each month in a press release issued close to the end of the month. Data are subsequently published monthly in *Agricultural Prices*, with revisions and a summary of the previous year published in July; the most recent of these is available at <http://usda.mannlib.cornell.edu/usda/current/AgriPricSu>. Information can also be found at <http://www.nass.usda.gov>, under the general section heading of "Economics."

References

The indexes are discussed in "Revised Prices Received and Paid Indexes, United States, 1975–1993 for Base Periods 1910–1914 = 100 and 1990–1992 = 100," *NASS Statistical Bulletin* no. 917, February 1995.

CHAPTER 9: EMPLOYMENT COSTS, PRODUCTIVITY, AND PROFITS

Section 9a: Employment Cost Indexes

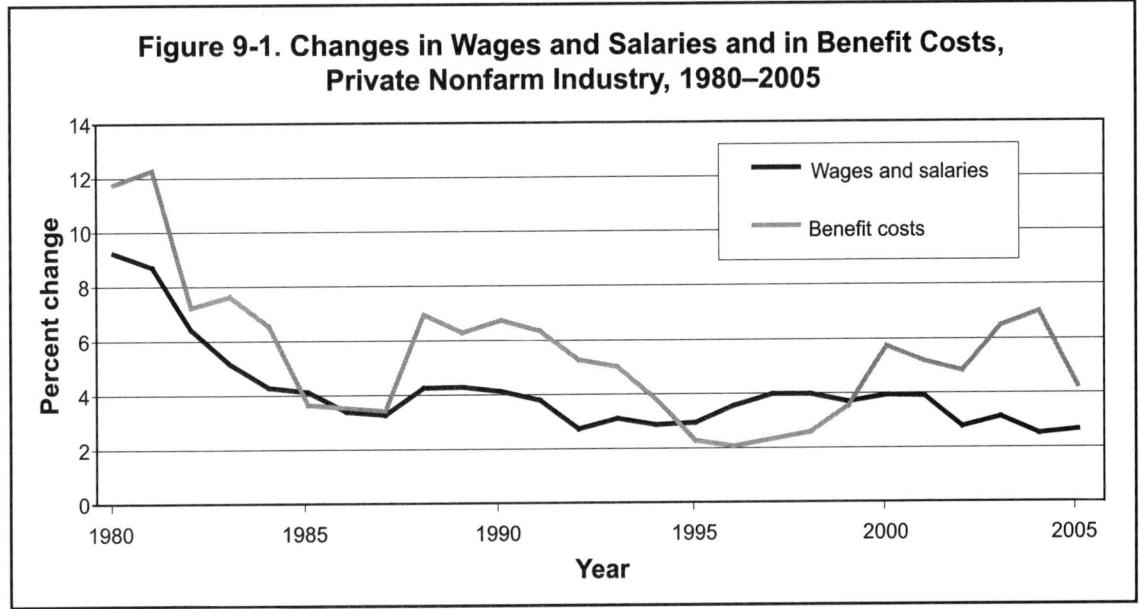

Figure 9-1. Changes in Wages and Salaries and in Benefit Costs, Private Nonfarm Industry, 1980–2005

- Between December 2000 and December 2005, average hourly wages and salaries for all private industry workers (excluding farm workers and private household workers) rose at a 2.9 percent annual rate, as measured in the Employment Cost Index (in current dollars, holding the mix of industries and occupations constant). (Table 9-2) The cost of employer-paid benefits rose at an annual rate of 5.4 percent, driven up by rising costs of medical benefits. (Table 9-3) As a result, the total compensation cost to the employer of an average hour of work in current dollars rose at a 3.6 percent annual rate. (Table 9-1)

- During the same 5-year December-to-December recession/recovery period, the Consumer Price Index rose at an average annual rate of 2.5 percent (Tables 8-1 and 20-2), implying a 1.1 percent rate of increase in real compensation and a 0.4 percent rate of increase in real wages and salaries. However, these real rates of increase fell far short of the 3.1 percent rate of increase in nonfarm worker productivity. About half of the gap between productivity growth and real labor compensation growth can be accounted for by differences between the productivity deflator and the CPI. (Table 9-4)

Table 9-1. Employment Cost Indexes (SIC)—Total Compensation

(December 2005 [not seasonally adjusted] = 100; annual values are for December, not seasonally adjusted; quarterly values, seasonally adjusted, except as noted.)

Year and quarter	All civilian workers [1,2]	State and local government workers [2]	All private industry workers [2]	Private industry workers excluding sales occupations [2,3]	Production and nonsupervisory occupations [3]	White-collar occupations [2]	Blue-collar occupations [2]	Service occupations [2]	Goods-producing industries Total [2]	Construction [2]	Manufacturing [2]	Service-providing industries Total [2]	Transportation and utilities	Wholesale trade	Retail trade	Finance, insurance, and real estate [2,3]	Services
1979	...	...	32.8	32.5	...	31.2	35.0	33.9	33.7	...	33.1	32.0	...	...	...	...	...
1980	...	...	35.9	35.9	...	34.2	38.5	37.1	37.0	...	36.4	35.1	...	...	...	...	...
1981	39.0	36.8	39.5	39.4	40.1	37.6	42.2	40.5	40.7	...	40.0	38.6	...	...	...	...	...
1982	41.5	39.4	42.0	42.0	42.8	40.1	44.7	43.9	43.2	...	42.4	41.1	...	...	...	...	...
1983	43.9	41.8	44.4	44.4	45.2	42.7	47.0	46.3	45.3	...	44.6	43.8	...	...	...	...	...
1984	46.2	44.6	46.6	46.7	47.3	44.8	49.0	49.4	47.4	...	46.9	46.0	...	...	...	...	...
1985	48.2	47.1	48.4	48.3	49.1	47.0	50.5	50.9	49.0	50.8	48.4	48.1	50.6	...	52.4	44.7	46.1
1986	49.9	49.6	49.9	49.9	50.5	48.6	51.9	52.4	50.5	52.3	50.0	49.6	51.8	48.5	53.5	46.1	48.1
1987	51.7	51.8	51.6	51.7	52.2	50.4	53.5	53.7	52.1	54.2	51.5	51.4	53.3	50.4	54.8	47.0	50.5
1988	54.2	54.7	54.1	54.1	54.8	52.9	55.9	56.5	54.4	56.5	53.8	54.0	54.9	52.5	58.0	50.0	53.5
1989	56.9	58.1	56.7	56.5	57.6	55.7	58.2	59.0	56.7	59.0	56.3	56.8	56.9	57.1	59.9	52.7	56.4
1990	59.7	61.5	59.3	59.3	60.1	58.4	60.7	61.8	59.4	60.9	59.1	59.4	59.1	58.2	62.5	54.9	59.9
1991	62.3	63.7	61.9	62.0	62.7	61.0	63.4	64.7	62.1	63.3	61.9	61.9	61.7	60.7	65.2	57.2	62.5
1992	64.4	66.0	64.1	64.2	64.9	63.1	65.6	66.7	64.5	65.6	64.3	63.9	63.9	62.5	66.9	57.9	65.2
1993	66.7	67.9	66.4	66.6	67.3	65.4	68.1	68.8	67.0	67.1	66.9	66.2	66.1	64.4	68.9	60.5	67.5
1994	68.7	69.9	68.5	68.6	69.2	67.5	70.0	70.8	69.0	69.6	69.0	68.1	68.7	66.4	70.8	61.8	69.4
1995	70.6	72.0	70.2	70.4	71.0	69.4	71.7	72.1	70.7	71.1	70.8	70.0	71.2	69.4	72.3	64.0	70.9
1996	72.6	73.9	72.4	72.4	73.1	71.7	73.6	74.2	72.7	72.9	72.9	72.3	73.4	71.5	75.1	65.5	73.1
1997	75.0	75.6	74.9	74.9	75.4	74.4	75.5	77.2	74.5	74.8	74.6	75.1	75.5	73.8	77.7	69.9	75.9
1998	77.6	77.8	77.5	77.2	78.1	77.3	77.6	79.4	76.5	77.4	76.6	78.0	78.4	78.0	80.0	74.1	78.2
1999	80.2	80.5	80.2	80.0	80.4	79.9	80.2	82.1	79.1	79.9	79.2	80.6	80.1	81.1	83.0	77.1	80.9
2000	83.6	82.9	83.6	83.6	84.0	83.6	83.6	85.3	82.6	84.6	82.3	84.2	83.5	84.4	86.4	81.0	84.5
2001	87.0	86.4	87.1	87.0	87.4	87.1	86.7	89.1	85.7	88.2	85.3	87.8	87.5	87.2	90.3	83.9	88.3
2002	90.0	89.9	90.0	89.9	90.2	89.9	89.8	92.0	88.9	90.0	88.5	90.5	91.0	91.1	91.9	87.6	90.7
2003	93.5	92.9	93.6	93.6	93.6	93.6	93.4	94.9	92.4	94.1	92.2	94.2	94.0	94.0	94.9	94.1	94.0
2004	96.9	96.1	97.1	97.2	97.2	96.9	97.5	97.7	96.8	96.4	96.7	97.3	97.6	96.5	97.1	96.7	97.5
2005	100.0	100.0	100.0	100.0	100.0	100.0	100.0	100.0	100.0	100.0	100.0	100.0	100.0	100.0	100.0	100.0	100.0
1998																	
1st quarter	75.6	76.0	75.4	75.5	76.1	75.1	76.0	77.7	75.1	75.4	75.1	75.8	76.4	75.4	78.5	71.1	76.4
2nd quarter	76.2	76.6	76.1	76.1	76.8	75.8	76.5	78.1	75.7	76.3	75.6	76.4	77.2	75.6	79.2	72.0	76.9
3rd quarter	77.0	77.2	76.9	76.9	77.6	76.7	77.1	78.9	76.2	76.8	76.2	77.4	77.9	76.9	80.0	73.3	77.7
4th quarter	77.5	77.7	77.5	77.2	78.1	77.4	77.7	79.3	76.6	77.6	76.7	78.1	78.4	78.1	80.2	74.1	78.3
1999																	
1st quarter	77.8	78.2	77.7	77.8	78.3	77.4	78.2	80.1	77.1	78.3	77.1	78.1	78.6	78.1	80.6	73.6	78.7
2nd quarter	78.6	78.8	78.5	78.6	79.1	78.3	78.8	80.7	77.7	78.8	77.6	79.1	79.3	78.9	82.0	75.8	79.3
3rd quarter	79.4	79.4	79.3	79.3	79.8	79.2	79.5	80.9	78.3	79.4	78.3	79.9	79.7	79.9	82.4	76.8	80.0
4th quarter	80.2	80.3	80.2	80.0	80.4	80.1	80.3	81.9	79.2	80.1	79.3	80.8	80.2	81.3	83.3	77.1	81.0
2000																	
1st quarter	81.2	81.0	81.3	81.1	81.7	81.2	81.4	82.6	80.5	81.3	80.4	81.8	81.0	82.1	84.4	79.0	81.9
2nd quarter	82.1	81.6	82.2	82.1	82.6	82.1	82.1	83.5	81.5	82.4	81.2	82.7	81.9	82.7	85.3	79.6	82.9
3rd quarter	82.9	82.0	83.0	82.9	83.4	83.0	83.0	84.2	82.3	83.6	82.0	83.5	82.8	83.1	86.1	80.7	83.7
4th quarter	83.6	82.7	83.8	83.6	84.0	83.8	83.8	85.1	82.8	84.7	82.6	84.4	83.6	84.5	86.7	81.0	84.6
2001																	
1st quarter	84.7	84.0	84.9	84.7	85.1	84.6	84.6	86.4	83.7	85.5	83.4	85.4	84.7	84.8	87.7	82.1	85.8
2nd quarter	85.5	84.9	85.7	85.5	85.8	85.5	85.1	87.1	84.6	86.5	84.0	86.2	85.7	86.2	88.2	82.9	86.5
3rd quarter	86.4	85.9	86.4	86.4	86.7	86.3	86.1	88.0	85.2	87.3	84.6	87.0	86.3	86.7	88.9	83.7	87.6
4th quarter	87.2	86.5	87.4	87.0	87.4	87.3	86.9	89.2	86.0	88.3	85.6	88.1	87.7	87.2	90.6	83.9	88.5
2002																	
1st quarter	88.0	87.2	88.1	88.0	88.3	88.0	87.7	90.1	86.7	88.9	86.2	88.8	88.6	88.5	90.5	85.9	89.1
2nd quarter	88.9	87.9	89.1	88.9	89.2	89.0	88.4	90.7	87.6	89.4	87.0	89.8	89.3	90.9	91.6	87.0	89.7
3rd quarter	89.5	89.1	89.6	89.5	89.8	89.5	89.1	91.6	88.3	90.0	87.8	90.3	90.3	90.7	91.9	87.4	90.3
4th quarter	90.2	90.0	90.3	89.9	90.2	90.2	90.1	92.1	89.2	91.1	89.0	90.8	91.2	91.1	92.1	87.6	90.9
2003																	
1st quarter	91.3	90.7	91.4	91.4	91.4	91.4	91.2	93.1	90.5	91.8	90.3	91.9	91.9	92.6	92.3	91.9	91.6
2nd quarter	92.1	91.6	92.3	92.2	92.2	92.1	91.9	93.6	91.3	92.8	91.0	92.7	92.9	93.6	92.7	92.7	92.3
3rd quarter	93.0	92.3	93.2	93.1	93.1	93.0	92.8	94.4	92.2	93.4	91.9	93.7	93.5	94.0	92.7	93.7	93.3
4th quarter	93.7	92.9	93.9	93.6	93.6	93.9	93.7	95.1	92.8	94.2	92.7	94.4	94.2	94.0	95.1	94.1	94.2
2004																	
1st quarter	94.7	93.7	95.0	95.0	95.2	94.7	95.3	96.0	94.4	95.0	94.5	95.2	95.7	95.0	95.6	94.9	95.0
2nd quarter	95.6	94.5	95.8	95.9	96.1	95.5	96.1	96.8	95.3	95.5	95.3	96.1	96.9	96.1	96.4	95.5	96.0
3rd quarter	96.4	95.2	96.7	96.7	96.9	96.4	97.0	97.3	96.3	96.2	96.5	96.8	97.5	97.2	96.7	96.1	96.9
4th quarter	97.1	96.0	97.4	97.2	97.2	97.2	97.8	97.8	97.1	96.5	97.3	97.5	97.9	96.5	97.3	96.7	97.7
2005																	
1st quarter	97.9	97.0	98.1	98.4	98.1	98.1	98.3	98.2	98.0	97.6	98.0	98.2	98.3	97.9	98.0	98.2	98.4
2nd quarter	98.6	97.8	98.8	99.1	98.8	98.7	98.9	98.9	98.9	98.5	98.9	98.8	98.7	98.0	98.5	99.3	99.0
3rd quarter	99.4	98.8	99.5	99.6	99.6	99.5	99.6	99.5	99.8	99.6	99.7	99.4	99.6	99.3	99.3	99.3	99.5
4th quarter	100.2	99.8	100.3	100.0	100.0	100.3	100.3	100.1	100.3	100.2	100.5	100.2	100.3	100.0	100.2	100.0	100.2

[1] Excludes farm workers, private household workers, and federal government employees.
[2] Roughly continuous and comparable with new NAICS-based series for 2006. See notes and definitions for more information.
[3] Not seasonally adjusted.
... = Not available.

Table 9-2. Employment Cost Indexes (SIC)—Wages and Salaries

(December 2005 [not seasonally adjusted] = 100; annual values are for December, not seasonally adjusted; quarterly values, seasonally adjusted, except as noted.)

Year and quarter	All civilian workers [1,2]	State and local government workers [2]	Private industry workers														
					By occupational group				By industry division								
									Goods-producing industries			Service-providing industries					
			All private industry workers [2]	Private industry workers excluding sales occupations [2,3]	Production and nonsupervisory occupations [3]	White-collar occupations [2]	Blue-collar occupations [2]	Service occupations [2]	Total [2]	Construction [2]	Manufacturing [2]	Total [2]	Transportation and utilities	Wholesale trade	Retail trade	Finance, insurance, and real estate [2,3]	Services
1979	...	...	36.1	36.1	36.8	34.1	39.4	37.9	38.2	41.4	37.5	34.9	39.1	33.7	39.7	32.8	31.7
1980	...	...	39.4	39.3	40.3	37.1	43.1	41.0	41.8	45.0	41.0	38.0	43.5	37.1	42.5	35.2	34.5
1981	42.3	40.1	42.8	42.9	43.9	40.4	46.8	44.4	45.4	49.0	44.5	41.4	47.1	40.0	45.6	38.8	38.1
1982	45.0	42.7	45.5	45.6	46.7	43.1	49.4	48.2	48.0	51.5	47.0	44.2	50.5	42.5	47.5	41.3	41.2
1983	47.3	45.0	47.8	47.9	48.9	45.7	51.3	50.4	49.9	53.0	49.0	46.7	53.0	45.1	49.5	44.3	43.9
1984	49.4	47.7	49.8	50.1	50.8	47.6	53.1	53.5	51.8	53.7	51.2	48.7	54.8	47.6	52.0	43.9	46.7
1985	51.5	50.3	51.8	51.9	52.9	50.0	55.0	54.8	53.6	55.3	53.0	51.0	56.9	49.7	54.5	47.9	48.4
1986	53.3	53.0	53.5	53.6	54.3	51.7	56.4	56.2	55.3	56.7	54.8	52.5	57.9	51.5	55.7	49.2	50.3
1987	55.2	55.2	55.2	55.5	56.0	53.6	58.1	57.6	57.1	58.6	56.6	54.3	59.1	53.6	57.2	49.8	53.0
1988	57.5	57.9	57.5	57.5	58.4	56.1	59.9	60.1	58.9	60.7	58.3	56.9	60.6	55.6	60.1	52.9	55.6
1989	60.1	61.0	59.9	59.8	61.0	58.7	62.0	62.3	61.2	62.8	60.6	59.5	62.2	60.7	62.0	55.7	58.3
1990	62.6	64.2	62.3	62.4	63.2	61.2	64.2	64.8	63.4	64.1	63.1	61.8	64.3	61.2	64.2	57.6	61.6
1991	64.9	66.4	64.6	64.7	65.4	63.5	66.4	67.4	65.8	66.0	65.6	64.1	66.6	63.6	66.6	59.6	63.8
1992	66.6	68.4	66.3	66.5	67.2	65.2	68.1	68.8	67.6	67.3	67.6	65.7	68.7	65.5	68.2	59.5	66.0
1993	68.7	70.2	68.3	68.5	69.2	67.4	70.0	70.3	69.6	68.6	69.7	67.8	70.9	67.1	70.2	62.1	68.0
1994	70.6	72.4	70.2	70.5	71.1	69.3	72.0	72.4	71.7	70.8	71.8	69.6	73.5	69.1	71.9	62.8	70.0
1995	72.7	74.7	72.2	72.5	73.0	71.3	74.1	74.0	73.7	72.5	73.9	71.7	76.0	72.4	73.6	65.1	71.7
1996	75.1	76.8	74.7	74.9	75.5	73.8	76.3	76.6	76.0	74.6	76.3	74.2	78.1	74.7	76.8	67.2	74.2
1997	77.9	78.9	77.6	77.7	78.3	77.0	78.8	79.9	78.3	77.1	78.6	77.4	80.7	77.0	79.7	71.8	77.5
1998	80.8	81.3	80.6	80.4	81.4	80.3	81.3	82.4	81.1	79.9	81.3	80.5	83.0	81.5	82.2	76.9	80.1
1999	83.6	84.2	83.5	83.4	83.8	83.1	84.0	85.1	83.8	82.5	84.1	83.4	84.8	84.5	85.2	79.8	83.0
2000	86.7	87.0	86.7	86.7	87.1	86.4	87.1	88.3	87.1	86.9	87.1	86.6	87.5	87.4	88.6	83.4	86.3
2001	90.0	90.2	90.0	90.0	90.4	89.6	90.5	91.8	90.2	90.4	90.2	89.9	91.7	89.3	91.9	85.8	90.0
2002	92.6	93.1	92.4	92.5	92.6	92.0	93.0	94.1	92.9	92.8	93.0	92.3	94.7	92.8	93.2	89.4	92.0
2003	95.2	95.0	95.2	95.4	95.1	95.2	95.2	96.2	95.1	95.1	95.2	95.3	96.2	95.3	95.5	95.9	94.8
2004	97.5	97.0	97.5	97.8	97.5	97.5	97.6	97.9	97.4	97.0	97.5	97.7	98.6	96.6	97.2	97.7	97.8
2005	100.0	100.0	100.0	100.0	100.0	100.0	100.0	100.0	100.0	100.0	100.0	100.0	100.0	100.0	100.0	100.0	100.0
1998																	
1st quarter	78.5	79.3	78.5	78.5	78.9	77.9	79.4	80.5	79.1	77.9	79.5	78.2	81.2	78.7	80.5	72.9	78.0
2nd quarter	79.2	79.9	79.1	79.2	79.7	78.5	80.1	81.0	79.9	78.9	80.0	78.8	81.6	79.0	81.2	74.1	78.7
3rd quarter	80.1	80.5	80.1	80.0	80.7	79.7	80.8	81.9	80.5	79.2	80.9	80.0	82.5	80.3	82.4	75.9	79.6
4th quarter	80.8	81.1	80.8	80.4	81.4	80.4	81.3	82.4	81.1	80.0	81.3	80.6	83.0	81.4	82.5	76.9	80.1
1999																	
1st quarter	81.1	81.6	81.0	81.2	81.6	80.5	81.9	83.3	81.7	80.8	82.0	80.8	83.2	81.3	83.1	75.4	80.9
2nd quarter	82.0	82.4	82.0	82.0	82.5	81.5	82.7	84.0	82.3	81.3	82.6	81.8	84.1	81.9	84.3	78.3	81.5
3rd quarter	82.8	83.2	82.7	82.7	83.1	82.3	83.5	84.1	83.0	82.1	83.4	82.6	84.5	83.2	84.6	79.4	82.1
4th quarter	83.6	84.0	83.5	83.4	83.8	83.2	84.0	85.1	83.8	82.6	84.1	83.5	84.8	84.5	85.4	79.8	83.1
2000																	
1st quarter	84.5	84.7	84.4	84.3	84.8	84.1	84.9	85.9	84.7	84.1	85.0	84.4	85.1	85.2	86.7	81.7	83.8
2nd quarter	85.3	85.4	85.3	85.2	85.7	85.0	85.7	86.8	85.7	85.1	85.9	85.2	86.0	85.9	87.4	82.2	84.9
3rd quarter	86.0	86.1	86.1	86.0	86.5	85.8	86.6	87.4	86.5	86.0	86.6	86.0	86.8	86.3	88.2	83.4	85.6
4th quarter	86.7	86.9	86.8	86.7	87.1	86.6	87.1	88.3	87.1	87.0	87.1	86.7	87.5	87.5	88.8	83.4	86.4
2001																	
1st quarter	87.8	87.7	87.8	87.8	88.1	87.4	88.2	89.2	88.1	87.9	88.3	87.6	88.4	87.4	89.6	84.6	87.5
2nd quarter	88.6	88.5	88.6	88.5	88.9	88.1	89.0	89.9	89.1	88.8	89.2	88.4	89.5	89.1	90.1	85.0	88.3
3rd quarter	89.3	89.5	89.2	89.4	89.7	88.7	90.0	90.6	89.6	89.6	89.6	89.0	90.1	88.9	90.7	85.7	89.3
4th quarter	90.1	90.0	90.1	90.0	90.4	89.8	90.5	91.8	90.2	90.5	90.2	90.0	91.7	89.3	92.1	85.8	90.1
2002																	
1st quarter	90.8	90.7	90.9	91.0	91.1	90.5	91.3	92.6	90.9	90.9	91.0	90.8	92.6	90.7	92.1	88.1	90.7
2nd quarter	91.6	91.3	91.7	91.7	91.9	91.4	92.1	93.1	91.8	91.4	91.9	91.7	93.4	93.0	93.1	89.1	91.3
3rd quarter	92.1	92.2	92.1	92.2	92.3	91.7	92.6	93.8	92.3	91.9	92.4	92.0	94.2	92.5	93.2	89.3	91.8
4th quarter	92.6	92.9	92.6	92.5	92.6	92.2	93.0	94.1	92.9	92.9	93.0	92.4	94.7	92.8	93.4	89.4	92.1
2003																	
1st quarter	93.5	93.4	93.5	93.6	93.3	93.3	93.7	94.8	93.7	93.1	93.9	93.4	95.2	94.2	93.4	94.1	92.6
2nd quarter	94.1	94.1	94.2	94.2	93.9	93.9	94.3	95.1	94.4	94.0	94.5	94.1	95.6	95.0	93.7	94.8	93.4
3rd quarter	94.8	94.5	94.9	95.0	94.7	94.7	94.9	95.7	94.9	94.7	94.9	94.9	95.8	95.0	95.3	95.7	94.3
4th quarter	95.2	94.8	95.3	95.4	95.1	95.4	95.2	96.2	95.1	95.2	95.2	95.4	96.2	95.3	95.6	95.9	94.9
2004																	
1st quarter	95.9	95.4	96.0	96.0	95.9	95.9	95.9	96.5	95.9	95.9	95.9	96.0	97.1	95.8	96.0	96.3	95.6
2nd quarter	96.4	95.9	96.5	96.6	96.5	96.4	96.6	97.1	96.5	96.3	96.6	96.6	97.8	96.8	96.5	96.4	96.4
3rd quarter	97.1	96.3	97.3	97.4	97.3	97.3	97.3	97.4	97.3	96.8	97.4	97.3	98.4	97.9	96.7	97.0	97.1
4th quarter	97.5	96.9	97.7	97.8	97.5	97.7	97.6	97.9	97.4	97.1	97.5	97.8	98.6	96.6	97.3	97.7	97.9
2005																	
1st quarter	98.1	97.6	98.2	98.4	98.2	98.3	98.1	98.4	98.1	97.6	98.3	98.3	98.4	97.8	97.9	98.5	98.6
2nd quarter	98.7	98.2	98.8	99.1	98.7	98.9	98.9	98.9	98.8	98.3	98.9	98.9	99.0	97.7	98.5	99.6	99.2
3rd quarter	99.3	98.9	99.4	99.6	99.5	99.4	99.5	99.5	99.5	99.2	99.5	99.4	99.6	99.0	99.3	99.5	99.4
4th quarter	100.0	99.8	100.1	100.0	100.0	100.2	100.0	100.0	100.0	100.1	100.0	100.1	100.0	100.0	100.1	100.0	100.1

[1]Excludes farm workers, private household workers, and federal government employees.
[2]Roughly continuous and comparable with new NAICS-based series for 2006. See notes and definitions for more information.
[3]Not seasonally adjusted.
. . . = Not available.

Table 9-3. Employment Cost Indexes (SIC)—Benefit Costs

(December 2005 [not seasonally adjusted] = 100; annual values are for December, not seasonally adjusted; quarterly values, seasonally adjusted.)

Year and quarter	All civilian workers [1,2]	State and local government workers [2]	All private industry workers [2]	By occupational group			By industry division			
				White-collar occupations [2]	Blue-collar occupations [2]	Service occupations [2]	Goods-producing industries		Service-providing industries [2]	Non-manufacturing
							Total [2]	Manufacturing [2]		
1979	. . .	. . .	25.7	24.7	27.4	. . .	26.0	25.8	25.4	25.6
1980	. . .	. . .	28.7	27.7	30.4	. . .	28.8	28.5	28.6	28.8
1981	31.8	. . .	32.2	31.1	34.0	. . .	32.4	32.1	31.9	32.2
1982	34.2	. . .	34.5	33.3	36.5	. . .	34.8	34.4	34.1	34.4
1983	36.8	. . .	37.1	35.8	39.1	. . .	37.2	36.9	36.8	37.1
1984	39.3	. . .	39.5	38.3	41.4	. . .	39.6	39.3	39.4	39.5
1985	40.8	. . .	40.9	40.0	42.5	41.2	40.8	40.4	40.9	41.1
1986	42.4	. . .	42.3	41.4	43.8	42.9	42.0	41.6	42.5	42.6
1987	44.0	. . .	43.7	42.9	45.3	43.9	43.2	42.7	44.2	44.3
1988	47.0	. . .	46.7	45.6	48.6	47.4	46.3	46.0	47.1	47.2
1989	50.1	52.2	49.6	48.6	51.2	50.5	48.8	48.7	50.2	50.1
1990	53.5	55.8	52.9	52.0	54.4	53.8	52.3	52.1	53.4	53.3
1991	56.5	58.0	56.2	55.2	57.8	57.7	55.5	55.2	56.7	56.6
1992	59.5	61.1	59.1	57.8	61.0	61.0	58.7	58.3	59.4	59.5
1993	62.2	62.9	62.0	60.5	64.4	64.4	62.0	61.8	62.0	62.1
1994	64.4	64.6	64.3	63.2	66.2	66.0	64.1	63.9	64.4	64.5
1995	65.8	66.3	65.7	64.8	67.2	66.6	65.2	65.0	66.0	65.9
1996	67.1	67.8	67.0	66.2	68.4	67.3	66.4	66.5	67.3	67.2
1997	68.5	68.6	68.5	68.0	69.4	69.6	67.3	67.4	69.2	69.0
1998	70.3	70.7	70.2	69.9	70.7	70.9	68.1	67.9	71.4	71.1
1999	72.6	72.7	72.6	72.3	73.0	73.4	70.5	70.3	73.8	73.4
2000	76.2	74.4	76.7	76.5	76.9	76.6	74.3	73.6	78.1	77.8
2001	80.2	78.5	80.6	81.1	79.5	81.3	77.3	76.3	82.5	82.3
2002	84.2	83.3	84.4	84.6	83.8	85.7	81.3	80.4	86.1	85.9
2003	89.5	88.4	89.8	89.7	89.8	91.3	87.4	86.7	91.2	91.0
2004	95.7	94.3	96.0	95.3	97.3	97.1	95.7	95.3	96.2	96.3
2005	100.0	100.0	100.0	100.0	100.0	100.0	100.0	100.0	100.0	100.0
1998										
1st quarter	68.8	69.1	68.7	68.5	69.5	70.2	67.2	67.4	69.8	69.5
2nd quarter	69.3	69.7	69.2	68.9	70.0	70.4	67.7	67.6	70.3	70.0
3rd quarter	69.8	70.3	69.6	69.4	70.4	70.9	68.0	67.9	70.9	70.6
4th quarter	70.3	70.7	70.2	70.1	70.7	71.0	68.2	68.0	71.6	71.2
1999										
1st quarter	70.4	71.0	70.2	70.0	71.0	71.6	68.5	68.2	71.4	71.2
2nd quarter	71.1	71.6	70.9	70.7	71.6	72.3	68.9	68.6	72.3	72.0
3rd quarter	71.6	71.6	71.6	71.5	72.2	72.7	69.6	69.4	73.1	72.8
4th quarter	72.7	72.7	72.6	72.6	73.2	73.5	70.7	70.6	74.0	73.7
2000										
1st quarter	73.9	73.3	74.0	73.9	74.8	73.8	72.2	72.2	75.3	75.0
2nd quarter	74.7	73.8	75.0	75.0	75.5	74.7	73.2	73.0	76.3	76.0
3rd quarter	75.5	73.6	75.9	76.0	76.4	75.7	74.1	73.8	77.2	77.0
4th quarter	76.4	74.3	76.8	76.9	77.2	76.9	74.7	74.2	78.4	78.1
2001										
1st quarter	77.4	75.3	77.8	78.1	77.6	77.9	75.1	74.4	79.5	79.2
2nd quarter	78.3	76.4	78.7	79.1	77.9	78.8	75.7	74.8	80.5	80.3
3rd quarter	79.4	77.6	79.8	80.3	79.0	80.1	76.6	75.5	81.7	81.5
4th quarter	80.5	78.4	81.0	81.6	79.9	81.6	77.8	76.9	82.9	82.7
2002										
1st quarter	81.1	79.1	81.5	81.9	80.8	82.5	78.4	77.5	83.4	83.2
2nd quarter	82.2	80.0	82.7	83.3	81.7	83.4	79.3	78.3	84.7	84.5
3rd quarter	83.3	81.7	83.7	84.0	83.0	85.1	80.5	79.6	85.6	85.3
4th quarter	84.5	83.2	84.8	85.2	84.3	86.0	81.9	81.1	86.5	86.3
2003										
1st quarter	86.1	84.4	86.5	86.6	86.0	87.9	84.1	83.7	87.9	87.7
2nd quarter	87.3	85.6	87.7	87.6	87.6	89.1	85.4	84.7	89.1	88.9
3rd quarter	88.7	87.1	89.1	89.1	89.1	90.3	86.9	86.4	90.5	90.1
4th quarter	90.0	88.2	90.4	90.4	90.4	91.7	88.1	87.6	91.7	91.5
2004										
1st quarter	92.0	89.7	92.5	91.6	93.7	94.4	91.6	91.9	93.0	92.7
2nd quarter	93.6	91.3	94.2	93.3	95.5	95.9	92.9	93.2	94.9	94.5
3rd quarter	94.7	92.8	95.2	94.5	96.5	96.9	94.3	95.0	95.7	95.4
4th quarter	96.2	94.1	96.7	96.0	97.9	97.6	96.6	96.3	96.7	96.8
2005										
1st quarter	97.4	95.6	97.9	97.5	98.6	97.9	97.8	97.6	97.9	97.9
2nd quarter	98.4	96.9	98.7	98.5	99.2	98.8	99.2	98.8	98.5	98.7
3rd quarter	99.5	98.4	99.8	99.8	100.0	99.6	100.4	100.1	99.5	99.7
4th quarter	100.5	99.8	100.7	100.8	100.6	100.6	100.9	101.1	100.6	100.5

[1]Excludes farm workers, private household workers, and federal government employees.
[2]Roughly continuous and comparable with new NAICS-based series for 2006. See notes and definitions for more information.
. . . = Not available.

Section 9b: Productivity and Related Data

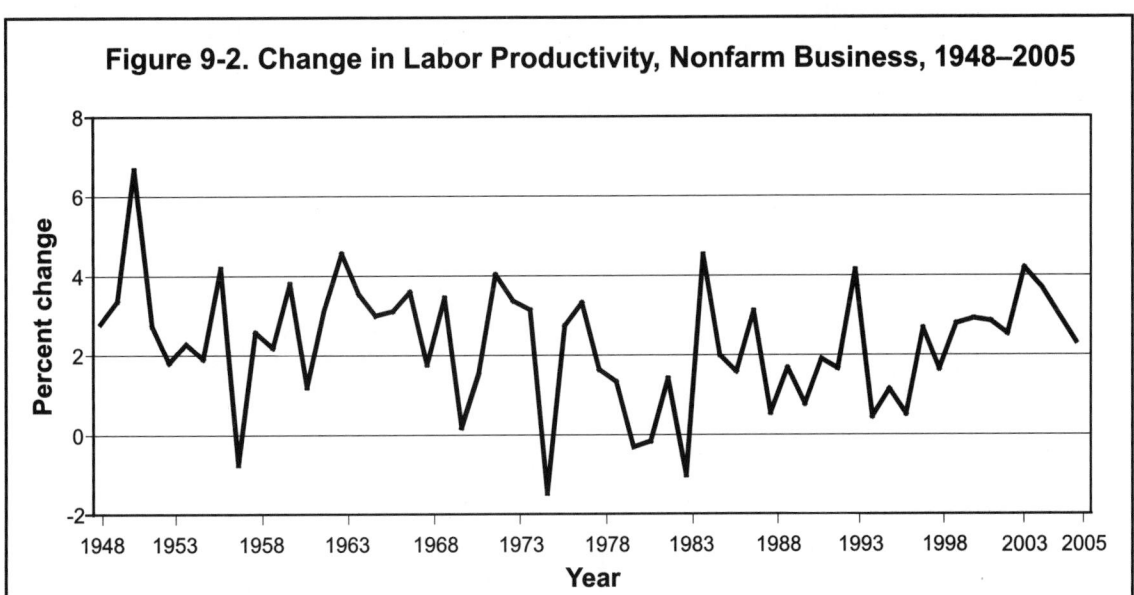

Figure 9-2. Change in Labor Productivity, Nonfarm Business, 1948–2005

- For most of the period since World War II, output per hour in nonfarm business typically grew little or declined in recession years. However, in 2001, productivity growth barely slowed. In 2002, productivity grew 4.1 percent. It slowed somewhat in following years, to 2.3 percent in 2005. Still, the record of the last 8 years—with productivity growth never falling below 2 percent and averaging 3 percent—is unmatched since the early 1960s. (Table 9-4)

- These productivity gains offset much of the increase in hourly labor compensation in recent years. For 2005, productivity growth of 2.3 percent and nominal compensation per hour growth of 4.4 percent meant that unit labor costs (the compensation cost of a unit of real output) rose only 2.0 percent, less than the 3.1 percent rise in the price of output (the implicit price deflator). In other words, labor costs were not putting any upward pressure on inflation. (Table 9-4)

- For nonfinancial businesses, unit profits and "unit nonlabor costs" (for example, depreciation and interest) can be calculated separately. Unit nonlabor costs rose rapidly in 2001—a typical effect of recession, since such costs cannot be reduced as fast as output declines—but have declined since then. Unit profits have increased at double-digit rates in each of the last four years, nearly doubling since 2001 and regaining all the ground lost between 1997 and 2001. (Table 9-4)

Table 9-4. Productivity and Related Data

(1992 = 100, seasonally adjusted.)

Year and quarter	Business sector								Nonfarm business sector							
	Output per hour of all persons	Output	Hours of all persons	Compensation per hour	Real compensation per hour	Unit labor costs	Unit nonlabor payments	Implicit price deflator	Output per hour of all persons	Output	Hours of all persons	Compensation per hour	Real compensation per hour	Unit labor costs	Unit nonlabor payments	Implicit price deflator
1947	32.2	20.4	63.4	7.0	40.7	21.8	18.6	20.6	37.0	20.1	54.2	7.5	43.3	20.2	17.8	19.3
1948	33.7	21.5	63.8	7.6	40.9	22.6	20.6	21.8	38.0	20.9	55.1	8.1	43.6	21.3	19.4	20.6
1949	34.5	21.3	61.8	7.7	42.0	22.4	20.4	21.6	39.3	20.8	53.0	8.3	45.4	21.2	20.0	20.8
1950	37.3	23.4	62.6	8.3	44.4	22.1	21.5	21.9	41.9	22.9	54.7	8.8	47.5	21.1	20.8	21.0
1951	38.5	24.9	64.6	9.0	45.1	23.5	23.7	23.6	43.0	24.6	57.2	9.6	47.8	22.3	22.5	22.4
1952	39.6	25.7	64.8	9.6	46.9	24.2	23.2	23.8	43.8	25.3	57.9	10.1	49.5	23.1	22.3	22.8
1953	41.0	26.9	65.6	10.2	49.5	24.9	22.6	24.0	44.8	26.6	59.3	10.7	51.9	23.9	22.2	23.3
1954	41.9	26.6	63.4	10.5	50.7	25.2	22.5	24.2	45.6	26.1	57.3	11.0	53.1	24.2	22.3	23.5
1955	43.6	28.7	65.8	10.8	52.2	24.8	24.0	24.5	47.5	28.3	59.6	11.4	55.3	24.1	23.7	23.9
1956	43.6	29.1	66.8	11.5	54.8	26.4	23.5	25.3	47.2	28.8	61.1	12.1	57.8	25.8	23.1	24.8
1957	45.0	29.6	65.8	12.3	56.5	27.2	24.2	26.1	48.4	29.4	60.7	12.8	59.2	26.6	23.8	25.6
1958	46.3	29.1	62.9	12.8	57.4	27.7	24.7	26.6	49.4	28.7	58.2	13.4	59.8	27.0	24.1	26.0
1959	48.0	31.4	65.5	13.3	59.4	27.8	25.2	26.8	51.3	31.2	60.9	13.9	61.8	27.1	25.0	26.3
1960	48.9	32.0	65.6	13.9	60.8	28.4	24.9	27.1	51.9	31.8	61.2	14.5	63.3	27.9	24.3	26.6
1961	50.6	32.7	64.6	14.4	62.5	28.5	25.3	27.3	53.5	32.4	60.6	15.0	64.8	28.0	24.8	26.8
1962	52.9	34.8	65.8	15.1	64.6	28.5	26.1	27.6	55.9	34.6	61.9	15.6	66.7	27.8	25.8	27.1
1963	55.0	36.4	66.2	15.6	66.1	28.4	26.6	27.7	57.8	36.2	62.6	16.1	68.1	27.8	26.3	27.3
1964	56.8	38.7	68.1	16.2	67.7	28.5	27.3	28.1	59.6	38.7	64.9	16.6	69.3	27.9	27.2	27.6
1965	58.8	41.4	70.4	16.8	69.1	28.6	28.4	28.5	61.4	41.4	67.4	17.1	70.5	27.9	28.1	28.0
1966	61.2	44.2	72.3	17.9	71.7	29.3	29.0	29.2	63.6	44.4	69.8	18.2	72.6	28.6	28.7	28.6
1967	62.5	45.1	72.1	19.0	73.5	30.3	29.5	30.0	64.7	45.1	69.7	19.2	74.5	29.7	29.2	29.5
1968	64.7	47.3	73.2	20.5	76.2	31.7	30.4	31.2	66.9	47.5	71.0	20.7	77.1	31.0	30.2	30.7
1969	65.0	48.8	75.0	21.9	77.3	33.7	30.8	32.6	67.0	48.9	73.0	22.1	78.1	33.0	30.5	32.1
1970	66.3	48.7	73.5	23.6	78.8	35.6	31.5	34.1	68.0	48.9	71.9	23.7	79.2	34.9	31.2	33.5
1971	69.0	50.6	73.3	25.1	80.2	36.3	34.1	35.5	70.7	50.7	71.7	25.2	80.7	35.7	33.8	35.0
1972	71.2	53.9	75.6	26.7	82.6	37.4	35.7	36.8	73.1	54.1	74.0	26.9	83.2	36.8	34.9	36.1
1973	73.4	57.6	78.5	28.9	84.3	39.4	37.5	38.7	75.3	58.0	77.0	29.1	84.7	38.6	35.3	37.4
1974	72.3	56.8	78.7	31.7	83.3	43.9	40.0	42.4	74.2	57.3	77.2	31.9	83.8	43.0	38.1	41.2
1975	74.8	56.3	75.3	34.9	84.1	46.7	46.3	46.6	76.2	56.3	73.9	35.1	84.5	46.0	44.9	45.6
1976	77.1	60.0	77.8	38.0	86.4	49.2	48.7	49.0	78.7	60.2	76.5	38.1	86.6	48.3	47.8	48.1
1977	78.5	63.3	80.7	41.0	87.6	52.2	51.5	52.0	80.0	63.6	79.5	41.2	88.0	51.5	50.7	51.2
1978	79.3	67.3	84.9	44.5	89.1	56.2	54.8	55.6	81.0	67.8	83.7	44.8	89.6	55.3	53.4	54.6
1979	79.3	69.6	87.7	48.9	89.3	61.6	58.2	60.4	80.7	70.0	86.6	49.1	89.7	60.8	56.5	59.2
1980	79.2	68.8	87.0	54.1	89.1	68.4	61.3	65.8	80.6	69.2	85.9	54.4	89.5	67.5	60.4	64.9
1981	80.8	70.7	87.6	59.3	89.3	73.5	69.1	71.8	81.7	70.7	86.6	59.7	89.8	73.1	67.7	71.1
1982	80.1	68.6	85.6	63.6	90.4	79.4	70.1	75.9	80.8	68.4	84.7	63.9	90.8	79.1	69.3	75.5
1983	83.0	72.3	87.1	66.3	90.3	79.8	76.3	78.5	84.5	72.9	86.3	66.6	90.9	78.9	76.1	77.9
1984	85.2	78.6	92.2	69.1	90.7	81.1	80.2	80.8	86.1	78.9	91.6	69.5	91.1	80.7	79.2	80.1
1985	87.1	82.2	94.3	72.5	92.0	83.2	82.0	82.7	87.5	82.2	94.0	72.6	92.2	83.0	81.5	82.5
1986	89.7	85.3	95.1	76.1	94.9	84.9	82.6	84.1	90.2	85.4	94.7	76.4	95.2	84.7	82.4	83.9
1987	90.1	88.3	97.9	79.0	95.2	87.6	83.1	85.9	90.6	88.4	97.6	79.2	95.5	87.4	82.8	85.7
1988	91.5	92.1	101.0	83.0	96.5	90.7	85.1	88.6	92.1	92.4	100.0	83.1	96.7	90.2	85.0	88.3
1989	92.4	95.4	103.0	85.2	95.0	92.2	91.3	91.9	92.8	95.7	103.0	85.3	95.1	91.9	90.9	91.5
1990	94.4	96.9	103.0	90.6	96.2	96.0	93.7	95.1	94.5	97.1	103.0	90.4	96.1	95.7	93.5	94.9
1991	95.9	96.1	100.0	95.1	97.4	99.1	96.7	98.2	96.1	96.3	100.0	95.0	97.4	98.9	96.8	98.1
1992	100.0	100.0	100.0	100.0	100.0	100.0	100.0	100.0	100.0	100.0	100.0	100.0	100.0	100.0	100.0	100.0
1993	100.4	103.1	102.7	102.2	99.7	101.8	102.6	102.1	100.4	103.4	102.9	102.0	99.5	101.6	103.1	102.1
1994	101.3	108.2	106.8	103.6	99.0	102.3	106.7	103.9	101.5	108.3	106.6	103.7	99.1	102.1	107.3	104.0
1995	101.5	111.4	109.7	105.8	98.7	104.2	108.3	105.7	102.0	111.8	109.6	105.9	98.8	103.8	109.3	105.8
1996	104.5	116.5	111.5	109.5	99.4	104.8	111.9	107.4	104.7	116.8	111.5	109.4	99.4	104.5	112.1	107.3
1997	106.5	122.7	115.2	113.0	100.5	106.1	113.8	109.0	106.4	122.8	115.4	112.8	100.3	106.0	114.5	109.1
1998	109.5	128.6	117.5	119.9	105.2	109.5	110.0	109.7	109.4	128.9	117.9	119.6	104.9	109.3	111.0	109.9
1999	112.8	135.2	119.8	125.8	108.0	111.5	109.4	110.7	112.5	135.6	120.5	125.2	107.5	111.3	110.9	111.1
2000	116.1	140.5	121.0	134.7	112.0	116.0	107.2	112.7	115.7	140.8	121.7	134.2	111.5	116.0	108.7	113.3
2001	119.1	141.0	118.4	140.4	113.5	117.9	110.0	114.9	118.6	141.3	119.2	139.5	112.8	117.7	111.6	115.4
2002	124.0	143.1	115.4	145.4	115.7	117.3	114.1	116.1	123.5	143.4	116.1	144.6	115.1	117.1	116.0	116.7
2003	128.7	147.5	114.6	151.2	117.7	117.5	118.3	117.8	128.0	147.8	115.4	150.4	117.1	117.5	119.6	118.3
2004	132.7	154.0	116.1	157.0	119.0	118.3	125.1	120.8	131.8	154.2	117.0	155.9	118.2	118.3	126.0	121.1
2005	135.7	159.8	117.7	163.8	120.2	120.7	130.3	124.3	134.9	160.0	118.7	162.7	119.3	120.7	132.2	124.9
2003																
1st quarter	125.8	144.4	114.8	148.0	115.7	117.7	116.5	117.3	125.1	144.6	115.5	147.3	115.1	117.7	118.2	117.9
2nd quarter	128.0	146.0	114.1	150.8	117.8	117.8	116.7	117.4	127.0	146.1	115.1	149.7	117.0	117.9	118.1	118.0
3rd quarter	130.8	149.7	114.5	152.5	118.4	116.6	120.2	118.0	130.1	150.0	115.3	151.7	117.8	116.6	121.5	118.4
4th quarter	130.3	150.1	115.2	153.6	118.9	117.9	119.5	118.5	129.9	150.6	115.9	152.9	118.4	117.7	120.5	118.7
2004																
1st quarter	131.4	151.7	115.5	154.4	118.5	117.5	122.9	119.5	130.5	151.9	116.4	153.4	117.8	117.6	123.6	119.8
2nd quarter	132.8	153.5	115.6	155.8	118.3	117.3	126.2	120.6	132.2	153.9	116.4	154.8	117.6	117.2	126.8	120.7
3rd quarter	133.0	154.8	116.4	157.5	119.1	118.5	125.5	121.1	132.2	155.1	117.3	156.6	118.3	118.4	126.4	121.4
4th quarter	133.5	155.8	116.7	160.1	120.0	119.9	125.8	122.1	132.4	156.0	117.8	158.7	118.9	119.9	127.0	122.5
2005																
1st quarter	134.5	157.4	117.0	161.6	120.4	120.1	127.9	123.0	133.5	157.6	118.0	160.4	119.5	120.1	129.4	123.5
2nd quarter	134.9	159.0	117.9	162.0	119.5	120.0	130.0	123.7	134.3	159.4	118.6	161.0	118.9	119.9	131.8	124.3
3rd quarter	136.6	160.9	117.8	165.2	120.3	121.0	131.1	124.7	135.8	161.3	118.8	164.1	119.5	120.9	133.1	125.3
4th quarter	136.7	161.7	118.3	166.5	120.3	121.8	132.3	125.7	135.8	162.0	119.3	165.3	119.4	121.7	134.3	126.4

Table 9-4. Productivity and Related Data—Continued

(1992 = 100, seasonally adjusted.)

Year and quarter	Nonfinancial corporations										Manufacturing					
	Output per hour of all employees	Output	Employee hours	Compensation per hour	Real compensation per hour	Unit costs			Unit profits	Implicit price deflator	Output per hour of all persons	Output	Hours of all persons	Compensation per hour	Real compensation per hour	Unit labor costs
						Total	Labor costs	Nonlabor costs								
1947	...	...	...	...	...	...	...	...	...	...	...	...	...	...	...	...
1948	...	...	...	...	...	...	...	...	...	...	...	...	...	...	...	...
1949	...	...	...	...	...	...	...	...	...	...	...	...	...	...	...	...
1950	...	...	...	...	...	...	...	...	...	...	...	...	...	...	...	...
1951	...	...	...	...	...	...	...	...	...	...	...	...	...	...	...	...
1952	...	...	...	...	...	...	...	...	...	...	...	...	...	...	...	...
1953	...	...	...	...	...	...	...	...	...	...	...	...	...	...	...	...
1954	...	...	...	...	...	...	...	...	...	...	...	...	...	...	...	...
1955	...	...	...	...	...	...	...	...	...	...	...	...	...	...	...	...
1956	...	...	...	...	...	...	...	...	...	...	...	...	...	...	...	...
1957	...	...	...	...	...	...	...	...	...	...	...	...	...	...	...	...
1958	52.8	25.4	48.0	15.0	67.2	27.1	28.4	23.5	47.2	28.9	...	...	...	...	...	...
1959	55.3	28.2	50.9	15.6	69.3	26.6	28.1	22.3	55.8	29.2	...	...	...	...	...	...
1960	56.2	29.1	51.7	16.2	70.8	27.3	28.8	23.3	50.2	29.4	...	...	...	...	...	...
1961	57.9	29.7	51.3	16.7	72.4	27.5	28.8	23.8	50.3	29.5	...	...	...	...	...	...
1962	60.4	32.2	53.3	17.4	74.4	27.3	28.7	23.4	54.5	29.7	...	...	...	...	...	...
1963	62.6	34.1	54.5	17.9	75.7	27.2	28.6	23.4	57.3	29.9	...	...	...	...	...	...
1964	63.6	36.5	57.4	18.2	76.2	27.2	28.7	23.3	59.7	30.1	...	...	...	...	...	...
1965	65.1	39.5	60.7	18.8	77.1	27.3	28.8	23.1	64.1	30.6	...	...	...	...	...	...
1966	66.2	42.3	63.9	19.8	79.2	28.2	29.9	23.3	63.6	31.3	...	...	...	...	...	...
1967	67.1	43.4	64.6	20.9	81.1	29.4	31.2	24.7	59.9	32.2	...	...	...	...	...	...
1968	69.5	46.1	66.4	22.5	83.8	30.7	32.4	26.2	60.0	33.4	...	...	...	...	...	...
1969	69.5	47.9	69.0	24.0	84.8	33.0	34.6	28.6	54.0	34.8	...	...	...	...	...	...
1970	69.8	47.4	67.9	25.7	85.9	35.6	36.9	32.2	44.4	36.4	...	...	...	...	...	...
1971	72.7	49.3	67.8	27.3	87.4	36.5	37.6	33.6	50.5	37.8	...	...	...	...	...	...
1972	74.2	53.1	71.6	28.8	89.2	37.5	38.8	33.9	54.1	39.0	...	...	...	...	...	...
1973	74.8	56.3	75.2	31.0	90.4	39.9	41.4	35.7	54.9	41.2	...	...	...	...	...	...
1974	73.3	55.3	75.5	33.9	89.2	44.9	46.3	41.1	48.4	45.2	...	...	...	...	...	...
1975	76.2	54.6	71.7	37.3	89.7	48.3	49.0	46.6	63.1	49.6	...	...	...	...	...	...
1976	78.6	58.9	75.0	40.3	91.8	50.0	51.3	46.4	71.4	51.9	...	...	...	...	...	...
1977	80.6	63.2	78.4	43.5	93.0	52.5	54.0	48.4	77.3	54.7	...	...	...	...	...	...
1978	81.7	67.4	82.5	47.6	95.1	56.4	58.2	51.2	79.1	58.4	...	...	...	...	...	...
1979	81.0	69.5	85.8	51.9	94.9	61.9	64.1	55.8	74.0	62.9	...	...	...	...	...	...
1980	80.8	68.8	85.2	57.2	94.1	69.2	70.8	64.9	66.9	69.0	...	...	...	...	...	...
1981	82.9	71.6	86.4	62.4	93.9	74.8	75.3	73.5	81.0	75.4	...	...	...	...	...	...
1982	83.1	69.9	84.1	66.5	94.4	80.4	80.0	81.3	75.2	79.9	...	...	...	...	...	...
1983	85.7	73.1	85.3	68.9	94.0	80.7	80.4	81.6	91.2	81.7	...	...	...	...	...	...
1984	87.8	79.7	90.8	71.9	94.3	81.7	81.9	81.3	108.0	84.1	...	...	...	...	...	...
1985	89.6	83.2	92.9	75.2	95.4	83.8	83.9	83.6	102.0	85.5	...	...	...	...	...	...
1986	91.4	85.2	93.2	78.9	98.3	86.3	86.3	86.3	90.2	86.6	...	...	...	...	...	...
1987	93.3	89.7	96.1	81.6	98.3	87.0	87.4	85.8	100.0	88.1	89.2	92.5	104.0	81.3	98.0	91.2
1988	95.7	94.9	99.1	84.9	98.7	88.2	88.7	86.8	112.0	90.3	91.0	97.4	107.0	84.1	97.8	92.4
1989	94.6	96.6	102.0	87.0	97.0	92.4	92.0	93.3	101.0	93.2	92.0	99.0	108.0	86.6	96.6	94.2
1990	95.4	97.8	103.0	91.1	96.8	96.0	95.5	97.3	96.9	96.1	93.9	98.6	105.0	90.5	96.1	96.3
1991	97.4	97.0	99.6	95.5	97.9	99.3	98.0	103.0	93.2	98.7	96.3	96.8	101.0	95.6	98.0	99.2
1992	100.0	100.0	100.0	100.0	100.0	100.0	100.0	100.0	100.0	100.0	100.0	100.0	100.0	100.0	100.0	100.0
1993	100.3	102.8	102.4	101.8	99.3	101.0	101.4	99.9	114.1	102.2	102.5	103.9	101.4	102.0	99.5	99.6
1994	102.2	109.2	106.8	103.5	98.9	101.2	101.3	100.8	131.7	103.9	106.1	110.0	103.8	105.3	100.6	99.3
1995	103.3	114.3	110.6	105.3	98.2	101.7	101.9	101.2	136.9	104.9	110.7	115.8	104.6	107.3	100.1	96.9
1996	107.1	120.6	112.6	108.5	98.5	100.9	101.3	100.0	150.0	105.3	115.0	119.8	104.2	109.3	99.3	95.1
1997	109.9	128.4	116.9	111.7	99.4	101.1	101.7	99.7	154.3	105.9	121.2	128.6	106.0	112.2	99.8	92.6
1998	113.7	135.8	119.5	118.3	103.8	102.9	104.1	99.5	137.0	105.9	127.9	135.3	105.7	118.8	104.2	92.8
1999	117.9	144.0	122.2	124.1	106.6	104.0	105.3	100.4	129.1	106.2	133.6	140.3	105.1	123.4	106.0	92.4
2000	122.4	151.5	123.7	133.0	110.5	107.4	108.6	104.2	108.7	107.5	139.4	144.1	103.4	134.7	112.0	96.7
2001	124.7	150.2	120.4	138.6	112.1	111.6	111.2	112.6	82.2	108.9	141.5	136.8	96.6	137.9	111.5	97.4
2002	129.7	151.5	116.7	143.6	114.3	110.7	110.7	110.8	98.0	109.6	151.4	135.9	89.8	147.8	117.7	97.6
2003	134.5	154.7	115.0	149.4	116.3	111.2	111.1	111.2	110.0	111.0	160.8	137.3	85.4	158.2	123.2	98.4
2004	139.4	162.5	116.6	154.3	116.9	110.3	110.7	109.2	138.8	112.8	163.8	139.1	84.9	161.4	122.3	98.5
2005	144.9	171.3	118.2	161.0	118.1	111.1	111.1	110.9	154.3	114.9	170.5	143.3	84.0	168.8	123.8	99.0
2003																
1st quarter	131.9	152.1	115.3	146.2	114.2	111.3	110.8	112.7	103.0	110.6	158.0	137.4	86.9	154.6	120.8	97.8
2nd quarter	133.6	153.4	114.8	148.8	116.2	111.3	111.4	111.2	105.9	110.8	159.7	136.5	85.5	157.2	122.8	98.5
3rd quarter	135.7	155.7	114.7	150.8	117.1	111.0	111.1	110.8	112.9	111.2	163.0	137.2	84.2	159.4	123.7	97.7
4th quarter	136.6	157.5	115.3	152.0	117.7	110.9	111.3	110.0	117.8	111.6	162.6	138.1	84.9	162.0	125.4	99.6
2004																
1st quarter	137.6	159.6	116.1	151.8	116.5	110.0	110.4	109.1	131.2	111.9	161.8	138.1	85.4	157.5	120.8	97.3
2nd quarter	138.6	161.1	116.2	153.2	116.4	110.2	110.5	109.3	139.2	112.8	163.3	138.9	85.0	159.8	121.4	97.8
3rd quarter	140.5	164.0	116.8	155.0	117.1	110.0	110.3	109.2	142.3	112.9	164.0	139.3	84.9	163.0	123.2	99.4
4th quarter	141.0	165.3	117.2	157.1	117.7	110.8	111.4	109.3	142.4	113.7	166.1	140.3	84.4	165.5	124.0	99.6
2005																
1st quarter	142.8	167.5	117.4	158.6	118.2	110.9	111.1	110.3	148.5	114.2	168.1	141.7	84.3	166.1	123.7	98.8
2nd quarter	144.5	170.6	118.1	159.3	117.6	110.2	110.2	110.2	159.0	114.8	169.7	142.2	83.8	167.8	123.8	98.9
3rd quarter	145.6	172.3	118.3	162.4	118.3	111.9	111.6	112.6	149.9	115.3	171.2	143.1	83.6	170.7	124.3	99.7
4th quarter	146.7	174.7	119.1	163.6	118.2	111.3	111.5	110.5	159.6	115.6	173.2	146.3	84.5	170.9	123.4	98.7

. . . = Not available.

Section 9c: Profits by Industry

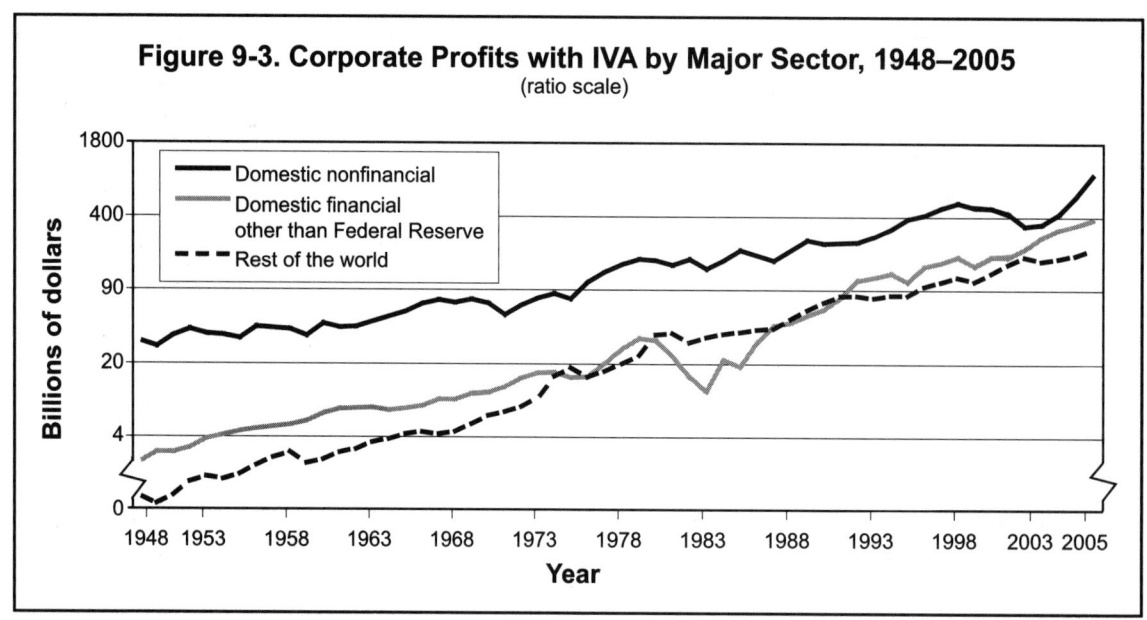

Figure 9-3. Corporate Profits with IVA by Major Sector, 1948–2005
(ratio scale)

- Total profits of U.S. corporations, with IVA (the inventory valuation adjustment) but without the CCAdj (capital consumption adjustment), rose at a 6.9 percent annual rate between 1948 and 2005. (Tables 9-5 and 9-6) This was equal to the rate of increase in total national income over the same period. Another component of the capital share of income—net interest—has increased at a 9.6 percent rate over the last 57 years. (Table 1-11)

- Profits rose 107 percent in the four years from 2001 through 2005, after sinking 11 percent from the previous high in 1997 through 2001. The domestic financial sector (other than the Federal Reserve) had increasing profits even during the general recession, and from 2001 to 2005, its profits rose 82 percent. Domestic nonfinancial corporations saw profits rise 180 percent over the same four years. (Tables 9-5 and 9-6)

- An examination of the NAICS industries shown in Table 9-6 back to 1998—the first years for which the new classification system is available—indicates that a majority of the nonfinancial industry groups have now regained the profits totals of 1998. The lagging industries are utilities, machinery, electrical equipment, and motor vehicles—the last of which has lost billions of dollars in each of the past five years. (Table 9-6)

Table 9-5. Corporate Profits with Inventory Valuation Adjustment by Industry Group (SIC Basis)

(Billions of dollars.)   NIPA Tables 6.16B, 6.16C

Classification basis, year, and quarter	Total	Domestic industries											
		Financial			Nonfinancial								
							Manufacturing						
								Durable goods					
		Total	Federal Reserve banks	Other financial	Total	Total	Primary metal industries	Fabricated metal products	Industrial machinery and equipment	Electronic and other electric equipment	Motor vehicles and equipment	Other durable goods
1972 SIC BASIS												
1948	33.7	32.5	0.2	2.5	29.7	17.5	1.6	0.8	1.3	0.6	1.4	1.8
1949	31.5	30.3	0.2	3.1	27.0	16.2	1.5	0.7	1.3	0.8	2.1	1.7
1950	38.3	37.0	0.2	3.1	33.7	21.0	2.3	1.1	1.6	1.2	3.1	2.6
1951	43.6	41.8	0.3	3.4	38.1	24.7	3.1	1.3	2.3	1.3	2.4	2.8
1952	41.2	39.3	0.3	4.1	34.9	21.7	1.9	1.0	2.3	1.5	2.4	2.6
1953	40.7	38.9	0.4	4.4	34.0	22.0	2.5	1.0	1.9	1.4	2.6	2.6
1954	39.0	37.1	0.3	4.8	32.0	19.9	1.7	0.9	1.7	1.2	2.1	2.9
1955	48.1	45.8	0.3	5.0	40.5	26.1	2.9	1.1	1.7	1.1	4.1	3.5
1956	47.8	44.9	0.5	5.2	39.3	24.8	3.0	1.1	2.1	1.2	2.2	3.1
1957	47.5	44.4	0.6	5.4	38.5	24.1	3.1	1.1	2.0	1.5	2.6	3.1
1958	42.7	40.2	0.6	5.9	33.7	19.5	1.9	0.9	1.5	1.3	0.9	2.9
1959	53.5	50.8	0.7	6.9	43.2	26.5	2.3	1.1	2.2	1.7	3.0	3.5
1960	51.5	48.3	0.9	7.5	39.9	23.8	2.0	0.8	1.8	1.3	3.0	2.7
1961	51.8	48.5	0.8	7.6	40.2	23.4	1.6	1.0	1.9	1.3	2.5	2.9
1962	57.0	53.3	0.9	7.7	44.7	26.3	1.6	1.2	2.4	1.5	4.0	3.4
1963	62.1	58.1	1.0	7.3	49.8	29.7	2.0	1.3	2.6	1.6	4.9	4.0
1964	68.6	64.1	1.1	7.6	55.4	32.6	2.5	1.5	3.3	1.7	4.6	4.4
1965	78.9	74.2	1.3	8.0	64.9	39.8	3.1	2.1	4.0	2.7	6.2	5.2
1966	84.6	80.1	1.7	9.1	69.3	42.6	3.6	2.4	4.6	3.0	5.2	5.2
1967	82.0	77.2	2.0	9.2	66.0	39.2	2.7	2.5	4.2	3.0	4.0	4.9
1968	88.8	83.2	2.5	10.3	70.4	41.9	1.9	2.3	4.2	2.9	5.5	5.6
1969	85.5	78.9	3.1	10.5	65.3	37.3	1.4	2.0	3.8	2.3	4.8	4.9
1970	74.4	67.3	3.5	11.9	52.0	27.5	0.8	1.1	3.1	1.3	1.3	2.9
1971	88.3	80.4	3.3	14.3	62.8	35.1	0.8	1.5	3.1	2.0	5.2	4.1
1972	101.2	91.7	3.3	15.8	72.6	41.9	1.7	2.2	4.5	2.9	6.0	5.6
1973	115.3	100.4	4.5	16.0	79.9	47.2	2.3	2.7	4.9	3.2	5.9	6.2
1974	109.5	92.1	5.7	14.5	71.9	41.4	5.0	1.8	3.3	0.6	0.7	4.0
1975	135.0	120.4	5.6	14.6	100.2	55.2	2.8	3.3	5.1	2.6	2.3	4.7
1976	165.6	149.0	5.9	19.1	124.1	71.3	2.1	3.9	6.9	3.8	7.4	7.3
1977	194.7	175.6	6.1	25.8	143.7	79.3	1.0	4.5	8.6	5.9	9.4	8.5
1978	222.4	199.6	7.6	31.9	160.0	90.5	3.6	5.0	10.7	6.7	9.0	10.5
1979	231.8	197.2	9.4	30.9	156.8	89.6	3.5	5.3	9.5	5.6	4.7	8.5
1980	211.4	175.9	11.8	22.2	141.9	78.3	2.7	4.4	8.0	5.2	-4.3	2.7
1981	219.1	189.4	14.4	14.7	160.3	91.1	3.1	4.5	9.0	5.2	0.3	-2.6
1982	191.0	158.5	15.2	10.8	132.4	67.1	-4.7	2.7	3.1	1.7	0.0	2.1
1983	226.5	191.4	14.6	20.9	155.9	76.2	-4.9	3.1	4.0	3.5	5.3	8.4
1984	264.6	228.1	16.4	18.0	193.7	91.8	-0.4	4.7	6.0	5.1	9.2	14.6
1985	257.5	219.4	16.3	29.5	173.5	84.3	-0.9	4.9	5.7	2.6	7.4	10.1
1986	253.0	213.5	15.5	41.2	156.8	57.9	0.9	5.2	0.8	2.7	4.6	12.1
1987	301.4	253.4	15.7	44.1	193.5	86.3	2.6	5.5	5.4	5.9	3.7	17.6
1987 SIC BASIS												
1987	301.4	253.4	15.7	44.1	193.5	86.3	2.6	5.5	5.4	5.9	3.7	17.6
1988	363.9	306.9	17.6	51.1	238.2	121.2	6.0	6.5	11.1	7.7	6.2	16.5
1989	367.4	300.3	20.2	57.8	222.3	110.9	6.4	6.4	12.2	9.3	2.7	14.2
1990	396.6	320.5	21.4	73.0	226.1	113.1	3.5	6.0	11.8	8.5	-1.9	15.9
1991	427.9	351.4	20.3	103.9	227.3	98.0	1.5	5.3	5.7	10.0	-5.4	17.3
1992	458.3	385.2	17.8	111.9	255.4	99.5	0.0	6.2	7.5	10.4	-1.0	17.4
1993	513.1	436.1	16.2	120.6	299.3	115.6	0.4	7.4	7.5	15.2	6.0	19.4
1994	564.6	487.6	18.1	101.8	367.7	147.0	2.3	11.1	9.1	22.8	7.8	21.3
1995	656.0	563.2	22.5	139.7	401.0	173.7	7.1	11.8	14.8	21.5	0.0	25.8
1996	736.1	634.2	22.1	150.5	461.6	188.8	5.6	14.5	16.9	20.1	4.2	29.2
1997	812.3	701.4	23.8	169.2	508.4	209.0	6.3	17.0	16.7	25.3	4.8	33.0
1998	738.5	635.5	25.2	140.7	469.6	173.5	6.5	16.4	19.5	8.9	5.9	30.1
1999	776.8	655.3	26.3	170.1	458.9	175.2	2.4	16.2	12.4	5.3	7.3	35.3
2000	759.3	613.6	30.8	173.0	409.8	166.3	1.2	15.4	16.3	4.7	-1.5	28.8
1998												
1st quarter	752.0	643.1	25.0	147.9	470.2	178.5	6.9	14.9	14.4	12.2	6.4	28.8
2nd quarter	732.5	626.3	25.2	136.4	464.7	170.1	6.2	16.7	19.5	8.3	3.5	27.4
3rd quarter	743.5	647.3	25.4	136.9	485.0	176.6	6.1	18.5	20.4	6.6	4.5	31.3
4th quarter	725.9	625.3	25.1	141.8	458.4	168.8	6.8	15.7	23.7	8.3	9.3	32.9
1999												
1st quarter	771.3	657.3	24.9	163.0	469.5	175.0	3.8	15.9	9.8	4.3	8.9	33.9
2nd quarter	773.2	656.5	25.5	157.8	473.2	182.5	3.1	15.7	12.8	4.9	6.1	37.8
3rd quarter	766.8	648.3	26.2	175.3	446.8	174.2	1.5	16.2	12.3	6.9	7.3	34.3
4th quarter	796.1	659.1	28.6	184.5	446.0	169.1	1.2	17.1	14.7	4.9	6.7	35.3
2000												
1st quarter	766.8	635.7	30.0	179.5	426.2	172.6	2.1	18.8	12.6	2.5	1.2	33.3
2nd quarter	773.5	634.9	30.5	164.5	440.0	186.1	2.0	16.2	16.1	8.7	0.3	33.7
3rd quarter	756.3	611.7	31.1	171.1	409.5	164.9	0.5	15.2	18.1	3.4	-2.4	27.3
4th quarter	740.7	572.1	31.7	176.8	363.6	141.6	0.3	11.3	18.1	4.1	-5.2	21.0

Table 9-5. Corporate Profits with Inventory Valuation Adjustment by Industry Group (SIC Basis) —Continued

(Billions of dollars.)

NIPA Tables 6.16B, 6.16C

Classification basis, year, and quarter	Manufacturing—Continued / Nondurable goods					Transportation and public utilities				Wholesale trade	Retail trade	Other nonfinancial	Rest of the world
	Total	Food and kindred products	Chemicals and allied products	Petroleum and coal products	Other nondurable goods	Total	Transportation	Communications	Electric, gas, and sanitary services				
1972 SIC BASIS													
1948	10.0	1.9	1.7	2.8	3.7	3.0	1.5	0.4	1.1	2.4	3.2	3.5	1.3
1949	8.1	1.6	1.8	1.9	2.8	3.0	1.2	0.5	1.4	1.9	2.8	3.1	1.1
1950	9.0	1.6	2.3	2.3	2.7	4.1	1.9	0.7	1.5	2.1	3.0	3.5	1.3
1951	11.4	1.4	2.8	2.8	4.4	4.7	1.9	1.0	1.8	2.6	2.6	3.6	1.7
1952	10.0	1.8	2.3	2.3	3.6	5.0	1.9	1.1	2.0	2.3	2.7	3.3	1.9
1953	10.0	1.8	2.2	2.7	3.3	5.0	1.6	1.2	2.2	1.8	2.3	3.0	1.8
1954	9.5	1.6	2.2	2.8	2.9	4.7	1.0	1.3	2.4	1.7	2.3	3.3	2.0
1955	11.8	2.2	3.0	3.0	3.6	5.7	1.5	1.7	2.5	2.4	2.9	3.5	2.4
1956	12.0	1.8	2.8	3.3	4.1	5.9	1.4	1.8	2.7	2.2	2.6	3.9	2.8
1957	10.8	1.8	2.8	2.6	3.6	5.9	1.1	2.0	2.7	2.2	2.6	3.8	3.1
1958	10.2	2.1	2.5	2.1	3.4	5.9	0.9	2.3	2.7	2.2	2.6	3.5	2.5
1959	12.9	2.5	3.5	2.6	4.3	7.1	1.1	2.8	3.1	2.9	3.3	3.4	2.7
1960	12.2	2.2	3.1	2.6	4.2	7.5	0.9	3.0	3.6	2.5	2.8	3.3	3.1
1961	12.1	2.4	3.3	2.3	4.2	7.9	1.0	3.2	3.7	2.5	3.0	3.4	3.3
1962	12.3	2.4	3.2	2.2	4.4	8.5	1.0	3.6	3.9	2.8	3.4	3.6	3.8
1963	13.3	2.7	3.7	2.2	4.7	9.5	1.4	3.9	4.2	2.8	3.6	4.1	4.1
1964	14.5	2.7	4.1	2.4	5.3	10.2	1.6	4.0	4.6	3.4	4.5	4.7	4.5
1965	16.5	2.9	4.6	2.9	6.1	11.0	2.1	4.3	4.6	3.8	4.9	5.4	4.7
1966	18.6	3.3	4.9	3.4	6.9	12.0	2.3	4.8	4.9	4.0	4.9	5.9	4.5
1967	18.0	3.3	4.3	4.0	6.4	10.9	1.3	4.8	4.8	4.1	5.7	6.1	4.8
1968	19.4	3.2	5.3	3.8	7.1	11.0	1.0	5.1	4.9	4.6	6.4	6.6	5.6
1969	18.1	3.1	4.6	3.4	7.0	10.7	0.7	5.4	4.6	4.9	6.4	6.1	6.6
1970	17.0	3.2	3.9	3.7	6.1	8.3	-0.1	4.8	3.6	4.4	6.0	5.8	7.1
1971	18.5	3.6	4.5	3.8	6.6	8.9	0.7	4.1	4.1	5.2	7.2	6.4	7.9
1972	19.2	3.0	5.3	3.3	7.6	9.5	1.5	3.9	4.0	6.9	7.4	7.0	9.5
1973	22.0	2.5	6.2	5.4	7.9	9.1	1.3	4.3	3.4	8.2	6.6	8.7	14.9
1974	26.1	2.6	5.3	10.9	7.3	7.6	2.0	4.1	1.5	11.5	2.3	9.1	17.5
1975	34.5	8.6	6.4	10.1	9.5	11.0	1.0	4.3	5.7	13.8	8.2	12.0	14.6
1976	39.9	7.1	8.2	13.5	11.1	15.3	3.0	5.7	6.5	12.9	10.5	14.0	16.5
1977	41.4	6.9	7.8	13.1	13.6	18.6	3.7	6.6	8.3	15.6	12.4	17.8	19.1
1978	45.1	6.2	8.3	15.8	14.8	21.8	4.1	8.6	9.1	15.6	12.3	19.8	22.9
1979	52.5	5.8	7.2	24.8	14.7	17.0	3.5	7.5	6.0	18.8	9.8	21.6	34.6
1980	59.5	6.1	5.7	34.7	13.1	18.4	2.7	7.7	8.0	17.2	6.2	21.8	35.5
1981	71.6	9.2	8.0	40.0	14.5	20.3	1.7	8.6	10.0	22.4	9.9	16.7	29.7
1982	62.1	7.3	5.1	34.7	15.0	23.1	-0.1	8.6	14.6	19.6	13.4	9.2	32.6
1983	56.7	6.3	7.4	23.9	19.1	29.5	3.2	9.9	16.4	21.0	18.7	10.4	35.1
1984	52.6	6.8	8.2	17.6	20.1	40.1	6.1	12.8	21.3	29.5	21.1	11.1	36.6
1985	54.6	8.8	6.6	18.7	20.5	33.8	1.8	14.2	17.8	23.9	22.2	9.2	38.1
1986	31.7	7.5	7.5	-4.7	21.3	35.8	3.4	17.6	14.7	24.1	23.5	15.5	39.5
1987	45.6	11.4	14.4	-1.5	21.3	41.9	3.4	19.4	19.1	18.6	23.4	23.4	48.0
1987 SIC BASIS													
1987	45.6	11.4	14.4	-1.5	21.3	41.9	3.4	19.4	19.1	18.6	23.4	23.4	48.0
1988	67.1	12.0	18.6	12.7	23.7	48.4	7.9	19.5	21.1	20.1	20.3	28.3	57.0
1989	59.7	11.1	18.2	6.5	23.9	43.3	1.3	18.2	23.9	21.8	20.8	25.5	67.1
1990	69.2	14.3	16.8	16.4	21.7	44.2	-0.4	20.1	24.5	19.2	20.7	29.0	76.1
1991	63.6	18.1	16.2	7.3	22.0	53.3	2.3	23.5	27.5	21.7	26.7	27.5	76.5
1992	59.0	18.2	16.0	-0.9	25.6	58.4	2.3	27.7	28.4	25.1	32.6	39.7	73.1
1993	59.7	16.4	15.9	2.7	24.7	69.5	7.0	32.9	29.6	26.3	39.1	48.9	76.9
1994	72.6	19.9	23.2	1.2	28.3	83.2	10.5	36.7	36.1	30.9	46.2	60.4	77.1
1995	92.8	27.1	27.9	7.1	30.6	85.8	11.5	33.6	40.8	27.3	43.1	71.2	92.8
1996	98.2	22.1	26.4	15.0	34.7	91.3	15.7	35.0	40.7	39.8	51.9	89.7	101.9
1997	105.9	24.6	32.3	17.3	31.7	84.2	19.0	25.5	39.7	47.6	64.2	103.4	110.9
1998	86.2	21.9	26.5	6.7	31.1	78.9	21.6	21.4	35.8	52.3	73.4	91.5	103.0
1999	96.4	28.1	25.2	4.3	38.9	56.8	15.8	4.6	36.3	52.6	74.6	99.7	121.5
2000	101.5	25.7	16.0	29.1	30.7	43.8	15.2	1.3	27.3	56.9	70.1	72.8	145.7
1998													
1st quarter	94.9	23.6	30.5	9.4	31.3	76.8	20.6	22.1	34.1	50.2	71.3	93.4	108.8
2nd quarter	88.5	24.6	22.9	8.9	32.1	81.0	21.5	24.0	35.5	52.6	72.5	88.6	106.2
3rd quarter	89.2	25.8	24.9	7.3	31.3	86.7	24.2	25.1	37.4	57.5	73.8	90.4	96.2
4th quarter	72.0	13.6	27.6	1.3	29.6	71.0	20.3	14.5	36.3	48.8	76.0	93.8	100.5
1999													
1st quarter	98.5	28.5	31.8	0.6	37.6	62.6	16.8	9.2	36.6	54.8	79.4	97.7	113.9
2nd quarter	102.1	28.6	31.8	4.0	37.7	52.1	16.0	3.4	32.8	53.1	79.0	106.6	116.6
3rd quarter	95.8	27.0	22.1	8.2	38.5	52.5	13.5	1.3	37.6	49.3	69.6	101.2	118.5
4th quarter	89.1	28.2	14.9	4.4	41.6	59.9	17.0	4.5	38.4	53.3	70.5	93.2	137.0
2000													
1st quarter	102.1	28.3	20.0	15.3	38.6	47.5	14.7	-0.3	33.0	52.4	75.5	78.3	131.1
2nd quarter	109.2	25.4	17.4	33.8	32.7	42.4	19.4	-3.4	26.4	63.2	70.8	77.4	138.5
3rd quarter	102.8	28.2	13.3	33.9	27.4	43.2	15.7	0.4	27.1	62.9	70.3	68.3	144.6
4th quarter	91.9	21.0	13.2	33.4	24.3	42.2	11.2	8.4	22.6	48.9	63.9	67.0	168.6

Table 9-6. Corporate Profits with Inventory Valuation Adjustment by Industry Group (NAICS Basis)

(Billions of dollars.) NIPA Table 6.16D

Year and quarter	Total	Domestic industries												
		Financial			Nonfinancial									
								Manufacturing						
									Durable goods					
		Total	Federal Reserve banks	Other financial	Total	Utilities	Total	Fabricated metal products	Machinery	Computer and electronic products	Electrical equipment, appliances, and components	Motor vehicles, bodies and trailers, and parts	Other durable goods
1998	738.5	635.5	25.2	140.2	470.1	32.7	157.0	16.7	15.6	3.9	6.1	6.4	34.6
1999	776.8	655.3	26.3	168.0	461.1	33.1	150.6	16.5	12.4	-6.5	6.3	7.3	36.4
2000	759.3	613.6	30.8	169.4	413.4	24.4	144.3	15.5	8.2	4.0	5.6	-1.0	27.7
2001	719.2	549.5	28.3	199.3	322.0	24.7	52.6	9.9	2.7	-48.5	1.9	-9.2	17.8
2002	766.2	610.4	23.7	252.7	334.0	10.6	48.2	8.9	1.7	-35.3	-0.1	-5.0	20.0
2003	894.5	729.0	20.1	297.2	411.8	11.6	76.0	7.9	1.5	-15.6	2.1	-12.3	10.5
2004	1 104.5	928.2	20.0	324.1	584.0	16.2	150.2	12.3	7.0	-6.7	0.2	-11.2	29.7
2005	1 486.1	1 289.1	26.6	362.5	900.1	30.3	254.8	20.6	13.8	3.9	5.7	-17.9	47.7
2003													
1st quarter	833.6	684.4	21.8	279.8	382.8	11.5	63.6	7.1	-0.3	-20.5	1.6	-6.0	11.5
2nd quarter	847.8	688.9	20.8	286.5	381.6	10.5	55.2	8.8	1.6	-19.0	1.9	-13.5	6.9
3rd quarter	912.9	749.8	19.5	306.9	423.5	11.0	77.0	6.9	1.4	-16.4	2.3	-15.5	9.7
4th quarter	983.6	793.0	18.2	315.5	459.2	13.2	108.2	9.1	3.4	-6.5	2.6	-14.1	13.7
2004													
1st quarter	1 061.7	876.9	19.0	335.2	522.7	13.6	127.7	9.8	4.7	-8.7	0.4	-7.2	18.8
2nd quarter	1 097.2	927.4	19.1	334.8	573.5	15.5	147.4	11.7	6.4	-5.7	0.4	-13.4	30.2
3rd quarter	1 086.9	904.3	20.1	268.4	615.8	15.7	155.0	12.3	9.0	-6.2	-1.5	-10.3	32.4
4th quarter	1 172.1	1 004.3	21.9	358.2	624.2	20.0	170.7	15.4	7.9	-6.3	1.5	-13.8	37.6
2005													
1st quarter	1 453.1	1 270.0	23.1	410.7	836.3	29.5	235.5	17.4	12.1	-1.8	3.2	-15.8	45.5
2nd quarter	1 487.4	1 302.2	25.9	365.7	910.5	30.9	264.0	21.2	13.7	2.8	7.2	-10.8	52.2
3rd quarter	1 444.9	1 221.5	26.9	290.6	904.1	22.4	260.7	22.8	14.5	6.7	6.7	-19.8	44.5
4th quarter	1 559.1	1 362.8	30.4	382.9	949.4	38.3	258.9	21.2	15.0	8.0	5.6	-25.3	48.5

Year and quarter	Domestic industries—Continued										Rest of the world, net
	Nonfinancial—Continued										
	Manufacturing—Continued										
	Nondurable goods					Wholesale trade	Retail trade	Transportation and warehousing	Information	Other nonfinancial	
	Total	Food and beverage and tobacco products	Petroleum and coal products	Chemical products	Other nondurable goods						
1998	73.6	21.8	4.9	25.1	21.8	53.2	66.4	21.0	20.1	119.8	103.0
1999	78.3	30.7	1.8	23.0	22.7	55.5	65.2	16.1	10.5	130.1	121.5
2000	84.3	25.4	26.9	14.2	17.8	59.7	59.6	14.9	-17.6	128.2	145.7
2001	78.0	28.0	29.6	12.6	7.8	52.1	71.0	1.3	-25.6	145.9	169.7
2002	58.1	24.9	1.6	18.4	13.2	49.3	79.4	-0.9	-8.5	155.8	155.8
2003	81.9	23.6	23.3	19.5	15.5	55.2	86.8	7.3	3.2	171.7	165.5
2004	118.9	22.4	49.3	23.8	23.4	69.9	89.3	11.8	37.7	208.8	176.3
2005	181.0	28.5	70.4	45.3	36.8	97.6	113.7	21.0	77.5	305.2	197.0
2003											
1st quarter	70.3	20.6	18.2	17.2	14.3	47.3	80.9	3.5	-5.1	181.0	149.2
2nd quarter	68.6	23.6	15.0	17.5	12.4	47.2	89.7	8.6	1.8	168.7	158.9
3rd quarter	88.6	23.1	26.9	22.1	16.5	61.0	89.5	8.0	11.3	165.7	163.1
4th quarter	100.1	27.0	33.3	21.0	18.8	65.4	87.3	9.0	4.8	171.2	190.6
2004											
1st quarter	109.8	24.7	42.1	22.1	20.9	64.5	96.6	13.5	10.8	196.0	184.8
2nd quarter	117.9	20.8	52.2	22.2	22.7	64.8	91.5	18.2	39.0	197.2	169.8
3rd quarter	119.3	22.5	43.7	27.8	25.3	81.2	82.5	10.1	55.4	216.0	182.6
4th quarter	128.4	21.7	59.0	23.1	24.7	69.3	86.7	5.6	45.8	226.0	167.8
2005											
1st quarter	175.0	29.4	65.1	47.1	33.3	88.2	102.6	19.9	68.6	291.9	183.0
2nd quarter	177.8	26.7	66.4	46.4	38.3	102.1	107.3	22.0	79.9	304.3	185.2
3rd quarter	185.2	29.3	74.2	43.3	38.4	94.1	115.9	23.1	77.8	310.1	223.4
4th quarter	186.0	28.6	76.0	44.4	37.0	105.9	129.1	19.0	83.6	314.6	196.3

NOTES AND DEFINITIONS

General note on data on compensation per hour

This chapter includes two data series with similar names—the Employment Cost Index for total compensation and the index of compensation per hour—which often display different behavior. Both are compiled and published by the Bureau of Labor Statistics (BLS), but the definitions, sources, and methods of compilation are different. Users should be aware of these differences, and of the consequent differences in the appropriate uses and interpretations for each of the two series.

The *Employment Cost Index (ECI)* (Tables 9-1 through 9-3) measures changes in hourly compensation for "all civilian workers," which is not as broad as it sounds, as it excludes federal government workers, farm workers, and private household workers. Indexes are also published for subgroups including state and local workers, "all private industry" (again excluding farm and private household workers), and a number of industry and occupational subgroups.

The ECI is calculated and published separately for *total compensation* and for the two major components of hourly compensation, *wages and salaries* and the employer cost of employee *benefits*. It is constructed by analogy with the Consumer Price Index. That is, it holds the composition of employment constant in order to isolate hourly compensation trends that take place for individual occupations, which are then aggregated, using relative importance weights. It is based on a sample survey. It may be revised from time to time, due to updated classification, weighting, and seasonal adjustments. However, it is not subject to major benchmark revision of the underlying wage, salary, and benefit observations. By design, it excludes any representation of employee stock options. As it is based on a sample survey, the ECI is measured "from the bottom up," aggregating from individual employers' reports to higher levels. The ECI is frequently, and appropriately, used as the best available measure of the general trend of wages and of the extent of inflationary pressure exerted on prices by labor costs.

The *compensation per hour* component of the "Productivity and Costs" report is calculated and published for total compensation in total business, nonfarm business, nonfinancial corporations, and manufacturing. The nonfarm business category is similar in scope to the "all private industry" category in the ECI. These measures are compiled "from the top down," starting with aggregate estimates of compensation and hours, then dividing the former by the latter. Compensation per hour is affected by changes in the composition of employment. If the composition of employment shifts toward higher-paid employees and/or industries, compensation per hour will rise even if there is no increase in hourly compensation for any individual worker.

In addition, *compensation per hour* includes the value of exercised stock options as expensed by companies. Also included are other transitory payments, many of which may be of little relevance to the typical worker or to ongoing production costs. These values are not reported immediately. Instead, they are incorporated when later, more comprehensive reports are received. This process can lead to dramatic revisions. For example, the fourth-quarter 2004 increase in compensation per hour in nonfarm business was initially reported at an annual rate of 3.1 percent. Four months later, the reported rate for the same time period was 10.2 percent. The rate of increase from a year earlier was revised from 3.6 to 5.9 percent. According to Federal Reserve Chairman Alan Greenspan, in testimony before the Joint Economic Committee on June 9, 2005, this reflected "a large but apparently transitory surge in bonuses and the proceeds of stock option exercises," not a potentially inflationary acceleration in the rate of labor compensation increase.

These characteristics suggest that *compensation per hour* should not be considered a reliable or appropriate indicator of wage or compensation trends for typical workers. It is useful in conjunction with the productivity series, because aggregate productivity is subject to the same composition shifts, as higher-productivity industries also tend to have higher-paid employees. Hence, the measure of *unit labor costs* (derived by dividing compensation per hour by output per hour in this system) is not distorted when the composition of output shifts toward higher-productivity industries. The shift affects the numerator and denominator of the ratio similarly. However, both compensation and unit labor costs can still be distorted by transitory payments, such as those discussed above.

TABLES 9-1 THROUGH 9-3
EMPLOYMENT COST INDEXES

SOURCE: U.S. DEPARTMENT OF LABOR, BUREAU OF LABOR STATISTICS (BLS)

The Employment Cost Index (ECI) is a quarterly measure of the change in the cost of labor, independent of the influence of employment shifts among occupations and industries. It uses a fixed market basket of labor—similar in concept to the Consumer Price Index's fixed market basket of goods and services—to measure changes over time in employer costs of employing labor. Data are quarterly in all cases and are reported for the final month of each quarter. These measures have been completely converted to a base of December 2005 (not seasonally adjusted) = 100.

Care should be used in comparing the ECI with other data sets. The ECI category called "all private industry" in fact excludes farm and household workers (it is sometimes, and more precisely, called "private nonfarm industry"), and the category "all civilian workers" excludes federal government, farm, and household workers, all of whom fall outside the scope of the ECI survey.

The official data for 1979 through 2005 presented here are based on the 1987 Standard Industrial Classification (SIC) and 1990 Occupational Classification System (OCS). Beginning with March 2006, the ECI is compiled based on the North American Industry Classification System (NAICS) and the 2000 Standard Occupational Classification Manual (SOC). For most of the broad categories shown in this volume—indicated by footnote 3 in Tables 9-1 through 9-3—the old SIC categories are, roughly, comparable and continuous with the data for 2006. A number of new industry and occupational categories are now published which are not continuous with the old series shown here, and some of the categories published here are not being continued into 2006 because they are deemed to be obsolete and no longer meaningful. See the box that follows for important information on consistent use of old and new data.

The indexes through 2005 shown in this volume are internally consistent and may be used as continuous series. They should not, however, be directly compared with the new NAICS-based data for 2006 and subsequent years, even in the case of the aggregate categories deemed to be "continuous." For example, a user seeking to calculate the change from the second quarter of 2005 to the second quarter of 2006 in a given series should not compare the published index for 2006:2 with the SIC-based number shown here for 2005:2. Instead, the user should use a NAICS-based value for 2005:2. NAICS-based values are available at <http://www.bls.gov> from 2001 through 2005. These are the values used by BLS to calculate the percent changes that are published in the Employment Cost Index releases.

Definitions

Total compensation comprises wages, salaries, and the employer's costs for employee benefits. Excluded from wages and salaries and employee benefits are the value of stock option exercises and items such as payment-in-kind, free room and board, and tips.

Wages and salaries consists of straight-time earnings per hour before payroll deductions, including production bonuses, incentive earnings, commissions, and cost-of-living adjustments. These wage rates exclude premium pay for overtime and for work on weekends and holidays, shift differentials, and nonproduction bonuses such as lump-sum payments provided in lieu of wage increases.

Benefits includes the cost to employers for paid leave—vacations, holidays, sick leave, and other leave; for supplemental pay—premium pay for work in addition to the regular work schedule (such as overtime, weekends, and holidays), shift differentials, and nonproduction bonuses (such as referral bonuses and lump-sum payments provided in lieu of wage increases); for insurance benefits—life,

health, short-term disability, and long-term disability; for retirement and savings benefits—defined benefit and defined contribution plans; and for legally required benefits—Social Security, Medicare, federal and state unemployment insurance, and workers' compensation. Severance pay and supplemental unemployment benefit (SUB) plans are included in the data through December 2005 but have been dropped beginning with March 2006. The combined cost of these two benefits accounts for less than one-tenth of one percent of compensation, and according to BLS, dropping these benefits will have virtually no impact on the index.

Private industry workers are workers in private nonfarm industry. Excluded are proprietors, the self-employed, and private household workers.

Civilian workers include private nonfarm industry workers and workers in state and local government. Federal workers are not included.

Notes on the data

Employee benefit costs are calculated as cents per hour worked for benefits ranging from employer payments for Social Security to paid time off for holidays.

The data are collected from probability samples of around 50,000 occupational observations in about 11,300 sample establishments in private industry, and around 3,500 occupations within about 800 establishments in state and local governments. Samples are rotated over approximately five years.

Currently, the sample establishments are classified in industry categories based on the NAICS. Within an establishment, specific job categories are selected and classified into approximately 800 occupational classifications according to the SOC. Similar procedures were followed under the previous classification systems. Data are collected each quarter for the pay periods that include the 12th day of March, June, September, and December.

Aggregate indexes are calculated using fixed employment weights. Beginning with March 2006, ECI weights are based on fixed employment counts for 2002 from BLS Occupational Statistics. ECI measures were based on 1990 employment counts from March 1995 through December 2005 and 1980 census employment counts from June 1986 through December 1994. Prior to June 1986, they were based on 1970 census employment counts. Use of fixed weights ensures that changes in the indexes reflect only changes in hourly compensation, not employment shifts among industries or occupations with different levels of wages and compensation. This feature distinguishes the ECI from other compensation series, such as average hourly earnings (see Table 10-11 and its notes and definitions) and the compensation per hour component of the productivity series (see Table 9-4 and its notes and definitions, and the general note above), each of which is affected by such employment shifts.

Data availability

Data for wages and salaries for the private nonfarm economy are available beginning with data for 1975; data for compensation begin at 1980. The series for state and local government and for the civilian nonfarm economy begin at 1981. All data are available on the BLS Web site at <http://www.bls.gov>.

Wage and salary change and compensation cost change data also are available by major occupational and industry groups, as well as by region and collective bargaining status. Wage and salary change information is available from 1975 to the present for most of these series. Compensation cost change data are available from 1980 to the present for most series. For 10 occupational and industry series, benefit cost change data are available from the early 1980s to the present. For state and local governments and the civilian economy (state and local governments plus private industry), wage and salary change and compensation cost change data are available for major occupational and industry series. BLS provides data for all these series from June 1981 to the present.

Updates are available about four weeks after the end of the reference quarter. Reference quarters end in March, June, September, and December.

References

Explanatory notes including references are included in each quarter's ECI news release, available on the BLS Internet site. The March 2006 revision is described in "Change Has Come to the ECI," on the BLS Web site, and a series of articles in the *Monthly Labor Review* for April 2006. Earlier references include: Chapter 8, "National Compensation Measures," *BLS Handbook of Methods*, Bulletin 2490 (April 1997); "Employment Cost Indexes, 1975–1999," BLS Bulletin 2532 (includes details on the sample design and seasonal adjustment methodology); and the following *Monthly Labor Review* articles: "Is the ECI Sensitive to the Method of Aggregation" (June 1997); "Employment Cost Index Rebased to June 1989" (April 1990); "Measuring the Precision of the Employment Cost Index" (March 1989); "Employment Cost Index to Replace Hourly Earnings Index" (July 1988); and "Estimation Procedures for the Employment Cost Index," May 1982.

TABLES 9-4 AND 19-13
PRODUCTIVITY AND RELATED DATA

SOURCE: U.S. DEPARTMENT OF LABOR, BUREAU OF LABOR STATISTICS (BLS)

Productivity measures relate real physical output to real input. They encompass a family of measures that includes single-factor input measures, such as output per unit of labor input or output per unit of capital input, as well as measures of multifactor productivity (output per unit of combined labor and capital inputs). The indexes published in this book are indexes of labor productivity expressed in terms of output per hour. (A larger group of BLS productivity measures is published in Bernan's *Handbook of U.S. Labor Statistics*.) Data are provided here for four sectors of the economy: business, nonfarm business, the nonfinancial corporate sector, and manufacturing. All data are presented as indexes, with base year 1992 = 100.

Definitions

Output per hour of all persons (labor productivity) is the value of goods and services in constant prices produced per hour of labor input. By definition, nonfinancial corporations include no self-employed persons. Productivity in this sector is expressed as *output per hour of all employees*.

Compensation per hour is the wages and salaries of employees plus employers' contributions for social insurance and private benefit plans and wages, salaries, and supplementary payments for the self-employed—the sum of these divided by hours at work. Included in compensation is the value of exercised stock options that companies report as a charge against earnings. These are not reported quarterly; consequently, recent values are estimated based on extrapolation. They are revised to actual values when the data become available.

Real compensation per hour is compensation per hour deflated by the CPI-U-RS for the period 1978 through 2005. For explanation of the CPI-U-RS, see the notes and definitions for Tables 8-2 and 8-3. Changes in the CPI-W are used for data before 1978.

Unit labor costs are the current-dollar labor costs expended in the production of a unit of output. They are derived by dividing compensation by output.

Unit nonlabor payments include profits, depreciation, interest, rental income of persons, and indirect taxes per unit of output. They are computed by subtracting current-dollar compensation of all persons from current-dollar value of output and dividing by output.

Unit nonlabor costs are available for nonfinancial corporations only. They contain all the components of unit nonlabor payments except unit profits (and rental income of persons, which for nonfinancial corporations is zero by definition).

Hours of all persons are the total hours at work (employment multiplied by the average workweek) of payroll workers, self-employed persons, and unpaid family workers. In the case of the data for nonfinancial corporations, there are no self-employed persons and the data represent *employee hours*.

Notes on the data

Output for the business sector is equal to constant-dollar gross domestic product minus the following: the rental value of owner-occupied dwellings; the output of non-profit institutions; the output of paid employees of private households; and general government output. The measures are derived from national income and product account (NIPA) data supplied by the U.S. Department of Commerce's Bureau of Economic Analysis (BEA). For manufacturing, BLS produces annual estimates of sectoral output. Quarterly manufacturing output indexes derived from the Federal Reserve Board of Governors' monthly indexes of industrial production (see Chapter 2) are adjusted to these annual measures by the BLS, and are used to project the quarterly values in the current period.

Nonfinancial corporate output excludes unincorporated businesses and financial corporations from business sector output. It accounted for approximately 54 percent of the value of GDP in 1996. Unit profits and unit nonlabor costs can be calculated separately for this sector and are shown here.

Compensation and hours data are developed from BLS and BEA data. The primary source for hours and employment is the BLS Current Employment Statistics (CES) program (see the notes and definitions for Tables 10-7 through 10-12). The CES provides data on hours paid for production or nonsupervisory workers. The BLS Office of Productivity and Technology estimates the paid hours of nonproduction and supervisory workers, using data from the Current Population Survey (CPS). Weekly paid hours are adjusted to hours at work using the annual BLS Hours at Work survey, conducted for this purpose. For paid employees, hours at work differ from hours paid, in that they exclude paid vacation and holidays, paid sick leave, and other paid personal or administrative leave.

Although the labor productivity measures relate output to labor input, they do not measure the contribution of labor or any other specific factor of production. They instead reflect the joint effect of many influences, including changes in technology; capital investment; level of output; utilization of capacity, energy, and materials; the organization of production; managerial skill; and the characteristics and efforts of the work force.

Revisions

Data for recent years are revised frequently to take account of revisions in the output and labor input measures that underlie the estimates. Customarily, all revisions to source data are reflected in the release following the source data revision. Data in this volume reflect the midyear 2006 revisions of the NIPAs and all revisions in labor input and compensation up through that time.

Data availability

Series are available quarterly and annually. Quarterly measures are based entirely on seasonally adjusted data. For some detailed manufacturing series (not shown here), only annual averages are available. Productivity indexes are published early in the second and third months of each quarter, reflecting new data for preceding quarters. Complete historical data are available on the BLS Web site at <http://www.bls.gov>.

BLS also publishes productivity estimates for a number of individual industries. A release on "Productivity and Costs by Industry" is available on the BLS Web site at <http://www.bls.gov>.

References

Chapter 10 "Productivity Measures: Business Sector and Major Subsectors," *BLS Handbook of Methods,* Bulletin 2490 (April 1997); and the following *Monthly Labor Review* articles: "Alternative Measures of Supervisory Employee Hours and Productivity Growth" (April 2004); "Possible Measurement Bias in Aggregate Productivity Growth" (February 1999); "Improvements to the Quarterly Productivity Measures" (October 1995); "Hours of Work: A New Base for BLS Productivity Statistics" (February 1990); and "New Sector Definitions for Productivity Series" (October 1976).

TABLE 9-5 AND 9-6
CORPORATE PROFITS WITH INVENTORY VALUATION ADJUSTMENT BY INDUSTRY GROUP

Source: U.S. Department of Commerce, Bureau of Economic Analysis

These profits measures are derived from the national income and product accounts (NIPAs). See the notes and definitions for Chapter 1 for definitions. Note that this industry breakdown of profits incorporates the inventory valuation adjustment (IVA), which eliminates any capital gain element in profits arising from changes in the prices at which inventories are valued, but does not incorporate the capital consumption adjustment (CCAdj), which adjusts historical costs of fixed capital to replacement costs and uses actual rather than tax-based service lives. The reason is that the CCAdj is calculated at an aggregate level, whereas the IVA is calculated at an industry level.

Beginning in 1998, data are compiled on the NAICS basis, as shown in Table 9-6. Data for earlier years based on the December 2003 revision—including an overlap for the years 1998 through 2000—are based on the older Standard Industrial Classification system (SIC) and are shown back to 1948 in Table 9-5 on that basis; these have not been revised and are as shown in previous years' *Business Statistics.* See Chapter 14 for an outline and discussion of NAICS and its relation to SIC.

CHAPTER 10: EMPLOYMENT, HOURS, AND EARNINGS

Section 10a: Labor Force, Employment, and Unemployment

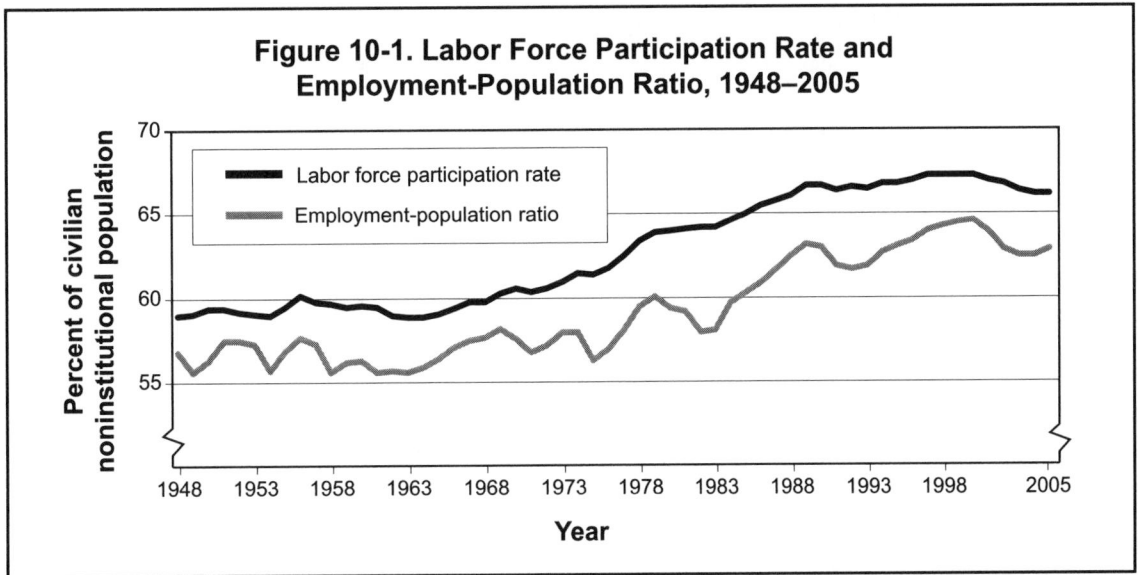

Figure 10-1. Labor Force Participation Rate and Employment-Population Ratio, 1948–2005

- The employment-population ratio increased in 2005 after a decline that was as severe and long-lasting as in any other postwar recession. (Tables 10-3 and 20-3)

- The labor force participation rate, which usually rises during cyclical recoveries, declined through early 2004 and has since leveled off. (Tables 10-1 and 20-3)

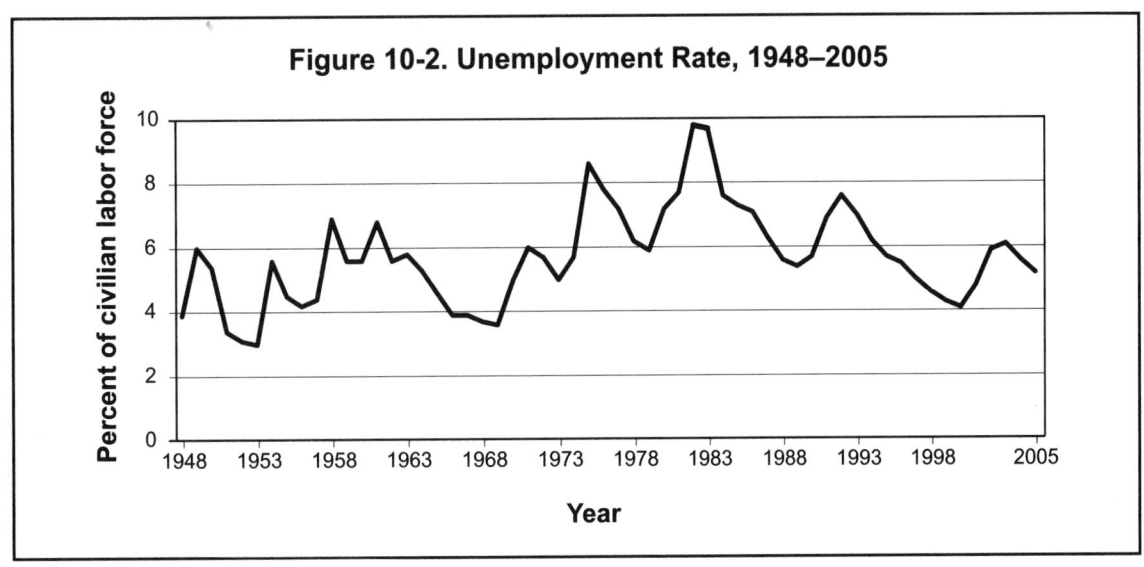

Figure 10-2. Unemployment Rate, 1948–2005

- The unemployment rate declined in 2004 and 2005. In 2004, this was due to the decline in the participation rate. In 2005, it reflected the increase in employment relative to population, coupled with the leveling-off of the labor force participation rate. (Tables 10-4 and 20-3)

Table 10-1. Civilian Population and Labor Force [1]

(Thousands of persons, 16 years of age and over; percent.)

Year and month	Civilian noninstitutional population	Not seasonally adjusted			Seasonally adjusted							
		Civilian labor force			Civilian labor force (thousands)				Participation rate (percent) [2]			
		Total	Employed	Unemployed	Total	Persons 20 years and over		Both sexes, 16 to 19 years	Total	Persons 20 years and over		Both sexes, 16 to 19 years
						Men	Women			Men	Women	
1960	117 245	69 628	65 778	3 852	69 628	43 603	21 185	4 841	59.4	86.0	37.6	47.5
1961	118 771	70 459	65 746	4 714	70 459	43 860	21 664	4 936	59.3	85.7	38.0	46.9
1962	120 153	70 614	66 702	3 911	70 614	43 831	21 868	4 916	58.8	84.8	37.8	46.1
1963	122 416	71 833	67 762	4 070	71 833	44 222	22 473	5 139	58.7	84.4	38.3	45.2
1964	124 485	73 091	69 305	3 786	73 091	44 604	23 098	5 388	58.7	84.2	38.9	44.5
1965	126 513	74 455	71 088	3 366	74 455	44 857	23 686	5 910	58.9	83.9	39.4	45.7
1966	128 058	75 770	72 895	2 875	75 770	44 788	24 431	6 558	59.2	83.6	40.1	48.2
1967	129 874	77 347	74 372	2 975	77 347	45 354	25 475	6 521	59.6	83.4	41.1	48.4
1968	132 028	78 737	75 920	2 817	78 737	45 852	26 266	6 619	59.6	83.1	41.6	48.3
1969	134 335	80 734	77 902	2 832	80 734	46 351	27 413	6 970	60.1	82.8	42.7	49.4
1970	137 085	82 771	78 678	4 093	82 771	47 220	28 301	7 249	60.4	82.6	43.3	49.9
1971	140 216	84 382	79 367	5 016	84 382	48 009	28 904	7 470	60.2	82.1	43.3	49.7
1972	144 126	87 034	82 153	4 882	87 034	49 079	29 901	8 054	60.4	81.6	43.7	51.9
1973	147 096	89 429	85 064	4 365	89 429	49 932	30 991	8 507	60.8	81.3	44.4	53.7
1974	150 120	91 949	86 794	5 156	91 949	50 879	32 201	8 871	61.3	81.0	45.3	54.8
1975	153 153	93 775	85 846	7 929	93 775	51 494	33 410	8 870	61.2	80.3	46.0	54.0
1976	156 150	96 158	88 752	7 406	96 158	52 288	34 814	9 056	61.6	79.8	47.0	54.5
1977	159 033	99 009	92 017	6 991	99 009	53 348	36 310	9 351	62.3	79.7	48.1	56.0
1978	161 910	102 251	96 048	6 202	102 251	54 471	38 128	9 652	63.2	79.8	49.6	57.8
1979	164 863	104 962	98 824	6 137	104 962	55 615	39 708	9 638	63.7	79.8	50.6	57.9
1980	167 745	106 940	99 303	7 637	106 940	56 455	41 106	9 378	63.8	79.4	51.3	56.7
1981	170 130	108 670	100 397	8 273	108 670	57 197	42 485	8 988	63.9	79.0	52.1	55.4
1982	172 271	110 204	99 526	10 678	110 204	57 980	43 699	8 526	64.0	78.7	52.7	54.1
1983	174 215	111 550	100 834	10 717	111 550	58 744	44 636	8 171	64.0	78.5	53.1	53.5
1984	176 383	113 544	105 005	8 539	113 544	59 701	45 900	7 943	64.4	78.3	53.7	53.9
1985	178 206	115 461	107 150	8 312	115 461	60 277	47 283	7 901	64.8	78.1	54.7	54.5
1986	180 587	117 834	109 597	8 237	117 834	61 320	48 589	7 926	65.3	78.1	55.5	54.7
1987	182 753	119 865	112 440	7 425	119 865	62 095	49 783	7 988	65.6	78.0	56.2	54.7
1988	184 613	121 669	114 968	6 701	121 669	62 768	50 870	8 031	65.9	77.9	56.8	55.3
1989	186 393	123 869	117 342	6 528	123 869	63 704	52 212	7 954	66.5	78.1	57.7	55.9
1990	189 164	125 840	118 793	7 047	125 840	64 916	53 131	7 792	66.5	78.2	58.0	53.7
1991	190 925	126 346	117 718	8 628	126 346	65 374	53 708	7 265	66.2	77.7	57.9	51.6
1992	192 805	128 105	118 492	9 613	128 105	66 213	54 796	7 096	66.4	77.7	58.5	51.3
1993	194 838	129 200	120 259	8 940	129 200	66 642	55 388	7 170	66.3	77.3	58.5	51.5
1994	196 814	131 056	123 060	7 996	131 056	66 921	56 655	7 481	66.6	76.8	59.3	52.7
1995	198 584	132 304	124 900	7 404	132 304	67 324	57 215	7 765	66.6	76.7	59.4	53.5
1996	200 591	133 943	126 708	7 236	133 943	68 044	58 094	7 806	66.8	76.8	59.9	52.3
1997	203 133	136 297	129 558	6 739	136 297	69 166	59 198	7 932	67.1	77.0	60.5	51.6
1998	205 220	137 673	131 463	6 210	137 673	69 715	59 702	8 256	67.1	76.8	60.4	52.8
1999	207 753	139 368	133 488	5 880	139 368	70 194	60 840	8 333	67.1	76.7	60.7	52.0
2000	212 577	142 583	136 891	5 692	142 583	72 010	62 301	8 271	67.1	76.7	60.6	52.0
2001	215 092	143 734	136 933	6 801	143 734	72 816	63 016	7 902	66.8	76.5	60.6	49.6
2002	217 570	144 863	136 485	8 378	144 863	73 630	63 648	7 585	66.6	76.3	60.5	47.4
2003	221 168	146 510	137 736	8 774	146 510	74 623	64 716	7 170	66.2	75.9	60.6	44.5
2004	223 357	147 401	139 252	8 149	147 401	75 364	64 923	7 114	66.0	75.8	60.3	43.9
2005	226 082	149 320	141 730	7 591	149 320	76 443	65 714	7 164	66.0	75.8	60.4	43.7
2004												
January	222 161	146 068	136 924	9 144	146 817	75 205	64 427	7 184	66.1	76.1	60.1	44.4
February	222 357	146 154	137 384	8 770	146 681	74 947	64 670	7 064	66.0	75.7	60.3	43.7
March	222 550	146 525	137 691	8 834	146 849	75 075	64 841	6 933	66.0	75.8	60.4	42.8
April	222 757	146 260	138 423	7 837	146 800	74 921	64 797	7 082	65.9	75.5	60.3	43.7
May	222 967	146 659	138 867	7 792	147 021	75 058	64 826	7 137	65.9	75.6	60.3	44.0
June	223 196	148 478	139 861	8 616	147 427	75 340	65 059	7 029	66.1	75.8	60.5	43.3
July	223 422	149 217	140 700	8 518	147 773	75 533	65 065	7 175	66.1	75.9	60.4	44.2
August	223 677	148 166	140 226	7 940	147 558	75 536	64 902	7 120	66.0	75.8	60.2	43.9
September	223 941	147 186	139 641	7 545	147 476	75 480	64 931	7 065	65.9	75.7	60.2	43.5
October	224 192	147 978	140 447	7 531	147 808	75 591	65 063	7 155	65.9	75.7	60.2	44.0
November	224 422	148 246	140 581	7 665	148 250	75 852	65 189	7 208	66.1	75.8	60.3	44.3
December	224 640	147 877	140 278	7 599	148 173	75 726	65 227	7 219	66.0	75.6	60.3	44.3
2005												
January	224 837	147 125	138 682	8 444	147 956	75 650	65 260	7 046	65.8	75.5	60.2	43.2
February	225 041	147 649	139 100	8 549	148 271	75 929	65 284	7 058	65.9	75.7	60.2	43.3
March	225 236	147 745	139 759	7 986	148 217	75 965	65 080	7 172	65.8	75.6	60.0	43.9
April	225 441	148 274	140 939	7 335	148 839	76 202	65 461	7 176	66.0	75.8	60.3	43.9
May	225 670	148 878	141 591	7 287	149 201	76 445	65 528	7 228	66.1	76.0	60.3	44.2
June	225 911	150 327	142 456	7 870	149 243	76 471	65 582	7 189	66.1	75.9	60.3	43.9
July	226 153	151 122	143 283	7 839	149 605	76 619	65 813	7 172	66.2	76.0	60.4	43.7
August	226 421	150 469	143 142	7 327	149 792	76 787	65 778	7 228	66.2	76.0	60.3	44.0
September	226 693	149 838	142 579	7 259	150 083	76 792	66 129	7 163	66.2	75.9	60.6	43.6
October	226 959	150 304	143 340	6 964	150 043	76 780	66 175	7 088	66.1	75.8	60.6	43.0
November	227 204	150 239	142 968	7 271	150 183	76 722	66 223	7 238	66.1	75.7	60.6	43.9
December	227 425	149 874	142 918	6 956	150 153	76 786	66 215	7 152	66.0	75.7	60.5	43.3

[1]Changes in survey design, population estimates, and methodology in 1994 and several other years affect year-to-year comparisons. See notes and definitions for more information.
[2]Labor force as a percent of the demographic group's civilian noninstitutional population.

Table 10-2. Civilian Employment [1]

(Thousands of persons, 16 years of age and over; seasonally adjusted, except as noted.)

Year and month	Total	By age and sex			Agricultural	By class of worker						
		Persons 20 years and over		Both sexes, 16 to 19 years		Nonagricultural industries						
							Wage and salary				Self-employed	Unpaid family workers [2]
									Private industries			
		Men	Women			Total	Total	Government	Private households [2]	Other private industries		
1960	65 778	41 543	20 105	4 129	5 458	60 318	53 418	7 935	. . .	. . .	6 303	598
1961	65 746	41 342	20 296	4 108	5 200	60 546	53 601	8 175	. . .	. . .	6 308	639
1962	66 702	41 815	20 693	4 195	4 944	61 759	54 963	8 691	. . .	. . .	6 193	603
1963	67 762	42 251	21 257	4 255	4 687	63 076	56 387	9 082	. . .	. . .	6 114	573
1964	69 305	42 886	21 903	4 516	4 523	64 782	58 026	9 350	. . .	. . .	6 179	576
1965	71 088	43 422	22 630	5 036	4 361	66 726	60 031	9 608	. . .	. . .	6 097	600
1966	72 895	43 668	23 510	5 721	3 979	68 915	62 362	10 323	. . .	. . .	5 991	564
1967	74 372	44 294	24 397	5 682	3 844	70 527	64 848	11 146	. . .	. . .	5 174	505
1968	75 920	44 859	25 281	5 781	3 817	72 103	66 519	11 590	. . .	. . .	5 102	485
1969	77 902	45 388	26 397	6 117	3 606	74 296	68 528	12 025	. . .	. . .	5 252	517
1970	78 678	45 581	26 952	6 144	3 463	75 215	69 491	12 431	. . .	. . .	5 221	502
1971	79 367	45 912	27 246	6 208	3 394	75 972	70 120	12 799	. . .	. . .	5 327	522
1972	82 153	47 130	28 276	6 746	3 484	78 669	72 785	13 393	. . .	. . .	5 365	519
1973	85 064	48 310	29 484	7 271	3 470	81 594	75 580	13 655	. . .	. . .	5 474	540
1974	86 794	48 922	30 424	7 448	3 515	83 279	77 094	14 124	. . .	. . .	5 697	489
1975	85 846	48 018	30 726	7 104	3 408	82 438	76 249	14 675	. . .	. . .	5 705	483
1976	88 752	49 190	32 226	7 336	3 331	85 421	79 175	15 132	. . .	. . .	5 783	464
1977	92 017	50 555	33 775	7 688	. . .	88 734	82 121	15 361	. . .	. . .	6 114	498
1978	96 048	52 143	35 836	8 070	3 387	92 661	85 753	15 525	. . .	. . .	6 429	479
1979	98 824	53 308	37 434	8 083	3 347	95 477	88 222	15 635	. . .	. . .	6 791	463
1980	99 303	53 101	38 492	7 710	3 364	95 938	88 525	15 912	. . .	. . .	7 000	413
1981	100 397	53 582	39 590	7 225	3 368	97 030	89 543	15 689	. . .	. . .	7 097	390
1982	99 526	52 891	40 086	6 549	3 401	96 125	88 462	15 516	. . .	. . .	7 262	401
1983	100 834	53 487	41 004	6 342	3 383	97 450	89 500	15 537	. . .	. . .	7 575	376
1984	105 005	55 769	42 793	6 444	3 321	101 685	93 565	15 770	. . .	. . .	7 785	335
1985	107 150	56 562	44 154	6 434	3 179	103 971	95 871	16 031	. . .	. . .	7 811	289
1986	109 597	57 569	45 556	6 472	3 163	106 434	98 299	16 342	. . .	. . .	7 881	255
1987	112 440	58 726	47 074	6 640	3 208	109 232	100 771	16 800	. . .	. . .	8 201	260
1988	114 968	59 781	48 383	6 805	3 169	111 800	103 021	17 114	. . .	. . .	8 519	260
1989	117 342	60 837	49 745	6 759	3 199	114 142	105 259	17 469	. . .	. . .	8 605	279
1990	118 793	61 678	50 535	6 581	3 223	115 570	106 598	17 769	. . .	. . .	8 719	253
1991	117 718	61 178	50 634	5 906	3 269	114 449	105 373	17 934	. . .	. . .	8 851	226
1992	118 492	61 496	51 328	5 669	3 247	115 245	106 437	18 136	. . .	. . .	8 575	233
1993	120 259	62 355	52 099	5 805	3 115	117 144	107 966	18 579	. . .	. . .	8 959	218
1994	123 060	63 294	53 606	6 161	3 409	119 651	110 517	18 293	. . .	. . .	9 003	131
1995	124 900	64 085	54 396	6 419	3 440	121 460	112 448	18 362	. . .	. . .	8 902	110
1996	126 708	64 897	55 311	6 500	3 443	123 264	114 171	18 217	. . .	. . .	8 971	122
1997	129 558	66 284	56 613	6 661	3 399	126 159	116 983	18 131	. . .	. . .	9 056	120
1998	131 463	67 135	57 278	7 051	3 378	128 085	119 019	18 383	. . .	. . .	8 962	103
1999	133 488	67 761	58 555	7 172	3 281	130 207	121 323	18 903	. . .	. . .	8 790	95
2000	136 891	69 634	60 067	7 189	2 464	134 427	125 114	19 248	718	105 148	9 205	108
2001	136 933	69 776	60 417	6 740	2 299	134 635	125 407	19 335	694	105 378	9 121	107
2002	136 485	69 734	60 420	6 332	2 311	134 174	125 156	19 636	757	104 764	8 923	95
2003	137 736	70 415	61 402	5 919	2 275	135 461	126 015	19 634	764	105 616	9 344	101
2004	139 252	71 572	61 773	5 907	2 232	137 020	127 463	19 983	779	106 701	9 467	90
2005	141 730	73 050	62 702	5 978	2 197	139 532	129 931	20 357	812	108 761	9 509	93
2004												
January	138 472	71 340	61 168	5 964	2 211	136 205	126 638	19 758	811	106 142	9 491	96
February	138 495	71 105	61 495	5 895	2 227	136 294	126 775	19 530	791	106 253	9 441	111
March	138 452	71 192	61 487	5 774	2 189	136 291	126 979	19 981	767	106 198	9 180	116
April	138 659	71 134	61 614	5 912	2 250	136 420	127 155	19 886	727	106 481	9 200	75
May	138 843	71 173	61 745	5 926	2 296	136 524	127 038	19 764	683	106 593	9 386	87
June	139 181	71 541	61 802	5 838	2 251	136 816	127 318	19 963	803	106 548	9 397	108
July	139 591	71 782	61 909	5 899	2 242	137 329	127 710	19 823	818	107 195	9 531	70
August	139 558	71 780	61 864	5 914	2 317	137 227	127 533	20 078	864	106 560	9 708	98
September	139 495	71 733	61 883	5 878	2 223	137 391	127 741	20 178	787	106 807	9 513	90
October	139 768	71 870	61 970	5 928	2 163	137 675	127 905	20 195	728	106 987	9 678	81
November	140 276	72 140	62 113	6 023	2 192	138 045	128 352	20 334	779	107 255	9 560	66
December	140 133	72 037	62 169	5 927	2 190	137 944	128 352	20 308	789	107 338	9 493	80
2005												
January	140 234	72 092	62 236	5 906	2 138	138 076	128 438	20 312	800	107 372	9 545	104
February	140 285	72 246	62 220	5 818	2 161	138 111	128 312	20 097	777	107 249	9 707	127
March	140 601	72 513	62 129	5 960	2 199	138 416	128 567	20 326	762	107 433	9 738	98
April	141 196	72 855	62 426	5 915	2 253	138 926	128 980	20 423	777	107 699	9 878	87
May	141 571	73 108	62 515	5 948	2 216	139 322	129 564	20 772	722	108 059	9 689	57
June	141 750	73 178	62 552	6 020	2 321	139 333	129 791	20 450	841	108 523	9 471	72
July	142 111	73 345	62 744	6 022	2 332	139 772	130 186	20 473	911	108 952	9 479	111
August	142 425	73 479	62 901	6 045	2 157	140 294	131 028	20 436	950	109 621	9 273	110
September	142 435	73 331	63 074	6 030	2 140	140 421	130 937	20 255	861	109 858	9 359	88
October	142 625	73 500	63 162	5 964	2 126	140 577	131 123	20 330	813	109 986	9 356	84
November	142 611	73 441	63 170	6 000	2 154	140 427	131 001	20 224	750	110 039	9 274	109
December	142 779	73 468	63 249	6 061	2 130	140 638	131 170	20 192	782	110 261	9 370	66

[1]Changes in survey design, population estimates, and methodology in 1994 and several other years affect year-to-year comparisons. See notes and definitions for more information.
[2]Not seasonally adjusted.
. . . = Not available.

Table 10-3. Civilian Employment and Unemployment [1]

(Thousands of persons, percent; seasonally adjusted.)

Year and month	Employment-population ratio, percent				Multiple jobholders		Employed and at work part time		Unemployment (thousands)				
	Total	Persons 20 years and over		Both sexes, 16 to 19 years	Total (thousands)	Percent of total employed	Economic reasons	Non-economic reasons	Total	Long-term [2]	Persons 20 years and over		Both sexes, 16 to 19 years
		Men	Women								Men	Women	
1960	56.1	81.9	35.7	40.5	. . .	. . .	2 855	6 845	3 852	957	2 060	1 080	712
1961	55.4	80.8	35.6	39.1	. . .	. . .	3 142	7 121	4 714	1 532	2 518	1 368	828
1962	55.5	80.9	35.8	39.4	. . .	. . .	2 661	7 527	3 911	1 119	2 016	1 175	721
1963	55.4	80.6	36.3	37.4	. . .	. . .	2 620	7 746	4 070	1 088	1 971	1 216	884
1964	55.7	80.9	36.9	37.3	. . .	. . .	2 455	8 155	3 786	973	1 718	1 195	872
1965	56.2	81.2	37.6	38.9	. . .	. . .	2 209	8 466	3 366	755	1 435	1 056	874
1966	56.9	81.5	38.6	42.1	. . .	. . .	1 960	8 112	2 875	526	1 120	921	837
1967	57.3	81.5	39.3	42.2	. . .	. . .	2 163	8 701	2 975	448	1 060	1 078	839
1968	57.5	81.3	40.0	42.2	. . .	. . .	1 970	9 075	2 817	412	993	985	838
1969	58.0	81.1	41.1	43.4	. . .	. . .	2 056	9 652	2 832	375	963	1 015	853
1970	57.4	79.7	41.2	42.3	. . .	. . .	2 446	9 999	4 093	663	1 638	1 349	1 106
1971	56.6	78.5	40.9	41.3	. . .	. . .	2 688	10 152	5 016	1 187	2 097	1 658	1 262
1972	57.0	78.4	41.3	43.5	. . .	. . .	2 648	10 612	4 882	1 167	1 948	1 625	1 308
1973	57.8	78.6	42.2	45.9	. . .	. . .	2 554	10 972	4 365	826	1 624	1 507	1 235
1974	57.8	77.9	42.8	46.0	. . .	. . .	2 988	11 153	5 156	955	1 957	1 777	1 422
1975	56.1	74.8	42.3	43.3	. . .	. . .	3 804	11 228	7 929	2 505	3 476	2 684	1 767
1976	56.8	75.1	43.5	44.2	. . .	. . .	3 607	11 607	7 406	2 366	3 098	2 588	1 719
1977	57.9	75.6	44.8	46.1	. . .	. . .	3 608	12 120	6 991	1 942	2 794	2 535	1 663
1978	59.3	76.4	46.6	48.3	. . .	. . .	3 516	12 650	6 202	1 414	2 328	2 292	1 583
1979	59.9	76.5	47.7	48.5	. . .	. . .	3 577	12 893	6 137	1 241	2 308	2 276	1 555
1980	59.2	74.6	48.1	46.6	. . .	. . .	4 321	13 067	7 637	1 871	3 353	2 615	1 669
1981	59.0	74.0	48.6	44.6	. . .	. . .	4 768	13 025	8 273	2 285	3 615	2 895	1 763
1982	57.8	71.8	48.4	41.5	. . .	. . .	6 170	12 953	10 678	3 485	5 089	3 613	1 977
1983	57.9	71.4	48.8	41.5	. . .	. . .	6 266	12 911	10 717	4 210	5 257	3 632	1 829
1984	59.5	73.2	50.1	43.7	. . .	. . .	5 744	13 169	8 539	2 737	3 932	3 107	1 499
1985	60.1	73.3	51.0	44.4	. . .	. . .	5 590	13 489	8 312	2 305	3 715	3 129	1 468
1986	60.7	73.3	52.0	44.6	. . .	. . .	5 588	13 935	8 237	2 232	3 751	3 032	1 454
1987	61.5	73.8	53.1	45.5	. . .	. . .	5 401	14 395	7 425	1 983	3 369	2 709	1 347
1988	62.3	74.2	54.0	46.8	. . .	. . .	5 206	14 963	6 701	1 610	2 987	2 487	1 226
1989	63.0	74.5	54.9	47.5	. . .	. . .	4 894	15 393	6 528	1 375	2 867	2 467	1 194
1990	62.8	74.3	55.2	45.3	. . .	. . .	5 204	15 341	7 047	1 525	3 239	2 596	1 212
1991	61.7	72.7	54.6	42.0	. . .	. . .	6 161	15 172	8 628	2 357	4 195	3 074	1 359
1992	61.5	72.1	54.8	41.0	. . .	. . .	6 520	14 918	9 613	3 408	4 717	3 469	1 427
1993	61.7	72.3	55.0	41.7	. . .	. . .	6 481	15 240	8 940	3 094	4 287	3 288	1 365
1994	62.5	72.6	56.2	43.4	7 260	5.9	4 625	17 638	7 996	2 860	3 627	3 049	1 320
1995	62.9	73.0	56.5	44.2	7 693	6.2	4 473	17 734	7 404	2 363	3 239	2 819	1 346
1996	63.2	73.2	57.0	43.5	7 832	6.2	4 315	17 770	7 236	2 316	3 146	2 783	1 306
1997	63.8	73.7	57.8	43.4	7 955	6.1	4 068	18 149	6 739	2 062	2 882	2 585	1 271
1998	64.1	73.9	58.0	45.1	7 926	6.0	3 665	18 530	6 210	1 637	2 580	2 424	1 205
1999	64.3	74.0	58.5	44.7	7 802	5.8	3 357	18 758	5 880	1 480	2 433	2 285	1 162
2000	64.4	74.2	58.4	45.2	7 604	5.6	3 227	18 814	5 692	1 318	2 376	2 235	1 081
2001	63.7	73.3	58.1	42.3	7 357	5.4	3 715	18 790	6 801	1 752	3 040	2 599	1 162
2002	62.7	72.3	57.5	39.6	7 291	5.3	4 213	18 843	8 378	2 904	3 896	3 228	1 253
2003	62.3	71.7	57.5	36.8	7 315	5.3	4 701	19 014	8 774	3 378	4 209	3 314	1 251
2004	62.3	71.9	57.4	36.4	7 473	5.4	4 567	19 380	8 149	3 072	3 791	3 150	1 208
2005	62.7	72.4	57.6	36.5	7 546	5.3	4 350	19 491	7 591	2 619	3 392	3 013	1 186
2004													
January	62.3	72.2	57.1	36.9	7 336	5.3	4 711	19 101	8 345	3 350	3 866	3 259	1 220
February	62.3	71.8	57.4	36.4	7 091	5.1	4 535	19 030	8 186	3 233	3 841	3 175	1 169
March	62.2	71.9	57.3	35.7	7 298	5.3	4 720	19 086	8 397	3 315	3 883	3 354	1 159
April	62.2	71.7	57.4	36.5	7 344	5.3	4 588	19 074	8 140	2 978	3 787	3 183	1 170
May	62.3	71.7	57.4	36.6	7 346	5.3	4 641	19 566	8 178	3 068	3 885	3 082	1 211
June	62.4	72.0	57.4	36.0	7 396	5.3	4 481	19 881	8 247	3 099	3 799	3 257	1 191
July	62.5	72.1	57.5	36.4	7 509	5.4	4 471	19 675	8 182	2 935	3 751	3 156	1 276
August	62.4	72.0	57.4	36.4	7 667	5.5	4 444	19 558	8 000	2 918	3 757	3 038	1 206
September	62.3	71.9	57.3	36.2	7 589	5.4	4 410	19 368	7 981	2 938	3 747	3 048	1 187
October	62.3	71.9	57.4	36.5	7 805	5.6	4 776	19 609	8 040	3 019	3 721	3 093	1 226
November	62.5	72.1	57.4	37.0	7 623	5.4	4 525	19 449	7 974	2 970	3 712	3 076	1 186
December	62.4	71.9	57.4	36.4	7 628	5.4	4 465	19 484	8 040	2 926	3 689	3 058	1 292
2005													
January	62.4	71.9	57.5	36.2	7 446	5.3	4 395	19 088	7 723	2 821	3 558	3 024	1 140
February	62.3	72.0	57.4	35.7	7 539	5.4	4 291	19 531	7 986	2 862	3 683	3 064	1 240
March	62.4	72.2	57.3	36.5	7 552	5.4	4 367	19 437	7 616	2 793	3 453	2 952	1 212
April	62.6	72.5	57.5	36.2	7 547	5.3	4 321	19 527	7 644	2 688	3 347	3 036	1 261
May	62.7	72.6	57.5	36.4	7 457	5.3	4 375	19 407	7 629	2 650	3 337	3 013	1 280
June	62.7	72.6	57.5	36.8	7 701	5.4	4 457	19 214	7 493	2 388	3 294	3 030	1 169
July	62.8	72.7	57.6	36.7	7 581	5.3	4 411	19 539	7 494	2 483	3 274	3 070	1 150
August	62.9	72.7	57.7	36.8	7 497	5.3	4 450	19 548	7 367	2 672	3 307	2 877	1 183
September	62.8	72.5	57.8	36.7	7 616	5.3	4 565	19 581	7 648	2 584	3 461	3 055	1 133
October	62.8	72.6	57.8	36.2	7 564	5.3	4 240	19 696	7 418	2 477	3 281	3 013	1 124
November	62.8	72.4	57.8	36.4	7 545	5.3	4 175	19 612	7 572	2 492	3 282	3 053	1 238
December	62.8	72.4	57.8	36.7	7 473	5.2	4 138	19 582	7 375	2 417	3 318	2 966	1 091

[1]Changes in survey design, population estimates, and methodology in 1994 and several other years affect year-to-year comparisons. See notes and definitions for more information.
[2]Fifteen weeks and over.
. . . = Not available.

Table 10-4. Unemployment Rates [1]

(Unemployment as a percent of the civilian labor force in group; seasonally adjusted, except as noted.)

Year and month	All civilian workers	By age and sex			By race				Hispanic or Latino ethnicity	By marital status		
		20 years and over		Both sexes, 16 to 19 years	White	Black and other	Black or African American	Asian [2]		Married men, spouse present	Married women, spouse present	Women who maintain families [2]
		Men	Women									
1960	5.5	4.7	5.1	14.7	5.0	10.2	...	...	...	3.7	5.2	...
1961	6.7	5.7	6.3	16.8	6.0	12.4	...	...	...	4.6	6.4	...
1962	5.5	4.6	5.4	14.7	4.9	10.9	...	...	...	3.6	5.4	...
1963	5.7	4.5	5.4	17.2	5.0	10.8	...	...	...	3.4	5.4	...
1964	5.2	3.9	5.2	16.2	4.6	9.6	...	...	...	2.8	5.1	...
1965	4.5	3.2	4.5	14.8	4.1	8.1	...	...	...	2.4	4.5	...
1966	3.8	2.5	3.8	12.8	3.4	7.3	...	...	...	1.9	3.7	...
1967	3.8	2.3	4.2	12.9	3.4	7.4	...	...	...	1.8	4.5	4.9
1968	3.6	2.2	3.8	12.7	3.2	6.7	...	...	...	1.6	3.9	4.4
1969	3.5	2.1	3.7	12.2	3.1	6.4	...	...	...	1.5	3.9	4.4
1970	4.9	3.5	4.8	15.3	4.5	8.2	...	...	...	2.6	4.9	5.4
1971	5.9	4.4	5.7	16.9	5.4	9.9	...	...	...	3.2	5.7	7.3
1972	5.6	4.0	5.4	16.2	5.1	10.0	10.4	...	...	2.8	5.4	7.2
1973	4.9	3.3	4.9	14.5	4.3	9.0	9.4	...	7.5	2.3	4.7	7.1
1974	5.6	3.8	5.5	16.0	5.0	9.9	10.5	...	8.1	2.7	5.3	7.0
1975	8.5	6.8	8.0	19.9	7.8	13.8	14.8	...	12.2	5.1	7.9	10.0
1976	7.7	5.9	7.4	19.0	7.0	13.1	14.0	...	11.5	4.2	7.1	10.1
1977	7.1	5.2	7.0	17.8	6.2	13.1	14.0	...	10.1	3.6	6.5	9.4
1978	6.1	4.3	6.0	16.4	5.2	11.9	12.8	...	9.1	2.8	5.5	8.5
1979	5.8	4.2	5.7	16.1	5.1	11.3	12.3	...	8.3	2.8	5.1	8.3
1980	7.1	5.9	6.4	17.8	6.3	13.1	14.3	...	10.1	4.2	5.8	9.2
1981	7.6	6.3	6.8	19.6	6.7	14.2	15.6	...	10.4	4.3	6.0	10.4
1982	9.7	8.8	8.3	23.2	8.6	17.3	18.9	...	13.8	6.5	7.4	11.7
1983	9.6	8.9	8.1	22.4	8.4	17.8	19.5	...	13.7	6.5	7.0	12.2
1984	7.5	6.6	6.8	18.9	6.5	14.4	15.9	...	10.7	4.6	5.7	10.3
1985	7.2	6.2	6.6	18.6	6.2	13.7	15.1	...	10.5	4.3	5.6	10.4
1986	7.0	6.1	6.2	18.3	6.0	13.1	14.5	...	10.6	4.4	5.2	9.8
1987	6.2	5.4	5.4	16.9	5.3	11.6	13.0	...	8.8	3.9	4.3	9.2
1988	5.5	4.8	4.9	15.3	4.7	10.4	11.7	...	8.2	3.3	3.9	8.1
1989	5.3	4.5	4.7	15.0	4.5	10.0	11.4	...	8.0	3.0	3.7	8.1
1990	5.6	5.0	4.9	15.5	4.8	10.1	11.4	...	8.2	3.4	3.8	8.3
1991	6.8	6.4	5.7	18.7	6.1	11.1	12.5	...	10.0	4.4	4.5	9.3
1992	7.5	7.1	6.3	20.1	6.6	12.7	14.2	...	11.6	5.1	5.0	10.0
1993	6.9	6.4	5.9	19.0	6.1	11.7	13.0	...	10.8	4.4	4.6	9.7
1994	6.1	5.4	5.4	17.6	5.3	10.5	11.5	...	9.9	3.7	4.1	8.9
1995	5.6	4.8	4.9	17.3	4.9	9.6	10.4	...	9.3	3.3	3.9	8.0
1996	5.4	4.6	4.8	16.7	4.7	9.3	10.5	...	8.9	3.0	3.6	8.2
1997	4.9	4.2	4.4	16.0	4.2	8.8	10.0	...	7.7	2.7	3.1	8.1
1998	4.5	3.7	4.1	14.6	3.9	7.8	8.9	...	7.2	2.4	2.9	7.2
1999	4.2	3.5	3.8	13.9	3.7	7.0	8.0	...	6.4	2.2	2.7	6.4
2000	4.0	3.3	3.6	13.1	3.5	6.7	7.6	3.6	5.7	2.0	2.7	5.9
2001	4.7	4.2	4.1	14.7	4.2	7.7	8.6	4.5	6.6	2.7	3.1	6.6
2002	5.8	5.3	5.1	16.5	5.1	9.2	10.2	5.9	7.5	3.6	3.7	8.0
2003	6.0	5.6	5.1	17.5	5.2	...	10.8	6.0	7.7	3.8	3.7	8.5
2004	5.5	5.0	4.9	17.0	4.8	...	10.4	4.4	7.0	3.1	3.5	8.0
2005	5.1	4.4	4.6	16.6	4.4	...	10.0	4.0	6.0	2.8	3.3	7.8
2004												
January	5.7	5.1	5.1	17.0	5.0	...	10.3	5.2	7.3	3.3	3.7	8.3
February	5.6	5.1	4.9	16.6	4.9	...	9.6	4.7	7.4	3.3	3.6	8.1
March	5.7	5.2	5.2	16.7	5.1	...	10.2	4.2	7.4	3.2	3.7	8.4
April	5.5	5.1	4.9	16.5	4.9	...	9.8	4.4	7.1	3.2	3.7	7.5
May	5.6	5.2	4.8	17.0	4.9	...	10.0	4.2	7.0	3.2	3.3	7.4
June	5.6	5.0	5.0	16.9	5.0	...	10.2	5.0	6.7	3.2	3.7	8.2
July	5.5	5.0	4.8	17.8	4.8	...	11.1	4.3	6.9	3.3	3.4	9.0
August	5.4	5.0	4.7	16.9	4.7	...	10.5	3.6	6.9	3.1	3.5	8.3
September	5.4	5.0	4.7	16.8	4.7	...	10.4	4.3	7.0	3.0	3.1	8.2
October	5.4	4.9	4.8	17.1	4.6	...	10.8	4.8	6.7	3.0	3.1	7.8
November	5.4	4.9	4.7	16.5	4.6	...	10.7	4.2	6.6	3.0	3.4	7.7
December	5.4	4.9	4.7	17.9	4.6	...	10.8	4.1	6.5	3.0	3.4	7.1
2005												
January	5.2	4.7	4.6	16.2	4.5	...	10.5	4.2	6.2	3.0	3.2	8.2
February	5.4	4.9	4.7	17.6	4.6	...	10.8	4.5	6.3	2.9	3.2	8.0
March	5.1	4.5	4.5	16.9	4.4	...	10.3	3.9	5.7	2.9	3.0	8.0
April	5.1	4.4	4.6	17.6	4.4	...	10.3	3.9	6.4	2.6	3.3	7.7
May	5.1	4.4	4.6	17.7	4.4	...	10.0	3.9	5.9	2.7	3.2	7.9
June	5.0	4.3	4.6	16.3	4.3	...	10.3	4.0	5.8	2.6	3.3	8.2
July	5.0	4.3	4.7	16.0	4.3	...	9.4	5.2	5.5	2.7	3.4	8.8
August	4.9	4.3	4.4	16.4	4.2	...	9.7	3.6	5.8	2.9	3.2	7.2
September	5.1	4.5	4.6	15.8	4.5	...	9.5	4.1	6.5	2.7	3.4	7.6
October	4.9	4.3	4.6	15.9	4.4	...	9.1	3.1	5.9	2.6	3.3	7.3
November	5.0	4.3	4.6	17.1	4.2	...	10.6	3.6	6.1	2.6	3.3	7.2
December	4.9	4.3	4.5	15.2	4.3	...	9.3	3.8	6.0	2.6	3.2	6.9

[1]Changes in survey design, population estimates, and methodology in 1994 and several other years affect year-to-year comparisons. See notes and definitions for more information.
[2]Not seasonally adjusted.
. . . = Not available.

Table 10-5. Unemployment Rates and Related Data [1]

(Seasonally adjusted.)

Year and month	Unemployment rates by reason for unemployment (percent of total civilian labor force)					Duration of unemployment		Augmented unemployment measures	
	Total	Job losers and persons who completed temporary jobs	Job leavers	Reentrants	New entrants	Average (mean) weeks unemployed	Median weeks unemployed	Persons not in labor force who currently want a job (thousands)	Augmented unemployment rate [2]
1960	5.5	. . .	. . .	. . .	. . .	12.8	. . .	. . .	. . .
1961	6.7	. . .	. . .	. . .	. . .	15.6	. . .	. . .	. . .
1962	5.5	. . .	. . .	. . .	. . .	14.7	. . .	. . .	. . .
1963	5.7	. . .	. . .	. . .	. . .	14.0	. . .	. . .	. . .
1964	5.2	. . .	. . .	. . .	. . .	13.3	. . .	. . .	. . .
1965	4.5	. . .	. . .	. . .	. . .	11.8	. . .	. . .	. . .
1966	3.8	. . .	. . .	. . .	. . .	10.4	. . .	. . .	. . .
1967	3.8	1.6	0.6	1.2	0.5	8.7	2.3	. . .	. . .
1968	3.6	1.4	0.5	1.2	0.5	8.4	4.5	. . .	. . .
1969	3.5	1.3	0.5	1.2	0.5	7.8	4.4	. . .	. . .
1970	4.9	2.2	0.7	1.5	0.6	8.6	4.9	3 907	9.2
1971	5.9	2.8	0.7	1.7	0.7	11.3	6.3	4 441	10.6
1972	5.6	2.4	0.7	1.7	0.8	12.0	6.2	4 476	10.2
1973	4.9	1.9	0.8	1.5	0.7	10.0	5.2	4 474	9.4
1974	5.6	2.4	0.8	1.6	0.7	9.8	5.2	4 541	10.0
1975	8.5	4.7	0.9	2.0	0.9	14.2	8.4	5 292	13.3
1976	7.7	3.8	0.9	2.0	0.9	15.8	8.2	5 217	12.5
1977	7.1	3.2	0.9	2.0	1.0	14.3	7.0	5 777	12.2
1978	6.1	2.5	0.9	1.8	0.9	11.9	5.9	5 459	10.8
1979	5.8	2.5	0.8	1.7	0.8	10.8	5.4	5 439	10.5
1980	7.1	3.7	0.8	1.8	0.8	11.9	6.5	5 682	11.8
1981	7.6	3.9	0.8	1.9	0.9	13.7	6.9	5 819	12.3
1982	9.7	5.7	0.8	2.2	1.1	15.6	8.7	6 563	14.8
1983	9.6	5.6	0.7	2.2	1.1	20.0	10.1	6 484	14.6
1984	7.5	3.9	0.7	1.9	1.0	18.2	7.9	6 054	12.2
1985	7.2	3.6	0.8	2.0	0.9	15.6	6.8	5 908	11.7
1986	7.0	3.4	0.9	1.8	0.9	15.0	6.9	5 848	11.4
1987	6.2	3.0	0.8	1.6	0.8	14.5	6.5	5 721	10.5
1988	5.5	2.5	0.8	1.5	0.7	13.5	5.9	5 370	9.5
1989	5.3	2.4	0.8	1.5	0.5	11.9	4.8	5 312	9.2
1990	5.6	2.7	0.8	1.5	0.5	12.0	5.3	5 481	9.5
1991	6.8	3.7	0.8	1.7	0.6	13.7	6.8	5 745	10.9
1992	7.5	4.2	0.8	1.8	0.7	17.7	8.7	6 172	11.8
1993	6.9	3.8	0.8	1.7	0.7	18.0	8.3	6 346	11.3
1994	6.1	2.9	0.6	2.1	0.5	18.8	9.2	6 218	10.4
1995	5.6	2.6	0.6	1.9	0.4	16.6	8.3	5 670	9.5
1996	5.4	2.5	0.6	1.9	0.4	16.7	8.3	5 451	9.1
1997	4.9	2.2	0.6	1.7	0.4	15.8	8.0	4 941	8.3
1998	4.5	2.1	0.5	1.5	0.4	14.5	6.7	4 812	7.7
1999	4.2	1.9	0.6	1.4	0.3	13.4	6.4	4 568	7.3
2000	4.0	1.8	0.5	1.4	0.3	12.6	5.9	4 413	6.9
2001	4.7	2.4	0.6	1.4	0.3	13.1	6.8	4 590	7.7
2002	5.8	3.2	0.6	1.6	0.4	16.6	9.1	4 677	8.7
2003	6.0	3.3	0.6	1.7	0.4	19.2	10.1	4 726	8.9
2004	5.5	2.8	0.6	1.6	0.5	19.6	9.8	4 852	8.5
2005	5.1	2.5	0.6	1.6	0.4	18.4	8.9	4 985	8.2
2004									
January	5.7	3.0	0.6	1.7	0.5	19.8	10.6	4 756	8.6
February	5.6	2.9	0.6	1.6	0.5	20.2	10.2	4 751	8.5
March	5.7	3.1	0.6	1.7	0.4	19.8	10.2	4 794	8.7
April	5.5	3.0	0.6	1.6	0.4	19.6	9.4	4 673	8.5
May	5.6	2.9	0.6	1.7	0.5	19.8	9.9	4 686	8.5
June	5.6	2.8	0.6	1.7	0.4	19.9	10.8	4 658	8.5
July	5.5	2.9	0.6	1.6	0.5	18.8	8.9	4 682	8.4
August	5.4	2.7	0.6	1.6	0.5	19.2	9.4	4 953	8.5
September	5.4	2.7	0.6	1.6	0.5	19.6	9.6	4 907	8.5
October	5.4	2.7	0.6	1.6	0.5	19.6	9.5	5 300	8.7
November	5.4	2.7	0.6	1.6	0.5	19.8	9.7	5 196	8.6
December	5.4	2.7	0.6	1.6	0.5	19.4	9.4	4 957	8.5
2005									
January	5.2	2.7	0.6	1.6	0.4	19.2	9.3	4 974	8.3
February	5.4	2.6	0.6	1.6	0.5	19.1	9.2	4 985	8.5
March	5.1	2.5	0.6	1.6	0.5	19.3	9.2	4 973	8.2
April	5.1	2.5	0.6	1.6	0.5	19.6	8.9	5 103	8.3
May	5.1	2.5	0.6	1.6	0.5	18.6	9.1	4 717	8.0
June	5.0	2.5	0.6	1.5	0.4	17.2	9.1	5 265	8.3
July	5.0	2.4	0.6	1.6	0.4	17.7	8.9	4 997	8.1
August	4.9	2.3	0.6	1.6	0.4	18.9	9.4	4 829	7.9
September	5.1	2.5	0.6	1.6	0.4	18.2	8.5	4 945	8.1
October	4.9	2.3	0.6	1.6	0.4	18.0	8.6	4 994	8.0
November	5.0	2.3	0.6	1.7	0.5	17.6	8.5	4 887	8.0
December	4.9	2.3	0.6	1.6	0.4	17.3	8.5	5 167	8.1

[1]Changes in survey design, population estimates, and methodology in 1994 and several other years affect year-to-year comparisons. See notes and definitions for more information.
[2]See notes and definitions.
. . . = Not available.

Table 10-6. Insured Unemployment

(Averages of weekly data; thousands of persons, except as noted.)

Year and month	State programs, seasonally adjusted			Federal programs, not seasonally adjusted					
				Initial claims		Persons claiming benefits			
	Initial claims	Insured unemployment	Insured unemployment rate (percent)¹	Federal employees	Newly discharged veterans	Federal employees	Newly discharged veterans	Railroad retirement	Extended benefits
1967	227	1 206	. . .	. . .	. . .	. . .	. . .	. . .	. . .
1968	197	1 088	. . .	. . .	. . .	. . .	. . .	. . .	. . .
1969	196	1 092	. . .	. . .	. . .	. . .	. . .	. . .	. . .
1970	297	1 848	. . .	. . .	. . .	. . .	. . .	. . .	. . .
1971	296	2 152	4.1	. . .	. . .	. . .	. . .	. . .	. . .
1972	263	1 844	3.5	. . .	. . .	. . .	. . .	. . .	. . .
1973	244	1 629	2.7	. . .	. . .	. . .	. . .	. . .	. . .
1974	352	2 278	3.5	. . .	. . .	. . .	. . .	. . .	. . .
1975	474	3 965	6.0	. . .	. . .	. . .	. . .	. . .	. . .
1976	383	2 978	4.5	. . .	. . .	. . .	. . .	. . .	. . .
1977	374	2 644	3.9	. . .	. . .	. . .	. . .	. . .	. . .
1978	341	2 337	3.3	. . .	. . .	. . .	. . .	. . .	. . .
1979	383	2 428	3.0	. . .	. . .	. . .	. . .	. . .	. . .
1980	488	3 365	3.9	. . .	. . .	. . .	. . .	. . .	. . .
1981	451	3 032	3.5	. . .	. . .	. . .	. . .	. . .	. . .
1982	586	4 094	4.7	. . .	. . .	. . .	. . .	. . .	. . .
1983	441	3 337	3.9	. . .	. . .	. . .	. . .	. . .	. . .
1984	374	2 452	2.8	. . .	. . .	. . .	. . .	. . .	. . .
1985	392	2 584	2.9	. . .	. . .	20.24	17.11	. . .	. . .
1986	378	2 632	2.8	2.13	2.52	21.29	17.71	. . .	9.51
1987	325	2 273	2.4	2.19	2.57	22.91	18.13	13.28	1.17
1988	309	2 075	2.1	2.32	2.74	22.17	15.09	10.37	0.61
1989	330	2 174	2.1	2.14	2.31	22.17	15.09	10.37	0.61
1990	385	2 539	2.4	2.45	2.54	23.89	18.43	10.56	2.36
1991	447	3 338	3.2	2.55	2.93	30.50	22.12	10.73	32.16
1992	409	3 208	3.1	2.75	4.95	32.10	60.25	8.77	4.61
1993	344	2 768	2.6	2.55	3.94	32.06	54.90	7.40	7.59
1994	340	2 667	2.5	2.54	3.02	32.21	37.65	6.21	31.09
1995	359	2 590	2.4	4.57	2.51	31.68	29.78	5.48	14.27
1996	352	2 552	2.3	7.33	2.13	29.84	24.30	5.40	5.53
1997	322	2 300	2.0	2.01	1.75	23.58	19.66	4.00	5.35
1998	317	2 213	1.9	1.64	1.41	19.60	15.68	3.19	6.43
1999	298	2 186	1.8	1.48	1.18	16.85	14.25	3.24	3.05
2000	299	2 112	1.7	1.73	1.05	18.60	12.54	3.92	0.58
2001	406	3 017	2.4	1.47	1.15	18.57	13.98	. . .	0.57
2002	404	3 570	2.8	1.46	1.22	17.54	16.07	. . .	10.79
2003	402	3 532	2.8	1.56	1.46	18.22	19.68	. . .	22.30
2004	343	2 929	2.3	1.50	1.89	18.14	26.90	. . .	4.22
2005	332	2 662	2.1	1.46	2.03	16.92	27.58	. . .	1.69
2003									
January	390	3 418	2.7	1.93	1.49	22.74	20.74	. . .	24.93
February	406	3 446	2.7	1.25	1.27	20.63	20.68	. . .	17.30
March	427	3 535	2.8	1.06	1.27	18.03	19.70	. . .	17.63
April	435	3 612	2.9	1.10	1.16	15.32	18.04	. . .	16.94
May	428	3 692	2.9	1.18	1.08	13.34	16.99	. . .	16.06
June	419	3 685	2.9	1.68	1.20	13.88	16.58	. . .	15.38
July	409	3 605	2.9	2.02	1.35	16.61	16.74	. . .	13.87
August	400	3 590	2.8	1.32	1.66	18.30	17.84	. . .	20.02
September	398	3 579	2.8	1.66	1.77	18.14	19.50	. . .	32.18
October	386	3 512	2.8	1.74	1.89	19.51	21.51	. . .	33.33
November	367	3 393	2.7	1.87	1.56	19.82	23.16	. . .	30.46
December	361	3 296	2.6	1.94	1.84	22.34	24.70	. . .	29.52
2004									
January	354	3 164	2.5	1.92	2.03	24.16	27.65	. . .	20.93
February	356	3 131	2.5	1.20	1.72	21.53	28.43	. . .	9.27
March	345	3 043	2.4	1.04	1.65	19.52	27.81	. . .	2.36
April	348	2 985	2.4	1.11	1.62	16.91	26.54	. . .	2.48
May	341	2 947	2.3	1.15	1.79	14.53	25.51	. . .	2.28
June	346	2 922	2.3	1.49	1.92	14.00	25.29	. . .	2.01
July	338	2 893	2.3	1.89	2.10	16.16	25.64	. . .	0.17
August	341	2 877	2.3	1.35	2.18	17.90	26.49	. . .	0.01
September	341	2 855	2.3	1.33	2.20	16.59	26.57	. . .	0.00
October	339	2 798	2.2	1.69	2.04	17.32	27.63	. . .	0.01
November	334	2 757	2.2	1.82	1.66	18.24	27.31	. . .	0.00
December	331	2 757	2.2	1.90	1.69	20.93	28.26	. . .	0.00
2005									
January	336	2 716	2.1	1.82	1.94	22.13	27.91	. . .	0.00
February	322	2 687	2.1	1.15	1.80	19.75	26.95	. . .	0.00
March	341	2 664	2.1	0.96	1.97	17.38	26.01	. . .	1.44
April	332	2 625	2.1	1.04	2.08	14.56	25.89	. . .	2.63
May	335	2 606	2.1	1.08	1.92	12.65	26.92	. . .	2.70
June	326	2 616	2.1	1.42	2.14	12.74	26.70	. . .	1.22
July	321	2 601	2.0	1.80	2.06	15.24	28.46	. . .	0.00
August	317	2 593	2.0	1.30	2.20	17.34	29.21	. . .	0.00
September	380	2 713	2.1	1.34	2.07	16.00	28.50	. . .	0.00
October	347	2 784	2.2	1.67	2.07	16.20	28.15	. . .	0.00
November	316	2 688	2.1	1.88	1.92	17.40	26.98	. . .	0.00
December	312	2 637	2.1	1.83	2.12	20.63	28.93	. . .	5.24

¹Insured unemployed as a percent of employment covered by state programs.
. . . = Not available.

Section 10b: Payroll Employment, Hours, and Earnings

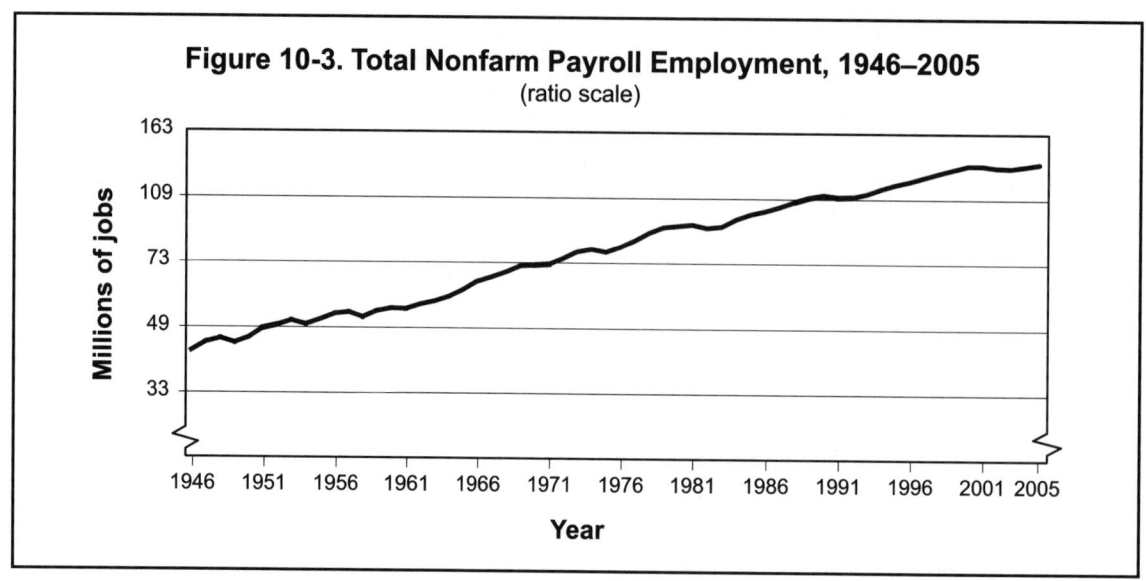

Figure 10-3. Total Nonfarm Payroll Employment, 1946–2005
(ratio scale)

- The number of jobs on nonfarm payrolls rose 1.5 percent in 2005, following a 1.1 percent increase in 2004, and surpassed the 2001 level of employment. However, the growth still fell short of longer-term rates. Between 1948 and 2000, job growth averaged 2.1 percent per year. (Tables 10-7 and 20-4)

- Job growth in 2004 and 2005 was led by private service-providing industries. In the government sector, only local governments significantly increased their employment. In the goods-producing sector, employment increased in mining and construction but continued to decline in manufacturing. (Table 10-7)

- The diffusion index shows the percentage of industries in which employment is stagnant or falling. Diffusion indexes below 50 percent are indicative of recession. In the short recession of 1980, and even in the severe recession of 1982, this index was below 50 only for a year or so. In 1990–1991, it remained there for two years, and in the latest recession, it held there for three years running. However, job growth became more pervasive by early 2004, and the most recent data continue to show employment gains for about 60 percent of private nonfarm industries. (Table 10-7)

Table 10-7. Nonfarm Payroll Employment by NAICS Supersector

(Thousands; seasonally adjusted, except as noted.)

Year and month	Total	Private							Service-providing				
		Total	Goods-producing						Total	Private			
			Total	Natural resources and mining	Construc-tion	Manufacturing				Total	Trade, transportation, and utilities		
						Total	Durable	Nondurable			Total	Wholesale trade	Retail trade
1960	54 296	45 832	19 182	771	2 973	15 438	9 071	6 367	35 114	26 650	11 147	2 690	5 589
1961	54 105	45 399	18 647	728	2 908	15 011	8 711	6 300	35 458	26 752	11 040	2 681	5 560
1962	55 659	46 655	19 203	709	2 997	15 498	9 099	6 399	36 455	27 451	11 215	2 737	5 672
1963	56 764	47 423	19 385	694	3 060	15 631	9 226	6 405	37 379	28 038	11 367	2 780	5 781
1964	58 391	48 680	19 733	697	3 148	15 888	9 414	6 474	38 658	28 947	11 677	2 856	5 977
1965	60 874	50 683	20 595	694	3 284	16 617	9 973	6 644	40 279	30 089	12 139	2 967	6 262
1966	64 020	53 110	21 740	690	3 371	17 680	10 803	6 878	42 280	31 370	12 611	3 080	6 530
1967	65 931	54 406	21 882	679	3 305	17 897	10 952	6 945	44 049	32 524	12 950	3 158	6 711
1968	68 023	56 050	22 292	671	3 410	18 211	11 137	7 074	45 731	33 759	13 334	3 236	6 977
1969	70 512	58 181	22 893	683	3 637	18 573	11 396	7 177	47 619	35 288	13 853	3 344	7 295
1970	71 006	58 318	22 179	677	3 654	17 848	10 762	7 086	48 827	36 139	14 144	3 418	7 463
1971	71 335	58 323	21 602	658	3 770	17 174	10 229	6 944	49 734	36 721	14 318	3 424	7 657
1972	73 798	60 333	22 299	672	3 957	17 669	10 630	7 039	51 499	38 034	14 788	3 547	8 038
1973	76 912	63 050	23 450	693	4 167	18 589	11 414	7 176	53 462	39 600	15 349	3 688	8 371
1974	78 389	64 086	23 364	755	4 095	18 514	11 432	7 082	55 025	40 721	15 693	3 823	8 536
1975	77 069	62 250	21 318	802	3 608	16 909	10 266	6 643	55 751	40 932	15 606	3 810	8 600
1976	79 502	64 501	22 025	832	3 662	17 531	10 640	6 891	57 477	42 476	16 128	3 920	8 966
1977	82 593	67 334	22 972	865	3 940	18 167	11 132	7 035	59 620	44 362	16 765	4 055	9 359
1978	86 826	71 014	24 156	902	4 322	18 932	11 770	7 162	62 670	46 858	17 658	4 280	9 879
1979	89 932	73 864	24 997	1 008	4 562	19 426	12 220	7 206	64 935	48 868	18 303	4 485	10 180
1980	90 528	74 154	24 263	1 077	4 454	18 733	11 679	7 054	66 265	49 891	18 413	4 557	10 244
1981	91 289	75 109	24 118	1 180	4 304	18 634	11 611	7 023	67 172	50 991	18 604	4 634	10 364
1982	89 677	73 695	22 550	1 163	4 024	17 363	10 610	6 753	67 127	51 145	18 457	4 575	10 372
1983	90 280	74 269	22 110	997	4 065	17 048	10 326	6 722	68 171	52 160	18 668	4 559	10 635
1984	94 530	78 371	23 435	1 014	4 501	17 920	11 050	6 870	71 095	54 936	19 653	4 788	11 223
1985	97 511	80 978	23 585	974	4 793	17 819	11 034	6 784	73 926	57 393	20 379	4 915	11 733
1986	99 474	82 636	23 318	829	4 937	17 552	10 795	6 757	76 156	59 318	20 795	4 935	12 078
1987	102 088	84 932	23 470	771	5 090	17 609	10 767	6 842	78 618	61 462	21 302	5 003	12 419
1988	105 345	87 806	23 909	770	5 233	17 906	10 969	6 938	81 436	63 897	21 974	5 153	12 808
1989	108 014	90 087	24 045	750	5 309	17 985	11 004	6 981	83 969	66 042	22 510	5 284	13 108
1990	109 487	91 072	23 723	765	5 263	17 695	10 736	6 959	85 764	67 349	22 666	5 268	13 182
1991	108 374	89 829	22 588	739	4 780	17 068	10 219	6 849	85 787	67 241	22 281	5 185	12 896
1992	108 726	89 940	22 095	689	4 608	16 799	9 945	6 854	86 631	67 845	22 125	5 110	12 828
1993	110 844	91 855	22 219	666	4 779	16 774	9 900	6 873	88 625	69 636	22 378	5 093	13 021
1994	114 291	95 016	22 774	659	5 095	17 021	10 131	6 890	91 517	72 242	23 128	5 247	13 491
1995	117 298	97 866	23 156	641	5 274	17 241	10 372	6 869	94 142	74 710	23 834	5 433	13 897
1996	119 708	100 169	23 410	637	5 536	17 237	10 485	6 752	96 299	76 759	24 239	5 522	14 143
1997	122 776	103 113	23 886	654	5 813	17 419	10 704	6 716	98 890	79 227	24 700	5 664	14 389
1998	125 930	106 021	24 354	645	6 149	17 560	10 910	6 650	101 576	81 667	25 186	5 795	14 609
1999	128 993	108 686	24 465	598	6 545	17 322	10 830	6 492	104 528	84 221	25 771	5 893	14 970
2000	131 785	110 996	24 649	599	6 787	17 263	10 876	6 388	107 136	86 346	26 225	5 933	15 280
2001	131 826	110 707	23 873	606	6 826	16 441	10 335	6 107	107 952	86 834	25 983	5 773	15 239
2002	130 341	108 828	22 557	583	6 716	15 259	9 483	5 775	107 784	86 271	25 497	5 652	15 025
2003	129 999	108 416	21 816	572	6 735	14 510	8 963	5 547	108 182	86 599	25 287	5 608	14 917
2004	131 435	109 814	21 882	591	6 976	14 315	8 924	5 391	109 553	87 932	25 533	5 663	15 058
2005	133 463	111 660	22 133	625	7 277	14 232	8 953	5 278	111 330	89 527	25 909	5 750	15 254
2004													
January	130 420	108 887	21 712	576	6 846	14 290	8 860	5 430	108 708	87 175	25 357	5 625	14 964
February	130 475	108 933	21 703	576	6 847	14 280	8 863	5 417	108 772	87 230	25 366	5 620	14 974
March	130 821	109 231	21 768	584	6 896	14 288	8 873	5 415	109 053	87 463	25 450	5 630	15 029
April	131 073	109 457	21 813	588	6 908	14 317	8 902	5 415	109 260	87 644	25 471	5 648	15 039
May	131 340	109 749	21 877	591	6 946	14 340	8 925	5 415	109 463	87 872	25 510	5 653	15 059
June	131 418	109 843	21 885	591	6 962	14 332	8 931	5 401	109 533	87 958	25 542	5 658	15 071
July	131 456	109 875	21 904	595	6 977	14 332	8 935	5 397	109 552	87 971	25 535	5 664	15 057
August	131 587	109 958	21 940	595	6 997	14 348	8 966	5 382	109 647	88 018	25 550	5 670	15 057
September	131 764	110 109	21 952	597	7 026	14 329	8 957	5 372	109 812	88 157	25 593	5 684	15 075
October	132 102	110 404	21 984	595	7 069	14 320	8 961	5 359	110 118	88 420	25 638	5 690	15 108
November	132 235	110 517	22 002	599	7 095	14 308	8 956	5 352	110 233	88 515	25 672	5 696	15 136
December	132 395	110 679	22 016	601	7 121	14 294	8 956	5 338	110 379	88 663	25 695	5 702	15 139
2005													
January	132 471	110 756	21 988	605	7 115	14 268	8 943	5 325	110 483	88 768	25 724	5 702	15 156
February	132 736	110 995	22 052	610	7 166	14 276	8 963	5 313	110 684	88 943	25 787	5 713	15 198
March	132 876	111 129	22 077	616	7 193	14 268	8 959	5 309	110 799	89 052	25 822	5 726	15 211
April	133 104	111 336	22 119	620	7 243	14 256	8 959	5 297	110 985	89 217	25 861	5 731	15 233
May	133 210	111 437	22 126	620	7 255	14 251	8 964	5 287	111 084	89 311	25 897	5 742	15 249
June	133 357	111 590	22 133	623	7 277	14 233	8 953	5 280	111 243	89 457	25 908	5 748	15 256
July	133 617	111 795	22 131	624	7 283	14 224	8 946	5 278	111 486	89 664	25 976	5 755	15 309
August	133 792	111 941	22 146	627	7 306	14 213	8 950	5 263	111 646	89 795	25 985	5 759	15 312
September	133 840	111 985	22 143	631	7 325	14 187	8 933	5 254	111 697	89 842	25 944	5 762	15 267
October	133 877	112 025	22 179	636	7 347	14 196	8 952	5 244	111 698	89 846	25 945	5 768	15 259
November	134 231	112 351	22 264	641	7 409	14 214	8 960	5 254	111 967	90 087	26 006	5 783	15 292
December	134 376	112 498	22 282	644	7 416	14 222	8 970	5 252	112 094	90 216	26 015	5 784	15 300

Table 10-7. Nonfarm Payroll Employment by NAICS Supersector—Continued

(Thousands; seasonally adjusted, except as noted.)

Year and month	Information	Financial activities	Professional and business services	Education and health services	Leisure and hospitality	Other services	Total	Federal Total	Federal Department of Defense [1]	State Total	State Education	Local Total	Local Education	Diffusion index, 6-month span, private industry [2]
1960	1 728	2 532	3 694	2 937	3 460	1 152	8 464	2 381	681	1 536	448	4 547	2 314	. . .
1961	1 693	2 590	3 744	3 030	3 468	1 188	8 706	2 391	683	1 607	474	4 708	2 411	. . .
1962	1 723	2 656	3 885	3 172	3 557	1 243	9 004	2 455	697	1 669	511	4 881	2 522	. . .
1963	1 735	2 731	3 990	3 288	3 639	1 288	9 341	2 473	687	1 747	557	5 121	2 674	. . .
1964	1 766	2 811	4 137	3 438	3 772	1 346	9 711	2 463	676	1 856	609	5 392	2 839	. . .
1965	1 824	2 878	4 306	3 587	3 951	1 404	10 191	2 495	679	1 996	679	5 700	3 031	. . .
1966	1 908	2 961	4 517	3 770	4 127	1 475	10 910	2 690	741	2 141	775	6 080	3 297	. . .
1967	1 955	3 087	4 720	3 986	4 269	1 558	11 525	2 852	802	2 302	873	6 371	3 490	. . .
1968	1 991	3 234	4 918	4 191	4 453	1 638	11 972	2 871	801	2 442	958	6 660	3 649	. . .
1969	2 048	3 404	5 156	4 428	4 670	1 731	12 330	2 893	815	2 533	1 042	6 904	3 785	. . .
1970	2 041	3 532	5 267	4 577	4 789	1 789	12 687	2 865	756	2 664	1 104	7 158	3 912	. . .
1971	2 009	3 651	5 328	4 675	4 914	1 827	13 012	2 828	731	2 747	1 149	7 437	4 091	. . .
1972	2 056	3 784	5 523	4 863	5 121	1 900	13 465	2 815	720	2 859	1 188	7 790	4 262	. . .
1973	2 135	3 920	5 774	5 092	5 341	1 990	13 862	2 794	696	2 923	1 205	8 146	4 433	. . .
1974	2 160	4 023	5 974	5 322	5 471	2 078	14 303	2 858	698	3 039	1 267	8 407	4 584	. . .
1975	2 061	4 047	6 034	5 497	5 544	2 144	14 820	2 882	704	3 179	1 323	8 758	4 722	. . .
1976	2 111	4 155	6 287	5 756	5 794	2 244	15 001	2 863	693	3 273	1 371	8 865	4 786	. . .
1977	2 185	4 348	6 587	6 052	6 065	2 359	15 258	2 859	676	3 377	1 385	9 023	4 859	79.7
1978	2 287	4 599	6 972	6 427	6 411	2 505	15 812	2 893	661	3 474	1 367	9 446	4 958	76.2
1979	2 375	4 843	7 312	6 767	6 631	2 637	16 068	2 894	649	3 541	1 378	9 633	4 989	57.9
1980	2 361	5 025	7 544	7 072	6 721	2 755	16 375	3 000	645	3 610	1 398	9 765	5 090	37.5
1981	2 382	5 163	7 782	7 357	6 840	2 865	16 180	2 922	655	3 640	1 420	9 619	5 095	58.0
1982	2 317	5 209	7 848	7 515	6 874	2 924	15 982	2 884	690	3 640	1 433	9 458	5 049	36.8
1983	2 253	5 334	8 039	7 766	7 078	3 021	16 011	2 915	699	3 662	1 450	9 434	5 020	78.2
1984	2 398	5 553	8 464	8 193	7 489	3 186	16 159	2 943	716	3 734	1 488	9 482	5 076	72.6
1985	2 437	5 815	8 871	8 657	7 869	3 366	16 533	3 014	738	3 832	1 540	9 687	5 221	57.6
1986	2 445	6 128	9 211	9 061	8 156	3 523	16 838	3 044	736	3 893	1 561	9 901	5 358	57.6
1987	2 507	6 385	9 608	9 515	8 446	3 699	17 156	3 089	736	3 967	1 586	10 100	5 469	69.5
1988	2 585	6 500	10 090	10 063	8 778	3 907	17 540	3 124	719	4 076	1 621	10 339	5 590	66.3
1989	2 622	6 562	10 555	10 616	9 062	4 116	17 927	3 136	735	4 182	1 668	10 609	5 740	53.7
1990	2 688	6 614	10 848	10 984	9 288	4 261	18 415	3 196	722	4 305	1 730	10 914	5 902	43.4
1991	2 677	6 558	10 714	11 506	9 256	4 249	18 545	3 110	702	4 355	1 768	11 081	5 994	45.0
1992	2 641	6 540	10 970	11 891	9 437	4 240	18 787	3 111	702	4 408	1 799	11 267	6 076	62.8
1993	2 668	6 709	11 495	12 303	9 732	4 350	18 989	3 063	670	4 488	1 834	11 438	6 206	70.7
1994	2 738	6 867	12 174	12 807	10 100	4 428	19 275	3 018	657	4 576	1 882	11 682	6 329	80.4
1995	2 843	6 827	12 844	13 289	10 501	4 572	19 432	2 949	627	4 635	1 919	11 849	6 453	68.5
1996	2 940	6 969	13 462	13 683	10 777	4 690	19 539	2 877	597	4 606	1 911	12 056	6 592	77.5
1997	3 084	7 178	14 335	14 087	11 018	4 825	19 664	2 806	588	4 582	1 904	12 276	6 759	79.9
1998	3 218	7 462	15 147	14 446	11 232	4 976	19 909	2 772	550	4 612	1 922	12 525	6 921	69.4
1999	3 419	7 648	15 957	14 798	11 543	5 087	20 307	2 769	525	4 709	1 983	12 829	7 120	68.9
2000	3 631	7 687	16 666	15 109	11 862	5 168	20 790	2 865	510	4 786	2 031	13 139	7 294	59.0
2001	3 629	7 807	16 476	15 645	12 036	5 258	21 118	2 764	504	4 905	2 113	13 449	7 479	33.5
2002	3 395	7 847	15 976	16 199	11 986	5 372	21 513	2 766	499	5 029	2 243	13 718	7 654	35.3
2003	3 188	7 977	15 987	16 588	12 173	5 401	21 583	2 761	486	5 002	2 255	13 820	7 709	40.3
2004	3 118	8 031	16 395	16 953	12 493	5 409	21 621	2 730	473	4 982	2 238	13 909	7 765	59.0
2005	3 066	8 141	16 882	17 342	12 802	5 386	21 803	2 724	485	5 021	2 250	14 058	7 864	60.6
2004														
January	3 141	7 980	16 151	16 775	12 366	5 405	21 533	2 728	470	4 959	2 229	13 846	7 716	49.8
February	3 143	7 989	16 155	16 794	12 378	5 405	21 542	2 730	467	4 970	2 239	13 842	7 711	52.3
March	3 137	7 998	16 190	16 843	12 425	5 420	21 590	2 728	466	4 974	2 242	13 888	7 751	54.7
April	3 133	8 013	16 301	16 881	12 424	5 421	21 616	2 751	467	4 972	2 239	13 893	7 758	60.8
May	3 134	8 033	16 381	16 917	12 474	5 423	21 591	2 726	469	4 966	2 228	13 899	7 763	63.3
June	3 138	8 040	16 400	16 934	12 483	5 421	21 575	2 728	475	4 958	2 217	13 889	7 753	63.8
July	3 123	8 021	16 429	16 965	12 485	5 413	21 581	2 725	477	4 971	2 230	13 885	7 754	63.1
August	3 106	8 036	16 435	16 993	12 490	5 408	21 629	2 731	478	4 983	2 234	13 915	7 769	63.5
September	3 093	8 063	16 470	16 999	12 537	5 402	21 655	2 734	476	4 990	2 240	13 931	7 781	59.0
October	3 092	8 054	16 574	17 074	12 591	5 397	21 698	2 729	475	5 003	2 249	13 966	7 808	61.3
November	3 088	8 057	16 577	17 104	12 621	5 396	21 718	2 736	478	5 010	2 251	13 972	7 811	55.9
December	3 080	8 076	16 630	17 141	12 643	5 398	21 716	2 726	480	5 010	2 248	13 980	7 813	55.6
2005														
January	3 068	8 091	16 638	17 176	12 673	5 398	21 715	2 721	479	5 013	2 248	13 981	7 816	55.4
February	3 063	8 097	16 711	17 188	12 703	5 394	21 741	2 727	480	5 016	2 249	13 998	7 830	57.7
March	3 067	8 096	16 745	17 211	12 722	5 389	21 747	2 730	482	5 015	2 247	14 002	7 829	57.4
April	3 072	8 100	16 780	17 241	12 770	5 393	21 768	2 729	482	5 018	2 247	14 021	7 839	58.8
May	3 065	8 101	16 794	17 291	12 778	5 385	21 773	2 725	483	5 017	2 247	14 031	7 842	55.2
June	3 062	8 114	16 844	17 333	12 802	5 386	21 786	2 727	489	5 016	2 244	14 043	7 851	58.6
July	3 061	8 136	16 898	17 368	12 833	5 392	21 822	2 726	490	5 023	2 249	14 073	7 878	60.8
August	3 065	8 155	16 932	17 413	12 860	5 385	21 851	2 725	489	5 024	2 252	14 102	7 901	59.5
September	3 071	8 172	16 997	17 451	12 826	5 381	21 855	2 725	485	5 026	2 255	14 104	7 892	60.6
October	3 058	8 201	16 991	17 440	12 840	5 371	21 852	2 724	486	5 022	2 248	14 106	7 895	57.7
November	3 064	8 217	17 061	17 481	12 881	5 377	21 880	2 728	486	5 032	2 257	14 120	7 899	58.5
December	3 066	8 223	17 121	17 507	12 898	5 386	21 878	2 713	485	5 036	2 258	14 129	7 907	60.6

[1] Not seasonally adjusted.
[2] See notes and definitions for explanation. September value used to represent year.
. . . = Not available.

Table 10-8. Production or Nonsupervisory Workers on Private Nonfarm Payrolls by NAICS Supersector

(Thousands, seasonally adjusted.)

Year and month	Total private	Natural resources and mining	Construc-tion	Manu-facturing	Trade, transportation, and utilities			Information	Financial activities	Profes-sional and business services	Education and health services	Leisure and hospitality	Other services
					Total	Wholesale trade	Retail trade						
1960	. . .	596	2 651	12 074	. . .	. . .	. . .	. . .	. . .	. . .	. . .	. . .	. . .
1961	. . .	556	2 582	11 612	. . .	. . .	. . .	. . .	. . .	. . .	. . .	. . .	. . .
1962	. . .	538	2 656	11 986	. . .	. . .	. . .	. . .	. . .	. . .	. . .	. . .	. . .
1963	. . .	525	2 719	12 051	. . .	. . .	. . .	. . .	. . .	. . .	. . .	. . .	. . .
1964	40 575	526	2 794	12 298	10 303	. . .	. . .	1 217	2 390	3 360	3 303	3 278	1 107
1965	42 302	523	2 906	12 905	10 702	. . .	. . .	1 268	2 434	3 515	3 443	3 443	1 161
1966	44 292	517	2 977	13 703	11 095	. . .	. . .	1 334	2 492	3 715	3 623	3 607	1 230
1967	45 185	501	2 903	13 714	11 369	. . .	. . .	1 365	2 585	3 890	3 818	3 734	1 306
1968	46 519	491	2 986	13 908	11 688	. . .	. . .	1 394	2 700	4 067	4 008	3 898	1 379
1969	48 246	501	3 177	14 147	12 152	. . .	. . .	1 438	2 841	4 252	4 196	4 089	1 452
1970	48 180	496	3 158	13 490	12 388	. . .	. . .	1 422	2 922	4 321	4 305	4 185	1 494
1971	48 151	474	3 238	13 034	12 502	. . .	. . .	1 392	2 978	4 354	4 372	4 286	1 521
1972	49 971	494	3 425	13 497	12 954	2 920	7 257	1 437	3 066	4 518	4 531	4 467	1 583
1973	52 235	502	3 576	14 227	13 437	3 041	7 551	1 504	3 164	4 748	4 747	4 664	1 666
1974	52 846	550	3 469	14 040	13 700	3 148	7 673	1 516	3 217	4 907	4 941	4 766	1 740
1975	51 010	581	2 990	12 576	13 578	3 121	7 714	1 416	3 227	4 939	5 088	4 821	1 795
1976	52 916	606	2 999	13 127	14 038	3 212	8 048	1 459	3 300	5 153	5 309	5 046	1 880
1977	55 207	636	3 209	13 591	14 579	3 323	8 396	1 514	3 452	5 404	5 561	5 284	1 978
1978	58 188	658	3 544	14 150	15 329	3 509	8 861	1 586	3 645	5 717	5 874	5 588	2 099
1979	60 403	737	3 760	14 458	15 843	3 667	9 113	1 650	3 825	5 993	6 157	5 772	2 209
1980	60 372	785	3 623	13 667	15 907	3 708	9 158	1 626	3 957	6 197	6 442	5 850	2 318
1981	60 960	861	3 469	13 492	16 004	3 753	9 238	1 633	4 052	6 396	6 694	5 944	2 414
1982	59 465	834	3 208	12 315	15 821	3 662	9 254	1 564	4 055	6 421	6 812	5 976	2 458
1983	60 005	698	3 240	12 121	15 999	3 639	9 494	1 502	4 128	6 581	7 032	6 161	2 542
1984	63 316	714	3 614	12 821	16 797	3 821	9 964	1 631	4 289	6 918	7 368	6 491	2 672
1985	65 436	686	3 868	12 648	17 427	3 935	10 399	1 660	4 476	7 258	7 770	6 817	2 827
1986	66 802	577	3 984	12 449	17 769	3 941	10 704	1 663	4 698	7 532	8 107	7 066	2 957
1987	68 700	541	4 088	12 537	18 196	3 989	10 986	1 717	4 861	7 859	8 488	7 310	3 104
1988	71 029	545	4 199	12 765	18 771	4 132	11 306	1 775	4 894	8 256	8 956	7 587	3 280
1989	72 927	526	4 257	12 805	19 230	4 235	11 565	1 807	4 931	8 648	9 432	7 833	3 459
1990	73 684	538	4 115	12 669	19 032	4 198	11 308	1 866	4 973	8 889	9 748	8 299	3 555
1991	72 520	515	3 674	12 164	18 640	4 122	11 008	1 871	4 911	8 748	10 212	8 247	3 539
1992	72 786	478	3 546	12 020	18 506	4 071	10 931	1 871	4 908	8 971	10 555	8 406	3 526
1993	74 591	462	3 704	12 070	18 752	4 072	11 104	1 896	5 057	9 451	10 908	8 667	3 623
1994	77 382	461	3 973	12 361	19 392	4 196	11 502	1 928	5 183	10 078	11 338	8 979	3 689
1995	79 845	458	4 113	12 566	19 984	4 361	11 841	2 007	5 165	10 645	11 765	9 330	3 812
1996	81 773	461	4 325	12 532	20 325	4 423	12 057	2 096	5 279	11 161	12 123	9 565	3 907
1997	84 158	479	4 546	12 673	20 698	4 523	12 274	2 181	5 415	11 896	12 478	9 780	4 013
1998	86 316	473	4 807	12 729	21 059	4 605	12 440	2 217	5 605	12 566	12 791	9 947	4 124
1999	88 430	438	5 105	12 524	21 576	4 673	12 772	2 351	5 728	13 184	13 089	10 216	4 219
2000	90 336	446	5 295	12 428	21 965	4 686	13 040	2 502	5 737	13 790	13 362	10 516	4 296
2001	89 983	457	5 332	11 677	21 709	4 555	12 952	2 530	5 810	13 588	13 846	10 662	4 373
2002	88 393	436	5 196	10 768	21 337	4 474	12 774	2 398	5 872	13 049	14 311	10 576	4 449
2003	87 658	420	5 123	10 190	21 078	4 396	12 655	2 347	5 967	12 910	14 532	10 666	4 426
2004	88 937	440	5 309	10 072	21 319	4 444	12 788	2 371	5 989	13 287	14 771	10 955	4 425
2005	90 944	471	5 566	10 062	21 788	4 572	13 007	2 390	6 084	13 797	15 103	11 252	4 432
2004													
January	87 967	425	5 209	10 025	21 116	4 386	12 689	2 337	5 950	13 025	14 632	10 836	4 412
February	87 977	425	5 197	10 012	21 130	4 386	12 702	2 342	5 948	13 029	14 647	10 840	4 407
March	88 234	433	5 241	10 026	21 194	4 396	12 739	2 343	5 954	13 076	14 666	10 881	4 420
April	88 493	436	5 236	10 061	21 221	4 414	12 747	2 361	5 962	13 184	14 706	10 904	4 422
May	88 792	441	5 280	10 091	21 270	4 427	12 774	2 373	5 977	13 261	14 729	10 942	4 428
June	88 934	440	5 294	10 086	21 326	4 435	12 809	2 380	5 998	13 279	14 745	10 953	4 433
July	89 050	443	5 315	10 107	21 332	4 448	12 796	2 385	5 987	13 322	14 776	10 956	4 427
August	89 188	446	5 336	10 123	21 364	4 458	12 811	2 387	5 998	13 344	14 815	10 940	4 435
September	89 343	450	5 356	10 101	21 404	4 472	12 822	2 384	6 019	13 384	14 817	10 999	4 429
October	89 591	443	5 392	10 091	21 446	4 485	12 839	2 388	6 016	13 479	14 866	11 042	4 428
November	89 736	449	5 411	10 080	21 496	4 497	12 869	2 385	6 018	13 496	14 889	11 082	4 430
December	89 851	451	5 434	10 066	21 504	4 506	12 861	2 382	6 031	13 519	14 926	11 104	4 434
2005													
January	89 997	453	5 422	10 054	21 580	4 508	12 902	2 375	6 042	13 538	14 964	11 133	4 436
February	90 233	457	5 477	10 054	21 637	4 525	12 938	2 370	6 051	13 608	14 976	11 166	4 437
March	90 394	461	5 494	10 054	21 679	4 539	12 958	2 379	6 048	13 655	15 004	11 183	4 437
April	90 635	465	5 534	10 053	21 734	4 546	12 988	2 388	6 049	13 698	15 034	11 240	4 440
May	90 725	466	5 552	10 059	21 774	4 561	13 007	2 384	6 047	13 709	15 070	11 227	4 437
June	90 921	471	5 568	10 054	21 815	4 570	13 034	2 388	6 064	13 766	15 108	11 249	4 438
July	91 104	471	5 570	10 050	21 873	4 577	13 081	2 387	6 081	13 817	15 141	11 276	4 438
August	91 245	475	5 591	10 054	21 895	4 587	13 088	2 390	6 091	13 857	15 168	11 293	4 431
September	91 263	477	5 606	10 048	21 822	4 594	13 008	2 406	6 100	13 906	15 193	11 277	4 428
October	91 291	481	5 627	10 069	21 824	4 598	13 001	2 400	6 125	13 907	15 165	11 274	4 419
November	91 693	485	5 690	10 103	21 908	4 616	13 050	2 408	6 148	13 999	15 207	11 326	4 419
December	91 803	487	5 678	10 123	21 904	4 621	13 042	2 408	6 159	14 044	15 226	11 346	4 428

. . . = Not available.

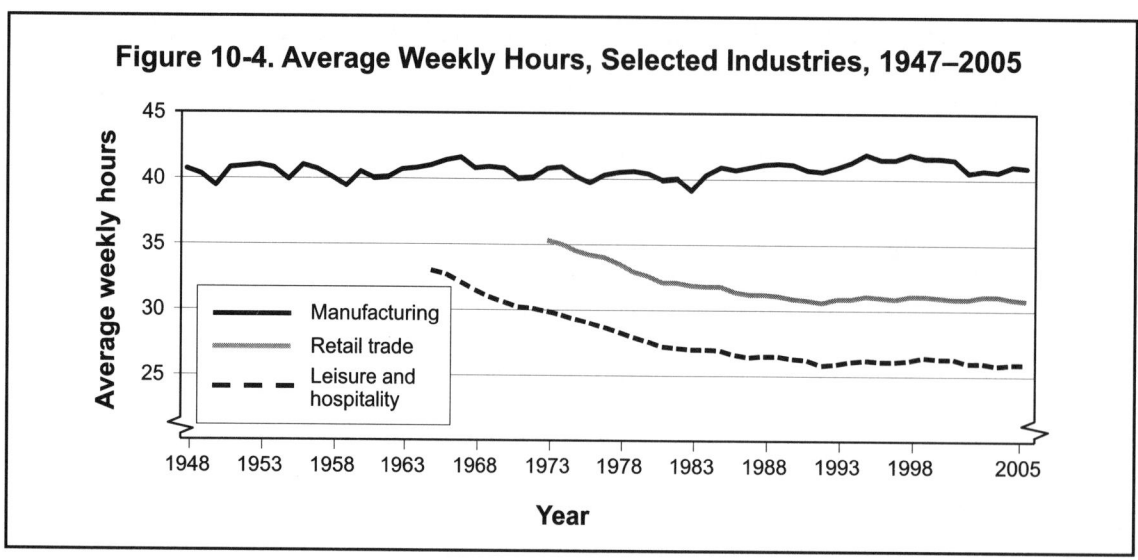

Figure 10-4. Average Weekly Hours, Selected Industries, 1947–2005

- The hours per week worked at the average private nonfarm production or nonsupervisory job have trended downward, falling from 38.5 hours in 1964 to 33.8 hours in 2005. It should be noted that these are hours per job, not hours per person. A worker with two half-time jobs would enter this average as two workers with 20 hours per week each, not as one worker with a 40 hour work week. (Table 10-9)

- The downtrend in the all-industry average reflects increases in the number of part-time jobs, as well as the increasing importance of retail trade, leisure and hospitality (restaurants, hotels, and motels), and other service-providing industries in which such jobs are frequently found. As shown by the graph above, manufacturing—which accounts for a steadily declining share of employment—displays no long-term downtrend in the workweek; if anything, factory workers have worked longer hours on average since the early 1980s. There was also no downtrend for construction or for natural resources and mining. However, a downtrend has occurred in recent decades for retail trade and for leisure and hospitality. These industries already had shorter workweeks, and have recently accounted for an increasing share of total employment. (Tables 10-7, 10-9, and 20-4)

Table 10-9. Average Weekly Hours of Production or Nonsupervisory Workers on Private Nonfarm Payrolls by NAICS Supersector

(Hours per week, seasonally adjusted.)

Year and month	Total private	Natural resources and mining	Construc-tion	Manufacturing		Trade, transportation, and utilities			Informa-tion	Financial activities	Profes-sional and business services	Education and health services	Leisure and hospitality	Other services
				Average weekly hours	Overtime hours	Total	Wholesale trade	Retail trade						
1960	. . .	41.9	37.2	39.8	2.5	. . .	. . .	. . .	. . .	. . .	. . .	. . .	. . .	. . .
1961	. . .	42.1	37.4	39.9	2.4	. . .	. . .	. . .	. . .	. . .	. . .	. . .	. . .	. . .
1962	. . .	42.5	37.5	40.5	2.8	. . .	. . .	. . .	. . .	. . .	. . .	. . .	. . .	. . .
1963	. . .	43.0	37.8	40.6	2.8	. . .	. . .	. . .	. . .	. . .	. . .	. . .	. . .	. . .
1964	38.5	43.4	37.7	40.8	3.1	39.7	. . .	. . .	38.2	37.2	37.4	35.5	32.8	36.3
1965	38.6	43.7	37.9	41.2	3.6	39.6	. . .	. . .	38.3	37.1	37.3	35.2	32.5	36.1
1966	38.5	44.1	38.1	41.4	3.9	39.1	. . .	. . .	38.3	37.2	37.0	34.9	31.9	35.8
1967	37.9	43.9	38.1	40.6	3.3	38.5	. . .	. . .	37.6	36.9	36.6	34.5	31.3	35.4
1968	37.7	44.0	37.8	40.7	3.5	38.2	. . .	. . .	37.6	36.8	36.3	34.1	30.8	35.0
1969	37.5	44.3	38.4	40.6	3.6	37.9	. . .	. . .	37.6	36.9	36.3	34.1	30.4	35.0
1970	37.0	43.9	37.8	39.8	2.9	37.6	. . .	. . .	37.2	36.6	35.9	33.8	30.0	34.7
1971	36.8	43.7	37.6	39.9	2.9	37.4	. . .	. . .	37.0	36.4	35.5	33.3	29.9	34.2
1972	36.9	44.0	37.0	40.6	3.4	37.4	39.8	35.1	37.3	36.4	35.5	33.3	29.7	34.2
1973	36.9	43.8	37.2	40.7	3.8	37.2	39.6	34.8	37.3	36.4	35.5	33.3	29.4	34.1
1974	36.4	43.7	37.1	40.0	3.2	36.8	39.2	34.3	37.0	36.3	35.3	33.1	29.1	33.9
1975	36.0	43.7	36.9	39.5	2.6	36.4	39.1	34.0	36.6	36.2	35.1	33.0	28.8	33.8
1976	36.1	44.2	37.3	40.1	3.1	36.3	39.1	33.8	36.7	36.2	34.9	32.7	28.5	33.6
1977	35.9	44.7	37.0	40.3	3.4	36.0	39.2	33.3	36.8	36.2	34.7	32.5	28.1	33.4
1978	35.8	44.9	37.3	40.4	3.6	35.6	39.2	32.7	36.8	36.1	34.6	32.3	27.7	33.2
1979	35.6	44.7	37.5	40.2	3.3	35.4	39.2	32.4	36.6	35.9	34.4	32.2	27.4	33.0
1980	35.2	44.9	37.5	39.7	2.8	35.0	38.8	31.9	36.3	36.0	34.3	32.1	27.0	33.0
1981	35.2	45.1	37.4	39.8	2.8	34.9	38.9	31.9	36.3	36.0	34.3	32.1	26.9	33.0
1982	34.7	44.1	37.2	38.9	2.3	34.6	38.7	31.7	35.8	36.0	34.2	32.1	26.8	33.0
1983	34.9	43.9	37.6	40.1	2.9	34.6	38.8	31.6	36.2	35.9	34.4	32.1	26.8	33.0
1984	35.1	44.6	38.2	40.7	3.4	34.7	38.9	31.6	36.6	36.2	34.3	32.0	26.7	32.9
1985	34.9	44.6	38.2	40.5	3.3	34.4	38.8	31.2	36.5	36.1	34.2	31.9	26.4	32.8
1986	34.7	43.6	37.9	40.7	3.4	34.1	38.7	31.0	36.4	36.1	34.3	32.0	26.2	32.9
1987	34.7	43.5	38.2	40.9	3.7	34.1	38.5	31.0	36.5	36.0	34.3	32.0	26.3	32.8
1988	34.6	43.3	38.2	41.0	3.8	33.8	38.5	30.9	36.1	35.6	34.2	32.0	26.3	32.9
1989	34.5	44.1	38.3	40.9	3.8	33.8	38.4	30.7	36.1	35.6	34.2	32.0	26.1	32.9
1990	34.3	45.0	38.3	40.5	3.8	33.7	38.4	30.6	35.8	35.5	34.2	31.9	26.0	32.8
1991	34.1	45.3	38.1	40.4	3.8	33.7	38.4	30.4	35.6	35.5	34.0	31.9	25.6	32.7
1992	34.2	44.6	38.0	40.7	4.0	33.8	38.6	30.7	35.8	35.6	34.0	32.0	25.7	32.6
1993	34.3	44.9	38.4	41.1	4.4	34.1	38.5	30.7	36.0	35.5	34.0	32.0	25.9	32.6
1994	34.5	45.3	38.8	41.7	5.0	34.3	38.8	30.9	36.0	35.5	34.1	32.0	26.0	32.7
1995	34.3	45.3	38.8	41.3	4.7	34.1	38.6	30.8	36.0	35.5	34.0	32.0	25.9	32.6
1996	34.3	46.0	38.9	41.3	4.8	34.1	38.6	30.7	36.4	35.5	34.1	31.9	25.9	32.5
1997	34.5	46.2	38.9	41.7	5.1	34.3	38.8	30.9	36.3	35.7	34.3	32.2	26.0	32.7
1998	34.5	44.9	38.8	41.4	4.8	34.2	38.6	30.9	36.6	36.0	34.3	32.2	26.2	32.6
1999	34.3	44.2	39.0	41.4	4.8	33.9	38.6	30.8	36.7	35.8	34.4	32.1	26.1	32.5
2000	34.3	44.4	39.2	41.3	4.7	33.8	38.8	30.7	36.8	35.9	34.5	32.2	26.1	32.5
2001	34.0	44.6	38.7	40.3	4.0	33.5	38.4	30.7	36.9	35.8	34.2	32.3	25.8	32.3
2002	33.9	43.2	38.4	40.5	4.2	33.6	38.0	30.9	36.5	35.6	34.2	32.4	25.8	32.0
2003	33.7	43.6	38.4	40.4	4.2	33.6	37.9	30.9	36.2	35.5	34.1	32.3	25.6	31.4
2004	33.7	44.5	38.3	40.8	4.6	33.5	37.8	30.7	36.3	35.5	34.2	32.4	25.7	31.0
2005	33.8	45.6	38.6	40.7	4.6	33.4	37.7	30.6	36.5	35.9	34.2	32.6	25.7	30.9
2004														
January	33.7	44.2	38.1	40.9	4.5	33.6	37.9	30.9	36.3	35.6	34.1	32.4	25.7	31.1
February	33.8	44.2	38.4	41.0	4.5	33.7	38.0	30.9	36.4	35.5	34.3	32.4	25.8	31.1
March	33.7	44.2	38.9	40.9	4.6	33.5	38.0	30.7	36.3	35.5	34.1	32.3	25.7	31.1
April	33.7	44.1	38.1	40.8	4.5	33.5	38.0	30.7	36.3	35.5	34.2	32.4	25.7	31.0
May	33.8	44.1	38.2	41.1	4.6	33.5	37.9	30.7	36.3	35.9	34.3	32.4	25.7	31.1
June	33.6	44.0	37.9	40.7	4.6	33.3	37.6	30.5	36.6	35.5	34.0	32.4	25.6	30.9
July	33.7	44.2	38.3	40.8	4.6	33.5	37.9	30.6	36.3	35.5	34.2	32.6	25.6	31.0
August	33.7	44.3	38.1	40.9	4.6	33.5	37.7	30.7	36.5	35.5	34.3	32.5	25.6	31.0
September	33.8	44.7	38.4	40.8	4.6	33.6	37.8	30.7	36.3	35.5	34.6	32.5	25.6	31.0
October	33.7	44.9	38.1	40.6	4.5	33.6	37.7	30.8	36.3	35.7	34.3	32.5	25.7	30.9
November	33.7	45.1	38.4	40.4	4.4	33.5	37.7	30.7	36.3	35.7	34.2	32.4	25.6	30.9
December	33.8	45.3	38.6	40.5	4.5	33.6	37.7	30.8	36.4	35.8	34.1	32.5	25.8	30.9
2005														
January	33.7	45.8	37.8	40.7	4.5	33.5	37.7	30.7	36.4	35.9	34.2	32.6	25.7	30.9
February	33.7	45.1	38.3	40.6	4.6	33.5	37.8	30.7	36.4	35.8	34.0	32.6	25.7	30.9
March	33.7	45.2	38.4	40.4	4.5	33.4	37.7	30.6	36.5	35.9	34.0	32.6	25.7	30.9
April	33.8	45.6	39.1	40.5	4.4	33.5	37.8	30.7	36.5	36.0	34.2	32.6	25.8	31.1
May	33.7	45.7	38.4	40.4	4.4	33.4	37.7	30.6	36.7	36.0	34.2	32.6	25.8	30.9
June	33.7	45.6	38.6	40.4	4.4	33.3	37.6	30.5	36.4	36.1	34.1	32.6	25.8	31.0
July	33.8	45.9	38.2	40.5	4.5	33.3	37.6	30.5	36.6	36.1	34.3	32.7	25.8	31.0
August	33.7	45.9	38.3	40.6	4.6	33.2	37.5	30.4	36.5	36.0	34.1	32.5	25.7	30.9
September	33.8	45.9	38.2	40.7	4.5	33.3	37.7	30.5	36.6	36.0	34.3	32.7	25.8	30.9
October	33.8	46.0	38.5	41.0	4.6	33.3	37.8	30.4	36.7	36.1	34.3	32.7	25.7	30.9
November	33.8	45.0	39.2	40.8	4.6	33.4	37.8	30.6	36.5	35.9	34.3	32.5	25.7	30.9
December	33.8	45.6	38.7	40.8	4.5	33.4	37.9	30.5	36.6	35.9	34.3	32.5	25.6	30.9

. . . = Not available.

Table 10-10. Indexes of Aggregate Weekly Hours of Production or Nonsupervisory Workers on Private Nonfarm Payrolls by NAICS Supersector

(2002 = 100, seasonally adjusted.)

Year and month	Total private	Natural resources and mining	Construc-tion	Manu-facturing	Trade, transportation, and utilities			Information	Financial activities	Profes-sional and business services	Education and health services	Leisure and hospitality	Other services
					Total	Wholesale trade	Retail trade						
1960	...	132.8	49.4	110.2	...	...	...	...	...	...	...	...	...
1961	...	124.2	48.4	106.3	...	...	...	...	...	...	...	...	...
1962	...	121.5	49.8	111.3	...	...	...	...	...	...	...	...	...
1963	...	120.0	51.4	112.2	...	...	...	...	...	...	...	...	...
1964	52.2	121.3	52.8	115.1	57.0	...	...	53.0	42.5	28.2	25.3	39.4	28.2
1965	54.6	121.6	55.2	122.0	59.0	...	...	55.5	43.3	29.4	26.2	41.0	29.4
1966	56.9	121.1	56.8	130.1	60.5	...	...	58.3	44.3	30.8	27.3	42.2	30.9
1967	57.2	117.0	55.4	127.8	61.1	...	...	58.6	45.7	31.9	28.4	42.9	32.4
1968	58.5	114.9	56.5	130.1	62.2	...	...	59.9	47.6	33.1	29.5	44.1	33.9
1969	60.5	118.1	61.0	131.9	64.3	...	...	61.7	50.2	34.6	30.9	45.6	35.6
1970	59.5	115.7	59.8	123.3	64.9	...	...	60.4	51.1	34.7	31.3	46.1	36.3
1971	59.1	109.9	61.0	119.2	65.1	...	...	58.7	51.9	34.7	31.4	46.9	36.5
1972	61.6	115.6	63.4	125.7	67.5	68.4	64.4	61.1	53.4	36.0	32.6	48.6	37.9
1973	64.3	117.0	66.7	132.9	69.6	71.0	66.4	64.1	55.1	37.8	34.1	50.3	39.9
1974	64.3	127.7	64.5	128.9	70.2	72.7	66.7	64.0	55.8	38.8	35.3	50.8	41.4
1975	61.3	134.9	55.2	113.9	68.9	71.8	66.4	59.1	55.9	38.9	36.2	50.9	42.6
1976	63.8	142.4	56.0	120.8	70.9	73.9	68.8	61.1	57.1	40.3	37.5	52.8	44.3
1977	66.3	151.1	59.4	125.8	73.1	76.7	70.7	63.5	59.7	42.1	39.0	54.4	46.3
1978	69.5	156.9	66.2	131.2	76.1	81.0	73.4	66.6	63.0	44.3	40.9	56.6	48.8
1979	71.8	175.2	70.6	133.3	78.3	84.6	74.7	69.0	65.8	46.3	42.7	57.9	51.2
1980	71.0	187.2	68.0	124.4	77.6	84.8	74.0	67.4	68.1	47.7	44.6	57.9	53.6
1981	71.6	206.2	64.9	123.1	78.0	86.0	74.5	67.6	69.8	49.2	46.3	58.7	55.8
1982	69.0	195.5	59.7	109.9	76.4	83.4	74.2	64.0	69.8	49.2	47.1	58.7	56.8
1983	70.0	162.8	61.0	111.6	77.2	83.3	76.0	62.1	70.9	50.7	48.8	60.5	58.9
1984	74.3	169.3	69.1	119.6	81.2	87.5	79.8	68.0	74.2	53.2	50.9	63.6	61.7
1985	76.2	162.7	73.9	117.5	83.5	89.9	82.2	69.1	77.3	55.6	53.5	66.1	65.1
1986	77.5	133.5	75.5	116.3	84.5	89.8	83.9	69.1	81.2	57.8	55.9	68.0	68.2
1987	79.7	125.2	78.1	117.8	86.5	90.5	86.3	71.4	83.7	60.3	58.5	70.5	71.5
1988	82.1	125.6	80.4	120.2	88.6	93.6	88.5	73.1	83.4	63.3	61.8	73.0	75.7
1989	84.1	123.2	81.7	120.3	90.5	95.9	90.0	74.4	83.9	66.3	65.2	74.9	79.8
1990	84.4	128.6	78.8	117.7	89.5	94.9	87.5	76.2	84.5	68.1	67.2	78.9	81.8
1991	82.6	123.8	70.1	112.8	87.4	93.3	84.8	76.1	83.3	66.7	70.2	77.3	81.2
1992	83.1	113.3	67.5	112.4	87.3	92.4	85.1	76.5	83.5	68.4	72.9	79.3	80.6
1993	85.5	110.3	71.3	113.9	89.0	92.4	86.3	78.0	85.9	71.9	75.4	82.2	82.8
1994	89.2	111.0	77.3	118.3	92.7	95.8	89.8	79.2	88.0	77.0	78.3	85.6	84.5
1995	91.6	110.2	79.9	119.0	95.1	99.2	92.3	82.5	87.8	81.2	81.2	88.5	87.1
1996	93.8	112.7	84.3	118.8	96.6	100.7	93.7	86.9	89.8	85.2	83.4	90.8	89.1
1997	97.1	117.6	88.6	121.4	98.8	103.4	95.9	90.4	92.6	91.5	86.7	93.4	91.9
1998	99.4	112.8	93.4	121.0	100.3	104.8	97.2	92.6	96.5	96.7	88.9	95.5	94.3
1999	101.5	102.9	99.7	118.9	101.9	106.2	99.5	98.5	98.0	101.7	90.6	97.9	96.3
2000	103.6	105.1	104.0	117.7	103.5	107.1	101.3	104.9	98.5	106.6	92.8	100.6	97.8
2001	102.1	108.3	103.2	108.1	101.5	102.9	100.5	106.6	99.5	104.0	96.6	100.7	99.1
2002	100.0	100.0	100.0	100.0	100.0	100.0	100.0	100.0	100.0	100.0	100.0	100.0	100.0
2003	98.7	97.4	98.4	94.5	98.6	98.0	98.9	97.0	101.5	98.7	101.4	100.1	97.5
2004	100.2	104.0	101.7	94.3	99.6	98.9	99.4	98.2	101.9	101.8	103.3	103.0	96.1
2005	102.6	114.2	107.5	93.9	101.5	101.6	100.6	99.6	104.6	105.8	106.2	106.2	96.1
2004													
January	99.0	99.8	99.4	94.1	98.9	97.9	99.2	96.8	101.4	99.5	102.3	102.1	96.3
February	99.4	99.8	99.9	94.2	99.3	98.2	99.3	97.3	101.0	100.2	102.4	102.5	96.1
March	99.3	101.7	102.1	94.1	99.0	98.4	99.0	97.1	101.1	99.9	102.2	102.5	96.4
April	99.6	102.2	99.9	94.2	99.1	98.8	99.1	97.8	101.3	101.1	102.8	102.7	96.2
May	100.3	103.3	101.0	95.2	99.3	98.8	99.3	98.3	102.7	101.9	102.9	103.1	96.6
June	99.8	102.9	100.5	94.2	99.0	98.2	98.9	99.4	101.9	101.2	103.1	102.8	96.1
July	100.3	104.1	101.9	94.6	99.6	99.3	99.1	98.8	101.7	102.1	103.9	102.8	96.3
August	100.4	105.0	101.8	95.0	99.8	99.0	99.6	99.4	101.9	102.6	103.9	102.7	96.4
September	100.9	106.9	103.0	94.6	100.3	99.5	99.6	98.7	102.3	103.8	103.9	103.2	96.3
October	100.9	105.7	102.9	94.0	100.5	99.6	100.1	98.9	102.8	103.6	104.2	104.0	96.0
November	101.0	107.6	104.0	93.5	100.4	99.8	100.0	98.8	102.8	103.4	104.1	104.0	96.0
December	101.5	108.6	105.0	93.6	100.7	100.1	100.3	98.9	103.3	103.3	104.6	105.0	96.1
2005													
January	101.3	110.3	102.6	93.9	100.8	100.1	100.3	98.6	103.8	103.8	105.2	104.9	96.2
February	101.6	109.5	105.0	93.7	101.0	100.7	100.5	98.4	103.7	103.7	105.3	105.2	96.2
March	101.8	110.7	105.6	93.2	100.9	100.8	100.4	99.1	103.9	104.1	105.5	105.3	96.2
April	102.4	112.7	108.3	93.4	101.5	101.2	100.9	99.5	104.2	105.0	105.7	106.3	96.9
May	102.2	113.2	106.7	93.3	101.4	101.3	100.7	99.8	104.2	105.1	106.0	106.2	96.2
June	102.4	114.1	107.6	93.2	101.3	101.2	100.6	99.2	104.8	105.2	106.2	106.4	96.5
July	102.9	114.9	106.5	93.4	101.5	101.4	101.0	99.7	105.1	106.2	106.8	106.6	96.5
August	102.7	115.9	107.2	93.7	101.3	101.3	100.7	99.5	104.9	105.9	106.3	106.4	96.0
September	103.1	116.3	107.2	93.9	101.3	102.0	100.4	100.5	105.1	106.9	107.2	106.6	96.0
October	103.1	117.6	108.5	94.7	101.3	102.3	100.0	100.5	105.8	106.9	107.0	106.2	95.8
November	103.5	116.0	111.7	94.6	102.0	102.8	101.1	100.3	105.6	107.6	106.6	106.7	95.8
December	103.7	118.0	110.0	94.8	102.0	103.1	100.7	100.6	105.8	108.0	106.7	106.5	96.0

... = Not available.

Table 10-11. Average Hourly Earnings of Production or Nonsupervisory Workers on Private Nonfarm Payrolls by NAICS Supersector

(Dollars, seasonally adjusted.)

Year and month	Total private	Natural resources and mining	Construction	Manu-facturing	Trade, transportation, and utilities			Information	Financial activities	Professional and business services	Education and health services	Leisure and hospitality	Other services
					Total	Wholesale trade	Retail trade						
1960	. . .	2.55	2.65	2.15	. . .	. . .	. . .	. . .	. . .	. . .	. . .	. . .	. . .
1961	. . .	2.59	2.78	2.20	. . .	. . .	. . .	. . .	. . .	. . .	. . .	. . .	. . .
1962	. . .	2.65	2.89	2.27	. . .	. . .	. . .	. . .	. . .	. . .	. . .	. . .	. . .
1963	. . .	2.70	2.99	2.34	. . .	. . .	. . .	. . .	. . .	. . .	. . .	. . .	. . .
1964	2.53	2.76	3.08	2.41	2.85	. . .	. . .	4.35	2.29	3.17	2.01	1.06	1.14
1965	2.63	2.87	3.23	2.49	2.94	. . .	. . .	4.47	2.38	3.28	2.12	1.14	1.25
1966	2.73	3.00	3.41	2.60	3.04	. . .	. . .	4.56	2.47	3.39	2.23	1.23	1.37
1967	2.85	3.14	3.63	2.71	3.15	. . .	. . .	4.68	2.58	3.51	2.36	1.34	1.49
1968	3.02	3.30	3.92	2.89	3.32	. . .	. . .	4.85	2.75	3.65	2.49	1.49	1.62
1969	3.22	3.54	4.30	3.07	3.48	. . .	. . .	5.05	2.92	3.84	2.68	1.64	1.81
1970	3.40	3.77	4.74	3.23	3.65	. . .	. . .	5.25	3.07	4.04	2.88	1.78	2.01
1971	3.63	3.99	5.17	3.45	3.86	. . .	. . .	5.53	3.23	4.26	3.11	1.90	2.24
1972	3.90	4.28	5.55	3.70	4.23	4.58	3.52	5.87	3.37	4.50	3.33	2.03	2.46
1973	4.14	4.59	5.89	3.97	4.45	4.80	3.69	6.17	3.55	4.72	3.54	2.15	2.67
1974	4.43	5.09	6.29	4.31	4.74	5.11	3.92	6.52	3.80	5.01	3.82	2.34	2.95
1975	4.73	5.68	6.78	4.71	5.02	5.45	4.14	6.92	4.08	5.29	4.09	2.52	3.21
1976	5.06	6.19	7.17	5.09	5.31	5.75	4.36	7.37	4.30	5.60	4.39	2.71	3.51
1977	5.44	6.70	7.56	5.55	5.67	6.12	4.65	7.84	4.58	5.95	4.72	2.96	3.84
1978	5.87	7.44	8.11	6.05	6.10	6.61	5.00	8.34	4.93	6.32	5.07	3.25	4.19
1979	6.33	8.20	8.71	6.57	6.55	7.12	5.34	8.86	5.31	6.71	5.44	3.54	4.56
1980	6.84	8.97	9.37	7.15	7.04	7.68	5.71	9.47	5.82	7.22	5.93	3.89	5.05
1981	7.43	9.89	10.24	7.86	7.55	8.28	6.09	10.21	6.34	7.80	6.49	4.26	5.61
1982	7.86	10.64	11.04	8.36	7.91	8.81	6.34	10.76	6.82	8.30	7.00	4.52	6.11
1983	8.19	11.14	11.36	8.70	8.23	9.27	6.60	11.18	7.32	8.70	7.39	4.76	6.51
1984	8.48	11.54	11.56	9.05	8.45	9.61	6.73	11.50	7.65	8.98	7.67	4.87	6.79
1985	8.73	11.87	11.75	9.40	8.60	9.88	6.83	11.81	7.97	9.28	7.98	4.98	7.10
1986	8.92	12.14	11.92	9.59	8.74	10.07	6.93	12.08	8.37	9.55	8.25	5.07	7.38
1987	9.13	12.17	12.15	9.77	8.92	10.32	7.02	12.36	8.73	9.85	8.57	5.17	7.69
1988	9.43	12.45	12.52	10.05	9.15	10.71	7.23	12.63	9.07	10.22	8.96	5.37	8.08
1989	9.80	12.91	12.98	10.35	9.46	11.12	7.46	12.99	9.54	10.69	9.46	5.62	8.58
1990	10.19	13.40	13.42	10.78	9.83	11.58	7.71	13.40	9.99	11.14	10.00	5.88	9.08
1991	10.50	13.82	13.65	11.13	10.08	11.95	7.89	13.90	10.42	11.50	10.49	6.06	9.39
1992	10.76	14.09	13.81	11.40	10.30	12.21	8.12	14.29	10.86	11.78	10.87	6.20	9.66
1993	11.03	14.12	14.04	11.70	10.55	12.57	8.36	14.86	11.36	11.96	11.21	6.32	9.90
1994	11.32	14.41	14.38	12.04	10.80	12.93	8.61	15.32	11.82	12.15	11.50	6.46	10.18
1995	11.64	14.78	14.73	12.34	11.10	13.34	8.85	15.68	12.28	12.53	11.80	6.62	10.51
1996	12.03	15.10	15.11	12.75	11.46	13.80	9.21	16.30	12.71	13.00	12.17	6.82	10.85
1997	12.49	15.57	15.67	13.14	11.90	14.41	9.59	17.14	13.22	13.57	12.56	7.13	11.29
1998	13.00	16.20	16.23	13.45	12.39	15.07	10.05	17.67	13.93	14.27	13.00	7.48	11.79
1999	13.47	16.33	16.80	13.85	12.82	15.62	10.45	18.40	14.47	14.85	13.44	7.76	12.26
2000	14.00	16.55	17.48	14.32	13.31	16.28	10.86	19.07	14.98	15.52	13.95	8.11	12.73
2001	14.53	17.00	18.00	14.76	13.70	16.77	11.29	19.80	15.59	16.33	14.64	8.35	13.27
2002	14.95	17.19	18.52	15.29	14.02	16.98	11.67	20.20	16.17	16.81	15.21	8.58	13.72
2003	15.35	17.56	18.95	15.74	14.34	17.36	11.90	21.01	17.14	17.21	15.64	8.76	13.84
2004	15.67	18.07	19.23	16.15	14.58	17.65	12.08	21.40	17.52	17.48	16.15	8.91	13.98
2005	16.11	18.73	19.46	16.56	14.93	18.16	12.36	22.07	17.94	18.07	16.72	9.14	14.33
2004													
January	15.48	17.86	19.10	15.94	14.44	17.52	11.94	21.15	17.38	17.28	15.88	8.83	13.85
February	15.52	17.94	19.16	15.96	14.49	17.53	11.97	21.24	17.36	17.27	15.94	8.87	13.87
March	15.54	18.02	19.15	16.01	14.46	17.52	11.98	21.26	17.43	17.31	15.99	8.88	13.90
April	15.58	17.97	19.20	16.08	14.52	17.59	12.00	21.28	17.46	17.33	16.05	8.86	13.93
May	15.63	18.01	19.23	16.08	14.55	17.63	12.03	21.43	17.51	17.41	16.10	8.87	13.95
June	15.65	18.18	19.20	16.11	14.58	17.66	12.07	21.31	17.48	17.46	16.15	8.87	13.98
July	15.68	18.09	19.21	16.14	14.60	17.69	12.08	21.40	17.50	17.49	16.20	8.90	13.99
August	15.74	18.05	19.24	16.21	14.62	17.69	12.12	21.52	17.55	17.62	16.24	8.92	14.01
September	15.77	18.05	19.26	16.30	14.66	17.73	12.19	21.62	17.60	17.60	16.27	8.94	14.06
October	15.79	18.09	19.29	16.28	14.66	17.76	12.16	21.52	17.65	17.66	16.30	8.98	14.08
November	15.81	18.22	19.30	16.30	14.68	17.81	12.20	21.51	17.63	17.67	16.33	9.02	14.12
December	15.84	18.37	19.28	16.35	14.71	17.85	12.22	21.61	17.71	17.73	16.37	9.01	14.13
2005													
January	15.88	18.43	19.23	16.38	14.78	17.88	12.31	21.73	17.69	17.81	16.41	9.04	14.17
February	15.91	18.40	19.28	16.42	14.77	17.93	12.29	21.57	17.74	17.85	16.47	9.05	14.20
March	15.95	18.25	19.34	16.43	14.81	17.95	12.31	21.72	17.81	17.88	16.55	9.06	14.24
April	16.00	18.55	19.38	16.48	14.86	18.03	12.35	21.92	17.85	17.94	16.58	9.09	14.26
May	16.03	18.58	19.37	16.54	14.87	18.01	12.36	21.92	17.81	17.98	16.64	9.10	14.30
June	16.07	18.66	19.43	16.56	14.89	18.10	12.35	22.04	17.87	18.03	16.69	9.12	14.31
July	16.14	18.74	19.52	16.58	15.00	18.22	12.45	22.17	17.95	18.11	16.76	9.13	14.35
August	16.16	18.88	19.51	16.65	14.98	18.21	12.41	22.21	17.92	18.14	16.79	9.16	14.39
September	16.19	19.03	19.54	16.60	14.98	18.26	12.35	22.32	18.01	18.15	16.84	9.22	14.40
October	16.28	19.04	19.58	16.71	15.05	18.32	12.43	22.65	18.09	18.30	16.90	9.22	14.46
November	16.28	18.95	19.59	16.68	15.04	18.45	12.35	22.40	18.20	18.29	16.95	9.24	14.46
December	16.35	19.12	19.65	16.70	15.10	18.56	12.39	22.60	18.27	18.42	17.00	9.27	14.47

. . . = Not available.

Table 10-12. Average Weekly Earnings of Production or Nonsupervisory Workers on Private Nonfarm Payrolls by NAICS Supersector

(Dollars, seasonally adjusted.)

Year and month	Total private	Natural resources and mining	Construc-tion	Manu-facturing	Trade, transportation, and utilities Total	Wholesale trade	Retail trade	Information	Financial activities	Profes-sional and business services	Education and health services	Leisure and hospitality	Other services
1960	. . .	106.85	98.58	85.57	. . .	. . .	. . .	. . .	. . .	. . .	. . .	. . .	. . .
1961	. . .	109.04	103.97	87.78	. . .	. . .	. . .	. . .	. . .	. . .	. . .	. . .	. . .
1962	. . .	112.63	108.38	91.94	. . .	. . .	. . .	. . .	. . .	. . .	. . .	. . .	. . .
1963	. . .	116.10	113.02	95.00	. . .	. . .	. . .	. . .	. . .	. . .	. . .	. . .	. . .
1964	97.41	119.78	116.12	98.33	113.15	. . .	. . .	166.17	85.19	118.56	71.36	34.77	41.38
1965	101.52	125.42	122.42	102.59	116.42	. . .	. . .	171.20	88.30	122.34	74.62	37.05	45.13
1966	105.11	132.30	129.92	107.64	118.86	. . .	. . .	174.65	91.88	125.43	77.83	39.24	49.05
1967	108.02	137.85	138.30	110.03	121.28	. . .	. . .	175.97	95.20	128.47	81.42	41.94	52.75
1968	113.85	145.20	148.18	117.62	126.82	. . .	. . .	182.36	101.20	132.50	84.91	45.89	56.70
1969	120.75	156.82	165.12	124.64	131.89	. . .	. . .	189.88	107.75	139.39	91.39	49.86	63.35
1970	125.80	165.50	179.17	128.55	137.24	. . .	. . .	195.30	112.36	145.04	97.34	53.40	69.75
1971	133.58	174.36	194.39	137.66	144.36	. . .	. . .	204.61	117.57	151.23	103.56	56.81	76.61
1972	143.91	188.32	205.35	150.22	158.20	182.28	123.55	218.95	122.67	159.75	110.89	60.29	84.13
1973	152.77	201.04	219.11	161.58	165.54	190.08	128.41	230.14	129.22	167.56	117.88	63.21	91.05
1974	161.25	222.43	233.36	172.40	174.43	200.31	134.46	241.24	137.94	176.85	126.44	68.09	100.01
1975	170.28	248.22	250.18	186.05	182.73	213.10	140.76	253.27	147.70	185.68	134.97	72.58	108.50
1976	182.67	273.60	267.44	204.11	192.75	224.83	147.37	270.48	155.66	195.44	143.55	77.24	117.94
1977	195.30	299.49	279.72	223.67	204.12	239.90	154.85	288.51	165.80	206.47	153.40	83.18	128.26
1978	210.15	334.06	302.50	244.42	217.16	259.11	163.50	306.91	177.97	218.67	163.76	90.03	139.11
1979	225.35	366.54	326.63	264.11	231.87	279.10	173.02	324.28	190.63	230.82	175.17	97.00	150.48
1980	240.77	402.75	351.38	283.86	246.40	297.98	182.15	343.76	209.52	247.65	190.35	105.03	166.65
1981	261.54	446.04	382.98	312.83	263.50	322.09	194.27	370.62	228.24	267.54	208.33	114.59	185.13
1982	272.74	469.22	410.69	325.20	273.69	340.95	200.98	385.21	245.52	283.86	224.70	121.14	201.63
1983	285.83	489.05	427.14	348.87	284.76	359.68	208.56	404.72	262.79	299.28	237.22	127.57	214.83
1984	297.65	514.68	441.59	368.34	293.22	373.83	212.67	420.90	276.93	308.01	245.44	130.03	223.39
1985	304.68	529.40	448.85	380.70	295.84	383.34	213.10	431.07	287.72	317.38	254.56	131.47	232.88
1986	309.52	529.30	451.77	390.31	298.03	389.71	214.83	439.71	302.16	327.57	264.00	132.83	242.80
1987	316.81	529.40	464.13	399.59	304.17	397.32	217.62	451.14	314.28	337.86	274.24	135.97	252.23
1988	326.28	539.09	478.26	412.05	309.27	412.34	223.41	455.94	322.89	349.52	286.72	141.23	265.83
1989	338.10	569.33	497.13	423.32	319.75	427.01	229.02	468.94	339.62	365.60	302.72	146.68	282.28
1990	349.29	602.54	513.43	436.16	331.55	444.48	235.62	479.50	354.65	380.61	319.27	152.47	297.91
1991	358.06	625.42	520.41	449.73	339.19	459.27	240.15	495.20	369.57	391.09	334.55	155.16	306.91
1992	367.83	629.02	525.13	464.43	348.68	470.51	249.63	512.01	386.01	400.64	348.29	159.54	315.08
1993	378.40	634.77	539.81	480.80	359.33	484.46	256.89	535.25	403.02	406.20	359.08	163.45	322.69
1994	390.73	653.14	558.53	502.12	370.38	501.17	265.77	551.28	419.20	414.16	368.14	168.00	332.44
1995	399.53	670.32	571.57	509.26	378.79	515.14	272.56	564.98	436.12	426.44	377.73	171.43	342.36
1996	412.74	695.07	588.48	526.55	390.64	533.29	282.76	592.68	451.49	442.81	388.27	176.48	352.62
1997	431.25	720.11	609.48	548.22	407.57	559.39	295.97	622.40	472.37	465.51	404.65	185.81	368.63
1998	448.04	727.28	629.75	557.12	423.30	582.21	310.34	646.52	500.95	490.00	418.82	195.82	384.25
1999	462.49	721.74	655.11	573.17	434.31	602.77	321.63	675.32	517.57	510.99	431.35	202.87	398.77
2000	480.41	734.92	685.78	590.65	449.88	631.40	333.38	700.89	537.37	535.07	449.29	211.79	413.41
2001	493.20	757.92	695.89	595.19	459.53	643.45	346.16	731.11	558.02	557.84	473.39	215.19	428.64
2002	506.07	741.97	711.82	618.75	471.27	644.38	360.81	738.17	575.51	574.66	492.74	221.26	439.76
2003	517.30	765.94	726.83	635.99	481.14	657.29	367.15	760.81	609.08	587.02	505.69	224.30	434.41
2004	528.36	803.82	735.55	658.59	488.42	667.09	371.13	777.05	622.87	597.56	523.78	228.65	433.04
2005	543.65	853.89	750.63	673.61	498.59	684.91	377.68	805.89	644.71	618.46	544.80	235.29	443.06
2004													
January	521.68	789.41	727.71	651.95	485.18	664.01	368.95	767.75	618.73	589.25	514.51	226.93	430.74
February	524.58	792.95	735.74	654.36	488.31	666.14	369.87	773.14	616.28	592.36	516.46	228.85	431.36
March	523.70	796.48	744.94	654.81	484.41	665.76	367.79	771.74	618.77	590.27	516.48	228.22	432.29
April	525.05	792.48	731.52	656.06	486.42	668.42	368.40	772.46	619.83	592.69	520.02	227.70	431.83
May	528.29	794.24	734.59	660.89	487.43	668.18	369.32	777.91	628.61	597.16	521.64	227.96	433.85
June	525.84	799.92	727.68	655.68	485.51	664.02	368.14	779.95	620.54	593.64	523.26	227.07	431.98
July	528.42	799.58	735.74	658.51	489.10	670.45	369.65	776.82	621.25	598.16	528.12	227.84	433.69
August	530.44	799.62	733.04	662.99	489.77	666.91	372.08	785.48	623.03	604.37	527.80	228.35	434.31
September	533.03	806.84	739.58	665.04	492.58	670.19	374.23	784.81	624.80	608.96	528.78	228.86	435.86
October	532.12	812.24	734.95	660.97	492.58	669.55	374.53	781.18	630.11	605.74	529.75	230.79	435.07
November	532.80	821.72	741.12	658.52	491.78	671.44	374.54	780.81	629.39	604.31	529.09	230.91	436.31
December	535.39	832.16	744.21	662.18	494.26	672.95	376.38	786.60	634.02	604.59	532.03	232.46	436.62
2005													
January	535.16	844.09	726.89	666.67	495.13	674.08	377.92	790.97	635.07	609.10	534.97	232.33	437.85
February	536.17	829.84	738.42	666.65	494.80	677.75	377.30	785.15	635.09	606.90	536.92	232.59	438.78
March	537.52	824.90	742.66	663.77	494.65	676.72	376.69	792.78	639.38	607.92	539.53	232.84	440.02
April	540.80	845.88	757.76	667.44	497.81	681.53	379.15	800.08	642.60	613.55	540.51	234.52	443.49
May	540.21	849.11	743.81	668.22	496.66	678.98	378.22	804.46	641.16	614.92	542.46	234.78	441.87
June	541.56	850.90	750.00	669.02	495.84	680.56	376.68	802.26	645.11	614.82	544.09	235.30	443.61
July	545.53	860.17	745.66	671.49	499.50	685.07	379.73	811.42	648.00	621.17	548.05	235.55	444.85
August	544.59	866.59	747.23	675.99	497.34	682.88	377.26	810.67	645.12	618.57	545.68	235.41	444.65
September	547.22	873.48	746.43	675.62	498.83	688.40	376.68	816.91	648.36	622.55	550.67	237.88	444.96
October	550.26	875.84	753.83	685.11	501.17	692.50	377.87	831.26	653.05	627.69	552.63	236.95	446.81
November	550.26	852.75	767.93	680.54	502.34	697.41	377.91	817.60	653.38	627.35	550.88	237.47	446.81
December	552.63	871.87	760.46	681.36	504.34	703.42	377.90	827.16	655.89	631.81	552.50	237.31	447.12

. . . = Not available.

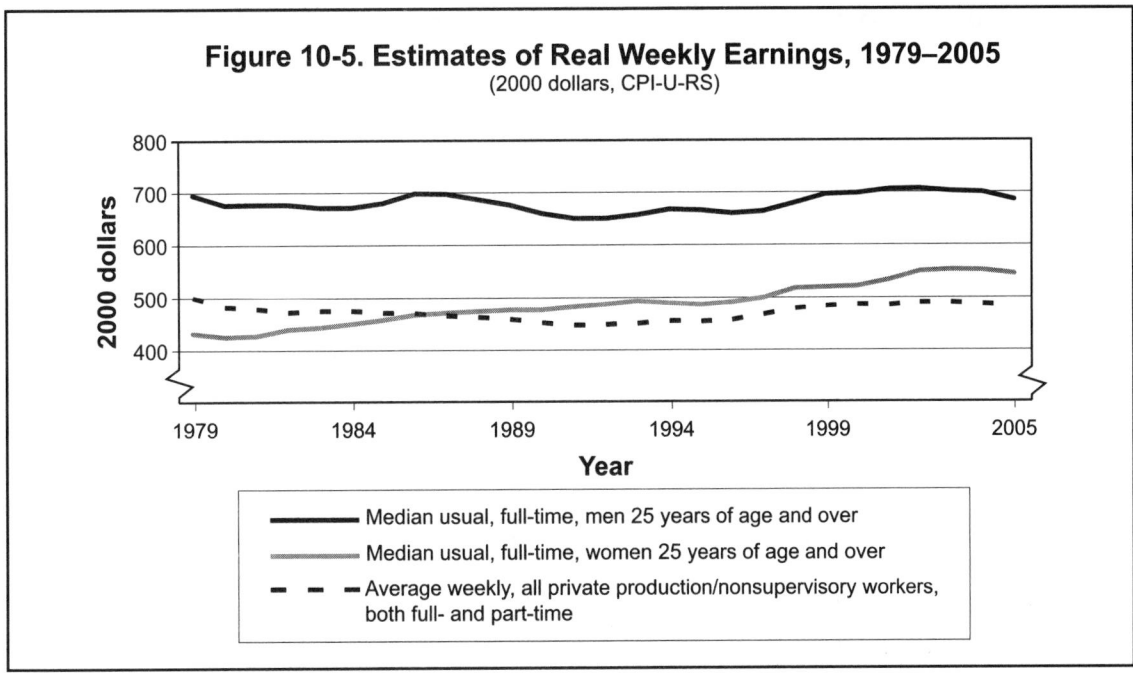

Figure 10-5. Estimates of Real Weekly Earnings, 1979–2005
(2000 dollars, CPI-U-RS)

Legend:
- Median usual, full-time, men 25 years of age and over
- Median usual, full-time, women 25 years of age and over
- Average weekly, all private production/nonsupervisory workers, both full- and part-time

- New in this edition of *Business Statistics* are data on median usual weekly earnings of full-time wage and salary workers. (Table 10-13) These data are derived quarterly from the Current Population Survey, not from the payroll survey that provides the data shown in Table 10-12. This means that they are collected from individual households in the CPS sample, instead of from employers, making it possible to tabulate by sex and other demographic characteristics; to identify full-time workers and measure them separately from part-time workers; and to identify the median worker. As a result, they provide better approximations of the paychecks of typical breadwinners than do the payroll data on average weekly earnings.

- In the graph above, median weekly earnings for men over 25 years of age and women over 25 years of age have been converted to constant year-2000 dollars using the CPI-U-RS—a price index developed to measure prices more consistently than the official Consumer Price Index (CPI). The CPI-U-RS is used to convert current-dollar figures to constant dollars in Census income reports and BLS productivity and costs reports. (See the notes and definitions for Chapters 8, 3, and 9.) They are compared with average weekly earnings from the payroll survey deflated with the same price index. (Tables 10-13, 10-12, and 8-2)

- Women still earn less than men, but the gap is narrowing. Women 25 years of age and over who worked full time earned 79 cents for every dollar earned by men 25 years of age and over in 2005, up from 62 cents in 1979. (Table 10-13)

- The median man of 25 years of age or over who worked full time earned significantly more than average weekly earnings throughout the period. However, his earnings, like average weekly earnings, failed to increase in real terms. (Tables 10-13, 10-12, and 8-2)

- On the other hand, women who worked full time saw their median weekly earnings increase 27 percent in real terms, or 0.9 percent per year, over the 1979–2005 period. (Table 10-13)

Table 10-13. Median Usual Weekly Earnings of Full-Time Wage and Salary Workers

(Dollars, not seasonally adjusted.)

Year and quarter	Total, 16 years and over	Sex and age						Race and ethnicity			
		Men, 16 years and over			Women, 16 years and over			White	Black or African American	Asian	Hispanic or Latino ethnicity
		Total	16–24 years	25 years and over	Total	16–24 years	25 years and over				
1979	240	291	196	314	182	154	194	247	198	. . .	. . .
1980	261	312	208	339	201	167	212	268	212	. . .	. . .
1981	283	339	218	371	219	180	233	290	234	. . .	. . .
1982	302	364	224	393	238	191	254	309	245	. . .	. . .
1983	313	378	223	406	252	197	267	319	261	. . .	. . .
1984	326	391	231	422	265	203	282	336	269	. . .	. . .
1985	343	406	240	442	277	210	296	355	277	. . .	. . .
1986	358	419	245	462	290	218	308	370	291	. . .	277
1987	373	433	257	477	303	226	321	383	301	. . .	284
1988	385	449	261	487	315	235	335	394	314	. . .	290
1989	399	468	271	500	328	246	351	409	319	. . .	298
1990	412	481	282	512	346	254	369	424	329	. . .	304
1991	426	493	285	523	366	266	387	442	348	. . .	312
1992	440	501	284	536	380	267	400	458	357	. . .	322
1993	459	510	288	555	393	273	415	475	369	. . .	331
1994	467	522	294	576	399	276	421	484	371	. . .	324
1995	479	538	303	588	406	275	428	494	383	. . .	329
1996	490	557	307	599	418	284	444	506	387	. . .	339
1997	503	579	317	615	431	292	462	519	400	. . .	351
1998	523	598	334	639	456	305	485	545	426	. . .	370
1999	549	618	356	668	473	324	497	573	445	. . .	385
2000	576	641	375	693	493	344	516	590	474	615	399
2001	596	670	391	720	512	353	543	610	491	639	417
2002	608	679	391	732	529	367	568	623	498	658	424
2003	620	695	398	744	552	371	584	636	514	693	440
2004	638	713	400	762	573	375	599	657	525	708	456
2005	651	722	409	771	585	381	612	672	520	753	471
1997											
1st quarter	504	582	319	615	427	289	456	519	399	. . .	349
2nd quarter	499	572	316	609	428	289	457	515	397	. . .	352
3rd quarter	499	573	312	614	429	291	463	515	397	. . .	352
4th quarter	511	587	323	621	440	299	470	528	410	. . .	354
1998											
1st quarter	521	596	337	629	455	304	480	543	418	. . .	364
2nd quarter	515	590	335	627	446	305	474	532	420	. . .	365
3rd quarter	520	593	323	639	455	299	489	540	430	. . .	382
4th quarter	541	614	342	664	471	311	495	565	439	. . .	372
1999											
1st quarter	538	612	360	655	468	331	488	560	443	. . .	387
2nd quarter	543	617	344	665	467	316	494	569	432	. . .	375
3rd quarter	546	614	347	668	474	323	500	569	454	. . .	392
4th quarter	568	633	377	661	483	331	506	586	450	. . .	383
2000											
1st quarter	575	649	369	697	488	341	511	590	459	. . .	395
2nd quarter	566	640	371	694	485	333	508	584	467	. . .	388
3rd quarter	575	640	378	700	491	335	519	590	463	. . .	402
4th quarter	585	658	385	708	502	360	522	601	480	. . .	399
2001											
1st quarter	592	668	384	718	508	358	535	610	477	. . .	407
2nd quarter	595	667	394	716	514	348	547	609	495	. . .	417
3rd quarter	595	674	389	725	507	350	542	610	489	. . .	418
4th quarter	605	683	400	731	517	361	550	621	486	. . .	419
2002											
1st quarter	611	682	406	729	533	375	570	625	510	651	420
2nd quarter	605	677	398	732	520	355	559	622	500	648	420
3rd quarter	603	671	376	729	527	360	570	620	484	665	420
4th quarter	613	686	390	737	542	384	576	630	495	667	435
2003											
1st quarter	620	695	396	741	551	384	581	636	516	718	447
2nd quarter	616	692	391	743	547	366	582	631	509	678	430
3rd quarter	618	689	396	742	550	366	585	633	509	692	444
4th quarter	625	704	409	750	561	372	588	646	522	680	441
2004											
1st quarter	634	711	410	757	567	387	592	652	521	712	450
2nd quarter	639	714	397	763	572	370	601	655	536	720	451
3rd quarter	632	704	400	759	571	371	602	651	531	701	458
4th quarter	647	722	396	768	578	371	603	671	519	698	467
2005											
1st quarter	653	729	401	775	586	380	610	677	513	738	470
2nd quarter	643	713	407	762	580	374	608	663	518	743	473
3rd quarter	649	716	407	768	585	379	615	667	520	761	462
4th quarter	659	731	418	778	588	389	614	682	533	767	479

. . . = Not available.

NOTES AND DEFINITIONS

General note on employment data

This chapter includes two different data sets measuring employment. Both are compiled and published by the Bureau of Labor Statistics (BLS), but each set has different characteristics. Users should be aware of these dissimilarities and the consequent differences in the appropriate uses and interpretations of data from the two systems. These differences are discussed below and at the front of this book, in the "Measures of Employment" section of "Topics of Current Interest."

One set of employment estimates comes from the Current Population Survey (CPS), a large sample survey of U.S. households. The numbers in the sample are blown up to match the latest estimates of the total U.S. population. These are the most comprehensive estimates in their scope—that is, in the universe that they are designed to measure. These estimates represent all civilian workers, including the following groups that are excluded by definition from the other set of estimates: farm workers, household workers (domestic servants), nonagricultural self-employed workers, and nonagricultural unpaid family workers.

However, official CPS data are characterized by periodic discontinuities, which occur when new benchmarks for Census measures of the total population are introduced. These updates take place in a single month, usually January, and the official data for previous months are typically not modified to provide a smooth transition. Therefore, shorter-term comparisons (for a year or two or for a business cycle phase) will be misleading if such a discontinuity is included in the period. For example, the current estimates of population, labor force, employment, and employment in numbers of persons from January 2005 and subsequent months are not directly comparable with the data for 2004. Furthermore, there are similar but larger "breaks" between December 2003 and January 2004 and between December 1999 and January 2000. Such discontinuities occur throughout the history of the series.

> For users who would like monthly data in which these discontinuities have been smoothed, the Bureau of Labor Statistics now makes available unofficial smoothed estimates of total labor force and total employment from January 1990 through December 2005 on its Web site. In this edition of *Business Statistics*, these two series are included in Table 20-3A in Chapter 20, "Selected Historical Data."

The CPS is a count of persons employed, rather than a count of jobs. A person is counted in these data only once, no matter how many jobs he or she may hold. The CPS count is limited to persons 16 years of age and over.

The second set of employment estimates—the payroll survey—comes from a very large sample survey of employers, the Current Employment Statistics (CES) survey. It is benchmarked annually to a survey of all employers. Benchmark data are introduced with a smooth adjustment back to the previous benchmark, thus preserving the continuity of the series and making it more appropriate for measurement of employment change over a year or two, or a business cycle, or other short- to medium-length periods. The scope of the survey is wage and salary workers on nonfarm payrolls, and it is a count of jobs. Thus, a person with more than one job is counted as employed in each job. Workers are not classified by age; as a result, there may be some persons younger than 16 years of age in the job count.

Persons with a job but not at work (absent due to bad weather, work stoppages, personal reasons, and the like) are included in the household survey. However, they are excluded from the payroll survey if on leave without pay for the entire payroll period.

In addition to the differences in definitions and scope between the two series, there are also differences in sample design, collection methodology, and the sampling variability inherent in the surveys.

The payroll survey provides the most reliable and detailed information on the breakdown of employment by industry (for example, the data shown in Table 16-1).

The CPS employment estimates provide the best information on the breakdown of employment by demographic characteristics, such as sex, age, race, and Hispanic ethnicity; by education levels; and by occupation. A few of these breakdowns are shown in *Business Statistics*. Many more breakdowns, in richer detail, can be found in the *Handbook of U.S. Labor Statistics*, also published by Bernan Press.

TABLES 10-1 THROUGH 10-5 AND 20-3
LABOR FORCE, EMPLOYMENT, AND UNEMPLOYMENT

SOURCE: U.S. DEPARTMENT OF LABOR, BUREAU OF LABOR STATISTICS (BLS)

Labor force, employment, and unemployment data are derived from the Current Population Survey (CPS), a sample survey of households conducted each month by the Census Bureau for BLS. The data pertain to the U.S. civilian noninstitutional population 16 years of age and over.

Due to changes in questionnaire design and survey methodology, data for 1994 and subsequent years are not fully comparable with data for 1993 and earlier years. Additionally, discontinuities in the reported number of persons in the population, as well as in the numbers of employed and unemployed persons and the number of persons in the labor force, are introduced whenever periodic updates are made to U.S. population estimates. Population controls based on Census 2000 were introduced beginning with the data for January 2000. These data are therefore not comparable with data for

December 1999 and earlier. Data for 1990 through 1999 incorporate 1990 census–based population controls and are not comparable with the preceding years. An additional large population adjustment was introduced in January 2004, making the data from that time forward not comparable with data for December 2003 and earlier; another smaller adjustment was introduced in January 2005. Other discontinuities have been introduced in various earlier years, usually with January data. See "Notes on the Data," below, for additional information.

For the most part, these population adjustments distort comparisons involving the numbers of persons in the population, labor force, and employment. They generally have negligible effects on the percentages that comprise the most important features of the CPS: the unemployment rates, the labor force participation rates, and the employment-population ratios.

BLS now makes available unofficial smoothed data for the total number of persons in the civilian labor force and the number of persons employed for 1990 through 2005, which introduce the population adjustments gradually within the period shown. These data are shown in Table 20-3A.

Beginning with the data for January 2000, data classified by industry and occupation use the 2002 North American Industry Classification System (NAICS—see Chapter 14 for more information) and the 2000 Standard Occupational Classification System. This creates breaks in the time series between December 1999 and January 2000 for occupational and industry data at all levels of aggregation. Since the recent history is so short, most industry and occupation data have been dropped from this volume in favor of other important and economically meaningful data for which a longer history can be supplied. However, detailed employment data by occupation and industry can be found in Bernan Press's *Handbook of U.S. Labor Statistics*.

Race and ethnic origin

Data for two broad racial categories are available beginning in 1954: *White* and *Black and other*. The latter includes Asians and all other "nonwhite" races. Data for Blacks only are available beginning with 1972; this category is now labeled *Black or African American*. Data for *Asians* are shown beginning with 2000. Persons in the remaining race categories—American Indian or Alaska Native, Native Hawaiian or Other Pacific Islander, and persons who selected more than one race category beginning in 2003 (see below)—are included in the estimates of total employment and unemployment, but are not shown separately because their numbers are too small to yield quality estimates.

Hispanic or Latino ethnicity, previously labeled *Hispanic origin*, is not a racial category and is established in a survey question separate from the question about race. Hispanics may be of any race.

In January 2003, changes that affected classification by race and Hispanic origin were introduced. These changes caused discontinuities in ethnic group data between December 2002 and January 2003.

- Individuals in the sample are now asked whether they are of Hispanic ethnicity before being asked about their race. Prior to 2003, individuals were asked their ethnic origin after they were asked about their race. Furthermore, respondents are now asked directly if they are Spanish, Hispanic, or Latino. Previously, they were identified based on their or their ancestors' country of origin.

- Individuals in the sample are now allowed to choose more than one race category. Before 2003, they were required to select a single primary race. This change had no impact on the size of the overall civilian noninstitutional population and labor force. It did reduce the population and labor force levels of Whites and Blacks beginning in January 2003, as individuals who reported more than one race are now excluded from those groups.

BLS has estimated, based on a special survey, that these changes reduced the population and labor force levels for Whites by about 950,000 and 730,000 persons, respectively, and for Blacks by about 320,000 and 240,000 persons, respectively, while having little or no impact on either of their unemployment rates. The changes did not affect the size of the Hispanic population or labor force, but they did cause an increase of about half a percentage point in the Hispanic unemployment rate.

Definitions

The employment status of the civilian population is surveyed each month with respect to a specific week in midmonth—not for the entire month. This is known as the "reference week"; it will be referred to frequently in the definitions that follow. For a precise definition and explanation of the reference week, see "Notes on the Data," which follows these definitions.

The *civilian noninstitutional population* comprises all civilians 16 years of age and over who are not inmates of penal or mental institutions, sanitariums, or homes for the aged, infirm, or needy.

Civilian employment includes those civilians who (1) worked for pay or profit at any time during the week that includes the 12th day of the month (the reference week), or who worked for 15 hours or more as an unpaid worker in a family-operated enterprise; or (2) were temporarily absent from regular jobs because of vacation, illness, industrial dispute, bad weather, or similar reasons. Each employed person is counted only once; those who hold more than one job are counted as being in the job at which they worked the greatest number of hours during the reference week.

Unemployed persons are all civilians who were not employed (according to the above definition) during the reference week, but who were available for work—except for temporary illness—and who had made specific efforts to find employment sometime during the previous four weeks. Persons who did not look for work because they were on layoff are also counted as unemployed.

The *civilian labor force* comprises all civilians classified as employed or unemployed.

Civilians 16 years of age and over in the noninstitutional population who are not classified as employed or unemployed are defined as *not in the labor force*. This group includes those engaged in own-home housework; in school; unable to work because of long-term illness, retirement, or age; seasonal workers for whom the reference week fell in an "off" season (not reported as unemployed); persons who became discouraged and gave up the search for work; and the voluntarily idle. Also included are those doing only incidental work (less than 15 hours) in a family-operated business during the reference week.

Persons not in the labor force who currently want a job consists of persons who are not employed and not counted as unemployed under the criteria given above, but who did want a job at the time of the survey.

The civilian *labor force participation rate* represents the percentage of the civilian noninstitutional population (age 16 years and over) that is in the civilian labor force.

The *employment-population ratio* represents the percentage of the civilian noninstitutional population (age 16 years and over) that is employed. This is traditionally called a "ratio," although it is traditionally expressed as a percent and therefore would be more appropriately called a "rate."

An analysis is shown of employment by *class of worker*, including a breakdown of total employment into *agricultural* and *nonagricultural industries*. Employment in *nonagricultural industries* includes *wage and salary workers*, the *self-employed*, and *unpaid family workers*.

Wage and salary workers receive wages, salaries, commissions, tips, and/or pay in kind. This category includes owners of self-owned incorporated businesses.

Self-employed workers are those who work for profit or for fees in their own business, profession, trade, or farm. This category includes only unincorporated businesses; workers whose businesses are incorporated are considered wage and salary workers since they are paid employees of a corporation, even if they are the corporation's president and sole employee.

Wage and salary employment is comprised of *government* and *private industry* workers. Domestic workers and other employees of *private households*, who are not included in the payroll employment series, are shown separately from all other private industries. The series for *government* and *other private industries* wage and salary workers are the closest in scope to similar categories in the payroll employment series.

Multiple jobholders are employed persons who, during the reference week, either had two or more jobs as a wage and salary worker, were self-employed and also held a wage and salary job, or worked as an unpaid family worker and also held a wage and salary job. Excluded are self-employed persons with multiple businesses and persons with multiple jobs as unpaid family workers. Multiple jobholders are counted as being in the job at which they worked the greatest number of hours during the reference week.

Employed and at work part time excludes employed persons who were absent from their jobs during the entire reference week for reasons such as vacation, illness, or industrial dispute.

At work part time for economic reasons ("involuntary" part time) refers to individuals who worked 1 to 34 hours during the reference week because of slack work, unfavorable business conditions, an inability to find full-time work, or seasonal declines in demand. To be included in this category, they must also indicate that they want and are available for full-time work.

At work part time for noneconomic reasons ("voluntary" part time) refers to persons who usually work part time and were at work for 1 to 34 hours during the reference week for reasons such as illness, other medical limitations, family obligations, education, retirement, Social Security limits on earnings, or working in an industry where the workweek is less than 35 hours. It also includes respondents who gave an economic reason but were not available for, or did not want, full-time work. At work part time for noneconomic reasons excludes persons who usually work full time, but who worked only 1 to 34 hours during the reference week for reasons such as holidays, illness, and bad weather.

The long-term unemployed are persons currently unemployed (searching or on layoff) who have been unemployed for 15 consecutive weeks or longer. If a person ceases to look for work for two weeks or more, or becomes temporarily employed, the continuity of long-term unemployment is broken. If he or she starts searching for work or is laid off again, the monthly CPS will record the length of his or her unemployment from the time the search recommenced or since the latest layoff.

The civilian *unemployment rate* is the number of unemployed persons as a percentage of the civilian labor force. The unemployment rates for groups within the civilian population (such as males 20 years of age and over) are the number of unemployed in a group as a percentage of that group's labor force.

Unemployment rates by reason provides a breakdown of the total unemployment rate. Each unemployed person is classified into one of four groups.

Job losers and persons who completed temporary jobs includes persons on temporary layoff, permanent job losers, and persons who completed temporary jobs and began looking for work after those jobs ended. These three categories are shown separately without seasonal adjustment in the "Employment Situation" news release and on the BLS Web site. They are combined, under the title shown here, for the purpose of seasonal adjustment.

Job leavers terminated their employment voluntarily and immediately began looking for work.

Reentrants are persons who previously worked, but were out of the labor force prior to beginning their current job search.

New entrants are persons who have never worked.

Each of these categories is expressed as a proportion of the entire civilian labor force, so that the sum of the four rates equals the unemployment rate for all civilian workers (with the exception of possible discrepancies due to rounding or separate seasonal adjustment).

Median and *average weeks unemployed* are summary measures of the length of time that persons classified as unemployed have been looking for work. For persons on layoff, the duration represents the number of full weeks of the layoff. The *average (mean)* number of weeks is computed by aggregating all the weeks of unemployment experienced by all unemployed persons during their current spell of unemployment and dividing by the number of unemployed. The *median* number of weeks unemployed is the number of weeks of unemployment experienced by the person at the midpoint of the distribution of all unemployed persons, as ranked by duration of unemployment.

The *augmented unemployment rate* is a broader measure of potential labor availability, based on BLS data and used by the Federal Reserve Board. The numbers shown here as percentages have been calculated by the editor of *Business Statistics* using the Federal Reserve definition. The numerator (augmented unemployment) is the number of unemployed plus those who are *not in the labor force and want a job*. The denominator (the augmented labor force) is the number in the civilian labor force plus the number of those who are not in the labor force and want a job.

Notes on the data

The CPS data are collected by trained interviewers from about 60,000 sample households selected to represent the U.S. civilian noninstitutional population. Sample size was about 60,000 households from mid-1989 to mid-1995, but, for budgetary reasons, was reduced in two stages to about 50,000 households, beginning in January 1996. This sample size was maintained from 1996 through 2000. The sample size was increased back to 60,000 households beginning with the data for July 2001, as part of a plan to meet the requirements of the State Children's Health Insurance Program legislation. The CPS provides data for other data series in addition to the BLS employment status data, such as household income (see Chapter 3) and health insurance.

The employment status data collected are based on the activity or status reported for the calendar week, Sunday through Saturday, that includes the 12th day of the month (the reference week). Households are interviewed in the week following the reference week. Sample households are phased in and out of the sample on a rotating basis. Consequently, three-fourths of the sample is the same for any two consecutive months. One-half of the sample is the same as that from the same month a year earlier.

Data relating to 1994 and subsequent years are not strictly comparable with data for 1993 and earlier years because of a major redesign of the survey questionnaire and collection methodology. The redesign includes new and revised questions for the classification of individuals as employed or unemployed, the collection of new data on multiple job holding, a change in the definition of discouraged workers, and the implementation of a more completely automated data collection.

The 1994 redesign of the CPS was the most extensive since its redesign in 1967. However, there are many other significant periods of year-to-year noncomparability in the labor force data. These typically result from the introduction of new decennial census data into the CPS estimation procedures, expansions of the sample, or other improvements made to increase the reliability of the estimates. Each change introduces a new discontinuity, usually between December of the previous year and January of the newly altered year. The discontinuities are usually minor or negligible with respect to figures expressed as nation-wide percentages (such as the unemployment rate or the labor force participation rate), but can be significant with respect to levels (such as labor force and employment in thousands of persons). A list of the dates of the major discontinuities follows, with BLS estimates of their quantitative impact on the national totals. (There are likely to be larger impacts on population subgroups.) The discontinuities occur in January unless otherwise indicated. Note that some of the changes caused adjustments that were carried back to an earlier year.

- 1953: 1950 census data introduced. Labor force and employment were raised by about 350,000.

- 1960: Alaska and Hawaii included. The labor force was increased by about 300,000, mainly in nonagricultural employment.

- 1962: 1960 census data introduced. Labor force and employment were reduced by about 200,000.

• 1972: 1970 census data introduced. Labor force and employment were raised by about 300,000.

• March 1973: Further 1970 census data were introduced, reducing White labor force and employment by about 150,000 and raising Black and other labor force and employment by approximately 210,000.

• July 1975: Adjustment for Vietnamese refugee inflow, raising total and Black and other population by 76,000.

• 1978: Sample expansion and revised estimation procedures increased labor force and employment by about 250,000.

• 1982: Change in estimation procedures introduced. To avoid major breaks, many series were reestimated back to 1970. This did not smooth the breaks that occurred between 1972 and 1979.

• 1986, with revisions carried back to 1980: Adjustment for better estimates of immigration, raising labor force by nearly 400,000 and employment by 350,000, mainly among Hispanics.

• 1994: 1990 census data introduced and carried back to 1990, when employment was increased by about 880,000, and the unemployment rate was raised by about 0.1 percentage point.

• 1997: New estimates of immigration and emigration, raising labor force and employment by about 300,000, again mainly among Hispanics.

• 1998: New population estimates and estimation procedures, reducing labor force and employment by around 250,000.

• 1999: New information on immigration, raising labor force and employment by around 60,000, but lowering Hispanic employment by about 200,000.

• 2000: Census 2000 data introduced, using the 2002 NAICS and the 2000 Standard Occupational Classification System. The labor force was increased by 1.6 million in January 2000, growing to 2.5 million by December 2002.

• 2003: Further population estimates introduced (based on an annual population update and therefore not carried back to 2000), raising the labor force by 614,000.

• 2004: Population controls updated to reflect revised migration estimates, reducing labor force and employment by around 400,000, mostly among Hispanics.

• 2005: Updated migration and vital statistics data decreased labor force and employment by around 45,000.

• 2006: Updated migration and vital statistics decreased labor force and employment by about 125,000.

For further information on these changes, see the BLS publication *Employment and Earnings*, February 2006.

The monthly labor force, employment, and unemployment data are seasonally adjusted by the census X-12-ARIMA method. All seasonally adjusted civilian labor force and unemployment rate statistics, as well as major employment and unemployment estimates, are computed by aggregating independently adjusted series. For example, the seasonally adjusted level of total unemployment is the sum of the seasonally adjusted levels of unemployment for the four sex-age groups (men and women age 16 to 19 years, and men and women age 20 years and over). Seasonally adjusted employment is the sum of the seasonally adjusted levels of employment for the same four groups. The seasonally adjusted civilian labor force is the sum of all eight components. Finally, the seasonally adjusted civilian worker unemployment rate is calculated by taking total seasonally adjusted unemployment as a percent of the total seasonally adjusted civilian labor force. Seasonal adjustment factors are revised at the end of each year to reflect recent experience. The revisions also affect the preceding four years. See *Employment and Earnings*, January 2006, for further information.

Breakdowns other than the basic age/sex classification described above—such as the employment data by class of worker in Table 10-2—will not necessarily add to totals, due to independent seasonal adjustment.

Data availability

Data for each month are usually released on the first Friday of the following month in the "Employment Situation" press release, which also includes data from the establishment survey (Tables 10-7 through 10-12). The press release and data are available on the BLS Web site at <http://www.bls.gov>. Data are subsequently published in the BLS monthly periodical *Employment and Earnings*, which contains detailed explanatory notes. Selected data are published each month in the *Monthly Labor Review*, which also features frequent articles analyzing developments in the labor force, employment, and unemployment.

Monthly and annual data are available beginning with 1948. Historical unadjusted data are published in *Labor Force Statistics Derived from the Current Population Survey* (BLS Bulletin 2307). Historical seasonally adjusted data are available from BLS upon request. Complete historical data are available on the BLS Web site at <http://www.bls.gov>.

Seasonal adjustment factors are revised each year for the five previous years, with the release of December data in early January. New population controls are introduced with the release of January data in early February.

References

Comprehensive descriptive material can be found in *Employment and Earnings*, a monthly BLS publication. Historical background on the CPS, as well as a description of the 1994 redesign, can be found in three articles from the September 1993 edition *Monthly Labor Review*: "Why Is It Necessary to Change?"; "Redesigning the Questionnaire"; and "Evaluating Changes in the Estimates." The redesign is also described in the February 1994 issue of *Employment and Earnings*. See also Chapter 1, "Labor Force Data Derived from the Current Population Survey," *BLS Handbook of Methods*, Bulletin 2490 (April 1997).

TABLE 20-3A
LABOR FORCE AND EMPLOYMENT ESTIMATES SMOOTHED FOR POPULATION ADJUSTMENTS

SOURCE: U.S. DEPARTMENT OF LABOR, BUREAU OF LABOR STATISTICS (BLS)

This table presents seasonally adjusted monthly estimates of total civilian labor force and total civilian employment in which discontinuities caused by the introduction of new population controls in the official series—as described above—have been smoothed. They are taken from the article "Labor Force and Employment Estimates Smoothed for Population Adjustments, 1990–2005," posted on the BLS Web site on February 2, 2006. The method of smoothing is described in Marisa L. Di Natale's "Creating Comparabil-ity in CPS Employment Series," available on the BLS Web site at <http://www.bls.gov/cps/cpscomp.pdf>. BLS notes that these series do not match the official estimates in BLS publications, which are also the data shown in all other tables in this volume.

TABLE 10-6
INSURED UNEMPLOYMENT

SOURCE: U.S. DEPARTMENT OF LABOR, EMPLOYMENT AND TRAINING ADMINISTRATION

Definitions

State programs of unemployment insurance cover operations of regular programs under state unemployment insurance laws. In 1976, the law was amended to extend coverage (effective January 1, 1978) to include virtually all state and local government employees, as well as many agricultural and domestic workers. Benefits under state programs are financed by taxes levied by the states on employers.

Federal programs are those directly financed by the federal government. They include unemployment benefits for *federal employees* (Unemployment Compensation for Federal Employees, or UCFE), *newly discharged veterans* (Unemployment Compensation for Ex-Service Members, or UCX), *railroad retirement*, and *extended benefits*, which are sometimes enacted by Congress in times of widespread or protracted unemployment.

UCX pays benefits based on service to veterans who were on active duty and honorably separated. In the case of both UCFE and UCX, state laws determine the benefit amounts, number of weeks benefits can be paid, and other eligibility conditions.

An *initial claim* is the first claim in a benefit year filed by a worker after losing his or her job, or the first claim filed at the beginning of a subsequent period of unemployment in the same benefit year. The initial claim establishes the starting date for any insured unemployment that may result if the claimant is unemployed for one week or longer. Transitional claims (filed by claimants as they start a new benefit year in a continuing spell of unemployment) are excluded; therefore, these data more closely represent instances of new unemployment and are widely followed as a leading indicator of job market conditions.

Insured unemployment and *persons claiming benefits* both describe the average number of persons receiving benefits in the indicated month or year.

The *insured unemployment rate* for state programs is the level of insured unemployment as a percentage of employment covered by state programs.

Monthly averages in this book are averages, calculated by the editor, of the weekly data published by the Employment and Training Administration. Annual data are averages of the monthly data.

Data availability

Data are published in weekly press releases from the Employment and Training Administration. These releases are available on their Web site at <http://www.doleta.gov>, under "Labor Market Data." Historical data on weekly claims are available at the Department of Labor's Information Technology Support Center at <http:// www.itsc.state.md.us>.

TABLES 10-7, 10-8, 16-1, 16-2, AND 20-4
NONFARM PAYROLL EMPLOYMENT

SOURCE: U.S. DEPARTMENT OF LABOR, BUREAU OF LABOR STATISTICS (BLS)

These nonfarm employment data, as well as the hours and earnings data in Tables 10-9 through 10-12, 16-3 through 16-7, and 20-4, are compiled from payroll records. Information is reported monthly on a voluntary basis to BLS and its cooperating state agencies by a large sample of establishments, which represent all industries except farming.

The survey, originally based on a stratified quota sample, has been replaced on a phased-in basis by a stratified probability sample. The new sampling procedure went into effect for wholesale trade in June 2000; for mining, construction, and manufacturing in June 2001; and for retail trade, transportation and public utilities, and finance, insurance, and real estate in June 2002. The phase-in was completed in June 2003, upon its extension to the service industries. The phase-in schedule was slightly different for the state and area series.

The sample has always been very large. Currently, it includes approximately 160,000 businesses and government agencies covering about 400,000 individual worksites, accounting for about one-third of total benchmark employment of payroll workers. The sample is drawn from a sampling frame of over 8 million unemployment insurance tax accounts.

These data, formally known as the Current Employment Statistics (CES) survey, are often referred to as the "establishment data" or the "payroll data." They are also known as the BLS-790 survey. Beginning in 2003, the data by industry conform to the definitions in the new North American Industry Classification System (NAICS). BLS has reconstructed historical time series to conform with NAICS, to ensure that all published series have a NAICS-based history extending back to at least January 1990. NAICS-based history extends back to January 1939 for total nonfarm and other high-level aggregates. For more detailed series, the starting date for NAICS data varies depending on the scope of the definitional changes between the old Standard Industrial Classification (SIC) and NAICS.

Definitions

An *establishment* is an economic unit that produces goods or services (such as a factory or store) at a single location and is engaged in one type of economic activity.

Employment comprises all persons who received pay (including holiday and sick pay) for any part of the payroll period that contains the 12th day of the month. Included are all full-time and part-time workers in nonfarm establishments, including salaried officers of corporations. Persons holding more than one job are counted in each establishment that reports them. Not covered are proprietors, the self-employed, unpaid volunteer and family workers, farm workers, domestic workers in households, and military personnel. Employees of the Central Intelligence Agency, the Defense Intelligence Agency, the National Geospatial-Intelligence Agency, and the National Security Agency are not included.

Persons on an establishment payroll who are on paid sick leave (when pay is received directly from the employer), on paid holiday or vacation, or who work during a portion of the pay period despite being unemployed or on strike during the rest of the period, are counted as employed. Not counted as employed are persons who are laid off, on leave without pay, on strike for the entire period, or hired but not paid during the period.

Intermittent workers are counted if they performed any service during the month. BLS considers regular full-time teachers (private and government) to be employed during the summer vacation period, regardless of whether they are specifically paid during those months.

The *government* division includes federal, state, and local activities such as legislative, executive, and judicial functions, as well as the U.S. Postal Service and all government-owned and government-operated business enterprises, establishments, and institutions (arsenals, navy yards, hospitals, state-owned utilities, and so forth), and government force account construction. However, as indicated earlier, certain national-security-related agencies are not included.

The monthly *diffusion index of employment change*, currently based on 278 private nonfarm NAICS industries, represents the percentage of those industries in which the seasonally adjusted level of employment in that month was higher than six months earlier, plus one-half of the percentage of industries with unchanged employment. For example, the diffusion index reported for September represents the change from March to September. *Business Statistics* uses the September value to represent the year, since it spans the year's midpoint. Diffusion indexes measure the dispersion of economic gains and losses, with values below 50 percent associated with recessions.

Production or nonsupervisory workers include all production and related workers in mining and manufacturing, construction workers in construction, and nonsupervisory workers in transportation, communication, electric, gas, and sanitary services; wholesale and retail trade; finance, insurance, and real estate; and services. These groups account for about four-fifths of the total employment on private nonagricultural payrolls.

Production and related workers include working supervisors and all nonsupervisory workers (including group leaders and trainees) engaged in fabricating, processing, assembling, inspecting, receiving, storing, handling, packing, warehousing, shipping, trucking, hauling, maintenance, repair, janitorial, guard services, product development, auxiliary production for plant's own use (such as a power plant), record keeping, and other services closely associated with these production operations.

Construction workers include the following employees in the construction division of the NAICS: working supervisors, qualified craft workers, mechanics, apprentices, laborers, and the like, who are engaged in new work, alterations, demolition, repair, maintenance, and other tasks, whether working at the site of construction or working in shops or yards at jobs (such as precutting and preassembling) ordinarily performed by members of the construction trades.

Nonsupervisory employees include employees (not above the working supervisory level) such as office and clerical workers, repairers, salespersons, operators, drivers, physicians, lawyers, accountants, nurses, social workers, research aides, teachers, drafters, photographers, beauticians, musicians, restaurant workers, custodial workers, attendants, line installers and repairers, laborers, janitors, guards, and other employees at similar occupational levels whose services are closely associated with those of the employees listed.

Notes on the data

Benchmark adjustments. The establishment survey data are adjusted annually to comprehensive counts of employment, called "benchmarks." Benchmark information on employment by industry is compiled by state agencies from reports of establishments covered under state unemployment insurance laws, in an annual compilation of administrative data known as the ES-202. These tabulations cover about 97 percent of all employees on nonfarm payrolls. Benchmark data for the residual are obtained from alternate sources, primarily from the Railroad Retirement Board records and the Census Bureau's *County Business Patterns*. The latest benchmark adjustment, which is incorporated into the data in this volume, lowered the not seasonally adjusted employment level in March 2005 by 158,000 jobs, a revision of 0.12 percent.

The estimates for the benchmark month are compared with new benchmark levels, industry by industry. If revisions are necessary, the monthly series of estimates between benchmark periods are adjusted by graduated amounts between the new benchmark and the preceding one ("wedged-back"), and the new benchmark level for each industry is then carried forward month by month based on the sample.

More specifically, the month-to-month changes for each estimation cell are based on changes in a matched sample for that cell, plus an estimate of net business births and deaths. The matched sample for each pair of months consists of establishments that have reported data for both months (which automatically excludes establishments that have gone out of business by the second month). Since new businesses are not immediately incorporated in the sample, a model-based estimate of net births and deaths in that estimating cell is added. The model-based estimate is based on past benchmark revisions.

Not seasonally adjusted data for all months since the last benchmark to which the series has been adjusted are subject to revision.

The data include Alaska and Hawaii beginning in 1959. This inclusion resulted in an increase of 212,000 (0.4 percent) in total nonfarm employment for the March 1959 benchmark month.

Seasonal adjustment. The seasonal movements that recur periodically—such as warm and cold weather, holidays, and vacations—are generally the largest single component of month-to-month changes in employment. After adjusting the data to remove such seasonal variation, the basic trends are more evident. BLS uses Census X-12-ARIMA software to produce the seasonal factors and perform concurrent seasonal adjustment. New factors are developed each month using the most current data. For many series, a special procedure called REGARIMA is also used to adjust for regular, predictable events not always associated with the same calendar month, including the length of the interval (four or five weeks) between the survey weeks, the presence or absence of religious holidays in the April survey reference period, the occasional occurrence of Labor Day in the September reference period, and variations in local government employment due to the presence or absence of poll workers.

Seasonal adjustment factors are directly applied to the component levels. Seasonally adjusted totals for employment series are then obtained by aggregating the seasonally adjusted components directly, while hours and earnings series represent weighted averages of the seasonally adjusted component series. Seasonally adjusted data are not published for a small number of series characterized by small seasonal components relative to their trend and/or irregular components. However, these series are used in aggregating to broader seasonally adjusted levels.

Revisions of the seasonally adjusted data, usually for the most recent five-year period, are made once a year coincident with the benchmark revisions. This means that these revisions typically extend back farther than the benchmark revisions.

Data availability

Employment data by industry division are available beginning with 1919. Data for each month usually are released on the first Friday of the following month in a press release that also contains data from the household survey (Tables 10-1 through 10-5). Data are subsequently published in the BLS monthly periodical *Employment and Earnings*, which features detailed explanatory notes. Selected data are published each month in the *Monthly Labor Review*, which contains frequent articles analyzing developments in the labor force, employment, and unemployment. Press releases and complete historical data are available on the BLS Web site at <http://www.bls.gov>.

Benchmark revisions and revised seasonally adjusted data for recent years are made each year with the release of January data in early February. Before 2004, the benchmark revisions were not made until June; the acceleration is due to earlier availability of the benchmark ES-202 data.

References

The extensive changes incorporated in June 2003 are described in "Recent Changes in the National Current Employment Statistics Survey," *Monthly Labor Review*, June 2003, and in the "Explanatory Notes" in any subsequent issue of *Employment and Earnings*. The revisions made beginning with the January 2006 data are described in "BLS National Establishment Estimates Revised to

Incorporate March 2005 Benchmarks," *Employment and Earnings*, February 2006. Descriptive material is available on the BLS Web site. See also Chapter 2, "Employment, Hours, and Earnings from the Establishment Survey," *BLS Handbook of Methods*, Bulletin 2490 (April 1997).

TABLES 10-9, 10-10, 16-3, 16-6, AND 20-4
AVERAGE HOURS PER WEEK; AGGREGATE EMPLOYEE HOURS

SOURCE: U.S. DEPARTMENT OF LABOR, BUREAU OF LABOR STATISTICS (BLS)

See the notes and definitions for Tables 10-7 and 10-8 for an overall description of the "establishment" or "payroll" survey that is the source of hours data.

Definitions

Average weekly hours represents the average hours paid per production or nonsupervisory worker during the pay period that contains the 12th of the month. Included are hours paid for holidays and vacations, as well as those paid for sick leave when pay is received directly from the firm.

Average weekly hours are different from standard or scheduled hours. Factors such as unpaid absenteeism, labor turnover, part-time work, and work stoppages can cause average weekly hours to be lower than scheduled hours of work for an establishment.

Average weekly hours pertain to jobs, not to persons; thus, a person with half-time jobs in two different establishments is represented in this series as two jobs that have 20-hour workweeks, not as one person with a 40-hour workweek.

Overtime hours represent the portion of average weekly hours worked in excess of regular hours, for which overtime premiums were paid. Weekend and holiday hours are included only if overtime premiums were paid. Hours for which only shift differential, hazard, incentive, or other similar types of premiums were paid are excluded.

Production or nonsupervisory workers. See the notes and definitions for Tables 10-7 and 10-8.

Aggregate hours provide a partial time series measure, in index-number form, of labor input to the industry. Data pertain to production and nonsupervisory workers in non-farm establishments. The indexes are obtained by multiplying seasonally adjusted production or nonsupervisory worker employment by seasonally adjusted average weekly hours, dividing the resulting series by their monthly averages for the 2002 period, and multiplying the results by 100, so that the annual average for 2002 equals 100. For total private, goods-producing, service-providing, and major industry divisions, the indexes are obtained by summing the seasonally adjusted aggregate weekly employee hours for the component industries, dividing by the monthly average for the 2002 period, and multiplying by 100.

Notes on the data

Benchmark adjustments. Independent benchmarks are not available for the hours and earnings series. At the time of the annual adjustment of the employment series to new benchmarks, the levels of hours and earnings may be affected by the revised employment weights (which are used in computing the industry averages for hours and earnings), as well as by the changes in seasonal adjustment factors introduced with the benchmark revision.

Method of computing industry series. Average weekly hours for individual industries are computed by dividing production or nonsupervisory worker hours (reported by establishments classified in each industry) by the number of production or nonsupervisory workers reported for the same establishments. Estimates for divisions and major industry groups are averages (weighted by employment) of the figures for component industries.

Seasonal adjustment. Hours and earnings series are seasonally adjusted by applying factors directly to the corresponding unadjusted series. Data for some industries are not seasonally adjusted because the seasonal component is small relative to the trend-cycle and/or irregular components. Consequently, they cannot be separated with sufficient precision.

REGARIMA modeling is used to correct for reporting and processing errors associated with the number of weekdays in a month. This is of particular importance for average weekly hours in the service-providing industries other than retail trade. For this reason, BLS advises that calculations of over-the-year changes (for example, the change for the current month from a year earlier) should use seasonally adjusted data, since the actual not-seasonally-adjusted monthly data may be distorted.

Data availability

See the data availability for Tables 10-7 and 10-8.

References

See the references for Tables 10-7 and 10-8.

TABLES 10-11, 10-12, 16-4, 16-5, AND 20-4
HOURLY AND WEEKLY EARNINGS

SOURCE: U.S. DEPARTMENT OF LABOR, BUREAU OF LABOR STATISTICS (BLS)

See the notes and definitions for Tables 10-7 and 10-8 for an overall description of the "establishment" or "payroll" survey that is the source of these earnings data.

Definitions

Earnings are the payments that production or nonsupervisory workers receive during the survey period (before deductions for taxes and other items), including premium pay for overtime or late-shift work, but excluding irregular bonuses, tips, and other special payments.

Production or nonsupervisory workers. See the notes and definitions for Tables 10-7 and 10-8.

Notes on the data

The hours and earnings series are based on reports of gross payroll and corresponding paid hours for full- and part-time production and related workers, construction workers, or nonsupervisory workers who received pay for any part of the pay period that contained the 12th of the month.

Total payrolls are before deductions, such as for the employee share of old-age and unemployment insurance, group insurance, withholding taxes, bonds, and union dues. The payroll figures also include pay for overtime, holidays, vacations, and sick leave (paid directly by the employer for the period reported). Excluded from the payroll figures are fringe benefits (health and other types of insurance and contributions to retirement, paid by the employer, and the employer share of payroll taxes); bonuses (unless earned and paid regularly each pay period); other pay not earned in the pay period reported (retroactive pay); tips; and the value of free rent, fuel, meals, or other payment in kind. The exclusion of tips is particularly significant for hotels, motels, and eating and drinking places.

Average hourly earnings data reflect not only changes in basic hourly and incentive wage rates, but also such variable factors as premium pay for overtime and late-shift work and changes in output of workers paid on an incentive basis. Shifts in the volume of employment between relatively high-paid and low-paid work also affect the general average of hourly earnings.

Averages of hourly earnings should not be confused with wage rates, which represent the rates stipulated for a given unit of work or time, while earnings refer to the actual return to the worker for a stated period of time. The earnings series do not represent total labor cost to the employer because of the exclusion of irregular bonuses, retroactive items, the cost of employer-provided benefits, payroll taxes paid by employers, and earnings for those employees not covered under the production or nonsupervisory worker definition.

Average weekly earnings are not the amounts available to workers for spending, since they do not reflect deductions, such as those for income taxes and Social Security taxes. It should also be noted that they represent earnings per job, not per worker (since a worker may have more than one job) and not per family (since a family may have more than one worker). A person with two half-time jobs will be reflected as two earners with low weekly earnings rather than as one person with the total earnings from his or her two jobs.

Method of computing industry series. Average hourly earnings are obtained by dividing the reported total production or nonsupervisory worker payroll by the total production or nonsupervisory worker hours. Estimates for both hours and hourly earnings for nonfarm divisions and major industry groups are employment-weighted averages of the figures for component industries.

Average weekly earnings are computed by multiplying average hourly earnings by average weekly hours. In addition to the factors mentioned above, which exert varying influences upon average hourly earnings, average weekly earnings are affected by changes in the length of the workweek, part-time work, work stoppages, labor turnover, and absenteeism. Persistent long-term uptrends in the proportion of part-time workers in retail trade and many of the service industries have reduced average workweeks (as measured here), and have similarly affected the average weekly earnings series.

Benchmark adjustments. Independent benchmarks are not available for the hours and earnings series. At the time of the annual adjustment of the employment series to new benchmarks, the levels of hours and earnings may be affected by the revised employment weights (which are used in computing the industry averages for hours and earnings), as well as by the changes in seasonal adjustment factors that were also introduced with the benchmark revision.

Seasonal adjustment. Hours and earnings series are seasonally adjusted by applying factors directly to the corresponding unadjusted series; seasonally adjusted average weekly earnings are the product of seasonally adjusted hourly earnings and weekly hours.

REGARIMA modeling is used to correct for reporting and processing errors associated with variations in the number of weekdays in a month. This is of particular importance for average hourly earnings in wholesale trade, financial activities, professional and business services, and other services. For this reason, BLS advises that calculations of over-the-year changes, for example the change for the current month from a year earlier, should use seasonally adjusted data, since the actual not-seasonally-adjusted monthly data may be distorted.

Data availability

See the data availability for Tables 10-7 and 10-8.

References

See the references for Tables 10-7 and 10-8.

TABLE 10-13
MEDIAN USUAL WEEKLY EARNINGS OF FULL-TIME WAGE AND SALARY WORKERS

Source: U.S. Department of Labor, Bureau of Labor Statistics (BLS)

These data are from the Current Population Survey, which was previously described in the notes for Tables 10-1 through 10-5. Because they are earnings per worker, not per job, and are limited to full-time workers, the data are not distorted by the increasing proportion of part-time workers, as the CES earnings data are.

Definitions

Full-time wage and salary workers are those who receive wages, salaries, commissions, tips, pay in kind, or piece rates, and usually work 35 hours or more per week at their sole or principal job. Self-employed persons are excluded. The number of full-time wage and salary workers was about 103.5 million in the first quarter of 2006, which was 73 percent of total civilian employment.

Usual weekly earnings are earnings before taxes and other deductions and include any overtime pay, commissions, or tips usually received. In the case of multiple jobholders they refer to the main job. The wording of the question was changed in January 1994 to better deal with persons who found it easier to report earnings on other than a weekly basis. Such reports are then converted to the weekly equivalent. According to BLS, "the term 'usual' is as perceived by the respondent. If the respondent asks for a definition of usual, interviewers are instructed to define the term as more than half the weeks worked during the past 4 or 5 months."

The *median* is the amount that divides a given earnings distribution into two equal groups, one having earnings above the median and the other having earnings below the median.

See the notes for Tables 10-1 through 10-5 for the definitions of race and ethnic categories.

Data availability

These data become available about 3 weeks after the end of each quarter in the "Usual Weekly Earnings of Wage and Salary Workers" press release, available on the BLS Web site at <http://www.bls.gov/cps>. Recent data are available at that location. Also available are greater detail by demographic and age groups, by occupation, by union status, and by education; distributional data, by deciles and quartiles; earnings for part-time workers; and earnings in 1982 dollars using the CPI-U. Further historical data are available upon request from BLS by telephone at (202) 691-6378.

CHAPTER 11: ENERGY

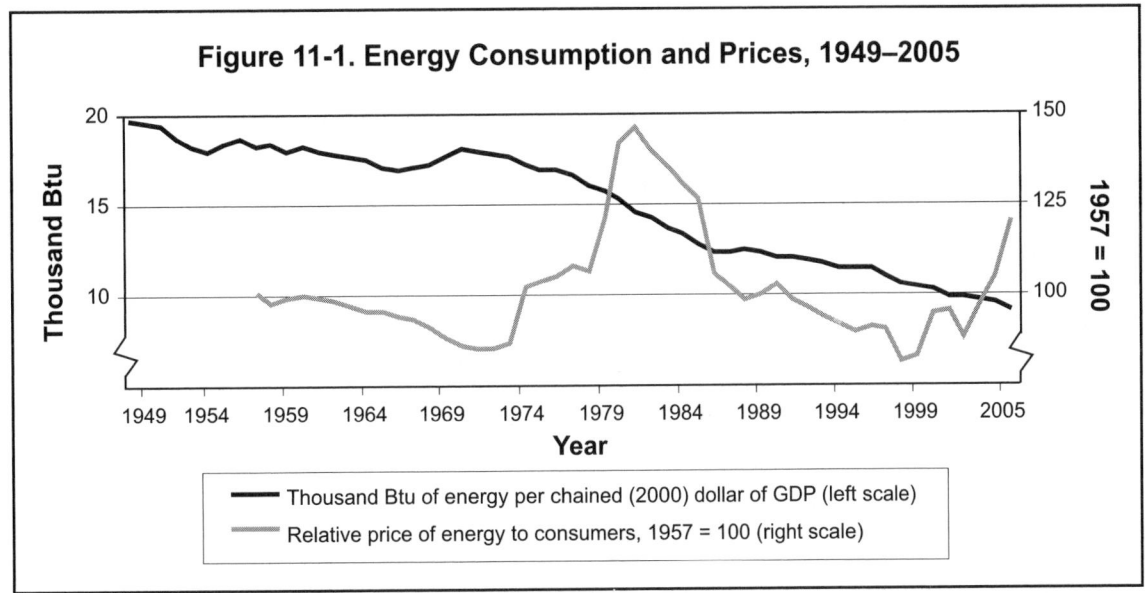

Figure 11-1. Energy Consumption and Prices, 1949–2005

Legend:
— Thousand Btu of energy per chained (2000) dollar of GDP (left scale)
— Relative price of energy to consumers, 1957 = 100 (right scale)

- U.S. energy consumption has more than tripled since 1949, but real gross domestic product (GDP) is more than six times what it was in that year. Consequently, there has been a downward trend in energy use per dollar of real GDP, which can also be described as an increase in the energy efficiency of national production. (Table 11-2) This trend may seem surprising in light of the continued increases in motor vehicle use, air-conditioning, air travel, and other consumer uses of energy. Evidently, these increases are more than offset by factors such as the rising share of services and high-tech goods in GDP and the declining relative importance of energy-intensive processes such as primary metals production.

- As the figure suggests, there have been dramatic upswings and downswings in relative energy prices over the last three decades, with apparently muted effects on the consistent, downward energy/GDP trend. (Tables 11-2 and 8-1)

- Between 1973 and 2005, the greatest savings in energy relative to GDP were achieved in industrial use, which actually fell between those years, despite increases of 154 percent in real GDP and 115 percent in industrial production. More modest economies relative to GDP growth were achieved in the use of energy for residential and commercial purposes, which rose 63 percent, and in transportation use, which rose 51 percent. (Table 11-1)

- Consumption of petroleum and natural gas per dollar of real GDP rose between 1949 and the early 1970s, but has been declining since then. Use of other forms of energy per real dollar has been declining for the entire postwar period. (Table 11-2)

- Net imports supplied 30 percent of total U.S. energy consumption in 2005, compared with 17 percent in 1973 and none in 1949 (when the United States exported more energy than it imported). In 2005, nuclear electric power supplied 8 percent of total consumption; hydroelectric and biomass (wood, waste, and ethanol) power each supplied less than 3 percent of total consumption. (Table 11-1)

Table 11-1. Energy Supply and Consumption

(Quadrillion Btu.)

Year and month	Imports	Exports	Production, by source								Consumption, by end-use sector			
			Total [1]	Coal	Natural gas	Crude oil	Natural gas plant liquids	Nuclear electric power	Hydro-electric power	Biomass [2]	Total	Residential and commercial	Industrial	Transportation
1949	1.448	1.592	31.722	11.974	5.377	10.683	0.714	0.000	1.425	1.549	31.982	9.275	14.717	7.990
1950	1.913	1.465	35.540	14.060	6.233	11.447	0.823	0.000	1.415	1.562	34.616	9.890	16.233	8.493
1951	1.892	2.622	38.751	14.419	7.416	13.037	0.920	0.000	1.424	1.535	36.974	10.263	17.669	9.042
1952	2.146	2.365	37.917	12.734	7.964	13.281	0.998	0.000	1.466	1.474	36.748	10.443	17.302	9.003
1953	2.313	1.866	38.181	12.278	8.339	13.671	1.062	0.000	1.413	1.419	37.664	10.340	18.201	9.123
1954	2.348	1.696	36.518	10.542	8.682	13.427	1.113	0.000	1.360	1.394	36.639	10.590	17.146	8.903
1955	2.790	2.286	40.148	12.370	9.345	14.410	1.240	0.000	1.360	1.424	40.208	11.185	19.472	9.551
1956	3.207	2.945	42.622	13.306	10.002	15.180	1.283	0.000	1.435	1.416	41.754	11.698	20.196	9.860
1957	3.529	3.439	42.983	13.061	10.605	15.178	1.289	0.000	1.516	1.334	41.787	11.686	20.205	9.897
1958	3.884	2.050	40.133	10.783	10.942	14.204	1.287	0.002	1.592	1.323	41.645	12.333	19.307	10.005
1959	4.076	1.534	41.949	10.778	11.952	14.933	1.383	0.002	1.548	1.353	43.466	12.800	20.316	10.349
1960	4.188	1.477	42.804	10.817	12.656	14.935	1.461	0.006	1.608	1.320	45.087	13.667	20.823	10.597
1961	4.437	1.377	43.280	10.447	13.105	15.206	1.549	0.020	1.656	1.295	45.739	14.032	20.937	10.770
1962	4.994	1.473	44.877	10.901	13.717	15.522	1.593	0.026	1.816	1.300	47.828	14.839	21.768	11.221
1963	5.087	1.835	47.174	11.849	14.513	15.966	1.709	0.038	1.771	1.323	49.646	15.261	22.730	11.655
1964	5.447	1.815	49.056	12.524	15.298	16.164	1.803	0.040	1.886	1.337	51.817	15.730	24.090	11.998
1965	5.892	1.829	50.676	13.055	15.775	16.521	1.883	0.043	2.059	1.335	54.017	16.509	25.075	12.434
1966	6.146	1.829	53.534	13.468	17.011	17.561	1.996	0.064	2.062	1.369	57.017	17.517	26.397	13.102
1967	6.159	2.115	56.379	13.825	17.943	18.651	2.177	0.088	2.347	1.340	58.908	18.541	26.616	13.752
1968	6.905	1.998	58.225	13.609	19.068	19.308	2.321	0.142	2.349	1.419	62.419	19.665	27.888	14.866
1969	7.676	2.126	60.541	13.863	20.446	19.556	2.420	0.154	2.648	1.440	65.621	21.000	29.114	15.506
1970	8.342	2.632	63.501	14.607	21.666	20.401	2.512	0.239	2.634	1.431	67.844	22.105	29.641	16.098
1971	9.535	2.151	62.723	13.186	22.280	20.033	2.544	0.413	2.824	1.432	69.289	22.959	29.601	16.729
1972	11.387	2.118	63.920	14.092	22.208	20.041	2.598	0.584	2.864	1.503	72.704	24.036	30.953	17.716
1973	14.613	2.033	63.585	13.992	22.187	19.493	2.569	0.910	2.861	1.529	75.708	24.437	32.653	18.612
1974	14.304	2.203	62.372	14.074	21.210	18.575	2.471	1.272	3.177	1.540	73.991	24.046	31.819	18.119
1975	14.032	2.323	61.357	14.989	19.640	17.729	2.374	1.900	3.155	1.499	71.999	24.308	29.447	18.244
1976	16.760	2.172	61.602	15.654	19.480	17.262	2.327	2.111	2.976	1.713	76.012	25.476	31.429	19.099
1977	19.948	2.052	62.052	15.755	19.565	17.454	2.327	2.702	2.333	1.838	78.000	25.866	32.307	19.820
1978	19.106	1.920	63.137	14.910	19.485	18.434	2.245	3.024	2.937	2.038	79.986	26.637	32.733	20.615
1979	19.460	2.855	65.948	17.540	20.076	18.104	2.286	2.776	2.931	2.152	80.903	26.469	33.962	20.471
1980	15.796	3.695	67.232	18.598	19.908	18.249	2.254	2.739	2.900	2.476	78.280	26.433	32.152	19.696
1981	13.719	4.307	67.008	18.377	19.699	18.146	2.307	3.008	2.758	2.591	76.343	25.991	30.836	19.513
1982	11.861	4.608	66.607	18.639	18.319	18.309	2.191	3.131	3.266	2.648	73.286	26.490	27.704	19.088
1983	11.752	3.693	64.151	17.247	16.593	18.392	2.184	3.203	3.527	2.876	73.146	26.456	27.511	19.176
1984	12.471	3.786	68.889	19.719	18.008	18.848	2.274	3.553	3.386	2.937	76.793	27.296	29.643	19.851
1985	11.781	4.196	67.758	19.325	16.980	18.992	2.241	4.076	2.970	2.975	76.580	27.504	28.958	20.122
1986	14.151	4.021	67.131	19.509	16.541	18.376	2.149	4.380	3.071	2.885	76.826	27.571	28.375	20.877
1987	15.398	3.812	67.606	20.141	17.136	17.675	2.215	4.754	2.635	2.821	79.223	28.182	29.519	21.524
1988	17.296	4.366	68.976	20.738	17.599	17.279	2.260	5.587	2.334	2.962	82.869	29.665	30.818	22.382
1989	18.766	4.661	69.407	21.346	17.847	16.117	2.158	5.602	2.837	3.105	84.999	30.972	31.396	22.622
1990	18.817	4.752	70.791	22.456	18.326	15.571	2.175	6.104	3.046	2.687	84.730	30.230	31.931	22.589
1991	18.335	5.141	70.434	21.594	18.229	15.701	2.306	6.422	3.016	2.727	84.667	30.928	31.543	22.195
1992	19.372	4.937	69.999	21.629	18.375	15.223	2.363	6.479	2.617	2.870	86.015	30.785	32.688	22.542
1993	21.273	4.258	68.335	20.249	18.584	14.494	2.408	6.410	2.892	2.836	87.652	32.096	32.683	22.883
1994	22.390	4.061	70.720	22.111	19.348	14.103	2.391	6.694	2.683	2.948	89.292	32.225	33.569	23.503
1995	22.260	4.511	71.135	22.029	19.082	13.887	2.442	7.075	3.205	3.018	91.200	33.286	33.950	23.960
1996	23.702	4.633	72.474	22.684	19.344	13.723	2.530	7.087	3.590	3.098	94.226	34.795	34.916	24.511
1997	25.215	4.514	72.462	23.211	19.394	13.658	2.495	6.597	3.640	3.037	94.800	34.805	35.181	24.808
1998	26.581	4.299	72.841	23.935	19.613	13.235	2.420	7.068	3.297	2.843	95.200	35.055	34.792	25.357
1999	27.252	3.715	71.715	23.186	19.341	12.451	2.528	7.610	3.268	2.886	96.837	36.024	34.699	26.108
2000	28.973	4.006	71.289	22.623	19.662	12.358	2.611	7.862	2.811	2.922	98.976	37.636	34.633	26.705
2001	30.157	3.770	71.910	23.490	20.205	12.282	2.547	8.033	2.242	2.666	96.498	37.507	32.713	26.273
2002	29.407	3.668	70.859	22.622	19.439	12.163	2.559	8.143	2.689	2.746	97.967	38.397	32.719	26.846
2003	31.060	4.054	70.136	21.970	19.691	12.026	2.346	7.959	2.825	2.812	98.273	38.583	32.655	27.039
2004	33.543	4.433	70.388	22.714	19.264	11.503	2.466	8.222	2.690	2.982	100.414	39.017	33.482	27.916
2005	34.304	4.581	69.159	23.010	18.791	10.840	2.323	8.133	2.715	2.781	99.781	39.804	31.932	28.040
2004														
January	2.624	0.299	6.041	1.913	1.650	1.002	0.208	0.738	0.230	0.254	9.422	4.349	2.846	2.226
February	2.562	0.312	5.588	1.772	1.530	0.935	0.194	0.668	0.210	0.237	8.794	3.887	2.711	2.197
March	2.843	0.388	6.008	1.941	1.665	1.008	0.211	0.660	0.230	0.246	8.464	3.350	2.787	2.329
April	2.689	0.410	5.754	1.877	1.604	0.962	0.199	0.611	0.209	0.246	7.819	2.808	2.728	2.287
May	2.875	0.390	5.833	1.784	1.635	0.998	0.206	0.677	0.241	0.243	7.991	2.811	2.829	2.351
June	2.832	0.390	5.921	1.942	1.593	0.939	0.194	0.706	0.253	0.245	7.996	2.924	2.722	2.349
July	2.940	0.372	6.009	1.888	1.643	0.981	0.209	0.750	0.234	0.256	8.418	3.202	2.783	2.429
August	2.944	0.375	6.013	1.948	1.636	0.959	0.215	0.741	0.216	0.253	8.375	3.121	2.824	2.427
September	2.665	0.362	5.696	1.913	1.522	0.881	0.201	0.687	0.206	0.241	7.851	2.864	2.691	2.295
October	2.873	0.351	5.776	1.895	1.606	0.927	0.210	0.652	0.189	0.252	7.989	2.792	2.793	2.405
November	2.812	0.350	5.713	1.888	1.566	0.939	0.209	0.615	0.210	0.245	8.089	2.988	2.842	2.260
December	2.884	0.434	6.036	1.953	1.613	0.973	0.210	0.715	0.263	0.263	9.208	3.921	2.925	2.361
2005														
January	2.787	0.366	5.986	1.906	1.647	0.970	0.209	0.728	0.244	0.238	9.305	4.228	2.829	2.246
February	2.664	0.376	5.529	1.829	1.504	0.888	0.194	0.635	0.218	0.223	8.285	3.595	2.573	2.117
March	2.844	0.415	6.086	2.077	1.653	0.988	0.215	0.641	0.232	0.233	8.695	3.577	2.764	2.355
April	2.765	0.411	5.718	1.897	1.591	0.955	0.204	0.571	0.229	0.223	7.715	2.808	2.609	2.302
May	2.869	0.446	5.866	1.833	1.621	0.988	0.213	0.656	0.273	0.231	7.855	2.780	2.666	2.409
June	2.912	0.462	5.913	1.939	1.591	0.944	0.199	0.689	0.268	0.230	8.160	3.076	2.703	2.379
July	2.974	0.396	5.903	1.868	1.606	0.943	0.202	0.737	0.261	0.239	8.563	3.433	2.674	2.452
August	2.923	0.403	5.988	1.989	1.612	0.948	0.198	0.740	0.216	0.240	8.618	3.427	2.723	2.464
September	2.718	0.309	5.383	1.945	1.395	0.733	0.165	0.695	0.175	0.227	7.749	2.998	2.457	2.293
October	2.986	0.312	5.419	1.905	1.475	0.764	0.177	0.638	0.181	0.230	7.741	2.839	2.523	2.380
November	2.899	0.306	5.577	1.932	1.515	0.824	0.181	0.656	0.193	0.228	7.911	2.990	2.669	2.252
December	2.964	0.379	5.791	1.889	1.583	0.894	0.168	0.748	0.223	0.238	9.186	4.053	2.743	2.390

[1]Includes categories not shown separately.
[2]Wood, waste, and alcohol fuels (ethanol blended into motor gasoline).

Table 11-2. Energy Consumption Per Dollar of Real Gross Domestic Product

Year	Energy consumption (quadrillion Btu)			Gross domestic product (billions of chained [2000] dollars)	Energy consumption per dollar of GDP (thousand Btu per chained [2000] dollar)		
	Total	Petroleum and natural gas	Other energy		Total	Petroleum and natural gas	Other energy
1949	31.982	17.028	14.954	1 634.6	19.57	10.42	9.15
1950	34.616	19.284	15.332	1 777.3	19.48	10.85	8.63
1951	36.974	21.477	15.497	1 915.0	19.31	11.21	8.09
1952	36.748	22.505	14.243	1 988.3	18.48	11.32	7.16
1953	37.664	23.462	14.202	2 079.5	18.11	11.28	6.83
1954	36.639	24.169	12.470	2 065.4	17.74	11.70	6.04
1955	40.208	26.253	13.955	2 212.8	18.17	11.86	6.31
1956	41.754	27.551	14.203	2 255.8	18.51	12.21	6.30
1957	41.787	28.122	13.665	2 301.1	18.16	12.22	5.94
1958	41.645	29.190	12.455	2 279.2	18.27	12.81	5.46
1959	43.466	31.040	12.426	2 441.3	17.80	12.71	5.09
1960	45.087	32.305	12.782	2 501.8	18.02	12.91	5.11
1961	45.739	33.143	12.596	2 560.0	17.87	12.95	4.92
1962	47.828	34.780	13.048	2 715.2	17.61	12.81	4.81
1963	49.646	36.104	13.542	2 834.0	17.52	12.74	4.78
1964	51.817	37.589	14.228	2 998.6	17.28	12.54	4.74
1965	54.017	39.014	15.003	3 191.1	16.93	12.23	4.70
1966	57.017	41.396	15.621	3 399.1	16.77	12.18	4.60
1967	58.908	43.228	15.680	3 484.6	16.91	12.41	4.50
1968	62.419	46.189	16.230	3 652.7	17.09	12.65	4.44
1969	65.621	49.016	16.605	3 765.4	17.43	13.02	4.41
1970	67.844	51.315	16.529	3 771.9	17.99	13.60	4.38
1971	69.289	53.030	16.259	3 898.6	17.77	13.60	4.17
1972	72.704	55.645	17.059	4 105.0	17.71	13.56	4.16
1973	75.708	57.352	18.356	4 341.5	17.44	13.21	4.23
1974	73.991	55.187	18.804	4 319.6	17.13	12.78	4.35
1975	71.999	52.678	19.321	4 311.2	16.70	12.22	4.48
1976	76.012	55.520	20.492	4 540.9	16.74	12.23	4.51
1977	78.000	57.053	20.947	4 750.5	16.42	12.01	4.41
1978	79.986	57.966	22.021	5 015.0	15.95	11.56	4.39
1979	80.903	57.789	23.114	5 173.4	15.64	11.17	4.47
1980	78.289	54.596	23.693	5 161.7	15.17	10.58	4.59
1981	76.342	51.859	24.483	5 291.7	14.43	9.80	4.63
1982	73.253	48.736	24.516	5 189.3	14.12	9.39	4.72
1983	73.101	47.411	25.690	5 423.8	13.48	8.74	4.74
1984	76.736	49.558	27.178	5 813.6	13.20	8.52	4.67
1985	76.469	48.756	27.713	6 053.7	12.63	8.05	4.58
1986	76.782	48.904	27.878	6 263.6	12.26	7.81	4.45
1987	79.225	50.609	28.616	6 475.1	12.24	7.82	4.42
1988	82.844	52.774	30.070	6 742.7	12.29	7.83	4.46
1989	84.957	53.923	31.034	6 981.4	12.17	7.72	4.45
1990	84.704	53.282	31.422	7 112.5	11.91	7.49	4.42
1991	84.643	52.994	31.649	7 100.5	11.92	7.46	4.46
1992	85.992	54.362	31.630	7 336.6	11.72	7.41	4.31
1993	87.619	55.193	32.524	7 532.7	11.63	7.33	4.32
1994	89.283	56.512	32.879	7 835.5	11.39	7.21	4.20
1995	91.250	57.338	34.028	8 031.7	11.36	7.14	4.24
1996	94.256	58.954	35.385	8 328.9	11.32	7.08	4.25
1997	94.768	59.594	35.280	8 703.5	10.89	6.85	4.05
1998	95.192	59.869	35.440	9 066.9	10.50	6.60	3.91
1999	96.836	60.970	35.988	9 470.3	10.23	6.44	3.80
2000	98.961	62.320	36.781	9 817.0	10.08	6.35	3.75
2001	96.472	61.239	35.379	9 890.7	9.75	6.19	3.58
2002	97.870	62.030	36.015	10 048.8	9.74	6.17	3.58
2003	98.273	62.014	36.497	10 320.6	9.52	6.01	3.54
2004	100.414	63.630	37.084	10 755.7	9.34	5.92	3.45
2005	99.876	63.063	37.153	11 134.8	8.97	5.66	3.34

NOTES AND DEFINITIONS

TABLES 11-1 AND 11-2
ENERGY SUPPLY AND CONSUMPTION

SOURCES: U.S. DEPARTMENT OF ENERGY, ENERGY INFORMATION ADMINISTRATION (EIA); U.S. DEPARTMENT OF COMMERCE, BUREAU OF ECONOMIC ANALYSIS (BEA)

Definitions

The *British thermal unit (Btu)* is a measure used to combine data for different energy sources into a consistent aggregate. It is the amount of energy required to raise the temperature of 1 pound of water 1 degree Fahrenheit when the water is near a temperature of 39.2 degrees Fahrenheit. To illustrate one of the factors used to convert volumes to Btu, conventional motor gasoline has a heat content of 5.253 million Btu per barrel. For further information, see Appendix A in the Energy Information Administration's (EIA) *Monthly Energy Review*.

Production: Crude oil includes lease condensates.

Hydroelectric power includes conventional electrical utility and industrial generation.

Biomass includes wood, waste, and alcohol fuels (ethanol blended into motor gasoline).

Energy production components not shown in this volume, which account for the difference between total production and the sum of the categories shown, include energy generated for distribution from geothermal, solar, and wind sources and an allowance for net hydroelectric energy losses related to pumped storage.

The sum of domestic energy *production* and net imports of energy (*imports* minus *exports*) does not exactly equal domestic energy *consumption*. The difference is attributed to inventory changes; losses and gains in conversion, transportation, and distribution; the addition of blending compounds; shipments of anthracite to U.S. armed forces in Europe; and adjustments to account for discrepancies between reporting systems.

Consumption by end-use sector is based on total, not net, consumption.

References and notes on the data

These data are published each month in Tables 1.1, 1.2, 1.8, and 2.1 in the *Monthly Energy Review*. Annual data before 1973 are published each year in the *Annual Energy Review*. The last printed edition of *Monthly Energy Review* will be issued in December 2006. Both publications, along with all current and historical data, will continue to be available on the EIA Web site at <http://www.eia.doe.gov>.

The real gross domestic product (GDP) data used to calculate energy consumption per dollar of real GDP are from the Bureau of Economic Analysis; see Table 1-2 and the applicable notes and definitions in this volume of *Business Statistics*.

CHAPTER 12: MONEY, ASSETS, LIABILITIES, AND ASSET MARKETS

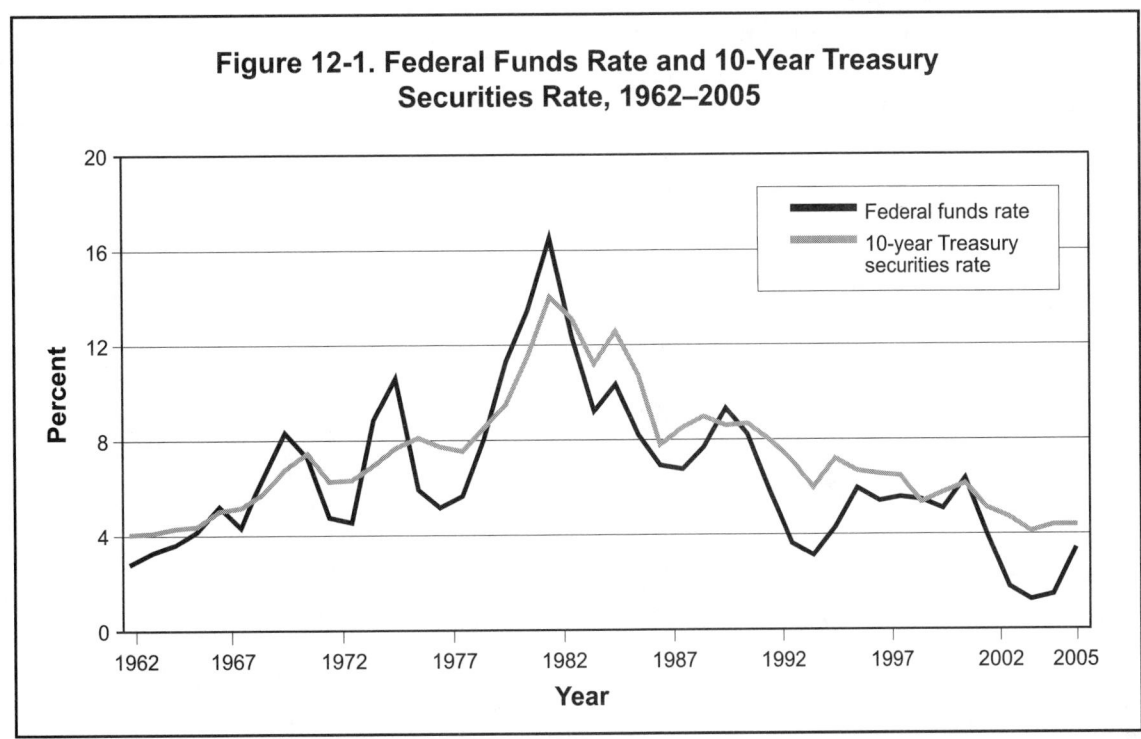

Figure 12-1. Federal Funds Rate and 10-Year Treasury Securities Rate, 1962–2005

- Inflation has fallen back to the levels of the early postwar period (see Chapter 8), and, as the figure shows, the same has happened with interest rates. (Table 12-9)

- Comparisons of interest rates and other financial data over the half-century span are not always straightforward, because financial institutions and instruments have changed. In particular, interest rates were held low until 1952 because the Federal Reserve was pegging Treasury bill and bond rates. Rates before 1953 are therefore not shown in Table 12-9 and are not available for many series. Since then, rates have been free to reflect changing degrees of monetary tightness, as well as changing inflation expectations and fluctuating views of the productivity of capital.

- In the short-term markets, where Federal Reserve policy governs the nominal price of overnight money, the federal funds rate in 2003 and 2004 was even lower than in years such as 1958, when the economy was slack and inflation expectations were nonexistent. Since inflation in recent years was around 2 percent, the real federal funds rate was negative. After mid-2004, Federal Reserve policy makers have increased this rate, gradually but steadily, back to 2001 levels. (Table 12-9)

- In the longer-term market, the 10-year Treasury rate in 2003 and 2004 was at levels last seen in the early 1960s. Since then, it has increased only slightly, and mortgage rates (which tend to reflect changes in the 10-year Treasury rate) have also changed little. For longer-denomination Treasuries and corporate and state and local bonds, rates were still declining in 2005. (Table 12-9)

Table 12-1. Money Stock Measures

(Billions of dollars, monthly data are averages of daily figures, annual data are for December.)

Year and month	Seasonally adjusted			Not seasonally adjusted		
	M1	M2	M3	M1	M2	M3
1959	140.0	297.8	299.7	143.6	300.6	302.4
1960	140.7	312.4	315.2	144.5	315.3	318.0
1961	145.2	335.5	340.8	149.2	338.5	343.7
1962	147.8	362.7	371.3	151.9	365.8	374.0
1963	153.3	393.2	405.9	157.5	396.4	408.7
1964	160.3	424.7	442.4	164.9	428.3	445.5
1965	167.8	459.2	482.1	172.6	463.1	485.5
1966	172.0	480.2	505.4	176.9	483.7	508.6
1967	183.3	524.8	557.9	188.4	528.0	560.9
1968	197.4	566.8	607.2	202.8	569.7	610.0
1969	203.9	587.9	615.9	209.4	590.1	618.2
1970	214.4	626.5	677.1	220.1	627.8	678.2
1971	228.3	710.3	776.0	234.5	711.2	776.6
1972	249.2	802.3	885.9	256.1	803.1	886.2
1973	262.9	855.5	985.0	270.2	856.5	985.2
1974	274.2	902.1	1 069.9	281.8	903.5	1 070.8
1975	287.1	1 016.2	1 170.2	295.3	1 017.8	1 173.3
1976	306.2	1 152.0	1 309.9	314.5	1 153.5	1 313.6
1977	330.9	1 270.3	1 470.4	340.0	1 273.0	1 476.2
1978	357.3	1 366.0	1 644.5	367.9	1 370.8	1 652.6
1979	381.8	1 473.7	1 808.7	393.2	1 479.0	1 815.2
1980	408.5	1 599.8	1 995.5	419.5	1 604.8	2 000.8
1981	436.7	1 755.4	2 254.5	447.0	1 760.3	2 259.0
1982	474.8	1 910.3	2 460.6	485.8	1 918.2	2 469.1
1983	521.4	2 126.5	2 697.4	533.3	2 137.0	2 708.5
1984	551.6	2 310.0	2 990.6	564.6	2 322.0	3 004.6
1985	619.8	2 495.7	3 208.1	633.3	2 507.7	3 221.6
1986	724.7	2 732.3	3 499.1	739.8	2 745.0	3 513.3
1987	750.2	2 831.5	3 686.5	765.4	2 843.4	3 698.7
1988	786.7	2 994.5	3 928.8	803.1	3 006.8	3 941.1
1989	792.9	3 158.5	4 077.1	810.6	3 171.5	4 089.5
1990	824.7	3 278.8	4 154.7	842.7	3 292.0	4 166.1
1991	897.1	3 379.7	4 210.3	915.6	3 393.4	4 222.8
1992	1 025.0	3 433.1	4 222.6	1 045.6	3 449.3	4 237.6
1993	1 129.7	3 484.3	4 285.6	1 153.3	3 504.3	4 304.5
1994	1 150.3	3 497.6	4 369.8	1 174.2	3 518.6	4 389.0
1995	1 126.8	3 640.6	4 636.3	1 152.1	3 663.8	4 658.8
1996	1 080.0	3 815.8	4 985.5	1 104.5	3 836.1	5 008.0
1997	1 072.2	4 031.6	5 460.9	1 096.9	4 052.8	5 489.2
1998	1 094.9	4 379.5	6 051.9	1 120.2	4 402.1	6 087.9
1999	1 123.1	4 641.1	6 551.5	1 148.0	4 667.5	6 597.1
2000	1 087.6	4 920.7	7 117.6	1 111.6	4 952.0	7 173.8
2001	1 182.1	5 429.8	8 035.4	1 208.3	5 464.3	8 105.8
2002	1 219.0	5 773.6	8 568.0	1 245.0	5 805.1	8 633.5
2003	1 304.1	6 059.4	8 872.3	1 332.0	6 091.7	8 927.8
2004	1 372.1	6 408.1	9 433.0	1 401.3	6 442.9	9 482.2
2005	1 368.5	6 664.8	10 154.0	1 396.5	6 702.3	10 201.4
2003						
January	1 225.8	5 803.0	8 588.1	1 224.9	5 792.3	8 602.0
February	1 237.6	5 843.2	8 628.7	1 224.9	5 819.2	8 635.5
March	1 238.2	5 861.3	8 648.8	1 244.5	5 881.2	8 694.4
April	1 251.8	5 901.7	8 686.0	1 259.0	5 938.2	8 714.2
May	1 270.4	5 958.7	8 741.9	1 266.0	5 937.6	8 728.4
June	1 279.2	5 998.3	8 791.6	1 284.1	5 994.4	8 792.3
July	1 290.0	6 048.8	8 888.7	1 287.3	6 039.0	8 850.5
August	1 294.6	6 097.4	8 918.2	1 291.6	6 097.5	8 902.7
September	1 295.7	6 076.7	8 906.5	1 285.7	6 068.3	8 871.7
October	1 297.0	6 064.4	8 896.8	1 288.4	6 050.5	8 852.1
November	1 296.5	6 058.0	8 880.3	1 293.3	6 074.4	8 894.6
December	1 304.1	6 059.4	8 872.3	1 332.0	6 091.7	8 927.8
2004						
January	1 305.0	6 067.6	8 930.2	1 301.5	6 050.0	8 930.7
February	1 319.7	6 112.6	9 000.3	1 306.4	6 081.7	8 993.9
March	1 329.4	6 153.8	9 080.7	1 337.7	6 161.4	9 108.2
April	1 337.1	6 195.9	9 149.6	1 343.0	6 231.3	9 178.3
May	1 336.2	6 262.1	9 243.8	1 333.3	6 245.4	9 236.2
June	1 340.3	6 270.1	9 275.7	1 347.4	6 269.6	9 281.4
July	1 343.3	6 278.0	9 282.7	1 338.6	6 275.8	9 257.1
August	1 354.1	6 300.3	9 314.4	1 352.3	6 295.7	9 299.9
September	1 359.7	6 329.4	9 351.8	1 348.9	6 327.0	9 333.8
October	1 360.7	6 353.3	9 359.4	1 351.1	6 347.7	9 329.1
November	1 374.2	6 389.1	9 395.1	1 370.8	6 398.8	9 396.0
December	1 372.1	6 408.1	9 433.0	1 401.3	6 442.9	9 482.2
2005						
January	1 365.8	6 422.4	9 487.2	1 361.3	6 401.7	9 479.3
February	1 369.1	6 443.9	9 531.6	1 354.9	6 403.9	9 511.8
March	1 372.6	6 463.7	9 565.3	1 381.7	6 466.5	9 584.7
April	1 363.3	6 468.1	9 620.9	1 369.2	6 511.0	9 660.5
May	1 370.3	6 479.2	9 665.0	1 368.3	6 457.9	9 654.6
June	1 374.2	6 506.0	9 725.3	1 382.1	6 508.9	9 734.3
July	1 369.3	6 527.7	9 762.4	1 363.9	6 530.8	9 745.7
August	1 376.8	6 558.8	9 864.6	1 375.6	6 554.4	9 852.8
September	1 372.4	6 588.6	9 950.8	1 361.0	6 585.9	9 938.7
October	1 374.3	6 619.0	10 032.0	1 363.8	6 612.6	10 005.7
November	1 375.1	6 638.2	10 078.5	1 373.1	6 651.5	10 077.2
December	1 368.5	6 664.8	10 154.0	1 396.5	6 702.3	10 201.4

Table 12-2. Selected Components of the Money Stock

(Billions of dollars, monthly data are averages of daily figures, seasonally adjusted, annual data are for December.)

Year and month	Currency	Demand deposits	Other checkable deposits	Repurchase agreements	Euro-dollars	Money market funds		Savings deposits		Small time deposits		Large time deposits	
						Retail	Institutional	At banks	At thrifts	At banks	At thrifts	At banks	At thrifts
1959	28.8	110.8	0.0	0.0	0.7	0.0	0.0	54.8	91.7	8.9	2.5	1.2	0.0
1960	28.7	111.6	0.0	0.0	0.8	0.0	0.0	58.3	100.8	9.7	2.8	2.0	0.0
1961	29.3	115.5	0.0	0.0	1.5	0.0	0.0	64.2	111.3	11.1	3.7	3.9	0.0
1962	30.3	117.1	0.0	0.0	1.6	0.0	0.0	71.3	123.4	15.5	4.6	7.0	0.0
1963	32.2	120.6	0.1	0.0	1.9	0.0	0.0	76.8	137.6	19.9	5.7	10.8	0.0
1964	33.9	125.8	0.1	0.0	2.4	0.0	0.0	82.9	152.4	22.4	6.8	15.2	0.0
1965	36.0	131.3	0.1	0.0	1.8	0.0	0.0	92.4	164.5	26.7	7.8	21.2	0.0
1966	38.0	133.4	0.1	0.0	2.2	0.0	0.0	89.9	163.3	38.7	16.3	23.1	0.0
1967	40.0	142.5	0.1	0.0	2.2	0.0	0.0	94.1	169.6	50.7	27.1	30.9	0.0
1968	43.0	153.6	0.1	0.0	2.9	0.0	0.0	96.1	172.8	63.5	37.1	37.4	0.0
1969	45.7	157.3	0.2		4.9	2.7	0.0	0.0	93.8	169.8	71.6	48.8	20.4	0.0
1970	48.6	164.7	0.1	3.0	2.4	0.0	0.0	98.6	162.3	79.3	71.9	44.4	0.7
1971	52.0	175.1	0.2	5.2	2.9	0.0	0.0	112.8	179.4	94.7	95.1	56.1	1.5
1972	56.2	191.6	0.2	6.6	3.8	0.0	0.0	124.8	196.6	108.2	123.5	70.8	2.5
1973	60.8	200.3	0.3	12.8	5.8	0.1	0.0	128.0	198.7	116.8	149.0	107.4	3.6
1974	67.0	205.1	0.4	14.5	8.5	1.4	0.2	136.8	201.8	123.1	164.8	139.3	5.4
1975	72.8	211.3	0.9	13.8	10.0	2.4	0.5	161.2	227.6	142.3	195.5	123.3	6.4
1976	79.5	221.5	2.7	24.0	15.2	1.8	0.6	201.8	251.4	155.5	235.2	110.3	7.8
1977	87.4	236.4	4.2	32.2	21.7	1.8	1.0	218.8	273.4	167.5	278.0	135.0	10.2
1978	0.0	249.5	8.5	44.4	35.1	5.8	3.5	216.5	265.4	185.1	335.8	179.1	16.5
1979	104.8	256.6	16.8	48.8	52.7	33.9	10.4	195.0	228.8	235.5	398.7	190.9	32.2
1980	115.3	261.2	28.1	58.1	61.4	62.5	16.0	185.7	214.5	286.2	442.3	215.2	45.0
1981	122.5	231.4	78.7	67.8	88.8	151.7	38.2	159.0	184.9	347.7	475.4	250.5	53.8
1982	132.5	234.1	104.1	71.8	104.2	184.5	48.8	190.1	210.0	379.9	471.0	261.9	63.7
1983	146.2	238.5	132.1	97.3	116.6	136.1	40.9	363.2	321.7	350.9	433.1	219.4	96.7
1984	156.1	243.4	147.1	107.3	108.9	164.9	62.3	389.3	315.4	387.9	500.9	255.1	147.1
1985	167.8	267.0	179.5	121.2	104.2	174.9	65.3	456.6	358.6	386.4	499.3	269.9	151.8
1986	180.4	302.9	235.2	145.8	115.7	208.4	86.2	533.5	407.4	369.4	489.0	268.6	150.4
1987	196.7	287.7	259.2	178.0	121.5	222.8	93.7	534.8	402.6	391.7	529.3	299.1	162.7
1988	212.0	287.1	280.6	196.5	131.7	244.3	93.8	542.4	383.9	451.2	585.9	337.8	174.5
1989	222.3	278.6	285.1	169.1	109.4	320.6	112.0	541.1	352.6	533.8	617.6	366.6	161.5
1990	246.5	276.8	293.7	151.5	103.3	357.7	139.6	581.4	341.6	610.7	562.7	360.5	121.1
1991	267.1	289.7	332.6	131.1	92.3	372.4	188.5	664.9	379.7	602.3	463.3	335.1	83.5
1992	292.2	340.0	384.6	141.5	79.5	352.8	212.8	754.2	433.1	508.1	360.0	288.4	67.3
1993	321.6	385.4	414.7	172.6	72.8	353.1	216.8	785.4	434.1	467.9	314.1	277.5	61.6
1994	354.0	383.6	404.2	196.3	86.3	380.9	210.8	752.7	397.3	502.5	313.8	314.1	64.8
1995	372.2	389.0	356.6	198.3	94.0	448.2	264.4	774.7	359.5	574.8	356.5	364.7	74.2
1996	394.1	401.6	275.5	210.3	114.6	516.0	324.2	905.6	367.3	593.3	353.6	443.3	77.8
1997	424.5	393.8	245.4	253.9	147.5	591.4	396.9	1 022.5	377.3	625.4	342.8	546.2	84.9
1998	459.8	377.0	249.6	293.2	150.2	727.4	545.1	1 188.0	417.1	626.2	325.8	595.6	88.0
1999	517.8	353.4	243.3	334.9	170.8	823.3	642.6	1 288.6	451.6	634.9	319.6	667.3	91.6
2000	531.2	309.9	238.2	362.3	195.2	910.5	796.6	1 424.1	453.8	699.8	345.0	734.3	102.5
2001	581.1	335.7	257.4	373.7	211.4	960.1	1 205.4	1 739.4	573.4	635.1	339.7	687.7	114.5
2002	626.2	306.0	279.1	473.4	230.7	883.3	1 256.1	2 060.9	717.9	590.1	302.4	698.2	117.5
2003	662.3	324.5	309.5	494.8	295.3	776.2	1 123.1	2 337.8	831.5	536.4	273.4	764.5	120.7
2004	697.3	340.2	327.1	492.6	379.1	699.5	1 073.9	2 632.0	887.5	545.1	271.8	909.3	161.5
2005	723.4	320.5	317.3	564.3	423.9	701.0	1 142.4	2 771.7	850.0	633.9	339.8	1 122.9	230.7
2004													
January	663.9	319.5	313.8	504.8	302.4	762.5	1 124.4	2 367.3	825.9	534.9	272.1	794.4	121.4
February	665.6	327.7	318.6	521.0	310.1	754.2	1 121.5	2 398.0	836.2	533.2	271.3	798.5	122.4
March	667.4	332.2	322.0	526.1	316.0	744.6	1 129.3	2 424.8	853.1	530.9	270.9	816.7	124.8
April	670.2	337.4	321.7	520.0	324.9	737.3	1 133.1	2 465.4	857.5	528.6	269.9	832.0	128.2
May	673.6	332.7	322.2	522.3	327.0	739.3	1 137.3	2 520.2	872.8	526.6	267.1	848.9	132.8
June	677.8	329.2	325.6	536.9	329.5	734.0	1 131.7	2 524.0	879.4	526.4	266.1	860.7	133.4
July	684.9	324.9	325.9	526.5	337.0	723.5	1 117.8	2 535.8	881.9	527.1	266.5	874.0	137.6
August	686.5	332.6	327.4	524.7	343.8	718.7	1 111.4	2 543.4	886.9	529.9	267.3	879.0	143.5
September	689.9	337.5	324.7	526.7	354.1	712.3	1 100.0	2 562.8	893.4	533.5	267.7	881.5	148.0
October	692.9	334.0	326.3	510.2	367.6	703.8	1 081.1	2 593.4	889.0	537.1	269.4	885.1	151.3
November	697.7	340.0	328.8	501.0	370.8	699.6	1 076.5	2 616.8	887.3	541.3	269.9	891.9	156.2
December	697.3	340.2	327.1	492.6	379.1	699.5	1 073.9	2 632.0	887.5	545.1	271.8	909.3	161.5
2005													
January	699.0	335.4	323.8	473.1	390.4	699.5	1 067.9	2 640.1	887.6	552.4	276.7	957.1	167.7
February	700.8	338.5	322.2	489.3	393.2	695.7	1 059.6	2 654.1	883.7	559.9	281.4	965.7	173.6
March	702.9	339.1	323.2	487.8	402.0	693.8	1 054.9	2 664.9	878.1	569.9	284.5	971.5	179.5
April	703.9	328.2	323.6	483.8	402.7	695.5	1 063.0	2 673.5	867.4	577.7	290.7	1 006.8	188.7
May	705.7	332.4	324.7	504.7	404.0	691.5	1 063.4	2 662.9	870.2	587.6	296.7	1 015.8	192.7
June	708.4	338.7	319.7	504.3	399.7	690.0	1 074.8	2 673.6	868.7	597.5	302.0	1 037.2	198.6
July	710.0	334.2	317.7	517.6	406.0	690.4	1 084.5	2 691.2	862.4	608.2	306.2	1 020.9	202.7
August	712.8	336.7	320.0	525.1	415.6	688.9	1 097.1	2 697.9	865.2	617.7	312.4	1 056.6	209.3
September	716.1	329.2	319.7	534.2	419.5	693.6	1 113.3	2 719.5	859.3	626.4	317.4	1 076.6	216.0
October	717.4	330.7	318.8	545.4	419.0	697.9	1 125.3	2 735.0	858.2	622.9	330.7	1 098.1	223.9
November	720.1	328.4	319.3	555.3	422.6	699.8	1 126.7	2 744.2	855.1	627.2	336.8	1 102.0	229.9
December	723.4	320.5	317.3	564.3	423.9	701.0	1 142.4	2 771.7	850.0	633.9	339.8	1 122.9	230.7

Table 12-3. Aggregate Reserves of Depository Institutions and Monetary Base

(Millions of dollars, monthly data are averages of daily figures, adjusted for seasonality and changes in reserve requirements, annual data are for December.)

Year and month	Reserves				Monetary base
	Total	Nonborrowed	Nonborrowed plus extended credit [1]	Required	
1959	11 109	10 168	10 168	10 603	40 880
1960	11 247	11 172	11 172	10 503	40 977
1961	11 499	11 366	11 366	10 915	41 853
1962	11 604	11 344	11 344	11 033	42 957
1963	11 730	11 397	11 397	11 239	45 003
1964	12 011	11 747	11 747	11 605	47 161
1965	12 316	11 872	11 872	11 892	49 620
1966	12 223	11 690	11 690	11 884	51 565
1967	13 180	12 952	12 952	12 805	54 579
1968	13 767	13 021	13 021	13 341	58 357
1969	14 168	13 049	13 049	13 882	61 569
1970	14 558	14 225	14 225	14 309	65 013
1971	15 230	15 104	15 104	15 049	69 108
1972	16 645	15 595	15 595	16 361	75 167
1973	17 021	15 723	15 723	16 717	81 073
1974	17 550	16 823	16 970	17 292	87 535
1975	17 822	17 692	17 704	17 556	93 887
1976	18 388	18 335	18 335	18 115	101 515
1977	18 990	18 420	18 420	18 800	110 324
1978	19 753	18 885	18 885	19 521	120 445
1979	20 720	19 248	19 248	20 279	131 143
1980	22 015	20 325	20 328	21 501	142 004
1981	22 443	21 807	21 956	22 124	149 021
1982	23 600	22 966	23 152	23 100	160 127
1983	25 367	24 593	24 595	24 806	175 467
1984	26 913	23 727	26 331	26 078	187 238
1985	31 569	30 250	30 749	30 505	203 562
1986	38 840	38 014	38 317	37 667	223 425
1987	38 913	38 135	38 618	37 893	239 837
1988	40 453	38 738	39 982	39 392	256 892
1989	40 486	40 221	40 241	39 545	267 755
1990	41 766	41 440	41 463	40 101	293 287
1991	45 515	45 323	45 324	44 526	317 557
1992	54 421	54 297	54 298	53 267	350 919
1993	60 567	60 485	60 485	59 497	386 594
1994	59 454	59 245	59 245	58 295	418 325
1995	56 483	56 226	56 226	55 193	434 585
1996	50 183	50 028	50 028	48 766	452 081
1997	46 873	46 549	46 549	45 189	479 946
1998	45 129	45 012	45 012	43 615	513 892
1999	41 958	41 638	41 638	40 661	593 938
2000	38 674	38 464	38 464	37 246	584 945
2001	41 390	41 323	41 323	39 739	635 480
2002	40 359	40 279	40 279	38 350	681 462
2003	42 699	42 654	...	41 657	720 128
2004	46 625	46 562	...	44 716	758 988
2005	45 312	45 143	...	43 403	787 091
2004					
January	42 776	42 670	...	41 884	721 675
February	42 893	42 851	...	41 697	723 800
March	44 658	44 607	...	42 851	726 638
April	45 723	45 638	...	43 916	730 530
May	45 664	45 552	...	43 977	734 347
June	46 014	45 834	...	44 081	738 914
July	46 103	45 859	...	44 384	746 118
August	45 513	45 262	...	43 930	747 691
September	46 331	45 996	...	44 676	751 981
October	46 337	46 158	...	44 581	754 674
November	46 258	46 075	...	44 475	759 101
December	46 625	46 562	...	44 716	758 988
2005					
January	47 170	47 108	...	45 431	760 418
February	45 890	45 848	...	44 396	763 316
March	46 627	46 577	...	44 847	765 822
April	46 290	46 158	...	44 619	766 849
May	45 805	45 665	...	44 273	768 301
June	46 277	46 028	...	44 503	771 108
July	46 235	45 810	...	44 493	773 167
August	45 232	44 869	...	43 618	775 426
September	46 194	45 862	...	44 159	778 753
October	45 488	45 205	...	43 592	780 785
November	45 423	45 297	...	43 635	784 153
December	45 312	45 143	...	43 403	787 091

[1] Extended credit program discontinued January 9, 2003. See notes and definitions for more information.
... = Not available.

Table 12-4. Commercial Banks: Bank Credit and Selected Liabilities

(All commercial banks in the United States, billions of dollars, seasonally adjusted, annual data are for December.)

Year and month	Bank credit Total	Securities in bank credit Total	U.S. Treasury and agency securities	Other securities	Loans and leases in bank credit Total	Commercial and industrial	Real estate Total	Revolving home equity	Other real estate
1950	120.4	72.2	65.1	7.1	48.2	17.6	12.9	...	...
1951	126.5	72.4	64.5	8.0	54.1	21.3	14.1	...	...
1952	134.1	74.3	66.3	7.9	59.8	23.6	15.0	...	...
1953	139.7	77.0	67.7	9.4	62.7	23.6	16.1	...	...
1954	150.8	85.8	74.9	10.8	65.0	22.9	17.6	...	...
1955	152.2	76.5	65.6	10.9	75.7	27.2	19.9	...	...
1956	158.0	73.2	62.1	11.1	84.9	33.0	21.7	...	...
1957	162.7	73.5	61.0	12.4	89.2	34.7	22.3	...	...
1958	184.1	85.9	70.5	15.4	98.2	35.4	25.1	...	...
1959	189.5	77.4	61.9	15.5	112.1	39.5	28.1	...	...
1960	197.6	79.5	63.9	15.6	118.1	42.4	28.7	...	...
1961	213.1	88.2	70.4	17.9	124.8	44.1	30.2	...	...
1962	231.0	92.2	70.7	21.5	138.8	47.7	34.0	...	...
1963	250.7	92.6	67.4	25.2	158.1	52.5	38.9	...	...
1964	270.4	94.7	66.7	28.1	175.6	58.7	43.5	...	...
1965	297.1	96.1	64.3	31.9	201.0	69.5	48.9	...	...
1966	318.6	97.2	61.0	36.2	221.4	79.3	53.8	...	...
1967	350.5	111.4	70.7	40.6	239.2	86.5	58.2	...	...
1968	390.5	121.9	73.8	48.1	268.6	96.5	64.8	...	...
1969	401.6	112.4	64.2	48.2	289.2	106.9	69.9	...	...
1970	434.4	129.7	73.4	56.3	304.6	111.6	72.9	...	...
1971	485.2	147.5	79.8	67.7	337.6	118.0	81.7	...	...
1972	555.3	160.6	85.4	75.2	394.7	133.6	98.8	...	...
1973	638.6	168.4	89.7	78.7	470.1	162.8	119.4	0.0	119.4
1974	701.7	173.8	87.9	85.9	527.9	193.0	132.5	0.0	132.5
1975	732.9	206.7	117.9	88.9	526.2	184.3	137.2	0.0	137.2
1976	790.7	228.6	137.3	91.3	562.1	186.3	151.3	0.0	151.3
1977	876.0	236.3	137.4	98.9	639.7	205.8	178.0	0.0	178.0
1978	989.4	242.2	138.4	103.8	747.2	239.0	213.5	0.0	213.5
1979	1 111.4	260.7	147.2	113.4	850.7	282.2	245.0	0.0	245.0
1980	1 207.1	296.8	173.2	123.6	910.3	314.5	265.7	0.0	265.7
1981	1 302.7	311.1	181.8	129.3	991.6	353.3	287.5	0.0	287.5
1982	1 412.3	338.6	204.7	133.9	1 073.7	396.4	303.8	0.0	303.8
1983	1 566.7	403.8	263.4	140.4	1 163.0	419.1	334.8	0.0	334.8
1984	1 733.4	406.6	262.9	143.7	1 326.9	479.4	380.8	0.0	380.8
1985	1 922.2	455.9	273.8	182.2	1 466.3	506.5	431.0	0.0	431.0
1986	2 106.6	510.0	312.8	197.2	1 596.5	544.0	499.9	0.0	499.9
1987	2 255.3	535.0	338.9	196.1	1 720.2	575.0	595.7	32.2	563.5
1988	2 433.8	562.1	366.7	195.4	1 871.7	612.0	676.6	42.6	634.0
1989	2 602.6	585.0	400.3	184.7	2 017.6	642.5	769.4	53.5	715.9
1990	2 749.1	634.9	456.5	178.4	2 114.2	644.8	856.7	66.4	790.3
1991	2 855.7	747.5	567.8	179.8	2 108.1	622.2	882.9	74.3	808.6
1992	2 952.8	842.1	665.7	176.4	2 110.7	597.9	905.9	78.5	827.4
1993	3 110.6	915.9	731.6	184.2	2 194.8	588.7	946.8	78.1	868.7
1994	3 315.5	939.9	722.3	217.7	2 375.5	648.2	1 010.3	80.5	929.8
1995	3 598.3	984.2	701.8	282.4	2 614.0	721.7	1 089.0	84.5	1 004.5
1996	3 755.2	984.9	703.1	281.9	2 770.3	782.0	1 141.5	90.9	1 050.6
1997	4 099.4	1 100.3	756.5	343.8	2 999.1	851.9	1 243.8	105.0	1 138.8
1998	4 534.5	1 239.6	798.5	441.1	3 294.9	945.5	1 334.1	103.9	1 230.2
1999	4 766.3	1 285.7	816.4	469.2	3 480.6	997.3	1 472.6	101.5	1 371.1
2000	5 222.1	1 351.4	793.6	557.8	3 870.7	1 086.3	1 652.7	130.0	1 522.7
2001	5 423.9	1 490.3	850.2	640.1	3 933.6	1 025.2	1 779.9	155.7	1 624.2
2002	5 891.2	1 724.5	1 030.7	693.8	4 166.6	962.0	2 023.1	213.5	1 809.6
2003	6 258.6	1 851.7	1 105.9	745.8	4 406.9	902.5	2 216.9	280.7	1 936.1
2004	6 798.4	1 939.6	1 151.9	787.7	4 858.8	927.6	2 547.6	399.7	2 148.0
2005	7 501.6	2 052.1	1 140.5	911.6	5 449.5	1 043.8	2 910.1	446.4	2 463.7
2004									
January	6 325.5	1 860.2	1 108.0	752.2	4 465.4	898.8	2 240.7	291.2	1 949.5
February	6 441.2	1 930.5	1 168.9	761.6	4 510.7	897.1	2 264.9	297.5	1 967.4
March	6 517.6	1 978.3	1 203.8	774.5	4 539.3	888.9	2 305.7	308.0	1 997.7
April	6 535.7	1 950.8	1 199.9	750.9	4 585.0	883.4	2 364.0	317.8	2 046.3
May	6 547.0	1 927.1	1 188.0	739.1	4 619.9	883.4	2 400.4	327.8	2 072.7
June	6 588.7	1 932.2	1 189.4	742.8	4 656.4	887.7	2 414.3	337.9	2 076.4
July	6 605.8	1 910.0	1 181.9	728.1	4 695.8	894.8	2 424.0	347.8	2 076.2
August	6 637.3	1 917.9	1 183.4	734.5	4 719.4	903.2	2 441.8	358.9	2 082.9
September	6 707.1	1 926.5	1 177.8	748.7	4 780.6	907.5	2 467.7	370.1	2 097.5
October	6 721.3	1 920.6	1 149.4	771.2	4 800.6	909.3	2 500.4	384.1	2 116.3
November	6 762.3	1 922.1	1 144.4	777.7	4 840.2	917.9	2 525.6	394.0	2 131.7
December	6 798.4	1 939.6	1 151.9	787.7	4 858.8	927.6	2 547.6	399.7	2 148.0
2005									
January	6 892.9	1 995.9	1 183.9	812.0	4 897.0	939.9	2 570.8	407.0	2 163.8
February	6 993.5	2 038.8	1 215.3	823.4	4 954.7	949.8	2 600.0	409.7	2 190.3
March	7 080.8	2 055.6	1 217.2	838.5	5 025.1	960.1	2 656.4	418.2	2 238.2
April	7 106.1	2 041.2	1 193.9	847.3	5 064.9	972.0	2 684.7	422.9	2 261.8
May	7 158.7	2 066.9	1 198.5	868.4	5 091.8	983.1	2 691.3	426.8	2 264.5
June	7 215.3	2 051.5	1 172.6	878.9	5 163.8	988.2	2 734.9	431.4	2 303.5
July	7 281.1	2 062.9	1 178.6	884.3	5 218.2	1 002.6	2 788.7	438.5	2 350.2
August	7 361.6	2 069.0	1 175.3	893.6	5 292.7	1 011.3	2 825.4	442.0	2 383.4
September	7 410.1	2 078.1	1 167.4	910.7	5 332.0	1 016.5	2 841.8	443.0	2 398.8
October	7 429.3	2 072.8	1 161.9	910.9	5 356.5	1 026.2	2 866.5	443.1	2 423.5
November	7 449.9	2 060.1	1 144.3	915.7	5 389.9	1 033.4	2 882.7	445.0	2 437.8
December	7 501.6	2 052.1	1 140.5	911.6	5 449.5	1 043.8	2 910.1	446.4	2 463.7

. . . = Not available.

Table 12-4. Commercial Banks: Bank Credit and Selected Liabilities—Continued

(All commercial banks in the United States, billions of dollars, seasonally adjusted, annual data are for December.)

Year and month	Bank credit—Continued				Selected liabilities		
	Loans and leases in bank credit—Continued					Borrowings	
	Consumer	Security	Other loans and leases	Deposits	Total	From banks in the United States	From others
1950	10.2	3.1	4.3	. . .	. . .	. . .	. . .
1951	10.7	2.7	5.2	. . .	. . .	. . .	. . .
1952	12.7	3.2	5.3	. . .	. . .	. . .	. . .
1953	14.7	3.6	4.8	. . .	. . .	. . .	. . .
1954	14.9	4.4	5.1	. . .	. . .	. . .	. . .
1955	17.3	5.1	6.1	. . .	. . .	. . .	. . .
1956	19.1	4.8	6.2	. . .	. . .	. . .	. . .
1957	20.0	4.6	7.6	. . .	. . .	. . .	. . .
1958	20.4	4.7	12.7	. . .	. . .	. . .	. . .
1959	24.1	5.0	15.4	. . .	. . .	. . .	. . .
1960	26.3	5.2	15.6	. . .	. . .	. . .	. . .
1961	27.6	6.1	16.8	. . .	. . .	. . .	. . .
1962	30.3	6.6	20.2	. . .	. . .	. . .	. . .
1963	34.2	7.9	24.6	. . .	. . .	. . .	. . .
1964	39.5	8.3	25.7	. . .	. . .	. . .	. . .
1965	45.0	8.0	29.7	. . .	. . .	. . .	. . .
1966	47.7	8.3	32.4	. . .	. . .	. . .	. . .
1967	51.2	9.6	33.8	. . .	. . .	. . .	. . .
1968	57.7	10.5	39.2	. . .	. . .	. . .	. . .
1969	62.6	10.0	39.8	. . .	. . .	. . .	. . .
1970	65.3	10.4	44.5	. . .	. . .	. . .	. . .
1971	73.3	10.9	53.9	. . .	. . .	. . .	. . .
1972	85.4	14.4	62.5	. . .	. . .	. . .	. . .
1973	98.3	11.2	78.4	651.6	70.5	44.1	26.4
1974	102.1	10.6	89.6	718.9	76.3	47.8	28.6
1975	104.6	12.7	87.5	759.3	72.1	45.1	27.0
1976	115.9	17.7	91.0	815.5	95.5	56.3	39.2
1977	138.1	20.7	97.2	899.4	111.7	61.8	49.9
1978	164.6	19.1	110.9	996.7	138.4	72.6	65.8
1979	184.5	17.4	121.6	1 069.3	176.6	97.4	79.2
1980	179.2	17.2	133.6	1 181.6	212.3	118.1	94.2
1981	182.7	20.2	148.0	1 247.4	256.0	142.3	113.7
1982	188.2	23.6	161.7	1 365.5	282.2	153.9	128.3
1983	213.2	26.5	169.4	1 478.8	282.8	149.1	133.7
1984	253.6	34.1	179.0	1 607.0	316.9	165.8	151.1
1985	294.5	42.9	191.4	1 752.1	372.6	192.4	180.1
1986	314.5	38.6	199.5	1 911.2	410.2	213.3	196.9
1987	327.7	34.8	187.0	1 971.7	427.2	222.2	204.9
1988	354.9	40.3	187.9	2 111.3	489.3	250.2	239.1
1989	375.3	40.9	189.4	2 236.0	550.7	280.9	269.8
1990	380.8	44.4	187.5	2 336.4	574.8	294.8	280.0
1991	363.8	53.9	185.3	2 462.4	496.6	221.2	275.4
1992	356.1	63.4	187.3	2 494.0	499.1	212.1	287.1
1993	387.4	86.4	185.5	2 528.3	537.1	213.5	323.6
1994	447.9	75.8	193.2	2 530.3	624.4	257.1	367.3
1995	491.1	83.2	228.9	2 665.0	700.4	289.8	410.6
1996	512.2	75.3	259.4	2 867.4	734.1	302.4	431.7
1997	502.5	94.4	306.6	3 123.4	861.3	311.9	549.5
1998	496.9	145.3	373.1	3 340.6	1 028.7	325.5	703.2
1999	490.8	149.8	370.1	3 546.7	1 133.4	352.4	781.0
2000	539.9	177.3	414.4	3 865.1	1 248.1	383.7	864.4
2001	557.1	146.0	425.4	4 239.6	1 255.8	409.0	846.8
2002	587.6	190.2	403.6	4 509.5	1 413.4	423.7	989.7
2003	644.6	217.7	425.3	4 768.2	1 475.1	388.4	1 086.7
2004	696.7	215.8	471.1	5 329.1	1 575.4	400.0	1 175.4
2005	707.5	263.9	524.2	5 766.5	1 733.4	366.3	1 367.1
2004							
January	653.2	236.6	436.0	4 814.4	1 519.5	388.7	1 130.8
February	654.5	246.3	447.9	4 842.4	1 583.1	419.4	1 163.7
March	657.8	246.2	440.6	4 928.6	1 551.5	398.2	1 153.3
April	657.3	240.7	439.5	4 981.7	1 579.4	431.7	1 147.7
May	659.5	235.2	441.4	5 055.6	1 552.7	424.3	1 128.4
June	662.1	248.9	443.5	5 115.1	1 586.4	433.3	1 153.2
July	691.1	238.1	447.8	5 155.3	1 603.6	459.5	1 144.2
August	691.1	232.1	451.3	5 174.1	1 588.4	446.7	1 141.6
September	693.5	247.5	464.4	5 201.5	1 611.6	458.9	1 152.7
October	690.8	241.6	458.6	5 234.3	1 597.6	441.9	1 155.7
November	687.2	236.8	472.7	5 288.8	1 589.9	425.5	1 164.4
December	696.7	215.8	471.1	5 329.1	1 575.4	400.0	1 175.4
2005							
January	704.3	200.5	481.5	5 377.7	1 551.3	365.0	1 186.2
February	701.0	220.5	483.4	5 389.6	1 596.0	380.1	1 215.9
March	707.6	226.2	474.9	5 448.9	1 618.6	371.3	1 247.3
April	709.3	223.9	475.0	5 497.8	1 620.4	380.2	1 240.1
May	703.9	237.1	476.4	5 510.9	1 641.1	368.5	1 272.5
June	706.6	248.4	485.7	5 553.0	1 636.8	367.6	1 269.2
July	710.4	232.5	484.0	5 582.9	1 633.1	348.5	1 284.7
August	716.8	245.4	493.8	5 647.8	1 678.5	353.1	1 325.4
September	720.2	246.7	506.7	5 681.1	1 682.0	357.5	1 324.5
October	710.4	242.2	511.1	5 705.2	1 678.0	351.5	1 326.5
November	711.9	248.0	513.8	5 733.4	1 709.4	368.5	1 340.9
December	707.5	263.9	524.2	5 766.5	1 733.4	366.3	1 367.1

. . . = Not available.

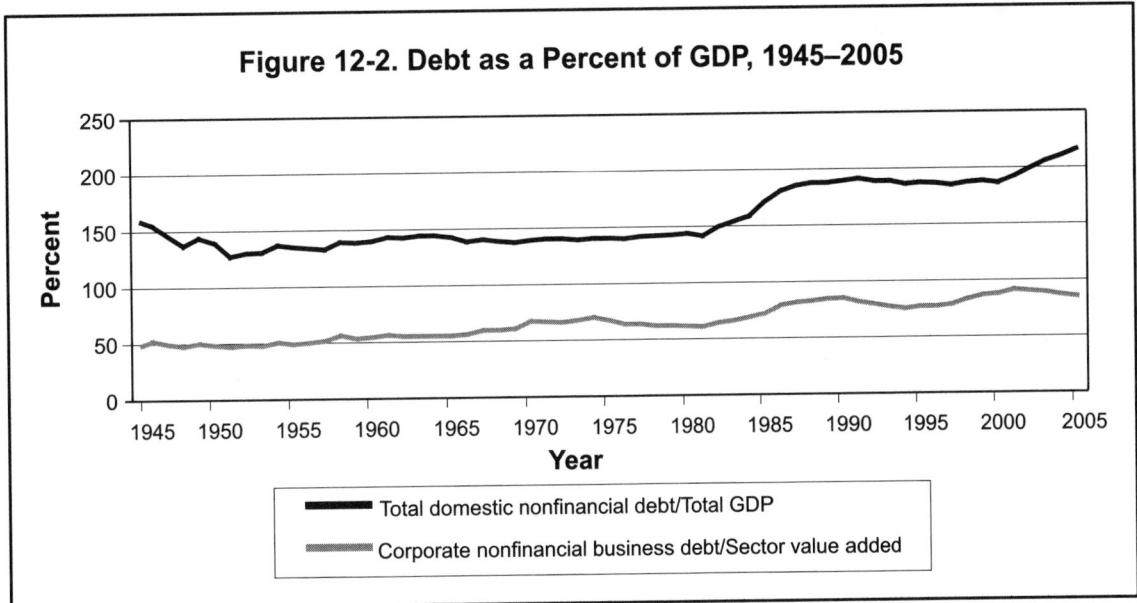

Figure 12-2. Debt as a Percent of GDP, 1945–2005

- After a pause during the 1990s, the ratio of the total debt owed by all domestic nonfinancial sectors at the end of the year to the year's gross domestic product (GDP) rose in each year of the new century to successive new peacetime records. Over the last five years, households, state and local governments, and the federal government all increased their debt by more than the growth in the value of GDP. (Tables 12-5 and 1-1)

- Household debt was the fastest-growing sector. Household debt can also be assessed relative to aggregate personal disposable income; it reached a level higher than a year's aggregate disposable personal income (DPI) in 2001 and continued to climb during the subsequent three years. (Tables 12-5 and 4-1)

- The debt of nonfinancial business grew no faster than aggregate GDP. Debt of corporate nonfinancial business can also be compared with its own contribution to GDP (value added), as seen in the lower line in Figure 12-2. This ratio reached a postwar high in 2001 but has declined each year since then. (Tables 12-5 and 1-13)

Table 12-5. Credit Market Debt Outstanding, by Borrower and Lender

(Billions of dollars, except as noted; end of period; not seasonally adjusted.)

Year and quarter	Total	Domestic financial sectors			Domestic nonfinancial sectors							Nonfinancial business		
					Total		Federal government			Households			Corporate	
		Total	Federal govern-ment-related	Private	Billions of dollars	Percent of GDP	Total	Treasury securities	Budget agency securities and mortgages	Billions of dollars	Percent of DPI	Total	Total	Percent of sector value added
1945	355.0	1.9	0.9	1.0	348.1	156.0	251.5	251.2	0.3	28.0	18.4	56.0	44.6	46.7
1946	350.8	3.0	1.2	1.8	339.8	152.9	228.0	227.9	0.1	35.2	21.8	63.9	49.8	50.1
1947	367.7	3.8	1.3	2.5	351.6	144.0	220.8	220.7	0.1	43.9	25.6	72.6	56.6	46.9
1948	382.2	5.3	1.6	3.7	363.2	134.9	215.1	214.2	0.9	52.4	27.5	80.0	62.7	45.3
1949	397.5	6.1	1.4	4.7	377.5	141.2	217.7	216.7	1.0	60.2	31.6	83.0	64.2	47.7
1950	425.3	8.5	1.8	6.7	402.8	137.1	216.5	216.1	0.4	72.9	34.7	92.1	70.3	45.9
1951	449.2	9.6	2.1	7.5	425.0	125.3	216.1	215.8	0.2	81.5	35.3	103.9	78.7	44.8
1952	484.9	11.1	2.2	8.9	458.7	128.0	221.4	220.8	0.6	93.9	38.6	112.6	84.9	46.3
1953	516.9	12.7	2.2	10.5	488.0	128.6	228.4	226.2	2.3	106.1	41.0	117.7	89.1	45.5
1954	542.0	12.3	2.1	10.1	513.2	134.9	230.8	228.5	2.3	117.4	44.4	123.9	92.6	48.0
1955	582.3	15.3	3.2	12.1	550.5	132.7	230.0	228.4	1.6	138.0	48.7	136.4	101.2	46.5
1956	611.8	17.9	4.0	13.9	576.5	131.8	224.1	222.8	1.4	152.9	50.5	149.1	110.8	47.6
1957	643.0	20.8	5.1	15.7	603.5	130.9	221.9	220.1	1.8	165.3	51.7	161.3	120.4	49.5
1958	682.0	21.0	5.2	15.8	640.2	137.0	231.1	229.0	2.1	176.1	53.3	172.3	127.6	53.8
1959	739.0	27.7	7.5	20.2	689.9	136.2	238.0	236.2	1.8	198.1	56.5	187.1	136.3	51.2
1960	780.5	32.5	8.1	24.4	724.7	137.7	236.0	234.0	1.9	215.6	59.0	201.0	145.2	52.5
1961	828.8	34.9	8.9	26.0	768.4	141.1	243.2	240.7	2.5	232.3	60.8	215.2	152.7	53.8
1962	888.4	39.4	10.5	28.9	821.4	140.3	250.0	246.8	3.3	254.3	62.8	233.3	163.1	52.6
1963	954.5	46.6	12.0	34.6	877.0	142.0	253.8	250.7	3.2	281.2	66.1	252.8	173.7	52.7
1964	1 028.8	53.0	12.7	40.3	940.9	141.8	259.9	255.9	4.0	310.3	67.1	275.0	187.5	52.7
1965	1 107.3	61.9	15.1	46.8	1 008.0	140.2	261.5	257.0	4.5	338.7	68.0	304.6	207.6	53.1
1966	1 187.8	72.9	20.3	52.5	1 075.5	136.5	265.1	259.3	5.8	361.2	67.2	339.1	232.1	54.1
1967	1 268.4	73.6	20.4	53.2	1 151.5	138.3	278.1	268.2	9.9	380.4	66.1	375.6	258.1	57.2
1968	1 373.4	84.0	24.4	59.6	1 243.3	136.6	290.6	277.6	13.0	412.8	66.1	413.8	285.1	57.3
1969	1 491.2	111.5	33.8	77.7	1 330.4	135.1	287.4	276.8	10.6	442.7	65.7	462.0	317.8	58.8
1970	1 600.0	127.8	43.6	84.1	1 420.2	136.8	299.5	289.9	9.6	458.7	62.3	511.7	360.5	64.6
1971	1 750.7	138.9	49.5	89.3	1 555.2	138.0	324.4	315.9	8.5	501.6	62.6	562.5	388.4	64.4
1972	1 935.1	162.8	57.9	104.8	1 711.2	138.2	339.4	330.1	9.3	559.3	64.4	631.8	425.9	63.6
1973	2 172.7	209.8	77.9	131.9	1 895.5	137.1	346.3	336.7	9.6	630.8	64.5	723.6	489.7	65.2
1974	2 409.5	258.3	98.6	159.7	2 069.9	138.0	358.2	348.8	9.4	685.7	64.0	817.8	546.2	67.4
1975	2 619.1	260.4	108.9	151.6	2 261.8	138.1	443.9	434.9	8.9	738.3	62.2	860.3	567.4	64.7
1976	2 904.9	283.9	123.1	160.8	2 505.3	137.3	513.1	503.7	9.3	822.3	63.1	932.1	608.7	61.5
1977	3 293.0	337.8	145.5	192.3	2 826.6	139.2	569.4	560.9	8.4	950.0	66.2	1 051.1	683.8	61.1
1978	3 779.4	412.5	182.6	229.9	3 211.2	139.9	621.9	614.9	7.0	1 109.1	69.0	1 184.7	757.6	59.5
1979	4 276.4	504.9	231.8	273.1	3 603.0	140.6	657.6	652.1	5.6	1 277.9	71.2	1 345.2	842.0	59.5
1980	4 725.1	578.1	276.6	301.5	3 953.5	141.7	735.0	730.0	5.0	1 398.3	69.6	1 475.8	907.9	59.1
1981	5 258.0	682.4	324.0	358.3	4 361.7	139.4	820.5	815.9	4.5	1 508.8	67.2	1 660.3	1 025.7	58.7
1982	5 769.6	778.1	388.9	389.2	4 783.4	147.0	981.8	978.1	3.7	1 578.1	65.2	1 809.7	1 115.7	61.8
1983	6 466.1	882.7	456.6	426.1	5 359.2	151.5	1 167.0	1 163.4	3.6	1 734.7	66.5	1 996.4	1 227.7	63.5
1984	7 431.5	1 052.4	531.2	521.2	6 146.2	156.3	1 364.2	1 360.8	3.4	1 945.7	66.8	2 322.7	1 435.9	66.2
1985	8 627.2	1 257.3	631.7	625.6	7 127.3	168.9	1 589.9	1 586.6	3.3	2 274.9	73.2	2 584.7	1 613.2	70.1
1986	9 816.1	1 593.6	810.3	783.3	7 970.6	178.6	1 805.9	1 802.2	3.6	2 532.4	77.1	2 880.2	1 838.2	77.0
1987	10 830.0	1 895.5	977.6	917.9	8 675.4	183.0	1 949.8	1 944.6	5.2	2 749.1	79.5	3 134.0	2 033.3	79.5
1988	11 871.2	2 145.8	1 098.4	1 047.4	9 455.7	185.3	2 104.9	2 082.3	22.6	3 035.7	81.0	3 422.1	2 234.2	80.6
1989	12 843.9	2 399.3	1 247.8	1 151.4	10 156.7	185.2	2 251.2	2 227.0	24.2	3 329.2	82.8	3 635.9	2 401.0	82.4
1990	13 771.3	2 613.6	1 418.4	1 195.2	10 839.4	186.8	2 498.1	2 465.8	32.4	3 594.6	83.9	3 759.2	2 530.5	83.2
1991	14 426.1	2 769.6	1 564.2	1 205.4	11 306.1	188.6	2 776.4	2 757.8	18.6	3 783.9	84.8	3 667.2	2 473.9	79.8
1992	15 218.2	3 024.1	1 720.4	1 303.6	11 821.7	186.5	3 080.3	3 061.6	18.8	3 983.3	83.8	3 663.0	2 499.3	77.2
1993	16 189.4	3 321.0	1 885.7	1 435.3	12 400.2	186.3	3 336.5	3 309.9	26.6	4 217.0	85.9	3 693.6	2 548.0	75.0
1994	17 209.5	3 791.1	2 173.4	1 617.7	12 975.3	183.5	3 492.3	3 465.6	26.7	4 536.0	88.0	3 839.7	2 681.3	73.1
1995	18 457.8	4 233.2	2 377.7	1 855.4	13 657.1	184.6	3 636.7	3 608.5	28.2	4 858.2	89.8	4 115.4	2 908.1	75.0
1996	19 774.1	4 746.9	2 609.2	2 137.8	14 369.9	183.8	3 781.7	3 755.1	26.6	5 187.1	91.2	4 369.7	3 090.2	75.2
1997	21 154.1	5 298.9	2 822.8	2 476.1	15 131.5	182.2	3 804.8	3 778.3	26.5	5 492.0	91.7	4 758.9	3 378.5	76.8
1998	23 266.7	6 323.8	3 294.4	3 029.4	16 159.7	184.7	3 752.2	3 723.7	28.5	5 918.0	92.5	5 345.8	3 775.4	81.1
1999	25 318.7	7 339.6	3 887.7	3 451.8	17 230.9	185.9	3 681.0	3 652.7	28.3	6 414.7	95.8	5 952.9	4 183.1	84.5
2000	27 028.0	8 121.7	4 319.7	3 802.0	18 091.8	184.3	3 385.1	3 357.8	27.3	7 006.0	97.4	6 503.0	4 525.0	85.8
2001	29 266.4	9 185.7	4 962.3	4 223.3	19 217.9	189.8	3 379.5	3 352.7	26.8	7 661.1	102.3	6 873.9	4 723.1	89.2
2002	31 724.1	10 052.6	5 509.0	4 543.6	20 599.2	196.8	3 637.0	3 609.8	27.3	8 469.5	108.2	7 045.3	4 738.6	88.2
2003	34 611.6	11 047.3	6 083.3	4 964.0	22 319.8	203.6	4 033.1	4 008.2	24.9	9 465.7	116.0	7 253.5	4 842.6	87.1
2004	37 695.1	11 938.9	6 201.3	5 737.5	24 331.5	207.7	4 395.0	4 370.7	24.3	10 574.0	121.8	7 679.7	5 017.8	84.6
2005	41 032.1	12 921.5	6 251.9	6 669.5	26 644.6	213.9	4 701.9	4 678.0	23.8	11 815.4	130.8	8 273.1	5 293.0	83.1
2003														
1st quarter	32 262.4	10 285.3	5 633.5	4 651.8	20 902.0	195.2	3 700.6	3 673.7	26.9	8 631.4	108.2	7 095.6	4 766.7	87.6
2nd quarter	33 063.0	10 514.0	5 744.1	4 769.9	21 434.3	197.9	3 806.9	3 779.9	27.0	8 926.6	110.4	7 171.4	4 815.8	87.5
3rd quarter	33 707.7	10 766.6	5 941.2	4 825.3	21 863.1	197.2	3 914.5	3 887.5	27.0	9 213.5	111.5	7 197.5	4 813.3	85.9
4th quarter	34 611.6	11 047.3	6 083.3	4 964.0	22 319.8	198.9	4 033.1	4 008.2	24.9	9 465.7	113.7	7 253.5	4 842.6	85.2
2004														
1st quarter	35 243.5	11 204.8	6 104.4	5 100.4	22 765.0	199.2	4 168.9	4 143.8	25.1	9 657.0	113.9	7 332.7	4 882.2	84.5
2nd quarter	35 899.9	11 428.1	6 170.7	5 257.4	23 203.1	199.2	4 209.6	4 185.4	24.2	9 938.1	115.5	7 420.6	4 905.8	83.4
3rd quarter	36 667.0	11 642.4	6 214.1	5 428.2	23 730.9	201.1	4 292.9	4 268.7	24.2	10 257.7	117.8	7 527.6	4 939.9	82.4
4th quarter	37 695.1	11 938.9	6 201.3	5 737.5	24 331.5	203.3	4 395.0	4 370.7	24.3	10 574.0	118.4	7 679.7	5 017.8	82.5
2005														
1st quarter	38 367.0	12 087.5	6 153.8	5 933.6	24 840.0	204.1	4 559.6	4 535.6	24.1	10 756.9	121.0	7 790.6	5 078.5	82.0
2nd quarter	39 172.8	12 375.3	6 221.7	6 221.1	25 335.6	205.2	4 516.8	4 493.1	23.7	11 088.1	123.6	7 955.0	5 150.9	81.4
3rd quarter	39 932.5	12 484.8	6 141.4	6 343.4	25 965.2	206.5	4 589.6	4 566.0	23.6	11 463.2	126.7	8 098.7	5 210.0	81.1
4th quarter	41 032.1	12 921.5	6 251.9	6 669.5	26 644.6	209.3	4 701.9	4 678.0	23.8	11 815.4	127.9	8 273.1	5 293.0	81.0

Table 12-5. Credit Market Debt Outstanding, by Borrower and Lender—Continued

(Billions of dollars, except as noted; end of period; not seasonally adjusted.)

Year and quarter	Nonfarm noncorporate	Farm	State and local governments	Foreign credit market debt held in United States	Total	Total	Federal government	Government-sponsored enterprises	Federally related mortgage pools	State and local governments	State and local retirement funds	Total, selected sectors	Monetary authority
1945	4.8	6.6	12.6	5.0	355.0	17.2	5.2	2.0	0.0	7.5	2.5	218.5	24.3
1946	7.2	7.0	12.7	8.0	350.8	20.0	8.3	2.1	0.0	6.8	2.8	219.0	23.5
1947	8.5	7.4	14.3	12.3	367.7	25.5	12.6	2.3	0.0	7.5	3.1	228.5	22.6
1948	9.2	8.1	15.7	13.7	382.2	28.3	13.9	2.7	0.0	8.2	3.5	235.7	23.5
1949	10.2	8.5	16.6	13.9	397.5	30.6	15.3	2.6	0.0	8.6	4.1	245.0	19.0
1950	12.3	9.5	21.2	14.0	425.3	33.2	16.0	3.1	0.0	9.4	4.7	262.3	20.7
1951	14.3	10.8	23.6	14.7	449.2	36.2	17.2	3.5	0.0	10.1	5.4	280.9	23.6
1952	16.1	11.6	30.8	15.1	484.9	40.6	18.8	3.6	0.1	11.7	6.4	303.8	24.1
1953	17.1	11.5	35.8	16.3	516.9	44.9	20.8	3.7	0.1	12.6	7.7	323.5	25.3
1954	18.9	12.3	41.1	16.6	542.0	47.3	20.5	4.0	0.1	13.5	9.2	347.0	25.0
1955	21.5	13.7	46.1	16.6	582.3	51.4	21.1	5.0	0.1	14.7	10.5	369.8	24.4
1956	23.7	14.6	50.4	17.4	611.8	55.6	21.8	6.0	0.1	15.9	11.7	391.3	24.7
1957	25.2	15.6	55.0	18.8	643.0	59.1	22.4	7.3	0.2	15.9	13.3	411.7	23.8
1958	27.7	17.0	60.7	20.8	682.0	62.8	23.9	7.7	0.2	16.1	15.0	445.4	26.3
1959	31.9	18.9	66.7	21.4	739.0	70.1	25.7	9.9	0.2	17.5	16.8	472.5	26.7
1960	35.8	20.0	72.2	23.2	780.5	76.0	26.7	11.1	0.2	19.1	18.9	504.1	27.0
1961	41.0	21.6	77.8	25.5	828.8	82.0	28.4	12.1	0.3	20.1	21.1	542.9	28.8
1962	46.4	23.9	83.8	27.5	888.4	89.4	30.4	13.7	0.4	21.7	23.2	589.2	30.5
1963	52.6	26.4	89.2	30.8	954.5	96.6	31.9	15.3	0.5	23.3	25.6	640.7	33.7
1964	58.5	29.0	95.6	35.0	1 028.8	104.7	34.7	16.0	0.6	25.0	28.3	698.1	36.6
1965	64.7	32.3	103.2	37.5	1 107.3	115.5	37.6	18.3	0.9	27.5	31.3	761.4	40.6
1966	71.5	35.5	110.0	39.5	1 187.8	129.8	42.7	23.3	1.3	27.5	34.9	807.8	43.7
1967	78.7	38.8	117.4	43.3	1 268.4	138.5	47.3	23.3	2.0	27.6	38.3	873.4	49.1
1968	87.1	41.6	126.1	46.1	1 373.4	154.4	52.3	26.5	2.5	31.4	41.6	947.0	53.0
1969	99.6	44.6	138.3	49.2	1 491.2	175.6	55.4	35.1	3.2	36.4	45.5	1 004.5	57.2
1970	103.6	47.6	150.3	52.1	1 600.0	191.5	58.2	43.9	4.8	35.1	49.6	1 078.8	62.2
1971	122.6	51.6	166.7	56.6	1 750.7	201.1	60.3	45.0	9.5	33.4	52.9	1 190.5	69.6
1972	149.0	56.8	180.7	61.1	1 935.1	223.0	62.2	49.0	14.4	40.1	57.4	1 336.4	71.2
1973	168.5	65.4	194.8	67.4	2 172.7	260.2	64.9	64.4	18.0	49.8	63.1	1 503.9	80.5
1974	198.4	73.3	208.2	81.2	2 409.5	304.7	72.2	85.3	21.5	56.4	69.4	1 641.7	85.3
1975	210.7	82.1	219.4	96.9	2 619.1	347.5	87.1	89.8	28.5	63.8	78.3	1 773.4	93.5
1976	231.2	92.2	237.8	115.7	2 904.9	398.6	93.7	94.5	40.7	82.0	87.7	1 968.8	100.3
1977	261.3	105.9	256.2	128.6	3 293.0	471.6	103.6	101.4	56.8	110.6	99.2	2 227.8	108.9
1978	304.8	122.2	295.6	155.7	3 779.4	582.6	120.6	128.1	70.4	147.5	116.0	2 526.1	117.4
1979	357.5	145.7	322.2	168.5	4 276.4	696.0	141.4	158.1	94.8	175.2	126.6	2 841.3	124.5
1980	406.4	161.5	344.4	193.4	4 725.1	804.5	165.5	184.5	114.0	193.4	147.2	3 108.5	128.0
1981	456.8	177.8	372.1	214.0	5 258.0	931.1	189.9	217.7	129.0	225.6	169.0	3 415.5	136.9
1982	509.5	184.5	413.8	208.1	5 769.6	1 058.9	205.8	233.7	178.5	250.1	190.7	3 658.8	144.5
1983	580.3	188.4	461.1	224.1	6 466.1	1 177.7	215.3	236.4	244.8	282.4	198.8	4 065.9	159.2
1984	698.8	187.9	513.6	232.8	7 431.5	1 339.7	232.6	265.9	289.0	319.0	233.2	4 624.5	167.6
1985	798.0	173.4	677.9	242.5	8 627.2	1 618.0	251.2	291.0	367.9	455.6	252.4	5 202.4	186.0
1986	886.0	156.0	752.1	251.9	9 816.1	1 920.0	258.0	307.6	531.6	525.8	297.1	5 917.1	205.5
1987	956.3	144.4	842.6	259.0	10 830.0	2 155.5	242.8	330.9	669.4	583.6	328.8	6 459.6	226.5
1988	1 054.2	133.7	893.0	269.8	11 871.2	2 295.9	217.4	364.2	745.3	618.6	350.5	7 000.3	240.6
1989	1 100.5	134.4	940.4	287.9	12 843.9	2 484.3	209.4	359.9	869.5	664.1	381.5	7 439.7	233.3
1990	1 093.3	135.4	987.4	318.2	13 771.3	2 742.2	243.1	373.9	1 019.9	703.4	402.0	7 801.9	241.4
1991	1 058.5	134.8	1 078.6	350.4	14 426.1	2 951.5	251.0	388.9	1 156.5	750.6	404.6	8 060.5	272.5
1992	1 028.4	135.3	1 095.1	372.4	15 218.2	3 163.2	239.0	458.1	1 272.0	752.3	441.8	8 439.7	300.4
1993	1 007.9	137.6	1 153.1	468.2	16 189.4	3 386.6	229.6	546.7	1 356.8	784.9	468.6	9 031.3	336.7
1994	1 015.9	142.4	1 107.3	443.1	17 209.5	3 563.5	214.6	667.9	1 472.4	729.9	478.7	9 506.9	368.2
1995	1 062.0	145.2	1 046.8	567.6	18 457.8	3 689.7	207.8	762.8	1 570.7	638.6	509.8	10 229.5	380.8
1996	1 130.7	148.8	1 031.5	657.2	19 774.1	3 895.3	206.6	833.8	1 711.7	604.8	538.4	10 825.4	393.1
1997	1 225.4	155.0	1 075.9	723.6	21 154.1	4 173.6	209.8	934.2	1 826.3	605.0	598.3	11 657.5	431.4
1998	1 405.3	165.2	1 143.7	783.2	23 266.7	4 868.2	221.6	1 251.5	2 019.0	714.6	661.5	12 825.6	452.5
1999	1 599.6	170.3	1 182.3	748.2	25 318.7	5 619.9	261.1	1 538.8	2 293.5	819.4	707.0	13 928.9	478.1
2000	1 796.5	181.6	1 197.7	814.5	27 028.0	6 195.2	272.7	1 794.4	2 493.2	891.5	743.2	14 801.7	511.8
2001	1 958.7	192.1	1 303.4	862.9	29 266.4	6 884.0	278.7	2 099.1	2 831.8	985.0	689.4	15 893.0	551.7
2002	2 106.7	200.0	1 447.3	1 072.3	31 724.1	7 480.1	288.2	2 323.2	3 158.6	1 071.4	638.7	17 120.4	629.4
2003	2 203.2	207.6	1 567.6	1 245.5	34 611.6	8 108.2	285.6	2 559.7	3 489.1	1 124.0	649.9	18 353.3	666.7
2004	2 442.8	219.1	1 682.8	1 424.8	37 695.1	8 299.8	288.8	2 605.9	3 542.2	1 185.8	677.1	19 996.7	717.8
2005	2 748.4	231.7	1 854.3	1 466.0	41 032.1	8 461.3	286.1	2 540.5	3 677.0	1 283.1	674.6	21 895.1	744.2
2003													
1st quarter	2 130.4	198.4	1 474.5	1 075.1	32 262.4	7 589.3	283.7	2 389.8	3 226.6	1 065.5	623.6	17 426.3	641.5
2nd quarter	2 152.7	202.9	1 529.5	1 114.7	33 063.0	7 672.9	281.7	2 419.4	3 289.1	1 085.9	596.8	17 897.7	652.1
3rd quarter	2 178.4	205.7	1 537.6	1 078.1	33 707.7	7 932.4	286.7	2 549.7	3 371.3	1 100.0	624.6	18 037.0	656.1
4th quarter	2 203.2	207.6	1 567.6	1 245.5	34 611.6	8 108.2	285.6	2 559.7	3 489.1	1 124.0	649.9	18 353.3	666.7
2004													
1st quarter	2 244.9	205.6	1 606.4	1 273.7	35 243.5	8 175.6	286.7	2 555.7	3 510.2	1 145.8	677.3	18 756.9	674.1
2nd quarter	2 302.2	212.5	1 634.8	1 268.7	35 899.9	8 257.8	283.7	2 603.8	3 523.5	1 152.6	694.1	19 117.5	687.4
3rd quarter	2 370.2	217.5	1 652.8	1 293.8	36 667.0	8 305.1	289.3	2 631.3	3 543.6	1 162.5	678.4	19 434.0	700.3
4th quarter	2 442.8	219.1	1 682.8	1 424.8	37 695.1	8 299.8	288.8	2 605.9	3 542.2	1 185.8	677.1	19 996.7	717.8
2005													
1st quarter	2 495.9	216.2	1 732.9	1 439.5	38 367.0	8 325.7	288.8	2 581.4	3 547.1	1 216.3	692.1	20 392.8	717.3
2nd quarter	2 580.0	224.1	1 775.6	1 462.0	39 192.8	8 345.2	284.6	2 571.2	3 567.9	1 235.3	686.2	20 834.5	724.7
3rd quarter	2 657.9	230.8	1 813.6	1 482.6	39 932.5	8 344.8	288.3	2 503.2	3 616.6	1 265.2	671.5	21 338.9	736.4
4th quarter	2 748.4	231.7	1 854.3	1 466.0	41 032.1	8 461.3	286.1	2 540.5	3 677.0	1 283.1	674.6	21 895.1	744.2

Table 12-5. Credit Market Debt Outstanding, by Borrower and Lender—Continued

(Billions of dollars, except as noted; end of period; not seasonally adjusted.)

Year and quarter	Commercial banks	Savings institutions	Credit unions	Life insurance companies	Property-casualty insurance companies	Private pension funds	Money market mutual funds	Mutual funds	Asset-backed security issuers	Finance companies	Households	Foreign holdings in United States	All other financial and nonfinancial sectors
1945	117.7	23.9	0.2	41.2	3.5	3.9	0.0	0.2	0.0	3.6	91.0	3.1	25.2
1946	111.6	26.7	0.2	44.4	4.1	4.1	0.0	0.3	0.0	4.1	90.3	2.4	19.1
1947	114.9	29.1	0.3	47.4	4.8	4.4	0.0	0.3	0.0	4.7	91.5	3.0	19.2
1948	113.2	31.2	0.5	50.9	5.7	4.7	0.0	0.3	0.0	5.7	93.7	3.1	21.4
1949	119.0	33.6	0.6	54.4	6.4	5.0	0.0	0.4	0.0	6.6	94.6	3.4	23.9
1950	125.6	36.7	0.7	57.9	7.2	5.3	0.0	0.4	0.0	7.8	96.2	4.8	28.8
1951	132.8	39.5	0.8	61.6	7.8	6.0	0.0	0.5	0.0	8.3	96.9	4.9	30.3
1952	141.4	44.1	1.1	65.9	8.7	7.2	0.0	0.5	0.0	10.8	104.6	5.1	30.7
1953	145.2	49.5	1.4	70.6	9.9	8.5	0.0	0.5	0.0	12.5	109.6	5.8	33.1
1954	154.9	55.5	1.6	75.4	10.8	9.8	0.0	0.7	0.0	13.2	109.5	6.4	31.9
1955	159.2	63.2	2.0	80.5	11.5	11.2	0.0	0.8	0.0	17.0	117.6	6.7	36.8
1956	164.8	70.2	2.4	85.6	11.9	12.7	0.0	1.1	0.0	18.0	124.9	7.3	32.7
1957	170.1	77.0	2.9	90.5	12.6	14.5	0.0	1.2	0.0	19.3	131.9	7.5	32.8
1958	185.0	85.5	3.1	95.5	13.4	16.2	0.0	1.5	0.0	19.0	132.7	7.5	33.6
1959	189.7	95.1	3.8	100.5	14.6	17.9	0.0	1.8	0.0	22.4	142.8	11.7	41.9
1960	199.7	104.2	4.5	105.6	15.5	19.7	0.0	2.0	0.0	25.9	150.9	12.6	36.8
1961	215.9	115.3	4.9	110.9	16.5	21.2	0.0	2.4	0.0	27.0	154.9	13.1	35.9
1962	235.2	128.3	5.6	116.9	18.0	22.9	0.0	2.6	0.0	29.2	158.2	14.8	36.7
1963	252.8	144.5	6.3	123.3	18.7	24.8	0.0	2.8	0.0	33.7	159.8	15.9	41.5
1964	276.1	160.2	7.2	130.3	19.5	27.2	0.0	3.2	0.0	37.9	166.2	16.9	42.9
1965	305.1	173.5	8.2	137.8	20.6	29.1	0.0	3.9	0.0	42.7	170.0	17.4	43.0
1966	323.1	181.7	9.4	145.9	22.0	31.9	0.0	5.1	0.0	44.9	190.0	17.3	42.9
1967	359.8	195.0	10.2	153.3	23.5	32.8	0.0	4.3	0.0	45.5	195.2	20.0	41.3
1968	398.7	208.9	11.7	160.7	25.4	33.8	0.0	4.1	0.0	50.6	203.5	22.6	45.9
1969	418.3	221.5	13.8	167.6	27.0	34.6	0.0	5.1	0.0	59.2	241.4	23.2	46.6
1970	455.3	236.8	15.2	174.6	30.9	36.6	0.0	5.7	0.0	61.5	242.4	35.0	52.3
1971	506.5	271.7	17.2	182.8	34.6	35.0	0.0	5.5	0.0	67.6	233.2	62.8	63.0
1972	575.7	314.5	20.1	192.5	38.3	40.5	0.0	6.0	0.0	77.5	230.0	73.2	72.5
1973	662.4	348.0	23.7	204.8	41.8	46.8	0.0	6.6	0.0	89.4	254.7	74.7	79.2
1974	737.5	369.7	26.4	217.7	46.4	55.6	0.8	7.4	0.0	94.8	299.5	79.8	83.8
1975	768.8	415.2	31.7	234.6	53.7	71.2	1.5	8.0	0.0	95.0	320.7	88.3	89.2
1976	833.2	477.5	38.4	258.3	66.2	77.8	2.1	8.4	0.0	106.6	331.3	99.4	106.9
1977	924.6	548.1	45.6	285.8	83.7	88.2	1.9	12.3	0.0	128.6	358.0	135.8	99.7
1978	1 052.6	614.4	52.0	318.9	100.2	98.7	5.1	12.5	0.0	154.2	405.6	162.3	102.7
1979	1 181.8	671.9	53.8	352.0	113.7	120.8	24.9	14.5	0.0	183.4	485.0	150.8	103.3
1980	1 289.9	722.7	53.0	385.1	123.5	151.4	42.0	17.1	0.0	195.8	519.6	171.1	121.3
1981	1 398.2	748.7	55.0	419.8	132.0	178.6	107.5	20.2	0.0	218.6	544.9	198.7	167.9
1982	1 482.9	756.7	57.3	463.2	137.0	225.4	137.6	25.4	0.0	228.8	610.8	242.0	199.3
1983	1 626.1	879.5	69.4	513.8	138.6	267.5	119.7	34.9	3.0	254.0	703.4	265.8	253.3
1984	1 800.1	1 018.6	85.0	570.1	150.3	305.9	164.1	53.9	19.8	289.0	821.3	344.0	301.9
1985	1 989.5	1 097.6	98.4	646.6	176.5	329.0	178.2	129.9	34.8	335.9	984.2	428.2	394.3
1986	2 187.6	1 191.0	113.9	734.5	219.2	333.6	213.1	259.9	71.4	387.6	1 014.8	552.8	411.3
1987	2 323.0	1 310.3	131.3	823.1	258.6	347.2	215.0	291.1	113.2	420.2	1 193.6	606.5	414.8
1988	2 479.5	1 409.3	148.8	927.2	287.9	369.2	225.5	304.5	147.6	460.4	1 399.2	714.4	461.4
1989	2 647.4	1 316.0	156.0	1 028.3	317.5	420.8	293.7	327.2	201.1	498.3	1 488.4	854.8	576.6
1990	2 772.5	1 176.5	166.6	1 134.5	344.0	464.3	371.3	360.1	250.3	520.4	1 750.1	926.4	550.7
1991	2 853.3	1 013.2	179.4	1 218.9	376.6	489.7	403.9	440.2	299.5	513.3	1 839.4	963.2	611.4
1992	2 948.6	937.4	197.1	1 304.4	389.4	515.7	408.6	566.4	357.9	513.8	1 890.0	1 051.0	674.4
1993	3 090.8	914.1	218.7	1 415.4	422.7	551.9	429.0	725.9	437.8	488.3	1 874.4	1 194.2	702.9
1994	3 254.3	920.8	246.8	1 487.5	446.4	591.5	459.0	718.8	501.0	512.7	2 183.3	1 277.6	678.1
1995	3 520.1	913.3	263.0	1 587.5	468.7	608.4	545.5	771.3	611.6	559.2	2 182.0	1 593.5	763.1
1996	3 707.7	933.2	288.5	1 657.0	491.2	602.3	634.3	820.2	711.6	586.3	2 344.0	1 946.1	763.2
1997	4 031.9	928.5	305.2	1 751.1	515.3	646.8	721.9	901.1	824.0	600.3	2 265.0	2 211.9	846.1
1998	4 336.1	965.5	324.2	1 828.0	521.1	639.7	970.5	1 028.4	1 074.4	685.2	2 336.6	2 358.7	877.7
1999	4 648.3	1 032.6	351.7	1 886.0	518.2	746.9	1 155.3	1 076.8	1 242.9	792.0	2 441.1	2 400.9	927.9
2000	5 006.2	1 088.8	379.7	1 943.9	509.4	621.9	1 317.5	1 103.1	1 390.6	928.8	2 232.5	2 751.9	1 046.6
2001	5 210.5	1 133.2	421.2	2 074.8	518.4	585.8	1 584.9	1 229.7	1 604.2	978.6	2 117.9	3 192.2	1 179.5
2002	5 614.9	1 166.6	465.4	2 307.8	558.3	572.3	1 567.1	1 368.4	1 787.8	1 082.3	2 196.7	3 708.0	1 218.9
2003	5 960.8	1 292.6	516.6	2 488.3	625.2	629.5	1 471.3	1 506.4	1 990.8	1 205.0	2 544.2	4 138.2	1 467.7
2004	6 543.0	1 485.4	556.4	2 661.4	698.8	624.2	1 346.3	1 623.0	2 320.4	1 420.0	2 766.1	4 929.3	1 703.3
2005	7 189.8	1 616.6	592.6	2 765.4	765.8	637.7	1 336.2	1 747.1	2 962.7	1 537.1	3 045.4	5 604.6	2 025.7
2003													
1st quarter	5 673.6	1 214.1	479.1	2 377.0	572.3	593.4	1 532.2	1 416.0	1 847.6	1 079.4	2 124.2	3 798.2	1 324.5
2nd quarter	5 831.3	1 238.5	494.8	2 436.5	584.7	598.7	1 541.3	1 481.4	1 908.8	1 129.5	2 194.3	3 975.9	1 322.2
3rd quarter	5 831.8	1 261.0	506.4	2 471.6	601.9	601.9	1 507.0	1 478.7	1 947.5	1 173.0	2 273.6	4 067.8	1 396.9
4th quarter	5 960.8	1 292.6	516.6	2 488.3	625.2	629.5	1 471.3	1 506.4	1 990.8	1 205.0	2 544.2	4 138.2	1 467.7
2004													
1st quarter	6 135.3	1 348.8	524.3	2 546.3	651.5	624.0	1 416.9	1 559.1	2 023.4	1 253.2	2 465.1	4 335.3	1 510.6
2nd quarter	6 270.2	1 391.2	541.3	2 586.1	667.8	622.5	1 353.6	1 559.1	2 121.9	1 316.2	2 518.5	4 552.9	1 453.3
3rd quarter	6 336.9	1 426.9	546.7	2 631.6	686.2	618.4	1 321.6	1 586.9	2 226.8	1 351.7	2 608.6	4 708.3	1 611.0
4th quarter	6 543.0	1 485.4	556.4	2 661.4	698.8	624.2	1 346.3	1 623.0	2 320.4	1 420.0	2 766.1	4 929.3	1 703.3
2005													
1st quarter	6 745.2	1 496.3	565.8	2 714.2	721.1	623.4	1 294.3	1 669.3	2 422.7	1 423.1	2 726.1	5 111.3	1 811.1
2nd quarter	6 909.7	1 550.2	579.0	2 733.2	733.4	624.5	1 245.1	1 697.3	2 595.7	1 441.7	2 824.1	5 299.6	1 869.4
3rd quarter	7 084.1	1 588.8	585.9	2 760.6	760.3	628.9	1 246.8	1 719.6	2 762.4	1 465.2	2 805.3	5 514.1	1 929.3
4th quarter	7 189.8	1 616.6	592.6	2 765.4	765.8	637.7	1 336.2	1 747.1	2 962.7	1 537.1	3 045.4	5 604.6	2 025.7

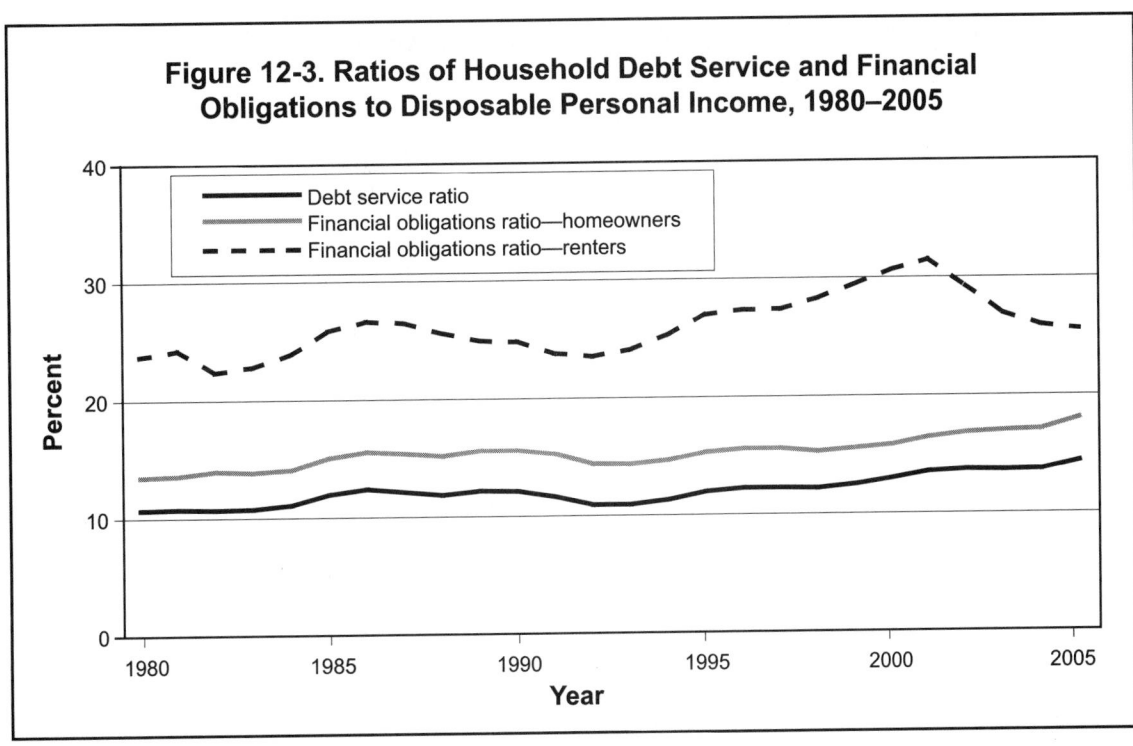

Figure 12-3. Ratios of Household Debt Service and Financial Obligations to Disposable Personal Income, 1980–2005

- The Federal Reserve calculates aggregate household debt service (payments of principal and interest) and total financial obligations as a percentage of aggregate disposable personal income (DPI) for the period 1980 to the present. These measures provide supplements to the ratio of the total level of household debt to DPI (shown in Table 12-5), which are important and needed because lengthening maturities and lower interest rates can mitigate much of the burden of a high level of debt. Unlike the debt/income ratio, the debt service ratio leveled off between 2002 and 2004, reflecting the decline in interest rates. However, the debt service ratio rose to a new record high in 2005. (Tables 12-5, 12-6, and 12-9)

- With increasing homeownership, a trend increase in the debt service ratio might be expected and no cause for concern. But other long-term trends have also come into play—increasing credit card use, increasing use of second mortgage (home equity) credit to finance purchases previously financed with consumer credit, and the increased use of auto leasing in place of auto purchase with consumer credit finance. To assess the financial condition of the personal sector while accounting for all of these trends, the Federal Reserve now makes available financial obligations ratios, which include all debt service, rental payments on primary residences, property taxes, homeowners' insurance, and automobile lease payments. Furthermore, the Federal Reserve estimates the breakdown between homeowners and renters in order to calculate a ratio for each group. (Table 12-6)

- Financial obligations ratios for both groups are, of course, higher than the ratio for debt service alone. Reflecting the lower average incomes of the renters' group, the ratio for renters is about double the ratio for homeowners. But the renters' ratio peaked in the fourth quarter of 2001 and has improved since then. The obligations of homeowners have continued to rise relative to their DPI. (Table 12-6)

- Additional evidence of the long-term trend toward more debt is seen in the ratio of aggregate household debt to aggregate household financial and tangible assets. This ratio leveled off in 2003 and 2004, due to the rapid increase in the value of homes, but resumed its rise in 2005. (Tables 12-6 and 12-10)

Table 12-6. Household Assets, Liabilities, Net Worth, Financial Obligations, and Delinquency Rates

(Billions of dollars, except as noted; end of period; not seasonally adjusted, except as noted.)

| Year and quarter | Financial assets of the household sector [1] | | | | | | | | | | | | | |
	Total [2]	Checkable deposits and currency	Time and savings deposits	Money market fund shares	U.S. savings bonds	Other Treasury securities	Agency- and GSE- backed securities	Municipal securities	Corporate and foreign bonds	Mortgages	Corporate equities	Mutual fund shares	Security credit	Life insurance reserves
1945	560.6	54.0	50.3	0.0	42.9	23.6	0.1	3.9	8.4	12.2	109.5	1.2	0.7	39.6
1946	601.7	58.9	56.6	0.0	44.2	21.0	0.1	3.8	7.5	13.7	101.3	1.3	0.7	43.4
1947	642.2	58.7	60.1	0.0	46.2	18.8	0.1	4.5	6.6	15.0	98.8	1.4	0.7	46.5
1948	664.2	56.3	62.3	0.0	47.8	18.0	0.1	4.6	6.7	16.2	97.5	1.4	0.7	49.4
1949	682.8	54.4	65.0	0.0	49.3	18.0	0.0	3.7	6.3	17.0	105.0	3.1	0.7	52.1
1950	736.0	56.9	67.4	0.0	49.6	16.9	0.1	5.5	6.0	17.6	128.7	3.3	1.0	55.0
1951	801.1	61.0	72.2	0.0	49.1	16.3	0.1	5.7	6.3	18.6	151.1	3.5	0.9	57.8
1952	830.0	63.1	79.6	0.0	49.2	18.2	0.0	11.0	6.0	19.2	151.0	3.9	0.7	60.7
1953	847.7	64.3	87.8	0.0	49.4	18.7	0.2	13.9	6.0	20.2	145.8	4.1	0.7	63.6
1954	926.1	66.0	96.9	0.0	50.0	16.1	0.1	16.0	4.9	21.4	198.8	6.1	1.0	66.3
1955	1 015.3	67.0	105.4	0.0	50.2	18.6	0.6	19.2	5.0	22.7	248.2	7.8	0.9	69.3
1956	1 083.9	68.7	114.7	0.0	50.1	20.1	1.0	21.9	6.1	24.3	271.0	9.0	0.9	72.7
1957	1 096.4	67.8	126.5	0.0	48.2	23.3	1.5	23.9	7.2	26.2	244.5	8.7	0.9	75.5
1958	1 224.3	70.1	140.3	0.0	47.7	20.9	0.8	24.6	7.9	28.8	322.3	13.2	1.2	78.5
1959	1 300.7	72.4	151.5	0.0	45.9	25.7	2.3	28.4	8.2	30.7	357.3	15.8	1.0	82.0
1960	1 349.0	74.1	163.4	0.0	45.6	26.6	1.0	31.0	10.6	33.5	359.8	17.0	1.1	85.2
1961	1 493.2	72.9	181.6	0.0	46.4	25.5	0.6	32.5	10.8	36.8	443.2	22.9	1.2	88.6
1962	1 535.2	72.5	207.4	0.0	47.0	26.8	0.2	32.1	10.2	39.0	431.2	20.9	1.2	92.4
1963	1 633.7	77.3	233.3	0.0	48.1	24.7	0.0	32.1	10.1	40.5	469.9	24.8	1.2	96.6
1964	1 788.2	79.9	259.3	0.0	49.1	24.5	0.2	34.9	10.3	42.0	544.1	28.4	1.7	101.1
1965	1 954.5	86.5	286.8	0.0	49.7	25.1	1.1	36.5	9.0	42.6	616.1	34.4	2.5	105.9
1966	1 977.2	88.9	305.5	0.0	50.2	28.8	5.9	41.2	11.1	44.6	548.3	33.9	2.7	110.6
1967	2 227.3	99.3	340.4	0.0	51.2	27.8	6.3	38.2	15.1	46.5	682.1	43.0	4.9	115.5
1968	2 491.4	108.7	370.8	0.0	51.9	29.9	6.1	36.5	18.0	49.0	815.3	49.5	7.0	120.3
1969	2 436.3	107.1	380.0	0.0	51.8	41.4	11.3	47.2	22.0	49.1	667.4	45.6	5.2	125.4
1970	2 528.1	114.3	421.5	0.0	52.1	31.0	15.9	47.1	29.7	50.0	650.2	44.5	4.4	130.7
1971	2 814.0	127.6	486.5	0.0	54.4	19.8	14.6	46.0	37.4	47.3	743.7	53.0	4.9	137.1
1972	3 221.7	139.1	558.0	0.0	57.7	19.7	8.9	47.7	38.5	48.2	921.4	56.4	5.0	143.9
1973	3 229.9	147.1	619.6	0.0	60.4	28.1	8.3	55.1	41.5	47.2	693.9	43.7	4.9	151.3
1974	3 204.1	151.7	674.6	2.4	63.3	32.9	13.7	62.2	54.4	50.5	445.0	31.8	3.9	158.4
1975	3 665.0	152.2	752.3	3.7	67.4	44.4	7.6	66.8	64.3	50.4	584.6	38.7	4.5	168.6
1976	4 149.2	162.2	853.5	3.4	72.0	30.7	11.7	72.9	74.3	52.8	731.6	41.4	5.7	177.8
1977	4 426.2	176.2	956.3	3.2	76.8	27.8	8.4	78.8	79.4	55.3	631.3	40.4	5.7	187.8
1978	4 956.6	190.2	1 056.6	8.9	80.7	29.6	9.5	104.2	73.0	62.4	640.0	41.1	8.5	199.4
1979	5 681.1	207.6	1 126.5	39.5	79.9	76.0	12.4	123.6	65.6	71.6	768.1	44.8	10.4	210.3
1980	6 554.9	221.4	1 244.9	64.4	72.5	101.3	18.8	130.1	57.4	87.2	1 010.4	52.1	16.2	220.6
1981	6 944.0	263.5	1 313.5	154.6	68.2	100.6	14.7	160.3	57.8	101.4	905.2	52.6	14.7	230.1
1982	7 533.9	277.6	1 423.6	188.1	68.3	117.4	14.6	201.1	49.8	110.9	966.3	65.1	17.8	238.0
1983	8 292.7	283.6	1 623.1	154.7	71.5	161.3	15.9	246.7	53.1	111.2	1 088.6	98.0	20.6	246.7
1984	8 813.6	296.0	1 849.0	199.2	74.5	205.9	29.5	290.4	52.8	102.5	1 008.7	117.5	21.6	252.8
1985	9 937.8	312.2	1 981.3	204.6	79.8	206.0	26.1	395.1	101.2	119.7	1 229.5	213.8	35.0	264.3
1986	11 050.4	425.4	2 072.1	243.4	93.3	181.1	27.0	410.9	130.8	115.5	1 494.0	378.7	44.0	282.6
1987	11 710.7	428.5	2 194.1	264.6	101.1	210.8	34.3	516.6	151.3	124.2	1 462.6	424.5	39.1	309.5
1988	12 849.4	425.7	2 373.7	282.7	109.6	288.1	54.1	586.0	141.8	125.9	1 757.1	439.1	40.9	335.7
1989	14 171.8	425.0	2 454.1	361.2	117.7	281.3	77.3	613.3	176.2	134.5	2 147.1	513.0	53.2	365.3
1990	14 562.7	413.4	2 485.2	391.7	126.2	382.4	118.7	647.7	238.0	143.5	1 960.2	511.5	62.4	391.7
1991	16 109.4	462.2	2 409.8	409.7	138.1	401.4	117.0	701.8	276.9	145.7	2 751.4	650.8	87.0	418.6
1992	16 911.5	570.5	2 302.4	368.3	157.3	475.0	113.2	672.2	279.7	139.9	3 074.0	816.8	76.2	447.7
1993	18 152.1	615.7	2 192.7	367.0	171.9	506.1	57.2	640.8	300.8	132.5	3 404.5	1 127.0	102.3	484.8
1994	18 821.0	582.2	2 167.2	377.4	179.9	695.5	175.2	594.1	345.2	123.7	3 249.0	1 137.5	109.0	520.3
1995	21 386.6	525.2	2 306.3	477.5	185.0	648.7	199.9	533.4	427.1	116.3	4 368.5	1 313.5	127.6	566.2
1996	23 798.5	455.6	2 451.1	533.7	187.0	707.2	300.1	493.0	472.3	108.7	5 154.6	1 644.8	162.9	610.6
1997	27 169.0	404.2	2 591.5	608.9	186.5	616.6	346.8	497.6	439.3	101.1	6 697.9	2 059.5	215.4	665.0
1998	29 992.9	415.2	2 685.0	706.8	186.6	552.8	410.0	498.7	510.0	98.2	7 559.7	2 489.2	276.7	718.3
1999	34 344.6	370.6	2 800.8	816.1	186.4	627.3	483.3	528.1	424.6	106.5	9 711.0	3 067.0	323.9	783.9
2000	32 959.6	279.1	3 062.4	959.8	184.8	399.1	508.3	531.2	394.6	117.3	8 035.6	2 855.9	412.4	819.1
2001	31 367.0	348.3	3 332.1	1 113.2	190.3	253.8	401.3	581.1	468.7	125.4	6 376.4	2 734.0	454.3	880.0
2002	29 060.0	345.6	3 656.2	1 070.0	194.9	92.2	242.5	678.7	741.9	136.2	4 535.9	2 420.4	412.7	920.9
2003	33 540.4	286.8	3 991.3	959.8	203.8	237.2	394.1	707.7	747.7	147.9	5 718.3	3 133.5	475.4	1 013.2
2004	36 442.9	319.0	4 353.9	903.5	204.4	359.3	435.7	741.0	729.5	160.2	5 811.1	3 659.2	578.3	1 060.4
2005	38 803.4	315.9	4 739.7	957.3	205.1	346.4	635.9	816.8	703.7	173.3	5 592.3	4 167.7	567.4	1 082.6
2003														
1st quarter	28 993.8	310.0	3 843.3	1 069.9	196.9	121.2	180.7	680.6	689.3	139.1	4 348.0	2 378.1	429.6	936.3
2nd quarter	30 848.7	298.2	3 872.6	1 016.7	199.1	202.5	123.1	708.3	710.6	142.0	4 939.9	2 711.3	515.1	959.7
3rd quarter	31 526.7	288.6	3 951.5	934.0	201.5	179.0	303.1	697.0	637.9	144.9	5 070.9	2 854.0	503.4	973.0
4th quarter	33 540.4	286.8	3 991.3	959.8	203.8	237.2	394.1	707.7	747.7	147.9	5 718.3	3 133.5	475.4	1 013.2
2004														
1st quarter	34 101.7	311.2	4 138.7	955.0	204.4	231.4	318.1	711.4	733.1	150.8	5 608.7	3 338.7	512.9	1 022.5
2nd quarter	34 555.4	288.0	4 231.0	924.5	204.6	249.3	355.7	731.0	706.0	154.1	5 664.7	3 358.2	533.9	1 031.9
3rd quarter	34 573.0	303.2	4 308.7	862.2	204.1	227.5	485.1	727.4	685.7	157.2	5 377.1	3 376.9	524.3	1 038.2
4th quarter	36 442.9	319.0	4 353.9	903.5	204.4	359.3	435.7	741.0	729.5	160.2	5 811.1	3 659.2	578.3	1 060.4
2005														
1st quarter	36 446.3	354.3	4 518.5	870.8	204.2	361.0	418.1	755.7	686.4	163.4	5 572.7	3 758.8	569.4	1 059.4
2nd quarter	36 998.1	331.5	4 555.1	866.4	204.2	308.5	488.2	789.3	715.3	166.9	5 488.2	3 828.2	583.2	1 067.2
3rd quarter	37 903.0	278.5	4 701.6	887.7	203.6	307.6	589.9	799.9	575.5	170.3	5 590.2	4 039.4	578.4	1 077.7
4th quarter	38 803.4	315.9	4 739.7	957.3	205.1	346.4	635.9	816.8	703.7	173.3	5 592.3	4 167.7	567.4	1 082.6

[1] Includes nonprofit organizations.
[2] Includes components not shown separately.

Table 12-6. Household Assets, Liabilities, Net Worth, Financial Obligations, and Delinquency Rates —Continued

(Billions of dollars, except as noted; end of period; not seasonally adjusted, except as noted.)

Year and quarter	Financial assets of the household sector [1] —Continued		Tangible assets of the household sector		Debt as a percent of total assets [1]	Total liabilities [1]	Net worth [1]	Ratios to disposable personal income (percent, seasonally adjusted)				Consumer credit card accounts held at banks (percent, seasonally adjusted)	
	Pension fund reserves	Equity in non-corporate business	Total [1]	Household real estate [3]				Household debt service	Household financial obligations			Delin-quency rate	Charge-off rate
									Total	Home-owners	Renters		
1945	13.5	195.5	181.4	116.0	3.8	30.3	711.6	...	...	...	...	...	...
1946	15.8	228.7	212.8	133.4	4.3	37.1	777.4	...	...	...	...	...	...
1947	18.3	261.2	272.5	177.5	4.8	46.1	868.7	...	...	...	...	...	...
1948	21.1	276.6	304.4	199.3	5.4	54.7	913.9	...	...	...	...	...	...
1949	24.3	278.6	330.1	216.5	5.9	63.0	950.0	...	...	...	...	...	...
1950	27.9	294.5	378.9	243.3	6.5	76.3	1 038.6	...	...	...	...	...	...
1951	33.5	320.6	420.3	270.9	6.7	85.3	1 136.1	...	...	...	...	...	...
1952	33.5	322.3	453.4	294.8	7.3	97.6	1 185.7	...	...	...	...	...	...
1953	38.5	322.1	482.3	315.1	8.0	110.4	1 219.7	...	...	...	...	...	...
1954	43.9	325.8	509.3	337.6	8.2	122.6	1 312.7	...	...	...	...	...	...
1955	52.0	334.9	553.8	367.4	8.8	143.9	1 425.2	...	...	...	...	...	...
1956	58.2	351.1	596.4	394.3	9.1	159.2	1 521.1	...	...	...	...	...	...
1957	64.6	363.1	631.3	417.2	9.6	171.6	1 556.1	...	...	...	...	...	...
1958	74.9	377.8	657.4	438.4	9.4	183.6	1 698.1	...	...	...	...	...	...
1959	85.0	379.2	692.5	463.6	9.9	206.1	1 787.0	...	...	...	...	...	...
1960	93.9	389.2	723.5	486.9	10.4	223.8	1 848.7	...	...	...	...	...	...
1961	107.2	405.8	755.2	511.1	10.3	241.9	2 006.5	...	...	...	...	...	...
1962	113.7	422.0	788.4	533.2	10.9	264.0	2 059.6	...	...	...	...	...	...
1963	128.0	426.6	823.6	553.2	11.4	292.9	2 164.3	...	...	...	...	...	...
1964	144.8	445.6	867.7	579.8	11.7	322.1	2 333.8	...	...	...	...	...	...
1965	162.0	471.7	913.1	605.6	11.8	351.5	2 516.1	...	...	...	...	...	...
1966	172.5	505.0	986.2	649.0	12.2	374.7	2 588.7	...	...	...	...	...	...
1967	195.6	529.5	1 053.6	685.7	11.6	397.8	2 883.1	...	...	...	...	...	...
1968	218.7	573.9	1 177.9	768.2	11.3	433.8	3 235.5	...	...	...	...	...	...
1969	230.9	607.5	1 283.3	832.4	11.9	461.4	3 258.3	...	...	...	...	...	...
1970	253.8	637.8	1 363.4	874.5	11.8	477.1	3 414.3	...	...	...	...	...	...
1971	293.5	703.5	1 487.9	957.2	11.7	523.8	3 778.1	...	...	...	...	...	...
1972	349.3	784.5	1 681.7	1 098.6	11.4	586.6	4 316.9	...	...	...	...	...	...
1973	358.5	919.3	1 905.8	1 251.4	12.3	655.0	4 480.7	...	...	...	...	...	...
1974	367.5	1 029.3	2 018.6	1 261.1	13.1	710.2	4 512.5	...	...	...	...	...	...
1975	467.0	1 128.7	2 237.4	1 413.7	12.5	764.9	5 137.5	...	...	...	...	...	...
1976	534.5	1 257.8	2 486.8	1 590.0	12.4	853.9	5 782.2	...	...	...	...	...	...
1977	589.9	1 420.1	2 885.7	1 886.8	13.0	984.9	6 327.1	...	...	...	...	...	...
1978	691.4	1 650.5	3 339.7	2 210.9	13.4	1 148.5	7 147.9	...	...	...	...	...	...
1979	801.1	1 915.6	3 882.2	2 603.3	13.4	1 319.7	8 243.6	...	...	...	...	...	...
1980	969.7	2 156.4	4 359.7	2 943.2	12.8	1 449.8	9 464.9	10.6	15.4	13.3	23.6	...	...
1981	1 063.5	2 313.8	4 823.0	3 293.0	12.8	1 561.3	10 205.6	10.6	15.6	13.5	24.1	...	...
1982	1 289.1	2 358.9	5 052.5	3 447.4	12.5	1 635.0	10 951.4	10.6	15.6	13.8	22.3	...	...
1983	1 535.8	2 418.6	5 307.2	3 602.8	12.8	1 803.0	11 796.8	10.6	15.6	13.7	22.7	...	...
1984	1 707.5	2 417.7	5 946.2	4 110.1	13.2	2 013.8	12 746.0	11.0	16.0	14.0	23.8	...	...
1985	2 088.6	2 472.2	6 633.9	4 658.4	13.7	2 365.1	14 206.7	11.8	17.1	14.9	25.7	...	2.98
1986	2 326.8	2 597.1	7 241.9	5 087.9	13.8	2 630.3	15 662.0	12.3	17.6	15.4	26.5	...	3.42
1987	2 504.8	2 690.3	7 813.7	5 501.8	14.1	2 837.3	16 687.1	12.0	17.4	15.3	26.3	...	3.26
1988	2 738.3	2 838.3	8 474.1	5 977.2	14.2	3 136.0	18 187.5	11.8	17.1	15.0	25.4	...	3.21
1989	3 169.0	2 960.0	9 138.8	6 473.7	14.3	3 445.6	19 865.0	12.0	17.3	15.5	24.8	...	3.26
1990	3 308.4	3 032.4	9 353.0	6 578.5	15.0	3 716.6	20 199.0	12.0	17.4	15.5	24.7	...	3.82
1991	3 824.8	2 987.7	9 594.4	6 786.6	14.7	3 930.9	21 772.9	11.5	17.0	15.2	23.7	5.30	4.65
1992	4 130.2	2 948.3	9 956.8	7 117.4	14.8	4 134.6	22 733.6	10.8	16.2	14.3	23.4	4.69	4.53
1993	4 605.6	3 076.9	10 318.6	7 366.1	14.8	4 397.5	24 073.2	10.8	16.2	14.2	23.9	3.90	3.34
1994	4 888.4	3 288.3	10 750.2	7 628.7	15.3	4 721.1	24 850.1	11.2	16.6	14.5	25.2	3.27	3.06
1995	5 715.3	3 464.8	11 226.9	7 969.6	14.9	5 055.4	27 558.2	11.8	17.4	15.2	26.9	3.93	3.93
1996	6 377.5	3 701.3	11 751.1	8 342.5	14.6	5 408.9	30 140.6	12.1	17.7	15.4	27.3	4.59	4.64
1997	7 354.8	3 930.2	12 367.7	8 755.8	13.9	5 759.8	33 776.8	12.1	17.7	15.5	27.3	4.78	5.50
1998	8 264.5	4 151.9	13 389.2	9 532.2	13.6	6 214.7	37 167.4	12.1	17.5	15.2	28.2	4.70	5.20
1999	9 265.2	4 360.2	14 524.0	10 429.3	13.1	6 792.9	42 075.7	12.4	17.9	15.5	29.3	4.50	4.53
2000	9 166.0	4 717.4	15 807.5	11 412.6	14.4	7 395.4	41 371.7	12.9	18.2	15.8	30.6	4.56	4.62
2001	8 766.4	4 806.3	17 019.9	12 481.2	15.8	8 009.5	40 377.4	13.4	18.9	16.3	31.4	4.68	6.25
2002	8 061.0	4 970.7	18 532.9	13 781.3	17.8	8 772.6	38 820.3	13.6	18.8	16.7	29.1	4.83	5.29
2003	9 502.7	5 401.1	20 247.5	15 269.4	17.6	9 806.0	43 981.9	13.5	18.5	16.9	26.8	4.41	5.71
2004	10 470.3	5 960.7	22 544.3	17 210.4	17.9	10 999.3	47 987.9	13.6	18.4	17.0	25.8	4.01	4.36
2005	11 009.4	6 734.7	25 218.7	19 491.9	18.5	12 210.9	51 811.2	14.3	19.2	17.9	25.4	3.50	5.66
2003													
1st quarter	8 001.3	5 070.5	18 904.5	14 101.1	18.0	8 946.9	38 951.3	13.6	18.8	16.8	28.5	4.68	5.47
2nd quarter	8 678.4	5 168.5	19 301.9	14 447.9	17.8	9 331.9	40 818.7	13.6	18.7	16.8	27.9	4.54	5.81
3rd quarter	8 881.5	5 288.1	19 746.7	14 834.0	18.0	9 598.4	41 675.0	13.4	18.5	16.7	27.1	4.24	5.51
4th quarter	9 502.7	5 401.1	20 247.5	15 269.4	17.6	9 806.0	43 981.9	13.5	18.5	16.9	26.8	4.41	5.71
2004													
1st quarter	9 724.9	5 498.3	20 748.5	15 686.8	17.6	10 016.1	44 834.1	13.5	18.4	16.8	26.3	4.22	5.11
2nd quarter	9 828.6	5 642.4	21 327.0	16 177.6	17.8	10 314.2	45 568.2	13.5	18.4	16.9	26.0	4.15	5.16
3rd quarter	9 830.1	5 793.2	21 908.3	16 690.1	18.2	10 627.9	45 853.4	13.6	18.6	17.1	25.9	4.08	4.80
4th quarter	10 470.3	5 960.7	22 544.3	17 210.4	17.9	10 999.3	47 987.9	13.6	18.4	17.0	25.8	4.01	4.36
2005													
1st quarter	10 304.1	6 138.1	23 158.9	17 725.3	18.0	11 185.1	48 420.2	13.9	18.8	17.4	25.9	3.73	4.44
2nd quarter	10 508.4	6 367.2	23 950.3	18 380.3	18.2	11 514.9	49 433.5	14.1	19.0	17.6	25.9	3.67	4.23
3rd quarter	10 786.1	6 559.3	24 579.4	18 937.3	18.3	11 884.3	50 598.1	14.3	19.2	17.9	25.6	3.90	4.48
4th quarter	11 009.4	6 734.7	25 218.7	19 491.9	18.5	12 210.9	51 811.2	14.3	19.2	17.9	25.4	3.50	5.66

[1] Includes nonprofit organizations.
[3] Excludes nonprofit organizations.
. . . = Not available.

Table 12-7. Mortgage Debt Outstanding

(Billions of dollars, except as noted; end of period; not seasonally adjusted.)

Year and quarter	Total	By type of property					By type of holder							
		Home		Multi-family residences	Commercial	Farm	Commercial banks	Savings institutions	Life insurance companies	Federal and related agencies	Mortgage pools or trusts			Other
		Billions of dollars	Percent of value of real estate								Total [1]	Federally related agencies	ABS issuers	
1945	36	19	16	5	7	5	5	10	7	2	0	0	0	12
1946	42	23	17	5	9	5	7	11	7	2	0	0	0	14
1947	49	28	16	6	10	5	9	14	9	2	0	0	0	16
1948	56	33	17	7	11	5	11	16	11	2	0	0	0	17
1949	63	37	17	8	12	6	12	18	13	2	0	0	0	18
1950	73	45	18	9	12	6	14	22	16	3	0	0	0	19
1951	83	52	19	11	13	7	15	25	19	3	0	0	0	20
1952	92	58	20	11	14	7	16	29	21	4	0	0	0	21
1953	101	66	21	12	16	8	17	34	23	5	0	0	0	22
1954	114	75	22	13	17	8	19	40	26	5	0	0	0	24
1955	130	88	24	13	19	9	21	48	29	5	0	0	0	26
1956	144	99	25	14	22	10	23	55	33	6	0	0	0	28
1957	157	107	26	15	24	10	23	60	35	7	0	0	0	30
1958	172	117	27	17	27	11	26	68	37	8	0	0	0	34
1959	191	130	28	19	30	12	28	77	39	10	0	0	0	37
1960	208	141	29	21	33	13	29	86	42	11	0	0	0	40
1961	229	154	30	24	37	14	30	96	44	12	0	0	0	46
1962	252	168	32	27	42	15	34	109	47	12	0	0	0	49
1963	279	185	33	30	47	17	39	125	51	11	1	1	0	53
1964	307	202	35	35	51	19	44	140	55	12	1	1	0	56
1965	334	219	36	38	56	21	50	153	60	13	1	1	0	59
1966	358	233	36	41	61	23	54	160	65	16	1	1	0	61
1967	382	246	36	45	66	25	59	170	68	19	2	2	0	65
1968	411	263	34	48	73	27	65	182	70	23	3	3	0	69
1969	440	279	33	53	79	29	71	194	72	28	3	3	0	72
1970	469	292	33	60	87	30	73	205	74	34	5	5	0	78
1971	518	318	33	70	97	32	83	231	75	37	10	10	0	82
1972	590	357	33	83	114	35	99	268	77	40	14	14	0	91
1973	666	400	32	93	134	40	119	300	81	47	18	18	0	101
1974	728	435	35	100	148	45	132	321	86	61	21	21	0	107
1975	786	474	34	101	161	50	136	351	89	73	29	29	0	108
1976	870	535	34	106	174	55	151	398	92	76	41	41	0	113
1977	999	628	33	114	193	64	179	459	97	84	57	57	0	123
1978	1 151	738	33	125	215	73	214	517	106	100	70	70	0	143
1979	1 317	856	33	135	239	87	245	565	118	121	95	95	0	172
1980	1 458	958	33	143	260	97	263	594	131	143	114	114	0	213
1981	1 579	1 030	31	142	300	107	284	612	138	160	129	129	0	256
1982	1 661	1 070	31	146	334	111	301	576	142	177	179	179	0	286
1983	1 850	1 186	33	161	389	114	331	627	151	188	245	245	0	309
1984	2 092	1 321	32	186	472	112	381	710	157	202	300	289	11	342
1985	2 372	1 519	33	206	542	106	431	766	172	213	393	368	25	398
1986	2 659	1 722	34	239	603	95	505	785	194	202	550	532	19	424
1987	2 961	1 921	35	259	694	88	595	824	212	189	702	669	32	440
1988	3 278	2 154	36	275	766	83	677	888	233	192	787	745	41	501
1989	3 548	2 379	37	288	801	80	771	873	254	198	923	870	53	530
1990	3 803	2 615	40	288	821	79	849	802	268	239	1 088	1 020	68	557
1991	3 953	2 782	41	285	807	79	881	705	260	266	1 271	1 156	115	569
1992	4 063	2 947	41	272	763	80	901	628	242	286	1 442	1 272	170	564
1993	4 196	3 106	42	269	740	81	948	598	224	326	1 565	1 357	208	535
1994	4 363	3 283	43	270	727	83	1 013	596	216	316	1 703	1 472	231	520
1995	4 550	3 451	43	276	739	85	1 090	597	213	308	1 819	1 571	248	523
1996	4 820	3 675	44	288	770	87	1 145	628	208	294	1 997	1 712	286	546
1997	5 133	3 910	45	300	833	91	1 245	632	207	285	2 175	1 826	348	589
1998	5 621	4 266	45	333	925	97	1 337	644	214	292	2 497	2 019	478	637
1999	6 233	4 691	45	375	1 064	103	1 495	668	231	320	2 845	2 294	552	674
2000	6 796	5 110	45	405	1 171	110	1 660	723	236	341	3 103	2 493	610	733
2001	7 486	5 640	45	446	1 282	118	1 790	758	243	373	3 543	2 832	711	779
2002	8 367	6 374	46	485	1 383	126	2 058	781	250	434	3 954	3 159	795	890
2003	9 374	7 174	47	555	1 510	134	2 256	870	261	537	4 456	3 489	967	993
2004	10 677	8 244	48	609	1 683	142	2 595	1 057	273	554	4 960	3 542	1 418	1 238
2005	12 146	9 380	48	680	1 938	148	2 957	1 153	285	555	5 780	3 677	2 103	1 416
2003														
1st quarter	8 572	6 543	46	495	1 407	128	2 099	815	251	456	4 058	3 227	832	892
2nd quarter	8 866	6 782	47	514	1 440	130	2 193	833	254	490	4 151	3 289	862	944
3rd quarter	9 142	7 007	47	531	1 472	132	2 264	851	257	525	4 274	3 371	903	971
4th quarter	9 374	7 174	47	555	1 510	134	2 256	870	261	537	4 456	3 489	967	993
2004														
1st quarter	9 639	7 393	47	564	1 546	135	2 329	926	262	543	4 554	3 510	1 043	1 024
2nd quarter	9 969	7 667	47	581	1 582	138	2 436	965	264	543	4 662	3 523	1 138	1 098
3rd quarter	10 341	7 980	48	593	1 627	141	2 517	1 008	268	548	4 843	3 544	1 299	1 157
4th quarter	10 677	8 244	48	609	1 683	142	2 595	1 057	273	554	4 960	3 542	1 418	1 238
2005														
1st quarter	10 935	8 445	48	622	1 726	143	2 689	1 068	275	555	5 082	3 547	1 535	1 266
2nd quarter	11 318	8 745	48	640	1 788	146	2 790	1 113	278	553	5 273	3 568	1 705	1 310
3rd quarter	11 750	9 087	48	658	1 856	148	2 895	1 141	281	553	5 522	3 617	1 905	1 358
4th quarter	12 146	9 380	48	680	1 938	148	2 957	1 153	285	555	5 780	3 677	2 103	1 416

[1] Outstanding principal balances of mortgage-backed securities issued or guaranteed by the holder indicated.

Table 12-8. Consumer Credit

(Outstanding at end of period, billions of dollars.)

Year and month	Seasonally adjusted			Not seasonally adjusted							
	Total	By major credit type		Total	By major holder						
		Revolving	Non-revolving		Commercial banks	Finance companies	Credit unions	Federal government and Sallie Mae	Savings institutions	Nonfinancial businesses	Securitized pools [1]
1950	23.2	0.0	23.2	23.9	9.7	5.3	0.3	0.0	0.9	7.7	0.0
1951	24.6	0.0	24.6	25.4	10.0	5.6	0.3	0.0	0.9	8.5	0.0
1952	29.7	0.0	29.7	30.5	12.3	7.1	0.6	0.0	0.9	9.7	0.0
1953	33.7	0.0	33.7	34.6	14.0	8.6	0.9	0.0	1.0	10.1	0.0
1954	35.0	0.0	35.0	36.0	14.3	9.1	1.1	0.0	1.1	10.5	0.0
1955	41.9	0.0	41.9	42.9	17.2	11.8	1.3	0.0	1.4	11.2	0.0
1956	45.4	0.0	45.4	46.6	18.9	12.7	1.7	0.0	1.5	11.8	0.0
1957	48.1	0.0	48.1	49.2	20.2	13.2	2.1	0.0	1.6	12.1	0.0
1958	48.4	0.0	48.4	49.5	20.7	12.3	2.3	0.0	1.8	12.3	0.0
1959	56.0	0.0	56.0	57.2	24.2	14.1	2.9	0.0	2.1	14.0	0.0
1960	60.0	0.0	60.0	61.2	26.4	15.4	3.4	0.0	2.4	13.5	0.0
1961	62.2	0.0	62.2	63.4	27.9	15.5	3.6	0.0	2.9	13.6	0.0
1962	68.1	0.0	68.1	69.3	30.6	17.3	4.1	0.0	3.0	14.3	0.0
1963	76.6	0.0	76.6	77.9	34.7	19.6	4.5	0.0	3.6	15.5	0.0
1964	86.0	0.0	86.0	87.4	39.8	21.6	5.4	0.0	3.7	16.8	0.0
1965	96.0	0.0	96.0	97.5	45.2	23.9	6.5	0.0	3.9	18.1	0.0
1966	101.8	0.0	101.8	103.4	48.2	24.8	7.5	0.0	4.0	19.0	0.0
1967	106.8	0.0	106.8	108.6	51.7	24.6	8.3	0.0	4.1	19.9	0.0
1968	117.4	2.0	115.4	119.3	58.5	26.1	9.7	0.0	4.3	20.8	0.0
1969	127.2	3.6	123.6	129.2	63.4	27.8	11.7	0.0	4.4	21.9	0.0
1970	131.6	5.0	126.6	133.7	65.6	27.6	13.0	0.0	4.4	23.0	0.0
1971	146.9	8.2	138.7	149.2	74.3	29.2	14.8	0.0	4.7	26.2	0.0
1972	166.2	9.4	156.8	168.8	87.0	31.9	17.0	0.0	5.1	27.8	0.0
1973	190.1	11.3	178.7	193.0	99.6	35.4	19.6	0.0	8.5	29.8	0.0
1974	198.9	13.2	185.7	201.9	103.0	36.1	21.9	0.0	9.1	31.8	0.0
1975	204.0	14.5	189.5	207.0	106.1	32.6	25.7	0.0	10.1	32.6	0.0
1976	225.7	16.5	209.2	229.0	118.0	33.7	31.2	0.0	10.8	35.2	0.0
1977	260.6	37.4	223.1	264.9	140.3	37.3	37.6	0.5	11.8	37.4	0.0
1978	306.1	45.7	260.4	311.3	166.5	44.4	45.2	0.9	13.1	41.2	0.0
1979	348.6	53.6	295.0	354.6	185.7	55.4	47.4	1.5	20.0	44.6	0.0
1980	351.9	55.0	297.0	358.0	180.2	62.2	44.1	2.6	22.7	46.2	0.0
1981	371.3	60.9	310.4	377.9	184.2	70.1	46.7	4.8	24.0	48.1	0.0
1982	389.8	66.3	323.5	396.7	190.9	75.3	48.8	6.4	26.6	48.7	0.0
1983	437.1	79.0	358.0	444.9	213.7	83.3	56.1	4.6	31.5	55.7	0.0
1984	517.3	100.4	416.9	526.6	258.8	89.9	67.9	5.6	44.2	60.2	0.0
1985	599.7	124.5	475.2	610.6	297.2	111.7	74.0	6.8	57.6	63.3	0.0
1986	654.8	141.1	513.7	666.4	320.2	134.0	77.1	8.2	62.9	64.0	0.0
1987	686.3	160.9	525.5	698.6	334.1	140.0	81.0	10.0	65.3	68.1	0.0
1988	731.9	184.6	547.3	745.2	360.8	144.7	88.3	13.2	66.8	71.4	0.0
1989	794.6	211.2	583.4	809.3	383.3	138.9	91.7	16.0	62.5	69.6	47.3
1990	808.2	238.6	569.6	824.4	382.0	133.4	91.6	19.2	49.6	71.9	76.7
1991	798.0	263.8	534.3	815.6	370.2	121.6	90.3	21.1	42.2	67.3	103.0
1992	801.1	278.4	527.7	824.8	362.9	118.1	91.7	24.2	37.4	70.3	120.3
1993	865.7	309.9	555.7	886.2	395.7	116.1	101.6	27.2	37.9	77.2	130.5
1994	997.1	365.6	631.6	1 021.0	458.8	134.4	119.6	37.1	38.5	86.6	146.1
1995	1 141.4	443.9	697.5	1 168.8	502.3	152.1	131.9	44.2	40.1	85.1	213.1
1996	1 253.3	507.5	745.8	1 273.8	527.5	154.9	144.1	51.3	44.7	77.7	273.5
1997	1 323.3	538.0	785.3	1 344.9	515.1	167.5	152.4	57.8	47.2	84.4	320.5
1998	1 419.4	579.5	839.9	1 442.1	512.0	183.3	155.4	65.7	52.4	79.3	393.9
1999	1 532.7	609.4	923.3	1 556.6	507.8	201.6	167.9	84.7	61.7	76.1	456.7
2000	1 722.4	683.0	1 039.4	1 748.6	551.1	234.4	184.4	104.0	64.8	81.5	528.4
2001	1 871.9	716.4	1 155.5	1 899.6	568.4	280.0	189.6	119.5	71.1	73.1	598.0
2002	1 985.0	748.9	1 236.1	2 013.0	602.6	307.5	195.7	129.6	68.7	74.8	634.1
2003	2 088.7	770.5	1 318.3	2 117.0	669.4	393.0	205.9	114.7	77.9	58.5	597.7
2004	2 204.1	801.0	1 403.2	2 233.9	704.3	492.3	215.4	98.4	91.3	58.5	573.8
2005	2 294.3	825.2	1 469.2	2 325.3	707.0	516.5	228.6	102.1	109.1	58.6	603.3
2004											
January	2 104.5	773.4	1 331.1	2 122.3	669.8	402.1	206.1	115.7	79.1	57.0	592.5
February	2 107.6	773.5	1 334.1	2 108.5	661.7	406.0	205.6	114.2	80.2	55.8	585.0
March	2 120.0	777.9	1 342.1	2 108.1	658.0	412.0	207.1	109.8	81.4	55.2	584.5
April	2 123.4	774.1	1 349.3	2 112.4	661.0	418.2	207.7	104.9	83.6	55.3	581.6
May	2 133.3	777.6	1 355.7	2 121.1	667.0	429.4	209.1	99.8	85.9	55.5	574.4
June	2 141.0	779.7	1 361.3	2 126.1	660.6	436.2	211.7	94.8	88.1	55.3	579.4
July	2 151.9	786.2	1 365.6	2 136.1	664.1	444.9	211.8	93.7	88.5	54.8	578.2
August	2 158.9	787.0	1 371.9	2 156.2	673.8	455.2	213.9	94.2	88.8	55.1	575.2
September	2 172.1	792.6	1 379.5	2 177.7	676.3	471.1	214.5	99.2	89.1	53.4	574.0
October	2 186.9	796.9	1 389.9	2 194.5	677.0	484.5	215.7	99.3	89.9	53.4	574.7
November	2 196.5	798.7	1 397.8	2 204.8	674.5	496.4	216.1	98.6	90.6	54.2	574.5
December	2 204.1	801.0	1 403.2	2 233.9	704.3	492.3	215.4	98.4	91.3	58.5	573.8
2005											
January	2 213.4	806.1	1 407.3	2 232.2	698.2	487.2	215.6	100.8	91.1	56.5	582.7
February	2 220.3	802.9	1 417.4	2 221.0	691.8	491.5	214.9	100.9	91.0	55.2	575.8
March	2 228.2	801.3	1 426.8	2 215.8	683.1	493.4	216.7	100.6	90.8	54.8	576.4
April	2 238.6	805.6	1 433.0	2 227.4	690.5	494.5	219.1	99.0	91.8	55.2	577.2
May	2 240.8	804.5	1 436.3	2 227.5	685.2	494.9	220.8	98.8	92.9	55.0	579.7
June	2 256.3	809.6	1 446.7	2 240.1	684.0	495.1	221.3	98.6	94.0	55.3	591.8
July	2 267.3	810.4	1 457.0	2 250.5	694.7	496.3	225.3	98.1	95.8	54.5	585.7
August	2 278.2	814.0	1 464.3	2 275.9	705.4	501.5	228.8	98.2	97.6	56.9	587.5
September	2 281.8	816.9	1 464.9	2 288.1	708.2	508.4	229.5	103.9	99.4	56.9	581.7
October	2 282.2	817.8	1 464.5	2 290.7	701.9	512.5	228.7	104.0	108.5	53.7	580.9
November	2 290.3	822.8	1 467.5	2 299.1	697.1	514.4	228.7	102.8	108.7	54.9	592.5
December	2 294.3	825.2	1 469.2	2 325.3	707.0	516.5	228.6	102.1	109.1	58.6	603.3

[1]Outstanding balances of pools upon which securities have been issued; these balances are no longer carried on the balance sheets of the loan originators.

Table 12-9. Selected Interest Rates and Bond Yields

(Percent per annum; interest rates are nominal [not adjusted for inflation], except as noted.)

Year and month	Short-term rates								Inflation: percent change from year earlier in PCE chain-type price index excluding food and energy	Real federal funds rate (nominal rate minus inflation)
	Federal funds	Federal Reserve discount rate [1]	Eurodollar deposits, 1-month	U.S. Treasury bills, secondary market, 3-month	U.S. Treasury bills, secondary market, 6-month	Commercial paper, 3-month [2]	CDs (secondary market), 3-month	Bank prime rate		
1955	1.79	. . .	. . .	1.72	. . .	. . .	. . .	3.16	1.21	0.58
1956	2.73	2.77	. . .	2.62	. . .	. . .	. . .	3.77	2.51	0.22
1957	3.11	3.12	. . .	3.22	. . .	. . .	. . .	4.20	2.99	0.12
1958	1.57	2.15	. . .	1.77	3.01	. . .	. . .	3.83	2.15	-0.58
1959	3.31	3.36	. . .	3.39	3.81	. . .	. . .	4.48	2.16	1.15
1960	3.21	3.53	. . .	2.87	3.20	. . .	. . .	4.82	1.67	1.54
1961	1.95	3.00	. . .	2.35	2.59	. . .	. . .	4.50	1.21	0.74
1962	2.71	3.00	. . .	2.77	2.90	. . .	. . .	4.50	1.25	1.46
1963	3.18	3.23	. . .	3.16	3.26	. . .	. . .	4.50	1.20	1.98
1964	3.50	3.55	. . .	3.55	3.68	. . .	3.92	4.50	1.45	2.05
1965	4.07	4.04	. . .	3.95	4.05	. . .	4.36	4.54	1.22	2.85
1966	5.11	4.50	. . .	4.86	5.06	. . .	5.45	5.63	2.09	3.02
1967	4.22	4.19	. . .	4.29	4.61	. . .	4.99	5.63	2.88	1.34
1968	5.66	5.17	. . .	5.34	5.47	. . .	5.82	6.31	4.25	1.41
1969	8.21	5.87	. . .	6.67	6.86	. . .	7.23	7.96	4.64	3.57
1970	7.17	5.95	. . .	6.39	6.51	. . .	7.55	7.91	4.53	2.64
1971	4.67	4.88	6.40	4.33	4.52	5.25	5.00	5.73	4.65	0.02
1972	4.44	4.50	5.00	4.06	4.47	4.66	4.66	5.25	3.24	1.20
1973	8.74	6.45	9.19	7.04	7.20	8.21	9.30	8.03	3.64	5.10
1974	10.51	7.83	10.79	7.85	7.95	10.05	10.29	10.81	7.51	3.00
1975	5.82	6.25	6.35	5.79	6.10	6.26	6.44	7.86	8.28	-2.46
1976	5.05	5.50	5.26	4.98	5.26	5.24	5.27	6.84	6.11	-1.06
1977	5.54	5.46	5.75	5.26	5.52	5.54	5.63	6.83	6.35	-0.81
1978	7.94	7.46	8.33	7.18	7.58	7.93	8.21	9.06	6.59	1.35
1979	11.20	10.29	11.66	10.05	10.04	10.95	11.20	12.67	6.97	4.23
1980	13.35	11.77	13.77	11.39	11.32	12.61	13.02	15.26	9.04	4.31
1981	16.39	13.42	16.72	14.04	13.81	15.34	15.93	18.87	8.71	7.68
1982	12.24	11.01	12.74	10.60	11.06	11.90	12.27	14.85	6.57	5.67
1983	9.09	8.50	9.38	8.62	8.74	8.88	9.07	10.79	5.27	3.82
1984	10.23	8.80	10.45	9.54	9.78	10.12	10.39	12.04	4.16	6.07
1985	8.10	7.69	8.12	7.47	7.65	7.95	8.04	9.93	3.83	4.27
1986	6.80	6.32	6.78	5.97	6.02	6.49	6.51	8.33	3.75	3.05
1987	6.66	5.66	6.88	5.78	6.03	6.82	6.87	8.21	3.70	2.96
1988	7.57	6.20	7.69	6.67	6.91	7.66	7.73	9.32	4.33	3.24
1989	9.21	6.93	9.16	8.11	8.03	8.99	9.09	10.87	4.13	5.08
1990	8.10	6.98	8.15	7.50	7.46	8.06	8.15	10.01	4.26	3.84
1991	5.69	5.45	5.81	5.38	5.44	5.87	5.83	8.46	3.91	1.78
1992	3.52	3.25	3.62	3.43	3.54	3.75	3.68	6.25	3.41	0.11
1993	3.02	3.00	3.07	3.00	3.12	3.22	3.17	6.00	2.56	0.46
1994	4.21	3.60	4.34	4.25	4.64	4.66	4.63	7.15	2.31	1.90
1995	5.83	5.21	5.86	5.49	5.56	5.93	5.92	8.83	2.23	3.60
1996	5.30	5.02	5.32	5.01	5.08	5.41	5.39	8.27	1.88	3.42
1997	5.46	5.00	5.52	5.06	5.18	5.52	5.62	8.44	1.61	3.85
1998	5.35	4.92	5.45	4.78	4.83	25.37	5.47	8.35	1.31	4.04
1999	4.97	4.62	5.15	4.64	4.75	5.21	5.33	8.00	1.49	3.48
2000	6.24	5.73	6.33	5.82	5.90	6.33	6.46	9.23	1.68	4.56
2001	3.88	3.40	3.81	3.40	3.34	3.65	3.71	6.91	1.90	1.98
2002	1.67	1.17	1.71	1.61	1.68	1.70	1.73	4.67	1.77	-0.10
2003	1.13	. . .	1.14	1.01	1.05	1.13	1.15	4.12	1.42	-0.29
2004	1.35	2.34	1.43	1.37	1.58	1.52	1.57	4.34	2.03	-0.68
2005	3.22	4.19	3.33	3.15	3.39	3.44	3.51	6.19	2.09	1.13
2004										
January	1.00	2.00	1.03	0.88	0.97	1.04	1.06	4.00	1.67	-0.67
February	1.01	2.00	1.02	0.93	0.99	1.03	1.05	4.00	1.77	-0.76
March	1.00	2.00	1.02	0.94	0.99	1.03	1.05	4.00	1.90	-0.90
April	1.00	2.00	1.02	0.94	1.09	1.06	1.08	4.00	2.02	-1.02
May	1.00	2.00	1.03	1.02	1.31	1.16	1.20	4.00	2.05	-1.05
June	1.03	2.01	1.18	1.27	1.60	1.39	1.46	4.01	2.17	-1.14
July	1.26	2.25	1.35	1.33	1.66	1.51	1.57	4.25	2.06	-0.80
August	1.43	2.43	1.52	1.48	1.72	1.65	1.68	4.43	2.02	-0.59
September	1.61	2.58	1.72	1.65	1.87	1.81	1.86	4.58	2.08	-0.47
October	1.76	2.75	1.84	1.76	2.00	1.97	2.04	4.75	2.15	-0.39
November	1.93	2.93	2.06	2.07	2.27	2.20	2.26	4.93	2.29	-0.36
December	2.16	3.15	2.32	2.19	2.43	2.38	2.45	5.15	2.21	-0.05
2005										
January	2.28	3.25	2.42	2.33	2.61	2.56	2.61	5.25	2.22	0.06
February	2.50	3.49	2.55	2.54	2.77	2.71	2.77	5.49	2.18	0.32
March	2.63	3.58	2.75	2.74	3.00	2.91	2.97	5.58	2.19	0.44
April	2.79	3.75	2.92	2.78	3.05	3.02	3.09	5.75	2.05	0.74
May	3.00	3.98	3.03	2.84	3.08	3.15	3.22	5.98	2.10	0.90
June	3.04	4.01	3.19	2.97	3.13	3.30	3.38	6.01	1.99	1.05
July	3.26	4.25	3.36	3.22	3.42	3.49	3.57	6.25	1.98	1.28
August	3.50	4.44	3.54	3.44	3.66	3.69	3.77	6.44	2.02	1.48
September	3.62	4.59	3.72	3.42	3.67	3.79	3.87	6.59	2.09	1.53
October	3.78	4.75	3.95	3.71	3.99	4.05	4.13	6.75	2.09	1.69
November	4.00	5.00	4.14	3.88	4.15	4.23	4.31	7.00	2.08	1.92
December	4.16	5.15	4.34	3.89	4.18	4.37	4.45	7.15	2.12	2.04

[1]Federal Reserve Bank of New York. Through 2002, represents the rate for adjustment credit. Beginning in 2003, represents the rate for primary credit. See notes and definitions for more information.
[2]Prior to September 1997, this series represents both nonfinancial and financial commercial paper rates. Beginning September 1997, rates for financial companies only are shown. See notes and definitions for more information.
. . . = Not available.

Table 12-9. Selected Interest Rates and Bond Yields—Continued

(Percent per annum; interest rates are nominal [not adjusted for inflation], except as noted.)

| Year and month | U.S. Treasury securities, constant maturities | | | | | Real rate on TIPS (indexed Treasury securities) | Bond yields | | | Fixed-rate first mortgages |
| | 1-year | 3-year | 10-year | 20-year | 30-year | | Domestic corporate (Moody's) | | State and local bonds (Bond Buyer) | |
							Aaa	Baa		
1955	. . .	. . .	. . .	. . .	. . .	. . .	3.05	3.53	2.48	. . .
1956	. . .	. . .	. . .	. . .	. . .	. . .	3.36	3.88	2.76	. . .
1957	. . .	. . .	. . .	. . .	. . .	. . .	3.89	4.71	3.28	. . .
1958	. . .	. . .	. . .	. . .	. . .	. . .	3.79	4.73	3.16	. . .
1959	. . .	. . .	. . .	. . .	. . .	. . .	4.38	5.05	3.56	. . .
1960	. . .	. . .	. . .	. . .	. . .	. . .	4.41	5.19	3.52	. . .
1961	. . .	. . .	. . .	. . .	. . .	. . .	4.35	5.08	3.45	. . .
1962	3.10	3.47	3.95	. . .	. . .	. . .	4.33	5.02	3.15	. . .
1963	3.36	3.67	4.00	. . .	. . .	. . .	4.26	4.86	3.17	. . .
1964	3.85	4.03	4.19	. . .	. . .	. . .	4.41	4.83	3.21	. . .
1965	4.15	4.22	4.28	. . .	. . .	. . .	4.49	4.87	3.26	. . .
1966	5.20	5.23	4.93	. . .	. . .	. . .	5.13	5.67	3.81	. . .
1967	4.88	5.03	5.07	. . .	. . .	. . .	5.51	6.23	3.94	. . .
1968	5.69	5.68	5.64	. . .	. . .	. . .	6.18	6.94	4.45	. . .
1969	7.12	7.02	6.67	. . .	. . .	. . .	7.03	7.81	5.72	. . .
1970	6.90	7.29	7.35	. . .	. . .	. . .	8.04	9.11	6.33	. . .
1971	4.89	5.66	6.16	. . .	. . .	. . .	7.39	8.56	5.47	. . .
1972	4.95	5.72	6.21	. . .	. . .	. . .	7.21	8.16	5.26	7.38
1973	7.32	6.96	6.85	. . .	. . .	. . .	7.44	8.24	5.19	8.04
1974	8.20	7.84	7.56	. . .	. . .	. . .	8.57	9.50	6.17	9.19
1975	6.78	7.50	7.99	. . .	. . .	. . .	8.83	10.61	7.05	9.04
1976	5.88	6.77	7.61	. . .	. . .	. . .	8.43	9.75	6.64	8.86
1977	6.08	6.68	7.42	. . .	7.75	. . .	8.02	8.97	5.68	8.84
1978	8.34	8.29	8.41	. . .	8.49	. . .	8.73	9.49	6.02	9.63
1979	10.65	9.70	9.43	. . .	9.28	. . .	9.63	10.69	6.52	11.19
1980	12.00	11.51	11.43	. . .	11.27	. . .	11.94	13.67	8.59	13.77
1981	14.80	14.46	13.92	. . .	13.45	. . .	14.17	16.04	11.33	16.63
1982	12.27	12.93	13.01	. . .	12.76	. . .	13.79	16.11	11.66	16.08
1983	9.58	10.45	11.10	. . .	11.18	. . .	12.04	13.55	9.51	13.23
1984	10.91	11.92	12.46	. . .	12.41	. . .	12.71	14.19	10.10	13.87
1985	8.42	9.64	10.62	. . .	10.79	. . .	11.37	12.72	9.10	12.42
1986	6.45	7.06	7.67	. . .	7.78	. . .	9.02	10.39	7.32	10.18
1987	6.77	7.68	8.39	. . .	8.59	. . .	9.38	10.58	7.64	10.20
1988	7.65	8.26	8.85	. . .	8.96	. . .	9.71	10.83	7.68	10.34
1989	8.53	8.55	8.49	. . .	8.45	. . .	9.26	10.18	7.23	10.32
1990	7.89	8.26	8.55	. . .	8.61	. . .	9.32	10.36	7.27	10.13
1991	5.86	6.82	7.86	. . .	8.14	. . .	8.77	9.80	6.92	9.25
1992	3.89	5.30	7.01	. . .	7.67	. . .	8.14	8.98	6.44	8.40
1993	3.43	4.44	5.87	6.29	6.59	. . .	7.22	7.93	5.60	7.33
1994	5.32	6.27	7.09	7.49	7.37	. . .	7.97	8.63	6.18	8.35
1995	5.94	6.25	6.57	6.95	6.88	. . .	7.59	8.20	5.95	7.95
1996	5.52	5.99	6.44	6.83	6.71	. . .	7.37	8.05	5.76	7.80
1997	5.63	6.10	6.35	6.69	6.61	. . .	7.27	7.87	5.52	7.60
1998	5.05	5.14	5.26	5.72	5.58	. . .	6.53	7.22	5.09	6.94
1999	5.08	5.49	5.65	6.20	5.87	. . .	7.05	7.88	5.43	7.43
2000	6.11	6.22	6.03	6.23	5.94	. . .	7.62	8.37	5.71	8.06
2001	3.49	4.09	5.02	5.63	5.49	. . .	7.08	7.95	5.15	6.97
2002	2.00	3.10	4.61	5.43	5.43	. . .	6.49	7.80	5.04	6.54
2003	1.24	2.10	4.01	4.96	. . .	2.54	5.66	6.76	4.75	5.82
2004	1.89	2.78	4.27	5.04	. . .	2.21	5.63	6.39	4.68	5.84
2005	3.62	3.93	4.29	4.64	. . .	1.94	5.23	6.06	4.40	5.86
2004										
January	1.24	2.27	4.15	5.01	. . .	2.24	5.54	6.44	4.61	5.74
February	1.24	2.25	4.08	4.94	. . .	2.15	5.50	6.27	4.55	5.64
March	1.19	2.00	3.83	4.72	. . .	1.93	5.33	6.11	4.41	5.45
April	1.43	2.57	4.35	5.16	. . .	2.28	5.73	6.46	4.82	5.83
May	1.78	3.10	4.72	5.46	. . .	2.45	6.04	6.75	5.07	6.27
June	2.12	3.26	4.73	5.45	. . .	2.43	6.01	6.78	5.05	6.29
July	2.10	3.05	4.50	5.24	. . .	2.36	5.82	6.62	4.87	6.06
August	2.02	2.88	4.28	5.07	. . .	2.26	5.65	6.46	4.70	5.87
September	2.12	2.83	4.13	4.89	. . .	2.18	5.46	6.27	4.56	5.75
October	2.23	2.85	4.10	4.85	. . .	2.15	5.47	6.21	4.49	5.72
November	2.50	3.09	4.19	4.89	. . .	2.11	5.52	6.20	4.52	5.73
December	2.67	3.21	4.23	4.88	. . .	2.00	5.47	6.15	4.48	5.75
2005										
January	2.86	3.39	4.22	4.77	. . .	1.96	5.36	6.02	4.41	5.71
February	3.03	3.54	4.17	4.61	. . .	1.83	5.20	5.82	4.35	5.63
March	3.30	3.91	4.50	4.89	. . .	1.93	5.40	6.06	4.57	5.93
April	3.32	3.79	4.34	4.75	. . .	1.86	5.33	6.05	4.46	5.86
May	3.33	3.72	4.14	4.56	. . .	1.80	5.15	6.01	4.31	5.72
June	3.36	3.69	4.00	4.35	. . .	1.77	4.96	5.86	4.23	5.58
July	3.64	3.91	4.18	4.48	. . .	1.96	5.06	5.95	4.31	5.70
August	3.87	4.08	4.26	4.53	. . .	1.98	5.09	5.96	4.32	5.82
September	3.85	3.96	4.20	4.51	. . .	1.89	5.13	6.03	4.29	5.77
October	4.18	4.29	4.46	4.74	. . .	2.05	5.35	6.30	4.48	6.07
November	4.33	4.43	4.54	4.83	. . .	2.11	5.42	6.39	4.57	6.33
December	4.35	4.39	4.47	4.73	. . .	2.09	5.37	6.32	4.46	6.27

. . . = Not available.

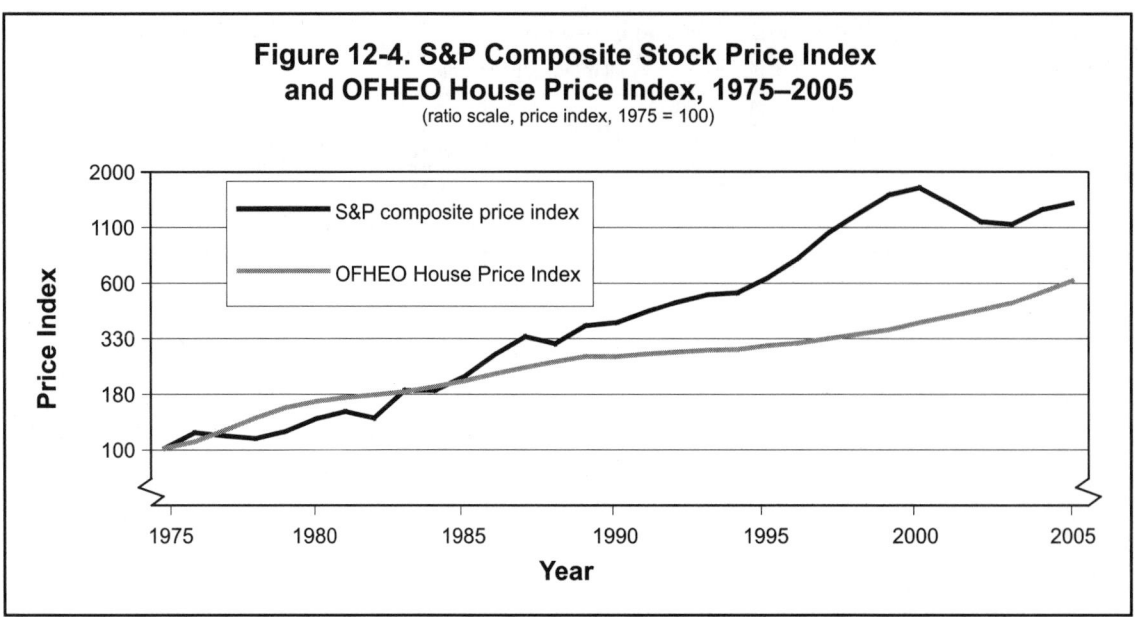

Figure 12-4. S&P Composite Stock Price Index and OFHEO House Price Index, 1975–2005
(ratio scale, price index, 1975 = 100)

• Prices of existing homes rose 13 percent from the fourth quarter of 2004 to the fourth quarter of 2005, exceeding the rates of appreciation experienced in the mid-1970s. Over the 30 years recorded by the new Office of Federal Housing Enterprise Oversight (OFHEO) House Price Index, average home prices increased sixfold, and did not decline in any year. (Table 12-10)

• However, the long-terms gains in housing prices were no match for those in the prices of common stocks. In the same 30-year period, the S&P 500 stock index, though more volatile than home prices, rose fourteen-fold. The annual average rates of appreciation were 9.2 percent for stocks and 6.2 percent for homes. (These simple average asset price comparisons do not take account of tax considerations, stock dividends, and the value of shelter provided by the owner-occupied home. Past history is no guarantee of future results.) (Table 12-10)

• Improvements in earnings caused stock price valuations to appear less out of line in 2005, judging by dividend-price and earnings-price ratios (which are inverses of valuation, since stock prices are the denominator rather than the numerator). The dividend-price ratio was the highest since 1996, though still low compared with years before that. The earnings-price ratio was the highest since 1995, and within the range of variation for years before that. (Table 12-10)

Table 12-10. Common Stock Prices and Yields; Existing House Prices

Year and month	Stock price indexes			Yields based on Standard and Poor's composite (percent)		OFHEO House Price Index	
	Dow Jones industrials (30 stocks)	Standard and Poor's composite (500 stocks) (1941–1943 = 10)	Nasdaq composite (Feb. 5, 1971 = 100)	Dividend-price ratio	Earnings-price ratio	Level at end of period (1980:I = 100)	Appreciation from same quarter one year earlier (percent)
1955	442.72	40.49	...	4.08	7.95	...	...
1956	493.01	46.62	...	4.09	7.55	...	...
1957	475.71	44.38	...	4.35	7.89	...	...
1958	491.66	46.24	...	3.97	6.23	...	...
1959	632.12	57.38	...	3.23	5.78	...	...
1960	618.04	55.85	...	3.47	5.90	...	...
1961	691.55	66.27	...	2.98	4.62	...	...
1962	639.76	62.38	...	3.37	5.82	...	...
1963	714.81	69.87	...	3.17	5.50	...	...
1964	834.05	81.37	...	3.01	5.32	...	...
1965	910.88	88.17	...	3.00	5.59	...	...
1966	873.60	85.26	...	3.40	6.63	...	...
1967	879.12	91.93	...	3.20	5.73	...	...
1968	906.00	98.70	...	3.07	5.67	...	...
1969	876.72	97.84	...	3.24	6.08	...	...
1970	753.19	83.22	...	3.83	6.45	...	...
1971	884.76	98.29	107.44	3.14	5.41	...	...
1972	950.71	109.20	128.52	2.84	5.50	...	...
1973	923.88	107.43	109.90	3.06	7.12	...	...
1974	759.37	82.85	76.29	4.47	11.59	...	...
1975	802.49	86.16	77.20	4.31	9.15	63.27	...
1976	974.92	102.01	89.90	3.77	8.90	68.10	7.63
1977	894.63	98.20	98.71	4.62	10.79	77.14	13.27
1978	820.23	96.02	117.53	5.28	12.03	87.51	13.44
1979	844.40	103.01	136.57	5.47	13.46	97.91	11.88
1980	891.41	118.78	168.61	5.26	12.66	104.65	6.88
1981	932.92	128.05	203.18	5.20	11.96	109.63	4.76
1982	884.36	119.71	188.97	5.81	11.60	112.03	2.19
1983	1 190.34	160.41	285.43	4.40	8.03	116.54	4.03
1984	1 178.48	160.46	248.88	4.64	10.02	122.77	5.35
1985	1 328.23	186.84	290.19	4.25	8.12	130.77	6.52
1986	1 792.76	236.34	366.96	3.49	6.09	141.42	8.14
1987	2 275.99	286.83	402.57	3.08	5.48	151.01	6.78
1988	2 060.82	265.79	374.43	3.64	8.01	160.36	6.19
1989	2 508.91	322.84	437.81	3.45	7.42	170.04	6.04
1990	2 678.94	334.59	409.17	3.61	6.47	170.48	0.26
1991	2 929.33	376.18	491.69	3.24	4.79	174.90	2.59
1992	3 284.29	415.74	599.26	2.99	4.22	178.19	1.88
1993	3 522.06	451.41	715.16	2.78	4.46	181.88	2.07
1994	3 793.77	460.42	751.65	2.82	5.83	183.39	0.83
1995	4 493.76	541.72	925.19	2.56	6.09	191.69	4.53
1996	5 742.89	670.50	1 164.96	2.19	5.24	196.64	2.58
1997	7 441.15	873.43	1 469.49	1.77	4.57	205.66	4.59
1998	8 625.52	1 085.50	1 794.91	1.49	3.46	215.90	4.98
1999	10 464.88	1 327.33	2 728.15	1.25	3.17	226.96	5.12
2000	10 734.90	1 427.22	3 783.67	1.15	3.63	244.10	7.55
2001	10 189.13	1 194.18	2 035.00	1.32	2.95	262.48	7.53
2002	9 226.43	993.94	1 539.73	1.61	2.92	281.97	7.43
2003	8 993.59	965.23	1 647.17	1.77	3.84	304.06	7.83
2004	10 317.39	1 130.65	1 986.53	1.72	4.89	340.29	11.92
2005	10 547.67	1 207.23	2 099.32	1.83	5.36	385.76	13.36
2004							
January	10 540.05	1 132.52	2 098.00	1.62	...	...	...
February	10 601.50	1 143.36	2 048.36	1.63	...	309.24	8.24
March	10 323.73	1 123.98	1 979.48	1.68	4.62	...	...
April	10 418.40	1 133.08	2 021.32	1.68	...	...	...
May	10 083.81	1 102.78	1 930.09	1.74	...	317.77	9.84
June	10 364.90	1 132.76	2 000.98	1.70	4.92	...	...
July	10 152.09	1 105.85	1 912.42	1.77	...	...	...
August	10 032.80	1 088.94	1 821.54	1.81	...	331.97	12.84
September	10 204.67	1 117.66	1 884.73	1.78	5.18	...	...
October	10 001.60	1 118.07	1 938.25	1.79	...	...	...
November	10 411.76	1 168.94	2 062.87	1.74	...	340.29	11.92
December	10 673.38	1 199.21	2 149.53	1.72	4.83	...	...
2005							
January	10 539.51	1 181.41	2 071.87	1.77	...	...	...
February	10 723.82	1 199.63	2 065.74	1.76	...	349.61	13.05
March	10 682.09	1 194.90	2 030.43	1.79	5.11	...	...
April	10 283.19	1 164.42	1 957.49	1.86	...	...	...
May	10 377.18	1 178.28	2 005.22	1.86	...	362.38	14.04
June	10 486.68	1 202.26	2 074.02	1.83	5.32	...	...
July	10 545.38	1 222.24	2 145.14	1.82	...	...	...
August	10 554.27	1 224.27	2 157.85	1.82	...	374.23	12.73
September	10 532.54	1 225.91	2 144.61	1.84	5.42	...	...
October	10 324.31	1 191.96	2 087.09	1.90	...	...	...
November	10 695.25	1 237.37	2 202.84	1.85	...	385.76	13.36
December	10 827.79	1 262.07	2 246.09	1.84	5.60	...	...

... = Not available.

NOTES AND DEFINITIONS

TABLES 12-1, 12-2, AND 20-5
MONEY STOCK MEASURES; SELECTED COMPONENTS OF THE MONEY STOCK

SOURCE: BOARD OF GOVERNORS OF THE FEDERAL RESERVE SYSTEM

Estimates of two monetary aggregates (M1 and M2) and the components of these measures are published weekly. The monthly data are averages of daily figures.

The Federal Reserve Board ceased publication of the M3 aggregate on March 23, 2006. Weekly publication was also discontinued for the following components of M3: large-denomination time deposits, repurchase agreements (RPs), and Eurodollars. The Board continues to publish institutional money market mutual funds as a memorandum item in this release. Measures of large-denomination time deposits continue to be published in the flow of funds accounts (Z.1 release) and in the H.8 release weekly for commercial banks.

The Board stated that "M3 does not appear to convey any additional information about economic activity that is not already embodied in M2 and has not played a role in the monetary policy process for many years. Consequently, the Board judged that the costs of collecting the underlying data and publishing M3 outweigh the benefits." ("Discontinuance of M3," H.6, Money Stock Measures [November 10, 2005, revised March 9, 2006]. <http://www.federalreserve.gov/releases/h6>. [Accessed November 6, 2006.])

Definitions

M1 consists of (1) currency, (2) traveler's checks of non-bank issuers (bank-issued traveler's checks are included in demand deposits), (3) demand deposits, and (4) other checkable deposits.

M2 consists of M1 plus savings deposits (including money market deposit accounts), small-denomination time deposits, and balances in retail money market mutual funds. It excludes individual retirement account (IRA) and Keogh balances at depository institutions and money market funds.

M3 consisted of M2 plus large-denomination time deposits, balances in institutional money funds, RP liabilities (overnight and term) issued by all depository institutions, and Eurodollars (overnight and term).

Currency consists of currency outside the U.S. Treasury, the Federal Reserve Banks, and the vaults of depository institutions.

Demand deposits consists of demand deposits at domestically chartered commercial banks, U.S. branches and agencies of foreign banks, and Edge Act corporations (excluding those amounts held by depository institutions, the U.S. government, and foreign banks and official institutions) less cash items in the process of collection and Federal Reserve float. A "demand deposit" is a deposit that the depositor has a right to withdraw at any time without prior notice to the depository institution—most commonly, a checking account. "Federal Reserve float" is Federal Reserve credit that appears on the books of the depository institution of both the check writer and the check receiver while a check is being processed.

Other checkable deposits consists of negotiable order of withdrawal (NOW) and automatic transfer service (ATS) balances at all depository institutions, credit union share draft balances, and demand deposits at thrift institutions.

Repurchase agreements (RPs) are commitments by depository institutions to repurchase securities (often government securities) purchased by a client from the institution. A repurchase agreement constitutes a ready source of liquidity for the client, similar in nature to other components of M2 and M3. Both overnight and longer-term repurchase agreements are included in the data.

Eurodollars are dollar-denominated deposits—both overnight and term—held by U.S. residents at foreign branches of U.S. banks worldwide and at all banking offices in the United Kingdom and Canada.

Savings deposits includes money market deposit accounts and other savings deposits at commercial banks and thrift institutions.

Small time deposits are deposits issued at commercial banks and thrift institutions in amounts less than $100,000. Retail RPs are included. All IRA and Keogh account balances at commercial banks and thrift institutions are subtracted from small time deposits.

Large time deposits are deposits issued in amounts of $100,000 or more at commercial banks and thrift institutions, excluding those booked at international banking facilities. Deposits held at commercial banks by money market mutual funds, depository institutions, the U.S. government, and foreign banks and official institutions also are excluded.

Notes on the data

Seasonal adjustment. Seasonally adjusted M1 is calculated by summing currency, travelers checks, demand deposits, and other checkable deposits (each seasonally adjusted separately). Seasonally adjusted M2 is computed by adjusting each of its non-M1 components and then adding this result to seasonally adjusted M1. Similarly, seasonally adjusted M3 was obtained by adjusting each of its non-M2 components and then adding this result to seasonally adjusted M2.

Revisions. Money stock measures are revised frequently and have a benchmark and seasonal factor review in the middle of the year; this review typically extends back a number of years. The monetary aggregates were redefined in major revisions introduced in 1980.

Data availability

Estimates are released weekly in Federal Reserve Statistical Release H.6, "Money Stock Measures." Historical data beginning with 1959 are available from Publications Services, Board of Governors of the Federal Reserve System. Current and historical data are available on the Federal Reserve Web site at <http://www.federalreserve.gov/releases/>.

References

The Board of Governors of the Federal Reserve System's "The Federal Reserve System: Purposes and Functions," Ninth edition, 2005, available online at <http://www.federalreserve/gov> in the "Feature Publications" category, includes a chapter discussing monetary policy and the monetary aggregates (pp. 15-25) and a glossary of terms as an appendix.

An explanation of the 1980 redefinition of the monetary aggregates is found in the *Federal Reserve Bulletin* for February 1980.

TABLES 12-3 AND 20-5
AGGREGATE RESERVES OF DEPOSITORY INSTITUTIONS AND MONETARY BASE

Source: Board of Governors of the Federal Reserve System

The data presented here are in millions of dollars, seasonally adjusted and adjusted for changes in reserve requirements ("break-adjusted") in order to provide a consistent gauge of the effect of Federal Reserve open-market operations. Break adjustment is required, as an observed increase in reserves will not represent an easing in monetary conditions if it is simply equal to the increase in reserves required by the Federal Reserve. Therefore, the mandated increases and decreases are deducted to provide the break-adjusted series. Monthly data are averages of daily figures. Annual data are for December.

Definitions

Total reserves consists of reserve balances with the Federal Reserve Banks plus vault cash used to satisfy reserve requirements. Seasonally adjusted, break-adjusted total reserves equal seasonally adjusted, break-adjusted required reserves plus unadjusted excess reserves.

Seasonally adjusted, break-adjusted *nonborrowed reserves* equal seasonally adjusted, break-adjusted total reserves less unadjusted total borrowings of depository institutions from the Federal Reserve.

Extended credit consisted of borrowing at the discount window under the terms and conditions established for the extended credit program to help depository institutions deal with sustained liquidity pressures. Since there was not the same need to repay such borrowing promptly as there was with traditional short-term adjustment credit, the money market impact of extended credit was similar to that of nonborrowed reserves. The extended credit program was significant in the 1980s but used infrequently in subsequent years. It ended with the 2002 revision of the discount window program, effective January 9, 2003. See the explanation of the discount rate in the notes and definitions for Table 12-9.

To adjust *required reserves* for discontinuities due to regulatory changes in reserve requirements, a multiplicative procedure is used to estimate what required reserves would have been in past periods, had current reserve requirements been in effect. Break-adjusted required reserves include required reserves against transactions deposits and personal time and savings deposits (but not reservable nondeposit liabilities).

The seasonally adjusted, break-adjusted *monetary base* consists of (1) seasonally adjusted, break-adjusted total reserves; plus (2) the seasonally adjusted currency component of the money stock; plus (3) the seasonally adjusted, break-adjusted difference between current vault cash and the amount applied to satisfy current reserve requirements for all quarterly reporters on the "Report of Transaction Accounts, Other Deposits and Vault Cash" and for all weekly reporters whose vault cash exceeds their required reserves.

Revisions

The data are revised annually around midyear to reflect the result of annual reviews of seasonal factors and break factors.

Data availability

Data are released weekly in Federal Reserve Release H.3, "Aggregate Reserves of Depository Institutions and the Monetary Base." Current and historical data are available on the Federal Reserve Web site at <http://www.federalreserve.gov/releases/>.

TABLE 12-4
COMMERCIAL BANKS: BANK CREDIT AND SELECTED LIABILITIES

Source: Board of Governors of the Federal Reserve System.

Definitions and notes on the data

The data are for all commercial banks in the United States. This category covers the following types of institutions in the 50 states and the District of Columbia: domestically chartered commercial banks that report weekly (large domestic), other domestically chartered commercial banks (small domestic), branches and agencies of foreign banks, and Edge Act and Agreement corporations (foreign related institutions). International Banking Facilities are excluded.

Data are collected weekly for Wednesday values, and monthly data are pro rata averages of Wednesday values. Annual data represent December figures. Data are complete for large domestic banks. Data for other institutions are estimated on the basis of weekly samples and end-of-quarter condition reports. Data are adjusted for breaks caused by the reclassifications of assets and liabilities.

Data before 1988 are based on previous versions of this survey—the G.7 release, "Loans and Securities at Commercial Banks," and the G.10 release, "Major Nondeposit Funds of Commercial Banks."

Most of the categories of credit and liabilities are self-explanatory. The component of *loans and leases in bank credit* labeled *security loans* consists of loans to purchase and carry securities and reverse repurchase agreements (RPs) with brokers, dealers, and others. In a reverse RP, a bank has provided liquidity to a borrower by buying a security, which the borrower promises to repurchase at a certain date.

Interbank loans, cash assets, and other assets are not components of bank credit and are omitted from Table 12-4. Interbank loans include loans made to commercial banks, reverse RPs with commercial banks, and federal funds sold to commercial banks.

Selected liabilities show *deposits* and *borrowings*. Two components of total liabilities, "net due to foreign offices" and "other liabilities," are omitted.

Revisions

Data are revised annually around midyear to reflect new benchmark information and revised seasonal factors.

Data availability

Federal Reserve Statistical Release H.8, "Assets and Liabilities of Commercial Banks in the United States," is issued each Friday around 4:30 p.m. (EST). Current and historical data are available on the Federal Reserve Web site at <http://www.federalreserve.gov/releases/>.

TABLE 12-5
CREDIT MARKET DEBT OUTSTANDING, BY BORROWER AND LENDER

Source: *Board of Governors of the Federal Reserve System*

The flow of funds accounts, compiled quarterly by the Federal Reserve Board, supplement the national income and product accounts (NIPAs) by providing a comprehensive and detailed accounting of financial transactions with a balance sheet for each financial and nonfinancial sector of the economy. Table 12-5 is taken from these accounts. It shows the *credit market debt outstanding owed* by the major sectors in the economy, and it shows the major lending sectors in the credit markets under *credit market assets held*. One purpose of these statistics is to show the comparative growth of the various lending sectors.

Aggregates of these data can include multiple layers of financial intermediation, such as banks making advances to finance companies that subsequently lend to households. Adding bank data to finance company data would involve duplication of such debt. In macroeconomic analysis, the most widely used flow of funds measure is the total debt of domestic nonfinancial sectors. By eliminating the financial sectors, this measure has little duplication due to financial intermediation. The Federal Reserve uses this along with the monetary aggregates as an indicator of monetary conditions.

Definitions and notes on the data

Quarterly data on debt outstanding are shown on an end-of-period basis, not adjusted for seasonal variation or for "breaks" or discontinuities in the series. Due to these discontinuities, caution should be used in interpreting changes in debt levels. Break-adjusted values of changes, representing best estimates of actual fund flows, can be found in the quarterly flow of funds report, along with a suggested method for calculating percentage changes.

The data on credit market debt exclude corporate equities and mutual fund shares. However, these instruments do appear as assets in the household sector accounts in Table 12-6.

Data for the current and preceding years are revised each year to reflect revisions in source data, including the NIPAs; the revisions are issued about a month after the release of the annual NIPA revisions.

Sectors owing debt

Domestic financial sectors:

Federal government-related sectors include government-sponsored enterprises (GSEs) such as Fannie Mae (originally the Federal National Mortgage Association), Freddie Mac (originally the Federal Home Loan Mortgage Corporation), and Ginnie Mae (originally the Government National Mortgage Association); agency and GSE-backed mortgage pools; and the monetary authority (Federal Reserve). However, the Federal Reserve usually owes no credit market debt.

The *private* sector includes commercial banks and bank holding companies, savings institutions, credit unions, life insurance companies, asset-backed securities (ABS) issuers, brokers and dealers, finance and mortgage companies, REITs (real estate investment trusts), and funding corporations.

Domestic nonfinancial sectors:

Federal government consists of all federal government agencies and funds included in the unified budget. However, the District of Columbia government is included in the state and local sector.

Treasury securities as shown here excludes securities issued by the Treasury but held by agencies within the U.S. government (e.g., in the Social Security trust funds). In this respect, it corresponds to the "Federal debt" shown in Table 6-17, except that the latter table uses a fiscal-year basis rather than a calendar-year basis. Federal government debt as shown here is smaller than the official total public debt and the "debt subject to limit." Both of these also include the securities held by U.S. government agencies. The value shown here is considered to be a more accurate measure of the effect of government borrowing in relation to the economy and credit markets than those obtained from the larger aggregates.

Budget agency securities and mortgages are those issued bygovernment-owned corporations and agencies, such as the Export-Import Bank, that issue securities individually. There are no mortgages currently included in the debt of agencies.

Households also includes personal trusts and nonprofit organizations.

State and local governments represent operating funds only. State and local government retirement funds are included in the financial sector.

Foreign credit market debt held in the United States shows the foreign credit market debt owed to U.S. residents. This debt is included along with the debt of domestic financial and nonfinancial sectors in total credit market debt outstanding.

Percentage measures:

Table 12-5 includes three measures of relative debt burdens, calculated by the editor.

Domestic nonfinancial debt as a percent of GDP is the total debt owed by domestic nonfinancial sectors as a percent of the current-dollar value of total gross domestic product. (Table 1-1)

Household debt as a percent of DPI is the value of debt owed by households as a percent of the current-dollar value of disposable personal income. (Table 4-1)

Corporate nonfinancial business debt as a percent of sector value added is the total debt owed by domestic corporate nonfinancial business as a percent of the current-dollar

gross value added of domestic corporate nonfinancial business. (Table 1-13)

For the annual ratios, debt outstanding at the end of the year is taken as a percent of the product or income data for the full preceding year. For the quarterly ratios, the debt outstanding at the end of the quarter is taken as a percent of the annual rate of the product or income flow for that quarter. This means that the end-year ratios will almost inevitably be higher than the corresponding end-quarter ratios and should therefore not be compared with them.

Credit market assets held by sector

Selected government-related sectors:

This grouping includes two nonfinancial and three financial sectors. The nonfinancial sectors are the *federal government*, as reflected in the U.S. Budget accounts, and the operations of *state and local governments*, including the District of Columbia. *State and local employee retirement funds* are shown separately and considered to be a financial sector. (The considerably smaller category of federal government retirement funds is also considered to be a financial sector. It is not included in this grouping of government-related sectors but is included at the end of the table in *all other financial and nonfinancial sectors*.) The other two government-related financial sectors are *government-sponsored enterprises (GSEs)* and *federally related mortgage pools*.

Government-sponsored enterprise (GSEs) are financial institutions that provide credit to housing, agricultre, and other specific areas of the economy, such as Federal Home Loan Banks, Fannie Mae, and Freddie Mac (see above for explanation of the latter two terms).

Federally related mortgage pools are entities established for bookkeeping purposes that record the issuance of pooled securities representing an interest in mortgages backed by federal agencies and GSEs. Rather than being composed of a group of institutions, the sector is made up of a set of contractual arrangements in regard to pooled mortgages.

Selected domestic financial sectors:

This grouping includes major financial sectors, such as *commercial banks*, *savings institutions*, and *credit unions*. The *monetary authority* (the Federal Reserve) has been put in this group because it is sometimes included in banking sector totals. Other important financial sectors are *life insurance companies*, *property-casualty insurance companies*, and *private pension funds*. Additional private financial sectors are *money market mutual funds*, which issue shares and invest in short-term liquid assets; *mutual funds*, whose investments are not restricted to the short-term area; *asset-backed security (ABS) issuers*, which issue debt obligations that are backed by pooled assets, a financial procedure similar to that of federally related mortgage pools; and *finance companies*, which provide credit to businesses and individuals.

Private domestic nonfinancial sectors:

Households were the dominant private domestic nonfinancial lenders in earlier years, but lending by domestic households has now been surpassed by foreign holdings of assets representing claims on U.S. entities.

A number of lending sectors of smaller importance, nonfinancial and financial, are included in the category *All other financial and nonfinancial*. One of those is nonfinancial business, a sector that is important on the borrowing side but not on the lending side.

Data availability

Debt estimates are released quarterly, about nine weeks following the end of the quarter. The data can be found in Federal Reserve Statistical Release Z.1, "Flow of Funds of the United States," available on the Federal Reserve Web site at <http://www.federalreserve.gov/releases>. The data in Table 12-5 are found in Tables L.1 and L.2 of that release. Current and historical data are also available on the same Federal Reserve Web site.

References

The *Guide to the Flow of Funds Accounts* can be ordered; ordering information is available on the Federal Reserve Web site. The *Federal Reserve Bulletin* for July 2001 includes an article entitled "The U.S. Flow of Funds Accounts and Their Uses."

TABLE 12-6
HOUSEHOLD ASSETS, LIABILITIES, NET WORTH, FINANCIAL OBLIGATIONS, AND DELINQUENCY RATES

SOURCE: BOARD OF GOVERNORS OF THE FEDERAL RESERVE SYSTEM

The quarterly data on household sector assets, liabilities, and net worth are also obtained from the Federal Reserve Board's flow of funds accounts, which are described above. These data appear in Table B.100 of the Z.1 statistical release, also cited above. The household credit ratios and rates are also compiled by the Federal Reserve.

The household debt service ratio relates required debt service (interest and principal) payments to disposable personal income (DPI). The financial obligations ratios include not only required debt payments, but also rental payments, automobile lease payments, homeowners' insurance, and property taxes. They are also expressed as a percentage of DPI. Unlike the debt service ratio, the financial obligations ratios are not distorted by the trend toward debt-financed homeownership in preference to rental or the trend toward auto leasing in preference to loan financing.

The delinquency and charge-off rates relate delinquent (past due 30 days or more) and charged-off consumer credit card credit at commercial banks to total bank holdings of that type of credit.

Definitions and notes on the data

Quarterly data on holdings of *financial assets* are shown on an end-of-period basis, not adjusted for seasonal variations. Data for the current and preceding years are revised annually to reflect revisions in source data. For most categories, the values for the household sector are calculated as residuals. That is, starting with known totals (such as total Treasury securities), amounts held by other sectors are subtracted and the remainders are assigned to the household sector.

Financial assets of the household sector include nonprofit organizations, which are difficult to estimate separately, but exclude holdings by unincorporated businesses.

The table shows total household ownership of *checkable deposits and currency, time and savings deposits, money market fund shares, U.S. savings bonds, other Treasury securities, agency- and GSE-backed securities, municipal securities, corporate and foreign bonds, mortgages, corporate equities* (at market value), *mutual fund shares* (with equities at market value and other assets at book value), *security credit, life insurance reserves, pension fund reserves*, and *equity in noncorporate business*. Note that the reserves of life insurance companies and pension funds, though held by institutions, are counted here as assets of the household sector. *Pension fund reserves* includes insurance and pension fund reserves of federal, state, and local government employee funds—but not the Social Security system—as well as private industry funds. Bank personal trusts were formerly included as a type of household financial asset. However, in the latest revision of the flow of funds accounts, the various assets in these trusts were instead included in the appropriate categories, such as bonds, equities, and so forth. Included in total *financial assets*, but not shown separately, are foreign deposits, open market paper, and claims on insurance companies, such as unearned premium reserves of other insurance companies and health insurance reserves of life insurance companies.

Tangible assets complete the asset side of the household balance sheet. Tangible assets comprise equipment and software owned by nonprofit organizations, real estate, and consumer durable goods. Household real estate includes farm homes, mobile homes, second homes not rented, vacant homes for sale, vacant land, and owner-occupied housing. It is valued at market value, while equipment, software, and consumer durables are valued at replacement (current) cost.

Debt as a percent of total assets is calculated by the editor as household credit market debt outstanding, from Table 12-5, as a percent of the total of tangible and financial assets in this table. It covers both households and non-profit organizations.

Total liabilities consists of household credit market debt, as shown in Table 12-5, plus security credit, trade payables of nonprofit organizations, and deferred and unpaid life insurance premiums.

Net worth is the sum of the value of financial and tangible assets minus total liabilities.

The *household debt-service* and *financial obligations ratios* are estimated on a quarterly basis by the Federal Reserve based on aggregate and consumer survey data. They are seasonally adjusted, unlike almost all of the other data in Table 12-6. Fourth-quarter values are shown to represent the calendar year. The denominator for the aggregate ratio is disposable personal income (DPI) from the NIPAs. (See Chapter 4.) The allocation of the NIPA data between *renters* and *homeowners* is estimated by the Federal Reserve based on data from its triennial Survey of Consumer Finances and the Census Bureau's Current Population Survey (CPS). (For more information on the CPS, see the notes and definitions for Chapters 3 and 10.)

Debt service payments are the minimum required monthly payments of principal and interest on mortgage debt (including home equity loans), revolving credit (credit card debt), and auto, student, mobile home, recreational vehicle, marine, and personal loans.

The *financial obligations ratios* include, in addition to debt service, rental payments on primary residences, property taxes, homeowners' insurance, and automobile lease payments.

Delinquency and *charge-off rates of credit card accounts held at banks* are compiled from the quarterly FFIEC (Federal Financial Institutions Examination Council) Consolidated Reports of Condition and Income (FFIEC 031 through 034) and pertain to all insured U.S.-chartered commercial banks. The delinquency rate concerns loans past due 30 days or more and still accruing interest as well as those in *nonaccrual status*, measured as a percentage of end-of-period loans. The *charge-off rate* is the value of net charge-offs (loans removed from the books and charged against loss reserves, minus recoveries) as a percentage of average loans outstanding over the quarter, annualized.

Data availability

Household balance sheet estimates are released quarterly, about nine weeks following the end of a quarter, in the Federal Reserve Statistical Release Z.1, "Flow of Funds Accounts of the United States." Further information on data availability is given in the notes to Table 12-5, a table that is also based on the flow of funds accounts.

The revised debt service ratio and the new financial obligations ratios are described in "Recent Changes to a Measure

of U.S. Household Debt Service," Federal Reserve Bulletin, October 2003. The data are estimated by the Federal Reserve about three months after the end of each quarter. Current and historical data are available on the Federal Reserve Web site at <http://www.federalreserve.gov/releases>.

Delinquency and charge-off rates of credit card accounts held at banks are also available on the Federal Reserve Web site, listed under "Charge-off and Delinquency Rates on Loans at Commercial Banks." Rates are posted approximately 60 days after the end of the quarter.

TABLE 12-7
MORTGAGE DEBT OUTSTANDING

SOURCE: BOARD OF GOVERNORS OF THE FEDERAL RESERVE SYSTEM

These data are also published in the Federal Reserve's Statistical Release Z.1, "Flow of Funds Accounts," Table L.217. They are based on reports from various government and private organizations.

Definitions and notes on the data

By type of property:

Home mortgages includes home equity loans; these are also shown separately in the flow of funds accounts.

Multifamily residences refers to mortgages on structures of five or more units.

By type of holder:

Federal and related agencies shows mortgages held directly by the federal government and GSEs (see notes and definitions for Table 12-5 above).

Mortgage pools or trusts show mortgages that were refinanced by their holders through the issuance of mortgage-backed securities. They are shown in two columns: refinancings by *federally related agencies*—mainly the Fannie Mae, Freddie Mac, and Ginnie Mae GSEs (see above)—and refinancings by private conduits (these are referred to as ABS issuers in the flow of funds accounts, which stands for issuers of asset-backed securities).

Other holders encompasses a variety of groups, including finance companies, individuals, state and local governments, credit unions, and others.

Home mortgage debt as a percent of the value of real estate is calculated by the editor, using total home mortgage debt as a percent of the value of household real estate, which is shown in Table 12-6.

Data availability

Mortgage debt data are compiled quarterly about nine weeks following the end of the quarter in Federal Reserve Statistical Release Z.1, "Flow of Funds Accounts of the United States." The release and current and historical data are available on the Federal Reserve Web site at <http://www.federalreserve.gov/releases>.

TABLE 12-8
CONSUMER CREDIT

SOURCE: BOARD OF GOVERNORS OF THE FEDERAL RESERVE SYSTEM

The consumer credit series cover most short- and intermediate-term credit extended to individuals through regular business channels, excluding loans secured by real estate (such as first and second mortgages and home equity credit). In October 2003, the scope of the statistics was expanded to incorporate student loans extended by the federal government and by SLM Holding Corporation (SLM), the parent company of Sallie Mae (Student Loan Marketing Association). The historical data have been revised back to 1977 to reflect this inclusion.

The failure to include home equity credit is an important limitation of this data set. The household debt series presented in Table 12-5 is more comprehensive, comprising both mortgage and consumer debt.

Consumer credit is categorized by major types of credit and by major holders.

Definitions and notes on the data

The major types of consumer credit are *revolving* and *nonrevolving*. *Revolving credit* includes credit arising from purchases on credit card plans of retail stores and banks, cash advances and check credit plans of banks, and some overdraft credit arrangements. *Nonrevolving credit* includes automobile loans, mobile home loans, and all other loans not included in revolving credit, such as loans for education, boats, trailers, or vacations. These loans may be secured or unsecured.

Debt secured by real estate (including first liens, junior liens, and home equity loans) is excluded. Credit extended to governmental agencies and nonprofit or charitable organizations, as well as credit extended to business or to individuals exclusively for business purposes, is excluded.

Categories of *holders* include *commercial banks*, *finance companies*, *credit unions*, *federal government and Sallie Mae*, *savings institutions*, *nonfinancial businesses*, and *pools of securitized assets*. Retailers and gasoline companies are included in the nonfinancial businesses category. *Pools of securitized assets* comprises the outstanding balances of pools upon which securities have been issued; these balances are no longer carried on the balance sheets of the loan originators.

The consumer credit series are based on comprehensive benchmark data that periodically become available. Current monthly estimates are brought forward from the latest benchmarks in accordance with weighted changes indicated by sample data. Classifications are made on a "holder" basis. Thus, installment paper sold by retail outlets is included in the figures for the banks and finance companies that purchased the paper.

The amount of outstanding credit represents the sum of the balances in the installment receivable accounts of financial institutions and retail outlets at the end of each month.

The estimates of the amount of credit outstanding include any finance and insurance charges included as part of the installment contract. Unearned income on loans is included in some cases when lenders cannot separate the components.

The seasonally adjusted data are adjusted for differences in the number of trading days and for seasonal influences. The seasonal factors used are derived through the X-11-ARIMA process.

Data availability

Current data are available monthly in the Federal Reserve Statistical Release G.19, "Consumer Credit," available along with all current and historical data on the Federal Reserve Web site at http://www.federalreserve.gov/releases/>. In the autumn of each year there is a revision of several years of past data reflecting benchmarking and seasonal factor review.

TABLES 12-9, 12-10 AND 20-6
INTEREST RATES, BOND YIELDS, STOCK PRICES AND YIELDS, AND EXISTING HOUSE PRICES

SOURCES: BOARD OF GOVERNORS OF THE FEDERAL RESERVE SYSTEM; BUREAU OF ECONOMIC ANALYSIS; MOODY'S INVESTORS SERVICE; THE BOND BUYER; DOW JONES, INC.; STANDARD AND POOR'S CORPORATION; NEW YORK STOCK EXCHANGE; OFHEO (OFFICE OF FEDERAL HOUSING ENTERPRISE OVERSIGHT)

Definitions and notes on the data

Interest rates and bond yields are percents per year and are averages of business day figures, except as noted. With two exceptions, they are nominal rates or yields not adjusted for inflation. Due to the attention now being given to "real" interest rates, *Business Statistics* now includes two estimates of an inflation-adjusted rate—one short-term and one long-term—in this table.

Real federal funds rate. There is no directly observable real short-term rate, but it can be approximated by subtracting some measure of the current inflation rate from the nominal rate. For Table 12-9, the editor has selected one widely-followed measure—the rate of change in the core PCE (personal consumption expenditures, excluding food and energy) chain price index—and calculated a "real" federal funds rate by subtracting the core inflation rate from the nominal rate. In the annual data, the inflation rate is the percentage change in the price index from the previous year; in the monthly data, it is the percentage change from the same month a year earlier. (The nominal federal funds rate is defined below.) As noted in Chapter 8, which includes and defines several different measures of inflation, other price indexes can be used as inflation indicators.

Real rate on TIPS. In recent years, the Treasury Department has begun to issue Treasury Inflation-Protected Securities (TIPS), which are marketable long-term bonds whose redemption value is increased by the change in the CPI-U from the date of purchase. (See the notes and definitions for Chapter 8.) The purchaser of these bonds, unlike with ordinary securities, is guaranteed that the real value of his or her principal will remain intact. He or she need not estimate future inflation in order to make a rational bid. Therefore, the observed purchase price represents a real rate of interest that purchasers and sellers are mutually willing to accept. The TIPS interest rate shown here is based on the unweighted average of the bid yields for all TIPS with remaining terms to maturity over 10 years.

The daily effective *federal funds rate* is a weighted average of rates on trades through New York brokers. Monthly figures include each calendar day in the month. Annualized figures use a 360-day year.

The *Federal Reserve discount rate* is the rate for discount window borrowing at the Federal Reserve Bank of New York. Monthly figures include each calendar day in the month. Annualized figures use a 360-day year.

Beginning in January 2003, the rules governing the discount window programs were revised. "Adjustment credit," which was extended at a below-market rate (as can be seen in Table 12-9), was replaced by a new type of credit called "primary credit." Primary credit is available for very short terms as a backup source of liquidity to depository institutions in generally sound financial condition, as judged by the lending Federal Reserve Bank. Primary credit is extended at a rate <u>above</u> the federal funds rate, eliminating the incentive for institutions to exploit the spread of money market rates over the discount rate.

Through December 2002, Table 12-9 displays the adjustment credit rate. Beginning in February 2003, the new primary credit rate is shown. The rule change, and the change in discount rates shown, did not entail a change in the stance of monetary policy, which continues to be measured by the level of the federal funds rate.

The *Eurodollar rate* shown is the bid rate for Eurodollar deposits at about 9:30 a.m. (EST) for 1-month deposits. Annualized figures use a 360-day year.

The *U.S. Treasury bills, 3-month rate* and the *U.S. Treasury bills, 6-month rate* are the yields on these securities based on their prices as traded in the secondary market. The rates are quoted on a discount basis. Annualized figures use a 360-day year.

Commercial paper, 3-month rates are interpolated from data on certain commercial paper trades settled by the Depository Trust Company. This company is a clearinghouse and custodian for nearly all domestic commercial paper activity. The trades, which are on a discount basis, represent sales of commercial paper by dealers or direct issuers. Annualized figures use a 360-day year. Prior to September 1997, the series represented both nonfinancial and financial commercial paper; since September 1997, only rates for financial companies have been shown. This introduces a slight discontinuity in this series between August and September 1997.

CDs (secondary market), 3-month rates are averages of dealer offering rates on nationally traded certificates of deposit. Annualized figures use a 360-day year.

The *bank prime rate* is one of several base rates used by banks to price short-term business loans. It is the rate posted by a majority of the top 25 (by assets in domestic offices) insured U.S.-chartered commercial banks. Monthly figures include each calendar day in the month. Annualized figures use a 360-day year.

The *inflation* column is the rate of change in the PCE chain-type price index, excluding food and energy. For monthly entries, it is the change from the same month a year earlier. This price index is calculated by the Bureau of Economic Analysis (BEA) and shown in Table 8-2. The inflation rate is shown along with other rates in Table 8-3; see the notes and definitions for that table.

U.S. Treasury securities. The rates shown for 1-year, 3-year, 10-year, 20-year, and 30-year securities are yields on actively traded issues adjusted to constant maturities. Yields on Treasury securities at "constant maturity" are interpolated by the Treasury Department from the daily yield curve. This curve, which relates the yield on a security to its time to maturity, is based on the closing market bid yields on actively traded Treasury securities in the over-the-counter market. These market yields are calculated from composites of quotations reported by U.S. Government securities dealers to the Federal Reserve Bank of New York. The constant maturity yield values are read from the yield curve at fixed maturities. For example, this method provides a yield for a 10-year maturity, even if no outstanding security has exactly 10 years remaining to maturity. The 30-year series was discontinued as of February 2002, because the Treasury Department was no longer issuing such bonds. (In 2005, the 30-year bond was revived.) The current 20-year series begins with 1993 and is not comparable with an earlier 20-year series. For further information, see the historical data series on the Federal Reserve Web site at <http://www.federal reserve.gov>.

Domestic corporate bond yields. The rates shown are for general obligation bonds based on Thursday figures, and are provided by Moody's Investors Service and republished by the Federal Reserve. The Aaa rates through December 6, 2001 are averages of Aaa utility and Aaa industrial bond rates. As of December 7, 2001, these rates are averages of Aaa industrial bonds only.

The *state and local bond yields* are the Bond Buyer index as republished by the Federal Reserve. The index is based on 20 state and local government general obligation bonds of mixed quality maturing in 20 years or less. Quotes are as of the Thursday of each week.

The *fixed rate mortgage* rates are primary market contract interest rates on commitments for fixed-rate conventional 30-year first mortgages. The rates are obtained by the Federal Reserve from the Federal Home Loan Mortgage Corporation (FHLMC, or Freddie Mac).

Stock price indexes. The *Dow Jones industrial* average is an average of 30 stocks compiled by Dow Jones, Inc. The *Standard and Poor's composite* is an index of 500 stocks based on 1941–1943 = 10 compiled by Standard and Poor's Corporation. The *dividend-price ratio* is compiled by Standard and Poor's, covering the 500 stocks in the S&P index. It represents aggregate cash dividends (based on the latest known annual rate) divided by aggregate market value based on Wednesday closing prices. The *earnings/price ratio* measures earnings (after taxes) for four quarters, ending with the indicated quarter, as a ratio to stock prices for the last day of that quarter. Monthly data are averages of weekly figures; annual data are averages of monthly or quarterly figures. The *Nasdaq composite index* is an average of over 5,000 stocks traded on the Nasdaq exchange.

OFHEO house price index. The value of single-family owner-occupied houses has been an increasingly important element in household economic well-being and credit expansion. The Office of Federal Housing Enterprise Oversight (OFHEO), a government agency charged with regulation of the government-sponsored mortgage finance institutions Fannie Mae and Freddie Mac, uses data from those institutions to compile a quarterly index of the value

of existing single-family homes. This index has been published since the fourth quarter of 1995. The data come from all properties for which a conventional, "conforming" mortgage has been purchased or securitized by Fannie Mae or Freddie Mac since January 1975. (A conforming mortgage is one no larger than the maximum that the insuring institution will insure.) Every new mortgage transaction that can be matched against a previous transaction for that property yields a rate of price change, which enters into the calculation of the index. This data set is very large, with about 30 million repeat transactions over the 30 years. Due to the size of this data set, the index can be calculated not only for the United States as a whole but also for regions, states, metropolitan statistical areas (MSAs) and metropolitan divisions (subdivisions of MSAs).

The OFHEO price index is subject to revision for preceding quarters and years, because each new transaction, when reported, affects the rate of price change since the last time that the property involved in the new transaction changed hands or was refinanced.

Data availability and references

Interest rates and bond yields are published weekly in the Federal Reserve's H.15 release, "Selected Interest Rates"; the release and current and historical data are available on the Federal Reserve Web site at <http://www.federalreserve.gov/releases/>. The starting dates for individual interest rate series vary; some date back to 1911, and many begin in the 1950s and 1960s.

Stock market data are published monthly in *Economic Indicators*, available by subscription from the Superintendent of Documents, Government Printing Office, Washington, DC 20402-9328, and annually in *Economic Report of the President*, available from the same source. Some historical interest rate data that are not available on the Federal Reserve Web site were taken from the *Economic Report of the President*.

The OFHEO house price indexes for the United States as a whole, regions, states, and metropolitan and sub-metropolitan groups are available on the OFHEO Web site at <http://www.ofheo.gov/hpi>. Explanatory material is also available on the OFHEO Web site.

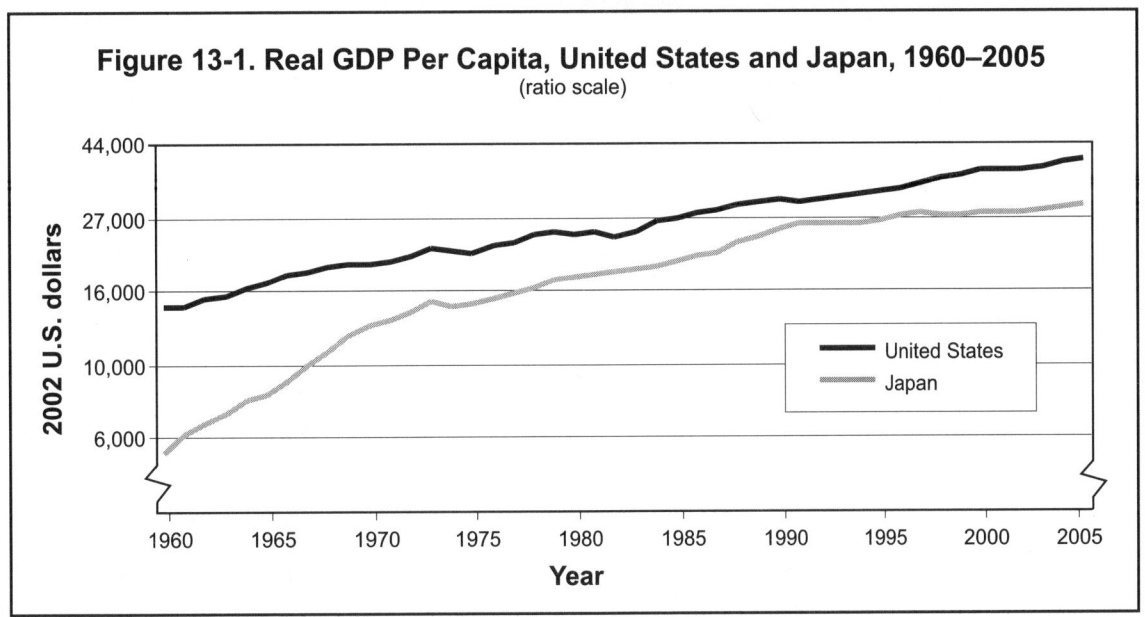

Figure 13-1. Real GDP Per Capita, United States and Japan, 1960–2005
(ratio scale)

- In the United States, gross domestic product (GDP) per capita grew at an annual rate of 2.3 percent between 1960 and 2000. The major industrial nations with the next-highest average levels of living in 1960—Germany, the United Kingdom, and Canada—grew at similar rates of 2.2 percent, 2.2 percent, and 2.4 percent, respectively. (Germany's growth would have been higher, perhaps 2.5 percent, without the effect of unification of West Germany with the poorer East Germany in 1991.) The industrial nations that were further behind in 1960—Japan, France, and Italy—grew at faster rates: 4.2 percent, 2.7 percent, and 3.1 percent, respectively. The growth paths of the United States and Japan are compared in Figure 13-1. (Table 13-2)

- In Japan and the four European countries compared in Tables 13-2 and 13-3, the growth rate in GDP per employed person—a measure of labor productivity—was very similar to the growth rate in GDP per capita. In other words, growth in productivity and in potential living standards was the same. In contrast, growth in GDP per employee was only 1.7 percent per year in the United States and 1.6 percent in Canada, significantly less than their per capita output growth rates, and less than productivity growth rates in Japan and the European countries. This means that in the two major North American economies, a significant fraction of the growth in GDP per capita was obtained from putting a larger proportion of the population to work, instead of from greater efficiency. (Tables 13-2 and 13-3)

- Japan experienced another year of deflation in 2005. The United States had the highest inflation rate (3.4 percent), while inflation in the other countries ranged from 1.8 to 2.8 percent. (Table 13-4)

- In 2005, the unemployment rate fell in the United States, Japan, Italy, and Canada; was little changed in France and the United Kingdom; and rose to 11.2 percent in Germany. (Table 13-5)

Table 13-1. International Comparisons: Growth Rates in Real Gross Domestic Product

(Percent change at annual rate.)

Area and country	1987–1996	1997	1998	1999	2000	2001	2002	2003	2004	2005 [1]
World	3.3	4.2	2.8	3.7	4.7	2.4	3.0	4.0	5.1	4.3
Advanced economies	3.0	3.5	2.6	3.5	3.9	1.2	1.5	1.9	3.3	2.5
United States	2.9	4.5	4.2	4.5	3.7	0.8	1.6	2.7	4.2	3.5
Japan	3.2	1.8	-1.0	-0.1	2.4	0.2	-0.3	1.4	2.7	2.0
United Kingdom	2.4	3.2	3.2	3.0	4.0	2.2	2.0	2.5	3.2	1.9
Canada	2.2	4.2	4.1	5.5	5.2	1.8	3.1	2.0	2.9	2.9
Euro area	. . .	2.6	2.8	2.7	3.8	1.7	0.9	0.7	2.0	1.2
Germany	2.6	1.7	2.0	1.9	3.1	1.2	0.1	-0.2	1.6	0.8
France	1.9	2.3	3.4	3.2	4.1	2.1	1.3	0.9	2.0	1.5
Italy	1.9	2.0	1.8	1.7	3.0	1.8	0.4	0.3	1.2	(2)
Spain	2.9	4.0	4.3	4.2	5.8	3.5	2.7	2.9	3.1	3.2
Netherlands	2.7	3.8	4.3	4.0	3.5	1.4	0.1	-0.1	1.7	0.7
Belgium	2.2	3.8	2.1	3.2	3.7	0.9	0.9	1.3	2.7	1.2
Austria	2.5	1.8	3.6	3.3	3.4	0.8	1.0	1.4	2.4	1.9
Finland	1.3	6.2	5.0	3.4	5.0	1.0	2.2	2.4	3.6	1.8
Greece	1.4	3.6	3.4	3.4	4.5	4.3	3.8	4.7	4.2	3.2
Portugal	4.0	4.0	4.6	3.8	3.4	1.7	0.4	-1.1	1.0	0.5
Ireland	5.2	10.8	8.5	10.7	9.2	6.2	6.1	4.4	4.5	5.0
Luxembourg	5.2	8.3	6.8	7.3	9.2	2.2	2.3	2.4	4.4	3.1
Memorandum:										
Major advanced economies [3]	2.7	3.3	2.8	3.1	3.5	1.0	1.1	1.8	3.2	2.5
Newly industrialized Asian economies [4]	7.9	5.5	-2.6	7.3	7.9	1.3	5.3	3.1	5.6	4.0
Other emerging market and developing countries	3.8	5.2	3.0	4.0	5.8	4.1	4.8	6.5	7.3	6.4
Regional groups										
Africa	2.2	3.4	3.2	2.8	3.3	4.1	3.6	4.6	5.3	4.5
Central and Eastern Europe	0.9	4.2	2.8	0.5	4.9	0.2	4.4	4.6	6.5	4.3
Commonwealth of Independent States [5]	. . .	1.1	-3.5	5.1	9.1	6.3	5.3	7.9	8.4	6.0
Russia	. . .	1.4	-5.3	6.3	10.0	5.1	4.7	7.3	7.2	5.5
Developing Asia	7.8	6.5	4.2	6.2	6.7	5.6	6.6	8.1	8.2	7.8
China	10.0	8.8	7.8	7.1	8.0	7.5	8.3	9.5	9.5	9.0
India	5.9	5.0	5.8	6.7	5.4	3.9	4.7	7.4	7.3	7.1
Middle East	3.4	4.7	4.2	2.0	4.9	3.7	4.2	6.5	5.5	5.4
Western Hemisphere	2.7	5.2	2.3	0.4	3.9	0.5	(2)	2.2	5.6	4.1
Brazil	2.1	3.3	0.1	0.8	4.4	1.3	1.9	0.5	4.9	3.3
Mexico	2.5	6.7	4.9	3.9	6.6	-0.2	0.8	1.4	4.4	3.0

[1]All figures are forecasts as published by the International Monetary Fund. For the United States, the latest Department of Commerce estimates are that real GDP grew 2.5 percent in 2003, 3.9 percent in 2004, and 3.2 percent in 2005.
[2]Figure is zero or negligible.
[3]Includes Canada, France, Germany, Italy, Japan, the United Kingdom, and the United States.
[4]Includes Hong Kong SAR (Special Administrative Region of China), Korea, Singapore, and Taiwan Province of China.
[5]Includes Mongolia, which is not a member of the Commonwealth of Independent States, but is included for reasons of geography and similarities in economic structure.
. . . = Not available.

Table 13-2. International Comparisons: Real Gross Domestic Product (GDP) Per Capita

(2002 U.S. dollars.)

Year	United States	Japan	Germany [1]	France	United Kingdom	Italy	Canada
1960	14 420	5 366	11 346	9 483	11 700	7 240	11 448
1961	14 516	6 003	11 715	9 901	11 888	7 782	11 573
1962	15 161	6 458	12 119	10 374	11 918	8 209	12 136
1963	15 598	6 954	12 340	10 733	12 451	8 606	12 520
1964	16 278	7 650	13 029	11 316	13 055	8 774	13 090
1965	17 107	7 919	13 575	11 757	13 270	8 985	13 686
1966	18 014	8 746	13 829	12 268	13 458	9 449	14 314
1967	18 267	9 602	13 755	12 743	13 713	10 055	14 479
1968	18 958	10 626	14 453	13 188	14 226	10 645	15 020
1969	19 351	11 756	15 384	13 997	14 462	11 231	15 595
1970	19 162	12 701	16 003	14 667	14 744	11 765	15 782
1971	19 557	13 079	16 323	15 225	14 966	11 922	16 123
1972	20 374	13 983	16 909	15 761	15 459	12 289	16 789
1973	21 342	14 897	17 628	16 486	16 526	13 086	17 778
1974	21 040	14 519	17 640	16 888	16 300	13 774	18 258
1975	20 797	14 785	17 483	16 764	16 211	13 415	18 392
1976	21 694	15 216	18 503	17 407	16 650	14 300	19 148
1977	22 468	15 735	19 070	17 887	17 065	14 629	19 580
1978	23 470	16 417	19 665	18 406	17 632	15 058	20 177
1979	23 944	17 173	20 485	18 973	18 087	15 936	20 818
1980	23 615	17 521	20 616	19 216	17 685	16 493	20 836
1981	23 970	17 906	20 598	19 386	17 422	16 611	21 212
1982	23 282	18 273	20 419	19 825	17 776	16 681	20 362
1983	24 115	18 442	20 851	20 150	18 396	16 884	20 709
1984	25 623	18 895	21 524	20 372	18 839	17 439	21 707
1985	26 445	19 734	22 016	20 677	19 458	17 934	22 538
1986	27 114	20 216	22 516	21 074	20 181	18 425	22 856
1987	27 780	20 883	22 845	21 448	21 054	19 018	23 514
1988	28 667	22 204	23 552	22 316	22 058	19 810	24 365
1989	29 402	23 292	24 164	23 059	22 470	20 478	24 557
1990	29 620	24 423	25 062	23 554	22 570	20 866	24 235
1991	29 179	25 141	23 576	23 733	22 184	21 152	23 446
1992	29 752	25 291	23 919	24 038	22 189	21 290	23 371
1993	30 152	25 278	23 556	23 672	22 677	21 150	23 655
1994	30 987	25 491	24 110	24 066	23 616	21 625	24 520
1995	31 389	25 940	24 493	24 510	24 223	22 220	24 948
1996	32 174	26 769	24 666	24 689	24 823	22 355	25 088
1997	33 221	27 179	25 063	25 148	25 541	22 722	25 889
1998	34 208	26 827	25 579	25 928	26 296	23 019	26 726
1999	35 324	26 750	26 075	26 639	26 997	23 417	27 976
2000	36 215	27 332	26 879	27 538	27 989	24 240	29 166
2001	36 110	27 309	27 162	27 863	28 502	24 666	29 369
2002	36 321	27 196	27 132	27 961	28 969	24 718	29 937
2003	36 937	27 511	27 068	28 082	29 583	24 459	30 255
2004	38 125	28 129	27 516	28 552	30 419	24 536	30 845
2005	39 103	28 865	27 772	28 717	30 887	24 376	31 459

[1]Data prior to 1991 are for West Germany only. In 1991, real GDP per capita in West Germany alone was $25,990 (2002 U.S. dollars).

Table 13-3. International Comparisons: Real Gross Domestic Product (GDP) Per Employed Person

(2002 U.S. dollars.)

Year	United States	Japan	Germany [1]	France	United Kingdom	Italy	Canada
1960	38 168	10 745	24 133	22 278	25 381	17 410	32 583
1961	39 041	11 861	24 903	23 508	25 734	18 719	33 089
1962	40 687	12 734	25 974	25 082	25 912	19 939	34 409
1963	41 883	13 736	26 641	26 213	27 180	21 413	35 346
1964	43 365	15 049	28 392	27 617	28 314	22 088	36 388
1965	45 044	15 659	29 743	28 848	28 687	23 380	37 372
1966	46 587	16 900	30 667	30 127	29 186	25 191	38 240
1967	46 654	18 393	31 602	31 459	30 259	26 667	38 293
1968	47 898	20 200	33 297	32 896	31 687	28 427	39 628
1969	48 190	22 396	35 233	34 668	32 358	30 379	40 497
1970	48 003	24 420	36 545	36 163	33 183	31 844	41 132
1971	49 425	25 313	37 510	37 723	33 887	32 412	42 446
1972	50 553	27 301	38 949	39 163	35 006	33 687	43 465
1973	51 760	28 842	40 365	40 730	36 939	35 610	44 404
1974	50 554	28 609	40 940	41 634	36 360	37 151	44 421
1975	51 027	29 566	41 543	41 883	36 302	36 371	44 639
1976	52 049	30 492	43 988	43 320	37 496	38 574	46 167
1977	52 570	31 453	45 175	44 345	38 387	39 510	46 930
1978	53 227	32 792	46 153	45 606	39 453	40 678	47 408
1979	53 413	34 238	47 306	46 975	40 114	42 700	47 376
1980	53 033	34 963	47 045	47 699	39 446	43 652	46 671
1981	53 768	35 717	47 142	48 578	39 904	44 053	46 732
1982	53 160	36 406	47 261	49 907	41 486	44 180	46 826
1983	54 846	36 442	48 787	51 151	43 268	44 590	47 706
1984	56 490	37 451	50 080	52 081	43 452	46 070	49 253
1985	57 661	39 142	50 718	53 544	44 439	46 948	50 198
1986	58 350	40 095	51 199	54 643	45 915	47 905	49 921
1987	58 818	41 452	51 583	55 488	47 075	49 339	50 563
1988	59 945	43 749	53 089	57 541	47 853	50 873	51 532
1989	60 843	45 394	54 224	58 820	47 658	52 270	51 715
1990	61 263	46 972	55 662	59 929	47 793	52 471	51 465
1991	61 733	47 578	48 826	60 617	48 417	52 249	51 217
1992	63 456	47 504	50 650	62 057	49 742	52 883	52 124
1993	64 289	47 442	50 918	62 175	51 440	54 020	53 088
1994	65 426	47 913	52 326	63 347	52 664	56 170	54 496
1995	66 140	48 809	53 194	64 173	54 202	57 832	55 048
1996	67 655	50 276	53 871	64 621	55 168	57 870	55 430
1997	69 184	50 643	54 894	65 764	55 922	58 667	56 523
1998	71 053	50 445	55 347	67 029	57 151	58 870	57 435
1999	73 117	50 807	55 706	67 828	58 098	59 258	59 105
2000	73 944	52 081	56 436	68 715	59 749	60 201	60 733
2001	74 472	52 493	56 886	68 767	60 577	60 082	61 066
2002	75 895	53 074	57 240	69 043	61 319	59 379	61 476
2003	77 237	53 939	57 685	69 703	62 263	58 343	61 286
2004	79 625	55 067	58 406	71 286	63 581	58 905	61 962
2005	81 024	56 313	59 052	71 942	64 134	58 813	62 916

[1]Data prior to 1991 are for West Germany only. In 1991, real GDP per employed person in West Germany alone was $57,051 (2002 U.S. dollars).

Table 13-4. International Comparisons: Consumer Price Indexes

(1982–1984 = 100, except as noted; not seasonally adjusted; percent changes are from previous year's average for annual data, from the same quarter of the previous year for quarterly data.)

Year and quarter	United States Index	United States Percent change	Japan Index	Japan Percent change	Germany [1] Index	Germany [1] Percent change	France Index	France Percent change	United Kingdom Index	United Kingdom Percent change	Italy Index	Italy Percent change	Canada Index	Canada Percent change
1950	24.1	...	14.8	...	34.5	...	11.1	...	9.8	...	...	...	21.6	...
1951	26.0	7.9	17.2	16.2	37.2	7.8	13.0	17.1	10.7	9.2	...	...	23.9	10.6
1952	26.5	1.9	18.0	4.7	38.0	2.2	14.6	12.3	11.7	9.3	...	...	24.5	2.5
1953	26.7	0.8	19.2	6.7	37.3	-1.8	14.4	-1.4	12.1	3.4	10.3	...	24.2	-1.2
1954	26.9	0.7	20.5	6.8	37.3	0.0	14.3	-0.7	12.3	1.7	10.6	2.9	24.4	0.8
1955	26.8	-0.4	20.2	-1.5	38.0	1.9	14.5	1.4	12.9	4.9	10.9	2.8	24.4	0.0
1956	27.2	1.5	20.3	0.5	39.0	2.6	14.8	2.1	13.5	4.7	11.2	2.8	24.8	1.6
1957	28.1	3.3	20.9	3.0	39.8	2.1	15.3	3.4	14.0	3.7	11.4	1.8	25.6	3.2
1958	28.9	2.8	20.8	-0.5	40.6	2.0	17.6	15.0	14.4	2.9	11.7	2.6	26.3	2.7
1959	29.1	0.7	21.1	1.4	41.0	1.0	18.7	6.2	14.5	0.7	11.7	0.0	26.6	1.1
1960	29.6	1.7	21.8	3.3	41.6	1.5	19.4	3.7	14.6	0.7	11.9	1.7	26.9	1.1
1961	29.9	1.0	23.0	5.5	42.6	2.4	20.0	3.1	15.1	3.4	12.2	2.5	27.1	0.7
1962	30.2	1.0	24.6	7.0	43.8	2.8	21.0	5.0	15.8	4.6	12.7	4.1	27.4	1.1
1963	30.6	1.3	26.4	7.3	45.1	3.0	22.0	4.8	16.1	1.9	13.7	7.9	27.9	1.8
1964	31.0	1.3	27.4	3.8	46.2	2.4	22.7	3.2	16.6	3.1	14.5	5.8	28.4	1.8
1965	31.5	1.6	29.5	7.7	47.8	3.5	23.3	2.6	17.4	4.8	15.2	4.8	29.1	2.5
1966	32.4	2.9	31.0	5.1	49.4	3.3	23.9	2.6	18.1	4.0	15.5	2.0	30.2	3.8
1967	33.4	3.1	32.3	4.2	50.1	1.4	24.6	2.9	18.5	2.2	16.1	3.9	31.3	3.6
1968	34.8	4.2	34.0	5.3	50.8	1.4	25.7	4.5	19.4	4.9	16.3	1.2	32.5	3.8
1969	36.7	5.5	35.8	5.3	51.8	2.0	27.3	6.2	20.5	5.7	16.7	2.5	34.0	4.6
1970	38.8	5.7	38.5	7.5	53.5	3.3	28.8	5.5	21.8	6.3	17.5	4.8	35.1	3.2
1971	40.5	4.4	40.9	6.2	56.2	5.0	30.3	5.2	23.8	9.2	18.4	5.1	36.2	3.1
1972	41.8	3.2	42.9	4.9	59.2	5.3	32.2	6.3	25.5	7.1	19.4	5.4	37.9	4.7
1973	44.4	6.2	47.9	11.7	63.2	6.8	34.6	7.5	27.9	9.4	21.6	11.3	40.7	7.4
1974	49.3	11.0	59.1	23.4	67.6	7.0	39.3	13.6	32.3	15.8	25.7	19.0	45.2	11.1
1975	53.8	9.1	66.0	11.7	71.7	6.1	43.9	11.7	40.1	24.1	30.0	16.7	50.1	10.8
1976	56.9	5.8	72.2	9.4	74.8	4.3	48.2	9.8	46.8	16.7	35.1	17.0	53.8	7.4
1977	60.6	6.5	78.1	8.2	77.4	3.5	52.7	9.3	54.2	15.8	41.0	16.8	58.1	8.0
1978	65.2	7.6	81.4	4.2	79.4	2.6	57.5	9.1	58.7	8.3	46.0	12.2	63.3	9.0
1979	72.6	11.3	84.4	3.7	82.4	3.8	63.6	10.6	66.6	13.5	52.8	14.8	69.1	9.2
1980	82.4	13.5	90.9	7.7	86.7	5.2	72.3	13.7	78.5	17.9	64.0	21.2	76.1	10.1
1981	90.9	10.3	95.4	5.0	92.2	6.3	82.0	13.4	87.9	12.0	75.4	17.8	85.6	12.5
1982	96.5	6.2	98.0	2.7	97.1	5.3	91.6	11.7	95.4	8.5	87.8	16.4	94.9	10.9
1983	99.6	3.2	99.8	1.8	100.2	3.2	100.5	9.7	99.8	4.6	100.7	14.7	100.4	5.8
1984	103.9	4.3	102.1	2.3	102.7	2.5	107.9	7.4	104.8	5.0	111.5	10.7	104.7	4.3
1985	107.6	3.6	104.2	2.1	104.7	1.9	114.2	5.8	111.1	6.0	121.8	9.2	108.9	4.0
1986	109.6	1.9	104.8	0.6	104.5	-0.2	117.2	2.6	114.9	3.4	129.0	5.9	113.4	4.1
1987	113.6	3.6	104.9	0.1	104.6	0.1	120.9	3.2	119.7	4.2	135.1	4.7	118.4	4.4
1988	118.3	4.1	105.7	0.8	105.7	1.1	124.2	2.7	125.6	4.9	141.9	5.0	123.2	4.1
1989	124.0	4.8	108.1	2.3	108.8	2.9	128.6	3.5	135.4	7.8	150.8	6.3	129.3	5.0
1990	130.7	5.4	111.4	3.1	111.7	2.7	133.0	3.4	148.2	9.5	160.5	6.4	135.5	4.8
1991	136.2	4.2	115.1	3.3	81.9	3.8	137.2	3.2	156.9	5.9	170.6	6.3	143.1	5.6
1992	140.3	3.0	117.0	1.7	86.1	5.1	140.6	2.5	162.7	3.7	179.4	5.2	145.3	1.5
1993	144.5	3.0	118.5	1.3	89.9	4.4	143.5	2.1	165.3	1.6	187.5	4.5	147.9	1.8
1994	148.2	2.6	119.3	0.7	92.3	2.7	145.9	1.7	169.3	2.4	195.0	4.0	148.2	0.2
1995	152.4	2.8	119.2	-0.1	93.9	1.7	148.4	1.7	175.2	3.5	205.1	5.2	151.4	2.2
1996	156.9	3.0	119.3	0.1	95.3	1.5	151.3	2.0	179.4	2.4	213.4	4.0	153.8	1.6
1997	160.5	2.3	121.5	1.8	97.1	1.9	153.2	1.3	185.1	3.2	217.7	2.0	156.2	1.6
1998	163.0	1.6	122.2	0.6	98.0	0.9	154.3	0.7	191.4	3.4	222.0	2.0	157.7	1.0
1999	166.6	2.2	121.8	-0.3	98.6	0.6	155.0	0.5	194.3	1.5	225.7	1.7	160.5	1.8
2000	172.2	3.4	121.0	-0.7	100.0	1.4	157.7	1.7	200.1	3.0	231.4	2.5	164.8	2.7
2001	177.1	2.8	120.1	-0.7	102.0	2.0	160.3	1.6	203.6	1.7	237.8	2.8	169.0	2.5
2002	179.9	1.6	119.1	-0.8	103.4	1.4	163.4	1.9	207.0	1.7	243.7	2.5	172.8	2.2
2003	184.0	2.3	118.7	-0.3	104.5	1.1	166.8	2.1	213.0	2.9	250.3	2.7	177.6	2.8
2004	188.9	2.7	118.7	0.0	106.2	1.6	170.3	2.1	219.4	3.0	255.8	2.2	180.9	1.9
2005	195.3	3.4	118.3	-0.3	108.3	2.0	173.3	1.8	225.6	2.8	260.8	2.0	184.9	2.2
2004														
1st quarter	...	1.8	...	-0.1	...	1.0	...	1.8	...	2.6	...	2.3	...	0.9
2nd quarter	...	2.9	...	-0.3	...	1.8	...	2.4	...	2.8	...	2.3	...	2.2
3rd quarter	...	2.7	...	-0.1	...	1.9	...	2.3	...	3.1	...	2.2	...	2.0
4th quarter	...	3.3	...	0.5	...	2.0	...	2.1	...	3.4	...	2.0	...	2.3
2005														
1st quarter	...	3.0	...	0.0	...	1.7	...	1.7	...	3.2	...	1.9	...	2.1
2nd quarter	...	2.9	...	-0.1	...	1.7	...	1.7	...	3.0	...	1.8	...	1.9
3rd quarter	...	3.8	...	-0.3	...	2.1	...	1.9	...	2.8	...	2.0	...	2.6
4th quarter	...	3.7	...	-0.7	...	2.2	...	1.6	...	2.4	...	2.2	...	2.3

[1]From 1950 through 1990, former West Germany only, 1982–1984 = 100. From 1991 forward, unified Germany, 2000 = 100. In 1991, the percent change is based on the 1991 index for former West Germany, which was 115.9.

... = Not available.

Table 13-5. International Comparisons: Unemployment Rates and Civilian Labor Forces [1]

(Quarterly data are seasonally adjusted.)

Year and quarter	United States Unemployment rate	United States Labor force (thousands)	Japan Unemployment rate	Japan Labor force (thousands)	Germany [2] Unemployment rate	Germany [2] Labor force (thousands)	France Unemployment rate	France Labor force (thousands)	United Kingdom Unemployment rate	United Kingdom Labor force (thousands)	Italy Unemployment rate	Italy Labor force (thousands)	Canada Unemployment rate	Canada Labor force (thousands)
1959	5.5	68 369	2.3	43 320	2.0	25 850	1.6	18 480	2.8	23 880	4.8	21 020	5.6	6 286
1960	5.5	69 628	1.7	44 120	1.1	25 990	1.5	18 520	2.2	24 130	3.7	20 820	6.5	6 462
1961	6.7	70 459	1.5	44 610	0.6	26 160	1.2	18 530	2.0	24 380	3.2	20 830	6.7	6 575
1962	5.5	70 614	1.3	45 040	0.6	26 210	1.4	18 720	2.7	24 720	2.8	20 680	5.5	6 670
1963	5.7	71 833	1.3	45 430	0.5	26 290	1.6	19 100	3.3	24 940	2.4	20 240	5.2	6 805
1964	5.2	73 091	1.2	46 040	0.4	26 270	1.2	19 430	2.5	25 070	2.7	20 220	4.4	6 994
1965	4.5	74 455	1.2	46 780	0.3	26 360	1.6	19 650	2.1	25 240	3.5	19 900	3.6	7 207
1966	3.8	75 770	1.4	47 850	0.3	26 290	1.6	19 850	2.3	25 320	3.7	19 620	3.4	7 493
1967	3.8	77 347	1.3	48 810	1.3	25 730	2.1	20 070	3.3	25 290	3.4	19 800	3.8	7 747
1968	3.6	78 737	1.2	49 690	1.1	25 690	2.7	20 190	3.2	25 180	3.5	19 780	4.5	7 951
1969	3.5	80 734	1.1	50 140	0.6	25 960	2.3	20 470	3.1	25 160	3.5	19 620	4.4	8 194
1970	4.9	82 771	1.2	50 730	0.5	26 240	2.5	20 800	3.1	25 110	3.2	19 720	5.7	8 395
1971	5.9	84 382	1.3	51 120	0.6	26 380	2.8	21 000	4.2	25 373	3.3	19 660	6.2	8 639
1972	5.6	87 034	1.4	51 320	0.7	26 470	2.9	21 150	4.4	25 501	3.8	19 450	6.2	8 897
1973	4.9	89 429	1.3	52 590	0.7	26 780	2.8	21 430	3.7	25 723	3.7	19 590	5.5	9 276
1974	5.6	91 949	1.4	52 440	1.6	26 660	2.9	21 660	3.7	25 798	3.1	19 900	5.3	9 639
1975	8.5	93 775	1.9	52 530	3.4	26 430	4.2	21 770	4.5	25 932	3.4	20 090	6.9	9 974
1976	7.7	96 158	2.0	53 100	3.4	26 290	4.6	22 050	5.4	26 024	3.9	20 290	6.9	10 368
1977	7.1	99 009	2.0	53 820	3.4	26 330	5.2	22 380	5.6	26 108	4.1	20 510	7.8	10 661
1978	6.1	102 251	2.3	54 610	3.3	26 520	5.4	22 540	5.5	26 227	4.1	20 570	8.1	11 022
1979	5.8	104 962	2.1	55 210	2.9	26 860	6.1	22 780	5.4	26 463	4.4	20 850	7.3	11 392
1980	7.1	106 940	2.0	55 740	2.8	27 260	6.5	22 930	6.9	26 750	4.4	21 120	7.3	11 725
1981	7.6	108 670	2.2	56 320	4.0	27 540	7.6	23 090	9.7	26 864	4.9	21 320	7.3	12 080
1982	9.7	110 204	2.4	56 980	5.6	27 710	8.3	23 320	10.8	26 656	5.4	21 410	10.7	12 145
1983	9.6	111 550	2.7	58 110	6.9	27 670	8.6	23 400	11.5	26 688	5.9	21 590	11.6	12 372
1984	7.5	113 544	2.8	58 480	7.1	27 800	10.0	23 560	11.8	27 355	5.9	21 670	10.9	12 588
1985	7.2	115 461	2.7	58 820	7.2	28 020	10.5	23 620	11.4	27 573	6.0	21 800	10.2	12 835
1986	7.0	117 834	2.8	59 410	6.6	28 240	10.6	23 760	11.4	27 739	7.5	22 290	9.3	13 089
1987	6.2	119 865	2.9	60 050	6.3	28 390	10.8	23 890	10.5	28 012	7.9	22 350	8.4	13 345
1988	5.5	121 669	2.5	60 860	6.3	28 610	10.3	23 980	8.6	28 350	7.9	22 660	7.4	13 590
1989	5.3	123 869	2.3	61 920	5.7	28 840	9.6	24 170	7.3	28 670	7.8	22 530	7.1	13 857
1990	5.6	125 840	2.1	63 050	5.0	29 410	8.6	24 159	7.1	28 766	7.0	22 670	7.7	14 047
1991	6.8	126 346	2.1	64 280	5.6	39 075	9.1	24 323	8.9	28 537	6.9	22 940	9.8	14 140
1992	7.5	128 105	2.2	65 040	6.7	39 005	10.0	24 443	10.0	28 207	7.3	22 910	10.6	14 150
1993	6.9	129 200	2.5	65 470	8.0	39 102	11.3	24 491	10.4	28 087	9.8	22 774	10.8	14 238
1994	6.1	131 056	2.9	65 780	8.5	39 074	11.9	24 672	8.7	28 118	10.7	22 595	9.6	14 347
1995	5.6	132 304	3.2	65 990	8.2	38 980	11.3	24 742	8.7	28 129	11.3	22 576	8.6	14 456
1996	5.4	133 943	3.4	66 450	9.0	39 142	11.8	24 982	8.1	28 239	11.3	22 677	8.8	14 623
1997	4.9	136 297	3.4	67 200	9.9	39 415	11.7	25 116	7.0	28 401	11.4	22 751	8.4	14 884
1998	4.5	137 673	4.1	67 240	9.3	39 752	11.2	25 434	6.3	28 474	11.5	23 002	7.7	15 135
1999	4.2	139 368	4.7	67 090	8.5	39 375	10.5	25 791	6.0	28 777	11.0	23 174	7.0	15 403
2000	4.0	142 583	4.8	66 990	7.8	39 302	9.1	26 099	5.5	28 952	10.2	23 359	6.1	15 637
2001	4.7	143 734	5.1	66 860	7.9	39 459	8.4	26 393	5.1	29 085	9.2	23 521	6.5	15 891
2002	5.8	144 863	5.4	66 240	8.6	39 413	9.0	26 710	5.2	29 335	8.7	23 726	7.0	16 366
2003	6.0	146 510	5.3	66 010	9.3	39 276	9.6	26 930	5.0	29 557	8.5	24 017	6.9	16 729
2004	5.5	147 401	4.8	65 770	10.3	39 711	9.8	26 969	4.8	29 776	8.1	24 066	6.4	16 955
2005	5.1	149 320	4.5	65 850	11.2	40 760	9.7	27 019	4.8	30 094	7.8	24 156	6.0	17 108
2004														
1st quarter	5.7	...	4.9	...	10.2	...	9.8	...	4.8	...	8.3	...	6.6	...
2nd quarter	5.6	...	4.7	...	10.3	...	9.8	...	4.8	...	8.1	...	6.5	...
3rd quarter	5.5	...	4.8	...	10.4	...	9.8	...	4.7	...	8.0	...	6.3	...
4th quarter	5.4	...	4.6	...	10.5	...	9.8	...	4.7	...	8.0	...	6.4	...
2005														
1st quarter	5.2	...	4.6	...	11.4	...	9.9	...	4.7	...	7.9	...	6.2	...
2nd quarter	5.1	...	4.4	...	11.4	...	9.8	...	4.7	...	7.9	...	6.0	...
3rd quarter	5.0	...	4.4	...	11.2	...	9.7	...	4.8	...	7.7	...	6.0	...
4th quarter	5.0	...	4.5	...	10.9	...	9.5	...	5.1	...	7.6	...	5.8	...

[1]Data for other countries adjusted to approximate U.S. concepts.
[2]Data prior to 1991 are for West Germany only. In 1991, the unemployment rate for West Germany alone was 4.3 percent.
. . . = Not available.

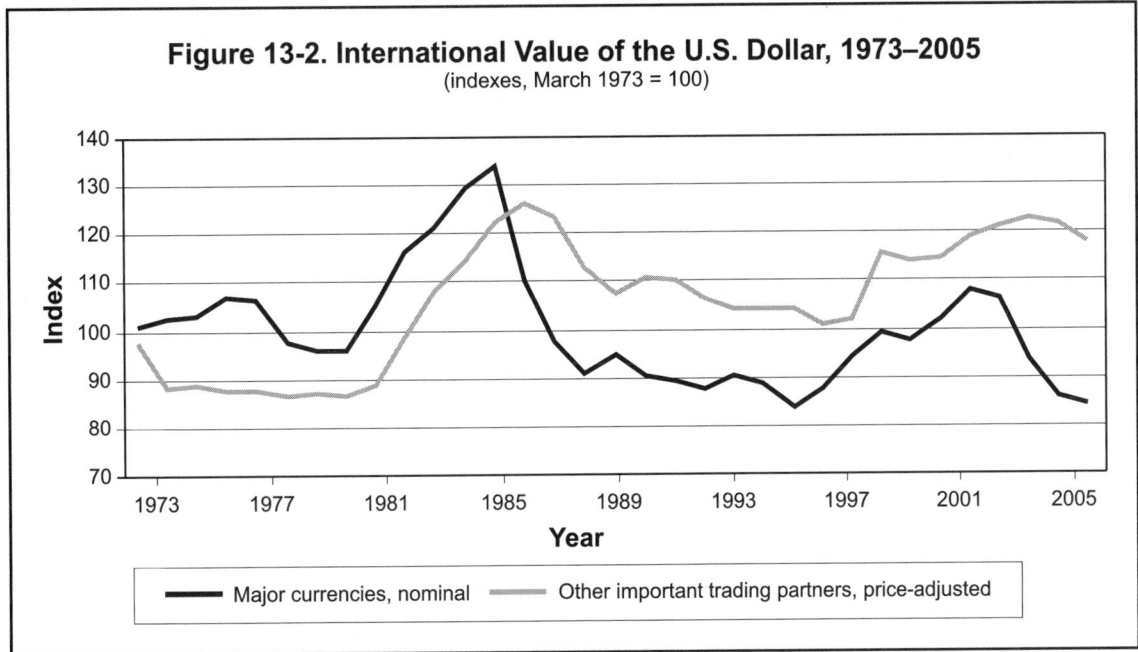

Figure 13-2. International Value of the U.S. Dollar, 1973–2005
(indexes, March 1973 = 100)

- The value of the U.S. dollar against the euro, the new European currency, rose between 1999 (when the euro was introduced) and 2001, but has dropped sharply since then. At the end of 2005, a dollar could be bought for just 0.84 euros, compared with 1.12 euros in 2001. This exchange rate is frequently quoted as dollars to one euro rather than euros to one dollar; in those terms, the euro was worth $1.19 in December 2005 but only $0.89 in 2001. The dollars-per-euro rate is higher when the <u>euro</u> is strong. In the method used in *Business Statistics*, the rate is higher when the <u>dollar</u> is strong for consistency with other measures shown in the table. (Table 13-6)

- Indexes of the dollar's international value against a group of currencies give a broader picture than the exchange rate against the euro or any other single currency. Figure 13-2 above displays two such indexes. One shows the dollar against a weighted average of seven major currencies—the euro, the British pound, the Canadian dollar, the Japanese yen, the Swiss franc, the Australian dollar, and the Swedish krona. These are all major industrial countries whose currencies are freely traded on world markets. Measured against these major currencies in terms of annual averages, the dollar depreciated 22 percent from 2001 to 2005—a big change but not as big as the 32 percent drop from 1985 to 1988. Dollar depreciation seems unsurprising in light of the large current-account deficits detailed in Chapter 7. (Table 13-6 and Chapter 7)

- However, the dollar has *not* depreciated significantly against the emerging-market currencies ("Other important trading partners") that account for much of the U.S. trade deficit. Therefore, currency adjustments are not bringing trade closer to balance in the way anticipated in basic economic theory. The reason is that many emerging-market countries, especially China, are able to control the international values of their currencies (through, for example, direct capital controls) and keep their currencies from appreciating relative to the dollar to maintain their competitiveness in the U.S. market. The result is that, between 2001 and 2005, the dollar fell 1 percent relative to "Other important trading partners" (OITP) in price-adjusted terms, and was actually higher in nominal terms. The price-adjusted OITP index is shown in Figure 13-2 because it is the preferred measure of competitiveness over the longer term, for reasons described in the notes and definitions. (Table 13-6)

Table 13-6. Exchange Rates

(Not seasonally adjusted.)

Year and month	Foreign currency per U.S. dollar						Trade-weighted exchange indexes of value of U.S. dollar [1]					
							Nominal				Price-adjusted	
	European currency unit	Japanese yen	German mark	Swiss franc	British pound	Canadian dollar	G-10 countries (March 1973 = 100)	Broad (January 1997 = 100)	Major currencies (March 1973 = 100)	Other important trading partners (January 1997 = 100)	Broad (March 1973 = 100)	Other important trading partners (March 1973 = 100)
1971	...	346.62	3.4673	4.1171	0.4092	1.0099	117.81	...	...	...	...	...
1972	...	303.11	3.1889	3.8186	0.4005	0.9908	109.07	...	...	...	...	...
1973	...	271.40	2.6719	3.1688	0.4084	1.0002	99.14	31.70	100.23	2.03	98.98	96.97
1974	...	291.94	2.5873	2.9805	0.4277	0.9781	101.41	32.58	102.05	2.14	95.72	87.81
1975	...	296.77	2.4614	2.5839	0.4521	1.0173	98.50	33.68	102.39	2.39	94.07	88.22
1976	...	296.48	2.5184	2.5002	0.5567	0.9861	105.63	35.83	106.42	2.70	93.97	86.99
1977	...	268.38	2.3225	2.4065	0.5733	1.0635	103.35	36.88	106.08	3.02	92.22	87.34
1978	...	210.46	2.0089	1.7907	0.5214	1.1408	92.39	35.09	97.21	3.18	86.56	86.15
1979	...	219.21	1.8331	1.6644	0.4720	1.1716	88.07	35.36	95.60	3.40	87.66	86.51
1980	...	226.58	1.8183	1.6772	0.4304	1.1694	87.39	36.35	95.35	3.75	89.13	85.73
1981	...	220.45	2.2606	1.9675	0.4978	1.1989	103.26	40.34	104.67	4.27	96.18	87.95
1982	...	249.05	2.4281	2.0319	0.5727	1.2339	116.50	46.83	115.76	5.52	105.48	98.32
1983	...	237.45	2.5545	2.1007	0.6601	1.2326	125.32	52.81	120.45	7.44	109.97	107.62
1984	...	237.59	2.8483	2.3500	0.7521	1.2952	138.34	60.11	128.75	9.78	117.09	113.92
1985	...	238.47	2.9443	2.4552	0.7792	1.3659	143.24	67.16	133.60	13.14	121.92	121.63
1986	...	168.50	2.1711	1.7979	0.6821	1.3898	112.27	62.35	109.86	16.49	106.51	125.71
1987	...	144.63	1.7976	1.4918	0.6117	1.3261	96.95	60.42	97.16	19.92	97.81	123.18
1988	...	128.14	1.7561	1.4643	0.5621	1.2309	92.75	60.92	90.41	24.07	91.24	112.55
1989	...	138.00	1.8792	1.6369	0.6111	1.1841	98.52	66.90	94.24	29.61	92.88	107.15
1990	...	144.82	1.6159	1.3901	0.5630	1.1670	89.05	71.41	89.87	40.10	91.23	110.09
1991	...	134.51	1.6585	1.4356	0.5667	1.1460	89.73	74.35	88.52	46.69	89.82	109.56
1992	...	126.75	1.5624	1.4064	0.5699	1.2088	86.64	76.91	87.02	53.13	87.93	105.96
1993	...	111.23	1.6537	1.4781	0.6662	1.2902	93.17	83.78	89.92	63.37	89.33	103.45
1994	...	102.19	1.6219	1.3667	0.6531	1.3659	91.32	90.87	88.42	80.54	89.16	103.52
1995	...	94.11	1.4331	1.1812	0.6337	1.3727	84.30	92.65	83.46	92.51	86.72	103.60
1996	...	108.81	1.5049	1.2361	0.6410	1.3637	87.34	97.46	87.24	98.24	88.76	100.56
1997	...	121.06	1.7339	1.4514	0.6106	1.3849	96.35	104.43	93.92	104.64	93.52	101.62
1998	...	130.99	1.7593	1.4506	0.6034	1.4836	98.82	115.89	98.41	125.89	101.46	114.94
1999	0.9387	113.73	1.8359	1.5045	0.6184	1.4858	...	116.04	96.84	129.20	100.84	113.64
2000	1.0864	107.80	...	1.6904	0.6611	1.4855	...	119.45	101.57	129.84	104.77	113.82
2001	1.1180	121.57	...	1.6891	0.6948	1.5487	...	125.93	107.65	135.91	110.84	118.39
2002	1.0612	125.22	...	1.5567	0.6667	1.5704	...	126.66	106.00	140.36	111.00	120.86
2003	0.8851	115.94	...	1.3450	0.6124	1.4008	...	119.09	93.01	143.54	104.27	122.47
2004	0.8049	108.15	...	1.2428	0.5458	1.3017	...	113.59	85.36	143.39	99.64	121.11
2005	0.8033	110.11	...	1.2459	0.5493	1.2115	...	110.81	83.79	138.90	98.10	117.34
2003												
January	0.9414	118.81	...	1.3765	0.6182	1.5414	...	123.42	98.77	144.42	107.61	122.85
February	0.9272	119.34	...	1.3602	0.6219	1.5121	...	123.27	97.71	145.90	107.70	124.06
March	0.9262	118.69	...	1.3614	0.6319	1.4761	...	122.79	97.01	145.92	107.63	124.71
April	0.9206	119.90	...	1.3783	0.6354	1.4582	...	121.81	96.66	143.98	106.65	122.86
May	0.8654	117.37	...	1.3111	0.6164	1.3840	...	117.84	92.15	141.75	103.17	121.18
June	0.8566	118.33	...	1.3196	0.6021	1.3525	...	117.19	91.06	142.07	102.88	122.04
July	0.8799	118.70	...	1.3611	0.6165	1.3821	...	118.41	92.92	141.84	104.10	121.97
August	0.8965	118.66	...	1.3811	0.6274	1.3963	...	119.72	94.07	143.19	105.42	123.29
September	0.8875	114.80	...	1.3743	0.6190	1.3634	...	118.38	92.27	142.96	104.16	122.77
October	0.8537	109.50	...	1.3222	0.5955	1.3221	...	116.03	88.79	143.26	101.69	122.08
November	0.8540	109.18	...	1.3318	0.5918	1.3130	...	115.90	88.48	143.52	100.91	121.00
December	0.8131	107.74	...	1.2643	0.5709	1.3128	...	114.33	86.21	143.66	99.31	120.88
2004												
January	0.7913	106.27	...	1.2391	0.5478	1.2958	...	112.43	84.38	142.10	97.94	119.47
February	0.7911	106.71	...	1.2448	0.5355	1.3299	...	112.97	84.95	142.49	98.60	119.73
March	0.8156	108.52	...	1.2778	0.5476	1.3286	...	114.09	86.45	142.66	99.91	120.42
April	0.8341	107.66	...	1.2969	0.5546	1.3420	...	114.91	87.44	143.00	100.71	120.87
May	0.8333	112.20	...	1.2839	0.5599	1.3789	...	116.78	88.99	145.09	102.74	123.42
June	0.8233	109.43	...	1.2503	0.5471	1.3578	...	115.67	87.55	144.80	102.06	123.58
July	0.8153	109.49	...	1.2452	0.5424	1.3225	...	114.85	86.42	144.75	101.10	122.85
August	0.8203	110.23	...	1.2623	0.5494	1.3127	...	115.02	86.67	144.73	101.08	122.45
September	0.8181	110.09	...	1.2629	0.5575	1.2881	...	114.55	86.18	144.39	100.55	121.74
October	0.7996	108.78	...	1.2330	0.5532	1.2469	...	112.94	84.23	143.78	99.24	121.23
November	0.7694	104.70	...	1.1711	0.5374	1.1968	...	110.07	81.00	142.24	96.55	119.57
December	0.7459	103.81	...	1.1465	0.5185	1.2189	...	108.84	80.11	140.65	95.17	117.94
2005												
January	0.7620	103.34	...	1.1792	0.5320	1.2248	...	109.45	81.05	140.45	95.96	117.77
February	0.7685	104.94	...	1.1918	0.5299	1.2401	...	109.66	81.81	139.55	96.05	116.28
March	0.7584	105.25	...	1.1756	0.5251	1.2160	...	109.05	80.88	139.70	96.01	117.36
April	0.7726	107.19	...	1.1954	0.5274	1.2359	...	109.99	82.22	139.67	97.37	118.17
May	0.7876	106.60	...	1.2172	0.5388	1.2555	...	110.48	83.34	138.87	97.63	117.40
June	0.8227	108.75	...	1.2665	0.5501	1.2402	...	111.62	84.92	138.92	98.76	117.73
July	0.8305	111.95	...	1.2945	0.5712	1.2229	...	112.12	85.73	138.78	99.41	117.54
August	0.8133	110.61	...	1.2629	0.5573	1.2043	...	110.69	84.20	137.80	98.44	117.10
September	0.8174	111.24	...	1.2671	0.5536	1.1777	...	110.62	83.82	138.31	99.07	118.42
October	0.8318	114.87	...	1.2880	0.5665	1.1774	...	111.70	85.12	138.78	99.95	118.28
November	0.8482	118.45	...	1.3110	0.5764	1.1815	...	112.51	86.58	138.26	99.82	116.48
December	0.8431	118.46	...	1.3053	0.5728	1.1615	...	111.79	85.83	137.72	98.72	115.56

[1]See notes and definitions for explanation of index categories.
. . . = Not available.

NOTES AND DEFINITIONS

TABLE 13-1
INTERNATIONAL COMPARISONS: GROWTH RATES IN REAL GROSS DOMESTIC PRODUCT

SOURCE: *ECONOMIC REPORT OF THE PRESIDENT, ANNUAL REPORT OF THE COUNCIL OF ECONOMIC ADVISERS, FEBRUARY 2006*

Table 13-1 is reprinted, with a footnote updated by the editor of *Business Statistics* providing later information on U.S. gross domestic product (GDP), from the 2006 *Annual Report of the U.S. Council of Economic Advisers*, where it appears as Table B-112. It is based on data from the Department of Commerce's Bureau of Economic Analysis (BEA) and the International Monetary Fund.

TABLES 13-2 AND 13-3
INTERNATIONAL COMPARISONS: REAL GROSS DOMESTIC PRODUCT PER CAPITA, REAL GROSS DOMESTIC PRODUCT PER EMPLOYED PERSON

SOURCE: *U.S. DEPARTMENT OF LABOR, BUREAU OF LABOR STATISTICS (BLS)*

Definitions and notes on the data

Real gross domestic product (GDP) per capita can be taken as a rough measure of potential economic welfare; that is, the potential standard of living available to a country's residents. Because income distributions are typically "skewed," GDP per capita (which is an average or "mean") should not be taken as a representation of the standard of living actually enjoyed by a typical ("median") individual. See the subsection entitled "Whose standard of living?" in the article "Using the Data: The U.S. Economy in the New Century" at the beginning of this volume.

Real gross domestic product per employed person is a rough measure of productivity (ignoring any differences in hours worked by employees).

The GDP, population, and employment measures for each country come from the country's own national accounts and population sources. Not all countries use annual chain-weighted methods such as those incorporated in U.S. GDP. (See notes and definitions for Chapter 1.) Some of the employment and population figures have been recalculated for greater comparability by the Bureau of Labor Statistics (BLS). GDP figures are converted from national currency values to U.S. dollar equivalents using purchasing power parities (PPPs) published by the OECD (Organisation for Economic Co-operation and Development) in the OECD-Eurostat PPP Program.

PPPs are currency conversion rates that allow output in different currency units to be expressed in a common unit of value (U.S. dollars in this case). They are preferable to international market exchange rates for this purpose.

According to BLS, "At best, market exchange rates represent only the relative prices of goods and services that are traded internationally, not the relative value of total domestic output, which also consists of goods, and particularly services, that are not traded internationally, or which are isolated from the effects of foreign trade. Market exchange rates also are affected by... currency traders' views of the stability of governments in various countries, relative interest rates among countries, and other incentives for holding financial assets in one currency rather than another."

Measuring PPPs is difficult and subject to error, and BLS emphasizes that statistics using PPPs should be used with caution: "The per capita GDPs of most OECD countries fall within a relatively narrow range, and changes in rankings can occur as a result of relatively minor adjustments to PPP estimates."

References

For more information, see: Department of Labor, Bureau of Labor Statistics, Office of Productivity and Technology, "Comparative Real Gross Domestic Product Per Capita and Per Employed Person, Fifteen Countries, 1960–2005" (June 16, 2006), available online at <http://www.bls.gov/fls>.

TABLE 13-4
INTERNATIONAL COMPARISONS: CONSUMER PRICE INDEXES

SOURCE: *U.S. DEPARTMENT OF LABOR, BUREAU OF LABOR STATISTICS (BLS)*

Notes on the data

These data are prepared by the BLS Office of Productivity and Technology, based on national consumer price indexes as published by each country. The most recent update was done on June 14, 2006, and is available at <http://www.bls.gov/fls>. The data are not adjusted for comparability across countries. National differences exist with respect to population coverage, frequency of market basket weight changes, and treatment of homeowner costs.

BLS links published indexes together to form historical series and rebases the foreign indexes to the U.S. base 1982–1984 = 100, except in the case of unified Germany. The data for Germany are for West Germany through 1990 for the price index level, which is on the 1982–1984 base, and through 1991 for the percent change in the price index. Index levels for unified Germany, with a comparison base of 2000 = 100, are shown from 1991 onward. The percent changes are based on unified Germany beginning in 1992.

For a description of the U.S. index, see the notes and definitions for Table 8-1.

TABLE 13-5
INTERNATIONAL COMPARISONS: UNEMPLOYMENT RATES AND CIVILIAN LABOR FORCES

SOURCE: U.S. DEPARTMENT OF LABOR, BUREAU OF LABOR STATISTICS (BLS)

Notes on the data

These data have been adjusted by BLS to approximate U.S. concepts and definitions. (See the notes and definitions for Tables 10-1 through 10-5.) The Germany data are for the former West Germany through 1990, and for unified Germany from 1991 to the present. Adding the former East Germany raised the 1991 unemployment rate from 4.3 percent for West Germany alone to 5.6 percent for unified Germany.

No adjustment is made to unemployment rates from Canada. Slight adjustments are made to those from Japan. Substantial adjustments were made to the Italian data prior to a 1992 definitional change. Before 1992, unemployment adjustment factors were based on annual household labor force surveys for France, Germany, and the United Kingdom.

The concept of "layoff" differs from country to country. In the United States and Canada, persons who are laid off are classified as unemployed. The employees do not remain on the payroll, receive no payments from their firms, and are frequently not rehired. However, in Europe and Japan, these people are classified as employed. In general, employers reduce hours or days worked, rather than letting people go for weeks without work. These workers continue to receive pay, which is supplemented by a subsidy for time not worked. Due to these differences, the strict U.S. definition of unemployment is not applied in these cases.

The adjusted statistics use the age at which compulsory schooling ends in each country instead of the U.S. standard of 16 years of age. Compulsory school ends at 16 years of age in France and in the United Kingdom since 1973; 15 years of age in Canada, Japan, Germany, Italy since 1993, and the United Kingdom before 1973; and 14 years of age in Italy before 1993. Data pertain to the noninstitutional population, except in Japan and Germany, where the institutionalized population of working age is included.

There are several breaks in the series due to changes in methodology or definitions. Among the more important of these breaks are ones for the United States (1994), France (1992), Germany (1983 and 1991), and Italy (1986, 1991, and 1993).

Data availability and references

The most recent compendium of annual data was issued by BLS on October 19, 2006. The compendium is updated biannually. Monthly updates to unemployment rates are also available on the Foreign Labor Statistics Web site at <http://www.bls.gov/fls/home.htm>.

TABLE 13-6
EXCHANGE RATES

SOURCE: BOARD OF GOVERNORS OF THE FEDERAL RESERVE SYSTEM

Definitions and notes on the data

This table shows measures of the U.S. dollar relative to foreign currencies—both to the currencies of some important individual countries and to average values for major groups of countries. In *Business Statistics*, all measures are defined as the foreign currency price of the U.S. dollar. Where its value is relatively high, the dollar is relatively "strong"—but less "competitive" (in the sense of price competition)—and the other currencies in question are relatively "weak" and more "competitive."

For consistency, this method is used in *Business Statistics* even in the case of currencies that are commonly quoted in the financial press and elsewhere as dollars per foreign currency unit instead of foreign currency units per dollar. Notably, this is the case for the new euro and for the British pound. Where *Business Statistics* shows the December 2005 value of the dollar as 0.8431 euros, the more usual statement—and the one found on the Federal Reserve release used as a source for this information—is that in December 2005, the euro was worth $1.1861 (1 divided by 0.8431). Where *Business Statistics* shows the December 2005 value of the dollar as 0.5728 British pounds, the more usual statement is that the pound was worth $1.7458. The Canadian dollar is also sometimes quoted relative to the U.S. dollar, rather than as shown here and in documents from the Federal Reserve.

The foreign exchange rates shown are averages of the daily noon buying rates in New York City for cable transfers payable in foreign currencies. Annual figures are averages of monthly data.

The introduction of the euro in January 1999 as the common currency for 11 European countries—Austria, Belgium, Finland, France, Germany, Ireland, Italy, Luxembourg, Netherlands, Portugal, and Spain—marked a major change in the international currency system. A 12th country, Greece, entered the European Monetary Union (EMU) in January 2001. The values of the currencies of these countries no longer fluctuate relative to each other, but the value of the euro still fluctuates relative to the dollar and to currencies for countries outside the EMU. The currency and coins of the individual countries continued to circulate from 1999 through the end of 2001; in January 2002, new euro currency and coins were introduced, replacing the currency and coins of the individual countries. Once a country has entered the monetary union, its value relative to the <u>dollar</u> continues to fluctuate—but only due to fluctuations in the value of the euro relative to the dollar.

There is no fully satisfactory historical equivalent to the euro. For comparisons over time, the Federal Reserve Board uses a "restated German mark," derived simply by dividing each historical value of the mark by the euro conversion factor, 1.95583. The G-10 dollar index described below includes five of the currencies that later merged into the euro, but also includes the currencies of Canada, Japan, the United Kingdom, Switzerland, and Sweden.

Trade-weighted indexes of the value of the dollar against groups of foreign currencies also appear in this table. In each case, weighted averages of the individual currency values of the dollar are set at 100 in a base period. The weights are based on goods trade only, and exclude trade in services. Base periods differ for different indexes.

The first four columns show the more familiar type of foreign exchange indexes, which use *nominal* values of each currency. The last two columns are *price-adjusted* (indexes of "real" exchange rates), aggregating values of the dollar in terms of each currency that have been adjusted for inflation, using each country's consumer price index.

Where any currency has had an episode of hyperinflation with consequent huge depreciation in terms of the dollar, the nominal index will not reflect the actual competitiveness of the dollar in terms of that currency over the longer term. As there have been hyperinflations in some of the countries making up the broad index and its "other important trading partners" component (see below), price-adjusted indexes are also shown for those two groupings in the final two columns.

The *G-10 Index (March 1973 = 100)*. This measure is an index of the exchange value of the U.S. dollar in terms of the weighted average currencies of the G-10 ("Other industrialized") countries, which are Belgium, Canada, France, Germany, Italy, Japan, the Netherlands, Sweden, Switzerland, and the United Kingdom. Unlike the three indexes that follow, the weights in this index—which represented "multilateral" (world market) trade shares—were fixed. The Federal Reserve stopped calculating this index as of December 1998.

The three newer indexes, introduced in December 1998, use weights that focus more directly on U.S. competitiveness and that change as trade flows shift. Each country's weight is based on an average of the country's share of U.S. imports, the country's share of U.S. exports, and the country's share of exports that go to other countries that are large importers of U.S. goods. The index formula uses geometric averaging.

The *broad index (January 1997 = 100)*. The new overall index includes currencies of all economies that have a share of U.S. non-oil goods imports or goods exports of at least 0.5 percent. These economies encompass the euro area and 25 other countries. The list of currencies and the weights are updated each year, though no changes have been made in the list of included countries. These countries are then classified in either the major currency index or the other important trading partners as outlined below.

The *major currency index (March 1973 = 100)*. This index serves purposes similar to those of the discontinued G-10 index, and its level and movements are similar. It is a measure of the competitiveness of U.S. products in the major industrial countries and a gauge of financial pressure on the dollar. The index includes countries whose currencies are traded in deep and relatively liquid financial markets and circulate widely outside the country of issue. These are also countries for which information on short- and long-term interest rates is readily available. As of February 2005, this index included the currencies of Canada, the euro countries, Japan, the United Kingdom, Switzerland, Australia, and Sweden. This list has not changed since the introduction of the new indexes in 1998.

The *other important trading partners (OITP) index (January 1997 = 100)*. This index captures the competitiveness of U.S. products in key emerging markets in Latin America, Asia, the Middle East, and Eastern Europe, whose currencies do not circulate widely outside the country of issue. Hyperinflations and large depreciations for some of these countries have led to a persistent upward trend in the nominal version of this index. Hence, the nominal OITP index is mainly useful for analysis of short-term developments, and the price-adjusted index is shown to give a more appropriate measure of longer-term competitiveness. As of February 2005, the countries included in this index were Mexico, China, Taiwan, South Korea, Singapore, Hong Kong, Malaysia, Brazil, Thailand, Indonesia, the Philippines, Russia, India, Saudi Arabia, Israel, Argentina, Venezuela, Chile, and Colombia.

Data availability and references

Current press releases and historical data on exchange rates and exchange rate indexes are available on the Federal Reserve Web site at <http://www.federalreserve.gov/releases/H10>. The dollar value indexes are described in the article "Indexes of the Foreign Exchange Value of the Dollar," *Federal Reserve Bulletin*, Winter 2005, available via a link from the "Currency Weights" area of the Federal Reserve Web site.

Additional information on exchange rates can be found on the Federal Reserve Bank of St. Louis Web site at <http:// www.stls.frb.org/fred/data/exchange.html>.

PART B

INDUSTRY PROFILES

THE STRUCTURE OF U.S. INDUSTRY: AN INTRODUCTION TO THE NORTH AMERICAN INDUSTRY CLASSIFICATION SYSTEM (NAICS)

This volume of *Business Statistics* incorporates data based on the new North American Industry Classification System (NAICS) for all of the major government statistical series that use classification by industry and have incorporated the new classification system.

Industry data collection is important because demands for goods and services are channeled into demands for labor and capital through the industries responsible for producing the requested goods and services. NAICS delineates industries that are better defined in relation to today's demands. It also groups together industries that are more closely related to each other by technology. Notable examples of these new features of NAICS include the more detailed data available on service industries, the more rational grouping of the Computer and electronic product manufacturing subsector, and the creation of the Information sector.

The editor has prepared a table of NAICS industry definitions to use as a guide to the contents of the new categories, which shows the NAICS two-digit industry sectors and their component three-digit subsectors. The table follows this introduction and precedes the chapters of statistical tables. Parenthetical listings of the component activities are shown in places where the short NAICS sector titles are not sufficiently self-explanatory.

For the user needing information as to how the new classifications do (and do not) relate to the old Standard Industrial Classification (SIC) system, a column showing a rough match between the 2002 NAICS and the 1987 SIC has been added to the table. It must be emphasized that this match is approximate, not exact, and does not reflect every aspect of the change in the classification systems. However, this column indicates just how thoroughly the SIC industries have been mixed and re-matched; it therefore explains why it has been difficult for the statistical agencies to produce longer spans of historical data on the new basis.

As a further illustration, the reader will note frequent references in this table to parts of SIC industries that have been parceled out among different NAICS industries. In some cases, the editor has included, in parentheses, the part of the old SIC industry contained in the new NAICS industry. See the entry of new NAICS subsector 711,

Performing arts and spectator sports, for an example. This subsector now contains dinner theaters, which used to be included in Eating places (a subdivision of Retail trade).

The reader may refer to Table 17-4, Manufacturers' Shipments, for an idea of the orders of magnitude of noncomparability among roughly matched industries. In this table—and in the three tables that follow, which were derived from the same survey—the editor has shown values for 1992 on both classification bases for roughly matching industries, such as Nonmetallic mineral products, Primary metals, Fabricated metal products, and Transportation equipment. Despite basic similarities in general definition between these industries in the old and new systems, the tabulated values can be quite different. As a result, it is evident that roughly matched industries cannot be viewed as continuous series.

NAICS industries are groupings of producing units—not of products as such—and are grouped according to similarity of production processes. This is done in order to collect consistent data on inputs and outputs, which are then used to measure important concepts, such as productivity and input-output parameters. Emphasis on the production process helps to explain a number of ways in which the NAICS differs from the SIC.

- Manufacturing activities at retail locations, such as bakeries, have been classified separately from retail activity and put into the Food manufacturing industry.

- Central administrative offices of companies have a new sector of their own, Management of companies and enterprises (sector 55). For example, the headquarters office of a food-producing corporation is considered part of the new sector instead of part of the Food manufacturing industry.

- Reproduction of packaged software, classified as a business service in the SIC, is now classified in sector 334, Computer and electronic product manufacturing, as a manufacturing process.

- Electronic markets and agents and brokers, formerly undifferentiated components of Wholesale trade industries, have a sector (425) of their own.

- Retail trade in NAICS (sectors 44 and 45) now includes establishments such as office supply stores, computer and software stores, building materials dealers, plumbing supply stores, and electrical supply stores, that display merchandise and use mass-media advertising to sell to individuals as well as to businesses, and that were formerly classified in Wholesale trade.

References

The reader needing more precise information on NAICS definitions and differences from the SIC should refer to *North American Industry Classification System: United States, 1997*, from the Executive Office of the President, Office of Management and Budget, which contains matches between the 1997 NAICS and the 1987 SIC; and *North American Industry Classification System: United States, 2002*, which contains matches showing the relatively few changes from the 1997 NAICS to the 2002 NAICS. Both volumes are available from Bernan Press. These volumes fully describe the development and application of the new classification system. They are the sources for the material presented in this volume. Information is also available on the NAICS Web site at <http://www.census.gov/naics>. Additional background information can also be found in Bernan Press's *Business Statistics of the United States: 2002* (8th edition), pp. xxiv–xxviii.

Table 14-1. NAICS Industry Definitions, with Rough Derivation from SIC

NAICS Code	NAICS 2-digit industry sector and 3-digit industry subsector	Roughly corresponding major component SIC industry group or industry
11	**AGRICULTURE, FORESTRY, FISHING, AND HUNTING**	Division A – Agriculture, forestry, and fishing; 241 – Logging
111	Crop production	
112	Animal production	
113	Forestry and logging	
114	Fishing, hunting, and trapping	
115	Agriculture and forestry support activities	
21	**MINING**	Division B – Mining
211	Oil and gas extraction	
212	Mining, except oil and gas (includes coal mining, mining for ores, and mining and quarrying of nonmetallic minerals)	
213	Support activities for mining (includes oil and gas well drilling and other support activities)	
22	**UTILITIES**	49 – Electric, gas, and sanitary services (with some exclusions)
221	Utilities (includes electric power generation, transmission, and distribution; natural gas distribution; and water, sewage, irrigation, steam, and air-conditioning systems)	
23	**CONSTRUCTION**	Division C – Construction
236	Construction of buildings	
237	Heavy and civil engineering construction	
238	Specialty trade contractors	
31-33	**MANUFACTURING**	Division D – Manufacturing (excluding 241 – Logging; 271, 272, 273, and 274 – Publishing; and with other exclusions and inclusions)
311	Food manufacturing	20 – Food and kindred products (excluding 208 – Beverages)
312	Beverage and tobacco product manufacturing	208 – Beverages; 21 – Tobacco products
313	Textile mills	221-4, 226, 228 – Yarns, fabrics, and finishing

Table 14-1. NAICS Industry Definitions, with Rough Derivation from SIC—Continued

NAICS Code	NAICS 2-digit industry sector and 3-digit industry subsector	Roughly corresponding major component SIC industry group or industry
314	Textile product mills (including household and miscellaneous products)	227 – Carpets and rugs; 229 – Miscellaneous textile products
315	Apparel manufacturing	23 – Apparel; 225 – Knitting mills
316	Leather and allied product manufacturing	31 – Leather and leather products
321	Wood product manufacturing	24 – Lumber and wood products (excluding 241 – Logging)
322	Paper manufacturing	26 – Paper and allied products
323	Printing and related support activities, including quick and instant	275-9 – Commercial printing and miscellaneous printing and trade services
324	Petroleum and coal products manufacturing (includes refineries, asphalt, oil and grease, and coke manufacturing)	29 – Petroleum and coal products
325	Chemical manufacturing (includes basic organic and inorganic chemicals; plastics materials; synthetic fibers and rubber; agricultural chemicals; pharmaceuticals and medicine; paint, adhesives, cleaning, and toilet preparations; and ink, explosives, and miscellaneous)	28 – Chemicals and allied products
326	Plastics and rubber products	30 – Rubber and miscellaneous plastics products
327	Nonmetallic mineral product manufacturing (includes pottery; plumbing fixtures; bricks and structural clay products; glass and products; cement and concrete; and lime, gypsum, and stone products)	32 – Stone, clay, and glass products
331	Primary metal manufacturing (primary and secondary ferrous and nonferrous metals; rolling, drawing, and extruding; and foundries)	33 – Primary metal industries
332	Fabricated metal product manufacturing (includes forging and stamping, cutlery, hardware, structural metal work, boilers, containers, machine shops, valves, fixtures, bearings, metal testing, small arms, ordnance, and ammunition)	34 – Fabricated metal products
333	Machinery manufacturing (includes machinery for agriculture, construction, mining, manufacturing, commercial, and service industries; metalworking machinery; turbine and power transmission; pumps and compressors; elevators and material handling; cranes; and miscellaneous general purpose machinery)	Parts of 35 – Industrial machinery and equipment, 36 – Electronic and other electric equipment, and 38 – Instruments and related products
334	Computer and electronic product manufacturing (includes electronic computers and equipment; communications equipment; audio and video equipment; semiconductors and other electronic components; electromedical equipment; navigation, measuring, and controlling instruments; reproducing software; and media manufacturing and reproducing)	Parts of 357 – Computer and office equipment, 36 – Electronic and other electric equipment, 38 – Instruments and related products, 73 – Business services, and 78 – Motion picture services
335	Electrical equipment and appliance manufacturing (includes electrical lighting, household appliances, electrical equipment, batteries, and wire and cable manufacturing)	Parts of 36 – Electronic and other electric equipment, and 335 – Nonferrous wire drawing
336	Transportation equipment manufacturing (includes motor vehicles and parts, truck trailers, aerospace products and parts, railroad rolling stock, ship and boat building and repairing, motorcycles, bicycles, military armored vehicles, and parts)	37 – Transportation equipment
337	Furniture and related product manufacturing	25 – Furniture and fixtures; parts of other industries
339	Miscellaneous manufacturing (includes medical equipment and supplies, jewelry, silverware, sporting goods, toys, games, office supplies, art supplies, burial caskets, and other goods)	Parts of 38 – Instruments, 39 – Miscellaneous, 25 – Furniture, and other industries

Table 14-1. NAICS Industry Definitions, with Rough Derivation from SIC—Continued

NAICS Code	NAICS 2-digit industry sector and 3-digit industry subsector	Roughly corresponding major component SIC industry group or industry
42	**WHOLESALE TRADE**	
423	Merchant wholesalers, durable goods	Parts of 50 – Wholesale trade—durable goods, and other industries
424	Merchant wholesalers, nondurable goods	Parts of 51 – Wholesale trade—nondurable goods, and other industries
425	Electronic markets and agents and brokers	Parts of 50 and 51 – Wholesale trade
44-45	**RETAIL TRADE**	
441	Motor vehicle and parts dealers	Parts of 55 – Automotive dealers and service stations, wholesale trade, and other industries
442	Furniture and home furnishings stores	Parts of 57 – Furniture and home furnishing stores, wholesale trade, and other industries
443	Electronics and appliance stores	5722 – Household appliance stores; 5734 – Computer and software stores; 5946 – Camera and photo supply stores; and parts of wholesale trade and other industries
444	Building material and garden supply stores	52 – Retail building materials and garden supplies, and parts of wholesale trade
445	Food and beverage stores	54 – Food stores, and 5921 – Liquor stores
446	Health and personal care stores	5912 – Drug stores and proprietary stores; and parts of wholesale trade, food stores, and miscellaneous stores
447	Gasoline stations (including stations with convenience stores)	Parts of 55 – Automotive dealers and service stations, and 54 – Food stores
448	Clothing and clothing accessories stores	56 – Apparel and accessory stores; 5944 – Jewelry stores; and 5948 – Luggage and leather goods stores
451	Sporting goods, hobby, book, and music stores	Parts of 59 – Miscellaneous retail, 57 – Furniture and home furnishing stores, and other industries
452	General merchandise stores (includes department stores, warehouse clubs, superstores, and other general merchandise)	53 – General merchandise, and parts of other retail
453	Miscellaneous store retailers (includes florists and office supply and stationery, gift, used merchandise, pet, manufactured and mobile home, tobacco, and miscellaneous other store retailers)	Parts of 59 – Miscellaneous retail, and other industries
454	Nonstore retailers (includes electronic shopping and auctions, mail order, vending machines, fuel, and other direct selling)	Parts of 59 – Miscellaneous retail, and 517 – Wholesale petroleum
48-49	**TRANSPORTATION AND WAREHOUSING**	
481	Air transportation	Parts of 45 – Transportation by air
482	Rail transportation	Parts of 40 – Railroad transportation
483	Water transportation	Parts of 44 – Water transportation
484	Truck transportation	Parts of 42 – Trucking and warehousing
485	Transit and ground passenger transportation	Parts of 41 – Local and suburban transportation

Table 14-1. NAICS Industry Definitions, with Rough Derivation from SIC—Continued

NAICS Code	NAICS 2-digit industry sector and 3-digit industry subsector	Roughly corresponding major component SIC industry group or industry
486	Pipeline transportation	46 – Pipelines, except natural gas; and parts of 492 – Gas production and distribution
487	Scenic and sightseeing transportation	Parts of 41 – Local and suburban, 44 – Water, 45 – Air, 47 – Transportation services, and 7999 – Amusement and recreation n.e.c.
488	Support activities for transportation	Parts of industries in transportation, communications, manufacturing, government (air traffic control), and services
491	Postal service	4311 – U.S. Postal Service, and part of 7389 – Business services n.e.c.
492	Couriers and messengers	4513 – Air couriers, and 4215 – Courier services except air
493	Warehousing and storage	Parts of 422 – Public warehousing and storage
51	**INFORMATION**	
511	Publishing industries, except Internet	
5111	Newspaper, book, and directory publishers	Parts of 271 – Newspapers, 272 – Periodicals, 273 – Books, 274 – Miscellaneous publishing, 277 – Greeting cards, and 733 – Mailing, reproduction, and stenographic services
5112	Software publishers	Part of 7372 – Prepackaged software
512	Motion picture and sound recording industries (includes music books and sheet music)	781 – Motion picture production and services; 783 – Motion picture theaters; and parts of 782 – Motion picture distribution and services, and other manufacturing and service industries
515	Broadcasting, except Internet	483 – Radio and television broadcasting; and part of 484 – Cable and other pay TV services
516	Internet publishing and broadcasting	Parts of publishing and service industries
517	Telecommunications	Parts of 481 – Telephone communications, 482 – Telegraph and other communications, and 484 – Cable and other pay TV services
518	ISPs, search portals, and data processing	7374 – Data processing and preparation; 7375 – Information retrieval services; and parts of other service industries
519	Other information services (includes news syndicates, libraries, archives, and other information services)	8231 – Libraries; and parts of other service industries
52	**FINANCE AND INSURANCE**	
521	Monetary authorities—central bank	6011 – Federal Reserve Banks
522	Credit intermediation and related activities (includes commercial banking, savings institutions, credit unions, credit card issuing, sales financing, consumer lending, real estate credit, trade financing, loan brokers, and processing and clearing)	Parts of 60 – Depository institutions, and 61 – Nondepository institutions
523	Securities, commodity contracts, and investments	62 – Security and commodity brokers, and parts of 60 – Depository institutions, 61 – Nondepository institutions, 63 – Insurance carriers, and 67 – Holding and other investment offices
524	Insurance carriers and related activities	64 – Insurance agents, brokers, and service; and parts of 63 – Insurance carriers
525	Funds, trusts, and other financial vehicles	672 – Investment offices; 6798 – Real estate investment trusts; and parts of 63 – Insurance carriers, and 673 – Trusts

n.e.c. = Not elsewhere classified.

Table 14-1. NAICS Industry Definitions, with Rough Derivation from SIC—Continued

NAICS Code	NAICS 2-digit industry sector and 3-digit industry subsector	Roughly corresponding major component SIC industry group or industry
53	REAL ESTATE AND RENTAL AND LEASING	
531	Real estate	Parts of 65 – Real estate, and 4225 – General warehousing and storage (mini-warehouses and self-storage units)
532	Rental and leasing services	7352 – Medical equipment rental; 7377 – Computer rental and leasing; 751 – Automotive rentals, no drivers; 7841 – Video tape rental; and parts of 4499 – Water transportation n.e.c., 4741 – Rental of railroad cars, 7299 – Miscellaneous personal services n.e.c., 735 – Miscellaneous equipment rental, 7922 – Theatrical producers and services, and 7999 – Amusement and recreation n.e.c.
533	Lessors of nonfinancial intangible assets (except copyrighted)	6794 – Patent owners and lessors, and part of 6792 – Oil royalty traders
54	PROFESSIONAL AND TECHNICAL SERVICES (includes legal, accounting, bookkeeping, architectural, engineering, design, computer design and programming, management and other consulting, scientific research and development, advertising and public relations, market research, polling, and other services)	741 – Veterinary services; 6541 – Title abstract offices, 731 – Advertising, 7221 – Photographic studios, portrait, 7921 – Tax return preparation, 7336 – Commercial art and graphic design, 7361 – Employment agencies, 7371 – Computer programming; 7373 – Computer systems design, 7376 – Computer facilities management, 8111 – Legal services, 871 – Engineering and architectural services, 873 – Research and testing; and parts of mining, 37 – Aircraft and guided missiles, 73 – Business services, 87 – Engineering and management services, and other industries
55	MANAGEMENT OF COMPANIES AND ENTERPRISES	671 – Holding companies, and establishments classified as auxilaries in producing industries
56	ADMINISTRATIVE AND WASTE SERVICES	
561	Administrative and support services (includes office administrative, employment placement, temporary help, telephone call centers, collection agencies, credit bureaus, court reporting, travel arrangement, investigation and security, services to buildings, and other support services)	782 – Lawn and garden services, 783 – Ornamental shrub and tree services, 4724 – Travel agencies, 4725 – Tour operators, 7217 – Carpet and upholstery cleaning, 732 – Credit reporting and collection, 7338 – Secretarial and court reporting, 734 – Services to buildings, 7363 – Help supply services, 7381 – Detective and armored car services, 7382 – Security systems, 8744 – Facilities support, and parts of 458 – Airfields, 472 – Passenger transportation arrangement, 495 – Sanitary services, 729 – Miscellaneous personal services, 73, Business services, 769 – Miscellaneous repair shops, 7819 – Services allied to motion pictures, 79 – Amusement and recreation services, 86 – Membership organizations, and 8741 – Management services
562	Waste management and remediation services	4953 – Refuse systems, and parts of 1799 – Special trade contractors, 4212 – Local trucking, 4959 – Sanitary services, 735 – Miscellaneous equipment rental and leasing (portable toilet rental), and 769 – Miscellaneous repair shops
61	EDUCATIONAL SERVICES	82 – Educational services, except 823 – Libraries; and parts of 7231 – Beauty shops, 7241 – Barber shops, 7911 – Dance studios, 7999 – Amusement and recreation n.e.c., and 8748 – Business consulting n.e.c. (educational testing services)
62	HEALTH CARE AND SOCIAL ASSISTANCE	
621	Ambulatory health care services	Offices and clinics for: 801 – Doctors, 802 – Dentists, 803 – Osteopaths, and 804 – Other health practicioners, 8071 – Medical laboratories, 8082 – Home health care services, 4119 – Ambulances; 4522 – Air ambulances, and parts of 809 – Health and allied services n.e.c.
622	Hospitals	806 – Hospitals
623	Nursing and residential care facilities	805 – Nursing and personal care facilities, and 836 – Residential care
624	Social assistance	8322 – Individual and family services, except parole and probation offices; 8331 – Job training; and 8351 – Child day care services

n.e.c. = Not elsewhere classified.

Table 14-1. NAICS Industry Definitions, with Rough Derivation from SIC—Continued

NAICS Code	NAICS 2-digit industry sector and 3-digit industry subsector	Roughly corresponding major component SIC industry group or industry
71	**ARTS, ENTERTAINMENT, AND RECREATION**	
711	Performing arts and spectator sports	7929 – Bands and other entertainment groups; 7941 – Professional sports clubs and promoters; 7948 – Racing; parts of 5812 – Eating places (dinner theaters) and 6512 – Building operators (stadium and arena owners); and agents, artists, writers, performers, correspondents, taxidermists, and antique restorers, previously classified as part of 738 – Miscellaneous business services; 76 – Miscellaneous repair services; 7819 – Motion picture services; 7999 – Amusement and recreation n.e.c.; and 8999 – Membership organizations, n.e.c.
712	Museums, historical sites, zoos, and parks	84 – Museums and botanical and zoological gardens; and part of 7999 – Amusement and recreation n.e.c. (caverns and miscellaneous commercial parks)
713	Amusements, gambling, and recreation	4493 – Marinas, 793 – Bowling centers, 7991 – Physical fitness facilities, 7992 – Public golf courses, 7995 – Coin operated amusements, 7996 – Amusement parks, 7997 – Membership sports and recreation clubs, and parts of 7911 – Dance studios, and 7999 – Amusement and recreation n.e.c.
72	**ACCOMMODATION AND FOOD SERVICES**	
721	Accommodation (includes hotels, motels, bed-and-breakfast inns, RV parks, camps, and rooming and boarding houses)	70 – Hotels and other lodging places
722	Food services and drinking places	5812 – Eating places (other than dinner theaters), 5813 – Drinking places, and parts of 4789 – Transportation services n.e.c. (contract dining car operations), 5641 – Retail bakeries, and 5963 – Direct selling (mobile food wagons)
81	**OTHER SERVICES, EXCEPT PUBLIC ADMINISTRATION**	
811	Repair and maintenance	753 – Automotive repair shops (other than tire retreading); 7542 – Carwashes; 7631 – Watch, clock, and jewelery repair; 7692 – Welding repair; and parts of 3732 – Boat repair, 7219 – Clothing alteration and repair, 7251 – Shoe repair, 7378 – Computer repair, 7549 – auto window tinting, 7622 – Radio and TV repair, 7623 – Refrigeration repair, 7629 – Electrical repair n.e.c., 7641 – Reupholstery and furniture repair, 7694 – Armature (rewinding), and 7699 – Repair services n.e.c.
812	Personal and laundry services	6553 – Cemetery subdividers and developers; 7211 – Power laundries; 7212 – Garment pressing and cleaners' agents; 7213 – Linen supply; 7215 – Coin-operated laundries and cleaning; 7216 – Drycleaning, except rugs; 7218 – Industrial launderers; 7261 – Funeral service and crematories; 7384 – Photofinishing laboratories; 7521 – Auto parking; and parts of 0752 – Pet care, 6531 – Real estate agents and managers (cemetery management), 7219 – Diaper and miscellaneous services, 7231 – Beauty shops, 7241 – Barber shops, 7251 – Shoe shine parlors, and 7389 – Business services n.e.c. (apparel pressing for the trade, bail bonding)
813	Membership associations and organizations	6732 – Educational, religious and charitable trusts; 8399 – Social services n.e.c. (voluntary health organizations, human rights organizations, environment, conservation, and wildlife, and other grant making, giving, and social advocacy organizations); 8611 – Business associations; 8621 – Professional organizations; 8631 – Labor organizations; 8651 – Political organizations; 8661 – Religious organizations; and parts of 6531 – Real estate agents and managers (condominium associations), 8641 – Civic and social organizations (all except tribal governments), and 8699 – Membership organizations n.e.c. (all except motor travel clubs)
814	Private households	8811 – Private households

n.e.c. = Not elsewhere classified.

Table 14-1.   NAICS Industry Definitions, with Rough Derivation from SIC—Continued

NAICS Code	NAICS 2-digit industry sector and 3-digit industry subsector	Roughly corresponding major component SIC industry group or industry
92	**PUBLIC ADMINISTRATION**	
921	Executive, legislative, and general government	91 – Executive, legislative, and general; 9311 – Finance, taxation, and monetary policy; and part of 8641 – Civic and social associations (tribal governments)
922	Justice, public order, and safety activities	92 – Justice, public order, and safety; and part of 8322 – Individual and family services (parole and probation)
923	Administration of human resource programs	94 – Administration of human resources
924	Administration of environmental programs	951 – Environmental quality
925	Community and housing program administration	953 – Housing and urban development
926	Administration of economic programs	9611 – Administration of general economic programs; 9631 – Regulation and administration of utilities; 9641 – Regulation of agricultural marketing; 9651 – Miscellaneous commercial regulation; and parts of 9621 – Regulation and administration of transportation (all except air traffic control)
927	Space research and technology	9661 – Space research and technology
928	National security and international affairs	97 – National security and international affairs

CHAPTER 15: PRODUCT AND INCOME BY INDUSTRY

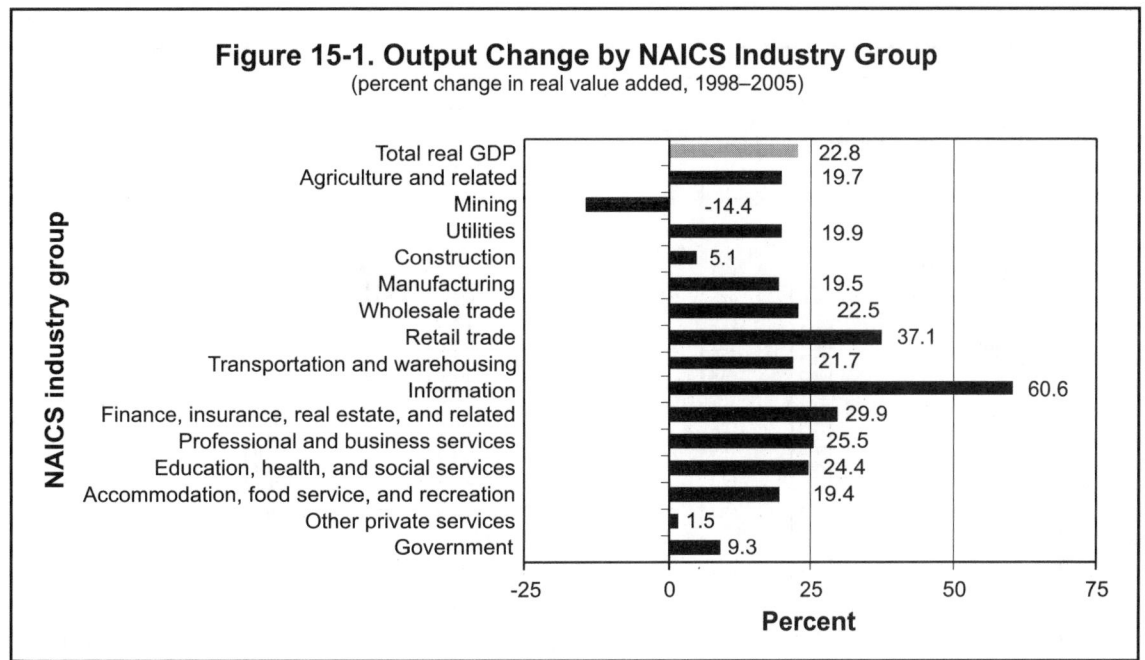

Figure 15-1. Output Change by NAICS Industry Group
(percent change in real value added, 1998–2005)

- Between 1998 and 2005, total real gross domestic product (GDP) rose 22.8 percent, with an average annual rate of 3.0 percent. In the figure above, the total GDP change is shown for comparison with the growth in component industry groups over the same years. This GDP growth may be lower than the potential national long-term growth rate, as the 2005 unemployment rate of 5.1 percent is somewhat higher than the 1998 rate of 4.5 percent. (Tables 15-3 and 10-4)

- Of the 15 industry groups represented in Table 15-3 and in the figure above, there were 5 that expanded significantly faster than the average. The fastest-growing industry was information, whose output rose 61 percent. Retail trade was next, with a 37 percent increase. The finance, insurance, and real estate industry group grew 30 percent; professional and business services grew 26 percent; and education, health, and social assistance grew 24 percent. (Table 15-3)

- Retail trade activity rose far more than U.S. output of agriculture and manufactured products. Retailers sell imported products as well as goods produced domestically. (Table 15-3)

- Table 15-4 can be used to assess the share of each industry group in total domestic factor income and the division of income in each industry between employee compensation and "gross operating surplus," which is the income accruing to land and capital. In 2004, the highest labor share was in education, and labor shares exceeding 70 percent were also found in durable goods manufacturing, retail trade, management, administrative and waste management (which includes temporary help), health care and social assistance, accommodation and food services, and other services. The new grouping called "information-communications-technology-producing industries" also falls in this labor-intensive category.

Table 15-1. Gross Domestic Product (Value Added) by SIC Industry Group, 1987–2000

(Billions of dollars; index numbers, 1996 = 100.)

Year and series definition	Gross domestic product	Private industries										
		Total	Agriculture, forestry, and fishing	Mining	Construc-tion	Manufacturing		Transpor-tation	Communi-cations	Electric, gas, and sanitary services	Wholesale trade	Retail trade
						Durable goods	Nondurable goods					
VALUE												
1987	4 742.5	4 081.4	88.9	92.2	219.3	516.8	371.8	158.8	125.5	141.9	308.9	434.5
1988	5 108.3	4 401.8	89.1	99.2	237.2	566.3	413.6	169.2	132.8	147.0	346.6	461.5
1989	5 489.1	4 735.5	102.0	97.1	245.8	582.7	434.9	172.2	137.4	159.0	364.7	492.7
1990	5 803.2	4 996.7	108.3	111.9	248.7	586.6	454.0	177.4	148.1	165.4	376.1	507.8
1991	5 986.2	5 129.1	102.9	96.7	232.7	575.5	468.0	186.1	155.7	176.5	395.6	523.7
1992	6 318.9	5 424.5	111.7	87.6	234.4	594.0	488.0	193.4	163.9	181.2	414.6	551.7
1993	6 642.3	5 717.5	108.3	88.4	248.9	632.8	498.6	206.0	178.6	188.7	432.5	578.0
1994	7 054.3	6 096.7	118.5	90.2	275.3	694.1	529.1	223.2	190.7	197.4	479.2	620.6
1995	7 400.5	6 411.1	109.8	95.7	290.3	729.8	559.2	233.4	202.3	206.9	500.6	646.8
1996	7 813.2	6 792.8	130.4	113.0	316.4	748.4	567.6	243.4	214.7	208.3	529.6	687.1
1997	8 318.4	7 253.6	130.0	118.9	338.2	791.2	588.4	261.8	220.8	205.9	566.8	740.5
1998	8 781.5	7 678.2	128.0	100.2	380.8	830.7	600.8	288.7	238.5	204.8	607.9	790.4
1999	9 274.3	8 123.0	127.7	104.1	425.4	853.8	627.5	301.9	257.2	211.0	645.3	831.7
2000	9 824.6	8 606.9	134.3	133.1	461.3	886.4	633.9	313.7	279.1	216.5	696.8	887.3
QUANTITY INDEX												
1987	78.2	76.7	84.6	87.2	88.0	72.3	90.2	66.7	61.8	79.6	66.8	74.5
1988	81.5	80.2	77.6	101.3	93.0	79.1	93.6	68.8	65.6	82.2	71.6	79.3
1989	84.4	83.2	85.4	91.0	93.6	78.8	92.5	70.9	68.1	87.7	75.4	81.9
1990	85.9	84.5	90.9	93.6	91.9	78.2	91.7	74.2	72.3	91.2	74.6	81.4
1991	85.5	84.0	93.0	89.5	84.9	74.7	90.0	76.4	75.5	94.1	78.7	80.7
1992	88.1	86.6	100.2	84.7	85.9	76.0	91.6	79.5	78.9	92.8	84.0	82.9
1993	90.4	89.0	94.0	89.4	88.2	80.2	92.6	82.7	84.8	92.8	85.4	84.7
1994	94.0	93.0	104.1	95.6	93.9	87.7	97.1	89.8	88.9	94.5	90.9	89.8
1995	96.6	95.8	94.4	99.9	94.7	95.5	100.5	92.5	94.3	99.5	91.2	93.4
1996	100.0	100.0	100.0	100.0	100.0	100.0	100.0	100.0	100.0	100.0	100.0	100.0
1997	104.4	105.3	110.1	103.5	102.6	108.6	101.3	102.3	101.4	97.0	110.3	108.5
1998	108.9	110.3	111.5	105.9	110.3	119.3	97.9	106.0	107.7	93.0	125.3	116.4
1999	113.4	115.6	118.5	101.5	116.2	126.8	100.6	110.4	118.9	100.3	133.8	123.2
2000	117.6	120.1	127.8	90.1	119.5	139.5	98.3	116.1	133.6	102.7	141.7	132.3

Year and series definition	Finance, insurance, and real estate [1]				Services [1]				Statistical discrepancy	Government		
	Total	Depository institutions	Real estate		Total	Business services	Health services	Other services		Total	Federal	State and local
			Nonfarm housing services	Other real estate								
VALUE												
1987	829.7	143.9	391.9	139.5	789.9	145.0	230.6	103.3	3.3	661.0	258.9	402.1
1988	893.7	147.6	424.3	162.0	887.9	166.9	253.6	119.8	-42.2	706.5	273.3	433.2
1989	954.5	157.2	456.7	174.0	976.0	183.7	280.7	135.8	16.3	753.6	287.1	466.5
1990	1 010.3	171.3	488.3	177.3	1 071.5	203.9	314.4	149.2	30.6	806.6	300.2	506.4
1991	1 072.2	193.9	515.5	173.6	1 123.8	205.3	345.3	150.0	19.6	857.1	322.4	534.7
1992	1 140.9	205.3	543.4	181.8	1 219.4	229.4	377.8	161.1	43.7	894.4	333.9	560.5
1993	1 205.3	200.9	558.1	193.5	1 287.7	247.6	394.5	170.6	63.8	924.8	336.2	588.6
1994	1 254.8	200.7	593.9	197.5	1 365.0	273.2	413.9	178.6	58.5	957.6	339.6	618.0
1995	1 347.2	227.4	628.9	203.7	1 462.4	302.0	433.1	194.4	26.5	989.5	342.3	647.2
1996	1 436.8	241.0	654.6	217.0	1 564.2	342.3	459.1	208.9	32.8	1 020.4	346.9	673.5
1997	1 569.9	273.9	679.1	241.0	1 691.5	395.5	472.2	229.7	29.7	1 064.8	354.7	710.1
1998	1 708.5	300.0	718.7	262.9	1 829.9	439.8	491.1	254.5	-31.0	1 103.3	359.9	743.4
1999	1 798.8	330.3	766.9	283.5	1 977.2	501.0	515.4	276.0	-38.8	1 151.3	369.8	781.5
2000	1 976.7	361.1	811.4	312.3	2 116.4	534.4	548.5	300.3	-128.5	1 217.7	389.5	828.2
QUANTITY INDEX												
1987	81.4	91.5	81.4	71.2	75.5	54.7	85.5	73.2	. . .	91.9	106.5	84.5
1988	84.2	90.3	84.2	83.5	80.2	61.0	86.9	79.9	. . .	94.2	107.4	87.5
1989	85.9	95.8	87.0	84.8	84.0	66.0	88.9	87.9	. . .	96.5	108.8	90.2
1990	87.0	101.2	88.6	84.3	87.1	70.5	92.2	91.6	. . .	98.8	110.9	92.7
1991	88.4	102.3	90.9	80.2	86.5	68.9	94.3	87.4	. . .	99.2	111.0	93.2
1992	90.3	97.4	93.0	87.9	89.0	74.4	96.4	86.8	. . .	99.5	110.2	94.1
1993	92.5	97.1	93.1	90.2	90.7	78.8	95.3	90.5	. . .	99.3	107.7	95.1
1994	93.8	94.6	96.5	90.5	93.2	86.2	95.5	92.0	. . .	99.6	105.8	96.4
1995	97.0	100.6	99.0	94.4	96.6	91.7	96.8	95.7	. . .	99.7	102.1	98.4
1996	100.0	100.0	100.0	100.0	100.0	100.0	100.0	100.0	. . .	100.0	100.0	100.0
1997	105.9	102.1	101.0	111.9	104.4	112.2	100.1	105.9	. . .	101.5	100.1	102.2
1998	112.9	106.4	103.5	123.9	108.6	120.0	100.4	114.2	. . .	102.6	100.2	103.9
1999	117.5	114.1	107.6	128.7	113.1	131.3	102.5	119.7	. . .	104.0	99.9	106.1
2000	124.8	119.2	110.4	136.2	116.7	134.4	106.3	126.3	. . .	106.7	102.3	108.9

Note: These data are reprinted without change from the 2006 edition of *Business Statistics* in order to provide data for years prior to those shown in Tables 15-2 and 15-3.

[1]Includes industries not shown separately.
. . . = Not available.

Table 15-2. Value Added (Gross Domestic Product) by NAICS Industry Group, in Current Dollars

(Billions of current dollars.)

NAICS industry	1999	2000	2001	2002	2003	2004	2005
Gross domestic product	9 268.4	9 817.0	10 128.0	10 469.6	10 971.2	11 734.3	12 487.1
Private industries	8 127.2	8 614.3	8 869.7	9 131.2	9 556.8	10 251.0	10 934.8
Agriculture, forestry, fishing, and hunting	93.8	98.0	97.9	95.4	114.2	141.6	119.1
Farms	68.8	71.5	73.1	70.8	88.0	112.2	...
Forestry, fishing, and related activities	25.0	26.5	24.8	24.6	26.2	29.4	...
Mining [1]	85.4	121.3	118.7	106.5	142.3	171.9	213.6
Oil and gas extraction	47.2	81.0	72.5	62.8	93.1	115.2	...
Mining, except oil and gas	27.5	27.0	27.1	26.8	27.4	30.6	...
Utilities	185.4	189.3	202.3	207.3	222.6	235.3	238.9
Construction	406.6	435.9	469.5	482.3	501.0	549.5	593.5
Manufacturing	1 373.1	1 426.2	1 341.3	1 352.6	1 369.2	1 420.1	1 496.5
Durable goods [1]	820.4	865.3	778.9	774.8	785.5	824.1	868.4
Computer and electronic products	162.8	185.6	136.9	124.2	125.6	132.6	...
Motor vehicles, bodies and trailers, and parts	115.4	118.1	103.7	118.9	129.9	120.1	...
Nondurable goods [1]	552.7	560.9	562.5	577.9	583.7	596.1	628.1
Food and beverage and tobacco products	153.6	154.8	167.1	172.9	170.6	167.9	...
Chemical products	157.1	157.1	157.2	174.4	181.8	186.0	...
Wholesale trade	577.7	591.7	607.1	615.4	633.0	694.7	733.1
Retail trade	635.5	662.4	691.6	719.6	751.0	790.4	828.6
Transportation and warehousing [1]	287.4	301.6	296.9	304.6	321.6	332.9	362.2
Air transportation	54.9	57.7	50.0	48.3	55.3	53.4	...
Rail transportation	24.7	25.5	25.6	26.2	27.1	29.0	...
Truck transportation	89.8	92.8	93.3	95.7	98.8	104.7	...
Transit and ground passenger transportation	14.4	14.5	15.1	15.7	16.2	16.8	...
Other transportation and support activities	64.8	70.2	71.4	73.4	76.4	83.2	...
Warehousing and storage	23.2	25.0	25.1	26.8	28.3	27.1	...
Information	439.3	458.3	476.9	483.0	491.8	538.7	578.3
Publishing industries (includes software)	118.7	116.7	118.7	119.0	118.8	125.3	...
Motion picture and sound recording industries	30.1	32.5	33.6	38.9	42.4	47.3	...
Broadcasting and telecommunications	253.8	271.3	283.2	278.9	280.4	312.0	...
Information and data processing services	36.7	37.7	41.5	46.2	50.1	54.1	...
Finance, insurance, real estate, rental, and leasing	1 798.4	1 931.0	2 059.2	2 141.9	2 260.4	2 412.9	2 574.4
Finance and insurance	679.8	740.5	782.6	822.7	885.2	927.4	1 011.5
Federal Reserve banks, credit intermediation, and related activities	308.0	319.0	360.1	417.4	451.8	464.7	...
Securities, commodity contracts, and investments	139.9	167.7	170.2	148.4	153.3	170.9	...
Insurance carriers and related activities	216.9	238.3	234.4	237.4	260.4	269.6	...
Funds, trusts, and other financial vehicles	15.0	15.5	18.0	19.5	19.7	22.2	...
Real estate and rental and leasing	1 118.6	1 190.5	1 276.6	1 319.2	1 375.2	1 485.5	1 562.9
Real estate	1 017.9	1 082.1	1 169.7	1 215.9	1 268.6	1 374.7	...
Rental and leasing services and lessors of intangible assets	100.6	108.3	106.9	103.3	106.6	110.8	...
Professional and business services	1 064.5	1 140.8	1 165.9	1 189.0	1 235.9	1 351.9	1 468.5
Professional, scientific, and technical services	613.9	675.1	698.8	705.2	727.4	784.3	862.4
Legal services	127.3	136.1	145.6	145.8	155.8	164.1	...
Computer systems design and related services	107.8	125.7	127.1	127.3	126.3	133.1	...
Miscellaneous professional, scientific, and technical services	378.8	413.3	426.2	432.2	445.3	487.2	...
Management of companies and enterprises	170.5	183.4	177.6	183.8	191.5	220.8	230.6
Administrative and waste management services	280.1	282.4	289.4	300.0	317.1	346.8	375.5
Administrative and support services	255.4	257.2	264.1	273.3	289.0	316.3	...
Waste management and remediation services	24.7	25.2	25.3	26.7	28.1	30.5	...
Educational services, health care, and social assistance	634.5	678.4	739.3	799.6	850.6	909.0	977.4
Educational services	72.8	79.2	85.1	93.3	99.6	106.3	113.1
Health care and social assistance	561.7	599.2	654.2	706.3	751.0	802.7	864.4
Ambulatory health care services	288.6	307.6	338.1	361.8	384.7	413.0	...
Hospitals and nursing and residential care facilities	225.6	238.6	258.0	281.1	299.0	318.8	...
Social assistance	47.6	53.0	58.1	63.4	67.3	70.9	...
Arts, entertainment, recreation, accommodation, and food services	327.8	350.1	361.5	381.5	398.8	424.3	455.9
Arts, entertainment, and recreation	83.8	88.7	95.7	102.4	106.3	111.6	117.9
Accommodation and food services	244.0	261.4	265.8	279.1	292.5	312.8	338.0
Accommodation	84.3	90.7	87.5	89.1	94.0	100.8	...
Food services and drinking places	159.7	170.8	178.3	190.0	198.5	212.0	...
Other services, except government	217.8	229.1	241.5	252.5	264.3	277.7	294.6
Government	1 141.2	1 202.7	1 258.3	1 338.4	1 414.5	1 483.3	1 552.3
Federal	361.9	378.7	385.7	417.3	447.1	475.9	494.8
General government	300.9	315.4	325.7	352.9	382.6	408.2	...
Government enterprises	61.0	63.4	60.0	64.5	64.5	67.7	...
State and local	779.4	823.9	872.6	921.1	967.4	1 007.4	1 057.5
General government	711.8	754.2	800.8	848.9	893.7	931.4	...
Government enterprises	67.6	69.7	71.9	72.2	73.7	75.9	...
Addenda:							
Private goods-producing industries [2]	1 958.9	2 081.5	2 027.5	2 036.9	2 126.7	2 283.1	2 422.7
Private services-producing industries [3]	6 168.3	6 532.8	6 842.2	7 094.3	7 430.0	7 967.9	8 512.1
Information-communications-technology-producing industries [4]	425.9	465.8	424.2	416.6	420.9	445.2	481.0

[1]Includes industries not shown separately.
[2]Consists of agriculture, forestry, fishing, and hunting; mining; construction; and manufacturing.
[3]Consists of utilities; wholesale trade; retail trade; transportation and warehousing; information; finance, insurance, real estate, rental, and leasing; professional and business services; educational services, health care, and social assistance; arts, entertainment, recreation, accommodation, and food services; and other services, except government.
[4]Consists of computer and electronic products; publishing industries (including software); information and data processing services; and computer systems design and related services.
. . . = Not available.

Table 15-3. Value Added (Gross Domestic Product) by NAICS Industry Group, in Constant Dollars

(Billions of chained [2000] dollars.)

NAICS industry	1999	2000	2001	2002	2003	2004	2005
Gross domestic product	9 470.3	9 817.0	9 890.7	10 048.8	10 320.6	10 755.7	11 134.8
Private industries	8 285.5	8 614.3	8 692.5	8 817.1	9 060.3	9 481.7	9 838.8
Agriculture, forestry, fishing, and hunting	87.4	98.0	91.8	96.8	104.2	106.0	101.3
Farms	62.9	71.5	65.6	70.1	76.0	75.9	. . .
Forestry, fishing, and related activities	24.5	26.5	26.3	26.7	28.1	30.5	. . .
Mining [1]	126.6	121.3	114.9	107.6	106.0	108.4	105.6
Oil and gas extraction	91.5	81.0	77.7	82.0	77.4	76.6	. . .
Mining, except oil and gas	26.7	27.0	25.8	24.2	24.3	25.1	. . .
Utilities	179.2	189.3	180.0	187.7	202.3	204.5	205.4
Construction	433.3	435.9	436.6	428.1	422.4	432.9	444.7
Manufacturing	1 342.1	1 426.2	1 346.9	1 384.4	1 410.4	1 478.1	1 536.6
Durable goods [1]	775.5	865.3	813.6	827.7	863.2	917.8	970.1
Computer and electronic products	125.4	185.6	181.9	185.8	215.0	260.3	. . .
Motor vehicles, bodies and trailers, and parts	114.6	118.1	104.6	127.5	143.2	139.2	. . .
Nondurable goods [1]	568.2	561.0	533.1	555.7	548.8	563.8	572.8
Food and beverage and tobacco products	155.1	154.8	156.0	153.7	153.3	155.8	. . .
Chemical products	157.1	157.1	153.1	170.5	172.9	173.6	. . .
Wholesale trade	594.1	591.7	633.1	639.4	653.6	683.7	692.0
Retail trade	633.9	662.4	708.6	724.0	749.9	797.7	821.1
Transportation and warehousing [1]	287.4	301.6	293.6	300.2	311.2	323.8	335.7
Air transportation	52.9	57.7	57.0	62.8	71.1	79.5	. . .
Rail transportation	24.8	25.5	24.8	24.4	24.7	25.7	. . .
Truck transportation	91.9	92.8	87.9	87.5	88.7	91.4	. . .
Transit and ground passenger transportation	14.7	14.5	14.5	14.6	14.4	14.4	. . .
Other transportation and support activities	66.2	70.2	69.4	70.6	72.0	75.5	. . .
Warehousing and storage	23.4	25.0	24.4	25.6	26.9	26.1	. . .
Information	437.5	458.3	476.8	487.0	500.0	563.8	605.6
Publishing industries (includes software)	121.2	116.7	115.7	115.4	118.8	130.8	. . .
Motion picture and sound recording industries	32.3	32.5	31.9	35.8	36.7	39.8	. . .
Broadcasting and telecommunications	248.3	271.3	289.1	291.8	296.7	340.2	. . .
Information and data processing services	36.2	37.7	40.2	43.7	47.2	53.0	. . .
Finance, insurance, real estate, rental, and leasing	1 834.3	1 931.0	2 005.4	2 023.6	2 093.3	2 173.1	2 262.5
Finance and insurance	678.1	740.5	772.8	790.0	837.0	845.3	902.0
Federal Reserve banks, credit intermediation, and related activities	328.4	319.0	345.9	381.2	409.9	406.6	. . .
Securities, commodity contracts, and investments	113.6	167.7	186.4	169.8	175.2	192.9	. . .
Insurance carriers and related activities	224.1	238.3	228.9	224.7	233.7	230.3	. . .
Funds, trusts, and other financial vehicles	20.4	15.5	12.6	12.0	14.1	14.9	. . .
Real estate and rental and leasing	1 157.0	1 190.5	1 232.6	1 233.9	1 257.2	1 328.0	1 361.2
Real estate	1 051.4	1 082.1	1 125.7	1 129.3	1 154.0	1 224.0	. . .
Rental and leasing services and lessors of intangible assets	105.6	108.3	106.8	104.3	102.7	103.3	. . .
Professional and business services	1 105.5	1 140.8	1 133.4	1 131.6	1 168.1	1 243.4	1 316.5
Professional, scientific, and technical services	623.9	675.1	679.1	668.8	684.2	732.7	784.1
Legal services	132.6	136.1	137.7	132.6	136.5	135.6	. . .
Computer systems design and related services	112.4	125.7	125.3	127.6	129.3	139.7	. . .
Miscellaneous professional, scientific, and technical services	379.0	413.3	416.1	408.8	418.5	458.8	. . .
Management of companies and enterprises	185.6	183.4	179.9	185.3	191.8	203.4	204.0
Administrative and waste management services	296.9	282.4	274.4	277.7	292.3	307.5	328.7
Administrative and support services	272.3	257.2	250.2	253.2	267.1	282.2	. . .
Waste management and remediation services	24.6	25.2	24.2	24.5	25.2	25.4	. . .
Educational services, health care, and social assistance	660.1	678.4	700.1	729.5	749.8	773.6	806.7
Educational services	77.1	79.2	79.1	81.2	82.1	82.7	83.4
Health care and social assistance	583.0	599.2	621.0	648.4	667.9	691.2	724.1
Ambulatory health care services	295.2	307.6	325.4	343.1	357.8	375.4	. . .
Hospitals and nursing and residential care facilities	237.6	238.6	239.8	245.6	247.8	250.9	. . .
Social assistance	50.2	53.0	55.9	60.1	63.2	66.7	. . .
Arts, entertainment, recreation, accommodation, and food services	339.0	350.1	347.6	353.7	364.1	375.2	390.6
Arts, entertainment, and recreation	87.9	88.7	91.5	94.7	95.4	97.3	99.4
Accommodation and food services	251.2	261.4	256.2	259.0	268.7	277.9	291.2
Accommodation	87.1	90.7	85.4	86.7	90.0	91.4	. . .
Food services and drinking places	164.1	170.8	170.8	172.3	178.7	186.4	. . .
Other services, except government	229.7	229.1	225.3	226.1	228.6	231.4	237.0
Government	1 178.7	1 202.7	1 212.2	1 232.4	1 248.0	1 260.0	1 274.3
Federal	373.0	378.7	372.5	380.0	387.1	393.1	397.3
General government	312.7	315.4	317.0	323.3	331.8	334.9	. . .
Government enterprises	60.4	63.4	55.7	56.9	55.6	58.5	. . .
State and local	805.7	823.9	839.7	852.4	860.8	866.8	876.9
General government	738.7	754.2	772.3	787.1	794.4	800.7	. . .
Government enterprises	67.0	69.7	67.5	65.4	66.6	66.2	. . .
Not allocated by industry [2]	-22.9	0.0	-16.3	-9.4	-8.4	-41.3	. . .
Addenda:							
Private goods-producing industries [3]	1 985.8	2 081.5	1 991.0	2 016.0	2 040.0	2 119.2	2 174.9
Private services-producing industries [4]	6 299.8	6 532.8	6 701.6	6 801.1	7 019.6	7 361.6	7 662.9
Information-communications-technology-producing industries [5]	390.1	465.8	464.0	473.4	505.0	570.1	638.0

[1]Includes industries not shown separately.
[2]The value of not allocated by industry reflects the difference between the first line and the sum of the most detailed lines, as well as the differences in source data used to estimate GDP by industry and the expenditures measure of real GDP.
[3]Consists of agriculture, forestry, fishing, and hunting; mining; construction; and manufacturing.
[4]Consists of utilities; wholesale trade; retail trade; transportation and warehousing; information; finance, insurance, real estate, rental, and leasing; professional and business services; educational services, health care, and social assistance; arts, entertainment, recreation, accommodation, and food services; and other services, except government.
[5]Consists of computer and electronic products; publishing industries (includes software); information and data processing services; and computer systems design and related services.
. . . = Not available.

Table 15-4. Gross Domestic Factor Income by NAICS Industry Group

(Billions of current dollars.)

NAICS industry	1998	1999	2000	2001	2002	2003	2004
Gross domestic factor income	8 142.5	8 638.6	9 152.4	9 454.6	9 745.2	10 216.5	10 924.9
Compensation of employees	5 023.9	5 362.3	5 787.3	5 947.2	6 096.6	6 326.7	6 693.4
Gross operating surplus	3 118.6	3 276.3	3 365.1	3 507.4	3 648.6	3 889.8	4 231.5
Private industries	7 037.0	7 486.2	7 939.2	8 185.2	8 393.7	8 788.0	9 426.9
Compensation of employees	4 107.7	4 407.0	4 776.4	4 882.4	4 957.6	5 118.0	5 421.5
Gross operating surplus	2 929.3	3 079.2	3 162.8	3 302.8	3 436.1	3 670.0	4 005.4
Agriculture, forestry, fishing, and hunting	107.9	106.8	112.1	110.6	99.2	121.8	145.9
Compensation of employees	31.2	33.0	34.6	36.1	36.4	36.1	39.3
Gross operating surplus	76.7	73.8	77.5	74.5	62.8	85.7	106.6
Mining	63.8	74.6	108.2	104.5	93.8	127.7	155.7
Compensation of employees	34.6	33.4	36.0	38.8	37.7	38.8	43.5
Gross operating surplus	29.2	41.2	72.2	65.7	56.1	88.9	112.2
Utilities	152.0	155.5	158.4	176.5	172.6	185.3	196.2
Compensation of employees	41.2	42.6	46.3	48.4	51.2	52.8	55.4
Gross operating surplus	110.8	112.9	112.1	128.1	121.4	132.5	140.8
Construction	370.0	401.8	430.9	464.3	476.5	494.7	542.7
Compensation of employees	254.3	282.8	309.2	327.6	332.7	337.2	360.1
Gross operating surplus	115.7	119.0	121.7	136.7	143.8	157.5	182.6
Durable goods manufacturing	794.2	807.5	851.7	764.9	760.0	770.2	807.7
Compensation of employees	546.2	570.4	621.2	584.2	570.8	590.5	600.5
Gross operating surplus	248.0	237.1	230.5	180.7	189.2	179.7	207.2
Nondurable goods manufacturing	512.4	527.7	533.8	534.7	548.2	553.7	564.8
Compensation of employees	279.1	283.8	297.6	292.6	303.5	308.5	314.7
Gross operating surplus	233.3	243.9	236.2	242.1	244.7	245.2	250.1
Wholesale trade	416.1	446.4	456.3	471.8	477.5	488.9	542.3
Compensation of employees	291.0	313.9	328.6	334.1	333.4	344.9	367.9
Gross operating surplus	125.1	132.5	127.7	137.7	144.1	144.0	174.4
Retail trade	474.4	502.6	522.0	549.0	572.6	596.4	625.5
Compensation of employees	342.3	368.2	396.6	410.5	422.3	433.1	451.5
Gross operating surplus	132.1	134.4	125.4	138.5	150.3	163.3	174.0
Transportation and warehousing	259.6	272.5	285.6	287.1	288.7	307.4	315.8
Compensation of employees	174.9	186.1	199.3	203.5	204.1	206.0	219.8
Gross operating surplus	84.7	86.4	86.3	83.6	84.6	101.4	96.0
Information	349.9	405.1	421.9	439.9	445.0	453.0	498.3
Compensation of employees	185.6	217.5	248.0	244.4	227.9	225.1	234.1
Gross operating surplus	164.3	187.6	173.9	195.5	217.1	227.9	264.2
Finance and insurance	613.3	650.7	710.4	751.2	789.2	848.8	888.6
Compensation of employees	344.5	370.7	409.3	437.0	448.0	471.1	510.5
Gross operating surplus	268.8	280.0	301.1	314.2	341.2	377.7	378.1
Real estate and rental and leasing	904.7	972.2	1 036.0	1 111.4	1 139.8	1 187.2	1 283.8
Compensation of employees	66.2	70.7	77.4	81.3	84.1	87.6	94.9
Gross operating surplus	838.5	901.5	958.6	1 030.1	1 055.7	1 099.6	1 188.9
Professional, scientific, and technical services	555.9	603.8	664.2	687.5	693.3	714.9	771.0
Compensation of employees	378.3	422.0	486.9	499.6	489.1	497.5	532.0
Gross operating surplus	177.6	181.8	177.3	187.9	204.2	217.4	239.0
Management of companies and enterprises	153.8	167.3	179.9	174.5	180.7	188.4	217.5
Compensation of employees	127.5	136.1	147.4	139.9	139.5	144.2	162.1
Gross operating surplus	26.3	31.2	32.5	34.6	41.2	44.2	55.4
Administrative and waste management services	247.7	273.3	274.8	281.7	292.0	308.8	338.0
Compensation of employees	193.9	213.1	211.7	217.0	222.9	230.1	250.4
Gross operating surplus	53.8	60.2	63.1	64.7	69.1	78.7	87.6
Educational services	66.6	71.8	78.2	83.9	92.0	98.3	105.0
Compensation of employees	61.2	65.9	72.0	78.1	85.5	91.6	97.6
Gross operating surplus	5.4	5.9	6.2	5.8	6.5	6.7	7.4
Health care and social assistance	527.3	554.7	591.9	646.4	697.8	742.1	793.3
Compensation of employees	425.9	447.1	478.8	516.2	553.8	589.6	629.5
Gross operating surplus	101.4	107.6	113.1	130.2	144.0	152.5	163.8
Arts, entertainment, and recreation	69.1	75.1	79.7	86.2	92.5	95.7	100.2
Compensation of employees	44.5	48.4	53.6	56.9	59.9	63.0	66.2
Gross operating surplus	24.6	26.7	26.1	29.3	32.6	32.7	34.0
Accommodation and food services	201.2	214.0	229.5	233.7	246.2	257.7	275.6
Compensation of employees	143.7	152.8	164.7	170.6	177.8	185.4	197.5
Gross operating surplus	57.5	61.2	64.8	63.1	68.4	72.3	78.1
Other services, except government	197.2	203.0	213.5	225.5	235.7	246.8	259.1
Compensation of employees	141.5	148.5	157.2	165.6	176.7	184.7	194.0
Gross operating surplus	55.7	54.5	56.3	59.9	59.0	62.1	65.1
Government	1 105.5	1 152.3	1 213.1	1 269.3	1 351.5	1 428.4	1 498.0
Compensation of employees	916.2	955.3	1 010.8	1 064.8	1 139.0	1 208.6	1 271.9
Gross operating surplus	189.3	197.0	202.3	204.5	212.5	219.8	226.1
Addenda:							
Private goods-producing industries [1]	1 848.3	1 918.3	2 036.8	1 979.0	1 978.0	2 068.0	2 216.7
Compensation of employees	1 145.4	1 203.4	1 298.7	1 279.3	1 281.2	1 311.1	1 358.1
Gross operating surplus	702.9	714.9	738.1	699.7	696.8	756.9	858.6
Private services-producing industries [2]	5 188.7	5 567.9	5 902.5	6 206.2	6 415.8	6 720.0	7 210.3
Compensation of employees	2 962.3	3 203.6	3 477.8	3 603.1	3 676.4	3 806.9	4 063.5
Gross operating surplus	2 226.4	2 364.3	2 424.7	2 603.1	2 739.4	2 913.1	3 146.8
Information-communications-technology-producing industries [3]	378.5	418.9	458.1	416.3	408.5	412.5	436.2
Compensation of employees	275.2	320.3	388.8	364.1	330.2	323.5	339.1
Gross operating surplus	103.3	98.6	69.3	52.2	78.3	89.0	97.1

[1]Consists of agriculture, forestry, fishing, and hunting; mining; construction; and manufacturing.
[2]Consists of utilities; wholesale trade; retail trade; transportation and warehousing; information; finance, insurance, real estate, rental, and leasing; professional and business services; educational services, health care, and social assistance; arts, entertainment, recreation, accommodation, and food services; and other services, except government.
[3]Consists of computer and electronic products; publishing industries (includes software); information and data processing services; and computer systems design and related services.

NOTES AND DEFINITIONS

TABLES 15-1 THROUGH 15-4

VALUE ADDED (GROSS DOMESTIC PRODUCT) AND GROSS FACTOR INCOME BY INDUSTRY

Source: U.S. Department of Commerce, Bureau of Economic Analysis (BEA)

In the introduction to the notes and definitions for Chapter 1, it was observed that gross domestic product (GDP), while primarily measured as the sum of final demands for goods and services, is also the sum of the values created by each industry in the economy. The industry accounts in the national income and product accounts (NIPAs) are designed to measure the contribution of each major industry to GDP. They are only calculated on an annual basis; no quarterly data are available.

Industry GDP data from 1987 through 2000, classified by the old Standard Industrial Classification (SIC) system and using an unrevised methodology, are reprinted from earlier editions of *Business Statistics* and are shown in Table 15-1.

In June 2004, BEA released a comprehensive revision and updating of the industry accounts for 1998 to 2003, using improved methods for integrating the industry accounts with annual input-output accounts and final-demand GDP calculations, and incorporating the new North American Industry Classification System (NAICS). These data have been revised and updated in subsequent years; full data are now available for 1994 through 2004, and preliminary estimates at a higher level of industry detail are available for 2005. Two important measures from these accounts—value added in current dollars and in chained (2000) dollars—are shown for 1998 through 2005 in Tables 15-2 and 15-3. See Chapter 14 for the relationship of NAICS to SIC.

Additionally, in Table 15-4, the editor presents for 1998 through 2004 a variation of current-dollar value added, called "gross domestic factor income," that enables users to obtain a clearer picture of the quantitative impact of each industry on the economy and of the shares of capital and labor in each industry.

The 2004 revision incorporated a change in terminology. An industry's contribution to total GDP, formerly referred to as "gross product originating" (GPO) or "gross product by industry," is now called "value added." This is consistent with the use of the term "value added" in most economic writing. However, it should not be confused with a concept known as "Census value added," which is used in U.S. censuses and surveys of manufactures. Census value added is calculated at the individual establishment level and does not exclude purchased business services. This means that census value added is not a true measure of economic value added.

Definitions and notes on the data

An industry's *value added*, or GPO, is equal to the market value of its gross output (which consists of the value, including taxes, of sales or receipts and other operating income plus the value of inventory change) minus the value of its intermediate inputs (energy, raw materials, semifinished goods, and services that are purchased from domestic industries or from foreign sources).

In concept, this is also equal to the sum of *compensation of employees, taxes on production and imports less subsidies,* and *gross operating surplus*. (See Chapter 1 and its notes and definitions for more information.)

Compensation of employees consists of wage and salary accruals and supplements to wages and salaries. This approximates the labor share of production, subject to the note below about proprietors' income.

Taxes on production and imports less subsidies. Although this is shown in BEA source data as a single net line item, it represents two separate adjustments.

Taxes on production and imports are included in the market value of the goods and services sold to final consumers and therefore in the consumer valuation of those goods. Since they are not part of the payments to the labor and capital inputs in the producing industries, they must be <u>added</u> to the sum of the returns to those inputs in order to account for the total value to consumers. Taxes that fall into this classification include property taxes, sales and excise taxes, and Customs duties.

BEA allocates these taxes to the industry level at which they are assessed by law. Most sales taxes are considered as part of the value added by retail trade. Some sales taxes, most fuel taxes, and all customs duties are attributed to wholesale trade. Residential real property taxes, including those on owner-occupied dwellings, are attributed to the real estate industry.

Subsidies to business by government are included in the labor and/or capital payments made by that industry. Since they are payments to the industry in addition to the market values paid by consumers, they are *subtracted* from the values of the labor and capital inputs to make them consistent with the market values as defined in value added. The role of subsidies is obvious in the data for the agricultural sector, where the net "taxes on production and imports less subsidies" has a negative sign: farm subsidies more than offset this industry's taxes on production and imports, which mainly consist of only property taxes, as sales, excise, and import taxes are not levied on farms.

For private sector businesses, *gross operating surplus* consists of business income (corporate profits before tax, proprietors' income, and rental income of persons), net interest and miscellaneous payments, business current transfer payments (net), and capital consumption allowances. For government, households, and institutions, it consists of consumption of fixed capital and (for government) government enterprises' current surplus. This approximates the share of the value of production ascribable to capital and land as measured in the NIPAs accounts; however, as BEA notes, "An unknown portion [of proprietors' income] reflects the labor contribution of proprietors." (*Survey of Current Business*, June 2004, p. 27, footnote 7.) Another aspect to be noted is that gross operating surplus includes the return to owner-occupied housing in the real estate sector. Because there is no employee compensation attributed to owner-occupied housing in the NIPAs, the capital share in that industry as measured by gross operating surplus is very large.

Value added in constant dollars. The preferred method for measuring real value added by industry is known as "double deflation." This entails constructing constant-dollar measures of the gross output of the industry and subtracting constant-dollar measures of the intermediate inputs to the industry from those values. In the new methodology, this is used for all industries. The results are shown in Table 15-3 in chained (2000) dollars. See the notes and definitions for Chapter 1 for an explanation of chained-dollar methodology. In the older methodology (used for the years 1987 through 2000 in Table 15-1), the double-deflation method is used to calculate real output for most industry groups, and the real output series (also based on chained dollars) are expressed as quantity indexes, 1996 = 100.

Gross domestic factor income (not a category published as such in the NIPAs) is calculated by the editor as value added minus "taxes on production and imports less subsidies." The effect of this procedure is to take out the specified taxes, and to leave in the subsidies embedded in the labor and gross operating surplus components. The editor believes that this provides a valuable alternative basis for assessing the importance of different industries in the economy and the shares of labor and capital in each industry's output.

The reasoning followed by the editor is based on the facts that more than half of these taxes are sales, excise, and import taxes, and the assignment of these taxes to industries is economically arbitrary. BEA assigns them to the industry with the legal liability to pay, not to the entity bearing the major incidence of the tax. Yet economists can demonstrate that most of the burdens of sales and excise taxes and import duties are not borne by the factors in the industry—they are passed on to consumers. In addition, because the wholesale and retail trade industries are classified as "services-producing," the allocation of those taxes has a very peculiar result: taxes on goods are represented as paid by "service" industries. The process adopted in Table 15-4, which excludes these taxes and focuses on "gross domestic factor income," has the effect (for example) of keeping the wholesale trade industry from appearing to be both larger and more heavily taxed than it really is.

Data availability and references

The latest estimates shown here were published in "Annual Industry Accounts: Advance Estimates for 2005," *Survey of Current Business*, May 2006. They do not reflect the mid-2006 revisions of the NIPAs that are shown in Chapter 1 of *Business Statistics*. The estimates for 1998–2003 were published and described in "Improved Annual Industry Accounts for 1998–2003," *Survey of Current Business*, June 2004. They were updated in "Annual Industry Accounts for 2001–2003," *Survey of Current Business*, January 2005.

Further background is given in "Preview of the Comprehensive Revision of the Annual Industry Accounts," *Survey of Current Business*, March 2004.

For the earlier estimates, concepts and methodology were described in "Improved Estimates of Gross Product by Industry for 1947–1998," *Survey of Current Business*, June 2000.

Revised estimates for 2003 through 2005 were published in "Annual Industry Accounts: Revised Estimates for 2003–2005," *Survey of Current Business*, December 2006. They were released too late to be included in this edition of *Business Statistics*.

Data and *Survey of Current Business* articles are available on the BEA Web site at <http://www.bea.gov>.

CHAPTER 16: EMPLOYMENT, HOURS, AND EARNINGS BY NAICS INDUSTRY

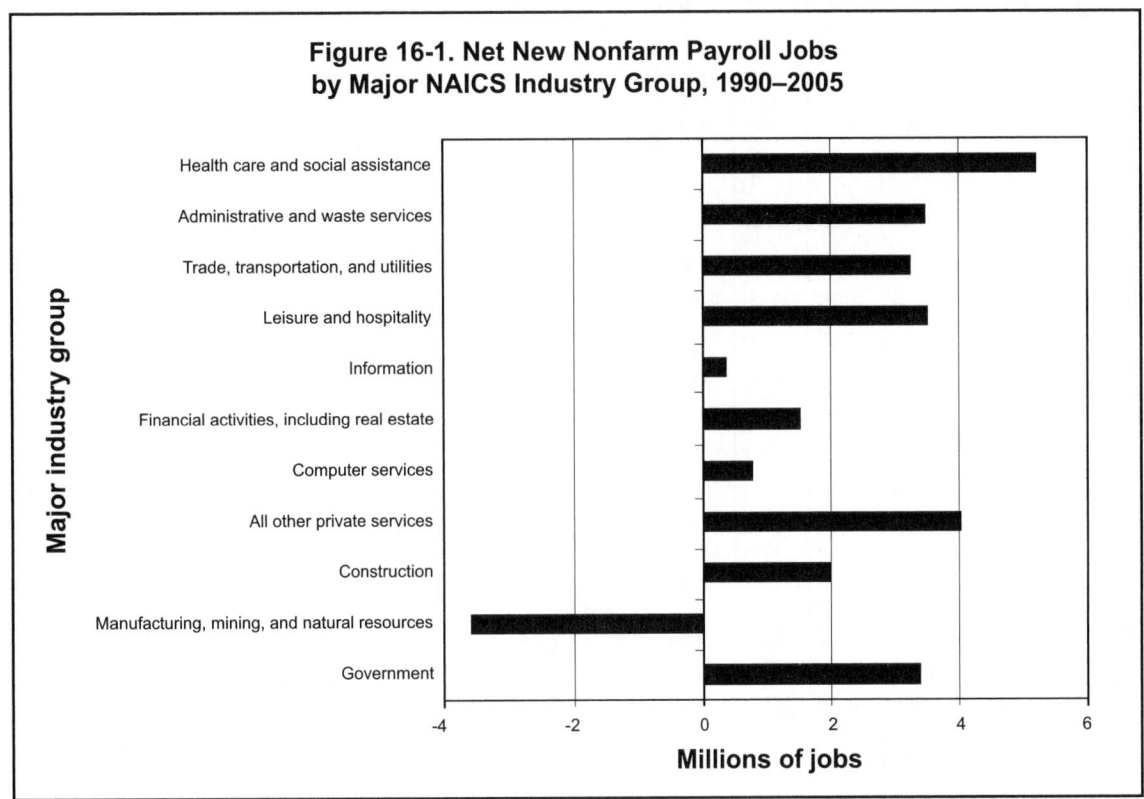

Figure 16-1. Net New Nonfarm Payroll Jobs by Major NAICS Industry Group, 1990–2005

- Between 1990 and 2005, U.S. industries added a net total of 24 million jobs. Manufacturing, mining, and natural resources lost 3.6 million employees, but 27.6 million employees were added in other industries. (Table 16-1)

- Of the major groups shown in the figure, health care and social assistance was the single greatest source of new jobs. This sector provided 5.2 million net new jobs, of which 1.1 million were in social assistance and the rest in health care.

- Administrative and waste services added 3.5 million net new jobs, of which 1.4 million were in the temporary help sector.

- Leisure and hospitality created 3.5 million net new jobs, with 2.6 million at food services and drinking places.

- Government provided 3.4 million net jobs—3.1 million at the local government level and 0.7 million at the state government level, partly offset by a loss of about half a million jobs in federal government.

- Trade, transportation, and utilities added 3.2 million net new jobs, with 2.1 million of them in retail trade.

- In 2005, the average workweek was 40 hours or more in most of the goods-producing industries. In manufacturing—the only sector for which overtime data are collected—more than 4 hours of the typical workweek were worked at overtime rates. Retail trade and some service industries, especially leisure and hospitality, had much shorter average workweeks; this indicated the presence of many part-time jobs. (Table 16-3)

- Average hourly earnings in 2005 ranged from less than $10 in the leisure and hospitality sector to over $20 in transportation equipment manufacturing, petroleum and coal products, utilities, and information. (Table 16-4)

Table 16-1. Nonfarm Employment by NAICS Sector and Industry

(Wage and salary workers on nonfarm payrolls, thousands.)

Industry	1990	1991	1992	1993	1994	1995	1996	1997	1998	1999	2000	2001	2002	2003
TOTAL NONFARM	109 487	108 374	108 726	110 844	114 291	117 298	119 708	122 776	125 930	128 993	131 785	131 826	130 341	129 999
Total Private	91 072	89 829	89 940	91 855	95 016	97 866	100 169	103 113	106 021	108 686	110 996	110 707	108 828	108 416
Goods-Producing	23 723	22 588	22 095	22 219	22 774	23 156	23 410	23 886	24 354	24 465	24 649	23 873	22 557	21 816
Natural resources and mining	765	739	689	666	659	641	637	654	645	598	599	606	583	572
Logging	84.6	78.7	78.7	81.0	82.0	82.5	80.7	82.1	80.0	80.8	79.0	73.5	70.4	69.4
Mining	680.1	660.5	609.8	584.9	576.5	558.1	556.4	571.3	564.7	517.4	520.2	532.5	512.2	502.7
Oil and gas extraction	190.2	191.0	182.2	170.9	162.4	151.7	146.9	144.1	140.8	131.2	124.9	123.7	121.9	120.2
Mining, except oil and gas [1]	302.2	285.1	271.8	250.9	255.2	252.4	249.4	249.5	243.1	234.5	224.8	218.7	210.6	202.7
Coal mining	136.0	125.6	117.5	100.2	103.5	96.7	90.5	89.4	85.3	78.6	72.2	74.3	74.4	70.0
Support activities for mining	187.6	184.5	155.7	163.1	158.8	154.0	160.1	177.7	180.8	151.7	170.6	190.1	179.8	179.8
Construction	5 263	4 780	4 608	4 779	5 095	5 274	5 536	5 813	6 149	6 545	6 787	6 826	6 716	6 735
Construction of buildings	1 413.0	1 252.9	1 187.3	1 227.4	1 300.8	1 325.4	1 380.2	1 435.4	1 508.8	1 586.3	1 632.5	1 588.9	1 574.8	1 575.8
Heavy and civil engineering	813.0	759.1	734.2	738.4	761.7	774.7	800.1	824.9	865.3	908.7	937.0	953.0	930.6	903.1
Specialty trade contractors	3 037.3	2 768.4	2 686.0	2 813.6	3 032.5	3 174.1	3 355.1	3 552.6	3 775.1	4 049.6	4 217.0	4 283.9	4 210.4	4 255.7
Manufacturing	17 695	17 068	16 799	16 774	17 021	17 241	17 237	17 419	17 560	17 322	17 263	16 441	15 259	14 510
Durable goods	10 736	10 219	9 945	9 900	10 131	10 372	10 485	10 704	10 910	10 830	10 876	10 335	9 483	8 963
Wood products	540.6	498.5	501.9	524.1	560.6	573.7	582.8	595.4	609.2	620.3	613.0	574.1	554.9	537.6
Nonmetallic mineral products	528.4	494.7	487.3	491.1	505.3	513.1	517.3	525.7	535.3	540.8	554.2	544.5	516.0	494.2
Primary metals	688.6	656.1	630.3	618.4	630.4	641.7	639.3	638.8	641.5	625.0	621.8	570.9	509.4	477.4
Fabricated metal products	1 610	1 541.3	1 497.2	1 509.5	1 565.3	1 623.4	1 647.5	1 695.8	1 739.5	1 728.4	1 752.6	1 676.4	1 548.5	1 478.9
Machinery	1 407.8	1 345.8	1 309.1	1 328.8	1 379.2	1 440.2	1 466.8	1 493.7	1 511.9	1 466.1	1 454.7	1 368.3	1 229.5	1 149.4
Computer and electronic products [1]	1 902.5	1 809.3	1 707.3	1 656.0	1 651.1	1 688.4	1 746.6	1 803.3	1 830.9	1 780.5	1 820.0	1 748.8	1 507.2	1 355.2
Computer and peripheral equipment	367.4	348.6	328.5	305.7	297.7	295.6	304.6	316.7	322.1	310.1	301.9	286.2	250.0	224.0
Communications equipment	231.5	220.6	209.7	210.3	218.0	232.8	237.6	243.9	246.4	237.4	247.7	233.9	185.8	154.9
Semiconductors and electronic components	574.0	546.6	519.4	519.4	535.4	571.0	606.6	639.8	649.8	630.5	676.3	645.4	524.5	461.1
Electronic instruments	626.3	590.0	548.5	517.6	493.4	482.0	489.1	493.9	500.2	489.6	478.6	475.1	450.0	429.7
Electrical equipment and appliances	633.1	597.7	579.4	575.8	588.5	592.8	591.0	586.3	591.6	588.0	590.9	556.9	496.5	459.6
Transportation equipment [1]	2 133.3	2 028.2	1 976.9	1 913.7	1 936.1	1 977.2	1 973.7	2 026.2	2 077.0	2 087.3	2 055.8	1 937.9	1 828.9	1 774.1
Motor vehicles and parts	1 054.2	1 017.6	1 047.0	1 077.8	1 168.5	1 241.5	1 240.3	1 253.9	1 271.5	1 312.5	1 313.6	1 212.9	1 151.2	1 125.3
Furniture and related products	601.4	561.0	562.8	575.4	600.2	606.7	603.8	615.1	641.2	664.8	679.7	642.4	604.1	572.9
Miscellaneous manufacturing	690.4	686.6	692.5	707.4	713.8	714.5	715.6	723.1	731.7	729.0	733.0	714.5	688.3	663.3
Nondurable goods	6 959	6 849	6 854	6 873	6 890	6 869	6 752	6 716	6 650	6 492	6 388	6 107	5 775	5 547
Food manufacturing	1 507.3	1 515.2	1 518.3	1 534.6	1 539.2	1 560.0	1 562.0	1 557.9	1 554.9	1 549.8	1 553.1	1 551.2	1 525.7	1 517.5
Beverage and tobacco products	217.7	214.7	208.5	207.1	204.6	202.6	204.4	206.3	208.9	208.3	207.0	209.0	207.4	199.6
Textile mills	491.8	479.9	479.0	478.7	477.6	468.5	443.2	436.2	424.5	397.1	378.2	332.9	290.9	261.3
Textile product mills	209.3	199.4	202.0	207.3	218.6	219.0	216.3	217.0	217.1	217.3	216.3	205.7	194.6	179.3
Apparel	929.1	902.6	905.2	882.5	856.3	814.1	743.1	700.2	639.0	555.6	496.8	426.5	359.7	312.3
Leather and allied products	133.2	124.4	120.8	118.1	113.9	104.9	94.2	89.5	82.9	74.9	68.8	58.0	50.2	44.5
Paper and paper products	647.2	638.5	639.6	639.7	639.4	639.5	631.4	630.6	624.9	615.6	604.7	577.6	546.6	516.2
Printing and related support activities	808.6	792.3	780.2	785.2	802.2	817.3	815.8	821.1	827.9	814.6	806.8	768.4	706.6	680.5
Petroleum and coal products	152.8	154.8	152.3	146.2	144.0	140.4	137.3	136.0	134.5	127.8	123.2	121.1	118.1	114.3
Chemicals	1 035.7	1 024.1	1 028.9	1 024.9	1 004.7	987.9	984.5	986.8	992.6	982.5	980.4	959.0	927.5	906.1
Plastics and rubber products	825.9	803.2	819.0	849.0	889.4	915.1	920.1	934.1	942.8	948.3	952.2	897.4	848.0	815.4
Service-Providing	85 764	85 787	86 631	88 625	91 517	94 142	96 299	98 890	101 576	104 528	107 136	107 952	107 784	108 182
Private Service-Providing	67 349	67 241	67 845	69 636	72 242	74 710	76 759	79 227	81 667	84 221	86 346	86 834	86 271	86 599
Trade, transportation, and utilities	22 666	22 281	22 125	22 378	23 128	23 834	24 239	24 700	25 186	25 771	26 225	25 983	25 497	25 287
Wholesale trade	5 268.4	5 185.3	5 109.7	5 093.2	5 247.3	5 433.1	5 522.0	5 663.9	5 795.2	5 892.5	5 933.2	5 772.7	5 652.3	5 607.5
Durable goods	2 833.7	2 766.6	2 698.8	2 687.0	2 786.0	2 908.8	2 977.8	3 071.9	3 162.4	3 219.6	3 250.7	3 130.4	3 007.9	2 940.6
Nondurable goods	1 900.2	1 891.3	1 891.5	1 888.3	1 927.0	1 969.3	1 977.5	2 007.9	2 032.7	2 061.1	2 064.8	2 031.3	2 015.0	2 004.6
Electronic markets, agents, and brokers	534.5	527.4	519.4	517.9	534.4	555.0	566.7	584.1	600.1	611.8	617.7	611.1	629.4	662.2

[1] Includes other industries, not shown separately.

Table 16-1. Nonfarm Employment by NAICS Sector and Industry—Continued

(Wage and salary workers on nonfarm payrolls, thousands.)

Industry	2004	2005	2005, seasonally adjusted											
			January	February	March	April	May	June	July	August	September	October	November	December
TOTAL NONFARM	131 435	133 463	132 471	132 736	132 876	133 104	133 210	133 376	133 617	133 792	133 840	133 877	134 231	134 376
Total Private	109 814	111 660	110 756	110 995	111 129	111 336	111 437	111 590	111 795	111 941	111 985	112 025	112 351	112 498
Goods-Producing	21 882	22 133	21 988	22 052	22 077	22 119	22 126	22 133	22 131	22 146	22 143	22 179	22 264	22 282
Natural resources and mining	591	625	605	610	616	620	620	623	624	627	631	636	641	644
Logging	67.6	64.2	66.9	66.7	68.1	65.3	64.0	63.7	63.8	63.4	62.7	62.1	62.1	62.0
Mining	523.0	560.7	537.7	543.1	547.9	554.5	556.1	559.7	559.9	563.1	567.9	573.8	579.3	582.1
Oil and gas extraction	123.4	125.9	124.0	123.3	124.8	124.4	125.2	125.3	126.1	126.2	126.5	127.4	128.9	128.7
Mining, except oil and gas [1]	205.1	212.1	207.8	209.4	208.9	211.1	211.9	213.9	212.7	212.6	212.7	214.5	215.0	214.3
Coal mining	70.6	73.8	72.3	72.5	72.3	72.9	72.7	73.5	74.1	73.7	74.5	75.1	75.1	75.4
Support activities for mining	194.6	222.7	205.9	210.4	214.2	219.0	219.0	220.5	221.1	224.3	228.7	231.9	235.4	239.1
Construction	6 976	7 277	7 115	7 166	7 193	7 243	7 255	7 277	7 283	7 306	7 325	7 347	7 409	7 416
Construction of buildings	1 630.0	1 694.6	1 675.6	1 683.3	1 685.2	1 686.5	1 686.7	1 689.1	1 691.8	1 699.8	1 697.6	1 702.4	1 722.4	1 727.2
Heavy and civil engineering	907.4	952.8	922.3	928.8	931.0	940.5	947.1	961.2	961.0	961.4	963.9	965.3	977.1	974.8
Specialty trade contractors	4 438.6	4 629.1	4 517.5	4 554.3	4 576.8	4 615.7	4 621.5	4 626.6	4 629.8	4 645.1	4 663.3	4 679.2	4 709.4	4 714.3
Manufacturing	14 315	14 232	14 268	14 276	14 268	14 256	14 251	14 233	14 224	14 213	14 187	14 196	14 214	14 222
Durable goods	8 924	8 953	8 943	8 963	8 959	8 959	8 964	8 953	8 946	8 950	8 933	8 952	8 960	8 970
Wood products	549.6	554.9	556.8	556.9	559.3	555.6	551.8	553.9	553.6	553.7	552.2	550.7	556.7	558.9
Nonmetallic mineral products	505.5	503.2	505.5	505.6	504.6	507.1	504.0	504.5	501.8	501.5	501.1	500.8	502.0	500.7
Primary metals	466.8	468.7	467.4	468.7	468.8	468.7	469.1	468.2	468.1	468.0	469.7	470.5	471.5	469.4
Fabricated metal products	1 497.1	1 519.0	1 512.3	1 512.4	1 515.0	1 516.1	1 519.1	1 519.5	1 521.1	1 521.9	1 521.7	1 520.8	1 524.1	1 526.7
Machinery	1 143.0	1 161.8	1 150.1	1 152.1	1 156.2	1 159.0	1 161.1	1 161.8	1 165.0	1 164.3	1 163.4	1 174.5	1 164.4	1 166.9
Computer and electronic products [1]	1 322.8	1 320.4	1 317.5	1 317.3	1 315.3	1 317.7	1 317.6	1 322.2	1 322.8	1 323.6	1 322.8	1 323.5	1 322.0	1 322.2
Computer and peripheral equipment	210.0	206.5	204.6	205.0	204.6	205.4	205.8	207.8	207.6	207.8	207.4	207.9	206.3	205.7
Communications equipment	148.4	148.1	149.2	148.3	147.0	147.5	147.5	147.6	147.6	147.6	147.9	148.2	148.0	149.2
Semiconductors and electronic components	454.1	451.1	450.9	451.2	451.2	451.0	450.5	451.4	451.4	451.7	451.8	450.7	450.6	451.0
Electronic instruments	431.4	438.1	435.4	435.1	435.0	435.9	436.0	438.0	439.1	440.1	440.6	441.6	442.0	441.7
Electrical equipment and appliances	445.1	435.6	440.7	439.5	438.5	437.1	438.2	435.0	434.3	434.5	431.8	431.1	434.3	434.4
Transportation equipment [1]	1 765.7	1 772.3	1 766.6	1 785.7	1 781.9	1 781.5	1 786.8	1 772.1	1 761.3	1 765.2	1 753.7	1 765.5	1 771.8	1 776.7
Motor vehicles and parts	1 112.8	1 098.2	1 103.7	1 115.8	1 110.7	1 107.5	1 109.5	1 093.4	1 080.2	1 087.1	1 098.4	1 088.4	1 092.4	1 092.1
Furniture and related products	573.3	563.3	571.7	570.2	568.4	565.0	563.7	562.6	561.3	561.3	561.3	560.5	558.4	558.0
Miscellaneous manufacturing	655.5	654.0	654.2	654.9	652.2	650.8	652.1	653.6	656.9	655.9	655.0	653.6	654.7	655.8
Nondurable goods	5 391	5 278	5 325	5 313	5 309	5 297	5 287	5 280	5 278	5 263	5 254	5 244	5 254	5 252
Food manufacturing	1 493.7	1 472.0	1 484.7	1 482.6	1 482.8	1 476.8	1 475.2	1 475.2	1 474.7	1 468.6	1 461.4	1 458.5	1 465.0	1 466.0
Beverage and tobacco products	194.6	191.9	193.0	192.9	192.0	191.6	191.9	191.0	190.8	189.9	191.0	192.4	193.4	192.3
Textile mills	236.9	217.9	227.4	225.5	223.7	219.6	220.2	219.3	217.5	216.2	214.7	213.2	210.9	209.0
Textile product mills	175.7	172.3	172.8	172.0	171.5	171.6	172.2	171.3	172.0	172.0	173.0	173.8	174.5	173.9
Apparel	285.5	260.2	271.6	269.3	265.5	265.0	261.4	260.1	259.4	257.1	255.1	251.8	253.7	253.5
Leather and allied products	41.8	39.5	40.1	39.8	39.5	39.5	39.0	39.1	39.5	39.7	39.5	39.6	39.5	39.7
Paper and paper products	495.5	484.4	490.2	490.1	490.4	488.0	486.8	485.1	484.6	483.2	480.5	478.5	478.5	478.1
Printing and related support activities	662.6	648.1	653.0	651.6	650.9	650.9	649.1	648.6	646.4	645.3	646.4	645.1	644.8	644.0
Petroleum and coal products	111.7	112.7	111.8	112.0	111.6	113.0	113.7	113.2	113.3	113.6	113.0	113.1	112.3	112.3
Chemicals	887.0	879.2	878.0	876.4	877.9	878.5	877.9	878.4	879.4	878.3	880.3	879.3	881.5	884.0
Plastics and rubber products	805.7	800.3	802.0	800.7	803.1	802.1	800.0	798.8	800.1	799.2	799.5	799.1	799.4	798.9
Service-Providing	109 553	111 330	110 483	110 684	110 799	110 985	111 084	111 243	111 486	111 646	111 697	111 698	111 967	112 094
Private Service-Providing	87 932	89 527	88 768	88 943	89 052	89 217	89 311	89 457	89 664	89 795	89 842	89 846	90 087	90 216
Trade, transportation, and utilities	25 533	25 909	25 724	25 787	25 822	25 861	25 897	25 908	25 976	25 985	25 944	25 945	26 006	26 015
Wholesale trade	5 662.9	5 749.5	5 701.7	5 712.6	5 726.4	5 730.8	5 742.5	5 747.9	5 755.3	5 759.3	5 762.3	5 767.8	5 782.7	5 783.8
Durable goods	2 950.5	2 992.0	2 969.7	2 972.6	2 979.2	2 981.6	2 986.7	2 990.8	2 993.4	2 995.4	2 997.8	3 002.3	3 010.5	3 017.6
Nondurable goods	2 010.0	2 022.3	2 012.1	2 016.2	2 020.6	2 020.8	2 022.7	2 022.1	2 023.6	2 023.1	2 022.1	2 021.7	2 028.9	2 023.9
Electronic markets, agents, and brokers	702.4	735.2	719.9	723.8	726.6	728.4	733.1	735.0	738.3	740.8	742.4	743.8	743.3	742.3

[1] Includes other industries, not shown separately.

Table 16-1. Nonfarm Employment by NAICS Sector and Industry—Continued

(Wage and salary workers on nonfarm payrolls, thousands.)

Industry	1990	1991	1992	1993	1994	1995	1996	1997	1998	1999	2000	2001	2002	2003
Retail trade	13 182.3	12 896.4	12 827.9	13 020.5	13 490.8	13 896.7	14 142.5	14 388.9	14 609.3	14 970.1	15 279.8	15 238.6	15 025.1	14 917.3
Motor vehicle and parts dealers [1]	1 494.4	1 435.1	1 428.1	1 475.3	1 564.7	1 627.1	1 685.6	1 723.4	1 740.9	1 796.6	1 846.9	1 854.6	1 879.4	1 882.9
Automobile dealers	983.3	938.3	934.8	970.4	1 031.8	1 071.6	1 113.0	1 134.5	1 142.0	1 179.7	1 216.5	1 225.1	1 252.8	1 254.4
Furniture and home furnishings stores	431.5	412.8	410.3	418.6	441.6	461.2	474.2	484.7	499.1	524.4	543.5	541.2	538.7	547.3
Electronics and appliance stores	382.3	381.1	378.1	386.9	417.0	448.7	470.2	494.0	510.2	542.2	564.4	554.5	525.3	512.2
Building material and garden supply stores	890.9	863.0	872.1	891.9	946.2	981.8	1 007.2	1 043.1	1 062.3	1 101.0	1 142.1	1 151.8	1 176.5	1 185.0
Food and beverage stores	2 778.8	2 767.9	2 743.9	2 774.8	2 825.0	2 879.8	2 927.8	2 956.9	2 965.7	2 984.5	2 993.0	2 950.5	2 881.6	2 838.4
Health and personal care stores	792.0	788.5	780.2	778.6	797.0	811.9	826.4	853.3	876.0	898.2	927.6	951.5	938.8	938.1
Gasoline stations	910.2	889.3	876.4	881.2	902.3	922.3	946.4	956.2	961.3	943.5	935.7	925.3	895.9	882.0
Clothing and clothing accessories stores	1 313.0	1 275.8	1 249.1	1 259.9	1 261.7	1 246.3	1 220.6	1 235.9	1 268.6	1 306.6	1 321.6	1 321.1	1 312.5	1 304.5
Sporting goods, hobby, book, and music stores	532.0	527.7	534.4	545.2	577.6	605.8	614.0	626.2	635.4	664.3	685.7	679.2	661.3	646.5
General merchandise stores [1]	2 499.8	2 416.7	2 414.2	2 450.2	2 541.0	2 635.4	2 657.3	2 657.6	2 686.5	2 751.8	2 819.8	2 842.2	2 812.0	2 822.4
Department stores	1 493.9	1 440.8	1 445.2	1 486.8	1 560.4	1 629.8	1 645.0	1 653.5	1 679.2	1 709.2	1 755.0	1 768.3	1 684.0	1 620.6
Miscellaneous store retailers	738.2	734.7	736.8	752.9	795.7	841.1	874.3	913.2	950.3	985.5	1 007.1	993.3	959.5	930.7
Nonstore retailers	419.2	403.7	404.5	404.9	421.2	435.4	438.5	444.5	453.0	471.6	492.4	473.5	443.7	427.3
Transportation and warehousing	3 475.6	3 462.8	3 461.8	3 553.8	3 701.0	3 837.8	3 935.3	4 026.5	4 168.0	4 300.3	4 410.3	4 372.0	4 223.6	4 185.4
Air transportation	529.2	525.4	519.6	516.6	511.2	510.9	525.7	542.0	562.7	586.3	614.4	615.3	563.5	528.3
Rail transportation	271.8	255.6	248.1	242.2	234.6	232.5	225.2	221.0	225.0	228.8	231.7	226.7	217.8	217.7
Water transportation	56.8	57.4	56.7	52.8	52.3	50.8	51.0	50.7	50.5	51.7	56.0	54.0	52.6	54.5
Truck transportation	1 122.4	1 104.6	1 107.4	1 154.8	1 206.2	1 249.1	1 282.4	1 308.2	1 354.4	1 391.5	1 405.8	1 386.8	1 339.3	1 325.6
Transit and ground passenger transportation	274.2	283.9	287.9	299.9	316.6	327.9	339.1	349.6	362.7	371.0	372.1	374.8	380.8	382.2
Pipeline transportation	59.8	60.7	60.1	58.7	57.0	53.6	51.4	49.7	48.1	46.9	46.0	45.4	41.7	40.2
Scenic and sightseeing transportation	15.7	16.5	17.7	19.3	21.3	22.0	23.2	24.5	25.4	26.1	27.5	29.1	25.6	26.6
Support activities for transportation	364.1	376.6	369.9	381.8	404.7	430.4	445.8	473.4	496.8	518.1	537.4	539.2	524.7	520.3
Couriers and messengers	375.0	378.9	388.8	414.3	466.2	516.8	539.9	546.0	568.2	585.9	605.0	587.0	560.9	561.7
Warehousing and storage	406.6	403.2	405.6	413.4	431.0	443.8	451.8	461.5	474.2	494.1	514.4	513.8	516.7	528.3
Utilities	740.0	736.1	726.0	710.7	689.3	666.2	639.6	620.9	613.4	608.5	601.3	599.4	596.2	577.0
Information	2 688	2 677	2 641	2 668	2 738	2 843	2 940	3 084	3 218	3 419	3 631	3 629	3 395	3 188
Publishing industries, except Internet	870.6	863.4	854.2	873.1	891.0	910.7	927.2	955.5	982.3	1 004.8	1 035.0	1 020.7	964.1	924.8
Motion picture and sound recording industries	254.6	258.9	254.3	259.6	278.4	311.1	334.7	353.0	369.5	384.4	382.6	376.8	387.9	376.2
Broadcasting, except Internet	283.8	281.2	279.7	284.0	290.1	298.1	309.1	313.0	321.2	329.4	343.5	344.6	334.1	324.3
Internet publishing and broadcasting	16.7	16.2	16.1	16.4	16.9	18.6	21.0	23.5	27.1	37.1	50.5	45.5	33.7	29.2
Telecommunications	980.3	973.1	946.0	942.2	961.1	975.7	997.0	1 059.5	1 107.8	1 179.7	1 262.6	1 302.1	1 186.5	1 082.3
ISPs, search portals, and data processing	252.2	251.7	258.5	263.1	268.0	291.2	311.6	338.8	369.1	439.3	510.1	493.6	441.0	402.4
Other information services	29.9	32.9	32.3	29.4	32.8	38.2	39.4	40.1	41.4	43.8	46.2	46.1	47.3	48.7
Financial activities	6 614	6 558	6 540	6 709	6 867	6 827	6 969	7 178	7 462	7 648	7 687	7 807	7 847	7 977
Finance and insurance	4 978.6	4 937.3	4 914.7	5 035.5	5 135.2	5 071.7	5 154.2	5 305.1	5 532.0	5 668.4	5 680.4	5 773.1	5 817.3	5 922.6
Monetary authorities–central bank	24.0	24.2	23.7	23.4	23.4	23.0	22.8	22.1	21.7	22.6	22.8	23.0	23.4	22.6
Credit intermediation and related activities [1]	2 424.8	2 352.4	2 317.3	2 360.7	2 375.7	2 314.4	2 368.2	2 433.6	2 531.9	2 591.0	2 547.8	2 597.7	2 686.0	2 792.4
Depository credit intermediation [1]	1 908.5	1 830.7	1 769.0	1 760.5	1 736.7	1 700.2	1 691.4	1 696.6	1 708.9	1 709.7	1 681.2	1 701.2	1 733.0	1 748.5
Commercial banking	1 361.8	1 333.7	1 302.8	1 308.7	1 297.4	1 281.7	1 275.1	1 277.9	1 286.0	1 281.2	1 250.5	1 258.4	1 278.1	1 280.1
Securities, commodity contracts, investments	457.9	455.0	475.7	507.9	553.4	562.2	589.6	636.1	692.2	737.3	804.5	830.5	789.4	757.7
Insurance carriers and related activities	2 016.1	2 048.2	2 039.5	2 082.5	2 118.8	2 108.2	2 108.0	2 143.6	2 209.4	2 236.1	2 220.6	2 233.7	2 233.2	2 266.0
Funds, trusts, and other financial vehicles	55.7	57.5	58.5	61.0	63.9	63.9	65.6	69.8	76.9	81.5	84.8	88.3	85.4	83.9
Real estate and rental and leasing	1 634.9	1 620.8	1 625.5	1 673.8	1 731.5	1 755.4	1 814.3	1 872.8	1 930.3	1 979.0	2 006.8	2 034.5	2 029.6	2 053.9
Real estate	1 106.8	1 107.6	1 114.5	1 146.1	1 183.2	1 178.9	1 205.8	1 240.7	1 274.2	1 299.0	1 312.2	1 339.5	1 352.9	1 383.6
Rental and leasing services	514.2	499.4	496.4	511.0	529.9	557.4	587.7	609.5	630.8	653.1	666.8	666.3	649.1	643.1
Lessors of nonfinancial intangible assets	13.9	13.9	14.6	16.7	18.4	19.0	20.8	22.6	25.3	26.8	27.8	28.7	27.6	27.3

[1]Includes other industries, not shown separately.

Table 16-1. Nonfarm Employment by NAICS Sector and Industry—Continued

(Wage and salary workers on nonfarm payrolls, thousands.)

Industry	2004	2005	2005, seasonally adjusted											
			January	February	March	April	May	June	July	August	September	October	November	December
Retail trade	15 058.2	15 254.9	15 156.7	15 198.1	15 211.1	15 233.5	15 249.4	15 256.3	15 309.8	15 312.9	15 267.0	15 259.6	15 292.9	15 300.3
Motor vehicle and parts dealers [1]	1 902.3	1 918.9	1 910.4	1 913.5	1 915.5	1 918.1	1 919.9	1 918.8	1 925.9	1 927.6	1 929.4	1 921.5	1 914.3	1 914.7
Automobile dealers	1 257.3	1 260.6	1 256.2	1 257.2	1 259.7	1 262.0	1 264.1	1 262.0	1 266.5	1 266.2	1 268.9	1 260.5	1 254.5	1 252.4
Furniture and home furnishings stores	563.4	577.8	570.9	571.7	572.3	575.8	579.1	575.8	578.5	578.8	580.9	581.5	583.3	583.0
Electronics and appliance stores	516.2	532.8	521.4	520.3	528.0	523.6	527.8	531.1	534.0	537.3	539.9	540.5	541.2	540.5
Building material and garden supply stores	1 227.1	1 272.3	1 251.9	1 269.3	1 269.4	1 268.0	1 269.1	1 271.7	1 279.3	1 277.8	1 272.3	1 273.1	1 281.6	1 290.9
Food and beverage stores	2 821.6	2 813.6	2 813.8	2 815.4	2 814.2	2 819.6	2 820.2	2 822.1	2 822.6	2 810.7	2 803.0	2 809.5	2 806.6	2 805.9
Health and personal care stores	941.1	955.2	943.7	948.3	947.1	952.7	955.7	955.1	954.1	960.4	953.8	959.3	964.7	966.1
Gasoline stations	875.6	871.3	868.8	870.7	870.3	871.6	872.1	869.0	874.6	876.2	873.9	874.6	869.1	869.6
Clothing and clothing accessories stores	1 364.3	1 414.1	1 383.5	1 390.1	1 394.4	1 396.4	1 401.1	1 410.9	1 430.7	1 430.8	1 414.2	1 413.5	1 434.5	1 448.1
Sporting goods, hobby, book, and music stores	641.3	642.1	645.5	643.2	643.9	645.6	644.2	644.1	642.7	643.0	631.3	638.7	641.5	640.0
General merchandise stores [1]	2 863.1	2 919.1	2 909.4	2 918.7	2 920.9	2 925.9	2 924.4	2 920.6	2 931.1	2 931.3	2 927.4	2 910.6	2 920.4	2 906.9
Department stores	1 605.3	1 602.8	1 602.4	1 604.7	1 601.5	1 604.6	1 603.4	1 603.1	1 613.5	1 611.4	1 610.9	1 590.6	1 595.2	1 595.6
Miscellaneous store retailers	913.5	902.9	906.2	905.9	903.8	903.8	904.2	905.2	903.1	903.9	902.2	899.1	897.3	899.0
Nonstore retailers	428.8	434.9	431.2	431.0	431.3	432.4	431.6	431.9	433.2	435.1	438.7	437.7	438.4	435.6
Transportation and warehousing	4 248.6	4 346.7	4 308.5	4 319.3	4 330.1	4 340.2	4 348.4	4 347.6	4 353.0	4 353.9	4 355.4	4 358.4	4 370.2	4 371.6
Air transportation	514.5	501.3	509.8	508.4	507.4	507.6	506.8	505.6	503.6	501.6	495.1	493.7	488.9	486.9
Rail transportation	225.7	228.3	228.0	228.6	228.8	228.8	229.4	229.1	228.9	228.4	228.2	228.1	227.8	227.3
Water transportation	56.4	60.6	57.8	58.0	58.7	59.3	59.7	60.0	60.2	61.0	61.8	62.6	63.6	63.7
Truck transportation	1 351.7	1 393.0	1 375.3	1 380.3	1 385.0	1 389.0	1 392.2	1 396.0	1 396.3	1 394.4	1 397.4	1 402.0	1 403.7	1 404.0
Transit and ground passenger transportation	384.9	388.5	389.8	388.5	387.6	387.6	387.5	381.5	387.3	386.7	388.0	388.5	394.9	392.2
Pipeline transportation	38.4	37.6	38.0	38.0	37.8	37.8	37.6	37.5	37.4	37.6	37.6	37.2	37.2	37.0
Scenic and sightseeing transportation	27.2	29.9	24.3	26.1	28.0	28.8	29.7	30.6	31.4	31.7	31.8	31.5	31.4	31.1
Support activities for transportation	535.1	550.6	547.2	549.7	551.3	550.1	551.8	549.4	549.5	549.2	551.9	549.8	553.9	556.2
Couriers and messengers	556.6	571.7	563.2	564.4	566.2	571.0	571.2	571.2	571.3	574.1	573.8	576.3	576.8	579.7
Warehousing and storage	558.1	585.2	575.1	577.3	579.3	580.2	582.5	586.7	587.1	589.2	589.8	588.7	592.0	593.5
Utilities	563.8	557.6	557.2	557.3	554.8	556.0	556.2	556.2	557.7	559.1	558.9	559.4	560.1	559.7
Information	3 118	3 066	3 068	3 063	3 067	3 072	3 065	3 062	3 061	3 065	3 071	3 058	3 064	3 066
Publishing industries, except Internet	909.1	903.7	902.0	903.5	905.0	902.1	901.5	902.7	905.9	904.8	904.4	903.7	902.8	902.5
Motion picture and sound recording industries	385.0	379.3	370.1	366.2	373.0	384.0	379.8	376.6	375.9	381.2	390.6	379.3	383.5	387.7
Broadcasting, except Internet	325.0	326.6	326.8	325.9	326.0	325.7	325.2	327.3	328.3	329.1	326.7	327.6	325.7	325.1
Internet publishing and broadcasting	29.9	30.4	30.9	30.4	30.4	30.6	30.5	30.5	29.9	30.1	30.4	30.1	30.1	30.4
Telecommunications	1 034.6	998.7	1 009.7	1 007.3	1 003.9	1 002.5	1 000.2	998.6	996.8	994.2	993.4	991.2	995.1	993.3
ISPs, search portals, and data processing	383.7	376.8	377.7	379.2	378.3	377.3	377.8	376.4	373.6	375.6	376.1	376.9	376.7	377.8
Other information services	50.8	50.1	50.9	50.9	50.6	50.0	49.9	50.3	50.7	50.1	49.7	49.4	49.9	49.6
Financial activities	8 031	8 141	8 091	8 097	8 096	8 100	8 101	8 114	8 136	8 155	8 172	8 201	8 217	8 223
Finance and insurance	5 949.0	6 012.0	5 984.4	5 984.9	5 982.6	5 982.9	5 983.8	5 989.8	6 002.5	6 014.7	6 029.1	6 053.3	6 066.7	6 068.2
Monetary authorities–central bank	21.8	20.8	20.8	20.7	20.8	20.8	20.8	20.8	20.7	20.7	20.7	20.7	20.9	21.0
Credit intermediation and related activities [1]	2 817.0	2 865.8	2 841.0	2 846.2	2 847.5	2 849.7	2 851.8	2 856.6	2 866.1	2 871.4	2 880.9	2 892.9	2 895.8	2 894.2
Depository credit intermediation [1]	1 751.5	1 774.4	1 757.9	1 761.7	1 762.6	1 763.5	1 765.9	1 768.0	1 773.5	1 778.5	1 783.5	1 790.8	1 793.3	1 793.2
Commercial banking	1 280.8	1 297.9	1 288.1	1 292.2	1 293.3	1 292.3	1 292.8	1 295.3	1 296.9	1 300.0	1 302.8	1 306.9	1 309.0	1 306.0
Securities, commodity contracts, investments	766.1	783.2	779.6	780.4	782.7	781.7	780.7	778.4	779.6	783.4	786.2	790.5	790.7	790.4
Insurance carriers and related activities	2 258.6	2 255.4	2 254.7	2 250.4	2 244.5	2 246.4	2 245.1	2 247.0	2 249.3	2 252.9	2 255.1	2 262.1	2 271.8	2 274.8
Funds, trusts, and other financial vehicles	85.4	86.8	88.3	87.2	87.1	84.3	85.4	87.0	86.8	86.3	86.2	87.1	87.5	87.8
Real estate and rental and leasing	2 081.9	2 129.3	2 106.9	2 112.2	2 113.7	2 117.0	2 116.7	2 124.6	2 133.3	2 139.8	2 143.3	2 147.5	2 150.2	2 154.5
Real estate	1 415.1	1 455.8	1 433.8	1 437.6	1 439.5	1 441.9	1 444.9	1 451.5	1 458.8	1 464.8	1 469.0	1 474.7	1 478.4	1 481.6
Rental and leasing services	641.1	646.4	647.1	648.5	648.1	648.2	644.5	646.2	647.4	647.8	646.8	645.1	643.9	645.0
Lessors of nonfinancial intangible assets	25.7	27.1	26.0	26.1	26.1	26.9	27.3	26.9	27.1	27.2	27.5	27.7	27.9	27.9

[1] Includes other industries, not shown separately.

Table 16-1. Nonfarm Employment by NAICS Sector and Industry—Continued

(Wage and salary workers on nonfarm payrolls, thousands.)

Industry	1990	1991	1992	1993	1994	1995	1996	1997	1998	1999	2000	2001	2002	2003
Professional and business services	10 848	10 714	10 970	11 495	12 174	12 844	13 462	14 335	15 147	15 957	16 666	16 476	15 976	15 987
Professional and technical services [1]	4 556.7	4 526.5	4 593.5	4 708.2	4 843.6	5 101.3	5 337.1	5 655.5	6 021.0	6 375.4	6 733.9	6 902.2	6 675.6	6 629.5
Legal services	943.6	946.0	949.8	963.9	965.6	959.2	968.4	987.5	1 021.1	1 051.4	1 065.7	1 091.3	1 115.3	1 142.1
Accounting and bookkeeping services	664.1	655.4	657.8	654.2	670.1	706.3	729.8	761.2	802.0	837.6	866.4	872.2	837.3	815.3
Architectural and engineering services	941.5	906.2	901.8	922.7	952.0	997.1	1 024.5	1 063.4	1 114.8	1 168.1	1 237.9	1 274.7	1 246.1	1 226.9
Computer systems design and related services	409.7	419.9	444.9	484.8	531.4	611.2	701.4	826.7	974.9	1 132.9	1 254.3	1 297.8	1 152.8	1 116.6
Management and technical consulting services	323.6	331.6	358.1	385.4	416.8	474.8	517.1	568.4	619.2	649.0	704.9	746.2	734.4	744.9
Management of companies and enterprises	1 667.4	1 638.1	1 623.4	1 640.1	1 665.9	1 685.8	1 702.7	1 729.7	1 756.1	1 773.8	1 796.0	1 779.0	1 705.4	1 687.2
Administrative and waste services	4 624.3	4 549.3	4 752.6	5 146.5	5 664.1	6 056.8	6 422.1	6 949.9	7 369.3	7 807.4	8 136.0	7 794.9	7 595.2	7 669.8
Administrative and support services [1]	4 394.9	4 317.0	4 515.9	4 897.8	5 403.4	5 783.4	6 140.0	6 659.4	7 069.9	7 496.9	7 823.1	7 477.6	7 276.8	7 347.7
Employment services [1]	1 493.7	1 448.7	1 592.5	1 865.1	2 226.5	2 425.2	2 600.8	2 927.2	3 217.0	3 551.5	3 817.0	3 437.1	3 246.5	3 299.5
Temporary help services	1 155.8	1 123.4	1 212.5	1 388.8	1 632.2	1 743.8	1 849.0	2 059.7	2 245.2	2 469.6	2 635.6	2 337.7	2 193.7	2 224.2
Business support services	504.6	503.3	524.5	549.0	574.4	629.8	678.3	733.9	772.2	780.5	786.7	779.7	756.6	749.7
Services to buildings and dwellings	1 174.6	1 150.9	1 159.7	1 197.9	1 267.2	1 302.4	1 361.5	1 424.1	1 460.0	1 534.7	1 570.5	1 606.2	1 606.1	1 636.1
Waste management and remediation services	229.4	232.4	236.7	248.6	260.7	273.3	282.0	290.5	299.3	310.5	312.9	317.3	318.3	322.1
Education and health services	10 984	11 506	11 891	12 303	12 807	13 289	13 683	14 087	14 446	14 798	15 109	15 645	16 199	16 588
Educational services	1 688.0	1 736.6	1 713.1	1 755.4	1 894.9	2 010.2	2 077.6	2 155.0	2 232.9	2 320.4	2 390.4	2 510.6	2 642.8	2 695.1
Health care and social assistance	9 295.8	9 769.8	10 178.0	10 548.1	10 911.7	11 278.4	11 604.9	11 932.2	12 213.5	12 477.1	12 718.0	13 134.0	13 555.7	13 892.6
Health care	8 210.7	8 617.7	8 954.8	9 253.6	9 529.7	9 808.9	10 092.6	10 358.0	10 540.9	10 690.9	10 857.8	11 188.1	11 536.0	11 817.1
Ambulatory health care services [1]	2 841.6	3 028.4	3 199.9	3 385.5	3 578.8	3 767.5	3 939.9	4 093.0	4 161.2	4 226.6	4 320.3	4 461.5	4 633.2	4 786.4
Offices of physicians	1 278.0	1 345.2	1 401.1	1 442.0	1 480.9	1 540.4	1 603.8	1 660.5	1 723.6	1 786.6	1 839.9	1 911.2	1 967.8	2 002.5
Outpatient care centers	260.5	271.4	286.5	303.1	314.5	328.8	340.2	352.1	363.3	375.4	386.4	399.7	413.0	426.8
Home health care services	287.5	340.7	393.4	463.8	553.2	621.8	667.2	702.8	659.5	629.6	633.3	638.6	679.8	732.6
Hospitals	3 512.6	3 617.3	3 711.4	3 740.0	3 724.0	3 733.7	3 772.8	3 821.6	3 892.4	3 935.5	3 954.3	4 050.9	4 159.6	4 244.6
Nursing and residential care facilities [1]	1 856.4	1 972.0	2 043.5	2 128.1	2 227.0	2 307.7	2 379.9	2 443.4	2 487.3	2 528.8	2 583.2	2 675.8	2 743.3	2 786.2
Nursing care facilities	1 169.8	1 240.2	1 273.4	1 319.3	1 377.1	1 413.0	1 448.4	1 474.6	1 489.3	1 501.0	1 513.6	1 546.8	1 573.2	1 579.8
Social assistance [1]	1 085.1	1 152.2	1 223.3	1 294.4	1 381.9	1 469.5	1 512.3	1 574.2	1 672.6	1 786.2	1 860.2	1 945.9	2 019.7	2 075.4
Child day care services	387.8	413.2	446.5	468.9	510.0	557.1	559.2	570.4	615.1	673.7	695.8	714.6	744.1	755.3
Leisure and hospitality	9 288	9 256	9 437	9 732	10 100	10 501	10 777	11 018	11 232	11 543	11 862	12 036	11 986	12 173
Arts, entertainment, and recreation	1 132.0	1 177.0	1 236.3	1 301.9	1 375.6	1 459.4	1 522.1	1 599.9	1 645.2	1 709.1	1 787.9	1 824.4	1 782.6	1 812.9
Performing arts and spectator sports	272.7	282.7	289.5	286.8	296.1	307.7	328.6	349.6	350.0	361.1	381.8	382.3	363.7	371.7
Museums, historical sites, zoos, and parks	68.0	71.0	75.0	78.3	81.8	83.9	88.9	93.8	97.4	103.1	110.4	115.0	114.0	114.7
Amusements, gambling, and recreation	791.3	823.4	871.8	936.8	997.7	1 067.8	1 104.5	1 156.5	1 197.9	1 244.9	1 295.7	1 327.1	1 305.0	1 326.5
Accommodation and food services	8 155.6	8 078.9	8 200.5	8 430.4	8 724.1	9 041.6	9 254.3	9 417.9	9 586.2	9 833.7	10 073.5	10 211.3	10 203.2	10 359.8
Accommodation	1 616.0	1 574.3	1 561.5	1 580.5	1 615.3	1 652.5	1 698.9	1 729.5	1 773.5	1 831.7	1 884.4	1 852.2	1 778.6	1 775.4
Food services and drinking places	6 539.6	6 504.6	6 639.0	6 849.9	7 108.7	7 389.1	7 555.4	7 688.5	7 812.7	8 002.0	8 189.1	8 359.1	8 424.6	8 584.4
Other services	4 261	4 249	4 240	4 350	4 428	4 572	4 690	4 825	4 976	5 087	5 168	5 258	5 372	5 401
Repair and maintenance	1 009.0	960.0	964.0	998.0	1 023.5	1 078.9	1 135.5	1 169.3	1 189.2	1 222.0	1 241.5	1 256.5	1 246.9	1 233.6
Personal and laundry services	1 119.9	1 109.2	1 098.9	1 116.0	1 120.3	1 143.9	1 165.7	1 180.4	1 205.6	1 220.3	1 242.9	1 255.0	1 257.2	1 263.5
Membership associations and organizations	2 132.2	2 179.5	2 177.1	2 236.4	2 284.5	2 348.9	2 389.1	2 474.9	2 581.3	2 644.4	2 683.3	2 746.4	2 867.8	2 903.6
Government	18 415	18 545	18 787	18 989	19 275	19 432	19 539	19 664	19 909	20 307	20 790	21 118	21 513	21 583
Federal	3 196	3 110	3 111	3 063	3 018	2 949	2 877	2 806	2 772	2 769	2 865	2 764	2 766	2 761
Federal, except U.S. Postal Service	2 370.5	2 296.2	2 310.7	2 269.4	2 197.2	2 098.8	2 009.8	1 940.2	1 891.3	1 879.5	1 984.8	1 891.0	1 923.8	1 952.4
U.S. Postal Service	825.1	813.2	800.0	793.2	820.6	849.9	867.2	866.0	880.5	889.7	879.7	873.0	842.4	808.6
State government	4 305	4 355	4 408	4 488	4 576	4 635	4 606	4 582	4 612	4 709	4 786	4 905	5 029	5 002
State government education	1 729.9	1 767.6	1 798.6	1 834.1	1 881.9	1 919.0	1 910.7	1 904.0	1 922.2	1 983.2	2 030.6	2 112.9	2 242.8	2 254.7
State government, excluding education	2 574.6	2 587.3	2 609.7	2 653.8	2 693.6	2 715.5	2 695.1	2 677.9	2 690.2	2 725.6	2 755.9	2 791.8	2 786.3	2 747.6
Local government	10 914	11 081	11 267	11 438	11 682	11 849	12 056	12 276	12 525	12 829	13 139	13 449	13 718	13 820
Local government education	5 902.1	5 994.1	6 075.9	6 206.3	6 329.4	6 453.1	6 592.3	6 758.5	6 920.9	7 120.4	7 293.9	7 479.3	7 654.4	7 709.4
Local government, excluding education	5 012.4	5 086.9	5 191.6	5 231.9	5 352.2	5 396.0	5 464.1	5 516.9	5 603.9	5 708.6	5 844.6	5 970.0	6 063.2	6 110.2

[1]Includes other industries, not shown separately.

Table 16-1. Nonfarm Employment by NAICS Sector and Industry—Continued

(Wage and salary workers on nonfarm payrolls, thousands.)

Industry	2004	2005	2005, seasonally adjusted											
			January	February	March	April	May	June	July	August	September	October	November	December
Professional and business services	16 395	16 882	16 638	16 711	16 745	16 780	16 794	16 844	16 898	16 932	16 997	16 991	17 061	17 121
Professional and technical services [1]	6 774.0	7 013.0	6 911.1	6 936.6	6 949.8	6 966.9	6 977.0	7 000.3	7 024.7	7 043.9	7 062.2	7 074.8	7 087.2	7 118.9
Legal services	1 163.1	1 164.1	1 164.3	1 164.8	1 165.2	1 165.0	1 166.2	1 165.6	1 167.5	1 166.9	1 159.5	1 159.2	1 160.0	1 160.8
Accounting and bookkeeping services	805.9	840.0	828.9	829.3	830.0	833.3	829.8	837.3	841.3	845.5	848.9	851.0	847.5	859.0
Architectural and engineering services	1 258.2	1 307.2	1 277.5	1 284.0	1 287.6	1 291.5	1 295.6	1 302.0	1 307.8	1 314.6	1 324.3	1 326.1	1 335.3	1 335.6
Computer systems design and related services	1 148.6	1 189.3	1 174.8	1 176.7	1 178.4	1 180.3	1 182.0	1 187.1	1 189.2	1 191.7	1 195.9	1 204.4	1 204.9	1 212.1
Management and technical consulting services	789.9	843.6	818.7	825.3	830.1	833.9	836.2	841.4	847.6	851.0	852.9	855.5	861.4	865.4
Management of companies and enterprises	1 724.4	1 751.6	1 747.3	1 748.7	1 750.6	1 752.5	1 753.3	1 755.6	1 757.1	1 756.6	1 754.2	1 749.9	1 743.2	1 756.7
Administrative and waste services	7 896.0	8 117.0	7 979.5	8 026.1	8 044.4	8 060.8	8 063.2	8 087.9	8 116.0	8 131.5	8 180.5	8 165.8	8 230.5	8 245.1
Administrative and support services [1]	7 567.4	7 782.8	7 644.4	7 689.6	7 708.6	7 727.2	7 732.9	7 754.3	7 778.4	7 794.6	7 846.5	7 835.6	7 897.8	7 911.0
Employment services [1]	3 428.5	3 575.3	3 482.6	3 507.1	3 515.1	3 532.6	3 534.9	3 550.6	3 561.5	3 582.2	3 628.2	3 617.2	3 663.7	3 671.0
Temporary help services	2 387.2	2 538.9	2 462.6	2 491.0	2 493.0	2 504.6	2 503.0	2 512.0	2 523.9	2 538.7	2 573.7	2 576.2	2 616.2	2 628.1
Business support services	757.8	759.8	762.7	765.2	764.8	765.6	764.5	760.8	759.5	759.4	757.2	752.7	754.7	751.8
Services to buildings and dwellings	1 693.7	1 729.8	1 700.0	1 710.5	1 713.0	1 715.9	1 718.8	1 727.2	1 738.5	1 735.3	1 735.4	1 741.1	1 755.4	1 751.1
Waste management and remediation services	328.6	334.2	335.1	336.5	335.8	333.6	330.3	333.6	337.6	336.9	334.0	330.2	332.7	334.1
Education and health services	16 953	17 342	17 176	17 188	17 211	17 241	17 291	17 333	17 368	17 413	17 451	17 440	17 481	17 507
Educational services	2 762.5	2 818.9	2 817.3	2 801.8	2 804.2	2 805.8	2 812.6	2 820.6	2 820.4	2 832.4	2 844.9	2 815.9	2 820.2	2 827.5
Health care and social assistance	14 190.2	14 522.9	14 358.7	14 385.8	14 407.2	14 435.5	14 478.2	14 512.8	14 547.4	14 580.3	14 605.8	14 624.5	14 661.2	14 679.6
Health care	12 055.3	12 313.1	12 182.9	12 205.6	12 220.9	12 243.8	12 276.4	12 302.8	12 334.3	12 361.1	12 382.9	12 392.7	12 423.8	12 435.8
Ambulatory health care services [1]	4 952.3	5 110.0	5 040.8	5 053.3	5 061.0	5 074.4	5 089.9	5 104.7	5 121.8	5 137.7	5 145.1	5 152.9	5 172.7	5 181.4
Offices of physicians	2 047.8	2 101.1	2 070.0	2 074.3	2 074.4	2 084.3	2 095.2	2 098.9	2 104.2	2 111.8	2 115.3	2 119.8	2 128.4	2 135.8
Outpatient care centers	450.5	473.5	462.7	464.3	466.2	467.8	469.5	471.2	474.7	476.5	479.3	480.6	482.4	484.1
Home health care services	776.6	814.1	804.1	806.5	809.4	809.0	809.6	815.1	817.1	819.6	820.5	820.8	824.3	822.1
Hospitals	4 284.7	4 346.9	4 305.7	4 311.7	4 317.8	4 325.5	4 333.8	4 344.6	4 353.5	4 361.0	4 366.8	4 371.7	4 379.2	4 382.5
Nursing and residential care facilities [1]	2 818.4	2 856.2	2 836.4	2 840.6	2 842.1	2 843.9	2 852.7	2 853.5	2 859.0	2 863.4	2 871.0	2 868.1	2 871.9	2 871.9
Nursing care facilities	1 576.9	1 579.3	1 575.7	1 576.3	1 577.9	1 576.6	1 577.5	1 578.8	1 579.9	1 580.9	1 582.2	1 578.9	1 582.5	1 582.5
Social assistance [1]	2 134.8	2 209.8	2 175.8	2 180.2	2 186.3	2 191.7	2 201.8	2 210.0	2 213.1	2 218.2	2 222.9	2 231.8	2 237.4	2 243.8
Child day care services	764.7	784.5	773.9	775.2	777.3	777.7	780.4	784.7	786.6	785.7	787.8	793.2	792.9	793.3
Leisure and hospitality	12 493	12 802	12 673	12 703	12 722	12 770	12 778	12 802	12 833	12 860	12 826	12 840	12 881	12 898
Arts, entertainment, and recreation	1 849.6	1 890.7	1 859.6	1 861.0	1 865.4	1 879.9	1 884.3	1 890.9	1 894.9	1 903.1	1 895.1	1 897.8	1 907.5	1 905.9
Performing arts and spectator sports	367.5	369.1	365.2	365.7	367.7	371.7	369.7	372.0	372.2	372.9	372.2	365.0	362.8	362.1
Museums, historical sites, zoos, and parks	118.3	120.7	118.4	117.5	119.5	120.5	121.1	121.5	121.3	121.1	123.2	121.6	121.0	121.6
Amusements, gambling, and recreation	1 363.8	1 400.9	1 376.0	1 377.8	1 378.2	1 387.7	1 393.5	1 397.4	1 401.4	1 409.1	1 399.7	1 411.2	1 423.7	1 422.2
Accommodation and food services	10 643.2	10 911.4	10 813.3	10 841.8	10 856.1	10 889.9	10 893.4	10 911.3	10 937.9	10 956.6	10 931.2	10 942.4	10 973.9	10 992.8
Accommodation	1 789.5	1 812.0	1 808.8	1 809.9	1 807.6	1 814.2	1 812.1	1 812.7	1 813.2	1 817.9	1 814.5	1 812.9	1 811.1	1 809.2
Food services and drinking places	8 853.7	9 099.4	9 004.5	9 031.9	9 048.5	9 075.7	9 081.3	9 098.6	9 124.7	9 138.7	9 116.7	9 129.5	9 162.8	9 183.1
Other services	5 409	5 386	5 398	5 394	5 389	5 393	5 385	5 394	5 392	5 385	5 381	5 371	5 377	5 386
Repair and maintenance	1 228.8	1 236.2	1 235.5	1 237.4	1 237.7	1 237.5	1 237.1	1 240.9	1 240.9	1 235.6	1 230.8	1 227.1	1 232.0	1 241.4
Personal and laundry services	1 272.9	1 272.9	1 276.6	1 276.3	1 276.2	1 278.7	1 274.9	1 274.1	1 271.3	1 271.7	1 271.3	1 270.3	1 271.1	1 270.3
Membership associations and organizations	2 907.5	2 877.1	2 885.8	2 880.0	2 874.8	2 876.6	2 873.3	2 879.3	2 879.6	2 877.9	2 879.2	2 873.2	2 873.6	2 874.5
Government	21 621	21 803	21 715	21 741	21 747	21 768	21 773	21 786	21 822	21 851	21 855	21 852	21 880	21 878
Federal	2 730	2 724	2 721	2 727	2 730	2 729	2 725	2 727	2 726	2 725	2 725	2 724	2 728	2 713
Federal, except U.S. Postal Service	1 947.5	1 950.8	1 946.0	1 952.3	1 956.0	1 955.3	1 950.6	1 951.5	1 950.7	1 950.4	1 949.9	1 949.5	1 953.1	1 941.2
U.S. Postal Service	782.1	773.4	775.0	774.6	774.0	773.5	774.7	775.7	775.5	774.6	774.7	774.1	774.9	772.1
State government	4 982	5 021	5 013	5 016	5 015	5 018	5 017	5 016	5 023	5 024	5 026	5 022	5 032	5 036
State government education	2 238.1	2 249.7	2 247.6	2 249.1	2 246.7	2 247.0	2 247.0	2 244.4	2 249.0	2 251.5	2 255.1	2 248.1	2 256.6	2 258.1
State government, excluding education	2 743.9	2 770.9	2 765.5	2 767.2	2 767.8	2 770.6	2 770.0	2 771.9	2 773.8	2 772.1	2 771.1	2 773.5	2 775.8	2 777.4
Local government	13 909	14 058	13 981	13 998	14 002	14 021	14 031	14 043	14 073	14 102	14 104	14 106	14 120	14 129
Local government education	7 765.2	7 864.1	7 816.3	7 830.2	7 829.2	7 838.6	7 841.5	7 851.1	7 878.0	7 900.9	7 891.9	7 894.9	7 899.3	7 906.9
Local government, excluding education	6 144.1	6 193.7	6 164.4	6 167.9	6 172.9	6 182.1	6 189.4	6 192.3	6 195.0	6 200.6	6 212.1	6 211.5	6 220.6	6 222.2

[1]Includes other industries, not shown separately.

Table 16-2. Production or Nonsupervisory Workers on Private Nonfarm Payrolls by NAICS Industry

(Wage and salary workers on nonfarm payrolls, thousands.)

Industry	1990	1991	1992	1993	1994	1995	1996	1997	1998	1999	2000	2001	2002	2003
Total Private	73 684	72 520	72 786	74 591	77 382	79 845	81 773	84 158	86 316	88 430	90 336	89 983	88 393	87 658
Goods-Producing	17 322	16 352	16 043	16 236	16 795	17 137	17 318	17 698	18 008	18 067	18 169	17 466	16 400	15 732
Natural resources and mining	538	515	478	462	461	458	461	479	473	438	446	457	436	420
Construction	4 115	3 674	3 546	3 704	3 973	4 113	4 325	4 546	4 807	5 105	5 295	5 332	5 196	5 123
Manufacturing	12 669	12 164	12 020	12 070	12 361	12 566	12 532	12 673	12 729	12 524	12 428	11 677	10 768	10 190
Durable goods	7 396	7 000	6 852	6 879	7 132	7 351	7 425	7 597	7 720	7 650	7 658	7 163	6 529	6 152
Wood products	449.9	412.8	417.0	436.8	468.7	477.5	484.9	496.6	507.9	514.4	505.6	468.3	448.7	433.0
Nonmetallic mineral products	413.2	384.1	378.4	380.7	392.3	399.7	404.8	412.5	420.6	426.0	439.5	427.1	398.8	374.7
Primary metals	525.1	496.9	478.7	473.3	487.4	500.3	500.3	501.6	505.3	491.9	490.0	446.9	396.2	370.3
Fabricated metal products	1 190.1	1 131.6	1 101.0	1 116.9	1 172.0	1 223.0	1 241.6	1 285.3	1 319.6	1 304.9	1 325.8	1 253.5	1 147.0	1 092.5
Machinery	937.6	883.6	856.3	874.1	921.1	968.5	983.2	1 005.5	1 014.7	977.0	959.9	889.1	785.4	730.9
Computer and electronic products	980.2	925.6	876.3	856.4	863.9	890.3	915.2	951.1	964.7	932.9	949.3	875.8	744.1	672.7
Electrical equipment and appliances	465.2	435.6	425.0	421.8	434.7	438.4	433.9	427.7	431.8	433.2	433.1	402.2	351.9	319.5
Transportation equipment [1]	1 472.5	1 405.5	1 387.7	1 366.1	1 414.6	1 471.1	1 480.0	1 520.8	1 529.2	1 525.4	1 496.7	1 397.7	1 309.3	1 268.5
Motor vehicles and parts	869.5	840.1	868.0	896.4	978.4	1 048.9	1 052.4	1 062.4	1 050.2	1 075.8	1 073.0	986.8	931.0	906.3
Furniture and related products	475.2	440.0	442.8	454.2	475.7	480.0	477.9	489.7	512.1	532.4	544.3	509.0	474.8	444.2
Miscellaneous manufacturing	487.2	484.2	489.1	498.2	502.1	502.2	503.3	506.6	514.3	512.2	513.2	493.1	472.5	445.3
Nondurable goods	5 273	5 164	5 168	5 192	5 229	5 215	5 107	5 076	5 009	4 873	4 770	4 514	4 239	4 038
Food manufacturing	1 165.0	1 174.2	1 182.0	1 195.3	1 200.4	1 221.0	1 227.7	1 227.7	1 227.6	1 228.7	1 227.9	1 221.3	1 202.3	1 192.5
Beverage and tobacco products	117.2	116.9	116.2	117.6	118.2	117.3	120.1	121.4	122.5	120.1	116.9	115.6	119.5	106.4
Textile mills	417.9	407.2	406.0	403.9	403.3	393.2	371.7	367.1	357.2	333.7	315.2	275.8	242.2	216.9
Textile product mills	170.1	160.9	163.0	167.2	176.0	176.3	173.4	174.7	173.9	173.4	171.8	163.9	153.7	141.3
Apparel	830.0	805.1	809.8	788.0	763.1	719.3	650.2	611.5	549.9	471.8	415.4	351.2	294.3	248.6
Leather and allied products	116.6	107.5	104.4	101.4	97.2	88.5	78.5	73.6	67.0	59.9	55.4	46.8	40.0	34.9
Paper and paper products	493.2	488.4	489.9	490.9	492.8	493.8	487.5	488.7	484.1	474.0	467.5	446.3	421.4	392.7
Printing and related support activities	597.6	581.7	573.6	579.7	591.4	599.1	594.0	597.0	598.4	585.1	575.7	544.4	492.6	471.2
Petroleum and coal products	97.5	97.4	96.8	93.0	90.9	88.8	87.2	87.8	87.1	84.6	83.1	80.9	78.0	74.4
Chemicals	620.3	599.7	586.2	590.1	595.6	598.4	595.1	593.3	600.6	595.2	587.7	562.2	531.9	524.9
Plastics and rubber products	647.7	624.8	639.8	664.7	699.6	719.8	721.3	732.7	740.4	747.0	753.6	705.3	662.7	634.3
Private Service-Providing	56 362	56 168	56 743	58 355	60 587	62 708	64 455	66 460	68 308	70 363	72 167	72 517	71 993	71 926
Trade, transportation, and utilities	19 032	18 640	18 506	18 752	19 392	19 984	20 325	20 698	21 059	21 576	21 965	21 709	21 337	21 078
Wholesale trade	4 198.3	4 122.2	4 070.7	4 072.2	4 196.4	4 360.8	4 423.2	4 523.2	4 605.0	4 673.1	4 686.4	4 555.1	4 473.5	4 395.9
Retail trade	11 308.4	11 007.9	10 931.4	11 104.0	11 502.1	11 841.0	12 056.7	12 273.6	12 439.8	12 771.5	13 039.8	12 952.3	12 774.0	12 654.9
Transportation and warehousing	2 940.8	2 928.4	2 934.3	3 019.4	3 152.8	3 260.2	3 339.3	3 406.8	3 521.6	3 641.9	3 753.2	3 718.2	3 611.3	3 563.1
Utilities	584.9	581.5	569.5	556.5	540.9	521.8	505.5	493.8	492.2	489.2	485.1	482.8	478.4	463.7
Information	1 866	1 871	1 871	1 896	1 928	2 007	2 096	2 181	2 217	2 351	2 502	2 530	2 398	2 347
Financial activities	4 973	4 911	4 908	5 057	5 183	5 165	5 279	5 415	5 605	5 728	5 737	5 810	5 872	5 967
Professional and business services	8 889	8 748	8 971	9 451	10 078	10 645	11 161	11 896	12 566	13 184	13 790	13 588	13 049	12 910
Education and health services	9 748	10 212	10 555	10 908	11 338	11 765	12 123	12 478	12 791	13 089	13 362	13 846	14 311	14 532
Leisure and hospitality	8 299	8 247	8 406	8 667	8 979	9 330	9 565	9 780	9 947	10 216	10 516	10 662	10 576	10 666
Other services	3 555	3 539	3 526	3 623	3 689	3 812	3 907	4 013	4 124	4 219	4 296	4 373	4 449	4 426

[1]Includes other industries, not shown separately.

Table 16-2. Production or Nonsupervisory Workers on Private Nonfarm Payrolls by NAICS Industry —Continued

(Wage and salary workers on nonfarm payrolls, thousands.)

Industry	2004	2005	2005, seasonally adjusted											
			January	February	March	April	May	June	July	August	September	October	November	December
Total Private	88 937	90 944	89 997	90 233	90 394	90 635	90 725	90 921	91 104	91 245	91 263	91 291	91 693	91 803
Goods-Producing	15 821	16 099	15 929	15 988	16 009	16 052	16 077	16 093	16 091	16 120	16 131	16 177	16 278	16 288
Natural resources and mining	440	471	453	457	461	465	466	471	471	475	477	481	485	487
Construction	5 309	5 566	5 422	5 477	5 494	5 534	5 552	5 568	5 570	5 591	5 606	5 627	5 690	5 678
Manufacturing	10 072	10 062	10 054	10 054	10 054	10 053	10 059	10 054	10 050	10 054	10 048	10 069	10 103	10 123
Durable goods	6 139	6 217	6 169	6 181	6 186	6 195	6 205	6 208	6 204	6 222	6 218	6 249	6 274	6 299
Wood products	443.9	449.7	450.2	450.4	450.9	449.6	446.4	447.9	447.5	447.9	450.0	449.2	452.6	455.4
Nonmetallic mineral products	387.8	385.5	389.1	387.9	386.7	388.1	385.3	387.3	384.4	384.4	382.9	382.5	383.5	382.7
Primary metals	363.7	364.9	363.7	364.8	364.9	364.6	364.4	364.3	364.4	364.4	363.3	365.6	366.5	367.5	367.1
Fabricated metal products	1 108.6	1 126.9	1 121.9	1 120.8	1 124.2	1 125.5	1 126.4	1 127.5	1 127.0	1 128.5	1 128.7	1 125.6	1 134.2	1 138.0
Machinery	728.3	746.6	734.0	735.5	738.9	743.3	746.7	748.0	751.1	749.3	749.6	756.9	750.9	754.3
Computer and electronic products	655.8	702.1	667.4	671.6	677.0	684.1	687.5	694.9	702.2	710.7	719.1	727.7	734.9	740.9
Electrical equipment and appliances	307.2	301.5	305.1	304.1	302.7	300.5	301.7	300.7	300.9	300.9	299.7	300.1	301.7	302.4
Transportation equipment [1]	1 264.4	1 276.9	1 264.9	1 275.8	1 275.4	1 279.2	1 285.7	1 276.2	1 264.6	1 273.0	1 261.8	1 280.1	1 288.5	1 296.9
Motor vehicles and parts	902.9	894.9	898.1	908.0	904.7	901.7	903.9	890.2	871.6	884.4	898.0	891.2	892.6	894.5
Furniture and related products	443.9	433.9	440.2	438.5	437.3	434.0	433.8	433.6	433.0	432.8	432.3	431.8	431.0	431.8
Miscellaneous manufacturing	435.4	428.7	432.0	431.9	428.3	426.0	426.7	427.9	429.3	430.3	428.3	428.4	429.1	429.1
Nondurable goods	3 933	3 846	3 885	3 873	3 868	3 858	3 854	3 846	3 846	3 832	3 830	3 820	3 829	3 824
Food manufacturing	1 177.8	1 165.8	1 174.4	1 172.5	1 173.4	1 169.1	1 168.4	1 168.0	1 166.5	1 163.0	1 159.5	1 156.0	1 162.6	1 160.7
Beverage and tobacco products	106.5	111.5	107.1	107.5	107.8	109.0	110.9	111.8	112.2	112.7	113.1	115.7	116.1	115.3
Textile mills	193.9	174.4	183.4	182.0	180.0	176.4	176.9	175.6	173.9	172.6	171.3	169.8	167.8	166.2
Textile product mills	140.8	139.6	137.8	137.4	137.9	138.5	139.5	139.4	140.1	139.9	141.8	143.1	143.2	141.9
Apparel	224.9	200.5	211.4	209.9	206.1	204.5	201.3	200.4	201.5	197.0	195.4	191.4	193.9	193.5
Leather and allied products	32.7	30.8	31.4	31.0	30.9	30.6	30.3	30.3	30.7	31.0	31.1	30.9	30.8	31.0
Paper and paper products	373.7	365.2	368.9	368.8	368.9	367.3	367.1	365.1	365.0	364.5	363.4	361.4	361.6	361.3
Printing and related support activities	459.5	448.5	453.6	450.3	448.3	450.3	449.6	448.9	447.5	446.3	446.9	446.1	446.8	447.6
Petroleum and coal products	76.7	75.7	77.6	77.4	76.6	77.0	77.1	76.7	75.7	75.1	74.5	74.7	73.7	73.6
Chemicals	520.2	514.6	515.9	515.0	514.6	514.2	513.9	513.9	515.2	513.3	515.7	512.8	515.1	516.2
Plastics and rubber products	626.4	619.0	623.2	621.1	623.8	621.4	618.5	616.3	617.4	616.4	617.7	617.6	617.8	616.9
Private Service-Providing	73 116	74 844	74 068	74 245	74 385	74 583	74 648	74 828	75 013	75 125	75 132	75 114	75 415	75 515
Trade, transportation, and utilities	21 319	21 788	21 580	21 637	21 679	21 734	21 774	21 815	21 873	21 895	21 822	21 824	21 908	21 904
Wholesale trade	4 443.5	4 572.0	4 507.8	4 524.8	4 538.8	4 546.1	4 561.0	4 569.7	4 577.1	4 587.0	4 593.7	4 597.6	4 616.1	4 620.6
Retail trade	12 788.1	13 007.3	12 902.0	12 938.0	12 958.4	12 988.1	13 006.7	13 033.6	13 081.1	13 088.4	13 008.5	13 000.7	13 050.1	13 042.2
Transportation and warehousing	3 637.1	3 762.1	3 726.0	3 731.5	3 740.3	3 756.4	3 761.9	3 767.0	3 768.1	3 771.4	3 771.3	3 776.3	3 790.6	3 792.0
Utilities	449.9	446.0	443.8	442.6	441.5	443.4	444.0	444.4	446.4	448.1	448.5	449.3	451.1	449.4
Information	2 371	2 390	2 375	2 370	2 379	2 388	2 384	2 388	2 387	2 390	2 406	2 400	2 408	2 408
Financial activities	5 989	6 084	6 042	6 051	6 048	6 049	6 047	6 064	6 081	6 091	6 100	6 125	6 148	6 159
Professional and business services	13 287	13 797	13 538	13 608	13 655	13 698	13 709	13 766	13 817	13 857	13 906	13 907	13 999	14 044
Education and health services	14 771	15 103	14 964	14 976	15 004	15 034	15 070	15 108	15 141	15 168	15 193	15 165	15 207	15 226
Leisure and hospitality	10 955	11 252	11 133	11 166	11 183	11 240	11 227	11 249	11 276	11 293	11 277	11 274	11 326	11 346
Other services	4 425	4 432	4 436	4 437	4 437	4 440	4 437	4 438	4 438	4 431	4 428	4 419	4 419	4 428

[1] Includes other industries, not shown separately.

Table 16-3. Average Weekly Hours of Production or Nonsupervisory Workers on Private Nonfarm Payrolls by NAICS Industry

(Hours.)

Industry	1990	1991	1992	1993	1994	1995	1996	1997	1998	1999	2000	2001	2002	2003
Total Private	34.3	34.1	34.2	34.3	34.5	34.3	34.3	34.5	34.5	34.3	34.3	34.0	33.9	33.7
Goods-Producing	40.1	40.1	40.2	40.6	41.1	40.8	40.8	41.1	40.8	40.8	40.7	39.9	39.9	39.8
Natural resources and mining	45.0	45.3	44.6	44.9	45.3	45.3	46.0	46.2	44.9	44.2	44.4	44.6	43.2	43.6
Construction	38.3	38.1	38.0	38.4	38.8	38.8	38.9	38.9	38.8	39.0	39.2	38.7	38.4	38.4
Manufacturing	40.5	40.4	40.7	41.1	41.7	41.3	41.3	41.7	41.4	41.4	41.3	40.3	40.5	40.4
Overtime hours	3.8	3.8	4.0	4.4	5.0	4.7	4.8	5.1	4.8	4.8	4.7	4.0	4.2	4.2
Durable goods	41.1	40.9	41.3	41.9	42.6	42.1	42.1	42.6	42.1	41.9	41.8	40.6	40.8	40.8
Overtime hours	3.9	3.7	3.9	4.5	5.3	5.0	5.0	5.4	5.0	5.0	4.8	3.9	4.2	4.3
Wood products	40.4	40.2	40.9	41.2	41.7	41.0	41.2	41.4	41.4	41.3	41.0	40.2	39.9	40.4
Nonmetallic mineral products	40.9	40.5	41.0	41.5	42.2	41.8	42.0	41.9	42.2	42.1	41.6	41.6	42.0	42.2
Primary metals	42.0	41.5	42.4	43.1	44.1	43.4	43.6	44.3	43.5	43.8	44.2	42.4	42.4	42.3
Fabricated metal products	41.0	40.8	41.2	41.6	42.3	41.9	41.9	42.3	41.9	41.7	41.9	40.6	40.6	40.7
Machinery	42.1	41.9	42.4	43.2	43.9	43.5	43.3	44.0	43.1	42.3	42.3	40.9	40.5	40.8
Computer and electronic products	41.3	40.9	41.4	41.8	42.2	42.2	41.9	42.5	41.8	41.5	41.4	39.8	39.7	40.4
Electrical equipment and appliances	41.2	41.5	41.8	42.4	43.0	41.9	42.1	42.1	41.8	41.8	41.6	39.8	40.1	40.6
Transportation equipment	42.0	41.9	41.9	43.0	44.3	43.7	43.8	44.2	43.2	43.6	43.3	41.9	42.5	41.9
Motor vehicles and parts	41.4	41.5	41.6	43.3	44.8	43.8	43.8	43.9	42.6	43.8	43.4	41.6	42.6	42.0
Furniture and related products	38.0	37.8	38.7	39.0	39.3	38.5	38.3	39.1	39.4	39.3	39.2	38.3	39.2	38.9
Miscellaneous manufacturing	39.0	39.1	39.3	39.2	39.4	39.2	39.1	39.7	39.2	39.3	39.0	38.8	38.6	38.4
Nondurable goods	39.6	39.7	40.0	40.1	40.5	40.1	40.1	40.5	40.5	40.4	40.3	39.9	40.1	39.8
Overtime hours	3.8	3.9	4.1	4.2	4.5	4.3	4.4	4.6	4.5	4.6	4.4	4.1	4.2	4.1
Food manufacturing	39.3	39.2	39.2	39.3	39.8	39.6	39.5	39.8	40.1	40.2	40.1	39.6	39.6	39.3
Beverage and tobacco products	38.9	38.8	38.7	38.3	39.3	39.3	39.7	40.0	40.3	41.0	42.0	40.9	39.4	39.1
Textile mills	40.2	40.7	41.3	41.6	41.9	40.9	40.8	41.6	41.0	41.0	41.4	40.0	40.6	39.1
Textile product mills	39.0	39.1	39.2	39.8	39.9	39.1	39.2	39.6	39.5	39.4	39.0	38.6	39.2	39.6
Apparel	34.8	35.4	35.6	35.5	35.5	35.7	35.3	35.2	35.5	35.5	35.4	35.7	36.0	36.7	35.6
Leather and allied products	37.4	37.6	37.9	38.4	38.2	37.7	37.8	38.2	37.4	37.2	37.5	36.4	37.5	39.3
Paper and paper products	43.6	43.6	43.8	43.8	44.2	43.4	43.5	43.9	43.6	43.6	42.8	42.1	41.9	41.5
Printing and related support activities	38.7	38.6	39.0	39.2	39.6	39.1	39.1	39.5	39.3	39.1	39.2	38.7	38.4	38.2
Petroleum and coal products	44.4	43.9	43.6	44.0	44.3	43.7	43.7	43.1	43.6	42.6	42.7	43.8	43.0	44.5
Chemicals	42.8	43.1	43.3	43.2	43.4	43.3	43.3	43.4	43.2	42.7	42.2	41.9	42.3	42.4
Plastics and rubber products	40.6	40.5	41.2	41.4	41.8	41.1	41.0	41.4	41.3	41.3	40.8	40.0	40.6	40.4
Private Service-Providing	32.5	32.4	32.5	32.5	32.7	32.6	32.6	32.8	32.8	32.7	32.7	32.5	32.5	32.4
Trade, transportation, and utilities	33.7	33.7	33.8	34.1	34.3	34.1	34.1	34.3	34.2	33.9	33.8	33.5	33.6	33.6
Wholesale trade	38.4	38.4	38.6	38.5	38.8	38.6	38.6	38.8	38.6	38.6	38.8	38.4	38.0	37.9
Retail trade	30.6	30.4	30.7	30.7	30.9	30.8	30.7	30.9	30.9	30.8	30.7	30.7	30.9	30.9
Transportation and warehousing	37.7	37.4	37.4	38.9	39.5	38.9	39.1	39.4	38.7	37.6	37.4	36.7	36.8	36.8
Utilities	41.5	41.5	41.7	42.1	42.3	42.3	42.0	42.0	42.0	42.0	42.0	41.4	40.9	41.1
Information	35.8	35.6	35.8	36.0	36.0	36.0	36.4	36.3	36.6	36.7	36.8	36.9	36.5	36.2
Financial activities	35.5	35.5	35.6	35.5	35.5	35.5	35.5	35.7	36.0	35.8	35.9	35.8	35.6	35.5
Professional and business services	34.2	34.0	34.0	34.0	34.1	34.0	34.1	34.3	34.3	34.4	34.5	34.2	34.2	34.1
Education and health services	31.9	31.9	32.0	32.0	32.0	32.0	31.9	32.2	32.2	32.1	32.2	32.3	32.4	32.3
Leisure and hospitality	26.0	25.6	25.7	25.9	26.0	25.9	25.9	26.0	26.2	26.1	26.1	25.8	25.8	25.6
Other services	32.8	32.7	32.6	32.6	32.7	32.6	32.5	32.7	32.6	32.5	32.5	32.3	32.0	31.4

Table 16-3. Average Weekly Hours of Production or Nonsupervisory Workers on Private Nonfarm Payrolls by NAICS Industry—Continued

(Hours.)

Industry	2004	2005	2005, seasonally adjusted											
			January	February	March	April	May	June	July	August	September	October	November	December
Total Private	33.7	33.8	33.7	33.7	33.7	33.8	33.7	33.7	33.8	33.7	33.8	33.8	33.8	33.8
Goods-Producing	40.0	40.1	39.8	39.9	39.9	40.2	39.9	39.9	39.9	39.9	40.0	40.3	40.4	40.2
Natural resources and mining	44.5	45.6	45.8	45.1	45.2	45.6	45.7	45.6	45.9	45.9	45.9	46.0	45.0	45.6
Construction	38.3	38.6	37.8	38.3	38.4	39.1	38.4	38.6	38.2	38.3	38.2	38.5	39.2	38.7
Manufacturing	40.8	40.7	40.7	40.6	40.4	40.5	40.4	40.4	40.5	40.6	40.7	41.0	40.8	40.8
Overtime hours	4.6	4.6	4.5	4.6	4.5	4.4	4.4	4.4	4.5	4.6	4.5	4.6	4.6	4.5
Durable goods	41.3	41.1	41.1	41.0	40.8	40.9	40.8	40.9	41.0	41.1	41.2	41.6	41.3	41.2
Overtime hours	4.7	4.6	4.6	4.7	4.5	4.5	4.4	4.5	4.6	4.7	4.6	4.8	4.7	4.5
Wood products	40.7	40.0	40.8	39.9	39.6	39.5	39.7	39.6	39.6	39.6	39.6	40.8	40.5	40.1
Nonmetallic mineral products	42.3	42.2	42.0	42.0	41.7	41.9	41.9	41.9	41.7	41.6	41.9	42.6	43.5	42.7
Primary metals	43.1	43.1	43.0	43.1	42.8	42.6	42.5	42.7	43.1	43.2	43.4	43.5	43.5	43.5
Fabricated metal products	41.1	41.0	40.9	40.8	40.7	40.8	40.8	40.7	40.9	40.9	40.8	41.6	41.2	41.1
Machinery	41.9	42.1	42.0	41.9	42.0	42.0	41.9	41.9	42.0	42.0	42.1	42.2	42.0	41.9
Computer and electronic products	40.4	40.0	39.9	39.8	39.4	39.8	39.8	39.8	40.1	39.9	40.2	40.5	40.3	40.3
Electrical equipment and appliances	40.7	40.6	40.2	40.0	40.1	40.2	40.2	40.3	40.8	40.9	41.3	41.4	41.0	40.9
Transportation equipment	42.5	42.5	42.3	42.3	42.0	42.2	41.8	42.1	42.3	42.7	42.7	43.0	42.7	42.6
Motor vehicles and parts	42.6	42.3	42.2	42.4	41.8	41.9	41.4	42.0	42.1	42.9	42.7	42.9	42.4	42.2
Furniture and related products	39.5	39.2	39.5	39.4	39.5	39.3	39.1	39.1	39.2	39.2	39.3	39.2	38.5	38.3
Miscellaneous manufacturing	38.5	38.7	38.6	38.6	38.8	38.9	38.6	38.7	38.3	38.7	38.8	39.0	38.6	38.5
Nondurable goods	40.0	39.9	40.0	39.9	39.7	39.9	39.7	39.7	39.7	39.7	39.9	40.1	40.0	40.2
Overtime hours	4.4	4.4	4.4	4.4	4.4	4.3	4.3	4.3	4.3	4.4	4.4	4.4	4.4	4.6
Food manufacturing	39.3	39.0	38.9	39.3	38.8	39.0	38.9	38.8	39.0	38.8	38.8	38.9	39.0	39.3
Beverage and tobacco products	39.2	40.0	40.4	39.8	40.1	40.3	38.9	40.0	40.0	40.0	39.5	40.8	40.1	40.0
Textile mills	40.1	40.3	40.3	39.8	39.9	40.2	40.3	40.4	40.2	40.1	39.9	40.2	40.6	41.0
Textile product mills	38.9	39.0	39.5	39.4	39.4	39.0	38.8	37.8	38.2	38.7	38.7	38.8	39.6	40.0
Apparel	36.0	35.7	35.9	35.8	36.0	36.0	35.1	35.4	35.5	35.8	35.8	36.1	35.9	35.6
Leather and allied products	38.4	38.4	37.2	37.4	37.2	37.8	38.4	38.7	39.0	38.6	38.5	38.7	39.5	39.4
Paper and paper products	42.1	42.5	42.5	42.1	42.1	42.2	42.3	42.3	42.3	42.4	42.8	42.9	42.5	42.6
Printing and related support activities	38.4	38.4	38.6	38.5	38.3	38.3	38.3	38.2	38.4	38.4	38.6	38.5	38.3	38.4
Petroleum and coal products	44.9	45.6	44.6	44.7	45.1	46.1	45.8	45.8	45.4	45.2	47.4	47.3	45.8	44.5
Chemicals	42.8	42.3	42.8	42.3	42.2	42.4	42.3	42.1	42.1	41.6	42.0	42.9	42.3	42.5
Plastics and rubber products	40.4	40.0	40.0	40.1	39.8	39.8	39.7	39.7	39.6	39.9	40.0	40.0	40.1	40.5
Private Service-Providing	32.3	32.4	32.4	32.4	32.4	32.5	32.4	32.4	32.4	32.3	32.4	32.4	32.4	32.4
Trade, transportation, and utilities	33.5	33.4	33.5	33.5	33.4	33.5	33.4	33.3	33.3	33.2	33.3	33.3	33.4	33.4
Wholesale trade	37.8	37.7	37.7	37.8	37.7	37.8	37.7	37.6	37.6	37.5	37.7	37.8	37.8	37.9
Retail trade	30.7	30.6	30.7	30.7	30.6	30.7	30.6	30.5	30.5	30.4	30.5	30.4	30.6	30.5
Transportation and warehousing	37.2	37.0	37.5	37.3	37.2	37.3	37.1	37.0	37.0	36.9	36.6	36.7	36.8	36.7
Utilities	40.9	41.1	41.0	40.6	40.3	41.1	40.9	41.2	41.2	41.2	41.2	41.3	41.2	41.4
Information	36.3	36.5	36.4	36.4	36.5	36.5	36.7	36.4	36.6	36.5	36.6	36.7	36.5	36.6
Financial activities	35.5	35.9	35.9	35.8	35.9	36.0	36.0	36.1	36.1	36.0	36.0	36.1	35.9	35.9
Professional and business services	34.2	34.2	34.2	34.0	34.0	34.2	34.2	34.1	34.3	34.1	34.3	34.3	34.3	34.3
Education and health services	32.4	32.6	32.6	32.6	32.6	32.6	32.6	32.6	32.7	32.5	32.7	32.7	32.5	32.5
Leisure and hospitality	25.7	25.7	25.7	25.7	25.7	25.8	25.8	25.8	25.8	25.7	25.8	25.7	25.7	25.6
Other services	31.0	30.9	30.9	30.9	30.9	31.1	30.9	31.0	31.0	30.9	30.9	30.9	30.9	30.9

Table 16-4. Average Hourly Earnings of Production or Nonsupervisory Workers on Private Nonfarm Payrolls by NAICS Industry

(Dollars.)

Industry	1990	1991	1992	1993	1994	1995	1996	1997	1998	1999	2000	2001	2002	2003
Total Private	10.19	10.50	10.76	11.03	11.32	11.64	12.03	12.49	13.00	13.47	14.00	14.53	14.95	15.35
Goods-Producing	11.46	11.76	11.99	12.28	12.63	12.96	13.38	13.82	14.23	14.71	15.27	15.78	16.33	16.80
Natural resources and mining	13.40	13.82	14.09	14.12	14.41	14.78	15.10	15.57	16.20	16.33	16.55	17.00	17.19	17.56
Construction	13.42	13.65	13.81	14.04	14.38	14.73	15.11	15.67	16.23	16.80	17.48	18.00	18.52	18.95
Manufacturing	10.78	11.13	11.40	11.70	12.04	12.34	12.75	13.14	13.45	13.85	14.32	14.76	15.29	15.74
Excluding overtime [1]	10.29	10.63	10.86	11.10	11.36	11.68	12.05	12.38	12.71	13.09	13.55	14.06	14.54	14.96
Durable goods	11.40	11.81	12.09	12.41	12.78	13.05	13.45	13.83	14.07	14.46	14.93	15.38	16.02	16.45
Wood products	8.82	9.03	9.24	9.41	9.66	9.92	10.24	10.53	10.85	11.18	11.63	11.99	12.33	12.71
Nonmetallic mineral products	11.11	11.34	11.57	11.83	12.11	12.39	12.80	13.17	13.59	13.97	14.53	14.86	15.40	15.76
Primary metals	12.97	13.37	13.72	14.08	14.47	14.75	15.12	15.40	15.66	16.00	16.64	17.06	17.68	18.13
Fabricated metal products	10.64	10.97	11.16	11.40	11.64	11.91	12.26	12.64	12.97	13.34	13.77	14.19	14.68	15.01
Machinery	11.73	12.12	12.40	12.73	12.94	13.14	13.49	13.94	14.24	14.77	15.22	15.49	15.92	16.30
Computer and electronic products	10.89	11.35	11.64	11.95	12.19	12.29	12.75	13.24	13.85	14.37	14.73	15.42	16.20	16.69
Electrical equipment and appliances	10.00	10.30	10.50	10.65	10.94	11.25	11.80	12.24	12.51	12.90	13.23	13.78	13.98	14.36
Transportation equipment	14.44	15.12	15.59	16.22	16.94	17.21	17.67	18.00	17.92	18.24	18.89	19.48	20.64	21.23
Motor vehicles and parts	15.00	15.67	15.92	16.56	17.38	17.72	18.14	18.43	18.21	18.49	19.11	19.66	21.09	21.68
Furniture and related products	8.52	8.74	9.00	9.24	9.51	9.75	10.08	10.50	10.88	11.27	11.72	12.14	12.61	12.98
Miscellaneous manufacturing	8.87	9.16	9.44	9.65	9.90	10.23	10.60	10.89	11.18	11.56	11.93	12.46	12.91	13.30
Nondurable goods	9.87	10.18	10.45	10.70	10.96	11.30	11.68	12.04	12.45	12.85	13.31	13.75	14.15	14.63
Food manufacturing	9.04	9.32	9.59	9.82	10.00	10.27	10.50	10.77	11.09	11.40	11.77	12.18	12.55	12.80
Beverage and tobacco products	13.24	13.65	14.07	14.30	14.97	15.40	15.73	16.00	16.03	16.54	17.40	17.67	17.73	17.96
Textile mills	8.17	8.49	8.82	9.12	9.35	9.63	9.88	10.22	10.58	10.90	11.23	11.40	11.73	11.99
Textile product mills	7.53	7.77	8.03	8.27	8.45	8.76	9.12	9.45	9.75	10.18	10.43	10.60	10.96	11.23
Apparel	6.22	6.43	6.60	6.74	6.95	7.22	7.45	7.76	8.05	8.35	8.60	8.82	9.10	9.56
Leather and allied products	7.18	7.43	7.68	7.88	8.23	8.50	8.94	9.31	9.68	9.93	10.35	10.69	11.66	11.66
Paper and paper products	12.06	12.45	12.78	13.13	13.49	13.94	14.38	14.76	15.20	15.58	15.91	16.38	16.85	17.33
Printing and related support activities	11.11	11.32	11.53	11.67	11.89	12.08	12.41	12.78	13.20	13.67	14.09	14.48	14.93	15.37
Petroleum and coal products	17.00	17.90	18.83	19.43	19.96	20.24	20.18	21.10	21.75	22.22	22.80	22.90	23.04	23.63
Chemicals	12.85	13.30	13.70	13.97	14.33	14.86	15.37	15.78	16.23	16.40	17.09	17.57	17.97	18.50
Plastics and rubber products	9.76	10.07	10.35	10.55	10.66	10.86	11.17	11.48	11.79	12.25	12.69	13.21	13.55	14.18
Private Service-Providing	9.71	10.05	10.33	10.60	10.87	11.19	11.57	12.05	12.59	13.07	13.60	14.16	14.56	14.96
Trade, transportation, and utilities	9.83	10.08	10.30	10.55	10.80	11.10	11.46	11.90	12.39	12.82	13.31	13.70	14.02	14.34
Wholesale trade	11.58	11.95	12.21	12.57	12.93	13.34	13.80	14.41	15.07	15.62	16.28	16.77	16.98	17.36
Retail trade	7.71	7.89	8.12	8.36	8.61	8.85	9.21	9.59	10.05	10.45	10.86	11.29	11.67	11.90
Transportation and warehousing	12.50	12.61	12.77	12.71	12.84	13.18	13.45	13.78	14.12	14.55	15.05	15.33	15.76	16.25
Utilities	16.14	16.70	17.17	17.95	18.66	19.19	19.78	20.59	21.48	22.03	22.75	23.58	23.96	24.77
Information	13.40	13.90	14.29	14.86	15.32	15.68	16.30	17.14	17.67	18.40	19.07	19.80	20.20	21.01
Financial activities	9.99	10.42	10.86	11.36	11.82	12.28	12.71	13.22	13.93	14.47	14.98	15.59	16.17	17.14
Professional and business services	11.14	11.50	11.78	11.96	12.15	12.53	13.00	13.57	14.27	14.85	15.52	16.33	16.81	17.21
Education and health services	10.00	10.49	10.87	11.21	11.50	11.80	12.17	12.56	13.00	13.44	13.95	14.64	15.21	15.64
Leisure and hospitality	5.88	6.06	6.20	6.32	6.46	6.62	6.82	7.13	7.48	7.76	8.11	8.35	8.58	8.76
Other services	9.08	9.39	9.66	9.90	10.18	10.51	10.85	11.29	11.79	12.26	12.73	13.27	13.72	13.84

[1]Derived by assuming that overtime hours are paid at the rate of time and one-half.

Table 16-4. Average Hourly Earnings of Production or Nonsupervisory Workers on Private Nonfarm Payrolls by NAICS Industry—Continued

(Dollars.)

Industry	2004	2005	2005, seasonally adjusted											
			January	February	March	April	May	June	July	August	September	October	November	December
Total Private	15.67	16.11	15.88	15.91	15.95	16.00	16.03	16.07	16.14	16.16	16.19	16.28	16.28	16.35
Goods-Producing	17.19	17.60	17.37	17.43	17.45	17.52	17.55	17.59	17.63	17.68	17.66	17.74	17.74	17.77
Natural resources and mining	18.07	18.73	18.43	18.40	18.25	18.55	18.58	18.66	18.74	18.88	19.03	19.04	18.95	19.12
Construction	19.23	19.46	19.23	19.28	19.34	19.38	19.37	19.43	19.52	19.51	19.54	19.58	19.59	19.65
Manufacturing	16.15	16.56	16.38	16.42	16.43	16.48	16.54	16.56	16.58	16.65	16.60	16.71	16.68	16.70
Excluding overtime [1]	15.29	15.69	15.52	15.54	15.56	15.63	15.69	15.70	15.71	15.76	15.73	15.82	15.79	15.83
Durable goods	16.82	17.34	17.11	17.17	17.17	17.24	17.29	17.32	17.36	17.45	17.38	17.51	17.50	17.52
Wood products	13.03	13.16	. . .	. . .	. . .	. . .	. . .	. . .	. . .	. . .	. . .	. . .	. . .	. . .
Nonmetallic mineral products	16.25	16.61	. . .	. . .	. . .	. . .	. . .	. . .	. . .	. . .	. . .	. . .	. . .	. . .
Primary metals	18.57	18.94	. . .	. . .	. . .	. . .	. . .	. . .	. . .	. . .	. . .	. . .	. . .	. . .
Fabricated metal products	15.31	15.80	. . .	. . .	. . .	. . .	. . .	. . .	. . .	. . .	. . .	. . .	. . .	. . .
Machinery	16.68	17.03	. . .	. . .	. . .	. . .	. . .	. . .	. . .	. . .	. . .	. . .	. . .	. . .
Computer and electronic products	17.27	18.40	. . .	. . .	. . .	. . .	. . .	. . .	. . .	. . .	. . .	. . .	. . .	. . .
Electrical equipment and appliances	14.90	15.25	. . .	. . .	. . .	. . .	. . .	. . .	. . .	. . .	. . .	. . .	. . .	. . .
Transportation equipment	21.49	22.10	. . .	. . .	. . .	. . .	. . .	. . .	. . .	. . .	. . .	. . .	. . .	. . .
Motor vehicles and parts	21.71	22.27	. . .	. . .	. . .	. . .	. . .	. . .	. . .	. . .	. . .	. . .	. . .	. . .
Furniture and related products	13.16	13.44	. . .	. . .	. . .	. . .	. . .	. . .	. . .	. . .	. . .	. . .	. . .	. . .
Miscellaneous manufacturing	13.84	14.08	. . .	. . .	. . .	. . .	. . .	. . .	. . .	. . .	. . .	. . .	. . .	. . .
Nondurable goods	15.05	15.27	15.19	15.20	15.22	15.22	15.31	15.29	15.27	15.30	15.30	15.35	15.29	15.31
Food manufacturing	12.98	13.04	. . .	. . .	. . .	. . .	. . .	. . .	. . .	. . .	. . .	. . .	. . .	. . .
Beverage and tobacco products	19.14	18.79	. . .	. . .	. . .	. . .	. . .	. . .	. . .	. . .	. . .	. . .	. . .	. . .
Textile mills	12.13	12.38	. . .	. . .	. . .	. . .	. . .	. . .	. . .	. . .	. . .	. . .	. . .	. . .
Textile product mills	11.39	11.66	. . .	. . .	. . .	. . .	. . .	. . .	. . .	. . .	. . .	. . .	. . .	. . .
Apparel	9.75	10.24	. . .	. . .	. . .	. . .	. . .	. . .	. . .	. . .	. . .	. . .	. . .	. . .
Leather and allied products	11.63	11.50	. . .	. . .	. . .	. . .	. . .	. . .	. . .	. . .	. . .	. . .	. . .	. . .
Paper and paper products	17.91	17.98	. . .	. . .	. . .	. . .	. . .	. . .	. . .	. . .	. . .	. . .	. . .	. . .
Printing and related support activities	15.71	15.75	. . .	. . .	. . .	. . .	. . .	. . .	. . .	. . .	. . .	. . .	. . .	. . .
Petroleum and coal products	24.39	24.54	. . .	. . .	. . .	. . .	. . .	. . .	. . .	. . .	. . .	. . .	. . .	. . .
Chemicals	19.17	19.67	. . .	. . .	. . .	. . .	. . .	. . .	. . .	. . .	. . .	. . .	. . .	. . .
Plastics and rubber products	14.59	14.82	. . .	. . .	. . .	. . .	. . .	. . .	. . .	. . .	. . .	. . .	. . .	. . .
Private Service-Providing	15.26	15.71	15.49	15.51	15.56	15.60	15.63	15.67	15.75	15.76	15.80	15.89	15.89	15.97
Trade, transportation, and utilities	14.58	14.93	14.78	14.77	14.81	14.86	14.87	14.89	15.00	14.98	14.98	15.05	15.04	15.10
Wholesale trade	17.65	18.16	17.88	17.93	17.95	18.03	18.01	18.10	18.22	18.21	18.26	18.32	18.45	18.56
Retail trade	12.08	12.36	12.31	12.29	12.31	12.35	12.36	12.35	12.45	12.41	12.35	12.43	12.35	12.39
Transportation and warehousing	16.52	16.71	16.55	16.51	16.61	16.60	16.64	16.66	16.75	16.78	16.82	16.82	16.85	16.87
Utilities	25.61	26.70	26.13	26.09	26.29	26.42	26.47	26.39	26.98	26.84	26.95	27.17	27.15	27.34
Information	21.40	22.07	21.73	21.57	21.72	21.92	21.92	22.04	22.17	22.21	22.32	22.65	22.40	22.60
Financial activities	17.52	17.94	17.69	17.74	17.81	17.85	17.81	17.87	17.95	17.92	18.01	18.09	18.20	18.27
Professional and business services	17.48	18.07	17.81	17.85	17.88	17.94	17.98	18.03	18.11	18.14	18.15	18.30	18.29	18.42
Education and health services	16.15	16.72	16.41	16.47	16.55	16.58	16.64	16.69	16.76	16.79	16.84	16.90	16.95	17.00
Leisure and hospitality	8.91	9.14	9.04	9.05	9.06	9.09	9.10	9.12	9.13	9.16	9.22	9.22	9.24	9.27
Other services	13.98	14.33	14.17	14.20	14.24	14.26	14.30	14.31	14.35	14.39	14.40	14.46	14.46	14.47

[1]Derived by assuming that overtime hours are paid at the rate of time and one-half.
. . . = Not available.

Table 16-5. Average Weekly Earnings of Production or Nonsupervisory Workers on Private Nonfarm Payrolls by NAICS Industry

(Dollars.)

Industry	1990	1991	1992	1993	1994	1995	1996	1997	1998	1999	2000	2001	2002	2003
Total Private	349.29	358.06	367.83	378.40	390.73	399.53	412.74	431.25	448.04	462.49	480.41	493.20	506.07	517.30
Goods-Producing	459.55	471.32	482.58	498.82	519.58	528.62	546.48	568.43	580.99	599.99	621.86	630.04	651.61	669.13
Natural resources and mining	602.54	625.42	629.02	634.77	653.14	670.32	695.07	720.11	727.28	721.74	734.92	757.92	741.97	765.94
Construction	513.43	520.41	525.13	539.81	558.53	571.57	588.48	609.48	629.75	655.11	685.78	695.89	711.82	726.83
Manufacturing	436.16	449.73	464.43	480.80	502.12	509.26	526.55	548.22	557.12	573.17	590.65	595.19	618.75	635.99
Durable goods	468.43	483.28	499.59	519.92	544.66	549.49	566.53	589.10	591.68	606.67	624.38	624.54	652.97	671.21
Wood products	356.38	362.69	377.76	387.38	402.86	406.51	422.32	435.78	449.78	461.61	477.23	481.36	492.00	514.10
Nonmetallic mineral products	453.98	459.20	474.55	490.54	510.92	517.68	537.81	552.02	572.96	587.53	604.88	618.79	646.91	664.92
Primary metals	545.22	555.37	581.34	606.37	637.69	639.70	658.68	681.47	681.64	700.76	734.62	723.95	749.32	767.60
Fabricated metal products	436.12	447.98	459.64	474.21	492.07	498.48	513.57	534.48	543.20	555.86	576.68	576.60	596.38	610.37
Machinery	493.39	507.96	525.53	549.98	568.12	571.25	584.69	613.49	613.87	625.40	643.92	632.77	645.55	664.79
Computer and electronic products	450.09	464.25	482.09	499.15	514.92	518.25	534.42	562.69	579.70	596.25	609.70	613.07	642.87	674.72
Electrical equipment and appliances	412.42	426.96	439.04	451.28	470.21	471.63	496.69	515.73	522.51	538.98	550.56	548.00	560.24	583.23
Transportation equipment	606.87	633.87	652.95	697.16	750.67	751.74	773.95	795.82	774.82	796.25	817.98	817.08	877.87	889.48
Motor vehicles and parts	621.68	650.36	662.82	717.68	779.29	776.41	794.09	808.28	775.56	809.31	828.73	818.68	898.54	910.02
Furniture and related products	324.08	330.49	348.03	360.63	373.87	375.06	385.68	410.38	428.50	443.38	459.69	464.57	494.01	505.30
Miscellaneous manufacturing	346.02	358.56	370.75	378.28	389.79	400.85	414.13	431.89	437.99	454.56	465.02	483.44	499.13	510.82
Nondurable goods	390.65	404.17	417.95	429.15	443.82	452.83	467.88	487.04	503.99	519.91	536.82	548.41	566.84	582.61
Food manufacturing	355.61	364.90	375.69	386.04	398.54	406.66	414.74	428.58	444.81	458.63	472.09	481.67	496.91	502.92
Beverage and tobacco products	515.73	530.09	544.25	547.60	588.39	605.00	624.82	639.69	646.26	679.06	730.35	721.68	698.39	702.45
Textile mills	328.11	345.48	364.45	379.74	391.64	394.17	403.08	425.53	434.15	447.38	459.69	456.64	476.52	469.33
Textile product mills	293.77	303.81	314.47	329.26	336.96	342.17	356.90	373.95	385.13	401.01	406.24	408.56	429.01	444.70
Apparel	216.10	227.76	235.20	239.45	248.33	254.85	261.90	275.61	286.07	295.20	307.00	317.15	333.66	340.12
Leather and allied products	268.32	279.41	291.11	302.85	314.18	319.98	337.86	355.63	361.87	369.80	388.46	388.83	412.99	457.83
Paper and paper products	525.71	542.26	560.27	575.49	596.19	604.74	625.38	647.55	662.20	679.24	681.34	690.06	705.62	719.73
Printing and related support activities	429.93	437.00	450.02	457.91	470.74	472.37	484.99	504.46	518.32	534.15	552.15	560.89	573.05	587.58
Petroleum and coal products	754.13	786.05	821.72	855.36	883.81	883.68	881.24	908.50	949.28	947.60	973.53	1 003.34	990.88	1 052.32
Chemicals	550.25	573.27	593.17	603.71	622.46	644.30	666.00	685.26	700.53	700.45	721.90	735.54	759.53	783.95
Plastics and rubber products	396.07	408.22	426.56	436.96	445.87	445.91	458.15	474.87	487.00	505.31	517.74	528.69	549.85	572.26
Private Service-Providing	315.49	325.31	335.46	345.03	354.97	364.14	376.72	394.77	412.78	427.30	445.00	460.32	472.88	483.89
Trade, transportation, and utilities	331.55	339.19	348.68	359.33	370.38	378.79	390.64	407.57	423.30	434.31	449.88	459.53	471.27	481.14
Wholesale trade	444.48	459.27	470.51	484.46	501.17	515.14	533.29	559.39	582.21	602.77	631.40	643.45	644.38	657.29
Retail trade	235.62	240.15	249.63	256.89	265.77	272.56	282.76	295.97	310.34	321.63	333.38	346.16	360.81	367.15
Transportation and warehousing	471.72	471.12	478.02	494.36	507.27	513.37	525.60	542.55	546.86	547.97	562.31	562.70	579.75	598.41
Utilities	670.40	693.40	716.36	756.35	789.98	811.52	830.74	865.26	902.94	924.59	955.66	977.18	979.09	1 017.27
Information	479.50	495.20	512.01	535.25	551.28	564.98	592.68	622.40	646.52	675.32	700.89	731.11	738.17	760.81
Financial activities	354.65	369.57	386.01	403.02	419.20	436.12	451.49	472.37	500.95	517.57	537.37	558.02	575.51	609.08
Professional and business services	380.61	391.09	400.64	406.20	414.16	426.44	442.81	465.51	490.00	510.99	535.07	557.84	574.66	587.02
Education and health services	319.27	334.55	348.29	359.08	368.14	377.73	388.27	404.65	418.82	431.35	449.29	473.39	492.74	505.69
Leisure and hospitality	152.47	155.16	159.54	163.45	168.00	171.43	176.48	185.81	195.82	202.87	211.79	215.19	221.26	224.30
Other services	297.91	306.91	315.08	322.69	332.44	342.36	352.62	368.63	384.25	398.77	413.41	428.64	439.76	434.41

Table 16-5. Average Weekly Earnings of Production or Nonsupervisory Workers on Private Nonfarm Payrolls by NAICS Industry—Continued

(Dollars.)

Industry	2004	2005	2005, seasonally adjusted											
			January	February	March	April	May	June	July	August	September	October	November	December
Total Private	528.36	543.65	535.16	536.17	537.52	540.80	540.21	541.56	545.53	544.59	547.22	550.26	550.26	552.63
Goods-Producing	688.17	705.28	691.33	695.46	696.26	704.30	700.25	701.84	703.44	705.43	706.40	714.92	716.70	714.35
Natural resources and mining	803.82	853.89	844.09	829.84	824.90	845.88	849.11	850.90	860.17	866.59	873.48	875.84	852.75	871.87
Construction	735.55	750.63	726.89	738.42	742.66	757.76	743.81	750.00	745.66	747.23	746.43	753.83	767.93	760.46
Manufacturing	658.59	673.61	666.67	666.65	663.77	667.44	668.22	669.02	671.49	675.99	675.62	685.11	680.54	681.36
Durable goods	694.13	713.05	703.22	703.97	700.54	705.12	705.43	708.39	711.76	717.20	716.06	728.42	722.75	721.82
Wood products	530.15	526.91	. . .	. . .	. . .	. . .	. . .	. . .	. . .	. . .	. . .	. . .	. . .	. . .
Nonmetallic mineral products	688.20	700.62	. . .	. . .	. . .	. . .	. . .	. . .	. . .	. . .	. . .	. . .	. . .	. . .
Primary metals	799.78	815.52	. . .	. . .	. . .	. . .	. . .	. . .	. . .	. . .	. . .	. . .	. . .	. . .
Fabricated metal products	628.80	647.32	. . .	. . .	. . .	. . .	. . .	. . .	. . .	. . .	. . .	. . .	. . .	. . .
Machinery	699.59	716.48	. . .	. . .	. . .	. . .	. . .	. . .	. . .	. . .	. . .	. . .	. . .	. . .
Computer and electronic products	697.83	735.82	. . .	. . .	. . .	. . .	. . .	. . .	. . .	. . .	. . .	. . .	. . .	. . .
Electrical equipment and appliances	606.97	619.19	. . .	. . .	. . .	. . .	. . .	. . .	. . .	. . .	. . .	. . .	. . .	. . .
Transportation equipment	912.98	938.37	. . .	. . .	. . .	. . .	. . .	. . .	. . .	. . .	. . .	. . .	. . .	. . .
Motor vehicles and parts	924.72	941.17	. . .	. . .	. . .	. . .	. . .	. . .	. . .	. . .	. . .	. . .	. . .	. . .
Furniture and related products	519.62	527.11	. . .	. . .	. . .	. . .	. . .	. . .	. . .	. . .	. . .	. . .	. . .	. . .
Miscellaneous manufacturing	533.07	545.19	. . .	. . .	. . .	. . .	. . .	. . .	. . .	. . .	. . .	. . .	. . .	. . .
Nondurable goods	602.53	609.13	607.60	606.48	604.23	607.28	607.81	607.01	606.22	607.41	610.47	615.54	611.60	615.46
Food manufacturing	509.55	508.03	. . .	. . .	. . .	. . .	. . .	. . .	. . .	. . .	. . .	. . .	. . .	. . .
Beverage and tobacco products	751.20	752.39	. . .	. . .	. . .	. . .	. . .	. . .	. . .	. . .	. . .	. . .	. . .	. . .
Textile mills	486.68	498.47	. . .	. . .	. . .	. . .	. . .	. . .	. . .	. . .	. . .	. . .	. . .	. . .
Textile product mills	443.12	455.19	. . .	. . .	. . .	. . .	. . .	. . .	. . .	. . .	. . .	. . .	. . .	. . .
Apparel	351.56	366.11	. . .	. . .	. . .	. . .	. . .	. . .	. . .	. . .	. . .	. . .	. . .	. . .
Leather and allied products	446.66	442.16	. . .	. . .	. . .	. . .	. . .	. . .	. . .	. . .	. . .	. . .	. . .	. . .
Paper and paper products	754.14	763.36	. . .	. . .	. . .	. . .	. . .	. . .	. . .	. . .	. . .	. . .	. . .	. . .
Printing and related support activities	603.97	604.80	. . .	. . .	. . .	. . .	. . .	. . .	. . .	. . .	. . .	. . .	. . .	. . .
Petroleum and coal products	1 095.00	1 117.94	. . .	. . .	. . .	. . .	. . .	. . .	. . .	. . .	. . .	. . .	. . .	. . .
Chemicals	819.73	831.40	. . .	. . .	. . .	. . .	. . .	. . .	. . .	. . .	. . .	. . .	. . .	. . .
Plastics and rubber products	589.84	592.50	. . .	. . .	. . .	. . .	. . .	. . .	. . .	. . .	. . .	. . .	. . .	. . .
Private Service-Providing	493.30	508.66	501.88	502.52	504.14	507.00	506.41	507.71	510.30	509.05	511.92	514.84	514.84	517.43
Trade, transportation, and utilities	488.42	498.59	495.13	494.80	494.65	497.81	496.66	495.84	499.50	497.34	498.83	501.17	502.34	504.34
Wholesale trade	667.09	684.91	674.08	677.75	676.72	681.53	678.98	680.56	685.07	682.88	688.40	692.50	697.41	703.42
Retail trade	371.13	377.68	377.92	377.30	376.69	379.15	378.22	376.68	379.73	377.26	376.68	377.87	377.91	377.90
Transportation and warehousing	614.82	618.64	620.63	615.82	617.89	619.18	617.34	616.42	619.75	619.18	615.61	617.29	620.08	619.13
Utilities	1 048.44	1 097.16	1 071.33	1 059.25	1 059.49	1 085.86	1 082.62	1 087.27	1 111.58	1 105.81	1 110.34	1 122.12	1 118.58	1 131.88
Information	777.05	805.89	790.97	785.15	792.78	800.08	804.46	802.26	811.42	810.67	816.91	831.26	817.60	827.16
Financial activities	622.87	644.71	635.07	635.09	639.38	642.60	641.16	645.11	648.00	645.12	648.36	653.05	653.38	655.89
Professional and business services	597.56	618.46	609.10	606.90	607.92	613.55	614.92	614.82	621.17	618.57	622.55	627.69	627.35	631.81
Education and health services	523.78	544.80	534.97	536.92	539.53	540.51	542.46	544.09	548.05	545.68	550.67	552.63	550.88	552.50
Leisure and hospitality	228.65	235.29	232.33	232.59	232.84	234.52	234.78	235.30	235.55	235.41	237.88	236.95	237.47	237.31
Other services	433.04	443.06	437.85	438.78	440.02	443.49	441.87	443.61	444.85	444.65	444.96	446.81	446.81	447.12

. . . = Not available.

Table 16-6. Indexes of Aggregate Weekly Hours of Production or Nonsupervisory Workers on Private Nonfarm Payrolls by NAICS Industry

(2002 = 100.)

Industry	1990	1991	1992	1993	1994	1995	1996	1997	1998	1999	2000	2001	2002	2003
Total Private	84.4	82.6	83.1	85.5	89.2	91.6	93.8	97.1	99.4	101.5	103.6	102.1	100.0	98.7
Goods-Producing	106.1	100.1	98.7	100.8	105.6	106.8	108.1	111.2	112.3	112.6	113.1	106.6	100.0	95.8
Natural resources and mining	128.6	123.8	113.3	110.3	111.0	110.2	112.7	117.6	112.8	102.9	105.1	108.3	100.0	97.4
Construction	78.8	70.1	67.5	71.3	77.3	79.9	84.3	88.6	93.4	99.7	104.0	103.2	100.0	98.4
Manufacturing	117.7	112.8	112.4	113.9	118.3	119.0	118.8	121.4	121.0	118.9	117.7	108.1	100.0	94.5
Durable goods	114.2	107.6	106.4	108.2	114.2	116.3	117.5	121.6	122.0	120.6	120.4	109.3	100.0	94.3
Wood products	101.5	92.6	95.2	100.5	109.1	109.3	111.6	114.8	117.5	118.6	115.8	105.0	100.0	97.8
Nonmetallic mineral products	100.8	92.8	92.6	94.2	98.8	99.7	101.5	103.2	105.8	106.9	109.1	106.1	100.0	94.3
Primary metals	131.5	122.9	120.8	121.4	128.0	129.3	129.9	132.3	131.1	128.4	128.9	113.0	100.0	93.4
Fabricated metal products	104.7	99.1	97.3	99.7	106.3	109.9	111.6	116.6	118.6	116.7	119.1	109.3	100.0	95.3
Machinery	123.9	116.3	113.9	118.6	127.0	132.3	133.8	139.0	137.4	129.9	127.6	114.1	100.0	93.6
Computer and electronic products	137.2	128.1	122.9	121.1	123.5	127.1	129.9	136.8	136.7	131.1	133.0	117.9	100.0	92.1
Electrical equipment and appliances	136.0	128.0	125.9	126.8	132.5	130.3	129.4	127.7	127.8	128.3	127.8	113.4	100.0	92.0
Transportation equipment	111.1	105.8	104.4	105.5	112.6	115.4	116.4	120.7	118.7	119.5	116.4	105.3	100.0	95.4
Motor vehicles and parts	90.9	87.9	91.1	97.9	110.6	115.9	116.1	117.5	112.8	118.7	117.3	103.6	100.0	95.9
Furniture and related products	97.2	89.5	92.1	95.3	100.5	99.3	98.3	102.9	108.5	112.6	114.8	104.8	100.0	93.0
Miscellaneous manufacturing	104.0	103.8	105.2	106.9	108.2	107.7	107.7	110.0	110.3	110.3	109.5	104.8	100.0	93.6
Nondurable goods	123.0	120.8	121.7	122.6	124.7	123.1	120.5	120.9	119.4	116.1	113.3	106.0	100.0	94.7
Food manufacturing	96.2	96.6	97.3	98.7	100.5	101.6	101.8	102.6	103.4	103.8	103.5	101.5	100.0	98.4
Beverage and tobacco products	96.9	96.4	95.4	95.6	98.7	97.9	101.4	103.1	104.9	104.7	104.2	100.3	100.0	88.4
Textile mills	170.4	168.4	170.3	170.8	171.6	163.5	154.1	155.2	148.9	139.1	132.4	112.2	100.0	86.3
Textile product mills	110.3	104.5	106.0	110.6	116.6	114.4	112.8	114.8	114.1	113.5	111.1	105.0	100.0	92.9
Apparel	267.4	264.2	267.5	259.4	252.6	235.4	211.9	201.4	181.2	154.7	137.4	117.1	100.0	81.9
Leather and allied products	290.0	268.9	263.5	259.1	246.9	221.8	197.5	187.1	166.6	148.3	138.4	113.3	100.0	91.3
Paper and paper products	121.8	120.6	121.7	121.9	123.5	121.4	120.1	121.5	119.5	117.1	113.4	106.6	100.0	92.4
Printing and related support activities	122.3	118.7	118.4	120.3	123.8	123.9	122.8	124.6	124.3	120.9	119.4	111.5	100.0	95.3
Petroleum and coal products	128.9	127.5	126.0	122.0	120.0	115.5	113.5	112.7	113.4	107.6	105.8	105.6	100.0	98.7
Chemicals	118.2	115.0	112.9	113.4	115.1	115.4	114.7	114.6	115.4	113.1	110.4	104.7	100.0	98.9
Plastics and rubber products	97.7	94.2	98.1	102.4	108.8	109.9	110.1	112.7	113.8	114.6	114.3	105.0	100.0	95.2
Private Service-Providing	78.3	77.8	78.8	81.2	84.6	87.3	89.7	93.1	95.8	98.4	101.0	100.8	100.0	99.5
Trade, transportation, and utilities	89.5	87.4	87.3	89.0	92.7	95.1	96.6	98.8	100.3	101.9	103.5	101.5	100.0	98.6
Wholesale trade	94.9	93.3	92.4	92.4	95.8	99.2	100.7	103.4	104.8	106.2	107.1	102.9	100.0	98.0
Retail trade	87.5	84.8	85.1	86.3	89.8	92.3	93.7	95.9	97.2	99.5	101.3	100.5	100.0	98.9
Transportation and warehousing	83.5	82.4	82.7	88.4	93.8	95.6	98.3	101.0	102.7	103.2	105.6	102.8	100.0	98.8
Utilities	124.3	123.5	121.6	119.9	117.1	112.9	108.6	106.1	105.8	105.0	104.2	102.4	100.0	97.4
Information	76.2	76.1	76.5	78.0	79.2	82.5	86.9	90.4	92.6	98.5	104.9	106.6	100.0	97.0
Financial activities	84.5	83.3	83.5	85.9	88.0	87.8	89.8	92.6	96.5	98.0	98.5	99.5	100.0	101.5
Professional and business services	68.1	66.7	68.4	71.9	77.0	81.2	85.2	91.5	96.7	101.7	106.6	104.0	100.0	98.7
Education and health services	67.2	70.2	72.9	75.4	78.3	81.2	83.4	86.7	88.9	90.6	92.8	96.6	100.0	101.4
Leisure and hospitality	78.9	77.3	79.3	82.2	85.6	88.5	90.8	93.4	95.5	97.9	100.6	100.7	100.0	100.1
Other services	81.8	81.2	80.6	82.8	84.5	87.1	89.1	91.9	94.3	96.3	97.8	99.1	100.0	97.5

Table 16-6. Indexes of Aggregate Weekly Hours of Production or Nonsupervisory Workers on Private Nonfarm Payrolls by NAICS Industry—Continued

(2002 = 100.)

Industry	2004	2005	2005, seasonally adjusted											
			January	February	March	April	May	June	July	August	September	October	November	December
Total Private	100.2	102.6	101.3	101.6	101.8	102.4	102.2	102.4	102.9	102.7	103.1	103.1	103.5	103.7
Goods-Producing	96.8	98.6	96.9	97.5	97.6	98.6	98.0	98.1	98.1	98.3	98.6	99.6	100.5	100.1
Natural resources and mining	104.0	114.2	110.3	109.5	110.7	112.7	113.2	114.1	114.9	115.9	116.3	117.6	116.0	118.0
Construction	101.7	107.5	102.6	105.0	105.6	108.3	106.7	107.6	106.5	107.2	107.2	108.5	111.7	110.0
Manufacturing	94.3	93.9	93.9	93.7	93.2	93.4	93.3	93.2	93.4	93.7	93.9	94.7	94.6	94.8
Durable goods	95.2	96.1	95.3	95.2	94.8	95.2	95.1	95.4	95.6	96.1	96.3	97.7	97.4	97.5
Wood products	100.9	100.5	102.6	100.4	99.7	99.2	99.0	99.1	99.0	99.1	99.5	102.4	102.4	102.0
Nonmetallic mineral products	98.0	97.0	97.5	97.2	96.2	97.0	96.3	96.8	95.6	95.4	95.7	97.2	99.5	97.5
Primary metals	93.3	93.6	93.2	93.7	93.0	92.5	92.3	92.7	93.6	93.8	94.5	95.0	95.2	95.1
Fabricated metal products	97.7	99.0	98.5	98.1	98.2	98.5	98.6	98.5	98.9	99.0	98.8	100.5	100.3	100.4
Machinery	95.9	98.7	96.8	96.8	97.5	98.0	98.3	98.4	99.1	98.8	99.1	100.3	99.0	99.3
Computer and electronic products	89.7	95.0	90.2	90.5	90.3	92.2	92.6	93.6	95.3	96.0	97.9	99.8	100.3	101.1
Electrical equipment and appliances	88.7	86.8	87.0	86.2	86.1	85.6	86.0	85.9	87.0	87.3	87.8	88.1	87.7	87.7
Transportation equipment	96.5	97.3	96.1	96.9	96.2	96.9	96.5	96.5	96.0	97.6	96.7	98.8	98.8	99.2
Motor vehicles and parts	97.0	95.4	95.6	97.1	95.3	95.3	94.4	94.3	92.5	95.7	96.7	96.4	95.4	95.2
Furniture and related products	94.3	91.5	93.5	92.9	92.9	91.7	91.2	91.2	91.3	91.2	91.3	91.0	89.2	88.9
Miscellaneous manufacturing	91.8	90.9	91.3	91.3	91.0	90.7	90.2	90.7	90.0	91.2	91.0	91.5	90.7	90.5
Nondurable goods	92.7	90.3	91.5	91.0	90.4	90.7	90.1	89.9	89.9	89.6	90.0	90.2	90.2	90.5
Food manufacturing	97.1	95.4	96.0	96.8	95.6	95.8	95.5	95.2	95.6	94.8	94.5	94.5	95.2	95.8
Beverage and tobacco products	88.8	94.8	91.9	90.9	91.8	93.3	91.6	95.0	95.3	95.8	94.9	100.3	98.9	98.0
Textile mills	79.0	71.4	75.1	73.6	73.0	72.0	72.4	72.1	71.0	70.3	69.3	69.4	69.2	69.2
Textile product mills	91.0	90.6	90.4	89.9	90.3	89.7	89.9	87.5	88.9	89.9	91.2	92.2	94.2	94.3
Apparel	75.1	66.4	70.3	69.6	68.8	68.2	65.5	65.8	66.3	65.4	64.8	64.0	64.5	63.9
Leather and allied products	83.6	78.8	77.7	77.1	76.4	77.0	77.4	78.0	79.6	79.6	79.6	79.6	81.0	81.2
Paper and paper products	89.2	87.9	88.8	88.0	88.0	87.8	88.0	87.5	87.5	87.6	88.1	87.9	87.1	87.2
Printing and related support activities	93.4	91.1	92.6	91.7	90.8	91.2	91.1	90.7	90.9	90.6	91.2	90.8	90.5	90.9
Petroleum and coal products	102.6	102.9	103.2	103.2	103.0	105.8	105.3	104.7	102.5	101.2	105.3	105.3	100.6	97.6
Chemicals	99.0	96.8	98.2	96.9	96.6	97.0	96.7	96.2	96.5	95.0	96.4	97.9	96.9	97.6
Plastics and rubber products	94.2	92.0	92.7	92.6	92.3	92.0	91.3	91.0	90.9	91.5	91.9	91.9	92.1	92.9
Private Service-Providing	101.1	103.6	102.6	102.9	103.1	103.6	103.4	103.7	103.9	103.8	104.1	104.1	104.5	104.6
Trade, transportation, and utilities	99.6	101.5	100.8	101.0	100.9	101.5	101.4	101.3	101.5	101.3	101.3	101.3	102.0	102.0
Wholesale trade	98.9	101.6	100.1	100.7	100.8	101.2	101.3	101.2	101.4	101.3	102.0	102.3	102.8	103.1
Retail trade	99.4	100.6	100.3	100.5	100.4	100.9	100.7	100.6	101.0	100.7	100.4	100.0	101.1	100.7
Transportation and warehousing	101.9	104.9	105.2	104.8	104.8	105.5	105.1	104.9	105.0	104.8	103.9	104.3	105.0	104.8
Utilities	94.2	93.7	93.1	91.9	91.0	93.2	92.9	93.7	94.1	94.4	94.5	94.9	95.1	95.2
Information	98.2	99.6	98.6	98.4	99.1	99.5	99.8	99.2	99.7	99.5	100.5	100.5	100.3	100.6
Financial activities	101.9	104.6	103.8	103.7	103.9	104.2	104.2	104.8	105.1	104.9	105.1	105.8	105.6	105.8
Professional and business services	101.8	105.8	103.8	103.7	104.1	105.0	105.1	105.2	106.2	105.9	106.9	106.9	107.6	108.0
Education and health services	103.3	106.2	105.2	105.3	105.5	105.7	106.0	106.2	106.8	106.3	107.2	107.0	106.6	106.7
Leisure and hospitality	103.0	106.2	104.9	105.2	105.3	106.3	106.2	106.4	106.6	106.4	106.6	106.2	106.7	106.5
Other services	96.1	96.1	96.2	96.2	96.2	96.9	96.2	96.5	96.5	96.0	96.0	96.0	95.8	96.0

Table 16-7. Indexes of Aggregate Weekly Payrolls of Production or Nonsupervisory Workers on Private Nonfarm Payrolls by NAICS Industry

(2002 = 100.)

Industry	1990	1991	1992	1993	1994	1995	1996	1997	1998	1999	2000	2001	2002	2003
Total Private	57.5	58.0	59.8	63.1	67.6	71.3	75.4	81.1	86.5	91.4	97.0	99.2	100.0	101.4
Goods-Producing	74.5	72.1	72.4	75.8	81.7	84.8	88.6	94.1	97.9	101.4	105.7	103.0	100.0	98.5
Natural resources and mining	100.2	99.5	92.8	90.6	93.0	94.8	99.0	106.5	106.3	97.8	101.2	107.1	100.0	99.5
Construction	57.1	51.7	50.3	54.1	60.0	63.6	68.8	74.9	81.8	90.4	98.2	100.3	100.0	100.7
Manufacturing	82.9	82.1	83.8	87.1	93.2	96.1	99.0	104.3	106.4	107.7	110.2	104.3	100.0	97.3
Durable goods	81.3	79.3	80.3	83.9	91.1	94.7	98.7	105.0	107.1	108.9	112.2	104.9	100.0	96.9
Nondurable goods	85.7	86.9	89.9	92.7	96.6	98.3	99.4	102.9	105.1	105.5	106.6	103.0	100.0	97.9
Private Service-Providing	52.2	53.7	55.9	59.1	63.2	67.1	71.3	77.1	82.8	88.3	94.3	98.1	100.0	102.2
Trade, transportation, and utilities	62.8	62.9	64.2	67.0	71.4	75.3	79.0	83.9	88.6	93.2	98.3	99.2	100.0	100.9
Wholesale trade	64.7	65.7	66.4	68.4	73.0	77.9	81.8	87.8	93.0	97.7	102.7	101.7	100.0	100.2
Retail trade	57.8	57.4	59.2	61.9	66.3	70.0	74.0	78.8	83.8	89.1	94.3	97.3	100.0	100.8
Transportation and warehousing	66.3	65.9	67.0	71.3	76.4	79.9	83.8	88.3	92.0	95.3	100.8	99.9	100.0	101.8
Utilities	83.7	86.1	87.1	89.9	91.2	90.4	89.7	91.2	94.9	96.6	99.0	100.7	100.0	100.7
Information	50.5	52.3	54.1	57.3	60.0	64.1	70.2	76.7	81.0	89.7	99.1	104.5	100.0	100.9
Financial activities	52.2	53.7	56.1	60.3	64.3	66.7	70.5	75.7	83.1	87.7	91.2	95.9	100.0	107.5
Professional and business services	45.1	45.6	47.9	51.2	55.7	60.5	65.9	73.8	82.1	89.8	98.4	101.1	100.0	101.1
Education and health services	44.1	48.4	52.1	55.5	59.2	63.0	66.8	71.6	76.0	80.1	85.1	92.9	100.0	104.2
Leisure and hospitality	54.1	54.7	57.3	60.5	64.5	68.4	72.1	77.7	83.2	88.6	95.2	98.1	100.0	102.2
Other services	54.1	55.5	56.8	59.8	62.7	66.7	70.4	75.6	81.0	86.0	90.8	95.8	100.0	98.3

Table 16-7. Indexes of Aggregate Weekly Payrolls of Production or Nonsupervisory Workers on Private Nonfarm Payrolls by NAICS Industry—Continued

(2002 = 100.)

Industry	2004	2005	2005, seasonally adjusted											
			January	February	March	April	May	June	July	August	September	October	November	December
Total Private	105.0	110.5	107.7	108.2	108.6	109.6	109.6	110.1	111.1	111.1	111.6	112.3	112.8	113.4
Goods-Producing	101.9	106.3	103.0	104.0	104.3	105.8	105.3	105.7	105.9	106.4	106.6	108.2	109.2	108.9
Natural resources and mining	109.3	124.3	118.2	117.2	117.5	121.6	122.3	123.9	125.2	127.2	128.8	130.2	127.8	131.2
Construction	105.6	113.0	106.6	109.3	110.3	113.4	111.7	112.9	112.3	113.0	113.1	114.7	118.1	116.7
Manufacturing	99.6	101.7	100.6	100.6	100.2	100.7	100.9	101.0	101.3	102.0	101.9	103.5	103.2	103.5
Durable goods	100.0	104.0	101.8	102.1	101.6	102.5	102.7	103.2	103.6	104.7	104.4	106.8	106.4	106.7
Nondurable goods	98.6	97.5	98.2	97.8	97.3	97.5	97.5	97.2	97.0	96.9	97.3	97.9	97.5	98.0
Private Service-Providing	105.9	111.8	109.2	109.6	110.2	111.1	111.0	111.6	112.4	112.3	113.0	113.6	114.0	114.8
Trade, transportation, and utilities	103.5	108.0	106.3	106.5	106.6	107.6	107.5	107.6	108.7	108.3	108.3	108.8	109.4	109.9
Wholesale trade	102.8	108.6	105.4	106.4	106.6	107.5	107.4	107.9	108.8	108.7	109.7	110.4	111.7	112.8
Retail trade	103.0	106.6	105.8	105.9	105.9	106.8	106.7	106.5	107.8	107.1	106.3	106.6	107.0	106.9
Transportation and warehousing	106.8	111.2	110.5	109.8	110.4	111.1	110.9	110.9	111.5	111.5	110.9	111.3	112.3	112.1
Utilities	100.7	104.5	101.5	100.1	99.9	102.8	102.6	103.2	105.9	105.8	106.3	107.6	107.7	108.6
Information	104.1	108.8	106.1	105.1	106.5	107.9	108.3	108.2	109.4	109.4	111.0	112.7	111.2	112.5
Financial activities	110.4	116.1	113.5	113.7	114.4	115.0	114.7	115.8	116.6	116.3	117.0	118.4	118.9	119.5
Professional and business services	105.9	113.8	110.0	110.1	110.7	112.1	112.4	112.9	114.5	114.3	115.4	116.4	117.1	118.3
Education and health services	109.7	116.7	113.5	114.0	114.8	115.2	115.9	116.6	117.7	117.4	118.6	118.8	118.8	119.3
Leisure and hospitality	107.1	113.1	110.5	111.0	111.3	112.7	112.6	113.1	113.5	113.6	114.6	114.2	114.9	115.1
Other services	97.9	100.4	99.3	99.5	99.8	100.6	100.2	100.6	100.9	100.7	100.7	100.9	100.9	101.2

NOTES AND DEFINITIONS

TABLES 16-1 THROUGH 16-7
EMPLOYMENT, HOURS, AND EARNINGS BY NAICS INDUSTRY

SOURCE: *U.S. DEPARTMENT OF LABOR, BUREAU OF LABOR STATISTICS*

See the notes and definitions for Tables 10-7 through 10-12 regarding definitions of *employment, production or nonsupervisory workers, average weekly hours, overtime hours, average hourly earnings, average weekly earnings*, and the *indexes of aggregate weekly hours.*

Indexes of aggregate weekly payrolls for private nonfarm production or nonsupervisory workers are calculated at the basic industry level as the product of average hourly earnings and aggregate weekly hours. At higher levels, payroll aggregates are the sum of the component aggregates. Index levels are calculated by dividing the current month's aggregate by the average of the 12 monthly figures for 2002.

See Chapter 14 for information on the North American Industry Classification System (NAICS).

Figure 17-1. New Orders for Durable Goods, 1959–2005
(ratio scale)

- The value of new orders for durable goods at U.S. manufacturing firms is a sensitive indicator of the business cycle, as shown in the figure above. From 2000 to 2003, the annual average of new orders dropped 12 percent, the longest and deepest decline in the postwar period. However, by 2005, orders had recovered to above the 2000 level. (Table 17-6)

- As a percentage of the total supply of petroleum and products (domestic crude oil and natural gas liquids production plus net imports), net imports rose from 10.4 percent in 1955 to 64.5 percent in 2005. (Table 17-1)

- For the housing sector, 2005 was the best year since 1972. Over 2 million units were started, of which 1.7 million were single-family structures. (Table 17-3)

- Sales of cars and light trucks in 2005 were little changed from 2004 and 2.3 percent below the high reached in 2000. Domestic unit sales were down 6.5 percent from 2000, while imports rose 18.9 percent. Sales of "light trucks" (trucks 14,000 pounds and under, a category which includes sport utility and similar vehicles) were 23 percent of total car and light truck sales in 1976, but rose to 55 percent of these sales in 2005. (Table 17-8)

- Sales by electronic shopping and mail order grew from 1.9 percent of total retail sales in 1992 to 4.3 percent in 2005. (Table 17-9) E-commerce alone grew from 0.9 percent of total retail sales in 2000 to 2.4 percent in 2005. (Table 17-10)

- E-commerce accounted for only 1.1 percent of total revenues for surveyed service industries as a whole in 2005, despite making up nearly one-quarter of the travel and reservation business. (Table 17-16)

Table 17-1. Petroleum and Petroleum Products—Prices, Imports, Domestic Production, and Stocks

(Not seasonally adjusted.)

Year and month	Crude oil futures price (dollars per barrel) Current dollars	2000 dollars	Total energy-related petroleum products (thousands of barrels)	Crude petroleum Thousands of barrels Total	Average per day	Unit price (dollars per barrel)	Exports	Petroleum and products Imports	Net imports	Domestic production Crude oil	Natural gas plant liquids	Crude oil and petroleum products	Crude petroleum Total	Strategic petroleum reserve
1955	...	...	...	...	...	...	368	1 248	880	6 807	771	715	266	...
1956	...	...	...	...	...	...	430	1 436	1 006	7 151	800	780	266	...
1957	...	...	...	...	...	...	568	1 574	1 006	7 170	808	841	282	...
1958	...	...	...	...	...	...	276	1 700	1 424	6 710	808	789	263	...
1959	...	...	...	...	...	...	211	1 780	1 569	7 054	879	808	257	...
1960	...	...	...	...	...	...	202	1 815	1 613	7 035	929	779	240	...
1961	...	...	...	...	...	...	174	1 917	1 743	7 183	991	825	245	...
1962	...	...	...	...	...	...	168	2 082	1 914	7 332	1 021	834	252	...
1963	...	...	...	...	...	...	208	2 123	1 915	7 542	1 098	836	237	...
1964	...	...	...	...	...	...	202	2 259	2 057	7 614	1 154	839	230	...
1965	...	...	...	...	...	...	187	2 468	2 281	7 804	1 210	836	220	...
1966	...	...	...	...	...	...	198	2 573	2 375	8 295	1 284	881	238	...
1967	...	...	...	...	...	...	307	2 537	2 230	8 810	1 409	944	249	...
1968	...	...	...	...	...	...	231	2 840	2 609	9 096	1 504	998	272	...
1969	...	...	...	...	...	...	233	3 166	2 933	9 238	1 590	980	265	...
1970	...	...	...	...	...	...	259	3 419	3 160	9 637	1 660	1 018	276	...
1971	...	...	...	...	...	...	224	3 926	3 702	9 463	1 693	1 044	260	...
1972	...	...	...	...	...	...	222	4 741	4 519	9 441	1 744	959	246	...
1973	...	...	...	1 392 970	3 816	3.30	231	6 256	6 025	9 208	1 738	1 008	242	...
1974	...	...	...	1 367 081	3 745	11.17	221	6 112	5 891	8 774	1 688	1 074	265	...
1975	...	...	...	1 584 730	4 342	11.59	209	6 056	5 847	8 375	1 633	1 133	271	...
1976	...	...	...	2 050 424	5 618	12.43	223	7 313	7 090	8 132	1 604	1 112	285	...
1977	...	...	...	2 519 806	6 904	13.33	243	8 807	8 564	8 245	1 618	1 312	348	7
1978	...	...	...	2 392 350	6 554	13.43	362	8 363	8 001	8 707	1 567	1 278	376	67
1979	...	...	...	2 467 315	6 760	18.68	471	8 456	7 985	8 552	1 584	1 341	430	91
1980	...	...	...	1 977 247	5 417	31.36	544	6 909	6 365	8 597	1 573	1 392	466	108
1981	...	...	...	1 763 072	4 830	35.13	595	5 996	5 401	8 572	1 609	1 484	594	230
1982	...	...	...	1 420 753	3 892	33.39	815	5 113	4 298	8 649	1 550	1 430	644	294
1983	30.66	49.11	...	1 293 819	3 545	29.51	739	5 051	4 312	8 688	1 559	1 454	723	379
1984	29.44	45.44	...	1 319 683	3 616	27.68	722	5 437	4 715	8 879	1 630	1 556	796	451
1985	27.89	41.67	...	1 260 856	3 454	26.20	781	5 067	4 286	8 971	1 609	1 519	814	493
1986	15.05	21.95	...	1 634 567	4 478	13.90	785	6 224	5 439	8 680	1 551	1 593	843	512
1987	19.15	26.99	...	1 744 977	4 781	16.80	764	6 678	5 914	8 349	1 595	1 607	890	541
1988	15.96	21.64	...	1 887 860	5 172	13.69	815	7 402	6 587	8 140	1 625	1 597	890	560
1989	19.58	25.44	...	2 146 552	5 881	16.49	859	8 061	7 202	7 613	1 546	1 581	921	580
1990	24.50	30.44	...	2 216 604	6 073	19.75	857	8 018	7 161	7 355	1 559	1 621	908	586
1991	21.50	25.77	2 828 953	2 146 064	5 880	17.46	1 001	7 627	6 626	7 417	1 659	1 617	893	569
1992	20.58	23.98	2 947 582	2 294 570	6 269	16.80	950	7 888	6 938	7 171	1 697	1 592	893	575
1993	18.48	21.05	3 257 008	2 543 374	6 968	15.13	1 003	8 620	7 617	6 847	1 736	1 647	922	587
1994	17.19	19.17	3 416 045	2 704 196	7 409	14.23	942	8 996	8 054	6 662	1 727	1 653	929	592
1995	18.40	20.09	3 361 882	2 767 312	7 582	15.81	949	8 835	7 886	6 560	1 762	1 563	895	592
1996	22.03	23.55	3 622 385	2 893 647	7 906	18.98	981	9 478	8 497	6 465	1 830	1 507	850	566
1997	20.61	21.67	3 802 574	3 069 430	8 409	17.67	1 003	10 162	9 159	6 452	1 817	1 560	868	563
1998	14.40	15.00	4 088 027	3 242 711	8 884	11.49	945	10 708	9 763	6 252	1 759	1 647	895	571
1999	19.30	19.78	4 081 181	3 228 092	8 844	15.76	940	10 852	9 912	5 881	1 850	1 493	852	567
2000	30.26	30.26	4 314 825	3 399 239	9 288	26.44	1 040	11 459	10 419	5 822	1 911	1 468	826	541
2001	25.95	25.42	4 475 026	3 471 067	9 510	21.40	971	11 871	10 900	5 801	1 868	1 586	862	550
2002	26.15	25.26	4 337 075	3 418 021	9 364	22.61	984	11 530	10 546	5 746	1 880	1 548	877	599
2003	30.99	29.35	4 654 638	3 676 006	10 071	26.98	1 027	12 264	11 237	5 681	1 719	1 568	907	638
2004	41.47	38.27	4 917 591	3 820 979	10 440	34.48	1 048	13 145	12 097	5 419	1 809	1 645	961	676
2005	56.70	50.86	5 004 339	3 754 669	10 287	46.81	1 165	13 714	12 549	5 178	1 717	1 698	1 008	685
2004														
January	34.22	32.03	395 226	309 876	9 996	28.57	748	12 014	11 266	5 570	1 802	1 556	913	641
February	34.50	32.18	380 038	288 494	9 948	29.17	1 046	12 658	11 612	5 556	1 799	1 557	931	647
March	36.72	34.13	429 420	329 991	10 645	30.66	1 024	13 349	12 325	5 607	1 828	1 571	949	652
April	36.62	33.99	393 788	311 663	10 389	31.00	1 153	12 883	11 730	5 527	1 783	1 580	962	658
May	40.28	37.22	398 862	317 854	10 253	33.14	1 052	13 375	12 323	5 548	1 780	1 610	966	661
June	38.05	35.07	432 235	344 729	11 491	33.74	1 070	13 561	12 491	5 398	1 738	1 631	967	662
July	40.81	37.59	414 258	324 108	10 455	33.38	1 080	13 570	12 490	5 458	1 812	1 646	960	666
August	44.88	41.31	437 516	333 756	10 766	36.54	1 091	13 689	12 598	5 333	1 863	1 654	948	669
September	45.94	42.23	377 861	297 013	9 900	37.52	961	12 676	11 715	5 062	1 797	1 642	943	670
October	53.09	48.56	408 187	313 249	10 105	41.84	1 078	13 438	12 360	5 156	1 820	1 637	957	670
November	48.48	44.25	439 794	329 660	10 989	41.19	992	13 409	12 417	5 396	1 868	1 656	961	673
December	43.26	39.49	410 406	320 586	10 341	36.46	1 284	13 088	11 804	5 413	1 817	1 645	961	676
2005														
January	46.85	42.70	419 291	325 786	10 509	35.27	917	12 991	12 074	5 441	1 812	1 647	966	680
February	48.05	43.67	387 899	293 425	10 479	36.93	1 256	13 749	12 493	5 494	1 868	1 663	984	682
March	54.63	49.43	418 418	324 180	10 457	41.28	1 308	13 230	11 922	5 601	1 872	1 661	1 008	688
April	53.22	47.99	413 267	315 528	10 518	44.78	1 330	13 476	12 146	5 556	1 840	1 702	1 030	692
May	49.87	44.95	420 464	319 982	10 322	43.04	1 380	14 006	12 626	5 581	1 849	1 730	1 030	694
June	56.42	50.85	430 594	327 865	10 929	44.41	1 477	14 270	12 793	5 460	1 785	1 740	1 024	696
July	59.03	52.98	419 157	312 106	10 068	49.07	1 259	13 925	12 666	5 240	1 748	1 743	1 017	699
August	64.99	58.09	433 073	329 039	10 614	52.85	1 295	13 848	12 553	5 218	1 724	1 716	1 010	701
September	65.55	58.05	389 645	277 589	9 253	57.42	844	13 229	12 385	4 204	1 491	1 704	1 000	694
October	62.27	55.02	432 162	300 884	9 706	56.21	854	14 208	13 354	4 534	1 544	1 716	1 007	685
November	58.34	51.75	422 459	314 028	10 468	52.16	961	14 096	13 135	4 837	1 621	1 729	1 008	686
December	59.45	52.74	417 910	314 259	10 137	49.79	1 106	13 548	12 442	4 984	1 459	1 698	1 008	685

. . . = Not available.

Table 17-2. New Construction Put in Place

(Billions of dollars, monthly data are at seasonally adjusted annual rates.)

Year and month	Total	Private											
		Total [1]	Residential	Office	Commercial		Health care	Educational	Amusement and recreation	Transportation	Communication	Power	Manufacturing
					Total [1]	Multi-retail							
1964	75.1	54.9	30.5	...	...	...	...	...	...	...	...	...	...
1965	81.9	60.0	30.2	...	...	...	...	...	...	...	...	...	...
1966	85.8	61.9	28.6	...	...	...	...	...	...	...	...	...	...
1967	87.2	61.8	28.7	...	...	...	...	...	...	...	...	...	...
1968	96.8	69.4	34.2	...	...	...	...	...	...	...	...	...	...
1969	104.9	77.2	37.2	...	...	...	...	...	...	...	...	...	...
1970	105.9	78.0	35.9	...	...	...	...	...	...	...	...	...	...
1971	122.4	92.7	48.5	...	...	...	...	...	...	...	...	...	...
1972	139.1	109.1	60.7	...	...	...	...	...	...	...	...	...	...
1973	153.8	121.4	65.1	...	...	...	...	...	...	...	...	...	...
1974	155.2	117.0	56.0	...	...	...	...	...	...	...	...	...	...
1975	152.6	109.3	51.6	...	...	...	...	...	...	...	...	...	...
1976	172.1	128.2	68.3	...	...	...	...	...	...	...	...	...	...
1977	200.5	157.4	92.0	...	...	...	...	...	...	...	...	...	...
1978	239.9	189.7	109.8	...	...	...	...	...	...	...	...	...	...
1979	272.9	216.2	116.4	...	...	...	...	...	...	...	...	...	...
1980	273.9	210.3	100.4	...	...	...	...	...	...	...	...	...	...
1981	289.1	224.4	99.2	...	...	...	...	...	...	...	...	...	...
1982	279.3	216.3	84.7	...	...	...	...	...	...	...	...	...	...
1983	311.9	248.4	125.8	...	...	...	...	...	...	...	...	...	...
1984	370.2	300.0	155.0	...	...	...	...	...	...	...	...	...	...
1985	403.4	325.6	160.5	...	...	...	...	...	...	...	...	...	...
1986	433.5	348.9	190.7	...	...	...	...	...	...	...	...	...	...
1987	446.6	356.0	199.7	...	...	...	...	...	...	...	...	...	...
1988	462.0	367.3	204.5	...	...	...	...	...	...	...	...	...	...
1989	477.5	379.3	204.3	...	...	...	...	...	...	...	...	...	...
1990	476.8	369.3	191.1	...	...	...	...	...	...	...	...	...	...
1991	432.6	322.5	166.3	...	...	...	...	...	...	...	...	...	...
1992	463.7	347.8	199.4	...	...	...	...	...	...	...	...	...	...
1993	491.0	375.1	225.1	20.0	34.4	11.5	14.9	4.8	4.6	4.7	9.8	23.6	23.4
1994	539.2	419.0	258.6	20.4	39.6	12.2	15.4	5.0	5.1	4.7	10.1	21.0	28.8
1995	557.8	427.9	247.4	23.0	44.1	12.0	15.3	5.7	5.9	4.8	11.1	22.0	35.4
1996	615.9	476.6	281.1	26.5	49.4	13.3	15.4	7.0	7.0	5.8	11.8	17.4	38.1
1997	653.4	502.7	289.0	32.8	53.1	12.2	17.4	8.8	8.5	6.2	12.5	16.4	37.6
1998	706.3	552.0	314.6	40.4	55.7	13.3	17.7	9.8	8.6	7.3	12.5	21.7	40.5
1999	769.5	599.7	350.6	45.1	59.4	15.2	18.4	9.8	9.6	6.5	18.4	22.0	35.1
2000	835.3	649.8	374.5	52.4	64.1	14.9	19.5	11.7	8.8	6.9	18.8	29.3	37.6
2001	868.3	662.2	388.3	49.7	63.6	16.4	19.5	12.8	7.8	7.1	19.6	31.5	37.8
2002	876.8	659.7	421.9	35.3	59.0	15.6	22.4	13.1	7.5	6.8	18.4	32.6	22.7
2003	926.9	702.9	475.9	30.6	57.5	15.4	24.2	13.4	7.8	6.6	12.1	33.6	21.4
2004	...	804.2	564.8	32.9	64.1	18.8	26.3	12.7	8.4	6.8	12.4	30.4	23.7
2005	...	899.0	642.3	36.8	69.1	23.0	27.7	12.8	7.7	7.3	13.3	29.0	30.9
2003													
January	897.8	674.5	448.9	30.8	56.7	14.9	23.1	13.0	6.5	6.8	11.8	37.9	19.6
February	892.9	671.8	448.0	29.4	55.2	14.4	24.1	12.8	7.0	7.0	11.4	38.1	19.7
March	886.3	670.9	444.2	29.4	55.8	14.8	24.0	13.1	7.5	6.6	12.1	38.1	20.7
April	895.1	676.8	452.4	28.7	56.1	15.2	24.0	12.9	7.7	6.5	12.0	36.7	20.6
May	907.3	685.7	455.0	28.8	57.1	14.8	24.4	13.9	7.8	6.5	12.2	34.1	22.1
June	923.0	696.0	465.9	30.2	58.6	15.8	24.6	13.9	8.1	6.6	12.3	33.8	22.4
July	932.0	705.2	482.4	30.0	59.1	15.6	23.9	13.9	7.8	6.4	12.6	28.0	21.5
August	940.8	711.4	484.0	30.9	61.0	16.1	23.9	13.8	7.7	6.4	11.8	30.5	21.9
September	942.8	714.5	484.1	30.9	57.8	15.5	23.7	14.1	8.2	6.6	12.2	34.7	22.4
October	954.9	724.6	494.7	33.2	58.1	16.0	24.4	13.5	8.5	6.6	11.6	31.2	22.8
November	957.4	732.9	509.7	32.6	57.3	16.2	24.8	12.9	8.1	6.3	12.3	27.9	21.7
December	973.0	753.8	525.6	32.4	57.4	15.7	25.7	13.3	8.2	6.5	12.3	33.0	21.0
2004													
January	973.8	753.0	524.2	30.5	59.0	16.3	24.4	12.9	7.6	6.8	10.5	38.0	21.3
February	974.2	756.8	527.4	32.0	59.9	17.0	25.1	12.4	7.8	7.2	11.9	30.6	22.7
March	999.5	769.5	536.3	32.4	60.4	17.7	26.3	12.7	8.0	7.0	11.9	31.8	21.7
April	...	782.4	547.1	32.9	62.7	18.3	26.9	12.9	8.2	6.6	12.0	30.3	21.7
May	...	792.0	556.8	32.7	64.7	18.8	27.0	12.6	8.9	6.6	12.0	26.7	22.4
June	...	795.5	562.1	32.5	66.3	19.1	26.8	12.5	8.6	6.7	11.8	24.7	21.0
July	...	810.1	569.4	34.3	68.1	20.3	26.7	12.5	8.6	6.9	12.1	26.5	22.6
August	...	831.0	585.9	33.0	66.2	19.7	26.3	12.6	8.8	6.8	12.6	33.0	23.5
September	...	826.5	579.4	32.5	66.5	19.9	26.5	12.8	8.6	6.8	13.0	33.0	24.1
October	...	832.3	584.4	33.1	65.5	19.5	26.0	12.9	8.9	6.8	13.7	32.2	26.2
November	...	832.1	584.9	33.6	64.9	19.4	26.7	12.9	8.6	6.9	12.9	30.3	27.6
December	...	842.4	598.7	33.8	63.6	19.5	26.3	12.7	8.5	6.9	13.4	27.8	28.3
2005													
January	...	853.6	605.6	35.9	65.1	19.8	27.0	12.7	8.3	7.0	14.2	27.6	28.7
February	...	868.2	616.7	38.0	65.8	20.3	26.7	12.7	8.3	6.4	14.2	28.2	29.0
March	...	880.5	626.9	36.6	67.5	21.7	26.5	12.7	8.0	6.7	13.5	29.2	29.7
April	...	878.9	627.8	37.4	68.5	21.6	26.1	12.7	7.6	7.1	13.6	26.5	29.3
May	...	891.9	636.0	37.1	69.7	22.3	26.8	12.7	7.3	7.4	13.7	31.0	28.9
June	...	891.5	642.2	36.7	67.5	22.0	27.0	12.9	7.3	7.3	13.4	27.4	29.3
July	...	895.5	646.6	34.9	67.8	23.8	28.3	12.8	7.0	7.1	13.3	27.1	29.6
August	...	902.7	650.8	35.6	69.1	23.6	29.3	12.8	7.2	7.3	13.4	24.3	31.6
September	...	917.3	655.0	37.4	69.7	23.9	30.0	13.2	7.9	7.5	13.2	29.3	31.9
October	...	924.0	659.3	37.0	71.7	24.6	28.5	12.9	7.7	7.7	13.0	30.7	33.0
November	...	931.3	663.1	36.9	72.7	25.4	28.0	12.6	7.9	7.9	13.0	32.7	34.0
December	...	940.2	665.6	39.0	74.8	27.2	28.7	13.2	8.0	8.2	12.5	32.2	34.9

[1] Includes categories not shown separately.
... = Not available.

Table 17-2. New Construction Put in Place—Continued

(Billions of dollars, monthly data are at seasonally adjusted annual rates.)

Year and month	Total	Public												Federal
		State and local												
		Total [1]	Residential	Office	Health care	Educa-tional	Public safety	Amuse-ment and recreation	Transpor-tation	Power	Highway and street	Sewage and waste disposal	Water supply	
1964	20.2	16.5	...	...	...	...	...	...	...	...	...	...	...	3.7
1965	21.9	18.0	...	...	...	...	...	...	...	...	...	...	...	3.9
1966	23.8	20.0	...	...	...	...	...	...	...	...	...	...	...	3.8
1967	25.4	22.1	...	...	...	...	...	...	...	...	...	...	...	3.3
1968	27.4	24.2	...	...	...	...	...	...	...	...	...	...	...	3.2
1969	27.8	24.6	...	...	...	...	...	...	...	...	...	...	...	3.2
1970	27.9	24.8	...	...	...	...	...	...	...	...	...	...	...	3.1
1971	29.7	25.9	...	...	...	...	...	...	...	...	...	...	...	3.8
1972	30.0	25.8	...	...	...	...	...	...	...	...	...	...	...	4.2
1973	32.3	27.6	...	...	...	...	...	...	...	...	...	...	...	4.7
1974	38.1	33.0	...	...	...	...	...	...	...	...	...	...	...	5.1
1975	43.3	37.2	...	...	...	...	...	...	...	...	...	...	...	6.1
1976	44.0	37.2	...	...	...	...	...	...	...	...	...	...	...	6.8
1977	43.1	36.0	...	...	...	...	...	...	...	...	...	...	...	7.1
1978	50.1	42.0	...	...	...	...	...	...	...	...	...	...	...	8.1
1979	56.6	48.1	...	...	...	...	...	...	...	...	...	...	...	8.6
1980	63.6	54.0	...	...	...	...	...	...	...	...	...	...	...	9.6
1981	64.7	54.3	...	...	...	...	...	...	...	...	...	...	...	10.4
1982	63.1	53.1	...	...	...	...	...	...	...	...	...	...	...	10.0
1983	63.5	52.9	...	...	...	...	...	...	...	...	...	...	...	10.6
1984	70.2	59.0	...	...	...	...	...	...	...	...	...	...	...	11.2
1985	77.8	65.8	...	...	...	...	...	...	...	...	...	...	...	12.0
1986	84.6	72.2	...	...	...	...	...	...	...	...	...	...	...	12.4
1987	90.6	76.6	...	...	...	...	...	...	...	...	...	...	...	14.1
1988	94.7	82.5	...	...	...	...	...	...	...	...	...	...	...	12.3
1989	98.2	86.0	...	...	...	...	...	...	...	...	...	...	...	12.2
1990	107.5	95.4	...	...	...	...	...	...	...	...	...	...	...	12.1
1991	110.1	97.3	...	...	...	...	...	...	...	...	...	...	...	12.8
1992	115.8	101.5	...	...	...	...	...	...	...	...	...	...	...	14.4
1993	116.0	101.5	3.7	3.2	2.7	19.2	5.2	4.9	8.8	3.2	34.4	8.9	5.1	14.4
1994	120.2	105.8	3.4	3.6	2.9	20.5	5.4	5.6	8.6	2.8	37.3	8.7	4.7	14.4
1995	129.9	114.2	4.0	3.9	3.2	25.7	5.9	6.1	9.0	2.9	37.6	8.4	4.7	15.8
1996	139.3	123.9	4.2	4.4	3.4	28.6	6.7	6.1	10.0	2.5	39.5	9.8	5.6	15.3
1997	150.7	136.6	4.3	4.6	3.5	33.8	6.7	6.9	9.7	3.1	43.0	10.5	6.5	14.1
1998	154.3	140.0	4.3	4.6	2.9	35.0	7.6	7.7	10.2	2.5	44.8	9.9	6.7	14.3
1999	169.7	155.7	4.6	4.5	3.2	41.1	7.9	9.2	11.3	3.2	49.2	10.5	7.0	14.0
2000	185.5	171.4	4.2	6.3	3.9	45.6	8.1	10.6	14.2	3.9	53.1	10.2	7.0	14.2
2001	206.1	191.0	5.0	7.2	3.8	51.3	7.8	11.8	16.1	4.0	59.1	11.1	9.0	15.1
2002	217.2	200.6	5.3	8.2	4.5	54.6	7.7	12.0	17.7	4.4	58.3	12.9	9.8	16.6
2003	224.0	206.1	5.4	8.2	5.4	56.8	7.8	11.2	17.4	6.6	58.0	13.7	10.2	17.9
2004	230.5	212.2	6.3	8.2	6.9	60.1	7.5	10.6	17.6	6.0	59.0	14.4	10.1	18.3
2005	244.7	227.0	6.7	7.4	8.0	64.7	8.5	10.5	17.9	7.1	64.8	15.0	10.9	17.7
2003														
January	223.3	205.9	5.4	8.3	4.9	54.2	7.6	12.3	17.5	6.9	60.8	12.8	10.1	17.3
February	221.1	203.4	5.5	8.6	5.3	53.0	7.7	11.4	18.3	6.7	58.7	13.2	10.4	17.6
March	215.4	199.0	5.2	8.2	5.2	55.0	7.8	11.4	17.3	6.9	54.8	12.6	10.2	16.4
April	218.3	199.8	5.1	8.0	5.0	54.6	7.6	11.6	17.8	6.6	55.5	12.9	9.9	18.5
May	221.6	202.9	5.4	7.8	5.2	56.8	7.7	12.4	17.7	6.1	55.1	13.3	10.1	18.8
June	227.0	208.4	5.5	7.8	5.4	57.9	7.8	11.6	18.1	7.3	56.8	13.6	10.3	18.6
July	226.9	208.8	5.5	8.8	5.3	58.7	8.1	11.1	17.3	6.3	57.2	13.6	10.3	18.1
August	229.4	210.8	5.7	8.6	5.5	58.2	7.9	10.7	17.5	7.1	58.6	14.0	10.8	18.5
September	228.3	210.0	5.6	8.6	5.6	57.0	7.9	10.4	17.6	5.5	61.6	14.1	10.2	18.4
October	230.3	211.6	5.5	8.1	5.6	58.4	8.4	10.6	17.2	7.6	59.8	14.3	10.2	18.7
November	224.5	207.4	5.4	8.1	5.8	58.6	8.0	10.8	16.8	5.7	58.6	14.5	10.4	17.1
December	219.2	202.7	5.4	7.7	5.7	57.9	7.8	10.1	15.8	5.5	57.4	14.7	10.2	16.5
2004														
January	220.8	203.5	5.5	7.7	6.0	56.9	7.3	11.7	16.7	5.3	56.7	14.4	10.7	17.3
February	217.4	200.9	5.5	8.0	6.0	57.0	7.2	10.8	16.6	4.9	55.2	14.2	10.4	16.5
March	230.0	211.7	5.8	8.6	6.3	59.4	7.4	10.6	17.6	4.8	61.0	14.4	10.8	18.3
April	232.0	212.7	6.2	8.2	6.7	59.2	7.5	10.9	17.5	5.3	61.2	14.4	10.5	19.4
May	231.4	212.3	6.6	8.2	6.7	60.0	7.5	10.9	16.8	5.5	59.8	15.3	9.9	19.1
June	233.8	215.9	6.6	8.1	7.1	62.5	7.5	10.7	16.9	6.5	60.5	14.2	10.0	17.9
July	235.6	217.1	6.8	8.2	7.1	61.9	7.6	10.8	18.3	6.1	59.0	14.9	10.9	18.6
August	232.5	213.5	6.7	8.3	7.1	60.8	7.7	10.6	17.9	6.7	57.8	14.5	10.1	19.1
September	229.7	210.6	6.6	8.3	6.9	60.9	7.4	10.7	17.6	7.5	54.8	14.0	10.1	19.2
October	228.3	212.3	6.0	8.3	7.1	60.0	7.3	10.2	18.5	6.1	59.0	14.5	9.5	16.0
November	235.8	217.3	6.5	8.2	7.3	60.0	7.7	9.9	18.4	7.2	62.9	14.3	9.5	18.6
December	232.9	214.2	6.5	8.4	8.1	60.3	7.8	10.0	18.2	5.9	60.8	13.9	9.7	18.7
2005														
January	231.4	213.9	6.4	8.1	7.5	60.2	8.1	9.8	18.0	7.4	60.4	13.6	9.8	17.5
February	236.8	218.8	7.0	8.0	7.4	60.5	8.0	10.0	17.8	6.6	65.5	13.7	9.8	18.0
March	239.1	221.3	6.7	8.0	7.6	63.0	7.9	10.1	17.6	7.0	64.4	13.4	10.6	17.8
April	238.2	222.2	6.9	7.7	8.0	65.0	8.0	9.7	17.6	6.2	62.4	14.2	11.1	16.0
May	245.6	229.4	6.9	7.0	8.8	66.2	8.2	10.8	16.8	9.0	63.6	15.0	11.3	16.2
June	248.4	230.2	6.9	7.3	7.9	67.0	8.7	10.5	17.1	8.6	64.3	15.0	11.0	18.2
July	245.8	227.7	6.6	7.2	8.1	65.7	8.2	10.8	17.5	7.7	64.1	15.5	10.7	18.1
August	247.6	229.4	6.7	6.8	8.2	65.0	8.5	10.7	18.3	7.1	65.5	15.1	11.6	18.2
September	244.7	227.3	6.2	6.8	8.3	63.4	9.4	10.2	18.4	6.8	65.4	15.2	11.2	17.4
October	248.5	229.6	7.0	7.0	8.4	65.2	9.1	10.6	18.2	6.3	65.4	15.6	11.2	18.9
November	251.7	233.5	7.0	7.4	8.2	66.8	9.3	10.7	18.2	5.8	66.9	15.9	11.4	18.3
December	254.3	235.5	6.9	7.3	7.8	68.2	8.7	11.4	18.1	6.5	67.0	16.6	11.0	18.7

[1]Includes categories not shown separately.
. . . = Not available.

Table 17-3. Housing Starts and Building Permits; New House Sales and Prices

Year and month	Housing starts and building permits										New house sales and prices			
	New private housing units (thousands)									Shipments of manufactured homes (thousands, seasonally adjusted annual rate)	Seasonally adjusted		Median sales price (dollars)	Price index (1996 = 100)
	Started (not seasonally adjusted)			Seasonally adjusted annual rate							Sold (thousands, annual rate)	For sale, end-of-period (thousands)		
				Started			Authorized by building permits [2]							
	Total [1]	One-family structures	Five units or more	Total [1]	One-family structures	Five units or more	Total [1]	One-family structures	Five units or more					
1959	1 517	1 234	. . .	1 517	1 234	. . .	1 208	938	193	120	. . .	. . .	. . .	. . .
1960	1 252	995	. . .	1 252	995	. . .	998	746	187	104	. . .	. . .	. . .	. . .
1961	1 313	974	. . .	1 313	974	. . .	1 064	723	274	90	. . .	. . .	. . .	. . .
1962	1 463	991	. . .	1 463	991	. . .	1 187	716	383	118	. . .	. . .	. . .	. . .
1963	1 603	1 012	. . .	1 603	1 012	. . .	1 335	750	466	151	560	264	18 000	17.8
1964	1 529	970	450	1 529	970	450	1 286	720	465	191	565	250	18 900	18.0
1965	1 473	964	422	1 473	964	422	1 241	710	446	216	575	226	20 000	18.3
1966	1 165	779	325	1 165	779	325	972	563	348	217	461	194	21 400	19.1
1967	1 292	844	376	1 292	844	376	1 141	651	418	240	487	187	22 700	19.6
1968	1 508	899	527	1 508	899	527	1 353	695	574	318	490	213	24 700	20.7
1969	1 467	811	571	1 467	811	571	1 322	625	612	413	448	222	25 600	22.2
1970	1 434	813	536	1 434	813	536	1 352	647	617	401	485	220	23 400	22.8
1971	2 052	1 151	781	2 052	1 151	781	1 925	906	886	492	656	287	25 200	24.1
1972	2 357	1 309	906	2 357	1 309	906	2 219	1 033	1 037	576	718	409	27 600	25.6
1973	2 045	1 132	795	2 045	1 132	795	1 820	882	820	580	634	418	32 500	27.9
1974	1 338	888	382	1 338	888	382	1 074	644	366	338	519	346	35 900	30.5
1975	1 160	892	204	1 160	892	204	939	676	200	213	549	313	39 300	33.7
1976	1 538	1 162	289	1 538	1 162	289	1 296	894	310	246	646	353	44 200	36.6
1977	1 987	1 451	414	1 987	1 451	414	1 690	1 126	443	266	819	402	48 800	41.3
1978	2 020	1 433	462	2 020	1 433	462	1 800	1 183	487	276	817	414	55 700	47.3
1979	1 745	1 194	429	1 745	1 194	429	1 552	982	445	277	709	397	62 900	54.0
1980	1 292	852	330	1 292	852	330	1 191	710	366	222	545	337	64 600	59.5
1981	1 084	705	288	1 084	705	288	986	564	319	241	436	275	68 900	64.2
1982	1 062	663	320	1 062	663	320	1 000	546	366	240	412	253	69 300	65.7
1983	1 703	1 068	522	1 703	1 068	522	1 605	902	570	296	623	301	75 300	67.1
1984	1 750	1 084	544	1 750	1 084	544	1 682	922	617	295	639	353	79 900	69.8
1985	1 742	1 072	576	1 742	1 072	576	1 733	957	657	284	688	346	84 300	70.7
1986	1 805	1 179	542	1 805	1 179	542	1 769	1 078	584	244	750	357	92 000	73.4
1987	1 620	1 146	409	1 620	1 146	409	1 535	1 024	421	233	671	366	104 500	77.4
1988	1 488	1 081	348	1 488	1 081	348	1 456	994	386	218	676	368	112 500	80.3
1989	1 376	1 003	318	1 376	1 003	318	1 338	932	340	198	650	365	120 000	83.5
1990	1 193	895	260	1 193	895	260	1 111	794	263	188	534	321	122 900	85.1
1991	1 014	840	138	1 014	840	138	949	754	152	171	509	284	120 000	86.2
1992	1 200	1 030	139	1 200	1 030	139	1 095	911	138	210	610	265	121 500	87.3
1993	1 288	1 126	133	1 288	1 126	133	1 199	986	160	254	666	293	126 500	91.1
1994	1 457	1 198	224	1 457	1 198	224	1 372	1 068	241	304	670	336	130 000	95.5
1995	1 354	1 076	244	1 354	1 076	244	1 332	997	272	340	667	370	133 900	98.2
1996	1 477	1 161	271	1 477	1 161	271	1 426	1 070	290	363	757	322	140 000	100.0
1997	1 474	1 134	296	1 474	1 134	296	1 441	1 062	310	354	804	281	146 000	102.9
1998	1 617	1 271	303	1 617	1 271	303	1 612	1 188	356	373	886	294	152 500	105.5
1999	1 641	1 302	307	1 641	1 302	307	1 664	1 247	351	348	880	308	161 000	110.7
2000	1 569	1 231	299	1 569	1 231	299	1 592	1 198	329	250	877	298	169 000	115.4
2001	1 603	1 273	293	1 603	1 273	293	1 637	1 236	335	193	908	308	175 200	119.5
2002	1 705	1 359	308	1 705	1 359	308	1 748	1 333	341	168	973	339	187 600	124.8
2003	1 848	1 499	315	1 848	1 499	315	1 889	1 461	346	131	1 086	370	195 000	131.9
2004	1 956	1 610	303	1 956	1 610	303	2 070	1 613	366	131	1 203	422	221 000	141.9
2005	2 068	1 716	311	2 068	1 716	311	2 155	1 682	389	147	1 283	509	240 900	153.1
2004														
January	124	100	23	1 911	1 560	322	1 952	1 539	320	122	1 165	374	209 500	. . .
February	126	102	22	1 846	1 481	336	1 966	1 564	315	123	1 159	372	219 600	139.6
March	174	144	28	1 998	1 632	334	2 066	1 648	318	133	1 276	381	209 600	. . .
April	180	150	26	2 003	1 646	320	2 070	1 617	359	129	1 186	383	222 300	. . .
May	188	159	24	1 981	1 652	272	2 150	1 675	386	129	1 241	383	211 700	141.6
June	172	147	23	1 828	1 526	276	2 020	1 615	322	129	1 180	383	215 700	. . .
July	182	152	24	2 002	1 675	263	2 112	1 620	386	129	1 088	400	212 400	. . .
August	186	155	24	2 024	1 691	266	2 056	1 609	364	127	1 175	405	218 100	142.9
September	164	132	29	1 905	1 555	319	2 041	1 586	375	134	1 214	410	211 600	. . .
October	181	143	34	2 072	1 660	370	2 097	1 593	417	136	1 305	413	229 200	. . .
November	138	111	24	1 782	1 458	285	2 079	1 572	415	135	1 179	418	224 500	146.6
December	140	115	21	2 042	1 714	281	2 082	1 613	379	133	1 242	422	229 600	. . .
2005														
January	143	114	25	2 137	1 736	355	2 144	1 651	414	148	1 193	440	223 100	. . .
February	149	121	24	2 213	1 796	365	2 121	1 636	396	137	1 252	446	237 300	148.9
March	156	133	20	1 856	1 578	244	2 084	1 600	404	128	1 324	446	229 300	. . .
April	185	152	29	2 079	1 680	351	2 177	1 671	430	131	1 270	445	236 300	. . .
May	198	170	24	2 034	1 717	280	2 111	1 669	360	128	1 311	450	228 300	153.6
June	193	163	27	2 078	1 724	316	2 188	1 690	412	129	1 272	455	226 100	. . .
July	188	158	26	2 070	1 740	294	2 206	1 722	385	127	1 367	464	229 200	. . .
August	192	159	30	2 075	1 713	319	2 205	1 706	412	125	1 271	477	240 100	154.0
September	188	154	28	2 158	1 790	310	2 240	1 778	375	137	1 253	487	240 400	. . .
October	180	151	27	2 046	1 726	287	2 131	1 717	333	192	1 346	490	243 900	. . .
November	161	133	24	2 131	1 795	298	2 191	1 716	394	208	1 236	500	237 900	156.1
December	136	108	26	2 002	1 633	338	2 107	1 642	381	182	1 259	509	238 600	. . .

[1]Includes structures with 2 to 4 units, not shown separately.
[2]Data beginning with 2004 cover 20,000 permit-issuing places; 1994 through 2003: 19,000 places; 1984 through 1993: 17,000 places; 1978 through 1983: 16,000 places; 1972 through 1977: 14,000 places; 1971: 13,000 places.
. . . = Not available.

Table 17-4. Manufacturers' Shipments

(Millions of dollars, adjusted for trading-day and calendar-month variation, but without seasonal adjustment.)

| Classification basis, year, and month | Total | NAICS durable goods industries | | Primary metals | | Fabricated metal products | Machinery | Computers and electronic products | Electrical equipment, appliances, and components | Transportation equipment | |
		Total ¹	Nonmetallic mineral products	Total	Iron and steel mills					Total	Motor vehicles and parts
SIC Basis ²											
1958	326 971	162 632	9 543	26 541	15 533	21 359		41 129		39 223	20 411
1959	363 437	187 168	11 052	31 381	18 251	23 723		47 386		45 502	26 239
1960	370 535	190 440	10 879	31 307	18 140	23 947		48 426		47 631	29 263
1961	371 067	187 217	10 782	30 610	17 196	23 701		49 376		44 221	25 222
1962	400 294	206 958	11 298	32 543	18 073	26 162		53 993		52 146	31 979
1963	420 690	219 058	12 000	34 398	18 954	26 847		56 450		56 379	35 328
1964	447 968	235 327	12 652	38 876	21 625	28 866		62 425		58 151	36 557
1965	491 938	266 318	13 652	43 975	23 965	32 378		71 268		68 213	45 162
1966	538 436	295 405	14 301	47 943	24 551	36 775		83 483		72 500	45 058
1967	557 836	302 795	14 116	45 139	23 123	40 054		86 946		72 535	40 337
1968	602 744	331 490	15 465	48 717	24 908	43 638		90 742		83 527	49 465
1969	642 013	352 836	16 499	53 534	26 412	46 104		98 144		85 175	50 943
1970	633 663	337 876	16 454	51 995	25 189	44 210		98 301		74 539	42 538
1971	670 877	359 089	18 220	51 585	25 791	45 478		98 822		88 857	58 247
1972	756 321	407 844	20 875	58 490	28 712	51 487		113 658		94 706	63 923
1973	875 173	475 621	23 141	72 791	36 301	58 804		132 776		110 587	74 799
1974	1 017 477	530 074	25 503	95 686	49 718	67 212		151 725		108 244	68 631
1975	1 039 065	523 178	26 233	80 890	42 281	68 411		152 422		113 503	70 033
1976	1 185 563	607 475	29 618	93 082	46 764	77 560		170 998		141 028	95 380
1977	1 358 416	710 017	34 209	103 267	50 670	89 938		200 594		166 954	117 747
1978	1 522 858	812 776	40 238	118 175	59 228	101 245		232 598		188 773	131 999
1979	1 727 234	911 124	44 287	137 488	67 414	113 494		269 375		201 623	131 378
1980	1 852 689	929 027	44 473	134 057	61 612	116 071		293 428		186 516	104 560
1981	2 017 544	1 004 725	46 220	142 072	70 254	123 535		323 186		205 223	116 981
1982	1 960 214	950 541	43 515	104 874	46 928	119 236		312 501		201 347	112 270
1983	2 070 564	1 025 770	47 697	109 240	46 398	123 083		314 584		245 392	148 296
1984	2 288 184	1 175 276	53 101	120 315	51 978	138 107		373 437		284 523	181 993
1985	2 334 456	1 215 352	55 821	112 265	48 904	143 268		382 359		307 380	193 445
1986	2 335 881	1 238 859	59 254	107 865	45 718	143 063		378 385		322 688	198 811
1987	2 475 906	1 297 532	61 477	120 248	51 815	147 367		388 958		332 936	205 923
1988	2 695 432	1 421 501	63 145	149 837	64 294	159 505		431 666		354 849	222 353
1989	2 840 375	1 477 900	63 729	155 718	64 783	164 073		450 810		369 675	233 232
1990	2 912 228	1 485 313	63 728	148 787	62 826	165 064		455 265		370 328	217 295
1991	2 878 167	1 451 998	59 957	136 378	57 267	159 760		446 786		367 235	209 210
1992	3 004 727	1 541 866	62 521	138 287	58 449	166 532		475 426		399 270	238 384
NAICS Basis											
1992	2 904 024	1 518 862	61 902	123 789	55 947	170 403	186 589	273 728	81 813	433 611	279 197
1993	3 020 497	1 604 544	64 957	126 988	59 632	177 967	201 076	286 457	87 646	453 437	310 178
1994	3 238 112	1 764 061	70 598	142 976	67 087	194 113	224 920	320 769	95 531	494 745	364 840
1995	3 479 677	1 902 815	74 865	160 774	72 019	212 444	246 277	370 679	101 051	508 271	379 551
1996	3 597 188	1 978 597	81 308	157 638	71 814	222 995	257 459	399 516	105 283	516 030	387 394
1997	3 834 699	2 147 384	86 465	168 118	76 900	242 812	270 687	439 380	112 116	575 307	421 573
1998	3 899 813	2 231 588	92 501	166 109	75 871	253 720	280 651	443 768	116 024	612 882	439 590
1999	4 031 887	2 326 736	96 153	156 648	70 087	257 071	276 904	467 059	118 313	676 328	498 716
2000	4 208 584	2 373 688	97 329	156 598	70 470	268 213	291 548	510 639	125 443	639 861	471 180
2001	4 022 901	2 203 102	94 460	137 469	60 803	258 918	268 457	434 427	116 919	613 837	439 905
2002	3 965 245	2 168 434	93 755	137 789	62 737	257 475	256 215	391 274	105 393	634 614	463 808
2003	3 972 114	2 130 238	96 349	136 839	61 175	244 662	253 600	353 667	101 770	645 759	485 921
2004	4 259 207	2 251 915	101 870	178 996	92 693	259 874	269 203	361 938	104 244	659 930	494 622
2005	4 544 839	2 385 367	112 321	194 247	96 789	275 301	295 315	394 644	112 096	666 790	481 835
2004											
January	308 683	159 913	7 054	12 294	5 720	18 490	18 545	25 439	7 283	48 297	38 119
February	328 449	177 144	7 131	13 091	6 147	19 602	19 644	27 572	7 976	58 000	43 640
March	376 085	208 119	8 556	15 257	7 335	22 907	25 330	33 127	9 270	66 254	50 264
April	347 512	184 752	8 715	14 776	7 350	21 465	23 160	27 106	8 387	55 305	43 185
May	353 637	185 597	8 496	14 718	7 484	21 862	22 000	27 873	8 594	55 870	41 682
June	376 859	203 499	9 027	15 718	8 287	22 956	24 815	33 063	9 341	60 325	44 509
July	328 841	163 381	8 748	14 415	7 847	20 994	21 547	26 633	8 094	38 045	26 492
August	367 620	192 013	9 390	16 206	8 770	23 063	21 717	29 157	8 915	56 024	42 364
September	376 301	202 874	8 992	16 275	8 791	23 239	24 025	34 053	9 711	58 823	43 453
October	371 527	192 976	9 107	16 057	8 595	22 625	23 037	30 091	8 678	56 626	43 293
November	360 308	186 583	8 683	15 362	8 280	21 790	21 048	31 126	8 929	52 903	39 441
December	363 385	195 064	7 971	14 827	8 087	20 881	24 335	36 698	9 066	53 458	38 180
2005											
January	337 367	174 035	7 878	16 131	8 523	20 557	21 496	27 883	7 888	47 888	36 757
February	348 981	185 001	7 950	16 160	8 506	21 393	22 424	29 117	8 488	53 665	40 824
March	394 746	211 365	9 228	17 656	9 183	23 530	26 445	36 350	9 500	59 675	42 759
April	372 036	194 694	9 373	16 666	8 484	22 919	25 120	29 277	8 855	55 213	40 813
May	380 690	198 370	9 675	16 351	8 241	23 580	24 718	30 338	9 187	56 788	41 952
June	400 071	214 937	9 994	16 381	7 987	24 426	26 614	36 784	9 960	61 015	43 976
July	345 443	169 094	9 266	14 031	6 721	21 237	22 681	28 393	8 526	38 810	26 362
August	395 980	204 570	10 382	16 433	7 877	24 416	24 371	32 329	9 807	58 191	43 655
September	403 254	215 367	10 021	16 642	8 024	24 376	25 831	37 806	10 566	60 661	45 387
October	394 000	206 589	10 187	16 848	8 017	24 121	25 159	32 541	9 788	59 105	44 462
November	382 519	199 737	9 650	15 938	7 658	22 756	23 813	33 031	9 834	55 966	38 311
December	389 752	211 608	8 717	15 010	7 568	21 990	26 643	40 795	9 697	59 813	36 577

¹Includes categories not shown separately.
²Data are for SIC industries roughly similar to the NAICS industries indicated in the column headings.

Table 17-4. Manufacturers' Shipments—Continued

(Millions of dollars, adjusted for trading-day and calendar-month variation, but without seasonal adjustment.)

Classification basis, year, and month	Total [1]	Food products	Beverage and tobacco products [3]	Textiles	Textile products	Apparel	Paper products	Chemical products	Petroleum and coal products	Plastics and rubber products
SIC Basis [2]										
1958	164 339	59 738	3 868	12 417		...	12 707	23 093	15 188	7 310
1959	176 269	60 781	4 049	14 067		...	14 077	26 358	15 806	8 395
1960	180 095	62 468	4 367	13 791		...	14 308	26 509	16 349	8 483
1961	183 850	64 542	4 487	14 016		...	14 524	27 175	16 359	8 511
1962	193 336	66 935	4 531	15 185		...	15 382	29 266	16 716	9 335
1963	201 632	68 469	4 521	15 744		...	16 192	31 682	17 506	10 076
1964	212 641	71 594	4 653	17 000		...	17 019	34 148	17 855	10 749
1965	225 620	74 250	4 649	18 299		...	18 394	37 289	18 588	11 966
1966	243 031	79 665	4 772	19 600		...	20 211	40 569	19 857	13 181
1967	255 041	83 961	4 903	19 816		...	20 777	42 037	21 435	13 908
1968	271 254	87 328	4 937	21 970		...	22 093	45 491	22 548	15 585
1969	289 177	93 385	4 992	22 978		...	24 188	48 096	23 721	16 935
1970	295 787	98 535	5 350	22 614		...	24 573	49 195	24 200	16 754
1971	311 788	103 637	5 528	24 034		...	25 182	51 681	26 198	18 409
1972	348 477	115 054	5 919	28 065		...	28 004	58 130	27 918	21 662
1973	399 552	135 585	6 341	31 073		...	32 495	66 003	33 903	25 191
1974	487 403	161 884	7 139	32 790		...	41 514	85 387	57 229	28 828
1975	515 887	172 054	8 058	31 065		...	41 497	91 710	67 496	28 128
1976	578 088	180 830	8 786	36 387		...	47 939	106 467	80 022	32 880
1977	648 399	192 913	9 051	40 550		...	51 881	120 905	94 702	40 944
1978	710 082	215 989	9 951	42 281		...	56 777	132 262	100 967	44 823
1979	816 110	235 976	10 602	45 137		...	64 957	151 887	144 156	48 694
1980	923 662	256 191	12 194	47 256		...	72 553	168 220	192 969	49 157
1981	1 012 819	272 140	13 130	50 260		...	79 970	186 909	217 681	55 178
1982	1 009 673	280 529	16 061	47 516		...	79 698	176 254	203 404	57 307
1983	1 044 794	289 314	16 268	53 733		...	84 817	189 552	187 788	62 870
1984	1 112 908	304 584	17 473	56 336		...	95 525	205 963	184 488	72 938
1985	1 119 104	308 606	18 559	54 605		...	94 679	204 790	176 574	75 590
1986	1 097 022	318 203	19 146	57 188		...	99 865	205 711	122 605	78 379
1987	1 178 374	329 725	20 757	62 787		...	108 989	229 546	130 414	86 634
1988	1 273 931	354 084	23 809	64 627		...	122 882	261 238	131 682	95 485
1989	1 362 475	380 160	25 875	67 265		...	131 896	283 196	146 487	101 236
1990	1 426 915	391 728	29 856	65 533		...	132 424	292 802	173 389	105 250
1991	1 426 169	397 893	31 943	65 440		...	130 131	298 545	159 144	105 804
1992	1 462 861	406 964	35 198	70 753		...	133 201	305 420	150 227	113 593
NAICS Basis										
1992	1 385 162	358 494	85 687	52 923	24 763	61 535	127 122	319 501	150 095	113 827
1993	1 415 953	373 612	79 227	55 375	25 623	63 210	126 982	330 760	144 731	122 807
1994	1 474 051	379 786	83 434	58 607	27 233	64 894	136 922	350 098	143 339	134 288
1995	1 576 862	393 204	88 945	59 885	27 976	65 214	166 051	376 995	151 431	145 084
1996	1 618 591	404 173	94 033	59 796	28 515	64 237	152 860	385 919	174 181	149 773
1997	1 687 315	421 737	96 971	58 707	31 052	68 018	150 296	415 617	177 394	159 161
1998	1 668 225	428 479	102 359	57 416	31 137	64 932	154 984	416 742	137 957	163 736
1999	1 705 151	426 001	106 920	54 306	32 689	62 305	156 915	420 321	162 620	171 885
2000	1 834 896	435 229	111 692	52 112	33 654	60 339	165 298	449 159	235 134	178 236
2001	1 819 799	456 692	117 422	45 141	34 165	56 545	159 150	442 790	222 356	178 127
2002	1 796 811	467 353	104 579	43 152	34 933	53 201	157 834	441 494	211 910	177 592
2003	1 841 876	482 815	106 873	42 557	30 827	40 624	149 271	477 360	237 010	176 345
2004	2 007 292	511 450	112 270	40 258	33 254	33 495	153 969	528 215	312 884	182 547
2005	2 159 472	532 496	114 800	36 012	34 326	33 879	158 053	553 657	404 591	196 206
2004										
January	148 770	38 786	8 069	3 137	2 465	2 526	12 265	39 499	20 807	13 734
February	151 305	39 428	8 287	3 468	2 743	2 926	12 057	39 971	20 853	13 861
March	167 966	41 376	9 722	3 589	2 855	2 977	12 892	46 500	23 382	16 229
April	162 760	41 133	9 279	3 418	2 749	2 586	12 307	43 360	24 458	15 551
May	168 040	42 094	9 864	3 472	2 752	2 677	12 586	43 975	27 290	15 427
June	173 360	42 978	10 383	3 487	2 898	2 724	13 691	46 181	26 303	16 250
July	165 460	41 132	9 595	3 150	2 814	2 774	12 810	43 070	27 456	14 768
August	175 607	44 607	9 997	3 450	3 000	2 952	13 482	45 050	28 698	15 940
September	173 427	44 646	9 624	3 558	2 818	2 883	13 116	44 749	27 600	15 665
October	178 551	46 201	9 338	3 378	2 919	3 121	13 030	45 920	30 049	15 729
November	173 725	45 533	9 109	3 144	2 782	2 923	12 811	45 478	28 463	14 872
December	168 321	43 536	9 003	3 007	2 459	2 426	12 922	44 462	27 525	14 521
2005										
January	163 332	42 117	8 191	2 974	2 540	2 446	12 964	43 338	26 286	14 748
February	163 980	42 474	8 354	3 235	2 762	2 762	12 797	42 813	25 952	15 148
March	183 381	44 625	9 038	3 240	2 881	2 728	13 748	49 441	32 333	16 946
April	177 342	42 080	9 343	3 207	2 877	2 505	13 142	47 235	32 561	16 541
May	182 320	44 680	10 388	3 159	2 819	2 637	13 618	47 158	33 103	16 926
June	185 134	45 177	10 368	3 311	2 971	2 898	14 047	47 014	34 233	17 133
July	176 349	42 271	9 903	2 798	2 864	2 830	12 749	44 313	35 866	15 352
August	191 410	45 340	10 683	2 978	3 041	3 013	13 307	47 929	39 775	17 262
September	187 887	46 057	9 664	2 910	3 086	2 933	12 717	45 847	39 333	17 040
October	187 411	46 179	9 681	2 860	3 025	3 179	13 032	46 056	37 786	17 212
November	182 782	46 522	9 649	2 762	2 908	3 244	12 947	47 105	33 061	16 548
December	178 144	44 974	9 538	2 578	2 552	2 704	12 985	45 408	34 302	15 350

[1]Includes categories not shown separately.
[2]Data are for SIC industries roughly similar to the NAICS industries indicated in the column headings.
[3]SIC tobacco only, 1958–1992.
. . . = Not available.

Table 17-4. Manufacturers' Shipments—Continued

(Millions of dollars, seasonally adjusted.)

Classification basis, year, and month	Total	NAICS durable goods industries										
		Total¹	Nonmetallic mineral products	Primary metals		Fabricated metal products	Machinery	Computers and electronic products	Electrical equipment, appliances, and components	Transportation equipment	
				Total	Iron and steel mills					Total	Motor vehicles and parts
SIC Basis²											
1958	326 971	162 632	9 543	26 541	15 533	21 359		41 129		39 223	20 411
1959	363 437	187 168	11 052	31 381	18 251	23 723		47 386		45 502	26 239
1960	370 535	190 440	10 879	31 307	18 140	23 947		48 426		47 631	29 263
1961	371 067	187 217	10 782	30 610	17 196	23 701		49 376		44 221	25 222
1962	400 294	206 958	11 298	32 543	18 073	26 162		53 993		52 146	31 979
1963	420 690	219 058	12 000	34 398	18 954	26 847		56 450		56 379	35 328
1964	447 968	235 327	12 652	38 876	21 625	28 866		62 425		58 151	36 557
1965	491 938	266 318	13 652	43 975	23 965	32 378		71 268		68 213	45 162
1966	538 436	295 405	14 301	47 943	24 551	36 775		83 483		72 500	45 058
1967	557 836	302 795	14 116	45 139	23 123	40 054		86 946		72 535	40 337
1968	602 744	331 490	15 465	48 717	24 908	43 638		90 742		83 527	49 465
1969	642 013	352 836	16 499	53 534	26 412	46 104		98 144		85 175	50 943
1970	633 663	337 876	16 454	51 995	25 189	44 210		98 301		74 539	42 538
1971	670 877	359 089	18 220	51 585	25 791	45 478		98 822		88 857	58 247
1972	756 321	407 844	20 875	58 490	28 712	51 487		113 658		94 706	63 923
1973	875 173	475 621	23 141	72 791	36 301	58 804		132 776		110 587	74 799
1974	1 017 477	530 074	25 503	95 686	49 718	67 212		151 725		108 244	68 631
1975	1 039 065	523 178	26 233	80 890	42 281	68 411		152 422		113 503	70 033
1976	1 185 563	607 475	29 618	93 082	46 764	77 560		170 998		141 028	95 380
1977	1 358 416	710 017	34 209	103 267	50 670	89 938		200 594		166 954	117 747
1978	1 522 858	812 776	40 238	118 175	59 228	101 245		232 598		188 773	131 999
1979	1 727 234	911 124	44 287	137 488	67 414	113 494		269 375		201 623	131 378
1980	1 852 689	929 027	44 473	134 057	61 612	116 071		293 428		186 516	104 560
1981	2 017 544	1 004 725	46 220	142 072	70 254	123 535		323 186		205 223	116 981
1982	1 960 214	950 541	43 515	104 874	46 928	119 236		312 501		201 347	112 270
1983	2 070 564	1 025 770	47 697	109 240	46 398	123 083		314 584		245 392	148 296
1984	2 288 184	1 175 276	53 101	120 315	51 978	138 107		373 437		284 593	181 993
1985	2 334 456	1 215 352	55 821	112 265	48 904	143 268		382 359		307 380	193 445
1986	2 335 881	1 238 859	59 254	107 865	45 718	143 063		378 385		322 688	198 811
1987	2 475 906	1 297 532	61 477	120 248	51 815	147 367		388 958		332 936	205 923
1988	2 695 432	1 421 501	63 145	149 837	64 294	159 505		431 666		354 849	222 353
1989	2 840 375	1 477 900	63 729	155 718	64 783	164 073		450 810		369 675	233 232
1990	2 912 228	1 485 313	63 728	148 787	62 826	165 064		455 265		370 328	217 295
1991	2 878 167	1 451 998	59 957	136 378	57 267	159 760		446 786		367 235	209 210
1992	3 004 727	1 541 866	62 521	138 287	58 449	166 532		475 426		399 270	238 384
NAICS Basis											
1992	2 904 024	1 518 862	61 902	123 789	55 947	170 403	186 589	273 728	81 813	433 611	279 197
1993	3 020 497	1 604 544	64 957	126 988	59 632	177 967	201 076	286 457	87 646	453 437	310 178
1994	3 238 112	1 764 061	70 598	142 976	67 087	194 113	224 920	320 769	95 531	494 745	364 840
1995	3 479 677	1 902 815	74 865	160 774	72 019	212 444	246 277	370 679	101 051	508 271	379 551
1996	3 597 188	1 978 597	81 308	157 638	71 814	222 995	257 459	399 516	105 283	516 030	387 394
1997	3 834 699	2 147 384	86 465	168 118	76 900	242 812	270 687	439 380	112 116	575 307	421 573
1998	3 899 813	2 231 588	92 501	166 109	75 871	253 720	280 651	443 768	116 024	612 882	439 590
1999	4 031 887	2 326 736	96 153	156 648	70 087	257 071	276 904	467 059	118 313	676 328	498 716
2000	4 208 584	2 373 688	97 329	156 598	70 470	268 213	291 548	510 639	125 443	639 861	471 180
2001	4 022 901	2 203 102	94 460	137 469	60 803	258 918	268 457	434 427	116 919	613 837	439 905
2002	3 965 245	2 168 434	93 755	137 789	62 737	257 475	256 215	391 274	105 393	634 614	463 808
2003	3 972 114	2 130 238	96 349	136 839	61 175	244 662	253 600	353 667	101 770	645 759	485 921
2004	4 259 207	2 251 915	101 870	178 996	92 693	259 874	269 203	361 938	104 244	659 930	494 622
2005	4 544 839	2 385 367	112 321	194 247	96 789	275 301	295 315	394 644	112 096	666 790	481 835
2004											
January	336 614	178 236	7 818	12 431	5 813	20 133	20 702	29 639	8 341	53 960	40 884
February	335 410	179 773	7 789	12 869	6 073	20 010	20 297	29 096	8 337	56 503	42 059
March	350 352	188 150	8 493	14 020	6 757	21 628	22 377	28 980	8 553	58 250	44 304
April	349 784	186 081	8 449	14 216	7 063	21 495	22 162	30 009	8 713	54 848	41 742
May	350 536	184 518	8 270	14 408	7 326	21 442	21 430	29 754	8 623	54 303	40 213
June	353 807	186 524	8 438	15 030	7 896	21 590	22 620	28 911	8 607	55 001	41 146
July	355 115	185 961	8 608	15 640	8 462	21 992	22 820	30 420	8 873	51 533	37 965
August	361 169	190 231	8 642	15 880	8 587	22 001	22 474	30 646	8 800	54 933	40 746
September	357 564	189 202	8 572	16 000	8 628	22 144	23 283	29 860	8 729	54 156	40 337
October	362 961	189 305	8 626	15 676	8 470	21 851	23 309	31 113	8 715	53 790	39 636
November	365 335	190 644	8 839	16 075	8 672	22 430	22 747	31 290	8 831	53 849	40 436
December	366 981	194 544	8 958	16 589	8 929	22 402	24 208	31 201	8 846	54 808	41 656
2005											
January	370 898	195 828	8 857	16 529	8 769	22 495	24 068	32 546	8 996	54 885	40 749
February	366 998	193 084	8 915	16 263	8 569	22 472	23 775	31 725	9 130	53 386	40 009
March	373 656	194 324	9 157	16 337	8 517	22 676	23 789	31 862	9 000	53 854	39 229
April	372 619	195 263	9 193	16 130	8 276	22 688	23 662	32 548	9 042	54 402	38 892
May	376 001	196 826	9 284	15 808	7 936	22 931	24 225	32 533	9 199	55 111	40 202
June	374 870	196 360	9 345	15 720	7 647	22 992	24 173	32 211	9 254	54 831	40 213
July	375 769	195 197	9 292	15 467	7 382	22 494	24 290	32 519	9 366	54 004	39 403
August	384 246	200 373	9 450	15 906	7 614	23 049	24 884	33 687	9 517	56 148	40 858
September	383 109	200 206	9 557	16 288	7 837	23 245	25 015	32 948	9 540	55 514	41 486
October	385 959	203 274	9 699	16 517	7 913	23 317	25 456	33 506	9 773	56 629	40 868
November	387 360	204 068	9 799	16 665	8 017	23 410	25 783	33 561	9 717	56 552	39 371
December	394 485	210 500	9 908	17 062	8 478	23 855	26 551	34 709	9 634	60 042	40 624

¹Includes categories not shown separately.
²Data are for SIC industries roughly similar to the NAICS industries indicated in the column headings.

Table 17-4. Manufacturers' Shipments—Continued

(Millions of dollars, seasonally adjusted.)

Classification basis, year, and month	Total [1]	Food products	Beverage and tobacco products [3]	Textiles	Textile products	Apparel	Paper products	Chemical products	Petroleum and coal products	Plastics and rubber products
SIC Basis [2]										
1958	164 339	59 738	3 868	12 417		...	12 707	23 093	15 188	7 310
1959	176 269	60 781	4 049	14 067		...	14 077	26 358	15 806	8 395
1960	180 095	62 468	4 367	13 791		...	14 308	26 509	16 349	8 483
1961	183 850	64 542	4 487	14 016		...	14 524	27 175	16 359	8 511
1962	193 336	66 935	4 531	15 185		...	15 382	29 266	16 716	9 335
1963	201 632	68 469	4 521	15 744		...	16 192	31 682	17 506	10 076
1964	212 641	71 594	4 653	17 000		...	17 019	34 148	17 855	10 749
1965	225 620	74 250	4 649	18 299		...	18 394	37 289	18 588	11 966
1966	243 031	79 665	4 772	19 600		...	20 211	40 569	19 857	13 181
1967	255 041	83 961	4 903	19 816		...	20 777	42 037	21 435	13 908
1968	271 254	87 328	4 937	21 970		...	22 093	45 491	22 548	15 585
1969	289 177	93 385	4 992	22 978		...	24 188	48 096	23 721	16 935
1970	295 787	98 535	5 350	22 614		...	24 573	49 195	24 200	16 754
1971	311 788	103 637	5 528	24 034		...	25 182	51 681	26 198	18 409
1972	348 477	115 054	5 919	28 065		...	28 004	58 130	27 918	21 662
1973	399 552	135 585	6 341	31 073		...	32 495	66 003	33 903	25 191
1974	487 403	161 884	7 139	32 790		...	41 514	85 387	57 229	28 828
1975	515 887	172 054	8 058	31 065		...	41 497	91 710	67 496	28 128
1976	578 088	180 830	8 786	36 387		...	47 939	106 467	80 022	32 880
1977	648 399	192 913	9 051	40 550		...	51 881	120 905	94 702	40 944
1978	710 082	215 989	9 951	42 281		...	56 777	132 262	100 967	44 823
1979	816 110	235 976	10 602	45 137		...	64 957	151 887	144 156	48 694
1980	923 662	256 191	12 194	47 256		...	72 553	168 220	192 969	49 157
1981	1 012 819	272 140	13 130	50 260		...	79 970	186 909	217 681	55 178
1982	1 009 673	280 529	16 061	47 516		...	79 698	176 254	203 404	57 307
1983	1 044 794	289 314	16 268	53 733		...	84 817	189 552	187 788	62 870
1984	1 112 908	304 584	17 473	56 336		...	95 525	205 963	184 488	72 938
1985	1 119 104	308 606	18 559	54 605		...	94 679	204 790	176 574	75 590
1986	1 097 022	318 203	19 146	57 188		...	99 865	205 711	122 605	78 379
1987	1 178 374	329 725	20 757	62 787		...	108 989	229 546	130 414	86 634
1988	1 273 931	354 084	23 809	64 627		...	122 882	261 238	131 682	95 485
1989	1 362 475	380 160	25 875	67 265		...	131 896	283 196	146 487	101 236
1990	1 426 915	391 728	29 856	65 533		...	132 424	292 802	173 389	105 250
1991	1 426 169	397 893	31 943	65 440		...	130 131	298 545	159 144	105 804
1992	1 462 861	406 964	35 198	70 753		...	133 201	305 420	150 227	113 593
NAICS Basis										
1992	1 385 162	358 494	85 687	52 923	24 763	61 535	127 122	319 501	150 095	113 827
1993	1 415 923	373 612	79 227	55 375	25 623	63 210	126 982	330 760	144 731	122 807
1994	1 474 051	379 786	83 434	58 607	27 233	64 894	136 922	350 098	143 339	134 288
1995	1 576 862	393 204	88 945	59 885	27 976	65 214	166 051	376 995	151 431	145 084
1996	1 618 591	404 173	94 033	59 796	28 515	64 237	152 860	385 919	174 181	149 773
1997	1 687 315	421 737	96 971	58 707	31 052	68 018	150 296	415 617	177 394	159 161
1998	1 668 225	428 479	102 359	57 416	31 137	64 932	154 984	416 742	137 957	163 736
1999	1 705 151	426 001	106 920	54 306	32 689	62 305	156 915	420 321	162 620	171 885
2000	1 834 896	435 229	111 692	52 112	33 654	60 339	165 298	449 159	235 134	178 236
2001	1 819 799	456 692	117 422	45 141	34 165	56 545	159 150	442 790	222 356	178 127
2002	1 796 811	467 353	104 579	43 152	34 933	53 201	157 834	441 494	211 910	177 592
2003	1 841 876	482 815	106 873	42 557	30 827	40 624	149 271	477 360	237 010	176 345
2004	2 007 292	511 450	112 270	40 258	33 254	33 495	153 969	528 215	312 884	182 547
2005	2 159 472	532 496	114 800	36 012	34 326	33 879	158 053	553 657	404 591	196 206
2004										
January	158 378	40 668	8 952	3 469	2 785	2 920	12 608	41 326	22 924	14 672
February	155 637	39 653	8 783	3 365	2 701	2 789	12 290	41 201	22 838	14 049
March	162 202	40 496	9 774	3 379	2 758	2 887	12 458	42 939	24 148	15 181
April	163 703	42 385	9 292	3 446	2 711	2 841	12 524	42 959	24 291	15 082
May	166 018	42 384	9 253	3 414	2 730	2 842	12 569	43 785	25 913	14 941
June	167 283	42 557	9 795	3 276	2 742	2 659	13 092	44 093	25 212	15 372
July	169 154	43 260	9 264	3 435	2 782	2 742	12 954	44 829	26 137	15 347
August	170 938	43 920	9 551	3 315	2 795	2 706	13 192	45 217	26 597	15 461
September	168 362	43 277	9 478	3 329	2 706	2 735	12 978	43 991	26 182	15 339
October	173 656	44 177	9 366	3 271	2 805	2 771	12 918	45 869	28 891	15 315
November	174 691	44 154	9 299	3 240	2 814	2 732	12 991	45 934	29 783	15 476
December	172 437	43 180	9 260	3 279	2 840	2 807	13 022	45 192	28 766	15 838
2005										
January	175 070	44 238	9 107	3 252	2 861	2 826	13 395	45 871	29 292	15 895
February	173 914	44 242	9 016	3 238	2 828	2 755	13 426	45 332	29 080	15 826
March	179 332	43 475	9 152	3 101	2 817	2 740	13 460	45 879	34 437	16 124
April	177 356	43 931	9 322	3 165	2 810	2 673	13 381	46 453	31 571	15 944
May	179 175	44 765	9 785	3 143	2 817	2 781	13 457	46 377	31 793	16 205
June	178 510	44 688	9 781	3 123	2 821	2 825	13 376	45 053	32 609	16 242
July	180 572	44 308	9 611	3 036	2 835	2 785	13 036	46 396	34 529	16 152
August	183 873	44 443	10 122	2 829	2 866	2 788	12 864	47 524	36 119	16 441
September	182 903	44 709	9 515	2 739	2 932	2 796	12 610	45 470	37 513	16 759
October	182 685	44 247	9 704	2 792	2 904	2 852	12 951	46 297	36 264	16 809
November	183 292	44 940	9 841	2 832	2 942	3 002	13 130	47 335	34 396	17 105
December	183 985	44 874	9 814	2 816	2 908	3 094	13 209	46 525	36 144	16 989

[1]Includes categories not shown separately.
[2]Data are for SIC industries roughly similar to the NAICS industries indicated in the column headings.
[3]SIC tobacco only, 1958–1992.
... = Not available.

Table 17-4. Manufacturers' Shipments—Continued

(Millions of dollars, seasonally adjusted.)

Classification basis, year, and month	Construction materials and supplies	Information technology industries	By topical categories						
			Capital goods				Consumer goods		
			Total	Nondefense		Defense	Total	Durable	Nondurable
				Total	Excluding aircraft and parts				
SIC Basis [2]									
1958	23 286	...	46 552	...	...	...	...	...	...
1959	26 278	...	51 234	...	...	...	...	...	...
1960	25 886	...	52 171	...	...	...	...	...	...
1961	25 498	...	53 762	...	...	...	...	...	...
1962	27 019	...	58 711	...	...	...	...	...	...
1963	28 545	...	61 186	...	...	...	...	...	...
1964	30 692	...	64 837	...	...	...	...	...	...
1965	33 287	...	71 621	...	...	...	...	...	...
1966	35 643	...	84 792	...	...	...	...	...	...
1967	36 210	...	94 101	...	...	...	...	...	...
1968	39 621	...	99 702	72 405	...	27 297	...	...	...
1969	42 493	...	105 773	79 568	...	26 205	...	...	...
1970	41 945	...	102 285	78 907	...	23 378	...	...	...
1971	45 559	...	98 643	79 148	...	19 495	...	...	...
1972	54 119	...	107 198	87 762	...	19 436	...	...	...
1973	62 228	...	124 912	103 997	...	20 915	...	...	...
1974	69 146	...	143 828	122 674	...	21 154	...	...	...
1975	66 984	...	149 687	126 363	...	23 324	...	...	...
1976	77 948	...	162 172	135 540	...	26 632	...	...	...
1977	91 883	...	185 541	155 956	...	29 585	...	...	...
1978	106 017	...	217 165	186 427	...	30 738	...	...	...
1979	118 024	...	254 754	222 069	...	32 685	...	...	...
1980	118 429	...	287 132	246 797	...	40 335	...	...	...
1981	122 844	...	317 628	269 774	...	47 854	...	...	...
1982	115 777	...	312 298	252 098	...	60 200	...	...	...
1983	127 781	...	316 125	242 297	...	73 828	...	...	...
1984	141 230	...	361 205	278 900	...	82 305	...	...	...
1985	147 103	...	388 763	293 420	...	95 343	...	...	...
1986	154 113	...	396 158	289 969	...	106 189	...	...	...
1987	164 865	...	404 738	295 334	...	109 404	...	...	...
1988	175 594	...	438 089	333 402	...	104 687	...	...	...
1989	180 083	...	450 863	350 870	...	99 993	...	...	...
1990	180 604	...	473 175	370 804	...	102 371	...	...	...
1991	171 876	...	467 419	369 796	...	97 623	...	...	...
1992	184 498	...	481 257	389 448	...	91 809	...	...	...
NAICS Basis									
1992	281 232	236 015	566 268	471 485	435 696	94 783	1 098 480	253 111	845 369
1993	303 391	241 680	580 859	493 875	463 753	86 984	1 127 629	274 813	852 816
1994	332 734	264 092	616 435	538 203	512 327	78 232	1 192 098	314 931	877 167
1995	353 198	291 885	666 167	590 578	565 729	75 589	1 256 611	324 036	932 575
1996	371 401	311 028	704 635	630 932	605 295	73 703	1 292 955	328 402	964 553
1997	399 880	349 846	779 232	702 971	665 074	76 261	1 358 516	360 193	998 323
1998	418 756	362 564	821 736	747 046	695 717	74 690	1 351 812	373 404	978 408
1999	434 138	374 384	839 754	768 799	713 042	70 955	1 424 828	412 646	1 012 182
2000	444 812	399 751	875 396	808 345	757 617	67 051	1 500 532	391 463	1 109 069
2001	430 226	357 327	804 226	731 280	680 413	72 946	1 499 818	377 514	1 122 304
2002	432 419	314 988	752 898	674 464	633 454	78 434	1 499 041	395 817	1 103 224
2003	426 625	277 281	715 491	631 666	600 469	83 825	1 560 671	416 418	1 144 253
2004	459 478	283 889	746 038	654 931	624 559	91 107	1 679 985	419 372	1 260 613
2005	488 096	307 279	821 519	730 842	683 934	90 677	1 793 004	422 668	1 370 336
2004									
January	35 182	23 177	59 129	51 740	49 612	7 389	133 888	34 521	99 367
February	35 144	22 746	59 894	51 242	48 866	8 652	133 154	35 582	97 572
March	38 336	22 892	61 210	53 719	51 023	7 491	138 422	37 285	101 137
April	38 566	23 730	61 405	53 918	51 721	7 487	137 801	35 117	102 684
May	38 297	23 215	60 908	53 139	50 452	7 769	138 662	33 883	104 779
June	38 102	22 718	61 284	54 056	51 655	7 228	139 891	34 681	105 210
July	38 586	23 788	62 314	54 696	52 513	7 618	137 654	31 253	106 401
August	39 333	24 152	63 056	55 340	52 683	7 716	142 164	34 415	107 749
September	38 920	23 533	62 946	55 568	52 938	7 378	138 985	34 058	104 927
October	38 371	24 500	64 103	56 552	53 785	7 551	143 674	34 055	109 619
November	39 083	24 315	62 830	55 336	53 121	7 494	145 380	34 787	110 593
December	39 816	24 305	64 742	57 395	54 431	7 347	143 476	36 072	107 404
2005									
January	39 545	24 959	65 712	58 349	56 189	7 363	144 206	34 464	109 742
February	39 462	24 840	64 867	57 366	55 293	7 501	143 961	34 757	109 204
March	40 163	25 121	65 861	58 423	55 520	7 438	148 172	34 353	113 819
April	39 963	25 267	66 961	59 451	55 800	7 510	146 163	34 211	111 952
May	40 259	25 448	67 617	59 943	56 815	7 674	148 553	34 975	113 578
June	40 644	25 248	67 242	59 522	56 334	7 720	148 256	35 262	112 994
July	39 922	25 386	66 873	59 594	56 443	7 279	149 698	34 948	114 750
August	40 634	26 128	69 299	61 701	57 689	7 598	153 199	35 557	117 642
September	41 464	25 464	67 723	60 034	57 298	7 689	153 396	36 501	116 895
October	41 752	26 266	70 523	62 999	58 406	7 524	152 474	35 787	116 687
November	42 182	26 068	72 073	64 498	58 656	7 575	151 192	35 327	115 865
December	42 685	26 866	75 392	67 553	59 746	7 839	153 378	36 371	117 007

[2]Data are for SIC industries roughly similar to the NAICS industries indicated in the column headings.
. . . = Not available.

Table 17-5. Manufacturers' Inventories

(Current cost basis, end of period; seasonally adjusted, except as noted; millions of dollars.)

Classification basis, year, and month	Total, not seasonally adjusted [1]	Total	NAICS durable goods industries — Total [1]	Non-metallic mineral products	Primary metals — Total	Primary metals — Iron and steel mills	Fabricated metal products	Machinery	Computers and electronic products	Electrical equipment, appliances, and components	Transportation equipment — Total	Transportation equipment — Motor vehicles and parts	Durables total by stage of fabrication — Materials and supplies	Work in progress	Finished goods
SIC Basis [2]															
1958	49 995	50 203	30 194	1 217	5 153	3 287	4 186	8 630			6 650	1 815	9 970	12 408	7 816
1959	52 671	52 913	32 012	1 351	5 109	3 109	4 244	9 682			6 943	2 211	10 709	13 086	8 217
1960	53 580	53 786	32 337	1 429	5 488	3 385	4 292	9 804			6 415	2 080	10 306	12 809	9 222
1961	54 730	54 871	32 496	1 439	5 792	3 684	4 269	9 890			6 207	2 082	10 246	13 211	9 039
1962	58 060	58 172	34 565	1 460	5 702	3 494	4 387	11 212			6 628	2 334	10 794	14 124	9 647
1963	59 922	60 029	35 776	1 498	5 749	3 459	4 534	11 352			7 111	2 463	11 053	14 835	9 888
1964	63 293	63 410	38 421	1 590	5 953	3 560	5 011	12 573			7 707	2 899	11 946	16 158	10 317
1965	68 028	68 207	42 189	1 669	6 199	3 617	5 696	14 340			8 430	3 289	13 298	18 055	10 836
1966	77 745	77 986	49 852	1 784	7 031	4 075	6 347	17 242			10 454	3 470	15 464	21 908	12 480
1967	84 388	84 646	54 896	1 827	7 553	4 417	6 729	18 279			12 852	3 516	16 423	24 933	13 540
1968	90 235	90 560	58 732	1 918	7 547	4 207	7 506	18 925			14 413	3 879	17 344	27 213	14 175
1969	97 749	98 145	64 598	2 051	8 066	4 451	7 666	21 480			15 942	4 067	18 636	30 282	15 680
1970	101 246	101 599	66 651	2 239	8 995	4 990	7 907	22 910			14 648	4 178	19 149	29 745	17 757
1971	102 267	102 567	66 136	2 302	9 084	4 926	8 098	22 402			13 799	4 173	19 679	28 550	17 907
1972	107 900	108 121	70 067	2 430	9 617	5 387	8 408	23 670			14 775	4 670	20 807	30 713	18 547
1973	124 327	124 499	81 192	2 712	10 034	5 302	9 864	28 943			16 458	5 708	25 944	35 490	19 758
1974	157 595	157 625	101 493	3 403	13 447	6 820	13 387	36 420			19 197	6 688	35 070	42 530	23 893
1975	159 844	159 708	102 590	3 594	15 742	8 597	13 091	35 266			19 620	6 101	33 903	43 227	25 460
1976	174 867	174 636	111 988	3 841	17 699	10 035	14 304	37 839			20 886	7 814	37 457	46 074	28 457
1977	188 435	188 378	120 877	4 095	18 261	10 004	15 527	41 204			22 443	9 078	40 186	50 226	30 465
1978	209 113	211 691	138 181	4 710	19 420	10 719	17 296	48 249			26 170	10 357	45 198	58 848	34 135
1979	239 101	242 157	160 734	5 183	22 446	12 012	19 145	57 030			31 638	10 978	52 670	69 325	38 739
1980	261 700	265 215	174 788	5 674	23 055	12 153	19 532	62 796			35 900	9 864	55 173	76 945	42 670
1981	279 453	283 413	186 443	6 106	25 794	13 359	20 209	67 260			37 527	9 047	57 998	80 998	47 447
1982	307 212	311 852	200 444	6 506	24 174	12 556	21 440	73 008			43 005	8 534	59 136	86 707	54 601
1983	307 675	312 379	199 854	6 628	22 308	11 065	21 752	71 508			43 791	10 433	60 325	86 899	52 630
1984	334 236	339 516	221 330	7 042	22 444	11 087	23 330	80 396			50 770	11 680	66 031	98 251	57 048
1985	329 555	334 749	218 193	7 040	19 974	9 709	22 880	77 075			52 634	11 809	63 904	98 162	56 127
1986	317 567	322 654	211 997	7 093	18 436	8 567	22 094	71 041			53 363	11 445	61 331	97 000	53 666
1987	332 619	338 109	220 799	7 154	19 076	8 620	22 920	73 000			56 461	11 937	63 562	102 393	54 844
1988	363 300	369 374	242 468	7 496	22 422	10 495	24 950	79 352			63 202	12 310	69 611	112 958	59 899
1989	384 539	391 212	257 513	7 792	22 838	10 942	25 427	83 965			70 968	12 503	72 435	122 251	62 827
1990	397 850	405 073	263 209	8 205	22 560	11 045	25 044	82 586			77 640	13 504	73 559	124 130	65 520
1991	383 509	390 950	250 019	7 928	20 703	10 236	23 922	78 861			73 019	13 163	70 834	114 960	64 225
1992	374 906	382 510	238 105	8 006	19 981	9 809	23 815	77 797			63 290	13 081	69 459	104 424	64 222
NAICS Basis															
1992	369 673	378 900	238 162	8 002	17 968	9 618	26 106	36 232	44 620	12 251	66 388	17 110	69 787	104 152	64 223
1993	370 775	379 829	238 781	7 579	17 972	9 596	26 293	37 087	44 036	12 480	64 292	18 228	72 705	101 917	64 159
1994	390 540	400 087	253 185	7 830	20 112	10 433	28 199	40 885	47 164	13 770	64 835	20 196	78 615	106 470	68 100
1995	414 969	425 032	267 472	8 434	21 463	11 291	30 300	44 665	53 697	14 173	63 106	20 758	82 320	106 601	75 337
1996	420 680	430 679	272 595	8 736	21 796	11 700	31 295	45 410	50 978	13 937	68 058	21 143	86 294	110 499	75 802
1997	433 451	443 768	281 154	9 004	22 566	12 302	32 435	45 959	55 270	14 090	68 840	20 745	92 357	109 879	78 918
1998	438 845	449 216	290 765	9 031	22 135	12 432	32 870	47 159	52 079	14 020	79 942	21 239	93 682	115 156	81 927
1999	452 803	463 744	296 615	9 446	22 151	12 153	33 481	47 452	54 963	14 007	79 694	22 662	98 003	114 057	84 555
2000	470 084	481 847	306 889	9 999	22 051	12 444	34 832	50 599	65 532	15 029	71 856	22 919	106 307	111 166	89 416
2001	436 622	441 477	279 825	9 226	19 790	11 054	31 800	47 468	54 080	13 799	69 210	20 358	104 346	103 378	82 101
2002	428 086	439 473	272 146	8 987	19 536	11 465	32 136	45 378	49 513	12 603	68 226	21 119	88 990	99 617	83 539
2003	395 920	406 816	264 080	9 388	18 595	9 809	30 628	38 667	40 872	11 481	61 868	21 462	81 676	89 223	75 941
2004	423 197	434 863	263 936	9 867	24 392	14 113	33 970	41 170	42 673	12 184	61 935	22 733	91 975	90 438	81 583
2005	439 763	452 049	273 123	10 230	25 310	14 110	34 514	43 388	42 697	12 886	64 933	23 442	94 076	94 817	84 230
2004															
January	404 436	406 509	246 140	9 349	18 752	9 929	30 499	38 599	39 945	11 499	61 997	22 107	81 803	89 001	75 336
February	411 466	408 482	246 676	9 375	18 967	9 966	30 631	38 758	39 866	11 346	61 983	22 123	82 320	88 920	75 436
March	409 471	410 172	247 637	9 331	19 401	10 215	30 679	38 842	40 461	11 405	61 457	22 156	83 479	88 530	75 628
April	414 109	412 022	248 965	9 301	19 722	10 462	30 631	38 894	41 004	11 390	61 865	22 235	84 878	88 778	75 265
May	418 428	415 301	250 495	9 382	20 028	10 646	31 036	39 291	41 029	11 560	61 582	22 270	85 099	88 887	76 509
June	416 879	419 234	252 923	9 351	20 498	11 073	31 371	39 654	41 521	11 718	62 037	22 694	86 198	89 453	77 272
July	425 050	422 632	255 141	9 392	20 826	11 266	31 872	39 929	41 822	11 880	62 503	22 652	87 659	89 939	77 543
August	428 689	425 771	257 220	9 495	21 533	11 907	32 466	40 214	41 848	12 090	62 324	22 820	88 168	89 985	79 067
September	425 924	426 248	258 214	9 547	22 272	12 535	32 831	40 332	41 850	12 141	61 727	23 137	88 690	89 033	80 491
October	432 651	430 115	260 501	9 786	23 371	13 398	33 073	40 369	42 501	12 117	61 477	22 900	90 339	89 619	80 543
November	434 877	434 423	263 152	9 867	23 973	13 796	33 376	41 048	42 356	12 122	62 466	23 076	91 513	90 650	80 989
December	423 197	434 863	263 936	9 867	24 392	14 113	33 970	41 170	42 673	12 184	61 935	22 733	91 915	90 438	81 583
2005															
January	438 233	440 532	267 152	9 914	25 031	14 636	34 253	41 701	42 986	12 245	62 770	23 378	93 406	91 209	82 537
February	446 217	442 953	268 951	10 018	25 259	14 932	34 605	41 956	42 690	12 282	63 820	23 561	93 187	92 413	83 351
March	444 842	445 178	269 998	10 014	25 884	15 258	34 750	42 069	41 909	12 373	64 441	23 906	93 501	92 116	84 381
April	448 148	445 674	270 107	10 032	25 949	15 210	34 913	42 437	41 596	12 481	64 002	24 062	93 724	91 755	84 628
May	448 310	444 876	270 748	10 060	26 054	15 212	34 981	42 725	41 651	12 452	64 294	23 991	93 733	92 160	84 855
June	442 488	444 891	269 244	10 108	25 807	15 027	34 642	42 512	41 148	12 457	63 873	23 935	93 475	91 672	84 097
July	450 132	447 555	271 254	10 202	25 649	14 848	34 549	43 163	41 766	12 498	64 542	23 590	93 263	92 990	85 001
August	449 306	446 434	270 358	10 191	25 469	14 577	34 316	43 363	41 661	12 466	63 740	23 672	92 842	92 218	85 298
September	445 763	446 221	270 229	10 142	25 279	14 284	34 196	43 418	41 785	12 619	63 872	23 195	92 727	93 124	84 398
October	451 922	449 332	271 604	10 062	25 251	14 279	34 195	43 281	42 240	12 671	64 883	23 704	93 335	93 513	84 756
November	450 385	449 992	273 273	10 076	25 216	14 158	34 412	43 464	43 107	12 751	65 029	23 780	94 022	93 997	85 254
December	439 763	452 049	273 123	10 230	25 310	14 110	34 514	43 388	42 697	12 886	64 933	23 442	94 076	94 817	84 230

[1] Includes categories not shown separately.
[2] Data are for SIC industries roughly similar to the NAICS industries indicated in the column headings. Data prior to 1982 are not comparable to subsequent periods due to changes in inventory valuation methods; see notes and definitions for more information.

Table 17-5. Manufacturers' Inventories—Continued

(Current cost basis, end of period; seasonally adjusted, except as noted; millions of dollars.)

Classification basis, year, and month	Total [1]	Food products	Beverage and tobacco products [3]	Textiles	Textile products	Apparel	Paper products	Chemical products	Petroleum and coal products	Plastics and rubber products	Materials and supplies	Work in process	Finished goods
SIC Basis [2]													
1958	40 018	10 604	3 964	4 296		...	2 860	5 990	3 268	2 066	17 352	5 654	17 012
1959	41 802	10 676	4 164	4 476		...	3 012	6 378	3 400	2 260	18 188	5 884	17 730
1960	42 898	10 984	4 386	4 602		...	3 086	6 596	3 334	2 326	18 194	5 894	18 810
1961	44 750	11 754	4 820	4 836		...	3 152	6 802	3 430	2 344	19 010	6 216	19 524
1962	47 214	12 396	4 808	5 170		...	3 404	7 318	3 572	2 554	19 672	6 608	20 934
1963	48 506	12 898	4 628	5 242		...	3 522	7 550	3 552	2 672	20 018	6 840	21 648
1964	49 978	13 258	4 612	5 364		...	3 566	7 918	3 520	2 860	20 334	7 062	22 582
1965	52 036	12 970	4 558	5 736		...	3 876	8 784	3 522	3 098	20 974	7 650	23 412
1966	56 268	13 946	4 412	6 090		...	4 340	9 902	3 616	3 542	22 394	8 452	25 422
1967	59 500	14 968	4 550	6 362		...	4 472	10 612	3 922	3 680	23 520	8 862	27 118
1968	63 656	16 018	4 436	7 220		...	4 618	11 084	4 070	4 036	24 656	9 704	29 296
1969	67 094	16 658	4 376	7 340		...	4 798	12 346	4 170	4 430	25 506	10 240	31 348
1970	69 896	17 476	4 104	7 352		...	5 470	13 498	4 322	4 772	26 336	10 542	33 018
1971	72 862	18 516	4 198	7 732		...	5 656	13 846	4 520	4 906	27 372	11 356	34 134
1972	76 108	19 346	4 710	8 112		...	5 792	14 158	4 284	5 390	29 354	11 996	34 758
1973	43 307	11 627	2 426	4 592		...	3 317	7 553	2 476	3 103	18 147	6 729	18 431
1974	56 132	14 625	3 024	5 044		...	4 816	11 579	3 945	4 023	23 744	8 189	24 199
1975	57 118	14 467	3 290	4 794		...	4 849	12 073	4 426	4 085	23 565	8 834	24 719
1976	62 648	15 695	3 416	5 232		...	5 299	13 319	4 711	4 581	25 847	9 929	26 872
1977	67 501	16 329	3 511	5 649		...	5 667	14 633	5 439	5 116	27 387	10 961	29 153
1978	73 510	18 073	3 669	5 935		...	6 114	16 018	5 330	5 801	29 619	12 085	31 806
1979	81 423	19 879	3 517	6 148		...	6 926	17 690	7 458	6 399	32 814	13 910	34 699
1980	90 427	21 710	3 721	6 648		...	7 802	20 066	9 693	6 435	36 606	15 884	37 937
1981	96 970	21 483	4 436	6 896		...	8 593	22 438	10 420	6 968	38 165	16 194	42 611
1982	111 408	23 016	6 873	6 723		...	9 022	24 448	17 009	7 748	44 039	18 612	48 757
1983	112 525	23 609	6 746	7 514		...	9 192	24 698	14 843	8 070	44 816	18 691	49 018
1984	118 186	24 182	6 533	7 827		...	10 299	26 420	14 260	8 904	45 692	19 328	53 166
1985	116 556	24 015	5 943	7 439		...	10 140	26 119	13 975	9 213	44 106	19 442	53 008
1986	110 657	23 884	5 449	7 191		...	10 254	25 743	8 791	9 285	42 335	18 124	50 198
1987	117 310	24 860	5 331	7 939		...	11 163	26 585	9 973	10 065	45 319	19 270	52 721
1988	126 906	27 122	5 286	8 384		...	12 495	29 792	9 196	11 367	49 396	20 559	56 951
1989	133 699	28 459	5 570	8 721		...	13 404	31 725	10 743	11 533	50 674	21 653	61 372
1990	141 864	29 714	5 974	8 732		...	13 640	34 001	13 432	12 292	52 645	22 817	66 402
1991	140 931	30 099	6 342	8 844		...	13 796	34 529	11 671	12 121	53 011	22 815	65 105
1992	144 405	30 996	6 668	8 710		...	14 010	35 720	11 350	12 541	54 007	23 532	66 866
NAICS Basis													
1992	140 738	26 451	11 635	6 468	3 514	8 920	13 452	37 530	11 667	12 660	53 201	23 330	64 207
1993	141 048	26 625	11 290	6 840	3 641	10 094	13 465	37 817	10 479	12 846	54 310	23 327	63 411
1994	146 902	27 565	10 961	7 192	3 930	10 491	13 746	38 863	11 310	14 298	57 189	24 411	65 302
1995	157 560	29 273	11 434	7 624	4 113	10 485	16 609	42 019	11 491	15 310	60 774	25 781	71 005
1996	158 084	29 588	12 382	7 239	4 094	8 783	15 292	43 328	12 782	15 800	59 141	26 466	72 477
1997	162 614	29 945	13 805	6 890	4 547	9 663	15 200	45 262	12 183	16 171	60 185	28 506	73 923
1998	158 451	29 208	13 910	6 939	4 220	9 475	14 825	45 563	9 692	16 189	58 222	27 069	73 160
1999	167 129	30 480	13 817	6 901	4 417	9 808	15 167	48 499	12 183	17 232	61 073	28 768	77 288
2000	174 958	31 759	14 039	6 482	4 910	9 516	15 339	52 437	13 829	18 024	61 469	30 053	83 436
2001	168 056	33 197	14 461	5 798	4 592	8 205	14 750	50 400	12 102	16 659	58 200	27 541	82 315
2002	167 327	34 030	14 172	5 089	4 632	7 642	14 579	50 649	12 621	15 903	55 822	29 613	81 892
2003	159 976	31 284	14 659	4 296	3 324	4 813	13 625	48 787	16 792	15 737	56 365	26 952	76 659
2004	170 927	31 790	14 897	3 987	3 015	4 475	14 294	54 044	20 204	17 299	59 758	28 673	82 496
2005	178 926	32 597	15 756	3 590	3 129	4 636	14 244	54 876	25 081	18 302	63 405	28 097	87 424
2004													
January	160 369	31 177	14 693	4 230	3 239	4 726	13 572	48 728	17 685	15 755	56 672	27 421	76 276
February	161 806	31 176	14 892	4 192	3 199	4 560	13 511	49 809	18 112	15 694	57 530	27 780	76 496
March	162 535	31 394	14 772	4 188	3 180	4 521	13 438	50 426	18 174	15 857	57 555	28 207	76 773
April	163 057	31 319	14 702	4 163	3 163	4 429	13 413	51 023	18 327	15 935	57 858	28 458	76 741
May	164 806	31 658	14 658	4 139	3 128	4 383	13 592	51 369	19 172	15 985	57 828	27 855	79 123
June	166 311	31 820	14 845	4 112	3 125	4 416	13 628	51 933	19 503	16 248	58 044	28 511	79 756
July	167 491	31 928	14 763	4 102	3 121	4 426	13 850	52 038	20 037	16 537	58 927	28 090	80 474
August	168 551	31 764	15 218	4 086	3 096	4 453	13 946	52 622	19 849	16 763	59 070	28 185	81 296
September	168 034	31 705	15 182	4 065	3 109	4 462	13 961	52 040	19 730	16 993	58 852	27 763	81 419
October	169 614	31 618	15 050	4 019	3 086	4 471	14 198	52 155	20 892	17 240	59 507	28 238	81 869
November	171 271	31 491	14 984	4 009	3 054	4 471	14 303	53 098	21 663	17 324	59 922	28 431	82 918
December	170 927	31 790	14 897	3 987	3 015	4 475	14 294	54 044	20 204	17 299	59 758	28 673	82 496
2005													
January	173 380	31 496	15 144	3 930	3 072	4 628	14 522	54 165	21 665	17 969	60 532	28 155	84 693
February	174 002	31 609	15 090	3 875	3 090	4 662	14 625	54 185	22 001	18 018	60 627	28 756	84 619
March	175 180	31 769	15 117	3 806	3 094	4 658	14 607	54 318	22 749	18 176	61 248	29 187	84 745
April	175 567	32 403	15 134	3 763	3 053	4 693	14 654	53 801	23 018	18 181	61 391	28 458	85 718
May	174 128	32 092	15 131	3 745	3 054	4 683	14 620	53 685	22 038	18 258	61 440	27 664	85 024
June	175 647	32 192	15 063	3 697	3 051	4 659	14 633	54 240	23 071	18 199	61 432	28 027	86 188
July	176 301	32 309	15 278	3 645	3 028	4 624	14 581	53 477	24 382	18 166	61 566	27 896	86 839
August	176 076	32 323	15 188	3 572	3 043	4 687	14 492	53 083	24 680	18 239	61 986	27 903	86 187
September	175 992	32 485	15 022	3 593	3 020	4 710	14 396	53 255	24 810	17 876	61 718	28 072	86 202
October	177 728	32 563	15 715	3 595	3 069	4 739	14 387	53 184	25 760	17 975	62 222	28 584	86 922
November	176 719	32 582	15 786	3 562	3 023	4 662	14 238	53 198	24 753	18 202	61 707	28 590	86 422
December	178 926	32 597	15 756	3 590	3 129	4 636	14 244	54 876	25 081	18 302	63 405	28 097	87 424

[1]Includes categories not shown separately.
[2]Data are for SIC industries roughly similar to the NAICS industries indicated in the column headings. Data prior to 1982 are not comparable to subsequent periods due to changes in inventory valuation methods; see notes and definitions for more information.
[3]SIC tobacco only, 1958–1992.
. . . = Not available.

Table 17-5. Manufacturers' Inventories—Continued

(Current cost basis, end of period; seasonally adjusted, except as noted; millions of dollars.)

Classification basis, year, and month	Construction materials and supplies	Information technology industries	Capital goods — Total	Capital goods — Nondefense Total	Capital goods — Nondefense Excluding aircraft and parts	Defense	Consumer goods — Total	Consumer goods — Durable	Consumer goods — Nondurable
SIC Basis [2]									
1958	7 524	...	22 762	...	...	...	...	...	...
1959	7 956	...	23 918	...	...	...	...	...	...
1960	8 158	...	23 474	...	...	...	...	...	...
1961	8 184	...	23 302	...	...	...	...	...	...
1962	8 446	...	25 920	...	...	...	...	...	...
1963	8 590	...	26 360	...	...	...	...	...	...
1964	9 102	...	28 534	...	...	...	...	...	...
1965	9 736	...	31 686	...	...	...	...	...	...
1966	10 650	...	39 582	...	...	...	...	...	...
1967	10 862	...	46 998	...	...	...	...	...	...
1968	11 610	...	51 418	36 316	...	15 102	...	...	...
1969	12 756	...	57 304	41 766	...	15 538	...	...	...
1970	13 734	...	55 718	45 620	...	10 098	...	...	...
1971	14 290	...	53 174	44 910	...	8 264	...	...	...
1972	15 206	...	55 334	46 674	...	8 660	...	...	...
1973	8 696	...	32 032	27 460	...	4 572	...	...	...
1974	11 076	...	39 605	34 583	...	5 022	...	...	...
1975	11 267	...	40 181	34 289	...	5 892	...	...	...
1976	12 540	...	41 046	34 449	...	6 597	...	...	...
1977	13 509	...	44 014	37 781	...	6 233	...	...	...
1978	15 100	...	52 237	45 660	...	6 577	...	...	...
1979	16 908	...	63 816	55 393	...	8 423	...	...	...
1980	17 513	...	74 531	63 692	...	10 839	...	...	...
1981	18 328	...	81 112	67 616	...	13 496	...	...	...
1982	18 580	...	92 601	73 748	...	18 853	...	...	...
1983	19 309	...	89 562	68 420	...	21 142	...	...	...
1984	20 552	...	102 615	75 466	...	27 149	...	...	...
1985	20 555	...	102 843	71 763	...	31 080	...	...	...
1986	20 348	...	99 104	67 631	...	31 473	...	...	...
1987	21 158	...	103 167	68 734	...	34 433	...	...	...
1988	22 925	...	114 207	77 448	...	36 759	...	...	...
1989	23 326	...	124 850	86 897	...	37 953	...	...	...
1990	23 714	...	128 997	90 894	...	38 103	...	...	...
1991	22 509	...	121 629	88 958	...	32 671	...	...	...
1992	22 779	...	110 261	84 351	...	25 910	...	...	...
NAICS Basis									
1992	36 751	40 299	120 620	97 493	79 040	23 127	103 328	20 878	82 450
1993	38 292	39 246	118 522	97 214	79 670	21 308	104 846	21 852	82 994
1994	40 892	41 638	123 470	103 461	85 851	20 009	109 611	23 967	85 644
1995	43 416	46 964	129 779	111 640	94 745	18 139	116 513	25 282	91 231
1996	44 113	43 643	132 890	115 321	93 542	17 569	116 505	24 801	91 704
1997	45 692	48 189	137 675	122 634	98 893	15 041	119 805	24 959	94 846
1998	46 460	45 437	145 229	127 192	97 420	18 037	117 520	24 946	92 574
1999	48 471	46 223	146 436	126 352	99 652	20 084	124 331	26 102	98 229
2000	50 517	52 844	149 321	131 862	110 302	17 459	130 952	27 222	103 730
2001	46 208	43 944	137 420	119 284	98 433	18 136	127 011	24 568	102 443
2002	47 538	39 406	128 111	109 813	90 967	18 298	129 248	25 951	103 297
2003	45 881	35 024	114 599	99 286	81 498	15 313	124 112	24 953	99 159
2004	50 367	36 889	116 986	101 745	86 361	15 241	130 697	26 230	104 467
2005	52 690	36 014	121 047	105 952	89 413	15 095	135 917	26 687	109 230
2004									
January	45 837	34 184	113 182	98 208	80 664	14 974	124 820	25 497	99 323
February	46 143	34 050	113 322	98 132	80 762	15 190	126 011	25 358	100 653
March	46 482	34 146	113 105	98 163	81 004	14 942	126 679	25 394	101 285
April	46 611	34 519	113 230	98 381	81 137	14 849	127 403	25 613	101 790
May	47 129	34 667	113 651	98 690	81 967	14 961	128 663	25 558	103 105
June	47 445	35 131	114 553	99 392	82 810	15 161	130 001	25 980	104 021
July	48 089	35 285	115 151	100 370	83 273	14 781	130 479	26 036	104 443
August	48 861	35 633	115 383	100 800	83 866	14 583	130 902	26 339	104 563
September	49 455	35 956	114 890	100 329	84 394	14 561	130 332	26 529	103 803
October	49 783	36 273	115 162	100 536	84 882	14 626	130 992	26 535	104 457
November	50 253	36 377	116 805	102 000	85 991	14 805	131 849	26 377	105 472
December	50 367	36 889	116 986	101 745	86 361	15 241	130 697	26 230	104 467
2005									
January	51 200	37 045	117 670	102 461	87 064	15 209	132 500	26 304	106 196
February	51 927	36 882	118 415	103 267	87 276	15 148	132 566	26 235	106 331
March	52 429	36 504	118 293	103 717	87 488	14 576	133 166	26 373	106 793
April	52 612	36 226	117 561	103 098	87 642	14 463	133 867	26 604	107 263
May	52 768	36 317	118 103	103 471	87 693	14 632	132 290	26 670	105 620
June	52 323	35 532	117 225	102 884	87 492	14 341	133 745	26 598	107 147
July	52 353	35 911	119 243	104 582	88 691	14 661	134 869	26 574	108 295
August	52 246	35 922	119 369	104 928	89 018	14 441	135 513	27 010	108 503
September	51 847	35 715	120 169	105 511	89 189	14 658	135 104	26 457	108 647
October	52 049	35 747	120 319	105 477	89 063	14 842	136 945	26 851	110 094
November	52 100	36 458	121 093	106 200	89 902	14 893	135 827	27 118	108 709
December	52 690	36 014	121 047	105 952	89 413	15 095	135 917	26 687	109 230

[2]Data are for SIC industries roughly similar to the NAICS industries indicated in the column headings. Data prior to 1982 are not comparable to subsequent periods due to changes in inventory valuation methods; see notes and definitions for more information.
... = Not available.

Table 17-6. Manufacturers' New Orders

(Net, millions of dollars, seasonally adjusted.)

Classification basis, year, and month	Total [1]	NAICS durable goods industries											
		Total [1]	Primary metals			Fabricated metal products	Machinery	Computers and electronic products	Electrical equipment, appliances, and components	Transportation equipment			
			Total [1]	Iron and steel mills	Aluminum and nonferrous metal products					Total [1]	Motor vehicles and parts	Non-defense aircraft and parts	Defense aircraft and parts
SIC Basis [2]													
1959	368 255	191 744	34 503	21 009	...	24 102		49 044		44 712	...	...	
1960	362 759	183 455	26 354	13 603	...	23 410		47 245		47 481	...	...	
1961	373 400	189 032	32 069	18 647	...	24 225		49 867		43 138	...	...	
1962	401 255	208 351	31 179	16 635	...	26 364		54 722		53 728	...	...	
1963	426 084	224 048	34 780	19 122	...	27 903		58 745		57 625	...	...	
1964	459 210	246 088	41 521	23 758	...	30 360		66 005		61 607	...	...	
1965	505 792	279 432	43 380	22 590	...	33 998		76 429		73 803	...	...	
1966	556 494	313 954	49 111	25 134	...	38 501		89 417		80 607	...	...	
1967	564 616	309 632	45 100	23 435	...	41 618		87 944		75 979	...	...	
1968	607 127	336 614	48 089	24 416	...	45 158		91 468		85 893	...	...	
1969	648 289	358 509	54 880	27 247	...	47 446		102 664		83 945	...	...	
1970	624 541	328 079	51 793	25 521	...	43 990		96 439		67 380	...	17 417	
1971	671 134	358 856	51 284	25 571	...	44 305		98 525		89 900	...	22 459	
1972	770 056	420 455	61 447	30 996	...	52 879		119 643		96 501	...	20 963	
1973	912 279	511 525	78 395	39 413	...	64 733		147 437		118 194	...	26 669	
1974	1 047 811	562 339	98 831	51 047	...	74 281		164 985		114 081	...	29 934	
1975	1 022 133	503 485	75 034	38 611	...	64 349		147 473		109 050	...	26 869	
1976	1 194 759	615 680	94 491	47 212	...	76 372		174 459		143 502	...	31 851	
1977	1 382 309	732 422	105 689	52 103	...	92 028		206 245		175 446	...	40 625	
1978	1 579 715	867 335	124 741	62 648	...	105 182		246 832		213 539	...	54 600	
1979	1 771 603	953 796	139 783	66 968	...	117 428		281 974		223 226	...	67 818	
1980	1 877 053	952 701	134 416	62 473	...	116 195		295 085		202 584	...	72 514	
1981	2 015 982	1 003 845	137 286	67 457	...	123 245		324 629		203 482	...	63 530	
1982	1 944 671	936 764	98 445	43 013	...	113 399		296 904		209 325	...	73 365	
1983	2 106 726	1 057 677	113 884	49 123	...	122 760		321 010		261 359	...	86 952	
1984	2 314 256	1 201 964	118 354	50 719	...	141 650		377 650		295 202	...	91 620	
1985	2 346 410	1 228 268	112 276	49 079	...	142 300		381 747		311 482	...	100 889	
1986	2 340 899	1 243 761	108 218	46 408	...	143 541		372 849		327 541	...	107 993	
1987	2 510 890	1 329 712	125 989	54 763	...	150 716		394 381		348 224	...	114 835	
1988	2 737 716	1 464 916	152 578	64 002	...	158 170		439 266		389 635	...	137 443	
1989	2 872 514	1 512 664	152 814	62 752	...	160 037		449 533		411 434	...	153 430	
1990	2 931 275	1 507 001	149 338	63 369	...	163 285		454 642		395 737	...	150 329	
1991	2 866 841	1 438 187	134 657	56 366	...	158 401		441 109		363 366	...	132 645	
1992	2 977 116	1 515 694	136 849	58 002	...	165 793		476 574		377 147	...	110 830	
NAICS Basis [3]													
1992	...	...			...		...			...			...
1993	2 960 015	1 544 062	128 895	62 580	53 733	175 990	202 848	248 104	88 263	427 966	311 928	38 427	32 569
1994	3 199 686	1 725 635	146 503	67 619	64 594	196 567	232 226	274 776	96 919	487 253	367 306	39 309	31 524
1995	3 426 503	1 849 641	159 957	72 600	72 264	214 488	251 307	311 275	101 409	508 133	378 886	57 454	27 736
1996	3 567 384	1 948 793	158 066	71 301	70 657	227 447	258 405	327 288	104 837	552 024	385 712	72 094	32 520
1997	3 779 835	2 092 520	171 407	78 577	74 974	247 839	272 998	363 635	113 411	581 780	422 427	85 797	23 280
1998	3 808 143	2 139 918	160 743	72 378	71 274	253 847	278 100	372 433	115 711	600 205	440 934	84 150	23 854
1999	3 957 242	2 252 091	156 968	70 924	68 469	258 116	278 277	402 216	120 774	660 215	499 527	81 619	25 717
2000	4 161 472	2 326 576	153 625	68 181	67 122	270 021	294 608	436 415	126 196	663 326	468 470	99 249	31 326
2001	3 917 225	2 097 426	135 902	60 463	58 835	255 179	263 754	352 220	113 930	605 854	438 837	75 024	36 587
2002	3 866 899	2 070 088	136 421	62 839	58 236	253 809	246 231	316 275	104 845	627 219	464 370	63 890	39 414
2003	3 900 807	2 058 931	139 030	63 061	61 193	244 335	258 145	281 435	101 309	639 000	487 464	49 852	40 274
2004	4 208 065	2 200 773	183 267	95 815	70 376	264 364	271 736	289 773	105 329	667 728	495 364	71 573	30 988
2005	4 549 636	2 390 164	197 739	99 243	79 574	281 683	304 955	324 505	114 951	720 083	483 467	139 146	36 575
2004													
January	329 514	171 136	12 948	6 089	5 617	21 373	20 520	22 906	8 257	51 839	40 700	3 502	2 043
February	331 032	175 395	13 756	6 619	5 806	20 947	20 487	23 616	8 554	55 730	42 366	4 588	3 290
March	350 328	188 126	14 926	7 359	6 130	22 420	23 608	24 688	8 861	59 185	44 495	5 392	2 341
April	345 714	182 011	14 486	7 468	5 651	22 517	21 899	23 673	9 343	55 537	42 066	4 922	2 207
May	346 304	180 286	15 207	7 940	5 821	21 391	22 209	24 250	8 783	53 543	40 637	5 502	2 267
June	349 156	181 873	15 383	8 170	5 839	21 673	22 661	22 904	8 300	56 166	41 407	4 807	4 733
July	353 303	184 149	16 545	9 166	5 882	21 639	22 361	22 702	8 866	57 614	37 901	10 693	2 547
August	354 522	183 584	16 492	9 169	5 867	22 380	22 127	23 374	9 010	54 762	41 019	5 845	2 385
September	353 494	185 132	15 850	8 556	5 817	21 650	23 721	26 366	8 987	53 360	40 454	5 383	1 959
October	355 853	182 197	15 040	7 766	5 840	22 600	23 695	24 734	8 549	52 536	39 035	4 930	2 872
November	363 462	188 771	15 962	8 621	5 847	22 761	22 912	24 304	9 143	57 621	40 267	8 767	2 641
December	361 954	189 517	16 481	8 817	6 175	22 498	24 877	25 278	8 434	55 561	41 524	6 620	1 658
2005													
January	362 878	187 808	15 881	8 114	6 187	22 877	24 615	26 279	9 209	53 234	40 424	4 624	2 391
February	364 034	190 120	16 226	8 643	6 146	22 963	24 604	26 584	9 277	54 079	40 078	6 510	2 604
March	366 164	186 832	16 163	8 254	6 404	22 851	23 917	27 583	8 967	50 525	39 075	4 510	1 787
April	366 204	188 848	15 696	7 685	6 383	23 060	24 507	26 053	9 155	53 641	39 091	6 622	2 281
May	381 214	202 039	15 550	7 491	6 393	23 625	24 431	26 250	9 459	65 342	40 478	17 495	2 490
June	382 988	204 478	15 380	7 302	6 546	23 830	25 835	28 538	9 530	64 419	40 194	12 556	2 474
July	373 785	193 213	15 472	7 415	6 436	22 778	24 685	26 377	9 357	57 542	39 615	10 093	2 542
August	385 870	201 997	16 848	8 534	6 853	23 786	25 735	28 623	10 116	59 235	41 014	11 504	2 741
September	381 665	198 762	17 676	8 771	7 237	24 263	25 797	27 257	10 162	55 820	42 034	6 945	2 655
October	387 884	205 199	17 790	9 212	6 944	23 881	26 463	26 692	9 999	61 924	41 375	10 732	6 102
November	397 596	214 304	17 822	8 909	7 275	23 882	27 034	26 884	9 871	70 625	39 147	23 302	3 650
December	400 150	216 165	17 631	9 008	7 032	24 356	27 791	27 133	10 006	71 580	40 991	22 094	4 828

[1]Includes categories not shown separately.
[2]Data are for SIC industries roughly similar to the NAICS industries indicated in the column headings.
[3]Data exclude semiconductors. See notes and definitions for more information.
. . . = Not available.

Table 17-6. Manufacturers' New Orders—Continued

(Net, millions of dollars, seasonally adjusted.)

Classification basis, year, and month	Construction materials and supplies	Information technology industries	Capital goods Total	Capital goods Nondefense Total	Capital goods Nondefense Excluding aircraft and parts	Defense	Consumer goods Total	Consumer goods Durable	Consumer goods Nondurable
SIC Basis [2]									
1959	...	...	...	...	...	...	...	...	...
1960	...	...	...	...	...	...	...	...	...
1961	...	...	...	...	...	...	...	...	...
1962	...	...	...	...	...	...	...	...	...
1963	...	...	...	...	...	...	...	...	...
1964	...	...	...	...	...	...	...	...	...
1965	...	...	...	...	...	...	...	...	...
1966	...	...	...	...	...	...	...	...	...
1967	...	...	...	...	...	...	...	...	...
1968	...	...	...	...	...	...	...	...	...
1969	...	...	...	84 549	...	23 790	...	...	...
1970	...	...	...	72 866	...	21 311	...	...	...
1971	...	...	...	80 185	...	18 787	...	...	...
1972	...	...	...	92 943	...	20 467	...	...	...
1973	...	...	...	119 108	...	23 409	...	...	...
1974	...	...	...	139 131	...	26 033	...	...	...
1975	...	...	...	118 635	...	24 765	...	...	...
1976	...	...	...	137 875	...	30 616	...	...	...
1977	...	...	...	164 168	...	34 624	...	...	...
1978	...	...	...	211 056	...	41 511	...	...	...
1979	...	...	...	253 844	...	33 795	...	...	...
1980	...	...	...	253 619	...	58 256	...	...	...
1981	...	...	...	261 666	...	58 881	...	...	...
1982	...	...	...	230 555	...	81 415	...	...	...
1983	...	...	...	235 489	...	96 105	...	...	...
1984	...	...	...	284 022	...	103 504	...	...	...
1985	...	...	...	294 544	...	109 505	...	...	...
1986	...	...	...	287 786	...	111 879	...	...	...
1987	...	...	...	313 127	...	111 639	...	...	...
1988	...	...	...	373 294	...	102 728	...	...	...
1989	...	...	...	395 855	...	93 398	...	...	...
1990	...	...	...	399 966	...	96 638	...	...	...
1991	...	...	...	365 655	...	87 213	...	...	...
1992	...	...	...	378 293	...	76 155	...	...	...
NAICS Basis [3]									
1992	...	...	...	...	...	...	...	...	...
1993	304 264	239 387	561 097	488 166	466 433	72 931	1 128 447	275 631	852 816
1994	335 962	265 010	616 252	542 094	523 461	74 158	1 192 584	315 417	877 167
1995	355 161	297 605	680 857	612 132	576 769	68 725	1 256 721	324 146	932 575
1996	373 536	310 074	737 268	648 797	607 174	88 471	1 293 537	328 984	964 553
1997	403 860	352 700	792 859	728 362	676 119	64 497	1 360 010	361 687	998 323
1998	419 330	365 723	809 727	745 600	698 279	64 127	1 352 708	374 300	978 408
1999	435 034	389 160	840 603	772 703	728 089	67 900	1 425 617	413 435	1 012 182
2000	446 792	409 500	910 933	831 335	767 754	79 598	1 501 810	392 741	1 109 069
2001	426 392	347 051	781 508	698 785	663 396	82 723	1 498 197	375 893	1 122 304
2002	431 760	308 181	725 304	647 124	615 525	78 180	1 498 851	395 627	1 103 224
2003	425 288	272 614	714 445	627 150	604 513	87 295	1 561 641	417 388	1 144 253
2004	462 478	286 039	761 726	664 570	623 449	97 156	1 680 496	419 883	1 260 613
2005	494 225	314 559	888 344	805 784	698 118	82 560	1 791 838	421 502	1 370 336
2004									
January	35 975	22 405	57 360	49 547	48 040	7 813	133 929	34 562	99 367
February	35 890	23 165	59 933	50 766	48 568	9 167	132 815	35 243	97 572
March	38 939	24 318	64 720	55 657	53 336	9 063	138 624	37 487	101 137
April	39 852	23 375	61 769	53 618	50 950	8 151	137 450	34 766	102 684
May	38 446	23 665	60 326	53 767	50 912	6 559	139 108	34 329	104 779
June	37 742	22 475	62 698	53 745	51 262	8 953	139 824	34 614	105 210
July	37 963	22 957	67 557	60 251	52 163	7 306	137 526	31 125	106 401
August	39 651	22 855	61 760	54 078	50 784	7 682	142 313	34 564	107 749
September	38 224	26 336	65 720	57 136	54 811	8 584	139 184	34 257	104 927
October	38 906	24 921	64 787	54 832	52 508	9 955	143 719	34 100	109 619
November	39 197	24 057	67 334	59 772	53 492	7 562	146 111	35 518	110 593
December	40 049	24 584	65 524	59 285	55 092	6 239	143 057	35 653	107 404
2005									
January	39 602	25 539	65 728	59 780	57 596	5 948	143 707	33 965	109 742
February	39 839	25 584	67 145	60 480	56 586	6 665	144 001	34 797	109 204
March	40 498	26 533	64 867	57 938	56 055	6 929	147 932	34 113	113 819
April	40 142	25 283	67 250	61 138	57 149	6 112	146 245	34 293	111 952
May	40 769	25 306	78 419	71 923	57 067	6 496	149 004	35 426	113 578
June	41 250	27 809	77 591	68 934	58 710	8 657	147 895	34 901	112 994
July	40 035	25 531	71 700	64 853	57 206	6 847	149 741	34 991	114 750
August	41 449	27 667	74 927	68 293	59 678	6 634	153 759	36 117	117 642
September	42 589	26 723	69 248	62 793	58 709	6 455	153 352	36 457	116 895
October	42 272	26 247	76 490	67 432	59 601	9 058	152 695	36 008	116 687
November	43 221	26 032	87 036	80 435	59 474	6 601	150 932	35 067	115 865
December	43 332	26 226	86 154	79 966	60 749	6 188	152 218	35 211	117 007

[2]Data are for SIC industries roughly similar to the NAICS industries indicated in the column headings.
[3]Data exclude semiconductors. See notes and definitions for more information.
. . . = Not available.

Table 17-7. Manufacturers' Unfilled Orders, Durable Goods Industries

(End of period, millions of dollars, seasonally adjusted, except as noted.)

Classification basis, year, and month	Not seasonally adjusted, total	Seasonally adjusted, NAICS industries							
		Total [1]	Primary metals			Fabricated metal products	Machinery	Computers and electronic products	Electrical equipment, appliances, and components
			Total [1]	Iron and steel mills	Aluminum and nonferrous metal products				
SIC Basis [2]									
1958	44 090	43 807	5 019	3 521	1 151	4 222		10 539	
1959	48 666	48 369	8 018	6 143	1 382	4 615		12 228	
1960	41 681	41 650	3 334	1 877	1 156	4 079		11 028	
1961	43 496	43 582	4 791	3 314	1 131	4 634		11 540	
1962	44 889	45 170	3 518	1 957	1 169	4 858		12 282	
1963	49 879	50 346	3 952	2 170	1 319	5 955		14 602	
1964	60 640	61 315	6 686	4 386	1 696	7 484		18 203	
1965	73 754	74 459	6 086	3 003	2 238	9 111		23 395	
1966	92 303	93 002	7 267	3 601	2 753	10 814		29 339	
1967	99 140	99 735	7 228	3 921	2 572	12 346		30 296	
1968	104 263	104 393	6 591	3 416	2 472	13 813		30 969	
1969	109 936	110 161	7 991	4 283	2 876	15 128		35 490	
1970	100 139	100 412	7 796	4 617	2 663	14 877		33 618	
1971	99 906	100 225	7 478	4 380	2 552	13 688		33 318	
1972	112 517	113 034	10 470	6 681	3 116	15 077		39 344	
1973	148 421	149 204	16 129	9 794	4 962	21 019		54 070	
1974	180 686	181 519	19 225	11 054	5 952	28 100		67 403	
1975	160 993	161 664	13 266	7 345	4 015	24 008		62 437	
1976	169 198	169 857	14 684	7 776	4 891	22 810		65 905	
1977	191 603	193 323	17 298	9 435	5 483	25 152		72 025	
1978	246 162	248 281	23 969	12 932	7 393	29 137		86 452	
1979	288 834	291 321	26 320	12 485	9 457	33 131		99 105	
1980	312 508	315 202	26 815	13 418	10 096	33 296		100 730	
1981	311 628	314 707	22 024	10 589	8 784	33 036		102 123	
1982	297 851	300 798	15 500	6 574	7 418	27 117		86 503	
1983	329 758	333 114	20 400	9 431	9 594	26 752		93 145	
1984	356 446	359 651	18 362	8 103	8 694	30 254		97 433	
1985	369 362	372 097	18 331	8 248	8 361	29 197		96 882	
1986	374 264	376 699	18 590	8 897	7 783	29 633		91 209	
1987	406 444	408 688	24 340	11 828	10 300	32 973		96 609	
1988	449 859	452 150	27 079	11 508	12 974	31 661		104 285	
1989	484 623	487 098	24 120	9 479	11 824	27 629		102 985	
1990	506 311	509 124	24 768	10 120	11 258	25 859		102 373	
1991	492 500	495 802	23 075	9 290	10 609	24 516		96 800	
1992	466 328	469 381	21 636	8 897	9 925	23 725		97 999	
NAICS Basis [3]									
1992	447 770	450 885	18 745	9 241	7 251	29 838	41 260	84 500	12 146
1993	422 314	425 834	20 806	12 372	6 401	27 886	43 083	81 208	12 786
1994	430 982	434 942	24 355	12 875	9 336	30 366	50 618	82 431	14 239
1995	443 497	447 475	23 466	13 419	7 989	32 405	55 839	88 839	14 593
1996	484 865	488 842	23 820	12 810	8 723	36 928	56 879	87 886	14 094
1997	508 480	513 057	27 217	14 540	9 957	42 106	59 343	90 845	15 421
1998	491 858	496 160	21 652	10 853	8 291	42 252	56 620	94 756	15 089
1999	500 749	505 543	22 026	11 719	8 226	43 393	57 960	113 783	17 629
2000	544 517	549 530	18 927	9 297	7 191	45 231	60 995	130 769	18 420
2001	507 149	511 562	17 272	8 890	5 923	41 382	56 026	116 712	15 331
2002	474 349	478 479	15 782	8 911	4 495	37 623	46 023	107 143	14 758
2003	469 686	473 758	17 928	10 742	4 685	37 320	50 528	101 532	14 276
2004	491 237	495 278	22 170	13 806	5 612	42 051	53 176	101 920	15 395
2005	572 428	576 197	25 613	16 189	6 596	48 579	62 919	108 275	18 335
2004									
January	475 438	472 360	18 445	11 018	4 890	38 560	50 346	100 501	14 192
February	479 995	473 758	19 332	11 564	5 164	39 497	50 536	100 797	14 409
March	488 370	479 555	20 238	12 166	5 442	40 289	51 767	102 326	14 717
April	489 543	481 450	20 508	12 571	5 343	41 311	51 504	101 955	15 347
May	488 915	483 410	21 307	13 185	5 433	41 260	52 283	102 643	15 507
June	486 387	484 593	21 660	13 459	5 547	41 343	52 324	102 470	15 200
July	488 912	489 086	22 565	14 163	5 685	40 990	51 865	101 057	15 193
August	485 066	488 682	23 177	14 745	5 705	41 369	51 518	100 028	15 403
September	483 146	490 646	23 027	14 673	5 588	40 875	51 956	102 568	15 661
October	480 887	489 839	22 391	13 969	5 660	41 624	52 342	102 490	15 495
November	484 933	494 279	22 278	13 918	5 579	41 955	52 507	101 817	15 807
December	491 237	495 278	22 170	13 806	5 612	42 051	53 176	101 920	15 395
2005									
January	497 402	494 002	21 522	13 151	5 638	42 433	53 723	102 397	15 608
February	503 639	497 135	21 485	13 225	5 608	42 924	54 552	103 353	15 755
March	504 271	495 283	21 311	12 962	5 721	43 099	54 680	104 714	15 722
April	502 912	495 196	20 877	12 371	5 783	43 471	55 525	104 547	15 835
May	511 753	506 606	20 619	11 926	5 843	44 165	55 731	104 461	16 095
June	522 432	520 750	20 279	11 581	5 873	45 003	57 393	106 814	16 371
July	524 711	525 165	20 284	11 614	5 795	45 287	57 788	107 071	16 362
August	529 479	533 449	21 226	12 534	5 937	46 024	58 639	108 667	16 961
September	530 691	538 467	22 614	13 468	6 327	47 042	59 421	109 438	17 583
October	537 434	546 785	23 887	14 767	6 310	47 606	60 428	109 017	17 809
November	553 943	563 614	25 044	15 659	6 547	48 078	61 679	108 933	17 963
December	572 428	576 197	25 613	16 189	6 596	48 579	62 919	108 275	18 335

[1] Includes categories not shown separately.
[2] Data are for SIC industries roughly similar to the NAICS industries indicated in the column headings.
[3] Data excludes semiconductors. See notes and definitions for more information.

Table 17-7. Manufacturers' Unfilled Orders, Durable Goods Industries—Continued

(End of period, millions of dollars, seasonally adjusted, except as noted.)

Classification basis, year, and month	Transportation equipment				By topical categories						
							Capital goods				
								Nondefense			
	Total[1]	Motor vehicles and parts	Non-defense aircraft and parts	Defense aircraft and parts	Construction materials and supplies	Information technology industries	Total	Total	Excluding aircraft and parts	Defense	Consumer durable goods
SIC Basis[2]											
1958	19 094	...	...		3 149		...	...	...	...	...
1959	18 342	...	...		3 642		...	...	...	...	...
1960	18 217	...	...		3 094		...	...	...	...	...
1961	17 202	...	...		3 449		...	...	...	...	...
1962	18 844	...	...		3 480		...	...	...	...	...
1963	20 151	...	...		4 127		...	...	...	...	...
1964	23 664	...	...		5 182		...	...	...	...	...
1965	29 262	...	...		5 823		...	...	...	...	...
1966	37 376	...	...		6 728		...	...	...	...	...
1967	40 807	...	...		7 521		...	...	...	...	...
1968	43 023	...	...		8 205		...	47 608	...	23 152	...
1969	41 812	...	...		8 873		...	52 591	...	20 809	...
1970	34 720	...	26 198		8 880	...	...	46 544	...	18 804	...
1971	35 793	...	26 259		8 073	...	...	47 576	...	18 158	...
1972	37 627	...	26 151		8 810	...	...	52 781	...	19 261	...
1973	45 248	...	27 842		12 311	...	...	67 947	...	21 756	...
1974	51 118	...	30 506		15 125	...	...	84 495	...	26 558	...
1975	46 633	...	28 244		12 694	...	...	76 773	...	27 936	...
1976	49 078	...	29 421		11 592	...	...	79 121	...	31 826	...
1977	57 101	...	37 325		12 821	...	...	87 552	...	36 692	...
1978	81 782	...	54 417		14 408	...	...	112 277	...	47 425	...
1979	103 555	...	74 034		15 360	...	...	144 114	...	48 656	...
1980	119 700	...	88 051		15 410	...	...	150 973	...	66 636	...
1981	118 008	...	86 794		15 213	...	...	142 802	...	77 793	...
1982	125 879	...	93 703		11 981	...	...	121 082	...	99 052	...
1983	141 637	...	105 504		12 673	...	...	114 280	...	121 177	...
1984	152 189	...	117 923		13 102	...	...	119 424	...	142 324	...
1985	156 155	...	127 282		13 124	...	...	120 687	...	156 188	...
1986	161 145	...	133 565		13 677	...	...	118 429	...	161 705	...
1987	176 588	...	144 987		14 140	...	...	136 171	...	163 786	...
1988	211 575	...	174 721		14 557	...	...	176 069	...	161 878	...
1989	253 517	...	217 557		13 992	...	...	221 152	...	155 314	...
1990	279 082	...	242 208		14 021	...	...	250 314	...	149 844	...
1991	275 260	...	242 798		14 828	...	...	246 093	...	139 666	...
1992	253 076	...	222 194		14 706	...	...	234 817	...	124 047	...
NAICS Basis[3]											
1992	258 720	11 587	127 145	49 504	20 979	80 284	318 410	179 371	92 893	139 039	3 831
1993	233 346	13 360	110 616	46 567	21 871	78 049	298 944	173 856	95 709	125 088	4 666
1994	225 817	15 880	100 870	44 563	25 201	79 091	299 031	177 983	107 072	121 048	5 194
1995	225 468	15 187	109 142	42 213	27 237	84 932	313 870	199 601	118 264	114 269	5 296
1996	261 297	13 486	130 295	45 081	29 462	84 091	346 497	217 462	120 267	129 035	5 846
1997	267 615	14 346	143 284	40 802	33 590	87 204	360 403	243 035	131 675	117 368	7 367
1998	254 841	15 636	137 494	37 650	34 225	90 555	348 297	241 431	134 160	106 866	8 260
1999	238 644	16 386	126 560	35 536	35 184	105 642	349 541	245 683	149 582	103 858	9 071
2000	262 079	13 663	138 493	42 398	37 262	115 650	385 236	268 714	159 946	116 522	10 367
2001	254 256	12 582	123 042	51 205	33 310	105 237	362 324	235 802	142 480	126 522	8 745
2002	246 977	13 141	110 930	56 166	32 634	98 367	334 672	208 275	124 357	126 397	8 522
2003	240 220	14 691	98 892	58 853	31 253	93 689	333 757	203 814	128 411	129 943	9 475
2004	247 740	15 438	107 642	49 609	34 351	95 731	349 424	213 567	127 529	135 857	9 984
2005	300 348	17 050	166 170	46 219	40 674	103 150	415 836	288 099	141 920	127 737	8 817
2004											
January	238 099	14 507	97 724	57 600	32 046	92 917	331 988	201 621	126 839	130 367	9 516
February	237 326	14 814	97 545	56 354	32 792	93 336	332 027	201 145	126 541	130 882	9 177
March	238 261	15 005	97 628	55 113	33 395	94 762	335 537	203 083	128 854	132 454	9 379
April	238 950	15 329	97 865	54 077	34 681	94 407	335 901	202 783	128 083	133 118	9 028
May	238 190	15 753	97 861	52 982	34 830	94 857	335 319	203 411	128 543	131 908	9 474
June	239 355	16 014	97 348	54 466	34 470	94 614	336 733	203 100	128 150	133 633	9 407
July	245 436	15 950	102 989	53 812	33 847	93 783	341 976	208 655	127 800	133 321	9 279
August	245 265	16 223	103 251	52 808	34 165	92 486	340 680	207 393	125 901	133 287	9 428
September	244 469	16 340	103 068	51 664	33 469	95 289	343 454	208 961	127 774	134 493	9 627
October	243 215	15 739	102 409	51 281	34 004	95 710	344 138	207 241	126 497	136 897	9 672
November	246 987	15 570	106 185	50 840	34 118	95 452	348 642	211 677	126 868	136 965	10 403
December	247 740	15 438	107 642	49 609	34 351	95 731	349 424	213 567	127 529	135 857	9 984
2005											
January	246 089	15 113	107 196	48 531	34 408	96 311	349 440	214 998	128 936	134 442	9 485
February	246 782	15 182	109 013	47 903	34 785	97 055	351 718	218 112	130 229	133 606	9 525
March	243 453	15 028	107 565	46 342	35 120	98 467	350 724	217 627	130 764	133 097	9 285
April	242 692	15 227	107 562	45 220	35 299	98 483	351 013	219 314	132 113	131 699	9 367
May	252 923	15 503	119 124	44 285	35 809	98 341	361 815	231 294	132 365	130 521	9 818
June	262 511	15 484	125 708	43 564	36 415	100 902	372 164	240 706	134 741	131 458	9 457
July	266 049	15 696	129 743	43 007	36 528	101 047	376 991	245 965	135 504	131 026	9 500
August	269 136	15 852	134 688	42 332	37 343	102 586	382 619	252 557	137 493	130 062	10 060
September	269 442	16 400	136 454	41 593	38 468	103 845	384 144	255 316	138 904	128 828	10 016
October	274 737	16 907	139 813	44 577	38 988	103 826	390 111	259 749	140 099	130 362	10 237
November	288 810	16 683	154 558	44 801	40 027	103 790	405 074	275 686	140 917	129 388	9 977
December	300 348	17 050	166 170	46 219	40 674	103 150	415 836	288 099	141 920	127 737	8 817

[1]Includes categories not shown separately.
[2]Data are for SIC industries roughly similar to the NAICS industries indicated in the column headings.
[3]Data exclude semiconductors. See notes and definitions for more information.
. . . = Not available.

Table 17-8. Motor Vehicle Sales and Inventories

(Number of units, as noted.)

Year and month	Retail sales of new passenger cars						Retail inventories of new domestic passenger cars (thousands of units, end of period)		
	Thousands of units, not seasonally adjusted			Millions of units, seasonally adjusted annual rate					
	Total	Domestic	Imports	Total	Domestic	Imports	Not seasonally adjusted	Seasonally adjusted	Inventory to sales ratio
1970	8 402.6	7 119.4	1 283.2	8.403	7.119	1.283	...	...	...
1971	10 227.8	8 661.8	1 566.0	10.228	8.662	1.566	...	...	...
1972	10 873.3	9 252.6	1 620.7	10.873	9.253	1.621	1 311.0	1 379.0	1.700
1973	11 350.1	9 588.6	1 761.5	11.350	9.589	1.762	1 600.0	1 654.0	2.500
1974	8 773.7	7 361.8	1 411.9	8.774	7.362	1.412	1 672.0	1 730.0	3.400
1975	8 537.8	6 950.9	1 586.9	8.538	6.951	1.587	1 419.0	1 468.0	2.200
1976	9 994.0	8 492.0	1 502.0	9.994	8.492	1.502	1 465.0	1 494.0	1.900
1977	11 046.0	8 971.2	2 074.8	11.046	8.971	2.075	1 731.0	1 743.0	2.300
1978	11 164.0	9 163.9	2 000.1	11.164	9.164	2.000	1 729.0	1 731.0	2.300
1979	10 558.8	8 230.1	2 328.7	10.559	8.230	2.329	1 691.0	1 667.0	2.400
1980	8 981.8	6 581.4	2 400.4	8.982	6.581	2.401	1 448.0	1 440.0	2.600
1981	8 534.3	6 208.8	2 325.5	8.534	6.209	2.326	1 471.0	1 495.0	3.600
1982	7 979.4	5 758.2	2 221.2	7.980	5.758	2.221	1 126.0	1 127.0	2.200
1983	9 178.6	6 793.0	2 385.6	9.179	6.793	2.386	1 352.0	1 350.0	2.000
1984	10 390.2	7 951.7	2 438.5	10.390	7.952	2.439	1 415.0	1 411.0	2.100
1985	10 978.4	8 204.7	2 773.7	10.978	8.205	2.774	1 630.0	1 619.0	2.500
1986	11 405.7	8 215.0	3 190.7	11.406	8.215	3.191	1 499.0	1 515.0	2.000
1987	10 170.9	7 080.9	3 090.0	10.171	7.081	3.090	1 680.0	1 716.0	2.800
1988	10 545.6	7 539.4	3 006.2	10.546	7.539	3.006	1 601.0	1 601.0	2.300
1989	9 776.8	7 078.1	2 698.7	9.777	7.078	2.699	1 669.0	1 687.0	3.100
1990	9 300.2	6 896.9	2 403.3	9.300	6.897	2.403	1 408.0	1 418.0	2.600
1991	8 175.0	6 136.9	2 038.1	8.175	6.137	2.038	1 283.0	1 296.0	2.600
1992	8 214.4	6 276.6	1 937.8	8.214	6.277	1.938	1 276.0	1 288.0	2.300
1993	8 517.7	6 734.0	1 783.7	8.518	6.734	1.784	1 345.5	1 392.3	2.489
1994	8 990.4	7 255.2	1 735.2	8.990	7.255	1.735	1 378.6	1 409.6	2.335
1995	8 636.2	7 128.8	1 507.4	8.637	7.129	1.508	1 639.2	1 665.9	2.810
1996	8 526.8	7 253.7	1 273.1	8.527	7.254	1.273	1 441.4	1 485.4	2.463
1997	8 272.5	6 906.2	1 366.3	8.273	6.907	1.366	1 316.8	1 356.4	2.360
1998	8 142.1	6 763.9	1 378.2	8.143	6.764	1.378	1 270.5	1 336.0	2.381
1999	8 696.5	6 981.7	1 714.8	8.697	6.982	1.715	1 318.1	1 392.3	2.394
2000	8 852.1	6 832.8	2 019.3	8.852	6.833	2.019	1 330.5	1 360.8	2.400
2001	8 422.1	6 322.7	2 099.4	8.422	6.323	2.099	1 108.2	1 147.3	2.198
2002	8 102.4	5 871.3	2 231.1	8.102	5.871	2.231	1 105.6	1 156.2	2.368
2003	7 614.5	5 527.1	2 087.4	7.615	5.527	2.087	1 143.6	1 254.1	2.726
2004	7 504.5	5 349.9	2 154.6	7.505	5.350	2.155	1 086.3	1 224.0	2.751
2005	7 667.2	5 480.4	2 186.8	7.667	5.480	2.187	929.5	1 076.0	2.360
2003									
January	543.2	385.5	157.7	8.115	5.824	2.291	1 220.5	1 225.0	2.524
February	581.1	418.4	162.7	7.526	5.320	2.206	1 250.3	1 232.2	2.780
March	695.7	503.3	192.4	7.670	5.494	2.176	1 242.8	1 232.2	2.692
April	653.0	475.8	177.2	7.442	5.412	2.030	1 228.9	1 241.1	2.752
May	726.9	534.9	192.0	7.305	5.327	1.978	1 201.0	1 268.1	2.857
June	688.6	514.4	174.2	7.688	5.646	2.042	1 185.8	1 280.2	2.721
July	680.1	494.1	186.0	7.625	5.574	2.051	1 026.1	1 278.4	2.752
August	738.1	535.2	202.9	7.871	5.764	2.107	965.7	1 244.0	2.590
September	596.0	433.8	162.2	7.627	5.531	2.096	1 014.0	1 270.1	2.756
October	573.8	417.4	156.4	7.249	5.294	1.955	1 111.2	1 283.1	2.908
November	557.7	398.3	159.4	7.796	5.662	2.134	1 145.5	1 258.3	2.667
December	580.3	416.0	164.3	7.462	5.480	1.982	1 131.0	1 236.4	2.707
2004									
January	495.4	360.8	134.6	7.131	5.219	1.912	1 170.2	1 240.8	2.853
February	582.2	426.0	156.2	7.603	5.459	2.144	1 197.7	1 243.4	2.733
March	692.0	503.0	189.0	7.751	5.596	2.155	1 211.5	1 226.8	2.631
April	644.0	455.9	188.1	7.291	5.177	2.114	1 218.5	1 261.0	2.923
May	742.9	539.9	203.0	7.871	5.638	2.233	1 127.5	1 239.8	2.639
June	669.4	478.3	191.1	7.241	5.099	2.142	1 120.4	1 230.4	2.896
July	682.0	490.1	191.9	7.496	5.414	2.082	933.0	1 207.3	2.676
August	636.0	454.0	182.0	7.244	5.192	2.052	940.8	1 216.4	2.811
September	605.8	434.6	171.2	7.341	5.257	2.084	968.0	1 219.3	2.783
October	584.9	398.1	186.8	7.497	5.131	2.366	1 038.2	1 235.7	2.890
November	517.8	353.2	164.6	7.480	5.218	2.262	1 076.7	1 206.5	2.775
December	652.1	456.0	196.1	8.110	5.800	2.310	1 032.6	1 160.5	2.401
2005									
January	486.3	349.0	137.3	7.369	5.298	2.071	1 081.8	1 142.2	2.587
February	571.4	413.5	157.9	7.501	5.317	2.184	1 123.7	1 153.7	2.604
March	718.5	516.8	201.7	7.740	5.536	2.204	1 081.9	1 134.4	2.459
April	714.6	510.1	204.5	7.912	5.658	2.254	1 023.4	1 087.3	2.306
May	690.1	494.8	195.3	7.554	5.351	2.203	957.6	1 068.5	2.396
June	706.2	506.1	200.1	7.506	5.291	2.215	959.3	1 074.7	2.438
July	712.3	509.0	203.3	8.098	5.792	2.306	752.1	1 048.4	2.172
August	697.8	499.5	198.3	7.756	5.564	2.192	740.8	1 022.1	2.204
September	646.7	463.5	183.2	7.922	5.690	2.232	741.8	1 004.5	2.118
October	562.6	397.0	165.6	7.302	5.162	2.140	834.3	1 044.8	2.429
November	540.7	384.4	156.3	7.636	5.537	2.099	925.4	1 067.4	2.313
December	620.0	436.7	183.3	7.711	5.568	2.143	932.4	1 064.0	2.293

... = Not available.

Table 17-8. Motor Vehicle Sales and Inventories—Continued

(Number of units, as noted.)

Year and month	Retail sales of new trucks and buses								Unit sales of cars and light trucks (millions of units, seasonally adjusted annual rate)		
	Thousands of units, not seasonally adjusted				Millions of units, seasonally adjusted annual rate						
	Total	0–10,000 pounds		10,001 pounds and over	Total	0–10,000 pounds		10,001 pounds and over	Total	Domestic	Imports
		Domestic	Imports			Domestic	Imports				
1970	1 745.8	1 408.5	0.0	337.3	. . .	1.408	. . .	0.335	. . .	8.528	. . .
1971	2 031.9	1 693.0	0.0	338.9	. . .	1.700	. . .	0.339	. . .	10.362	. . .
1972	2 559.9	2 122.5	0.0	437.4	. . .	2.116	. . .	0.437	. . .	11.369	. . .
1973	3 005.1	2 509.4	0.0	495.7	. . .	2.513	. . .	0.495	. . .	12.102	. . .
1974	2 604.0	2 180.1	0.0	423.9	. . .	2.176	. . .	0.424	. . .	9.538	. . .
1975	2 350.9	2 052.6	0.0	298.3	. . .	2.055	. . .	0.298	12.950	9.006	. . .
1976	3 300.5	2 738.3	237.5	324.7	3.296	2.733	0.239	0.324	12.950	11.225	1.741
1977	3 813.0	3 112.8	323.1	377.1	3.818	3.116	0.324	0.378	14.492	12.088	2.398
1978	4 256.8	3 481.1	335.9	439.8	4.249	3.469	0.340	0.440	14.975	12.633	2.340
1979	3 589.7	2 730.2	469.4	390.1	3.599	2.740	0.469	0.390	13.775	10.970	2.798
1980	2 487.4	1 731.1	484.6	271.7	2.482	1.731	0.480	0.271	11.192	8.312	2.881
1981	2 255.6	1 581.7	447.6	226.3	2.255	1.585	0.444	0.226	10.558	7.794	2.770
1982	2 562.8	1 967.5	410.4	184.9	2.569	1.971	0.413	0.185	10.375	7.729	2.634
1983	3 117.3	2 465.2	463.3	188.8	3.130	2.480	0.461	0.189	12.117	9.273	2.846
1984	4 093.1	3 207.2	607.7	278.2	4.085	3.199	0.609	0.278	14.200	11.150	3.047
1985	4 741.7	3 618.4	828.3	295.0	4.759	3.634	0.831	0.295	15.433	11.838	3.604
1986	4 912.1	3 671.4	967.2	273.5	4.918	3.676	0.969	0.273	16.042	11.891	4.160
1987	4 991.5	3 792.0	912.2	287.3	4.977	3.783	0.907	0.288	14.867	10.864	3.997
1988	5 231.9	4 199.7	697.9	334.3	5.225	4.194	0.697	0.334	15.433	11.733	3.703
1989	5 055.9	4 113.6	630.3	312.0	5.065	4.123	0.629	0.313	14.542	11.201	3.328
1990	4 837.0	3 956.8	602.7	277.5	4.841	3.960	0.602	0.278	13.867	10.857	3.006
1991	4 355.4	3 605.6	528.8	221.0	4.360	3.612	0.528	0.221	12.317	9.748	2.566
1992	4 892.2	4 247.0	395.9	249.3	4.894	4.247	0.398	0.248	12.867	10.524	2.336
1993	5 667.8	5 000.5	364.5	302.8	5.658	4.991	0.365	0.302	13.867	11.725	2.148
1994	6 407.3	5 658.2	396.3	352.8	6.408	5.659	0.395	0.354	15.042	12.914	2.130
1995	6 469.8	5 690.9	390.5	388.4	6.486	5.703	0.393	0.390	14.742	12.832	1.900
1996	6 921.8	6 131.8	430.9	359.1	6.914	6.127	0.429	0.357	15.083	13.381	1.702
1997	7 217.6	6 270.4	571.2	376.2	7.229	6.283	0.570	0.376	15.117	13.190	1.936
1998	7 815.8	6 745.3	646.2	424.3	7.788	6.720	0.644	0.425	15.500	13.484	2.022
1999	8 704.2	7 420.0	762.9	521.3	8.713	7.429	0.763	0.521	16.892	14.411	2.478
2000	8 953.5	7 650.8	840.8	461.9	8.951	7.649	0.841	0.461	17.342	14.481	2.861
2001	9 046.3	7 718.4	977.8	350.1	9.043	7.715	0.978	0.350	17.100	14.038	3.078
2002	9 035.6	7 646.9	1 066.3	322.4	9.035	7.647	1.066	0.322	16.800	13.518	3.298
2003	9 357.0	7 801.4	1 227.2	328.4	9.356	7.802	1.227	0.328	16.633	13.329	3.315
2004	9 792.4	8 114.6	1 246.2	431.6	9.790	8.115	1.246	0.429	16.883	13.465	3.401
2005	9 777.4	8 065.4	1 215.5	496.5	9.779	8.065	1.215	0.498	16.950	13.546	3.402
2003											
January	564.8	463.9	80.8	20.1	8.585	7.180	1.126	0.279	16.400	13.004	3.417
February	658.0	553.5	82.9	21.6	8.607	7.176	1.135	0.296	15.800	12.496	3.341
March	782.6	648.3	109.2	25.1	8.834	7.248	1.295	0.291	16.200	12.742	3.471
April	783.7	652.9	102.2	28.6	9.299	7.742	1.246	0.311	16.400	13.154	3.276
May	874.2	730.7	115.9	27.6	9.151	7.636	1.209	0.306	16.200	12.963	3.187
June	813.8	683.0	102.4	28.4	9.319	7.731	1.267	0.321	16.700	13.377	3.309
July	858.7	714.5	114.9	29.3	9.493	7.888	1.265	0.340	16.800	13.462	3.316
August	918.0	760.7	130.0	27.3	10.386	8.743	1.313	0.330	17.900	14.507	3.420
September	733.4	609.7	95.5	28.2	9.667	8.030	1.288	0.349	16.900	13.561	3.384
October	759.8	633.4	95.5	30.9	9.242	7.708	1.188	0.346	16.100	13.002	3.143
November	727.7	607.5	93.5	26.7	9.777	8.184	1.219	0.374	17.200	13.846	3.353
December	882.3	743.3	104.4	34.6	9.917	8.352	1.175	0.390	17.000	13.832	3.157
2004											
January	654.1	538.0	89.0	27.1	9.614	8.008	1.217	0.389	16.400	13.227	3.129
February	721.5	603.1	89.2	29.2	9.469	7.851	1.220	0.398	16.700	13.310	3.364
March	847.0	702.5	106.9	37.6	9.514	7.851	1.255	0.408	16.900	13.447	3.410
April	811.6	677.8	97.5	36.3	9.569	8.022	1.153	0.394	16.500	13.199	3.267
May	918.0	772.1	110.3	35.6	10.209	8.547	1.249	0.413	17.700	14.185	3.482
June	811.4	669.8	104.5	37.1	8.836	7.218	1.214	0.404	15.700	12.317	3.356
July	907.1	751.2	119.7	36.2	9.976	8.279	1.267	0.430	17.000	13.693	3.349
August	827.3	680.4	109.7	37.2	9.847	8.194	1.212	0.441	16.700	13.386	3.264
September	864.3	728.7	99.1	36.5	10.562	8.863	1.251	0.448	17.500	14.120	3.335
October	785.3	643.8	103.2	38.3	9.929	8.160	1.309	0.460	17.000	13.291	3.675
November	713.4	583.7	94.7	35.0	9.816	8.094	1.262	0.460	16.800	13.312	3.524
December	931.4	763.5	122.4	45.5	10.144	8.291	1.346	0.507	17.700	14.091	3.656
2005											
January	609.6	491.7	82.6	35.3	9.486	7.765	1.194	0.527	16.300	13.063	3.265
February	714.7	588.4	90.9	35.4	9.464	7.736	1.245	0.483	16.500	13.053	3.429
March	897.5	745.9	108.2	43.4	9.647	7.965	1.208	0.474	16.900	13.501	3.412
April	827.4	678.2	106.6	42.6	9.808	8.086	1.244	0.478	17.200	13.744	3.498
May	847.2	700.0	105.7	41.5	9.694	7.997	1.225	0.472	16.800	13.348	3.428
June	1 013.8	858.1	109.4	46.3	10.757	9.000	1.254	0.503	17.800	14.291	3.469
July	1 133.4	971.2	120.8	41.4	13.111	11.265	1.335	0.511	20.700	17.057	3.641
August	826.3	670.4	112.6	43.3	9.554	7.850	1.212	0.492	16.800	13.414	3.404
September	720.2	589.9	89.3	41.0	9.049	7.433	1.114	0.502	16.500	13.123	3.346
October	621.6	493.1	87.4	41.1	7.985	6.335	1.155	0.495	14.800	11.497	3.295
November	660.0	531.6	89.2	39.2	8.890	7.211	1.167	0.512	16.000	12.748	3.266
December	905.7	746.9	112.8	46.0	9.898	8.141	1.231	0.526	17.100	13.709	3.374

. . . = Not available.

Table 17-9. Retail and Food Services Sales

(All retail establishments and food services; millions of dollars; not seasonally adjusted.)

Classification basis, year, and month	Retail and food services, total [1]	Retail (NAICS industry categories)											Food services and drinking places
		GAFO (department store type goods), total [2]	Motor vehicles and parts	Furniture and home furnishings	Electronics and appliances	Building materials and garden	Food and beverages	Health and personal care	Gasoline	Clothing and accessories	General merchandise	Nonstore retailers	
SIC Basis [3]													
1967	297 084	. . .	56 094	13 605	. . .	13 435	70 456	11 359	22 362	17 900	40 124	. . .	22 518
1968	329 336	. . .	64 314	15 257	. . .	15 602	75 899	12 378	24 750	19 707	44 019	. . .	25 279
1969	352 457	. . .	67 745	16 152	. . .	17 175	81 258	13 200	26 301	21 384	46 559	. . .	27 173
1970	374 989	. . .	65 241	17 043	. . .	18 080	89 990	14 567	28 903	22 095	49 163	. . .	30 476
1971	413 969	. . .	80 718	18 183	. . .	20 924	94 002	15 143	30 620	24 178	54 365	. . .	32 321
1972	458 267	. . .	92 335	21 199	. . .	24 123	100 589	16 139	33 072	26 367	59 656	. . .	35 738
1973	511 570	. . .	104 893	24 244	. . .	27 466	111 817	17 190	36 942	29 109	65 825	. . .	40 290
1974	541 686	. . .	97 551	25 982	. . .	27 347	126 312	18 595	43 054	30 077	69 540	. . .	44 606
1975	587 704	. . .	107 348	27 046	. . .	27 299	138 665	19 995	47 603	32 398	73 759	. . .	51 067
1976	655 859	. . .	130 169	30 300	. . .	33 259	148 218	21 710	52 037	34 706	79 500	. . .	57 331
1977	722 109	. . .	150 129	33 308	. . .	38 913	158 444	23 381	56 638	37 165	87 824	. . .	63 370
1978	804 019	. . .	168 065	36 832	. . .	45 170	175 425	25 607	59 889	42 649	97 215	. . .	71 828
1979	896 561	. . .	178 641	42 417	. . .	51 016	197 985	28 455	73 521	46 070	103 817	. . .	82 110
1980	956 921	. . .	164 149	44 238	. . .	50 794	220 224	30 951	94 093	49 296	108 955	. . .	90 058
1981	1 038 163	. . .	181 903	46 900	. . .	52 230	236 188	33 999	103 072	53 998	120 534	. . .	98 118
1982	1 068 747	. . .	192 440	46 761	. . .	50 994	246 122	36 440	97 440	55 570	124 624	. . .	104 593
1983	1 170 163	. . .	229 979	54 691	. . .	58 739	256 018	40 591	102 927	60 192	135 959	. . .	113 281
1984	1 286 914	. . .	273 320	61 432	. . .	67 077	271 909	44 011	107 565	64 341	150 283	. . .	121 321
1985	1 375 027	. . .	303 199	68 287	. . .	71 196	285 062	46 994	113 341	70 195	158 636	. . .	127 949
1986	1 449 636	. . .	326 138	75 714	. . .	77 104	297 019	50 546	102 093	75 626	169 397	. . .	139 415
1987	1 541 299	. . .	342 896	78 072	. . .	83 454	309 461	54 142	104 769	79 322	181 970	. . .	153 461
1988	1 656 202	. . .	372 570	85 390	. . .	91 056	325 493	57 842	110 341	85 307	192 521	. . .	167 993
1989	1 758 971	. . .	386 011	91 301	. . .	92 379	347 045	63 343	122 882	92 341	206 306	. . .	177 829
1990	1 844 611	. . .	387 605	91 545	. . .	94 640	368 333	70 558	138 504	95 819	215 514	. . .	190 149
1991	1 855 937	. . .	372 647	91 676	. . .	91 496	374 523	75 540	137 295	97 441	226 730	. . .	194 424
1992	1 951 589	. . .	406 935	96 947	. . .	100 838	377 099	77 788	136 950	104 212	246 420	. . .	200 164
NAICS Basis													
1992	2 019 131	534 367	419 353	52 467	42 763	131 244	371 451	89 782	156 556	120 346	247 968	78 657	203 415
1993	2 158 299	571 790	473 948	55 587	48 760	141 220	375 440	92 671	162 587	125 001	266 088	85 977	216 051
1994	2 335 650	617 379	542 235	60 551	57 413	157 497	385 265	96 442	171 416	129 341	285 278	96 460	225 629
1995	2 456 129	651 071	580 842	63 601	64 919	164 831	391 312	101 719	181 294	131 593	300 589	103 705	233 625
1996	2 609 561	683 678	628 687	67 848	68 515	176 972	402 020	109 646	194 601	136 851	315 398	117 963	242 896
1997	2 732 043	714 453	655 013	72 863	70 211	191 345	410 288	118 769	199 856	140 565	331 454	126 397	258 040
1998	2 859 332	759 063	689 679	77 569	74 686	202 724	417 433	129 699	191 887	149 433	351 186	134 113	272 227
1999	3 093 569	816 827	765 549	84 451	79 138	218 611	434 599	142 829	212 682	160 043	380 291	152 022	285 013
2000	3 294 217	863 903	797 568	91 328	82 363	229 320	445 666	155 372	249 975	167 968	404 344	180 688	305 461
2001	3 385 577	883 866	816 941	91 644	80 395	239 707	463 330	166 678	251 537	167 583	427 586	180 805	317 852
2002	3 466 136	913 925	820 269	94 610	83 897	248 888	465 794	180 143	250 770	172 617	446 648	189 535	331 814
2003	3 615 170	948 246	841 215	97 528	86 957	265 052	477 130	192 224	273 566	178 778	468 734	203 902	349 693
2004	3 849 748	1 007 937	864 848	105 477	94 989	298 935	495 717	198 588	320 793	190 204	497 231	224 699	372 440
2005	4 115 815	1 061 836	895 250	111 293	100 440	326 993	519 292	208 376	388 261	201 682	525 726	249 011	396 637
2003													
January	268 714	65 262	62 179	7 218	6 529	17 335	38 718	15 528	21 148	10 819	31 551	17 562	26 104
February	259 408	64 565	61 063	6 744	6 029	15 721	35 709	14 765	20 784	11 673	32 243	16 382	25 600
March	293 827	72 112	71 907	7 660	6 372	20 089	38 880	15 838	23 787	13 461	36 248	16 995	29 185
April	294 374	71 421	72 425	7 422	5 893	24 214	38 658	15 723	22 753	13 699	36 036	15 708	28 278
May	312 557	77 089	76 750	8 134	6 569	25 796	41 239	16 150	23 209	14 742	38 845	15 428	30 928
June	301 279	73 967	74 625	7 815	6 644	25 166	39 193	15 486	22 694	13 505	37 293	14 865	29 772
July	310 240	74 822	78 453	8 143	6 832	24 631	41 332	15 986	23 876	13 858	37 202	15 078	30 604
August	317 350	82 360	77 602	8 458	7 428	22 914	40 945	15 983	24 822	15 526	40 204	15 566	31 837
September	294 054	72 980	70 040	8 099	6 808	23 032	38 676	15 692	23 210	13 569	35 278	16 671	31 373
October	304 326	77 645	68 028	8 444	6 961	24 367	40 127	16 050	23 419	14 601	38 673	18 444	30 207
November	301 337	89 140	61 558	9 117	8 349	20 960	40 050	15 686	21 730	16 554	44 743	18 218	28 823
December	357 704	126 883	66 585	10 274	12 543	20 827	43 603	18 897	22 134	26 771	60 418	22 985	29 844
2004													
January	281 439	70 727	60 980	7 761	7 217	18 280	40 279	16 309	22 482	11 787	34 379	18 944	28 566
February	282 542	72 599	65 067	7 732	7 005	18 158	37 487	15 625	22 239	13 340	35 934	17 991	28 674
March	318 957	77 927	78 464	8 638	7 286	25 080	39 958	17 143	25 225	14 750	38 291	18 886	31 039
April	315 088	77 423	73 074	8 128	6 705	28 409	40 230	16 512	25 810	15 052	38 907	17 442	30 778
May	328 356	80 928	77 327	8 250	7 177	28 623	42 308	16 491	28 145	15 373	41 351	16 275	32 069
June	321 186	78 262	75 185	8 592	7 437	28 914	40 896	16 345	27 991	14 227	38 951	16 642	31 303
July	328 304	80 072	78 682	9 052	7 482	26 579	42 988	16 256	28 895	14 658	39 639	16 310	33 044
August	326 783	83 429	76 245	9 040	7 851	26 117	41 109	16 315	28 407	15 582	40 221	17 704	32 087
September	314 067	77 277	73 467	8 595	7 346	25 615	40 770	15 907	27 124	14 218	37 565	18 167	30 427
October	320 416	82 135	68 682	8 874	7 316	25 342	41 585	16 326	29 384	15 567	41 148	19 297	32 144
November	324 778	92 982	65 193	9 749	8 962	24 306	41 536	16 354	27 666	17 230	46 312	21 159	29 863
December	387 832	134 176	72 482	11 066	13 205	23 512	46 541	19 005	27 425	28 420	64 533	25 882	32 446
2005													
January	294 114	73 097	62 072	8 016	7 567	20 270	41 149	16 714	25 847	12 079	36 105	20 267	29 672
February	296 367	74 916	67 265	8 081	7 483	20 279	38 414	16 289	25 388	13 905	36 977	19 009	29 624
March	340 568	82 785	81 155	8 910	7 827	26 326	42 860	17 876	29 949	15 763	41 027	21 350	32 641
April	337 663	81 163	78 518	8 544	7 145	29 950	41 668	16 932	31 247	15 741	40 805	19 030	33 487
May	347 570	84 275	79 111	8 792	7 540	31 891	43 796	17 448	31 954	16 032	42 706	18 620	33 997
June	353 605	84 515	86 159	9 127	7 806	31 404	43 309	17 020	32 752	15 621	42 701	18 663	33 575
July	354 414	83 701	88 314	9 125	7 788	27 808	44 635	16 852	34 884	15 271	42 106	17 503	34 952
August	358 936	88 966	81 938	9 808	8 362	29 133	43 824	17 448	37 284	16 757	42 843	20 240	34 324
September	336 696	82 063	70 038	9 446	7 807	28 813	43 050	16 971	37 330	15 015	40 059	20 266	32 935
October	339 826	87 041	64 203	9 355	7 781	28 657	43 508	17 281	37 594	16 579	43 906	21 510	34 025
November	346 993	98 987	65 360	10 506	9 528	27 583	43 776	17 396	32 054	18 479	49 509	23 607	32 220
December	409 063	140 327	71 117	11 583	13 806	25 499	49 303	20 149	31 978	30 440	66 982	28 945	35 185

[1] Includes store categories not shown separately.
[2] Includes furniture, home furnishings, electronics, appliances, clothing, sporting goods, hobby, book, music, general merchandise, office supplies, stationery, and gifts.
[3] Data are for SIC industries roughly similar to the NAICS industries indicated in the column headings.
. . . = Not available.

Table 17-9. Retail and Food Services Sales—Continued

(All retail establishments and food services; millions of dollars; seasonally adjusted.)

Classification basis, year, and month	Total	Retail (NAICS industry categories)						Food and beverages			Health and personal care	Gasoline
		Total	GAFO (department store type goods)²	Motor vehicles and parts	Furniture and home furnishings	Electronics and appliances	Building materials and garden	Total	Groceries	Beer, wine, and liquor		
SIC Basis ³												
1967	297 084	...	...	56 094	13 605	...	13 435	70 456	65 036	6 652	11 359	22 362
1968	329 336	...	...	64 314	15 257	...	15 602	75 899	69 873	7 258	12 378	24 750
1969	352 457	...	...	67 745	16 152	...	17 175	81 258	74 836	7 739	13 200	26 301
1970	374 989	...	...	65 241	17 043	...	18 080	89 990	82 556	8 412	14 567	28 903
1971	413 969	...	...	80 718	18 183	...	20 924	94 002	86 419	9 294	15 143	30 620
1972	458 267	...	...	92 335	21 199	...	24 123	100 589	92 856	9 814	16 139	33 072
1973	511 570	...	...	104 893	24 244	...	27 466	111 817	103 555	10 288	17 190	36 942
1974	541 686	...	...	97 551	25 982	...	27 347	126 312	117 182	11 087	18 595	43 054
1975	587 704	...	...	107 348	27 046	...	27 299	138 665	129 087	11 896	19 995	47 603
1976	655 859	...	...	130 169	30 300	...	33 259	148 218	137 992	12 442	21 710	52 037
1977	722 109	...	...	150 129	33 308	...	38 913	158 444	148 116	13 031	23 381	56 638
1978	804 019	...	...	168 065	36 832	...	45 170	175 425	164 234	13 630	25 607	59 889
1979	896 561	...	...	178 641	42 417	...	51 016	197 985	185 318	15 194	28 455	73 521
1980	956 921	...	...	164 149	44 238	...	50 794	220 224	205 630	16 882	30 951	94 093
1981	1 038 163	...	...	181 903	46 900	...	52 230	236 188	220 580	17 702	33 999	103 072
1982	1 068 747	...	...	192 440	46 761	...	50 994	246 122	230 696	18 146	36 440	97 440
1983	1 170 163	...	...	229 979	54 691	...	58 739	256 018	240 402	19 121	40 591	102 927
1984	1 286 914	...	...	273 320	61 432	...	67 077	271 909	258 465	18 273	44 011	107 565
1985	1 375 027	...	...	303 199	68 287	...	71 196	285 062	269 546	19 532	46 994	113 341
1986	1 449 636	...	...	326 138	75 714	...	77 104	297 019	280 833	19 929	50 546	102 093
1987	1 541 299	...	...	342 896	78 072	...	83 454	309 461	290 979	19 826	54 142	104 769
1988	1 656 202	...	...	372 570	85 390	...	91 056	325 493	307 173	19 638	57 842	110 341
1989	1 758 971	...	...	386 011	91 301	...	92 379	347 045	328 072	20 099	63 343	122 882
1990	1 844 611	...	...	387 605	91 545	...	94 640	368 333	348 243	21 722	70 558	138 504
1991	1 855 937	...	...	372 647	91 676	...	91 496	374 523	354 331	22 454	75 540	137 295
1992	1 951 589	...	...	406 935	96 947	...	100 838	377 099	358 148	21 698	77 788	136 950
NAICS Basis												
1992	2 019 131	1 815 716	534 367	419 353	52 467	42 763	131 244	371 451	337 925	21 825	89 782	156 556
1993	2 158 299	1 942 248	571 790	473 948	55 587	48 760	141 220	375 440	341 855	21 675	92 671	162 587
1994	2 335 650	2 110 021	617 379	542 235	60 551	57 413	157 497	385 265	351 056	22 240	96 442	171 416
1995	2 456 129	2 222 504	651 071	580 842	63 601	64 919	164 831	391 312	356 932	22 145	101 719	181 294
1996	2 609 561	2 366 665	683 678	628 687	67 848	68 515	176 972	402 020	366 075	23 300	109 646	194 601
1997	2 732 043	2 474 003	714 453	655 013	72 863	70 211	191 345	410 288	373 072	24 222	118 769	199 856
1998	2 859 332	2 587 105	759 063	689 679	77 569	74 686	202 724	417 433	378 675	25 533	129 699	191 887
1999	3 093 569	2 808 556	816 827	765 549	84 451	79 138	218 611	434 599	394 724	26 635	142 829	212 682
2000	3 294 217	2 988 756	863 903	797 568	91 328	82 363	229 320	445 666	402 988	28 668	155 372	249 975
2001	3 385 577	3 067 725	883 866	816 941	91 644	80 395	239 707	463 330	418 596	29 783	166 678	251 537
2002	3 466 160	3 134 322	913 925	820 269	94 610	83 897	248 888	465 794	420 288	30 061	180 143	250 770
2003	3 615 170	3 265 477	948 246	841 215	97 528	86 957	265 052	477 130	429 962	30 676	192 224	273 566
2004	3 849 748	3 477 308	1 007 937	864 848	105 477	94 989	298 935	495 717	445 104	32 576	198 588	320 793
2005	4 115 815	3 719 178	1 061 836	895 250	111 293	100 440	326 993	519 292	463 905	34 967	208 376	388 261
2003												
January	295 636	267 507	76 707	69 872	7 889	6 884	21 287	39 418	35 629	2 470	15 451	23 037
February	291 896	263 887	76 081	66 850	7 544	6 758	20 106	39 420	35 660	2 466	15 493	23 780
March	297 198	268 669	76 966	69 188	7 913	6 846	21 306	39 478	35 658	2 502	15 681	24 100
April	296 078	267 629	77 168	69 660	7 955	6 924	21 138	39 619	35 762	2 525	15 676	22 640
May	296 682	267 642	78 092	69 558	8 094	7 095	21 535	39 110	35 261	2 498	15 741	21 772
June	299 042	269 854	78 813	69 242	8 166	7 163	22 086	39 771	35 917	2 503	15 932	21 905
July	303 559	274 189	79 658	71 086	8 184	7 290	22 591	40 109	36 183	2 550	16 197	22 293
August	308 256	278 334	80 845	73 059	8 212	7 446	22 636	40 077	36 061	2 603	16 309	22 899
September	305 668	276 305	80 677	70 929	8 315	7 438	22 715	40 107	36 067	2 628	16 312	22 867
October	304 568	274 601	80 022	69 790	8 336	7 519	23 092	40 080	35 991	2 643	16 424	22 240
November	308 662	278 512	80 928	71 920	8 411	7 581	23 096	40 071	36 031	2 615	16 477	23 068
December	307 042	277 228	81 413	69 942	8 387	7 644	22 960	40 099	36 024	2 642	16 605	23 397
2004												
January	309 206	278 913	82 308	69 349	8 473	7 628	22 873	40 595	36 492	2 642	16 244	24 437
February	312 136	281 729	82 530	71 418	8 506	7 659	22 953	40 360	36 261	2 634	16 075	24 960
March	317 446	286 775	83 348	72 434	8 752	7 748	25 173	40 735	36 614	2 642	16 547	25 352
April	313 959	283 486	82 521	69 897	8 684	7 823	24 895	40 753	36 609	2 682	16 414	25 479
May	319 870	289 241	83 377	72 905	8 496	7 875	24 789	41 002	36 812	2 711	16 393	27 037
June	313 578	282 889	82 920	66 758	8 723	7 919	24 923	41 063	36 862	2 701	16 560	26 940
July	319 699	288 672	83 983	71 407	9 016	7 941	24 962	41 093	36 884	2 713	16 470	26 681
August	319 188	288 365	83 603	71 059	8 837	7 930	25 174	41 282	37 063	2 720	16 614	26 352
September	325 247	293 879	84 426	74 717	8 797	8 000	25 345	41 534	37 298	2 734	16 604	26 566
October	327 054	295 509	84 814	74 488	8 892	7 976	25 185	41 677	37 397	2 775	16 659	27 958
November	327 663	296 162	85 079	73 009	8 839	8 059	25 303	42 010	37 713	2 745	16 722	29 000
December	331 941	299 943	85 548	75 490	8 997	8 044	25 971	42 106	37 827	2 722	16 759	28 778
2005												
January	330 643	298 703	85 878	73 446	9 027	8 140	26 144	42 337	38 060	2 709	16 934	28 655
February	333 908	301 567	87 032	74 414	9 009	8 348	26 006	42 384	37 977	2 810	17 074	29 249
March	334 358	302 294	86 545	74 070	8 982	8 280	26 294	42 501	38 049	2 828	16 944	30 467
April	339 841	307 011	87 715	75 438	9 080	8 306	26 915	42 899	38 354	2 849	17 155	30 694
May	338 488	305 736	87 662	74 036	9 120	8 262	27 110	42 999	38 457	2 860	17 241	30 725
June	343 692	310 743	88 690	76 435	9 247	8 347	27 360	43 108	38 531	2 903	17 209	31 372
July	351 454	318 480	88 352	83 123	9 264	8 351	27 083	43 260	38 649	2 916	17 391	32 663
August	345 111	311 980	88 727	73 900	9 377	8 375	27 334	43 515	38 888	2 928	17 431	34 080
September	346 551	313 080	89 244	71 241	9 570	8 465	27 804	43 732	39 005	2 958	17 623	36 137
October	347 443	313 688	90 352	70 082	9 459	8 524	28 306	43 992	39 219	2 984	17 670	35 736
November	349 630	315 571	90 274	73 392	9 508	8 540	28 754	44 003	39 175	3 017	17 842	33 529
December	351 070	316 810	90 174	74 403	9 440	8 440	28 650	44 182	39 357	3 026	17 878	33 520

²Includes furniture, home furnishings, electronics, appliances, clothing, sporting goods, hobby, book, music, general merchandise, office supplies, stationery, and gifts.
³Data are for SIC industries roughly similar to the NAICS industries indicated in the column headings.
... = Not available.

Table 17-9. Retail and Food Services Sales—Continued

(All retail establishments and food services; millions of dollars; seasonally adjusted, except as noted.)

Classification basis, year, and month	Clothing and accessories Total [1]	Men's clothing	Women's clothing	Family clothing [4]	Shoes	Sporting goods, hobby, book, and music	General merchandise Total	Department stores [5]	Other general merchandise	Miscel- laneous store retailers	Nonstore retailers Total [1]	Electronic shopping and mail order	Food services and drinking places
SIC Basis [3]													
1967	17 900	3 519	6 812	3 569	3 606	...	40 124	29 183	...	...	...	...	22 518
1968	19 707	3 916	7 435	3 897	4 062	...	44 019	32 431	...	...	...	...	25 279
1969	21 384	4 382	7 842	4 204	4 577	...	46 559	34 754	...	...	...	...	27 173
1970	22 095	4 544	8 239	4 363	4 458	...	49 163	36 167	...	...	...	...	30 476
1971	24 178	4 903	9 222	5 046	4 524	...	54 365	40 472	...	...	...	...	32 321
1972	26 367	5 684	9 739	5 525	4 884	...	59 656	44 451	...	...	...	...	35 738
1973	29 109	6 193	10 732	5 959	5 600	...	65 825	49 342	...	...	...	...	40 290
1974	30 077	6 190	11 338	6 360	5 405	...	69 540	52 059	...	...	...	...	44 606
1975	32 398	6 619	12 438	6 725	5 751	...	73 759	55 702	...	...	...	...	51 067
1976	34 706	6 815	13 426	7 201	8 249	...	79 500	61 500	...	...	...	...	57 331
1977	37 165	7 042	12 537	7 972	7 058	...	87 824	68 856	...	...	...	...	63 370
1978	42 649	7 537	15 995	8 559	8 305	...	97 215	76 137	...	...	...	...	71 828
1979	46 070	7 763	17 030	9 397	9 693	...	103 817	81 161	...	...	...	...	82 110
1980	49 296	7 664	17 592	10 843	10 530	...	108 955	85 464	...	...	...	...	90 058
1981	53 998	7 910	19 060	12 251	11 821	...	120 534	95 638	...	...	...	...	98 118
1982	55 570	7 803	20 017	13 660	11 419	...	124 624	99 841	...	...	...	...	104 593
1983	60 192	7 958	21 847	15 384	11 949	...	135 959	108 637	...	...	...	...	113 281
1984	64 341	8 206	23 764	16 443	12 306	...	150 283	120 487	...	...	...	...	121 321
1985	70 195	8 458	26 149	17 827	13 054	...	158 636	126 412	...	...	...	...	127 949
1986	75 626	8 646	28 600	19 336	13 947	...	169 397	134 486	...	...	...	...	139 415
1987	79 322	9 017	29 208	21 472	14 594	...	181 970	144 017	...	...	...	...	153 461
1988	85 307	9 826	30 567	23 902	15 444	...	192 521	151 523	...	...	...	...	167 993
1989	92 341	10 507	32 231	26 375	17 290	...	206 306	160 524	...	...	...	...	177 829
1990	95 819	10 450	32 812	28 398	18 043	...	215 514	165 808	...	...	...	...	190 149
1991	97 441	10 435	32 865	30 521	17 504	...	226 730	172 922	...	...	...	...	194 424
1992	104 212	10 197	35 750	33 222	18 122	...	246 420	186 423	...	...	...	...	200 164
NAICS Basis													
1992	120 346	10 185	31 840	33 159	18 630	49 296	247 968	177 089	70 879	55 833	78 657	35 252	203 415
1993	125 001	9 968	32 377	35 311	19 042	52 368	266 088	187 685	78 403	62 601	85 977	40 725	216 051
1994	129 341	10 039	30 611	38 118	19 921	57 538	285 278	198 945	86 333	70 585	96 460	47 093	225 629
1995	131 593	9 322	28 723	40 014	20 354	60 922	300 589	205 920	94 669	77 177	103 705	52 741	233 625
1996	136 851	9 554	28 266	42 275	21 248	64 055	315 398	212 203	103 195	84 109	117 963	61 174	242 896
1997	140 565	10 077	27 851	45 259	21 463	65 573	331 454	220 108	111 346	91 669	126 397	70 136	258 040
1998	149 433	10 204	28 363	50 169	22 251	68 939	351 186	223 290	127 896	99 757	134 113	80 366	272 227
1999	160 043	9 675	29 581	55 333	22 704	72 764	380 291	230 304	149 987	105 577	152 022	94 361	285 013
2000	167 968	9 515	31 480	58 928	22 888	76 112	404 344	232 475	171 869	108 052	180 688	113 877	305 461
2001	167 583	8 632	31 487	60 165	22 897	77 138	427 586	228 377	199 209	104 381	180 805	114 844	317 852
2002	172 617	8 119	31 280	64 305	23 215	76 988	446 648	220 743	225 905	104 163	189 535	122 313	331 814
2003	178 778	8 488	32 525	67 272	23 219	77 335	468 734	214 427	254 307	103 056	203 902	131 171	349 693
2004	190 204	9 060	34 718	71 991	23 751	80 211	497 231	215 657	281 574	105 616	224 699	147 123	372 440
2005	201 682	9 437	36 735	77 268	24 628	81 853	525 726	214 658	311 068	111 001	249 011	161 578	396 637
2003													
January	14 560	675	2 643	3 908	1 872	6 402	37 767	17 798	19 969	8 640	16 300	10 433	28 129
February	14 196	664	2 578	3 929	1 893	6 240	38 164	17 776	20 388	8 456	16 880	10 580	28 009
March	14 482	676	2 616	5 046	1 924	6 198	38 336	17 671	20 665	8 489	16 652	10 546	28 529
April	14 431	688	2 588	5 064	1 861	6 364	38 267	17 682	20 585	8 505	16 450	10 664	28 449
May	14 696	704	2 642	5 421	1 895	6 311	38 574	17 859	20 715	8 624	16 532	10 655	29 040
June	14 888	709	2 659	5 141	1 918	6 486	38 815	17 892	20 923	8 628	16 772	10 892	29 188
July	15 134	708	2 753	5 473	1 963	6 387	39 376	18 128	21 248	8 628	16 914	11 014	29 370
August	15 094	732	2 718	5 959	1 995	6 712	40 079	18 242	21 837	8 724	17 087	11 057	29 922
September	15 226	729	2 789	5 198	1 975	6 564	39 919	18 151	21 768	8 543	17 370	11 253	29 363
October	15 065	719	2 759	5 723	1 945	6 450	39 443	17 859	21 584	8 657	17 505	11 345	29 967
November	15 288	719	2 806	6 710	1 977	6 538	39 894	17 751	22 143	8 621	17 547	11 300	30 150
December	15 426	739	2 894	9 700	1 979	6 577	40 091	17 790	22 301	8 649	17 451	11 340	29 814
2004													
January	15 546	735	2 852	4 245	1 983	6 661	40 663	17 827	22 836	8 655	17 789	11 680	30 293
February	15 652	744	2 878	4 566	2 005	6 658	40 699	18 010	22 689	8 496	18 293	11 891	30 407
March	16 002	745	2 908	5 579	2 030	6 588	40 975	18 046	22 929	8 639	17 830	11 953	30 671
April	15 485	737	2 807	5 576	1 982	6 554	40 639	17 751	22 888	8 767	18 096	11 970	30 473
May	15 739	735	2 880	5 642	1 965	6 552	41 399	17 894	23 505	8 955	18 099	12 177	30 629
June	15 586	734	2 875	5 290	1 948	6 629	40 767	17 690	23 077	8 635	18 386	12 104	30 689
July	15 736	751	2 860	5 802	1 956	6 755	41 224	17 870	23 354	8 693	18 694	12 193	31 027
August	15 630	751	2 832	6 087	1 933	6 780	41 147	17 809	23 338	8 695	18 865	12 314	30 823
September	15 884	753	2 900	5 460	1 974	6 810	41 586	18 025	23 561	8 844	19 192	12 378	31 368
October	16 086	764	2 962	6 191	1 984	6 705	41 837	17 984	23 853	8 851	19 195	12 491	31 545
November	16 030	775	2 910	7 073	1 937	6 736	42 099	17 960	24 139	9 015	19 340	12 501	31 501
December	16 061	778	2 913	10 480	1 999	6 654	42 525	18 127	24 398	9 043	19 515	12 648	31 998
2005													
January	16 212	768	2 949	4 409	1 984	6 627	42 617	17 962	24 655	8 906	19 658	12 792	31 940
February	16 708	802	2 994	4 888	2 083	6 719	42 946	18 097	24 849	9 036	19 674	12 753	32 341
March	16 255	798	2 994	6 081	1 929	6 759	42 903	17 861	25 042	9 046	19 793	12 796	32 064
April	16 775	783	3 033	5 963	2 028	6 788	43 429	18 050	25 379	9 107	20 425	13 152	32 830
May	16 585	792	3 027	5 951	2 032	6 853	43 423	17 823	25 600	9 254	20 128	13 198	32 752
June	16 848	798	3 084	5 956	2 035	6 768	44 048	18 139	25 909	9 289	20 712	13 435	32 949
July	16 681	783	3 062	6 131	2 034	6 848	43 774	17 780	25 994	9 317	20 725	13 560	32 974
August	16 758	787	3 069	6 592	2 023	6 873	43 904	17 734	26 170	9 204	21 229	13 737	33 131
September	16 724	763	3 079	5 775	2 056	6 767	44 267	17 640	26 627	9 418	21 332	13 667	33 471
October	17 190	780	3 117	6 644	2 132	6 921	44 768	17 938	26 830	9 505	21 535	13 904	33 755
November	17 165	787	3 149	7 563	2 152	6 824	44 792	17 989	26 803	9 494	21 728	14 120	34 059
December	17 134	779	3 113	11 315	2 109	6 908	44 812	17 793	27 019	9 353	22 090	14 285	34 260

[1] Includes store categories not shown separately.
[3] Data are for SIC industries roughly similar to the NAICS industries indicated in the column headings.
[4] Not seasonally adjusted.
[5] Excluding leased departments.
... = Not available.

Table 17-10. Quarterly U.S. Retail Sales: Total and E-Commerce

Year and quarter	Retail sales (millions of dollars)		E-commerce as a percent of total sales	Percent change from prior quarter		Percent change from same quarter a year ago	
	Total	E-commerce		Total sales	E-commerce sales	Total sales	E-commerce sales
Not Seasonally Adjusted							
1999							
4th quarter	768 726	5 293	0.7	8.3	. . .	8.8	. . .
2000							
1st quarter	696 048	5 594	0.8	-9.5	5.7	10.9	. . .
2nd quarter	753 211	6 103	0.8	8.2	9.1	7.2	. . .
3rd quarter	746 875	6 944	0.9	-0.8	13.8	5.3	. . .
4th quarter	792 622	9 124	1.2	6.1	31.4	3.1	72.4
2001							
1st quarter	704 757	7 931	1.1	-11.1	-13.1	1.3	41.8
2nd quarter	779 011	7 873	1.0	10.5	-0.7	3.4	29.0
3rd quarter	756 128	7 810	1.0	-2.9	-0.8	1.2	12.5
4th quarter	827 829	10 903	1.3	9.5	39.6	4.4	19.5
2002							
1st quarter	717 302	9 721	1.4	-13.4	-10.8	1.8	22.6
2nd quarter	790 486	10 161	1.3	10.2	4.5	1.5	29.1
3rd quarter	792 657	10 836	1.4	0.3	6.6	4.8	38.7
4th quarter	833 877	14 283	1.7	5.2	31.8	0.7	31.0
2003							
1st quarter	741 060	12 334	1.7	-11.1	-13.6	3.3	26.9
2nd quarter	819 232	12 851	1.6	10.5	4.2	3.6	26.5
3rd quarter	830 692	13 761	1.7	1.4	7.1	4.8	27.0
4th quarter	874 493	17 698	2.0	5.3	28.6	4.9	23.9
2004							
1st quarter	794 659	15 897	2.0	-9.1	-10.2	7.2	28.9
2nd quarter	870 480	16 065	1.8	9.5	1.1	6.3	25.0
3rd quarter	873 596	16 952	1.9	0.4	5.5	5.2	23.2
4th quarter	938 573	21 992	2.3	7.4	29.7	7.3	24.3
2005							
1st quarter	839 112	19 529	2.3	-10.6	-11.2	5.6	22.8
2nd quarter	937 779	20 141	2.1	11.8	3.1	7.7	25.4
3rd quarter	947 835	21 276	2.2	1.1	5.6	8.5	25.5
4rd quarter	994 452	27 080	2.7	4.9	27.3	6.0	23.1
2006							
1st quarter	906 465	24 521	2.7	-8.8	-9.4	8.0	25.6
Seasonally Adjusted							
1999							
4th quarter	724 737	4 615	0.6	2.2	. . .	9.0	. . .
2000							
1st quarter	742 622	5 838	0.8	2.5	26.5	9.3	. . .
2nd quarter	741 410	6 495	0.9	-0.2	11.3	7.0	. . .
3rd quarter	748 083	7 353	1.0	0.9	13.2	5.5	. . .
4th quarter	753 134	7 876	1.0	0.7	7.1	3.9	70.7
2001							
1st quarter	756 906	8 254	1.1	0.5	4.8	1.9	41.4
2nd quarter	765 398	8 394	1.1	1.1	1.7	3.2	29.2
3rd quarter	759 464	8 314	1.1	-0.8	-1.0	1.5	13.1
4th quarter	785 912	9 419	1.2	3.5	13.3	4.4	19.6
2002							
1st quarter	773 165	10 094	1.3	-1.6	7.2	2.1	22.3
2nd quarter	779 761	10 835	1.4	0.9	7.3	1.9	29.1
3rd quarter	790 081	11 559	1.5	1.3	6.7	4.0	39.0
4th quarter	791 997	12 317	1.6	0.2	6.6	0.8	30.8
2003							
1st quarter	800 063	12 772	1.6	1.0	3.7	3.5	26.5
2nd quarter	805 125	13 679	1.7	0.6	7.1	3.3	26.2
3rd quarter	828 828	14 630	1.8	2.9	7.0	4.9	26.6
4th quarter	830 341	15 372	1.9	0.2	5.1	4.8	24.8
2004							
1st quarter	847 417	16 407	1.9	2.1	6.7	5.9	28.5
2nd quarter	855 616	17 091	2.0	1.0	4.2	6.3	24.9
3rd quarter	870 916	18 024	2.1	1.8	5.5	5.1	23.2
4th quarter	891 614	19 146	2.1	2.4	6.2	7.4	24.6
2005							
1st quarter	902 564	20 118	2.2	1.2	5.1	6.5	22.6
2nd quarter	923 223	21 410	2.3	2.3	6.4	7.9	25.3
3rd quarter	943 540	22 656	2.4	2.2	5.8	8.3	25.7
4rd quarter	946 069	23 569	2.5	0.3	4.0	6.1	23.1
2006							
1st quarter	976 110	25 218	2.6	3.2	7.0	8.1	25.4

. . . = Not available.

Table 17-11. Retail Inventories

(All retail stores; end of period, millions of dollars.)

Year and month	Not seasonally adjusted			Seasonally adjusted (NAICS industry categories)							General merchandise	
	Total	Excluding motor vehicles and parts	Motor vehicles and parts	Total	Excluding motor vehicles and parts	Motor vehicles and parts	Furniture, home furnishings, electronics, and appliances	Building materials and garden	Food and beverages	Clothing and accessories	Total	Department stores[1]
SIC Basis[2]												
1967	...	...	...	...	...	...	...	...	...	...	...	...
1968	...	...	...	...	...	...	...	...	...	...	...	...
1969	...	...	...	...	...	...	...	...	...	...	...	...
1970	...	...	...	...	...	...	...	...	...	...	...	...
1971	...	...	...	...	...	...	...	...	...	...	...	...
1972	53 791	42 126	11 665	55 079	43 224	11 855	4 414	4 268	5 981	5 200	11 743	8 214
1973	61 835	47 565	14 270	63 237	48 881	14 356	4 800	4 844	6 946	5 791	13 137	9 016
1974	69 644	52 874	16 770	71 067	54 330	16 737	5 439	5 131	8 043	6 071	13 647	9 632
1975	70 273	53 795	16 478	71 744	55 397	16 347	5 717	5 474	8 069	6 029	13 521	9 848
1976	77 617	58 994	18 623	79 273	60 853	18 420	6 115	6 481	8 709	6 516	14 886	11 037
1977	87 411	65 269	22 142	89 444	67 565	21 879	6 610	7 502	9 362	7 646	17 307	13 145
1978	100 242	74 752	25 490	102 694	77 506	25 188	7 876	8 397	10 193	8 914	19 853	14 829
1979	108 408	81 152	27 256	111 098	84 165	26 933	8 681	8 981	11 343	9 514	21 033	15 686
1980	117 857	92 190	25 667	121 078	95 525	25 553	9 207	9 685	13 390	10 929	23 171	16 814
1981	129 073	100 936	28 137	132 719	104 693	28 026	9 795	10 180	14 649	12 234	25 951	19 279
1982	130 797	102 360	28 437	134 628	106 276	28 352	9 714	10 203	15 248	12 392	26 548	19 645
1983	143 513	110 483	33 030	147 833	114 914	32 919	11 217	11 716	16 282	13 466	28 651	21 196
1984	162 773	123 493	39 280	167 812	128 808	39 004	12 433	12 890	17 624	14 641	34 392	25 750
1985	176 941	130 542	46 399	181 881	136 083	45 798	13 762	13 683	19 283	15 689	34 683	25 525
1986	181 651	135 461	46 190	186 510	141 264	45 246	14 340	14 033	19 612	16 067	35 743	26 412
1987	203 210	145 410	57 800	207 836	151 675	56 161	15 050	14 868	19 898	17 280	38 285	28 450
1988	214 824	153 909	60 915	219 047	160 140	58 907	16 311	16 157	21 601	18 079	39 179	29 987
1989	233 143	166 707	66 436	237 234	173 162	64 072	17 280	17 122	23 543	19 422	43 107	33 678
1990	236 152	170 635	65 517	239 815	176 708	63 107	17 442	17 015	25 038	19 690	42 377	33 387
1991	239 478	176 344	63 134	243 389	182 508	60 881	17 649	16 718	25 580	20 263	45 764	36 110
1992	248 198	181 697	66 501	252 185	188 051	64 134	17 934	17 234	25 738	22 249	48 630	38 033
NAICS Basis												
1992	256 810	185 195	71 615	261 369	192 066	69 303	16 208	21 144	27 467	27 467	49 783	38 333
1993	274 748	196 932	77 816	279 526	204 233	75 293	18 138	22 667	27 558	28 193	53 700	40 854
1994	300 517	211 758	88 759	305 442	219 514	85 928	20 421	24 905	28 171	29 602	56 830	42 136
1995	318 021	221 462	96 559	322 925	229 379	93 546	21 839	26 384	28 776	29 382	59 550	43 455
1996	328 912	228 456	100 456	333 915	236 579	97 336	22 278	27 497	29 718	29 864	60 611	44 124
1997	339 565	234 858	104 707	344 593	243 104	101 489	22 135	28 947	29 949	31 167	60 735	44 309
1998	351 996	245 964	106 032	357 267	254 464	102 803	22 682	30 966	30 901	32 383	61 566	43 438
1999	379 738	260 474	119 264	385 087	269 141	115 946	23 980	33 215	32 628	33 648	64 325	43 855
2000	401 530	269 618	131 912	407 035	278 443	128 592	25 356	34 643	32 029	36 505	64 942	42 707
2001	389 125	266 980	122 145	394 966	275 375	119 591	24 072	34 764	33 008	35 191	64 798	40 525
2002	410 704	272 304	138 400	416 499	280 650	135 849	25 275	36 771	32 668	36 773	65 927	38 825
2003	426 945	277 930	149 015	432 268	285 995	146 273	26 442	38 315	32 290	37 617	66 628	36 992
2004	455 858	297 976	157 882	461 202	306 342	154 860	29 220	42 839	33 198	40 349	70 976	37 566
2005	468 689	311 501	157 188	473 865	320 040	153 825	30 320	46 207	33 636	42 409	74 208	37 840
2003												
January	410 297	269 583	140 714	418 329	280 383	137 946	25 199	36 191	32 529	37 224	65 725	38 549
February	418 083	272 881	145 202	422 017	281 709	140 308	25 291	36 906	32 672	37 362	65 503	38 221
March	427 470	279 097	148 373	423 888	282 413	141 475	25 061	37 034	32 778	37 573	65 679	38 256
April	429 218	278 853	150 365	424 147	282 095	142 052	25 081	36 765	32 680	37 366	66 500	38 881
May	422 432	274 698	147 734	423 073	280 439	142 634	24 996	36 706	32 582	37 423	65 634	38 109
June	419 066	273 163	145 903	423 546	280 714	142 832	25 431	36 904	32 480	37 232	65 622	37 947
July	410 823	276 060	134 763	425 044	282 378	142 666	25 479	36 943	32 698	37 412	65 928	37 742
August	406 288	278 708	127 580	421 431	281 578	139 853	25 567	37 286	32 644	37 453	65 187	37 191
September	422 139	291 005	131 134	426 040	284 100	141 940	25 799	38 114	32 967	37 373	66 127	37 605
October	447 852	308 027	139 825	429 241	285 262	143 979	26 492	37 980	32 530	37 284	66 819	37 813
November	459 575	313 082	146 493	431 489	286 165	145 324	26 509	38 132	32 372	37 690	66 384	37 178
December	426 945	277 930	149 015	432 268	285 995	146 273	26 442	38 315	32 290	37 617	66 628	36 992
2004												
January	424 509	275 182	149 327	432 632	285 859	146 773	26 213	38 188	32 380	37 724	66 928	37 175
February	431 786	278 436	153 350	435 262	287 218	148 044	26 424	38 662	32 261	37 906	67 294	37 162
March	445 001	286 262	158 739	440 187	289 373	150 814	26 924	39 021	32 354	38 099	67 741	37 159
April	451 991	288 417	163 574	445 237	291 413	153 824	27 123	39 606	32 553	38 596	67 844	37 273
May	446 601	287 421	159 180	446 814	293 269	153 545	27 390	40 217	32 883	39 017	67 905	37 201
June	447 844	287 357	160 487	452 185	294 945	157 240	27 335	40 609	33 012	38 944	68 607	37 242
July	440 527	288 990	151 537	456 257	295 638	160 619	27 577	41 160	33 059	38 829	68 475	37 179
August	442 861	294 253	148 608	461 058	297 549	163 509	28 004	41 456	33 012	39 245	68 752	37 208
September	453 005	305 577	147 428	458 549	298 572	159 977	28 047	41 339	33 099	39 405	68 992	37 073
October	475 099	323 636	151 463	456 832	300 566	156 266	28 015	42 093	33 144	39 702	69 244	37 340
November	489 937	331 480	158 457	460 562	303 513	157 049	28 374	42 276	33 326	40 068	70 331	37 534
December	455 858	297 976	157 882	461 202	306 342	154 860	29 220	42 839	33 198	40 349	70 976	37 566
2005												
January	453 354	297 226	156 128	461 831	308 355	153 476	29 033	43 818	33 314	40 962	71 508	37 777
February	459 350	300 537	158 813	463 277	309 983	153 294	28 983	43 934	33 275	41 421	71 787	37 840
March	469 839	307 635	162 204	464 569	310 711	153 858	29 057	43 733	33 186	41 619	72 822	38 563
April	471 997	308 336	163 661	465 273	311 461	153 812	29 323	43 556	33 334	41 569	72 857	37 854
May	466 530	306 979	159 551	466 650	313 021	153 629	29 754	43 993	33 392	41 598	73 078	37 607
June	459 561	306 885	152 676	464 220	314 612	149 608	30 050	44 213	33 557	42 117	72 948	37 642
July	441 084	307 003	134 081	456 505	314 315	142 190	29 997	44 414	33 389	41 995	72 775	37 702
August	444 252	312 719	131 533	460 907	316 168	144 739	29 964	44 669	33 489	42 095	73 641	37 756
September	460 489	324 330	136 159	464 680	316 991	147 689	29 887	44 977	33 112	42 262	73 818	37 853
October	484 966	340 592	144 374	465 932	316 765	149 167	29 854	45 096	33 465	42 360	73 647	37 717
November	500 295	346 579	153 716	470 209	317 843	152 366	29 925	45 720	33 619	42 192	73 797	37 636
December	468 689	311 501	157 188	473 865	320 040	153 825	30 320	46 207	33 636	42 409	74 208	37 840

[1]Excluding leased departments.
[2]Data are for SIC industries roughly similar to the NAICS industries indicated in the column headings.
. . . = Not available.

Table 17-12. Merchant Wholesalers—Sales and Inventories

(Millions of dollars.)

Classification basis, year, and month	Not seasonally adjusted — Sales Total	Durable goods establishments	Nondurable goods establishments	Inventories (current cost, end of period) Total	Durable goods establishments	Nondurable goods establishments	Seasonally adjusted — Sales Total	Durable goods establishments	Nondurable goods establishments	Inventories (current cost, end of period) Total	Durable goods establishments	Nondurable goods establishments
SIC Basis[1]												
1972	358 388	168 879	189 509	. . .	. . .	. . .	358 388	168 879	189 509	. . .	. . .	. . .
1973	457 378	208 554	248 824	. . .	. . .	. . .	457 378	208 554	248 824	. . .	. . .	. . .
1974	575 786	255 863	319 923	. . .	. . .	. . .	575 786	255 863	319 923	. . .	. . .	. . .
1975	559 606	235 723	323 883	. . .	. . .	. . .	559 606	235 723	323 883	. . .	. . .	. . .
1976	608 381	263 605	344 776	. . .	. . .	. . .	608 381	263 605	344 776	. . .	. . .	. . .
1977	673 633	304 721	368 912	. . .	. . .	. . .	673 633	304 721	368 912	. . .	. . .	. . .
1978	796 961	372 176	424 785	. . .	. . .	. . .	796 961	372 176	424 785	. . .	. . .	. . .
1979	948 614	436 254	512 360	. . .	. . .	. . .	948 614	436 254	512 360	. . .	. . .	. . .
1980	1 117 187	486 509	630 678	124 015	78 849	45 166	1 117 187	486 509	630 678	122 631	79 372	43 259
1981	1 214 156	525 607	688 549	130 709	85 371	45 338	1 214 156	525 607	688 549	129 654	85 856	43 798
1982	1 142 535	480 318	662 217	128 514	84 806	43 708	1 142 535	480 318	662 217	127 428	85 222	42 206
1983	1 190 705	523 080	667 625	131 306	84 709	46 597	1 190 705	523 080	667 625	130 075	85 180	44 895
1984	1 346 392	622 361	724 031	143 458	94 895	48 563	1 346 392	622 361	724 031	142 452	95 474	46 978
1985	1 361 507	651 864	709 643	148 403	96 659	51 744	1 361 507	651 864	709 643	147 409	97 371	50 038
1986	1 379 514	681 691	697 823	154 081	101 369	52 712	1 379 514	681 691	697 823	153 574	102 349	51 225
1987	1 475 613	730 592	745 021	164 310	106 820	57 490	1 475 613	730 592	745 021	163 903	108 112	55 791
1988	1 614 249	801 751	812 498	179 828	115 613	64 215	1 614 249	801 751	812 498	178 801	117 045	61 756
1989	1 725 123	851 550	873 573	187 897	120 701	67 196	1 725 123	851 550	873 573	187 009	122 237	64 772
1990	1 794 072	880 767	913 305	196 881	124 839	72 042	1 794 072	880 767	913 305	195 833	126 461	69 372
1991	1 779 673	860 138	919 535	201 777	125 921	75 856	1 779 673	860 138	919 535	200 448	127 399	73 049
1992	1 849 798	908 917	940 881	209 675	130 044	79 631	1 849 798	908 917	940 881	208 302	131 509	76 793
NAICS Basis												
1992	1 767 130	861 182	905 948	197 793	121 809	75 984	1 767 130	861 182	905 948	196 914	123 435	73 479
1993	1 848 215	939 945	908 270	205 815	127 094	78 721	1 848 215	939 945	908 270	204 842	128 851	75 991
1994	1 974 899	1 037 638	937 261	222 826	139 941	82 885	1 974 899	1 037 638	937 261	221 978	141 975	80 003
1995	2 158 980	1 141 701	1 017 279	239 275	151 709	87 566	2 158 980	1 141 701	1 017 279	238 392	154 089	84 303
1996	2 284 343	1 190 342	1 094 001	241 396	154 207	87 189	2 284 343	1 190 342	1 094 001	241 078	156 682	84 396
1997	2 377 845	1 256 384	1 121 461	258 900	165 371	93 529	2 377 845	1 256 384	1 121 461	258 496	168 041	90 455
1998	2 427 120	1 306 545	1 120 575	272 575	175 994	96 581	2 427 120	1 306 545	1 120 575	272 292	178 871	93 421
1999	2 599 159	1 406 371	1 192 788	290 693	187 828	102 865	2 599 159	1 406 371	1 192 788	290 418	190 946	99 472
2000	2 814 554	1 486 673	1 327 881	310 370	198 705	111 665	2 814 554	1 486 673	1 327 881	309 809	201 981	107 828
2001	2 785 152	1 422 195	1 362 957	299 498	182 720	116 778	2 785 152	1 422 195	1 362 957	298 380	185 735	112 645
2002	2 835 528	1 421 503	1 414 025	303 925	182 399	121 526	2 835 528	1 421 503	1 414 025	302 478	185 355	117 123
2003	2 962 284	1 448 944	1 513 340	310 050	184 890	125 160	2 962 284	1 448 944	1 513 340	308 017	187 777	120 240
2004	3 296 520	1 654 621	1 641 899	340 023	209 954	130 069	3 296 520	1 654 621	1 641 899	338 232	213 021	125 211
2005	3 550 116	1 760 675	1 789 441	364 121	225 652	138 469	3 550 116	1 760 675	1 789 441	362 084	228 938	133 146
2003												
January	234 899	110 834	124 065	305 570	183 654	121 916	243 451	118 336	125 115	302 097	184 703	117 394
February	223 359	104 953	118 406	304 580	186 599	117 981	243 472	116 335	127 137	303 177	186 178	116 999
March	250 734	121 753	128 981	305 407	186 997	118 410	246 129	118 879	127 250	304 130	186 652	117 478
April	245 416	120 200	125 216	304 902	188 919	115 983	241 225	118 254	122 971	304 682	187 298	117 384
May	243 012	119 006	124 006	299 796	186 759	113 037	240 652	118 333	122 319	303 000	186 198	116 802
June	247 028	123 958	123 070	300 465	186 400	114 065	243 947	119 860	124 087	302 299	185 521	116 778
July	250 622	123 725	126 897	301 887	186 880	115 007	246 711	121 126	125 585	302 344	184 567	117 777
August	243 934	119 290	124 644	298 395	183 983	114 412	246 616	120 377	126 239	301 798	183 838	117 960
September	253 452	127 475	125 977	300 811	183 444	117 367	247 909	122 424	125 485	303 308	184 262	119 046
October	269 044	133 085	135 959	307 632	184 651	122 981	251 270	123 757	127 513	305 575	184 938	120 637
November	238 951	117 207	121 744	308 362	184 215	124 147	253 710	125 210	128 500	306 578	185 410	121 168
December	261 833	127 458	134 375	310 050	184 890	125 160	256 027	125 876	130 151	308 017	187 777	120 240
2004												
January	241 216	114 822	126 394	311 941	187 553	124 388	256 242	125 425	130 817	307 919	188 519	119 400
February	243 002	118 371	124 631	314 425	191 700	122 725	261 473	129 371	132 102	312 217	191 100	121 117
March	292 064	147 232	144 832	315 909	193 322	122 587	270 417	135 370	135 047	313 783	192 810	120 973
April	276 250	139 490	136 760	314 487	195 286	119 201	271 106	136 552	134 554	314 008	193 677	120 331
May	267 373	133 290	134 083	314 197	197 421	116 776	272 786	136 934	135 852	317 787	196 935	120 852
June	284 751	146 836	137 915	318 617	200 353	118 264	273 497	137 946	135 551	320 674	199 349	121 325
July	270 427	137 587	132 840	325 124	204 923	120 201	274 139	138 810	135 329	325 825	202 499	123 326
August	282 599	143 155	139 444	325 586	206 190	119 396	277 381	140 210	137 171	329 171	206 181	122 990
September	282 554	143 429	139 125	327 563	206 654	120 909	277 244	138 631	138 613	330 116	207 823	122 293
October	283 115	142 301	140 814	335 661	209 732	125 929	279 416	140 278	139 138	334 219	210 200	124 019
November	282 566	141 509	141 057	339 146	211 087	128 059	283 522	142 210	141 312	338 210	212 497	125 713
December	290 603	146 599	144 004	340 023	209 954	130 069	285 440	144 861	140 579	338 232	213 021	125 211
2005												
January	261 694	127 746	133 948	345 868	214 849	131 019	286 021	143 509	142 512	342 184	215 788	126 396
February	262 074	129 525	132 549	346 434	217 968	128 466	285 820	143 110	142 710	344 289	217 159	127 130
March	308 917	155 550	153 367	347 410	217 896	129 514	286 447	142 707	143 740	345 152	217 165	127 987
April	288 907	143 573	145 334	348 861	220 186	128 675	290 863	144 624	146 239	348 400	218 461	129 939
May	293 194	145 322	147 872	345 438	219 756	125 682	290 853	144 788	146 065	349 180	219 217	129 963
June	303 694	153 941	149 753	349 037	222 087	126 950	292 456	145 075	147 381	351 151	221 032	130 119
July	282 006	139 060	142 946	350 787	224 546	126 241	294 673	145 184	149 489	351 621	221 963	129 658
August	313 760	155 203	158 557	349 492	222 202	127 290	298 721	148 152	150 569	353 223	222 090	131 133
September	311 155	154 542	156 613	352 710	221 467	131 243	304 949	149 107	155 842	355 881	222 924	132 957
October	312 923	153 798	159 125	358 252	225 246	133 006	308 013	151 656	156 357	357 061	225 800	131 261
November	304 446	150 112	154 334	359 547	225 855	133 692	306 416	151 594	154 822	358 711	227 352	131 359
December	307 346	152 303	155 043	364 121	225 652	138 469	309 975	154 012	155 963	362 084	228 938	133 146

[1]Data are for SIC industries roughly similar to the NAICS industries indicated in the column headings.

. . . = Not available.

Table 17-13. Selected Service Industries—Receipts of Taxable Firms, 1986–1998, by SIC Industry

(By kind of business and SIC code, millions of dollars.)

Year	Arrangement of passenger transportation (472)	Real estate agents and managers (653)	Hotels, rooming houses, camps and other lodging places, except on membership basis (70, ex. 704)	Personal services (72)	Business services (73)	Automotive repair, services, and parking (75)	Miscellaneous repair services (76)	Motion pictures (78)
1986	7 465	48 360	47 634	39 587	170 250	53 867	22 478	23 740
1987	8 196	52 919	53 630	43 247	188 856	58 278	24 599	27 754
1988	9 521	58 980	58 637	48 329	223 369	66 053	27 659	31 746
1989	11 041	62 325	61 229	51 832	251 648	70 961	30 064	36 173
1990	12 276	63 023	64 225	54 736	280 699	73 722	32 848	39 982
1991	11 438	63 180	65 284	54 620	287 214	71 542	32 401	42 838
1992	11 926	73 115	71 038	59 597	309 439	78 511	35 238	45 662
1993	12 396	79 206	74 149	62 597	337 403	84 324	36 772	49 799
1994	13 125	80 947	79 555	66 105	375 067	91 865	40 683	53 504
1995	14 192	82 667	84 093	70 607	425 075	99 227	44 870	57 184
1996	15 354	90 186	88 961	73 905	484 242	106 638	46 101	60 279
1997	16 461	99 854	94 139	77 712	548 434	111 444	47 895	62 865
1998	17 038	108 639	100 650	82 798	638 500	119 978	52 365	66 229

Year	Amusement and recreation services (79)	Health services (80)	Legal services (81)	Vocational schools (824)	Social services (83)	Museums, art galleries, and botanical and zoological gardens (84)	Engineering, accounting, research, management, and related services (87)
1986	33 984	173 885	63 390	3 327	. . .	. . .	127 885
1987	36 646	196 212	72 115	3 400	. . .	. . .	139 897
1988	41 272	221 741	81 636	4 263	. . .	. . .	160 446
1989	44 539	241 558	89 144	4 577	. . .	. . .	183 528
1990	50 126	271 212	97 640	4 519	15 509	144	198 395
1991	51 654	293 907	100 027	4 183	16 365	154	202 696
1992	57 699	321 653	108 443	4 429	18 201	192	215 624
1993	63 651	335 108	112 145	4 507	20 146	222	222 853
1994	68 453	351 419	114 603	4 710	22 498	231	235 447
1995	77 452	376 279	116 000	5 285	24 858	247	263 835
1996	85 733	398 353	124 659	6 190	27 694	273	292 260
1997	92 837	420 361	133 015	7 031	30 150	322	321 679
1998	97 512	444 727	141 827	8 268	31 970	388	360 823

. . . = Not available.

Table 17-14. Selected Service Industries—Revenue of Tax-Exempt Firms, 1986–1998, by SIC Industry

(By kind of business and SIC code, millions of dollars.)

Year	Camps and membership lodging (703, 704)	Selected amusement and recreation services (792, 7991, 7997, 7999)	Health services (80)	Legal aid societies and similar legal services (81)	Libraries (823)	Vocational schools (824)	Social services (83)	Museums, art galleries, and botanical and zoological gardens (84)	Selected membership organizations (86 [pt])	Research, development, and testing services (873)	Commercial, physical, and biological research (8731)	Non-commercial research organizations (8733)	Management and public relations services (874, excluding 8744)
1986	. . .	5 070	. . .	563	. . .	. . .	. . .	. . .	. . .	7 125	. . .	. . .	791
1987	. . .	5 858	. . .	665	. . .	. . .	. . .	. . .	. . .	8 304	. . .	. . .	902
1988	. . .	6 506	. . .	775	. . .	. . .	. . .	. . .	. . .	9 014	. . .	. . .	1 201
1989	. . .	7 163	. . .	944	. . .	. . .	. . .	. . .	. . .	9 975	. . .	. . .	1 494
1990	798	7 922	267 858	1 088	476	507	45 255	2 871	31 458	11 035	. . .	. . .	1 933
1991	782	8 160	298 168	1 162	481	486	49 055	3 048	33 288	11 463	. . .	. . .	2 150
1992	808	8 993	324 416	1 161	527	549	53 673	3 199	36 256	12 534	. . .	. . .	2 246
1993	817	10 279	345 081	1 190	606	569	59 052	3 615	39 426	13 180	. . .	. . .	2 588
1994	836	11 560	363 112	1 241	655	612	63 493	3 972	41 907	13 919	. . .	. . .	3 119
1995	846	12 778	385 210	1 278	730	696	70 303	4 295	45 873	14 493	5 951	7 688	3 732
1996	877	13 299	401 047	1 259	754	772	75 240	4 729	48 897	14 906	5 703	8 293	4 821
1997	929	14 600	414 990	1 446	850	871	83 235	6 231	51 098	16 839	5 950	9 953	6 583
1998	993	15 360	436 078	1 599	934	943	90 458	6 566	55 955	18 732	6 770	10 753	7 761

. . . = Not available.

Table 17-15. Selected Service Industries—Revenue, by NAICS Industry

(Millions of dollars; employer and nonemployer firms, except as noted.)

NAICS code	Kind of business	1998	1999	2000	2001	2002	2003	2004
	Total for Selected Service Industries	3 759 984	4 082 942	4 442 227	4 539 960	4 643 495	4 851 593	5 192 418
484	Truck transportation	170 762	181 000	192 523	190 387	192 943	200 443	222 015
492	Couriers and messengers	51 250	54 178	60 268	61 113	60 980	62 945	65 505
493	Warehousing and storage	13 177	14 011	14 929	15 586	16 945	17 896	18 254
51	Information	707 049	789 663	871 491	891 678	899 396	916 728	964 343
511	Publishing industries [1]	212 688	231 687	246 800	247 090	246 043	247 635	260 348
512	Motion picture and sound recording industries [1]	60 389	66 720	71 560	72 904	78 250	83 113	88 267
513	Broadcasting and telecommunications [1]	383 457	428 460	473 503	487 451	485 607	492 997	512 896
514	Information services and data processing services [1]	44 302	55 777	72 009	76 531	81 946	84 464	93 572
5231	Securities and commodity contracts intermediation and brokerage	213 055	256 534	302 440	252 870	217 669	230 627	256 174
532	Rental and leasing services	88 061	96 222	103 945	102 599	100 626	102 194	108 897
54	Professional, scientific, and technical services (except notaries and landscape architectural services)	758 515	829 733	911 320	947 450	961 540	1 002 014	1 076 415
56	Administrative and support and waste management and remediation services (except landscaping services)	344 658	380 852	415 933	410 942	419 179	438 173	468 937
561	Administrative and support services	297 930	330 363	363 839	358 379	366 785	382 434	408 997
562	Waste management and remediation services	46 728	50 489	52 094	52 564	52 394	55 739	59 939
62	Health care and social assistance	971 521	1 013 111	1 072 561	1 157 852	1 253 127	1 334 868	1 432 989
621	Ambulatory health care services	403 295	420 346	446 946	483 312	520 680	560 641	605 682
622	Hospitals	391 557	406 717	423 888	455 261	500 113	529 202	569 444
623	Nursing and residential care facilities	104 927	107 544	114 169	122 030	128 650	134 877	140 095
624	Social assistance	71 742	78 504	87 558	97 249	103 684	110 149	117 769
71	Arts, entertainment, and recreation	129 005	136 507	145 113	152 224	161 904	170 356	178 924
711	Performing arts, spectator sports, and related industries	56 785	60 098	64 163	67 632	73 094	75 891	77 427
712	Museums, historical sites, and similar institutions	8 358	8 757	9 402	9 282	8 674	9 150	9 763
713	Amusement, gambling, and recreation industries	63 862	67 652	71 548	75 310	80 136	85 315	91 734
81	Other services (except public administration; religious, labor, and political organizations; and private households)	312 932	331 132	351 707	357 259	359 187	375 349	400 010
811	Repair and maintenance	122 254	127 832	134 133	139 783	141 123	147 209	153 298
812	Personal and laundry services	86 724	92 032	97 973	101 655	105 100	109 859	116 847
813	Religious, grantmaking, civic, professional, and similar organizations (except religious, labor, and political organizations)	103 954	111 268	119 601	115 822	112 964	118 281	129 866

[1]Employer firms only.

Table 17-16. Selected Service Industries—Revenue [1]—Total and E-Commerce, by NAICS Industry

(Millions of dollars, percent.)

NAICS code	Kind of business	Value of revenue, 2003		Value of revenue, 2004	
		Total	E-commerce revenue	Total	E-commerce revenue
	Total for Selected Service Industries [1]	5 113 554	51 435	5 473 772	59 206
	Selected transportation and warehousing	245 767	4 385	265 941	4 964
484	Truck transportation	168 487	3 264	185 944	4 027
492	Couriers and messengers	59 825	1 006	62 246	764
493	Warehousing and storage	17 455	B	17 751	B
51	Information	908 209	13 483	955 084	15 131
511	Publishing industries	247 635	6 533	260 348	6 355
513	Broadcasting and telecommunications	492 997	2 461	512 896	2 378
51419	Online information services	27 628	2 763	32 390	4 393
	Selected finance	311 525	6 015	349 166	6 963
5231	Securities and commodity contracts intermediation and brokerage	225 299	5 934	250 080	6 871
532	Rental and leasing services	96 387	B	102 756	B
	Selected professional, scientific, and technical services	900 759	8 281	965 669	9 569
5415	Computer systems design and related services	171 394	5 522	173 171	4 834
	Selected administrative and support and waste management and remediation services	414 606	10 168	443 507	10 385
5615	Travel arrangement and reservation services	26 593	5 965	28 199	6 268
62	Health care and social assistance services	1 289 368	B	1 383 439	B
71	Arts, entertainment, and recreation services	149 346	B	158 545	B
72	Accommodation and food services	484 174	B	517 495	B
	Selected other services	313 413	1 860	332 170	2 279
811	Repair and maintenance	123 079	232	127 823	226
813	Religious, grantmaking, civic, professional, and similar organizations	118 281	1 304	129 866	1 526

NAICS code	Kind of business	E-commerce as percent of total revenue						
		1998	1999	2000	2001	2002	2003	2004
	Total for Selected Service Industries [1]	0.4	0.6	0.8	0.8	0.8	1.0	1.1
	Selected transportation and warehousing	0.8	0.9	1.1	1.2	1.4	1.8	1.9
484	Truck transportation	0.4	0.5	0.8	0.9	1.4	1.9	2.2
492	Couriers and messengers	1.1	1.2	1.2	1.1	1.5	1.7	1.2
493	Warehousing and storage	B	B	B	B	B	B	B
51	Information	0.4	0.7	1.1	1.2	1.3	1.5	1.6
511	Publishing industries	0.8	1.4	2.0	2.1	2.3	2.6	2.4
513	Broadcasting and telecommunications	0.1	0.2	0.4	0.5	0.5	0.5	0.5
51419	Online information services	3.6	5.1	6.4	5.7	5.7	10.0	13.6
	Selected finance	0.9	1.4	1.8	1.3	1.6	1.9	2.0
5231	Securities and commodity contracts intermediation and brokerage	1.3	2.0	2.5	1.9	2.5	2.6	2.7
532	Rental and leasing services	B	B	B	B	B	B	B
	Selected professional, scientific, and technical services	0.4	0.6	0.7	0.6	0.8	0.9	1.0
5415	Computer systems design and related services	1.2	1.8	1.9	1.9	2.5	3.2	2.8
	Selected administrative and support and waste management and remediation services	1.4	1.9	2.4	2.4	2.5	2.5	2.3
5615	Travel arrangement and reservation services	18.3	21.1	23.4	23.9	24.2	22.4	22.2
62	Health care and social assistance services	B	B	B	B	B	B	B
71	Arts, entertainment, and recreation services	B	B	B	B	B	B	B
72	Accommodation and food services	B	B	B	B	B	B	B
	Selected other services	0.1	0.1	0.2	0.2	0.3	0.6	0.7
811	Repair and maintenance	0.1	0.1	0.2	0.2	0.2	0.2	0.2
813	Religious, grantmaking, civic, professional, and similar organizations	0.1	0.1	0.2	0.3	0.5	1.1	1.2

[1]Includes data only for businesses with paid employees, except for accommodation and food services, which also includes businesses without paid employees. Note that accommodation and food services were not included in Table 17-14.
B = Data do not meet publication standards because of high sampling variability or poor response quality. Unpublished estimates derived from this table by subtraction should be used with caution and not be attributed to the U.S. Census Bureau.

Table 17-17. Selected Services—Quarterly Estimated Revenue for Employer Firms

(Millions of dollars; not seasonally adjusted.)

NAICS code	Kind of business	2003 4th quarter	2004 1st quarter	2004 2nd quarter	2004 3rd quarter	2004 4th quarter	2005 1st quarter	2005 2nd quarter	2005 3rd quarter	2005 4th quarter
51	**Information**	242 929	228 835	238 361	237 464	250 423	238 729	246 452	247 405	258 920
511	Publishing industries	68 995	61 267	63 988	65 071	70 022	64 220	68 158	69 866	74 116
51111	Newspaper publishers	12 431	11 565	12 200	11 918	12 916	12 005	12 714	12 446	13 227
51112	Periodical publishers	10 332	9 345	10 628	10 898	10 889	9 765	10 903	11 391	11 864
5111 (pt)	Book, database and directory, and other publishers	15 026	13 465	13 937	14 983	15 343	14 420	14 996	16 736	15 638
5112	Software publishers	31 206	26 892	27 223	27 272	30 874	28 030	29 545	29 293	33 387
512	Motion picture and sound recording industries	25 528	21 408	22 536	19 963	24 360	21 158	20 729	19 770	22 517
513	Broadcasting and telecommunications	124 688	123 679	128 335	129 113	131 769	129 633	133 066	132 308	135 905
5131	Radio and television broadcasting	12 913	11 636	13 579	12 871	14 007	12 114	12 672	11 654	13 614
5132	Cable networks and program distribution	24 076	24 688	26 002	26 390	27 610	27 670	29 343	29 102	30 104
5133	Telecommunications	87 699	87 355	88 754	89 852	90 152	89 849	91 051	91 552	92 187
51331	Wired telecommunications carriers	54 195	53 487	53 003	52 411	52 275	51 225	50 782	50 336	50 202
51332	Wireless telecommunications carriers (except satellite)	29 224	29 758	31 388	33 084	33 372	33 771	35 461	36 570	37 195
5133 (pt)	Other telecommunications	4 280	4 110	4 363	4 357	4 505	4 853	4 808	4 646	4 790
514	Information services and data processing services	23 718	22 481	23 502	23 317	24 272	23 718	24 499	25 461	26 382
5141	Information services	8 583	8 563	8 941	8 940	9 798	9 509	9 607	9 920	10 357
5142	Data processing services	15 135	13 918	14 561	14 377	14 474	14 209	14 892	15 541	16 025
54	**Professional, Scientific, and Technical Services**	231 424	231 261	244 082	235 304	255 067	250 812	261 301	255 216	277 489
5412	Accounting, tax preparation, bookkeeping, and payroll services	21 452	27 852	24 102	19 667	21 262	30 388	25 723	20 698	22 723
5413	Architectural, engineering, and related services	40 544	42 599	47 419	43 846	46 209	44 529	47 739	49 729	53 031
5415	Computer system design and related services	41 827	43 223	42 488	42 969	44 491	44 380	46 406	45 832	46 541
5416	Management, scientific, and technical consulting services	28 301	28 196	30 840	30 711	32 570	32 580	34 384	34 503	37 432
5418	Advertising and related services	15 531	14 758	15 659	15 766	17 400	15 868	17 606	17 508	19 122
541 (pt)	Other professional, scientific, and technical services	83 769	74 633	83 574	82 345	93 135	83 067	89 443	86 946	98 640
56	**Administrative and Support and Waste Management and Remediation Services**	102 242	103 463	109 633	112 784	117 626	112 211	117 826	119 750	124 300
561	Administrative and support services	88 560	90 156	95 502	97 168	102 038	98 498	103 069	103 582	107 535
5613	Employment services	33 300	32 706	36 016	37 045	39 950	37 595	38 573	40 085	41 352
5615	Travel arrangement and reservation services	6 151	6 594	7 486	7 134	6 985	7 462	8 414	7 950	8 077
561 (pt)	Other administrative and support services	49 109	50 856	52 000	52 989	55 103	53 441	56 082	55 547	58 106
562	Waste management and remediation services	13 682	13 307	14 131	15 616	15 588	13 713	14 757	16 168	16 765
62 (pt)	**Selected Health Care Services**	. . .	. . .	. . .	. . .	188 932	192 528	193 831	195 775	197 271
622	Hospitals	. . .	. . .	. . .	. . .	153 354	157 494	157 959	159 486	160 129
623	Nursing and residential care facilities	. . .	. . .	. . .	. . .	35 578	35 034	35 872	36 289	37 142

. . . = Not available.

NOTES AND DEFINITIONS

TABLE 17-1
PETROLEUM AND PETROLEUM PRODUCTS—PRICES, IMPORTS, DOMESTIC PRODUCTION, AND STOCKS

SOURCES: FUTURES PRICES—U.S. DEPARTMENT OF ENERGY, ENERGY INFORMATION ADMINISTRATION (EIA), AND U.S. DEPARTMENT OF COMMERCE, BUREAU OF ECONOMIC ANALYSIS (BEA); IMPORTS—U.S. DEPARTMENT OF COMMERCE, CENSUS BUREAU; SUPPLY (NET IMPORTS AND DOMESTIC PRODUCTION) AND STOCKS—EIA.

Definitions and notes on the data

The *crude oil futures price* in *current dollars per barrel* is the price for next-month delivery in Cushing, Oklahoma (a pipeline hub), of light, sweet crude oil, as determined by trading on the New York Mercantile Exchange (NYMEX). Official daily closing prices are reported each day at 2:30 p.m., and are tabulated weekly in Table 16 of *EIA's Weekly Petroleum Status Report*. The monthly averages shown in this volume are the average prices for the nearest future from each trading day of the month. For example, for most days in January, the futures contract priced will be for February; for the last few days in January, the February contract will have expired and the March contract will be quoted. The annual averages are averages of the monthly averages.

The *crude oil futures price* in *2000 dollars* is calculated by the editor and divides the current-dollar price by the chain price index for total personal consumption expenditures (PCE), with the average for the year 2000 set at 1.0000. The PCE chain price index is compiled by the Bureau of Economic Analysis (BEA). It is described in the notes and definitions for Chapter 1 and is also presented in Chapter 8 and discussed in its notes and definitions.

The imports data in Columns 3 through 6 of this table are those published as Exhibit 16, "Imports of Energy-related Petroleum Products, Including Crude Petroleum," in the monthly Census-BEA foreign trade press release. *Total energy-related petroleum products* includes the following Standard International Trade Classification (SITC) commodity groupings: crude oil, petroleum preparations, and liquefied propane and butane gas.

The data in Columns 7 through 11, on exports, imports, and net imports (imports minus exports) of petroleum and products and domestic production of crude oil and natural gas plant liquids (all expressed as thousands of barrels per day), and in Columns 12 through 14, depicting stocks of crude oil in millions of barrels, are derived from the Department of Energy's weekly petroleum supply reporting system. They are published in EIA's *Monthly Energy Review* and can be found in Tables 3.1a, 3.1b, and 3.2b. Stock totals are as of the end of the period.

Geographic coverage includes the 50 states and the District of Columbia.

Data availability

Data on futures prices, petroleum supply and stocks are available from the EIA Web site at <http://www.eia.doe.gov>, under the categories "Publications and Reports/Monthly Energy Review" and "Petroleum/Weekly Petroleum Status Report." The *Monthly Energy Review* is no longer published in printed form.

See the notes and definitions for Tables 7-9 through 7-14 for information about the availability of import data.

TABLE 17-2
CONSTRUCTION PUT IN PLACE

SOURCE: U.S. DEPARTMENT OF COMMERCE, CENSUS BUREAU

The Census Bureau's estimates of the value of new construction put in place are intended to provide monthly estimates of the total dollar value of construction work done in the United States.

Definitions and notes on the data

The estimates cover all construction work done each month on new private residential and nonresidential buildings and structures, public construction, and improvements to existing buildings and structures. Included are the cost of labor, materials, and equipment rental; cost of architectural and engineering work; overhead costs assigned to the project; interest and taxes paid during construction; and contractor's profits.

The total value put in place for a given period is the sum of the value of work done on all projects underway during this period, regardless of when work on each individual project was started or when payment was made to the contractors. For some categories, estimates are derived by distributing the total construction cost of the project by means of historic construction progress patterns. Published estimates represent payments made during a period for some categories.

The statistics on the value of construction put in place result from direct measurement and indirect estimation. A series results from direct measurement when it is based on reports of the actual value of construction progress or construction expenditures obtained in a complete census or a sample survey. All other series are developed by indirect estimation using related construction statistics. On an annual basis, estimates for series directly measured monthly, quarterly, or annually accounted for about 71 percent of total construction in 1998 (private multifamily residential, private residential improvements, private nonresidential buildings, farm nonresidential construction, public utility construction, all other private construction, and virtually all of public construction). On a monthly basis, directly measured data are available for about 55 percent of the value in place estimates.

Beginning in 1993, the Construction Expenditures Branch of the Census Bureau's Manufacturing and Construction Division began collecting these data using a new classification system, which bases project types on their end usage instead of on building/nonbuilding types. Data collection on this system for federal construction began in January 2002.

With the changes in project classifications, data presented in these tables for 1993 to date are not directly comparable with data for previous years, except at aggregate levels. For that reason, *Business Statistics* shows earlier historical data only at these aggregate levels. Although some categories, such as lodging, office, education, and religion, have the same names as categories in previously published data, there have been changes within the classifications that make these values noncomparable. For example, private medical office buildings were classified as "office" buildings previously, but are categorized as "health care" under the new classification.

The seasonally adjusted data are obtained by removing normal seasonal movement from the unadjusted data to bring out underlying trends and business cycles, which is accomplished by using the Census X-12-ARIMA method. Seasonal adjustment accounts for month-to-month variations resulting from normal or average changes in any phenomena affecting the data, such as weather conditions, the differing lengths of months, and the varying number of holidays, weekdays, and weekends within each month. It does not adjust for abnormal conditions within each month or for year-to-year variations in weather. The seasonally adjusted annual rate is the seasonally adjusted monthly rate multiplied by 12.

Residential consists of new houses, town houses, apartments, and condominiums for sale or rent; these dwellings are built by the owner or for the owner on contract. It includes improvements inside and outside residential structures, such as remodeling, additions, major replacements, and additions of swimming pools and garages. Manufactured housing, houseboats, and maintenance and repair work are not included.

Office includes general office buildings, administration buildings, professional buildings, and financial institution buildings. Office buildings at manufacturing sites are classified as *manufacturing*, but office buildings owned by manufacturing companies but not at such a site are included in the *office* category. In the state and local government category, office includes capitols, city halls, courthouses, and similar buildings.

Commercial includes buildings and structures used by the retail, wholesale, farm, and selected service industries. One of the subgroups of this category is *multi-retail*, which consists of department and variety stores, shopping centers and malls, and warehouse-type retail stores.

Health care includes hospitals, medical buildings, nursing homes, adult daycare centers, and similar institutions.

Educational includes schools at all levels, higher education facilities, trade schools, libraries, museums, and similar institutions.

Amusement and recreation includes theme and amusement parks, sports structures not located at educational institutions, fitness centers and health clubs, neighborhood centers, camps, movie theaters, and similar establishments.

Transportation includes airport facilities; rail facilities, track, and bridges; bus, rail, maritime, and air terminals; and docks, marinas, and similar structures.

Communication includes telephone, television, and radio distribution and maintenance structures.

Power includes electricity production and distribution and gas and crude oil transmission, storage, and distribution.

Manufacturing includes all buildings and structures at manufacturing sites but not the installation of production machinery or special-purpose equipment.

Included in *total private construction*, but not shown separately in these pages, are lodging facilities (hotels and motels), religious structures, and private public safety, sewage and waste disposal, water supply, highway and street, and conservation and development spending.

Included in *total state and local construction*, but not shown separately in these pages, are state and local construction of commercial buildings, conservation and development (dams, levees, jetties, and dredging), lodging, religious facilities, and communication structures.

Public safety includes correctional facilities, police and sheriffs' stations, fire stations, and similar establishments.

Highway and street includes pavement, lighting, retaining walls, bridges, tunnels, toll facilities, and maintenance and rest facilities.

Sewage and waste disposal includes sewage systems, solid waste disposal, and recycling.

Water supply includes water supply, transmission, and storage facilities.

Among the data sources for construction expenditures are the Census Bureau's Survey of Construction, Building Permits Survey, Consumer Expenditure Survey (conducted for the Bureau of Labor Statistics), Annual Capital Expenditures Survey, and Construction Progress Reporting Survey; also included are data from the F.W. Dodge Division of the McGraw-Hill Information Systems Company, the U.S. Department of Agriculture, and utility regulatory agencies.

Data availability

Each month's "Construction Spending" press release is released on the last workday of the following month. The release, more detailed data, and a discussion of methodologies can be found on the Census Bureau's Web site at <http://www.census.gov/constructionspending>.

TABLE 17-3
HOUSING STARTS AND BUILDING PERMITS; NEW HOUSE SALES AND PRICES

SOURCES: U.S. DEPARTMENT OF COMMERCE, CENSUS BUREAU

These data are mainly found in two major Census Bureau reports, "New Residential Construction" and "New Residential Sales." They cover new housing units intended for occupancy and maintained by the occupants, excluding hotels, motels, and group residential structures. Manufactured home units are reported in a separate survey.

Definitions

A *housing unit* is a house, an apartment, or a group of rooms or single room intended for occupancy as separate living quarters. Occupants must live separately from other individuals in the building and have direct access to the housing unit from the outside of the building or through a common hall. Each apartment unit in an apartment building is counted as one housing unit. As of January 2000, a previous requirement for residents to have the capability to eat separately has been eliminated. (Based on the old definition, some senior housing projects were excluded from the multifamily housing statistics because individual units did not have their own eating facilities.) Housing starts exclude group quarters such as dormitories or rooming houses, transient accommodations such as motels, and manufactured homes. Publicly owned housing units are excluded, but units in structures built by private developers with subsidies or for sale to local public housing authorities are both classified as private housing.

The *start* of construction of a privately owned housing unit is when excavation begins for the footings or foundation of a building primarily intended as a housekeeping residential structure and designed for nontransient occupancy. All housing units in a multifamily building are defined as being started when excavation for the building begins.

One-family structures includes fully detached, semi-detached, row houses, and town houses. In the case of attached units, each must be separated from the adjacent unit by a ground-to-roof wall to be classified as a one-unit structure and must not share facilities such as heating or water supply. Units built one on top of another and those built side-by-side without a ground-to-roof wall and/or with common facilities are classified by the number of units in the structure.

Apartment buildings are defined as buildings containing *five units or more*. The type of ownership is not the criterion—a condominium apartment building is not classified as one-family structures but as a multifamily structure.

A *manufactured* home is a movable dwelling, 8 feet or more wide and 40 feet or more long, designed to be towed on its own chassis with transportation gear integral to the unit when it leaves the factory, and without need of a permanent foundation. Multiwides and expandable manufactured homes are included. Excluded are travel trailers, motor homes, and modular housing. The shipments figures are based on reports submitted by manufacturers on the number of homes actually shipped during the survey month. Shipments to dealers may not necessarily be placed for residential use in the same month as they are shipped. The number of manufactured "homes" used for nonresidential purposes (for example, those used for offices) is not known.

Units authorized by building permits represents the approximately 97 percent of housing in permit-requiring areas.

The *start* occurs when excavation begins for the footing or foundation. Starts are estimated for all areas, regardless of whether permits are required.

New house *sales* are reported only for new single-family residential structures. The sales transaction must intend to include both house and land. Excluded are houses built for rent, houses built by the owner, and houses built by a contractor on the owner's land. A sale is reported when a deposit is taken or a sales agreement is signed; this can occur prior to a permit being issued.

A house is *for sale* when a permit to build has been issued (or work begun in non-permit areas) and a sales contract has not been signed nor a deposit accepted.

The *sales price* used in this survey is the price agreed upon between the purchaser and the seller at the time the first sales contract is signed or deposit made. It includes the price of the improved lot. The *median sales price* is the sales price of the house that falls on the middle point of a distribution by price of the total number of houses sold. Half of the houses sold have a sales price lower than the median; half have a price higher than the median. Changes in the *sales price* data reflect changes in the distribution of houses by region, size, and the like, as well as changes in the prices of houses with identical characteristics.

The *price index* measures the change in price of a new single-family house of constant physical characteristics, using the characteristics of houses built in 1996. Characteristics held constant include floor area, whether inside or outside a metropolitan area, number of bedrooms, number of bathrooms, number of fireplaces, type of parking facility, type of foundation, presence of a deck, construction method, exterior wall material, type of heating, and presence of air-conditioning. The indexes are calculated separately for attached and detached houses and combined with base period weights. The price measured includes the value of the lot.

Notes on the data

Monthly permit authorizations are based on data collected by a mail survey from a sample of 8,500 permit-issuing places, selected from a universe of 20,000 such places in the United States. Data for 1994 through 2003 represented 19,000 places; data for 1984 through 1993 represented 17,000 places; data for 1978 through 1983 represented 16,000 places; data for 1972 through 1977 represented 14,000 places; and data for 1971 represented 13,000 places.

Housing starts and sales data are obtained from the Survey of Construction, for which Census Bureau field representatives sample both permit-issuing and non-permit-issuing places.

Effective with the January 2005 data release, the Survey of Construction implemented a new sample of building permit offices, replacing a previous sample selected in 1985. As a result, writes the Census Bureau, "Data users should use caution when analyzing year over year changes in housing prices and characteristics between 2004 and 2005." In the newer sample, land may be more abundant, lot sizes larger, and sales prices lower.

For 2004, the permit data were compiled for both the new 20,000 place universe and the old 19,000 place universe. Ratios of the new estimates to the old were calculated by state for total housing units, structures by number of units, and valuation. For the United States as a whole, the new estimate was 100.9 percent of the old estimate. The complete table of ratios can be found on the Census Bureau Web site at <http://www.census.gov/const/www/permitsindex>.

Effective with the data for April 2001, the Census Bureau made changes to the methodology used for new house sales, including discontinuing an adjustment for construction in areas in which building permits are required without a permit being issued. It was believed that such unauthorized construction has virtually ceased. The upward adjustment was not phased out but dropped completely in revised estimates as of January 1999. The total effect of these changes was to lower the number of sales by about 2.9 percent relative to those published for earlier years.

The data used in the price index are collected in the Survey of Construction, through monthly interviews with the builders or owners. The size of the sample is currently about 20,000 observations per year.

Data availability and references

Housing starts and building permit data have been collected monthly by the Census Bureau since 1959.

The monthly report for "New Residential Construction" (permits, starts, and completions) is issued in the middle of the following month. The monthly report and associated descriptions and historical data can be found at <http://www.census.gov/newresconst>.

The monthly report for "New Residential Sales" (sales, houses for sale, and prices) is issued toward the end of the following month. The monthly report and associated descriptions and historical data can be found at <http://www.census.gov/newhomesales>.

The manufactured housing data (not seasonally adjusted) and background information can be found at <http://www.manufacturedhousing.org/statistics>. Data with and without seasonal adjustment can be found at <http://www.census.gov/const/mhs/shiphist>.

Data and background on the price index for new one-family houses can be found at <http://www.census.gov/const/price_sold>.

TABLES 17-4 THROUGH 17-7
MANUFACTURERS' SHIPMENTS, INVENTORIES, AND ORDERS

SOURCE: U.S. DEPARTMENT OF COMMERCE, CENSUS BUREAU

These data are from the Census Bureau's monthly M3 survey, a sample-based survey that provides measures of changes in the value of domestic manufacturing activity and indications of future production commitments. The sample includes most companies with $500 million or more in annual shipments, along with a selection of smaller companies. Currently, reported monthly data represent approximately 60 percent of shipments at the total manufacturing level.

One important technology industry, semiconductors, is represented in the shipments and inventories data in this report but not in new or unfilled orders. This affects the new and unfilled orders totals for computers and electronic products, durable goods industries, and total manufacturing. Based on shipments data, semiconductors accounted for about 15 percent of computers and electronic products, 3 percent of durable goods industries, and 1.5 percent of total manufacturing. Since semiconductors are intermediate materials and components rather than finished final products, the absence of these data does not distort new and unfilled orders data for important final demand categories, such as capital goods and information technology.

The Census Bureau now compiles this survey on the North American Industry Classification System (NAICS), and has restated historical data on the NAICS basis back to January 1992. To allow the user to observe the difference between levels of activity implied by the two systems, and to "link" the new data to older data if a longer time series is required, *Business Statistics* is republishing (on the same page with the new data) the previous SIC-based annual data up through 1992, providing an overlap with the new data in that year. Link factors can be calculated as the ratio of the 1992 NAICS value to the value of the most closely related Standard Industrial Classification (SIC) category. The SIC values multiplied by these link factors will yield a roughly comparable series without discontinuity. Where overlapping 1992 values are not available, as in the case of new orders, the link factor calculated from shipments can be used for an approximation.

Classification changes in NAICS

There were three major changes from SIC to NAICS that affected the level and trend of manufacturing as a whole: publishing was moved out of manufacturing to the new information industry; some research and development activities were moved out of aerospace manufacturing; and logging was moved out of manufacturing to the agriculture, forestry, fishing, and hunting group. A few relatively small activities, the two largest of which are dental laboratories and retail bakeries, have been shifted into manufacturing based on similarity of production process.

In addition, there was a major rearrangement of industries within manufacturing, yielding groupings that are more relevant in today's economy. Three new industry groups—NAICS 333, Machinery; 334, Computers and electronic products; and 335, Electrical equipment, Appliances, and Components have been formed, mainly from individual industries that were previously represented in SIC 35, Industrial Machinery (which included computers); SIC 36, Electronic and Electric Equipment; and SIC 38, Instruments. Other notable features in NAICS include moving beverages out of the Food group into a new Beverages and tobacco group and replacement of the old Textile mill products group with two new groups, Textile mills and Textile products.

In many cases, the changes are so pervasive that it is not possible to match major SIC and NAICS industries. In Tables 17-4 through 17-7, SIC industries for 1992 and earlier years have been roughly aligned with the new NAICS categories, but a comparison of the old with the new data for 1992 indicates that in many cases, even after this alignment, the old and new industry groupings are still substantially different.

Definitions and notes on the data

Shipments. The value of shipments data represent net selling values, f.o.b. (free on board) plant, after discounts and allowances and excluding freight charges and excise taxes. For multi-establishment companies, the M3 reports are typically company- or division-level reports that encompass groups of plants or products. The data reported are usually net sales and receipts from customers and do not include the value of interplant transfers. The reported sales are used to calculate month-to-month changes that bring forward the estimates for the entire industry (that is, estimates of the statistical "universe") that have been developed from the Annual Survey of Manufactures (ASM). The value of products made elsewhere under contract from materials owned by the plant is also included in shipments, along with receipts for contract work performed for others, resales, miscellaneous activities such as the sale of scrap and refuse, and installation and repair work performed by employees of the plant.

Inventories. Inventory data are requested from respondents by three stages of fabrication: finished goods, work in process, and raw materials and supplies. Response to the stage of fabrication inquiries is lower than for total inventories; not all companies keep their monthly data at this level of detail. It should be noted that a product considered to be a finished good in one industry, such as steel mill shapes, may be reported as a raw material in another industry, such as stamping plants. For some purposes, this difference in definitions is an advantage. When a factory accumulates inventory that it considers to be raw materials, it can be expected that that accumulation is intentional. But when a factory—whether a materials-making or a final-product producer—has a buildup of finished goods inventories, it may indicate involuntary accumulation as a result of sales falling short of expectations. Hence, the two types of accumulation can have different economic interpretations, even if they represent identical types of goods.

Like total inventories, stage of fabrication inventories are benchmarked to the ASM data. Stage of fabrication data are benchmarked at the major group level, as opposed to the level of total inventories, which is benchmarked at the individual industry level.

New orders, as reported in the monthly survey, is net of order cancellations and includes orders received and filled during the month as well as orders received for future delivery. New orders also includes the value of contract changes that increase or decrease the value of the unfilled orders to which they relate. Orders are defined to include those supported by binding legal documents such as signed contracts, letters of award, or letters of intent, although this definition may not be strictly applicable in some industries.

Unfilled orders includes new orders (as defined above) that have not been reflected as shipments. Generally, unfilled orders at the end of the reporting period are equal to unfilled orders at the beginning of the period plus net new orders received less net shipments.

Series are adjusted for seasonal variation and variation in the number of trading days in the month using the X-12-ARIMA version of the Census Bureau's seasonal adjustment program.

Benchmarking and revisions

The M3 series are periodically benchmarked and their seasonal adjustment factors recalculated. In the latest benchmark, published in May 2006 and available on the

Census Bureau Web site, the shipments and inventory data were benchmarked to the 2004 ASM, new and unfilled orders were adjusted to be consistent with the benchmarked shipments and inventory data, and other corrections were made. Seasonal adjustment factors were also revised and updated for all series.

Data availability and references

Data have been collected monthly since 1958.

The "Advance Report on Durable Goods Manufacturers' Shipments, Inventories and Orders" report is available as a press release about 18 working days after the end of each month. It includes seasonally adjusted and not seasonally adjusted estimates of shipments, new orders, unfilled orders, and inventories for durable goods industries.

The monthly "Manufacturers' Shipments, Inventories, and Orders" reports is released on the 23rd working day after the end of the month. Content includes revisions to the advance durable goods data, estimates for nondurable goods industries, tabulations by market category, and ratios of shipments to inventories and to unfilled orders. Revisions may affect selected data for the two previous months.

Press releases, historical data, descriptions of the survey, and extensive documentation of the new NAICS including comparisons with the SIC are available on the Census Bureau Web site at <http://www.census.gov>.

TABLE 17-8
MOTOR VEHICLE SALES AND INVENTORIES

SOURCE: U.S. DEPARTMENT OF COMMERCE, BUREAU OF ECONOMIC ANALYSIS (BEA)

Retail sales and *inventories of cars, trucks, and buses.* These estimates are prepared by the Bureau of Economic Analysis (BEA), based on data from the American Automobile Manufacturers Association, Ward's Automotive Reports, and other sources. Seasonal adjustments are recalculated annually. Data are available on the BEA Web site at <http://www.bea.gov> as a part of the national income and product accounts data set; they are found under the "Supplemental Estimates" heading. They are also available on the STAT-USA subscription Web site at <http://www.stat-usa.gov>.

In these tables, unlike in some other tables that include inventories in *Business Statistics*, the yearly values shown for inventories and the inventory to sales ratio are annual averages of monthly figures.

TABLES 17-9 AND 17-11
RETAIL SALES AND INVENTORIES

SOURCE: U.S. DEPARTMENT OF COMMERCE, CENSUS BUREAU

Every month, the Census Bureau prepares estimates of retail sales and inventories by kind of business, based on a mail-out/mail-back survey of a sample of companies with one or more establishments that sell merchandise and related services to final consumers.

Retail sales and inventories are now compiled using the new NAICS classification system, which replaced the old SIC system. Historical data have been restated on the NAICS basis back to January 1992. To allow the user to observe the difference between levels of activity implied by the two systems and to "link" the new data to older data if a longer time series is required, *Business Statistics* is republishing (on the same page with the new data) the previous SIC-based annual data through 1992; this provides an overlap with the new data in that year.

Classification changes in NAICS

• In NAICS, Eating and drinking places and Mobile food services have been reclassified out of retail trade and into sector 72, Accommodation and food services, which also includes Hotels. The retail sales survey still collects and publishes sales data for *Food services and drinking places*. It no longer includes them in the *Retail* total, but they are included in a new *Retail and food services* total.

• Some activities, such as retail bakeries, are shifted to Manufacturing, based on use of the same production processes.

• Partly offsetting these losses, a significant number of businesses are shifted from Wholesale to Retail trade, including a number of sellers of lumber; construction and lawn equipment; electrical, plumbing, and farm supplies; computers; and office supplies. Establishments which are designed to attract walk-in customers and which use mass-media advertising are now classified as Retail, even if they also serve business and institutional clients.

Data are published under the NAICS system for a new group consisting of *Sporting goods, hobby, book, and music stores*. In addition, total sales of *Nonstore retailers* and a subgroup of nonstores—*Electronic shopping and mail order houses*—are now published. *Store retailers* operate fixed point-of-sale locations designed to attract walk-in customers, display merchandise, use mass-media advertising, and may provide after-sales services. *Nonstore retailers*, on the other hand, sell by "infomercials," paper and electronic catalogs, door-to-door and in-home selling, portable stalls, or vending machines.

Subtotals of durable and nondurable goods are no longer published. They were always imprecise for retail sales, since general merchandise stores (including department stores) were included in nondurable goods, yet obviously sold substantial quantities of durable goods.

For further information about SIC and NAICS, see Chapter 14.

Definitions

Sales is the value of merchandise sold for cash or credit at retail or wholesale. Services that are incidental to the sale of merchandise, and excise taxes that are paid by the manufacturer or wholesaler and passed along to the retailer, are also included. Sales are net, after deductions for refunds and merchandise returns. They exclude sales taxes collected directly from customers and paid directly to a local, state, or federal tax agency. The sales estimates include only sales by establishments primarily engaged in retail trade, and are not intended to measure the total sales for a given commodity or merchandise line.

Inventories is the value of stocks of goods held for sale through retail stores, valued at cost, as of the last day of the report period. Stocks may be held either at the store or at warehouses that maintain supplies primarily intended for distribution to retail stores within the organization.

Inventory data prior to 1980 are not comparable to later years, due to changes in valuation methods. Prior to 1980, inventories are the book values of merchandise on hand at the end of the period. They are valued according to the valuation method used by each respondent. Thus the aggregates are a mixture of LIFO (last in, first out) and non-LIFO values. Beginning with 1980, inventories are valued using methods other than LIFO in order to better reflect the current costs of goods held as inventory.

Leased departments consists of the operations of one company conducted within the establishment of another company, such as jewelry counters or optical centers within department stores. The values for sales and inventories at department stores in Tables 17-9 and 17-10 exclude sales of leased departments.

GAFO (department store type goods) is a special aggregate grouping of sales at general merchandise stores and at other stores that sell merchandise normally sold in department stores—clothing and accessories, furniture and home furnishings, electronics, appliances, sporting goods, hobby, book, music, office supplies, stationery, and gifts.

Notes on the data

The new NAICS-based data have been benchmarked to the 2002, 1997, and 1992 Economic Censuses and the Annual Retail Trade Survey for 2004 and previous years. Each year, the monthly series are benchmarked to the latest annual survey and new factors are incorporated to adjust for seasonal, trading-day, and holiday variations, using the Census Bureau's X-12-ARIMA program.

At the time of the latest benchmark revision, issued in March 2006, some components were revised back to 1992 to reflect new classification rules for the boundary between the Retail trade and Wholesale trade sectors.

The survey sample is stratified by kind of business and estimated sales. All firms with sales above applicable size cutoffs are included. Firms are selected randomly from the remaining strata. The sample used for the end-of-month inventory estimates is a sub-sample of the monthly sales sample, about one-third of the size of the whole sample.

New samples, designed to produce NAICS estimates, were introduced with the 1999 Annual Retail Trade Survey and the March 2001 Monthly Retail Trade Survey. On November 30, 2006, another new sample was introduced, affecting the data for September 2006 and the following months.

Data availability and references

An "Advance Monthly Retail Sales" report is released about nine working days after the close of the reference month, based on responses from a sub-sample of the complete retail sample.

The revised and more complete monthly "Retail Trade, Sales, and Inventories" reports are released six weeks after the close of the reference month. They contain preliminary figures for the current month and final figures for the prior 12 months. Statistics include retail sales, inventories, and ratios of inventories to sales. Data are both seasonally adjusted and unadjusted.

The "Annual Benchmark Report for Retail Trade" is released each spring. It includes updated seasonal adjustment factors; revised and benchmarked monthly estimates of sales and inventories; monthly data for the most recent 10 or more years; detailed annual estimates and ratios for the United States by kind of business; and comparable prior-year statistics and year-to-year changes. The latest such report is U.S. Census Bureau, Current Business Reports, Series BR-05A, *Annual Revision of Monthly Retail and Food Services: Shipments and Inventories—January 1992 through February 2006*, issued in March 2006 and available on the Census Bureau Web site at <http://www.census.gov>, along with the latest data releases and complete historical data.

TABLE 17-10
QUARTERLY RETAIL SALES:
TOTAL AND E-COMMERCE

SOURCE: U.S. DEPARTMENT OF COMMERCE, CENSUS BUREAU

Beginning with the fourth quarter of 1999, the Census Bureau has conducted a quarterly survey of retail e-commerce sales from the Monthly Retail Trade Survey sample. (The monthly survey does not report electronic shopping separately; it is combined with mail order.) E-commerce sales are the sales of goods and services in which an order is placed by the buyer or the price and terms of sale are negotiated over the Internet or an extranet, Electronic Data Interchange (EDI) network, e-mail, or other online system. Payment may or may not be made online. The quarterly release is issued around the 20th of February, May, August, and November, and is available along with full historical data on the Census Bureau Web site at <http://www.census.gov>.

These estimates reflect the NAICS definition of retail sales, which excludes food service. Online travel services, financial brokers and dealers, and ticket sales agencies are not classified as retail and are not included in these estimates; they are, however, included in the annual survey of selected services. See Table 17-16 for more information.

TABLE 17-12
MERCHANT WHOLESALERS:
SALES AND INVENTORIES

SOURCE: *U.S. DEPARTMENT OF COMMERCE, CENSUS BUREAU*

These data are based on a monthly mail-out/mail-back sample survey conducted by the Census Bureau.

These data are now based on the new NAICS classification system, which replaced the old SIC system. Historical data have been restated on the NAICS basis back to January 1992. To allow the user to observe the difference between levels of activity implied by the two systems, and to "link" the new data to older data if a longer time series is required, *Business Statistics* is republishing (on the same page with the new data) the previous SIC-based annual data up through 1992, providing an overlap with the new data in that year.

Classification changes in NAICS

NAICS shifts a significant number of businesses from the Wholesale to the Retail sector. An important new criterion for classification concerns whether or not the establishment is intended to solicit walk-in traffic. If it is, and if it uses mass-media advertising, it is now classified as Retail, even if it also serves business and institutional clients. (See the notes on retail trade, above, for the major categories involved in this shift.)

In the latest benchmark revision, some components were revised back to 1992 to reflect new classification rules for the boundary between the Retail trade and Wholesale trade sectors.

Definitions

Merchant wholesalers includes merchant wholesalers that take title of the goods they sell, as well as jobbers, industrial distributors, exporters, and importers. Excluded are non-merchant wholesalers such as manufacturer sales branches and offices; agents; merchandise or commodity brokers; and commission merchants.

Notes on the data

Inventory data prior to 1980 are not comparable to later years because of changes in valuation methods, and are not included in this book. Prior to 1980, inventories are book values of stocks on hand at the end of the period and

are valued according to the valuation method used by each respondent. Thus, the aggregates are a mixture of LIFO (last in, first out) and non-LIFO values. Beginning with 1980, inventories are valued using methods other than LIFO in order to better reflect the current costs of goods held as inventory.

A survey has been conducted monthly since 1946. New samples are drawn every 5 years, most recently in 2001. The samples are updated every quarter to add new businesses and to drop companies that are no longer active.

Data availability and references

"Monthly Wholesale Trade, Sales and Inventories" reports are released six weeks after the close of the reference month. They contain preliminary current-month figures and final figures for the previous month. Statistics include sales, inventories, and stock/sale ratios, along with standard errors. Data are both seasonally adjusted and unadjusted.

The "Annual Benchmark Report for Wholesale Trade" is released each spring. It contains estimated annual sales, monthly and year-end inventories, inventory/sales ratios, purchases, gross margins, and gross margin/sales ratios by kind of business. Annual estimates are benchmarked to the most recent census of wholesale trade. This report also presents the results of a benchmarking operation that revises monthly sales and inventory estimates, and revised data for both seasonally adjusted and unadjusted values are published.

Data and documentation are available on the Census Bureau Web site at <http://www.census.gov>.

A new sample was introduced in November 2006, with revisions for previous months in 2006 and September 2005 based on the new sample. These revisions are not included in this volume of *Business Statistics*.

TABLES 17-13 THROUGH 17-16
SELECTED SERVICE INDUSTRIES— RECEIPTS
AND REVENUE

SOURCE: *U.S. DEPARTMENT OF COMMERCE, CENSUS BUREAU*

The Census Service Annual Survey provides annual estimates of revenues of taxable and tax-exempt firms for selected service industries. The survey is based on a sample of establishments.

For 1986 through 1998, the data were collected using the old Standard Industrial Classification System (SIC) and were tabulated separately for taxable and nontaxable firms. These data are shown in Tables 17-13 and 17-14 and are unchanged from the 2006 edition of *Business Statistics*.

Data from 1998 through 2004 were collected using the North American Industry Classification System (NAICS), and the data for each industry include both taxable and nontaxable firms. These data are shown in Tables 17-15 and 17-16. They have been adjusted to reflect the results of the 2002 Economic Census.

See Chapter 14 for information on comparability of industries in the new and old classification systems.

Notes on the data

In the SIC estimates for 1986 through 1998, separate estimates were developed for taxable and nontaxable firms in camps and membership lodging; selected amusement and recreation services; selected health services; legal services; libraries; vocational schools; social services; museums, art galleries, botanical gardens, and zoos; research, development, and testing services; and selected management and public relations services. Firms considered tax-exempt include membership lodging, membership organizations, and noncommercial research organizations. Firms in all remaining SIC categories were defined as taxable. For tax-exempt firms, employer firms only were sampled; for all other kinds of business, data represent combined estimates for employer and nonemployer firms. Government-operated hospitals were included, while all other government establishments were excluded.

In Table 17-16, total and e-commerce revenues are reported for the service industries represented in Table 17-15. They are also reported for NAICS industry 72, Accommodation and food services, which is not represented in Table 17-15.

Data availability and references

Data for the latest year and revisions of previous years are published annually as *Current Business Reports, Service Annual Survey*. They are available on the Census Bureau Web site at <http://www.census.gov>. The e-commerce estimates can be found at <http://www.census.gov/eos/www/ebusiness>.

TABLE 17-17
SELECTED SERVICES, QUARTERLY:
ESTIMATED REVENUE FOR EMPLOYER FIRMS

SOURCE: U.S. DEPARTMENT OF COMMERCE, CENSUS BUREAU

New Census data on quarterly revenue for selected service industries are based on information collected from a probability sample of approximately 6,000 employer firms (firms with employees) chosen from the sample from the larger Service Annual Survey (see notes on Tables 17-13 through 17-16 above) and expanded to represent totals for the selected industries. Industries are defined according to the 2002 NAICS.

These data have not been collected long enough to provide the data required for calculation of seasonal adjustment factors. However, there do seem to be some seasonal patterns of an expected type in the data so far collected. For example, revenues for the employment services industry rise in the fourth quarter and drop back in the first quarter, reflecting temporary hiring for the holiday season. Accounting, tax preparation, and related services rise in the first quarter and drop back thereafter, undoubtedly because of the tax season. Users should primarily rely on comparisons with year-earlier data.

Data availability and references

The quarterly release "U.S. Government Estimates of Quarterly Revenue for Selected Services" is available on the Census Web site at <http://www.census.gov/qss> around the middle of the third month following the end of the quarter. Information about the survey and its reliability is included in this release.

PART C

HISTORICAL DATA

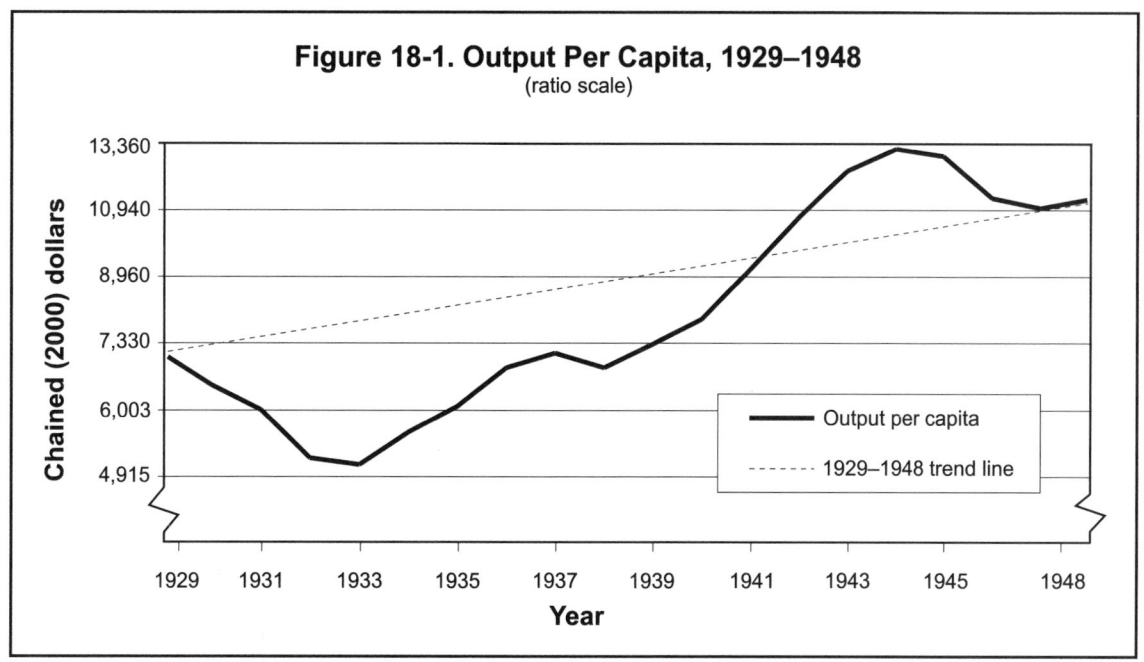

Figure 18-1. Output Per Capita, 1929–1948
(ratio scale)

- In 1929, a year of peak business activity and low unemployment, gross domestic product (GDP) per capita in the United States—revalued to 2000 prices—was $7,099. Over the next four years, per capita real GDP would contract to just over $5,000. Production recovered after 1933, but the 1929 peak was not seen again until 1937. (Tables 18-2 and 18-4)

- Production surged during World War II; most of the increase in output was war materiel, but real consumer spending also increased during the war years. In 1948, with the postwar demobilization complete, output per capita (in 2000 prices) was $11,206, 58 percent higher than in 1929. The average annual growth rate in GDP per capita from 1929 to 1948 was 2.4 percent—but as Figure 18-1 indicates, most of the 1930s was spent far below this trend line. (Table 18-2)

- Prices declined throughout the 1929–1933 contraction. While this would seem to moderate the impact of falling incomes on individuals, it was in fact catastrophic for the economy. Falling prices and the anticipation of further decline destroy any incentive to invest immediately, as prices are expected to be still lower in the future. Even very low nominal interest rates become prohibitively high in real terms. Real gross private domestic investment collapsed by 1932 to just one-eighth of its 1929 level. (Tables 18-2 and 18-4)

- The personal saving rate was 4.5 percent in 1929; by 1932, it was negative, as people spent their assets to keep their living standards from declining too steeply. Personal saving was back to the 1929 rate by 1935. (Table 18-1)

- Worker incomes increased during the wartime boom as employment, average hours, and hourly wages all rose. Consumption spending opportunities were limited by rationing and production controls. (For example, passenger cars were simply not produced, as assembly lines were converted to building military vehicles.) This, along with "war bond" savings drives, contributed to a huge increase in personal saving, which peaked at 26.1 percent of disposable income in 1944. By 1947, the personal saving rate had returned to 4.3 percent, almost equal to its 1929 level. (Tables 18-1 and 18-4)

Table 18-1. National Income and Product Accounts, 1929–1948

(Billions of current dollars, except as noted.)

Classification	1929	1930	1931	1932	1933	1934	1935	1936	1937	1938
Gross domestic product, total	103.6	91.2	76.5	58.7	56.4	66.0	73.3	83.8	91.9	86.1
Personal consumption expenditures, total	77.4	70.1	60.7	48.7	45.9	51.5	55.9	62.2	66.8	64.3
Durable goods	9.2	7.2	5.5	3.6	3.5	4.2	5.1	6.3	6.9	5.7
Nondurable goods	37.7	34.0	29.0	22.7	22.3	26.7	29.3	32.9	35.2	34.0
Services	30.5	29.0	26.2	22.3	20.2	20.5	21.5	23.0	24.7	24.6
Gross private domestic fixed investment, total	14.9	11.0	7.0	3.6	3.1	4.3	5.6	7.5	9.5	7.7
Nonresidential, total	11.0	8.6	5.3	2.9	2.5	3.3	4.3	5.8	7.5	5.5
Structures	5.5	4.4	2.6	1.4	1.1	1.2	1.4	1.9	2.7	2.1
Equipment and software	5.5	4.2	2.6	1.5	1.4	2.1	2.8	3.9	4.8	3.4
Residential	4.0	2.4	1.8	0.8	0.6	0.9	1.3	1.7	2.1	2.1
Change in private inventories	1.5	-0.2	-1.1	-2.4	-1.4	-0.6	1.1	1.2	2.6	-0.6
Net exports of goods and services	0.4	0.3	0.0	0.0	0.1	0.3	-0.2	-0.1	0.1	1.0
Exports	5.9	4.4	2.9	2.0	2.0	2.6	2.8	3.0	4.0	3.8
Imports	5.6	4.1	2.9	1.9	1.9	2.2	3.0	3.2	4.0	2.8
Government consumption expenditures and gross investment, total	9.4	10.0	9.9	8.7	8.7	10.5	10.9	13.1	12.8	13.8
Federal	1.7	1.8	1.9	1.8	2.3	3.3	3.4	5.6	5.1	5.7
National defense	0.9	0.9	0.9	0.9	0.9	0.8	1.0	1.2	1.3	1.4
State and local	7.6	8.2	8.0	6.9	6.4	7.2	7.5	7.5	7.7	8.1
Gross national product	104.4	91.9	77.0	59.1	56.7	66.3	73.6	84.0	92.2	86.5
National income, total	94.2	83.1	67.6	51.3	48.9	58.3	66.3	75.0	83.6	76.8
Compensation of employees	51.1	46.9	39.8	31.1	29.6	34.3	37.4	42.9	48.0	45.0
Proprietors' income with IVA and CCAdj	14.2	11.1	8.5	5.1	5.4	7.1	10.2	10.4	12.6	10.6
Farm	5.8	4.0	3.1	1.8	2.3	2.7	5.0	4.0	5.7	4.1
Nonfarm	8.4	7.0	5.3	3.3	3.1	4.4	5.2	6.4	6.9	6.6
Rental income of persons with CCAdj	6.2	5.5	4.5	3.6	2.9	2.6	2.6	2.8	3.0	3.6
Corporate profits with IVA and CCAdj	10.8	7.5	2.9	-0.2	-0.1	2.5	4.0	6.2	7.1	5.0
Net interest and miscellaneous payments	4.6	4.8	4.8	4.5	4.0	4.0	4.1	3.8	3.7	3.6
Taxes on production and imports	6.8	7.0	6.7	6.6	6.9	7.6	8.0	8.5	8.9	8.9
Less: Subsidies less current surplus of government enterprises	0.0	0.0	0.1	0.1	0.1	0.4	0.5	0.2	0.2	0.4
Business current transfer payments (net)	0.5	0.5	0.5	0.6	0.5	0.5	0.5	0.5	0.5	0.4
Personal income, total	85.1	76.3	65.3	49.9	46.9	53.7	60.4	68.7	74.1	68.4
Less: Personal current taxes	1.7	1.6	1.0	0.7	0.8	0.9	1.1	1.3	1.9	1.9
Equals: Disposable personal income (DPI)	83.4	74.7	64.3	49.2	46.1	52.8	59.3	67.4	72.2	66.6
Less: Personal outlays	79.6	71.6	61.8	49.7	46.8	52.3	56.7	63.1	67.9	65.3
Equals: Personal saving	3.8	3.1	2.5	-0.5	-0.7	0.5	2.6	4.3	4.3	1.3
As a percentage of DPI	4.5	4.1	3.9	-0.9	-1.5	1.0	4.3	6.3	6.0	2.0
Gross saving	19.3	15.0	8.3	3.3	3.3	6.4	9.6	11.5	16.2	11.7
Net saving	9.9	5.8	-0.3	-4.2	-3.9	-1.2	2.1	3.6	7.5	2.8
Net private saving	7.4	4.2	0.9	-3.6	-3.4	-0.2	2.8	4.5	5.2	2.1
Net government saving, federal	1.0	0.2	-2.1	-1.3	-0.9	-2.2	-1.9	-3.2	0.2	-1.3
Net government saving, state and local	1.5	1.3	1.0	0.7	0.4	1.2	1.1	2.3	2.0	2.0
Consumption of fixed capital, private	8.4	8.3	7.7	6.7	6.3	6.5	6.5	6.6	7.4	7.6
Consumption of fixed capital, government	1.0	0.9	0.9	0.8	0.9	1.1	1.1	1.2	1.3	1.4
Gross domestic investment, total	19.3	13.9	8.9	3.4	3.7	6.4	9.5	12.8	15.9	11.3
Private	16.5	10.8	5.9	1.3	1.7	3.7	6.7	8.6	12.2	7.1
Government	2.8	3.2	3.0	2.1	1.9	2.7	2.8	4.1	3.8	4.2
Net lending or net borrowing (-), NIPAs	0.8	0.7	0.2	0.2	0.2	0.4	-0.1	-0.1	0.2	1.2
Net domestic investment	9.9	4.7	0.3	-4.1	-3.5	-1.2	1.9	4.9	7.3	2.3
Gross saving as a percentage of gross national income	18.6	16.3	10.9	5.6	5.8	9.7	13.0	13.9	17.5	13.7
Net saving as a percentage of gross national income	9.6	6.3	-0.3	-7.2	-7.0	-1.8	2.8	4.4	8.1	3.2

Table 18-1. National Income and Product Accounts, 1929–1948—Continued

(Billions of current dollars, except as noted.)

Classification	1939	1940	1941	1942	1943	1944	1945	1946	1947	1948
Gross domestic product, total	92.2	101.4	126.7	161.9	198.6	219.8	223.1	222.3	244.2	269.2
Personal consumption expenditures, total	67.2	71.3	81.1	89.0	99.9	108.7	120.0	144.3	162.0	175.0
Durable goods	6.7	7.8	9.7	6.9	6.5	6.7	8.0	15.8	20.4	22.9
Nondurable goods	35.1	37.0	42.9	50.8	58.6	64.3	71.9	82.7	90.9	96.6
Services	25.4	26.5	28.5	31.4	34.8	37.6	40.1	45.8	50.7	55.6
Gross private domestic fixed investment, total	9.1	11.2	13.8	8.5	6.9	8.7	12.3	25.1	35.5	42.4
Nonresidential, total	6.1	7.7	9.7	6.3	5.4	7.4	10.6	17.3	23.5	26.8
Structures	2.2	2.6	3.3	2.2	1.8	2.4	3.3	7.4	8.1	9.5
Equipment and software	3.9	5.2	6.4	4.1	3.7	5.0	7.3	9.9	15.3	17.3
Residential	3.0	3.5	4.1	2.2	1.4	1.4	1.7	7.8	12.1	15.6
Change in private inventories	0.2	2.4	4.3	1.9	-0.7	-0.9	-1.5	6.0	-0.6	5.7
Net exports of goods and services	0.8	1.5	1.0	-0.3	-2.2	-2.0	-0.8	7.2	10.8	5.5
Exports	4.0	4.9	5.5	4.4	4.0	4.9	6.8	14.2	18.7	15.5
Imports	3.1	3.4	4.4	4.6	6.3	6.9	7.5	7.0	7.9	10.1
Government consumption expenditures and gross investment, total	14.8	15.0	26.5	62.7	94.8	105.3	93.0	39.6	36.4	40.6
Federal	6.0	6.5	18.0	54.1	86.5	97.0	84.1	28.9	22.7	24.2
National defense	1.5	2.5	14.3	51.1	84.2	94.5	82.0	25.2	18.2	18.3
State and local	8.8	8.6	8.6	8.6	8.4	8.4	9.0	10.8	13.7	16.3
Gross national product	92.5	101.7	127.2	162.3	198.9	220.1	223.4	222.9	245.3	270.6
National income, total	82.2	91.2	116.0	149.8	184.5	198.2	198.4	198.5	216.6	243.0
Compensation of employees	48.1	52.2	64.8	85.3	109.6	121.3	123.3	119.6	130.1	142.0
Proprietors' income with IVA and CCAdj	11.2	12.3	16.7	23.4	28.3	29.4	30.8	35.6	34.5	39.3
Farm	4.1	4.1	6.1	9.7	11.6	11.5	11.8	14.2	14.4	16.7
Nonfarm	7.1	8.2	10.6	13.7	16.7	18.0	19.0	21.4	20.2	22.6
Rental income of persons with CCAdj	3.8	3.9	4.5	5.5	6.1	6.5	6.7	7.1	7.2	7.9
Corporate profits with IVA and CCAdj	6.6	9.8	15.5	20.6	24.9	24.9	20.3	17.8	23.7	31.2
Net interest and miscellaneous payments	3.6	3.3	3.3	3.2	2.9	2.4	2.3	1.9	2.5	2.6
Taxes on production and imports	9.1	9.8	11.1	11.5	12.4	13.7	15.1	16.8	18.1	19.7
Less: Subsidies less current surplus of government enterprises	0.7	0.6	0.3	0.4	0.4	0.9	1.0	1.2	0.2	0.3
Business current transfer payments (net)	0.4	0.5	0.5	0.5	0.6	0.8	0.9	0.7	0.7	0.7
Personal income, total	72.9	78.5	96.1	123.5	152.2	166.0	171.7	178.6	191.0	209.8
Less: Personal current taxes	1.5	1.7	2.3	4.9	16.7	17.7	19.4	17.2	19.8	19.2
Equals: Disposable personal income (DPI)	71.4	76.8	93.8	118.6	135.4	148.3	152.2	161.4	171.2	190.6
Less: Personal outlays	68.2	72.4	82.3	90.0	100.8	109.7	121.2	145.9	163.8	177.3
Equals: Personal saving	3.2	4.4	11.5	28.6	34.6	38.7	31.1	15.5	7.4	13.4
As a percentage of DPI	4.5	5.7	12.2	24.1	25.6	26.1	20.4	9.6	4.3	7.0
Gross saving	13.6	18.5	29.8	39.8	44.9	39.9	29.8	38.4	46.6	58.0
Net saving	4.6	9.0	19.0	26.4	28.6	20.5	8.7	15.1	20.2	29.9
Net private saving	4.6	7.4	14.9	33.6	41.2	45.8	36.1	18.6	13.5	25.1
Net government saving, federal	-2.1	-0.3	2.2	-8.7	-14.1	-26.9	-29.0	-5.0	5.3	3.6
Net government saving, state and local	2.0	2.0	1.9	1.5	1.5	1.6	1.6	1.5	1.4	1.2
Consumption of fixed capital, private	7.6	7.9	8.8	9.9	10.0	10.5	10.9	12.5	15.7	18.4
Consumption of fixed capital, government	1.4	1.5	2.0	3.5	6.2	8.9	10.1	10.8	10.7	9.7
Gross domestic investment, total	13.8	18.0	28.9	39.0	45.2	44.4	35.0	34.6	39.6	55.1
Private	9.3	13.6	18.1	10.4	6.1	7.8	10.8	31.1	35.0	48.1
Government	4.5	4.4	10.8	28.5	39.1	36.6	24.1	3.5	4.6	7.0
Net lending or net borrowing (-), NIPAs	1.0	1.5	1.3	-0.1	-2.1	-2.0	-1.3	4.9	9.3	2.4
Net domestic investment	4.8	8.6	18.1	25.6	28.9	25.1	13.9	11.3	13.2	27.0
Gross saving as a percentage of gross national income	14.9	18.4	23.5	24.4	22.4	18.3	13.6	17.3	19.2	21.4
Net saving as a percentage of gross national income	5.0	9.0	15.0	16.2	14.3	9.4	4.0	6.8	8.3	11.0

Table 18-2. NIPA Data on Real Output, Prices, and Employment, 1929–1948

Classification	1929	1930	1931	1932	1933	1934	1935	1936	1937	1938
POPULATION										
Population (midperiod, thousands)	121 878	123 188	124 149	124 949	125 690	126 485	127 362	128 181	128 961	129 969
BILLIONS OF CHAINED (2000) DOLLARS (Except as noted)										
Real gross domestic product, total	865.2	790.7	739.9	643.7	635.5	704.2	766.9	866.6	911.1	879.7
Per capita (2000 dollars)	7 099	6 418	5 960	5 152	5 056	5 567	6 021	6 761	7 065	6 769
Personal consumption expenditures	661.4	626.1	606.9	553.0	541.0	579.3	614.8	677.0	702.0	690.7
Gross private domestic investment	91.3	60.9	38.3	11.5	17.0	30.7	56.9	72.9	91.1	60.2
Exports	34.9	28.9	24.0	18.8	18.9	21.0	22.2	23.3	29.3	29.0
Imports	44.3	38.5	33.6	27.9	29.1	29.7	38.9	38.4	43.3	33.6
Government	120.6	132.9	138.5	133.8	129.2	145.7	149.7	174.7	167.3	180.2
Disposable personal income	712.7	666.8	643.5	558.4	542.3	594.5	652.2	733.6	758.6	715.5
Per capita (2000 dollars)	5 848	5 413	5 183	4 469	4 315	4 700	5 121	5 723	5 882	5 505
CHAIN-TYPE PRICE INDEXES, 2000 = 100										
Gross domestic product	11.94	11.48	10.33	9.15	8.91	9.35	9.53	9.64	10.00	9.81
Percent change	. . .	-3.9	-10.0	-11.5	-2.6	4.9	2.0	1.2	3.7	-1.9
Personal consumption expenditures	11.70	11.20	10.00	8.81	8.49	8.88	9.10	9.18	9.52	9.30
Percent change	. . .	-4.2	-10.8	-11.9	-3.6	4.6	2.4	1.0	3.6	-2.3
EMPLOYMENT, NIPA DATA (1942 SIC): FULL-TIME AND PART-TIME EMPLOYEES (Thousands)										
Total	37 699	35 590	32 724	29 445	30 940	34 238	35 577	38 599	39 701	38 322
Domestic industries	37 699	35 590	32 723	29 444	30 939	34 237	35 576	38 598	39 700	38 321
Private industries	34 088	31 811	28 590	25 071	25 038	27 417	28 426	30 548	32 508	30 124
Agriculture, forestry, and fisheries	3 556	3 337	3 252	3 028	2 995	2 986	3 013	3 106	3 083	2 949
Mining	993	932	813	672	693	822	840	897	955	859
Contract construction	1 484	1 366	1 198	907	703	866	866	1 104	1 082	1 055
Manufacturing	10 428	9 309	7 895	6 678	7 204	8 364	8 904	9 645	10 591	9 131
Durable goods	5 238	4 457	3 497	2 724	2 893	3 587	3 941	4 460	5 130	4 085
Nondurable goods	5 190	4 852	4 398	3 954	4 311	4 777	4 963	5 185	5 461	5 046
Transportation and public utilities	3 989	3 742	3 282	2 826	2 684	2 774	2 808	2 973	3 140	2 837
Wholesale trade	1 757	1 693	1 530	1 380	1 377	1 492	1 507	1 612	1 770	1 767
Retail trade and automobile services	4 684	4 469	4 148	3 688	3 699	4 075	4 200	4 543	4 904	4 780
Finance, insurance, and real estate	1 520	1 491	1 423	1 358	1 309	1 332	1 352	1 401	1 445	1 436
Services	5 677	5 472	5 049	4 534	4 374	4 766	4 936	5 267	5 538	5 310
Government	3 611	3 779	4 133	4 373	5 901	6 820	7 150	8 050	7 192	8 197
Federal	981	1 034	1 019	1 006	1 470	2 227	2 209	4 993	4 085	4 987
General government	644	695	683	673	1 135	1 868	1 835	4 612	3 698	4 583
Civilian, except work relief	267	310	296	290	294	357	449	521	517	507
Military [1]	377	385	387	383	370	371	396	438	474	504
Work relief	. . .	. . .	. . .	. . .	471	1 140	990	3 653	2 707	3 572
Government enterprises	337	339	336	333	335	359	374	381	387	404
State and local	2 630	2 745	3 114	3 367	4 431	4 593	4 941	3 057	3 107	3 210
General government	2 509	2 618	2 984	3 249	4 317	4 473	4 815	2 922	2 967	3 070
Public education	1 067	1 095	1 105	1 093	1 069	1 069	1 097	1 118	1 149	1 180
Nonschool, except work relief	1 442	1 503	1 580	1 564	1 524	1 570	1 621	1 713	1 762	1 871
Work relief	. . .	20	299	592	1 724	1 834	2 097	91	56	19
Government enterprises	121	127	130	118	114	120	126	135	140	140
Rest of the world	0	0	1	1	1	1	1	1	1	1

[1] Includes Coast Guard.
. . . = Not available.

Table 18-2. NIPA Data on Real Output, Prices, and Employment, 1929–1948—Continued

Classification	1939	1940	1941	1942	1943	1944	1945	1946	1947	1948
POPULATION										
Population (midperiod, thousands)	131 028	132 122	133 402	134 860	136 739	138 397	139 928	141 389	144 126	146 631
BILLIONS OF CHAINED (2000) DOLLARS (Except as noted)										
Real gross domestic product, total	950.7	1 034.1	1 211.1	1 435.4	1 670.9	1 806.5	1 786.3	1 589.4	1 574.5	1 643.2
Per capita (2000 dollars)	7 256	7 827	9 079	10 644	12 220	13 053	12 766	11 241	10 925	11 206
Personal consumption expenditures	729.1	767.1	821.9	803.1	826.1	850.2	902.7	1 012.9	1 031.6	1 054.4
Gross private domestic investment	77.4	107.9	131.7	69.6	41.1	50.8	67.0	172.1	165.3	211.2
Exports	30.6	34.8	35.7	23.6	19.9	21.4	29.9	64.6	73.7	58.0
Imports	35.3	36.2	44.5	40.4	50.9	53.3	56.7	47.0	44.6	52.0
Government	196.0	201.5	335.1	788.6	1 173.3	1 320.5	1 152.9	396.8	337.2	361.7
Disposable personal income	774.9	826.5	950.7	1 069.9	1 119.9	1 160.7	1 145.3	1 132.7	1 090.3	1 148.4
Per capita (2000 dollars)	5 914	6 255	7 127	7 934	8 190	8 387	8 185	8 011	7 565	7 832
CHAIN-TYPE PRICE INDEXES, 2000 = 100										
Gross domestic product	9.69	9.77	10.40	11.26	11.88	12.16	12.48	13.93	15.49	16.37
Percent change	-1.2	0.9	6.5	8.2	5.6	2.4	2.6	11.7	11.2	5.7
Personal consumption expenditures	9.22	9.29	9.86	11.08	12.09	12.78	13.29	14.25	15.70	16.60
Percent change	-0.9	0.8	6.1	12.3	9.1	5.7	4.0	7.2	10.2	5.7
EMPLOYMENT, NIPA DATA (1942 SIC): FULL-TIME AND PART-TIME EMPLOYEES (Thousands)										
Total	39 633	41 437	45 785	50 219	55 995	57 221	55 548	49 643	49 936	51 332
Domestic industries	39 632	41 435	45 782	50 214	56 016	57 276	55 614	49 690	49 941	51 325
Private industries	31 612	33 518	37 210	39 728	40 723	39 749	38 183	40 379	42 458	43 431
Agriculture, forestry, and fisheries	2 859	2 809	2 779	2 692	2 563	2 372	2 259	2 343	2 427	2 498
Mining	832	927	975	985	917	879	829	871	933	981
Contract construction	1 219	1 285	1 774	2 131	1 566	1 110	1 135	1 739	2 062	2 278
Manufacturing	9 967	10 882	13 137	15 284	17 402	17 050	15 186	14 493	15 205	15 276
Durable goods	4 609	5 367	6 999	8 846	10 924	10 722	8 933	7 742	8 330	8 309
Nondurable goods	5 358	5 515	6 138	6 438	6 478	6 328	6 253	6 751	6 875	6 967
Transportation and public utilities	2 943	3 064	3 311	3 458	3 652	3 822	3 926	4 113	4 173	4 212
Wholesale trade	1 833	1 899	2 014	1 916	1 808	1 828	1 927	2 286	2 480	2 573
Retail trade and automobile services	4 992	5 321	5 754	5 623	5 570	5 529	5 717	6 769	7 061	7 223
Finance, insurance, and real estate	1 470	1 518	1 559	1 531	1 475	1 447	1 477	1 692	1 744	1 811
Services	5 497	5 813	5 907	6 108	5 770	5 712	5 727	6 073	6 373	6 579
Government	8 020	7 917	8 572	10 486	15 293	17 527	17 431	9 311	7 483	7 894
Federal	4 754	4 652	5 281	7 252	12 155	14 405	14 258	5 902	3 808	4 007
General government	4 342	4 227	4 829	6 765	11 611	13 885	13 722	5 294	3 268	3 437
Civilian, except work relief	560	642	944	1 702	2 497	2 520	2 420	1 822	1 436	1 428
Military [1]	566	793	1 693	4 154	9 029	11 365	11 302	3 472	1 832	2 009
Work relief	3 216	2 792	2 192	909	85	. . .	. . .	. . .	. . .	. . .
Government enterprises	412	425	452	487	544	520	536	608	540	570
State and local	3 266	3 265	3 291	3 234	3 138	3 122	3 173	3 409	3 675	3 887
General government	3 123	3 104	3 119	3 063	2 965	2 956	3 007	3 236	3 481	3 657
Public education	1 207	1 194	1 256	1 264	1 256	1 256	1 273	1 347	1 445	1 504
Nonschool, except work relief	1 877	1 872	1 846	1 794	1 709	1 700	1 734	1 889	2 036	2 153
Work relief	39	38	17	5	. . .	. . .	. . .	. . .	. . .	. . .
Government enterprises	143	161	172	171	173	166	166	173	194	230
Rest of the world	1	2	3	5	-21	-55	-66	-47	-5	7

[1]Includes Coast Guard.
. . . = Not available.

Table 18-3. Fixed Assets: Current-Cost Values and Quantity Indexes, 1929–1948

Classification	1929	1930	1931	1932	1933	1934	1935	1936	1937	1938
CURRENT-COST NET STOCK OF FIXED ASSETS (Billions of dollars, year end)										
Total	285.7	273.4	236.2	218.3	233.8	240.1	244.2	270.7	285.3	287.9
Private, total	245.0	233.7	200.1	182.6	192.0	194.2	195.5	216.5	228.1	228.7
Nonresidential										
Equipment and software	33.4	32.1	29.4	26.5	26.2	26.4	25.9	27.9	30.2	30.3
Structures	91.8	87.3	77.2	72.2	74.0	75.2	75.4	83.9	86.6	85.2
Residential	119.8	114.3	93.5	83.9	91.7	92.7	94.2	104.7	111.3	113.1
Government, total	40.8	39.7	36.1	35.7	41.8	45.9	48.7	54.2	57.2	59.2
Nonresidential										
Equipment and software	2.4	2.3	2.3	2.3	2.3	2.6	2.8	3.0	3.2	3.3
Structures	38.4	37.3	33.8	33.4	39.4	43.2	45.8	51.1	53.8	55.6
Residential	0.0	0.0	0.0	0.0	0.0	0.0	0.0	0.1	0.2	0.2
Private and government fixed assets, total	285.7	273.4	236.2	218.3	233.8	240.1	244.2	270.7	285.3	287.9
Nonresidential										
Equipment and software	35.8	34.5	31.8	28.8	28.6	29.0	28.7	30.9	33.4	33.6
Structures	130.1	124.6	110.9	105.6	113.5	118.4	121.3	134.9	140.4	140.9
Residential	119.8	114.3	93.5	84.0	91.7	92.7	94.2	104.8	111.5	113.4
Government, by level										
Federal	7.9	7.4	6.8	6.7	7.6	8.6	9.8	11.4	12.6	13.3
State and local	32.9	32.2	29.3	29.0	34.2	37.2	38.8	42.8	44.6	45.9
CHAIN-TYPE QUANTITY INDEXES FOR NET STOCK OF FIXED ASSETS (Index numbers, 2000 = 100)										
Total	14.77	15.07	15.20	15.14	15.02	15.01	15.08	15.32	15.59	15.77
Private, total	16.54	16.78	16.79	16.58	16.34	16.20	16.15	16.24	16.41	16.45
Nonresidential										
Equipment and software	6.95	7.04	6.87	6.49	6.16	5.97	5.94	6.12	6.42	6.42
Structures	23.63	24.21	24.36	24.20	23.94	23.72	23.56	23.54	23.65	23.62
Residential	17.58	17.70	17.76	17.68	17.57	17.51	17.53	17.61	17.71	17.81
Government, total	9.70	10.25	10.81	11.26	11.57	11.98	12.42	13.13	13.72	14.39
Nonresidential										
Equipment and software	2.47	2.47	2.50	2.49	2.48	2.62	2.81	2.92	3.04	3.23
Structures	12.69	13.45	14.23	14.87	15.30	15.81	16.36	17.29	18.04	18.90
Residential	0.03	0.06	0.09	0.12	0.14	0.17	0.25	0.70	1.32	1.57
Private and government fixed assets, total	14.77	15.07	15.20	15.14	15.02	15.01	15.08	15.32	15.59	15.77
Nonresidential										
Equipment and software	5.75	5.82	5.69	5.40	5.14	5.03	5.04	5.19	5.44	5.47
Structures	18.73	19.39	19.80	19.98	20.02	20.14	20.31	20.72	21.12	21.49
Residential	17.20	17.32	17.38	17.30	17.20	17.14	17.16	17.25	17.36	17.47
Government, by level										
Federal	6.69	6.74	6.88	7.10	7.54	8.15	9.00	9.80	10.53	11.23
State and local	10.97	11.72	12.46	13.00	13.26	13.59	13.88	14.56	15.10	15.77

Table 18-3. Fixed Assets: Current-Cost Values and Quantity Indexes, 1929–1948—Continued

Classification	1939	1940	1941	1942	1943	1944	1945	1946	1947	1948
CURRENT-COST NET STOCK OF FIXED ASSETS (Billions of dollars, year end)										
Total	294.6	319.4	363.9	416.1	463.3	496.6	539.9	633.7	729.8	774.6
Private, total	233.0	251.7	279.3	299.1	314.0	326.7	351.5	433.4	515.4	560.0
Nonresidential										
Equipment and software	31.1	33.6	38.7	39.8	40.3	40.5	46.8	56.3	68.0	82.2
Structures	85.2	90.0	100.8	108.7	110.3	111.5	120.4	150.0	180.0	189.8
Residential	116.7	128.1	139.9	150.6	163.5	174.7	184.3	227.1	267.4	288.0
Government, total	61.6	67.6	84.5	117.0	149.3	169.9	188.4	200.3	214.4	214.6
Nonresidential										
Equipment and software	3.6	4.0	7.7	20.9	45.4	65.5	75.8	70.7	62.0	52.2
Structures	57.7	63.1	75.8	94.4	101.3	101.6	109.6	125.7	146.8	157.4
Residential	0.3	0.5	1.0	1.7	2.6	2.8	3.0	4.0	5.6	5.0
Private and government fixed assets, total	294.6	319.4	363.9	416.1	463.3	496.6	539.9	633.7	729.8	774.6
Nonresidential										
Equipment and software	34.7	37.6	46.4	60.7	85.7	106.0	122.6	127.0	130.1	134.4
Structures	142.9	153.1	176.6	203.1	211.6	213.0	230.0	275.7	326.8	347.3
Residential	117.0	128.7	140.9	152.3	166.0	177.6	187.3	231.1	273.0	293.0
Government, by level										
Federal	14.0	15.7	24.4	49.7	80.8	103.0	118.9	122.4	121.1	113.0
State and local	47.6	51.9	60.2	67.4	68.5	66.9	69.5	77.9	93.3	101.6
CHAIN-TYPE QUANTITY INDEXES FOR NET STOCK OF FIXED ASSETS (Index numbers, 2000 = 100)										
Total	16.04	16.39	17.05	18.13	19.35	20.36	20.81	20.70	20.83	21.14
Private, total	16.59	16.84	17.16	17.13	16.99	16.96	17.08	17.62	18.35	19.16
Nonresidential										
Equipment and software	6.50	6.78	7.17	7.11	7.00	7.12	7.61	8.17	9.13	10.04
Structures	23.63	23.70	23.85	23.71	23.45	23.30	23.33	23.88	24.33	24.90
Residential	18.05	18.34	18.67	18.72	18.66	18.60	18.53	19.03	19.73	20.60
Government, total	15.15	15.85	17.73	22.68	28.64	33.50	35.16	32.54	30.29	28.63
Nonresidential										
Equipment and software	3.43	3.63	6.71	19.63	44.69	68.65	76.96	63.17	50.32	39.61
Structures	19.87	20.70	22.12	24.80	25.87	26.18	26.33	26.11	26.13	26.39
Residential	2.04	3.42	6.19	9.25	13.15	14.09	14.31	15.88	16.37	16.67
Private and government fixed assets, total	16.04	16.39	17.05	18.13	19.35	20.36	20.81	20.70	20.83	21.14
Nonresidential										
Equipment and software	5.57	5.82	6.65	8.64	12.27	15.83	17.42	15.98	14.98	14.26
Structures	21.92	22.33	23.04	24.17	24.51	24.57	24.66	24.87	25.14	25.57
Residential	17.71	18.03	18.41	18.52	18.55	18.51	18.45	18.97	19.67	20.52
Government, by level										
Federal	11.86	12.83	18.75	37.26	60.90	80.63	87.70	77.36	67.93	60.29
State and local	16.58	17.17	17.49	17.53	17.37	17.19	17.04	17.05	17.25	17.59

Table 18-4. Price and Production Indexes and Labor Force Data, 1929–1948

Classification	1929	1930	1931	1932	1933	1934	1935	1936	1937	1938
CONSUMER AND PRODUCER PRICE INDEXES										
Consumer prices, all items; 1982–1984 = 100:										
All urban consumers (CPI-U)	17.1	16.7	15.2	13.7	13.0	13.4	13.7	13.9	14.4	14.1
Percent change	0.0	-2.3	-9.0	-9.9	-5.1	3.1	2.2	1.5	3.6	-2.1
Urban wage earners and clerical workers (CPI-W)	17.2	16.8	15.3	13.7	13.0	13.5	13.8	13.9	14.4	14.2
Producer prices, 1982 = 100:										
All commodities	16.4	14.9	12.6	11.2	11.4	12.9	13.8	13.9	14.9	13.5
Farm products	26.4	22.4	16.4	12.2	13.0	16.5	19.8	20.4	21.8	17.3
Industrial commodities	15.6	14.5	12.8	11.9	12.1	13.3	13.3	13.5	14.5	13.9
INDEXES OF INDUSTRIAL PRODUCTION (2002 = 100)										
Total	8.5	7.1	5.8	4.6	5.4	5.9	6.8	8.0	8.8	6.9
Products	...	...	...	...	...	...	...	...	...	...
Consumer goods	...	...	...	...	...	...	...	...	...	...
Materials	...	...	...	...	...	...	...	...	...	...
Manufacturing (SIC)	8.2	6.8	5.5	4.3	5.1	5.6	6.5	7.8	8.5	6.5
EMPLOYMENT STATUS OF THE CIVILIAN NONINSTITUTIONAL POPULATION, 14 YEARS AND OVER (Thousands of persons, except as noted)										
Civilian noninstitutional population	...	...	...	...	...	...	...	...	...	...
Civilian labor force	49 180	49 820	50 420	51 000	51 590	52 230	52 870	53 440	54 000	54 610
Participation rate, percent	...	...	...	...	...	...	...	...	...	...
Employment, total	47 630	45 480	42 400	38 940	38 760	40 890	42 260	44 410	46 300	44 220
Ratio, employment to population, percent	...	...	...	...	...	...	...	...	...	...
Agricultural	10 450	10 340	10 290	10 170	10 090	9 900	10 110	10 000	9 820	9 690
Nonagricultural	37 180	35 140	32 110	28 770	28 670	30 990	32 150	34 410	36 480	34 530
Unemployment	1 550	4 340	8 020	12 060	12 830	11 340	10 610	9 030	7 700	10 390
Percent of civilian labor force	3.2	8.7	15.9	23.6	24.9	21.7	20.1	16.9	14.3	19.0
Unemployment rate counting persons on work relief as employed, percent of civilian labor force [1]	3.2	8.7	15.3	22.5	20.6	16.0	14.2	9.9	9.1	12.5
NONFARM PAYROLL EMPLOYMENT (NAICS) (Thousands of persons, except as noted)										
Total	...	...	...	...	...	...	...	...	...	...
Private, total	...	...	...	...	...	...	...	...	...	...
Goods-producing, total	...	...	...	...	...	...	...	...	...	...
Natural resources and mining	...	...	...	...	...	...	...	...	...	...
Construction	...	...	...	...	...	...	...	...	...	...
Manufacturing, total	...	...	...	...	...	...	...	...	...	...
Durable goods	...	...	...	...	...	...	...	...	...	...
Nondurable goods, total	...	...	...	...	...	...	...	...	...	...
Private service-providing, total	...	...	...	...	...	...	...	...	...	...
Trade, transportation, and utilities, total	...	...	...	...	...	...	...	...	...	...
Wholesale trade	...	...	...	...	...	...	...	...	...	...
Retail trade	...	...	...	...	...	...	...	...	...	...
Information	...	...	...	...	...	...	...	...	...	...
Financial activities	...	...	...	...	...	...	...	...	...	...
Professional and business services	...	...	...	...	...	...	...	...	...	...
Education and health services	...	...	...	...	...	...	...	...	...	...
Leisure and hospitality	...	...	...	...	...	...	...	...	...	...
Other services	...	...	...	...	...	...	...	...	...	...
Government, total	...	...	...	...	...	...	...	...	...	...
Federal, total	...	...	...	...	...	...	...	...	...	...
Department of Defense, total	...	...	...	...	...	...	...	...	...	...
Service-providing	...	...	...	...	...	...	...	...	...	...
Manufacturing, production workers:										
Total (thousands)	...	...	...	...	...	...	...	...	...	...
Average weekly hours (number of hours per week)	...	...	...	...	...	...	...	...	...	...
Index of aggregate weekly hours (2002 = 100)	...	...	...	...	...	...	...	...	...	...
Average hourly earnings (dollars)	...	...	...	...	...	...	...	...	...	...
Average weekly earnings (dollars)	...	...	...	...	...	...	...	...	...	...

[1]Darby, Michael. 1976. "Three-and-a-Half Million U.S. Employees Have Been Mislaid." *Journal of Political Economy* 84(1).
. . . = Not available.

Table 18-4. Price and Production Indexes and Labor Force Data, 1929–1948—*Continued*

Classification	1939	1940	1941	1942	1943	1944	1945	1946	1947	1948
CONSUMER AND PRODUCER PRICE INDEXES										
Consumer prices, all items; 1982–1984 = 100:										
All urban consumers (CPI-U)	13.9	14.0	14.7	16.3	17.3	17.6	18.0	19.5	22.3	24.1
Percent change	-1.4	0.7	5.0	10.9	6.1	1.7	2.3	8.3	14.4	8.1
Urban wage earners and clerical workers (CPI-W)	14.0	14.1	14.8	16.4	17.4	17.7	18.1	19.6	22.5	24.2
Producer prices, 1982 = 100:										
All commodities	13.3	13.5	15.1	17.0	17.8	17.9	18.2	20.8	25.6	27.7
Farm products	16.5	17.1	20.8	26.7	30.9	31.2	32.4	37.5	45.1	48.5
Industrial commodities	13.9	14.1	15.1	16.2	16.5	16.7	17.0	18.6	22.7	24.6
INDEXES OF INDUSTRIAL PRODUCTION (2002 = 100)										
Total	8.5	9.8	12.4	14.2	17.3	18.6	16.0	13.8	15.5	16.1
Products	8.5	9.6	12.1	13.8	17.1	18.7	15.8	13.8	15.4	16.1
Consumer goods	11.6	12.3	14.8	13.7	13.9	14.6	15.0	18.0	19.1	19.7
Materials	8.3	10.0	12.5	14.5	17.1	18.0	15.8	13.4	15.2	15.8
Manufacturing (SIC)	7.8	9.2	11.7	13.7	17.0	18.4	15.4	12.8	14.3	14.8
EMPLOYMENT STATUS OF THE CIVILIAN NONINSTITUTIONAL POPULATION, 14 YEARS AND OVER (Thousands of persons, except as noted)										
Civilian noninstitutional population	...	99 840	99 900	98 640	94 640	93 220	94 090	103 070	106 018	...
Civilian labor force	55 230	55 640	55 910	56 410	55 540	54 630	53 860	57 520	60 168	...
Participation rate, percent	...	55.7	56.0	57.2	58.7	58.6	57.2	55.8	56.8	...
Employment, total	45 750	47 520	50 350	53 750	54 470	53 960	52 820	55 250	57 812	...
Ratio, employment to population, percent	...	47.6	50.4	54.5	57.6	57.9	56.1	53.6	54.5	...
Agricultural	9 610	9 540	9 100	9 250	9 080	8 950	8 580	8 320	8 256	...
Nonagricultural	36 140	37 980	41 250	44 500	45 390	45 010	44 240	46 930	49 557	...
Unemployment	9 480	8 120	5 560	2 660	1 070	670	1 040	2 270	2 356	...
Percent of civilian labor force	17.2	14.6	9.9	4.7	1.9	1.2	1.9	3.9	3.9	...
Unemployment rate counting persons on work relief as employed, percent of civilian labor force [1]	11.3	9.5	6.0	3.1	1.8	...	...	...	...	...
NONFARM PAYROLL EMPLOYMENT (NAICS) (Thousands of persons, except as noted)										
Total	30 645	32 407	36 600	40 213	42 574	42 006	40 510	41 759	43 945	44 954
Private, total	26 606	28 156	31 874	34 621	36 353	35 819	34 428	36 054	38 379	39 213
Goods-producing, total	11 511	12 378	14 940	17 275	18 738	17 981	16 308	16 122	17 314	17 579
Natural resources and mining	856	927	967	1 010	958	926	864	885	976	1 014
Construction	1 205	1 352	1 852	2 234	1 627	1 152	1 190	1 724	2 051	2 241
Manufacturing, total	9 450	10 099	12 121	14 030	16 153	15 903	14 255	13 513	14 287	14 324
Durable goods	4 654	5 261	6 778	8 502	10 583	10 372	8 732	7 535	8 079	8 028
Nondurable goods, total	4 796	4 839	5 343	5 528	5 570	5 531	5 523	5 978	6 208	6 296
Private service-providing, total	15 094	15 778	16 934	17 347	17 615	17 839	18 121	19 932	21 064	21 634
Trade, transportation, and utilities, total	6 739	7 043	7 550	7 607	7 628	7 805	8 048	8 945	9 452	9 716
Wholesale trade	1 508	1 571	1 679	1 635	1 566	1 585	1 672	1 962	2 116	2 230
Retail trade	3 158	3 324	3 552	3 522	3 479	3 516	3 624	4 118	4 393	4 524
Information	1 141	1 196	1 342	1 470	1 605	1 635	1 581	1 594	1 658	1 669
Financial activities	1 386	1 424	1 466	1 455	1 431	1 414	1 435	1 619	1 674	1 742
Professional and business services	1 976	2 073	2 265	2 410	2 518	2 523	2 495	2 666	2 828	2 893
Education and health services	1 405	1 470	1 566	1 632	1 660	1 667	1 698	1 885	2 015	2 077
Leisure and hospitality	1 896	1 995	2 130	2 133	2 122	2 142	2 200	2 485	2 650	2 726
Other services	553	578	616	641	652	654	664	737	788	812
Government, total	4 040	4 251	4 726	5 592	6 222	6 187	6 082	5 705	5 567	5 742
Federal, total	950	1 045	1 406	2 322	3 047	3 071	2 945	2 365	1 985	1 954
Department of Defense, total	132	182	375	920	1 361	1 352	1 234	746	499	511
Service-providing	19 134	20 029	21 660	22 938	23 837	24 026	24 203	25 637	26 631	27 376
Manufacturing, production workers:										
Total (thousands)	8 163	8 737	10 641	12 447	14 407	14 031	12 445	11 781	12 453	12 383
Average weekly hours (number of hours per week)	37.7	38.2	40.7	43.2	45.1	45.4	43.6	40.4	40.5	40.1
Index of aggregate weekly hours (2002 = 100)	70.7	76.7	99.5	123.5	149.2	146.1	124.7	109.2	115.7	114.0
Average hourly earnings (dollars)	0.49	0.53	0.61	0.74	0.86	0.91	0.90	0.95	1.10	1.20
Average weekly earnings (dollars)	18.47	20.25	24.83	31.97	38.79	41.31	39.24	38.38	44.55	48.12

[1]Darby, Michael. 1976. "Three-and-a-Half Million U.S. Employees Have Been Mislaid." *Journal of Political Economy* 84(1).
. . . = Not available.

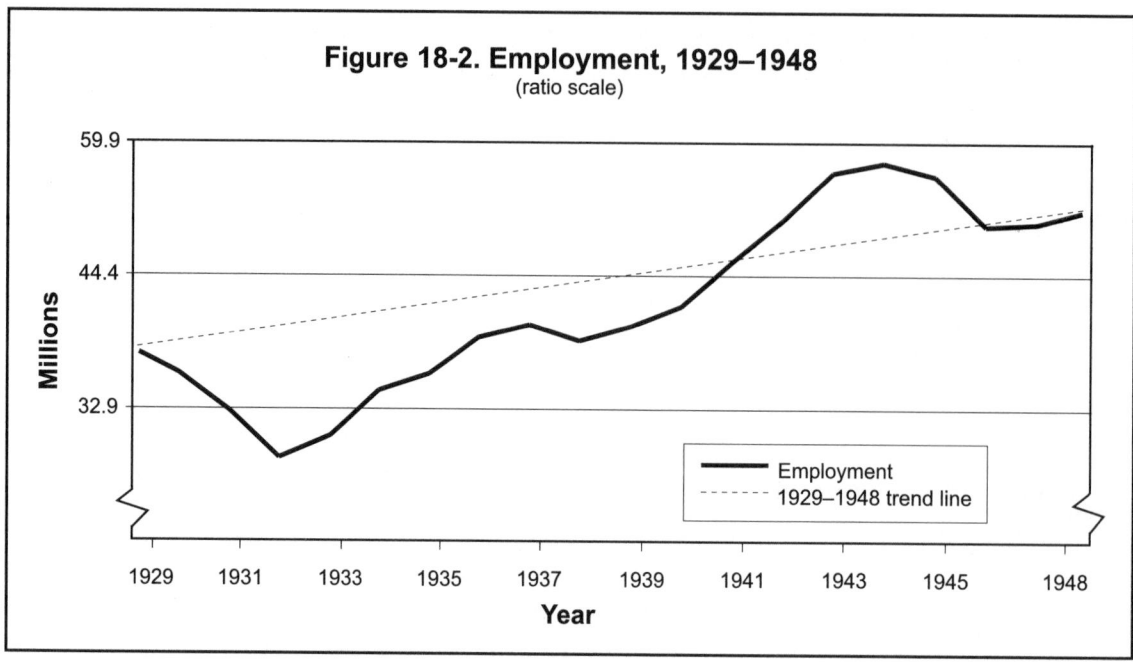

Figure 18-2. Employment, 1929–1948
(ratio scale)

- One-fifth of all the jobs held in the U.S. economy in 1929—8.25 million jobs—were gone by 1932. Employment was back to its 1929 level by 1936, but this total was not enough to fully employ a growing labor force; an unemployment rate as low as the one in 1929 would not be seen until after the United States entered World War II. Figure 18-2 displays a broad measure of employment, shown in Table 18-2, that includes the armed forces and work relief jobs. (Tables 18-2 and 18-4)

- In Table 18-4, civilian labor force data—available only from 1939 onward—are shown. Civilian employment rose by 8.7 million from 1939 to 1943, despite the withdrawal of members of the armed forces from the civilian population base. The unemployed found work, and women and others who had not previously sought jobs entered the labor force. The rise in nonfarm payroll jobs was even greater at 11.9 million. Workers left agriculture, household service, and other less productive activities (which are included in civilian employment but not in the payroll series) for factory jobs making armaments, for government positions, and for other payroll employment.

- Unemployment fell to 1.2 percent of the labor force in 1944. When the demobilization was over, unemployment only increased to 3.9 percent in 1946 and 1947, compared with the prewar (1939) rate of 17.2 percent. (This rate drops to 11.3 percent if work relief is counted as employment instead of unemployment.) (Table 18-4)

- Prices rose at an accelerating rate early in the war. Under price controls and rationing, inflation subsided in 1944 and 1945, but rose again when the controls were lifted. (Table 18-4)

Table 18-5. Federal Budget, 1929–1948

(Fiscal years, billions of dollars, percent.)

Classification	1929	1930	1931	1932	1933	1934	1935	1936	1937	1938
Receipts	3.9	4.1	3.1	1.9	2.0	3.0	3.6	3.9	5.4	6.8
Outlays	3.1	3.3	3.6	4.7	4.6	6.5	6.4	8.2	7.6	6.8
National defense	...	...	...	...	...	...	...	...	...	...
Surplus or deficit (-)	0.7	0.7	-0.5	-2.7	-2.6	-3.6	-2.8	-4.3	-2.2	-0.1
Fiscal year GDP	...	97.4	83.8	67.6	57.6	61.2	69.6	78.5	87.8	89.0
As percent of GDP										
Receipts	...	4.2	3.7	2.8	3.5	4.8	5.2	5.0	6.1	7.6
Outlays	...	3.4	4.3	6.9	8.0	10.7	9.2	10.5	8.6	7.7
National defense	...	...	...	...	...	...	...	...	...	...
Surplus or deficit (-)	...	0.8	-0.6	-4.0	-4.5	-5.9	-4.0	-5.5	-2.5	-0.1
Debt held by the public, end of year										
Billions of dollars	...	...	...	...	...	...	...	...	...	...
Percent of GDP	...	...	...	...	...	...	...	...	...	...

Classification	1939	1940	1941	1942	1943	1944	1945	1946	1947	1948
Receipts	6.3	6.5	8.7	14.6	24.0	43.7	45.2	39.3	38.5	41.6
Outlays	9.1	9.5	13.7	35.1	78.6	91.3	92.7	55.2	34.5	29.8
National defense	...	1.7	6.4	25.7	66.7	79.1	83.0	42.7	12.8	9.1
Surplus or deficit (-)	-2.8	-2.9	-4.9	-20.5	-54.6	-47.6	-47.6	-15.9	4.0	11.8
Fiscal year GDP	89.1	96.8	114.1	144.3	180.3	209.2	221.4	222.7	233.2	256.0
As percent of GDP										
Receipts	7.1	6.8	7.6	10.1	13.3	20.9	20.4	17.6	16.5	16.2
Outlays	10.3	9.8	12.0	24.3	43.6	43.6	41.9	24.8	14.8	11.6
National defense	...	1.7	5.6	17.8	37.0	37.8	37.5	19.2	5.5	3.6
Surplus or deficit (-)	-3.2	-3.0	-4.3	-14.2	-30.3	-22.7	-21.5	-7.2	1.7	4.6
Debt held by the public, end of year										
Billions of dollars	...	42.8	48.2	67.8	127.8	184.8	235.2	241.9	224.3	216.3
Percent of GDP	...	44.2	42.3	47.0	70.9	88.3	106.2	108.6	96.2	84.5

. . . = Not available.

NOTES AND DEFINITIONS

General note on the chronology of the 1930s and 1940s

See the notes and definitions for Table 1-8 for the business cycle peaks and troughs occurring in this period, as determined by the National Bureau of Economic Research (NBER).

The NBER chronology may seem surprising to readers who are looking for "The Great Depression" and are not familiar with the NBER approach to business cycles. As NBER perceives it, a downtrend in economic activity began in August 1929 (before the stock market crash) and lasted until March 1933. This period has been called the "Great Contraction" and was the longest period of economic decline since the 1870s. The NBER chronology also states that this period was nearly three times as long as any recession since then. For the rest of the 1930s—except a 13-month recession in 1937–1938—the economy is viewed by the NBER as being in an expansion phase. The NBER chronology does not use the term "depression."

On the other hand, the term "The Great Depression" is often colloquially used for the entire 1929–1939 period, even though the economy was expanding for most of the period following March 1933. It is true that economic activity during that time, though increasing, remained below the levels of the 1920s and below the likely capacity of the economy. This is suggested in Figures 18-1 and 18-2.

It should also be noted that NBER construes the entire period from June 1938 through February 1945 as a business cycle expansion. The recovery from the 1937–1938 recession merged into a further, continued rise in activity that reflected the outbreak of war in Europe in September 1939 and a consequent preparedness effort in the United States. The United States entered the war after being attacked by Japan in December 1941, launching an all-out war production effort at that time.

The February 1945 end of the "wartime" expansion (as defined by NBER) preceded the end of the war, as the European war ended in May 1945 and the Pacific war concluded in August 1945. A brief demobilization recession occurred from February to October 1945, followed by the first postwar expansion, which lasted from October 1945 to November 1948.

TABLES 18-1 AND 18-2
NATIONAL INCOME AND PRODUCT ACCOUNTS (NIPAS) AND RELATED DATA, 1929–1948

For most of these data, the sources, definitions, and availability are the same as for the identically titled series in Part A. Specific references to the appropriate chapter's notes and definitions are given below.

Gross domestic product and its components in current and constant dollars, gross national product, national income and its components, population and per capita data, and chain-type price indexes: See the notes and definitions for Chapter 1.

Personal income and its disposition and disposable personal income: See the notes and definitions for Chapter 4.

Saving and investment: See the notes and definitions for Chapter 5.

Employment, NIPA data, full-time and part-time employees: As seen in Table 18-4, payroll employment data from the Bureau of Labor Statistics (BLS) are not available for the years before 1939, and the civilian employment estimates do not include work-relief employees. In order to provide fuller information on employment, this table presents estimates from the national income and product accounts (NIPA) for the total number of full-time and part-time employees. Like the BLS payroll data, these estimates are a count of jobs rather than of persons employed, and persons with two jobs will appear as two persons employed in these data. These estimates include numbers of the armed forces and employees of Depression-era work-relief programs in the total, and also show them as separate categories. The issue of counting work-relief jobs is discussed below.

TABLE 18-3
FIXED ASSETS: CURRENT-COST VALUES AND QUANTITY INDEXES, 1929–1948

See the notes and definitions for Tables 5-5 and 5-6.

TABLE 18-4
PRICE AND PRODUCTION INDEXES AND LABOR DATA, 1929–1948

Consumer and producer price indexes: See the notes and definitions for Chapter 8.

Indexes of industrial production: See the notes and definitions for Chapter 2.

Civilian noninstitutional population, labor force, employment, and unemployment are as defined in the notes and definitions for Chapter 10 with the following exceptions:

• The data for 1929 through 1947 in Chapter 18 pertain to persons 14 years of age and over. The data in Chapter 10 from 1947 to the present are for persons 16 years of age and over. The differences made by this change in definitions can be observed in the two different sets of data— one from this table, the other from Tables 10-1 through 10-5—for the overlap year, 1947. In that year, the unemployment rates are the same (3.9 percent) for both age definitions. However, the labor force participation rate and the employment/population ratio are higher when the 14- and 15-year-olds are excluded.

• The Census Bureau began the monthly survey of households that provides labor force data in 1942, and the

Census of Population supplied data for 1940. For earlier years, data for the labor force, employment, and unemployment are retrospective estimates made by BLS.

• The 1940 census and the BLS data for 1931 through 1942 did not treat government work relief employment as employment; persons engaged in such work were counted as unemployed. Michael Darby calculated an alternative unemployment rate in which such workers are counted as employed, and this rate is also shown in Table 18-4. It would appear that the Darby rate is more consistent with the NIPA total employment data. Furthermore, the NIPA data on gross domestic product (GDP) include, as output, the work done by relief workers, and the buildings they constructed are included in investment and capital stock.

BLS data for 1940 through 1947 are published on the BLS Web site at <http://www.bls.gov>. The data for 1929 through 1939 were published in *Employment and Earnings*, May 1972, and in U.S. Commerce Department,

Bureau of Economic Analysis, *Long-Term Economic Growth, 1860–1970* (June 1973), p. 163.

The Darby alternative unemployment rate is found in Michael Darby, "Three-and-a-Half Million U.S. Employees Have Been Mislaid," *Journal of Political Economy*, February 1976, vol. 84, no. 1. It is also displayed and discussed in Robert A. Margo, "Employment and Unemployment in the 1930s," *Journal of Economic Perspectives*, vol. 7, no. 2, Spring 1993.

Nonfarm employment and its components, and number, hours, and earnings for manufacturing production workers: See the notes and definitions for Chapter 10. Note that because age is not specified in the Current Employment Survey, these data include any workers under 16 years of age and have always done so.

TABLE 18-5
FEDERAL BUDGET, 1929–1948

See notes and definitions for Tables 6-16 and 6-17.

Table 19-1. Gross Domestic Product

(Billions of dollars, quarterly data are at seasonally adjusted annual rates.)

NIPA Tables 1.1.5, 1.4.5

Year and quarter	Gross domestic product	Personal consumption expenditures	Gross private domestic investment				Exports and imports of goods and services			Government consumption expenditures and gross investment			Addendum: Final sales of domestic product
			Total	Fixed investment		Change in private inventories	Net exports	Exports	Imports	Total	Federal	State and local	
				Nonresidential	Residential								
1946	222.3	144.3	31.1	17.3	7.8	6.0	7.2	14.2	7.0	39.6	28.9	10.8	216.3
1947	244.2	162.0	35.0	23.5	12.1	-0.6	10.8	18.7	7.9	36.4	22.7	13.7	244.7
1948	269.2	175.0	48.1	26.8	15.6	5.7	5.5	15.5	10.1	40.6	24.2	16.3	263.5
1949	267.3	178.5	36.9	24.9	14.6	-2.7	5.2	14.5	9.2	46.7	27.7	19.0	270.0
1947													
1st quarter	237.2	156.3	33.7	22.8	10.4	0.5	10.9	18.4	7.5	36.3	23.4	13.0	236.7
2nd quarter	240.5	160.2	32.4	23.2	10.4	-1.2	11.3	19.5	8.2	36.6	23.3	13.4	241.7
3rd quarter	244.6	163.7	32.7	23.3	12.3	-2.9	11.8	19.4	7.7	36.4	22.4	14.0	247.5
4th quarter	254.4	167.8	41.0	24.5	15.1	1.5	9.3	17.6	8.3	36.3	21.6	14.7	252.9
1948													
1st quarter	260.4	170.5	45.0	26.2	15.2	3.6	7.3	16.9	9.6	37.6	22.4	15.2	256.7
2nd quarter	267.3	174.3	48.1	26.0	16.3	5.9	5.2	15.2	10.0	39.7	23.8	15.9	261.5
3rd quarter	273.9	177.2	50.2	27.0	16.1	7.2	4.9	15.4	10.5	41.4	24.6	16.8	266.7
4th quarter	275.2	178.1	49.1	28.1	15.0	6.0	4.5	14.6	10.1	43.5	26.0	17.5	269.2
1949													
1st quarter	270.0	177.0	40.9	26.6	14.0	0.4	6.5	16.1	9.6	45.6	27.6	18.0	269.6
2nd quarter	266.2	178.6	34.0	25.5	13.7	-5.1	6.3	15.6	9.4	47.3	28.6	18.7	271.4
3rd quarter	267.7	178.0	37.3	24.1	14.5	-1.3	5.2	14.1	8.9	47.2	27.7	19.5	269.0
4th quarter	265.2	180.4	35.2	23.5	16.3	-4.7	3.0	12.1	9.1	46.6	26.9	19.7	269.9
1950													
1st quarter	275.2	183.1	44.4	24.2	18.1	2.0	2.2	11.7	9.5	45.6	25.5	20.0	273.2
2nd quarter	284.6	187.0	49.9	26.6	20.4	2.8	1.6	11.9	10.2	46.1	25.7	20.4	281.7
3rd quarter	302.0	200.7	56.1	29.6	22.3	4.2	-0.7	12.3	13.0	45.9	24.9	21.0	297.8
4th quarter	313.4	198.1	65.9	30.6	21.3	14.0	-0.2	13.5	13.7	49.5	27.9	21.6	299.3
1951													
1st quarter	329.0	209.4	62.1	30.9	20.8	10.4	0.2	15.0	14.9	57.4	35.2	22.1	318.6
2nd quarter	336.7	205.1	64.8	31.8	18.2	14.8	1.9	17.1	15.2	64.7	41.8	22.9	321.9
3rd quarter	343.6	207.8	59.4	32.5	17.2	9.7	3.7	18.1	14.3	72.6	49.2	23.4	333.8
4th quarter	348.0	211.8	54.4	32.2	17.5	4.7	4.2	18.2	14.0	77.6	53.9	23.7	343.3
1952													
1st quarter	351.3	213.1	55.2	32.4	18.0	4.7	3.7	18.7	15.0	79.2	55.4	23.8	346.5
2nd quarter	352.2	217.3	49.9	32.9	18.5	-1.5	2.0	16.6	14.6	83.1	58.5	24.6	353.7
3rd quarter	358.5	219.8	53.9	29.8	18.5	5.6	0.0	15.2	15.3	84.9	60.5	24.4	353.0
4th quarter	371.4	227.9	57.1	32.5	19.4	5.3	-1.0	15.3	16.3	87.4	62.4	25.0	366.1
1953													
1st quarter	378.4	231.5	57.9	34.3	19.7	3.9	-0.7	15.1	15.8	89.7	63.9	25.8	374.5
2nd quarter	382.0	233.3	58.1	34.8	19.8	3.6	-1.3	15.2	16.4	91.8	66.2	25.6	378.4
3rd quarter	381.1	234.0	57.4	35.9	19.2	2.3	-0.6	15.8	16.3	90.3	64.0	26.3	378.8
4th quarter	375.9	233.5	52.3	35.4	18.9	-2.0	-0.3	15.2	15.5	90.5	63.6	26.9	377.9
1954													
1st quarter	375.3	235.5	51.5	34.5	19.0	-2.0	-0.4	14.4	14.8	88.6	60.8	27.8	377.3
2nd quarter	376.0	238.3	51.2	34.3	20.3	-3.4	0.3	16.4	16.2	86.2	57.7	28.5	379.4
3rd quarter	380.8	240.7	54.7	35.0	21.8	-2.1	0.6	15.9	15.3	84.8	55.4	29.5	382.9
4th quarter	389.5	245.5	57.8	34.9	23.2	-0.3	1.1	16.6	15.5	85.0	55.2	29.8	389.8
1955													
1st quarter	402.6	251.8	64.2	35.4	25.0	3.8	1.1	17.3	16.2	85.4	54.6	30.8	398.8
2nd quarter	410.9	256.9	68.1	37.9	25.6	4.6	-0.2	16.9	17.1	86.0	54.7	31.3	406.3
3rd quarter	419.5	261.1	70.0	40.4	25.2	4.3	0.7	18.1	17.4	87.7	55.8	31.8	415.2
4th quarter	426.0	265.1	73.9	42.5	24.2	7.2	0.2	18.3	18.1	86.8	54.4	32.4	418.8
1956													
1st quarter	428.3	266.7	73.0	42.9	23.7	6.4	0.4	19.4	18.9	88.2	54.7	33.5	421.9
2nd quarter	434.2	269.4	71.4	43.9	23.9	3.6	1.9	20.9	19.0	91.5	57.1	34.4	430.6
3rd quarter	439.3	272.6	72.5	45.4	23.5	3.6	2.6	21.8	19.3	91.6	56.4	35.1	435.7
4th quarter	448.1	278.0	71.2	45.9	23.0	2.2	4.5	23.1	18.5	94.4	58.5	35.8	445.9
1957													
1st quarter	457.2	282.4	71.8	47.0	22.6	2.2	4.8	24.9	20.1	98.2	61.1	37.1	455.1
2nd quarter	459.2	284.7	71.9	47.1	22.2	2.7	4.1	24.4	20.3	98.4	60.5	38.0	456.5
3rd quarter	466.4	289.3	73.2	48.4	22.0	2.8	4.0	23.8	19.8	99.9	61.2	38.7	463.6
4th quarter	461.5	291.0	64.9	47.5	21.9	-4.5	3.4	23.0	19.6	102.3	62.7	39.6	466.1
1958													
1st quarter	454.0	290.5	60.5	43.6	20.9	-4.0	1.1	20.5	19.5	101.8	61.2	40.6	458.0
2nd quarter	458.1	293.4	58.7	42.0	21.0	-4.2	0.5	20.5	20.1	105.4	63.9	41.6	462.3
3rd quarter	471.7	298.5	65.5	41.4	22.5	1.5	0.9	20.6	19.7	106.9	64.2	42.7	470.2
4th quarter	485.0	302.3	73.2	43.1	24.9	5.2	-0.3	20.6	20.8	109.7	66.0	43.7	479.8
1959													
1st quarter	495.4	310.0	76.2	44.5	27.8	3.9	0.4	21.8	21.4	108.9	64.3	44.5	491.5
2nd quarter	508.4	316.0	82.2	46.1	28.8	7.3	0.0	22.6	22.5	110.2	65.5	44.7	501.2
3rd quarter	509.3	321.2	76.4	47.8	28.3	0.4	0.6	23.5	22.9	111.0	66.2	44.8	508.9
4th quarter	513.2	323.3	79.3	47.7	27.5	4.1	0.6	23.1	22.5	110.0	65.4	44.6	509.1
1960													
1st quarter	526.9	326.9	89.1	49.5	28.4	11.2	2.7	26.0	23.3	108.3	62.4	45.8	515.7
2nd quarter	521.1	332.7	79.7	50.3	26.1	3.2	4.2	27.6	23.5	109.5	62.4	47.2	522.9
3rd quarter	528.9	332.7	78.7	49.0	25.3	4.3	4.2	27.0	22.9	113.4	65.3	48.1	524.6
4th quarter	523.6	334.6	68.1	48.6	25.3	-5.8	5.8	27.5	21.7	115.1	66.3	48.8	529.4

Table 19-1. Gross Domestic Product—Continued

(Billions of dollars, quarterly data are at seasonally adjusted annual rates.)

NIPA Tables 1.1.5, 1.4.5

Year and quarter	Gross domestic product	Personal consumption expenditures	Gross private domestic investment				Exports and imports of goods and services			Government consumption expenditures and gross investment			Addendum: Final sales of domestic product
			Total	Fixed investment		Change in private inventories	Net exports	Exports	Imports	Total	Federal	State and local	
				Nonresidential	Residential								
1961													
1st quarter	527.9	335.1	70.3	47.5	25.3	-2.5	5.8	27.5	21.7	116.7	66.0	50.7	530.5
2nd quarter	539.0	340.1	75.8	48.4	25.5	1.8	5.5	27.4	21.9	117.6	66.8	50.8	537.2
3rd quarter	549.4	343.0	82.4	48.8	26.9	6.7	3.9	27.2	23.3	120.2	68.6	51.6	542.8
4th quarter	562.5	350.3	84.2	50.4	27.8	6.0	4.4	28.3	23.9	123.6	70.2	53.4	556.6
1962													
1st quarter	576.0	355.6	89.4	51.6	28.4	9.4	4.0	28.3	24.3	127.2	73.4	53.8	566.6
2nd quarter	583.2	361.2	87.9	53.2	29.2	5.4	5.8	30.7	24.9	128.3	73.9	54.4	577.8
3rd quarter	590.0	365.1	89.3	53.9	29.2	6.2	3.8	29.0	25.1	131.8	76.6	55.2	583.8
4th quarter	593.3	371.3	86.0	53.5	29.1	3.4	2.8	28.4	25.6	133.2	77.1	56.1	589.9
1963													
1st quarter	602.4	374.9	90.5	53.4	30.2	6.9	3.9	29.1	25.2	133.2	75.5	57.6	595.6
2nd quarter	611.2	379.0	92.2	55.1	32.2	4.8	6.5	32.4	25.9	133.4	74.9	58.5	606.3
3rd quarter	623.9	386.0	95.0	56.8	32.5	5.7	3.9	30.6	26.7	139.0	78.8	60.2	618.2
4th quarter	633.5	390.7	97.4	58.7	33.7	5.1	5.4	32.2	26.8	139.9	78.4	61.5	628.4
1964													
1st quarter	649.6	400.3	100.7	60.1	35.4	5.1	7.3	34.2	27.0	141.3	78.6	62.7	644.5
2nd quarter	658.8	408.3	100.6	61.9	34.2	4.5	7.1	34.8	27.7	142.9	78.4	64.5	654.4
3rd quarter	670.5	417.2	102.5	64.1	33.7	4.7	6.4	34.8	28.4	144.4	78.9	65.5	665.8
4th quarter	675.6	419.8	104.6	65.7	33.8	5.0	6.9	36.2	29.3	144.3	77.8	66.5	670.6
1965													
1st quarter	695.7	430.5	115.7	70.3	33.9	11.5	4.6	33.1	28.5	144.9	77.1	67.8	684.1
2nd quarter	708.1	437.4	115.8	73.1	34.2	8.6	7.5	39.1	31.7	147.4	77.5	69.9	699.6
3rd quarter	725.2	446.6	119.7	76.1	34.3	9.3	4.9	36.9	32.0	154.0	81.6	72.5	715.9
4th quarter	747.5	460.6	121.8	79.7	34.5	7.6	5.5	39.5	33.9	159.6	85.5	74.1	739.9
1966													
1st quarter	770.8	471.0	131.7	83.0	34.8	13.9	4.4	39.4	35.0	163.6	87.6	76.0	756.9
2nd quarter	779.9	476.1	130.7	85.2	33.2	12.3	5.2	41.5	36.2	167.9	90.0	77.9	767.6
3rd quarter	793.4	485.3	130.2	86.4	31.9	11.9	2.2	40.4	38.2	175.7	95.8	79.9	781.5
4th quarter	807.1	491.1	132.7	87.0	29.2	16.5	3.6	42.4	38.8	179.8	96.8	83.0	790.6
1967													
1st quarter	817.9	495.4	129.3	85.6	28.3	15.4	4.6	44.0	39.4	188.7	103.2	85.4	802.5
2nd quarter	822.5	504.5	123.7	85.7	31.6	6.3	4.5	43.5	39.0	189.7	102.9	86.8	816.1
3rd quarter	837.1	511.8	128.5	85.8	33.4	9.3	2.9	42.4	39.5	194.0	105.6	88.3	827.9
4th quarter	852.8	519.3	132.9	88.4	36.0	8.4	2.2	43.9	41.7	198.4	107.4	90.9	844.4
1968													
1st quarter	879.9	537.3	137.2	91.9	36.9	8.4	1.1	45.5	44.4	204.3	110.3	94.0	871.5
2nd quarter	904.2	551.2	143.4	91.2	38.2	14.1	1.9	47.4	45.4	207.7	110.7	97.0	890.2
3rd quarter	919.4	567.4	139.7	93.2	38.9	7.7	1.3	49.5	48.2	211.1	111.8	99.2	911.7
4th quarter	936.3	576.3	144.4	97.4	40.9	6.0	1.1	49.2	48.2	214.6	112.7	102.0	930.3
1969													
1st quarter	961.0	588.5	155.7	101.0	43.2	11.5	0.2	44.0	43.8	216.6	112.2	104.4	949.5
2nd quarter	976.3	599.9	155.7	103.0	43.4	9.2	1.2	53.9	52.7	219.5	112.1	107.4	967.0
3rd quarter	996.5	610.2	160.3	106.9	43.2	10.2	1.0	53.3	52.4	224.9	115.4	109.5	986.3
4th quarter	1 004.6	622.2	154.1	107.6	40.7	5.8	3.3	56.5	53.1	225.0	113.7	111.3	998.9
1970													
1st quarter	1 017.3	633.3	150.7	108.1	40.7	1.8	3.4	56.9	53.5	229.9	115.0	114.9	1 015.5
2nd quarter	1 033.2	643.3	153.9	109.4	39.4	5.1	5.4	60.6	55.2	230.7	112.7	118.0	1 028.2
3rd quarter	1 050.7	655.3	156.1	110.6	40.4	5.1	3.8	60.3	56.4	235.6	112.8	122.7	1 045.6
4th quarter	1 052.9	662.0	148.9	107.9	45.0	-4.0	3.2	61.1	57.9	238.9	113.3	125.6	1 056.9
1971													
1st quarter	1 098.3	681.0	171.3	110.4	48.6	12.3	4.4	63.1	58.7	241.6	112.9	128.7	1 086.1
2nd quarter	1 119.1	695.1	178.8	113.4	54.6	10.9	-0.2	63.1	63.3	245.3	113.5	131.8	1 108.2
3rd quarter	1 139.3	707.5	183.4	114.8	58.3	10.2	-0.1	65.4	65.5	248.5	114.7	133.8	1 129.1
4th quarter	1 151.7	723.8	179.2	118.0	61.5	-0.3	-1.7	60.3	61.9	250.3	113.6	136.8	1 152.0
1972													
1st quarter	1 190.6	741.2	193.2	123.3	66.6	3.2	-3.5	68.6	72.2	259.7	119.8	139.9	1 187.3
2nd quarter	1 225.9	759.8	206.5	126.3	68.2	12.0	-4.3	67.2	71.4	263.9	122.6	141.3	1 213.9
3rd quarter	1 249.7	778.3	212.4	129.1	69.6	13.7	-2.6	71.5	74.1	261.6	116.9	144.8	1 236.0
4th quarter	1 287.0	803.1	218.4	136.6	74.3	7.5	-3.1	76.1	79.2	268.6	119.4	149.2	1 279.5
1973													
1st quarter	1 335.5	827.7	232.5	144.1	77.9	10.6	-1.4	84.0	85.4	276.7	123.4	153.3	1 325.0
2nd quarter	1 371.9	843.3	246.0	152.1	75.8	18.2	2.5	91.9	89.5	280.1	123.3	156.8	1 353.7
3rd quarter	1 391.2	861.8	241.8	157.0	75.0	9.8	6.4	97.6	91.1	281.2	120.4	160.8	1 381.4
4th quarter	1 432.3	876.9	257.6	159.9	72.7	25.0	9.0	107.6	98.7	288.8	122.9	165.9	1 407.3
1974													
1st quarter	1 447.0	895.1	244.1	162.6	69.0	12.5	6.4	116.7	110.3	301.4	128.6	172.8	1 434.5
2nd quarter	1 485.3	923.7	252.3	167.4	67.5	17.4	-2.7	126.7	129.4	312.1	131.1	180.9	1 467.9
3rd quarter	1 514.2	952.5	245.4	172.5	67.4	5.6	-7.0	126.6	133.6	323.2	136.1	187.1	1 508.6
4th quarter	1 553.4	962.4	255.8	175.4	60.0	20.4	0.0	136.6	136.6	335.1	142.5	192.6	1 532.9
1975													
1st quarter	1 570.0	988.6	218.7	171.0	57.7	-10.0	16.5	141.4	124.9	346.3	144.0	202.2	1 580.0
2nd quarter	1 605.6	1 017.4	216.8	170.8	59.9	-14.0	21.6	136.8	115.2	349.8	144.9	204.9	1 619.6
3rd quarter	1 663.1	1 051.3	237.8	174.6	64.6	-1.4	12.0	134.1	122.1	362.0	151.4	210.6	1 664.5
4th quarter	1 714.6	1 080.2	247.6	178.6	68.7	0.3	13.8	142.5	128.7	372.9	156.0	216.9	1 714.2

Table 19-1. Gross Domestic Product—Continued

(Billions of dollars, quarterly data are at seasonally adjusted annual rates.)

NIPA Tables 1.1.5, 1.4.5

Year and quarter	Gross domestic product	Personal consumption expenditures	Gross private domestic investment				Exports and imports of goods and services			Government consumption expenditures and gross investment			Addendum: Final sales of domestic product
			Total	Fixed investment		Change in private inventories	Net exports	Exports	Imports	Total	Federal	State and local	
				Nonresidential	Residential								
1976													
1st quarter	1 772.6	1 114.0	274.8	183.9	76.2	14.7	4.7	143.6	138.9	379.1	156.3	222.8	1 757.9
2nd quarter	1 804.9	1 133.7	291.6	188.5	80.7	22.4	-0.5	146.6	147.1	380.1	157.8	222.3	1 782.4
3rd quarter	1 838.3	1 163.1	296.5	195.1	80.6	20.8	-4.1	151.8	155.8	382.8	159.9	223.0	1 817.5
4th quarter	1 885.3	1 196.9	304.9	201.9	92.5	10.5	-6.6	156.1	162.7	390.0	164.9	225.2	1 874.8
1977													
1st quarter	1 939.3	1 232.5	326.6	214.2	97.6	14.8	-21.1	155.4	176.4	401.4	169.8	231.5	1 924.5
2nd quarter	2 006.0	1 260.4	354.9	223.8	111.7	19.5	-21.1	161.9	183.0	411.8	174.8	237.0	1 986.6
3rd quarter	2 066.8	1 291.7	378.4	232.5	115.0	30.9	-20.6	162.3	182.9	417.3	176.5	240.8	2 035.9
4th quarter	2 111.6	1 329.8	385.5	244.5	116.9	24.1	-29.6	157.8	187.4	425.8	180.6	245.3	2 087.5
1978													
1st quarter	2 150.0	1 359.9	396.8	250.4	121.0	25.5	-38.7	164.6	203.3	431.9	183.0	249.0	2 124.5
2nd quarter	2 275.6	1 417.6	430.9	276.0	130.6	24.3	-22.6	186.2	208.8	449.8	189.2	260.6	2 251.4
3rd quarter	2 336.2	1 448.7	451.4	290.6	135.8	25.0	-23.8	191.3	215.1	459.9	192.4	267.4	2 311.2
4th quarter	2 417.0	1 487.9	472.8	305.3	139.0	28.5	-16.4	205.4	221.8	472.7	199.1	273.6	2 388.5
1979													
1st quarter	2 464.4	1 523.6	481.1	318.8	138.5	23.9	-18.2	211.7	229.8	477.8	202.3	275.5	2 440.5
2nd quarter	2 527.6	1 564.3	493.0	324.9	140.6	27.4	-22.2	220.9	243.1	492.5	207.9	284.6	2 500.2
3rd quarter	2 600.7	1 618.6	497.9	342.3	143.5	12.1	-23.0	234.3	257.3	507.3	211.8	295.5	2 588.6
4th quarter	2 660.5	1 662.2	499.5	349.6	141.4	8.6	-26.8	253.7	280.5	525.5	220.5	305.0	2 651.9
1980													
1st quarter	2 725.3	1 709.1	505.2	361.3	134.0	9.9	-35.8	268.5	304.3	546.8	231.7	315.1	2 715.4
2nd quarter	2 729.3	1 711.2	470.4	350.9	111.7	7.8	-15.2	277.4	292.6	562.8	243.0	319.8	2 721.5
3rd quarter	2 786.6	1 770.1	443.5	361.1	116.3	-33.9	5.5	284.7	279.2	567.6	243.6	324.0	2 820.5
4th quarter	2 916.9	1 838.1	497.9	376.2	130.8	-9.1	-6.7	292.5	299.2	587.5	256.8	330.8	2 926.0
1981													
1st quarter	3 052.7	1 893.7	563.1	393.1	131.3	38.8	-14.3	305.5	319.7	610.1	266.5	343.6	3 014.0
2nd quarter	3 085.9	1 925.5	551.4	410.8	128.9	11.7	-13.5	308.4	322.0	622.5	278.7	343.8	3 074.2
3rd quarter	3 178.7	1 965.1	592.8	428.4	120.4	44.0	-7.6	302.3	309.9	628.4	281.4	347.0	3 134.8
4th quarter	3 196.4	1 979.9	582.2	447.8	109.6	24.8	-14.8	304.7	319.4	649.0	294.2	354.8	3 171.6
1982													
1st quarter	3 186.8	2 018.0	526.4	443.1	104.8	-21.5	-16.3	293.2	309.5	658.6	298.7	359.9	3 208.2
2nd quarter	3 242.7	2 044.4	530.8	432.0	102.9	-4.2	-4.4	294.7	299.1	671.9	305.1	366.8	3 246.9
3rd quarter	3 276.2	2 092.4	528.7	419.5	103.5	5.8	-29.7	279.6	309.3	684.7	312.3	372.4	3 270.4
4th quarter	3 314.4	2 154.2	483.0	411.3	111.5	-39.8	-29.6	265.3	294.9	706.8	327.1	379.7	3 354.2
1983													
1st quarter	3 382.9	2 194.1	496.6	400.5	131.2	-35.1	-24.6	270.7	295.3	716.7	332.9	383.8	3 417.9
2nd quarter	3 484.1	2 258.2	542.2	402.9	147.0	-7.7	-45.4	272.5	318.0	729.1	342.1	387.0	3 491.8
3rd quarter	3 589.3	2 328.6	577.7	419.5	162.4	-4.2	-65.2	278.2	343.4	748.2	354.2	394.0	3 593.5
4th quarter	3 690.4	2 381.3	640.7	446.0	170.8	23.9	-71.4	286.6	358.0	739.8	342.5	397.3	3 666.5
1984													
1st quarter	3 809.6	2 427.6	709.7	460.1	176.6	73.0	-95.0	293.0	388.0	767.4	359.3	408.0	3 736.6
2nd quarter	3 908.6	2 486.3	735.1	484.4	181.4	69.3	-104.3	302.2	406.5	791.5	374.0	417.4	3 839.3
3rd quarter	3 978.2	2 524.9	753.5	500.7	181.4	71.3	-103.9	305.7	409.6	803.6	375.3	428.4	3 906.8
4th quarter	4 036.3	2 574.3	744.3	513.3	183.0	48.0	-107.8	308.6	416.4	825.5	388.8	436.7	3 988.3
1985													
1st quarter	4 119.5	2 645.7	720.0	520.5	183.3	16.2	-91.9	305.4	397.3	845.7	398.1	447.6	4 103.3
2nd quarter	4 178.4	2 690.1	735.3	528.5	185.1	21.6	-115.4	303.1	418.6	868.5	407.7	460.8	4 156.8
3rd quarter	4 261.3	2 758.7	727.2	522.2	188.8	16.3	-118.6	295.6	414.2	894.0	420.8	473.2	4 245.0
4th quarter	4 321.8	2 786.7	762.2	533.6	195.5	33.1	-134.9	304.0	438.9	907.8	424.7	483.1	4 288.7
1986													
1st quarter	4 385.6	2 830.3	763.8	527.2	206.3	30.3	-127.6	312.2	439.8	919.2	421.5	497.7	4 355.3
2nd quarter	4 425.7	2 862.0	753.0	517.5	219.8	15.7	-130.0	314.4	444.4	940.7	434.8	505.9	4 410.0
3rd quarter	4 493.9	2 933.5	732.5	513.5	226.1	-7.0	-139.5	320.4	459.8	967.4	452.1	515.3	4 500.9
4th quarter	4 546.1	2 973.2	736.7	521.2	228.3	-12.7	-133.8	335.2	469.0	970.0	446.2	523.9	4 558.8
1987													
1st quarter	4 613.8	3 008.0	765.0	506.8	230.1	28.0	-141.3	336.8	478.1	982.1	451.9	530.2	4 585.8
2nd quarter	4 690.0	3 075.3	767.6	518.2	232.9	16.5	-147.6	355.1	502.7	994.6	459.1	535.5	4 673.5
3rd quarter	4 767.8	3 141.6	769.5	534.2	234.2	1.0	-146.0	371.7	517.7	1 002.7	461.0	541.7	4 766.8
4th quarter	4 886.3	3 176.0	837.8	537.2	237.5	63.1	-145.9	392.0	537.9	1 018.4	468.2	550.2	4 823.2
1988													
1st quarter	4 951.9	3 256.8	797.6	546.2	234.4	17.0	-124.7	418.5	543.2	1 022.9	460.9	561.3	4 934.9
2nd quarter	5 062.8	3 316.4	820.4	562.3	238.4	19.7	-107.4	439.1	546.6	1 033.5	459.7	573.8	5 043.2
3rd quarter	5 146.6	3 384.0	825.7	567.5	240.0	18.2	-100.5	452.9	553.3	1 037.4	456.8	580.5	5 128.5
4th quarter	5 253.7	3 457.2	842.6	579.1	244.4	19.1	-109.0	465.8	574.8	1 062.9	471.8	591.1	5 234.7
1989													
1st quarter	5 367.1	3 511.3	884.1	591.3	244.6	48.2	-98.2	484.0	582.3	1 070.0	470.1	599.9	5 318.9
2nd quarter	5 454.1	3 573.9	878.2	601.9	240.2	36.0	-91.6	505.7	597.3	1 093.6	482.2	611.5	5 418.1
3rd quarter	5 531.9	3 630.9	870.3	621.9	238.4	10.0	-79.3	508.4	587.7	1 109.9	489.7	620.2	5 521.9
4th quarter	5 584.3	3 677.8	867.3	615.8	234.8	16.6	-83.5	515.2	598.7	1 122.7	486.9	635.8	5 567.7
1990													
1st quarter	5 716.4	3 762.6	880.0	626.9	239.2	13.9	-83.6	537.6	621.1	1 157.4	501.4	655.9	5 702.4
2nd quarter	5 797.7	3 815.9	882.5	617.9	230.9	33.7	-70.9	546.3	617.2	1 170.2	506.7	663.5	5 764.0
3rd quarter	5 849.4	3 879.6	866.8	626.1	218.8	21.9	-78.5	555.9	634.3	1 181.5	505.8	675.7	5 827.6
4th quarter	5 848.8	3 901.7	814.6	618.9	207.0	-11.3	-79.0	569.7	648.7	1 211.5	519.2	692.3	5 860.1

Table 19-1. Gross Domestic Product—Continued

(Billions of dollars, quarterly data are at seasonally adjusted annual rates.)

NIPA Tables 1.1.5, 1.4.5

Year and quarter	Gross domestic product	Personal consumption expenditures	Gross private domestic investment				Exports and imports of goods and services			Government consumption expenditures and gross investment			Addendum: Final sales of domestic product
			Total	Fixed investment		Change in private inventories	Net exports	Exports	Imports	Total	Federal	State and local	
				Nonresidential	Residential								
1991													
1st quarter	5 888.0	3 914.2	787.9	608.2	195.2	-15.6	-41.5	574.6	616.1	1 227.4	530.4	697.0	5 903.5
2nd quarter	5 964.3	3 970.3	784.0	601.4	200.7	-18.1	-24.3	592.3	616.6	1 234.3	532.9	701.4	5 982.4
3rd quarter	6 035.6	4 015.7	805.2	594.1	210.3	0.8	-22.7	602.6	625.3	1 237.5	527.3	710.2	6 034.8
4th quarter	6 095.8	4 044.1	834.4	589.0	214.2	31.2	-21.4	617.8	639.2	1 238.6	520.5	718.1	6 064.5
1992													
1st quarter	6 196.1	4 142.5	810.2	585.6	224.4	0.2	-14.2	627.4	641.6	1 257.6	526.8	730.7	6 195.9
2nd quarter	6 290.1	4 193.1	865.4	607.1	235.1	23.2	-33.7	628.0	661.7	1 265.3	530.0	735.3	6 266.9
3rd quarter	6 380.5	4 264.3	876.8	619.0	237.3	20.5	-39.6	641.8	681.4	1 278.9	539.6	739.3	6 360.0
4th quarter	6 484.3	4 341.1	906.6	636.7	248.6	21.3	-45.5	644.1	689.6	1 282.1	539.3	742.8	6 463.0
1993													
1st quarter	6 542.7	4 379.3	931.3	642.8	252.6	35.9	-50.0	645.1	695.1	1 282.1	528.9	753.2	6 506.8
2nd quarter	6 612.1	4 446.7	942.3	660.3	257.9	24.1	-65.2	654.3	719.6	1 288.3	524.7	763.6	6 588.0
3rd quarter	6 674.6	4 510.7	943.4	667.5	269.3	6.6	-70.9	651.6	722.5	1 291.5	521.7	769.8	6 668.0
4th quarter	6 800.2	4 574.9	996.5	695.7	284.1	16.7	-74.0	672.3	746.3	1 302.8	525.7	777.2	6 783.5
1994													
1st quarter	6 911.0	4 643.9	1 043.2	704.8	293.1	45.3	-77.6	681.2	758.8	1 301.5	513.3	788.2	6 865.7
2nd quarter	7 030.6	4 702.8	1 106.7	720.5	304.7	81.5	-94.6	706.3	801.0	1 315.7	516.2	799.5	6 949.1
3rd quarter	7 115.1	4 778.6	1 092.9	734.7	304.8	53.4	-99.7	737.2	836.9	1 343.4	528.6	814.8	7 061.7
4th quarter	7 232.2	4 847.9	1 145.5	765.6	304.8	75.1	-102.4	758.8	861.2	1 341.3	518.5	822.8	7 157.1
1995													
1st quarter	7 298.3	4 879.0	1 160.6	797.7	301.7	61.2	-102.7	780.7	883.4	1 361.4	523.5	837.9	7 237.1
2nd quarter	7 337.7	4 946.7	1 132.6	805.5	293.4	33.7	-114.3	797.7	912.0	1 372.7	523.3	849.3	7 304.0
3rd quarter	7 432.1	5 011.0	1 126.2	811.2	303.8	11.2	-78.2	830.9	909.1	1 373.0	520.3	852.7	7 420.8
4th quarter	7 522.5	5 066.4	1 156.6	825.8	312.4	18.3	-70.3	839.6	909.8	1 369.8	509.7	860.1	7 504.2
1996													
1st quarter	7 624.1	5 142.8	1 170.0	841.4	321.8	6.8	-84.2	848.2	932.4	1 395.6	527.8	867.8	7 617.3
2nd quarter	7 776.6	5 232.0	1 227.9	860.5	336.9	30.5	-97.0	859.6	956.6	1 413.7	533.6	880.0	7 746.2
3rd quarter	7 866.2	5 286.4	1 279.9	889.0	339.7	51.1	-116.7	860.8	977.5	1 416.6	522.8	893.8	7 815.1
4th quarter	8 000.4	5 366.1	1 283.3	910.7	337.9	34.7	-87.1	905.6	992.7	1 438.1	525.3	912.8	7 965.8
1997													
1st quarter	8 113.8	5 448.8	1 315.4	930.1	340.8	44.4	-103.0	919.7	1 022.7	1 452.7	523.5	929.2	8 069.4
2nd quarter	8 250.4	5 484.6	1 385.2	950.0	346.8	88.5	-88.3	955.5	1 043.8	1 468.9	535.6	933.3	8 162.0
3rd quarter	8 381.9	5 589.8	1 419.5	995.7	351.3	72.5	-99.6	975.6	1 075.2	1 472.2	532.8	939.4	8 309.4
4th quarter	8 471.2	5 666.4	1 439.1	998.9	357.5	82.7	-115.3	970.6	1 085.9	1 481.1	531.7	949.4	8 388.6
1998													
1st quarter	8 586.7	5 733.4	1 505.5	1 024.0	365.9	115.5	-129.2	965.2	1 094.4	1 477.0	520.3	956.7	8 471.2
2nd quarter	8 657.9	5 834.2	1 474.6	1 049.1	378.6	46.9	-162.4	949.6	1 112.0	1 511.5	534.4	977.1	8 611.0
3rd quarter	8 789.5	5 924.2	1 507.8	1 054.3	392.8	60.7	-174.2	938.3	1 112.5	1 531.7	530.5	1 001.2	8 728.8
4th quarter	8 953.8	6 026.2	1 548.6	1 082.7	406.0	59.9	-174.0	970.6	1 144.6	1 553.1	536.6	1 016.4	8 893.9
1999													
1st quarter	9 066.6	6 101.7	1 596.7	1 101.0	413.5	82.2	-207.5	960.1	1 167.6	1 575.6	540.6	1 035.0	8 984.4
2nd quarter	9 174.1	6 237.2	1 589.9	1 130.1	421.7	38.1	-252.1	972.8	1 224.9	1 599.1	545.9	1 053.2	9 136.0
3rd quarter	9 313.5	6 337.2	1 628.3	1 151.5	427.8	49.1	-285.2	1 000.5	1 285.7	1 633.2	560.0	1 073.2	9 264.4
4th quarter	9 519.5	6 453.7	1 687.7	1 153.0	436.5	98.2	-297.2	1 031.6	1 328.8	1 675.3	576.8	1 098.5	9 421.3
2000													
1st quarter	9 629.4	6 613.9	1 672.3	1 193.9	448.5	29.9	-346.4	1 055.1	1 401.5	1 689.6	565.3	1 124.3	9 599.6
2nd quarter	9 822.8	6 688.1	1 781.7	1 236.5	448.8	96.3	-366.9	1 091.8	1 458.7	1 720.0	586.6	1 133.4	9 726.5
3rd quarter	9 862.1	6 783.9	1 749.0	1 247.5	443.1	58.4	-400.7	1 122.4	1 523.1	1 729.9	581.2	1 148.6	9 803.7
4th quarter	9 953.6	6 871.6	1 738.9	1 250.3	447.2	41.4	-403.9	1 115.8	1 519.7	1 746.9	582.0	1 164.9	9 912.2
2001													
1st quarter	10 021.5	6 955.8	1 675.3	1 229.6	455.6	-9.9	-392.9	1 100.7	1 493.7	1 783.3	596.2	1 187.2	10 031.4
2nd quarter	10 128.9	7 017.5	1 647.7	1 187.1	467.6	-7.0	-361.7	1 060.5	1 422.2	1 825.4	610.9	1 214.5	10 136.0
3rd quarter	10 135.1	7 058.5	1 613.0	1 167.2	477.6	-31.8	-361.9	1 003.5	1 365.3	1 825.6	614.3	1 211.2	10 166.9
4th quarter	10 226.3	7 188.4	1 521.4	1 123.2	476.3	-78.2	-351.6	966.6	1 318.2	1 868.2	630.1	1 238.1	10 304.5
2002													
1st quarter	10 333.3	7 230.3	1 564.1	1 085.2	487.2	-8.3	-373.1	976.4	1 349.5	1 912.0	654.9	1 257.2	10 341.6
2nd quarter	10 426.6	7 323.0	1 571.4	1 067.8	501.0	2.6	-416.1	1 008.2	1 424.3	1 948.3	675.2	1 273.1	10 424.0
3rd quarter	10 527.4	7 396.6	1 592.9	1 061.4	505.4	26.0	-433.8	1 022.9	1 456.7	1 971.8	682.0	1 289.8	10 501.4
4th quarter	10 591.1	7 453.1	1 600.1	1 050.7	522.1	27.3	-474.6	1 016.2	1 490.8	2 012.5	706.6	1 305.9	10 563.9
2003													
1st quarter	10 705.6	7 548.1	1 606.4	1 044.0	539.3	23.0	-499.3	1 012.4	1 511.7	2 050.3	725.9	1 324.4	10 682.6
2nd quarter	10 831.8	7 628.4	1 617.1	1 067.4	553.2	-3.5	-501.3	1 010.8	1 512.1	2 087.7	762.2	1 325.5	10 835.4
3rd quarter	11 086.1	7 782.6	1 690.5	1 093.3	585.4	11.8	-495.2	1 040.7	1 535.9	2 108.2	764.8	1 343.3	11 074.3
4th quarter	11 219.5	7 855.3	1 742.3	1 104.8	611.6	25.9	-501.8	1 099.1	1 600.9	2 123.7	772.8	1 350.9	11 193.6
2004													
1st quarter	11 430.9	8 018.0	1 781.9	1 112.1	631.8	38.0	-543.4	1 135.1	1 678.5	2 174.4	808.2	1 366.3	11 392.9
2nd quarter	11 649.3	8 148.1	1 892.2	1 137.6	675.2	79.3	-606.2	1 166.3	1 772.5	2 215.1	823.8	1 391.4	11 569.9
3rd quarter	11 799.4	8 265.0	1 917.7	1 170.0	692.9	54.8	-630.7	1 185.3	1 815.9	2 247.3	838.4	1 409.0	11 744.6
4th quarter	11 970.3	8 414.8	1 960.2	1 201.5	701.4	57.3	-672.7	1 225.8	1 898.5	2 268.0	833.2	1 434.8	11 913.0
2005													
1st quarter	12 173.2	8 519.7	2 013.5	1 230.0	724.1	59.4	-676.2	1 254.0	1 930.2	2 316.2	862.9	1 453.3	12 113.8
2nd quarter	12 346.1	8 674.6	2 009.1	1 251.8	764.9	-7.6	-686.4	1 293.8	1 980.2	2 348.9	868.4	1 480.5	12 353.7
3rd quarter	12 573.5	8 847.3	2 052.6	1 276.7	791.2	-15.3	-728.8	1 312.4	2 041.2	2 402.4	895.8	1 506.6	12 588.8
4th quarter	12 730.5	8 927.8	2 154.5	1 304.3	801.5	48.6	-775.4	1 352.4	2 127.8	2 423.6	886.2	1 537.4	12 681.9

Table 19-2. Real Gross Domestic Product

(Billions of chained [2000] dollars, quarterly data are at seasonally adjusted annual rates.)

NIPA Tables 1.1.6, 1.4.6

Year and quarter	Gross domestic product	Personal consumption expenditures	Gross private domestic investment Total	Fixed investment Nonresidential	Residential	Change in private inventories	Net exports	Exports	Imports	Government Total	Federal	State and local	Addendum: Final sales of domestic product
1946	1 589.4	1 012.9	172.1	. . .	. . .	. . .	. . .	64.6	47.0	396.8	. . .	. . .	1 566.4
1947	1 574.5	1 031.6	165.3	. . .	. . .	. . .	. . .	73.7	44.6	337.2	. . .	. . .	1 598.5
1948	1 643.2	1 054.4	211.2	. . .	. . .	. . .	. . .	58.0	52.0	361.7	. . .	. . .	1 628.1
1949	1 634.6	1 083.5	161.2	. . .	. . .	. . .	. . .	57.5	50.2	404.9	. . .	. . .	1 666.7
1947													
1st quarter	1 570.5	1 017.2	170.2	. . .	. . .	. . .	. . .	78.3	46.0	335.4	. . .	. . .	1 584.0
2nd quarter	1 568.7	1 034.0	156.7	. . .	. . .	. . .	. . .	77.5	46.9	337.4	. . .	. . .	1 594.5
3rd quarter	1 568.0	1 037.5	151.6	. . .	. . .	. . .	. . .	73.7	41.6	340.5	. . .	. . .	1 607.6
4th quarter	1 590.9	1 037.7	182.6	. . .	. . .	. . .	. . .	65.3	43.9	335.4	. . .	. . .	1 607.8
1948													
1st quarter	1 616.1	1 042.6	202.6	. . .	. . .	. . .	. . .	62.3	49.5	342.0	. . .	. . .	1 614.6
2nd quarter	1 644.6	1 054.3	215.8	. . .	. . .	. . .	. . .	56.4	51.4	358.4	. . .	. . .	1 625.6
3rd quarter	1 654.1	1 056.1	218.3	. . .	. . .	. . .	. . .	57.7	54.1	365.5	. . .	. . .	1 628.8
4th quarter	1 658.0	1 064.8	207.9	. . .	. . .	. . .	. . .	55.7	53.2	381.0	. . .	. . .	1 643.4
1949													
1st quarter	1 633.2	1 066.1	174.8	. . .	. . .	. . .	. . .	62.3	51.6	391.7	. . .	. . .	1 649.4
2nd quarter	1 628.4	1 082.6	150.9	. . .	. . .	. . .	. . .	61.8	50.9	409.5	. . .	. . .	1 671.2
3rd quarter	1 646.7	1 085.0	164.3	. . .	. . .	. . .	. . .	56.7	48.8	413.7	. . .	. . .	1 670.4
4th quarter	1 629.9	1 100.2	154.9	. . .	. . .	. . .	. . .	49.1	49.5	404.7	. . .	. . .	1 675.7
1950													
1st quarter	1 696.8	1 118.9	194.2	. . .	. . .	. . .	. . .	48.3	50.9	397.9	. . .	. . .	1 703.0
2nd quarter	1 747.3	1 136.8	215.5	. . .	. . .	. . .	. . .	48.9	53.7	404.3	. . .	. . .	1 748.1
3rd quarter	1 815.8	1 195.3	234.8	. . .	. . .	. . .	. . .	50.1	66.3	396.7	. . .	. . .	1 811.4
4th quarter	1 848.9	1 160.1	266.2	. . .	. . .	. . .	. . .	54.1	66.4	422.3	. . .	. . .	1 792.7
1951													
1st quarter	1 871.3	1 187.4	237.9	. . .	. . .	. . .	. . .	56.9	66.4	467.2	. . .	. . .	1 844.6
2nd quarter	1 903.1	1 154.5	244.0	. . .	. . .	. . .	. . .	62.5	64.2	531.4	. . .	. . .	1 854.0
3rd quarter	1 941.1	1 167.9	225.3	. . .	. . .	. . .	. . .	64.0	58.8	591.5	. . .	. . .	1 915.3
4th quarter	1 944.4	1 174.9	206.1	. . .	. . .	. . .	. . .	63.4	57.2	623.9	. . .	. . .	1 943.7
1952													
1st quarter	1 964.7	1 178.1	210.9	. . .	. . .	. . .	. . .	66.8	63.9	643.7	. . .	. . .	1 960.4
2nd quarter	1 966.0	1 200.7	193.3	. . .	. . .	. . .	. . .	59.4	63.6	665.3	. . .	. . .	1 991.3
3rd quarter	1 978.8	1 206.0	203.5	. . .	. . .	. . .	. . .	54.7	67.4	672.0	. . .	. . .	1 971.5
4th quarter	2 043.8	1 248.3	218.1	. . .	. . .	. . .	. . .	55.2	73.4	684.1	. . .	. . .	2 036.6
1953													
1st quarter	2 082.3	1 263.4	222.5	. . .	. . .	. . .	. . .	54.2	71.7	707.1	. . .	. . .	2 080.8
2nd quarter	2 098.1	1 271.2	223.3	. . .	. . .	. . .	. . .	54.5	75.4	722.6	. . .	. . .	2 097.4
3rd quarter	2 085.4	1 268.2	218.0	. . .	. . .	. . .	. . .	56.7	75.1	713.9	. . .	. . .	2 092.3
4th quarter	2 052.5	1 259.7	201.0	. . .	. . .	. . .	. . .	54.8	71.4	711.9	. . .	. . .	2 080.4
1954													
1st quarter	2 042.4	1 264.3	199.1	. . .	. . .	. . .	. . .	52.4	67.3	692.6	. . .	. . .	2 068.1
2nd quarter	2 044.3	1 280.1	198.5	. . .	. . .	. . .	. . .	59.9	73.3	668.0	. . .	. . .	2 075.7
3rd quarter	2 066.9	1 297.1	208.7	. . .	. . .	. . .	. . .	58.0	68.9	651.9	. . .	. . .	2 095.9
4th quarter	2 107.8	1 324.0	218.2	. . .	. . .	. . .	. . .	60.6	69.6	647.8	. . .	. . .	2 130.4
1955													
1st quarter	2 168.5	1 353.5	241.6	. . .	. . .	. . .	. . .	62.9	73.7	647.1	. . .	. . .	2 170.9
2nd quarter	2 204.0	1 379.1	256.8	. . .	. . .	. . .	. . .	61.4	77.9	640.5	. . .	. . .	2 199.1
3rd quarter	2 233.4	1 396.1	260.4	. . .	. . .	. . .	. . .	65.5	79.1	644.5	. . .	. . .	2 231.1
4th quarter	2 245.3	1 413.3	266.0	. . .	. . .	. . .	. . .	65.8	82.0	630.5	. . .	. . .	2 235.5
1956													
1st quarter	2 234.8	1 415.5	257.1	. . .	. . .	. . .	. . .	68.9	85.4	630.0	. . .	. . .	2 230.3
2nd quarter	2 252.5	1 420.2	254.1	. . .	. . .	. . .	. . .	73.5	85.0	643.3	. . .	. . .	2 255.1
3rd quarter	2 249.8	1 423.4	251.2	. . .	. . .	. . .	. . .	76.0	85.8	637.3	. . .	. . .	2 255.9
4th quarter	2 286.5	1 442.8	248.4	. . .	. . .	. . .	. . .	79.4	81.9	653.6	. . .	. . .	2 294.6
1957													
1st quarter	2 300.3	1 452.7	244.3	. . .	. . .	. . .	. . .	84.6	88.4	667.2	. . .	. . .	2 314.8
2nd quarter	2 294.6	1 455.1	244.1	. . .	. . .	. . .	. . .	82.1	89.1	662.8	. . .	. . .	2 305.9
3rd quarter	2 317.0	1 467.0	249.9	. . .	. . .	. . .	. . .	79.8	87.3	668.0	. . .	. . .	2 323.6
4th quarter	2 292.5	1 467.8	228.7	. . .	. . .	. . .	. . .	77.3	87.5	680.2	. . .	. . .	2 323.4
1958													
1st quarter	2 230.2	1 447.3	211.9	. . .	. . .	. . .	. . .	69.7	88.8	672.5	. . .	. . .	2 263.4
2nd quarter	2 243.4	1 458.9	206.7	. . .	. . .	. . .	. . .	70.0	92.5	689.4	. . .	. . .	2 274.9
3rd quarter	2 295.2	1 482.2	223.8	. . .	. . .	. . .	. . .	70.2	91.3	693.6	. . .	. . .	2 307.2
4th quarter	2 348.0	1 500.9	244.5	. . .	. . .	. . .	. . .	70.1	96.4	708.3	. . .	. . .	2 350.4
1959													
1st quarter	2 392.9	1 525.9	258.0	. . .	. . .	. . .	. . .	74.7	98.3	703.7	. . .	. . .	2 396.9
2nd quarter	2 455.8	1 551.7	279.8	. . .	. . .	. . .	. . .	77.2	103.3	714.4	. . .	. . .	2 440.3
3rd quarter	2 453.9	1 569.2	260.1	. . .	. . .	. . .	. . .	79.6	104.5	723.4	. . .	. . .	2 471.1
4th quarter	2 462.6	1 571.4	268.8	. . .	. . .	. . .	. . .	77.4	101.8	715.6	. . .	. . .	2 462.3
1960													
1st quarter	2 517.4	1 585.6	298.5	. . .	. . .	. . .	. . .	87.2	105.6	701.3	. . .	. . .	2 488.1
2nd quarter	2 504.8	1 605.1	268.0	. . .	. . .	. . .	. . .	92.7	106.3	707.0	. . .	. . .	2 511.5
3rd quarter	2 508.7	1 598.5	266.4	. . .	. . .	. . .	. . .	90.4	103.1	724.1	. . .	. . .	2 507.9
4th quarter	2 476.2	1 600.3	233.6	. . .	. . .	. . .	. . .	92.2	98.3	729.1	. . .	. . .	2 519.8

. . . = Not available.

Table 19-2. Real Gross Domestic Product—Continued

(Billions of chained [2000] dollars, quarterly data are at seasonally adjusted annual rates.) **NIPA Tables 1.1.6, 1.4.6**

Year and quarter	Gross domestic product	Personal consumption expenditures	Gross private domestic investment Total	Fixed investment Nonresidential	Fixed investment Residential	Change in private inventories	Net exports	Exports	Imports	Government Total	Federal	State and local	Addendum: Final sales of domestic product
1961													
1st quarter	2 491.2	1 600.2	239.4	. . .	. . .	. . .	. . .	91.6	97.8	738.6	. . .	. . .	2 522.0
2nd quarter	2 538.0	1 624.2	257.3	. . .	. . .	. . .	. . .	90.3	99.0	740.3	. . .	. . .	2 549.1
3rd quarter	2 579.1	1 632.1	279.0	. . .	. . .	. . .	. . .	89.8	105.6	754.9	. . .	. . .	2 568.9
4th quarter	2 631.8	1 664.9	283.7	. . .	. . .	. . .	. . .	92.6	108.1	771.4	. . .	. . .	2 627.3
1962													
1st quarter	2 679.1	1 682.7	300.6	. . .	. . .	. . .	. . .	92.4	111.4	785.2	. . .	. . .	2 659.5
2nd quarter	2 708.4	1 703.1	297.7	. . .	. . .	. . .	. . .	101.3	113.8	789.4	. . .	. . .	2 704.5
3rd quarter	2 733.3	1 717.0	302.9	. . .	. . .	. . .	. . .	95.6	115.2	807.3	. . .	. . .	2 725.6
4th quarter	2 740.0	1 741.5	292.6	. . .	. . .	. . .	. . .	93.5	116.6	808.5	. . .	. . .	2 744.5
1963													
1st quarter	2 775.9	1 753.1	308.9	. . .	. . .	. . .	. . .	95.7	113.9	803.6	. . .	. . .	2 762.8
2nd quarter	2 810.6	1 770.0	313.4	. . .	. . .	. . .	. . .	106.9	116.6	802.6	. . .	. . .	2 809.7
3rd quarter	2 863.5	1 794.0	323.7	. . .	. . .	. . .	. . .	101.2	119.6	837.0	. . .	. . .	2 859.4
4th quarter	2 885.8	1 809.3	327.8	. . .	. . .	. . .	. . .	106.3	119.2	829.4	. . .	. . .	2 889.5
1964													
1st quarter	2 950.5	1 845.2	341.2	. . .	. . .	. . .	. . .	112.8	119.1	832.3	. . .	. . .	2 952.7
2nd quarter	2 984.8	1 877.9	339.7	. . .	. . .	. . .	. . .	114.7	121.8	837.8	. . .	. . .	2 988.1
3rd quarter	3 025.5	1 912.6	347.7	. . .	. . .	. . .	. . .	113.8	125.0	838.3	. . .	. . .	3 025.4
4th quarter	3 033.6	1 918.0	350.3	. . .	. . .	. . .	. . .	117.2	128.4	835.9	. . .	. . .	3 033.2
1965													
1st quarter	3 108.2	1 960.3	385.8	. . .	. . .	. . .	. . .	104.5	123.8	834.0	. . .	. . .	3 081.0
2nd quarter	3 150.2	1 982.0	385.7	. . .	. . .	. . .	. . .	124.2	138.4	844.6	. . .	. . .	3 136.6
3rd quarter	3 214.1	2 016.0	399.5	. . .	. . .	. . .	. . .	117.1	139.0	873.8	. . .	. . .	3 195.5
4th quarter	3 291.8	2 072.7	401.4	. . .	. . .	. . .	. . .	125.5	145.8	892.7	. . .	. . .	3 282.4
1966													
1st quarter	3 372.3	2 103.2	435.2	. . .	. . .	. . .	. . .	123.3	149.5	908.7	. . .	. . .	3 337.0
2nd quarter	3 384.0	2 109.0	427.3	. . .	. . .	. . .	. . .	128.7	153.2	924.8	. . .	. . .	3 352.4
3rd quarter	3 406.3	2 133.1	423.1	. . .	. . .	. . .	. . .	123.9	161.8	949.7	. . .	. . .	3 380.2
4th quarter	3 433.7	2 142.0	425.2	. . .	. . .	. . .	. . .	128.0	163.7	965.1	. . .	. . .	3 389.6
1967													
1st quarter	3 464.1	2 154.6	413.4	. . .	. . .	. . .	. . .	130.4	166.1	1 006.1	. . .	. . .	3 424.2
2nd quarter	3 464.3	2 183.4	395.8	. . .	. . .	. . .	. . .	129.3	164.8	1 000.6	. . .	. . .	3 460.2
3rd quarter	3 491.8	2 194.5	407.2	. . .	. . .	. . .	. . .	126.1	167.1	1 011.0	. . .	. . .	3 477.8
4th quarter	3 518.2	2 207.8	416.0	. . .	. . .	. . .	. . .	129.7	175.9	1 018.0	. . .	. . .	3 508.2
1968													
1st quarter	3 590.7	2 260.3	425.2	. . .	. . .	. . .	. . .	133.5	186.2	1 035.6	. . .	. . .	3 581.7
2nd quarter	3 651.6	2 295.1	442.3	. . .	. . .	. . .	. . .	136.1	189.1	1 040.3	. . .	. . .	3 617.7
3rd quarter	3 676.5	2 338.2	427.9	. . .	. . .	. . .	. . .	144.1	200.4	1 042.6	. . .	. . .	3 669.4
4th quarter	3 692.0	2 348.6	432.3	. . .	. . .	. . .	. . .	142.3	198.7	1 043.3	. . .	. . .	3 692.2
1969													
1st quarter	3 750.2	2 375.0	460.8	. . .	. . .	. . .	. . .	125.2	180.0	1 044.4	. . .	. . .	3 730.5
2nd quarter	3 760.9	2 390.0	457.1	. . .	. . .	. . .	. . .	153.3	215.5	1 040.0	. . .	. . .	3 748.6
3rd quarter	3 784.2	2 401.0	467.8	. . .	. . .	. . .	. . .	149.6	212.7	1 041.4	. . .	. . .	3 767.6
4th quarter	3 766.3	2 419.8	442.7	. . .	. . .	. . .	. . .	154.8	210.3	1 026.0	. . .	. . .	3 768.1
1970													
1st quarter	3 760.0	2 434.4	428.7	. . .	. . .	. . .	. . .	156.1	209.7	1 020.5	. . .	. . .	3 778.0
2nd quarter	3 767.1	2 445.7	430.2	. . .	. . .	. . .	. . .	163.0	213.8	1 007.3	. . .	. . .	3 771.0
3rd quarter	3 800.5	2 467.1	437.5	. . .	. . .	. . .	. . .	162.5	213.3	1 011.8	. . .	. . .	3 804.6
4th quarter	3 759.8	2 460.1	411.9	. . .	. . .	. . .	. . .	164.0	216.7	1 011.8	. . .	. . .	3 797.2
1971													
1st quarter	3 864.1	2 507.4	465.6	. . .	. . .	. . .	. . .	164.6	214.1	995.4	. . .	. . .	3 844.7
2nd quarter	3 885.9	2 530.5	479.9	. . .	. . .	. . .	. . .	164.3	230.2	992.3	. . .	. . .	3 871.3
3rd quarter	3 916.7	2 550.7	486.3	. . .	. . .	. . .	. . .	171.0	235.3	991.5	. . .	. . .	3 905.2
4th quarter	3 927.9	2 593.2	471.3	. . .	. . .	. . .	. . .	156.7	219.3	984.1	. . .	. . .	3 952.5
1972													
1st quarter	3 997.7	2 627.6	504.4	. . .	. . .	. . .	. . .	173.3	251.4	987.7	. . .	. . .	4 006.9
2nd quarter	4 092.1	2 677.3	535.4	. . .	. . .	. . .	. . .	168.2	242.5	993.8	. . .	. . .	4 073.0
3rd quarter	4 131.1	2 718.4	542.9	. . .	. . .	. . .	. . .	178.4	247.5	973.3	. . .	. . .	4 109.6
4th quarter	4 198.7	2 781.7	545.5	. . .	. . .	. . .	. . .	185.9	258.7	979.4	. . .	. . .	4 204.8
1973													
1st quarter	4 305.3	2 832.0	580.4	. . .	. . .	. . .	. . .	199.6	270.6	988.9	. . .	. . .	4 296.4
2nd quarter	4 355.1	2 830.5	607.4	. . .	. . .	. . .	. . .	209.2	262.8	983.1	. . .	. . .	4 317.4
3rd quarter	4 331.9	2 840.6	583.6	. . .	. . .	. . .	. . .	209.9	255.6	970.5	. . .	. . .	4 322.6
4th quarter	4 373.3	2 832.2	606.2	. . .	. . .	. . .	. . .	220.2	257.5	977.6	. . .	. . .	4 327.3
1974													
1st quarter	4 335.4	2 807.8	566.9	. . .	. . .	. . .	. . .	223.0	248.7	998.1	. . .	. . .	4 322.7
2nd quarter	4 347.9	2 819.0	564.7	. . .	. . .	. . .	. . .	233.9	261.9	1 004.7	. . .	. . .	4 328.7
3rd quarter	4 305.8	2 831.6	533.0	. . .	. . .	. . .	. . .	221.3	257.4	1 006.2	. . .	. . .	4 316.3
4th quarter	4 288.9	2 790.8	537.9	. . .	. . .	. . .	. . .	227.0	254.8	1 009.8	. . .	. . .	4 254.5
1975													
1st quarter	4 237.6	2 814.6	443.8	. . .	. . .	. . .	. . .	228.7	229.3	1 022.1	. . .	. . .	4 287.8
2nd quarter	4 268.6	2 860.5	427.7	. . .	. . .	. . .	. . .	222.0	210.9	1 014.2	. . .	. . .	4 331.0
3rd quarter	4 340.9	2 901.2	463.9	. . .	. . .	. . .	. . .	218.2	228.4	1 032.2	. . .	. . .	4 370.1
4th quarter	4 397.8	2 931.4	477.2	. . .	. . .	. . .	. . .	230.6	240.6	1 040.9	. . .	. . .	4 421.1

. . . = Not available.

Table 19-2. Real Gross Domestic Product—Continued

(Billions of chained [2000] dollars, quarterly data are at seasonally adjusted annual rates.)   **NIPA Tables 1.1.6, 1.4.6**

Year and quarter	Gross domestic product	Personal consumption expenditures	Gross private domestic investment				Exports and imports of goods and services			Government consumption expenditures and gross investment			Addendum: Final sales of domestic product
			Total	Fixed investment		Change in private inventories	Net exports	Exports	Imports	Total	Federal	State and local	
				Nonresidential	Residential								
1976													
1st quarter	4 496.8	2 989.7	526.4	. . .	. . .	. . .	. . .	229.0	255.7	1 043.4	. . .	. . .	4 482.1
2nd quarter	4 530.3	3 016.3	549.3	. . .	. . .	. . .	. . .	231.3	266.8	1 032.0	. . .	. . .	4 496.3
3rd quarter	4 552.0	3 047.9	550.0	. . .	. . .	. . .	. . .	238.0	277.6	1 026.6	. . .	. . .	4 523.7
4th quarter	4 584.6	3 088.0	553.1	. . .	. . .	. . .	. . .	240.4	286.8	1 025.8	. . .	. . .	4 587.1
1977													
1st quarter	4 640.0	3 124.6	580.9	. . .	. . .	. . .	. . .	236.6	300.4	1 035.1	. . .	. . .	4 631.5
2nd quarter	4 731.1	3 141.5	625.5	. . .	. . .	. . .	. . .	243.0	303.2	1 045.8	. . .	. . .	4 705.5
3rd quarter	4 815.8	3 171.4	659.8	. . .	. . .	. . .	. . .	244.8	299.0	1 047.7	. . .	. . .	4 755.2
4th quarter	4 815.3	3 219.1	641.9	. . .	. . .	. . .	. . .	237.0	303.2	1 044.4	. . .	. . .	4 794.1
1978													
1st quarter	4 830.8	3 237.3	654.0	. . .	. . .	. . .	. . .	242.6	323.5	1 046.1	. . .	. . .	4 799.5
2nd quarter	5 021.2	3 306.4	699.3	. . .	. . .	. . .	. . .	267.8	324.5	1 074.3	. . .	. . .	4 989.9
3rd quarter	5 070.7	3 320.8	720.6	. . .	. . .	. . .	. . .	270.8	328.8	1 082.9	. . .	. . .	5 036.0
4th quarter	5 137.4	3 347.8	736.6	. . .	. . .	. . .	. . .	281.6	333.4	1 092.7	. . .	. . .	5 100.6
1979													
1st quarter	5 147.4	3 365.3	737.1	. . .	. . .	. . .	. . .	281.8	332.4	1 082.9	. . .	. . .	5 117.8
2nd quarter	5 152.3	3 364.0	735.1	. . .	. . .	. . .	. . .	282.5	334.2	1 094.4	. . .	. . .	5 117.9
3rd quarter	5 189.4	3 397.3	720.6	. . .	. . .	. . .	. . .	292.7	329.1	1 095.9	. . .	. . .	5 192.3
4th quarter	5 204.7	3 407.1	707.2	. . .	. . .	. . .	. . .	311.0	336.3	1 103.1	. . .	. . .	5 216.9
1980													
1st quarter	5 221.3	3 401.7	701.6	. . .	. . .	. . .	. . .	319.8	336.6	1 120.8	. . .	. . .	5 227.3
2nd quarter	5 115.9	3 325.8	638.7	. . .	. . .	. . .	. . .	325.8	312.1	1 124.3	. . .	. . .	5 126.2
3rd quarter	5 107.4	3 362.0	590.3	. . .	. . .	. . .	. . .	325.1	289.6	1 108.8	. . .	. . .	5 193.5
4th quarter	5 202.1	3 406.8	650.6	. . .	. . .	. . .	. . .	323.2	305.2	1 107.7	. . .	. . .	5 239.7
1981													
1st quarter	5 307.5	3 421.3	716.0	. . .	. . .	. . .	. . .	329.2	318.2	1 122.5	. . .	. . .	5 261.7
2nd quarter	5 266.1	3 422.1	682.2	. . .	. . .	. . .	. . .	331.1	318.7	1 124.9	. . .	. . .	5 272.8
3rd quarter	5 329.8	3 435.7	724.7	. . .	. . .	. . .	. . .	324.0	315.1	1 122.3	. . .	. . .	5 278.5
4th quarter	5 263.4	3 409.7	696.4	. . .	. . .	. . .	. . .	325.5	324.2	1 132.7	. . .	. . .	5 247.4
1982													
1st quarter	5 177.1	3 432.2	623.7	. . .	. . .	. . .	. . .	311.4	314.9	1 131.5	. . .	. . .	5 232.9
2nd quarter	5 204.9	3 444.3	622.9	. . .	. . .	. . .	. . .	313.3	309.8	1 138.2	. . .	. . .	5 230.5
3rd quarter	5 185.2	3 470.8	615.8	. . .	. . .	. . .	. . .	299.4	324.1	1 146.0	. . .	. . .	5 196.6
4th quarter	5 189.8	3 533.9	561.5	. . .	. . .	. . .	. . .	285.7	311.4	1 165.8	. . .	. . .	5 273.3
1983													
1st quarter	5 253.8	3 568.5	581.3	. . .	. . .	. . .	. . .	290.3	318.5	1 174.6	. . .	. . .	5 329.2
2nd quarter	5 372.3	3 639.5	637.7	. . .	. . .	. . .	. . .	291.2	343.0	1 184.6	. . .	. . .	5 404.6
3rd quarter	5 478.4	3 704.1	680.1	. . .	. . .	. . .	. . .	295.6	369.7	1 205.2	. . .	. . .	5 505.1
4th quarter	5 590.5	3 762.5	750.7	. . .	. . .	. . .	. . .	301.5	387.9	1 184.8	. . .	. . .	5 577.0
1984													
1st quarter	5 699.8	3 794.9	830.1	. . .	. . .	. . .	. . .	307.8	419.0	1 196.6	. . .	. . .	5 614.4
2nd quarter	5 797.9	3 849.3	858.0	. . .	. . .	. . .	. . .	315.5	436.6	1 222.4	. . .	. . .	5 717.5
3rd quarter	5 854.3	3 879.1	878.3	. . .	. . .	. . .	. . .	322.4	447.9	1 231.4	. . .	. . .	5 770.2
4th quarter	5 902.4	3 930.2	864.3	. . .	. . .	. . .	. . .	329.0	461.1	1 257.9	. . .	. . .	5 854.6
1985													
1st quarter	5 956.9	3 996.2	835.2	. . .	. . .	. . .	. . .	329.2	450.9	1 272.2	. . .	. . .	5 953.0
2nd quarter	6 007.8	4 032.6	849.8	. . .	. . .	. . .	. . .	328.0	473.1	1 300.8	. . .	. . .	5 998.5
3rd quarter	6 101.7	4 109.1	840.5	. . .	. . .	. . .	. . .	323.2	468.5	1 334.6	. . .	. . .	6 095.8
4th quarter	6 148.6	4 118.4	873.5	. . .	. . .	. . .	. . .	332.9	486.7	1 342.6	. . .	. . .	6 121.2
1986													
1st quarter	6 207.4	4 152.7	871.6	. . .	. . .	. . .	. . .	343.6	486.5	1 357.1	. . .	. . .	6 184.1
2nd quarter	6 232.0	4 196.7	852.2	. . .	. . .	. . .	. . .	347.3	507.1	1 385.9	. . .	. . .	6 230.5
3rd quarter	6 291.7	4 269.5	825.4	. . .	. . .	. . .	. . .	355.2	521.2	1 417.5	. . .	. . .	6 317.8
4th quarter	6 323.4	4 296.7	826.6	. . .	. . .	. . .	. . .	368.5	525.4	1 409.6	. . .	. . .	6 355.0
1987													
1st quarter	6 365.0	4 298.6	852.0	. . .	. . .	. . .	. . .	368.7	522.0	1 413.2	. . .	. . .	6 344.4
2nd quarter	6 435.0	4 357.3	853.2	. . .	. . .	. . .	. . .	383.6	535.1	1 423.1	. . .	. . .	6 431.4
3rd quarter	6 493.4	4 406.3	854.1	. . .	. . .	. . .	. . .	400.1	545.5	1 425.6	. . .	. . .	6 510.8
4th quarter	6 606.8	4 417.1	920.6	. . .	. . .	. . .	. . .	414.9	558.0	1 445.1	. . .	. . .	6 542.5
1988													
1st quarter	6 639.1	4 490.6	868.8	. . .	. . .	. . .	. . .	437.8	555.6	1 436.7	. . .	. . .	6 637.2
2nd quarter	6 723.5	4 522.7	889.9	. . .	. . .	. . .	. . .	450.0	549.1	1 439.9	. . .	. . .	6 716.4
3rd quarter	6 759.4	4 560.5	895.6	. . .	. . .	. . .	. . .	458.3	561.9	1 438.0	. . .	. . .	6 749.5
4th quarter	6 848.6	4 614.0	907.5	. . .	. . .	. . .	. . .	472.4	578.8	1 465.9	. . .	. . .	6 835.1
1989													
1st quarter	6 918.1	4 631.2	942.3	. . .	. . .	. . .	. . .	485.9	577.2	1 456.7	. . .	. . .	6 873.3
2nd quarter	6 963.5	4 653.0	931.3	. . .	. . .	. . .	. . .	507.1	585.8	1 479.2	. . .	. . .	6 933.6
3rd quarter	7 013.1	4 697.3	920.4	. . .	. . .	. . .	. . .	513.0	586.5	1 493.0	. . .	. . .	7 015.3
4th quarter	7 030.9	4 718.8	910.8	. . .	. . .	. . .	. . .	521.4	594.2	1 501.0	. . .	. . .	7 026.8
1990													
1st quarter	7 112.1	4 757.1	920.0	603.9	321.0	14.1	-63.8	543.6	607.3	1 524.2	659.9	861.9	7 110.6
2nd quarter	7 130.3	4 773.0	920.1	593.5	308.6	33.9	-63.6	550.5	614.1	1 526.8	660.7	863.6	7 103.8
3rd quarter	7 130.8	4 792.6	898.4	597.2	291.1	22.8	-58.1	555.1	613.2	1 526.7	654.9	869.4	7 118.3
4th quarter	7 076.9	4 758.3	841.8	585.8	275.0	-9.3	-33.2	560.7	593.8	1 542.2	660.7	878.9	7 101.3

. . . = Not available.

Table 19-2. Real Gross Domestic Product—Continued

(Billions of chained [2000] dollars, quarterly data are at seasonally adjusted annual rates.)

NIPA Tables 1.1.6, 1.4.6

Year and quarter	Gross domestic product	Personal consumption expenditures	Gross private domestic investment Total	Fixed investment Nonresidential	Fixed investment Residential	Change in private inventories	Net exports	Exports	Imports	Gov't Total	Gov't Federal	Gov't State and local	Addendum: Final sales of domestic product
1991													
1st quarter	7 040.8	4 738.1	807.3	570.7	258.6	-14.4	-18.3	563.2	581.5	1 548.4	665.8	880.0	7 071.5
2nd quarter	7 086.5	4 779.4	803.5	565.3	264.7	-18.1	-14.3	583.8	598.1	1 553.7	667.7	883.5	7 120.2
3rd quarter	7 120.7	4 800.1	823.5	559.9	275.7	-0.1	-16.0	597.8	613.9	1 546.6	655.5	888.6	7 134.6
4th quarter	7 154.1	4 795.9	854.7	556.9	281.7	30.7	-9.6	611.6	621.2	1 540.4	642.8	895.2	7 133.8
1992													
1st quarter	7 228.2	4 875.0	835.8	554.5	296.1	1.8	-4.7	621.9	626.6	1 552.3	643.1	906.9	7 239.3
2nd quarter	7 297.9	4 903.0	890.7	576.5	307.4	22.9	-20.2	622.2	642.4	1 550.7	642.6	905.8	7 284.3
3rd quarter	7 369.5	4 951.8	900.2	588.2	308.2	19.6	-15.9	635.6	651.4	1 559.0	650.1	906.6	7 360.5
4th quarter	7 450.7	5 009.4	929.1	606.0	318.6	21.5	-23.0	639.1	662.1	1 559.3	650.4	906.6	7 440.3
1993													
1st quarter	7 459.7	5 027.3	950.3	609.6	320.1	36.7	-37.4	639.9	677.2	1 543.0	630.5	910.4	7 431.2
2nd quarter	7 497.5	5 071.9	957.8	625.9	323.8	24.3	-48.6	647.4	696.0	1 541.4	621.4	918.0	7 483.7
3rd quarter	7 536.0	5 127.3	957.8	632.8	335.0	7.0	-59.4	645.7	705.1	1 537.0	612.5	922.7	7 540.6
4th quarter	7 637.4	5 172.9	1 007.3	659.3	351.9	14.5	-63.0	667.0	730.1	1 542.7	614.1	926.9	7 633.7
1994													
1st quarter	7 715.1	5 230.3	1 050.6	665.9	358.8	46.3	-73.8	672.8	746.5	1 527.1	595.8	929.6	7 677.5
2nd quarter	7 815.7	5 268.0	1 112.0	679.3	370.9	83.0	-83.0	695.0	778.1	1 533.7	592.6	939.6	7 737.2
3rd quarter	7 859.5	5 305.7	1 092.4	692.0	367.0	51.7	-79.0	721.0	800.0	1 558.8	606.8	950.4	7 814.3
4th quarter	7 951.6	5 358.7	1 143.2	722.6	362.3	73.4	-81.9	737.3	819.2	1 545.5	590.5	953.7	7 882.3
1995													
1st quarter	7 973.7	5 367.2	1 154.6	752.1	354.2	60.8	-86.0	750.5	836.5	1 551.9	589.4	961.2	7 918.7
2nd quarter	7 988.0	5 411.7	1 123.8	757.4	342.9	34.6	-87.7	761.0	848.7	1 558.2	588.3	968.7	7 962.3
3rd quarter	8 053.1	5 458.8	1 113.1	762.5	353.6	7.9	-57.1	794.5	851.7	1 553.2	582.7	969.2	8 055.0
4th quarter	8 112.0	5 496.1	1 144.4	777.9	361.6	16.2	-53.1	806.6	859.7	1 535.5	560.6	974.1	8 104.8
1996													
1st quarter	8 169.2	5 544.6	1 160.2	797.1	371.1	3.0	-68.2	816.4	884.6	1 544.9	572.3	971.6	8 175.4
2nd quarter	8 303.1	5 604.9	1 220.0	820.0	386.8	24.5	-81.2	830.3	911.4	1 570.3	583.6	985.6	8 285.8
3rd quarter	8 372.7	5 640.7	1 280.8	847.3	385.7	57.5	-104.3	837.3	941.6	1 565.1	569.6	994.7	8 319.9
4th quarter	8 470.6	5 687.6	1 276.1	870.1	381.8	29.9	-64.9	889.5	954.4	1 579.2	568.5	1 010.0	8 444.7
1997													
1st quarter	8 536.1	5 749.1	1 302.9	892.2	383.1	34.7	-89.0	905.7	994.7	1 581.6	561.2	1 019.8	8 507.3
2nd quarter	8 665.8	5 775.8	1 389.6	914.3	387.9	94.2	-93.1	941.8	1 034.8	1 598.1	573.6	1 024.0	8 574.6
3rd quarter	8 773.7	5 870.7	1 417.5	961.1	389.7	72.3	-108.8	964.2	1 073.0	1 598.5	569.9	1 028.0	8 705.7
4th quarter	8 838.4	5 931.4	1 440.7	969.0	393.6	83.4	-127.6	963.2	1 090.9	1 597.9	565.7	1 031.8	8 758.6
1998													
1st quarter	8 936.2	5 996.8	1 515.8	1 001.6	401.8	116.9	-163.7	967.4	1 131.1	1 589.1	551.9	1 037.0	8 821.1
2nd quarter	8 995.3	6 092.1	1 491.7	1 032.5	412.9	50.4	-205.1	957.0	1 162.1	1 621.4	565.9	1 055.2	8 948.7
3rd quarter	9 098.9	6 165.7	1 525.8	1 042.4	424.1	64.2	-223.9	952.9	1 176.9	1 636.0	561.1	1 074.9	9 038.4
4th quarter	9 237.1	6 248.8	1 563.0	1 074.7	434.3	58.9	-222.3	988.7	1 211.0	1 651.1	566.1	1 084.9	9 182.2
1999													
1st quarter	9 315.5	6 311.3	1 606.6	1 094.0	438.1	79.5	-262.1	980.1	1 242.2	1 662.2	562.9	1 099.3	9 239.7
2nd quarter	9 392.6	6 409.7	1 607.8	1 127.3	441.8	41.7	-295.2	991.2	1 286.4	1 672.3	565.3	1 107.0	9 353.7
3rd quarter	9 502.2	6 476.7	1 647.4	1 154.4	444.5	50.8	-313.9	1 017.4	1 331.3	1 693.1	576.7	1 116.3	9 453.5
4th quarter	9 671.1	6 556.8	1 708.4	1 157.3	449.9	103.5	-313.7	1 044.1	1 357.9	1 720.2	589.9	1 130.2	9 569.3
2000													
1st quarter	9 695.6	6 661.3	1 678.0	1 196.7	454.5	26.9	-350.6	1 060.9	1 411.5	1 707.3	568.2	1 139.2	9 668.8
2nd quarter	9 847.9	6 703.3	1 788.6	1 238.6	450.4	99.3	-374.5	1 092.0	1 466.5	1 730.5	591.2	1 139.3	9 748.4
3rd quarter	9 836.6	6 768.0	1 742.6	1 245.2	441.2	56.2	-395.6	1 120.0	1 515.6	1 721.5	578.6	1 142.9	9 780.4
4th quarter	9 887.7	6 825.0	1 732.7	1 247.9	441.6	43.5	-397.2	1 112.3	1 509.5	1 727.1	577.2	1 149.9	9 844.3
2001													
1st quarter	9 875.6	6 853.1	1 670.3	1 234.4	444.0	-7.8	-398.2	1 097.2	1 495.4	1 749.6	588.5	1 161.1	9 883.2
2nd quarter	9 905.9	6 870.3	1 637.4	1 190.2	450.1	-2.5	-385.2	1 060.6	1 445.8	1 783.0	601.4	1 181.6	9 908.2
3rd quarter	9 871.1	6 900.5	1 592.6	1 169.3	452.1	-29.9	-398.4	1 008.7	1 407.1	1 776.1	601.5	1 174.6	9 899.9
4th quarter	9 910.0	7 017.6	1 493.4	1 128.2	447.8	-86.7	-414.5	980.3	1 394.9	1 812.7	614.2	1 198.5	9 992.3
2002													
1st quarter	9 977.3	7 042.2	1 541.7	1 090.3	459.0	-10.2	-441.3	992.8	1 434.0	1 832.0	623.2	1 208.9	9 986.8
2nd quarter	10 031.6	7 083.5	1 549.0	1 073.3	469.5	2.6	-458.9	1 018.0	1 476.9	1 853.4	641.7	1 211.8	10 028.4
3rd quarter	10 090.7	7 123.2	1 570.9	1 068.0	471.8	28.0	-472.2	1 025.2	1 497.4	1 863.9	646.5	1 217.5	10 063.5
4th quarter	10 095.8	7 148.2	1 567.0	1 054.5	479.3	29.5	-513.0	1 017.2	1 530.2	1 885.8	662.3	1 223.6	10 067.3
2003													
1st quarter	10 126.0	7 184.9	1 561.8	1 047.5	484.1	24.3	-507.2	1 003.3	1 510.5	1 879.3	662.5	1 216.9	10 100.9
2nd quarter	10 212.7	7 249.3	1 574.4	1 074.5	496.3	-2.7	-526.9	999.0	1 525.9	1 907.5	693.0	1 214.4	10 213.7
3rd quarter	10 398.7	7 352.9	1 639.7	1 098.8	521.8	10.5	-513.8	1 026.3	1 540.0	1 914.5	693.7	1 220.8	10 385.9
4th quarter	10 467.0	7 394.3	1 676.5	1 106.5	535.2	25.0	-527.8	1 075.8	1 603.6	1 918.0	699.0	1 219.0	10 440.0
2004													
1st quarter	10 566.3	7 479.8	1 696.4	1 111.2	539.2	35.9	-548.5	1 094.8	1 643.2	1 931.8	711.3	1 220.4	10 528.7
2nd quarter	10 671.5	7 534.4	1 781.9	1 130.7	564.1	74.7	-593.9	1 111.3	1 705.2	1 942.6	715.7	1 226.8	10 596.1
3rd quarter	10 753.3	7 607.1	1 790.8	1 158.8	568.6	50.8	-599.4	1 124.3	1 723.7	1 948.7	724.5	1 224.1	10 700.1
4th quarter	10 822.9	7 687.1	1 813.4	1 182.3	567.7	52.0	-621.9	1 151.3	1 773.1	1 939.3	714.9	1 224.3	10 768.2
2005													
1st quarter	10 913.8	7 739.4	1 849.6	1 199.7	582.8	55.2	-626.4	1 164.5	1 790.9	1 947.2	720.8	1 226.3	10 856.5
2nd quarter	11 001.8	7 819.8	1 832.6	1 214.8	609.9	-7.4	-606.1	1 191.0	1 797.1	1 952.6	721.6	1 230.9	11 005.3
3rd quarter	11 115.1	7 895.3	1 855.9	1 232.4	620.4	-12.7	-607.6	1 200.5	1 808.1	1 968.8	738.2	1 230.5	11 123.5
4th quarter	11 163.8	7 910.2	1 927.0	1 248.2	618.9	43.5	-636.6	1 228.4	1 865.0	1 963.5	729.6	1 233.7	11 115.5

Table 19-3. Contributions to Percent Change in Real Gross Domestic Product

(Percent; percentage points.)

NIPA Table 1.1.2

Year and quarter	Percent change at seasonally adjusted annual rate, GDP	Personal consumption expenditures	Gross private domestic investment				Exports and imports of goods and services			Government consumption expenditures and gross investment		
			Total	Fixed investment		Change in private inventories	Net exports	Exports	Imports	Total	Federal	State and local
				Nonresidential	Residential							
1946	-11.0	6.36	7.46	2.24	2.39	2.84	3.82	3.25	0.57	-28.67	-29.06	0.39
1947	-0.9	1.20	-0.57	1.31	1.06	-2.93	1.08	0.91	0.17	-2.65	-3.32	0.68
1948	4.4	1.47	4.00	0.51	0.98	2.50	-2.18	-1.63	-0.55	1.08	0.71	0.37
1949	-0.5	1.79	-4.22	-0.93	-0.44	-2.85	0.08	-0.05	0.13	1.83	0.90	0.93
1947												
1st quarter	. . .	. . .	. . .	. . .	. . .	. . .	. . .	. . .	. . .	. . .	. . .	. . .
2nd quarter	-0.5	4.55	-4.65	-0.58	-0.84	-3.24	-0.68	-0.43	-0.25	0.36	0.04	0.31
3rd quarter	-0.2	1.07	-1.65	-0.73	2.78	-3.70	-0.19	-1.75	1.56	0.66	0.00	0.66
4th quarter	6.0	-0.06	11.09	1.32	4.20	5.57	-4.15	-3.48	-0.67	-0.86	-1.24	0.39
1948												
1st quarter	6.5	1.32	6.71	2.72	-0.27	4.26	-2.74	-1.24	-1.50	1.25	1.28	-0.03
2nd quarter	7.3	3.04	4.21	-1.40	1.36	4.26	-2.94	-2.35	-0.59	2.97	2.24	0.73
3rd quarter	2.3	0.36	0.96	0.14	-0.74	1.56	-0.30	0.48	-0.78	1.31	0.83	0.49
4th quarter	1.0	1.94	-2.95	1.08	-1.74	-2.30	-0.58	-0.82	0.24	2.54	1.95	0.59
1949												
1st quarter	-5.8	0.28	-10.72	-2.04	-1.78	-6.90	2.75	2.33	0.41	1.70	0.74	0.96
2nd quarter	-1.2	3.69	-7.96	-1.54	-0.34	-6.08	0.05	-0.17	0.22	3.02	1.54	1.48
3rd quarter	4.6	0.18	4.97	-1.86	1.75	5.08	-1.33	-1.91	0.59	0.75	-0.42	1.17
4th quarter	-4.0	3.32	-2.95	-0.60	2.67	-5.02	-2.88	-2.70	-0.18	-1.50	-2.05	0.56
1950												
1st quarter	17.4	4.16	14.93	1.12	3.10	10.72	-0.55	-0.22	-0.33	-1.08	-1.86	0.78
2nd quarter	12.5	4.18	7.64	3.40	2.76	1.47	-0.50	0.23	-0.73	1.18	0.91	0.27
3rd quarter	16.6	14.05	6.52	3.53	1.66	1.32	-2.80	0.44	-3.25	-1.13	-1.15	0.02
4th quarter	7.5	-7.70	9.90	-0.06	-1.36	11.32	1.26	1.31	-0.05	4.04	4.02	0.01
1951												
1st quarter	4.9	6.42	-9.05	-1.04	-1.46	-6.55	0.76	0.81	-0.05	6.78	7.06	-0.28
2nd quarter	7.0	-6.92	1.76	0.54	-3.43	4.65	2.38	1.82	0.56	9.75	9.29	0.46
3rd quarter	8.2	2.95	-5.78	0.45	-1.38	-4.85	2.05	0.52	1.53	9.02	8.89	0.13
4th quarter	0.7	1.39	-5.75	-0.75	0.18	-5.17	0.22	-0.15	0.37	4.81	4.86	-0.04
1952												
1st quarter	4.2	0.24	1.51	0.21	0.59	0.71	-0.63	1.23	-1.85	3.11	3.02	0.10
2nd quarter	0.3	4.54	-5.15	0.44	0.37	-5.97	-2.16	-2.18	0.02	3.06	2.46	0.60
3rd quarter	2.6	0.92	3.08	-3.29	-0.21	6.58	-2.31	-1.31	-1.00	0.93	1.67	-0.74
4th quarter	13.8	8.94	4.38	3.20	1.17	0.01	-1.26	0.22	-1.48	1.75	1.07	0.68
1953												
1st quarter	7.7	3.03	1.17	1.95	0.34	-1.11	0.25	-0.18	0.42	3.28	2.67	0.61
2nd quarter	3.1	1.39	0.19	0.26	0.06	-0.13	-0.68	0.17	-0.85	2.18	2.23	-0.04
3rd quarter	-2.4	-0.74	-1.29	0.84	-0.78	-1.34	0.73	0.71	0.03	-1.10	-1.84	0.74
4th quarter	-6.2	-1.78	-4.35	-0.42	-0.16	-3.77	0.25	-0.55	0.80	-0.26	-0.93	0.67
1954												
1st quarter	-2.0	0.66	-0.30	-1.09	0.21	0.58	0.14	-0.76	0.90	-2.45	-3.50	1.05
2nd quarter	0.4	2.99	-0.08	-0.37	1.31	-1.03	0.70	2.16	-1.46	-3.25	-3.37	0.12
3rd quarter	4.5	3.25	3.00	1.04	1.36	0.60	0.38	-0.61	0.99	-2.13	-2.99	0.86
4th quarter	8.2	5.35	2.83	-0.09	1.49	1.43	0.54	0.73	-0.20	-0.54	-0.68	0.15
1955												
1st quarter	12.0	5.84	6.68	0.69	1.86	4.13	-0.38	0.58	-0.96	-0.12	-1.41	1.28
2nd quarter	6.7	4.79	4.11	2.32	0.35	1.44	-1.35	-0.43	-0.91	-0.83	-1.24	0.41
3rd quarter	5.4	3.17	0.93	1.93	-0.55	-0.45	0.78	1.08	-0.31	0.56	0.61	-0.05
4th quarter	2.2	3.07	1.40	1.06	-1.05	1.39	-0.57	0.04	-0.61	-1.74	-1.92	0.19
1956												
1st quarter	-1.9	0.31	-2.16	-0.69	-0.57	-0.90	0.05	0.79	-0.74	-0.03	-0.37	0.33
2nd quarter	3.2	0.75	-0.76	0.63	-0.15	-1.24	1.34	1.28	0.06	1.87	1.46	0.41
3rd quarter	-0.5	0.47	-0.70	0.33	-0.44	-0.59	0.48	0.66	-0.18	-0.73	-0.90	0.16
4th quarter	6.7	3.43	-0.69	-0.09	-0.33	-0.27	1.73	0.93	0.80	2.22	1.88	0.34
1957												
1st quarter	2.4	1.59	-0.89	0.30	-0.30	-0.90	-0.01	1.35	-1.36	1.77	0.94	0.83
2nd quarter	-1.0	0.33	-0.09	-0.10	-0.48	0.49	-0.73	-0.57	-0.16	-0.51	-0.80	0.29
3rd quarter	4.0	2.06	1.46	0.91	-0.25	0.80	-0.26	-0.57	0.32	0.72	0.22	0.49
4th quarter	-4.2	0.07	-5.24	-1.03	-0.03	-4.19	-0.64	-0.57	-0.07	1.65	0.80	0.85
1958												
1st quarter	-10.4	-3.29	-4.21	-2.72	-0.69	-0.80	-2.05	-1.81	-0.24	-0.87	-1.84	0.98
2nd quarter	2.4	2.01	-1.33	-1.61	0.05	0.23	-0.64	0.11	-0.75	2.34	1.80	0.53
3rd quarter	9.6	4.14	4.58	-0.54	1.36	3.76	0.29	0.10	0.20	0.55	-0.26	0.82
4th quarter	9.5	3.13	5.44	1.35	2.10	1.99	-0.97	-0.01	-0.96	1.94	1.24	0.69
1959												
1st quarter	7.9	3.94	3.89	1.11	2.37	0.41	0.76	1.18	-0.42	-0.72	-1.02	0.30
2nd quarter	10.9	4.26	5.69	1.14	0.83	3.73	-0.31	0.63	-0.94	1.32	1.21	0.11
3rd quarter	-0.3	2.72	-4.42	1.14	-0.43	-5.13	0.37	0.59	-0.23	1.03	0.99	0.04
4th quarter	1.4	0.33	2.07	-0.15	-0.63	2.86	-0.04	-0.49	0.45	-0.95	-0.77	-0.18
1960												
1st quarter	9.2	2.47	6.70	1.49	0.65	4.57	1.70	2.30	-0.60	-1.63	-2.24	0.62
2nd quarter	-2.0	3.13	-6.92	0.58	-1.76	-5.74	1.15	1.26	-0.10	0.66	-0.20	0.85
3rd quarter	0.6	-0.99	-0.46	-0.94	-0.60	1.08	0.01	-0.54	0.54	2.07	1.52	0.55
4th quarter	-5.1	0.31	-7.21	-0.18	-0.03	-7.00	1.26	0.43	0.83	0.58	0.16	0.42

. . . = Not available.

Table 19-3. Contributions to Percent Change in Real Gross Domestic Product—Continued

(Percent; percentage points.) NIPA Table 1.1.2

Year and quarter	Percent change at seasonally adjusted annual rate, GDP	Personal consumption expenditures	Gross private domestic investment				Exports and imports of goods and services			Government consumption expenditures and gross investment		
			Total	Fixed investment		Change in private inventories	Net exports	Exports	Imports	Total	Federal	State and local
				Nonresidential	Residential							
1961												
1st quarter	2.4	-0.03	1.40	-0.76	0.07	2.08	-0.07	-0.14	0.07	1.12	-0.08	1.20
2nd quarter	7.7	3.89	4.14	0.77	0.07	3.30	-0.48	-0.28	-0.20	0.19	0.45	-0.26
3rd quarter	6.6	1.25	4.84	0.30	1.03	3.51	-1.17	-0.11	-1.06	1.74	1.41	0.32
4th quarter	8.4	5.15	1.11	1.20	0.66	-0.75	0.21	0.62	-0.40	1.95	0.88	1.07
1962												
1st quarter	7.4	2.69	3.66	0.82	0.36	2.48	-0.56	-0.05	-0.51	1.59	1.86	-0.27
2nd quarter	4.4	3.02	-0.56	1.05	0.62	-2.23	1.51	1.88	-0.37	0.47	0.20	0.27
3rd quarter	3.7	2.03	1.10	0.46	-0.02	0.65	-1.38	-1.17	-0.21	1.99	1.52	0.48
4th quarter	1.0	3.53	-2.05	-0.26	-0.03	-1.77	-0.63	-0.42	-0.21	0.13	-0.28	0.41
1963												
1st quarter	5.3	1.74	3.30	-0.06	0.73	2.63	0.88	0.46	0.41	-0.53	-1.25	0.72
2nd quarter	5.1	2.43	0.88	1.13	1.44	-1.70	1.90	2.29	-0.38	-0.12	-0.46	0.35
3rd quarter	7.7	3.45	2.02	1.11	0.39	0.52	-1.53	-1.11	-0.42	3.80	2.76	1.04
4th quarter	3.1	2.10	0.80	1.19	0.63	-1.02	1.05	0.99	0.06	-0.81	-1.35	0.54
1964												
1st quarter	9.3	5.00	2.64	0.93	1.32	0.38	1.30	1.27	0.02	0.33	-0.25	0.58
2nd quarter	4.7	4.42	-0.25	0.95	-1.10	-0.09	-0.02	0.35	-0.37	0.58	-0.31	0.89
3rd quarter	5.6	4.66	1.46	1.29	-0.33	0.50	-0.60	-0.16	-0.44	0.06	-0.36	0.43
4th quarter	1.1	0.71	0.44	0.81	-0.36	0.00	0.17	0.62	-0.45	-0.24	-0.66	0.42
1965												
1st quarter	10.2	5.68	6.36	2.72	0.07	3.56	-1.65	-2.29	0.64	-0.18	-0.56	0.38
2nd quarter	5.5	2.83	-0.09	1.52	0.15	-1.77	1.68	3.59	-1.91	1.10	0.08	1.02
3rd quarter	8.4	4.36	2.34	1.59	0.08	0.67	-1.31	-1.23	-0.07	2.96	1.82	1.14
4th quarter	10.0	7.18	0.32	1.77	-0.41	-1.04	0.62	1.48	-0.86	1.91	1.31	0.60
1966												
1st quarter	10.1	3.74	5.68	1.88	0.42	3.38	-0.82	-0.36	-0.46	1.55	1.05	0.50
2nd quarter	1.4	0.67	-1.22	0.65	-1.47	-0.40	0.45	0.89	-0.45	1.49	1.19	0.31
3rd quarter	2.7	2.80	-0.65	0.51	-0.55	-0.61	-1.82	-0.80	-1.02	2.33	1.86	0.46
4th quarter	3.3	1.02	0.32	-0.12	-1.70	2.14	0.48	0.68	-0.20	1.44	0.38	1.06
1967												
1st quarter	3.6	1.44	-1.83	-0.91	-0.43	-0.49	0.16	0.41	-0.25	3.82	3.30	0.52
2nd quarter	0.0	3.25	-2.69	-0.15	1.58	-4.11	-0.03	-0.20	0.17	-0.51	-0.74	0.23
3rd quarter	3.2	1.27	1.73	-0.21	0.77	1.17	-0.74	-0.51	-0.24	0.97	0.80	0.17
4th quarter	3.1	1.49	1.32	0.84	0.94	-0.46	-0.41	0.58	-0.99	0.65	-0.09	0.74
1968												
1st quarter	8.5	5.97	1.38	1.34	0.11	-0.06	-0.54	0.60	-1.15	1.70	0.93	0.77
2nd quarter	7.0	3.85	2.57	-0.73	0.43	2.87	0.10	0.42	-0.31	0.45	-0.39	0.84
3rd quarter	2.7	4.59	-2.06	0.52	0.30	-2.89	0.01	1.22	-1.21	0.22	-0.40	0.62
4th quarter	1.7	1.09	0.63	1.18	0.21	-0.77	-0.10	-0.27	0.17	0.07	-0.30	0.37
1969												
1st quarter	6.5	2.80	4.16	1.23	0.65	2.28	-0.58	-2.53	1.94	0.10	-0.26	0.36
2nd quarter	1.1	1.54	-0.49	0.45	-0.19	-0.75	0.50	4.08	-3.58	-0.39	-0.75	0.36
3rd quarter	2.5	1.13	1.51	1.14	-0.14	0.52	-0.25	-0.53	0.28	0.12	0.03	0.09
4th quarter	-1.9	1.92	-3.44	-0.25	-1.27	-1.92	0.98	0.74	0.24	-1.34	-1.25	-0.09
1970												
1st quarter	-0.7	1.46	-1.90	-0.23	0.03	-1.70	0.26	0.19	0.08	-0.50	-0.91	0.41
2nd quarter	0.8	1.17	0.20	-0.23	-1.08	1.51	0.57	0.98	-0.41	-1.18	-1.43	0.25
3rd quarter	3.6	2.23	1.00	0.20	0.81	-0.01	-0.03	-0.08	0.05	0.40	-0.64	1.04
4th quarter	-4.2	-0.66	-3.42	-1.61	1.61	-3.43	-0.12	0.21	-0.33	0.00	-0.24	0.24
1971												
1st quarter	11.6	5.09	7.60	0.32	0.96	6.33	0.36	0.09	0.26	-1.42	-1.64	0.22
2nd quarter	2.3	2.34	1.86	0.57	1.80	-0.51	-1.63	-0.05	-1.59	-0.28	-0.60	0.32
3rd quarter	3.2	2.03	0.83	0.18	0.97	-0.32	0.43	0.92	-0.49	-0.08	-0.19	0.12
4th quarter	1.1	4.14	-1.98	0.92	0.79	-3.69	-0.35	-1.93	1.57	-0.67	-1.27	0.60
1972												
1st quarter	7.3	3.34	4.54	1.49	1.44	1.62	-0.89	2.23	-3.12	0.31	0.15	0.16
2nd quarter	9.8	4.83	4.22	0.78	0.45	2.99	0.21	-0.68	0.89	0.55	0.65	-0.10
3rd quarter	3.9	3.77	1.05	0.68	0.05	0.32	0.82	1.30	-0.48	-1.78	-2.16	0.38
4th quarter	6.7	5.83	0.45	2.17	0.80	-2.53	-0.11	0.95	-1.07	0.55	-0.11	0.66
1973												
1st quarter	10.6	4.61	4.47	2.02	0.80	1.65	0.59	1.73	-1.14	0.88	0.67	0.22
2nd quarter	4.7	-0.14	3.36	1.75	-1.19	2.80	1.96	1.20	0.75	-0.47	-0.55	0.08
3rd quarter	-2.1	0.87	-2.72	0.73	-0.95	-2.50	0.78	0.06	0.71	-1.04	-1.52	0.48
4th quarter	3.9	-0.72	2.84	0.34	-1.03	3.53	1.17	1.39	-0.22	0.59	0.02	0.57
1974												
1st quarter	-3.4	-2.09	-4.40	-0.07	-1.48	-2.84	1.38	0.37	1.01	1.69	1.07	0.62
2nd quarter	1.2	1.07	-0.34	-0.11	-0.82	0.59	-0.15	1.56	-1.71	0.58	-0.07	0.65
3rd quarter	-3.8	1.15	-3.85	-0.51	-0.58	-2.76	-1.24	-1.85	0.61	0.12	0.18	-0.06
4th quarter	-1.6	-3.45	0.33	-1.27	-2.33	3.93	1.26	0.90	0.36	0.31	0.29	0.03
1975												
1st quarter	-4.7	2.15	-11.74	-2.70	-0.93	-8.11	3.84	0.23	3.61	1.08	-0.40	1.48
2nd quarter	3.0	4.21	-2.11	-1.13	0.32	-1.30	1.52	-1.05	2.56	-0.65	-0.28	-0.37
3rd quarter	6.9	3.69	4.53	0.39	1.06	3.08	-2.86	-0.57	-2.29	1.59	0.94	0.65
4th quarter	5.4	2.68	1.64	0.37	0.69	0.58	0.26	1.81	-1.56	0.77	0.11	0.67

Table 19-3. Contributions to Percent Change in Real Gross Domestic Product—Continued

(Percent; percentage points.)   NIPA Table 1.1.2

Year and quarter	Percent change at seasonally adjusted annual rate, GDP	Personal consumption expenditures	Gross private domestic investment				Exports and imports of goods and services			Government consumption expenditures and gross investment		
			Total	Fixed investment		Change in private inventories	Net exports	Exports	Imports	Total	Federal	State and local
				Nonresidential	Residential							
1976												
1st quarter	9.3	5.03	6.17	0.73	1.63	3.80	-2.12	-0.23	-1.89	0.24	-0.33	0.56
2nd quarter	3.0	2.23	2.76	0.47	0.50	1.79	-1.04	0.33	-1.37	-0.93	-0.06	-0.86
3rd quarter	1.9	2.63	0.12	0.89	-0.29	-0.47	-0.39	0.94	-1.33	-0.43	-0.09	-0.34
4th quarter	2.9	3.39	0.34	0.83	2.24	-2.73	-0.77	0.34	-1.11	-0.06	0.10	-0.15
1977												
1st quarter	4.9	3.14	3.07	1.74	0.62	0.71	-2.08	-0.51	-1.57	0.78	0.31	0.47
2nd quarter	8.1	1.43	5.23	1.33	2.40	1.50	0.55	0.87	-0.33	0.89	0.60	0.29
3rd quarter	7.4	2.46	3.98	0.99	-0.07	3.06	0.77	0.25	0.53	0.15	0.20	-0.05
4th quarter	0.0	3.69	-1.94	1.56	-0.30	-3.20	-1.53	-1.03	-0.50	-0.27	-0.34	0.07
1978												
1st quarter	1.3	1.35	1.63	0.51	0.10	1.02	-1.83	0.67	-2.50	0.12	0.11	0.01
2nd quarter	16.7	5.68	5.56	4.18	1.14	0.23	3.23	3.34	-0.11	2.27	0.85	1.42
3rd quarter	4.0	1.06	2.45	1.71	0.31	0.43	-0.12	0.35	-0.48	0.61	0.11	0.50
4th quarter	5.4	2.01	1.85	1.62	-0.08	0.31	0.80	1.31	-0.50	0.71	0.29	0.43
1979												
1st quarter	0.8	1.34	-0.03	1.04	-0.54	-0.53	0.14	0.03	0.10	-0.67	0.04	-0.71
2nd quarter	0.4	-0.12	-0.18	-0.21	-0.43	0.46	-0.10	0.09	-0.19	0.78	0.39	0.40
3rd quarter	2.9	2.42	-1.50	1.56	-0.27	-2.79	1.87	1.24	0.63	0.12	-0.05	0.16
4th quarter	1.2	0.68	-1.40	0.10	-0.86	-0.64	1.39	2.22	-0.84	0.51	0.01	0.50
1980												
1st quarter	1.3	-0.45	-0.49	0.55	-1.65	0.61	1.02	0.97	0.05	1.19	1.00	0.19
2nd quarter	-7.8	-5.56	-6.62	-2.68	-3.61	-0.33	4.09	0.75	3.35	0.26	0.87	-0.61
3rd quarter	-0.7	2.72	-5.29	0.38	0.28	-5.95	3.04	-0.07	3.10	-1.14	-0.47	-0.67
4th quarter	7.6	3.44	6.58	1.11	1.66	3.82	-2.30	-0.20	-2.10	-0.08	0.12	-0.20
1981												
1st quarter	8.4	1.15	7.08	0.86	-0.31	6.53	-0.92	0.83	-1.75	1.09	0.74	0.36
2nd quarter	-3.1	0.07	-3.50	1.06	-0.58	-3.99	0.18	0.26	-0.08	0.18	1.04	-0.86
3rd quarter	4.9	1.01	4.46	1.32	-1.28	4.43	-0.36	-0.82	0.46	-0.17	-0.03	-0.14
4th quarter	-4.9	-1.83	-2.89	1.33	-1.55	-2.67	-0.92	0.17	-1.09	0.76	0.40	0.36
1982												
1st quarter	-6.4	1.64	-7.46	-1.28	-0.78	-5.40	-0.52	-1.67	1.15	-0.06	0.08	-0.13
2nd quarter	2.2	0.88	-0.05	-1.98	-0.42	2.35	0.83	0.20	0.63	0.50	0.36	0.14
3rd quarter	-1.5	1.93	-0.68	-1.82	-0.04	1.18	-3.32	-1.62	-1.70	0.57	0.57	0.00
4th quarter	0.4	4.60	-5.61	-1.07	0.92	-5.46	-0.08	-1.56	1.48	1.44	1.13	0.31
1983												
1st quarter	5.0	2.48	2.20	-1.00	2.26	0.94	-0.29	0.51	-0.80	0.63	0.47	0.16
2nd quarter	9.3	5.25	5.88	0.52	1.86	3.50	-2.53	0.10	-2.63	0.73	0.85	-0.11
3rd quarter	8.1	4.71	4.26	2.05	1.70	0.51	-2.31	0.47	-2.79	1.47	1.11	0.36
4th quarter	8.4	4.22	6.83	3.03	0.79	3.01	-1.21	0.63	-1.84	-1.39	-1.36	-0.03
1984												
1st quarter	8.1	2.34	7.29	1.59	0.54	5.17	-2.35	0.66	-3.01	0.82	0.31	0.51
2nd quarter	7.1	3.83	2.34	2.44	0.35	-0.45	-0.91	0.77	-1.68	1.80	1.22	0.58
3rd quarter	3.9	2.06	1.65	1.67	-0.17	0.15	-0.38	0.67	-1.05	0.61	-0.15	0.76
4th quarter	3.3	3.42	-1.28	1.22	0.02	-2.52	-0.58	0.61	-1.19	1.77	1.28	0.49
1985												
1st quarter	3.8	4.30	-2.40	0.61	-0.06	-2.95	0.90	0.01	0.89	0.95	0.42	0.52
2nd quarter	3.5	2.35	1.24	0.73	0.14	0.36	-2.00	-0.12	-1.87	1.86	0.96	0.90
3rd quarter	6.4	4.95	-0.72	-0.76	0.23	-0.18	-0.02	-0.44	0.42	2.19	1.33	0.86
4th quarter	3.1	0.57	2.71	0.84	0.42	1.45	-0.68	0.81	-1.49	0.50	-0.01	0.51
1986												
1st quarter	3.9	2.10	-0.06	-0.68	0.78	-0.16	0.95	0.85	0.10	0.89	-0.21	1.10
2nd quarter	1.6	2.69	-1.50	-1.22	1.05	-1.33	-1.37	0.28	-1.65	1.77	1.22	0.55
3rd quarter	3.9	4.48	-2.08	-0.70	0.31	-1.68	-0.47	0.63	-1.10	1.95	1.51	0.44
4th quarter	2.0	1.65	0.12	0.44	-0.04	-0.28	0.72	1.06	-0.33	-0.46	-0.59	0.13
1987												
1st quarter	2.7	0.10	2.09	-1.26	-0.06	3.41	0.23	0.02	0.21	0.25	0.27	-0.02
2nd quarter	4.5	3.64	0.09	1.03	0.09	-1.02	0.11	1.19	-1.08	0.63	0.60	0.03
3rd quarter	3.7	3.00	0.06	1.40	-0.06	-1.29	0.45	1.31	-0.86	0.17	0.08	0.09
4th quarter	7.2	0.66	5.17	-0.11	0.10	5.18	0.15	1.16	-1.02	1.21	0.62	0.58
1988												
1st quarter	2.0	4.33	-3.88	0.34	-0.42	-3.80	1.98	1.78	0.20	-0.46	-1.01	0.55
2nd quarter	5.2	1.92	1.57	1.11	0.15	0.31	1.48	0.96	0.52	0.21	-0.35	0.56
3rd quarter	2.1	2.20	0.40	0.23	0.01	0.15	-0.35	0.64	-1.00	-0.09	-0.25	0.16
4th quarter	5.4	3.15	0.85	0.47	0.17	0.21	-0.22	1.07	-1.29	1.61	1.10	0.51
1989												
1st quarter	4.1	0.99	2.48	0.75	-0.12	1.85	1.15	1.02	0.12	-0.49	-0.72	0.23
2nd quarter	2.6	1.25	-0.78	0.62	-0.54	-0.86	0.92	1.57	-0.64	1.25	0.80	0.45
3rd quarter	2.9	2.51	-0.76	1.26	-0.19	-1.84	0.38	0.43	-0.05	0.76	0.35	0.41
4th quarter	1.0	1.20	-0.66	-0.67	-0.36	0.37	0.05	0.60	-0.55	0.43	-0.17	0.60
1990												
1st quarter	4.7	2.19	0.60	0.58	0.17	-0.16	0.64	1.57	-0.93	1.28	0.54	0.74
2nd quarter	1.0	0.85	0.03	-0.77	-0.64	1.43	0.02	0.48	-0.47	0.14	0.05	0.09
3rd quarter	0.0	1.06	-1.42	0.25	-0.92	-0.76	0.39	0.31	0.08	0.00	-0.30	0.30
4th quarter	-3.0	-1.92	-3.70	-0.84	-0.83	-2.03	1.81	0.39	1.42	0.82	0.31	0.51

Table 19-3. Contributions to Percent Change in Real Gross Domestic Product—Continued

(Percent; percentage points.) NIPA Table 1.1.2

Year and quarter	Percent change at seasonally adjusted annual rate, GDP	Personal consump-tion expen-ditures	Gross private domestic investment				Exports and imports of goods and services			Government consumption expenditures and gross investment		
			Total	Fixed investment		Change in private inventories	Net exports	Exports	Imports	Total	Federal	State and local
				Nonresi-dential	Residential							
1991												
1st quarter	-2.0	-1.18	-2.25	-1.14	-0.87	-0.24	1.08	0.18	0.90	0.33	0.27	0.06
2nd quarter	2.6	2.29	-0.22	-0.41	0.31	-0.12	0.26	1.43	-1.16	0.29	0.11	0.18
3rd quarter	1.9	1.14	1.31	-0.40	0.56	1.15	-0.12	0.95	-1.07	-0.38	-0.65	0.27
4th quarter	1.9	-0.24	2.02	-0.23	0.30	1.94	0.43	0.92	-0.49	-0.32	-0.67	0.35
1992												
1st quarter	4.2	4.50	-1.26	-0.19	0.72	-1.79	0.32	0.68	-0.37	0.65	0.02	0.64
2nd quarter	3.9	1.56	3.45	1.50	0.56	1.39	-1.01	0.02	-1.03	-0.08	-0.03	-0.06
3rd quarter	4.0	2.70	0.58	0.78	0.03	-0.24	0.26	0.86	-0.60	0.44	0.40	0.04
4th quarter	4.5	3.14	1.80	1.18	0.51	0.11	-0.47	0.22	-0.70	0.02	0.02	0.00
1993												
1st quarter	0.5	0.92	1.34	0.25	0.07	1.03	-0.93	0.05	-0.98	-0.85	-1.04	0.19
2nd quarter	2.0	2.37	0.48	1.04	0.18	-0.75	-0.72	0.46	-1.18	-0.08	-0.47	0.38
3rd quarter	2.1	2.95	0.01	0.44	0.54	-0.96	-0.67	-0.10	-0.56	-0.22	-0.46	0.24
4th quarter	5.5	2.47	2.97	1.69	0.83	0.45	-0.25	1.29	-1.53	0.29	0.08	0.21
1994												
1st quarter	4.1	3.07	2.47	0.39	0.34	1.74	-0.65	0.34	-0.99	-0.76	-0.90	0.14
2nd quarter	5.3	1.98	3.56	0.81	0.58	2.17	-0.56	1.31	-1.86	0.33	-0.16	0.49
3rd quarter	2.3	1.94	-1.11	0.75	-0.18	-1.68	0.20	1.49	-1.29	1.23	0.71	0.52
4th quarter	4.8	2.71	2.89	1.82	-0.22	1.29	-0.19	0.93	-1.12	-0.64	-0.80	0.16
1995												
1st quarter	1.1	0.39	0.69	1.68	-0.38	-0.61	-0.26	0.72	-0.98	0.28	-0.06	0.34
2nd quarter	0.7	2.21	-1.68	0.29	-0.53	-1.44	-0.11	0.59	-0.70	0.31	-0.05	0.36
3rd quarter	3.3	2.37	-0.58	0.29	0.50	-1.37	1.75	1.92	-0.17	-0.24	-0.27	0.03
4th quarter	3.0	1.87	1.70	0.88	0.38	0.44	0.21	0.68	-0.47	-0.82	-1.06	0.24
1996												
1st quarter	2.9	2.46	0.76	1.09	0.44	-0.77	-0.85	0.56	-1.42	0.49	0.59	-0.10
2nd quarter	6.7	3.02	3.17	1.29	0.73	1.15	-0.71	0.77	-1.48	1.23	0.56	0.67
3rd quarter	3.4	1.74	3.14	1.48	-0.05	1.71	-1.23	0.38	-1.61	-0.25	-0.66	0.40
4th quarter	4.8	2.28	-0.25	1.20	-0.18	-1.27	2.09	2.75	-0.66	0.64	-0.05	0.69
1997												
1st quarter	3.1	2.89	1.40	1.14	0.06	0.21	-1.22	0.82	-2.03	0.06	-0.34	0.40
2nd quarter	6.2	1.27	4.39	1.14	0.22	3.03	-0.18	1.81	-1.99	0.73	0.57	0.16
3rd quarter	5.1	4.42	1.38	2.34	0.08	-1.04	-0.73	1.10	-1.83	0.01	-0.15	0.16
4th quarter	3.0	2.78	1.12	0.37	0.17	0.57	-0.87	-0.04	-0.83	0.01	-0.15	0.16
1998												
1st quarter	4.5	2.98	3.53	1.57	0.35	1.61	-1.65	0.20	-1.85	-0.41	-0.66	0.25
2nd quarter	2.7	4.25	-1.12	1.44	0.47	-3.04	-1.86	-0.48	-1.38	1.40	0.61	0.79
3rd quarter	4.7	3.29	1.57	0.45	0.48	0.64	-0.82	-0.19	-0.63	0.66	-0.19	0.85
4th quarter	6.2	3.71	1.71	1.49	0.44	-0.22	0.13	1.59	-1.46	0.64	0.20	0.44
1999												
1st quarter	3.4	2.68	1.96	0.87	0.16	0.93	-1.67	-0.39	-1.28	0.46	-0.14	0.60
2nd quarter	3.4	4.23	0.05	1.47	0.16	-1.57	-1.35	0.48	-1.83	0.41	0.09	0.32
3rd quarter	4.8	2.90	1.72	1.19	0.11	0.42	-0.75	1.12	-1.87	0.88	0.49	0.39
4th quarter	7.3	3.47	2.65	0.12	0.23	2.30	0.01	1.13	-1.11	1.17	0.58	0.59
2000												
1st quarter	1.0	4.38	-1.30	1.64	0.19	-3.13	-1.53	0.70	-2.23	-0.56	-0.93	0.36
2nd quarter	6.4	1.78	4.65	1.76	-0.16	3.05	-0.98	1.30	-2.27	0.96	0.96	0.01
3rd quarter	-0.5	2.62	-1.84	0.28	-0.38	-1.74	-0.87	1.14	-2.01	-0.37	-0.51	0.15
4th quarter	2.1	2.29	-0.36	0.11	0.02	-0.49	-0.07	-0.31	0.24	0.22	-0.07	0.29
2001												
1st quarter	-0.5	1.07	-2.44	-0.52	0.10	-2.01	-0.04	-0.59	0.56	0.92	0.46	0.46
2nd quarter	1.2	0.67	-1.28	-1.76	0.25	0.23	0.49	-1.45	1.94	1.35	0.52	0.83
3rd quarter	-1.4	1.20	-1.76	-0.83	0.08	-1.02	-0.56	-2.04	1.48	-0.28	0.00	-0.28
4th quarter	1.6	4.71	-3.95	-1.63	-0.18	-2.14	-0.66	-1.11	0.45	1.48	0.51	0.97
2002												
1st quarter	2.7	1.01	1.92	-1.50	0.46	2.95	-0.97	0.47	-1.44	0.79	0.36	0.43
2nd quarter	2.2	1.64	0.30	-0.66	0.43	0.53	-0.62	0.96	-1.58	0.88	0.76	0.12
3rd quarter	2.4	1.57	0.87	-0.21	0.09	0.98	-0.49	0.27	-0.76	0.43	0.20	0.23
4th quarter	0.2	0.97	-0.14	-0.52	0.30	0.08	-1.52	-0.31	-1.21	0.89	0.64	0.25
2003												
1st quarter	1.2	1.41	-0.16	-0.24	0.20	-0.12	0.21	-0.53	0.74	-0.26	0.01	-0.27
2nd quarter	3.5	2.53	0.51	1.01	0.51	-1.01	-0.73	-0.16	-0.57	1.16	1.26	-0.10
3rd quarter	7.5	4.13	2.56	0.92	1.08	0.56	0.51	1.02	-0.51	0.29	0.03	0.26
4th quarter	2.7	1.59	1.39	0.29	0.55	0.56	-0.47	1.81	-2.29	0.14	0.21	-0.07
2004												
1st quarter	3.9	3.30	0.74	0.18	0.16	0.40	-0.73	0.69	-1.42	0.55	0.49	0.06
2nd quarter	4.0	2.07	3.17	0.69	1.03	1.44	-1.62	0.60	-2.22	0.43	0.18	0.25
3rd quarter	3.1	2.74	0.32	0.97	0.18	-0.84	-0.20	0.46	-0.66	0.24	0.34	-0.10
4th quarter	2.6	2.97	0.82	0.81	-0.04	0.05	-0.81	0.96	-1.77	-0.37	-0.38	0.01
2005												
1st quarter	3.4	1.94	1.32	0.59	0.63	0.09	-0.16	0.47	-0.63	0.31	0.23	0.08
2nd quarter	3.3	2.90	-0.60	0.50	1.10	-2.20	0.70	0.90	-0.20	0.20	0.00	0.20
3rd quarter	4.2	2.80	0.80	0.60	0.40	-0.20	-0.10	0.30	-0.40	0.60	0.70	0.00
4th quarter	1.8	0.53	2.51	0.52	-0.06	2.05	-1.07	0.97	-2.04	-0.21	-0.33	0.13

Table 19-4. Chain-Type Quantity Indexes for Gross Domestic Product and Domestic Purchases

(Index numbers, 2000 = 100.)

NIPA Tables 1.1.3, 1.4.3, 2.3.3

Year and quarter	Gross domestic product, total	Personal consumption expenditures		Private fixed investment			Exports and imports of goods and services		Government consumption expenditures and gross investment			Gross domestic purchases
		Total	Excluding food and energy	Total	Nonresidential	Residential	Exports	Imports	Total	Federal	State and local	
1946	16.2	15.0	11.2	9.0	7.1	16.6	5.9	3.2	23.0	43.0	11.6	15.4
1947	16.0	15.3	11.7	10.8	8.2	21.3	6.7	3.0	19.6	31.8	13.2	15.1
1948	16.7	15.6	12.2	11.9	8.7	25.5	5.3	3.5	21.0	34.3	14.0	16.1
1949	16.7	16.1	12.6	10.9	7.9	23.6	5.2	3.4	23.5	37.6	16.2	16.0
1947												
1st quarter	16.0	15.1	. . .	10.6	8.3	19.6	7.1	3.1	19.5	32.0	12.9	15.0
2nd quarter	16.0	15.3	. . .	10.3	8.2	18.6	7.1	3.2	19.6	32.1	13.0	15.0
3rd quarter	16.0	15.4	. . .	10.7	8.0	21.5	6.7	2.8	19.8	32.1	13.3	15.0
4th quarter	16.2	15.4	. . .	11.6	8.3	25.6	6.0	3.0	19.5	31.0	13.6	15.4
1948												
1st quarter	16.5	15.5	. . .	12.0	8.8	25.3	5.7	3.4	19.9	32.0	13.5	15.8
2nd quarter	16.8	15.6	. . .	12.0	8.5	26.8	5.1	3.5	20.8	33.9	13.9	16.2
3rd quarter	16.8	15.7	. . .	11.9	8.5	26.0	5.3	3.7	21.2	34.7	14.2	16.3
4th quarter	16.9	15.8	. . .	11.7	8.8	24.1	5.1	3.6	22.1	36.5	14.5	16.3
1949												
1st quarter	16.6	15.8	. . .	11.0	8.3	22.2	5.7	3.5	22.8	37.3	15.1	16.0
2nd quarter	16.6	16.1	. . .	10.7	8.0	21.9	5.6	3.4	23.8	38.7	16.0	15.9
3rd quarter	16.8	16.1	. . .	10.7	7.6	23.7	5.2	3.3	24.0	38.3	16.6	16.1
4th quarter	16.6	16.3	. . .	11.0	7.5	26.6	4.5	3.4	23.5	36.3	17.0	16.1
1950												
1st quarter	17.3	16.6	. . .	11.8	7.7	29.7	4.4	3.4	23.1	34.6	17.4	16.8
2nd quarter	17.8	16.9	. . .	12.8	8.4	32.5	4.5	3.6	23.5	35.4	17.5	17.3
3rd quarter	18.5	17.7	. . .	13.8	9.1	34.3	4.6	4.5	23.0	34.1	17.5	18.1
4th quarter	18.8	17.2	. . .	13.5	9.1	32.7	4.9	4.5	24.5	38.2	17.6	18.4
1951												
1st quarter	19.1	17.6	. . .	13.0	8.9	31.0	5.2	4.5	27.1	45.6	17.4	18.6
2nd quarter	19.4	17.1	. . .	12.4	9.0	26.8	5.7	4.4	30.9	55.4	17.7	18.8
3rd quarter	19.8	17.3	. . .	12.2	9.1	25.1	5.8	4.0	34.4	64.9	17.8	19.1
4th quarter	19.8	17.4	. . .	12.1	8.9	25.3	5.8	3.9	36.2	70.1	17.7	19.1
1952												
1st quarter	20.0	17.5	. . .	12.2	9.0	26.0	6.1	4.3	37.4	73.3	17.8	19.3
2nd quarter	20.0	17.8	. . .	12.4	9.1	26.5	5.4	4.3	38.6	76.2	18.2	19.5
3rd quarter	20.2	17.9	. . .	11.6	8.2	26.2	5.0	4.6	39.0	78.2	17.7	19.7
4th quarter	20.8	18.5	. . .	12.5	9.0	27.6	5.0	5.0	39.7	79.4	18.1	20.4
1953												
1st quarter	21.2	18.7	. . .	13.0	9.5	28.0	4.9	4.9	41.1	82.4	18.5	20.8
2nd quarter	21.4	18.9	. . .	13.1	9.5	28.1	5.0	5.1	42.0	85.0	18.4	21.0
3rd quarter	21.2	18.8	. . .	13.1	9.7	27.0	5.2	5.1	41.5	82.7	18.9	20.8
4th quarter	20.9	18.7	. . .	13.0	9.6	26.8	5.0	4.8	41.4	81.6	19.4	20.5
1954												
1st quarter	20.8	18.8	. . .	12.8	9.3	27.1	4.8	4.6	40.2	77.2	20.1	20.4
2nd quarter	20.8	19.0	. . .	13.0	9.2	28.9	5.5	5.0	38.8	73.0	20.2	20.4
3rd quarter	21.1	19.2	. . .	13.5	9.5	30.6	5.3	4.7	37.9	69.4	20.7	20.6
4th quarter	21.5	19.6	. . .	13.8	9.5	32.5	5.5	4.7	37.6	68.6	20.8	20.9
1955												
1st quarter	22.1	20.1	. . .	14.3	9.6	35.0	5.7	5.0	37.6	66.9	21.7	21.6
2nd quarter	22.5	20.5	. . .	15.0	10.2	35.5	5.6	5.3	37.2	65.4	22.0	22.0
3rd quarter	22.8	20.7	. . .	15.3	10.8	34.7	6.0	5.4	37.4	66.1	22.0	22.2
4th quarter	22.9	21.0	. . .	15.3	11.1	33.3	6.0	5.6	36.6	63.6	22.1	22.4
1956												
1st quarter	22.8	21.0	. . .	15.0	10.9	32.4	6.3	5.8	36.6	63.1	22.3	22.3
2nd quarter	22.9	21.1	. . .	15.1	11.0	32.2	6.7	5.8	37.4	64.8	22.6	22.4
3rd quarter	22.9	21.1	. . .	15.1	11.1	31.5	6.9	5.8	37.0	63.6	22.7	22.3
4th quarter	23.3	21.4	. . .	15.0	11.1	31.1	7.2	5.5	38.0	65.9	22.9	22.6
1957												
1st quarter	23.4	21.6	. . .	15.0	11.2	30.6	7.7	6.0	38.8	67.1	23.5	22.7
2nd quarter	23.4	21.6	. . .	14.8	11.1	29.9	7.5	6.0	38.5	66.0	23.7	22.7
3rd quarter	23.6	21.8	. . .	15.0	11.4	29.5	7.3	5.9	38.8	66.3	24.1	22.9
4th quarter	23.4	21.8	. . .	14.7	11.1	29.4	7.1	5.9	39.5	67.2	24.6	22.7
1958												
1st quarter	22.7	21.5	. . .	13.8	10.3	28.3	6.4	6.0	39.1	64.8	25.3	22.2
2nd quarter	22.9	21.6	. . .	13.4	9.8	28.3	6.4	6.3	40.0	66.9	25.7	22.4
3rd quarter	23.4	22.0	. . .	13.6	9.7	30.4	6.4	6.2	40.3	66.6	26.3	22.9
4th quarter	23.9	22.3	. . .	14.4	10.1	33.6	6.4	6.5	41.1	68.1	26.8	23.5
1959												
1st quarter	24.4	22.6	18.2	15.3	10.4	37.5	6.8	6.7	40.9	67.0	27.0	23.9
2nd quarter	25.0	23.0	18.6	15.8	10.7	38.8	7.0	7.0	41.5	68.6	27.0	24.5
3rd quarter	25.0	23.3	18.8	16.0	11.0	38.1	7.3	7.1	42.0	70.0	27.1	24.5
4th quarter	25.1	23.3	18.8	15.8	11.0	37.0	7.1	6.9	41.6	69.0	26.9	24.6
1960												
1st quarter	25.6	23.5	19.0	16.3	11.4	38.0	8.0	7.2	40.7	65.9	27.4	25.0
2nd quarter	25.5	23.8	19.3	16.0	11.6	34.9	8.5	7.2	41.1	65.6	28.1	24.8
3rd quarter	25.6	23.7	19.3	15.6	11.3	33.8	8.2	7.0	42.1	67.7	28.5	24.9
4th quarter	25.2	23.7	19.3	15.5	11.2	33.8	8.4	6.7	42.3	67.9	28.8	24.5

. . . = Not available.

Table 19-4. Chain-Type Quantity Indexes for Gross Domestic Product and Domestic Purchases—Continued

(Index numbers, 2000 = 100.)

NIPA Tables 1.1.3, 1.4.3, 2.3.3

Year and quarter	Gross domestic product, total	Personal consumption expenditures Total	Excluding food and energy	Private fixed investment Total	Nonresi-dential	Residential	Exports and imports of goods and services Exports	Imports	Government consumption expenditures and gross investment Total	Federal	State and local	Gross domestic purchases
1961												
1st quarter	25.4	23.7	19.2	15.3	11.0	33.9	8.4	6.6	42.9	67.8	29.7	24.6
2nd quarter	25.9	24.1	19.6	15.6	11.2	34.0	8.2	6.7	43.0	68.4	29.5	25.1
3rd quarter	26.3	24.2	19.7	15.9	11.3	35.9	8.2	7.2	43.8	70.4	29.8	25.6
4th quarter	26.8	24.7	20.3	16.5	11.7	37.1	8.4	7.3	44.8	71.6	30.6	26.1
1962												
1st quarter	27.3	25.0	20.5	16.8	12.0	37.7	8.4	7.5	45.6	74.3	30.4	26.6
2nd quarter	27.6	25.3	20.8	17.3	12.3	38.9	9.2	7.7	45.9	74.6	30.6	26.8
3rd quarter	27.8	25.5	21.0	17.5	12.5	38.9	8.7	7.8	46.9	76.8	31.0	27.2
4th quarter	27.9	25.8	21.4	17.4	12.4	38.8	8.5	7.9	47.0	76.4	31.3	27.3
1963												
1st quarter	28.3	26.0	21.6	17.6	12.4	40.2	8.7	7.7	46.7	74.5	31.9	27.6
2nd quarter	28.6	26.3	21.9	18.4	12.8	43.1	9.8	7.9	46.6	73.8	32.2	27.8
3rd quarter	29.2	26.6	22.2	18.9	13.2	43.9	9.2	8.1	48.6	77.9	33.1	28.4
4th quarter	29.4	26.8	22.4	19.5	13.6	45.3	9.7	8.1	48.2	75.9	33.5	28.6
1964												
1st quarter	30.1	27.4	23.0	20.2	13.9	48.1	10.3	8.1	48.3	75.5	34.0	29.1
2nd quarter	30.4	27.9	23.4	20.2	14.3	45.6	10.5	8.3	48.7	75.0	34.8	29.5
3rd quarter	30.8	28.4	23.8	20.5	14.8	44.9	10.4	8.5	48.7	74.4	35.2	29.9
4th quarter	30.9	28.5	23.9	20.6	15.1	44.1	10.7	8.7	48.6	73.3	35.6	30.0
1965												
1st quarter	31.7	29.1	24.5	21.6	16.1	44.2	9.5	8.4	48.4	72.4	35.9	30.9
2nd quarter	32.1	29.4	24.7	22.2	16.7	44.6	11.3	9.4	49.1	72.5	36.8	31.2
3rd quarter	32.7	29.9	25.2	22.8	17.3	44.7	10.7	9.4	50.8	75.5	37.9	31.9
4th quarter	33.5	30.8	25.9	23.3	18.0	43.8	11.5	9.9	51.9	77.6	38.4	32.7
1966												
1st quarter	34.4	31.2	26.4	24.2	18.8	44.8	11.2	10.1	52.8	79.3	38.9	33.5
2nd quarter	34.5	31.3	26.4	23.9	19.1	41.2	11.7	10.4	53.7	81.4	39.2	33.6
3rd quarter	34.7	31.7	26.8	23.8	19.4	39.8	11.3	11.0	55.2	84.7	39.6	34.0
4th quarter	35.0	31.8	27.0	23.1	19.3	35.7	11.7	11.1	56.1	85.4	40.7	34.2
1967												
1st quarter	35.3	32.0	27.1	22.6	18.9	34.6	11.9	11.3	58.4	91.3	41.2	34.5
2nd quarter	35.3	32.4	27.5	23.2	18.8	38.5	11.8	11.2	58.1	90.0	41.4	34.5
3rd quarter	35.6	32.6	27.8	23.4	18.7	40.5	11.5	11.3	58.7	91.4	41.5	34.9
4th quarter	35.8	32.8	27.8	24.1	19.1	42.8	11.8	11.9	59.1	91.2	42.3	35.2
1968												
1st quarter	36.6	33.5	28.6	24.7	19.7	43.1	12.2	12.6	60.2	92.8	43.0	35.9
2nd quarter	37.2	34.1	29.0	24.6	19.4	44.2	12.4	12.8	60.4	92.0	43.8	36.5
3rd quarter	37.5	34.7	29.6	24.9	19.6	45.0	13.1	13.6	60.6	91.2	44.5	36.8
4th quarter	37.6	34.8	29.8	25.5	20.2	45.5	13.0	13.5	60.6	90.7	44.9	37.0
1969												
1st quarter	38.2	35.2	30.1	26.3	20.8	47.1	11.4	12.2	60.7	90.2	45.2	37.6
2nd quarter	38.3	35.5	30.3	26.5	21.0	46.6	14.0	14.6	60.4	88.7	45.6	37.7
3rd quarter	38.5	35.6	30.5	26.9	21.6	46.3	13.6	14.4	60.5	88.8	45.7	37.9
4th quarter	38.4	35.9	30.7	26.2	21.5	42.9	14.1	14.3	59.6	86.4	45.6	37.6
1970												
1st quarter	38.3	36.1	30.8	26.1	21.4	43.0	14.2	14.2	59.3	84.7	46.0	37.6
2nd quarter	38.4	36.3	30.9	25.6	21.3	40.1	14.9	14.5	58.5	82.0	46.3	37.6
3rd quarter	38.7	36.6	31.2	26.0	21.4	42.2	14.8	14.5	58.8	80.8	47.3	37.9
4th quarter	38.3	36.5	31.0	26.0	20.6	46.7	15.0	14.7	58.8	80.4	47.6	37.5
1971												
1st quarter	39.4	37.2	31.8	26.6	20.8	49.2	15.0	14.5	57.8	77.3	47.8	38.5
2nd quarter	39.6	37.5	32.2	27.7	21.1	54.1	15.0	15.6	57.6	76.2	48.1	38.9
3rd quarter	39.9	37.8	32.6	28.2	21.1	56.8	15.6	15.9	57.6	75.8	48.2	39.2
4th quarter	40.0	38.5	33.3	29.0	21.6	59.0	14.3	14.9	57.2	73.5	48.8	39.3
1972												
1st quarter	40.7	39.0	33.8	30.3	22.3	63.0	15.8	17.0	57.4	73.8	49.0	40.1
2nd quarter	41.7	39.7	34.4	30.9	22.7	64.2	15.3	16.4	57.7	74.9	48.9	41.0
3rd quarter	42.1	40.3	35.0	31.2	23.0	64.3	16.3	16.8	56.5	70.9	49.3	41.3
4th quarter	42.8	41.3	35.9	32.6	24.2	66.6	17.0	17.5	56.9	70.7	50.0	42.0
1973												
1st quarter	43.9	42.0	36.8	34.0	25.4	68.9	18.2	18.3	57.4	71.8	50.2	43.0
2nd quarter	44.4	42.0	36.9	34.3	26.4	65.4	19.1	17.8	57.1	70.7	50.3	43.3
3rd quarter	44.1	42.1	37.0	34.2	26.9	62.6	19.1	17.3	56.4	67.7	50.8	43.0
4th quarter	44.5	42.0	37.0	33.9	27.1	59.6	20.1	17.5	56.8	67.8	51.4	43.3
1974												
1st quarter	44.2	41.7	37.0	33.1	27.0	55.2	20.3	16.9	58.0	69.9	52.1	42.7
2nd quarter	44.3	41.8	37.1	32.6	27.0	52.8	21.3	17.8	58.4	69.8	52.8	42.8
3rd quarter	43.9	42.0	37.1	32.0	26.7	51.1	20.2	17.4	58.4	70.1	52.7	42.6
4th quarter	43.7	41.4	36.4	30.2	25.9	44.4	20.7	17.3	58.7	70.7	52.8	42.3
1975												
1st quarter	43.2	41.8	36.8	28.4	24.3	41.6	20.9	15.5	59.4	69.9	54.3	41.4
2nd quarter	43.5	42.4	37.3	28.0	23.7	42.5	20.2	14.3	58.9	69.3	53.9	41.5
3rd quarter	44.2	43.0	38.0	28.7	23.9	45.5	19.9	15.5	60.0	71.0	54.6	42.6
4th quarter	44.8	43.5	38.6	29.2	24.1	47.5	21.0	16.3	60.5	71.2	55.3	43.1

Table 19-4. Chain-Type Quantity Indexes for Gross Domestic Product and Domestic Purchases—Continued

(Index numbers, 2000 = 100.)

NIPA Tables 1.1.3, 1.4.3, 2.3.3

Year and quarter	Gross domestic product											Gross domestic purchases
	Gross domestic product, total	Personal consumption expenditures		Private fixed investment			Exports and imports of goods and services		Government consumption expenditures and gross investment			
		Total	Excluding food and energy	Total	Nonresidential	Residential	Exports	Imports	Total	Federal	State and local	
1976												
1st quarter	45.8	44.4	39.3	30.4	24.6	52.3	20.9	17.3	60.6	70.6	55.9	44.3
2nd quarter	46.1	44.8	39.6	30.9	24.9	53.8	21.1	18.1	59.9	70.4	54.9	44.7
3rd quarter	46.4	45.2	40.0	31.2	25.4	52.9	21.7	18.8	59.6	70.2	54.5	45.0
4th quarter	46.7	45.8	40.5	32.8	25.9	59.7	21.9	19.4	59.6	70.4	54.4	45.4
1977												
1st quarter	47.3	46.4	41.0	34.0	26.9	61.5	21.6	20.4	60.1	71.0	54.9	46.2
2nd quarter	48.2	46.6	41.5	35.9	27.7	68.5	22.2	20.5	60.7	72.1	55.2	47.1
3rd quarter	49.1	47.1	42.0	36.4	28.3	68.3	22.3	20.3	60.9	72.6	55.2	47.8
4th quarter	49.1	47.8	42.8	37.1	29.3	67.4	21.6	20.5	60.7	71.8	55.3	48.0
1978												
1st quarter	49.2	48.0	43.0	37.4	29.5	67.8	22.1	21.9	60.8	72.1	55.3	48.3
2nd quarter	51.1	49.1	44.3	40.1	32.0	71.0	24.4	22.0	62.4	73.8	56.9	49.8
3rd quarter	51.7	49.3	44.5	41.2	33.2	72.0	24.7	22.3	62.9	74.1	57.5	50.3
4th quarter	52.3	49.7	44.8	42.1	34.2	71.7	25.7	22.6	63.5	74.7	58.1	50.9
1979												
1st quarter	52.4	49.9	45.0	42.4	35.0	70.1	25.7	22.5	62.9	74.8	57.1	51.0
2nd quarter	52.5	49.9	45.2	42.1	34.9	68.8	25.8	22.6	63.6	75.8	57.6	51.0
3rd quarter	52.9	50.4	45.8	42.9	36.0	67.9	26.7	22.3	63.7	75.6	57.8	51.2
4th quarter	53.0	50.6	45.8	42.5	36.1	65.4	28.4	22.8	64.1	75.6	58.5	51.1
1980												
1st quarter	53.2	50.5	45.7	41.9	36.5	60.4	29.2	22.8	65.1	78.0	58.8	51.2
2nd quarter	52.1	49.3	44.5	38.2	34.6	49.2	29.7	21.1	65.3	80.0	58.0	49.6
3rd quarter	52.0	49.9	45.3	38.6	34.9	50.0	29.7	19.6	64.4	78.9	57.2	49.2
4th quarter	53.0	50.6	46.2	40.1	35.6	54.9	29.5	20.7	64.3	79.2	57.0	50.4
1981												
1st quarter	54.1	50.8	46.5	40.4	36.2	53.9	30.0	21.6	65.2	80.8	57.4	51.6
2nd quarter	53.6	50.8	46.3	40.7	36.9	52.1	30.2	21.6	65.3	83.2	56.3	51.1
3rd quarter	54.3	51.0	46.7	40.7	37.8	48.1	29.6	21.4	65.2	83.1	56.1	51.8
4th quarter	53.6	50.6	46.1	40.6	38.7	43.2	29.7	22.0	65.8	84.0	56.5	51.3
1982												
1st quarter	52.7	50.9	46.5	39.3	37.8	40.7	28.4	21.3	65.7	84.2	56.4	50.5
2nd quarter	53.0	51.1	46.6	37.9	36.4	39.4	28.6	21.0	66.1	84.9	56.6	50.7
3rd quarter	52.8	51.5	47.1	36.9	35.2	39.3	27.3	22.0	66.6	86.2	56.6	50.9
4th quarter	52.9	52.4	48.2	36.8	34.5	42.2	26.1	21.1	67.7	88.8	56.9	51.0
1983												
1st quarter	53.5	53.0	48.8	37.6	33.9	49.3	26.5	21.6	68.2	89.8	57.2	51.6
2nd quarter	54.7	54.0	49.9	39.1	34.3	55.2	26.6	23.2	68.8	91.7	57.0	53.1
3rd quarter	55.8	55.0	50.8	41.4	35.8	60.6	27.0	25.1	70.0	94.3	57.5	54.5
4th quarter	56.9	55.8	51.9	43.8	38.1	63.2	27.5	26.3	68.8	91.0	57.4	55.7
1984												
1st quarter	58.1	56.3	52.6	45.2	39.4	65.0	28.1	28.4	69.5	91.8	58.1	57.1
2nd quarter	59.1	57.1	53.3	47.1	41.3	66.2	28.8	29.6	71.0	94.7	58.8	58.2
3rd quarter	59.6	57.6	53.8	48.1	42.7	65.5	29.4	30.4	71.5	94.3	59.9	58.8
4th quarter	60.1	58.3	54.7	49.0	43.7	65.6	30.0	31.2	73.1	97.4	60.5	59.4
1985												
1st quarter	60.7	59.3	55.7	49.3	44.2	65.4	30.0	30.6	73.9	98.5	61.3	59.8
2nd quarter	61.2	59.8	56.4	49.9	44.9	65.9	29.9	32.1	75.6	100.9	62.5	60.6
3rd quarter	62.2	61.0	57.7	49.5	44.2	66.8	29.5	31.7	77.5	104.3	63.7	61.5
4th quarter	62.6	61.1	57.7	50.5	44.9	68.3	30.4	33.0	78.0	104.2	64.5	62.0
1986												
1st quarter	63.2	61.6	58.3	50.6	44.3	71.3	31.3	33.0	78.8	103.7	66.1	62.5
2nd quarter	63.5	62.3	59.0	50.4	43.2	75.2	31.7	34.4	80.5	107.0	66.9	62.9
3rd quarter	64.1	63.4	60.3	50.1	42.6	76.4	32.4	35.3	82.3	111.0	67.5	63.6
4th quarter	64.4	63.8	60.6	50.5	43.0	76.2	33.6	35.6	81.9	109.3	67.7	63.8
1987												
1st quarter	64.8	63.8	60.7	49.5	41.8	76.0	33.6	35.4	82.1	110.0	67.7	64.1
2nd quarter	65.6	64.7	61.6	50.4	42.8	76.4	35.0	36.3	82.7	111.6	67.8	64.8
3rd quarter	66.1	65.4	62.5	51.4	44.2	76.1	36.5	37.0	82.8	111.7	67.9	65.3
4th quarter	67.3	65.5	62.6	51.4	44.1	76.5	37.8	37.8	83.9	113.4	68.8	66.4
1988												
1st quarter	67.6	66.6	63.6	51.4	44.5	74.9	39.9	37.6	83.4	110.3	69.6	66.4
2nd quarter	68.5	67.1	64.0	52.4	45.6	75.5	41.0	37.2	83.6	109.2	70.5	67.0
3rd quarter	68.9	67.7	64.5	52.6	45.8	75.5	41.8	38.1	83.5	108.4	70.7	67.4
4th quarter	69.8	68.5	65.3	53.1	46.3	76.2	43.1	39.2	85.1	111.6	71.5	68.3
1989												
1st quarter	70.5	68.7	65.6	53.6	47.1	75.7	44.3	39.1	84.6	109.4	71.9	68.8
2nd quarter	70.9	69.0	66.1	53.7	47.7	73.4	46.3	39.7	85.9	111.8	72.6	69.1
3rd quarter	71.4	69.7	66.8	54.6	49.1	72.6	46.8	39.7	86.7	112.9	73.3	69.5
4th quarter	71.6	70.0	66.9	53.7	48.4	71.1	47.6	40.3	87.2	112.3	74.2	69.7
1990												
1st quarter	72.4	70.6	67.8	54.4	49.0	71.8	49.6	41.2	88.5	114.0	75.4	70.3
2nd quarter	72.6	70.8	67.8	53.2	48.2	69.1	50.2	41.6	88.7	114.2	75.6	70.5
3rd quarter	72.6	71.1	68.0	52.6	48.5	65.1	50.6	41.6	88.7	113.2	76.1	70.5
4th quarter	72.1	70.6	67.6	51.1	47.5	61.5	51.1	40.2	89.6	114.2	76.9	69.6

Table 19-4. Chain-Type Quantity Indexes for Gross Domestic Product and Domestic Purchases—Continued

(Index numbers, 2000 = 100.)

NIPA Tables 1.1.3, 1.4.3, 2.3.3

Year and quarter	Gross domestic product											Gross domestic purchases
	Gross domestic product, total	Personal consumption expenditures		Private fixed investment			Exports and imports of goods and services		Government consumption expenditures and gross investment			
		Total	Excluding food and energy	Total	Nonresidential	Residential	Exports	Imports	Total	Federal	State and local	
1991												
1st quarter	71.7	70.3	67.4	49.3	46.3	57.9	51.4	39.4	89.9	115.0	77.0	69.1
2nd quarter	72.2	70.9	67.8	49.3	45.9	59.2	53.3	40.5	90.2	115.4	77.3	69.5
3rd quarter	72.5	71.2	68.2	49.4	45.4	61.7	54.5	41.6	89.8	113.3	77.8	69.9
4th quarter	72.9	71.2	68.3	49.5	45.2	63.0	55.8	42.1	89.5	111.1	78.3	70.1
1992												
1st quarter	73.6	72.3	69.6	50.0	45.0	66.3	56.7	42.5	90.2	111.1	79.4	70.8
2nd quarter	74.3	72.8	70.2	52.0	46.8	68.8	56.8	43.5	90.1	111.0	79.3	71.6
3rd quarter	75.1	73.5	71.0	52.8	47.7	69.0	58.0	44.1	90.6	112.3	79.3	72.3
4th quarter	75.9	74.3	71.7	54.4	49.2	71.3	58.3	44.9	90.6	112.4	79.3	73.2
1993												
1st quarter	76.0	74.6	72.1	54.7	49.5	71.6	58.4	45.9	89.6	108.9	79.7	73.4
2nd quarter	76.4	75.3	72.8	56.0	50.8	72.5	59.1	47.2	89.5	107.4	80.3	73.9
3rd quarter	76.8	76.1	73.5	57.0	51.4	75.0	58.9	47.8	89.3	105.8	80.7	74.4
4th quarter	77.8	76.8	74.3	59.5	53.5	78.7	60.8	49.5	89.6	106.1	81.1	75.5
1994												
1st quarter	78.6	77.6	75.3	60.3	54.0	80.3	61.4	50.6	88.7	102.9	81.3	76.3
2nd quarter	79.6	78.2	75.7	61.7	55.1	83.0	63.4	52.7	89.1	102.4	82.2	77.4
3rd quarter	80.1	78.7	76.4	62.3	56.2	82.1	65.8	54.2	90.5	104.8	83.2	77.8
4th quarter	81.0	79.5	77.4	64.0	58.7	81.1	67.3	55.5	89.8	102.0	83.5	78.8
1995												
1st quarter	81.2	79.6	77.5	65.5	61.0	79.3	68.5	56.7	90.1	101.8	84.1	79.0
2nd quarter	81.4	80.3	78.2	65.2	61.5	76.7	69.4	57.5	90.5	101.6	84.8	79.2
3rd quarter	82.0	81.0	79.0	66.1	61.9	79.1	72.5	57.7	90.2	100.7	84.8	79.5
4th quarter	82.6	81.6	79.7	67.5	63.1	80.9	73.6	58.3	89.2	96.9	85.2	80.0
1996												
1st quarter	83.2	82.3	80.4	69.2	64.7	83.0	74.5	59.9	89.7	98.9	85.0	80.7
2nd quarter	84.6	83.2	81.4	71.5	66.6	86.5	75.7	61.8	91.2	100.8	86.2	82.2
3rd quarter	85.3	83.7	82.2	73.1	68.8	86.3	76.4	63.8	90.9	98.4	87.0	83.1
4th quarter	86.3	84.4	82.9	74.3	70.6	85.4	81.1	64.7	91.7	98.2	88.4	83.7
1997												
1st quarter	87.0	85.3	83.9	75.8	72.4	85.7	82.6	67.4	91.9	97.0	89.2	84.6
2nd quarter	88.3	85.7	84.4	77.4	74.2	86.8	85.9	70.1	92.8	99.1	89.6	85.9
3rd quarter	89.4	87.1	86.0	80.4	78.0	87.2	87.9	72.7	92.8	98.5	90.0	87.1
4th quarter	90.0	88.0	87.0	81.1	78.7	88.1	87.9	73.9	92.8	97.7	90.3	87.9
1998												
1st quarter	91.0	89.0	88.1	83.5	81.3	89.9	88.2	76.6	92.3	95.4	90.7	89.3
2nd quarter	91.6	90.4	89.5	86.0	83.8	92.4	87.3	78.7	94.2	97.8	92.3	90.3
3rd quarter	92.7	91.5	90.7	87.3	84.6	94.9	86.9	79.7	95.0	96.9	94.1	91.5
4th quarter	94.1	92.7	92.2	89.8	87.2	97.2	90.2	82.1	95.9	97.8	94.9	92.8
1999												
1st quarter	94.9	93.6	93.2	91.2	88.8	98.0	89.4	84.2	96.6	97.2	96.2	94.0
2nd quarter	95.7	95.1	94.7	93.4	91.5	98.9	90.4	87.2	97.1	97.7	96.9	95.0
3rd quarter	96.8	96.1	95.8	95.2	93.7	99.5	92.8	90.2	98.3	99.6	97.7	96.3
4th quarter	98.5	97.3	97.0	95.7	93.9	100.7	95.2	92.0	99.9	101.9	98.9	97.9
2000												
1st quarter	98.8	98.8	98.9	98.3	97.1	101.7	96.8	95.6	99.2	98.2	99.7	98.5
2nd quarter	100.3	99.5	99.4	100.6	100.5	100.8	99.6	99.4	100.5	102.1	99.7	100.3
3rd quarter	100.2	100.4	100.5	100.4	101.1	98.7	102.2	102.7	100.0	100.0	100.0	100.4
4th quarter	100.7	101.3	101.2	100.6	101.3	98.8	101.5	102.3	100.3	99.7	100.6	100.9
2001												
1st quarter	100.6	101.7	101.7	100.0	100.2	99.3	100.1	101.3	101.6	101.7	101.6	100.8
2nd quarter	100.9	101.9	102.3	97.7	96.6	100.7	96.7	98.0	103.6	103.9	103.4	100.9
3rd quarter	100.6	102.4	102.8	96.6	94.9	101.2	92.0	95.3	103.2	103.9	102.8	100.7
4th quarter	100.9	104.1	104.7	93.9	91.6	100.2	89.4	94.5	105.3	106.1	104.9	101.3
2002												
1st quarter	101.6	104.5	105.1	92.4	88.5	102.7	90.6	97.2	106.4	107.7	105.8	102.2
2nd quarter	102.2	105.1	105.6	92.1	87.1	105.1	92.9	100.1	107.7	110.9	106.0	102.9
3rd quarter	102.8	105.7	106.3	91.9	86.7	105.6	93.5	101.5	108.3	111.7	106.5	103.6
4th quarter	102.8	106.1	106.6	91.6	85.6	107.2	92.8	103.7	109.5	114.4	107.1	104.0
2003												
1st quarter	103.1	106.6	107.1	91.5	85.0	108.3	91.5	102.4	109.2	114.5	106.5	104.2
2nd quarter	104.0	107.6	108.3	93.8	87.2	111.1	91.1	103.4	110.8	119.7	106.3	105.3
3rd quarter	105.9	109.1	109.9	96.9	89.2	116.8	93.6	104.4	111.2	119.9	106.8	107.0
4th quarter	106.6	109.7	110.6	98.2	89.8	119.8	98.1	108.7	111.4	120.8	106.7	107.8
2004												
1st quarter	107.6	111.0	111.9	98.8	90.2	120.7	99.9	111.3	112.2	122.9	106.8	108.9
2nd quarter	108.7	111.8	112.8	101.5	91.8	126.2	101.4	115.5	112.8	123.7	107.3	110.4
3rd quarter	109.5	112.9	114.1	103.4	94.1	127.2	102.6	116.8	113.2	125.2	107.1	111.3
4th quarter	110.2	114.1	115.1	104.7	96.0	127.0	105.0	120.2	112.6	123.5	107.1	112.2
2005												
1st quarter	111.2	114.8	115.7	106.7	97.4	130.4	106.2	121.4	113.1	124.5	107.3	113.1
2nd quarter	112.1	116.0	117.0	109.3	98.6	136.5	108.6	121.8	113.4	124.7	107.7	113.8
3rd quarter	113.2	117.2	118.1	111.0	100.0	138.8	109.5	122.5	114.4	127.5	107.7	114.9
4th quarter	113.7	117.4	118.2	111.8	101.3	138.5	112.1	126.4	114.0	126.1	108.0	115.7

Table 19-5. Chain-Type Price Indexes for Gross Domestic Product and Domestic Purchases

(Index numbers, 2000 = 100.)

NIPA Tables 1.1.4, 1.6.4, 2.3.4

Year and quarter	Gross domestic product, total	Personal consumption expenditures		Private fixed investment			Exports and imports of goods and services		Government consumption expenditures and gross investment			Gross domestic purchases
		Total	Excluding food and energy	Total	Nonresidential	Residential	Exports	Imports	Total	Federal	State and local	
1946	13.9	14.2	14.4	16.7	19.9	10.6	21.9	14.9	10.0	11.6	8.1	13.6
1947	15.5	15.7	15.6	19.6	23.2	12.6	25.4	17.8	10.8	12.3	9.1	15.1
1948	16.4	16.6	16.5	21.3	25.2	13.7	26.8	19.3	11.2	12.2	10.2	16.0
1949	16.4	16.5	16.6	21.7	25.8	13.9	25.2	18.4	11.5	12.7	10.3	16.1
1947												
1st quarter	15.1	15.4	...	18.7	22.2	11.9	23.4	16.3	10.8	12.6	8.8	14.8
2nd quarter	15.3	15.5	...	19.4	22.9	12.6	25.1	17.5	10.9	12.5	9.0	15.0
3rd quarter	15.6	15.8	...	19.9	23.6	12.9	26.3	18.4	10.7	12.1	9.2	15.2
4th quarter	15.9	16.2	...	20.3	24.0	13.2	27.0	19.0	10.8	12.1	9.5	15.5
1948												
1st quarter	16.1	16.4	...	20.6	24.1	13.4	27.2	19.5	11.0	12.1	9.8	15.7
2nd quarter	16.3	16.5	...	21.0	24.8	13.6	27.0	19.5	11.1	12.1	10.0	15.9
3rd quarter	16.6	16.8	...	21.7	25.7	13.9	26.7	19.3	11.3	12.3	10.4	16.2
4th quarter	16.6	16.7	...	21.9	26.1	13.9	26.3	19.0	11.4	12.3	10.5	16.2
1949												
1st quarter	16.5	16.6	...	21.9	25.9	14.1	25.8	18.6	11.6	12.8	10.4	16.2
2nd quarter	16.4	16.5	...	21.8	25.8	14.0	25.3	18.4	11.6	12.8	10.3	16.1
3rd quarter	16.3	16.4	...	21.6	25.7	13.7	24.9	18.3	11.4	12.5	10.2	16.0
4th quarter	16.3	16.4	...	21.5	25.6	13.7	24.7	18.4	11.5	12.8	10.2	16.0
1950												
1st quarter	16.2	16.4	...	21.5	25.6	13.7	24.3	18.7	11.5	12.8	10.1	15.9
2nd quarter	16.3	16.5	...	21.9	25.8	14.1	24.3	19.1	11.4	12.6	10.2	16.0
3rd quarter	16.6	16.8	...	22.5	26.4	14.6	24.5	19.8	11.6	12.6	10.5	16.4
4th quarter	16.9	17.1	...	22.9	27.3	14.6	25.0	20.7	11.7	12.6	10.8	16.6
1951												
1st quarter	17.5	17.6	...	23.7	28.2	15.0	26.5	22.4	12.3	13.4	11.1	17.2
2nd quarter	17.6	17.8	...	24.0	28.7	15.2	27.4	23.6	12.2	13.1	11.3	17.3
3rd quarter	17.6	17.8	...	24.2	29.0	15.3	28.3	24.3	12.3	13.1	11.6	17.4
4th quarter	17.8	18.0	...	24.5	29.3	15.4	28.7	24.4	12.4	13.3	11.7	17.6
1952												
1st quarter	17.9	18.1	...	24.6	29.4	15.5	28.0	23.4	12.3	13.1	11.7	17.6
2nd quarter	17.9	18.1	...	24.7	29.5	15.6	27.9	23.0	12.5	13.3	11.8	17.7
3rd quarter	18.1	18.2	...	24.7	29.4	15.8	27.8	22.6	12.6	13.4	12.1	17.8
4th quarter	18.1	18.3	...	24.7	29.4	15.7	27.8	22.2	12.8	13.6	12.1	17.9
1953												
1st quarter	18.2	18.3	...	24.7	29.4	15.7	27.9	22.0	12.7	13.4	12.2	17.9
2nd quarter	18.2	18.4	...	24.8	29.7	15.7	27.9	21.8	12.7	13.5	12.2	17.9
3rd quarter	18.3	18.5	...	25.0	29.9	15.9	27.8	21.7	12.6	13.4	12.2	18.0
4th quarter	18.3	18.5	...	25.0	29.9	15.8	27.7	21.7	12.7	13.5	12.1	18.0
1954												
1st quarter	18.4	18.6	...	25.0	30.0	15.7	27.5	22.0	12.8	13.6	12.1	18.1
2nd quarter	18.4	18.6	...	25.1	30.1	15.8	27.4	22.1	12.9	13.6	12.4	18.2
3rd quarter	18.4	18.6	...	25.1	29.9	15.9	27.4	22.2	13.0	13.8	12.4	18.2
4th quarter	18.5	18.5	...	25.1	30.0	15.9	27.4	22.2	13.1	13.9	12.5	18.2
1955												
1st quarter	18.5	18.6	...	25.1	29.9	16.0	27.5	21.9	13.2	14.1	12.4	18.2
2nd quarter	18.6	18.6	...	25.3	30.0	16.1	27.6	22.0	13.4	14.5	12.5	18.3
3rd quarter	18.8	18.7	...	25.6	30.5	16.3	27.7	22.0	13.6	14.6	12.7	18.5
4th quarter	18.9	18.8	...	26.0	31.2	16.3	27.9	22.1	13.8	14.8	12.8	18.6
1956												
1st quarter	19.1	18.8	...	26.5	32.1	16.4	28.1	22.1	14.0	15.0	13.1	18.8
2nd quarter	19.3	19.0	...	26.8	32.3	16.6	28.4	22.3	14.2	15.2	13.3	18.9
3rd quarter	19.5	19.2	...	27.2	33.2	16.7	28.7	22.4	14.4	15.3	13.5	19.2
4th quarter	19.6	19.3	...	27.4	33.6	16.6	29.1	22.7	14.4	15.4	13.7	19.3
1957												
1st quarter	19.8	19.4	...	27.7	34.2	16.6	29.5	22.7	14.7	15.7	13.8	19.5
2nd quarter	20.0	19.6	...	27.8	34.3	16.6	29.7	22.8	14.9	15.8	14.0	19.6
3rd quarter	20.1	19.7	...	28.0	34.6	16.7	29.8	22.6	15.0	16.0	14.1	19.8
4th quarter	20.2	19.8	...	28.1	34.9	16.6	29.8	22.4	15.0	16.1	14.1	19.9
1958												
1st quarter	20.4	20.1	...	27.9	34.5	16.6	29.5	21.9	15.1	16.3	14.0	20.0
2nd quarter	20.5	20.1	...	28.0	34.7	16.6	29.3	21.7	15.3	16.5	14.1	20.1
3rd quarter	20.6	20.1	...	28.0	34.7	16.6	29.3	21.6	15.4	16.7	14.2	20.2
4th quarter	20.6	20.1	...	28.1	34.8	16.6	29.4	21.6	15.5	16.8	14.3	20.2
1959												
1st quarter	20.7	20.3	20.9	28.1	34.9	16.6	29.2	21.8	15.5	16.6	14.5	20.3
2nd quarter	20.7	20.4	21.0	28.2	35.1	16.6	29.2	21.8	15.4	16.5	14.5	20.3
3rd quarter	20.8	20.5	21.1	28.3	35.2	16.6	29.5	21.9	15.3	16.3	14.5	20.4
4th quarter	20.9	20.6	21.2	28.4	35.3	16.6	29.8	22.1	15.4	16.4	14.5	20.5
1960												
1st quarter	20.9	20.6	21.3	28.4	35.3	16.7	29.8	22.1	15.4	16.4	14.6	20.5
2nd quarter	21.0	20.7	21.3	28.5	35.3	16.8	29.8	22.1	15.5	16.4	14.7	20.6
3rd quarter	21.1	20.8	21.4	28.4	35.3	16.8	29.9	22.2	15.7	16.7	14.8	20.7
4th quarter	21.2	20.9	21.5	28.4	35.2	16.8	29.8	22.1	15.8	16.9	14.8	20.8

. . . = Not available.

Table 19-5. Chain-Type Price Indexes for Gross Domestic Product and Domestic Purchases—Continued

(Index numbers, 2000 = 100.)   NIPA Tables 1.1.4, 1.6.4, 2.3.4

Year and quarter	Gross domestic product, total	Personal consumption expenditures		Private fixed investment			Exports and imports of goods and services		Government consumption expenditures and gross investment			Gross domestic purchases
		Total	Excluding food and energy	Total	Nonresidential	Residential	Exports	Imports	Total	Federal	State and local	
1961												
1st quarter	21.2	20.9	21.5	28.3	35.1	16.7	30.0	22.2	15.8	16.8	14.9	20.8
2nd quarter	21.2	20.9	21.6	28.3	35.1	16.8	30.4	22.1	15.9	16.9	15.0	20.8
3rd quarter	21.3	21.0	21.7	28.3	35.0	16.8	30.3	22.1	15.9	16.8	15.1	20.9
4th quarter	21.4	21.0	21.7	28.3	35.1	16.8	30.5	22.1	16.0	16.9	15.3	20.9
1962												
1st quarter	21.5	21.1	21.8	28.3	35.1	16.8	30.6	21.8	16.2	17.1	15.5	21.0
2nd quarter	21.5	21.2	21.9	28.4	35.1	16.8	30.3	21.9	16.3	17.1	15.5	21.1
3rd quarter	21.6	21.3	22.0	28.4	35.1	16.8	30.3	21.8	16.3	17.2	15.6	21.2
4th quarter	21.7	21.3	22.0	28.3	35.1	16.8	30.3	21.9	16.5	17.4	15.7	21.2
1963												
1st quarter	21.7	21.4	22.1	28.3	35.1	16.8	30.4	22.1	16.6	17.5	15.8	21.3
2nd quarter	21.8	21.4	22.1	28.3	35.1	16.7	30.3	22.2	16.6	17.5	15.9	21.3
3rd quarter	21.8	21.5	22.2	28.2	35.1	16.5	30.3	22.3	16.6	17.5	15.9	21.4
4th quarter	21.9	21.6	22.3	28.3	35.1	16.6	30.3	22.5	16.9	17.9	16.0	21.5
1964												
1st quarter	22.0	21.7	22.4	28.2	35.1	16.5	30.4	22.7	17.0	18.0	16.1	21.6
2nd quarter	22.1	21.7	22.5	28.4	35.3	16.7	30.4	22.8	17.1	18.1	16.2	21.7
3rd quarter	22.2	21.8	22.5	28.4	35.3	16.8	30.6	22.7	17.2	18.3	16.3	21.8
4th quarter	22.3	21.9	22.6	28.8	35.5	17.2	30.9	22.8	17.3	18.3	16.3	21.9
1965												
1st quarter	22.4	22.0	22.7	28.8	35.5	17.1	31.6	23.0	17.4	18.4	16.5	21.9
2nd quarter	22.5	22.1	22.7	28.8	35.6	17.2	31.5	22.9	17.5	18.5	16.6	22.0
3rd quarter	22.6	22.2	22.8	28.9	35.7	17.1	31.5	23.1	17.6	18.7	16.7	22.1
4th quarter	22.7	22.2	22.9	29.2	35.9	17.6	31.4	23.3	17.9	19.1	16.9	22.3
1966												
1st quarter	22.9	22.4	23.0	29.1	35.8	17.4	32.0	23.4	18.0	19.1	17.1	22.4
2nd quarter	23.1	22.6	23.1	29.6	36.2	18.0	32.2	23.7	18.2	19.1	17.4	22.6
3rd quarter	23.3	22.8	23.3	29.6	36.3	17.9	32.6	23.6	18.5	19.6	17.6	22.8
4th quarter	23.5	22.9	23.5	29.9	36.6	18.3	33.2	23.7	18.6	19.6	17.9	23.0
1967												
1st quarter	23.6	23.0	23.6	30.1	36.8	18.3	33.7	23.7	18.8	19.5	18.2	23.1
2nd quarter	23.8	23.1	23.8	30.2	37.0	18.4	33.7	23.7	19.0	19.8	18.4	23.3
3rd quarter	24.0	23.3	24.0	30.4	37.2	18.5	33.7	23.7	19.2	20.0	18.6	23.5
4th quarter	24.2	23.5	24.2	30.8	37.6	18.9	33.8	23.7	19.5	20.4	18.8	23.7
1968												
1st quarter	24.5	23.8	24.5	31.1	37.8	19.2	34.1	23.8	19.7	20.5	19.1	24.0
2nd quarter	24.8	24.0	24.8	31.4	38.2	19.4	34.8	24.0	20.0	20.8	19.4	24.2
3rd quarter	25.0	24.3	25.1	31.6	38.5	19.4	34.4	24.1	20.2	21.2	19.5	24.5
4th quarter	25.4	24.5	25.4	32.3	39.1	20.1	34.6	24.2	20.6	21.5	19.9	24.8
1969												
1st quarter	25.6	24.8	25.6	32.6	39.4	20.5	35.1	24.3	20.7	21.5	20.2	25.1
2nd quarter	26.0	25.1	25.9	33.0	39.8	20.8	35.2	24.5	21.1	21.8	20.6	25.4
3rd quarter	26.3	25.4	26.2	33.3	40.2	20.9	35.7	24.6	21.6	22.5	21.0	25.8
4th quarter	26.7	25.7	26.5	33.7	40.7	21.2	36.5	25.3	21.9	22.7	21.4	26.1
1970												
1st quarter	27.1	26.0	26.8	33.9	41.1	21.2	36.5	25.5	22.5	23.5	21.8	26.5
2nd quarter	27.4	26.3	27.1	34.7	41.8	22.0	37.2	25.8	22.9	23.7	22.3	26.8
3rd quarter	27.7	26.6	27.4	34.6	42.1	21.4	37.1	26.5	23.3	24.1	22.7	27.1
4th quarter	28.0	26.9	27.8	35.0	42.6	21.6	37.2	26.7	23.6	24.4	23.1	27.4
1971												
1st quarter	28.4	27.2	28.1	35.6	43.2	22.1	38.3	27.4	24.3	25.2	23.6	27.9
2nd quarter	28.8	27.5	28.4	36.1	43.8	22.6	38.4	27.5	24.7	25.7	24.0	28.2
3rd quarter	29.1	27.7	28.7	36.6	44.1	23.0	38.2	27.8	25.1	26.1	24.3	28.5
4th quarter	29.3	27.9	28.9	36.9	44.4	23.4	38.5	28.2	25.4	26.7	24.5	28.8
1972												
1st quarter	29.8	28.2	29.2	37.4	44.9	23.7	39.6	28.7	26.3	28.1	25.0	29.2
2nd quarter	30.0	28.4	29.4	37.6	45.2	23.8	39.9	29.5	26.6	28.3	25.3	29.4
3rd quarter	30.3	28.6	29.6	38.0	45.5	24.2	40.1	29.9	26.9	28.5	25.7	29.7
4th quarter	30.6	28.9	29.8	38.5	45.8	24.9	41.0	30.6	27.4	29.2	26.1	30.1
1973												
1st quarter	31.0	29.2	30.0	38.9	46.2	25.3	42.1	31.5	28.0	29.7	26.7	30.5
2nd quarter	31.5	29.8	30.4	39.6	46.8	25.9	44.0	34.0	28.5	30.1	27.3	31.1
3rd quarter	32.1	30.3	30.7	40.4	47.5	26.8	46.6	35.6	29.0	30.7	27.7	31.6
4th quarter	32.7	31.0	31.1	40.9	48.0	27.2	49.0	38.2	29.5	31.3	28.2	32.2
1974												
1st quarter	33.4	31.9	31.6	41.7	48.8	27.9	52.4	44.3	30.2	31.8	29.0	33.1
2nd quarter	34.1	32.8	32.4	42.9	50.4	28.5	54.2	49.4	31.1	32.5	30.0	34.0
3rd quarter	35.2	33.6	33.3	44.6	52.5	29.4	57.2	52.0	32.1	33.5	31.0	35.0
4th quarter	36.2	34.5	34.1	46.4	54.9	30.2	60.1	53.7	33.2	34.9	31.9	36.1
1975												
1st quarter	37.1	35.1	34.7	48.1	57.1	31.0	61.8	54.5	33.9	35.6	32.6	36.8
2nd quarter	37.6	35.6	35.3	49.2	58.6	31.5	61.6	54.6	34.5	36.1	33.3	37.4
3rd quarter	38.3	36.2	35.8	49.8	59.3	31.8	61.5	53.4	35.1	36.8	33.8	38.1
4th quarter	39.0	36.9	36.4	50.5	60.1	32.4	61.8	53.5	35.8	37.9	34.3	38.7

Table 19-5. Chain-Type Price Indexes for Gross Domestic Product and Domestic Purchases—Continued

(Index numbers, 2000 = 100.) NIPA Tables 1.1.4, 1.6.4, 2.3.4

Year and quarter	Gross domestic product											Gross domestic purchases
	Gross domestic product, total	Personal consumption expenditures		Private fixed investment			Exports and imports of goods and services		Government consumption expenditures and gross investment			
		Total	Excluding food and energy	Total	Nonresidential	Residential	Exports	Imports	Total	Federal	State and local	
1976												
1st quarter	39.4	37.3	36.9	51.0	60.8	32.6	62.7	54.4	36.3	38.3	34.9	39.2
2nd quarter	39.9	37.6	37.4	51.9	61.6	33.6	63.4	55.2	36.8	38.7	35.4	39.6
3rd quarter	40.4	38.2	38.0	52.6	62.4	34.1	63.8	56.2	37.3	39.3	35.8	40.2
4th quarter	41.1	38.8	38.6	53.5	63.3	34.7	64.9	56.8	38.0	40.5	36.2	40.8
1977												
1st quarter	41.8	39.5	39.2	54.6	64.6	35.5	65.7	58.7	38.8	41.4	36.9	41.6
2nd quarter	42.5	40.1	39.8	55.7	65.6	36.5	66.6	60.4	39.4	41.9	37.6	42.3
3rd quarter	43.0	40.7	40.4	56.9	66.8	37.7	66.3	61.2	39.8	42.1	38.2	43.0
4th quarter	43.8	41.3	41.0	58.1	67.9	38.8	66.6	61.8	40.8	43.4	38.8	43.7
1978												
1st quarter	44.5	42.0	41.7	59.3	68.9	40.0	67.9	62.8	41.3	43.9	39.4	44.4
2nd quarter	45.4	42.9	42.4	60.5	70.1	41.2	69.6	64.4	41.9	44.3	40.1	45.3
3rd quarter	46.1	43.6	43.1	61.7	71.2	42.2	70.8	65.4	42.5	44.9	40.7	46.0
4th quarter	47.1	44.5	43.8	62.9	72.5	43.4	73.1	66.6	43.3	46.1	41.2	46.9
1979												
1st quarter	47.9	45.3	44.4	64.2	74.0	44.2	75.2	69.1	44.1	46.7	42.2	47.8
2nd quarter	49.1	46.5	45.3	65.9	75.7	45.7	78.3	72.7	45.0	47.4	43.2	49.0
3rd quarter	50.1	47.7	46.1	67.5	77.3	47.2	80.1	78.2	46.3	48.4	44.7	50.3
4th quarter	51.1	48.8	47.1	68.9	78.7	48.3	81.6	83.4	47.6	50.4	45.6	51.5
1980												
1st quarter	52.2	50.2	48.2	70.5	80.5	49.6	84.0	90.4	48.8	51.3	46.9	52.9
2nd quarter	53.4	51.5	49.3	72.1	82.4	50.8	85.2	93.6	50.0	52.5	48.2	54.2
3rd quarter	54.6	52.7	50.4	73.7	84.1	51.9	87.6	96.2	51.2	53.3	49.5	55.4
4th quarter	56.1	54.0	51.6	75.3	85.8	53.2	90.5	97.8	53.0	56.1	50.8	56.9
1981												
1st quarter	57.6	55.3	52.7	77.3	88.3	54.4	92.8	100.4	54.4	57.0	52.4	58.4
2nd quarter	58.6	56.3	53.7	79.1	90.5	55.2	93.2	101.0	55.3	57.9	53.4	59.4
3rd quarter	59.7	57.2	54.7	80.4	92.1	55.9	93.3	98.4	56.0	58.5	54.1	60.4
4th quarter	60.7	58.1	55.7	81.9	94.0	56.8	93.6	98.6	57.3	60.5	54.9	61.4
1982												
1st quarter	61.6	58.8	56.5	83.1	95.3	57.6	94.2	98.3	58.2	61.4	55.9	62.2
2nd quarter	62.3	59.4	57.3	84.0	96.3	58.5	94.1	96.6	59.0	62.1	56.7	62.9
3rd quarter	63.2	60.3	58.2	84.5	96.8	59.0	93.4	95.4	59.8	62.6	57.6	63.7
4th quarter	63.9	61.0	59.1	84.6	96.8	59.2	92.9	94.7	60.6	63.7	58.3	64.4
1983												
1st quarter	64.4	61.5	59.9	84.2	96.1	59.5	93.3	92.7	61.0	64.0	58.8	64.8
2nd quarter	64.9	62.1	60.3	83.9	95.5	59.7	93.6	92.7	61.6	64.4	59.4	65.2
3rd quarter	65.5	62.9	61.3	83.7	95.1	60.0	94.1	92.9	62.1	64.9	60.0	65.8
4th quarter	66.0	63.3	61.8	83.9	95.0	60.5	95.0	92.3	62.4	65.0	60.5	66.2
1984												
1st quarter	66.8	64.0	62.4	83.9	94.9	60.9	95.2	92.6	64.1	67.7	61.5	67.1
2nd quarter	67.4	64.6	63.1	84.3	95.2	61.3	95.8	93.1	64.8	68.3	62.1	67.6
3rd quarter	68.0	65.1	63.7	84.6	95.3	61.9	94.8	91.4	65.3	68.8	62.6	68.1
4th quarter	68.4	65.5	64.2	84.8	95.4	62.4	93.8	90.3	65.6	69.0	63.1	68.5
1985												
1st quarter	69.2	66.2	65.0	85.1	95.6	62.7	92.8	88.1	66.5	69.9	63.9	69.1
2nd quarter	69.5	66.7	65.5	85.2	95.7	62.9	92.4	88.5	66.8	69.8	64.5	69.5
3rd quarter	69.9	67.1	66.0	85.5	96.0	63.3	91.4	88.4	67.0	69.7	65.0	69.9
4th quarter	70.3	67.7	66.6	86.1	96.4	64.0	91.3	90.2	67.6	70.4	65.6	70.5
1986												
1st quarter	70.7	68.2	67.3	86.5	96.6	64.8	90.9	90.4	67.7	70.3	65.9	70.9
2nd quarter	71.0	68.2	67.9	87.1	97.3	65.4	90.5	87.6	67.9	70.3	66.2	71.0
3rd quarter	71.5	68.7	68.6	87.9	98.0	66.3	90.2	88.2	68.3	70.4	66.8	71.5
4th quarter	72.0	69.2	69.2	88.5	98.4	67.0	91.0	89.3	68.8	70.5	67.7	72.0
1987												
1st quarter	72.5	70.0	69.8	88.8	98.4	67.7	91.4	91.6	69.5	71.0	68.5	72.7
2nd quarter	72.9	70.6	70.4	88.9	98.3	68.2	92.6	94.0	69.9	71.1	69.1	73.2
3rd quarter	73.5	71.3	71.1	89.0	98.2	68.8	93.0	95.0	70.3	71.3	69.8	73.8
4th quarter	73.9	71.9	71.8	89.8	98.9	69.4	94.5	96.4	70.5	71.4	70.0	74.3
1988												
1st quarter	74.6	72.5	72.6	90.6	99.8	70.1	95.6	97.8	71.2	72.2	70.6	75.0
2nd quarter	75.3	73.3	73.5	91.1	100.3	70.7	97.6	99.5	71.8	72.7	71.2	75.7
3rd quarter	76.2	74.2	74.3	91.6	100.7	71.1	98.8	98.5	72.1	72.8	71.8	76.4
4th quarter	76.8	74.9	75.1	92.4	101.7	71.8	98.6	99.3	72.5	73.0	72.3	77.1
1989												
1st quarter	77.6	75.8	75.9	92.9	102.1	72.3	99.6	100.9	73.5	74.3	73.0	77.9
2nd quarter	78.3	76.8	76.6	93.5	102.5	73.2	99.7	102.0	73.9	74.5	73.7	78.8
3rd quarter	78.9	77.3	77.2	93.9	102.9	73.4	99.1	100.2	74.4	75.0	74.1	79.2
4th quarter	79.4	77.9	77.9	94.3	103.4	73.9	98.8	100.7	74.8	74.9	74.9	79.8
1990												
1st quarter	80.4	79.1	78.8	94.9	103.9	74.5	98.9	102.2	75.9	76.0	76.1	80.9
2nd quarter	81.3	79.9	79.9	95.2	104.2	74.8	99.2	100.5	76.7	76.7	76.8	81.6
3rd quarter	82.1	81.0	80.6	95.8	104.9	75.1	100.2	103.4	77.4	77.3	77.7	82.5
4th quarter	82.7	82.0	81.3	96.4	105.7	75.3	101.6	109.2	78.6	78.6	78.8	83.5

Table 19-5. Chain-Type Price Indexes for Gross Domestic Product and Domestic Purchases—Continued

(Index numbers, 2000 = 100.) NIPA Tables 1.1.4, 1.6.4, 2.3.4

Year and quarter	Gross domestic product, total	Personal consumption expenditures		Private fixed investment			Exports and imports of goods and services		Government consumption expenditures and gross investment			Gross domestic purchases
		Total	Excluding food and energy	Total	Nonresidential	Residential	Exports	Imports	Total	Federal	State and local	
1991												
1st quarter	83.7	82.6	82.2	97.1	106.7	75.5	102.0	105.9	79.3	79.7	79.2	84.2
2nd quarter	84.2	83.1	82.9	97.1	106.5	75.8	101.4	103.1	79.4	79.8	79.4	84.5
3rd quarter	84.8	83.7	83.6	97.0	106.2	76.3	100.8	101.8	80.0	80.4	79.9	85.1
4th quarter	85.2	84.3	84.4	96.7	105.9	76.0	101.0	102.9	80.4	81.0	80.2	85.6
1992												
1st quarter	85.8	85.0	85.2	96.5	105.7	75.8	100.9	102.4	81.0	81.9	80.6	86.1
2nd quarter	86.2	85.5	85.8	96.6	105.4	76.5	100.9	103.0	81.6	82.5	81.2	86.6
3rd quarter	86.6	86.1	86.4	96.7	105.3	77.0	101.0	104.6	82.0	83.0	81.5	87.1
4th quarter	87.0	86.7	87.0	96.9	105.2	78.0	100.8	104.2	82.2	82.9	81.9	87.5
1993												
1st quarter	87.7	87.1	87.5	97.4	105.5	78.9	100.8	102.6	83.1	83.9	82.7	88.1
2nd quarter	88.2	87.7	88.2	97.7	105.5	79.7	101.1	103.4	83.6	84.4	83.2	88.6
3rd quarter	88.6	88.0	88.6	98.0	105.5	80.4	100.9	102.5	84.0	85.2	83.4	88.9
4th quarter	89.0	88.4	89.0	98.1	105.5	80.8	100.8	102.2	84.5	85.6	83.8	89.3
1994												
1st quarter	89.6	88.8	89.5	98.6	105.8	81.7	101.3	101.7	85.2	86.2	84.8	89.8
2nd quarter	90.0	89.3	90.1	99.0	106.1	82.2	101.6	103.0	85.8	87.1	85.1	90.3
3rd quarter	90.5	90.1	90.8	99.3	106.2	83.0	102.3	104.7	86.2	87.1	85.7	90.9
4th quarter	91.0	90.5	91.2	99.6	106.0	84.1	102.9	105.2	86.8	87.8	86.3	91.3
1995												
1st quarter	91.6	90.9	91.7	100.0	106.1	85.2	104.0	105.6	87.7	88.8	87.2	91.9
2nd quarter	91.9	91.4	92.2	100.3	106.4	85.6	104.8	107.5	88.1	89.0	87.7	92.3
3rd quarter	92.3	91.8	92.6	100.4	106.4	85.9	104.6	106.7	88.4	89.3	88.0	92.7
4th quarter	92.7	92.2	93.1	100.4	106.2	86.4	104.1	105.8	89.2	90.9	88.3	93.1
1996												
1st quarter	93.3	92.8	93.5	100.1	105.6	86.7	103.9	105.4	90.3	92.2	89.3	93.6
2nd quarter	93.6	93.4	93.9	99.8	104.9	87.1	103.5	105.0	90.0	91.5	89.3	93.9
3rd quarter	94.1	93.7	94.3	100.1	104.9	88.1	102.8	103.8	90.5	91.8	89.9	94.3
4th quarter	94.5	94.4	94.8	100.1	104.7	88.5	101.8	104.0	91.1	92.4	90.4	94.8
1997												
1st quarter	95.0	94.8	95.1	99.9	104.2	89.0	101.5	102.8	91.8	93.3	91.1	95.2
2nd quarter	95.3	95.0	95.6	99.8	103.9	89.4	101.5	100.8	91.9	93.4	91.1	95.3
3rd quarter	95.5	95.2	95.8	99.8	103.6	90.2	101.2	100.2	92.1	93.5	91.4	95.5
4th quarter	95.9	95.5	96.1	99.6	103.1	90.8	100.8	99.5	92.7	94.0	92.1	95.8
1998												
1st quarter	96.1	95.6	96.4	99.1	102.2	91.1	99.8	96.7	93.0	94.3	92.3	95.8
2nd quarter	96.3	95.8	96.7	98.8	101.6	91.7	99.2	95.7	93.2	94.4	92.6	95.9
3rd quarter	96.6	96.1	97.0	98.8	101.1	92.6	98.5	94.5	93.6	94.6	93.2	96.1
4th quarter	96.9	96.4	97.4	98.7	100.7	93.5	98.2	94.5	94.1	94.8	93.7	96.4
1999												
1st quarter	97.3	96.7	97.7	98.9	100.6	94.4	98.0	94.0	94.8	96.1	94.2	96.8
2nd quarter	97.7	97.3	98.2	98.9	100.2	95.4	98.1	95.3	95.6	96.6	95.2	97.3
3rd quarter	98.0	97.9	98.5	98.8	99.7	96.3	98.3	96.6	96.5	97.1	96.1	97.8
4th quarter	98.5	98.4	99.0	98.9	99.6	97.0	98.8	97.9	97.4	97.8	97.2	98.4
2000												
1st quarter	99.3	99.3	99.6	99.5	99.8	98.7	99.5	99.3	99.0	99.5	98.7	99.3
2nd quarter	99.8	99.8	99.9	99.8	99.8	99.6	100.0	99.5	99.4	99.2	99.5	99.7
3rd quarter	100.2	100.2	100.1	100.3	100.2	100.4	100.2	100.5	100.5	100.4	100.5	100.3
4th quarter	100.7	100.7	100.5	100.5	100.2	101.3	100.3	100.7	101.1	100.8	101.3	100.7
2001												
1st quarter	101.5	101.5	101.2	100.4	99.6	102.6	100.3	99.9	101.9	101.3	102.2	101.4
2nd quarter	102.3	102.1	101.7	100.9	99.7	103.9	100.0	98.4	102.4	101.6	102.8	102.0
3rd quarter	102.7	102.3	102.1	101.4	99.8	105.6	99.5	97.1	102.8	102.1	103.1	102.2
4th quarter	103.1	102.4	102.7	101.4	99.6	106.4	98.6	94.6	103.1	102.6	103.3	102.4
2002												
1st quarter	103.6	102.7	103.0	101.3	99.5	106.2	98.4	94.1	104.4	105.1	104.0	102.8
2nd quarter	103.9	103.4	103.5	101.5	99.5	106.7	99.0	96.5	105.1	105.2	105.1	103.4
3rd quarter	104.3	103.8	104.0	101.5	99.4	107.1	99.8	97.3	105.8	105.5	105.9	103.8
4th quarter	104.9	104.3	104.3	102.3	99.6	109.0	99.9	97.4	106.7	106.7	106.7	104.4
2003												
1st quarter	105.7	105.1	104.6	103.1	99.7	111.4	100.9	100.1	109.1	109.6	108.8	105.4
2nd quarter	106.1	105.2	104.9	102.9	99.3	111.5	101.2	99.1	109.4	110.0	109.1	105.6
3rd quarter	106.6	105.9	105.4	103.2	99.5	112.2	101.4	99.7	110.1	110.3	110.0	106.2
4th quarter	107.2	106.2	105.8	104.1	99.8	114.3	102.2	99.8	110.7	110.6	110.8	106.7
2004												
1st quarter	108.2	107.2	106.5	105.2	100.1	117.2	103.7	102.2	112.6	113.6	112.0	107.8
2nd quarter	109.2	108.2	107.1	106.4	100.6	119.8	105.0	104.0	114.0	115.1	113.4	108.9
3rd quarter	109.7	108.7	107.5	107.3	101.0	121.9	105.4	105.4	115.3	115.7	115.1	109.6
4th quarter	110.6	109.5	108.2	108.3	101.6	123.6	106.5	107.1	117.0	116.6	117.2	110.6
2005												
1st quarter	111.6	110.1	108.8	109.2	102.5	124.3	107.7	107.8	119.0	119.7	118.5	111.4
2nd quarter	112.2	110.9	109.3	109.9	103.1	125.5	108.6	110.2	120.3	120.4	120.3	112.4
3rd quarter	113.1	112.1	109.7	111.0	103.6	127.6	109.3	112.9	122.0	121.4	122.4	113.6
4th quarter	114.0	112.9	110.4	112.2	104.5	129.5	110.1	114.1	123.4	121.5	124.6	114.5

Table 19-6. Personal Income and Its Disposition

(Billions of current dollars, except as noted, percent; quarterly data are at seasonally adjusted annual rates.)   NIPA Table 2.1

Year and quarter	Personal income							Less: Personal current taxes	Equals: Disposable personal income	Less: Personal outlays	Equals: Personal saving		Disposable personal income, billions of chained (2000) dollars
	Total	Compen-sation of employees, received	Proprietors' income with IVA and CCAdj	Rental income of persons with CCAdj	Personal income receipts on assets	Personal current transfer receipts	Less: Contribu-tions for govern-ment social insurance				Billions of dollars	Percent of disposable personal income	
1946	178.6	119.6	35.6	7.1	12.3	10.6	6.6	17.2	161.4	145.9	15.5	9.6	1 132.7
1947	191.0	130.1	34.5	7.2	13.9	10.8	5.6	19.8	171.2	163.8	7.4	4.3	1 090.3
1948	209.8	141.9	39.3	7.9	15.1	10.3	4.6	19.2	190.6	177.3	13.4	7.0	1 148.4
1949	207.1	141.9	34.7	8.2	16.0	11.2	4.9	16.7	190.4	180.9	9.5	5.0	1 155.8
1947													
1st quarter	187.6	127.2	36.6	7.0	13.4	9.7	6.3	19.2	168.4	158.1	10.3	6.1	1 096.0
2nd quarter	185.7	128.7	32.4	7.1	13.8	9.6	6.0	19.5	166.2	161.9	4.3	2.6	1 072.8
3rd quarter	193.7	130.0	33.9	7.3	14.2	13.5	5.2	19.7	174.0	165.6	8.4	4.8	1 102.8
4th quarter	197.0	134.3	35.3	7.5	14.2	10.5	4.8	20.8	176.2	169.7	6.5	3.7	1 089.7
1948													
1st quarter	202.3	137.8	36.1	7.7	14.9	10.7	4.8	21.2	181.1	172.7	8.4	4.6	1 107.3
2nd quarter	208.3	139.4	40.4	7.9	14.7	10.4	4.6	18.9	189.3	176.5	12.8	6.8	1 145.3
3rd quarter	214.3	144.6	41.0	7.9	15.2	10.1	4.6	18.2	196.1	179.5	16.6	8.5	1 168.4
4th quarter	214.4	145.8	39.7	8.0	15.6	9.8	4.5	18.4	196.0	180.4	15.6	8.0	1 171.9
1949													
1st quarter	208.3	143.9	35.5	7.9	15.7	10.5	5.2	17.8	190.5	179.2	11.3	5.9	1 147.6
2nd quarter	207.0	142.2	34.9	8.0	15.9	11.0	5.1	17.0	190.0	181.0	9.0	4.7	1 151.4
3rd quarter	206.3	141.0	34.2	8.3	16.0	11.5	4.8	16.3	190.0	180.4	9.6	5.0	1 158.1
4th quarter	207.0	140.5	34.2	8.5	16.5	11.8	4.5	15.8	191.2	183.0	8.2	4.3	1 165.7
1950													
1st quarter	221.6	144.6	35.7	8.8	17.7	20.2	5.3	16.6	205.0	185.7	19.3	9.4	1 252.8
2nd quarter	222.4	150.6	36.3	9.0	18.0	13.8	5.3	17.6	204.8	189.7	15.1	7.4	1 245.4
3rd quarter	231.3	159.0	38.8	9.2	19.0	10.8	5.5	18.9	212.4	203.6	8.8	4.1	1 264.8
4th quarter	240.7	166.8	39.5	9.5	19.6	11.1	5.8	22.5	218.2	201.1	17.1	7.8	1 277.4
1951													
1st quarter	249.6	174.8	42.1	9.7	18.6	11.1	6.6	24.4	225.2	212.4	12.8	5.7	1 276.9
2nd quarter	256.9	180.7	42.5	10.0	19.1	11.4	6.7	26.4	230.6	208.1	22.5	9.8	1 297.5
3rd quarter	260.1	183.0	42.7	10.3	19.2	11.6	6.6	27.8	232.4	210.8	21.6	9.3	1 305.9
4th quarter	265.5	187.0	43.6	10.5	19.5	11.6	6.7	29.6	235.8	214.8	21.1	8.9	1 308.5
1952													
1st quarter	267.5	191.3	41.9	10.8	19.1	11.4	6.9	30.9	236.7	216.2	20.4	8.6	1 308.1
2nd quarter	271.4	192.7	43.1	11.1	19.8	11.5	6.8	31.8	239.6	220.5	19.1	8.0	1 323.9
3rd quarter	278.2	196.6	44.9	11.4	20.0	12.3	6.9	32.3	246.0	223.2	22.8	9.3	1 349.7
4th quarter	284.3	204.1	42.7	11.7	20.5	12.3	7.1	33.1	251.2	231.5	19.7	7.8	1 376.0
1953													
1st quarter	289.0	208.0	43.1	12.0	20.6	12.4	7.1	33.4	255.6	235.3	20.3	7.9	1 395.0
2nd quarter	293.0	211.4	42.4	12.3	21.7	12.3	7.1	33.4	259.6	237.3	22.2	8.6	1 414.5
3rd quarter	293.1	211.6	41.7	12.6	21.9	12.5	7.2	33.2	259.9	238.2	21.8	8.4	1 408.7
4th quarter	292.4	210.1	41.4	12.9	22.1	12.9	7.1	32.9	259.4	237.7	21.7	8.4	1 399.8
1954													
1st quarter	292.4	208.1	42.7	13.2	23.0	13.5	8.1	30.2	262.2	239.7	22.5	8.6	1 407.5
2nd quarter	291.9	207.7	42.0	13.4	22.7	14.1	8.0	30.0	262.0	242.5	19.5	7.4	1 407.4
3rd quarter	294.0	208.3	42.4	13.6	23.4	14.5	8.1	30.0	264.0	245.2	18.8	7.1	1 422.7
4th quarter	299.4	212.6	42.2	13.7	23.9	15.2	8.1	30.5	269.0	249.9	19.1	7.1	1 450.6
1955													
1st quarter	305.3	216.9	43.5	13.8	24.7	15.3	8.9	31.4	273.9	256.3	17.5	6.4	1 471.9
2nd quarter	313.2	223.1	44.5	13.8	25.2	15.6	9.0	32.4	280.7	261.6	19.1	6.8	1 506.9
3rd quarter	320.5	229.1	44.7	13.9	26.1	15.9	9.2	33.4	287.2	266.1	21.1	7.3	1 535.3
4th quarter	325.5	233.6	44.5	14.0	26.7	16.0	9.3	34.2	291.3	270.3	21.0	7.2	1 552.7
1956													
1st quarter	330.9	238.0	44.9	14.1	27.4	16.3	9.9	35.4	295.5	272.1	23.4	7.9	1 568.4
2nd quarter	336.7	242.6	45.4	14.1	27.9	16.6	10.0	36.2	300.4	274.9	25.5	8.5	1 583.9
3rd quarter	341.6	245.7	46.2	14.2	28.3	17.1	10.0	36.9	304.7	278.2	26.5	8.7	1 590.6
4th quarter	349.2	251.6	46.9	14.3	29.2	17.3	10.1	37.9	311.3	283.7	27.7	8.9	1 615.9
1957													
1st quarter	353.3	255.3	47.0	14.4	29.8	18.2	11.4	38.6	314.7	288.3	26.5	8.4	1 618.9
2nd quarter	357.8	257.0	47.8	14.5	30.5	19.4	11.4	39.0	318.9	290.6	28.2	8.9	1 629.5
3rd quarter	362.1	259.7	48.7	14.6	31.0	19.6	11.5	39.2	322.9	295.3	27.7	8.6	1 637.5
4th quarter	361.5	258.1	47.9	14.9	31.1	20.8	11.3	38.8	322.7	297.0	25.8	8.0	1 628.2
1958													
1st quarter	362.0	254.6	50.2	15.2	31.3	22.1	11.3	38.2	323.8	296.6	27.3	8.4	1 613.2
2nd quarter	364.3	254.2	50.3	15.3	31.8	23.9	11.3	37.7	326.6	299.4	27.2	8.3	1 623.7
3rd quarter	372.6	262.2	50.0	15.5	32.1	24.2	11.4	38.9	333.6	304.4	29.2	8.8	1 656.8
4th quarter	377.2	267.2	50.1	15.6	32.2	23.7	11.5	39.4	337.8	308.3	29.5	8.7	1 677.1
1959													
1st quarter	383.8	274.5	50.4	15.6	33.0	24.0	13.7	40.8	343.0	315.9	27.1	7.9	1 688.6
2nd quarter	392.4	281.6	50.7	16.0	34.0	23.9	13.9	42.0	350.5	322.1	28.4	8.1	1 721.0
3rd quarter	394.6	282.3	50.5	16.4	35.1	24.2	13.9	42.7	352.0	327.6	24.4	6.9	1 719.5
4th quarter	400.3	285.5	50.9	16.7	36.3	24.8	13.9	43.7	356.6	329.9	26.7	7.5	1 733.2
1960													
1st quarter	406.7	294.0	50.2	16.9	37.4	24.6	16.4	45.3	361.4	333.6	27.8	7.7	1 753.2
2nd quarter	411.2	296.9	50.9	17.0	37.5	25.3	16.5	46.0	365.2	339.7	25.5	7.0	1 761.8
3rd quarter	413.4	297.6	50.9	17.2	38.1	26.0	16.5	46.5	366.9	339.8	27.0	7.4	1 762.8
4th quarter	414.7	297.1	51.2	17.4	38.5	27.0	16.4	46.4	368.3	342.0	26.3	7.1	1 761.2

Table 19-6. Personal Income and Its Disposition—Continued

(Billions of current dollars, except as noted, percent; quarterly data are at seasonally adjusted annual rates.) **NIPA Table 2.1**

Year and quarter	Personal income							Less: Personal current taxes	Equals: Disposable personal income	Less: Personal outlays	Equals: Personal saving		Disposable personal income, billions of chained (2000) dollars
	Total	Compensation of employees, received	Proprietors' income with IVA and CCAdj	Rental income of persons with CCAdj	Personal income receipts on assets	Personal current transfer receipts	Less: Contributions for government social insurance				Billions of dollars	Percent of disposable personal income	
1961													
1st quarter	418.8	298.0	52.4	17.6	38.7	28.8	16.7	46.5	372.3	342.6	29.8	8.0	1 777.6
2nd quarter	424.8	302.2	52.6	17.8	39.5	29.7	16.9	46.9	377.9	347.5	30.4	8.0	1 804.6
3rd quarter	431.8	307.2	53.4	18.0	40.5	29.9	17.1	47.4	384.4	350.5	33.9	8.8	1 829.2
4th quarter	440.6	313.8	54.6	18.2	41.9	29.4	17.3	48.1	392.5	357.9	34.5	8.8	1 865.4
1962													
1st quarter	447.4	320.4	55.4	18.5	42.0	30.0	18.9	49.4	398.0	363.3	34.7	8.7	1 883.4
2nd quarter	454.8	326.4	55.2	18.7	43.6	30.0	19.1	50.9	403.8	369.1	34.7	8.6	1 904.1
3rd quarter	459.4	329.2	55.2	18.9	44.9	30.4	19.2	52.3	407.1	373.2	33.9	8.3	1 914.7
4th quarter	465.2	332.6	55.7	19.1	45.9	31.2	19.3	53.6	411.6	379.7	31.9	7.8	1 930.4
1963													
1st quarter	470.2	337.5	56.0	19.3	46.1	32.6	21.3	54.1	416.1	383.6	32.6	7.8	1 946.0
2nd quarter	475.0	342.4	55.8	19.5	47.1	31.7	21.5	54.3	420.7	387.9	32.7	7.8	1 964.3
3rd quarter	482.0	347.4	56.3	19.6	48.4	32.0	21.8	54.6	427.4	395.3	32.1	7.5	1 986.4
4th quarter	491.3	353.6	57.7	19.6	49.9	32.5	22.0	55.2	436.1	400.3	35.8	8.2	2 019.6
1964													
1st quarter	500.8	360.0	58.1	19.6	51.5	33.6	22.0	53.8	447.1	410.1	37.0	8.3	2 060.6
2nd quarter	510.0	367.4	59.0	19.6	53.1	33.2	22.3	49.7	460.3	418.4	41.9	9.1	2 116.8
3rd quarter	519.4	374.6	59.6	19.7	54.6	33.5	22.5	51.6	467.8	427.7	40.1	8.6	2 144.6
4th quarter	528.1	380.8	60.8	19.6	55.8	33.7	22.7	53.2	474.8	430.5	44.4	9.3	2 169.4
1965													
1st quarter	538.6	387.3	62.2	19.9	57.1	35.0	22.9	57.0	481.7	441.3	40.4	8.4	2 193.3
2nd quarter	547.8	394.1	63.4	20.1	58.8	34.6	23.2	58.4	489.4	448.7	40.7	8.3	2 217.4
3rd quarter	561.7	402.3	64.2	20.3	60.3	38.1	23.6	57.0	504.7	458.1	46.6	9.2	2 278.4
4th quarter	574.8	414.3	65.9	20.3	61.4	36.9	24.0	58.3	516.5	472.2	44.3	8.6	2 324.3
1966													
1st quarter	586.9	426.7	69.4	20.7	62.6	37.8	30.4	61.5	525.3	482.8	42.5	8.1	2 345.9
2nd quarter	596.5	437.8	67.4	20.6	63.6	37.9	30.8	65.6	530.9	488.3	42.6	8.0	2 351.7
3rd quarter	609.6	449.0	67.6	20.9	64.5	39.6	31.9	67.9	541.7	497.6	44.1	8.1	2 381.3
4th quarter	622.8	457.2	68.3	20.9	65.5	43.1	32.2	70.6	552.2	503.6	48.5	8.8	2 408.6
1967													
1st quarter	633.3	463.3	69.1	21.1	67.5	46.1	33.6	71.2	562.2	508.2	53.9	9.6	2 445.0
2nd quarter	640.4	469.0	68.9	21.2	68.7	47.2	34.6	70.9	569.5	517.9	51.6	9.1	2 464.5
3rd quarter	654.1	478.7	71.0	21.2	69.8	48.7	35.2	73.8	580.3	524.9	55.3	9.5	2 488.1
4th quarter	665.4	489.7	70.5	21.1	70.1	50.0	36.0	75.9	589.5	532.6	57.0	9.7	2 506.1
1968													
1st quarter	684.7	504.5	72.2	20.9	72.4	52.4	37.6	78.6	606.2	550.9	55.3	9.1	2 549.8
2nd quarter	704.2	517.6	73.6	20.9	74.7	55.9	38.4	81.7	622.5	565.1	57.4	9.2	2 592.3
3rd quarter	722.0	531.4	75.4	21.0	76.0	57.3	39.1	91.9	630.2	581.9	48.3	7.7	2 597.1
4th quarter	737.2	543.8	76.0	20.8	77.6	58.7	39.7	95.9	641.3	591.2	50.2	7.8	2 613.7
1969													
1st quarter	751.2	555.9	76.2	21.1	80.5	60.4	42.9	102.6	648.6	603.9	44.7	6.9	2 617.5
2nd quarter	769.2	569.8	77.4	21.1	83.0	61.5	43.7	105.7	663.5	616.0	47.5	7.2	2 643.5
3rd quarter	789.5	586.6	78.1	21.3	85.3	62.9	44.6	104.1	685.4	626.7	58.7	8.6	2 696.6
4th quarter	804.0	598.2	77.9	21.2	87.7	64.3	45.3	105.6	698.4	639.2	59.2	8.5	2 716.1
1970													
1st quarter	814.7	606.1	77.6	21.2	89.6	66.1	46.0	104.6	710.1	650.7	59.4	8.4	2 729.4
2nd quarter	836.1	616.3	77.1	20.9	91.9	76.1	46.3	105.5	730.5	660.9	69.6	9.5	2 777.4
3rd quarter	848.2	622.5	79.1	21.5	95.4	76.3	46.7	100.7	747.5	673.2	74.4	10.0	2 814.6
4th quarter	856.1	623.9	79.7	21.8	97.1	80.1	46.5	101.5	754.6	680.2	74.5	9.9	2 804.4
1971													
1st quarter	876.1	641.6	81.8	21.7	99.5	82.0	50.5	98.3	777.8	699.6	78.2	10.1	2 863.6
2nd quarter	898.6	653.5	83.9	22.3	100.3	89.6	51.0	100.7	797.9	714.1	83.7	10.5	2 904.6
3rd quarter	911.3	663.5	85.2	22.7	101.7	89.6	51.3	102.3	809.0	727.1	81.9	10.1	2 916.4
4th quarter	928.0	674.8	88.3	23.1	102.4	91.3	51.9	105.5	822.5	743.9	78.5	9.5	2 946.8
1972													
1st quarter	956.1	702.6	88.5	23.7	105.2	94.3	58.1	119.8	836.4	761.8	74.6	8.9	2 965.0
2nd quarter	972.3	716.2	91.8	20.7	107.6	94.9	58.8	123.4	848.9	780.9	68.0	8.0	2 991.5
3rd quarter	998.6	729.9	96.5	24.6	111.1	96.0	59.5	124.3	874.3	799.8	74.5	8.5	3 053.6
4th quarter	1 043.8	751.9	106.7	24.6	114.6	106.4	60.4	127.1	916.7	825.0	91.6	10.0	3 175.0
1973													
1st quarter	1 064.8	781.6	106.0	24.5	117.2	109.1	73.6	126.4	938.4	849.9	88.5	9.4	3 210.5
2nd quarter	1 094.6	801.1	111.1	24.5	121.1	111.5	74.7	129.2	965.4	866.0	99.4	10.3	3 240.3
3rd quarter	1 122.6	819.9	114.4	23.5	127.6	113.3	76.1	134.1	988.5	884.9	103.6	10.5	3 258.3
4th quarter	1 161.0	842.5	122.4	24.5	132.6	116.5	77.6	140.0	1 021.0	901.6	119.4	11.7	3 297.6
1974													
1st quarter	1 177.8	860.7	115.9	24.7	137.7	121.9	83.1	142.8	1 035.0	918.7	116.3	11.2	3 246.6
2nd quarter	1 203.9	881.9	108.8	24.0	144.0	129.9	84.7	148.9	1 055.0	947.8	107.2	10.2	3 219.9
3rd quarter	1 241.8	904.6	112.9	24.4	149.1	137.1	86.4	154.9	1 086.9	977.4	109.4	10.1	3 231.1
4th quarter	1 267.1	915.7	114.7	24.2	154.7	144.3	86.6	157.6	1 109.5	987.9	121.5	11.0	3 217.3
1975													
1st quarter	1 284.0	919.4	113.2	24.1	159.0	155.9	87.6	158.0	1 126.0	1 015.5	110.5	9.8	3 205.7
2nd quarter	1 314.2	931.7	115.4	23.8	159.9	171.5	88.0	121.1	1 193.2	1 044.5	148.6	12.5	3 354.6
3rd quarter	1 351.9	957.6	122.4	23.7	163.1	174.8	89.8	152.8	1 199.1	1 079.1	120.0	10.0	3 309.1
4th quarter	1 390.1	987.5	126.9	23.2	166.7	177.6	91.8	158.5	1 231.5	1 108.3	123.2	10.0	3 342.0

Table 19-6. Personal Income and Its Disposition—Continued

(Billions of current dollars, except as noted, percent; quarterly data are at seasonally adjusted annual rates.)   NIPA Table 2.1

Year and quarter	Personal income							Less: Personal current taxes	Equals: Disposable personal income	Less: Personal outlays	Equals: Personal saving		Disposable personal income, billions of chained (2000) dollars
	Total	Compensation of employees, received	Proprietors' income with IVA and CCAdj	Rental income of persons with CCAdj	Personal income receipts on assets	Personal current transfer receipts	Less: Contributions for government social insurance				Billions of dollars	Percent of disposable personal income	
1976													
1st quarter	1 425.6	1 022.3	127.6	22.9	170.4	181.4	98.9	162.1	1 263.5	1 141.8	121.7	9.6	3 390.9
2nd quarter	1 453.5	1 046.0	129.9	21.9	176.3	179.7	100.4	169.0	1 284.5	1 161.6	122.9	9.6	3 417.5
3rd quarter	1 491.5	1 070.7	133.7	22.1	180.8	186.4	102.2	175.8	1 315.8	1 191.4	124.4	9.5	3 448.0
4th quarter	1 528.5	1 098.0	137.4	22.2	186.2	188.5	103.8	182.4	1 346.1	1 225.9	120.2	8.9	3 473.0
1977													
1st quarter	1 561.0	1 126.9	140.4	22.2	190.2	190.6	109.3	188.4	1 372.5	1 262.7	109.8	8.0	3 479.7
2nd quarter	1 606.6	1 164.3	141.6	20.6	201.0	191.1	112.1	195.3	1 411.3	1 291.8	119.5	8.5	3 517.4
3rd quarter	1 652.4	1 196.8	143.3	20.0	210.5	196.2	114.3	198.2	1 454.3	1 323.9	130.3	9.0	3 570.6
4th quarter	1 712.8	1 233.7	157.5	19.8	219.5	199.0	116.7	208.1	1 504.6	1 363.2	141.4	9.4	3 642.1
1978													
1st quarter	1 750.7	1 269.6	157.8	21.4	224.9	203.1	126.2	211.7	1 538.9	1 394.9	144.0	9.4	3 663.5
2nd quarter	1 811.9	1 318.3	167.3	20.9	230.6	204.9	130.1	222.8	1 589.0	1 454.2	134.8	8.5	3 706.3
3rd quarter	1 866.5	1 355.2	170.4	22.7	237.4	213.6	132.8	236.0	1 630.5	1 486.7	143.8	8.8	3 737.6
4th quarter	1 921.7	1 400.2	171.2	23.3	246.2	216.9	136.0	247.0	1 674.8	1 527.3	147.5	8.8	3 768.3
1979													
1st quarter	1 979.1	1 445.2	178.2	25.0	257.1	222.5	148.8	253.4	1 725.8	1 563.8	162.0	9.4	3 811.7
2nd quarter	2 021.9	1 478.4	178.2	22.1	267.0	227.1	150.9	261.8	1 760.2	1 605.5	154.6	8.8	3 785.2
3rd quarter	2 088.5	1 519.0	181.3	21.8	277.7	242.7	154.2	274.6	1 813.9	1 661.3	152.6	8.4	3 807.2
4th quarter	2 159.2	1 561.2	182.7	26.3	297.2	248.9	157.1	285.0	1 874.2	1 706.8	167.4	8.9	3 841.5
1980													
1st quarter	2 228.2	1 602.7	176.1	29.8	324.0	258.7	163.1	284.2	1 944.0	1 759.2	184.9	9.5	3 869.4
2nd quarter	2 246.8	1 625.1	161.0	25.4	334.6	263.9	163.2	291.6	1 955.2	1 761.2	194.0	9.9	3 800.0
3rd quarter	2 322.8	1 657.4	173.5	26.6	336.0	295.9	166.6	301.6	2 021.2	1 819.7	201.6	10.0	3 839.0
4th quarter	2 433.7	1 722.1	185.9	38.2	360.1	299.3	171.8	318.2	2 115.5	1 890.1	225.4	10.7	3 920.8
1981													
1st quarter	2 492.2	1 774.5	188.5	36.7	378.2	305.9	191.6	330.3	2 161.9	1 950.2	211.6	9.8	3 905.7
2nd quarter	2 544.9	1 808.0	179.6	36.5	405.6	309.3	194.1	342.1	2 202.8	1 984.6	218.3	9.9	3 915.0
3rd quarter	2 645.9	1 846.2	186.3	37.8	445.5	327.9	197.7	356.3	2 289.6	2 027.5	262.2	11.5	4 003.1
4th quarter	2 682.1	1 874.2	177.4	41.0	458.5	330.4	199.4	352.1	2 330.1	2 044.9	285.1	12.2	4 012.8
1982													
1st quarter	2 711.6	1 898.0	170.2	40.1	474.7	335.7	207.2	351.9	2 359.7	2 086.6	273.1	11.6	4 013.3
2nd quarter	2 758.2	1 917.2	175.1	37.6	491.7	344.9	208.4	359.1	2 399.1	2 116.4	282.7	11.8	4 041.9
3rd quarter	2 796.7	1 937.0	176.1	39.6	492.3	361.5	209.8	349.5	2 447.2	2 167.1	280.1	11.4	4 059.6
4th quarter	2 834.7	1 951.1	183.9	38.0	494.7	377.3	210.2	356.0	2 478.7	2 231.5	247.2	10.0	4 066.2
1983													
1st quarter	2 871.5	1 979.2	188.0	38.0	506.4	380.2	220.4	350.3	2 521.2	2 274.0	247.2	9.8	4 100.4
2nd quarter	2 923.3	2 018.5	189.4	38.3	514.4	386.4	223.6	359.0	2 564.3	2 341.0	223.3	8.7	4 132.7
3rd quarter	2 980.0	2 059.9	190.2	35.8	539.3	381.9	227.2	344.9	2 635.1	2 414.5	220.6	8.4	4 191.6
4th quarter	3 068.0	2 114.6	202.4	39.0	558.2	386.5	232.2	355.1	2 712.9	2 469.6	243.3	9.0	4 286.5
1984													
1st quarter	3 166.0	2 184.6	231.6	37.8	569.7	393.4	251.0	360.7	2 805.3	2 517.2	288.2	10.3	4 385.5
2nd quarter	3 255.3	2 235.2	245.9	36.3	596.0	397.8	255.8	370.0	2 885.4	2 578.9	306.5	10.6	4 467.0
3rd quarter	3 338.6	2 281.5	248.7	40.8	627.1	400.5	259.9	383.6	2 955.0	2 620.5	334.5	11.3	4 539.8
4th quarter	3 397.9	2 320.3	247.1	45.8	638.9	408.9	263.1	395.5	3 002.4	2 672.5	330.0	11.0	4 583.9
1985													
1st quarter	3 464.0	2 366.0	263.3	44.1	646.4	419.6	275.4	431.8	3 032.2	2 748.5	283.7	9.4	4 580.0
2nd quarter	3 505.6	2 403.3	261.2	43.3	654.5	422.1	278.8	388.1	3 117.5	2 798.6	318.9	10.2	4 673.4
3rd quarter	3 536.5	2 441.1	261.1	41.0	648.6	427.5	282.8	421.1	3 115.4	2 869.7	245.7	7.9	4 640.4
4th quarter	3 600.6	2 489.2	263.6	39.3	666.6	430.4	288.4	428.5	3 172.2	2 900.4	271.8	8.6	4 688.0
1986													
1st quarter	3 659.1	2 522.7	264.5	38.3	688.9	442.7	297.9	425.8	3 233.4	2 945.6	287.7	8.9	4 744.2
2nd quarter	3 698.0	2 545.3	271.3	36.2	697.5	448.5	300.7	428.9	3 269.1	2 978.6	290.5	8.9	4 793.8
3rd quarter	3 746.2	2 581.4	283.9	31.7	698.7	455.4	305.1	438.9	3 307.2	3 050.8	256.4	7.8	4 813.6
4th quarter	3 786.2	2 631.1	282.9	27.9	697.1	457.3	310.1	455.5	3 330.7	3 091.8	238.9	7.2	4 813.4
1987													
1st quarter	3 847.3	2 678.6	291.7	31.7	699.3	462.5	316.5	450.3	3 397.1	3 124.0	273.0	8.0	4 854.6
2nd quarter	3 900.6	2 721.1	298.5	29.3	704.3	467.6	320.2	511.2	3 389.4	3 191.3	198.1	5.8	4 802.3
3rd quarter	3 973.0	2 767.3	304.7	34.7	722.1	468.7	324.5	488.5	3 484.5	3 258.9	225.6	6.5	4 887.3
4th quarter	4 068.6	2 833.9	313.9	38.1	742.3	471.7	331.2	506.5	3 562.1	3 293.4	268.7	7.5	4 954.1
1988													
1st quarter	4 139.6	2 883.1	333.4	39.1	747.1	489.0	352.1	501.1	3 638.5	3 376.1	262.4	7.2	5 016.9
2nd quarter	4 208.2	2 945.5	339.5	37.2	752.5	492.6	359.1	496.9	3 711.3	3 437.6	273.7	7.4	5 061.3
3rd quarter	4 292.6	2 994.2	350.2	38.4	775.3	498.8	364.4	505.7	3 786.9	3 506.8	280.0	7.4	5 103.3
4th quarter	4 374.5	3 045.9	343.2	47.6	802.1	506.0	370.3	516.3	3 858.2	3 582.7	275.5	7.1	5 149.2
1989													
1st quarter	4 506.2	3 092.8	367.0	46.1	849.9	530.2	379.8	551.3	3 954.9	3 640.9	314.0	7.9	5 216.3
2nd quarter	4 558.5	3 122.1	360.1	46.5	875.1	537.6	382.8	565.1	3 993.4	3 708.1	285.3	7.1	5 199.1
3rd quarter	4 608.8	3 158.3	359.0	41.5	888.3	548.0	386.4	570.0	4 038.8	3 769.0	269.7	6.7	5 224.9
4th quarter	4 677.8	3 207.7	367.0	38.3	898.6	557.9	391.8	578.2	4 099.5	3 820.1	279.5	6.8	5 259.9
1990													
1st quarter	4 778.8	3 272.8	376.4	44.5	911.4	577.8	404.1	580.6	4 198.2	3 905.6	292.6	7.0	5 307.9
2nd quarter	4 860.8	3 330.5	379.7	47.7	922.3	588.8	408.3	592.7	4 268.1	3 960.9	307.2	7.2	5 338.7
3rd quarter	4 924.5	3 370.2	385.1	54.0	930.9	598.4	414.1	598.8	4 325.7	4 027.8	297.8	6.9	5 343.6
4th quarter	4 950.2	3 379.2	381.1	56.4	931.3	616.1	413.9	598.9	4 351.3	4 051.3	300.0	6.9	5 306.6

Table 19-6. Personal Income and Its Disposition—Continued

(Billions of current dollars, except as noted, percent; quarterly data are at seasonally adjusted annual rates.)　　　　**NIPA Table 2.1**

| Year and quarter | Personal income | | | | | | Less: Contributions for government social insurance | Less: Personal current taxes | Equals: Disposable personal income | Less: Personal outlays | Equals: Personal saving | | Disposable personal income, billions of chained (2000) dollars |
	Total	Compensation of employees, received	Proprietors' income with IVA and CCAdj	Rental income of persons with CCAdj	Personal income receipts on assets	Personal current transfer receipts					Billions of dollars	Percent of disposable personal income	
1991													
1st quarter	4 965.7	3 394.4	367.9	55.9	932.0	640.0	424.5	578.5	4 387.1	4 066.7	320.4	7.3	5 310.5
2nd quarter	5 025.5	3 426.9	374.2	58.3	934.1	659.8	427.7	583.7	4 441.8	4 124.1	317.7	7.2	5 347.1
3rd quarter	5 071.7	3 461.5	377.2	61.6	935.0	669.1	432.6	588.0	4 483.7	4 170.0	313.7	7.0	5 359.6
4th quarter	5 140.9	3 498.5	389.2	65.3	927.0	696.9	435.9	596.4	4 544.5	4 199.8	344.7	7.6	5 389.4
1992													
1st quarter	5 238.0	3 566.8	409.5	71.6	914.1	724.8	448.7	586.6	4 651.4	4 292.0	359.4	7.7	5 473.9
2nd quarter	5 321.0	3 617.0	425.3	79.8	909.3	743.2	453.7	604.9	4 716.1	4 342.3	373.8	7.9	5 514.6
3rd quarter	5 382.5	3 659.9	432.4	70.8	907.2	769.9	457.8	613.9	4 768.6	4 418.5	350.1	7.3	5 537.4
4th quarter	5 506.5	3 761.0	443.1	89.9	912.7	759.4	459.6	636.9	4 869.6	4 488.7	380.9	7.8	5 619.2
1993													
1st quarter	5 419.5	3 666.6	444.6	90.9	907.7	777.8	468.1	617.9	4 801.6	4 529.2	272.4	5.7	5 512.1
2nd quarter	5 542.3	3 780.5	456.3	95.3	903.8	782.3	475.9	641.2	4 901.1	4 596.9	304.3	6.2	5 590.2
3rd quarter	5 579.6	3 821.2	448.9	94.3	897.5	797.8	480.1	655.3	4 924.3	4 659.8	264.5	5.4	5 597.4
4th quarter	5 692.8	3 911.4	465.5	101.7	898.4	802.4	486.6	672.1	5 020.8	4 725.7	295.1	5.9	5 677.2
1994													
1st quarter	5 668.9	3 873.2	460.9	105.7	905.2	822.6	498.7	670.2	4 998.7	4 795.4	203.3	4.1	5 629.9
2nd quarter	5 813.7	3 973.4	475.1	120.9	931.0	819.6	506.5	695.6	5 118.1	4 859.3	258.8	5.1	5 733.1
3rd quarter	5 891.0	4 009.0	475.9	126.2	967.1	823.3	510.5	693.5	5 197.5	4 941.2	256.3	4.9	5 770.8
4th quarter	5 996.5	4 062.8	481.3	125.9	999.8	843.8	517.1	703.4	5 293.1	5 013.7	279.4	5.3	5 850.9
1995													
1st quarter	6 072.3	4 118.6	483.1	122.6	1 006.7	867.2	525.9	721.4	5 350.9	5 048.1	302.9	5.7	5 886.4
2nd quarter	6 119.2	4 153.2	484.9	122.3	1 012.2	876.8	530.1	742.9	5 376.3	5 123.3	253.0	4.7	5 881.7
3rd quarter	6 174.6	4 197.5	493.9	119.6	1 014.7	884.1	535.2	747.5	5 427.1	5 196.8	230.3	4.2	5 912.1
4th quarter	6 243.0	4 238.7	506.7	124.1	1 032.0	881.6	540.0	764.4	5 478.6	5 260.9	217.6	4.0	5 943.3
1996													
1st quarter	6 371.1	4 291.7	526.0	131.1	1 056.1	910.7	544.4	796.6	5 574.5	5 338.0	236.5	4.2	6 010.0
2nd quarter	6 490.5	4 359.0	547.9	130.7	1 073.2	931.9	552.2	833.9	5 656.6	5 433.6	223.0	3.9	6 059.8
3rd quarter	6 566.0	4 419.1	545.5	132.1	1 100.2	928.0	558.9	838.5	5 727.5	5 492.6	234.9	4.1	6 111.3
4th quarter	6 654.6	4 477.8	553.6	132.0	1 127.4	929.4	565.3	859.4	5 795.3	5 576.0	219.2	3.8	6 142.5
1997													
1st quarter	6 773.1	4 556.4	569.6	130.0	1 146.7	946.2	575.8	895.7	5 877.4	5 663.7	213.7	3.6	6 201.3
2nd quarter	6 847.0	4 617.9	566.8	129.5	1 168.7	946.4	582.2	910.4	5 936.7	5 706.0	230.6	3.9	6 251.9
3rd quarter	6 956.7	4 693.4	579.9	128.2	1 192.4	952.9	590.0	935.9	6 020.8	5 816.1	204.7	3.4	6 323.3
4th quarter	7 083.7	4 790.8	587.9	127.4	1 219.0	959.4	600.7	963.3	6 120.5	5 896.2	224.3	3.7	6 406.6
1998													
1st quarter	7 247.1	4 894.1	606.2	131.0	1 257.6	969.7	611.5	991.2	6 255.9	5 964.2	291.7	4.7	6 543.4
2nd quarter	7 376.0	4 977.6	619.2	135.7	1 287.6	975.8	619.9	1 018.3	6 357.7	6 072.3	285.4	4.5	6 638.6
3rd quarter	7 485.8	5 062.2	632.6	141.6	1 298.8	979.1	628.5	1 037.7	6 448.1	6 167.6	280.5	4.3	6 710.9
4th quarter	7 583.0	5 146.4	653.3	141.6	1 288.8	989.8	636.8	1 061.0	6 522.1	6 272.5	249.6	3.8	6 763.0
1999													
1st quarter	7 658.4	5 242.8	664.3	145.2	1 249.4	1 009.5	652.8	1 071.7	6 586.7	6 346.3	240.4	3.6	6 812.9
2nd quarter	7 728.8	5 297.3	672.0	147.6	1 255.4	1 013.3	656.8	1 090.2	6 638.6	6 489.5	149.1	2.2	6 822.1
3rd quarter	7 823.7	5 371.2	680.6	144.5	1 262.3	1 027.4	662.4	1 115.5	6 708.2	6 593.2	115.0	1.7	6 856.0
4th quarter	7 998.8	5 496.5	696.1	152.1	1 289.7	1 038.1	673.8	1 152.5	6 846.2	6 716.6	129.7	1.9	6 955.6
2000													
1st quarter	8 266.2	5 694.1	709.3	153.8	1 349.9	1 054.6	695.5	1 207.0	7 059.2	6 888.0	171.2	2.4	7 109.7
2nd quarter	8 372.3	5 727.2	726.5	148.5	1 385.6	1 080.8	696.3	1 231.1	7 141.2	6 970.0	171.3	2.4	7 157.5
3rd quarter	8 514.4	5 837.4	735.6	148.2	1 406.2	1 094.8	707.7	1 248.0	7 266.4	7 076.3	190.1	2.6	7 249.3
4th quarter	8 565.8	5 871.9	742.1	150.5	1 406.5	1 106.0	711.2	1 256.6	7 309.3	7 168.1	141.2	1.9	7 259.6
2001													
1st quarter	8 688.7	5 946.2	769.4	155.3	1 397.4	1 149.6	729.2	1 296.6	7 392.1	7 253.5	138.6	1.9	7 283.0
2nd quarter	8 719.9	5 944.6	770.6	161.7	1 388.7	1 185.7	731.5	1 312.3	7 407.6	7 318.8	88.7	1.2	7 252.1
3rd quarter	8 733.1	5 939.3	773.4	176.4	1 373.3	1 202.6	731.9	1 110.3	7 622.8	7 361.2	261.6	3.4	7 452.2
4th quarter	8 754.8	5 938.3	774.2	176.2	1 360.3	1 237.8	731.9	1 230.0	7 524.8	7 484.4	40.5	0.5	7 346.0
2002													
1st quarter	8 814.7	6 025.3	763.0	172.1	1 340.6	1 260.9	747.1	1 063.2	7 751.5	7 526.1	225.4	2.9	7 549.9
2nd quarter	8 892.0	6 091.5	763.5	167.7	1 336.5	1 284.0	751.1	1 050.3	7 841.7	7 620.5	221.2	2.8	7 585.2
3rd quarter	8 895.4	6 114.5	769.1	142.9	1 327.4	1 292.7	751.1	1 050.0	7 845.4	7 692.4	153.0	2.0	7 555.5
4th quarter	8 925.5	6 133.4	778.1	129.2	1 328.5	1 307.1	750.9	1 043.8	7 881.7	7 742.4	139.3	1.8	7 559.3
2003													
1st quarter	8 998.2	6 191.0	779.1	137.4	1 329.1	1 327.0	765.4	1 022.7	7 975.5	7 826.4	149.1	1.9	7 591.7
2nd quarter	9 111.3	6 275.4	801.6	130.5	1 334.9	1 344.0	775.0	1 023.7	8 087.6	7 913.7	173.9	2.2	7 685.7
3rd quarter	9 203.6	6 340.8	823.5	116.3	1 339.5	1 365.5	782.1	942.6	8 261.0	8 067.0	194.0	2.3	7 804.8
4th quarter	9 341.3	6 434.3	840.8	147.6	1 343.1	1 367.6	791.9	1 015.4	8 326.0	8 143.5	182.5	2.2	7 837.3
2004													
1st quarter	9 497.7	6 525.4	877.5	140.1	1 366.1	1 399.3	810.8	1 016.0	8 481.6	8 302.7	178.9	2.1	7 912.4
2nd quarter	9 640.5	6 611.7	910.2	132.0	1 389.8	1 416.7	819.8	1 033.4	8 607.1	8 438.7	168.3	2.0	7 958.8
3rd quarter	9 767.9	6 714.6	915.1	112.7	1 415.7	1 441.7	831.8	1 061.6	8 706.3	8 565.1	141.2	1.6	8 013.3
4th quarter	10 019.4	6 809.4	941.5	123.4	1 539.8	1 448.4	843.1	1 088.2	8 931.2	8 722.3	208.9	2.3	8 158.8
2005													
1st quarter	10 048.8	6 889.6	952.8	118.5	1 464.3	1 487.3	863.6	1 157.9	8 890.9	8 838.5	52.5	0.6	8 076.6
2nd quarter	10 161.5	6 953.7	965.8	102.8	1 500.5	1 510.1	871.5	1 191.8	8 969.7	9 000.4	-30.8	-0.3	8 085.8
3rd quarter	10 262.7	7 093.6	967.3	-11.5	1 532.7	1 569.0	888.5	1 215.0	9 047.7	9 180.3	-132.6	-1.5	8 074.1
4th quarter	10 483.7	7 184.4	996.8	81.5	1 580.2	1 539.8	898.9	1 247.6	9 236.1	9 264.5	-28.5	-0.3	8 183.3

Table 19-7. Per Capita Product and Income, Population, and Inventories to Sales Ratios

(Seasonally adjusted.) NIPA Tables 5.7.5A, 5.7.5B, 5.7.6A, 5.7.6B, 7.1

Year and quarter	Chained (2000) dollars per capita		Population (mid-period, thousands)	Ratio, inventories at end of quarter to monthly rate of sales during the quarter					
	Gross domestic product	Disposable personal income		Total private inventories to final sales of domestic business		Nonfarm inventories to final sales of domestic business		Nonfarm inventories to final sales of goods and structures	
				Current dollars	Chained (2000) dollars	Current dollars	Chained (2000) dollars	Current dollars	Chained (2000) dollars
1946	11 241	8 011	141 389	. . .	. . .	. . .	. . .	. . .	. . .
1947	10 925	7 565	144 126	. . .	. . .	. . .	. . .	. . .	. . .
1948	11 206	7 832	146 631	. . .	. . .	. . .	. . .	. . .	. . .
1949	10 957	7 747	149 188	. . .	. . .	. . .	. . .	. . .	. . .
1947									
1st quarter	10 971	7 656	143 156	5.81	3.73	2.78	2.21	3.43	3.38
2nd quarter	10 908	7 460	143 803	5.77	3.70	2.78	2.21	3.42	3.38
3rd quarter	10 854	7 634	144 462	5.89	3.62	2.72	2.17	3.34	3.33
4th quarter	10 962	7 508	145 135	6.16	3.60	2.77	2.19	3.38	3.34
1948									
1st quarter	11 087	7 597	145 761	5.87	3.62	2.83	2.22	3.45	3.37
2nd quarter	11 238	7 826	146 341	5.89	3.67	2.86	2.24	3.49	3.42
3rd quarter	11 254	7 950	146 973	5.75	3.74	2.93	2.28	3.59	3.49
4th quarter	11 228	7 937	147 659	5.62	3.77	2.96	2.30	3.63	3.51
1949									
1st quarter	11 013	7 739	148 298	5.54	3.76	2.93	2.30	3.61	3.52
2nd quarter	10 937	7 733	148 891	5.27	3.68	2.79	2.24	3.44	3.42
3rd quarter	11 013	7 745	149 529	5.28	3.67	2.78	2.23	3.43	3.40
4th quarter	10 851	7 760	150 211	5.12	3.60	2.73	2.17	3.36	3.30
1950									
1st quarter	11 248	8 305	150 852	5.15	3.56	2.72	2.16	3.36	3.27
2nd quarter	11 542	8 226	151 385	5.17	3.49	2.71	2.14	3.33	3.24
3rd quarter	11 943	8 319	152 039	5.11	3.34	2.69	2.07	3.27	3.10
4th quarter	12 106	8 364	152 724	5.70	3.53	3.00	2.24	3.68	3.39
1951									
1st quarter	12 204	8 328	153 336	5.84	3.55	3.08	2.27	3.73	3.42
2nd quarter	12 362	8 428	153 947	5.88	3.67	3.21	2.39	3.93	3.64
3rd quarter	12 551	8 444	154 655	5.79	3.65	3.16	2.40	3.87	3.64
4th quarter	12 513	8 421	155 389	5.76	3.62	3.11	2.40	3.78	3.61
1952									
1st quarter	12 591	8 384	156 033	5.68	3.66	3.13	2.43	3.81	3.66
2nd quarter	12 551	8 452	156 644	5.54	3.62	3.04	2.38	3.72	3.60
3rd quarter	12 578	8 579	157 324	5.54	3.71	3.11	2.45	3.82	3.71
4th quarter	12 932	8 706	158 043	5.16	3.61	3.02	2.39	3.69	3.59
1953									
1st quarter	13 125	8 793	158 648	4.99	3.56	2.99	2.36	3.65	3.54
2nd quarter	13 176	8 883	159 234	4.92	3.57	3.02	2.38	3.71	3.57
3rd quarter	13 037	8 806	159 963	4.92	3.59	3.06	2.39	3.76	3.59
4th quarter	12 771	8 710	160 713	4.96	3.61	3.04	2.39	3.75	3.59
1954									
1st quarter	12 655	8 721	161 389	4.95	3.59	3.01	2.37	3.72	3.57
2nd quarter	12 616	8 685	162 044	4.84	3.54	2.95	2.32	3.65	3.50
3rd quarter	12 696	8 739	162 792	4.78	3.47	2.90	2.27	3.61	3.43
4th quarter	12 885	8 868	163 585	4.67	3.40	2.85	2.23	3.54	3.35
1955									
1st quarter	13 201	8 960	164 266	4.61	3.34	2.82	2.20	3.51	3.31
2nd quarter	13 364	9 137	164 926	4.50	3.33	2.84	2.21	3.48	3.27
3rd quarter	13 480	9 267	165 674	4.41	3.30	2.85	2.21	3.52	3.29
4th quarter	13 487	9 327	166 481	4.36	3.33	2.91	2.24	3.61	3.36
1956									
1st quarter	13 367	9 381	167 190	4.43	3.36	2.97	2.28	3.69	3.43
2nd quarter	13 418	9 436	167 869	4.51	3.37	3.00	2.30	3.72	3.45
3rd quarter	13 339	9 431	168 654	4.44	3.36	2.99	2.31	3.71	3.47
4th quarter	13 490	9 533	169 497	4.41	3.33	2.99	2.30	3.74	3.48
1957									
1st quarter	13 514	9 511	170 218	4.38	3.33	2.99	2.30	3.71	3.46
2nd quarter	13 425	9 534	170 915	4.42	3.36	3.01	2.33	3.74	3.51
3rd quarter	13 496	9 538	171 684	4.39	3.35	2.99	2.33	3.72	3.50
4th quarter	13 292	9 441	172 463	4.39	3.36	2.98	2.32	3.74	3.52
1958									
1st quarter	12 883	9 319	173 116	4.60	3.44	3.00	2.36	3.78	3.58
2nd quarter	12 909	9 343	173 781	4.58	3.44	2.96	2.33	3.73	3.55
3rd quarter	13 150	9 492	174 535	4.51	3.37	2.88	2.27	3.65	3.47
4th quarter	13 391	9 565	175 340	4.44	3.33	2.87	2.25	3.62	3.42
1959									
1st quarter	13 592	9 592	176 045	4.31	3.25	2.80	2.21	3.54	3.36
2nd quarter	13 896	9 738	176 727	4.28	3.24	2.83	2.23	3.59	3.40
3rd quarter	13 827	9 689	177 481	4.19	3.21	2.81	2.22	3.57	3.38
4th quarter	13 814	9 722	178 268	4.20	3.26	2.87	2.27	3.67	3.48
1960									
1st quarter	14 009	9 756	179 694	4.24	3.27	2.90	2.30	3.70	3.51
2nd quarter	13 890	9 770	180 335	4.16	3.26	2.88	2.30	3.68	3.51
3rd quarter	13 853	9 734	181 094	4.22	3.30	2.92	2.33	3.73	3.55
4th quarter	13 612	9 682	181 915	4.17	3.27	2.86	2.29	3.67	3.51

. . . = Not available.

Table 19-7. Per Capita Product and Income, Population, and Inventories to Sales Ratios—Continued

(Seasonally adjusted.)

NIPA Tables 5.7.5A, 5.7.5B, 5.7.6A, 5.7.6B, 7.1

Year and quarter	Chained (2000) dollars per capita		Population (mid-period, thousands)	Ratio, inventories at end of quarter to monthly rate of sales during the quarter					
	Gross domestic product	Disposable personal income		Total private inventories to final sales of domestic business		Nonfarm inventories to final sales of domestic business		Nonfarm inventories to final sales of goods and structures	
				Current dollars	Chained (2000) dollars	Current dollars	Chained (2000) dollars	Current dollars	Chained (2000) dollars
1961									
1st quarter	13 640	9 733	182 634	4.14	3.25	2.83	2.27	3.63	3.48
2nd quarter	13 843	9 843	183 337	4.06	3.23	2.80	2.25	3.63	3.48
3rd quarter	14 009	9 936	184 103	4.12	3.25	2.82	2.27	3.63	3.50
4th quarter	14 234	10 089	184 894	4.07	3.20	2.78	2.24	3.58	3.45
1962									
1st quarter	14 439	10 150	185 553	4.10	3.22	2.79	2.27	3.60	3.48
2nd quarter	14 545	10 226	186 203	4.04	3.19	2.77	2.26	3.58	3.48
3rd quarter	14 623	10 243	186 926	4.12	3.21	2.80	2.29	3.61	3.50
4th quarter	14 599	10 286	187 680	4.09	3.21	2.79	2.29	3.60	3.51
1963									
1st quarter	14 742	10 334	188 299	4.07	3.23	2.80	2.30	3.61	3.53
2nd quarter	14 878	10 398	188 906	4.00	3.19	2.76	2.27	3.58	3.50
3rd quarter	15 100	10 475	189 631	3.95	3.17	2.76	2.28	3.56	3.49
4th quarter	15 160	10 609	190 362	3.91	3.15	2.75	2.27	3.56	3.49
1964									
1st quarter	15 451	10 791	190 954	3.81	3.09	2.71	2.24	3.50	3.44
2nd quarter	15 581	11 051	191 560	3.75	3.07	2.70	2.24	3.50	3.45
3rd quarter	15 737	11 155	192 256	3.74	3.05	2.70	2.24	3.49	3.43
4th quarter	15 723	11 244	192 938	3.75	3.07	2.73	2.26	3.54	3.49
1965									
1st quarter	16 066	11 337	193 467	3.77	3.07	2.74	2.28	3.55	3.50
2nd quarter	16 238	11 430	193 994	3.78	3.05	2.73	2.27	3.54	3.49
3rd quarter	16 512	11 705	194 647	3.74	3.04	2.73	2.27	3.53	3.48
4th quarter	16 857	11 903	195 279	3.73	2.99	2.70	2.24	3.47	3.42
1966									
1st quarter	17 227	11 983	195 763	3.76	3.00	2.71	2.26	3.47	3.43
2nd quarter	17 241	11 981	196 277	3.83	3.06	2.77	2.33	3.58	3.56
3rd quarter	17 302	12 096	196 877	3.87	3.09	2.82	2.37	3.63	3.61
4th quarter	17 387	12 197	197 481	3.88	3.16	2.89	2.44	3.74	3.75
1967									
1st quarter	17 498	12 351	197 967	3.91	3.22	2.95	2.50	3.84	3.85
2nd quarter	17 456	12 418	198 455	3.90	3.21	2.93	2.49	3.80	3.83
3rd quarter	17 546	12 502	199 012	3.89	3.24	2.95	2.52	3.83	3.88
4th quarter	17 629	12 557	199 572	3.87	3.25	2.96	2.54	3.86	3.92
1968									
1st quarter	17 954	12 749	199 995	3.85	3.22	2.92	2.51	3.80	3.86
2nd quarter	18 217	12 932	200 452	3.84	3.24	2.90	2.52	3.79	3.90
3rd quarter	18 291	12 921	200 997	3.79	3.22	2.87	2.51	3.75	3.87
4th quarter	18 319	12 969	201 538	3.76	3.23	2.87	2.53	3.76	3.91
1969									
1st quarter	18 569	12 961	201 955	3.77	3.22	2.88	2.53	3.75	3.90
2nd quarter	18 580	13 060	202 419	3.81	3.25	2.88	2.56	3.78	3.95
3rd quarter	18 643	13 285	202 986	3.80	3.28	2.92	2.59	3.82	4.01
4th quarter	18 500	13 341	203 584	3.85	3.30	2.95	2.62	3.89	4.08
1970									
1st quarter	18 424	13 374	204 086	3.83	3.29	2.94	2.61	3.88	4.06
2nd quarter	18 401	13 567	204 721	3.83	3.31	2.94	2.62	3.89	4.10
3rd quarter	18 501	13 702	205 419	3.82	3.29	2.94	2.62	3.91	4.10
4th quarter	18 240	13 605	206 130	3.78	3.29	2.94	2.63	3.92	4.13
1971									
1st quarter	18 688	13 850	206 763	3.81	3.28	2.93	2.63	3.91	4.12
2nd quarter	18 739	14 008	207 362	3.81	3.29	2.92	2.63	3.90	4.12
3rd quarter	18 830	14 021	208 000	3.76	3.29	2.90	2.63	3.88	4.11
4th quarter	18 826	14 124	208 642	3.73	3.24	2.86	2.59	3.83	4.07
1972									
1st quarter	19 115	14 177	209 142	3.69	3.20	2.82	2.57	3.77	4.02
2nd quarter	19 520	14 270	209 637	3.72	3.18	2.81	2.55	3.74	3.98
3rd quarter	19 655	14 528	210 181	3.73	3.17	2.81	2.55	3.76	3.99
4th quarter	19 924	15 066	210 737	3.72	3.09	2.75	2.50	3.66	3.90
1973									
1st quarter	20 386	15 202	211 192	3.81	3.02	2.77	2.47	3.65	3.83
2nd quarter	20 576	15 309	211 663	4.00	3.06	2.84	2.50	3.74	3.88
3rd quarter	20 415	15 356	212 191	4.07	3.08	2.85	2.51	3.77	3.91
4th quarter	20 560	15 503	212 708	4.18	3.13	2.96	2.57	3.91	4.01
1974									
1st quarter	20 340	15 232	213 144	4.25	3.18	3.10	2.63	4.10	4.10
2nd quarter	20 355	15 074	213 602	4.27	3.22	3.26	2.67	4.33	4.18
3rd quarter	20 107	15 088	214 147	4.46	3.25	3.37	2.70	4.49	4.24
4th quarter	19 976	14 985	214 700	4.49	3.37	3.52	2.82	4.73	4.50
1975									
1st quarter	19 697	14 901	215 135	4.28	3.33	3.38	2.76	4.56	4.41
2nd quarter	19 794	15 555	215 652	4.24	3.26	3.28	2.70	4.44	4.32
3rd quarter	20 070	15 299	216 289	4.17	3.22	3.22	2.66	4.34	4.24
4th quarter	20 281	15 412	216 848	4.02	3.17	3.14	2.62	4.24	4.17

Table 19-7. Per Capita Product and Income, Population, and Inventories to Sales Ratios—Continued

(Seasonally adjusted.)

NIPA Tables 5.7.5A, 5.7.5B, 5.7.6A, 5.7.6B, 7.1

Year and quarter	Chained (2000) dollars per capita		Population (mid-period, thousands)	Ratio, inventories at end of quarter to monthly rate of sales during the quarter					
				Total private inventories to final sales of domestic business		Nonfarm inventories to final sales of domestic business		Nonfarm inventories to final sales of goods and structures	
	Gross domestic product	Disposable personal income		Current dollars	Chained (2000) dollars	Current dollars	Chained (2000) dollars	Current dollars	Chained (2000) dollars
1976									
1st quarter	20 692	15 604	217 314	3.96	3.14	3.12	2.60	4.21	4.13
2nd quarter	20 803	15 693	217 776	4.08	3.17	3.19	2.64	4.31	4.20
3rd quarter	20 849	15 792	218 338	4.01	3.19	3.21	2.66	4.37	4.23
4th quarter	20 942	15 864	218 917	3.93	3.14	3.17	2.63	4.32	4.21
1977									
1st quarter	21 146	15 858	219 427	3.66	3.14	3.18	2.63	4.34	4.20
2nd quarter	21 509	15 991	219 956	3.69	3.11	3.14	2.61	4.26	4.14
3rd quarter	21 833	16 188	220 573	3.75	3.13	3.14	2.62	4.28	4.18
4th quarter	21 769	16 465	221 201	3.86	3.13	3.14	2.62	4.29	4.18
1978									
1st quarter	21 788	16 523	221 719	4.01	3.18	3.20	2.67	4.41	4.28
2nd quarter	22 589	16 674	222 281	3.90	3.06	3.10	2.58	4.21	4.08
3rd quarter	22 745	16 766	222 933	3.92	3.06	3.11	2.58	4.20	4.07
4th quarter	22 978	16 854	223 583	3.95	3.06	3.12	2.58	4.20	4.06
1979									
1st quarter	22 964	17 005	224 152	4.13	3.09	3.20	2.61	4.30	4.10
2nd quarter	22 926	16 843	224 737	4.17	3.13	3.27	2.64	4.42	4.18
3rd quarter	23 021	16 890	225 418	4.15	3.08	3.26	2.60	4.38	4.07
4th quarter	23 018	16 989	226 117	4.17	3.08	3.33	2.60	4.47	4.08
1980									
1st quarter	23 026	17 064	226 754	4.23	3.09	3.43	2.61	4.63	4.10
2nd quarter	22 499	16 711	227 389	4.38	3.20	3.55	2.71	4.84	4.29
3rd quarter	22 394	16 833	228 070	4.32	3.10	3.48	2.64	4.75	4.18
4th quarter	22 748	17 145	228 689	4.23	3.05	3.42	2.60	4.69	4.13
1981									
1st quarter	23 161	17 044	229 155	4.24	3.09	3.46	2.63	4.73	4.15
2nd quarter	22 929	17 046	229 674	4.23	3.10	3.45	2.63	4.74	4.18
3rd quarter	23 143	17 382	230 301	4.18	3.15	3.46	2.67	4.76	4.23
4th quarter	22 795	17 379	230 903	4.15	3.20	3.47	2.71	4.80	4.31
1982									
1st quarter	22 373	17 344	231 395	4.17	3.20	3.45	2.70	4.79	4.31
2nd quarter	22 444	17 429	231 906	4.13	3.20	3.41	2.70	4.76	4.31
3rd quarter	22 302	17 460	232 498	4.10	3.25	3.41	2.73	4.82	4.40
4th quarter	22 267	17 446	233 074	3.95	3.15	3.28	2.64	4.67	4.26
1983									
1st quarter	22 496	17 557	233 546	3.87	3.08	3.18	2.58	4.56	4.18
2nd quarter	22 956	17 659	234 028	3.80	3.02	3.13	2.54	4.49	4.11
3rd quarter	23 352	17 867	234 603	3.72	2.95	3.11	2.51	4.46	4.05
4th quarter	23 774	18 228	235 153	3.68	2.91	3.07	2.49	4.39	3.98
1984									
1st quarter	24 192	18 614	235 605	3.76	2.95	3.13	2.53	4.48	4.04
2nd quarter	24 559	18 922	236 082	3.74	2.96	3.14	2.53	4.49	4.04
3rd quarter	24 737	19 183	236 657	3.73	2.99	3.16	2.57	4.53	4.09
4th quarter	24 880	19 322	237 232	3.70	2.98	3.14	2.56	4.50	4.07
1985									
1st quarter	25 064	19 270	237 673	3.59	2.93	3.05	2.52	4.40	4.02
2nd quarter	25 224	19 622	238 176	3.53	2.93	3.03	2.51	4.38	4.02
3rd quarter	25 553	19 433	238 789	3.45	2.90	2.97	2.48	4.30	3.98
4th quarter	25 685	19 584	239 387	3.49	2.92	2.99	2.50	4.36	4.03
1986									
1st quarter	25 879	19 779	239 861	3.40	2.91	2.92	2.50	4.27	4.01
2nd quarter	25 927	19 944	240 368	3.36	2.91	2.90	2.50	4.25	4.02
3rd quarter	26 111	19 976	240 962	3.28	2.86	2.84	2.46	4.15	3.95
4th quarter	26 180	19 928	241 539	3.23	2.84	2.80	2.44	4.12	3.92
1987									
1st quarter	26 301	20 059	242 009	3.30	2.87	2.85	2.48	4.22	4.02
2nd quarter	26 534	19 802	242 520	3.28	2.83	2.84	2.46	4.20	3.97
3rd quarter	26 709	20 102	243 120	3.24	2.79	2.81	2.42	4.14	3.90
4th quarter	27 108	20 327	243 721	3.31	2.84	2.88	2.47	4.25	3.99
1988									
1st quarter	27 186	20 543	244 208	3.28	2.80	2.84	2.44	4.22	3.94
2nd quarter	27 475	20 682	244 716	3.27	2.77	2.84	2.43	4.20	3.91
3rd quarter	27 549	20 800	245 354	3.28	2.76	2.84	2.44	4.22	3.94
4th quarter	27 844	20 934	245 966	3.27	2.75	2.84	2.43	4.22	3.92
1989									
1st quarter	28 070	21 165	246 460	3.30	2.76	2.87	2.44	4.28	3.94
2nd quarter	28 190	21 048	247 017	3.27	2.77	2.86	2.45	4.25	3.94
3rd quarter	28 313	21 094	247 698	3.20	2.73	2.81	2.43	4.16	3.89
4th quarter	28 308	21 177	248 374	3.22	2.75	2.82	2.44	4.22	3.94
1990									
1st quarter	28 570	21 322	248 936	3.16	2.72	2.77	2.42	4.11	3.88
2nd quarter	28 554	21 379	249 711	3.16	2.75	2.76	2.45	4.16	3.97
3rd quarter	28 455	21 324	250 595	3.19	2.76	2.81	2.46	4.24	4.00
4th quarter	28 141	21 101	251 482	3.21	2.77	2.81	2.46	4.27	4.02

Table 19-7. Per Capita Product and Income, Population, and Inventories to Sales Ratios—Continued

(Seasonally adjusted.)   NIPA Tables 5.7.5A, 5.7.5B, 5.7.6A, 5.7.6B, 7.1

Year and quarter	Chained (2000) dollars per capita		Population (mid-period, thousands)	Ratio, inventories at end of quarter to monthly rate of sales during the quarter					
	Gross domestic product	Disposable personal income		Total private inventories to final sales of domestic business		Nonfarm inventories to final sales of domestic business		Nonfarm inventories to final sales of goods and structures	
				Current dollars	Chained (2000) dollars	Current dollars	Chained (2000) dollars	Current dollars	Chained (2000) dollars
1991									
1st quarter	27 911	21 052	252 258	3.16	2.79	2.76	2.48	4.21	4.05
2nd quarter	28 003	21 129	253 063	3.07	2.76	2.69	2.45	4.12	4.02
3rd quarter	28 038	21 104	253 965	3.03	2.75	2.68	2.45	4.12	4.03
4th quarter	28 074	21 149	254 835	3.04	2.77	2.69	2.46	4.17	4.07
1992									
1st quarter	28 281	21 417	255 585	2.98	2.72	2.61	2.41	4.07	3.98
2nd quarter	28 459	21 505	256 439	2.97	2.71	2.61	2.40	4.08	3.98
3rd quarter	28 632	21 514	257 386	2.95	2.69	2.59	2.39	4.06	3.95
4th quarter	28 848	21 757	258 277	2.90	2.67	2.55	2.36	3.99	3.90
1993									
1st quarter	28 798	21 279	259 039	2.93	2.69	2.57	2.39	4.04	3.96
2nd quarter	28 856	21 515	259 826	2.91	2.68	2.56	2.39	4.02	3.94
3rd quarter	28 905	21 469	260 714	2.87	2.66	2.53	2.38	4.00	3.93
4th quarter	29 201	21 706	261 547	2.83	2.63	2.50	2.35	3.92	3.86
1994									
1st quarter	29 419	21 468	262 250	2.84	2.64	2.49	2.35	3.92	3.87
2nd quarter	29 715	21 797	263 020	2.84	2.66	2.52	2.37	3.96	3.89
3rd quarter	29 785	21 870	263 870	2.84	2.66	2.52	2.36	3.96	3.88
4th quarter	30 043	22 106	264 678	2.87	2.67	2.54	2.38	3.99	3.88
1995									
1st quarter	30 046	22 180	265 388	2.91	2.69	2.59	2.40	4.07	3.91
2nd quarter	30 014	22 100	266 142	2.92	2.69	2.62	2.41	4.13	3.95
3rd quarter	30 161	22 143	267 000	2.88	2.65	2.58	2.39	4.08	3.91
4th quarter	30 289	22 191	267 820	2.86	2.63	2.56	2.38	4.05	3.88
1996									
1st quarter	30 427	22 385	268 487	2.82	2.61	2.53	2.35	3.99	3.84
2nd quarter	30 838	22 506	269 251	2.79	2.58	2.49	2.33	3.93	3.79
3rd quarter	30 995	22 624	270 128	2.79	2.59	2.48	2.33	3.92	3.79
4th quarter	31 258	22 667	270 991	2.74	2.56	2.45	2.30	3.87	3.74
1997									
1st quarter	31 416	22 823	271 709	2.72	2.56	2.43	2.31	3.83	3.73
2nd quarter	31 803	22 944	272 487	2.71	2.59	2.42	2.33	3.84	3.78
3rd quarter	32 092	23 129	273 391	2.68	2.57	2.39	2.32	3.78	3.74
4th quarter	32 228	23 361	274 246	2.68	2.60	2.41	2.34	3.82	3.78
1998									
1st quarter	32 501	23 798	274 950	2.68	2.63	2.41	2.38	3.84	3.84
2nd quarter	32 627	24 079	275 703	2.64	2.62	2.39	2.37	3.79	3.82
3rd quarter	32 900	24 265	276 564	2.60	2.62	2.36	2.37	3.74	3.81
4th quarter	33 299	24 380	277 400	2.56	2.59	2.33	2.35	3.67	3.75
1999									
1st quarter	33 497	24 498	278 103	2.56	2.61	2.33	2.37	3.69	3.80
2nd quarter	33 682	24 464	278 864	2.55	2.59	2.32	2.35	3.67	3.77
3rd quarter	33 967	24 507	279 751	2.56	2.59	2.34	2.36	3.71	3.78
4th quarter	34 467	24 789	280 592	2.59	2.60	2.37	2.37	3.76	3.79
2000									
1st quarter	34 467	25 274	281 304	2.58	2.58	2.36	2.36	3.75	3.76
2nd quarter	34 920	25 380	282 015	2.60	2.60	2.38	2.38	3.79	3.81
3rd quarter	34 781	25 633	282 812	2.61	2.61	2.40	2.40	3.83	3.84
4th quarter	34 866	25 599	283 591	2.63	2.62	2.41	2.40	3.85	3.86
2001									
1st quarter	34 740	25 620	284 269	2.62	2.61	2.38	2.39	3.82	3.84
2nd quarter	34 762	25 449	284 964	2.58	2.61	2.35	2.39	3.76	3.84
3rd quarter	34 545	26 080	285 742	2.54	2.61	2.32	2.39	3.72	3.84
4th quarter	34 589	25 640	286 509	2.44	2.55	2.23	2.33	3.57	3.74
2002									
1st quarter	34 743	26 291	287 171	2.45	2.56	2.24	2.34	3.61	3.77
2nd quarter	34 850	26 352	287 846	2.45	2.55	2.25	2.34	3.64	3.78
3rd quarter	34 962	26 178	288 619	2.48	2.56	2.26	2.35	3.68	3.79
4th quarter	34 888	26 123	289 375	2.51	2.58	2.28	2.37	3.73	3.85
2003									
1st quarter	34 914	26 176	290 025	2.53	2.57	2.30	2.36	3.78	3.83
2nd quarter	35 129	26 437	290 717	2.48	2.54	2.26	2.33	3.71	3.78
3rd quarter	35 675	26 776	291 485	2.44	2.49	2.21	2.28	3.59	3.66
4th quarter	35 818	26 819	292 226	2.45	2.49	2.22	2.28	3.62	3.67
2004									
1st quarter	36 081	27 018	292 853	2.47	2.48	2.23	2.28	3.66	3.67
2nd quarter	36 355	27 113	293 539	2.51	2.49	2.26	2.28	3.70	3.69
3rd quarter	36 538	27 228	294 301	2.51	2.49	2.28	2.28	3.73	3.66
4th quarter	36 683	27 654	295 037	2.52	2.49	2.29	2.28	3.76	3.67
2005									
1st quarter	36 916	27 319	295 643	2.53	2.48	2.30	2.28	3.77	3.66
2nd quarter	37 132	27 290	296 289	2.48	2.43	2.25	2.24	3.67	3.56
3rd quarter	37 421	27 183	297 027	2.47	2.40	2.25	2.20	3.66	3.51
4th quarter	37 494	27 484	297 748	2.51	2.42	2.28	2.22	3.74	3.55

Table 19-8. National Income by Type of Income

(Billions of dollars, quarterly data are at seasonally adjusted annual rates.)

NIPA Tables 1.7.5, 1.12

Year and quarter	National income, total	Compensation of employees			Proprietors' income with IVA and CCAdj		Rental income of persons with CCAdj	Corporate profits with IVA and CCAdj	Net interest and miscellaneous payments	Taxes on production and imports	Less: Subsidies	Business current transfer payments, net	Addendum: Net national factor income
		Total	Wage and salary accruals	Supplements to wages and salaries	Farm	Nonfarm							
1946	198.5	119.6	112.0	7.6	14.2	21.4	7.1	17.8	1.9	16.8	1.2	0.7	182.1
1947	216.6	130.1	123.1	7.0	14.4	20.2	7.2	23.7	2.5	18.1	0.2	0.7	198.0
1948	243.0	142.0	135.6	6.4	16.7	22.6	7.9	31.2	2.6	19.7	0.3	0.7	222.9
1949	238.0	141.9	134.7	7.1	12.0	22.7	8.2	29.1	2.9	20.9	0.3	0.7	216.6
1947													
1st quarter	211.7	127.2	119.7	7.5	16.0	20.6	7.0	20.6	2.3	17.7	0.3	0.7	193.7
2nd quarter	213.0	128.7	121.5	7.2	12.4	20.0	7.1	24.1	2.4	17.7	0.2	0.7	194.7
3rd quarter	216.6	130.1	123.4	6.6	14.1	19.8	7.3	24.2	2.6	18.0	0.2	0.7	198.0
4th quarter	225.2	134.3	127.8	6.5	14.9	20.3	7.5	25.9	2.6	19.0	0.1	0.7	205.5
1948													
1st quarter	233.7	137.9	131.4	6.5	14.5	21.6	7.7	29.9	2.5	19.0	0.2	0.7	214.1
2nd quarter	242.3	139.6	133.2	6.4	18.0	22.5	7.9	31.6	2.6	19.7	0.1	0.7	222.0
3rd quarter	247.2	144.5	138.1	6.4	17.9	23.1	7.9	30.8	2.6	20.0	0.4	0.7	226.9
4th quarter	248.9	145.9	139.5	6.4	16.4	23.2	8.0	32.3	2.6	20.3	0.6	0.7	228.5
1949													
1st quarter	241.9	144.1	137.0	7.1	12.7	22.8	7.9	31.0	2.7	20.4	0.3	0.7	221.2
2nd quarter	237.6	141.9	134.6	7.2	12.1	22.7	8.0	28.7	2.8	20.8	0.2	0.7	216.2
3rd quarter	238.1	141.0	133.9	7.1	11.6	22.6	8.3	29.9	2.9	21.3	0.3	0.7	216.4
4th quarter	234.5	140.5	133.4	7.0	11.5	22.7	8.5	26.7	3.0	21.2	0.2	0.8	212.8
1950													
1st quarter	244.2	144.6	137.1	7.5	12.2	23.4	8.8	30.2	3.1	21.6	0.4	0.7	222.4
2nd quarter	255.7	150.6	142.9	7.8	12.2	24.1	9.0	33.8	3.2	22.5	0.6	0.8	233.0
3rd quarter	273.4	159.0	150.8	8.2	13.1	25.7	9.2	38.5	3.2	24.4	0.5	0.9	248.6
4th quarter	284.3	166.9	158.3	8.6	13.9	25.6	9.5	41.6	3.2	23.4	0.8	1.0	260.7
1951													
1st quarter	295.9	175.0	165.5	9.4	15.0	27.1	9.7	40.4	3.4	25.1	0.9	1.1	270.5
2nd quarter	301.7	180.6	170.8	9.7	15.4	27.1	10.0	40.6	3.6	24.1	0.8	1.2	277.2
3rd quarter	306.9	183.7	173.8	9.9	15.1	27.6	10.3	41.2	3.8	24.5	0.6	1.2	281.7
4th quarter	312.9	186.5	176.2	10.2	15.6	27.9	10.5	42.5	3.8	25.3	0.7	1.3	286.9
1952													
1st quarter	314.8	191.5	181.2	10.3	13.7	28.2	10.8	39.8	3.9	26.1	0.5	1.3	287.9
2nd quarter	316.5	192.8	182.4	10.4	14.5	28.6	11.1	37.8	4.0	26.9	0.4	1.3	288.8
3rd quarter	322.4	196.3	185.7	10.6	15.9	28.9	11.4	37.6	4.1	27.3	0.4	1.2	294.2
4th quarter	333.6	204.1	193.3	10.8	13.0	29.6	11.7	41.9	4.2	28.2	0.3	1.2	304.5
1953													
1st quarter	339.9	208.0	196.9	11.1	13.0	30.1	12.0	42.6	4.5	28.8	0.3	1.3	310.2
2nd quarter	342.9	211.3	200.1	11.3	12.4	30.0	12.3	41.8	4.6	29.2	0.1	1.3	312.5
3rd quarter	341.5	211.5	200.3	11.2	11.7	30.0	12.6	40.7	4.8	29.3	0.3	1.2	311.3
4th quarter	333.7	210.0	198.7	11.3	11.5	29.9	12.9	33.8	5.0	29.2	-0.2	1.1	303.1
1954													
1st quarter	335.4	208.1	196.4	11.7	12.8	29.9	13.2	36.1	5.2	28.7	-0.3	1.0	305.3
2nd quarter	335.5	207.7	196.0	11.7	11.6	30.4	13.4	37.3	5.5	28.8	0.3	1.0	306.0
3rd quarter	338.9	208.3	196.3	11.9	11.7	30.6	13.6	39.2	5.7	28.8	-0.1	1.0	309.1
4th quarter	347.9	212.6	200.4	12.2	10.6	31.6	13.7	42.8	6.0	29.3	-0.3	1.0	317.3
1955													
1st quarter	360.0	217.1	204.2	12.9	10.9	32.6	13.8	48.0	6.1	30.3	-0.2	1.2	328.4
2nd quarter	370.1	223.6	210.3	13.3	11.2	33.3	13.8	49.3	6.3	31.2	-0.1	1.3	337.5
3rd quarter	377.0	228.6	214.7	13.9	10.6	34.1	13.9	49.9	6.2	32.0	-0.4	1.5	343.2
4th quarter	383.6	233.6	219.5	14.1	9.9	34.7	14.0	51.0	6.3	32.5	-0.2	1.6	349.4
1956													
1st quarter	387.2	238.0	223.3	14.8	10.1	34.8	14.1	48.9	6.6	33.1	-0.1	1.7	352.5
2nd quarter	392.9	242.6	227.5	15.1	10.3	35.2	14.1	48.8	6.8	33.6	0.2	1.7	357.7
3rd quarter	397.0	245.7	230.0	15.8	10.8	35.4	14.2	47.9	7.1	34.6	0.5	1.8	361.1
4th quarter	405.2	251.6	235.4	16.2	10.8	36.1	14.3	48.6	7.0	35.7	0.8	1.8	368.4
1957													
1st quarter	412.1	255.3	238.3	17.1	9.8	37.1	14.4	50.4	7.7	36.2	0.9	1.9	374.9
2nd quarter	414.4	257.0	239.6	17.4	10.4	37.4	14.5	49.4	8.0	36.6	0.8	1.9	376.7
3rd quarter	418.4	259.7	241.8	17.8	10.9	37.8	14.6	48.8	8.2	37.0	0.6	1.9	380.0
4th quarter	412.1	258.1	240.1	18.1	10.6	37.3	14.9	44.8	8.2	36.8	0.5	1.9	373.9
1958													
1st quarter	407.2	255.2	237.4	17.9	13.2	37.0	15.2	39.5	9.0	36.8	0.6	1.9	369.0
2nd quarter	408.4	254.8	236.9	17.9	12.9	37.4	15.3	40.0	9.5	37.4	0.8	1.8	370.0
3rd quarter	418.9	260.9	242.6	18.3	12.0	38.0	15.5	44.2	9.8	37.8	1.0	1.8	380.4
4th quarter	432.5	267.2	248.4	18.8	11.2	38.9	15.6	50.4	9.9	39.0	1.2	1.7	393.1
1959													
1st quarter	445.0	274.5	254.0	20.5	10.8	39.6	15.6	54.5	8.8	39.8	1.1	1.7	403.7
2nd quarter	459.8	281.6	260.6	21.1	9.8	40.9	16.0	59.6	9.8	40.3	0.9	1.8	417.7
3rd quarter	456.6	282.3	260.9	21.4	9.3	41.2	16.4	54.2	9.8	41.8	1.1	1.8	413.2
4th quarter	461.9	285.5	263.9	21.6	10.0	40.9	16.7	54.4	10.1	42.5	1.1	1.8	417.6
1960													
1st quarter	474.8	294.1	270.8	23.3	9.5	40.6	16.9	58.0	10.2	43.7	1.0	1.8	429.3
2nd quarter	474.8	296.9	273.4	23.5	10.4	40.5	17.0	53.9	10.1	44.4	1.3	1.8	428.9
3rd quarter	475.8	297.6	274.0	23.7	10.8	40.1	17.2	52.8	10.7	44.9	1.0	1.9	429.3
4th quarter	474.0	297.1	273.3	23.8	11.1	40.0	17.4	50.4	11.2	45.3	1.2	1.9	427.2

Table 19-8. National Income by Type of Income—Continued

(Billions of dollars, quarterly data are at seasonally adjusted annual rates.)

NIPA Tables 1.7.5, 1.12

Year and quarter	National income, total	Compensation of employees			Proprietors' income with IVA and CCAdj		Rental income of persons with CCAdj	Corporate profits with IVA and CCAdj	Net interest and miscella-neous payments	Taxes on production and imports	Less: Subsidies	Business current transfer payments, net	Addendum: Net national factor income
		Total	Wage and salary accruals	Supple-ments to wages and salaries	Farm	Nonfarm							
1961													
1st quarter	476.1	298.0	273.8	24.2	11.3	41.0	17.6	49.5	11.6	45.8	1.6	2.0	429.1
2nd quarter	485.8	302.2	277.6	24.6	10.7	41.9	17.8	53.8	12.2	46.5	2.0	2.0	438.6
3rd quarter	495.2	307.2	282.3	24.9	10.8	42.5	18.0	56.1	12.6	47.3	2.2	2.0	447.3
4th quarter	509.2	313.8	288.4	25.4	11.3	43.3	18.2	60.0	13.4	48.4	2.3	2.1	460.0
1962													
1st quarter	520.2	320.4	293.3	27.2	11.7	43.7	18.5	62.6	13.1	49.4	2.3	2.2	470.0
2nd quarter	526.9	326.4	298.7	27.6	10.9	44.3	18.7	61.9	14.1	50.0	2.4	2.2	476.3
3rd quarter	532.9	329.2	301.2	28.0	10.5	44.8	18.9	63.2	14.6	50.9	2.2	2.3	481.1
4th quarter	540.3	332.6	304.2	28.4	11.0	44.7	19.1	65.4	15.0	51.4	2.2	2.3	487.9
1963													
1st quarter	546.7	337.5	308.0	29.5	11.2	44.8	19.3	65.4	14.6	52.1	2.0	2.6	492.8
2nd quarter	556.1	342.4	312.4	30.0	10.6	45.3	19.5	68.7	14.8	53.0	2.2	2.6	501.3
3rd quarter	564.6	347.4	316.8	30.6	10.4	45.9	19.6	70.1	15.3	54.0	2.3	2.7	508.9
4th quarter	574.9	353.6	322.2	31.3	10.9	46.8	19.6	71.7	15.8	54.7	2.4	2.8	518.4
1964													
1st quarter	587.7	360.0	328.2	31.8	9.6	48.5	19.6	76.1	16.6	55.7	2.7	2.9	530.4
2nd quarter	597.4	367.4	334.8	32.5	9.3	49.7	19.6	76.1	17.1	56.8	2.9	2.9	539.2
3rd quarter	608.9	374.7	341.4	33.3	9.1	50.5	19.7	77.3	17.9	57.9	2.6	3.3	549.1
4th quarter	616.7	380.7	346.7	34.0	10.2	50.6	19.6	76.4	18.1	58.8	2.7	3.4	555.6
1965													
1st quarter	635.1	387.3	352.8	34.5	11.2	51.0	19.9	84.3	19.0	60.2	2.9	3.6	572.8
2nd quarter	646.1	394.1	358.9	35.2	11.8	51.6	20.1	86.4	19.5	60.4	3.0	3.6	583.5
3rd quarter	657.0	402.3	366.2	36.1	12.0	52.2	20.3	87.6	20.0	60.6	3.0	3.6	594.5
4th quarter	675.6	414.3	377.1	37.2	12.3	53.6	20.3	91.6	20.0	61.9	3.1	3.6	612.1
1966													
1st quarter	695.1	426.7	385.8	40.9	14.6	54.7	20.7	94.7	21.1	61.4	3.6	3.6	632.6
2nd quarter	704.6	437.8	395.9	41.9	12.4	55.0	20.6	93.4	21.9	62.9	3.9	3.5	641.1
3rd quarter	715.9	449.0	406.1	42.8	12.1	55.5	20.9	91.7	22.7	63.8	4.1	3.5	651.8
4th quarter	728.3	457.1	413.5	43.7	12.0	56.3	20.9	93.0	23.8	65.0	4.2	3.5	663.1
1967													
1st quarter	734.7	463.3	418.8	44.4	11.7	57.3	21.1	90.5	24.7	65.6	4.0	3.6	668.5
2nd quarter	741.8	469.0	423.6	45.4	10.9	57.9	21.2	89.5	25.5	66.9	3.9	3.7	674.1
3rd quarter	757.6	478.7	432.0	46.6	11.8	59.2	21.2	91.0	25.8	68.8	3.7	3.8	687.6
4th quarter	773.4	489.7	441.6	48.1	11.4	59.1	21.1	94.3	26.2	70.7	3.7	3.9	701.7
1968													
1st quarter	794.3	504.5	454.2	50.3	11.5	60.7	20.9	95.5	26.6	73.5	4.0	4.1	719.6
2nd quarter	815.1	517.6	465.9	51.7	11.1	62.5	20.9	99.4	27.0	75.5	4.2	4.3	738.3
3rd quarter	833.6	531.4	478.3	53.1	11.6	63.7	21.0	99.6	27.1	77.8	4.2	4.4	754.4
4th quarter	849.6	543.8	489.4	54.4	11.8	64.2	20.8	100.7	27.7	79.2	4.2	4.6	769.0
1969													
1st quarter	866.2	555.9	499.1	56.8	11.4	64.8	21.1	100.4	30.5	80.7	4.3	4.9	784.0
2nd quarter	882.1	569.8	511.4	58.4	12.4	65.1	21.1	97.2	32.1	83.0	4.5	5.0	797.6
3rd quarter	900.7	586.6	526.4	60.1	12.9	65.1	21.3	94.5	33.7	85.3	4.7	5.0	814.1
4th quarter	909.7	598.2	536.5	61.8	13.9	64.0	21.2	89.5	34.6	86.8	4.7	5.0	821.4
1970													
1st quarter	914.5	608.6	545.1	63.5	13.4	64.3	21.2	82.0	36.0	88.6	4.7	4.8	825.4
2nd quarter	926.1	614.2	549.1	65.1	12.2	64.9	20.9	85.7	38.1	90.6	4.8	4.6	836.0
3rd quarter	941.3	622.2	555.7	66.4	13.0	66.2	21.5	85.8	40.5	92.6	4.7	4.4	849.1
4th quarter	941.8	623.9	556.3	67.6	12.3	67.4	21.8	80.9	41.9	94.2	4.8	4.3	848.3
1971													
1st quarter	979.3	641.6	570.2	71.4	13.2	68.6	21.7	94.4	43.1	97.8	4.8	4.3	882.6
2nd quarter	999.0	653.7	580.3	73.4	13.1	70.8	22.3	96.6	44.0	99.1	4.8	4.3	900.5
3rd quarter	1 016.3	664.1	588.8	75.3	12.7	72.5	22.7	98.9	44.1	101.8	4.5	4.3	915.0
4th quarter	1 037.6	676.3	599.0	77.3	13.9	74.4	23.1	102.2	44.3	103.8	4.6	4.4	934.2
1972													
1st quarter	1 069.0	701.1	618.0	83.2	12.9	75.7	23.7	107.2	45.2	104.7	6.1	4.7	965.7
2nd quarter	1 088.7	715.8	630.5	85.3	15.1	76.6	20.7	108.0	46.5	106.9	6.2	4.8	982.7
3rd quarter	1 120.0	729.7	642.4	87.3	17.0	79.5	24.6	113.0	48.9	109.0	7.2	5.0	1 012.6
4th quarter	1 167.2	753.9	664.3	89.7	22.2	84.5	24.6	120.2	51.1	111.6	7.1	5.2	1 056.4
1973													
1st quarter	1 205.3	781.7	683.4	98.3	21.7	84.3	24.5	127.2	51.3	114.7	5.9	5.7	1 090.7
2nd quarter	1 229.4	800.8	700.1	100.7	27.1	84.0	24.5	123.8	52.8	116.3	5.7	6.1	1 113.0
3rd quarter	1 257.8	819.9	716.2	103.7	29.4	85.0	23.5	124.0	56.8	118.5	4.7	5.9	1 138.6
4th quarter	1 297.0	842.5	735.4	107.1	37.4	85.0	24.5	127.0	60.0	119.8	4.6	6.1	1 176.5
1974													
1st quarter	1 308.9	860.7	748.2	112.5	28.4	87.5	24.7	120.0	64.4	120.9	3.6	6.6	1 185.6
2nd quarter	1 329.6	881.4	765.3	116.1	19.8	89.0	24.0	118.3	69.1	124.2	2.9	6.9	1 201.6
3rd quarter	1 357.6	903.1	783.1	120.0	21.2	91.7	24.4	114.5	72.4	127.2	3.2	7.3	1 227.3
4th quarter	1 372.5	915.8	792.5	123.3	23.4	91.4	24.2	110.4	77.3	127.8	3.6	7.7	1 242.4
1975													
1st quarter	1 380.6	919.5	791.9	127.6	19.4	93.8	24.1	112.4	80.7	129.0	4.2	8.7	1 249.9
2nd quarter	1 412.3	931.7	800.4	131.4	19.9	95.5	23.8	125.3	80.8	133.2	4.3	9.5	1 277.0
3rd quarter	1 473.2	957.7	821.3	136.4	23.5	98.9	23.7	147.3	82.2	138.4	4.6	9.7	1 333.3
4th quarter	1 517.4	987.6	845.8	141.9	24.1	102.8	23.2	154.3	82.8	141.3	4.9	9.8	1 374.8

Table 19-8. National Income by Type of Income—Continued

(Billions of dollars, quarterly data are at seasonally adjusted annual rates.)

NIPA Tables 1.7.5, 1.12

Year and quarter	National income, total	Compensation of employees			Proprietors' income with IVA and CCAdj		Rental income of persons with CCAdj	Corporate profits with IVA and CCAdj	Net interest and miscellaneous payments	Taxes on production and imports	Less: Subsidies	Business current transfer payments, net	Addendum: Net national factor income
		Total	Wage and salary accruals	Supplements to wages and salaries	Farm	Nonfarm							
1976													
1st quarter	1 567.4	1 022.4	871.2	151.1	19.2	108.4	22.9	167.1	82.5	141.9	5.1	9.8	1 422.4
2nd quarter	1 593.2	1 046.1	889.4	156.8	16.7	113.2	21.9	161.8	85.2	145.1	4.8	9.8	1 445.0
3rd quarter	1 626.0	1 070.8	908.4	162.4	15.9	117.8	22.1	162.4	86.6	147.9	5.1	9.5	1 475.6
4th quarter	1 660.7	1 098.1	929.9	168.1	16.1	121.3	22.2	162.1	87.9	151.5	5.5	9.0	1 507.7
1977													
1st quarter	1 706.2	1 127.0	950.0	177.0	15.7	124.6	22.2	170.7	90.5	155.0	5.8	8.6	1 550.7
2nd quarter	1 775.3	1 164.4	980.9	183.5	13.9	127.8	20.6	191.9	98.6	158.2	5.9	8.2	1 617.2
3rd quarter	1 833.1	1 196.9	1 007.5	189.4	11.5	131.8	20.0	207.1	105.1	161.7	6.4	8.3	1 672.4
4th quarter	1 881.1	1 233.7	1 038.2	195.6	21.7	135.8	19.8	200.1	110.1	164.5	10.3	8.6	1 721.7
1978													
1st quarter	1 917.3	1 269.7	1 064.2	205.5	18.3	139.5	21.4	191.7	111.3	167.2	8.7	9.6	1 751.9
2nd quarter	2 012.2	1 318.4	1 106.4	212.0	20.6	146.7	20.9	218.7	113.9	173.3	8.4	10.2	1 839.1
3rd quarter	2 058.2	1 355.7	1 138.0	217.7	20.4	150.0	22.7	222.8	115.3	170.0	8.3	10.9	1 886.8
4th quarter	2 121.9	1 400.6	1 176.2	224.3	19.1	152.1	23.3	233.3	119.6	174.2	10.4	11.5	1 948.0
1979													
1st quarter	2 177.9	1 445.3	1 210.2	235.1	23.3	154.8	25.0	223.8	126.6	176.7	8.4	12.5	1 998.8
2nd quarter	2 216.0	1 477.5	1 236.3	241.2	21.4	156.8	22.1	224.8	132.8	178.8	8.8	12.9	2 035.3
3rd quarter	2 269.9	1 518.9	1 270.9	248.1	21.9	159.4	21.8	223.7	140.8	181.2	8.1	13.3	2 086.6
4th quarter	2 332.4	1 561.4	1 305.8	255.5	20.5	162.2	26.3	220.7	155.4	184.9	8.9	13.4	2 146.5
1980													
1st quarter	2 386.8	1 602.5	1 338.4	264.1	12.9	163.2	29.8	216.7	171.3	189.9	9.2	13.5	2 196.5
2nd quarter	2 371.2	1 625.1	1 354.9	270.3	2.7	158.3	25.4	185.8	176.9	197.2	9.6	13.8	2 174.2
3rd quarter	2 434.0	1 657.9	1 381.0	276.9	11.5	162.0	26.6	192.3	180.1	204.7	10.1	14.1	2 230.5
4th quarter	2 565.3	1 721.6	1 436.3	285.3	18.3	167.6	38.2	209.7	199.0	211.0	10.3	16.1	2 354.3
1981													
1st quarter	2 656.9	1 774.5	1 474.7	299.8	17.3	171.2	36.7	223.7	201.9	231.2	10.6	16.9	2 425.3
2nd quarter	2 702.3	1 808.0	1 502.4	305.7	17.8	161.8	36.5	218.8	221.4	235.9	10.7	17.1	2 464.3
3rd quarter	2 798.7	1 846.4	1 535.1	311.3	23.0	163.3	37.8	238.6	251.0	237.8	11.1	17.8	2 560.1
4th quarter	2 811.5	1 874.2	1 557.8	316.4	16.7	160.7	41.0	223.3	255.1	239.2	13.5	18.4	2 571.0
1982													
1st quarter	2 815.6	1 897.9	1 573.2	324.6	14.1	156.1	40.1	201.1	266.4	237.8	14.0	19.5	2 575.7
2nd quarter	2 864.2	1 917.3	1 587.1	330.2	12.6	162.5	37.6	214.4	278.3	238.7	13.6	20.1	2 622.7
3rd quarter	2 883.8	1 937.1	1 602.3	334.8	11.8	164.3	39.6	214.8	271.4	242.2	13.0	20.4	2 639.0
4th quarter	2 893.7	1 951.1	1 612.2	338.9	13.8	170.1	38.0	208.4	268.4	246.7	19.4	20.6	2 649.7
1983													
1st quarter	2 959.1	1 979.2	1 629.5	349.7	12.8	175.2	38.0	230.4	274.8	251.1	19.8	21.0	2 710.4
2nd quarter	3 040.0	2 017.2	1 661.8	355.4	7.6	181.8	38.3	260.9	275.6	261.6	21.5	21.6	2 781.4
3rd quarter	3 117.8	2 059.5	1 699.0	360.6	-0.1	190.2	35.8	277.3	290.0	267.9	22.1	22.7	2 852.8
4th quarter	3 219.9	2 114.5	1 748.1	366.4	3.5	198.9	39.0	288.3	300.8	274.2	21.5	24.6	2 945.0
1984													
1st quarter	3 358.1	2 184.8	1 794.0	390.8	19.2	212.4	37.8	314.3	303.3	282.1	21.2	27.6	3 071.7
2nd quarter	3 458.5	2 235.4	1 837.9	397.5	20.9	225.0	36.3	324.2	321.7	288.2	20.9	29.6	3 163.6
3rd quarter	3 526.4	2 281.5	1 877.3	404.1	20.1	228.6	40.8	314.5	340.0	292.7	20.8	31.1	3 225.5
4th quarter	3 586.2	2 320.9	1 911.1	409.7	22.2	225.0	45.8	321.4	343.2	298.0	21.1	32.1	3 278.5
1985													
1st quarter	3 652.6	2 366.2	1 946.2	419.9	22.6	240.7	44.1	322.7	343.2	301.5	21.0	33.1	3 339.5
2nd quarter	3 700.1	2 402.2	1 976.3	426.0	20.3	240.9	43.3	326.7	341.3	306.1	20.9	39.0	3 374.7
3rd quarter	3 746.8	2 441.1	2 009.3	431.8	19.1	242.0	41.0	343.3	334.5	312.2	21.2	33.5	3 421.0
4th quarter	3 794.1	2 489.2	2 050.1	439.1	21.2	242.4	39.3	328.5	346.3	314.3	21.9	33.8	3 466.8
1986													
1st quarter	3 856.3	2 522.7	2 076.3	446.4	19.4	245.2	38.3	327.1	365.1	317.8	23.0	42.8	3 517.7
2nd quarter	3 874.1	2 545.3	2 093.8	451.5	19.8	251.5	36.2	320.6	368.6	319.8	24.1	35.1	3 542.1
3rd quarter	3 916.8	2 581.4	2 124.0	457.4	25.6	258.3	31.7	313.7	369.9	326.5	25.4	33.8	3 580.7
4th quarter	3 962.1	2 631.1	2 165.2	466.0	25.6	257.3	27.9	316.6	363.4	330.7	26.7	34.6	3 621.9
1987													
1st quarter	4 035.8	2 678.6	2 207.7	470.8	26.5	265.1	31.7	327.9	361.9	336.3	28.2	34.3	3 691.8
2nd quarter	4 124.5	2 721.1	2 244.9	476.2	28.6	269.9	29.3	363.6	361.5	344.7	30.4	34.8	3 774.0
3rd quarter	4 218.3	2 767.6	2 285.4	482.2	28.8	275.9	34.7	387.5	368.2	352.7	31.2	33.1	3 862.7
4th quarter	4 316.4	2 833.7	2 344.9	488.7	30.7	283.3	38.1	396.3	373.8	357.8	31.0	33.1	3 955.8
1988													
1st quarter	4 410.8	2 883.1	2 381.5	501.6	33.3	300.1	39.1	408.2	379.8	365.5	30.3	32.3	4 043.6
2nd quarter	4 503.2	2 945.5	2 435.5	510.0	27.5	312.0	37.2	427.5	373.9	373.0	29.7	33.0	4 123.6
3rd quarter	4 591.3	2 994.2	2 476.0	518.3	28.9	321.3	38.4	436.0	385.6	378.1	29.1	34.5	4 204.5
4th quarter	4 692.2	3 045.9	2 518.8	527.1	17.6	325.5	47.6	458.8	402.1	383.0	28.4	36.2	4 297.5
1989													
1st quarter	4 775.4	3 092.8	2 555.5	537.3	36.7	330.3	46.1	437.1	425.8	391.6	27.8	38.1	4 368.8
2nd quarter	4 803.9	3 122.1	2 576.9	545.2	32.4	327.7	46.5	428.1	433.0	397.8	27.2	38.3	4 389.7
3rd quarter	4 840.7	3 158.3	2 605.0	553.3	30.0	329.0	41.5	421.0	437.1	404.3	26.9	40.9	4 417.0
4th quarter	4 886.6	3 207.7	2 648.1	559.7	32.9	334.1	38.3	420.3	432.5	403.7	27.1	39.7	4 465.8
1990													
1st quarter	4 999.4	3 272.8	2 701.2	571.6	34.7	341.8	44.5	433.6	436.6	419.9	26.9	39.4	4 563.9
2nd quarter	5 090.7	3 330.5	2 749.8	580.7	32.5	347.3	47.7	457.8	441.1	420.0	26.7	39.1	4 656.8
3rd quarter	5 121.3	3 370.2	2 781.3	588.9	31.3	353.8	54.0	430.4	440.7	427.4	26.7	39.1	4 680.4
4th quarter	5 145.2	3 379.4	2 783.7	595.6	29.0	352.0	56.4	429.4	450.3	434.7	26.8	40.0	4 696.6

Table 19-8. National Income by Type of Income—Continued

(Billions of dollars, quarterly data are at seasonally adjusted annual rates.)

NIPA Tables 1.7.5, 1.12

Year and quarter	National income, total	Compensation of employees			Proprietors' income with IVA and CCAdj		Rental income of persons with CCAdj	Corporate profits with IVA and CCAdj	Net interest and miscellaneous payments	Taxes on production and imports	Less: Subsidies	Business current transfer payments, net	Addendum: Net national factor income
		Total	Wage and salary accruals	Supplements to wages and salaries	Farm	Nonfarm							
1991													
1st quarter	5 165.9	3 394.5	2 786.7	607.9	26.0	341.9	55.9	456.0	429.8	444.7	26.9	40.6	4 704.1
2nd quarter	5 199.7	3 426.5	2 809.6	616.9	27.7	346.5	58.3	449.4	420.6	452.0	27.0	39.7	4 729.0
3rd quarter	5 246.9	3 461.5	2 834.3	627.2	24.5	352.7	61.6	447.8	418.8	461.6	27.3	39.6	4 766.8
4th quarter	5 298.9	3 498.5	2 861.4	637.2	28.8	360.4	65.3	451.6	403.8	471.7	27.9	39.6	4 808.3
1992													
1st quarter	5 432.6	3 566.8	2 911.7	655.0	33.0	376.5	71.6	492.4	397.5	476.7	28.4	39.3	4 937.7
2nd quarter	5 506.4	3 617.0	2 950.1	666.9	35.5	389.8	79.8	494.8	390.4	481.5	29.0	38.9	5 007.3
3rd quarter	5 486.7	3 659.9	2 982.3	677.6	35.2	397.2	70.8	428.5	382.7	486.3	30.2	48.0	4 974.3
4th quarter	5 625.3	3 698.0	3 014.0	684.0	34.3	408.8	89.9	501.6	383.3	490.7	31.9	43.5	5 115.9
1993													
1st quarter	5 663.8	3 738.7	3 042.7	696.0	28.8	415.9	90.9	505.1	381.0	490.1	35.2	42.3	5 160.4
2nd quarter	5 750.9	3 782.5	3 074.2	708.3	35.1	421.2	95.3	536.2	371.6	498.3	37.3	40.2	5 241.9
3rd quarter	5 779.8	3 823.2	3 105.5	717.6	25.5	423.4	94.3	539.3	359.2	505.3	37.4	39.8	5 264.8
4th quarter	5 898.9	3 861.2	3 134.3	727.0	35.5	429.9	101.7	587.0	351.1	520.1	35.7	40.3	5 366.6
1994													
1st quarter	5 931.9	3 929.6	3 190.9	738.7	40.9	420.0	105.7	526.7	353.9	532.3	33.3	48.5	5 376.8
2nd quarter	6 091.1	3 978.1	3 231.5	746.6	35.9	439.3	120.9	597.1	357.9	544.6	32.1	40.3	5 529.2
3rd quarter	6 181.8	4 013.7	3 262.9	750.8	31.4	444.5	126.2	625.2	370.9	550.6	31.6	42.0	5 611.9
4th quarter	6 284.2	4 067.5	3 313.7	753.8	27.6	453.7	125.9	652.2	382.9	555.1	31.7	42.3	5 709.8
1995													
1st quarter	6 356.3	4 134.9	3 379.2	755.7	20.9	462.2	122.6	657.4	379.1	555.2	33.3	45.4	5 777.2
2nd quarter	6 408.0	4 169.5	3 412.6	757.0	19.0	465.9	122.3	683.9	369.2	554.0	33.8	46.7	5 829.8
3rd quarter	6 492.1	4 213.8	3 455.1	758.7	22.0	471.8	119.6	720.6	360.1	559.5	34.3	47.6	5 908.0
4th quarter	6 559.3	4 255.1	3 495.7	759.4	28.8	477.9	124.1	724.9	359.8	564.2	34.6	47.8	5 970.6
1996													
1st quarter	6 677.0	4 295.3	3 532.7	762.6	36.7	489.3	131.1	768.1	359.9	571.1	34.6	48.0	6 080.4
2nd quarter	6 796.6	4 362.7	3 596.8	765.9	43.9	504.0	130.7	780.9	370.2	578.1	34.5	48.4	6 192.4
3rd quarter	6 876.8	4 422.7	3 653.9	768.8	33.4	512.1	132.1	787.1	379.8	582.0	34.2	48.8	6 267.2
4th quarter	7 010.0	4 481.5	3 709.5	772.0	35.2	518.2	132.0	808.5	394.9	593.3	33.9	67.0	6 370.3
1997													
1st quarter	7 114.6	4 553.5	3 777.7	775.8	39.1	530.5	130.0	835.2	404.3	596.0	33.4	46.8	6 492.6
2nd quarter	7 220.0	4 615.0	3 833.7	781.3	29.8	537.0	129.5	861.2	409.0	610.6	32.7	47.3	6 581.5
3rd quarter	7 361.1	4 690.5	3 900.5	790.0	34.5	545.3	128.2	895.5	416.9	616.9	32.5	53.3	6 710.9
4th quarter	7 473.0	4 787.8	3 986.8	801.0	33.4	554.5	127.4	881.9	432.3	624.3	32.9	52.1	6 817.4
1998													
1st quarter	7 573.3	4 893.4	4 075.7	817.6	29.6	576.6	131.0	811.9	464.7	629.2	33.5	59.8	6 907.3
2nd quarter	7 687.5	4 976.9	4 146.4	830.5	27.7	591.5	135.7	794.0	488.5	635.8	34.2	60.8	7 014.3
3rd quarter	7 823.1	5 061.5	4 218.3	843.2	27.4	605.1	141.6	807.1	498.8	643.4	35.7	63.3	7 141.6
4th quarter	7 927.3	5 145.7	4 290.4	855.3	32.8	620.4	141.6	793.5	496.2	651.0	38.2	75.1	7 230.2
1999													
1st quarter	8 074.2	5 248.0	4 380.9	867.0	34.9	629.4	145.2	844.2	480.6	657.9	41.3	64.2	7 382.2
2nd quarter	8 161.3	5 302.5	4 425.4	877.1	29.3	642.7	147.6	849.3	490.6	667.5	44.0	65.4	7 462.0
3rd quarter	8 254.7	5 376.3	4 486.1	890.2	25.6	655.1	144.5	842.3	498.8	679.6	45.6	68.1	7 542.6
4th quarter	8 456.4	5 501.7	4 593.2	908.5	24.6	671.5	152.1	869.3	511.5	691.2	45.8	71.8	7 730.7
2000													
1st quarter	8 680.5	5 694.1	4 760.0	934.1	23.2	686.1	153.8	832.6	548.3	697.6	44.4	81.3	7 938.1
2nd quarter	8 750.4	5 727.2	4 783.2	944.0	23.8	702.7	148.5	833.0	560.6	706.9	44.4	85.0	7 995.8
3rd quarter	8 858.3	5 837.4	4 874.9	962.5	23.0	712.6	148.2	811.8	564.3	712.2	44.3	88.9	8 097.2
4th quarter	8 891.7	5 871.9	4 898.8	973.1	20.7	721.4	150.5	794.3	563.0	718.7	44.1	93.1	8 121.9
2001													
1st quarter	8 987.6	5 946.2	4 961.1	985.1	21.9	747.5	155.3	778.7	565.2	725.1	52.3	98.3	8 214.7
2nd quarter	9 001.5	5 944.6	4 951.4	993.2	19.2	751.5	161.7	783.1	569.9	726.3	58.4	104.8	8 229.9
3rd quarter	8 890.3	5 939.3	4 935.2	1 004.1	17.7	755.7	176.4	714.5	565.5	725.6	67.3	65.7	8 169.1
4th quarter	9 039.9	5 938.3	4 923.4	1 014.8	20.0	754.1	176.2	793.0	564.8	737.6	43.1	102.5	8 246.4
2002													
1st quarter	9 131.1	6 025.3	4 961.2	1 064.2	8.9	754.1	172.1	829.4	545.8	746.0	39.9	91.1	8 335.6
2nd quarter	9 211.7	6 091.5	4 989.4	1 102.1	4.0	759.4	167.7	864.3	519.3	757.9	37.0	85.8	8 406.2
3rd quarter	9 247.5	6 114.5	4 988.5	1 126.0	11.0	758.1	142.9	895.4	507.0	771.6	38.3	81.4	8 428.9
4th quarter	9 326.7	6 133.4	4 984.5	1 148.9	18.4	759.7	129.2	956.1	511.5	775.5	38.3	78.8	8 508.4
2003													
1st quarter	9 406.7	6 202.4	5 032.4	1 170.0	21.8	757.4	137.4	923.6	529.1	787.5	42.0	84.1	8 571.7
2nd quarter	9 537.9	6 289.0	5 098.7	1 190.3	30.5	771.2	130.5	956.2	529.6	800.2	55.6	83.8	8 706.9
3rd quarter	9 699.3	6 365.8	5 159.3	1 206.6	32.1	791.5	116.3	1 016.2	526.4	812.9	46.5	84.1	8 848.4
4th quarter	9 885.4	6 444.3	5 220.4	1 223.9	32.5	808.3	147.6	1 076.5	513.7	828.0	47.3	83.3	9 022.8
2004													
1st quarter	10 084.3	6 521.9	5 276.4	1 245.5	38.1	839.4	140.1	1 158.1	501.8	845.4	43.7	85.4	9 199.5
2nd quarter	10 207.0	6 590.2	5 328.1	1 262.1	39.5	870.6	132.0	1 183.3	493.4	858.2	42.8	86.1	9 309.0
3rd quarter	10 243.5	6 689.6	5 408.1	1 281.5	32.9	882.2	112.7	1 154.0	475.7	867.2	44.3	79.1	9 347.1
4th quarter	10 488.6	6 799.4	5 495.8	1 303.5	34.3	907.3	123.4	1 234.9	469.4	885.2	47.8	91.2	9 568.6
2005													
1st quarter	10 702.3	6 889.6	5 555.7	1 333.9	33.9	918.9	118.5	1 320.0	483.7	901.6	52.3	97.6	9 764.5
2nd quarter	10 795.4	6 953.7	5 601.3	1 352.4	28.7	937.1	102.8	1 342.9	477.1	920.2	55.6	99.9	9 842.2
3rd quarter	10 643.2	7 093.6	5 715.2	1 378.4	29.7	937.7	-11.5	1 266.3	482.9	930.2	58.1	0.2	9 798.7
4th quarter	11 106.2	7 184.4	5 787.0	1 397.4	28.7	968.1	81.5	1 393.5	490.0	937.3	63.1	99.1	10 146.2

Table 19-9. Saving and Investment

(Billions of dollars, percent; quarterly data are at seasonally adjusted annual rates.)

NIPA Tables 1.7.5, 5.1

Year and quarter	Gross saving Total	Net saving Private	Net saving Government Federal	Net saving Government State and local	Consumption of fixed capital Total	Consumption of fixed capital Private	Consumption of fixed capital Government Federal	Consumption of fixed capital Government State and local	Gross domestic investment Total	Gross domestic investment Private	Gross domestic investment Government	Net lending or net borrowing (-), NIPAs	Net domestic investment	Gross national income	Net saving as a percentage of gross national income
1946	38.4	18.6	-5.0	1.5	23.3	12.5	9.3	1.5	34.6	31.1	3.5	4.9	11.3	221.8	6.8
1947	46.6	13.5	5.3	1.4	26.4	15.7	8.8	1.8	39.6	35.0	4.6	9.3	13.2	243.0	8.3
1948	58.0	25.1	3.6	1.2	28.1	18.4	7.6	2.1	55.1	48.1	7.0	2.4	27.0	271.1	11.0
1949	45.6	21.1	-5.7	1.5	28.7	20.0	6.6	2.1	46.6	36.9	9.7	0.9	17.9	266.7	6.3
1947															
1st quarter	46.6	13.4	5.9	1.6	25.6	14.6	9.3	1.7	38.0	33.7	4.3	9.4	12.3	237.4	8.8
2nd quarter	44.0	11.2	5.2	1.6	26.0	15.4	8.9	1.8	36.7	32.4	4.3	9.9	10.6	239.0	7.5
3rd quarter	45.1	15.3	2.0	1.1	26.7	16.1	8.7	1.9	37.4	32.7	4.7	10.1	10.7	243.3	7.6
4th quarter	50.7	14.2	7.9	1.3	27.2	16.9	8.4	1.9	46.2	41.0	5.1	7.8	19.0	252.3	9.3
1948															
1st quarter	55.4	19.3	7.7	1.0	27.4	17.4	8.0	2.0	51.2	45.0	6.2	4.9	23.9	261.0	10.7
2nd quarter	59.1	25.1	5.1	1.2	27.8	18.1	7.6	2.1	54.8	48.1	6.7	3.0	27.0	270.1	11.6
3rd quarter	58.6	27.6	1.4	1.2	28.4	18.8	7.5	2.1	57.4	50.2	7.1	0.9	28.9	275.7	11.0
4th quarter	58.9	28.5	0.2	1.5	28.8	19.4	7.2	2.2	57.1	49.1	8.0	0.8	28.3	277.7	10.8
1949															
1st quarter	51.1	24.1	-3.4	1.5	28.9	19.6	7.1	2.2	49.5	40.9	8.6	2.2	20.6	270.8	8.2
2nd quarter	44.0	20.4	-6.5	1.4	28.7	19.8	6.8	2.1	43.6	34.0	9.5	1.7	14.8	266.4	5.7
3rd quarter	46.0	22.3	-6.5	1.6	28.6	20.1	6.4	2.1	47.6	37.3	10.3	0.6	19.1	266.7	6.5
4th quarter	41.3	17.5	-6.2	1.3	28.6	20.3	6.2	2.1	45.5	35.2	10.4	-1.0	16.9	263.1	4.8
1950															
1st quarter	48.7	27.6	-8.4	1.0	28.5	20.6	5.9	2.0	53.4	44.4	9.0	-1.0	24.9	272.8	7.4
2nd quarter	56.6	24.3	2.8	0.7	28.8	21.0	5.8	2.1	59.2	49.9	9.4	-1.3	30.4	284.6	9.8
3rd quarter	63.0	18.2	13.5	1.8	29.6	21.7	5.7	2.1	66.4	56.1	10.2	-2.7	36.8	302.9	11.0
4th quarter	74.1	27.4	14.2	1.8	30.8	22.6	5.9	2.3	76.5	65.9	10.6	-2.5	45.7	315.1	13.7
1951															
1st quarter	70.8	18.8	17.2	2.7	32.1	23.7	6.0	2.4	75.0	62.1	13.0	-1.7	42.9	328.0	11.8
2nd quarter	77.4	32.0	10.0	2.5	32.9	24.3	6.0	2.5	81.1	64.8	16.2	0.3	48.2	334.6	13.3
3rd quarter	75.5	34.2	5.3	2.4	33.6	24.9	6.1	2.6	78.4	59.4	19.0	2.2	44.8	340.5	12.3
4th quarter	76.4	33.4	6.0	2.7	34.3	25.4	6.3	2.7	76.7	54.4	22.3	2.7	42.3	347.2	12.1
1952															
1st quarter	77.1	32.4	6.9	2.9	34.9	25.8	6.5	2.6	77.1	55.2	21.9	3.6	42.1	349.7	12.0
2nd quarter	70.8	29.6	3.4	2.4	35.5	26.0	6.7	2.7	71.8	49.9	22.0	1.2	36.4	352.0	10.0
3rd quarter	73.1	32.8	1.1	3.3	36.0	26.2	7.0	2.8	76.4	53.9	22.5	-1.0	40.4	358.3	10.4
4th quarter	75.7	32.2	3.5	3.4	36.5	26.5	7.2	2.8	80.1	57.1	22.9	-1.2	43.6	370.1	10.6
1953															
1st quarter	77.0	32.9	4.3	2.9	37.0	26.7	7.4	2.8	81.8	57.9	23.9	-1.3	44.8	376.8	10.6
2nd quarter	77.4	33.2	2.6	4.0	37.6	27.1	7.6	2.8	82.8	58.1	24.6	-1.8	45.2	380.5	10.5
3rd quarter	77.2	32.2	3.5	3.5	38.1	27.6	7.7	2.8	81.7	57.4	24.3	-1.1	43.6	379.6	10.3
4th quarter	68.8	30.1	-3.2	3.6	38.4	27.7	7.8	2.8	75.4	52.3	23.1	-0.9	37.1	372.1	8.2
1954															
1st quarter	71.9	32.7	-3.3	3.6	38.9	28.1	8.0	2.8	75.3	51.5	23.8	-0.4	36.4	374.3	8.8
2nd quarter	72.0	31.0	-1.9	3.3	39.7	28.6	8.2	2.9	74.4	51.2	23.2	0.4	34.7	375.2	8.6
3rd quarter	72.6	30.8	-1.3	3.0	40.2	28.9	8.3	2.9	76.4	54.7	21.7	0.0	36.2	379.1	8.6
4th quarter	77.0	33.2	0.0	3.1	40.7	29.3	8.5	3.0	79.2	57.8	21.4	1.0	38.5	388.6	9.3
1955															
1st quarter	81.7	34.2	3.6	3.0	40.9	29.4	8.6	2.9	85.2	64.2	21.0	0.6	44.3	401.0	10.2
2nd quarter	88.1	36.6	6.7	3.3	41.4	29.9	8.6	3.0	90.0	68.1	21.9	-0.2	48.5	411.5	11.3
3rd quarter	89.1	38.0	4.9	3.8	42.5	30.6	8.7	3.2	90.7	70.0	20.7	0.9	48.3	419.4	11.1
4th quarter	93.1	38.0	7.8	3.9	43.4	31.3	8.9	3.2	94.1	73.9	20.3	0.5	50.7	427.1	11.6
1956															
1st quarter	96.7	39.0	8.5	4.3	44.8	32.4	9.1	3.4	94.7	73.0	21.8	1.0	49.9	432.1	12.0
2nd quarter	97.7	40.6	6.7	4.5	45.9	33.2	9.2	3.5	93.7	71.4	22.2	2.3	47.8	438.7	11.8
3rd quarter	101.3	42.0	7.8	4.5	47.0	34.1	9.3	3.6	96.4	72.5	23.9	3.1	49.4	444.0	12.2
4th quarter	101.9	42.4	7.3	4.3	47.9	34.8	9.4	3.7	94.9	71.2	23.7	4.6	47.0	453.1	11.9
1957															
1st quarter	102.1	42.5	6.1	4.8	48.6	35.2	9.6	3.7	96.0	71.8	24.2	5.6	47.4	460.7	11.6
2nd quarter	102.0	44.0	4.3	4.3	49.4	35.8	9.7	3.9	95.8	71.9	23.9	4.9	46.4	463.8	11.3
3rd quarter	101.9	43.1	4.4	4.1	50.3	36.5	9.8	3.9	97.9	73.2	24.6	5.0	47.6	468.7	11.0
4th quarter	92.6	39.3	-1.5	3.6	51.2	37.4	9.9	3.9	89.6	64.9	24.7	3.7	38.4	463.3	8.9
1958															
1st quarter	88.8	38.3	-3.2	2.7	51.1	37.5	9.8	3.9	85.6	60.5	25.1	1.6	34.5	458.3	8.2
2nd quarter	84.4	38.2	-8.3	2.6	51.9	38.2	9.8	4.0	84.0	58.7	25.3	0.9	32.0	460.3	7.1
3rd quarter	91.1	42.4	-6.4	2.6	52.5	38.5	9.9	4.1	92.8	65.5	27.3	1.2	40.3	471.5	8.2
4th quarter	99.0	46.2	-3.5	3.6	52.6	38.5	10.0	4.1	101.5	73.2	28.2	0.0	48.8	485.2	9.6
1959															
1st quarter	104.7	46.1	3.2	3.1	52.4	38.1	10.1	4.2	106.7	76.2	30.5	-1.4	54.3	497.4	10.5
2nd quarter	111.3	49.8	5.2	3.6	52.7	38.3	10.2	4.2	111.7	82.2	29.5	-2.0	59.0	512.6	11.4
3rd quarter	103.0	42.8	2.9	4.2	53.2	38.7	10.3	4.3	105.8	76.4	29.3	-0.5	52.6	509.8	9.8
4th quarter	105.8	45.6	2.1	4.3	53.8	39.1	10.4	4.3	107.1	79.3	27.8	-0.8	53.3	515.7	10.1
1960															
1st quarter	118.3	47.6	11.7	4.3	54.7	39.9	10.5	4.3	116.8	89.1	27.7	1.8	62.0	529.6	12.0
2nd quarter	110.8	43.0	8.2	4.2	55.3	40.4	10.6	4.4	107.2	79.7	27.5	2.5	51.9	530.2	10.5
3rd quarter	111.0	44.2	6.6	4.3	55.9	40.8	10.6	4.5	107.7	78.7	29.0	3.8	51.8	531.7	10.4
4th quarter	105.2	42.3	2.2	4.4	56.3	41.1	10.7	4.5	97.0	68.1	28.9	4.8	40.7	530.3	9.2

Table 19-9. Saving and Investment—Continued

(Billions of dollars, percent; quarterly data are at seasonally adjusted annual rates.)

NIPA Tables 1.7.5, 5.1

Year and quarter	Gross saving	Net saving			Consumption of fixed capital				Gross domestic investment and net lending, NIPAs				Net domestic invest-ment	Gross national income	Net saving as a percent-age of gross national income
	Total	Private	Government		Total	Private	Government		Gross domestic investment			Net lending or net borrow-ing (-), NIPAs			
			Federal	State and local			Federal	State and local	Total	Private	Govern-ment				
1961															
1st quarter	108.2	45.0	2.5	4.1	56.6	41.3	10.8	4.6	101.7	70.3	31.4	5.4	45.1	532.7	9.7
2nd quarter	110.2	48.4	0.8	4.0	57.0	41.5	10.8	4.6	105.7	75.8	30.0	4.1	48.8	542.8	9.8
3rd quarter	117.1	52.7	2.5	4.5	57.4	41.7	10.9	4.7	113.5	82.4	31.2	3.8	56.2	552.6	10.8
4th quarter	121.8	54.7	4.7	4.6	57.8	42.0	11.0	4.8	117.0	84.2	32.8	3.8	59.2	567.1	11.3
1962															
1st quarter	124.5	58.8	2.4	4.9	58.3	42.2	11.3	4.9	122.4	89.4	33.0	3.1	64.1	578.5	11.4
2nd quarter	123.9	57.9	2.2	5.0	58.8	42.5	11.3	5.0	120.6	87.9	32.7	4.9	61.8	585.7	11.1
3rd quarter	125.7	57.5	3.1	5.5	59.6	42.9	11.6	5.1	123.0	89.3	33.7	4.2	63.5	592.5	11.2
4th quarter	125.7	57.5	2.4	5.5	60.4	43.4	11.8	5.1	119.7	86.0	33.7	3.3	59.3	600.7	10.9
1963															
1st quarter	128.5	57.6	4.2	5.4	61.4	44.2	12.0	5.2	123.5	90.5	33.0	4.0	62.1	608.0	11.0
2nd quarter	133.1	59.1	6.3	5.5	62.1	44.7	12.1	5.3	125.0	92.2	32.8	5.4	62.9	618.2	11.5
3rd quarter	133.6	58.9	5.9	6.0	62.8	45.2	12.2	5.4	129.8	95.0	34.8	4.7	67.0	627.4	11.3
4th quarter	137.6	63.1	5.2	5.9	63.4	45.7	12.2	5.5	131.3	97.4	33.9	6.0	67.9	638.3	11.6
1964															
1st quarter	140.0	67.7	2.0	6.4	63.8	46.0	12.3	5.6	134.9	100.7	34.2	8.3	71.0	651.5	11.7
2nd quarter	140.3	72.0	-2.6	6.3	64.6	46.5	12.3	5.7	135.2	100.6	34.6	6.8	70.6	662.0	11.4
3rd quarter	143.5	70.4	1.3	6.5	65.3	47.2	12.4	5.8	137.2	102.5	34.8	7.6	71.9	674.2	11.6
4th quarter	149.7	73.7	3.3	6.4	66.4	48.0	12.4	5.9	139.5	104.6	34.9	7.4	73.1	683.1	12.2
1965															
1st quarter	157.1	75.9	7.6	6.2	67.4	48.9	12.5	6.0	149.9	115.7	34.2	5.8	82.5	702.5	12.8
2nd quarter	158.7	76.7	6.8	6.5	68.7	49.9	12.6	6.2	150.6	115.8	34.8	7.1	81.9	714.7	12.6
3rd quarter	158.8	82.6	-0.4	6.6	70.0	51.0	12.7	6.3	156.1	119.7	36.5	6.0	86.2	727.0	12.2
4th quarter	159.2	81.6	-0.6	6.8	71.4	52.2	12.8	6.4	158.5	121.8	36.7	6.0	87.1	747.0	11.8
1966															
1st quarter	167.5	81.8	5.0	7.7	73.0	53.5	12.9	6.6	170.4	131.7	38.7	4.8	97.4	768.1	12.3
2nd quarter	167.3	81.0	3.5	8.0	74.8	54.9	13.0	6.8	168.9	130.7	38.2	4.0	94.1	779.4	11.9
3rd quarter	167.3	81.4	1.4	8.0	76.5	56.1	13.4	7.0	170.4	130.2	40.3	2.8	93.9	792.4	11.5
4th quarter	172.7	88.2	-0.9	7.3	78.1	57.4	13.6	7.2	174.7	132.7	42.0	4.0	96.6	806.4	11.7
1967															
1st quarter	168.0	90.9	-9.7	7.5	79.3	58.3	13.7	7.3	172.8	129.3	43.4	4.4	93.5	814.0	10.9
2nd quarter	164.3	87.2	-10.4	6.9	80.6	59.3	13.9	7.4	165.7	123.7	42.0	3.6	85.1	822.5	10.2
3rd quarter	171.8	91.7	-8.5	6.4	82.2	60.4	14.1	7.6	171.7	128.5	43.2	3.2	89.5	839.7	10.7
4th quarter	177.9	95.7	-8.8	7.2	83.8	61.7	14.4	7.8	176.2	132.9	43.3	2.9	92.3	857.2	11.0
1968															
1st quarter	176.1	89.5	-6.0	7.2	85.4	62.8	14.6	8.1	180.3	137.2	43.1	1.8	94.9	879.7	10.3
2nd quarter	181.9	93.9	-7.4	8.2	87.2	64.3	14.7	8.2	187.4	143.4	44.0	2.4	100.3	902.3	10.5
3rd quarter	182.3	84.2	1.5	7.4	89.1	65.9	14.9	8.3	183.6	139.7	43.8	1.7	94.4	922.7	10.1
4th quarter	187.6	86.1	2.7	7.2	91.6	68.0	15.1	8.6	187.9	144.4	43.6	1.0	96.3	941.3	10.2
1969															
1st quarter	196.0	79.7	14.6	7.4	94.4	70.2	15.2	8.9	201.1	155.7	45.4	1.8	106.7	960.5	10.6
2nd quarter	196.3	80.2	11.5	7.8	96.8	72.2	15.4	9.2	199.1	155.7	43.4	0.8	102.2	978.9	10.2
3rd quarter	202.9	89.8	5.6	8.5	99.0	74.1	15.5	9.4	203.9	160.3	43.6	1.6	104.9	999.7	10.4
4th quarter	198.1	85.3	3.2	8.2	101.4	76.0	15.7	9.7	194.8	154.1	40.7	2.9	93.4	1 011.0	9.6
1970															
1st quarter	191.9	82.5	-2.3	8.2	103.5	77.6	15.9	10.0	193.5	150.7	42.8	4.0	90.0	1 018.0	8.7
2nd quarter	194.1	96.4	-15.8	7.7	105.8	79.4	16.0	10.4	196.5	153.9	42.6	5.5	90.7	1 031.9	8.6
3rd quarter	195.7	100.2	-19.4	7.1	107.7	80.8	16.2	10.7	200.1	156.1	44.1	3.8	92.4	1 049.0	8.4
4th quarter	189.0	97.0	-23.1	5.4	109.8	82.3	16.3	11.1	193.7	148.9	44.8	2.7	84.0	1 051.5	7.5
1971															
1st quarter	203.1	109.7	-23.6	5.0	112.0	84.1	16.5	11.4	212.9	171.3	41.7	4.6	100.9	1 091.3	8.3
2nd quarter	206.9	117.0	-30.1	6.0	113.9	85.7	16.5	11.7	220.6	178.8	41.8	0.3	106.7	1 113.0	8.4
3rd quarter	211.4	118.0	-29.1	6.5	116.0	87.6	16.5	11.9	225.7	183.4	42.3	-0.1	109.6	1 132.4	8.4
4th quarter	214.3	118.4	-30.6	8.4	118.1	89.5	16.4	12.2	220.5	179.2	41.3	-2.5	102.4	1 155.7	8.3
1972															
1st quarter	222.1	114.5	-22.6	9.1	121.1	92.0	16.6	12.4	235.5	193.2	42.3	-4.7	114.4	1 190.0	8.5
2nd quarter	229.4	108.7	-27.7	18.7	129.7	100.5	16.5	12.6	249.4	206.5	42.9	-4.3	119.7	1 218.4	8.2
3rd quarter	237.8	118.1	-16.6	10.1	126.1	96.6	16.6	12.9	253.5	212.4	41.1	-3.1	127.3	1 246.1	9.0
4th quarter	260.8	137.7	-30.7	24.6	129.2	99.2	16.8	13.3	262.7	218.4	44.3	-2.3	133.5	1 296.4	10.2
1973															
1st quarter	274.0	137.6	-14.7	18.9	132.2	101.7	16.8	13.7	280.0	232.5	47.5	2.6	147.8	1 337.6	10.6
2nd quarter	283.4	143.5	-14.7	15.7	138.9	107.8	17.0	14.1	292.8	246.0	46.7	5.9	153.9	1 368.3	10.6
3rd quarter	293.9	148.7	-10.1	14.6	140.8	109.2	17.2	14.5	287.4	241.8	45.6	13.0	146.6	1 398.6	10.9
4th quarter	316.7	163.5	-5.7	13.6	145.2	113.0	17.2	15.0	305.1	257.6	47.5	15.8	159.9	1 442.3	11.9
1974															
1st quarter	308.2	154.0	-8.3	11.8	150.8	117.5	17.4	15.9	295.6	244.1	51.5	17.0	144.7	1 459.7	10.8
2nd quarter	298.6	140.1	-10.8	10.6	158.7	123.8	17.8	17.1	308.8	252.3	56.5	3.2	150.1	1 488.3	9.4
3rd quarter	298.8	133.0	-10.5	10.0	166.3	129.4	18.5	18.4	303.4	245.4	58.0	1.0	137.1	1 523.8	8.7
4th quarter	300.2	146.5	-25.4	4.9	174.2	135.9	19.0	19.3	314.9	255.8	59.0	5.3	140.7	1 546.7	8.1
1975															
1st quarter	280.4	146.2	-47.2	0.6	180.7	141.6	19.3	19.9	281.3	218.7	62.6	19.2	100.6	1 561.3	6.4
2nd quarter	278.7	194.4	-104.2	2.6	185.9	146.3	19.5	20.1	274.8	216.8	58.1	23.0	88.9	1 598.2	5.8
3rd quarter	308.9	177.3	-62.0	3.6	190.1	149.8	19.9	20.3	301.7	237.8	63.9	20.0	111.6	1 663.3	7.1
4th quarter	320.0	185.4	-62.8	3.1	194.3	153.3	20.4	20.6	315.5	247.6	67.8	23.3	121.2	1 711.7	7.3

Table 19-9. Saving and Investment—Continued

(Billions of dollars, percent; quarterly data are at seasonally adjusted annual rates.)

NIPA Tables 1.7.5, 5.1

Year and quarter	Gross saving Total	Net saving Private	Government Federal	Government State and local	Consumption of fixed capital Total	Consumption of fixed capital Private	Government Federal	Government State and local	Gross domestic investment Total	Gross domestic investment Private	Gross domestic investment Government	Net lending or net borrowing (-), NIPAs	Net domestic investment	Gross national income	Net saving as a percentage of gross national income
1976															
1st quarter	337.3	186.0	-52.4	5.7	198.0	156.3	20.8	20.9	345.2	274.8	70.4	14.9	147.2	1 765.4	7.9
2nd quarter	342.9	181.4	-48.1	6.5	203.0	160.7	21.2	21.2	357.4	291.6	65.8	10.8	154.4	1 796.2	7.8
3rd quarter	343.7	181.9	-51.7	6.3	207.1	164.2	21.6	21.3	361.8	296.5	65.3	4.2	154.7	1 833.1	7.4
4th quarter	344.6	176.0	-54.8	11.0	212.5	168.8	22.0	21.6	368.9	304.9	64.0	5.6	156.5	1 873.2	7.1
1977															
1st quarter	353.5	169.0	-45.3	9.6	220.2	175.6	22.6	22.0	393.5	326.6	66.9	-6.3	173.3	1 926.4	6.9
2nd quarter	392.9	193.1	-39.4	11.8	227.4	182.1	23.0	22.4	424.0	354.9	69.1	-7.0	196.6	2 002.7	8.3
3rd quarter	418.0	215.0	-45.2	15.7	232.5	186.6	23.1	22.8	446.0	378.4	67.6	-5.9	213.5	2 065.6	9.0
4th quarter	425.8	216.9	-46.5	15.5	239.9	193.1	23.7	23.2	452.0	385.5	66.5	-16.9	212.0	2 121.1	8.8
1978															
1st quarter	434.5	215.0	-46.3	16.9	249.0	201.1	24.3	23.6	463.2	396.8	66.4	-23.0	214.2	2 166.3	8.6
2nd quarter	472.8	217.4	-25.5	23.0	257.8	208.8	24.8	24.2	507.9	430.9	77.0	-10.7	250.1	2 270.0	9.5
3rd quarter	490.8	227.4	-19.4	16.1	266.8	216.8	25.3	24.8	532.0	451.4	80.7	-9.2	265.2	2 325.0	9.6
4th quarter	514.0	234.3	-14.7	18.7	275.6	224.7	25.6	25.4	557.0	472.8	84.2	1.1	281.3	2 397.5	9.9
1979															
1st quarter	533.1	240.2	-6.1	14.5	284.4	232.5	25.9	26.1	560.2	481.1	79.1	0.6	275.8	2 462.3	10.1
2nd quarter	533.2	231.5	-6.2	11.9	296.0	242.4	26.6	27.0	578.4	493.0	85.4	-0.1	282.4	2 512.0	9.4
3rd quarter	536.5	227.7	-11.9	13.9	306.7	251.3	27.4	27.9	591.6	497.9	93.7	5.1	284.9	2 576.6	8.9
4th quarter	544.3	240.0	-20.8	11.6	313.4	256.5	28.0	28.9	595.2	499.5	95.7	0.1	281.8	2 645.9	8.7
1980															
1st quarter	548.6	242.8	-30.9	10.6	326.0	267.4	28.7	30.0	606.9	505.2	101.7	-7.9	280.9	2 712.8	8.2
2nd quarter	526.9	238.3	-54.7	5.5	337.8	276.9	29.7	31.1	570.3	470.4	99.9	12.7	232.6	2 709.0	7.0
3rd quarter	533.4	246.6	-68.7	7.5	348.1	285.3	30.4	32.4	541.3	443.5	97.9	31.0	193.3	2 782.1	6.7
4th quarter	588.8	277.6	-60.2	11.5	359.9	294.9	31.4	33.6	599.4	497.9	101.5	9.6	239.5	2 925.2	7.8
1981															
1st quarter	619.5	275.6	-39.3	11.7	371.5	304.3	32.4	34.8	670.7	563.1	107.6	4.5	299.2	3 028.4	8.2
2nd quarter	629.5	281.8	-43.4	8.0	383.2	313.9	33.4	35.9	656.9	551.4	105.5	3.1	273.7	3 085.5	8.0
3rd quarter	688.8	338.7	-51.1	7.7	393.5	322.4	34.3	36.8	698.0	592.8	105.2	10.0	304.4	3 192.3	9.3
4th quarter	680.7	353.2	-79.4	2.8	404.1	331.1	35.2	37.7	691.5	582.2	109.3	7.6	287.4	3 215.6	8.6
1982															
1st quarter	644.0	330.8	-100.4	-0.7	414.3	339.5	36.3	38.5	633.2	526.4	106.7	4.0	218.9	3 229.9	7.1
2nd quarter	668.6	352.1	-105.9	-1.4	423.8	347.2	37.3	39.3	643.6	530.8	112.8	20.8	219.8	3 288.0	7.4
3rd quarter	633.4	349.1	-143.8	-2.6	430.7	352.6	38.1	40.0	641.0	528.7	112.3	-10.7	210.3	3 314.5	6.1
4th quarter	570.3	312.8	-177.3	-4.0	438.8	359.8	38.7	40.3	600.4	483.0	117.4	-14.0	161.6	3 332.5	3.9
1983															
1st quarter	587.7	332.4	-173.2	-7.4	436.0	356.0	39.4	40.6	614.5	496.6	117.9	-4.7	178.5	3 395.1	4.5
2nd quarter	595.8	322.9	-169.4	3.0	439.4	358.5	40.2	40.7	662.0	542.2	119.7	-24.5	222.6	3 479.4	4.5
3rd quarter	598.3	325.2	-185.7	9.8	449.0	366.6	41.4	41.0	703.5	577.7	125.8	-44.7	254.5	3 566.8	4.2
4th quarter	655.6	354.4	-163.8	14.2	450.8	367.4	42.1	41.3	768.7	640.7	128.0	-53.5	317.9	3 670.7	5.6
1984															
1st quarter	738.4	410.0	-153.9	22.5	459.8	374.9	43.3	41.6	842.6	709.7	133.0	-75.3	382.8	3 817.9	7.3
2nd quarter	768.6	437.0	-164.0	26.7	468.9	382.6	44.2	42.1	872.2	735.1	137.1	-84.6	403.3	3 927.4	7.6
3rd quarter	792.9	466.8	-171.7	21.1	476.7	389.2	45.0	42.6	892.6	753.5	139.1	-87.0	415.9	4 003.1	7.9
4th quarter	793.9	466.4	-182.8	25.4	484.9	395.8	46.1	43.0	892.5	744.3	148.3	-99.9	407.7	4 071.1	7.6
1985															
1st quarter	783.6	412.3	-147.0	24.7	493.6	403.1	46.9	43.7	869.2	720.0	149.1	-85.8	375.5	4 146.3	7.0
2nd quarter	779.6	451.7	-197.3	24.0	501.2	409.4	47.5	44.3	893.3	735.3	157.9	-107.6	392.1	4 201.3	6.6
3rd quarter	748.2	388.4	-174.3	21.7	512.5	419.0	48.6	44.9	892.2	727.2	165.0	-117.4	379.8	4 259.3	5.5
4th quarter	758.5	401.1	-181.3	19.0	519.6	424.4	49.5	45.7	925.3	762.2	163.1	-131.3	405.7	4 313.7	5.5
1986															
1st quarter	771.5	405.0	-180.7	26.7	520.5	424.1	50.0	46.4	928.9	763.8	165.1	-124.5	408.4	4 376.8	5.7
2nd quarter	744.4	398.5	-202.1	20.5	527.5	428.9	51.2	47.4	923.5	753.0	170.5	-138.1	396.0	4 401.6	4.9
3rd quarter	705.8	355.4	-207.1	22.8	534.8	434.3	52.2	48.3	913.6	732.5	181.1	-146.5	378.8	4 451.6	3.8
4th quarter	712.4	329.4	-173.3	13.8	542.5	440.0	53.1	49.4	913.0	736.7	176.2	-146.6	370.5	4 504.6	3.8
1987															
1st quarter	754.6	378.4	-180.5	6.0	550.7	446.3	54.2	50.1	943.8	765.0	178.9	-147.2	393.1	4 586.5	4.4
2nd quarter	773.6	322.6	-126.0	19.4	557.7	451.9	54.7	51.0	951.3	767.6	183.7	-150.7	393.6	4 682.2	4.6
3rd quarter	803.6	361.1	-134.4	12.2	564.8	457.3	55.5	51.9	957.4	769.5	187.9	-150.4	392.6	4 783.0	5.0
4th quarter	855.4	407.7	-139.1	12.1	574.6	465.4	56.5	52.7	1 024.4	837.8	186.7	-153.3	449.8	4 891.0	5.7
1988															
1st quarter	872.8	417.6	-142.4	13.6	584.0	472.8	57.7	53.6	979.1	797.6	181.5	-123.1	395.0	4 994.8	5.8
2nd quarter	909.9	434.8	-131.0	13.2	592.9	479.8	58.7	54.4	1 006.7	820.4	186.3	-106.0	413.8	5 096.1	6.2
3rd quarter	933.7	439.3	-128.0	21.2	601.2	486.3	59.7	55.2	1 012.0	825.7	186.3	-102.4	410.8	5 192.6	6.4
4th quarter	943.7	444.4	-136.4	23.6	612.2	495.1	60.9	56.1	1 033.1	842.6	190.4	-115.4	420.9	5 304.3	6.3
1989															
1st quarter	982.0	445.7	-111.4	26.6	621.2	502.3	62.0	57.0	1 075.2	884.1	191.1	-98.3	454.0	5 396.6	6.7
2nd quarter	938.6	409.7	-128.6	27.2	630.4	509.5	62.9	58.0	1 073.2	878.2	195.1	-91.0	442.9	5 434.3	5.7
3rd quarter	933.0	392.0	-139.5	22.8	657.7	534.7	63.9	59.1	1 072.5	870.3	202.2	-79.7	414.8	5 498.4	5.0
4th quarter	925.0	391.4	-140.9	6.7	667.8	541.8	65.1	60.9	1 069.6	867.3	202.3	-82.9	401.8	5 554.3	4.6
1990															
1st quarter	929.7	418.2	-168.6	15.8	664.2	536.7	66.2	61.2	1 092.4	880.0	212.4	-79.5	428.2	5 663.6	4.7
2nd quarter	963.1	448.9	-171.4	10.1	675.5	545.8	67.2	62.5	1 096.2	882.5	213.7	-69.5	420.7	5 766.2	5.0
3rd quarter	935.0	405.2	-164.9	6.1	688.5	556.5	68.3	63.8	1 082.6	866.8	215.8	-80.4	394.1	5 809.8	4.2
4th quarter	934.0	418.5	-183.1	-3.1	701.7	567.2	69.8	64.7	1 035.6	814.6	221.0	-77.0	333.9	5 846.9	4.0

Table 19-9. Saving and Investment—Continued

(Billions of dollars, percent; quarterly data are at seasonally adjusted annual rates.)

NIPA Tables 1.7.5, 5.1

Year and quarter	Gross saving Total	Net saving Private	Net saving Government Federal	Net saving Government State and local	Consumption of fixed capital Total	Consumption of fixed capital Private	Consumption of fixed capital Government Federal	Consumption of fixed capital Government State and local	Gross domestic investment Total	Gross domestic investment Private	Gross domestic investment Government	Net lending or net borrowing (-), NIPAs	Net domestic investment	Gross national income	Net saving as a percentage of gross national income
1991															
1st quarter	1 017.3	465.9	-158.4	-7.0	716.8	580.2	70.9	65.6	1 004.3	787.9	216.4	52.9	287.6	5 882.6	5.1
2nd quarter	954.6	449.2	-211.7	-6.2	723.3	585.0	71.7	66.6	1 005.3	784.0	221.3	18.3	282.0	5 923.0	3.9
3rd quarter	932.1	437.1	-232.7	-0.2	727.8	587.7	72.7	67.4	1 027.2	805.2	222.0	-25.3	299.4	5 974.7	3.4
4th quarter	952.5	472.1	-252.1	-3.3	735.9	594.5	73.4	68.0	1 055.9	834.4	221.5	-10.0	320.1	6 034.8	3.6
1992															
1st quarter	959.0	520.8	-288.5	-0.3	726.9	584.7	73.7	68.5	1 037.3	810.2	227.1	-11.2	310.4	6 159.6	3.8
2nd quarter	971.1	530.6	-291.7	2.1	730.2	586.3	74.4	69.5	1 090.1	865.4	224.6	-35.3	359.9	6 236.6	3.9
3rd quarter	942.3	454.7	-316.1	-3.8	807.5	662.4	74.9	70.2	1 098.2	876.8	221.3	-42.4	290.7	6 294.2	2.1
4th quarter	920.5	466.0	-293.4	4.8	743.1	596.0	75.9	71.2	1 126.0	906.6	219.4	-60.9	382.9	6 368.4	2.8
1993															
1st quarter	954.2	498.6	-300.6	-9.9	766.1	616.7	77.1	72.4	1 148.0	931.3	216.7	-46.9	381.9	6 430.0	2.9
2nd quarter	970.8	472.7	-268.0	-1.7	767.8	616.7	77.7	73.4	1 163.4	942.3	221.1	-68.8	395.5	6 518.8	3.1
3rd quarter	943.5	432.5	-274.0	-0.3	785.3	632.8	78.3	74.2	1 160.9	943.4	217.6	-71.6	375.6	6 565.1	2.4
4th quarter	981.3	430.4	-251.3	15.7	786.5	632.6	78.7	75.2	1 217.2	996.5	220.7	-99.5	430.6	6 685.4	2.9
1994															
1st quarter	1 040.4	395.3	-232.2	4.2	873.1	716.3	79.1	77.7	1 255.1	1 043.2	211.9	-80.1	382.0	6 805.0	2.5
2nd quarter	1 064.1	441.4	-190.3	6.4	806.6	649.2	79.9	77.4	1 324.9	1 106.7	218.2	-106.1	518.3	6 897.7	3.7
3rd quarter	1 070.7	444.0	-211.3	17.8	820.2	661.1	80.3	78.8	1 321.6	1 092.9	228.7	-114.8	501.4	7 002.0	3.6
4th quarter	1 107.7	474.8	-215.5	13.5	834.9	673.6	81.3	79.9	1 372.1	1 145.5	226.6	-126.7	537.2	7 119.0	3.8
1995															
1st quarter	1 166.1	516.9	-215.2	10.2	854.3	691.2	81.7	81.4	1 392.1	1 160.6	231.5	-101.4	537.8	7 210.6	4.3
2nd quarter	1 161.3	485.7	-195.3	0.4	870.6	706.2	81.8	82.6	1 368.7	1 132.6	236.1	-107.3	498.1	7 278.5	4.0
3rd quarter	1 187.1	488.8	-198.7	13.4	883.6	718.1	81.8	83.7	1 357.0	1 126.2	230.8	-89.5	473.4	7 375.7	4.1
4th quarter	1 223.7	473.2	-178.7	24.3	904.9	737.9	82.1	84.9	1 389.1	1 156.6	232.5	-69.6	484.2	7 464.3	4.3
1996															
1st quarter	1 238.9	495.0	-182.1	23.7	902.2	734.3	82.0	85.9	1 409.1	1 170.0	239.1	-84.0	506.9	7 579.2	4.4
2nd quarter	1 273.8	483.6	-143.1	21.9	911.5	742.8	82.0	86.7	1 473.4	1 227.9	245.5	-98.4	561.9	7 708.1	4.7
3rd quarter	1 308.3	491.0	-133.1	27.2	923.2	753.4	82.1	87.7	1 526.2	1 279.9	246.3	-123.1	603.0	7 800.0	4.9
4th quarter	1 343.6	486.3	-108.7	30.4	935.5	764.7	82.1	88.7	1 532.0	1 283.3	248.7	-98.4	596.5	7 945.5	5.1
1997															
1st quarter	1 380.9	489.3	-89.2	29.6	951.2	779.1	82.3	89.8	1 567.9	1 315.4	252.5	-110.9	616.7	8 065.8	5.3
2nd quarter	1 450.5	516.5	-69.1	36.4	966.7	793.1	82.5	91.1	1 640.0	1 385.2	254.7	-87.1	673.3	8 186.7	5.9
3rd quarter	1 495.1	503.5	-35.0	44.4	982.1	807.6	82.5	92.0	1 672.7	1 419.5	253.3	-106.1	690.7	8 343.2	6.1
4th quarter	1 517.8	503.9	-30.0	46.1	997.8	821.4	82.9	93.5	1 687.2	1 439.1	248.1	-141.0	689.4	8 470.8	6.1
1998															
1st quarter	1 573.5	503.7	13.0	48.6	1 008.2	831.4	82.4	94.4	1 751.7	1 505.5	246.2	-145.4	743.5	8 581.5	6.6
2nd quarter	1 577.2	480.0	28.9	46.7	1 021.6	843.6	82.7	95.3	1 733.5	1 474.6	258.9	-181.8	711.9	8 709.1	6.4
3rd quarter	1 629.4	482.1	60.4	49.7	1 037.3	857.6	82.8	96.8	1 780.9	1 507.8	273.1	-210.0	743.7	8 860.4	6.7
4th quarter	1 614.8	445.2	53.0	63.0	1 053.6	872.2	83.2	98.2	1 819.8	1 548.6	271.2	-215.4	766.3	8 980.9	6.2
1999															
1st quarter	1 696.7	498.8	79.4	49.0	1 069.5	886.1	83.9	99.6	1 871.1	1 596.7	274.4	-221.6	801.6	9 143.7	6.9
2nd quarter	1 650.6	413.7	104.6	45.3	1 087.0	901.2	84.5	101.3	1 874.2	1 589.9	284.4	-262.7	787.2	9 248.3	6.1
3rd quarter	1 648.1	368.1	107.8	52.0	1 120.3	932.3	85.1	102.8	1 916.6	1 628.3	288.3	-300.8	796.4	9 375.0	5.6
4th quarter	1 701.6	395.3	122.7	55.3	1 128.3	937.6	85.8	104.8	1 987.8	1 687.7	300.1	-329.9	859.5	9 584.7	6.0
2000															
1st quarter	1 784.5	362.8	212.7	55.9	1 153.1	959.6	86.7	106.8	1 975.6	1 672.3	303.3	-363.6	822.6	9 833.6	6.4
2nd quarter	1 772.4	354.5	181.4	59.5	1 177.0	981.0	87.0	109.0	2 085.7	1 781.7	304.0	-381.9	908.7	9 927.4	6.0
3rd quarter	1 795.1	355.0	191.2	49.0	1 199.9	1 001.6	87.4	110.9	2 054.0	1 749.0	305.0	-424.3	854.1	10 058.2	5.9
4th quarter	1 730.0	300.8	172.5	35.4	1 221.3	1 021.1	87.6	112.5	2 044.5	1 738.9	305.6	-419.9	823.3	10 113.0	5.0
2001															
1st quarter	1 745.3	315.7	156.6	32.5	1 240.5	1 038.4	87.9	114.2	1 988.5	1 675.3	313.2	-412.0	748.0	10 228.0	4.9
2nd quarter	1 704.0	283.8	123.6	25.8	1 270.8	1 067.0	88.3	115.6	1 981.6	1 647.7	333.9	-377.4	710.7	10 272.3	4.2
3rd quarter	1 647.9	412.4	-88.6	-8.6	1 332.7	1 121.3	88.4	122.9	1 929.3	1 613.0	316.3	-353.7	596.6	10 223.0	3.1
4th quarter	1 533.1	286.5	-4.7	-30.6	1 281.8	1 075.2	88.2	118.4	1 854.0	1 521.4	332.7	-342.9	572.2	10 321.8	2.4
2002															
1st quarter	1 535.7	497.4	-208.5	-35.3	1 282.0	1 073.1	88.6	120.3	1 903.1	1 564.1	339.0	-422.2	621.1	10 413.1	2.4
2nd quarter	1 512.6	500.9	-241.4	-35.1	1 288.2	1 077.5	88.6	122.1	1 915.4	1 571.4	343.9	-460.7	627.2	10 499.9	2.1
3rd quarter	1 461.5	445.4	-247.3	-31.4	1 294.9	1 082.4	88.8	123.7	1 939.7	1 592.9	346.8	-465.1	644.8	10 542.4	1.6
4th quarter	1 446.6	473.3	-294.6	-34.9	1 302.7	1 088.4	89.4	124.9	1 947.4	1 600.1	347.4	-490.7	644.7	10 629.4	1.4
2003															
1st quarter	1 402.6	436.9	-290.2	-61.2	1 317.0	1 101.1	89.7	126.2	1 954.6	1 606.4	348.2	-532.5	637.6	10 723.7	0.8
2nd quarter	1 435.6	498.9	-365.5	-27.2	1 329.5	1 111.7	90.6	127.2	1 969.6	1 617.1	352.5	-519.2	640.1	10 867.3	1.0
3rd quarter	1 445.6	562.6	-451.4	-8.2	1 342.6	1 123.6	90.7	128.3	2 053.4	1 690.5	362.8	-513.2	710.7	11 041.9	0.9
4th quarter	1 552.2	561.5	-381.5	15.2	1 357.0	1 136.7	90.7	129.5	2 102.6	1 742.3	360.3	-496.9	745.6	11 242.4	1.7
2004															
1st quarter	1 532.7	575.2	-401.0	-14.7	1 373.2	1 150.3	91.8	131.2	2 140.2	1 781.9	358.3	-565.4	767.0	11 457.6	1.4
2nd quarter	1 525.8	525.6	-380.6	-13.6	1 394.5	1 166.4	93.8	134.3	2 263.8	1 892.2	371.7	-651.4	869.3	11 601.5	1.1
3rd quarter	1 575.4	443.4	-380.6	-22.3	1 534.9	1 301.9	94.5	138.6	2 293.6	1 917.7	375.9	-655.1	758.7	11 778.4	0.3
4th quarter	1 540.6	465.2	-365.7	-0.9	1 442.0	1 203.1	96.2	142.7	2 339.9	1 960.2	379.7	-733.4	897.9	11 930.6	0.8
2005															
1st quarter	1 608.4	417.2	-287.6	10.9	1 467.8	1 225.7	97.5	144.7	2 397.1	2 013.5	383.6	-762.1	929.3	12 170.1	1.2
2nd quarter	1 565.0	351.1	-289.6	12.4	1 491.1	1 244.9	98.2	147.9	2 404.4	2 009.1	395.3	-753.6	913.3	12 286.5	0.6
3rd quarter	1 653.5	170.9	-396.0	-19.3	1 898.0	1 632.3	99.8	165.9	2 452.9	2 052.6	400.3	-717.2	554.9	12 541.2	-1.9
4th quarter	1 621.2	339.5	-263.6	-17.2	1 562.5	1 307.5	100.7	154.3	2 563.6	2 154.5	409.1	-870.2	1 001.1	12 668.7	0.5

Table 19-10. Federal Government Current Receipts and Expenditures

(National income and product accounts, calendar years, billions of dollars, quarterly data are at seasonally adjusted annual rates.)

NIPA Table 3.2

Year and quarter	Current receipts														
		Tax receipts								Contribu-tions for govern-ment social insurance	Income receipts on assets			Current transfer receipts	Current surplus of govern-ment enter-prises
				Taxes on production and imports		Taxes on corporate income									
	Total	Total [1]	Personal current taxes	Total [1]	Excise taxes	Total	Federal Reserve banks	Other		Total	Interest receipts	Rents and royalties		
1946	39.5	32.7	16.4	7.7	7.2	8.6	0.0	8.6	6.5	...	...	...	0.3	...
1947	42.8	37.1	18.8	7.7	7.2	10.7	0.1	10.6	5.4	...	...	...	0.3	...
1948	42.4	37.6	18.1	7.8	7.4	11.8	0.2	11.6	4.4	...	...	...	0.3	...
1949	37.9	32.8	15.4	7.9	7.5	9.6	0.2	9.4	4.7	...	...	...	0.3	...
1947														
1st quarter	43.4	36.9	18.2	7.8	...	10.9	0.1	10.9	6.2	...	...	...	0.3	...
2nd quarter	42.5	36.4	18.5	7.5	...	10.4	0.1	10.3	5.8	...	...	...	0.3	...
3rd quarter	41.6	36.3	18.7	7.4	...	10.2	0.1	10.1	5.0	...	...	...	0.3	...
4th quarter	43.8	38.9	19.8	7.9	...	11.1	0.1	11.0	4.6	...	...	...	0.3	...
1948														
1st quarter	44.0	39.1	20.1	7.5	...	11.5	0.1	11.4	4.6	...	...	...	0.3	...
2nd quarter	42.5	37.8	17.8	7.9	...	12.1	0.1	12.0	4.3	...	...	...	0.3	...
3rd quarter	41.6	36.9	17.1	7.9	...	11.9	0.2	11.7	4.4	...	...	...	0.3	...
4th quarter	41.4	36.7	17.3	7.9	...	11.5	0.2	11.3	4.3	...	...	...	0.3	...
1949														
1st quarter	39.9	34.6	16.5	7.8	...	10.4	0.2	10.2	5.0	...	...	...	0.3	...
2nd quarter	37.9	32.7	15.6	7.9	...	9.1	0.2	8.9	4.9	...	...	...	0.3	...
3rd quarter	37.4	32.5	14.9	8.1	...	9.5	0.2	9.3	4.6	...	...	...	0.3	...
4th quarter	36.2	31.5	14.5	7.7	...	9.3	0.2	9.2	4.3	...	...	...	0.3	...
1950														
1st quarter	41.4	36.1	15.2	7.9	...	13.0	0.2	12.9	5.1	...	...	...	0.2	...
2nd quarter	45.5	40.2	16.1	8.5	...	15.6	0.2	15.4	5.1	...	...	...	0.2	...
3rd quarter	51.8	46.3	17.4	9.8	...	19.1	0.2	18.9	5.3	...	...	...	0.2	...
4th quarter	56.5	50.7	21.0	8.8	...	20.9	0.2	20.7	5.6	...	...	...	0.2	...
1951														
1st quarter	64.5	57.9	22.8	9.8	...	25.3	0.2	25.0	6.4	...	...	...	0.3	...
2nd quarter	61.6	54.9	24.7	8.8	...	21.4	0.3	21.1	6.5	...	...	...	0.3	...
3rd quarter	60.9	54.3	26.1	8.8	...	19.4	0.3	19.1	6.3	...	...	...	0.3	...
4th quarter	64.6	57.9	27.9	9.3	...	20.7	0.3	20.4	6.4	...	...	...	0.3	...
1952														
1st quarter	64.7	57.8	29.1	9.8	...	19.0	0.3	18.7	6.7	...	...	...	0.3	...
2nd quarter	64.8	58.0	30.0	10.1	...	17.9	0.3	17.6	6.6	...	...	...	0.3	...
3rd quarter	65.3	58.4	30.4	10.1	...	17.8	0.3	17.5	6.6	...	...	...	0.3	...
4th quarter	68.4	61.4	31.2	10.5	...	19.7	0.3	19.3	6.8	...	...	...	0.3	...
1953														
1st quarter	70.1	63.1	31.5	10.8	...	20.8	0.3	20.4	6.8	...	...	...	0.3	...
2nd quarter	70.5	63.3	31.5	11.0	...	20.9	0.3	20.5	6.8	...	...	...	0.3	...
3rd quarter	69.5	62.4	31.2	10.7	...	20.4	0.4	20.0	6.9	...	...	...	0.3	...
4th quarter	64.3	57.3	31.0	10.4	...	15.9	0.3	15.6	6.7	...	...	...	0.3	...
1954														
1st quarter	61.6	53.6	28.1	9.7	...	15.7	0.3	15.4	7.8	...	...	...	0.3	...
2nd quarter	61.7	53.7	27.9	9.6	...	16.2	0.3	15.9	7.7	...	...	...	0.3	...
3rd quarter	62.3	54.3	27.9	9.3	...	17.1	0.3	16.9	7.7	...	...	...	0.3	...
4th quarter	64.4	56.3	28.3	9.5	...	18.4	0.2	18.2	7.8	...	...	...	0.3	...
1955														
1st quarter	68.3	59.5	29.0	10.0	...	20.4	0.2	20.2	8.5	...	...	...	0.3	...
2nd quarter	70.3	61.3	30.1	10.5	...	20.7	0.2	20.4	8.7	...	...	...	0.3	...
3rd quarter	72.0	62.8	31.0	10.6	...	21.2	0.3	20.9	8.9	...	...	...	0.3	...
4th quarter	73.7	64.5	31.8	10.6	...	22.0	0.3	21.7	8.9	...	...	...	0.3	...
1956														
1st quarter	74.2	64.3	32.7	10.6	...	21.0	0.4	20.6	9.5	...	...	...	0.4	...
2nd quarter	75.6	65.6	33.6	10.6	...	21.4	0.4	21.0	9.6	...	...	...	0.4	...
3rd quarter	75.4	65.4	34.2	11.0	...	20.1	0.4	19.7	9.6	...	...	...	0.4	...
4th quarter	78.2	68.1	35.2	11.7	...	21.2	0.4	20.8	9.8	...	...	...	0.4	...
1957														
1st quarter	80.4	69.0	35.7	11.6	...	21.7	0.5	21.3	11.0	...	...	...	0.4	...
2nd quarter	79.9	68.5	36.1	11.6	...	20.8	0.5	20.3	11.0	...	...	...	0.4	...
3rd quarter	79.9	68.4	36.3	11.7	...	20.4	0.6	19.8	11.1	...	...	...	0.4	...
4th quarter	77.1	65.8	35.9	11.3	...	18.6	0.6	18.0	10.9	...	...	...	0.4	...
1958														
1st quarter	73.6	62.2	35.2	11.1	...	16.0	0.6	15.4	10.9	...	...	...	0.4	...
2nd quarter	73.5	62.2	34.7	11.2	...	16.3	0.6	15.8	10.9	...	...	...	0.4	...
3rd quarter	76.7	65.3	35.9	11.1	...	18.4	0.5	17.9	11.0	...	...	...	0.4	...
4th quarter	80.4	68.9	36.2	11.5	...	21.1	0.5	20.7	11.1	...	...	...	0.4	...
1959														
1st quarter	84.9	71.4	37.2	11.9	10.9	22.3	0.7	21.6	13.3	0.0	...	0.0	0.4	-0.1
2nd quarter	88.6	74.9	38.3	12.1	11.0	24.4	0.8	23.6	13.5	0.0	...	0.0	0.4	-0.1
3rd quarter	86.8	73.2	38.7	12.5	11.4	21.9	1.0	20.9	13.4	0.0	...	0.0	0.4	-0.2
4th quarter	87.4	73.7	39.7	12.5	11.4	21.4	1.2	20.2	13.5	0.0	...	0.0	0.4	-0.1
1960														
1st quarter	95.6	78.2	41.1	13.3	12.1	23.6	0.9	22.7	16.0	1.3	1.3	0.0	0.4	-0.2
2nd quarter	94.3	76.8	41.8	13.2	12.1	21.7	0.9	20.8	16.0	1.3	1.2	0.0	0.4	-0.2
3rd quarter	93.7	76.2	42.3	13.1	12.1	20.7	0.9	19.8	16.0	1.5	1.4	0.0	0.4	-0.4
4th quarter	92.2	74.8	42.1	12.9	11.9	19.7	0.8	18.9	15.9	1.4	1.4	0.0	0.4	-0.4

[1] Includes components not shown separately.
. . . = Not available.

Table 19-10. Federal Government Current Receipts and Expenditures—Continued

(National income and product accounts, calendar years, billions of dollars, quarterly data are at seasonally adjusted annual rates.)

NIPA Table 3.2

| Year and quarter | Current expenditures [1] | | | | | | | | | | Net federal government saving, NIPA (surplus + / deficit -) | | |
| | Total | Consumption expenditures | Government social benefits | | Other current transfer payments | | Interest payments | | | Subsidies | Total | Social insurance funds | Other |
			Total [1]	To persons	Total [1]	Grants-in-aid to state and local governments	Total	To persons and business	To the rest of the world				
1946	44.5	27.0	8.7	8.7	3.3	1.0	4.0	...	0.0	1.6	-5.0	3.2	-8.2
1947	37.6	20.9	8.4	8.4	3.6	1.6	4.1	...	0.0	0.6	5.3	3.2	2.1
1948	38.8	21.2	7.2	7.2	5.6	1.7	4.2	...	0.0	0.6	3.6	2.4	1.2
1949	43.5	23.3	8.2	8.2	7.0	1.9	4.3	...	0.0	0.7	-5.7	1.5	-7.2
1947													
1st quarter	37.5	21.7	7.7	7.7	3.2	1.4	4.2	...	0.0	0.7	5.9	...	...
2nd quarter	37.3	21.6	7.3	7.3	3.6	1.7	4.1	...	0.0	0.6	5.2	...	...
3rd quarter	39.7	20.6	10.7	10.7	3.8	1.6	4.1	...	0.0	0.5	2.0	...	...
4th quarter	35.8	19.6	7.8	7.8	3.8	1.6	4.1	...	0.0	0.5	7.9	...	...
1948													
1st quarter	36.3	19.6	7.5	7.5	4.6	1.6	4.1	...	0.0	0.5	7.7	...	...
2nd quarter	37.4	21.0	7.2	7.2	4.6	1.7	4.1	...	0.0	0.4	5.1	...	...
3rd quarter	40.2	21.8	7.0	7.0	6.6	1.8	4.1	...	0.0	0.7	1.4	...	...
4th quarter	41.2	22.5	7.0	7.0	6.4	1.9	4.2	...	0.0	1.0	0.2	...	...
1949													
1st quarter	43.3	23.8	7.7	7.7	6.9	1.7	4.3	...	0.0	0.7	-3.4	...	...
2nd quarter	44.4	24.4	8.2	8.2	7.1	1.7	4.3	...	0.0	0.5	-6.5	...	...
3rd quarter	43.9	23.0	8.5	8.5	7.4	2.1	4.3	...	0.0	0.7	-6.5	...	...
4th quarter	42.3	22.2	8.5	8.5	6.6	1.9	4.4	...	0.0	0.7	-6.2	...	...
1950													
1st quarter	49.8	22.1	16.6	16.6	5.8	1.9	4.4	...	0.0	0.9	-8.4	...	...
2nd quarter	42.8	22.1	9.6	9.6	5.7	1.9	4.4	...	0.0	1.0	2.8	...	...
3rd quarter	38.3	20.6	7.2	7.2	5.0	1.9	4.5	...	0.0	0.9	13.5	...	...
4th quarter	42.3	23.6	7.5	7.5	5.4	1.9	4.5	...	0.0	1.3	14.2	...	...
1951													
1st quarter	47.3	28.8	7.5	7.5	5.1	2.0	4.6	...	0.0	1.3	17.2	...	...
2nd quarter	51.6	32.7	7.9	7.9	5.2	2.1	4.6	...	0.0	1.3	10.0	...	...
3rd quarter	55.5	37.4	8.1	8.1	5.1	1.9	4.6	...	0.0	1.1	5.3	...	...
4th quarter	58.7	38.7	8.0	8.0	5.4	2.1	4.7	...	0.0	1.2	6.0	...	...
1952													
1st quarter	57.8	40.8	7.7	7.7	3.8	2.0	4.6	...	0.0	1.0	6.9	...	...
2nd quarter	61.4	43.8	7.6	7.6	4.5	2.1	4.6	...	0.0	0.9	3.4	...	...
3rd quarter	64.2	45.3	8.5	8.5	4.8	2.3	4.6	...	0.1	0.9	1.1	...	...
4th quarter	64.9	46.9	8.5	8.5	3.9	2.3	4.7	...	0.1	0.8	3.5	...	...
1953													
1st quarter	65.8	47.7	8.6	8.6	3.9	1.8	4.7	...	0.1	0.9	4.3	...	...
2nd quarter	67.8	49.2	8.4	8.4	4.8	2.7	4.7	...	0.1	0.6	2.6	...	...
3rd quarter	66.1	47.6	8.6	8.6	4.2	2.3	4.7	...	0.1	0.8	3.5	...	...
4th quarter	67.5	48.8	9.2	9.2	4.2	2.3	4.8	...	0.1	0.4	-3.2	...	...
1954													
1st quarter	65.0	45.9	9.9	9.9	4.1	2.3	4.8	...	0.1	0.3	-3.3	...	...
2nd quarter	63.6	43.6	10.5	10.5	3.7	2.3	4.8	...	0.1	0.9	-1.9	...	...
3rd quarter	63.7	43.1	10.9	10.9	4.3	2.4	4.8	...	0.1	0.6	-1.3	...	...
4th quarter	64.3	43.2	11.4	11.4	4.4	2.3	4.8	...	0.1	0.4	0.0	...	...
1955													
1st quarter	64.7	43.3	11.4	11.4	4.8	2.3	4.7	...	0.1	0.6	3.6	...	...
2nd quarter	63.6	42.8	11.4	11.4	4.4	2.4	4.6	...	0.1	0.8	6.7	...	...
3rd quarter	67.1	45.2	11.6	11.6	4.4	2.5	4.8	...	0.1	0.5	4.9	...	...
4th quarter	65.9	44.4	11.6	11.6	4.3	2.4	4.9	...	0.1	0.7	7.8	...	...
1956													
1st quarter	65.7	43.9	11.9	11.9	4.2	2.4	4.9	...	0.1	0.8	8.5	...	...
2nd quarter	68.8	46.1	12.1	12.1	4.4	2.5	5.1	...	0.1	1.0	6.7	...	...
3rd quarter	67.6	43.9	12.5	12.5	4.5	2.6	5.2	...	0.2	1.4	7.8	...	...
4th quarter	70.9	46.3	12.6	12.6	4.6	2.7	5.7	...	0.2	1.7	7.3	...	...
1957													
1st quarter	74.3	49.1	13.4	13.4	4.6	2.9	5.4	...	0.2	1.7	6.1	...	...
2nd quarter	75.5	49.0	14.5	14.5	4.8	2.8	5.6	...	0.2	1.6	4.3	...	...
3rd quarter	75.5	49.1	14.6	14.6	4.7	2.9	5.7	...	0.2	1.5	4.4	...	...
4th quarter	78.6	50.7	15.7	15.7	4.9	3.1	5.9	...	0.2	1.4	-1.5	...	...
1958													
1st quarter	76.8	49.1	16.8	16.8	4.6	2.9	5.4	...	0.2	1.5	-3.2	-1.3	-1.9
2nd quarter	81.8	51.8	18.6	18.6	5.1	3.3	5.2	...	0.1	1.7	-8.3	-3.6	-4.7
3rd quarter	83.1	50.6	19.0	19.0	5.1	3.2	5.3	...	0.1	1.9	-6.4	-3.5	-3.0
4th quarter	83.9	52.0	18.3	18.3	5.9	4.0	5.6	...	0.2	2.0	-3.5	-2.4	-1.1
1959													
1st quarter	81.7	48.3	18.4	18.4	7.5	3.5	6.4	...	0.2	1.1	3.2	-0.6	3.8
2nd quarter	83.4	50.2	18.3	18.3	8.1	3.9	5.9	...	0.2	0.9	5.2	-0.3	5.5
3rd quarter	83.9	50.7	18.5	18.5	7.2	3.8	6.3	...	0.3	1.1	2.9	-0.7	3.6
4th quarter	85.3	50.7	19.1	19.1	7.8	3.8	6.7	...	0.4	1.1	2.1	-1.2	3.3
1960													
1st quarter	83.9	48.1	19.1	18.9	7.1	3.9	8.6	8.2	0.4	1.0	11.7	1.3	10.3
2nd quarter	86.0	48.6	19.6	19.5	8.0	4.0	8.5	8.2	0.3	1.3	8.2	0.8	7.4
3rd quarter	87.1	50.6	20.3	20.1	6.9	4.0	8.2	7.9	0.3	1.0	6.6	0.2	6.4
4th quarter	90.0	51.7	21.2	21.0	7.7	4.2	8.1	7.8	0.3	1.2	2.2	-0.8	3.0

[1]Includes components not shown separately.
. . . = Not available.

Table 19-10. Federal Government Current Receipts and Expenditures—Continued

(National income and product accounts, calendar years, billions of dollars, quarterly data are at seasonally adjusted annual rates.)

NIPA Table 3.2

| Year and quarter | Total | Tax receipts | | | | | | | Contributions for government social insurance | Income receipts on assets | | | Current transfer receipts | Current surplus of government enterprises |
| | | Total [1] | Personal current taxes | Taxes on production and imports | | Taxes on corporate income | | | | Total | Interest receipts | Rents and royalties | | |
				Total [1]	Excise taxes	Total	Federal Reserve banks	Other						
1961														
1st quarter	92.2	74.6	42.2	12.9	11.9	19.4	0.7	18.7	16.3	1.4	1.4	0.1	0.5	-0.5
2nd quarter	94.1	76.4	42.5	13.1	12.1	20.7	0.7	20.1	16.4	1.5	1.4	0.1	0.5	-0.6
3rd quarter	96.0	78.0	42.8	13.2	12.1	22.0	0.7	21.3	16.6	1.4	1.4	0.1	0.5	-0.5
4th quarter	99.5	81.0	43.4	13.6	12.5	23.9	0.7	23.2	16.8	1.6	1.5	0.1	0.5	-0.3
1962														
1st quarter	101.0	80.9	44.6	14.0	12.8	22.3	0.8	21.5	18.4	1.6	1.5	0.1	0.5	-0.4
2nd quarter	102.5	82.2	46.0	14.0	12.8	22.1	0.8	21.3	18.6	1.8	1.7	0.1	0.5	-0.5
3rd quarter	104.9	84.5	47.2	14.4	13.2	22.7	0.8	21.9	18.6	1.7	1.6	0.1	0.5	-0.5
4th quarter	106.1	85.7	48.4	14.3	13.1	22.8	0.8	22.0	18.7	1.7	1.6	0.1	0.5	-0.5
1963														
1st quarter	109.1	86.3	48.8	14.4	13.2	22.9	0.8	22.0	20.7	1.7	1.7	0.1	0.6	-0.3
2nd quarter	111.4	88.4	49.0	14.7	13.5	24.5	0.9	23.6	20.9	1.7	1.7	0.1	0.6	-0.3
3rd quarter	112.5	89.3	49.1	14.8	13.6	25.2	0.9	24.3	21.1	1.8	1.7	0.1	0.6	-0.3
4th quarter	114.1	90.5	49.6	15.0	13.7	25.8	0.9	24.8	21.4	1.8	1.7	0.1	0.6	-0.2
1964														
1st quarter	112.7	89.1	48.0	15.0	13.8	25.9	1.5	24.4	21.4	1.9	1.8	0.1	0.6	-0.2
2nd quarter	109.0	85.3	43.7	15.4	14.1	26.0	1.6	24.4	21.6	1.8	1.7	0.1	0.5	-0.2
3rd quarter	111.7	87.6	45.4	15.5	14.2	26.5	1.6	24.9	21.8	2.0	1.9	0.1	0.9	-0.6
4th quarter	113.6	89.1	46.9	15.9	14.5	26.1	1.7	24.5	22.0	1.6	1.5	0.1	1.0	-0.2
1965														
1st quarter	119.5	94.6	50.5	16.4	15.0	27.5	1.2	26.3	22.2	2.0	1.9	0.1	1.0	-0.3
2nd quarter	121.4	96.2	51.9	15.7	14.1	28.4	1.3	27.1	22.4	2.0	1.9	0.1	1.0	-0.2
3rd quarter	119.8	94.3	50.4	14.8	13.1	28.9	1.3	27.6	22.8	2.0	1.9	0.1	1.1	-0.4
4th quarter	123.1	97.6	51.5	15.0	13.3	30.8	1.4	29.4	23.2	1.7	1.6	0.1	1.1	-0.5
1966														
1st quarter	132.5	100.2	54.4	13.9	12.1	31.7	1.5	30.2	29.6	2.0	1.9	0.1	1.1	-0.5
2nd quarter	137.3	104.6	58.0	14.7	12.8	31.7	1.6	30.2	30.0	2.0	1.9	0.1	1.1	-0.6
3rd quarter	139.7	106.1	59.8	14.6	12.7	31.4	1.7	29.7	31.1	2.1	2.0	0.1	1.2	-0.8
4th quarter	142.3	108.2	62.2	14.9	13.0	30.9	1.8	29.0	31.4	2.3	2.1	0.1	1.2	-0.7
1967														
1st quarter	143.2	107.7	62.9	15.0	13.0	29.7	1.9	27.8	32.8	2.3	2.2	0.2	1.0	-0.7
2nd quarter	144.3	107.5	62.6	15.2	13.3	29.4	1.9	27.5	33.7	2.5	2.4	0.2	1.1	-0.6
3rd quarter	147.8	110.3	65.2	15.3	13.5	29.6	1.9	27.8	34.4	2.5	2.4	0.2	1.1	-0.5
4th quarter	152.2	114.0	66.9	15.5	13.5	31.4	2.0	29.4	35.1	2.6	2.4	0.2	1.2	-0.8
1968														
1st quarter	160.9	120.6	68.8	16.2	14.1	35.2	2.3	33.0	36.7	2.9	2.7	0.2	1.1	-0.4
2nd quarter	165.6	124.4	71.4	16.8	14.6	35.9	2.4	33.5	37.5	2.9	2.7	0.2	1.1	-0.3
3rd quarter	176.8	134.8	81.0	17.3	15.0	36.1	2.5	33.5	38.1	3.1	2.9	0.2	1.1	-0.3
4th quarter	181.5	139.3	84.5	17.5	15.1	37.0	2.6	34.4	38.7	2.8	2.6	0.2	1.1	-0.4
1969														
1st quarter	191.0	145.9	90.7	17.4	15.4	37.4	2.8	34.6	41.9	2.6	2.4	0.2	1.1	-0.5
2nd quarter	194.1	148.1	93.3	17.9	15.3	36.5	3.0	33.5	42.7	2.6	2.5	0.2	1.1	-0.5
3rd quarter	191.9	144.8	90.8	18.3	15.8	35.3	3.1	32.2	43.6	2.7	2.5	0.2	1.2	-0.4
4th quarter	193.3	145.4	91.9	18.0	15.6	35.1	3.3	31.8	44.2	2.8	2.6	0.2	1.2	-0.3
1970														
1st quarter	187.2	139.2	90.6	18.0	15.5	30.3	3.4	27.0	44.9	2.9	2.7	0.2	1.2	-1.0
2nd quarter	188.1	140.5	91.4	18.2	15.8	30.5	3.5	27.0	45.2	3.1	2.8	0.2	1.2	-1.8
3rd quarter	184.7	136.5	86.3	18.3	15.8	31.5	3.6	27.9	45.6	3.1	2.8	0.3	1.1	-1.5
4th quarter	183.8	135.9	87.2	18.3	15.7	30.1	3.5	26.6	45.4	3.1	2.9	0.3	1.1	-1.7
1971														
1st quarter	188.5	136.8	83.6	19.5	16.9	33.3	3.4	29.9	49.3	3.2	2.9	0.3	1.1	-2.0
2nd quarter	191.4	138.2	85.1	18.8	16.1	33.9	3.3	30.7	49.9	3.5	3.1	0.3	1.1	-1.3
3rd quarter	191.8	138.7	86.3	19.0	15.8	33.1	3.4	29.8	50.1	3.5	3.1	0.4	1.1	-1.6
4th quarter	195.1	141.1	88.2	19.1	15.1	33.5	3.4	30.1	50.7	3.7	3.3	0.4	1.1	-1.5
1972														
1st quarter	214.1	154.0	100.3	18.3	15.2	35.0	3.2	31.8	56.9	3.5	3.2	0.4	1.2	-1.5
2nd quarter	217.5	156.4	102.4	18.4	15.6	35.2	3.2	32.0	57.5	3.5	3.2	0.4	1.3	-1.2
3rd quarter	220.4	158.4	103.1	18.6	15.7	36.3	3.2	33.1	58.2	3.7	3.3	0.4	1.3	-1.1
4th quarter	228.2	164.7	105.3	19.1	15.9	39.9	3.3	36.6	59.0	3.7	3.3	0.4	1.3	-0.6
1973														
1st quarter	243.5	167.6	104.5	19.7	16.2	43.0	3.7	39.3	72.2	3.8	3.4	0.4	1.4	-1.4
2nd quarter	247.6	170.7	106.9	20.0	16.7	43.5	4.2	39.4	73.3	3.8	3.4	0.4	1.5	-1.8
3rd quarter	250.8	173.4	111.0	19.8	16.7	42.2	4.6	37.6	74.5	3.7	3.3	0.4	1.1	-1.9
4th quarter	259.6	180.9	116.0	20.2	17.0	44.3	4.9	39.4	76.0	3.8	3.3	0.5	1.1	-2.2
1974														
1st quarter	267.2	182.3	119.5	19.9	16.5	42.5	5.1	37.4	81.5	4.0	3.5	0.5	1.3	-2.0
2nd quarter	277.6	190.2	124.8	20.2	16.7	44.8	5.5	39.3	83.1	4.2	3.6	0.5	1.4	-1.2
3rd quarter	288.4	199.8	129.7	20.4	16.5	49.3	5.8	43.5	84.7	4.2	3.7	0.6	1.5	-1.8
4th quarter	284.9	196.6	132.0	20.3	16.5	43.9	5.8	38.1	84.8	4.3	3.8	0.6	1.5	-2.3
1975														
1st quarter	278.3	189.6	132.3	19.9	15.8	37.0	5.5	31.5	85.9	4.5	3.9	0.6	1.5	-3.1
2nd quarter	245.1	156.1	94.6	21.5	16.3	39.6	5.4	34.2	86.2	4.8	4.2	0.6	1.5	-3.4
3rd quarter	288.5	198.0	125.7	23.5	16.6	48.3	5.2	43.2	87.9	5.1	4.5	0.6	1.5	-3.9
4th quarter	296.8	204.4	130.4	24.1	16.8	49.4	5.5	43.9	89.9	5.2	4.5	0.6	1.5	-4.1

[1] Includes components not shown separately.

Table 19-10. Federal Government Current Receipts and Expenditures—Continued

(National income and product accounts, calendar years, billions of dollars, quarterly data are at seasonally adjusted annual rates.)

NIPA Table 3.2

Year and quarter	Total	Consumption expenditures	Government social benefits Total [1]	Government social benefits To persons	Other current transfer payments Total [1]	Other current transfer payments Grants-in-aid to state and local governments	Interest payments Total	Interest payments To persons and business	Interest payments To the rest of the world	Subsidies	Net saving Total	Net saving Social insurance funds	Net saving Other
1961													
1st quarter	89.7	49.8	22.9	22.7	7.5	4.2	7.9	7.6	0.3	1.6	2.5	-2.1	4.6
2nd quarter	93.4	51.2	23.7	23.4	8.7	4.5	7.8	7.6	0.3	2.0	0.8	-2.7	3.5
3rd quarter	93.5	52.2	23.7	23.5	7.5	4.6	7.9	7.6	0.3	2.2	2.5	-2.7	5.2
4th quarter	94.9	53.3	23.1	22.9	8.1	4.7	8.0	7.7	0.3	2.3	4.7	-1.8	6.5
1962													
1st quarter	98.6	56.0	23.6	23.3	8.5	4.9	8.2	7.9	0.3	2.3	2.4	-0.6	3.1
2nd quarter	100.3	56.9	23.4	23.1	9.1	4.9	8.6	8.2	0.3	2.4	2.2	-0.3	2.5
3rd quarter	101.7	58.9	23.7	23.5	8.1	5.2	8.8	8.5	0.3	2.2	3.1	-0.5	3.6
4th quarter	103.7	59.6	24.3	24.1	8.6	5.2	9.0	8.6	0.4	2.2	2.4	-0.8	3.2
1963													
1st quarter	104.9	59.5	25.5	25.3	8.8	5.3	9.0	8.7	0.4	2.0	4.2	-0.2	4.3
2nd quarter	105.0	59.1	24.4	24.2	10.1	5.5	9.2	8.8	0.4	2.2	6.3	1.1	5.2
3rd quarter	106.7	61.8	24.6	24.3	8.6	5.8	9.4	9.0	0.4	2.3	5.9	1.2	4.7
4th quarter	108.9	62.7	25.0	24.8	9.2	6.1	9.6	9.2	0.4	2.4	5.2	1.2	4.0
1964													
1st quarter	110.7	62.7	25.8	25.5	9.6	6.5	9.8	9.4	0.4	2.7	2.0	0.5	1.5
2nd quarter	111.6	62.9	25.2	24.9	10.7	6.5	9.9	9.5	0.4	2.9	-2.6	1.3	-3.9
3rd quarter	110.4	63.4	25.3	25.1	9.0	6.2	10.1	9.7	0.4	2.6	1.3	1.5	-0.2
4th quarter	110.3	62.1	25.4	25.1	9.8	6.6	10.2	9.7	0.5	2.7	3.3	1.7	1.6
1965													
1st quarter	111.9	62.3	26.5	26.2	9.8	6.5	10.3	9.9	0.5	2.9	7.6	0.9	6.7
2nd quarter	114.6	63.1	26.2	25.7	11.8	7.1	10.5	10.1	0.5	3.0	6.8	1.6	5.1
3rd quarter	120.2	66.7	29.5	29.2	10.5	7.5	10.6	10.1	0.5	3.0	-0.4	-1.2	0.8
4th quarter	123.7	70.8	28.2	27.9	10.8	7.6	10.8	10.3	0.5	3.1	-0.6	0.5	-1.1
1966													
1st quarter	127.4	71.3	29.0	28.7	12.6	9.0	11.0	10.5	0.5	3.5	5.0	6.4	-1.4
2nd quarter	133.8	74.5	28.6	28.3	15.3	10.1	11.5	10.9	0.5	3.9	3.5	6.7	-3.2
3rd quarter	138.3	78.6	30.2	29.8	13.6	10.5	11.8	11.2	0.6	4.0	1.4	6.2	-4.8
4th quarter	143.2	79.1	33.1	32.8	14.5	10.7	12.3	11.7	0.6	4.2	-0.9	4.7	-5.6
1967													
1st quarter	152.9	85.2	35.9	35.6	15.3	11.1	12.5	12.0	0.5	4.0	-9.7	3.7	-13.4
2nd quarter	154.7	86.2	36.4	36.1	15.8	11.6	12.4	11.8	0.6	3.8	-10.4	4.3	-14.7
3rd quarter	156.3	87.3	37.5	36.9	15.3	11.6	12.6	12.0	0.6	3.7	-8.5	4.0	-12.5
4th quarter	161.0	89.9	37.9	37.6	16.4	12.7	13.1	12.5	0.7	3.7	-8.8	4.6	-13.4
1968													
1st quarter	166.9	93.7	39.6	39.3	15.6	11.8	13.8	13.1	0.7	4.0	-6.0	4.6	-10.5
2nd quarter	173.0	94.5	42.2	41.8	17.6	13.3	14.5	13.8	0.7	4.2	-7.4	2.9	-10.3
3rd quarter	175.2	95.9	43.2	42.8	17.0	12.6	14.9	14.3	0.7	4.2	1.5	2.6	-1.1
4th quarter	178.9	97.5	43.9	43.5	18.2	13.2	15.1	14.4	0.7	4.2	2.7	2.7	0.0
1969													
1st quarter	176.4	95.4	44.9	44.6	16.6	13.1	15.1	14.3	0.8	4.3	14.6	5.1	9.4
2nd quarter	182.5	97.6	45.7	45.3	19.2	14.0	15.6	14.8	0.8	4.4	11.5	5.5	6.1
3rd quarter	186.2	100.2	46.5	46.1	19.0	15.1	15.9	15.1	0.8	4.6	5.6	6.0	-0.3
4th quarter	190.1	100.3	47.4	47.0	21.0	16.1	16.7	15.9	0.8	4.6	3.2	6.2	-3.0
1970													
1st quarter	189.5	99.8	48.6	48.3	21.5	17.5	17.3	16.4	0.8	4.7	-2.3	6.6	-8.8
2nd quarter	204.0	98.0	57.9	57.5	23.6	18.8	17.5	16.6	1.0	4.8	-15.8	-1.3	-14.5
3rd quarter	204.1	98.4	57.4	56.9	25.0	20.1	18.2	17.0	1.1	4.7	-19.4	0.5	-19.9
4th quarter	206.9	98.3	60.3	59.8	25.5	20.8	18.0	16.9	1.2	4.8	-23.1	-1.7	-21.4
1971													
1st quarter	212.0	101.0	61.5	61.0	27.0	21.6	17.9	16.5	1.3	4.7	-23.6	1.3	-24.9
2nd quarter	221.5	101.9	68.4	67.9	28.8	23.2	17.6	16.0	1.6	4.8	-30.1	-5.1	-25.0
3rd quarter	221.0	102.0	67.7	67.2	28.7	23.5	18.0	15.9	2.1	4.5	-29.1	-4.1	-25.1
4th quarter	225.7	103.0	68.7	68.2	31.3	24.7	18.2	15.9	2.4	4.6	-30.6	-4.2	-26.4
1972													
1st quarter	236.6	108.3	70.7	70.2	33.2	25.7	18.3	15.8	2.5	6.1	-22.6	0.1	-22.7
2nd quarter	245.2	109.4	70.7	70.2	40.3	33.9	18.6	16.0	2.6	6.2	-27.7	0.8	-28.5
3rd quarter	237.0	105.9	70.7	70.3	34.4	26.8	18.8	16.1	2.7	7.1	-16.6	2.0	-18.5
4th quarter	258.9	107.0	81.2	80.6	46.4	40.4	19.4	16.5	2.9	7.0	-30.7	-5.4	-25.3
1973													
1st quarter	258.2	108.5	82.8	82.2	40.1	35.6	21.0	17.6	3.5	5.9	-14.7	6.1	-20.8
2nd quarter	262.3	109.2	84.2	83.6	40.8	34.7	22.4	18.5	3.9	5.6	-14.7	5.7	-20.4
3rd quarter	260.9	107.8	85.7	85.1	39.2	33.9	23.5	19.5	4.0	4.6	-10.1	5.7	-15.8
4th quarter	265.3	109.9	87.9	87.3	38.7	34.9	24.3	20.3	4.0	4.5	-5.7	5.6	-11.3
1974													
1st quarter	275.5	114.0	94.5	94.1	38.9	34.6	24.8	20.8	4.0	3.5	-8.3	9.1	-17.4
2nd quarter	288.4	114.6	101.3	100.7	43.5	35.4	25.6	21.4	4.2	2.8	-10.8	4.1	-14.8
3rd quarter	298.9	119.0	107.1	106.4	41.7	36.8	26.7	22.4	4.3	3.1	-10.5	1.8	-12.3
4th quarter	310.4	124.3	112.6	112.0	43.1	38.2	26.9	22.4	4.5	3.5	-25.4	-2.2	-23.3
1975													
1st quarter	325.5	125.8	121.2	120.5	47.1	40.7	27.3	22.4	4.9	4.1	-47.2	-9.1	-38.1
2nd quarter	349.3	128.2	134.9	134.2	54.1	45.8	28.1	23.7	4.4	4.1	-104.2	-14.9	-89.3
3rd quarter	350.5	130.2	137.4	136.8	49.3	46.5	29.3	24.8	4.5	4.4	-62.0	-21.1	-40.8
4th quarter	359.6	134.0	138.6	137.8	51.5	47.5	31.0	26.6	4.4	4.8	-62.8	-19.6	-43.2

[1] Includes components not shown separately.

Table 19-10. Federal Government Current Receipts and Expenditures—Continued

(National income and product accounts, calendar years, billions of dollars, quarterly data are at seasonally adjusted annual rates.)

NIPA Table 3.2

Year and quarter	Current receipts Total	Tax receipts Total [1]	Personal current taxes	Taxes on production and imports Total [1]	Excise taxes	Taxes on corporate income Total	Federal Reserve banks	Other	Contributions for government social insurance	Income receipts on assets Total	Interest receipts	Rents and royalties	Current transfer receipts	Current surplus of government enterprises
1976														
1st quarter	312.1	210.0	132.7	21.0	16.7	55.7	5.8	49.9	96.9	5.7	5.0	0.7	1.5	-2.0
2nd quarter	319.0	215.4	138.4	21.5	17.0	54.8	5.8	49.0	98.3	5.9	5.2	0.7	1.6	-2.2
3rd quarter	326.6	221.2	144.2	21.9	17.1	54.4	5.9	48.5	100.0	6.1	5.4	0.7	1.6	-2.3
4th quarter	332.5	225.9	149.7	21.9	17.3	53.5	6.0	47.5	101.4	5.8	5.1	0.7	1.7	-2.3
1977														
1st quarter	347.0	234.7	154.9	22.2	17.1	56.9	5.9	51.0	106.8	6.5	5.6	0.8	1.7	-2.6
2nd quarter	360.8	245.7	160.6	22.7	17.4	61.7	6.0	55.7	109.4	6.7	5.8	0.9	1.8	-2.7
3rd quarter	367.4	250.2	162.3	23.4	17.6	63.8	5.9	57.9	111.5	6.9	5.9	1.0	2.1	-3.2
4th quarter	378.5	259.1	170.8	23.4	17.9	64.1	6.0	58.1	113.6	6.8	5.8	1.0	2.1	-3.2
1978														
1st quarter	388.7	258.9	173.1	24.2	17.8	60.7	6.3	54.4	123.0	7.6	6.6	1.0	2.3	-3.1
2nd quarter	417.1	282.1	182.7	25.6	18.5	72.8	6.6	66.2	126.8	8.4	7.3	1.1	2.4	-2.5
3rd quarter	434.7	295.7	195.1	25.8	18.5	73.9	7.2	66.7	129.3	8.7	7.6	1.1	2.5	-1.5
4th quarter	453.5	310.7	204.9	26.6	19.1	78.2	7.9	70.3	132.4	9.4	8.2	1.2	2.6	-1.5
1979														
1st quarter	469.1	313.3	211.3	26.2	18.6	74.8	8.2	66.6	145.0	9.9	8.6	1.3	2.7	-1.8
2nd quarter	480.3	322.4	219.7	26.2	18.7	75.4	8.8	66.5	147.0	10.2	8.7	1.4	2.8	-2.1
3rd quarter	492.4	330.9	229.2	25.7	18.4	74.8	9.5	65.3	150.3	10.9	9.4	1.6	2.9	-2.6
4th quarter	503.1	338.3	238.3	25.9	18.6	72.7	10.6	62.1	153.2	11.6	9.9	1.7	3.0	-2.9
1980														
1st quarter	517.2	345.7	237.6	28.0	20.7	78.6	11.6	67.0	159.5	12.1	10.2	2.0	3.1	-3.2
2nd quarter	514.3	341.2	243.6	33.9	27.0	62.1	12.3	49.8	160.3	13.0	10.8	2.2	3.2	-3.4
3rd quarter	533.6	357.3	252.2	36.5	29.3	67.0	11.0	56.0	162.8	14.2	11.8	2.5	3.2	-3.8
4th quarter	563.3	379.5	266.6	37.7	30.4	73.6	11.9	61.7	167.9	15.3	12.5	2.8	4.6	-3.9
1981														
1st quarter	606.6	401.9	277.8	51.0	43.2	71.5	13.0	58.5	187.9	16.6	13.5	3.1	3.9	-3.7
2nd quarter	616.1	406.4	288.4	52.2	43.8	64.3	13.6	50.7	190.3	17.5	14.2	3.4	3.5	-1.7
3rd quarter	631.9	419.0	300.8	49.5	40.7	67.2	14.5	52.7	193.7	18.8	15.2	3.6	3.7	-3.3
4th quarter	623.2	405.0	295.3	48.5	39.1	59.8	15.0	44.8	195.5	20.2	16.4	3.8	3.9	-1.4
1982														
1st quarter	616.5	388.4	294.6	43.9	34.8	48.6	15.1	33.5	203.2	21.6	17.7	3.9	4.9	-1.5
2nd quarter	622.7	393.2	301.1	40.4	31.7	50.4	15.7	34.7	204.3	22.0	18.1	3.9	5.2	-2.0
3rd quarter	611.9	381.7	289.1	40.5	32.2	50.8	15.4	35.4	205.8	22.4	18.5	3.8	5.4	-3.3
4th quarter	615.2	383.7	295.2	40.7	32.4	46.3	14.6	31.7	206.1	22.7	19.0	3.7	5.5	-2.8
1983														
1st quarter	622.1	379.8	289.0	41.5	33.8	48.2	13.9	34.3	216.3	23.2	19.7	3.5	5.5	-2.8
2nd quarter	647.7	401.8	294.7	45.7	36.7	60.2	13.9	46.3	219.6	23.3	19.8	3.4	5.8	-2.8
3rd quarter	641.1	391.5	276.8	45.9	36.2	67.6	14.3	53.3	223.1	24.0	20.6	3.4	6.1	-3.5
4th quarter	658.4	401.2	284.4	46.2	36.1	69.4	14.8	54.6	228.3	24.9	21.4	3.5	6.6	-2.6
1984														
1st quarter	692.5	416.4	287.4	47.4	36.5	80.3	15.4	64.8	246.5	25.5	21.7	3.8	7.1	-3.0
2nd quarter	705.2	423.0	294.1	48.0	35.8	79.5	15.7	63.8	251.2	27.0	23.1	3.9	7.3	-3.1
3rd quarter	711.8	426.1	306.9	47.9	35.7	70.1	16.3	53.8	255.2	26.8	22.9	3.9	7.3	-3.7
4th quarter	726.6	437.4	317.3	47.8	35.5	71.0	16.7	54.3	258.4	27.3	23.5	3.9	7.3	-3.8
1985														
1st quarter	779.8	476.7	352.6	46.8	34.5	75.9	18.2	57.7	270.7	27.7	23.9	3.8	7.9	-3.2
2nd quarter	743.6	429.5	307.1	46.0	34.4	74.5	18.2	56.3	274.1	28.3	24.7	3.6	13.6	-2.0
3rd quarter	781.1	467.3	339.6	47.2	35.1	78.4	17.5	60.8	277.9	30.0	26.6	3.4	8.0	-2.1
4th quarter	788.6	469.1	344.7	45.8	33.1	76.3	17.3	59.0	283.2	30.5	27.4	3.1	7.9	-2.2
1986														
1st quarter	799.2	469.3	341.3	44.8	32.0	81.7	18.7	63.0	292.4	31.5	28.8	2.7	8.0	-2.0
2nd quarter	802.6	470.1	343.9	43.3	29.8	81.4	17.9	63.4	294.9	31.1	28.6	2.5	8.2	-1.7
3rd quarter	816.8	479.2	351.4	44.1	29.8	81.9	17.3	64.6	298.9	32.9	30.6	2.3	7.3	-1.5
4th quarter	842.2	499.9	363.7	43.9	29.7	90.3	17.2	73.1	303.6	30.1	27.8	2.2	9.4	-0.8
1987														
1st quarter	842.3	494.3	357.9	44.4	29.5	90.2	17.2	73.0	309.7	29.3	26.9	2.4	10.0	-1.0
2nd quarter	911.8	560.1	409.7	46.1	30.3	102.3	17.7	84.6	313.2	28.8	26.4	2.4	11.2	-1.5
3rd quarter	906.2	552.6	394.4	46.7	31.3	109.5	18.0	91.5	317.2	27.9	25.5	2.3	10.7	-2.1
4th quarter	926.2	568.9	408.0	47.7	31.8	110.7	18.1	92.7	323.5	25.9	23.6	2.3	11.0	-3.2
1988														
1st quarter	940.0	556.5	401.7	50.0	33.7	102.7	16.7	85.9	344.1	33.9	31.7	2.2	10.1	-4.5
2nd quarter	949.9	561.6	399.6	49.8	33.6	109.5	16.6	92.8	350.8	28.2	26.2	2.0	10.5	-1.3
3rd quarter	961.3	568.1	401.6	50.7	34.2	113.4	17.5	95.9	355.9	27.9	26.0	1.9	11.1	-1.7
4th quarter	981.8	580.5	408.7	50.7	33.9	119.0	18.6	100.4	361.6	29.9	28.0	1.9	11.6	-1.7
1989														
1st quarter	1 028.2	618.5	437.9	51.3	34.2	126.3	21.2	105.1	371.1	28.4	26.5	1.9	11.8	-1.6
2nd quarter	1 030.8	618.1	446.8	49.7	32.2	119.1	22.1	97.0	374.0	28.2	26.2	2.0	12.0	-1.4
3rd quarter	1 038.5	619.2	455.5	50.5	32.8	110.5	21.5	89.0	377.4	30.3	28.1	2.2	13.1	-1.5
4th quarter	1 052.0	630.9	465.8	49.4	31.8	113.0	21.8	91.1	382.6	27.4	25.1	2.3	12.8	-1.7
1990														
1st quarter	1 057.5	626.9	461.3	50.8	33.1	112.1	22.6	89.6	394.6	27.5	25.1	2.5	12.3	-3.8
2nd quarter	1 075.8	643.0	470.1	51.3	33.5	118.7	23.2	95.5	398.5	26.8	24.3	2.6	12.7	-5.1
3rd quarter	1 093.2	653.9	475.1	51.6	34.2	124.2	24.7	99.5	403.9	27.2	24.6	2.7	13.7	-5.5
4th quarter	1 099.5	647.3	474.3	52.0	35.0	117.5	24.0	93.5	403.4	39.3	36.6	2.7	15.5	-6.0

[1] Includes components not shown separately.

Table 19-10. Federal Government Current Receipts and Expenditures—Continued

(National income and product accounts, calendar years, billions of dollars, quarterly data are at seasonally adjusted annual rates.)

NIPA Table 3.2

Year and quarter	Current expenditures [1]										Net federal government saving, NIPA (surplus + / deficit -)		
	Total	Consumption expenditures	Government social benefits		Other current transfer payments		Interest payments			Subsidies	Total	Social insurance funds	Other
			Total [1]	To persons	Total [1]	Grants-in-aid to state and local governments	Total	To persons and business	To the rest of the world				
1976													
1st quarter	364.5	134.2	141.8	141.0	51.3	48.7	32.4	28.0	4.4	5.0	-52.4	-14.9	-37.5
2nd quarter	367.1	136.5	140.1	139.3	52.7	49.5	33.2	28.8	4.4	4.7	-48.1	-12.5	-35.6
3rd quarter	378.3	136.6	145.8	145.0	57.0	50.4	34.1	29.5	4.6	4.9	-51.7	-17.3	-34.3
4th quarter	387.3	141.4	148.1	147.3	57.2	54.4	35.4	30.7	4.7	5.3	-54.8	-17.9	-37.0
1977													
1st quarter	392.3	145.3	150.3	149.4	55.6	52.5	35.6	30.8	4.8	5.6	-45.3	-14.4	-30.9
2nd quarter	400.2	149.5	149.3	148.6	59.4	55.5	36.4	31.3	5.1	5.7	-39.4	-12.0	-27.3
3rd quarter	412.6	151.6	154.9	154.1	62.8	59.1	37.2	31.6	5.6	6.2	-45.2	-14.7	-30.5
4th quarter	425.0	156.5	157.1	156.2	62.2	59.2	39.2	32.6	6.6	10.1	-46.5	-14.2	-32.3
1978													
1st quarter	435.1	158.3	159.1	158.3	67.3	63.5	41.9	34.1	7.8	8.5	-46.3	-5.6	-40.7
2nd quarter	442.6	162.1	158.6	157.7	70.1	66.1	43.8	35.4	8.4	8.1	-25.5	-1.4	-24.1
3rd quarter	454.2	164.0	166.5	165.6	69.3	65.5	46.4	37.8	8.6	8.0	-19.4	-6.3	-13.2
4th quarter	468.1	168.9	169.0	168.0	70.9	67.1	49.2	39.3	9.8	10.1	-14.7	-5.0	-9.7
1979													
1st quarter	475.3	173.2	173.1	172.2	68.4	64.4	52.3	41.2	11.1	8.1	-6.1	4.9	-11.0
2nd quarter	486.5	178.0	176.4	175.4	69.3	65.0	54.4	43.4	11.0	8.5	-6.2	4.5	-10.7
3rd quarter	504.2	177.3	190.8	189.8	72.0	67.6	56.4	45.3	11.1	7.8	-11.9	-4.2	-7.6
4th quarter	524.0	187.5	194.6	193.6	73.7	68.4	59.7	48.4	11.3	8.5	-20.8	-4.5	-16.3
1980													
1st quarter	548.1	195.8	202.5	201.5	75.8	69.3	65.3	52.9	12.3	8.9	-30.9	-2.3	-28.6
2nd quarter	569.0	207.1	207.6	206.6	75.2	70.8	69.7	57.8	11.9	9.3	-54.7	-7.6	-47.0
3rd quarter	602.4	208.1	235.9	234.8	78.7	73.4	70.0	57.8	12.1	9.7	-68.7	-27.7	-41.0
4th quarter	623.5	219.0	236.9	235.7	83.8	75.8	73.9	59.5	14.4	9.9	-60.2	-24.3	-35.9
1981													
1st quarter	645.8	228.1	241.1	239.9	79.5	74.4	87.0	70.8	16.2	10.2	-39.3	-7.3	-32.0
2nd quarter	659.5	237.1	242.2	241.0	79.8	74.5	90.1	72.7	17.4	10.3	-43.4	-6.2	-37.2
3rd quarter	683.0	238.3	260.0	258.7	78.2	71.9	96.0	78.3	17.7	10.7	-51.1	-19.9	-31.2
4th quarter	702.6	249.7	262.2	260.9	75.2	69.2	102.4	84.6	17.9	13.1	-79.4	-22.0	-57.4
1982													
1st quarter	716.8	255.2	265.5	264.6	76.0	68.8	106.5	87.7	18.8	13.5	-100.4	-18.8	-81.6
2nd quarter	728.7	256.5	272.8	271.6	76.1	70.4	110.2	91.9	18.3	13.1	-105.9	-25.5	-80.4
3rd quarter	755.7	265.1	288.2	286.9	75.2	69.0	114.9	94.9	19.9	12.5	-143.8	-38.9	-104.9
4th quarter	792.6	276.6	303.3	301.9	78.3	69.8	115.5	95.4	20.1	18.9	-177.3	-52.0	-125.3
1983													
1st quarter	795.3	280.5	302.9	301.6	75.5	70.6	117.0	98.2	18.9	19.4	-173.2	-41.7	-131.5
2nd quarter	817.2	287.3	308.2	306.9	78.4	72.7	121.0	102.3	18.7	21.0	-169.4	-44.2	-125.3
3rd quarter	826.8	296.3	302.1	300.8	78.8	71.8	127.5	108.5	19.0	21.7	-185.7	-33.5	-152.2
4th quarter	822.2	282.0	304.2	302.9	82.0	71.2	132.8	113.4	19.4	21.0	-163.8	-29.8	-134.0
1984													
1st quarter	846.3	297.2	307.1	305.9	82.0	75.4	139.6	119.8	19.8	20.7	-153.9	-13.0	-140.8
2nd quarter	869.2	310.5	309.2	307.9	84.3	77.4	145.0	124.7	20.3	20.5	-164.0	-9.5	-154.5
3rd quarter	883.5	313.2	309.8	308.6	84.8	75.1	155.2	133.5	21.6	20.4	-171.7	-5.2	-166.5
4th quarter	909.4	319.1	315.8	314.6	92.9	78.8	161.5	138.6	22.9	20.7	-182.8	-7.2	-175.6
1985													
1st quarter	926.8	329.3	324.0	322.7	88.6	79.1	164.3	141.3	23.0	20.7	-147.0	-1.9	-145.1
2nd quarter	940.9	334.5	324.9	323.7	90.9	80.0	169.0	146.1	22.9	20.6	-197.3	1.1	-198.4
3rd quarter	955.5	342.1	328.3	327.1	94.1	81.2	170.1	146.8	23.3	20.9	-174.3	1.7	-176.0
4th quarter	969.9	347.7	329.3	328.0	97.1	83.1	174.2	150.9	23.3	21.6	-181.3	6.1	-187.4
1986													
1st quarter	979.9	347.2	339.2	337.7	93.6	84.8	177.2	152.7	24.5	22.7	-180.7	6.8	-187.5
2nd quarter	1 004.7	357.1	342.9	341.4	102.5	89.0	178.5	154.2	24.2	23.8	-202.1	6.1	-208.2
3rd quarter	1 023.9	365.8	348.6	347.2	106.1	91.8	178.4	153.7	24.8	25.1	-207.1	4.8	-211.9
4th quarter	1 015.6	362.9	350.4	348.3	97.3	84.9	178.5	153.5	25.0	26.5	-173.3	8.0	-181.4
1987													
1st quarter	1 022.8	369.6	354.5	353.0	91.1	82.1	179.7	153.9	25.8	27.9	-180.5	11.2	-191.7
2nd quarter	1 037.8	372.3	358.5	357.1	95.4	85.8	181.5	155.5	26.0	30.1	-126.0	11.5	-137.5
3rd quarter	1 040.5	372.3	358.9	357.4	93.4	83.9	185.2	159.1	26.1	30.9	-134.4	15.7	-150.1
4th quarter	1 065.3	382.8	360.7	359.2	99.0	83.8	191.8	164.9	26.9	30.7	-139.1	22.2	-161.3
1988													
1st quarter	1 082.4	381.5	375.6	374.0	99.4	89.5	195.9	167.0	28.9	29.9	-142.4	31.4	-173.8
2nd quarter	1 080.9	379.9	376.7	375.1	98.6	90.0	196.2	165.3	30.9	29.4	-131.0	38.5	-169.5
3rd quarter	1 089.3	377.0	380.1	378.5	103.3	93.1	200.1	167.2	32.9	28.7	-128.0	42.1	-170.1
4th quarter	1 118.2	391.4	383.9	382.3	109.9	93.8	205.0	170.9	34.1	28.0	-136.4	46.7	-183.2
1989													
1st quarter	1 139.6	389.0	404.4	402.8	105.3	94.9	213.5	176.6	36.9	27.4	-111.4	41.8	-153.2
2nd quarter	1 159.4	400.5	408.8	407.2	104.2	95.6	219.1	181.0	38.1	26.8	-128.6	42.6	-171.3
3rd quarter	1 178.0	403.0	414.3	412.6	113.3	101.4	220.9	181.8	39.1	26.5	-139.5	42.9	-182.4
4th quarter	1 192.9	404.5	421.4	419.7	116.5	101.4	223.9	184.6	39.3	26.7	-140.9	45.2	-186.1
1990													
1st quarter	1 226.0	414.9	437.6	435.9	117.7	106.5	229.2	189.2	40.1	26.5	-168.6	43.8	-212.4
2nd quarter	1 247.2	418.1	443.5	441.7	125.7	110.3	233.6	193.1	40.5	26.4	-171.4	43.5	-214.9
3rd quarter	1 258.1	416.4	448.0	446.2	125.9	112.6	241.5	200.6	40.9	26.4	-164.9	45.8	-210.7
4th quarter	1 282.6	429.7	459.5	457.8	121.7	116.3	245.5	203.9	41.6	26.4	-183.1	39.0	-222.2

[1] Includes components not shown separately.

Table 19-10. Federal Government Current Receipts and Expenditures—Continued

(National income and product accounts, calendar years, billions of dollars, quarterly data are at seasonally adjusted annual rates.)

NIPA Table 3.2

Year and quarter	Total	Tax receipts		Taxes on production and imports		Taxes on corporate income			Contributions for government social insurance	Income receipts on assets			Current transfer receipts	Current surplus of government enterprises
		Total [1]	Personal current taxes	Total [1]	Excise taxes	Total	Federal Reserve banks	Other		Total	Interest receipts	Rents and royalties		
1991														
1st quarter	1 087.0	627.5	457.3	60.1	43.6	107.4	21.5	85.9	413.5	32.4	29.6	2.8	17.1	-3.5
2nd quarter	1 095.7	632.6	459.2	61.7	45.6	109.0	20.8	88.2	416.3	30.1	27.3	2.8	17.7	-1.0
3rd quarter	1 107.1	638.5	461.9	62.2	45.5	111.8	20.5	91.3	420.8	30.4	27.7	2.8	18.3	-0.9
4th quarter	1 115.3	645.6	467.0	64.6	46.7	111.6	20.3	91.2	423.7	27.5	24.8	2.7	18.6	-0.1
1992														
1st quarter	1 126.8	645.8	459.1	64.0	46.3	120.0	17.8	102.2	436.1	26.5	23.9	2.6	18.4	0.1
2nd quarter	1 143.7	658.8	468.0	63.5	45.5	124.7	17.4	107.3	440.7	25.8	23.2	2.5	18.2	0.2
3rd quarter	1 137.6	649.2	477.2	62.3	43.6	107.1	16.2	90.9	444.5	25.0	22.5	2.5	18.6	0.3
4th quarter	1 180.6	687.8	496.8	65.0	46.1	123.3	15.7	107.5	446.0	25.5	23.0	2.5	22.3	-1.1
1993														
1st quarter	1 174.4	674.6	481.4	62.5	43.9	127.8	16.4	111.4	454.3	26.9	24.3	2.6	21.0	-2.5
2nd quarter	1 218.1	709.6	502.8	65.1	44.9	139.0	16.0	123.1	461.9	26.9	24.2	2.7	20.8	-1.1
3rd quarter	1 226.8	715.5	511.7	65.7	45.2	135.4	15.7	119.7	465.8	26.5	23.8	2.7	20.8	-1.9
4th quarter	1 270.9	753.9	526.1	73.4	53.5	151.6	15.8	135.8	472.2	24.6	21.8	2.7	21.9	-1.6
1994														
1st quarter	1 272.4	741.0	523.3	75.9	55.3	138.9	18.6	120.3	484.1	23.9	21.1	2.8	23.3	0.1
2nd quarter	1 326.8	789.4	553.7	79.0	57.8	153.5	19.5	134.0	491.9	23.4	20.6	2.8	22.0	0.1
3rd quarter	1 331.0	789.4	542.3	80.9	58.9	163.1	20.9	142.1	496.0	23.4	20.7	2.7	22.7	-0.5
4th quarter	1 353.0	807.8	551.4	81.7	59.8	171.4	22.9	148.6	502.7	22.8	20.2	2.6	21.1	-1.4
1995														
1st quarter	1 373.8	817.7	564.6	76.9	56.9	172.6	22.8	149.8	511.9	22.9	20.6	2.3	20.5	0.8
2nd quarter	1 407.3	848.1	590.6	76.1	56.1	177.7	23.8	154.0	516.3	23.8	21.5	2.3	19.5	-0.4
3rd quarter	1 415.2	852.5	586.8	75.8	56.1	185.8	23.6	162.1	521.8	23.1	20.6	2.5	18.9	-1.1
4th quarter	1 429.8	862.0	601.8	74.8	55.1	181.2	23.3	157.8	526.8	25.0	22.2	2.8	17.6	-1.6
1996														
1st quarter	1 470.5	896.1	631.3	73.0	52.9	187.2	19.9	167.3	531.4	26.4	22.9	3.5	18.1	-1.6
2nd quarter	1 519.0	936.4	668.1	71.5	52.2	192.0	20.0	172.0	539.6	26.4	22.6	3.8	18.3	-1.7
3rd quarter	1 529.5	937.5	669.2	72.1	52.4	190.9	20.1	170.8	546.6	27.7	23.5	4.2	18.8	-1.1
4th quarter	1 577.0	959.6	685.2	76.3	58.6	192.4	20.3	172.0	553.5	27.2	22.8	4.4	37.2	-0.5
1997														
1st quarter	1 600.2	990.0	718.0	72.3	53.3	194.9	20.0	174.9	564.5	27.0	22.5	4.5	19.3	-0.6
2nd quarter	1 636.3	1 017.7	733.5	80.1	59.6	199.3	20.5	178.8	571.3	27.0	22.4	4.5	19.6	0.8
3rd quarter	1 672.8	1 046.8	751.8	80.3	60.5	209.6	20.9	188.8	579.4	25.7	21.3	4.5	20.4	0.5
4th quarter	1 703.1	1 067.9	774.0	80.1	60.8	208.2	21.3	186.9	590.2	23.9	19.6	4.4	20.4	0.7
1998														
1st quarter	1 731.4	1 086.0	796.1	79.9	60.5	205.2	26.4	178.9	600.9	22.5	18.3	4.1	21.2	1.0
2nd quarter	1 758.1	1 104.9	816.5	80.5	60.9	202.8	26.6	176.2	609.4	21.8	17.9	3.9	21.4	0.7
3rd quarter	1 792.4	1 131.4	836.3	81.8	62.0	207.7	26.8	181.0	618.2	20.9	17.2	3.7	21.8	0.1
4th quarter	1 813.2	1 145.1	854.5	82.1	62.6	201.3	26.6	174.7	626.7	20.8	17.4	3.5	21.8	-1.4
1999														
1st quarter	1 843.6	1 157.5	864.1	81.7	63.5	206.3	24.0	182.3	643.0	20.8	17.7	3.2	21.9	0.4
2nd quarter	1 869.5	1 179.2	879.7	82.1	64.2	211.4	24.6	186.8	647.1	21.2	17.9	3.4	22.1	-0.2
3rd quarter	1 900.2	1 203.9	899.5	84.2	64.5	213.9	25.3	188.5	652.6	21.5	18.0	3.5	22.5	-0.4
4th quarter	1 951.6	1 242.4	928.7	87.5	66.5	220.2	27.7	192.5	663.9	22.3	18.4	3.8	24.2	-1.2
2000														
1st quarter	2 035.7	1 301.9	975.4	86.7	66.7	233.0	24.7	208.3	685.3	24.5	20.1	4.4	24.8	-0.8
2nd quarter	2 044.9	1 309.4	987.4	88.9	67.0	225.5	25.0	200.6	685.6	25.5	20.7	4.8	25.3	-0.9
3rd quarter	2 066.8	1 322.6	1 011.7	88.1	66.5	215.6	25.6	189.9	696.5	25.0	19.6	5.4	25.8	-3.1
4th quarter	2 068.0	1 320.4	1 021.7	87.5	66.5	203.7	26.1	177.6	699.4	25.9	19.9	6.0	26.7	-4.5
2001														
1st quarter	2 089.2	1 323.0	1 047.3	87.6	65.8	180.7	29.6	151.1	716.4	26.4	19.8	6.6	27.2	-3.8
2nd quarter	2 080.5	1 315.6	1 045.7	86.9	66.3	176.6	28.0	148.7	718.1	25.2	18.6	6.7	27.3	-5.7
3rd quarter	1 895.4	1 132.0	881.0	84.2	64.3	159.7	26.6	133.2	717.9	24.4	17.9	6.5	27.1	-6.1
4th quarter	1 999.6	1 238.1	1 004.1	84.6	64.4	141.6	24.3	117.4	717.6	23.5	17.3	6.2	26.6	-6.2
2002														
1st quarter	1 845.9	1 071.3	843.1	84.9	66.3	136.3	25.0	111.3	732.1	21.1	15.8	5.3	25.7	-4.3
2nd quarter	1 854.1	1 077.5	835.2	87.7	68.0	147.4	25.3	122.1	735.5	20.1	15.0	5.1	24.9	-3.9
3rd quarter	1 856.1	1 075.4	825.8	88.5	67.9	153.9	24.4	129.5	735.0	19.8	15.2	4.7	24.5	1.4
4th quarter	1 856.6	1 078.0	818.0	88.0	67.2	164.2	23.2	141.0	734.4	19.9	15.5	4.4	24.0	0.3
2003														
1st quarter	1 888.9	1 092.7	804.4	90.0	68.5	190.8	23.9	166.9	747.6	19.8	15.0	4.7	24.2	4.6
2nd quarter	1 903.3	1 097.0	810.4	89.5	68.3	186.5	22.8	163.7	755.9	23.0	16.6	6.4	24.7	2.7
3rd quarter	1 817.3	1 004.5	708.2	88.8	67.3	199.6	21.4	178.2	761.7	24.2	16.9	7.3	25.4	1.5
4th quarter	1 910.2	1 089.1	774.7	90.3	68.8	214.3	20.0	194.3	770.3	24.8	17.2	7.6	25.7	0.4
2004														
1st quarter	1 945.4	1 108.6	776.0	93.6	71.4	229.4	17.2	212.2	787.8	22.2	15.3	7.0	26.7	0.1
2nd quarter	1 985.6	1 141.0	791.4	94.0	71.1	246.5	17.2	229.3	795.8	21.7	15.2	6.5	27.4	-0.3
3rd quarter	2 013.0	1 156.9	810.8	95.1	71.6	242.8	18.1	224.6	807.1	22.0	15.7	6.3	28.2	-1.3
4th quarter	2 059.9	1 194.3	827.5	95.8	71.4	259.3	19.8	239.5	817.9	22.5	15.9	6.5	28.6	-3.4
2005														
1st quarter	2 214.5	1 328.0	891.2	97.9	73.0	327.6	18.6	309.0	838.3	22.8	16.2	6.7	29.1	-3.7
2nd quarter	2 240.3	1 344.3	910.9	102.7	77.4	321.4	20.9	300.5	846.1	23.8	16.2	7.6	30.5	-4.5
3rd quarter	2 182.4	1 364.2	941.0	102.4	77.0	309.5	21.7	287.8	863.2	22.8	15.7	7.1	-61.7	-6.0
4th quarter	2 349.8	1 428.4	968.4	101.6	75.9	347.1	24.6	322.5	873.8	22.3	15.3	6.9	30.6	-5.4

[1]Includes components not shown separately.

Table 19-10. Federal Government Current Receipts and Expenditures—Continued

(National income and product accounts, calendar years, billions of dollars, quarterly data are at seasonally adjusted annual rates.)

NIPA Table 3.2

| Year and quarter | Current expenditures [1] | | Government social benefits | | Other current transfer payments | | Interest payments | | | Subsidies | Net federal government saving, NIPA (surplus + / deficit -) | | |
	Total	Consumption expenditures	Total [1]	To persons	Total [1]	Grants-in-aid to state and local governments	Total	To persons and business	To the rest of the world		Total	Social insurance funds	Other
1991													
1st quarter	1 245.4	443.8	480.9	479.1	46.1	122.8	248.2	206.4	41.8	26.5	-158.4	29.7	-188.1
2nd quarter	1 307.4	442.2	491.2	489.3	96.0	128.1	251.0	210.1	40.9	26.6	-211.7	25.0	-236.6
3rd quarter	1 339.8	438.1	495.0	493.1	129.0	134.9	250.7	209.7	41.1	26.9	-232.7	27.1	-259.7
4th quarter	1 367.4	433.9	509.5	506.5	142.7	140.6	253.9	214.1	39.7	27.5	-252.1	20.9	-273.1
1992													
1st quarter	1 415.3	439.2	539.5	538.0	156.9	143.2	251.7	212.6	39.2	28.0	-288.5	8.8	-297.3
2nd quarter	1 435.4	441.1	551.2	548.5	161.9	146.2	252.6	213.3	39.3	28.6	-291.7	4.5	-296.3
3rd quarter	1 453.7	450.1	555.5	553.5	166.6	152.4	251.8	212.6	39.1	29.8	-316.1	6.5	-322.6
4th quarter	1 473.9	450.3	560.7	559.1	182.5	154.6	248.9	210.2	38.8	31.6	-293.4	6.2	-299.6
1993													
1st quarter	1 475.0	442.7	574.1	572.7	169.9	156.3	253.4	214.6	38.8	34.8	-300.6	3.6	-304.3
2nd quarter	1 486.1	440.0	580.4	578.4	174.8	159.3	253.9	215.2	38.7	36.9	-268.0	5.8	-273.8
3rd quarter	1 500.8	441.2	585.4	583.4	183.0	165.0	254.2	214.3	39.8	37.0	-274.0	4.9	-278.9
4th quarter	1 522.2	443.7	589.5	587.5	201.6	174.1	252.0	211.9	40.1	35.4	-251.3	8.3	-259.5
1994													
1st quarter	1 504.6	437.8	600.4	599.0	183.0	171.2	250.4	209.7	40.7	32.9	-232.2	13.4	-245.5
2nd quarter	1 517.2	438.4	604.3	602.9	185.3	171.6	257.5	215.1	42.3	31.7	-190.3	18.1	-208.4
3rd quarter	1 542.3	446.7	610.0	606.3	190.1	174.9	264.3	219.8	44.6	31.2	-211.3	18.0	-229.3
4th quarter	1 568.6	440.4	615.7	613.9	207.9	181.2	273.2	224.0	49.1	31.4	-215.5	22.4	-237.9
1995													
1st quarter	1 589.0	442.9	631.9	630.7	198.0	185.0	283.1	234.8	48.3	33.0	-215.2	20.7	-235.9
2nd quarter	1 602.6	442.6	640.3	638.2	196.0	184.9	290.2	237.5	52.7	33.5	-195.3	17.9	-213.2
3rd quarter	1 613.9	443.5	646.0	643.9	197.1	185.1	293.4	237.4	56.0	34.0	-198.7	18.6	-217.3
4th quarter	1 608.5	432.8	652.6	650.5	194.0	181.6	294.9	236.6	58.3	34.3	-178.7	18.8	-197.5
1996													
1st quarter	1 652.6	443.6	672.0	669.7	205.8	186.1	296.9	237.2	59.7	34.3	-182.1	8.6	-190.6
2nd quarter	1 662.1	447.6	678.5	676.4	207.0	195.0	294.8	232.0	62.8	34.2	-143.1	11.7	-154.9
3rd quarter	1 662.6	442.2	682.2	680.1	206.0	193.2	298.3	231.2	67.2	33.9	-133.1	16.3	-149.4
4th quarter	1 685.7	451.7	687.4	685.3	214.2	190.3	298.9	227.6	71.4	33.5	-108.7	19.2	-127.8
1997													
1st quarter	1 689.4	453.2	702.8	700.7	202.9	192.4	297.5	223.1	74.4	33.0	-89.2	20.9	-110.1
2nd quarter	1 705.4	461.7	706.0	703.7	206.1	195.5	299.3	221.6	77.7	32.3	-69.1	25.6	-94.7
3rd quarter	1 707.8	457.2	707.7	705.7	209.7	198.4	301.1	220.4	80.7	32.1	-35.0	33.0	-68.0
4th quarter	1 733.1	458.5	708.9	706.7	231.2	208.2	302.0	220.3	81.7	32.4	-30.0	42.8	-72.8
1998													
1st quarter	1 718.4	447.7	716.7	714.4	218.7	207.9	302.3	220.9	81.3	33.1	13.0	46.2	-33.2
2nd quarter	1 729.2	457.9	718.0	715.6	218.2	208.1	301.2	220.1	81.2	33.7	28.9	54.8	-25.8
3rd quarter	1 732.0	451.0	720.5	718.3	225.9	213.0	299.3	220.1	79.2	35.3	60.4	62.1	-1.7
4th quarter	1 760.2	461.8	721.4	719.1	246.6	222.0	292.6	217.1	75.5	37.7	53.0	72.9	-19.9
1999													
1st quarter	1 764.2	467.0	733.4	731.0	238.5	227.0	284.4	210.6	73.8	40.9	79.4	85.5	-6.1
2nd quarter	1 764.8	463.9	736.5	734.2	237.4	223.7	283.3	210.4	72.9	43.6	104.6	89.5	15.1
3rd quarter	1 792.4	477.6	739.3	736.9	250.2	237.6	280.1	205.2	75.0	45.2	107.8	95.3	12.5
4th quarter	1 828.9	491.8	742.9	740.6	265.9	243.2	282.8	206.2	76.5	45.4	122.7	105.9	16.9
2000													
1st quarter	1 823.0	485.7	756.1	753.7	252.1	239.0	285.1	205.6	79.6	43.9	212.7	117.7	95.0
2nd quarter	1 863.5	505.1	771.8	769.3	257.0	242.8	285.7	203.5	82.2	43.8	181.4	105.3	76.1
3rd quarter	1 875.5	501.5	776.8	774.2	271.1	255.0	282.5	198.6	83.9	43.7	191.2	114.1	77.1
4th quarter	1 895.5	505.0	785.1	782.6	282.2	252.6	279.6	193.5	86.2	43.5	172.5	112.2	60.2
2001													
1st quarter	1 932.6	518.4	817.3	814.6	278.1	266.5	274.5	188.6	85.9	44.3	156.6	102.6	54.0
2nd quarter	1 956.9	528.0	831.2	828.5	290.1	278.3	263.7	178.7	85.0	44.0	123.6	95.2	28.4
3rd quarter	1 984.0	532.7	849.4	846.7	286.1	272.8	253.3	173.4	80.0	62.5	-88.6	80.9	-169.5
4th quarter	2 004.3	548.4	867.6	865.0	305.8	286.6	242.8	164.0	78.8	39.7	-4.7	69.3	-74.1
2002													
1st quarter	2 054.4	571.3	896.4	893.7	318.7	291.4	229.9	150.8	79.1	38.1	-208.5	64.9	-273.4
2nd quarter	2 095.5	585.0	922.8	920.1	317.9	303.1	233.3	155.6	77.7	36.5	-241.4	46.1	-287.5
3rd quarter	2 103.4	591.4	927.0	924.3	320.6	306.6	227.7	151.8	76.0	36.7	-247.3	44.0	-291.3
4th quarter	2 151.1	618.5	932.2	929.5	336.3	317.2	225.4	151.5	73.9	38.7	-294.6	40.6	-335.1
2003													
1st quarter	2 179.0	636.9	948.0	945.3	337.0	311.9	216.6	144.1	72.5	41.9	-290.2	42.4	-332.6
2nd quarter	2 268.8	668.4	964.0	961.1	367.4	342.2	212.4	141.2	71.2	55.2	-365.5	37.4	-402.9
3rd quarter	2 268.8	669.1	972.7	969.8	369.4	345.9	210.0	135.3	74.7	47.5	-451.4	36.7	-488.1
4th quarter	2 291.7	676.5	981.5	978.6	374.8	354.2	212.5	135.4	77.1	46.4	-381.5	39.4	-420.8
2004													
1st quarter	2 346.4	712.2	1 003.7	1 000.8	373.0	339.5	215.6	136.4	79.2	43.4	-401.0	45.1	-446.1
2nd quarter	2 366.3	722.6	1 012.3	1 009.3	372.2	349.8	215.3	127.6	87.7	42.4	-380.6	49.2	-429.8
3rd quarter	2 393.6	734.8	1 022.2	1 019.2	367.8	345.7	224.8	133.1	91.7	43.9	-380.6	53.3	-433.9
4th quarter	2 425.6	728.3	1 035.6	1 032.4	386.6	361.2	227.7	132.5	95.2	47.4	-365.7	53.8	-419.5
2005													
1st quarter	2 502.0	758.0	1 065.9	1 062.9	395.2	355.9	230.9	128.8	102.2	51.9	-287.6	50.5	-338.1
2nd quarter	2 529.9	760.8	1 076.4	1 073.3	385.4	359.8	252.1	142.5	109.6	55.2	-289.6	49.4	-338.9
3rd quarter	2 578.5	784.3	1 087.8	1 084.7	393.5	361.9	255.2	137.9	117.2	57.7	-396.0	64.0	-460.0
4th quarter	2 613.3	771.1	1 096.7	1 093.5	405.7	366.8	277.1	151.8	125.3	62.7	-263.6	68.5	-332.0

[1]Includes components not shown separately.

Table 19-11. State and Local Government Current Receipts and Expenditures

(National income and product accounts, calendar years, billions of dollars, quarterly data are at seasonally adjusted annual rates.)

NIPA Table 3.3

Year and quarter	Total	Current receipts											
		Current tax receipts								Contributions for government social insurance	Income receipts on assets		
		Total	Personal current taxes		Taxes on production and imports				Taxes on corporate income		Total ¹	Interest receipts	Rents and royalties
			Total ¹	Income taxes	Total	Sales taxes	Property taxes	Other					
1946	12.6	10.5	0.9	0.4	9.1	2.9	4.8	1.4	0.5	0.2	0.4	0.3	0.1
1947	14.9	12.0	1.0	0.5	10.4	3.5	5.3	1.6	0.6	0.2	0.4	0.3	0.1
1948	16.8	13.7	1.1	0.6	11.9	4.1	5.9	1.8	0.7	0.2	0.5	0.3	0.2
1949	18.3	15.0	1.4	0.7	13.0	4.3	6.6	2.1	0.6	0.2	0.5	0.3	0.2
1947													
1st quarter	14.1	11.5	1.0	. . .	9.9	. . .	. . .	. . .	0.6	0.2	0.4	. . .	0.1
2nd quarter	14.7	11.8	1.0	. . .	10.2	. . .	. . .	. . .	0.6	0.2	0.4	. . .	0.1
3rd quarter	15.1	12.2	1.0	. . .	10.6	. . .	. . .	. . .	0.6	0.2	0.4	. . .	0.1
4th quarter	15.6	12.7	1.0	. . .	11.1	. . .	. . .	. . .	0.6	0.2	0.4	. . .	0.1
1948													
1st quarter	16.1	13.2	1.1	. . .	11.4	. . .	. . .	. . .	0.7	0.2	0.5	. . .	0.2
2nd quarter	16.6	13.6	1.1	. . .	11.7	. . .	. . .	. . .	0.7	0.2	0.5	. . .	0.2
3rd quarter	17.0	13.9	1.1	. . .	12.1	. . .	. . .	. . .	0.7	0.2	0.5	. . .	0.2
4th quarter	17.3	14.1	1.1	. . .	12.3	. . .	. . .	. . .	0.7	0.2	0.5	. . .	0.2
1949													
1st quarter	17.7	14.6	1.3	. . .	12.6	. . .	. . .	. . .	0.7	0.2	0.5	. . .	0.2
2nd quarter	17.9	14.8	1.4	. . .	12.9	. . .	. . .	. . .	0.6	0.2	0.5	. . .	0.2
3rd quarter	18.7	15.2	1.4	. . .	13.2	. . .	. . .	. . .	0.6	0.2	0.5	. . .	0.2
4th quarter	18.8	15.4	1.4	. . .	13.4	. . .	. . .	. . .	0.6	0.2	0.5	. . .	0.2
1950													
1st quarter	19.2	15.8	1.5	. . .	13.7	. . .	. . .	. . .	0.6	0.2	0.5	. . .	0.2
2nd quarter	19.7	16.1	1.5	. . .	14.0	. . .	. . .	. . .	0.7	0.2	0.5	. . .	0.2
3rd quarter	20.4	16.9	1.5	. . .	14.6	. . .	. . .	. . .	0.9	0.2	0.5	. . .	0.2
4th quarter	20.6	17.1	1.5	. . .	14.6	. . .	. . .	. . .	0.9	0.2	0.6	. . .	0.2
1951													
1st quarter	21.7	17.9	1.6	. . .	15.3	. . .	. . .	. . .	1.0	0.2	0.6	. . .	0.2
2nd quarter	21.6	17.8	1.7	. . .	15.3	. . .	. . .	. . .	0.9	0.2	0.6	. . .	0.2
3rd quarter	21.9	18.1	1.7	. . .	15.6	. . .	. . .	. . .	0.8	0.2	0.6	. . .	0.2
4th quarter	22.5	18.6	1.7	. . .	16.0	. . .	. . .	. . .	0.8	0.2	0.6	. . .	0.2
1952													
1st quarter	22.9	19.0	1.8	. . .	16.3	. . .	. . .	. . .	0.8	0.3	0.6	. . .	0.2
2nd quarter	23.4	19.4	1.8	. . .	16.8	. . .	. . .	. . .	0.8	0.3	0.7	. . .	0.2
3rd quarter	24.0	19.8	1.8	. . .	17.2	. . .	. . .	. . .	0.8	0.3	0.7	. . .	0.2
4th quarter	24.6	20.4	1.8	. . .	17.7	. . .	. . .	. . .	0.9	0.3	0.7	. . .	0.2
1953													
1st quarter	24.6	20.7	1.9	. . .	18.0	. . .	. . .	. . .	0.9	0.3	0.7	. . .	0.3
2nd quarter	25.8	21.0	1.9	. . .	18.2	. . .	. . .	. . .	0.9	0.3	0.7	. . .	0.3
3rd quarter	25.8	21.4	2.0	. . .	18.6	. . .	. . .	. . .	0.8	0.3	0.7	. . .	0.3
4th quarter	25.9	21.4	2.0	. . .	18.8	. . .	. . .	. . .	0.7	0.3	0.7	. . .	0.3
1954													
1st quarter	26.4	21.7	2.1	. . .	19.0	. . .	. . .	. . .	0.7	0.3	0.8	. . .	0.3
2nd quarter	26.6	22.0	2.1	. . .	19.2	. . .	. . .	. . .	0.7	0.3	0.8	. . .	0.3
3rd quarter	27.1	22.4	2.1	. . .	19.5	. . .	. . .	. . .	0.8	0.3	0.8	. . .	0.3
4th quarter	27.6	22.8	2.1	. . .	19.9	. . .	. . .	. . .	0.8	0.3	0.8	. . .	0.3
1955													
1st quarter	28.3	23.6	2.4	. . .	20.3	. . .	. . .	. . .	0.9	0.3	0.8	. . .	0.3
2nd quarter	29.0	24.0	2.4	. . .	20.7	. . .	. . .	. . .	0.9	0.3	0.8	. . .	0.3
3rd quarter	29.8	24.7	2.4	. . .	21.3	. . .	. . .	. . .	1.0	0.3	0.9	. . .	0.3
4th quarter	30.4	25.3	2.4	. . .	21.9	. . .	. . .	. . .	1.0	0.3	0.9	. . .	0.3
1956													
1st quarter	31.3	26.1	2.7	. . .	22.4	. . .	. . .	. . .	1.0	0.4	0.9	. . .	0.3
2nd quarter	32.0	26.8	2.7	. . .	23.0	. . .	. . .	. . .	1.1	0.4	1.0	. . .	0.3
3rd quarter	32.8	27.3	2.7	. . .	23.6	. . .	. . .	. . .	1.0	0.4	1.0	. . .	0.3
4th quarter	33.4	27.8	2.7	. . .	24.1	. . .	. . .	. . .	1.1	0.4	1.0	. . .	0.3
1957													
1st quarter	34.4	28.5	2.9	. . .	24.6	. . .	. . .	. . .	1.1	0.4	1.1	. . .	0.3
2nd quarter	34.7	28.9	2.9	. . .	25.0	. . .	. . .	. . .	1.0	0.4	1.1	. . .	0.3
3rd quarter	35.3	29.3	2.9	. . .	25.4	. . .	. . .	. . .	1.0	0.4	1.1	. . .	0.3
4th quarter	35.6	29.3	2.9	. . .	25.5	. . .	. . .	. . .	0.9	0.4	1.1	. . .	0.3
1958													
1st quarter	35.7	29.7	3.0	1.8	25.8	9.8	13.4	2.7	0.9	0.4	1.1	0.7	0.4
2nd quarter	36.5	30.1	3.0	1.8	26.1	9.8	13.6	2.7	0.9	0.4	1.1	0.8	0.4
3rd quarter	37.2	30.8	3.1	1.8	26.7	10.0	13.9	2.8	1.0	0.4	1.1	0.8	0.4
4th quarter	38.9	31.7	3.1	1.8	27.4	10.3	14.2	3.0	1.2	0.4	1.2	0.8	0.4
1959													
1st quarter	39.1	32.7	3.6	2.0	27.9	10.7	14.4	2.8	1.2	0.4	1.1	0.8	0.3
2nd quarter	40.1	33.2	3.7	2.1	28.2	10.9	14.5	2.9	1.3	0.4	1.1	0.8	0.3
3rd quarter	41.3	34.4	4.0	2.4	29.3	11.4	14.9	2.9	1.1	0.4	1.1	0.9	0.3
4th quarter	42.1	35.1	4.0	2.4	30.0	11.5	15.4	3.0	1.1	0.4	1.2	0.9	0.3
1960													
1st quarter	43.3	36.0	4.2	2.5	30.4	11.8	15.6	3.1	1.4	0.4	1.3	1.1	0.3
2nd quarter	44.2	36.7	4.2	2.5	31.2	12.1	16.0	3.1	1.3	0.4	1.4	1.1	0.3
3rd quarter	44.8	37.3	4.3	2.6	31.8	12.3	16.5	3.1	1.2	0.5	1.3	1.0	0.3
4th quarter	45.5	37.9	4.3	2.6	32.4	12.4	16.9	3.1	1.1	0.5	1.3	1.0	0.3

¹Includes components not shown separately.
. . . = Not available.

Table 19-11. State and Local Government Current Receipts and Expenditures—Continued

(National income and product accounts, calendar years, billions of dollars, quarterly data are at seasonally adjusted annual rates.)

NIPA Table 3.3

Year and quarter	Current receipts—Continued				Current surplus of government enterprises	Current expenditures					Net state and local government saving, NIPA (surplus + / deficit -)		
	Current transfer receipts												
	Total	Federal grants-in-aid	From business, net	From persons		Total [1]	Consumption expenditures	Government social benefits to persons	Interest payments	Subsidies	Total	Social insurance funds	Other
1946	1.2	1.0	0.1	0.2	0.4	11.1	9.2	1.5	0.5	. . .	1.5	0.1	1.4
1947	1.8	1.6	0.1	0.2	0.4	13.5	10.9	2.0	0.5	. . .	1.4	0.1	1.4
1948	2.0	1.7	0.1	0.2	0.3	15.5	12.3	2.7	0.5	. . .	1.2	0.1	1.1
1949	2.2	1.9	0.1	0.3	0.4	16.8	13.7	2.7	0.5	. . .	1.5	0.1	1.4
1947													
1st quarter	1.6	1.4	0.1	0.2	0.4	12.5	10.3	1.6	0.5	. . .	1.6	. . .	. . .
2nd quarter	1.9	1.7	0.1	0.2	0.4	13.1	10.7	1.9	0.5	. . .	1.6	. . .	. . .
3rd quarter	1.9	1.6	0.1	0.2	0.4	14.0	11.1	2.4	0.5	. . .	1.1	. . .	. . .
4th quarter	1.9	1.6	0.1	0.2	0.4	14.3	11.5	2.3	0.5	. . .	1.3	. . .	. . .
1948													
1st quarter	1.9	1.6	0.1	0.2	0.4	15.1	11.8	2.8	0.5	. . .	1.0	. . .	. . .
2nd quarter	2.0	1.7	0.1	0.2	0.3	15.4	12.0	2.8	0.5	. . .	1.2	. . .	. . .
3rd quarter	2.1	1.8	0.1	0.3	0.3	15.8	12.5	2.7	0.5	. . .	1.2	. . .	. . .
4th quarter	2.2	1.9	0.1	0.3	0.3	15.8	13.0	2.4	0.5	. . .	1.5	. . .	. . .
1949													
1st quarter	2.1	1.7	0.1	0.3	0.4	16.2	13.3	2.5	0.5	. . .	1.5	. . .	. . .
2nd quarter	2.0	1.7	0.1	0.3	0.4	16.5	13.4	2.6	0.5	. . .	1.4	. . .	. . .
3rd quarter	2.5	2.1	0.1	0.3	0.4	17.1	13.8	2.7	0.5	. . .	1.6	. . .	. . .
4th quarter	2.3	1.9	0.1	0.3	0.4	17.5	14.1	2.9	0.5	. . .	1.3	. . .	. . .
1950													
1st quarter	2.3	1.9	0.1	0.3	0.4	18.2	14.5	3.2	0.6	. . .	1.0	. . .	. . .
2nd quarter	2.3	1.9	0.1	0.3	0.4	18.9	14.7	3.7	0.6	. . .	0.7	. . .	. . .
3rd quarter	2.3	1.9	0.1	0.3	0.4	18.6	15.0	3.0	0.6	. . .	1.8	. . .	. . .
4th quarter	2.3	1.9	0.1	0.3	0.4	18.8	15.3	2.9	0.6	. . .	1.8	. . .	. . .
1951													
1st quarter	2.5	2.0	0.1	0.3	0.5	19.0	15.6	2.8	0.6	. . .	2.7	. . .	. . .
2nd quarter	2.5	2.1	0.1	0.3	0.5	19.1	15.9	2.6	0.6	. . .	2.5	. . .	. . .
3rd quarter	2.4	1.9	0.1	0.3	0.5	19.5	16.2	2.6	0.6	. . .	2.4	. . .	. . .
4th quarter	2.6	2.1	0.1	0.3	0.5	19.8	16.6	2.6	0.7	. . .	2.7	. . .	. . .
1952													
1st quarter	2.5	2.0	0.1	0.3	0.5	20.0	16.5	2.8	0.7	. . .	2.9	. . .	. . .
2nd quarter	2.5	2.1	0.1	0.3	0.5	21.0	17.3	3.0	0.7	. . .	2.4	. . .	. . .
3rd quarter	2.7	2.3	0.1	0.3	0.5	20.7	17.1	2.9	0.7	. . .	3.3	. . .	. . .
4th quarter	2.7	2.3	0.1	0.3	0.5	21.2	17.5	2.9	0.7	. . .	3.4	. . .	. . .
1953													
1st quarter	2.3	1.8	0.1	0.3	0.5	21.7	18.0	2.9	0.7	. . .	2.9	. . .	. . .
2nd quarter	3.2	2.7	0.1	0.3	0.5	21.8	18.0	3.0	0.8	. . .	4.0	. . .	. . .
3rd quarter	2.8	2.3	0.1	0.4	0.6	22.3	18.4	3.1	0.8	. . .	3.5	. . .	. . .
4th quarter	2.8	2.3	0.2	0.4	0.6	22.3	18.5	2.9	0.8	. . .	3.6	. . .	. . .
1954													
1st quarter	2.9	2.3	0.2	0.4	0.6	22.8	18.9	3.0	0.9	. . .	3.6	. . .	. . .
2nd quarter	2.8	2.3	0.2	0.4	0.7	23.4	19.4	3.0	0.9	. . .	3.3	. . .	. . .
3rd quarter	2.9	2.4	0.2	0.4	0.7	24.1	20.1	3.1	0.9	. . .	3.0	. . .	. . .
4th quarter	2.9	2.3	0.2	0.4	0.7	24.5	20.4	3.1	1.0	. . .	3.1	. . .	. . .
1955													
1st quarter	2.8	2.3	0.2	0.4	0.8	25.3	21.1	3.2	1.0	. . .	3.0	. . .	. . .
2nd quarter	2.9	2.4	0.2	0.4	0.8	25.7	21.3	3.3	1.1	. . .	3.3	. . .	. . .
3rd quarter	3.1	2.5	0.2	0.4	0.9	26.0	21.7	3.3	1.1	. . .	3.8	. . .	. . .
4th quarter	3.0	2.4	0.2	0.4	0.9	26.5	22.1	3.2	1.1	. . .	3.9	. . .	. . .
1956													
1st quarter	3.0	2.4	0.2	0.4	0.9	27.0	22.6	3.3	1.2	. . .	4.3	. . .	. . .
2nd quarter	3.1	2.5	0.2	0.4	0.9	27.6	23.1	3.2	1.2	. . .	4.5	. . .	. . .
3rd quarter	3.3	2.6	0.2	0.4	0.9	28.3	23.8	3.3	1.3	. . .	4.5	. . .	. . .
4th quarter	3.3	2.7	0.2	0.5	0.9	29.0	24.4	3.4	1.3	. . .	4.3	. . .	. . .
1957													
1st quarter	3.6	2.9	0.2	0.5	0.9	29.6	24.8	3.5	1.3	. . .	4.8	. . .	. . .
2nd quarter	3.5	2.8	0.2	0.5	0.9	30.4	25.5	3.5	1.4	. . .	4.3	. . .	. . .
3rd quarter	3.7	2.9	0.2	0.5	0.9	31.3	26.2	3.6	1.4	. . .	4.1	. . .	. . .
4th quarter	3.8	3.1	0.2	0.5	0.9	32.0	26.8	3.7	1.5	. . .	3.6	. . .	. . .
1958													
1st quarter	3.6	2.9	0.2	0.5	0.9	33.0	27.6	4.0	1.5	. . .	2.7	0.1	2.6
2nd quarter	4.1	3.3	0.2	0.5	0.9	33.9	28.4	4.0	1.5	. . .	2.6	0.0	2.5
3rd quarter	3.9	3.2	0.2	0.5	0.9	34.6	29.0	4.0	1.6	. . .	2.6	0.0	2.6
4th quarter	4.7	4.0	0.2	0.5	0.9	35.3	29.5	4.1	1.6	. . .	3.6	0.0	3.6
1959													
1st quarter	3.9	3.5	0.1	0.3	1.0	36.1	30.0	4.3	1.7	0.0	3.1	0.0	3.0
2nd quarter	4.3	3.9	0.1	0.3	1.1	36.5	30.5	4.3	1.7	0.0	3.6	0.0	3.5
3rd quarter	4.2	3.8	0.1	0.3	1.2	37.1	30.9	4.3	1.8	0.0	4.2	0.0	4.1
4th quarter	4.2	3.8	0.1	0.3	1.2	37.8	31.5	4.4	1.9	0.0	4.3	0.0	4.3
1960													
1st quarter	4.3	3.9	0.2	0.3	1.2	39.0	32.5	4.4	2.1	0.0	4.3	0.0	4.3
2nd quarter	4.4	4.0	0.2	0.3	1.3	40.0	33.4	4.5	2.1	0.0	4.2	0.0	4.2
3rd quarter	4.5	4.0	0.2	0.3	1.3	40.5	33.8	4.6	2.0	0.0	4.3	0.0	4.3
4th quarter	4.7	4.2	0.2	0.3	1.3	41.2	34.5	4.7	2.0	0.0	4.4	0.0	4.3

[1] Includes components not shown separately.
. . . = Not available.

Table 19-11. State and Local Government Current Receipts and Expenditures—Continued

(National income and product accounts, calendar years, billions of dollars, quarterly data are at seasonally adjusted annual rates.)

NIPA Table 3.3

Year and quarter	Current receipts Total	Current tax receipts Total	Personal current taxes Total [1]	Personal current taxes Income taxes	Taxes on production and imports Total	Taxes on production and imports Sales taxes	Taxes on production and imports Property taxes	Taxes on production and imports Other	Taxes on corporate income	Contributions for government social insurance	Income receipts on assets Total [1]	Income receipts on assets Interest receipts	Income receipts on assets Rents and royalties
1961													
1st quarter	46.5	38.4	4.3	2.6	32.9	12.6	17.2	3.2	1.2	0.5	1.4	1.0	0.4
2nd quarter	47.6	39.2	4.5	2.7	33.4	12.8	17.5	3.2	1.2	0.5	1.4	1.1	0.4
3rd quarter	48.6	40.1	4.6	2.9	34.1	13.2	17.7	3.2	1.3	0.5	1.4	1.1	0.4
4th quarter	49.6	41.0	4.7	3.0	34.8	13.6	18.0	3.2	1.4	0.5	1.4	1.1	0.4
1962													
1st quarter	50.7	41.8	4.9	3.1	35.5	13.9	18.3	3.2	1.5	0.5	1.5	1.1	0.4
2nd quarter	51.5	42.4	5.0	3.1	36.0	13.9	18.7	3.3	1.5	0.5	1.5	1.1	0.4
3rd quarter	52.5	43.1	5.1	3.2	36.5	14.0	19.2	3.3	1.5	0.6	1.6	1.2	0.4
4th quarter	53.3	43.8	5.2	3.3	37.1	14.2	19.6	3.3	1.5	0.6	1.5	1.1	0.4
1963													
1st quarter	54.1	44.4	5.3	3.3	37.6	14.3	19.9	3.4	1.5	0.6	1.5	1.1	0.4
2nd quarter	55.3	45.2	5.3	3.3	38.3	14.7	20.1	3.5	1.6	0.6	1.6	1.2	0.4
3rd quarter	56.8	46.3	5.5	3.5	39.1	15.3	20.4	3.5	1.7	0.6	1.7	1.3	0.4
4th quarter	57.9	47.1	5.6	3.6	39.8	15.6	20.6	3.5	1.7	0.7	1.7	1.3	0.4
1964													
1st quarter	59.7	48.3	5.8	3.7	40.7	16.1	21.0	3.6	1.8	0.7	1.8	1.4	0.4
2nd quarter	60.7	49.2	6.0	4.0	41.4	16.3	21.4	3.7	1.8	0.7	2.0	1.5	0.4
3rd quarter	61.7	50.5	6.2	4.1	42.4	16.7	21.9	3.7	1.9	0.7	1.9	1.5	0.4
4th quarter	62.9	51.1	6.4	4.2	42.9	16.7	22.4	3.8	1.8	0.7	2.0	1.5	0.4
1965													
1st quarter	64.1	52.2	6.5	4.3	43.8	17.2	22.8	3.8	1.9	0.7	2.1	1.6	0.4
2nd quarter	65.9	53.2	6.5	4.4	44.7	17.8	23.1	3.9	1.9	0.8	2.2	1.8	0.4
3rd quarter	67.3	54.4	6.6	4.4	45.8	18.5	23.3	4.0	2.0	0.8	2.2	1.7	0.4
4th quarter	68.9	55.7	6.8	4.5	46.8	19.2	23.6	4.0	2.1	0.8	2.3	1.8	0.4
1966													
1st quarter	71.8	56.9	7.1	4.8	47.5	19.5	23.9	4.1	2.3	0.8	2.5	2.0	0.5
2nd quarter	74.1	58.0	7.6	5.2	48.2	19.7	24.3	4.2	2.3	0.8	2.6	2.0	0.5
3rd quarter	76.1	59.5	8.0	5.6	49.2	20.2	24.7	4.3	2.2	0.8	2.7	2.2	0.5
4th quarter	77.7	60.6	8.4	6.0	50.1	20.4	25.2	4.5	2.2	0.8	2.7	2.2	0.5
1967													
1st quarter	79.2	61.6	8.3	5.9	50.7	20.4	25.8	4.4	2.6	0.9	2.8	2.2	0.6
2nd quarter	80.7	62.5	8.3	5.9	51.7	20.7	26.6	4.4	2.6	0.9	2.8	2.2	0.6
3rd quarter	83.3	64.8	8.7	6.2	53.5	21.8	27.3	4.5	2.6	0.9	3.1	2.5	0.6
4th quarter	86.8	67.0	9.0	6.5	55.2	22.7	28.1	4.4	2.7	0.9	3.3	2.7	0.6
1968													
1st quarter	89.3	70.2	9.7	7.1	57.2	23.8	28.9	4.5	3.2	0.9	3.4	2.6	0.7
2nd quarter	92.9	72.3	10.3	7.6	58.7	24.6	29.6	4.6	3.3	0.9	3.4	2.7	0.7
3rd quarter	94.6	74.6	10.8	8.1	60.4	25.6	30.3	4.6	3.3	1.0	3.5	2.8	0.7
4th quarter	97.3	76.5	11.4	8.5	61.8	26.2	30.9	4.6	3.4	1.0	3.7	3.0	0.7
1969													
1st quarter	100.1	79.0	11.9	8.9	63.3	27.1	31.6	4.7	3.8	1.0	4.0	3.2	0.8
2nd quarter	103.4	81.1	12.3	9.3	65.1	28.1	32.3	4.7	3.7	1.0	4.2	3.5	0.8
3rd quarter	107.5	83.9	13.4	10.3	67.0	29.1	33.1	4.7	3.5	1.0	4.5	3.7	0.8
4th quarter	110.9	85.9	13.7	10.5	68.8	29.9	34.1	4.8	3.4	1.1	4.7	3.9	0.8
1970													
1st quarter	115.1	88.4	14.0	10.8	70.6	30.6	35.1	4.9	3.8	1.1	4.9	4.1	0.8
2nd quarter	118.6	90.3	14.1	10.9	72.4	31.3	36.2	4.9	3.7	1.1	5.1	4.3	0.8
3rd quarter	122.2	92.5	14.3	11.0	74.3	32.1	37.2	5.0	3.8	1.1	5.2	4.4	0.8
4th quarter	124.5	94.0	14.4	11.0	76.0	32.6	38.2	5.2	3.6	1.1	5.3	4.5	0.8
1971													
1st quarter	128.5	97.1	14.7	11.3	78.3	33.6	39.2	5.5	4.1	1.1	5.4	4.5	0.9
2nd quarter	133.2	100.0	15.6	12.2	80.2	34.5	40.1	5.6	4.2	1.2	5.5	4.6	0.9
3rd quarter	136.7	103.2	16.0	12.5	82.8	36.1	40.9	5.8	4.4	1.2	5.5	4.6	0.9
4th quarter	141.3	106.5	17.3	13.8	84.7	37.3	41.6	5.9	4.5	1.2	5.5	4.6	0.9
1972													
1st quarter	147.2	110.9	19.5	15.9	86.4	38.1	42.2	6.1	5.0	1.3	5.7	4.7	1.0
2nd quarter	159.4	114.5	21.0	17.3	88.5	39.4	42.8	6.3	5.0	1.3	5.8	4.8	1.0
3rd quarter	154.9	116.8	21.2	17.5	90.4	40.3	43.6	6.5	5.2	1.3	6.0	5.0	1.0
4th quarter	172.3	120.1	21.8	18.1	92.5	41.4	44.4	6.7	5.7	1.4	6.3	5.3	1.0
1973													
1st quarter	171.0	123.0	21.9	18.0	95.1	43.0	45.3	6.8	6.0	1.4	6.9	5.8	1.1
2nd quarter	172.4	124.7	22.3	18.4	96.3	43.3	46.1	6.9	6.1	1.5	7.4	6.3	1.1
3rd quarter	175.1	127.6	23.1	19.1	98.7	44.9	46.8	7.0	5.9	1.5	8.0	6.9	1.1
4th quarter	178.9	129.7	24.0	19.9	99.6	45.1	47.3	7.2	6.1	1.6	8.7	7.5	1.1
1974													
1st quarter	180.4	130.6	23.3	19.2	101.0	45.7	47.8	7.5	6.3	1.6	9.4	8.1	1.3
2nd quarter	185.8	134.7	24.1	19.9	104.0	47.8	48.5	7.7	6.6	1.6	10.0	8.7	1.3
3rd quarter	192.0	139.3	25.2	21.0	106.8	49.7	49.3	7.8	7.3	1.7	10.5	9.2	1.3
4th quarter	194.0	139.6	25.6	21.3	107.5	49.4	50.3	7.8	6.5	1.7	10.8	9.5	1.3
1975													
1st quarter	198.3	140.9	25.7	21.4	109.0	49.5	51.6	7.9	6.1	1.8	11.2	9.9	1.3
2nd quarter	207.6	144.8	26.5	22.1	111.7	50.8	52.8	8.1	6.6	1.8	11.3	9.9	1.3
3rd quarter	213.8	150.3	27.2	22.7	114.9	52.6	54.0	8.3	8.2	1.9	11.2	9.8	1.3
4th quarter	218.6	153.9	28.2	23.6	117.3	53.8	55.2	8.2	8.4	2.0	11.0	9.6	1.3

[1] Includes components not shown separately.

Table 19-11. State and Local Government Current Receipts and Expenditures—Continued

(National income and product accounts, calendar years, billions of dollars, quarterly data are at seasonally adjusted annual rates.)

NIPA Table 3.3

Year and quarter	Current receipts—Continued				Current surplus of government enterprises	Current expenditures					Net state and local government saving, NIPA (surplus + / deficit -)		
	Current transfer receipts					Total [1]	Consumption expenditures	Government social benefits to persons	Interest payments	Subsidies	Total	Social insurance funds	Other
	Total	Federal grants-in-aid	From business, net	From persons									
1961													
1st quarter	4.9	4.2	0.2	0.4	1.3	42.4	35.5	4.9	2.0	0.0	4.1	0.0	4.1
2nd quarter	5.2	4.5	0.2	0.4	1.4	43.6	36.5	4.9	2.2	0.0	4.0	0.0	4.0
3rd quarter	5.3	4.6	0.2	0.4	1.3	44.1	36.8	5.0	2.3	0.0	4.5	0.0	4.4
4th quarter	5.4	4.7	0.2	0.5	1.4	45.0	37.5	5.1	2.4	0.0	4.6	0.0	4.6
1962													
1st quarter	5.6	4.9	0.2	0.5	1.3	45.8	38.1	5.2	2.4	0.0	4.9	0.0	4.9
2nd quarter	5.6	4.9	0.2	0.5	1.4	46.5	38.7	5.3	2.4	0.0	5.0	0.0	5.0
3rd quarter	5.9	5.2	0.2	0.5	1.4	47.0	39.2	5.3	2.5	0.0	5.5	0.0	5.5
4th quarter	5.9	5.2	0.2	0.5	1.5	47.8	39.9	5.5	2.4	0.0	5.5	0.0	5.5
1963													
1st quarter	6.0	5.3	0.3	0.5	1.6	48.7	40.7	5.6	2.5	0.0	5.4	0.0	5.3
2nd quarter	6.2	5.5	0.3	0.5	1.6	49.7	41.5	5.7	2.6	0.0	5.5	0.0	5.5
3rd quarter	6.5	5.8	0.3	0.5	1.7	50.8	42.3	5.7	2.7	0.0	6.0	0.0	6.0
4th quarter	6.8	6.1	0.3	0.5	1.6	52.0	43.3	5.8	2.9	0.0	5.9	0.0	5.8
1964													
1st quarter	7.3	6.5	0.3	0.5	1.6	53.2	44.4	6.0	2.9	0.0	6.4	0.0	6.4
2nd quarter	7.3	6.5	0.3	0.5	1.6	54.5	45.3	6.1	3.0	0.0	6.3	0.0	6.2
3rd quarter	7.0	6.2	0.3	0.5	1.7	55.3	46.2	6.2	2.8	0.0	6.5	0.1	6.4
4th quarter	7.4	6.6	0.3	0.5	1.7	56.5	47.2	6.4	2.9	0.0	6.4	0.1	6.3
1965													
1st quarter	7.4	6.5	0.3	0.5	1.7	57.8	48.3	6.5	3.0	0.0	6.2	0.1	6.1
2nd quarter	7.9	7.1	0.3	0.5	1.7	59.3	49.5	6.6	3.2	0.0	6.5	0.1	6.4
3rd quarter	8.3	7.5	0.3	0.5	1.7	60.8	50.9	6.7	3.2	0.0	6.6	0.1	6.5
4th quarter	8.5	7.6	0.3	0.6	1.7	62.1	52.1	6.8	3.2	0.0	6.8	0.1	6.7
1966													
1st quarter	10.0	9.0	0.3	0.6	1.6	64.0	53.7	7.0	3.3	0.0	7.7	0.1	7.6
2nd quarter	11.1	10.1	0.3	0.7	1.6	66.1	55.2	7.5	3.4	0.0	8.0	0.1	7.9
3rd quarter	11.5	10.5	0.3	0.8	1.6	68.2	56.9	7.7	3.5	0.0	8.0	0.1	7.9
4th quarter	11.8	10.7	0.3	0.8	1.6	70.4	58.7	8.2	3.5	0.0	7.3	0.1	7.1
1967													
1st quarter	12.4	11.1	0.5	0.9	1.6	71.7	60.0	8.4	3.3	0.0	7.5	0.1	7.4
2nd quarter	12.9	11.6	0.5	0.9	1.6	73.9	61.5	8.9	3.4	0.0	6.9	0.1	6.7
3rd quarter	13.0	11.6	0.5	0.9	1.5	76.9	63.5	9.5	3.8	0.0	6.4	0.1	6.2
4th quarter	14.2	12.7	0.5	1.0	1.5	79.6	65.3	10.1	4.3	0.0	7.2	0.1	7.1
1968													
1st quarter	13.2	11.8	0.5	1.0	1.6	82.1	67.4	10.6	4.0	0.0	7.2	0.1	7.0
2nd quarter	14.8	13.3	0.5	1.0	1.5	84.7	69.2	11.4	4.1	0.0	8.2	0.1	8.1
3rd quarter	14.1	12.6	0.5	1.0	1.5	87.2	71.3	11.7	4.2	0.0	7.4	0.1	7.3
4th quarter	14.7	13.2	0.5	1.0	1.5	90.1	73.6	12.1	4.3	0.0	7.2	0.2	7.1
1969													
1st quarter	14.7	13.1	0.5	1.0	1.5	92.7	75.9	12.6	4.2	0.0	7.4	0.1	7.3
2nd quarter	15.6	14.0	0.5	1.1	1.5	95.6	78.4	12.8	4.3	0.0	7.8	0.2	7.6
3rd quarter	16.7	15.1	0.5	1.1	1.5	99.0	81.2	13.4	4.4	0.0	8.5	0.2	8.3
4th quarter	17.7	16.1	0.5	1.1	1.5	102.6	83.9	14.0	4.6	0.0	8.2	0.2	8.1
1970													
1st quarter	19.2	17.5	0.6	1.1	1.5	106.9	87.3	14.7	4.9	0.0	8.2	0.2	8.0
2nd quarter	20.6	18.8	0.6	1.2	1.5	110.8	90.0	15.6	5.2	0.0	7.7	0.2	7.5
3rd quarter	21.9	20.1	0.6	1.2	1.5	115.1	93.0	16.6	5.4	0.0	7.1	0.2	7.0
4th quarter	22.6	20.8	0.6	1.3	1.5	119.1	95.8	17.5	5.8	0.0	5.4	0.2	5.2
1971													
1st quarter	23.5	21.6	0.6	1.3	1.4	123.5	99.0	18.3	6.2	0.0	5.0	0.2	4.8
2nd quarter	25.1	23.2	0.6	1.4	1.3	127.1	101.6	19.1	6.4	0.0	6.0	0.2	5.8
3rd quarter	25.5	23.5	0.6	1.4	1.4	130.2	104.2	19.6	6.7	0.0	6.5	0.2	6.2
4th quarter	26.8	24.7	0.6	1.5	1.4	132.9	106.1	20.3	6.9	0.0	8.4	0.2	8.2
1972													
1st quarter	28.0	25.7	0.7	1.6	1.5	138.1	109.1	21.2	7.2	0.0	9.1	0.2	8.8
2nd quarter	36.2	33.9	0.7	1.6	1.6	140.7	111.6	21.6	7.4	0.1	18.7	0.3	18.4
3rd quarter	29.1	26.8	0.7	1.7	1.6	144.8	114.6	22.5	7.6	0.1	10.1	0.3	9.9
4th quarter	42.8	40.4	0.7	1.7	1.6	147.6	117.3	22.5	7.8	0.1	24.6	0.3	24.4
1973													
1st quarter	38.1	35.6	0.9	1.7	1.6	152.1	120.7	23.2	8.1	0.1	18.9	0.3	18.7
2nd quarter	37.2	34.7	0.9	1.7	1.5	156.6	124.2	24.0	8.3	0.1	15.7	0.3	15.4
3rd quarter	36.5	33.9	0.9	1.7	1.4	160.5	127.7	24.2	8.6	0.1	14.6	0.3	14.3
4th quarter	37.6	34.9	0.9	1.8	1.3	165.3	131.4	25.0	8.8	0.1	13.6	0.3	13.3
1974													
1st quarter	37.6	34.6	1.1	1.8	1.2	168.6	136.0	23.4	9.1	0.1	11.8	0.4	11.4
2nd quarter	38.4	35.4	1.1	1.9	1.0	175.2	140.9	24.7	9.4	0.1	10.6	0.4	10.3
3rd quarter	39.9	36.8	1.1	2.0	0.7	182.0	146.3	25.9	9.8	0.1	10.0	0.4	9.6
4th quarter	41.4	38.2	1.1	2.1	0.5	189.1	151.8	27.1	10.1	0.1	4.9	0.4	4.5
1975													
1st quarter	44.1	40.7	1.2	2.2	0.3	197.7	157.8	29.2	10.5	0.1	0.6	0.4	0.2
2nd quarter	49.4	45.8	1.2	2.3	0.4	205.0	163.5	30.5	10.9	0.2	2.6	0.5	2.1
3rd quarter	50.2	46.5	1.2	2.4	0.3	210.3	167.9	31.0	11.3	0.2	3.6	0.5	3.1
4th quarter	51.3	47.5	1.2	2.6	0.5	215.5	171.1	32.6	11.6	0.2	3.1	0.5	2.6

[1] Includes components not shown separately.

Table 19-11. State and Local Government Current Receipts and Expenditures—Continued

(National income and product accounts, calendar years, billions of dollars, quarterly data are at seasonally adjusted annual rates.)

NIPA Table 3.3

Year and quarter	Total	Current receipts											
		Current tax receipts							Taxes on corporate income	Contributions for government social insurance	Income receipts on assets		
		Total	Personal current taxes		Taxes on production and imports						Total ¹	Interest receipts	Rents and royalties
			Total ¹	Income taxes	Total	Sales taxes	Property taxes	Other					
1976													
1st quarter	225.8	160.0	29.5	24.8	120.9	55.9	56.4	8.5	9.7	2.0	10.5	9.1	1.3
2nd quarter	230.2	163.7	30.6	25.8	123.5	57.2	57.7	8.7	9.6	2.1	10.4	9.0	1.3
3rd quarter	234.9	167.3	31.6	26.7	126.0	58.0	58.9	9.2	9.7	2.2	10.3	9.0	1.3
4th quarter	243.8	171.9	32.6	27.7	129.6	60.0	60.0	9.6	9.6	2.3	10.5	9.1	1.3
1977													
1st quarter	247.9	176.9	33.5	28.6	132.9	61.8	61.5	9.5	10.5	2.5	10.9	9.6	1.3
2nd quarter	256.3	181.6	34.7	29.8	135.5	63.1	62.8	9.6	11.4	2.7	11.4	10.1	1.3
3rd quarter	265.2	186.1	35.9	30.9	138.3	64.7	63.8	9.8	11.8	2.9	11.9	10.6	1.3
4th quarter	270.4	190.3	37.3	32.2	141.1	66.4	64.6	10.0	12.0	3.0	12.5	11.2	1.3
1978													
1st quarter	277.7	192.1	38.6	33.4	143.0	67.3	65.3	10.4	10.5	3.2	13.2	11.8	1.3
2nd quarter	289.5	200.2	40.1	34.7	147.7	70.8	66.1	10.9	12.4	3.3	14.1	12.7	1.3
3rd quarter	287.5	197.6	40.9	35.4	144.2	72.0	61.3	10.9	12.5	3.5	15.1	13.7	1.3
4th quarter	295.5	202.7	42.1	36.5	147.6	74.0	62.3	11.3	13.1	3.6	16.2	14.9	1.3
1979													
1st quarter	298.8	206.3	42.0	36.3	150.6	75.4	63.2	12.0	13.7	3.8	18.2	16.2	1.9
2nd quarter	302.8	208.4	42.1	36.3	152.6	76.3	64.0	12.3	13.8	3.9	19.5	17.5	1.9
3rd quarter	312.8	214.6	45.4	39.6	155.6	77.9	64.8	12.8	13.6	3.9	20.8	18.8	1.9
4th quarter	319.0	218.8	46.6	40.7	159.0	79.6	65.6	13.8	13.2	4.0	22.0	20.0	1.9
1980													
1st quarter	328.0	224.5	46.6	40.4	161.9	81.2	66.5	14.2	16.1	3.6	24.3	21.1	3.1
2nd quarter	329.5	224.1	48.0	41.7	163.3	80.8	67.8	14.7	12.8	2.9	25.6	22.4	3.1
3rd quarter	341.5	231.5	49.4	43.0	168.2	83.5	69.5	15.2	14.0	3.8	26.9	23.7	3.1
4th quarter	353.7	240.0	51.6	45.2	173.3	86.0	71.5	15.8	15.1	4.0	28.3	25.1	3.1
1981													
1st quarter	363.5	249.5	52.5	46.0	180.2	89.6	73.9	16.7	16.8	3.7	29.9	26.5	3.3
2nd quarter	368.1	252.5	53.7	47.0	183.7	89.6	76.2	17.9	15.2	3.8	31.4	27.9	3.3
3rd quarter	374.0	259.5	55.5	48.8	188.3	91.8	78.0	18.5	15.7	3.9	32.7	29.2	3.3
4th quarter	375.3	261.6	56.8	49.9	190.7	92.1	80.2	18.4	14.1	4.0	33.9	30.4	3.3
1982													
1st quarter	380.8	265.4	57.3	50.2	193.9	92.9	82.4	18.5	14.1	4.0	35.2	31.6	3.5
2nd quarter	389.1	270.6	58.1	50.9	198.3	95.5	84.5	18.3	14.3	4.0	36.3	32.6	3.5
3rd quarter	395.0	276.5	60.4	53.1	201.7	97.0	86.3	18.4	14.4	4.1	37.3	33.6	3.5
4th quarter	400.8	280.1	60.8	53.4	206.0	99.3	87.9	18.7	13.3	4.1	38.1	34.5	3.5
1983													
1st quarter	407.6	283.7	61.3	53.7	209.6	101.5	89.3	18.8	12.8	4.0	39.5	35.4	4.0
2nd quarter	423.6	295.9	64.3	56.5	216.0	106.2	90.9	18.9	15.7	4.1	40.7	36.4	4.2
3rd quarter	436.4	307.5	68.1	60.2	222.0	109.9	92.7	19.5	17.4	4.1	42.0	37.5	4.4
4th quarter	446.9	316.4	70.7	62.7	228.0	113.1	94.6	20.3	17.7	4.3	43.5	38.8	4.6
1984													
1st quarter	465.3	328.0	73.3	65.0	234.7	116.8	96.8	21.1	20.1	4.5	44.9	40.0	4.7
2nd quarter	478.1	336.0	75.8	67.4	240.3	119.9	98.8	21.6	19.9	4.7	46.7	41.7	4.9
3rd quarter	481.6	339.0	76.8	68.1	244.7	122.0	100.7	22.0	17.5	4.8	48.6	43.4	5.0
4th quarter	495.6	346.1	78.2	69.3	250.2	125.3	102.5	22.3	17.7	4.8	50.5	45.3	5.1
1985													
1st quarter	506.6	353.9	79.3	70.2	254.7	127.3	104.5	22.9	20.0	4.7	52.9	47.6	5.1
2nd quarter	516.4	360.6	80.9	71.8	260.0	130.6	106.5	23.0	19.6	4.8	54.5	49.1	5.2
3rd quarter	526.1	367.5	81.5	72.2	265.1	132.8	108.5	23.8	20.9	4.9	55.4	49.8	5.4
4th quarter	535.2	372.7	83.7	74.3	268.5	133.8	110.6	24.1	20.5	5.2	56.7	50.9	5.7
1986													
1st quarter	552.7	378.9	84.5	75.0	273.0	136.1	112.6	24.3	21.4	5.5	57.7	51.3	6.2
2nd quarter	554.8	383.6	85.0	75.4	276.6	137.8	114.9	23.8	22.0	5.8	58.3	51.9	6.3
3rd quarter	567.1	392.2	87.5	77.7	282.3	142.0	117.3	23.0	22.4	6.1	58.7	52.3	6.3
4th quarter	572.0	403.5	91.8	81.8	286.8	143.5	119.8	23.5	24.8	6.4	58.9	52.6	6.2
1987													
1st quarter	570.8	405.0	92.4	82.1	291.9	145.1	122.5	24.2	20.7	6.7	58.5	52.4	6.0
2nd quarter	593.2	423.7	101.5	90.9	298.5	148.6	125.1	24.8	23.7	7.0	58.0	52.2	5.6
3rd quarter	594.1	425.5	94.1	83.4	306.0	152.9	127.7	25.4	25.5	7.3	58.0	52.7	5.2
4th quarter	604.1	434.2	98.4	87.5	310.0	154.7	130.3	25.1	25.7	7.7	58.1	53.3	4.6
1988													
1st quarter	616.4	438.9	99.4	88.3	315.5	157.8	132.4	25.3	24.0	8.0	59.0	54.2	4.7
2nd quarter	626.2	446.8	97.2	85.8	323.3	162.3	134.9	26.1	25.8	8.3	59.9	55.2	4.5
3rd quarter	643.4	458.1	104.1	92.5	327.4	163.7	137.7	25.9	26.6	8.5	61.0	56.5	4.3
4th quarter	656.2	467.7	107.6	95.8	332.4	165.8	141.0	25.6	27.8	8.7	62.2	57.8	4.2
1989													
1st quarter	673.4	480.2	113.4	101.3	340.3	168.7	145.0	26.6	26.6	8.8	64.1	59.7	4.2
2nd quarter	687.0	491.0	118.2	105.8	348.1	172.9	148.4	26.9	24.6	8.9	65.2	60.9	4.1
3rd quarter	694.5	491.0	114.5	102.1	353.8	174.6	151.5	27.7	22.7	9.0	66.3	62.0	4.1
4th quarter	694.3	489.8	112.4	99.8	354.3	173.2	154.5	26.6	23.1	9.3	67.2	63.0	4.0
1990													
1st quarter	721.5	509.9	119.3	106.6	369.1	183.7	156.6	28.7	21.5	9.5	67.5	63.5	3.8
2nd quarter	730.6	514.0	122.6	109.5	368.7	181.2	159.7	27.9	22.7	9.9	68.4	64.4	3.8
3rd quarter	744.3	523.0	123.7	110.8	375.7	185.3	163.1	27.3	23.6	10.2	69.6	64.3	5.0
4th quarter	754.7	529.6	124.6	111.5	382.7	186.9	166.7	29.1	22.2	10.5	68.3	64.0	4.0

¹Includes components not shown separately.

Table 19-11. State and Local Government Current Receipts and Expenditures—Continued

(National income and product accounts, calendar years, billions of dollars, quarterly data are at seasonally adjusted annual rates.)

NIPA Table 3.3

| Year and quarter | Current receipts—Continued | | | | | Current expenditures | | | | | Net state and local government saving, NIPA (surplus + / deficit -) | | |
| | Current transfer receipts | | | | Current surplus of government enterprises | Total [1] | Consumption expenditures | Government social benefits to persons | Interest payments | Subsidies | Total | Social insurance funds | Other |
	Total	Federal grants-in-aid	From business, net	From persons									
1976													
1st quarter	52.7	48.7	1.4	2.7	0.5	220.1	174.5	33.4	12.0	0.2	5.7	0.5	5.2
2nd quarter	53.6	49.5	1.4	2.8	0.4	223.7	177.8	33.4	12.4	0.2	6.5	0.6	5.9
3rd quarter	54.7	50.4	1.4	2.9	0.3	228.6	180.9	34.7	12.7	0.2	6.3	0.6	5.7
4th quarter	58.8	54.4	1.4	3.0	0.3	232.8	184.6	35.0	13.0	0.2	11.0	0.7	10.3
1977													
1st quarter	57.2	52.5	1.6	3.2	0.3	238.3	189.2	35.7	13.3	0.2	9.6	0.8	8.8
2nd quarter	60.3	55.5	1.6	3.3	0.3	244.5	193.3	37.5	13.5	0.2	11.8	0.9	10.9
3rd quarter	64.1	59.1	1.6	3.3	0.3	249.5	198.2	37.3	13.8	0.2	15.7	1.1	14.7
4th quarter	64.2	59.2	1.6	3.4	0.4	254.9	202.8	37.7	14.1	0.2	15.5	1.2	14.3
1978													
1st quarter	68.8	63.5	1.9	3.5	0.4	260.9	207.2	39.2	14.3	0.2	16.9	1.3	15.5
2nd quarter	71.6	66.1	1.9	3.6	0.3	266.5	210.7	41.0	14.6	0.2	23.0	1.4	21.6
3rd quarter	71.1	65.5	1.9	3.7	0.2	271.4	215.2	41.3	15.1	0.2	16.1	1.5	14.5
4th quarter	72.8	67.1	1.9	3.8	0.1	276.8	219.6	41.7	15.6	0.3	18.7	1.7	17.1
1979													
1st quarter	70.5	64.4	2.2	4.0	0.0	284.3	225.5	42.4	16.4	0.3	14.5	1.7	12.9
2nd quarter	71.2	65.0	2.2	4.1	-0.2	290.9	229.2	43.5	17.0	0.3	11.9	1.8	10.1
3rd quarter	74.0	67.6	2.2	4.2	-0.4	298.9	236.3	44.5	17.6	0.3	13.9	1.8	12.1
4th quarter	74.9	68.4	2.2	4.3	-0.6	307.4	242.4	46.9	18.0	0.3	11.6	1.8	9.8
1980													
1st quarter	76.2	69.3	2.5	4.4	-0.7	317.3	249.3	49.1	18.4	0.3	10.6	1.4	9.2
2nd quarter	77.9	70.8	2.5	4.6	-0.9	324.0	255.8	49.0	19.0	0.3	5.5	0.7	4.8
3rd quarter	80.7	73.4	2.5	4.8	-1.4	334.0	261.6	52.4	19.6	0.4	7.5	1.5	6.0
4th quarter	83.3	75.8	2.5	5.0	-1.9	342.2	267.0	54.3	20.4	0.4	11.5	1.6	9.9
1981													
1st quarter	82.6	74.4	2.9	5.4	-2.3	351.8	274.4	55.6	21.4	0.4	11.7	1.3	10.4
2nd quarter	83.0	74.5	2.9	5.6	-2.6	360.0	279.9	57.4	22.3	0.4	8.0	1.3	6.7
3rd quarter	80.5	71.9	2.9	5.8	-2.5	366.4	284.9	57.7	23.3	0.4	7.7	1.3	6.4
4th quarter	78.1	69.2	2.9	6.0	-2.2	372.5	290.1	57.7	24.3	0.4	2.8	1.3	1.5
1982													
1st quarter	78.2	68.8	3.2	6.1	-2.0	381.5	296.6	59.0	25.4	0.4	-0.7	1.3	-2.0
2nd quarter	79.9	70.4	3.2	6.3	-1.7	390.6	302.6	61.0	26.5	0.5	-1.4	1.2	-2.7
3rd quarter	78.7	69.0	3.3	6.4	-1.5	397.7	307.4	62.1	27.7	0.5	-2.6	1.2	-3.9
4th quarter	79.7	69.8	3.3	6.6	-1.2	404.8	312.8	62.6	29.0	0.5	-4.0	1.2	-5.2
1983													
1st quarter	81.1	70.6	3.6	6.8	-0.8	415.0	318.4	65.8	30.4	0.5	-7.4	1.2	-8.6
2nd quarter	83.3	72.7	3.6	7.0	-0.4	420.6	322.1	66.3	31.7	0.4	3.0	1.2	1.8
3rd quarter	82.7	71.8	3.6	7.3	0.0	426.6	326.0	67.2	33.0	0.4	9.8	1.2	8.5
4th quarter	82.4	71.2	3.7	7.5	0.2	432.7	329.8	68.3	34.1	0.4	14.2	1.3	12.9
1984													
1st quarter	87.1	75.4	4.0	7.8	0.7	442.8	337.2	69.9	35.2	0.4	22.5	1.4	21.1
2nd quarter	89.6	77.4	4.2	8.0	1.1	451.4	343.9	70.6	36.4	0.4	26.7	1.5	25.3
3rd quarter	87.7	75.1	4.3	8.3	1.6	460.5	351.3	71.3	37.6	0.4	21.1	1.5	19.7
4th quarter	91.6	78.8	4.3	8.5	2.5	470.2	358.2	72.8	38.8	0.4	25.4	1.4	24.0
1985													
1st quarter	92.2	79.1	4.3	8.7	2.9	481.9	367.3	74.9	39.4	0.3	24.7	1.3	23.4
2nd quarter	93.4	80.0	4.4	9.1	3.2	492.4	376.0	76.3	39.8	0.3	24.0	1.2	22.8
3rd quarter	95.0	81.2	4.4	9.4	3.4	504.5	386.9	78.1	39.2	0.3	21.7	1.3	20.4
4th quarter	97.4	83.1	4.5	9.7	3.3	516.2	397.0	79.8	39.2	0.3	19.0	1.5	17.6
1986													
1st quarter	107.6	84.8	12.6	10.2	3.1	526.0	406.9	81.6	37.2	0.3	26.7	1.6	25.0
2nd quarter	104.2	89.0	4.7	10.5	2.9	534.3	413.1	83.6	37.2	0.3	20.5	1.8	18.7
3rd quarter	107.4	91.8	4.8	10.8	2.7	544.3	420.5	85.3	38.3	0.3	22.8	2.0	20.8
4th quarter	100.7	84.9	4.8	11.0	2.5	558.2	430.9	86.9	40.1	0.3	13.8	2.1	11.8
1987													
1st quarter	97.9	82.1	4.8	11.0	2.6	564.8	433.7	88.3	42.6	0.3	6.0	2.1	3.9
2nd quarter	101.7	85.8	4.8	11.1	2.8	573.8	438.7	89.9	44.9	0.3	19.4	2.1	17.3
3rd quarter	100.1	83.9	4.9	11.2	3.1	581.9	442.5	91.6	47.6	0.3	12.2	2.2	9.9
4th quarter	100.2	83.8	5.0	11.4	3.9	592.0	448.9	93.1	49.7	0.3	12.1	2.3	9.8
1988													
1st quarter	106.2	89.5	5.1	11.6	4.2	602.8	459.2	95.3	48.0	0.3	13.6	2.4	11.2
2nd quarter	107.1	90.0	5.2	11.9	4.6	613.0	467.2	97.3	48.1	0.3	13.2	2.5	10.7
3rd quarter	110.7	93.1	5.5	12.1	5.0	622.2	474.0	99.5	48.3	0.4	21.2	2.6	18.6
4th quarter	112.0	93.8	5.7	12.5	5.6	632.6	481.1	101.9	49.3	0.4	23.6	2.6	21.0
1989													
1st quarter	114.0	94.9	6.1	13.0	6.3	646.8	489.8	104.2	52.3	0.4	26.6	2.5	24.1
2nd quarter	115.2	95.6	6.3	13.3	6.6	659.8	498.1	107.3	54.0	0.4	27.2	2.4	24.8
3rd quarter	121.5	101.4	6.5	13.5	6.8	671.7	504.8	111.0	55.6	0.4	22.8	2.3	20.6
4th quarter	121.9	101.4	6.7	13.9	6.2	687.6	515.9	114.8	56.5	0.4	6.7	2.1	4.5
1990													
1st quarter	127.8	106.5	7.2	14.0	6.8	705.7	530.0	118.8	56.5	0.4	15.8	2.0	13.8
2nd quarter	131.7	110.3	6.9	14.5	6.7	720.5	538.5	124.2	57.5	0.4	10.1	2.0	8.2
3rd quarter	134.9	112.6	7.0	15.2	6.6	738.2	549.3	130.3	58.3	0.4	6.1	2.0	4.1
4th quarter	139.6	116.3	7.2	16.0	6.7	757.8	560.8	137.4	59.2	0.4	-3.1	2.0	-5.0

[1] Includes components not shown separately.

Table 19-11. State and Local Government Current Receipts and Expenditures—Continued

(National income and product accounts, calendar years, billions of dollars, quarterly data are at seasonally adjusted annual rates.)

NIPA Table 3.3

Year and quarter	Total	Current tax receipts Total	Personal current taxes Total¹	Income taxes	Taxes on production and imports Total	Sales taxes	Property taxes	Other	Taxes on corporate income	Contributions for government social insurance	Income receipts on assets Total¹	Interest receipts	Rents and royalties
1991													
1st quarter	763.0	528.5	121.2	108.0	384.6	184.8	171.2	28.6	22.7	11.0	68.8	64.1	4.3
2nd quarter	778.8	538.2	124.5	111.2	390.3	187.9	174.7	27.7	23.4	11.4	68.3	63.5	4.5
3rd quarter	798.2	549.7	126.1	112.2	399.3	193.1	177.8	28.4	24.2	11.8	67.7	62.7	4.6
4th quarter	816.6	560.8	129.4	115.5	407.1	196.9	180.5	29.7	24.2	12.2	67.1	62.0	4.7
1992													
1st quarter	824.3	564.4	127.5	112.7	412.6	200.6	182.9	29.1	24.4	12.6	66.9	61.1	5.3
2nd quarter	842.7	580.4	136.9	122.3	418.0	201.6	184.4	32.0	25.5	13.0	65.0	60.0	4.6
3rd quarter	851.7	582.6	136.7	121.9	424.0	207.4	185.4	31.3	21.8	13.3	64.1	59.1	4.6
4th quarter	863.9	591.6	140.2	124.6	425.7	207.7	186.0	32.0	25.8	13.6	63.1	58.1	4.6
1993													
1st quarter	862.5	588.6	136.5	121.8	427.6	210.9	184.8	31.8	24.6	13.8	62.0	57.0	4.6
2nd quarter	875.9	598.5	138.3	123.9	433.2	214.7	185.9	32.6	27.0	14.1	61.4	56.3	4.5
3rd quarter	893.2	609.5	143.6	128.7	439.6	217.4	187.8	34.4	26.3	14.2	61.0	55.8	4.5
4th quarter	916.1	622.3	145.9	130.5	446.7	222.5	190.5	33.7	29.7	14.4	60.9	55.8	4.5
1994													
1st quarter	920.9	629.9	146.9	131.4	456.4	225.7	196.0	34.7	26.5	14.6	61.6	56.4	4.5
2nd quarter	931.4	636.9	141.9	125.8	465.5	230.9	198.8	35.8	29.5	14.6	62.4	57.1	4.5
3rd quarter	952.3	652.1	151.2	135.1	469.7	233.1	200.8	35.8	31.2	14.5	63.8	58.5	4.5
4th quarter	966.9	658.0	152.0	136.7	473.4	235.9	201.9	35.6	32.6	14.4	65.0	59.6	4.5
1995													
1st quarter	980.9	665.6	156.8	140.6	478.3	240.4	200.8	37.2	30.5	14.0	66.5	61.1	4.5
2nd quarter	979.1	661.6	152.4	136.1	477.9	239.6	201.6	36.8	31.3	13.7	67.6	62.3	4.5
3rd quarter	997.6	677.2	160.6	144.2	483.7	243.7	203.0	37.0	32.8	13.5	69.1	63.5	4.5
4th quarter	1 003.3	684.1	162.6	146.0	489.4	247.3	204.9	37.2	32.0	13.2	70.4	64.7	4.5
1996													
1st quarter	1 021.7	695.8	165.3	149.0	498.1	252.4	208.1	37.6	32.4	13.0	71.4	65.6	4.6
2nd quarter	1 042.6	705.7	165.9	149.6	506.5	255.7	210.9	40.0	33.3	12.7	72.6	66.7	4.6
3rd quarter	1 049.1	712.4	169.3	152.8	509.9	256.8	213.7	39.4	33.1	12.3	73.9	67.8	4.7
4th quarter	1 059.7	724.5	174.2	157.8	517.0	259.9	216.7	40.5	33.3	11.9	75.1	69.0	4.7
1997													
1st quarter	1 073.4	734.3	177.8	160.7	523.7	262.8	220.0	40.9	32.8	11.3	76.5	70.3	4.8
2nd quarter	1 084.0	741.0	176.9	159.6	530.5	266.8	222.6	41.2	33.5	10.9	77.4	71.1	4.8
3rd quarter	1 106.5	756.0	184.1	166.8	536.6	270.5	224.8	41.3	35.3	10.6	78.3	71.9	4.8
4th quarter	1 125.8	768.5	189.2	171.6	544.3	274.5	226.8	43.0	34.9	10.5	79.1	72.8	4.7
1998													
1st quarter	1 137.5	779.5	195.1	177.2	549.3	277.5	227.7	44.1	35.2	10.6	79.8	73.5	4.6
2nd quarter	1 150.5	791.8	201.8	183.6	555.3	281.4	229.7	44.2	34.7	10.4	80.3	74.1	4.6
3rd quarter	1 165.3	798.6	201.4	183.2	561.6	285.4	232.0	44.2	35.5	10.3	81.2	74.9	4.6
4th quarter	1 199.4	809.7	206.5	188.0	568.9	291.1	234.7	43.1	34.3	10.1	82.4	76.0	4.7
1999													
1st quarter	1 205.1	818.6	207.6	188.8	576.1	292.9	238.3	45.0	34.9	9.8	83.0	76.5	4.8
2nd quarter	1 217.1	831.4	210.4	191.6	585.4	298.8	241.3	45.3	35.6	9.7	84.4	77.7	5.0
3rd quarter	1 249.6	847.3	216.0	196.9	595.4	305.4	244.3	45.7	35.9	9.7	86.0	79.0	5.2
4th quarter	1 275.0	864.3	223.8	204.7	603.7	309.3	247.2	47.1	36.8	9.9	87.7	80.4	5.5
2000													
1st quarter	1 294.4	880.3	231.6	212.2	610.9	313.3	249.9	47.7	37.8	10.3	90.4	82.7	5.9
2nd quarter	1 319.0	898.4	243.7	224.5	618.0	315.7	252.9	49.4	36.7	10.7	91.9	83.9	6.2
3rd quarter	1 330.5	895.4	236.3	216.6	624.1	317.0	256.1	51.1	35.0	11.2	92.8	84.5	6.4
4th quarter	1 333.9	898.8	234.8	215.7	631.2	320.3	259.5	51.5	32.8	11.8	93.7	85.1	6.7
2001													
1st quarter	1 367.2	919.1	249.2	230.1	637.5	322.8	262.6	52.1	32.4	12.7	91.6	83.1	6.6
2nd quarter	1 397.4	937.9	266.6	246.9	639.4	320.5	266.5	52.4	31.9	13.5	89.9	81.4	6.6
3rd quarter	1 354.8	899.9	229.3	209.5	641.4	317.7	271.3	52.4	29.2	14.0	87.7	79.3	6.5
4th quarter	1 372.5	906.2	225.8	205.9	652.9	323.5	276.7	52.7	27.4	14.4	85.9	77.5	6.4
2002													
1st quarter	1 379.7	910.3	220.1	200.3	661.1	324.2	282.9	54.0	29.1	15.0	82.3	73.8	6.4
2nd quarter	1 396.4	916.5	215.1	194.6	670.2	328.1	288.3	53.8	31.2	15.6	79.0	70.5	6.5
3rd quarter	1 422.7	940.1	224.2	203.5	683.2	333.9	292.9	56.4	32.8	16.1	76.5	67.9	6.6
4th quarter	1 441.7	949.0	225.8	204.9	687.5	334.5	296.5	56.6	35.6	16.5	75.0	66.2	6.8
2003													
1st quarter	1 435.8	949.2	218.3	197.1	697.5	338.3	300.7	58.5	33.3	17.8	74.0	64.5	7.3
2nd quarter	1 474.2	956.8	213.2	191.4	710.7	344.7	305.2	60.7	32.9	19.1	73.0	63.1	7.7
3rd quarter	1 516.8	994.4	234.4	211.7	724.1	350.5	310.1	63.5	35.9	20.4	72.5	62.2	8.1
4th quarter	1 549.9	1 017.4	240.6	217.7	737.7	357.3	315.4	65.0	39.1	21.7	72.2	61.7	8.3
2004													
1st quarter	1 552.9	1 032.3	240.1	216.9	751.8	363.8	321.6	66.5	40.4	23.1	72.2	61.6	8.5
2nd quarter	1 582.9	1 049.8	242.0	219.0	764.1	368.5	327.1	68.5	43.7	24.0	72.9	62.1	8.6
3rd quarter	1 590.9	1 065.6	250.8	227.5	772.1	369.8	332.6	69.7	42.7	24.7	73.4	62.3	8.8
4th quarter	1 643.6	1 095.7	260.7	236.9	789.4	379.3	337.8	72.3	45.6	25.2	74.6	62.5	9.0
2005													
1st quarter	1 672.2	1 129.2	266.7	242.8	803.8	387.5	342.8	73.5	58.7	25.3	74.4	62.9	9.2
2nd quarter	1 702.9	1 155.6	280.9	256.9	817.5	393.7	347.9	76.0	57.1	25.3	75.0	63.2	9.4
3rd quarter	1 697.8	1 156.6	274.0	249.5	827.9	397.9	353.0	76.9	54.7	25.3	75.6	63.6	9.6
4th quarter	1 729.6	1 176.3	279.3	254.3	835.7	397.2	358.1	80.5	61.3	25.2	76.3	64.0	9.8

¹Includes components not shown separately.

Table 19-11. State and Local Government Current Receipts and Expenditures—Continued

(National income and product accounts, calendar years, billions of dollars, quarterly data are at seasonally adjusted annual rates.)

NIPA Table 3.3

Year and quarter	Current receipts—Continued				Current surplus of government enterprises	Current expenditures					Net state and local government saving, NIPA (surplus + / deficit -)		
	Current transfer receipts					Total [1]	Consumption expenditures	Government social benefits to persons	Interest payments	Subsidies	Total	Social insurance funds	Other
	Total	Federal grants-in-aid	From business, net	From persons									
1991													
1st quarter	147.8	122.8	7.8	17.2	6.9	769.9	567.1	141.5	60.9	0.4	-7.0	2.1	-9.1
2nd quarter	153.9	128.1	7.6	18.2	7.0	785.0	570.8	152.2	61.6	0.4	-6.2	2.3	-8.5
3rd quarter	162.0	134.9	7.9	19.2	7.1	798.4	577.4	158.6	62.0	0.4	-0.2	2.4	-2.6
4th quarter	169.2	140.6	8.5	20.1	7.3	819.9	583.2	173.8	62.5	0.4	-3.3	2.6	-5.9
1992													
1st quarter	173.1	143.2	8.9	21.0	7.3	824.6	591.3	170.5	62.4	0.4	-0.3	2.8	-3.0
2nd quarter	176.8	146.2	8.9	21.7	7.5	840.6	599.5	178.6	62.0	0.4	2.1	3.0	-0.9
3rd quarter	183.8	152.4	9.2	22.2	7.9	855.5	607.5	185.8	61.9	0.4	-3.8	3.3	-7.1
4th quarter	187.3	154.6	10.0	22.7	8.2	859.1	612.4	185.0	61.3	0.4	4.8	3.5	1.3
1993													
1st quarter	189.4	156.3	10.1	23.0	8.7	872.5	622.6	188.9	60.6	0.4	-9.9	3.8	-13.7
2nd quarter	193.0	159.3	10.4	23.3	8.9	877.6	627.3	189.7	60.3	0.4	-1.7	4.1	-5.8
3rd quarter	199.3	165.0	10.6	23.7	9.2	893.6	632.8	200.6	59.9	0.4	-0.3	4.3	-4.7
4th quarter	209.2	174.1	11.0	24.1	9.2	900.5	638.5	201.7	59.9	0.4	15.7	4.5	11.1
1994													
1st quarter	207.3	171.2	11.4	24.7	7.5	916.7	651.8	203.6	60.9	0.4	4.2	4.6	-0.4
2nd quarter	208.5	171.6	11.8	25.1	9.0	925.0	659.1	203.9	61.6	0.3	6.4	4.7	1.7
3rd quarter	212.5	174.9	12.1	25.4	9.4	934.5	668.0	203.7	62.5	0.3	17.8	4.7	13.1
4th quarter	219.5	181.2	12.5	25.8	10.0	953.4	674.3	215.7	63.1	0.3	13.5	4.6	8.9
1995													
1st quarter	223.9	185.0	12.9	26.0	11.0	970.8	687.0	220.4	63.1	0.3	10.2	4.4	5.8
2nd quarter	224.5	184.9	13.3	26.3	11.7	978.7	694.0	220.7	63.7	0.3	0.4	4.2	-3.8
3rd quarter	225.5	185.1	13.7	26.6	12.4	984.3	698.7	220.7	64.5	0.3	13.4	3.9	9.4
4th quarter	222.7	181.6	14.1	27.0	13.0	979.0	704.5	208.8	65.4	0.3	24.3	3.7	20.6
1996													
1st quarter	227.8	186.1	14.5	27.2	13.7	998.1	712.9	218.2	66.6	0.3	23.7	3.4	20.2
2nd quarter	237.6	195.0	15.0	27.6	14.0	1 020.7	720.5	232.2	67.7	0.3	21.9	3.0	18.8
3rd quarter	236.5	193.2	15.4	27.9	14.0	1 021.9	728.2	224.8	68.5	0.3	27.2	2.6	24.6
4th quarter	234.4	190.3	15.8	28.3	13.8	1 029.3	737.7	221.7	69.5	0.4	30.4	2.2	28.3
1997													
1st quarter	238.1	192.4	16.3	29.5	13.2	1 043.8	747.0	226.0	70.4	0.4	29.6	1.5	28.1
2nd quarter	242.2	195.5	16.6	30.1	12.6	1 047.7	752.5	223.7	71.1	0.4	36.4	1.2	35.2
3rd quarter	249.6	198.4	20.6	30.6	12.0	1 062.0	761.7	228.0	71.8	0.4	44.4	1.0	43.4
4th quarter	256.5	208.2	17.2	31.0	11.3	1 079.7	774.4	232.4	72.4	0.5	46.1	1.0	45.1
1998													
1st quarter	257.9	207.9	18.8	31.2	9.7	1 088.9	783.1	232.2	73.1	0.5	48.6	1.5	47.1
2nd quarter	257.7	208.1	18.0	31.6	10.2	1 103.7	794.7	235.2	73.4	0.5	46.7	1.7	45.1
3rd quarter	264.8	213.0	19.6	32.1	10.5	1 115.6	807.6	233.9	73.7	0.4	49.7	1.8	47.9
4th quarter	286.6	222.0	31.8	32.8	10.6	1 136.4	820.0	241.7	74.2	0.4	63.0	1.8	61.2
1999													
1st quarter	282.8	227.0	22.4	33.5	10.8	1 156.1	834.3	247.7	73.8	0.4	49.0	1.7	47.3
2nd quarter	280.9	223.7	22.8	34.3	10.7	1 171.8	850.8	246.3	74.2	0.4	45.3	1.7	43.6
3rd quarter	296.1	237.6	23.2	35.3	10.4	1 197.6	867.3	255.1	74.8	0.4	52.0	1.7	50.3
4th quarter	303.3	243.2	23.7	36.4	9.8	1 219.7	883.3	260.3	75.6	0.4	55.3	1.7	53.5
2000													
1st quarter	304.7	239.0	28.0	37.6	8.8	1 238.5	900.6	260.4	77.0	0.5	55.9	1.7	54.2
2nd quarter	310.0	242.8	28.6	38.7	8.0	1 259.5	910.8	269.6	78.5	0.5	59.5	1.9	57.7
3rd quarter	323.8	255.0	29.1	39.8	7.3	1 281.6	923.4	277.4	80.3	0.6	49.0	2.1	46.8
4th quarter	323.0	252.6	29.6	40.8	6.6	1 298.5	936.3	279.2	82.4	0.6	35.4	2.4	33.0
2001													
1st quarter	338.2	266.5	30.1	41.6	5.5	1 334.7	951.7	290.7	84.2	8.0	32.5	2.6	29.9
2nd quarter	351.5	278.3	30.5	42.7	4.6	1 371.6	963.6	308.3	85.3	14.4	25.8	2.7	23.1
3rd quarter	350.0	272.8	33.3	43.9	3.2	1 363.4	976.6	295.9	86.0	4.8	-8.6	2.6	-11.2
4th quarter	363.3	286.6	31.5	45.2	2.8	1 403.1	987.1	326.0	86.6	3.4	-30.6	2.4	-33.0
2002													
1st quarter	369.5	291.4	32.0	46.1	2.7	1 415.0	1 001.8	324.9	86.5	1.8	-35.3	2.1	-37.4
2nd quarter	382.5	303.1	32.4	47.0	2.7	1 431.5	1 019.4	325.4	86.2	0.6	-35.1	1.8	-36.9
3rd quarter	387.4	306.6	32.9	47.9	2.6	1 454.2	1 033.6	333.0	85.9	1.7	-31.4	1.6	-33.0
4th quarter	399.3	317.2	33.3	48.8	2.0	1 476.6	1 046.7	344.7	85.7	-0.4	-34.9	1.4	-36.2
2003													
1st quarter	394.0	311.9	32.6	49.5	0.7	1 497.0	1 065.2	345.3	86.4	0.1	-61.2	2.3	-63.5
2nd quarter	425.5	342.2	33.2	50.2	-0.2	1 501.4	1 066.7	347.2	87.1	0.3	-27.2	3.2	-30.4
3rd quarter	430.6	345.9	33.8	51.0	-1.1	1 525.0	1 076.2	361.8	88.1	-1.0	-8.2	4.3	-12.5
4th quarter	440.5	354.2	34.5	51.8	-1.8	1 534.8	1 086.9	357.8	89.2	0.9	15.2	5.3	9.9
2004													
1st quarter	427.6	339.5	35.3	52.8	-2.3	1 567.6	1 103.9	372.9	90.3	0.4	-14.7	6.6	-21.3
2nd quarter	439.5	349.8	35.9	53.8	-3.3	1 596.5	1 120.9	383.7	91.5	0.4	-13.6	7.4	-21.0
3rd quarter	431.4	345.7	31.0	54.8	-4.3	1 613.2	1 136.6	384.0	92.3	0.4	-22.3	7.9	-30.2
4th quarter	453.4	361.2	36.4	55.7	-5.2	1 644.5	1 160.0	391.2	93.0	0.4	-0.9	8.1	-9.0
2005													
1st quarter	448.7	355.9	36.1	56.7	-5.4	1 661.2	1 174.6	393.4	92.8	0.4	10.9	7.8	3.1
2nd quarter	453.8	359.8	36.3	57.7	-6.8	1 690.5	1 192.8	403.8	93.5	0.4	12.4	7.6	4.9
3rd quarter	462.0	361.9	41.4	58.8	-21.7	1 717.2	1 217.8	404.5	94.5	0.4	-19.3	7.2	-26.6
4th quarter	459.8	366.8	33.1	59.9	-7.9	1 746.8	1 243.4	407.3	95.8	0.4	-17.2	6.8	-24.0

[1] Includes components not shown separately.

Table 19-12. U.S. International Transactions

(Millions of dollars, seasonally adjusted.)

Year and quarter	Exports of goods, services, and income				Imports of goods, services, and income [1]				Unilateral current transfers, net [2]	U.S.-owned assets abroad, net [3]					
										Total	U.S. official reserve assets, net	U.S. government assets other than official reserve assets, net	U.S. private assets, net		
	Total	Goods	Services	Income receipts	Total	Goods	Services	Income payments					Total	Direct investment	Foreign securities
1960															
1st quarter	7 355	4 685	1 543	1 127	-6 050	-3 812	-1 907	-331	-955	-1 066	159	-237	-988	-664	-266
2nd quarter	7 762	4 916	1 715	1 131	-6 078	-3 858	-1 906	-314	-1 154	-1 156	175	-339	-992	-586	-166
3rd quarter	7 650	5 031	1 453	1 166	-5 925	-3 648	-1 970	-307	-889	-956	740	-160	-1 536	-754	-111
4th quarter	7 791	5 018	1 580	1 193	-5 619	-3 440	-1 892	-287	-1 064	-923	1 071	-365	-1 629	-936	-120
1961															
1st quarter	7 827	5 095	1 481	1 251	-5 599	-3 394	-1 912	-293	-989	-1 320	371	-381	-1 310	-774	-135
2nd quarter	7 773	4 806	1 758	1 209	-5 659	-3 438	-1 922	-299	-1 208	-1 029	-320	471	-1 180	-551	-246
3rd quarter	7 757	5 038	1 468	1 251	-6 026	-3 809	-1 900	-317	-887	-1 928	-212	-486	-1 230	-737	-124
4th quarter	8 047	5 169	1 590	1 288	-6 171	-3 896	-1 939	-336	-1 043	-1 260	768	-513	-1 515	-592	-257
1962															
1st quarter	8 015	5 077	1 666	1 272	-6 256	-3 966	-1 971	-319	-1 113	-1 301	427	-406	-1 322	-545	-196
2nd quarter	8 719	5 336	2 004	1 379	-6 402	-4 080	-1 992	-330	-1 272	-1 461	-163	-381	-917	-716	-308
3rd quarter	8 295	5 331	1 567	1 397	-6 455	-4 116	-2 005	-334	-879	-279	881	8	-1 168	-811	-87
4th quarter	8 315	5 037	1 709	1 569	-6 567	-4 098	-2 126	-343	-1 016	-1 134	390	-306	-1 218	-779	-378
1963															
1st quarter	8 428	5 063	1 849	1 516	-6 478	-4 064	-2 057	-357	-1 107	-1 922	32	-482	-1 472	-980	-522
2nd quarter	9 244	5 599	2 150	1 495	-6 674	-4 226	-2 066	-382	-1 371	-2 631	124	-654	-2 101	-874	-536
3rd quarter	8 832	5 671	1 620	1 541	-6 893	-4 372	-2 122	-399	-918	-887	227	-86	-1 028	-721	-100
4th quarter	9 275	5 939	1 731	1 605	-6 926	-4 386	-2 118	-422	-999	-1 831	-5	-440	-1 386	-908	53
1964															
1st quarter	9 885	6 242	1 922	1 721	-6 982	-4 416	-2 140	-426	-993	-2 086	-51	-288	-1 747	-822	20
2nd quarter	9 975	6 199	2 088	1 688	-7 179	-4 598	-2 142	-439	-1 269	-2 018	303	-386	-1 935	-970	-206
3rd quarter	10 009	6 423	1 851	1 735	-7 349	-4 756	-2 153	-440	-935	-2 255	70	-414	-1 911	-1 018	2
4th quarter	10 299	6 637	1 982	1 680	-7 594	-4 930	-2 186	-478	-1 043	-3 200	-151	-592	-2 457	-949	-494
1965															
1st quarter	9 689	5 768	2 047	1 874	-7 395	-4 711	-2 187	-497	-1 037	-1 576	843	-374	-2 045	-1 606	-198
2nd quarter	11 263	6 876	2 448	1 939	-8 208	-5 428	-2 269	-511	-1 478	-1 270	69	-536	-803	-1 250	-147
3rd quarter	10 625	6 643	2 120	1 862	-8 307	-5 516	-2 263	-528	-1 013	-1 454	42	-254	-1 242	-1 030	-209
4th quarter	11 149	7 174	2 212	1 763	-8 802	-5 855	-2 393	-554	-1 058	-1 416	271	-441	-1 246	-1 125	-205
1966															
1st quarter	11 190	7 242	2 124	1 824	-9 068	-6 012	-2 483	-573	-1 140	-1 465	424	-321	-1 568	-1 115	-437
2nd quarter	11 726	7 169	2 705	1 852	-9 390	-6 195	-2 601	-594	-1 547	-1 967	68	-504	-1 531	-1 373	-115
3rd quarter	11 470	7 290	2 301	1 879	-9 912	-6 576	-2 693	-643	-1 073	-1 681	83	-339	-1 425	-1 314	-115
4th quarter	12 068	7 609	2 487	1 972	-10 098	-6 710	-2 717	-671	-1 194	-2 208	-5	-380	-1 823	-1 616	-53
1967															
1st quarter	12 439	7 751	2 731	1 957	-10 248	-6 708	-2 866	-674	-1 315	-1 203	1 027	-643	-1 587	-1 186	-265
2nd quarter	12 275	7 693	2 666	1 916	-10 136	-6 475	-2 986	-675	-1 472	-2 339	-419	-543	-1 377	-964	-261
3rd quarter	12 134	7 530	2 540	2 064	-10 262	-6 526	-3 059	-677	-1 309	-3 155	-375	-551	-2 229	-1 359	-419
4th quarter	12 506	7 692	2 731	2 083	-10 833	-7 157	-2 955	-721	-1 199	-3 060	-180	-685	-2 195	-1 297	-363
1968															
1st quarter	13 016	7 998	2 816	2 202	-11 571	-7 796	-2 997	-778	-1 249	-1 299	912	-706	-1 505	-981	-449
2nd quarter	13 577	8 324	2 936	2 317	-11 885	-8 051	-2 990	-844	-1 363	-2 427	-135	-632	-1 660	-1 172	-283
3rd quarter	14 195	8 745	3 039	2 411	-12 611	-8 612	-3 129	-870	-1 445	-3 447	-572	-568	-2 307	-1 573	-318
4th quarter	14 126	8 559	3 129	2 438	-12 604	-8 532	-3 185	-887	-1 573	-3 803	-1 075	-368	-2 360	-1 568	-519
1969															
1st quarter	12 921	7 468	2 884	2 569	-11 622	-7 444	-3 174	-1 004	-1 177	-2 595	-45	-406	-2 144	-1 556	-366
2nd quarter	15 492	9 536	3 283	2 673	-13 978	-9 527	-3 303	-1 148	-1 645	-3 428	-298	-632	-2 498	-1 663	-498
3rd quarter	15 439	9 400	3 245	2 794	-14 072	-9 380	-3 368	-1 324	-1 319	-3 361	-685	-703	-1 973	-1 548	-546
4th quarter	16 279	10 010	3 394	2 875	-14 329	-9 456	-3 481	-1 392	-1 593	-2 199	-151	-459	-1 589	-1 192	-139
1970															
1st quarter	16 461	10 258	3 235	2 968	-14 458	-9 587	-3 449	-1 422	-1 383	-2 611	481	-399	-2 693	-1 958	-306
2nd quarter	17 419	10 744	3 645	3 030	-14 861	-9 766	-3 690	-1 405	-1 586	-1 725	1 025	-348	-2 402	-2 144	80
3rd quarter	17 267	10 665	3 625	2 977	-15 141	-10 049	-3 715	-1 377	-1 611	-2 146	802	-423	-2 525	-1 718	-517
4th quarter	17 241	10 802	3 666	2 773	-15 443	-10 464	-3 668	-1 311	-1 576	-1 989	1 040	-419	-2 610	-1 771	-333
1971															
1st quarter	17 980	10 920	4 048	3 012	-15 551	-10 600	-3 724	-1 227	-1 746	-2 747	868	-573	-3 042	-2 033	-408
2nd quarter	18 163	10 878	4 087	3 198	-16 764	-11 614	-3 867	-1 283	-1 283	-2 534	839	-567	-2 806	-1 949	-368
3rd quarter	18 676	11 548	3 972	3 156	-17 460	-12 171	-3 861	-1 428	-1 752	-3 390	1 377	-387	-4 380	-2 308	-346
4th quarter	17 564	9 973	4 251	3 340	-16 639	-11 194	-3 948	-1 497	-2 098	-3 084	-18	-355	-2 711	-1 327	9
1972															
1st quarter	19 757	11 833	4 473	3 451	-19 153	-13 501	-4 173	-1 479	-2 297	-3 585	620	-212	-3 993	-2 187	-476
2nd quarter	19 427	11 618	4 233	3 576	-19 105	-13 254	-4 228	-1 623	-2 011	-2 125	-60	-271	-1 794	-1 481	-318
3rd quarter	20 788	12 351	4 634	3 803	-19 767	-14 022	-4 095	-1 650	-2 306	-3 952	96	-518	-3 530	-2 435	203
4th quarter	22 015	13 579	4 503	3 933	-21 212	-15 020	-4 371	-1 821	-1 933	-4 125	50	-566	-3 609	-1 644	-28
1973															
1st quarter	24 681	15 474	4 579	4 628	-23 000	-16 285	-4 613	-2 102	-1 536	-7 886	213	-572	-7 527	-3 785	55
2nd quarter	27 127	17 112	4 828	5 187	-24 301	-17 168	-4 741	-2 392	-1 953	-4 154	11	-423	-3 742	-2 691	-86
3rd quarter	29 329	18 271	5 145	5 913	-24 841	-17 683	-4 640	-2 518	-1 751	-3 189	-23	-608	-2 558	-2 159	-196
4th quarter	31 912	20 553	5 279	6 080	-26 855	-19 363	-4 849	-2 643	-1 674	-7 646	-43	-1 042	-6 561	-2 718	-445
1974															
1st quarter	34 698	22 614	5 189	6 895	-29 643	-21 952	-4 985	-2 706	-3 443	-5 914	-246	1 389	-7 057	900	-600
2nd quarter	37 295	24 500	5 691	7 104	-34 710	-26 346	-5 359	-3 005	-2 475	-10 318	-358	267	-10 227	-1 790	-272
3rd quarter	37 385	24 629	5 633	7 123	-36 004	-27 368	-5 360	-3 276	-1 676	-7 694	-1 002	-354	-6 338	-4 385	-282
4th quarter	39 105	26 563	6 078	6 464	-36 918	-28 145	-5 675	-3 098	-1 656	-10 818	139	-938	-10 019	-3 776	-699

[1] A minus sign indicates imports of goods or services or income payments.
[2] A minus sign indicates net unilateral transfers to foreigners.
[3] A minus sign indicates financial outflows or increases in U.S. official assets.

Table 19-12. U.S. International Transactions—Continued

(Millions of dollars, seasonally adjusted.)

Year and quarter	U.S.-owned assets abroad, net [3] —Continued		Foreign-owned assets in the United States, net [4]									Statistical discrepancy [5]	Balance on goods and services	Balance on current account
	U.S. private assets, net—Continued				Other foreign assets in the United States, net									
	U.S. claims		Total	Foreign official assets in the United States, net	Total	Direct invest-ment	U.S. Treasury securities and U.S. currency flows	U.S. securities other than U.S. Treasury securities	U.S. liabilities					
	On unaffiliated foreigners reported by U.S. nonbanking concerns	Reported by U.S. banks, not included elsewhere							To unaffiliated foreigners reported by U.S. nonbanking concerns	Reported by U.S. banks, not included elsewhere				
1960														
1st quarter	38	-96	926	380	546	89	-100	170	-1	388	-210	509	350
2nd quarter	-100	-140	912	435	477	102	-143	118	-50	450	-286	867	530
3rd quarter	-51	-620	381	283	98	93	-99	5	-11	110	-261	866	836
4th quarter	-281	-292	77	377	-300	31	-22	-11	-28	-270	-262	1 266	1 108
1961														
1st quarter	-117	-284	435	438	-3	68	-82	104	73	-166	-354	1 270	1 239
2nd quarter	-164	-219	620	-307	927	86	-38	152	72	655	-497	1 204	906
3rd quarter	-149	-220	934	673	261	58	83	3	14	103	150	797	844
4th quarter	-128	-538	715	-41	756	99	188	66	67	336	-288	924	833
1962														
1st quarter	-186	-395	737	. . .	737	89	193	145	-14	324	-82	806	646
2nd quarter	-5	112	675	503	172	130	-51	7	-64	150	-259	1 268	1 045
3rd quarter	-181	-89	-277	178	-455	59	-109	-23	16	-398	-405	777	961
4th quarter	17	-78	779	591	188	68	-99	6	-47	260	-377	522	732
1963														
1st quarter	-27	57	1 191	946	245	40	25	14	-36	202	-112	791	843
2nd quarter	-108	-583	1 527	910	617	108	-109	119	69	430	-95	1 457	1 199
3rd quarter	47	-254	205	56	149	105	1	52	11	-20	-339	797	1 021
4th quarter	245	-776	295	75	220	-22	-66	102	-80	286	186	1 166	1 350
1964														
1st quarter	-206	-739	462	393	69	87	32	-42	0	-8	-286	1 608	1 910
2nd quarter	-166	-593	630	227	403	109	-108	14	19	369	-139	1 547	1 527
3rd quarter	-532	-363	769	275	494	56	-65	-30	37	496	-239	1 365	1 725
4th quarter	-204	-810	1 781	763	1 018	70	-5	-27	19	961	-243	1 503	1 662
1965														
1st quarter	286	-527	208	-202	410	184	60	57	3	106	111	917	1 257
2nd quarter	165	429	-330	-194	-136	-21	64	-243	63	1	23	1 627	1 577
3rd quarter	-19	16	587	115	472	147	-149	-227	49	652	-438	984	1 305
4th quarter	-91	175	280	421	-141	104	-106	54	63	-256	-153	1 138	1 289
1966														
1st quarter	-159	143	458	-164	622	143	-102	173	68	340	25	871	982
2nd quarter	-68	25	961	-57	1 018	133	-316	518	78	605	217	1 078	789
3rd quarter	-105	109	909	-342	1 251	-37	66	107	195	920	287	322	485
4th quarter	-110	-44	1 332	-111	1 443	187	-4	108	135	1 017	100	669	776
1967														
1st quarter	-107	-29	401	708	-307	169	-6	133	219	-822	-74	908	876
2nd quarter	-69	-83	1 884	1 100	784	174	-61	329	66	276	-212	898	667
3rd quarter	-40	-411	2 513	548	1 965	127	-36	520	164	1 190	79	485	563
4th quarter	-563	28	2 584	1 098	1 486	228	-32	34	135	1 121	2	311	474
1968														
1st quarter	-231	156	1 374	-533	1 907	367	22	855	207	456	-271	21	196
2nd quarter	-567	362	2 192	-2 007	4 199	133	86	1 122	478	2 380	-94	219	329
3rd quarter	-213	-203	2 809	442	2 367	148	-8	1 124	315	788	499	43	139
4th quarter	-191	-82	3 550	1 321	2 229	160	36	1 312	474	247	304	-29	-51
1969														
1st quarter	-132	-90	3 664	-1 117	4 781	359	-125	1 388	90	3 069	-1 191	-266	122
2nd quarter	-21	-316	3 896	-766	4 662	267	-35	365	181	3 884	-337	-11	-131
3rd quarter	141	-20	3 833	1 256	2 577	261	79	396	345	1 496	-520	-103	48
4th quarter	-114	-144	1 311	-672	1 983	376	13	981	176	437	531	467	357
1970														
1st quarter	-366	-63	2 160	2 830	-670	592	16	304	222	-1 804	-169	457	620
2nd quarter	-73	-265	848	694	154	212	-35	374	534	-931	-95	933	972
3rd quarter	-157	-133	1 940	1 411	529	357	1	720	510	-1 059	-309	526	515
4th quarter	0	-506	1 413	1 975	-562	303	99	792	748	-2 504	354	336	222
1971														
1st quarter	-355	-246	3 092	5 178	-2 086	196	179	559	-62	-2 958	-1 028	644	683
2nd quarter	-131	-358	5 154	5 630	-476	140	1 862	196	-34	-2 640	-2 211	-516	-409
3rd quarter	-337	-1 389	8 726	10 367	-1 641	-293	-795	626	79	-1 258	-4 800	-512	-536
4th quarter	-406	-987	5 997	5 704	293	324	-1 270	908	386	-55	-1 740	-918	-1 173
1972														
1st quarter	-248	-1 082	4 367	2 762	1 605	-136	-3	1 059	-14	699	911	-1 368	-1 693
2nd quarter	-185	190	4 277	1 103	3 174	373	-83	961	250	1 673	-463	-1 631	-1 689
3rd quarter	-241	-1 057	6 382	4 740	1 642	310	-12	718	216	410	-1 145	-1 132	-1 285
4th quarter	-380	-1 557	6 437	1 871	4 566	403	59	1 769	363	1 972	-1 182	-1 309	-1 130
1973														
1st quarter	-809	-2 988	10 743	9 937	806	631	-119	1 718	246	-1 670	-3 002	-845	145
2nd quarter	-202	-763	3 056	-403	3 458	835	-185	489	54	2 265	225	31	873
3rd quarter	-502	299	2 168	-772	2 940	539	-205	1 173	454	979	-1 716	1 093	2 737
4th quarter	-870	-2 528	2 423	-2 736	5 159	795	293	662	281	3 128	1 840	1 620	3 383
1974														
1st quarter	-2 113	-5 244	6 514	-1 138	7 652	1 784	336	712	354	4 466	-2 212	866	1 612
2nd quarter	-588	-7 577	9 962	4 434	5 528	539	60	363	390	4 176	246	-1 514	110
3rd quarter	273	-1 944	9 303	3 062	6 241	1 610	400	227	239	3 765	-1 314	-2 466	-295
4th quarter	-793	-4 751	9 563	4 188	5 375	828	1 001	-925	861	3 610	724	-1 179	531

[3]A minus sign indicates financial outflows or increases in U.S. official assets.
[4]A minus sign indicates financial outflows or decreases in foreign official assets in the United States.
[5]Sum of credits and debits with the sign reversed.
. . . = Not available.

Table 19-12. U.S. International Transactions—Continued

(Millions of dollars, seasonally adjusted.)

Year and quarter	Exports of goods, services, and income				Imports of goods, services, and income [1]				Unilateral current transfers, net [2]	U.S.-owned assets abroad, net [3]					
										Total	U.S. official reserve assets, net	U.S. government assets other than official reserve assets, net	U.S. private assets, net		
	Total	Goods	Services	Income receipts	Total	Goods	Services	Income payments					Total	Direct investment	Foreign securities
1975															
1st quarter	40 047	27 480	6 454	6 113	-33 797	-24 980	-5 580	-3 237	-2 043	-10 576	-327	-877	-9 372	-4 022	-1 931
2nd quarter	38 675	25 866	6 807	6 002	-31 284	-22 832	-5 309	-3 143	-2 377	-9 591	-28	-875	-8 688	-3 990	-985
3rd quarter	38 347	26 109	5 886	6 352	-33 078	-24 487	-5 379	-3 212	-1 189	-5 099	-333	-745	-4 021	-1 495	-938
4th quarter	40 868	27 633	6 351	6 884	-34 588	-25 886	-5 729	-2 973	-1 467	-14 436	-161	-977	-13 298	-4 736	-2 393
1976															
1st quarter	41 183	27 575	6 556	7 052	-37 464	-28 176	-5 883	-3 405	-1 153	-12 364	-777	-749	-10 838	-3 923	-2 467
2nd quarter	42 309	28 256	6 660	7 393	-39 494	-30 182	-5 980	-3 332	-1 167	-11 701	-1 580	-914	-9 207	-2 017	-1 405
3rd quarter	43 818	29 056	7 311	7 451	-41 737	-32 213	-6 231	-3 293	-2 165	-10 618	-408	-1 428	-8 782	-3 327	-2 751
4th quarter	44 780	29 858	7 444	7 478	-43 416	-33 657	-6 478	-3 281	-1 201	-16 588	207	-1 124	-15 671	-2 682	-2 262
1977															
1st quarter	44 916	29 668	7 494	7 754	-46 360	-36 585	-6 676	-3 099	-1 243	-1 198	-420	-1 062	284	-1 880	-749
2nd quarter	46 796	30 852	7 901	8 043	-48 401	-38 063	-6 940	-3 398	-1 426	-12 182	-24	-885	-11 273	-3 783	-1 784
3rd quarter	47 125	30 752	7 991	8 382	-48 511	-38 005	-6 894	-3 612	-1 371	-6 297	112	-1 001	-5 408	-2 762	-2 177
4th quarter	45 818	29 544	8 098	8 176	-50 495	-39 254	-7 133	-4 108	-1 185	-15 109	-43	-746	-14 320	-3 466	-749
1978															
1st quarter	48 847	30 470	8 704	9 673	-54 471	-42 487	-7 612	-4 372	-1 396	-15 219	187	-1 009	-14 397	-4 771	-1 115
2nd quarter	54 213	35 674	8 772	9 767	-56 513	-43 419	-7 768	-5 326	-1 477	-5 606	248	-1 257	-4 597	-3 720	-1 094
3rd quarter	56 058	36 523	9 203	10 332	-58 300	-44 422	-8 248	-5 630	-1 425	-9 703	115	-1 394	-8 424	-2 753	-510
4th quarter	61 399	39 408	9 673	12 318	-60 587	-45 674	-8 561	-6 352	-1 491	-30 601	182	-999	-29 784	-4 812	-907
1979															
1st quarter	64 530	41 475	9 664	13 391	-63 492	-47 582	-8 649	-7 261	-1 462	-7 841	-2 446	-1 094	-4 301	-5 465	-908
2nd quarter	68 445	43 885	9 713	14 847	-67 584	-50 778	-8 960	-7 846	-1 552	-15 565	322	-970	-14 917	-7 220	-492
3rd quarter	74 411	47 104	9 936	17 371	-71 856	-54 002	-9 329	-8 525	-1 632	-27 156	2 779	-779	-29 156	-7 166	-2 331
4th quarter	80 577	51 975	10 378	18 224	-78 726	-59 645	-9 751	-9 330	-1 949	-14 353	-649	-904	-12 800	-5 370	-995
1980															
1st quarter	85 274	54 237	10 997	20 040	-86 559	-65 815	-10 335	-10 409	-2 174	-12 662	-2 116	-1 441	-9 105	-5 188	-787
2nd quarter	83 441	55 967	11 491	15 983	-82 734	-62 274	-10 106	-10 354	-1 648	-24 724	502	-1 159	-24 067	-2 659	-1 387
3rd quarter	86 148	55 830	12 543	17 775	-79 906	-59 010	-10 292	-10 604	-1 909	-19 666	-1 109	-1 382	-17 175	-4 156	-944
4th quarter	89 578	58 216	12 554	18 808	-84 577	-62 651	-10 760	-11 166	-2 618	-28 761	-4 279	-1 178	-23 304	-7 219	-450
1981															
1st quarter	94 665	60 317	13 684	20 664	-91 024	-67 004	-11 360	-12 660	-2 678	-21 922	-3 436	-1 361	-17 125	-2 044	-473
2nd quarter	96 294	60 141	14 392	21 761	-92 303	-67 181	-11 447	-13 675	-2 763	-24 158	-905	-1 491	-21 762	-5 709	-1 564
3rd quarter	95 013	58 031	14 835	22 147	-89 787	-64 407	-11 236	-14 144	-3 145	-17 945	-4	-1 268	-16 673	-1 124	-697
4th quarter	94 958	58 555	14 446	21 957	-91 082	-66 475	-11 460	-13 147	-3 117	-49 028	262	-976	-48 314	-745	-2 966
1982															
1st quarter	94 006	55 163	16 032	22 811	-90 336	-63 502	-12 749	-14 085	-3 955	-36 335	-1 089	-800	-34 446	. . .	-628
2nd quarter	96 060	55 344	16 187	24 529	-88 318	-60 580	-13 096	-14 642	-3 953	-42 754	-1 132	-1 727	-39 895	1 074	-471
3rd quarter	90 925	52 089	16 003	22 833	-90 938	-63 696	-12 794	-14 448	-4 027	-23 547	-794	-2 524	-20 229	903	-3 397
4th quarter	85 993	48 561	15 857	21 575	-86 379	-59 864	-13 109	-13 406	-4 611	-25 246	-1 950	-1 080	-22 217	-3 838	-3 488
1983															
1st quarter	86 146	49 198	16 239	20 709	-85 097	-59 757	-12 951	-12 389	-3 566	-28 890	-787	-1 136	-26 967	-862	-1 549
2nd quarter	87 214	49 340	16 093	21 781	-91 096	-64 783	-13 557	-12 756	-3 951	-2 974	16	-1 263	-1 727	-1 842	-2 813
3rd quarter	89 919	50 324	16 308	23 287	-98 481	-70 370	-14 133	-13 978	-4 339	-12 191	529	-1 171	-11 549	-4 861	-1 308
4th quarter	92 831	52 937	15 671	24 223	-102 822	-73 991	-14 337	-14 494	-5 453	-22 318	-953	-1 436	-19 929	-4 962	-1 093
1984															
1st quarter	96 000	52 991	17 353	25 656	-112 576	-79 740	-16 131	-16 705	-4 354	-8 338	-657	-2 033	-5 648	-1 837	758
2nd quarter	100 257	54 626	18 045	27 586	-119 220	-83 798	-16 885	-18 537	-4 476	-25 714	-566	-1 342	-23 811	-1 967	-764
3rd quarter	102 296	55 893	17 936	28 467	-120 533	-83 918	-17 168	-19 447	-5 147	15 298	-799	-1 392	17 489	-3 209	-1 106
4th quarter	101 361	56 416	17 834	27 111	-121 591	-84 962	-17 564	-19 065	-6 359	-21 618	-1 110	-720	-19 789	-9 396	-3 644
1985															
1st quarter	97 794	54 866	18 227	24 701	-116 249	-80 319	-17 707	-18 223	-5 064	-5 491	-233	-760	-4 498	-2 783	-2 474
2nd quarter	97 437	54 154	18 214	25 069	-120 891	-84 565	-18 276	-18 050	-5 235	-2 340	-356	-1 053	-931	-4 374	-2 219
3rd quarter	94 771	52 836	17 961	23 974	-120 285	-83 909	-18 151	-18 225	-5 789	-5 776	-121	-453	-5 202	-4 469	-1 572
4th quarter	97 612	54 059	18 756	24 797	-126 349	-89 295	-18 732	-18 322	-5 911	-31 146	-3 148	-555	-27 444	-7 073	-1 217
1986															
1st quarter	100 332	53 536	21 052	25 744	-129 342	-89 220	-19 855	-20 267	-5 199	-17 406	-115	-266	-17 025	-9 781	-5 930
2nd quarter	102 206	56 828	20 912	24 466	-131 690	-91 743	-19 066	-20 881	-6 208	-24 945	16	-230	-24 731	-7 298	-1 051
3rd quarter	101 288	55 645	21 969	23 674	-132 879	-92 801	-20 448	-19 630	-6 458	-32 615	280	-1 554	-31 341	-4 975	181
4th quarter	103 275	57 335	22 761	23 179	-136 232	-94 661	-20 778	-20 793	-6 269	-36 753	132	29	-36 914	-1 938	2 529
1987															
1st quarter	104 750	56 696	23 602	24 452	-138 887	-96 023	-21 273	-21 591	-5 128	8 177	1 956	-5	6 226	-6 547	-1 749
2nd quarter	111 642	60 202	24 740	26 700	-146 125	-100 648	-22 537	-22 940	-5 502	-26 738	3 419	-168	-29 989	-7 541	-287
3rd quarter	116 688	64 217	24 986	27 485	-151 111	-104 412	-22 833	-23 866	-5 706	-27 791	32	310	-28 133	-8 795	-1 159
4th quarter	123 968	69 093	25 329	29 546	-158 324	-108 682	-24 146	-25 496	-6 926	-32 943	3 742	868	-37 553	-12 150	-2 056
1988															
1st quarter	134 932	75 655	26 598	32 679	-161 810	-109 963	-24 503	-27 344	-6 074	2 892	1 502	-1 597	2 987	-5 037	-4 504
2nd quarter	139 984	79 542	27 567	32 875	-163 265	-110 836	-24 282	-28 147	-5 615	-23 428	39	-854	-22 613	-2 594	1 318
3rd quarter	143 879	80 941	28 453	34 485	-165 901	-110 901	-24 588	-30 412	-5 902	-49 965	-7 380	1 960	-44 545	-7 791	-1 500
4th quarter	149 068	84 092	28 302	36 674	-172 770	-115 489	-25 157	-32 124	-7 685	-36 074	1 925	3 457	-41 456	-7 105	-3 294
1989															
1st quarter	155 853	86 322	30 576	38 955	-178 297	-118 709	-25 140	-34 448	-6 048	-53 703	-4 000	961	-50 664	-12 136	-2 225
2nd quarter	163 435	91 482	31 110	40 843	-182 850	-121 012	-25 241	-36 597	-5 753	-8 202	-12 095	-306	4 199	-7 686	-6 192
3rd quarter	163 560	90 743	32 316	40 501	-178 980	-117 459	-25 792	-35 729	-6 630	-51 678	-5 996	489	-46 171	-8 704	-9 149
4th quarter	165 444	91 369	33 087	40 988	-181 480	-120 485	-26 306	-34 689	-7 739	-61 803	-3 202	87	-58 688	-14 922	-4 504

[1] A minus sign indicates imports of goods or services or income payments.
[2] A minus sign indicates net unilateral transfers to foreigners.
[3] A minus sign indicates financial outflows or increases in U.S. official assets.
. . . = Not available.

Table 19-12. U.S. International Transactions—Continued

(Millions of dollars, seasonally adjusted.)

Year and quarter	U.S. private assets, net—Continued — U.S. claims — On unaffiliated foreigners reported by U.S. nonbanking concerns	Reported by U.S. banks, not included elsewhere	Foreign-owned assets in the United States, net — Total	Foreign official assets in the United States, net	Other foreign assets in the United States, net — Total	Direct investment	U.S. Treasury securities and U.S. currency flows	U.S. securities other than U.S. Treasury securities	U.S. liabilities — To unaffiliated foreigners reported by U.S. nonbanking concerns	Reported by U.S. banks, not included elsewhere	Statistical discrepancy [5]	Balance on goods and services	Balance on current account
1975													
1st quarter	353	-3 772	2 788	3 419	-631	278	892	344	359	-2 504	3 581	3 374	4 207
2nd quarter	112	-3 825	4 371	2 244	2 127	870	10	385	55	807	206	4 532	5 014
3rd quarter	-939	-649	2 991	-1 731	4 722	86	2 424	737	-163	1 638	-1 972	2 129	4 080
4th quarter	-883	-5 286	7 021	3 095	3 926	1 369	764	1 038	68	687	2 602	2 369	4 813
1976													
1st quarter	-747	-3 701	7 769	3 699	4 070	1 471	737	1 036	154	672	2 029	72	2 566
2nd quarter	-999	-4 786	8 453	4 039	4 414	1 086	-91	134	-231	3 516	1 600	-1 246	1 648
3rd quarter	616	-3 320	9 120	2 958	6 162	999	3 325	64	-184	1 958	1 582	-2 077	-84
4th quarter	-1 166	-9 561	12 677	6 997	5 680	790	312	51	-317	4 844	3 748	-2 833	163
1977													
1st quarter	-771	3 684	3 062	5 554	-2 492	980	1 181	749	-98	-5 304	823	-6 099	-2 687
2nd quarter	-1 124	-4 582	14 781	7 888	6 893	965	-799	589	-102	6 240	432	-6 250	-3 031
3rd quarter	1 310	-1 779	14 676	8 257	6 419	1 023	1 651	337	768	2 640	-5 622	-6 156	-2 757
4th quarter	-1 355	-8 750	20 703	15 117	5 586	761	401	763	518	3 143	268	-8 745	-5 862
1978													
1st quarter	-2 241	-6 270	18 684	15 448	3 236	1 356	1 381	396	507	-404	3 555	-10 925	-7 020
2nd quarter	315	-98	1 551	-5 113	6 664	2 313	1 493	1 082	304	1 472	7 832	-6 741	-3 777
3rd quarter	-29	-5 132	17 582	4 903	12 679	2 620	-368	296	912	9 219	-4 212	-6 944	-3 667
4th quarter	-1 898	-22 167	29 220	18 440	10 780	1 608	2 672	480	166	5 854	2 060	-5 154	-679
1979													
1st quarter	-3 854	5 926	2 707	-8 697	11 404	1 554	2 964	409	-296	6 773	5 558	-5 092	-424
2nd quarter	716	-7 921	7 663	-9 775	17 438	3 354	743	524	799	12 018	8 593	-6 140	-691
3rd quarter	-1 826	-17 833	25 349	6 036	19 313	3 382	2 402	166	210	13 153	884	-6 291	923
4th quarter	-50	-6 385	5 134	-1 228	6 362	3 588	951	252	908	663	9 317	-7 043	-98
1980													
1st quarter	-1 927	-1 203	9 582	-7 413	16 995	3 321	4 300	2 435	340	6 599	6 539	-10 916	-3 459
2nd quarter	144	-20 165	11 373	7 731	3 643	5 756	229	496	1 671	-4 509	14 292	-4 922	-941
3rd quarter	365	-12 440	14 930	7 564	7 366	4 713	222	263	1 252	916	403	-929	4 333
4th quarter	-2 605	-13 030	26 726	7 614	19 112	3 128	2 394	2 263	3 590	7 737	-348	-2 641	2 383
1981													
1st quarter	-2 944	-11 664	9 819	5 502	4 317	3 146	2 486	2 357	121	-3 793	11 140	-4 363	963
2nd quarter	513	-15 002	15 364	-3 159	18 523	5 294	1 641	3 512	13	8 063	7 566	-4 095	1 228
3rd quarter	458	-15 310	17 531	-5 992	23 523	5 505	-248	704	1 084	16 478	-1 667	-2 777	2 081
4th quarter	-2 404	-42 199	43 519	8 609	34 910	11 251	2 248	332	-301	21 380	4 750	-4 934	759
1982													
1st quarter	2 220	-33 343	27 240	-3 265	30 505	. . .	1 297	1 263	-65	25 856	9 325	-5 056	-285
2nd quarter	-1 095	-39 403	35 260	1 534	33 726	2 945	4 193	2 486	-2 023	26 125	3 653	-2 145	3 789
3rd quarter	3 670	-21 405	18 663	2 694	15 969	2 849	2 091	555	-282	10 756	8 876	-8 398	-4 040
4th quarter	2 028	-16 919	15 424	2 629	12 795	4 685	3 446	1 781	-13	2 896	14 775	-8 555	-4 997
1983													
1st quarter	-4 253	-20 303	16 266	-38	16 304	1 254	3 713	2 873	-2 763	11 227	15 090	-7 271	-2 517
2nd quarter	-590	3 518	16 325	1 612	14 713	3 287	4 616	2 470	-64		-5 570	-12 907	-7 833
3rd quarter	-1 764	-3 616	20 420	-2 689	23 109	4 059	2 308	1 777	1 311	13 654	4 619	-17 871	-12 901
4th quarter	-4 347	-9 527	35 682	6 960	28 722	1 771	3 452	1 044	1 398	21 057	2 027	-19 720	-15 444
1984													
1st quarter	-3 012	-1 557	23 302	-2 956	26 258	4 858	2 450	1 333	6 092	11 525	5 910	-25 527	-20 930
2nd quarter	-934	-20 146	42 689	-156	42 845	8 625	8 036	362	4 232	21 590	6 411	-28 012	-23 439
3rd quarter	3 987	17 817	7 568	-884	8 452	4 432	1 447	1 662		-5 192	458	-27 257	-23 384
4th quarter	492	-7 241	44 192	7 136	37 056	6 552	10 512	9 426	4 640	5 926	3 953	-28 276	-26 589
1985													
1st quarter	475	284	18 342	-10 962	29 304	4 913	3 390	9 615	-720	12 106	10 597	-24 933	-23 519
2nd quarter	2 337	3 325	29 334	8 502	20 832	4 376	6 888	7 194	1 724	650	1 619	-30 473	-28 689
3rd quarter	-2 779	3 847	38 263	2 506	35 757	4 839	9 136	11 669	2 801	7 312	-1 265	-31 263	-31 303
4th quarter	-10 375	-8 779	60 179	-1 165	61 344	5 618	6 219	22 484	6 046	20 977	5 528	-35 212	-34 648
1986													
1st quarter	-6 230	4 916	41 489	2 712	38 777	3 431	6 420	18 730	696	9 500	10 042	-34 487	-34 209
2nd quarter	-2 722	-13 660	53 710	15 918	37 792	5 520	4 620	22 752	1 635	3 265	6 851	-33 069	-35 692
3rd quarter	-7 638	-18 909	70 876	15 789	55 087	8 746	-854	17 107	1 947	28 141	-282	-35 635	-38 049
4th quarter	-5 183	-32 322	63 933	1 229	62 704	17 723	-2 277	12 380	-953	35 831	11 975	-35 343	-39 226
1987													
1st quarter	-5 715	20 237	42 247	14 199	28 048	12 883	-2 326	18 372	6 151	-7 032	-11 246	-36 998	-39 265
2nd quarter	712	-22 873	57 331	10 444	46 887	8 593	-731	15 960	5 595	17 470	9 301	-38 243	-39 985
3rd quarter	-1 319	-16 860	83 145	764	82 381	20 763	-1 835	12 676	6 656	44 121	-15 319	-38 042	-40 129
4th quarter	-724	-22 623	65 910	19 980	45 930	16 230	2 649	-4 888	-39	31 978	8 222	-38 406	-41 282
1988													
1st quarter	-3 454	15 982	32 028	24 925	7 103	8 425	6 511	2 423	12 593	-22 849	-2 077	-32 213	-32 952
2nd quarter	-9 954	-11 383	74 531	6 006	68 525	13 717	7 673	9 702	6 742	30 691	-22 325	-28 009	-28 896
3rd quarter	-5 217	-30 037	52 797	-1 974	54 771	13 778	4 743	7 464	6 399	22 387	24 962	-26 095	-27 924
4th quarter	-2 568	-28 489	87 166	10 801	76 365	21 815	7 112	6 764	7 159	33 515	-19 841	-28 252	-31 387
1989													
1st quarter	-9 293	-27 010	66 666	7 700	58 966	18 584	10 961	8 544	6 637	14 240	15 401	-26 951	-28 492
2nd quarter	-5 767	23 844	10 980	-5 114	16 094	15 325	4 789	9 365	12 000	-25 385	22 257	-23 661	-25 168
3rd quarter	-5 924	-22 394	74 068	13 060	61 008	11 519	12 744	10 270	-1 121	27 596	-479	-20 192	-22 050
4th quarter	-6 662	-32 600	73 215	-7 142	80 357	22 846	7 024	10 588	4 570	35 329	12 427	-22 335	-23 775

[3] A minus sign indicates financial outflows or increases in U.S. official assets.
[4] A minus sign indicates financial outflows or decreases in foreign official assets in the United States.
[5] Sum of credits and debits with the sign reversed.
. . . = Not available.

Table 19-12. U.S. International Transactions—Continued

(Millions of dollars, seasonally adjusted.)

Year and quarter	Exports of goods, services, and income				Imports of goods, services, and income [1]				Unilateral current transfers, net [2]	U.S.-owned assets abroad, net [3]					
										Total	U.S. official reserve assets, net	U.S. government assets other than official reserve assets, net	U.S. private assets, net		
	Total	Goods	Services	Income receipts	Total	Goods	Services	Income payments					Total	Direct investment	Foreign securities
1990															
1st quarter	171 856	95 070	35 016	41 770	-188 962	-124 947	-28 173	-35 842	-6 540	37 828	-3 177	-756	41 761	-10 391	-8 580
2nd quarter	174 266	96 273	35 988	42 005	-186 146	-121 782	-28 764	-35 600	-7 644	-37 204	371	-796	-36 779	-4 651	-11 037
3rd quarter	176 466	97 227	37 402	41 837	-190 664	-124 132	-29 923	-36 609	-7 339	-43 716	1 739	-338	-45 117	-17 898	-1 037
4th quarter	184 389	98 831	39 428	46 130	-193 514	-127 577	-30 795	-35 142	-5 133	-38 142	-1 092	4 205	-41 255	-4 240	-8 111
1991															
1st quarter	181 296	101 258	37 891	42 147	-186 167	-122 326	-29 801	-34 040	14 828	-10 570	-353	549	-10 766	-14 318	-9 960
2nd quarter	180 627	102 674	40 745	37 208	-181 695	-120 103	-29 660	-31 932	3 593	745	1 014	-423	154	-1 230	-12 021
3rd quarter	181 647	104 238	41 860	35 549	-182 800	-122 448	-29 200	-31 152	-3 033	-15 900	3 878	3 256	-23 034	-9 356	-12 550
4th quarter	183 993	105 913	43 766	34 314	-183 906	-126 143	-29 799	-27 964	-5 488	-38 664	1 226	-459	-39 431	-12 987	-11 142
1992															
1st quarter	186 444	108 062	44 164	34 218	-185 468	-127 962	-29 762	-27 744	-7 210	-11 428	-1 057	-259	-10 112	-20 695	-8 668
2nd quarter	186 873	107 941	44 133	34 799	-190 414	-132 484	-29 443	-28 487	-8 349	-16 235	1 464	-302	-17 397	-10 268	-8 196
3rd quarter	188 127	110 847	44 609	32 671	-193 313	-136 048	-30 175	-27 090	-7 982	-13 570	1 952	-392	-15 130	-5 157	-13 059
4th quarter	189 201	112 781	44 343	32 077	-196 427	-140 034	-30 182	-26 211	-11 561	-33 177	1 542	-715	-34 004	-12 145	-19 243
1993															
1st quarter	191 422	112 099	45 984	33 339	-197 860	-142 331	-29 996	-25 533	-8 339	-21 491	-983	487	-20 995	-14 982	-28 208
2nd quarter	193 169	113 257	46 457	33 455	-204 737	-146 800	-30 661	-27 276	-9 111	-45 843	822	-304	-46 361	-23 264	-29 833
3rd quarter	194 153	112 982	46 707	34 464	-205 549	-147 763	-30 922	-26 864	-9 906	-52 975	-544	-194	-52 237	-13 155	-51 940
4th quarter	200 170	118 605	46 766	34 799	-215 772	-152 500	-32 202	-31 070	-12 456	-80 243	-673	-340	-79 230	-32 550	-36 272
1994															
1st quarter	204 240	118 833	48 362	37 045	-220 726	-156 303	-32 809	-31 614	-8 495	-39 740	-59	399	-40 080	-28 554	-19 540
2nd quarter	211 812	122 251	49 978	39 583	-231 476	-163 200	-33 023	-35 253	-8 914	-45 677	3 537	477	-49 691	-14 932	-11 834
3rd quarter	222 795	128 947	50 667	43 181	-244 319	-171 342	-33 624	-39 353	-10 084	-31 948	-165	-323	-31 460	-17 316	-13 368
4th quarter	230 930	132 828	51 391	46 711	-254 602	-177 845	-33 603	-43 154	-12 773	-61 574	2 033	-943	-62 664	-19 367	-18 448
1995															
1st quarter	241 117	138 370	52 173	50 574	-263 108	-183 966	-34 426	-44 716	-9 443	-64 771	-5 318	-553	-58 900	-19 325	-8 596
2nd quarter	248 705	142 520	53 163	53 022	-271 587	-189 910	-35 097	-46 580	-9 131	-118 089	-2 722	-225	-115 142	-15 078	-27 964
3rd quarter	255 495	146 536	56 436	52 523	-272 929	-187 685	-35 604	-49 640	-9 543	-47 311	-1 893	252	-45 670	-21 772	-42 116
4th quarter	259 310	147 778	57 408	54 124	-272 501	-187 813	-36 272	-48 416	-9 956	-122 091	191	-458	-121 824	-42 573	-43 718
1996															
1st quarter	263 221	150 552	57 442	55 227	-279 419	-194 445	-37 090	-47 884	-11 242	-80 431	17	-210	-80 238	-23 759	-43 538
2nd quarter	266 995	152 861	59 350	54 784	-287 312	-200 070	-37 606	-49 636	-9 523	-68 123	-523	-568	-67 032	-15 096	-30 579
3rd quarter	266 854	151 856	58 664	56 334	-293 261	-202 367	-38 836	-52 058	-9 651	-91 580	7 489	105	-99 174	-23 129	-33 178
4th quarter	280 655	156 844	64 029	59 782	-299 487	-206 231	-39 023	-54 233	-12 603	-173 272	-315	-316	-172 641	-29 898	-42 020
1997															
1st quarter	287 279	162 670	62 515	62 094	-313 370	-214 188	-40 405	-58 777	-9 967	-152 729	4 480	-76	-157 133	-29 544	-24 352
2nd quarter	299 679	170 249	64 292	65 138	-318 220	-217 306	-40 879	-60 035	-10 267	-93 152	-236	-298	-92 618	-24 883	-31 275
3rd quarter	303 542	173 155	64 855	65 532	-325 472	-220 853	-42 078	-62 541	-10 666	-119 387	-730	377	-119 034	-21 217	-51 401
4th quarter	300 762	172 292	64 429	64 041	-329 536	-224 123	-42 571	-62 842	-14 160	-120 209	-4 524	65	-115 750	-29 161	-9 824
1998															
1st quarter	302 195	171 060	64 690	66 445	-333 832	-227 353	-43 304	-63 175	-12 053	-74 438	-444	-80	-73 914	-41 844	-19 451
2nd quarter	298 846	165 559	66 174	67 113	-337 534	-228 197	-44 627	-64 710	-12 361	-138 628	-1 945	-483	-136 200	-44 689	-42 961
3rd quarter	293 115	164 054	64 786	64 275	-338 440	-227 430	-45 784	-65 226	-13 140	-58 520	-2 025	188	-56 683	-20 479	7 783
4th quarter	300 835	169 743	67 106	63 986	-345 530	-234 123	-46 965	-64 442	-15 633	-82 245	-2 369	-47	-79 829	-35 634	-75 575
1999															
1st quarter	300 183	164 302	68 755	67 126	-351 199	-238 715	-47 703	-64 781	-11 885	-84 623	4 068	118	-88 809	-68 498	2 696
2nd quarter	307 288	166 144	70 138	71 006	-366 741	-250 093	-49 234	-67 414	-12 260	-182 426	1 159	-392	-183 193	-50 190	-69 682
3rd quarter	319 936	172 989	71 185	75 762	-388 190	-264 363	-50 818	-73 009	-11 987	-123 490	1 951	-686	-124 755	-64 062	-39 790
4th quarter	332 407	180 530	71 842	80 035	-403 076	-276 809	-51 435	-74 832	-14 295	-113 524	1 569	3 710	-118 803	-42 185	-15 460
2000															
1st quarter	341 683	185 253	73 127	83 303	-427 173	-293 664	-54 240	-79 269	-12 859	-207 606	-554	-127	-206 925	-34 934	-32 542
2nd quarter	355 307	191 227	75 335	88 745	-440 926	-301 569	-55 245	-84 112	-13 368	-107 301	2 020	-570	-108 751	-52 029	-38 171
3rd quarter	360 295	198 811	74 662	86 822	-453 693	-312 780	-57 353	-83 560	-14 208	-84 847	-346	114	-84 615	-39 618	-32 363
4th quarter	364 231	196 703	75 479	92 049	-456 232	-316 395	-56 914	-82 923	-18 212	-160 771	-1 410	-358	-159 003	-32 633	-24 832
2001															
1st quarter	350 489	193 976	74 564	81 949	-442 851	-309 396	-56 420	-77 035	-15 171	-216 194	190	77	-216 461	-35 381	-25 355
2nd quarter	334 968	185 030	74 110	75 828	-417 089	-290 214	-57 578	-69 297	-15 802	-86 702	-1 343	-783	-84 576	-26 783	-50 200
3rd quarter	311 110	172 648	70 579	67 883	-401 111	-277 881	-54 863	-68 367	-2 941	32 858	-3 559	77	36 340	-44 327	11 639
4th quarter	296 582	167 058	66 932	62 592	-369 764	-268 409	-52 930	-48 425	-17 374	-112 577	-199	143	-112 521	-35 857	-26 728
2002															
1st quarter	300 892	165 171	70 799	64 922	-391 610	-273 155	-55 981	-62 474	-18 326	-84 841	390	133	-85 364	-48 155	-9 012
2nd quarter	312 379	172 131	72 292	67 956	-416 841	-291 124	-56 586	-69 131	-14 764	-139 712	-1 843	42	-137 911	-36 163	-20 735
3rd quarter	318 631	174 241	73 650	70 740	-423 115	-297 169	-57 979	-67 967	-14 599	-70 987	-1 416	-27	2 335	-33 165	4 884
4th quarter	313 475	170 879	75 558	67 038	-422 661	-303 272	-60 522	-58 867	-15 897	-70 987	-812	197	-70 372	-36 979	-23 705
2003															
1st quarter	316 991	173 423	73 068	70 500	-436 556	-310 042	-60 666	-65 848	-17 598	-82 375	83	53	-82 511	-22 716	-31 947
2nd quarter	319 380	174 438	72 428	72 514	-433 578	-310 279	-59 822	-63 477	-16 905	-158 245	-170	310	-158 385	-46 590	-32 734
3rd quarter	330 049	177 796	76 404	75 849	-444 630	-313 786	-63 389	-67 455	-16 961	-847	-611	483	-719	-40 689	-27 677
4th quarter	352 733	187 758	80 780	84 195	-462 697	-326 610	-66 398	-69 689	-17 747	-84 954	2 221	-309	-86 866	-39 899	-54 364
2004															
1st quarter	362 895	194 056	83 313	85 526	-486 179	-344 010	-69 507	-72 662	-22 554	-309 212	557	727	-310 496	-56 127	-30 045
2nd quarter	375 770	199 617	85 276	90 877	-521 646	-364 709	-71 573	-85 364	-20 895	-135 173	1 122	-2	-136 293	-53 196	-38 702
3rd quarter	384 648	204 340	85 349	94 959	-534 451	-373 143	-73 218	-88 090	-16 524	-144 528	429	484	-145 441	-38 774	-47 988
4th quarter	403 536	209 503	90 488	103 545	-568 283	-391 064	-76 013	-101 206	-21 609	-278 884	697	501	-280 082	-96 026	-29 814

[1] A minus sign indicates imports of goods or services or income payments.
[2] A minus sign indicates net unilateral transfers to foreigners.
[3] A minus sign indicates financial outflows or increases in U.S. official assets.

Table 19-12. U.S. International Transactions—Continued

(Millions of dollars, seasonally adjusted.)

Year and quarter	U.S.-owned assets abroad, net [3]—Continued / U.S. private assets, net—Continued / U.S. claims — On unaffiliated foreigners reported by U.S. nonbanking concerns	Reported by U.S. banks, not included elsewhere	Foreign-owned assets in the United States, net [4] — Total	Foreign official assets in the United States, net	Other foreign assets in the United States, net — Total	Direct invest-ment	U.S. Treasury securities and U.S. currency flows	U.S. securities other than U.S. Treasury securities	U.S. liabilities — To unaffiliated foreigners reported by U.S. nonbanking concerns	Reported by U.S. banks, not included elsewhere	Statistical discrep-ancy [5]	Balance on goods and services	Balance on current account
1990													
1st quarter	3 019	57 713	-22 824	-6 421	-16 403	15 774	1 709	1 311	12 904	-48 101	8 661	-23 034	-23 646
2nd quarter	-5 069	-16 022	41 215	6 207	35 008	13 773	6 257	2 114	6 713	6 151	15 356	-18 285	-19 524
3rd quarter	-15 514	-10 668	63 231	13 937	49 294	8 313	6 044	-2 874	16 838	20 973	1 857	-19 426	-21 537
4th quarter	-10 260	-18 644	59 949	20 186	39 763	10 635	2 256	1 041	8 678	17 153	-667	-20 113	-14 258
1991													
1st quarter	-40	13 552	8 347	5 569	2 778	4 076	9 539	5 023	-586	-15 274	-6 793	-12 978	9 957
2nd quarter	7 902	5 503	12 678	-4 913	17 591	13 378	15 661	14 872	-2 549	-23 771	-16 021	-6 344	2 525
3rd quarter	3 341	-4 469	33 236	3 854	29 382	-1 354	3 004	10 310	4 761	12 661	-9 364	-5 550	-4 186
4th quarter	-106	-15 196	56 549	12 879	43 670	7 072	6 022	4 939	-4 741	30 378	-12 659	-6 263	-5 401
1992													
1st quarter	7 562	11 689	31 079	20 988	10 091	2 086	1 986	4 569	5 689	-4 239	-13 280	-5 498	-6 234
2nd quarter	-6 620	7 687	50 304	20 879	29 425	5 916	11 331	10 467	3 954	-2 243	-22 004	-9 853	-11 890
3rd quarter	-3 737	6 823	35 469	-7 524	42 993	2 898	11 008	2 531	4 854	21 702	-8 600	-10 767	-13 168
4th quarter	2 408	-5 024	53 809	6 133	47 676	8 922	26 206	12 476	-924	996	-1 731	-13 092	-18 787
1993													
1st quarter	-6 130	28 325	25 099	10 937	14 162	8 060	16 363	9 694	-215	-19 740	11 927	-14 244	-14 777
2nd quarter	-725	7 461	59 038	17 466	41 572	11 386	5 608	15 205	6 531	2 842	7 634	-17 747	-20 679
3rd quarter	5 896	6 962	85 694	19 073	66 621	11 688	9 658	17 782	288	27 205	-11 185	-18 996	-21 302
4th quarter	1 725	-12 133	112 210	24 277	87 933	20 229	11 652	37 411	3 885	14 756	-3 750	-19 331	-28 058
1994													
1st quarter	-2 215	10 229	90 280	10 568	79 712	5 883	15 412	21 070	5 856	31 491	-25 401	-21 917	-24 981
2nd quarter	-20 966	-1 959	56 842	9 455	47 387	5 767	-798	12 352	4 269	25 797	18 424	-23 994	-28 578
3rd quarter	-960	184	81 934	19 358	62 576	13 709	10 361	13 389	-1 620	26 737	-17 982	-25 352	-31 608
4th quarter	-12 195	-12 654	76 933	202	76 731	20 762	32 699	10 160	-7 203	20 313	21 244	-27 229	-36 445
1995													
1st quarter	-2 631	-28 348	97 915	21 956	75 959	9 924	34 410	12 400	17 764	1 461	-1 535	-27 849	-31 434
2nd quarter	-24 580	-47 520	122 149	37 072	85 077	11 888	30 338	15 851	11 864	15 136	27 999	-29 324	-32 013
3rd quarter	13 729	4 489	116 366	39 302	77 064	16 764	37 194	26 218	13 493	-16 605	-41 441	-20 317	-26 977
4th quarter	-31 804	-3 729	102 132	11 550	90 582	19 200	1 902	22 780	16 516	30 184	43 175	-18 899	-23 147
1996													
1st quarter	-15 210	2 269	85 255	51 771	33 484	28 518	13 646	20 356	4 350	-33 386	22 794	-23 541	-27 440
2nd quarter	-22 000	643	101 405	13 503	87 902	16 184	29 514	24 686	15 259	2 259	-3 264	-25 465	-29 840
3rd quarter	-9 090	-33 777	144 109	23 020	121 089	15 257	37 116	29 719	28 925	3 072	-16 285	-30 683	-36 058
4th quarter	-40 033	-60 690	220 326	38 430	181 896	26 542	77 108	28 511	5 202	44 533	-15 426	-24 381	-31 435
1997													
1st quarter	-38 112	-65 125	173 005	27 763	145 242	28 626	32 537	38 490	25 055	20 534	15 997	-29 408	-36 058
2nd quarter	-9 885	-26 575	140 719	-6 019	146 738	23 150	38 750	45 651	6 461	32 726	-18 479	-28 424	-28 808
3rd quarter	-22 173	-24 243	167 223	23 474	143 749	17 865	42 709	52 544	25 550	5 081	-14 940	-24 921	-32 596
4th quarter	-51 590	-25 175	225 860	-26 182	252 042	35 960	41 221	24 724	59 452	90 685	-62 485	-29 973	-42 934
1998													
1st quarter	-7 822	-4 797	79 170	11 072	68 098	19 759	-5 789	63 237	39 833	-48 942	39 152	-34 907	-43 690
2nd quarter	-20 363	-28 187	155 055	-10 235	165 290	20 391	24 163	56 146	30 722	33 868	34 813	-41 091	-51 049
3rd quarter	-15 658	-28 329	75 963	-46 640	122 603	23 490	2 195	6 628	14 976	75 314	-44 374	-44 374	-58 465
4th quarter	5 639	25 741	113 381	25 900	87 481	115 405	18 634	30 304	-62 391	-20 471	29 376	-44 239	-60 328
1999													
1st quarter	-47 211	24 204	109 283	4 381	104 902	28 759	-10 887	49 157	51 307	-13 434	38 437	-53 361	-62 901
2nd quarter	-27 021	-36 300	247 860	-757	248 617	140 759	-8 355	70 205	16 928	29 080	6 470	-63 045	-71 713
3rd quarter	-13 663	-7 240	156 858	12 625	144 233	50 758	8 382	86 202	-8 777	7 668	47 062	-71 007	-80 241
4th quarter	-9 809	-51 349	226 210	27 294	198 916	69 169	-11 230	93 270	16 789	30 918	-23 359	-75 872	-84 964
2000													
1st quarter	-79 800	-59 649	248 698	22 542	226 156	52 094	-17 860	129 306	72 433	-9 817	57 480	-89 524	-98 349
2nd quarter	-25 287	6 736	247 559	6 952	240 607	91 669	-21 894	88 189	28 796	53 847	-41 033	-90 252	-98 987
3rd quarter	-14 121	1 487	246 185	11 354	234 831	79 979	-12 656	122 138	16 914	28 456	-53 462	-96 660	-107 606
4th quarter	-19 582	-81 956	304 456	1 910	302 546	97 534	-12 258	120 256	52 529	44 485	-33 193	-101 127	-110 213
2001													
1st quarter	-46 769	-108 956	332 155	21 333	310 822	59 145	-15 348	129 474	112 097	25 454	-8 127	-97 276	-107 533
2nd quarter	-7 507	-86	207 866	-19 965	227 831	59 338	-9 144	108 537	-173	69 273	-22 928	-88 652	-97 923
3rd quarter	1 824	67 204	22 936	15 653	7 283	13 783	205	60 748	-23 171	-44 282	37 481	-89 517	-92 942
4th quarter	43 932	-93 868	219 902	11 038	208 864	34 755	33 692	95 126	-22 643	67 934	-16 446	-87 349	-90 556
2002													
1st quarter	-27 798	-399	174 113	12 801	161 312	24 485	14 852	73 750	57 788	-9 563	20 093	-93 166	-109 044
2nd quarter	-13 680	-67 333	231 296	53 312	177 984	7 194	26 013	99 689	17 805	27 283	27 975	-103 287	-119 226
3rd quarter	-7 443	38 059	161 785	18 328	143 457	13 929	56 616	43 282	7 515	22 115	-43 195	-107 257	-119 083
4th quarter	-1 101	-8 587	230 618	31 504	199 114	38 763	24 435	66 578	12 763	56 575	-34 131	-117 357	-125 083
2003													
1st quarter	1 757	-29 605	242 159	50 622	191 537	37 193	12 030	52 209	68 460	21 645	-22 171	-124 217	-137 163
2nd quarter	-15 829	-63 232	220 780	66 889	153 891	-5 420	51 175	81 187	15 129	11 820	70 191	-123 235	-131 103
3rd quarter	21 261	46 386	130 592	64 595	65 997	-1 514	37 906	15 354	9 137	5 114	2 661	-122 975	-131 542
4th quarter	-26 040	33 437	271 239	96 169	175 070	33 703	6 984	71 955	3 800	58 628	-58 190	-124 470	-127 711
2004													
1st quarter	-55 101	-169 223	438 930	147 627	291 303	23 627	30 176	47 862	42 419	147 219	16 577	-136 148	-145 838
2nd quarter	-4 969	-39 426	314 152	79 944	234 208	33 007	73 592	87 270	2 840	37 499	-11 809	-151 389	-166 771
3rd quarter	-3 501	-55 178	260 132	71 285	188 847	36 844	355	86 577	13 353	51 718	51 646	-156 672	-166 327
4th quarter	-56 446	-97 796	437 006	88 953	348 053	39 683	13 644	159 784	34 638	100 304	28 716	-167 086	-186 356

[3] A minus sign indicates financial outflows or increases in U.S. official assets.
[4] A minus sign indicates financial outflows or decreases in foreign official assets in the United States.
[5] Sum of credits and debits with the sign reversed.

Table 19-13. Productivity and Related Data

(1992 = 100, seasonally adjusted.)

Year and quarter	Business sector								Nonfarm business sector							
	Output per hour of all persons	Output	Hours of all persons	Compensation per hour	Real compensation per hour	Unit labor costs	Unit nonlabor payments	Implicit price deflator	Output per hour of all persons	Output	Hours of all persons	Compensation per hour	Real compensation per hour	Unit labor costs	Unit nonlabor payments	Implicit price deflator
1947	32.2	20.4	63.4	7.0	40.7	21.8	18.6	20.6	37.0	20.1	54.2	7.5	43.3	20.2	17.8	19.3
1948	33.7	21.5	63.8	7.6	40.9	22.6	20.6	21.8	38.0	20.9	55.1	8.1	43.6	21.3	19.4	20.6
1949	34.5	21.3	61.8	7.7	42.0	22.4	20.4	21.6	39.3	20.8	53.0	8.3	45.4	21.2	20.0	20.8
1947																
1st quarter	32.1	20.2	63.1	6.8	40.6	21.2	17.9	20.0	36.5	19.7	54.0	7.2	43.2	19.9	16.7	18.7
2nd quarter	32.3	20.3	63.0	7.0	41.0	21.5	18.0	20.2	37.4	20.2	54.0	7.4	43.3	19.7	17.7	19.0
3rd quarter	32.1	20.4	63.5	7.0	40.4	21.9	18.8	20.7	36.3	19.7	54.2	7.5	43.3	20.7	18.2	19.8
4th quarter	32.4	20.7	63.9	7.3	40.8	22.4	19.4	21.3	37.8	20.7	54.7	7.7	43.2	20.4	18.6	19.7
1948																
1st quarter	33.2	21.1	63.6	7.4	40.5	22.3	20.2	21.5	37.9	20.9	55.0	7.9	43.4	20.8	18.8	20.1
2nd quarter	33.9	21.6	63.6	7.5	40.4	22.1	21.0	21.7	37.9	20.9	55.0	8.0	43.3	21.2	19.2	20.4
3rd quarter	33.8	21.7	64.2	7.7	40.8	22.8	20.9	22.1	38.0	21.0	55.4	8.2	43.5	21.6	19.5	20.8
4th quarter	34.0	21.7	63.8	7.9	42.2	23.1	20.3	22.1	38.2	21.0	54.9	8.3	44.5	21.7	20.0	21.1
1949																
1st quarter	33.9	21.3	62.9	7.7	41.7	22.8	20.5	21.9	38.6	20.8	54.0	8.3	45.1	21.6	19.8	21.0
2nd quarter	34.0	21.2	62.4	7.6	41.2	22.3	20.5	21.6	39.0	20.7	53.1	8.3	45.0	21.3	19.8	20.8
3rd quarter	35.0	21.5	61.3	7.7	42.2	22.0	20.6	21.5	39.9	21.0	52.5	8.4	45.6	20.9	20.3	20.7
4th quarter	35.1	21.2	60.6	7.8	42.8	22.3	20.1	21.5	39.7	20.7	52.3	8.4	45.7	21.1	19.9	20.6
1950																
1st quarter	36.7	22.3	60.7	8.1	44.4	22.0	20.3	21.4	41.0	21.6	52.7	8.6	47.0	20.9	20.4	20.7
2nd quarter	37.0	23.0	62.1	8.2	44.5	22.0	20.7	21.5	41.5	22.4	54.0	8.7	47.5	21.0	20.4	20.8
3rd quarter	37.7	24.0	63.7	8.3	44.4	22.0	22.0	22.0	42.5	23.6	55.7	8.9	47.6	20.9	21.1	21.0
4th quarter	37.9	24.3	64.1	8.5	44.5	22.4	22.7	22.5	42.5	23.9	56.2	9.1	47.9	21.5	21.4	21.4
1951																
1st quarter	37.8	24.5	64.7	8.8	44.2	23.2	23.6	23.3	42.6	24.3	57.2	9.4	47.2	22.0	22.2	22.1
2nd quarter	38.0	24.8	65.1	9.0	44.9	23.7	23.4	23.6	42.5	24.5	57.6	9.5	47.6	22.5	22.1	22.3
3rd quarter	39.2	25.2	64.3	9.2	45.8	23.4	23.8	23.5	43.5	24.8	57.0	9.7	48.4	22.3	22.8	22.5
4th quarter	39.0	25.2	64.5	9.2	45.5	23.7	24.0	23.8	43.6	24.9	57.1	9.8	48.3	22.6	22.7	22.6
1952																
1st quarter	39.1	25.4	64.8	9.3	45.8	23.9	23.5	23.7	43.7	25.1	57.4	10.0	48.8	22.8	22.4	22.7
2nd quarter	39.5	25.3	64.1	9.5	46.6	24.1	23.0	23.7	43.7	25.0	57.2	10.0	49.1	23.0	22.1	22.6
3rd quarter	39.6	25.5	64.3	9.7	46.9	24.4	23.2	24.0	43.5	25.1	57.6	10.1	49.2	23.3	22.2	22.9
4th quarter	40.2	26.5	65.9	9.9	47.9	24.6	23.0	24.0	44.3	26.2	59.2	10.4	50.4	23.5	22.4	23.1
1953																
1st quarter	40.8	27.0	66.2	10.1	48.9	24.7	22.8	24.0	44.6	26.7	59.8	10.5	51.1	23.6	22.4	23.1
2nd quarter	41.1	27.2	66.1	10.2	49.3	24.7	22.7	24.0	44.8	26.8	59.9	10.7	51.6	23.8	22.3	23.3
3rd quarter	41.1	27.0	65.6	10.3	49.8	25.1	22.4	24.1	45.0	26.7	59.3	10.8	51.9	23.9	22.3	23.3
4th quarter	41.0	26.5	64.5	10.3	49.6	25.1	22.4	24.1	44.8	26.1	58.3	10.9	52.3	24.2	21.8	23.4
1954																
1st quarter	41.0	26.3	64.1	10.4	49.8	25.3	22.3	24.2	44.9	25.8	57.6	11.0	52.7	24.4	21.8	23.4
2nd quarter	41.6	26.3	63.2	10.5	50.7	25.3	22.1	24.1	45.2	25.8	57.1	11.0	52.8	24.3	22.1	23.5
3rd quarter	42.2	26.6	63.0	10.6	50.9	25.0	22.7	24.2	46.0	26.2	56.9	11.1	53.4	24.1	22.4	23.5
4th quarter	42.8	27.1	63.4	10.7	51.8	25.0	22.8	24.2	46.5	26.8	57.6	11.2	54.0	24.0	22.8	23.6
1955																
1st quarter	43.5	28.1	64.6	10.7	51.5	24.5	23.9	24.3	47.4	27.8	58.5	11.3	54.4	23.7	23.6	23.7
2nd quarter	43.8	28.6	65.2	10.8	52.3	24.7	23.8	24.3	47.5	28.2	59.3	11.4	55.0	23.9	23.5	23.8
3rd quarter	43.7	29.0	66.2	10.8	52.3	24.7	24.2	24.5	47.7	28.6	59.9	11.5	55.7	24.1	23.8	24.0
4th quarter	43.4	29.1	67.0	10.9	52.8	25.2	24.1	24.8	47.5	28.8	60.7	11.6	56.2	24.5	23.8	24.2
1956																
1st quarter	43.3	28.9	66.8	11.2	54.1	25.9	23.5	25.0	46.9	28.6	61.0	11.8	57.0	25.2	23.2	24.5
2nd quarter	43.5	29.1	67.0	11.5	54.9	26.3	23.1	25.1	47.1	28.8	61.2	12.1	57.8	25.6	22.9	24.6
3rd quarter	43.5	29.0	66.7	11.6	54.9	26.6	23.5	25.5	47.1	28.7	60.9	12.2	58.0	26.0	23.1	24.9
4th quarter	44.4	29.5	66.5	11.8	55.6	26.7	23.7	25.6	47.5	29.1	61.2	12.4	58.5	26.2	23.2	25.1
1957																
1st quarter	44.6	29.7	66.5	12.1	56.3	27.0	24.1	25.9	48.1	29.5	61.3	12.6	58.9	26.3	23.9	25.4
2nd quarter	44.7	29.5	66.1	12.2	56.4	27.3	24.1	26.1	47.9	29.3	61.2	12.8	59.0	26.6	23.7	25.5
3rd quarter	45.2	29.8	66.1	12.3	56.4	27.2	24.5	26.2	48.6	29.6	60.9	12.9	59.2	26.6	24.1	25.6
4th quarter	45.6	29.5	64.5	12.5	57.1	27.4	24.1	26.2	48.8	29.1	59.6	13.1	59.7	26.8	23.8	25.7
1958																
1st quarter	45.2	28.4	62.8	12.6	57.0	28.0	24.0	26.5	48.0	28.0	58.3	13.1	59.2	27.4	23.2	25.8
2nd quarter	45.9	28.5	62.3	12.7	56.7	27.6	24.5	26.5	48.9	28.1	57.4	13.3	59.3	27.1	23.8	25.9
3rd quarter	46.7	29.3	62.7	12.9	57.8	27.6	25.0	26.6	49.9	29.0	58.1	13.4	60.2	26.9	24.4	26.0
4th quarter	47.2	30.1	63.7	13.0	58.3	27.6	25.5	26.8	50.7	29.9	59.0	13.6	60.8	26.8	25.0	26.1
1959																
1st quarter	47.6	30.8	64.7	13.2	58.9	27.7	25.3	26.8	50.8	30.5	60.1	13.7	61.2	27.0	25.0	26.2
2nd quarter	47.9	31.7	66.2	13.2	58.9	27.6	25.4	26.8	51.5	31.5	61.3	13.8	61.7	26.9	25.1	26.2
3rd quarter	48.2	31.6	65.6	13.4	59.4	27.8	25.2	26.8	51.5	31.4	61.1	13.9	61.8	27.1	25.0	26.3
4th quarter	48.3	31.7	65.5	13.6	59.8	28.1	24.9	26.9	51.4	31.4	61.1	14.1	62.0	27.4	24.8	26.4
1960																
1st quarter	49.7	32.4	65.3	13.9	61.3	28.0	25.3	27.0	52.5	32.3	61.5	14.4	63.2	27.3	25.0	26.5
2nd quarter	48.7	32.1	66.0	13.9	60.7	28.5	24.8	27.1	51.8	31.9	61.6	14.4	63.2	27.9	24.2	26.5
3rd quarter	48.8	32.1	65.9	13.8	60.6	28.4	25.0	27.1	51.9	31.8	61.2	14.5	63.6	28.0	24.4	26.6
4th quarter	48.4	31.5	65.1	14.0	60.8	28.9	24.4	27.2	51.2	31.1	60.7	14.6	63.4	28.5	23.8	26.7

Table 19-13. Productivity and Related Data—Continued

(1992 = 100, seasonally adjusted.)

Year and quarter	Nonfinancial corporations					Unit costs					Manufacturing					
	Output per hour of all employees	Output	Employee hours	Compensation per hour	Real compensation per hour	Total	Labor costs	Nonlabor costs	Unit profits	Implicit price deflator	Output per hour of all persons	Output	Hours of all persons	Compensation per hour	Real compensation per hour	Unit labor costs
1947	...	...	...	...	...	...	...	...	...	...	...	...	...	...	...	...
1948	...	...	...	...	...	...	...	...	...	...	...	...	...	...	...	...
1949	...	...	...	...	...	...	...	...	...	...	...	...	...	...	...	...
1947																
1st quarter	...	...	...	...	...	...	...	...	...	...	...	...	...	...	...	...
2nd quarter	...	...	...	...	...	...	...	...	...	...	...	...	...	...	...	...
3rd quarter	...	...	...	...	...	...	...	...	...	...	...	...	...	...	...	...
4th quarter	...	...	...	...	...	...	...	...	...	...	...	...	...	...	...	...
1948																
1st quarter	...	...	...	...	...	...	...	...	...	...	...	...	...	...	...	...
2nd quarter	...	...	...	...	...	...	...	...	...	...	...	...	...	...	...	...
3rd quarter	...	...	...	...	...	...	...	...	...	...	...	...	...	...	...	...
4th quarter	...	...	...	...	...	...	...	...	...	...	...	...	...	...	...	...
1949																
1st quarter	...	...	...	...	...	...	...	...	...	...	...	...	...	...	...	...
2nd quarter	...	...	...	...	...	...	...	...	...	...	...	...	...	...	...	...
3rd quarter	...	...	...	...	...	...	...	...	...	...	...	...	...	...	...	...
4th quarter	...	...	...	...	...	...	...	...	...	...	...	...	...	...	...	...
1950																
1st quarter	...	...	...	...	...	...	...	...	...	...	...	...	...	...	...	...
2nd quarter	...	...	...	...	...	...	...	...	...	...	...	...	...	...	...	...
3rd quarter	...	...	...	...	...	...	...	...	...	...	...	...	...	...	...	...
4th quarter	...	...	...	...	...	...	...	...	...	...	...	...	...	...	...	...
1951																
1st quarter	...	...	...	...	...	...	...	...	...	...	...	...	...	...	...	...
2nd quarter	...	...	...	...	...	...	...	...	...	...	...	...	...	...	...	...
3rd quarter	...	...	...	...	...	...	...	...	...	...	...	...	...	...	...	...
4th quarter	...	...	...	...	...	...	...	...	...	...	...	...	...	...	...	...
1952																
1st quarter	...	...	...	...	...	...	...	...	...	...	...	...	...	...	...	...
2nd quarter	...	...	...	...	...	...	...	...	...	...	...	...	...	...	...	...
3rd quarter	...	...	...	...	...	...	...	...	...	...	...	...	...	...	...	...
4th quarter	...	...	...	...	...	...	...	...	...	...	...	...	...	...	...	...
1953																
1st quarter	...	...	...	...	...	...	...	...	...	...	...	...	...	...	...	...
2nd quarter	...	...	...	...	...	...	...	...	...	...	...	...	...	...	...	...
3rd quarter	...	...	...	...	...	...	...	...	...	...	...	...	...	...	...	...
4th quarter	...	...	...	...	...	...	...	...	...	...	...	...	...	...	...	...
1954																
1st quarter	...	...	...	...	...	...	...	...	...	...	...	...	...	...	...	...
2nd quarter	...	...	...	...	...	...	...	...	...	...	...	...	...	...	...	...
3rd quarter	...	...	...	...	...	...	...	...	...	...	...	...	...	...	...	...
4th quarter	...	...	...	...	...	...	...	...	...	...	...	...	...	...	...	...
1955																
1st quarter	...	...	...	...	...	...	...	...	...	...	...	...	...	...	...	...
2nd quarter	...	...	...	...	...	...	...	...	...	...	...	...	...	...	...	...
3rd quarter	...	...	...	...	...	...	...	...	...	...	...	...	...	...	...	...
4th quarter	...	...	...	...	...	...	...	...	...	...	...	...	...	...	...	...
1956																
1st quarter	...	...	...	...	...	...	...	...	...	...	...	...	...	...	...	...
2nd quarter	...	...	...	...	...	...	...	...	...	...	...	...	...	...	...	...
3rd quarter	...	...	...	...	...	...	...	...	...	...	...	...	...	...	...	...
4th quarter	...	...	...	...	...	...	...	...	...	...	...	...	...	...	...	...
1957																
1st quarter	...	...	...	...	...	...	...	...	...	...	...	...	...	...	...	...
2nd quarter	...	...	...	...	...	...	...	...	...	...	...	...	...	...	...	...
3rd quarter	...	...	...	...	...	...	...	...	...	...	...	...	...	...	...	...
4th quarter	...	...	...	...	...	...	...	...	...	...	...	...	...	...	...	...
1958																
1st quarter	51.5	24.8	48.2	14.8	66.7	27.4	28.7	23.7	42.8	28.7	...	...	...	...	...	...
2nd quarter	52.2	24.7	47.3	14.9	66.6	27.3	28.5	24.1	43.7	28.8	...	...	...	...	...	...
3rd quarter	53.2	25.5	47.9	15.1	67.6	27.1	28.4	23.6	48.1	29.0	...	...	...	...	...	...
4th quarter	54.3	26.5	48.8	15.3	68.2	26.7	28.1	22.8	53.8	29.1	...	...	...	...	...	...
1959																
1st quarter	54.8	27.4	50.1	15.3	68.5	26.4	28.0	22.1	56.9	29.1	...	...	...	...	...	...
2nd quarter	55.9	28.7	51.4	15.5	69.2	26.1	27.8	21.5	60.1	29.1	...	...	...	...	...	...
3rd quarter	55.1	28.1	51.1	15.6	69.3	26.8	28.4	22.5	53.6	29.2	...	...	...	...	...	...
4th quarter	55.5	28.4	51.2	15.8	69.7	27.0	28.4	22.9	52.6	29.3	...	...	...	...	...	...
1960																
1st quarter	56.5	29.4	52.1	16.1	70.8	26.8	28.4	22.5	54.8	29.3	...	...	...	...	...	...
2nd quarter	55.9	29.1	52.1	16.2	70.8	27.3	28.9	23.1	50.1	29.4	...	...	...	...	...	...
3rd quarter	56.1	29.1	51.8	16.2	70.9	27.4	28.9	23.6	49.2	29.4	...	...	...	...	...	...
4th quarter	56.3	28.8	51.1	16.3	70.9	27.7	29.0	24.1	46.6	29.4	...	...	...	...	...	...

. . . = Not available.

Table 19-13. Productivity and Related Data—Continued

(1992 = 100, seasonally adjusted.)

Year and quarter	Business sector								Nonfarm business sector							
	Output per hour of all persons	Output	Hours of all persons	Compensation per hour	Real compensation per hour	Unit labor costs	Unit nonlabor payments	Implicit price deflator	Output per hour of all persons	Output	Hours of all persons	Compensation per hour	Real compensation per hour	Unit labor costs	Unit nonlabor payments	Implicit price deflator
1961																
1st quarter	48.9	31.7	64.8	14.1	61.2	28.8	24.5	27.2	51.9	31.3	60.3	14.7	63.9	28.4	24.0	26.8
2nd quarter	50.6	32.4	64.0	14.4	62.6	28.5	25.2	27.3	53.3	32.1	60.2	14.9	64.8	28.0	24.8	26.8
3rd quarter	51.1	33.0	64.5	14.5	62.8	28.4	25.5	27.3	54.1	32.7	60.5	15.0	65.0	27.8	25.2	26.8
4th quarter	51.7	33.6	65.1	14.7	63.4	28.4	25.7	27.4	54.6	33.5	61.3	15.1	65.4	27.7	25.3	26.8
1962																
1st quarter	52.2	34.3	65.8	14.8	63.8	28.4	26.1	27.5	55.5	34.2	61.5	15.4	66.2	27.7	25.7	27.0
2nd quarter	52.5	34.7	66.1	15.0	64.3	28.6	25.8	27.6	55.4	34.5	62.3	15.5	66.4	27.9	25.6	27.1
3rd quarter	53.2	35.0	65.8	15.1	64.7	28.4	26.3	27.6	56.1	34.9	62.1	15.6	66.6	27.8	26.0	27.1
4th quarter	53.7	35.1	65.3	15.3	65.3	28.5	26.1	27.6	56.5	34.9	61.7	15.7	67.1	27.9	25.9	27.1
1963																
1st quarter	54.1	35.6	65.8	15.4	65.4	28.5	26.2	27.7	56.8	35.3	62.1	15.9	67.5	28.0	25.9	27.2
2nd quarter	54.4	36.1	66.2	15.5	65.6	28.4	26.4	27.7	57.4	35.9	62.5	16.0	67.8	27.8	26.1	27.2
3rd quarter	55.6	36.8	66.2	15.7	66.2	28.3	26.9	27.7	58.6	36.7	62.7	16.1	68.0	27.6	26.7	27.2
4th quarter	55.7	37.1	66.6	15.9	66.7	28.5	27.0	27.9	58.6	37.0	63.2	16.3	68.6	27.9	26.6	27.4
1964																
1st quarter	56.5	38.1	67.4	16.0	66.9	28.3	27.4	27.9	59.2	38.1	64.3	16.3	68.3	27.6	27.2	27.4
2nd quarter	56.6	38.5	68.0	16.1	67.3	28.4	27.3	28.0	59.6	38.5	64.6	16.5	69.0	27.7	27.3	27.5
3rd quarter	57.2	39.1	68.4	16.3	68.0	28.5	27.4	28.1	60.0	39.1	65.0	16.7	69.7	27.8	27.4	27.7
4th quarter	56.9	39.1	68.8	16.4	68.2	28.9	27.1	28.2	59.5	39.0	65.7	16.8	69.9	28.3	26.8	27.8
1965																
1st quarter	57.8	40.3	69.6	16.6	68.6	28.7	27.8	28.4	60.3	40.2	66.7	16.9	70.0	28.0	27.6	27.9
2nd quarter	57.9	40.8	70.5	16.7	68.5	28.8	27.9	28.5	60.6	40.8	67.4	17.0	70.0	28.1	27.7	27.9
3rd quarter	59.3	41.7	70.4	16.9	69.2	28.5	28.6	28.5	61.7	41.7	67.5	17.2	70.5	27.9	28.3	28.0
4th quarter	60.2	42.9	71.2	17.1	69.7	28.3	29.1	28.6	62.9	42.9	68.2	17.4	71.2	27.7	28.7	28.1
1966																
1st quarter	61.3	44.0	71.9	17.5	70.7	28.5	29.3	28.8	63.7	44.1	69.1	17.8	71.7	27.9	28.8	28.2
2nd quarter	61.0	44.1	72.4	17.8	71.3	29.2	28.8	29.0	63.3	44.2	69.8	18.0	72.2	28.5	28.5	28.5
3rd quarter	61.0	44.3	72.5	18.1	71.8	29.6	28.8	29.3	63.4	44.5	70.1	18.3	72.6	28.8	28.5	28.7
4th quarter	61.5	44.5	72.3	18.4	72.4	29.9	29.2	29.6	63.8	44.7	70.0	18.5	73.0	29.0	29.1	29.1
1967																
1st quarter	62.1	44.9	72.3	18.5	72.8	29.8	29.5	29.7	64.4	45.0	69.9	18.8	73.8	29.2	29.2	29.2
2nd quarter	62.6	44.8	71.6	18.9	73.7	30.1	29.3	29.8	64.6	44.8	69.4	19.1	74.5	29.6	29.1	29.4
3rd quarter	62.6	45.1	72.0	19.1	73.8	30.5	29.5	30.1	64.8	45.1	69.7	19.4	74.8	29.9	29.2	29.6
4th quarter	62.8	45.4	72.4	19.3	73.9	30.8	29.7	30.4	65.0	45.5	70.0	19.6	75.1	30.2	29.4	29.9
1968																
1st quarter	64.2	46.5	72.4	19.9	75.4	31.0	30.2	30.7	66.5	46.6	70.1	20.2	76.4	30.4	30.0	30.2
2nd quarter	64.9	47.3	73.0	20.3	76.0	31.3	30.7	31.0	67.1	47.5	70.8	20.5	77.0	30.6	30.5	30.6
3rd quarter	64.9	47.6	73.4	20.7	76.5	31.8	30.4	31.3	67.0	47.8	71.3	20.9	77.2	31.1	30.2	30.8
4th quarter	64.8	47.8	73.8	21.1	77.0	32.5	30.4	31.7	66.9	48.0	71.7	21.3	77.8	31.8	30.2	31.2
1969																
1st quarter	65.0	48.7	74.9	21.2	76.4	32.6	31.2	32.1	67.5	48.9	72.4	21.6	77.9	32.0	30.9	31.6
2nd quarter	64.9	48.7	75.0	21.7	77.2	33.4	30.9	32.5	66.9	48.9	73.1	21.9	77.9	32.7	30.5	31.9
3rd quarter	65.1	49.0	75.3	22.2	77.7	34.1	30.7	32.8	66.9	49.1	73.4	22.3	78.2	33.3	30.5	32.3
4th quarter	64.9	48.6	74.9	22.6	78.2	34.9	30.4	33.2	66.6	48.8	73.2	22.7	78.5	34.1	30.0	32.6
1970																
1st quarter	65.2	48.6	74.5	23.1	78.5	35.4	30.4	33.5	66.8	48.7	72.9	23.2	78.7	34.7	30.0	33.0
2nd quarter	66.0	48.7	73.8	23.4	78.4	35.4	31.5	34.0	67.9	48.8	71.9	23.6	78.9	34.7	31.3	33.4
3rd quarter	67.2	49.2	73.3	23.8	79.0	35.5	32.0	34.2	68.9	49.3	71.6	24.0	79.5	34.7	31.6	33.6
4th quarter	66.8	48.5	72.6	24.1	78.9	36.1	32.0	34.6	68.3	48.5	71.0	24.2	79.2	35.4	31.8	34.1
1971																
1st quarter	68.7	50.1	72.9	24.6	79.7	35.8	33.6	35.0	70.4	50.2	71.4	24.7	80.1	35.1	33.3	34.4
2nd quarter	68.8	50.4	73.4	24.9	79.9	36.2	34.1	35.4	70.6	50.5	71.6	25.1	80.6	35.5	33.7	34.9
3rd quarter	69.6	50.9	73.2	25.3	80.6	36.4	34.6	35.7	71.2	51.0	71.6	25.5	81.0	35.7	34.3	35.2
4th quarter	69.0	51.0	73.9	25.5	80.6	37.0	34.2	35.9	70.6	51.1	72.4	25.7	81.0	36.3	33.7	35.4
1972																
1st quarter	69.7	52.2	74.9	26.1	81.8	37.5	34.5	36.4	71.6	52.5	73.2	26.3	82.3	36.7	34.2	35.8
2nd quarter	71.4	53.7	75.3	26.4	82.3	37.1	35.7	36.5	73.1	53.9	73.8	26.6	82.9	36.4	35.1	35.9
3rd quarter	71.6	54.3	75.8	26.7	82.6	37.4	36.1	36.9	73.5	54.5	74.2	27.0	83.4	36.7	35.2	36.2
4th quarter	72.3	55.3	76.5	27.3	83.6	37.8	36.4	37.3	74.1	55.5	75.0	27.6	84.2	37.2	35.0	36.4
1973																
1st quarter	73.7	57.1	77.5	28.1	84.7	38.2	36.8	37.7	75.8	57.6	76.1	28.3	85.1	37.3	35.4	36.6
2nd quarter	73.9	57.9	78.4	28.6	84.2	38.7	37.5	38.2	75.8	58.3	76.9	28.7	84.7	37.9	35.5	37.0
3rd quarter	72.9	57.5	78.8	29.2	84.3	40.0	37.4	39.0	75.1	58.2	77.4	29.3	84.6	39.0	34.9	37.5
4th quarter	73.2	58.1	79.3	29.8	83.9	40.6	38.4	39.8	74.7	58.1	77.8	29.9	84.4	40.1	35.4	38.4
1974																
1st quarter	72.2	57.2	79.3	30.3	83.0	42.0	38.4	40.6	74.6	57.7	77.5	30.6	83.9	41.1	35.9	39.2
2nd quarter	72.5	57.4	79.1	31.3	83.4	43.1	39.2	41.7	74.4	57.8	77.7	31.4	83.8	42.3	37.7	40.6
3rd quarter	71.9	56.6	78.7	32.3	83.6	44.9	39.9	43.0	73.6	57.0	77.4	32.3	83.9	43.9	38.3	41.9
4th quarter	72.5	56.2	77.5	33.0	83.0	45.5	42.4	44.3	74.3	56.6	76.1	33.2	83.5	44.6	40.5	43.1
1975																
1st quarter	73.5	55.2	75.1	34.0	83.8	46.3	44.0	45.4	74.9	55.2	73.7	34.1	84.0	45.5	42.8	44.5
2nd quarter	74.7	55.6	74.5	34.7	84.4	46.4	45.5	46.1	76.1	55.6	73.0	34.8	84.7	45.7	44.4	45.2
3rd quarter	75.4	56.7	75.2	35.2	83.9	46.6	47.5	47.0	76.9	56.7	73.7	35.4	84.5	46.0	45.9	46.0
4th quarter	75.6	57.6	76.3	35.9	84.2	47.6	48.0	47.7	76.9	57.7	75.0	36.1	84.5	46.9	46.3	46.7

Table 19-13. Productivity and Related Data—Continued

(1992 = 100, seasonally adjusted.)

Year and quarter	Output per hour of all employees	Output	Employee hours	Compensation per hour	Real compensation per hour	Unit costs Total	Unit costs Labor costs	Unit costs Nonlabor costs	Unit profits	Implicit price deflator	Output per hour of all persons	Output	Hours of all persons	Compensation per hour	Real compensation per hour	Unit labor costs
1961																
1st quarter	56.4	28.5	50.6	16.4	71.3	27.9	29.1	24.5	45.5	29.5	...	...	...	...	...	...
2nd quarter	57.8	29.4	50.8	16.6	72.3	27.5	28.8	23.9	49.8	29.5	...	...	...	...	...	...
3rd quarter	58.3	30.0	51.4	16.8	72.6	27.4	28.8	23.6	51.3	29.5	...	...	...	...	...	...
4th quarter	59.2	30.9	52.2	17.0	73.2	27.2	28.7	23.2	54.1	29.6	...	...	...	...	...	...
1962																
1st quarter	59.9	31.5	52.6	17.2	73.8	27.2	28.6	23.1	55.6	29.7	...	...	...	...	...	...
2nd quarter	60.0	32.0	53.4	17.3	74.1	27.3	28.8	23.3	53.4	29.7	...	...	...	...	...	...
3rd quarter	60.5	32.4	53.6	17.4	74.4	27.4	28.8	23.5	53.9	29.7	...	...	...	...	...	...
4th quarter	61.3	32.9	53.6	17.6	75.0	27.3	28.7	23.6	55.1	29.8	...	...	...	...	...	...
1963																
1st quarter	61.6	33.2	53.9	17.7	75.0	27.3	28.7	23.6	54.9	29.8	...	...	...	...	...	...
2nd quarter	62.3	34.0	54.5	17.8	75.4	27.1	28.5	23.4	57.5	29.8	...	...	...	...	...	...
3rd quarter	62.9	34.4	54.7	18.0	75.7	27.1	28.6	23.3	58.0	29.9	...	...	...	...	...	...
4th quarter	63.3	34.8	55.0	18.2	76.4	27.2	28.7	23.3	58.7	30.1	...	...	...	...	...	...
1964																
1st quarter	63.1	35.7	56.5	18.0	75.3	27.0	28.5	23.1	60.8	30.1	...	...	...	...	...	...
2nd quarter	63.4	36.2	57.1	18.2	75.9	27.2	28.6	23.2	59.9	30.1	...	...	...	...	...	...
3rd quarter	64.0	37.0	57.7	18.4	76.5	27.2	28.7	23.2	59.6	30.1	...	...	...	...	...	...
4th quarter	63.7	37.2	58.4	18.4	76.6	27.5	29.0	23.6	58.5	30.3	...	...	...	...	...	...
1965																
1st quarter	64.6	38.5	59.5	18.5	76.7	27.2	28.7	23.2	63.5	30.4	...	...	...	...	...	...
2nd quarter	64.7	39.0	60.4	18.6	76.5	27.3	28.8	23.2	64.1	30.6	...	...	...	...	...	...
3rd quarter	65.2	39.8	61.0	18.8	77.1	27.3	28.9	23.2	63.9	30.6	...	...	...	...	...	...
4th quarter	65.8	40.8	62.0	19.1	77.9	27.4	29.0	23.0	64.9	30.7	...	...	...	...	...	...
1966																
1st quarter	66.2	41.7	63.0	19.3	78.0	27.5	29.2	23.0	65.9	30.9	...	...	...	...	...	...
2nd quarter	66.1	42.2	63.8	19.6	78.7	28.0	29.7	23.2	64.2	31.2	...	...	...	...	...	...
3rd quarter	66.1	42.5	64.3	20.0	79.4	28.4	30.2	23.5	62.0	31.4	...	...	...	...	...	...
4th quarter	66.4	42.9	64.6	20.3	79.9	28.7	30.6	23.7	62.4	31.7	...	...	...	...	...	...
1967																
1st quarter	66.4	42.8	64.5	20.5	80.5	29.1	30.9	24.1	60.3	31.8	...	...	...	...	...	...
2nd quarter	67.1	43.0	64.1	20.8	81.2	29.2	31.0	24.5	59.3	31.9	...	...	...	...	...	...
3rd quarter	67.3	43.4	64.6	21.1	81.4	29.6	31.3	24.9	59.3	32.2	...	...	...	...	...	...
4th quarter	67.8	44.1	65.1	21.3	81.6	29.8	31.5	25.3	60.8	32.6	...	...	...	...	...	...
1968																
1st quarter	68.7	44.9	65.4	21.9	83.0	30.2	31.9	25.7	59.7	32.9	...	...	...	...	...	...
2nd quarter	69.4	45.9	66.1	22.3	83.6	30.5	32.1	26.0	60.8	33.2	...	...	...	...	...	...
3rd quarter	69.8	46.6	66.7	22.7	83.8	30.8	32.5	26.4	59.7	33.4	...	...	...	...	...	...
4th quarter	70.0	47.1	67.3	23.1	84.5	31.4	33.0	26.9	59.8	33.9	...	...	...	...	...	...
1969																
1st quarter	69.7	47.5	68.2	23.3	84.3	31.9	33.5	27.6	58.3	34.3	...	...	...	...	...	...
2nd quarter	69.5	47.9	68.9	23.8	84.6	32.6	34.2	28.2	55.7	34.6	...	...	...	...	...	...
3rd quarter	69.5	48.2	69.4	24.3	85.1	33.3	34.9	28.8	53.1	35.0	...	...	...	...	...	...
4th quarter	69.2	48.0	69.4	24.7	85.5	34.1	35.8	29.7	49.2	35.5	...	...	...	...	...	...
1970																
1st quarter	68.8	47.4	69.0	25.1	85.4	35.1	36.5	31.0	44.0	35.9	...	...	...	...	...	...
2nd quarter	69.6	47.4	68.2	25.5	85.6	35.4	36.7	31.8	46.4	36.4	...	...	...	...	...	...
3rd quarter	70.5	47.8	67.8	26.0	86.2	35.6	36.8	32.3	45.0	36.5	...	...	...	...	...	...
4th quarter	70.4	47.0	66.8	26.3	86.0	36.4	37.4	33.6	42.0	36.9	...	...	...	...	...	...
1971																
1st quarter	72.2	48.5	67.2	26.8	86.9	36.1	37.1	33.3	49.7	37.3	...	...	...	...	...	...
2nd quarter	72.4	49.0	67.6	27.2	87.4	36.5	37.5	33.6	50.2	37.7	...	...	...	...	...	...
3rd quarter	72.9	49.5	67.9	27.5	87.6	36.7	37.7	33.9	50.6	37.9	...	...	...	...	...	...
4th quarter	73.2	50.4	68.7	27.8	87.8	36.8	37.9	33.8	51.7	38.2	...	...	...	...	...	...
1972																
1st quarter	73.5	51.5	70.1	28.2	88.5	37.1	38.4	33.6	53.1	38.6	...	...	...	...	...	...
2nd quarter	74.0	52.6	71.2	28.6	88.9	37.4	38.6	34.1	52.0	38.7	...	...	...	...	...	...
3rd quarter	74.2	53.3	71.9	28.9	89.1	37.6	38.9	33.9	54.2	39.1	...	...	...	...	...	...
4th quarter	75.0	54.8	73.0	29.5	90.2	37.9	39.3	34.0	56.9	39.6	...	...	...	...	...	...
1973																
1st quarter	75.5	56.1	74.2	30.1	90.5	38.3	39.8	34.2	57.8	40.1	...	...	...	...	...	...
2nd quarter	75.0	56.2	75.0	30.6	90.3	39.4	40.9	35.3	54.1	40.7	...	...	...	...	...	...
3rd quarter	74.5	56.2	75.4	31.3	90.5	40.5	42.0	36.3	53.2	41.6	...	...	...	...	...	...
4th quarter	74.4	56.6	76.1	32.0	90.1	41.4	43.0	37.0	54.5	42.6	...	...	...	...	...	...
1974																
1st quarter	73.5	55.9	76.1	32.6	89.2	42.7	44.3	38.5	49.7	43.3	...	...	...	...	...	...
2nd quarter	73.7	56.0	76.0	33.5	89.3	43.9	45.4	39.8	49.2	44.4	...	...	...	...	...	...
3rd quarter	73.1	55.3	75.7	34.5	89.4	45.7	47.2	41.7	47.4	45.8	...	...	...	...	...	...
4th quarter	72.8	54.1	74.3	35.3	88.9	47.4	48.5	44.4	47.3	47.4	...	...	...	...	...	...
1975																
1st quarter	74.1	53.0	71.5	36.2	89.3	48.3	48.9	46.7	50.6	48.5	...	...	...	...	...	...
2nd quarter	76.0	53.7	70.7	36.9	89.9	48.2	48.6	47.0	59.3	49.2	...	...	...	...	...	...
3rd quarter	77.2	55.3	71.7	37.6	89.7	48.0	48.7	46.3	70.4	50.0	...	...	...	...	...	...
4th quarter	77.3	56.2	72.7	38.4	89.9	48.7	49.6	46.4	71.4	50.8	...	...	...	...	...	...

. . . = Not available.

Table 19-13. Productivity and Related Data—Continued

(1992 = 100, seasonally adjusted.)

Year and quarter	Business sector								Nonfarm business sector							
	Output per hour of all persons	Output	Hours of all persons	Compensation per hour	Real compensation per hour	Unit labor costs	Unit nonlabor payments	Implicit price deflator	Output per hour of all persons	Output	Hours of all persons	Compensation per hour	Real compensation per hour	Unit labor costs	Unit nonlabor payments	Implicit price deflator
1976																
1st quarter	76.6	59.3	77.4	36.8	85.3	48.0	48.3	48.2	78.1	59.5	76.2	36.9	85.4	47.2	47.2	47.2
2nd quarter	77.1	59.8	77.6	37.5	86.2	48.7	48.5	48.6	78.8	60.1	76.2	37.6	86.4	47.8	47.6	47.7
3rd quarter	77.2	60.1	77.9	38.3	86.5	49.6	48.7	49.3	78.9	60.4	76.5	38.5	86.9	48.7	47.8	48.4
4th quarter	77.7	60.7	78.1	39.2	87.3	50.5	49.5	50.1	79.1	60.9	77.0	39.3	87.5	49.6	48.6	49.3
1977																
1st quarter	78.0	61.6	78.9	39.9	87.3	51.1	50.5	50.9	79.6	61.9	77.8	40.0	87.4	50.2	49.6	50.0
2nd quarter	78.2	63.1	80.7	40.5	87.1	51.8	51.2	51.6	79.9	63.4	79.3	40.8	87.6	51.0	50.5	50.8
3rd quarter	79.2	64.4	81.3	41.4	87.7	52.2	52.0	52.1	80.8	64.7	80.1	41.6	88.1	51.5	51.5	51.5
4th quarter	78.3	64.3	82.1	42.1	88.0	53.8	52.4	53.2	79.7	64.4	80.9	42.3	88.4	53.1	51.2	52.4
1978																
1st quarter	78.0	64.4	82.5	43.3	89.1	55.5	51.6	54.0	79.7	64.8	81.3	43.5	89.6	54.6	50.4	53.1
2nd quarter	79.6	67.5	84.9	44.0	88.7	55.3	54.7	55.1	81.3	68.0	83.6	44.3	89.2	54.5	53.3	54.0
3rd quarter	79.7	68.2	85.6	44.9	88.8	56.3	55.6	56.0	81.3	68.6	84.3	45.1	89.3	55.5	54.3	55.1
4th quarter	80.0	69.2	86.5	46.0	89.3	57.5	56.9	57.3	81.8	69.8	85.4	46.2	89.8	56.5	55.6	56.2
1979																
1st quarter	79.5	69.2	87.1	47.3	89.8	59.5	56.2	58.3	81.0	69.6	86.0	47.5	90.2	58.6	54.4	57.1
2nd quarter	79.3	69.3	87.4	48.3	89.4	60.9	58.0	59.8	80.8	69.7	86.3	48.5	89.7	60.0	56.4	58.7
3rd quarter	79.3	69.9	88.1	49.4	89.1	62.3	59.1	61.1	80.7	70.2	87.0	49.6	89.4	61.5	57.4	60.0
4th quarter	79.1	69.9	88.4	50.5	88.9	63.9	59.4	62.2	80.6	70.3	87.2	50.8	89.4	63.1	57.8	61.1
1980																
1st quarter	79.6	70.0	88.0	52.1	88.9	65.5	60.3	63.6	80.9	70.4	87.0	52.3	89.2	64.7	59.3	62.7
2nd quarter	78.7	68.0	86.5	53.5	89.1	68.0	59.9	64.5	80.0	68.4	85.5	53.7	89.4	67.1	60.0	64.5
3rd quarter	78.8	67.9	86.2	54.8	89.2	69.6	61.1	66.4	80.3	68.3	85.1	55.1	89.6	68.6	60.2	65.5
4th quarter	79.6	69.4	87.3	56.2	89.4	70.6	63.8	68.1	81.2	69.9	86.2	56.6	89.9	69.7	62.1	66.9
1981																
1st quarter	81.1	71.1	87.7	57.7	89.2	71.1	67.9	69.9	82.4	71.4	86.6	58.1	89.8	70.5	66.5	69.0
2nd quarter	80.4	70.4	87.6	58.7	89.3	73.1	68.0	71.2	81.3	70.5	86.7	59.1	89.8	72.7	66.5	70.4
3rd quarter	81.4	71.3	87.6	60.0	89.4	73.7	70.5	72.5	82.0	71.1	86.6	60.4	90.0	73.6	68.9	71.9
4th quarter	80.2	70.1	87.3	60.9	89.2	75.9	70.0	73.7	81.0	69.9	86.3	61.3	89.7	75.7	69.0	73.2
1982																
1st quarter	79.8	68.5	85.9	62.5	90.4	78.3	68.3	74.6	80.5	68.3	84.9	62.9	90.9	78.1	67.4	74.2
2nd quarter	80.0	68.9	86.1	63.1	90.4	78.9	69.7	75.5	80.6	68.7	85.2	63.4	90.7	78.6	69.0	75.1
3rd quarter	80.0	68.5	85.6	64.0	90.2	80.0	70.5	76.5	80.8	68.4	84.6	64.4	90.6	79.7	69.6	76.0
4th quarter	80.8	68.5	84.8	64.9	90.4	80.3	71.8	77.1	81.5	68.3	83.9	65.2	90.9	80.0	71.3	76.8
1983																
1st quarter	81.6	69.5	85.2	65.4	90.6	80.2	73.4	77.7	82.5	69.6	84.4	65.8	91.2	79.8	72.6	77.2
2nd quarter	83.0	71.5	86.1	66.0	90.4	79.5	75.6	78.1	84.4	72.0	85.3	66.4	90.9	78.7	75.3	77.4
3rd quarter	83.3	73.2	87.8	66.3	90.0	79.6	77.7	78.9	85.2	74.1	87.0	66.8	90.6	78.3	77.8	78.1
4th quarter	84.0	75.0	89.2	67.2	90.4	80.0	78.3	79.4	85.6	75.9	88.6	67.5	90.8	78.8	78.3	78.6
1984																
1st quarter	84.4	76.8	91.0	68.0	90.3	80.6	79.0	80.0	85.5	77.2	90.3	68.3	90.7	79.9	77.9	79.2
2nd quarter	85.1	78.4	92.1	68.7	90.3	80.7	80.4	80.6	86.1	78.7	91.5	69.0	90.8	80.2	79.3	79.8
3rd quarter	85.5	79.2	92.6	69.6	90.9	81.4	80.5	81.1	86.4	79.4	91.9	70.0	91.3	81.0	79.6	80.5
4th quarter	85.8	79.8	93.1	70.2	90.9	81.9	80.8	81.5	86.5	80.0	92.5	70.5	91.3	81.5	79.8	80.9
1985																
1st quarter	86.1	80.7	93.8	71.1	91.3	82.6	81.6	82.3	86.6	80.8	93.3	71.4	91.6	82.4	80.7	81.8
2nd quarter	86.4	81.5	94.3	71.7	91.3	83.0	81.8	82.6	86.8	81.5	93.9	71.9	91.6	82.8	81.3	82.3
3rd quarter	87.9	83.0	94.4	72.8	92.1	82.9	82.6	82.8	88.0	82.8	94.1	72.9	92.2	82.9	82.5	82.8
4th quarter	88.2	83.6	94.8	74.2	92.9	84.1	81.8	83.2	88.4	83.6	94.6	74.2	93.0	84.0	81.4	83.0
1986																
1st quarter	89.1	84.5	94.8	75.0	93.5	84.2	82.5	83.6	89.5	84.5	94.5	75.2	93.7	84.0	82.4	83.4
2nd quarter	89.6	84.8	94.6	75.6	94.8	84.4	82.9	83.8	90.2	85.0	94.2	75.9	95.0	84.1	82.8	83.6
3rd quarter	90.1	85.7	95.1	76.3	95.1	84.7	83.1	84.1	90.6	85.8	94.7	76.6	95.4	84.6	82.7	83.9
4th quarter	89.8	86.1	95.8	77.6	96.0	86.4	81.9	84.7	90.3	86.2	95.4	77.9	96.4	86.2	81.6	84.5
1987																
1st quarter	89.4	86.6	96.9	77.7	95.1	86.9	82.1	85.1	89.9	86.8	96.6	78.0	95.4	86.8	81.8	84.9
2nd quarter	90.0	87.8	97.5	78.5	95.0	87.2	82.9	85.6	90.6	88.0	97.1	78.7	95.3	87.0	82.6	85.4
3rd quarter	90.1	88.4	98.1	79.3	95.1	88.0	83.4	86.3	90.6	88.6	97.8	79.6	95.4	87.8	83.1	86.1
4th quarter	91.0	90.2	99.1	80.3	95.5	88.3	83.9	86.7	91.4	90.3	98.8	80.5	95.8	88.1	83.6	86.4
1988																
1st quarter	91.2	90.5	99.2	81.6	96.4	89.5	83.9	87.4	91.6	90.6	98.9	81.8	96.6	89.3	83.4	87.1
2nd quarter	91.4	91.9	100.6	82.6	96.6	90.4	84.2	88.1	91.9	92.2	100.3	82.7	96.7	90.0	84.1	87.8
3rd quarter	91.6	92.3	100.7	83.6	96.7	91.3	85.6	89.1	92.2	92.7	100.6	83.7	96.7	90.8	85.2	88.7
4th quarter	91.8	93.6	101.9	84.1	96.3	91.5	86.8	89.8	92.7	94.3	101.7	84.2	96.4	90.8	87.1	89.4
1989																
1st quarter	92.0	94.6	102.9	84.3	95.7	91.7	89.2	90.8	92.4	94.8	102.7	84.5	95.8	91.5	88.4	90.3
2nd quarter	92.3	95.2	103.1	84.7	94.6	91.8	91.4	91.7	92.6	95.5	103.1	84.7	94.6	91.5	91.1	91.3
3rd quarter	92.6	95.9	103.5	85.3	94.6	92.1	92.4	92.2	93.0	96.1	103.3	85.4	94.7	91.8	92.3	92.0
4th quarter	92.8	96.0	103.5	86.4	95.0	93.2	92.2	92.8	93.2	96.3	103.4	86.5	95.1	92.8	91.7	92.4
1990																
1st quarter	93.8	97.2	103.6	88.3	95.5	94.1	93.4	93.8	94.0	97.4	103.6	88.1	95.4	93.7	93.0	93.5
2nd quarter	94.5	97.3	103.0	90.2	96.8	95.5	93.8	94.9	94.7	97.6	103.1	90.0	96.6	95.1	93.5	94.5
3rd quarter	95.0	97.1	102.2	91.6	96.7	96.4	94.2	95.6	95.0	97.3	102.4	91.4	96.4	96.2	93.9	95.4
4th quarter	94.2	96.0	101.9	92.3	95.9	98.0	93.5	96.3	94.3	96.1	101.9	92.2	95.8	97.7	93.6	96.2

Table 19-13. Productivity and Related Data—Continued

(1992 = 100, seasonally adjusted.)

Year and quarter	Output per hour of all employees	Output	Employee hours	Compensation per hour	Real compensation per hour	Unit costs Total	Unit costs Labor costs	Unit costs Nonlabor costs	Unit profits	Implicit price deflator	Output per hour of all persons	Output	Hours of all persons	Compensation per hour	Real compensation per hour	Unit labor costs
1976																
1st quarter	78.4	58.2	74.3	39.1	90.5	48.7	49.9	45.4	75.7	51.1	. . .	. . .	. . .	. . .	. . .	. . .
2nd quarter	78.4	58.7	74.8	39.8	91.5	49.5	50.8	46.1	71.3	51.5	. . .	. . .	. . .	. . .	. . .	. . .
3rd quarter	78.8	59.3	75.3	40.7	92.0	50.3	51.7	46.5	70.3	52.1	. . .	. . .	. . .	. . .	. . .	. . .
4th quarter	78.7	59.5	75.6	41.6	92.8	51.5	52.9	47.5	68.5	53.0	. . .	. . .	. . .	. . .	. . .	. . .
1977																
1st quarter	78.8	60.4	76.6	42.1	92.2	52.1	53.5	48.2	70.2	53.7	. . .	. . .	. . .	. . .	. . .	. . .
2nd quarter	80.4	62.9	78.2	43.0	92.5	52.0	53.5	47.9	77.8	54.3	. . .	. . .	. . .	. . .	. . .	. . .
3rd quarter	82.1	64.9	79.0	44.0	93.2	52.0	53.6	47.9	82.4	54.7	. . .	. . .	. . .	. . .	. . .	. . .
4th quarter	81.1	64.8	79.9	44.9	93.8	53.8	55.3	49.6	78.5	56.0	. . .	. . .	. . .	. . .	. . .	. . .
1978																
1st quarter	81.0	64.8	80.1	46.0	94.7	55.4	56.8	51.4	71.0	56.8	. . .	. . .	. . .	. . .	. . .	. . .
2nd quarter	82.3	67.7	82.3	47.1	94.8	55.5	57.2	51.0	81.6	57.9	. . .	. . .	. . .	. . .	. . .	. . .
3rd quarter	81.6	67.9	83.2	48.0	95.0	56.6	58.8	50.7	81.0	58.8	. . .	. . .	. . .	. . .	. . .	. . .
4th quarter	81.9	69.0	84.3	49.2	95.5	57.8	60.1	51.7	82.3	60.0	. . .	. . .	. . .	. . .	. . .	. . .
1979																
1st quarter	81.5	69.4	85.1	50.3	95.5	59.4	61.7	53.1	77.2	61.0	. . .	. . .	. . .	. . .	. . .	. . .
2nd quarter	81.0	69.3	85.5	51.3	95.0	61.1	63.3	55.0	75.4	62.4	. . .	. . .	. . .	. . .	. . .	. . .
3rd quarter	80.7	69.5	86.2	52.4	94.5	62.8	65.0	56.7	72.3	63.6	. . .	. . .	. . .	. . .	. . .	. . .
4th quarter	80.8	69.8	86.4	53.6	94.4	64.2	66.4	58.2	71.1	64.8	. . .	. . .	. . .	. . .	. . .	. . .
1980																
1st quarter	80.9	69.8	86.2	55.1	94.0	66.1	68.1	60.7	69.4	66.4	. . .	. . .	. . .	. . .	. . .	. . .
2nd quarter	80.0	67.8	84.8	56.5	94.0	68.9	70.6	64.4	59.6	68.1	. . .	. . .	. . .	. . .	. . .	. . .
3rd quarter	80.6	67.9	84.3	57.8	94.1	70.4	71.8	66.4	65.0	69.9	. . .	. . .	. . .	. . .	. . .	. . .
4th quarter	81.6	69.8	85.5	59.4	94.4	71.5	72.8	68.2	73.4	71.7	. . .	. . .	. . .	. . .	. . .	. . .
1981																
1st quarter	82.1	70.7	86.1	60.7	93.9	72.8	73.9	69.9	78.7	73.4	. . .	. . .	. . .	. . .	. . .	. . .
2nd quarter	82.5	71.4	86.5	61.8	93.8	74.2	74.8	72.6	78.7	74.6	. . .	. . .	. . .	. . .	. . .	. . .
3rd quarter	83.9	72.8	86.7	63.1	93.9	74.9	75.2	74.2	87.2	76.0	. . .	. . .	. . .	. . .	. . .	. . .
4th quarter	82.9	71.5	86.3	64.1	93.8	77.2	77.3	77.1	79.1	77.4	. . .	. . .	. . .	. . .	. . .	. . .
1982																
1st quarter	83.1	70.5	84.8	65.5	94.7	79.0	78.8	79.5	73.5	78.5	. . .	. . .	. . .	. . .	. . .	. . .
2nd quarter	83.2	70.3	84.6	66.0	94.5	79.7	79.4	80.7	78.0	79.6	. . .	. . .	. . .	. . .	. . .	. . .
3rd quarter	83.0	69.7	84.0	66.8	94.1	80.9	80.6	81.8	78.0	80.6	. . .	. . .	. . .	. . .	. . .	. . .
4th quarter	83.0	69.0	83.0	67.5	94.1	81.9	81.3	83.5	71.2	81.0	. . .	. . .	. . .	. . .	. . .	. . .
1983																
1st quarter	84.2	70.2	83.4	67.9	94.1	81.2	80.6	82.7	79.6	81.0	. . .	. . .	. . .	. . .	. . .	. . .
2nd quarter	85.6	72.2	84.4	68.6	94.0	80.5	80.1	81.4	90.1	81.3	. . .	. . .	. . .	. . .	. . .	. . .
3rd quarter	86.3	74.2	85.9	69.1	93.7	80.4	80.1	81.4	96.2	81.8	. . .	. . .	. . .	. . .	. . .	. . .
4th quarter	86.7	75.9	87.6	70.1	94.3	80.9	80.9	81.0	98.0	82.5	. . .	. . .	. . .	. . .	. . .	. . .
1984																
1st quarter	87.1	77.8	89.3	70.6	93.7	80.8	81.0	80.3	108.5	83.3	. . .	. . .	. . .	. . .	. . .	. . .
2nd quarter	87.7	79.5	90.6	71.4	93.9	81.3	81.5	80.7	110.0	83.8	. . .	. . .	. . .	. . .	. . .	. . .
3rd quarter	88.0	80.2	91.2	72.5	94.6	82.2	82.4	81.9	105.9	84.3	. . .	. . .	. . .	. . .	. . .	. . .
4th quarter	88.3	81.2	92.0	73.1	94.6	82.6	82.8	82.2	106.0	84.7	. . .	. . .	. . .	. . .	. . .	. . .
1985																
1st quarter	88.6	81.8	92.4	73.9	94.9	83.4	83.4	83.3	103.4	85.2	. . .	. . .	. . .	. . .	. . .	. . .
2nd quarter	88.9	82.6	93.0	74.5	94.8	83.9	83.8	84.2	100.4	85.4	. . .	. . .	. . .	. . .	. . .	. . .
3rd quarter	90.5	84.1	93.0	75.5	95.5	83.3	83.5	83.0	107.1	85.5	. . .	. . .	. . .	. . .	. . .	. . .
4th quarter	90.7	84.4	93.1	76.9	96.3	84.6	84.8	84.0	98.2	85.8	. . .	. . .	. . .	. . .	. . .	. . .
1986																
1st quarter	91.2	85.0	93.2	77.7	96.8	85.3	85.2	85.8	93.3	86.1	. . .	. . .	. . .	. . .	. . .	. . .
2nd quarter	91.1	84.6	92.9	78.4	98.2	86.1	86.0	86.2	90.7	86.5	. . .	. . .	. . .	. . .	. . .	. . .
3rd quarter	91.3	84.9	93.0	79.2	98.7	86.7	86.8	86.6	88.3	86.9	. . .	. . .	. . .	. . .	. . .	. . .
4th quarter	92.1	86.1	93.5	80.3	99.3	87.0	87.2	86.5	88.4	87.1	. . .	. . .	. . .	. . .	. . .	. . .
1987																
1st quarter	91.9	87.1	94.7	80.5	98.5	87.3	87.6	86.5	91.5	87.7	87.3	90.1	103.1	80.6	98.5	92.2
2nd quarter	93.0	88.9	95.6	81.0	98.1	86.8	87.2	85.9	98.8	87.9	89.0	91.5	102.9	80.9	98.0	91.0
3rd quarter	94.0	90.7	96.5	81.8	98.1	86.5	87.0	85.1	105.9	88.2	89.7	93.0	103.6	81.7	98.0	91.1
4th quarter	94.3	91.9	97.4	82.8	98.6	87.2	87.8	85.7	104.1	88.7	90.6	95.5	105.4	82.0	97.5	90.5
1988																
1st quarter	95.5	93.2	97.7	83.7	98.8	87.2	87.6	85.8	109.5	89.2	90.3	95.9	106.2	82.9	97.9	91.8
2nd quarter	95.7	94.5	98.8	84.6	98.9	87.8	88.4	86.2	109.9	89.8	90.8	97.0	106.8	83.5	97.6	92.0
3rd quarter	95.6	95.0	99.4	85.5	98.8	88.9	89.5	87.2	110.9	90.8	91.0	97.5	107.1	84.4	97.6	92.7
4th quarter	96.2	96.8	100.6	85.9	98.4	88.9	89.3	87.9	116.0	91.3	91.9	99.0	107.7	85.6	98.0	93.1
1989																
1st quarter	95.0	96.6	101.6	86.3	97.9	90.8	90.8	90.8	105.1	92.1	92.4	99.9	108.1	85.9	97.5	93.0
2nd quarter	94.2	96.2	102.1	86.4	96.5	92.1	91.8	92.8	102.8	93.0	91.8	99.2	108.1	85.7	95.8	93.4
3rd quarter	94.5	96.7	102.3	87.0	96.5	92.8	92.1	94.6	101.3	93.5	91.4	98.5	107.8	86.6	96.1	94.8
4th quarter	94.7	97.1	102.6	88.3	97.1	93.8	93.3	95.2	95.8	94.0	92.3	98.3	106.6	88.2	97.0	95.6
1990																
1st quarter	94.1	97.4	103.5	88.8	96.1	94.7	94.4	95.4	98.1	95.0	93.1	98.8	106.1	88.3	95.6	94.9
2nd quarter	95.6	98.4	103.0	90.7	97.3	95.2	94.9	95.9	103.2	95.9	93.5	99.1	106.0	90.0	96.5	96.3
3rd quarter	95.7	97.9	102.3	92.1	97.2	96.7	96.3	98.0	94.9	96.6	94.6	99.1	104.8	91.2	96.2	96.4
4th quarter	96.2	97.6	101.4	92.9	96.5	97.4	96.5	99.9	91.5	96.9	94.6	97.5	103.0	92.4	96.0	97.7

. . . = Not available.

Table 19-13. Productivity and Related Data—Continued

(1992 = 100, seasonally adjusted.)

Year and quarter	Business sector								Nonfarm business sector							
	Output per hour of all persons	Output	Hours of all persons	Compensation per hour	Real compensation per hour	Unit labor costs	Unit nonlabor payments	Implicit price deflator	Output per hour of all persons	Output	Hours of all persons	Compensation per hour	Real compensation per hour	Unit labor costs	Unit nonlabor payments	Implicit price deflator
1991																
1st quarter	94.4	95.2	100.8	93.0	96.2	98.5	95.3	97.3	94.5	95.3	100.8	92.9	96.1	98.3	95.5	97.3
2nd quarter	95.8	95.9	100.2	94.7	97.5	98.9	96.2	97.9	95.9	96.1	100.2	94.7	97.4	98.7	96.3	97.8
3rd quarter	96.4	96.5	100.1	95.7	97.9	99.3	97.3	98.6	96.6	96.6	100.0	95.7	97.9	99.1	97.7	98.6
4th quarter	97.1	97.0	99.9	96.8	98.3	99.7	97.7	99.0	97.2	97.1	99.9	96.7	98.3	99.5	97.8	98.9
1992																
1st quarter	98.9	98.3	99.4	98.7	99.6	99.8	98.6	99.4	98.8	98.3	99.4	98.6	99.5	99.8	98.7	99.4
2nd quarter	99.5	99.4	99.9	99.3	99.6	99.8	99.6	99.7	99.5	99.3	99.8	99.4	99.7	99.9	99.5	99.7
3rd quarter	100.4	100.5	100.0	100.8	100.5	100.4	99.9	100.2	100.4	100.5	100.0	100.8	100.5	100.4	99.7	100.2
4th quarter	101.2	101.9	100.7	101.2	100.1	100.0	101.9	100.7	101.3	102.0	100.7	101.2	100.2	100.0	102.0	100.7
1993																
1st quarter	100.4	101.8	101.4	101.6	100.0	101.2	101.8	101.4	100.5	102.1	101.6	101.4	99.8	100.9	102.4	101.5
2nd quarter	100.0	102.5	102.5	102.0	99.7	102.1	101.7	101.9	99.9	102.7	102.8	101.8	99.5	101.9	102.0	101.9
3rd quarter	100.1	103.1	103.0	102.5	99.7	102.3	102.3	102.3	100.3	103.5	103.3	102.2	99.5	101.9	103.0	102.3
4th quarter	101.1	105.0	103.9	102.8	99.4	101.7	104.6	102.8	101.0	105.2	104.1	102.6	99.1	101.5	104.8	102.7
1994																
1st quarter	101.6	106.3	104.6	103.8	100.1	102.2	105.0	103.2	101.7	106.3	104.5	103.7	100.0	102.0	105.2	103.2
2nd quarter	101.4	107.9	106.5	103.4	99.2	102.0	106.1	103.6	101.6	108.0	106.3	103.5	99.3	101.9	106.5	103.6
3rd quarter	100.8	108.5	107.7	103.4	98.4	102.6	107.0	104.2	100.9	108.5	107.6	103.4	98.4	102.5	107.7	104.4
4th quarter	101.6	110.1	108.4	103.9	98.4	102.2	108.7	104.6	101.9	110.3	108.2	104.0	98.5	102.1	109.5	104.8
1995																
1st quarter	101.1	110.4	109.1	104.8	98.7	103.6	107.7	105.2	101.6	110.7	108.9	104.8	98.7	103.2	109.0	105.3
2nd quarter	101.2	110.5	109.3	105.3	98.4	104.1	107.9	105.5	101.8	110.9	109.0	105.5	98.5	103.6	109.3	105.7
3rd quarter	101.3	111.7	110.2	106.0	98.6	104.6	108.4	106.0	101.9	112.2	110.1	106.1	98.7	104.1	109.3	106.0
4th quarter	102.3	112.8	110.3	107.0	99.1	104.6	109.2	106.3	102.7	113.3	110.2	107.0	99.1	104.2	109.8	106.2
1996																
1st quarter	103.4	113.9	110.2	108.0	99.2	104.5	110.7	106.8	103.7	114.2	110.1	108.1	99.3	104.2	110.8	106.7
2nd quarter	104.6	116.0	111.0	109.1	99.4	104.4	112.2	107.3	104.8	116.3	111.0	109.2	99.4	104.2	112.0	107.0
3rd quarter	104.9	117.2	111.7	110.1	99.8	105.0	111.8	107.5	105.1	117.5	111.8	110.0	99.6	104.7	112.3	107.5
4th quarter	105.1	118.8	113.1	110.6	99.4	105.2	112.8	108.0	105.3	119.2	113.2	110.4	99.3	104.9	113.2	108.0
1997																
1st quarter	104.8	119.9	114.4	111.2	99.4	106.1	113.1	108.7	104.9	120.1	114.5	111.1	99.4	105.9	113.3	108.6
2nd quarter	106.2	122.1	115.0	112.0	99.9	105.5	114.3	108.8	106.2	122.2	115.1	112.0	99.9	105.5	115.1	109.0
3rd quarter	107.2	123.9	115.5	113.3	100.6	105.7	114.9	109.1	107.1	124.0	115.8	113.1	100.4	105.6	115.7	109.3
4th quarter	107.7	124.9	116.0	115.4	102.0	107.2	113.1	109.4	107.5	125.1	116.3	115.0	101.6	107.0	114.1	109.6
1998																
1st quarter	108.5	126.5	116.6	117.6	103.7	108.3	111.5	109.5	108.4	126.8	117.0	117.2	103.4	108.2	112.4	109.7
2nd quarter	108.7	127.4	117.2	119.1	104.8	109.6	109.4	109.5	108.7	127.7	117.5	118.8	104.5	109.3	110.5	109.8
3rd quarter	110.0	129.0	117.3	121.0	106.0	110.0	109.3	109.7	109.9	129.4	117.7	120.8	105.7	109.9	110.4	110.1
4th quarter	110.6	131.5	118.8	121.8	106.2	110.1	109.7	109.9	110.5	131.8	119.3	121.4	105.9	109.9	110.7	110.2
1999																
1st quarter	111.8	132.7	118.6	124.3	108.0	111.2	108.8	110.3	111.5	133.0	119.3	123.7	107.4	110.9	109.8	110.5
2nd quarter	112.0	133.9	119.5	124.7	107.6	111.3	109.1	110.5	111.7	134.3	120.2	124.1	107.0	111.1	110.7	111.0
3rd quarter	112.8	135.7	120.3	125.8	107.7	111.5	109.7	110.8	112.4	136.1	121.0	125.2	107.1	111.3	111.4	111.3
4th quarter	114.6	138.5	120.8	128.2	108.9	111.8	111.0	111.1	114.4	138.9	121.4	127.8	108.5	111.7	111.8	111.7
2000																
1st quarter	114.2	138.6	121.4	132.6	111.6	116.1	105.3	112.1	113.9	138.8	121.9	132.3	111.3	116.1	106.6	112.6
2nd quarter	116.4	141.1	121.2	133.2	111.2	114.4	109.5	112.6	116.0	141.4	121.9	132.6	110.8	114.4	111.0	113.1
3rd quarter	116.1	140.8	121.3	135.8	112.3	116.9	106.3	112.9	115.7	141.1	121.9	135.2	111.9	116.9	107.8	113.5
4th quarter	117.4	141.5	120.6	136.7	112.3	116.5	108.0	113.3	116.8	141.8	121.4	136.0	111.8	116.4	109.6	113.9
2001																
1st quarter	117.2	141.1	120.4	139.0	113.1	118.6	106.4	114.1	116.7	141.4	121.2	138.3	112.5	118.5	108.0	114.6
2nd quarter	118.8	141.4	119.1	140.0	113.2	117.9	109.9	114.9	118.3	141.9	119.9	139.1	112.4	117.6	111.7	115.4
3rd quarter	119.3	140.3	117.7	140.8	113.5	118.0	110.4	115.2	118.8	140.8	118.5	139.8	112.7	117.7	112.0	115.6
4th quarter	121.1	141.0	116.3	141.8	114.4	117.0	113.1	115.6	120.6	141.2	117.1	141.0	113.7	116.8	114.7	116.0
2002																
1st quarter	122.8	141.9	115.5	143.8	115.6	117.1	113.2	115.6	122.7	142.5	116.1	143.1	115.1	116.7	115.0	116.0
2nd quarter	123.4	142.6	115.5	145.5	116.1	117.9	112.6	115.9	123.0	143.0	116.3	144.7	115.5	117.7	114.8	116.6
3rd quarter	124.8	143.8	115.2	146.1	116.0	117.1	114.7	116.2	124.2	144.1	116.0	145.3	115.3	117.0	116.6	116.9
4th quarter	124.8	144.0	115.4	146.2	115.3	117.1	116.0	116.7	124.2	144.1	116.0	145.4	114.7	117.1	117.7	117.3
2003																
1st quarter	125.8	144.4	114.8	148.0	115.7	117.7	116.5	117.3	125.1	144.6	115.5	147.3	115.1	117.7	118.2	117.9
2nd quarter	128.0	146.0	114.1	150.8	117.8	117.8	116.7	117.4	127.0	146.1	115.1	149.7	117.0	117.9	118.1	118.0
3rd quarter	130.8	149.7	114.5	152.5	118.4	116.6	120.2	118.0	130.1	150.0	115.3	151.7	117.8	116.6	121.5	118.4
4th quarter	130.3	150.1	115.2	153.6	118.9	117.9	119.5	118.5	129.9	150.6	115.9	152.9	118.4	117.7	120.5	118.7
2004																
1st quarter	131.4	151.7	115.5	154.4	118.5	117.5	122.9	119.5	130.5	151.9	116.4	153.4	117.8	117.6	123.6	119.8
2nd quarter	132.8	153.5	115.6	155.8	118.3	117.3	126.2	120.6	132.2	153.9	116.4	154.8	117.6	117.2	126.8	120.7
3rd quarter	133.0	154.8	116.4	157.5	119.1	118.5	125.5	121.1	132.2	155.1	117.3	156.6	118.3	118.4	126.6	121.4
4th quarter	133.5	155.8	116.7	160.1	120.0	119.9	125.8	122.1	132.4	156.0	117.8	158.7	118.9	119.9	127.0	122.5
2005																
1st quarter	134.5	157.4	117.0	161.6	120.4	120.1	127.9	123.0	133.5	157.6	118.0	160.4	119.5	120.1	129.4	123.5
2nd quarter	134.9	159.0	117.9	162.0	119.5	120.0	130.0	123.7	134.3	159.4	118.6	161.0	118.9	119.9	131.8	124.3
3rd quarter	136.6	160.9	117.8	165.2	120.3	121.0	131.1	124.7	135.8	161.3	118.8	164.1	119.5	120.9	133.1	125.3
4th quarter	136.7	161.7	118.3	166.5	120.3	121.8	132.3	125.7	135.8	162.0	119.3	165.3	119.4	121.7	134.3	126.4

Table 19-13. Productivity and Related Data—Continued

(1992 = 100, seasonally adjusted.)

Year and quarter	Nonfinancial corporations					Unit costs					Manufacturing					
	Output per hour of all employees	Output	Employee hours	Compensation per hour	Real compensation per hour	Total	Labor costs	Nonlabor costs	Unit profits	Implicit price deflator	Output per hour of all persons	Output	Hours of all persons	Compensation per hour	Real compensation per hour	Unit labor costs
1991																
1st quarter	96.6	96.8	100.2	93.5	96.7	98.3	96.8	102.4	94.3	98.0	94.4	95.4	101.1	93.7	96.9	99.3
2nd quarter	97.5	96.8	99.3	95.2	97.9	99.1	97.7	102.9	93.7	98.6	95.8	96.0	100.2	95.3	98.0	99.4
3rd quarter	97.7	97.1	99.4	96.2	98.3	99.7	98.5	103.0	92.8	99.1	97.3	97.8	100.4	96.3	98.5	98.9
4th quarter	98.0	97.5	99.4	97.1	98.7	100.0	99.1	102.5	91.9	99.3	97.6	98.0	100.4	97.0	98.5	99.3
1992																
1st quarter	99.4	98.9	99.4	98.6	99.6	99.6	99.2	100.9	96.7	99.4	98.1	98.0	99.9	98.4	99.3	100.3
2nd quarter	99.7	99.8	100.1	99.4	99.7	99.7	99.7	99.9	100.6	99.8	99.4	99.8	100.4	99.5	99.8	100.1
3rd quarter	100.0	99.8	99.8	100.9	100.6	100.6	100.8	100.1	95.3	100.2	101.3	100.7	99.4	101.2	100.9	99.8
4th quarter	100.8	101.5	100.7	101.2	100.1	100.0	100.3	99.2	107.3	100.7	101.2	101.5	100.4	101.0	99.9	99.8
1993																
1st quarter	99.5	100.8	101.2	101.1	99.6	101.3	101.6	100.6	104.1	101.6	102.0	102.9	100.8	100.9	99.4	98.9
2nd quarter	100.3	102.4	102.1	101.6	99.3	100.8	101.3	99.4	113.4	101.9	102.0	103.4	101.4	101.5	99.2	99.5
3rd quarter	100.3	103.1	102.7	102.0	99.2	101.2	101.6	100.1	112.9	102.3	102.2	103.8	101.6	102.3	99.6	100.1
4th quarter	101.1	104.8	103.6	102.3	98.9	100.7	101.2	99.6	125.7	103.0	103.6	105.6	101.9	103.3	99.9	99.7
1994																
1st quarter	101.9	106.3	104.4	103.6	99.9	101.8	101.7	102.0	120.2	103.4	104.4	106.7	102.2	104.8	101.0	100.3
2nd quarter	102.1	108.5	106.3	103.3	99.1	100.9	101.2	99.9	131.5	103.6	105.9	109.2	103.1	104.9	100.6	99.1
3rd quarter	102.0	109.8	107.6	103.3	98.3	101.1	101.2	100.8	134.7	104.1	106.3	110.8	104.2	105.4	100.3	99.1
4th quarter	102.8	112.0	109.0	103.8	98.4	100.9	101.0	100.5	140.0	104.4	107.6	113.4	105.4	106.1	100.5	98.6
1995																
1st quarter	102.4	112.5	109.8	104.7	98.6	101.9	102.2	101.3	132.7	104.7	109.1	115.2	105.6	105.5	99.3	96.7
2nd quarter	102.8	113.4	110.3	105.0	98.1	102.0	102.2	101.6	132.4	104.7	110.3	115.2	104.5	107.0	100.0	97.0
3rd quarter	103.7	115.2	111.1	105.4	98.1	101.5	101.7	100.9	141.0	105.0	111.2	115.9	104.2	108.1	100.5	97.1
4th quarter	104.4	116.2	111.3	106.1	98.2	101.5	101.7	101.1	141.2	105.1	112.4	116.9	104.1	108.7	100.6	96.7
1996																
1st quarter	105.7	117.5	111.1	107.1	98.4	101.1	101.4	100.5	148.3	105.3	113.7	116.7	102.7	108.7	99.9	95.6
2nd quarter	106.7	119.6	112.1	108.2	98.5	101.1	101.4	100.0	149.9	105.4	114.2	119.0	104.2	109.0	99.3	95.5
3rd quarter	107.7	121.7	113.0	109.0	98.7	100.8	101.2	99.7	149.4	105.1	115.5	120.9	104.7	109.6	99.3	94.9
4th quarter	108.3	123.6	114.2	109.5	98.5	100.7	101.1	99.7	152.2	105.3	116.6	122.5	105.1	110.1	99.0	94.4
1997																
1st quarter	108.4	125.3	115.6	110.4	98.7	101.4	101.8	100.2	152.7	106.0	118.2	125.2	105.9	110.2	98.5	93.2
2nd quarter	109.2	127.2	116.5	110.9	99.0	101.1	101.6	99.9	152.9	105.8	119.9	126.9	105.8	111.5	99.5	93.0
3rd quarter	110.6	129.7	117.3	111.9	99.4	100.8	101.2	99.7	158.5	106.0	122.5	129.5	105.8	112.7	100.1	92.0
4th quarter	111.3	131.5	118.2	113.7	100.4	101.3	102.1	99.2	153.1	105.9	124.4	132.7	106.7	114.5	101.1	92.0
1998																
1st quarter	111.9	132.9	118.7	116.2	102.5	102.5	103.8	99.1	139.7	105.9	125.9	134.2	106.5	116.6	102.8	92.5
2nd quarter	113.1	134.7	119.1	117.7	103.5	102.7	104.0	99.1	136.6	105.8	126.7	134.4	106.1	118.3	104.0	93.3
3rd quarter	114.8	137.0	119.4	119.4	104.6	102.7	104.0	99.1	139.8	106.0	129.1	135.1	104.7	120.0	105.0	92.9
4th quarter	114.8	138.6	120.8	120.0	104.7	103.5	104.6	100.5	132.2	106.1	130.0	137.3	105.6	120.2	104.9	92.5
1999																
1st quarter	117.0	141.6	121.1	123.1	106.9	103.6	105.2	99.2	133.3	106.3	131.9	138.5	105.0	121.3	105.4	91.9
2nd quarter	117.6	143.2	121.8	123.4	106.4	103.5	104.9	99.7	133.6	106.2	132.9	139.7	105.1	122.1	105.3	91.9
3rd quarter	117.7	144.4	122.7	124.1	106.2	104.3	105.5	101.0	126.2	106.2	133.0	140.4	105.6	123.5	105.7	92.9
4th quarter	119.1	146.9	123.3	125.9	107.0	104.6	105.7	101.5	123.4	106.3	136.4	142.7	104.6	126.8	107.7	92.9
2000																
1st quarter	121.3	150.3	123.9	130.6	109.9	106.1	107.7	101.9	114.6	106.9	138.4	144.1	104.1	133.2	112.1	96.3
2nd quarter	122.0	151.1	123.9	131.4	109.7	106.6	107.7	103.5	115.9	107.4	139.4	145.2	104.1	132.5	110.7	95.0
3rd quarter	122.9	152.4	124.0	134.0	110.8	107.9	109.0	104.8	107.4	107.8	139.0	144.2	103.8	135.9	112.4	97.8
4th quarter	123.2	152.3	123.6	135.5	111.3	109.1	110.0	106.5	97.0	108.0	140.1	142.9	102.0	136.7	112.3	97.6
2001																
1st quarter	123.7	151.9	122.8	136.7	111.2	110.2	110.5	109.2	87.4	108.1	139.7	140.1	100.3	138.1	112.4	98.8
2nd quarter	124.6	151.1	121.3	138.0	111.5	111.0	110.8	111.6	86.9	108.9	140.7	137.9	98.0	137.4	111.0	97.6
3rd quarter	124.9	149.4	119.6	139.2	112.2	112.2	111.5	114.1	79.0	109.2	141.4	135.5	95.8	137.0	110.4	96.9
4th quarter	125.7	148.2	117.9	140.7	113.5	113.0	111.9	115.7	75.5	109.6	144.5	133.6	92.5	139.0	112.1	96.2
2002																
1st quarter	127.3	149.3	117.2	141.6	113.9	111.7	111.2	113.0	85.8	109.4	147.9	134.3	90.8	144.6	116.2	97.7
2nd quarter	129.4	151.3	117.0	143.5	114.5	110.9	111.0	110.7	94.5	109.4	150.5	136.0	90.4	147.6	117.8	98.1
3rd quarter	130.6	152.2	116.5	144.5	114.6	110.5	110.6	110.0	100.3	109.5	152.9	136.9	89.5	149.1	118.3	97.5
4th quarter	131.7	153.0	116.2	144.9	114.3	110.0	110.1	109.6	111.2	110.1	154.5	136.5	88.4	150.2	118.5	97.2
2003																
1st quarter	131.9	152.1	115.3	146.2	114.2	111.3	110.8	112.7	103.0	110.6	158.0	137.4	86.9	154.6	120.8	97.8
2nd quarter	133.6	153.4	114.8	148.8	116.2	111.3	111.4	111.2	105.9	110.8	159.7	136.5	85.5	157.2	122.8	98.5
3rd quarter	135.7	155.7	114.7	150.8	117.1	111.0	111.1	110.8	112.9	111.2	163.0	137.2	84.2	159.4	123.7	97.7
4th quarter	136.6	157.5	115.3	152.0	117.7	110.9	111.3	110.0	117.8	111.6	162.6	138.1	84.9	162.0	125.4	99.6
2004																
1st quarter	137.6	159.6	116.1	151.8	116.5	110.0	110.4	109.1	131.2	111.9	161.8	138.1	85.4	157.5	120.8	97.3
2nd quarter	138.6	161.1	116.2	153.2	116.4	110.2	110.5	109.3	139.2	112.8	163.3	138.9	85.0	159.8	121.4	97.8
3rd quarter	140.5	164.0	116.8	155.0	117.1	110.0	110.3	109.2	142.3	112.9	164.0	139.3	84.9	163.0	123.2	99.4
4th quarter	141.0	165.3	117.2	157.1	117.7	110.8	111.4	109.3	142.4	113.7	166.1	140.3	84.4	165.5	124.0	99.6
2005																
1st quarter	142.8	167.5	117.4	158.6	118.2	110.9	111.1	110.3	148.5	114.2	168.1	141.7	84.3	166.1	123.7	98.8
2nd quarter	144.5	170.6	118.1	159.3	117.6	110.2	110.2	110.2	159.0	114.6	169.7	142.2	83.8	167.8	123.8	98.9
3rd quarter	145.6	172.3	118.3	162.4	118.3	111.9	111.6	112.6	149.9	115.3	171.2	143.1	83.6	170.7	124.3	99.7
4th quarter	146.7	174.7	119.1	163.6	118.2	111.3	111.5	110.5	159.6	115.6	173.2	146.3	84.5	170.9	123.4	98.7

NOTES AND DEFINITIONS

TABLES 19-1 THROUGH 19-11
SELECTED NATIONAL INCOME
AND PRODUCT ACCOUNT DATA

See the notes and definitions for Tables 1-1 through 1-7 and 1-9 through 1-13.

For *personal income and its disposition* (Table 19-6), see the notes and definitions for Table 4-1.

For *inventories to sales ratios* (Table 19-7), see the notes and definitions for Table 5-7.

For *federal* and *state and local government current receipts and expenditures* (Tables 19-10 and 19-11), see the notes and definitions for Tables 6-1 and 6-8. Some of the detailed data shown in these tables is not available for earlier years and is listed below.

• In Table 19-10, from 1947 through 1958, only total *taxes on production and imports* is available. Separate quarterly data on *excise taxes* and on customs duties (the other component of the total, not shown here) are not available.

• In Table 19-10, prior to 1960, *interest receipts* are not shown separately, but have been subtracted from total *interest payments*.

• In Table 19-10, prior to 1959, the *current surplus of government enterprises* is not shown separately as a current receipt, and the expenditure category *subsidies* is presented net of the current surplus of government enterprises. In the case of the federal government, subsidies are substantial and government enterprise activity relatively minor.

• In Table 19-11, prior to 1959, the *current surplus of government enterprises* category of current receipts is presented net of expenditures for *subsidies*, which are not shown separately. This is the reverse of the treatment in Table 19-10, reflecting the reality that subsidies by state and local governments are usually minor compared with their enterprise activities.

TABLE 19-12
U.S. INTERNATIONAL TRANSACTIONS

See the notes and definitions for Table 7-6.

TABLE 19-13
PRODUCTIVITY AND RELATED DATA

See the notes and definitions for Table 9-4.

Table 20-1. Industrial Production and Capacity Utilization

(Seasonally adjusted; 2002 = 100, except as noted.)

Year and month	Total industry	Manufac-turing (SIC)	Consumer goods Total	Durable	Nondurable	Business equipment	Defense and space equipment	Construction supplies	Business supplies	Materials	Cap. util. Total industry	Cap. util. Manufac-turing (SIC)
1947	15.5	14.3	19.1	12.4	22.6	8.6	9.5	23.4	12.5	15.2	...	...
1948	16.1	14.8	19.7	12.9	23.2	8.9	11.1	25.0	13.0	15.8	...	82.5
1949	15.2	14.0	19.6	12.3	23.4	7.8	11.6	22.9	12.9	14.4	...	74.2
1950	17.6	16.3	22.3	16.4	25.4	8.3	13.6	27.6	14.4	17.3	...	82.8
1951	19.1	17.6	22.1	14.2	26.3	10.2	33.5	28.8	15.2	19.1	...	85.8
1952	19.9	18.3	22.6	13.8	27.3	11.5	47.1	28.5	15.2	19.4	...	85.4
1953	21.5	20.0	24.0	16.1	28.1	12.0	56.4	30.6	16.2	21.5	...	89.3
1954	20.4	18.7	23.8	15.0	28.4	10.5	49.7	30.2	16.4	19.9	...	80.1
1955	23.0	21.1	26.6	18.4	30.6	11.4	45.5	34.7	18.3	23.5	...	87.0
1956	24.0	21.9	27.5	17.9	32.6	13.2	44.5	35.7	19.4	24.1	...	86.1
1957	24.3	22.2	28.2	17.8	33.6	13.7	46.4	35.2	19.7	24.1	...	83.6
1958	22.8	20.6	28.0	15.9	34.6	11.6	46.6	34.0	19.5	21.7	...	75.0
1959	25.5	23.2	30.7	18.7	37.0	13.0	49.1	38.1	21.2	25.0	...	81.6
1960	26.0	23.7	31.8	19.8	38.2	13.4	50.5	37.2	22.0	25.4	...	80.1
1961	26.2	23.8	32.5	19.5	39.4	13.0	51.3	37.5	22.6	25.4	...	77.3
1962	28.4	25.9	34.7	22.0	41.3	14.1	59.4	39.8	24.0	27.7	...	81.4
1963	30.1	27.4	36.6	23.9	43.2	14.8	64.1	41.7	25.6	29.5	...	83.5
1964	32.1	29.3	38.7	25.7	45.3	16.6	62.0	44.2	27.4	31.8	...	85.6
1965	35.3	32.5	41.7	30.1	47.2	19.0	68.6	46.9	29.2	35.5	...	89.5
1966	38.4	35.4	43.8	31.9	49.5	22.0	80.7	48.9	31.5	38.7	...	91.1
1967	39.2	36.1	44.9	30.7	52.0	22.4	92.0	50.2	33.1	38.3	87.0	87.2
1947												
January	15.3	14.1	18.9	11.7	22.8	8.2	9.7	22.2	12.4	14.9	...	...
February	15.4	14.2	18.9	12.1	22.5	8.3	9.6	22.9	12.5	15.0	...	...
March	15.5	14.2	18.9	12.3	22.4	8.4	9.4	23.1	12.5	15.5	...	...
April	15.3	14.3	18.9	12.4	22.3	8.5	9.5	23.3	12.6	15.2	...	...
May	15.4	14.2	18.7	12.3	22.1	8.5	9.4	23.6	12.6	15.2	...	...
June	15.4	14.2	18.7	12.4	22.1	8.6	9.3	23.7	12.4	15.1	...	...
July	15.3	14.1	18.8	12.2	22.3	8.4	9.2	23.1	12.5	14.9	...	...
August	15.4	14.2	19.0	12.0	22.6	8.6	9.2	23.4	12.4	14.9	...	...
September	15.5	14.2	19.1	12.4	22.7	8.7	9.2	23.6	12.4	15.1	...	...
October	15.7	14.4	19.4	12.6	23.0	8.8	9.5	23.6	12.5	15.2	...	...
November	15.9	14.6	19.7	13.0	23.3	8.8	9.6	24.1	12.7	15.6	...	...
December	15.9	14.7	19.8	13.2	23.2	8.8	9.8	24.1	12.9	15.4	...	...
1948												
January	16.0	14.7	19.7	13.0	23.1	8.9	9.9	25.2	12.9	15.5	...	84.4
February	16.1	14.7	19.7	12.8	23.4	8.9	10.3	24.9	13.1	15.5	...	84.0
March	15.9	14.7	19.5	12.9	23.0	8.9	10.5	25.0	13.0	15.4	...	83.4
April	15.9	14.7	19.7	12.8	23.3	8.9	10.8	24.8	12.9	15.3	...	82.8
May	16.2	14.9	19.6	12.6	23.3	8.8	10.5	25.1	13.0	16.1	...	83.3
June	16.4	15.0	19.9	13.1	23.5	9.0	10.9	24.8	13.1	16.1	...	83.6
July	16.4	15.0	19.9	13.4	23.2	9.0	11.1	25.4	13.0	16.2	...	83.4
August	16.3	15.0	19.7	13.2	23.1	9.0	11.3	25.4	13.2	16.0	...	82.7
September	16.2	14.8	19.6	12.8	23.1	8.9	11.7	25.0	13.1	16.0	...	81.5
October	16.3	14.9	19.8	13.3	23.2	8.8	11.9	25.6	13.1	16.1	...	81.7
November	16.1	14.7	19.6	12.8	23.3	8.8	12.1	24.8	13.1	15.9	...	80.2
December	16.0	14.6	19.4	12.3	23.1	8.7	12.1	24.6	13.2	15.8	...	79.3
1949												
January	15.8	14.4	19.1	11.9	23.0	8.5	11.9	23.9	12.9	15.5	...	77.9
February	15.7	14.3	19.1	11.7	23.1	8.5	11.9	23.4	12.7	15.5	...	76.9
March	15.4	14.2	19.2	11.7	23.3	8.3	11.9	23.1	12.7	14.8	...	75.9
April	15.3	13.9	19.2	11.7	23.2	8.1	11.7	22.8	12.7	14.6	...	74.2
May	15.1	13.8	19.2	11.7	23.3	8.0	11.9	22.5	12.8	14.2	...	73.2
June	15.0	13.8	19.4	11.9	23.3	7.8	11.9	22.5	12.8	14.0	...	73.1
July	15.0	13.8	19.6	12.3	23.4	7.7	11.9	22.2	12.8	14.0	...	73.1
August	15.2	14.0	19.8	12.5	23.7	7.6	11.7	22.4	12.8	14.2	...	73.6
September	15.3	14.2	20.1	13.0	23.7	7.6	11.5	23.1	13.1	14.4	...	74.8
October	14.7	13.7	20.1	13.2	23.8	7.2	11.1	22.4	13.2	13.0	...	71.7
November	15.1	13.8	19.8	12.4	23.7	7.0	11.1	23.1	13.2	14.2	...	72.0
December	15.4	14.2	19.6	12.3	23.6	7.0	11.0	24.1	13.2	14.8	...	73.6
1950												
January	15.7	14.5	20.4	13.7	24.0	7.2	10.9	23.8	13.4	15.0	...	74.9
February	15.7	14.6	20.5	13.7	24.0	7.4	10.9	24.8	13.7	14.7	...	75.4
March	16.2	14.9	20.9	14.3	24.3	7.5	11.0	25.4	13.7	15.7	...	76.4
April	16.8	15.5	21.5	15.3	24.7	7.7	11.3	26.7	14.0	16.3	...	79.2
May	17.2	15.9	22.0	16.1	24.9	8.0	11.7	26.9	14.1	16.8	...	81.0
June	17.7	16.3	22.6	17.4	25.1	8.3	12.0	27.9	14.2	17.5	...	83.1
July	18.2	16.9	23.2	18.2	25.6	8.6	12.7	28.6	14.6	17.9	...	85.5
August	18.8	17.5	24.0	18.7	26.6	9.1	14.0	29.1	14.9	18.5	...	88.4
September	18.7	17.3	23.4	17.9	26.2	8.9	15.4	29.2	14.8	18.7	...	87.2
October	18.8	17.4	23.2	17.5	26.0	9.0	16.6	29.5	15.0	18.9	...	87.5
November	18.8	17.4	23.1	17.1	26.1	9.1	17.7	29.5	15.1	18.7	...	87.0
December	19.1	17.7	23.5	17.0	26.9	9.3	19.2	29.6	15.3	19.0	...	88.1
1951												
January	19.2	17.8	23.6	16.7	27.2	9.4	21.3	29.8	15.5	18.8	...	88.3
February	19.3	17.8	23.6	16.7	27.2	9.5	24.7	29.5	15.3	18.9	...	88.3
March	19.4	17.9	23.2	16.6	26.6	9.6	28.0	29.6	15.5	19.3	...	88.4
April	19.4	18.0	22.8	15.8	26.5	9.9	30.7	29.5	15.9	19.4	...	88.2
May	19.4	17.8	22.4	15.0	26.2	10.0	31.7	29.3	15.7	19.6	...	87.4
June	19.3	17.8	22.1	14.3	26.2	10.1	33.4	29.1	15.4	19.7	...	86.6
July	19.0	17.5	21.4	12.8	26.0	10.2	35.3	28.4	15.3	19.3	...	84.9
August	18.8	17.3	20.9	12.0	25.7	10.3	36.5	28.3	15.1	19.0	...	83.6
September	18.9	17.3	21.1	12.5	25.7	10.5	37.6	28.2	15.0	19.1	...	83.7
October	18.9	17.3	21.0	12.4	25.7	10.7	39.2	28.0	14.7	18.8	...	83.1
November	19.0	17.4	21.3	12.6	26.0	10.9	41.4	27.7	14.7	18.9	...	83.6
December	19.2	17.6	21.5	12.8	26.2	11.0	42.3	27.8	14.8	18.9	...	83.9

. . . = Not available.

Table 20-1. Industrial Production and Capacity Utilization—Continued

(Seasonally adjusted; 2002 = 100, except as noted.)

Year and month	Total industry	Manufac-turing (SIC)	Market groups								Capacity utilization (output as percentage of capacity)	
			Consumer goods			Business equipment	Defense and space equipment	Construction supplies	Business supplies	Materials	Total industry	Manufac-turing (SIC)
			Total	Durable	Nondurable							
1952												
January	19.4	17.7	21.7	12.7	26.5	11.3	43.1	28.2	14.8	19.4	. . .	84.4
February	19.5	17.8	21.8	12.7	26.8	11.5	43.5	28.4	14.8	19.2	. . .	84.6
March	19.5	17.9	21.9	12.9	26.8	11.6	43.6	28.2	14.9	19.2	. . .	84.7
April	19.4	17.8	21.9	12.8	26.9	11.5	44.1	27.8	14.8	18.8	. . .	83.6
May	19.2	17.7	21.9	13.2	26.6	11.6	45.5	27.4	14.7	18.6	. . .	83.1
June	19.0	17.5	22.5	13.4	27.5	11.6	47.0	27.2	15.0	17.5	. . .	81.9
July	18.7	17.2	22.1	12.1	27.6	11.1	47.2	27.1	15.1	17.1	. . .	79.8
August	19.9	18.4	22.6	13.3	27.7	11.3	48.0	29.0	15.2	19.3	. . .	85.1
September	20.6	19.0	23.1	14.6	27.7	11.5	48.8	29.3	15.5	20.6	. . .	87.7
October	20.8	19.3	23.5	15.1	27.9	11.7	50.4	29.7	15.7	20.5	. . .	88.8
November	21.3	19.7	24.0	16.1	28.2	11.8	51.4	30.2	15.8	21.1	. . .	90.2
December	21.4	19.8	24.0	16.1	28.1	11.9	53.0	30.3	15.8	21.1	. . .	90.5
1953												
January	21.4	19.9	24.2	16.7	28.1	12.0	53.7	30.8	15.5	21.0	. . .	90.5
February	21.6	20.1	24.4	16.9	28.3	12.1	54.9	31.3	15.9	21.5	. . .	91.1
March	21.7	20.2	24.4	17.1	28.1	12.1	55.9	31.4	16.2	21.8	. . .	91.4
April	21.8	20.3	24.3	16.9	28.3	12.2	56.7	31.5	16.3	22.0	. . .	91.5
May	21.9	20.4	24.5	17.0	28.4	12.1	57.7	30.8	16.4	22.4	. . .	91.7
June	21.9	20.3	24.1	16.4	28.3	12.0	58.0	30.6	16.4	22.4	. . .	90.7
July	22.1	20.4	24.1	16.3	28.2	12.2	58.5	31.0	16.4	22.7	. . .	91.0
August	22.0	20.4	24.0	16.1	28.1	12.1	58.1	30.9	16.4	22.1	. . .	90.6
September	21.6	19.9	23.7	15.5	27.9	12.0	58.0	30.3	16.3	21.6	. . .	88.3
October	21.4	19.7	23.7	15.3	28.1	12.0	57.5	30.4	16.2	20.9	. . .	87.2
November	20.9	19.2	23.3	14.8	27.8	11.6	53.7	29.9	16.1	20.3	. . .	84.7
December	20.4	18.7	22.9	14.3	27.5	11.4	54.2	29.2	15.9	19.9	. . .	82.3
1954												
January	20.2	18.6	23.0	14.0	27.9	11.1	53.1	29.7	15.9	19.6	. . .	81.3
February	20.3	18.5	23.3	14.4	28.1	10.9	52.7	29.8	16.0	19.6	. . .	80.8
March	20.1	18.4	23.3	14.4	28.1	10.8	52.0	29.6	16.0	19.4	. . .	80.2
April	20.0	18.3	23.3	14.5	27.9	10.6	51.1	29.6	16.1	19.4	. . .	79.4
May	20.1	18.4	23.5	14.8	28.0	10.6	50.4	30.0	16.1	19.6	. . .	79.8
June	20.2	18.5	23.6	14.9	28.1	10.4	49.6	29.3	16.2	19.9	. . .	79.9
July	20.2	18.5	23.7	14.8	28.4	10.4	49.4	29.2	16.0	20.0	. . .	79.4
August	20.2	18.4	23.7	14.9	28.4	10.3	48.4	29.1	16.1	19.8	. . .	78.8
September	20.2	18.5	23.9	15.0	28.7	10.2	47.9	30.5	16.6	19.7	. . .	79.2
October	20.5	18.7	24.0	15.2	28.8	10.2	47.4	31.5	16.8	20.1	. . .	79.7
November	20.8	19.1	24.5	15.6	29.2	10.4	47.2	31.8	17.0	20.5	. . .	80.9
December	21.1	19.3	25.0	16.2	29.5	10.4	46.4	32.1	17.2	20.8	. . .	81.8
1955												
January	21.6	19.8	25.5	17.4	29.6	10.5	46.1	32.6	17.4	21.6	. . .	83.5
February	21.8	20.0	25.6	17.6	29.6	10.7	46.1	33.0	17.6	22.1	. . .	84.1
March	22.3	20.5	26.1	18.0	30.1	10.8	45.9	34.1	18.1	22.7	. . .	85.8
April	22.6	20.8	26.3	18.3	30.3	11.1	45.8	34.4	18.0	23.1	. . .	86.7
May	23.0	21.1	26.7	18.8	30.5	11.3	45.8	34.5	18.3	23.6	. . .	87.9
June	23.0	21.2	26.4	18.4	30.4	11.4	45.4	35.1	18.4	23.6	. . .	87.6
July	23.2	21.2	26.5	18.7	30.4	11.5	45.3	35.1	18.4	23.9	. . .	87.7
August	23.1	21.2	26.6	18.7	30.4	11.5	45.0	35.1	18.2	23.9	. . .	87.3
September	23.3	21.4	26.7	18.7	30.7	11.6	45.1	35.4	18.7	24.2	. . .	87.5
October	23.7	21.7	27.2	18.9	31.5	12.1	44.9	35.4	18.8	24.4	. . .	88.4
November	23.8	21.7	27.3	18.7	31.7	12.2	44.8	35.8	19.1	24.3	. . .	88.3
December	23.8	22.0	27.5	18.6	32.0	12.4	45.0	36.0	19.0	24.5	. . .	89.0
1956												
January	24.0	21.9	27.5	18.4	32.2	12.5	44.5	36.6	19.1	24.6	. . .	88.2
February	23.8	21.8	27.4	18.1	32.2	12.7	44.0	36.4	19.2	24.1	. . .	87.4
March	23.8	21.7	27.4	18.1	32.2	12.8	43.1	36.4	19.3	24.1	. . .	87.0
April	24.0	22.0	27.5	18.4	32.2	13.2	43.4	36.2	19.5	24.2	. . .	87.8
May	23.8	21.8	27.3	17.9	32.3	13.1	43.5	35.7	19.4	23.8	. . .	86.3
June	23.5	21.6	27.3	17.5	32.4	13.2	43.5	35.3	19.3	23.5	. . .	85.3
July	22.8	20.7	27.3	17.5	32.6	13.2	43.5	33.4	19.4	21.6	. . .	81.5
August	23.8	21.7	27.5	17.5	32.8	13.3	44.0	35.1	19.4	23.6	. . .	84.9
September	24.3	22.0	27.5	17.3	32.8	13.4	44.5	36.1	19.4	24.8	. . .	86.0
October	24.5	22.3	27.7	17.5	33.0	13.5	45.6	35.8	19.6	25.2	. . .	86.5
November	24.3	22.2	27.5	17.2	32.9	13.7	46.3	35.5	19.6	24.6	. . .	85.8
December	24.7	22.5	27.8	18.0	32.9	13.9	47.3	36.2	19.7	25.1	. . .	86.8
1957												
January	24.6	22.4	27.9	18.0	33.0	14.1	47.5	35.6	19.8	24.6	. . .	86.2
February	24.8	22.7	28.3	18.3	33.4	14.4	47.8	36.7	19.8	24.8	. . .	87.0
March	24.8	22.6	28.3	18.2	33.6	14.3	47.7	36.1	19.7	24.7	. . .	86.4
April	24.4	22.3	28.0	17.7	33.5	14.0	47.9	35.4	19.7	24.4	. . .	85.0
May	24.4	22.2	28.1	17.6	33.5	13.8	47.2	35.2	19.9	24.2	. . .	84.2
June	24.4	22.4	28.2	17.9	33.6	13.9	47.4	35.4	19.7	24.4	. . .	84.6
July	24.6	22.4	28.3	17.8	33.9	13.9	46.9	35.5	19.8	24.5	. . .	84.3
August	24.6	22.4	28.5	18.2	33.8	13.9	47.0	35.2	19.8	24.6	. . .	84.2
September	24.4	22.2	28.5	18.2	33.9	13.7	46.0	35.0	19.8	24.2	. . .	83.2
October	24.0	21.8	28.0	17.5	33.6	13.3	44.9	34.6	19.6	23.9	. . .	81.4
November	23.4	21.3	28.0	17.5	33.5	13.0	43.4	34.2	19.4	23.0	. . .	79.4
December	23.0	20.9	27.8	16.7	33.8	12.6	43.1	33.6	19.3	22.2	. . .	77.5

. . . = Not available.

Table 20-1. Industrial Production and Capacity Utilization—Continued

(Seasonally adjusted; 2002 = 100, except as noted.)

Year and month	Total industry	Manufac-turing (SIC)	Consumer goods Total	Durable	Nondurable	Business equipment	Defense and space equipment	Construction supplies	Business supplies	Materials	Capacity utilization Total industry	Manufac-turing (SIC)
1958												
January	22.5	20.5	27.4	16.0	33.7	12.3	43.6	33.2	19.2	21.6	. . .	75.7
February	22.1	20.0	27.2	15.5	33.7	11.9	43.9	32.1	19.2	20.9	. . .	73.8
March	21.8	19.8	27.0	15.0	33.7	11.6	44.8	32.0	19.2	20.3	. . .	72.7
April	21.4	19.4	26.7	14.4	33.7	11.4	45.5	31.6	19.1	19.8	. . .	71.3
May	21.6	19.7	27.1	14.9	34.0	11.1	46.0	32.6	19.0	20.1	. . .	71.9
June	22.2	20.3	27.7	15.3	34.5	11.1	47.3	33.9	19.2	20.9	. . .	73.9
July	22.5	20.4	28.1	15.5	35.0	11.2	47.3	33.7	19.3	21.5	. . .	74.3
August	23.0	20.9	28.2	15.8	35.0	11.4	47.8	35.2	19.5	22.1	. . .	75.7
September	23.2	21.1	27.9	14.7	35.2	11.5	48.1	35.3	19.8	22.7	. . .	76.2
October	23.5	21.2	28.1	15.5	35.2	11.6	48.0	35.3	20.1	23.1	. . .	76.4
November	24.2	22.0	29.5	18.1	35.6	11.9	48.4	36.6	20.2	23.7	. . .	79.1
December	24.2	22.0	29.6	18.2	35.7	11.9	48.5	36.2	20.1	23.8	. . .	79.0
1959												
January	24.6	22.4	29.9	18.2	36.1	12.2	48.7	36.9	20.6	24.2	. . .	80.2
February	25.0	22.8	30.2	18.3	36.5	12.3	48.2	37.9	20.8	24.9	. . .	81.4
March	25.4	23.2	30.2	18.7	36.3	12.5	48.4	38.9	20.9	25.6	. . .	82.5
April	25.9	23.7	30.6	18.8	36.9	12.8	48.8	40.0	20.9	26.3	. . .	84.0
May	26.3	24.0	30.8	19.2	36.9	13.2	49.1	40.3	21.0	27.0	. . .	84.9
June	26.4	24.0	30.6	19.3	36.7	13.5	49.3	40.2	21.2	26.8	. . .	84.8
July	25.7	23.6	31.0	19.7	37.0	13.6	49.5	38.6	21.4	25.2	. . .	83.0
August	24.9	22.6	31.1	19.2	37.4	13.4	49.2	36.1	21.4	23.3	. . .	79.5
September	24.8	22.6	31.0	18.6	37.6	13.3	49.5	35.7	21.5	23.3	. . .	79.0
October	24.7	22.4	30.8	19.0	37.1	13.2	49.4	35.9	21.5	23.0	. . .	78.2
November	24.8	22.6	30.2	16.7	37.6	13.0	49.3	37.1	21.4	23.9	. . .	78.5
December	26.3	24.1	31.2	18.8	37.8	13.2	49.7	40.0	21.6	26.5	. . .	83.6
1960												
January	27.0	24.8	32.1	20.9	37.9	13.7	50.1	39.7	21.9	27.3	. . .	85.6
February	26.8	24.6	31.8	20.6	37.6	13.8	50.4	39.3	21.9	26.9	. . .	84.6
March	26.5	24.3	31.8	20.2	37.9	13.8	50.6	38.1	21.9	26.5	. . .	83.2
April	26.3	24.1	32.0	20.1	38.3	13.7	50.3	38.1	22.2	25.9	. . .	82.3
May	26.3	23.9	32.2	20.3	38.4	13.7	50.9	37.7	22.3	25.6	. . .	81.5
June	26.0	23.7	32.0	20.1	38.2	13.5	49.6	37.0	22.1	25.2	. . .	80.2
July	25.9	23.6	31.7	19.4	38.3	13.4	50.8	37.4	22.1	25.2	. . .	79.7
August	25.9	23.5	31.8	19.6	38.3	13.2	51.1	36.4	21.9	25.1	. . .	79.1
September	25.6	23.3	31.6	19.3	38.2	13.1	50.9	36.1	21.8	24.7	. . .	77.9
October	25.6	23.2	32.0	19.5	38.6	13.0	50.4	36.2	21.9	24.6	. . .	77.5
November	25.2	22.8	31.4	18.9	38.2	12.9	50.6	35.8	21.9	24.0	. . .	75.8
December	24.7	22.4	31.2	18.3	38.1	12.7	49.8	35.3	21.5	23.3	. . .	74.3
1961												
January	24.7	22.4	30.9	17.6	38.2	12.7	50.4	35.0	21.9	23.5	. . .	74.1
February	24.7	22.3	31.1	17.5	38.5	12.6	50.0	34.9	21.9	23.4	. . .	73.5
March	24.9	22.5	31.1	17.5	38.5	12.6	49.9	35.7	22.1	23.6	. . .	73.9
April	25.4	23.0	31.8	18.8	38.9	12.7	50.0	36.6	22.2	24.3	. . .	75.4
May	25.8	23.4	32.2	19.4	39.1	12.8	50.0	36.8	22.3	25.0	. . .	76.4
June	26.1	23.7	32.5	20.0	39.3	12.9	50.0	37.6	22.5	25.4	. . .	77.3
July	26.4	24.0	32.8	20.4	39.5	12.9	50.4	38.2	22.7	25.7	. . .	78.1
August	26.7	24.4	33.1	20.4	39.8	13.0	50.6	38.6	22.9	26.2	. . .	79.0
September	26.6	24.2	32.5	19.3	39.6	13.2	51.7	38.9	22.8	26.3	. . .	78.2
October	27.1	24.7	33.4	20.3	40.3	13.2	52.9	39.2	23.1	26.8	. . .	79.6
November	27.6	25.1	34.0	21.2	40.7	13.5	54.1	38.9	23.3	27.1	. . .	80.8
December	27.8	25.4	34.0	21.6	40.7	13.6	55.1	39.2	23.5	27.5	. . .	81.6
1962												
January	27.6	25.1	33.8	21.1	40.5	13.5	55.7	37.4	23.5	27.3	. . .	80.2
February	28.0	25.5	34.0	21.3	40.8	13.7	56.7	39.6	23.7	27.7	. . .	81.4
March	28.2	25.7	34.3	21.6	41.0	13.9	57.5	40.1	23.7	27.8	. . .	81.9
April	28.2	25.8	34.6	22.1	41.1	14.0	58.0	39.5	23.7	27.7	. . .	81.7
May	28.2	25.7	34.7	22.3	41.3	14.0	58.4	39.5	24.1	27.4	. . .	81.3
June	28.1	25.6	34.5	21.9	41.2	14.1	58.9	39.8	24.0	27.3	. . .	80.9
July	28.4	25.9	35.1	22.3	41.7	14.2	60.1	39.6	24.0	27.5	. . .	81.5
August	28.4	25.9	34.7	22.0	41.3	14.4	60.9	40.3	24.1	27.6	. . .	81.4
September	28.6	26.1	34.9	22.3	41.6	14.4	61.1	40.8	24.4	27.8	. . .	81.8
October	28.7	26.1	34.9	22.4	41.4	14.4	61.2	40.1	24.3	27.8	. . .	81.4
November	28.8	26.3	35.1	22.4	41.6	14.4	61.9	40.3	24.5	28.0	. . .	81.8
December	28.8	26.3	35.2	22.6	41.8	14.3	62.1	40.6	24.3	27.9	. . .	81.7
1963												
January	29.0	26.5	35.7	22.8	42.4	14.3	65.0	39.6	24.5	28.0	. . .	81.9
February	29.3	26.7	36.1	23.1	42.8	14.5	64.6	39.7	24.8	28.4	. . .	82.4
March	29.5	26.9	36.2	23.1	43.0	14.4	64.2	40.2	24.5	28.8	. . .	82.6
April	29.8	27.2	36.4	23.3	43.2	14.5	64.1	41.5	25.3	29.1	. . .	83.5
May	30.1	27.5	36.4	23.7	43.0	14.5	64.1	42.4	25.6	29.8	. . .	84.0
June	30.2	27.6	36.6	24.1	43.1	14.5	64.1	42.3	25.5	29.9	. . .	83.9
July	30.1	27.5	36.5	24.1	42.9	14.8	63.4	42.1	25.6	29.6	. . .	83.3
August	30.2	27.6	36.8	24.1	43.4	15.1	63.7	42.2	25.8	29.3	. . .	83.5
September	30.5	27.8	36.9	24.6	43.3	15.1	63.9	41.9	26.1	29.9	. . .	83.8
October	30.7	28.0	37.2	24.6	43.6	15.3	63.9	42.6	26.3	30.1	. . .	84.3
November	30.8	28.1	37.2	24.8	43.6	15.5	63.7	43.1	26.6	30.3	. . .	84.3
December	30.8	28.1	37.5	24.9	43.9	15.4	63.9	42.4	26.4	30.1	. . .	84.0

. . . = Not available.

Table 20-1. Industrial Production and Capacity Utilization—Continued

(Seasonally adjusted; 2002 = 100, except as noted.)

Year and month	Total industry	Manufac-turing (SIC)	Consumer goods Total	Durable	Nondurable	Business equipment	Defense and space equipment	Construction supplies	Business supplies	Materials	Capacity utilization Total industry	Manufac-turing (SIC)
1964												
January	31.0	28.4	37.8	25.0	44.4	15.8	63.2	42.7	26.6	30.3	. . .	84.5
February	31.2	28.5	37.7	25.1	44.2	15.7	62.7	43.8	26.8	30.8	. . .	84.7
March	31.2	28.5	37.6	24.9	44.1	15.9	62.5	43.9	26.9	30.8	. . .	84.4
April	31.7	29.0	38.5	25.6	45.1	16.3	62.4	44.1	27.3	31.2	. . .	85.6
May	31.9	29.2	38.8	25.7	45.5	16.5	61.3	44.3	27.6	31.4	. . .	85.6
June	32.0	29.2	38.7	26.0	45.2	16.5	60.9	44.0	27.6	31.6	. . .	85.4
July	32.2	29.5	39.3	26.4	45.8	16.8	60.8	44.9	27.6	31.7	. . .	85.9
August	32.4	29.6	39.2	26.6	45.5	16.8	61.1	44.4	27.5	32.3	. . .	86.1
September	32.6	29.8	38.8	26.0	45.3	16.9	61.5	44.1	27.5	32.8	. . .	86.2
October	32.1	29.3	38.0	23.3	45.9	16.8	61.9	44.2	27.6	32.2	. . .	84.6
November	33.1	30.2	39.4	26.5	46.0	17.3	62.6	45.3	27.8	33.2	. . .	86.8
December	33.5	30.8	40.2	28.0	46.3	17.6	63.0	44.7	28.0	33.6	. . .	88.0
1965												
January	33.9	31.1	40.8	28.5	46.9	17.6	63.7	45.0	28.3	34.0	. . .	88.6
February	34.1	31.3	40.9	28.9	46.8	17.9	64.4	46.2	28.4	34.1	. . .	88.7
March	34.5	31.7	41.3	29.7	46.9	18.1	65.6	46.6	28.7	34.7	. . .	89.3
April	34.7	31.9	41.2	29.6	46.8	18.3	66.4	45.9	28.7	35.0	. . .	89.3
May	34.9	32.1	41.4	29.8	47.0	18.6	67.8	46.4	29.0	35.2	. . .	89.4
June	35.2	32.3	41.6	30.1	47.1	18.8	68.7	46.4	29.1	35.6	. . .	89.5
July	35.5	32.8	41.6	30.3	46.9	19.2	69.8	47.7	29.1	35.9	. . .	90.3
August	35.7	32.9	41.5	30.0	47.1	19.2	70.3	47.2	29.4	36.2	. . .	89.9
September	35.8	32.9	42.1	30.6	47.7	19.5	70.5	46.8	29.4	36.0	. . .	89.6
October	36.1	33.2	42.4	30.8	47.8	19.8	71.4	47.5	29.7	36.3	. . .	89.8
November	36.3	33.4	42.6	31.1	48.1	20.2	72.0	48.2	29.9	36.2	. . .	89.6
December	36.7	33.9	42.8	31.7	48.0	20.6	72.7	49.2	30.4	36.6	. . .	90.5
1966												
January	37.1	34.2	43.1	31.8	48.3	21.0	74.2	49.2	30.4	37.1	. . .	90.9
February	37.3	34.4	43.2	31.7	48.6	21.0	75.4	48.7	30.7	37.5	. . .	90.9
March	37.8	34.9	43.5	32.0	48.9	21.4	76.0	49.7	31.0	38.2	. . .	91.6
April	37.9	35.1	43.6	32.6	48.8	21.6	77.6	49.7	30.8	38.1	. . .	91.5
May	38.3	35.3	43.6	32.1	49.1	21.8	79.1	49.9	31.2	38.5	. . .	91.6
June	38.5	35.5	43.8	32.1	49.4	22.0	80.2	49.2	31.6	38.8	. . .	91.5
July	38.7	35.7	43.8	31.5	49.7	22.4	81.3	49.7	32.0	38.9	. . .	91.4
August	38.7	35.7	43.6	31.0	49.8	22.5	82.4	48.2	31.8	39.2	. . .	91.1
September	39.1	36.0	43.8	31.1	49.9	22.7	83.5	48.2	32.0	39.6	. . .	91.2
October	39.3	36.4	44.7	32.8	50.3	22.7	84.8	48.2	32.0	39.8	. . .	91.6
November	39.1	36.0	44.4	31.8	50.6	22.3	86.3	48.3	32.1	39.2	. . .	90.1
December	39.1	36.2	44.3	31.4	50.6	22.7	87.2	48.2	32.2	39.2	. . .	90.0
1967												
January	39.3	36.3	44.7	30.7	51.8	22.5	88.7	49.5	32.8	39.0	89.4	89.8
February	38.9	35.9	44.1	29.8	51.4	22.5	89.7	49.1	32.6	38.3	88.0	88.4
March	38.7	35.7	44.3	30.1	51.4	22.5	90.6	49.1	32.6	37.6	87.1	87.5
April	39.0	35.9	45.0	30.3	52.5	22.5	91.5	49.0	32.9	37.9	87.5	87.7
May	38.7	35.7	44.2	29.9	51.4	22.6	92.2	49.8	32.4	37.5	86.4	86.6
June	38.7	35.6	44.3	29.6	51.8	22.4	92.0	50.1	32.6	37.4	86.0	86.1
July	38.6	35.5	44.2	30.0	51.4	22.0	92.5	50.3	32.7	37.4	85.4	85.3
August	39.3	36.1	44.7	30.3	51.9	22.4	92.7	50.8	33.6	38.5	86.6	86.5
September	39.3	36.1	44.7	30.2	52.1	22.3	92.9	51.2	33.7	38.3	86.1	86.1
October	39.6	36.4	45.3	30.8	52.7	22.1	93.7	50.9	33.9	38.7	86.4	86.4
November	40.2	37.1	46.3	32.5	53.1	22.7	93.8	51.3	34.0	39.2	87.3	87.5
December	40.6	37.5	47.1	33.8	53.5	22.9	93.8	51.2	33.9	39.7	87.8	88.0
1968												
January	40.5	37.4	46.4	32.8	53.1	23.0	93.4	51.6	34.0	39.9	87.4	87.4
February	40.7	37.5	46.7	33.3	53.2	23.0	94.5	52.1	34.3	39.9	87.3	87.4
March	40.8	37.6	47.0	33.2	53.7	23.2	92.7	52.2	34.3	40.0	87.3	87.2
April	40.9	37.6	46.9	33.3	53.6	23.1	90.8	52.5	34.6	40.3	87.1	86.9
May	41.3	38.1	47.1	33.7	53.7	23.4	92.1	52.7	35.0	40.9	87.7	87.6
June	41.5	38.2	47.4	34.0	54.0	23.4	92.6	52.7	35.1	41.1	87.7	87.4
July	41.4	38.1	47.3	33.7	54.0	23.2	92.6	52.8	35.1	41.1	87.2	86.7
August	41.5	38.3	47.9	34.2	54.6	23.4	92.8	53.0	35.5	40.8	87.1	86.8
September	41.7	38.3	48.1	34.5	54.6	23.6	92.7	52.6	35.6	41.0	87.1	86.5
October	41.8	38.5	48.4	35.0	54.8	23.8	90.3	52.6	35.8	41.1	86.9	86.6
November	42.3	39.1	49.0	35.8	55.3	23.8	91.2	53.8	36.2	41.7	87.7	87.5
December	42.5	39.1	48.7	36.1	54.6	24.1	90.7	54.8	36.4	41.9	87.6	87.1
1969												
January	42.7	39.3	49.0	36.0	55.1	24.4	90.9	55.2	36.6	42.1	87.8	87.3
February	43.0	39.6	49.4	36.0	55.7	24.4	90.2	55.7	36.4	42.6	88.1	87.6
March	43.3	39.9	49.7	36.2	56.2	24.7	90.6	55.9	37.6	42.8	88.5	88.0
April	43.2	39.8	49.0	35.2	55.6	24.9	89.9	55.4	37.1	42.9	87.8	87.3
May	43.0	39.6	48.6	34.8	55.3	24.7	89.7	55.0	37.4	42.8	87.2	86.6
June	43.4	39.8	49.2	35.9	55.4	25.0	88.4	55.3	37.7	43.4	87.7	86.8
July	43.6	40.1	50.1	35.9	56.8	25.3	88.1	54.8	37.5	43.4	87.9	87.1
August	43.7	40.2	50.0	36.3	56.4	25.2	86.8	54.8	37.7	43.8	87.7	86.9
September	43.7	40.1	49.6	36.0	56.0	25.4	86.3	54.8	37.6	44.0	87.4	86.4
October	43.7	40.2	49.6	36.2	55.9	25.5	85.5	55.0	37.7	44.0	87.1	86.2
November	43.3	39.8	49.2	34.7	56.3	24.9	83.9	54.6	37.5	43.7	86.0	85.0
December	43.2	39.5	49.2	34.5	56.5	24.8	82.9	54.3	37.9	43.5	85.5	84.2

. . . = Not available.

Table 20-1. Industrial Production and Capacity Utilization—Continued

(Seasonally adjusted; 2002 = 100, except as noted.)

Year and month	Total industry	Manufac- turing (SIC)	Consumer goods Total	Durable	Nondurable	Business equipment	Defense and space equipment	Construction supplies	Business supplies	Materials	Total industry	Manufac- turing (SIC)
1970												
January	42.4	38.7	48.4	32.7	56.4	24.5	81.7	52.6	37.9	42.5	83.6	82.1
February	42.4	38.7	48.9	33.1	56.8	24.6	80.4	52.4	37.6	42.2	83.3	81.9
March	42.3	38.6	48.8	33.4	56.5	24.6	78.6	52.9	37.8	42.1	82.9	81.4
April	42.2	38.5	49.0	33.4	56.8	24.6	76.9	53.4	37.6	41.8	82.5	80.8
May	42.2	38.4	49.3	33.5	57.3	24.6	75.2	53.5	37.5	41.7	82.1	80.4
June	42.0	38.3	49.4	34.1	57.0	24.4	73.9	53.3	37.5	41.5	81.6	79.9
July	42.1	38.4	49.5	34.2	57.2	24.4	72.7	53.9	37.6	41.7	81.5	79.9
August	42.1	38.1	48.7	33.1	56.5	24.3	72.1	53.6	37.3	42.2	81.1	79.1
September	41.8	37.8	48.5	32.2	56.8	23.8	71.4	53.5	37.6	41.9	80.3	78.2
October	40.9	36.9	47.9	30.3	57.1	23.0	70.4	53.0	37.4	40.8	78.5	76.2
November	40.7	36.7	47.6	30.4	56.6	22.9	69.8	52.3	37.5	40.6	77.8	75.5
December	41.6	37.7	49.6	34.0	57.5	23.2	69.1	52.9	37.5	41.5	79.3	77.3
1971												
January	42.0	38.0	50.4	35.3	57.8	22.7	69.6	53.0	37.7	42.1	79.7	77.7
February	41.9	38.0	50.4	36.1	57.2	22.8	67.9	53.3	38.1	41.8	79.3	77.5
March	41.8	37.9	50.5	36.1	57.4	22.5	67.3	53.1	37.8	41.9	79.0	77.2
April	42.1	38.1	50.9	36.4	57.9	22.4	67.4	53.6	38.1	42.2	79.3	77.4
May	42.3	38.4	51.0	36.9	57.6	22.3	68.2	53.8	38.2	42.7	79.5	77.7
June	42.5	38.5	51.3	37.2	58.0	22.4	67.2	54.4	38.1	42.9	79.6	77.7
July	42.3	38.6	52.1	37.9	58.9	22.4	66.6	54.9	39.0	41.8	79.2	77.6
August	42.1	38.1	51.5	37.6	58.1	22.7	66.7	54.0	38.6	41.6	78.5	76.5
September	42.8	38.9	52.0	37.5	59.0	23.3	66.0	56.0	39.2	42.4	79.6	77.9
October	43.1	39.5	52.7	38.2	59.6	23.5	65.6	56.8	39.5	42.5	80.0	78.8
November	43.3	39.6	53.1	38.6	60.1	23.6	65.0	56.9	39.9	42.6	80.1	78.9
December	43.8	40.0	53.5	38.7	60.5	23.7	64.1	57.9	40.0	43.5	80.9	79.4
1972												
January	44.8	41.0	54.3	39.9	61.1	24.5	63.8	59.5	40.7	44.8	82.6	81.2
February	45.2	41.3	54.6	40.0	61.4	24.8	64.0	59.7	41.4	45.3	83.1	81.6
March	45.6	41.6	54.6	39.8	61.7	25.1	64.7	60.2	41.9	45.7	83.5	82.0
April	46.0	42.0	55.2	40.9	61.8	25.5	65.0	60.8	41.9	46.2	84.2	82.7
May	46.0	42.1	55.0	40.6	61.7	25.6	64.3	61.1	42.1	46.3	84.0	82.6
June	46.2	42.3	55.0	40.6	61.8	25.8	64.4	61.7	42.5	46.3	84.0	82.8
July	46.2	42.3	55.5	41.5	61.8	25.8	64.4	62.6	42.5	46.0	83.8	82.6
August	46.8	42.9	56.1	41.9	62.6	26.3	64.3	63.0	43.0	46.7	84.7	83.4
September	47.1	43.2	56.3	42.3	62.7	26.5	64.8	63.5	43.0	47.2	85.1	83.8
October	47.8	43.8	57.2	43.3	63.4	27.0	65.0	64.5	43.7	47.7	86.0	84.8
November	48.3	44.4	57.6	44.2	63.4	27.5	66.9	64.9	43.9	48.4	86.8	85.7
December	48.9	45.0	58.1	45.1	63.5	27.8	68.0	64.8	44.0	49.2	87.5	86.5
1973												
January	49.2	45.3	57.9	44.9	63.5	28.1	68.9	65.5	44.3	49.6	87.7	86.8
February	49.9	46.0	58.7	45.7	64.1	28.8	70.5	66.7	44.8	50.3	88.8	88.0
March	49.9	46.1	58.8	45.8	64.3	29.0	70.2	67.1	44.8	50.2	88.5	87.8
April	49.8	46.0	58.2	45.1	63.8	29.2	69.8	66.9	44.8	50.3	88.1	87.4
May	50.2	46.3	58.6	45.0	64.5	29.6	70.1	67.3	45.1	50.6	88.4	87.7
June	50.2	46.3	58.2	44.9	63.9	29.9	70.8	67.3	45.1	50.7	88.2	87.4
July	50.4	46.5	58.1	44.9	63.7	30.3	72.3	67.9	45.4	50.9	88.3	87.6
August	50.3	46.4	57.5	43.5	63.8	30.4	72.4	68.0	45.4	50.9	87.9	87.0
September	50.8	46.8	58.5	45.0	64.3	30.9	72.5	67.9	45.4	51.2	88.4	87.5
October	51.1	47.2	58.7	44.7	64.9	31.3	74.0	67.8	45.9	51.5	88.7	87.9
November	51.4	47.5	58.9	44.7	65.2	31.4	73.5	68.2	45.9	51.9	88.9	88.3
December	51.2	47.5	57.8	43.8	64.1	31.6	72.8	68.9	45.5	52.1	88.4	88.1
1974												
January	50.9	47.1	57.0	41.5	64.3	31.6	72.3	68.9	45.5	51.7	87.5	87.1
February	50.7	47.0	56.8	41.3	64.1	31.5	73.1	68.1	45.3	51.6	87.0	86.5
March	50.7	46.9	56.9	41.4	64.2	31.7	73.0	68.3	45.4	51.4	86.7	86.2
April	50.6	46.8	56.7	41.2	64.1	31.6	72.9	67.7	45.5	51.4	86.4	85.7
May	51.0	47.1	57.2	41.2	64.8	31.9	73.2	68.0	45.7	51.7	86.7	85.9
June	50.9	47.1	57.5	41.8	64.9	31.8	72.2	67.6	45.9	51.5	86.4	85.8
July	50.9	47.0	57.3	41.7	64.8	31.8	73.1	66.3	45.5	51.7	86.2	85.4
August	50.4	46.7	57.3	41.6	64.8	31.8	74.7	65.5	45.3	50.8	85.2	84.5
September	50.5	46.7	56.8	41.5	64.0	32.3	75.0	65.1	45.1	51.0	85.1	84.4
October	50.3	46.3	56.9	41.0	64.4	32.3	76.1	64.0	44.9	50.7	84.5	83.6
November	48.6	44.9	55.2	39.0	63.1	31.8	75.8	61.9	43.9	48.5	81.6	80.9
December	46.9	42.9	53.5	35.8	62.5	30.4	75.0	59.1	43.0	46.6	78.6	77.1
1975												
January	46.3	42.1	52.3	34.3	61.5	29.8	76.0	58.8	42.3	46.2	77.4	75.4
February	45.2	40.8	51.6	33.3	61.0	28.7	71.8	56.9	41.5	45.1	75.3	73.1
March	44.7	40.3	51.7	33.8	61.0	28.2	72.5	54.8	40.9	44.4	74.4	72.0
April	44.7	40.2	52.8	35.0	61.9	27.9	72.1	54.3	41.0	44.2	74.3	71.7
May	44.6	40.3	53.1	36.0	61.7	27.6	75.5	54.4	40.8	43.9	74.1	71.6
June	44.9	40.6	53.8	36.4	62.6	27.3	76.7	54.1	40.9	44.2	74.4	72.1
July	45.4	41.2	55.2	38.2	63.6	27.6	75.7	54.9	41.3	44.4	75.1	73.0
August	45.8	41.6	55.5	38.7	63.8	27.4	75.1	55.5	41.7	45.1	75.6	73.6
September	46.4	42.3	56.3	39.5	64.5	27.8	77.4	56.1	41.9	45.7	76.5	74.7
October	46.6	42.5	56.4	39.4	64.7	27.8	76.8	56.4	42.1	46.0	76.6	74.8
November	46.7	42.6	56.6	39.4	65.1	27.7	73.7	56.7	42.2	46.2	76.6	74.9
December	47.3	43.2	57.1	40.1	65.4	28.1	76.1	56.8	42.6	46.9	77.4	75.7

Table 20-1. Industrial Production and Capacity Utilization—Continued

(Seasonally adjusted; 2002 = 100, except as noted.)

Year and month	Total industry	Manufac-turing (SIC)	Market groups								Capacity utilization (output as percentage of capacity)	
			Consumer goods			Business equipment	Defense and space equipment	Construction supplies	Business supplies	Materials	Total industry	Manufac-turing (SIC)
			Total	Durable	Nondurable							
1976												
January	48.0	43.7	57.9	40.8	66.2	28.5	76.5	58.2	43.0	47.6	78.4	76.6
February	48.4	44.3	58.0	41.3	66.2	28.6	76.1	59.1	43.1	48.3	78.9	77.4
March	48.4	44.4	57.9	41.2	66.0	28.6	76.1	58.2	43.3	48.5	78.8	77.4
April	48.8	44.7	58.1	41.2	66.2	29.0	74.6	59.1	43.6	48.9	79.2	77.8
May	49.0	44.9	58.6	41.3	67.0	29.2	73.8	59.7	43.7	48.9	79.3	78.0
June	49.0	45.0	58.3	41.1	66.7	29.3	73.1	60.1	43.4	49.0	79.2	77.8
July	49.2	45.3	58.7	41.4	67.1	29.6	71.1	61.4	44.1	49.1	79.4	78.2
August	49.6	45.6	58.8	42.0	67.0	30.1	71.1	60.8	44.2	49.6	79.8	78.5
September	49.7	45.7	58.8	41.6	67.1	30.1	70.9	61.1	45.2	49.7	79.8	78.5
October	49.8	45.7	59.3	42.1	67.6	30.3	70.9	61.1	45.4	49.5	79.8	78.3
November	50.5	46.3	60.4	43.5	68.4	31.2	70.2	61.5	45.7	50.1	80.8	79.1
December	51.0	46.8	61.0	44.6	68.7	31.6	69.1	61.8	46.1	50.7	81.4	79.8
1977												
January	50.8	46.6	60.9	44.5	68.6	31.7	68.0	60.8	45.9	50.2	80.7	79.3
February	51.5	47.5	61.6	45.0	69.4	32.5	67.8	62.2	46.5	51.0	81.7	80.5
March	52.2	48.2	61.7	46.2	68.7	32.9	66.3	63.6	46.8	52.0	82.5	81.5
April	52.6	48.7	62.0	46.6	69.0	33.4	66.6	65.1	47.3	52.4	83.1	82.1
May	53.0	49.1	62.1	46.8	69.0	33.9	66.5	66.0	47.8	52.9	83.5	82.5
June	53.4	49.4	62.5	47.7	69.1	34.6	66.4	66.5	48.2	53.1	83.8	82.9
July	53.6	49.5	62.7	47.7	69.3	35.0	66.3	66.6	48.4	53.1	83.8	82.8
August	53.6	49.8	62.8	47.7	69.5	35.3	65.5	67.1	48.7	53.0	83.7	83.0
September	53.9	49.9	62.8	47.9	69.3	35.6	65.5	66.8	48.8	53.4	83.8	82.9
October	54.0	50.0	63.4	47.9	70.3	35.5	60.0	66.9	48.8	53.6	83.8	82.9
November	54.0	50.1	63.4	47.9	70.3	35.5	59.0	67.2	48.9	53.7	83.6	82.8
December	54.1	50.6	63.9	48.1	71.0	36.2	63.1	67.8	49.2	53.1	83.5	83.4
1978												
January	53.4	49.9	62.3	45.5	70.2	35.6	63.8	66.5	49.1	52.6	82.1	82.0
February	53.6	50.0	63.3	46.6	71.1	36.3	60.6	66.3	49.2	52.5	82.3	82.1
March	54.6	50.9	64.6	48.1	72.1	37.1	65.9	67.6	49.9	53.3	83.5	83.2
April	55.7	51.7	65.1	49.0	72.3	38.0	65.5	69.1	50.0	54.9	85.0	84.3
May	55.9	51.9	64.6	48.3	72.0	37.9	65.6	69.0	50.3	55.4	85.1	84.3
June	56.3	52.3	65.0	48.7	72.4	38.6	66.2	69.6	50.8	55.7	85.5	84.8
July	56.3	52.2	64.7	48.8	71.9	38.8	66.2	69.6	50.7	55.7	85.2	84.5
August	56.5	52.5	64.6	48.5	71.9	39.4	66.9	69.8	50.8	55.9	85.3	84.6
September	56.6	52.7	64.7	48.2	72.2	39.7	67.0	70.0	50.9	56.0	85.3	84.7
October	57.1	53.1	64.7	48.4	72.1	40.6	66.7	70.7	51.2	56.6	85.8	85.2
November	57.6	53.6	64.9	48.5	72.3	41.4	66.3	71.1	51.4	57.0	86.3	85.8
December	57.9	54.1	65.0	48.7	72.5	41.9	67.0	72.4	51.8	57.3	86.6	86.2
1979												
January	57.5	53.6	64.8	49.0	72.0	42.3	67.2	70.5	51.8	56.5	85.8	85.2
February	57.8	53.9	64.4	48.4	71.7	43.1	68.8	71.0	52.3	57.0	86.1	85.4
March	58.0	54.1	64.7	48.3	72.2	43.4	68.1	71.9	52.5	57.1	86.2	85.6
April	57.5	53.3	63.5	46.0	71.8	42.7	66.7	70.7	52.3	56.8	85.1	84.1
May	57.8	53.9	63.9	47.3	71.6	43.7	67.7	71.0	52.4	57.0	85.5	84.8
June	57.8	54.0	63.6	46.8	71.4	43.9	68.3	71.3	52.1	57.1	85.3	84.7
July	57.7	54.0	63.1	46.2	71.0	44.3	69.6	71.3	52.2	56.9	85.0	84.6
August	57.3	53.3	62.4	44.1	71.3	43.7	70.6	70.6	52.4	56.5	84.2	83.2
September	57.4	53.5	62.8	45.7	70.8	44.9	71.2	70.7	51.8	56.2	84.1	83.2
October	57.7	53.6	62.9	45.4	71.2	44.3	73.5	71.2	52.3	56.7	84.4	83.3
November	57.7	53.5	62.7	44.6	71.4	44.3	75.3	70.9	52.5	56.6	84.1	82.8
December	57.7	53.7	62.8	44.5	71.6	44.6	76.8	71.3	52.6	56.6	84.1	82.9
1980												
January	58.0	53.9	62.5	43.6	71.7	45.3	77.9	71.1	52.2	57.0	84.3	83.0
February	58.0	53.9	62.7	43.3	72.3	45.6	81.5	70.0	52.2	56.8	84.1	82.8
March	57.8	53.4	62.3	42.5	72.1	45.2	82.2	69.2	52.1	56.8	83.7	81.9
April	56.7	52.4	61.3	40.7	71.7	44.7	82.9	66.0	51.3	55.4	81.9	80.1
May	55.2	50.7	60.0	38.2	71.2	43.9	83.1	63.3	50.2	53.8	79.6	77.4
June	54.5	50.0	59.7	37.6	71.2	43.3	83.8	62.0	49.6	52.8	78.5	76.0
July	54.2	49.5	59.8	37.5	71.3	43.4	84.6	61.5	49.8	52.1	77.8	75.2
August	54.3	49.9	60.1	37.8	71.6	43.3	84.8	62.4	50.0	52.2	77.9	75.5
September	55.2	50.7	60.6	39.6	71.2	44.0	85.0	64.0	50.7	53.3	79.0	76.5
October	55.9	51.5	61.0	40.3	71.5	44.7	86.2	65.3	50.8	54.0	79.8	77.6
November	56.9	52.5	61.4	41.3	71.3	45.5	87.3	66.7	51.4	55.2	81.0	78.9
December	57.2	52.7	61.3	40.8	71.7	45.6	87.6	66.6	52.0	55.8	81.3	78.9
1981												
January	56.9	52.5	61.3	40.6	71.8	45.9	87.4	66.4	52.0	55.1	80.7	78.4
February	56.6	52.1	61.1	40.4	71.6	45.3	86.8	65.7	51.5	54.9	80.1	77.7
March	56.9	52.3	61.1	41.0	71.2	45.8	87.0	66.0	51.6	55.3	80.4	77.8
April	56.6	52.6	61.3	41.5	71.2	46.1	87.1	66.0	51.8	54.5	79.8	78.0
May	57.0	52.9	62.0	42.2	71.8	46.3	88.1	66.0	52.5	54.8	80.2	78.2
June	57.3	52.7	61.6	41.9	71.3	46.1	89.0	65.0	52.7	55.6	80.4	77.7
July	57.7	52.8	62.0	42.1	71.8	46.2	90.3	65.1	53.0	56.0	80.7	77.7
August	57.7	52.8	62.0	41.8	72.1	46.2	91.5	65.0	52.7	56.0	80.6	77.6
September	57.3	52.6	61.4	40.8	71.8	46.2	93.4	64.5	52.7	55.5	79.9	77.0
October	56.9	52.1	61.8	40.6	72.5	45.9	95.3	62.6	52.4	54.7	79.1	76.1
November	56.3	51.5	61.7	39.8	72.9	45.3	97.9	61.7	52.1	53.8	78.1	75.0
December	55.7	50.6	61.1	38.2	73.0	44.5	100.7	60.6	52.1	53.1	77.0	73.6

Table 20-1. Industrial Production and Capacity Utilization—Continued

(Seasonally adjusted; 2002 = 100, except as noted.)

Year and month	Total industry	Manufac-turing (SIC)	Consumer goods Total	Consumer goods Durable	Consumer goods Nondurable	Business equipment	Defense and space equipment	Construction supplies	Business supplies	Materials	Cap. util. Total industry	Cap. util. Manufac-turing (SIC)
1982												
January	54.6	49.4	60.1	37.1	72.1	42.9	100.7	58.5	51.4	52.2	75.4	71.8
February	55.7	50.8	61.7	38.5	73.7	44.3	105.9	60.6	52.4	52.8	76.6	73.5
March	55.3	50.4	61.3	38.3	73.2	43.7	107.3	59.3	52.1	52.5	75.9	72.8
April	54.8	50.0	61.3	39.1	72.7	43.3	108.1	58.9	51.9	51.8	75.1	72.1
May	54.4	49.9	61.3	39.1	72.7	43.1	109.6	59.1	51.6	51.2	74.4	71.8
June	54.2	49.8	61.6	39.4	73.0	42.2	109.7	58.6	51.6	51.0	74.0	71.5
July	54.0	49.7	61.7	39.6	73.1	42.1	111.0	58.5	51.6	50.6	73.6	71.3
August	53.6	49.3	61.6	39.1	73.2	41.1	110.5	58.5	51.6	50.1	72.9	70.6
September	53.3	49.2	61.5	38.5	73.5	40.8	112.0	58.7	51.6	49.8	72.5	70.2
October	52.9	48.6	61.6	38.0	74.0	39.9	111.8	57.8	51.5	49.2	71.8	69.4
November	52.7	48.3	61.5	38.0	73.7	39.5	111.9	57.5	51.4	49.0	71.4	68.8
December	52.2	48.1	60.7	37.9	72.5	39.8	111.0	56.9	51.2	48.6	70.7	68.4
1983												
January	53.2	49.2	61.9	39.5	73.4	39.8	110.1	59.1	51.8	49.7	72.0	70.0
February	52.9	49.2	61.2	39.4	72.3	39.6	108.4	58.7	51.8	49.5	71.5	69.9
March	53.4	49.7	61.5	40.0	72.4	40.1	108.7	59.5	52.6	50.0	72.1	70.5
April	54.0	50.2	62.7	40.8	73.8	40.1	107.7	60.3	53.2	50.6	72.9	71.3
May	54.4	50.9	63.0	41.7	73.7	40.6	107.8	61.4	53.2	51.0	73.4	72.2
June	54.7	51.3	63.2	42.4	73.6	40.9	107.1	62.5	53.5	51.3	73.8	72.7
July	55.6	52.0	64.1	43.4	74.4	41.8	108.7	63.8	54.2	52.2	74.9	73.8
August	56.2	52.4	64.7	44.2	74.8	42.1	109.3	64.0	54.8	52.9	75.7	74.3
September	57.0	53.4	65.5	45.0	75.6	43.3	110.3	64.8	55.8	53.6	76.8	75.7
October	57.5	54.1	65.2	45.5	74.7	43.9	112.1	65.9	56.0	54.4	77.5	76.5
November	57.7	54.2	65.1	45.5	74.7	44.2	112.3	65.7	56.2	54.7	77.6	76.7
December	58.0	54.4	65.2	46.5	74.2	44.6	113.5	65.9	56.3	54.9	77.9	76.8
1984												
January	59.2	55.4	66.6	47.6	75.7	45.6	116.6	66.3	57.4	56.0	79.5	78.1
February	59.4	56.0	66.4	47.8	75.3	46.1	119.2	67.8	57.5	56.4	79.7	78.9
March	59.7	56.2	66.7	47.9	75.6	46.6	119.5	67.4	58.0	56.6	80.0	79.1
April	60.1	56.5	66.8	47.8	76.0	47.1	122.2	67.8	58.0	57.0	80.4	79.4
May	60.4	56.7	66.6	47.4	75.8	47.4	122.8	68.1	58.8	57.4	80.7	79.5
June	60.6	56.9	66.5	47.5	75.6	48.0	123.9	68.5	59.2	57.5	80.8	79.6
July	60.8	57.2	66.5	48.1	75.3	48.6	122.6	68.3	59.4	57.7	80.9	79.8
August	60.9	57.3	66.1	48.4	74.5	49.3	126.6	68.6	59.4	57.6	80.9	79.8
September	60.8	57.2	66.0	47.7	74.7	49.5	129.3	68.9	59.4	57.4	80.6	79.4
October	60.7	57.4	66.5	47.3	75.7	49.9	130.6	68.5	59.7	56.9	80.3	79.5
November	60.9	57.6	66.7	48.1	75.6	50.3	130.0	68.4	59.9	57.1	80.5	79.6
December	61.0	57.8	67.0	48.6	75.8	50.6	131.8	69.2	59.5	56.9	80.4	79.6
1985												
January	60.8	57.6	66.6	48.0	75.5	50.4	132.4	67.9	59.6	57.0	79.9	79.1
February	61.1	57.4	67.1	47.6	76.5	50.1	134.0	68.1	60.2	57.2	80.1	78.6
March	61.2	57.9	67.0	48.1	76.1	50.6	136.2	69.9	60.1	57.1	80.0	79.0
April	61.1	57.7	66.7	47.5	75.9	50.1	136.9	69.9	60.5	57.1	79.7	78.6
May	61.1	57.8	66.7	47.5	76.0	50.2	137.7	70.2	60.6	57.1	79.6	78.5
June	61.2	57.9	67.0	47.5	76.5	50.3	139.6	70.6	60.3	57.0	79.4	78.4
July	60.8	57.6	66.7	47.5	76.0	50.0	138.4	70.3	59.8	56.6	78.7	77.7
August	61.1	57.9	67.0	48.0	76.2	50.2	141.0	70.5	60.4	56.7	78.9	78.0
September	61.3	58.0	67.5	47.9	76.9	50.0	141.9	70.4	60.9	57.0	79.1	77.9
October	61.1	57.8	67.4	47.7	76.8	50.0	143.8	70.5	60.4	56.7	78.6	77.6
November	61.3	58.2	67.7	48.8	76.7	50.4	146.0	70.4	60.5	56.8	78.8	77.9
December	61.9	58.4	68.4	49.0	77.8	50.3	146.7	70.2	61.4	57.5	79.4	78.1
1986												
January	62.2	59.1	69.2	50.3	78.2	50.4	148.4	71.8	61.8	57.6	79.7	78.9
February	61.7	58.7	68.5	49.9	77.4	49.7	145.5	71.1	61.3	57.4	79.0	78.2
March	61.4	58.6	68.3	49.9	77.1	49.8	146.9	71.3	61.0	56.8	78.4	77.9
April	61.4	58.8	68.7	49.7	77.8	49.4	147.2	72.0	61.5	56.6	78.3	78.1
May	61.5	58.9	69.1	49.9	78.3	49.3	147.6	72.5	62.0	56.7	78.4	78.2
June	61.3	58.7	69.2	50.5	78.1	48.7	147.9	71.6	62.5	56.4	78.0	77.8
July	61.7	59.0	69.6	51.1	78.5	49.1	149.2	72.1	62.5	56.8	78.4	78.1
August	61.6	59.2	69.6	51.3	78.2	49.2	149.0	72.8	62.6	56.5	78.2	78.2
September	61.7	59.3	69.6	51.7	78.1	49.1	148.5	72.9	62.7	56.7	78.3	78.3
October	61.9	59.5	70.0	51.8	78.5	48.9	148.7	72.8	63.2	57.0	78.5	78.4
November	62.2	59.8	70.5	52.4	78.9	49.0	149.7	73.0	63.2	57.3	78.8	78.7
December	62.8	60.3	71.1	53.4	79.4	49.5	149.7	73.5	64.1	57.8	79.3	79.2
1987												
January	62.6	60.1	70.4	53.1	78.5	49.6	151.1	74.2	63.6	57.7	79.0	78.9
February	63.4	61.0	71.3	53.9	79.3	50.8	151.0	75.5	64.1	58.3	79.8	79.8
March	63.5	61.0	71.5	53.6	79.8	50.5	151.0	75.2	64.5	58.5	79.8	79.7
April	63.8	61.3	71.4	53.3	79.9	50.9	150.9	75.6	65.2	59.0	80.1	79.9
May	64.3	61.8	71.9	53.6	80.5	51.4	150.6	76.2	66.0	59.3	80.6	80.4
June	64.6	62.0	72.0	53.1	81.0	51.9	150.1	76.3	66.3	59.6	80.8	80.5
July	65.0	62.5	72.4	52.9	81.7	52.1	149.6	76.5	66.7	60.1	81.2	80.9
August	65.4	62.7	72.9	53.4	82.2	52.6	151.1	77.1	66.9	60.5	81.6	81.1
September	65.6	63.1	72.5	53.9	81.3	53.4	151.8	77.5	67.0	60.7	81.7	81.5
October	66.6	64.1	73.8	55.7	82.3	54.6	150.9	78.6	67.6	61.6	82.8	82.6
November	66.9	64.5	73.9	55.6	82.5	55.1	151.9	78.6	67.6	62.1	83.1	83.0
December	67.2	64.8	74.0	55.2	82.9	55.6	153.0	79.1	67.8	62.4	83.4	83.4

Table 20-1. Industrial Production and Capacity Utilization—Continued

(Seasonally adjusted; 2002 = 100, except as noted.)

Year and month	Total industry	Manufac-turing (SIC)	Consumer goods Total	Consumer goods Durable	Consumer goods Nondurable	Business equipment	Defense and space equipment	Construction supplies	Business supplies	Materials	Capacity utilization Total industry	Capacity utilization Manufac-turing (SIC)
1988												
January	67.2	64.7	74.4	55.0	83.5	55.6	157.1	77.9	68.0	62.2	83.4	83.2
February	67.5	64.8	74.7	54.9	84.1	55.7	153.8	78.4	68.5	62.4	83.6	83.2
March	67.6	65.0	74.7	55.5	83.8	56.2	152.9	78.8	68.4	62.7	83.7	83.4
April	68.0	65.5	75.1	56.7	83.7	56.7	151.0	78.5	68.5	63.0	84.1	84.0
May	67.9	65.4	74.9	56.8	83.3	56.9	151.0	78.7	68.0	63.1	84.0	83.9
June	68.1	65.5	74.9	57.0	83.2	57.4	149.6	78.1	68.2	63.3	84.2	84.0
July	68.2	65.6	74.9	55.7	83.9	57.1	151.2	78.3	68.6	63.5	84.3	84.0
August	68.5	65.7	75.5	56.2	84.5	57.3	150.9	77.8	69.2	63.8	84.6	84.0
September	68.3	65.9	75.0	57.4	83.1	57.8	151.3	78.1	68.6	63.5	84.3	84.2
October	68.7	66.3	75.6	58.0	83.8	58.5	151.8	78.4	69.0	63.8	84.7	84.7
November	68.8	66.5	75.7	58.7	83.5	58.6	151.2	78.8	69.0	63.9	84.8	84.8
December	69.1	66.8	76.1	59.3	83.7	58.8	152.0	78.8	69.2	64.3	85.0	85.0
1989												
January	69.3	67.3	76.0	60.6	82.9	59.3	152.0	80.1	69.2	64.4	85.1	85.5
February	69.0	66.6	76.0	59.9	83.4	59.1	152.3	78.1	69.5	63.9	84.6	84.5
March	69.2	66.5	76.2	59.1	84.1	58.7	151.2	78.4	70.2	64.2	84.7	84.3
April	69.1	66.6	76.1	59.5	83.7	59.2	153.4	78.3	69.6	64.1	84.5	84.2
May	68.7	66.0	75.3	58.2	83.2	58.3	153.8	77.6	69.3	63.9	83.8	83.3
June	68.7	66.1	75.4	57.5	83.7	58.9	153.4	77.8	69.6	63.6	83.6	83.2
July	68.0	65.4	73.7	55.6	82.2	58.5	154.0	77.8	69.0	63.3	82.7	82.1
August	68.7	66.0	74.9	57.7	82.9	59.5	155.0	77.7	69.3	63.6	83.3	82.7
September	68.5	65.8	74.7	57.7	82.5	59.3	154.1	77.5	69.5	63.4	82.8	82.2
October	68.4	65.7	74.9	56.6	83.4	58.3	148.7	77.8	69.6	63.5	82.6	81.9
November	68.6	65.8	75.1	57.0	83.6	58.8	146.8	77.7	70.0	63.7	82.7	81.9
December	69.1	65.9	76.5	57.6	85.3	60.2	149.3	76.9	70.4	63.5	83.1	81.8
1990												
January	68.7	65.8	74.7	54.3	84.4	59.9	149.6	78.6	70.9	63.4	82.4	81.5
February	69.3	66.7	75.6	57.8	83.9	60.6	149.5	78.8	70.7	64.0	82.9	82.4
March	69.6	67.0	76.2	58.8	84.2	61.0	148.3	78.8	71.2	64.2	83.2	82.6
April	69.6	66.9	76.0	57.6	84.5	61.0	147.7	78.1	71.3	64.4	83.0	82.3
May	69.6	66.9	75.8	58.0	84.1	61.4	145.8	77.5	71.6	64.4	82.9	82.1
June	69.8	67.1	76.6	58.8	84.9	61.4	145.1	77.7	71.4	64.5	82.9	82.2
July	69.7	66.9	76.1	57.2	84.8	61.6	146.1	77.1	71.7	64.5	82.7	81.8
August	69.9	67.2	76.2	57.1	85.1	61.8	144.3	77.0	71.6	64.9	82.8	81.9
September	70.0	67.1	76.9	57.4	86.1	61.7	143.5	76.7	71.7	64.8	82.8	81.7
October	69.5	66.6	75.7	55.5	85.3	61.5	144.5	75.8	71.5	64.5	82.0	81.0
November	68.7	65.9	74.8	52.5	85.5	60.2	142.5	75.8	71.2	63.7	80.9	79.9
December	68.2	65.4	74.4	51.7	85.2	59.8	143.2	75.4	70.8	63.2	80.2	79.2
1991												
January	67.9	64.8	74.7	51.7	85.7	59.2	141.6	72.5	70.5	62.8	79.7	78.4
February	67.4	64.4	74.0	50.5	85.3	58.9	140.4	72.3	69.9	62.5	79.1	77.7
March	67.1	64.0	74.1	50.8	85.2	58.9	139.5	71.3	69.1	62.0	78.6	77.1
April	67.2	64.2	74.0	51.8	84.7	58.9	136.0	71.9	69.5	62.2	78.6	77.3
May	67.9	64.7	75.3	52.8	86.1	59.5	133.2	72.0	70.2	62.8	79.3	77.7
June	68.6	65.4	76.5	54.2	87.1	60.2	134.0	73.3	70.7	63.2	80.0	78.5
July	68.6	65.6	76.1	55.1	85.9	60.1	132.6	73.0	70.2	63.7	79.9	78.6
August	68.7	65.8	76.1	54.4	86.4	60.2	133.7	73.8	70.7	63.7	79.9	78.7
September	69.3	66.4	77.2	56.6	87.0	60.9	133.2	74.2	71.0	64.1	80.5	79.4
October	69.2	66.3	77.0	56.4	86.7	60.3	133.9	73.4	70.8	64.2	80.2	79.1
November	69.1	66.2	77.0	56.4	86.7	60.3	133.1	74.0	70.9	64.0	80.0	78.9
December	68.9	66.1	76.1	56.0	85.5	60.5	131.6	74.0	70.9	64.0	79.7	78.7
1992												
January	68.5	65.8	75.3	53.7	85.6	59.4	130.3	74.2	70.8	64.0	79.1	78.1
February	69.0	66.3	76.1	55.8	85.6	60.8	129.0	74.8	70.8	64.3	79.5	78.6
March	69.5	66.9	76.8	57.0	86.1	61.0	128.5	75.2	71.3	64.8	80.0	79.2
April	70.0	67.2	77.5	58.1	86.6	61.6	126.1	75.8	71.8	65.2	80.4	79.4
May	70.3	67.7	78.0	59.9	86.4	62.2	125.4	76.4	72.0	65.3	80.6	79.8
June	70.3	67.9	77.6	59.2	86.2	62.4	125.4	76.0	71.9	65.5	80.5	79.8
July	70.8	68.4	78.6	60.8	86.8	62.8	123.8	76.5	72.4	66.0	81.0	80.3
August	70.5	68.2	78.7	60.3	87.2	62.5	123.9	76.7	72.3	65.3	80.4	79.8
September	70.6	68.2	78.3	59.9	86.8	62.7	124.0	76.6	72.5	65.8	80.5	79.7
October	71.1	68.6	79.3	61.1	87.8	62.9	123.2	76.8	72.8	66.1	80.9	80.0
November	71.4	68.8	79.5	61.6	87.8	63.4	123.2	76.6	73.0	66.4	81.0	80.1
December	71.5	68.7	79.6	62.4	87.5	63.6	123.2	76.8	73.3	66.3	81.0	79.8
1993												
January	71.8	69.5	80.0	63.5	87.5	64.2	122.7	77.1	73.4	66.7	81.2	80.5
February	72.1	69.6	80.0	63.2	87.8	64.0	121.3	78.3	73.8	67.1	81.4	80.4
March	72.1	69.5	80.1	63.6	87.7	64.1	119.8	77.7	74.4	67.0	81.3	80.2
April	72.3	69.8	80.3	64.2	87.7	64.5	119.7	78.0	74.4	67.2	81.4	80.4
May	72.0	69.7	79.8	64.4	86.8	64.5	118.7	78.9	74.0	67.0	81.0	80.2
June	72.2	69.7	80.0	64.1	87.3	64.0	117.9	78.9	74.1	67.4	81.1	80.0
July	72.5	69.9	80.8	64.1	88.4	63.9	118.8	79.3	74.3	67.4	81.2	80.1
August	72.5	69.9	80.8	63.7	88.7	63.6	117.1	79.6	74.4	67.5	81.1	79.9
September	72.8	70.3	81.0	65.0	88.4	64.4	117.6	80.0	74.7	67.8	81.4	80.3
October	73.3	70.9	81.4	66.7	88.2	65.4	117.1	80.8	74.8	68.3	81.8	80.7
November	73.6	71.2	81.6	67.3	88.0	65.7	116.5	81.5	74.9	68.8	82.0	80.9
December	74.0	71.6	81.8	67.8	88.1	66.0	115.5	82.5	75.4	69.3	82.3	81.2

Table 20-1. Industrial Production and Capacity Utilization—Continued

(Seasonally adjusted; 2002 = 100, except as noted.)

Year and month	Total industry	Manufac-turing (SIC)	Consumer goods Total	Consumer goods Durable	Consumer goods Nondurable	Business equipment	Defense and space equipment	Construction supplies	Business supplies	Materials	Capacity utilization Total industry	Capacity utilization Manufac-turing (SIC)
1994												
January	74.4	71.8	82.5	69.1	88.6	66.4	114.0	82.2	75.9	69.4	82.5	81.3
February	74.4	71.8	82.7	69.1	88.8	65.7	112.3	81.6	75.9	69.7	82.3	81.1
March	75.1	72.7	83.3	69.7	89.5	66.6	113.4	83.1	76.4	70.4	83.0	82.0
April	75.5	73.3	83.4	70.4	89.2	67.1	113.4	84.2	76.7	70.9	83.2	82.4
May	76.0	73.9	84.0	70.8	89.9	67.3	112.0	85.0	76.9	71.4	83.5	82.8
June	76.5	74.1	84.7	71.6	90.7	67.7	110.6	85.1	77.5	71.9	83.8	82.8
July	76.7	74.5	84.4	71.8	90.1	68.5	110.1	86.0	77.3	72.3	83.8	82.9
August	77.0	75.0	85.3	73.1	90.7	68.5	108.9	85.9	77.4	72.7	83.9	83.2
September	77.2	75.2	84.7	73.2	89.9	68.7	109.7	86.6	77.7	73.0	83.8	83.1
October	77.9	75.9	85.6	73.8	90.9	69.8	110.4	87.0	78.4	73.5	84.2	83.6
November	78.3	76.5	85.5	73.5	90.9	70.5	111.5	87.3	78.7	74.3	84.5	84.0
December	79.2	77.4	86.2	74.4	91.5	71.1	111.7	88.0	79.2	75.3	85.0	84.5
1995												
January	79.4	77.7	86.3	75.2	91.3	71.7	111.4	88.1	79.5	75.6	85.0	84.5
February	79.4	77.6	86.5	75.0	91.7	71.9	110.2	87.0	79.6	75.6	84.7	84.1
March	79.6	77.8	86.4	74.7	91.7	72.4	110.0	86.9	79.9	75.8	84.5	83.9
April	79.5	77.7	86.1	74.4	91.4	72.7	109.7	86.4	79.8	75.9	84.1	83.4
May	79.7	77.7	86.2	73.6	91.9	72.9	109.1	85.7	80.2	76.0	83.9	83.0
June	79.9	78.0	86.7	74.2	92.3	73.4	109.6	85.9	80.5	76.0	83.8	82.9
July	79.6	77.5	86.3	72.8	92.4	73.2	108.5	85.8	80.4	75.6	83.1	82.0
August	80.7	78.5	87.8	75.5	93.2	74.8	108.4	86.5	81.4	76.5	83.9	82.6
September	81.0	79.1	87.9	76.5	92.9	75.6	107.0	87.9	81.3	76.9	83.8	82.9
October	80.9	79.1	87.2	75.6	92.3	75.3	106.5	87.7	81.6	77.0	83.3	82.4
November	81.1	79.2	87.5	75.7	92.7	75.6	104.2	87.7	82.0	77.3	83.2	82.1
December	81.4	79.5	87.8	76.3	92.9	76.5	103.7	88.5	81.9	77.5	83.2	82.0
1996												
January	80.7	78.7	86.6	73.9	92.3	75.9	101.7	86.7	81.4	77.2	82.1	80.8
February	82.0	79.9	88.1	76.1	93.4	77.8	104.9	87.9	82.3	78.1	83.0	81.6
March	81.8	79.6	87.5	73.6	93.7	77.4	104.8	89.0	82.3	78.1	82.5	81.0
April	82.5	80.6	88.4	77.5	93.3	78.5	104.5	89.5	82.3	78.8	82.9	81.5
May	83.1	81.1	88.5	77.9	93.3	79.2	104.6	90.3	83.2	79.6	83.1	81.7
June	83.8	82.0	89.4	79.7	93.7	80.2	103.9	91.8	83.4	80.2	83.5	82.1
July	83.7	82.2	88.7	80.1	92.5	80.9	104.5	91.2	83.4	80.1	83.0	81.9
August	84.2	82.7	88.5	79.4	92.6	81.9	105.2	92.2	84.3	80.9	83.2	82.1
September	84.7	83.3	89.3	79.6	93.7	82.4	105.5	92.5	84.7	81.2	83.3	82.2
October	84.7	83.2	88.9	78.2	93.6	82.4	105.1	92.7	84.9	81.5	82.9	81.8
November	85.6	84.0	90.0	79.5	94.7	83.9	104.8	93.4	85.6	82.0	83.3	82.1
December	86.1	84.8	90.3	80.9	94.5	85.8	104.3	92.9	86.1	82.5	83.5	82.4
1997												
January	86.3	84.9	90.1	80.6	94.3	86.4	102.7	92.0	86.7	82.9	83.3	82.2
February	87.3	86.1	90.5	81.8	94.4	87.9	102.7	93.8	87.5	84.2	83.9	82.8
March	88.0	87.1	91.2	82.9	94.9	89.3	102.1	94.8	87.9	84.7	84.1	83.3
April	88.0	86.8	90.2	80.4	94.6	89.3	102.0	94.4	88.2	85.1	83.6	82.5
May	88.5	87.5	90.8	81.3	95.0	90.3	101.7	95.1	88.8	85.5	83.6	82.7
June	88.9	88.1	90.8	82.7	94.3	91.5	101.5	94.8	89.1	86.1	83.5	82.7
July	89.3	88.4	90.8	80.5	95.4	91.6	101.6	95.0	89.8	86.7	83.5	82.4
August	90.4	89.8	92.2	84.1	95.7	94.3	102.0	95.6	90.0	87.6	84.0	83.1
September	91.3	90.6	93.0	85.2	96.4	94.6	102.0	96.1	91.2	88.6	84.3	83.3
October	92.0	91.2	94.2	85.4	98.1	95.7	102.1	96.6	92.1	88.8	84.3	83.3
November	92.8	92.3	94.5	87.6	97.5	97.9	101.8	97.1	92.5	89.9	84.6	83.6
December	93.2	92.7	94.1	87.5	97.0	98.9	103.6	98.2	92.8	90.4	84.4	83.4
1998												
January	93.6	93.4	94.6	88.0	97.4	100.1	104.3	98.7	92.6	90.7	84.2	83.4
February	93.7	93.5	94.3	87.8	97.2	100.1	104.7	99.1	92.9	90.9	83.7	82.9
March	93.7	93.3	94.6	88.1	97.4	99.9	104.0	98.5	93.6	90.8	83.3	82.2
April	94.2	93.9	95.2	88.6	98.0	100.4	103.7	99.0	93.9	91.2	83.1	82.1
May	94.7	94.3	95.5	89.0	98.3	101.2	105.0	100.2	94.6	91.7	83.1	81.9
June	94.2	93.7	94.4	84.6	98.6	102.0	105.2	99.9	94.8	91.1	82.2	80.9
July	93.9	93.4	93.4	80.9	98.9	101.5	106.4	100.3	95.4	90.9	81.5	80.1
August	96.0	95.8	96.5	91.5	98.7	104.6	107.2	100.7	96.0	92.6	82.8	81.7
September	95.8	95.5	95.6	90.7	97.7	104.8	106.2	100.2	96.1	92.8	82.3	81.0
October	96.5	96.4	96.1	92.5	97.6	106.1	108.1	101.4	96.4	93.5	82.5	81.4
November	96.4	96.6	95.4	92.2	96.8	106.3	108.1	101.5	96.7	93.6	82.1	81.1
December	96.7	97.0	95.3	92.9	96.3	106.2	107.4	102.8	96.6	94.3	81.9	81.1
1999												
January	97.1	97.3	96.4	93.2	97.8	106.1	107.3	102.1	97.3	94.6	82.0	80.9
February	97.6	98.1	96.7	94.0	97.8	106.6	107.8	102.1	97.5	95.2	82.0	81.1
March	97.8	98.0	96.5	93.4	97.7	106.4	106.9	101.3	97.9	95.9	81.8	80.7
April	98.0	98.3	96.2	94.2	97.0	107.1	105.7	101.5	98.2	96.4	81.7	80.6
May	98.8	99.3	97.3	95.3	98.1	108.9	104.6	101.9	98.7	97.0	82.0	81.1
June	98.7	99.1	96.3	94.7	97.0	108.7	103.4	102.0	98.8	97.5	81.7	80.5
July	99.4	99.6	96.0	94.9	96.4	109.7	103.1	102.6	99.6	98.8	81.9	80.6
August	99.9	100.3	97.3	97.2	97.3	109.7	103.0	102.6	99.7	98.9	82.0	80.8
September	99.4	99.8	96.5	95.8	96.7	109.1	100.1	102.7	99.7	98.7	81.3	80.1
October	100.7	101.4	98.2	98.6	98.1	109.8	100.2	103.9	100.7	100.0	82.1	80.9
November	101.3	102.1	98.1	97.6	98.4	109.9	98.1	104.6	101.4	101.2	82.2	81.2
December	102.2	103.0	99.2	97.6	99.8	110.8	96.7	105.5	102.2	102.1	82.6	81.5

Table 20-1. Industrial Production and Capacity Utilization—Continued

(Seasonally adjusted; 2002 = 100, except as noted.)

Year and month	Total industry	Manufac- turing (SIC)	Market groups								Capacity utilization (output as percentage of capacity)	
			Consumer goods			Business equipment	Defense and space equipment	Construction supplies	Business supplies	Materials	Total industry	Manufac- turing (SIC)
			Total	Durable	Nondurable							
2000												
January	102.4	103.3	98.0	99.6	97.4	112.6	96.2	106.1	102.7	102.7	82.5	81.3
February	102.8	103.6	98.6	99.5	98.2	113.9	94.1	106.2	102.8	102.9	82.5	81.2
March	103.1	104.2	98.2	99.0	98.0	115.4	93.1	106.2	103.5	103.5	82.5	81.4
April	103.9	104.9	99.2	100.3	98.8	116.9	91.3	106.6	104.6	103.9	82.7	81.6
May	104.2	104.9	99.5	100.2	99.2	117.5	90.5	105.0	104.8	104.4	82.7	81.2
June	104.2	105.0	99.6	100.0	99.4	117.2	91.1	104.6	104.7	104.6	82.5	81.0
July	103.9	105.0	98.9	97.6	99.5	117.7	93.0	105.2	104.7	104.1	82.0	80.6
August	103.6	104.3	98.7	98.3	98.9	116.8	90.9	104.5	104.4	103.9	81.4	79.8
September	104.0	104.7	99.8	99.4	100.0	117.8	86.7	104.6	104.1	104.1	81.5	79.8
October	103.7	104.4	98.7	97.5	99.2	118.3	91.1	104.2	103.8	103.9	80.9	79.2
November	103.6	104.0	99.0	95.2	100.5	118.2	94.1	103.8	104.0	103.5	80.7	78.7
December	103.2	103.3	99.5	93.6	101.8	117.0	94.3	102.5	103.6	102.7	80.1	77.8
2001												
January	102.4	102.5	98.5	92.1	101.0	116.4	97.1	102.7	103.1	101.5	79.2	77.0
February	101.6	101.8	97.6	92.0	99.7	115.4	97.1	101.6	101.8	101.1	78.4	76.2
March	101.3	101.4	97.6	94.3	98.9	114.4	99.0	101.8	101.0	100.6	77.9	75.7
April	101.2	101.3	98.1	94.4	99.6	112.4	100.2	101.7	100.6	100.5	77.6	75.4
May	100.4	100.4	98.1	95.2	99.2	110.1	99.7	100.9	99.8	99.6	76.9	74.6
June	99.9	99.9	98.0	94.8	99.3	109.0	100.8	100.3	99.4	98.7	76.3	74.0
July	99.5	99.6	97.9	95.7	98.8	108.1	102.2	100.3	99.4	98.2	75.9	73.7
August	99.2	99.0	97.8	94.2	99.1	106.0	101.1	99.3	99.0	98.3	75.4	73.1
September	98.8	98.7	97.3	93.7	98.7	104.2	101.3	99.3	99.0	98.1	75.0	72.7
October	98.3	98.1	97.5	92.4	99.5	102.7	101.3	98.1	98.4	97.6	74.5	72.2
November	97.9	97.9	97.6	94.2	98.9	101.8	101.0	97.9	97.7	96.9	74.0	72.0
December	97.9	98.2	98.1	96.1	99.0	100.8	100.7	99.0	98.1	96.7	73.9	72.1
2002												
January	98.6	98.7	99.1	96.6	100.1	100.8	99.8	98.9	97.9	97.6	74.3	72.5
February	98.4	98.6	98.4	96.8	99.0	100.4	99.7	99.4	97.9	98.0	74.1	72.3
March	99.3	99.4	99.5	97.7	100.2	100.7	99.1	100.5	99.1	98.8	74.7	72.9
April	99.7	99.5	99.5	98.9	99.7	99.7	98.9	100.3	99.8	99.9	74.9	73.0
May	100.1	100.0	99.7	99.5	99.8	100.1	98.7	100.8	100.3	100.2	75.2	73.3
June	101.0	101.0	101.0	100.9	101.1	100.6	99.5	101.2	100.9	101.2	75.8	74.0
July	100.7	100.6	100.6	101.4	100.3	99.7	99.0	99.6	100.8	101.1	75.6	73.7
August	100.7	100.8	100.4	101.4	100.0	100.3	99.6	100.2	100.8	101.2	75.6	73.9
September	100.7	100.8	100.6	101.7	100.2	99.6	100.3	100.5	100.9	101.0	75.6	73.9
October	100.3	100.2	100.2	100.4	100.1	99.4	101.2	99.9	101.1	100.3	75.3	73.4
November	100.5	100.4	101.0	103.0	100.1	99.6	100.6	99.6	100.4	100.6	75.5	73.6
December	100.1	100.0	100.1	101.7	99.4	99.2	103.6	99.0	100.0	100.3	75.2	73.3
2003												
January	100.5	100.3	100.5	103.8	99.2	99.0	103.7	99.1	101.4	100.8	75.5	73.5
February	100.6	100.1	100.9	101.8	100.6	99.4	104.1	98.1	101.0	100.5	75.6	73.4
March	100.4	100.3	101.0	101.9	100.7	99.7	103.4	97.8	101.2	100.0	75.4	73.5
April	99.6	99.5	100.3	101.6	99.8	98.3	103.1	96.9	99.8	99.5	74.9	72.9
May	99.5	99.4	100.0	101.5	99.4	98.2	103.5	98.1	100.1	99.3	74.9	72.8
June	99.8	99.9	100.5	103.2	99.4	98.8	103.9	98.8	99.8	99.4	75.1	73.2
July	100.3	100.2	101.3	105.1	99.7	99.1	104.5	98.4	100.3	99.8	75.4	73.4
August	100.4	100.1	100.9	103.7	99.8	100.3	105.4	99.3	100.3	99.8	75.5	73.4
September	101.0	101.0	101.8	107.3	99.6	100.9	106.2	99.2	100.3	100.6	76.0	74.0
October	101.1	101.1	101.1	105.3	99.4	100.9	107.1	100.2	100.7	101.1	76.1	74.1
November	102.0	102.3	102.0	106.5	100.2	102.8	107.8	101.6	101.7	101.7	76.8	75.0
December	102.3	102.3	102.2	106.5	100.4	102.9	107.2	102.0	101.7	102.1	76.9	75.1
2004												
January	102.7	102.6	102.7	108.2	100.5	103.7	106.4	102.4	101.7	102.5	77.2	75.3
February	103.5	103.6	103.4	107.9	101.5	105.3	108.6	102.3	102.8	103.2	77.8	76.0
March	103.2	103.7	102.5	107.2	100.6	105.7	109.5	102.7	102.2	103.1	77.6	76.1
April	104.0	104.6	103.2	107.9	101.3	107.2	110.9	103.5	103.2	103.8	78.1	76.7
May	105.0	105.5	103.8	107.1	102.5	108.3	112.1	104.9	104.1	104.9	78.8	77.3
June	104.4	104.9	102.4	105.1	101.3	108.8	112.0	104.6	103.8	104.5	78.4	76.9
July	105.0	105.7	102.3	105.0	101.2	111.3	114.2	105.7	104.3	105.1	78.8	77.4
August	105.3	106.4	103.2	107.2	101.7	110.9	114.6	105.7	104.5	105.2	79.0	77.9
September	105.1	106.0	102.6	105.4	101.4	111.3	116.1	104.9	104.2	105.1	78.7	77.5
October	105.8	106.9	103.6	107.7	101.9	112.6	116.7	106.1	104.7	105.6	79.2	78.1
November	106.0	106.9	103.7	107.3	102.2	112.9	117.6	105.7	105.0	105.9	79.3	78.0
December	106.7	107.5	104.1	107.3	102.9	114.1	119.0	106.1	106.2	106.5	79.7	78.3
2005												
January	106.9	108.1	103.9	106.3	102.9	115.2	119.4	106.0	106.7	106.8	79.8	78.6
February	107.4	108.6	104.7	109.7	102.8	115.9	121.6	106.4	106.1	107.0	80.0	78.9
March	107.3	108.2	104.6	107.7	103.4	116.3	122.5	106.2	106.5	106.8	79.9	78.5
April	107.2	108.3	104.1	106.0	103.3	116.8	124.5	107.3	106.7	106.5	79.7	78.4
May	107.4	108.7	104.6	107.1	103.5	117.9	124.1	107.5	106.7	106.5	79.8	78.6
June	108.3	109.0	105.8	108.5	104.7	118.4	124.9	106.9	107.6	107.3	80.3	78.7
July	108.3	109.1	105.2	107.1	104.4	120.0	126.8	107.5	107.4	107.2	80.2	78.6
August	108.6	109.5	105.6	110.1	103.9	120.1	127.4	108.2	107.9	107.4	80.3	78.8
September	107.2	108.9	106.4	112.7	103.9	115.1	124.6	109.8	107.8	104.5	79.1	78.2
October	108.4	110.9	106.5	113.1	103.9	123.1	127.8	112.4	108.4	104.9	79.9	79.4
November	109.4	111.7	105.7	110.1	103.9	125.8	128.6	113.4	109.1	106.9	80.5	79.9
December	110.4	112.2	106.6	109.0	105.5	126.4	129.9	113.1	110.3	108.3	81.1	80.1

Table 20-2. Summary Consumer and Producer Price Indexes

(Seasonally adjusted.)

Year and month	Consumer Price Index, all urban consumers, 1982–1984 = 100							Producer Price Index, 1982 = 100					
								Finished goods		Intermediate materials, supplies, and components		Crude materials for further processing	
	All items	All items less food and energy	Food	Energy	Apparel	Transportation	Medical care	Total	Less food and energy	Total	Less food and energy	Total	Crude nonfood less energy
1946	19.5	. . .	19.8	. . .	34.4	16.7	12.5	. . .	. . .	23.3	. . .	. . .	. . .
1947	22.3	. . .	24.1	. . .	39.9	18.5	13.5	26.4	. . .	23.3	. . .	31.7	. . .
1948	24.1	. . .	26.1	. . .	42.5	20.6	14.4	28.5	. . .	25.2	. . .	34.7	. . .
1949	23.8	. . .	25.0	. . .	40.8	22.1	14.8	27.7	. . .	24.2	. . .	30.1	. . .
1950	24.1	. . .	25.4	. . .	40.3	22.7	15.1	28.2	. . .	25.3	. . .	32.7	. . .
1951	26.0	. . .	28.2	. . .	43.9	24.1	15.9	30.8	. . .	28.4	. . .	37.6	. . .
1952	26.5	. . .	28.7	. . .	43.5	25.7	16.7	30.6	. . .	27.5	. . .	34.5	. . .
1953	26.7	. . .	28.3	. . .	43.1	26.5	17.3	30.3	. . .	27.7	. . .	31.9	. . .
1954	26.9	. . .	28.2	. . .	43.1	26.1	17.8	30.4	. . .	27.9	. . .	31.6	. . .
1955	26.8	. . .	27.8	. . .	42.9	25.8	18.2	30.5	. . .	28.4	. . .	30.4	. . .
1956	27.2	. . .	28.0	. . .	43.7	26.2	18.9	31.3	. . .	29.6	. . .	30.6	. . .
1957	28.1	28.9	28.9	21.5	44.5	27.7	19.7	32.5	. . .	30.3	. . .	31.2	. . .
1958	28.9	29.6	30.2	21.5	44.6	28.6	20.6	33.2	. . .	30.4	. . .	31.9	. . .
1959	29.1	30.2	29.7	21.9	45.0	29.8	21.5	33.1	. . .	30.8	. . .	31.1	. . .
1947													
January	21.5	. . .	22.8	. . .	38.4	17.9	13.2	. . .	. . .	. . .	. . .	. . .	. . .
February	21.6	. . .	23.1	. . .	38.8	17.9	13.3	. . .	. . .	. . .	. . .	. . .	. . .
March	22.0	. . .	23.8	. . .	39.4	18.1	13.3	. . .	. . .	. . .	. . .	. . .	. . .
April	22.0	. . .	23.5	. . .	39.7	18.3	13.4	26.0	. . .	23.1	. . .	30.7	. . .
May	22.0	. . .	23.4	. . .	39.8	18.3	13.5	26.1	. . .	23.0	. . .	30.4	. . .
June	22.1	. . .	23.5	. . .	40.0	18.4	13.5	26.2	. . .	23.2	. . .	30.6	. . .
July	22.2	. . .	23.8	. . .	40.0	18.5	13.5	26.2	. . .	23.2	. . .	31.0	. . .
August	22.4	. . .	24.1	. . .	40.1	18.5	13.6	26.3	. . .	23.3	. . .	31.6	. . .
September	22.8	. . .	24.8	. . .	40.2	18.7	13.7	26.7	. . .	23.7	. . .	32.4	. . .
October	22.9	. . .	24.9	. . .	40.4	18.8	13.8	26.8	. . .	24.0	. . .	33.7	. . .
November	23.1	. . .	25.2	. . .	40.6	19.0	13.8	27.1	. . .	24.3	. . .	33.9	. . .
December	23.4	. . .	25.7	. . .	41.0	19.1	13.9	27.7	. . .	24.5	. . .	35.3	. . .
1948													
January	23.7	. . .	26.1	. . .	41.3	19.6	14.0	28.1	. . .	25.0	. . .	36.2	. . .
February	23.7	. . .	25.9	. . .	41.8	19.5	14.0	27.9	. . .	24.7	. . .	34.4	. . .
March	23.5	. . .	25.3	. . .	42.0	19.6	14.1	28.0	. . .	24.8	. . .	33.5	. . .
April	23.8	. . .	26.0	. . .	42.1	19.9	14.3	28.1	. . .	25.1	. . .	34.2	. . .
May	24.0	. . .	26.3	. . .	42.5	19.9	14.3	28.4	. . .	25.1	. . .	35.3	. . .
June	24.2	. . .	26.5	. . .	42.4	20.0	14.4	28.6	. . .	25.4	. . .	36.2	. . .
July	24.4	. . .	26.7	. . .	42.7	21.0	14.5	28.8	. . .	25.4	. . .	36.1	. . .
August	24.4	. . .	26.5	. . .	43.1	21.3	14.6	28.9	. . .	25.5	. . .	35.5	. . .
September	24.4	. . .	26.3	. . .	43.1	21.4	14.5	28.8	. . .	25.5	. . .	34.9	. . .
October	24.3	. . .	26.1	. . .	43.1	21.5	14.6	28.7	. . .	25.5	. . .	33.8	. . .
November	24.2	. . .	25.7	. . .	43.0	21.6	14.7	28.5	. . .	25.4	. . .	33.5	. . .
December	24.0	. . .	25.5	. . .	43.0	21.6	14.7	28.5	. . .	25.2	. . .	33.0	. . .
1949													
January	24.0	. . .	25.4	. . .	42.2	21.6	14.7	28.3	. . .	25.2	. . .	32.0	. . .
February	23.9	. . .	25.3	. . .	41.8	21.8	14.8	28.0	. . .	24.8	. . .	30.9	. . .
March	23.9	. . .	25.3	. . .	41.6	21.9	14.8	28.0	. . .	24.7	. . .	30.8	. . .
April	23.9	. . .	25.3	. . .	41.3	22.0	14.8	27.9	. . .	24.5	. . .	30.2	. . .
May	23.9	. . .	25.2	. . .	41.1	22.2	14.8	27.8	. . .	24.3	. . .	30.1	. . .
June	23.9	. . .	25.3	. . .	41.0	22.1	14.8	27.7	. . .	24.1	. . .	29.7	. . .
July	23.7	. . .	24.8	. . .	40.8	22.2	14.8	27.5	. . .	24.1	. . .	29.2	. . .
August	23.7	. . .	24.8	. . .	40.5	22.3	14.9	27.4	. . .	23.9	. . .	29.2	. . .
September	23.8	. . .	25.0	. . .	40.2	22.2	14.9	27.4	. . .	23.9	. . .	29.5	. . .
October	23.7	. . .	24.8	. . .	39.9	22.3	14.9	27.3	. . .	23.8	. . .	29.5	. . .
November	23.7	. . .	24.8	. . .	39.8	22.3	14.9	27.2	. . .	23.7	. . .	29.6	. . .
December	23.6	. . .	24.5	. . .	39.8	22.5	14.9	27.2	. . .	23.8	. . .	29.6	. . .
1950													
January	23.5	. . .	24.3	. . .	39.7	22.4	14.9	27.2	. . .	23.8	. . .	29.6	. . .
February	23.6	. . .	24.7	. . .	39.7	22.4	15.0	27.2	. . .	23.9	. . .	30.5	. . .
March	23.6	. . .	24.6	. . .	39.7	22.4	15.0	27.3	. . .	24.1	. . .	30.3	. . .
April	23.6	. . .	24.6	. . .	39.7	22.4	15.0	27.3	. . .	24.2	. . .	30.5	. . .
May	23.8	. . .	24.8	. . .	39.7	22.5	15.0	27.5	. . .	24.6	. . .	31.6	. . .
June	23.9	. . .	25.1	. . .	39.7	22.5	15.0	27.6	. . .	24.7	. . .	32.1	. . .
July	24.1	. . .	25.6	. . .	39.9	22.7	15.1	28.0	. . .	25.3	. . .	33.3	. . .
August	24.2	. . .	25.8	. . .	40.1	22.9	15.1	28.6	. . .	25.6	. . .	34.0	. . .
September	24.3	. . .	25.8	. . .	40.6	22.9	15.2	28.9	. . .	26.2	. . .	34.5	. . .
October	24.5	. . .	26.0	. . .	41.2	22.9	15.3	29.0	. . .	26.7	. . .	34.5	. . .
November	24.6	. . .	26.1	. . .	41.5	23.0	15.3	29.4	. . .	26.9	. . .	35.4	. . .
December	25.0	. . .	26.9	. . .	41.9	23.2	15.4	30.0	. . .	27.8	. . .	36.7	. . .
1951													
January	25.4	. . .	27.6	. . .	42.6	23.3	15.4	30.5	. . .	28.5	. . .	38.2	. . .
February	25.8	. . .	28.5	. . .	43.3	23.6	15.5	30.8	. . .	28.7	. . .	39.6	. . .
March	25.9	. . .	28.4	. . .	43.5	23.8	15.7	30.9	. . .	28.8	. . .	39.1	. . .
April	25.9	. . .	28.2	. . .	43.8	23.9	15.7	30.9	. . .	28.8	. . .	39.1	. . .
May	26.0	. . .	28.3	. . .	43.9	24.0	15.8	31.1	. . .	28.8	. . .	38.4	. . .
June	25.9	. . .	28.0	. . .	43.9	24.1	15.8	31.0	. . .	28.7	. . .	38.1	. . .
July	25.9	. . .	27.9	. . .	44.0	24.1	15.8	30.8	. . .	28.4	. . .	36.8	. . .
August	25.9	. . .	27.8	. . .	44.0	24.2	15.9	30.7	. . .	28.0	. . .	36.2	. . .
September	26.0	. . .	27.9	. . .	44.8	24.4	15.9	30.6	. . .	28.0	. . .	35.9	. . .
October	26.2	. . .	28.4	. . .	44.7	24.5	16.0	30.8	. . .	27.9	. . .	36.7	. . .
November	26.3	. . .	28.6	. . .	44.4	24.8	16.1	30.9	. . .	27.9	. . .	36.4	. . .
December	26.5	. . .	28.9	. . .	44.3	24.9	16.3	30.9	. . .	27.8	. . .	36.6	. . .

. . . = Not available.

Table 20-2. Summary Consumer and Producer Price Indexes—Continued

(Seasonally adjusted.)

Year and month	Consumer Price Index, all urban consumers, 1982–1984 = 100							Producer Price Index, 1982 = 100					
								Finished goods		Intermediate materials, supplies, and components		Crude materials for further processing	
	All items	All items less food and energy	Food	Energy	Apparel	Transportation	Medical care	Total	Less food and energy	Total	Less food and energy	Total	Crude nonfood less energy
1952													
January	26.4	...	28.9	...	43.9	25.0	16.3	30.8	...	27.8	...	35.8	...
February	26.4	...	28.6	...	43.9	25.2	16.4	30.7	...	27.7	...	35.5	...
March	26.4	...	28.5	...	43.7	25.3	16.5	30.9	...	27.6	...	35.0	...
April	26.5	...	28.7	...	43.6	25.5	16.5	30.7	...	27.5	...	34.9	...
May	26.5	...	28.7	...	43.6	25.6	16.5	30.7	...	27.5	...	34.8	...
June	26.5	...	28.6	...	43.5	25.8	16.8	30.7	...	27.6	...	34.6	...
July	26.7	...	28.9	...	43.5	26.0	16.9	30.8	...	27.5	...	34.6	...
August	26.7	...	28.9	...	43.4	25.9	16.9	30.7	...	27.6	...	34.7	...
September	26.6	...	28.7	...	43.3	26.0	16.9	30.6	...	27.6	...	33.8	...
October	26.7	...	28.8	...	43.1	26.1	16.9	30.5	...	27.5	...	33.8	...
November	26.7	...	28.8	...	43.0	26.2	16.9	30.4	...	27.4	...	33.7	...
December	26.7	...	28.6	...	43.0	26.2	17.0	30.2	...	27.3	...	32.9	...
1953													
January	26.6	...	28.4	...	43.0	26.3	17.0	30.3	...	27.4	...	32.5	...
February	26.6	...	28.3	...	43.0	26.2	17.0	30.2	...	27.4	...	32.4	...
March	26.6	...	28.3	...	43.0	26.3	17.0	30.3	...	27.5	...	32.4	...
April	26.7	...	28.1	...	43.1	26.4	17.1	30.2	...	27.5	...	31.6	...
May	26.7	...	28.2	...	43.2	26.4	17.2	30.3	...	27.6	...	31.8	...
June	26.8	...	28.4	...	43.3	26.5	17.3	30.4	...	27.7	...	31.4	...
July	26.8	...	28.2	...	43.3	26.6	17.3	30.5	...	28.0	...	32.3	...
August	26.8	...	28.3	...	43.2	26.7	17.4	30.4	...	27.9	...	31.8	...
September	26.9	...	28.4	...	43.2	26.7	17.5	30.4	...	27.9	...	32.0	...
October	27.0	...	28.4	...	43.2	26.6	17.5	30.4	...	27.9	...	31.4	...
November	26.8	...	28.1	...	43.3	26.3	17.6	30.3	...	27.8	...	31.2	...
December	26.9	...	28.3	...	43.2	26.2	17.6	30.4	...	27.8	...	31.7	...
1954													
January	26.9	...	28.5	...	43.3	26.5	17.6	30.5	...	27.9	...	32.0	...
February	27.0	...	28.5	...	43.2	26.3	17.7	30.4	...	27.9	...	32.0	...
March	26.9	...	28.4	...	43.0	26.3	17.7	30.4	...	27.9	...	32.1	...
April	26.9	...	28.4	...	43.0	26.4	17.8	30.6	...	27.9	...	32.2	...
May	26.9	...	28.4	...	43.1	26.4	17.8	30.6	...	27.9	...	32.1	...
June	26.9	...	28.4	...	43.2	26.4	17.8	30.4	...	27.8	...	31.5	...
July	26.9	...	28.4	...	43.1	26.0	17.8	30.5	...	27.9	...	31.4	...
August	26.8	...	28.3	...	43.0	25.9	17.9	30.4	...	27.9	...	31.3	...
September	26.8	...	28.0	...	42.9	25.9	17.9	30.3	...	27.8	...	31.5	...
October	26.7	...	27.9	...	42.9	25.4	17.9	30.2	...	27.8	...	31.2	...
November	26.8	...	27.9	...	42.9	25.8	18.0	30.3	...	27.9	...	31.4	...
December	26.8	...	27.8	...	42.9	25.8	18.0	30.3	...	27.9	...	30.8	...
1955													
January	26.8	...	27.8	...	42.8	25.9	18.0	30.4	...	27.9	...	31.1	...
February	26.8	...	28.0	...	42.8	25.9	18.1	30.5	...	28.0	...	31.0	...
March	26.8	...	28.0	...	42.7	25.9	18.1	30.3	...	28.0	...	30.7	...
April	26.8	...	28.0	...	42.8	25.6	18.1	30.4	...	28.1	...	31.0	...
May	26.8	...	27.9	...	42.8	25.7	18.2	30.4	...	28.1	...	30.2	...
June	26.7	...	27.7	...	42.8	25.8	18.2	30.5	...	28.2	...	30.7	...
July	26.8	...	27.7	...	42.8	25.7	18.2	30.4	...	28.4	...	30.4	...
August	26.7	...	27.6	...	42.9	25.6	18.3	30.4	...	28.5	...	30.1	...
September	26.8	...	27.8	...	43.0	25.7	18.3	30.5	...	28.8	...	30.4	...
October	26.8	...	27.7	...	43.0	25.8	18.4	30.6	...	28.9	...	30.4	...
November	26.9	...	27.6	...	43.0	26.0	18.5	30.6	...	28.9	...	29.4	...
December	26.9	...	27.6	...	43.1	25.8	18.6	30.7	...	29.0	...	29.5	...
1956													
January	26.8	...	27.5	...	43.2	25.8	18.6	30.7	...	29.1	...	29.4	...
February	26.9	...	27.5	...	43.5	25.8	18.7	30.8	...	29.2	...	29.9	...
March	26.9	...	27.5	...	43.5	25.8	18.7	30.9	...	29.4	...	29.8	...
April	26.9	...	27.6	...	43.6	25.8	18.8	31.0	...	29.5	...	30.3	...
May	27.0	...	27.8	...	43.6	26.0	18.8	31.2	...	29.6	...	30.7	...
June	27.2	...	28.1	...	43.6	26.0	18.8	31.4	...	29.6	...	30.5	...
July	27.3	...	28.4	...	43.8	26.2	18.9	31.3	...	29.4	...	30.5	...
August	27.3	...	28.2	...	43.9	26.3	19.0	31.4	...	29.7	...	31.0	...
September	27.4	...	28.2	...	44.0	26.4	19.1	31.6	...	29.8	...	31.0	...
October	27.5	...	28.3	...	44.0	27.0	19.1	31.8	...	30.0	...	31.0	...
November	27.5	...	28.4	...	44.1	26.9	19.1	31.9	...	30.0	...	31.1	...
December	27.6	...	28.5	...	44.3	27.0	19.2	31.9	...	30.1	...	31.7	...
1957													
January	27.7	28.5	28.4	21.3	44.3	27.2	19.3	32.1	...	30.3	...	31.3	...
February	27.8	28.6	28.7	21.4	44.3	27.4	19.3	32.2	...	30.3	...	31.0	...
March	27.9	28.7	28.6	21.5	44.5	27.5	19.4	32.1	...	30.3	...	30.9	...
April	27.9	28.8	28.6	21.6	44.4	27.7	19.5	32.3	...	30.2	...	30.8	...
May	28.0	28.8	28.7	21.6	44.5	27.6	19.6	32.3	...	30.2	...	30.7	...
June	28.1	28.9	28.9	21.6	44.5	27.7	19.7	32.5	...	30.3	...	31.5	...
July	28.2	29.0	29.1	21.5	44.5	27.8	19.7	32.6	...	30.3	...	32.0	...
August	28.3	29.0	29.4	21.4	44.6	27.8	19.8	32.6	...	30.4	...	32.0	...
September	28.3	29.1	29.2	21.4	44.5	27.9	19.8	32.6	...	30.4	...	31.2	...
October	28.3	29.2	29.2	21.4	44.6	27.5	19.9	32.7	...	30.3	...	31.0	...
November	28.4	29.3	29.2	21.5	44.7	28.3	20.0	32.9	...	30.4	...	31.1	...
December	28.5	29.3	29.2	21.5	44.6	28.1	20.1	33.0	...	30.4	...	31.5	...

. . . = Not available.

Table 20-2. Summary Consumer and Producer Price Indexes—Continued

(Seasonally adjusted.)

Year and month	Consumer Price Index, all urban consumers, 1982–1984 = 100							Producer Price Index, 1982 = 100					
								Finished goods		Intermediate materials, supplies, and components		Crude materials for further processing	
	All items	All items less food and energy	Food	Energy	Apparel	Transportation	Medical care	Total	Less food and energy	Total	Less food and energy	Total	Crude nonfood less energy
1958													
January	28.6	29.3	29.8	21.6	44.8	28.1	20.2	33.2	...	30.4	...	31.4	...
February	28.7	29.4	29.9	21.3	44.7	28.2	20.2	33.2	...	30.3	...	31.9	...
March	28.9	29.5	30.5	21.4	44.7	28.3	20.3	33.4	...	30.3	...	32.3	...
April	28.9	29.5	30.6	21.4	44.7	28.3	20.4	33.2	...	30.2	...	31.8	...
May	28.9	29.5	30.5	21.5	44.7	28.4	20.5	33.2	...	30.3	...	32.4	...
June	28.9	29.6	30.3	21.5	44.8	28.4	20.6	33.3	...	30.3	...	32.0	...
July	28.9	29.6	30.2	21.6	44.7	28.7	20.7	33.2	...	30.3	...	32.1	...
August	28.9	29.6	30.1	21.7	44.7	28.8	20.7	33.2	...	30.4	...	31.9	...
September	28.9	29.7	30.0	21.7	44.5	28.9	20.9	33.2	...	30.4	...	31.6	...
October	28.9	29.7	30.0	21.7	44.5	28.9	21.0	33.2	...	30.4	...	31.9	...
November	29.0	29.8	30.0	21.4	44.7	29.1	21.0	33.2	...	30.5	...	32.1	...
December	29.0	29.9	29.9	21.4	44.7	29.2	21.1	33.1	...	30.6	...	31.6	...
1959													
January	29.0	29.9	30.0	21.4	44.8	29.3	21.1	33.1	...	30.6	...	31.6	...
February	29.0	29.9	29.8	21.6	44.7	29.4	21.2	33.2	...	30.7	...	31.4	...
March	29.0	30.0	29.7	21.7	44.7	29.6	21.3	33.2	...	30.7	...	31.5	...
April	29.0	30.0	29.5	21.8	44.8	29.7	21.3	33.2	...	30.7	...	31.7	...
May	29.0	30.1	29.5	21.8	44.9	29.7	21.4	33.3	...	30.9	...	31.5	...
June	29.1	30.2	29.7	21.9	45.0	29.8	21.5	33.2	...	30.9	...	31.3	...
July	29.2	30.2	29.6	21.8	45.1	29.9	21.5	33.1	...	30.8	...	31.0	...
August	29.2	30.2	29.6	21.9	45.2	29.9	21.6	33.0	...	30.8	...	30.7	...
September	29.2	30.3	29.7	21.9	45.3	30.0	21.7	33.4	...	30.8	...	30.9	...
October	29.4	30.4	29.7	22.2	45.3	30.1	21.7	33.1	...	30.8	...	30.7	...
November	29.4	30.4	29.7	22.2	45.3	30.1	21.8	33.0	...	30.9	...	30.5	...
December	29.4	30.5	29.6	22.3	45.3	30.1	21.8	33.0	...	30.9	...	30.3	...
1960													
January	29.4	30.5	29.6	22.3	45.3	30.0	21.9	33.1	...	30.8	...	30.4	...
February	29.4	30.6	29.5	22.2	45.5	30.0	22.0	33.1	...	30.9	...	30.4	...
March	29.4	30.6	29.6	22.3	45.5	29.9	22.1	33.4	...	30.9	...	30.7	...
April	29.5	30.6	30.0	22.4	45.6	29.9	22.2	33.4	...	30.8	...	30.8	...
May	29.6	30.6	30.0	22.3	45.7	29.8	22.2	33.4	...	30.8	...	30.8	...
June	29.6	30.7	30.0	22.4	45.7	29.8	22.2	33.4	...	30.9	...	30.4	...
July	29.6	30.6	29.9	22.5	45.8	29.8	22.3	33.5	...	30.8	...	30.4	...
August	29.6	30.6	30.0	22.5	45.8	29.8	22.3	33.4	...	30.8	...	29.8	...
September	29.6	30.6	30.1	22.6	45.9	29.6	22.4	33.4	...	30.8	...	30.0	...
October	29.8	30.8	30.3	22.5	46.0	29.6	22.4	33.7	...	30.8	...	30.2	...
November	29.8	30.8	30.5	22.7	45.9	29.6	22.5	33.7	...	30.7	...	30.2	...
December	29.8	30.7	30.5	22.6	45.9	29.7	22.6	33.6	...	30.7	...	30.3	...
1961													
January	29.8	30.8	30.5	22.7	46.0	29.7	22.6	33.6	...	30.6	...	30.4	...
February	29.8	30.8	30.5	22.6	46.0	29.8	22.7	33.7	...	30.7	...	30.5	...
March	29.8	30.9	30.5	22.6	46.0	29.8	22.7	33.6	...	30.8	...	30.3	...
April	29.8	30.9	30.4	22.2	45.9	29.8	22.8	33.4	...	30.7	...	30.2	...
May	29.8	30.9	30.3	22.4	46.0	30.0	22.8	33.3	...	30.6	...	29.9	...
June	29.8	31.0	30.2	22.5	46.0	30.1	22.9	33.3	...	30.5	...	29.5	...
July	29.9	31.0	30.3	22.5	46.1	30.3	22.9	33.3	...	30.5	...	29.7	...
August	29.9	31.1	30.3	22.5	46.1	30.4	23.0	33.4	...	30.5	...	30.5	...
September	30.0	31.1	30.3	22.6	46.2	30.5	23.1	33.3	...	30.5	...	30.3	...
October	30.0	31.1	30.3	22.4	46.2	30.5	23.1	33.3	...	30.4	...	30.3	...
November	30.0	31.2	30.3	22.5	46.1	30.4	23.1	33.4	...	30.5	...	30.2	...
December	30.0	31.2	30.3	22.4	46.1	30.3	23.2	33.4	...	30.6	...	30.6	...
1962													
January	30.0	31.2	30.4	22.4	46.0	30.4	23.2	33.5	...	30.5	...	30.6	...
February	30.1	31.2	30.5	22.6	46.1	30.5	23.3	33.6	...	30.6	...	30.5	...
March	30.2	31.3	30.6	22.4	46.2	30.5	23.4	33.5	...	30.6	...	30.5	...
April	30.2	31.3	30.7	22.7	46.2	30.9	23.4	33.5	...	30.6	...	30.1	...
May	30.2	31.4	30.6	22.7	46.2	30.9	23.5	33.4	...	30.6	...	30.1	...
June	30.2	31.4	30.5	22.5	46.3	30.9	23.5	33.4	...	30.6	...	29.9	...
July	30.2	31.4	30.4	22.3	46.4	30.6	23.6	33.4	...	30.6	...	30.2	...
August	30.3	31.5	30.6	22.4	46.2	30.8	23.6	33.5	...	30.6	...	30.5	...
September	30.4	31.5	30.9	22.8	46.6	31.0	23.6	33.8	...	30.6	...	31.2	...
October	30.4	31.5	30.8	22.7	46.7	30.9	23.7	33.6	...	30.5	...	30.8	...
November	30.4	31.5	30.9	22.7	46.5	30.9	23.7	33.6	...	30.5	...	31.0	...
December	30.4	31.6	30.7	22.8	46.4	30.9	23.8	33.5	...	30.5	...	30.6	...
1963													
January	30.4	31.5	31.0	22.8	46.6	30.6	23.9	33.4	...	30.5	...	30.3	...
February	30.5	31.6	31.1	22.7	46.7	30.7	23.9	33.4	...	30.5	...	30.0	...
March	30.5	31.7	31.0	22.7	46.7	30.8	23.9	33.3	...	30.5	...	29.6	...
April	30.5	31.7	30.9	22.6	46.8	30.8	23.9	33.3	...	30.5	...	29.8	...
May	30.5	31.7	30.9	22.6	46.7	30.9	24.0	33.4	...	30.7	...	29.6	...
June	30.6	31.8	31.0	22.5	46.8	30.9	24.1	33.5	...	30.7	...	29.9	...
July	30.7	31.8	31.2	22.7	46.9	30.9	24.1	33.4	...	30.7	...	30.0	...
August	30.8	31.9	31.2	22.6	47.0	31.0	24.2	33.4	...	30.7	...	29.9	...
September	30.7	31.9	31.1	22.5	47.0	31.0	24.2	33.4	...	30.7	...	29.8	...
October	30.8	32.0	31.0	22.7	47.1	31.2	24.2	33.5	...	30.8	...	29.9	...
November	30.8	32.0	31.2	22.6	47.2	31.1	24.3	33.5	...	30.8	...	30.2	...
December	30.9	32.1	31.3	22.6	47.2	31.2	24.3	33.4	...	30.8	...	29.4	...

. . . = Not available.

Table 20-2. Summary Consumer and Producer Price Indexes—Continued

(Seasonally adjusted.)

Year and month	Consumer Price Index, all urban consumers, 1982–1984 = 100							Producer Price Index, 1982 = 100					
								Finished goods		Intermediate materials, supplies, and components		Crude materials for further processing	
	All items	All items less food and energy	Food	Energy	Apparel	Transportation	Medical care	Total	Less food and energy	Total	Less food and energy	Total	Crude nonfood less energy
1964													
January	30.9	32.2	31.4	22.8	47.2	31.4	24.4	33.5	. . .	30.8	. . .	29.8	. . .
February	30.9	32.2	31.4	22.2	47.2	31.3	24.4	33.5	. . .	30.8	. . .	29.4	. . .
March	30.9	32.2	31.4	22.6	47.2	31.4	24.4	33.4	. . .	30.8	. . .	29.5	. . .
April	31.0	32.2	31.4	22.5	47.3	31.3	24.5	33.5	. . .	30.8	. . .	29.5	. . .
May	31.0	32.2	31.4	22.5	47.3	31.3	24.5	33.5	. . .	30.7	. . .	29.4	. . .
June	31.0	32.3	31.4	22.6	47.3	31.4	24.6	33.5	. . .	30.6	. . .	29.0	. . .
July	31.0	32.3	31.5	22.5	47.4	31.3	24.6	33.5	. . .	30.7	. . .	29.2	. . .
August	31.0	32.3	31.4	22.6	47.4	31.4	24.7	33.6	. . .	30.6	. . .	29.4	. . .
September	31.1	32.3	31.6	22.5	47.2	31.3	24.7	33.6	. . .	30.7	. . .	30.1	. . .
October	31.1	32.4	31.6	22.5	47.2	31.3	24.7	33.6	. . .	30.8	. . .	29.8	. . .
November	31.2	32.5	31.7	22.5	47.3	31.4	24.8	33.6	. . .	30.8	. . .	29.9	. . .
December	31.2	32.5	31.7	22.6	47.4	31.7	24.8	33.6	. . .	30.9	. . .	29.8	. . .
1965													
January	31.3	32.6	31.6	22.8	47.5	31.9	24.8	33.6	. . .	30.9	. . .	29.5	. . .
February	31.3	32.6	31.5	22.7	47.5	31.8	24.9	33.7	. . .	30.9	. . .	29.9	. . .
March	31.3	32.6	31.7	22.6	47.5	31.8	25.0	33.7	. . .	31.0	. . .	30.0	. . .
April	31.4	32.7	31.8	22.9	47.6	31.9	25.0	34.0	. . .	31.1	. . .	30.4	. . .
May	31.5	32.7	32.1	23.0	47.7	32.0	25.1	34.1	. . .	31.1	. . .	30.8	. . .
June	31.6	32.7	32.6	23.1	47.8	31.9	25.1	34.2	. . .	31.2	. . .	31.6	. . .
July	31.6	32.7	32.5	23.0	47.7	31.9	25.3	34.1	. . .	31.2	. . .	31.2	. . .
August	31.6	32.7	32.4	23.0	47.8	31.9	25.3	34.2	. . .	31.3	. . .	31.5	. . .
September	31.6	32.8	32.3	23.1	47.8	31.9	25.3	34.3	. . .	31.3	. . .	31.4	. . .
October	31.6	32.8	32.5	23.0	47.9	31.8	25.4	34.4	. . .	31.3	. . .	31.8	. . .
November	31.8	32.9	32.6	23.1	48.0	31.9	25.5	34.5	. . .	31.4	. . .	32.1	. . .
December	31.8	33.0	32.8	23.1	48.1	32.0	25.5	34.7	. . .	31.4	. . .	32.7	. . .
1966													
January	31.9	33.0	33.0	23.1	48.3	31.9	25.6	34.7	. . .	31.4	. . .	33.1	. . .
February	32.1	33.1	33.5	23.2	48.4	32.0	25.6	35.0	. . .	31.6	. . .	33.7	. . .
March	32.2	33.1	33.8	23.2	48.5	32.1	25.8	35.0	. . .	31.7	. . .	33.5	. . .
April	32.3	33.3	33.8	23.2	48.7	32.2	25.9	35.1	. . .	31.8	. . .	33.3	. . .
May	32.4	33.4	33.7	23.2	48.8	32.1	26.0	35.1	. . .	32.0	. . .	33.0	. . .
June	32.4	33.5	33.7	23.3	48.9	32.2	26.1	34.9	. . .	32.0	. . .	33.0	. . .
July	32.4	33.6	33.5	23.4	49.1	32.5	26.3	35.1	. . .	32.2	. . .	33.4	. . .
August	32.6	33.7	34.0	23.3	49.1	32.6	26.4	35.4	. . .	32.3	. . .	33.5	. . .
September	32.8	33.8	34.1	23.4	49.4	32.6	26.7	35.6	. . .	32.2	. . .	33.4	. . .
October	32.8	34.0	34.2	23.4	49.6	32.7	26.9	35.5	. . .	32.1	. . .	32.9	. . .
November	32.9	34.0	34.1	23.5	49.7	32.8	27.1	35.5	. . .	32.2	. . .	32.3	. . .
December	32.9	34.1	34.0	23.5	49.9	32.6	27.2	35.4	. . .	32.2	. . .	32.1	. . .
1967													
January	32.9	34.2	33.9	23.6	50.1	32.6	27.4	35.4	. . .	32.2	. . .	32.2	. . .
February	33.0	34.2	33.8	23.7	50.3	32.8	27.5	35.3	. . .	32.1	. . .	31.5	. . .
March	33.0	34.3	33.8	23.6	50.4	32.8	27.6	35.3	. . .	32.1	. . .	31.1	. . .
April	33.1	34.4	33.7	23.9	50.6	33.0	27.8	35.3	. . .	32.1	. . .	30.7	. . .
May	33.1	34.5	33.7	23.9	50.7	33.1	27.9	35.4	. . .	32.1	. . .	31.1	. . .
June	33.3	34.6	34.0	23.8	50.9	33.1	28.1	35.7	. . .	32.2	. . .	31.4	. . .
July	33.4	34.7	34.1	23.8	51.1	33.3	28.2	35.7	. . .	32.2	. . .	31.3	. . .
August	33.5	34.9	34.3	23.9	51.3	33.4	28.3	35.8	. . .	32.2	. . .	31.3	. . .
September	33.6	35.0	34.3	24.0	51.3	33.7	28.5	35.8	. . .	32.3	. . .	31.2	. . .
October	33.7	35.1	34.4	23.9	51.5	33.6	28.7	35.9	. . .	32.3	. . .	31.3	. . .
November	33.9	35.2	34.5	24.0	51.6	33.9	28.8	35.9	. . .	32.4	. . .	31.1	. . .
December	34.0	35.4	34.6	23.9	51.9	33.9	29.0	36.0	. . .	32.6	. . .	31.5	. . .
1968													
January	34.1	35.5	34.6	24.0	52.1	34.1	29.1	36.1	. . .	32.6	. . .	31.4	. . .
February	34.2	35.7	34.8	24.1	52.4	34.2	29.2	36.2	. . .	32.7	. . .	31.5	. . .
March	34.3	35.8	34.9	24.1	52.7	34.2	29.4	36.3	. . .	32.8	. . .	31.6	. . .
April	34.4	35.9	35.0	24.0	53.0	34.1	29.5	36.5	. . .	32.8	. . .	31.7	. . .
May	34.5	36.0	35.1	24.1	53.3	34.1	29.6	36.5	. . .	32.8	. . .	31.5	. . .
June	34.7	36.2	35.2	24.2	53.5	34.3	29.7	36.6	. . .	32.9	. . .	31.3	. . .
July	34.9	36.4	35.3	24.2	53.9	34.3	29.9	36.7	. . .	33.0	. . .	31.6	. . .
August	35.0	36.5	35.4	24.3	54.2	34.4	30.0	36.8	. . .	33.0	. . .	31.7	. . .
September	35.1	36.7	35.6	24.3	54.5	34.4	30.2	37.0	. . .	33.1	. . .	31.9	. . .
October	35.3	36.9	35.9	24.3	54.8	34.5	30.4	37.0	. . .	33.2	. . .	32.1	. . .
November	35.4	37.1	35.9	24.4	54.9	34.7	30.6	37.1	. . .	33.2	. . .	32.8	. . .
December	35.6	37.2	36.0	24.3	55.2	34.5	30.8	37.1	. . .	33.4	. . .	32.4	. . .
1969													
January	35.7	37.3	36.1	24.4	55.5	34.7	30.9	37.2	. . .	33.6	. . .	32.6	. . .
February	35.8	37.6	36.1	24.4	55.7	35.2	31.2	37.2	. . .	33.7	. . .	32.3	. . .
March	36.1	37.8	36.2	24.7	55.9	35.8	31.4	37.4	. . .	33.9	. . .	32.7	. . .
April	36.3	38.1	36.4	24.9	56.2	35.8	31.6	37.6	. . .	33.8	. . .	33.1	. . .
May	36.4	38.1	36.6	24.8	56.4	35.5	31.8	37.8	. . .	33.9	. . .	34.0	. . .
June	36.6	38.3	37.0	25.0	56.7	35.6	31.9	38.0	. . .	34.0	. . .	34.5	. . .
July	36.8	38.5	37.3	24.9	57.0	35.6	32.1	38.1	. . .	34.0	. . .	34.1	. . .
August	36.9	38.7	37.5	24.9	57.0	35.7	32.2	38.2	. . .	34.2	. . .	34.4	. . .
September	37.1	38.9	37.7	25.0	57.4	35.6	32.5	38.3	. . .	34.2	. . .	34.4	. . .
October	37.3	39.1	37.8	25.0	57.6	35.9	32.3	38.5	. . .	34.4	. . .	34.8	. . .
November	37.5	39.2	38.2	25.0	57.9	36.0	32.5	38.8	. . .	34.6	. . .	35.2	. . .
December	37.7	39.4	38.6	25.1	58.0	36.2	32.6	38.9	. . .	34.7	. . .	35.1	. . .

. . . = Not available.

Table 20-2. Summary Consumer and Producer Price Indexes—Continued

(Seasonally adjusted.)

Year and month	Consumer Price Index, all urban consumers, 1982–1984 = 100							Producer Price Index, 1982 = 100					
								Finished goods		Intermediate materials, supplies, and components		Crude materials for further processing	
	All items	All items less food and energy	Food	Energy	Apparel	Transportation	Medical care	Total	Less food and energy	Total	Less food and energy	Total	Crude nonfood less energy
1970													
January	37.9	39.6	38.7	25.1	58.2	36.6	32.8	39.1	...	35.0	...	35.1	...
February	38.1	39.8	38.9	25.1	58.5	36.7	33.0	39.0	...	35.0	...	35.2	...
March	38.3	40.1	38.9	25.0	58.5	36.6	33.2	39.1	...	34.9	...	35.6	...
April	38.5	40.4	39.0	25.5	58.7	37.1	33.5	39.1	...	35.1	...	35.5	...
May	38.6	40.5	39.2	25.4	58.8	37.2	33.7	39.1	...	35.2	...	35.0	...
June	38.8	40.8	39.2	25.3	59.0	37.4	33.9	39.2	...	35.3	...	35.0	...
July	38.9	40.9	39.2	25.5	59.1	37.6	34.1	39.2	...	35.5	...	35.1	...
August	39.0	41.1	39.2	25.4	59.3	37.5	34.3	39.2	...	35.5	...	34.7	...
September	39.2	41.3	39.4	25.6	59.6	37.7	34.5	39.6	...	35.6	...	35.5	...
October	39.4	41.5	39.5	25.9	59.8	38.1	34.6	39.6	...	35.8	...	35.5	...
November	39.6	41.8	39.5	26.0	60.1	38.5	34.8	39.8	...	35.9	...	35.1	...
December	39.8	42.0	39.5	26.2	60.3	38.9	35.1	39.8	...	35.9	...	34.5	...
1971													
January	39.9	42.1	39.4	26.3	60.4	39.2	35.2	39.9	...	36.0	...	34.8	...
February	39.9	42.2	39.5	26.2	60.6	39.4	35.4	40.1	...	36.1	...	35.9	...
March	40.0	42.2	39.8	26.2	60.6	39.4	35.6	40.2	...	36.3	...	35.4	...
April	40.1	42.4	40.1	26.1	60.7	39.4	35.8	40.3	...	36.3	...	36.0	...
May	40.3	42.6	40.3	26.2	61.1	39.4	36.0	40.5	...	36.5	...	36.0	...
June	40.5	42.8	40.5	26.3	61.2	39.6	36.2	40.6	...	36.7	...	36.2	...
July	40.6	42.9	40.6	26.3	61.3	39.6	36.4	40.4	...	36.9	...	35.9	...
August	40.7	43.0	40.6	26.8	61.1	39.7	36.5	40.7	...	37.2	...	35.8	...
September	40.8	43.0	40.6	26.9	61.3	39.5	36.7	40.7	...	37.2	...	35.7	...
October	40.9	43.1	40.7	27.0	61.4	39.5	36.5	40.7	...	37.1	...	36.4	...
November	41.0	43.2	40.9	26.9	61.5	39.4	36.6	40.8	...	37.2	...	37.0	...
December	41.1	43.3	41.3	27.0	61.6	39.4	36.7	41.1	...	37.4	...	37.2	...
1972													
January	41.2	43.5	41.1	27.0	61.7	39.7	36.8	41.0	...	37.5	...	37.8	...
February	41.4	43.6	41.7	26.8	61.9	39.6	36.9	41.3	...	37.7	...	38.1	...
March	41.4	43.6	41.6	26.9	61.9	39.6	37.0	41.3	...	37.8	...	38.1	...
April	41.5	43.8	41.6	26.9	62.1	39.6	37.1	41.3	...	37.9	...	38.7	...
May	41.6	43.9	41.7	27.0	62.2	39.7	37.2	41.5	...	38.0	...	39.3	...
June	41.7	44.0	41.9	27.0	62.2	39.7	37.3	41.7	...	38.0	...	39.4	...
July	41.8	44.1	42.1	27.1	62.2	39.8	37.3	41.8	...	38.1	...	40.0	...
August	41.9	44.3	42.2	27.3	62.0	40.0	37.4	42.0	...	38.2	...	40.3	...
September	42.1	44.3	42.5	27.6	62.5	40.2	37.4	42.2	...	38.5	...	40.5	...
October	42.2	44.4	42.8	27.7	62.8	40.1	37.8	42.0	...	38.7	...	40.9	...
November	42.4	44.4	43.0	27.9	63.0	40.3	37.8	42.3	...	39.0	...	42.0	...
December	42.5	44.6	43.2	27.8	63.2	40.4	37.9	42.7	...	39.6	...	43.8	...
1973													
January	42.7	44.6	44.0	27.9	63.2	40.4	38.0	43.0	...	39.8	...	45.0	...
February	43.0	44.8	44.6	28.2	63.4	40.6	38.1	43.5	...	40.4	...	47.1	...
March	43.4	45.0	45.8	28.3	63.8	40.7	38.2	44.4	...	41.1	...	49.3	...
April	43.7	45.1	46.5	28.6	64.2	41.0	38.3	44.7	...	41.3	...	50.1	...
May	43.9	45.3	47.1	28.8	64.4	41.0	38.5	45.0	...	42.2	...	52.5	...
June	44.2	45.4	47.6	29.2	64.6	41.2	38.6	45.5	...	43.0	...	55.0	...
July	44.2	45.5	47.7	29.2	64.6	41.2	38.6	45.4	...	42.3	...	52.5	...
August	45.0	45.7	50.5	29.4	64.9	41.2	38.7	47.0	...	43.5	...	64.1	...
September	45.2	46.0	50.4	29.4	65.2	41.1	38.9	46.9	...	43.0	...	60.9	...
October	45.6	46.3	50.7	30.3	65.4	41.4	39.6	46.8	...	43.4	...	58.5	...
November	45.9	46.5	51.4	31.5	65.7	41.8	39.7	47.2	...	43.8	...	59.0	...
December	46.3	46.7	51.9	32.5	66.0	42.2	39.9	47.6	...	44.8	...	59.1	...
1974													
January	46.8	46.9	52.5	34.1	66.3	42.8	40.1	48.8	49.7	45.9	47.5	63.3	86.3
February	47.3	47.2	53.6	35.4	67.0	43.4	40.3	49.7	50.0	46.8	48.1	64.3	86.5
March	47.8	47.6	54.2	36.9	67.5	44.2	40.7	50.2	50.5	48.1	49.5	62.3	88.3
April	48.1	47.9	54.1	37.6	68.2	44.7	41.0	50.7	51.1	49.0	50.9	60.6	89.7
May	48.6	48.5	54.5	38.3	68.7	45.3	41.4	51.3	52.2	50.6	52.5	58.3	83.8
June	49.0	49.0	54.5	38.6	69.2	45.9	42.1	51.3	53.1	51.5	53.7	55.4	82.9
July	49.3	49.5	54.3	38.9	69.5	46.4	42.6	52.7	54.0	53.4	55.2	59.8	84.2
August	49.9	50.2	55.1	39.2	70.8	46.6	43.2	53.7	55.0	55.8	57.0	62.9	85.5
September	50.6	50.7	56.2	39.3	71.0	47.0	43.7	54.3	55.7	55.9	57.6	60.9	82.5
October	51.0	51.2	56.8	39.2	71.2	47.3	44.1	55.3	56.7	57.2	58.2	63.2	80.6
November	51.5	51.6	57.5	39.4	71.7	47.6	44.4	56.4	57.4	57.8	58.8	64.2	77.6
December	51.9	52.0	58.2	39.6	71.7	47.9	44.8	56.4	57.9	57.8	59.1	61.5	71.6
1975													
January	52.3	52.3	58.4	40.0	71.8	48.0	45.3	56.7	58.3	58.0	59.6	59.6	69.8
February	52.6	52.8	58.5	40.3	72.0	48.3	45.8	56.6	58.7	57.8	59.8	57.9	69.2
March	52.8	53.0	58.4	40.6	72.1	48.7	46.3	56.6	59.0	57.4	59.7	57.1	68.2
April	53.0	53.3	58.3	41.0	72.1	48.8	46.7	57.1	59.2	57.5	59.7	59.5	67.7
May	53.1	53.5	58.6	41.3	72.2	48.9	47.0	57.4	59.3	57.3	59.7	61.2	68.8
June	53.5	53.8	59.2	41.7	72.2	49.4	47.4	57.9	59.5	57.3	59.8	61.5	66.5
July	54.0	54.0	60.3	42.5	72.6	50.2	47.8	58.4	59.8	57.5	59.9	62.4	66.5
August	54.2	54.2	60.3	42.8	72.6	50.6	48.1	58.9	59.9	58.0	60.1	63.0	67.7
September	54.6	54.5	60.7	43.2	72.7	51.4	48.5	59.3	60.2	58.2	60.3	64.5	71.2
October	54.9	54.8	61.3	43.5	73.0	51.7	48.9	59.8	60.6	58.8	61.0	65.1	71.5
November	55.3	55.2	61.7	43.9	73.2	52.4	48.8	60.0	61.0	59.0	61.4	64.4	71.9
December	55.6	55.5	62.1	44.1	73.4	52.6	49.3	60.1	61.4	59.2	61.8	64.0	73.1

. . . = Not available.

Table 20-2. Summary Consumer and Producer Price Indexes—Continued

(Seasonally adjusted.)

Year and month	Consumer Price Index, all urban consumers, 1982–1984 = 100							Producer Price Index, 1982 = 100					
								Finished goods		Intermediate materials, supplies, and components		Crude materials for further processing	
	All items	All items less food and energy	Food	Energy	Apparel	Transportation	Medical care	Total	Less food and energy	Total	Less food and energy	Total	Crude nonfood less energy
1976													
January	55.8	55.9	61.9	44.5	73.7	53.0	49.7	60.0	61.7	59.4	62.1	63.0	72.4
February	55.9	56.2	61.3	44.4	74.0	53.3	50.2	59.9	61.9	59.6	62.3	62.1	73.8
March	56.0	56.5	60.9	44.1	74.2	53.8	50.7	60.0	62.2	59.8	62.6	61.5	74.5
April	56.1	56.7	60.9	43.9	74.3	54.0	51.0	60.3	62.3	60.0	62.8	63.9	78.1
May	56.4	57.0	61.1	44.1	74.6	54.3	51.4	60.4	62.4	60.3	63.2	63.6	80.6
June	56.7	57.2	61.3	44.4	74.9	54.8	51.8	60.5	62.8	60.8	63.6	65.2	82.8
July	57.0	57.6	61.6	44.8	75.3	55.1	52.3	60.7	63.1	61.1	63.9	64.8	87.3
August	57.3	57.9	61.8	45.2	75.8	55.4	52.6	60.9	63.5	61.3	64.3	63.6	84.1
September	57.6	58.2	62.1	45.7	76.1	56.0	53.0	61.1	63.9	61.9	64.7	63.4	84.4
October	57.9	58.5	62.4	46.1	76.2	56.6	53.2	61.4	64.1	62.0	65.0	63.0	82.2
November	58.1	58.7	62.3	46.8	76.5	57.0	53.9	61.9	64.6	62.4	65.3	63.4	81.8
December	58.4	58.9	62.5	47.5	76.8	57.3	54.2	62.4	64.9	62.8	65.6	64.5	81.1
1977													
January	58.7	59.3	62.7	48.1	77.2	57.8	54.6	62.5	65.1	63.0	65.8	64.3	78.7
February	59.3	59.7	63.9	48.1	77.6	58.2	54.9	63.2	65.4	63.3	65.9	65.7	79.7
March	59.6	60.0	64.2	48.4	77.5	58.7	55.5	63.7	65.7	63.9	66.4	66.6	81.5
April	60.0	60.3	65.0	48.6	77.6	59.0	56.0	64.0	65.9	64.4	66.7	68.3	82.1
May	60.2	60.6	65.3	48.9	78.1	59.1	56.5	64.4	66.1	64.9	67.1	67.6	82.5
June	60.5	61.0	65.7	48.9	78.5	59.1	57.0	64.6	66.5	64.9	67.4	65.5	79.7
July	60.8	61.2	65.9	49.1	79.1	59.0	57.3	64.8	66.8	65.1	67.9	64.7	78.8
August	61.1	61.5	66.2	49.5	79.2	58.9	57.7	65.2	67.3	65.4	68.2	63.9	79.2
September	61.3	61.8	66.4	49.8	79.1	59.1	58.2	65.5	67.8	65.7	68.7	63.7	79.2
October	61.6	62.0	66.6	50.5	79.3	59.3	58.4	65.9	68.2	65.8	68.8	64.0	78.5
November	62.0	62.3	67.1	51.3	79.8	59.5	58.6	66.4	68.8	66.3	69.1	65.4	78.4
December	62.3	62.7	67.4	51.6	80.1	59.8	59.0	66.7	69.0	66.6	69.4	66.4	80.1
1978													
January	62.7	63.1	67.9	51.1	80.1	60.1	59.3	67.0	69.2	66.9	69.8	67.3	80.3
February	63.0	63.4	68.6	50.6	79.5	60.2	59.9	67.5	69.5	67.4	70.3	68.4	80.6
March	63.4	63.8	69.5	51.0	79.9	60.3	60.2	67.8	69.9	67.8	70.6	69.8	80.3
April	63.9	64.3	70.6	51.4	80.7	60.4	60.7	68.6	70.6	68.1	71.1	72.1	82.2
May	64.5	64.7	71.6	51.7	81.3	60.7	61.1	69.1	71.1	68.7	71.6	72.8	84.6
June	65.0	65.2	72.7	51.9	81.6	61.1	61.5	69.7	71.7	69.2	72.2	74.6	87.4
July	65.5	65.6	73.0	52.1	81.5	61.6	61.9	70.3	72.3	69.4	72.5	74.2	89.6
August	65.9	66.1	73.3	52.6	81.7	62.0	62.4	70.4	72.8	69.9	73.2	73.7	90.4
September	66.5	66.7	73.6	53.2	81.9	62.6	62.8	71.1	73.5	70.5	73.7	75.1	92.3
October	67.1	67.2	74.2	54.1	82.4	63.3	63.3	71.4	73.4	71.3	74.5	77.0	94.7
November	67.5	67.6	74.7	54.9	82.6	63.9	63.8	72.0	74.1	71.9	75.2	77.4	96.3
December	67.9	68.0	75.1	55.9	82.6	64.5	64.1	72.8	74.7	72.4	75.6	78.0	96.8
1979													
January	68.5	68.5	76.4	55.8	83.0	64.6	64.8	73.7	75.3	73.1	76.3	80.1	96.4
February	69.2	69.2	77.7	55.9	83.3	65.2	65.2	74.4	75.9	73.7	77.0	82.1	99.6
March	69.9	69.8	78.4	57.4	83.6	66.4	65.7	75.0	76.4	74.6	77.8	83.8	104.2
April	70.6	70.3	79.0	59.5	84.0	67.8	66.1	75.8	77.0	75.7	78.9	84.4	105.1
May	71.4	70.8	79.7	62.0	84.5	69.1	66.6	76.2	77.4	76.6	79.6	84.7	106.7
June	72.2	71.3	80.0	64.7	84.7	70.5	67.1	76.6	78.0	77.5	80.1	85.6	111.6
July	73.0	71.9	80.5	67.3	84.8	71.7	67.7	77.4	78.5	78.7	81.1	86.5	109.4
August	73.7	72.7	80.4	69.7	85.0	72.7	68.2	78.2	78.8	79.8	81.8	85.5	106.4
September	74.4	73.3	80.9	71.9	85.6	73.5	68.7	79.5	79.7	81.1	82.7	87.9	106.5
October	75.2	74.0	81.5	73.5	86.1	74.0	69.2	80.4	80.4	82.4	83.9	88.8	108.9
November	76.0	74.8	82.0	74.8	86.6	74.7	69.8	81.4	81.0	83.2	84.5	90.0	111.3
December	76.9	75.7	82.8	76.8	87.3	75.8	70.6	82.2	81.7	84.0	85.2	91.2	111.3
1980													
January	78.0	76.7	83.3	79.1	88.1	78.0	71.4	83.4	83.3	86.0	87.2	90.9	112.6
February	79.0	77.5	83.4	81.9	88.7	79.8	72.3	84.6	84.2	87.6	88.2	92.6	115.3
March	80.1	78.6	84.1	84.5	89.7	81.8	73.0	85.5	84.7	88.2	88.6	90.8	111.7
April	80.9	79.5	84.7	85.4	90.1	82.2	73.6	86.2	85.5	88.5	88.8	88.3	109.9
May	81.7	80.1	85.2	86.4	90.3	82.8	74.2	86.6	85.7	89.0	89.1	89.5	107.2
June	82.5	81.0	85.7	86.5	90.6	82.7	74.7	87.3	86.6	89.8	89.8	90.1	106.1
July	82.6	80.8	86.6	86.7	90.9	83.1	75.2	88.7	87.7	90.5	90.3	94.6	109.6
August	83.2	81.3	88.0	87.2	91.4	83.7	75.6	89.7	88.4	91.5	91.1	99.0	112.4
September	83.9	82.1	89.1	87.5	92.0	84.6	76.3	90.1	88.8	91.9	91.4	100.4	116.2
October	84.7	83.0	89.8	88.0	92.7	85.3	76.9	90.8	89.6	92.8	92.1	102.2	118.2
November	85.6	83.9	90.8	88.8	93.1	86.1	77.3	91.4	90.1	93.5	92.6	103.5	119.8
December	86.4	84.9	91.3	90.7	93.3	86.8	77.8	91.8	90.4	94.4	93.7	102.7	119.3
1981													
January	87.2	85.4	91.6	92.1	93.4	88.5	78.6	92.8	91.4	95.6	94.7	103.4	113.3
February	88.0	85.9	92.1	95.2	93.9	90.7	79.2	93.6	92.0	96.1	94.9	104.2	106.2
March	88.6	86.4	92.6	97.4	94.3	91.8	79.9	94.7	92.6	97.1	95.6	103.8	108.9
April	89.1	87.0	92.8	97.6	94.7	91.7	80.7	95.7	93.5	98.3	96.6	104.2	111.9
May	89.7	87.8	92.8	97.9	94.8	92.2	81.4	96.0	94.0	98.7	97.1	103.8	113.7
June	90.5	88.6	93.2	97.3	95.0	92.7	82.3	96.5	94.6	99.0	97.7	104.9	115.5
July	91.5	89.8	93.9	97.3	95.4	93.5	83.4	96.7	94.8	99.2	98.4	105.0	116.4
August	92.2	90.7	94.4	97.8	95.9	93.9	84.3	96.8	95.3	99.7	98.9	104.0	115.5
September	93.1	91.8	94.8	98.6	96.1	94.6	85.1	97.2	95.9	99.7	99.3	102.7	112.6
October	93.4	92.1	95.0	99.2	96.4	95.5	85.9	97.6	96.5	99.8	99.5	101.2	110.8
November	93.8	92.5	95.1	100.5	96.4	96.2	86.8	97.9	97.0	99.9	99.7	99.7	107.5
December	94.1	93.0	95.3	101.5	96.7	96.4	87.5	98.3	97.6	100.0	99.8	98.8	106.0

Table 20-2. Summary Consumer and Producer Price Indexes—Continued

(Seasonally adjusted.)

Year and month	Consumer Price Index, all urban consumers, 1982–1984 = 100							Producer Price Index, 1982 = 100					
								Finished goods		Intermediate materials, supplies, and components		Crude materials for further processing	
	All items	All items less food and energy	Food	Energy	Apparel	Transportation	Medical care	Total	Less food and energy	Total	Less food and energy	Total	Crude nonfood less energy
1982													
January	94.4	93.3	95.6	100.6	96.7	96.7	88.2	98.9	98.1	100.4	99.9	99.7	101.2
February	94.7	93.8	96.3	98.0	97.0	96.2	88.8	98.8	98.1	100.3	100.0	100.0	100.7
March	94.7	93.9	96.2	96.6	97.3	95.8	89.6	98.8	98.7	99.9	99.9	99.7	100.0
April	95.0	94.7	96.4	94.2	97.5	94.5	90.5	99.0	99.0	99.7	99.8	100.2	101.1
May	95.9	95.4	97.2	95.7	97.6	95.1	91.3	99.0	99.4	99.7	100.1	101.9	102.2
June	97.0	96.1	98.1	98.4	97.7	97.2	92.2	99.8	99.9	99.8	100.0	101.8	101.0
July	97.5	96.7	98.2	99.3	98.1	98.1	93.0	100.2	100.1	100.0	99.8	100.7	101.4
August	97.7	97.1	98.0	99.8	98.1	98.2	93.9	100.6	100.6	99.9	99.7	99.8	100.0
September	97.7	97.2	98.2	100.3	98.1	98.0	94.7	100.7	100.8	100.0	100.2	99.2	98.9
October	98.1	97.5	98.2	101.7	98.3	98.2	95.5	101.0	101.3	99.9	100.2	98.7	97.7
November	98.0	97.3	98.2	102.5	98.3	98.2	96.5	101.4	101.6	100.1	100.2	99.2	96.3
December	97.7	97.2	98.2	102.8	98.2	97.7	97.2	101.8	102.2	100.1	100.3	98.8	95.9
1983													
January	97.9	97.6	98.1	99.6	98.6	97.6	97.9	101.0	101.8	99.8	100.3	98.8	97.3
February	98.0	98.0	98.2	97.7	99.1	96.9	98.8	101.1	102.2	100.0	100.8	100.0	99.8
March	98.1	98.2	98.8	96.8	99.1	96.5	99.0	101.0	102.5	99.7	100.8	100.5	102.2
April	98.8	98.6	99.2	98.9	99.3	97.8	99.4	101.1	102.4	99.5	100.9	101.2	102.1
May	99.2	98.9	99.5	100.4	99.9	98.6	99.9	101.4	102.6	99.8	101.0	100.9	103.4
June	99.4	99.2	99.6	100.6	100.3	99.0	100.4	101.6	102.8	100.2	101.3	100.5	104.8
July	99.8	99.8	99.6	100.9	100.9	99.6	100.8	101.6	103.1	100.5	101.8	99.5	106.2
August	100.1	100.1	99.7	101.2	101.0	100.4	101.4	101.9	103.5	100.9	102.0	102.2	108.4
September	100.4	100.5	100.0	101.0	100.8	100.7	101.8	102.2	103.5	101.6	102.3	103.3	109.0
October	100.8	101.0	100.3	100.8	100.6	101.1	102.3	102.2	103.6	101.7	102.5	103.2	109.1
November	101.1	101.5	100.3	100.5	100.9	101.5	102.8	102.0	103.8	101.8	102.8	102.3	109.9
December	101.4	101.8	100.6	100.0	101.1	101.5	103.4	102.3	104.1	101.9	103.1	103.5	111.2
1984													
January	102.1	102.5	102.0	100.2	101.5	102.0	104.0	103.0	104.5	102.1	103.4	104.6	111.5
February	102.6	102.8	102.7	101.4	101.2	102.2	105.0	103.4	104.7	102.5	103.8	103.8	113.8
March	102.9	103.2	102.9	101.4	101.3	102.9	105.2	103.8	105.2	103.0	104.4	105.7	114.8
April	103.3	103.7	102.9	101.7	101.2	103.3	105.8	103.9	105.3	103.2	104.5	105.2	115.1
May	103.5	104.1	102.7	101.6	101.4	103.7	106.2	103.8	105.3	103.4	104.6	104.5	115.7
June	103.7	104.5	103.1	100.8	101.3	103.9	106.7	103.8	105.5	103.6	104.8	103.3	114.1
July	104.1	105.0	103.3	100.5	101.9	103.7	107.2	104.0	105.7	103.4	104.9	104.0	112.0
August	104.4	105.4	103.9	100.1	102.5	103.8	107.7	103.8	105.9	103.2	105.1	103.3	109.6
September	104.7	105.8	103.8	100.6	102.7	104.1	108.1	103.8	106.2	103.1	105.0	102.8	110.5
October	105.1	106.2	104.0	101.1	103.0	104.8	108.7	103.6	105.9	103.2	105.1	101.5	108.5
November	105.3	106.4	104.1	100.8	103.0	104.9	109.3	104.0	106.2	103.3	105.3	101.9	107.7
December	105.5	106.8	104.5	100.1	103.1	104.7	109.8	104.0	106.3	103.2	105.3	101.4	107.3
1985													
January	105.7	107.1	104.7	100.3	103.2	105.1	110.2	104.0	106.9	103.1	105.3	99.9	107.4
February	106.3	107.7	105.2	100.3	104.1	105.6	110.8	104.1	107.3	102.8	105.3	99.4	107.2
March	106.8	108.1	105.5	101.3	104.5	106.3	111.4	104.1	107.6	102.7	105.2	97.6	107.0
April	107.0	108.4	105.4	102.3	104.5	106.8	112.0	104.6	107.6	102.9	105.2	96.7	107.4
May	107.2	108.8	105.2	102.2	104.4	106.5	112.6	104.9	107.8	103.2	105.3	95.8	105.3
June	107.5	109.1	105.5	102.2	105.1	106.5	113.3	104.6	108.2	102.6	105.5	95.2	103.6
July	107.7	109.4	105.5	102.2	105.2	106.6	113.9	104.7	108.4	102.3	105.3	94.9	104.3
August	107.9	109.8	105.6	101.2	105.3	106.2	114.6	104.5	108.5	102.3	105.3	92.9	103.6
September	108.1	110.0	105.8	101.2	105.5	106.2	115.2	103.8	107.9	102.2	105.2	91.8	103.3
October	108.5	110.5	105.8	101.2	105.7	106.5	115.8	104.9	108.9	102.3	105.1	94.1	103.7
November	109.0	111.1	106.5	101.8	106.0	107.0	116.5	105.5	109.1	102.5	105.1	95.7	103.0
December	109.5	111.4	107.3	102.4	106.1	107.5	117.1	106.0	109.1	102.9	105.1	95.5	102.4
1986													
January	109.9	111.9	107.5	102.6	106.1	108.0	118.0	105.5	109.3	102.4	105.0	94.2	103.6
February	109.7	112.2	107.3	99.5	105.4	107.0	118.8	104.1	109.5	101.2	104.9	90.5	103.5
March	109.1	112.5	107.5	92.6	105.0	103.6	119.7	102.8	109.6	99.9	105.0	88.2	103.8
April	108.7	112.9	107.7	87.2	105.0	101.0	120.4	102.3	110.1	98.9	104.7	85.6	103.9
May	109.0	113.1	108.2	87.2	104.9	101.4	121.2	102.8	110.2	98.7	104.6	86.5	104.1
June	109.4	113.4	108.3	88.8	104.9	102.3	121.8	103.1	110.5	98.6	104.7	86.2	104.7
July	109.5	113.8	109.1	85.6	105.5	101.1	122.5	102.3	110.7	98.0	104.8	86.4	105.3
August	109.6	114.2	110.1	83.6	106.4	100.1	123.2	102.7	110.8	98.0	104.9	86.7	99.7
September	110.0	114.6	110.2	84.4	106.9	100.6	124.0	102.9	110.7	98.5	105.1	86.6	100.3
October	110.2	115.0	110.5	82.8	106.6	100.5	124.7	103.5	111.8	98.3	105.1	87.4	102.0
November	110.4	115.3	111.1	82.1	106.9	100.8	125.5	103.4	112.0	98.3	105.2	87.6	102.8
December	110.8	115.6	111.4	82.5	107.2	101.1	126.2	103.6	112.1	98.5	105.3	86.9	104.1
1987													
January	111.4	115.9	111.8	85.4	108.0	102.6	126.7	104.1	112.5	99.0	105.6	89.3	105.4
February	111.8	116.2	112.2	87.4	108.6	103.5	127.2	104.4	112.3	99.8	105.9	90.2	106.2
March	112.2	116.6	112.4	87.6	109.2	103.8	127.8	104.5	112.4	99.9	106.2	90.5	106.5
April	112.7	117.3	112.6	87.6	109.8	104.3	128.6	105.1	112.9	100.3	106.5	92.5	107.5
May	113.0	117.7	113.2	87.1	110.3	104.4	129.2	105.2	113.0	100.8	107.0	93.8	110.0
June	113.5	117.9	113.9	88.5	110.3	105.1	130.0	105.5	113.1	101.4	107.5	94.5	113.2
July	113.8	118.3	113.7	89.2	110.3	105.9	130.6	105.7	113.3	101.9	107.9	95.6	115.9
August	114.3	118.7	113.9	90.5	111.0	106.6	131.2	105.9	113.6	102.4	108.3	96.5	119.1
September	114.7	119.2	114.3	90.3	111.6	106.9	131.9	106.2	113.9	102.6	108.9	96.0	122.8
October	115.0	119.8	114.5	89.6	112.3	107.0	132.4	106.0	114.0	103.1	109.6	95.8	126.6
November	115.4	120.1	114.5	90.0	113.0	107.3	133.0	106.0	114.2	103.5	110.1	95.1	127.5
December	115.6	120.4	115.1	89.5	112.7	107.2	133.5	105.8	114.3	103.8	110.7	94.9	127.9

Table 20-2. Summary Consumer and Producer Price Indexes—Continued

(Seasonally adjusted.)

| Year and month | Consumer Price Index, all urban consumers, 1982–1984 = 100 | | | | | | | Producer Price Index, 1982 = 100 | | | | | |
| | | | | | | | | Finished goods | | Intermediate materials, supplies, and components | | Crude materials for further processing | |
	All items	All items less food and energy	Food	Energy	Apparel	Transportation	Medical care	Total	Less food and energy	Total	Less food and energy	Total	Crude nonfood less energy
1988													
January	116.0	120.9	115.6	88.8	113.2	107.0	134.4	106.4	115.0	104.1	111.8	94.2	129.4
February	116.2	121.2	115.6	88.7	112.1	107.0	135.2	106.3	115.3	104.4	112.2	95.2	131.7
March	116.5	121.7	115.8	88.4	113.4	107.0	135.8	106.6	115.6	104.8	112.8	94.1	133.0
April	117.2	122.3	116.4	88.8	115.1	107.5	136.7	107.0	115.9	105.5	113.6	95.4	132.1
May	117.5	122.7	116.9	88.5	115.1	107.9	137.6	107.2	116.2	106.2	114.3	95.8	130.7
June	118.0	123.2	117.6	88.9	115.5	108.3	138.3	107.5	116.6	107.4	114.9	97.0	131.1
July	118.5	123.6	118.8	89.4	115.9	108.8	139.1	108.4	117.2	108.3	115.8	96.7	133.2
August	119.0	124.0	119.4	90.1	114.5	109.7	139.8	108.8	117.7	108.5	116.3	97.0	134.3
September	119.5	124.7	120.1	89.8	116.3	109.9	140.5	109.0	118.1	108.7	116.8	97.0	133.3
October	119.9	125.2	120.3	89.8	117.5	110.0	141.4	109.2	118.4	108.6	117.3	96.6	133.6
November	120.3	125.6	120.5	89.8	117.7	110.2	142.0	109.6	118.7	108.8	118.0	95.2	136.0
December	120.7	126.0	121.1	89.6	118.2	110.4	142.7	110.0	119.2	109.4	118.6	98.1	137.6
1989													
January	121.2	126.5	121.6	90.3	118.4	110.9	143.8	111.1	119.9	110.8	119.5	102.0	140.6
February	121.6	126.9	122.5	90.8	117.1	111.7	144.9	111.9	120.5	111.3	119.9	101.7	140.3
March	122.2	127.4	123.2	91.8	118.1	112.4	145.8	112.3	120.7	111.9	120.2	102.9	140.6
April	123.1	127.8	123.9	96.6	118.6	115.0	146.6	113.1	120.8	112.5	120.5	104.1	140.3
May	123.7	128.3	124.7	97.4	118.9	115.8	147.5	114.0	121.6	112.6	120.6	104.5	139.8
June	124.1	128.8	125.1	96.9	118.7	115.7	148.6	114.0	122.2	112.5	120.6	103.2	137.9
July	124.5	129.2	125.6	96.7	118.3	115.4	149.6	113.8	122.1	112.2	120.3	103.5	135.9
August	124.5	129.5	125.9	94.9	117.1	114.5	150.6	113.4	122.7	111.8	120.2	101.2	136.8
September	124.8	129.9	126.3	93.8	118.7	113.9	151.8	114.0	123.1	112.1	120.2	102.5	137.5
October	125.4	130.6	126.8	94.4	119.6	114.5	152.8	114.6	123.5	112.2	120.3	102.7	137.9
November	125.9	131.1	127.4	93.9	120.0	114.4	154.1	114.8	123.9	112.0	120.0	103.5	134.9
December	126.3	131.6	127.8	94.2	119.8	114.7	154.9	115.5	124.2	112.2	119.8	105.1	132.8
1990													
January	127.5	132.1	129.7	98.9	119.9	117.0	156.0	117.7	124.5	113.7	120.0	106.7	132.7
February	128.0	132.7	130.8	98.2	122.0	117.2	157.1	117.6	124.9	112.8	119.9	106.8	131.6
March	128.6	133.5	131.0	97.6	123.8	117.3	158.3	117.5	125.3	112.9	120.2	105.1	133.9
April	128.9	134.0	130.8	97.5	124.1	117.7	159.6	117.4	125.5	113.1	120.5	102.7	137.0
May	129.1	134.4	131.1	96.7	124.0	117.5	160.8	117.5	126.0	113.1	120.6	103.1	138.0
June	129.9	135.1	132.1	97.3	124.2	118.0	162.0	117.6	126.4	112.9	120.4	100.6	137.3
July	130.5	135.8	132.8	97.1	124.2	118.5	163.4	117.9	126.6	112.8	120.6	101.0	138.0
August	131.6	136.6	133.2	101.6	124.5	120.7	164.8	119.2	127.1	114.0	120.8	110.5	140.1
September	132.5	137.1	133.6	106.5	125.4	123.2	165.9	120.7	127.7	115.8	121.5	115.8	139.9
October	133.4	137.6	134.1	110.8	125.4	125.6	167.3	121.9	128.0	117.4	122.1	125.8	138.4
November	133.7	138.0	134.5	111.2	125.4	126.1	168.7	122.6	128.4	117.7	122.3	117.8	135.7
December	134.2	138.6	134.6	111.0	126.2	126.9	169.8	122.0	128.6	116.9	122.1	110.8	133.8
1991													
January	134.7	139.5	135.0	108.5	126.9	125.5	171.0	122.6	129.5	116.9	122.4	113.3	134.2
February	134.8	140.2	135.1	104.5	127.3	123.9	172.1	121.8	129.8	115.9	122.1	104.1	133.7
March	134.8	140.5	135.3	101.9	127.0	122.7	173.2	121.3	130.1	114.7	121.7	100.5	131.8
April	135.1	140.9	136.1	101.2	127.5	122.5	174.3	121.3	130.4	114.2	121.5	100.2	131.7
May	135.6	141.3	136.6	102.1	128.0	123.2	175.2	121.6	130.6	114.1	121.3	100.9	130.4
June	136.0	141.8	137.4	101.1	127.9	123.4	176.4	121.4	130.7	113.9	121.3	99.2	126.1
July	136.2	142.3	136.7	100.7	128.7	123.3	177.4	121.1	131.0	113.6	121.1	99.4	125.4
August	136.6	142.9	136.2	101.1	129.9	124.0	178.8	121.3	131.3	113.8	121.0	99.1	125.8
September	137.0	143.4	136.4	101.5	130.0	124.1	179.9	121.5	131.8	114.0	121.0	98.4	125.7
October	137.2	143.7	136.2	101.6	130.1	123.9	180.9	121.9	132.3	114.0	121.1	100.8	125.4
November	137.8	144.2	136.7	102.4	131.0	124.5	181.9	122.4	132.5	114.1	121.1	100.7	124.4
December	138.2	144.7	137.0	103.1	130.7	125.1	183.1	122.3	132.6	114.0	121.1	98.2	123.4
1992													
January	138.3	145.1	136.6	101.5	130.9	124.6	184.3	122.0	133.0	113.4	121.0	97.2	123.4
February	138.6	145.4	137.1	101.2	131.0	124.5	185.6	122.3	133.1	113.8	121.3	98.6	125.2
March	139.1	145.9	137.6	101.2	131.3	125.0	186.8	122.4	133.4	113.9	121.5	97.1	127.7
April	139.4	146.3	137.5	101.4	130.7	125.6	187.9	122.5	133.8	114.1	121.7	98.1	128.4
May	139.7	146.8	137.2	102.0	131.6	125.9	188.7	122.9	134.3	114.5	121.8	100.3	129.1
June	140.1	147.1	137.6	103.3	132.1	126.4	189.6	123.4	134.1	115.1	122.0	101.6	128.8
July	140.5	147.6	137.4	103.7	132.7	126.9	190.6	123.3	134.3	115.2	122.1	101.6	129.6
August	140.8	147.9	138.4	103.5	132.3	127.0	191.5	123.4	134.3	115.1	122.3	100.7	130.4
September	141.1	148.1	138.9	103.6	132.2	127.0	192.4	123.7	134.6	115.3	122.4	102.8	130.4
October	141.7	148.8	138.9	104.3	132.5	128.1	193.5	124.2	134.9	115.3	122.4	102.8	128.9
November	142.1	149.2	138.7	105.1	132.7	128.7	194.5	124.1	135.1	115.1	122.4	102.5	128.2
December	142.3	149.6	138.8	105.3	132.8	128.9	195.3	124.2	135.2	115.1	122.5	101.3	130.5
1993													
January	142.8	150.1	139.1	105.0	132.8	129.2	196.4	124.4	135.6	115.4	122.9	101.7	135.0
February	143.1	150.6	139.6	104.3	134.0	129.6	197.4	124.7	135.9	115.9	123.5	101.2	136.8
March	143.3	150.8	139.6	104.9	134.0	129.4	198.1	125.0	136.1	116.3	123.8	101.7	137.0
April	143.8	151.4	140.0	104.9	134.0	129.6	199.1	125.7	136.5	116.6	124.0	103.2	138.4
May	144.2	151.8	141.0	104.3	133.5	129.9	200.5	125.7	136.6	116.3	123.7	105.6	140.3
June	144.3	152.1	140.6	103.9	133.0	129.9	201.3	125.2	136.4	116.3	123.7	103.8	140.3
July	144.5	152.3	140.6	103.4	133.8	130.1	202.2	125.1	136.6	116.3	123.7	101.6	142.1
August	144.8	152.8	141.1	103.4	134.0	130.5	202.8	123.9	134.9	116.2	123.9	100.8	140.4
September	145.0	152.9	141.4	103.0	133.7	130.4	203.6	124.1	134.9	116.3	124.0	101.2	140.7
October	145.6	153.4	142.0	105.3	133.8	132.0	204.5	124.2	135.0	116.4	124.0	103.7	142.6
November	146.0	153.9	142.3	104.4	134.4	132.2	205.1	124.4	135.3	116.5	124.3	103.0	144.1
December	146.3	154.3	142.8	103.7	134.1	132.1	205.8	124.4	135.7	116.2	124.5	101.7	145.3

Table 20-2. Summary Consumer and Producer Price Indexes—Continued

(Seasonally adjusted.)

Year and month	Consumer Price Index, all urban consumers, 1982–1984 = 100							Producer Price Index, 1982 = 100					
								Finished goods		Intermediate materials, supplies, and components		Crude materials for further processing	
	All items	All items less food and energy	Food	Energy	Apparel	Transportation	Medical care	Total	Less food and energy	Total	Less food and energy	Total	Crude nonfood less energy
1994													
January	146.3	154.5	142.9	102.8	133.3	131.7	206.4	124.8	136.3	116.5	124.7	103.8	148.3
February	146.7	154.8	142.7	104.1	133.2	132.3	207.2	125.0	136.3	116.9	124.9	102.1	151.0
March	147.1	155.3	142.7	104.3	133.8	132.6	207.9	125.1	136.4	117.1	125.1	103.8	151.5
April	147.2	155.5	143.0	103.7	133.5	132.8	209.0	125.1	136.6	117.1	125.3	103.8	150.7
May	147.5	155.9	143.3	102.8	134.0	132.4	209.7	125.1	137.0	117.2	125.6	102.2	149.7
June	147.9	156.4	143.8	103.1	134.8	133.2	210.5	125.2	137.2	117.8	126.3	102.7	151.2
July	148.4	156.7	144.6	104.5	134.2	134.4	211.3	125.7	137.3	118.3	126.7	101.7	155.5
August	149.0	157.1	145.1	106.7	133.2	136.0	212.2	126.2	137.6	119.1	127.4	101.6	158.8
September	149.3	157.5	145.3	106.1	133.6	136.1	213.1	125.9	137.7	119.6	128.4	99.7	160.5
October	149.4	157.8	145.3	105.7	133.0	136.2	214.1	125.5	137.4	120.1	129.3	98.6	161.3
November	149.8	158.2	145.6	106.1	132.5	136.7	215.0	126.1	137.6	121.0	130.3	99.8	166.6
December	150.1	158.3	146.8	105.9	132.1	137.1	215.9	126.6	137.9	121.5	131.0	101.1	169.9
1995													
January	150.5	159.0	146.7	105.7	132.2	137.4	216.6	126.9	138.4	122.8	132.6	102.1	174.5
February	150.9	159.4	147.3	105.8	131.9	137.9	217.4	127.2	138.7	123.7	133.7	102.9	176.5
March	151.2	159.9	147.1	105.5	132.2	138.4	218.1	127.4	139.0	124.3	134.3	102.3	177.8
April	151.8	160.4	148.1	105.6	131.9	139.2	218.6	127.7	139.3	125.0	135.2	103.7	180.2
May	152.1	160.7	148.2	105.8	131.6	139.7	219.2	127.8	139.7	125.2	135.5	102.4	179.6
June	152.4	161.1	148.3	106.7	131.3	140.6	219.9	127.8	139.8	125.5	135.7	103.0	179.5
July	152.6	161.4	148.5	105.8	131.4	139.9	220.6	128.0	140.2	125.6	136.1	101.6	176.4
August	152.9	161.8	148.6	105.6	132.5	139.4	221.6	127.9	140.2	125.6	136.1	99.7	173.4
September	153.1	162.2	149.1	104.1	132.3	139.1	222.4	128.1	140.2	125.5	136.2	102.0	170.9
October	153.5	162.7	149.5	104.4	132.4	139.5	223.0	128.4	141.0	125.4	135.8	101.9	166.6
November	153.7	163.0	149.6	103.4	132.0	139.1	223.7	128.7	141.3	125.2	135.5	104.1	163.6
December	153.9	163.1	149.9	104.4	132.2	139.1	224.3	129.3	141.5	125.4	135.2	106.5	162.3
1996													
January	154.7	163.7	150.4	106.9	132.7	140.4	225.2	129.7	141.5	125.5	134.8	109.8	162.6
February	155.0	164.0	150.8	107.1	132.2	140.9	225.7	129.7	141.6	125.0	134.4	111.6	162.1
March	155.5	164.4	151.4	108.3	132.6	141.5	226.2	130.5	141.6	125.3	134.1	109.8	158.2
April	156.1	164.6	152.0	111.2	131.8	142.9	226.8	130.9	141.6	125.7	133.8	114.2	156.7
May	156.4	165.0	151.9	112.0	131.8	143.5	227.4	130.9	142.0	126.2	134.0	114.6	157.6
June	156.7	165.4	152.9	110.3	131.6	143.4	228.0	131.3	142.2	125.8	133.9	112.2	154.6
July	157.0	165.7	153.4	110.1	131.3	143.0	228.6	131.2	142.2	125.5	133.6	114.6	152.2
August	157.2	166.0	153.9	109.7	130.6	143.0	229.1	131.6	142.3	125.6	133.6	115.3	152.5
September	157.7	166.5	154.6	109.8	131.3	143.6	229.7	131.7	142.2	126.1	134.0	112.7	153.5
October	158.2	166.8	155.5	110.5	131.3	143.9	230.3	132.4	142.3	126.0	133.7	111.9	153.3
November	158.7	167.2	156.1	111.8	131.6	144.6	231.0	132.5	142.1	125.8	133.7	115.7	153.0
December	159.1	167.4	156.3	113.9	131.9	145.7	231.2	132.9	142.3	126.4	133.9	122.5	153.6
1997													
January	159.4	167.8	155.9	115.2	132.3	145.6	231.8	133.0	142.5	126.6	134.1	127.5	156.2
February	159.7	168.1	156.5	115.0	133.0	145.2	232.2	132.7	142.4	126.5	134.1	116.6	157.6
March	159.8	168.4	156.6	113.0	132.4	145.0	233.0	132.6	142.6	126.1	134.2	107.5	158.7
April	159.9	168.9	156.5	111.0	133.0	144.3	233.5	131.8	142.6	125.6	134.1	107.8	155.8
May	159.9	169.2	156.6	108.8	133.3	143.3	234.1	131.5	142.4	125.4	134.2	109.1	157.0
June	160.2	169.4	156.9	110.0	133.1	143.6	234.4	131.3	142.4	125.4	134.2	106.2	156.9
July	160.4	169.7	157.2	109.1	133.3	143.3	234.7	130.9	142.2	125.1	134.2	106.2	155.7
August	160.8	169.8	157.7	110.9	132.7	144.1	235.1	131.4	142.3	125.3	134.3	106.8	156.8
September	161.2	170.2	158.0	112.4	132.9	144.8	235.5	131.6	142.6	125.5	134.3	108.4	155.8
October	161.5	170.6	158.3	111.8	132.7	144.7	236.1	131.9	142.6	125.4	134.3	113.4	156.7
November	161.7	170.8	158.6	111.4	132.7	143.9	236.9	131.6	142.4	125.6	134.4	115.8	156.5
December	161.8	171.2	158.7	109.8	133.0	143.7	237.8	131.4	142.3	125.4	134.4	108.8	154.2
1998													
January	162.0	171.6	159.5	107.5	133.1	143.0	238.1	130.7	142.4	124.6	134.3	102.8	150.4
February	162.0	171.9	159.4	105.1	133.0	142.4	238.8	130.6	142.6	124.2	134.2	100.8	150.1
March	162.0	172.2	159.7	103.3	132.7	141.5	239.4	130.5	143.3	123.7	134.1	99.5	148.7
April	162.2	172.5	159.7	102.4	132.3	140.9	240.3	130.7	143.4	123.6	134.0	100.6	147.3
May	162.6	172.9	160.3	103.2	132.7	141.2	241.2	130.5	143.5	123.5	133.9	99.6	146.2
June	162.8	173.2	160.2	103.6	133.3	141.4	241.8	130.4	143.5	123.1	133.6	97.1	145.9
July	163.2	173.5	160.6	103.3	133.5	141.7	242.5	130.7	143.8	123.0	133.5	97.4	143.4
August	163.4	174.0	161.0	102.1	135.1	141.6	243.3	130.4	143.8	122.7	133.4	93.6	139.4
September	163.5	174.2	161.1	101.3	133.1	141.2	244.1	130.4	144.0	122.3	133.1	91.4	137.6
October	163.9	174.4	162.0	101.5	132.7	141.4	244.8	130.9	144.2	122.2	132.7	93.9	134.0
November	164.1	174.8	162.2	101.1	132.7	141.3	245.3	130.8	144.3	122.0	132.5	93.6	131.6
December	164.4	175.4	162.4	100.1	132.0	140.9	245.9	131.3	145.8	121.3	132.2	90.2	129.4
1999													
January	164.7	175.6	163.0	99.7	131.5	140.8	246.5	131.7	145.6	121.2	132.0	91.0	128.7
February	164.7	175.6	163.3	99.2	130.8	140.0	247.3	131.2	145.7	120.8	131.8	89.0	130.5
March	164.8	175.7	163.3	100.4	130.4	140.7	247.9	131.5	145.7	121.1	131.9	89.6	129.6
April	165.9	176.3	163.5	105.5	131.7	143.6	248.7	132.1	145.7	121.9	132.0	91.3	128.7
May	166.0	176.5	163.8	104.9	131.7	143.4	249.3	132.3	145.7	122.2	132.4	96.8	130.5
June	166.0	176.6	163.7	104.5	131.7	143.0	250.0	132.4	145.8	122.6	132.8	97.0	131.6
July	166.7	177.1	163.9	106.7	131.5	144.6	250.9	132.7	145.8	123.4	133.3	97.3	133.6
August	167.1	177.3	164.2	109.5	130.9	145.9	251.7	133.5	145.7	124.1	133.6	102.4	136.3
September	167.8	177.8	164.6	111.8	131.2	147.0	252.5	134.5	146.5	124.6	133.9	106.4	138.8
October	168.1	178.1	165.0	112.0	131.4	147.6	253.1	134.4	146.9	124.9	134.3	103.8	142.5
November	168.4	178.4	165.3	111.5	131.0	147.5	253.9	134.9	146.9	125.4	134.5	109.7	144.4
December	168.8	178.7	165.5	113.8	131.3	148.8	254.9	135.2	147.0	125.8	134.7	104.4	147.6

Table 20-2. Summary Consumer and Producer Price Indexes—Continued

(Seasonally adjusted.)

Year and month	Consumer Price Index, all urban consumers, 1982–1984 = 100							Producer Price Index, 1982 = 100					
								Finished goods		Intermediate materials, supplies, and components		Crude materials for further processing	
	All items	All items less food and energy	Food	Energy	Apparel	Transportation	Medical care	Total	Less food and energy	Total	Less food and energy	Total	Crude nonfood less energy
2000													
January	169.3	179.3	165.6	115.0	130.7	149.1	255.6	135.2	146.8	126.4	135.1	106.8	150.5
February	170.0	179.4	166.2	118.8	130.4	150.0	256.5	136.6	147.3	127.5	135.5	111.0	151.3
March	171.0	180.0	166.5	124.3	130.3	153.6	257.7	137.3	147.4	128.4	136.0	113.2	150.5
April	170.9	180.3	166.7	120.9	129.8	152.1	258.4	136.9	147.4	128.3	136.5	111.3	148.8
May	171.2	180.7	167.3	120.0	129.7	152.0	259.2	137.0	147.8	128.2	136.6	115.1	147.8
June	172.2	181.1	167.4	126.8	129.3	155.0	260.3	138.1	147.8	129.3	136.9	124.8	145.1
July	172.7	181.5	168.3	127.3	128.9	154.6	261.2	138.2	148.1	129.6	137.1	122.1	142.8
August	172.7	181.9	168.7	123.8	128.9	153.2	262.4	137.9	148.2	129.3	136.9	117.6	141.2
September	173.6	182.3	168.9	129.2	129.5	155.2	263.3	139.0	148.6	130.3	137.0	125.6	142.9
October	173.9	182.6	169.0	129.6	129.2	154.7	264.1	139.5	148.5	130.7	137.1	130.2	142.1
November	174.2	183.1	169.2	129.2	129.2	155.0	264.7	140.2	148.7	130.7	136.9	129.1	139.6
December	174.6	183.3	170.0	130.1	129.1	155.1	265.6	140.5	148.9	131.3	136.9	141.1	139.5
2001													
January	175.6	183.9	170.3	135.0	129.4	155.4	267.2	141.7	149.5	132.1	137.1	165.6	138.7
February	176.0	184.4	171.2	134.1	129.6	155.2	268.3	141.9	149.2	131.8	137.3	141.7	136.5
March	176.1	184.7	171.7	131.7	129.5	154.2	269.4	141.2	149.5	131.0	137.4	132.4	135.0
April	176.4	185.1	172.1	132.3	128.2	154.8	270.4	142.0	149.8	130.9	137.3	133.0	131.3
May	177.3	185.3	172.4	138.4	127.4	157.6	271.3	142.3	150.1	131.1	137.3	130.5	130.9
June	177.7	186.0	173.1	136.9	127.4	157.3	272.4	141.8	150.2	130.9	137.1	119.9	129.7
July	177.4	186.4	173.6	129.6	127.3	154.0	272.8	140.1	150.5	129.4	136.4	113.3	130.6
August	177.4	186.7	174.0	127.3	126.4	153.4	274.3	140.7	150.5	129.1	135.9	112.3	128.4
September	178.1	187.1	174.2	130.9	125.8	156.0	275.2	141.3	150.7	129.3	135.9	107.2	128.8
October	177.6	187.4	174.8	122.9	125.8	152.9	276.3	139.0	149.8	127.6	135.4	97.4	126.5
November	177.5	188.1	174.9	116.9	125.4	150.2	277.4	138.5	150.2	127.0	135.1	102.7	126.2
December	177.4	188.4	174.7	113.9	124.9	149.2	278.2	138.0	150.4	126.1	134.8	95.5	125.7
2002													
January	177.7	188.7	175.3	114.3	124.5	149.3	279.8	137.7	150.1	125.6	134.7	99.8	126.2
February	178.0	189.1	175.7	113.4	124.7	148.6	280.4	138.0	150.2	125.4	134.6	98.4	127.7
March	178.6	189.2	176.1	118.2	125.4	150.8	281.4	138.9	150.1	126.3	135.0	103.8	128.1
April	179.3	189.7	176.3	121.8	125.2	152.7	282.7	139.0	150.4	127.3	135.3	108.2	130.9
May	179.4	190.0	175.8	121.5	124.7	152.6	283.9	138.4	150.3	127.0	135.3	109.2	134.2
June	179.6	190.2	175.9	121.3	123.9	152.5	284.6	138.8	150.6	127.3	135.6	105.2	138.3
July	180.0	190.5	176.1	122.5	123.3	153.3	286.3	138.6	150.1	127.7	136.0	106.4	140.6
August	180.5	191.1	176.1	123.3	124.2	154.0	287.3	138.7	149.9	128.1	136.2	108.2	139.9
September	180.8	191.4	176.5	124.1	123.4	154.4	288.1	139.0	150.3	128.9	136.5	110.7	140.0
October	181.2	191.5	176.4	126.6	123.0	155.4	289.8	139.9	150.5	128.8	136.7	112.6	140.1
November	181.5	191.9	177.0	126.2	123.0	155.2	291.1	139.9	150.4	129.9	136.8	116.6	141.1
December	181.7	192.1	177.2	126.6	122.7	155.1	292.1	139.7	149.5	129.9	136.7	118.9	141.3
2003													
January	182.3	192.4	177.0	130.4	122.1	156.4	292.7	141.1	149.9	131.3	137.2	128.1	143.2
February	183.3	192.4	178.2	138.5	121.7	159.5	293.0	142.6	149.9	133.7	138.1	134.3	147.7
March	184.1	192.4	178.5	145.9	120.8	161.6	293.4	144.2	150.8	136.3	138.6	152.2	147.0
April	183.3	192.5	178.5	137.8	120.4	158.2	294.0	142.2	150.0	133.1	138.3	127.9	145.5
May	183.2	192.9	178.8	132.6	120.2	156.0	295.2	141.9	150.1	132.5	138.4	130.0	146.0
June	183.4	193.0	179.7	132.5	120.6	155.8	296.1	142.7	150.2	133.1	138.4	136.0	146.5
July	183.8	193.4	179.8	133.6	120.9	156.4	297.3	142.8	150.3	133.3	138.2	132.3	148.9
August	184.5	193.6	180.5	137.8	120.8	158.4	298.4	143.6	150.6	133.9	138.4	130.8	151.5
September	185.0	193.7	180.8	142.4	120.8	159.8	299.7	143.9	150.6	133.8	138.7	134.6	156.1
October	184.9	194.0	181.6	137.6	121.1	157.6	300.5	144.6	151.1	134.1	139.1	138.0	160.4
November	184.7	194.0	182.6	133.9	120.7	155.6	301.4	144.7	151.1	134.3	139.3	137.5	165.8
December	185.1	194.2	183.5	135.3	120.2	155.7	302.9	145.2	151.1	135.1	139.6	142.0	171.6
2004													
January	185.9	194.6	183.4	140.4	120.1	158.0	303.8	145.7	151.4	136.4	140.4	148.6	179.3
February	186.5	194.8	183.9	144.0	119.9	159.5	305.2	145.6	151.4	137.5	141.7	150.2	188.9
March	187.3	195.4	184.3	146.8	120.6	161.3	306.6	146.3	151.8	138.4	142.8	152.8	193.5
April	187.5	195.9	184.7	145.8	120.7	160.8	307.7	147.4	152.0	140.2	144.5	155.6	186.0
May	188.6	196.2	186.0	152.0	121.0	163.6	308.6	148.6	152.3	142.0	145.6	160.7	177.5
June	189.2	196.6	186.5	154.6	121.2	164.3	309.8	148.5	152.8	142.5	146.1	162.6	177.2
July	189.2	196.8	186.8	152.7	120.8	163.4	310.8	148.4	152.5	143.2	146.8	162.2	196.2
August	189.4	197.0	187.0	152.3	120.2	163.0	311.8	148.5	152.9	144.6	148.3	161.6	200.0
September	189.7	197.6	186.9	151.8	120.0	163.2	312.9	148.6	153.2	144.8	149.5	154.3	197.8
October	190.8	197.9	187.9	158.3	120.3	166.8	314.0	150.8	153.7	146.3	150.1	160.6	204.7
November	191.2	198.3	188.3	159.4	120.4	167.0	314.6	152.2	154.1	147.6	150.7	172.1	208.0
December	191.2	198.5	188.3	157.6	120.0	166.0	315.8	151.5	154.5	147.5	151.2	166.8	206.4
2005													
January	191.4	199.0	188.6	155.2	120.3	165.2	317.0	151.7	155.4	148.3	152.3	163.9	203.3
February	192.1	199.4	188.6	159.2	120.0	167.0	318.4	152.4	155.5	149.2	153.1	162.7	199.1
March	193.2	200.0	189.0	165.1	120.6	169.8	319.8	153.6	155.7	150.6	153.7	170.3	198.2
April	194.1	200.2	190.4	170.7	120.1	172.1	320.7	154.4	156.1	151.6	153.8	174.9	202.5
May	194.0	200.5	190.6	167.2	120.0	170.4	321.9	154.1	156.4	151.1	153.4	169.5	196.7
June	193.9	200.6	190.6	165.7	119.3	170.1	322.6	154.2	156.3	151.4	153.3	166.6	189.7
July	195.1	201.0	190.9	174.4	118.6	173.7	323.8	155.4	156.8	152.9	153.5	175.1	190.9
August	196.2	201.2	191.1	183.3	119.4	177.7	324.2	156.2	156.8	153.7	153.4	181.3	199.6
September	198.6	201.5	191.5	205.0	119.3	186.6	325.2	158.4	157.1	157.3	154.9	200.3	210.8
October	199.1	202.0	192.0	205.0	118.9	184.4	327.0	159.6	156.6	162.0	157.1	211.7	207.6
November	197.8	202.5	192.5	188.3	119.0	175.4	328.7	158.8	156.8	159.9	157.8	208.8	212.6
December	197.7	202.8	192.7	184.3	118.7	174.1	329.4	159.9	156.8	160.3	158.4	201.4	216.6

Table 20-3. Summary Labor Force, Employment, and Unemployment

(Thousands of persons, percent, seasonally adjusted, except as noted.)

Year and month	Civilian noninstitutional population [1]	Civilian labor force		Employment, thousands of persons					Employment-population ratio, percent	Unemployment		
		Thousands of persons	Participation rate (percent)	By age and sex			By industry			Thousands of persons		Rate, percent
				Men, 20 years and over	Women, 20 years and over	Both sexes, 16 to 19 years	Agricultural	Nonagricultural		Total	Unemployed 15 weeks and over	
1947	101 827	59 350	58.3	57 038			7 890	49 148	56.0	2 311	. . .	3.9
1948	103 068	60 621	58.8	39 382	14 936	4 026	7 629	50 714	56.6	2 276	309	3.8
1949	103 994	61 286	58.9	38 803	15 137	3 712	7 658	49 993	55.4	3 637	684	5.9
1950	104 995	62 208	59.2	39 394	15 824	3 703	7 160	51 758	56.1	3 288	782	5.3
1951	104 621	62 017	59.2	39 626	16 570	3 767	6 726	53 235	57.3	2 055	303	3.3
1952	105 231	62 138	59.0	39 578	16 958	3 719	6 500	53 749	57.3	1 883	232	3.0
1953	107 056	63 015	58.9	40 296	17 164	3 720	6 260	54 919	57.1	1 834	210	2.9
1954	108 321	63 643	58.8	39 634	17 000	3 475	6 205	53 904	55.5	3 532	812	5.5
1955	109 683	65 023	59.3	40 526	18 002	3 642	6 450	55 722	56.7	2 852	702	4.4
1956	110 954	66 552	60.0	41 216	18 767	3 818	6 283	57 514	57.5	2 750	533	4.1
1957	112 265	66 929	59.6	41 239	19 052	3 778	5 947	58 123	57.1	2 859	560	4.3
1958	113 727	67 639	59.5	40 411	19 043	3 582	5 586	57 450	55.4	4 602	1 452	6.8
1959	115 329	68 369	59.3	41 267	19 524	3 838	5 565	59 065	56.0	3 740	1 040	5.5
1948												
January	102 603	60 095	58.6	39 386	14 556	4 119	8 077	49 984	56.6	2 034	311	3.4
February	102 698	60 524	58.9	39 480	14 621	4 095	7 696	50 500	56.7	2 328	283	3.8
March	102 771	60 070	58.5	39 098	14 481	4 092	7 333	50 338	56.1	2 399	292	4.0
April	102 831	60 677	59.0	39 157	15 001	4 133	7 557	50 734	56.7	2 386	324	3.9
May	102 923	59 972	58.3	39 139	14 712	4 003	7 141	50 713	56.2	2 118	329	3.5
June	102 992	60 957	59.2	39 392	15 213	4 138	7 591	51 152	57.0	2 214	322	3.6
July	103 216	61 181	59.3	39 607	15 348	4 013	7 602	51 366	57.1	2 213	295	3.6
August	103 240	60 806	58.9	39 510	14 994	3 952	7 562	50 894	56.6	2 350	332	3.9
September	103 291	60 815	58.9	39 324	15 207	3 982	7 865	50 648	56.6	2 302	298	3.8
October	103 361	60 646	58.7	39 522	14 956	3 909	7 626	50 761	56.5	2 259	324	3.7
November	103 424	60 702	58.7	39 459	15 054	3 904	7 624	50 793	56.5	2 285	282	3.8
December	103 468	61 169	59.1	39 539	15 137	4 064	7 984	50 756	56.8	2 429	305	4.0
1949												
January	103 529	60 771	58.7	39 233	14 991	3 951	7 790	50 385	56.2	2 596	315	4.3
February	103 559	61 057	59.0	39 117	15 117	3 974	8 022	50 186	56.2	2 849	374	4.7
March	103 665	61 073	58.9	39 015	15 069	3 959	8 008	50 035	56.0	3 030	414	5.0
April	103 739	61 007	58.8	38 993	14 978	3 776	7 911	49 836	55.7	3 260	483	5.3
May	103 845	61 259	59.0	38 701	15 066	3 785	8 067	49 485	55.4	3 707	602	6.1
June	103 930	60 948	58.6	38 632	15 003	3 537	7 802	49 370	55.0	3 776	705	6.2
July	104 042	61 301	58.9	38 405	15 244	3 541	8 021	49 169	55.0	4 111	848	6.7
August	104 121	61 590	59.2	38 610	15 181	3 606	7 604	49 793	55.1	4 193	917	6.8
September	104 219	61 633	59.1	38 744	15 129	3 711	7 297	50 287	55.3	4 049	973	6.6
October	104 338	62 185	59.6	38 394	15 260	3 615	6 814	50 455	54.9	4 916	1 000	7.9
November	104 421	62 005	59.4	38 860	15 422	3 727	7 497	50 512	55.6	3 996	1 056	6.4
December	104 524	61 908	59.2	38 908	15 300	3 637	7 379	50 466	55.3	4 063	961	6.6
1950												
January	104 619	61 661	58.9	38 780	15 255	3 600	7 065	50 570	55.1	4 026	947	6.5
February	104 737	61 687	58.9	38 818	15 339	3 594	7 057	50 694	55.1	3 936	947	6.4
March	104 844	61 604	58.8	38 851	15 366	3 511	7 116	50 612	55.1	3 876	912	6.3
April	104 943	62 158	59.2	39 100	15 831	3 652	7 264	51 319	55.8	3 575	920	5.8
May	105 014	62 083	59.1	39 416	15 628	3 605	7 277	51 372	55.8	3 434	890	5.5
June	105 104	62 419	59.4	39 476	15 953	3 623	7 285	51 767	56.2	3 367	868	5.4
July	105 194	62 121	59.1	39 517	15 793	3 691	7 126	51 875	56.1	3 120	769	5.0
August	105 282	62 596	59.5	39 879	16 124	3 794	7 248	52 549	56.8	2 799	633	4.5
September	105 269	62 349	59.2	39 865	15 902	3 808	6 992	52 583	56.6	2 774	648	4.4
October	105 096	62 428	59.4	39 737	16 175	3 891	7 371	52 432	56.9	2 625	545	4.2
November	104 979	62 286	59.3	39 668	16 195	3 834	7 163	52 534	56.9	2 589	507	4.2
December	104 872	62 068	59.2	39 536	16 149	3 744	6 760	52 669	56.7	2 639	482	4.3
1951												
January	104 844	61 941	59.1	39 595	16 279	3 762	6 828	52 808	56.9	2 305	438	3.7
February	104 604	61 778	59.1	39 695	16 257	3 709	6 738	52 923	57.0	2 117	386	3.4
March	104 629	62 526	59.8	40 013	16 557	3 831	6 858	53 543	57.7	2 125	355	3.4
April	104 541	61 808	59.1	39 804	16 426	3 659	6 722	53 167	57.3	1 919	294	3.1
May	104 491	62 044	59.4	39 752	16 581	3 855	6 752	53 436	57.6	1 856	269	3.0
June	104 488	61 615	59.0	39 538	16 368	3 714	6 529	53 091	57.1	1 995	258	3.2
July	104 504	62 106	59.4	39 483	16 898	3 775	6 601	53 555	57.6	1 950	260	3.1
August	104 536	61 927	59.2	39 508	16 665	3 821	6 790	53 204	57.4	1 933	249	3.1
September	104 588	61 780	59.1	39 416	16 504	3 793	6 558	53 155	57.1	2 067	223	3.3
October	104 690	62 204	59.4	39 555	16 674	3 781	6 636	53 374	57.3	2 194	269	3.5
November	104 740	62 014	59.2	39 504	16 669	3 663	6 699	53 137	57.1	2 178	316	3.5
December	104 810	62 457	59.6	39 691	16 946	3 860	7 065	53 432	57.7	1 960	269	3.1
1952												
January	104 862	62 432	59.5	39 714	17 001	3 745	7 148	53 312	57.7	1 972	282	3.2
February	104 868	62 419	59.5	39 772	16 935	3 755	7 020	53 442	57.7	1 957	248	3.1
March	104 860	61 721	58.9	39 580	16 627	3 701	6 468	53 440	57.1	1 813	234	2.9
April	104 906	61 720	58.8	39 542	16 659	3 708	6 525	53 384	57.1	1 811	242	2.9
May	104 996	62 058	59.1	39 588	16 844	3 763	6 334	53 861	57.3	1 863	219	3.0
June	105 118	62 103	59.1	39 558	16 837	3 824	6 529	53 690	57.3	1 884	210	3.0
July	105 246	61 962	58.9	39 496	16 778	3 697	6 334	53 637	57.0	1 991	194	3.2
August	105 346	61 877	58.7	39 289	16 867	3 634	6 174	53 616	56.8	2 087	211	3.4
September	105 436	62 457	59.2	39 386	17 477	3 658	6 537	53 984	57.4	1 936	249	3.1
October	105 591	61 971	58.7	39 451	17 032	3 649	6 363	53 769	56.9	1 839	230	3.0
November	105 706	62 491	59.1	39 549	17 450	3 749	6 509	54 239	57.5	1 743	216	2.8
December	105 812	62 621	59.2	40 011	17 181	3 762	6 361	54 593	57.6	1 667	238	2.7

[1]Not seasonally adjusted.
. . . = Not available.

Table 20-3. Summary Labor Force, Employment, and Unemployment—Continued

(Thousands of persons, percent, seasonally adjusted, except as noted.)

| Year and month | Civilian noninstitutional population [1] | Civilian labor force | | Employment, thousands of persons | | | | | Employment-population ratio, percent | Unemployment | | Rate (percent) |
| | | Thousands of persons | Participation rate (percent) | By age and sex | | | By industry | | | Thousands of persons | | |
				Men, 20 years and over	Women, 20 years and over	Both sexes, 16 to 19 years	Agricultural	Nonagricultural		Total	Unemployed 15 weeks and over	
1953												
January	106 594	63 439	59.5	40 256	17 482	3 862	6 642	54 958	57.8	1 839	268	2.9
February	106 678	63 520	59.5	40 546	17 321	4 017	6 463	55 421	58.0	1 636	208	2.6
March	106 744	63 657	59.6	40 648	17 397	3 965	6 420	55 590	58.1	1 647	213	2.6
April	106 826	63 167	59.1	40 346	17 242	3 856	6 362	55 082	57.5	1 723	180	2.7
May	106 910	62 615	58.6	40 323	16 983	3 713	5 937	55 082	57.1	1 596	176	2.5
June	106 978	63 063	58.9	40 358	17 301	3 797	6 361	55 095	57.4	1 607	213	2.5
July	107 034	63 057	58.9	40 378	17 341	3 678	6 267	55 130	57.4	1 660	168	2.6
August	107 132	62 816	58.6	40 352	17 108	3 691	6 319	54 832	57.1	1 665	177	2.7
September	107 253	62 727	58.5	40 192	17 063	3 651	6 198	54 708	56.8	1 821	178	2.9
October	107 383	62 867	58.5	40 155	17 236	3 502	6 096	54 797	56.7	1 974	190	3.1
November	107 504	62 949	58.6	40 163	16 974	3 601	6 345	54 393	56.5	2 211	259	3.5
December	107 623	62 795	58.3	39 885	16 599	3 493	5 929	54 048	55.7	2 818	309	4.5
1954												
January	107 763	63 101	58.6	39 834	16 574	3 616	6 073	53 951	55.7	3 077	372	4.9
February	107 880	63 994	59.3	39 899	17 162	3 602	6 590	54 073	56.2	3 331	532	5.2
March	107 987	63 793	59.1	39 497	17 022	3 667	6 395	53 791	55.7	3 607	765	5.7
April	108 080	63 934	59.2	39 613	17 015	3 557	6 142	54 043	55.7	3 749	774	5.9
May	108 184	63 675	58.9	39 467	16 975	3 466	6 210	53 698	55.4	3 767	879	5.9
June	108 267	63 343	58.5	39 476	16 894	3 422	6 162	53 630	55.2	3 551	880	5.6
July	108 344	63 302	58.4	39 467	16 777	3 399	6 222	53 421	55.0	3 659	932	5.8
August	108 440	63 707	58.7	39 582	16 868	3 403	6 087	53 766	55.2	3 854	1 002	6.0
September	108 546	64 209	59.2	39 702	17 133	3 447	6 453	53 829	55.5	3 927	1 017	6.1
October	108 668	63 936	58.8	39 618	17 209	3 443	6 242	54 028	55.5	3 666	1 009	5.7
November	108 798	63 759	58.6	39 745	17 213	3 399	5 934	54 423	55.5	3 402	975	5.3
December	108 892	63 312	58.1	39 763	17 121	3 232	5 848	54 268	55.2	3 196	827	5.0
1955												
January	109 059	63 910	58.6	39 937	17 375	3 441	6 113	54 640	55.7	3 157	882	4.9
February	109 078	63 696	58.4	39 964	17 413	3 350	5 854	54 873	55.7	2 969	826	4.7
March	109 254	63 882	58.5	40 111	17 415	3 438	6 242	54 722	55.8	2 918	816	4.6
April	109 377	64 564	59.0	40 120	17 867	3 528	6 363	55 152	56.2	3 049	811	4.7
May	109 544	64 381	58.8	40 410	17 665	3 559	6 327	55 307	56.3	2 747	734	4.3
June	109 680	64 482	58.8	40 444	17 837	3 500	6 243	55 538	56.3	2 701	668	4.2
July	109 792	65 145	59.3	40 751	18 123	3 639	6 438	56 075	56.9	2 632	640	4.0
August	109 882	65 581	59.7	40 747	18 377	3 673	6 575	56 222	57.1	2 784	535	4.2
September	109 977	65 628	59.7	40 920	18 285	3 745	6 819	56 131	57.2	2 678	558	4.1
October	110 085	65 821	59.8	40 858	18 327	3 806	6 728	56 263	57.2	2 830	572	4.3
November	110 177	66 037	59.9	40 936	18 422	3 899	6 655	56 602	57.4	2 780	564	4.2
December	110 296	66 445	60.2	41 063	18 630	3 991	6 653	57 031	57.7	2 761	581	4.2
1956												
January	110 390	66 419	60.2	41 203	18 691	3 859	6 590	57 163	57.8	2 666	561	4.0
February	110 478	66 124	59.9	41 175	18 582	3 761	6 457	57 061	57.5	2 606	545	3.9
March	110 582	66 175	59.8	41 199	18 496	3 716	6 221	57 190	57.3	2 764	521	4.2
April	110 650	66 264	59.9	41 289	18 629	3 696	6 460	57 154	57.5	2 650	476	4.0
May	110 810	66 722	60.2	41 166	18 844	3 851	6 375	57 486	57.6	2 861	506	4.3
June	110 903	66 702	60.1	41 196	18 748	3 876	6 335	57 485	57.5	2 882	516	4.3
July	111 019	66 752	60.1	41 216	18 718	3 866	6 320	57 480	57.5	2 952	523	4.4
August	111 099	66 673	60.0	41 265	18 864	3 843	6 280	57 692	57.6	2 701	543	4.1
September	111 222	66 714	60.0	41 221	19 019	3 839	6 375	57 704	57.6	2 635	577	3.9
October	111 335	66 546	59.8	41 261	18 928	3 786	6 137	57 838	57.5	2 571	530	3.9
November	111 432	66 657	59.8	41 208	18 846	3 742	5 997	57 799	57.3	2 861	575	4.3
December	111 526	66 700	59.8	41 192	18 859	3 859	5 806	58 104	57.3	2 790	567	4.2
1957												
January	111 626	66 428	59.5	41 168	18 740	3 724	5 790	57 842	57.0	2 796	509	4.2
February	111 711	66 879	59.9	41 341	19 115	3 801	6 125	58 132	57.5	2 622	530	3.9
March	111 824	66 913	59.8	41 500	19 066	3 838	5 963	58 441	57.6	2 509	514	3.7
April	111 933	66 647	59.5	41 345	18 937	3 765	5 836	58 211	57.2	2 600	516	3.9
May	112 031	66 695	59.5	41 334	18 897	3 754	5 999	57 986	57.1	2 710	538	4.1
June	112 172	67 052	59.8	41 411	18 973	3 812	6 002	58 194	57.2	2 856	526	4.3
July	112 317	67 336	60.0	41 472	19 262	3 806	6 401	58 139	57.5	2 796	535	4.2
August	112 421	66 706	59.3	41 243	19 020	3 696	5 898	58 061	56.9	2 747	542	4.1
September	112 554	67 064	59.6	41 213	19 116	3 792	5 728	58 393	57.0	2 943	559	4.4
October	112 710	67 066	59.5	41 069	19 160	3 817	5 875	58 171	56.8	3 020	650	4.5
November	112 874	67 123	59.5	40 853	19 082	3 734	5 686	57 983	56.4	3 454	674	5.1
December	113 013	67 398	59.6	40 884	19 285	3 753	6 037	57 885	56.6	3 476	731	5.2
1958												
January	113 138	67 095	59.3	40 617	19 035	3 568	5 831	57 389	55.9	3 875	879	5.8
February	113 234	67 201	59.3	40 336	18 951	3 611	5 654	57 244	55.5	4 303	1 005	6.4
March	113 337	67 223	59.3	40 180	18 968	3 583	5 561	57 170	55.3	4 492	1 128	6.7
April	113 415	67 647	59.6	40 129	18 969	3 533	5 602	57 029	55.2	5 016	1 387	7.4
May	113 534	67 895	59.8	40 253	18 978	3 643	5 647	57 227	55.4	5 021	1 493	7.4
June	113 647	67 674	59.5	40 208	19 008	3 514	5 510	57 220	55.2	4 944	1 677	7.3
July	113 727	67 824	59.6	40 270	19 039	3 436	5 525	57 220	55.2	5 079	1 796	7.5
August	113 835	68 037	59.8	40 343	19 103	3 566	5 673	57 339	55.4	5 025	1 888	7.4
September	113 977	68 002	59.7	40 564	19 033	3 584	5 453	57 728	55.4	4 821	1 795	7.1
October	114 138	68 045	59.6	40 699	19 091	3 685	5 563	57 912	55.6	4 570	1 708	6.7
November	114 283	67 658	59.2	40 684	19 157	3 629	5 571	57 899	55.5	4 188	1 570	6.2
December	114 429	67 740	59.2	40 666	19 170	3 713	5 521	58 028	55.5	4 191	1 490	6.2

[1] Not seasonally adjusted.

Table 20-3. Summary Labor Force, Employment, and Unemployment—Continued

(Thousands of persons, percent, seasonally adjusted, except as noted.)

| Year and month | Civilian noninstitutional population [1] | Civilian labor force | | Employment, thousands of persons | | | | | Employ-ment-population ratio, percent | Unemployment | | |
| | | Thousands of persons | Participa-tion rate (percent) | By age and sex | | | By industry | | | Thousands of persons | | Rate (percent) |
				Men, 20 years and over	Women, 20 years and over	Both sexes, 16 to 19 years	Agricultural	Nonagri-cultural		Total	Unem-ployed 15 weeks and over	
1959												
January	114 582	67 936	59.3	40 769	19 292	3 807	5 481	58 387	55.7	4 068	1 396	6.0
February	114 712	67 649	59.0	40 699	19 167	3 818	5 429	58 255	55.5	3 965	1 277	5.9
March	114 849	68 068	59.3	41 079	19 379	3 809	5 677	58 590	56.0	3 801	1 210	5.6
April	114 986	68 339	59.4	41 419	19 498	3 851	5 893	58 875	56.3	3 571	1 039	5.2
May	115 144	68 178	59.2	41 355	19 565	3 779	5 792	58 907	56.2	3 479	965	5.1
June	115 287	68 278	59.2	41 387	19 658	3 804	5 712	59 137	56.3	3 429	963	5.0
July	115 429	68 539	59.4	41 596	19 595	3 820	5 564	59 447	56.3	3 528	889	5.1
August	115 555	68 432	59.2	41 485	19 568	3 791	5 442	59 402	56.1	3 588	889	5.2
September	115 668	68 545	59.3	41 351	19 531	3 888	5 447	59 323	56.0	3 775	895	5.5
October	115 798	68 821	59.4	41 362	19 702	3 847	5 355	59 556	56.1	3 910	883	5.7
November	115 916	68 533	59.1	41 062	19 594	3 874	5 480	59 050	55.7	4 003	982	5.8
December	116 040	68 994	59.5	41 651	19 717	3 973	5 458	59 883	56.3	3 653	920	5.3
1960												
January	116 594	68 962	59.1	41 637	19 686	4 024	5 458	59 889	56.0	3 615	915	5.2
February	116 702	68 949	59.1	41 729	19 765	4 126	5 443	60 177	56.2	3 329	841	4.8
March	116 827	68 399	58.5	41 320	19 388	3 965	4 959	59 714	55.4	3 726	959	5.4
April	116 910	69 579	59.5	41 641	20 110	4 208	5 471	60 488	56.4	3 620	896	5.2
May	117 033	69 626	59.5	41 668	20 186	4 203	5 359	60 698	56.4	3 569	797	5.1
June	117 167	69 934	59.7	41 553	20 290	4 325	5 416	60 752	56.5	3 766	854	5.4
July	117 281	69 745	59.5	41 490	20 257	4 162	5 542	60 367	56.2	3 836	921	5.5
August	117 431	69 841	59.5	41 503	20 316	4 076	5 520	60 375	56.1	3 946	927	5.6
September	117 521	70 151	59.7	41 604	20 493	4 170	5 755	60 512	56.4	3 884	982	5.5
October	117 643	69 884	59.4	41 464	20 076	4 092	5 436	60 196	55.8	4 252	1 189	6.1
November	117 829	70 439	59.8	41 543	20 384	4 182	5 513	60 596	56.1	4 330	1 223	6.1
December	118 001	70 395	59.7	41 416	20 332	4 030	5 622	60 156	55.7	4 617	1 142	6.6
1961												
January	118 155	70 447	59.6	41 363	20 325	4 088	5 422	60 354	55.7	4 671	1 328	6.6
February	118 250	70 420	59.6	41 177	20 392	4 019	5 472	60 116	55.5	4 832	1 416	6.9
March	118 358	70 703	59.7	41 273	20 459	4 118	5 406	60 444	55.6	4 853	1 463	6.9
April	118 503	70 267	59.3	41 206	20 145	4 023	5 037	60 337	55.2	4 893	1 598	7.0
May	118 638	70 452	59.4	41 139	20 261	4 049	5 099	60 350	55.2	5 003	1 686	7.1
June	118 767	70 878	59.7	41 349	20 446	4 198	5 220	60 773	55.6	4 885	1 651	6.9
July	118 889	70 536	59.3	41 245	20 252	4 111	5 153	60 455	55.2	4 928	1 830	7.0
August	119 006	70 534	59.3	41 362	20 279	4 211	5 366	60 486	55.3	4 682	1 649	6.6
September	119 107	70 217	59.0	41 400	20 112	4 029	5 021	60 520	55.0	4 676	1 531	6.7
October	119 202	70 492	59.1	41 509	20 338	4 072	5 203	60 716	55.3	4 573	1 481	6.5
November	119 153	70 376	59.1	41 556	20 330	4 195	5 090	60 991	55.5	4 295	1 388	6.1
December	119 214	70 077	58.8	41 534	20 287	4 079	4 992	60 908	55.3	4 177	1 361	6.0
1962												
January	119 300	70 189	58.8	41 547	20 501	4 060	5 094	61 014	55.4	4 081	1 235	5.8
February	119 360	70 409	59.0	41 745	20 693	4 100	5 289	61 249	55.7	3 871	1 244	5.5
March	119 476	70 414	58.9	41 696	20 567	4 230	5 157	61 336	55.7	3 921	1 162	5.6
April	119 702	70 278	58.7	41 647	20 567	4 158	5 009	61 363	55.4	3 906	1 122	5.6
May	119 813	70 551	58.9	41 847	20 558	4 283	4 964	61 724	55.7	3 863	1 134	5.5
June	119 943	70 514	58.8	41 761	20 547	4 362	4 943	61 727	55.6	3 844	1 079	5.5
July	120 128	70 302	58.5	41 671	20 592	4 220	4 840	61 643	55.3	3 819	1 049	5.4
August	120 323	70 981	59.0	41 900	20 841	4 227	4 866	62 102	55.7	4 013	1 081	5.7
September	120 653	71 153	59.0	42 020	20 982	4 190	4 867	62 325	55.7	3 961	1 096	5.6
October	120 856	70 917	58.7	42 086	20 856	4 172	4 816	62 298	55.5	3 803	1 022	5.4
November	121 045	70 871	58.5	41 985	20 794	4 068	4 831	62 016	55.2	4 024	1 051	5.7
December	121 236	70 854	58.4	41 934	20 831	4 182	4 647	62 300	55.2	3 907	1 068	5.5
1963												
January	121 463	71 146	58.6	41 938	20 933	4 201	4 882	62 190	55.2	4 074	1 122	5.7
February	121 633	71 262	58.6	41 876	21 046	4 102	4 652	62 372	55.1	4 238	1 137	5.9
March	121 824	71 423	58.6	42 047	21 162	4 142	4 696	62 655	55.3	4 072	1 087	5.7
April	121 986	71 697	58.8	42 131	21 281	4 230	4 670	62 972	55.5	4 055	1 071	5.7
May	122 162	71 832	58.8	42 145	21 225	4 245	4 729	62 886	55.3	4 217	1 157	5.9
June	122 352	71 626	58.5	42 268	21 185	4 196	4 642	63 007	55.3	3 977	1 067	5.6
July	122 521	71 956	58.7	42 427	21 268	4 210	4 694	63 211	55.4	4 051	1 070	5.6
August	122 667	71 786	58.5	42 400	21 185	4 323	4 604	63 304	55.4	3 878	1 114	5.4
September	122 821	72 131	58.7	42 500	21 317	4 357	4 650	63 524	55.5	3 957	1 069	5.5
October	123 014	72 281	58.8	42 437	21 456	4 401	4 702	63 592	55.5	3 987	1 071	5.5
November	123 192	72 418	58.8	42 415	21 553	4 299	4 694	63 573	55.4	4 151	1 054	5.7
December	123 360	72 188	58.5	42 427	21 481	4 305	4 629	63 584	55.3	3 975	1 007	5.5
1964												
January	123 560	72 356	58.6	42 510	21 462	4 355	4 603	63 724	55.3	4 029	1 057	5.6
February	123 707	72 683	58.8	42 579	21 652	4 520	4 563	64 188	55.6	3 932	1 015	5.4
March	123 857	72 713	58.7	42 600	21 685	4 478	4 366	64 397	55.5	3 950	1 039	5.4
April	124 019	73 274	59.1	42 885	22 110	4 361	4 414	64 942	55.9	3 918	934	5.3
May	124 204	73 395	59.1	43 025	22 103	4 503	4 603	65 028	56.1	3 764	975	5.1
June	124 386	73 032	58.7	42 760	21 995	4 463	4 556	64 662	55.6	3 814	1 047	5.2
July	124 567	73 007	58.6	42 998	21 846	4 555	4 591	64 808	55.7	3 608	1 002	4.9
August	124 731	73 118	58.6	42 963	22 002	4 498	4 573	64 890	55.7	3 655	934	5.0
September	124 920	73 290	58.7	43 009	21 863	4 706	4 619	64 959	55.7	3 712	917	5.1
October	125 108	73 308	58.6	43 023	21 984	4 575	4 550	65 032	55.6	3 726	903	5.1
November	125 291	73 286	58.5	43 171	21 954	4 610	4 496	65 239	55.7	3 551	922	4.8
December	125 468	73 465	58.6	43 109	22 136	4 569	4 322	65 492	55.6	3 651	873	5.0

[1] Not seasonally adjusted.

Table 20-3. Summary Labor Force, Employment, and Unemployment—Continued

(Thousands of persons, percent, seasonally adjusted, except as noted.)

Year and month	Civilian noninstitutional population [1]	Civilian labor force		Employment, thousands of persons					Employment-population ratio, percent	Unemployment		
		Thousands of persons	Participation rate (percent)	By age and sex			By industry			Thousands of persons		Rate (percent)
				Men, 20 years and over	Women, 20 years and over	Both sexes, 16 to 19 years	Agricultural	Nonagricultural		Total	Unemployed 15 weeks and over	
1965												
January	125 647	73 569	58.6	43 237	22 282	4 478	4 271	65 726	55.7	3 572	793	4.9
February	125 810	73 857	58.7	43 279	22 276	4 572	4 322	65 805	55.7	3 730	919	5.1
March	125 985	73 949	58.7	43 370	22 373	4 696	4 318	66 121	55.9	3 510	796	4.7
April	126 155	74 228	58.8	43 397	22 416	4 820	4 424	66 209	56.0	3 595	796	4.8
May	126 320	74 466	59.0	43 579	22 494	4 961	4 724	66 310	56.2	3 432	736	4.6
June	126 499	74 412	58.8	43 487	22 759	4 779	4 444	66 581	56.1	3 387	786	4.6
July	126 573	74 761	59.1	43 489	22 841	5 130	4 390	67 070	56.5	3 301	683	4.4
August	126 756	74 616	58.9	43 447	22 783	5 132	4 355	67 007	56.3	3 254	733	4.4
September	126 906	74 502	58.7	43 371	22 684	5 231	4 271	67 015	56.2	3 216	732	4.3
October	127 043	74 838	58.9	43 461	22 819	5 415	4 418	67 277	56.4	3 143	672	4.2
November	127 171	74 797	58.8	43 447	22 829	5 448	4 093	67 631	56.4	3 073	645	4.1
December	127 294	75 093	59.0	43 513	22 983	5 566	4 159	67 903	56.6	3 031	659	4.0
1966												
January	127 394	75 186	59.0	43 495	23 098	5 605	4 077	68 121	56.7	2 988	623	4.0
February	127 514	74 954	58.8	43 528	23 089	5 517	4 078	68 056	56.6	2 820	594	3.8
March	127 626	75 075	58.8	43 576	23 109	5 503	4 069	68 119	56.6	2 887	583	3.8
April	127 744	75 338	59.0	43 679	23 227	5 604	4 108	68 402	56.8	2 828	575	3.8
May	127 879	75 447	59.0	43 710	23 282	5 505	3 930	68 567	56.7	2 950	534	3.9
June	127 983	75 647	59.1	43 662	23 359	5 754	3 967	68 808	56.9	2 872	475	3.8
July	128 102	75 736	59.1	43 574	23 422	5 864	3 920	68 940	56.9	2 876	427	3.8
August	128 240	76 046	59.3	43 636	23 605	5 905	3 921	69 225	57.0	2 900	464	3.8
September	128 359	76 056	59.3	43 718	23 881	5 659	3 952	69 306	57.1	2 798	488	3.7
October	128 494	76 199	59.3	43 776	23 881	5 744	3 912	69 489	57.1	2 798	494	3.7
November	128 627	76 610	59.6	43 804	24 130	5 906	3 945	69 895	57.4	2 770	464	3.6
December	128 730	76 641	59.5	43 820	24 025	5 884	3 906	69 823	57.3	2 912	488	3.8
1967												
January	128 909	76 639	59.5	44 029	23 872	5 770	3 890	69 781	57.1	2 968	489	3.9
February	129 032	76 521	59.3	43 997	23 919	5 690	3 723	69 883	57.0	2 915	459	3.8
March	129 190	76 328	59.1	43 922	23 832	5 685	3 757	69 682	56.8	2 889	436	3.8
April	129 344	76 777	59.4	44 061	24 161	5 660	3 748	70 134	57.1	2 895	428	3.8
May	129 515	76 773	59.3	44 100	24 172	5 572	3 658	70 186	57.0	2 929	417	3.8
June	129 722	77 270	59.6	44 230	24 303	5 745	3 689	70 589	57.3	2 992	422	3.9
July	129 918	77 464	59.6	44 364	24 416	5 740	3 833	70 687	57.4	2 944	412	3.8
August	130 187	77 712	59.7	44 410	24 600	5 757	3 963	70 804	57.4	2 945	441	3.8
September	130 392	77 812	59.7	44 535	24 683	5 636	3 851	71 003	57.4	2 958	448	3.8
October	130 582	78 194	59.9	44 610	24 802	5 639	4 008	71 043	57.5	3 143	472	4.0
November	130 754	78 191	59.8	44 625	24 914	5 586	3 933	71 192	57.5	3 066	490	3.9
December	130 936	78 491	59.9	44 719	25 104	5 650	4 076	71 397	57.6	3 018	485	3.8
1968												
January	131 112	77 578	59.2	44 606	24 581	5 513	3 908	70 792	57.0	2 878	503	3.7
February	131 277	78 230	59.6	44 659	24 881	5 689	3 959	71 270	57.3	3 001	468	3.8
March	131 412	78 256	59.6	44 663	25 019	5 697	3 904	71 475	57.4	2 877	447	3.7
April	131 553	78 270	59.5	44 753	25 072	5 736	3 875	71 686	57.4	2 709	393	3.5
May	131 712	78 847	59.9	44 841	25 513	5 753	3 814	72 293	57.8	2 740	395	3.5
June	131 872	79 120	60.0	44 914	25 466	5 802	3 806	72 376	57.8	2 938	405	3.7
July	132 053	78 970	59.8	44 935	25 347	5 805	3 820	72 267	57.6	2 883	426	3.7
August	132 251	78 811	59.6	44 897	25 201	5 945	3 736	72 307	57.5	2 768	393	3.5
September	132 446	78 858	59.5	44 893	25 445	5 834	3 758	72 414	57.5	2 686	375	3.4
October	132 617	78 913	59.5	44 884	25 475	5 865	3 741	72 483	57.5	2 689	386	3.4
November	132 903	79 209	59.6	44 996	25 674	5 824	3 758	72 736	57.6	2 715	357	3.4
December	133 120	79 463	59.7	45 262	25 712	5 804	3 746	73 032	57.7	2 685	351	3.4
1969												
January	133 324	79 523	59.6	45 154	25 777	5 874	3 704	73 101	57.6	2 718	339	3.4
February	133 465	80 019	60.0	45 339	26 092	5 896	3 770	73 557	57.9	2 692	358	3.4
March	133 639	80 079	59.9	45 305	26 115	5 947	3 668	73 699	57.9	2 712	353	3.4
April	133 821	80 281	60.0	45 262	26 233	6 028	3 629	73 894	57.9	2 758	386	3.4
May	134 027	80 125	59.8	45 278	26 283	5 851	3 706	73 706	57.8	2 713	387	3.4
June	134 213	80 696	60.1	45 313	26 429	6 138	3 663	74 217	58.0	2 816	368	3.5
July	134 414	80 827	60.1	45 305	26 516	6 138	3 548	74 411	58.0	2 868	377	3.5
August	134 597	81 106	60.3	45 513	26 556	6 181	3 613	74 637	58.1	2 856	373	3.5
September	134 774	81 290	60.3	45 447	26 572	6 231	3 551	74 699	58.1	3 040	391	3.7
October	135 012	81 494	60.4	45 488	26 658	6 299	3 517	74 928	58.1	3 049	374	3.7
November	135 239	81 397	60.2	45 505	26 652	6 384	3 477	75 064	58.1	2 856	392	3.5
December	135 489	81 624	60.2	45 577	26 832	6 331	3 409	75 331	58.1	2 884	413	3.5
1970												
January	135 713	81 981	60.4	45 654	26 908	6 218	3 422	75 358	58.0	3 201	431	3.9
February	135 957	82 151	60.4	45 627	26 828	6 243	3 439	75 259	57.9	3 453	470	4.2
March	136 179	82 498	60.6	45 668	26 933	6 262	3 499	75 364	57.9	3 635	534	4.4
April	136 416	82 727	60.6	45 679	27 114	6 137	3 568	75 362	57.9	3 797	602	4.6
May	136 686	82 483	60.3	45 666	26 739	6 159	3 547	75 017	57.5	3 919	591	4.8
June	136 928	82 484	60.2	45 554	26 904	5 955	3 555	74 858	57.3	4 071	657	4.9
July	137 196	82 901	60.4	45 516	27 083	6 127	3 517	75 209	57.4	4 175	662	5.0
August	137 455	82 880	60.3	45 495	27 011	6 118	3 418	75 206	57.2	4 256	705	5.1
September	137 717	82 954	60.2	45 535	26 784	6 179	3 451	75 047	57.0	4 456	788	5.4
October	137 988	83 276	60.4	45 508	27 058	6 119	3 337	75 348	57.0	4 591	771	5.5
November	138 264	83 548	60.4	45 540	27 020	6 090	3 372	75 278	56.9	4 898	871	5.9
December	138 529	83 670	60.4	45 466	27 038	6 090	3 380	75 214	56.7	5 076	1 102	6.1

[1]Not seasonally adjusted.

Table 20-3. Summary Labor Force, Employment, and Unemployment—Continued

(Thousands of persons, percent, seasonally adjusted, except as noted.)

Year and month	Civilian noninsti-tutional population [1]	Civilian labor force		Employment, thousands of persons					Employ-ment-population ratio, percent	Unemployment		
		Thousands of persons	Participa-tion rate (percent)	By age and sex			By industry			Thousands of persons		Rate (percent)
				Men, 20 years and over	Women, 20 years and over	Both sexes, 16 to 19 years	Agricultural	Nonagri-cultural		Total	Unem-ployed 15 weeks and over	
1971												
January	138 795	83 850	60.4	45 527	27 173	6 164	3 393	75 471	56.8	4 986	1 113	5.9
February	139 021	83 603	60.1	45 455	27 040	6 205	3 288	75 412	56.6	4 903	1 068	5.9
March	139 285	83 575	60.0	45 520	26 967	6 101	3 356	75 232	56.4	4 987	1 098	6.0
April	139 566	83 946	60.1	45 789	26 984	6 214	3 574	75 413	56.6	4 959	1 149	5.9
May	139 826	84 135	60.2	45 917	27 056	6 166	3 449	75 690	56.6	4 996	1 173	5.9
June	140 090	83 706	59.8	45 879	27 013	5 865	3 334	75 423	56.2	4 949	1 167	5.9
July	140 343	84 340	60.1	46 000	27 054	6 251	3 386	75 919	56.5	5 035	1 251	6.0
August	140 596	84 673	60.2	46 041	27 171	6 327	3 395	76 144	56.6	5 134	1 261	6.1
September	140 869	84 731	60.1	46 090	27 390	6 209	3 367	76 322	56.6	5 042	1 239	6.0
October	141 146	84 872	60.1	46 132	27 538	6 248	3 405	76 513	56.6	4 954	1 268	5.8
November	141 393	85 458	60.4	46 209	27 721	6 367	3 410	76 887	56.8	5 161	1 277	6.0
December	141 666	85 625	60.4	46 280	27 791	6 400	3 371	77 100	56.8	5 154	1 283	6.0
1972												
January	142 736	85 978	60.2	46 471	27 956	6 532	3 366	77 593	56.7	5 019	1 257	5.8
February	143 017	86 036	60.2	46 600	28 016	6 492	3 358	77 750	56.7	4 928	1 292	5.7
March	143 263	86 611	60.5	46 821	28 126	6 626	3 438	78 135	56.9	5 038	1 232	5.8
April	143 483	86 614	60.4	46 863	28 114	6 678	3 382	78 273	56.9	4 959	1 203	5.7
May	143 760	86 809	60.4	46 950	28 184	6 753	3 412	78 475	57.0	4 922	1 168	5.7
June	144 033	87 006	60.4	47 147	28 175	6 761	3 402	78 681	57.0	4 923	1 141	5.7
July	144 285	87 143	60.4	47 244	28 225	6 761	3 461	78 769	57.0	4 913	1 154	5.6
August	144 522	87 517	60.6	47 321	28 382	6 875	3 603	78 975	57.1	4 939	1 156	5.6
September	144 761	87 392	60.4	47 394	28 417	6 732	3 568	78 975	57.0	4 849	1 131	5.5
October	144 988	87 491	60.3	47 354	28 438	6 824	3 634	78 982	57.0	4 875	1 123	5.6
November	145 211	87 592	60.3	47 529	28 567	6 894	3 517	79 473	57.2	4 602	1 040	5.3
December	145 446	87 943	60.5	47 747	28 698	6 955	3 596	79 804	57.3	4 543	1 006	5.2
1973												
January	145 720	87 487	60.0	47 701	28 596	6 864	3 456	79 705	57.1	4 326	947	4.9
February	145 943	88 364	60.5	47 884	28 995	7 033	3 415	80 497	57.5	4 452	894	5.0
March	146 230	88 846	60.8	48 117	29 110	7 225	3 469	80 983	57.8	4 394	889	4.9
April	146 459	89 018	60.8	48 098	29 304	7 157	3 407	81 152	57.7	4 459	809	5.0
May	146 719	88 977	60.6	48 068	29 432	7 148	3 376	81 272	57.7	4 329	816	4.9
June	146 981	89 548	60.9	48 244	29 505	7 436	3 509	81 676	58.0	4 363	779	4.9
July	147 233	89 604	60.9	48 452	29 592	7 255	3 540	81 759	57.9	4 305	756	4.8
August	147 471	89 509	60.7	48 353	29 578	7 273	3 425	81 779	57.8	4 305	788	4.8
September	147 731	89 838	60.8	48 408	29 710	7 370	3 342	82 146	57.9	4 350	785	4.8
October	147 980	90 131	60.9	48 631	29 885	7 471	3 424	82 563	58.1	4 144	793	4.6
November	148 219	90 716	61.2	48 764	30 071	7 485	3 593	82 727	58.2	4 396	832	4.8
December	148 479	90 890	61.2	48 902	29 991	7 508	3 658	82 743	58.2	4 489	767	4.9
1974												
January	148 753	91 199	61.3	49 107	29 893	7 555	3 756	82 799	58.2	4 644	799	5.1
February	148 982	91 485	61.4	49 057	30 146	7 551	3 824	82 930	58.2	4 731	829	5.2
March	149 225	91 453	61.3	48 986	30 293	7 540	3 726	83 093	58.2	4 634	849	5.1
April	149 478	91 287	61.1	48 853	30 376	7 440	3 582	83 087	58.0	4 618	889	5.1
May	149 750	91 596	61.2	49 039	30 424	7 428	3 529	83 362	58.0	4 705	880	5.1
June	150 012	91 868	61.2	48 946	30 512	7 483	3 386	83 555	58.0	4 927	926	5.4
July	150 248	92 212	61.4	48 883	30 869	7 397	3 436	83 713	58.0	5 063	924	5.5
August	150 493	92 059	61.2	48 950	30 662	7 425	3 429	83 608	57.8	5 022	960	5.5
September	150 753	92 488	61.4	48 978	30 569	7 504	3 460	83 591	57.7	5 437	1 021	5.9
October	151 009	92 518	61.3	48 959	30 570	7 466	3 431	83 564	57.6	5 523	1 072	6.0
November	151 256	92 766	61.3	48 833	30 424	7 369	3 405	83 221	57.3	6 140	1 128	6.6
December	151 494	92 780	61.2	48 458	30 431	7 255	3 361	82 783	56.9	6 636	1 326	7.2
1975												
January	151 755	93 128	61.4	48 086	30 343	7 198	3 401	82 226	56.4	7 501	1 555	8.1
February	151 990	92 776	61.0	47 927	30 215	7 114	3 361	81 895	56.1	7 520	1 841	8.1
March	152 217	93 165	61.2	47 776	30 334	7 077	3 358	81 829	56.0	7 978	2 074	8.6
April	152 443	93 399	61.3	47 759	30 410	7 020	3 315	81 874	55.9	8 210	2 442	8.8
May	152 704	93 884	61.5	47 835	30 483	7 133	3 560	81 891	56.0	8 433	2 643	9.0
June	152 976	93 575	61.2	47 754	30 618	6 983	3 368	81 987	55.8	8 220	2 843	8.8
July	153 309	94 021	61.3	48 050	30 794	7 050	3 457	82 437	56.0	8 127	2 943	8.6
August	153 580	94 162	61.3	48 239	30 966	7 029	3 429	82 805	56.1	7 928	2 862	8.4
September	153 848	94 202	61.2	48 126	30 979	7 174	3 508	82 771	56.1	7 923	2 906	8.4
October	154 082	94 267	61.2	48 165	31 121	7 084	3 397	82 973	56.1	7 897	2 689	8.4
November	154 338	94 250	61.1	48 203	31 135	7 118	3 331	83 125	56.0	7 794	2 789	8.3
December	154 589	94 409	61.1	48 266	31 268	7 131	3 259	83 406	56.1	7 744	2 868	8.2
1976												
January	154 853	94 934	61.3	48 592	31 595	7 213	3 387	84 013	56.4	7 534	2 713	7.9
February	155 066	94 998	61.3	48 721	31 680	7 271	3 304	84 368	56.5	7 326	2 519	7.7
March	155 306	95 215	61.3	48 836	31 842	7 307	3 296	84 689	56.7	7 230	2 441	7.6
April	155 529	95 746	61.6	49 097	31 951	7 368	3 438	84 978	56.8	7 330	2 210	7.7
May	155 765	95 847	61.5	49 193	32 147	7 454	3 367	85 427	57.0	7 053	2 115	7.4
June	156 027	95 885	61.5	49 010	32 267	7 286	3 310	85 253	56.8	7 322	2 332	7.6
July	156 276	96 583	61.8	49 236	32 334	7 523	3 358	85 735	57.0	7 490	2 316	7.8
August	156 525	96 741	61.8	49 417	32 437	7 369	3 380	85 843	57.0	7 518	2 378	7.8
September	156 779	96 553	61.6	49 485	32 390	7 298	3 278	85 895	56.9	7 380	2 296	7.6
October	156 993	96 704	61.6	49 524	32 412	7 338	3 316	85 958	56.9	7 430	2 292	7.7
November	157 235	97 254	61.9	49 561	32 753	7 320	3 263	86 371	57.0	7 620	2 354	7.8
December	157 438	97 348	61.8	49 599	32 914	7 290	3 251	86 552	57.0	7 545	2 375	7.8

[1] Not seasonally adjusted.

Table 20-3. Summary Labor Force, Employment, and Unemployment—Continued

(Thousands of persons, percent, seasonally adjusted, except as noted.)

Year and month	Civilian noninstitutional population [1]	Civilian labor force		Employment, thousands of persons					Employment-population ratio, percent	Unemployment		
				By age and sex			By industry			Thousands of persons		
		Thousands of persons	Participation rate (percent)	Men, 20 years and over	Women, 20 years and over	Both sexes, 16 to 19 years	Agricultural	Nonagricultural		Total	Unemployed 15 weeks and over	Rate (percent)
1977												
January	157 688	97 208	61.6	49 738	32 872	7 318	3 185	86 743	57.0	7 280	2 200	7.5
February	157 913	97 785	61.9	49 838	32 997	7 507	3 222	87 120	57.2	7 443	2 174	7.6
March	158 131	98 115	62.0	50 031	33 246	7 531	3 212	87 596	57.4	7 307	2 057	7.4
April	158 371	98 330	62.1	50 185	33 470	7 616	3 313	87 958	57.6	7 059	1 936	7.2
May	158 657	98 665	62.2	50 280	33 851	7 623	3 432	88 322	57.8	6 911	1 928	7.0
June	158 929	99 093	62.4	50 544	33 678	7 737	3 340	88 619	57.9	7 134	1 918	7.2
July	159 185	98 913	62.1	50 597	33 749	7 738	3 247	88 837	57.8	6 829	1 907	6.9
August	159 430	99 366	62.3	50 745	33 809	7 887	3 260	89 181	58.0	6 925	1 836	7.0
September	159 674	99 453	62.3	50 825	34 218	7 659	3 201	89 501	58.1	6 751	1 853	6.8
October	159 915	99 815	62.4	51 046	34 187	7 819	3 272	89 780	58.2	6 763	1 789	6.8
November	160 129	100 576	62.8	51 316	34 536	7 909	3 375	90 386	58.6	6 815	1 804	6.8
December	160 377	100 491	62.7	51 492	34 668	7 945	3 320	90 785	58.7	6 386	1 717	6.4
1978												
January	160 617	100 873	62.8	51 542	34 948	7 894	3 434	90 950	58.8	6 489	1 643	6.4
February	160 831	100 837	62.7	51 578	35 118	7 823	3 320	91 199	58.8	6 318	1 584	6.3
March	161 038	101 092	62.8	51 635	35 310	7 810	3 351	91 404	58.8	6 337	1 531	6.3
April	161 263	101 574	63.0	51 912	35 546	7 936	3 349	92 045	59.2	6 180	1 502	6.1
May	161 518	101 896	63.1	52 050	35 597	8 122	3 325	92 444	59.3	6 127	1 420	6.0
June	161 795	102 371	63.3	52 240	35 828	8 275	3 483	92 860	59.5	6 028	1 352	5.9
July	162 034	102 399	63.2	52 190	35 764	8 136	3 441	92 649	59.3	6 309	1 373	6.2
August	162 259	102 511	63.2	52 228	35 856	8 347	3 401	93 030	59.4	6 080	1 242	5.9
September	162 502	102 795	63.3	52 284	36 274	8 112	3 400	93 270	59.5	6 125	1 308	6.0
October	162 783	103 080	63.3	52 448	36 525	8 160	3 409	93 724	59.7	5 947	1 319	5.8
November	163 017	103 562	63.5	52 802	36 559	8 124	3 284	94 201	59.8	6 077	1 242	5.9
December	163 272	103 809	63.6	52 807	36 686	8 088	3 396	94 185	59.8	6 228	1 269	6.0
1979												
January	163 516	104 057	63.6	53 072	36 697	8 179	3 305	94 643	59.9	6 109	1 250	5.9
February	163 726	104 502	63.8	53 233	36 904	8 192	3 373	94 956	60.1	6 173	1 297	5.9
March	164 027	104 589	63.8	53 120	37 159	8 201	3 368	95 112	60.0	6 109	1 365	5.8
April	164 162	104 172	63.5	53 085	36 944	8 074	3 291	94 812	59.8	6 069	1 272	5.8
May	164 459	104 171	63.3	53 178	37 134	8 019	3 272	95 059	59.8	5 840	1 239	5.6
June	164 721	104 638	63.5	53 309	37 221	8 149	3 331	95 348	59.9	5 959	1 171	5.7
July	164 970	105 002	63.6	53 384	37 514	8 108	3 335	95 671	60.0	5 996	1 123	5.7
August	165 198	105 096	63.6	53 336	37 548	7 892	3 374	95 402	59.8	6 320	1 203	6.0
September	165 431	105 530	63.8	53 510	37 798	8 032	3 371	95 969	60.0	6 190	1 172	5.9
October	165 813	105 700	63.7	53 478	37 931	7 995	3 325	96 079	59.9	6 296	1 219	6.0
November	166 051	105 812	63.7	53 435	38 065	8 074	3 436	96 138	60.0	6 238	1 239	5.9
December	166 300	106 258	63.9	53 555	38 259	8 119	3 400	96 533	60.1	6 325	1 277	6.0
1980												
January	166 544	106 562	64.0	53 501	38 367	8 011	3 316	96 563	60.0	6 683	1 353	6.3
February	166 759	106 697	64.0	53 686	38 389	7 920	3 397	96 598	60.0	6 702	1 358	6.3
March	166 984	106 442	63.7	53 353	38 406	7 954	3 418	96 295	59.7	6 729	1 457	6.3
April	167 197	106 591	63.8	53 035	38 427	7 771	3 326	95 907	59.4	7 358	1 694	6.9
May	167 407	106 929	63.9	52 915	38 335	7 695	3 382	95 563	59.1	7 984	1 740	7.5
June	167 643	106 780	63.7	52 712	38 312	7 658	3 296	95 386	58.9	8 098	1 760	7.6
July	167 932	107 159	63.8	52 733	38 374	7 689	3 319	95 477	58.8	8 363	1 995	7.8
August	168 103	107 105	63.7	52 815	38 511	7 498	3 234	95 590	58.8	8 281	2 162	7.7
September	168 297	107 098	63.6	52 866	38 595	7 616	3 443	95 634	58.9	8 021	2 309	7.5
October	168 503	107 405	63.7	53 094	38 620	7 603	3 372	95 945	58.9	8 088	2 306	7.5
November	168 695	107 568	63.8	53 210	38 795	7 540	3 396	96 149	59.0	8 023	2 329	7.5
December	168 883	107 352	63.6	53 333	38 737	7 564	3 492	96 142	59.0	7 718	2 406	7.2
1981												
January	169 104	108 026	63.9	53 392	39 042	7 521	3 429	96 526	59.1	8 071	2 389	7.5
February	169 280	108 242	63.9	53 445	39 280	7 466	3 345	96 846	59.2	8 051	2 344	7.4
March	169 453	108 553	64.1	53 662	39 464	7 445	3 365	97 206	59.4	7 982	2 276	7.4
April	169 641	108 925	64.2	53 886	39 628	7 542	3 529	97 527	59.6	7 869	2 231	7.2
May	169 829	109 222	64.3	53 879	39 759	7 410	3 369	97 679	59.5	8 174	2 221	7.5
June	170 042	108 396	63.7	53 576	39 682	7 040	3 334	96 964	59.0	8 098	2 250	7.5
July	170 246	108 556	63.8	53 814	39 683	7 196	3 296	97 397	59.1	7 863	2 166	7.2
August	170 399	108 725	63.8	53 718	39 723	7 248	3 379	97 310	59.1	8 036	2 241	7.4
September	170 593	108 294	63.5	53 625	39 342	7 097	3 361	96 703	58.7	8 230	2 261	7.6
October	170 809	109 024	63.8	53 482	39 843	7 053	3 412	96 966	58.8	8 646	2 303	7.9
November	170 996	109 236	63.9	53 335	39 908	6 964	3 415	96 792	58.6	9 029	2 345	8.3
December	171 166	108 912	63.6	53 149	39 708	6 788	3 227	96 418	58.2	9 267	2 374	8.5
1982												
January	171 335	109 089	63.7	53 103	39 821	6 768	3 393	96 299	58.2	9 397	2 409	8.6
February	171 489	109 467	63.8	53 172	39 859	6 731	3 375	96 387	58.2	9 705	2 758	8.9
March	171 667	109 567	63.8	53 054	39 936	6 682	3 372	96 300	58.1	9 895	2 965	9.0
April	171 844	109 820	63.9	53 081	39 848	6 647	3 351	96 225	57.9	10 244	3 086	9.3
May	172 026	110 451	64.2	53 234	40 121	6 761	3 434	96 682	58.2	10 335	3 276	9.4
June	172 190	110 081	63.9	52 933	40 219	6 391	3 331	96 212	57.8	10 538	3 451	9.6
July	172 364	110 342	64.0	52 896	40 228	6 369	3 402	96 091	57.7	10 849	3 555	9.8
August	172 511	110 514	64.1	52 797	40 336	6 500	3 408	96 225	57.8	10 881	3 696	9.8
September	172 690	110 721	64.1	52 760	40 275	6 469	3 385	96 119	57.6	11 217	3 889	10.1
October	172 881	110 744	64.1	52 624	40 105	6 486	3 489	95 726	57.4	11 529	4 185	10.4
November	173 058	111 050	64.2	52 537	40 111	6 464	3 510	95 602	57.3	11 938	4 485	10.8
December	173 199	111 083	64.1	52 497	40 164	6 371	3 414	95 618	57.2	12 051	4 662	10.8

[1]Not seasonally adjusted.

Table 20-3. Summary Labor Force, Employment, and Unemployment—Continued

(Thousands of persons, percent, seasonally adjusted, except as noted.)

Year and month	Civilian noninstitutional population [1]	Civilian labor force		Employment, thousands of persons					Employment-population ratio, percent	Unemployment		
		Thousands of persons	Participation rate (percent)	By age and sex			By industry			Thousands of persons		Rate (percent)
				Men, 20 years and over	Women, 20 years and over	Both sexes, 16 to 19 years	Agricultural	Nonagricultural		Total	Unemployed 15 weeks and over	
1983												
January	173 354	110 695	63.9	52 487	40 268	6 406	3 439	95 722	57.2	11 534	4 668	10.4
February	173 505	110 634	63.8	52 453	40 336	6 300	3 382	95 707	57.1	11 545	4 641	10.4
March	173 656	110 587	63.7	52 615	40 368	6 196	3 360	95 819	57.1	11 408	4 612	10.3
April	173 794	110 828	63.8	52 814	40 542	6 204	3 341	96 219	57.3	11 268	4 370	10.2
May	173 953	110 796	63.7	52 922	40 538	6 182	3 328	96 314	57.3	11 154	4 538	10.1
June	174 125	111 879	64.3	53 515	40 695	6 423	3 462	97 171	57.8	11 246	4 470	10.1
July	174 306	111 756	64.1	53 835	41 041	6 332	3 481	97 727	58.1	10 548	4 329	9.4
August	174 440	112 231	64.3	53 837	41 314	6 457	3 502	98 106	58.2	10 623	4 070	9.5
September	174 602	112 298	64.3	53 983	41 650	6 383	3 347	98 669	58.4	10 282	3 854	9.2
October	174 779	111 926	64.0	54 146	41 597	6 296	3 303	98 736	58.4	9 887	3 648	8.8
November	174 951	112 228	64.1	54 499	41 788	6 442	3 291	99 438	58.7	9 499	3 535	8.5
December	175 121	112 327	64.1	54 662	41 852	6 482	3 332	99 664	58.8	9 331	3 379	8.3
1984												
January	175 533	112 209	63.9	54 975	41 812	6 414	3 293	99 908	58.8	9 008	3 254	8.0
February	175 679	112 615	64.1	55 213	42 196	6 415	3 353	100 471	59.1	8 791	2 991	7.8
March	175 824	112 713	64.1	55 281	42 328	6 358	3 233	100 734	59.1	8 746	2 881	7.8
April	175 969	113 098	64.3	55 373	42 512	6 451	3 291	101 045	59.3	8 762	2 858	7.7
May	176 123	113 649	64.5	55 661	43 071	6 461	3 343	101 850	59.7	8 456	2 884	7.4
June	176 284	113 817	64.6	55 996	42 944	6 651	3 383	102 208	59.9	8 226	2 612	7.2
July	176 440	113 972	64.6	55 921	42 979	6 535	3 344	102 091	59.8	8 537	2 638	7.5
August	176 583	113 682	64.4	55 930	42 885	6 348	3 286	101 877	59.6	8 519	2 604	7.5
September	176 763	113 857	64.4	56 095	42 967	6 428	3 393	102 097	59.7	8 367	2 538	7.3
October	176 956	114 019	64.4	56 183	43 052	6 403	3 194	102 444	59.7	8 381	2 526	7.4
November	177 135	114 170	64.5	56 274	43 244	6 454	3 394	102 578	59.8	8 198	2 438	7.2
December	177 306	114 581	64.6	56 313	43 472	6 438	3 385	102 838	59.9	8 358	2 401	7.3
1985												
January	177 384	114 725	64.7	56 184	43 589	6 529	3 317	102 985	59.9	8 423	2 284	7.3
February	177 516	114 876	64.7	56 216	43 787	6 552	3 317	103 238	60.0	8 321	2 389	7.2
March	177 667	115 328	64.9	56 356	44 035	6 598	3 250	103 739	60.2	8 339	2 394	7.2
April	177 799	115 331	64.9	56 374	44 000	6 562	3 306	103 630	60.1	8 395	2 393	7.3
May	177 944	115 234	64.8	56 531	43 905	6 496	3 280	103 652	60.1	8 302	2 292	7.2
June	178 096	114 965	64.6	56 288	43 958	6 259	3 161	103 344	59.8	8 460	2 310	7.4
July	178 263	115 320	64.7	56 435	43 975	6 397	3 143	103 664	59.9	8 513	2 329	7.4
August	178 405	115 291	64.6	56 655	44 103	6 337	3 121	103 974	60.0	8 196	2 258	7.1
September	178 572	115 905	64.9	56 845	44 395	6 417	3 064	104 593	60.3	8 248	2 242	7.1
October	178 770	116 145	65.0	56 969	44 565	6 313	3 051	104 796	60.3	8 298	2 295	7.1
November	178 940	116 135	64.9	56 972	44 617	6 418	3 062	104 945	60.4	8 128	2 207	7.0
December	179 112	116 354	65.0	56 995	44 889	6 332	3 141	105 075	60.4	8 138	2 208	7.0
1986												
January	179 670	116 682	64.9	57 637	44 944	6 306	3 287	105 600	60.6	7 795	2 089	6.7
February	179 821	116 882	65.0	57 269	44 804	6 407	3 083	105 397	60.3	8 402	2 308	7.2
March	179 985	117 220	65.1	57 353	44 960	6 524	3 200	105 637	60.5	8 383	2 261	7.2
April	180 148	117 316	65.1	57 358	45 081	6 513	3 153	105 799	60.5	8 364	2 162	7.1
May	180 311	117 528	65.2	57 287	45 289	6 513	3 150	105 939	60.5	8 439	2 232	7.2
June	180 503	118 084	65.4	57 471	45 621	6 484	3 193	106 383	60.7	8 508	2 320	7.2
July	180 682	118 129	65.4	57 514	45 837	6 459	3 141	106 669	60.8	8 319	2 269	7.0
August	180 828	118 150	65.3	57 597	45 926	6 492	3 082	106 933	60.8	8 135	2 276	6.9
September	180 997	118 395	65.4	57 630	45 972	6 483	3 171	106 914	60.8	8 310	2 318	7.0
October	181 186	118 516	65.4	57 660	46 046	6 567	3 128	107 145	60.9	8 243	2 188	7.0
November	181 363	118 634	65.4	57 941	46 070	6 464	3 220	107 255	60.9	8 159	2 202	6.9
December	181 547	118 611	65.3	58 185	46 132	6 411	3 148	107 580	61.0	7 883	2 161	6.6
1987												
January	181 827	118 845	65.4	58 264	46 219	6 470	3 143	107 810	61.0	7 892	2 168	6.6
February	181 998	119 122	65.5	58 279	46 444	6 534	3 208	108 049	61.1	7 865	2 117	6.6
March	182 179	119 270	65.5	58 362	46 549	6 497	3 214	108 194	61.2	7 862	2 070	6.6
April	182 344	119 336	65.4	58 503	46 746	6 545	3 246	108 548	61.3	7 542	2 091	6.3
May	182 533	120 008	65.7	58 713	47 052	6 669	3 345	109 089	61.6	7 574	2 104	6.3
June	182 703	119 644	65.5	58 581	47 102	6 563	3 216	109 030	61.4	7 398	2 087	6.2
July	182 885	119 902	65.6	58 740	47 229	6 665	3 235	109 399	61.6	7 268	1 921	6.1
August	183 002	120 318	65.7	58 810	47 322	6 925	3 112	109 945	61.8	7 261	1 878	6.0
September	183 161	120 011	65.5	58 964	47 285	6 660	3 189	109 720	61.6	7 102	1 866	5.9
October	183 311	120 509	65.7	59 073	47 533	6 676	3 219	110 063	61.8	7 227	1 794	6.0
November	183 470	120 540	65.7	59 210	47 622	6 673	3 145	110 360	61.9	7 035	1 797	5.8
December	183 620	120 729	65.7	59 217	47 781	6 795	3 213	110 580	62.0	6 936	1 767	5.7
1988												
January	183 822	120 969	65.8	59 346	47 862	6 808	3 247	110 769	62.0	6 953	1 714	5.7
February	183 969	121 156	65.9	59 535	47 919	6 773	3 201	111 026	62.1	6 929	1 738	5.7
March	184 111	120 913	65.7	59 393	48 090	6 554	3 169	110 868	61.9	6 876	1 744	5.7
April	184 232	121 251	65.8	59 832	48 147	6 671	3 224	111 426	62.2	6 601	1 563	5.4
May	184 374	121 071	65.7	59 644	47 946	6 702	3 121	111 171	62.0	6 779	1 647	5.6
June	184 562	121 473	65.8	59 751	48 146	7 030	3 111	111 816	62.3	6 546	1 531	5.4
July	184 729	121 665	65.9	59 888	48 186	6 986	3 060	112 000	62.3	6 605	1 601	5.4
August	184 830	122 125	66.1	59 877	48 467	6 938	3 119	112 163	62.4	6 843	1 639	5.6
September	184 962	121 960	65.9	59 980	48 511	6 865	3 165	112 191	62.4	6 604	1 569	5.4
October	185 114	122 206	66.0	60 023	48 859	6 756	3 231	112 407	62.5	6 568	1 562	5.4
November	185 244	122 637	66.2	60 042	49 254	6 804	3 241	112 859	62.7	6 537	1 468	5.3
December	185 402	122 622	66.1	60 059	49 257	6 788	3 194	112 910	62.6	6 518	1 490	5.3

[1] Not seasonally adjusted.

Table 20-3. Summary Labor Force, Employment, and Unemployment—Continued

(Thousands of persons, percent, seasonally adjusted, except as noted.)

Year and month	Civilian noninstitutional population [1]	Civilian labor force		Employment, thousands of persons					Employment-population ratio, percent	Unemployment		
				By age and sex			By industry			Thousands of persons		
		Thousands of persons	Participation rate (percent)	Men, 20 years and over	Women, 20 years and over	Both sexes, 16 to 19 years	Agricultural	Nonagricultural		Total	Unemployed 15 weeks and over	Rate (percent)
1989												
January	185 644	123 390	66.5	60 477	49 529	6 702	3 287	113 421	62.9	6 682	1 480	5.4
February	185 777	123 135	66.3	60 588	49 497	6 691	3 234	113 542	62.9	6 359	1 304	5.2
March	185 897	123 227	66.3	60 795	49 503	6 724	3 198	113 824	62.9	6 205	1 353	5.0
April	186 024	123 565	66.4	60 764	49 565	6 768	3 162	113 935	62.9	6 468	1 397	5.2
May	186 181	123 474	66.3	60 795	49 583	6 721	3 125	113 974	62.9	6 375	1 348	5.2
June	186 329	123 995	66.5	61 054	49 542	6 822	3 068	114 350	63.0	6 577	1 300	5.3
July	186 483	123 967	66.5	60 947	49 693	6 832	3 227	114 245	63.0	6 495	1 435	5.2
August	186 598	124 166	66.5	60 915	49 804	6 936	3 284	114 371	63.1	6 511	1 302	5.2
September	186 726	123 944	66.4	60 668	50 015	6 671	3 219	114 135	62.8	6 590	1 360	5.3
October	186 871	124 211	66.5	60 958	49 871	6 752	3 215	114 366	62.9	6 630	1 392	5.3
November	187 017	124 637	66.6	60 958	50 221	6 733	3 132	114 780	63.0	6 725	1 418	5.4
December	187 165	124 497	66.5	61 068	50 116	6 646	3 188	114 642	63.0	6 667	1 375	5.4
1990												
January	188 413	125 833	66.8	61 742	50 436	6 903	3 210	115 871	63.2	6 752	1 412	5.4
February	188 516	125 710	66.7	61 805	50 438	6 816	3 188	115 871	63.2	6 651	1 350	5.3
March	188 630	125 801	66.7	61 832	50 463	6 908	3 260	115 943	63.2	6 598	1 331	5.2
April	188 778	125 649	66.6	61 579	50 457	6 816	3 231	115 621	63.0	6 797	1 376	5.4
May	188 913	125 893	66.6	61 778	50 646	6 727	3 266	115 885	63.1	6 742	1 415	5.4
June	189 058	125 573	66.4	61 762	50 550	6 671	3 245	115 738	62.9	6 590	1 436	5.2
July	189 188	125 732	66.5	61 683	50 514	6 613	3 192	115 618	62.8	6 922	1 534	5.5
August	189 342	125 990	66.5	61 715	50 635	6 452	3 197	115 605	62.7	7 188	1 607	5.7
September	189 528	125 892	66.4	61 608	50 587	6 329	3 206	115 318	62.5	7 368	1 695	5.9
October	189 710	125 995	66.4	61 606	50 616	6 314	3 270	115 266	62.5	7 459	1 689	5.9
November	189 872	126 070	66.4	61 545	50 541	6 220	3 189	115 117	62.3	7 764	1 831	6.2
December	190 017	126 142	66.4	61 506	50 530	6 205	3 245	114 996	62.2	7 901	1 804	6.3
1991												
January	190 163	125 955	66.2	61 383	50 472	6 085	3 208	114 732	62.0	8 015	1 866	6.4
February	190 271	126 020	66.2	61 117	50 523	6 115	3 270	114 485	61.9	8 265	1 955	6.6
March	190 381	126 238	66.3	61 144	50 422	6 086	3 177	114 475	61.8	8 586	2 137	6.8
April	190 517	126 548	66.4	61 280	50 760	6 069	3 241	114 868	62.0	8 439	2 206	6.7
May	190 650	126 176	66.2	61 052	50 457	5 931	3 275	114 165	61.6	8 736	2 252	6.9
June	190 800	126 331	66.2	61 147	50 585	5 907	3 300	114 339	61.7	8 692	2 533	6.9
July	190 946	126 154	66.1	61 179	50 636	5 753	3 319	114 249	61.6	8 586	2 388	6.8
August	191 116	126 150	66.0	61 122	50 601	5 761	3 313	114 171	61.5	8 666	2 460	6.9
September	191 302	126 650	66.2	61 279	50 864	5 785	3 319	114 609	61.6	8 722	2 497	6.9
October	191 497	126 642	66.1	61 174	50 811	5 815	3 289	114 511	61.5	8 842	2 638	7.0
November	191 657	126 701	66.1	61 201	50 759	5 810	3 296	114 474	61.4	8 931	2 718	7.0
December	191 798	126 664	66.0	61 074	50 728	5 664	3 146	114 320	61.2	9 198	2 892	7.3
1992												
January	191 953	127 261	66.3	61 116	51 095	5 767	3 155	114 823	61.5	9 283	3 060	7.3
February	192 067	127 207	66.2	61 062	51 033	5 658	3 239	114 514	61.3	9 454	3 182	7.4
March	192 204	127 604	66.4	61 363	51 204	5 577	3 236	114 908	61.5	9 460	3 196	7.4
April	192 354	127 841	66.5	61 468	51 323	5 635	3 245	115 181	61.6	9 415	3 130	7.4
May	192 503	128 119	66.6	61 513	51 245	5 617	3 213	115 162	61.5	9 744	3 444	7.6
June	192 663	128 459	66.7	61 537	51 383	5 499	3 297	115 122	61.5	10 040	3 758	7.8
July	192 826	128 563	66.7	61 641	51 458	5 614	3 285	115 428	61.6	9 850	3 614	7.7
August	193 018	128 613	66.6	61 681	51 386	5 759	3 279	115 547	61.6	9 787	3 579	7.6
September	193 229	128 501	66.5	61 663	51 359	5 698	3 274	115 446	61.4	9 781	3 504	7.6
October	193 442	128 026	66.2	61 550	51 373	5 705	3 254	115 374	61.3	9 398	3 505	7.3
November	193 621	128 441	66.3	61 644	51 535	5 697	3 207	115 669	61.4	9 565	3 397	7.4
December	193 784	128 554	66.3	61 721	51 524	5 752	3 259	115 738	61.4	9 557	3 651	7.4
1993												
January	193 962	128 400	66.2	61 895	51 505	5 675	3 222	115 853	61.4	9 325	3 346	7.3
February	194 108	128 458	66.2	61 963	51 573	5 739	3 125	116 150	61.4	9 183	3 190	7.1
March	194 248	128 598	66.2	62 007	51 808	5 727	3 119	116 423	61.5	9 056	3 115	7.0
April	194 398	128 584	66.1	62 032	51 732	5 710	3 074	116 400	61.5	9 110	3 014	7.1
May	194 549	129 264	66.4	62 309	51 996	5 810	3 100	117 015	61.7	9 149	3 101	7.1
June	194 719	129 411	66.5	62 409	52 183	5 698	3 108	117 182	61.8	9 121	3 141	7.0
July	194 882	129 397	66.4	62 497	52 088	5 882	3 126	117 341	61.8	8 930	3 046	6.9
August	195 063	129 619	66.4	62 634	52 294	5 928	3 026	117 830	62.0	8 763	3 026	6.8
September	195 259	129 268	66.2	62 437	52 241	5 876	3 174	117 380	61.7	8 714	3 042	6.7
October	195 444	129 573	66.3	62 614	52 379	5 830	3 084	117 739	61.8	8 750	3 029	6.8
November	195 625	129 711	66.3	62 732	52 531	5 906	3 157	118 012	61.9	8 542	2 986	6.6
December	195 794	129 941	66.4	62 760	52 813	5 891	3 116	118 348	62.0	8 477	2 968	6.5
1994												
January	195 953	130 596	66.6	62 798	53 052	6 116	3 302	118 664	62.2	8 630	3 060	6.6
February	196 090	130 669	66.6	62 708	53 266	6 112	3 339	118 747	62.3	8 583	3 118	6.6
March	196 213	130 400	66.5	62 780	53 099	6 051	3 354	118 576	62.1	8 470	3 055	6.5
April	196 363	130 621	66.5	62 906	53 274	6 110	3 428	118 862	62.3	8 331	2 921	6.4
May	196 510	130 779	66.6	63 116	53 624	6 124	3 409	119 455	62.5	7 915	2 836	6.1
June	196 693	130 561	66.4	63 041	53 393	6 200	3 299	119 335	62.3	7 927	2 735	6.1
July	196 859	130 652	66.4	63 034	53 531	6 141	3 333	119 373	62.3	7 946	2 822	6.1
August	197 043	131 275	66.6	63 294	53 744	6 304	3 451	119 891	62.6	7 933	2 750	6.0
September	197 248	131 421	66.6	63 631	53 991	6 065	3 430	120 257	62.7	7 734	2 746	5.9
October	197 430	131 744	66.7	63 818	54 071	6 223	3 490	120 622	62.9	7 632	2 955	5.8
November	197 607	131 891	66.7	64 080	54 168	6 268	3 574	120 942	63.0	7 375	2 666	5.6
December	197 765	131 951	66.7	64 359	54 054	6 308	3 577	121 144	63.1	7 230	2 488	5.5

[1]Not seasonally adjusted.

Table 20-3. Summary Labor Force, Employment, and Unemployment—Continued

(Thousands of persons, percent, seasonally adjusted, except as noted.)

Year and month	Civilian noninsti-tutional population [1]	Civilian labor force		Employment, thousands of persons					Employ-ment-population ratio, percent	Unemployment		
		Thousands of persons	Participa-tion rate (percent)	By age and sex			By industry			Thousands of persons		Rate (percent)
				Men, 20 years and over	Women, 20 years and over	Both sexes, 16 to 19 years	Agricultural	Nonagri-cultural		Total	Unem-ployed 15 weeks and over	
1995												
January	197 753	132 038	66.8	64 185	54 087	6 391	3 519	121 144	63.0	7 375	2 396	5.6
February	197 886	132 115	66.8	64 378	54 226	6 324	3 620	121 308	63.1	7 187	2 345	5.4
March	198 007	132 108	66.7	64 321	54 141	6 493	3 634	121 321	63.1	7 153	2 287	5.4
April	198 148	132 590	66.9	64 165	54 366	6 414	3 566	121 379	63.1	7 645	2 473	5.8
May	198 286	131 851	66.5	63 829	54 272	6 320	3 349	121 072	62.7	7 430	2 577	5.6
June	198 453	131 949	66.5	63 992	54 020	6 510	3 461	121 061	62.7	7 427	2 266	5.6
July	198 615	132 343	66.6	63 962	54 476	6 378	3 379	121 437	62.8	7 527	2 311	5.7
August	198 801	132 336	66.6	63 875	54 434	6 543	3 374	121 478	62.8	7 484	2 391	5.7
September	199 005	132 611	66.6	64 179	54 507	6 447	3 285	121 848	62.9	7 478	2 306	5.6
October	199 192	132 716	66.6	64 272	54 692	6 424	3 438	121 950	62.9	7 328	2 272	5.5
November	199 355	132 614	66.5	63 931	54 850	6 407	3 338	121 850	62.8	7 426	2 339	5.6
December	199 508	132 511	66.4	64 041	54 674	6 373	3 352	121 736	62.7	7 423	2 331	5.6
1996												
January	199 634	132 616	66.4	64 180	54 580	6 365	3 483	121 642	62.7	7 491	2 371	5.6
February	199 773	132 952	66.6	64 398	54 844	6 397	3 547	122 092	62.9	7 313	2 307	5.5
March	199 921	133 180	66.6	64 506	54 994	6 362	3 489	122 373	63.0	7 318	2 454	5.5
April	200 101	133 409	66.7	64 481	55 067	6 446	3 406	122 588	63.0	7 415	2 455	5.6
May	200 278	133 667	66.7	64 683	55 034	6 527	3 473	122 771	63.0	7 423	2 403	5.6
June	200 459	133 697	66.7	64 940	55 177	6 485	3 424	123 178	63.2	7 095	2 355	5.3
July	200 641	134 284	66.9	65 068	55 362	6 517	3 433	123 514	63.3	7 337	2 297	5.5
August	200 847	134 054	66.7	65 216	55 525	6 431	3 395	123 777	63.3	6 882	2 267	5.1
September	201 061	134 515	66.9	65 169	55 669	6 698	3 448	124 088	63.4	6 979	2 220	5.2
October	201 273	134 921	67.0	65 460	55 750	6 680	3 463	124 427	63.5	7 031	2 268	5.2
November	201 463	135 007	67.0	65 320	55 896	6 555	3 356	124 415	63.4	7 236	2 159	5.4
December	201 636	135 113	67.0	65 435	55 849	6 576	3 445	124 415	63.4	7 253	2 124	5.4
1997												
January	202 285	135 456	67.0	65 679	56 024	6 595	3 449	124 849	63.4	7 158	2 162	5.3
February	202 389	135 400	66.9	65 758	55 955	6 585	3 353	124 945	63.4	7 102	2 140	5.2
March	202 513	135 891	67.1	65 974	56 270	6 647	3 419	125 472	63.6	7 000	2 110	5.2
April	202 674	136 016	67.1	66 092	56 347	6 704	3 462	125 681	63.7	6 873	2 176	5.1
May	202 832	136 119	67.1	66 328	56 446	6 690	3 437	126 027	63.8	6 655	2 121	4.9
June	203 000	136 211	67.1	66 308	56 573	6 531	3 409	126 003	63.7	6 799	2 085	5.0
July	203 166	136 477	67.2	66 422	56 785	6 615	3 422	126 400	63.9	6 655	2 119	4.9
August	203 364	136 618	67.2	66 508	56 852	6 650	3 359	126 651	63.9	6 608	2 004	4.8
September	203 570	136 675	67.1	66 483	56 931	6 605	3 392	126 627	63.9	6 656	2 074	4.9
October	203 767	136 633	67.1	66 511	56 982	6 686	3 312	126 867	63.9	6 454	1 950	4.7
November	203 941	136 961	67.2	66 765	57 039	6 849	3 386	127 267	64.1	6 308	1 817	4.6
December	204 098	137 155	67.2	66 643	57 219	6 817	3 405	127 274	64.0	6 476	1 901	4.7
1998												
January	204 238	137 095	67.1	66 750	56 941	7 035	3 299	127 389	64.0	6 368	1 833	4.6
February	204 400	137 112	67.1	66 856	56 992	6 959	3 284	127 522	64.0	6 306	1 809	4.6
March	204 547	137 236	67.1	66 721	57 080	7 014	3 146	127 650	64.0	6 422	1 772	4.7
April	204 731	137 150	67.0	67 151	57 074	6 985	3 334	127 852	64.1	5 941	1 476	4.3
May	204 899	137 372	67.0	67 164	57 155	7 007	3 360	127 959	64.1	6 047	1 490	4.4
June	205 085	137 455	67.0	67 054	57 156	7 033	3 380	127 874	64.0	6 212	1 613	4.5
July	205 270	137 588	67.0	67 119	57 192	7 018	3 455	127 913	64.0	6 259	1 577	4.5
August	205 479	137 570	67.0	66 985	57 332	7 074	3 509	127 970	63.9	6 179	1 626	4.5
September	205 699	138 286	67.2	67 254	57 520	7 212	3 500	128 399	64.2	6 300	1 688	4.6
October	205 919	138 279	67.2	67 433	57 529	7 036	3 593	128 389	64.1	6 280	1 582	4.5
November	206 104	138 381	67.1	67 591	57 638	7 052	3 375	128 897	64.2	6 100	1 590	4.4
December	206 270	138 634	67.2	67 548	57 840	7 214	3 246	129 320	64.3	6 032	1 559	4.4
1999												
January	206 719	139 003	67.2	67 679	58 256	7 092	3 233	129 802	64.4	5 976	1 490	4.3
February	206 873	138 967	67.2	67 498	58 129	7 229	3 246	129 647	64.2	6 111	1 551	4.4
March	207 036	138 730	67.0	67 660	58 132	7 155	3 238	129 656	64.2	5 783	1 472	4.2
April	207 236	138 959	67.1	67 542	58 260	7 153	3 336	129 615	64.2	6 004	1 480	4.3
May	207 427	139 107	67.1	67 539	58 440	7 331	3 335	129 937	64.3	5 796	1 505	4.2
June	207 632	139 329	67.1	67 700	58 641	7 037	3 386	129 982	64.2	5 951	1 624	4.3
July	207 828	139 439	67.1	67 731	58 490	7 193	3 346	130 146	64.2	6 025	1 513	4.3
August	208 038	139 430	67.0	67 768	58 707	7 117	3 234	130 366	64.2	5 838	1 455	4.2
September	208 265	139 622	67.0	67 882	58 735	7 090	3 173	130 434	64.2	5 915	1 449	4.2
October	208 483	139 771	67.0	67 840	58 921	7 232	3 229	130 758	64.3	5 778	1 438	4.1
November	208 666	140 025	67.1	68 094	59 018	7 198	3 343	130 989	64.4	5 716	1 378	4.1
December	208 832	140 177	67.1	68 217	59 056	7 251	3 260	131 257	64.4	5 653	1 375	4.0
2000												
January	211 410	142 267	67.3	69 419	59 842	7 298	2 613	133 863	64.6	5 708	1 380	4.0
February	211 576	142 456	67.3	69 505	59 887	7 206	2 731	133 912	64.6	5 858	1 300	4.1
March	211 772	142 434	67.3	69 482	59 977	7 241	2 579	134 022	64.6	5 733	1 312	4.0
April	212 018	142 751	67.3	69 519	60 358	7 393	2 505	134 806	64.7	5 481	1 261	3.8
May	212 242	142 388	67.1	69 399	59 951	7 280	2 480	134 144	64.4	5 758	1 325	4.0
June	212 466	142 591	67.1	69 629	60 027	7 284	2 445	134 528	64.5	5 651	1 242	4.0
July	212 677	142 278	66.9	69 525	60 011	6 995	2 408	134 196	64.2	5 747	1 343	4.0
August	212 916	142 514	66.9	69 823	59 719	7 120	2 433	134 311	64.2	5 853	1 394	4.1
September	213 163	142 518	66.9	69 700	60 083	7 110	2 384	134 489	64.2	5 625	1 290	3.9
October	213 405	142 622	66.8	69 762	60 238	7 088	2 319	134 808	64.2	5 534	1 337	3.9
November	213 540	142 962	66.9	69 910	60 269	7 143	2 330	134 921	64.3	5 639	1 315	3.9
December	213 736	143 248	67.0	69 939	60 503	7 172	2 389	135 194	64.4	5 634	1 329	3.9

[1]Not seasonally adjusted.

Table 20-3. Summary Labor Force, Employment, and Unemployment—Continued

(Thousands of persons, percent, seasonally adjusted, except as noted.)

Year and month	Civilian noninstitutional population [1]	Civilian labor force		Employment, thousands of persons					Employmentpopulation ratio, percent	Unemployment		
		Thousands of persons	Participation rate (percent)	By age and sex			By industry			Thousands of persons		Rate (percent)
				Men, 20 years and over	Women, 20 years and over	Both sexes, 16 to 19 years	Agricultural	Nonagricultural		Total	Unemployed 15 weeks and over	
2001												
January	213 888	143 788	67.2	70 051	60 619	7 101	2 353	135 323	64.4	6 017	1 374	4.2
February	214 110	143 675	67.1	69 941	60 612	7 034	2 366	135 273	64.3	6 088	1 492	4.2
March	214 305	143 931	67.2	69 874	60 901	7 025	2 347	135 362	64.3	6 132	1 522	4.3
April	214 525	143 567	66.9	69 918	60 521	6 852	2 335	135 028	64.0	6 276	1 497	4.4
May	214 732	143 320	66.7	69 881	60 507	6 711	2 353	134 745	63.8	6 222	1 501	4.3
June	214 950	143 361	66.7	69 701	60 364	6 816	2 090	134 758	63.7	6 480	1 525	4.5
July	215 180	143 662	66.8	69 818	60 477	6 787	2 308	134 810	63.7	6 580	1 647	4.6
August	215 420	143 301	66.5	69 600	60 299	6 358	2 301	133 964	63.3	7 044	1 860	4.9
September	215 665	143 995	66.8	69 930	60 267	6 652	2 321	134 577	63.5	7 146	1 952	5.0
October	215 903	144 097	66.7	69 624	60 170	6 598	2 323	134 116	63.2	7 705	2 086	5.3
November	216 117	144 246	66.7	69 441	60 178	6 614	2 210	133 966	63.0	8 014	2 325	5.6
December	216 315	144 324	66.7	69 547	60 100	6 396	2 288	133 755	62.9	8 281	2 458	5.7
2002												
January	216 506	143 858	66.4	69 289	60 053	6 351	2 369	133 256	62.7	8 165	2 575	5.7
February	216 663	144 604	66.7	69 505	60 466	6 414	2 386	134 084	62.9	8 219	2 610	5.7
March	216 823	144 474	66.6	69 477	60 180	6 553	2 365	133 782	62.8	8 263	2 730	5.7
April	217 006	144 717	66.7	69 592	60 193	6 344	2 376	133 830	62.7	8 589	2 844	5.9
May	217 198	144 931	66.7	70 006	60 216	6 328	2 263	134 299	62.9	8 382	2 942	5.8
June	217 407	144 802	66.6	69 782	60 282	6 359	2 187	134 137	62.8	8 379	3 002	5.8
July	217 630	144 818	66.5	69 823	60 285	6 322	2 353	134 023	62.7	8 388	2 944	5.8
August	217 866	145 052	66.6	69 957	60 562	6 216	2 126	134 627	62.8	8 318	2 902	5.7
September	218 107	145 573	66.7	70 201	60 693	6 416	2 282	135 143	63.0	8 263	2 987	5.7
October	218 340	145 347	66.6	69 950	60 681	6 384	2 435	134 627	62.8	8 332	3 053	5.7
November	218 548	145 072	66.4	69 601	60 714	6 196	2 268	134 196	62.5	8 561	3 080	5.9
December	218 741	145 091	66.3	69 593	60 687	6 120	2 342	134 082	62.4	8 691	3 298	6.0
2003												
January	219 897	145 914	66.4	69 894	61 452	6 084	2 315	135 059	62.5	8 484	3 153	5.8
February	220 114	146 001	66.3	70 202	61 127	6 037	2 224	135 218	62.4	8 636	3 166	5.9
March	220 317	145 944	66.2	70 244	61 279	5 928	2 260	135 160	62.4	8 493	3 173	5.8
April	220 540	146 449	66.4	70 343	61 349	5 937	2 163	135 537	62.4	8 822	3 338	6.0
May	220 768	146 478	66.3	70 253	61 372	5 926	2 185	135 389	62.3	8 926	3 287	6.1
June	221 014	147 003	66.5	70 175	61 700	5 900	2 224	135 418	62.3	9 228	3 506	6.3
July	221 252	146 535	66.2	70 224	61 435	5 852	2 229	135 138	62.2	9 024	3 597	6.2
August	221 507	146 507	66.1	70 262	61 456	5 875	2 294	135 262	62.1	8 914	3 609	6.1
September	221 779	146 580	66.1	70 596	61 163	5 860	2 334	135 426	62.1	8 961	3 524	6.1
October	222 039	146 778	66.1	70 694	61 495	5 833	2 428	135 668	62.2	8 755	3 448	6.0
November	222 279	147 109	66.2	70 939	61 532	5 987	2 381	136 068	62.3	8 651	3 451	5.9
December	222 509	146 808	66.0	71 135	61 437	5 836	2 239	136 172	62.2	8 399	3 389	5.7
2004												
January	222 161	146 817	66.1	71 340	61 168	5 964	2 211	136 205	62.3	8 345	3 350	5.7
February	222 357	146 681	66.0	71 105	61 495	5 895	2 227	136 294	62.3	8 186	3 233	5.6
March	222 550	146 849	66.0	71 192	61 487	5 774	2 189	136 291	62.2	8 397	3 315	5.7
April	222 757	146 800	65.9	71 134	61 614	5 912	2 250	136 420	62.2	8 140	2 978	5.5
May	222 967	147 021	65.9	71 173	61 745	5 926	2 296	136 524	62.3	8 178	3 068	5.6
June	223 196	147 427	66.1	71 541	61 802	5 838	2 251	136 816	62.4	8 247	3 099	5.6
July	223 422	147 773	66.1	71 782	61 909	5 899	2 242	137 329	62.5	8 182	2 935	5.5
August	223 677	147 558	66.0	71 780	61 864	5 914	2 317	137 227	62.4	8 000	2 918	5.4
September	223 941	147 476	65.9	71 733	61 883	5 878	2 223	137 391	62.3	7 981	2 938	5.4
October	224 192	147 808	65.9	71 870	61 970	5 928	2 163	137 675	62.3	8 040	3 019	5.4
November	224 422	148 250	66.1	72 140	62 113	6 023	2 192	138 045	62.5	7 974	2 970	5.4
December	224 640	148 173	66.0	72 037	62 169	5 927	2 190	137 944	62.4	8 040	2 926	5.4
2005												
January	224 837	147 956	65.8	72 092	62 236	5 906	2 138	138 076	62.4	7 723	2 821	5.2
February	225 041	148 271	65.9	72 246	62 220	5 818	2 161	138 111	62.3	7 986	2 862	5.4
March	225 236	148 217	65.8	72 513	62 129	5 960	2 199	138 416	62.4	7 616	2 793	5.1
April	225 441	148 839	66.0	72 855	62 426	5 915	2 253	138 926	62.6	7 644	2 688	5.1
May	225 670	149 201	66.1	73 108	62 515	5 948	2 216	139 322	62.7	7 629	2 650	5.1
June	225 911	149 243	66.1	73 178	62 552	6 020	2 321	139 333	62.7	7 493	2 388	5.0
July	226 153	149 605	66.2	73 345	62 744	6 022	2 332	139 772	62.8	7 494	2 483	5.0
August	226 421	149 792	66.2	73 479	62 901	6 045	2 157	140 294	62.9	7 367	2 672	4.9
September	226 693	150 083	66.2	73 331	63 074	6 030	2 140	140 421	62.8	7 648	2 584	5.1
October	226 959	150 043	66.1	73 500	63 162	5 964	2 126	140 577	62.8	7 418	2 477	4.9
November	227 204	150 183	66.1	73 441	63 170	6 000	2 154	140 427	62.8	7 572	2 492	5.0
December	227 425	150 153	66.0	73 468	63 249	6 061	2 130	140 638	62.8	7 375	2 417	4.9

[1]Not seasonally adjusted.

Table 20-3A. Labor Force and Employment Estimates Smoothed for Population Adjustments

(Thousands of persons, seasonally adjusted.)

Year	January	February	March	April	May	June	July	August	September	October	November	December
Civilian Labor Force												
1990	125 845	125 734	125 837	125 697	125 953	125 645	125 816	126 087	126 001	126 116	126 203	126 287
1991	126 112	126 189	126 420	126 742	126 382	126 549	126 384	126 392	126 905	126 909	126 981	126 956
1992	127 566	127 524	127 934	128 184	128 475	128 829	128 945	129 008	128 908	128 444	128 872	128 998
1993	128 856	128 926	129 079	129 077	129 772	129 932	129 931	130 166	129 826	130 145	130 296	130 539
1994	131 210	131 296	131 038	131 272	131 444	131 237	131 341	131 980	132 139	132 477	132 637	132 710
1995	132 811	132 901	132 906	133 404	132 673	132 784	133 193	133 199	133 489	133 607	133 517	133 426
1996	133 545	133 896	134 138	134 381	134 654	134 697	135 302	135 083	135 560	135 982	136 082	136 202
1997	136 560	136 517	137 025	137 164	137 281	137 387	137 668	137 824	137 894	137 865	138 209	138 418
1998	138 370	138 401	138 539	138 465	138 703	138 800	138 947	138 942	139 679	139 685	139 801	140 070
1999	140 456	140 433	140 207	140 452	140 615	140 852	140 977	140 981	141 189	141 353	141 623	141 790
2000	142 272	142 467	142 450	142 773	142 415	142 623	142 316	142 557	142 566	142 676	143 021	143 313
2001	143 870	143 777	144 005	143 655	143 410	143 454	143 757	143 392	144 103	144 205	144 365	144 435
2002	144 018	144 804	144 631	144 870	145 091	144 966	144 971	145 181	145 742	145 498	145 240	145 261
2003	145 508	145 662	145 551	145 986	146 002	146 540	146 004	145 915	146 022	146 179	146 513	146 213
2004	146 691	146 552	146 717	146 666	146 884	147 287	147 630	147 413	147 328	147 657	148 096	148 017
2005	147 847	148 160	148 105	148 724	149 084	149 124	149 484	149 669	149 958	149 916	150 055	150 023
Civilian Employment, Total												
1990	119 093	119 082	119 238	118 898	119 209	119 052	118 891	118 894	118 628	118 651	118 432	118 379
1991	118 089	117 915	117 823	118 293	117 634	117 845	117 785	117 712	118 169	118 052	118 033	117 740
1992	118 265	118 050	118 454	118 748	118 709	118 764	119 071	119 195	119 101	119 020	119 280	119 413
1993	119 503	119 715	119 995	119 938	120 594	120 781	120 970	121 373	121 081	121 363	121 722	122 031
1994	122 547	122 679	122 534	122 908	123 497	123 277	123 362	124 013	124 372	124 811	125 230	125 448
1995	125 402	125 681	125 720	125 722	125 207	125 321	125 629	125 677	125 972	126 241	126 052	125 963
1996	126 013	126 542	126 779	126 924	127 189	127 562	127 922	128 161	128 540	128 909	128 801	128 904
1997	129 358	129 370	129 981	130 247	130 584	130 544	130 970	131 172	131 194	131 368	131 859	131 898
1998	131 958	132 053	132 072	132 484	132 614	132 545	132 643	132 718	133 333	133 359	133 655	133 994
1999	134 436	134 276	134 381	134 402	134 775	134 855	134 905	135 097	135 227	135 529	135 862	136 092
2000	136 564	136 608	136 717	137 291	136 656	136 971	136 567	136 703	136 940	137 140	137 379	137 676
2001	137 846	137 685	137 861	137 382	137 180	136 966	137 169	136 344	136 954	136 505	136 356	136 170
2002	135 826	136 576	136 333	136 279	136 695	136 569	136 569	136 859	137 475	137 176	136 697	136 584
2003	137 024	137 061	137 039	137 203	137 103	137 328	137 012	137 048	137 113	137 486	137 941	137 877
2004	138 355	138 375	138 330	138 534	138 716	139 051	139 458	139 423	139 357	139 628	140 133	139 988
2005	140 132	140 181	140 495	141 088	141 461	141 638	141 997	142 309	142 318	142 506	142 490	142 656

Table 20-4. Nonfarm Payroll Employment, Hours, and Earnings

(Wage and salary workers on nonfarm payrolls, seasonally adjusted.)

Year and month	All wage and salary workers (thousands)					Production or nonsupervisory workers on private payrolls							
	Total	Private				Number (thousands)		Average hours per week		Average hourly earnings, dollars		Average weekly earnings, dollars	
		Total	Goods-producing		Service-providing	Total private	Manufacturing	Total private	Manufacturing	Total private	Manufacturing	Total private	Manufacturing
			Total	Manufacturing									
1946	41 759	36 054	16 122	13 513	25 637	. . .	11 781	. . .	40.4	. . .	0.95	. . .	38.38
1947	43 945	38 379	17 314	14 287	26 631	. . .	12 453	. . .	40.5	. . .	1.10	. . .	44.55
1948	44 954	39 213	17 579	14 324	27 376	. . .	12 383	. . .	40.1	. . .	1.20	. . .	48.12
1949	43 843	37 893	16 464	13 281	27 379	. . .	11 355	. . .	39.2	. . .	1.25	. . .	49.00
1950	45 287	39 167	17 343	14 013	27 945	. . .	12 032	. . .	40.6	. . .	1.32	. . .	53.59
1951	47 930	41 427	18 703	15 070	29 227	. . .	12 808	. . .	40.7	. . .	1.45	. . .	59.02
1952	48 909	42 182	18 928	15 291	29 981	. . .	12 797	. . .	40.8	. . .	1.53	. . .	62.42
1953	50 310	43 552	19 733	16 131	30 577	. . .	13 437	. . .	40.6	. . .	1.63	. . .	66.18
1954	49 093	42 235	18 515	15 002	30 578	. . .	12 300	. . .	39.7	. . .	1.66	. . .	65.90
1955	50 744	43 722	19 234	15 524	31 510	. . .	12 735	. . .	40.8	. . .	1.74	. . .	70.99
1956	52 473	45 087	19 799	15 858	32 674	. . .	12 869	. . .	40.5	. . .	1.84	. . .	74.52
1957	52 959	45 235	19 669	15 798	33 290	. . .	12 640	. . .	39.9	. . .	1.93	. . .	77.01
1958	51 426	43 480	18 319	14 656	33 107	. . .	11 532	. . .	39.2	. . .	1.99	. . .	78.01
1959	53 374	45 182	19 163	15 325	34 211	. . .	12 089	. . .	40.3	. . .	2.08	. . .	83.82
1946													
January	39 839	34 054	15 031	12 719	24 808	. . .	10 990	. . .	40.9	. . .	0.86	. . .	35.17
February	39 250	33 472	14 308	11 922	24 942	. . .	10 292	. . .	40.4	. . .	0.85	. . .	34.34
March	40 192	34 434	15 017	12 545	25 175	. . .	10 989	. . .	40.6	. . .	0.89	. . .	36.13
April	40 908	35 147	15 439	13 200	25 469	. . .	11 616	. . .	40.4	. . .	0.92	. . .	37.17
May	41 348	35 616	15 875	13 389	25 473	. . .	11 758	. . .	39.8	. . .	0.93	. . .	37.01
June	41 732	36 052	16 206	13 598	25 526	. . .	11 905	. . .	40.0	. . .	0.94	. . .	37.60
July	42 153	36 471	16 461	13 771	25 692	. . .	12 065	. . .	40.2	. . .	0.96	. . .	38.59
August	42 642	36 961	16 728	13 981	25 914	. . .	12 241	. . .	40.6	. . .	0.98	. . .	39.79
September	42 908	37 239	16 912	14 135	25 996	. . .	12 311	. . .	40.4	. . .	0.99	. . .	40.00
October	43 094	37 430	17 002	14 182	26 092	. . .	12 302	. . .	40.4	. . .	1.00	. . .	40.40
November	43 396	37 757	17 157	14 310	26 239	. . .	12 421	. . .	40.3	. . .	1.02	. . .	41.11
December	43 379	37 751	17 164	14 301	26 215	. . .	12 419	. . .	40.5	. . .	1.02	. . .	41.31
1947													
January	43 545	37 926	17 213	14 328	26 332	. . .	12 445	. . .	40.5	. . .	1.03	. . .	41.72
February	43 563	37 957	17 200	14 278	26 363	. . .	12 487	. . .	40.4	. . .	1.04	. . .	42.02
March	43 605	38 017	17 196	14 259	26 409	. . .	12 518	. . .	40.3	. . .	1.06	. . .	42.72
April	43 491	37 933	17 178	14 240	26 313	. . .	12 531	. . .	40.5	. . .	1.06	. . .	42.93
May	43 637	38 086	17 176	14 189	26 461	. . .	12 449	. . .	40.4	. . .	1.08	. . .	43.63
June	43 808	38 284	17 253	14 200	26 555	. . .	12 389	. . .	40.4	. . .	1.10	. . .	44.44
July	43 742	38 218	17 106	14 076	26 636	. . .	12 265	. . .	40.4	. . .	1.10	. . .	44.44
August	43 958	38 439	17 280	14 200	26 678	. . .	12 370	. . .	40.0	. . .	1.11	. . .	44.40
September	44 201	38 662	17 398	14 315	26 803	. . .	12 430	. . .	40.5	. . .	1.11	. . .	44.96
October	44 415	38 849	17 499	14 393	26 916	. . .	12 464	. . .	40.5	. . .	1.13	. . .	45.77
November	44 486	38 901	17 517	14 414	26 969	. . .	12 494	. . .	40.5	. . .	1.14	. . .	46.17
December	44 578	38 973	17 563	14 428	27 015	. . .	12 526	. . .	40.8	. . .	1.16	. . .	47.33
1948													
January	44 686	39 062	17 625	14 438	27 061	. . .	12 520	. . .	40.5	. . .	1.16	. . .	46.98
February	44 537	38 922	17 447	14 339	27 090	. . .	12 437	. . .	40.2	. . .	1.16	. . .	46.63
March	44 680	39 057	17 544	14 364	27 136	. . .	12 489	. . .	40.4	. . .	1.16	. . .	46.86
April	44 369	38 726	17 302	14 183	27 067	. . .	12 304	. . .	40.1	. . .	1.17	. . .	46.92
May	44 795	39 114	17 508	14 235	27 287	. . .	12 344	. . .	40.2	. . .	1.18	. . .	47.44
June	45 032	39 296	17 633	14 318	27 399	. . .	12 402	. . .	40.3	. . .	1.19	. . .	47.96
July	45 160	39 386	17 649	14 359	27 511	. . .	12 417	. . .	40.2	. . .	1.21	. . .	48.64
August	45 175	39 384	17 655	14 353	27 520	. . .	12 397	. . .	40.2	. . .	1.23	. . .	49.45
September	45 294	39 489	17 741	14 441	27 553	. . .	12 450	. . .	40.1	. . .	1.24	. . .	49.72
October	45 250	39 421	17 683	14 390	27 567	. . .	12 364	. . .	39.8	. . .	1.25	. . .	49.75
November	45 194	39 325	17 599	14 292	27 595	. . .	12 302	. . .	39.8	. . .	1.26	. . .	50.15
December	45 028	39 140	17 417	14 086	27 611	. . .	12 127	. . .	39.6	. . .	1.26	. . .	49.90
1949													
January	44 675	38 781	17 170	13 867	27 505	. . .	11 905	. . .	39.4	. . .	1.26	. . .	49.64
February	44 500	38 607	17 019	13 734	27 481	. . .	11 792	. . .	39.4	. . .	1.26	. . .	49.64
March	44 238	38 323	16 848	13 581	27 390	. . .	11 654	. . .	39.1	. . .	1.26	. . .	49.27
April	44 230	38 282	16 685	13 439	27 545	. . .	11 517	. . .	38.8	. . .	1.25	. . .	48.50
May	43 982	38 020	16 492	13 269	27 490	. . .	11 352	. . .	38.9	. . .	1.25	. . .	48.63
June	43 739	37 783	16 351	13 178	27 388	. . .	11 266	. . .	39.0	. . .	1.26	. . .	49.14
July	43 530	37 568	16 222	13 067	27 308	. . .	11 168	. . .	39.2	. . .	1.26	. . .	49.39
August	43 621	37 636	16 327	13 158	27 294	. . .	11 251	. . .	39.2	. . .	1.25	. . .	49.00
September	43 784	37 794	16 403	13 225	27 381	. . .	11 284	. . .	39.4	. . .	1.25	. . .	49.25
October	42 950	36 980	15 739	12 891	27 211	. . .	10 940	. . .	39.6	. . .	1.24	. . .	49.10
November	43 244	37 294	16 040	12 882	27 204	. . .	10 964	. . .	39.1	. . .	1.24	. . .	48.48
December	43 516	37 564	16 217	13 062	27 299	. . .	11 173	. . .	39.4	. . .	1.25	. . .	49.25
1950													
January	43 530	37 596	16 255	13 161	27 275	. . .	11 258	. . .	39.6	. . .	1.27	. . .	50.29
February	43 298	37 372	16 035	13 169	27 263	. . .	11 262	. . .	39.7	. . .	1.26	. . .	50.02
March	43 952	37 874	16 482	13 290	27 470	. . .	11 362	. . .	39.7	. . .	1.28	. . .	50.82
April	44 376	38 282	16 718	13 471	27 658	. . .	11 528	. . .	40.3	. . .	1.29	. . .	51.99
May	44 717	38 674	17 080	13 780	27 637	. . .	11 855	. . .	40.3	. . .	1.30	. . .	52.39
June	45 084	39 062	17 288	13 923	27 796	. . .	11 979	. . .	40.6	. . .	1.30	. . .	52.78
July	45 453	39 363	17 464	14 072	27 989	. . .	12 107	. . .	40.9	. . .	1.31	. . .	53.58
August	46 187	40 000	17 917	14 461	28 270	. . .	12 476	. . .	41.3	. . .	1.33	. . .	54.93
September	46 442	40 214	18 040	14 561	28 402	. . .	12 519	. . .	40.8	. . .	1.33	. . .	54.26
October	46 712	40 463	18 249	14 737	28 463	. . .	12 659	. . .	41.1	. . .	1.36	. . .	55.90
November	46 778	40 516	18 288	14 762	28 490	. . .	12 682	. . .	41.0	. . .	1.37	. . .	56.17
December	46 855	40 541	18 283	14 782	28 572	. . .	12 710	. . .	40.9	. . .	1.39	. . .	56.85

. . . = Not available.

Table 20-4. Nonfarm Payroll Employment, Hours, and Earnings—Continued

(Wage and salary workers on nonfarm payrolls, seasonally adjusted.)

Year and month	All wage and salary workers (thousands) Total	Private Total	Goods-producing Total	Goods-producing Manufacturing	Service-providing	Number (thousands) Total private	Number (thousands) Manufacturing	Average hours per week Total private	Average hours per week Manufacturing	Average hourly earnings, dollars Total private	Average hourly earnings, dollars Manufacturing	Average weekly earnings, dollars Total private	Average weekly earnings, dollars Manufacturing
1951													
January	47 289	40 937	18 518	14 950	28 771	. . .	12 816	. . .	41.0	. . .	1.40	. . .	57.40
February	47 577	41 195	18 666	15 076	28 911	. . .	12 929	. . .	40.9	. . .	1.41	. . .	57.67
March	47 871	41 461	18 754	15 125	29 117	. . .	12 936	. . .	41.0	. . .	1.42	. . .	58.22
April	47 856	41 405	18 810	15 166	29 046	. . .	12 960	. . .	41.0	. . .	1.43	. . .	58.63
May	47 952	41 535	18 829	15 164	29 123	. . .	12 941	. . .	41.0	. . .	1.44	. . .	59.04
June	48 067	41 568	18 826	15 176	29 241	. . .	12 934	. . .	40.9	. . .	1.45	. . .	59.31
July	48 061	41 523	18 747	15 110	29 314	. . .	12 848	. . .	40.6	. . .	1.45	. . .	58.87
August	48 008	41 489	18 709	15 061	29 299	. . .	12 772	. . .	40.4	. . .	1.46	. . .	58.98
September	47 955	41 403	18 622	14 996	29 333	. . .	12 659	. . .	40.4	. . .	1.46	. . .	58.98
October	48 009	41 432	18 630	14 973	29 379	. . .	12 615	. . .	40.3	. . .	1.47	. . .	59.24
November	48 149	41 523	18 617	14 999	29 532	. . .	12 628	. . .	40.4	. . .	1.48	. . .	59.79
December	48 308	41 620	18 698	15 045	29 610	. . .	12 667	. . .	40.7	. . .	1.49	. . .	60.64
1952													
January	48 299	41 710	18 719	15 067	29 580	. . .	12 675	. . .	40.8	. . .	1.49	. . .	60.79
February	48 522	41 872	18 813	15 105	29 709	. . .	12 689	. . .	40.8	. . .	1.49	. . .	60.79
March	48 504	41 842	18 775	15 127	29 729	. . .	12 695	. . .	40.6	. . .	1.51	. . .	61.31
April	48 616	41 954	18 806	15 162	29 810	. . .	12 713	. . .	40.3	. . .	1.51	. . .	60.85
May	48 645	41 951	18 784	15 143	29 861	. . .	12 676	. . .	40.5	. . .	1.51	. . .	61.16
June	48 286	41 574	18 419	14 828	29 867	. . .	12 353	. . .	40.6	. . .	1.51	. . .	61.31
July	48 144	41 407	18 268	14 707	29 876	. . .	12 233	. . .	40.2	. . .	1.50	. . .	60.30
August	48 922	42 204	18 928	15 279	29 994	. . .	12 764	. . .	40.7	. . .	1.53	. . .	62.27
September	49 319	42 585	19 206	15 553	30 113	. . .	13 007	. . .	41.1	. . .	1.55	. . .	63.71
October	49 598	42 782	19 312	15 690	30 286	. . .	13 122	. . .	41.2	. . .	1.56	. . .	64.27
November	49 816	43 015	19 473	15 843	30 343	. . .	13 262	. . .	41.2	. . .	1.58	. . .	65.10
December	50 164	43 229	19 610	15 973	30 554	. . .	13 375	. . .	41.2	. . .	1.58	. . .	65.10
1953													
January	50 145	43 351	19 721	16 067	30 424	. . .	13 447	. . .	41.1	. . .	1.59	. . .	65.35
February	50 339	43 542	19 841	16 158	30 498	. . .	13 529	. . .	41.0	. . .	1.61	. . .	66.01
March	50 474	43 690	19 909	16 270	30 565	. . .	13 620	. . .	41.2	. . .	1.61	. . .	66.33
April	50 432	43 662	19 908	16 293	30 524	. . .	13 629	. . .	40.9	. . .	1.62	. . .	66.26
May	50 491	43 774	19 930	16 341	30 561	. . .	13 645	. . .	41.0	. . .	1.62	. . .	66.42
June	50 522	43 788	19 909	16 343	30 613	. . .	13 636	. . .	40.9	. . .	1.63	. . .	66.67
July	50 536	43 813	19 910	16 353	30 626	. . .	13 653	. . .	40.7	. . .	1.64	. . .	66.75
August	50 487	43 733	19 834	16 278	30 653	. . .	13 564	. . .	40.7	. . .	1.64	. . .	66.75
September	50 365	43 616	19 726	16 151	30 639	. . .	13 419	. . .	40.1	. . .	1.65	. . .	66.17
October	50 242	43 478	19 578	15 991	30 664	. . .	13 244	. . .	40.1	. . .	1.65	. . .	66.17
November	49 906	43 157	19 315	15 728	30 591	. . .	12 990	. . .	40.0	. . .	1.65	. . .	66.00
December	49 702	42 959	19 173	15 581	30 529	. . .	12 847	. . .	39.7	. . .	1.65	. . .	65.51
1954													
January	49 467	42 707	18 963	15 440	30 504	. . .	12 706	. . .	39.5	. . .	1.65	. . .	65.18
February	49 381	42 598	18 880	15 307	30 501	. . .	12 593	. . .	39.7	. . .	1.65	. . .	65.51
March	49 158	42 362	18 748	15 197	30 410	. . .	12 493	. . .	39.6	. . .	1.65	. . .	65.34
April	49 177	42 371	18 602	15 065	30 575	. . .	12 361	. . .	39.7	. . .	1.65	. . .	65.51
May	48 965	42 136	18 476	14 974	30 489	. . .	12 282	. . .	39.7	. . .	1.67	. . .	66.30
June	48 896	42 050	18 400	14 910	30 496	. . .	12 220	. . .	39.7	. . .	1.67	. . .	66.30
July	48 834	41 966	18 280	14 799	30 554	. . .	12 121	. . .	39.7	. . .	1.66	. . .	65.90
August	48 825	41 933	18 251	14 772	30 574	. . .	12 089	. . .	39.8	. . .	1.66	. . .	66.07
September	48 881	41 987	18 261	14 805	30 620	. . .	12 104	. . .	39.9	. . .	1.66	. . .	66.23
October	48 944	42 044	18 321	14 841	30 623	. . .	12 142	. . .	39.7	. . .	1.67	. . .	66.30
November	49 179	42 215	18 438	14 913	30 741	. . .	12 206	. . .	40.1	. . .	1.68	. . .	67.37
December	49 331	42 374	18 508	14 967	30 823	. . .	12 254	. . .	40.1	. . .	1.68	. . .	67.37
1955													
January	49 497	42 544	18 609	15 034	30 888	. . .	12 309	. . .	40.4	. . .	1.69	. . .	68.28
February	49 644	42 721	18 726	15 138	30 918	. . .	12 408	. . .	40.6	. . .	1.70	. . .	69.02
March	49 963	43 025	18 910	15 258	31 053	. . .	12 524	. . .	40.7	. . .	1.71	. . .	69.60
April	50 246	43 287	19 067	15 375	31 179	. . .	12 626	. . .	40.8	. . .	1.71	. . .	69.77
May	50 512	43 521	19 223	15 493	31 289	. . .	12 731	. . .	41.1	. . .	1.73	. . .	71.10
June	50 790	43 770	19 331	15 585	31 459	. . .	12 810	. . .	40.8	. . .	1.73	. . .	70.58
July	50 985	43 936	19 376	15 614	31 609	. . .	12 818	. . .	40.7	. . .	1.75	. . .	71.23
August	51 112	44 089	19 432	15 679	31 680	. . .	12 866	. . .	40.7	. . .	1.76	. . .	71.63
September	51 262	44 195	19 427	15 668	31 835	. . .	12 830	. . .	40.7	. . .	1.77	. . .	72.04
October	51 431	44 313	19 482	15 740	31 949	. . .	12 896	. . .	41.0	. . .	1.77	. . .	72.57
November	51 592	44 509	19 554	15 813	32 038	. . .	12 967	. . .	41.1	. . .	1.78	. . .	73.16
December	51 805	44 673	19 608	15 859	32 197	. . .	13 009	. . .	40.9	. . .	1.78	. . .	72.80
1956													
January	51 975	44 808	19 665	15 882	32 310	. . .	13 011	. . .	40.8	. . .	1.78	. . .	72.62
February	52 167	44 955	19 731	15 889	32 436	. . .	12 986	. . .	40.7	. . .	1.79	. . .	72.85
March	52 295	45 043	19 691	15 829	32 604	. . .	12 905	. . .	40.6	. . .	1.80	. . .	73.08
April	52 375	45 099	19 811	15 909	32 564	. . .	12 970	. . .	40.5	. . .	1.82	. . .	73.71
May	52 506	45 139	19 825	15 893	32 681	. . .	12 925	. . .	40.4	. . .	1.83	. . .	73.93
June	52 583	45 216	19 905	15 835	32 678	. . .	12 836	. . .	40.3	. . .	1.83	. . .	73.75
July	51 954	44 549	19 390	15 468	32 564	. . .	12 435	. . .	40.3	. . .	1.82	. . .	73.35
August	52 632	45 181	19 922	15 893	32 710	. . .	12 860	. . .	40.3	. . .	1.85	. . .	74.56
September	52 600	45 119	19 860	15 863	32 740	. . .	12 822	. . .	40.5	. . .	1.87	. . .	75.74
October	52 781	45 262	19 918	15 937	32 863	. . .	12 908	. . .	40.6	. . .	1.88	. . .	76.33
November	52 822	45 269	19 886	15 916	32 936	. . .	12 864	. . .	40.4	. . .	1.88	. . .	75.95
December	52 930	45 346	19 926	15 957	33 004	. . .	12 882	. . .	40.6	. . .	1.91	. . .	77.55

. . . = Not available.

Table 20-4. Nonfarm Payroll Employment, Hours, and Earnings—Continued

(Wage and salary workers on nonfarm payrolls, seasonally adjusted.)

Year and month	All wage and salary workers (thousands)					Production or nonsupervisory workers on private payrolls							
	Total	Private				Number (thousands)		Average hours per week		Average hourly earnings, dollars		Average weekly earnings, dollars	
		Total	Goods-producing		Service-providing	Total private	Manufac-turing	Total private	Manufac-turing	Total private	Manufac-turing	Total private	Manufac-turing
			Total	Manufac-turing									
1957													
January	52 888	45 268	19 833	15 970	33 055	. . .	12 881	. . .	40.4	. . .	1.90	. . .	76.76
February	53 098	45 452	19 933	15 998	33 165	. . .	12 885	. . .	40.5	. . .	1.91	. . .	77.36
March	53 156	45 484	19 936	15 994	33 220	. . .	12 855	. . .	40.4	. . .	1.92	. . .	77.57
April	53 238	45 537	19 887	15 970	33 351	. . .	12 811	. . .	40.0	. . .	1.91	. . .	76.40
May	53 149	45 436	19 834	15 931	33 315	. . .	12 762	. . .	40.0	. . .	1.92	. . .	76.80
June	53 066	45 364	19 777	15 873	33 289	. . .	12 697	. . .	40.0	. . .	1.92	. . .	76.80
July	53 122	45 368	19 735	15 854	33 387	. . .	12 669	. . .	40.0	. . .	1.93	. . .	77.20
August	53 128	45 371	19 728	15 867	33 400	. . .	12 673	. . .	40.0	. . .	1.94	. . .	77.60
September	52 932	45 183	19 545	15 710	33 387	. . .	12 528	. . .	39.7	. . .	1.95	. . .	77.42
October	52 765	44 997	19 421	15 599	33 344	. . .	12 437	. . .	39.4	. . .	1.96	. . .	77.22
November	52 557	44 788	19 260	15 466	33 297	. . .	12 301	. . .	39.2	. . .	1.96	. . .	76.83
December	52 385	44 539	19 111	15 332	33 274	. . .	12 170	. . .	39.1	. . .	1.95	. . .	76.25
1958													
January	52 077	44 256	18 902	15 130	33 175	. . .	11 969	. . .	38.9	. . .	1.95	. . .	75.86
February	51 576	43 744	18 529	14 908	33 047	. . .	11 757	. . .	38.7	. . .	1.95	. . .	75.47
March	51 300	43 452	18 335	14 670	32 965	. . .	11 532	. . .	38.8	. . .	1.96	. . .	76.05
April	51 026	43 158	18 120	14 506	32 906	. . .	11 373	. . .	38.9	. . .	1.96	. . .	76.24
May	50 913	43 019	18 008	14 414	32 905	. . .	11 294	. . .	38.9	. . .	1.97	. . .	76.63
June	50 912	42 986	17 984	14 408	32 928	. . .	11 300	. . .	39.1	. . .	1.98	. . .	77.42
July	51 037	43 065	18 038	14 450	32 999	. . .	11 349	. . .	39.3	. . .	1.98	. . .	77.81
August	51 233	43 221	18 147	14 524	33 086	. . .	11 412	. . .	39.5	. . .	2.01	. . .	79.40
September	51 506	43 490	18 331	14 658	33 175	. . .	11 556	. . .	39.5	. . .	2.00	. . .	79.00
October	51 485	43 454	18 218	14 503	33 267	. . .	11 394	. . .	39.6	. . .	2.00	. . .	79.20
November	51 943	43 915	18 610	14 827	33 333	. . .	11 702	. . .	39.9	. . .	2.03	. . .	81.00
December	52 088	43 988	18 592	14 877	33 496	. . .	11 743	. . .	39.9	. . .	2.04	. . .	81.40
1959													
January	52 481	44 376	18 796	14 998	33 685	. . .	11 849	. . .	40.2	. . .	2.04	. . .	82.01
February	52 687	44 571	18 890	15 115	33 797	. . .	11 950	. . .	40.3	. . .	2.05	. . .	82.62
March	53 016	44 884	19 069	15 259	33 947	. . .	12 078	. . .	40.4	. . .	2.07	. . .	83.63
April	53 320	45 178	19 269	15 385	34 051	. . .	12 185	. . .	40.5	. . .	2.08	. . .	84.24
May	53 549	45 396	19 378	15 487	34 171	. . .	12 277	. . .	40.7	. . .	2.08	. . .	84.66
June	53 678	45 535	19 462	15 554	34 216	. . .	12 330	. . .	40.6	. . .	2.09	. . .	84.85
July	53 803	45 630	19 529	15 623	34 274	. . .	12 366	. . .	40.3	. . .	2.09	. . .	84.23
August	53 337	45 156	19 049	15 202	34 288	. . .	11 936	. . .	40.4	. . .	2.07	. . .	83.63
September	53 428	45 189	19 052	15 254	34 376	. . .	11 984	. . .	40.4	. . .	2.08	. . .	84.03
October	53 359	45 094	18 925	15 158	34 434	. . .	11 864	. . .	40.1	. . .	2.07	. . .	83.01
November	53 635	45 351	19 108	15 300	34 527	. . .	11 991	. . .	39.9	. . .	2.07	. . .	82.59
December	54 175	45 807	19 425	15 573	34 750	. . .	12 254	. . .	40.3	. . .	2.11	. . .	85.03
1960													
January	54 274	45 967	19 491	15 687	34 783	. . .	12 362	. . .	40.6	. . .	2.13	. . .	86.48
February	54 513	46 187	19 605	15 765	34 908	. . .	12 434	. . .	40.3	. . .	2.14	. . .	86.24
March	54 458	45 933	19 373	15 707	35 085	. . .	12 362	. . .	40.0	. . .	2.14	. . .	85.60
April	54 812	46 278	19 446	15 654	35 366	. . .	12 299	. . .	40.0	. . .	2.14	. . .	85.60
May	54 472	46 040	19 374	15 575	35 098	. . .	12 218	. . .	40.1	. . .	2.14	. . .	85.81
June	54 347	45 915	19 240	15 466	35 107	. . .	12 102	. . .	39.9	. . .	2.14	. . .	85.39
July	54 303	45 861	19 170	15 413	35 133	. . .	12 047	. . .	39.9	. . .	2.14	. . .	85.39
August	54 272	45 800	19 105	15 360	35 167	. . .	11 986	. . .	39.7	. . .	2.15	. . .	85.36
September	54 228	45 734	19 057	15 330	35 171	. . .	11 956	. . .	39.4	. . .	2.16	. . .	85.10
October	54 144	45 642	18 952	15 231	35 192	. . .	11 846	. . .	39.7	. . .	2.16	. . .	85.75
November	53 962	45 446	18 799	15 112	35 163	. . .	11 726	. . .	39.3	. . .	2.15	. . .	84.50
December	53 743	45 146	18 548	14 947	35 195	. . .	11 556	. . .	38.4	. . .	2.16	. . .	82.94
1961													
January	53 683	45 119	18 508	14 863	35 175	. . .	11 473	. . .	39.3	. . .	2.16	. . .	84.89
February	53 556	44 969	18 418	14 801	35 138	. . .	11 414	. . .	39.4	. . .	2.16	. . .	85.10
March	53 662	45 051	18 438	14 802	35 224	. . .	11 410	. . .	39.5	. . .	2.16	. . .	85.32
April	53 626	44 997	18 432	14 825	35 194	. . .	11 444	. . .	39.5	. . .	2.18	. . .	86.11
May	53 783	45 119	18 523	14 932	35 260	. . .	11 544	. . .	39.7	. . .	2.19	. . .	86.94
June	53 977	45 289	18 618	14 981	35 359	. . .	11 593	. . .	40.0	. . .	2.20	. . .	88.00
July	54 124	45 400	18 640	15 029	35 484	. . .	11 639	. . .	40.0	. . .	2.21	. . .	88.40
August	54 299	45 535	18 725	15 093	35 574	. . .	11 701	. . .	40.1	. . .	2.22	. . .	89.02
September	54 387	45 591	18 730	15 080	35 657	. . .	11 679	. . .	39.5	. . .	2.20	. . .	86.90
October	54 521	45 716	18 805	15 143	35 716	. . .	11 731	. . .	40.3	. . .	2.23	. . .	89.87
November	54 743	45 931	18 927	15 259	35 816	. . .	11 842	. . .	40.7	. . .	2.23	. . .	90.76
December	54 871	46 035	18 981	15 309	35 890	. . .	11 872	. . .	40.4	. . .	2.24	. . .	90.50
1962													
January	54 891	46 040	18 936	15 322	35 955	. . .	11 865	. . .	40.0	. . .	2.25	. . .	90.00
February	55 187	46 309	19 109	15 411	36 078	. . .	11 950	. . .	40.4	. . .	2.26	. . .	91.30
March	55 276	46 375	19 109	15 451	36 167	. . .	11 970	. . .	40.6	. . .	2.26	. . .	91.76
April	55 601	46 679	19 258	15 524	36 343	. . .	12 034	. . .	40.6	. . .	2.26	. . .	91.76
May	55 626	46 668	19 253	15 513	36 373	. . .	12 011	. . .	40.6	. . .	2.27	. . .	92.16
June	55 644	46 644	19 186	15 518	36 458	. . .	12 006	. . .	40.5	. . .	2.26	. . .	91.53
July	55 746	46 720	19 248	15 522	36 498	. . .	12 004	. . .	40.5	. . .	2.27	. . .	91.94
August	55 838	46 775	19 251	15 517	36 587	. . .	11 990	. . .	40.5	. . .	2.28	. . .	92.34
September	55 977	46 888	19 305	15 568	36 672	. . .	12 033	. . .	40.5	. . .	2.28	. . .	92.34
October	56 041	46 927	19 301	15 569	36 740	. . .	12 034	. . .	40.3	. . .	2.29	. . .	92.29
November	56 055	46 910	19 260	15 530	36 795	. . .	11 977	. . .	40.5	. . .	2.29	. . .	92.75
December	56 027	46 901	19 219	15 520	36 808	. . .	11 961	. . .	40.3	. . .	2.29	. . .	92.29

. . . = Not available.

Table 20-4. Nonfarm Payroll Employment, Hours, and Earnings—Continued

(Wage and salary workers on nonfarm payrolls, seasonally adjusted.)

Year and month	All wage and salary workers (thousands)					Production or nonsupervisory workers on private payrolls							
	Total	Private				Number (thousands)		Average hours per week		Average hourly earnings, dollars		Average weekly earnings, dollars	
		Total	Goods-producing		Service-providing	Total private	Manufacturing	Total private	Manufacturing	Total private	Manufacturing	Total private	Manufacturing
			Total	Manufacturing									
1963													
January	56 116	46 912	19 257	15 545	36 859	. . .	11 974	. . .	40.5	. . .	2.30	. . .	93.15
February	56 231	47 000	19 228	15 542	37 003	. . .	11 965	. . .	40.5	. . .	2.31	. . .	93.56
March	56 322	47 077	19 233	15 564	37 089	. . .	11 990	. . .	40.5	. . .	2.32	. . .	93.96
April	56 580	47 316	19 343	15 602	37 237	. . .	12 029	. . .	40.5	. . .	2.32	. . .	93.96
May	56 616	47 328	19 399	15 641	37 217	. . .	12 066	. . .	40.5	. . .	2.33	. . .	94.37
June	56 658	47 356	19 371	15 624	37 287	. . .	12 050	. . .	40.7	. . .	2.34	. . .	95.24
July	56 795	47 461	19 423	15 646	37 372	. . .	12 080	. . .	40.6	. . .	2.35	. . .	95.41
August	56 910	47 542	19 437	15 644	37 473	. . .	12 060	. . .	40.6	. . .	2.34	. . .	95.00
September	57 078	47 661	19 483	15 674	37 595	. . .	12 088	. . .	40.6	. . .	2.36	. . .	95.82
October	57 284	47 805	19 517	15 714	37 767	. . .	12 131	. . .	40.7	. . .	2.36	. . .	96.05
November	57 255	47 771	19 456	15 675	37 799	. . .	12 072	. . .	40.7	. . .	2.37	. . .	96.46
December	57 360	47 863	19 493	15 712	37 867	. . .	12 108	. . .	40.6	. . .	2.38	. . .	96.63
1964													
January	57 487	47 925	19 406	15 715	38 081	39 914	12 132	38.2	40.1	2.50	2.38	95.50	95.44
February	57 752	48 171	19 570	15 742	38 182	40 123	12 165	38.5	40.7	2.50	2.38	96.25	96.87
March	57 898	48 287	19 587	15 770	38 311	40 171	12 190	38.5	40.6	2.50	2.38	96.25	96.63
April	57 923	48 279	19 593	15 785	38 330	40 208	12 211	38.6	40.7	2.52	2.40	97.27	97.68
May	58 089	48 419	19 630	15 812	38 459	40 332	12 231	38.6	40.8	2.52	2.40	97.27	97.92
June	58 221	48 552	19 682	15 839	38 539	40 448	12 255	38.6	40.8	2.53	2.41	97.66	98.33
July	58 412	48 735	19 740	15 887	38 672	40 624	12 309	38.5	40.8	2.53	2.41	97.41	98.33
August	58 620	48 888	19 810	15 948	38 810	40 770	12 354	38.5	40.9	2.55	2.42	98.18	98.98
September	58 903	49 117	19 943	16 073	38 960	41 026	12 479	38.5	40.9	2.55	2.44	98.18	99.80
October	58 794	48 949	19 723	15 821	39 071	40 827	12 224	38.5	40.7	2.55	2.40	98.18	97.68
November	59 217	49 338	20 026	16 096	39 191	41 157	12 477	38.6	41.0	2.56	2.42	98.82	99.22
December	59 420	49 523	20 111	16 176	39 309	41 308	12 551	38.7	41.2	2.58	2.44	99.85	100.53
1965													
January	59 583	49 646	20 173	16 245	39 410	41 453	12 603	38.7	41.3	2.58	2.45	99.85	101.19
February	59 800	49 826	20 216	16 291	39 584	41 583	12 644	38.7	41.3	2.59	2.46	100.23	101.60
March	60 003	49 993	20 292	16 353	39 711	41 675	12 701	38.7	41.3	2.60	2.47	100.62	102.01
April	60 258	50 207	20 317	16 418	39 941	41 886	12 752	38.7	41.2	2.60	2.47	100.62	101.76
May	60 492	50 398	20 444	16 477	40 048	42 044	12 792	38.8	41.3	2.62	2.49	101.66	102.84
June	60 690	50 562	20 522	16 554	40 168	42 183	12 854	38.6	41.2	2.62	2.49	101.13	102.59
July	60 963	50 762	20 611	16 669	40 352	42 364	12 962	38.6	41.2	2.63	2.49	101.52	102.59
August	61 228	50 957	20 726	16 732	40 502	42 537	12 994	38.5	41.1	2.64	2.50	101.64	102.75
September	61 490	51 152	20 808	16 802	40 682	42 726	13 046	38.6	41.1	2.65	2.51	102.29	103.16
October	61 718	51 340	20 895	16 864	40 823	42 870	13 100	38.5	41.2	2.66	2.52	102.41	103.82
November	61 997	51 561	21 021	16 962	40 976	43 045	13 175	38.6	41.3	2.67	2.52	103.06	104.08
December	62 321	51 822	21 151	17 051	41 170	43 270	13 243	38.6	41.3	2.68	2.53	103.45	104.49
1966													
January	62 528	51 987	21 214	17 143	41 314	43 401	13 301	38.6	41.5	2.68	2.54	103.45	105.41
February	62 796	52 185	21 315	17 288	41 481	43 552	13 426	38.7	41.7	2.69	2.56	104.10	106.75
March	63 191	52 499	21 515	17 400	41 676	43 801	13 508	38.7	41.6	2.70	2.56	104.49	106.50
April	63 436	52 677	21 568	17 517	41 868	43 959	13 598	38.7	41.8	2.71	2.58	104.88	107.84
May	63 711	52 890	21 675	17 625	42 036	44 138	13 678	38.5	41.5	2.72	2.58	104.72	107.07
June	64 110	53 208	21 846	17 733	42 264	44 390	13 753	38.5	41.4	2.72	2.58	104.72	106.81
July	64 301	53 327	21 872	17 760	42 429	44 484	13 758	38.4	41.2	2.74	2.60	105.22	107.12
August	64 507	53 501	21 972	17 882	42 535	44 596	13 843	38.4	41.4	2.75	2.61	105.60	108.05
September	64 645	53 582	21 948	17 886	42 697	44 659	13 841	38.3	41.2	2.76	2.63	105.71	108.36
October	64 854	53 727	21 991	17 956	42 863	44 789	13 906	38.4	41.3	2.77	2.64	106.37	109.03
November	65 019	53 816	21 988	17 981	43 031	44 834	13 918	38.3	41.2	2.78	2.65	106.47	109.18
December	65 199	53 943	22 008	17 998	43 191	44 916	13 906	38.2	40.9	2.78	2.64	106.20	107.98
1967													
January	65 407	54 092	22 057	18 033	43 350	45 050	13 925	38.3	41.1	2.79	2.65	106.86	108.92
February	65 427	54 074	21 987	17 978	43 440	44 967	13 853	37.9	40.4	2.81	2.67	106.50	107.87
March	65 530	54 133	21 919	17 940	43 611	44 991	13 797	37.9	40.5	2.81	2.67	106.50	108.14
April	65 467	54 032	21 842	17 878	43 625	44 871	13 712	37.8	40.4	2.82	2.68	106.60	108.27
May	65 618	54 144	21 779	17 832	43 839	44 961	13 664	37.8	40.4	2.83	2.69	106.97	108.68
June	65 750	54 216	21 761	17 812	43 989	45 004	13 632	37.8	40.4	2.84	2.69	107.35	108.68
July	65 887	54 343	21 772	17 784	44 115	45 105	13 602	37.8	40.5	2.86	2.71	108.11	109.76
August	66 142	54 552	21 887	17 905	44 255	45 267	13 681	37.8	40.6	2.87	2.73	108.49	110.84
September	66 163	54 540	21 775	17 794	44 388	45 236	13 559	37.8	40.6	2.88	2.73	108.86	110.84
October	66 225	54 583	21 779	17 800	44 446	45 278	13 587	37.8	40.6	2.89	2.74	109.24	111.24
November	66 703	55 008	21 996	17 985	44 707	45 701	13 777	37.9	40.6	2.91	2.75	110.29	111.65
December	66 900	55 165	22 037	18 025	44 863	45 800	13 782	37.7	40.7	2.92	2.77	110.08	112.74
1968													
January	66 805	55 011	21 917	18 040	44 888	45 655	13 798	37.6	40.4	2.94	2.81	110.54	113.52
February	67 214	55 395	22 117	18 054	45 097	45 980	13 793	37.8	40.8	2.95	2.82	111.51	115.06
March	67 296	55 454	22 119	18 067	45 177	46 041	13 803	37.7	40.8	2.97	2.84	111.97	115.87
April	67 555	55 677	22 207	18 131	45 348	46 239	13 858	37.6	40.3	2.98	2.85	112.05	114.86
May	67 652	55 747	22 255	18 190	45 397	46 267	13 900	37.7	40.9	3.00	2.87	113.10	117.38
June	67 904	55 917	22 264	18 228	45 640	46 402	13 921	37.8	40.9	3.01	2.88	113.78	117.79
July	68 126	56 108	22 329	18 265	45 797	46 562	13 953	37.7	40.8	3.03	2.89	114.23	117.91
August	68 338	56 286	22 350	18 254	45 978	46 669	13 903	37.7	40.7	3.03	2.89	114.23	117.62
September	68 487	56 420	22 390	18 252	46 097	46 792	13 914	37.7	40.9	3.06	2.92	115.36	119.43
October	68 720	56 619	22 419	18 293	46 301	46 989	13 974	37.7	41.0	3.07	2.94	115.74	120.54
November	68 985	56 878	22 512	18 346	46 473	47 244	14 028	37.5	40.9	3.09	2.96	115.88	121.06
December	69 245	57 100	22 617	18 410	46 628	47 384	14 044	37.5	40.7	3.11	2.97	116.63	120.88

. . . = Not available.

Table 20-4. Nonfarm Payroll Employment, Hours, and Earnings—Continued

(Wage and salary workers on nonfarm payrolls, seasonally adjusted.)

Year and month	All wage and salary workers (thousands)					Production or nonsupervisory workers on private payrolls							
	Total	Private				Number (thousands)		Average hours per week		Average hourly earnings, dollars		Average weekly earnings, dollars	
		Total	Goods-producing		Service-providing	Total private	Manufacturing	Total private	Manufacturing	Total private	Manufacturing	Total private	Manufacturing
			Total	Manufacturing									
1969													
January	69 438	57 229	22 644	18 432	46 794	47 528	14 086	37.7	40.8	3.12	2.99	117.62	121.99
February	69 698	57 474	22 755	18 502	46 943	47 697	14 134	37.5	40.4	3.14	3.00	117.75	121.20
March	69 906	57 677	22 813	18 558	47 093	47 852	14 169	37.6	40.8	3.15	3.01	118.44	122.81
April	70 072	57 827	22 815	18 554	47 257	47 959	14 144	37.7	41.0	3.17	3.03	119.51	124.23
May	70 328	58 044	22 899	18 588	47 429	48 122	14 161	37.6	40.7	3.19	3.04	119.94	123.73
June	70 636	58 277	22 981	18 640	47 655	48 330	14 206	37.5	40.7	3.20	3.05	120.00	124.14
July	70 730	58 390	22 990	18 642	47 740	48 434	14 194	37.5	40.6	3.22	3.08	120.75	125.05
August	71 005	58 632	23 111	18 767	47 894	48 616	14 287	37.5	40.6	3.24	3.10	121.50	125.86
September	70 918	58 539	22 988	18 620	47 930	48 524	14 159	37.5	40.6	3.26	3.12	122.25	126.67
October	71 119	58 689	22 976	18 613	48 143	48 669	14 174	37.4	40.5	3.28	3.13	122.67	126.77
November	71 088	58 640	22 840	18 467	48 248	48 589	14 035	37.5	40.5	3.29	3.14	123.38	127.17
December	71 240	58 763	22 884	18 485	48 356	48 638	14 013	37.5	40.6	3.30	3.15	123.75	127.89
1970													
January	71 176	58 680	22 726	18 424	48 450	48 564	13 964	37.3	40.4	3.31	3.16	123.46	127.66
February	71 302	58 784	22 747	18 361	48 555	48 600	13 897	37.3	40.2	3.33	3.17	124.21	127.43
March	71 453	58 850	22 738	18 360	48 715	48 690	13 917	37.2	40.1	3.35	3.19	124.62	127.92
April	71 348	58 643	22 552	18 207	48 796	48 479	13 785	37.0	39.8	3.36	3.19	124.32	126.96
May	71 122	58 454	22 336	18 029	48 786	48 287	13 616	37.0	39.8	3.38	3.22	125.06	128.16
June	71 028	58 361	22 241	17 930	48 787	48 226	13 554	36.9	39.8	3.39	3.24	125.09	128.95
July	71 055	58 358	22 195	17 877	48 860	48 242	13 527	37.0	40.0	3.41	3.25	126.17	130.00
August	70 932	58 221	22 105	17 779	48 827	48 089	13 449	37.0	39.8	3.43	3.26	126.91	129.75
September	70 949	58 208	21 988	17 692	48 961	48 101	13 401	36.8	39.6	3.45	3.29	126.96	130.28
October	70 519	57 726	21 477	17 173	49 042	47 619	12 905	36.8	39.5	3.46	3.26	127.33	128.77
November	70 409	57 579	21 345	17 024	49 064	47 466	12 781	36.7	39.5	3.47	3.26	127.35	128.77
December	70 790	57 945	21 673	17 309	49 117	47 778	13 062	36.8	39.5	3.50	3.32	128.80	131.14
1971													
January	70 866	57 988	21 594	17 280	49 272	47 859	13 069	36.8	39.9	3.52	3.36	129.54	134.06
February	70 805	57 928	21 514	17 216	49 291	47 779	13 033	36.7	39.7	3.54	3.39	129.92	134.58
March	70 859	57 951	21 491	17 154	49 368	47 819	12 984	36.7	39.8	3.56	3.39	130.65	134.92
April	71 037	58 092	21 552	17 149	49 485	47 966	12 993	36.8	39.9	3.57	3.41	131.38	136.06
May	71 247	58 277	21 645	17 225	49 602	48 153	13 081	36.7	40.0	3.60	3.43	132.12	137.20
June	71 253	58 245	21 568	17 139	49 685	48 109	13 012	36.8	39.9	3.62	3.45	133.22	137.66
July	71 316	58 305	21 564	17 126	49 752	48 167	13 001	36.7	40.0	3.63	3.46	133.22	138.40
August	71 368	58 327	21 570	17 115	49 798	48 164	12 993	36.7	39.8	3.66	3.48	134.32	138.50
September	71 620	58 552	21 650	17 154	49 970	48 362	13 038	36.7	39.7	3.67	3.48	134.69	138.16
October	71 642	58 527	21 604	17 126	50 038	48 305	13 027	36.8	39.9	3.68	3.50	135.42	139.65
November	71 844	58 696	21 684	17 166	50 160	48 442	13 064	36.9	40.0	3.69	3.49	136.16	139.60
December	72 108	58 918	21 741	17 202	50 367	48 613	13 078	36.9	40.2	3.73	3.55	137.64	142.71
1972													
January	72 445	59 179	21 865	17 283	50 580	49 035	13 173	36.9	40.2	3.80	3.57	140.22	143.51
February	72 652	59 354	21 915	17 361	50 737	49 143	13 235	36.9	40.4	3.82	3.61	140.96	145.84
March	72 945	59 616	22 036	17 447	50 909	49 437	13 316	36.9	40.4	3.84	3.63	141.70	146.65
April	73 163	59 805	22 099	17 508	51 064	49 561	13 373	36.9	40.5	3.86	3.65	142.43	147.83
May	73 467	60 051	22 222	17 602	51 245	49 745	13 451	36.8	40.5	3.87	3.67	142.42	148.64
June	73 760	60 355	22 282	17 641	51 478	49 997	13 475	36.9	40.6	3.88	3.68	143.17	149.41
July	73 709	60 227	22 162	17 556	51 547	49 842	13 387	36.8	40.5	3.90	3.69	143.52	149.45
August	74 137	60 607	22 400	17 741	51 737	50 156	13 562	36.8	40.6	3.92	3.73	144.26	151.44
September	74 268	60 693	22 456	17 774	51 812	50 224	13 572	36.9	40.6	3.94	3.75	145.39	152.25
October	74 672	61 066	22 613	17 893	52 059	50 552	13 681	37.0	40.7	3.97	3.78	146.89	153.85
November	74 965	61 322	22 688	18 005	52 277	50 790	13 783	36.9	40.7	3.98	3.79	146.86	154.25
December	75 270	61 586	22 772	18 158	52 498	51 054	13 902	36.8	40.6	4.01	3.83	147.57	155.50
1973													
January	75 620	61 930	22 955	18 276	52 665	51 349	14 006	36.8	40.4	4.03	3.86	148.30	155.94
February	76 017	62 306	23 160	18 410	52 857	51 686	14 127	36.9	40.9	4.04	3.87	149.08	158.28
March	76 286	62 541	23 262	18 493	53 024	51 901	14 181	37.0	40.9	4.06	3.88	150.22	158.69
April	76 456	62 679	23 316	18 530	53 140	51 982	14 192	36.9	40.8	4.08	3.91	150.55	159.53
May	76 646	62 829	23 382	18 564	53 264	52 082	14 217	36.9	40.7	4.10	3.93	151.29	159.95
June	76 886	63 014	23 485	18 606	53 401	52 234	14 253	36.9	40.7	4.12	3.95	152.03	160.77
July	76 911	63 046	23 522	18 598	53 389	52 238	14 232	36.9	40.7	4.15	3.98	153.14	161.99
August	77 166	63 262	23 559	18 629	53 607	52 393	14 251	36.9	40.6	4.16	4.00	153.50	162.40
September	77 281	63 389	23 548	18 609	53 733	52 410	14 213	36.8	40.7	4.19	4.03	154.19	164.02
October	77 605	63 628	23 641	18 702	53 964	52 655	14 289	36.7	40.6	4.21	4.05	154.51	164.43
November	77 909	63 874	23 719	18 773	54 190	52 847	14 342	36.9	40.6	4.23	4.07	156.09	165.24
December	78 035	63 965	23 779	18 820	54 256	52 954	14 386	36.7	40.6	4.25	4.09	155.98	166.05
1974													
January	78 104	64 014	23 709	18 788	54 395	52 896	14 340	36.6	40.5	4.26	4.10	155.92	166.05
February	78 253	64 118	23 718	18 727	54 535	52 971	14 269	36.6	40.4	4.29	4.13	157.01	166.85
March	78 295	64 143	23 687	18 700	54 608	52 951	14 223	36.6	40.4	4.31	4.15	157.75	167.66
April	78 384	64 193	23 670	18 702	54 714	53 003	14 225	36.4	39.5	4.34	4.16	157.98	164.32
May	78 547	64 326	23 635	18 688	54 912	53 095	14 199	36.5	40.3	4.39	4.25	160.24	171.28
June	78 602	64 363	23 591	18 690	55 011	53 107	14 197	36.5	40.2	4.43	4.30	161.70	172.86
July	78 634	64 346	23 462	18 656	55 172	53 044	14 152	36.5	40.1	4.45	4.33	162.43	173.63
August	78 619	64 291	23 396	18 570	55 223	53 025	14 089	36.5	40.2	4.49	4.38	163.89	176.08
September	78 614	64 192	23 274	18 492	55 340	52 915	14 025	36.4	40.0	4.53	4.42	164.89	176.80
October	78 627	64 143	23 118	18 364	55 509	52 836	13 884	36.3	40.0	4.56	4.48	165.53	179.20
November	78 259	63 727	22 773	18 077	55 486	52 413	13 607	36.1	39.5	4.57	4.49	164.98	177.36
December	77 657	63 098	22 303	17 693	55 354	51 856	13 259	36.1	39.3	4.60	4.52	166.06	177.64

Table 20-4. Nonfarm Payroll Employment, Hours, and Earnings—Continued

(Wage and salary workers on nonfarm payrolls, seasonally adjusted.)

Year and month	All wage and salary workers (thousands)					Production or nonsupervisory workers on private payrolls							
	Total	Private				Number (thousands)		Average hours per week		Average hourly earnings, dollars		Average weekly earnings, dollars	
		Total	Goods-producing		Service-providing	Total private	Manufac-turing	Total private	Manufac-turing	Total private	Manufac-turing	Total private	Manufac-turing
			Total	Manufac-turing									
1975													
January	77 297	62 673	21 974	17 344	55 323	51 439	12 933	36.1	39.2	4.61	4.54	166.42	177.97
February	76 919	62 172	21 512	17 004	55 407	50 934	12 622	35.9	38.9	4.63	4.58	166.22	178.16
March	76 649	61 895	21 274	16 853	55 375	50 666	12 483	35.7	38.8	4.66	4.63	166.36	179.64
April	76 463	61 668	21 109	16 759	55 354	50 439	12 407	35.8	39.0	4.66	4.63	166.83	180.57
May	76 623	61 796	21 097	16 746	55 526	50 558	12 406	35.9	39.0	4.68	4.65	168.01	181.35
June	76 519	61 735	21 018	16 690	55 501	50 537	12 371	35.9	39.2	4.72	4.68	169.45	183.46
July	76 768	61 907	20 981	16 678	55 787	50 726	12 374	35.9	39.4	4.73	4.71	169.81	185.57
August	77 154	62 284	21 176	16 824	55 978	51 070	12 538	36.1	39.7	4.77	4.75	172.20	188.58
September	77 232	62 408	21 284	16 904	55 948	51 183	12 617	36.1	39.8	4.79	4.78	172.92	190.24
October	77 535	62 635	21 384	16 984	56 151	51 376	12 687	36.1	39.9	4.81	4.80	173.64	191.52
November	77 679	62 776	21 442	17 025	56 237	51 458	12 700	36.1	39.9	4.85	4.83	175.09	192.72
December	78 017	63 071	21 602	17 140	56 415	51 759	12 811	36.2	40.2	4.87	4.86	176.29	195.37
1976													
January	78 506	63 537	21 799	17 287	56 707	52 182	12 945	36.3	40.3	4.89	4.90	177.51	197.47
February	78 817	63 836	21 893	17 384	56 924	52 430	13 030	36.3	40.4	4.93	4.94	178.96	199.58
March	79 049	64 062	21 980	17 470	57 069	52 615	13 092	36.0	40.2	4.95	4.98	178.20	200.20
April	79 293	64 308	22 050	17 541	57 243	52 810	13 160	36.0	39.6	4.97	4.98	178.92	197.21
May	79 311	64 340	21 988	17 513	57 323	52 802	13 130	36.1	40.3	5.01	5.04	180.86	203.11
June	79 376	64 413	21 982	17 521	57 394	52 830	13 121	36.1	40.2	5.03	5.07	181.58	203.81
July	79 546	64 553	21 988	17 558	57 558	52 973	13 124	36.1	40.3	5.06	5.11	182.67	205.93
August	79 704	64 697	22 038	17 596	57 666	53 072	13 195	36.0	40.2	5.11	5.16	183.96	207.43
September	79 892	64 921	22 142	17 665	57 750	53 268	13 253	36.0	40.2	5.14	5.20	185.04	209.04
October	79 905	64 877	22 037	17 548	57 868	53 165	13 109	35.9	40.0	5.16	5.19	185.24	207.60
November	80 237	65 164	22 207	17 682	58 030	53 362	13 199	35.9	40.1	5.20	5.25	186.68	210.53
December	80 448	65 373	22 261	17 719	58 187	53 543	13 230	35.9	39.9	5.22	5.29	187.40	211.07
1977													
January	80 692	65 636	22 320	17 803	58 372	53 756	13 305	35.6	39.4	5.25	5.35	186.90	210.79
February	80 987	65 931	22 478	17 843	58 509	54 016	13 331	36.0	40.2	5.29	5.36	190.44	215.47
March	81 391	66 341	22 672	17 941	58 719	54 390	13 424	35.9	40.3	5.32	5.40	190.99	217.62
April	81 730	66 655	22 807	18 024	58 923	54 670	13 490	36.0	40.4	5.36	5.45	192.96	220.18
May	82 089	66 957	22 919	18 107	59 170	54 940	13 567	36.0	40.5	5.39	5.49	194.04	222.35
June	82 488	67 281	23 046	18 192	59 442	55 195	13 622	36.0	40.5	5.42	5.54	195.12	224.37
July	82 836	67 537	23 106	18 259	59 730	55 395	13 670	35.9	40.4	5.45	5.58	195.66	225.43
August	83 074	67 746	23 124	18 276	59 950	55 543	13 679	35.9	40.4	5.47	5.61	196.37	226.64
September	83 532	68 129	23 244	18 334	60 288	55 859	13 714	35.9	40.4	5.50	5.65	197.45	228.26
October	83 794	68 331	23 279	18 356	60 515	56 004	13 722	36.0	40.6	5.55	5.69	199.80	231.01
November	84 173	68 658	23 371	18 419	60 802	56 281	13 771	35.9	40.5	5.58	5.72	200.32	231.66
December	84 408	68 870	23 371	18 531	61 037	56 466	13 861	35.8	40.4	5.60	5.75	200.48	232.30
1978													
January	84 595	68 984	23 374	18 593	61 221	56 547	13 917	35.3	39.5	5.65	5.83	199.45	230.29
February	84 948	69 277	23 453	18 639	61 495	56 768	13 950	35.6	39.9	5.68	5.86	202.21	233.81
March	85 461	69 730	23 649	18 699	61 812	57 176	13 992	35.8	40.5	5.72	5.88	204.78	238.14
April	86 163	70 366	24 008	18 772	62 155	57 709	14 037	35.8	40.4	5.78	5.93	206.92	239.57
May	86 509	70 675	24 082	18 848	62 427	57 941	14 096	35.8	40.4	5.81	5.96	208.00	240.78
June	86 951	71 099	24 238	18 919	62 713	58 263	14 129	35.9	40.6	5.86	6.01	210.37	244.01
July	87 205	71 304	24 300	18 951	62 905	58 422	14 152	35.9	40.6	5.89	6.06	211.45	246.04
August	87 481	71 590	24 374	19 006	63 107	58 626	14 187	35.8	40.5	5.92	6.09	211.94	246.65
September	87 618	71 799	24 444	19 068	63 174	58 819	14 241	35.8	40.5	5.96	6.15	213.37	249.08
October	87 954	72 096	24 548	19 142	63 406	59 017	14 291	35.8	40.5	6.02	6.20	215.52	251.10
November	88 391	72 497	24 678	19 257	63 713	59 397	14 388	35.7	40.6	6.05	6.26	215.99	254.16
December	88 674	72 763	24 758	19 334	63 916	59 599	14 459	35.7	40.5	6.09	6.31	217.41	255.56
1979													
January	88 811	72 874	24 740	19 388	64 071	59 659	14 497	35.6	40.4	6.13	6.36	218.23	256.94
February	89 054	73 107	24 784	19 409	64 270	59 840	14 501	35.7	40.5	6.17	6.40	220.27	259.20
March	89 480	73 524	24 998	19 453	64 482	60 216	14 526	35.8	40.6	6.21	6.45	222.32	261.87
April	89 418	73 441	24 958	19 450	64 460	60 067	14 515	35.3	39.3	6.21	6.43	219.21	252.70
May	89 790	73 800	25 071	19 509	64 719	60 368	14 551	35.6	40.2	6.27	6.52	223.21	262.10
June	90 108	74 063	25 161	19 553	64 947	60 583	14 566	35.6	40.2	6.31	6.56	224.64	263.71
July	90 214	74 064	25 163	19 531	65 051	60 558	14 536	35.6	40.2	6.35	6.59	226.06	264.92
August	90 296	74 067	25 059	19 406	65 237	60 516	14 397	35.6	40.1	6.39	6.63	227.48	265.86
September	90 323	74 195	25 088	19 442	65 235	60 629	14 440	35.6	40.1	6.44	6.67	229.26	267.47
October	90 480	74 344	25 038	19 390	65 442	60 746	14 384	35.6	40.2	6.46	6.71	229.98	269.74
November	90 574	74 401	24 947	19 299	65 627	60 778	14 295	35.6	40.1	6.50	6.74	231.40	270.27
December	90 669	74 489	24 970	19 301	65 699	60 860	14 300	35.5	40.1	6.56	6.80	232.88	272.68
1980													
January	90 800	74 599	24 949	19 282	65 851	60 896	14 241	35.4	40.0	6.56	6.82	232.22	272.80
February	90 879	74 653	24 874	19 219	66 005	60 964	14 170	35.4	40.1	6.62	6.88	234.35	275.89
March	90 991	74 695	24 818	19 217	66 173	60 987	14 165	35.3	39.9	6.69	6.95	236.16	277.31
April	90 846	74 263	24 507	18 973	66 339	60 540	13 914	35.2	39.8	6.71	6.97	236.19	277.41
May	90 415	73 961	24 234	18 726	66 181	60 194	13 632	35.1	39.3	6.75	7.02	236.93	275.89
June	90 095	73 654	23 968	18 490	66 127	59 892	13 405	35.0	39.2	6.81	7.10	238.35	278.32
July	89 832	73 414	23 698	18 276	66 134	59 693	13 227	34.9	39.1	6.85	7.16	239.07	279.96
August	90 092	73 682	23 860	18 414	66 232	59 908	13 349	35.1	39.5	6.90	7.24	242.19	285.98
September	90 205	73 875	23 931	18 445	66 274	60 075	13 396	35.1	39.6	6.94	7.30	243.59	289.08
October	90 485	74 099	24 012	18 506	66 473	60 239	13 437	35.2	39.8	7.01	7.38	246.75	293.72
November	90 741	74 350	24 123	18 601	66 618	60 449	13 528	35.3	39.9	7.08	7.47	249.92	298.05
December	90 936	74 563	24 182	18 640	66 754	60 606	13 550	35.3	40.1	7.12	7.52	251.34	301.55

Table 20-4. Nonfarm Payroll Employment, Hours, and Earnings—Continued

(Wage and salary workers on nonfarm payrolls, seasonally adjusted.)

Year and month	All wage and salary workers (thousands)					Production or nonsupervisory workers on private payrolls							
	Total	Private				Number (thousands)		Average hours per week		Average hourly earnings, dollars		Average weekly earnings, dollars	
		Total	Goods-producing		Service-providing	Total private	Manufac-turing	Total private	Manufac-turing	Total private	Manufac-turing	Total private	Manufac-turing
			Total	Manufac-turing									
1981													
January	91 031	74 671	24 152	18 639	66 879	60 710	13 545	35.4	40.1	7.18	7.58	254.17	303.96
February	91 098	74 752	24 118	18 613	66 980	60 736	13 518	35.2	39.8	7.22	7.62	254.14	303.28
March	91 202	74 910	24 203	18 647	66 999	60 875	13 550	35.3	40.0	7.28	7.68	256.98	307.20
April	91 276	75 016	24 151	18 711	67 125	60 973	13 594	35.3	40.1	7.32	7.76	258.40	311.18
May	91 286	75 088	24 148	18 766	67 138	60 973	13 633	35.3	40.2	7.36	7.81	259.81	313.96
June	91 482	75 323	24 290	18 789	67 192	61 134	13 632	35.2	40.0	7.41	7.85	260.83	314.00
July	91 594	75 419	24 302	18 785	67 292	61 222	13 629	35.2	39.9	7.45	7.89	262.24	314.81
August	91 558	75 448	24 258	18 748	67 300	61 216	13 573	35.2	40.0	7.52	7.97	264.70	318.80
September	91 471	75 440	24 210	18 712	67 261	61 235	13 565	35.0	39.6	7.56	8.03	264.60	317.99
October	91 371	75 302	24 051	18 566	67 320	61 066	13 399	35.1	39.6	7.58	8.06	266.06	319.18
November	91 162	75 084	23 875	18 409	67 287	60 817	13 235	35.1	39.4	7.63	8.08	267.81	318.35
December	90 884	74 811	23 656	18 223	67 228	60 511	13 033	34.9	39.2	7.63	8.09	266.29	317.13
1982													
January	90 557	74 516	23 362	18 047	67 195	60 206	12 874	34.1	37.3	7.71	8.26	262.91	308.10
February	90 551	74 540	23 361	17 981	67 190	60 277	12 831	35.1	39.6	7.72	8.21	270.97	325.12
March	90 422	74 398	23 214	17 857	67 208	60 140	12 727	34.9	39.1	7.75	8.24	270.48	322.18
April	90 141	74 131	22 996	17 683	67 145	59 867	12 566	34.8	39.1	7.76	8.28	270.05	323.75
May	90 096	74 093	22 884	17 588	67 212	59 840	12 506	34.8	39.1	7.82	8.33	272.14	325.70
June	89 853	73 837	22 643	17 430	67 210	59 589	12 365	34.8	39.2	7.84	8.37	272.83	328.10
July	89 510	73 620	22 434	17 278	67 076	59 411	12 261	34.8	39.2	7.88	8.40	274.22	329.28
August	89 352	73 422	22 268	17 160	67 084	59 203	12 153	34.7	39.0	7.93	8.43	275.17	328.77
September	89 171	73 248	22 146	17 074	67 025	59 069	12 104	34.8	39.0	7.93	8.45	275.96	329.55
October	88 894	72 938	21 879	16 853	67 015	58 750	11 880	34.6	38.9	7.95	8.44	275.07	328.32
November	88 770	72 793	21 736	16 722	67 034	58 613	11 766	34.6	39.0	7.97	8.46	275.76	329.94
December	88 756	72 775	21 688	16 690	67 068	58 585	11 746	34.7	39.0	8.01	8.49	277.95	331.11
1983													
January	88 981	72 958	21 757	16 705	67 224	58 813	11 783	34.8	39.3	8.05	8.52	280.14	334.84
February	88 903	72 899	21 676	16 706	67 227	58 792	11 794	34.5	39.3	8.09	8.59	279.11	337.59
March	89 076	73 071	21 649	16 711	67 427	58 958	11 817	34.7	39.6	8.09	8.59	280.72	340.16
April	89 352	73 362	21 729	16 794	67 623	59 201	11 894	34.8	39.7	8.12	8.61	282.58	341.82
May	89 629	73 624	21 829	16 885	67 800	59 444	11 987	34.9	40.0	8.16	8.64	284.78	345.60
June	90 007	73 987	21 949	16 960	68 058	59 806	12 054	34.9	40.1	8.18	8.66	285.48	347.27
July	90 425	74 414	22 103	17 059	68 322	60 189	12 155	34.9	40.3	8.22	8.71	286.88	351.01
August	90 117	74 101	22 207	17 118	67 910	59 820	12 200	34.9	40.3	8.19	8.71	285.83	351.01
September	91 231	75 189	22 381	17 255	68 850	60 849	12 318	35.0	40.6	8.25	8.76	288.75	355.66
October	91 502	75 516	22 546	17 367	68 956	61 095	12 408	35.2	40.6	8.30	8.80	292.16	357.28
November	91 854	75 857	22 698	17 479	69 156	61 378	12 503	35.1	40.6	8.31	8.84	291.68	358.90
December	92 210	76 202	22 803	17 551	69 407	61 664	12 553	35.1	40.5	8.32	8.87	292.03	359.24
1984													
January	92 657	76 647	22 942	17 630	69 715	61 906	12 617	35.1	40.6	8.37	8.91	293.79	361.75
February	93 136	77 111	23 146	17 728	69 990	62 329	12 703	35.3	41.1	8.36	8.92	295.11	366.61
March	93 411	77 381	23 209	17 806	70 202	62 516	12 768	35.1	40.7	8.40	8.96	294.84	364.67
April	93 774	77 699	23 305	17 872	70 469	62 801	12 814	35.2	40.8	8.44	8.98	297.09	366.38
May	94 082	77 979	23 389	17 916	70 693	63 012	12 840	35.1	40.7	8.43	8.99	295.89	365.89
June	94 461	78 334	23 497	17 967	70 964	63 296	12 871	35.1	40.6	8.47	9.03	297.30	366.62
July	94 773	78 601	23 571	18 013	71 202	63 517	12 901	35.1	40.6	8.51	9.05	298.70	367.43
August	95 014	78 790	23 608	18 034	71 406	63 654	12 906	35.0	40.5	8.51	9.09	297.85	368.15
September	95 325	79 070	23 617	18 019	71 708	63 874	12 880	35.1	40.5	8.55	9.12	300.11	369.36
October	95 611	79 337	23 626	18 024	71 985	64 083	12 868	34.9	40.5	8.54	9.15	298.05	370.58
November	95 960	79 649	23 639	18 016	72 321	64 325	12 846	35.0	40.4	8.56	9.19	299.60	371.28
December	96 087	79 805	23 673	18 023	72 414	64 441	12 848	35.1	40.5	8.60	9.22	301.86	373.41
1985													
January	96 353	80 017	23 672	18 009	72 681	64 657	12 833	34.9	40.3	8.60	9.27	300.14	373.58
February	96 477	80 128	23 621	17 966	72 856	64 758	12 784	34.8	40.1	8.63	9.29	300.32	372.53
March	96 823	80 428	23 661	17 939	73 162	65 007	12 758	34.9	40.4	8.66	9.32	302.23	376.53
April	97 018	80 588	23 644	17 886	73 374	65 113	12 701	34.9	40.5	8.68	9.35	302.93	378.68
May	97 292	80 818	23 632	17 855	73 660	65 307	12 673	34.9	40.4	8.69	9.37	303.28	378.55
June	97 437	80 939	23 592	17 819	73 845	65 382	12 635	34.9	40.5	8.73	9.39	304.68	380.30
July	97 626	81 006	23 549	17 776	74 077	65 432	12 596	34.8	40.4	8.73	9.42	303.80	380.57
August	97 819	81 200	23 546	17 756	74 273	65 615	12 593	34.8	40.6	8.76	9.43	304.85	382.86
September	98 023	81 385	23 528	17 718	74 495	65 750	12 556	34.8	40.6	8.79	9.44	305.89	383.26
October	98 210	81 556	23 529	17 708	74 681	65 917	12 556	34.8	40.7	8.78	9.46	305.54	385.02
November	98 419	81 745	23 520	17 697	74 899	66 069	12 545	34.8	40.7	8.81	9.49	306.59	386.24
December	98 587	81 893	23 518	17 693	75 069	66 197	12 550	34.9	40.9	8.86	9.55	309.21	390.60
1986													
January	98 710	81 995	23 530	17 686	75 180	66 293	12 546	35.0	40.7	8.84	9.53	309.40	387.87
February	98 817	82 058	23 485	17 663	75 332	66 365	12 530	34.8	40.7	8.87	9.56	308.68	389.09
March	98 910	82 155	23 428	17 624	75 482	66 403	12 498	34.8	40.7	8.88	9.58	309.02	389.91
April	99 098	82 333	23 427	17 616	75 671	66 531	12 495	34.7	40.5	8.88	9.56	308.14	387.18
May	99 223	82 433	23 349	17 593	75 874	66 606	12 474	34.8	40.7	8.89	9.59	309.37	390.31
June	99 130	82 351	23 263	17 530	75 867	66 533	12 424	34.7	40.7	8.90	9.58	308.83	389.91
July	99 448	82 669	23 235	17 497	76 213	66 810	12 389	34.6	40.6	8.91	9.60	308.29	389.76
August	99 561	82 761	23 225	17 489	76 336	66 909	12 399	34.7	40.7	8.93	9.61	309.87	391.13
September	99 907	82 997	23 216	17 498	76 691	67 108	12 411	34.6	40.7	8.93	9.60	308.98	390.72
October	100 094	83 125	23 208	17 477	76 886	67 206	12 396	34.6	40.6	8.95	9.62	309.67	390.57
November	100 280	83 275	23 204	17 472	77 076	67 344	12 407	34.7	40.7	8.99	9.64	311.95	392.35
December	100 484	83 463	23 237	17 478	77 247	67 493	12 425	34.6	40.8	9.00	9.66	311.40	394.13

Table 20-4. Nonfarm Payroll Employment, Hours, and Earnings—Continued

(Wage and salary workers on nonfarm payrolls, seasonally adjusted.)

Year and month	All wage and salary workers (thousands)					Production or nonsupervisory workers on private payrolls							
	Total	Private				Number (thousands)		Average hours per week		Average hourly earnings, dollars		Average weekly earnings, dollars	
		Total	Goods-producing		Service-providing	Total private	Manufac-turing	Total private	Manufac-turing	Total private	Manufac-turing	Total private	Manufac-turing
			Total	Manufac-turing									
1987													
January	100 655	83 610	23 232	17 465	77 423	67 614	12 405	34.7	40.8	9.01	9.67	312.65	394.54
February	100 887	83 851	23 296	17 499	77 591	67 845	12 438	34.9	41.2	9.04	9.69	315.50	399.23
March	101 136	84 072	23 307	17 507	77 829	67 991	12 446	34.7	41.0	9.06	9.71	314.38	398.11
April	101 474	84 365	23 342	17 525	78 132	68 237	12 465	34.7	40.8	9.07	9.71	314.73	396.17
May	101 701	84 589	23 390	17 542	78 311	68 426	12 481	34.8	41.0	9.10	9.73	316.68	398.93
June	101 872	84 748	23 390	17 537	78 482	68 552	12 482	34.7	40.9	9.10	9.74	315.77	398.37
July	102 218	85 058	23 455	17 593	78 763	68 798	12 521	34.7	41.0	9.11	9.74	316.12	399.34
August	102 388	85 216	23 506	17 630	78 882	68 926	12 560	34.9	40.9	9.17	9.80	320.03	400.82
September	102 617	85 482	23 566	17 691	79 051	69 139	12 614	34.7	40.8	9.18	9.85	318.55	401.88
October	103 109	85 840	23 655	17 729	79 454	69 416	12 637	34.8	41.1	9.21	9.84	320.51	404.42
November	103 340	86 041	23 711	17 775	79 629	69 594	12 678	34.8	41.0	9.26	9.87	322.25	404.67
December	103 634	86 287	23 772	17 809	79 862	69 826	12 707	34.6	41.0	9.27	9.89	320.74	405.49
1988													
January	103 728	86 363	23 668	17 790	80 060	69 833	12 684	34.6	41.1	9.28	9.91	321.09	407.30
February	104 180	86 791	23 769	17 823	80 411	70 228	12 706	34.7	41.1	9.28	9.92	322.02	407.71
March	104 456	87 009	23 824	17 844	80 632	70 371	12 712	34.5	40.9	9.30	9.94	320.85	406.55
April	104 701	87 249	23 880	17 874	80 821	70 578	12 733	34.6	41.0	9.35	9.99	323.51	409.59
May	104 928	87 447	23 896	17 892	81 032	70 693	12 747	34.6	41.0	9.40	10.02	325.24	410.82
June	105 291	87 776	23 951	17 916	81 340	71 000	12 767	34.6	41.1	9.41	10.04	325.59	412.64
July	105 514	88 020	23 966	17 926	81 548	71 210	12 774	34.7	41.1	9.44	10.05	327.57	413.06
August	105 635	88 091	23 926	17 891	81 709	71 273	12 752	34.5	40.9	9.45	10.07	326.03	411.86
September	105 975	88 341	23 942	17 914	82 033	71 456	12 764	34.5	41.0	9.50	10.12	327.75	414.92
October	106 243	88 573	23 987	17 966	82 256	71 649	12 812	34.7	41.1	9.55	10.16	331.39	417.58
November	106 582	88 836	24 030	18 003	82 552	71 872	12 851	34.5	41.1	9.57	10.19	330.17	418.81
December	106 871	89 135	24 054	18 025	82 817	72 144	12 864	34.6	40.9	9.59	10.20	331.81	417.18
1989													
January	107 133	89 359	24 097	18 057	83 036	72 361	12 882	34.7	41.1	9.64	10.23	334.51	420.45
February	107 391	89 579	24 080	18 055	83 311	72 545	12 880	34.5	41.2	9.67	10.26	333.62	422.71
March	107 583	89 761	24 069	18 060	83 514	72 663	12 878	34.5	41.1	9.69	10.29	334.31	422.92
April	107 756	89 916	24 100	18 055	83 656	72 788	12 867	34.6	41.1	9.74	10.28	337.00	422.51
May	107 874	89 998	24 089	18 040	83 785	72 826	12 852	34.4	41.0	9.72	10.30	334.37	422.30
June	107 991	90 079	24 052	18 013	83 939	72 906	12 822	34.4	40.9	9.76	10.33	335.74	422.50
July	108 030	90 125	24 027	17 980	84 003	72 943	12 790	34.5	40.9	9.81	10.36	338.45	423.72
August	108 077	90 088	24 048	17 964	84 029	72 931	12 790	34.5	40.9	9.82	10.39	338.79	424.95
September	108 326	90 299	24 000	17 922	84 326	73 080	12 745	34.4	40.8	9.86	10.41	339.18	424.73
October	108 437	90 404	23 997	17 895	84 440	73 176	12 723	34.6	40.8	9.92	10.43	343.23	425.54
November	108 714	90 657	24 009	17 886	84 705	73 392	12 713	34.4	40.7	9.92	10.44	341.25	424.91
December	108 809	90 734	23 949	17 881	84 860	73 468	12 705	34.3	40.5	9.97	10.49	341.97	424.85
1990													
January	109 144	90 993	23 981	17 796	85 163	73 701	12 739	34.4	40.5	10.00	10.51	344.00	425.66
February	109 397	91 220	24 074	17 896	85 323	73 901	12 848	34.3	40.6	10.06	10.64	345.06	431.98
March	109 618	91 324	24 025	17 870	85 593	73 963	12 823	34.4	40.7	10.10	10.70	347.44	435.49
April	109 652	91 275	23 966	17 845	85 686	73 928	12 806	34.3	40.6	10.12	10.68	347.12	433.61
May	109 801	91 202	23 887	17 796	85 914	73 839	12 755	34.3	40.6	10.14	10.74	347.80	436.04
June	109 820	91 264	23 847	17 774	85 973	73 824	12 736	34.4	40.7	10.19	10.77	350.54	438.34
July	109 773	91 213	23 746	17 704	86 027	73 773	12 675	34.3	40.6	10.21	10.81	350.20	438.89
August	109 569	91 112	23 646	17 647	85 923	73 705	12 622	34.2	40.5	10.23	10.80	349.87	437.40
September	109 485	91 048	23 572	17 610	85 913	73 606	12 601	34.2	40.5	10.27	10.87	351.23	440.24
October	109 321	90 878	23 470	17 574	85 851	73 466	12 576	34.1	40.4	10.29	10.92	350.89	441.17
November	109 175	90 725	23 283	17 428	85 892	73 316	12 439	34.2	40.2	10.31	10.89	352.60	437.78
December	109 118	90 650	23 203	17 395	85 915	73 250	12 413	34.2	40.3	10.33	10.93	353.29	440.48
1991													
January	108 998	90 524	23 060	17 329	85 938	73 103	12 351	34.1	40.2	10.36	10.97	353.28	440.99
February	108 698	90 216	22 903	17 214	85 795	72 815	12 243	34.1	40.1	10.38	10.98	353.96	440.30
March	108 542	90 054	22 780	17 141	85 762	72 666	12 191	34.0	40.0	10.40	11.00	353.60	440.00
April	108 325	89 840	22 687	17 093	85 638	72 496	12 158	34.0	40.1	10.44	11.03	354.96	442.30
May	108 203	89 705	22 617	17 069	85 586	72 395	12 142	34.0	40.1	10.47	11.08	355.98	444.31
June	108 283	89 722	22 569	17 042	85 714	72 417	12 134	34.1	40.5	10.51	11.13	358.39	450.77
July	108 233	89 635	22 508	17 016	85 725	72 383	12 132	34.1	40.5	10.53	11.17	359.07	452.39
August	108 252	89 685	22 493	17 025	85 759	72 435	12 151	34.1	40.6	10.54	11.18	359.41	453.91
September	108 285	89 742	22 467	17 011	85 818	72 453	12 143	34.1	40.6	10.57	11.22	360.44	455.53
October	108 293	89 700	22 416	16 997	85 877	72 421	12 138	34.2	40.6	10.58	11.25	361.84	456.75
November	108 235	89 608	22 315	16 960	85 920	72 350	12 103	34.1	40.6	10.60	11.26	361.46	457.16
December	108 261	89 620	22 274	16 916	85 987	72 394	12 074	34.1	40.7	10.63	11.26	362.48	458.28
1992													
January	108 313	89 625	22 213	16 839	86 100	72 422	12 009	34.1	40.6	10.63	11.24	362.48	456.34
February	108 242	89 553	22 144	16 831	86 098	72 406	12 018	34.1	40.7	10.66	11.30	363.51	459.91
March	108 301	89 586	22 127	16 805	86 174	72 421	12 006	34.1	40.7	10.69	11.33	364.53	461.13
April	108 457	89 718	22 131	16 830	86 326	72 570	12 029	34.3	40.9	10.71	11.36	367.35	464.62
May	108 584	89 831	22 134	16 834	86 450	72 684	12 045	34.2	40.9	10.73	11.39	366.97	465.85
June	108 640	89 878	22 096	16 825	86 544	72 725	12 041	34.1	40.8	10.75	11.41	366.58	465.53
July	108 714	89 897	22 077	16 822	86 637	72 731	12 047	34.2	40.8	10.77	11.43	368.33	466.34
August	108 851	89 968	22 044	16 782	86 807	72 815	12 020	34.2	40.8	10.81	11.47	369.70	467.98
September	108 888	90 059	22 021	16 762	86 867	72 921	12 005	34.3	40.8	10.81	11.46	370.78	467.57
October	109 061	90 233	22 028	16 750	87 033	73 076	12 001	34.2	40.8	10.84	11.47	370.73	467.98
November	109 205	90 364	22 042	16 758	87 163	73 219	12 008	34.2	40.9	10.86	11.49	371.41	469.94
December	109 418	90 540	22 075	16 768	87 343	73 411	12 029	34.2	40.9	10.88	11.51	372.10	470.76

Table 20-4. Nonfarm Payroll Employment, Hours, and Earnings—Continued

(Wage and salary workers on nonfarm payrolls, seasonally adjusted.)

Year and month	All wage and salary workers (thousands)					Production or nonsupervisory workers on private payrolls							
	Total	Private				Number (thousands)		Average hours per week		Average hourly earnings, dollars		Average weekly earnings, dollars	
		Total	Goods-producing		Service-providing	Total private	Manufacturing	Total private	Manufacturing	Total private	Manufacturing	Total private	Manufacturing
			Total	Manufacturing									
1993													
January	109 725	90 824	22 132	16 790	87 593	73 678	12 056	34.3	41.1	10.92	11.55	374.56	474.71
February	109 962	91 060	22 189	16 806	87 773	73 940	12 075	34.3	41.1	10.93	11.58	374.90	475.94
March	109 916	91 009	22 142	16 795	87 774	73 855	12 074	34.1	40.8	10.98	11.58	374.42	472.46
April	110 223	91 285	22 130	16 771	88 093	74 077	12 055	34.4	41.5	10.98	11.63	377.71	482.65
May	110 496	91 545	22 189	16 766	88 307	74 332	12 056	34.3	41.1	11.01	11.66	377.64	479.23
June	110 660	91 691	22 165	16 742	88 495	74 438	12 038	34.3	41.0	11.02	11.67	377.99	478.47
July	110 960	91 900	22 186	16 742	88 774	74 615	12 041	34.4	41.1	11.04	11.69	379.78	480.46
August	111 119	92 091	22 203	16 741	88 916	74 793	12 049	34.3	41.2	11.07	11.72	379.70	482.86
September	111 359	92 318	22 251	16 768	89 108	74 981	12 081	34.4	41.3	11.09	11.77	381.50	486.10
October	111 638	92 596	22 306	16 778	89 332	75 229	12 093	34.4	41.3	11.11	11.79	382.18	486.93
November	111 901	92 833	22 347	16 800	89 554	75 443	12 116	34.4	41.3	11.14	11.83	383.22	488.58
December	112 203	93 094	22 413	16 815	89 790	75 662	12 142	34.4	41.4	11.17	11.88	384.25	491.83
1994													
January	112 473	93 326	22 463	16 853	90 010	75 875	12 181	34.4	41.4	11.19	11.89	384.94	492.25
February	112 665	93 515	22 451	16 862	90 214	76 075	12 199	34.2	40.9	11.23	11.98	384.07	489.98
March	113 133	93 943	22 549	16 896	90 584	76 436	12 234	34.5	41.7	11.23	11.95	387.44	498.32
April	113 490	94 267	22 640	16 932	90 850	76 734	12 275	34.5	41.7	11.26	11.96	388.47	498.73
May	113 829	94 565	22 704	16 962	91 125	77 013	12 305	34.5	41.8	11.28	11.98	389.16	500.76
June	114 139	94 865	22 765	17 011	91 374	77 265	12 353	34.5	41.8	11.30	12.00	389.85	501.60
July	114 498	95 197	22 808	17 027	91 690	77 566	12 369	34.6	41.8	11.33	12.02	392.02	502.44
August	114 801	95 495	22 877	17 082	91 924	77 802	12 429	34.5	41.7	11.34	12.05	391.23	502.49
September	115 155	95 818	22 947	17 114	92 208	78 069	12 460	34.4	41.6	11.37	12.09	391.13	502.94
October	115 361	96 017	22 974	17 144	92 387	78 253	12 490	34.5	41.8	11.42	12.12	393.99	506.62
November	115 786	96 419	23 051	17 187	92 735	78 600	12 527	34.5	41.8	11.43	12.15	394.34	507.87
December	116 056	96 668	23 096	17 218	92 960	78 839	12 559	34.5	41.8	11.46	12.16	395.37	508.29
1995													
January	116 377	96 980	23 144	17 259	93 233	79 086	12 593	34.5	41.8	11.47	12.19	395.72	509.54
February	116 588	97 181	23 102	17 264	93 486	79 240	12 601	34.4	41.7	11.52	12.25	396.29	510.83
March	116 808	97 381	23 151	17 263	93 657	79 423	12 600	34.4	41.5	11.54	12.25	396.98	508.38
April	116 971	97 537	23 174	17 278	93 797	79 560	12 609	34.3	41.2	11.56	12.25	396.51	504.70
May	116 962	97 544	23 121	17 260	93 841	79 577	12 592	34.2	41.2	11.58	12.28	396.04	505.94
June	117 189	97 744	23 140	17 250	94 049	79 740	12 575	34.3	41.2	11.62	12.31	398.57	507.17
July	117 260	97 823	23 119	17 218	94 141	79 811	12 538	34.3	41.1	11.66	12.38	399.94	508.82
August	117 538	98 109	23 165	17 241	94 373	80 059	12 568	34.3	41.2	11.68	12.39	400.62	510.47
September	117 777	98 347	23 207	17 246	94 570	80 253	12 566	34.3	41.2	11.71	12.41	401.65	511.29
October	117 926	98 462	23 205	17 215	94 721	80 373	12 535	34.3	41.2	11.75	12.44	403.03	512.53
November	118 070	98 607	23 198	17 207	94 872	80 451	12 517	34.3	41.3	11.77	12.45	403.71	514.19
December	118 210	98 744	23 208	17 230	95 002	80 604	12 548	34.2	40.9	11.79	12.49	403.22	510.84
1996													
January	118 192	98 742	23 194	17 206	94 998	80 529	12 520	33.8	39.7	11.84	12.60	400.19	500.22
February	118 627	99 142	23 280	17 229	95 347	80 914	12 531	34.3	41.3	11.86	12.56	406.80	518.73
March	118 882	99 350	23 275	17 192	95 607	81 092	12 489	34.3	41.1	11.88	12.50	407.48	513.75
April	119 047	99 532	23 316	17 204	95 731	81 259	12 505	34.2	41.2	11.94	12.69	408.35	522.83
May	119 376	99 847	23 357	17 221	96 019	81 515	12 514	34.3	41.3	11.96	12.70	410.23	524.51
June	119 647	100 119	23 399	17 226	96 248	81 733	12 526	34.4	41.5	12.02	12.76	413.49	529.54
July	119 875	100 328	23 417	17 222	96 458	81 921	12 516	34.3	41.4	12.04	12.79	412.97	529.51
August	120 078	100 574	23 479	17 255	96 599	82 118	12 543	34.3	41.5	12.08	12.82	414.34	532.03
September	120 296	100 729	23 498	17 253	96 798	82 243	12 544	34.4	41.6	12.12	12.85	416.93	534.56
October	120 534	100 980	23 546	17 268	96 988	82 476	12 558	34.4	41.4	12.14	12.84	417.62	531.58
November	120 826	101 261	23 583	17 276	97 243	82 664	12 561	34.4	41.5	12.19	12.88	419.34	534.52
December	121 003	101 432	23 599	17 285	97 404	82 831	12 569	34.4	41.7	12.23	12.95	420.71	540.02
1997													
January	121 232	101 639	23 619	17 298	97 613	82 973	12 579	34.3	41.4	12.27	12.99	420.86	537.79
February	121 526	101 928	23 686	17 316	97 840	83 252	12 592	34.5	41.6	12.30	13.00	424.35	540.80
March	121 843	102 235	23 738	17 339	98 105	83 478	12 613	34.5	41.8	12.35	13.04	426.08	545.07
April	122 134	102 531	23 767	17 351	98 367	83 727	12 618	34.6	41.8	12.37	13.04	428.00	545.07
May	122 396	102 795	23 809	17 362	98 587	83 943	12 630	34.5	41.7	12.42	13.06	428.49	544.60
June	122 642	102 982	23 834	17 387	98 808	84 080	12 649	34.4	41.6	12.45	13.09	428.28	544.54
July	122 918	103 232	23 860	17 387	99 058	84 320	12 645	34.5	41.6	12.48	13.09	430.56	544.54
August	122 911	103 294	23 951	17 451	98 960	84 264	12 697	34.6	41.6	12.55	13.17	434.23	547.87
September	123 417	103 738	23 997	17 466	99 420	84 659	12 710	34.4	41.7	12.58	13.17	435.27	549.19
October	123 756	104 018	24 053	17 513	99 703	84 869	12 746	34.5	41.8	12.65	13.28	436.43	555.10
November	124 063	104 302	24 111	17 555	99 952	85 053	12 774	34.6	41.8	12.70	13.32	439.42	556.78
December	124 361	104 595	24 183	17 587	100 178	85 288	12 798	34.6	42.0	12.73	13.35	440.46	560.70
1998													
January	124 629	104 859	24 264	17 621	100 365	85 438	12 819	34.6	41.9	12.77	13.34	441.84	558.95
February	124 814	105 028	24 283	17 627	100 531	85 605	12 828	34.6	41.7	12.82	13.39	443.57	558.36
March	124 962	105 170	24 264	17 637	100 698	85 629	12 822	34.5	41.5	12.87	13.43	444.02	557.35
April	125 240	105 424	24 339	17 636	100 901	85 845	12 813	34.5	41.3	12.91	13.41	445.40	553.83
May	125 641	105 766	24 361	17 624	101 280	86 124	12 790	34.5	41.5	12.95	13.45	446.78	558.18
June	125 846	105 967	24 386	17 607	101 460	86 274	12 772	34.4	41.4	12.97	13.43	446.17	556.00
July	125 967	106 037	24 237	17 421	101 730	86 271	12 553	34.5	41.4	12.99	13.34	448.16	552.28
August	126 322	106 363	24 421	17 564	101 901	86 572	12 705	34.5	41.4	13.07	13.46	450.92	557.24
September	126 543	106 558	24 420	17 558	102 123	86 735	12 713	34.4	41.3	13.10	13.53	450.64	558.79
October	126 735	106 734	24 406	17 512	102 329	86 885	12 676	34.5	41.4	13.13	13.52	452.99	559.73
November	127 020	106 976	24 395	17 466	102 625	87 039	12 631	34.5	41.5	13.16	13.54	454.02	561.91
December	127 364	107 285	24 454	17 449	102 910	87 307	12 622	34.5	41.5	13.19	13.56	455.06	562.74

Table 20-4. Nonfarm Payroll Employment, Hours, and Earnings—Continued

(Wage and salary workers on nonfarm payrolls, seasonally adjusted.)

Year and month	All wage and salary workers (thousands)					Production or nonsupervisory workers on private payrolls								
	Total	Private				Number (thousands)		Average hours per week		Average hourly earnings, dollars		Average weekly earnings, dollars	
		Total	Goods-producing		Service-providing	Total private	Manufac-turing	Total private	Manufac-turing	Total private	Manufac-turing	Total private	Manufac-turing
			Total	Manufac-turing									
1999													
January	127 477	107 393	24 400	17 426	103 077	87 355	12 604	34.4	41.3	13.25	13.59	455.80	561.27
February	127 873	107 729	24 433	17 394	103 440	87 676	12 574	34.4	41.3	13.28	13.63	456.83	562.92
March	127 997	107 829	24 378	17 368	103 619	87 731	12 562	34.3	41.3	13.32	13.69	456.88	565.40
April	128 379	108 142	24 423	17 342	103 956	87 963	12 539	34.4	41.3	13.37	13.75	459.93	567.88
May	128 593	108 364	24 445	17 333	104 148	88 168	12 535	34.4	41.4	13.42	13.81	461.65	571.73
June	128 850	108 578	24 433	17 294	104 417	88 328	12 504	34.4	41.3	13.45	13.85	462.68	572.01
July	129 145	108 806	24 485	17 319	104 660	88 506	12 530	34.4	41.5	13.50	13.91	464.40	577.27
August	129 338	108 963	24 468	17 288	104 870	88 632	12 502	34.4	41.5	13.54	13.95	465.78	578.93
September	129 525	109 121	24 485	17 281	105 040	88 757	12 496	34.4	41.5	13.60	14.01	467.84	581.42
October	129 947	109 490	24 508	17 275	105 439	89 082	12 484	34.4	41.4	13.62	14.00	468.53	579.60
November	130 242	109 746	24 562	17 283	105 680	89 316	12 488	34.4	41.4	13.64	14.00	469.22	579.60
December	130 536	109 996	24 579	17 277	105 957	89 525	12 490	34.4	41.4	13.68	14.07	470.59	582.50
2000													
January	130 781	110 210	24 629	17 285	106 152	89 697	12 494	34.4	41.5	13.73	14.12	472.31	585.98
February	130 901	110 302	24 609	17 285	106 292	89 768	12 481	34.4	41.4	13.78	14.14	474.03	586.81
March	131 377	110 644	24 705	17 302	106 672	90 040	12 491	34.3	41.4	13.83	14.18	474.37	587.05
April	131 662	110 860	24 689	17 299	106 973	90 259	12 477	34.4	41.5	13.89	14.23	477.82	590.55
May	131 882	110 735	24 644	17 276	107 238	90 160	12 463	34.3	41.3	13.92	14.23	477.46	587.70
June	131 839	110 952	24 673	17 297	107 166	90 325	12 469	34.3	41.3	13.97	14.29	479.17	590.18
July	132 015	111 148	24 720	17 325	107 295	90 491	12 480	34.3	41.5	14.02	14.32	480.89	594.28
August	132 004	111 167	24 683	17 287	107 321	90 487	12 428	34.2	41.1	14.05	14.37	480.51	590.61
September	132 122	111 387	24 644	17 232	107 478	90 640	12 384	34.2	41.0	14.11	14.40	482.56	590.40
October	132 110	111 367	24 636	17 215	107 474	90 619	12 358	34.3	41.2	14.17	14.48	486.03	596.58
November	132 326	111 566	24 625	17 204	107 701	90 751	12 337	34.2	41.1	14.22	14.51	486.32	596.36
December	132 484	111 680	24 575	17 181	107 909	90 798	12 307	34.0	40.3	14.26	14.50	484.84	584.35
2001													
January	132 454	111 622	24 523	17 101	107 931	90 774	12 228	34.2	40.6	14.27	14.48	488.03	587.89
February	132 546	111 644	24 476	17 030	108 070	90 715	12 157	34.0	40.5	14.35	14.54	487.90	588.87
March	132 511	111 565	24 409	16 936	108 102	90 662	12 087	34.1	40.4	14.40	14.58	491.04	589.03
April	132 214	111 219	24 250	16 801	107 964	90 422	11 981	34.0	40.5	14.44	14.64	490.96	592.92
May	132 187	111 156	24 120	16 658	108 067	90 349	11 858	34.0	40.4	14.48	14.70	492.32	593.88
June	132 029	110 916	23 964	16 511	108 065	90 132	11 734	34.0	40.4	14.52	14.74	493.68	595.50
July	131 941	110 763	23 840	16 386	108 101	90 060	11 641	34.0	40.6	14.54	14.81	494.36	601.29
August	131 803	110 579	23 675	16 240	108 128	89 919	11 499	33.9	40.3	14.58	14.83	494.26	597.65
September	131 549	110 301	23 544	16 123	108 005	89 643	11 405	33.8	40.2	14.62	14.89	494.16	598.58
October	131 172	109 896	23 372	15 972	107 800	89 312	11 287	33.7	40.1	14.64	14.89	493.37	597.09
November	130 879	109 551	23 211	15 827	107 668	88 991	11 175	33.8	40.1	14.69	14.95	496.52	599.50
December	130 705	109 352	23 090	15 710	107 615	88 884	11 079	33.8	40.2	14.73	15.01	497.87	603.40
2002													
January	130 581	109 206	22 961	15 584	107 620	88 879	10 996	33.8	40.2	14.73	15.05	497.87	605.01
February	130 478	109 077	22 889	15 514	107 589	88 804	10 949	33.8	40.2	14.77	15.11	499.23	607.42
March	130 441	109 003	22 787	15 441	107 654	88 780	10 905	33.8	40.5	14.80	15.15	500.24	613.58
April	130 335	108 887	22 694	15 391	107 641	88 613	10 861	33.9	40.5	14.82	15.17	502.40	614.39
May	130 326	108 790	22 602	15 336	107 724	88 444	10 824	33.9	40.5	14.86	15.23	503.75	616.82
June	130 377	108 831	22 578	15 298	107 799	88 391	10 797	33.9	40.7	14.92	15.27	505.79	621.49
July	130 277	108 765	22 519	15 259	107 758	88 259	10 770	33.8	40.5	14.96	15.29	505.65	619.25
August	130 295	108 724	22 451	15 179	107 844	88 194	10 699	33.9	40.5	15.00	15.33	508.50	620.87
September	130 250	108 693	22 401	15 128	107 849	88 159	10 672	33.9	40.5	15.05	15.38	510.20	622.89
October	130 309	108 735	22 312	15 058	107 997	88 187	10 628	33.8	40.4	15.10	15.45	510.38	624.18
November	130 315	108 733	22 280	14 993	108 035	88 127	10 580	33.8	40.3	15.13	15.47	511.39	623.44
December	130 161	108 559	22 181	14 911	107 980	87 950	10 520	33.8	40.5	15.19	15.53	513.42	628.97
2003													
January	130 247	108 614	22 133	14 854	108 114	87 971	10 478	33.8	40.3	15.19	15.58	513.42	627.87
February	130 125	108 492	22 019	14 780	108 106	87 867	10 416	33.7	40.3	15.27	15.62	514.60	629.49
March	129 907	108 296	21 955	14 726	107 952	87 569	10 357	33.8	40.4	15.27	15.64	516.13	631.86
April	129 853	108 258	21 870	14 615	107 983	87 532	10 258	33.6	40.1	15.25	15.63	512.40	626.76
May	129 827	108 252	21 821	14 555	108 006	87 490	10 218	33.6	40.1	15.31	15.68	514.42	628.77
June	129 854	108 250	21 792	14 494	108 062	87 519	10 168	33.6	40.3	15.34	15.72	515.42	633.52
July	129 857	108 250	21 711	14 410	108 146	87 519	10 104	33.6	40.1	15.39	15.74	517.10	631.17
August	129 859	108 279	21 697	14 373	108 162	87 548	10 075	33.6	40.2	15.40	15.78	517.44	634.36
September	129 953	108 432	21 692	14 348	108 261	87 640	10 056	33.6	40.5	15.40	15.83	517.44	641.12
October	130 076	108 525	21 680	14 328	108 396	87 719	10 048	33.7	40.6	15.41	15.81	519.32	641.89
November	130 172	108 617	21 693	14 315	108 479	87 774	10 041	33.8	40.8	15.45	15.88	522.21	647.90
December	130 255	108 701	21 680	14 297	108 575	87 821	10 031	33.6	40.7	15.45	15.92	519.12	647.94
2004													
January	130 420	108 887	21 712	14 290	108 708	87 967	10 025	33.7	40.9	15.48	15.94	521.68	651.95
February	130 475	108 933	21 703	14 280	108 772	87 977	10 012	33.8	41.0	15.52	15.96	524.58	654.36
March	130 821	109 231	21 768	14 288	109 053	88 234	10 026	33.7	40.9	15.54	16.01	523.70	654.81
April	131 073	109 457	21 813	14 317	109 260	88 493	10 061	33.7	40.8	15.58	16.08	525.05	656.06
May	131 340	109 749	21 877	14 340	109 463	88 792	10 091	33.8	41.1	15.63	16.08	528.29	660.89
June	131 418	109 843	21 885	14 332	109 533	88 934	10 086	33.6	40.7	15.65	16.11	525.84	655.68
July	131 456	109 875	21 904	14 332	109 552	89 050	10 107	33.7	40.8	15.68	16.14	528.42	658.51
August	131 587	109 958	21 940	14 348	109 647	89 188	10 123	33.7	40.9	15.74	16.21	530.44	662.99
September	131 764	110 109	21 952	14 329	109 812	89 343	10 101	33.8	40.8	15.77	16.30	533.03	665.04
October	132 102	110 404	21 984	14 320	110 118	89 591	10 091	33.7	40.6	15.79	16.28	532.12	660.97
November	132 235	110 517	22 002	14 308	110 233	89 736	10 080	33.7	40.4	15.81	16.30	532.80	658.52
December	132 395	110 679	22 016	14 294	110 379	89 851	10 066	33.8	40.5	15.84	16.35	535.39	662.18

Table 20-5. Money Stock, Reserves, and Monetary Base

(Averages of daily figures, seasonally adjusted.)

Year and month	Money stock measures, billions of dollars			Reserves, adjusted for change in reserve requirements, millions of dollars				
	M1	M2	M3	Total	Nonborrowed	Nonborrowed plus extended credit [1]	Required	Monetary base
1959								
January	138.9	286.6	288.8	11 112	10 560	10 560	10 614	40 425
February	139.4	287.7	289.9	11 129	10 624	10 624	10 675	40 605
March	139.7	289.2	291.4	11 081	10 482	10 482	10 621	40 615
April	139.7	290.1	292.3	11 116	10 424	10 424	10 684	40 694
May	140.7	292.2	294.4	11 058	10 317	10 317	10 637	40 731
June	141.2	294.1	296.3	10 972	10 043	10 043	10 566	40 750
July	141.7	295.2	297.4	11 109	10 148	10 148	10 693	40 896
August	141.9	296.4	298.5	11 168	10 177	10 177	10 720	40 992
September	141.0	296.7	298.8	11 128	10 202	10 202	10 686	41 034
October	140.5	296.5	298.5	11 057	10 150	10 150	10 616	40 903
November	140.4	297.1	299.1	11 052	10 194	10 194	10 609	40 822
December	140.0	297.8	299.7	11 109	10 168	10 168	10 603	40 880
1960								
January	140.0	298.2	300.1	11 081	10 194	10 194	10 567	40 794
February	139.9	298.5	300.4	10 884	10 074	10 074	10 430	40 666
March	139.8	299.4	301.4	10 796	10 155	10 155	10 373	40 616
April	139.6	300.1	302.2	10 767	10 161	10 161	10 341	40 621
May	139.6	300.9	303.0	10 840	10 344	10 344	10 396	40 639
June	139.6	302.3	304.5	10 885	10 451	10 451	10 406	40 689
July	140.2	304.1	306.4	10 994	10 615	10 615	10 493	40 794
August	141.3	306.9	309.3	11 078	10 782	10 782	10 536	40 895
September	141.2	308.4	311.0	11 147	10 932	10 932	10 520	41 040
October	140.9	309.5	312.2	11 216	11 049	11 049	10 554	41 097
November	140.9	310.9	313.6	11 299	11 166	11 166	10 556	41 130
December	140.7	312.4	315.2	11 247	11 172	11 172	10 503	40 977
1961								
January	141.1	314.1	317.1	11 324	11 259	11 259	10 553	40 960
February	141.6	316.5	319.9	11 229	11 096	11 096	10 580	40 945
March	141.9	318.3	321.9	11 108	11 038	11 038	10 563	40 851
April	142.1	319.9	323.8	11 123	11 066	11 066	10 507	40 823
May	142.7	322.2	326.5	11 035	10 940	10 940	10 480	40 791
June	142.9	324.3	328.9	11 087	11 024	11 024	10 497	40 902
July	142.9	325.6	330.5	11 124	11 070	11 070	10 508	40 980
August	143.5	327.6	332.7	11 234	11 169	11 169	10 655	41 227
September	143.8	329.5	334.8	11 289	11 251	11 251	10 709	41 417
October	144.1	331.1	336.5	11 413	11 342	11 342	10 881	41 651
November	144.8	333.4	338.8	11 482	11 384	11 384	10 891	41 782
December	145.2	335.5	340.8	11 499	11 366	11 366	10 915	41 853
1962								
January	145.2	337.5	343.0	11 490	11 403	11 403	10 867	41 864
February	145.7	340.1	346.1	11 301	11 233	11 233	10 799	41 810
March	146.0	343.1	349.4	11 259	11 170	11 170	10 788	41 923
April	146.4	345.5	352.1	11 330	11 258	11 258	10 838	42 096
May	146.8	347.5	354.2	11 384	11 323	11 323	10 867	42 194
June	146.6	349.3	356.3	11 328	11 226	11 226	10 855	42 259
July	146.5	350.8	358.0	11 394	11 302	11 302	10 860	42 398
August	146.6	352.8	360.1	11 355	11 231	11 231	10 826	42 491
September	146.3	354.9	362.5	11 383	11 303	11 303	10 893	42 537
October	146.7	357.2	365.1	11 450	11 387	11 387	10 972	42 700
November	147.3	359.8	368.0	11 492	11 372	11 372	10 936	42 861
December	147.8	362.7	371.3	11 604	11 344	11 344	11 033	42 957
1963								
January	148.3	365.2	374.2	11 567	11 421	11 421	11 062	43 008
February	148.9	367.9	377.2	11 456	11 290	11 290	10 995	43 155
March	149.2	370.7	380.2	11 404	11 255	11 255	10 970	43 289
April	149.7	373.3	383.1	11 449	11 319	11 319	10 992	43 444
May	150.4	376.1	386.2	11 426	11 216	11 216	10 996	43 586
June	150.4	378.4	388.8	11 398	11 139	11 139	10 981	43 780
July	151.3	381.1	391.5	11 530	11 232	11 232	11 075	44 058
August	151.8	383.6	394.5	11 484	11 155	11 155	11 039	44 149
September	152.0	386.0	397.3	11 503	11 184	11 184	11 075	44 339
October	152.6	388.3	400.0	11 457	11 137	11 137	11 060	44 444
November	153.7	391.5	403.8	11 547	11 198	11 198	11 106	44 744
December	153.3	393.2	405.9	11 730	11 397	11 397	11 239	45 003
1964								
January	153.7	395.2	408.5	11 643	11 369	11 369	11 204	45 042
February	154.3	397.6	411.3	11 547	11 261	11 261	11 150	45 112
March	154.5	399.8	413.6	11 563	11 285	11 285	11 177	45 371
April	154.8	401.7	415.8	11 537	11 326	11 326	11 185	45 470
May	155.3	404.2	418.9	11 523	11 263	11 263	11 169	45 651
June	155.6	407.1	422.1	11 595	11 326	11 326	11 220	45 959
July	156.8	410.1	425.5	11 651	11 387	11 387	11 275	46 143
August	157.8	413.4	429.2	11 795	11 480	11 480	11 374	46 410
September	158.7	416.9	433.0	11 863	11 518	11 518	11 432	46 714
October	159.2	419.1	435.9	11 888	11 567	11 567	11 490	46 823
November	160.0	422.1	439.3	11 998	11 598	11 598	11 591	47 106
December	160.3	424.7	442.4	12 011	11 747	11 747	11 605	47 161

[1]Extended credit program discontinued January 9, 2003. See notes and definitions for more information.

Table 20-5. Money Stock, Reserves, and Monetary Base—Continued

(Averages of daily figures, seasonally adjusted.)

Year and month	Money stock measures, billions of dollars			Reserves, adjusted for change in reserve requirements, millions of dollars				
	M1	M2	M3	Total	Nonborrowed	Nonborrowed plus extended credit [1]	Required	Monetary base
1965								
January	160.7	427.5	445.8	11 952	11 653	11 653	11 537	47 281
February	160.9	430.4	449.1	11 883	11 479	11 479	11 472	47 500
March	161.5	433.2	452.0	11 884	11 472	11 472	11 518	47 584
April	162.0	435.4	454.5	12 043	11 571	11 571	11 701	47 721
May	161.7	437.1	456.4	11 912	11 417	11 417	11 578	47 799
June	162.2	440.1	459.9	12 005	11 467	11 467	11 643	48 061
July	163.1	442.9	463.3	12 073	11 544	11 544	11 720	48 281
August	163.7	445.8	466.8	12 079	11 531	11 531	11 682	48 453
September	164.9	449.5	471.1	12 071	11 517	11 517	11 662	48 712
October	166.0	452.6	474.9	12 118	11 630	11 630	11 759	49 029
November	166.7	455.7	478.3	12 087	11 655	11 655	11 735	49 234
December	167.8	459.2	482.1	12 316	11 872	11 872	11 892	49 620
1966								
January	169.1	462.0	485.1	12 295	11 875	11 875	11 916	49 850
February	169.6	464.6	487.8	12 193	11 711	11 711	11 846	50 054
March	170.5	467.2	490.8	12 164	11 604	11 604	11 822	50 171
April	171.8	469.3	494.0	12 258	11 621	11 621	11 903	50 439
May	171.3	470.1	495.4	12 263	11 575	11 575	11 922	50 591
June	171.6	471.2	497.1	12 256	11 549	11 549	11 901	50 754
July	170.3	470.9	497.8	12 371	11 629	11 629	11 993	51 019
August	170.8	472.6	499.6	12 165	11 430	11 430	11 798	50 989
September	172.0	475.4	502.3	12 229	11 460	11 460	11 858	51 154
October	171.2	475.7	501.4	12 199	11 465	11 465	11 867	51 200
November	171.4	477.3	502.0	12 205	11 598	11 598	11 820	51 422
December	172.0	480.2	505.4	12 223	11 690	11 690	11 884	51 565
1967								
January	171.9	481.6	509.1	12 334	11 924	11 924	11 931	51 876
February	173.0	485.1	514.5	12 280	11 916	11 916	11 911	52 173
March	174.8	489.7	519.9	12 438	12 237	12 237	12 024	52 494
April	174.2	492.1	522.6	12 488	12 342	12 342	12 138	52 517
May	175.7	497.2	527.7	12 418	12 329	12 329	12 053	52 682
June	177.0	502.0	533.1	12 457	12 351	12 351	12 104	52 867
July	178.1	506.3	537.7	12 722	12 607	12 607	12 304	53 165
August	179.7	510.8	542.5	12 678	12 598	12 598	12 313	53 347
September	180.7	514.7	546.8	12 846	12 758	12 758	12 504	53 670
October	181.6	518.2	550.2	13 088	12 959	12 959	12 752	54 044
November	182.4	521.2	553.9	13 131	12 999	12 999	12 773	54 241
December	183.3	524.8	557.9	13 180	12 952	12 952	12 805	54 579
1968								
January	184.3	527.4	560.4	13 239	12 993	12 993	12 852	54 892
February	184.7	530.4	563.6	13 188	12 815	12 815	12 801	55 171
March	185.5	533.2	567.0	13 186	12 527	12 527	12 849	55 436
April	186.6	535.7	569.2	13 117	12 432	12 432	12 782	55 692
May	188.0	538.9	572.3	13 130	12 389	12 389	12 771	55 872
June	189.4	542.6	575.9	13 251	12 557	12 557	12 923	56 323
July	190.5	545.6	580.6	13 455	12 928	12 928	13 105	56 626
August	191.8	549.4	585.6	13 440	12 875	12 875	13 110	56 976
September	192.7	553.6	590.6	13 435	12 931	12 931	13 074	57 160
October	194.0	557.6	595.8	13 529	13 086	13 086	13 283	57 477
November	196.0	562.4	601.7	13 649	13 104	13 104	13 340	57 887
December	197.4	566.8	607.2	13 767	13 021	13 021	13 341	58 357
1969								
January	198.7	569.3	607.9	13 629	12 893	12 893	13 383	58 597
February	199.3	571.9	609.1	13 714	12 879	12 879	13 460	58 917
March	200.0	574.4	610.8	13 653	12 751	12 751	13 434	58 999
April	200.7	575.7	611.5	13 471	12 468	12 468	13 304	59 062
May	200.8	576.5	611.6	13 844	12 470	12 470	13 589	59 552
June	201.3	578.5	612.1	13 795	12 410	12 410	13 491	59 794
July	201.7	579.5	610.1	13 491	12 239	12 239	13 266	59 713
August	201.7	580.1	607.7	13 784	12 565	12 565	13 547	60 137
September	202.1	582.1	608.5	13 822	12 743	12 743	13 549	60 357
October	202.9	583.4	608.9	13 904	12 754	12 754	13 741	60 633
November	203.6	585.4	613.5	14 172	12 969	12 969	13 943	61 229
December	203.9	587.9	615.9	14 168	13 049	13 049	13 882	61 569
1970								
January	206.2	589.6	616.1	14 087	13 128	13 128	13 914	61 792
February	205.0	586.3	613.3	14 099	13 019	13 019	13 891	61 931
March	205.7	587.3	615.7	14 071	13 173	13 173	13 908	62 205
April	206.7	588.4	619.5	14 209	13 364	13 364	14 057	62 653
May	207.2	591.5	624.3	14 007	13 040	13 040	13 850	62 977
June	207.6	595.2	627.1	14 078	13 197	13 197	13 888	63 189
July	208.0	599.1	635.7	14 159	12 799	12 799	13 993	63 444
August	209.9	604.9	644.8	14 282	13 445	13 445	14 108	63 725
September	211.8	611.2	654.4	14 447	13 847	13 847	14 203	64 087
October	212.9	616.4	662.3	14 480	14 017	14 017	14 274	64 303
November	213.7	621.1	669.3	14 470	14 055	14 055	14 236	64 574
December	214.4	626.5	677.1	14 558	14 225	14 225	14 309	65 013

[1]Extended credit program discontinued January 9, 2003. See notes and definitions for more information.

Table 20-5. Money Stock, Reserves, and Monetary Base—Continued

(Averages of daily figures, seasonally adjusted.)

Year and month	Money stock measures, billions of dollars			Reserves, adjusted for change in reserve requirements, millions of dollars				
	M1	M2	M3	Total	Nonborrowed	Nonborrowed plus extended credit [1]	Required	Monetary base
1971								
January	215.5	633.0	685.5	14 604	14 240	14 240	14 371	65 545
February	217.4	641.0	695.8	14 819	14 488	14 488	14 565	66 037
March	218.8	649.9	706.5	14 798	14 479	14 479	14 603	66 378
April	220.0	658.4	713.7	14 759	14 606	14 606	14 591	66 731
May	222.0	666.7	723.3	14 982	14 698	14 698	14 763	67 315
June	223.5	673.0	730.1	15 057	14 564	14 564	14 855	67 678
July	224.9	679.6	738.3	15 125	14 302	14 302	14 941	68 155
August	225.6	685.5	744.0	15 190	14 380	14 380	14 994	68 413
September	226.5	692.5	751.7	15 423	14 928	14 928	15 234	68 751
October	227.2	698.4	760.2	15 211	14 854	14 854	15 049	68 603
November	227.8	704.6	768.3	15 247	14 864	14 864	15 010	68 894
December	228.3	710.3	776.0	15 230	15 104	15 104	15 049	69 108
1972								
January	230.1	717.7	783.8	15 369	15 347	15 347	15 163	69 853
February	232.3	725.7	792.9	15 363	15 331	15 331	15 211	70 368
March	234.3	733.5	800.6	15 480	15 382	15 382	15 291	70 820
April	235.6	738.4	807.9	15 651	15 534	15 534	15 495	71 031
May	235.9	743.4	816.1	15 739	15 628	15 628	15 600	71 525
June	236.6	749.7	824.6	15 909	15 809	15 809	15 706	71 817
July	238.8	759.5	835.5	15 835	15 597	15 597	15 642	72 173
August	240.9	768.7	846.6	16 010	15 623	15 623	15 822	72 623
September	243.2	778.3	856.4	16 000	15 459	15 459	15 788	72 984
October	245.0	786.9	865.8	16 193	15 637	15 637	15 981	73 644
November	246.4	793.9	875.8	16 441	15 833	15 833	16 088	74 370
December	249.2	802.3	885.9	16 645	15 595	15 595	16 361	75 167
1973								
January	251.5	810.3	896.3	16 708	15 548	15 548	16 450	75 925
February	252.2	814.1	906.1	16 714	15 120	15 120	16 516	76 160
March	251.7	815.3	915.0	16 923	15 099	15 099	16 714	76 663
April	252.7	819.7	922.4	16 731	15 020	15 020	16 508	76 962
May	254.9	826.8	932.3	16 672	14 829	14 830	16 533	77 393
June	256.7	833.3	940.7	16 746	14 895	14 903	16 528	77 842
July	257.5	836.5	950.3	16 988	15 035	15 067	16 705	78 531
August	257.7	838.8	959.0	16 796	14 631	14 657	16 624	78 781
September	257.9	839.3	965.8	16 735	14 883	14 909	16 505	79 316
October	259.0	842.6	972.0	16 924	15 448	15 464	16 672	80 173
November	261.0	848.9	977.3	16 978	15 585	15 585	16 753	80 479
December	262.9	855.5	985.0	17 021	15 723	15 723	16 717	81 073
1974								
January	263.8	859.7	993.9	17 222	16 171	16 174	17 060	81 850
February	265.3	864.2	1 002.4	17 125	15 933	15 933	16 941	82 341
March	266.7	870.1	1 010.7	17 131	15 817	15 817	16 997	82 835
April	267.2	872.9	1 020.8	17 298	15 561	15 561	17 116	83 621
May	267.6	874.6	1 029.2	17 423	14 833	15 491	17 263	84 432
June	268.5	877.8	1 037.8	17 367	14 361	15 587	17 169	84 895
July	269.3	881.4	1 043.9	17 486	14 185	15 615	17 323	85 439
August	270.1	884.1	1 048.6	17 391	14 055	15 592	17 203	85 974
September	271.0	887.9	1 052.9	17 385	14 102	15 731	17 204	86 377
October	272.3	893.3	1 058.5	17 349	15 536	16 021	17 228	86 513
November	273.7	898.6	1 063.7	17 453	16 201	16 361	17 248	87 043
December	274.2	902.1	1 069.9	17 550	16 823	16 970	17 292	87 535
1975								
January	273.9	906.3	1 075.5	17 273	16 874	17 010	17 126	87 756
February	275.0	914.1	1 082.7	17 271	17 123	17 176	17 077	88 192
March	276.4	925.0	1 090.0	17 439	17 333	17 370	17 239	88 916
April	276.2	935.1	1 095.8	17 498	17 387	17 398	17 340	89 116
May	279.2	947.9	1 105.9	17 353	17 288	17 291	17 198	89 610
June	282.4	963.0	1 118.7	17 715	17 488	17 504	17 513	90 817
July	283.7	975.1	1 128.7	17 632	17 331	17 351	17 445	91 373
August	284.1	983.1	1 135.1	17 660	17 449	17 461	17 465	91 700
September	285.7	991.5	1 145.9	17 834	17 438	17 452	17 643	92 119
October	285.4	997.8	1 153.8	17 587	17 397	17 408	17 380	92 448
November	286.8	1 006.9	1 163.8	17 849	17 789	17 794	17 566	93 373
December	287.1	1 016.2	1 170.2	17 822	17 692	17 704	17 556	93 887
1976								
January	288.4	1 026.6	1 181.6	17 616	17 537	17 549	17 376	94 281
February	290.8	1 040.3	1 193.5	17 806	17 725	17 734	17 587	95 039
March	292.7	1 050.0	1 204.6	17 875	17 821	17 824	17 651	95 786
April	294.7	1 060.8	1 216.7	17 719	17 675	17 675	17 564	96 479
May	295.9	1 072.1	1 227.6	17 940	17 826	17 826	17 731	97 251
June	296.2	1 077.6	1 236.1	17 946	17 820	17 820	17 732	97 732
July	297.2	1 086.3	1 245.6	17 846	17 714	17 714	17 612	98 234
August	299.0	1 098.7	1 259.2	18 053	17 953	17 953	17 846	98 888
September	299.6	1 110.8	1 268.2	18 009	17 948	17 948	17 808	99 446
October	302.0	1 125.0	1 280.8	18 077	17 983	17 983	17 858	100 066
November	303.6	1 138.2	1 294.5	18 340	18 268	18 268	18 083	100 892
December	306.2	1 152.0	1 309.9	18 388	18 335	18 335	18 115	101 515

[1]Extended credit program discontinued January 9, 2003. See notes and definitions for more information.

Table 20-5. Money Stock, Reserves, and Monetary Base—Continued

(Averages of daily figures, seasonally adjusted.)

Year and month	Money stock measures, billions of dollars			Reserves, adjusted for change in reserve requirements, millions of dollars				
	M1	M2	M3	Total	Nonborrowed	Nonborrowed plus extended credit [1]	Required	Monetary base
1977								
January	308.3	1 165.2	1 322.5	18 421	18 353	18 353	18 156	102 237
February	311.5	1 177.6	1 335.5	18 299	18 227	18 227	18 100	102 654
March	313.9	1 188.5	1 348.4	18 405	18 301	18 301	18 190	103 337
April	316.0	1 199.6	1 360.6	18 479	18 406	18 406	18 287	104 076
May	317.2	1 209.0	1 374.0	18 585	18 379	18 379	18 377	104 630
June	318.8	1 217.8	1 387.6	18 471	18 208	18 208	18 324	105 186
July	320.2	1 226.7	1 400.4	18 748	18 425	18 425	18 473	106 394
August	322.3	1 237.0	1 415.2	18 919	17 858	17 858	18 719	107 185
September	324.5	1 246.2	1 428.0	18 873	18 247	18 247	18 664	107 923
October	326.4	1 254.0	1 441.8	18 963	17 658	17 658	18 753	108 750
November	328.6	1 262.4	1 457.1	19 012	18 150	18 150	18 761	109 560
December	330.9	1 270.3	1 470.4	18 990	18 420	18 420	18 800	110 324
1978								
January	334.4	1 279.7	1 486.3	19 290	18 806	18 806	19 023	111 449
February	335.3	1 285.5	1 498.1	19 561	19 155	19 155	19 319	112 450
March	337.0	1 292.2	1 513.0	19 286	18 958	18 958	19 087	112 778
April	339.9	1 300.4	1 528.6	19 408	18 851	18 851	19 260	113 377
May	344.9	1 310.5	1 544.3	19 655	18 443	18 443	19 436	114 418
June	346.9	1 318.5	1 555.4	19 868	18 774	18 774	19 691	115 376
July	347.6	1 324.1	1 567.0	20 118	18 801	18 801	19 921	116 273
August	349.6	1 333.5	1 583.2	19 912	18 772	18 772	19 744	116 904
September	352.2	1 345.0	1 597.2	19 994	18 934	18 934	19 801	118 112
October	353.3	1 352.3	1 611.1	20 109	18 832	18 832	19 947	119 044
November	355.4	1 359.1	1 630.2	19 872	19 169	19 169	19 650	119 733
December	357.3	1 366.0	1 644.5	19 753	18 885	18 885	19 521	120 445
1979								
January	358.6	1 371.6	1 656.8	19 821	18 818	18 818	19 606	121 272
February	359.9	1 377.8	1 669.2	19 396	18 423	18 423	19 187	121 504
March	362.5	1 387.8	1 683.2	19 429	18 439	18 439	19 271	122 065
April	368.0	1 402.1	1 700.8	19 504	18 587	18 587	19 328	122 819
May	369.6	1 410.2	1 711.0	19 553	17 788	17 788	19 412	123 487
June	373.4	1 423.0	1 728.1	19 808	18 390	18 390	19 587	124 635
July	377.2	1 434.8	1 743.3	19 992	18 822	18 822	19 782	125 810
August	378.8	1 446.6	1 761.6	20 008	18 923	18 923	19 786	127 079
September	379.3	1 454.1	1 783.1	20 007	18 667	18 667	19 816	128 309
October	380.8	1 460.4	1 796.7	20 375	18 353	18 353	20 103	129 458
November	380.8	1 465.9	1 798.9	20 398	18 492	18 492	20 153	130 369
December	381.8	1 473.7	1 808.7	20 720	19 248	19 248	20 279	131 143
1980								
January	385.8	1 482.7	1 823.0	20 693	19 452	19 452	20 442	131 998
February	390.1	1 494.6	1 841.7	20 682	19 027	19 027	20 471	132 785
March	388.5	1 499.8	1 850.2	20 703	17 879	17 978	20 517	133 607
April	383.8	1 502.2	1 854.2	20 629	18 174	18 726	20 432	134 740
May	384.8	1 512.3	1 867.0	20 440	19 421	20 164	20 262	134 998
June	389.1	1 529.2	1 884.4	20 575	20 196	20 503	20 372	135 679
July	394.0	1 545.5	1 903.2	20 796	20 401	20 654	20 511	136 637
August	399.2	1 561.5	1 920.8	21 011	20 352	20 594	20 709	137 977
September	404.8	1 574.0	1 935.2	21 232	19 921	20 011	20 977	139 220
October	409.0	1 584.8	1 953.6	21 147	19 837	19 837	20 941	140 150
November	410.7	1 595.7	1 975.3	22 150	20 091	20 091	21 629	141 566
December	408.5	1 599.8	1 995.5	22 015	20 325	20 328	21 501	142 004
1981								
January	411.3	1 606.9	2 020.6	21 673	20 278	20 348	21 298	141 462
February	414.8	1 618.7	2 039.5	21 840	20 536	20 557	21 489	142 270
March	419.0	1 636.6	2 058.1	22 072	21 072	21 086	21 791	143 029
April	427.4	1 659.3	2 086.4	22 187	20 849	20 857	22 018	143 917
May	424.7	1 664.2	2 102.7	22 442	20 219	20 224	22 184	144 587
June	425.2	1 670.3	2 118.4	22 326	20 289	20 295	21 988	145 001
July	427.0	1 681.9	2 137.9	22 329	20 650	20 653	21 989	145 839
August	426.9	1 694.3	2 157.1	22 356	20 936	21 017	22 064	146 467
September	427.0	1 706.0	2 179.4	22 487	21 031	21 332	22 073	146 941
October	428.4	1 721.8	2 204.7	22 296	21 115	21 553	22 018	147 062
November	431.2	1 736.1	2 226.7	22 338	21 675	21 840	21 993	147 749
December	436.7	1 755.4	2 254.5	22 443	21 807	21 956	22 124	149 021
1982								
January	442.7	1 770.4	2 275.7	22 669	21 152	21 349	22 251	149 991
February	441.9	1 774.5	2 284.4	22 551	20 762	20 994	22 248	150 459
March	442.8	1 786.5	2 303.0	22 452	20 898	21 206	22 091	150 660
April	447.2	1 804.0	2 328.5	22 337	20 769	21 014	22 064	151 606
May	446.7	1 815.4	2 343.1	22 402	21 285	21 461	22 043	152 868
June	447.5	1 826.0	2 359.7	22 368	21 164	21 268	22 060	153 861
July	448.0	1 834.3	2 372.2	22 182	21 490	21 541	21 868	154 385
August	451.4	1 849.4	2 396.6	22 348	21 833	21 926	22 036	155 470
September	456.9	1 863.3	2 413.0	22 686	21 752	21 871	22 302	156 629
October	464.5	1 874.7	2 435.0	22 889	22 412	22 553	22 485	157 716
November	471.5	1 888.4	2 447.4	23 354	22 733	22 921	22 952	158 667
December	474.8	1 910.3	2 460.6	23 600	22 966	23 152	23 100	160 127

[1]Extended credit program discontinued January 9, 2003. See notes and definitions for more information.

Table 20-5. Money Stock, Reserves, and Monetary Base—Continued

(Averages of daily figures, seasonally adjusted.)

Year and month	Money stock measures, billions of dollars			Reserves, adjusted for change in reserve requirements, millions of dollars				
	M1	M2	M3	Total	Nonborrowed	Nonborrowed plus extended credit [1]	Required	Monetary base
1983								
January	477.2	1 963.3	2 488.9	23 226	22 697	22 854	22 678	161 136
February	484.3	2 000.5	2 517.8	23 901	23 319	23 597	23 466	163 170
March	490.6	2 018.6	2 534.1	24 414	23 621	23 939	23 981	165 052
April	493.2	2 031.9	2 553.9	24 900	23 890	24 295	24 424	166 549
May	500.0	2 046.4	2 569.5	24 860	23 907	24 420	24 411	167 842
June	504.0	2 056.7	2 585.0	25 277	23 641	24 599	24 797	169 393
July	507.8	2 067.8	2 596.0	25 356	23 903	24 480	24 848	170 129
August	510.5	2 076.9	2 609.8	25 376	23 830	24 320	24 929	171 208
September	512.8	2 086.1	2 626.3	25 435	23 994	24 509	24 937	172 411
October	517.1	2 102.2	2 646.1	25 454	24 610	24 866	24 949	173 584
November	519.0	2 115.4	2 673.9	25 396	24 491	24 497	24 867	174 605
December	521.4	2 126.5	2 697.4	25 367	24 593	24 595	24 806	175 467
1984								
January	525.1	2 141.2	2 714.9	25 451	24 736	24 740	24 838	176 896
February	527.5	2 161.4	2 742.6	25 829	25 262	25 266	24 923	177 839
March	531.4	2 178.4	2 771.9	25 763	24 811	24 838	25 095	178 866
April	535.0	2 194.9	2 801.2	25 691	24 457	24 501	25 218	179 894
May	536.7	2 207.5	2 828.4	25 882	22 894	22 931	25 313	180 729
June	540.2	2 218.5	2 850.2	26 094	22 793	24 666	25 334	181 996
July	540.9	2 226.9	2 871.8	25 980	20 056	25 064	25 351	182 994
August	541.0	2 233.6	2 886.0	26 039	18 023	25 066	25 359	183 760
September	543.1	2 247.5	2 904.7	26 089	18 847	25 306	25 440	184 645
October	543.7	2 262.1	2 930.2	26 259	20 242	25 299	25 641	185 226
November	547.5	2 284.8	2 957.9	26 518	21 901	25 738	25 820	186 113
December	551.6	2 310.0	2 990.6	26 913	23 727	26 331	26 078	187 238
1985								
January	557.0	2 336.0	3 018.0	27 077	25 682	26 732	26 334	188 082
February	563.6	2 357.5	3 040.7	27 596	26 307	27 110	26 746	189 636
March	566.6	2 369.5	3 056.6	27 590	25 997	27 056	26 916	190 317
April	570.4	2 378.9	3 062.5	27 870	26 548	27 416	27 134	191 360
May	575.2	2 393.2	3 078.8	28 155	26 821	27 355	27 402	192 699
June	582.2	2 416.2	3 103.6	28 848	27 644	28 309	27 926	194 751
July	589.1	2 433.0	3 112.7	29 141	28 034	28 541	28 301	195 951
August	596.2	2 447.5	3 131.4	29 652	28 580	29 149	28 818	198 006
September	603.3	2 459.9	3 149.7	30 030	28 741	29 397	29 333	199 301
October	607.8	2 471.6	3 167.1	30 490	29 303	29 932	29 746	200 745
November	612.2	2 481.2	3 182.3	30 916	29 175	29 706	29 998	202 119
December	619.8	2 495.7	3 208.1	31 569	30 250	30 749	30 505	203 562
1986								
January	621.5	2 505.7	3 232.8	31 563	30 793	31 290	30 481	204 227
February	625.2	2 516.1	3 250.7	31 658	30 775	31 267	30 645	205 315
March	633.5	2 536.2	3 277.2	32 090	31 330	31 848	31 207	206 917
April	640.9	2 561.0	3 307.7	32 517	31 625	32 259	31 745	208 129
May	652.0	2 588.4	3 331.0	33 265	32 389	32 974	32 387	210 149
June	660.6	2 608.6	3 353.0	33 947	33 144	33 674	33 028	211 794
July	670.3	2 630.5	3 381.9	34 657	33 916	34 294	33 784	213 409
August	678.7	2 650.3	3 407.8	35 191	34 319	34 784	34 451	215 271
September	687.4	2 671.9	3 435.3	35 621	34 613	35 183	34 932	216 769
October	694.9	2 691.9	3 455.6	36 262	35 420	35 917	35 545	218 645
November	705.4	2 705.5	3 467.1	37 270	36 519	36 937	36 369	220 698
December	724.7	2 732.3	3 499.1	38 840	38 014	38 317	37 667	223 425
1987								
January	730.2	2 748.1	3 524.7	39 244	38 664	38 889	38 173	225 338
February	730.7	2 751.8	3 534.3	39 006	38 450	38 733	37 813	226 564
March	733.8	2 757.7	3 542.6	38 827	38 300	38 564	37 907	227 093
April	743.9	2 771.9	3 562.7	39 533	38 540	38 811	38 677	228 961
May	745.8	2 777.2	3 578.2	39 812	38 776	39 064	38 744	230 515
June	743.2	2 778.8	3 593.4	39 462	38 685	38 958	38 228	231 312
July	743.1	2 783.3	3 599.2	39 080	38 408	38 602	38 221	231 981
August	744.9	2 792.3	3 620.1	39 208	38 561	38 693	38 157	233 513
September	747.5	2 803.6	3 642.5	39 118	38 178	38 586	38 333	234 715
October	756.2	2 819.2	3 667.9	39 826	38 883	39 333	38 737	237 107
November	753.3	2 824.0	3 681.5	39 334	38 709	39 103	38 394	238 800
December	750.2	2 831.5	3 686.5	38 913	38 135	38 618	37 893	239 837
1988								
January	756.2	2 852.4	3 709.1	39 464	38 383	38 754	38 213	241 821
February	757.8	2 875.4	3 737.2	39 406	39 010	39 215	38 268	242 802
March	761.8	2 895.7	3 762.1	39 266	37 514	38 993	38 321	243 751
April	768.1	2 915.7	3 788.5	39 622	36 628	39 252	38 737	245 761
May	771.8	2 931.2	3 814.6	39 958	37 380	39 487	38 911	247 440
June	778.4	2 943.4	3 834.2	40 277	37 195	39 748	39 382	249 157
July	781.4	2 953.1	3 850.3	40 514	37 075	39 613	39 623	250 995
August	783.3	2 958.3	3 864.5	40 470	37 229	39 882	39 500	252 076
September	783.8	2 963.2	3 876.3	40 343	37 503	39 562	39 326	253 370
October	783.2	2 971.5	3 890.1	40 422	38 123	39 904	39 370	254 574
November	784.8	2 986.4	3 909.0	40 548	37 687	40 009	39 374	255 678
December	786.7	2 994.5	3 928.8	40 453	38 738	39 982	39 392	256 892

[1]Extended credit program discontinued January 9, 2003. See notes and definitions for more information.

Table 20-5. Money Stock, Reserves, and Monetary Base—Continued

(Averages of daily figures, seasonally adjusted.)

Year and month	Money stock measures, billions of dollars			Reserves, adjusted for change in reserve requirements, millions of dollars				
	M1	M2	M3	Total	Nonborrowed	Nonborrowed plus extended credit [1]	Required	Monetary base
1989								
January	785.8	2 997.7	3 937.0	40 422	38 773	39 811	39 278	257 922
February	783.8	2 998.1	3 940.8	40 339	38 852	39 901	39 184	258 309
March	783.1	3 005.7	3 961.5	39 844	38 032	39 366	38 926	259 139
April	779.2	3 011.9	3 970.8	39 533	37 244	38 950	38 719	259 553
May	775.0	3 017.5	3 974.9	39 301	37 580	38 778	38 258	260 264
June	773.5	3 033.6	3 995.2	39 085	37 595	38 512	38 177	261 102
July	777.8	3 058.2	4 017.4	39 438	38 744	38 850	38 455	262 227
August	779.4	3 080.4	4 027.5	39 397	38 722	38 764	38 505	262 859
September	781.0	3 098.7	4 035.2	39 673	38 980	39 002	38 728	263 748
October	786.6	3 120.7	4 047.5	40 163	39 607	39 629	39 123	264 899
November	788.0	3 139.4	4 063.1	40 170	39 820	39 841	39 221	265 649
December	792.9	3 158.5	4 077.1	40 486	40 221	40 241	39 545	267 755
1990								
January	795.3	3 172.8	4 089.2	40 731	40 291	40 317	39 688	269 569
February	798.0	3 185.6	4 095.6	40 743	39 295	39 830	39 743	271 142
March	801.6	3 196.6	4 098.3	40 650	38 526	40 477	39 769	273 045
April	806.3	3 208.4	4 105.8	40 845	39 236	40 621	39 974	275 229
May	804.2	3 206.6	4 107.8	40 750	39 419	40 291	39 796	276 758
June	808.8	3 219.2	4 115.1	40 666	39 785	40 131	39 879	278 947
July	810.1	3 229.9	4 127.8	40 575	39 818	40 098	39 707	281 005
August	815.7	3 247.6	4 144.2	40 873	39 946	40 074	39 997	284 096
September	820.0	3 260.2	4 151.5	41 090	40 466	40 472	40 177	287 275
October	819.8	3 265.0	4 155.9	40 808	40 398	40 416	39 968	289 202
November	822.2	3 269.6	4 151.8	40 970	40 740	40 765	40 043	291 128
December	824.7	3 278.8	4 154.7	41 766	41 440	41 463	40 101	293 287
1991								
January	827.1	3 294.6	4 177.2	42 295	41 761	41 787	40 153	297 784
February	832.7	3 311.8	4 193.9	42 072	41 820	41 854	40 267	300 917
March	838.8	3 329.3	4 201.5	41 807	41 566	41 619	40 623	302 724
April	843.2	3 340.4	4 209.0	41 859	41 628	41 714	40 833	303 027
May	848.8	3 350.6	4 208.4	42 410	42 107	42 194	41 376	304 189
June	856.7	3 359.1	4 209.2	42 709	42 369	42 377	41 716	305 487
July	861.4	3 362.7	4 202.5	42 983	42 376	42 422	42 080	307 225
August	866.7	3 361.6	4 197.1	43 395	42 631	42 931	42 308	309 318
September	870.3	3 361.9	4 191.2	43 555	42 910	43 212	42 625	310 687
October	878.0	3 366.9	4 195.4	44 005	43 744	43 756	42 950	312 707
November	887.5	3 372.0	4 201.2	44 613	44 505	44 507	43 722	314 938
December	897.1	3 379.7	4 210.3	45 515	45 323	45 324	44 526	317 557
1992								
January	910.4	3 388.2	4 215.8	46 372	46 139	46 139	45 381	319 645
February	925.2	3 407.1	4 236.2	47 610	47 532	47 534	46 557	322 585
March	936.9	3 411.8	4 238.4	48 274	48 182	48 184	47 249	324 360
April	943.9	3 407.2	4 226.1	49 035	48 945	48 947	47 908	326 695
May	950.4	3 404.6	4 220.5	49 336	49 181	49 181	48 333	328 750
June	954.3	3 400.6	4 218.7	49 270	49 040	49 040	48 346	330 183
July	963.2	3 401.2	4 218.9	49 755	49 471	49 471	48 780	333 219
August	973.7	3 405.7	4 227.1	50 478	50 228	50 228	49 540	336 935
September	987.9	3 417.1	4 235.7	51 392	51 105	51 105	50 380	340 775
October	1 003.7	3 431.1	4 234.9	52 765	52 622	52 622	51 704	344 572
November	1 015.8	3 434.2	4 230.8	53 749	53 645	53 645	52 707	347 651
December	1 025.0	3 433.1	4 222.6	54 421	54 297	54 298	53 267	350 919
1993								
January	1 030.3	3 427.2	4 204.5	54 971	54 805	54 806	53 708	353 704
February	1 033.5	3 423.6	4 207.7	54 686	54 640	54 641	53 593	355 397
March	1 038.7	3 421.0	4 211.1	54 969	54 878	54 878	53 737	357 846
April	1 047.8	3 420.8	4 212.6	55 359	55 286	55 287	54 255	360 879
May	1 065.8	3 444.2	4 241.9	56 651	56 530	56 530	55 656	364 910
June	1 075.0	3 449.6	4 242.1	57 082	56 901	56 901	56 191	367 899
July	1 084.4	3 450.0	4 238.9	57 729	57 485	57 485	56 662	371 425
August	1 094.3	3 454.6	4 240.4	58 183	57 830	57 830	57 231	374 604
September	1 104.2	3 461.2	4 249.6	58 867	58 440	58 440	57 784	378 291
October	1 112.9	3 465.3	4 256.5	59 595	59 309	59 309	58 517	381 559
November	1 124.2	3 479.4	4 275.3	60 301	60 212	60 212	59 184	384 069
December	1 129.7	3 484.3	4 285.6	60 567	60 485	60 485	59 497	386 594
1994								
January	1 131.6	3 485.1	4 282.4	60 893	60 820	60 820	59 436	390 210
February	1 136.4	3 486.4	4 268.7	60 513	60 442	60 442	59 367	393 260
March	1 140.4	3 492.8	4 279.6	60 296	60 241	60 241	59 315	396 038
April	1 141.0	3 497.2	4 290.4	60 500	60 376	60 376	59 361	398 878
May	1 143.3	3 505.5	4 300.8	59 968	59 768	59 768	59 103	401 448
June	1 145.0	3 492.0	4 297.3	60 045	59 712	59 712	58 931	404 428
July	1 149.8	3 497.8	4 318.3	60 315	59 857	59 858	59 205	407 773
August	1 150.1	3 495.5	4 319.7	59 952	59 484	59 484	58 949	409 632
September	1 151.6	3 496.6	4 329.4	59 796	59 309	59 309	58 751	411 788
October	1 149.8	3 495.0	4 339.7	59 368	58 987	58 987	58 576	413 997
November	1 150.6	3 498.0	4 355.4	59 403	59 154	59 154	58 415	416 758
December	1 150.3	3 497.6	4 369.8	59 454	59 245	59 245	58 295	418 325

[1]Extended credit program discontinued January 9, 2003. See notes and definitions for more information.

Table 20-5. Money Stock, Reserves, and Monetary Base—Continued

(Averages of daily figures, seasonally adjusted.)

Year and month	Money stock measures, billions of dollars			Reserves, adjusted for change in reserve requirements, millions of dollars				
	M1	M2	M3	Total	Nonborrowed	Nonborrowed plus extended credit [1]	Required	Monetary base
1995								
January	1 151.2	3 503.4	4 393.7	59 410	59 274	59 278	58 071	421 019
February	1 147.1	3 500.6	4 396.5	58 644	58 585	58 585	57 683	421 630
March	1 146.4	3 501.9	4 415.7	58 201	58 132	58 132	57 386	424 679
April	1 148.9	3 510.0	4 436.5	57 969	57 858	57 858	57 216	427 888
May	1 144.7	3 533.1	4 476.0	57 642	57 492	57 492	56 768	430 563
June	1 143.8	3 558.6	4 514.6	57 376	57 104	57 104	56 393	430 193
July	1 144.8	3 577.2	4 540.2	57 815	57 444	57 444	56 711	430 693
August	1 145.0	3 599.4	4 575.5	57 536	57 254	57 254	56 532	431 322
September	1 141.2	3 611.2	4 596.4	57 307	57 030	57 030	56 338	431 899
October	1 136.8	3 623.3	4 613.6	56 725	56 480	56 480	55 640	432 649
November	1 133.6	3 630.9	4 624.4	56 314	56 109	56 109	55 360	432 949
December	1 126.8	3 640.6	4 636.3	56 483	56 226	56 226	55 193	434 585
1996								
January	1 122.9	3 658.5	4 670.3	55 881	55 843	55 843	54 417	434 812
February	1 118.0	3 672.6	4 700.6	54 617	54 583	54 583	53 761	432 590
March	1 121.8	3 698.0	4 734.7	55 292	55 271	55 271	54 153	435 872
April	1 124.2	3 709.5	4 753.0	55 175	55 085	55 085	54 052	436 960
May	1 115.8	3 718.9	4 788.1	54 036	53 908	53 908	53 130	437 491
June	1 114.3	3 732.0	4 811.0	54 139	53 753	53 753	53 031	440 073
July	1 111.6	3 747.5	4 837.4	53 374	53 006	53 006	52 356	442 573
August	1 100.9	3 756.0	4 857.3	52 159	51 825	51 825	51 201	444 688
September	1 095.6	3 766.0	4 885.4	51 309	50 942	50 942	50 262	446 032
October	1 085.2	3 780.1	4 925.6	50 037	49 750	49 750	49 030	446 864
November	1 082.1	3 795.2	4 946.3	49 776	49 562	49 562	48 724	448 784
December	1 080.0	3 815.8	4 985.5	50 183	50 028	50 028	48 766	452 081
1997								
January	1 080.1	3 829.7	5 013.0	49 680	49 635	49 635	48 456	453 523
February	1 077.4	3 840.8	5 045.3	48 712	48 670	48 670	47 681	454 525
March	1 070.7	3 855.7	5 079.8	47 847	47 690	47 690	46 681	456 228
April	1 062.6	3 872.6	5 120.7	47 348	47 087	47 087	46 339	457 897
May	1 062.9	3 884.5	5 146.8	46 637	46 394	46 394	45 374	459 509
June	1 065.2	3 901.7	5 176.9	46 907	46 540	46 540	45 593	462 162
July	1 065.3	3 921.4	5 235.2	46 735	46 325	46 325	45 518	464 706
August	1 073.7	3 951.4	5 291.5	46 908	46 310	46 310	45 653	466 996
September	1 066.9	3 970.9	5 333.7	46 251	45 813	45 813	44 950	469 206
October	1 065.3	3 988.5	5 376.2	45 958	45 689	45 689	44 544	471 817
November	1 069.3	4 010.1	5 417.2	46 411	46 258	46 258	44 742	475 929
December	1 072.2	4 031.6	5 460.9	46 873	46 549	46 549	45 189	479 946
1998								
January	1 073.4	4 055.6	5 508.6	46 687	46 477	46 477	44 894	482 061
February	1 077.4	4 088.0	5 545.5	45 740	45 682	45 682	44 208	483 225
March	1 076.6	4 114.3	5 610.7	45 854	45 813	45 813	44 503	484 941
April	1 076.4	4 137.5	5 647.1	46 127	46 055	46 055	44 739	486 896
May	1 077.6	4 158.5	5 687.0	45 514	45 361	45 361	44 241	488 839
June	1 076.1	4 184.3	5 728.4	45 413	45 162	45 162	43 798	491 865
July	1 074.5	4 200.7	5 749.6	44 889	44 631	44 631	43 519	494 676
August	1 074.1	4 224.6	5 814.7	44 954	44 683	44 683	43 423	497 881
September	1 078.6	4 266.9	5 883.9	44 847	44 596	44 596	43 152	502 607
October	1 084.7	4 307.9	5 953.6	44 884	44 710	44 710	43 312	506 852
November	1 093.4	4 347.6	6 010.3	44 824	44 741	44 741	43 205	510 345
December	1 094.9	4 379.5	6 051.9	45 129	45 012	45 012	43 615	513 892
1999								
January	1 096.3	4 401.6	6 080.9	44 474	44 268	44 268	42 988	516 404
February	1 096.1	4 427.6	6 134.1	44 207	44 091	44 091	43 011	520 260
March	1 096.0	4 437.5	6 132.3	44 032	43 968	43 968	42 764	524 613
April	1 102.1	4 468.8	6 172.7	43 507	43 341	43 341	42 347	528 337
May	1 101.8	4 486.5	6 200.4	43 745	43 618	43 618	42 523	533 195
June	1 098.5	4 507.8	6 237.5	43 110	42 966	42 966	41 815	537 004
July	1 098.0	4 531.7	6 268.7	42 131	41 822	41 822	41 007	540 534
August	1 098.0	4 553.0	6 299.2	42 249	41 906	41 906	41 090	544 840
September	1 095.9	4 568.0	6 323.0	42 207	41 869	41 869	40 998	550 330
October	1 101.7	4 587.1	6 378.4	41 727	41 446	41 446	40 576	557 808
November	1 110.8	4 612.7	6 465.0	41 918	41 683	41 683	40 589	571 625
December	1 123.1	4 641.1	6 551.5	41 958	41 638	41 638	40 661	593 938
2000								
January	1 121.4	4 667.8	6 605.5	42 138	41 765	41 765	40 119	590 917
February	1 108.8	4 683.1	6 642.2	40 901	40 793	40 793	39 789	572 526
March	1 107.6	4 712.4	6 704.0	40 344	40 165	40 165	39 134	571 265
April	1 114.9	4 762.5	6 767.3	40 323	40 018	40 018	39 165	571 970
May	1 105.7	4 754.9	6 776.9	40 456	40 094	40 094	39 484	573 485
June	1 103.6	4 772.1	6 823.6	40 121	39 642	39 642	39 004	575 701
July	1 103.5	4 784.9	6 875.2	40 020	39 451	39 451	38 877	577 035
August	1 100.2	4 819.1	6 945.0	39 773	39 194	39 194	38 755	577 809
September	1 098.6	4 851.6	7 003.5	39 756	39 279	39 279	38 638	578 403
October	1 098.0	4 869.2	7 027.0	39 498	39 079	39 079	38 348	580 520
November	1 091.9	4 878.4	7 038.3	39 611	39 328	39 328	38 304	582 362
December	1 087.6	4 920.7	7 117.6	38 674	38 464	38 464	37 246	584 945

[1]Extended credit program discontinued January 9, 2003. See notes and definitions for more information.

Table 20-5. Money Stock, Reserves, and Monetary Base—Continued

(Averages of daily figures, seasonally adjusted.)

Year and month	Money stock measures, billions of dollars			Reserves, adjusted for change in reserve requirements, millions of dollars				
	M1	M2	M3	Total	Nonborrowed	Nonborrowed plus extended credit [1]	Required	Monetary base
2001								
January	1 096.6	4 975.8	7 237.2	37 765	37 692	37 692	36 380	587 906
February	1 101.2	5 015.1	7 308.5	38 428	38 377	38 377	36 921	589 547
March	1 108.8	5 075.1	7 372.0	38 284	38 226	38 226	36 884	592 167
April	1 117.4	5 136.1	7 507.8	38 342	38 291	38 291	37 065	595 396
May	1 119.7	5 135.8	7 564.1	38 529	38 316	38 316	37 509	598 757
June	1 126.5	5 175.0	7 644.7	38 960	38 730	38 730	37 597	602 076
July	1 140.4	5 208.1	7 691.9	39 447	39 165	39 165	38 040	607 958
August	1 150.1	5 243.2	7 696.3	40 029	39 846	39 846	38 822	615 542
September	1 203.5	5 353.5	7 853.2	58 141	54 757	54 757	39 125	639 637
October	1 165.2	5 344.2	7 897.8	45 616	45 489	45 489	44 290	630 304
November	1 170.7	5 384.4	7 973.0	41 141	41 057	41 057	39 699	629 976
December	1 182.1	5 429.8	8 035.4	41 390	41 323	41 323	39 739	635 480
2002								
January	1 189.6	5 455.1	8 063.9	41 469	41 419	41 419	40 074	641 105
February	1 190.3	5 482.6	8 109.3	41 632	41 602	41 602	40 261	646 006
March	1 191.6	5 490.2	8 117.3	40 884	40 805	40 805	39 463	649 776
April	1 188.7	5 494.4	8 142.6	40 585	40 514	40 514	39 373	653 832
May	1 190.2	5 519.5	8 175.1	39 529	39 417	39 417	38 268	657 861
June	1 191.9	5 541.3	8 190.8	39 198	39 056	39 056	37 960	663 030
July	1 200.9	5 590.0	8 244.2	39 284	39 092	39 092	37 906	668 564
August	1 186.2	5 629.8	8 298.1	39 961	39 627	39 627	38 353	670 264
September	1 194.4	5 655.7	8 331.5	39 049	38 820	38 820	37 563	671 387
October	1 203.1	5 703.2	8 368.9	39 246	39 103	39 103	37 711	673 804
November	1 208.0	5 747.4	8 498.8	39 998	39 726	39 726	38 359	676 976
December	1 219.0	5 773.6	8 568.0	40 359	40 279	40 279	38 350	681 462
2003								
January	1 225.8	5 803.0	8 588.1	40 542	40 515	. . .	38 835	685 012
February	1 237.6	5 843.2	8 628.7	41 105	41 080	. . .	39 139	690 401
March	1 238.2	5 861.3	8 648.8	41 010	40 988	. . .	39 375	694 695
April	1 251.8	5 901.7	8 686.0	40 635	40 606	. . .	39 092	698 198
May	1 270.4	5 958.7	8 741.9	41 018	40 963	. . .	39 396	701 552
June	1 279.2	5 998.3	8 791.6	42 375	42 214	. . .	40 330	703 827
July	1 290.0	6 048.8	8 888.7	43 100	42 969	. . .	41 164	705 476
August	1 294.6	6 097.4	8 918.2	45 872	45 544	. . .	42 104	709 627
September	1 295.7	6 076.7	8 906.5	44 225	44 045	. . .	42 714	710 911
October	1 297.0	6 064.4	8 896.8	43 526	43 418	. . .	42 050	714 737
November	1 296.5	6 058.0	8 880.3	43 131	43 063	. . .	41 638	717 655
December	1 304.1	6 059.4	8 872.3	42 699	42 654	. . .	41 657	720 128
2004								
January	1 305.0	6 067.6	8 930.2	42 776	42 670	. . .	41 884	721 675
February	1 319.7	6 112.6	9 000.3	42 893	42 851	. . .	41 697	723 800
March	1 329.4	6 153.8	9 080.7	44 658	44 607	. . .	42 851	726 638
April	1 337.1	6 195.9	9 149.6	45 723	45 638	. . .	43 916	730 530
May	1 336.2	6 262.1	9 243.8	45 664	45 552	. . .	43 977	734 347
June	1 340.3	6 270.1	9 275.7	46 014	45 834	. . .	44 081	738 914
July	1 343.3	6 278.0	9 282.7	46 103	45 859	. . .	44 384	746 118
August	1 354.1	6 300.3	9 314.4	45 513	45 262	. . .	43 930	747 691
September	1 359.7	6 329.4	9 351.8	46 331	45 996	. . .	44 676	751 981
October	1 360.7	6 353.3	9 359.4	46 337	46 158	. . .	44 581	754 674
November	1 374.2	6 389.1	9 395.1	46 258	46 075	. . .	44 475	759 101
December	1 372.1	6 408.1	9 433.0	46 625	46 562	. . .	44 716	758 988
2005								
January	1 365.8	6 422.4	9 487.2	47 170	47 108	. . .	45 431	760 418
February	1 369.1	6 443.9	9 531.6	45 890	45 848	. . .	44 396	763 316
March	1 372.6	6 463.7	9 565.3	46 627	46 577	. . .	44 847	765 822
April	1 363.3	6 468.1	9 620.9	46 290	46 158	. . .	44 619	766 849
May	1 370.3	6 479.2	9 665.0	45 805	45 665	. . .	44 273	768 301
June	1 374.2	6 506.0	9 725.3	46 277	46 028	. . .	44 503	771 108
July	1 369.3	6 527.7	9 762.4	46 235	45 810	. . .	44 493	773 167
August	1 376.8	6 558.8	9 864.6	45 232	44 869	. . .	43 618	775 426
September	1 372.4	6 588.6	9 950.8	46 194	45 862	. . .	44 159	778 753
October	1 374.3	6 619.0	10 032.0	45 488	45 205	. . .	43 592	780 785
November	1 375.1	6 638.2	10 078.5	45 423	45 297	. . .	43 635	784 153
December	1 368.5	6 664.8	10 154.0	45 312	45 143	. . .	43 403	787 091

[1]Extended credit program discontinued January 9, 2003. See notes and definitions for more information.
. . . = Not available.

Table 20-6. Interest Rates, Bond Yields, and Stock Price Indexes

(Not seasonally adjusted.)

Year and month	Percent per annum											Stock price indexes		
	Short-term rates					U.S. Treasury securities		Bond yields				Dow Jones industrials (30 stocks)	Standard and Poor's composite (500 stocks) [2]	Nasdaq composite [3]
	Federal funds	Federal Reserve discount rate [1]	U.S. Treasury bills, 3-month	U.S. Treasury bills, 6-month	Bank prime rate	1-year	10-year	Domestic corporate (Moody's)		State and local bonds (Bond Buyer)	Fixed-rate first mortgages			
								Aaa	Baa					
1945	...	1.00	0.38	...	1.50	...	...	2.62	3.29	...	...	169.82	15.16	...
1946	...	1.00	0.38	...	1.50	...	...	2.53	3.05	...	...	191.65	17.08	...
1947	...	1.00	0.60	...	1.63	...	...	2.61	3.24	...	...	177.58	15.17	...
1948	...	1.34	1.04	...	1.88	...	...	2.82	3.47	...	...	179.95	15.53	...
1949	...	1.50	1.10	...	2.00	...	...	2.66	3.42	...	...	179.48	15.23	...
1950	...	1.59	1.22	...	2.07	...	...	2.62	3.24	...	...	216.31	18.40	...
1951	...	1.75	1.55	...	2.56	...	...	2.86	3.41	...	...	257.64	22.34	...
1952	...	1.75	1.77	...	3.00	...	...	2.96	3.52	...	...	270.76	24.50	...
1953	...	1.99	1.94	...	3.17	...	...	3.20	3.73	2.74	...	275.97	24.73	...
1954	...	1.60	0.95	...	3.05	1.05	2.40	2.90	3.51	2.39	...	333.94	29.69	...
1945														
January	...	...	0.38	...	...	...	...	2.69	3.46	...	...	153.95	13.49	...
February	...	...	0.38	...	...	...	...	2.65	3.41	...	...	157.24	13.94	...
March	...	...	0.38	...	...	...	...	2.62	3.38	...	...	157.31	13.93	...
April	...	...	0.38	...	...	...	...	2.61	3.36	...	...	160.34	14.28	...
May	...	...	0.38	...	...	...	...	2.62	3.32	...	...	165.52	14.82	...
June	...	...	0.38	...	...	...	...	2.61	3.29	...	...	167.37	15.09	...
July	...	...	0.38	...	...	...	...	2.60	3.26	...	...	163.92	14.78	...
August	...	...	0.38	...	...	...	...	2.61	3.26	...	...	166.17	14.83	...
September	...	...	0.38	...	...	...	...	2.62	3.24	...	...	177.85	15.84	...
October	...	...	0.38	...	...	...	...	2.62	3.20	...	...	185.06	16.50	...
November	...	...	0.38	...	...	...	...	2.62	3.15	...	...	190.34	17.04	...
December	...	...	0.38	...	...	...	...	2.61	3.10	...	...	192.68	17.33	...
1946														
January	...	...	0.38	...	...	...	...	2.54	3.01	...	...	199.23	18.02	...
February	...	...	0.38	...	...	...	...	2.48	2.95	...	...	198.56	18.07	...
March	...	...	0.38	...	...	...	...	2.47	2.94	...	...	194.23	17.53	...
April	...	...	0.38	...	...	...	...	2.46	2.96	...	...	205.71	18.66	...
May	...	...	0.38	...	...	...	...	2.51	3.02	...	...	206.80	18.70	...
June	...	...	0.38	...	...	...	...	2.49	3.03	...	...	207.33	18.58	...
July	...	...	0.38	...	...	...	...	2.48	3.03	...	...	202.28	18.05	...
August	...	...	0.38	...	...	...	...	2.51	3.03	...	...	199.45	17.70	...
September	...	...	0.38	...	...	...	...	2.58	3.10	...	...	172.74	15.09	...
October	...	...	0.38	...	...	...	...	2.60	3.15	...	...	169.47	14.75	...
November	...	...	0.38	...	...	...	...	2.59	3.17	...	...	168.74	14.69	...
December	...	...	0.38	...	...	...	...	2.61	3.17	...	...	174.29	15.13	...
1947														
January	...	...	0.38	...	...	...	...	2.57	3.13	...	...	176.15	15.21	...
February	...	...	0.38	...	...	...	...	2.55	3.12	...	...	181.43	15.80	...
March	...	...	0.38	...	...	...	...	2.55	3.15	...	...	176.69	15.16	...
April	...	...	0.38	...	...	...	...	2.53	3.16	...	...	171.23	14.60	...
May	...	...	0.38	...	...	...	...	2.53	3.17	...	...	168.63	14.34	...
June	...	...	0.38	...	...	...	...	2.55	3.21	...	...	173.76	14.84	...
July	...	...	0.64	...	...	...	...	2.55	3.18	...	...	183.53	15.77	...
August	...	...	0.74	...	...	...	...	2.56	3.17	...	...	180.08	15.46	...
September	...	...	0.79	...	...	...	...	2.61	3.23	...	...	176.81	15.06	...
October	...	...	0.84	...	...	...	...	2.70	3.35	...	...	181.95	15.45	...
November	...	...	0.92	...	...	...	...	2.77	3.44	...	...	181.52	15.27	...
December	...	...	0.95	...	...	...	...	2.86	3.52	...	...	179.24	15.03	...
1948														
January	...	...	0.97	...	...	...	...	2.86	3.52	...	...	176.30	14.83	...
February	...	...	0.99	...	...	...	...	2.85	3.53	...	...	168.64	14.10	...
March	...	...	1.00	...	...	...	...	2.83	3.53	...	...	169.77	14.30	...
April	...	...	1.00	...	...	...	...	2.78	3.47	...	...	180.05	15.40	...
May	...	...	1.00	...	...	...	...	2.76	3.38	...	...	186.51	16.15	...
June	...	...	1.00	...	...	...	...	2.76	3.34	...	...	191.06	16.82	...
July	...	...	1.00	...	...	...	...	2.81	3.37	...	...	187.07	16.42	...
August	...	...	1.03	...	...	...	...	2.84	3.44	...	...	181.77	15.94	...
September	...	...	1.09	...	...	...	...	2.84	3.45	...	...	180.34	15.76	...
October	...	...	1.12	...	...	...	...	2.84	3.50	...	...	185.16	16.19	...
November	...	...	1.14	...	...	...	...	2.84	3.53	...	...	176.76	15.29	...
December	...	...	1.15	...	...	...	...	2.79	3.53	...	...	176.30	15.19	...
1949														
January	...	...	1.16	...	2.00	...	...	2.71	3.46	...	...	179.63	15.36	...
February	...	...	1.16	...	2.00	...	...	2.71	3.45	...	...	174.54	14.77	...
March	...	...	1.16	...	2.00	...	...	2.70	3.47	...	...	175.87	14.91	...
April	...	...	1.16	...	2.00	...	...	2.70	3.45	...	...	175.63	14.89	...
May	...	...	1.15	...	2.00	...	...	2.71	3.45	...	...	173.93	14.78	...
June	...	...	1.16	...	2.00	...	...	2.71	3.47	...	...	165.60	13.97	...
July	...	...	0.98	...	2.00	...	...	2.67	3.46	...	...	173.34	14.76	...
August	...	...	1.02	...	2.00	...	...	2.62	3.40	...	...	179.25	15.29	...
September	...	...	1.06	...	2.00	...	...	2.60	3.37	...	...	180.92	15.49	...
October	...	...	1.04	...	2.00	...	...	2.61	3.36	...	...	186.57	15.89	...
November	...	...	1.06	...	2.00	...	...	2.60	3.35	...	...	191.49	16.11	...
December	...	...	1.10	...	2.00	...	...	2.58	3.31	...	...	196.78	16.54	...

[1]Federal Reserve Bank of New York. Through 2002, represents the rate for adjustment credit. Beginning in 2003, represents the rate for primary credit. See notes and definitions for more information.
[2]1941–1943 = 10.
[3]February 5, 1971 = 100.
... = Not available.

Table 20-6. Interest Rates, Bond Yields, and Stock Price Indexes—Continued

(Not seasonally adjusted.)

Year and month	Percent per annum											Stock price indexes		
	Short-term rates					U.S. Treasury securities		Bond yields				Dow Jones industrials (30 stocks)	Standard and Poor's composite (500 stocks) [2]	Nasdaq composite [3]
	Federal funds	Federal Reserve discount rate [1]	U.S. Treasury bills, 3-month	U.S. Treasury bills, 6-month	Bank prime rate	1-year	10-year	Domestic corporate (Moody's)		State and local bonds (Bond Buyer)	Fixed-rate first mortgages			
								Aaa	Baa					
1950														
January	. . .	1.50	1.09	. . .	2.00	. . .	. . .	2.57	3.24	. . .	. . .	199.75	16.88	. . .
February	. . .	1.50	1.13	. . .	2.00	. . .	. . .	2.58	3.24	. . .	. . .	203.31	17.21	. . .
March	. . .	1.50	1.14	. . .	2.00	. . .	. . .	2.58	3.24	. . .	. . .	206.25	17.35	. . .
April	. . .	1.50	1.16	. . .	2.00	. . .	. . .	2.60	3.23	. . .	. . .	212.76	17.84	. . .
May	. . .	1.50	1.17	. . .	2.00	. . .	. . .	2.61	3.25	. . .	. . .	219.30	18.44	. . .
June	. . .	1.50	1.17	. . .	2.00	. . .	. . .	2.62	3.28	. . .	. . .	221.02	18.74	. . .
July	. . .	1.50	1.17	. . .	2.00	. . .	. . .	2.65	3.32	. . .	. . .	205.31	17.38	. . .
August	. . .	1.59	1.21	. . .	2.00	. . .	. . .	2.61	3.23	. . .	. . .	216.61	18.43	. . .
September	. . .	1.75	1.31	. . .	2.08	. . .	. . .	2.64	3.21	. . .	. . .	223.20	19.08	. . .
October	. . .	1.75	1.33	. . .	2.25	. . .	. . .	2.67	3.22	. . .	. . .	229.24	19.87	. . .
November	. . .	1.75	1.36	. . .	2.25	. . .	. . .	2.67	3.22	. . .	. . .	229.08	19.83	. . .
December	. . .	1.75	1.37	. . .	2.25	. . .	. . .	2.67	3.20	. . .	. . .	229.18	19.75	. . .
1951														
January	. . .	1.75	1.39	. . .	2.44	. . .	. . .	2.66	3.17	. . .	. . .	244.41	21.21	. . .
February	. . .	1.75	1.39	. . .	2.50	. . .	. . .	2.66	3.16	. . .	. . .	253.16	22.00	. . .
March	. . .	1.75	1.42	. . .	2.50	. . .	. . .	2.78	3.23	. . .	. . .	249.36	21.63	. . .
April	. . .	1.75	1.52	. . .	2.50	. . .	. . .	2.87	3.35	. . .	. . .	253.02	21.92	. . .
May	. . .	1.75	1.58	. . .	2.50	. . .	. . .	2.89	3.40	. . .	. . .	254.45	21.93	. . .
June	. . .	1.75	1.50	. . .	2.50	. . .	. . .	2.94	3.49	. . .	. . .	249.32	21.55	. . .
July	. . .	1.75	1.59	. . .	2.50	. . .	. . .	2.94	3.53	. . .	. . .	253.61	21.93	. . .
August	. . .	1.75	1.64	. . .	2.50	. . .	. . .	2.88	3.50	. . .	. . .	264.93	22.89	. . .
September	. . .	1.75	1.65	. . .	2.50	. . .	. . .	2.84	3.46	. . .	. . .	273.37	23.48	. . .
October	. . .	1.75	1.61	. . .	2.62	. . .	. . .	2.89	3.50	. . .	. . .	269.85	23.36	. . .
November	. . .	1.75	1.61	. . .	2.75	. . .	. . .	2.96	3.56	. . .	. . .	259.65	22.71	. . .
December	. . .	1.75	1.73	. . .	2.85	. . .	. . .	3.01	3.61	. . .	. . .	266.15	23.41	. . .
1952														
January	. . .	1.75	1.69	. . .	3.00	. . .	. . .	2.98	3.59	. . .	. . .	271.64	24.19	. . .
February	. . .	1.75	1.57	. . .	3.00	. . .	. . .	2.93	3.53	. . .	. . .	264.72	23.75	. . .
March	. . .	1.75	1.66	. . .	3.00	. . .	. . .	2.96	3.51	. . .	. . .	264.45	23.81	. . .
April	. . .	1.75	1.62	. . .	3.00	. . .	. . .	2.93	3.50	. . .	. . .	262.46	23.74	. . .
May	. . .	1.75	1.71	. . .	3.00	. . .	. . .	2.93	3.49	. . .	. . .	261.63	23.73	. . .
June	. . .	1.75	1.70	. . .	3.00	. . .	. . .	2.94	3.50	. . .	. . .	268.39	24.38	. . .
July	. . .	1.75	1.82	. . .	3.00	. . .	. . .	2.95	3.50	. . .	. . .	276.05	25.08	. . .
August	. . .	1.75	1.88	. . .	3.00	. . .	. . .	2.94	3.51	. . .	. . .	276.70	25.18	. . .
September	. . .	1.75	1.79	. . .	3.00	. . .	. . .	2.95	3.52	. . .	. . .	272.41	24.78	. . .
October	. . .	1.75	1.78	. . .	3.00	. . .	. . .	3.01	3.54	. . .	. . .	267.78	24.26	. . .
November	. . .	1.75	1.86	. . .	3.00	. . .	. . .	2.98	3.53	. . .	. . .	276.38	25.03	. . .
December	. . .	1.75	2.13	. . .	3.00	. . .	. . .	2.97	3.51	. . .	. . .	285.96	26.04	. . .
1953														
January	. . .	1.88	2.04	. . .	3.00	. . .	. . .	3.02	3.51	2.44	. . .	288.45	26.18	. . .
February	. . .	2.00	2.02	. . .	3.00	. . .	. . .	3.07	3.53	2.59	. . .	283.96	25.86	. . .
March	. . .	2.00	2.08	. . .	3.00	. . .	. . .	3.12	3.57	2.65	. . .	286.79	25.99	. . .
April	. . .	2.00	2.18	. . .	3.03	2.36	2.83	3.23	3.65	2.67	. . .	275.29	24.71	. . .
May	. . .	2.00	2.20	. . .	3.25	2.48	3.05	3.34	3.78	2.82	. . .	276.84	24.84	. . .
June	. . .	2.00	2.23	. . .	3.25	2.45	3.11	3.40	3.86	3.03	. . .	266.89	23.95	. . .
July	. . .	2.00	2.10	. . .	3.25	2.38	2.93	3.28	3.86	2.95	. . .	270.33	24.29	. . .
August	. . .	2.00	2.09	. . .	3.25	2.28	2.95	3.24	3.85	2.90	. . .	272.20	24.39	. . .
September	. . .	2.00	1.88	. . .	3.25	2.20	2.87	3.29	3.88	2.87	. . .	261.90	23.27	. . .
October	. . .	2.00	1.40	. . .	3.25	1.79	2.66	3.16	3.82	2.71	. . .	270.72	23.97	. . .
November	. . .	2.00	1.43	. . .	3.25	1.67	2.68	3.11	3.75	2.60	. . .	277.09	24.50	. . .
December	. . .	2.00	1.63	. . .	3.25	1.66	2.59	3.13	3.74	2.59	. . .	281.15	24.83	. . .
1954														
January	. . .	2.00	1.21	. . .	3.25	1.41	2.48	3.06	3.71	2.50	. . .	286.64	25.46	. . .
February	. . .	1.79	0.98	. . .	3.25	1.14	2.47	2.95	3.61	2.42	. . .	292.13	26.02	. . .
March	. . .	1.75	1.05	. . .	3.13	1.13	2.37	2.86	3.51	2.39	. . .	299.16	26.57	. . .
April	. . .	1.63	1.01	. . .	3.00	0.96	2.29	2.85	3.47	2.47	. . .	310.93	27.63	. . .
May	. . .	1.50	0.78	. . .	3.00	0.85	2.37	2.88	3.47	2.49	. . .	322.85	28.73	. . .
June	. . .	1.50	0.65	. . .	3.00	0.82	2.38	2.90	3.49	2.47	. . .	327.91	28.96	. . .
July	0.80	1.50	0.71	. . .	3.00	0.84	2.30	2.89	3.50	2.32	. . .	341.27	30.13	. . .
August	1.22	1.50	0.89	. . .	3.00	0.88	2.36	2.87	3.49	2.26	. . .	346.06	30.73	. . .
September	1.06	1.50	1.01	. . .	3.00	1.03	2.38	2.89	3.47	2.31	. . .	352.71	31.45	. . .
October	0.85	1.50	0.99	. . .	3.00	1.17	2.43	2.87	3.46	2.34	. . .	358.29	32.18	. . .
November	0.83	1.50	0.95	. . .	3.00	1.14	2.48	2.89	3.45	2.32	. . .	375.71	33.44	. . .
December	1.28	1.50	1.17	. . .	3.00	1.21	2.51	2.90	3.45	2.36	. . .	393.84	34.97	. . .
1955														
January	1.39	1.50	1.26	. . .	3.00	1.39	2.61	2.93	3.45	2.40	. . .	398.43	35.60	. . .
February	1.29	1.50	1.18	. . .	3.00	1.57	2.65	2.93	3.47	2.43	. . .	410.26	36.79	. . .
March	1.35	1.50	1.33	. . .	3.00	1.59	2.68	3.02	3.48	2.44	. . .	408.91	36.50	. . .
April	1.43	1.63	1.62	. . .	3.00	1.75	2.75	3.01	3.49	2.41	. . .	423.00	37.76	. . .
May	1.43	1.75	1.49	. . .	3.00	1.90	2.76	3.04	3.50	2.38	. . .	421.55	37.60	. . .
June	1.64	1.75	1.43	. . .	3.00	1.91	2.78	3.05	3.51	2.41	. . .	440.83	39.78	. . .
July	1.68	1.75	1.62	. . .	3.00	2.02	2.90	3.06	3.52	2.54	. . .	462.17	42.69	. . .
August	1.96	1.97	1.88	. . .	3.23	2.37	2.97	3.11	3.56	2.60	. . .	457.31	42.43	. . .
September	2.18	2.18	2.09	. . .	3.25	2.36	2.97	3.13	3.59	2.58	. . .	476.44	44.34	. . .
October	2.24	2.25	2.26	. . .	3.40	2.39	2.88	3.10	3.59	2.51	. . .	452.65	42.11	. . .
November	2.35	2.36	2.22	. . .	3.50	2.48	2.89	3.10	3.58	2.45	. . .	476.60	44.95	. . .
December	2.48	2.50	2.56	. . .	3.50	2.73	2.96	3.15	3.62	2.57	. . .	484.58	45.37	. . .

[1]Federal Reserve Bank of New York. Through 2002, represents the rate for adjustment credit. Beginning in 2003, represents the rate for primary credit. See notes and definitions for more information.
[2]1941–1943 = 10.
[3]February 5, 1971 = 100.
. . . = Not available.

Table 20-6. Interest Rates, Bond Yields, and Stock Price Indexes—Continued

(Not seasonally adjusted.)

	Percent per annum											Stock price indexes		
	Short-term rates					U.S. Treasury securities		Bond yields						
								Domestic corporate (Moody's)		State and local bonds (Bond Buyer)	Fixed-rate first mortgages	Dow Jones industrials (30 stocks)	Standard and Poor's composite (500 stocks) [2]	Nasdaq composite [3]
Year and month	Federal funds	Federal Reserve discount rate [1]	U.S. Treasury bills, 3-month	U.S. Treasury bills, 6-month	Bank prime rate	1-year	10-year	Aaa	Baa					
1956														
January	2.45	2.50	2.46	...	3.50	2.58	2.90	3.11	3.60	2.50	...	474.75	44.15	...
February	2.50	2.50	2.37	...	3.50	2.49	2.84	3.08	3.58	2.44	...	475.53	44.43	...
March	2.50	2.50	2.31	...	3.50	2.61	2.96	3.10	3.60	2.57	...	502.67	47.49	...
April	2.62	2.65	2.61	...	3.65	2.92	3.18	3.24	3.68	2.70	...	511.05	48.05	...
May	2.75	2.75	2.65	...	3.75	2.94	3.07	3.28	3.73	2.68	...	495.21	46.54	...
June	2.71	2.75	2.53	...	3.75	2.74	3.00	3.26	3.76	2.54	...	485.33	46.27	...
July	2.75	2.75	2.33	...	3.75	2.76	3.11	3.28	3.80	2.65	...	509.75	48.78	...
August	2.73	2.81	2.61	...	3.84	3.10	3.33	3.43	3.93	2.80	...	511.69	48.49	...
September	2.95	3.00	2.85	...	4.00	3.35	3.38	3.56	4.07	2.93	...	495.03	46.84	...
October	2.96	3.00	2.96	...	4.00	3.28	3.34	3.59	4.17	2.95	...	483.81	46.24	...
November	2.88	3.00	3.00	...	4.00	3.44	3.49	3.69	4.24	3.16	...	479.36	45.76	...
December	2.94	3.00	3.23	...	4.00	3.68	3.59	3.75	4.37	3.22	...	492.02	46.44	...
1957														
January	2.84	3.00	3.21	...	4.00	3.37	3.46	3.77	4.49	3.18	...	485.90	45.43	...
February	3.00	3.00	3.16	...	4.00	3.38	3.34	3.67	4.47	3.00	...	466.83	43.47	...
March	2.96	3.00	3.14	...	4.00	3.42	3.41	3.66	4.43	3.09	...	472.77	44.03	...
April	3.00	3.00	3.11	...	4.00	3.49	3.48	3.67	4.44	3.13	...	485.42	45.05	...
May	3.00	3.00	3.04	...	4.00	3.48	3.60	3.74	4.52	3.27	...	500.83	46.78	...
June	3.00	3.00	3.32	...	4.00	3.65	3.80	3.91	4.63	3.41	...	505.29	47.55	...
July	2.99	3.00	3.16	...	4.00	3.81	3.93	3.99	4.73	3.39	...	514.65	48.51	...
August	3.24	3.15	3.40	...	4.42	4.01	3.93	4.10	4.82	3.54	...	487.97	45.84	...
September	3.47	3.50	3.58	...	4.50	4.07	3.92	4.12	4.93	3.53	...	471.80	43.98	...
October	3.50	3.50	3.59	...	4.50	4.01	3.97	4.10	4.99	3.42	...	443.38	41.24	...
November	3.28	3.23	3.34	...	4.50	3.57	3.72	4.08	5.09	3.37	...	436.73	40.35	...
December	2.98	3.00	3.10	...	4.50	3.18	3.21	3.81	5.03	3.04	...	436.96	40.33	...
1958														
January	2.72	2.94	2.60	...	4.34	2.65	3.09	3.60	4.83	2.91	...	445.69	41.12	...
February	1.67	2.75	1.56	...	4.00	1.99	3.05	3.59	4.66	3.02	...	444.16	41.26	...
March	1.20	2.35	1.35	...	4.00	1.84	2.98	3.63	4.68	3.06	...	450.15	42.11	...
April	1.26	2.03	1.13	...	3.83	1.45	2.88	3.60	4.67	2.96	...	446.91	42.34	...
May	0.63	1.75	1.05	...	3.50	1.37	2.92	3.57	4.62	2.92	...	460.04	43.70	...
June	0.93	1.75	0.88	...	3.50	1.23	2.97	3.57	4.55	2.97	...	471.98	44.75	...
July	0.68	1.75	0.96	...	3.50	1.61	3.20	3.67	4.53	3.09	...	488.30	45.98	...
August	1.53	1.75	1.69	...	3.50	2.50	3.54	3.85	4.67	3.35	...	507.55	47.70	...
September	1.76	1.91	2.48	...	3.83	3.05	3.76	4.09	4.87	3.54	...	521.81	48.96	...
October	1.80	2.00	2.79	...	4.00	3.19	3.80	4.11	4.92	3.45	...	539.85	50.95	...
November	2.27	2.40	2.76	...	4.00	3.10	3.74	4.09	4.87	3.32	...	557.11	52.50	...
December	2.42	2.50	2.81	3.01	4.00	3.29	3.86	4.08	4.85	3.33	...	566.44	53.49	...
1959														
January	2.48	2.50	2.84	3.09	4.00	3.36	4.02	4.12	4.87	3.42	...	592.30	55.62	...
February	2.43	2.50	2.71	3.13	4.00	3.54	3.96	4.14	4.89	3.36	...	590.72	54.77	...
March	2.80	2.92	2.85	3.13	4.00	3.61	3.99	4.13	4.85	3.30	...	609.13	56.15	...
April	2.96	3.00	2.96	3.27	4.00	3.72	4.12	4.23	4.86	3.39	...	617.00	57.10	...
May	2.90	3.05	2.85	3.33	4.23	3.96	4.31	4.37	4.96	3.57	...	630.80	57.96	...
June	3.39	3.50	3.25	3.52	4.50	4.07	4.34	4.46	5.04	3.71	...	631.52	57.46	...
July	3.47	3.50	3.24	3.82	4.50	4.39	4.40	4.47	5.08	3.71	...	662.81	59.74	...
August	3.50	3.50	3.36	3.87	4.50	4.42	4.43	4.43	5.09	3.58	...	660.58	59.40	...
September	3.76	3.83	4.00	4.70	5.00	5.00	4.68	4.52	5.18	3.78	...	635.49	57.05	...
October	3.98	4.00	4.12	4.53	5.00	4.80	4.53	4.57	5.28	3.62	...	637.35	57.00	...
November	4.00	4.00	4.21	4.54	5.00	4.81	4.53	4.56	5.26	3.55	...	646.43	57.23	...
December	3.99	4.00	4.57	4.85	5.00	5.14	4.69	4.58	5.28	3.70	...	671.36	59.06	...
1960														
January	3.99	4.00	4.44	4.74	5.00	5.03	4.72	4.61	5.34	3.72	...	655.39	58.03	...
February	3.97	4.00	3.96	4.30	5.00	4.66	4.49	4.56	5.34	3.60	...	624.89	55.78	...
March	3.84	4.00	3.44	3.61	5.00	4.02	4.25	4.49	5.25	3.57	...	614.70	55.02	...
April	3.92	4.00	3.25	3.55	5.00	4.04	4.28	4.45	5.20	3.56	...	619.98	55.73	...
May	3.85	4.00	3.39	3.58	5.00	4.21	4.35	4.46	5.28	3.60	...	615.63	55.22	...
June	3.32	3.65	2.64	2.74	5.00	3.36	4.15	4.45	5.26	3.55	...	644.39	57.26	...
July	3.23	3.50	2.40	2.71	5.00	3.20	3.90	4.41	5.22	3.50	...	625.83	55.84	...
August	2.98	3.18	2.29	2.59	4.85	2.95	3.80	4.28	5.08	3.33	...	624.47	56.51	...
September	2.60	3.00	2.49	2.83	4.50	3.07	3.80	4.25	5.01	3.42	...	598.10	54.81	...
October	2.47	3.00	2.43	2.73	4.50	3.04	3.89	4.30	5.11	3.53	...	582.47	53.73	...
November	2.44	3.00	2.39	2.66	4.50	3.08	3.93	4.31	5.08	3.40	...	601.14	55.47	...
December	1.98	3.00	2.27	2.50	4.50	2.86	3.84	4.35	5.10	3.40	...	609.54	56.80	...
1961														
January	1.45	3.00	2.30	2.47	4.50	2.81	3.84	4.32	5.10	3.39	...	632.20	59.72	...
February	2.54	3.00	2.41	2.60	4.50	2.93	3.78	4.27	5.07	3.31	...	650.02	62.17	...
March	2.02	3.00	2.42	2.54	4.50	2.88	3.74	4.22	5.02	3.45	...	670.57	64.12	...
April	1.49	3.00	2.33	2.47	4.50	2.88	3.78	4.25	5.01	3.48	...	684.90	65.83	...
May	1.98	3.00	2.29	2.45	4.50	2.87	3.71	4.27	5.01	3.43	...	693.03	66.50	...
June	1.73	3.00	2.36	2.54	4.50	3.06	3.88	4.33	5.03	3.52	...	691.46	65.62	...
July	1.17	3.00	2.27	2.45	4.50	2.92	3.92	4.41	5.09	3.51	...	690.67	65.44	...
August	2.00	3.00	2.40	2.66	4.50	3.06	4.04	4.45	5.11	3.52	...	718.64	67.79	...
September	1.88	3.00	2.30	2.68	4.50	3.06	3.98	4.45	5.12	3.53	...	711.02	67.26	...
October	2.26	3.00	2.35	2.66	4.50	3.05	3.92	4.42	5.13	3.42	...	703.01	68.00	...
November	2.61	3.00	2.46	2.70	4.50	3.07	3.94	4.39	5.11	3.41	...	724.74	71.08	...
December	2.33	3.00	2.62	2.88	4.50	3.18	4.06	4.42	5.10	3.47	...	728.44	71.74	...

[1] Federal Reserve Bank of New York. Through 2002, represents the rate for adjustment credit. Beginning in 2003, represents the rate for primary credit. See notes and definitions for more information.
[2] 1941–1943 = 10.
[3] February 5, 1971 = 100.
... = Not available.

Table 20-6. Interest Rates, Bond Yields, and Stock Price Indexes—Continued

(Not seasonally adjusted.)

Year and month	Percent per annum											Stock price indexes		
	Short-term rates					U.S. Treasury securities		Bond yields			Fixed-rate first mortgages	Dow Jones industrials (30 stocks)	Standard and Poor's composite (500 stocks)[2]	Nasdaq composite[3]
	Federal funds	Federal Reserve discount rate[1]	U.S. Treasury bills, 3-month	U.S. Treasury bills, 6-month	Bank prime rate	1-year	10-year	Domestic corporate (Moody's)		State and local bonds (Bond Buyer)				
								Aaa	Baa					
1962														
January	2.15	3.00	2.75	2.94	4.50	3.28	4.08	4.42	5.08	3.34	. . .	705.15	69.07	. . .
February	2.37	3.00	2.76	2.93	4.50	3.28	4.04	4.42	5.07	3.21	. . .	711.95	70.22	. . .
March	2.85	3.00	2.72	2.87	4.50	3.06	3.93	4.39	5.04	3.14	. . .	714.20	70.29	. . .
April	2.78	3.00	2.74	2.83	4.50	2.99	3.84	4.33	5.02	3.06	. . .	690.29	68.05	. . .
May	2.36	3.00	2.70	2.78	4.50	3.03	3.87	4.28	5.00	3.11	. . .	643.71	62.99	. . .
June	2.68	3.00	2.72	2.80	4.50	3.03	3.91	4.28	5.02	3.25	. . .	572.65	55.63	. . .
July	2.71	3.00	2.94	3.08	4.50	3.29	4.01	4.34	5.05	3.27	. . .	581.79	56.97	. . .
August	2.93	3.00	2.84	2.99	4.50	3.20	3.98	4.35	5.06	3.23	. . .	602.50	58.52	. . .
September	2.90	3.00	2.79	2.93	4.50	3.06	3.98	4.32	5.03	3.11	. . .	597.02	58.00	. . .
October	2.90	3.00	2.75	2.84	4.50	2.98	3.93	4.28	4.99	3.02	. . .	580.67	56.17	. . .
November	2.94	3.00	2.80	2.89	4.50	3.00	3.92	4.25	4.96	3.04	. . .	628.83	60.04	. . .
December	2.93	3.00	2.86	2.91	4.50	3.01	3.86	4.24	4.92	3.07	. . .	648.38	62.64	. . .
1963														
January	2.92	3.00	2.91	2.96	4.50	3.04	3.83	4.21	4.91	3.10	. . .	672.10	65.06	. . .
February	3.00	3.00	2.92	2.98	4.50	3.01	3.92	4.19	4.89	3.15	. . .	679.74	65.92	. . .
March	2.98	3.00	2.90	2.95	4.50	3.03	3.93	4.19	4.88	3.05	. . .	674.63	65.67	. . .
April	2.90	3.00	2.91	2.98	4.50	3.11	3.97	4.21	4.87	3.10	. . .	707.12	68.76	. . .
May	3.00	3.00	2.92	3.01	4.50	3.12	3.93	4.22	4.85	3.11	. . .	720.84	70.14	. . .
June	2.99	3.00	3.00	3.08	4.50	3.20	3.99	4.23	4.84	3.21	. . .	719.15	70.11	. . .
July	3.02	3.24	3.14	3.31	4.50	3.48	4.02	4.26	4.84	3.22	. . .	700.75	69.07	. . .
August	3.49	3.50	3.32	3.44	4.50	3.53	4.00	4.29	4.83	3.13	. . .	714.16	70.98	. . .
September	3.48	3.50	3.38	3.50	4.50	3.57	4.08	4.31	4.84	3.20	. . .	738.53	72.85	. . .
October	3.50	3.50	3.45	3.58	4.50	3.64	4.11	4.32	4.83	3.20	. . .	747.53	73.03	. . .
November	3.48	3.50	3.52	3.65	4.50	3.74	4.12	4.33	4.84	3.30	. . .	743.24	72.62	. . .
December	3.38	3.50	3.52	3.66	4.50	3.81	4.13	4.35	4.85	3.27	. . .	759.96	74.17	. . .
1964														
January	3.48	3.50	3.53	3.64	4.50	3.79	4.17	4.39	4.83	3.22	. . .	777.07	76.45	. . .
February	3.48	3.50	3.53	3.67	4.50	3.78	4.15	4.36	4.83	3.14	. . .	793.02	77.39	. . .
March	3.43	3.50	3.55	3.72	4.50	3.91	4.22	4.38	4.83	3.28	. . .	812.19	78.80	. . .
April	3.47	3.50	3.48	3.66	4.50	3.91	4.23	4.40	4.85	3.28	. . .	820.96	79.94	. . .
May	3.50	3.50	3.48	3.60	4.50	3.84	4.20	4.41	4.85	3.20	. . .	823.13	80.72	. . .
June	3.50	3.50	3.48	3.56	4.50	3.83	4.17	4.41	4.85	3.20	. . .	817.65	80.24	. . .
July	3.42	3.50	3.48	3.56	4.50	3.72	4.19	4.40	4.83	3.18	. . .	844.25	83.22	. . .
August	3.50	3.50	3.51	3.61	4.50	3.74	4.19	4.41	4.82	3.19	. . .	835.31	82.00	. . .
September	3.45	3.50	3.53	3.68	4.50	3.84	4.20	4.42	4.82	3.23	. . .	863.55	83.41	. . .
October	3.36	3.50	3.58	3.72	4.50	3.86	4.19	4.42	4.81	3.25	. . .	875.27	84.85	. . .
November	3.52	3.62	3.62	3.81	4.50	3.91	4.15	4.43	4.81	3.18	. . .	880.03	85.44	. . .
December	3.85	4.00	3.86	3.95	4.50	4.02	4.18	4.44	4.81	3.13	. . .	866.73	83.96	. . .
1965														
January	3.90	4.00	3.83	3.94	4.50	3.94	4.19	4.43	4.80	3.06	. . .	889.91	86.12	. . .
February	3.98	4.00	3.93	4.00	4.50	4.03	4.21	4.41	4.78	3.09	. . .	894.42	86.75	. . .
March	4.04	4.00	3.94	4.00	4.50	4.06	4.21	4.42	4.78	3.17	. . .	896.45	86.83	. . .
April	4.09	4.00	3.93	3.99	4.50	4.04	4.20	4.43	4.80	3.15	. . .	907.72	87.97	. . .
May	4.10	4.00	3.90	3.95	4.50	4.03	4.21	4.44	4.81	3.17	. . .	927.50	89.28	. . .
June	4.04	4.00	3.81	3.86	4.50	3.99	4.21	4.46	4.85	3.24	. . .	878.07	85.04	. . .
July	4.09	4.00	3.83	3.90	4.50	3.98	4.20	4.48	4.88	3.27	. . .	873.44	84.91	. . .
August	4.12	4.00	3.84	3.95	4.50	4.07	4.25	4.49	4.88	3.24	. . .	887.71	86.49	. . .
September	4.01	4.00	3.91	4.07	4.50	4.20	4.29	4.52	4.91	3.35	. . .	922.20	89.38	. . .
October	4.08	4.00	4.03	4.19	4.50	4.30	4.35	4.56	4.93	3.40	. . .	944.78	91.39	. . .
November	4.10	4.00	4.08	4.24	4.50	4.37	4.45	4.60	4.95	3.45	. . .	953.31	92.15	. . .
December	4.32	4.42	4.36	4.55	4.92	4.72	4.62	4.68	5.02	3.54	. . .	955.20	91.73	. . .
1966														
January	4.42	4.50	4.60	4.71	5.00	4.88	4.61	4.74	5.06	3.52	. . .	985.93	93.32	. . .
February	4.60	4.50	4.67	4.82	5.00	4.94	4.83	4.78	5.12	3.64	. . .	977.15	92.69	. . .
March	4.65	4.50	4.63	4.78	5.35	4.97	4.87	4.92	5.32	3.72	. . .	926.43	88.88	. . .
April	4.67	4.50	4.61	4.74	5.50	4.90	4.75	4.96	5.41	3.56	. . .	943.46	91.60	. . .
May	4.90	4.50	4.64	4.81	5.50	4.93	4.78	4.98	5.48	3.65	. . .	890.71	86.78	. . .
June	5.17	4.50	4.54	4.65	5.52	4.97	4.81	5.07	5.58	3.77	. . .	888.83	86.06	. . .
July	5.30	4.50	4.86	4.93	5.75	5.17	5.02	5.16	5.68	3.95	. . .	875.89	85.84	. . .
August	5.53	4.50	4.93	5.27	5.88	5.54	5.22	5.31	5.83	4.12	. . .	817.55	80.65	. . .
September	5.40	4.50	5.36	5.79	6.00	5.82	5.18	5.49	6.09	4.12	. . .	791.66	77.81	. . .
October	5.53	4.50	5.39	5.62	6.00	5.58	5.01	5.41	6.10	3.93	. . .	778.11	77.13	. . .
November	5.76	4.50	5.34	5.54	6.00	5.54	5.16	5.35	6.13	3.86	. . .	806.56	80.99	. . .
December	5.40	4.50	5.01	5.07	6.00	5.20	4.84	5.39	6.18	3.86	. . .	800.88	81.33	. . .
1967														
January	4.94	4.50	4.76	4.74	5.96	4.75	4.58	5.20	5.97	3.54	. . .	830.55	84.45	. . .
February	5.00	4.50	4.56	4.59	5.75	4.71	4.63	5.03	5.82	3.52	. . .	851.12	87.36	. . .
March	4.53	4.50	4.29	4.22	5.71	4.35	4.54	5.13	5.85	3.55	. . .	858.12	89.42	. . .
April	4.05	4.10	3.86	3.89	5.50	4.11	4.59	5.11	5.83	3.60	. . .	868.66	90.96	. . .
May	3.94	4.00	3.64	3.80	5.50	4.15	4.85	5.24	5.96	3.89	. . .	883.74	92.59	. . .
June	3.98	4.00	3.48	3.89	5.50	4.48	5.02	5.44	6.15	3.96	. . .	872.66	91.43	. . .
July	3.79	4.00	4.31	4.72	5.50	5.01	5.16	5.58	6.26	4.02	. . .	888.51	93.01	. . .
August	3.90	4.00	4.27	4.83	5.50	5.13	5.28	5.62	6.33	3.99	. . .	912.48	94.49	. . .
September	3.99	4.00	4.45	4.96	5.50	5.24	5.30	5.65	6.40	4.12	. . .	923.46	95.81	. . .
October	3.88	4.00	4.59	5.07	5.50	5.37	5.48	5.82	6.52	4.29	. . .	907.55	95.66	. . .
November	4.13	4.18	4.76	5.25	5.68	5.61	5.75	6.07	6.72	4.34	. . .	865.44	92.66	. . .
December	4.51	4.50	5.01	5.49	6.00	5.71	5.70	6.19	6.93	4.43	. . .	887.20	95.30	. . .

[1]Federal Reserve Bank of New York. Through 2002, represents the rate for adjustment credit. Beginning in 2003, represents the rate for primary credit. See notes and definitions for more information.
[2]1941–1943 = 10.
[3]February 5, 1971 = 100.
. . . = Not available.

Table 20-6. Interest Rates, Bond Yields, and Stock Price Indexes—Continued

(Not seasonally adjusted.)

Year and month	Percent per annum											Stock price indexes		
	Short-term rates					U.S. Treasury securities		Bond yields				Dow Jones industrials (30 stocks)	Standard and Poor's composite (500 stocks) [2]	Nasdaq composite [3]
	Federal funds	Federal Reserve discount rate [1]	U.S. Treasury bills, 3-month	U.S. Treasury bills, 6-month	Bank prime rate	1-year	10-year	Domestic corporate (Moody's)		State and local bonds (Bond Buyer)	Fixed-rate first mortgages			
								Aaa	Baa					
1968														
January	4.60	4.50	5.08	5.24	6.00	5.43	5.53	6.17	6.84	4.29	...	884.78	95.04	...
February	4.71	4.50	4.97	5.17	6.00	5.41	5.56	6.10	6.80	4.31	...	847.20	90.75	...
March	5.05	4.66	5.15	5.33	6.00	5.58	5.74	6.11	6.85	4.54	...	834.76	89.09	...
April	5.76	5.20	5.37	5.49	6.20	5.71	5.64	6.21	6.97	4.34	...	893.38	95.67	...
May	6.11	5.50	5.62	5.83	6.50	6.14	5.87	6.27	7.03	4.54	...	905.23	97.87	...
June	6.07	5.50	5.55	5.64	6.50	5.98	5.72	6.28	7.07	4.49	...	906.82	100.53	...
July	6.02	5.50	5.38	5.41	6.50	5.65	5.50	6.24	6.98	4.33	...	905.33	100.30	...
August	6.03	5.48	5.09	5.23	6.50	5.43	5.42	6.02	6.82	4.21	...	883.73	98.11	...
September	5.78	5.25	5.20	5.25	6.45	5.45	5.46	5.97	6.79	4.38	...	922.82	101.34	...
October	5.91	5.25	5.34	5.41	6.25	5.57	5.58	6.09	6.84	4.49	...	955.48	103.76	...
November	5.82	5.25	5.49	5.60	6.25	5.75	5.70	6.19	7.01	4.60	...	964.13	105.40	...
December	6.02	5.36	5.92	6.06	6.60	6.19	6.03	6.45	7.23	4.82	...	968.39	106.48	...
1969														
January	6.30	5.50	6.18	6.28	6.95	6.34	6.04	6.59	7.32	4.85	...	935.00	102.04	...
February	6.61	5.50	6.16	6.30	7.00	6.41	6.19	6.66	7.30	4.98	...	931.31	101.46	...
March	6.79	5.50	6.08	6.16	7.24	6.34	6.30	6.85	7.51	5.26	...	916.52	99.30	...
April	7.41	5.95	6.16	6.13	7.50	6.26	6.17	6.89	7.54	5.19	...	927.38	101.26	...
May	8.67	6.00	6.08	6.15	7.50	6.42	6.32	6.79	7.52	5.33	...	954.88	104.62	...
June	8.90	6.00	6.49	6.75	8.23	7.04	6.57	6.98	7.70	5.75	...	896.62	99.14	...
July	8.61	6.00	7.01	7.24	8.50	7.60	6.72	7.08	7.84	5.75	...	844.02	94.71	...
August	9.19	6.00	7.01	7.19	8.50	7.54	6.69	6.97	7.86	6.00	...	825.46	94.18	...
September	9.15	6.00	7.13	7.32	8.50	7.82	7.16	7.14	8.05	6.26	...	826.72	94.51	...
October	9.00	6.00	7.04	7.29	8.50	7.64	7.10	7.33	8.22	6.09	...	832.52	95.52	...
November	8.85	6.00	7.20	7.62	8.50	7.89	7.14	7.35	8.25	6.30	...	841.10	96.21	...
December	8.97	6.00	7.72	7.90	8.50	8.17	7.65	7.72	8.65	6.82	...	789.23	91.11	...
1970														
January	8.98	6.00	7.92	7.78	8.50	8.10	7.79	7.91	8.86	6.63	...	782.93	90.31	...
February	8.98	6.00	7.16	7.22	8.50	7.59	7.24	7.93	8.78	6.22	...	756.22	87.16	...
March	7.76	6.00	6.71	6.58	8.39	6.97	7.07	7.84	8.63	6.05	...	777.63	88.65	...
April	8.10	6.00	6.48	6.60	8.00	7.06	7.39	7.83	8.70	6.65	...	771.65	85.95	...
May	7.94	6.00	7.03	7.02	8.00	7.75	7.91	8.11	8.98	7.00	...	691.97	76.06	...
June	7.60	6.00	6.74	6.86	8.00	7.55	7.84	8.48	9.25	6.93	...	699.30	75.59	...
July	7.21	6.00	6.47	6.51	8.00	7.10	7.46	8.44	9.40	6.42	...	712.81	75.72	...
August	6.61	6.00	6.41	6.55	8.00	6.98	7.53	8.13	9.44	6.17	...	731.98	77.92	...
September	6.29	6.00	6.24	6.46	7.83	6.73	7.39	8.09	9.39	6.31	...	759.39	82.58	...
October	6.20	6.00	5.93	6.21	7.50	6.43	7.33	8.03	9.33	6.37	...	763.74	84.37	...
November	5.60	5.85	5.29	5.42	7.28	5.51	6.84	8.05	9.38	5.71	...	769.28	84.28	...
December	4.90	5.52	4.86	4.89	6.92	5.00	6.39	7.64	9.12	5.47	...	821.51	90.05	...
1971														
January	4.14	5.23	4.49	4.47	6.29	4.57	6.24	7.36	8.74	5.35	...	849.04	93.49	...
February	3.72	4.91	3.78	3.78	5.88	3.89	6.11	7.08	8.39	5.23	...	879.69	97.11	...
March	3.71	4.75	3.33	3.50	5.44	3.69	5.70	7.21	8.46	5.17	...	901.29	99.60	...
April	4.15	4.75	3.78	4.03	5.28	4.30	5.83	7.25	8.45	5.37	7.31	932.54	103.04	...
May	4.63	4.75	4.14	4.36	5.46	5.04	6.39	7.53	8.62	5.90	7.43	925.51	101.64	...
June	4.91	4.75	4.70	4.97	5.50	5.64	6.52	7.64	8.75	5.95	7.53	900.45	99.72	...
July	5.31	4.88	5.41	5.63	5.91	6.04	6.73	7.64	8.76	6.06	7.60	887.81	99.00	...
August	5.56	5.00	5.08	5.22	6.00	5.80	6.58	7.59	8.76	5.82	7.70	875.41	97.24	...
September	5.55	5.00	4.67	4.97	6.00	5.41	6.14	7.44	8.59	5.37	7.69	901.22	99.40	...
October	5.20	5.00	4.49	4.60	5.90	4.91	5.93	7.39	8.48	5.06	7.63	872.15	97.29	...
November	4.91	4.90	4.19	4.38	5.53	4.67	5.81	7.26	8.38	5.20	7.55	822.11	92.78	...
December	4.14	4.63	4.02	4.23	5.49	4.60	5.93	7.25	8.38	5.21	7.48	869.92	99.17	...
1972														
January	3.50	4.50	3.41	3.66	5.18	4.28	5.95	7.19	8.23	5.12	7.44	904.65	103.30	...
February	3.29	4.50	3.18	3.63	4.75	4.27	6.08	7.27	8.23	5.28	7.33	914.37	105.24	...
March	3.83	4.50	3.72	4.12	4.75	4.67	6.07	7.24	8.24	5.31	7.30	939.23	107.69	...
April	4.17	4.50	3.72	4.23	4.97	4.96	6.19	7.30	8.24	5.43	7.29	958.17	108.81	...
May	4.27	4.50	3.65	4.12	5.00	4.64	6.13	7.30	8.23	5.30	7.37	948.22	107.65	...
June	4.46	4.50	3.87	4.35	5.04	4.93	6.11	7.23	8.20	5.33	7.37	943.44	108.01	...
July	4.55	4.50	4.06	4.50	5.25	4.96	6.11	7.21	8.23	5.41	7.40	925.94	107.21	...
August	4.80	4.50	4.01	4.55	5.27	4.98	6.21	7.19	8.19	5.30	7.40	958.36	111.01	...
September	4.87	4.50	4.65	5.13	5.50	5.52	6.55	7.22	8.09	5.36	7.42	950.60	109.39	...
October	5.04	4.50	4.72	5.13	5.73	5.52	6.48	7.21	8.06	5.18	7.42	944.10	109.56	...
November	5.06	4.50	4.78	5.09	5.75	5.27	6.28	7.12	7.99	5.02	7.43	1 001.20	115.05	...
December	5.33	4.50	5.06	5.30	5.79	5.52	6.36	7.08	7.93	5.05	7.44	1 020.32	117.50	...
1973														
January	5.94	4.77	5.31	5.62	6.00	5.89	6.46	7.15	7.90	5.05	7.44	1 026.82	118.42	...
February	6.58	5.05	5.56	5.83	6.02	6.19	6.64	7.22	7.97	5.13	7.44	974.05	114.16	...
March	7.09	5.50	6.05	6.51	6.30	6.85	6.71	7.29	8.03	5.29	7.46	957.36	112.42	...
April	7.12	5.50	6.29	6.52	6.61	6.85	6.67	7.26	8.09	5.15	7.54	944.12	110.27	...
May	7.84	5.90	6.35	6.62	7.01	6.89	6.85	7.29	8.06	5.15	7.65	922.41	107.22	...
June	8.49	6.33	7.19	7.23	7.49	7.31	6.90	7.37	8.13	5.17	7.73	893.90	104.75	...
July	10.40	6.98	8.02	8.12	8.30	8.39	7.13	7.45	8.24	5.40	8.05	903.61	105.83	...
August	10.50	7.29	8.67	8.65	9.23	8.82	7.40	7.68	8.53	5.48	8.50	883.73	103.80	...
September	10.78	7.50	8.48	8.45	9.86	8.31	7.09	7.63	8.63	5.10	8.82	909.99	105.61	...
October	10.01	7.50	7.16	7.32	9.94	7.40	6.79	7.60	8.41	5.05	8.77	967.63	109.84	...
November	10.03	7.50	7.87	7.96	9.75	7.57	6.73	7.67	8.42	5.18	8.58	878.99	102.03	...
December	9.95	7.50	7.37	7.56	9.75	7.27	6.74	7.68	8.48	5.12	8.54	824.08	94.78	...

[1]Federal Reserve Bank of New York. Through 2002, represents the rate for adjustment credit. Beginning in 2003, represents the rate for primary credit. See notes and definitions for more information.
[2]1941–1943 = 10.
[3]February 5, 1971 = 100.
. . . = Not available.

Table 20-6. Interest Rates, Bond Yields, and Stock Price Indexes—Continued

(Not seasonally adjusted.)

Year and month	Percent per annum											Stock price indexes		
	Short-term rates					U.S. Treasury securities		Bond yields				Dow Jones industrials (30 stocks)	Standard and Poor's composite (500 stocks) [2]	Nasdaq composite [3]
	Federal funds	Federal Reserve discount rate [1]	U.S. Treasury bills, 3-month	U.S. Treasury bills, 6-month	Bank prime rate	1-year	10-year	Domestic corporate (Moody's)		State and local bonds (Bond Buyer)	Fixed-rate first mortgages			
								Aaa	Baa					
1974														
January	9.65	7.50	7.76	7.65	9.73	7.42	6.99	7.83	8.48	5.22	8.54	857.25	96.11	...
February	8.97	7.50	7.06	6.96	9.21	6.88	6.96	7.85	8.53	5.20	8.46	831.33	93.45	...
March	9.35	7.50	7.99	7.83	8.85	7.76	7.21	8.01	8.62	5.40	8.41	874.01	97.44	...
April	10.51	7.60	8.23	8.32	10.02	8.62	7.51	8.25	8.87	5.73	8.58	847.79	92.46	...
May	11.31	8.00	8.43	8.40	11.25	8.78	7.58	8.37	9.05	6.02	8.97	830.26	89.67	...
June	11.93	8.00	8.15	8.12	11.54	8.67	7.54	8.47	9.27	6.13	9.09	831.45	89.79	...
July	12.92	8.00	7.75	7.94	11.97	8.80	7.81	8.72	9.48	6.68	9.28	783.01	82.82	...
August	12.01	8.00	8.75	9.11	12.00	9.36	8.04	9.00	9.77	6.71	9.59	729.30	76.03	...
September	11.34	8.00	8.37	8.53	12.00	8.87	8.04	9.24	10.18	6.76	9.96	651.29	68.12	...
October	10.06	8.00	7.24	7.74	11.68	8.05	7.90	9.27	10.48	6.57	9.98	638.62	69.44	...
November	9.45	8.00	7.59	7.52	10.83	7.66	7.68	8.89	10.60	6.61	9.79	642.11	71.74	...
December	8.53	7.81	7.18	7.11	10.50	7.31	7.43	8.89	10.63	7.05	9.62	596.50	67.07	...
1975														
January	7.13	7.40	6.49	6.36	10.05	6.83	7.50	8.83	10.81	6.82	9.43	659.09	72.56	...
February	6.24	6.82	5.59	5.62	8.96	5.98	7.39	8.62	10.65	6.39	9.11	724.89	80.10	...
March	5.54	6.40	5.55	5.62	7.93	6.11	7.73	8.67	10.48	6.73	8.90	765.06	83.78	...
April	5.49	6.25	5.69	6.00	7.50	6.90	8.23	8.95	10.58	6.95	8.82	790.94	84.72	...
May	5.22	6.12	5.32	5.59	7.40	6.39	8.06	8.90	10.69	6.97	8.91	836.55	90.10	...
June	5.55	6.00	5.20	5.61	7.07	6.29	7.86	8.77	10.62	6.94	8.89	845.70	92.40	...
July	6.10	6.00	6.17	6.50	7.15	7.11	8.06	8.84	10.55	7.07	8.89	856.29	92.49	...
August	6.14	6.00	6.46	6.94	7.66	7.70	8.40	8.95	10.59	7.17	8.94	815.52	85.71	...
September	6.24	6.00	6.38	6.92	7.88	7.75	8.43	8.95	10.61	7.44	9.13	818.29	84.67	...
October	5.82	6.00	6.08	6.25	7.96	6.95	8.14	8.86	10.62	7.39	9.22	831.27	88.57	...
November	5.22	6.00	5.47	5.80	7.53	6.49	8.05	8.78	10.56	7.43	9.15	845.52	90.07	...
December	5.20	6.00	5.50	5.85	7.26	6.60	8.00	8.79	10.56	7.31	9.10	840.80	88.70	...
1976														
January	4.87	5.79	4.96	5.14	7.00	5.81	7.74	8.60	10.41	7.07	9.02	929.34	96.86	...
February	4.77	5.50	4.85	5.20	6.75	5.91	7.79	8.55	10.24	6.94	8.81	971.72	100.64	...
March	4.84	5.50	5.05	5.44	6.75	6.21	7.73	8.52	10.12	6.91	8.76	988.55	101.08	...
April	4.82	5.50	4.88	5.18	6.75	5.92	7.56	8.40	9.94	6.60	8.73	992.52	101.93	...
May	5.29	5.50	5.19	5.62	6.75	6.40	7.90	8.58	9.86	6.87	8.77	988.82	101.16	...
June	5.48	5.50	5.45	5.77	7.20	6.52	7.86	8.62	9.89	6.87	8.85	985.60	101.77	...
July	5.31	5.50	5.28	5.53	7.25	6.20	7.83	8.56	9.82	6.79	8.93	993.20	104.20	...
August	5.29	5.50	5.15	5.40	7.01	6.00	7.77	8.45	9.64	6.61	9.00	981.63	103.29	...
September	5.25	5.50	5.08	5.30	7.00	5.84	7.59	8.38	9.40	6.51	8.98	994.38	105.45	...
October	5.02	5.50	4.93	5.06	6.77	5.50	7.41	8.32	9.29	6.30	8.93	951.96	101.89	...
November	4.95	5.43	4.81	4.88	6.50	5.29	7.29	8.25	9.23	6.29	8.81	944.58	101.19	...
December	4.65	5.25	4.36	4.51	6.35	4.89	6.87	7.98	9.12	5.94	8.79	976.87	104.66	...
1977														
January	4.61	5.25	4.60	4.83	6.25	5.29	7.21	7.96	9.08	5.87	8.72	970.63	103.81	...
February	4.68	5.25	4.66	4.90	6.25	5.47	7.39	8.04	9.12	5.88	8.67	941.75	100.96	...
March	4.69	5.25	4.61	4.88	6.25	5.50	7.46	8.10	9.12	5.89	8.69	946.10	100.57	...
April	4.73	5.25	4.54	4.80	6.25	5.44	7.37	8.04	9.07	5.72	8.75	929.12	99.05	...
May	5.35	5.25	4.94	5.20	6.41	5.84	7.46	8.05	9.01	5.75	8.82	926.30	98.76	...
June	5.39	5.25	5.00	5.21	6.75	5.80	7.28	7.95	8.91	5.62	8.86	916.57	99.29	...
July	5.42	5.25	5.14	5.40	6.75	5.94	7.33	7.94	8.87	5.63	8.94	908.21	100.18	...
August	5.90	5.27	5.50	5.83	6.83	6.37	7.40	7.98	8.82	5.62	8.94	872.27	97.75	...
September	6.14	5.75	5.77	6.04	7.13	6.53	7.34	7.92	8.80	5.51	8.90	853.37	96.23	...
October	6.47	5.80	6.19	6.43	7.52	6.97	7.52	8.04	8.89	5.64	8.91	823.96	93.74	...
November	6.51	6.00	6.16	6.41	7.75	6.95	7.58	8.08	8.95	5.49	8.92	828.52	94.28	...
December	6.56	6.00	6.06	6.40	7.75	6.96	7.69	8.19	8.99	5.57	8.96	818.80	93.82	...
1978														
January	6.70	6.37	6.45	6.70	7.93	7.28	7.96	8.41	9.17	5.71	9.02	781.08	90.25	...
February	6.78	6.50	6.46	6.74	8.00	7.34	8.03	8.47	9.20	5.62	9.16	763.58	88.98	...
March	6.79	6.50	6.32	6.63	8.00	7.31	8.04	8.47	9.22	5.61	9.20	756.37	88.82	...
April	6.89	6.50	6.31	6.73	8.00	7.45	8.15	8.56	9.32	5.79	9.36	794.66	92.71	...
May	7.36	6.84	6.43	7.02	8.27	7.82	8.35	8.69	9.49	6.03	9.58	838.56	97.41	...
June	7.60	7.00	6.71	7.23	8.63	8.09	8.46	8.76	9.60	6.22	9.71	840.25	97.66	...
July	7.81	7.23	7.08	7.44	9.00	8.39	8.64	8.88	9.60	6.28	9.74	831.72	97.19	...
August	8.04	7.43	7.04	7.37	9.01	8.31	8.41	8.69	9.48	6.12	9.78	887.93	103.92	...
September	8.45	7.83	7.84	7.99	9.41	8.64	8.42	8.69	9.42	6.09	9.76	878.64	103.86	...
October	8.96	8.26	8.13	8.55	9.94	9.14	8.64	8.89	9.59	6.13	9.86	857.70	100.58	...
November	9.76	9.50	8.79	9.24	10.94	10.01	8.81	9.03	9.83	6.19	10.11	804.30	94.71	...
December	10.03	9.50	9.12	9.36	11.55	10.30	9.01	9.16	9.94	6.50	10.35	807.96	96.11	...
1979														
January	10.07	9.50	9.35	9.47	11.75	10.41	9.10	9.25	10.13	6.46	10.39	837.39	99.71	...
February	10.06	9.50	9.27	9.41	11.75	10.24	9.10	9.26	10.08	6.31	10.41	825.18	98.23	...
March	10.09	9.50	9.46	9.47	11.75	10.25	9.12	9.37	10.26	6.33	10.43	847.85	100.11	...
April	10.01	9.50	9.49	9.49	11.75	10.12	9.18	9.38	10.33	6.28	10.50	864.97	102.07	...
May	10.24	9.50	9.58	9.54	11.75	10.12	9.25	9.50	10.47	6.25	10.69	837.41	99.73	...
June	10.29	9.50	9.05	9.06	11.65	9.57	8.91	9.29	10.38	6.12	11.04	838.65	101.73	...
July	10.47	9.69	9.27	9.24	11.54	9.64	8.95	9.20	10.29	6.13	11.09	836.96	102.71	...
August	10.94	10.24	9.45	9.49	11.91	9.98	9.03	9.23	10.35	6.20	11.09	873.55	107.36	...
September	11.43	10.70	10.18	10.20	12.90	10.84	9.33	9.44	10.54	6.52	11.30	878.51	108.60	...
October	13.77	11.77	11.47	11.66	14.39	12.44	10.30	10.13	11.40	7.08	11.64	840.52	104.47	...
November	13.18	12.00	11.87	11.82	15.55	12.39	10.65	10.76	11.99	7.30	12.83	815.79	103.66	...
December	13.78	12.00	12.07	11.84	15.30	11.98	10.39	10.74	12.06	7.22	12.90	836.14	107.78	...

[1] Federal Reserve Bank of New York. Through 2002, represents the rate for adjustment credit. Beginning in 2003, represents the rate for primary credit. See notes and definitions for more information.
[2] 1941–1943 = 10.
[3] February 5, 1971 = 100.
... = Not available.

Table 20-6. Interest Rates, Bond Yields, and Stock Price Indexes—Continued

(Not seasonally adjusted.)

	Percent per annum												Stock price indexes		
	Short-term rates					U.S. Treasury securities		Bond yields				Dow Jones industrials (30 stocks)	Standard and Poor's composite (500 stocks) [2]	Nasdaq composite [3]
Year and month								Domestic corporate (Moody's)		State and local bonds (Bond Buyer)	Fixed-rate first mortgages			
	Federal funds	Federal Reserve discount rate [1]	U.S. Treasury bills, 3-month	U.S. Treasury bills, 6-month	Bank prime rate	1-year	10-year	Aaa	Baa					
1980														
January	13.82	12.00	12.04	11.84	15.25	12.06	10.80	11.09	12.42	7.35	12.88	860.75	110.87	...
February	14.13	12.52	12.82	12.86	15.63	13.92	12.41	12.38	13.57	8.16	13.04	878.22	115.34	...
March	17.19	13.00	15.53	15.03	18.31	15.82	12.75	12.96	14.45	9.16	15.28	803.57	104.69	...
April	17.61	13.00	14.00	12.88	19.77	13.30	11.47	12.04	14.19	8.63	16.33	786.35	102.97	...
May	10.98	12.94	9.15	8.65	16.57	9.39	10.18	10.99	13.17	7.59	14.26	828.20	107.69	...
June	9.47	11.40	7.00	7.30	12.63	8.16	9.78	10.58	12.71	7.63	12.71	869.86	114.55	...
July	9.03	10.87	8.13	8.06	11.48	8.65	10.25	11.07	12.65	8.13	12.19	909.79	119.83	...
August	9.61	10.00	9.26	9.41	11.12	10.24	11.10	11.64	13.15	8.67	12.56	947.33	123.50	...
September	10.87	10.17	10.32	10.57	12.23	11.52	11.51	12.02	13.70	8.94	13.20	946.68	126.51	...
October	12.81	11.00	11.58	11.63	13.79	12.49	11.75	12.31	14.23	9.11	13.79	949.17	130.22	...
November	15.85	11.47	13.89	13.50	16.06	14.15	12.68	12.97	14.64	9.56	14.21	971.09	135.65	...
December	18.90	12.87	15.66	14.64	20.35	14.88	12.84	13.21	15.14	10.20	14.79	945.97	133.48	...
1981														
January	19.08	13.00	14.73	14.08	20.16	14.08	12.57	12.81	15.03	9.66	14.90	962.14	132.97	...
February	15.93	13.00	14.91	14.05	19.43	14.57	13.19	13.35	15.37	10.09	15.13	945.51	128.40	...
March	14.70	13.00	13.48	12.81	18.05	13.71	13.12	13.33	15.34	10.16	15.40	987.18	133.19	...
April	15.72	13.00	13.63	13.45	17.15	14.32	13.68	13.88	15.56	10.62	15.58	1 004.86	134.43	...
May	18.52	13.87	16.29	15.29	19.61	16.20	14.10	14.32	15.95	10.77	16.40	979.53	131.73	...
June	19.10	14.00	14.56	14.09	20.03	14.86	13.47	13.75	15.80	10.67	16.70	996.27	132.28	...
July	19.04	14.00	14.70	14.74	20.39	15.72	14.28	14.38	16.17	11.14	16.83	947.95	129.13	...
August	17.82	14.00	15.61	15.52	20.50	16.72	14.94	14.89	16.34	12.26	17.29	926.26	129.63	...
September	15.87	14.00	14.95	14.92	20.08	16.52	15.32	15.49	16.92	12.92	18.16	853.39	118.27	...
October	15.08	14.00	13.87	13.82	18.45	15.38	15.15	15.40	17.11	12.83	18.45	853.26	119.80	...
November	13.31	13.03	11.27	11.30	16.84	12.41	13.39	14.22	16.39	11.89	17.83	860.43	122.92	...
December	12.37	12.10	10.93	11.52	15.75	12.85	13.72	14.23	16.55	12.91	16.92	878.29	123.79	...
1982														
January	13.22	12.00	12.41	12.83	15.75	14.32	14.59	15.18	17.10	13.28	17.40	853.42	117.28	...
February	14.78	12.00	13.78	13.61	16.56	14.73	14.43	15.27	17.18	12.97	17.60	833.16	114.50	...
March	14.68	12.00	12.49	12.77	16.50	13.95	13.86	14.58	16.82	12.82	17.16	812.34	110.84	...
April	14.94	12.00	12.82	12.80	16.50	13.98	13.87	14.46	16.78	12.58	16.89	844.93	116.31	...
May	14.45	12.00	12.15	12.16	16.50	13.34	13.62	14.26	16.64	11.95	16.68	846.74	116.35	...
June	14.15	12.00	12.11	12.70	16.50	14.07	14.30	14.81	16.92	12.44	16.70	804.37	109.70	...
July	12.59	11.81	11.92	11.88	16.26	13.24	13.95	14.61	16.80	12.28	16.82	818.41	109.38	...
August	10.12	10.68	9.01	9.88	14.39	11.43	13.06	13.71	16.32	11.23	16.27	832.11	109.65	...
September	10.31	10.00	8.20	9.37	13.50	10.85	12.34	12.94	15.63	10.66	15.43	917.27	122.43	...
October	9.71	9.68	7.75	8.29	12.52	9.32	10.91	12.12	14.73	9.68	14.61	988.73	132.66	...
November	9.20	9.35	8.04	8.34	11.85	9.16	10.55	11.68	14.30	10.06	13.83	1 027.76	138.10	...
December	8.95	8.73	8.02	8.16	11.50	8.91	10.54	11.83	14.14	9.96	13.62	1 033.10	139.37	...
1983														
January	8.68	8.50	7.81	7.93	11.16	8.62	10.46	11.79	13.94	9.50	13.25	1 064.31	144.27	...
February	8.51	8.50	8.13	8.23	10.98	8.92	10.72	12.01	13.95	9.58	13.04	1 087.40	146.80	...
March	8.77	8.50	8.30	8.37	10.50	9.04	10.51	11.73	13.61	9.20	12.80	1 129.58	151.88	...
April	8.80	8.50	8.25	8.30	10.50	8.98	10.40	11.51	13.29	9.04	12.78	1 168.43	157.71	...
May	8.63	8.50	8.19	8.22	10.50	8.90	10.38	11.46	13.09	9.11	12.63	1 212.86	164.10	...
June	8.98	8.50	8.82	8.89	10.50	9.66	10.85	11.74	13.37	9.52	12.87	1 221.47	166.39	...
July	9.37	8.50	9.12	9.26	10.50	10.20	11.38	12.15	13.39	9.53	13.42	1 213.94	166.96	...
August	9.56	8.50	9.39	9.51	10.89	10.53	11.85	12.51	13.64	9.72	13.81	1 189.22	162.42	...
September	9.45	8.50	9.05	9.15	11.00	10.16	11.65	12.37	13.55	9.58	13.73	1 237.04	167.16	...
October	9.48	8.50	8.71	8.83	11.00	9.81	11.54	12.25	13.46	9.66	13.54	1 252.20	167.65	...
November	9.34	8.50	8.71	8.93	11.00	9.94	11.69	12.41	13.61	9.74	13.44	1 250.00	165.23	...
December	9.47	8.50	8.96	9.17	11.00	10.11	11.83	12.57	13.75	9.89	13.42	1 257.65	164.36	...
1984														
January	9.56	8.50	8.93	9.01	11.00	9.90	11.67	12.20	13.65	9.63	13.37	1 258.89	166.39	...
February	9.59	8.50	9.03	9.18	11.00	10.04	11.84	12.08	13.59	9.64	13.23	1 164.45	157.25	...
March	9.91	8.50	9.08	9.66	11.21	10.59	12.32	12.57	13.99	9.94	13.39	1 161.98	157.44	...
April	10.29	8.87	9.69	9.84	11.93	10.90	12.63	12.81	14.31	9.96	13.65	1 152.72	157.60	...
May	10.32	9.00	9.90	10.31	12.39	11.66	13.41	13.28	14.74	10.49	13.94	1 143.42	156.55	...
June	11.06	9.00	9.94	10.51	12.60	12.08	13.56	13.55	15.05	10.67	14.42	1 121.14	153.12	...
July	11.23	9.00	10.13	10.52	13.00	12.03	13.36	13.44	15.15	10.42	14.67	1 113.29	151.08	...
August	11.64	9.00	10.49	10.61	13.00	11.82	12.72	12.87	14.63	9.99	14.47	1 212.82	164.42	...
September	11.30	9.00	10.41	10.47	12.97	11.58	12.52	12.66	14.35	10.10	14.35	1 213.52	166.11	...
October	9.99	9.00	9.97	9.87	12.58	10.90	12.16	12.63	13.94	10.25	14.13	1 199.30	164.82	...
November	9.43	8.83	8.79	8.81	11.77	9.82	11.57	12.29	13.48	10.17	13.64	1 211.31	166.27	247.00
December	8.38	8.37	8.16	8.28	11.06	9.33	11.50	12.13	13.40	9.95	13.18	1 188.96	164.48	242.53
1985														
January	8.35	8.00	7.76	8.00	10.61	9.02	11.38	12.08	13.26	9.51	13.08	1 238.16	171.61	260.85
February	8.50	8.00	8.17	8.39	10.50	9.29	11.51	12.13	13.23	9.65	12.92	1 283.23	180.88	285.52
March	8.58	8.00	8.57	8.90	10.50	9.86	11.86	12.56	13.69	9.77	13.17	1 268.84	179.42	280.43
April	8.27	8.00	8.00	8.23	10.50	9.14	11.43	12.23	13.51	9.42	13.20	1 266.38	180.62	280.90
May	7.97	7.81	7.56	7.65	10.31	8.46	10.85	11.72	13.15	9.01	12.91	1 279.41	184.90	287.51
June	7.53	7.50	7.01	7.09	9.78	7.80	10.16	10.94	12.40	8.69	12.22	1 314.00	188.89	290.45
July	7.88	7.50	7.05	7.20	9.50	7.86	10.31	10.97	12.43	8.81	12.03	1 343.17	192.54	302.04
August	7.90	7.50	7.18	7.32	9.50	8.05	10.33	11.05	12.50	9.08	12.19	1 326.19	188.31	298.25
September	7.92	7.50	7.08	7.27	9.50	8.07	10.37	11.07	12.48	9.27	12.19	1 317.95	184.06	287.94
October	7.99	7.50	7.17	7.33	9.50	8.01	10.24	11.02	12.36	9.08	12.14	1 351.58	186.18	285.37
November	8.05	7.50	7.20	7.30	9.50	7.88	9.78	10.55	11.99	8.54	11.78	1 432.89	197.45	304.36
December	8.27	7.50	7.07	7.14	9.50	7.67	9.26	10.16	11.58	8.42	11.26	1 517.02	207.26	320.24

[1]Federal Reserve Bank of New York. Through 2002, represents the rate for adjustment credit. Beginning in 2003, represents the rate for primary credit. See notes and definitions for more information.
[2]1941–1943 = 10.
[3]February 5, 1971 = 100.
. . . = Not available.

Table 20-6. Interest Rates, Bond Yields, and Stock Price Indexes—Continued

(Not seasonally adjusted.)

Year and month	Percent per annum											Stock price indexes		
	Short-term rates					U.S. Treasury securities		Bond yields						
								Domestic corporate (Moody's)		State and local bonds (Bond Buyer)	Fixed-rate first mortgages	Dow Jones industrials (30 stocks)	Standard and Poor's composite (500 stocks)[2]	Nasdaq composite[3]
	Federal funds	Federal Reserve discount rate[1]	U.S. Treasury bills, 3-month	U.S. Treasury bills, 6-month	Bank prime rate	1-year	10-year	Aaa	Baa					
1986														
January	8.14	7.50	7.04	7.16	9.50	7.73	9.19	10.05	11.44	8.08	10.88	1 534.85	208.19	328.54
February	7.86	7.50	7.03	7.11	9.50	7.61	8.70	9.67	11.11	7.44	10.71	1 652.74	219.37	348.79
March	7.48	7.10	6.59	6.57	9.10	7.03	7.78	9.00	10.50	7.08	10.08	1 757.36	232.33	368.28
April	6.99	6.83	6.06	6.08	8.83	6.44	7.30	8.79	10.19	7.19	9.94	1 807.06	237.98	382.54
May	6.85	6.50	6.12	6.19	8.50	6.65	7.71	9.09	10.29	7.54	10.14	1 801.81	238.46	388.49
June	6.92	6.50	6.21	6.27	8.50	6.73	7.80	9.13	10.34	7.87	10.68	1 867.71	245.30	398.60
July	6.56	6.16	5.84	5.86	8.16	6.27	7.30	8.88	10.16	7.51	10.51	1 809.92	240.18	385.90
August	6.17	5.82	5.57	5.55	7.90	5.93	7.17	8.72	10.18	7.21	10.20	1 843.45	245.00	375.62
September	5.89	5.50	5.19	5.35	7.50	5.77	7.45	8.89	10.20	7.11	10.01	1 813.48	238.27	358.26
October	5.85	5.50	5.18	5.26	7.50	5.72	7.43	8.86	10.24	7.08	9.97	1 817.06	237.36	355.05
November	6.04	5.50	5.35	5.41	7.50	5.80	7.25	8.68	10.07	6.84	9.70	1 883.65	245.09	358.08
December	6.91	5.50	5.49	5.55	7.50	5.87	7.11	8.49	9.97	6.87	9.31	1 924.09	248.61	354.90
1987														
January	6.43	5.50	5.45	5.44	7.50	5.78	7.08	8.36	9.72	6.66	9.20	2 065.13	264.51	384.24
February	6.10	5.50	5.59	5.59	7.50	5.96	7.25	8.38	9.65	6.61	9.08	2 202.34	280.93	411.71
March	6.13	5.50	5.56	5.60	7.50	6.03	7.25	8.36	9.61	6.65	9.04	2 292.61	292.47	432.19
April	6.37	5.50	5.76	5.90	7.75	6.50	8.02	8.85	10.04	7.55	9.83	2 302.66	289.32	422.75
May	6.85	5.50	5.75	6.05	8.14	7.00	8.61	9.33	10.51	8.00	10.60	2 291.12	289.12	416.64
June	6.73	5.50	5.69	5.99	8.25	6.80	8.40	9.32	10.52	7.79	10.54	2 384.02	301.38	423.70
July	6.58	5.50	5.78	5.76	8.25	6.68	8.45	9.42	10.61	7.72	10.28	2 481.73	310.09	429.01
August	6.73	5.50	6.00	6.15	8.25	7.03	8.76	9.67	10.80	7.82	10.33	2 655.02	329.36	448.45
September	7.22	5.95	6.32	6.64	8.70	7.67	9.42	10.18	11.31	8.26	10.89	2 570.81	318.66	442.82
October	7.29	6.00	6.40	6.69	9.07	7.59	9.52	10.52	11.62	8.70	11.26	2 224.58	280.16	385.05
November	6.69	6.00	5.81	6.19	8.78	6.96	8.86	10.01	11.23	7.95	10.65	1 931.88	245.01	318.76
December	6.77	6.00	5.80	6.36	8.75	7.17	8.99	10.11	11.29	7.96	10.65	1 910.07	240.96	314.55
1988														
January	6.83	6.00	5.90	6.25	8.75	6.99	8.67	9.88	11.07	7.69	10.43	1 947.35	250.48	339.29
February	6.58	6.00	5.69	5.93	8.51	6.64	8.21	9.40	10.62	7.49	9.89	1 980.65	258.13	353.58
March	6.58	6.00	5.69	5.91	8.50	6.71	8.37	9.39	10.57	7.74	9.93	2 044.32	265.74	375.55
April	6.87	6.00	5.92	6.21	8.50	7.01	8.72	9.67	10.90	7.81	10.20	2 036.14	262.61	377.23
May	7.09	6.00	6.27	6.56	8.84	7.40	9.09	9.90	11.04	7.91	10.46	1 988.91	256.12	371.88
June	7.51	6.00	6.50	6.71	9.00	7.49	8.92	9.86	11.00	7.78	10.46	2 104.95	270.68	385.99
July	7.75	6.00	6.73	6.99	9.29	7.75	9.06	9.96	11.11	7.76	10.43	2 104.23	269.05	391.43
August	8.01	6.37	7.02	7.39	9.84	8.17	9.26	10.11	11.21	7.79	10.60	2 051.28	263.73	379.60
September	8.19	6.50	7.23	7.43	10.00	8.09	8.98	9.82	10.90	7.66	10.48	2 080.07	267.97	382.17
October	8.30	6.50	7.34	7.50	10.00	8.11	8.80	9.51	10.41	7.46	10.30	2 144.33	277.40	385.02
November	8.35	6.50	7.68	7.86	10.05	8.48	8.96	9.45	10.48	7.46	10.27	2 099.04	271.02	372.90
December	8.76	6.50	8.09	8.22	10.50	8.99	9.11	9.57	10.65	7.61	10.61	2 148.59	276.51	375.80
1989														
January	9.12	6.50	8.29	8.36	10.50	9.05	9.09	9.62	10.65	7.35	10.73	2 234.68	285.41	389.33
February	9.36	6.59	8.48	8.55	10.93	9.25	9.17	9.64	10.61	7.44	10.65	2 304.31	294.01	404.09
March	9.85	7.00	8.83	8.85	11.50	9.57	9.36	9.80	10.67	7.59	11.03	2 283.10	292.71	404.00
April	9.84	7.00	8.70	8.65	11.50	9.36	9.18	9.79	10.61	7.49	11.05	2 348.92	302.25	417.14
May	9.81	7.00	8.40	8.41	11.50	8.98	8.86	9.57	10.46	7.25	10.77	2 439.57	313.93	435.99
June	9.53	7.00	8.22	7.93	11.07	8.44	8.28	9.10	10.03	7.02	10.20	2 494.89	323.73	447.63
July	9.24	7.00	7.92	7.61	10.98	7.89	8.02	8.93	9.87	6.96	9.88	2 554.04	331.93	446.70
August	8.99	7.00	7.91	7.74	10.50	8.18	8.11	8.96	9.88	7.06	9.99	2 691.12	346.61	461.83
September	9.02	7.00	7.72	7.74	10.50	8.22	8.19	9.01	9.91	7.26	10.13	2 693.14	347.33	469.28
October	8.84	7.00	7.63	7.62	10.50	7.99	8.01	8.92	9.81	7.22	9.95	2 692.01	347.40	469.69
November	8.55	7.00	7.65	7.49	10.50	7.77	7.87	8.89	9.81	7.14	9.77	2 642.50	340.22	454.69
December	8.45	7.00	7.64	7.42	10.50	7.72	7.84	8.86	9.82	6.98	9.74	2 728.47	348.57	449.02
1990														
January	8.23	7.00	7.64	7.55	10.11	7.92	8.21	8.99	9.94	7.10	9.90	2 679.24	339.97	439.35
February	8.24	7.00	7.76	7.70	10.00	8.11	8.47	9.22	10.14	7.22	10.20	2 614.19	330.45	424.53
March	8.28	7.00	7.87	7.85	10.00	8.35	8.59	9.37	10.21	7.29	10.27	2 700.13	338.47	436.10
April	8.26	7.00	7.78	7.84	10.00	8.40	8.79	9.46	10.30	7.39	10.37	2 708.27	338.18	429.00
May	8.18	7.00	7.78	7.76	10.00	8.32	8.76	9.47	10.41	7.35	10.48	2 793.82	350.25	442.60
June	8.29	7.00	7.74	7.63	10.00	8.10	8.48	9.26	10.22	7.24	10.16	2 894.84	360.39	462.31
July	8.15	7.00	7.66	7.52	10.00	7.94	8.47	9.24	10.20	7.19	10.04	2 934.23	360.03	455.83
August	8.13	7.00	7.44	7.38	10.00	7.78	8.75	9.41	10.41	7.32	10.10	2 681.89	330.75	396.33
September	8.20	7.00	7.38	7.32	10.00	7.76	8.89	9.56	10.64	7.43	10.18	2 550.69	315.41	368.57
October	8.11	7.00	7.19	7.16	10.00	7.55	8.72	9.53	10.74	7.49	10.18	2 460.54	307.12	338.02
November	7.81	7.00	7.07	7.03	10.00	7.31	8.39	9.30	10.62	7.18	10.01	2 518.58	315.29	347.72
December	7.31	6.79	6.81	6.70	10.00	7.05	8.08	9.05	10.43	7.09	9.67	2 610.92	328.75	370.21
1991														
January	6.91	6.50	6.30	6.28	9.52	6.64	8.09	9.04	10.45	7.08	9.64	2 587.60	325.49	376.67
February	6.25	6.00	5.95	5.93	9.05	6.27	7.85	8.83	10.07	6.91	9.37	2 863.05	362.26	442.59
March	6.12	6.00	5.91	5.92	9.00	6.40	8.11	8.93	10.09	7.10	9.50	2 920.12	372.28	469.10
April	5.91	5.98	5.67	5.71	9.00	6.24	8.04	8.86	9.94	7.02	9.49	2 925.55	379.68	496.32
May	5.78	5.50	5.51	5.61	8.50	6.13	8.07	8.86	9.86	6.95	9.47	2 928.43	377.99	490.93
June	5.90	5.50	5.60	5.75	8.50	6.36	8.28	9.01	9.96	7.13	9.62	2 968.14	378.29	490.38
July	5.82	5.50	5.58	5.70	8.50	6.31	8.27	9.00	9.89	7.05	9.57	2 978.19	380.23	489.37
August	5.66	5.50	5.39	5.39	8.50	5.78	7.90	8.75	9.65	6.90	9.24	3 006.09	389.40	513.25
September	5.45	5.20	5.25	5.25	8.20	5.57	7.65	8.61	9.51	6.80	9.01	3 010.36	387.20	520.56
October	5.21	5.00	5.03	5.04	8.00	5.33	7.53	8.55	9.49	6.68	8.86	3 019.74	386.88	528.92
November	4.81	4.58	4.60	4.61	7.58	4.89	7.42	8.48	9.45	6.73	8.71	2 986.13	385.92	536.58
December	4.43	4.11	4.12	4.10	7.21	4.38	7.09	8.31	9.26	6.69	8.50	2 958.66	388.51	544.10

[1]Federal Reserve Bank of New York. Through 2002, represents the rate for adjustment credit. Beginning in 2003, represents the rate for primary credit. See notes and definitions for more information.
[2]1941–1943 = 10.
[3]February 5, 1971 = 100.

Table 20-6. Interest Rates, Bond Yields, and Stock Price Indexes—Continued

(Not seasonally adjusted.)

	Percent per annum												Stock price indexes		
	Short-term rates					U.S. Treasury securities		Bond yields					Dow Jones industrials (30 stocks)	Standard and Poor's composite (500 stocks) [2]	Nasdaq composite [3]
Year and month								Domestic corporate (Moody's)		State and local bonds (Bond Buyer)	Fixed-rate first mortgages				
	Federal funds	Federal Reserve discount rate [1]	U.S. Treasury bills, 3-month	U.S. Treasury bills, 6-month	Bank prime rate	1-year	10-year	Aaa	Baa						
1992															
January	4.03	3.50	3.84	3.87	6.50	4.15	7.03	8.20	9.13	6.54	8.43	3 227.06	416.08	615.73
February	4.06	3.50	3.84	3.93	6.50	4.29	7.34	8.29	9.23	6.74	8.76	3 257.27	412.56	632.05
March	3.98	3.50	4.05	4.18	6.50	4.63	7.54	8.35	9.25	6.76	8.94	3 247.42	407.36	619.60
April	3.73	3.50	3.81	3.87	6.50	4.30	7.48	8.33	9.21	6.67	8.85	3 294.10	407.41	582.79
May	3.82	3.50	3.66	3.75	6.50	4.19	7.39	8.28	9.13	6.57	8.67	3 376.79	414.81	581.47
June	3.76	3.50	3.70	3.77	6.50	4.17	7.26	8.22	9.05	6.49	8.51	3 337.79	408.27	566.66
July	3.25	3.02	3.28	3.28	6.02	3.60	6.84	8.07	8.84	6.13	8.13	3 329.41	415.05	568.72
August	3.30	3.00	3.14	3.21	6.00	3.47	6.59	7.95	8.65	6.16	7.98	3 307.46	417.93	569.00
September	3.22	3.00	2.97	2.96	6.00	3.18	6.42	7.92	8.62	6.25	7.92	3 293.93	418.48	580.68
October	3.10	3.00	2.84	3.04	6.00	3.30	6.59	7.99	8.84	6.41	8.09	3 198.70	412.50	585.01
November	3.09	3.00	3.14	3.34	6.00	3.68	6.87	8.10	8.96	6.36	8.31	3 238.49	422.84	630.86
December	2.92	3.00	3.25	3.36	6.00	3.71	6.77	7.98	8.81	6.22	8.22	3 303.15	435.64	661.28
1993															
January	3.02	3.00	3.06	3.14	6.00	3.50	6.60	7.91	8.67	6.15	8.02	3 277.73	435.23	691.13
February	3.03	3.00	2.95	3.07	6.00	3.39	6.26	7.71	8.39	5.87	7.68	3 367.26	441.70	681.71
March	3.07	3.00	2.97	3.05	6.00	3.33	5.98	7.58	8.15	5.64	7.50	3 440.73	450.16	684.49
April	2.96	3.00	2.89	2.97	6.00	3.24	5.97	7.46	8.14	5.76	7.47	3 423.62	443.08	665.33
May	3.00	3.00	2.96	3.07	6.00	3.36	6.04	7.43	8.21	5.73	7.47	3 478.18	445.25	686.45
June	3.04	3.00	3.10	3.20	6.00	3.54	5.96	7.33	8.07	5.63	7.42	3 513.81	448.06	695.38
July	3.06	3.00	3.05	3.16	6.00	3.47	5.81	7.17	7.93	5.57	7.21	3 529.44	447.29	703.40
August	3.03	3.00	3.05	3.14	6.00	3.44	5.68	6.85	7.60	5.45	7.11	3 597.03	454.13	725.15
September	3.09	3.00	2.96	3.06	6.00	3.36	5.36	6.66	7.34	5.29	6.92	3 592.29	459.24	745.94
October	2.99	3.00	3.04	3.12	6.00	3.39	5.33	6.67	7.31	5.25	6.83	3 625.81	463.90	771.31
November	3.02	3.00	3.12	3.26	6.00	3.58	5.72	6.93	7.66	5.47	7.16	3 674.71	462.89	764.04
December	2.96	3.00	3.08	3.23	6.00	3.61	5.77	6.93	7.69	5.35	7.17	3 744.10	465.95	762.94
1994															
January	3.05	3.00	3.02	3.15	6.00	3.54	5.75	6.92	7.65	5.31	7.06	3 868.37	472.99	787.77
February	3.25	3.00	3.21	3.43	6.00	3.87	5.97	7.08	7.76	5.40	7.15	3 905.62	471.58	787.81
March	3.34	3.00	3.52	3.78	6.06	4.32	6.48	7.48	8.13	5.91	7.68	3 816.99	463.81	785.93
April	3.56	3.00	3.74	4.09	6.45	4.82	6.97	7.88	8.52	6.23	8.32	3 661.49	447.23	732.30
May	4.01	3.24	4.19	4.60	6.99	5.31	7.18	7.99	8.62	6.19	8.60	3 708.00	450.90	727.76
June	4.25	3.50	4.18	4.55	7.25	5.27	7.10	7.97	8.65	6.11	8.40	3 737.58	454.83	723.21
July	4.26	3.50	4.39	4.75	7.25	5.48	7.30	8.11	8.80	6.23	8.61	3 718.31	451.40	713.49
August	4.47	3.76	4.50	4.88	7.51	5.56	7.24	8.07	8.74	6.21	8.51	3 797.48	464.24	738.87
September	4.73	4.00	4.64	5.04	7.75	5.76	7.46	8.34	8.98	6.28	8.64	3 880.60	466.96	763.94
October	4.76	4.00	4.96	5.39	7.75	6.11	7.74	8.57	9.20	6.52	8.93	3 868.10	463.81	762.46
November	5.29	4.40	5.25	5.72	8.15	6.54	7.96	8.68	9.32	6.97	9.17	3 792.44	461.01	760.42
December	5.45	4.75	5.64	6.21	8.50	7.14	7.81	8.46	9.10	6.80	9.20	3 770.30	455.19	734.96
1995															
January	5.53	4.75	5.81	6.21	8.50	7.05	7.78	8.46	9.08	6.53	9.15	3 872.46	465.25	758.01
February	5.92	5.25	5.80	6.03	9.00	6.70	7.47	8.26	8.85	6.22	8.83	3 953.73	481.92	784.24
March	5.98	5.25	5.73	5.89	9.00	6.43	7.20	8.12	8.70	6.10	8.46	4 062.78	493.15	807.16
April	6.05	5.25	5.67	5.77	9.00	6.27	7.06	8.03	8.60	6.02	8.32	4 230.67	507.91	825.34
May	6.01	5.25	5.70	5.67	9.00	6.00	6.63	7.65	8.20	5.95	7.96	4 391.58	523.81	859.77
June	6.00	5.25	5.50	5.42	9.00	5.64	6.17	7.30	7.90	5.84	7.57	4 510.77	539.35	906.04
July	5.85	5.25	5.47	5.37	8.80	5.59	6.28	7.41	8.04	5.92	7.61	4 684.78	557.37	979.36
August	5.74	5.25	5.41	5.41	8.75	5.75	6.49	7.57	8.19	6.06	7.86	4 639.27	559.11	1 009.59
September	5.80	5.25	5.26	5.30	8.75	5.62	6.20	7.32	7.93	5.91	7.64	4 746.76	578.77	1 051.00
October	5.76	5.25	5.30	5.32	8.75	5.59	6.04	7.12	7.75	5.80	7.48	4 760.48	582.92	1 022.15
November	5.80	5.25	5.35	5.27	8.75	5.43	5.93	7.02	7.68	5.64	7.38	4 935.82	595.53	1 046.64
December	5.60	5.25	5.16	5.13	8.65	5.31	5.71	6.82	7.49	5.45	7.20	5 136.11	614.57	1 047.04
1996															
January	5.56	5.24	5.02	4.92	8.50	5.09	5.65	6.81	7.47	5.43	7.03	5 179.38	614.42	1 024.95
February	5.22	5.00	4.87	4.77	8.25	4.94	5.81	6.99	7.63	5.43	7.08	5 518.74	649.54	1 094.02
March	5.31	5.00	4.96	4.96	8.25	5.34	6.27	7.35	8.03	5.79	7.62	5 612.25	647.07	1 092.65
April	5.22	5.00	4.99	5.06	8.25	5.54	6.51	7.50	8.19	5.94	7.93	5 579.86	647.17	1 135.63
May	5.24	5.00	5.02	5.12	8.25	5.64	6.74	7.62	8.30	5.98	8.07	5 616.71	661.23	1 220.54
June	5.27	5.00	5.11	5.25	8.25	5.81	6.91	7.71	8.40	6.02	8.32	5 671.52	668.50	1 205.08
July	5.40	5.00	5.17	5.30	8.25	5.85	6.87	7.65	8.35	5.92	8.24	5 496.27	644.07	1 105.61
August	5.22	5.00	5.09	5.13	8.25	5.67	6.64	7.46	8.18	5.76	8.00	5 685.51	662.68	1 134.25
September	5.30	5.00	5.15	5.24	8.25	5.83	6.83	7.66	8.35	5.87	8.23	5 804.01	674.88	1 186.44
October	5.24	5.00	5.01	5.11	8.25	5.55	6.53	7.39	8.07	5.72	7.92	5 996.22	701.45	1 234.04
November	5.31	5.00	5.03	5.07	8.25	5.42	6.20	7.10	7.79	5.59	7.62	6 318.36	735.67	1 259.83
December	5.29	5.00	4.87	5.04	8.25	5.47	6.30	7.20	7.89	5.64	7.60	6 435.87	743.25	1 292.15
1997															
January	5.25	5.00	5.05	5.10	8.25	5.61	6.58	7.42	8.09	5.72	7.82	6 707.05	766.22	1 345.41
February	5.19	5.00	5.00	5.06	8.25	5.53	6.42	7.31	7.94	5.63	7.65	6 917.46	798.39	1 349.17
March	5.39	5.00	5.14	5.26	8.30	5.80	6.69	7.55	8.18	5.76	7.90	6 901.14	792.16	1 282.86
April	5.51	5.00	5.17	5.37	8.50	5.99	6.89	7.73	8.34	5.88	8.14	6 657.51	763.93	1 225.00
May	5.50	5.00	5.13	5.30	8.50	5.87	6.71	7.58	8.20	5.70	7.94	7 242.33	833.09	1 352.56
June	5.56	5.00	4.92	5.13	8.50	5.69	6.49	7.41	8.02	5.53	7.69	7 599.61	876.29	1 422.45
July	5.52	5.00	5.07	5.12	8.50	5.54	6.22	7.14	7.75	5.35	7.50	7 990.65	925.29	1 531.14
August	5.54	5.00	5.13	5.19	8.50	5.56	6.30	7.22	7.82	5.41	7.48	7 948.42	927.74	1 596.74
September	5.54	5.00	4.97	5.09	8.50	5.52	6.21	7.15	7.70	5.39	7.43	7 866.59	937.02	1 660.15
October	5.50	5.00	4.95	5.09	8.50	5.46	6.03	7.00	7.57	5.38	7.29	7 875.82	951.16	1 682.17
November	5.52	5.00	5.15	5.17	8.50	5.46	5.88	6.87	7.42	5.33	7.21	7 677.35	938.92	1 600.97
December	5.50	5.00	5.16	5.24	8.50	5.53	5.81	6.76	7.32	5.19	7.10	7 909.82	962.37	1 567.00

[1] Federal Reserve Bank of New York. Through 2002, represents the rate for adjustment credit. Beginning in 2003, represents the rate for primary credit. See notes and definitions for more information.
[2] 1941–1943 = 10.
[3] February 5, 1971 = 100.

Table 20-6. Interest Rates, Bond Yields, and Stock Price Indexes—Continued

(Not seasonally adjusted.)

Year and month	Percent per annum											Stock price indexes		
	Short-term rates					U.S. Treasury securities		Bond yields			Fixed-rate first mortgages	Dow Jones industrials (30 stocks)	Standard and Poor's composite (500 stocks) [2]	Nasdaq composite [3]
								Domestic corporate (Moody's)		State and local bonds (Bond Buyer)				
	Federal funds	Federal Reserve discount rate [1]	U.S. Treasury bills, 3-month	U.S. Treasury bills, 6-month	Bank prime rate	1-year	10-year	Aaa	Baa					
1998														
January	5.56	5.00	5.09	5.03	8.50	5.24	5.54	6.61	7.19	5.06	6.99	7 808.36	963.36	1 570.23
February	5.51	5.00	5.11	5.07	8.50	5.31	5.57	6.67	7.25	5.10	7.04	8 323.62	1 023.74	1 714.87
March	5.49	5.00	5.03	5.04	8.50	5.39	5.65	6.72	7.32	5.21	7.13	8 709.48	1 076.83	1 781.27
April	5.45	5.00	5.00	5.06	8.50	5.38	5.64	6.69	7.33	5.23	7.14	9 037.43	1 112.20	1 852.30
May	5.49	5.00	5.03	5.14	8.50	5.44	5.65	6.69	7.30	5.20	7.14	9 080.09	1 108.42	1 836.39
June	5.56	5.00	4.99	5.12	8.50	5.41	5.50	6.53	7.13	5.12	7.00	8 872.96	1 108.39	1 795.74
July	5.54	5.00	4.96	5.03	8.50	5.36	5.46	6.55	7.15	5.14	6.95	9 097.15	1 156.58	1 941.58
August	5.55	5.00	4.94	4.95	8.50	5.21	5.34	6.52	7.14	5.10	6.92	8 478.54	1 074.63	1 784.75
September	5.51	5.00	4.74	4.63	8.49	4.71	4.81	6.40	7.09	4.99	6.72	7 909.80	1 020.64	1 663.43
October	5.07	4.86	4.08	4.05	8.12	4.12	4.53	6.37	7.18	4.93	6.71	8 164.47	1 032.47	1 615.69
November	4.83	4.63	4.44	4.42	7.89	4.53	4.83	6.41	7.34	5.03	6.87	9 005.78	1 144.43	1 888.72
December	4.68	4.50	4.42	4.40	7.75	4.52	4.65	6.22	7.23	4.98	6.72	9 018.68	1 190.05	2 071.03
1999														
January	4.63	4.50	4.34	4.33	7.75	4.51	4.72	6.24	7.29	5.01	6.79	9 345.86	1 248.77	2 357.80
February	4.76	4.50	4.45	4.44	7.75	4.70	5.00	6.40	7.39	5.03	6.81	9 322.94	1 246.58	2 356.99
March	4.81	4.50	4.48	4.47	7.75	4.78	5.23	6.62	7.53	5.10	7.04	9 753.64	1 281.66	2 391.14
April	4.74	4.50	4.28	4.37	7.75	4.69	5.18	6.64	7.48	5.08	6.92	10 443.50	1 334.76	2 537.89
May	4.74	4.50	4.51	4.56	7.75	4.85	5.54	6.93	7.72	5.18	7.15	10 853.88	1 332.07	2 512.60
June	4.76	4.50	4.59	4.82	7.75	5.10	5.90	7.23	8.02	5.36	7.55	10 704.03	1 322.55	2 520.96
July	4.99	4.50	4.60	4.58	8.00	5.03	5.79	7.19	7.95	5.36	7.63	11 052.22	1 380.99	2 741.26
August	5.07	4.56	4.76	4.87	8.06	5.20	5.94	7.40	8.15	5.58	7.94	10 935.48	1 327.49	2 642.45
September	5.22	4.75	4.73	4.88	8.25	5.25	5.92	7.39	8.20	5.69	7.82	10 714.03	1 318.17	2 807.95
October	5.20	4.75	4.88	4.98	8.25	5.43	6.11	7.55	8.38	5.92	7.85	10 396.89	1 300.01	2 815.28
November	5.42	4.86	5.07	5.20	8.37	5.55	6.03	7.36	8.15	5.86	7.74	10 809.80	1 391.00	3 230.55
December	5.30	5.00	5.23	5.44	8.50	5.84	6.28	7.55	8.19	5.95	7.91	11 246.37	1 428.68	3 739.88
2000														
January	5.45	5.00	5.34	5.50	8.50	6.12	6.66	7.78	8.33	6.08	8.21	11 281.27	1 425.59	4 013.49
February	5.73	5.24	5.57	5.72	8.73	6.22	6.52	7.68	8.29	6.00	8.32	10 541.93	1 388.87	4 410.87
March	5.85	5.34	5.72	5.85	8.83	6.22	6.26	7.68	8.37	5.83	8.24	10 483.38	1 442.21	4 802.99
April	6.02	5.50	5.67	5.81	9.00	6.15	5.99	7.64	8.40	5.75	8.15	10 944.32	1 461.36	3 863.64
May	6.27	5.71	5.92	6.10	9.24	6.33	6.44	7.99	8.90	6.00	8.52	10 580.28	1 418.48	3 528.42
June	6.53	6.00	5.74	5.97	9.50	6.17	6.10	7.67	8.48	5.80	8.29	10 582.93	1 461.96	3 865.48
July	6.54	6.00	5.96	6.00	9.50	6.08	6.05	7.65	8.35	5.63	8.15	10 662.98	1 473.00	4 017.69
August	6.50	6.00	6.09	6.07	9.50	6.18	5.83	7.55	8.26	5.51	8.03	11 014.51	1 485.46	3 909.60
September	6.52	6.00	6.00	5.98	9.50	6.13	5.80	7.62	8.35	5.56	7.91	10 967.88	1 468.05	3 875.82
October	6.51	6.00	6.11	6.04	9.50	6.01	5.74	7.55	8.34	5.59	7.80	10 440.96	1 390.14	3 333.82
November	6.51	6.00	6.17	6.06	9.50	6.09	5.72	7.45	8.28	5.54	7.75	10 666.08	1 375.04	3 055.42
December	6.40	6.00	5.77	5.68	9.50	5.60	5.24	7.21	8.02	5.22	7.38	10 652.52	1 330.93	2 657.81
2001														
January	5.98	5.52	5.15	4.95	9.05	4.81	5.16	7.15	7.93	5.10	7.03	10 682.76	1 335.63	2 656.86
February	5.49	5.00	4.88	4.71	8.50	4.68	5.10	7.10	7.87	5.18	7.05	10 774.58	1 305.75	2 449.57
March	5.31	4.81	4.42	4.28	8.32	4.30	4.89	6.98	7.84	5.13	6.95	10 081.33	1 185.85	1 986.66
April	4.80	4.28	3.87	3.85	7.80	3.98	5.14	7.20	8.07	5.27	7.08	10 234.52	1 189.84	1 933.93
May	4.21	3.73	3.62	3.62	7.24	3.78	5.39	7.29	8.07	5.29	7.15	11 004.95	1 270.37	2 181.13
June	3.97	3.47	3.49	3.45	6.98	3.58	5.28	7.18	7.97	5.20	7.16	10 767.19	1 238.71	2 112.05
July	3.77	3.25	3.51	3.45	6.75	3.62	5.24	7.13	7.97	5.20	7.13	10 444.50	1 204.45	2 033.98
August	3.65	3.16	3.36	3.29	6.67	3.47	4.97	7.02	7.85	5.03	6.95	10 314.70	1 178.50	1 929.71
September	3.07	2.77	2.64	2.63	6.28	2.82	4.73	7.17	8.03	5.09	6.82	9 042.57	1 044.64	1 573.31
October	2.49	2.02	2.16	2.12	5.53	2.33	4.57	7.03	7.91	5.05	6.62	9 220.75	1 076.59	1 656.43
November	2.09	1.58	1.87	1.88	5.10	2.18	4.65	6.97	7.81	5.04	6.66	9 721.83	1 129.68	1 870.06
December	1.82	1.33	1.69	1.78	4.84	2.22	5.09	6.77	8.05	5.25	7.07	9 979.89	1 144.93	1 977.71
2002														
January	1.73	1.25	1.65	1.73	4.75	2.16	5.04	6.55	7.87	5.16	7.00	9 923.81	1 140.21	1 976.77
February	1.74	1.25	1.73	1.82	4.75	2.23	4.91	6.51	7.89	5.11	6.89	9 891.05	1 100.67	1 799.72
March	1.73	1.25	1.79	2.01	4.75	2.57	5.28	6.81	8.11	5.29	7.01	10 500.96	1 153.79	1 863.05
April	1.75	1.25	1.72	1.93	4.75	2.48	5.21	6.76	8.03	5.22	6.99	10 165.18	1 112.03	1 758.80
May	1.75	1.25	1.73	1.86	4.75	2.35	5.16	6.75	8.09	5.19	6.81	10 080.49	1 079.27	1 660.31
June	1.75	1.25	1.70	1.79	4.75	2.20	4.93	6.63	7.95	5.09	6.65	9 492.44	1 014.05	1 505.49
July	1.73	1.25	1.68	1.70	4.75	1.96	4.65	6.53	7.90	5.02	6.49	8 616.53	903.59	1 346.09
August	1.74	1.25	1.62	1.60	4.75	1.76	4.26	6.37	7.58	4.95	6.29	8 685.48	912.55	1 327.36
September	1.75	1.25	1.63	1.60	4.75	1.72	3.87	6.15	7.40	4.74	6.09	8 160.79	867.81	1 251.07
October	1.75	1.25	1.58	1.56	4.75	1.65	3.94	6.32	7.73	4.88	6.11	8 048.12	854.63	1 241.91
November	1.34	0.83	1.23	1.27	4.35	1.49	4.05	6.31	7.62	4.95	6.07	8 625.73	909.93	1 409.15
December	1.24	0.75	1.19	1.24	4.25	1.45	4.03	6.21	7.45	4.85	6.05	8 526.67	899.18	1 387.15
2003														
January	1.24	. . .	1.17	1.20	4.25	1.36	4.05	6.17	7.35	4.90	5.92	8 474.59	895.84	1 389.56
February	1.26	2.25	1.17	1.18	4.25	1.30	3.90	5.95	7.06	4.81	5.84	7 916.18	837.62	1 313.26
March	1.25	2.25	1.13	1.13	4.25	1.24	3.81	5.89	6.95	4.76	5.75	7 977.73	846.62	1 348.50
April	1.26	2.25	1.13	1.14	4.25	1.27	3.96	5.74	6.85	4.74	5.81	8 332.09	890.03	1 409.83
May	1.26	2.25	1.07	1.08	4.25	1.18	3.57	5.22	6.38	4.41	5.48	8 623.41	935.96	1 524.18
June	1.22	2.20	0.92	0.92	4.22	1.01	3.33	4.97	6.19	4.33	5.23	9 098.07	988.00	1 631.75
July	1.01	2.00	0.90	0.95	4.00	1.12	3.98	5.49	6.62	4.74	5.63	9 154.39	992.54	1 716.85
August	1.03	2.00	0.95	1.03	4.00	1.31	4.45	5.88	7.01	5.10	6.26	9 284.78	989.53	1 724.82
September	1.01	2.00	0.94	1.01	4.00	1.24	4.27	5.72	6.79	4.92	6.15	9 492.54	1 019.44	1 856.22
October	1.01	2.00	0.92	1.00	4.00	1.25	4.29	5.70	6.73	4.89	5.95	9 682.46	1 038.73	1 907.89
November	1.00	2.00	0.93	1.02	4.00	1.34	4.30	5.65	6.66	4.73	5.93	9 762.20	1 049.90	1 939.25
December	0.98	2.00	0.90	0.99	4.00	1.31	4.27	5.62	6.60	4.64	5.88	10 124.66	1 080.64	1 956.98

[1] Federal Reserve Bank of New York. Through 2002, represents the rate for adjustment credit. Beginning in 2003, represents the rate for primary credit. See notes and definitions for more information.
[2] 1941–1943 = 10.
[3] February 5, 1971 = 100.
. . . = Not available.

Table 20-6. Interest Rates, Bond Yields, and Stock Price Indexes—Continued

(Not seasonally adjusted.)

Year and month	Percent per annum											Stock price indexes		
	Short-term rates					U.S. Treasury securities		Bond yields						
								Domestic corporate (Moody's)		State and local bonds (Bond Buyer)	Fixed-rate first mortgages	Dow Jones industrials (30 stocks)	Standard and Poor's composite (500 stocks) [2]	Nasdaq composite [3]
	Federal funds	Federal Reserve discount rate [1]	U.S. Treasury bills, 3-month	U.S. Treasury bills, 6-month	Bank prime rate	1-year	10-year	Aaa	Baa					
2004														
January	1.00	2.00	0.88	0.97	4.00	1.24	4.15	5.54	6.44	4.61	5.74	10 540.05	1 132.52	2 098.00
February	1.01	2.00	0.93	0.99	4.00	1.24	4.08	5.50	6.27	4.55	5.64	10 601.50	1 143.36	2 048.36
March	1.00	2.00	0.94	0.99	4.00	1.19	3.83	5.33	6.11	4.41	5.45	10 323.73	1 123.98	1 979.48
April	1.00	2.00	0.94	1.09	4.00	1.43	4.35	5.73	6.46	4.82	5.83	10 418.40	1 133.08	2 021.32
May	1.00	2.00	1.02	1.31	4.00	1.78	4.72	6.04	6.75	5.07	6.27	10 083.81	1 102.78	1 930.09
June	1.03	2.01	1.27	1.60	4.01	2.12	4.73	6.01	6.78	5.05	6.29	10 364.90	1 132.76	2 000.98
July	1.26	2.25	1.33	1.66	4.25	2.10	4.50	5.82	6.62	4.87	6.06	10 152.09	1 105.85	1 912.42
August	1.43	2.43	1.48	1.72	4.43	2.02	4.28	5.65	6.46	4.70	5.87	10 032.80	1 088.94	1 821.54
September	1.61	2.58	1.65	1.87	4.58	2.12	4.13	5.46	6.27	4.56	5.75	10 204.67	1 117.66	1 884.73
October	1.76	2.75	1.76	2.00	4.75	2.23	4.10	5.47	6.21	4.49	5.72	10 001.60	1 118.07	1 938.25
November	1.93	2.93	2.07	2.27	4.93	2.50	4.19	5.52	6.20	4.52	5.73	10 411.76	1 168.94	2 062.87
December	2.16	3.15	2.19	2.43	5.15	2.67	4.23	5.47	6.15	4.48	5.75	10 673.38	1 199.21	2 149.53
2005														
January	2.28	3.25	2.33	2.61	5.25	2.86	4.22	5.36	6.02	4.41	5.71	10 539.51	1 181.41	2 071.87
February	2.50	3.49	2.54	2.77	5.49	3.03	4.17	5.20	5.82	4.35	5.63	10 723.82	1 199.63	2 065.74
March	2.63	3.58	2.74	3.00	5.58	3.30	4.50	5.40	6.06	4.57	5.93	10 682.09	1 194.90	2 030.43
April	2.79	3.75	2.78	3.05	5.75	3.32	4.34	5.33	6.05	4.46	5.86	10 283.19	1 164.42	1 957.49
May	3.00	3.98	2.84	3.08	5.98	3.33	4.14	5.15	6.01	4.31	5.72	10 377.18	1 178.28	2 005.22
June	3.04	4.01	2.97	3.13	6.01	3.36	4.00	4.96	5.86	4.23	5.58	10 486.68	1 202.26	2 074.02
July	3.26	4.25	3.22	3.42	6.25	3.64	4.18	5.06	5.95	4.31	5.70	10 545.38	1 222.24	2 145.14
August	3.50	4.44	3.44	3.66	6.44	3.87	4.26	5.09	5.96	4.32	5.82	10 554.27	1 224.27	2 157.85
September	3.62	4.59	3.42	3.67	6.59	3.85	4.20	5.13	6.03	4.29	5.77	10 532.54	1 225.91	2 144.61
October	3.78	4.75	3.71	3.99	6.75	4.18	4.46	5.35	6.30	4.48	6.07	10 324.31	1 191.96	2 087.09
November	4.00	5.00	3.88	4.15	7.00	4.33	4.54	5.42	6.39	4.57	6.33	10 695.25	1 237.37	2 202.84
December	4.16	5.15	3.89	4.18	7.15	4.35	4.47	5.37	6.32	4.46	6.27	10 827.79	1 262.07	2 246.09

[1] Federal Reserve Bank of New York. Through 2002, represents the rate for adjustment credit. Beginning in 2003, represents the rate for primary credit. See notes and definitions for more information.
[2] 1941–1943 = 10.
[3] February 5, 1971 = 100.

Table 20-7. Composite Indexes of Economic Activity and Selected Index Components

(Seasonally adjusted, except as noted.)

Year and month	Cyclical composite indexes, 1996 = 100				Selected components of leading index		Selected component of coincident index	Selected component of lagging index
	Leading	Coincident	Lagging	Ratio, coincident to lagging	Vendor performance (slower deliveries, diffusion index, percent)	Interest rate spread, 10-year Treasury bond less federal funds [1]	Personal income less transfer payments (billions of 1996 dollars)	Consumer installment credit outstanding (percent of personal income)
1959								
January	41.1	36.2	35.4	102.3	61.8	1.54	1 758.3	12.8
February	41.7	36.5	35.6	102.5	67.3	1.53	1 769.1	12.9
March	42.2	36.8	35.6	103.4	66.3	1.19	1 785.4	12.9
April	42.2	37.2	35.8	103.9	64.8	1.16	1 797.4	13.0
May	42.4	37.4	36.0	103.9	63.0	1.41	1 812.3	13.0
June	42.4	37.5	36.2	103.6	63.7	0.95	1 819.2	13.1
July	42.3	37.4	36.5	102.5	59.1	0.93	1 816.3	13.2
August	42.1	36.9	37.0	99.7	57.4	0.93	1 806.8	13.5
September	42.1	36.9	37.3	98.9	57.5	0.92	1 806.7	13.6
October	41.8	36.9	37.6	98.1	58.5	0.55	1 809.9	13.7
November	41.4	37.1	37.6	98.7	54.6	0.53	1 822.4	13.7
December	42.3	37.8	37.6	100.5	53.7	0.70	1 842.4	13.8
1960								
January	42.1	38.1	37.4	101.9	46.2	0.73	1 852.5	13.8
February	41.8	38.1	37.6	101.3	31.7	0.52	1 853.2	13.9
March	41.3	38.0	37.9	100.3	28.8	0.41	1 854.0	14.0
April	41.5	38.1	38.0	100.3	28.9	0.36	1 859.4	14.1
May	41.4	37.9	38.4	98.7	32.3	0.50	1 863.6	14.1
June	41.5	37.8	38.7	97.7	34.8	0.83	1 862.1	14.2
July	41.5	37.8	38.8	97.4	35.8	0.67	1 863.1	14.2
August	41.6	37.7	38.8	97.2	38.0	0.82	1 859.8	14.3
September	41.6	37.7	38.7	97.4	37.3	1.20	1 860.4	14.3
October	41.5	37.7	38.7	97.4	36.2	1.42	1 865.8	14.3
November	41.4	37.4	38.8	96.4	37.6	1.49	1 854.1	14.4
December	41.5	37.2	39.0	95.4	40.4	1.86	1 841.8	14.5
1961								
January	41.8	37.1	39.1	94.9	39.2	2.39	1 858.9	14.6
February	42.0	37.1	39.1	94.9	41.1	1.24	1 859.4	14.4
March	42.7	37.3	38.9	95.9	42.1	1.72	1 868.6	14.4
April	43.1	37.4	38.8	96.4	47.5	2.29	1 874.5	14.3
May	43.5	37.6	38.6	97.4	47.9	1.73	1 884.9	14.2
June	44.0	37.9	38.4	98.7	49.3	2.15	1 901.1	14.1
July	44.0	38.0	38.3	99.2	49.4	2.75	1 905.6	14.0
August	44.7	38.3	38.4	99.7	50.6	2.04	1 913.5	14.0
September	44.5	38.4	38.5	99.7	50.7	2.10	1 918.3	14.1
October	45.1	38.6	38.6	100.0	52.4	1.66	1 938.2	14.0
November	45.6	39.0	38.6	101.0	51.1	1.33	1 957.5	14.0
December	45.9	39.1	38.8	100.8	55.8	1.73	1 967.8	14.0
1962								
January	45.9	39.1	39.1	100.0	57.1	1.93	1 963.7	14.0
February	46.4	39.3	39.1	100.5	56.2	1.67	1 974.0	14.0
March	46.4	39.5	39.3	100.5	57.0	1.08	1 987.8	14.0
April	46.4	39.7	39.4	100.8	47.4	1.06	1 998.9	14.1
May	46.1	39.7	39.6	100.3	45.2	1.51	2 001.9	14.2
June	45.8	39.7	39.8	99.7	43.3	1.23	2 007.6	14.3
July	46.1	39.8	40.0	99.5	45.1	1.30	2 015.4	14.3
August	46.3	39.9	40.2	99.3	43.7	1.05	2 017.1	14.4
September	46.4	40.0	40.2	99.5	45.1	1.08	2 019.9	14.4
October	46.6	40.1	40.3	99.5	46.7	1.03	2 024.0	14.5
November	47.2	40.3	40.4	99.8	48.7	0.98	2 035.9	14.5
December	47.3	40.2	40.6	99.0	50.1	0.93	2 046.1	14.6
1963								
January	47.6	40.3	40.6	99.3	50.4	0.91	2 040.0	14.6
February	48.0	40.5	40.7	99.5	51.0	0.92	2 045.0	14.8
March	48.3	40.6	40.8	99.5	54.9	0.95	2 053.7	14.9
April	48.7	40.9	40.9	100.0	58.2	1.07	2 060.4	15.0
May	48.9	40.9	41.0	99.8	56.4	0.93	2 068.0	15.0
June	49.0	41.1	41.2	99.8	56.3	1.00	2 080.9	15.0
July	49.0	41.2	41.3	99.8	43.6	1.00	2 081.4	15.2
August	49.1	41.2	41.6	99.0	48.5	0.51	2 089.4	15.3
September	49.5	41.4	41.7	99.3	49.7	0.60	2 103.4	15.3
October	49.8	41.6	41.9	99.3	47.4	0.61	2 116.8	15.4
November	49.9	41.6	42.3	98.3	48.7	0.64	2 120.5	15.4
December	50.0	41.8	42.4	98.6	47.6	0.75	2 136.3	15.5
1964								
January	50.3	42.0	42.3	99.3	55.3	0.69	2 137.9	15.6
February	50.6	42.2	42.5	99.3	51.9	0.67	2 156.5	15.6
March	50.8	42.3	42.7	99.1	60.3	0.79	2 166.4	15.7
April	51.1	42.5	42.9	99.1	57.7	0.76	2 180.2	15.8
May	51.4	42.7	42.8	99.8	61.4	0.70	2 194.6	15.8
June	51.6	42.8	42.9	99.8	57.6	0.67	2 203.9	15.9
July	51.9	43.0	43.0	100.0	61.8	0.77	2 212.7	16.0
August	52.2	43.2	43.3	99.8	66.2	0.69	2 230.2	16.0
September	52.7	43.4	43.5	99.8	71.9	0.75	2 239.2	16.1
October	52.6	43.2	43.7	98.9	71.2	0.83	2 241.2	16.2
November	52.9	43.7	43.7	100.0	70.3	0.63	2 256.0	16.1
December	53.1	44.1	43.8	100.7	67.8	0.33	2 277.8	16.1

[1] Not seasonally adjusted.

Table 20-7. Composite Indexes of Economic Activity and Selected Index Components—Continued

(Seasonally adjusted, except as noted.)

Year and month	Cyclical composite indexes, 1996 = 100				Selected components of leading index		Selected component of coincident index	Selected component of lagging index
	Leading	Coincident	Lagging	Ratio, coincident to lagging	Vendor performance (slower deliveries, diffusion index, percent)	Interest rate spread, 10-year Treasury bond less federal funds [1]	Personal income less transfer payments (billions of 1996 dollars)	Consumer installment credit outstanding (percent of personal income)
1965								
January	53.6	44.3	44.1	100.5	68.5	0.29	2 281.5	16.2
February	53.6	44.4	44.5	99.8	68.1	0.23	2 293.2	16.4
March	53.9	44.7	44.6	100.2	65.9	0.17	2 304.1	16.4
April	54.0	44.9	44.9	100.0	69.4	0.11	2 313.6	16.6
May	54.2	45.1	45.2	99.8	68.9	0.11	2 327.4	16.6
June	54.2	45.2	45.3	99.8	69.3	0.17	2 333.8	16.7
July	54.3	45.6	45.4	100.4	65.1	0.11	2 349.2	16.7
August	54.4	45.7	45.6	100.2	65.4	0.13	2 361.2	16.7
September	54.6	45.9	45.8	100.2	61.2	0.28	2 379.7	16.4
October	55.1	46.3	46.0	100.7	59.1	0.27	2 404.5	16.6
November	55.6	46.6	46.2	100.9	65.1	0.35	2 421.8	16.6
December	56.0	46.9	46.4	101.1	73.5	0.30	2 434.3	16.6
1966								
January	56.0	47.1	46.6	101.1	74.9	0.19	2 440.4	16.7
February	56.1	47.3	46.9	100.9	80.1	0.23	2 450.8	16.6
March	56.6	47.7	47.1	101.3	86.4	0.22	2 462.2	16.6
April	56.4	47.7	47.4	100.6	79.3	0.08	2 463.2	16.7
May	55.8	47.9	47.8	100.2	74.6	-0.12	2 471.8	16.7
June	55.4	48.2	48.1	100.2	71.6	-0.36	2 487.0	16.6
July	55.2	48.3	48.5	99.6	73.1	-0.28	2 499.2	16.6
August	54.9	48.5	48.6	99.8	74.3	-0.31	2 505.8	16.5
September	54.7	48.7	48.7	100.0	72.4	-0.22	2 511.4	16.4
October	54.4	48.9	48.7	100.4	68.7	-0.52	2 523.2	16.3
November	54.2	48.9	49.1	99.6	62.6	-0.60	2 532.4	16.3
December	54.0	49.0	49.1	99.8	57.9	-0.56	2 528.7	16.3
1967								
January	54.3	49.2	49.3	99.8	48.2	-0.36	2 551.6	16.2
February	54.0	49.1	49.5	99.2	49.9	-0.37	2 549.9	16.2
March	54.1	49.2	49.6	99.2	38.0	0.01	2 560.3	16.1
April	54.2	49.2	49.8	98.8	36.9	0.54	2 560.7	16.2
May	54.7	49.2	49.7	99.0	34.4	0.91	2 565.2	16.1
June	55.2	49.4	50.1	98.6	36.5	1.04	2 575.2	16.1
July	55.5	49.4	50.1	98.6	40.9	1.37	2 587.8	16.0
August	56.2	49.8	50.0	99.6	44.8	1.38	2 598.3	16.0
September	56.3	49.8	50.1	99.4	46.5	1.31	2 600.8	16.0
October	56.4	49.8	50.2	99.2	51.1	1.60	2 596.8	16.0
November	56.7	50.4	50.2	100.4	51.4	1.62	2 612.3	16.0
December	57.2	50.7	50.3	100.8	49.9	1.19	2 638.3	15.9
1968								
January	57.2	50.7	50.3	100.8	50.6	0.93	2 640.8	15.8
February	57.6	50.9	50.6	100.6	53.9	0.85	2 662.3	15.8
March	57.9	51.1	50.8	100.6	54.0	0.69	2 674.9	15.7
April	57.4	51.2	51.0	100.4	49.0	-0.12	2 684.5	15.7
May	57.5	51.4	51.3	100.2	49.4	-0.24	2 699.9	15.7
June	57.7	51.6	51.5	100.2	49.9	-0.35	2 712.1	15.6
July	58.1	51.8	51.5	100.6	55.9	-0.52	2 729.0	15.6
August	57.6	51.9	51.8	100.2	47.8	-0.61	2 737.6	15.6
September	58.2	52.1	51.8	100.6	48.4	-0.32	2 749.7	15.6
October	58.8	52.3	52.0	100.6	53.3	-0.33	2 753.9	15.7
November	58.9	52.6	52.2	100.8	61.0	-0.12	2 765.2	15.8
December	58.9	52.7	52.5	100.4	58.3	0.01	2 775.0	15.8
1969								
January	59.2	52.9	52.8	100.2	63.6	-0.26	2 775.9	15.9
February	59.2	53.1	52.9	100.4	60.1	-0.42	2 786.6	15.9
March	59.0	53.3	53.2	100.2	60.5	-0.49	2 799.2	15.9
April	59.3	53.4	53.5	99.8	63.9	-1.24	2 808.9	15.9
May	58.7	53.5	53.9	99.3	64.9	-2.35	2 819.1	15.9
June	58.3	53.7	54.1	99.3	67.0	-2.33	2 828.6	15.9
July	57.7	53.9	54.2	99.4	65.7	-1.89	2 844.5	15.8
August	57.7	54.1	54.5	99.3	70.3	-2.50	2 862.8	15.8
September	57.6	54.2	54.6	99.3	68.9	-1.99	2 868.5	15.8
October	57.1	54.3	54.6	99.5	66.8	-1.90	2 875.1	15.8
November	56.6	54.2	54.7	99.1	64.1	-1.71	2 876.0	15.8
December	56.2	54.2	55.0	98.5	66.8	-1.32	2 878.5	15.7
1970								
January	55.4	53.9	55.4	97.3	57.9	-1.19	2 873.7	15.8
February	54.8	54.0	55.4	97.5	57.7	-1.74	2 875.4	15.7
March	54.4	54.0	55.6	97.1	49.3	-0.69	2 882.7	15.7
April	53.7	53.9	55.5	97.1	48.7	-0.71	2 889.8	15.3
May	54.1	53.9	55.4	97.3	67.2	-0.03	2 892.2	15.4
June	54.2	53.8	55.6	96.8	66.1	0.24	2 885.6	15.5
July	54.2	53.9	55.3	97.5	49.8	0.25	2 900.6	15.4
August	54.4	53.9	55.5	97.1	46.1	0.92	2 908.6	15.4
September	54.4	53.8	55.4	97.1	46.5	1.10	2 908.6	15.3
October	54.2	53.3	55.4	96.2	39.0	1.13	2 884.1	15.4
November	54.3	53.1	55.4	95.8	37.8	1.24	2 880.9	15.3
December	55.4	53.7	55.0	97.6	37.5	1.49	2 886.8	15.3

[1] Not seasonally adjusted.

Table 20-7. Composite Indexes of Economic Activity and Selected Index Components—Continued

(Seasonally adjusted, except as noted.)

Year and month	Cyclical composite indexes, 1996 = 100				Selected components of leading index		Selected component of coincident index	Selected component of lagging index
	Leading	Coincident	Lagging	Ratio, coincident to lagging	Vendor performance (slower deliveries, diffusion index, percent)	Interest rate spread, 10-year Treasury bond less federal funds [1]	Personal income less transfer payments (billions of 1996 dollars)	Consumer installment credit outstanding (percent of personal income)
1971								
January	56.0	54.0	54.9	98.4	39.8	2.10	2 919.5	15.4
February	56.6	54.0	54.9	98.4	44.2	2.39	2 919.6	15.4
March	57.1	54.0	54.8	98.5	45.0	1.99	2 930.9	15.4
April	57.5	54.2	54.6	99.3	48.9	1.68	2 938.0	15.4
May	57.9	54.4	54.6	99.6	49.4	1.76	2 948.4	15.4
June	58.1	54.5	54.4	100.2	47.9	1.61	2 947.8	15.2
July	58.2	54.5	54.7	99.6	47.4	1.42	2 949.6	15.5
August	58.5	54.6	55.1	99.1	49.7	1.02	2 966.9	15.5
September	58.8	54.8	55.1	99.5	48.9	0.59	2 968.9	15.6
October	59.0	55.0	55.0	100.0	50.9	0.73	2 979.2	15.6
November	59.3	55.2	55.0	100.4	50.9	0.90	2 993.9	15.7
December	60.3	55.6	55.0	101.1	53.3	1.79	3 018.8	15.7
1972								
January	60.9	56.1	54.3	103.3	55.2	2.45	3 038.7	15.6
February	61.6	56.2	54.3	103.5	52.6	2.79	3 054.1	15.6
March	62.0	56.6	54.6	103.7	57.1	2.24	3 070.7	15.6
April	62.1	56.9	54.8	103.8	55.0	2.02	3 093.4	15.7
May	62.3	57.1	55.0	103.8	56.1	1.86	3 105.9	15.8
June	62.6	57.2	55.3	103.4	57.7	1.65	3 074.4	16.1
July	63.2	57.3	55.5	103.2	61.7	1.56	3 124.4	15.9
August	64.2	57.9	55.4	104.5	62.9	1.41	3 157.7	15.9
September	64.8	58.1	55.3	105.1	65.5	1.68	3 172.6	15.9
October	65.3	58.7	55.5	105.8	73.0	1.44	3 221.9	15.7
November	65.7	59.2	55.6	106.5	74.5	1.22	3 248.0	15.7
December	66.3	59.6	55.6	107.2	80.7	1.03	3 268.8	15.8
1973								
January	66.5	59.8	56.2	106.4	83.7	0.52	3 255.3	16.1
February	66.6	60.2	56.7	106.2	85.2	0.06	3 275.6	16.1
March	66.2	60.3	57.1	105.6	87.5	-0.38	3 277.7	16.2
April	65.6	60.3	57.6	104.7	86.7	-0.45	3 281.5	16.2
May	65.4	60.5	57.9	104.5	86.6	-0.99	3 302.7	16.3
June	65.2	60.7	58.5	103.8	85.6	-1.59	3 314.5	16.3
July	64.8	60.9	58.8	103.6	85.2	-3.27	3 327.7	16.4
August	64.2	60.7	59.3	102.4	86.7	-3.10	3 315.7	16.4
September	64.0	61.0	59.5	102.5	90.1	-3.69	3 337.4	16.4
October	63.8	61.5	59.5	103.4	88.7	-3.22	3 369.4	16.3
November	63.5	61.8	59.7	103.5	96.8	-3.30	3 379.7	16.3
December	62.3	61.7	60.0	102.8	92.8	-3.21	3 371.8	16.2
1974								
January	61.8	61.6	60.5	101.8	91.8	-2.66	3 335.4	16.3
February	61.2	61.5	60.5	101.7	88.8	-2.01	3 313.2	16.3
March	61.3	61.4	60.7	101.2	88.9	-2.14	3 289.0	16.3
April	60.4	61.3	61.2	100.2	82.1	-3.00	3 270.3	16.4
May	60.1	61.5	61.7	99.7	74.5	-3.73	3 279.6	16.2
June	59.3	61.5	62.0	99.2	73.1	-4.39	3 284.4	16.2
July	58.6	61.6	62.4	98.7	69.2	-5.11	3 297.0	16.1
August	57.4	61.3	62.9	97.5	66.3	-3.97	3 280.8	16.1
September	55.9	61.3	63.2	97.0	51.8	-3.30	3 274.5	16.0
October	55.2	61.1	63.4	96.4	45.3	-2.16	3 279.9	15.8
November	54.2	60.5	63.5	95.3	34.0	-1.77	3 251.6	15.8
December	53.2	59.7	63.8	93.6	23.2	-1.10	3 236.3	15.6
1975								
January	52.9	59.3	63.5	93.4	19.5	0.37	3 224.6	15.6
February	53.0	58.9	63.1	93.3	15.9	1.15	3 205.3	15.5
March	53.3	58.4	62.8	93.0	17.3	2.19	3 203.6	15.4
April	54.6	58.4	62.2	93.9	21.7	2.74	3 199.0	15.3
May	55.4	58.5	61.6	95.0	22.7	2.84	3 215.1	15.2
June	56.0	58.6	60.3	97.2	24.9	2.31	3 220.8	14.6
July	56.9	58.9	60.3	97.7	28.7	1.96	3 222.8	14.8
August	57.1	59.3	60.0	98.8	35.1	2.26	3 253.0	14.6
September	57.6	59.5	59.9	99.3	43.8	2.19	3 265.8	14.6
October	58.1	59.7	60.0	99.5	44.8	2.32	3 282.2	14.5
November	58.4	59.8	59.9	99.8	46.8	2.83	3 291.5	14.5
December	58.7	60.2	60.0	100.3	41.2	2.80	3 293.1	14.6
1976								
January	60.1	60.8	60.0	101.3	54.0	2.87	3 316.7	14.5
February	61.1	61.1	60.0	101.8	56.1	3.02	3 340.0	14.5
March	61.3	61.3	60.0	102.2	56.7	2.89	3 358.5	14.5
April	61.5	61.6	60.0	102.7	57.3	2.74	3 379.8	14.6
May	61.9	61.7	60.0	102.8	58.3	2.61	3 392.7	14.5
June	62.1	61.8	59.9	103.2	58.6	2.38	3 392.5	14.6
July	62.7	62.0	60.0	103.3	54.0	2.52	3 408.5	14.6
August	63.0	62.2	60.0	103.7	55.2	2.48	3 421.8	14.5
September	63.4	62.3	60.2	103.5	52.6	2.34	3 428.5	14.6
October	63.4	62.3	60.5	103.0	49.0	2.39	3 433.3	14.6
November	63.9	62.8	60.5	103.8	47.2	2.34	3 463.9	14.6
December	64.7	63.2	60.5	104.5	53.3	2.22	3 472.3	14.6

[1]Not seasonally adjusted.

Table 20-7. Composite Indexes of Economic Activity and Selected Index Components—Continued

(Seasonally adjusted, except as noted.)

Year and month	Cyclical composite indexes, 1996 = 100				Selected components of leading index		Selected component of coincident index	Selected component of lagging index
	Leading	Coincident	Lagging	Ratio, coincident to lagging	Vendor performance (slower deliveries, diffusion index, percent)	Interest rate spread, 10-year Treasury bond less federal funds [1]	Personal income less transfer payments (billions of 1996 dollars)	Consumer installment credit outstanding (percent of personal income)
1977								
January	64.6	63.1	60.6	104.1	55.3	2.60	3 460.2	14.6
February	65.2	63.5	60.8	104.4	65.1	2.71	3 470.9	14.6
March	65.8	64.0	60.8	105.3	49.6	2.77	3 489.6	14.7
April	66.0	64.3	61.1	105.2	54.6	2.64	3 508.0	14.8
May	66.3	64.6	61.2	105.6	55.4	2.11	3 531.0	14.9
June	66.7	64.9	61.6	105.4	53.3	1.89	3 542.8	15.0
July	66.8	65.2	61.8	105.5	58.3	1.91	3 556.0	15.0
August	66.8	65.3	62.1	105.2	53.5	1.50	3 568.8	15.0
September	67.0	65.7	62.3	105.5	56.7	1.20	3 599.7	15.0
October	67.0	66.1	62.5	105.8	53.6	1.05	3 648.4	15.1
November	67.1	66.4	62.8	105.7	56.3	1.07	3 665.4	15.1
December	67.3	66.6	62.7	106.2	57.1	1.13	3 676.4	15.1
1978								
January	66.5	66.3	63.4	104.6	55.6	1.26	3 662.2	15.2
February	67.0	66.7	63.5	105.0	63.4	1.25	3 680.7	15.2
March	67.1	67.3	63.8	105.5	58.9	1.25	3 706.8	15.3
April	67.9	68.1	63.8	106.7	57.1	1.26	3 738.3	15.3
May	68.0	68.3	64.2	106.4	57.4	0.99	3 741.0	15.4
June	68.1	68.7	64.7	106.2	61.1	0.86	3 762.9	15.6
July	67.9	68.8	65.0	105.8	59.4	0.83	3 773.9	15.6
August	68.1	69.1	65.2	106.0	60.6	0.37	3 787.5	15.7
September	68.4	69.2	65.7	105.3	60.0	-0.03	3 802.9	15.7
October	68.6	69.5	65.8	105.6	64.7	-0.32	3 818.8	15.7
November	67.8	69.9	66.4	105.3	64.5	-0.95	3 831.5	15.8
December	67.3	70.2	66.7	105.2	63.5	-1.02	3 854.8	15.8
1979								
January	67.2	70.1	67.0	104.6	66.4	-0.97	3 861.1	15.8
February	67.2	70.3	67.4	104.3	64.0	-0.96	3 881.0	15.9
March	67.5	70.8	67.1	105.5	66.7	-0.97	3 895.8	15.9
April	66.4	70.3	68.1	103.2	75.6	-0.83	3 856.0	16.0
May	66.7	70.7	68.2	103.7	63.7	-0.99	3 856.0	16.1
June	66.4	70.8	68.8	102.9	61.4	-1.38	3 865.4	16.1
July	65.7	70.8	69.1	102.5	57.4	-1.52	3 869.4	16.0
August	65.6	70.8	69.6	101.7	52.9	-1.91	3 875.4	16.1
September	65.6	70.8	70.2	100.9	50.7	-2.10	3 876.1	16.1
October	64.7	71.0	70.6	100.6	46.9	-3.47	3 897.0	16.1
November	64.1	71.1	70.9	100.3	46.8	-2.53	3 917.2	16.0
December	63.7	71.2	71.1	100.1	42.2	-3.39	3 931.3	16.0
1980								
January	63.8	71.4	71.4	100.0	42.1	-3.02	3 933.7	15.8
February	63.7	71.3	71.7	99.4	46.0	-1.72	3 920.1	15.8
March	61.7	71.0	72.7	97.7	39.1	-4.44	3 905.9	15.7
April	60.1	70.4	73.5	95.8	36.9	-6.14	3 869.0	15.7
May	59.4	69.8	73.1	95.5	29.8	-0.80	3 845.1	15.5
June	60.5	69.5	72.5	95.9	32.4	0.31	3 846.8	15.3
July	61.4	69.4	71.2	97.5	36.3	1.22	3 832.4	15.1
August	62.3	69.7	70.4	99.0	40.1	1.49	3 848.6	15.0
September	63.2	70.1	69.8	100.4	41.2	0.64	3 868.0	14.8
October	63.7	70.8	69.5	101.9	46.5	-1.06	3 933.4	14.5
November	63.8	71.1	69.6	102.2	46.8	-3.17	3 957.4	14.4
December	62.9	71.4	70.4	101.4	50.1	-6.06	3 977.0	14.3
1981								
January	62.4	71.3	70.8	100.7	49.7	-6.51	3 954.2	14.3
February	61.6	71.2	71.0	100.3	48.5	-2.74	3 943.0	14.2
March	62.0	71.3	71.0	100.4	48.7	-1.58	3 952.7	14.2
April	62.5	71.3	71.1	100.3	51.2	-2.04	3 954.8	14.2
May	62.2	71.3	72.0	99.0	50.2	-4.42	3 968.5	14.2
June	61.3	71.6	72.2	99.2	47.9	-5.63	3 996.2	14.1
July	60.6	71.8	72.5	99.0	44.9	-4.76	4 037.8	13.9
August	60.5	71.9	72.7	98.9	49.6	-2.88	4 059.9	13.8
September	59.6	71.7	73.3	97.8	45.9	-0.55	4 060.5	13.9
October	58.9	71.5	73.2	97.7	37.7	0.07	4 056.2	13.9
November	58.7	71.2	73.1	97.4	40.5	0.08	4 051.4	13.8
December	58.8	70.8	72.9	97.1	41.2	1.35	4 042.3	13.8
1982								
January	58.5	70.4	73.2	96.2	40.1	1.37	4 031.0	13.9
February	59.1	70.8	72.7	97.4	40.8	-0.35	4 042.8	13.9
March	58.7	70.7	72.4	97.7	36.4	-0.82	4 047.9	13.8
April	59.2	70.5	72.6	97.1	38.2	-1.07	4 066.3	13.8
May	59.2	70.5	72.5	97.2	42.1	-0.83	4 074.3	13.8
June	58.9	70.2	72.7	96.6	45.2	0.15	4 055.2	13.8
July	59.2	69.9	72.6	96.3	45.8	1.36	4 043.1	13.7
August	59.0	69.7	72.5	96.1	45.3	2.94	4 040.8	13.7
September	59.9	69.6	72.4	96.1	45.9	2.03	4 032.7	13.7
October	60.4	69.3	72.0	96.2	46.5	1.20	4 023.7	13.7
November	60.9	69.2	71.4	96.9	46.9	1.35	4 026.0	13.6
December	61.6	69.1	70.7	97.7	48.6	1.59	4 041.2	13.7

[1] Not seasonally adjusted.

Table 20-7. Composite Indexes of Economic Activity and Selected Index Components—Continued

(Seasonally adjusted, except as noted.)

Year and month	Cyclical composite indexes, 1996 = 100				Selected components of leading index		Selected component of coincident index	Selected component of lagging index
	Leading	Coincident	Lagging	Ratio, coincident to lagging	Vendor performance (slower deliveries, diffusion index, percent)	Interest rate spread, 10-year Treasury bond less federal funds [1]	Personal income less transfer payments (billions of 1996 dollars)	Consumer installment credit outstanding (percent of personal income)
1983								
January	62.8	69.6	70.3	99.0	46.7	1.78	4 044.5	13.7
February	63.5	69.5	70.4	98.7	49.9	2.21	4 044.9	13.7
March	64.5	69.8	70.2	99.4	50.8	1.74	4 063.6	13.7
April	65.3	70.1	70.2	99.9	52.7	1.60	4 064.5	13.7
May	66.3	70.5	69.9	100.9	51.9	1.75	4 094.1	13.7
June	66.9	70.9	70.1	101.1	56.8	1.87	4 104.2	13.8
July	67.4	71.4	70.3	101.6	58.9	2.01	4 127.0	13.8
August	67.2	71.3	70.7	100.8	60.2	2.29	4 115.0	13.9
September	67.7	72.2	70.8	102.0	60.7	2.20	4 153.1	13.9
October	68.4	72.7	70.8	102.7	62.8	2.06	4 204.9	13.9
November	68.8	73.0	71.3	102.4	67.5	2.35	4 231.1	14.0
December	69.0	73.5	71.6	102.7	62.1	2.36	4 272.4	14.1
1984								
January	70.1	74.1	71.7	103.3	64.4	2.11	4 312.1	14.1
February	70.4	74.4	72.5	102.6	61.5	2.25	4 330.6	14.3
March	70.4	74.7	73.0	102.3	65.5	2.41	4 358.3	14.3
April	70.4	75.1	73.6	102.0	64.6	2.34	4 395.9	14.3
May	70.7	75.5	74.1	101.9	62.5	3.09	4 416.4	14.5
June	70.4	75.9	74.7	101.6	56.2	2.50	4 458.2	14.6
July	70.6	76.1	75.4	100.9	59.1	2.13	4 491.7	14.7
August	70.3	76.3	75.9	100.5	55.2	1.08	4 506.2	14.8
September	70.2	76.5	76.3	100.3	52.8	1.22	4 542.0	14.8
October	70.1	76.6	76.6	100.0	49.3	2.17	4 536.4	15.0
November	70.7	77.0	76.7	100.4	48.1	2.14	4 565.0	15.0
December	71.2	77.2	76.8	100.5	48.8	3.12	4 587.5	15.1
1985								
January	71.9	77.2	77.0	100.3	50.4	3.03	4 588.8	15.2
February	72.1	77.4	77.2	100.3	48.6	3.01	4 593.1	15.4
March	72.4	77.7	77.5	100.3	46.7	3.28	4 611.9	15.5
April	72.5	77.7	77.6	100.1	46.1	3.16	4 613.1	15.7
May	73.0	78.0	78.1	99.9	48.0	2.88	4 617.9	15.9
June	73.6	78.0	78.3	99.6	47.1	2.63	4 634.3	15.9
July	73.8	77.9	78.7	99.0	45.7	2.43	4 621.3	16.1
August	74.2	78.3	78.8	99.4	46.6	2.43	4 631.1	16.2
September	74.7	78.5	78.8	99.6	49.5	2.45	4 638.7	16.4
October	74.7	78.5	79.5	98.7	50.0	2.25	4 673.6	16.4
November	74.9	78.7	79.6	98.9	48.5	1.73	4 670.1	16.6
December	75.8	79.0	79.9	98.9	49.3	0.99	4 710.0	16.5
1986								
January	75.9	79.2	79.9	99.1	50.1	1.05	4 688.2	16.6
February	76.1	79.1	80.1	98.8	49.8	0.84	4 713.1	16.7
March	76.3	79.3	80.5	98.5	50.5	0.30	4 755.7	16.7
April	76.8	79.6	80.1	99.4	50.7	0.31	4 759.0	16.8
May	77.0	79.6	80.4	99.0	50.2	0.86	4 766.3	16.9
June	77.5	79.6	80.5	98.9	49.9	0.88	4 768.8	17.0
July	77.4	79.8	80.6	99.0	49.9	0.74	4 777.4	17.0
August	77.5	79.9	80.7	99.0	50.8	1.00	4 794.1	17.1
September	77.7	80.3	80.4	99.9	49.6	1.56	4 795.9	17.2
October	78.2	80.3	81.1	99.0	51.3	1.58	4 795.7	17.4
November	78.4	80.5	81.1	99.3	52.0	1.21	4 816.6	17.2
December	79.3	80.9	80.8	100.1	52.8	0.20	4 818.9	17.2
1987								
January	79.1	80.7	81.5	99.0	51.5	0.65	4 821.5	17.1
February	79.7	81.3	81.1	100.2	51.2	1.15	4 836.6	17.0
March	80.0	81.5	81.1	100.5	51.9	1.12	4 851.3	16.8
April	80.0	81.6	81.3	100.4	52.8	1.65	4 846.9	16.9
May	80.2	81.9	81.6	100.4	54.0	1.76	4 869.5	16.9
June	80.7	82.1	81.8	100.4	56.8	1.67	4 874.3	16.9
July	81.2	82.4	81.9	100.6	58.9	1.87	4 890.9	16.9
August	81.3	82.7	82.0	100.9	60.3	2.03	4 923.7	16.9
September	81.6	82.9	82.3	100.7	61.5	2.20	4 928.7	16.9
October	81.6	83.4	82.7	100.8	62.2	2.23	4 966.5	16.9
November	81.3	83.7	82.8	101.1	64.9	2.17	4 991.9	16.9
December	81.2	84.1	82.7	101.7	62.7	2.22	5 047.2	16.7
1988								
January	81.3	84.0	83.2	101.0	62.0	1.84	5 014.2	16.8
February	82.3	84.4	83.3	101.3	61.2	1.63	5 037.7	16.8
March	82.5	84.8	83.5	101.6	57.3	1.79	5 046.9	16.8
April	82.6	84.9	84.0	101.1	58.6	1.85	5 055.3	16.9
May	82.7	85.1	84.2	101.1	56.9	2.00	5 063.3	16.9
June	83.8	85.4	84.6	100.9	65.6	1.41	5 080.5	16.8
July	83.1	85.6	84.6	101.2	58.4	1.31	5 107.6	16.8
August	83.3	85.7	84.9	100.9	57.4	1.25	5 111.0	16.8
September	83.3	85.9	84.9	101.2	55.2	0.79	5 117.6	16.7
October	83.5	86.2	85.2	101.2	54.8	0.50	5 145.2	16.7
November	83.5	86.5	85.5	101.2	52.1	0.61	5 149.6	16.7
December	83.8	86.9	85.5	101.6	53.0	0.35	5 191.5	16.6

[1] Not seasonally adjusted.

Table 20-7. Composite Indexes of Economic Activity and Selected Index Components—Continued

(Seasonally adjusted, except as noted.)

Year and month	Cyclical composite indexes, 1996 = 100				Selected components of leading index		Selected component of coincident index	Selected component of lagging index
	Leading	Coincident	Lagging	Ratio, coincident to lagging	Vendor performance (slower deliveries, diffusion index, percent)	Interest rate spread, 10-year Treasury bond less federal funds [1]	Personal income less transfer payments (billions of 1996 dollars)	Consumer installment credit outstanding (percent of personal income)
1989								
January	84.0	87.2	85.9	101.5	53.9	-0.03	5 235.9	16.7
February	83.4	87.2	86.7	100.6	54.0	-0.19	5 240.4	16.7
March	82.6	87.3	87.2	100.1	52.5	-0.49	5 254.2	16.8
April	83.0	87.4	87.0	100.5	52.2	-0.66	5 244.3	16.8
May	82.3	87.3	87.9	99.3	49.1	-0.95	5 222.0	16.9
June	82.1	87.3	88.3	98.9	46.5	-1.25	5 237.4	16.9
July	82.1	87.2	88.6	98.4	46.1	-1.22	5 250.6	16.9
August	82.2	87.6	88.4	99.1	44.0	-0.88	5 255.8	16.9
September	82.3	87.6	88.4	99.1	43.9	-0.83	5 252.5	16.9
October	81.9	87.5	88.9	98.4	43.3	-0.83	5 265.3	16.9
November	82.1	87.9	88.9	98.9	42.5	-0.68	5 290.9	16.9
December	82.4	88.1	89.1	98.9	43.5	-0.61	5 300.6	16.9
1990								
January	82.5	88.1	88.7	99.3	48.2	-0.02	5 295.4	16.8
February	81.8	88.5	88.7	99.8	44.4	0.23	5 318.0	16.7
March	82.3	88.7	89.0	99.7	47.2	0.31	5 320.3	16.6
April	81.7	88.7	89.1	99.6	47.2	0.53	5 349.3	16.5
May	81.7	88.8	89.2	99.6	48.2	0.58	5 336.2	16.5
June	81.9	88.9	89.4	99.4	49.8	0.19	5 344.9	16.4
July	81.7	88.9	89.7	99.1	46.4	0.32	5 366.0	16.4
August	81.0	88.9	89.7	99.1	50.1	0.62	5 335.8	16.4
September	80.4	88.6	90.0	98.4	48.9	0.69	5 330.9	16.4
October	79.8	88.3	90.2	97.9	48.1	0.61	5 284.8	16.5
November	79.2	87.9	90.4	97.2	48.6	0.58	5 282.1	16.4
December	79.4	87.7	90.4	97.0	47.2	0.77	5 289.9	16.3
1991								
January	78.9	87.4	90.6	96.5	44.4	1.18	5 235.6	16.3
February	79.5	87.2	90.3	96.6	44.7	1.60	5 233.8	16.2
March	80.1	87.0	90.4	96.2	43.9	1.99	5 238.9	16.2
April	80.7	87.2	89.7	97.2	45.0	2.13	5 248.5	16.2
May	81.2	87.3	89.5	97.5	46.0	2.29	5 243.7	16.1
June	81.7	87.6	89.0	98.4	47.1	2.38	5 273.9	15.9
July	82.7	87.6	88.8	98.6	49.6	2.45	5 257.9	15.9
August	82.4	87.6	88.5	99.0	48.3	2.24	5 259.0	15.8
September	82.7	87.8	88.3	99.4	48.8	2.20	5 270.4	15.7
October	82.8	87.7	88.2	99.4	50.2	2.32	5 251.2	15.6
November	82.8	87.7	88.2	99.4	50.1	2.61	5 266.2	15.6
December	82.6	87.6	88.1	99.4	49.4	2.66	5 292.4	15.4
1992								
January	83.3	87.8	87.5	100.3	48.7	3.00	5 285.1	15.4
February	83.9	88.0	87.3	100.8	49.3	3.28	5 321.2	15.2
March	84.7	88.1	87.2	101.0	50.3	3.56	5 326.0	15.2
April	85.0	88.4	87.0	101.6	47.4	3.75	5 336.4	15.1
May	85.5	88.5	86.9	101.8	50.0	3.57	5 356.9	15.0
June	85.7	88.7	86.7	102.3	50.8	3.50	5 364.2	14.9
July	85.8	88.9	86.4	102.9	52.5	3.59	5 360.5	14.9
August	86.1	88.7	86.8	102.2	50.3	3.29	5 336.7	14.8
September	86.5	89.0	86.7	102.7	51.2	3.20	5 370.3	14.8
October	87.0	89.3	86.7	103.0	48.6	3.49	5 396.3	14.7
November	87.9	89.5	87.2	102.6	51.3	3.78	5 414.8	14.7
December	89.1	90.4	86.4	104.6	51.5	3.85	5 620.5	14.3
1993								
January	89.1	89.7	87.4	102.6	52.3	3.58	5 337.8	14.9
February	89.5	89.8	87.7	102.4	51.7	3.23	5 336.0	15.0
March	89.0	89.6	87.9	101.9	52.7	2.91	5 311.2	15.0
April	89.7	90.2	87.9	102.6	52.8	3.01	5 420.6	14.8
May	89.6	90.4	88.1	102.6	51.5	3.04	5 437.6	14.8
June	90.2	90.6	88.2	102.7	50.4	2.92	5 428.7	14.8
July	90.0	90.7	88.6	102.4	51.0	2.75	5 424.6	14.9
August	90.7	90.9	88.7	102.5	51.8	2.65	5 442.5	14.9
September	91.2	91.1	88.9	102.5	51.3	2.27	5 438.2	15.0
October	91.6	91.4	88.8	102.9	50.7	2.34	5 450.9	15.1
November	92.1	91.7	88.9	103.1	50.9	2.70	5 467.1	15.2
December	93.1	92.6	88.8	104.3	51.5	2.81	5 669.9	14.8
1994								
January	93.3	91.9	89.7	102.5	54.4	2.70	5 408.9	15.5
February	93.3	92.3	89.6	103.0	57.0	2.72	5 470.3	15.5
March	94.2	92.9	89.7	103.6	55.4	3.14	5 494.5	15.6
April	94.5	93.3	90.0	103.7	57.2	3.41	5 569.8	15.6
May	95.1	93.7	90.4	103.7	60.2	3.17	5 608.2	15.7
June	95.4	94.0	90.9	103.4	60.3	2.85	5 603.4	15.8
July	95.1	94.2	91.2	103.3	58.1	3.04	5 611.5	15.9
August	95.9	94.7	91.4	103.6	61.6	2.77	5 619.8	16.0
September	96.3	94.9	92.0	103.2	62.5	2.73	5 647.8	16.2
October	96.8	95.4	92.3	103.4	64.9	2.98	5 692.7	16.2
November	97.0	95.7	93.0	102.9	64.7	2.67	5 687.8	16.4
December	97.5	96.1	93.5	102.8	64.8	2.36	5 705.5	16.6

[1] Not seasonally adjusted.

Table 20-7. Composite Indexes of Economic Activity and Selected Index Components—Continued

(Seasonally adjusted, except as noted.)

Year and month	Cyclical composite indexes, 1996 = 100				Selected components of leading index		Selected component of coincident index	Selected component of lagging index
	Leading	Coincident	Lagging	Ratio, coincident to lagging	Vendor performance (slower deliveries, diffusion index, percent)	Interest rate spread, 10-year Treasury bond less federal funds [1]	Personal income less transfer payments (billions of 1996 dollars)	Consumer installment credit outstanding (percent of personal income)
1995								
January	97.3	96.4	94.2	102.3	62.7	2.25	5 721.4	16.7
February	97.1	96.5	94.9	101.7	60.7	1.55	5 725.0	16.8
March	96.5	96.6	95.3	101.4	56.9	1.22	5 730.6	17.0
April	96.5	96.6	96.1	100.5	56.3	1.01	5 735.1	17.1
May	96.4	96.7	96.6	100.1	53.3	0.62	5 725.7	17.3
June	96.8	97.0	97.2	99.8	51.8	0.17	5 744.1	17.4
July	97.0	96.9	97.6	99.3	51.3	0.43	5 752.9	17.5
August	97.5	97.4	97.7	99.7	49.1	0.75	5 756.1	17.7
September	97.8	97.7	98.2	99.5	50.0	0.40	5 779.9	17.9
October	97.6	97.7	98.4	99.3	48.4	0.28	5 790.1	17.9
November	97.7	98.0	98.7	99.3	45.3	0.13	5 820.9	18.2
December	98.1	98.3	98.8	99.5	47.5	0.11	5 836.8	18.2
1996								
January	96.8	98.0	99.1	98.9	47.8	0.09	5 843.3	18.2
February	98.0	98.8	99.1	99.7	49.5	0.59	5 897.6	18.2
March	98.6	98.9	99.2	99.7	49.6	0.96	5 918.9	18.3
April	99.0	99.2	99.3	99.9	49.4	1.29	5 923.7	18.4
May	99.6	99.7	99.6	100.1	49.9	1.50	5 948.3	18.4
June	100.4	100.0	99.7	100.3	52.8	1.64	5 991.6	18.4
July	100.6	100.1	100.3	99.8	50.8	1.47	5 988.0	18.6
August	100.7	100.5	100.3	100.2	51.9	1.42	6 017.4	18.6
September	101.1	100.8	100.6	100.2	50.0	1.53	6 040.9	18.6
October	101.2	101.0	100.7	100.3	50.9	1.29	6 045.0	18.6
November	101.9	101.4	100.9	100.5	51.2	0.89	6 066.5	18.6
December	101.9	101.6	101.3	100.3	52.0	1.01	6 092.2	18.6
1997								
January	102.2	101.5	101.6	99.9	49.7	1.33	6 119.1	18.6
February	103.5	102.1	101.6	100.5	52.1	1.23	6 147.6	18.7
March	103.8	102.4	101.8	100.6	53.1	1.30	6 176.6	18.6
April	103.8	102.6	102.3	100.3	53.4	1.38	6 185.6	18.7
May	104.6	102.9	102.7	100.2	55.0	1.21	6 216.0	18.7
June	105.1	103.3	102.8	100.5	54.6	0.93	6 239.7	18.7
July	106.1	103.8	102.8	101.0	54.7	0.70	6 271.8	18.6
August	106.0	104.0	103.2	100.8	55.2	0.76	6 312.5	18.6
September	106.7	104.6	103.6	101.0	54.8	0.67	6 331.5	18.6
October	107.2	104.9	103.9	101.0	54.9	0.53	6 364.5	18.6
November	107.6	105.5	104.3	101.2	55.2	0.36	6 415.9	18.5
December	107.3	105.8	104.5	101.2	53.9	0.31	6 451.4	18.6
1998								
January	107.6	106.3	104.8	101.4	53.0	-0.02	6 516.5	18.4
February	108.5	106.7	105.3	101.3	52.8	0.06	6 568.2	18.3
March	108.6	107.0	106.0	100.9	53.0	0.16	6 612.2	18.3
April	108.8	107.3	106.2	101.0	52.4	0.19	6 644.0	18.6
May	108.9	107.7	106.6	101.0	51.5	0.16	6 681.3	18.5
June	108.4	107.8	107.4	100.4	50.9	-0.06	6 722.8	18.5
July	108.8	107.8	107.7	100.1	50.2	-0.08	6 741.1	18.6
August	109.1	108.6	108.0	100.6	50.3	-0.21	6 774.3	18.5
September	109.0	108.8	108.2	100.6	50.8	-0.70	6 799.2	18.6
October	109.1	109.2	108.3	100.8	49.8	-0.54	6 811.5	18.6
November	110.2	109.5	108.4	101.0	50.4	0.00	6 843.8	18.6
December	110.4	109.8	108.5	101.2	48.5	-0.03	6 853.8	18.7
1999								
January	111.0	109.9	109.2	100.6	51.0	0.09	6 856.6	18.8
February	111.8	110.5	109.5	100.9	50.8	0.24	6 883.1	18.8
March	111.8	110.6	110.0	100.5	52.3	0.42	6 890.3	18.9
April	111.6	110.7	110.4	100.3	49.5	0.44	6 880.2	19.0
May	112.2	111.2	110.5	100.6	52.1	0.80	6 900.6	19.0
June	112.8	111.4	110.5	100.8	52.6	1.14	6 920.6	19.1
July	113.3	111.7	111.3	100.4	54.0	0.80	6 929.4	19.2
August	113.4	112.0	111.8	100.2	51.4	0.87	6 959.1	19.2
September	113.5	112.0	112.4	99.6	55.8	0.70	6 947.3	19.2
October	113.8	112.7	112.4	100.3	56.2	0.91	7 014.9	19.1
November	114.5	113.2	113.0	100.2	56.8	0.61	7 070.4	19.1
December	115.2	113.8	113.4	100.4	56.7	0.98	7 128.0	19.0
2000								
January	115.7	114.4	113.7	100.6	55.0	1.21	7 231.2	18.8
February	114.9	114.4	114.7	99.7	54.4	0.79	7 265.6	18.8
March	115.5	114.9	114.6	100.3	54.3	0.41	7 291.1	18.8
April	116.2	115.2	115.3	99.9	55.4	-0.03	7 297.3	18.9
May	115.3	115.3	115.7	99.7	55.4	0.17	7 297.6	19.0
June	115.5	115.5	116.7	99.0	54.5	-0.43	7 328.5	19.1
July	115.1	115.7	116.8	99.1	53.9	-0.49	7 387.8	19.2
August	114.9	115.7	117.5	98.5	53.5	-0.67	7 410.1	19.4
September	115.0	115.9	117.9	98.3	49.6	-0.72	7 407.9	19.5
October	114.5	115.8	118.7	97.6	51.1	-0.77	7 419.8	19.6
November	113.9	115.8	119.6	96.8	50.2	-0.79	7 412.5	19.8
December	113.0	115.8	119.5	96.9	52.8	-1.16	7 394.7	20.0

[1] Not seasonally adjusted.

Table 20-7. Composite Indexes of Economic Activity and Selected Index Components—Continued

(Seasonally adjusted, except as noted.)

Year and month	Cyclical composite indexes, 1996 = 100				Selected components of leading index		Selected component of coincident index	Selected component of lagging index
	Leading	Coincident	Lagging	Ratio, coincident to lagging	Vendor performance (slower deliveries, diffusion index, percent)	Interest rate spread, 10-year Treasury bond less federal funds [1]	Personal income less transfer payments (billions of 1996 dollars)	Consumer installment credit outstanding (percent of personal income)
2001								
January	113.0	115.6	118.1	97.9	49.8	-0.82	7 424.0	19.9
February	112.6	115.7	117.7	98.3	50.2	-0.39	7 428.6	20.0
March	112.1	115.5	117.6	98.2	47.7	-0.42	7 436.0	20.0
April	112.1	115.1	117.6	97.9	47.2	0.34	7 393.8	20.2
May	112.6	115.0	117.5	97.9	45.4	1.18	7 371.1	20.3
June	112.8	114.6	116.9	98.0	47.1	1.31	7 362.9	20.3
July	113.0	114.6	117.1	97.9	46.8	1.47	7 366.8	20.4
August	113.2	114.5	117.0	97.9	46.7	1.32	7 364.7	20.5
September	112.2	114.1	117.2	97.4	47.5	1.66	7 353.9	20.5
October	112.3	114.1	116.7	97.8	49.5	2.08	7 330.0	20.7
November	113.6	113.8	116.6	97.6	49.1	2.56	7 332.5	20.9
December	115.3	113.9	116.7	97.6	49.3	3.27	7 352.1	21.0
2002								
January	116.2	113.9	116.6	97.7	51.2	3.31	7 348.0	21.0
February	116.9	113.9	116.7	97.6	51.4	3.17	7 359.4	21.0
March	117.3	113.9	116.9	97.4	51.9	3.55	7 364.2	21.1
April	117.4	114.1	116.5	97.9	53.5	3.46	7 350.3	21.1
May	118.5	114.1	116.3	98.1	53.4	3.41	7 358.9	21.2
June	118.6	114.4	116.4	98.3	54.4	3.18	7 367.5	21.2
July	118.6	114.3	116.5	98.1	54.8	2.92	7 340.2	21.4
August	118.9	114.2	116.3	98.2	53.6	2.52	7 319.7	21.4
September	118.9	114.0	116.2	98.1	56.7	2.12	7 304.8	21.5
October	119.0	114.0	116.2	98.1	53.4	2.19	7 303.5	21.5
November	120.0	114.1	116.2	98.2	52.1	2.71	7 304.7	21.5
December	120.4	113.9	116.3	97.9	52.9	2.79	7 311.3	21.5
2003								
January	120.7	114.2	116.5	98.0	52.8	2.81	7 320.4	21.6
February	120.6	113.9	117.1	97.3	52.8	2.64	7 310.2	21.6
March	120.6	113.9	117.1	97.3	52.5	2.56	7 307.6	21.4
April	121.2	113.8	117.1	97.2	50.0	2.70	7 351.2	21.5
May	122.9	114.0	117.1	97.4	50.8	2.31	7 406.5	21.5
June	123.8	114.3	116.5	98.1	49.8	2.11	7 424.0	21.5
July	124.8	114.6	116.3	98.5	51.5	2.97	7 430.1	21.5
August	125.4	114.6	116.3	98.5	53.1	3.42	7 425.0	21.5
September	126.3	114.8	115.9	99.1	53.2	3.26	7 430.3	21.6
October	127.6	115.1	116.1	99.1	54.4	3.28	7 469.0	21.5
November	128.4	115.5	115.6	99.9	56.2	3.30	7 536.0	21.3
December	129.4	115.7	115.4	100.3	59.2	3.29	7 539.2	21.4
2004								
January	130.3	115.8	115.6	100.2	61.6	3.15	7 540.0	21.3
February	130.6	116.1	115.4	100.6	62.9	3.07	7 551.4	21.2
March	132.4	116.6	115.0	101.4	66.6	2.83	7 561.5	21.2
April	132.5	116.8	115.1	101.5	67.1	3.35	7 570.0	21.2
May	133.3	117.2	115.4	101.6	68.5	3.72	7 592.6	21.0
June	133.7	117.1	115.9	101.0	66.9	3.70	7 589.2	21.1
July	134.2	117.5	116.9	100.5	64.5	3.24	7 634.0	21.1
August	134.4	117.8	117.1	100.6	62.9	2.85	7 650.1	21.1
September	134.4	117.8	117.6	100.2	59.7	2.52	7 635.3	21.2
October	134.4	118.3	118.1	100.2	58.8	2.34	7 714.1	21.1
November	135.2	118.5	118.0	100.4	56.6	2.26	7 717.5	21.0
December	136.1	119.9	117.1	102.4	55.5	2.07	8 028.2	20.4
2005								
January	135.8	119.2	118.5	100.6	54.1	1.94	7 784.0	20.9
February	136.3	119.3	119.2	100.1	54.1	1.67	7 780.5	20.9
March	135.4	119.4	119.3	100.1	52.7	1.87	7 766.1	20.9
April	135.5	119.5	119.8	99.7	52.1	1.55	7 770.4	20.9
May	135.6	119.8	120.2	99.7	51.2	1.14	7 788.4	20.8
June	137.1	120.2	120.3	99.9	53.1	0.96	7 835.8	20.8
July	136.9	120.5	120.6	99.9	52.3	0.92	7 881.4	20.8
August	137.0	119.5	121.1	98.7	50.6	0.76	7 548.6	21.2
September	135.8	120.1	120.9	99.3	58.6	0.58	7 842.4	20.7
October	136.9	120.5	121.8	98.9	60.8	0.68	7 870.2	20.5
November	138.2	121.2	122.0	99.3	56.9	0.54	7 925.6	20.5
December	138.5	121.6	121.8	99.8	52.9	0.31	7 976.0	20.4

[1] Not seasonally adjusted.

NOTES AND DEFINITIONS

TABLE 20-1
INDUSTRIAL PRODUCTION AND CAPACITY UTILIZATION

See the notes and definitions for Tables 2-1 through 2-3.

TABLE 20-2
SUMMARY CONSUMER AND PRODUCER PRICE INDEXES

See the notes and definitions for Tables 8-1 through 8-6.

TABLE 20-3
SUMMARY LABOR FORCE, EMPLOYMENT, AND UNEMPLOYMENT

See the notes and definitions for Tables 10-1 through 10-5.

TABLE 20-3A
LABOR FORCE AND EMPLOYMENT ESTIMATES SMOOTHED FOR POPULATION ADJUSTMENTS

SOURCE: *U.S. DEPARTMENT OF LABOR, BUREAU OF LABOR STATISTICS (BLS)*

This table presents seasonally adjusted monthly estimates of total civilian labor force and total civilian employment in which discontinuities caused by the introduction of new population controls in the official series—as described in the notes and definitions for Tables 10-1 through 10-5—have been smoothed. They are taken from the article "Labor Force and Employment Estimates Smoothed for Population Adjustments, 1990–2005," which was posted on the Bureau of Labor Statistics (BLS) Web site on February 2, 2006. The method of smoothing is described in "Creating Comparability in CPS Employment Series," by Marisa L. Di Natale, available on the BLS Web site at <http://www.bls.gov/cps/cpscomp.pdf>. BLS notes that these series do not match the official estimates in BLS publications, which are also the data shown in all other tables in this volume.

TABLES 20-4
NONFARM PAYROLL EMPLOYMENT, HOURS, AND EARNINGS

See the notes and definitions for Tables 10-7 through 10-12.

TABLE 20-5
MONEY STOCK, RESERVES, AND MONETARY BASE

See the notes and definitions for Tables 12-1 through 12-3.

TABLE 20-6
INTEREST RATES, BOND YIELDS, AND STOCK PRICE INDEXES

See the notes and definitions for Tables 12-9 and 12-10.

TABLE 20-7
COMPOSITE INDEXES OF ECONOMIC ACTIVITY AND SELECTED INDEX COMPONENTS

See the notes and definitions for Table 1-8.

PART D

REGIONAL AND STATE DATA

CHAPTER 21: REGIONAL AND STATE DATA

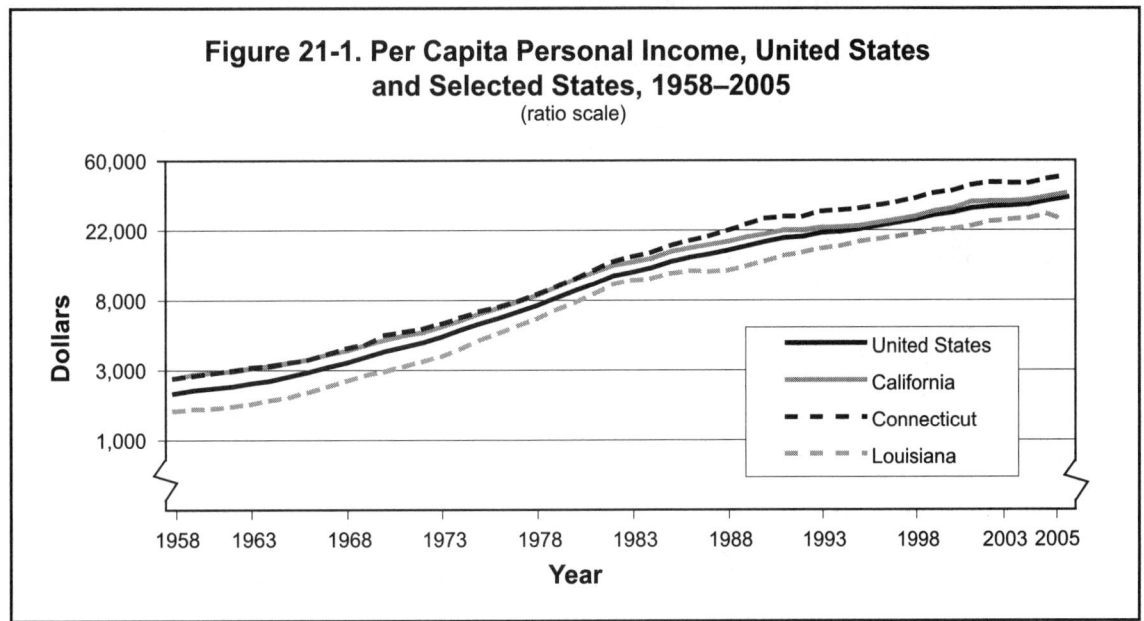

Figure 21-1. Per Capita Personal Income, United States and Selected States, 1958–2005
(ratio scale)

- Per capita personal income (total personal income divided by the size of the population) is one measure of the affluence of states and regions. To provide examples, Figure 21-1 shows the time path since 1958 for the U.S. total, for the largest state in terms of both population and total income (California), for the state with the highest per capita income in 2005 (Connecticut), and for the state with the lowest per capita income in 2005 (Louisiana, which displaced Mississippi in last place in 2005 because of Hurricane Katrina). (The District of Columbia, which is shown in Tables 21-1 and 21-2 in order to complete the coverage of the United States, has even higher per capita income than Connecticut. However, the District of Columbia is not really comparable with the states in many respects, as it consists entirely of a central city area.) (Table 21-2)

- These data are not adjusted to remove the effects of inflation or the effects of different costs of living in different states or regions. In addition, they are averages ("means") and—due to the skewed distribution of income—do not necessarily approximate the income of the typical, or "median," person in the state. State median household income data are shown in Table 3-16 of this volume. (See "Using the Data" at the beginning of this volume for a discussion of means and medians. The District of Columbia provides an extreme example of the difference. Despite its high per capita income, the District's median income is low and its poverty rate is high.) However, per capita income data can be useful for assessing and comparing the economic and fiscal capacities of the states.

- Quantity indexes for gross state product indicate that Nevada had the greatest output growth between 2000 and 2005—more than twice the national average—with Florida as the runner-up. Michigan and Louisiana had the weakest output growth. The fastest-growing states in the late-expansion period from 1997 to 2000 were Arizona, California, and Colorado, while Alaska and Hawaii were the only states with declines over those three years. (Table 21-1)

Table 21-1. Gross State Product by Region and State

(Billions of dollars; index numbers, 2000 = 100.)

Year	United States	New England							Mideast						
		Total	Connect-icut	Maine	Massa-chusetts	New Hamp-shire	Rhode Island	Vermont	Total	Delaware	District of Columbia	Maryland	New Jersey	New York	Pennsyl-vania
VALUE															
1977	1 986.1	103.4	29.3	7.6	49.6	6.3	7.3	3.4	402.8	6.0	15.1	35.4	66.6	179.2	100.4
1978	2 243.6	116.0	32.8	8.3	55.5	7.5	8.0	4.0	446.4	6.7	16.5	39.3	73.8	198.5	111.7
1979	2 491.4	128.7	36.4	9.2	61.4	8.4	8.9	4.5	488.6	7.3	18.0	43.2	82.1	215.7	122.3
1980	2 719.1	142.4	40.3	10.1	68.0	9.4	9.7	4.9	528.6	7.9	19.5	47.0	89.7	235.0	129.6
1981	3 064.6	159.3	45.1	11.1	76.2	10.6	10.8	5.5	585.6	8.9	21.4	52.7	99.9	261.3	141.4
1982	3 217.6	172.5	49.4	12.0	82.3	11.5	11.5	5.8	623.0	9.6	22.8	55.9	106.8	282.6	145.2
1983	3 451.3	190.4	54.4	13.1	91.4	12.7	12.4	6.4	676.2	10.7	24.3	61.8	119.0	305.2	155.2
1984	3 872.8	217.7	62.1	14.9	104.9	14.9	13.9	7.0	756.6	12.0	26.4	69.9	134.9	342.1	171.2
1985	4 155.0	239.0	67.4	16.1	115.6	16.9	15.3	7.7	814.6	13.2	28.5	77.3	147.6	366.8	181.2
1986	4 364.3	261.2	73.5	17.5	126.4	18.8	16.7	8.3	874.9	14.2	30.1	84.4	160.5	394.1	191.7
1987	4 663.3	287.7	81.3	19.3	138.5	21.5	17.9	9.3	945.8	15.6	32.2	92.1	175.7	423.8	206.5
1988	5 067.5	315.3	89.3	21.6	151.2	23.2	19.7	10.4	1 037.3	17.0	35.3	102.0	196.4	462.8	223.8
1989	5 385.8	331.2	94.6	22.8	157.7	23.9	20.9	11.3	1 089.7	19.0	37.7	108.5	206.4	481.3	236.7
1990	5 674.0	338.3	99.0	23.3	158.9	23.8	20.5	11.7	1 140.7	20.1	40.1	113.7	214.8	503.6	248.3
1991	5 857.3	341.9	100.2	23.4	160.2	24.8	21.6	11.7	1 168.7	21.9	41.8	116.2	221.7	508.9	258.1
1992	6 174.4	356.8	104.2	24.2	166.6	26.6	22.6	12.6	1 225.5	23.0	43.8	119.5	233.2	532.6	273.5
1993	6 453.5	368.8	106.3	25.0	173.2	27.6	23.6	13.1	1 271.7	23.6	45.7	124.7	243.4	549.2	285.0
1994	6 865.5	390.3	111.2	26.2	185.3	29.5	24.4	13.7	1 326.3	25.1	46.8	132.1	254.5	569.4	298.3
1995	7 232.7	415.4	120.8	27.6	195.3	32.1	25.7	13.9	1 387.7	27.5	47.1	137.4	266.7	594.4	314.5
1996	7 659.7	439.8	126.7	28.6	208.3	34.8	26.7	14.6	1 456.7	28.9	47.6	142.9	281.8	630.0	325.5
1997	8 171.0	472.0	137.5	29.9	223.0	37.1	29.0	15.5	1 539.2	31.3	49.4	152.3	296.1	668.1	342.0
1997 [1]	8 238.0	470.6	137.7	30.9	221.8	36.6	28.5	15.2	1 539.0	35.5	50.4	154.1	300.9	654.8	343.4
1998 [1]	8 679.7	497.8	145.4	31.7	236.1	39.1	29.5	15.9	1 613.3	36.8	51.7	162.0	314.1	686.9	361.8
1999 [1]	9 201.1	524.1	150.3	33.4	252.6	40.2	30.8	16.8	1 700.9	39.4	56.4	171.4	327.3	730.3	376.1
2000 [1]	9 749.1	565.8	160.4	35.5	274.9	43.5	33.6	17.8	1 792.1	41.5	58.7	180.4	344.8	777.2	389.6
2001 [1]	10 058.2	580.9	165.0	37.1	280.5	44.3	35.1	18.8	1 878.8	44.2	63.7	192.7	363.0	808.5	406.7
2002 [1]	10 398.4	591.7	166.1	38.6	284.4	46.2	36.9	19.6	1 934.6	45.3	67.7	204.1	372.8	821.6	423.1
2003 [1]	10 896.4	614.6	170.2	40.2	295.9	48.4	39.3	20.6	2 008.9	48.1	71.3	214.5	388.6	847.1	439.2
2004 [1]	11 655.3	654.3	182.5	43.3	312.7	52.1	41.8	22.0	2 141.3	52.3	77.5	230.7	410.3	906.8	463.8
2005 [1]	12 403.0	690.7	194.5	45.1	328.5	55.7	43.8	23.1	2 263.5	54.4	82.8	244.9	430.8	963.5	487.2
QUANTITY INDEX															
1977	47.7	42.3	43.6	51.4	41.7	29.4	51.0	41.3	54.2	44.3	80.8	49.4	45.7	54.9	59.9
1978	50.3	44.6	45.9	52.9	44.0	32.5	52.5	45.5	56.4	46.2	83.2	51.4	47.6	57.1	62.2
1979	51.8	46.3	47.7	54.3	45.6	34.4	54.2	47.5	57.7	46.5	84.3	52.7	49.5	58.2	63.4
1980	51.8	47.2	48.6	55.3	46.5	35.4	54.2	49.0	57.4	45.7	83.9	52.9	49.6	58.3	62.2
1981	53.2	48.4	49.7	55.9	47.8	36.7	55.5	50.6	58.3	46.6	82.7	54.1	50.7	59.3	62.4
1982	52.5	49.0	50.8	56.8	48.2	37.3	55.2	50.2	58.0	47.5	80.8	53.7	50.8	60.0	60.1
1983	54.0	51.6	53.2	59.2	51.1	39.7	56.7	52.3	60.0	51.0	81.4	56.3	54.2	61.4	61.6
1984	58.1	56.4	57.9	63.7	56.1	44.9	61.0	55.1	64.1	55.0	83.5	60.6	58.7	65.7	65.2
1985	60.6	59.9	60.9	67.0	59.8	49.2	64.8	58.7	66.3	58.7	85.1	64.5	61.9	67.5	66.9
1986	61.8	63.1	63.9	70.2	63.0	52.8	67.9	61.2	68.4	60.1	85.8	67.7	64.8	69.5	68.1
1987	64.4	67.8	69.1	74.9	67.3	58.9	70.6	66.3	72.0	64.4	88.6	71.4	69.0	72.9	71.7
1988	67.7	72.0	73.6	80.5	71.3	61.8	75.3	72.1	76.2	67.3	92.3	76.2	74.2	77.0	74.8
1989	69.2	72.7	74.7	82.0	71.6	61.3	77.1	75.1	77.0	72.2	94.4	78.0	75.1	77.2	76.1
1990	70.3	71.4	75.1	81.0	69.4	58.9	76.4	75.8	77.7	73.8	96.5	78.8	75.3	77.7	77.1
1991	70.0	69.5	73.2	78.4	67.3	59.2	73.6	73.4	76.5	76.3	94.6	77.3	74.8	75.4	77.3
1992	72.0	70.6	74.0	79.1	68.1	62.0	74.9	77.2	77.9	76.7	95.7	77.3	76.9	76.4	79.9
1993	73.3	71.0	73.3	79.3	68.9	62.9	76.0	78.2	78.7	76.7	96.7	78.4	78.0	76.7	81.0
1994	76.3	73.4	74.7	80.9	72.1	65.5	76.6	80.3	80.2	79.2	96.1	80.8	79.6	78.0	82.7
1995	78.8	76.4	79.2	82.5	74.4	70.5	78.9	80.2	81.9	83.5	93.2	81.8	81.5	79.6	85.3
1996	82.1	79.6	81.5	84.7	78.1	75.8	80.5	83.6	84.6	85.1	91.5	83.6	85.0	82.8	87.2
1997	86.3	84.0	86.7	87.5	82.2	80.1	85.6	87.3	87.7	88.6	92.4	87.3	87.7	86.3	90.2
1997 [1]	88.4	85.8	90.2	93.5	82.0	84.0	90.0	87.8	89.9	90.4	93.6	90.4	91.9	87.2	92.7
1998 [1]	92.4	90.4	94.0	93.9	87.5	90.9	92.0	91.1	92.8	93.7	93.9	93.7	94.5	89.9	96.6
1999 [1]	96.5	94.0	95.6	96.4	92.8	93.3	94.0	95.3	96.5	98.3	99.4	97.2	96.9	94.8	98.7
2000 [1]	100.0	100.0	100.0	100.0	100.0	100.0	100.0	100.0	100.0	100.0	100.0	100.0	100.0	100.0	100.0
2001 [1]	100.9	100.8	100.5	101.8	100.6	100.2	101.7	104.3	102.5	103.6	104.9	103.9	103.0	102.2	101.5
2002 [1]	102.4	100.5	98.9	103.3	100.0	102.4	103.9	106.3	103.3	103.5	107.0	107.3	103.8	101.9	103.4
2003 [1]	105.0	102.8	99.6	105.3	102.7	105.8	108.4	110.3	105.3	107.7	109.5	110.4	106.2	103.3	105.3
2004 [1]	109.4	107.0	104.0	110.2	106.4	111.5	112.4	115.2	109.4	113.3	114.7	115.6	109.5	108.0	108.2
2005 [1]	113.2	110.1	107.9	111.8	109.1	116.4	114.7	118.7	112.6	114.8	119.8	119.9	111.8	111.6	110.4

[1]NAICS basis, not continuous with previous years, which are based on the SIC. See notes and definitions.

Table 21-1. Gross State Product by Region and State—Continued

(Billions of dollars; index numbers, 2000 = 100.)

Year	Great Lakes						Plains							
	Total	Illinois	Indiana	Michigan	Ohio	Wisconsin	Total	Iowa	Kansas	Minnesota	Missouri	Nebraska	North Dakota	South Dakota
VALUE														
1977	390.7	115.7	47.8	88.3	97.9	41.0	149.1	26.4	20.5	36.4	41.7	13.7	5.3	5.2
1978	434.9	128.8	53.7	98.0	108.6	45.8	169.1	30.1	22.8	41.1	46.9	15.7	6.5	6.0
1979	470.5	139.9	57.8	103.8	118.3	50.6	188.2	32.8	26.3	46.4	51.4	17.3	7.3	6.8
1980	483.6	146.4	58.7	102.4	122.7	53.4	198.1	34.0	28.2	49.7	53.4	18.1	7.7	6.9
1981	530.7	160.8	64.6	113.0	134.2	58.0	222.1	37.9	32.0	55.0	58.7	20.8	10.0	7.8
1982	539.2	165.2	64.7	113.4	135.9	60.0	228.0	36.9	33.5	57.0	61.6	21.2	10.0	7.8
1983	577.7	173.5	69.0	125.5	146.1	63.7	239.7	37.0	35.2	61.0	66.5	21.7	10.1	8.2
1984	650.8	194.7	78.6	141.5	165.4	70.7	270.3	41.0	38.4	70.3	75.9	24.6	10.7	9.3
1985	690.7	206.5	81.8	151.8	176.0	74.6	283.6	42.4	40.8	74.8	79.4	25.8	10.7	9.7
1986	729.2	218.5	86.1	161.5	184.5	78.5	293.8	43.1	41.7	78.2	84.7	26.1	9.8	10.2
1987	763.8	230.6	91.2	166.9	192.8	82.4	310.6	45.1	43.9	83.9	89.8	26.8	10.3	10.7
1988	823.4	251.1	98.7	177.4	206.3	89.9	331.9	48.9	46.3	90.0	96.3	29.3	9.7	11.2
1989	872.2	265.2	106.5	186.7	218.5	95.4	353.2	52.8	48.3	96.2	102.0	31.4	10.7	11.9
1990	905.7	277.2	110.1	189.7	228.3	100.3	369.7	55.9	51.3	100.3	104.1	33.8	11.5	12.8
1991	934.3	286.6	113.8	194.3	234.7	104.9	385.5	57.7	53.3	103.8	109.5	35.6	11.7	13.8
1992	997.9	304.0	123.6	207.4	250.2	112.8	410.2	61.3	56.1	111.9	115.2	38.0	12.8	14.9
1993	1 046.9	317.2	130.6	221.3	258.3	119.6	421.9	62.7	57.9	114.9	118.3	39.1	12.9	16.0
1994	1 137.5	343.4	141.2	246.1	278.5	128.4	458.0	69.2	61.8	124.7	128.5	42.8	14.0	17.0
1995	1 186.1	359.7	148.0	251.0	293.3	134.1	481.3	71.9	63.7	131.4	137.5	44.5	14.5	17.8
1996	1 243.8	377.3	155.5	263.9	305.4	141.8	515.4	77.2	68.0	141.7	145.0	48.3	16.1	19.1
1997	1 318.3	401.1	164.2	278.8	325.4	148.8	546.5	81.9	72.5	152.2	154.5	49.8	16.1	19.5
1997 [1]	1 354.8	404.0	168.1	299.0	332.1	151.5	554.8	81.9	72.1	155.9	158.2	50.5	16.3	19.8
1998 [1]	1 421.6	423.9	178.9	309.4	348.7	160.7	578.6	83.7	76.0	164.9	164.3	52.1	16.9	20.8
1999 [1]	1 485.3	443.8	185.7	326.2	360.6	169.0	598.5	86.1	78.7	172.9	169.0	53.4	16.9	21.6
2000 [1]	1 543.6	464.2	194.4	337.2	372.0	175.7	631.1	90.2	82.8	185.1	176.7	55.5	17.8	23.1
2001 [1]	1 562.7	476.5	195.2	334.4	374.7	181.9	650.8	91.9	86.4	190.2	182.4	57.4	18.5	23.9
2002 [1]	1 620.4	487.1	205.0	349.8	389.8	188.6	680.1	97.4	89.6	198.6	188.4	59.9	19.9	26.4
2003 [1]	1 687.5	509.2	216.7	362.8	402.6	196.3	714.3	102.4	93.1	209.3	195.6	64.8	21.7	27.4
2004 [1]	1 762.7	533.7	229.4	366.6	425.2	207.7	760.0	110.2	98.9	224.6	205.8	68.0	22.7	29.7
2005 [1]	1 836.7	560.2	238.6	377.9	442.4	217.5	794.6	114.3	105.4	233.3	216.1	70.3	24.2	31.1
QUANTITY INDEX														
1977	57.7	56.7	54.5	63.7	58.9	50.8	52.3	58.6	56.7	43.4	55.6	52.5	62.3	48.1
1978	60.1	59.2	57.1	66.1	61.1	53.2	55.1	62.0	58.2	45.7	58.4	55.7	69.8	51.5
1979	60.7	60.0	57.3	65.3	62.1	54.9	57.0	63.2	61.8	47.8	59.8	57.2	71.8	53.8
1980	57.8	58.1	54.2	59.4	59.6	54.1	55.8	62.0	61.0	47.7	57.6	56.6	69.0	51.6
1981	58.2	58.8	54.9	59.6	60.1	54.3	57.7	64.2	62.9	49.1	58.1	60.0	79.4	54.6
1982	55.6	56.7	51.8	55.8	57.0	53.1	56.3	60.0	62.3	48.3	57.4	58.7	76.4	53.0
1983	57.3	57.2	52.9	59.5	59.2	54.0	56.5	57.2	62.4	49.6	59.1	57.0	74.5	52.2
1984	62.0	61.5	57.9	64.6	64.5	57.5	61.1	61.0	65.4	54.9	64.5	61.6	76.6	56.5
1985	64.1	63.2	59.1	67.6	66.9	59.6	63.0	62.6	68.2	57.3	65.5	64.3	77.2	58.9
1986	65.1	64.5	60.1	68.9	67.6	60.5	63.2	61.8	68.2	57.7	67.2	63.0	71.6	59.5
1987	66.8	66.6	62.3	69.5	69.3	61.9	65.2	63.1	70.3	60.5	69.5	63.2	73.3	60.8
1988	69.8	70.1	65.2	72.1	71.7	65.6	67.4	66.4	71.8	62.6	72.2	66.6	67.3	61.2
1989	71.2	71.4	67.7	73.0	73.1	66.9	69.1	68.9	72.3	64.4	73.6	68.7	71.2	62.2
1990	71.5	72.1	67.9	71.8	73.9	68.0	69.9	70.8	73.8	65.0	72.6	71.6	73.5	65.4
1991	71.1	71.9	67.9	70.6	73.3	68.9	70.7	71.1	74.5	65.0	73.6	73.7	73.3	68.7
1992	74.1	74.5	72.1	73.2	76.3	72.6	73.5	74.2	76.5	68.6	75.5	76.8	78.7	72.1
1993	75.8	75.7	74.3	75.9	76.8	75.3	73.7	74.2	76.8	68.6	75.5	77.1	77.5	75.8
1994	80.3	80.1	78.4	82.2	80.8	78.9	78.1	80.0	80.2	72.6	79.9	82.6	82.7	78.8
1995	82.2	82.3	80.8	82.3	83.5	80.4	80.4	82.1	81.1	74.6	83.8	84.1	84.0	80.9
1996	85.1	85.2	84.0	85.1	85.9	84.1	84.5	86.5	84.5	79.3	87.0	88.9	90.1	84.4
1997	89.0	89.2	87.7	88.9	90.4	87.6	88.8	91.6	89.2	84.3	91.3	91.2	90.0	86.3
1997 [1]	92.6	91.5	90.8	94.1	94.4	90.9	92.1	94.4	91.2	87.9	95.3	94.7	94.2	91.6
1998 [1]	95.7	94.8	95.2	95.8	97.5	95.0	95.1	95.8	95.9	92.2	97.1	96.8	98.7	95.2
1999 [1]	98.2	97.6	97.4	98.7	99.1	98.1	96.8	97.1	97.6	95.2	97.9	98.0	97.1	98.6
2000 [1]	100.0	100.0	100.0	100.0	100.0	100.0	100.0	100.0	100.0	100.0	100.0	100.0	100.0	100.0
2001 [1]	98.8	100.2	97.9	96.9	98.3	101.0	100.5	99.1	101.3	100.7	100.6	100.6	100.9	101.4
2002 [1]	100.7	100.4	101.2	99.9	100.4	102.6	103.0	102.9	103.0	103.3	101.8	102.6	106.0	102.8
2003 [1]	103.2	103.1	105.4	102.3	102.0	105.1	106.0	106.0	104.3	107.0	103.8	108.3	112.1	106.1
2004 [1]	105.3	105.4	108.9	101.5	105.1	108.5	109.6	110.6	107.6	111.9	106.5	109.5	112.5	106.8
2005 [1]	106.6	107.6	110.1	101.6	106.2	110.7	112.0	112.6	111.9	113.4	108.8	111.4	117.6	110.5

[1]NAICS basis, not continuous with previous years, which are based on the SIC. See notes and definitions.

Table 21-1. Gross State Product by Region and State—Continued

(Billions of dollars; index numbers, 2000 = 100.)

Year	Southeast												
	Total	Alabama	Arkansas	Florida	Georgia	Kentucky	Louisiana	Mississippi	North Carolina	South Carolina	Tennessee	Virginia	West Virginia
VALUE													
1977	389.5	26.5	15.0	66.3	40.9	28.6	39.6	16.0	44.0	20.3	33.7	44.0	14.7
1978	443.5	30.4	17.3	77.1	46.3	32.1	45.2	17.9	50.2	23.2	38.4	49.2	16.3
1979	494.8	33.5	18.9	88.2	51.6	35.2	51.8	20.2	54.9	25.8	42.4	54.4	17.7
1980	546.9	36.0	20.1	100.6	56.3	36.6	64.0	21.5	59.3	28.0	45.4	60.0	19.0
1981	621.0	40.1	22.7	115.3	63.7	40.7	77.6	24.3	66.4	31.5	50.7	67.6	20.5
1982	651.7	41.5	23.3	124.8	68.3	41.7	78.5	24.9	69.4	32.8	52.4	72.9	21.3
1983	707.2	45.2	25.0	139.5	76.6	43.4	77.3	26.2	78.2	36.3	57.5	81.0	21.0
1984	796.8	49.7	28.2	158.8	88.6	48.8	83.0	29.1	89.3	41.9	64.6	91.8	22.8
1985	858.2	53.7	29.1	173.8	98.7	51.5	84.8	30.6	98.0	44.9	69.3	100.4	23.6
1986	906.3	56.0	30.4	188.1	108.4	53.3	75.9	31.3	106.2	48.5	74.1	110.0	24.0
1987	976.6	60.6	32.2	206.9	116.8	56.6	76.5	33.6	114.1	53.2	81.2	120.1	24.7
1988	1 058.7	65.4	34.5	226.6	126.1	60.7	82.3	35.7	125.2	58.0	87.5	130.4	26.2
1989	1 125.2	67.9	36.6	243.3	133.1	64.7	86.2	37.3	134.6	62.0	91.9	140.2	27.3
1990	1 181.7	71.1	38.1	257.2	139.5	67.5	93.6	38.8	140.3	65.7	94.6	147.0	28.3
1991	1 234.4	75.3	41.0	267.9	146.3	70.5	94.3	40.8	146.5	68.4	101.4	152.7	29.4
1992	1 309.7	80.5	44.3	283.8	158.3	76.6	88.9	43.7	159.2	71.6	111.3	160.5	31.0
1993	1 384.0	83.5	46.6	302.1	169.0	80.4	93.2	46.7	167.2	75.5	118.9	168.6	32.4
1994	1 485.3	88.6	50.2	322.1	184.3	86.3	101.9	50.6	179.6	81.0	128.9	177.0	34.9
1995	1 575.5	94.0	53.3	340.5	199.1	90.5	109.2	53.8	191.6	86.1	135.7	185.5	36.4
1996	1 664.3	97.9	56.5	363.0	215.1	95.0	115.0	56.0	201.3	89.3	141.3	196.6	37.3
1997	1 768.9	102.5	58.7	384.0	230.4	101.8	121.7	58.3	218.4	94.9	151.0	208.6	38.5
1997 [1]	1 797.9	102.4	59.2	391.5	237.5	105.7	113.3	58.0	228.9	97.4	153.4	211.9	38.8
1998 [1]	1 901.5	106.7	61.9	417.2	255.6	108.8	118.1	60.5	242.9	102.9	160.9	226.6	39.5
1999 [1]	2 022.5	111.9	65.6	442.6	277.1	113.5	124.0	63.0	262.7	108.7	169.6	242.7	41.1
2000 [1]	2 114.5	114.6	66.8	471.3	290.9	111.9	131.5	64.3	273.7	112.5	174.9	260.7	41.5
2001 [1]	2 202.9	118.7	68.9	497.4	299.4	115.1	133.7	66.0	285.7	117.3	180.6	276.8	43.4
2002 [1]	2 288.9	123.8	72.2	522.7	306.7	120.7	134.3	68.1	296.4	121.6	191.5	285.8	45.0
2003 [1]	2 410.2	130.5	75.6	556.7	317.5	125.8	146.1	72.5	307.9	127.5	201.5	301.9	46.6
2004 [1]	2 592.6	141.4	82.7	609.4	339.7	133.0	160.2	77.1	324.0	131.5	216.8	327.0	49.9
2005 [1]	2 779.3	149.8	86.8	674.0	364.3	140.4	166.3	80.2	344.6	139.8	226.5	352.7	53.8
QUANTITY INDEX													
1977	44.2	52.2	49.3	35.2	33.3	53.1	73.1	54.4	40.2	40.5	43.9	44.8	73.7
1978	46.9	55.6	52.9	38.3	35.3	55.5	76.6	56.2	42.7	43.5	46.9	46.9	75.2
1979	48.4	57.1	53.6	40.9	37.0	56.9	75.7	58.3	44.0	45.4	48.4	48.5	76.0
1980	49.0	56.8	52.8	43.1	37.4	55.3	78.0	57.3	44.2	45.7	47.9	49.3	75.8
1981	50.6	57.8	54.7	45.1	38.8	56.9	80.5	59.3	45.7	47.3	49.1	50.7	74.8
1982	50.0	56.3	53.2	45.8	39.3	54.9	77.4	57.4	44.7	46.4	48.0	50.9	72.9
1983	51.9	58.9	54.9	48.5	41.9	54.7	76.5	58.5	47.0	49.3	50.6	53.2	70.1
1984	56.1	62.0	59.3	52.6	46.2	59.3	81.1	62.7	51.3	54.3	54.5	57.1	74.1
1985	58.7	65.2	60.1	55.4	49.8	61.4	82.5	64.7	54.7	56.4	56.7	60.0	74.8
1986	60.4	65.9	61.1	57.6	52.7	61.2	80.5	64.5	56.8	58.9	58.5	63.1	75.3
1987	63.3	69.5	63.1	61.3	55.1	63.7	80.2	68.3	59.1	62.9	62.4	66.7	76.1
1988	66.4	72.4	65.5	64.8	57.4	66.3	84.3	70.0	62.5	66.1	64.9	69.9	78.5
1989	67.9	72.4	66.9	67.1	58.5	68.2	83.8	70.6	64.4	68.3	65.7	72.3	79.3
1990	68.8	73.6	67.5	68.4	59.3	69.0	85.3	70.7	64.7	70.3	65.3	73.1	80.5
1991	69.3	75.5	70.5	68.6	60.0	69.4	85.0	72.1	64.6	70.7	67.5	72.6	81.1
1992	71.7	78.8	74.6	70.9	63.3	73.4	79.2	75.5	68.1	72.4	72.4	74.0	84.1
1993	73.9	79.7	76.6	73.3	65.9	75.4	80.6	78.4	70.0	74.7	75.3	75.8	86.4
1994	77.9	82.6	80.6	76.3	70.4	80.0	87.1	83.2	74.9	78.5	79.7	78.4	91.0
1995	80.9	85.2	83.9	78.9	74.3	82.8	91.5	87.1	78.6	81.3	82.2	80.4	93.3
1996	84.1	87.8	87.5	82.7	79.2	85.7	92.3	89.3	81.4	83.5	84.6	83.7	95.2
1997	88.0	90.8	90.5	86.1	83.5	90.9	95.6	91.7	87.1	87.9	89.1	87.1	96.9
1997 [1]	90.2	94.2	94.4	88.2	86.2	99.0	95.7	96.1	87.4	91.6	93.5	86.8	97.4
1998 [1]	94.2	96.6	96.2	92.4	91.5	101.1	102.4	98.5	91.7	95.2	96.2	91.1	98.4
1999 [1]	98.2	99.9	100.4	96.2	97.2	103.4	104.2	100.6	97.6	98.6	99.3	95.4	101.3
2000 [1]	100.0	100.0	100.0	100.0	100.0	100.0	100.0	100.0	100.0	100.0	100.0	100.0	100.0
2001 [1]	101.5	100.9	100.3	102.9	100.7	100.2	98.3	99.5	101.7	101.4	100.8	103.4	101.1
2002 [1]	103.2	103.2	103.1	105.5	101.1	103.2	98.6	100.5	103.2	102.8	104.7	104.0	102.4
2003 [1]	106.4	106.5	105.9	110.1	103.0	105.7	100.1	104.1	105.4	106.1	108.5	107.8	103.4
2004 [1]	111.4	111.9	112.3	117.3	107.7	108.8	104.6	107.1	108.4	106.8	114.3	114.1	106.8
2005 [1]	116.2	115.4	115.1	126.4	112.6	111.3	102.9	108.4	112.7	110.5	116.2	120.5	110.2

[1]NAICS basis, not continuous with previous years, which are based on the SIC. See notes and definitions.

Table 21-1. Gross State Product by Region and State—Continued

(Billions of dollars; index numbers, 2000 = 100.)

Year	Southwest					Rocky Mountain					
	Total	Arizona	New Mexico	Oklahoma	Texas	Total	Colorado	Idaho	Montana	Utah	Wyoming
VALUE											
1977	184.5	19.4	10.3	24.0	130.8	54.6	25.1	7.1	6.4	10.4	5.5
1978	211.6	23.0	11.7	27.2	149.7	63.9	29.2	8.4	7.5	12.1	6.7
1979	245.0	27.3	13.4	31.7	172.6	73.1	33.7	9.2	8.3	13.8	8.2
1980	288.9	30.4	16.0	37.8	204.6	83.1	38.2	9.8	9.0	15.4	10.6
1981	345.7	33.7	18.9	45.8	247.3	95.2	43.8	10.6	10.3	17.5	13.0
1982	367.0	35.0	19.7	49.8	262.5	99.8	47.4	10.6	10.4	18.5	12.9
1983	375.7	38.8	20.4	48.3	268.2	104.8	50.4	11.7	10.7	19.9	12.0
1984	412.8	45.2	22.1	52.0	293.5	114.7	55.9	12.5	11.2	22.4	12.7
1985	439.5	50.1	23.3	53.6	312.6	120.7	59.3	13.0	11.2	24.4	12.8
1986	425.6	55.2	22.4	49.2	298.8	120.1	60.1	13.1	11.2	24.6	11.1
1987	433.4	59.2	23.0	48.9	302.4	124.6	62.9	13.8	11.7	25.3	11.0
1988	471.7	63.6	23.8	52.7	331.6	132.0	66.3	15.1	11.9	27.4	11.3
1989	501.2	66.4	25.3	54.8	354.7	140.0	69.6	16.8	12.8	28.9	11.9
1990	538.0	69.3	26.9	57.7	384.1	150.0	74.2	17.8	13.4	31.4	13.2
1991	561.1	72.3	30.5	59.5	398.9	158.2	78.6	18.6	14.1	33.7	13.3
1992	596.3	79.7	32.6	62.0	422.1	169.5	85.1	20.3	15.0	35.7	13.3
1993	635.9	85.2	36.5	65.0	449.2	183.6	92.5	22.7	16.1	38.4	13.9
1994	681.7	95.3	41.1	67.1	478.1	198.5	100.4	24.8	17.0	42.2	14.1
1995	722.5	104.0	41.5	69.6	507.4	213.4	108.0	27.1	17.4	46.3	14.6
1996	781.7	113.1	43.7	74.9	550.0	229.4	116.0	28.2	18.0	51.4	15.7
1997	855.2	122.9	47.6	79.5	605.3	246.7	127.9	29.4	18.8	54.6	16.0
1997 [1]	852.3	127.4	47.4	78.0	599.5	252.0	132.9	28.5	19.1	56.6	14.9
1998 [1]	892.0	137.6	45.9	79.3	629.2	267.9	143.2	29.8	19.9	60.2	14.9
1999 [1]	949.7	148.5	49.0	83.2	669.0	289.1	156.3	32.7	20.4	63.8	15.9
2000 [1]	1 026.2	158.5	50.7	89.8	727.2	313.1	171.9	35.0	21.4	67.6	17.3
2001 [1]	1 073.3	165.4	51.4	94.3	762.2	325.2	178.1	35.6	22.5	70.1	18.9
2002 [1]	1 105.1	171.9	52.5	97.2	783.5	334.6	182.2	36.7	23.6	72.7	19.6
2003 [1]	1 172.1	182.4	57.5	103.8	828.5	350.8	188.9	38.5	25.5	76.2	21.8
2004 [1]	1 272.9	194.2	63.6	111.8	903.2	379.1	201.4	43.5	27.6	82.5	24.1
2005 [1]	1 388.0	215.8	69.3	120.5	982.4	410.4	216.1	47.2	29.9	89.8	27.4
QUANTITY INDEX											
1977	42.3	28.7	43.0	62.0	42.8	40.9	36.6	38.6	68.3	36.7	63.2
1978	44.8	31.7	45.4	64.8	45.2	44.2	39.6	41.9	73.3	39.6	69.3
1979	46.7	34.8	45.9	67.9	46.7	46.3	42.3	42.6	73.4	41.6	72.2
1980	48.5	35.7	47.5	71.2	48.5	47.8	43.7	43.0	73.7	42.6	79.5
1981	51.1	36.5	48.2	75.4	51.4	49.6	45.6	43.2	76.7	44.2	82.7
1982	51.3	35.5	47.6	77.7	51.7	49.2	46.6	41.4	73.6	43.9	78.0
1983	51.3	37.5	48.4	74.1	51.7	49.6	47.2	43.1	73.1	45.3	73.6
1984	54.7	41.8	51.0	77.8	55.0	52.4	50.0	44.2	74.1	49.0	77.6
1985	57.1	44.8	53.0	79.1	57.4	53.8	51.2	45.6	72.7	52.0	78.8
1986	55.8	47.5	52.1	74.0	55.6	52.8	50.5	44.5	71.9	51.2	74.9
1987	55.6	49.3	52.0	72.3	55.2	53.4	51.4	45.5	72.6	51.3	73.5
1988	58.8	51.2	52.4	76.0	58.8	54.9	52.6	48.0	71.4	53.8	76.1
1989	60.0	51.6	53.6	75.9	60.4	56.1	53.2	51.1	74.4	54.6	76.6
1990	61.5	52.1	54.6	76.4	62.3	57.9	54.6	52.7	75.4	57.5	80.3
1991	62.6	52.5	60.5	76.7	63.3	59.4	55.9	53.8	77.3	59.7	81.8
1992	65.4	56.6	63.7	78.4	65.8	62.3	59.1	57.5	81.0	61.8	82.0
1993	67.9	58.9	70.0	80.1	68.2	65.8	62.6	62.4	84.2	64.8	84.2
1994	71.6	64.4	78.2	81.3	71.5	69.7	66.5	66.8	86.6	69.5	85.5
1995	74.8	69.1	79.3	82.8	74.8	73.5	70.1	72.5	86.9	74.4	87.8
1996	79.2	74.6	82.5	86.9	79.0	77.5	73.8	74.7	88.4	81.5	90.3
1997	85.4	80.2	89.8	90.8	85.5	82.2	80.0	78.0	91.1	85.0	90.9
1997 [1]	86.5	80.8	90.8	92.2	86.8	83.9	80.5	81.7	94.1	88.5	91.8
1998 [1]	91.2	87.5	91.2	94.1	91.7	88.6	86.1	85.8	96.6	93.2	92.9
1999 [1]	96.0	94.4	98.7	96.8	96.1	94.4	92.7	93.6	97.9	97.1	98.0
2000 [1]	100.0	100.0	100.0	100.0	100.0	100.0	100.0	100.0	100.0	100.0	100.0
2001 [1]	102.5	103.1	100.4	102.3	102.5	101.6	101.7	100.7	101.4	101.0	104.5
2002 [1]	104.5	105.3	101.8	103.5	104.6	102.5	102.1	102.0	104.1	102.3	106.1
2003 [1]	106.6	110.2	105.8	105.6	106.0	104.8	103.5	105.2	109.0	105.0	109.5
2004 [1]	111.8	114.8	112.8	109.1	111.5	109.9	107.6	115.8	113.2	110.7	113.6
2005 [1]	117.3	124.8	118.0	112.3	116.3	115.4	112.1	124.4	119.3	117.2	119.2

[1]NAICS basis, not continuous with previous years, which are based on the SIC. See notes and definitions.

Table 21-1. Gross State Product by Region and State—Continued

(Billions of dollars; index numbers, 2000 = 100.)

Year	Far West						
	Total	Alaska	California	Hawaii	Nevada	Oregon	Washington
VALUE							
1977	311.5	7.5	228.5	9.4	7.5	22.3	36.3
1978	358.2	9.1	261.5	10.5	9.1	25.9	42.2
1979	402.6	10.9	291.9	11.9	10.6	29.0	48.4
1980	447.6	15.1	324.4	13.3	12.0	30.5	52.2
1981	504.9	21.7	365.2	14.5	13.6	32.0	58.0
1982	536.4	23.3	389.9	15.4	14.3	31.9	61.6
1983	579.5	22.5	423.9	16.8	15.4	34.0	66.8
1984	653.1	23.8	483.2	18.6	17.0	37.9	72.6
1985	708.7	26.2	528.0	20.0	18.5	40.1	75.9
1986	753.2	18.8	568.4	21.5	20.2	42.3	81.9
1987	820.8	22.3	620.2	23.3	22.4	45.0	87.7
1988	897.2	21.3	678.8	25.7	25.5	49.6	96.2
1989	973.1	23.4	734.4	28.4	28.6	53.3	105.1
1990	1 050.0	25.0	788.3	31.9	31.8	57.3	115.7
1991	1 073.3	22.2	801.2	33.6	33.6	60.1	122.7
1992	1 108.5	22.6	819.4	35.2	36.5	63.7	131.1
1993	1 140.6	23.0	833.7	35.9	40.0	69.2	138.8
1994	1 187.9	23.1	862.5	36.3	44.9	74.4	146.7
1995	1 250.8	24.8	909.0	36.6	49.0	80.1	151.3
1996	1 328.5	26.1	958.5	37.0	54.1	91.2	161.8
1997	1 424.3	26.9	1 028.6	37.9	58.9	97.5	174.4
1997 [1]	1 416.6	25.0	1 019.2	37.5	59.9	96.6	178.3
1998 [1]	1 507.0	23.2	1 085.9	37.5	63.6	101.0	195.8
1999 [1]	1 631.0	24.3	1 180.6	38.6	68.8	104.3	214.4
2000 [1]	1 762.5	27.0	1 287.1	40.2	73.7	112.4	222.0
2001 [1]	1 783.5	26.6	1 301.1	41.8	77.3	110.9	225.8
2002 [1]	1 843.0	29.2	1 340.4	43.5	81.3	117.1	231.5
2003 [1]	1 938.0	31.5	1 410.5	46.4	89.0	120.5	240.0
2004 [1]	2 092.3	36.0	1 519.2	50.2	99.1	134.6	253.1
2005 [1]	2 239.8	39.9	1 621.8	53.7	110.5	145.4	268.5
QUANTITY INDEX							
1977	40.9	66.3	40.8	61.4	26.7	38.7	41.3
1978	43.8	72.4	43.6	64.0	30.0	41.2	44.7
1979	45.7	76.0	45.2	67.6	32.2	42.9	47.6
1980	46.8	87.3	46.3	69.3	33.2	42.5	47.7
1981	48.2	100.6	47.9	68.0	34.4	41.2	48.9
1982	48.1	103.6	47.9	68.0	33.9	38.9	48.9
1983	49.7	101.0	49.8	70.4	34.9	39.2	49.9
1984	53.6	105.5	54.3	72.9	36.8	41.8	51.6
1985	56.3	117.3	57.4	74.9	38.4	43.0	52.2
1986	58.1	96.0	59.7	77.2	40.3	43.7	54.3
1987	61.5	112.2	63.3	80.8	42.7	45.0	56.4
1988	65.0	109.0	67.1	85.7	46.4	47.9	59.6
1989	67.9	112.7	69.9	91.3	50.3	49.4	62.7
1990	70.5	112.0	72.2	98.9	54.4	51.4	66.6
1991	69.6	100.2	70.8	99.8	55.5	52.2	68.1
1992	70.2	101.3	70.7	101.9	59.0	53.9	70.8
1993	70.2	100.3	70.0	101.1	63.2	56.6	72.7
1994	71.5	100.1	70.8	99.6	68.9	59.5	74.9
1995	73.9	105.0	73.4	98.3	73.1	63.1	75.3
1996	77.2	103.6	76.1	97.4	79.7	71.7	79.1
1997	81.5	104.8	80.5	97.6	84.8	76.5	84.0
1997 [1]	82.6	101.9	80.8	100.6	86.2	84.6	85.2
1998 [1]	87.8	99.0	86.1	98.4	90.7	89.7	92.0
1999 [1]	94.1	100.1	93.0	98.9	95.8	92.8	98.9
2000 [1]	100.0	100.0	100.0	100.0	100.0	100.0	100.0
2001 [1]	99.5	95.3	99.6	101.1	101.9	98.3	99.2
2002 [1]	101.1	103.7	100.9	102.2	104.6	102.3	99.6
2003 [1]	104.1	102.5	104.1	105.9	112.3	104.0	101.1
2004 [1]	109.6	109.9	109.5	111.1	121.1	113.9	103.9
2005 [1]	114.6	110.5	114.3	116.4	131.0	121.5	107.8

[1]NAICS basis, not continuous with previous years, which are based on the SIC. See notes and definitions.

Table 21-2. Personal Income and Employment by Region and State

(Millions of dollars, except as noted.)

Region or state and year	Personal income, total	Earnings by place of work			Less: Contributions for government social insurance	Plus: Adjustment for residence	Equals: Net earnings by place of residence	Plus: Dividends, interest, and rent	Plus: Personal current transfer receipts	Per capita (dollars)		Population (thousands)	Total employment (thousands)
		Nonfarm	Farm	Total						Personal income	Disposable personal income		
UNITED STATES													
1958	367 249	292 629	15 252	307 881	11 371	-204	296 306	47 413	23 529	2 109	1 888	174 153	. . .
1959	391 286	317 047	13 034	330 081	13 824	-217	316 040	50 939	24 306	2 209	1 970	177 136	. . .
1960	408 376	330 712	13 561	344 273	16 349	-285	327 639	54 997	25 740	2 269	2 014	179 972	. . .
1961	425 829	341 270	14 265	355 535	16 905	-279	338 351	58 028	29 450	2 327	2 070	182 976	. . .
1962	453 276	364 933	14 329	379 262	19 011	-233	360 018	62 866	30 392	2 440	2 164	185 739	. . .
1963	476 109	384 082	14 167	398 249	21 548	-208	376 493	67 407	32 209	2 527	2 238	188 434	. . .
1964	510 599	413 156	13 017	426 173	22 247	-207	403 719	73 376	33 504	2 672	2 400	191 085	. . .
1965	551 432	443 773	15 369	459 142	23 268	-152	435 722	79 532	36 178	2 850	2 553	193 457	. . .
1966	598 615	489 059	16 397	505 456	31 127	-143	474 186	84 812	39 617	3 062	2 723	195 499	. . .
1967	642 212	523 648	15 077	538 725	34 558	-143	504 024	90 174	48 014	3 254	2 885	197 375	. . .
1968	705 105	576 211	15 276	591 487	38 338	-170	552 979	96 032	56 094	3 538	3 104	199 312	. . .
1969	772 235	631 338	17 243	648 581	43 792	-163	604 626	105 287	62 322	3 836	3 321	201 298	91 057
1970	832 429	671 582	17 463	689 045	46 012	-175	642 858	114 838	74 733	4 085	3 582	203 799	91 282
1971	897 952	719 396	17 970	737 366	50 859	-198	686 309	123 395	88 248	4 342	3 853	206 818	91 586
1972	987 137	793 438	21 733	815 171	58 897	-229	756 045	132 962	98 130	4 717	4 129	209 275	94 317
1973	1 105 605	884 639	34 658	919 297	75 183	-244	843 870	148 887	112 848	5 231	4 607	211 349	98 433
1974	1 217 556	968 564	29 813	998 377	84 873	-264	913 240	170 677	133 639	5 707	5 002	213 334	100 118
1975	1 329 892	1 034 062	28 873	1 062 935	88 975	-313	973 647	185 821	170 424	6 172	5 489	215 457	98 907
1976	1 469 467	1 160 623	24 993	1 185 616	100 987	-339	1 084 290	200 695	184 482	6 754	5 965	217 554	101 597
1977	1 627 310	1 295 462	24 254	1 319 716	112 699	-377	1 206 640	225 919	194 751	7 405	6 509	219 761	105 049
1978	1 831 117	1 467 160	28 073	1 495 233	130 827	-410	1 363 996	256 812	210 309	8 245	7 215	222 098	109 689
1979	2 053 827	1 641 985	29 875	1 671 860	152 274	-398	1 519 188	298 510	236 129	9 146	7 952	224 569	113 289
1980	2 298 255	1 795 158	20 392	1 815 550	165 669	-454	1 649 427	368 611	280 217	10 114	8 802	227 225	114 231
1981	2 580 600	1 969 935	27 169	1 997 104	195 066	-443	1 801 595	459 858	319 147	11 246	9 746	229 466	115 304
1982	2 764 886	2 066 560	24 558	2 091 118	208 173	-520	1 882 425	527 092	355 369	11 935	10 410	231 664	114 557
1983	2 949 883	2 206 755	17 235	2 223 990	225 148	-508	1 998 334	567 273	384 276	12 618	11 114	233 792	116 057
1984	3 275 805	2 452 535	31 814	2 484 349	256 554	-579	2 227 216	647 861	400 728	13 891	12 294	235 825	121 091
1985	3 511 344	2 639 477	31 950	2 671 427	280 384	-603	2 390 440	695 617	425 287	14 758	13 008	237 924	124 510
1986	3 708 199	2 798 353	33 079	2 831 432	302 395	-575	2 528 462	728 615	451 122	15 442	13 626	240 133	126 970
1987	3 934 655	2 997 457	39 409	3 036 866	322 010	-608	2 714 248	752 842	467 565	16 240	14 226	242 289	130 400
1988	4 237 460	3 253 621	39 109	3 292 730	360 256	-651	2 931 823	809 089	496 548	17 331	15 271	244 499	134 507
1989	4 571 133	3 446 466	45 677	3 492 143	383 938	-664	3 107 541	920 199	543 393	18 520	16 231	246 819	137 200
1990	4 861 936	3 655 379	46 760	3 702 139	408 654	-737	3 292 748	973 575	595 613	19 477	17 108	249 623	139 381
1991	5 032 196	3 762 522	41 579	3 804 101	428 560	-788	3 374 753	991 122	666 321	19 892	17 578	252 981	138 606
1992	5 349 384	4 017 224	49 550	4 066 774	453 745	-797	3 612 232	987 898	749 254	20 854	18 478	256 514	139 162
1993	5 548 121	4 191 800	47 244	4 239 044	476 585	-798	3 761 661	996 465	789 995	21 346	18 862	259 919	141 779
1994	5 833 906	4 395 182	49 932	4 445 114	507 172	-860	3 937 082	1 069 567	827 257	22 172	19 550	263 126	145 224
1995	6 144 741	4 622 731	39 675	4 662 406	531 848	-893	4 129 665	1 137 710	877 366	23 076	20 286	266 278	148 983
1996	6 512 485	4 868 019	54 906	4 922 925	554 248	-914	4 367 763	1 219 791	924 931	24 175	21 089	269 394	152 150
1997	6 907 332	5 180 807	52 982	5 233 789	586 178	-969	4 646 642	1 309 556	951 134	25 334	21 941	272 647	155 608
1998	7 415 709	5 591 837	49 748	5 641 585	623 147	-1 022	5 017 416	1 419 686	978 607	26 883	23 163	275 854	159 628
1999	7 796 137	5 975 196	49 774	6 024 970	660 395	-1 030	5 363 545	1 410 543	1 022 049	27 939	23 974	279 040	162 955
2000	8 422 074	6 460 197	44 482	6 504 679	701 650	-1 060	5 801 969	1 536 284	1 083 821	29 845	25 470	282 193	166 759
2001	8 716 992	6 665 188	42 811	6 707 999	730 005	-1 093	5 976 901	1 546 360	1 193 731	30 574	26 239	285 108	167 015
2002	8 872 871	6 817 857	33 461	6 851 318	748 787	-1 162	6 101 369	1 485 161	1 286 341	30 810	27 162	287 985	166 633
2003	9 150 908	7 060 270	49 241	7 109 511	777 556	-1 198	6 330 757	1 468 652	1 351 499	31 463	28 024	290 850	167 547
2004	9 717 173	7 503 882	58 718	7 562 600	824 946	-1 228	6 736 426	1 553 960	1 426 787	33 090	29 519	293 657	170 483
2005	10 224 761	7 932 763	54 708	7 987 471	879 189	-1 264	7 107 018	1 591 151	1 526 592	34 495	30 441	296 410	174 220

. . . = Not available.

Table 21-2. Personal Income and Employment by Region and State—Continued

(Millions of dollars, except as noted.)

Region or state and year	Personal income, total	Derivation of personal income								Per capita (dollars)		Population (thousands)	Total employment (thousands)
		Earnings by place of work			Less: Contributions for government social insurance	Plus: Adjustment for residence	Equals: Net earnings by place of residence	Plus: Dividends, interest, and rent	Plus: Personal current transfer receipts	Personal income	Disposable personal income		
		Nonfarm	Farm	Total									
NEW ENGLAND													
1958	23 237	18 684	317	19 002	722	18	18 297	3 250	1 690	2 274	2 019	10 219	. . .
1959	24 798	20 248	248	20 496	872	20	19 644	3 468	1 686	2 376	2 103	10 437	. . .
1960	25 854	21 094	315	21 408	1 025	27	20 411	3 682	1 761	2 455	2 154	10 532	. . .
1961	27 111	21 999	266	22 265	1 073	28	21 220	3 914	1 977	2 542	2 241	10 666	. . .
1962	28 786	23 401	256	23 657	1 215	31	22 473	4 306	2 007	2 665	2 344	10 800	. . .
1963	30 043	24 325	248	24 573	1 357	36	23 252	4 665	2 126	2 735	2 400	10 986	. . .
1964	32 186	25 882	286	26 168	1 400	42	24 810	5 170	2 207	2 877	2 568	11 186	. . .
1965	34 527	27 608	337	27 945	1 450	44	26 539	5 658	2 330	3 048	2 712	11 329	. . .
1966	37 550	30 471	341	30 812	1 937	51	28 926	6 113	2 512	3 285	2 899	11 430	. . .
1967	40 858	32 904	237	33 141	2 133	58	31 066	6 710	3 082	3 534	3 107	11 562	. . .
1968	44 339	35 781	264	36 045	2 367	71	33 748	6 908	3 682	3 810	3 300	11 637	. . .
1969	49 110	38 952	292	39 244	2 634	850	37 460	7 541	4 110	4 185	3 580	11 735	5 516
1970	52 799	41 507	304	41 811	2 769	856	39 898	8 000	4 902	4 445	3 868	11 878	5 518
1971	56 146	43 683	281	43 964	3 008	884	41 840	8 432	5 874	4 680	4 130	11 996	5 454
1972	60 795	47 663	285	47 948	3 449	941	45 440	8 949	6 406	5 029	4 372	12 088	5 573
1973	66 585	52 617	395	53 013	4 355	997	49 655	9 734	7 195	5 481	4 795	12 148	5 783
1974	72 433	56 312	427	56 739	4 823	1 084	52 999	10 905	8 530	5 958	5 204	12 157	5 843
1975	77 693	58 564	310	58 874	4 913	1 171	55 131	11 426	11 135	6 381	5 657	12 176	5 685
1976	84 949	64 843	426	65 269	5 515	1 300	61 053	12 228	11 667	6 959	6 121	12 207	5 811
1977	93 075	71 649	382	72 030	6 127	1 453	67 356	13 611	12 109	7 593	6 663	12 257	6 007
1978	103 505	80 717	393	81 110	7 097	1 636	75 649	15 052	12 804	8 413	7 334	12 303	6 280
1979	115 950	90 631	376	91 006	8 287	1 868	84 587	17 099	14 264	9 392	8 123	12 345	6 515
1980	131 495	100 572	365	100 936	9 186	2 184	93 935	21 156	16 404	10 629	9 164	12 372	6 641
1981	147 313	110 056	468	110 524	10 801	2 360	102 084	26 458	18 771	11 846	10 151	12 436	6 692
1982	160 475	117 752	511	118 263	11 790	2 538	109 011	30 943	20 521	12 871	11 095	12 468	6 694
1983	173 474	128 988	477	129 465	13 042	2 671	119 094	32 462	21 918	13 829	12 050	12 544	6 828
1984	194 956	145 754	564	146 318	15 170	2 851	134 000	37 985	22 971	15 422	13 505	12 642	7 198
1985	210 807	159 769	554	160 324	16 763	3 009	146 570	40 070	24 166	16 546	14 396	12 741	7 447
1986	227 430	173 818	572	174 390	18 460	3 186	159 116	42 941	25 374	17 722	15 338	12 833	7 687
1987	247 610	191 880	637	192 517	20 144	3 353	175 726	45 790	26 095	19 119	16 431	12 951	7 828
1988	272 305	212 023	653	212 677	22 610	3 553	193 620	50 631	28 054	20 811	18 091	13 085	8 082
1989	291 087	221 728	601	222 329	23 600	3 478	202 207	57 540	31 340	22 083	19 157	13 182	8 072
1990	300 474	226 118	683	226 801	24 139	3 468	206 130	59 311	35 033	22 712	19 749	13 230	7 918
1991	304 280	225 468	629	226 097	24 576	3 464	204 986	58 851	40 443	22 969	20 068	13 248	7 585
1992	320 794	238 304	790	239 094	25 752	4 699	218 041	58 892	43 861	24 172	21 092	13 271	7 624
1993	330 058	247 633	733	248 366	26 959	4 136	225 544	59 163	45 351	24 752	21 510	13 334	7 748
1994	344 112	258 270	681	258 951	28 549	3 937	234 339	62 048	47 724	25 687	22 279	13 396	7 843
1995	361 504	270 708	604	271 313	30 077	4 736	245 972	64 974	50 558	26 832	23 136	13 473	7 938
1996	382 164	285 093	694	285 787	31 483	5 568	259 872	70 219	52 073	28 194	24 026	13 555	8 069
1997	404 990	304 268	598	304 867	33 623	5 185	276 428	74 302	54 260	29 687	25 007	13 642	8 228
1998	435 052	327 646	622	328 268	35 767	6 648	299 149	80 797	55 106	31 677	26 452	13 734	8 402
1999	458 387	351 831	674	352 505	38 053	6 557	321 009	80 582	56 796	33 126	27 510	13 838	8 562
2000	503 961	388 102	674	388 776	41 223	6 869	354 422	89 556	59 982	36 118	29 520	13 953	8 776
2001	524 402	402 212	596	402 808	42 658	6 275	366 425	92 812	65 165	37 342	30 826	14 043	8 835
2002	528 030	406 020	519	406 539	43 372	5 623	368 791	88 730	70 509	37 379	32 172	14 126	8 776
2003	539 130	415 605	554	416 159	43 825	5 563	377 897	86 996	74 237	37 983	33 028	14 194	8 754
2004	569 708	442 363	694	443 057	46 896	6 194	402 356	89 277	78 075	40 059	34 859	14 222	8 853
2005	595 013	461 010	697	461 708	49 188	6 585	419 105	93 118	82 790	41 785	35 891	14 240	8 976

. . . = Not available.

Table 21-2. Personal Income and Employment by Region and State—Continued

(Millions of dollars, except as noted.)

Region or state and year	Personal income, total	Derivation of personal income								Per capita (dollars)		Population (thousands)	Total employment (thousands)
		Earnings by place of work			Less: Contributions for government social insurance	Plus: Adjustment for residence	Equals: Net earnings by place of residence	Plus: Dividends, interest, and rent	Plus: Personal current transfer receipts	Personal income	Disposable personal income		
		Nonfarm	Farm	Total									
MIDEAST													
1958	90 864	75 901	985	76 886	3 047	-582	73 256	11 892	5 715	2 409	2 124	37 721	. . .
1959	96 289	81 169	787	81 955	3 679	-623	77 653	12 702	5 935	2 521	2 212	38 202	. . .
1960	100 494	84 920	890	85 810	4 353	-749	80 708	13 666	6 119	2 604	2 279	38 597	. . .
1961	104 502	87 673	893	88 565	4 580	-780	83 205	14 303	6 994	2 670	2 338	39 133	. . .
1962	110 533	92 962	721	93 683	5 116	-792	87 775	15 607	7 150	2 795	2 440	39 552	. . .
1963	115 398	96 647	783	97 431	5 641	-828	90 962	16 844	7 593	2 879	2 512	40 083	. . .
1964	123 680	103 129	790	103 919	5 691	-887	97 341	18 478	7 861	3 050	2 701	40 555	. . .
1965	132 265	109 860	884	110 743	5 938	-926	103 879	19 981	8 405	3 224	2 844	41 025	. . .
1966	142 545	120 014	903	120 916	7 889	-1 004	112 023	21 121	9 401	3 446	3 021	41 360	. . .
1967	153 635	128 437	961	129 398	8 607	-1 171	119 620	22 413	11 602	3 692	3 220	41 617	. . .
1968	168 522	140 404	912	141 316	9 391	-1 292	130 633	24 017	13 872	4 020	3 474	41 924	. . .
1969	181 847	152 341	1 093	153 435	11 063	-1 763	140 609	25 972	15 266	4 318	3 681	42 111	19 435
1970	196 035	162 686	1 051	163 737	11 648	-1 676	150 413	27 506	18 116	4 611	3 985	42 517	19 469
1971	209 754	172 600	959	173 559	12 763	-1 757	159 039	28 964	21 751	4 893	4 285	42 870	19 304
1972	226 753	187 174	952	188 126	14 524	-1 928	171 674	30 644	24 435	5 274	4 553	42 992	19 526
1973	246 067	204 210	1 373	205 582	18 181	-2 067	185 334	33 415	27 318	5 744	4 988	42 837	19 973
1974	267 975	219 769	1 272	221 041	20 147	-2 304	198 590	37 559	31 826	6 274	5 427	42 709	19 960
1975	289 442	231 378	1 180	232 557	20 828	-2 632	209 098	39 856	40 487	6 774	5 949	42 728	19 485
1976	313 595	251 815	1 263	253 078	22 884	-2 988	227 206	42 683	43 707	7 350	6 424	42 667	19 568
1977	341 719	275 240	1 081	276 321	24 856	-3 397	248 068	47 609	46 041	8 032	6 982	42 547	19 855
1978	375 225	304 666	1 290	305 957	28 197	-3 929	273 831	52 546	48 848	8 845	7 660	42 421	20 412
1979	413 568	335 719	1 499	337 218	32 242	-4 599	300 377	59 582	53 610	9 764	8 395	42 358	20 900
1980	461 074	366 473	1 115	367 589	35 077	-5 472	327 039	72 378	61 657	10 907	9 373	42 272	20 962
1981	513 728	400 069	1 477	401 546	40 900	-6 096	354 550	89 636	69 543	12 137	10 351	42 329	21 061
1982	555 698	423 565	1 441	425 007	43 908	-6 361	374 738	103 732	77 228	13 112	11 214	42 382	20 945
1983	592 905	451 999	1 072	453 071	47 823	-6 483	398 764	110 628	83 513	13 936	12 083	42 544	21 140
1984	655 004	499 159	1 879	501 037	54 352	-6 832	439 853	128 241	86 910	15 345	13 339	42 687	21 891
1985	700 965	537 095	1 993	539 089	59 534	-7 145	472 409	137 210	91 346	16 380	14 176	42 794	22 485
1986	745 867	576 142	2 176	578 318	64 727	-7 570	506 021	143 331	96 515	17 349	15 010	42 991	22 996
1987	797 403	624 822	2 275	627 096	69 438	-8 069	549 589	148 639	99 174	18 463	15 832	43 190	23 505
1988	868 226	685 292	2 183	687 475	78 001	-8 776	600 698	162 243	105 285	19 989	17 295	43 435	24 124
1989	935 223	723 215	2 551	725 765	82 280	-9 049	634 436	186 854	113 933	21 457	18 486	43 585	24 412
1990	989 039	762 655	2 443	765 098	86 817	-9 850	668 431	195 844	124 764	22 601	19 569	43 762	24 476
1991	1 016 388	773 800	2 066	775 866	89 611	-10 425	675 831	199 744	140 813	23 063	20 110	44 071	23 904
1992	1 069 395	820 468	2 600	823 069	94 257	-12 216	716 596	195 997	156 802	24 090	21 021	44 392	23 796
1993	1 095 679	845 769	2 537	848 306	97 857	-12 146	738 302	192 182	165 194	24 502	21 308	44 717	23 915
1994	1 133 109	872 295	2 302	874 598	102 909	-11 974	759 714	202 048	171 348	25 197	21 864	44 970	24 084
1995	1 189 144	911 867	1 783	913 650	106 722	-13 142	793 786	213 982	181 376	26 317	22 793	45 186	24 376
1996	1 252 041	955 150	2 727	957 877	109 947	-13 630	834 300	226 610	191 130	27 588	23 716	45 384	24 602
1997	1 319 270	1 009 108	1 877	1 010 985	114 752	-14 012	882 222	243 551	193 498	28 944	24 665	45 580	24 971
1998	1 404 640	1 081 158	2 370	1 083 528	121 047	-15 313	947 168	259 099	198 373	30 654	25 973	45 822	25 416
1999	1 467 261	1 145 465	2 430	1 147 895	127 305	-16 820	1 003 770	257 372	206 119	31 824	26 804	46 106	25 900
2000	1 580 733	1 231 448	2 699	1 234 147	135 130	-15 670	1 083 347	279 930	217 456	34 076	28 576	46 388	26 540
2001	1 627 895	1 266 667	2 540	1 269 207	141 240	-15 191	1 112 776	278 002	237 117	34 906	29 207	46 636	26 653
2002	1 648 005	1 291 272	1 851	1 293 123	144 909	-16 065	1 132 149	262 297	253 559	35 155	30 347	46 878	26 615
2003	1 690 170	1 329 062	2 636	1 331 699	149 478	-15 976	1 166 244	257 176	266 750	35 869	31 292	47 121	26 733
2004	1 798 714	1 412 745	3 270	1 416 015	155 959	-17 077	1 242 979	274 069	281 666	38 023	33 192	47 306	27 096
2005	1 884 242	1 486 049	3 296	1 489 345	164 633	-17 749	1 306 964	286 103	291 176	39 755	34 259	47 397	27 541

. . . = Not available.

Table 21-2. Personal Income and Employment by Region and State—Continued

(Millions of dollars, except as noted.)

Region or state and year	Personal income, total	Earnings by place of work			Less: Contributions for government social insurance	Plus: Adjustment for residence	Equals: Net earnings by place of residence	Plus: Dividends, interest, and rent	Plus: Personal current transfer receipts	Per capita (dollars)		Population (thousands)	Total employment (thousands)
		Nonfarm	Farm	Total						Personal income	Disposable personal income		
GREAT LAKES													
1958	79 768	64 987	2 400	67 388	2 492	-112	64 784	9 925	5 059	2 242	2 008	35 578	. . .
1959	85 126	70 816	1 903	72 719	3 045	-126	69 547	10 636	4 943	2 369	2 115	35 928	. . .
1960	88 445	73 432	1 976	75 408	3 656	-124	71 629	11 559	5 257	2 437	2 159	36 290	. . .
1961	90 551	73 553	2 402	75 954	3 617	-112	72 226	12 195	6 130	2 473	2 204	36 616	. . .
1962	96 107	78 602	2 309	80 911	4 043	-116	76 753	13 201	6 154	2 603	2 308	36 927	. . .
1963	100 629	82 530	2 311	84 842	4 561	-114	80 166	14 119	6 343	2 694	2 385	37 357	. . .
1964	108 246	89 273	1 999	91 273	4 762	-122	86 389	15 383	6 474	2 859	2 564	37 868	. . .
1965	118 260	97 093	2 587	99 680	4 946	-134	94 600	16 725	6 935	3 079	2 752	38 405	. . .
1966	128 663	107 168	2 921	110 089	6 742	-147	103 201	17 933	7 529	3 303	2 932	38 951	. . .
1967	135 549	112 492	2 495	114 987	7 271	-136	107 581	18 959	9 009	3 445	3 049	39 347	. . .
1968	147 984	123 164	2 399	125 563	7 985	-146	117 432	20 140	10 413	3 733	3 265	39 645	. . .
1969	161 216	134 765	2 823	137 588	9 310	287	128 564	21 319	11 332	4 040	3 475	39 904	17 785
1970	169 065	139 828	2 468	142 296	9 504	262	133 055	22 464	13 547	4 193	3 647	40 320	17 630
1971	181 621	149 081	2 856	151 936	10 425	334	141 845	23 673	16 103	4 471	3 941	40 622	17 549
1972	198 554	163 794	3 114	166 907	12 096	383	155 195	25 387	17 973	4 864	4 227	40 824	17 933
1973	222 988	183 726	5 158	188 884	15 629	435	173 689	28 362	20 937	5 446	4 759	40 947	18 710
1974	242 749	197 733	4 588	202 321	17 400	535	185 457	32 361	24 931	5 915	5 153	41 037	18 911
1975	261 436	205 408	5 752	211 160	17 671	628	194 118	35 288	32 030	6 360	5 614	41 105	18 399
1976	289 361	232 056	4 759	236 815	20 243	776	217 348	37 821	34 192	7 026	6 144	41 187	18 891
1977	321 800	260 950	4 757	265 707	22 759	959	243 908	42 176	35 716	7 782	6 770	41 353	19 508
1978	357 361	292 752	4 425	297 177	26 310	1 185	272 053	46 904	38 404	8 609	7 452	41 510	20 196
1979	394 863	321 395	5 134	326 529	29 955	1 405	297 979	53 456	43 428	9 489	8 182	41 611	20 520
1980	428 890	334 970	3 223	338 193	30 983	1 681	308 891	65 489	54 510	10 287	8 933	41 694	20 024
1981	468 448	357 480	3 605	361 085	35 487	1 440	327 038	80 802	60 608	11 248	9 729	41 648	19 862
1982	489 802	361 458	2 869	364 327	36 419	1 338	329 246	92 540	68 016	11 805	10 344	41 492	19 315
1983	514 149	380 781	-168	380 614	38 830	1 319	343 102	98 364	72 682	12 429	10 929	41 366	19 335
1984	568 589	421 539	4 319	425 858	44 244	1 423	383 037	111 096	74 456	13 736	12 136	41 393	20 120
1985	603 916	450 343	4 886	455 229	48 176	1 462	408 515	117 214	78 187	14 581	12 835	41 418	20 605
1986	634 420	475 878	4 409	480 287	51 707	1 531	430 111	122 456	81 853	15 304	13 487	41 455	21 050
1987	665 925	504 152	4 956	509 108	54 365	1 600	456 343	125 466	84 116	16 012	14 013	41 590	21 651
1988	711 001	546 216	3 304	549 520	60 533	1 724	490 711	132 499	87 791	17 042	14 974	41 721	22 219
1989	762 846	576 310	6 917	583 227	64 389	1 763	520 600	148 027	94 218	18 218	15 925	41 873	22 717
1990	804 166	605 942	5 825	611 767	68 063	1 966	545 671	155 614	102 881	19 105	16 725	42 091	23 093
1991	828 639	624 201	3 411	627 612	71 309	2 014	558 316	157 550	112 773	19 499	17 154	42 496	23 003
1992	884 713	669 058	5 717	674 776	75 713	2 245	601 308	159 796	123 609	20 621	18 213	42 903	23 126
1993	918 620	700 714	5 058	705 771	80 221	2 335	627 886	161 006	129 728	21 228	18 651	43 275	23 512
1994	975 700	745 488	5 695	751 183	86 536	2 549	667 196	174 775	133 729	22 384	19 607	43 590	24 215
1995	1 021 606	781 585	3 253	784 838	91 002	2 683	696 520	184 396	140 689	23 259	20 302	43 924	24 876
1996	1 073 297	812 452	6 713	819 165	93 998	2 994	728 161	197 605	147 531	24 261	21 032	44 239	25 274
1997	1 132 660	856 122	6 766	862 889	98 451	3 340	767 777	212 193	152 690	25 457	21 951	44 494	25 674
1998	1 207 487	916 993	5 562	922 556	103 148	3 466	822 873	229 877	154 737	26 996	23 179	44 728	26 131
1999	1 255 454	969 950	4 158	974 108	108 420	3 884	869 572	224 886	160 996	27 918	23 964	44 969	26 548
2000	1 333 971	1 024 233	4 264	1 028 498	111 902	4 245	920 840	242 503	170 627	29 496	25 332	45 226	26 986
2001	1 359 189	1 040 895	3 569	1 044 465	114 167	4 493	934 791	237 352	187 045	29 914	25 824	45 436	26 700
2002	1 386 117	1 068 457	1 999	1 070 457	116 016	4 570	959 010	228 113	198 993	30 381	26 778	45 625	26 454
2003	1 429 241	1 109 135	4 886	1 114 021	119 129	4 695	999 587	221 018	208 636	31 187	27 819	45 828	26 400
2004	1 479 761	1 148 032	7 640	1 155 672	124 843	4 932	1 035 761	227 420	216 579	32 171	28 770	45 996	26 638
2005	1 538 939	1 192 691	4 510	1 197 201	132 346	5 209	1 070 064	236 832	232 043	33 342	29 543	46 156	26 943

. . . = Not available.

Table 21-2. Personal Income and Employment by Region and State—Continued

(Millions of dollars, except as noted.)

Region or state and year	Personal income, total	Earnings by place of work			Less: Contributions for government social insurance	Plus: Adjustment for residence	Equals: Net earnings by place of residence	Plus: Dividends, interest, and rent	Plus: Personal current transfer receipts	Per capita (dollars)		Population (thousands)	Total employment (thousands)
		Nonfarm	Farm	Total						Personal income	Disposable personal income		
PLAINS													
1958	30 375	21 265	3 831	25 097	826	7	24 278	4 140	1 957	2 026	1 830	14 994	. . .
1959	31 179	22 993	2 664	25 657	1 000	8	24 665	4 417	2 097	2 052	1 852	15 195	. . .
1960	32 729	23 903	3 071	26 974	1 156	7	25 825	4 687	2 218	2 122	1 902	15 424	. . .
1961	33 917	24 786	2 983	27 769	1 211	6	26 564	4 888	2 464	2 178	1 953	15 570	. . .
1962	36 235	26 311	3 484	29 795	1 317	7	28 485	5 191	2 560	2 314	2 073	15 657	. . .
1963	37 686	27 544	3 414	30 959	1 493	3	29 469	5 521	2 696	2 398	2 145	15 715	. . .
1964	39 277	29 455	2 733	32 187	1 554	5	30 638	5 851	2 788	2 488	2 254	15 787	. . .
1965	43 108	31 395	4 048	35 443	1 632	4	33 815	6 272	3 021	2 725	2 463	15 819	. . .
1966	46 359	34 470	4 240	38 710	2 197	0	36 513	6 583	3 263	2 918	2 617	15 888	. . .
1967	48 663	36 961	3 623	40 583	2 549	-5	38 030	6 739	3 894	3 053	2 730	15 942	. . .
1968	53 037	40 516	3 625	44 141	2 837	-14	41 291	7 241	4 505	3 305	2 934	16 047	. . .
1969	58 083	44 468	4 157	48 626	3 164	-414	45 048	8 096	4 940	3 585	3 134	16 202	7 506
1970	62 780	47 467	4 378	51 845	3 342	-358	48 145	8 844	5 791	3 840	3 394	16 350	7 516
1971	67 510	50 815	4 554	55 369	3 697	-355	51 317	9 541	6 651	4 098	3 665	16 475	7 544
1972	74 631	55 480	6 091	61 571	4 228	-361	56 982	10 399	7 250	4 506	3 979	16 563	7 731
1973	87 442	61 770	11 224	72 994	5 405	-399	67 190	11 804	8 448	5 259	4 681	16 628	8 065
1974	92 655	68 191	7 590	75 782	6 194	-432	69 156	13 651	9 848	5 558	4 866	16 672	8 219
1975	101 551	73 769	7 410	81 179	6 600	-423	74 155	15 275	12 120	6 065	5 380	16 743	8 181
1976	109 353	83 446	4 328	87 774	7 518	-521	79 735	16 453	13 165	6 485	5 716	16 864	8 438
1977	121 183	92 400	5 110	97 510	8 276	-659	88 574	18 694	13 914	7 150	6 291	16 950	8 657
1978	137 405	104 056	7 733	111 789	9 619	-819	101 350	20 900	15 155	8 069	7 080	17 028	8 958
1979	151 909	116 763	6 495	123 259	11 228	-989	111 041	23 892	16 975	8 885	7 731	17 097	9 247
1980	164 453	126 038	1 769	127 807	12 066	-1 146	114 596	29 583	20 275	9 557	8 314	17 208	9 250
1981	186 200	135 956	5 340	141 296	13 919	-1 338	126 039	37 048	23 113	10 785	9 363	17 264	9 212
1982	198 366	140 880	3 935	144 815	14 702	-1 344	128 769	43 844	25 753	11 472	9 977	17 292	9 082
1983	208 000	149 764	1 509	151 273	15 683	-1 434	134 156	46 139	27 705	12 006	10 597	17 325	9 196
1984	232 330	165 627	6 435	172 062	17 725	-1 604	152 733	50 727	28 870	13 366	11 911	17 382	9 512
1985	245 609	175 442	7 372	182 814	19 127	-1 714	161 973	53 060	30 576	14 114	12 556	17 402	9 664
1986	256 417	183 830	7 972	191 802	20 442	-1 829	169 531	54 841	32 046	14 743	13 149	17 393	9 754
1987	269 790	195 341	9 709	205 050	21 670	-1 940	181 440	55 378	32 971	15 480	13 717	17 428	10 009
1988	282 070	208 831	7 312	216 144	24 068	-2 103	189 972	57 506	34 591	16 088	14 260	17 533	10 221
1989	302 898	221 060	9 071	230 131	25 672	-2 186	202 274	63 155	37 469	17 215	15 193	17 595	10 427
1990	320 841	233 098	10 157	243 255	27 311	-2 429	213 515	66 828	40 499	18 129	15 987	17 698	10 617
1991	333 016	242 685	7 919	250 604	28 836	-2 481	219 286	69 176	44 554	18 663	16 544	17 843	10 667
1992	355 443	260 395	10 305	270 700	30 671	-2 726	237 302	69 859	48 282	19 718	17 507	18 026	10 778
1993	364 761	272 319	6 124	278 443	32 318	-2 813	243 312	70 294	51 155	20 031	17 720	18 210	11 004
1994	389 452	288 145	10 081	298 225	34 685	-3 032	260 509	75 507	53 436	21 188	18 730	18 381	11 301
1995	406 860	303 842	5 682	309 524	36 499	-3 171	269 854	80 406	56 600	21 934	19 298	18 550	11 611
1996	437 288	320 004	13 336	333 340	38 271	-3 394	291 675	86 163	59 450	23 378	20 468	18 705	11 836
1997	460 385	339 516	10 525	350 041	40 508	-3 805	305 728	93 219	61 438	24 422	21 257	18 851	12 054
1998	492 324	365 434	9 778	375 212	43 015	-4 066	328 132	100 976	63 216	25 928	22 520	18 988	12 316
1999	511 507	387 838	7 398	395 236	45 317	-4 402	345 517	99 915	66 075	26 737	23 251	19 131	12 510
2000	545 882	412 558	7 075	419 634	47 513	-4 695	367 426	107 850	70 606	28 326	24 564	19 271	12 696
2001	562 733	425 963	5 678	431 641	49 299	-4 827	377 515	107 646	77 572	29 047	25 261	19 373	12 692
2002	576 806	439 790	3 700	443 490	50 533	-4 963	387 994	105 060	83 752	29 622	26 295	19 472	12 662
2003	599 339	455 456	9 137	464 593	51 944	-4 973	407 676	104 367	87 296	30 607	27 471	19 582	12 664
2004	633 538	481 979	11 754	493 733	54 284	-5 110	434 338	107 905	91 294	32 164	28 962	19 697	12 839
2005	661 089	504 681	10 458	515 139	57 969	-5 295	451 874	112 542	96 674	33 362	29 772	19 816	13 070

. . . = Not available.

Table 21-2. Personal Income and Employment by Region and State—Continued

(Millions of dollars, except as noted.)

Region or state and year	Personal income, total	Derivation of personal income								Per capita (dollars)		Population (thousands)	Total employment (thousands)
		Earnings by place of work			Less: Contributions for government social insurance	Plus: Adjustment for residence	Equals: Net earnings by place of residence	Plus: Dividends, interest, and rent	Plus: Personal current transfer receipts	Personal income	Disposable personal income		
		Nonfarm	Farm	Total									
SOUTHEAST													
1958	58 253	45 299	3 569	48 868	1 738	465	47 595	6 595	4 063	1 556	1 423	37 435	...
1959	62 411	49 084	3 459	52 543	2 106	505	50 942	7 122	4 347	1 637	1 489	38 115	...
1960	64 713	50 920	3 318	54 238	2 445	552	52 345	7 765	4 603	1 664	1 508	38 885	...
1961	68 143	52 712	3 735	56 446	2 510	578	54 514	8 334	5 295	1 723	1 565	39 544	...
1962	72 754	56 795	3 495	60 290	2 803	634	58 122	9 076	5 556	1 811	1 634	40 179	...
1963	77 570	60 759	3 716	64 475	3 284	691	61 881	9 788	5 901	1 904	1 717	40 742	...
1964	83 864	66 215	3 584	69 798	3 441	752	67 109	10 598	6 158	2 028	1 848	41 349	...
1965	91 117	72 211	3 464	75 675	3 675	854	72 854	11 540	6 723	2 177	1 976	41 857	...
1966	99 915	80 502	3 667	84 170	4 912	951	80 209	12 366	7 340	2 364	2 130	42 257	...
1967	108 436	87 252	3 664	90 916	5 655	1 104	86 365	13 325	8 746	2 545	2 291	42 611	...
1968	120 221	97 328	3 544	100 871	6 394	1 202	95 679	14 442	10 100	2 793	2 489	43 042	...
1969	133 396	107 868	4 024	111 892	7 217	1 134	105 808	16 202	11 386	3 071	2 698	43 440	19 085
1970	146 106	116 499	4 011	120 510	7 781	1 014	113 743	18 589	13 773	3 323	2 949	43 974	19 254
1971	161 148	127 812	4 227	132 039	8 838	988	124 189	20 686	16 273	3 580	3 202	45 013	19 635
1972	181 308	144 522	4 922	149 444	10 454	1 049	140 039	22 857	18 412	3 940	3 482	46 019	20 523
1973	207 012	164 064	7 235	171 299	13 505	1 118	158 913	26 278	21 821	4 405	3 915	46 992	21 636
1974	231 338	181 835	6 604	188 439	15 476	1 237	174 199	30 756	26 383	4 824	4 270	47 955	22 069
1975	253 040	193 691	5 947	199 638	16 283	1 478	184 832	33 964	34 244	5 187	4 675	48 788	21 642
1976	282 944	219 142	6 323	225 465	18 670	1 667	208 462	37 160	37 323	5 714	5 112	49 514	22 351
1977	314 833	246 134	5 721	251 855	20 907	1 900	232 848	42 236	39 748	6 258	5 581	50 312	23 208
1978	358 185	281 063	6 871	287 935	24 367	2 207	265 774	48 856	43 555	7 008	6 217	51 113	24 309
1979	404 319	315 506	6 775	322 281	28 409	2 574	296 446	57 632	50 241	7 779	6 860	51 977	25 020
1980	457 351	349 106	4 103	353 209	31 472	3 121	324 858	72 622	59 871	8 649	7 623	52 881	25 378
1981	518 648	385 765	6 570	392 335	37 325	3 556	358 566	91 563	68 520	9 671	8 495	53 627	25 676
1982	556 499	405 718	6 722	412 439	40 014	3 774	376 199	104 262	76 038	10 258	9 056	54 249	25 579
1983	600 314	437 897	4 862	442 759	43 707	3 836	402 888	114 568	82 858	10 943	9 740	54 856	26 113
1984	671 395	490 730	8 332	499 062	49 941	4 023	453 144	130 915	87 337	12 094	10 838	55 515	27 396
1985	723 822	530 457	7 382	537 838	54 907	4 222	487 154	143 419	93 250	12 880	11 476	56 199	28 243
1986	769 051	565 084	6 887	571 971	59 646	4 445	516 769	152 882	99 400	13 525	12 057	56 861	28 986
1987	821 022	608 702	8 255	616 958	63 886	4 748	557 820	159 675	103 527	14 270	12 660	57 536	29 714
1988	887 860	658 337	10 858	669 195	71 716	5 205	602 684	174 165	111 012	15 276	13 616	58 120	30 732
1989	964 369	698 612	11 314	709 926	77 054	5 561	638 432	202 339	123 598	16 419	14 573	58 733	31 473
1990	1 027 597	742 219	10 581	752 800	82 334	6 324	676 790	215 541	135 266	17 266	15 364	59 516	32 068
1991	1 074 251	768 714	12 167	780 881	86 845	6 868	700 903	220 417	152 931	17 756	15 887	60 501	31 940
1992	1 148 896	827 937	13 040	840 977	92 810	7 344	755 511	217 769	175 616	18 679	16 736	61 508	32 402
1993	1 206 516	874 804	12 636	887 440	98 854	7 742	796 328	225 313	184 875	19 295	17 248	62 531	33 414
1994	1 278 747	924 517	13 835	938 352	106 194	7 667	839 825	243 165	195 757	20 114	17 930	63 574	34 368
1995	1 354 691	977 844	12 425	990 270	112 353	8 006	885 923	258 650	210 118	20 970	18 645	64 602	35 493
1996	1 437 179	1 031 269	14 127	1 045 396	117 639	7 546	935 303	278 888	222 988	21 904	19 354	65 611	36 336
1997	1 523 242	1 093 453	14 329	1 107 781	124 948	8 337	991 170	300 536	231 535	22 853	20 070	66 655	37 295
1998	1 633 535	1 178 179	12 881	1 191 060	133 230	8 240	1 066 071	328 652	238 811	24 155	21 113	67 627	38 306
1999	1 716 450	1 258 627	13 444	1 272 072	141 274	9 685	1 140 483	326 126	249 841	25 032	21 854	68 569	39 177
2000	1 840 460	1 347 513	12 238	1 359 751	148 752	8 106	1 219 106	354 362	266 993	26 484	23 090	69 494	39 981
2001	1 922 935	1 401 277	13 008	1 414 285	155 921	8 024	1 266 388	361 369	295 178	27 348	23 936	70 313	40 027
2002	1 973 853	1 448 066	7 699	1 455 765	161 078	9 523	1 304 209	349 999	319 646	27 733	24 760	71 172	40 072
2003	2 042 954	1 507 838	11 961	1 519 799	164 754	9 343	1 364 389	344 310	334 255	28 350	25 577	72 061	40 483
2004	2 186 244	1 611 753	13 178	1 624 931	175 519	9 670	1 459 082	366 619	360 543	29 927	27 025	73 054	41 441
2005	2 306 347	1 713 457	13 760	1 727 217	188 356	9 915	1 548 777	359 989	397 582	31 123	27 834	74 103	42 491

... = Not available.

Table 21-2. Personal Income and Employment by Region and State—Continued

(Millions of dollars, except as noted.)

| Region or state and year | Personal income, total | Earnings by place of work | | | Less: Contributions for government social insurance | Plus: Adjustment for residence | Equals: Net earnings by place of residence | Plus: Dividends, interest, and rent | Plus: Personal current transfer receipts | Per capita (dollars) | | Population (thousands) | Total employment (thousands) |
		Nonfarm	Farm	Total						Personal income	Disposable personal income		
SOUTHWEST													
1958	25 372	19 745	1 627	21 372	708	3	20 666	3 267	1 438	1 866	1 686	13 598	...
1959	26 926	21 132	1 477	22 608	847	4	21 766	3 604	1 556	1 941	1 750	13 874	...
1960	27 935	21 939	1 458	23 397	1 005	5	22 397	3 894	1 645	1 962	1 764	14 235	...
1961	29 462	22 931	1 610	24 541	1 039	6	23 508	4 103	1 851	2 022	1 817	14 572	...
1962	30 964	24 374	1 393	25 767	1 131	9	24 645	4 324	1 995	2 074	1 858	14 930	...
1963	32 317	25 667	1 175	26 842	1 276	12	25 579	4 586	2 152	2 139	1 916	15 108	...
1964	34 600	27 667	1 113	28 781	1 329	14	27 465	4 889	2 247	2 265	2 059	15 278	...
1965	37 086	29 492	1 330	30 821	1 399	16	29 438	5 197	2 451	2 406	2 182	15 414	...
1966	40 256	32 568	1 389	33 957	1 881	17	32 093	5 489	2 674	2 586	2 327	15 567	...
1967	43 804	35 693	1 278	36 971	2 180	19	34 809	5 752	3 242	2 784	2 499	15 734	...
1968	48 805	39 886	1 410	41 296	2 450	24	38 869	6 123	3 812	3 051	2 710	15 998	...
1969	54 214	44 504	1 499	46 003	2 889	-71	43 044	6 920	4 250	3 320	2 912	16 328	7 219
1970	59 884	48 244	1 824	50 069	3 105	-84	46 880	7 968	5 037	3 603	3 197	16 621	7 311
1971	65 468	52 674	1 670	54 344	3 502	-88	50 754	8 830	5 883	3 834	3 443	17 077	7 457
1972	72 894	58 803	2 002	60 805	4 087	-106	56 612	9 690	6 592	4 165	3 698	17 503	7 807
1973	83 245	66 442	3 284	69 726	5 309	-119	64 298	11 110	7 836	4 639	4 139	17 943	8 215
1974	94 055	75 785	2 119	77 904	6 216	-80	71 608	13 094	9 354	5 124	4 528	18 354	8 511
1975	106 022	84 534	2 094	86 628	6 833	-47	79 748	14 446	11 827	5 643	5 060	18 789	8 633
1976	119 729	96 956	2 068	99 024	7 905	24	91 143	15 644	12 942	6 213	5 537	19 270	9 001
1977	134 097	110 113	1 847	111 959	9 030	-222	102 707	17 649	13 741	6 803	6 017	19 710	9 467
1978	154 990	128 346	1 666	130 011	10 769	-359	118 884	20 872	15 235	7 680	6 778	20 180	10 043
1979	179 873	148 041	2 960	151 001	12 999	-351	137 651	24 817	17 406	8 658	7 569	20 777	10 539
1980	207 566	169 583	1 510	171 092	14 993	-456	155 643	31 513	20 410	9 688	8 443	21 426	10 944
1981	243 542	196 004	2 820	198 824	18 612	-188	180 023	40 197	23 321	11 077	9 553	21 985	11 485
1982	266 878	211 431	2 338	213 769	20 507	-250	193 012	47 492	26 373	11 710	10 171	22 791	11 717
1983	282 870	221 074	2 388	223 462	21 383	-180	201 899	51 515	29 455	12 086	10 706	23 405	11 747
1984	313 020	244 032	2 649	246 681	24 036	-180	222 465	59 312	31 243	13 165	11 737	23 776	12 310
1985	337 065	261 602	2 557	264 159	26 108	-147	237 904	65 691	33 470	13 948	12 430	24 166	12 686
1986	344 430	265 084	2 559	267 643	26 812	-32	240 799	67 158	36 473	14 010	12 609	24 585	12 551
1987	354 107	271 650	3 504	275 153	27 210	59	248 002	67 579	38 526	14 309	12 814	24 748	12 860
1988	375 506	289 186	4 149	293 336	29 947	156	263 545	71 110	40 851	15 105	13 591	24 860	13 137
1989	402 842	306 386	4 078	310 464	31 925	238	278 777	78 949	45 116	16 060	14 378	25 083	13 331
1990	433 473	329 983	4 921	334 904	34 487	336	300 752	82 704	50 017	17 058	15 253	25 411	13 646
1991	454 182	346 721	4 471	351 193	37 087	293	314 399	84 341	55 442	17 524	15 752	25 917	13 850
1992	487 472	372 640	5 286	377 926	39 441	332	338 816	84 232	64 424	18 401	16 609	26 491	13 978
1993	514 272	396 136	6 178	402 314	41 994	380	360 700	84 645	68 927	18 966	17 091	27 116	14 427
1994	546 291	419 859	5 256	425 116	45 155	401	380 362	92 027	73 902	19 670	17 702	27 772	14 943
1995	580 621	446 364	4 263	450 627	47 850	381	403 158	98 193	79 269	20 430	18 351	28 420	15 498
1996	622 613	479 691	3 922	483 613	51 087	383	432 909	105 301	84 403	21 455	19 136	29 020	15 990
1997	674 420	523 385	5 083	528 468	55 200	372	473 640	112 833	87 948	22 765	20 174	29 625	16 588
1998	732 215	572 873	4 924	577 797	59 764	378	518 411	122 915	90 889	24 214	21 371	30 240	17 179
1999	776 129	614 351	7 023	621 375	63 353	467	558 488	122 930	94 711	25 177	22 236	30 827	17 543
2000	850 326	676 366	4 669	681 035	67 860	527	613 701	135 901	100 723	27 088	23 838	31 391	18 052
2001	892 795	710 498	5 229	715 727	71 681	383	644 430	136 517	111 848	27 963	24 724	31 928	18 216
2002	905 918	720 256	5 386	725 642	73 109	393	652 926	130 339	122 653	27 872	25 196	32 503	18 243
2003	939 815	746 752	5 858	752 610	76 154	437	676 892	132 073	130 850	28 427	25 941	33 061	18 444
2004	1 006 412	804 762	6 062	810 824	80 402	501	730 923	137 606	137 884	29 919	27 384	33 638	18 833
2005	1 084 380	869 326	6 080	875 407	87 227	427	788 606	144 578	151 196	31 637	28 715	34 276	19 462

. . . = Not available.

Table 21-2. Personal Income and Employment by Region and State—Continued

(Millions of dollars, except as noted.)

Region or state and year	Personal income, total	Earnings by place of work			Less: Contributions for government social insurance	Plus: Adjustment for residence	Equals: Net earnings by place of residence	Plus: Dividends, interest, and rent	Plus: Personal current transfer receipts	Per capita (dollars)		Population (thousands)	Total employment (thousands)
		Nonfarm	Farm	Total						Personal income	Disposable personal income		
ROCKY MOUNTAIN													
1958	8 406	6 292	704	6 995	252	-3	6 741	1 134	531	2 031	1 829	4 139	...
1959	8 885	6 793	578	7 372	291	-3	7 078	1 214	594	2 103	1 885	4 226	...
1960	9 390	7 247	580	7 827	354	-3	7 471	1 295	624	2 159	1 923	4 350	...
1961	9 938	7 744	525	8 269	382	-3	7 885	1 363	690	2 210	1 968	4 497	...
1962	10 720	8 224	711	8 935	412	-3	8 520	1 479	721	2 341	2 092	4 580	...
1963	11 050	8 605	623	9 228	478	-2	8 748	1 545	758	2 386	2 126	4 632	...
1964	11 554	9 109	509	9 617	491	-2	9 125	1 652	777	2 473	2 243	4 673	...
1965	12 423	9 584	726	10 310	499	-2	9 810	1 773	840	2 643	2 395	4 700	...
1966	13 175	10 328	693	11 022	646	-1	10 375	1 898	902	2 782	2 506	4 735	...
1967	14 009	10 942	707	11 650	720	-1	10 928	2 011	1 069	2 929	2 628	4 783	...
1968	15 230	11 979	747	12 726	803	-1	11 922	2 093	1 215	3 128	2 783	4 868	...
1969	16 945	13 223	881	14 104	884	15	13 235	2 364	1 345	3 428	3 003	4 943	2 216
1970	18 959	14 580	995	15 575	965	16	14 626	2 732	1 601	3 763	3 337	5 038	2 271
1971	21 075	16 293	959	17 252	1 105	19	16 166	3 038	1 871	4 058	3 621	5 194	2 343
1972	23 910	18 534	1 260	19 794	1 323	22	18 493	3 327	2 090	4 454	3 945	5 368	2 482
1973	27 460	21 163	1 742	22 905	1 732	22	21 195	3 823	2 442	4 968	4 399	5 527	2 646
1974	31 054	23 917	1 825	25 741	2 006	25	23 760	4 457	2 838	5 497	4 842	5 650	2 740
1975	34 301	26 568	1 373	27 942	2 181	37	25 797	4 974	3 529	5 933	5 293	5 782	2 778
1976	38 235	30 309	1 016	31 325	2 515	42	28 852	5 503	3 879	6 463	5 731	5 916	2 912
1977	42 875	34 583	675	35 258	2 873	44	32 429	6 301	4 146	7 053	6 225	6 079	3 060
1978	49 738	40 290	941	41 231	3 414	54	37 872	7 330	4 536	7 949	7 005	6 257	3 257
1979	56 617	46 043	731	46 773	4 095	54	42 733	8 734	5 150	8 793	7 695	6 439	3 406
1980	64 677	51 329	946	52 275	4 581	78	47 772	10 865	6 040	9 811	8 603	6 592	3 482
1981	73 822	57 702	1 039	58 740	5 544	49	53 245	13 518	7 059	10 949	9 552	6 743	3 571
1982	79 932	61 325	814	62 138	6 011	51	56 179	15 721	8 032	11 578	10 131	6 904	3 608
1983	85 115	64 682	1 132	65 814	6 402	53	59 465	16 820	8 830	12 099	10 771	7 035	3 654
1984	92 828	70 926	1 028	71 953	7 181	72	64 845	18 766	9 217	13 058	11 680	7 109	3 817
1985	97 850	74 902	831	75 733	7 736	90	68 087	19 988	9 775	13 651	12 184	7 168	3 882
1986	100 722	76 478	1 226	77 704	8 060	112	69 756	20 475	10 491	13 989	12 528	7 200	3 876
1987	104 000	78 751	1 569	80 320	8 246	137	72 212	20 659	11 129	14 433	12 871	7 206	3 908
1988	109 048	83 306	1 618	84 924	9 098	174	76 000	21 332	11 717	15 140	13 505	7 203	4 047
1989	118 433	88 587	2 194	90 781	9 785	209	81 205	24 296	12 932	16 372	14 524	7 234	4 142
1990	127 012	95 147	2 682	97 829	10 634	245	87 439	25 594	13 979	17 387	15 368	7 305	4 260
1991	134 339	101 315	2 427	103 742	11 630	275	92 386	26 574	15 379	17 967	15 926	7 477	4 364
1992	144 661	110 240	2 489	112 730	12 591	306	100 445	27 139	17 077	18 796	16 640	7 696	4 464
1993	156 042	119 490	3 211	122 701	13 759	338	109 281	28 341	18 420	19 656	17 367	7 939	4 657
1994	166 759	128 150	2 035	130 184	14 930	389	115 643	31 818	19 299	20 408	17 969	8 171	4 919
1995	179 084	136 956	1 965	138 920	15 894	453	123 479	34 611	20 994	21 371	18 790	8 380	5 080
1996	192 538	146 540	2 182	148 723	16 746	525	132 502	37 720	22 316	22 478	19 636	8 565	5 284
1997	206 054	157 536	2 191	159 727	17 842	595	142 480	40 740	22 835	23 560	20 448	8 746	5 475
1998	223 844	171 306	2 411	173 716	18 724	689	155 681	44 601	23 562	25 100	21 698	8 918	5 663
1999	239 693	186 425	2 798	189 223	20 083	791	169 932	44 939	24 822	26 356	22 713	9 094	5 815
2000	264 024	206 838	1 994	208 831	21 824	857	187 864	49 481	26 680	28 490	24 436	9 267	6 013
2001	279 678	218 558	2 523	221 082	22 884	922	199 120	51 284	29 275	29 639	25 689	9 436	6 057
2002	283 369	222 241	1 936	224 177	23 660	938	201 455	49 707	32 207	29 553	26 259	9 588	6 048
2003	289 429	227 030	2 103	229 133	24 548	958	205 543	50 093	33 793	29 793	26 733	9 715	6 075
2004	309 467	244 199	2 860	247 059	26 455	1 024	221 627	52 411	35 429	31 416	28 255	9 850	6 221
2005	329 271	262 082	2 781	264 862	28 870	1 090	237 082	54 161	38 028	32 898	29 289	10 009	6 422

. . . = Not available.

Table 21-2. Personal Income and Employment by Region and State—Continued

(Millions of dollars, except as noted.)

Region or state and year	Personal income, total	Earnings by place of work			Less: Contributions for government social insurance	Plus: Adjustment for residence	Equals: Net earnings by place of residence	Plus: Dividends, interest, and rent	Plus: Personal current transfer receipts	Per capita (dollars)		Population (thousands)	Total employment (thousands)
		Nonfarm	Farm	Total						Personal income	Disposable personal income		
FAR WEST													
1958	50 973	40 455	1 819	42 274	1 584	-1	40 689	7 209	3 076	2 490	2 229	20 469	. . .
1959	55 671	44 813	1 917	46 730	1 984	-1	44 745	7 777	3 148	2 631	2 349	21 159	. . .
1960	58 816	47 258	1 953	49 211	2 356	-2	46 854	8 449	3 513	2 716	2 400	21 659	. . .
1961	62 206	49 873	1 852	51 725	2 494	-2	49 229	8 928	4 049	2 780	2 460	22 378	. . .
1962	67 177	54 264	1 961	56 225	2 976	-4	53 245	9 682	4 250	2 906	2 569	23 114	. . .
1963	71 416	58 004	1 897	59 900	3 458	-6	56 436	10 340	4 640	2 999	2 649	23 811	. . .
1964	77 190	62 426	2 004	64 430	3 580	-7	60 843	11 355	4 992	3 165	2 844	24 389	. . .
1965	82 647	66 529	1 995	68 524	3 730	-8	64 786	12 387	5 474	3 318	2 982	24 908	. . .
1966	90 151	73 538	2 243	75 781	4 925	-10	70 846	13 309	5 996	3 562	3 180	25 311	. . .
1967	97 258	78 966	2 113	81 078	5 443	-11	75 624	14 264	7 370	3 773	3 357	25 779	. . .
1968	106 969	87 154	2 375	89 529	6 111	-14	83 404	15 068	8 496	4 090	3 600	26 151	. . .
1969	117 424	95 215	2 474	97 689	6 630	-201	90 858	16 873	9 693	4 409	3 844	26 635	12 295
1970	126 801	100 771	2 433	103 204	6 899	-205	96 099	18 736	11 966	4 679	4 150	27 101	12 313
1971	135 230	106 438	2 464	108 902	7 521	-222	101 159	20 230	13 842	4 905	4 400	27 570	12 301
1972	148 290	117 467	3 108	120 575	8 736	-228	111 611	21 709	14 970	5 312	4 687	27 918	12 742
1973	164 806	130 648	4 247	134 895	11 068	-231	123 596	24 360	16 850	5 818	5 173	28 328	13 405
1974	185 296	145 021	5 388	150 410	12 611	-328	137 471	27 894	19 931	6 434	5 701	28 801	13 865
1975	206 409	160 150	4 808	164 958	13 666	-524	150 768	30 591	25 051	7 034	6 308	29 346	14 104
1976	231 301	182 055	4 812	186 867	15 736	-640	170 491	33 204	27 606	7 728	6 872	29 929	14 625
1977	257 728	204 392	4 682	209 074	17 871	-454	190 750	37 643	29 335	8 435	7 456	30 553	15 287
1978	294 707	235 270	4 753	240 023	21 055	-385	218 583	44 352	31 772	9 420	8 274	31 285	16 235
1979	336 728	267 888	5 905	273 793	25 059	-360	248 374	53 298	35 056	10 534	9 196	31 965	17 141
1980	382 747	297 087	7 361	304 449	27 313	-444	276 692	65 005	41 051	11 676	10 198	32 780	17 549
1981	428 897	326 903	5 851	332 754	32 478	-226	300 050	80 635	48 212	12 828	11 219	33 434	17 744
1982	457 237	344 431	5 928	350 359	34 820	-268	315 271	88 558	53 408	13 414	11 834	34 086	17 618
1983	493 057	371 570	5 962	377 532	38 277	-290	338 966	96 777	57 314	14 202	12 585	34 716	18 044
1984	547 683	414 770	6 608	421 378	43 906	-332	377 140	110 819	59 724	15 506	13 759	35 321	18 847
1985	591 310	449 866	6 376	456 241	48 033	-379	407 829	118 965	64 516	16 408	14 491	36 037	19 498
1986	629 862	482 039	7 279	489 318	52 540	-418	436 360	124 532	68 970	17 109	15 112	36 815	20 070
1987	674 798	522 159	8 505	530 664	57 052	-496	473 116	129 655	72 026	17 927	15 676	37 641	20 926
1988	731 443	570 428	9 031	579 459	64 283	-583	514 592	139 604	77 247	18 978	16 721	38 542	21 944
1989	793 435	610 569	8 951	619 521	69 234	-677	549 609	159 037	84 789	20 070	17 510	39 534	22 626
1990	859 336	660 218	9 468	669 686	74 869	-796	594 021	172 139	93 175	21 160	18 510	40 610	23 304
1991	887 101	679 618	8 488	688 106	78 666	-795	608 645	174 471	103 985	21 413	18 881	41 428	23 293
1992	938 010	718 181	9 322	727 503	82 509	-781	644 213	174 213	119 583	22 214	19 711	42 226	22 994
1993	962 172	734 935	10 767	745 702	84 623	-771	660 308	175 520	126 345	22 482	19 937	42 798	23 102
1994	999 736	758 458	10 047	768 505	88 214	-797	679 494	188 179	132 063	23 104	20 458	43 271	23 551
1995	1 051 231	793 565	9 699	803 264	91 451	-840	710 973	202 498	137 761	24 031	21 186	43 745	24 111
1996	1 115 366	837 819	11 205	849 024	95 077	-906	753 041	217 285	145 040	25 169	21 950	44 314	24 760
1997	1 186 310	897 418	11 612	909 031	100 854	-980	807 197	232 181	146 931	26 331	22 751	45 054	25 324
1998	1 286 611	978 248	11 199	989 447	108 453	-1 065	879 930	252 769	153 913	28 093	24 115	45 798	26 214
1999	1 371 257	1 060 709	11 848	1 072 557	116 590	-1 192	954 775	253 792	162 690	29 486	24 949	46 506	26 901
2000	1 502 717	1 173 138	10 869	1 184 007	127 447	-1 298	1 055 262	276 701	170 754	31 835	26 517	47 203	27 715
2001	1 547 366	1 199 117	9 667	1 208 784	132 156	-1 172	1 075 456	281 378	190 532	32 276	27 293	47 941	27 834
2002	1 570 773	1 221 754	10 372	1 232 126	136 110	-1 181	1 094 835	270 916	205 022	32 307	28 350	48 620	27 765
2003	1 620 831	1 269 392	12 106	1 281 497	147 723	-1 244	1 132 529	272 618	215 684	32 884	29 101	49 289	27 994
2004	1 733 330	1 358 049	13 260	1 371 310	160 588	-1 362	1 209 359	298 652	225 318	34 741	30 767	49 893	28 561
2005	1 825 479	1 443 467	13 125	1 456 592	170 599	-1 447	1 284 546	303 829	237 103	36 209	31 630	50 415	29 314

. . . = Not available.

Table 21-2. Personal Income and Employment by Region and State—Continued

(Millions of dollars, except as noted.)

Region or state and year	Personal income, total	Earnings by place of work			Less: Contributions for government social insurance	Plus: Adjustment for residence	Equals: Net earnings by place of residence	Plus: Dividends, interest, and rent	Plus: Personal current transfer receipts	Per capita (dollars)		Population (thousands)	Total employment (thousands)
		Nonfarm	Farm	Total						Personal income	Disposable personal income		
ALABAMA													
1958	4 595	3 670	304	3 974	135	1	3 839	412	344	1 453	1 331	3 163	. . .
1959	4 837	3 934	248	4 181	159	1	4 024	451	363	1 510	1 382	3 204	. . .
1960	5 042	4 091	255	4 346	187	2	4 161	496	385	1 540	1 404	3 274	. . .
1961	5 199	4 193	245	4 438	194	2	4 247	523	429	1 568	1 435	3 316	. . .
1962	5 465	4 425	224	4 649	219	4	4 434	564	468	1 645	1 494	3 323	. . .
1963	5 821	4 695	271	4 966	259	6	4 713	613	496	1 734	1 577	3 358	. . .
1964	6 327	5 159	245	5 404	265	8	5 146	668	513	1 864	1 705	3 395	. . .
1965	6 884	5 625	254	5 879	273	10	5 616	718	551	1 999	1 825	3 443	. . .
1966	7 384	6 157	241	6 398	376	15	6 038	747	599	2 132	1 929	3 464	. . .
1967	7 801	6 524	206	6 730	429	21	6 323	787	690	2 256	2 040	3 458	. . .
1968	8 526	7 103	227	7 330	472	24	6 882	843	801	2 474	2 221	3 446	. . .
1969	9 384	7 734	277	8 011	551	137	7 597	895	891	2 728	2 412	3 440	1 411
1970	10 202	8 284	247	8 531	590	136	8 076	1 029	1 097	2 957	2 657	3 450	1 413
1971	11 199	9 013	276	9 289	655	144	8 778	1 136	1 284	3 202	2 889	3 497	1 423
1972	12 466	10 050	345	10 395	765	171	9 801	1 234	1 431	3 521	3 152	3 540	1 471
1973	14 103	11 284	532	11 816	983	188	11 021	1 401	1 681	3 939	3 527	3 581	1 526
1974	15 715	12 656	335	12 991	1 136	198	12 053	1 651	2 010	4 332	3 874	3 628	1 552
1975	17 537	13 669	410	14 079	1 221	204	13 061	1 876	2 600	4 765	4 307	3 681	1 543
1976	19 851	15 672	475	16 148	1 421	218	14 944	2 068	2 839	5 312	4 773	3 737	1 594
1977	21 914	17 571	380	17 951	1 595	247	16 603	2 317	2 995	5 793	5 199	3 783	1 651
1978	24 773	19 942	504	20 447	1 840	270	18 877	2 634	3 262	6 461	5 782	3 834	1 714
1979	27 615	22 041	516	22 557	2 102	297	20 753	3 061	3 801	7 137	6 355	3 869	1 739
1980	30 564	23 944	205	24 149	2 281	328	22 196	3 908	4 460	7 836	6 966	3 900	1 736
1981	34 004	25 812	485	26 297	2 648	427	24 076	4 920	5 008	8 678	7 698	3 919	1 724
1982	35 988	26 702	407	27 110	2 787	448	24 771	5 681	5 536	9 168	8 216	3 925	1 692
1983	38 491	28 731	289	29 020	3 053	441	26 409	6 087	5 996	9 784	8 766	3 934	1 722
1984	42 692	31 793	476	32 270	3 428	493	29 335	7 020	6 337	10 803	9 731	3 952	1 787
1985	45 944	34 347	462	34 809	3 740	503	31 572	7 678	6 694	11 566	10 352	3 973	1 831
1986	48 553	36 390	453	36 843	3 937	525	33 432	8 158	6 963	12 164	10 889	3 992	1 868
1987	51 502	38 824	537	39 361	4 163	533	35 731	8 652	7 119	12 826	11 419	4 015	1 923
1988	55 120	41 549	800	42 349	4 651	529	38 228	9 467	7 426	13 698	12 287	4 024	1 982
1989	59 911	43 962	934	44 896	4 972	548	40 472	11 047	8 391	14 865	13 266	4 030	2 019
1990	63 679	46 896	820	47 716	5 317	525	42 924	11 528	9 227	15 723	14 047	4 050	2 061
1991	67 250	49 183	1 097	50 280	5 674	555	45 161	11 899	10 191	16 406	14 714	4 099	2 073
1992	71 977	52 870	990	53 860	6 061	610	48 408	11 974	11 595	17 327	15 578	4 154	2 110
1993	74 863	55 245	1 001	56 246	6 437	659	50 468	12 097	12 298	17 764	15 941	4 214	2 172
1994	79 265	58 052	1 055	59 107	6 899	751	52 958	13 285	13 021	18 606	16 637	4 260	2 193
1995	83 534	60 851	798	61 649	7 276	827	55 200	14 302	14 033	19 441	17 344	4 297	2 256
1996	86 972	63 130	918	64 048	7 512	837	57 374	14 810	14 788	20 081	17 842	4 331	2 290
1997	91 419	65 943	998	66 940	7 863	938	60 015	15 979	15 425	20 930	18 528	4 368	2 335
1998	97 012	69 795	1 095	70 890	8 212	1 049	63 728	17 454	15 830	22 025	19 500	4 405	2 385
1999	100 662	73 138	1 307	74 445	8 569	1 116	66 992	17 154	16 517	22 722	20 095	4 430	2 405
2000	105 807	76 023	955	76 977	8 783	1 238	69 433	18 725	17 648	23 764	21 046	4 452	2 416
2001	110 421	79 205	1 242	80 448	9 146	1 252	72 554	18 739	19 129	24 717	21 994	4 467	2 393
2002	113 835	82 501	860	83 361	9 456	1 272	75 177	18 073	20 585	25 409	22 929	4 480	2 387
2003	118 585	85 886	1 250	87 136	9 668	1 333	78 801	18 033	21 750	26 341	23 983	4 502	2 397
2004	126 955	91 312	1 463	92 775	10 103	1 383	84 056	19 686	23 213	28 054	25 632	4 525	2 453
2005	135 018	97 349	1 382	98 731	10 888	1 455	89 298	20 629	25 090	29 623	26 851	4 558	2 511

. . . = Not available.

Table 21-2. Personal Income and Employment by Region and State—Continued

(Millions of dollars, except as noted.)

Region or state and year	Personal income, total	Earnings by place of work			Less: Contributions for government social insurance	Plus: Adjustment for residence	Equals: Net earnings by place of residence	Plus: Dividends, interest, and rent	Plus: Personal current transfer receipts	Per capita (dollars)		Population (thousands)	Total employment (thousands)
		Nonfarm	Farm	Total						Personal income	Disposable personal income		
ALASKA													
1958	559	533	2	535	22	0	513	25	21	2 494	. . .	224	. . .
1959	592	566	1	567	24	0	544	27	21	2 645	. . .	224	. . .
1960	701	673	2	675	28	-2	646	33	22	3 062	2 703	229	. . .
1961	698	664	2	666	28	-3	635	36	27	2 931	2 611	238	. . .
1962	731	697	1	698	29	-5	665	40	26	2 970	2 622	246	. . .
1963	790	758	1	758	33	-8	717	45	27	3 086	2 714	256	. . .
1964	890	855	1	856	37	-13	806	55	29	3 385	3 047	263	. . .
1965	963	926	1	927	41	-18	869	63	31	3 554	3 149	271	. . .
1966	1 034	995	1	997	48	-23	926	74	34	3 814	3 392	271	. . .
1967	1 133	1 095	1	1 096	53	-30	1 012	82	39	4 075	3 620	278	. . .
1968	1 231	1 199	2	1 201	67	-38	1 096	87	48	4 319	3 822	285	. . .
1969	1 412	1 377	1	1 378	94	-26	1 258	100	54	4 769	4 071	296	144
1970	1 602	1 564	2	1 566	105	-47	1 414	116	72	5 263	4 573	304	149
1971	1 772	1 729	2	1 730	118	-61	1 551	130	91	5 600	4 901	316	153
1972	1 945	1 904	2	1 905	134	-76	1 695	146	103	5 956	5 141	326	158
1973	2 274	2 113	2	2 115	165	-94	1 856	171	247	6 823	5 978	333	167
1974	2 809	2 839	2	2 841	241	-210	2 391	210	209	8 148	6 964	345	189
1975	3 963	4 479	4	4 482	407	-614	3 462	264	237	10 683	9 055	371	227
1976	4 767	5 631	4	5 635	526	-885	4 224	309	233	12 125	10 279	393	243
1977	4 929	5 213	5	5 218	463	-454	4 301	350	278	12 405	10 554	397	237
1978	5 028	5 078	5	5 083	434	-326	4 324	406	299	12 501	10 819	402	237
1979	5 334	5 318	3	5 321	467	-289	4 565	477	293	13 219	11 291	404	241
1980	6 025	5 962	3	5 965	527	-329	5 109	573	343	14 866	12 947	405	244
1981	6 934	6 965	2	6 967	666	-473	5 827	701	406	16 569	14 127	418	253
1982	8 335	8 057	3	8 060	775	-565	6 720	891	724	18 538	16 050	450	278
1983	9 365	8 985	2	8 987	851	-623	7 513	1 061	791	19 174	16 869	488	298
1984	10 019	9 678	2	9 680	947	-639	8 094	1 243	682	19 503	17 375	514	310
1985	10 821	10 137	2	10 139	969	-632	8 539	1 396	886	20 321	18 184	532	318
1986	10 780	9 835	7	9 841	918	-571	8 353	1 431	996	19 807	17 938	544	311
1987	10 440	9 294	9	9 303	859	-533	7 911	1 490	1 038	19 357	17 373	539	312
1988	10 789	9 583	11	9 594	930	-556	8 108	1 564	1 117	19 907	17 972	542	318
1989	11 834	10 444	5	10 449	1 027	-618	8 804	1 793	1 237	21 628	19 231	547	330
1990	12 617	11 042	8	11 050	1 097	-654	9 299	1 950	1 369	22 804	20 147	553	341
1991	13 207	11 579	8	11 588	1 164	-700	9 724	2 020	1 463	23 161	20 666	570	349
1992	14 004	12 222	8	12 230	1 228	-734	10 268	2 109	1 627	23 786	21 320	589	353
1993	14 709	12 689	11	12 699	1 305	-753	10 641	2 253	1 814	24 538	22 023	599	361
1994	15 113	12 874	12	12 886	1 357	-771	10 759	2 499	1 855	25 050	22 402	603	366
1995	15 415	12 990	13	13 003	1 366	-778	10 859	2 624	1 932	25 504	22 822	604	367
1996	15 704	13 041	14	13 055	1 365	-793	10 897	2 728	2 079	25 805	23 003	609	371
1997	16 402	13 389	16	13 405	1 400	-783	11 222	2 928	2 252	26 759	23 765	613	377
1998	17 085	13 884	17	13 900	1 448	-834	11 619	3 015	2 451	27 560	24 401	620	383
1999	17 557	14 132	20	14 152	1 464	-832	11 856	2 970	2 730	28 100	24 932	625	384
2000	18 741	14 859	15	14 874	1 527	-887	12 461	3 191	3 090	29 867	26 426	628	395
2001	20 050	16 202	16	16 218	1 629	-937	13 652	3 148	3 249	31 711	28 155	632	402
2002	20 722	17 037	17	17 053	1 703	-1 000	14 350	3 022	3 351	32 343	29 162	641	411
2003	21 134	17 692	15	17 707	1 821	-1 009	14 876	2 966	3 291	32 588	29 635	649	411
2004	22 207	18 952	15	18 968	1 932	-1 065	15 971	3 032	3 204	33 761	30 898	658	427
2005	23 515	20 132	14	20 146	2 085	-1 129	16 931	3 158	3 426	35 433	32 151	664	437

. . . = Not available.

Table 21-2. Personal Income and Employment by Region and State—Continued

(Millions of dollars, except as noted.)

Region or state and year	Personal income, total	Derivation of personal income									Per capita (dollars)		Population (thousands)	Total employment (thousands)
		Earnings by place of work			Less: Contributions for government social insurance	Plus: Adjustment for residence	Equals: Net earnings by place of residence	Plus: Dividends, interest, and rent	Plus: Personal current transfer receipts		Personal income	Disposable personal income		
		Nonfarm	Farm	Total										
ARIZONA														
1958	2 258	1 771	130	1 901	79	-2	1 820	303	135		1 893	1 710	1 193	. . .
1959	2 496	1 975	124	2 099	95	-2	2 001	342	153		1 979	1 776	1 261	. . .
1960	2 728	2 165	127	2 293	117	-2	2 173	389	166		2 065	1 843	1 321	. . .
1961	2 970	2 329	134	2 462	125	-2	2 335	440	194		2 111	1 895	1 407	. . .
1962	3 198	2 527	136	2 664	139	-2	2 523	463	212		2 174	1 943	1 471	. . .
1963	3 358	2 680	111	2 790	162	0	2 628	499	231		2 208	1 974	1 521	. . .
1964	3 600	2 853	129	2 981	167	*	2 814	536	250		2 314	2 105	1 556	. . .
1965	3 816	3 008	127	3 134	174	1	2 961	572	282		2 409	2 191	1 584	. . .
1966	4 161	3 369	120	3 489	232	0	3 257	600	305		2 578	2 333	1 614	. . .
1967	4 524	3 620	148	3 767	265	0	3 502	644	377		2 748	2 473	1 646	. . .
1968	5 188	4 101	191	4 292	312	2	3 982	770	435		3 084	2 754	1 682	. . .
1969	6 039	4 715	203	4 918	322	-26	4 570	977	492		3 477	3 053	1 737	711
1970	6 884	5 320	180	5 499	362	-29	5 108	1 183	593		3 835	3 385	1 795	747
1971	7 855	6 070	201	6 270	430	-28	5 812	1 333	711		4 143	3 701	1 896	786
1972	9 010	7 060	205	7 265	525	-32	6 708	1 485	817		4 485	3 965	2 009	850
1973	10 450	8 237	239	8 476	695	-31	7 750	1 715	984		4 917	4 396	2 125	925
1974	11 814	9 076	384	9 460	791	-41	8 628	1 996	1 189		5 311	4 721	2 224	955
1975	12 679	9 474	217	9 691	816	-47	8 828	2 190	1 661		5 545	5 045	2 286	935
1976	14 254	10 665	329	10 994	916	-47	10 031	2 399	1 825		6 071	5 487	2 348	976
1977	16 080	12 261	266	12 527	1 061	-56	11 409	2 746	1 924		6 625	5 945	2 427	1 048
1978	18 974	14 559	317	14 876	1 292	-69	13 515	3 289	2 171		7 536	6 705	2 518	1 149
1979	22 475	17 302	398	17 700	1 606	-71	16 023	3 981	2 471		8 518	7 530	2 639	1 241
1980	26 073	19 463	476	19 939	1 810	-80	18 049	5 055	2 969		9 524	8 458	2 738	1 285
1981	29 889	21 780	414	22 194	2 178	-14	20 003	6 396	3 490		10 636	9 365	2 810	1 317
1982	31 598	22 582	397	22 979	2 300	-6	20 672	7 032	3 893		10 934	9 668	2 890	1 320
1983	34 656	24 757	327	25 083	2 581	4	22 506	7 886	4 263		11 673	10 413	2 969	1 383
1984	39 524	28 362	527	28 890	3 019	8	25 878	9 075	4 571		12 886	11 526	3 067	1 511
1985	43 833	31 695	492	32 187	3 436	21	28 772	10 101	4 961		13 769	12 250	3 184	1 632
1986	47 730	34 645	472	35 117	3 825	41	31 332	10 956	5 442		14 427	12 851	3 308	1 712
1987	51 506	37 301	636	37 937	4 093	68	33 912	11 648	5 946		14 985	13 324	3 437	1 777
1988	55 246	40 178	763	40 942	4 571	110	36 480	12 244	6 522		15 627	13 971	3 535	1 847
1989	59 413	41 787	690	42 477	4 863	168	37 781	14 075	7 557		16 403	14 598	3 622	1 880
1990	62 649	44 065	653	44 718	5 151	228	39 795	14 485	8 369		17 005	15 131	3 684	1 910
1991	65 390	46 059	729	46 787	5 487	224	41 524	14 561	9 304		17 260	15 379	3 789	1 918
1992	69 609	49 518	673	50 190	5 855	250	44 586	14 323	10 700		17 777	15 906	3 916	1 940
1993	74 370	53 127	796	53 923	6 325	268	47 866	14 923	11 580		18 293	16 325	4 065	2 026
1994	81 555	58 376	585	58 961	7 003	281	52 239	16 941	12 375		19 212	17 103	4 245	2 158
1995	88 333	63 463	833	64 296	7 298	302	57 300	17 890	13 143		19 929	17 717	4 432	2 275
1996	95 514	69 410	752	70 162	8 213	331	62 279	19 267	13 968		20 823	18 306	4 587	2 406
1997	103 557	75 371	745	76 116	8 833	365	67 648	21 308	14 601		21 861	19 157	4 737	2 515
1998	113 370	83 272	871	84 143	9 576	410	74 977	23 290	15 103		23 216	20 250	4 883	2 631
1999	120 857	90 179	926	91 105	10 295	469	81 279	23 414	16 165		24 057	20 966	5 024	2 722
2000	132 558	99 949	684	100 633	11 159	522	89 997	25 454	17 107		25 660	22 326	5 166	2 819
2001	138 854	104 250	836	105 085	11 709	564	93 940	25 454	19 460		26 219	22 951	5 296	2 857
2002	144 150	107 778	1 074	108 852	12 093	550	97 309	25 188	21 653		26 507	23 772	5 438	2 877
2003	150 847	112 932	781	113 712	12 415	567	101 863	25 637	23 346		27 044	24 435	5 578	2 953
2004	164 413	123 386	905	124 291	13 431	618	111 477	27 689	25 246		28 644	25 836	5 740	3 070
2005	179 114	136 214	918	137 132	14 953	644	122 823	28 560	27 731		30 157	26 899	5 939	3 236

. . . = Not available.
* = Less than $50,000, but the estimates for this item are included in the total.

Table 21-2. Personal Income and Employment by Region and State—Continued

(Millions of dollars, except as noted.)

Region or state and year	Personal income, total	Derivation of personal income								Per capita (dollars)		Population (thousands)	Total employment (thousands)
		Earnings by place of work			Less: Contributions for government social insurance	Plus: Adjustment for residence	Equals: Net earnings by place of residence	Plus: Dividends, interest, and rent	Plus: Personal current transfer receipts	Personal income	Disposable personal income		
		Nonfarm	Farm	Total									
ARKANSAS													
1958	2 254	1 606	283	1 889	66	-1	1 823	222	209	1 306	1 209	1 726	. . .
1959	2 476	1 727	364	2 091	79	-1	2 011	240	225	1 410	1 302	1 756	. . .
1960	2 503	1 785	310	2 095	92	-2	2 001	262	240	1 399	1 289	1 789	. . .
1961	2 715	1 894	365	2 258	95	-2	2 161	286	269	1 504	1 387	1 806	. . .
1962	2 893	2 082	320	2 402	109	-3	2 290	315	288	1 561	1 424	1 853	. . .
1963	3 073	2 228	318	2 546	126	-4	2 415	348	310	1 639	1 496	1 875	. . .
1964	3 338	2 416	356	2 772	137	-5	2 631	381	326	1 760	1 629	1 897	. . .
1965	3 525	2 598	283	2 881	147	-6	2 728	440	357	1 861	1 714	1 894	. . .
1966	3 920	2 849	388	3 238	191	-5	3 042	487	391	2 064	1 880	1 899	. . .
1967	4 158	3 097	297	3 394	221	-5	3 168	523	468	2 188	1 992	1 901	. . .
1968	4 512	3 413	334	3 747	251	-7	3 488	499	525	2 372	2 137	1 902	. . .
1969	4 978	3 744	342	4 086	279	30	3 837	557	584	2 602	2 320	1 913	800
1970	5 458	3 997	411	4 408	297	20	4 131	643	683	2 828	2 535	1 930	805
1971	6 072	4 470	404	4 874	341	19	4 552	719	801	3 079	2 795	1 972	831
1972	6 854	5 090	477	5 567	406	18	5 178	783	893	3 396	3 070	2 018	867
1973	8 167	5 770	909	6 679	526	14	6 166	918	1 083	3 967	3 575	2 058	902
1974	9 156	6 492	827	7 319	610	7	6 716	1 125	1 315	4 359	3 899	2 100	927
1975	10 066	6 943	789	7 733	640	6	7 099	1 298	1 669	4 664	4 250	2 158	905
1976	11 175	8 051	636	8 687	746	-4	7 938	1 415	1 823	5 153	4 636	2 169	941
1977	12 481	9 058	721	9 778	849	-8	8 921	1 625	1 935	5 655	5 104	2 207	981
1978	14 489	10 332	1 171	11 503	990	-14	10 499	1 863	2 127	6 466	5 834	2 241	1 022
1979	15 924	11 480	988	12 469	1 137	-15	11 317	2 168	2 439	7 018	6 284	2 269	1 033
1980	17 221	12 474	363	12 837	1 227	-3	11 607	2 726	2 888	7 524	6 704	2 289	1 035
1981	19 545	13 435	845	14 280	1 430	-22	12 828	3 446	3 270	8 523	7 605	2 293	1 030
1982	20 511	13 892	638	14 530	1 506	-18	13 006	3 949	3 556	8 940	7 927	2 294	1 014
1983	21 884	15 108	412	15 520	1 642	-48	13 830	4 205	3 849	9 491	8 520	2 306	1 043
1984	24 523	16 870	876	17 746	1 873	-68	15 806	4 682	4 035	10 571	9 564	2 320	1 084
1985	26 203	17 956	858	18 815	2 010	-72	16 733	5 197	4 273	11 260	10 163	2 327	1 104
1986	27 307	18 898	798	19 696	2 153	-94	17 449	5 356	4 502	11 710	10 593	2 332	1 116
1987	28 308	19 854	931	20 785	2 262	-112	18 411	5 264	4 634	12 085	10 882	2 342	1 143
1988	30 223	21 094	1 343	22 436	2 517	-146	19 774	5 587	4 862	12 901	11 639	2 343	1 177
1989	32 334	22 306	1 229	23 535	2 686	-146	20 703	6 261	5 371	13 781	12 395	2 346	1 197
1990	34 076	23 763	1 013	24 776	2 875	-210	21 692	6 572	5 813	14 460	12 987	2 357	1 211
1991	36 043	25 233	1 102	26 334	3 074	-236	23 024	6 611	6 408	15 124	13 625	2 383	1 238
1992	39 162	27 465	1 393	28 859	3 347	-259	25 252	6 771	7 139	16 209	14 621	2 416	1 263
1993	40 822	28 886	1 315	30 201	3 564	-289	26 348	6 946	7 528	16 619	14 977	2 456	1 309
1994	43 272	30 657	1 452	32 108	3 859	-312	27 937	7 420	7 915	17 350	15 563	2 494	1 337
1995	45 829	32 388	1 496	33 883	4 070	-282	29 531	7 802	8 497	18 076	16 170	2 535	1 391
1996	48 679	33 700	1 910	35 610	4 223	-273	31 114	8 536	9 028	18 926	16 920	2 572	1 414
1997	50 955	35 253	1 887	37 140	4 427	-272	32 441	9 102	9 411	19 590	17 424	2 601	1 435
1998	53 810	37 573	1 615	39 188	4 659	-275	34 254	9 853	9 703	20 489	18 146	2 626	1 462
1999	56 052	39 646	1 813	41 459	4 884	-301	36 274	9 738	10 040	21 137	18 749	2 652	1 482
2000	58 726	41 852	1 218	43 070	5 065	-346	37 659	10 411	10 656	21 925	19 375	2 679	1 504
2001	61 967	43 936	1 313	45 249	5 296	-350	39 604	10 558	11 805	23 023	20 444	2 692	1 499
2002	63 234	45 600	527	46 127	5 455	-381	40 292	10 184	12 758	23 363	21 029	2 707	1 497
2003	66 463	47 301	1 917	49 217	5 698	-376	43 142	9 981	13 340	24 380	22 189	2 726	1 500
2004	70 903	50 535	2 089	52 624	5 995	-405	46 224	10 409	14 270	25 783	23 508	2 750	1 526
2005	74 040	53 538	1 055	54 593	6 379	-417	47 797	10 899	15 343	26 641	24 072	2 779	1 557

. . . = Not available.

Table 21-2. Personal Income and Employment by Region and State—Continued

(Millions of dollars, except as noted.)

Region or state and year	Personal income, total	Derivation of personal income								Per capita (dollars)		Population (thousands)	Total employment (thousands)
		Earnings by place of work			Less: Contributions for government social insurance	Plus: Adjustment for residence	Equals: Net earnings by place of residence	Plus: Dividends, interest, and rent	Plus: Personal current transfer receipts	Personal income	Disposable personal income		
		Nonfarm	Farm	Total									
CALIFORNIA													
1958	38 676	30 512	1 335	31 847	1 112	-4	30 731	5 721	2 223	2 599	2 312	14 880	. . .
1959	42 432	34 008	1 413	35 421	1 423	-5	33 992	6 167	2 273	2 743	2 432	15 467	. . .
1960	44 846	35 878	1 430	37 308	1 719	-6	35 583	6 679	2 584	2 826	2 497	15 870	. . .
1961	47 529	37 964	1 361	39 325	1 830	-6	37 488	7 042	2 999	2 881	2 549	16 497	. . .
1962	51 304	41 321	1 425	42 746	2 247	-7	40 492	7 633	3 179	3 005	2 655	17 072	. . .
1963	54 800	44 377	1 357	45 734	2 623	-7	43 104	8 179	3 517	3 102	2 740	17 668	. . .
1964	59 452	47 837	1 508	49 345	2 729	-8	46 608	9 031	3 812	3 275	2 945	18 151	. . .
1965	63 434	50 792	1 456	52 248	2 845	-10	49 393	9 829	4 213	3 413	3 069	18 585	. . .
1966	68 937	55 942	1 574	57 516	3 739	-12	53 765	10 519	4 653	3 656	3 268	18 858	. . .
1967	74 287	59 941	1 489	61 430	4 094	-14	57 323	11 210	5 755	3 874	3 450	19 176	. . .
1968	81 475	65 966	1 716	67 682	4 579	-16	63 087	11 744	6 643	4 201	3 699	19 394	. . .
1969	89 273	71 819	1 701	73 521	4 830	-132	68 559	13 099	7 616	4 529	3 958	19 711	9 033
1970	96 313	75 965	1 705	77 670	5 020	-116	72 534	14 479	9 300	4 810	4 275	20 023	9 057
1971	102 428	80 044	1 704	81 749	5 452	-126	76 170	15 564	10 694	5 034	4 526	20 346	9 036
1972	112 265	88 387	2 170	90 557	6 337	-129	84 090	16 654	11 520	5 454	4 815	20 585	9 369
1973	124 037	97 808	2 928	100 737	7 979	-116	92 642	18 638	12 757	5 944	5 298	20 868	9 844
1974	138 721	107 848	3 645	111 493	9 020	-131	102 342	21 263	15 116	6 552	5 819	21 173	10 163
1975	153 525	117 689	3 272	120 961	9 606	-21	111 333	23 200	18 992	7 129	6 411	21 537	10 287
1976	171 635	132 990	3 478	136 468	10 984	82	125 566	25 082	20 987	7 825	6 972	21 935	10 633
1977	191 542	149 938	3 545	153 483	12 566	-70	140 847	28 417	22 278	8 570	7 589	22 350	11 119
1978	218 788	172 547	3 490	176 037	14 800	-80	161 157	33 545	24 086	9 580	8 429	22 839	11 803
1979	250 061	196 345	4 575	200 920	17 658	-57	183 205	40 390	26 465	10 753	9 406	23 255	12 462
1980	284 455	218 407	5 591	223 999	19 245	-90	204 664	49 064	30 727	11 951	10 443	23 801	12 777
1981	319 962	241 392	4 357	245 749	23 075	248	222 921	60 883	36 159	13 175	11 537	24 286	12 969
1982	341 593	255 578	4 604	260 182	24 980	253	235 455	66 508	39 630	13 763	12 136	24 820	12 899
1983	369 132	277 336	4 235	281 571	27 658	261	254 174	72 635	42 324	14 556	12 871	25 360	13 219
1984	413 355	312 504	4 913	317 417	32 083	235	285 569	83 619	44 168	15 994	14 147	25 844	13 852
1985	448 335	340 854	4 952	345 807	35 345	182	310 644	89 931	47 760	16 956	14 918	26 441	14 359
1986	478 832	366 896	5 389	372 285	38 927	123	333 481	94 051	51 300	17 668	15 548	27 102	14 787
1987	515 252	399 627	6 612	406 238	42 578	40	363 700	98 032	53 520	18 549	16 142	27 777	15 394
1988	557 867	435 774	6 967	442 741	47 865	-3	394 873	105 733	57 261	19 599	17 202	28 464	16 133
1989	601 456	463 473	6 809	470 282	51 198	-20	419 064	119 685	62 706	20 585	17 899	29 218	16 550
1990	648 263	497 550	7 230	504 780	55 042	-79	449 660	129 702	68 901	21 638	18 871	29 960	16 965
1991	662 728	507 383	6 210	513 593	57 255	-69	456 269	129 807	76 651	21 750	19 154	30 471	16 870
1992	696 670	531 743	6 799	538 541	59 325	-71	479 146	128 895	88 629	22 492	19 957	30 975	16 510
1993	707 906	538 682	7 800	546 482	60 172	-3	486 306	128 042	93 558	22 635	20 067	31 275	16 484
1994	730 529	552 103	7 583	559 686	62 187	12	497 510	135 370	97 650	23 203	20 544	31 484	16 659
1995	765 806	576 839	7 281	584 120	64 041	-3	520 075	145 317	100 414	24 161	21 263	31 697	17 059
1996	810 448	607 170	8 183	615 354	66 134	-13	549 206	155 712	105 530	25 312	22 011	32 019	17 466
1997	860 545	650 342	8 753	659 095	70 388	-110	588 597	166 048	105 900	26 490	22 793	32 486	17 787
1998	936 009	711 197	8 260	719 456	75 771	-120	643 565	181 283	111 160	28 374	24 258	32 988	18 504
1999	999 228	772 928	9 163	782 091	82 306	-183	699 602	182 484	117 142	29 828	25 087	33 499	19 024
2000	1 103 842	866 034	8 089	874 122	91 271	-351	782 500	199 052	122 290	32 463	26 716	34 003	19 626
2001	1 135 304	883 356	7 168	890 523	95 774	-354	794 395	204 379	136 531	32 882	27 510	34 527	19 716
2002	1 147 716	896 771	7 778	904 549	98 694	-303	805 552	195 208	146 955	32 803	28 616	34 988	19 660
2003	1 184 455	931 629	8 957	940 586	106 614	-299	833 673	195 345	155 436	33 406	29 392	35 457	19 782
2004	1 264 422	996 163	9 939	1 006 101	116 447	-307	889 347	211 611	163 464	35 278	31 050	35 842	20 100
2005	1 332 919	1 056 331	9 864	1 066 194	123 354	-257	942 583	218 939	171 397	36 890	32 010	36 132	20 558

. . . = Not available.

Table 21-2. Personal Income and Employment by Region and State—Continued

(Millions of dollars, except as noted.)

Region or state and year	Personal income, total	Earnings by place of work			Less: Contributions for government social insurance	Plus: Adjustment for residence	Equals: Net earnings by place of residence	Plus: Dividends, interest, and rent	Plus: Personal current transfer receipts	Per capita (dollars)		Population (thousands)	Total employment (thousands)
		Nonfarm	Farm	Total						Personal income	Disposable personal income		
COLORADO													
1958	3 583	2 756	177	2 932	95	1	2 839	524	220	2 149	1 917	1 667	. . .
1959	3 857	2 992	156	3 148	109	1	3 040	558	259	2 256	2 016	1 710	. . .
1960	4 130	3 226	171	3 397	133	1	3 266	589	275	2 335	2 058	1 769	. . .
1961	4 446	3 492	172	3 665	150	1	3 516	629	302	2 411	2 126	1 844	. . .
1962	4 680	3 686	153	3 839	163	1	3 676	685	319	2 465	2 176	1 899	. . .
1963	4 899	3 885	137	4 022	191	0	3 832	728	339	2 530	2 235	1 936	. . .
1964	5 186	4 129	135	4 264	197	*	4 066	776	343	2 632	2 374	1 970	. . .
1965	5 541	4 323	210	4 534	197	0	4 336	830	375	2 791	2 513	1 985	. . .
1966	5 960	4 735	188	4 924	263	-1	4 660	893	407	2 970	2 655	2 007	. . .
1967	6 431	5 089	184	5 272	294	-1	4 977	970	483	3 132	2 789	2 053	. . .
1968	7 147	5 658	242	5 900	333	-2	5 565	1 033	549	3 371	2 969	2 120	. . .
1969	7 967	6 340	249	6 589	388	2	6 204	1 158	605	3 678	3 191	2 166	1 001
1970	9 003	7 073	287	7 361	427	2	6 935	1 337	730	4 048	3 558	2 224	1 032
1971	10 164	8 031	300	8 331	499	3	7 835	1 478	850	4 412	3 902	2 304	1 072
1972	11 509	9 226	331	9 557	606	4	8 956	1 611	943	4 786	4 174	2 405	1 149
1973	13 217	10 612	438	11 051	797	3	10 256	1 853	1 108	5 296	4 640	2 496	1 243
1974	14 861	11 793	533	12 326	905	4	11 426	2 152	1 284	5 848	5 101	2 541	1 276
1975	16 379	12 907	462	13 369	966	8	12 411	2 357	1 611	6 333	5 602	2 586	1 285
1976	18 137	14 577	334	14 911	1 104	9	13 816	2 562	1 759	6 890	6 066	2 632	1 340
1977	20 343	16 562	263	16 825	1 260	12	15 578	2 900	1 865	7 546	6 598	2 696	1 411
1978	23 488	19 364	205	19 569	1 505	20	18 085	3 373	2 031	8 490	7 400	2 767	1 505
1979	27 101	22 430	213	22 643	1 837	20	20 827	3 992	2 282	9 512	8 242	2 849	1 594
1980	31 259	25 394	285	25 679	2 101	28	23 606	5 007	2 646	10 746	9 320	2 909	1 654
1981	36 126	29 007	302	29 309	2 592	6	26 723	6 295	3 108	12 131	10 462	2 978	1 722
1982	39 663	31 705	181	31 886	2 901	3	28 988	7 153	3 523	12 955	11 156	3 062	1 765
1983	42 631	33 698	356	34 055	3 128	0	30 926	7 807	3 898	13 604	12 016	3 134	1 794
1984	46 846	37 094	421	37 516	3 537	8	33 986	8 752	4 108	14 778	13 111	3 170	1 856
1985	49 537	39 247	391	39 639	3 833	17	35 823	9 414	4 300	15 438	13 661	3 209	1 926
1986	51 108	40 374	393	40 768	4 039	23	36 751	9 742	4 614	15 786	14 010	3 237	1 925
1987	53 063	41 724	475	42 199	4 136	35	38 098	9 992	4 974	16 275	14 392	3 260	1 915
1988	55 884	44 002	576	44 578	4 510	50	40 119	10 531	5 234	17 130	15 185	3 262	1 981
1989	60 652	46 648	615	47 263	4 834	66	42 495	12 314	5 844	18 515	16 307	3 276	2 017
1990	64 748	49 807	912	50 719	5 235	91	45 576	12 915	6 256	19 575	17 201	3 308	2 054
1991	68 283	52 974	630	53 604	5 731	103	47 976	13 357	6 950	20 160	17 740	3 387	2 101
1992	73 794	57 765	669	58 434	6 212	117	52 339	13 665	7 791	21 109	18 569	3 496	2 149
1993	79 697	62 827	812	63 639	6 819	130	56 949	14 405	8 344	22 054	19 345	3 614	2 249
1994	85 671	67 176	566	67 742	7 376	147	60 513	16 341	8 817	23 004	20 120	3 724	2 362
1995	92 704	72 272	535	72 807	7 887	169	65 088	17 858	9 758	24 226	21 175	3 827	2 441
1996	100 233	78 009	671	78 680	8 425	187	70 442	19 492	10 299	25 570	22 174	3 920	2 537
1997	107 873	84 641	685	85 326	9 109	207	76 424	21 010	10 439	26 846	23 068	4 018	2 647
1998	118 493	93 252	787	94 039	9 537	233	84 736	23 100	10 657	28 784	24 565	4 117	2 751
1999	128 860	103 383	934	104 318	10 435	262	94 145	23 323	11 392	30 492	25 948	4 226	2 840
2000	144 394	117 038	567	117 605	11 567	290	106 328	25 955	12 111	33 371	28 236	4 327	2 950
2001	152 700	123 456	768	124 224	12 146	336	112 414	26 990	13 296	34 493	29 586	4 427	2 969
2002	153 066	124 150	541	124 692	12 556	346	112 482	25 626	14 958	34 027	29 950	4 498	2 941
2003	154 887	125 728	639	126 367	12 663	356	114 059	25 229	15 598	34 056	30 329	4 548	2 934
2004	164 586	134 596	737	135 332	13 642	380	122 071	26 337	16 179	35 766	31 945	4 602	2 987
2005	174 754	143 367	795	144 162	14 869	404	129 697	27 680	17 376	37 459	33 124	4 665	3 071

. . . = Not available.
* = Less than $50,000, but the estimates for this item are included in the total.

Table 21-2. Personal Income and Employment by Region and State—Continued

(Millions of dollars, except as noted.)

Region or state and year	Personal income, total	Derivation of personal income								Per capita (dollars)		Population (thou-sands)	Total employ-ment (thou-sands)
		Earnings by place of work			Less: Contribu-tions for govern-ment social insurance	Plus: Adjust-ment for residence	Equals: Net earnings by place of residence	Plus: Dividends, interest, and rent	Plus: Personal current transfer receipts	Personal income	Disposable personal income		
		Nonfarm	Farm	Total									
CONNECTICUT													
1958	6 396	5 121	67	5 188	184	-2	5 003	1 003	390	2 615	2 302	2 446	. . .
1959	6 839	5 552	58	5 610	230	-2	5 378	1 084	376	2 711	2 381	2 523	. . .
1960	7 117	5 787	63	5 849	278	3	5 575	1 154	389	2 798	2 437	2 544	. . .
1961	7 524	6 049	58	6 106	290	3	5 819	1 257	448	2 910	2 543	2 586	. . .
1962	8 042	6 479	59	6 538	320	3	6 221	1 381	441	3 038	2 652	2 647	. . .
1963	8 485	6 825	63	6 888	369	4	6 523	1 493	469	3 111	2 701	2 727	. . .
1964	9 112	7 299	61	7 360	379	5	6 985	1 632	495	3 257	2 883	2 798	. . .
1965	9 791	7 815	71	7 885	395	2	7 492	1 776	523	3 427	3 013	2 857	. . .
1966	10 753	8 747	73	8 820	553	0	8 267	1 923	564	3 704	3 230	2 903	. . .
1967	11 791	9 464	57	9 521	602	2	8 921	2 168	701	4 017	3 474	2 935	. . .
1968	12 576	10 196	67	10 264	671	7	9 600	2 122	854	4 243	3 604	2 964	. . .
1969	14 502	11 126	66	11 193	752	728	11 169	2 385	947	4 834	4 081	3 000	1 417
1970	15 432	11 725	71	11 796	783	722	11 735	2 552	1 146	5 078	4 405	3 039	1 414
1971	16 222	12 144	69	12 213	840	746	12 119	2 679	1 423	5 299	4 669	3 061	1 388
1972	17 478	13 231	68	13 299	968	785	13 115	2 857	1 505	5 694	4 943	3 070	1 416
1973	19 119	14 722	80	14 802	1 234	808	14 376	3 114	1 629	6 230	5 448	3 069	1 480
1974	20 906	15 985	83	16 068	1 395	841	15 514	3 474	1 918	6 797	5 942	3 076	1 511
1975	22 386	16 629	75	16 704	1 423	916	16 197	3 643	2 546	7 257	6 437	3 085	1 468
1976	24 327	18 206	82	18 289	1 577	1 011	17 723	3 895	2 708	7 883	6 908	3 086	1 493
1977	26 849	20 256	83	20 339	1 778	1 121	19 682	4 336	2 832	8 693	7 620	3 089	1 546
1978	29 896	22 830	80	22 910	2 062	1 273	22 121	4 855	2 920	9 660	8 383	3 095	1 616
1979	33 675	25 755	79	25 833	2 421	1 449	24 861	5 564	3 250	10 863	9 353	3 100	1 675
1980	38 470	28 754	83	28 837	2 682	1 695	27 850	6 884	3 737	12 357	10 587	3 113	1 709
1981	43 267	31 541	82	31 622	3 157	1 878	30 343	8 611	4 313	13 828	11 797	3 129	1 732
1982	46 731	33 642	108	33 750	3 431	2 035	32 354	9 582	4 796	14 887	12 683	3 139	1 731
1983	49 978	36 347	105	36 452	3 735	2 156	34 873	9 925	5 180	15 804	13 807	3 162	1 749
1984	55 880	40 799	129	40 928	4 304	2 309	38 932	11 532	5 416	17 572	15 437	3 180	1 831
1985	59 962	44 509	127	44 636	4 740	2 448	42 343	11 875	5 743	18 731	16 308	3 201	1 890
1986	64 552	48 289	140	48 429	5 210	2 609	45 827	12 650	6 075	20 024	17 335	3 224	1 948
1987	70 599	53 653	142	53 795	5 699	2 736	50 832	13 487	6 279	21 741	18 642	3 247	1 997
1988	77 821	59 457	156	59 613	6 394	2 923	56 142	14 902	6 777	23 784	20 660	3 272	2 053
1989	84 330	62 593	139	62 732	6 705	2 815	58 842	17 888	7 600	25 684	22 327	3 283	2 047
1990	87 251	64 508	182	64 689	6 927	2 780	60 542	18 214	8 495	26 504	23 121	3 292	2 018
1991	87 567	64 814	162	64 975	7 123	2 745	60 597	17 496	9 474	26 512	23 128	3 303	1 937
1992	93 615	68 000	187	68 187	7 344	3 958	64 801	17 646	11 168	28 362	24 471	3 301	1 917
1993	95 882	70 520	211	70 731	7 609	3 375	66 497	17 760	11 625	28 975	24 859	3 309	1 938
1994	98 467	72 709	187	72 896	7 970	3 139	68 065	18 343	12 059	29 693	25 468	3 316	1 920
1995	103 199	75 954	173	76 128	8 349	3 901	71 680	18 686	12 834	31 045	26 418	3 324	1 958
1996	108 189	79 217	162	79 379	8 695	4 689	75 373	19 607	13 210	32 424	27 105	3 337	1 989
1997	115 134	85 414	157	85 571	9 240	4 219	80 549	20 963	13 622	34 375	28 349	3 349	2 015
1998	123 918	91 518	182	91 699	9 733	5 609	87 575	22 535	13 807	36 822	30 068	3 365	2 043
1999	129 807	97 457	201	97 658	10 205	5 450	92 903	22 759	14 145	38 332	31 148	3 386	2 076
2000	141 570	106 464	191	106 655	10 785	5 678	101 549	25 164	14 858	41 489	33 383	3 412	2 114
2001	147 356	111 502	184	111 686	11 106	5 035	105 615	25 979	15 762	42 930	34 618	3 432	2 124
2002	146 997	112 370	169	112 540	11 641	4 379	105 277	24 790	16 930	42 505	35 801	3 458	2 118
2003	148 975	114 703	163	114 866	11 890	4 303	107 279	24 292	17 404	42 737	36 399	3 486	2 113
2004	158 896	122 213	182	122 395	12 326	4 826	114 895	25 605	18 395	45 412	38 650	3 499	2 140
2005	166 807	128 509	180	128 689	12 805	5 121	121 005	26 664	19 139	47 519	39 727	3 510	2 173

. . . = Not available.

Table 21-2. Personal Income and Employment by Region and State—Continued

(Millions of dollars, except as noted.)

Region or state and year	Personal income, total	Earnings by place of work			Less: Contributions for government social insurance	Plus: Adjustment for residence	Equals: Net earnings by place of residence	Plus: Dividends, interest, and rent	Plus: Personal current transfer receipts	Per capita (dollars)		Population (thousands)	Total employment (thousands)
		Nonfarm	Farm	Total						Personal income	Disposable personal income		
DELAWARE													
1958	1 156	917	35	952	32	-49	871	234	52	2 671	2 248	433	...
1959	1 207	974	30	1 004	42	-50	912	243	52	2 738	2 288	441	...
1960	1 264	1 023	34	1 057	53	-51	953	257	54	2 816	2 356	449	...
1961	1 300	1 049	29	1 079	51	-51	976	259	65	2 821	2 375	461	...
1962	1 377	1 114	32	1 147	58	-52	1 037	273	67	2 936	2 440	469	...
1963	1 475	1 209	26	1 234	69	-56	1 109	296	70	3 053	2 560	483	...
1964	1 598	1 308	26	1 333	68	-58	1 207	317	74	3 215	2 702	497	...
1965	1 762	1 444	35	1 478	69	-65	1 345	338	80	3 475	2 917	507	...
1966	1 860	1 584	26	1 609	99	-69	1 441	330	88	3 604	3 039	516	...
1967	1 983	1 683	32	1 715	117	-69	1 530	345	108	3 777	3 199	525	...
1968	2 173	1 848	29	1 878	119	-71	1 688	358	127	4 070	3 424	534	...
1969	2 382	1 992	55	2 047	139	-43	1 865	378	139	4 411	3 642	540	271
1970	2 530	2 132	35	2 167	147	-48	1 971	394	165	4 597	3 822	550	275
1971	2 765	2 349	38	2 387	168	-60	2 159	411	194	4 891	4 107	565	280
1972	3 040	2 606	49	2 655	196	-68	2 391	434	215	5 298	4 436	574	293
1973	3 392	2 928	96	3 023	253	-97	2 674	471	248	5 858	4 899	579	305
1974	3 695	3 171	82	3 253	282	-108	2 863	528	303	6 336	5 322	583	302
1975	3 969	3 340	91	3 432	293	-110	3 029	532	408	6 742	5 746	589	292
1976	4 355	3 693	84	3 776	325	-121	3 331	586	438	7 347	6 177	593	296
1977	4 696	3 989	56	4 045	352	-133	3 560	659	477	7 895	6 647	595	296
1978	5 155	4 431	60	4 492	402	-162	3 928	728	499	8 617	7 258	598	304
1979	5 677	4 876	54	4 929	460	-184	4 285	819	572	9 480	7 917	599	312
1980	6 394	5 412	12	5 424	512	-230	4 682	1 018	694	10 748	8 970	595	312
1981	7 051	5 814	42	5 856	592	-249	5 015	1 255	781	11 831	9 799	596	314
1982	7 593	6 231	65	6 296	648	-270	5 378	1 386	829	12 673	10 645	599	317
1983	8 172	6 723	78	6 801	704	-316	5 781	1 507	884	13 498	11 500	605	326
1984	9 046	7 399	96	7 495	780	-356	6 359	1 739	948	14 792	12 692	612	341
1985	9 884	8 096	104	8 200	865	-397	6 938	1 950	997	15 987	13 735	618	359
1986	10 484	8 526	143	8 669	926	-398	7 345	2 061	1 078	16 706	14 318	628	372
1987	11 293	9 338	114	9 452	1 007	-454	7 992	2 178	1 124	17 730	15 263	637	389
1988	12 308	10 204	181	10 386	1 144	-498	8 744	2 326	1 238	19 006	16 443	648	405
1989	13 655	11 136	192	11 327	1 255	-607	9 465	2 848	1 342	20 743	17 911	658	417
1990	14 343	11 826	139	11 966	1 333	-678	9 954	2 948	1 442	21 422	18 474	670	423
1991	15 089	12 312	130	12 442	1 406	-688	10 348	3 110	1 631	22 090	19 224	683	417
1992	15 754	13 178	114	13 292	1 448	-996	10 848	3 091	1 815	22 670	19 768	695	416
1993	16 224	13 504	109	13 613	1 510	-944	11 159	3 123	1 942	22 967	19 973	706	423
1994	16 884	14 216	120	14 337	1 611	-1 106	11 619	3 202	2 063	23 530	20 343	718	427
1995	17 811	14 687	87	14 774	1 701	-930	12 143	3 402	2 265	24 407	21 105	730	445
1996	19 063	15 455	120	15 575	1 790	-952	12 833	3 724	2 506	25 727	22 071	741	456
1997	19 895	16 449	95	16 544	1 895	-1 228	13 421	3 926	2 548	26 475	22 427	751	468
1998	21 565	17 776	140	17 916	1 983	-1 410	14 523	4 356	2 687	28 252	23 933	763	485
1999	22 416	19 089	139	19 228	2 131	-1 690	15 407	4 200	2 809	28 925	24 518	775	497
2000	24 277	20 358	122	20 480	2 233	-1 733	16 514	4 705	3 058	30 869	26 278	786	508
2001	25 537	21 620	184	21 804	2 370	-1 833	17 601	4 600	3 337	32 105	27 267	795	505
2002	26 530	22 457	139	22 595	2 439	-1 899	18 257	4 659	3 613	32 925	28 771	806	503
2003	27 496	23 344	206	23 550	2 477	-1 985	19 089	4 561	3 845	33 620	29 693	818	506
2004	29 454	24 849	227	25 077	2 608	-2 062	20 407	4 948	4 099	35 484	31 327	830	519
2005	31 281	26 526	307	26 833	2 807	-2 254	21 771	5 075	4 435	37 084	32 356	844	528

. . . = Not available.

Table 21-2. Personal Income and Employment by Region and State—Continued

(Millions of dollars, except as noted.)

Region or state and year	Personal income, total	Earnings by place of work			Less: Contributions for government social insurance	Plus: Adjustment for residence	Equals: Net earnings by place of residence	Plus: Dividends, interest, and rent	Plus: Personal current transfer receipts	Per capita (dollars)		Population (thousands)	Total employment (thousands)
		Nonfarm	Farm	Total						Personal income	Disposable personal income		
DISTRICT OF COLUMBIA													
1958	2 057	2 751	0	2 751	79	-1 049	1 623	327	106	2 717	2 360	757	. . .
1959	2 123	2 902	0	2 902	89	-1 139	1 673	340	109	2 789	2 383	761	. . .
1960	2 147	3 088	0	3 088	101	-1 321	1 666	369	112	2 806	2 384	765	. . .
1961	2 265	3 281	0	3 281	107	-1 410	1 765	376	123	2 911	2 513	778	. . .
1962	2 445	3 536	0	3 536	114	-1 496	1 926	393	127	3 103	2 668	788	. . .
1963	2 601	3 805	0	3 805	138	-1 612	2 055	411	135	3 259	2 828	798	. . .
1964	2 765	4 086	0	4 086	135	-1 749	2 202	423	140	3 465	3 055	798	. . .
1965	2 995	4 443	0	4 443	140	-1 903	2 399	446	150	3 758	3 335	797	. . .
1966	3 126	4 792	0	4 792	186	-2 090	2 516	449	160	3 952	3 467	791	. . .
1967	3 349	5 418	0	5 418	213	-2 498	2 706	450	192	4 234	3 739	791	. . .
1968	3 524	5 840	0	5 840	234	-2 767	2 839	456	230	4 530	3 991	778	. . .
1969	3 423	6 168	0	6 168	252	-3 208	2 708	481	234	4 492	3 842	762	678
1970	3 755	6 720	0	6 720	274	-3 512	2 934	519	302	4 973	4 276	755	674
1971	4 129	7 309	0	7 309	299	-3 828	3 182	572	375	5 500	4 791	751	669
1972	4 482	7 918	0	7 918	343	-4 161	3 414	622	447	6 027	5 218	744	671
1973	4 748	8 441	0	8 441	414	-4 449	3 578	658	512	6 472	5 588	734	664
1974	5 228	9 285	0	9 285	472	-4 910	3 904	729	595	7 254	6 290	721	676
1975	5 709	10 269	0	10 269	521	-5 523	4 225	744	741	8 038	7 007	710	680
1976	6 080	11 186	0	11 186	573	-6 095	4 518	794	768	8 732	7 494	696	677
1977	6 577	12 269	0	12 269	609	-6 741	4 919	871	787	9 647	8 371	682	683
1978	6 949	13 370	0	13 370	668	-7 527	5 175	965	810	10 371	8 904	670	696
1979	7 366	14 631	0	14 631	770	-8 486	5 375	1 088	903	11 236	9 512	656	709
1980	7 845	16 125	0	16 125	859	-9 728	5 538	1 283	1 025	12 291	10 450	638	707
1981	8 610	17 541	0	17 541	1 002	-10 675	5 864	1 614	1 133	13 519	11 349	637	696
1982	9 352	18 647	0	18 647	1 074	-11 326	6 247	1 838	1 267	14 747	12 452	634	681
1983	9 796	19 582	0	19 582	1 292	-11 702	6 588	1 883	1 325	15 490	13 204	632	676
1984	10 829	21 323	0	21 323	1 463	-12 630	7 231	2 185	1 414	17 098	14 596	633	699
1985	11 516	22 794	0	22 794	1 678	-13 423	7 693	2 408	1 415	18 148	15 475	635	713
1986	12 135	24 283	0	24 283	1 845	-14 271	8 166	2 500	1 469	19 013	16 245	638	733
1987	12 829	26 112	0	26 112	2 015	-15 322	8 775	2 540	1 514	20 141	17 067	637	746
1988	14 042	28 785	0	28 785	2 312	-16 846	9 626	2 789	1 626	22 273	19 061	630	769
1989	15 063	30 522	0	30 522	2 550	-17 953	10 019	3 418	1 626	24 133	20 667	624	777
1990	16 025	32 860	0	32 860	2 813	-19 150	10 897	3 393	1 734	26 473	22 858	605	788
1991	16 564	34 558	0	34 558	2 987	-20 356	11 215	3 371	1 978	27 567	24 027	601	774
1992	17 279	36 614	0	36 614	3 172	-21 744	11 698	3 395	2 186	28 916	25 315	598	768
1993	17 857	38 062	0	38 062	3 319	-22 634	12 110	3 354	2 394	29 996	26 358	595	767
1994	18 169	38 961	0	38 961	3 470	-23 190	12 301	3 432	2 437	30 835	26 876	589	747
1995	18 151	39 471	0	39 471	3 530	-23 538	12 403	3 374	2 373	31 266	27 245	581	740
1996	18 766	39 820	0	39 820	3 567	-23 410	12 843	3 343	2 580	32 786	28 275	572	721
1997	19 580	41 000	0	41 000	3 676	-24 077	13 247	3 757	2 575	34 488	29 380	568	717
1998	20 562	42 956	0	42 956	3 907	-25 176	13 873	3 980	2 709	36 379	30 608	565	721
1999	21 115	46 459	0	46 459	4 268	-27 665	14 527	3 862	2 726	37 030	30 716	570	735
2000	23 102	48 999	0	48 999	4 493	-28 346	16 160	4 124	2 818	40 456	33 408	571	757
2001	25 525	52 256	0	52 256	4 921	-28 871	18 465	4 094	2 966	44 834	37 671	569	760
2002	25 786	55 075	0	55 075	5 258	-31 181	18 635	3 859	3 292	45 670	39 510	565	774
2003	27 169	57 444	0	57 444	5 370	-32 141	19 932	3 834	3 402	48 703	42 468	558	777
2004	29 278	62 123	0	62 123	5 722	-34 635	21 767	4 060	3 451	52 825	46 088	554	786
2005	31 010	65 371	0	65 371	6 039	-36 219	23 113	4 158	3 739	56 329	48 432	551	795

. . . = Not available.

Table 21-2. Personal Income and Employment by Region and State—Continued

(Millions of dollars, except as noted.)

Region or state and year	Personal income, total	Earnings by place of work			Less: Contributions for government social insurance	Plus: Adjustment for residence	Equals: Net earnings by place of residence	Plus: Dividends, interest, and rent	Plus: Personal current transfer receipts	Per capita (dollars)		Population (thousands)	Total employment (thousands)
		Nonfarm	Farm	Total						Personal income	Disposable personal income		
FLORIDA													
1958	8 710	6 449	368	6 817	216	-1	6 600	1 531	580	1 881	1 708	4 630	. . .
1959	9 626	7 144	441	7 586	282	-1	7 302	1 668	655	2 002	1 811	4 808	. . .
1960	10 088	7 507	379	7 886	329	-1	7 556	1 817	715	2 016	1 822	5 004	. . .
1961	10 666	7 784	437	8 222	343	-1	7 877	1 959	829	2 034	1 839	5 243	. . .
1962	11 524	8 412	451	8 863	389	-1	8 474	2 122	928	2 111	1 907	5 458	. . .
1963	12 368	9 071	433	9 504	449	-1	9 055	2 302	1 011	2 198	1 985	5 628	. . .
1964	13 571	10 000	490	10 490	481	-1	10 008	2 508	1 055	2 347	2 137	5 781	. . .
1965	14 854	10 948	463	11 411	516	-1	10 894	2 788	1 171	2 495	2 265	5 954	. . .
1966	16 344	12 175	473	12 648	679	-1	11 967	3 071	1 306	2 678	2 426	6 104	. . .
1967	18 129	13 376	512	13 889	808	-2	13 079	3 422	1 628	2 904	2 608	6 242	. . .
1968	20 850	15 267	526	15 793	963	-4	14 826	4 089	1 936	3 241	2 875	6 433	. . .
1969	24 265	17 587	636	18 224	1 132	-22	17 070	5 002	2 194	3 654	3 215	6 641	2 857
1970	27 412	19 648	546	20 194	1 272	-20	18 903	5 865	2 645	4 004	3 566	6 845	2 966
1971	30 744	21 806	640	22 446	1 472	-14	20 960	6 598	3 187	4 292	3 846	7 163	3 082
1972	35 396	25 330	739	26 068	1 796	-11	24 261	7 382	3 753	4 707	4 148	7 520	3 338
1973	41 436	29 862	837	30 699	2 420	-10	28 269	8 608	4 559	5 227	4 634	7 927	3 666
1974	46 570	32 988	908	33 897	2 780	-1	31 116	9 957	5 496	5 599	4 981	8 317	3 766
1975	50 491	34 395	1 000	35 395	2 859	-9	32 527	10 783	7 181	5 911	5 362	8 542	3 676
1976	55 378	37 742	1 037	38 779	3 168	10	35 621	11 798	7 959	6 369	5 738	8 695	3 730
1977	62 064	42 319	1 035	43 354	3 570	22	39 806	13 548	8 710	6 982	6 273	8 889	3 929
1978	71 641	49 021	1 236	50 256	4 245	25	46 037	15 921	9 683	7 845	7 000	9 132	4 235
1979	82 755	56 229	1 312	57 541	5 105	22	52 458	19 076	11 221	8 738	7 743	9 471	4 457
1980	97 741	64 498	1 671	66 169	5 915	16	60 270	24 129	13 341	9 933	8 764	9 840	4 695
1981	113 537	73 001	1 405	74 406	7 194	111	67 323	30 619	15 595	11 139	9 811	10 193	4 881
1982	122 669	77 823	1 784	79 608	7 902	134	71 839	33 177	17 653	11 715	10 236	10 471	4 970
1983	136 037	85 908	2 474	88 382	8 777	160	79 765	36 964	19 309	12 655	11 331	10 750	5 185
1984	152 157	97 483	1 835	99 318	10 141	210	89 387	42 201	20 568	13 782	12 455	11 040	5 529
1985	166 837	107 129	1 841	108 970	11 349	255	97 876	46 765	22 196	14 698	13 130	11 351	5 809
1986	180 125	116 036	1 977	118 013	12 556	312	105 768	50 446	23 910	15 438	13 740	11 668	6 055
1987	194 991	127 575	2 145	129 719	13 658	373	116 434	53 207	25 351	16 253	14 440	11 997	6 140
1988	213 834	140 308	2 705	143 013	15 504	450	127 959	58 106	27 768	17 376	15 504	12 306	6 443
1989	238 049	149 588	2 484	152 072	16 800	531	135 803	70 930	31 317	18 836	16 792	12 638	6 654
1990	254 984	160 352	2 079	162 431	17 966	637	145 102	75 602	34 280	19 564	17 525	13 033	6 800
1991	264 449	165 073	2 458	167 531	18 866	683	149 348	76 318	38 783	19 780	17 842	13 370	6 775
1992	278 700	176 786	2 461	179 247	20 071	748	159 925	71 444	47 331	20 417	18 411	13 651	6 820
1993	293 167	188 108	2 534	190 641	21 391	803	170 054	75 621	47 492	21 050	18 942	13 927	7 061
1994	308 508	197 779	2 163	199 942	22 925	865	177 882	80 344	50 282	21 666	19 450	14 239	7 294
1995	329 885	210 690	2 183	212 873	24 318	933	189 489	86 064	54 333	22 691	20 321	14 538	7 554
1996	351 355	224 299	1 931	226 229	25 622	1 005	201 612	92 335	57 407	23 655	20 962	14 853	7 804
1997	372 094	236 991	2 117	239 108	27 216	1 101	212 993	99 454	59 647	24 502	21 513	15 186	8 068
1998	402 454	257 448	2 512	259 960	29 239	1 224	231 945	109 355	61 154	25 987	22 728	15 487	8 368
1999	423 834	277 556	2 928	280 484	31 118	1 351	250 717	109 423	63 693	26 894	23 509	15 759	8 656
2000	457 539	301 755	1 750	303 505	33 266	1 514	271 753	117 914	67 872	28 509	24 810	16 049	8 933
2001	478 637	313 257	2 053	315 310	35 508	1 572	281 373	122 897	74 367	29 273	25 617	16 351	9 112
2002	495 489	326 733	1 970	328 703	37 126	1 543	293 120	121 968	80 401	29 709	26 584	16 678	9 205
2003	515 600	344 546	1 765	346 311	37 854	1 527	309 984	120 125	85 492	30 341	27 548	16 993	9 410
2004	566 372	372 004	1 686	373 690	40 830	1 585	334 445	137 080	94 847	32 577	29 413	17 385	9 737
2005	606 612	405 929	1 953	407 882	44 917	1 631	364 596	142 911	99 105	34 099	30 416	17 790	10 134

. . . = Not available.

Table 21-2. Personal Income and Employment by Region and State—Continued

(Millions of dollars, except as noted.)

Region or state and year	Personal income, total	Earnings by place of work			Less: Contributions for government social insurance	Plus: Adjustment for residence	Equals: Net earnings by place of residence	Plus: Dividends, interest, and rent	Plus: Personal current transfer receipts	Per capita (dollars)		Population (thousands)	Total employment (thousands)
		Nonfarm	Farm	Total						Personal income	Disposable personal income		
GEORGIA													
1958	5 974	4 845	359	5 204	186	-11	5 007	589	379	1 570	1 436	3 804	. . .
1959	6 378	5 261	310	5 571	224	-13	5 334	644	401	1 649	1 503	3 868	. . .
1960	6 670	5 485	323	5 808	261	-15	5 532	721	417	1 686	1 525	3 956	. . .
1961	6 954	5 641	343	5 985	266	-16	5 703	777	473	1 732	1 569	4 015	. . .
1962	7 475	6 150	309	6 459	297	-20	6 142	846	488	1 830	1 647	4 086	. . .
1963	8 123	6 655	395	7 051	349	-24	6 678	924	522	1 947	1 752	4 172	. . .
1964	8 808	7 316	330	7 647	376	-29	7 242	1 019	547	2 069	1 875	4 258	. . .
1965	9 713	8 051	374	8 425	407	-35	7 983	1 129	601	2 242	2 027	4 332	. . .
1966	10 695	9 023	385	9 408	545	-43	8 820	1 219	656	2 442	2 193	4 379	. . .
1967	11 625	9 829	383	10 212	624	-52	9 535	1 309	781	2 637	2 378	4 408	. . .
1968	12 873	11 011	341	11 352	682	-62	10 608	1 334	930	2 872	2 558	4 482	. . .
1969	14 317	12 274	416	12 690	786	-76	11 828	1 427	1 063	3 146	2 743	4 551	2 119
1970	15 556	13 140	394	13 535	836	-69	12 629	1 628	1 299	3 378	2 989	4 605	2 121
1971	17 197	14 398	453	14 851	951	-65	13 835	1 817	1 545	3 651	3 266	4 710	2 167
1972	19 340	16 305	467	16 772	1 127	-57	15 588	2 012	1 740	4 023	3 549	4 807	2 253
1973	21 988	18 369	783	19 153	1 444	-55	17 653	2 325	2 009	4 481	3 984	4 907	2 356
1974	24 235	20 004	666	20 670	1 626	-55	18 989	2 736	2 510	4 852	4 312	4 995	2 374
1975	26 088	20 923	633	21 555	1 679	-45	19 832	2 931	3 326	5 157	4 673	5 059	2 313
1976	29 155	23 887	625	24 513	1 945	-77	22 492	3 117	3 547	5 688	5 107	5 126	2 400
1977	32 319	27 068	360	27 428	2 188	-97	25 143	3 496	3 680	6 201	5 535	5 212	2 503
1978	36 742	30 792	562	31 354	2 550	-79	28 724	4 015	4 002	6 951	6 163	5 286	2 622
1979	41 292	34 539	592	35 130	2 972	-97	32 062	4 670	4 560	7 659	6 711	5 391	2 705
1980	46 192	38 226	34	38 260	3 309	-114	34 837	5 901	5 454	8 420	7 409	5 486	2 747
1981	52 395	42 185	517	42 702	3 929	-28	38 745	7 431	6 218	9 409	8 246	5 568	2 785
1982	56 834	45 089	679	45 767	4 283	-69	41 416	8 627	6 792	10 059	8 872	5 650	2 802
1983	62 289	49 717	471	50 188	4 794	-112	45 282	9 631	7 376	10 874	9 574	5 728	2 886
1984	71 237	56 949	950	57 899	5 610	-176	52 113	11 242	7 882	12 209	10 814	5 835	3 081
1985	78 332	63 162	781	63 943	6 359	-193	57 390	12 490	8 451	13 137	11 561	5 963	3 224
1986	85 000	69 039	822	69 860	7 115	-238	62 507	13 491	9 001	13 970	12 305	6 085	3 354
1987	91 395	74 555	891	75 446	7 642	-238	67 566	14 383	9 446	14 721	12 894	6 208	3 455
1988	99 402	80 830	1 151	81 981	8 534	-232	73 215	15 990	10 198	15 738	13 860	6 316	3 568
1989	107 069	85 130	1 349	86 479	9 075	-192	77 211	18 537	11 321	16 701	14 648	6 411	3 633
1990	114 643	90 735	1 257	91 991	9 719	-113	82 159	19 906	12 577	17 603	15 464	6 513	3 689
1991	120 222	93 943	1 552	95 495	10 196	-129	85 170	20 604	14 449	18 070	15 985	6 653	3 645
1992	130 041	102 108	1 638	103 746	10 930	-179	92 637	21 206	16 198	19 075	16 909	6 817	3 722
1993	137 607	108 791	1 480	110 271	11 683	-166	98 422	21 819	17 366	19 719	17 402	6 978	3 891
1994	148 234	116 226	1 947	118 173	12 644	-214	105 315	24 283	18 637	20 711	18 252	7 157	4 046
1995	158 858	125 131	1 784	126 914	13 582	-297	113 036	25 942	19 880	21 677	19 043	7 328	4 215
1996	172 113	134 974	1 881	136 855	14 509	-350	121 996	28 738	21 378	22 945	20 029	7 501	4 362
1997	182 868	144 033	1 861	145 894	15 538	-434	129 922	31 166	21 779	23 795	20 630	7 685	4 477
1998	198 782	157 534	1 823	159 357	16 845	-552	141 960	34 433	22 389	25 279	21 792	7 864	4 640
1999	212 081	171 018	1 994	173 012	18 195	-582	154 235	34 086	23 761	26 359	22 695	8 046	4 778
2000	230 356	185 385	1 650	187 035	19 367	-728	166 940	37 570	25 845	27 989	24 054	8 230	4 892
2001	240 616	192 105	1 985	194 091	20 178	-766	173 148	38 767	28 702	28 592	24 695	8 416	4 908
2002	244 957	195 576	1 470	197 046	20 587	-801	175 659	36 731	32 568	28 544	25 226	8 582	4 893
2003	251 612	201 084	2 018	203 102	20 179	-848	182 075	36 658	32 878	28 766	25 683	8 747	4 950
2004	265 199	213 960	1 885	215 845	22 236	-876	192 733	37 290	35 175	29 737	26 622	8 918	5 052
2005	282 979	227 555	1 937	229 492	23 517	-921	205 055	39 798	38 127	31 191	27 704	9 073	5 197

. . . = Not available.

Table 21-2. Personal Income and Employment by Region and State—Continued

(Millions of dollars, except as noted.)

Region or state and year	Personal income, total	Earnings by place of work			Less: Contributions for government social insurance	Plus: Adjustment for residence	Equals: Net earnings by place of residence	Plus: Dividends, interest, and rent	Plus: Personal current transfer receipts	Per capita (dollars)		Population (thousands)	Total employment (thousands)
		Nonfarm	Farm	Total						Personal income	Disposable personal income		
HAWAII													
1958	1 168	963	64	1 027	40	0	986	140	42	1 931	. . .	605	. . .
1959	1 306	1 077	73	1 151	45	0	1 106	155	46	2 100	. . .	622	. . .
1960	1 496	1 216	81	1 297	52	0	1 245	203	48	2 330	2 005	642	. . .
1961	1 619	1 316	75	1 391	57	0	1 334	227	59	2 457	2 112	659	. . .
1962	1 736	1 403	78	1 481	61	0	1 421	248	67	2 538	2 222	684	. . .
1963	1 850	1 505	87	1 592	76	0	1 516	264	70	2 712	2 377	682	. . .
1964	2 013	1 647	88	1 735	82	0	1 653	289	70	2 876	2 556	700	. . .
1965	2 205	1 795	91	1 885	85	0	1 800	323	81	3 132	2 796	704	. . .
1966	2 410	1 983	95	2 077	113	0	1 964	351	95	3 394	2 982	710	. . .
1967	2 620	2 145	98	2 243	130	0	2 112	387	121	3 623	3 176	723	. . .
1968	2 949	2 442	117	2 559	152	0	2 407	402	140	4 018	3 495	734	. . .
1969	3 375	2 826	119	2 946	183	0	2 763	452	160	4 543	3 893	743	416
1970	3 886	3 238	133	3 371	212	0	3 160	520	206	5 094	4 389	763	434
1971	4 225	3 476	131	3 607	236	0	3 371	585	270	5 338	4 677	792	437
1972	4 653	3 840	132	3 971	274	0	3 697	633	322	5 687	4 918	818	453
1973	5 172	4 297	139	4 436	349	0	4 087	715	370	6 143	5 328	842	473
1974	5 945	4 740	343	5 084	401	0	4 683	818	444	6 928	6 040	858	485
1975	6 483	5 252	203	5 454	443	0	5 011	895	577	7 409	6 613	875	499
1976	7 041	5 736	173	5 909	485	0	5 425	943	674	7 891	6 991	892	505
1977	7 650	6 244	185	6 428	523	0	5 905	1 038	707	8 353	7 368	916	509
1978	8 465	6 935	168	7 103	597	0	6 506	1 200	759	9 114	7 976	929	527
1979	9 602	7 838	194	8 032	701	0	7 331	1 432	839	10 107	8 818	950	556
1980	11 073	8 781	377	9 158	781	0	8 377	1 733	962	11 443	10 007	968	575
1981	12 015	9 482	200	9 682	901	0	8 781	2 102	1 132	12 283	10 748	978	569
1982	12 715	10 103	235	10 338	952	0	9 386	2 102	1 227	12 794	11 408	994	568
1983	14 087	10 863	339	11 202	1 040	0	10 162	2 576	1 349	13 910	12 412	1 013	579
1984	15 352	11 896	240	12 136	1 140	0	10 996	2 933	1 423	14 935	13 374	1 028	585
1985	16 311	12 744	222	12 966	1 242	0	11 724	3 078	1 509	15 688	13 990	1 040	602
1986	17 225	13 543	257	13 799	1 348	0	12 452	3 202	1 572	16 377	14 568	1 052	616
1987	18 386	14 669	241	14 910	1 474	0	13 436	3 324	1 627	17 217	15 106	1 068	647
1988	20 161	16 240	264	16 504	1 697	0	14 807	3 616	1 739	18 671	16 358	1 080	674
1989	22 462	17 930	246	18 176	1 892	0	16 283	4 251	1 927	20 521	17 789	1 095	702
1990	24 704	19 964	261	20 225	2 113	0	18 112	4 505	2 087	22 186	19 269	1 113	730
1991	26 026	21 069	230	21 299	2 278	0	19 021	4 702	2 304	22 895	19 769	1 137	751
1992	27 910	22 533	217	22 750	2 429	0	20 321	4 526	3 063	24 089	21 223	1 159	753
1993	28 799	23 125	213	23 339	2 471	0	20 868	5 002	2 929	24 555	21 655	1 173	749
1994	29 424	23 199	210	23 409	2 503	0	20 906	5 347	3 172	24 777	21 869	1 188	744
1995	29 926	23 202	200	23 402	2 484	0	20 918	5 444	3 564	25 004	22 190	1 197	740
1996	30 122	23 261	197	23 459	2 460	0	20 999	5 461	3 663	25 024	22 086	1 204	739
1997	31 002	23 747	208	23 956	2 462	0	21 493	5 834	3 675	25 587	22 565	1 212	740
1998	31 757	24 192	221	24 413	2 492	0	21 921	6 100	3 736	26 132	22 967	1 215	742
1999	32 646	24 881	252	25 133	2 561	0	22 572	6 191	3 882	26 973	23 651	1 210	742
2000	34 451	26 266	212	26 478	2 668	0	23 810	6 567	4 074	28 422	24 842	1 212	763
2001	35 126	26 745	215	26 960	2 786	0	24 174	6 596	4 357	28 748	25 127	1 222	767
2002	36 370	28 382	223	28 605	2 991	0	25 614	6 045	4 711	29 464	26 173	1 234	770
2003	37 803	30 187	217	30 404	3 257	0	27 147	5 782	4 874	30 286	27 085	1 248	787
2004	41 178	32 768	212	32 980	3 350	0	29 629	6 346	5 202	32 626	29 190	1 262	810
2005	43 953	35 091	222	35 312	3 604	0	31 708	6 643	5 602	34 468	30 487	1 275	835

. . . = Not available.

Table 21-2. Personal Income and Employment by Region and State—Continued

(Millions of dollars, except as noted.)

Region or state and year	Personal income, total	Derivation of personal income								Per capita (dollars)		Population (thousands)	Total employment (thousands)
		Earnings by place of work			Less: Contributions for government social insurance	Plus: Adjustment for residence	Equals: Net earnings by place of residence	Plus: Dividends, interest, and rent	Plus: Personal current transfer receipts	Personal income	Disposable personal income		
		Nonfarm	Farm	Total									
IDAHO													
1958	1 165	824	164	988	37	-3	948	139	78	1 804	1 627	646	...
1959	1 236	884	164	1 048	43	-3	1 002	149	85	1 881	1 693	657	...
1960	1 263	913	156	1 069	50	-3	1 016	156	90	1 882	1 683	671	...
1961	1 336	971	156	1 127	56	-3	1 068	166	102	1 954	1 760	684	...
1962	1 430	1 046	165	1 210	62	-3	1 145	179	106	2 067	1 866	692	...
1963	1 459	1 062	171	1 233	69	-2	1 162	188	109	2 137	1 920	683	...
1964	1 507	1 141	132	1 273	70	-2	1 201	194	112	2 215	2 017	680	...
1965	1 728	1 247	229	1 477	76	-2	1 399	209	120	2 519	2 296	686	...
1966	1 753	1 322	177	1 499	93	-1	1 405	219	129	2 544	2 308	689	...
1967	1 865	1 387	204	1 591	107	-1	1 484	226	155	2 711	2 450	688	...
1968	1 989	1 515	184	1 698	121	-1	1 576	239	174	2 862	2 573	695	...
1969	2 290	1 675	250	1 925	127	12	1 810	286	194	3 239	2 887	707	315
1970	2 525	1 828	264	2 092	137	14	1 969	328	229	3 520	3 165	717	324
1971	2 755	2 001	247	2 248	154	15	2 108	378	269	3 730	3 354	739	332
1972	3 144	2 279	317	2 596	183	16	2 429	409	306	4 119	3 727	763	347
1973	3 658	2 588	450	3 038	240	18	2 816	491	351	4 677	4 200	782	365
1974	4 316	2 963	625	3 588	282	22	3 328	567	421	5 341	4 758	808	381
1975	4 626	3 367	383	3 750	316	28	3 462	640	524	5 560	4 999	832	393
1976	5 218	3 917	339	4 256	370	35	3 922	705	591	6 088	5 466	857	419
1977	5 715	4 417	236	4 653	418	35	4 271	818	627	6 469	5 793	883	435
1978	6 595	5 124	304	5 427	487	42	4 982	944	669	7 240	6 465	911	460
1979	7 264	5 665	227	5 892	567	48	5 372	1 110	781	7 789	6 942	933	470
1980	8 198	6 040	402	6 442	605	61	5 899	1 365	934	8 648	7 719	948	466
1981	9 032	6 497	423	6 920	702	53	6 271	1 690	1 071	9 387	8 297	962	463
1982	9 368	6 479	391	6 869	718	62	6 214	1 925	1 229	9 621	8 590	974	453
1983	10 143	7 008	581	7 589	782	64	6 871	1 972	1 300	10 330	9 293	982	464
1984	10 973	7 715	496	8 211	874	77	7 414	2 212	1 346	11 074	10 002	991	474
1985	11 572	8 162	454	8 617	933	84	7 767	2 362	1 442	11 641	10 490	994	476
1986	11 833	8 305	475	8 780	961	100	7 919	2 392	1 521	11 949	10 827	990	476
1987	12 366	8 689	592	9 282	995	109	8 396	2 404	1 566	12 554	11 348	985	490
1988	13 300	9 437	670	10 106	1 127	124	9 104	2 515	1 682	13 493	12 172	986	512
1989	14 647	10 188	876	11 065	1 235	139	9 969	2 855	1 824	14 729	13 143	994	529
1990	15 918	11 099	990	12 089	1 358	152	10 884	3 067	1 968	15 724	13 988	1 012	552
1991	16 692	11 780	816	12 596	1 482	174	11 289	3 210	2 194	16 030	14 280	1 041	570
1992	18 318	13 082	858	13 940	1 613	191	12 518	3 340	2 460	17 093	15 135	1 072	590
1993	20 073	14 337	1 080	15 416	1 767	210	13 860	3 568	2 644	18 103	16 066	1 109	616
1994	21 422	15 629	761	16 390	1 951	238	14 676	3 957	2 789	18 707	16 593	1 145	651
1995	22 871	16 455	836	17 291	2 074	281	15 498	4 350	3 023	19 426	17 206	1 177	672
1996	24 360	17 184	947	18 131	2 134	326	16 323	4 718	3 319	20 248	17 898	1 203	694
1997	25 367	17 966	779	18 745	2 223	369	16 891	5 068	3 408	20 648	18 173	1 229	713
1998	27 287	19 127	959	20 086	2 337	437	18 185	5 544	3 557	21 789	19 192	1 252	740
1999	29 068	20 676	1 046	21 722	2 480	504	19 746	5 546	3 776	22 786	19 988	1 276	759
2000	31 290	22 587	867	23 453	2 676	524	21 302	5 909	4 079	24 075	20 959	1 300	788
2001	33 054	23 441	1 043	24 484	2 723	530	22 291	6 195	4 568	25 019	21 909	1 321	796
2002	33 849	24 131	953	25 085	2 801	544	22 827	6 051	4 971	25 185	22 703	1 344	802
2003	34 687	24 930	749	25 679	3 024	549	23 204	6 227	5 256	25 354	23 005	1 368	813
2004	38 090	26 910	1 179	28 088	3 223	577	25 443	7 036	5 611	27 302	24 809	1 395	837
2005	40 584	29 095	1 026	30 121	3 510	614	27 225	7 344	6 015	28 398	25 586	1 429	868

. . . = Not available.

Table 21-2. Personal Income and Employment by Region and State—Continued

(Millions of dollars, except as noted.)

Region or state and year	Personal income, total	Earnings by place of work Nonfarm	Farm	Total	Less: Contributions for government social insurance	Plus: Adjustment for residence	Equals: Net earnings by place of residence	Plus: Dividends, interest, and rent	Plus: Personal current transfer receipts	Per capita (dollars) Personal income	Disposable personal income	Population (thousands)	Total employment (thousands)
ILLINOIS													
1958	24 601	20 156	856	21 012	704	-111	20 198	3 052	1 350	2 488	2 208	9 886	. . .
1959	26 130	21 778	657	22 435	852	-127	21 456	3 267	1 407	2 617	2 321	9 986	. . .
1960	26 950	22 507	636	23 143	1 073	-133	21 937	3 540	1 472	2 672	2 352	10 086	. . .
1961	27 971	22 922	800	23 723	1 088	-138	22 496	3 775	1 699	2 761	2 439	10 130	. . .
1962	29 527	24 220	785	25 004	1 195	-154	23 655	4 108	1 763	2 872	2 528	10 280	. . .
1963	30 678	25 126	805	25 931	1 329	-159	24 443	4 419	1 815	2 949	2 602	10 402	. . .
1964	32 775	26 982	651	27 633	1 337	-175	26 122	4 806	1 847	3 098	2 772	10 580	. . .
1965	35 524	28 969	888	29 857	1 356	-194	28 307	5 237	1 981	3 322	2 965	10 693	. . .
1966	38 473	31 888	960	32 848	1 820	-222	30 806	5 523	2 145	3 551	3 142	10 836	. . .
1967	40 917	33 884	922	34 806	1 986	-239	32 581	5 781	2 555	3 738	3 295	10 947	. . .
1968	43 848	36 625	680	37 306	2 192	-265	34 849	6 006	2 993	3 988	3 476	10 995	. . .
1969	47 931	39 958	897	40 854	2 717	93	38 230	6 465	3 236	4 342	3 715	11 039	5 179
1970	50 835	42 176	706	42 882	2 811	18	40 089	6 909	3 837	4 570	3 930	11 125	5 144
1971	54 555	44 885	870	45 755	3 075	-23	42 657	7 307	4 592	4 868	4 253	11 206	5 105
1972	59 248	48 794	980	49 774	3 518	-42	46 214	7 865	5 169	5 263	4 538	11 258	5 156
1973	66 374	54 070	1 822	55 892	4 491	-59	51 342	8 884	6 149	5 895	5 119	11 260	5 351
1974	72 753	59 101	1 649	60 750	5 079	-71	55 600	10 143	7 010	6 453	5 580	11 274	5 442
1975	79 270	62 185	2 439	64 625	5 196	-96	59 332	10 952	8 986	7 011	6 150	11 306	5 342
1976	86 597	69 306	1 693	70 999	5 882	-76	65 040	11 641	9 916	7 623	6 623	11 360	5 458
1977	95 420	76 897	1 695	78 592	6 516	-10	72 066	12 982	10 372	8 366	7 250	11 406	5 587
1978	105 497	85 870	1 482	87 352	7 467	78	79 963	14 494	11 039	9 226	7 972	11 434	5 748
1979	115 966	93 950	1 809	95 759	8 483	163	87 439	16 503	12 024	10 152	8 709	11 423	5 811
1980	125 838	99 447	350	99 797	8 955	262	91 104	20 148	14 585	11 005	9 464	11 435	5 688
1981	139 569	106 465	1 497	107 962	10 275	198	97 885	24 927	16 758	12 196	10 471	11 443	5 684
1982	147 604	109 368	899	110 267	10 717	126	99 676	29 528	18 401	12 921	11 284	11 423	5 583
1983	153 546	114 125	-498	113 627	11 259	90	102 458	31 385	19 703	13 459	11 829	11 409	5 542
1984	169 736	126 062	1 202	127 264	12 809	-15	114 440	35 223	20 073	14 873	13 150	11 412	5 746
1985	178 529	133 155	1 697	134 852	13 762	-83	121 007	36 571	20 951	15 661	13 801	11 400	5 814
1986	187 025	141 045	1 404	142 449	14 767	-142	127 540	37 776	21 710	16 424	14 487	11 387	5 927
1987	197 603	151 176	1 415	152 591	15 637	-230	136 723	38 717	22 163	17 347	15 145	11 391	6 072
1988	212 011	164 930	838	165 768	17 418	-361	147 989	41 099	22 923	18 613	16 346	11 390	6 232
1989	225 574	173 261	2 143	175 404	18 470	-376	156 558	44 657	24 358	19 770	17 247	11 410	6 342
1990	238 499	183 093	1 722	184 815	19 637	-281	164 897	47 026	26 576	20 824	18 168	11 453	6 440
1991	245 434	188 369	928	189 298	20 599	-294	168 405	48 337	28 693	21 215	18 634	11 569	6 416
1992	263 702	201 612	1 882	203 494	21 736	-337	181 421	49 557	32 724	22 550	19 905	11 694	6 397
1993	271 174	209 580	1 641	211 222	22 937	-497	187 788	49 132	34 254	22 962	20 164	11 810	6 487
1994	285 537	219 921	2 095	222 015	24 452	-515	197 048	53 003	35 486	23 969	20 964	11 913	6 658
1995	301 688	232 445	556	233 001	25 762	-778	206 461	57 378	37 849	25 123	21 920	12 008	6 822
1996	320 081	243 715	2 345	246 061	26 827	-831	218 403	61 828	39 850	26 449	22 924	12 102	6 925
1997	337 897	258 356	2 167	260 523	28 338	-874	231 312	65 874	40 712	27 729	23 849	12 186	7 029
1998	360 095	276 720	1 487	278 207	30 089	-853	247 265	71 525	41 305	29 343	25 103	12 272	7 185
1999	373 385	293 094	935	294 029	31 536	-1 049	261 445	69 859	42 081	30 212	25 763	12 359	7 282
2000	400 373	311 686	1 338	313 024	33 038	-1 343	278 642	76 913	44 818	32 185	27 412	12 440	7 416
2001	407 254	317 043	1 129	318 172	33 984	-1 505	282 683	76 281	48 290	32 532	27 866	12 519	7 371
2002	413 711	324 017	408	324 425	34 496	-1 457	288 472	73 143	52 096	32 869	28 821	12 587	7 284
2003	427 427	337 471	1 457	338 928	34 903	-1 389	302 635	70 081	54 710	33 789	30 069	12 650	7 261
2004	442 519	349 097	2 985	352 082	37 159	-1 477	313 446	72 808	56 265	34 811	31 033	12 712	7 316
2005	462 857	366 334	907	367 241	40 353	-1 511	325 377	76 071	61 409	36 264	31 973	12 763	7 425

. . . = Not available.

Table 21-2. Personal Income and Employment by Region and State—Continued

(Millions of dollars, except as noted.)

Region or state and year	Personal income, total	Derivation of personal income								Per capita (dollars)		Population (thousands)	Total employment (thousands)
		Earnings by place of work			Less: Contributions for government social insurance	Plus: Adjustment for residence	Equals: Net earnings by place of residence	Plus: Dividends, interest, and rent	Plus: Personal current transfer receipts	Personal income	Disposable personal income		
		Nonfarm	Farm	Total									
INDIANA													
1958	9 197	7 480	420	7 900	295	35	7 640	986	570	2 007	1 816	4 583	. . .
1959	9 790	8 186	294	8 479	356	41	8 164	1 055	571	2 122	1 908	4 613	. . .
1960	10 286	8 534	359	8 893	415	40	8 518	1 164	604	2 201	1 964	4 674	. . .
1961	10 590	8 584	455	9 039	411	43	8 671	1 227	692	2 239	2 010	4 730	. . .
1962	11 343	9 289	444	9 733	461	48	9 320	1 326	697	2 395	2 137	4 736	. . .
1963	11 909	9 775	460	10 236	526	48	9 757	1 428	724	2 482	2 201	4 799	. . .
1964	12 684	10 603	293	10 896	545	46	10 397	1 538	749	2 612	2 341	4 856	. . .
1965	14 029	11 559	544	12 103	581	49	11 571	1 653	806	2 850	2 551	4 922	. . .
1966	15 137	12 807	470	13 277	818	55	12 515	1 756	866	3 028	2 684	4 999	. . .
1967	15 860	13 426	423	13 849	916	59	12 992	1 856	1 011	3 139	2 775	5 053	. . .
1968	17 245	14 664	373	15 037	992	69	14 113	1 951	1 180	3 386	2 968	5 093	. . .
1969	18 956	16 014	541	16 555	1 097	25	15 483	2 194	1 279	3 686	3 186	5 143	2 327
1970	19 678	16 472	371	16 843	1 116	58	15 785	2 393	1 500	3 782	3 309	5 204	2 291
1971	21 408	17 530	588	18 118	1 229	118	17 008	2 609	1 790	4 078	3 607	5 250	2 290
1972	23 453	19 484	496	19 980	1 442	151	18 689	2 794	1 970	4 428	3 876	5 296	2 367
1973	27 049	21 954	1 218	23 172	1 865	195	21 502	3 211	2 335	5 076	4 487	5 329	2 483
1974	28 975	23 614	721	24 335	2 091	256	22 500	3 718	2 757	5 416	4 713	5 350	2 493
1975	31 211	24 291	1 085	25 376	2 122	301	23 555	4 144	3 512	5 833	5 170	5 351	2 405
1976	34 912	27 780	1 065	28 846	2 440	351	26 756	4 491	3 665	6 500	5 704	5 372	2 489
1977	38 717	31 429	712	32 141	2 757	413	29 798	5 070	3 849	7 163	6 263	5 405	2 578
1978	43 272	35 403	716	36 119	3 196	467	33 390	5 646	4 236	7 945	6 916	5 446	2 671
1979	47 781	38 926	655	39 581	3 636	544	36 489	6 425	4 867	8 727	7 565	5 475	2 713
1980	51 469	40 144	361	40 505	3 725	667	37 447	7 937	6 085	9 374	8 188	5 491	2 632
1981	56 488	43 131	291	43 422	4 306	716	39 832	9 856	6 800	10 307	8 961	5 480	2 611
1982	58 448	43 147	297	43 445	4 399	781	39 827	11 044	7 577	10 689	9 376	5 468	2 530
1983	61 123	45 482	-265	45 218	4 660	830	41 388	11 576	8 159	11 214	9 902	5 450	2 550
1984	68 027	50 091	738	50 829	5 257	993	46 565	12 904	8 558	12 463	11 055	5 458	2 653
1985	71 838	53 092	668	53 760	5 685	1 080	49 155	13 675	9 008	13 159	11 631	5 459	2 709
1986	75 378	55 967	564	56 532	6 093	1 177	51 615	14 251	9 512	13 820	12 243	5 454	2 769
1987	79 846	60 020	753	60 773	6 466	1 249	55 556	14 592	9 698	14 592	12 872	5 473	2 865
1988	84 969	64 859	274	65 132	7 244	1 375	59 263	15 428	10 277	15 472	13 654	5 492	2 953
1989	92 341	68 990	946	69 937	7 759	1 442	63 619	17 555	11 167	16 717	14 678	5 524	3 030
1990	97 213	72 440	838	73 278	8 221	1 513	66 570	18 516	12 127	17 491	15 368	5 558	3 090
1991	100 361	75 515	212	75 728	8 700	1 536	68 563	18 421	13 377	17 869	15 752	5 616	3 091
1992	108 029	80 908	771	81 679	9 257	1 752	74 173	18 631	15 224	19 037	16 844	5 675	3 139
1993	113 428	85 485	849	86 334	9 860	1 940	78 415	18 951	16 062	19 764	17 431	5 739	3 216
1994	120 278	90 848	766	91 614	10 664	2 091	83 042	20 481	16 756	20 761	18 225	5 794	3 306
1995	125 269	94 943	330	95 273	11 170	2 342	86 445	21 817	17 006	21 408	18 757	5 851	3 400
1996	132 103	98 763	1 144	99 907	11 546	2 486	90 847	23 246	18 010	22 368	19 528	5 906	3 439
1997	138 794	103 913	1 185	105 098	12 122	2 648	95 625	24 734	18 435	23 306	20 247	5 955	3 496
1998	149 336	112 167	763	112 931	12 830	2 679	102 779	27 448	19 109	24 894	21 572	5 999	3 567
1999	154 842	118 361	300	118 660	13 446	3 032	108 246	26 616	19 980	25 615	22 206	6 045	3 626
2000	165 285	124 719	553	125 272	13 888	3 374	114 757	28 997	21 531	27 132	23 647	6 092	3 673
2001	167 881	125 841	469	126 310	14 113	3 472	115 669	28 530	23 682	27 406	23 928	6 126	3 611
2002	172 474	130 509	116	130 624	14 505	3 426	119 546	27 685	25 243	28 023	24 927	6 155	3 585
2003	178 972	136 567	790	137 357	14 657	3 358	126 059	26 626	26 287	28 884	25 979	6 196	3 579
2004	187 781	142 882	1 518	144 400	15 391	3 469	132 477	27 552	27 752	30 158	27 227	6 227	3 629
2005	195 372	148 566	767	149 332	16 379	3 644	136 598	28 648	30 126	31 150	27 896	6 272	3 679

. . . = Not available.

Table 21-2. Personal Income and Employment by Region and State—Continued

(Millions of dollars, except as noted.)

Region or state and year	Personal income, total	Earnings by place of work			Less: Contributions for government social insurance	Plus: Adjustment for residence	Equals: Net earnings by place of residence	Plus: Dividends, interest, and rent	Plus: Personal current transfer receipts	Per capita (dollars)		Population (thousands)	Total employment (thousands)
		Nonfarm	Farm	Total						Personal income	Disposable personal income		
IOWA													
1958	5 394	3 437	1 005	4 442	135	27	4 335	729	331	1 992	1 803	2 708	. . .
1959	5 540	3 775	741	4 516	166	29	4 379	799	362	2 030	1 841	2 729	. . .
1960	5 674	3 889	720	4 609	186	33	4 457	833	385	2 059	1 850	2 756	. . .
1961	6 007	4 000	838	4 838	189	36	4 685	898	424	2 180	1 969	2 756	. . .
1962	6 271	4 184	870	5 054	203	39	4 890	938	444	2 281	2 060	2 750	. . .
1963	6 667	4 407	983	5 390	233	41	5 198	1 005	464	2 427	2 194	2 747	. . .
1964	6 984	4 727	905	5 633	247	44	5 430	1 075	479	2 543	2 318	2 746	. . .
1965	7 744	5 060	1 232	6 292	261	48	6 080	1 143	522	2 824	2 569	2 742	. . .
1966	8 428	5 626	1 328	6 955	352	52	6 655	1 207	566	3 051	2 746	2 762	. . .
1967	8 589	6 020	1 066	7 086	418	56	6 725	1 189	675	3 075	2 760	2 793	. . .
1968	9 226	6 491	1 009	7 500	457	60	7 103	1 340	782	3 292	2 931	2 803	. . .
1969	10 256	7 109	1 222	8 331	544	82	7 869	1 532	856	3 656	3 225	2 805	1 289
1970	10 931	7 541	1 197	8 738	568	89	8 259	1 680	992	3 865	3 436	2 829	1 295
1971	11 450	8 046	997	9 043	627	88	8 504	1 819	1 127	4 015	3 609	2 852	1 297
1972	12 835	8 774	1 464	10 237	720	94	9 611	2 008	1 216	4 487	3 968	2 861	1 316
1973	15 472	9 873	2 712	12 586	931	88	11 742	2 326	1 404	5 402	4 817	2 864	1 374
1974	16 035	11 078	1 694	12 772	1 094	84	11 762	2 647	1 626	5 591	4 853	2 868	1 407
1975	17 919	12 052	1 945	13 997	1 169	100	12 928	2 974	2 017	6 219	5 488	2 881	1 407
1976	19 111	13 718	1 204	14 922	1 324	92	13 689	3 207	2 215	6 582	5 758	2 904	1 455
1977	21 145	15 318	1 204	16 522	1 461	65	15 126	3 677	2 341	7 255	6 352	2 914	1 488
1978	24 433	16 950	2 412	19 362	1 675	61	17 748	4 104	2 581	8 370	7 352	2 919	1 514
1979	26 220	18 993	1 540	20 533	1 960	71	18 644	4 683	2 892	8 989	7 816	2 917	1 557
1980	27 930	20 155	683	20 838	2 067	92	18 863	5 661	3 405	9 585	8 320	2 914	1 541
1981	31 569	21 304	1 611	22 915	2 325	118	20 708	6 986	3 876	10 856	9 429	2 908	1 513
1982	32 477	21 296	797	22 093	2 354	192	19 931	8 126	4 419	11 245	9 870	2 888	1 476
1983	33 153	22 192	-7	22 185	2 430	206	19 961	8 456	4 737	11 550	10 226	2 871	1 479
1984	36 836	23 961	1 434	25 395	2 688	239	22 945	9 038	4 853	12 886	11 579	2 859	1 506
1985	38 171	24 690	1 729	26 419	2 815	278	23 882	9 139	5 151	13 490	12 122	2 830	1 503
1986	39 389	25 379	2 106	27 485	2 947	270	24 808	9 237	5 344	14 108	12 706	2 792	1 501
1987	41 242	27 165	2 442	29 606	3 158	266	26 714	9 068	5 460	14 905	13 297	2 767	1 523
1988	42 415	29 167	1 627	30 794	3 529	307	27 572	9 142	5 700	15 321	13 634	2 768	1 567
1989	45 981	30 999	2 366	33 365	3 774	315	29 906	9 985	6 091	16 596	14 707	2 771	1 611
1990	48 358	32 713	2 250	34 963	4 010	323	31 276	10 473	6 609	17 389	15 369	2 781	1 646
1991	49 808	34 164	1 730	35 894	4 221	373	32 047	10 663	7 098	17 804	15 785	2 798	1 665
1992	53 082	36 360	2 558	38 918	4 467	399	34 850	10 565	7 667	18 834	16 768	2 818	1 680
1993	53 098	38 164	846	39 010	4 718	380	34 672	10 408	8 018	18 716	16 590	2 837	1 702
1994	57 873	40 512	2 762	43 273	5 082	386	38 577	10 982	8 314	20 301	18 042	2 851	1 735
1995	60 012	42 462	1 817	44 279	5 345	446	39 380	11 848	8 785	20 929	18 559	2 867	1 796
1996	64 862	44 253	3 653	47 907	5 541	498	42 863	12 750	9 248	22 521	19 962	2 880	1 826
1997	68 297	46 672	3 610	50 283	5 838	578	45 023	13 731	9 543	23 623	20 794	2 891	1 852
1998	71 704	50 255	2 391	52 646	6 175	663	47 134	14 800	9 770	24 701	21 725	2 903	1 894
1999	73 285	53 167	1 402	54 569	6 422	737	48 885	14 310	10 090	25 118	22 076	2 918	1 914
2000	77 763	55 681	1 656	57 336	6 609	832	51 560	15 416	10 787	26 554	23 390	2 928	1 934
2001	79 456	57 013	1 290	58 302	6 820	783	52 265	15 556	11 635	27 106	23 928	2 931	1 916
2002	82 398	58 768	1 399	60 167	6 953	817	54 032	15 478	12 888	28 081	25 274	2 934	1 906
2003	84 055	61 259	1 544	62 804	7 240	856	56 420	14 679	12 956	28 577	25 918	2 941	1 898
2004	91 436	65 286	3 625	68 911	7 564	880	62 228	15 793	13 416	30 965	28 211	2 953	1 928
2005	94 316	68 770	2 436	71 206	8 039	898	64 065	15 996	14 254	31 795	28 722	2 966	1 967

. . . = Not available.

Table 21-2. Personal Income and Employment by Region and State—Continued

(Millions of dollars, except as noted.)

Region or state and year	Personal income, total	Derivation of personal income								Per capita (dollars)		Population (thousands)	Total employment (thousands)
		Earnings by place of work			Less: Contributions for government social insurance	Plus: Adjustment for residence	Equals: Net earnings by place of residence	Plus: Dividends, interest, and rent	Plus: Personal current transfer receipts	Personal income	Disposable personal income		
		Nonfarm	Farm	Total									

KANSAS

1958	4 469	3 025	524	3 548	121	147	3 575	636	258	2 086	1 889	2 142	...
1959	4 514	3 180	365	3 545	142	163	3 567	667	280	2 090	1 892	2 160	...
1960	4 693	3 241	435	3 676	161	173	3 688	703	302	2 150	1 930	2 183	...
1961	4 895	3 394	442	3 836	177	176	3 835	725	335	2 210	1 986	2 215	...
1962	5 101	3 579	414	3 993	183	192	4 002	754	345	2 286	2 046	2 231	...
1963	5 226	3 683	394	4 077	206	212	4 083	777	366	2 357	2 100	2 217	...
1964	5 494	3 928	360	4 288	213	234	4 309	806	379	2 487	2 260	2 209	...
1965	5 855	4 100	454	4 554	222	257	4 589	853	413	2 654	2 410	2 206	...
1966	6 277	4 496	469	4 966	293	292	4 965	869	444	2 853	2 554	2 200	...
1967	6 573	4 791	400	5 191	339	322	5 174	868	532	2 992	2 672	2 197	...
1968	7 143	5 257	395	5 651	376	353	5 628	899	616	3 223	2 850	2 216	...
1969	7 937	5 721	457	6 178	423	441	6 196	1 052	689	3 550	3 111	2 236	1 029
1970	8 583	6 035	599	6 633	444	439	6 629	1 151	803	3 818	3 372	2 248	1 017
1971	9 320	6 510	700	7 210	494	430	7 146	1 258	916	4 149	3 718	2 246	1 022
1972	10 411	7 208	956	8 163	575	453	8 041	1 386	984	4 616	4 096	2 256	1 048
1973	11 936	8 099	1 378	9 477	737	468	9 208	1 577	1 151	5 271	4 669	2 264	1 090
1974	12 943	9 079	1 049	10 127	856	483	9 754	1 865	1 323	5 707	4 997	2 268	1 122
1975	14 136	10 059	797	10 856	938	497	10 415	2 108	1 613	6 204	5 501	2 279	1 133
1976	15 432	11 388	575	11 963	1 070	514	11 407	2 245	1 780	6 713	5 947	2 299	1 169
1977	16 876	12 551	489	13 040	1 176	559	12 423	2 527	1 926	7 281	6 407	2 318	1 208
1978	18 712	14 255	273	14 528	1 375	604	13 757	2 854	2 102	8 021	7 033	2 333	1 252
1979	21 422	16 102	695	16 796	1 617	652	15 832	3 272	2 318	9 126	7 924	2 347	1 298
1980	23 578	17 658	97	17 755	1 760	729	16 724	4 098	2 756	9 953	8 629	2 369	1 312
1981	26 764	19 350	333	19 683	2 059	755	18 378	5 210	3 176	11 223	9 638	2 385	1 326
1982	28 988	20 045	570	20 615	2 184	778	19 209	6 215	3 564	12 072	10 413	2 401	1 310
1983	30 221	21 125	373	21 498	2 289	754	19 963	6 457	3 800	12 511	11 018	2 416	1 327
1984	33 274	23 302	740	24 042	2 569	799	22 272	7 085	3 918	13 726	12 216	2 424	1 370
1985	35 078	24 466	802	25 268	2 735	844	23 376	7 570	4 131	14 451	12 810	2 427	1 375
1986	36 501	25 581	930	26 510	2 901	826	24 436	7 731	4 334	15 005	13 399	2 433	1 375
1987	38 146	26 820	1 168	27 988	3 017	901	25 872	7 818	4 456	15 599	13 818	2 445	1 428
1988	40 070	28 412	1 136	29 549	3 319	911	27 140	8 254	4 675	16 275	14 422	2 462	1 440
1989	42 157	30 030	818	30 847	3 504	960	28 303	8 725	5 128	17 048	14 988	2 473	1 463
1990	44 876	31 495	1 372	32 867	3 708	975	30 134	9 174	5 568	18 085	15 971	2 481	1 483
1991	46 541	32 815	1 017	33 832	3 928	953	30 857	9 652	6 032	18 626	16 517	2 499	1 498
1992	49 867	35 362	1 395	36 757	4 178	967	33 546	9 637	6 685	19 692	17 554	2 532	1 511
1993	51 729	36 977	1 338	38 315	4 384	1 062	34 992	9 670	7 067	20 234	17 973	2 557	1 534
1994	54 164	38 811	1 397	40 208	4 671	932	36 469	10 383	7 312	20 990	18 609	2 581	1 561
1995	56 073	40 611	786	41 396	4 843	1 099	37 653	10 758	7 662	21 558	18 995	2 601	1 609
1996	59 729	42 595	1 484	44 079	5 057	1 159	40 180	11 579	7 970	22 845	20 036	2 615	1 642
1997	63 356	45 464	1 405	46 869	5 387	1 066	42 548	12 456	8 352	24 041	20 923	2 635	1 686
1998	67 800	49 032	1 290	50 322	5 757	1 096	45 661	13 654	8 485	25 483	22 171	2 661	1 734
1999	70 158	51 703	1 364	53 066	6 013	996	48 050	13 305	8 804	26 195	22 775	2 678	1 752
2000	74 570	55 091	705	55 796	6 259	1 103	50 640	14 437	9 492	27 694	24 047	2 693	1 771
2001	77 564	57 480	778	58 258	6 496	993	52 755	14 350	10 459	28 718	25 060	2 701	1 782
2002	78 606	58 959	250	59 209	6 626	991	53 575	13 818	11 214	28 980	25 825	2 712	1 773
2003	81 126	60 956	1 219	62 175	6 777	850	56 248	13 120	11 758	29 780	26 835	2 724	1 758
2004	85 596	65 385	992	66 377	7 160	764	59 981	13 424	12 192	31 312	28 325	2 734	1 780
2005	90 433	68 886	1 254	70 140	7 814	840	63 166	14 278	12 989	32 948	29 560	2 745	1 801

. . . = Not available.

Table 21-2. Personal Income and Employment by Region and State—Continued

(Millions of dollars, except as noted.)

Region or state and year	Personal income, total	Derivation of personal income								Per capita (dollars)		Population (thou-sands)	Total employ-ment (thou-sands)
		Earnings by place of work			Less: Contribu-tions for govern-ment social insurance	Plus: Adjust-ment for residence	Equals: Net earnings by place of residence	Plus: Dividends, interest, and rent	Plus: Personal current transfer receipts	Personal income	Disposable personal income		
		Nonfarm	Farm	Total									
KENTUCKY													
1958	4 532	3 344	361	3 705	142	83	3 646	507	379	1 531	1 385	2 961	. . .
1959	4 769	3 575	336	3 911	169	97	3 839	537	393	1 590	1 438	2 999	. . .
1960	4 921	3 675	319	3 994	184	97	3 907	585	429	1 618	1 461	3 041	. . .
1961	5 238	3 770	392	4 162	184	89	4 066	618	555	1 715	1 558	3 054	. . .
1962	5 563	4 108	391	4 500	209	92	4 383	676	504	1 807	1 628	3 079	. . .
1963	5 848	4 374	400	4 774	240	92	4 625	719	504	1 889	1 706	3 096	. . .
1964	6 112	4 670	293	4 963	245	99	4 817	765	530	1 953	1 775	3 129	. . .
1965	6 631	5 044	361	5 405	258	107	5 255	798	579	2 112	1 915	3 140	. . .
1966	7 243	5 621	377	5 997	339	116	5 775	842	627	2 302	2 064	3 147	. . .
1967	7 840	6 117	378	6 495	399	95	6 191	903	746	2 472	2 227	3 172	. . .
1968	8 577	6 777	369	7 146	445	104	6 805	929	843	2 684	2 395	3 195	. . .
1969	9 444	7 416	423	7 839	511	174	7 502	998	944	2 953	2 585	3 198	1 332
1970	10 229	7 993	388	8 381	549	164	7 996	1 129	1 104	3 166	2 801	3 231	1 336
1971	11 132	8 708	403	9 110	616	107	8 601	1 233	1 298	3 375	3 014	3 298	1 360
1972	12 329	9 651	501	10 152	716	101	9 538	1 351	1 441	3 696	3 256	3 336	1 392
1973	13 901	10 965	573	11 538	922	59	10 675	1 508	1 719	4 123	3 676	3 372	1 461
1974	15 670	12 264	657	12 921	1 063	26	11 883	1 736	2 051	4 586	4 010	3 417	1 496
1975	17 119	13 218	475	13 693	1 124	11	12 580	1 956	2 583	4 935	4 413	3 469	1 465
1976	19 247	15 045	550	15 595	1 293	-23	14 279	2 146	2 822	5 452	4 857	3 530	1 523
1977	21 702	17 051	675	17 727	1 454	1	16 273	2 471	2 959	6 071	5 363	3 575	1 579
1978	24 378	19 341	595	19 936	1 690	12	18 259	2 949	3 171	6 750	5 945	3 611	1 645
1979	27 686	21 634	667	22 301	1 950	4	20 355	3 634	3 697	7 598	6 696	3 644	1 668
1980	29 965	22 940	549	23 488	2 064	28	21 453	4 059	4 453	8 178	7 238	3 664	1 646
1981	33 296	24 726	928	25 654	2 396	-8	23 250	5 022	5 025	9 072	7 981	3 670	1 639
1982	35 477	25 629	895	26 524	2 528	-18	23 979	6 013	5 485	9 631	8 498	3 683	1 621
1983	36 630	26 730	224	26 954	2 655	12	24 311	6 379	5 941	9 915	8 796	3 694	1 629
1984	41 139	29 648	1 109	30 757	3 001	-65	27 691	7 230	6 218	11 132	9 978	3 695	1 683
1985	42 974	31 166	865	32 031	3 219	-76	28 736	7 731	6 506	11 631	10 379	3 695	1 706
1986	44 492	32 459	636	33 095	3 420	-48	29 626	8 055	6 811	12 065	10 775	3 688	1 742
1987	47 171	34 929	722	35 651	3 652	-78	31 920	8 207	7 044	12 807	11 388	3 683	1 775
1988	49 914	37 047	770	37 817	4 064	-91	33 663	8 782	7 469	13 564	12 072	3 680	1 827
1989	53 733	39 213	1 125	40 338	4 355	-138	35 845	9 698	8 190	14 612	12 920	3 677	1 877
1990	57 026	41 431	1 045	42 475	4 677	-101	37 697	10 361	8 968	15 437	13 621	3 694	1 918
1991	60 160	43 101	1 068	44 168	4 961	-142	39 065	10 831	10 264	16 162	14 347	3 722	1 915
1992	64 671	47 009	1 306	48 315	5 389	-413	42 513	10 982	11 176	17 175	15 251	3 765	1 962
1993	66 791	49 229	1 104	50 333	5 737	-424	44 172	11 012	11 606	17 520	15 527	3 812	2 006
1994	70 148	51 763	1 139	52 901	6 169	-538	46 194	11 785	12 169	18 225	16 110	3 849	2 047
1995	73 389	54 066	714	54 780	6 482	-573	47 725	12 581	13 084	18 879	16 625	3 887	2 123
1996	77 819	56 573	1 131	57 704	6 740	-641	50 323	13 607	13 889	19 854	17 443	3 920	2 155
1997	82 436	59 950	1 163	61 112	7 129	-657	53 326	14 482	14 627	20 855	18 218	3 953	2 203
1998	87 851	64 022	1 042	65 064	7 498	-595	56 970	15 845	15 035	22 043	19 218	3 985	2 244
1999	91 462	68 223	796	69 019	7 993	-686	60 340	15 528	15 593	22 763	19 834	4 018	2 291
2000	98 845	72 430	1 442	73 872	8 182	-719	64 972	17 137	16 736	24 412	21 344	4 049	2 332
2001	101 346	74 503	953	75 456	8 478	-976	66 002	17 191	18 153	24 920	21 770	4 067	2 305
2002	103 866	77 377	391	77 768	8 777	-1 073	67 918	16 449	19 498	25 404	22 575	4 089	2 292
2003	106 292	80 426	580	81 007	9 033	-1 342	70 631	15 513	20 148	25 819	23 118	4 117	2 301
2004	111 991	84 725	999	85 724	9 461	-1 452	74 811	15 506	21 674	27 039	24 333	4 142	2 337
2005	118 180	89 361	1 521	90 882	10 067	-1 667	79 148	16 126	22 907	28 317	25 303	4 173	2 381

. . . = Not available.

Table 21-2. Personal Income and Employment by Region and State—Continued

(Millions of dollars, except as noted.)

Region or state and year	Personal income, total	Derivation of personal income									Per capita (dollars)		Population (thou-sands)	Total employ-ment (thou-sands)
		Earnings by place of work			Less: Contribu-tions for govern-ment social insurance	Plus: Adjust-ment for residence	Equals: Net earnings by place of residence	Plus: Dividends, interest, and rent	Plus: Personal current transfer receipts	Personal income	Disposable personal income		
		Nonfarm	Farm	Total									

LOUISIANA

1958	5 162	4 114	187	4 301	140	-3	4 159	625	378	1 636	1 496	3 155	...
1959	5 412	4 279	203	4 482	159	-2	4 321	679	411	1 687	1 524	3 208	...
1960	5 510	4 356	183	4 539	185	-2	4 353	721	436	1 690	1 541	3 260	...
1961	5 723	4 464	215	4 679	187	-1	4 491	747	486	1 741	1 587	3 287	...
1962	6 038	4 747	202	4 949	208	0	4 740	794	504	1 805	1 641	3 345	...
1963	6 441	5 042	257	5 300	246	-1	5 054	852	535	1 907	1 726	3 377	...
1964	6 894	5 494	223	5 717	262	-1	5 455	885	554	2 001	1 830	3 446	...
1965	7 456	6 007	195	6 202	285	-1	5 915	943	598	2 133	1 952	3 496	...
1966	8 242	6 763	236	6 999	389	2	6 613	987	642	2 322	2 093	3 550	...
1967	9 024	7 405	265	7 670	432	4	7 242	1 030	752	2 520	2 278	3 581	...
1968	9 880	8 159	297	8 455	489	4	7 970	1 059	850	2 742	2 458	3 603	...
1969	10 453	8 655	239	8 894	568	3	8 328	1 164	961	2 888	2 569	3 619	1 440
1970	11 281	9 160	280	9 441	591	3	8 852	1 275	1 154	3 090	2 788	3 650	1 429
1971	12 299	9 931	318	10 249	657	-9	9 583	1 398	1 318	3 314	2 994	3 711	1 445
1972	13 462	10 934	345	11 280	756	-22	10 502	1 511	1 450	3 578	3 210	3 762	1 488
1973	15 076	12 125	576	12 701	960	-38	11 703	1 688	1 685	3 979	3 582	3 789	1 550
1974	17 188	13 722	609	14 331	1 117	-55	13 159	2 055	1 974	4 499	4 013	3 821	1 598
1975	19 297	15 506	416	15 921	1 242	-84	14 595	2 262	2 439	4 964	4 478	3 887	1 641
1976	21 951	17 920	452	18 372	1 453	-114	16 805	2 456	2 689	5 555	4 962	3 952	1 702
1977	24 561	20 222	452	20 674	1 625	-141	18 907	2 760	2 893	6 116	5 448	4 016	1 756
1978	28 160	23 540	369	23 909	1 929	-188	21 791	3 219	3 150	6 913	6 113	4 073	1 848
1979	32 076	26 737	498	27 235	2 273	-234	24 727	3 764	3 585	7 749	6 801	4 139	1 899
1980	37 067	30 700	169	30 869	2 595	-339	27 934	4 857	4 276	8 777	7 680	4 223	1 968
1981	42 887	35 149	261	35 411	3 182	-365	31 864	6 247	4 775	10 013	8 692	4 283	2 036
1982	45 962	36 735	260	36 995	3 383	-343	33 268	7 185	5 509	10 560	9 307	4 353	2 029
1983	47 894	37 172	228	37 400	3 376	-324	33 701	7 922	6 271	10 897	9 716	4 395	1 990
1984	51 348	39 558	318	39 875	3 661	-317	35 897	8 921	6 530	11 669	10 466	4 400	2 032
1985	53 398	40 512	226	40 738	3 773	-286	36 679	9 685	7 034	12 113	10 853	4 408	2 020
1986	52 905	39 217	230	39 447	3 665	-231	35 551	9 633	7 720	12 005	10 887	4 407	1 939
1987	53 052	39 221	393	39 614	3 621	-196	35 797	9 438	7 818	12 212	11 052	4 344	1 915
1988	55 908	41 436	627	42 062	3 989	-176	37 898	9 817	8 193	13 036	11 845	4 289	1 947
1989	59 437	43 499	461	43 961	4 215	-142	39 604	10 879	8 955	13 976	12 620	4 253	1 966
1990	64 052	47 034	381	47 414	4 569	-119	42 726	11 456	9 870	15 173	13 689	4 222	2 019
1991	67 628	49 404	448	49 852	4 912	-137	44 803	11 583	11 242	15 900	14 381	4 253	2 044
1992	72 000	52 211	554	52 765	5 126	-137	47 503	11 497	13 000	16 771	15 233	4 293	2 052
1993	75 161	54 150	566	54 717	5 360	-139	49 218	11 725	14 218	17 413	15 788	4 316	2 100
1994	80 043	57 071	659	57 729	5 785	-165	51 779	12 536	15 727	18 411	16 667	4 347	2 140
1995	83 535	59 857	675	60 532	6 073	-193	54 265	13 530	15 741	19 077	17 228	4 379	2 209
1996	87 036	62 305	870	63 175	6 355	-217	56 603	14 435	15 999	19 786	17 690	4 399	2 254
1997	91 432	65 945	715	66 660	6 742	-233	59 685	15 415	16 331	20 681	18 373	4 421	2 305
1998	96 677	70 309	453	70 762	7 137	-255	63 370	16 684	16 622	21 772	19 385	4 440	2 355
1999	98 200	71 733	616	72 349	7 217	-249	64 884	16 193	17 123	22 014	19 650	4 461	2 374
2000	103 151	74 913	502	75 415	7 380	-260	67 775	17 700	17 676	23 079	20 574	4 469	2 404
2001	110 256	79 924	467	80 392	7 845	-139	72 408	17 429	20 420	24 692	22 038	4 465	2 409
2002	112 744	82 480	232	82 712	8 114	-125	74 473	16 539	21 732	25 194	22 825	4 475	2 412
2003	115 873	85 717	676	86 393	8 207	-165	78 021	15 895	21 957	25 805	23 637	4 490	2 436
2004	122 050	90 682	544	91 226	8 487	-169	82 570	15 466	24 014	27 082	24 920	4 507	2 470
2005	111 201	88 527	491	89 018	8 899	-133	79 986	-5 066	36 281	24 582	22 529	4 524	2 463

. . . = Not available.

Table 21-2. Personal Income and Employment by Region and State—Continued

(Millions of dollars, except as noted.)

Region or state and year	Personal income, total	Earnings by place of work			Less: Contributions for government social insurance	Plus: Adjustment for residence	Equals: Net earnings by place of residence	Plus: Dividends, interest, and rent	Plus: Personal current transfer receipts	Per capita (dollars)		Population (thousands)	Total employment (thousands)
		Nonfarm	Farm	Total						Personal income	Disposable personal income		
MAINE													
1958	1 678	1 294	100	1 395	52	-20	1 322	215	141	1 778	1 626	944	. . .
1959	1 749	1 409	59	1 468	60	-24	1 383	219	148	1 828	1 674	957	. . .
1960	1 854	1 473	102	1 575	70	-28	1 477	224	152	1 901	1 724	975	. . .
1961	1 872	1 513	66	1 579	73	-29	1 477	228	167	1 882	1 707	995	. . .
1962	1 950	1 576	65	1 641	78	-30	1 533	245	172	1 962	1 773	994	. . .
1963	2 014	1 626	58	1 684	87	-30	1 567	267	181	2 028	1 843	993	. . .
1964	2 179	1 734	88	1 823	92	-31	1 700	295	184	2 195	2 011	993	. . .
1965	2 357	1 832	125	1 957	92	-30	1 834	331	192	2 364	2 168	997	. . .
1966	2 510	1 998	106	2 104	118	-33	1 953	347	210	2 513	2 300	999	. . .
1967	2 641	2 145	54	2 199	137	-35	2 027	365	248	2 630	2 396	1 004	. . .
1968	2 824	2 326	54	2 381	157	-38	2 185	360	279	2 841	2 557	994	. . .
1969	3 106	2 505	74	2 578	181	-23	2 375	419	312	3 131	2 782	992	443
1970	3 400	2 705	77	2 782	193	-18	2 571	459	370	3 411	3 068	997	446
1971	3 647	2 872	66	2 937	211	-17	2 709	500	438	3 591	3 278	1 016	443
1972	3 993	3 159	64	3 223	241	-20	2 962	541	490	3 859	3 502	1 035	453
1973	4 509	3 497	147	3 644	301	-11	3 332	593	583	4 309	3 875	1 046	470
1974	5 034	3 799	195	3 993	337	-6	3 650	681	703	4 749	4 278	1 060	478
1975	5 397	4 063	81	4 143	357	-19	3 767	732	899	5 029	4 578	1 073	475
1976	6 215	4 722	163	4 885	422	-23	4 440	800	975	5 702	5 170	1 090	498
1977	6 766	5 177	128	5 305	461	-25	4 819	1 038	908	6 121	5 556	1 105	513
1978	7 483	5 820	89	5 909	531	-23	5 355	1 013	1 115	6 708	6 053	1 115	532
1979	8 349	6 478	74	6 552	607	-17	5 929	1 160	1 260	7 422	6 658	1 125	546
1980	9 406	7 140	48	7 189	670	-14	6 504	1 431	1 471	8 347	7 464	1 127	555
1981	10 415	7 663	117	7 780	773	-50	6 956	1 782	1 677	9 193	8 153	1 133	554
1982	11 282	8 134	103	8 238	835	-49	7 354	2 089	1 839	9 925	8 739	1 137	556
1983	12 108	8 841	71	8 913	912	-40	7 961	2 157	1 989	10 577	9 432	1 145	568
1984	13 506	9 831	117	9 948	1 045	-30	8 873	2 534	2 099	11 687	10 481	1 156	591
1985	14 602	10 729	102	10 831	1 133	-9	9 689	2 693	2 221	12 556	11 209	1 163	610
1986	15 789	11 659	92	11 751	1 246	29	10 535	2 951	2 304	13 494	11 976	1 170	635
1987	17 231	12 834	135	12 969	1 362	48	11 655	3 219	2 357	14 546	12 789	1 185	658
1988	18 912	14 270	117	14 387	1 549	61	12 900	3 513	2 500	15 710	13 851	1 204	692
1989	20 499	15 283	124	15 406	1 657	60	13 810	3 997	2 693	16 803	14 827	1 220	708
1990	21 402	15 741	166	15 907	1 704	58	14 261	4 135	3 006	17 376	15 387	1 232	707
1991	21 681	15 603	121	15 724	1 721	75	14 078	4 144	3 459	17 526	15 627	1 237	683
1992	22 606	16 216	176	16 392	1 818	119	14 692	4 099	3 815	18 253	16 343	1 239	686
1993	23 156	16 678	157	16 835	1 925	179	15 088	4 049	4 018	18 639	16 688	1 242	697
1994	24 092	17 239	148	17 387	2 033	240	15 593	4 298	4 201	19 387	17 292	1 243	708
1995	25 044	17 679	123	17 802	2 110	310	16 002	4 613	4 429	20 140	17 965	1 243	710
1996	26 484	18 406	151	18 558	2 171	364	16 750	4 991	4 743	21 203	18 801	1 249	720
1997	27 830	19 332	106	19 438	2 290	436	17 584	5 279	4 967	22 179	19 509	1 255	733
1998	29 710	20 612	138	20 750	2 417	511	18 844	5 744	5 122	23 596	20 576	1 259	753
1999	31 016	21 939	154	22 092	2 555	580	20 118	5 619	5 279	24 484	21 343	1 267	770
2000	33 173	23 226	146	23 371	2 666	701	21 406	6 179	5 588	25 969	22 489	1 277	792
2001	35 107	24 719	117	24 837	2 812	726	22 751	6 338	6 018	27 292	23 717	1 286	797
2002	35 998	25 492	76	25 569	2 847	710	23 432	6 089	6 478	27 756	24 660	1 297	799
2003	37 588	26 595	98	26 692	2 892	706	24 507	6 048	7 033	28 732	25 812	1 308	802
2004	39 314	28 149	133	28 282	3 001	750	26 031	5 796	7 487	29 897	26 898	1 315	817
2005	40 714	29 018	120	29 138	3 140	789	26 786	5 772	8 156	30 808	27 468	1 322	822

. . . = Not available.

Table 21-2. Personal Income and Employment by Region and State—Continued

(Millions of dollars, except as noted.)

Region or state and year	Personal income, total	Derivation of personal income								Per capita (dollars)		Population (thousands)	Total employment (thousands)
		Earnings by place of work			Less: Contributions for government social insurance	Plus: Adjustment for residence	Equals: Net earnings by place of residence	Plus: Dividends, interest, and rent	Plus: Personal current transfer receipts	Personal income	Disposable personal income		
		Nonfarm	Farm	Total									
MARYLAND													
1958	6 580	5 040	103	5 143	188	466	5 422	848	311	2 207	1 940	2 982	. . .
1959	6 954	5 365	85	5 450	239	516	5 727	901	327	2 268	1 976	3 066	. . .
1960	7 312	5 622	93	5 715	289	582	6 008	964	340	2 349	2 041	3 113	. . .
1961	7 771	5 941	88	6 029	312	641	6 359	1 021	391	2 447	2 141	3 176	. . .
1962	8 403	6 417	84	6 500	350	720	6 870	1 117	416	2 575	2 226	3 263	. . .
1963	8 997	6 848	66	6 913	380	804	7 337	1 225	436	2 657	2 288	3 386	. . .
1964	9 822	7 435	85	7 520	396	886	8 010	1 352	460	2 813	2 460	3 492	. . .
1965	10 727	8 035	96	8 131	398	1 003	8 735	1 488	504	2 980	2 598	3 600	. . .
1966	11 841	9 015	77	9 093	526	1 117	9 684	1 600	557	3 205	2 754	3 695	. . .
1967	12 913	9 601	94	9 694	585	1 366	10 476	1 746	691	3 437	2 948	3 757	. . .
1968	14 305	10 668	86	10 755	641	1 528	11 641	1 837	826	3 750	3 128	3 815	. . .
1969	16 230	11 866	131	11 997	750	2 154	13 401	1 885	944	4 196	3 482	3 868	1 679
1970	17 951	12 944	120	13 064	815	2 512	14 761	2 064	1 126	4 558	3 857	3 938	1 702
1971	19 640	14 079	93	14 172	916	2 764	16 020	2 248	1 373	4 883	4 190	4 023	1 729
1972	21 555	15 481	127	15 608	1 059	3 000	17 549	2 433	1 574	5 282	4 457	4 081	1 781
1973	23 861	17 260	208	17 468	1 353	3 203	19 318	2 727	1 816	5 807	4 929	4 109	1 846
1974	26 329	18 949	163	19 112	1 531	3 478	21 058	3 166	2 105	6 370	5 369	4 133	1 868
1975	28 656	20 109	202	20 311	1 622	3 864	22 553	3 456	2 647	6 893	5 918	4 157	1 846
1976	31 444	22 281	173	22 454	1 806	4 179	24 827	3 767	2 850	7 537	6 473	4 172	1 866
1977	34 306	24 337	128	24 465	1 972	4 586	27 079	4 190	3 037	8 179	6 965	4 195	1 919
1978	38 027	27 080	182	27 262	2 258	4 953	29 957	4 720	3 350	9 029	7 673	4 212	2 003
1979	42 135	29 946	158	30 104	2 607	5 388	32 885	5 449	3 801	9 977	8 430	4 223	2 061
1980	47 296	32 846	56	32 902	2 861	5 961	36 002	6 767	4 526	11 187	9 511	4 228	2 075
1981	52 794	36 134	127	36 261	3 377	6 434	39 318	8 289	5 187	12 388	10 415	4 262	2 102
1982	57 330	38 006	142	38 149	3 613	7 008	41 544	10 013	5 774	13 386	11 336	4 283	2 090
1983	61 841	41 516	88	41 604	4 071	7 382	44 916	10 630	6 296	14 337	12 313	4 313	2 158
1984	68 984	46 396	263	46 659	4 672	8 079	50 065	12 282	6 636	15 803	13 558	4 365	2 253
1985	75 325	50 925	275	51 201	5 285	8 729	54 645	13 665	7 015	17 069	14 721	4 413	2 356
1986	81 069	55 292	285	55 577	5 863	9 361	59 075	14 510	7 484	18 068	15 593	4 487	2 443
1987	87 696	60 547	298	60 845	6 352	10 136	64 629	15 295	7 771	19 208	16 379	4 566	2 572
1988	95 867	66 462	364	66 826	7 276	11 230	70 780	16 800	8 288	20 582	17 765	4 658	2 668
1989	103 528	70 968	362	71 330	7 861	12 077	75 546	18 953	9 029	21 900	18 724	4 727	2 726
1990	109 686	75 228	351	75 579	8 417	12 546	79 708	20 088	9 890	22 852	19 591	4 800	2 760
1991	113 436	76 595	305	76 901	8 725	13 216	81 392	20 961	11 083	23 304	20 135	4 868	2 683
1992	118 847	79 974	353	80 327	9 032	14 068	85 363	21 012	12 472	24 139	20 951	4 923	2 656
1993	122 906	83 059	329	83 388	9 386	14 474	88 476	21 446	12 984	24 720	21 406	4 972	2 679
1994	128 523	86 718	311	87 029	9 944	14 942	92 026	22 861	13 636	25 587	22 085	5 023	2 726
1995	133 814	90 440	219	90 659	10 331	14 992	95 320	24 048	14 446	26 393	22 676	5 070	2 788
1996	140 035	93 880	398	94 279	10 678	15 347	98 947	25 566	15 522	27 393	23 396	5 112	2 827
1997	147 843	100 100	274	100 374	11 326	15 310	104 358	27 583	15 901	28 666	24 091	5 157	2 891
1998	157 784	106 978	331	107 309	12 034	16 649	111 924	29 550	16 310	30 317	25 610	5 204	2 947
1999	167 075	114 411	349	114 760	12 769	17 611	119 603	30 200	17 272	31 796	26 813	5 255	3 018
2000	181 957	124 081	354	124 435	13 613	19 892	130 715	32 998	18 245	34 257	28 800	5 312	3 092
2001	191 657	131 865	293	132 158	14 628	20 321	137 851	33 910	19 896	35 627	30 062	5 380	3 129
2002	198 824	138 561	179	138 740	15 339	20 996	144 396	32 939	21 488	36 533	31 526	5 442	3 162
2003	206 370	144 435	313	144 748	15 647	21 927	151 029	32 266	23 075	37 437	32 551	5 512	3 207
2004	221 284	154 091	416	154 508	16 923	23 958	161 542	35 688	24 054	39 790	34 626	5 561	3 259
2005	235 196	163 675	376	164 052	17 952	25 249	171 349	37 862	25 985	41 996	36 179	5 600	3 329

. . . = Not available.

Table 21-2. Personal Income and Employment by Region and State—Continued

(Millions of dollars, except as noted.)

Region or state and year	Personal income, total	Earnings by place of work			Less: Contributions for government social insurance	Plus: Adjustment for residence	Equals: Net earnings by place of residence	Plus: Dividends, interest, and rent	Plus: Personal current transfer receipts	Per capita (dollars)		Population (thousands)	Total employment (thousands)
		Nonfarm	Farm	Total						Personal income	Disposable personal income		
MASSACHUSETTS													
1958	11 553	9 446	67	9 513	353	-56	9 104	1 574	874	2 306	2 041	5 010	. . .
1959	12 350	10 226	59	10 285	427	-69	9 788	1 687	874	2 413	2 124	5 117	. . .
1960	12 869	10 657	68	10 725	499	-75	10 150	1 798	921	2 494	2 175	5 160	. . .
1961	13 510	11 151	60	11 211	528	-83	10 600	1 883	1 027	2 589	2 276	5 219	. . .
1962	14 303	11 829	60	11 889	617	-93	11 180	2 072	1 051	2 718	2 379	5 263	. . .
1963	14 866	12 229	60	12 289	679	-99	11 511	2 245	1 110	2 782	2 434	5 344	. . .
1964	15 890	12 952	62	13 014	697	-109	12 208	2 531	1 151	2 917	2 595	5 448	. . .
1965	16 966	13 749	68	13 818	714	-122	12 982	2 772	1 212	3 084	2 740	5 502	. . .
1966	18 318	15 028	71	15 099	942	-141	14 015	3 002	1 300	3 309	2 914	5 535	. . .
1967	19 937	16 197	56	16 252	1 032	-158	15 062	3 270	1 605	3 564	3 132	5 594	. . .
1968	21 805	17 670	64	17 735	1 138	-176	16 421	3 449	1 936	3 881	3 359	5 618	. . .
1969	23 734	19 262	66	19 328	1 259	-126	17 943	3 635	2 156	4 201	3 572	5 650	2 679
1970	25 568	20 590	69	20 659	1 323	-108	19 228	3 791	2 550	4 483	3 872	5 704	2 679
1971	27 271	21 783	63	21 846	1 443	-111	20 292	3 960	3 019	4 752	4 161	5 739	2 644
1972	29 436	23 667	62	23 729	1 647	-110	21 972	4 151	3 313	5 109	4 398	5 762	2 697
1973	32 081	26 017	70	26 088	2 069	-134	23 885	4 481	3 716	5 547	4 811	5 784	2 787
1974	34 754	27 700	69	27 769	2 269	-150	25 350	5 001	4 404	6 016	5 205	5 777	2 811
1975	37 217	28 668	68	28 737	2 290	-155	26 292	5 195	5 731	6 459	5 678	5 762	2 728
1976	40 233	31 440	76	31 516	2 550	-182	28 784	5 513	5 936	6 998	6 107	5 749	2 756
1977	43 770	34 557	79	34 636	2 811	-224	31 600	6 073	6 098	7 620	6 619	5 744	2 833
1978	48 413	38 736	103	38 839	3 242	-287	35 310	6 635	6 468	8 430	7 297	5 743	2 959
1979	53 926	43 372	90	43 461	3 788	-361	39 312	7 453	7 161	9 385	8 050	5 746	3 079
1980	60 920	48 178	105	48 283	4 217	-483	43 583	9 165	8 172	10 602	9 053	5 746	3 142
1981	68 062	52 825	116	52 940	4 985	-599	47 357	11 417	9 289	11 798	9 987	5 769	3 155
1982	74 684	56 835	131	56 966	5 488	-729	50 749	13 894	10 041	12 941	11 082	5 771	3 157
1983	81 246	62 745	164	62 909	6 135	-906	55 867	14 737	10 642	14 009	12 057	5 799	3 230
1984	91 835	71 536	182	71 719	7 218	-1 180	63 321	17 321	11 194	15 723	13 603	5 841	3 422
1985	99 445	78 467	160	78 627	7 995	-1 366	69 266	18 465	11 714	16 910	14 544	5 881	3 533
1986	107 119	85 208	175	85 383	8 777	-1 502	75 104	19 692	12 323	18 148	15 531	5 903	3 629
1987	116 181	93 682	153	93 835	9 558	-1 683	82 595	20 913	12 673	19 575	16 660	5 935	3 661
1988	127 622	103 283	173	103 456	10 690	-1 917	90 848	23 126	13 647	21 341	18 412	5 980	3 770
1989	134 399	107 024	152	107 175	11 056	-2 040	94 080	24 930	15 390	22 342	19 178	6 015	3 743
1990	138 782	108 597	151	108 748	11 227	-2 089	95 432	26 109	17 241	23 043	19 795	6 023	3 647
1991	141 024	108 226	171	108 396	11 401	-2 295	94 700	26 555	19 770	23 432	20 272	6 018	3 480
1992	147 930	114 834	171	115 005	11 992	-2 401	100 613	26 696	20 622	24 538	21 281	6 029	3 510
1993	152 578	119 513	166	119 679	12 610	-2 613	104 456	26 951	21 171	25 176	21 745	6 061	3 576
1994	160 322	125 587	151	125 738	13 431	-2 824	109 483	28 393	22 445	26 303	22 639	6 095	3 645
1995	168 623	132 142	148	132 289	14 231	-2 891	115 167	29 801	23 655	27 457	23 458	6 141	3 680
1996	178 797	140 371	169	140 540	15 029	-3 153	122 358	32 042	24 397	28 933	24 439	6 180	3 744
1997	189 885	149 449	169	149 619	16 164	-3 428	130 027	34 439	25 419	30 498	25 500	6 226	3 833
1998	203 987	161 510	107	161 617	17 279	-3 656	140 683	37 686	25 618	32 524	26 916	6 272	3 917
1999	216 221	175 021	106	175 127	18 592	-4 247	152 288	37 540	26 393	34 227	28 126	6 317	3 989
2000	240 209	195 723	116	195 839	20 551	-5 116	170 173	42 108	27 928	37 756	30 310	6 362	4 097
2001	249 095	200 623	97	200 721	21 152	-5 074	174 495	43 988	30 613	38 953	31 806	6 395	4 125
2002	249 954	200 721	115	200 836	21 040	-4 871	174 924	41 670	33 360	38 985	33 422	6 412	4 065
2003	254 206	203 611	110	203 721	21 024	-4 865	177 832	40 778	35 596	39 611	34 262	6 418	4 031
2004	267 821	216 748	129	216 878	23 099	-5 007	188 772	42 101	36 948	41 799	36 188	6 407	4 057
2005	279 635	224 729	121	224 850	24 289	-5 048	195 513	44 635	39 488	43 702	37 395	6 399	4 114

. . . = Not available.

Table 21-2. Personal Income and Employment by Region and State—Continued

(Millions of dollars, except as noted.)

Region or state and year	Personal income, total	Earnings by place of work			Less: Contributions for government social insurance	Plus: Adjustment for residence	Equals: Net earnings by place of residence	Plus: Dividends, interest, and rent	Plus: Personal current transfer receipts	Personal income	Disposable personal income	Population (thousands)	Total employment (thousands)
		Nonfarm	Farm	Total									
MICHIGAN													
1958	17 188	13 954	295	14 249	560	30	13 719	2 286	1 183	2 242	2 025	7 667	. . .
1959	18 278	15 158	220	15 378	695	34	14 717	2 488	1 073	2 353	2 115	7 767	. . .
1960	19 088	15 800	234	16 034	824	37	15 246	2 730	1 112	2 437	2 174	7 834	. . .
1961	19 156	15 411	293	15 704	786	38	14 956	2 868	1 332	2 427	2 183	7 893	. . .
1962	20 582	16 724	269	16 993	888	41	16 146	3 131	1 304	2 595	2 314	7 933	. . .
1963	22 021	18 018	292	18 310	1 038	44	17 317	3 377	1 327	2 733	2 429	8 058	. . .
1964	24 210	19 813	289	20 101	1 077	49	19 074	3 771	1 366	2 957	2 662	8 187	. . .
1965	26 937	22 103	268	22 371	1 122	54	21 303	4 158	1 476	3 223	2 890	8 357	. . .
1966	29 419	24 418	342	24 760	1 571	63	23 252	4 550	1 617	3 456	3 083	8 512	. . .
1967	30 765	25 205	271	25 476	1 652	68	23 892	4 871	2 002	3 565	3 175	8 630	. . .
1968	34 072	28 062	300	28 362	1 853	76	26 585	5 175	2 312	3 918	3 429	8 696	. . .
1969	36 523	30 769	345	31 115	2 203	107	29 019	4 945	2 559	4 159	3 571	8 781	3 640
1970	37 346	31 039	334	31 374	2 193	112	29 293	4 837	3 216	4 198	3 654	8 897	3 558
1971	40 372	33 744	305	34 049	2 446	104	31 706	4 827	3 839	4 500	3 951	8 972	3 571
1972	44 824	37 704	420	38 124	2 901	112	35 336	5 170	4 318	4 967	4 285	9 025	3 687
1973	50 345	42 829	555	43 384	3 794	138	39 728	5 691	4 925	5 550	4 824	9 072	3 858
1974	53 956	44 629	640	45 270	4 077	140	41 333	6 471	6 153	5 923	5 174	9 109	3 854
1975	57 435	45 633	570	46 204	4 087	154	42 271	7 088	8 076	6 306	5 595	9 108	3 695
1976	64 660	52 806	471	53 277	4 789	197	48 685	7 665	8 311	7 092	6 200	9 117	3 844
1977	72 818	60 448	552	61 000	5 485	223	55 737	8 547	8 534	7 952	6 888	9 157	4 016
1978	80 986	68 222	500	68 722	6 394	270	62 598	9 312	9 076	8 801	7 551	9 202	4 188
1979	89 110	74 493	534	75 027	7 197	310	68 140	10 504	10 467	9 635	8 269	9 249	4 234
1980	95 460	75 328	525	75 853	7 181	355	69 026	12 625	13 809	10 314	8 983	9 256	4 039
1981	102 206	79 421	505	79 927	8 188	384	72 123	15 456	14 627	11 098	9 634	9 209	3 992
1982	105 189	78 622	402	79 025	8 242	393	71 176	17 682	16 331	11 540	10 147	9 115	3 837
1983	111 468	83 679	214	83 893	8 948	427	75 372	18 812	17 284	12 320	10 797	9 048	3 881
1984	123 531	93 384	540	93 924	10 351	491	84 064	21 990	17 477	13 651	11 999	9 049	4 059
1985	134 083	102 618	653	103 271	11 659	512	92 124	23 920	18 039	14 773	12 895	9 076	4 257
1986	142 459	109 552	482	110 035	12 629	495	97 900	25 643	18 915	15 607	13 642	9 128	4 373
1987	147 486	113 544	660	114 204	12 973	512	101 743	26 291	19 452	16 053	13 984	9 187	4 511
1988	156 961	122 341	580	122 921	14 386	523	109 058	27 631	20 272	17 028	14 901	9 218	4 612
1989	168 637	129 411	967	130 378	15 261	517	115 634	31 067	21 937	18 225	15 878	9 253	4 742
1990	176 189	134 549	757	135 305	15 869	457	119 893	32 537	23 758	18 922	16 571	9 311	4 825
1991	181 655	137 697	645	138 343	16 406	472	122 409	32 558	26 688	19 324	17 028	9 400	4 754
1992	192 788	148 021	740	148 760	17 435	599	131 924	32 883	27 981	20 338	18 040	9 479	4 783
1993	201 574	155 626	742	156 368	18 536	663	138 494	33 204	29 876	21 129	18 567	9 540	4 843
1994	217 812	169 356	566	169 922	20 325	763	150 360	37 309	30 143	22 694	19 888	9 598	5 016
1995	227 466	177 753	711	178 464	21 386	734	157 812	38 018	31 635	23 508	20 487	9 676	5 175
1996	237 193	183 594	629	184 222	21 903	758	163 077	40 784	33 333	24 306	21 040	9 759	5 282
1997	248 821	191 430	655	192 086	22 969	849	169 966	43 479	35 376	25 367	21 857	9 809	5 363
1998	265 098	205 821	633	206 454	24 035	892	183 312	46 690	35 096	26 919	23 077	9 848	5 416
1999	278 062	218 175	838	219 013	25 441	995	194 567	45 859	37 635	28 095	24 099	9 897	5 519
2000	294 227	230 621	560	231 181	26 411	1 005	205 775	49 515	38 938	29 552	25 435	9 956	5 629
2001	299 542	233 516	359	233 875	26 358	1 063	208 580	47 635	43 327	29 946	26 000	10 003	5 540
2002	303 465	238 109	413	238 522	26 764	1 086	212 844	45 766	44 855	30 227	26 814	10 039	5 483
2003	313 724	246 604	576	247 180	27 444	1 201	220 937	45 494	47 293	31 129	27 931	10 078	5 462
2004	320 418	249 821	872	250 692	28 058	1 240	223 874	47 353	49 191	31 711	28 571	10 104	5 482
2005	331 304	256 749	856	257 605	29 201	1 296	229 700	49 431	52 173	32 735	29 275	10 121	5 515

. . . = Not available.

Table 21-2. Personal Income and Employment by Region and State—Continued

(Millions of dollars, except as noted.)

Region or state and year	Personal income, total	Earnings by place of work			Less: Contributions for government social insurance	Plus: Adjustment for residence	Equals: Net earnings by place of residence	Plus: Dividends, interest, and rent	Plus: Personal current transfer receipts	Per capita (dollars)		Population (thousands)	Total employment (thousands)
		Nonfarm	Farm	Total						Personal income	Disposable personal income		
MINNESOTA													
1958	6 645	4 886	594	5 480	179	1	5 302	879	464	2 006	1 800	3 313	. . .
1959	6 905	5 287	409	5 695	220	0	5 475	942	488	2 052	1 836	3 366	. . .
1960	7 332	5 575	505	6 080	260	-1	5 819	1 006	507	2 141	1 907	3 425	. . .
1961	7 706	5 818	529	6 347	269	-3	6 075	1 061	571	2 221	1 980	3 470	. . .
1962	8 129	6 263	456	6 719	303	-3	6 414	1 125	590	2 314	2 054	3 513	. . .
1963	8 620	6 521	608	7 128	339	-4	6 785	1 210	625	2 441	2 175	3 531	. . .
1964	8 968	6 979	390	7 370	348	-4	7 018	1 299	651	2 520	2 271	3 558	. . .
1965	9 914	7 531	641	8 172	372	-7	7 793	1 413	708	2 760	2 478	3 592	. . .
1966	10 749	8 308	721	9 028	522	-13	8 493	1 495	761	2 972	2 650	3 617	. . .
1967	11 562	9 035	633	9 668	601	-17	9 050	1 587	925	3 160	2 808	3 659	. . .
1968	12 731	10 001	672	10 673	683	-24	9 966	1 707	1 058	3 438	3 038	3 703	. . .
1969	14 157	11 177	709	11 886	782	-33	11 071	1 925	1 161	3 767	3 270	3 758	1 691
1970	15 411	11 948	863	12 811	826	-29	11 956	2 081	1 373	4 039	3 554	3 815	1 699
1971	16 417	12 736	786	13 522	911	-28	12 582	2 242	1 593	4 262	3 789	3 852	1 706
1972	17 845	13 821	946	14 767	1 038	-30	13 699	2 384	1 762	4 615	4 040	3 867	1 780
1973	21 033	15 462	2 165	17 628	1 336	-38	16 254	2 713	2 065	5 414	4 804	3 885	1 878
1974	22 671	17 045	1 626	18 671	1 528	-34	17 110	3 139	2 423	5 815	5 059	3 898	1 921
1975	24 432	18 413	1 247	19 660	1 615	-34	18 011	3 497	2 924	6 223	5 454	3 926	1 920
1976	26 580	20 697	767	21 464	1 847	-43	19 574	3 797	3 210	6 718	5 854	3 957	1 977
1977	29 978	22 914	1 485	24 398	2 045	-55	22 298	4 305	3 375	7 533	6 552	3 980	2 034
1978	33 703	26 160	1 605	27 765	2 412	-70	25 283	4 795	3 624	8 416	7 284	4 005	2 123
1979	37 603	29 778	1 221	30 998	2 858	-88	28 052	5 498	4 052	9 312	7 983	4 038	2 222
1980	41 898	32 485	934	33 418	3 111	-92	30 215	6 826	4 857	10 256	8 838	4 085	2 254
1981	46 460	35 134	1 018	36 152	3 609	-131	32 411	8 474	5 575	11 299	9 705	4 112	2 241
1982	49 807	36 680	804	37 484	3 842	-154	33 488	10 050	6 268	12 056	10 420	4 131	2 201
1983	52 586	39 255	107	39 362	4 165	-183	35 014	10 814	6 758	12 698	11 023	4 141	2 228
1984	59 664	44 180	1 421	45 601	4 800	-238	40 563	12 009	7 092	14 350	12 587	4 158	2 335
1985	63 458	47 404	1 322	48 726	5 238	-286	43 202	12 721	7 535	15 166	13 306	4 184	2 399
1986	67 102	50 169	1 622	51 791	5 657	-327	45 807	13 423	7 873	15 957	14 047	4 205	2 432
1987	71 516	53 912	2 125	56 036	6 067	-378	49 591	13 802	8 123	16 886	14 738	4 235	2 526
1988	75 230	58 303	1 237	59 540	6 819	-458	52 263	14 392	8 575	17 511	15 311	4 296	2 598
1989	82 088	62 152	2 022	64 174	7 304	-442	56 428	16 338	9 322	18 923	16 520	4 338	2 653
1990	87 318	66 158	1 916	68 073	7 823	-469	59 781	17 517	10 020	19 891	17 304	4 390	2 712
1991	90 050	68 981	1 159	70 140	8 310	-477	61 354	17 909	10 787	20 278	17 739	4 441	2 736
1992	96 401	74 824	1 396	76 220	8 954	-513	66 753	17 938	11 710	21 443	18 707	4 496	2 781
1993	98 571	77 927	177	78 104	9 436	-519	68 149	18 065	12 357	21 636	18 790	4 556	2 835
1994	105 971	82 409	1 287	83 696	10 146	-568	72 983	19 968	13 021	22 985	19 964	4 610	2 923
1995	112 209	87 062	503	87 565	10 708	-614	76 244	22 161	13 804	24 078	20 814	4 660	3 015
1996	121 195	92 732	1 886	94 618	11 367	-684	82 567	24 182	14 447	25 716	21 986	4 713	3 077
1997	128 388	98 786	1 152	99 938	12 044	-777	87 117	26 524	14 747	26 953	22 994	4 763	3 129
1998	139 553	107 639	1 556	109 195	12 946	-837	95 412	28 941	15 200	28 993	24 649	4 813	3 202
1999	146 722	115 346	1 071	116 418	13 821	-946	101 650	29 205	15 867	30 106	25 784	4 873	3 275
2000	157 964	124 400	1 016	125 416	14 734	-1 040	109 642	31 339	16 983	32 017	27 187	4 934	3 344
2001	162 578	128 707	448	129 156	15 342	-1 136	112 677	30 918	18 982	32 616	27 832	4 985	3 363
2002	166 968	132 755	569	133 323	15 723	-1 164	116 437	29 926	20 605	33 237	28 912	5 024	3 362
2003	173 756	137 466	1 265	138 732	16 197	-1 180	121 354	30 707	21 695	34 328	30 204	5 062	3 381
2004	184 571	146 064	1 588	147 652	17 048	-1 235	129 370	32 474	22 728	36 215	31 979	5 097	3 428
2005	191 568	151 046	1 937	152 983	17 969	-1 215	133 798	34 119	23 650	37 322	32 637	5 133	3 499

. . . = Not available.

Table 21-2. Personal Income and Employment by Region and State—Continued

(Millions of dollars, except as noted.)

Region or state and year	Personal income, total	Derivation of personal income									Per capita (dollars)		Population (thousands)	Total employment (thousands)
		Earnings by place of work			Less: Contributions for government social insurance	Plus: Adjustment for residence	Equals: Net earnings by place of residence	Plus: Dividends, interest, and rent	Plus: Personal current transfer receipts		Personal income	Disposable personal income		
		Nonfarm	Farm	Total										
MISSISSIPPI														
1958	2 396	1 758	271	2 029	72	9	1 966	226	204		1 149	1 076	2 086	. . .
1959	2 651	1 922	333	2 255	87	10	2 178	254	219		1 240	1 155	2 138	. . .
1960	2 680	1 990	278	2 268	101	12	2 179	268	233		1 228	1 136	2 182	. . .
1961	2 895	2 074	350	2 423	104	13	2 332	301	262		1 312	1 223	2 206	. . .
1962	3 023	2 228	294	2 522	115	15	2 422	328	273		1 348	1 245	2 243	. . .
1963	3 331	2 374	428	2 801	136	17	2 682	359	290		1 484	1 370	2 244	. . .
1964	3 454	2 543	366	2 909	143	20	2 785	366	303		1 541	1 434	2 241	. . .
1965	3 749	2 823	348	3 171	152	22	3 041	380	328		1 669	1 547	2 246	. . .
1966	4 078	3 158	343	3 501	197	23	3 327	391	360		1 816	1 670	2 245	. . .
1967	4 417	3 384	383	3 767	226	25	3 565	421	431		1 983	1 825	2 228	. . .
1968	4 834	3 768	361	4 129	252	32	3 908	437	489		2 179	1 994	2 219	. . .
1969	5 303	4 160	346	4 506	291	35	4 249	503	552		2 389	2 172	2 220	909
1970	5 813	4 432	391	4 823	311	36	4 549	575	689		2 617	2 369	2 221	917
1971	6 450	4 860	433	5 293	351	58	4 999	637	814		2 847	2 619	2 266	939
1972	7 352	5 594	490	6 084	422	73	5 735	699	918		3 187	2 889	2 307	979
1973	8 439	6 321	688	7 010	539	93	6 564	810	1 065		3 591	3 276	2 350	1 019
1974	9 308	7 013	510	7 523	616	123	7 029	966	1 313		3 913	3 534	2 379	1 031
1975	10 086	7 510	372	7 882	654	150	7 378	1 077	1 631		4 203	3 859	2 400	1 001
1976	11 529	8 587	572	9 159	757	182	8 584	1 167	1 779		4 744	4 321	2 430	1 039
1977	12 870	9 678	606	10 284	851	223	9 655	1 312	1 903		5 232	4 779	2 460	1 071
1978	14 345	10 993	449	11 442	984	279	10 737	1 513	2 095		5 766	5 206	2 488	1 102
1979	16 263	12 205	699	12 904	1 131	337	12 110	1 762	2 392		6 485	5 835	2 508	1 117
1980	17 695	13 168	178	13 346	1 216	425	12 555	2 275	2 865		7 007	6 305	2 525	1 114
1981	19 928	14 416	327	14 743	1 429	455	13 770	2 909	3 250		7 849	7 011	2 539	1 110
1982	21 064	14 802	421	15 223	1 505	473	14 191	3 298	3 575		8 238	7 494	2 557	1 083
1983	22 021	15 557	99	15 656	1 597	530	14 589	3 494	3 939		8 576	7 768	2 568	1 091
1984	24 278	16 979	473	17 452	1 777	594	16 270	3 935	4 074		9 417	8 581	2 578	1 121
1985	25 602	17 983	433	18 416	1 917	624	17 123	4 211	4 268		9 892	9 010	2 588	1 129
1986	26 440	18 749	198	18 946	2 045	609	17 511	4 409	4 520		10 194	9 323	2 594	1 136
1987	27 962	19 641	584	20 224	2 135	647	18 736	4 516	4 710		10 802	9 845	2 589	1 147
1988	29 832	20 962	731	21 693	2 387	688	19 994	4 819	5 019		11 561	10 576	2 580	1 176
1989	32 164	22 257	562	22 819	2 564	731	20 986	5 682	5 496		12 495	11 374	2 574	1 196
1990	33 754	23 567	433	24 001	2 712	754	22 042	5 754	5 958		13 089	11 910	2 579	1 210
1991	35 607	24 634	538	25 172	2 885	813	23 100	5 871	6 635		13 702	12 525	2 599	1 218
1992	38 199	26 425	641	27 066	3 073	832	24 824	5 926	7 449		14 559	13 319	2 624	1 241
1993	40 596	28 534	547	29 081	3 335	852	26 598	6 057	7 940		15 290	13 941	2 655	1 294
1994	43 805	30 802	818	31 620	3 668	854	28 805	6 598	8 402		16 291	14 801	2 689	1 343
1995	45 973	32 211	681	32 892	3 850	943	29 985	6 900	9 088		16 885	15 314	2 723	1 374
1996	48 646	33 488	1 067	34 555	3 977	986	31 565	7 416	9 665		17 702	16 004	2 748	1 398
1997	51 514	35 315	1 174	36 490	4 175	1 124	33 439	8 016	10 058		18 550	16 733	2 777	1 424
1998	54 820	37 875	958	38 833	4 421	1 204	35 616	8 889	10 315		19 545	17 593	2 805	1 462
1999	56 719	39 635	955	40 590	4 614	1 310	37 286	8 748	10 685		20 053	18 038	2 828	1 488
2000	59 837	41 267	724	41 991	4 707	1 506	38 790	9 547	11 500		21 005	18 935	2 849	1 493
2001	62 739	42 332	905	43 237	4 819	1 658	40 077	9 782	12 880		21 955	19 839	2 858	1 470
2002	63 979	43 834	334	44 168	5 009	1 724	40 883	9 207	13 889		22 321	20 424	2 866	1 473
2003	66 340	45 713	965	46 678	5 112	1 721	43 287	8 596	14 456		23 028	21 244	2 881	1 471
2004	69 454	48 264	1 186	49 451	5 376	1 817	45 891	8 059	15 504		23 943	22 243	2 901	1 493
2005	72 809	50 052	1 289	51 341	5 613	1 937	47 665	5 594	19 551		24 925	22 985	2 921	1 505

. . . = Not available.

Table 21-2. Personal Income and Employment by Region and State—Continued

(Millions of dollars, except as noted.)

Region or state and year	Personal income, total	Earnings by place of work			Less: Contributions for government social insurance	Plus: Adjustment for residence	Equals: Net earnings by place of residence	Plus: Dividends, interest, and rent	Plus: Personal current transfer receipts	Per capita (dollars)		Population (thousands)	Total employment (thousands)
		Nonfarm	Farm	Total						Personal income	Disposable personal income		
MISSOURI													
1958	8 692	6 822	559	7 381	260	-149	6 971	1 122	598	2 076	1 864	4 186	. . .
1959	9 211	7 372	468	7 840	311	-165	7 363	1 215	633	2 163	1 938	4 258	. . .
1960	9 483	7 623	437	8 060	358	-176	7 526	1 286	671	2 192	1 950	4 326	. . .
1961	9 796	7 793	476	8 269	375	-182	7 713	1 338	745	2 252	2 004	4 349	. . .
1962	10 325	8 265	478	8 743	408	-198	8 137	1 417	771	2 370	2 100	4 357	. . .
1963	10 840	8 771	430	9 202	469	-222	8 511	1 521	808	2 468	2 182	4 392	. . .
1964	11 452	9 403	326	9 730	491	-246	8 993	1 628	830	2 578	2 316	4 442	. . .
1965	12 449	10 084	525	10 609	517	-271	9 820	1 741	888	2 787	2 486	4 467	. . .
1966	13 314	11 094	408	11 502	695	-310	10 497	1 857	960	2 944	2 617	4 523	. . .
1967	14 170	11 852	396	12 249	796	-346	11 107	1 943	1 120	3 122	2 773	4 539	. . .
1968	15 683	13 052	472	13 524	898	-382	12 244	2 127	1 313	3 433	3 028	4 568	. . .
1969	16 551	14 162	442	14 604	954	-758	12 892	2 232	1 427	3 567	3 085	4 640	2 216
1970	18 037	15 085	516	15 600	1 004	-702	13 895	2 451	1 691	3 850	3 376	4 685	2 203
1971	19 431	16 087	563	16 649	1 108	-683	14 858	2 623	1 950	4 114	3 643	4 723	2 200
1972	21 140	17 456	704	18 161	1 261	-703	16 197	2 833	2 111	4 448	3 889	4 753	2 242
1973	23 542	19 089	1 206	20 295	1 584	-737	17 975	3 119	2 449	4 931	4 358	4 775	2 325
1974	25 235	20 650	627	21 277	1 766	-763	18 748	3 596	2 890	5 273	4 624	4 785	2 341
1975	27 602	21 920	687	22 607	1 841	-773	19 993	3 955	3 654	5 756	5 120	4 795	2 291
1976	30 433	24 747	460	25 208	2 095	-850	22 263	4 277	3 893	6 309	5 570	4 824	2 365
1977	33 839	27 557	706	28 263	2 330	-990	24 943	4 832	4 064	6 984	6 167	4 845	2 424
1978	37 743	30 825	905	31 730	2 695	-1 143	27 892	5 431	4 420	7 748	6 792	4 871	2 513
1979	42 199	34 195	1 164	35 359	3 087	-1 307	30 965	6 234	5 000	8 631	7 529	4 889	2 580
1980	45 893	36 617	225	36 843	3 284	-1 524	32 034	7 778	6 082	9 324	8 143	4 922	2 554
1981	51 359	39 478	759	40 237	3 795	-1 663	34 779	9 743	6 836	10 413	9 054	4 932	2 549
1982	54 839	41 306	338	41 644	4 051	-1 730	35 863	11 522	7 454	11 125	9 625	4 929	2 525
1983	58 534	44 455	-110	44 345	4 387	-1 758	38 199	12 327	8 008	11 840	10 468	4 944	2 571
1984	65 162	49 343	410	49 754	4 995	-1 886	42 873	13 930	8 359	13 097	11 642	4 975	2 679
1985	69 812	52 925	785	53 710	5 477	-2 003	46 230	14 765	8 817	13 962	12 364	5 000	2 753
1986	73 310	55 978	571	56 549	5 908	-2 052	48 589	15 438	9 282	14 595	12 937	5 023	2 816
1987	77 057	59 356	728	60 084	6 219	-2 177	51 687	15 811	9 559	15 239	13 466	5 057	2 854
1988	81 340	63 171	648	63 819	6 842	-2 265	54 712	16 541	10 087	16 006	14 179	5 082	2 905
1989	86 570	66 431	893	67 324	7 283	-2 395	57 646	17 997	10 927	16 988	14 975	5 096	2 960
1990	90 407	69 167	682	69 849	7 670	-2 626	59 553	19 014	11 839	17 627	15 536	5 129	2 993
1991	94 900	71 308	561	71 869	8 001	-2 639	61 229	19 883	13 789	18 353	16 312	5 171	2 962
1992	100 945	76 098	804	76 903	8 440	-2 814	65 648	20 548	14 749	19 349	17 240	5 217	2 977
1993	104 699	79 308	493	79 801	8 857	-2 922	68 022	20 881	15 796	19 862	17 654	5 271	3 061
1994	111 005	84 013	680	84 693	9 506	-2 917	72 270	22 179	16 556	20 848	18 466	5 324	3 134
1995	115 948	88 669	232	88 901	10 081	-3 143	75 678	22 666	17 604	21 559	19 013	5 378	3 218
1996	122 469	92 921	1 040	93 961	10 514	-3 277	80 170	23 802	18 497	22 548	19 777	5 432	3 277
1997	129 992	98 557	1 096	99 654	11 141	-3 484	85 029	25 766	19 197	23 716	20 701	5 481	3 349
1998	137 619	105 196	614	105 810	11 671	-3 691	90 448	27 453	19 718	24 923	21 683	5 522	3 405
1999	142 925	111 165	247	111 411	12 281	-3 767	95 363	26 837	20 725	25 697	22 345	5 562	3 450
2000	152 722	117 772	657	118 429	12 842	-4 056	101 530	29 030	22 162	27 241	23 676	5 606	3 497
2001	156 937	120 401	555	120 956	13 288	-3 938	103 729	28 768	24 439	27 809	24 177	5 643	3 481
2002	161 104	124 405	243	124 647	13 642	-4 036	106 969	27 904	26 231	28 358	25 223	5 681	3 471
2003	166 425	127 945	624	128 570	13 773	-3 859	110 938	27 961	27 527	29 102	26 182	5 719	3 476
2004	173 458	133 193	1 530	134 723	14 189	-3 791	116 743	27 686	29 029	30 117	27 195	5 760	3 512
2005	181 542	140 228	683	140 911	15 289	-4 006	121 617	28 865	31 060	31 299	28 001	5 800	3 574

. . . = Not available.

Table 21-2. Personal Income and Employment by Region and State—Continued

(Millions of dollars, except as noted.)

Region or state and year	Personal income, total	Derivation of personal income								Per capita (dollars)		Population (thousands)	Total employment (thousands)
		Earnings by place of work			Less: Contributions for government social insurance	Plus: Adjustment for residence	Equals: Net earnings by place of residence	Plus: Dividends, interest, and rent	Plus: Personal current transfer receipts	Personal income	Disposable personal income		
		Nonfarm	Farm	Total									
MONTANA													
1958	1 380	906	235	1 142	44	0	1 098	182	100	2 072	1 891	666	...
1959	1 352	956	146	1 102	51	0	1 052	193	107	2 021	1 806	669	...
1960	1 405	996	160	1 156	62	0	1 094	203	108	2 069	1 864	679	...
1961	1 402	1 041	107	1 149	62	*	1 086	198	117	2 014	1 801	696	...
1962	1 646	1 104	274	1 378	64	0	1 314	213	119	2 358	2 144	698	...
1963	1 631	1 153	209	1 362	72	0	1 290	220	121	2 319	2 094	703	...
1964	1 662	1 206	166	1 373	74	0	1 298	238	126	2 355	2 153	706	...
1965	1 787	1 282	187	1 470	76	0	1 394	259	134	2 531	2 300	706	...
1966	1 915	1 367	223	1 590	99	0	1 491	282	143	2 709	2 451	707	...
1967	1 952	1 408	188	1 596	108	0	1 487	296	169	2 785	2 510	701	...
1968	2 052	1 487	194	1 680	115	-1	1 565	296	191	2 932	2 642	700	...
1969	2 276	1 613	239	1 853	127	-1	1 724	342	209	3 279	2 872	694	298
1970	2 518	1 736	289	2 025	137	-1	1 886	390	241	3 611	3 215	697	301
1971	2 684	1 897	249	2 145	152	-1	1 992	411	280	3 774	3 404	711	307
1972	3 116	2 133	398	2 531	179	0	2 352	454	310	4 332	3 863	719	319
1973	3 628	2 389	573	2 961	229	0	2 733	535	360	4 987	4 432	727	333
1974	3 947	2 700	462	3 162	264	1	2 899	626	423	5 354	4 743	737	344
1975	4 347	3 012	396	3 409	285	3	3 126	707	514	5 802	5 190	749	344
1976	4 696	3 447	222	3 669	326	3	3 346	781	569	6 191	5 495	759	359
1977	5 104	3 886	68	3 954	371	4	3 588	903	613	6 617	5 835	771	372
1978	5 998	4 430	299	4 729	435	3	4 297	1 027	674	7 650	6 791	784	390
1979	6 466	4 887	115	5 003	500	6	4 509	1 197	759	8 193	7 171	789	397
1980	7 144	5 204	118	5 322	537	14	4 799	1 453	892	9 058	7 955	789	394
1981	8 124	5 659	223	5 881	626	25	5 281	1 811	1 032	10 214	9 007	795	396
1982	8 566	5 811	168	5 979	656	18	5 341	2 069	1 155	10 654	9 502	804	392
1983	9 009	6 143	123	6 265	701	9	5 573	2 170	1 266	11 067	9 912	814	400
1984	9 609	6 570	42	6 611	760	6	5 857	2 401	1 351	11 706	10 528	821	410
1985	9 793	6 745	-86	6 659	792	3	5 871	2 494	1 429	11 909	10 718	822	409
1986	10 148	6 704	233	6 938	810	-2	6 126	2 496	1 525	12 470	11 331	814	404
1987	10 448	6 895	314	7 209	833	-3	6 373	2 477	1 598	12 978	11 700	805	408
1988	10 640	7 260	106	7 366	931	0	6 435	2 519	1 686	13 296	11 917	800	419
1989	11 707	7 646	413	8 059	997	-2	7 059	2 801	1 847	14 641	13 043	800	427
1990	12 361	8 097	386	8 483	1 077	-4	7 402	2 935	2 024	15 448	13 795	800	436
1991	13 213	8 693	544	9 237	1 182	-11	8 043	3 045	2 125	16 318	14 656	810	447
1992	13 928	9 376	467	9 843	1 291	-2	8 550	3 087	2 291	16 867	15 115	826	459
1993	15 012	10 094	769	10 863	1 432	1	9 432	3 112	2 467	17 770	15 939	845	473
1994	15 384	10 634	366	11 001	1 518	6	9 489	3 343	2 552	17 861	15 939	861	497
1995	16 084	10 964	322	11 286	1 534	9	9 761	3 604	2 719	18 349	16 402	877	507
1996	16 880	11 402	295	11 697	1 538	12	10 171	3 835	2 874	19 047	16 983	886	523
1997	17 688	11 814	329	12 143	1 555	14	10 602	4 174	2 912	19 877	17 660	890	529
1998	18 857	12 596	337	12 932	1 598	18	11 353	4 489	3 015	21 130	18 738	892	540
1999	19 373	13 176	391	13 567	1 651	22	11 938	4 443	2 991	21 585	19 087	898	548
2000	20 716	14 077	244	14 321	1 733	26	12 614	4 763	3 339	22 929	20 233	904	559
2001	22 359	15 295	286	15 581	1 853	32	13 760	4 995	3 605	24 676	21 891	906	566
2002	22 819	15 794	180	15 973	1 948	31	14 056	4 974	3 789	25 065	22 597	910	572
2003	24 073	16 603	365	16 968	2 184	29	14 813	5 316	3 944	26 227	23 834	918	579
2004	25 670	17 941	494	18 435	2 332	33	16 136	5 331	4 204	27 694	25 178	927	597
2005	27 046	19 318	506	19 825	2 497	31	17 359	5 187	4 500	28 906	25 985	936	613

... = Not available.
* = Less than $50,000, but the estimates for this item are included in the total.

Table 21-2. Personal Income and Employment by Region and State—Continued

(Millions of dollars, except as noted.)

Region or state and year	Personal income, total	Derivation of personal income								Per capita (dollars)		Population (thousands)	Total employment (thousands)
		Earnings by place of work			Less: Contributions for government social insurance	Plus: Adjustment for residence	Equals: Net earnings by place of residence	Plus: Dividends, interest, and rent	Plus: Personal current transfer receipts	Personal income	Disposable personal income		
		Nonfarm	Farm	Total									
NEBRASKA													
1958	2 863	1 824	521	2 345	75	-9	2 261	442	160	2 070	1 891	1 383	. . .
1959	2 892	1 992	357	2 349	93	-9	2 247	471	174	2 070	1 885	1 397	. . .
1960	3 072	2 129	385	2 514	116	-11	2 387	500	185	2 168	1 957	1 417	. . .
1961	3 138	2 235	312	2 547	119	-11	2 417	516	205	2 170	1 943	1 446	. . .
1962	3 411	2 359	430	2 789	128	-10	2 652	544	216	2 330	2 109	1 464	. . .
1963	3 502	2 441	384	2 825	140	-9	2 676	597	229	2 373	2 140	1 476	. . .
1964	3 592	2 586	304	2 891	146	-8	2 736	619	236	2 423	2 214	1 482	. . .
1965	3 951	2 701	490	3 191	148	-8	3 035	659	258	2 686	2 462	1 471	. . .
1966	4 252	2 908	583	3 490	196	-8	3 287	685	280	2 920	2 655	1 456	. . .
1967	4 403	3 141	481	3 622	228	-8	3 386	676	341	3 022	2 734	1 457	. . .
1968	4 692	3 433	438	3 871	245	-8	3 618	679	394	3 198	2 868	1 467	. . .
1969	5 261	3 800	596	4 397	269	-100	4 028	804	430	3 570	3 140	1 474	704
1970	5 642	4 121	534	4 655	289	-107	4 259	885	498	3 792	3 363	1 488	715
1971	6 197	4 438	681	5 120	320	-110	4 689	946	562	4 120	3 719	1 504	728
1972	6 874	4 879	800	5 679	364	-119	5 196	1 059	619	4 527	4 014	1 518	748
1973	8 042	5 466	1 219	6 685	467	-123	6 095	1 207	741	5 261	4 678	1 529	775
1974	8 379	6 078	759	6 837	541	-133	6 164	1 369	847	5 449	4 785	1 538	793
1975	9 523	6 579	1 099	7 677	579	-140	6 959	1 528	1 036	6 178	5 535	1 541	790
1976	9 970	7 478	579	8 056	661	-147	7 248	1 620	1 103	6 437	5 743	1 549	811
1977	10 817	8 151	522	8 673	723	-146	7 805	1 838	1 174	6 959	6 128	1 554	831
1978	12 534	9 128	1 074	10 202	832	-169	9 201	2 030	1 303	8 030	7 111	1 561	855
1979	13 527	10 202	740	10 943	970	-198	9 775	2 300	1 451	8 647	7 555	1 564	877
1980	14 403	11 053	98	11 151	1 051	-215	9 885	2 824	1 693	9 160	8 015	1 572	879
1981	16 722	11 887	822	12 708	1 209	-255	11 244	3 526	1 952	10 593	9 351	1 579	874
1982	17 984	12 352	760	13 111	1 287	-262	11 562	4 272	2 151	11 370	9 889	1 582	864
1983	18 630	12 989	540	13 528	1 355	-276	11 897	4 405	2 327	11 759	10 498	1 584	870
1984	20 826	14 329	1 150	15 479	1 525	-328	13 627	4 758	2 441	13 109	11 846	1 589	889
1985	21 978	15 089	1 442	16 531	1 651	-353	14 527	4 859	2 593	13 869	12 527	1 585	902
1986	22 565	15 614	1 406	17 020	1 756	-351	14 913	4 942	2 710	14 333	12 942	1 574	902
1987	23 549	16 436	1 630	18 066	1 859	-347	15 860	4 916	2 772	15 032	13 521	1 567	930
1988	25 095	17 477	2 026	19 503	2 069	-380	17 054	5 148	2 893	15 969	14 355	1 571	953
1989	26 497	18 526	1 834	20 360	2 209	-389	17 761	5 633	3 102	16 825	15 022	1 575	971
1990	28 444	19 736	2 182	21 918	2 372	-382	19 164	5 915	3 365	17 983	16 031	1 582	994
1991	29 563	20 678	1 979	22 658	2 508	-420	19 730	6 226	3 608	18 524	16 566	1 596	998
1992	31 184	21 948	2 087	24 034	2 630	-458	20 947	6 313	3 924	19 349	17 329	1 612	1 005
1993	32 105	23 084	1 735	24 818	2 769	-472	21 577	6 341	4 187	19 750	17 656	1 626	1 027
1994	34 012	24 518	1 787	26 306	2 961	-479	22 865	6 779	4 367	20 751	18 515	1 639	1 068
1995	36 006	26 296	1 311	27 607	3 101	-524	23 982	7 377	4 647	21 730	19 290	1 657	1 077
1996	39 382	27 887	2 555	30 442	3 264	-579	26 599	7 822	4 961	23 530	20 879	1 674	1 103
1997	40 576	29 465	1 823	31 288	3 462	-653	27 173	8 272	5 131	24 061	21 132	1 686	1 118
1998	43 314	31 387	1 723	33 110	3 686	-684	28 741	9 096	5 477	25 542	22 392	1 696	1 144
1999	45 116	33 311	1 472	34 783	3 874	-762	30 146	9 148	5 822	26 465	23 175	1 705	1 166
2000	47 329	35 157	963	36 120	4 031	-825	31 263	9 991	6 075	27 625	24 089	1 713	1 183
2001	49 303	36 471	1 201	37 672	4 200	-833	32 639	9 998	6 666	28 682	25 122	1 719	1 182
2002	50 390	37 857	660	38 517	4 350	-869	33 299	10 023	7 069	29 182	26 132	1 727	1 180
2003	53 388	39 445	1 979	41 424	4 541	-920	35 962	10 002	7 424	30 718	27 848	1 738	1 182
2004	55 858	41 640	1 962	43 602	4 704	-951	37 946	10 188	7 724	31 961	28 992	1 748	1 199
2005	58 019	43 621	1 695	45 316	5 025	-986	39 306	10 603	8 111	32 988	29 635	1 759	1 218

. . . = Not available.

Table 21-2. Personal Income and Employment by Region and State—Continued

(Millions of dollars, except as noted.)

Region or state and year	Personal income, total	Earnings by place of work			Less: Contributions for government social insurance	Plus: Adjustment for residence	Equals: Net earnings by place of residence	Plus: Dividends, interest, and rent	Plus: Personal current transfer receipts	Personal income	Disposable personal income	Population (thousands)	Total employment (thousands)
		Nonfarm	Farm	Total									
NEVADA													
1958	705	595	22	617	26	-2	589	79	37	2 622	2 309	269	. . .
1959	776	663	19	682	30	-2	650	88	38	2 780	2 470	279	. . .
1960	851	730	14	744	36	-2	706	104	41	2 923	2 573	291	. . .
1961	941	805	13	817	40	-3	775	117	49	2 988	2 606	315	. . .
1962	1 134	985	18	1 004	50	-4	950	133	51	3 222	2 829	352	. . .
1963	1 276	1 127	20	1 147	66	-6	1 075	143	58	3 213	2 804	397	. . .
1964	1 387	1 222	11	1 234	67	-5	1 161	161	65	3 257	2 909	426	. . .
1965	1 487	1 285	13	1 299	66	-5	1 228	187	72	3 348	2 999	444	. . .
1966	1 570	1 359	18	1 377	80	-4	1 294	199	78	3 521	3 144	446	. . .
1967	1 668	1 429	17	1 446	86	-3	1 356	217	95	3 715	3 309	449	. . .
1968	1 935	1 642	19	1 661	100	-4	1 557	265	113	4 170	3 632	464	. . .
1969	2 164	1 888	32	1 921	132	-34	1 754	285	125	4 509	3 830	480	244
1970	2 435	2 096	34	2 130	144	-39	1 947	340	148	4 936	4 360	493	256
1971	2 719	2 322	35	2 357	165	-42	2 151	384	184	5 229	4 674	520	267
1972	3 043	2 589	42	2 631	194	-45	2 393	433	218	5 566	4 944	547	280
1973	3 474	2 976	56	3 032	256	-55	2 721	499	254	6 107	5 429	569	304
1974	3 873	3 277	34	3 311	287	-57	2 967	591	315	6 491	5 752	597	317
1975	4 365	3 622	33	3 655	312	-58	3 284	644	438	7 043	6 404	620	326
1976	5 009	4 191	35	4 226	367	-68	3 791	730	489	7 745	6 938	647	349
1977	5 786	4 919	27	4 946	438	-84	4 424	829	534	8 533	7 593	678	384
1978	6 996	6 029	23	6 052	552	-117	5 383	1 010	603	9 725	8 566	719	432
1979	8 157	7 005	9	7 014	678	-132	6 204	1 242	711	10 661	9 314	765	468
1980	9 480	7 965	57	8 022	775	-160	7 087	1 529	863	11 700	10 300	810	490
1981	10 809	8 927	27	8 954	928	-170	7 857	1 900	1 053	12 752	11 192	848	502
1982	11 594	9 228	32	9 261	951	-171	8 139	2 283	1 172	13 152	11 651	882	497
1983	12 317	9 778	26	9 804	1 048	-179	8 576	2 458	1 283	13 656	12 193	902	502
1984	13 521	10 716	35	10 751	1 190	-191	9 369	2 777	1 374	14 618	13 080	925	528
1985	14 723	11 601	28	11 630	1 313	-199	10 118	3 095	1 510	15 481	13 776	951	551
1986	15 856	12 531	27	12 559	1 458	-217	10 884	3 289	1 683	16 170	14 346	981	577
1987	17 260	13 799	48	13 847	1 621	-241	11 985	3 479	1 796	16 865	14 880	1 023	623
1988	19 531	15 800	64	15 864	1 878	-280	13 706	3 850	1 975	18 168	15 966	1 075	670
1989	22 019	17 627	78	17 705	2 125	-325	15 254	4 485	2 281	19 360	17 012	1 137	719
1990	24 837	19 831	81	19 912	2 387	-381	17 144	5 085	2 607	20 346	17 866	1 221	766
1991	26 910	20 891	73	20 964	2 551	-351	18 062	5 645	3 203	20 761	18 383	1 296	779
1992	29 844	23 028	70	23 098	2 779	-313	20 006	6 209	3 629	22 084	19 526	1 351	786
1993	32 143	25 017	117	25 134	3 041	-354	21 739	6 567	3 837	22 777	20 053	1 411	829
1994	35 641	27 653	81	27 734	3 398	-367	23 969	7 649	4 023	23 772	21 015	1 499	909
1995	39 250	30 519	69	30 588	3 736	-365	26 487	8 397	4 366	24 817	21 941	1 582	964
1996	43 466	33 715	72	33 787	4 041	-386	29 360	9 395	4 711	26 085	22 803	1 666	1 035
1997	47 388	36 638	72	36 710	4 310	-340	32 059	10 321	5 008	26 862	23 531	1 764	1 102
1998	52 371	40 341	95	40 436	4 582	-349	35 504	11 529	5 338	28 260	24 576	1 853	1 145
1999	56 462	44 151	89	44 240	4 831	-379	39 030	11 855	5 577	29 184	25 349	1 935	1 215
2000	61 428	47 304	97	47 401	4 701	-339	42 361	13 067	5 999	30 437	26 322	2 018	1 268
2001	64 367	49 386	102	49 487	4 988	-302	44 198	13 351	6 819	30 727	26 788	2 095	1 289
2002	66 632	50 914	81	50 995	5 256	-311	45 428	13 545	7 659	30 736	27 306	2 168	1 304
2003	71 226	54 600	86	54 686	5 598	-367	48 721	14 471	8 035	31 773	28 485	2 242	1 364
2004	79 453	60 696	117	60 813	6 091	-446	54 276	16 582	8 595	34 058	30 364	2 333	1 443
2005	86 403	67 202	114	67 317	6 809	-535	59 973	17 119	9 311	35 780	31 468	2 415	1 527

. . . = Not available.

Table 21-2. Personal Income and Employment by Region and State—Continued

(Millions of dollars, except as noted.)

Region or state and year	Personal income, total	Derivation of personal income								Per capita (dollars)		Population (thousands)	Total employment (thousands)
		Earnings by place of work			Less: Contributions for government social insurance	Plus: Adjustment for residence	Equals: Net earnings by place of residence	Plus: Dividends, interest, and rent	Plus: Personal current transfer receipts	Personal income	Disposable personal income		
		Nonfarm	Farm	Total									
NEW HAMPSHIRE													
1958	1 163	887	21	908	39	57	926	155	83	2 002	1 807	581	. . .
1959	1 265	976	16	992	46	70	1 016	163	86	2 122	1 912	596	. . .
1960	1 336	1 025	19	1 044	55	79	1 068	178	90	2 194	1 959	609	. . .
1961	1 407	1 068	20	1 089	56	85	1 118	188	102	2 277	2 040	618	. . .
1962	1 509	1 142	19	1 160	62	94	1 193	211	105	2 387	2 134	632	. . .
1963	1 569	1 185	17	1 202	68	100	1 234	223	113	2 418	2 150	649	. . .
1964	1 686	1 271	18	1 289	71	108	1 326	244	116	2 543	2 309	663	. . .
1965	1 822	1 365	21	1 386	75	119	1 430	268	123	2 695	2 435	676	. . .
1966	2 005	1 519	24	1 543	103	139	1 579	294	132	2 945	2 630	681	. . .
1967	2 191	1 668	17	1 685	116	154	1 723	313	155	3 143	2 805	697	. . .
1968	2 424	1 838	20	1 858	128	173	1 902	342	180	3 418	3 029	709	. . .
1969	2 705	1 992	21	2 012	129	232	2 116	386	203	3 736	3 295	724	334
1970	2 883	2 113	16	2 130	135	220	2 215	427	241	3 886	3 409	742	334
1971	3 123	2 270	14	2 284	150	230	2 364	467	292	4 098	3 662	762	336
1972	3 454	2 525	16	2 541	176	252	2 617	515	322	4 419	3 888	782	350
1973	3 905	2 882	21	2 902	229	284	2 957	568	380	4 870	4 340	802	374
1974	4 304	3 119	13	3 132	257	329	3 204	644	455	5 267	4 673	817	381
1975	4 655	3 266	17	3 283	266	359	3 375	694	586	5 608	5 049	830	370
1976	5 298	3 787	19	3 806	310	411	3 906	768	624	6 255	5 588	847	394
1977	5 992	4 304	18	4 322	353	480	4 449	883	660	6 873	6 109	872	418
1978	6 918	5 032	19	5 051	420	572	5 203	993	723	7 739	6 817	894	446
1979	7 933	5 762	21	5 784	503	681	5 962	1 144	827	8 700	7 653	912	469
1980	9 104	6 397	14	6 410	560	849	6 699	1 435	969	9 850	8 698	924	483
1981	10 323	7 062	23	7 084	669	959	7 375	1 812	1 135	11 021	9 703	937	494
1982	11 382	7 629	19	7 648	741	1 050	7 957	2 180	1 246	12 010	10 698	948	500
1983	12 517	8 563	17	8 580	841	1 174	8 913	2 274	1 331	13 064	11 631	958	520
1984	14 211	9 694	21	9 715	977	1 390	10 129	2 674	1 408	14 547	12 997	977	556
1985	15 763	10 930	24	10 954	1 125	1 513	11 342	2 947	1 474	15 815	14 018	997	589
1986	17 407	12 256	24	12 280	1 285	1 598	12 594	3 267	1 546	16 981	14 957	1 025	622
1987	19 252	13 814	43	13 856	1 430	1 723	14 150	3 524	1 579	18 261	16 067	1 054	639
1988	21 178	15 254	45	15 299	1 621	1 876	15 554	3 910	1 714	19 563	17 335	1 083	665
1989	22 615	15 864	34	15 898	1 700	1 968	16 166	4 531	1 918	20 475	18 157	1 105	665
1990	22 817	15 773	43	15 817	1 720	2 004	16 101	4 568	2 149	20 512	18 292	1 112	648
1991	23 518	15 619	44	15 663	1 740	2 190	16 113	4 543	2 863	21 189	19 031	1 110	621
1992	24 594	16 706	51	16 758	1 845	2 247	17 159	4 384	3 051	22 002	19 777	1 118	633
1993	25 273	17 449	43	17 492	1 924	2 370	17 938	4 383	2 953	22 376	20 016	1 129	647
1994	26 972	18 492	41	18 532	2 082	2 468	18 919	4 696	3 358	23 607	21 141	1 143	670
1995	28 647	19 637	36	19 673	2 228	2 456	19 901	5 131	3 615	24 748	22 094	1 158	685
1996	31 045	20 859	42	20 901	2 352	2 624	21 173	6 302	3 570	26 427	23 434	1 175	701
1997	32 420	22 536	39	22 575	2 536	2 829	22 869	5 830	3 721	27 257	23 770	1 189	722
1998	35 149	24 694	42	24 736	2 753	2 946	24 928	6 363	3 858	29 147	25 403	1 206	745
1999	37 125	26 424	45	26 469	2 929	3 410	26 949	6 244	3 932	30 380	26 278	1 222	763
2000	41 429	29 364	42	29 405	3 210	4 043	30 239	6 986	4 204	33 396	28 566	1 241	785
2001	42 624	30 315	38	30 353	3 354	4 015	31 014	7 044	4 566	33 868	29 220	1 259	795
2002	43 393	31 138	38	31 176	3 437	3 865	31 604	6 794	4 995	34 043	30 368	1 275	795
2003	44 549	32 470	42	32 512	3 426	3 867	32 952	6 517	5 080	34 598	31 221	1 288	804
2004	47 463	34 807	50	34 857	3 685	3 972	35 144	6 751	5 567	36 533	33 110	1 299	820
2005	49 561	36 626	48	36 674	3 894	4 026	36 806	6 993	5 762	37 835	33 928	1 310	836

. . . = Not available.

Table 21-2. Personal Income and Employment by Region and State—Continued

(Millions of dollars, except as noted.)

Region or state and year	Personal income, total	Earnings by place of work			Less: Contributions for government social insurance	Plus: Adjustment for residence	Equals: Net earnings by place of residence	Plus: Dividends, interest, and rent	Plus: Personal current transfer receipts	Per capita (dollars)		Population (thousands)	Total employment (thousands)
		Nonfarm	Farm	Total						Personal income	Disposable personal income		
NEW JERSEY													
1958	14 369	11 477	133	11 610	469	684	11 825	1 698	847	2 440	2 160	5 890	. . .
1959	15 456	12 474	105	12 580	557	769	12 792	1 809	855	2 570	2 279	6 015	. . .
1960	16 288	13 087	120	13 207	660	855	13 403	1 989	896	2 669	2 357	6 103	. . .
1961	17 112	13 633	119	13 752	694	912	13 970	2 118	1 024	2 731	2 411	6 265	. . .
1962	18 410	14 592	108	14 700	771	1 013	14 943	2 389	1 079	2 887	2 545	6 376	. . .
1963	19 320	15 227	106	15 333	869	1 088	15 552	2 608	1 159	2 958	2 605	6 531	. . .
1964	20 731	16 175	102	16 277	881	1 205	16 601	2 925	1 205	3 113	2 793	6 660	. . .
1965	22 283	17 303	118	17 421	934	1 317	17 804	3 194	1 285	3 293	2 932	6 767	. . .
1966	24 138	18 890	118	19 008	1 212	1 514	19 310	3 442	1 385	3 523	3 135	6 851	. . .
1967	26 025	20 250	104	20 354	1 345	1 680	20 689	3 694	1 642	3 757	3 319	6 928	. . .
1968	28 601	22 151	102	22 253	1 533	1 888	22 608	4 030	1 964	4 083	3 575	7 005	. . .
1969	32 013	24 081	104	24 186	1 827	3 117	25 476	4 325	2 212	4 512	3 913	7 095	3 061
1970	34 663	26 049	99	26 149	1 957	3 071	27 263	4 712	2 689	4 821	4 225	7 190	3 125
1971	37 285	27 829	93	27 922	2 168	3 155	28 908	5 100	3 276	5 120	4 549	7 282	3 119
1972	40 492	30 383	88	30 472	2 482	3 354	31 343	5 485	3 664	5 519	4 835	7 337	3 184
1973	44 253	33 599	126	33 725	3 128	3 511	34 109	6 012	4 132	6 033	5 331	7 335	3 288
1974	48 161	36 184	137	36 320	3 458	3 701	36 564	6 748	4 848	6 566	5 779	7 335	3 301
1975	51 810	37 723	96	37 819	3 541	3 983	38 261	7 211	6 338	7 057	6 299	7 341	3 191
1976	56 579	41 568	101	41 669	3 930	4 326	42 065	7 673	6 842	7 704	6 809	7 344	3 248
1977	62 009	45 747	111	45 858	4 313	4 720	46 265	8 526	7 218	8 446	7 383	7 342	3 325
1978	68 857	51 302	126	51 428	4 985	5 301	51 744	9 431	7 681	9 360	8 160	7 356	3 464
1979	76 525	56 860	126	56 985	5 744	6 057	57 298	10 684	8 544	10 379	8 956	7 373	3 555
1980	86 355	62 436	114	62 549	6 325	7 159	63 384	13 209	9 763	11 707	10 084	7 376	3 608
1981	96 485	68 287	148	68 436	7 378	7 797	68 854	16 668	10 963	13 025	11 188	7 407	3 643
1982	104 313	73 032	165	73 198	8 007	8 339	73 529	18 766	12 018	14 038	12 070	7 431	3 651
1983	112 659	79 741	191	79 932	8 979	8 573	79 526	20 155	12 978	15 086	13 118	7 468	3 753
1984	124 744	88 809	199	89 008	10 422	8 976	87 562	23 648	13 533	16 598	14 501	7 515	3 933
1985	133 915	96 368	226	96 594	11 391	9 355	94 558	25 171	14 186	17 701	15 321	7 566	4 049
1986	143 017	104 150	228	104 378	12 485	9 953	101 846	26 320	14 852	18 763	16 212	7 622	4 146
1987	154 440	114 160	260	114 420	13 605	10 505	111 321	27 770	15 350	20 134	17 237	7 671	4 248
1988	169 577	126 764	260	127 024	15 329	10 836	122 531	30 701	16 345	21 988	19 041	7 712	4 349
1989	181 461	133 204	254	133 458	15 980	10 339	127 816	36 138	17 506	23 487	20 354	7 726	4 386
1990	190 753	139 588	234	139 821	16 641	10 556	133 736	37 702	19 315	24 572	21 381	7 763	4 344
1991	194 174	140 848	220	141 068	17 191	10 647	134 524	37 633	22 016	24 847	21 700	7 815	4 204
1992	207 904	150 184	237	150 421	18 256	12 656	144 821	37 478	25 604	26 382	23 084	7 881	4 201
1993	213 222	156 037	268	156 305	18 953	13 077	150 429	36 017	26 776	26 824	23 357	7 949	4 228
1994	220 859	162 295	286	162 581	20 037	13 144	155 688	38 032	27 139	27 558	23 897	8 014	4 264
1995	233 937	170 507	284	170 790	20 840	14 226	164 176	40 712	29 049	28 941	25 158	8 083	4 330
1996	248 320	179 807	303	180 110	21 722	15 672	174 060	43 856	30 404	30 470	26 299	8 150	4 386
1997	263 420	189 111	248	189 359	22 502	18 451	185 309	47 048	31 063	32 051	27 411	8 219	4 446
1998	282 721	203 154	261	203 415	23 902	20 798	200 311	50 775	31 636	34 115	28 914	8 287	4 524
1999	294 385	213 763	234	213 997	25 071	22 436	211 362	50 143	32 881	35 215	29 600	8 360	4 595
2000	323 554	233 138	304	233 441	26 854	25 657	232 244	56 234	35 076	38 364	32 009	8 434	4 755
2001	332 951	238 171	269	238 440	27 970	27 219	237 689	56 587	38 676	39 148	32 822	8 505	4 789
2002	337 009	245 182	261	245 444	28 752	24 087	240 779	54 151	42 080	39 296	33 971	8 576	4 804
2003	343 435	252 269	257	252 526	29 130	24 558	247 955	51 940	43 540	39 749	34 751	8 640	4 846
2004	363 852	265 820	282	266 103	30 136	27 231	263 198	55 873	44 781	41 893	36 811	8 685	4 912
2005	382 041	278 250	277	278 527	31 673	29 115	275 969	59 029	47 044	43 822	38 019	8 718	4 998

. . . = Not available.

Table 21-2. Personal Income and Employment by Region and State—Continued

(Millions of dollars, except as noted.)

Region or state and year	Personal income, total	Derivation of personal income								Per capita (dollars)		Population (thousands)	Total employment (thousands)
		Earnings by place of work			Less: Contributions for government social insurance	Plus: Adjustment for residence	Equals: Net earnings by place of residence	Plus: Dividends, interest, and rent	Plus: Personal current transfer receipts	Personal income	Disposable personal income		
		Nonfarm	Farm	Total									
NEW MEXICO													
1958	1 630	1 322	113	1 435	45	-13	1 377	168	84	1 840	1 672	886	. . .
1959	1 754	1 448	99	1 546	54	-14	1 478	184	93	1 909	1 728	919	. . .
1960	1 807	1 494	86	1 580	61	-14	1 505	200	102	1 894	1 719	954	. . .
1961	1 891	1 533	101	1 634	61	-14	1 558	214	118	1 959	1 778	965	. . .
1962	1 965	1 622	82	1 703	66	-15	1 623	223	120	2 008	1 816	979	. . .
1963	2 029	1 672	85	1 757	74	-16	1 667	233	129	2 052	1 857	989	. . .
1964	2 144	1 785	65	1 850	78	-17	1 755	254	135	2 131	1 955	1 006	. . .
1965	2 272	1 877	77	1 954	81	-19	1 854	272	145	2 245	2 041	1 012	. . .
1966	2 393	1 967	99	2 066	104	-19	1 943	294	156	2 376	2 161	1 007	. . .
1967	2 481	2 040	89	2 129	121	-20	1 989	297	195	2 481	2 257	1 000	. . .
1968	2 683	2 182	101	2 284	124	-21	2 138	316	228	2 699	2 443	994	. . .
1969	2 942	2 399	107	2 506	152	-22	2 332	350	261	2 910	2 588	1 011	395
1970	3 262	2 592	131	2 723	163	-22	2 538	399	325	3 188	2 849	1 023	399
1971	3 601	2 856	129	2 986	188	-22	2 775	448	378	3 419	3 106	1 053	416
1972	4 043	3 225	136	3 362	221	-20	3 121	500	422	3 752	3 380	1 078	440
1973	4 551	3 610	179	3 789	283	-17	3 489	562	500	4 122	3 716	1 104	461
1974	5 143	4 078	147	4 225	328	-15	3 881	662	601	4 553	4 086	1 130	478
1975	5 876	4 596	176	4 772	367	-13	4 393	745	738	5 054	4 618	1 163	491
1976	6 601	5 263	123	5 386	421	-12	4 953	823	825	5 523	5 003	1 195	512
1977	7 429	5 981	134	6 116	481	-11	5 623	937	869	6 064	5 486	1 225	539
1978	8 515	6 872	167	7 039	565	-11	6 463	1 098	954	6 802	6 091	1 252	568
1979	9 666	7 746	206	7 952	667	-9	7 275	1 290	1 101	7 549	6 751	1 281	593
1980	10 929	8 561	179	8 740	740	-3	7 996	1 623	1 310	8 346	7 483	1 309	598
1981	12 415	9 637	128	9 765	893	-15	8 857	2 062	1 497	9 316	8 255	1 333	613
1982	13 559	10 281	115	10 396	972	-17	9 407	2 506	1 647	9 942	8 789	1 364	621
1983	14 594	10 921	126	11 046	1 035	-13	9 998	2 797	1 800	10 467	9 476	1 394	633
1984	16 030	12 030	145	12 176	1 165	-6	11 005	3 102	1 923	11 315	10 286	1 417	658
1985	17 376	12 929	207	13 136	1 272	1	11 865	3 450	2 060	12 080	10 958	1 438	678
1986	17 993	13 270	193	13 463	1 333	9	12 139	3 637	2 217	12 301	11 212	1 463	684
1987	18 769	13 784	240	14 024	1 376	24	12 671	3 753	2 345	12 695	11 443	1 479	703
1988	19 816	14 537	320	14 857	1 514	35	13 378	3 926	2 512	13 296	11 995	1 490	739
1989	21 173	15 319	381	15 700	1 614	43	14 129	4 246	2 797	14 078	12 637	1 504	754
1990	22 708	16 407	416	16 822	1 737	51	15 136	4 525	3 046	14 924	13 413	1 522	767
1991	24 302	17 549	402	17 951	1 887	64	16 128	4 783	3 391	15 625	14 088	1 555	790
1992	25 963	18 776	484	19 260	2 006	81	17 335	4 848	3 781	16 273	14 687	1 595	803
1993	27 753	20 215	533	20 748	2 167	99	18 680	4 977	4 096	16 959	15 254	1 636	831
1994	29 662	21 511	463	21 974	2 357	117	19 734	5 506	4 421	17 631	15 831	1 682	863
1995	31 701	22 924	397	23 321	2 524	130	20 926	5 925	4 849	18 426	16 566	1 720	905
1996	33 345	23 626	413	24 039	2 597	150	21 592	6 472	5 282	19 029	17 034	1 752	915
1997	34 961	24 728	559	25 287	2 722	173	22 739	6 804	5 418	19 698	17 529	1 775	929
1998	37 046	26 134	614	26 748	2 852	196	24 091	7 261	5 694	20 656	18 382	1 793	945
1999	38 046	26 974	726	27 700	2 967	224	24 957	7 061	6 028	21 042	18 681	1 808	951
2000	40 318	28 692	504	29 196	3 115	250	26 332	7 545	6 441	22 134	19 578	1 822	973
2001	44 138	31 234	712	31 946	3 337	251	28 860	8 080	7 198	24 085	21 493	1 833	978
2002	44 987	32 637	498	33 134	3 497	252	29 890	7 190	7 906	24 246	21 899	1 855	988
2003	46 698	34 212	529	34 741	3 606	258	31 392	6 882	8 424	24 849	22 637	1 879	1 013
2004	50 792	36 721	739	37 460	3 755	264	33 970	7 826	8 996	26 690	24 415	1 903	1 037
2005	53 826	39 122	705	39 827	4 047	284	36 064	8 105	9 657	27 912	25 380	1 928	1 064

. . . = Not available.

Table 21-2. Personal Income and Employment by Region and State—Continued

(Millions of dollars, except as noted.)

Region or state and year	Personal income, total	Earnings by place of work			Less: Contributions for government social insurance	Plus: Adjustment for residence	Equals: Net earnings by place of residence	Plus: Dividends, interest, and rent	Plus: Personal current transfer receipts	Per capita (dollars)		Population (thousands)	Total employment (thousands)
		Nonfarm	Farm	Total						Personal income	Disposable personal income		
NEW YORK													
1958	42 844	35 970	374	36 344	1 434	-589	34 321	5 925	2 597	2 581	2 263	16 601	. . .
1959	45 478	38 431	314	38 745	1 711	-663	36 371	6 385	2 721	2 726	2 373	16 685	. . .
1960	47 504	40 258	348	40 607	2 040	-738	37 828	6 882	2 794	2 821	2 452	16 838	. . .
1961	49 537	41 747	359	42 106	2 191	-792	39 123	7 207	3 207	2 904	2 511	17 061	. . .
1962	52 265	44 181	282	44 463	2 489	-879	41 095	7 875	3 295	3 021	2 615	17 301	. . .
1963	54 369	45 662	330	45 992	2 712	-945	42 335	8 485	3 549	3 114	2 696	17 461	. . .
1964	58 119	48 468	313	48 781	2 681	-1 042	45 058	9 338	3 723	3 304	2 902	17 589	. . .
1965	61 648	51 125	361	51 486	2 803	-1 129	47 554	10 079	4 016	3 476	3 042	17 734	. . .
1966	66 196	55 520	421	55 941	3 719	-1 284	50 938	10 623	4 636	3 710	3 226	17 843	. . .
1967	71 480	59 466	376	59 842	4 031	-1 429	54 382	11 198	5 900	3 985	3 437	17 935	. . .
1968	78 777	65 221	385	65 606	4 444	-1 611	59 551	12 012	7 213	4 364	3 736	18 051	. . .
1969	83 071	70 374	435	70 810	5 283	-3 370	62 156	13 177	7 738	4 588	3 866	18 105	8 496
1970	89 047	74 870	415	75 285	5 525	-3 320	66 440	13 696	8 912	4 874	4 182	18 272	8 468
1971	94 929	79 090	405	79 495	6 021	-3 426	70 047	14 132	10 750	5 169	4 499	18 365	8 348
1972	101 465	84 851	347	85 199	6 786	-3 682	74 731	14 735	11 999	5 529	4 758	18 352	8 350
1973	108 510	91 179	465	91 644	8 402	-3 900	79 342	15 873	13 295	5 964	5 159	18 195	8 468
1974	117 015	96 764	435	97 199	9 177	-4 124	83 898	17 692	15 425	6 475	5 582	18 073	8 395
1975	125 715	101 226	372	101 598	9 443	-4 471	87 683	18 518	19 514	6 972	6 100	18 032	8 175
1976	134 312	108 634	395	109 029	10 240	-4 915	93 875	19 655	20 782	7 472	6 514	17 975	8 128
1977	145 284	117 785	325	118 110	11 004	-5 468	101 638	21 900	21 746	8 138	7 069	17 852	8 202
1978	158 202	129 462	425	129 887	12 359	-6 121	111 407	24 010	22 785	8 928	7 721	17 720	8 381
1979	173 257	142 323	530	142 853	14 064	-6 979	121 810	27 111	24 336	9 825	8 437	17 634	8 591
1980	193 492	156 467	521	156 988	15 326	-8 203	133 459	32 079	27 955	11 015	9 424	17 567	8 622
1981	216 592	172 221	535	172 756	17 978	-8 989	145 788	39 247	31 556	12 329	10 454	17 568	8 700
1982	235 868	185 233	512	185 745	19 580	-9 865	156 300	45 045	34 523	13 409	11 352	17 590	8 710
1983	252 521	197 967	363	198 331	21 209	-10 334	166 787	48 380	37 353	14 277	12 282	17 687	8 771
1984	281 237	219 483	484	219 967	23 922	-11 005	185 040	56 657	39 540	15 848	13 687	17 746	9 058
1985	300 275	236 364	552	236 916	26 256	-11 661	198 999	59 537	41 739	16 877	14 473	17 792	9 293
1986	320 223	254 715	645	255 360	28 610	-12 570	214 180	61 820	44 223	17 956	15 381	17 833	9 494
1987	341 560	275 384	727	276 111	30 469	-13 388	232 255	63 931	45 375	19 115	16 212	17 869	9 552
1988	372 771	301 956	642	302 598	34 131	-14 183	254 284	70 236	48 252	20 777	17 818	17 941	9 768
1989	400 769	316 180	764	316 944	35 868	-13 782	267 294	80 513	52 962	22 286	18 986	17 983	9 841
1990	423 897	332 467	745	333 212	37 849	-14 083	281 280	84 547	58 069	23 523	20 183	18 021	9 817
1991	434 304	334 699	617	335 316	38 691	-14 151	282 475	86 538	65 291	23 965	20 750	18 123	9 567
1992	453 737	354 874	728	355 602	40 470	-17 429	297 702	83 690	72 344	24 867	21 525	18 247	9 494
1993	462 008	362 389	792	363 181	41 543	-17 363	304 275	80 922	76 811	25 143	21 650	18 375	9 516
1994	475 979	370 458	665	371 123	43 347	-17 370	310 406	85 003	80 570	25 785	22 197	18 459	9 551
1995	501 667	389 360	545	389 905	44 952	-19 760	325 193	90 770	85 704	27 082	23 268	18 524	9 601
1996	528 363	411 259	777	412 036	46 314	-22 529	343 193	95 589	89 580	28 424	24 212	18 588	9 686
1997	557 024	436 661	474	437 135	48 332	-25 017	363 785	103 491	89 748	29 857	25 245	18 657	9 819
1998	591 847	469 379	716	470 096	51 014	-28 639	390 443	108 539	92 864	31 555	26 461	18 756	10 015
1999	619 659	498 632	827	499 459	53 642	-30 402	415 415	108 354	95 889	32 816	27 296	18 883	10 220
2000	663 005	537 852	770	538 623	57 239	-34 495	446 888	115 784	100 334	34 897	28 881	18 999	10 455
2001	679 886	550 300	851	551 151	59 470	-35 416	456 264	113 585	110 036	35 612	29 161	19 091	10 491
2002	677 604	548 912	596	549 508	60 353	-31 537	457 618	103 078	116 908	35 357	30 083	19 165	10 415
2003	691 962	560 477	770	561 247	62 803	-31 959	466 484	102 458	123 020	35 987	30 988	19 228	10 460
2004	741 275	597 765	973	598 738	65 105	-35 495	498 137	110 774	132 364	38 446	33 024	19 281	10 599
2005	771 568	629 646	1 039	630 685	68 106	-37 847	524 732	114 958	131 878	40 072	33 876	19 255	10 760

. . . = Not available.

Table 21-2. Personal Income and Employment by Region and State—Continued

(Millions of dollars, except as noted.)

| Region or state and year | Personal income, total | Earnings by place of work | | | Less: Contributions for government social insurance | Plus: Adjustment for residence | Equals: Net earnings by place of residence | Plus: Dividends, interest, and rent | Plus: Personal current transfer receipts | Per capita (dollars) | | Population (thousands) | Total employment (thousands) |
		Nonfarm	Farm	Total						Personal income	Disposable personal income		
NORTH CAROLINA													
1958	6 552	5 065	625	5 690	214	9	5 485	666	400	1 497	1 383	4 376	. . .
1959	7 014	5 609	518	6 127	257	9	5 879	705	430	1 573	1 435	4 458	. . .
1960	7 414	5 879	600	6 478	306	9	6 181	776	457	1 621	1 473	4 573	. . .
1961	7 834	6 140	639	6 779	314	10	6 474	836	524	1 680	1 526	4 663	. . .
1962	8 416	6 653	621	7 275	346	10	6 939	924	552	1 788	1 615	4 707	. . .
1963	8 849	7 072	599	7 670	412	11	7 270	985	595	1 866	1 682	4 742	. . .
1964	9 596	7 687	628	8 316	435	11	7 892	1 081	623	1 998	1 823	4 802	. . .
1965	10 349	8 440	526	8 966	467	11	8 510	1 160	679	2 128	1 922	4 863	. . .
1966	11 484	9 499	611	10 110	617	10	9 504	1 243	738	2 346	2 107	4 896	. . .
1967	12 429	10 362	602	10 964	714	10	10 259	1 311	859	2 510	2 257	4 952	. . .
1968	13 702	11 642	514	12 156	825	12	11 343	1 377	981	2 738	2 429	5 004	. . .
1969	15 272	12 885	667	13 553	899	16	12 670	1 495	1 107	3 036	2 655	5 031	2 458
1970	16 661	13 881	666	14 546	971	13	13 589	1 734	1 337	3 267	2 879	5 099	2 469
1971	18 181	15 184	622	15 805	1 101	10	14 714	1 898	1 568	3 496	3 108	5 201	2 490
1972	20 569	17 280	743	18 023	1 308	4	16 720	2 094	1 756	3 884	3 409	5 296	2 602
1973	23 407	19 492	1 155	20 647	1 677	2	18 972	2 398	2 038	4 349	3 844	5 382	2 720
1974	25 830	21 304	1 101	22 405	1 900	8	20 513	2 784	2 532	4 730	4 155	5 461	2 743
1975	27 932	22 239	1 058	23 297	1 977	14	21 334	3 077	3 521	5 046	4 541	5 535	2 647
1976	31 206	25 131	1 141	26 272	2 271	15	24 016	3 409	3 781	5 579	4 966	5 593	2 754
1977	34 239	28 005	849	28 854	2 512	22	26 364	3 884	3 992	6 040	5 352	5 668	2 851
1978	38 715	31 757	1 133	32 890	2 922	21	29 989	4 424	4 303	6 744	5 950	5 740	2 948
1979	42 946	35 519	746	36 264	3 390	18	32 892	5 133	4 921	7 403	6 474	5 802	3 051
1980	48 344	38 941	639	39 580	3 727	23	35 875	6 599	5 870	8 195	7 172	5 899	3 060
1981	54 553	42 821	1 040	43 860	4 393	-20	39 448	8 334	6 772	9 158	8 000	5 957	3 082
1982	58 508	44 892	1 058	45 950	4 648	-30	41 272	9 694	7 542	9 720	8 615	6 019	3 051
1983	63 973	49 669	628	50 296	5 177	-49	45 070	10 770	8 132	10 527	9 304	6 077	3 138
1984	72 997	56 515	1 283	57 798	5 974	-83	51 741	12 659	8 596	11 842	10 517	6 164	3 306
1985	79 417	61 714	1 152	62 866	6 593	-147	56 126	14 075	9 217	12 699	11 245	6 254	3 410
1986	85 223	66 483	1 136	67 619	7 231	-210	60 179	15 243	9 802	13 481	11 928	6 322	3 512
1987	91 611	72 355	1 137	73 492	7 803	-292	65 397	16 016	10 198	14 306	12 552	6 404	3 631
1988	99 786	78 675	1 477	80 152	8 776	-351	71 025	17 733	11 028	15 398	13 589	6 481	3 774
1989	108 309	83 928	1 712	85 640	9 430	-403	75 807	20 186	12 316	16 497	14 460	6 565	3 864
1990	114 926	88 090	2 122	90 212	10 017	-447	79 748	21 605	13 573	17 246	15 196	6 664	3 928
1991	119 927	90 607	2 382	92 989	10 504	-430	82 055	22 291	15 581	17 677	15 648	6 784	3 889
1992	129 957	99 375	2 308	101 682	11 395	-451	89 836	22 782	17 339	18 842	16 720	6 897	3 989
1993	137 865	105 214	2 587	107 800	12 178	-467	95 155	23 608	19 101	19 575	17 325	7 043	4 113
1994	146 620	111 617	2 804	114 421	13 105	-520	100 797	25 958	19 865	20 400	17 982	7 187	4 227
1995	156 407	118 415	2 701	121 115	13 922	-592	106 601	27 715	22 091	21 295	18 716	7 345	4 380
1996	167 416	124 934	3 001	127 935	14 596	-648	112 691	30 754	23 972	22 320	19 548	7 501	4 487
1997	180 163	134 089	3 024	137 114	15 663	-716	120 735	34 165	25 263	23 530	20 508	7 657	4 631
1998	193 223	144 640	2 365	147 005	16 692	-704	129 609	37 408	26 206	24 743	21 400	7 809	4 746
1999	203 187	155 058	2 158	157 216	17 797	-771	138 648	36 606	27 933	25 560	22 136	7 949	4 850
2000	218 668	166 192	2 579	168 771	18 748	-885	149 137	39 633	29 898	27 068	23 396	8 078	4 925
2001	225 395	170 532	2 766	173 298	19 564	-781	152 953	39 156	33 286	27 493	23 837	8 198	4 885
2002	228 684	174 832	1 363	176 195	19 900	-779	155 515	37 195	35 975	27 510	24 330	8 313	4 878
2003	235 140	180 421	1 632	182 053	20 738	-711	160 605	37 038	37 498	27 919	24 934	8 422	4 890
2004	252 614	191 812	2 132	193 943	21 545	-744	171 655	40 760	40 199	29 579	26 518	8 540	4 991
2005	269 435	204 012	2 691	206 703	23 340	-784	182 579	43 632	43 223	31 029	27 548	8 683	5 113

. . . = Not available.

Table 21-2. Personal Income and Employment by Region and State—Continued

(Millions of dollars, except as noted.)

Region or state and year	Personal income, total	Derivation of personal income								Per capita (dollars)		Population (thousands)	Total employment (thousands)
		Earnings by place of work			Less: Contributions for government social insurance	Plus: Adjustment for residence	Equals: Net earnings by place of residence	Plus: Dividends, interest, and rent	Plus: Personal current transfer receipts	Personal income	Disposable personal income		
		Nonfarm	Farm	Total									
NORTH DAKOTA													
1958	1 156	624	321	945	31	-10	904	179	73	1 908	1 766	606	...
1959	1 069	680	185	865	34	-11	820	170	78	1 729	1 594	618	...
1960	1 185	706	269	974	41	-11	922	180	83	1 869	1 724	634	...
1961	1 077	735	140	875	43	-11	820	166	90	1 680	1 543	641	...
1962	1 516	796	472	1 268	47	-14	1 207	215	94	2 379	2 206	637	...
1963	1 401	847	321	1 168	56	-14	1 097	206	98	2 176	2 000	644	...
1964	1 392	913	235	1 148	59	-17	1 072	215	104	2 145	1 976	649	...
1965	1 621	971	376	1 347	62	-17	1 268	238	114	2 497	2 315	649	...
1966	1 638	1 023	343	1 366	74	-16	1 276	239	123	2 531	2 330	647	...
1967	1 640	1 052	305	1 357	89	-16	1 252	241	147	2 620	2 395	626	...
1968	1 708	1 121	280	1 402	95	-16	1 291	252	164	2 750	2 510	621	...
1969	1 910	1 227	379	1 605	103	-52	1 450	277	183	3 076	2 759	621	274
1970	1 999	1 367	300	1 667	115	-55	1 497	291	212	3 230	2 920	619	281
1971	2 314	1 500	428	1 928	130	-58	1 741	325	248	3 693	3 397	627	284
1972	2 769	1 681	661	2 342	148	-62	2 132	361	276	4 388	4 027	631	288
1973	3 914	1 901	1 521	3 422	190	-65	3 167	437	310	6 189	5 686	632	300
1974	3 878	2 155	1 153	3 308	225	-78	3 005	517	356	6 114	5 444	634	308
1975	4 063	2 443	934	3 377	257	-84	3 037	606	420	6 363	5 695	638	314
1976	3 990	2 796	470	3 266	295	-99	2 872	654	464	6 183	5 531	645	326
1977	4 160	3 038	266	3 304	304	-106	2 894	760	506	6 409	5 764	649	331
1978	5 258	3 471	855	4 326	355	-118	3 852	853	553	8 082	7 246	651	345
1979	5 392	3 890	491	4 382	414	-136	3 831	948	613	8 269	7 390	652	354
1980	5 174	4 232	-396	3 837	448	-153	3 235	1 216	723	7 907	6 932	654	356
1981	6 819	4 733	361	5 094	530	-176	4 388	1 601	830	10 340	9 098	660	360
1982	7 383	5 006	298	5 304	574	-179	4 551	1 902	930	11 036	9 929	669	361
1983	7 734	5 256	358	5 614	615	-182	4 817	1 882	1 035	11 430	10 361	677	366
1984	8 410	5 555	599	6 154	654	-188	5 312	1 988	1 110	12 358	11 252	680	368
1985	8 710	5 682	688	6 370	680	-188	5 502	2 029	1 179	12 866	11 731	677	365
1986	8 796	5 704	682	6 386	702	-184	5 500	2 011	1 285	13 137	12 032	670	359
1987	9 057	5 927	780	6 707	732	-186	5 789	1 924	1 344	13 699	12 489	661	365
1988	8 343	6 144	-70	6 074	798	-192	5 083	1 912	1 348	12 731	11 485	655	369
1989	9 338	6 373	426	6 798	846	-198	5 754	2 116	1 468	14 447	13 075	646	373
1990	10 166	6 714	751	7 465	908	-194	6 363	2 231	1 573	15 943	14 457	638	376
1991	10 351	7 091	594	7 685	978	-203	6 504	2 245	1 602	16 282	14 746	636	385
1992	11 277	7 550	1 021	8 570	1 044	-222	7 304	2 214	1 759	17 669	16 085	638	390
1993	11 351	8 033	602	8 635	1 131	-242	7 262	2 236	1 853	17 703	16 006	641	400
1994	12 255	8 481	994	9 475	1 207	-258	8 011	2 368	1 876	19 006	17 244	645	414
1995	12 221	8 888	404	9 292	1 255	-283	7 754	2 490	1 977	18 865	17 008	648	421
1996	13 702	9 354	1 272	10 627	1 312	-319	8 995	2 631	2 075	21 068	19 084	650	429
1997	13 440	9 791	336	10 127	1 357	-344	8 425	2 861	2 154	20 686	18 560	650	433
1998	14 810	10 390	950	11 340	1 414	-371	9 555	3 065	2 190	22 872	20 620	648	440
1999	14 934	10 837	658	11 495	1 446	-402	9 647	2 994	2 293	23 180	20 863	644	443
2000	16 097	11 360	962	12 322	1 503	-428	10 391	3 244	2 462	25 106	22 595	641	447
2001	16 465	12 059	542	12 601	1 559	-461	10 581	3 352	2 531	25 879	23 203	636	449
2002	16 743	12 584	314	12 898	1 600	-486	10 812	3 256	2 675	26 427	24 095	634	451
2003	18 137	13 262	1 243	14 505	1 766	-505	12 234	3 139	2 764	28 651	26 385	633	451
2004	18 467	14 327	611	14 938	1 891	-554	12 493	3 109	2 865	29 021	26 691	636	463
2005	19 883	15 197	1 126	16 322	2 000	-592	13 731	3 112	3 041	31 230	28 542	637	472

... = Not available.

Table 21-2. Personal Income and Employment by Region and State—Continued

(Millions of dollars, except as noted.)

Region or state and year	Personal income, total	Earnings by place of work			Less: Contributions for government social insurance	Plus: Adjustment for residence	Equals: Net earnings by place of residence	Plus: Dividends, interest, and rent	Plus: Personal current transfer receipts	Per capita (dollars)		Population (thousands)	Total employment (thousands)
		Nonfarm	Farm	Total						Personal income	Disposable personal income		
OHIO													
1958	20 843	17 271	378	17 649	700	-119	16 830	2 567	1 446	2 171	1 945	9 599	. . .
1959	22 308	18 960	261	19 221	860	-133	18 228	2 712	1 368	2 307	2 059	9 671	. . .
1960	23 209	19 579	327	19 906	1 002	-131	18 772	2 925	1 512	2 384	2 114	9 734	. . .
1961	23 635	19 548	365	19 914	984	-121	18 809	3 066	1 760	2 398	2 139	9 854	. . .
1962	24 920	20 810	328	21 138	1 125	-126	19 888	3 302	1 731	2 510	2 229	9 929	. . .
1963	25 946	21 726	325	22 051	1 236	-129	20 686	3 477	1 782	2 598	2 304	9 986	. . .
1964	27 708	23 369	297	23 666	1 354	-134	22 178	3 742	1 789	2 749	2 474	10 080	. . .
1965	30 005	25 317	350	25 667	1 408	-147	24 112	4 000	1 893	2 941	2 630	10 201	. . .
1966	32 757	27 971	487	28 458	1 864	-166	26 428	4 290	2 038	3 171	2 821	10 330	. . .
1967	34 362	29 268	322	29 590	1 957	-161	27 472	4 512	2 379	3 300	2 933	10 414	. . .
1968	37 916	32 238	407	32 645	2 133	-184	30 328	4 899	2 690	3 606	3 167	10 516	. . .
1969	41 407	35 347	409	35 757	2 360	-187	33 210	5 298	2 899	3 920	3 394	10 563	4 695
1970	43 597	36 742	426	37 167	2 409	-178	34 580	5 623	3 394	4 086	3 589	10 669	4 683
1971	46 381	38 669	407	39 076	2 605	-128	36 343	6 026	4 012	4 321	3 856	10 735	4 627
1972	50 350	42 095	497	42 592	2 987	-125	39 479	6 435	4 436	4 685	4 116	10 747	4 710
1973	56 071	47 155	658	47 813	3 865	-153	43 795	7 113	5 163	5 208	4 581	10 767	4 902
1974	61 593	50 967	784	51 752	4 312	-129	47 311	8 081	6 200	5 721	5 020	10 766	4 964
1975	65 710	52 665	802	53 468	4 338	-75	49 055	8 726	7 929	6 101	5 402	10 770	4 809
1976	72 585	58 965	777	59 742	4 944	-85	54 713	9 389	8 483	6 750	5 946	10 753	4 889
1977	80 707	66 238	664	66 902	5 557	-98	61 246	10 549	8 912	7 493	6 561	10 771	5 034
1978	89 417	73 903	613	74 515	6 407	-116	67 993	11 843	9 581	8 283	7 233	10 795	5 207
1979	99 084	81 302	745	82 047	7 332	-138	74 578	13 566	10 940	9 176	7 960	10 799	5 298
1980	108 500	85 191	559	85 750	7 615	-153	77 983	16 735	13 783	10 046	8 770	10 801	5 215
1981	118 192	91 268	155	91 423	8 706	-463	82 254	20 621	15 316	10 956	9 510	10 788	5 151
1982	123 709	92 078	260	92 338	8 892	-585	82 861	23 070	17 778	11 500	10 105	10 757	4 983
1983	131 008	97 188	-77	97 111	9 600	-706	86 805	25 186	19 017	12 201	10 737	10 738	4 978
1984	144 833	107 686	857	108 543	10 920	-841	96 782	28 427	19 624	13 488	11 941	10 738	5 183
1985	153 758	114 774	855	115 630	11 858	-930	102 842	29 995	20 921	14 323	12 641	10 735	5 316
1986	160 111	120 111	669	120 780	12 681	-964	107 135	31 178	22 157	14 955	13 220	10 730	5 430
1987	167 984	126 814	722	127 536	13 449	-1 001	113 086	31 871	23 026	15 612	13 688	10 760	5 582
1988	179 628	137 023	772	137 795	14 928	-1 053	121 815	33 627	24 186	16 634	14 648	10 799	5 720
1989	192 358	144 303	1 149	145 453	15 919	-1 092	128 441	38 088	25 828	17 763	15 559	10 829	5 843
1990	203 630	151 641	1 166	152 807	16 872	-1 079	134 856	40 065	28 709	18 743	16 446	10 864	5 905
1991	209 066	155 532	663	156 195	17 692	-1 082	137 421	40 360	31 285	19 100	16 824	10 946	5 882
1992	221 277	165 885	1 121	167 006	18 756	-1 284	146 967	40 372	33 938	20 062	17 709	11 029	5 893
1993	229 065	173 029	912	173 941	19 815	-1 346	152 780	41 056	35 230	20 634	18 149	11 101	5 998
1994	242 146	183 511	1 127	184 638	21 316	-1 485	161 837	43 717	36 592	21 712	19 067	11 152	6 175
1995	252 003	190 711	892	191 603	22 425	-1 408	167 769	45 671	38 563	22 495	19 675	11 203	6 341
1996	262 201	196 924	1 231	198 156	23 039	-1 367	173 749	48 328	40 124	23 322	20 217	11 243	6 437
1997	278 049	207 342	1 734	209 076	23 706	-1 451	183 918	52 712	41 419	24 656	21 308	11 277	6 541
1998	294 292	220 595	1 258	221 853	24 264	-1 567	196 022	56 190	42 079	26 017	22 405	11 312	6 660
1999	304 464	232 218	752	232 970	25 366	-1 597	206 007	55 044	43 413	26 859	23 164	11 335	6 747
2000	320 538	243 185	936	244 121	25 426	-1 526	217 168	57 209	46 161	28 207	24 263	11 364	6 836
2001	325 623	246 588	689	247 277	26 189	-1 405	219 684	55 602	50 337	28 601	24 681	11 385	6 759
2002	333 158	253 786	199	253 985	26 334	-1 438	226 212	53 187	53 758	29 212	25 652	11 405	6 691
2003	340 840	261 596	715	262 311	27 903	-1 440	232 967	51 287	56 586	29 815	26 464	11 432	6 664
2004	352 315	272 484	909	273 393	29 343	-1 424	242 626	50 676	59 013	30 769	27 337	11 450	6 730
2005	365 319	282 080	760	282 840	30 724	-1 438	250 678	52 287	62 354	31 867	28 057	11 464	6 792

. . . = Not available.

Table 21-2. Personal Income and Employment by Region and State—Continued

(Millions of dollars, except as noted.)

| Region or state and year | Personal income, total | Derivation of personal income | | | | | | | | Per capita (dollars) | | Population (thousands) | Total employment (thousands) |
| | | Earnings by place of work | | | Less: Contributions for government social insurance | Plus: Adjustment for residence | Equals: Net earnings by place of residence | Plus: Dividends, interest, and rent | Plus: Personal current transfer receipts | Personal income | Disposable personal income | | |
		Nonfarm	Farm	Total									
OKLAHOMA													
1958	4 085	3 022	326	3 348	113	4	3 239	514	331	1 802	1 636	2 267	. . .
1959	4 265	3 207	262	3 469	130	5	3 344	562	359	1 863	1 685	2 289	. . .
1960	4 488	3 303	331	3 634	150	7	3 491	619	378	1 921	1 736	2 336	. . .
1961	4 638	3 432	297	3 728	159	8	3 578	644	416	1 949	1 754	2 380	. . .
1962	4 836	3 659	236	3 895	178	11	3 728	668	441	1 993	1 791	2 427	. . .
1963	4 997	3 825	209	4 035	208	12	3 839	688	471	2 049	1 844	2 439	. . .
1964	5 355	4 116	204	4 320	207	14	4 127	737	491	2 189	1 989	2 446	. . .
1965	5 736	4 347	273	4 620	216	17	4 422	788	526	2 351	2 136	2 440	. . .
1966	6 142	4 734	263	4 996	286	21	4 731	827	584	2 503	2 261	2 454	. . .
1967	6 695	5 188	273	5 461	336	25	5 150	845	700	2 690	2 425	2 489	. . .
1968	7 341	5 777	216	5 993	384	31	5 640	912	789	2 933	2 626	2 503	. . .
1969	8 111	6 305	272	6 576	402	63	6 237	1 018	855	3 200	2 818	2 535	1 107
1970	8 919	6 802	355	7 157	431	65	6 791	1 147	981	3 475	3 098	2 566	1 120
1971	9 729	7 391	332	7 723	484	64	7 303	1 295	1 130	3 716	3 356	2 618	1 132
1972	10 675	8 155	413	8 568	558	73	8 084	1 351	1 240	4 017	3 574	2 657	1 183
1973	12 172	9 095	729	9 825	720	83	9 188	1 578	1 406	4 518	4 058	2 694	1 221
1974	13 600	10 387	446	10 832	846	107	10 094	1 842	1 663	4 977	4 400	2 732	1 256
1975	15 237	11 530	399	11 928	928	142	11 142	2 043	2 052	5 497	4 936	2 772	1 269
1976	16 879	12 960	333	13 293	1 054	177	12 416	2 217	2 245	5 978	5 339	2 823	1 305
1977	18 853	14 807	178	14 985	1 198	153	13 940	2 525	2 388	6 578	5 841	2 866	1 359
1978	21 405	17 011	167	17 178	1 417	149	15 911	2 923	2 571	7 348	6 456	2 913	1 428
1979	24 956	19 487	628	20 115	1 687	164	18 592	3 413	2 952	8 403	7 364	2 970	1 483
1980	28 906	22 648	257	22 905	1 964	171	21 113	4 383	3 410	9 506	8 279	3 041	1 551
1981	33 952	26 334	324	26 657	2 443	196	24 411	5 667	3 874	10 966	9 414	3 096	1 630
1982	37 938	28 875	483	29 358	2 741	201	26 817	6 753	4 368	11 833	10 086	3 206	1 678
1983	38 747	28 987	208	29 196	2 738	239	26 697	7 257	4 794	11 776	10 372	3 290	1 642
1984	41 833	31 099	368	31 467	2 968	288	28 787	8 072	4 974	12 732	11 328	3 286	1 672
1985	43 614	32 036	375	32 411	3 108	330	29 632	8 668	5 314	13 332	11 874	3 271	1 656
1986	43 291	31 358	638	31 996	3 118	378	29 256	8 388	5 647	13 309	12 100	3 253	1 595
1987	43 171	31 321	558	31 880	3 135	425	29 169	8 126	5 875	13 448	12 062	3 210	1 607
1988	45 023	32 621	760	33 381	3 457	473	30 397	8 414	6 212	14 216	12 753	3 167	1 617
1989	48 111	34 557	792	35 349	3 696	497	32 151	9 342	6 618	15 272	13 632	3 150	1 632
1990	50 971	36 644	847	37 490	3 966	560	34 084	9 765	7 121	16 187	14 280	3 149	1 664
1991	52 565	38 020	610	38 630	4 241	590	34 978	9 845	7 742	16 554	14 749	3 175	1 678
1992	55 958	40 450	815	41 266	4 469	610	37 406	9 876	8 676	17 376	15 553	3 221	1 690
1993	57 937	42 261	865	43 125	4 721	645	39 049	9 774	9 115	17 814	15 947	3 252	1 726
1994	60 283	43 590	821	44 412	4 979	701	40 133	10 474	9 676	18 374	16 410	3 281	1 759
1995	62 395	45 122	275	45 397	5 194	739	40 942	11 142	10 311	18 861	16 826	3 308	1 810
1996	65 944	47 523	373	47 896	5 379	767	43 284	11 886	10 773	19 743	17 523	3 340	1 861
1997	69 720	50 339	680	51 018	5 605	840	46 253	12 369	11 098	20 671	18 213	3 373	1 908
1998	74 118	53 674	572	54 246	5 882	874	49 238	13 431	11 448	21 766	19 161	3 405	1 957
1999	77 565	56 264	872	57 136	6 050	925	52 011	13 537	12 017	22 567	19 887	3 437	1 975
2000	84 310	60 883	715	61 598	6 355	1 008	56 251	15 290	12 770	24 407	21 517	3 454	2 015
2001	90 161	65 716	625	66 341	6 798	1 010	60 553	15 478	14 130	26 015	23 005	3 466	2 025
2002	90 178	65 338	774	66 112	7 012	1 043	60 143	14 914	15 121	25 861	23 254	3 487	2 007
2003	92 591	67 739	735	68 474	7 324	1 059	62 210	14 475	15 906	26 417	23 944	3 505	1 987
2004	99 963	73 780	801	74 581	7 937	1 120	67 764	15 589	16 610	28 370	25 783	3 524	2 019
2005	106 111	78 528	870	79 398	8 444	1 174	72 128	16 121	17 861	29 908	26 978	3 548	2 071

. . . = Not available.

Table 21-2. Personal Income and Employment by Region and State—Continued

(Millions of dollars, except as noted.)

Region or state and year	Personal income, total	Earnings by place of work			Less: Contributions for government social insurance	Plus: Adjustment for residence	Equals: Net earnings by place of residence	Plus: Dividends, interest, and rent	Plus: Personal current transfer receipts	Per capita (dollars)		Population (thousands)	Total employment (thousands)
		Nonfarm	Farm	Total						Personal income	Disposable personal income		
OREGON													
1958	3 596	2 826	175	3 001	145	-11	2 846	467	283	2 093	1 834	1 718	. . .
1959	3 896	3 120	178	3 297	180	-14	3 103	507	286	2 232	1 957	1 746	. . .
1960	4 021	3 238	172	3 410	207	-17	3 185	532	304	2 269	1 987	1 772	. . .
1961	4 170	3 321	159	3 480	211	-19	3 250	568	352	2 333	2 061	1 787	. . .
1962	4 441	3 554	170	3 724	232	-22	3 470	612	359	2 443	2 150	1 818	. . .
1963	4 678	3 792	161	3 953	266	-27	3 660	647	371	2 524	2 202	1 853	. . .
1964	5 041	4 123	148	4 270	271	-32	3 967	690	384	2 670	2 348	1 888	. . .
1965	5 492	4 484	166	4 650	276	-38	4 337	741	414	2 835	2 512	1 937	. . .
1966	5 929	4 883	193	5 076	352	-42	4 681	800	447	3 011	2 650	1 969	. . .
1967	6 296	5 141	183	5 324	392	-46	4 886	877	533	3 181	2 802	1 979	. . .
1968	6 864	5 632	182	5 814	444	-54	5 315	948	600	3 425	2 986	2 004	. . .
1969	7 554	6 145	224	6 369	483	-91	5 795	1 097	662	3 664	3 138	2 062	920
1970	8 242	6 542	214	6 756	506	-67	6 183	1 254	805	3 924	3 424	2 100	926
1971	9 027	7 143	203	7 345	569	-56	6 720	1 376	932	4 199	3 696	2 150	951
1972	10 110	8 062	257	8 320	680	-50	7 589	1 498	1 022	4 605	4 014	2 195	1 001
1973	11 442	9 112	369	9 481	881	-56	8 545	1 685	1 213	5 110	4 473	2 239	1 058
1974	13 010	10 141	475	10 615	1 004	-63	9 549	1 965	1 496	5 704	4 959	2 281	1 089
1975	14 389	10 975	391	11 367	1 057	-31	10 278	2 210	1 901	6 190	5 470	2 325	1 105
1976	16 374	12 735	368	13 103	1 235	-16	11 852	2 454	2 067	6 903	6 046	2 372	1 156
1977	18 371	14 488	318	14 805	1 421	-74	13 311	2 826	2 235	7 531	6 504	2 439	1 223
1978	21 122	16 878	315	17 192	1 694	-132	15 366	3 315	2 441	8 416	7 244	2 510	1 297
1979	24 001	19 107	387	19 494	1 989	-205	17 300	3 964	2 737	9 309	7 984	2 578	1 352
1980	26 710	20 445	474	20 919	2 125	-253	18 541	4 920	3 248	10 113	8 731	2 641	1 353
1981	28 882	21 280	403	21 683	2 367	-263	19 052	6 070	3 760	10 825	9 388	2 668	1 324
1982	29 672	21 153	290	21 443	2 400	-250	18 793	6 640	4 239	11 134	9 687	2 665	1 274
1983	31 490	22 284	296	22 580	2 559	-234	19 787	7 145	4 557	11 869	10 431	2 653	1 300
1984	34 350	24 480	397	24 877	2 892	-280	21 704	7 939	4 706	12 882	11 381	2 667	1 348
1985	36 197	25 930	423	26 353	3 073	-317	22 963	8 308	4 925	13 543	11 923	2 673	1 379
1986	37 965	27 265	545	27 809	3 264	-362	24 184	8 769	5 013	14 148	12 386	2 684	1 414
1987	39 999	29 155	512	29 667	3 451	-422	25 795	9 014	5 191	14 809	12 966	2 701	1 464
1988	43 446	32 087	702	32 789	3 936	-493	28 359	9 566	5 522	15 849	14 044	2 741	1 532
1989	47 580	34 664	666	35 330	4 270	-546	30 514	11 007	6 060	17 050	14 833	2 791	1 586
1990	51 515	37 807	694	38 501	4 615	-608	33 278	11 646	6 591	18 010	15 823	2 860	1 638
1991	54 256	39 622	706	40 328	4 936	-664	34 729	12 212	7 316	18 527	16 214	2 929	1 647
1992	57 547	42 441	716	43 158	5 291	-748	37 118	12 310	8 119	19 235	16 813	2 992	1 665
1993	61 349	45 294	860	46 154	5 661	-838	39 655	13 005	8 689	20 046	17 471	3 060	1 709
1994	65 735	48 530	759	49 289	6 127	-888	42 275	14 426	9 034	21 060	18 284	3 121	1 792
1995	70 990	51 716	678	52 394	6 591	-1 061	44 742	16 228	10 020	22 293	19 393	3 184	1 858
1996	75 975	55 840	819	56 659	7 245	-1 284	48 129	17 149	10 697	23 398	20 232	3 247	1 933
1997	80 854	59 858	945	60 802	7 703	-1 467	51 632	18 176	11 046	24 469	20 986	3 304	1 999
1998	85 629	63 656	877	64 533	8 097	-1 589	54 848	19 314	11 467	25 542	21 951	3 352	2 037
1999	89 873	67 936	829	68 765	8 477	-1 737	58 551	18 929	12 393	26 480	22 657	3 394	2 065
2000	96 402	73 256	849	74 105	9 090	-1 904	63 111	20 303	12 988	28 097	23 905	3 431	2 111
2001	99 020	74 810	763	75 572	9 158	-1 891	64 523	19 999	14 498	28 507	24 510	3 473	2 104
2002	101 882	77 128	783	77 912	9 301	-1 952	66 659	19 502	15 721	28 924	25 495	3 522	2 092
2003	104 660	79 832	977	80 810	10 161	-1 910	68 739	19 800	16 121	29 377	26 066	3 563	2 102
2004	110 695	84 960	1 181	86 141	10 964	-1 987	73 190	20 951	16 554	30 823	27 365	3 591	2 159
2005	117 149	90 616	1 241	91 857	11 563	-2 126	78 168	21 414	17 568	32 174	28 256	3 641	2 225

. . . = Not available.

Table 21-2. Personal Income and Employment by Region and State—Continued

(Millions of dollars, except as noted.)

Region or state and year	Personal income, total	Derivation of personal income									Per capita (dollars)		Population (thousands)	Total employment (thousands)
		Earnings by place of work			Less: Contributions for government social insurance	Plus: Adjustment for residence	Equals: Net earnings by place of residence	Plus: Dividends, interest, and rent	Plus: Personal current transfer receipts		Personal income	Disposable personal income		
		Nonfarm	Farm	Total										
PENNSYLVANIA														
1958	23 858	19 746	339	20 086	846	-45	19 195	2 861	1 803		2 158	1 925	11 058	. . .
1959	25 072	21 023	252	21 275	1 042	-57	20 177	3 024	1 871		2 232	1 986	11 234	. . .
1960	25 978	21 843	294	22 137	1 211	-75	20 851	3 205	1 922		2 293	2 036	11 329	. . .
1961	26 517	22 021	297	22 318	1 225	-81	21 012	3 322	2 183		2 328	2 080	11 392	. . .
1962	27 632	23 123	214	23 337	1 334	-97	21 905	3 560	2 167		2 433	2 161	11 355	. . .
1963	28 637	23 897	255	24 153	1 473	-106	22 573	3 818	2 245		2 507	2 222	11 424	. . .
1964	30 646	25 658	264	25 922	1 530	-129	24 264	4 124	2 259		2 660	2 388	11 519	. . .
1965	32 850	27 511	273	27 785	1 593	-149	26 043	4 438	2 370		2 827	2 530	11 620	. . .
1966	35 384	30 213	260	30 473	2 147	-193	28 133	4 676	2 575		3 034	2 694	11 664	. . .
1967	37 885	32 020	355	32 375	2 316	-222	29 837	4 980	3 068		3 243	2 883	11 681	. . .
1968	41 142	34 675	310	34 985	2 420	-258	32 307	5 323	3 512		3 504	3 089	11 741	. . .
1969	44 729	37 860	367	38 227	2 810	-413	35 003	5 726	4 000		3 810	3 311	11 741	5 250
1970	48 088	39 971	382	40 353	2 930	-379	37 044	6 121	4 923		4 071	3 566	11 812	5 226
1971	51 007	41 943	331	42 274	3 190	-362	38 722	6 501	5 783		4 292	3 802	11 884	5 159
1972	55 719	45 934	341	46 275	3 658	-372	42 246	6 935	6 537		4 680	4 060	11 905	5 247
1973	61 303	50 803	479	51 282	4 632	-336	46 314	7 675	7 315		5 158	4 504	11 885	5 402
1974	67 547	55 417	455	55 872	5 228	-341	50 302	8 695	8 550		5 693	4 947	11 864	5 419
1975	73 581	58 711	417	59 128	5 407	-374	53 347	9 395	10 840		6 184	5 460	11 898	5 302
1976	80 825	64 453	510	64 963	6 010	-362	58 591	10 207	12 027		6 799	5 984	11 887	5 353
1977	88 847	71 112	462	71 574	6 607	-361	64 606	11 463	12 778		7 478	6 545	11 882	5 429
1978	98 035	79 020	497	79 518	7 526	-372	71 620	12 692	13 723		8 263	7 205	11 865	5 564
1979	108 608	87 084	631	87 715	8 596	-395	78 724	14 431	15 452		9 147	7 935	11 874	5 672
1980	119 692	93 188	412	93 600	9 194	-431	83 975	18 022	17 695		10 085	8 769	11 868	5 638
1981	132 196	100 071	625	100 697	10 573	-413	89 710	22 563	19 923		11 148	9 628	11 859	5 605
1982	141 241	102 416	557	102 972	10 986	-246	91 740	26 684	22 817		11 924	10 389	11 845	5 495
1983	147 915	106 470	352	106 822	11 570	-86	95 166	28 072	24 677		12 495	11 020	11 838	5 455
1984	160 164	115 749	837	116 585	13 094	104	103 596	31 729	24 839		13 556	11 964	11 815	5 606
1985	170 050	122 548	836	123 384	14 059	251	109 576	34 479	25 995		14 447	12 738	11 771	5 714
1986	178 939	129 176	875	130 051	14 998	356	115 408	36 121	27 409		15 187	13 418	11 783	5 808
1987	189 585	139 281	876	140 157	15 991	453	124 619	36 926	28 040		16 052	14 096	11 811	5 998
1988	203 661	151 121	737	151 857	17 810	685	134 733	39 391	29 537		17 193	15 134	11 846	6 165
1989	220 748	161 204	980	162 184	18 766	878	144 296	44 984	31 467		18 603	16 334	11 866	6 265
1990	234 334	170 686	973	171 659	19 763	959	152 855	47 166	34 314		19 687	17 344	11 903	6 342
1991	242 822	174 787	794	175 581	20 611	908	155 877	48 130	38 814		20 265	17 949	11 982	6 259
1992	255 874	185 645	1 169	186 813	21 879	1 229	166 163	47 330	42 381		21 235	18 796	12 049	6 262
1993	263 462	192 717	1 039	193 756	23 147	1 243	171 853	47 321	44 289		21 738	19 236	12 120	6 302
1994	272 695	199 647	919	200 566	24 499	1 607	177 675	49 517	45 504		22 414	19 776	12 166	6 369
1995	283 764	207 402	648	208 051	25 368	1 868	184 551	51 675	47 539		23 262	20 443	12 198	6 471
1996	297 494	214 929	1 128	216 057	25 875	2 242	192 423	54 532	50 538		24 344	21 258	12 220	6 525
1997	311 509	225 787	786	226 573	27 021	2 549	202 101	57 746	51 662		25 475	22 096	12 228	6 631
1998	330 161	240 915	921	241 836	28 206	2 465	216 095	61 899	52 167		26 961	23 301	12 246	6 724
1999	342 611	253 111	881	253 992	29 424	2 889	227 456	60 613	54 542		27 937	24 101	12 264	6 836
2000	364 838	267 020	1 148	268 169	30 697	3 355	240 827	66 085	57 926		29 695	25 573	12 286	6 973
2001	372 339	272 455	943	273 398	31 880	3 389	244 907	65 227	62 205		30 281	26 135	12 296	6 979
2002	382 251	281 086	675	281 761	32 768	3 470	252 463	63 611	66 177		31 016	27 398	12 324	6 956
2003	393 738	291 093	1 090	292 182	34 052	3 624	261 755	62 117	69 867		31 843	28 388	12 365	6 936
2004	413 572	308 096	1 371	309 467	35 466	3 927	277 928	62 727	72 917		33 367	29 823	12 394	7 020
2005	433 146	322 580	1 297	323 877	38 056	4 208	290 030	65 022	78 094		34 848	30 851	12 430	7 131

. . . = Not available.

Table 21-2. Personal Income and Employment by Region and State—Continued

(Millions of dollars, except as noted.)

Region or state and year	Personal income, total	Earnings by place of work			Less: Contributions for government social insurance	Plus: Adjustment for residence	Equals: Net earnings by place of residence	Plus: Dividends, interest, and rent	Plus: Personal current transfer receipts	Per capita (dollars)		Population (thousands)	Total employment (thousands)
		Nonfarm	Farm	Total						Personal income	Disposable personal income		
RHODE ISLAND													
1958	1 793	1 443	8	1 450	75	44	1 418	225	149	2 090	1 865	858	. . .
1959	1 893	1 543	6	1 550	86	51	1 514	232	146	2 209	1 978	857	. . .
1960	1 934	1 581	7	1 589	96	54	1 547	237	150	2 262	2 012	855	. . .
1961	2 023	1 634	7	1 641	98	57	1 601	256	166	2 358	2 090	858	. . .
1962	2 169	1 751	7	1 758	108	63	1 713	287	169	2 490	2 215	871	. . .
1963	2 265	1 807	7	1 814	117	67	1 764	323	179	2 586	2 299	876	. . .
1964	2 416	1 933	8	1 940	122	73	1 892	340	184	2 729	2 459	885	. . .
1965	2 600	2 078	8	2 086	133	82	2 035	367	198	2 912	2 617	893	. . .
1966	2 840	2 296	9	2 305	162	96	2 239	383	218	3 159	2 818	899	. . .
1967	3 082	2 468	7	2 474	174	105	2 405	411	265	3 390	3 038	909	. . .
1968	3 367	2 700	8	2 708	200	116	2 625	434	308	3 652	3 235	922	. . .
1969	3 591	2 901	8	2 909	230	65	2 744	500	347	3 853	3 392	932	440
1970	3 902	3 117	9	3 126	245	66	2 948	531	423	4 104	3 653	951	440
1971	4 137	3 278	8	3 286	267	61	3 081	560	497	4 292	3 824	964	436
1972	4 510	3 614	8	3 621	306	56	3 371	593	546	4 619	4 066	976	447
1973	4 853	3 873	6	3 880	381	71	3 569	659	625	4 962	4 372	978	452
1974	5 142	3 973	9	3 982	410	88	3 660	749	734	5 393	4 744	954	439
1975	5 543	4 113	9	4 121	415	82	3 788	783	972	5 857	5 257	946	424
1976	6 090	4 631	9	4 641	472	89	4 257	840	993	6 408	5 699	950	442
1977	6 670	5 096	8	5 104	520	103	4 687	943	1 040	6 983	6 224	955	459
1978	7 317	5 661	9	5 670	597	102	5 176	1 031	1 111	7 644	6 714	957	475
1979	8 141	6 305	7	6 312	684	110	5 738	1 168	1 235	8 510	7 401	957	484
1980	9 181	6 882	8	6 890	746	124	6 268	1 484	1 428	9 677	8 476	949	486
1981	10 263	7 431	9	7 440	851	155	6 744	1 885	1 634	10 769	9 441	953	486
1982	11 036	7 803	27	7 831	902	209	7 137	2 105	1 794	11 566	10 196	954	477
1983	11 890	8 425	37	8 462	988	265	7 739	2 238	1 913	12 432	10 998	956	482
1984	13 183	9 384	32	9 416	1 135	334	8 615	2 603	1 965	13 705	12 183	962	507
1985	14 161	10 162	42	10 204	1 220	394	9 378	2 696	2 087	14 615	12 968	969	522
1986	15 174	10 991	43	11 034	1 336	419	10 118	2 886	2 171	15 526	13 697	977	541
1987	16 310	11 910	41	11 951	1 435	488	11 004	3 071	2 236	16 482	14 393	990	550
1988	17 980	13 160	42	13 202	1 603	563	12 162	3 427	2 391	18 045	15 865	996	564
1989	19 559	13 860	32	13 892	1 669	625	12 848	4 098	2 612	19 546	17 184	1 001	565
1990	20 126	14 136	31	14 167	1 716	665	13 117	4 123	2 887	20 006	17 639	1 006	555
1991	20 262	13 810	32	13 842	1 722	693	12 814	3 940	3 509	20 049	17 741	1 011	528
1992	21 129	14 666	30	14 696	1 835	712	13 573	3 902	3 654	20 867	18 541	1 013	534
1993	21 913	15 207	30	15 237	1 924	754	14 067	3 880	3 966	21 586	19 141	1 015	538
1994	22 450	15 657	26	15 683	2 011	828	14 500	4 007	3 943	22 097	19 553	1 016	538
1995	23 620	16 395	25	16 420	2 080	860	15 200	4 253	4 167	23 225	20 544	1 017	541
1996	24 609	16 919	24	16 943	2 113	929	15 759	4 623	4 227	24 106	21 213	1 021	544
1997	25 983	17 758	16	17 774	2 218	990	16 547	4 940	4 497	25 341	22 080	1 025	550
1998	27 501	18 856	16	18 872	2 348	1 074	17 598	5 315	4 587	26 670	23 111	1 031	558
1999	28 568	19 810	16	19 826	2 459	1 177	18 544	5 232	4 792	27 459	23 757	1 040	570
2000	30 697	21 255	16	21 271	2 619	1 344	19 996	5 713	4 988	29 214	25 059	1 051	584
2001	32 478	22 360	15	22 376	2 748	1 341	20 969	5 951	5 559	30 687	26 407	1 058	587
2002	33 635	23 231	18	23 249	2 875	1 305	21 679	6 057	5 899	31 478	27 742	1 069	589
2003	35 063	24 632	18	24 650	3 042	1 285	22 893	6 036	6 134	32 594	28 988	1 076	595
2004	36 652	25 968	20	25 989	3 170	1 363	24 182	5 918	6 552	33 940	30 207	1 080	603
2005	37 903	27 009	21	27 030	3 348	1 390	25 071	5 978	6 853	35 219	31 040	1 076	608

. . . = Not available.

Table 21-2. Personal Income and Employment by Region and State—Continued

(Millions of dollars, except as noted.)

Region or state and year	Personal income, total	Derivation of personal income								Per capita (dollars)		Population (thousands)	Total employment (thousands)
		Earnings by place of work			Less: Contributions for government social insurance	Plus: Adjustment for residence	Equals: Net earnings by place of residence	Plus: Dividends, interest, and rent	Plus: Personal current transfer receipts	Personal income	Disposable personal income		
		Nonfarm	Farm	Total									
SOUTH CAROLINA													
1958	3 014	2 438	182	2 620	95	13	2 538	287	189	1 308	1 211	2 304	. . .
1959	3 249	2 678	164	2 842	113	15	2 745	305	199	1 384	1 267	2 348	. . .
1960	3 416	2 824	168	2 991	135	17	2 874	333	210	1 428	1 306	2 392	. . .
1961	3 585	2 913	194	3 107	138	19	2 988	359	238	1 488	1 360	2 409	. . .
1962	3 853	3 153	183	3 336	153	22	3 205	395	253	1 590	1 444	2 423	. . .
1963	4 074	3 355	186	3 541	189	25	3 377	425	272	1 656	1 505	2 460	. . .
1964	4 389	3 645	178	3 823	202	30	3 650	455	284	1 773	1 625	2 475	. . .
1965	4 839	4 030	180	4 210	221	35	4 024	506	310	1 940	1 770	2 494	. . .
1966	5 433	4 611	194	4 804	290	43	4 557	533	342	2 156	1 947	2 520	. . .
1967	5 876	4 994	196	5 190	341	49	4 898	577	401	2 320	2 096	2 533	. . .
1968	6 519	5 618	154	5 772	386	57	5 443	605	471	2 547	2 283	2 559	. . .
1969	7 229	6 159	186	6 345	416	115	6 044	648	536	2 813	2 495	2 570	1 170
1970	7 928	6 657	187	6 844	448	116	6 511	748	669	3 051	2 738	2 598	1 196
1971	8 690	7 253	202	7 456	509	128	7 075	837	778	3 265	2 935	2 662	1 215
1972	9 766	8 206	212	8 417	599	145	7 963	927	876	3 592	3 168	2 718	1 262
1973	11 148	9 348	300	9 648	773	159	9 035	1 070	1 043	4 017	3 562	2 775	1 328
1974	12 652	10 492	339	10 830	897	174	10 107	1 228	1 318	4 450	3 939	2 843	1 365
1975	13 721	10 992	274	11 266	927	185	10 524	1 384	1 814	4 731	4 297	2 900	1 326
1976	15 460	12 649	232	12 880	1 088	220	12 013	1 528	1 919	5 256	4 713	2 941	1 376
1977	16 945	13 977	185	14 162	1 198	243	13 207	1 733	2 005	5 669	5 066	2 989	1 411
1978	19 167	15 871	243	16 114	1 389	261	14 985	1 978	2 204	6 303	5 616	3 041	1 467
1979	21 577	17 805	256	18 062	1 607	285	16 740	2 294	2 544	6 990	6 160	3 087	1 510
1980	24 270	19 666	33	19 699	1 777	320	18 242	2 939	3 088	7 743	6 846	3 135	1 527
1981	27 402	21 686	168	21 854	2 095	350	20 110	3 721	3 571	8 619	7 584	3 179	1 541
1982	29 155	22 456	192	22 649	2 199	383	20 832	4 401	3 922	9 089	8 081	3 208	1 518
1983	31 715	24 588	49	24 637	2 470	396	22 564	4 967	4 184	9 806	8 717	3 234	1 552
1984	35 810	27 767	266	28 033	2 850	443	25 627	5 769	4 414	10 945	9 789	3 272	1 631
1985	38 534	29 706	194	29 899	3 096	500	27 303	6 447	4 783	11 666	10 407	3 303	1 664
1986	40 900	31 674	88	31 762	3 393	564	28 934	6 922	5 045	12 235	10 915	3 343	1 706
1987	43 838	34 116	248	34 364	3 631	608	31 341	7 310	5 188	12 968	11 518	3 381	1 748
1988	47 510	37 151	347	37 498	4 110	628	34 016	7 959	5 535	13 924	12 439	3 412	1 820
1989	51 381	39 690	363	40 053	4 463	581	36 171	8 569	6 640	14 864	13 172	3 457	1 871
1990	55 647	42 754	295	43 049	4 817	505	38 737	9 845	7 064	15 894	14 095	3 501	1 926
1991	57 987	43 771	394	44 164	5 035	492	39 621	10 219	8 148	16 241	14 522	3 570	1 898
1992	61 377	46 294	376	46 671	5 305	502	41 867	10 391	9 119	16 953	15 186	3 620	1 910
1993	64 220	48 564	338	48 902	5 641	506	43 767	10 666	9 788	17 531	15 681	3 663	1 944
1994	68 050	50 654	484	51 138	5 982	611	45 767	11 730	10 553	18 365	16 384	3 705	1 992
1995	71 688	53 328	381	53 709	6 326	731	48 115	12 272	11 301	19 124	16 980	3 749	2 051
1996	76 144	55 854	463	56 318	6 540	851	50 628	13 319	12 197	20 058	17 724	3 796	2 094
1997	81 004	59 171	474	59 645	6 942	1 000	53 702	14 486	12 816	20 987	18 473	3 860	2 154
1998	86 854	63 512	341	63 853	7 403	1 074	57 524	15 912	13 418	22 161	19 440	3 919	2 209
1999	91 716	67 945	418	68 363	7 786	1 169	61 747	15 705	14 264	23 075	20 238	3 975	2 257
2000	98 270	71 951	489	72 441	8 132	1 398	65 707	17 289	15 274	24 424	21 501	4 024	2 291
2001	101 468	73 736	587	74 323	8 425	1 371	67 270	17 216	16 982	24 994	22 072	4 060	2 266
2002	104 046	76 089	190	76 279	8 721	1 390	68 948	16 654	18 445	25 361	22 794	4 103	2 259
2003	107 247	79 108	565	79 673	8 996	1 404	72 081	15 765	19 401	25 863	23 435	4 147	2 277
2004	113 668	83 629	576	84 205	9 433	1 483	76 256	16 464	20 948	27 077	24 579	4 198	2 319
2005	120 043	88 422	517	88 939	9 993	1 572	80 519	17 162	22 363	28 212	25 413	4 255	2 363

. . . = Not available.

Table 21-2. Personal Income and Employment by Region and State—Continued

(Millions of dollars, except as noted.)

Region or state and year	Personal income, total	Earnings by place of work			Less: Contributions for government social insurance	Plus: Adjustment for residence	Equals: Net earnings by place of residence	Plus: Dividends, interest, and rent	Plus: Personal current transfer receipts	Personal income	Disposable personal income	Population (thousands)	Total employment (thousands)
		Nonfarm	Farm	Total						Per capita (dollars)			
SOUTH DAKOTA													
1958	1 156	648	308	956	26	0	930	153	73	1 762	1 620	656	. . .
1959	1 048	707	140	847	34	0	814	153	82	1 571	1 454	667	. . .
1960	1 290	740	320	1 060	35	0	1 026	179	86	1 889	1 752	683	. . .
1961	1 297	811	246	1 057	39	0	1 019	184	94	1 872	1 723	693	. . .
1962	1 482	865	364	1 229	45	1	1 184	198	100	2 102	1 941	705	. . .
1963	1 429	875	293	1 168	51	1	1 118	205	106	2 018	1 853	708	. . .
1964	1 397	918	211	1 129	50	1	1 080	208	109	1 993	1 853	701	. . .
1965	1 574	950	330	1 279	51	2	1 230	226	119	2 275	2 124	692	. . .
1966	1 701	1 016	388	1 404	64	2	1 342	230	129	2 491	2 311	683	. . .
1967	1 726	1 070	340	1 411	77	3	1 336	236	154	2 573	2 383	671	. . .
1968	1 853	1 162	359	1 521	83	3	1 440	236	177	2 770	2 542	669	. . .
1969	2 010	1 272	353	1 625	90	6	1 541	275	194	3 009	2 739	668	303
1970	2 177	1 371	369	1 740	96	6	1 650	305	222	3 265	3 005	667	305
1971	2 381	1 498	400	1 897	107	6	1 797	329	255	3 546	3 304	671	306
1972	2 757	1 662	560	2 221	121	7	2 107	368	282	4 070	3 795	677	309
1973	3 502	1 879	1 022	2 901	159	7	2 749	426	327	5 158	4 776	679	323
1974	3 515	2 107	681	2 789	184	8	2 613	520	382	5 169	4 717	680	326
1975	3 877	2 303	701	3 004	201	10	2 814	607	456	5 689	5 271	681	326
1976	3 837	2 622	273	2 895	225	12	2 682	654	501	5 586	5 108	687	336
1977	4 368	2 871	439	3 310	238	13	3 085	755	528	6 339	5 875	689	342
1978	5 023	3 267	609	3 877	275	15	3 617	832	574	7 287	6 708	689	355
1979	5 545	3 603	644	4 247	323	16	3 941	956	648	8 048	7 387	689	360
1980	5 577	3 839	128	3 966	344	18	3 640	1 180	758	8 073	7 317	691	354
1981	6 507	4 070	437	4 507	391	14	4 130	1 508	869	9 437	8 582	690	349
1982	6 887	4 196	368	4 564	411	12	4 165	1 756	966	9 972	9 022	691	345
1983	7 142	4 492	249	4 741	442	5	4 304	1 798	1 040	10 306	9 486	693	354
1984	8 159	4 956	680	5 636	493	-2	5 141	1 918	1 099	11 701	10 887	697	364
1985	8 401	5 186	604	5 791	532	-5	5 254	1 978	1 169	12 029	11 172	698	367
1986	8 755	5 406	656	6 062	572	-11	5 478	2 060	1 217	12 578	11 691	696	368
1987	9 223	5 725	837	6 563	617	-19	5 926	2 040	1 257	13 251	12 251	696	383
1988	9 577	6 156	708	6 865	691	-26	6 148	2 116	1 313	13 717	12 669	698	390
1989	10 267	6 550	713	7 263	750	-36	6 476	2 360	1 431	14 737	13 548	697	398
1990	11 273	7 115	1 005	8 120	821	-56	7 243	2 505	1 525	16 172	14 822	697	412
1991	11 803	7 647	879	8 526	891	-69	7 567	2 599	1 638	16 774	15 396	704	423
1992	12 687	8 253	1 045	9 298	958	-85	8 255	2 645	1 787	17 799	16 328	713	434
1993	13 207	8 827	935	9 761	1 025	-99	8 638	2 693	1 877	18 289	16 682	722	445
1994	14 172	9 401	1 173	10 574	1 113	-128	9 333	2 849	1 989	19 392	17 775	731	467
1995	14 390	9 854	629	10 482	1 167	-152	9 163	3 106	2 121	19 501	17 777	738	475
1996	15 948	10 262	1 446	11 708	1 216	-192	10 300	3 396	2 252	21 488	19 661	742	482
1997	16 335	10 781	1 102	11 883	1 278	-191	10 413	3 609	2 313	21 949	19 849	744	488
1998	17 523	11 534	1 255	12 789	1 366	-243	11 180	3 967	2 376	23 488	21 251	746	497
1999	18 367	12 309	1 185	13 494	1 459	-258	11 777	4 116	2 474	24 475	22 019	750	509
2000	19 438	13 099	1 116	14 215	1 535	-280	12 400	4 393	2 645	25 720	23 163	756	519
2001	20 429	13 832	863	14 696	1 593	-235	12 867	4 703	2 859	26 949	24 329	758	517
2002	20 596	14 462	266	14 728	1 641	-216	12 871	4 655	3 070	27 087	24 829	760	519
2003	22 452	15 122	1 262	16 384	1 649	-216	14 519	4 760	3 173	29 364	27 315	765	518
2004	24 151	16 083	1 446	17 530	1 728	-223	15 578	5 233	3 341	31 340	29 154	771	529
2005	25 328	16 933	1 327	18 261	1 834	-235	16 192	5 568	3 568	32 642	30 148	776	538

. . . = Not available.

Table 21-2. Personal Income and Employment by Region and State—Continued

(Millions of dollars, except as noted.)

Region or state and year	Personal income, total	Derivation of personal income								Per capita (dollars)		Population (thousands)	Total employment (thousands)
		Earnings by place of work			Less: Contributions for government social insurance	Plus: Adjustment for residence	Equals: Net earnings by place of residence	Plus: Dividends, interest, and rent	Plus: Personal current transfer receipts	Personal income	Disposable personal income		
		Nonfarm	Farm	Total									
TENNESSEE													
1958	5 272	4 206	313	4 520	175	27	4 372	531	370	1 519	1 393	3 471	...
1959	5 657	4 589	305	4 893	207	23	4 709	562	386	1 606	1 471	3 522	...
1960	5 808	4 771	243	5 014	242	23	4 794	610	404	1 625	1 478	3 575	...
1961	6 144	4 966	290	5 256	247	22	5 031	654	459	1 696	1 547	3 622	...
1962	6 525	5 336	250	5 586	273	22	5 335	713	477	1 777	1 595	3 673	...
1963	6 912	5 687	273	5 959	323	22	5 658	751	502	1 859	1 687	3 718	...
1964	7 436	6 188	234	6 422	339	21	6 104	807	525	1 972	1 808	3 771	...
1965	8 109	6 756	250	7 006	363	21	6 664	867	578	2 135	1 949	3 798	...
1966	8 935	7 605	253	7 858	502	21	7 377	922	636	2 338	2 115	3 822	...
1967	9 577	8 150	215	8 366	564	35	7 836	978	763	2 482	2 252	3 859	...
1968	10 675	9 077	222	9 299	634	33	8 697	1 103	875	2 753	2 467	3 878	...
1969	11 487	9 905	252	10 157	659	-155	9 342	1 168	977	2 948	2 607	3 897	1 789
1970	12 480	10 539	265	10 804	695	-155	9 954	1 330	1 197	3 170	2 827	3 937	1 785
1971	13 776	11 592	262	11 854	789	-165	10 900	1 481	1 396	3 435	3 087	4 010	1 817
1972	15 518	13 153	321	13 475	937	-192	12 346	1 634	1 538	3 796	3 407	4 088	1 924
1973	17 714	14 916	488	15 403	1 211	-181	14 011	1 886	1 816	4 280	3 842	4 138	2 025
1974	19 663	16 476	312	16 788	1 383	-191	15 214	2 230	2 220	4 680	4 202	4 202	2 055
1975	21 405	17 344	244	17 588	1 430	-190	15 968	2 503	2 933	5 024	4 557	4 261	1 983
1976	24 104	19 654	366	20 021	1 639	-184	18 197	2 714	3 193	5 568	5 030	4 329	2 052
1977	26 795	22 168	294	22 463	1 846	-241	20 376	3 066	3 354	6 087	5 503	4 402	2 135
1978	30 593	25 576	312	25 888	2 151	-308	23 429	3 500	3 664	6 857	6 164	4 462	2 228
1979	34 236	28 396	333	28 730	2 480	-358	25 891	4 079	4 266	7 552	6 777	4 533	2 282
1980	37 994	30 627	188	30 815	2 675	-425	27 714	5 143	5 136	8 259	7 406	4 600	2 264
1981	42 404	33 394	352	33 746	3 142	-460	30 144	6 435	5 825	9 163	8 216	4 628	2 263
1982	45 249	34 683	297	34 979	3 338	-417	31 224	7 632	6 393	9 739	8 780	4 646	2 224
1983	48 130	37 357	-38	37 318	3 650	-430	33 238	8 022	6 869	10 329	9 331	4 660	2 247
1984	53 966	41 775	402	42 178	4 188	-430	37 559	9 213	7 194	11 515	10 468	4 687	2 354
1985	57 984	45 092	326	45 419	4 588	-447	40 384	9 952	7 648	12 297	11 140	4 715	2 411
1986	61 771	48 341	232	48 574	5 017	-487	43 069	10 493	8 209	13 035	11 819	4 739	2 490
1987	66 412	52 507	297	52 804	5 430	-520	46 855	10 907	8 650	13 885	12 531	4 783	2 593
1988	71 640	56 628	382	57 011	6 057	-534	50 420	11 925	9 294	14 856	13 464	4 822	2 680
1989	76 859	59 936	430	60 366	6 500	-560	53 306	13 327	10 225	15 833	14 298	4 854	2 753
1990	81 700	63 314	423	63 737	6 916	-595	56 226	14 157	11 317	16 692	15 122	4 894	2 796
1991	85 914	66 124	490	66 613	7 353	-592	58 668	14 403	12 842	17 298	15 728	4 967	2 795
1992	93 807	72 514	653	73 167	7 953	-432	64 782	14 590	14 435	18 577	16 893	5 050	2 855
1993	99 074	77 377	577	77 954	8 566	-562	68 825	14 785	15 463	19 284	17 504	5 138	2 960
1994	105 846	83 132	626	83 758	9 339	-666	73 752	15 881	16 212	20 233	18 318	5 231	3 079
1995	112 793	88 380	437	88 818	9 959	-757	78 102	17 027	17 665	21 174	19 132	5 327	3 164
1996	118 374	92 275	374	92 649	10 314	-732	81 602	18 221	18 551	21 854	19 628	5 417	3 214
1997	124 699	97 431	485	97 916	10 941	-935	86 039	19 343	19 317	22 676	20 290	5 499	3 288
1998	133 620	104 721	235	104 955	11 589	-1 088	92 278	21 026	20 316	23 989	21 452	5 570	3 373
1999	140 395	111 391	103	111 494	12 204	-1 285	98 006	21 138	21 252	24 898	22 293	5 639	3 435
2000	148 833	116 833	383	117 216	12 650	-1 456	103 110	22 659	23 065	26 097	23 409	5 703	3 496
2001	154 416	120 939	298	121 237	13 069	-1 517	106 651	22 614	25 150	26 870	24 155	5 747	3 459
2002	159 173	126 489	-15	126 474	13 656	-1 525	111 293	20 939	26 942	27 490	25 137	5 790	3 452
2003	165 622	131 745	200	131 944	14 086	-1 406	116 453	20 569	28 600	28 352	26 139	5 842	3 473
2004	174 726	140 201	131	140 331	14 745	-1 475	124 111	20 290	30 325	29 648	27 405	5 893	3 555
2005	184 566	147 430	365	147 794	15 403	-1 453	130 938	21 371	32 258	30 952	28 409	5 963	3 627

. . . = Not available.

Table 21-2. Personal Income and Employment by Region and State—Continued

(Millions of dollars, except as noted.)

Region or state and year	Personal income, total	Earnings by place of work			Less: Contributions for government social insurance	Plus: Adjustment for residence	Equals: Net earnings by place of residence	Plus: Dividends, interest, and rent	Plus: Personal current transfer receipts	Per capita (dollars)		Population (thousands)	Total employment (thousands)
		Nonfarm	Farm	Total						Personal income	Disposable personal income		
TEXAS													
1958	17 399	13 629	1 058	14 687	472	14	14 229	2 282	888	1 881	1 697	9 252	...
1959	18 411	14 502	992	15 495	567	14	14 942	2 517	951	1 958	1 765	9 405	...
1960	18 913	14 976	914	15 890	677	15	15 228	2 687	998	1 965	1 764	9 624	...
1961	19 964	15 638	1 078	16 716	695	15	16 036	2 806	1 122	2 033	1 824	9 820	...
1962	20 965	16 567	938	17 505	748	15	16 772	2 971	1 222	2 085	1 866	10 053	...
1963	21 932	17 491	769	18 260	831	16	17 444	3 166	1 321	2 159	1 930	10 159	...
1964	23 502	18 914	716	19 630	877	16	18 770	3 361	1 371	2 288	2 079	10 270	...
1965	25 263	20 260	853	21 113	929	18	20 201	3 564	1 498	2 434	2 206	10 378	...
1966	27 561	22 499	907	23 406	1 259	15	22 162	3 769	1 630	2 627	2 358	10 492	...
1967	30 103	24 846	768	25 614	1 458	13	24 169	3 966	1 969	2 840	2 543	10 599	...
1968	33 593	27 825	901	28 726	1 630	12	27 108	4 124	2 360	3 105	2 747	10 819	...
1969	37 122	31 086	917	32 003	2 013	-86	29 905	4 575	2 642	3 361	2 941	11 045	5 005
1970	40 820	33 530	1 159	34 689	2 150	-97	32 443	5 240	3 137	3 633	3 221	11 237	5 045
1971	44 282	36 357	1 008	37 365	2 400	-102	34 864	5 754	3 664	3 847	3 451	11 510	5 123
1972	49 166	40 363	1 248	41 611	2 784	-128	38 699	6 354	4 114	4 181	3 709	11 759	5 334
1973	56 072	45 501	2 136	47 636	3 610	-155	43 871	7 254	4 947	4 665	4 150	12 019	5 608
1974	63 498	52 244	1 143	53 387	4 251	-132	49 004	8 593	5 901	5 176	4 562	12 268	5 822
1975	72 230	58 934	1 302	60 236	4 722	-130	55 384	9 469	7 377	5 747	5 131	12 568	5 938
1976	81 994	68 068	1 282	69 351	5 514	-94	63 743	10 205	8 047	6 355	5 638	12 903	6 207
1977	91 735	77 063	1 269	78 332	6 290	-308	71 734	11 442	8 560	6 954	6 118	13 192	6 521
1978	106 096	89 904	1 015	90 918	7 495	-428	82 995	13 562	9 539	7 860	6 925	13 498	6 898
1979	122 776	103 506	1 727	105 234	9 039	-434	95 760	16 133	10 883	8 841	7 696	13 887	7 222
1980	141 659	118 911	598	119 509	10 479	-544	108 486	20 452	12 721	9 880	8 563	14 338	7 511
1981	167 287	138 253	1 954	140 207	13 099	-356	126 753	26 073	14 460	11 344	9 736	14 746	7 925
1982	183 782	149 693	1 344	151 037	14 494	-427	136 116	31 201	16 466	11 987	10 406	15 331	8 098
1983	194 872	156 409	1 728	158 137	15 029	-410	142 699	33 576	18 598	12 372	10 940	15 752	8 088
1984	215 633	172 540	1 609	174 149	16 884	-471	156 795	39 062	19 777	13 471	11 989	16 007	8 469
1985	232 242	184 943	1 482	186 424	18 291	-499	167 635	43 472	21 135	14 272	12 708	16 273	8 721
1986	235 416	185 811	1 256	187 067	18 535	-459	168 072	44 177	23 167	14 215	12 784	16 561	8 560
1987	240 661	189 243	2 070	191 313	18 606	-457	172 250	44 052	24 360	14 479	12 975	16 622	8 773
1988	255 422	201 850	2 306	204 156	20 405	-461	183 290	46 527	25 605	15 325	13 812	16 667	8 934
1989	274 145	214 722	2 215	216 937	21 751	-471	194 715	51 286	28 144	16 312	14 626	16 807	9 064
1990	297 146	232 867	3 006	235 873	23 633	-504	211 737	53 929	31 480	17 421	15 623	17 057	9 304
1991	311 926	245 094	2 731	247 824	25 471	-585	221 768	55 152	35 005	17 929	16 165	17 398	9 465
1992	335 941	263 896	3 314	267 209	27 111	-609	239 489	55 185	41 267	18 916	17 128	17 760	9 545
1993	354 213	280 534	3 984	284 518	28 782	-633	255 104	54 972	44 137	19 503	17 633	18 162	9 844
1994	374 791	296 382	3 387	299 769	30 815	-698	268 256	59 105	47 430	20 189	18 236	18 564	10 163
1995	398 192	314 855	2 758	317 613	32 834	-790	283 990	63 236	50 966	21 003	18 928	18 959	10 507
1996	427 810	339 131	2 385	341 516	34 898	-865	305 753	67 676	54 380	22 120	19 802	19 340	10 808
1997	466 182	372 947	3 099	376 046	38 041	-1 006	337 000	72 351	56 831	23 616	20 991	19 740	11 236
1998	507 681	409 793	2 867	412 660	41 453	-1 102	370 104	78 933	58 644	25 186	22 282	20 158	11 646
1999	539 661	440 935	4 499	445 434	44 041	-1 151	400 241	78 918	60 502	26 250	23 251	20 558	11 895
2000	593 139	486 842	2 765	489 607	47 231	-1 254	441 122	87 612	64 405	28 313	24 964	20 949	12 245
2001	619 642	509 298	3 058	512 355	49 836	-1 442	461 077	87 505	71 060	29 045	25 720	21 334	12 356
2002	626 604	514 504	3 039	517 543	50 507	-1 452	465 585	83 046	77 973	28 846	26 146	21 722	12 370
2003	649 680	531 870	3 814	535 683	52 809	-1 447	481 427	85 079	83 175	29 398	26 920	22 099	12 491
2004	691 245	570 874	3 617	574 492	55 279	-1 501	517 711	86 502	87 031	30 761	28 282	22 472	12 706
2005	745 329	615 463	3 587	619 050	59 782	-1 676	557 592	91 791	95 946	32 604	29 738	22 860	13 091

. . . = Not available.

Table 21-2. Personal Income and Employment by Region and State—Continued

(Millions of dollars, except as noted.)

Region or state and year	Personal income, total	Derivation of personal income									Per capita (dollars)		Population (thousands)	Total employment (thousands)
		Earnings by place of work			Less: Contributions for government social insurance	Plus: Adjustment for residence	Equals: Net earnings by place of residence	Plus: Dividends, interest, and rent	Plus: Personal current transfer receipts		Personal income	Disposable personal income		
		Nonfarm	Farm	Total										
UTAH														
1958	1 591	1 308	53	1 360	54	0	1 307	189	95		1 883	1 708	845	. . .
1959	1 710	1 415	49	1 464	62	1	1 402	207	101		1 965	1 770	870	. . .
1960	1 827	1 514	43	1 557	75	1	1 483	239	105		2 030	1 826	900	. . .
1961	1 951	1 628	34	1 662	79	1	1 583	250	117		2 084	1 869	936	. . .
1962	2 131	1 770	53	1 822	87	1	1 736	273	122		2 225	2 002	958	. . .
1963	2 214	1 867	40	1 907	105	1	1 803	279	132		2 273	2 041	974	. . .
1964	2 326	1 952	29	1 982	106	1	1 876	309	141		2 378	2 167	978	. . .
1965	2 462	2 043	46	2 089	109	1	1 982	329	152		2 485	2 266	991	. . .
1966	2 615	2 199	48	2 247	144	1	2 105	349	162		2 592	2 353	1 009	. . .
1967	2 763	2 311	62	2 373	159	1	2 216	356	191		2 711	2 454	1 019	. . .
1968	2 974	2 497	66	2 563	175	1	2 390	364	220		2 890	2 587	1 029	. . .
1969	3 238	2 694	73	2 766	176	2	2 593	397	248		3 093	2 734	1 047	444
1970	3 611	2 960	77	3 036	191	2	2 847	465	298		3 389	3 032	1 066	455
1971	4 023	3 280	76	3 356	218	3	3 141	530	353		3 655	3 296	1 101	467
1972	4 516	3 682	87	3 769	260	5	3 515	599	402		3 980	3 569	1 135	494
1973	5 052	4 137	129	4 266	339	8	3 936	645	472		4 323	3 873	1 169	523
1974	5 688	4 687	95	4 782	396	11	4 398	752	538		4 745	4 244	1 199	545
1975	6 392	5 211	66	5 277	433	14	4 859	860	673		5 180	4 693	1 234	553
1976	7 328	6 013	73	6 086	502	17	5 601	997	730		5 760	5 157	1 272	580
1977	8 356	6 910	63	6 972	575	22	6 419	1 151	786		6 348	5 671	1 316	613
1978	9 623	7 971	70	8 041	678	27	7 390	1 357	876		7 054	6 291	1 364	651
1979	11 035	9 048	81	9 129	810	36	8 354	1 683	998		7 792	6 923	1 416	679
1980	12 519	10 013	58	10 071	897	52	9 226	2 118	1 175		8 501	7 584	1 473	689
1981	14 206	11 235	41	11 276	1 082	54	10 247	2 582	1 377		9 374	8 325	1 515	699
1982	15 541	11 929	45	11 974	1 170	54	10 857	3 100	1 583		9 973	8 852	1 558	709
1983	16 803	12 704	36	12 739	1 268	43	11 514	3 564	1 726		10 535	9 469	1 595	721
1984	18 546	14 162	55	14 216	1 449	38	12 805	3 961	1 779		11 431	10 325	1 622	764
1985	19 794	15 128	55	15 183	1 579	40	13 644	4 217	1 932		12 048	10 849	1 643	793
1986	20 663	15 740	85	15 825	1 666	35	14 193	4 380	2 090		12 426	11 176	1 663	805
1987	21 361	16 368	129	16 497	1 729	25	14 792	4 328	2 241		12 729	11 392	1 678	835
1988	22 287	17 390	208	17 598	1 931	24	15 691	4 263	2 333		13 192	11 803	1 689	870
1989	23 891	18 574	202	18 777	2 095	22	16 703	4 613	2 575		14 005	12 546	1 706	903
1990	25 817	20 227	246	20 473	2 293	17	18 197	4 795	2 825		14 913	13 197	1 731	944
1991	27 573	21 772	228	22 000	2 518	11	19 493	5 106	3 106		15 492	13 786	1 780	967
1992	29 601	23 606	278	23 883	2 726	6	21 164	5 013	3 424		16 115	14 331	1 837	985
1993	31 810	25 462	303	25 765	2 956	7	22 817	5 244	3 750		16 756	14 857	1 898	1 032
1994	34 437	27 633	222	27 855	3 253	7	24 609	5 966	3 862		17 566	15 481	1 960	1 109
1995	37 218	30 017	170	30 187	3 545	1	26 643	6 434	4 141		18 478	16 210	2 014	1 158
1996	40 386	32 475	182	32 657	3 777	1	28 881	7 115	4 390		19 529	17 085	2 068	1 225
1997	43 667	35 231	206	35 436	4 050	1	31 387	7 681	4 599		20 600	17 977	2 120	1 277
1998	47 019	38 008	240	38 248	4 301	-5	33 943	8 258	4 818		21 708	18 937	2 166	1 317
1999	49 343	40 340	256	40 596	4 519	-1	36 076	8 188	5 078		22 393	19 488	2 203	1 349
2000	53 561	43 559	201	43 760	4 797	4	38 967	9 148	5 447		23 878	20 802	2 243	1 388
2001	56 594	45 996	277	46 273	5 030	18	41 261	9 372	5 961		24 738	21 693	2 288	1 393
2002	58 172	47 353	181	47 534	5 172	13	42 374	9 302	6 495		24 895	22 306	2 337	1 394
2003	59 367	48 459	210	48 669	5 436	21	43 254	9 251	6 862		24 958	22 504	2 379	1 409
2004	63 401	52 392	296	52 688	5 927	32	46 793	9 422	7 185		26 191	23 654	2 421	1 452
2005	67 906	56 798	256	57 053	6 522	40	50 571	9 582	7 753		27 497	24 571	2 470	1 510

. . . = Not available.

Table 21-2. Personal Income and Employment by Region and State—Continued

(Millions of dollars, except as noted.)

Region or state and year	Personal income, total	Earnings by place of work			Less: Contributions for government social insurance	Plus: Adjustment for residence	Equals: Net earnings by place of residence	Plus: Dividends, interest, and rent	Plus: Personal current transfer receipts	Per capita (dollars)		Population (thousands)	Total employment (thousands)
		Nonfarm	Farm	Total						Personal income	Disposable personal income		
VERMONT													
1958	653	493	54	547	19	-5	523	77	52	1 718	1 553	380	. . .
1959	703	542	50	592	22	-5	564	83	55	1 816	1 634	387	. . .
1960	744	571	56	626	27	-5	594	90	59	1 912	1 718	389	. . .
1961	774	584	55	639	28	-5	606	101	67	1 985	1 787	390	. . .
1962	813	624	46	670	31	-5	634	109	70	2 068	1 863	393	. . .
1963	843	653	43	696	36	-5	655	114	74	2 124	1 893	397	. . .
1964	903	693	49	742	38	-5	698	128	77	2 264	2 034	399	. . .
1965	990	770	45	814	41	-7	765	144	81	2 451	2 218	404	. . .
1966	1 124	883	58	941	58	-10	873	164	87	2 722	2 426	413	. . .
1967	1 217	962	46	1 008	71	-10	927	183	107	2 878	2 562	423	. . .
1968	1 342	1 050	50	1 100	74	-11	1 015	201	126	3 121	2 750	430	. . .
1969	1 473	1 167	57	1 224	83	-27	1 113	215	144	3 370	2 921	437	203
1970	1 614	1 256	61	1 318	89	-27	1 202	241	172	3 617	3 154	446	205
1971	1 745	1 337	60	1 397	98	-24	1 276	265	205	3 841	3 444	454	206
1972	1 924	1 467	67	1 534	111	-21	1 402	291	230	4 153	3 657	463	211
1973	2 118	1 626	71	1 697	141	-20	1 536	320	262	4 521	4 028	469	220
1974	2 293	1 736	58	1 794	155	-17	1 622	356	315	4 847	4 319	473	222
1975	2 494	1 826	60	1 886	162	-11	1 712	380	401	5 197	4 654	480	220
1976	2 786	2 056	77	2 133	184	-6	1 943	411	431	5 742	5 172	485	228
1977	3 028	2 259	65	2 325	203	-2	2 119	467	441	6 152	5 494	492	236
1978	3 478	2 637	94	2 731	244	-2	2 485	526	467	6 980	6 227	498	252
1979	3 924	2 960	104	3 064	284	5	2 785	609	530	7 760	6 878	506	261
1980	4 414	3 220	107	3 327	310	14	3 031	756	627	8 613	7 607	513	266
1981	4 983	3 535	122	3 657	366	18	3 309	950	724	9 664	8 505	516	271
1982	5 359	3 708	122	3 831	393	24	3 461	1 093	805	10 324	9 175	519	272
1983	5 735	4 067	82	4 150	431	22	3 740	1 131	864	10 959	9 764	523	279
1984	6 341	4 510	82	4 592	490	28	4 130	1 321	889	12 040	10 759	527	290
1985	6 873	4 972	100	5 071	549	30	4 552	1 394	928	12 968	11 528	530	302
1986	7 388	5 414	98	5 512	607	33	4 939	1 494	956	13 834	12 238	534	313
1987	8 037	5 987	123	6 110	661	41	5 490	1 576	971	14 875	13 053	540	323
1988	8 792	6 599	120	6 720	752	47	6 014	1 753	1 025	15 992	14 109	550	337
1989	9 685	7 105	121	7 226	814	50	6 461	2 097	1 126	17 365	15 268	558	344
1990	10 096	7 362	111	7 473	845	49	6 677	2 163	1 256	17 876	15 759	565	344
1991	10 227	7 396	100	7 497	869	56	6 684	2 173	1 369	17 985	15 951	569	337
1992	10 919	7 881	175	8 056	918	64	7 202	2 165	1 552	19 065	16 964	573	344
1993	11 257	8 265	127	8 392	967	72	7 498	2 140	1 619	19 485	17 310	578	352
1994	11 809	8 586	128	8 714	1 022	86	7 778	2 311	1 719	20 226	17 998	584	361
1995	12 370	8 901	100	9 001	1 079	100	8 022	2 490	1 858	21 002	18 697	589	365
1996	13 040	9 321	146	9 467	1 123	115	8 460	2 655	1 925	21 964	19 418	594	370
1997	13 738	9 779	111	9 890	1 175	138	8 853	2 850	2 035	23 002	20 160	597	375
1998	14 788	10 457	137	10 594	1 238	164	9 521	3 153	2 115	24 629	21 515	600	386
1999	15 650	11 180	153	11 333	1 313	187	10 207	3 188	2 255	25 881	22 577	605	394
2000	16 883	12 070	163	12 234	1 392	219	11 060	3 407	2 416	27 680	24 010	610	404
2001	17 742	12 692	144	12 836	1 486	232	11 582	3 513	2 647	28 951	25 223	613	408
2002	18 051	13 067	102	13 169	1 531	237	11 875	3 329	2 847	29 291	26 021	616	410
2003	18 749	13 595	123	13 718	1 552	268	12 434	3 325	2 989	30 284	27 290	619	409
2004	19 563	14 478	180	14 658	1 615	289	13 332	3 105	3 126	31 491	28 392	621	417
2005	20 393	15 120	208	15 327	1 712	308	13 923	3 077	3 393	32 731	29 206	623	424

. . . = Not available.

Table 21-2. Personal Income and Employment by Region and State—Continued

(Millions of dollars, except as noted.)

Region or state and year	Personal income, total	Earnings by place of work			Less: Contributions for government social insurance	Plus: Adjustment for residence	Equals: Net earnings by place of residence	Plus: Dividends, interest, and rent	Plus: Personal current transfer receipts	Per capita (dollars)		Population (thousands)	Total employment (thousands)
		Nonfarm	Farm	Total						Personal income	Disposable personal income		
VIRGINIA													
1958	6 872	5 383	258	5 641	184	361	5 818	723	331	1 756	1 579	3 914	. . .
1959	7 327	5 840	192	6 033	234	386	6 185	781	361	1 854	1 662	3 951	. . .
1960	7 598	5 992	212	6 203	268	432	6 367	859	373	1 906	1 693	3 986	. . .
1961	8 089	6 317	222	6 538	284	463	6 717	944	428	1 975	1 760	4 095	. . .
1962	8 741	6 829	219	7 047	317	512	7 242	1 046	452	2 091	1 853	4 180	. . .
1963	9 353	7 409	133	7 542	369	565	7 738	1 130	485	2 187	1 921	4 276	. . .
1964	10 338	8 118	219	8 337	383	615	8 569	1 258	512	2 373	2 126	4 357	. . .
1965	11 158	8 710	205	8 915	402	704	9 217	1 381	560	2 529	2 254	4 411	. . .
1966	12 078	9 592	153	9 745	544	779	9 981	1 486	610	2 710	2 395	4 456	. . .
1967	13 230	10 380	199	10 579	630	933	10 882	1 614	734	2 935	2 589	4 508	. . .
1968	14 683	11 639	176	11 816	696	1 008	12 128	1 701	855	3 221	2 819	4 558	. . .
1969	16 396	13 209	210	13 419	800	956	13 575	1 842	978	3 554	3 046	4 614	2 148
1970	17 658	14 220	210	14 430	871	851	14 411	2 068	1 179	3 789	3 265	4 660	2 158
1971	19 443	15 651	191	15 842	1 000	877	15 719	2 312	1 413	4 091	3 561	4 753	2 196
1972	21 655	17 464	251	17 715	1 167	933	17 480	2 553	1 621	4 485	3 849	4 828	2 263
1973	24 393	19 683	351	20 034	1 484	1 005	19 555	2 902	1 937	4 907	4 300	4 907	2 384
1974	27 300	21 863	312	22 175	1 701	1 134	21 608	3 391	2 301	5 484	4 710	4 978	2 451
1975	30 141	23 555	262	23 816	1 821	1 394	23 389	3 804	2 947	5 961	5 245	5 056	2 425
1976	33 619	26 394	233	26 627	2 071	1 617	26 173	4 227	3 219	6 550	5 730	5 133	2 501
1977	37 455	29 520	165	29 685	2 302	1 857	29 240	4 763	3 452	7 195	6 259	5 206	2 585
1978	42 386	33 282	286	33 568	2 621	2 191	33 137	5 432	3 816	8 021	6 936	5 284	2 697
1979	47 656	37 211	151	37 362	3 050	2 588	36 900	6 376	4 380	8 950	7 730	5 325	2 769
1980	54 457	41 357	64	41 421	3 388	3 164	41 198	8 052	5 208	10 144	8 770	5 368	2 802
1981	61 447	45 860	265	46 125	4 022	3 394	45 497	9 937	6 013	11 287	9 696	5 444	2 820
1982	66 758	49 328	119	49 447	4 381	3 464	48 530	11 657	6 572	12 154	10 521	5 493	2 832
1983	72 551	53 913	42	53 955	4 947	3 450	52 459	12 984	7 108	13 038	11 411	5 565	2 905
1984	81 186	60 988	321	61 309	5 702	3 561	59 168	14 498	7 520	14 385	12 677	5 644	3 054
1985	87 821	66 828	223	67 051	6 436	3 680	64 295	15 489	8 037	15 366	13 459	5 715	3 198
1986	94 892	72 660	270	72 930	7 211	3 835	69 555	16 820	8 517	16 328	14 311	5 812	3 335
1987	102 769	79 524	366	79 890	7 910	4 048	76 029	17 893	8 847	17 324	15 066	5 932	3 501
1988	111 768	86 420	520	86 939	8 962	4 431	82 408	19 911	9 449	18 514	16 190	6 037	3 582
1989	120 816	92 214	634	92 848	9 725	4 664	87 787	22 688	10 342	19 740	17 185	6 120	3 681
1990	127 129	96 150	670	96 819	10 329	5 419	91 909	23 997	11 223	20 449	17 872	6 217	3 726
1991	131 913	98 849	604	99 453	10 804	5 950	94 600	24 995	12 318	20 934	18 384	6 301	3 666
1992	139 901	104 961	658	105 619	11 403	6 420	100 636	25 388	13 876	21 811	19 200	6 414	3 684
1993	146 273	109 985	524	110 509	11 991	6 862	105 381	26 218	14 674	22 470	19 726	6 510	3 758
1994	153 654	115 007	629	115 636	12 705	6 853	109 783	28 374	15 497	23 305	20 389	6 593	3 842
1995	160 470	120 085	553	120 637	13 240	7 072	114 469	29 315	16 686	24 056	21 007	6 671	3 931
1996	169 001	126 723	570	127 292	13 902	6 519	119 910	31 117	17 974	25 034	21 761	6 751	4 012
1997	179 654	135 507	428	135 935	14 876	7 060	128 119	33 037	18 498	26 307	22 746	6 829	4 111
1998	191 711	145 903	436	146 339	15 969	6 758	137 128	35 425	19 158	27 780	23 662	6 901	4 185
1999	204 586	157 576	360	157 936	17 243	8 158	148 851	35 604	20 132	29 226	24 664	7 000	4 282
2000	220 845	171 986	521	172 507	18 568	6 275	160 214	39 100	21 531	31 087	26 215	7 104	4 407
2001	233 770	182 604	449	183 052	19 642	6 037	169 448	40 332	23 991	32 505	27 549	7 192	4 439
2002	240 534	187 668	408	188 076	20 303	7 555	175 328	39 648	25 557	33 013	28 712	7 286	4 440
2003	250 838	196 181	418	196 599	20 544	7 393	183 448	40 222	27 168	33 973	29 788	7 383	4 499
2004	267 066	212 953	488	213 441	22 315	7 654	198 780	39 684	28 602	35 698	31 363	7 481	4 613
2005	284 174	227 969	583	228 552	24 066	7 763	212 248	41 010	30 916	37 552	32 578	7 567	4 728

. . . = Not available.

Table 21-2. Personal Income and Employment by Region and State—Continued

(Millions of dollars, except as noted.)

| Region or state and year | Personal income, total | Derivation of personal income | | | | | | | | Per capita (dollars) | | Population (thousands) | Total employment (thousands) |
| | | Earnings by place of work | | | Less: Contributions for government social insurance | Plus: Adjustment for residence | Equals: Net earnings by place of residence | Plus: Dividends, interest, and rent | Plus: Personal current transfer receipts | Personal income | Disposable personal income | | |
		Nonfarm	Farm	Total									
WASHINGTON													
1958	6 270	5 026	221	5 246	239	16	5 023	778	469	2 261	2 019	2 773	. . .
1959	6 668	5 380	232	5 612	281	21	5 351	833	484	2 364	2 122	2 821	. . .
1960	6 901	5 523	253	5 777	313	25	5 489	898	514	2 417	2 163	2 855	. . .
1961	7 248	5 802	244	6 046	327	29	5 747	938	563	2 515	2 248	2 882	. . .
1962	7 832	6 304	268	6 572	357	34	6 248	1 017	567	2 662	2 375	2 942	. . .
1963	8 024	6 445	271	6 716	395	42	6 363	1 063	598	2 715	2 419	2 955	. . .
1964	8 406	6 742	248	6 990	394	51	6 647	1 128	631	2 839	2 582	2 961	. . .
1965	9 066	7 247	268	7 515	417	62	7 159	1 244	663	3 056	2 770	2 967	. . .
1966	10 272	8 376	362	8 738	593	71	8 216	1 367	689	3 360	3 011	3 057	. . .
1967	11 255	9 215	325	9 540	687	82	8 935	1 491	829	3 546	3 163	3 174	. . .
1968	12 515	10 273	339	10 612	769	99	9 942	1 622	951	3 827	3 390	3 270	. . .
1969	13 645	11 160	396	11 556	910	83	10 729	1 840	1 077	4 082	3 578	3 343	1 539
1970	14 323	11 365	344	11 709	913	65	10 861	2 028	1 435	4 191	3 748	3 417	1 491
1971	15 058	11 724	390	12 114	981	63	11 196	2 191	1 671	4 368	3 945	3 447	1 457
1972	16 275	12 685	505	13 190	1 117	73	12 146	2 344	1 784	4 722	4 218	3 447	1 481
1973	18 408	14 340	754	15 094	1 438	90	13 746	2 651	2 011	5 294	4 715	3 477	1 558
1974	20 939	16 177	889	17 065	1 659	133	15 540	3 048	2 351	5 902	5 262	3 548	1 622
1975	23 684	18 134	905	19 039	1 840	200	17 399	3 378	2 907	6 545	5 859	3 619	1 659
1976	26 475	20 773	752	21 526	2 140	247	19 633	3 686	3 156	7 174	6 407	3 691	1 739
1977	29 449	23 591	603	24 194	2 459	227	21 962	4 184	3 304	7 807	6 953	3 772	1 815
1978	34 308	27 803	752	28 555	2 977	270	25 848	4 876	3 583	8 828	7 781	3 886	1 939
1979	39 572	32 275	737	33 013	3 567	323	29 769	5 792	4 011	9 861	8 616	4 013	2 061
1980	45 004	35 527	859	36 386	3 862	389	32 913	7 185	4 907	10 832	9 486	4 155	2 110
1981	50 295	38 858	861	39 719	4 540	433	35 612	8 980	5 703	11 874	10 373	4 236	2 126
1982	53 328	40 311	764	41 075	4 762	465	36 778	10 134	6 416	12 470	11 106	4 277	2 101
1983	56 666	42 325	1 063	43 388	5 119	485	38 754	10 902	7 010	13 177	11 860	4 300	2 147
1984	61 086	45 497	1 020	46 518	5 653	543	41 408	12 308	7 370	14 063	12 720	4 344	2 224
1985	64 924	48 599	748	49 347	6 094	587	43 840	13 157	7 927	14 755	13 316	4 400	2 290
1986	69 203	51 969	1 055	53 024	6 627	608	47 006	13 791	8 406	15 542	14 052	4 453	2 365
1987	73 461	55 615	1 083	56 698	7 068	659	50 289	14 317	8 855	16 210	14 545	4 532	2 486
1988	79 648	60 944	1 023	61 967	7 976	749	54 740	15 274	9 634	17 166	15 461	4 640	2 617
1989	88 084	66 431	1 148	67 579	8 722	833	59 690	17 816	10 578	18 558	16 542	4 746	2 737
1990	97 399	74 023	1 195	75 218	9 615	926	66 528	19 251	11 620	19 865	17 676	4 903	2 863
1991	103 974	79 073	1 262	80 335	10 483	989	70 841	20 085	13 049	20 689	18 502	5 026	2 897
1992	112 035	86 214	1 513	87 727	11 457	1 085	77 354	20 165	14 516	21 709	19 441	5 161	2 928
1993	117 266	90 128	1 765	91 893	11 972	1 177	81 098	20 650	15 517	22 214	19 945	5 279	2 972
1994	123 294	94 099	1 402	95 501	12 642	1 217	84 076	22 888	16 329	22 938	20 528	5 375	3 082
1995	129 845	98 300	1 457	99 757	13 232	1 367	87 892	24 488	17 464	23 690	21 163	5 481	3 123
1996	139 650	104 792	1 919	106 711	13 831	1 570	94 451	26 841	18 359	25 073	22 202	5 570	3 215
1997	150 119	113 444	1 619	115 063	14 590	1 720	102 193	28 875	19 050	26 454	23 223	5 675	3 320
1998	163 762	124 979	1 731	126 710	16 062	1 827	112 474	31 528	19 760	28 384	24 615	5 770	3 402
1999	175 491	136 680	1 496	138 175	16 951	1 939	123 163	31 363	20 966	30 037	25 627	5 843	3 471
2000	187 853	145 419	1 607	147 026	18 189	2 182	131 019	34 521	22 314	31 779	27 309	5 911	3 551
2001	193 498	148 619	1 404	150 023	17 821	2 312	134 515	33 906	25 078	32 291	28 183	5 992	3 557
2002	197 452	151 522	1 490	153 012	18 165	2 385	137 232	33 595	26 625	32 549	29 202	6 066	3 527
2003	201 552	155 451	1 853	157 303	20 273	2 342	139 373	34 254	27 926	32 874	29 762	6 131	3 549
2004	215 376	164 511	1 797	166 308	21 804	2 443	146 947	40 130	28 298	34 699	31 556	6 207	3 623
2005	221 540	174 096	1 670	175 766	23 183	2 600	155 184	36 557	29 799	35 234	31 637	6 288	3 732

. . . = Not available.

Table 21-2. Personal Income and Employment by Region and State—Continued

(Millions of dollars, except as noted.)

Region or state and year	Personal income, total	Earnings by place of work			Less: Contributions for government social insurance	Plus: Adjustment for residence	Equals: Net earnings by place of residence	Plus: Dividends, interest, and rent	Plus: Personal current transfer receipts	Per capita (dollars)		Population (thousands)	Total employment (thousands)
		Nonfarm	Farm	Total						Personal income	Disposable personal income		
WEST VIRGINIA													
1958	2 921	2 421	58	2 479	114	-21	2 344	275	301	1 583	1 444	1 845	...
1959	3 014	2 526	45	2 571	135	-20	2 415	296	303	1 625	1 470	1 855	...
1960	3 062	2 566	49	2 615	155	-20	2 440	318	304	1 653	1 484	1 853	...
1961	3 101	2 557	42	2 599	153	-20	2 426	331	344	1 696	1 524	1 828	...
1962	3 238	2 673	31	2 703	168	-19	2 517	354	367	1 790	1 609	1 809	...
1963	3 378	2 798	24	2 821	186	-18	2 618	381	379	1 881	1 684	1 796	...
1964	3 601	2 977	23	2 999	173	-17	2 809	407	385	2 004	1 816	1 797	...
1965	3 850	3 180	24	3 205	184	-13	3 008	431	411	2 155	1 957	1 786	...
1966	4 080	3 450	14	3 463	244	-10	3 209	437	434	2 298	2 072	1 775	...
1967	4 329	3 634	28	3 662	268	-8	3 386	451	492	2 447	2 210	1 769	...
1968	4 590	3 854	22	3 876	298	2	3 579	467	544	2 603	2 325	1 763	...
1969	4 868	4 138	30	4 169	324	-79	3 766	503	599	2 788	2 443	1 746	652
1970	5 428	4 548	25	4 573	350	-82	4 141	566	722	3 108	2 752	1 747	660
1971	5 965	4 945	25	4 970	395	-100	4 474	620	870	3 369	2 999	1 770	670
1972	6 601	5 465	30	5 495	455	-114	4 926	678	997	3 673	3 256	1 797	684
1973	7 240	5 929	44	5 973	567	-117	5 288	765	1 186	4 010	3 579	1 805	700
1974	8 051	6 562	28	6 590	647	-131	5 812	897	1 343	4 438	3 916	1 814	711
1975	9 157	7 399	14	7 412	709	-158	6 545	1 012	1 600	4 975	4 407	1 841	717
1976	10 268	8 408	3	8 412	817	-195	7 400	1 115	1 753	5 469	4 821	1 877	739
1977	11 488	9 497	-2	9 495	915	-226	8 354	1 263	1 871	6 028	5 324	1 906	758
1978	12 796	10 617	12	10 629	1 056	-263	9 309	1 407	2 080	6 663	5 903	1 920	781
1979	14 293	11 710	17	11 727	1 211	-273	10 242	1 616	2 435	7 371	6 488	1 939	791
1980	15 841	12 567	8	12 575	1 297	-301	10 978	2 034	2 829	8 118	7 129	1 951	784
1981	17 249	13 280	-23	13 257	1 467	-280	11 511	2 542	3 196	8 827	7 765	1 954	764
1982	18 325	13 687	-29	13 659	1 552	-234	11 872	2 948	3 505	9 399	8 318	1 950	743
1983	18 700	13 448	-16	13 432	1 569	-191	11 672	3 143	3 885	9 614	8 555	1 945	724
1984	20 063	14 404	22	14 426	1 735	-139	12 551	3 544	3 968	10 408	9 303	1 928	735
1985	20 777	14 860	20	14 880	1 826	-118	12 936	3 698	4 143	10 896	9 729	1 907	735
1986	21 444	15 139	46	15 185	1 905	-91	13 189	3 856	4 400	11 392	10 221	1 882	735
1987	22 010	15 602	6	15 608	1 977	-26	13 605	3 883	4 523	11 849	10 624	1 858	742
1988	22 922	16 238	4	16 242	2 166	8	14 084	4 066	4 772	12 524	11 283	1 830	755
1989	24 305	16 886	31	16 917	2 268	87	14 736	4 535	5 034	13 454	12 034	1 807	762
1990	25 980	18 133	44	18 177	2 420	70	15 827	4 759	5 394	14 493	12 965	1 793	783
1991	27 152	18 794	34	18 828	2 580	41	16 289	4 793	6 071	15 095	13 554	1 799	784
1992	29 105	19 919	62	19 981	2 756	103	17 328	4 819	6 959	16 112	14 543	1 806	794
1993	30 077	20 721	64	20 785	2 971	106	17 919	4 758	7 400	16 548	14 936	1 818	806
1994	31 301	21 758	60	21 819	3 113	149	18 854	4 971	7 477	17 194	15 464	1 820	827
1995	32 328	22 444	23	22 467	3 255	194	19 406	5 202	7 721	17 727	15 924	1 824	844
1996	33 622	23 016	11	23 026	3 350	208	19 885	5 599	8 139	18 445	16 540	1 823	853
1997	35 005	23 825	3	23 827	3 435	360	20 753	5 890	8 363	19 243	17 200	1 819	864
1998	36 722	24 847	7	24 853	3 566	401	21 689	6 367	8 666	20 226	18 068	1 816	878
1999	37 557	25 707	-4	25 704	3 654	455	22 504	6 204	8 849	20 729	18 509	1 812	879
2000	39 582	26 926	26	26 951	3 905	568	23 615	6 676	9 292	21 899	19 535	1 807	887
2001	41 902	28 201	-10	28 192	3 952	663	24 902	6 689	10 312	23 261	20 775	1 801	883
2002	43 312	28 886	-31	28 855	3 974	722	25 603	6 413	11 296	24 002	21 745	1 805	884
2003	43 342	29 710	-24	29 686	4 639	813	25 859	5 917	11 566	23 941	21 820	1 810	879
2004	45 245	31 676	-2	31 674	4 993	868	27 549	5 924	11 772	24 962	22 850	1 813	896
2005	47 290	33 313	-24	33 290	5 273	932	28 948	5 924	12 418	26 029	23 620	1 817	910

. . . = Not available.

Table 21-2. Personal Income and Employment by Region and State—Continued

(Millions of dollars, except as noted.)

Region or state and year	Personal income, total	Derivation of personal income									Per capita (dollars)		Population (thousands)	Total employment (thousands)
		Earnings by place of work			Less: Contributions for government social insurance	Plus: Adjustment for residence	Equals: Net earnings by place of residence	Plus: Dividends, interest, and rent	Plus: Personal current transfer receipts		Personal income	Disposable personal income		
		Nonfarm	Farm	Total										
WISCONSIN														
1958	7 940	6 126	451	6 578	233	52	6 397	1 033	510		2 066	1 843	3 843	. . .
1959	8 620	6 733	472	7 205	282	59	6 982	1 113	524		2 215	1 969	3 891	. . .
1960	8 911	7 012	421	7 432	341	63	7 155	1 199	557		2 249	1 982	3 962	. . .
1961	9 199	7 087	487	7 575	348	67	7 294	1 260	646		2 295	2 040	4 009	. . .
1962	9 735	7 559	484	8 043	374	74	7 743	1 334	658		2 404	2 127	4 049	. . .
1963	10 074	7 884	430	8 314	433	81	7 962	1 417	695		2 450	2 159	4 112	. . .
1964	10 869	8 506	470	8 976	449	91	8 618	1 527	724		2 610	2 327	4 165	. . .
1965	11 765	9 146	537	9 683	479	104	9 307	1 678	779		2 780	2 469	4 232	. . .
1966	12 877	10 084	661	10 745	668	123	10 200	1 815	862		3 013	2 652	4 274	. . .
1967	13 645	10 709	557	11 266	759	137	10 644	1 938	1 063		3 171	2 769	4 303	. . .
1968	14 904	11 574	640	12 214	815	158	11 557	2 109	1 237		3 430	2 992	4 345	. . .
1969	16 398	12 676	630	13 307	934	249	12 622	2 418	1 359		3 746	3 212	4 378	1 944
1970	17 609	13 399	631	14 030	974	253	13 308	2 702	1 599		3 979	3 460	4 426	1 954
1971	18 906	14 252	686	14 938	1 070	264	14 132	2 904	1 870		4 239	3 737	4 460	1 957
1972	20 679	15 717	721	16 437	1 248	287	15 477	3 123	2 080		4 597	4 007	4 498	2 014
1973	23 149	17 717	907	18 624	1 615	313	17 322	3 462	2 365		5 123	4 476	4 518	2 116
1974	25 472	19 421	793	20 215	1 841	339	18 713	3 948	2 811		5 613	4 878	4 538	2 159
1975	27 810	20 632	855	21 488	1 928	345	19 905	4 378	3 527		6 086	5 345	4 570	2 148
1976	30 606	23 199	752	23 951	2 188	390	22 154	4 634	3 818		6 676	5 829	4 585	2 211
1977	34 137	25 939	1 133	27 072	2 444	432	25 061	5 027	4 049		7 400	6 437	4 613	2 293
1978	38 190	29 355	1 114	30 468	2 847	487	28 108	5 609	4 472		8 245	7 113	4 632	2 382
1979	42 922	32 724	1 391	34 115	3 307	526	31 334	6 457	5 131		9 199	7 958	4 666	2 465
1980	47 623	34 859	1 429	36 288	3 507	550	33 330	8 044	6 249		10 107	8 786	4 712	2 449
1981	51 994	37 195	1 157	38 352	4 011	604	34 945	9 943	7 107		11 001	9 506	4 726	2 424
1982	54 851	38 243	1 011	39 254	4 170	623	35 707	11 216	7 928		11 599	10 118	4 729	2 382
1983	57 004	40 307	457	40 764	4 363	677	37 079	11 405	8 520		12 073	10 632	4 721	2 385
1984	62 462	44 316	982	45 298	4 908	794	41 185	12 553	8 724		13 190	11 645	4 736	2 478
1985	65 709	46 704	1 012	47 716	5 212	883	43 387	13 053	9 269		13 840	12 219	4 748	2 509
1986	69 089	49 203	1 289	50 491	5 536	966	45 920	13 608	9 560		14 528	12 822	4 756	2 551
1987	73 006	52 599	1 405	54 004	5 840	1 071	49 235	13 994	9 777		15 280	13 406	4 778	2 621
1988	77 433	57 064	840	57 904	6 557	1 240	52 587	14 715	10 132		16 057	14 102	4 822	2 702
1989	83 936	60 344	1 712	62 056	6 980	1 272	56 348	16 660	10 927		17 283	15 140	4 857	2 759
1990	88 635	64 219	1 342	65 561	7 464	1 356	59 453	17 470	11 711		18 072	15 801	4 905	2 834
1991	92 124	67 086	963	68 049	7 912	1 381	61 518	17 875	12 731		18 557	16 260	4 964	2 860
1992	98 917	72 633	1 204	73 837	8 530	1 515	66 822	18 353	13 742		19 683	17 253	5 025	2 913
1993	103 379	76 993	914	77 907	9 073	1 575	70 409	18 663	14 306		20 331	17 768	5 085	2 969
1994	109 927	81 854	1 141	82 995	9 780	1 695	74 910	20 265	14 752		21 413	18 666	5 134	3 060
1995	115 180	85 733	764	86 497	10 258	1 793	78 032	21 513	15 636		22 215	19 310	5 185	3 140
1996	121 718	89 456	1 363	90 819	10 682	1 947	82 085	23 420	16 214		23 273	20 091	5 230	3 191
1997	129 099	95 081	1 024	96 106	11 316	2 167	86 957	25 394	16 748		24 514	21 034	5 266	3 245
1998	138 667	101 690	1 421	103 111	11 930	2 314	93 495	28 024	17 148		26 175	22 382	5 298	3 303
1999	144 702	108 102	1 333	109 435	12 631	2 502	99 306	27 509	17 887		27 135	23 236	5 333	3 374
2000	153 548	114 023	877	114 900	13 138	2 736	104 498	29 870	19 179		28 570	24 498	5 374	3 431
2001	158 888	117 907	923	118 830	13 522	2 868	108 176	29 303	21 409		29 400	25 324	5 404	3 419
2002	163 309	122 036	864	122 900	13 917	2 952	111 936	28 332	23 042		30 025	26 433	5 439	3 411
2003	168 278	126 897	1 348	128 245	14 222	2 966	116 989	27 530	23 759		30 754	27 322	5 472	3 435
2004	176 728	133 748	1 357	135 105	14 891	3 125	123 338	29 031	24 359		32 112	28 633	5 504	3 482
2005	184 087	138 962	1 220	140 182	15 690	3 218	127 711	30 396	25 980		33 251	29 375	5 536	3 532

. . . = Not available.

Table 21-2. Personal Income and Employment by Region and State—Continued

(Millions of dollars, except as noted.)

Region or state and year	Personal income, total	Earnings by place of work			Less: Contributions for government social insurance	Plus: Adjustment for residence	Equals: Net earnings by place of residence	Plus: Dividends, interest, and rent	Plus: Personal current transfer receipts	Per capita (dollars)		Population (thousands)	Total employment (thousands)
		Nonfarm	Farm	Total						Personal income	Disposable personal income		
WYOMING													
1958	687	498	75	573	23	-1	549	100	38	2 182	1 973	315	. . .
1959	730	546	64	610	27	-1	582	107	42	2 282	2 053	320	. . .
1960	765	597	50	647	34	-1	611	109	45	2 312	2 068	331	. . .
1961	803	611	56	667	34	-1	632	119	53	2 384	2 146	337	. . .
1962	832	619	66	685	35	-1	649	128	54	2 498	2 238	333	. . .
1963	848	638	66	703	40	-1	662	130	56	2 524	2 235	336	. . .
1964	874	681	46	727	43	-1	684	135	55	2 577	2 348	339	. . .
1965	904	688	52	741	41	-1	700	147	58	2 724	2 479	332	. . .
1966	931	705	57	762	48	0	714	155	61	2 882	2 606	323	. . .
1967	999	748	70	818	53	0	764	163	71	3 101	2 787	322	. . .
1968	1 066	822	62	884	59	0	825	161	81	3 291	2 946	324	. . .
1969	1 173	902	69	971	66	*	905	180	89	3 567	3 148	329	158
1970	1 303	983	78	1 060	72	0	989	212	103	3 904	3 466	334	159
1971	1 449	1 084	87	1 172	81	-1	1 090	240	119	4 261	3 811	340	165
1972	1 626	1 215	125	1 340	96	-3	1 242	255	129	4 689	4 240	347	172
1973	1 905	1 436	152	1 588	128	-7	1 453	299	152	5 390	4 806	353	182
1974	2 242	1 774	109	1 883	159	-14	1 711	360	172	6 151	5 388	365	194
1975	2 557	2 071	66	2 137	182	-16	1 939	411	208	6 722	5 986	380	203
1976	2 857	2 356	47	2 403	213	-23	2 167	458	232	7 224	6 383	395	214
1977	3 357	2 809	44	2 853	249	-30	2 574	529	254	8 157	7 210	412	231
1978	4 033	3 402	63	3 465	309	-39	3 118	630	286	9 361	8 254	431	250
1979	4 752	4 012	95	4 107	381	-56	3 670	752	331	10 517	9 137	452	267
1980	5 556	4 677	84	4 761	442	-77	4 243	922	392	11 718	10 216	474	280
1981	6 335	5 304	51	5 354	542	-88	4 724	1 140	471	12 883	11 159	492	290
1982	6 794	5 400	29	5 429	566	-85	4 779	1 474	541	13 417	11 831	506	288
1983	6 528	5 129	37	5 166	523	-62	4 581	1 306	640	12 791	11 409	510	275
1984	6 854	5 385	14	5 399	561	-56	4 782	1 440	633	13 576	12 208	505	277
1985	7 154	5 619	17	5 636	600	-55	4 982	1 501	672	14 317	12 871	500	278
1986	6 971	5 355	39	5 394	584	-43	4 767	1 464	740	14 064	12 754	496	265
1987	6 762	5 076	58	5 134	553	-28	4 553	1 458	751	14 177	12 801	477	260
1988	6 938	5 218	59	5 276	601	-23	4 652	1 504	782	14 918	13 463	465	265
1989	7 536	5 530	88	5 618	622	-16	4 979	1 714	842	16 440	14 729	458	267
1990	8 167	5 916	148	6 064	671	-12	5 381	1 881	906	18 002	16 149	454	272
1991	8 579	6 096	209	6 305	717	-2	5 586	1 988	1 005	18 680	16 816	459	279
1992	9 020	6 412	218	6 630	748	-7	5 874	2 034	1 112	19 346	17 430	466	282
1993	9 450	6 771	247	7 018	785	-10	6 224	2 012	1 215	19 976	17 925	473	286
1994	9 845	7 077	119	7 197	832	-9	6 356	2 211	1 278	20 498	18 364	480	299
1995	10 207	7 248	102	7 350	854	-7	6 489	2 366	1 352	21 039	18 848	485	302
1996	10 678	7 472	87	7 558	872	-2	6 685	2 559	1 434	21 875	19 159	488	306
1997	11 459	7 884	193	8 076	905	3	7 175	2 806	1 478	23 412	20 413	489	309
1998	12 189	8 323	88	8 411	952	6	7 465	3 209	1 515	24 836	21 613	491	315
1999	13 050	8 849	170	9 020	998	5	8 027	3 439	1 584	26 536	23 044	492	319
2000	14 063	9 576	115	9 692	1 051	13	8 653	3 706	1 704	28 460	24 497	494	328
2001	14 972	10 371	149	10 520	1 132	6	9 394	3 733	1 846	30 305	26 352	494	333
2002	15 463	10 813	81	10 894	1 182	4	9 716	3 754	1 994	30 986	27 754	499	337
2003	16 415	11 311	140	11 451	1 241	2	10 213	4 069	2 133	32 704	29 655	502	339
2004	17 720	12 360	155	12 515	1 331	1	11 185	4 285	2 250	35 028	31 840	506	349
2005	18 982	13 504	197	13 701	1 472	1	12 230	4 366	2 385	37 270	33 495	509	360

. . . = Not available.
* = Less than $50,000, but the estimates for this item are included in the total.

NOTES AND DEFINITIONS

TABLE 21-1
GROSS STATE PRODUCT BY REGION AND STATE

Source: U.S. Department of Commerce, Bureau of Economic Analysis (BEA)

Gross state product (GSP) is the sum of the value added in all industries in a state. Aside from minor definitional differences, the sum of the GSPs of all states is equal in concept for U.S. gross domestic product (GDP). (In practice, there are measurement differences as well as definitional differences.) For explanation of GDP, see the notes and definitions for Tables 1-1 through 1-13. GSP is only calculated on an annual basis.

Definitions and notes on the data

The value of an industry's GSP is equal to the market value of its gross output (which consists of sales or receipts and other operating income, taxes on production and imports, and inventory change) minus the value of its intermediate inputs (which consist of energy, raw materials, semifinished goods, and services that are purchased from domestic industries or foreign sources). In concept, this definition is equal to the sum of labor and property-type income earned in that industry in the production of GDP plus commodity taxes. Property-type income is the sum of corporate profits, proprietors' income, rental income of persons, net interest, capital consumption allowances, business transfer payments, and the current surplus of government enterprises less subsidies.

In practice, GSP, like national GDP by industry, is measured using the incomes data rather than data on gross output and intermediate inputs, which are not available on a sufficiently detailed and timely basis.

Therefore, the *value of gross state product* is defined as the sum of labor and property-type incomes originating in each of 63 industries in that state plus commodity taxes. Due to insufficient information, the nationwide statistical discrepancy—the difference between GDP measured as the sum of final demands and GDP measured as the sum of labor and property incomes and taxes on production and imports—is not allocated to individual industries or states.

The *quantity indexes* of gross state product are aggregates of the real output of each industry in the state, net of intermediate inputs, based on chained constant-dollar estimates and expressed as index numbers, 2000 = 100. They are derived by applying national implicit deflators calculated for each industry group to the current-dollar GSP estimates for that industry group, and then applying the chain-type index formula used in the national accounts to aggregate the industry groups to the state total.

To the extent that a state's output is produced and sold in national markets at relatively uniform prices, or sold locally at national prices, GSP captures the differences across states that reflect the relative differences in the mix of goods and services produced by the states. However, real GSP does not capture geographic differences in the prices of goods and services produced and sold locally.

Data availability and references

Data can be found on the Bureau of Economic Analysis (BEA) Web site <http://www.bea.gov>. GSP is now calculated on a North American Industry Classification System (NAICS) basis back through 1997. Data for earlier years, beginning with 1977, were calculated on the Standard Industrial Classification (SIC) basis. Since the 1997 values are not identical in the old and new systems, *Business Statistics* presents the data for earlier years, including 1997 values, so that users may link the earlier years data to current estimates.

The early estimates for 2005 and revised estimates for 1998 through 2004 that are shown here were presented in "Gross State Product: Advanced Estimates for 2005 and Revised Estimates for 1998–2004," *Survey of Current Business*, July 2006. Revised 2005 estimates will be updated on the Internet, and revised multiyear estimates using the standard methodology will be available in June 2007.

TABLE 21-2
PERSONAL INCOME AND EMPLOYMENT BY REGION AND STATE

Source: U.S. Department of Commerce, Bureau of Economic Analysis (BEA)

This table presents annual time-series data on personal income and employment for the United States as a whole, each individual state, the District of Columbia, and eight geographic regions for 1958 through 2005. In almost all respects, the data are consistent with the national personal income data as defined and presented in Chapters 1 and 4. BEA also publishes quarterly estimates of state personal income, which are not shown here.

The sum of state personal incomes for the United States shown in this table is somewhat smaller than U.S. personal income (as shown in the national income and product accounts [NIPAs], which are described in Chapters 1 and 4), due to slightly different definitions. The national total of the state estimates consists only of the income earned by persons who live in the United States and of foreign residents who work in the United States. The measure of personal income in the NIPAs is broader. It includes the earnings of federal civilian and military personnel stationed abroad (see below for a change in the definition of "stationed abroad") and of U.S. residents on foreign assignment for less than a year. It also includes the investment income received by federal retirement plans for federal workers stationed abroad. Earnings of foreign residents are included only if they live and work in the United States for a year or more. There are also statistical differences that reflect the variable timing of the availability of source data.

In the October 2005 *Survey of Current Business*, BEA announced "New Treatment of State Estimates of Military Compensation." (This information can be found in the article referenced below.) This announcement says, "BEA's state estimates of military compensation are based on troop data by base and national estimates of average pay from the Department of Defense (DOD). For 2001–2004, the DOD estimates of troops stationed at U.S. bases do not show a large decrease for troops sent to Afghanistan and Iraq. Those estimates reflect the DOD's new method of reporting active duty military personnel for the Army and the Air Force. The DOD now reports active duty regular military personnel according to the troops' home bases and reserve personnel according to the state of the reservists' bases. However, for the Marines, DOD continues to use an approach that reduces domestic base personnel figures when troops are sent overseas. Since BEA's state estimates of military earnings reflect the geographic distribution of military personnel as reported by the DOD, the surge in military earnings due to the activation of reservists and the special pay associated with the war is recorded in the states from which the forces were deployed. This practice is consistent with the pay being received by family members at home and with news reports of strong retail sales at affected military bases.... Since the Persian Gulf war, the demographics of the armed forces have evolved, and BEA has changed its military residency definition accordingly. The current Army has a larger proportion of mature troops with families to support, in contrast to the typical young, single soldiers of the past."

Definitions

A state's *personal income* is the personal income (as defined below) of persons resident in that state, not persons working in that state. Its derivation from source data on earnings by place of work is shown in the succeeding columns of Table 21-2 and is explained below.

Earnings by place of work includes wage and salary disbursements, all supplements to wages and salaries (including employer contributions for government social insurance and all other benefits), and farm and nonfarm proprietors' income paid to persons working in the state.

Contributions for government social insurance, which is subtracted from total earnings, includes both the employer and the employee contributions. Personal income is net of all contributions for government social insurance, though not of other taxes on wages or other income.

Adjustment for residence. BEA adjusts earnings by place of work to a place-of-residence basis, to account for interstate and international commuting. The difference between earnings by place of residence and earnings by place of work is shown in the "Adjustment for residence" column. This adjustment is a net figure, equaling income received by state (or area) residents from employment outside the state minus income paid to persons residing outside the state but working in the state. There is a negative adjustment for the United States as a whole, reflecting net payments to foreign residents working in the United States.

The effect of interstate commuting can be seen in its most extreme form by comparing the District of Columbia, with its 2005 adjustment for residence of negative $36 billion (representing net payments to persons living outside D.C.) with Maryland, with its adjustment for residence of positive $25 billion net from the District of Columbia and other employment sources outside the state in 2005.

Dividends, interest, and rent are as defined in U.S. personal income, including the capital consumption adjustment for rental income of persons.

Total employment is the total number of jobs, full-time plus part-time; each job that any person holds is counted at full weight. The employment estimates are on a place-of-work basis. Both wage and salary employment and self-employment are included. The main source for the wage and salary employment estimates is the Bureau of Labor Statistics estimates from unemployment insurance data (the ES-202 data), which also provides benchmarks for the payroll employment measures. (See Table 10-7 and its notes and definitions.) Self-employment is estimated mainly from individual and partnership federal income tax returns.

This concept of employment differs from the concept of employment in the Current Population Survey (CPS), which is derived from a monthly count of persons employed; any individual will appear only once in the CPS in a given month, no matter how many different jobs he or she might hold. (See the notes and definitions to Tables 10-1 through 10-5.) In addition, a self-employed individual who files more than one Schedule C income-tax filing will be counted more than once in the state figures. Finally, the state figures include members of the armed forces, who are not covered in the CPS. Due to these differences and other possible reporting inconsistencies, the BEA estimates are different from, and usually larger than, state employment estimates from the CPS.

The employment estimates correspond closely in coverage to the earnings estimates. However, the earnings estimates include the income of limited partnerships and of tax-exempt cooperatives, for which there are no corresponding employment estimates.

Per capita income is total income divided by the state's population. It is therefore an average or "mean," subject to the qualifications discussed in the "Using the Data" article at the beginning of this volume, under the "Whose Standard of Living?" heading. For recent data on median household income by state, which give a better idea of the income of typical residents of the state, see Table 3-16 in Chapter 3.

The states and the District of Columbia are divided into regions by BEA as follows:

- **New England**: Connecticut, Maine, Massachusetts, New Hampshire, Rhode Island, and Vermont

- **Mideast**: Delaware, District of Columbia, Maryland, New Jersey, New York, and Pennsylvania

- **Great Lakes**: Illinois, Indiana, Michigan, Ohio, and Wisconsin

- **Plains**: Iowa, Kansas, Minnesota, Missouri, Nebraska, North Dakota, and South Dakota

- **Southeast**: Alabama, Arkansas, Florida, Georgia, Kentucky, Louisiana, Mississippi, North Carolina, South Carolina, Tennessee, Virginia, and West Virginia

- **Southwest**: Arizona, New Mexico, Oklahoma, and Texas

- **Rocky Mountain**: Colorado, Idaho, Montana, Utah, and Wyoming

- **Far West**: Alaska, California, Hawaii, Nevada, Oregon, and Washington

These BEA regional groupings differ from the region and division definitions used by the Census Bureau.

Data availability and references

The most recent updates to state personal income appear in a BEA news release entitled "State Personal Income: Second Quarter 2006, Revised State Personal Income: 2003–2005" (September 26, 2006), available on the BEA Web site at <http://www.bea.gov/bea/rels.htm>. These estimates incorporated midyear population estimates released by the Census Bureau in December 2005.

The most recent comprehensive revision of state personal income, consistent with the 2003 comprehensive revision of the NIPAs, was presented in "Comprehensive Revision of State Personal Income: Preliminary Estimates for 2003, Revised Estimates for 1969–2002," *Survey of Current Business*, May 2004. A subsequent update was described in "State Personal Income: Second Quarter of 2005 and Revised Estimates for 2002–2005:I," *Survey of Current Business*, October 2005. A similar article is to be published in the October 2006 *Survey of Current Business*. These articles can be found on the BEA Web site at <http://www.bea.gov>. All current and historical data are available on the BEA Web site at <http://www.bea.gov/bea/regional/spi>.

Also included on the BEA Web site are some annual state data that go back even farther than shown here. Included are data on personal income, per capita personal income, and population back to 1929; disposable personal income and per capita disposable personal income back to 1948; and various levels of industry detail for income and wages and salaries within the state data back to 1929. For a complete listing, see the referenced article in the October 2005 issue of the *Survey of Current Business*.

INDEX

INDEX